Paradise Planned

Paradise Planned

The Garden Suburb and the Modern City

Robert A. M. Stern, David Fishman, and Jacob Tilove

THE MONACELLI PRESS

Published in the United States by The Monacelli Press

Library of Congress Cataloging-in-Publication Data

Stern, Robert A. M.
 Paradise planned : the garden suburb and the modern
city / Robert A.M. Stern, David Fishman, and Jacob
Tilove.
     pages cm.
ISBN 978-1-58093-326-1 (hardback)
1. Garden suburbs—History. I. Fishman, David.
II. Tilove, Jacob. III. Title.
 HT161.S74 2013
 307.7409--dc23
                            2013020286

Designed by Pentagram

Printed in China

www.monacellipress.com

Acknowledgments

Paradise Planned would not have been possible without the help of a great many people. The book had its origins in a 1981 special issue of *Architectural Design,* prepared in collaboration with John Montague Massengale. While limitations of space prevent us from recognizing everyone individually, *we* would like to give special thanks to our colleague Sarah Acheson, whose able support during the later stages of the book in finding, obtaining, and organizing the artwork was critical. We would also like to thank Kevin Adkisson, Emily Jones, Paul Needham, and Margaret Day for their valuable assistance during various stages of the project. We are also indebted to the many archives, libraries, universities, municipalities, local historical societies, and photographers that generously shared their knowledge and collections. As always, the collections and staff at Columbia University's libraries were a constant and indispensable resource.

It is a pleasure to acknowledge the professional team that has given the book its form. The wonderful design was conceived and implemented by Michael Bierut, Yve Ludwig, and Aron Fay at Pentagram. Elizabeth White skillfully orchestrated the editing and production process, assisted by Mikhaela Mahony and Michael Vagnetti. We are also grateful for the editorial contributions of Leslie Yudell. The support and vision of our publisher, Gianfranco Monacelli, was indispensable in bringing *Paradise Planned* to fruition.

Contents

Foreword

"No great town can long
exist without great suburbs."

—Frederick Law Olmsted, 1868[1]

Suburbs are an important and distinct part of modern culture, reflecting widely held insecurities largely brought on by rapid industrialization and dramatic demographic shifts. Not conforming to a single physical type, suburbs constitute a broad category encompassing many things: a political condition, a patchwork of land-use patterns, a lifestyle. At its most basic, the suburb is a pattern of inhabitation conveniently connected to the inner city but typically, although not necessarily, separate from its economic engines of production.

This book is about one particular type of suburb: the planned garden suburb, a type that has its roots in late-eighteenth-century England, flourished in England and the United States in the nineteenth century, then became an international phenomenon in the first two decades of the twentieth century. The impact of the garden suburb gradually diminished between the two world wars, but this type of community is now being revalued and reestablished as a development model as part of New Urbanism's Traditional Town movement. At its best, the planned garden suburb is a remarkable urbanistic achievement intended to evoke the physical structure of preindustrial-era villages, an incomparable work

Forest Hills Gardens.
RAMSA (2012)

of environmental art combining enlightened land planning, landscape, and architecture to shape neighborhoods and foster a sense of community.

Garden suburbs are valued by the public but little appreciated or even discussed by a majority of today's social scientists, planners, and architects. Recoiling against the sprawling land-use patterns and consequent environmental degradation brought about by the almost exclusive dependence since the 1940s on the automobile, these professionals have preferred to indiscriminately lump the garden suburb into a broad-based rejection of suburbanism as a whole. In deriding the suburb, the intelligentsia tends to consider only its basest form—that of placeless sprawl. Moreover, these observers see the popularity of the planned garden suburb with the prosperous classes as testimony to what they deem its inherent triviality, castigating it, and indeed all suburbs, as escapist, especially for the moneyed classes. Notwithstanding the claims of many among the intelligentsia, the stereotypical view of the planned garden suburb as exclusively catering to the moneyed classes does not hold true. Many examples were deliberately conceived to improve the lot of the average white- and blue-collar worker. It cannot be too often stated, and this book hopes to demonstrate, that whether built for the affluent or for the working class, the planned garden suburb has proven its enduring value and appeal as an attainable, inhabitable arcadia for everyman.

INTERPRETING THE GARDEN SUBURB

Historians, architects, and planners of the 1950s and 1960s have tended to denigrate the garden suburb if they bothered to discuss it at all.[2] There are some exceptions to this, most notably the American scholar-urbanist Lewis Mumford (1895–1990) who, in his magisterial book, *The City in History*, emphasized the inspired role the garden suburb plays in modern urbanism as a whole:

> *The ultimate outcome of [the] . . . suburban retreat on a large scale has proved to be a non-city, if not an anti-city, just because of the very isolation and separation . . . Yet none of the planning done within the nineteenth*

century, not even that done under Haussmann, compares in freshness of form and boldness of design with the best of the suburbs, from Olmsted's Riverside, near Chicago, to his Roland Park near Baltimore, from Llewellyn Park in New Jersey to Unwin and Parker's superb achievement at Hampstead Garden Suburb, in which the buildings were an integral part of the whole design. So charming was the physical environment of the better suburbs that for long it drew attention away from their social deficiencies and oversights. By getting away from the standard gridiron plan and high ground rents, by accepting the co-operation of nature instead of stamping out every trace of environmental character, the new planners and builders evolved a new form for the city, or at least, the rough outlines of a new form. This achievement deserves an historic monograph that has still to be written.[3]

Since Mumford's book was published in 1961, other historians, including Walter Creese (1919–2002), Mervyn Miller (b. 1942), and Gabriele Tagliaventi (b. 1960), and a few architect-urbanists, especially Andrés Duany (b. 1949) and Elizabeth Plater-Zyberk (b. 1950), whose accomplishments are discussed in the final chapter of this book, have taken up the garden suburb as a worthy historical topic.[4] But even this slow-growing literature of affirmation concentrates on relatively few representative examples, giving the impression that the garden suburb movement was something of a minor distraction in the history of the modern city. Such couldn't be further from the truth as we discovered for ourselves in researching this book. Suspecting that there were numerous excellently planned garden suburbs deeply appreciated by residents but overlooked by most historians, we were amazed to discover the wealth of examples not only in the United Kingdom and the United States but also in virtually every industrialized country in the world. Aided by the great resources of Columbia University's Avery Architectural Library and those recently made available on the internet, we have discovered innumerable little-known or largely forgotten examples and have been introduced to a vast literature documenting their early and subsequent histories, frequently written by local amateurs dedicated to sharing with others the pleasure they take in their own garden suburb communities.

STYLE AND THE GARDEN SUBURB

One reason the garden suburb has been treated so dismissively by many scholars is that, imbued with the prejudices of Modernist architects and theorists of architecture, they hold in contempt the scenographic use of stylistic precedent and therefore find it easy to characterize the architecture and urbanism of the garden suburb as trivial and fundamentally opposed to the realities of modern life. However, the co-opting of the past, as the historian T. J. Jackson Lears has made clear, is a quintessential characteristic of modernity, at once a reaction against and a complement to the dehumanizing character of mechanization.[5]

The evocation of vernacular styles, however, is more than a matter of packaging; it is an essential ingredient in the place-making process, helping to speed up the establishment of a sense of community by rooting "instant" developments in an evolving tradition. Important as architectural style is in the place-making process, so too are the patterns of streets and squares that evolved naturally in vernacular towns and are used to help structure many of the best garden suburbs.

The value of vernacular styles and planning principles was made vividly clear in the decades between the two world wars, when the idea of the garden suburb was co-opted by European Socialist governments and their planners, but drastically reconfigured in the form of siedlungen, or housing estates, which eschewed preindustrial-age vernacular styles and more significantly the village-based vocabulary of streets and squares in favor of a "collectivist" approach that valorized an aesthetic based on utilitarian functionalism and regimented uniformity. Although many of the social and environmental principles that lay behind the garden suburb movement remained intact in these housing estates, the sense of community was compromised, with particularly disastrous social consequences in Great Britain and the United States, where these developments were more often than not perceived as placeless and soulless.

WHY THE GARDEN SUBURB NOW?

This book attempts to be the comprehensive monographic treatment of the garden suburb that Lewis Mumford called for in *The City in History*. Our study is written with the intention of stimulating an appreciation of the garden suburb in its various types, but it is just as importantly intended as an activist work using historical scholarship to promote the garden suburb as a development model for the present and foreseeable future. By offering a new and long-overdue look at the garden suburb, we hope that architects, developers, and planners will reconceptualize the planning and design of the seemingly inevitable suburban development that takes place on greenfield sites on the fringes of metropolitan regions. But even more, we hope this book will make clear the garden suburb's value as a conceptual model for the redevelopment of the vast, virtually empty urban wastelands that lie within established cities in what can be called the "middle city," a deracinated zone between downtown and pre-automobile-era suburban development where neighborhoods in cities like Detroit, Cleveland, and St. Louis have been largely abandoned and now, virtually empty of people and buildings, have no discernible assets except the infrastructure of streets and the utility systems buried under them.[6]

We hope that what we have written about the garden suburb will not only draw attention to a largely overlooked phenomenon of architecture, landscape, and infrastructure but also encourage architects, planners, developers, and government officials in their work of going forward to add it to their inventory of ideas and thus help satisfy the hunger of the very many who wish to be Hamiltonian by day and Jeffersonian by night, that is to say, to combine the material and cultural advantages of city life with the restorative powers of dwelling amidst nature.

Origins

The word "suburb" evolved from the Latin *suburbium,* most likely adapted by the English from the Old French *suburbe* during the period of Gallic influences in the fourteenth century. Chaucer's casual use of the term in 1386 in the *Canterbury Tales* suggests that it had long acquired a definite meaning, probably extending back to the Roman Empire, with its high valuation of *rus in urbe.* Nonetheless, the suburb as we know it is a quintessentially modern phenomenon—the dependent dormitory town that could not exist without convenient transportation to easily carry its residents into and out of the city, where, typically, jobs are to be had and cultural pleasures pursued.[1]

The planned garden suburb, a village or enclave located within the catchments of a city, and sometimes directly embedded in the city itself, though a by-product of early-nineteenth-century industrialization, and especially efficient mechanically powered transportation, may be said to have a prehistory beginning in the eighteenth century with, for example, the clustering of lodges (1716–21) by Joseph Effner (1867–1745) around the forecourt of the Nymphenburg Palace in Munich. It was further defined with the booming expansion of London under George III, when horse-drawn stages for the newly prosperous merchant class, aided by the building of an extensive paved road system, fostered the development and rapid growth of small, once-remote villages, giving rise to enclaves such as the Paragon, Blackheath (1795) by Michael Searles (1750–1813) outside

London, and Blaise Hamlet (1811) by John Nash (1752–1835) outside Bristol.

Although these examples provided the formal basis for much that would follow, they were little more than fragments of a town planning ideal that would not grow into a full-fledged model of community design until the emergence of mechanized transportation beginning with steam ferries, which opened up outlying areas to suburban development, especially in New York, where Brooklyn Heights, across the East River, became the city's first suburb. But it was the development of extensive railroad systems that by the 1840s made it possible for upper-middle-class businessmen and professionals to live at some distance from their places of work, and it was the electrified trolley, coming in the late 1880s, that opened up the suburb to a wide spectrum of the middle and working classes.

ENGLISH BEGINNINGS 1750–1885

England's first garden villages were built in the countryside by estate owners who, in the process of improving their properties, endeavored to rebuild unsightly villages in situ or, just as often, relocate them so as to be either completely out of sight from their country houses or picturesquely fitted into the landscape to enhance distant views. Built to house estate workers, as Gillian Darley has noted in *Villages of Vision,* these villages represented

Regent's Development, Park Village West. Murray. TM (2013)

1. Ordnance Survey map. LLFH (1850)

2. Aerial view. GE (2009)

3. The Avenue. CRS

4. The Avenue. RIBA10 (c. 1910)

the first instance when architects were "required to turn their minds to the design and planning of small-scale rural communities and the type of housing previously considered as totally insignificant."[2] **Harewood** (1760), in Yorkshire's West Riding, designed by John Carr of York (1723–1807) for Edwin Lascelles (1713–1795), was, as John Jewell observed in 1819, "uniformly and modestly rebuilt, so as to exclude every appearance of filth or poverty," making it distinguishable "from almost every other village in the kingdom, by its regularity and cleanliness."[3] Carr's plan brought a measure of genteel sophistication to a rural setting, with stone houses visually united by arches, and a school, inn, doctor's house, and short-lived ribbon factory placed around a T-shaped intersection just outside the Harewood House gates. In his 1946 book, *The Anatomy of the Village*, Thomas Sharp called attention to Harewood village with its "subtle effect of . . . curving approach road which suddenly narrows where the village begins, thus creating the suggestion of a preliminary gateway; and, at the other end of the village, where the street has widened out a little, the curved narrowing towards the climax of the vista, the lodges and gates to the park of the great house."[4]

Lowther Village, commissioned in 1766 by Sir James Lowther (1736–1802), was even more incongruously urban given its remote location in Westmorland, "a particularly distant corner of Britain."[5] The only rural planning project to be realized by architects Robert

(1728–1792) and James (1732–1794) Adam, Lowther Village's tripartite plan positioned attached one- and two-room cottages around a central circus or circle flanked on the east and west by two Greek cross-shaped closes, superimposing, as Richard Warner observed in 1802, "the grandest features of city architecture, the Circus, the Crescent and the Square upon the mean scale of a peasant's cottage."[6] Only half the circus was built, along with a portion of the western close, as well as a U-shaped group that was not part of the original plan, in all providing more than ninety cottages, each with a backyard.

Milton Abbas (1775–76), in Dorset, was decidedly more picturesque, establishing the prototype for garden suburban imagery—that of the preindustrial vernacular village—reflecting the inclinations of landscape architect Lancelot "Capability" Brown (1716–1783), who planned the village with architect William Chambers (1723–1796), his fiercest critic, while they were both at work rebuilding the former Milton Abbey for its new owner, Joseph Damer (1718–1798).[7] Damer purchased the house and a cheek-by-jowl market town in 1752 but decided to relocate the town, with its population of almost 600, four inns, a well-known brewery, school, church, almshouses, and shops, to a new site about a mile away. Chambers and Brown submitted separate plans for the village, and while it remains unknown whose plan was followed, Chambers's falling out with Damer and his subsequent departure from the project hints that it may have been a

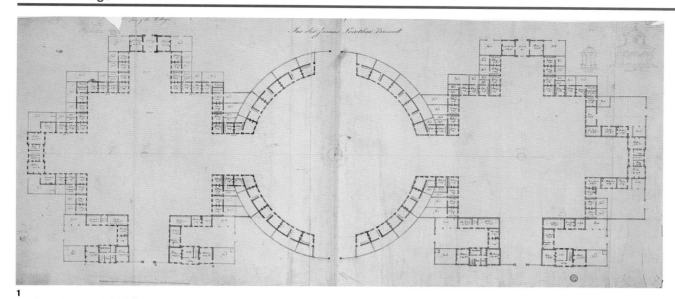

1. Plan, Robert and James Adam, 1766. SJS

2. Aerial view. GE (2009)

3. Western portion of the village. Bolton. HB (2002)

4. Eastern portion of the village. Bolton. HB (2002)

combination of the two, with Chambers's initial designs being further developed and carried out by Brown, who may have designed the cottages.[8] The new village featured forty semidetached, whitewashed thatch-roofed houses drawn from the Dorset vernacular lining a single 20-foot-wide road that curved gently through its valley setting. As Thomas Sharp noted, "the chief buildings punctuate the design; the church facing the almshouses at the centre; the vicarage facing the brewery at one end; the school, the inn and the hospital terminating the other end."[9] The inclusion of broad grassy verges on either side of the road allowed for a distance of 80 feet between house fronts. Each cottage had a rear garden beyond which allotments extended up the hillsides. A horse chestnut tree was planted between each pair of cottages, but the trees were later removed to let in more sunlight. Milton Abbas was completed in 1786 after the last tenants' leases expired in the old village. Writing in 1791, novelist and diarist Fanny Burney (known as Madam d'Arbley, following her marriage) found the relatively pristine houses to be misleading, "for the sight of common people and of the poor labouring or strolling in and about these dwellings, made them appear rather to be reduced from better days than flourish in a primitive or natural state."[10]

East Stratton (1806), in Hampshire, was another roadside village where, for Francis Baring MP (1740–1810), George Dance the Younger (1741–1825) designed nine semidetached cottages of brick, timber framing,

and thatch along one side of the road, each house entered from the side and set in a garden. "It is only the formalism that clearly marks his cottages out from the other traditionally designed houses in the village," writes Darley. "Externally there is little which would mark them apart . . . The general effect is strictly utilitarian with no alien Picturesque effects."[11]

Closer to London, estate owners catering to prosperous merchants desiring to establish a foothold in the country undertook the first planned suburbs, "new towns" such as Somers Town and Camden Town, but it is with surveyor Michael Searles's developments, the **Paragon, New Kent Road** (1787–91) and the **Paragon, Blackheath** (1794–1807), that a new typology, at once urban and arcadian, really began to take form.[12] The New Kent Road Paragon has its formal origins in the **Royal Crescent** (1767–75), the palace-like townhouse terrace designed by John Wood the Younger (1728–1782) in Bath, which "turned its back on the town, facing instead the distant horizon and bringing the landscape into direct visual contact with the dwelling complex itself," as John Archer has written, noting that despite this, the concept was "more of a visual pairing of *rus* with *urbe* than a successful integration of the two."[13] Although the Paragon on New Kent Road in the East End was demolished in 1898 to make way for a school, the Paragon in Blackheath survives, restored after World War II bomb damage. At Blackheath, Searles adopted the Royal Crescent's bold

Milton Abbas

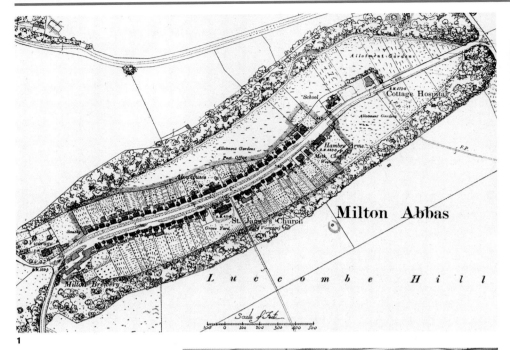

1

2

1. Map. TPR16

2. View over the lake. Smith. RIBAP (1964)

3. Aerial view. CUCAP (1950)

4. Church and cottage. TPR16 (c. 1916)

5. View from the church. Ives/Townsend. IT (2007)

3

4

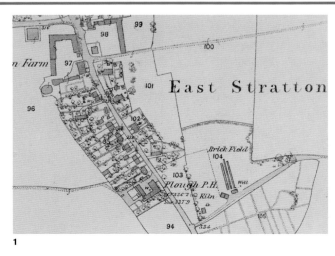

5

East Stratton

1. Ordnance Survey map. HRO (c. 1870)

2. Stratton Lane. EHC (2006)

1

2

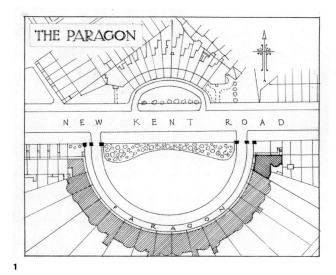

1. Block plan based on 1870 Ordnance Survey map. EH (1951)

2. View from New Kent Road. LMA (c. 1896)

Paragon, Blackheath

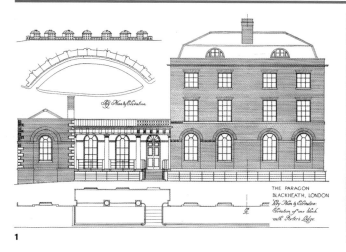

1. Plan and elevations. SHLGP

2. View across lawn. Stephen. POE (2012)

sweep of building and landscape but in a move reflecting bourgeois preference for freestanding houses, replaced Wood's singular terrace with seven four-story redbrick villas connected by one-story service ranges, with the center villa intended for single occupancy but the rest containing two dwellings each sharing a party wall. Crucial to the plan was a small park formed between the public road and the development's private access-way. The combination of the crescent of houses and the forecourt-like park together give a sense of cohesiveness that perfectly conveys urbanity without sacrificing village-like domesticity. At the rear, curved bay windows rise to the full height of each unit, overlooking the private, shared garden. "Stranded out in a void, far from the intimacy and assurance of surrounding streets," as Andrew Saint has written, "the house-pairs of The Paragon hang on to one another, hold hands, as it were, for moral support, by means of linking colonnades. This equivocal blend of dependence and independence is the essence of suburban architecture—perhaps, indeed, of the whole modern manner of life."[14]

Following on the Paragon, the design of the **Eyre Estate** (1794) in St. John's Wood, then on the outskirts of London, took the idea of the garden suburb a significant step further. It called for an arrangement of streets and squares, as well as a grand circus or circle, with semidetached, villa-like houses separated by large gardens, with additional gardens behind them, forming the building blocks of a new neighborhood, the planning of which, as John Summerson was to write, constituted "a revolution of striking significance and far-reaching effect."[15] Although the plan, prepared by surveyors John Spurrier (n.d.) and Josiah Phipps (n.d.), was not realized, the Eyre Estate was built out beginning in 1815 under the direction of John Shaw (1776–1832), to whom the idea and design of the detached and semidetached houses has been attributed.

Blaise Hamlet (1811), situated along an irregularly looped lane off a main road four miles north of Bristol in the west of England, is the first fully realized exemplar of the garden suburb.[16] Consisting of ten highly individualistic, neo-vernacular, medievalizing, freestanding cottages set in a deliberately random arrangement around a green—complete with village pump (incorporating a sundial) and many other "countrified" touches that fit squarely into the tradition of associationism characteristic of most suburban architecture to this day—Blaise Hamlet conjures up a prior, more "innocent"

Royal Crescent, Bath

1. Royal Crescent. Menneer. NM
(c. 1995)

1

Eyre Estate

1 Plan, Spurrier & Phipps,
1794. LMA

2. Map of St. John's Wood.
WAC (1890)

3. Clifton Hill. Rae. RR (2012)

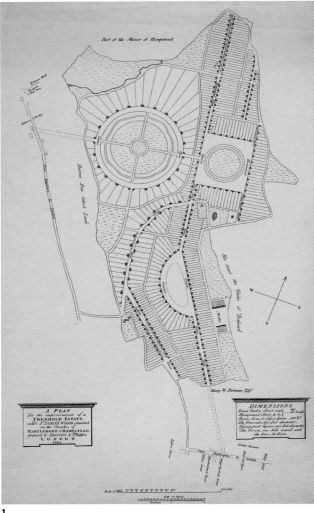

1

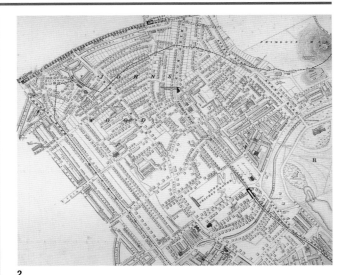

2

3

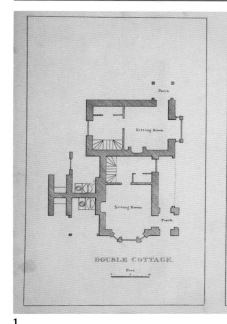

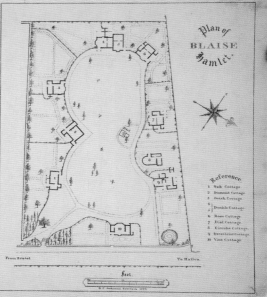

condition of community, making it, as architect George Godwin (1813–1888), writing to the editor of the *Civil Engineer and Architect's Journal* in 1839, put it, "certainly a spot [to] play at Arcadia."[17] The hamlet was designed for J. S. Harford (1754–1815), a Quaker banker, by John Nash, who persuaded his client to locate the development away from Harford's Blaise Castle, setting it instead in a wooded clearing where the residents, who were retired servants, might better enjoy peace, quiet, and privacy, a point made obvious by the decision to surround the house group by a stone wall entered through a single gate. At Blaise Hamlet, Nash laid out the road map for virtually all the garden suburbs that followed.

Whereas Blaise Hamlet was small, rural, altruistic, and all of one piece, Nash's **Regent's Development** (1811–32) was complex and commercial, a massive land-development scheme conceived as a speculative venture to extend the existing city of London into its rural periphery, combining various types of residential development with public open space and sophisticated new infrastructure in the form of a system of canals.[18] Undertaken for the Crown Estate, the Regent's Development incorporated existing urban fabric, most notably Robert and James Adam's Portland Place (1773), while pushing new streets through older districts to make possible what was at once both a real and a metaphoric journey from

1. Double cottage plan and site plan, John Nash, 1811. BMGA (1826)

2. Aerial view. GE (2007)

3. Cottages, J. Horner, 1838. RIBAD

4, 5. Cottages. CPSmith. GEO (2010)

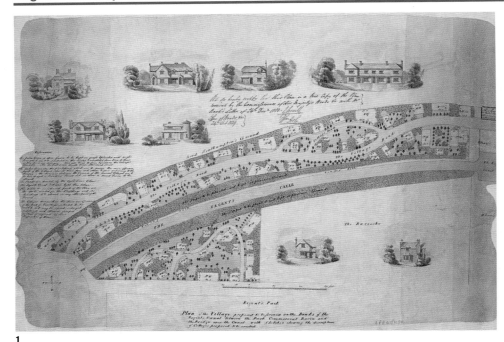

1

3

4

5

6

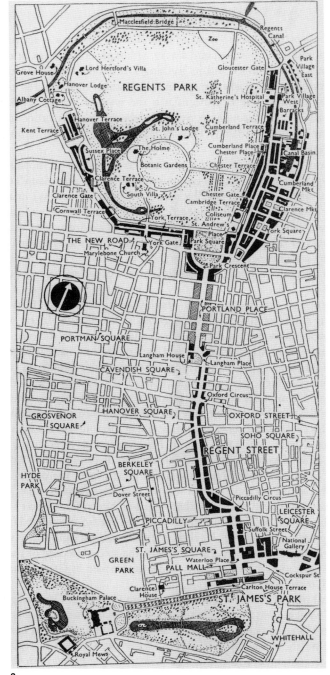

2

1. Plan of the Park Villages, with wash drawings of proposed villa types, John Nash, 1823. TNA

2. Map of Regent's Park and Regent Street connection to St. James Park. JS

3. St. Dunstan's Lodge, Decimus Burton, 1825. MI

4. Grove House, Decimus Burton, 1822. MI

5. St. John's Wood Lodge, John Raffield, 1817–18. MI

6. The Holme, Decimus Burton, 1818. MI

town to country. To help render explicit the journey's metaphor, Nash employed a variety of architectural languages, from the monumental classicism of Imperial Rome to rural vernaculars, including those of Tuscany and pre-Georgian England itself. Nash's Regent's Development is, as the architect-planner Steen Eiler Rasmussen (1898–1990) observed in his book, *London: The Unique City,* "the garden-city in embryo . . . an entire ideal suburb . . . founded on a small scale, which could provide for itself, with favourable conditions for its own industry, its own houses both for the upper and lower classes, its own supplies of goods, and its own large and beautiful park which was not only an ornament for the royal residential city but also a place in which the citizens could find recreation in playing games."[19]

Among Nash's greatest innovations, none would prove more significant for future planned suburban design than that of the controlled right-of-way. In this case it took the form of Lower and Upper Regent Streets, which, together with Portland Place, provided a monumental and direct link between an established green park, St. James's, and a new one, the 472-acre Regent's Park, conceived as a public pleasure ground, suggesting deep country far away from the city, but dotted with and surrounded by sound real estate development that would support its maintenance. Inside the park, twenty-eight detached villas were proposed but only eight were realized. Along its edges, the fronts of Bath-inspired terrace rows and crescents were set, Paragon-like, behind their own small private grassy enclosures, but positioned to

7

8

9

10

11

12

13

14

15

16

17

18

19

7. Cornwall Terrace, Decimus Burton, 1821–23. MI

8. Cumberland Terrace, John Nash, 1826. MI

9. Hanover Terrace, John Nash, 1822–23. MI

10. Ulster Terrace, John Nash, 1823–26. MI

11. Park Crescent, John Nash 1812–22. MI

12. Chester Terrace, John Nash, 1825. RAMSA (1977)

13. Chester Terrace. RAMSA (2010)

14. Cornwall Terrace. Cadman. FL (2006)

15. Park Village West. RAMSA (2004)

16. Park Village West. Yarham. GEO (2012)

17, 18. Park Village East. RAMSA (2008)

19. Park Village East, canal towpath and house backs. MI

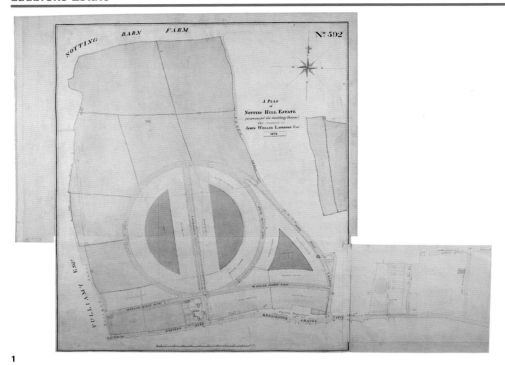

1

2

3

4

1. Plan, Thomas Allason, 1823.
LMA

2. Plan based on 1863–67
and 1894–95 Ordnance Surveys.
EH (1973)

3. Aerial view. GE (2010)

4. Stanley Crescent. OGS (2009)

take advantage of open views to the public park beyond. Stable mews were located at the rear. East of Regent's Park lay Albany Street, where Nash located military barracks and public markets as well as an ophthalmologic hospital. Several streets and squares opened off Albany Street, including York Square and Park Village East and Park Village West, containing comparatively modest-size houses intended for tradesmen and artisans. These villages, and their position in the overall plan, further shaped the development model that, as John Tyack has written, still constitutes what many people regard as "the most desirable setting for urban life," with the Park Villages constituting "the beau ideal of the arcadian middle-class suburb."[20]

Nash's original plan for the Park Villages (1823) called for virtually continuous open lawns punctuated by houses. The final design was more urban, with close-packed single and double villas. The villas have become widely emulated prototypes for scenographic suburban design. Nash was, as J. M. Richards has written, "if

not one of the first to approach architectural problems scenically, one of the first to suggest the scenic opportunities offered when relatively small units of domestic architecture were laid out as a single conception." What he pioneered at Blaise Hamlet he took much further at Park Village West, where on a plan of straight and curving streets Nash designed "toy-like villas, each different in design and each set off against a background of trees and hedges."[21]

The 500-acre Regent's Development, incomparable for the complexity of its urbanism, was at a scale that could only be undertaken with public—or in this case, royal—investment. Typically, in the 1820s and 1830s, the realization of garden suburbs would fall to individual entrepreneurs or business consortia, whose comparatively limited resources confined their projects to a much smaller canvas. In 1823 architect Thomas Allason (1790–1852) was commissioned by James Weller Ladbroke (1772–1847) to prepare plans for a residential development on 170 acres in the largely

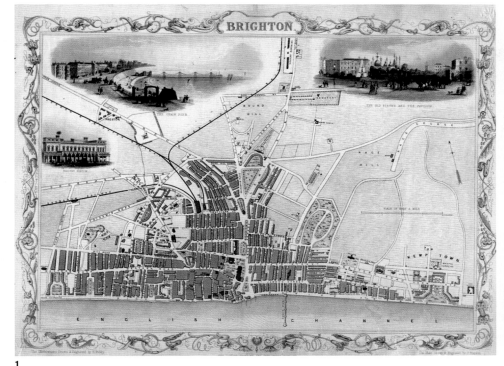

1

2

3

4

5

rural western reaches of London that he had recently inherited.[22] Inspired by the unrealized 1794 plan for the Eyre Estate and more directly by Nash's Regent's Development, the centerpiece of Allason's **Ladbroke Estate** was a large circus, 560 yards in diameter or about one mile in circumference, bisected by a wide north–south road and surrounded by detached villas on plots of nearly one acre. Allason also called for semidetached houses on radiating streets that would be built around "paddocks" or communal gardens. The financial crisis of 1825 halted development before any houses were built, and by the time building began in the early 1840s, the plan was revised, perhaps by architect James Thomson (1800–1883) in consultation with Allason. The north–south thoroughfare survived in the form of Ladbroke Grove, and the idea of communal garden space was also retained, most notably at Stanley Crescent, Kensington Park Gardens, and Stanley Gardens, all largely the work of architect Thomas Allom (1804–1872) in the 1850s.

Nash's influence was also strongly felt in the seaside resort of **Brighton**, where a building boom during the first decades of the nineteenth century, spilling over into Brighton's increasingly subsumed westerly neighbor, Hove, resulted in a proliferation of squares, crescents, and terraces to produce what Nicholas Antram and Richard Morrice have called "one of the great sequences of Regency and Early Victorian town planning in England."[23] Although Brighton received its first architecturally cohesive group of houses—and the first to face toward the sea—in 1798, when in emulation of Bath, J. B. Otto, a West Indian plantation owner, built Royal Crescent, the town's subsequent and more characteristic developments were the work of three architects: Amon Wilds (1762–1833), also a builder; his son Amon Henry Wilds (1790?–1857); and Charles Augustin Busby (1786–1834), who partnered with the younger Wilds for two years (1823–25) before practicing on his own. The architects' first significant work was Hanover Crescent (1814–23), featuring twenty-four Palladian villas set behind a private garden on the east side of the Level, an upland park. Facing northwest away from the sea, the two-story houses were arranged mostly in groups of three, with two-bay-wide units flanking a central three-bay unit. Single-story temple-fronted lodges stood at each of the crescent's entrances. The Wildses' next project, Richmond Terrace (1818), combining semidetached and single houses, was a short distance south, while the later Park Crescent (1849), consisting of forty-eight houses in a horseshoe configuration around a private garden, bordered the Level on

1. Plan, John Forbes, 1824. JHU (1826)

2. Entrance gates. FP (c. 1930s)

3. Clarence Square. Langhorn. FP (2011)

4. Pump Room. Rimell. GEO (2011)

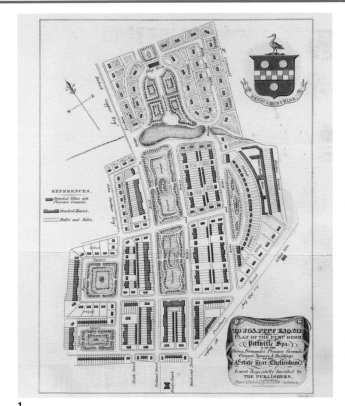

1

2

3

4

the north. Also included among the Wildses' and Busby's work are Regency Square (Amon Wilds and Amon H. Wilds, 1817–30), a seaward-facing square; Oriental Crescent (Amon H. Wilds, 1825–27); Montpelier Crescent (Amon H. Wilds, 1843–47), facing northwest away from the sea; and two Brighton suburbs: the monumentally scaled Kemp Town (Amon H. Wilds and Charles Busby, 1823–28), at Brighton's eastern edge—incorporating crescents, squares, and terraces that brought Nash's Regent's Park terraces to new proportions, extending for thirty or more bays and reaching five stories in height—and Brunswick Town (Charles Busby, 1824–30), in Hove, where two thirty-nine-bay terraces bordered a seaside park.

Pittville (1824), developed by banker Joseph Pitt (1759–1842) as a suburb of Cheltenham, was a spa almost 100 miles from London that had grown fashionable in the late eighteenth century.[24] Taking advantage of Cheltenham's booming economy, Pitt, who had previously developed Cheltenham's Royal Crescent, modeled on its predecessor in Bath, chose not to extend the spa town but instead to build a separate suburban enclave of 500 to 600 intermixed terraced houses and villas to be realized on about 100 acres of land. Plans developed by John

Forbes (b. 1795?), a local architect, called for a long garden at the center of the property, a residential crescent, and two squares as well as an ornamental lake. Though Forbes's plan largely consisted of rectangular blocks split by service mews, at the site's north end a looser arrangement of curving avenues lined with freestanding villas was adopted facing a park leading to the Pump Room (1830), which was the suburb's social center. Three sides of each house lot were to be defined by seven-foot-high brick walls, but the street frontage was to be treated as an ornamental pleasure ground, fenced with visually permeable iron railings, the design of which was to be approved by Pitt.

Leamington Spa, ninety-five miles from London, was another booming resort town where from 1827 to 1828 John Nash and James Morgan (1776?–1856) collaborated on a plan for the **Newbold Comyn Estate**, proposing villas, terraced houses, and walks on either side of the River Leam, with a linear garden, Holly Grove, at the site's north end, creating a mix that, according to John Archer, "was a far more complex integration of city and country than Nash's earlier work at Regent's Park."[25] **Calverley Park and Plain** (1827–50), near the fashionable resort at Tunbridge Wells, was laid out by the

Newbold Comyn Estate

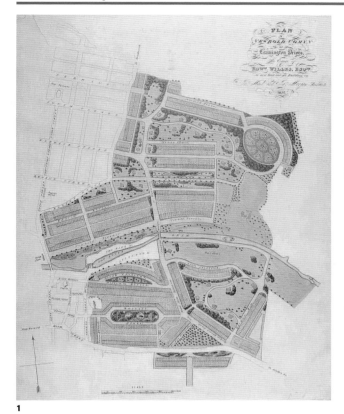

1. Plan, John Nash and James Morgan, 1827. WCRO

2. Newbold Terrace and Jephson Gardens from All Saint's Church tower. WCRO (1932)

3. Newbold Street. Brown. FL (2011)

Calverley Park and Plain

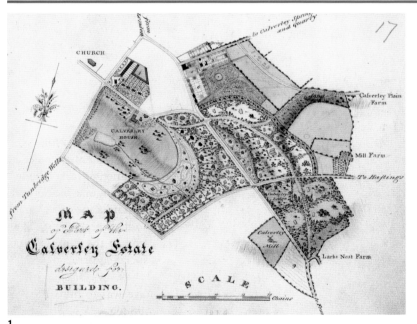

T. H. CLARKE, del.   B. & W. sc.

1. Plan, Decimus Burton, 1828. TW

2. Victoria Gate. DSTW (1832)

3. Calverley Promenade. CNG

4. Calverley Promenade. Murrain. PM

5. Park and villas. DSTW (1832)

1

2

3

4

architect Decimus Burton (1800–1881) as a middle-class village of detached and semidetached houses separated by hedgerows for privacy but with "open space in front" to "accommodate pleasure walks and command views of the distant hills."[26]

While Nash's Regent's Development was aristocratic in its spaciousness, Calverley Park, promoted by John Ward (1770–1855), a London merchant, was more modest, calling for twenty-four villas arranged along a 26-acre semicircular park to minimize views from one to the other while all sharing the distant scene of the valley below. Principally entered through Victoria Gate, a triumphal arch set between two lodges, the villa park was closed to outsiders until 1840, after which the public was freely admitted. The focal point of the plan was the Gothic-style Holy Trinity Church (1827–29) designed by Burton as a separate undertaking. Burton linked the park to the church with a "Parade" lined by semidetached villas. The development was notable for providing more than just villas. A crescent of shops, designed to recall the covered walks of the Parade at Tunbridge Wells, and an inn and a market hall were built, as well as artisans' houses, all in support of the establishment of a self-contained community.

By midcentury, the rapid expansion of efficient rail service made the countryside accessible to affluent commuters, typically middle-class businessmen and professionals anxious to reside away from overcrowded, smoke-filled, disease-breeding cities. Victoria Park, in Manchester, and Rock Park and Prince's Park, in Liverpool, are among the most significant early planned garden suburbs specifically geared to the requirements of daily commuters. In 1836–37, the Victoria Park Company was established on 140 acres two miles south of the center of Manchester. The prospectus promoted the site as entirely free of "manufacturers and their disagreeable effects."[27] Richard Lane (1795–1880), a prominent local architect and a founding member of the development company, drew up a scheme of 220 lots to be developed as **Victoria Park** with detached and semidetached residences mostly in a stripped version of Tudor Gothic. The plan also called for dedicated green spaces. A system of curving roads led from guarded entrance gates and lodges. Nine houses were built at the time the park opened in 1837; nineteen were completed by 1839, but only eight of these were occupied, leading to the development company's virtual collapse in 1842. Three years

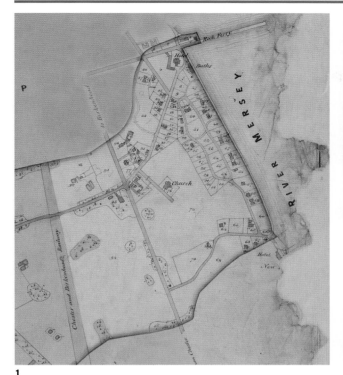

1

2

3

4

1. Tithe map. CRO (1844)

2. Road to the ferry. WAS

3. Houses seen from the River Mersey. Scales. LS (2011)

4. Rock Park Road. Benkid. WC (2009)

later a trust was formed to preserve the development, allowing for future villas and terraces, which continued to be built there until the 1880s.

Though Victoria Park was a distinctly upper-middle-class enclave, it was developed by high-minded citizens, including calico printer Richard Cobden (1804–1865), who was one of the reformers behind the Anti-Corn Law League. However, in most respects the development did not seek to overthrow the trappings of the aristocracy—but instead adapted the house and estate design of the landed gentry to the needs of the commuting bourgeoisie. In fact, as Robert Fishman points out, "The designation 'Park' referred unmistakably to the country estates of the aristocracy" and "in case the point was missed, the whole development was surrounded by walls similar to those which ringed a country estate and could be entered only via a gatehouse," an essential contradiction that "is not surprising if one considers that suburbia was not 'a retreat from urban society and its problems' [as Cobden had written] but a new way of expressing dominance within that society. Suburbia proved to be the perfect setting in which the older symbolism of aristocratic power

could be appropriated by the middle classes." Fishman also points out a "crucial ambiguity in the . . . plan": the "conflict between the self-sufficiency of each house and the environment of the whole." While the overall plan anticipated a "relatively open design, with the lawns and gardens of each house contributing to a unified effect," the homeowners argued for, and were granted permission to build, walls along their properties.[28]

The **Rock Park Estate** (1837), a gated community connected by ferry to Liverpool, was intended principally as a summer resort.[29] As planned by Jonathan Bennison (n.d.), a surveyor, Rock Park, consisting of detached and semidetached houses, allowed for "no trade or business 'other than the learned professions' to be carried on."[30] The writer Nathaniel Hawthorne, who lived there for three years while serving as American consul in Liverpool, delighted in Rock Park's "new and neat residences for city people . . . springing up with fine names—Eldon Terrace, Rose Cottage, Belvoir Villa." Hawthorne was impressed with the privacy that came from the existence of a "small Gothic structure of stone" at each entrance staffed by attendants who barred the way to all who were "ragged or ill-looking," collecting

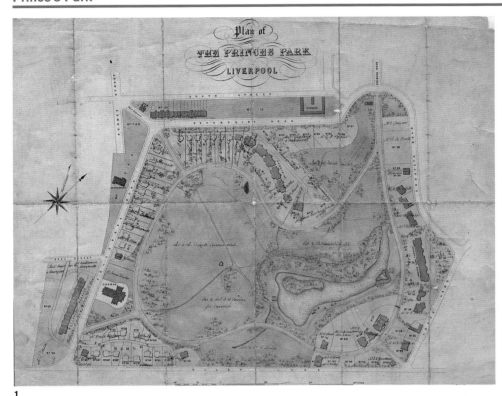

1. Plan, Joseph Paxton and James Pennethorne. LRO (1857)

2. Aerial view. GE (2007)

3. Aerial view. LRO (1921)

4. Villa on the north side of the park. Scales. LS (2012)

tolls from nonresidents and thereby virtually eliminating "all unnecessary passage of carriages."[31]

Prince's Park (1842), Liverpool, the work of Joseph Paxton (1803–1865) and James Pennethorne (1801–1871), was developed by iron merchant and philanthropist Richard Vaughan Yates (1785–1856) on 97 acres of meadow and farmland about a mile and a half from the city center.[32] The plan for Prince's Park, Paxton's first venture in town design, devoted about 40 acres to public open space, with the rest given over to a combination of terrace rows and, lining a serpentine road, single villas backing up to the lake and wooded landscape. According to Paxton's biographer, Kate Colquhoun, his involvement in the project proved to be a "marketing coup" for the developer. Echoing the premise of London's Regent's Development, Prince's Park provided "exclusive housing built around the edges of the park on individual plots sold for profit. While the land plots sold far slower than

Yates had expected, and most of the proposed terraces were never built, the project enabled Paxton to try out ideas he had been developing for years, in particular the making of a clear distinction between vehicular and pedestrian traffic, the inclusion of water in the overall plan, the landscaping of open meadow, and the juxtaposition between private and open space, wide views and winding paths. Prince's Park was the prototype of all his future park design."[33]

The idea of the planned suburban villa park was carried to even more elaborate scale at **Birkenhead Park** (1843–47), Liverpool, where marshland was transformed into a picturesque public pleasure ground surrounded by villas and terrace houses that, as at Prince's Park, were intended to pay for the public improvement.[34] Laid out by Joseph Paxton for a commission chaired by Sir William Jackson (1805–1876), Birkenhead Park was located across the Mersey River from Liverpool, to which it was

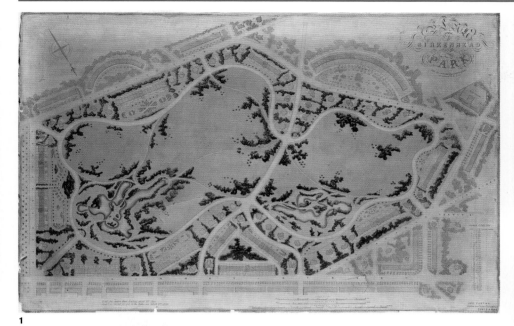

accessible by ferry. Jackson and a few colleagues had assembled the land at their own expense, which they then sold back to the town. In the course of shaping the 185-acre development, lakes were dug and the excavated earth used to create artificial hills. Paxton's plan called for 60 acres devoted to a combination of villas and terraces, "ingeniously arranged," as Nikolaus Pevsner wrote, "so as almost everywhere to avoid rigid straight rows—an interesting development of Nash's Regent's Park."[35] The lots came with deed restrictions governing the development and maintenance of the property and the selection of building materials. The park was bisected by only one road and many pedestrian paths were tunneled under it.

The project's long-term gestation led to a coarsening of the initial intentions, with only sixty villas built and no terraces, but in its initial stage it was greeted by the *Edinburgh Journal* as "one of the greatest wonders of the age."[36] Later, Frederick Law Olmsted (1822–1903), who visited Birkenhead Park in 1850 and would remember what he saw when he designed Central Park with Calvert Vaux (1824–1895) in 1858, would say that "in democratic America there was nothing to be thought of as comparable with this People's Garden."[37]

In 1852 the sixth Duke of Devonshire commissioned Paxton, his head gardener for more than a decade and a close friend, to lay out a villa park on 100 acres in the largely undeveloped spa town of Buxton, Derbyshire.[38] Similar to but smaller in scale than Birkenhead Park, **Buxton Park** featured serpentine drives and an oval park surrounded by detached houses on unusually large plots. In addition to forty-seven villas, Paxton's plan also called for a pair of semidetached houses and three terrace groups. The park, with its carriage drives, public walks, and cricket ground, was the only element of the scheme to be realized, the residential component most likely being too ambitious for the still sleepy town. As the 2007 Buxton Conservation Area report states, "It is likely that the original scheme was simply not economically feasible in the 1850s. The number of permanent residents with money to spare to afford to develop such enormous plots would have been small, particularly bearing in mind that it would be a further decade before the railway reached Buxton, bringing the town within a relatively comfortable and fast journey to Manchester and other large cites."[39] Significant residential development at Buxton did not begin until the mid-1870s, a decade after Paxton's death.

Somerleyton (1844), about twenty miles southeast of Norwich, in many ways a reiteration of Blaise Hamlet, designed by the sculptor and occasional architect John Thomas (1813–1862) for the builder and civil engineer Samuel Morton Peto (1809–1889), has been

1. Plan, Joseph Paxton, 1844. BRL

2. Aerial view. GE (2007)

3. Boathouse. Scales. LS (2012)

4. Gatehouse. Scales. LS (2012)

5. Entrance. Scales. LS (2012)

6. Ashville Road. Garvin. AG (2008)

1. Plan, Joseph Paxton, 1852. BUX

2. Aerial view of park and houses. BUX (1935)

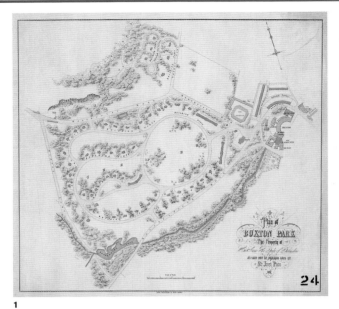

1

2

1

2

3

1. Cottages facing the green. CRS

2. Cottage. Felix. FL (2010)

3. Aerial view. GE (2006)

described by Nikolaus Pevsner as "a weird village" with a square green, with its pump and school building faced by twenty-eight cottages intended for workers on the estate, and "houses . . . of brick or sham timber-framing, of a great variety of shapes, and thatched."[40] While Blaise Hamlet and Somerleyton are set in the deep country, **Holly Village** (1865) adapts their example to a distinctly suburban location just a few miles from Central London, where Baroness Burdett-Coutts (1814–1906), heir to a banking fortune and a generous philanthropist, lived at Holly Lodge, her Highgate estate.[41] Designed by Henry Darbishire (1839–1908), the baroness's favorite architect, Holly Village, located on the southern edge of Holly Lodge, consisted of eight elaborately detailed yellow-brick detached and semidetached Gothic-style houses and a gatehouse, grouped around a green. The houses were originally intended for estate workers, but that plan was soon abandoned and they were let. In 1907, when Hampstead Garden Suburb (see p. 350) was taking shape, Charles G. Harper drew attention to Holly Village as, "on a small scale, the

'Garden suburb' of its age," urging "those who would see, in a manner, what the 'Garden suburb' at Golder's Green will be, on a larger scale," to visit it.[42]

In response to an extreme shortage of faculty housing at Oxford, three garden suburbs in miniature, Park Town, Walton Manor, and Norham Manor, were developed by a consortium formed in 1853.[43] The developments, extending the town into farmlands owned by St. John's College, took place over time, with S. L. Seckham (1827–1900) hired to plan and design the first new community, **Park Town** (1853), on a long, narrow nine-acre site surrounded by open fields owned by the college. Though the late-Georgian imagery and formality of both plan and architecture of Park Town may have seemed old fashioned to a community absorbed in the Gothic Revival, Seckham's ingenious combination of detached villas with formal gardens and terraced crescents of row-houses north and south of an elliptical central garden proved successful as a real estate development. It led to the college's next ventures in town development, **Walton Manor** (1860) and **Norham Manor** (1860), also designed

1

2

3

4

1. Aerial view. GE (1999)

2. Gatehouse. EH (1870–1900)

3. The green. Osley. GEO (2011)

4. The green. Gougeon. FL (2010)

by Seckham for farmland sites between Oxford and Park Town, where a more medievalizing effect was achieved. Walton Manor, a conventional gridiron subdivision interrupted by a triangular church green, was owned by St. John's College and hence all work was supervised by them to maintain general standards (the only fixed building regulations on record are a prohibition against roughcast stone or cement exteriors, and a ban on high walls between lots). Most of the accommodation consisted of detached villas on properties large enough to provide small gardens on both sides as well as front and rear. Servants' quarters and artisans' cottages, built in larger groups, were carefully separated both geographically and stylistically from the dons' houses.

Norham Manor was more interesting, with a plan that was to combine a variety of house types, including large detached villas screening the suburb from the main road and terraces running along the border of Park Town. Gently curved roads were to provide maximum visual privacy between houses. Without shops or a church, the suburb was to be strictly residential and very private. It is not clear whether credit for this plan should be given to Seckham or to William Wilkinson (1819–1901), who took over in 1860. Sadly, as realized, the scheme was considerably simpler, with one looping road along the periphery, a cross road within, and two access points but only one gate lodge.

By midcentury, planned garden suburbs, promising a way for families to enjoy the aesthetic ideal of country living while paying for it with the economic benefits that came from city business, were becoming commonplace, with many artistically notable examples, such as **St. Margaret's** (1854) in Twickenham, west of London near Richmond, which John Archer judges "on an aesthetic basis" as probably "the best example of *rus in urbe* in a suburban subdivision in Britain."[44] St. Margaret's, a project of the Conservative Land Society, was located on the Thames River, across which, a short distance away, lay Richmond and Richmond station, providing train service to Central London. The plan, whose designer is unknown, balanced development and open space, with small parks interwoven between the houses, the backs opening to small parks linked to each other by grade-separated passages similar to those at Prince's Park and Birkenhead Park, giving many residents, as Archer writes, access "to something much more elaborate than residents of almost any other contemporary suburban development: a fully developed landscape of leisure, extending some distance, including lawns, trees, plantings, a lake, and bridges . . . By intertwining the pleasure ground so thoroughly with dwellings and roadways, the plan turned the focus of the estate inward . . . stressing connections between the rear of the dwelling and the interior leisure domain," an idea that, as Archer has

Park Town

1. Plan, S. L. Seckham, 1853.
BODPT

2, 3. Park Town. RAMSA (2009)

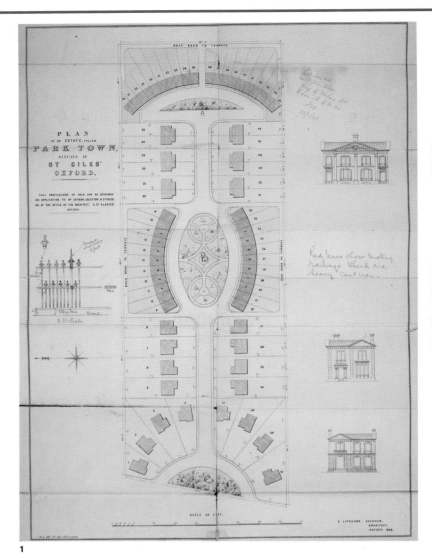

Walton Manor

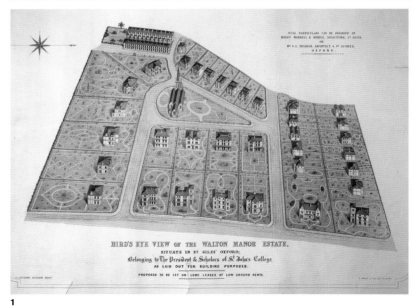

1

2

1. Bird's-eye view, S. L. Seckham,
c. 1854. SJC1

2. Revised scheme, S. L. Seckham,
1860. SJC2

observed, would not resurface until the development of Radburn, New Jersey, in 1929 (see p. 275).[45] Archer goes on to state:

> On a broader scale, the St. Margaret's plan also positioned the dwelling to serve as an instrument of negotiation among the ideals of urban and rural, and the interests of the bourgeois resident. If urbanity could be identified with the Richmond railway line running from left to right across the advertising poster, or located in Richmond itself, a mile's walk across the river, and the best of rural retirement was found in the gates and private landscape of the interior pleasure grounds, then the rows of dwellings and yards that separated the roadways from the pleasure grounds served as a kind of transition zone, in part protecting the parkland from corruption or encroachment, and in part affording the resident a place for decompression in passing from the urban world into the rural. The rows of dwellings also amounted to a lengthy linear filter around the enclosed interior parkland, isolating and protecting it in its aesthetic perfection from contact with the material corruptions of the world beyond, just as it protected the residents themselves in their pursuit of retirement, leisure, and recreation from contact with the mundane activities in surrounding streets and the world beyond. In other words the dwelling was not only an apparatus in its own right that articulated certain dimensions of the bourgeois self, but it also became an intermediary, transitional apparatus for negotiating the passage of that self back and forth between the realms of urbs and rus. Still, the realm of rus remained most distinctly oppositional to that of urbs. Instead of wedding each to the other, the apparatus of the subdivision was at least as effective at demarcating each from the other.[46]

With **Bedford Park** (1875) the planned garden village comes into its full maturity, "a self-contained residential unit with its own activities, social, cultural and religious, as expressed in its public buildings," as T. Affleck Greeves has written.[47] No designer's name is attached to the plan, although Jonathan T. Carr (1875–1915), Bedford Park's developer, or his architect William Street-Wilson (1856–1928) may have been its author. Carr was a cloth merchant and land speculator who in 1875 bought 24 acres of what had been part of a large estate belonging to his father-in-law. The property included Bedford House (1793), two additional eighteenth-century houses, and an arboretum. According to Andrew Saint, Carr was "a risk-taker, haphazard about business and architectural detail . . . but . . . also a social idealist who hoped and in part managed to create an egalitarian, secular, middle-class community with what we would now call 'leisure facilities'—club, pub, tennis courts, and art school, as well as the inevitable church."[48] Although Bedford Park enjoys

Norham Manor

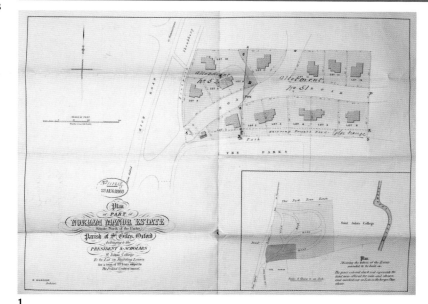

1

2

3

4

1. Plan, William Wilkinson, 1860. SJC3

2. Bird's-eye view. BOD1 (1860)

3, 4. Typical streets. RAMSA (2009)

1. Bird's-eye view. CLS (1854)

2. Plan from sale catalogue, 1854. RLS

3. Aerial view. GE (2010)

4. St. Peter's Road. Hamilton. FL (2012)

5. The Avenue. RLS

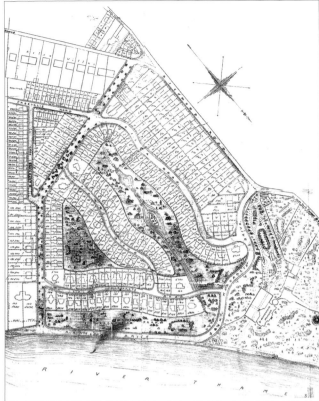

a reputation as a path-breaking garden suburb, Mark Girouard argues that there "is no evidence" that Carr set out with such high ambitions: "He certainly envisaged an estate of houses of good architectural quality for middle-class people of modest means." But had he had more in mind at the outset, "it seems unlikely that he would have called it Bedford Park, for 'Park' was a popular suffix for suburban developments and had genteel rather than progressive connotations."[49] Carr promoted the development as particularly suited to artists and aesthetes; he emphasized the architecture of the public buildings and houses as part of his marketing campaign and, as Saint points out, he innovated the practice of commissioning houses for specific sites as part of an overall strategy

that included tree preservation. Bedford Park, as Bridget Cherry has written, "was the first example where the relaxed, informal mood of a market town or village was adopted for a completely speculatively built suburb."[50]

The powerful impact of Bedford Park's plan is something of an enigma. The plan is simplicity itself, and seems almost inevitable, not "composed." A network of streets emanates from Acton Green and the Turnham Green railroad station, which together serve to focus the village where three main roads converge. Minor roads such as Queen Anne's Gardens, as well as those fringing the green, follow a more complex trajectory as they weave through trees of the former estate, creating angled intersections and T-junctions. These enhance the picturesque effect of the development, as does the design of the houses with their variegated rooflines, abundant chimneys, and white-painted bay windows.

Not every historian is convinced that Bedford Park deserves serious consideration as a garden suburb. For example, Walter Creese argued that the long and narrow blocks of the plan disqualify it from the garden suburb category. But Creese acknowledged that the village's wide streets—the principal streets were 60 feet wide; lesser streets were 40 feet wide—and the generous 15- to 20-foot setbacks of the houses from them "represented the beginning of the essentially modern and middle-class search for some effective compromise between street and home, dynamic and static, public and private, big scale and little elements in the suburban picture, in a delayed and removed reaction to the larger problems of the bigger city." Most of all, what makes Bedford Park important, Creese pointed out, is not the plan but the relationship between the placement of the houses in their narrow lots, the quality of their design, and their relationship to each other. Taken together, they transformed the "character of the street itself, which represents a cultural break" with the dense pattern of the typical English town without losing the sense of the street as a contained space as did Olmsted's plan for Riverside (see p. 122). For Creese, Bedford Park's plan and landscaping combined to produce a "revolutionary consciousness of space brought alive by light filtering through the trees."[51]

The Regent's Development, relying on a variety of compositional and stylistic tropes, was the first to present a wholly convincing picture of urban evolution from city to country. But Bedford Park was the first to present a new residential village as a development intended to evoke the preindustrial Old English village, with houses designed to look like seventeenth- and eighteenth-century brick-and-tile vernacular examples easily found in the nearby so-called home counties—Surrey in particular. Four years after the first houses began to be realized, a local observer wrote, "the whole place has the snug, warm look of having been inhabited for at least a century."[52] As Creese wisely observed, Bedford Park expressed "the English dual requirement, the seeking of new images through the restoration of old values," a hallmark of all the suburban developments that preceded it and almost all that would follow.[53]

After a false start, when E. W. Godwin (1833–1886) prepared schemes for some model houses, Carr consulted Maurice B. Adams (1849–1933), editor of the *Building News,* before asking Richard Norman Shaw (1831–1912) to take over as architect. As Mark Girouard writes, Shaw "created the architectural character of Bedford Park, one which delighted and surprised the visitors who, emerging from Turnham Green station, felt themselves to be in a village or small country town where nothing had happened for at least a hundred years. In fact none of the houses bore more than a superficial resemblance to anything built in the 17th or 18th centuries; their apparent artlessness concealed a great deal of sophistication."[54]

Shaw served as estate architect until 1880 and then continued as design consultant until 1886. Godwin, Adams, Shaw, and E. J. May (1853–1941), whom Shaw recommended as his successor, designed individual houses and a few short terraces. They also developed about thirty prototype designs for detached and semidetached houses which were arrayed across the village in a way that ensured each street a measure of individuality. But, as Girouard emphasizes, "the general effect" was "unified" because May, Adams, and William Street-Wilson, who adopted some of Godwin's designs, "although capable designers with an individuality of their own, were all strongly under the influence of Norman Shaw."[55]

Carr began with 24 acres, but by January 1880 he controlled 100. By 1883, 333 houses had been built; the number would rise to 400 by decade's end. The clubhouse opened in May 1879; the church of St. Michael and All Angels was consecrated in 1880; the Tabard Inn, a freestyle interpretation in what may be described as the Tudorbethan manner, provided dining and overnight accommodation and was also realized in 1880; and the Chiswick School of Art, designed by Adams, was completed in 1881, by which time Bedford Park, with over twenty studios and its club and school of art, had become an artists' haven, even though the majority of those living in the 490 houses on the 113 acres eventually assembled were more conventionally employed.

Bedford Park's greatest contribution to the evolution of the garden suburb may not lie in its planning or its architecture, but in the way the developer promoted the project. Although much of what makes Bedford Park important had already been adopted by the American developers of Riverside, Andrew Saint points out that for the English, Bedford Park was a breakthrough: "The church, the club, the inn, the stores and the tennis court were no longer erected by a squire to admonish the tenants of their grateful duties and loyalties, but built by a 'promoter' to service the leisure and the options of an independent community. Just like the poster of advertisement devised for the station on the new line out to Turnham Green, these facilities 'sold' Bedford Park." Carr catered to a rising category of the middle class by building houses that were for the most part "cheap, unornamented and small," but also "decidedly charming," houses "where the cultured classes, leisured but without large income or many servants, could dwell in mutual daily intercourse, unembarrassed by the excesses of villadom."[56]

Bedford Park had a significant impact on garden suburb and garden city planning in England, the United States, and Europe. Raymond Unwin (1863–1940) surely knew of it when he began his work on New Earswick (see p. 228). Hermann Muthesius (1861–1927), the German architect attached to his country's embassy in London in order to study English domestic architecture, noting that "no American passing through London could miss seeing" it, went on to assess Bedford Park's importance in his pioneering survey, *Das englische Haus* (1904):

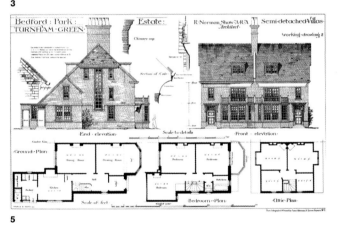

1. Plan, 1877. CLLC (c. 1932)

2. Bath Road. Berry F. Berry, artist. CLLC (1882)

3. Tower House and Queen Anne's Grove. S. N. Trautschold, artist. CLLC (1882)

4. House designs, Richard Norman Shaw, 1877. BN77

5. Plans for semidetached villas, Richard Norman Shaw, 1877. BN77

The success of the experiment exceeded all expectations. The ground was parceled out in such a way as to preserve as many as possible of the fine old trees and there was no reluctance to leave old trees standing at the roadside or to carry the pavement round them. Streets were pleasantly winding and care was taken to see that the houses faced in the best possible direction—south-east to south—and every house had its small or not so small garden shaped as agreeably as possible. Most of the houses were detached, a few were semi-detached and there were also a few terraced houses, for the planners were aware that where extreme cheapness was required, this could only be achieved with terraced housing. A carefully calculated variety—which yet managed to avoid the trivial and the picturesque, into which such attempts may easily degenerate—ensured that even the terraced houses made a pleasant impression . . . The estate was a complete revelation to the contemporary world. These streets with their cheerful little houses nestling amid the greenery seemed to bespeak quiet comfort and a refreshing joie-de-vivre. Such a thing had never been dreamt of before.[57]

In the last analysis, as Ian Fletcher has written, "What was admired about Bedford Park was primarily the country quality, rather than the complex of buildings; not so much its sense of community expressed in its co-operative stores and clubhouse, as its insinuation into the landscape . . . Bedford Park was rus in urbe."[58]

Shaftesbury Park Estate (1872–77), Battersea, London, is worth consideration as a complement to Bedford Park.[59] Its street plan by J. G. W. Buckle (d. 1921) is conventional, providing only one public open space, a central green that was built over in 1877 when the

Bedford Park

6

8

7

9

10

11

6. Bath Road, showing Tabard Inn on right. Lemere. EH (1881)

7. Bath Road stores. Smith. RIBAP (1961)

8. Bedford Road. Lemere. EH (1881)

9. Bedford Road. RAMSA (1977)

10. The Avenue. Cadman. FL (2008)

11. Tabard Inn. Cadman. FL (2008)

Shaftesbury Park Estate

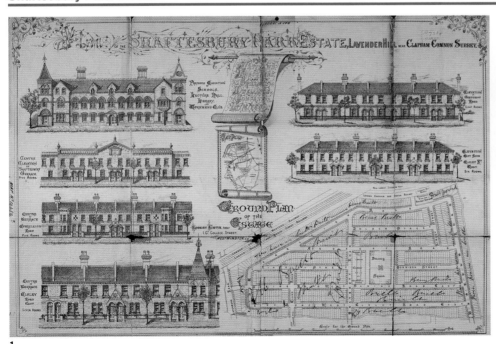

1

2

1. Plan and elevations, Robert Austin, 1872–77. LMA

2. Eland and Ellsley Roads. Kereshun. AK (2011)

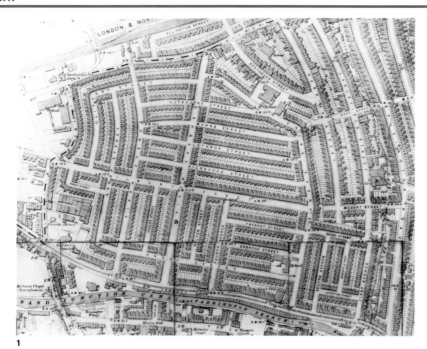

1. Ordnance Survey map. WAC (1894)

2. Fifth Avenue and Ilbert Street. EH (1997)

3. Barfett Street. WAC (1910)

4. Queen's Park Hall, Rowland Plumbe, c. 1880. WAC (c. 1911)

5. Kilburn Lane. Kereshun. AK (2011)

developers had financial problems. Conventional, also, is the architecture of the small terraced houses designed by Robert Austin (n.d.) on a 40-acre site. But the estate is significant as a pioneer philanthropic enterprise built for working-class families by the Artisans', Labourers' and General Dwellings Company, and as the progenitor of its complement, **Queen's Park** (1874–83), Paddington, London, developed by the same sponsors who intended "to provide the labouring man with an increase of the comforts and convenience of life whilst providing full compensation for the capitalist."[60] Located on 80 acres purchased from All Souls College, Oxford, Queen's Park, designed initially by Buckle and Austin, with later work by architect Rowland Plumbe (1838–1919), included more than 2,000 terraced houses deployed in long rows, hugging straight and gently curving streets. In addition to the yellow- and redbrick two-story houses, designed in "a minimum Gothic" style, according to Bridget Cherry, the development also included a meeting hall and Methodist church designed by Plumbe in the early 1880s.[61] While the layout at Queen's Park "seems more

rigid than at Shaftesbury Park," as John Nelson Tarn has written, both are nonetheless "rather more spacious than was usual at that time and the little front gardens, with pollarded trees set in the pavement in front of them, are without parallel in this kind of housing before the advent of the garden suburb."[62]

Noel Park (1883–1907), Wood Green, Hornsey, also undertaken by the Artisans', Labourers' and General Dwellings Company, is another significant example of a workers' development conceived along garden suburb lines.[63] A 100-acre estate planned with a grid of tree-lined streets laid out by Plumbe, Noel Park anticipates the charm of many workers' villages that were to follow, yet Plumbe provided a variety of house types which, according to Tarn, "had the double advantage of providing a choice for tenants and also a chance for architectural diversity."[64] The estate now forms a gateway to the London County Council's White Hart Lane Estate (see p. 382), revealing the dramatic contrast in town planning and house design that took place in a quarter century.

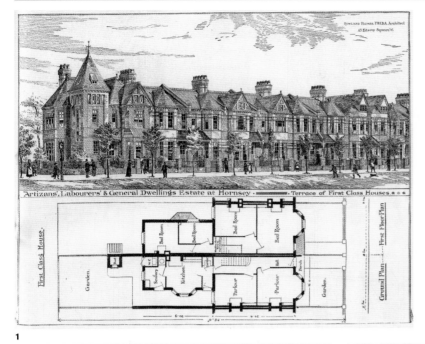

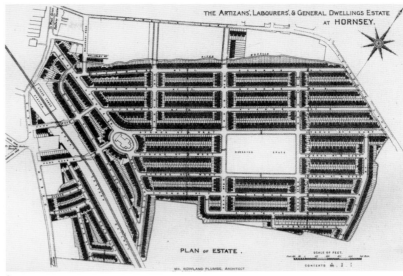

A RARE FRENCH EXAMPLE

Arguably, and surprisingly, as Theodore Turak has written, "the idea of a semi-self-sufficient, politically independent regulated community associated with a large city probably originated with the French," when in 1833 the banker Jacques Laffitte (1767–1844) sold off lots in the park of his château (1630–51) to create the *colonie paysagère* (landscaped colony) that in 1882 was named Maisons-Laffitte.[65] But the decision to adapt his land subdivision layout to the plan of the original Baroque garden did not permit the "romantic ambience" of the English estate models Laffitte probably had in mind, so the distinction of France's first fully considered garden village—and indeed, despite claims on behalf of Olmsted's Riverside, possibly the world's first—probably falls to **Le Vésinet** (1858).[66]

Located ten miles west of the Gare St. Lazare, Le Vésinet was developed to take advantage of newly instituted railroad service to Paris, making the location a twenty-six-minute trip from the city and setting the stage for the development of the suburb by the duc de Morny (1811–1865), Emperor Napoleon III's illegitimate half-brother. Le Vésinet was named after the forest in which it was developed—a royal hunting ground in the ancien régime that had been divided up during the Revolution. With the decision under the Second Empire to return confiscated land to private ownership, the duc de Morny was able to assemble 1,077 acres of land before turning over the management of the project to Alphonse Pallu (1808–1880), a successful, progressive businessman who took control in 1856 and began selling lots in 1858. By 1867, Le Vésinet was an established fact on the Parisian scene. According to a publication from that year, Pallu and his collaborators, "through a metamorphosis . . . created a great and beautiful park . . . with rivers, cascades and the rest. But the park is not a promenade. Under its great trees it had been erected with the rapidity of American cities, a new city, a city composed of lovely country houses. These chalets, these villas, these cottages belong to people who range from the very fashionable to simple bourgeoisie, unpretentious clerks, and artisans who come to pass the

1. Terrace of First Class Houses, Rowland Plumbe, 1883. TB83

2. Plan, Rowland Plumbe, 1883. TB83

3. Gladstone Avenue. Kereshun. AK (2011)

4. Moselle and Gladstone Avenues. Kereshun. AK (2011)

5. Aerial view looking down Farrant Avenue. Irid. WC (2009)

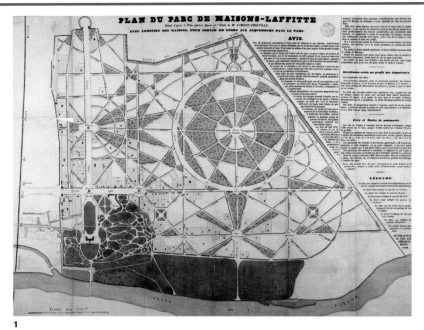

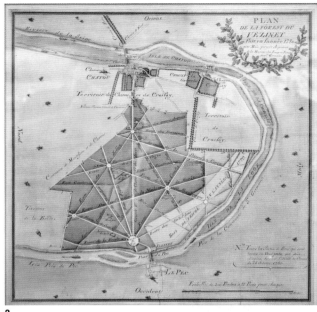

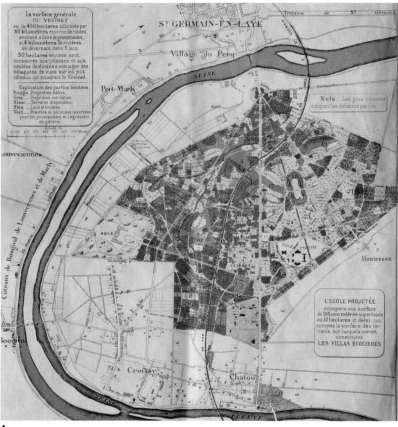

1. Maisons-Laffitte plan, 1843.
BHVP

2. Plan de la Forest du Vésinet,
1780. SHV

3. Bird's-eye view. SHV (1858)

4. General plan, Paul de Lavenne
and Pierre-Joseph Olive, 1858.
SHV (1876)

summer season. Many live there the year round. The terrain has been sold at low prices, with 'easy payment.'"[67] By 1875 Le Vésinet's population had reached 1,500.

Exhibiting a reformist's zeal, Pallu guided the planning, with regulations controlling public and private property development and keeping ownership of utilities under the control of his company. Pallu retained landscape architect Paul de Lavenne, the comte de Choulot (1794–1864), who, assisted by architect Pierre-Joseph Olive (1817–1899), laid out the streets and parks. Choulot, a Legitimist, had spent time in exile in England, where he became familiar with important landscapes, including Hyde Park and its serpentine lake, which was used as the basis for Le Vésinet's series of small ponds connected by meandering streams and bordered by public paths threaded through the property to form the back edges of many house lots. To keep the water well-flushed, a steam engine was constructed at Croissy to pump water from the Seine. Because the local soil was very porous, the lake and stream beds were concretized and then made to seem natural through the extensive and artful use of rocks and plants.

Choulot retained the straight paths of the old hunting preserve, developing some as boulevards, such as the principal artery, Boulevard Carnot, which linked the two commercial areas, the *rond-point* of Le Pecq in the northwest with the gridded town center at the railroad station. He then overlaid the forest's axial paths with a lacy network of curving streets, replacing most of the regular rows of trees with naturalistic arrangements along curving roads in the English manner.

Long greenswards, which Choulot called *coulées,* literally "paths," aerated the plan, enhancing the general sense of openness that is the development's hallmark. Facing the *coulées* and streamside lanes, walls were restricted to slightly more than three feet in height, although high walls or fences were permitted elsewhere on most properties. To further enhance the sense of countryside, houses facing the *"coulées, pelouses, tapis verts, lacs et rivières"* had to be set back at least 33 feet from the property lines.[68] The overall effect of the naturalistic design is nothing short of magical. Le Vésinet is perhaps the most beautiful garden suburb of all.

CHAPTER TWO

The Garden Suburb in America 1850–1940

From the early nineteenth century, suburban development was part and parcel of the growth of American cities, especially in the industrializing Northern states. For example, New York City's first suburb was the independent village of Brooklyn, across the East River, which was made accessible for daily commuters in 1814 when Robert Fulton inaugurated ferry service. As an island city, New York had limited land available for residential development catering to the middle class—the rich were housed along Fifth Avenue, the island's spine, farthest from the waterfront where the poor were forced to live side-by-side with industry. The commuter ferries, with many connecting to railroad lines, opened up the rural hinterlands on Long Island and in New Jersey.

By the 1880s, about 300,000 people commuted on a daily basis between New York and its suburbs, leading one observer, James Richardson, to write in *Scribner's Monthly* in 1874: "From a domestic point of view, New York . . . is a city of paradoxes. It is full of palatial dwellings and homeless people [boarders] . . . paying for unsocial subsistence a price that, under a wiser system, might give them every domestic comfort the heart could wish. Thousands who would live in the city could they find suitable homes here, and who would be worth millions to the city, are driven to the surrounding country to build up Jersey and all the regions round about; while no small proportion of those who must remain" find themselves "herded" into hotels and boardinghouses, "a manner of living which violates the very first requirements of the life we most affect, namely, individual privacy and family seclusion."[1]

Suburban living rapidly increased in popularity as a direct consequence of the economic depression that followed the Panic of 1873, with "the dullness of trade and scarcity of money" driving "thousands and tens of thousands into the adjacent country—Westchester County, Long Island, Staten Island, and New Jersey, where comparatively low rents prevailed . . . so that the continuous region from twenty to thirty miles around is little else than a vast dormitory of New York."[2] As a result of the Panic, many city houses went unrented as did rooms in hotels and boardinghouses. But the suburbs remained popular. While the rich could move to new houses farther uptown, or to elaborate apartments in the new French flats, by 1878 it was pretty much agreed, as the journalist Raymond Westbrook wrote in the *Atlantic Monthly*, that "the middle class are hardly expected to stay on the island at all." Already they were "spread out into the country by rail, [forming] vast settlements of ornamental cottages, while New York itself is given up to the rich and poor."[3]

Though the suburbs offered to those who could afford the cost of transportation and the time of travel involved an affordable and comfortable alternative to living on Manhattan Island, they seemed to many a badge of failure, a kind of retreat from the city's sophistication to a smaller-scaled, provincial urbanism such as one could find elsewhere in the country's interior but

Station Square, Forest Hills Gardens. RAMSA (2012)

that one did not associate with life in New York City. Social stigma aside, however, there was little choice for many middle-class people other than the grinding daily commute between the outer reaches of Brooklyn, the so-called Annexed District (the modern borough of the Bronx), Queens, and Staten Island, or towns in New Jersey and Westchester County, and New York's business district.[4] Other middle-class families chose to remain in New York even though their living conditions were poorer than they might be in the suburbs. *Harper's New Monthly* pointed out in 1882: "Myriads of inmates of the squalid, distressing tenement-houses, in which morality was as impossible as happiness, would not give them up, despite their horrors, for clean, orderly, wholesome habitations in the suburbs, could they be transported there and back free of charge. They are in some unaccountable way terribly in love with their own wretchedness."[5] But to many, the suburbs did offer better middle-class living conditions. Westbrook argued that "in everything except proximity to their business, —and there is not so much difference even here, . . . the suburban people, in their spacious houses, designed often by the best professional skill, and affording in their interiors light for works of art and room for the varied activities of a refined life, have the best of it."[6]

THE GARDEN ENCLAVE

Despite deep connections to English practice, the garden suburb reached its full flowering first in the United States during the second half of the nineteenth century, constituting two distinct typologies: garden villages and garden enclaves. Garden villages are independent entities connected to the city by railroad, streetcar, or automobile, with community attributes such as shops and civic buildings in addition to their residential components. The plan of the garden enclave, often called the residence park when it is organized along naturalistic lines and the private place when it is within the city, has strong antecedents in the pattern of London residential squares under the control of single property owners, such as the Paragon and Holly Village, to name but a few discussed in the first chapter of this book. Whether residence park or private place, the character of the garden enclave is almost always the result of coordinated land-use planning—controlling setbacks, landscape, and the like—in order to stand apart from its immediate surroundings. Conceived as tranquil, identifiable, well-ordered physical entities, garden enclaves consist almost exclusively of house sites.

Llewellyn Park (1853), New Jersey, is the preeminent examplar of the American garden enclave, located about twelve miles west of Manhattan Island, constituting in most ways the template for the type that would proliferate for the next seventy-five years.[7] As a residence park, it was not a true village but a gated development of houses in a naturalistic setting. Llewellyn Park can be seen as part of nineteenth-century America's obsession with nature. But it more particularly reflected a reaction on the part of the rising upper middle class against what they perceived as the increased incivility of urban life, attributed by Alexis de Tocqueville in his two-volume book *Democracy in America* to the "individualism . . . that disposes each citizen to isolate himself from the mass of those like him and to withdraw to one side with his family and his friends, so that after having thus created a little society for his own use, he willingly abandons society at large to itself."[8] This seemingly unchecked individualism wrecked deplorable conditions on the public space of the city, its streets, and common grounds. With little sense of individual responsibility for the upkeep of public space or for traditional standards of behavior or decorum in them, cities, traditionally emblems of civilized behavior, threatened to degenerate into settings for mayhem.

Llewellyn Park was founded by pharmaceutical magnate Llewellyn S. Haskell (1815–1872). Unlike the individualistic anti-urbanists whom Tocqueville described, Haskell was not against cities but intent on their reform: for example, he was an ardent supporter of the proposal to create Central Park. At the same time, he preferred to live outside the city. As a consequence of his ambivalence, Haskell's motivations in establishing Llewellyn Park seem somewhat conflicted. His new residence park was to be a refuge from but not a rejection of city life for a wide group of like-minded intellectuals and friends, including Washington Irving, William Cullen Bryant, and the architect Alexander Jackson Davis (1803–1892).

Ironically, though Haskell treasured the ideal of rural life, living in the country had not been a notable success for him. In fact he abandoned his country estate in Belleville, New Jersey, on the swampy Passaic River, after concluding that it was at least partly to blame for the deaths of four of his five sons and his own bouts with rheumatism. The Belleville estate included a villa designed by Davis featuring a salon, dining room, and parlor labeled, respectively, mind, body, and soul. Haskell believed better air was to be found at higher ground nearby on Orange Mountain, where, on February 20, 1853, he bought a 21.5-acre farm near a mineral spring that had been a popular resort destination in the 1820s, commissioning Davis to transform the existing house into a villa.

By the 1840s Orange was already on its way to becoming a haven for monied commuters, a neighborhood of estates made more village-like as a result of the decision of Matthias Ogden Halsted (1792–1866) to occupy only a portion of a 100-acre farm there, parceling off the remaining land to his city friends. At his own expense Halsted built a depot on the newly opened Morris and Essex Railroad that in turn agreed to have one inbound train in the morning and one outbound train in the evening stop there, making possible a relatively easy hour-long commute to and from New York via rail and ferry. It was approximately the same amount of time it took a rush-hour horse car to go from lower Manhattan

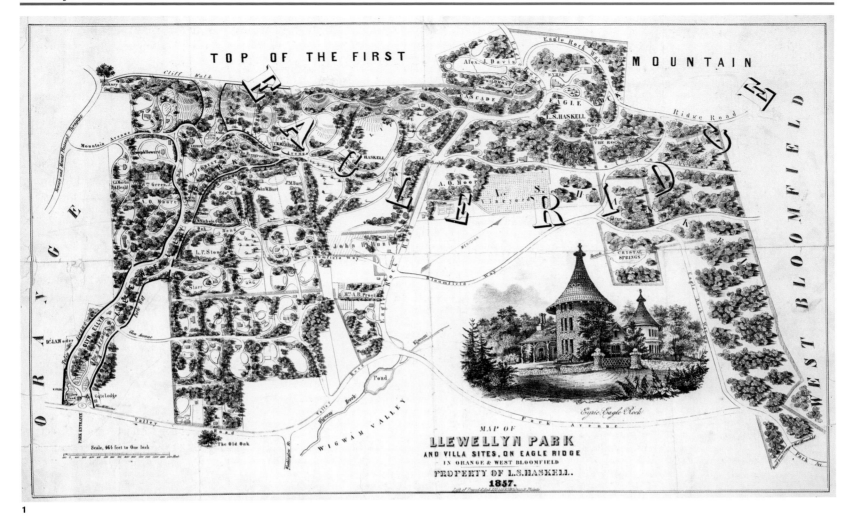

1

to the fashionable uptown residential neighborhood of Murray Hill.

But Haskell had more in mind than establishing his own country seat, and with other investors he assembled about 350 acres of land for which he conceived, probably on the advice of Davis, a gated residence park filled with "country homes for city people," ranging in size from grand villas down to modest cottages, thereby providing for a varied community of residents who included powerful business leaders, journalists, and clergymen.[9] Davis, who was a disciple of and sometime collaborator with Andrew Jackson Downing (1815–1852), was known for promoting the "American Style," also known as the Cottage Style—that is, houses sheathed in wide plank siding overlaid with wooden battens and sheltered by deep roof eaves supported by brackets.[10] Generous verandas, towers, and cupolas, all composed "naturalistically," completed the picturesque effect. Davis also had some experience with planned suburban development. With his former partner, Ithiel Town (1784–1844), he was responsible for four houses in New Haven's Hillhouse Avenue development (1828–29), including that of the developer, James Hillhouse (1754–1832).[11] Hillhouse Avenue—originally named Temple Avenue until the son of its developer moved there in 1830, twenty-eight years after his father conceived the real estate scheme—was

a quarter-mile-long parcel planned to accommodate houses set back 50 feet from the right-of-way on comparatively narrow lots that guaranteed a sense of closure along the street. With its "broad grass verges and long rows of trees," the much-admired Hillhouse Avenue became, according to Vincent Scully, "a kind of model for some of the finest suburbs and garden cities in the United States."[12] In addition to Haskell and Davis, two landscape gardeners, Eugene A. Baumann (1817–1869) and Howard Daniels (1815–1863), probably also contributed to Llewellyn Park's layout. Baumann, recently arrived from France, had a reputation as a designer of small suburban sites, and Daniels's submission to the 1858 competition for Central Park had received an honorable mention.

Set behind a barrier of evergreen plantings and fencing, Llewellyn Park seemed to a contemporary journalist as "if its residents had thrown up an abatis against an insurrection of visitors from the town."[13] The development included a 50-acre linear strip of common parkland known initially as Llewellyn Park but after about 1860 as the Ramble, which served as the community's spine. A picturesque ravine crisscrossed by paths and bridges, the Ramble contained a miniature waterfall and ornamental ponds. Two roads bounded it, Tulip Avenue and Park Way, the first use of the term that

1. Plan, 1857. MMA

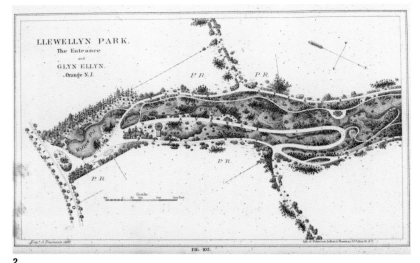

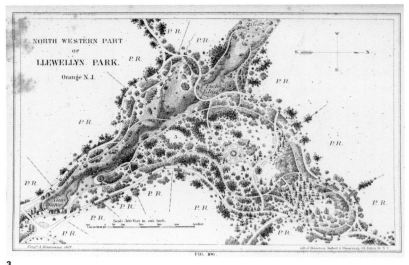

2

3

4

5

6

2. Plan, entrance and Glen Ellyn, 1856. CHG

3. Plan, northwestern section, 1856. CHG

4. Aerial view. GE (2006)

5. Entrance. NJIC (1857)

6. Llewellyn Haskell cottage, Andrew Jackson Downing, 1854. NJIC

7. View from Eagle Rock. NJIC

8. Drive through the Ramble. CRS

7

8

Frederick Law Olmsted would later adopt to describe a new kind of highway. Ten miles of curving streets encircled the Ramble and branched out to the house sites, laid out in a largely unmanicured landscape that flew in the face of conventional practice. By common consent, hedges rather than fences were used to demarcate property lines, a decision that Olmsted was to criticize in an 1869 letter to Edward Everett Hale: "The point I stand for is that no house is [a] fit place for a family that has not both public *& private outside apartments*. Consequently, I am bound to regard the fence as a sort of outer wall of the house. I think that the want of fences, of distinct family separation out of the house, is the real cause of the ill-success or want of great success of . . . Llewellyn

Park."[14] Ironically, the sometimes contradictory Olmsted would ban fences at Riverside (1869), his model suburban village (see p. 122). To preserve Llewellyn Park's pastoral character, covenants not only protected the park area but also stipulated that no house be built on less than one acre. Many sites were larger.

Haskell's interests in health and the spiritual life attracted like-minded residents. Soon the place became known as a haven for freethinkers, "famous," as an original resident, Edward D. Page, wrote, "for its long-haired men and short-haired women."[15] As early as 1857, the editors of *The Crayon*, the leading New York art magazine, recognized the unique nature of the enterprise, describing it as "the first development, so far as we know, of an idea which may mark a new era in Country Life and Landscape Gardening in this country." Deeming the location a "happy one," the editors praised the plan, writing that "this irregularity of form gives great variety of surface and feeling of size, and it furnishes secluded and quiet nooks and most pleasant surprises. Carefully preserving its natural attractions, the Landscape Gardener's Art developes [sic] others: what is artificial is made not only to harmonize with the rustic character of the design, but made with regard to permanence, impressing us as if here, at least, was one work to remain for our children. There are no shams to gratify mistaken economy and offend good taste; but, on the contrary, though simple and rustic, all is honest and pure."[16]

At Llewellyn Park, environmental considerations tended to trump architecture. Although some elaborate villas were built there in the early years, the development had a fair share of modest dwellings that would be replaced by elaborate versions in the years leading up to World War I. It was not architecture but landscape, or more particularly, nature, that remained paramount in most people's perception of Llewellyn Park. The balance between architecture and landscape was such that the *New York Times* repeated an account from the *Independent* documenting the visit to Llewellyn Park of Theodore Tilton, the well-known editor and Swedenborgian who compared the gated enclave to the "project of the ancient architects to carve Mount Athos into a statue of a king, holding a city in his right hand, and a basin of rivers in his left," transforming what had been "a rough, shaggy mountain side . . . into an enchanted ground, or fairy land."[17]

By 1860, despite reverses suffered in the Panic of 1857, Haskell owned 500 acres of land. The Civil War interrupted development, but by 1870 he had added another 250 acres, intended to provide sites for one hundred families, thirty of whom were already in residence elsewhere in the community. But the tastes of the post–Civil War bonanza economy era had evolved away from simple cottage styles to the mansarded grandeur of the French Second Empire, and even Davis succumbed to their shifting winds—the Mrs. Elwood Byerly house (1868) was one of his best efforts in the new manner. The depression of the 1870s slowed things to a near halt, but with the return of prosperity in the 1880s, large new houses began to go up. Haskell did not live to see this phase in Llewellyn Park's development, which in many ways contradicted his original vision; he was seriously injured in a railroad accident in 1865. An early casualty of the economic turmoil of the 1870s, he had already been forced to surrender much of his control by the time he died in 1872.

In 1855, at about the same time Haskell was at work on Llewellyn Park, architect Thomas Dixon (1819–1886) purchased 300 heavily wooded hilly acres four miles from the Baltimore city line with the intention of subdividing the property into a small number of relatively large house lots.[18] Connected by railroad to the city, the development, dubbed **Dixon's Hill**, was not gated but, like

9. Gatehouse. Garvin. AG (1975)

10, 11. Typical streets. RAMSA (2012)

Llewellyn Park, was a residence park with curving streets circling the hill, dividing the site into irregularly sized plots at various elevations. Development activity stalled during the Civil War, but by 1880 Dixon had built and sold thirty-five houses, designing most himself. With his partner Charles L. Carson (1847–1891) he also designed the subdivision's only nonresidential building, a Stick Style Presbyterian church (1878) on Thornbury Road.

In about 1875, David Nelson Skillings (1818–1880), a lumber dealer, subdivided his 25-acre estate in Winchester, Massachusetts, a suburban town eight miles northwest of Boston, into a residence park named **Rangeley**, retaining ownership of the land and building houses that he first leased to friends and relatives

Dixon's Hill

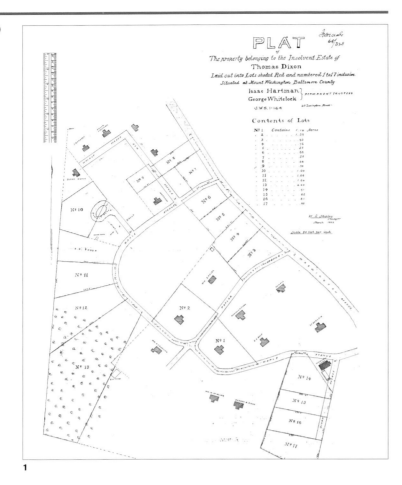

1

Rangeley

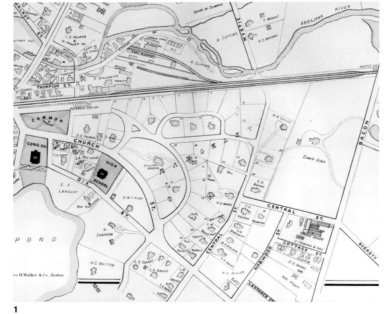

1

2

3

and later to hand-picked Boston businessmen and professionals.[19] Skillings enlisted Boston architect George Dutton Rand (1833–1910) to plan the neighborhood of winding roads and park-like open spaces that directly abutted the Winchester station of the Boston and Lowell Railroad. Rand designed most of Rangeley's stylistically eclectic houses as well as Rangeley Hall (1877), a Queen Anne Revival social center and kindergarten. His land plan called for contiguous backyards, undivided by fence or hedge, to act as a public park. According to architectural historian Maureen Meister, Skillings and Rand, in addition to being influenced by Llewellyn Park, would likely have considered Oak Bluffs (see p. 302) as a model as well as the mill village of South Manchester, Connecticut (see p. 798), near Hartford, where Rand had worked between 1861 and 1869, and which was also owned by a single entity, provided a community hall, and featured a naturalistic landscape.

Horace William Shaler Cleveland (1814–1900) was among the most skilled of the multitude of landscape architects, civil engineers, and local surveyors who contributed to the evolution of the garden enclave in the post–Civil War era. During the 1830s, Cleveland had prepared surveys of Illinois and other Western states for railroad companies and real estate speculators, using those connections to secure work when he moved from Boston to Chicago in 1869. In 1871 he was hired by William Robbins (1824–1889), a businessman who acquired his wealth in the California gold rush, to plan the **Robbins Park Addition** in Hinsdale, Illinois, sixteen miles west of Chicago on the Chicago, Burlington and Quincy Railroad. Robbins himself had developed the town of Hinsdale after purchasing 700 acres of vacant land during the previous decade and donating a right-of-way and depot to the railroad.[20] After building his own country house in 1864, Robbins began subdividing the property to create the town of Hinsdale, laying out a grid of streets, first north of the railroad tracks, then in 1866 expanding south of the railroad tracks with a 480-acre addition constituting, in effect, a suburban enclave for a barely realized town. His decision to abandon the gridiron plan in favor of a more naturalistic one of curving streets must have been influenced by Olmsted's Riverside while his choice of Cleveland as landscape architect may have stemmed from the designer's work at Highland Park (see p. 127). In laying out the Robbins Park Addition, Cleveland acknowledged Hinsdale's grid at its edges, positioning entrances at regular intervals. But toward the center, he allowed tree-lined roads, one of which featured a planted median, to follow the site's natural valleys, preserving the hills for houses. The lots ranged from one-half to five acres, and street frontages were between 30 and 300 feet, providing for an anticipated range of incomes.

In *A Few Hints on Landscape Gardening in the West* (1871), Cleveland described the rationale behind his design:

> *The adjacent portion of the town had previously been laid out in squares, but owing to the*

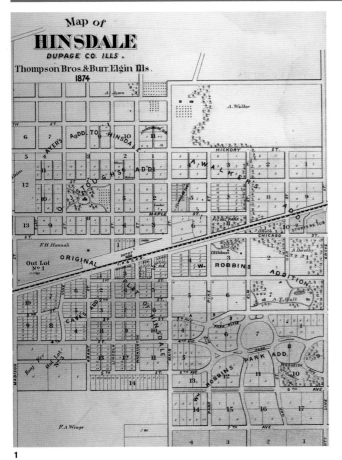

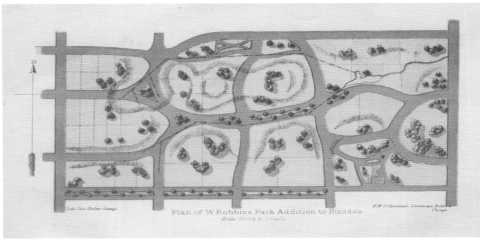

1. Map of Hinsdale showing Robbins Park Addition. HA (1874)

2. Plan, H. W. S. Cleveland, 1871. CHM

3. Elm and Fourth Streets. HHS

4. Fourth Street. Miller. HHS (2012)

5. Third Street. Miller. HHS (2012)

inequalities of surface of this tract, much of its beauty and convenience would have been sacrificed by continuing the streets in straight lines across it. It comprises a series of irregular and prettily shaped hills, divided by low wet sloughs. The course of these sloughs . . . [dictated] the course of the drains, which were constructed throughout the two principal branches, concentrating the drainage in a little ornamental pond. The principal roads were then constructed along the line of these drains, winding around the base of the hills or ascending their sides by easy grades to connect with other roads beyond the tract. By this arrangement the roads occupy the portions which are of least value for building sites, while as they wind around the hills they open a series of pretty views . . . The highest and pleasantest building sites are reserved in the lots, which all slope toward the roads, so that any lot may be drained directly into the roadside mains without crossing an adjoining lot.[21]

Robbins was apparently pleased with Cleveland's work, providing a written testimonial to his planner: "Everyone who sees" the Robbins Park Addition "says the plan suits the ground, and I am well pleased that I adopted your method instead of the rectangular plan I had previously used."[22]

The bonanza economy of the early 1870s led to a veritable explosion of suburban development, with Cleveland dominating the Midwest scene. In 1871, he planned the unrealized **South Park** on the steep, heavily

South Park

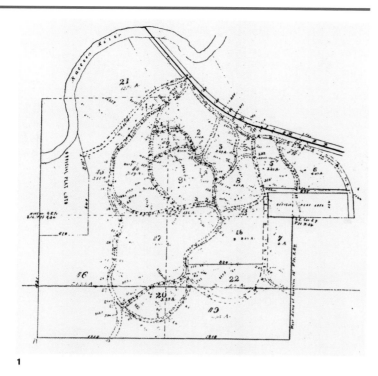

1

Brookside and Oak Hill

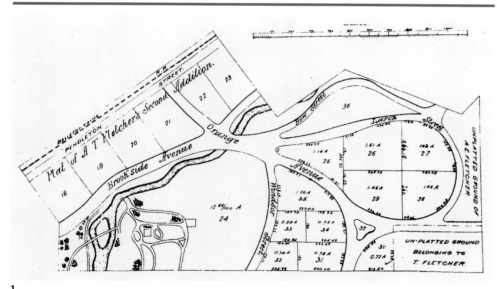

1

2

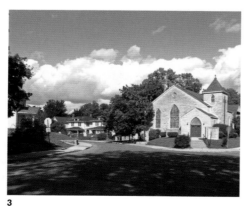

3

forested bluffs above the Raccoon River, just south of Des Moines, Iowa, aiming to "skillfully" develop the site's "advantages and beauty."[23] In northeastern Indianapolis, for the heirs of a deceased landowner, Cleveland laid out another residence park, **Brookside** and **Oak Hill** (also known as the A. E. Fletcher Third Addition and now known as Windsor Park), comprising 1,500 acres.[24] Brookside's (1870) intended large lots were eventually subdivided, factories were erected nearby, and according to Cleveland's biographer, Virginia Luckhardt, "industry continued to intrude." By the 1980s the area had "been further split by an expressway so that the original charm designed into the area . . . has been all but obliterated."[25]

In 1873, Cleveland and William M. R. French (1843–1914), a landscape architect and brother of sculptor Daniel Chester French (1850–1931), planned a subdivision for former Minnesota Governor William R. Marshall (1825–1896) and his brother-in-law Nathaniel P. Langford (1832–1911), who had purchased 1,200 acres of land between the growing cities of Minneapolis and St. Paul from the federal government, intending it for "wealthy families ensconced in suburban villas tastefully sited on lots ranging from five to 25 acres."[26] Even with the luxury of such large acreage, **St. Anthony Park** was a residence park with none of the features of a village. Its development faltered during the Panic of 1873 and then suffered as the wealthy began moving west from Minneapolis toward the Lake District instead of east. Although Cleveland's plan was discarded, enough of the picturesque character he originally intended for it, if in diminished form, survived the railroad's arrival in 1885, though its right-of-way split the site in half, with each side replatted. The northern portion was laid out by a group of Virginia land speculators, the southern section by a syndicate led by the St. Anthony Park Company. The railroad spurred residential construction in the north, where a majority of the housing stock was built between 1890 and 1930, but industry, attracted by a second railroad line, dominated in the south.

The growth of the Twin Cities led to several other residence parks, known locally as Tangletowns because of their winding roads and hilly sites. In 1886, Cleveland laid out the 220-acre **Washburn Park** for W. D. Washburn (1831–1912), a flour milling baron and railroad builder, adjacent to Minnehaha Creek about five miles south of Minneapolis, with small one-quarter- to one-half-acre lots.[27] Other examples of the type in Minneapolis include Lake Iris Park (1883), Macalester Park (1883), Prospect Park, (1884), and Warrendale (1884), all of which employed "the free-flowing English landscape garden tradition of curved streets, lakes and parks."[28]

Across the Raccoon River from Horace Cleveland's South Park, in Des Moines, Iowa, Jacob Weidenmann (1829–1893), a Swiss-born landscape architect who had worked in Olmsted's office, laid out **Polk and Hubbell Park** (1885).[29] The site occupied a portion of the grounds of Terrace Hill (1869), a mansion, now the governor's residence, designed by W. W. Boyington (1818–1898) for Iowa's first millionaire, Benjamin Franklin Allen. When

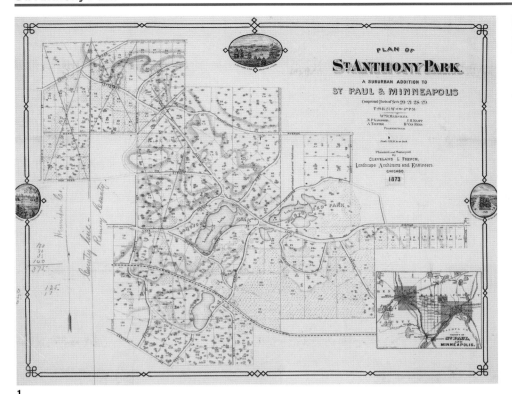

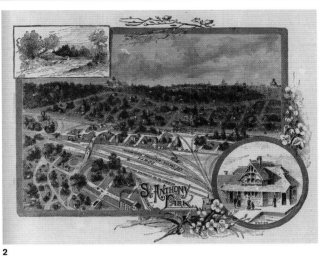

1. Plan, H. W. S. Cleveland and William M. R. French, 1873. RCHS

2. Bird's-eye view. MHSL (1886)

Allen went bankrupt in 1875, real estate broker Frederick Marion Hubbell (1839–1930) and his partner, attorney Jefferson S. Polk (1831–1907), acquired the property with the intention of surrounding the mansion and its out-buildings with a residence park. Weidenmann's plan for the site, which he deemed "forty-five acres of a most unfavorable undulation of high priced land," called for a loop road around Terrace Hill with seventy-five house lots averaging one-half to three-quarters of an acre and a network of meandering tree-lined drives extending across the grounds to the south and west.[30] Weidenmann placed a park and pond next to the planned depot of a branch of the Des Moines and North Western Railroad that was never built; the area was eventually given over to house sites.

In 1876, Frederick Law Olmsted, as part of the inte-grated system of parks and parkways (1868–98) that he designed with Calvert Vaux for Buffalo, New York, pro-posed that a residential enclave, **Parkside**, be developed around the north and east edges of The Park (now Del-aware Park), the city's principal open space about two miles north of downtown.[31] Intending Parkside to serve as a low-density buffer between The Park and the prevailing "formal tree-planted streets of the city proper," Olmsted also anticipated a symbiotic relationship between the pri-vately developed subdivision and the municipally funded park system, expecting increased tax revenues from the property to help fund the parks, an idea that he picked up from Joseph Paxton's Birkenhead Park of 1850, as histo-rian Francis R. Kowsky has noted.[32]

Prepared in collaboration with George Kent Radford (1827–1908), chief engineer of Buffalo's park and parkway system, Olmsted's naturalistic plan of roughly concentric tree-lined streets curving around the edges of the park was not realized until the late 1880s and 1890s, after a rail line had been constructed and "just as the city was becoming more industrialized, more ethnic," as Kowsky observed. In a 1981 guidebook to Buffalo architecture, Kowsky positioned Parkside as an "in-town, quasi-sub-urban" district "for the city's wealthier classes, who were seeking refuge from the changes occurring 'downtown.'"[33] In 1885, the developers, a group of local landowners incorporated as the Parkside Land Improvement Com-pany, asked Olmsted and his nephew and adopted son, John Charles (1852–1920), to revisit their original design, increasing the number of lots by reducing their size (the original plan featured lots of up to an acre) while soften-ing the curvature of the streets. To the detriment of the plan, additional changes were made between 1888 and 1890 without the Olmsteds' involvement, notably the addition of at least four streets running perpendicular to the park, cutting through the loop roads to create a more conventional arrangement of rectangular blocks. The western portion of the neighborhood, developed during the 1920s on the former grounds of the Pan American Exposition (1901), benefited from restrictive covenants dictating setbacks and minimum construction costs, but not all of the area was subjected to the rules, and portions were developed without regard to the Olmsted plan.

Rochelle Park (1885) is a garden enclave set within the existing suburban town of New Rochelle, a small city in Westchester County that was "just forty-five min-utes from Broadway," as George M. Cohan (1878–1942) was to put it in a popular song of the pre–World War I era.[34] With its clearly defined boundaries and self-contained internal circulation system that made only

1. Plan, H. W .S. Cleveland, 1886. HCL

2, 3. Typical streets. SDate. SD (2010)

4. Aerial view. SDate. SD (2006)

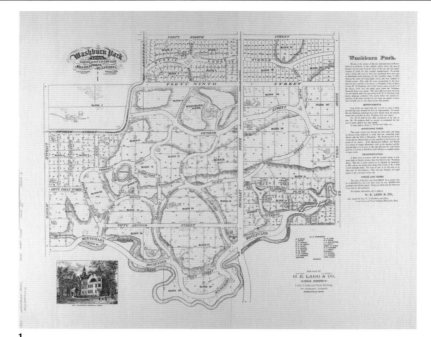

1

2

3

4

Polk and Hubbell Park

1. Plan, Jacob Weidenmann, 1885. PCR

2. Aerial view. GE (2006)

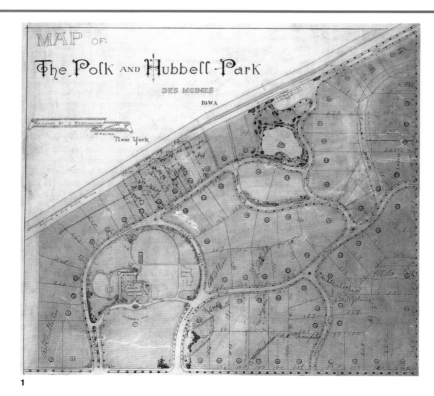

1

2

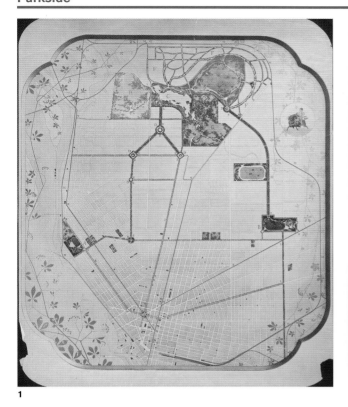

1. Map of Buffalo showing Parkside at the top. FLO

2. Aerial view. GE (2002)

3. Typical street. Garvin. AG (2009).

1

2

3

two connections to the city's street system, Rochelle Park was intended to foster a sense of separateness from New Rochelle. The enclave builds up on precedents that include Jacob Weidenmann's unrealized **Hill Park Estate** (1857) on Staten Island, a 103-acre residence park that was to incorporate two parks for the exclusive use of residents who would occupy houses on lots ranging from two to nine acres.[35] Although traversed by a public road, the roads within Hill Park Estate were to be private, ensuring exclusivity. As well, the example of Llewellyn Park lay behind Rochelle Park, as Samuel Swift observed in 1904: "If Llewellyn Park be an expression of idealistic aims of a wise dreamer, then Rochelle Park may be declared an embodiment of commercial expediency . . . The case of Rochelle Park might be matched within the land tributary to any one of a dozen American cities; while Llewellyn Park and our exclusive and fashionable communities are the products of exceptional conditions."[36]

Although New Rochelle contains other subdivisions similar to Rochelle Park, including Lather's Hill (1858), named for its developer Richard Lather, where a group of four houses was built by Alexander Jackson Davis, none of these developments have the scope of Rochelle Park, occupying 75 acres of former farmland that had been purchased under foreclosure by the Manhattan Life Insurance Company.[37] Bound on one side by the tracks of the New York, New Haven, and Hartford Railroad, Rochelle Park's site was varied but largely inhospitable, including swampland and craggy rock outcroppings. It posed a challenge for the landscape architect Nathan F. Barrett (1845–1919), who, according to Swift, had as his "watchword . . . the commercial value of sentiment,"

and for his associate Horace Crosby (1839–1914), a civil engineer.[38] Barrett, designer of Pullman (see p. 244) as well as Section 2 of Chevy Chase, Maryland (see p. 147), devoted nearly one-third of Rochelle Park's land to roads and open spaces: six acres for parkland, including an open meadow called the Lawn, and 15 or more acres for the streets, sidewalks, and planting borders, leaving some 115 building plots averaging a scant half-acre each. The location of the New Rochelle train station, a ten-minute walk to the southwest, dictated the diagonal orientation of the principal street, the Boulevard, the formality of which was counterbalanced by the Serpentine, an avenue that looped its way through the community. Together, these streets embodied a dialogue between the organic or naturalistic approach on the one hand and the geometric, classicizing one on the other that was highly unusual in a time when sides tended to be chosen in matters of composition and expression. Although no gates were provided, stone walls with terminal posts designed by Edward A. Sargent (1842–1914), an English-born architect at the time basing his practice on Staten Island, clearly defined Rochelle Park's borders, "giving more the idea of a large private estate than a public park," according to the *New York Daily Graphic*.[39] Within, the Rochelle Park Community Association maintained a tennis court on the Lawn and lawn bowls on the long rectilinear space at the end of the Boulevard known as the Court.

Rochelle Park was intended for the middle class. The lots were comparatively small, 100-by-200 feet, with houses expected to cost from $3,500 to $5,000. While there was no formal program of architectural review, house designs were prepared by Sargent.

1

2

1. Plan, Nathan F. Barrett and Horace Crosby, 1885. NRPL

2. Manhattan Avenue. NRPL (1889)

3. Main entrance. NRPL (1889)

4. The Boulevard. RAMSA (2012)

5. Intersection of the Boulevard and the Court. RAMSA (2012)

6. View across the lawn. RAMSA (2012)

7. Rochelle Heights, Cortlandt Avenue. RAMSA. (2012)

8. Rochelle Heights, Hamilton Avenue entrance gates. RAMSA (2012)

3

4

5

6

7

8

Promoted for its views over Long Island Sound and its convenience to New York, Rochelle Park was praised as "attractive" in an article published in the *Real Estate Record and Builders' Guide* in 1887, signed by "Wanderer" (probably the architectural critic Montgomery Schuyler, who lived nearby),[40] and the *Daily Graphic* wrote that there was "no comparison in the advantages of this situation over New Jersey towns with the inconveniences and delays experienced in crossing" the Hudson River by ferry.[41] So attractive to home buyers was Rochelle Park that it stimulated a building boom in New Rochelle with more houses completed between 1885 and 1887 than had been built there in the previous fifteen years.

The success of Rochelle Park led to the development of the estate property to its north, marketed as Rochelle Heights (1905). As laid out by the architectural firm of Horace B. Mann (1868–1937) and Perry R. MacNeille (1872–1931), who would soon work on many planned industrial villages such as Goodyear Heights (see p. 837) and Jefferson Rouge (see p. 845), the development, also marked by an imposing stone gateway at Hamilton Avenue, was larger and more diverse, with lots varying in size, but with no significant area dedicated to public space.[42]

Park Hill (1888), Yonkers, New York, came into being as the result of the opening of a station on the Putnam Railroad's Rapid Transit Division connecting New York City with Getty Square in Yonkers.[43] The enclave

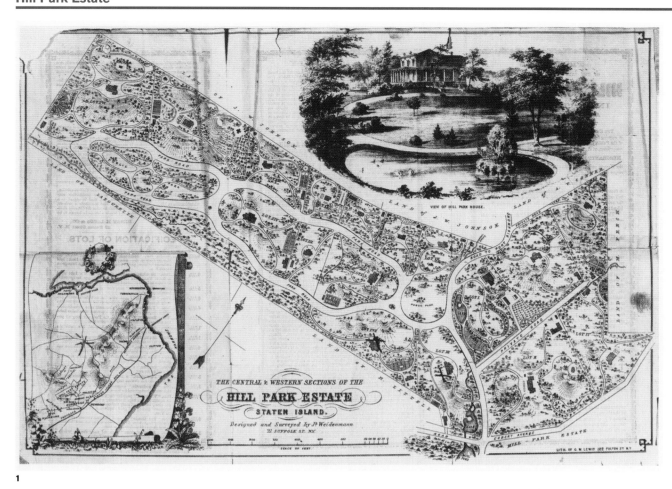

1

began with 12 acres purchased by the Parkhill Association, a group of businessmen who named their venture after Robert Parkhill Getty, a prominent Yonkers citizen and landowner. Soon afterward, the association was acquired by the newly established American Real Estate Company, which immediately began to promote the development as "The Beautiful Suburb," while constructing a country club and a passenger elevator—actually a hydraulic-powered tram—connecting the new railroad station with the hilltop development perched 325 feet above. Two hotels were initially intended to serve the community, the most prominent of which, the seven-story Hendrick Hudson, occupied a rocky outcropping overlooking the river. A private elevator drilled through the rock connected to the train station below. Regrettably, the hotel burned in March 1901, shortly before its planned opening.

As Park Hill prospered, the developers acquired adjoining properties, laying out additional winding streets. Eventually there were Park Hill, Park Hill South, and Lowerre Summit Park, constituting what was considered a single neighborhood. Because of the steep terrain, horses and carriages were liveried away from individual houses, a pattern that continued with the introduction of automobiles. Most residents walked to the train station or to the elevator that connected to it. While many well-known architects were commissioned to design houses in Park Hill, no one knows who laid out the plan of roads.

Fieldston (1910), in the New York City borough of the Bronx, like Forest Hills Gardens (see p. 140), owes its development to the realization of rapid transit connections with Manhattan's business district.[44] The extension of the Broadway subway to Van Cortlandt Park in 1908 made the hitherto relatively isolated area accessible to Manhattan, leading to the development of 140 rugged acres planned by Albert E. Wheeler (1879?–1969), an engineer, who laid out contour-hugging, picturesquely curving tree-lined streets that were held privately by the Delafield family. The Delafields were developers of the enclave who had banded together with other landowners in the area to halt the city's plans to extend the street grid in favor of providing modest houses and streets of great charm in a "private park devoted exclusively to country homes."[45] Wheeler's plan gave shape to irregular blocks with lots ranging in size from less than a quarter of an acre to one acre. The curving 100-foot-wide Fieldston Road was treated as a boulevard, divided in its center by a median dotted with trees. Its intersection with West 246th Street was handled as a circle, the geometry of which was reflected in the angled facades of the bordering houses. The pace of development was slow, and in 1923, when only eighty lots had been sold, the developers threatened to sell off the undeveloped land, jeopardizing the integrity of the neighborhood and leading concerned residents to band together and buy up the remaining property, incorporating themselves as

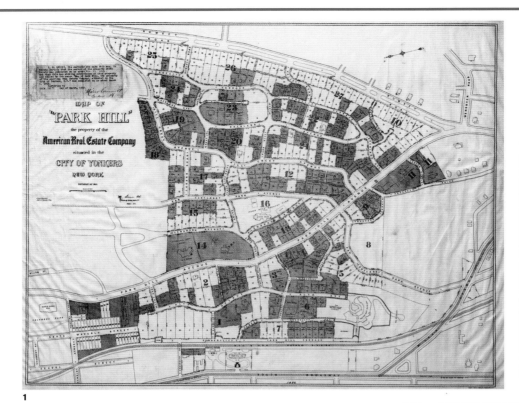

1. Map. WCA (1915)

2. Undercliff Street. WCHS (c. 1912)

3. Rockland Avenue. WCHS

4. Edgecliff Terrace. Dzikowski (FDZ) (2011)

the Fieldston Property Owners Association, managed by Wheeler, in order to carry out the estate's policies. Moreover, they retained Wheeler to help orchestrate Fieldston's future, extending protective covenants and establishing an architectural committee to review new house designs.

Many of Fieldston's houses were built by Edward Delafield, who usually hired Dwight James Baum (1886–1939), the architect who also renovated Delafield's family mansion, Fieldston Hill, in 1916, and designed the local country club in 1924.[46] Baum's work was notable for its charming details, sure sense of scale, and stylistic diversity. His own house in Fieldston had complex hipped roofs, a brick base, and a stucco second floor that made it a convincingly American version of the English Free Vernacular style of C. F. A. Voysey (1857–1941) and M. H. Baillie Scott (1865–1945). Mann & MacNeille also

designed numerous Fieldston houses, working in a half-timbered cottage mode, as well as the Barnard School, which together with the Horace Mann and Riverdale Schools made the suburb the city's headquarters for the newly fashionable "country-day school."[47] By 1940 most of the area was built out with about 250 houses.

In 1884, a consortium of five local landowners commissioned Frederick Law Olmsted and John Charles Olmsted to create a plan for Brookline Hills, a 1,500-acre residential subdivision located in Brookline, Massachusetts, a suburb of Boston.[48] Olmsted senior had recently moved to Brookline, setting up both his home and office at Fairsted, 99 Warren Street, a historic farmhouse that he nearly doubled in size. Although a new resident, Olmsted was familiar with the general vicinity, having worked on the design of both the Boston and Brookline park systems since the mid-1870s. The tract

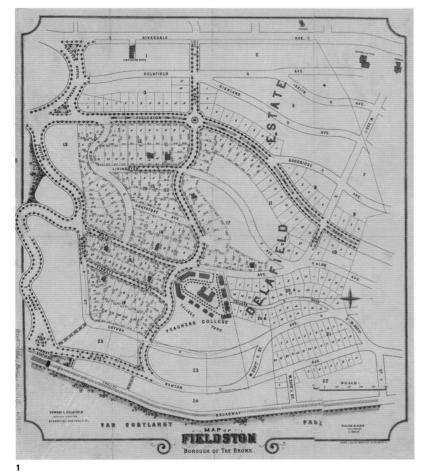

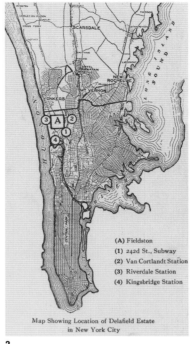

1. Plan, Albert E. Wheeler, 1910. NYPLMD (1912)

2. Locator map. NYPLMD (1912)

3. Advertisement. RERG (1913)

4. Fieldston Road. Garvin. AG (2012)

5. Baum house, Dwight James Baum, 1915. AA15

6. Goodridge Avenue, looking toward Fieldston Road. Garvin. AG (2012)

under consideration for development, like other parts of Brookline, had initially been developed as a summer retreat for wealthy Bostonians, with several large estates built in the first decades of the nineteenth century. The construction of a substantial reservoir in 1844 and the arrival three years later of train service to Boston with the opening of a station on the Newton Highlands branch of the Boston and Albany Railroad made the area convenient to daily commuters. Still, at the time of Olmsted's plan, the tract, rising 240 feet above the reservoir, remained largely undeveloped.

The name Brookline Hills was quickly dropped, as were both Mount Vernon and Henshaw Hill, before the developers settled on **Fisher Hill**, named in honor of Francis Fisher, a prominent Boston merchant who built an estate (1852) at the corner of Boylston Street and Chestnut Hill Avenue. The initial investors included George A. Goddard (1844–1920) of the Goddard Land Company, early landowners in the area; banker Henry Lee Higginson (1834–1919); real estate investor Jacob Pierce (b. 1853); architect Arthur Rotch (1850–1894); and dry goods magnate Joseph H. White (1823–1915). Concerned that the picturesque nature of the area was in jeopardy as the result of encroaching development, the developers turned to Olmsted, in the words of Jacob Pierce, to make sure that Fisher Hill would "remain unblemished by any structure not in harmony with the high character [they] wished the neighborhood to maintain."[49]

Olmsted's curvilinear plan for the hilly site, bound by Boylston Street on the south, Chestnut Hill Avenue on the west, the tracks of the Boston and Albany Railroad on the north, and Cypress Street on the east, complemented the topography and provided for relatively large lot sizes. The looping tree-lined roads were reminiscent

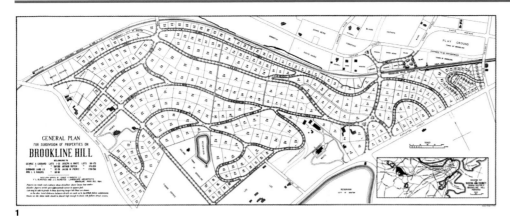

1. Plan, Frederick Law Olmsted and John Charles Olmsted, 1884. FLO

2. Aerial view. GE (2005)

3. Cotswold Road. Garvin. AG (1995)

4. John Batchelder house, Shepley, Rutan & Coolidge, 1893. ARB99

of those at Riverside, but the plan called for no public park space. Although an approved plan was in place by December 1884, and the suburb was faithfully laid out according to Olmsted's specifications, development did not begin in earnest until the 1890s and then rapidly expanded in the first years of the new century. A number of prominent firms were active in the area, including Peabody & Stearns, Shepley, Rutan & Coolidge, Kilham, Hopkins & Greeley, and Chapman & Frazer.

Fisher Hill became the most prestigious neighborhood in Brookline. But by 1914 the community, concerned that increasing land values were raising development pressures, signed a covenant prohibiting the construction of apartments, two-family houses, and public garages. The agreement remained in place until 1940, by which time the town had adopted strict zoning regulations so that since then, as landscape architect Linda Olson Pehlke has observed, "The neighborhood has remained substantially unchanged, making Fisher Hill the most intact Olmsted designed subdivision in the country."[50] In addition to the specific deed restrictions, Fisher Hill's preservation can be credited to Olmsted's plan of winding streets that had the effect of discouraging through traffic, with the only direct route to Brookline's major east–west arteries, Boylston and Beacon Streets, located on the site's border at Chestnut Hill Avenue. Alexander Garvin has observed that "From the street, Fisher Hill has the look of other Olmsted subdivisions. It is from the rear, however, that its exceptional features are revealed. The curving roadways of Fisher Hill were laid out to hug the contours of the

site so that many of the houses can open out to the view below, which in most cases overlooks the nearby city of Boston."[51]

On a far more modest scale, but employing a similar plan of curving tree-lined streets, Olmsted designed **Philbrick Estate**, another garden enclave in suburban Brookline, laying out in 1889 the property of Edward S. Philbrick (1827–1889), a civil engineer.[52] Located at the top of the neighborhood now known as Pill Hill because of the large number of doctors who have lived in the area, Olmsted's work was confined to the picturesque loop composed of Maple Street and Upland Road as well as a portion of Walnut Street. Although a landscaped island intended for Walnut Street went unrealized, the plan was otherwise carried out to Olmsted's design. As at Fisher Hill, the developers, the Brookline Land Company, instructed Olmsted to safeguard the "high class" character of the neighborhood and prevent "any occupation or erection of any building, which could work injury or annoyance to residents."[53]

Olmsted also performed preliminary work on plans for at least three other Brookline enclaves, including projects for Chestnut Hill (1888), Corey Hill (1889), and a triangular parcel of land bound by Pond Avenue and Jamaica and Highland Roads (1894), but these languished and no detailed schemes were produced.[54] However, Olmsted could claim at least partial credit for an additional realized Brookline enclave, **Aspinwall Hill**, which has a somewhat convoluted history.[55] Plans for a subdivision on 56 acres were first introduced in 1857 by civil engineer J. Herbert Shedd (1834–1915), who

PLAN FOR THE SUBDIVISION OF THE
ESTATE OF EDWARD S. PHILBRICK
BROOKLINE, MASS.

1

2

1. Plan, Frederick Law Olmsted, 1889. FLO

2. Upland Road. RAMSA (2011)

proposed a series of terraces with a modest green space at the top. Nothing came of the scheme and more than twenty years later, in 1880, before his move to Brookline, Olmsted was hired to prepare a plan for William Aspinwall (1819–1892) of the Aspinwall Land Company, who controlled a majority of the still-undeveloped tract, home to only two early-nineteenth-century houses. The two other owners of the site were William Bowditch (1819–1909) and Boston University, which controlled the key Beacon Street frontage. Angering both Bowditch and Boston University, Olmsted worked with Aspinwall's son, Thomas (1853–1918), a principal in the civil engineering firm of Aspinwall & Lincoln, to produce a preliminary study for the entirety of the site that envisioned a curvilinear scheme similar to the one he later proposed at Fisher Hill, a not surprising solution considering the similarity of the two sites.

To counter Aspinwall and Olmsted's proposal, Bowditch and Boston University hired Bowditch's son, Ernest W. Bowditch (1850–1918), a landscape gardener and civil engineer, to prepare alternate plans. Born and raised in Brookline, and educated at MIT, where he studied chemistry and mining, Ernest Bowditch had worked with Olmsted many times before, preparing topographical surveys. But Bowditch did not respect Olmsted, believing that the famous practitioner had prospered at the expense of local professionals. In an unpublished memoir written a year before he died, Bowditch characterized Olmsted's plan as "a handsome scheme—not very much studied, that wasted a much larger area of land in street than was necessary for the most economical

development of the land." Bowditch's revised plan (1885) of winding and looping tree-lined roads, which he claimed "saved . . . one-quarter of the land that Olmsted had proposed to dedicate to the public," was embraced by Aspinwall, and Olmsted was dropped from the project.[56] But landscape historian Cynthia Zaitzevsky writes that "it is difficult to see that much land was 'wasted' in streets" in Olmsted's scheme, and furthermore, she notes, Bowditch's reworking "appears more cramped and contorted than any of Olmsted's studies."[57] With all of the landholders in agreement, the first houses were built at the end of 1885 following the Bowditch plan. After the extension of the West End Street Railway to Beacon Street in 1889, development picked up considerably, with many large Queen Anne and Colonial Revival houses built in the early 1890s. Lacking Fisher Hill's severe deed restrictions, by the late 1890s Aspinwall Hill was home to two- and three-family houses crowded along Rawson Road and apartment buildings on Addington Road.

Bowditch, whose most prominent project was for Pierre Lorillard at Tuxedo Park, New York (see p. 295), was responsible for two additional Boston area suburban enclaves. At **Allston Park** (1890), located within Boston's city limits, he struggled to insert naturalistic planning into the surrounding grid.[58] The modest development was organized in successively larger oval portions featuring slightly curving streets. To further differentiate itself from its surroundings, Allston Park had strict deed restrictions, allowing only single-family residences, albeit on small lots, and mandating that each house have a stone foundation and cost more than $4,000 to

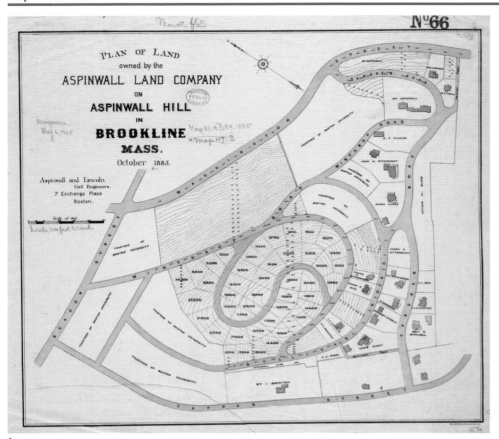

1. Plan, Ernest W. Bowditch, 1885. FLO

2. Aerial view. GE (2008)

3. Harry Hartley house, Chapman & Frazer, 1902. AR10

4. Colbourne Crescent. RAMSA (2011)

5. Colbourne Path. RAMSA (2011)

6. View from Corey Hill. ISUL

build. Bowditch had far more room to maneuver at **Newton Terraces** (1890), situated in Waban, one of thirteen villages in the suburban city of Newton, about twelve miles west of Boston.[59] The area had recently become accessible to commuters with the opening in 1886 of a new station on the Boston and Albany line, one of the last projects designed by Henry Hobson Richardson (1838–1886), offering frequent service to Boston. The site's south border was the Charles River. Bowditch's plan of winding, tree-lined streets, providing house lots that were roughly four times larger than those at Allston Park, resulted in a mazelike pattern of streets. At the center, Bowditch included a modest amount of public park space.

In 1911, inspired by the Sage Foundation's work at Forest Hills Gardens in New York, the Boston Dwelling House Company, which had only recently been founded by public-spirited citizens, acquired the Minot

estate, a beautifully landscaped 30-acre site near the terminal of Boston's elevated railroad system in Forest Hills, a recently annexed portion of the city.[60] The Olmsted Brothers, in association with Robert A. Pope (b. 1884), were retained to lay out **Woodbourne**, an affordable suburban enclave calling for low but monumental apartment houses along Hyde Park, the principal through street, to shelter clusters of single, double, and group houses, each having its own garden but also sharing common open spaces reserved for playgrounds and greenswards. The development, according to Robert Campbell, "is a hilly enclave of little streets that climb and twist among mostly stucco cottages," with 150 houses planned.[61] The firm of Walter Harrington Kilham (1868–1948) and James Cleveland Hopkins (1873–1938) were the architects of the single-family housing and the apartments, built between 1912 and 1914, that were conceived as alternatives to the ubiquitous Boston tenement

Allston Park

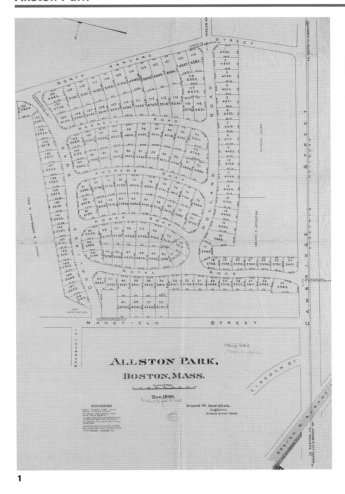

1

2

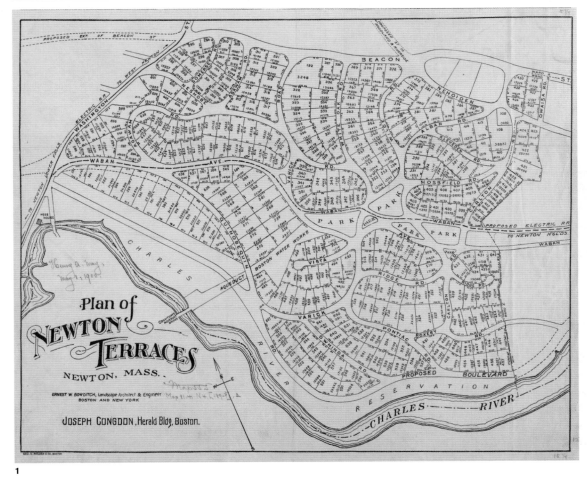

3

1. Plan, Ernest W. Bowditch, 1890. BPL

2. Aerial view. GE (2005)

3. Holman Street. Berman. DB (2012)

Newton Terraces

1

2

3

1. Plan, Ernest W. Bowditch, 1890. BPL

2. Alban Road. RAMSA (2011)

3. Waban Avenue. RAMSA (2011)

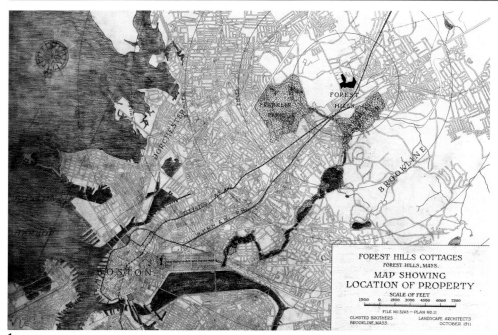

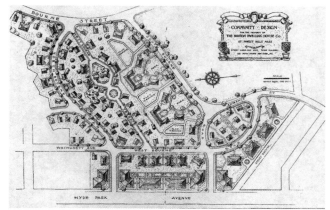

1

2

3

4

5

6

1. Locator map. FLO (1911)

2. Plan for first part of development, Olmsted Brothers and Robert A. Pope, c. 1911. BR13

3. Hyde Park Avenue apartment buildings, Kilham & Hopkins, 1914. WA18

4. Aerial view. GE (2008)

5. Florian Street. Berman. DB (2012)

6. Southbourne Road houses, Kilham & Hopkins, 1914. WA18

type, the so-called "three-decker." Richard Heath has noted that the apartment houses, which were demolished in 1976, "were distinguished by dignified facades, shaded corner entrances and recessed balconies. They formed a formal gateway to the cottages . . . (Sometime in their existence they caused the area to be nicknamed 'White City' because of their color)."[62]

On the western outskirts of Cleveland, Ohio, Ernest Bowditch designed the small suburban enclave of **Clifton Park** (1894), bound on the west by the Rocky River, on the north by Lake Erie, and on the east by the suburban town of Lakewood.[63] Although much of the Lake Erie waterfront around Cleveland was taken over by industry, the site of Clifton Park had been passed over because of steep, 75-foot-high bluffs that made it ideal for dramatically sited houses. Clifton Park was first conceived in 1866 as a summer resort and amusement grounds by a group of Clevelanders who by 1869 had built the Rocky River Railroad, which bound the site on the south. The resort enjoyed some popularity but after the Panic of 1873, slumping profits led initially to

the platting of a subdivision of about eighty lots that did not go forward and subsequently to Bowditch's plan of ninety-six lots averaging one acre each along naturalistic looping roads covering almost 200 acres. Lots on the interior of the site were later reduced in size, while the lakefront properties attracted luxurious houses. In addition to the small triangular parklets that were created by intersecting streets, a beach with a bathing pavilion was provided at the juncture of the river and the lake, a lakefront park was reserved between houses along the bluffs, and a lagoon was later dredged to serve as a marina.

The first houses were rustic seasonal cottages built mainly between 1899 and 1903. By 1918 the nearly complete Clifton Park still conveyed a natural feel, leading I. T. Frary to observe in *Architectural Record* that the neighborhood "which a generation ago was used as a picnic resort, is still thickly wooded with forest trees which have been carefully preserved . . . The winding roads and the heavy screen of trees, by cutting off continuous vistas in any direction, give an exaggerated impression of its extent."[64] Unfortunately, the enclave was bisected during

Clifton Park

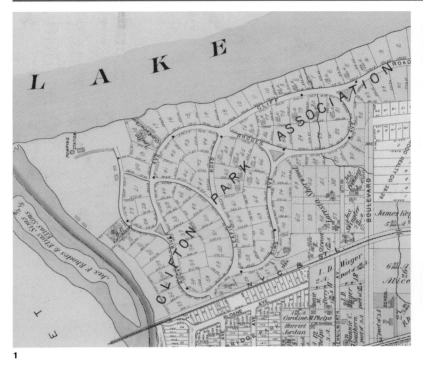

1. Map. CPL (1898)

2. Aerial view. GE (2010)

3. Lake Road. CSU (c. 1917)

4. Clifton Beach. CSU (c. 1913)

Country Club

1. Entrance gates, Country Club Place. DPL41 (1905–10)

2. Typical street. DPL5 (1906–20)

3. Entrance gates, Country Club Place. DPL77 (1930–40)

4. Gilpin Street, Country Club Place. AHP (1978)

5. Entrance gates, Country Club Place. Beall. WC (2008)

the 1930s by the east–west course of Clifton Boulevard, interrupting many of Bowditch's through streets that were curtailed as dead ends or culs-de-sac.

A number of noteworthy garden enclaves were built in the West. In Denver, Colorado, the **Country Club** neighborhood was founded in 1902 by the owners of the Denver Country Club, who purchased 240 acres of John Jacob Riethmann's wheat farm, two miles southeast of the Colorado capital's downtown, and began transforming the southern half of the land into a golf course and club grounds and the northern half into a series of residential neighborhoods.[65] The four contiguous subdivisions that were built over the next twenty-five years accommodate roughly 380 houses on a 120-acre L-shaped site between Downing and University Streets and First and Fourth Avenues, extending north to Sixth Avenue from east of High Street to University Boulevard. The first section to be built, Park Club Place (1905), set behind redbrick piers on Fourth Avenue, did not markedly differ from Denver's surrounding

1. Plan, William S. Ladd, 1891. OHS47

2. Aerial view showing Laurelhurst in distance. OHS71 (before 1919)

3. Aerial view. GE (2006)

4. Central *rond-point*. OHS28

5, 6. Typical streets. Massey. JCM (2012)

1

2

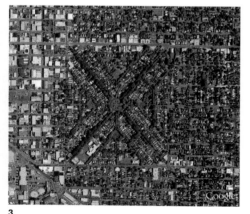

3

4

5

6

residential areas, which were characterized by houses set back on raised front yards on lots averaging 50 feet wide and 125 feet deep. The next phase, the 40-acre Country Club Place (also known as Country Club Addition, 1903–6), a collaboration between Frederick Law Olmsted Jr. (1870–1957) and the Canadian-born Denver architect William Ellsworth Fisher (1871–1937), assisted by his brother and partner Arthur A. Fisher (1878–1965), was notable for broad landscaped malls dividing Franklin, Gilpin, and High Streets—resulting in one less street than its predecessor—as well as William Fisher's Mission-style stucco and red-tile entrance gates on East Fourth Avenue, which, more so than the eclectic houses within, earned the neighborhood its nickname, "Spanish Suburb." Farther east, Country Club Annex was laid out between 1924 and 1927 and built primarily in the 1930s, 1940s, and 1950s with rectangular blocks similar to the first section but with larger lots and houses. The last phase, Park Lane Square, north of Fourth Avenue, was the first to break from the grid, with a rotary and the looping Circle Drive laid out in 1926 by Dutch-born landscape architect Saco Rienk DeBoer (1883–1974), who provided fifty-eight lots. Also known as New Country Club, the enclave, geared toward the automobile and, with no sidewalks, discouraging foot traffic, was entered through elaborate brick gateways on its north, west, and east boundaries and protected by deed restrictions defining minimum construction costs, outlawing nonresidential uses, and limiting the enclave to white residents.

Ladd's Addition, in southeast Portland, Oregon, was designed in 1891 by William S. Ladd (1826–1893), a businessman and one-time mayor, as a "residential section for cultured people."[66] The 126-acre neighborhood (1903–30) was situated along a streetcar line. Broad, elm-lined streets populated by comfortably planned, eclectically styled houses set back 15 to 20 feet from the street are familiar suburban features, but Ladd's scheme, inspired by L'Enfant's plan for Washington, D.C., was distinctly atypical of garden enclave planning and was carried out against the advice of the civil engineers whom Ladd had originally hired to survey the property. It consisted of a central *rond-point* acting as a hub to a series of streets and service alleys leading to individual garages that fanned out on the diagonal for approximately two blocks in each direction, where they collided with Portland's gridiron. Development lagged following Ladd's death in 1893 and the national financial panic but picked up in earnest after the Lewis & Clark Centennial Exposition in 1905. A former associate of the Olmsted Brothers and Portland Parks Superintendent Emanuel T. Mische (1870–1934) designed the four rose gardens called for in the plan.

In 1908, Ladd's son, William Mead Ladd (1855–1931), developed the **Laurelhurst** neighborhood in Portland with a plan of gently curving and concentric arcing streets laid out around intersecting north–south and east–west axes.[67] As planned by civil engineer George Cottrell (n.d.), the 427-acre suburb with 117 blocks

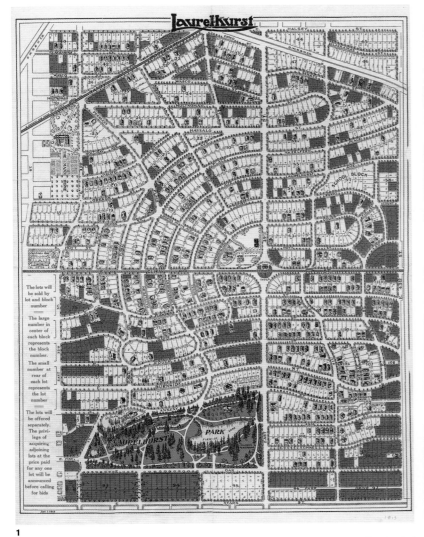

1. Sales map. OHS40 (1919)

2. Aerial view. OHS73

3. Glisan Street showing entrance gate and streetcar tracks. OHS85 (1921)

4. Typical street. Schechter. DS (2012)

5. Promotional brochure. OHS6 (1912)

6. Entrance gate, Glisan Street. Schechter. DS (2012)

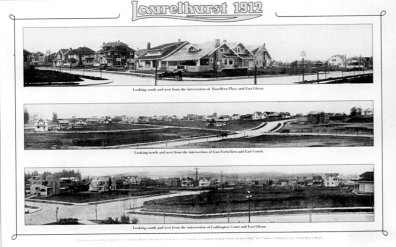

divided into 50-by-100-foot lots included a 32-acre park. In 1910, a streetcar line was completed along the east–west Glisan Street, connecting the neighborhood to downtown Portland two miles away, but Laurelhurst was built with automobiles in mind, and houses were provided with garages. Within the suburb, there were distinct neighborhoods, notably Fernhaven Court, a single block of bungalows bisected by a 20-foot-wide paved serpentine alley accessing garages and service entrances, "avoiding the necessity of cutting up and ruining the [front] lawns with runways."[68] Another notable block featured a planned cluster of nine houses (only five were built) designed in 1917 by the firm of Ellis F. Lawrence (1879–1946) and William G. Holford (1878–1970) with houses set back on their lots, several sharing driveways that led to side and rear garages.

1. Real estate advertisement with map. FLO (1907)

2. Aerial view. SMA (1971)

3. Lake Washington Boulevard. UWL (c. 1911)

4. Mount Baker Drive. SMA (1924)

5. Sierra Drive. Garvin. AG (1998)

In Seattle, the leading city of the Pacific Northwest, **Mount Baker Park Addition** (1906–7) was a 200-acre planned community facing Lake Washington, with streetcar service to downtown.[69] The area, treated as part of the Olmsted Brothers' 1908 supplement to their 1903 plan for Seattle's parks and boulevards, was laid out by Edward O. Schwagerl (1842–1910). It consisted of gridded streets connected to the Seattle network and curvilinear streets and boulevards, including Mount Baker and Hunter Boulevards, that respected the topography. Schwagerl was a native of Bavaria who had worked for Jacob Weidenmann in Hartford, Connecticut, then practiced landscape design in Omaha, St. Louis, Cleveland, and Tacoma before becoming Seattle's superintendent of

public parks in 1892. The largest real estate subdivision to be incorporated in the Olmsted plan, Mount Baker Park Addition, was, according to Davis A. Rash, "the first to include both boulevards and extensive park grounds as an integral part of the design."[70]

At the northern edge of Seattle, twelve miles from downtown, the **Highlands** (1909), perched 450 feet above Puget Sound on a spectacular 340-acre sloping hillside interrupted by shelves and ravines, was laid out by Alexander MacDougall (n.d.), an engineer closely associated with John Olmsted and James Frederick Dawson (1874–1941), who ringed the development with a golf course and provided fifty house lots of varying sizes.[71] Responding to the topography and

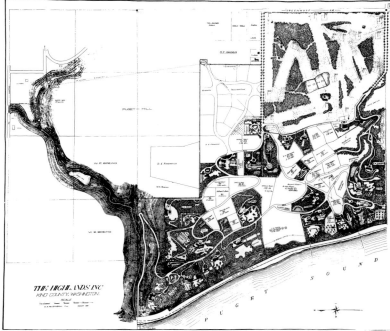

to the dramatic views, a system of switchback roads, typically with 5 percent grades, was geared to automobiles. Aside from the golf course and some reserved, otherwise unbuildable sites, there is virtually no sense of shared communal space at the Highlands, and most house sites—none smaller than five acres—are treated as clearings in the dense second-growth conifer forest. Significantly, the Highlands is fenced in and access is controlled through a single gate, placing it in the tradition of Llewellyn and Tuxedo Parks.

Broadmoor, like the Highlands, was a gated enclave organized around a golf course.[72] In 1920 the Puget Mill Company, which had logged the area south of Union Bay for more than six decades, divided a 460-acre tract three miles northeast of downtown Seattle in two, selling the western 260 acres to the city at a deep discount for a municipal park but holding on to the remaining 200 acres in order to develop, in collaboration with several local businessmen, a "country club within the city" providing large, secluded houses for the wealthy.[73] The lumber company hired local engineer Clyde D. Pike (1887–1948) and prolific golf-course architect Arthur Vernon Macan (1882–1964), a gifted amateur golfer whose playing career had ended with the loss of his left leg in World War I,

to lay out the subdivision, bound by marshland on the north, Thirty-seventh Avenue on the east, Madison Street on the south, and Washington Park on the west.

Pike and Macan set 85 acres aside for the single-family houses that were located within the 115 acres of the U-shaped eighteen-hole golf course that surrounded the residential component on three sides. At the fourth side, forming the southern border, they located the main entrance flanked by imposing brick piers. A second gated entrance was placed in the northwest corner of the site, providing more direct access to the golf course. The long and narrow parcel intended for the houses was subdivided into 400 lots placed primarily along gently curving north–south streets geared to the automobile.

The golf course, initially intended only for residents and their guests, was completed in 1927, joined the following year by a clubhouse designed by John Graham (1873–1955). Architect Dwight James Baum, best known for houses in Riverdale and Fieldston, New York, writing in the September 1929 issue of *American Architect*, declared that Broadmoor has "many attractive homes" designed in a wide variety of styles by leading Seattle-based architects such as Arthur L. Loveless (1873–1971) and George W. Stoddard (1896–1967).[74] About a quarter

1. Plan, Alexander MacDougall, 1909. HIGH (1931)

2–4. Typical streets. Wilder. HIGH (2012)

1. Plan, Clyde D. Pike and Arthur Vernon Macan, 1924. SMA

2. Aerial view. GE (2007)

3. Typical street. SMA (1930)

4. Main entrance, Madison Street. AMA29 (c. 1929)

5. Typical view. Mabel. JMA (2008)

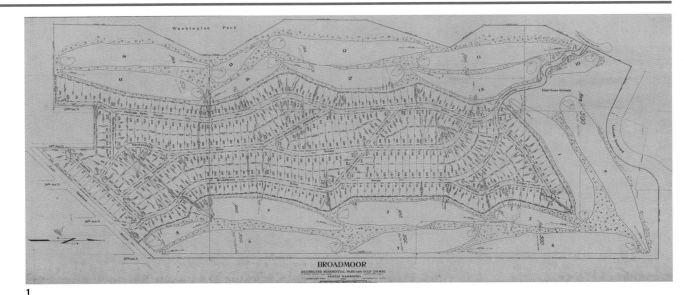

of the lots were sold before the Depression halted development, and progress did not resume in earnest until after World War II, at which time membership in the golf club was opened to those living beyond the subdivision's gates. To this day Broadmoor remains a fenced-in preserve for the city's elite. Seattle-based, Zimbabwean-born writer and critic Charles Mudede recently compared Seattle's two most exclusive neighborhoods, observing that "Broadmoor is very different from the Highlands. It has the feel of new money where the Highlands has the sedative ease of old money. The differences associated with these class conditions can easily be read in the design of the two communities. When racing down Madison how can one miss Broadmoor and its elaborate

brick entrance? It stands boastfully there for everyone to see. The Highlands, on the other hand, is totally hidden; without clear direction one will never find it."[75]

One of the most dramatic stories of urban growth in the early twentieth century is that of San Francisco, which reemerged from the devastating earthquake of 1906 to become the nation's most sophisticated metropolis west of the Mississippi. In 1910, the announcement of plans to build a tunnel through the San Miguel Hills, bringing streetcar service to the city's western edge, near the Pacific Ocean, spurred the construction of several notable garden enclaves. The 2.27-mile-long Twin Peaks Tunnel, the country's longest railway tunnel west of New York City, would significantly reduce commuting

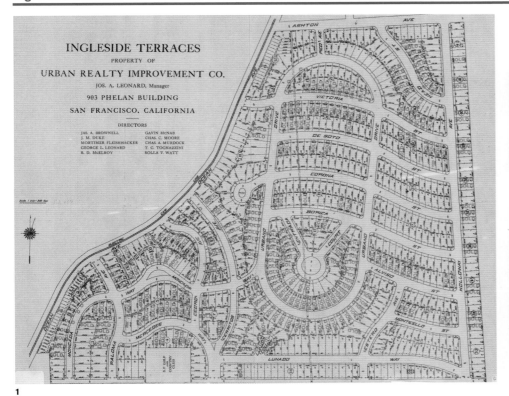

times and, combined with the new system of boulevards that connected the area to downtown via Golden Gate Park, open up for development the remote and largely undeveloped southwestern section of the city.

Developer and architect Joseph A. Leonard (1850–1929) was one of the first to take advantage of plans for the tunnel, purchasing a 148-acre parcel formerly home to the Ingleside Horseracing Track, which had operated from 1885 to 1905 but failed to reopen after the 1906 earthquake.[76] Leonard named the new subdivision **Ingleside Terraces** (1910) and the site, about six miles from downtown and bound by Ocean Avenue to the north, Junipero Serra Boulevard to the west, Holloway Avenue to the south, and Ashton Avenue to the east, enjoyed unspoiled views of Lake Merced and the Pacific Ocean beyond.

Working with civil engineer E. J. Morser (n.d.), Leonard laid out 613 single-family house sites along a gently curved, contour-hugging street grid occasionally punctuated by culs-de-sac. The plan provided generous lots ranging from 50 to 80 feet wide and 120 to 200 feet deep, allowing for substantial yards on all sides. Leonard also stipulated that no fences or high hedges be built, in an effort to keep an open feel for the community. Several modest parks were included in the plan as well as a home for the San Francisco Golf and Country Club in the northwest part of the enclave. Leonard adapted one element from the site's history, transforming the mile-long former racetrack into the oval-shaped Urbano Drive, named for the developer's Urban Realty Improvement Company. A stone sundial that served as the community's focus was placed on Entrada Court, a plaza at the western end of the oval. The functioning sundial, which Leonard claimed was the largest in the world, featured a 26-foot-high gnomon rising out of a pool graced by two bronze seals and surrounded by a broad dial of Roman numerals. Adding to the development's appeal were wide sidewalks, trellised lampposts, and along Junipero Serra Boulevard and Ocean Avenue, stone entrance gates carrying wrought-iron arches displaying the subdivision's name.

1. Plat map showing sold lots, Joseph A. Leonard and E. J. Morser, 1910. ESML

2. Moncada Way. SFHC (c. 1912)

3. Streetcar and entrance gates, Ocean Avenue and Victoria Street. SFHC (1912)

4. Streetlamp. SFHC (c. 1912)

5. Entrance gates, Ocean Avenue and Victoria Street. Mendelson. JM (2012)

6. Sundial, Entrada Court. Mendelson. JM (2012)

1. Plan, James Frederick Dawson, 1912–14. FLO

2. St. Francis Boulevard, showing fountain designed by John Galen Howard. Moulin. FLO (c. 1916)

3. Typical street. EDA (1920)

4. St. Francis Boulevard and Santa Ana Avenue. EDA (c. 1912)

Ingleside Terraces, promoted by Leonard as "San Francisco's Great Park of Restricted Residences,"[77] was geared toward an affluent clientele and, typical of the time, included covenants governing who could purchase houses in the suburb, banning people of "African, Japanese, Chinese, or of any Mongolian descent."[78] Leonard, and later his son George, were responsible for the design of many of the early Arts and Crafts–style bungalows, including Leonard's own at 90 Cedro Avenue. Despite an official opening on October 10, 1913, the day that the sundial was dedicated, the construction of houses did not begin in earnest until after the completion of

the Twin Peaks Tunnel in 1918, with the first phase of building largely concluded by 1924. A second phase of development, begun five years later after Joseph Leonard's death, was characterized by larger, predominantly Mediterranean-style dwellings; lost with Leonard's passing was the restriction on fences and hedges.

St. Francis Wood (1912), located one mile north of Ingleside Terraces, was planned for an even wealthier group of homeowners.[79] The 175-acre site was heavily forested and its spectacular downward southwest slope toward the Pacific Ocean encouraged the developer, Duncan McDuffie (1877–1951), to conceive, in his own

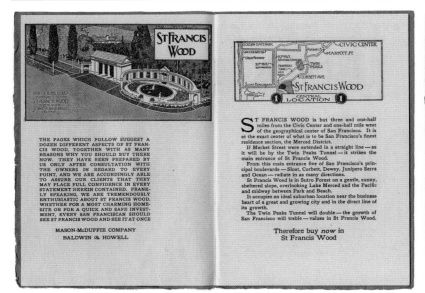

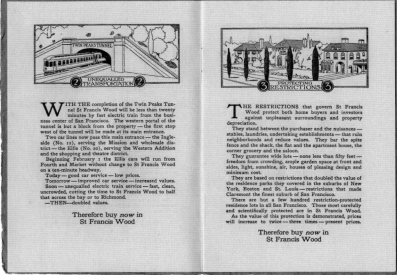

5

6

7

8

9

10

11

5, 6. Promotional brochure. CHS (c.1912)

7. Entrance, St. Francis Boulevard. Mendelson. JM (2012)

8. Typical street. Mendelson. JM (2012)

9. San Benito Way and St. Francis Boulevard. Mendelson. JM (2012)

10. St. Francis Plaza, showing fountain by Henry H. Gutterson. Mendelson. JM (2012)

11. Pedestrian path. Mendelson. JM (2012)

words, a "residence park"[80] to prove "to San Franciscans the possibility of creating 'rus in urbe.'"[81] MIT and Beaux-Arts-trained John Galen Howard (1864–1931), one of San Francisco's leading architects, designed the sales office that formed the development's gateway as well as many ornamental details, including lamp standards cast from Venetian models and the special, Roman-style pavement. In 1913, when Howard became professor of architecture at the University of California, forcing him to retire from private practice, the job of supervising architect was turned over to one of his close associates, Henry H. Gutterson (1884–1954).

The plan of St. Francis Wood was the work of James Frederick Dawson, of the Olmsted Brothers, who revised an initial design prepared under Howard's guidance by C. L. Huggins (n.d.), a civil engineer, widening the principal street, St. Francis Boulevard, from 100 feet to 150 feet to accommodate a planted mall. The revised plan called for 50-by-100-foot lots and underground utilities. The central block was interrupted by a *rond-point* with a fountain designed by Howard, from which St. Francis Boulevard rose eastward to its conclusion at St. Francis Plaza, where a terrace was embellished by a fountain designed by Gutterson. As at Ingleside Terraces, the

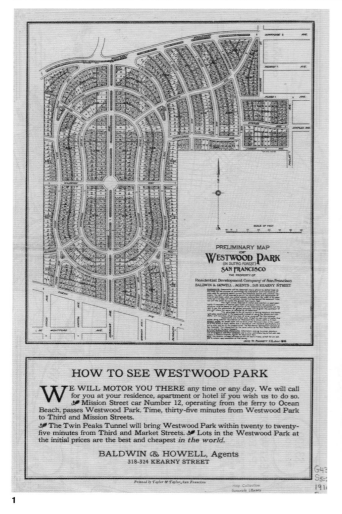

1. Promotional brochure with plan, John M. Punnett, 1916. BLUCB

2. Aerial view. MTD (1929)

3. Typical street. MOU (c. 1917)

4. Entrance gates, Monterey Boulevard and Miramar Avenue. MOU (c. 1917) (2012)

5. Advertisement featuring Ida McCain, *San Francisco Chronicle*, June 5, 1920. FAWA

6. Plymouth Avenue. Mendelson. JM (2012)

7. Entrance gates, Monterey Boulevard and Miramar Avenue. Mendelson. JM (2012)

construction of houses did not take off until after the Twin Peaks Tunnel opening, making the architecture of the suburb a reflection of 1920s taste. By 1932, according to McDuffie, Werner Hegemann (1881–1936), the German planner with wide knowledge of American practice, considered St. Francis Wood to be "the most distinguished residential suburb not alone in California, but in America."[82]

In 1916, less than a mile southwest of St. Francis Wood, the developer Archibald S. Baldwin (1848–1924) announced plans for **Westwood Park**, a subdivision intended to be "a modern residence park which was to be a model home community for the family of average means," as a promotional brochure put it.[83] Bound by Monterey Boulevard to the north, Faxon Street to the west, Ocean Avenue to the south, and Phelan Avenue to the east, the undeveloped tract was subdivided by engineer John M. Punnett (n.d.) into 650 single-family

house sites, the majority of which were 25 feet wide. Punnett's plan of curving streets with a prominent oval-shaped portion was reminiscent of the design of Ingleside Terraces. In this case the oval was bisected by a broad boulevard with a planted median, Miramar Avenue, one of the few straight streets in the enclave. Charles F. Strothoff (1891?–1963) was the designer of close to three-quarters of the houses in Westwood Park, mostly Arts and Crafts–style bungalows completed between 1918 and 1923. Ida McCain (1884–1966) was another architect active in the suburb. A rare female practitioner, her image was used as a promotional tool in advertisements published in the *San Francisco Chronicle*. In one such piece that ran on June 5, 1920, a caricature of "Expert Bungalow Designer" McCain holding a T-square and compass was accompanied by a caption exclaiming, "I'll design a bungalow specially for YOU."[84] The subdivision incorporated a few commercial buildings, including a grocery store, and featured stone entrance gates and elaborate lampposts designed by another leading San Francisco architect, the Missouri-born Louis Christian Mullgardt (1866–1942), who had received his architectural training working in St. Louis, Boston, and Chicago firms.

Archibald Baldwin was also the developer of a more upscale enclave, **Westwood Highlands** (1924), located adjacent and to the north of Westwood Park on a hilly site bound by Monterey Boulevard on the south, Yerba Buena Avenue on the west, Hazelwood and Brentwood Avenues on the north, and Ridgewood Avenue on the east.[85] Baldwin again hired Punnett to plat the subdivision, and he responded with a topographically sympathetic curvilinear arrangement of streets that provided for 283 single-family houses on generous and irregularly sized lots. Also returning as architect was Charles Strothoff, although he was given more freedom here than at Westwood Park, designing larger Tudor- and Mediterranean-style houses as well as Arts and Crafts bungalows between 1924 and 1929. For Westwood Highlands, Baldwin eschewed monumental stone gates, instead marking the Monterey Boulevard entrances to the community with eight modest wrought-iron signs attached to lampposts.

Eighteen miles south of San Francisco, in San Mateo County, Francis Newlands (1848–1917), the developer of Chevy Chase, Maryland undertook **Burlingame Park** (1893), a new enclave that would provide, as a real estate prospectus put it, a "complete change of climate" from San Francisco's cold summers and combine "the charms of the country with all the conveniences of the city."[86] Optimistically labeled the "Tuxedo Park of the West," Burlingame Park was little more than a neighborhood within the city named for General Anson Burlingame (1820–1870), ambassador to China, who had previously owned the land and in 1868 had planned a suburban retreat for wealthy San Franciscans. That plan died with Burlingame in 1870, and the property fell to Newlands, who retained Richard Hammond (n.d.), a civil engineer, to lay out an initial section on a flat, open portion of the site in 1893. The plan called for curving roads but was otherwise of no particular distinction. When sales proved sluggish, the Burlingame Country Club, with polo grounds said to be superior to those in Newport, Rhode Island, was founded to attract buyers. Country club members partially financed the construction of a train depot (1894) and A. Page Brown (1859–1896), a San Francisco architect who had worked in the office of McKim, Mead & White before moving west, designed model summer cottages as well as the first clubhouse (1894). A second subdivision was platted by engineer Michael O'Shaughnessy (1864–1934) on a hillier part of the site near the country club, where sales were brisker. John McLaren (1846–1943), superintendent of Golden Gate Park, prepared a lush landscape plan for the entirety of Burlingame Park.

Although scholarly attention has largely been focused on San Francisco's garden enclaves, a number were realized in Southern California, including

Westwood Highlands

1. Aerial view showing Westwood Highlands, top center, and Westwood Park, bottom center. GE (1938)

2. Monterey Boulevard and Plymouth Avenue. MTD (1927)

3. Brentwood Avenue. Anom. FL (2007)

Burlingame Park

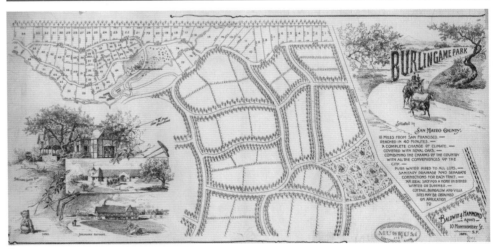

1. Sales map. SMCHM (1894)

2. Entrance. BURL (c. 1915)

1. Advertisement and plan,
Thomas Jordan, 1923. LAPL

2. Aerial view. GE (2010)

3. View from Deronda Drive.
BLP (1925)

1

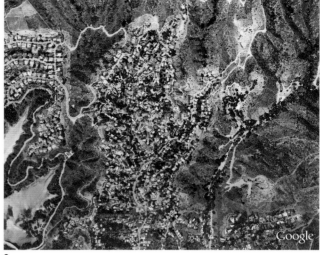

2

3

Hollywoodland (1923), occupying 500 acres in the foothills north of Hollywood, which has largely been overlooked because the signboard proclaiming its name has become an internationally recognized symbol of the motion picture industry and has obscured its original purpose as advertising for a new residential enclave.[87] Hollywoodland was developed by five partners, including Harry Chandler (1864–1944), publisher of the *Los Angeles Times*, who came up with the idea of erecting the giant sign high above the subdivision on the side of Mt. Lee, spelling out the development's name in 50-foot-high sheet-metal letters illuminated at night by 4,000 20-watt bulbs. Hollywoodland, located between Griffith Park on the east and Lake Hollywood on the west, was planned by Thomas Jordan (n.d.) of the Los Angeles–based Engineering Service Company, with roads twisting through wooded canyons and knolls, supported by impressive granite retaining walls built by Italian stonemasons who also constructed six sets of stairs—one with a cascading fountain down its center—to help pedestrians negotiate the terrain. The entrance, on Beachwood Drive, was flanked by gray sandstone gatehouses arching over the sidewalks, one a rather squat box and the other a more

whimsical miniature castle with a high tower, faux chimney, and narrow window. Inside the gates, at the intersection of Beachwood and Westshire Drives, a sales office took the form of a Tudor cottage designed by John DeLario (1888–1950), an architect who led the development's design review board. Until the sponsors sold their interest in the 1940s, house styles were limited to French Norman, Tudor, Mediterranean, and Spanish. DeLario employed the latter in numerous Hollywoodland houses as well a two-story retail building (1925) in a largely unrealized commercial center just inside the gates.

Hollywoodland got off to a strong start. Within ninety days seven miles of roadways were built to entice automobile owners. Within a year, a program was initiated to reforest the site with cedar, pine, fir, redwood, and cypress trees. In addition to tennis courts, putting greens, and a riding club with miles of bridle paths, the developers provided a bus to shuttle residents and domestic help between the entrance and the houses. By the end of the decade Hollywoodland was well established and well known, but the Depression prevented full realization of the original vision for the 1,800-acre project extending over Mt. Lee. The advertising sign, an immediate and

4. Entrance and gatehouses, Beachwood and Westshire Drives. BLP (1925)

5. Commercial building, John DeLario, 1925, Beachwood Drive. BLP (1925)

6. Typical street. LAPL

7. View showing Hollywoodland sign in distance. LAPL

4

5

6

7

enduring icon, was donated to the city in 1944 and five years later the letters "L-A-N-D" were removed.

In 1926, intent on developing an upscale automobile-oriented residential subdivision, Robert C. Gillis (1863–1947), president of the Santa Monica Land and Water Company, purchased 247 acres in Pacific Palisades, California, founded four years earlier as a district within the city of Los Angeles and located 20 miles west of its downtown and four miles north of the city of Santa Monica.[88] Gillis purchased the picturesque site on a bluff overlooking the Pacific Ocean from the heirs of railroad magnate Collis P. Huntington (1821–1900), who had failed in his effort to build a private estate and commercial seaport at the mouth of Potrero Canyon. Huntington had purchased the tract from Abbot Kinney (1850–1920), developer of Venice, California (see p. 321), who also had failed in his plans to develop a subdivision on the site in the late 1880s but had made a lasting contribution to it by planting hundreds of eucalyptus trees. Landscape architect Mark Daniels (1881–1952), former landscape engineer of Yosemite National Park and director of the National Park Service, and engineer W. W. Williams (n.d.) were commissioned to prepare the plan

for **Huntington Palisades**, named in honor of the site's former owner. Partially protected by natural barriers and bound by Beverly Boulevard (now Sunset Boulevard) on the north, Chautauqua Boulevard on the east, the Pacific Ocean on the south, and Potrero Canyon on the west, Huntington Palisades was promoted as a "carefully restricted" development occupying the "last of the city's mountain shoreline."[89]

In the more intensely developed northern portion of the site within walking distance of the modest village of Pacific Palisades, Daniels and Williams laid out semicircular streets bisected by Pampas Ricas Boulevard, the enclave's 100-foot-wide main thoroughfare with a planted median leading from El Cerco Place, an oval-shaped group of houses, to the principal entrance at Sunset Boulevard. The southern parcel featured curvilinear 60-foot-wide streets that followed the topography of the site while sparing the eucalyptus trees planted forty years earlier. Daniels and Williams divided the site into 226 lots ranging in size from one-quarter of an acre to a little over a full acre, with the largest houses occupying sites along the mesa's rim. In order to control development, Gillis imposed several restrictions, establishing

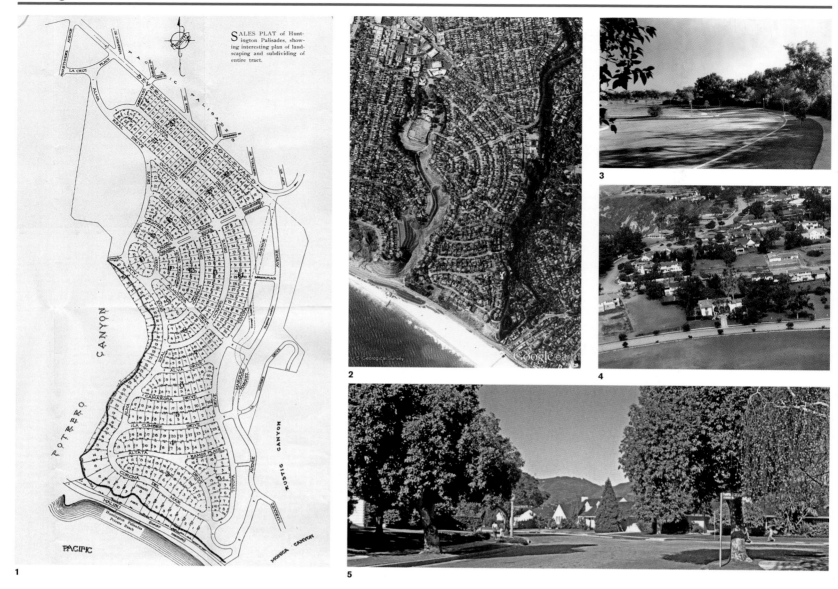

1. Plat map, Mark Daniels and W. W. Williams, 1926. SMLW

2. Aerial view. GE (2007)

3. Alma Real Drive. SMLW

4. Aerial view of Altata and Alma Real Drives. SMLW (c. 1950)

5. Ocampo Drive and Pampas Ricas Boulevard. Garvin. AG (1976)

minimum construction costs and requiring that only single-family houses, none taller than two stories, be built. Setback requirements were instituted and hedges were limited in height to five feet. Membership in a private bathing club, enjoying 300 feet of beach frontage, was an amenity offered to each resident.

In June 1929, the *Los Angeles Times* reported that fifteen houses had been completed in Huntington Palisades, with several more under construction, including a handsome two-story design by Paul R. Williams (1894–1980) and a Spanish Colonial–style house from the firm of George E. Gable (1892–1953) and C. Stanley Wyant (1890–1964). The economic turmoil that soon followed, however, stymied development for the next fifteen years. When construction resumed after the end of World War II, picking up considerable steam in the late 1950s and early 1960s, despite changing tastes in residential architecture, Huntington Palisades was able to maintain its essential character with the original plan and building restrictions continuing to hold sway. Historian Robert Fogelson admired the subdivision's "romantic scheme of curved streets,"[90] while Kevin Starr, the prolific historian

of California's past, praised the "intricately platted" development "which took maximum advantage of sweeping mountain views."[91]

By the 1910s sophisticated garden enclaves were not only cropping up in major cities and their suburbs but also in minor cities. Walter Burley Griffin (1876–1937), the American architect most famous for his competition-winning design (1912) of the Australian capital, Canberra (see p. 646), took on several such projects in the United States, where despite a considerable boost in the wake of his Australian success, his commissions tended to be for small, Midwestern enclaves.[92] Nonetheless, Griffin's decision to permanently relocate to Australia in 1914, combined with the economic slowdown accompanying the outbreak of war in Europe, meant that few of his garden enclaves would be realized. For the utopistic **Emory Hills** (c. 1911), in Wheaton, Illinois, twenty-eight miles west of Chicago, Griffin subdivided 20 acres into nine farms of varying sizes, arranged around a circular loop road and arcing tangential drives, with the intention of allowing Chicago commuters "to make use of their limited hours of freedom in a more substantial form of recreation than mere pleasure seeking."[93] The farms were to provide a "maximum convenience for the work of each plot for a minimum of expense in equipment and help," with a premium being placed on "health and enjoyment of mind and body before pecuniary profits."[94] Griffin's plan grouped the houses together with outbuildings to form small compounds arranged on their sites to take advantage of distant views but also to block out the railroad tracks to the east and "other features of the town life" that "tend to be somewhat in evidence."[95]

Griffin's **Ridge Quadrangles** (c. 1912) was another utopistic development.[96] Intended to house 200 families (1,000 people) on a rectangular site in Evanston, Illinois, bound by Dobson and Ridge Boulevards and Barton and Harvard Streets, Ridge Quadrangles was influenced by Unwin's diagrams suggesting layouts for blocks of cooperative dwellings published in *The Art of Building a Home* (1901) and *Nothing Gained by Overcrowding* (1912). A railroad line three blocks from the site was to provide primary transport for commuters to Chicago, but a parking garage, part of a building called a "community service station," was also included in the plan, one of the earliest examples of such a provision. Griffin reimagined the site, which had previously been laid out in keeping with the surrounding grid, with two long east–west oriented rectangular blocks, as three blocks formed by a T-shaped intersection with a circular pool in the center. By setting the detached and semidetached houses back and forth from the street, Griffin opened up views for each residence and allowed for individual front and rear gardens as well as shared "campuses" of one and five acres on the block interior.

Griffin's curvilinear plan for the **Clarke Resubdivision** (c. 1912), on a 20-acre parcel in Grinnell, Iowa, whose previous layout as an extension of the city grid was deemed infeasible due to drainage problems, allowed roads to wind along the prairie's natural ravines and reserved as house sites those spots that would offer the best views.[97] The design not only solved the drainage issues but increased the number of lots from fifty-seven to sixty-six while at the same time providing all but two lots with 75-foot frontages as compared with mostly 50-foot frontages in the previous plan. Griffin narrowed the streets as they entered the enclave, bringing all but one together in a five-point intersection. As Andrés Duany has written, the site plan displayed "the combination, preferred by Prairie School architects, of having both roads and buildings affected by the topography but not entirely determined by it in lockstep . . . The buildings are freely located on the best part of each lot but they are all disposed orthogonally."[98] The project was only partially realized, but elements reappeared in Griffin's later plan for Castlecrag, outside Sydney, Australia (see p. 652).

Griffin's most fully realized American suburban plan was for the residence park of **Rock Crest–Rock Glen**, in Mason City, Iowa, only three blocks from the center of the burgeoning farming and industrial town, on both sides of a sweeping bend of the Willow Creek Valley.[99]

Emory Hills

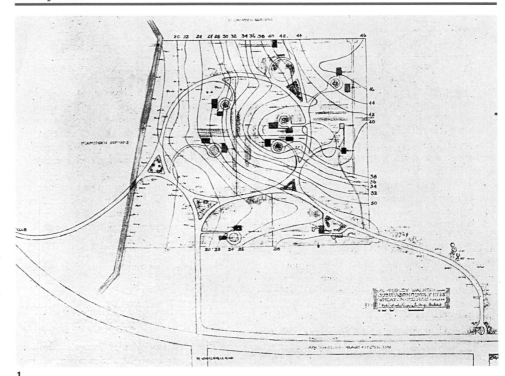

1. Plan, Walter Burley Griffin, c. 1911. WA13

Ridge Quadrangles

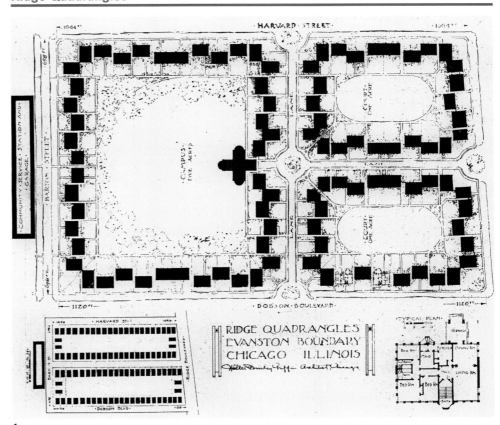

1. Plan, Walter Burley Griffin, c. 1912. WA13

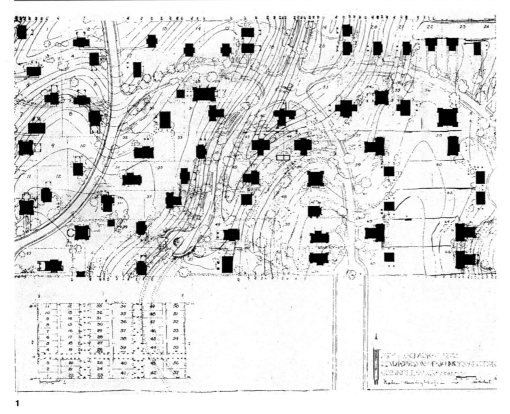

1

1. Plan, Walter Burley Griffin, c. 1912. WA13

Rock Crest referred to the bluffs and terraces on the south and east banks of the creek, while Rock Glen described the opposite bank where meadows gently sloped upward from the creek. The site, which had long been passed over because of its challenging terrain, was far from its pure natural state; it had been quarried for stone, a retired gristmill sat along the creek, and portions of the glen had been used as a dump.

The development was undertaken by two Mason City lawyers, James Blythe (1856–1938) and J. E. E. Markley (1857–1939), along with the builder and self-styled architect Joshua G. Melson (1865–1945). Blythe and Markley were responsible for bringing Frank Lloyd Wright (1867–1959) to Mason City to design the City National Bank and Park Inn Hotel (1907–9). They are thought to have wanted Wright to prepare a plan for their 18-acre Rock Crest–Rock Glen site, but when the architect eloped to Europe in 1909, the developers asked Griffin to undertake the job, agreeing to his terms that no changes to the land be made without prior approval. Griffin's plan, presented in 1912, placed twenty houses around the perimeter of the site in order to preserve for communal use the creek and its banks, which would become "the tranquil, luminescent focus of the community," according to planning historian Christopher Vernon.[100] Griffin described his house designs as being "as unique as their sites, cut into rock or perched on the crest or nestled in the cove as the case may be."[101] Of the eight houses that were originally built, five were completed to Griffin's designs, the most spectacular of which, the J. G. Melson house (1912), fit into a cavity in the limestone Rock Crest bluff, constructed in rough limestone ashlar so that its river facade seemed to grow naturally out of the cliff wall.

Washington Highlands (1916), a garden enclave in the town of Wauwatosa, itself a suburb of Milwaukee, Wisconsin, eventually accommodated 281 families on a 133-acre farm formerly belonging to Gustav Pabst, the prominent Milwaukee brewer.[102] Conceived by local developers Richter, Dick & Reuteman as a membership community with private parks and playing fields, it was planned by Werner Hegemann and Elbert Peets (1886–1968), assisted by Joseph Hudnut (1886–1968). Hegemann, a German-born city planner and multidisciplinary scholar trained in Europe and the United States, had served as secretary of the international city planning exhibitions in Berlin and Düsseldorf in 1910 and published a two-volume study of city planning, *Der Städtebau*, in 1911 and 1913, giving lectures on the subject in the United States shortly thereafter. Peets, a Harvard-educated American landscape architect and expert on European Renaissance and American Colonial city planning, had practiced for a year with the Boston firm of Pray, Hubbard & White, before leaving to collaborate with Hegemann on the design of the company town of Kohler, Wisconsin (1916) which shortly preceded Washington Highlands. The two would also collaborate on the monumental planning study, *The American Vitruvius: An Architect's Handbook of Civic Art* (1922).

The Washington Highlands site had remained undeveloped even as its surroundings were built up with gridded additions beginning in 1891, when the Pabst family granted a right-of-way to streetcar companies along Pabst Avenue (now West Lloyd Street), forming the development's northern boundary, with Eighth Avenue (now Sixty-eighth Street) on the west, Spring Avenue (now Sixtieth Street) on the east, and East Milwaukee Avenue on the south. The project was devised as a "secluded" enclave enclosed by hedges, walls, and gateways, with existing trees preserved to the fullest extent possible and interconnected parks meandering across the site. A promotional brochure touted Washington Highlands as a "new type of Subdivision—the super-subdivision it might be called," modeled on those examples in "Baltimore, New York, Kansas City and San Francisco [that] have acquired fame all over the country for setting new standards of beauty and convenience."[103] The developers highlighted its role as "by far the largest restricted area in Milwaukee," and their application of "the best principles and ideas in real estate in America and foreign countries," but they were careful to point out that "no one of the general public need feel to be excluded from its privileges . . . The environment of a thrifty workingman can and ought to be made just as beautiful as that of a millionaire: This is the *DEMOCRACY OF THE MODERN GARDEN CITY*."[104]

Although Washington Highlands was accessible by streetcar, the developers used renderings featuring cars comfortably navigating the streets to attract affluent automobile owners. The principal street, Washington Circle, was a horseshoe-shaped divided boulevard whose

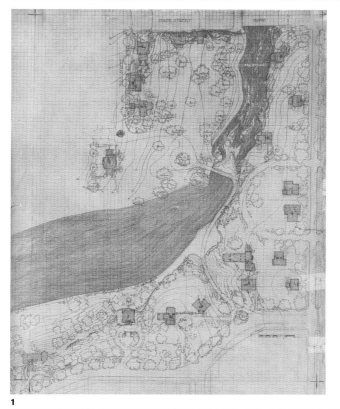

1. Plan, Walter Burley Griffin, c. 1912. NLA00

2. J. G. Melson house, Walter Burley Griffin, 1912, rendering by Marion Mahony Griffin. WA13

3. Hand-colored perspective rendering by Marion Mahony Griffin. NLA97 (c. 1912)

4. Sam Schneider house, Walter Burley Griffin, 1915. Ewing. FL (2006)

geometry was echoed in many of the surrounding roads. Mount Vernon Avenue, becoming Washington Boulevard as it extended east from the suburb to Washington Park and then linking to Milwaukee's street grid, was "not an ordinary street, but . . . the final link in the finest chain of boulevards of Milwaukee, making a *direct connection of smooth pavements between the heart of the Washington Highlands and the heart of the city of Milwaukee.*" Interestingly, Hegemann called for a forced perspective on Mount Vernon Avenue, narrowing its width and condensing the hedges and trees along its edges in a pattern "dear to the great masters of old Italian garden craft."[105] Parcels were set aside for schools, and the original plan suggested specific placement of small-scale apartment groups along the edges.

Describing the project in 1923, Hegemann and Peets explained that the design "was made shortly after the international competition for laying out a quarter section of land in the neighboring city of Chicago (see p. 162) had been decided in favor of an informal design. The conception of a curved street, in fact of anything deviating from the routine, had at that time become so pleasing to the popular imagination, that the dealers in real estate asked their architect first of all to give them a curved street, which in their mind was identical with city planning: the help of an outside town planning architect being required only for the purpose of deviating from the straight streets of the existing gridiron plan. Fortunately for the designer, the topography was difficult and justified curves."[106] The neighborhood's success led the developers to commission Hegemann and Peets to plan a nearby subdivision called **Grand Circle** (1918) on a flat site bordered by a trolley on one side.[107] Though at first glance the circular plan seems arbitrary, it notably provides for automobiles by placing a central garage court accessible by each of the fourteen houses on the inner ring.

Wawaset Park (1918–21), in Wilmington, Delaware, sponsored by the chemical conglomerate DuPont, was located in close proximity to Union Park Gardens (see p. 873), an industrial workers' village designed by John Nolen (1869–1937), but Wawaset was intended for DuPont managers, scientists, and executives.[108] In early 1918 the company purchased a flat, featureless

1

2

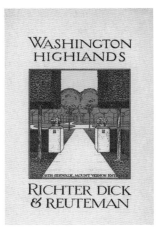

3

4

58-acre site just west of downtown, bound by West Seventh Street and Greenhill, Pennsylvania, and Woodlawn Avenues, formerly home to Schuetzen Park, a horse racing and automobile track that also hosted the state fair. The company selected Edward L. Palmer Jr. (1877–1952) to plan the strictly residential subdivision based on the recommendation of Frank H. McCormick, a DuPont employee who had lived in a Palmer-designed house in Roland Park, Maryland, where the architect also served as company architect in the Baltimore development's second phase. Palmer's Olmsted-inspired plan for Wawaset Park featured a main entrance via Riverview Avenue at the northern end of the site that quickly branched off into Nottingham and Blackshire Roads, which ultimately connected near the southern end of the site, creating a large oval within the subdivision's rectangular boundaries. Within the oval, Palmer grouped row, semidetached, and detached houses on four short, curving streets and included two circles and a cul-de-sac surrounded by rowhouses. West Eleventh Street, a wide boulevard with a generous landscaped median, ran east–west through the site as a continuation of the Wilmington grid. The extensive tree-planting program adopted to relieve the barren site was another significant component of the plan.

Palmer was also the architect of ninety-five brick, stucco, and stone houses completed at Wawaset Park by 1921, including the groups of rowhouses surrounding Bedford Court as well as those along Crawford Circle and the *rond-point* created by the intersection of Nottingham and Blackshire Roads, later named Palmer Square in his honor. Although DuPont offered generous financing for the mortgages, sales were not particularly brisk, and the company soon offered the houses as well as unimproved lots to buyers outside the company. To maintain control of the upscale development, plans for any new house or alterations to existing dwellings had to be approved by the Wawaset Park Maintenance Corporation. Between the mid-1920s and early 1930s, another one hundred houses, primarily larger Tudor- and Georgian-style detached houses, were completed in Wawaset Park, along with one five-story brick apartment house (Wallace E. Hance, 1932). Photographs taken at the subdivision's inception are not particularly flattering, with the two- and three-story buildings overwhelming the bare site, but Palmer's extensive landscaping scheme eventually took hold, transforming Wawaset Park into a leafy enclave.

John Nolen was responsible for the plan of **Seneca Heights** (1920), a garden enclave comprising 140 houses

Grand Circle

1

2

Wawaset Park

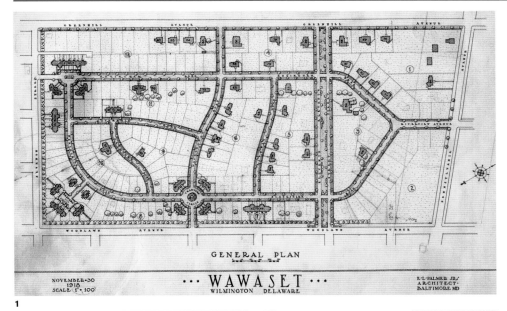

1

2

3

4

5

on 200 acres less than one mile from the business center of Olean, New York, a small industrial city whose boom beginning in the 1860s was tied to the production of oil, for which the city was named.[109] Occupying a recently stabilized sloping site above the Allegheny River in the foothills of the Allegheny Mountains, the town was organized around a 50-foot-wide tree-lined spine leading southeast from a public square near the river past a large central plot reserved for a school. Secondary streets, including three culs-de-sac that Nolen hoped would "give an air of homelike seclusion and quietude to the localities," were 42 feet wide and lined with 6- and 7-foot-wide planting strips to accommodate trees.[110] In some areas, the steep incline led to the inclusion of landscaped pedestrian footpaths and steps. Alleyways

were not provided behind the houses, which were screened from one another by trees. The Olean Housing Corporation, established to develop the town, relied heavily on the local population, which donated its time and resources to the project to build the five-, six-, and seven-room single-family and double houses designed by Alfred C. Bossom (1881–1965), an English architect, then resident in the United States.

In the 1920s, automobile-oriented garden enclaves were being planned to meet the expectations of an affluent upper middle class who preferred to commute in private automobiles rather than use public transportation. Usually constructed at the outer edge, where land was cheap, many of these enclaves were little more than developers' subdivisions, with little sense of place,

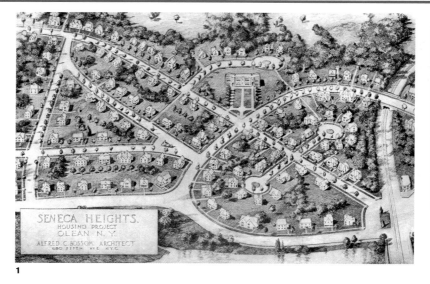

1. Bird's-eye view, Alfred C. Bossom. A21

2. Aerial view. CRS

Palmer Woods

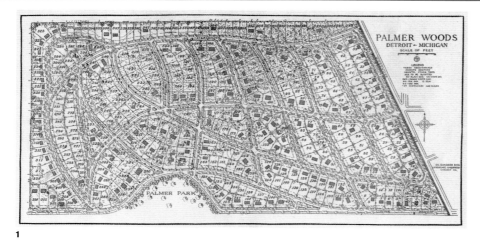

1. Plan, Ossian Cole Simonds, 1915. BHC

2. Typical street. RAMSA (2012)

as Sinclair Lewis made clear in his 1922 novel, *Babbitt*, whose title character resides in a Dutch Colonial house in Floral Heights, an upscale neighborhood in the fictitious Midwestern city of Zenith, where "a stranger suddenly dropped into the business-center . . . could not have told whether he was in a city of Oregon or Georgia, Ohio or Maine, Oklahoma or Manitoba."[111] For example, in Detroit, where the automobile industry was based, the 188-acre suburb of **Palmer Woods** was developed in 1915 by Charles W. Burton (1848–1945) and laid out by landscape gardener Ossian Cole Simonds (1855–1932). The site was buffered from the surrounding city by a cemetery on the north and Palmer Park and its golf links on the south.[112] Three hundred houses, built mainly between 1915 and 1940, were set among lushly landscaped drives shaped to create picturesque vistas, attracting Detroit's elite, many of whom were automobile executives.

In 1920 developer R. H. Wilkinson Jr. (b. 1876) purchased the 1,000-acre Perkins estate, reserving 300 acres just east of the steel town of Warren, Ohio, fourteen miles northwest of Youngstown, for a residence park and golf course, initially named the Country Club District in deference to the development in Kansas City, but also known as **Perkinswood**.[113] Wilkinson hired landscape architect William Pitkin Jr. (1884–1972), who had earlier planned two industrial villages, Eclipse Park, Wisconsin (see p. 840) and a development for automobile workers outside Flint, Michigan (see p. 842), to prepare a plan for the relatively flat, well-treed site. Many of the most substantial houses faced the golf course but, grouped in roughly oval-shaped blocks or placed along straight and curving north–south streets, the remainder of the houses were evenly set back behind generous front lawns. In his 1921 three-volume history of Youngstown and the surrounding Mahoning Valley, Joseph G. Butler Jr., who was also Wilkinson's investment partner in the subdivision, described the nascent development as the "Shaker Heights of Warren."[114] Boosterism aside, Butler's assessment rings true as the development quickly became the city's most exclusive neighborhood.

In 1922 the Detroit-based architect Leonard B. Willeke (1889–1970) was hired to rework a 12-acre estate in Cincinnati's East Walnut Hills district into the **Green Hills and Far Hills Subdivision** (1923), placing twenty-eight houses on small lots around the property's existing mansion.[115] The enclave consisted of two entrance roads leading to a loop, within which six houses were placed with ten more around the perimeter. To the east of the

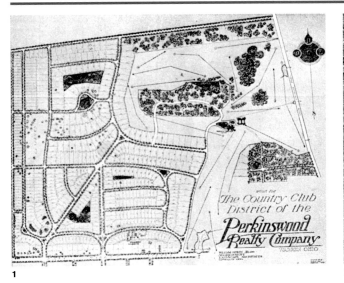

1. Plan, William Pitkin Jr., 1920. NRE26

2. Aerial view. GE (2006)

1

2

Green Hills and Far Hills Subdivision

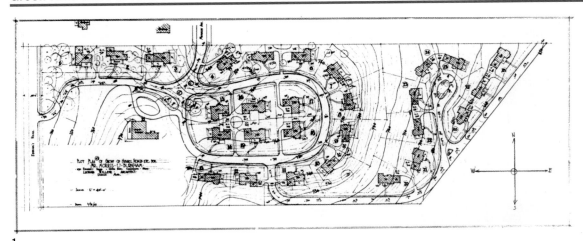

1

2

1. Plan, Leonard B. Willeke, 1923. TWB

2. Advertisement in the *Cincinnati Enquirer*, September 30, 1923. BHL

central circle, detached houses sharing common driveways were to extend along an unrealized cul-de-sac. While three houses were completed according to designs by Willeke and his collaborator Moritz Sax (b. 1873), the original developer's death left the site for other builders to fill out.

Earle S. Draper (1894–1994) designed the high-end garden enclave of **Forest Hills** (1917), North Carolina, in the city of Durham, home to tobacco and textile companies, a growing number of banks and insurance companies, as well as Trinity College, which would change its name to Duke University in 1924.[116] In 1917 the New Hope Realty Company, led by insurance executive and former Durham mayor W. J. Griswold, purchased 242 heavily wooded, undeveloped acres a little over a mile southwest of the downtown business district with the intention of creating a suburb geared toward the rising number of professionals working in the prosperous city. Draper's plan, in marked contrast to Durham's prevailing gridiron pattern, divided the site into 331 generously sized, irregularly shaped lots surrounding a nine-hole golf course. Curvilinear streets followed the topography of the hilly site, while Hope Valley Road (renamed University Drive), the main thoroughfare,

with a landscaped median, extended northeast to southwest through the center of the tract. The plan also included a "colored" section intended for 115 building lots, east of the New Hope Valley Railway tracks.

Progress was stymied by the war, and before any construction began at Forest Hills, the developers went bankrupt, selling the property in 1922 to local businessmen James O. Cobb and J. Fuller Glass who reincorporated the New Hope Realty Company but trimmed the site to 150 acres, now roughly bound by Bivins and Wells Streets on the north, Kent Street on the west, Forestwood and Beverly Drives on the south, and the railroad tracks on the east. The new developers, after dropping the "colored" section, maintained Draper's basic plan and hired local architect George Watts Carr (1892–1975) to design the first houses as well as the modest Colonial-style clubhouse (1923). The most interesting of the speculatively developed Colonial-, Tudor-, and Georgian-style houses were grouped around Carolina Circle and the oval-shaped Hermitage Court, whose name was most likely taken from the Nolen-designed 1911 subdivision near Charlotte's Myers Park. Lots were also sold to individuals, with surprisingly few restrictions placed on new construction except that houses

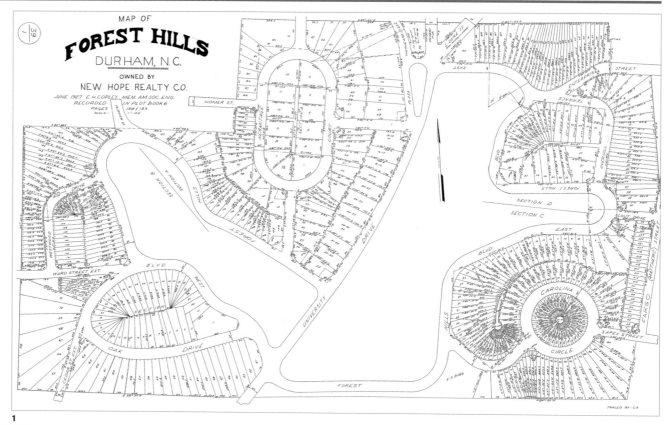

1

2

3

had to be set back at least 30 feet from the street and no plots could be subdivided. More modest houses, including some bungalows, lined University Drive. Picturesque Forest Hills, characterized by historians Catherine W. Bishir and Michael T. Southern as Durham's "first true automobile suburb," quickly became the city's most sought after residential neighborhood.[117]

A few more than one hundred houses were completed before the New Hope Realty Company again went bankrupt, this time due to the effects of the stock market crash and the Depression. Durham banker James Sprunt Hill took over the development and donated the clubhouse and golf course to the city, which converted the facilities into a 39-acre public park. A second wave of house construction, similar in spirit to the first, began in the late 1930s under Hill's direction. Another one hundred houses were completed over the next decade, many again designed by George Watts Carr along with another local practitioner, H. Raymond Weeks (1901–1956). Forest Hills retained its sylvan setting and exclusive character after this round of development.

Khakum Wood (1925), in Greenwich, Connecticut, planned by Brooklyn-born landscape architect Edward Clark Whiting (1881–1962), who spent his career in the Olmsted Brothers office, where he became partner in 1920, was laid out on the 175-acre estate of architect, housing reformer, and historian I. N. Phelps Stokes (1867–1944), whose own residence (1908–12), after which the development was named, incorporated a half-timbered Tudor manor house (1597) relocated from Ipswich, England.[118] The land was subdivided into forty-three residential lots ranging in size from about two to six acres, with Stokes's house remaining on a 23-acre parcel until its demolition after his death. Whiting, incorporating two ponds and a large lake, situated houses to take advantage of views that were carefully indicated on the original plan. A main drive and several culs-de-sac were "laid out as lightly as possible on the topography," as Andrés Duany has noted, "not as shortcuts, but as long and meandering as necessary. The resulting inefficiency is economically feasible only when the roads are detailed in a rural manner: narrow and

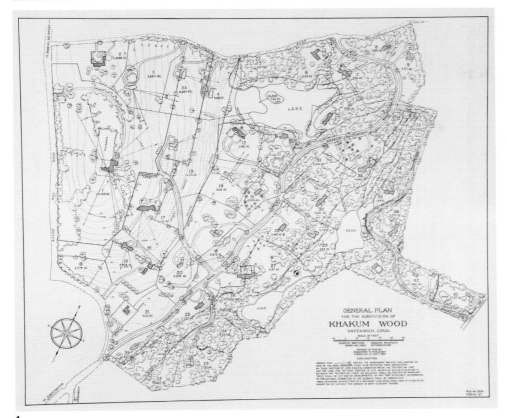

1

3

with drainage by swales." As a result, Khakum Wood, "seventy-five years after its design, looks like there has been no design applied at all."[119]

In San Antonio, Texas, **Olmos Park Estates** (1927), at the northern edge of the city, was developed by oilman Herman Charles Thorman (1884–1954) on a hilly 1,600-acre tract on the west bank of Olmos Creek that had been undevelopable because of frequent flooding until the completion in 1926 of the 1,941-foot Olmos Dam.[120] The dam not only kept the land dry but also supported a roadway that served as an important new crosstown link to the east side of the creek, where the suburb of **Alamo Heights**, laid out in 1891 by a Denver, Colorado–based engineer, had begun to flourish in the early 1920s.[121] Olmos Park and Alamo Heights, in addition to the adjacent Terrell Hills, another restricted suburb that deviated from the gridiron plan and began to be developed in the 1930s, were incorporated as independent municipalities, forming small "island cities" after 1944 when San Antonio annexed thousands of acres around them.[122] Olmos Park's plan, the work of an anonymous engineer, provided no sidewalks and was almost entirely geared toward the automobile and to a concept of introspective exclusivity. Alameda Circle, a traffic rotary with five streets radiating outward, contributed to a street plan that discouraged through traffic. As one resident described it, Olmos Park "was really a little town on the edge of a big town and was situated where it was 'out of the way'—and because of the street layout, nobody went thru' it or even came into it except us."[123] Typical restrictive covenants governed building materials, minimum construction costs, and lot sizes and excluded black residents as well as nonresidential uses, positioning the neighborhood as an exclusive enclave.

In 1925 J. P. Stephenson (1866–1937), a Dallas entrepreneur, and F. N. Drane (1862–1938), a real estate investor based in Corsicana, Texas, purchased a 150-acre parcel five miles north of downtown Dallas and just west of Highland Park with the intention of creating a strictly residential, upscale development that would take its inspiration from English precedent, with single-family houses grouped around commonly shared parkland.[124] The developers' original name for the subdivision was Greenaway Parks in honor of Kate Greenaway (1846–1901), the English author and illustrator whose children's books are filled with drawings of picturesque landscapes, but the name was soon simplified to **Greenway Parks**. Stephenson and Drane selected architect David R. Williams (1890–1962) to prepare the plan, perhaps attracted to the native Texan because of his work in Mexico for American oil companies, especially Aguila Colony (1922), Tampico, which eschewed a standard grid in favor of a scheme that placed houses and public facilities around a common green.[125] Except for an existing dirt road, Mockingbird Lane, at the southern end of the parcel, Greenway Parks' site, otherwise bound by Inwood Road on the west, University Boulevard on the north, and the tracks of the St. Louis Southwestern Railway on the east, was unimproved and vacant.

Williams bisected the site, intended for 300 houses, with the 110-foot-wide north–south Greenway Boulevard, with 70- to 150-foot-wide, 130-foot-deep house lots

1. Plan, Edward Clark Whiting, 1926. FLO (1937)

2, 3. Typical streets. RAMSA (2012)

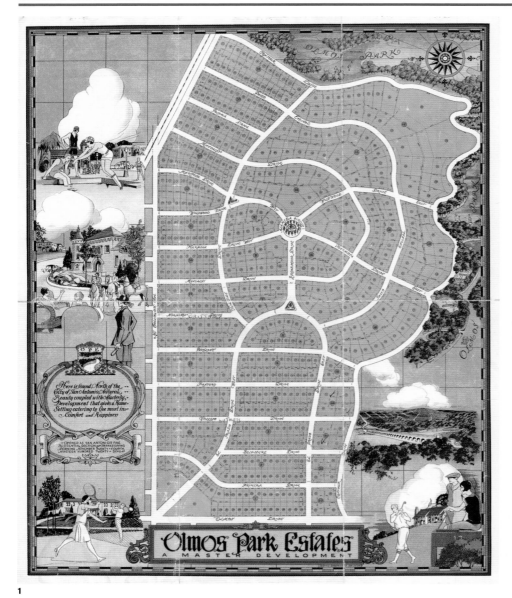

1. Advertising brochure and map. SACS (1927)

2. Aerial view. COP (1927)

3. Alameda Circle. Porterfield. EP (2011)

4. West El Prado Drive. Porterfield. EP (2011)

located on gently curving east–west streets. The tree-lined Greenway Boulevard branched off into two separate roads at both ends, creating two triangular parks. The highlights of the plan were the 100- to 200-foot-wide, block-long central common greens separating houses in the southern half of the site, representing 27 percent of the entire tract. Williams hoped that front doors would face the generously sized, shared parks, but this desire was only partially realized because the developers refused to mandate this provision when they sold plots to individuals building their own houses. The northern part of the site, planned for more modest houses, substituted 15-foot-wide alleys for the wide greens. Before proceeding with Williams's plan, Ferguson and Drane sought the advice of J. C. Nichols (1880–1950), developer of Kansas City's Country Club District (see p. 167), who gave it his seal of approval.

Although Williams would design a house (1929) for Drane in Corsicana and go on to become an influential practitioner and leader of the so-called Texas regionalist movement, his work at Greenway Parks was

limited to the formation of its plan. Between 1927 and 1932 a number of other Texas architects, including James Cheek (1895–1970) of the firm Fooshee & Cheek, Clyde H. Griesenbeck (1892–1970), Ralph Bryan (1892–1965), and Fonzie Robertson (1890–1970) completed fifty Colonial-, Spanish Colonial-, Tudor-, Mediterranean-, and Arts and Crafts–style houses in the subdivision, the majority built by individuals who purchased lots but were required to get the approval of the developers before proceeding.

THE PRIVATE PLACE IDEA

Among garden enclaves, those constituting "private places" are the most unusual. First developed in St. Louis in the 1850s as what architectural historian Charles Savage has called "the only defense against inadequate municipal protection available to the residents of the city," private places represent the most systematically thought-through examples of the garden enclave type,

Alamo Heights

1

2

3

1. Census map. USNA (1940)

2, 3. Typical streets. Williams. SWLD (2012)

Greenway Parks

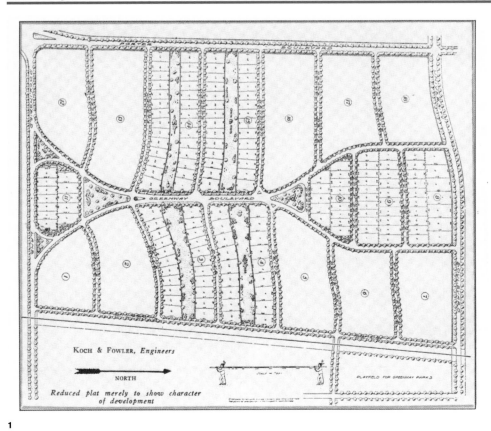

1

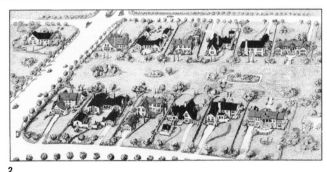

2

3

1. Plan, David R. Williams, 1925. GPHA

2. Bird's-eye view showing common green. GPHA

3. Typical street. Rene. WC (2012)

many with highly articulated street hierarchies as well as sophisticated development controls.[126] Proliferating just before the turn of the twentieth century and spreading to cities throughout the country, including Brooklyn, New York, New Orleans, Louisiana, Clearwater, Florida, and Houston, Texas, private places are not owned by the host city but by the property owners themselves, who, as members of a street association, fund physical maintenance, including that of trees, streets, parks, lighting, and sewers, and pay for security and maintenance personnel. Private places typically consist of a grand boulevard entered at one or both ends past ornamental gates. The boulevard is frequently divided by a generously planted mall that, as the noted urbanist Alexander Garvin points out in his history of American planning, contributes to the homeowners' illusion of life "opposite a garden because the island's landscaping usually blocks the view of the houses facing their own."[127] Lining the boulevard, large houses, often built on relatively small lots, are typically set back uniformly from the street in accord with strict development controls established by the street association to foster an impression of openness far beyond the realities of the situation. The closure of some private places to through traffic adds to the feel of a quiet refuge apart from, yet embedded into, the city.

The historian James Neal Primm has observed that private places constitute an urban equivalent to the great country estates that were being developed in post–Civil War America. The historical evolution of the private place type should be seen as a reflection of what Primm has described as the

> *increasingly ambitious efforts of the wealthy, the socially secure, and the socially aspiring to wall out the world, to exclude from their line of sight and smell all that was unpleasant in city living. The noise and smoke of industry; the swarming masses of the poor; the stifling heat of the treeless downtown streets; the risk of epidemic disease— all these could be avoided, or at least minimized by distance and enforced isolation . . . Large country estates limited socialization; in the city the private place was the answer.*[128]

Primm's observations of 1988 echo those of S. L. Sherer, writing in 1904, who summed up the "the idea of private places" as the promotion of a "union of house and garden essential to the art of living rightly . . . It imparts a measure of privacy to homelife . . . and serves to protect a neighborhood from many annoyances that necessarily surround localities where restrictions do not pertain. And . . . it encourages the building of houses of a higher standard of architectural excellence, and this makes for a better life."[129]

Alexander Garvin charts the evolution of St. Louis's private places, which established the model that by the early twentieth century became a distinct type. The first private places "were within walking distance of the business district. As the city became an increasingly important industrial metropolis, those citizens with enough money to select among different residential locations chose to move away from downtown congestion, noise, and grime. This move was accelerated during the 1880s by the introduction of mass transit. Whereas pedestrian St. Louis had extended westward from the Mississippi River for a distance of only 1½ miles, the trolley (well known to fans of the movie *Meet Me in St. Louis*) allowed settlement to extend along radial streetcar lines for a distance of about 6 miles. Developers lost no time in creating new private places on this newly accessible, cheaper suburban land."[130]

Lucas Place, planned by James H. Lucas (1800–1873) in 1851, was the first private place in St. Louis, conforming to the grid as it ran for two blocks up the slope from 14th to 16th Street (it was extended two additional blocks to 18th Street in 1853, and in 1859 was extended again to Jefferson Avenue).[131] At its eastern end, Missouri Park, given to the city by the Lucas family, prevented through traffic from invading the neighborhood. While the plan of Lucas Place did not differ physically from that of the typical St. Louis street, its innovative internal regulations prohibiting any commercial development and reserving part of the property exclusively for schools and churches ensured the development's distinction from its surroundings. Traffic was confined to pleasure vehicles; buildings had to be set back 25 feet from the building line; and the street was itself owned by its residents, who shared in the responsibility for its maintenance. Lucas Place had no gates and though one end was terminated by a park, the other led, as Charles Savage has written, into "the less developed adjacent areas."[132] Yet its combination of covenants and restrictions were enough to set it apart from the random character of the developing city at its edges.

Benton Place (1868) introduced what would become the typical pattern of St. Louis's private places.[133] Located north of Lafayette Square, a former common pasture that had been turned into a public park in 1836, Benton Place, developed by Montgomery Blair (1813–1883), postmaster general in Abraham Lincoln's cabinet, was arranged by Julius Pitzman (1837–1923), a German-born civil engineer, to provide a series of lots facing the park across Park Avenue and to open up the center of the property with a single road leading past a gated entry before encircling a lushly planted elliptical green space. The plan called for forty-nine lots, each 25 feet wide. Most lots backed up to a service alley that opened to both the public and private streets. The introduction of the service alley and of the landscaped central mall marked a significant advance over Lucas Place, as did the fact that the private road was in effect a cul-de-sac, eliminating through traffic.

The grandest private place, **Vandeventer Place**, begun in 1870, was developed by Charles H. Peck (1817–1899), a builder, real estate entrepreneur, and sometime architect, in conjunction with Napoleon Mullikin, Joseph McCune, and the heirs of Peter L. Vandeventer.[134] Its spacious plan and lush landscaping

Lucas Place

1. Bird's-eye view. CCHM (1875)

2. North side of Lucas Place between 15th and 16th Streets. CCHM (1885)

Benton Place

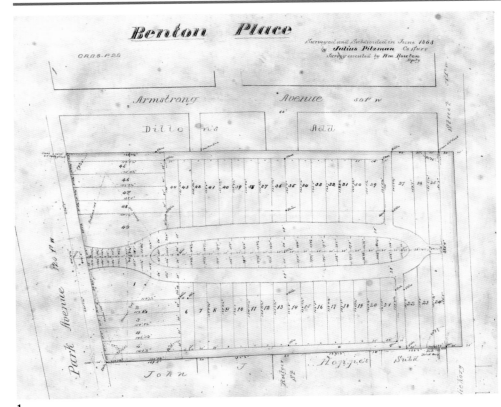

1

2

3

1. Plan, Julius Pitzman, 1868. PCSE

2. Benton Place. Garvin. AG (2010)

3. Benton Place. Naffziger. CN (2012)

make it "pivotal in the history of the private places," as Charles Savage has noted.[135] Julius Pitzman connected the new enclave to the city grid but marked the entrance with a fountain and provided an internal focus in the form of a 50-foot-wide landscaped center mall flanked by 30-foot-wide roadways, creating an elongated version of the Benton Place ellipse. Set on high ground, northwest of Lucas Place, Vandeventer Place was entered from the west side of Grand Avenue. No churches, schools, or museums were permitted, nor were any commercial uses. All deliveries were confined to service alleys. The development was bisected by one street, which was dedicated to public use in perpetuity. Strict deed restrictions were imposed. Houses on the eighty-six lots, each 50 feet wide and 143 feet deep, were required to be set back 30 feet from the street, including a 12-foot-wide strip between curb and lawn that contained a sidewalk. From the first, many of the lots were combined, with some owners merging as many as five lots, so that in contrast with previous private places, where the house architecture was rather urban in character, Vandeventer Place seemed almost ruralesque, with lavish, "artistic" houses designed by such notable architects as Peabody & Stearns, Burnham & Root, and Henry Hobson Richardson, whose fortresslike John R. Lionberger house (1886), 27 Vandeventer Place, was probably the most distinctive.[136] Louis C. Mullgardt, of Stewart, McClure & Mullgardt, designed the exedral east and west gates at the entrance road, flanked by smaller gates on each side for pedestrians.

Vandeventer Place was "no diminutive cul-de-sac like Benton" but a street and a garden combined to ensure the

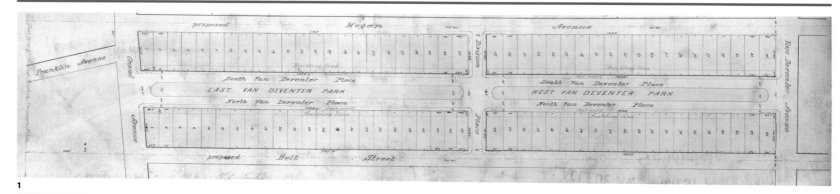

1. Plan, Julius Pitzman, 1870. PCSE

2. Bird's-eye view. PSL (1875)

3. John R. Lionberger residence,
H. H. Richardson, 1886.
Schankman. MHM (1946)

4. View looking over Vandeventer
Place from Grand Avenue. MHM
(c. 1902)

privacy and security of its residents.[137] It proved, as Savage has written, that a private place "need not be limited to a block in length, that it could be superimposed on the city's grid plan, and that it was unnecessary to restrict it to a cul-de-sac, lined with narrow-fronted lots."[138] Sadly, as industry encroached around its flanks, pushing fashionable neighborhoods farther west, Vandeventer's fortunes declined, and with the expiration of the covenants it was demolished in two campaigns between 1948 and 1958, with only the fountain, the east gate, and the porch of the Lionberger house preserved at other locations.

Shaw Place (1878), just west of Grand Avenue, was planned by George I. Barnett (1815–1898), who also designed all ten of its two-story houses in red brick with limestone trim.[139] The plan is similar but more generous than that of Benton Place, with a north–south landscaped cul-de-sac-like mall around which the houses are grouped. **Clifton Heights** (1885), the next in the sequence, has a looping, naturalistic road pattern that

may be traceable to its origins not as a conventional real estate development but as a Methodist Church retreat, similar to Oak Bluffs on Martha's Vineyard (see p. 302). Clifton Heights was developed by a group of Methodist investors and their pastor, the Reverend Benjamin St. James Fry (1824–1892), who commissioned Julius Pitzman to survey and plat their 35-acre tract.[140] Pitzman's plan made the most of the steeply sloping topography, reserving a flat portion to serve as a village green, Clifton Park, in which was located a small pond.

Pitzman returned to the more conventional gridiron plan at **West Cabanne Place** (1888), which was advertised as "an ideal quiet suburban home" that would "become a second Vandeventer Place."[141] The gently sloping former Cabanne family farm, like Clifton Heights, was at the city's farthest edge, but connected to the center by a narrow gauge railway. More than most of the private places, the houses of West Cabanne Place exhibited an architectural coherence, with many excellent examples

Shaw Place

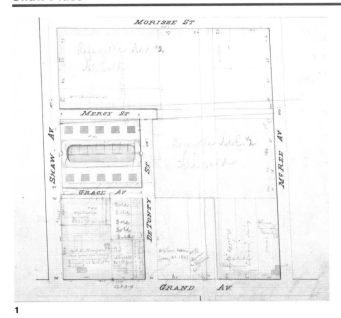

1. Plat map, 1878. MBG

2. Shaw Place. Naffziger. CN (2012)

Clifton Heights

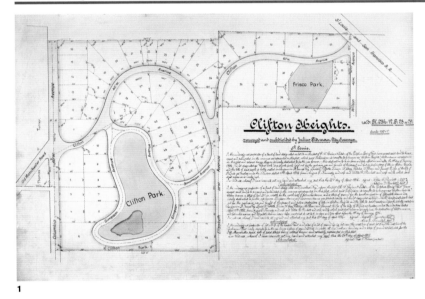

1. Plan, Julius Pitzman, 1885. PCSE

2. View across pond. Naffziger. CN (2012)

of the Shingle Style, including one of H. H. Richardson's masterpieces, the Henry S. Potter house (1886), which was razed in 1958.

West Cabanne Place's rectilinear plan was not as advanced as some preceding it—with no boulevard and no service streets. But the next private place development, the **Forest Park Addition** (1888), contained two boulevards: Westmoreland Place, developed by four businessmen, George C. Capen, William L. Huse, Thomas H. West, and Edwards Whitaker, and Portland Place, undertaken by George Warren Brown, F. W. Carter, Samuel Kennard, and Lewis B. Tebbets.[142] Laid out by Pitzman, Forest Park Addition, on the 78-acre Griswold tract, was, according to Savage, "the fullest and finest development" of the private place type in St. Louis.[143] The addition was bordered on its south by the newly established Forest Park. Portland Place and Westmoreland Place ran east–west through Pitzman's plan, with a narrow north–south street, Lake Avenue,

located just to the west of center, running south from Portland Place to Forest Park Terrace, which became known as Lindell Boulevard in 1906. The proximity of Forest Park vastly enhanced the development's appeal as did the extension of cable car service to Kings Highway and Maryland Avenue, just opposite the Westmoreland Place gates. Restrictions were more severe than in earlier developments. Buildings had to be at least 40 feet from the street curb, but towers and balconies and porches could be 12 feet closer. Only one house was permitted on each of the 100-by-195-foot lots, and the design of each house had to be approved by the association.

Westmoreland Place and Portland Place were entered through elaborate gates. The firm of William Sylvester Eames (1857–1915) and Thomas Crane Young (1858–1934), who designed six of the houses at the eastern end of Westmoreland Place, also designed the low, tawny limestone, red-tile hip-roofed gatehouses (1889) that supported wrought-iron gates and a wrought-iron arch at its eastern

West Cabanne Place

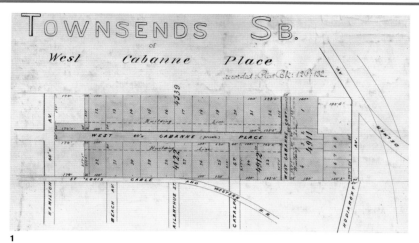

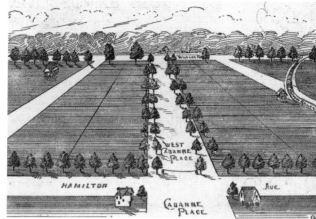

1. Plan, Julius Pitzman, 1888. PCSE

2. Advertisement from *The Spectator*, 1887. SAV

3, 4. West Cabanne Place. Naffziger. CN (2012)

Forest Park Addition

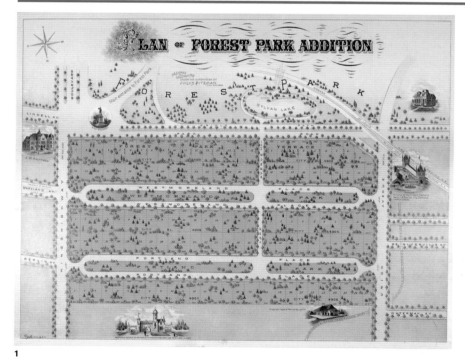

1. Plan, Julius Pitzman, 1887. PCSE

2. East gate, Portland Place, Theodore C. Link. CRS

3. Portland Place. Garvin. AG (2003)

4. Westmoreland Place. Garvin. AG (1997)

5. East gate, Westmoreland Place, Eames & Young, 1889. RAMSA

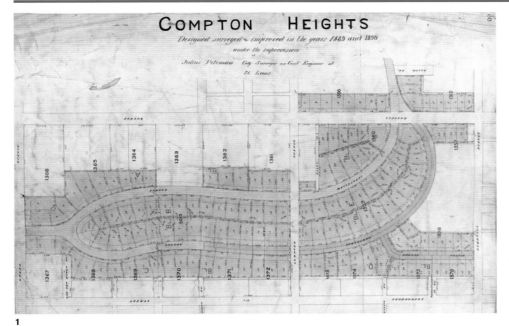

1. Plan, Julius Pitzman, 1890. PCSE

2. Hawthorne Boulevard from Grand Avenue. Boehl. MHM (1890)

3. Longfellow Boulevard. Naffziger. CN (2012)

4. Entrance gates. Naffziger. CN (2012)

5. Street sign. Naffziger. CN (2012)

entrance. Theodore C. Link (1850–1923) designed both the east and west gates of Portland Place. The east gate took the form of an octagonal gray-brick and rough-ashlar-limestone tower rising to a steeply pitched eight-sided roof, as well as two lych-gates set in flanking brick and stone walls.

Julius Pitzman took the private place type even further toward rurality in his design for **Compton Heights** (1889–90) by capitalizing on existing topography to create a looping, winding street plan that broke decisively with the city grid.[144] Ornamental street signs helped to reinforce the identity of Compton Heights, though it was Pitzman's lima bean–shaped plan, providing two gently curving streets, Longfellow and Hawthorne Boulevards, which follow the hilly topography over a ten-block-long parcel, that really set the enclave apart. According to Savage, "Pitzman's previous experience was maximized on Compton Heights." While Clifton Heights had "challenged his topographical planning skills," at Compton Heights, he allowed the terrain to shape the plan and in so doing made the avenues, which were open to the public on a limited basis, inherently unfavorable to through traffic so that residents could enjoy their privacy but benefit from city maintenance.[145] **Lewis Place** (1890) was another Pitzman design, with smaller than usual building lots.[146] It did not succeed in part because a railroad

switching yard was established just outside its monumental triumphal entrance arch (1895), designed by Barnett, Haynes & Barnett in yellow brick and limestone, that led to Lewis Park, a broad landscaped boulevard which formed the development's spine.

Flora Boulevard (1890), just west of Compton Heights, was conceived by its developer Henry Shaw as an approach to the Missouri Botanical Garden.[147] Originally intended as a conventional subdivision, it was recast as a private place, and Pitzman was hired to plat the property's north side. The six-block-long Flora Boulevard, divided by a wide median, was entered from Grand Avenue through an elaborate gateway ensemble, with no gatehouse or triumphal arch but with a statue of Flora set within a pedimented arch (Weber & Groves, c. 1898).

Bell Place consisted of about one hundred 100-by-95-foot lots arranged along two parallel avenues, Washington Terrace (1892) and Kingsbury Place (1902), entered through extraordinarily elaborate gateways.[148] The rust-colored Roman brick and brownstone clock-tower gatehouse at the eastern end of Washington Terrace, based on medieval German precedents, was designed by George R. Mann (1856–1939) in association with Harvey Ellis (1852–1904).[149] Kingsbury Place, the second phase of the development, had smaller lots. Its gateway (1901), by Barnett, Haynes & Barnett, was

Lewis Place

1. Plan, Julius Pitzman, 1890. PCSE

2. Entrance arch. Naffziger. CN (2012)

3. Lewis Place. Naffziger. CN (2011)

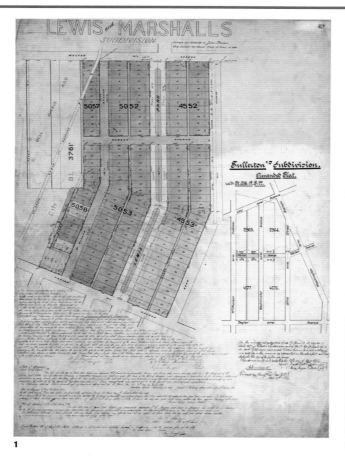

1

2

3

Flora Boulevard

1

2

3

1. Flora Boulevard from Grand Avenue showing gateway, Weber & Groves, c. 1898, after removal of statue of Flora. Ross. MHM (1960)

2, 3. Flora Boulevard. Naffziger. CN (2012)

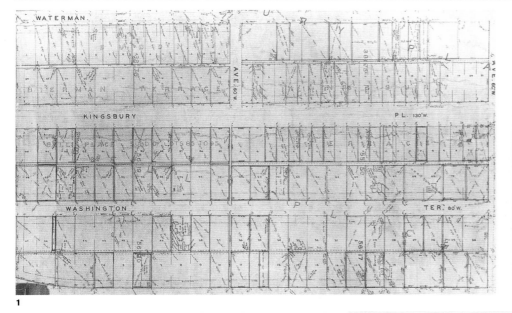

1. Plat map, Julius Pitzman. PCSE

2. Aerial view. GE (2010)

3. Washington Terrace, east entrance showing gate designed by George R. Mann in association with Harvey Ellis. MHM (c. 1889)

4. Washington Terrace, east entrance. MHM (1920)

5. Washington Terrace, west entrance gates. MHM (c. 1885)

6. Kingsbury Place, east entrance gate, Barnett, Haynes & Barnett, 1901. WA12

7. Washington Terrace. Garvin. AG (2010)

elaborately classical in the manner of the Modern French or Beaux-Arts baroque made popular by the Exposition Universelle in Paris in 1900.

Private places flourished around the turn of the century—Windermere Place (1895), Hortense Place (1905), Lenox Place (1904), Beverly Place (1905), and Parkview (1905)—but their layouts were less sophisticated than those that preceded them.[150] In the first decades of the twentieth century, the private place tradition of St. Louis followed the westward trend of population to the suburbs outside the city limits. Several fashionable enclaves were built in Clayton, Missouri, a western

suburb, during the 1910s and 1920s, beginning with the contiguous developments of Brentmoor Park (1910), West Brentmoor (1911), and Forest Ridge (1913), the first independent projects to be commissioned from the young architect-planner Henry Wright (1878–1936).[151] Connected to the city by an interurban trolley, they occupied an L-shaped site at the intersection of Big Bend and Wydown Boulevards. Born in Lawrence, Kansas, Wright, who would be closely associated with the garden suburb movement in America as an architect and teacher, established his firm in 1909, seven years after moving to St. Louis to open an office for the Kansas

1. Composite plan showing Southmoor, left, Forest Ridge, center, Brentmoor Park, right, and West Brentmoor, top. Henry Wright. AR13

2. Plat of Brentmoor Park, Henry Wright. AR13

3. Gregg residence, Howard Van Doren Shaw. AR13

4. Dana residence, Klipstein & Rathmann, left, and Bemis residence, Henry Wright. AR13

5. Davis residence, Cope & Stewardson, left. AR13

6. Entrance gates. Naffziger. CN (2012)

7. Streetcar waiting station. Naffziger. CN (2012)

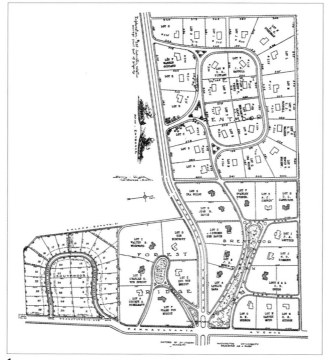

1

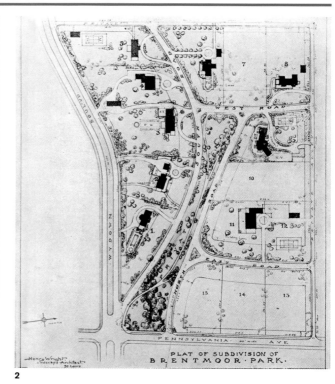

2

3

4

5

6

7

City planner George E. Kessler (1862–1923).[152] Listed in business directories as an architect, landscape architect, landscape gardener, and consulting engineer, Wright took on all aspects of the Brentmoor projects, including site planning, the design of individual houses and their grounds, the installation of utilities, and the placement of roads and drives.

Beginning with the 33.8-acre **Brentmoor Park**, Wright abandoned the fundamental dialogue between urban and suburban character hitherto present in St. Louis's private places in favor of a virtually uninhibited naturalistic suburbanity. What was only implied in Pitzman's design for Compton Heights was revealed in Brentmoor Park as a break with the grand public gesture, pointing to an even more insular environment that would complement the trend toward viewing the suburb as an escape rather than a refuge from community life. The original site included a small valley running down its length that Wright dedicated as a park, around which he grouped most of the fifteen one-and-a-half-to two-acre housing sites. Entering through stone gates on Wydown Boulevard, the houses were accessed from a central loop road, with rear service roads discreetly hidden away.

1. Entrance to Forest Ridge Drive showing streetcar waiting station. Persons. MHM (1920s)

2. Typical house. Naffziger. CN (2012)

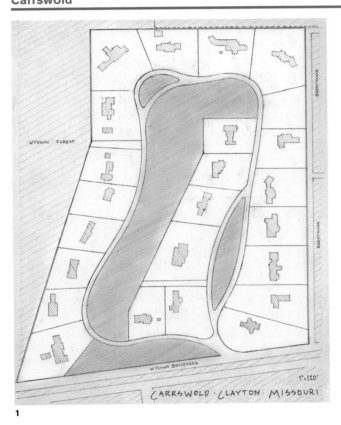

1. Plan. CRS (2012)

2. Entrance showing streetcar waiting station. Naffziger. CN (2012)

3. Median park. Naffziger. CN (2012)

West Brentmoor's relatively level 49.8-acre site prompted a simpler plan, with an oval road. **Forest Ridge** was the most luxurious of the three, its 20 acres divided into just six lots positioned around a central open plateau. Both Forest Ridge and Brentmoor Park, on either side of Wydown Boulevard, provided tile-roofed red-granite trolley shelters. Charles W. Fullgraf (1884–1957), a landscape contractor particularly skilled in moving mature trees, helped transform the bare site into a lushly planted environment.[153]

Brentmoor Park and West Brentmoor were developed by the Brenttract Realty Company, headed by J. Herndon Smith (1871–1928), an investment banker, and Joseph Dickson Jr. (b. 1876), a lawyer, who followed the private place model by selling lots to individual buyers while turning over the streets and common areas to a group of trustees chosen by the property owners. Forest Ridge was developed by the owners of the six sites, who drew straws to determine which lot they would build on. Wright was asked to design four houses—one in Brentmoor Park and three in Forest Ridge—while some of the best-known architects of the day were also called upon, including the Chicagoan Howard Van Doren Shaw (1869–1926), who designed three houses in Brentmoor Park. James P. Jamieson (1867–1941), of the Philadelphia firm of Cope & Stewardson, who had been sent to St. Louis in 1899 to supervise the construction of the Collegiate Gothic campus of the newly founded Washington University and established his own practice in the city in 1912, also designed a house in the development. Wright designed a fourth subdivision south of Forest Ridge, as well, known as Southmoor (c. 1913), approximating Forest Ridge in size but carved into thirty lots that were placed around a U-shaped drive providing two entrances on Pennsylvania Avenue.[154]

Carrswold, occupying the 35-acre former Robert E. Carr estate that had been purchased for development by a group of ten local businessmen in 1922, was contiguous with the west side of West Brentmoor.[155] As designed by Jens Jensen (1860–1951), a Danish-born Chicago landscape architect who was instrumental in developing the so-called Prairie Style of landscape architecture, emphasizing native vegetation and local landforms, Carrswold featured twenty-three houses on generously sized lots and 10 acres dedicated to common open space. The single looping drive, Carrswold, flanked at its entrance by stone walls that tied into a small pavilion providing a trolley waiting area, enclosed a central oval lawn, half of which was given over to six houses and the other half protected as park space. The remainder of the houses sat toward the site's perimeter. The loop road forked in two locations to embrace broad, commonly owned median parks, sited so that only four of the enclave's houses faced each other directly. Covenants mandated two-story houses and banned street-facing garage doors. Jensen required that the front 15 feet of each lot be planted by the Carrswold trustees to ensure that the drive be sufficiently shadowed, creating the impression that the houses, set back on open lawns, were placed within sunlit clearings. Between 1924 and 1931, nineteen houses were built, fifteen of which were designed by the prominent St. Louis firm of Raymond E. Maritz (1893–1973) and W. Ridgely Young (1893–1948), which had also designed ten houses in Brentmoor.

The influence of the St. Louis private places was widespread, especially in the Midwest. **Woodruff Place** (1872), occupying 77 acres just east of downtown Indianapolis, was built by civil engineer-turned-real estate developer James Orton Woodruff (1840–1879), a native of Auburn, New York, who had moved to the Indiana capital in 1870 to direct the completion of the city's waterworks before being swept into real estate speculation.[156] Woodruff platted the rectangular site, bound by Tenth and Michigan Streets and East and West Drives, with three 82-foot-wide north–south boulevards—East, West, and Middle Drives—intersected by Cross Drive, the enclave's only cross street, marking each intersection with an ornate multitiered fountain, one of which is believed to have been previously installed at the Centennial Exposition in Philadelphia. In addition to the fountains—as well as six others that were placed around the neighborhood—ninety statues, urns, and planters were positioned along the landscaped malls, while the entire perimeter of the development was defined by a stone balustrade.

The original plan called for 181 lots (261 were eventually created) averaging 80 by 170 feet. Woodruff's own house (c. 1875), designed by William LeBaron Jenney (1832–1907), was the first to be built but was later demolished. Progress had just gotten under way when the Panic of 1873 slowed things down, but the early residents incorporated Woodruff Place in 1876. The Panic bankrupted Woodruff, who left Indianapolis around 1877 for the East Coast.

New residents began to settle in Woodruff Place during the late 1880s, with a majority of the houses being built between 1898 and 1910 during a wave of prosperity that saw the construction of carriage houses and servants quarters along the enclave's rear alleys. A town hall was built in the 1920s, and in the 1930s the board of trustees established restrictions governing land use and building heights in order to preserve the character that was being threatened as wealthier residents moved away from Indianapolis's expanding center. But the restrictions failed to mandate single-family use, and duplexes and small apartment houses were built while existing houses were divided into apartments. The neighborhood declined during the 1950s and 1960s and lost its independence in 1962 when it was annexed by Indianapolis, at which point the fountains and statues fell into disrepair. Woodruff Place was added to the National Register of Historic Places in 1972, when architectural historian Wesley I. Shank could still note that the enclave remained "largely unchanged from the turn of the century."[157] The neighborhood has seen steady improvement in recent years.

In Fort Wayne, Indiana, **Forest Park Place** (1910), roughly one-and-a-half miles northeast of downtown, was undertaken by Louis F. Curdes (1863–1934), a prominent real estate developer who had initially platted the area in 1905 as the Forest Park Addition. It was a typical extension of the city grid providing 756 lots, but after experiencing slow sales despite its location on two streetcar lines, Curdes reconceived the eastern third of the site according to the private place model, calling for substantially larger lots along a 130-foot-wide boulevard, Forest Park Boulevard, that featured a broad, landscaped median and paved sidewalks.[158] Stone gates marked the two entrances on Lake Avenue and East State Boulevard. Curdes retained some mature trees and planted new shade trees, while lot owners contributed to a fund for grass cutting. Deed restrictions allowed only one dwelling per lot, banned nonresidential uses, established minimum construction costs and setbacks—houses had to be at least 140 feet from the center line of the boulevard—and required that house designs gain the approval of a committee chosen by the first forty purchasers. The revised plan was a success, attracting prominent members of Fort Wayne society and encouraging Curdes to develop the Driving Park Addition (1913) as an extension of Forest Park Boulevard one block north to Dodge

1. Aerial view. GE (2005)

2. Entrance to Woodruff Place, lithograph. LOCP (1905)

3. Middle Drive. IHS1 (1928)

4. East Drive IHS2 (1928)

5–7. Typical streets. Roberts. BR (2012)

8. Perimeter balustrade. Roberts. BR (2012)

Avenue, where he widened the median and provided ornamental streetlights.

Shawnee Place, one mile south of downtown Fort Wayne, geared toward the middle class, was completed in 1916 by the Wildwood Builders Company, headed by husband and wife Lee J. (1874–1953) and Joel Roberts (1873–1916) Ninde. The latter, a self-trained architect and one of the state's first female practitioners, designed the enclave's forty-six houses in collaboration with Grace Crosby (1874?–1962), another of Indiana's pioneer women architects.[159] The Nindes divided the rectangular, topographically bowl-shaped eight-and-a-half-acre site, bordered by Killea Street, West Wildwood Avenue, Webster Street, and Hoagland Avenue, with Shawnee Drive, an 80-foot-wide tree-lined boulevard comprising two 18-foot-wide roadways flanking a 20-foot-wide landscaped median. Half of the houses, occupying 40-by-100-foot lots and setback 20 feet from the curb, faced the boulevard while the other half faced outward along the development's east and west edges. Ornamental concrete light standards were placed at the entrance on Shawnee Drive and as gateways to a pedestrian path that crossed the development from east to west, meeting at a decorative fountain in the center of the boulevard.

Kansas City, Missouri, took up the St. Louis model beginning in 1888 with the **Hyde Park** subdivision, which had as its principal asset a 7.8-acre gully transformed into a fenced-in recreational park designed exclusively for residents' use by George Kessler that was later incorporated into the city's extensive public park and parkway

Forest Park Place

1. Projected Forest Park Place.
CRS (1910)

2. Forest Park Place.
Quinn. ARCH

Forest Park Boulevard, Fort Wayne, Ind., looking North from Lake Avenue.

Copyrighted by L. F. Curdes 1910.

1

2

Shawnee Place

1. Entrance to Shawnee
Place. CRS

2. Shawnee Place. AC 16

3. Shawnee Place. Quinn.
ARCH (2010)

13436. Shawnee Place, Fort Wayne, Ind.

1

2

3

system also laid out by Kessler.[160] **Janssen Place** (1897–1917), developed within Hyde Park by Arthur E. Stilwell (1859–1928), founder of the Kansas City Southern Railroad, in collaboration with a group of Dutch investors, and designed by George A. Mathews (1860–1903), a Kansas City architect, was modeled on St. Louis's Vandeventer Place, containing thirty-two lots facing a broad private boulevard, entered through a classical Arkansas limestone gateway designed by Mathews.[161]

Though not technically a private place, Kansas City's **Rockhill District**, located south of downtown and north of Brush Creek, was begun in 1895 but developed in earnest between 1900 and 1910 by William Rockhill Nelson (1841–1915), a newspaperman who had founded the *Kansas City Evening Star* in 1880 after an earlier career in real estate and construction.[162] Nelson, a proponent of the park and parkway system and a devotee of the City Beautiful movement, undertook the development on some of the 275 acres he had acquired around his residence, Oak Hall. To get people to the site, in 1900 Nelson built Rockhill Road, a wide, divided boulevard with a trolley line located next to the street rather than down the center in order to keep the tracks out of sight. In laying out the new district's straight and curving roads that followed the site's contours, Nelson may have been assisted, according to historian William S. Worley, by his friend George Kessler.[163]

Nelson built large speculative houses in the vicinity of Oak Hall as well as modest-size dwellings that he rented to employees of his newspaper. The workers' houses were aligned on only one side of the street to provide better views, and the designs were kept consistent within each block but varied from one block to the next. Locally quarried limestone, used to build rubble walls around each block, came to characterize the neighborhood. The stone was also used for foundations and as a cladding in conjunction with wood siding on the workers' houses. In addition to a plant nursery developed to supply the neighborhood's gardeners, Nelson built a community parking garage that provided shuttle service to and from the houses. After Nelson's death the property passed to his heirs and eventually to a trust that sold it off. Over time, the expansion of the University of Missouri-Kansas City and other institutions, including the Nelson-Atkins Museum of Art, which was built on the site of Oak Hall, encroached on the enclave, but a portion remains intact and was listed on the National Register of Historic Places in 1975.

The private place idea reached Detroit in 1892, when Joseph R. McLaughlin (b. 1851) and Edmund J. Owen (n.d.) platted the so-called McLaughlin and Owen Subdivision, consisting of the parallel East Boston and East Chicago (later renamed Arden Park) Boulevards, each with grassy medians stretching for three blocks between Woodward and Oakland Avenues.[164] Stone and brick walls with gateposts demarcated the Woodward Avenue entrances, where lots were also preserved as open space. Most of the development occurred after 1910, when the project was bought and renamed **Arden Park–East**

Boston by real estate broker Max Broock (1870–1915). Ninety-two houses representing a diversity of styles were built, set back uniformly from the street, serviced by rear alleys, and mandated to be two-and-a-half-stories tall and clad in brick or stone. Two churches were also allowed, but a ban on commercial enterprises staved off the encroaching city.

In Chicago, **Chatham Fields** (1914–16), a subdivision on the city's south side, between Seventy-ninth and Eighty-third Streets, South Park and South Cottage Grove Avenues, was designed by architect Edward H. Bennett (1874–1954), Daniel Burnham's chief planner and consulting architect to the Chicago Plan Commission. The developer, William H. Harmon, intended Chatham Fields as a "Modern Home Community" for moderate-income families, convenient to the "Loop" via two trolley lines from the development's main entrance gates at Eighty-first Street and Cottage Grove Avenue.[165] Eighty-first Street was embellished by a landscaped mall that continued one-and-a-half miles through the development. Land-use controls were established, and the development undertook to maintain street plantings for seven years, drawing upon funds contributed by purchasers who were assessed five dollars per lot. According to Robert Bruegmann, as a result of the rules established in Chatham Fields, "strict zoning codes and property standards became a characteristic feature" of the surrounding community of Chatham as it developed during the 1920s.[166]

Nineteen miles north of Chicago, near the southern border of Winnetka, Illinois, Walter Burley Griffin, upon returning from a visit to Canberra, Australia (see p. 646), in 1912, was commissioned to design the **Trier Center Neighborhood** (1912), an enclave of thirty-five small houses on a flat, rectangular nine-acre site scattered with trees and wild roses near a stop on the Chicago and Northwestern Railroad and a station on the Chicago-Milwaukee electric line.[167] It seemed a prime opportunity for Griffin to implement many of his planning ideas, and he took a financial stake in the development in which he also planned to build a residence for himself. The neighborhood took its name from New Trier High School (1909), adjacent to the east, designed by Dwight Perkins (1867–1941) to function as what Griffin called a "complete domestic social center" for the township. Organized in quadrangles and providing playgrounds and athletic fields, a restaurant, an auditorium, a theater, a gymnasium, and a natatorium, the program recognized "a new function which our public school buildings have begun to assume to make them count for the older members of the family as well as the children."[168] The Trier Center houses were to be built from thirteen distinct designs on lots averaging 64 by 149 feet. The estimated cost of each house, including its lot, ranged from $6,500 to $6,800, an "exceedingly low price even for that time," according to Mark L. Peisch.[169]

The plan called for two narrow streets—one entering from the west and one from the south—bordered on each side by three-foot-wide planting strips and

Hyde Park

1. View across Harrison Parkway and Gleed Terrace. MVSC (1931)

2. Hyde Park. LOCP (c. 1909)

Janssen Place

1. Entrance to Janssen Place. MVSC

2. Entrance gate. Fischer. WEFJ (2011)

3, 4. Janssen Place. Fischer. WEFJ (2011)

Rockhill District

1. Rockhill Boulevard with Oak Hall in background. MVSC

2. Workers' houses on Pierce Street between Rockhill Road and Locust Street. Storck. MVSC (1977)

1

2

Arden Park–East Boston

1

2

3

1. Plat map. AOM (1892)

2. Typical street. RAMSA (2012)

3. Entrance to Arden Park Boulevard. RAMSA (2012)

four-foot-wide sidewalks and meeting in a traffic circle with a reflecting pool. Unlike most private places, however, Trier Center would "not separate itself by aristocratic pillars or imposing entrances from the democratic village with which it wants to be integral."[170] Despite the site's featurelessness, Griffin, relying on architecture, site planning, and landscaping, aimed "to secure that garden charm which alone justifies living out in the suburbs; the architecture of the houses is reduced to a minimum of scale, height and obtrusiveness." He dictated fireproof masonry construction with minimal ornament and "maximum suitability to . . . embellishment with luxuriant growth not only over walls but roofs also."[171] The houses were to be grouped in pairs and connected by walled service courts or garages and other outbuildings in an effort "to obviate the petty spottiness and monotony of isolated single little houses . . . [and to] help convert each house that alone would be an unmitigated box into an appropriate link of a rambling, cozy, private community home of separated wings, bays and pavilions, such as might constitute the dream of the useless overgrown Castle in Spain toward which each of us is so often selfishly and aristocratically inclined."[172] Shared driveways reduced the perceived number of houses, while the pairs were staggered across the street from one another and set back and forth from the lot line to allow long views of common space and a lush landscape created by the installation of some 10,000 trees, shrubs, and vines—one of the few components of the plan to be implemented.

Griffin's relocation to Australia in 1914 hampered Trier Center's development. Only a portion of the street pattern was realized, as well as one house (1914) designed by Barry Byrne (1883–1967), Griffin's partner who took over much of his American work. According to Donald Leslie Johnson, the neighborhood, Griffin's "first statement on how to resolve the problem of easy access to private and community space and segregation from vehicular traffic . . . prefigured" Clarence S. Stein and Henry Wright's Radburn (see p. 275) in four distinct ways: "First the communal space in the center was surrounded and enclosed by houses . . . Second, a common driveway provided a shared parking space for two houses in many instances. Third, the living spaces of the houses were oriented to the internal community space. Fourth, the placement of the houses was essential to Griffin's plan . . . Only the addition of more houses about a common driveway was necessary to define more precisely the cul-de-sac concept."[173]

One of the last of the private places, and one of the most picturesque, **Sessions Village** (1927–32), in the city of Bexley, Ohio, three miles east of downtown Columbus, was developed by D. W. Fulton, Webb I. Vorys, and J. M. Rankin, who entrusted Robert R. "Roy" Reeves (1886–1937) of the firm Miller & Reeves with responsibility for the planning of the enclave as well as the thirteen French Norman–style houses that press against the edges of its two narrow streets, with walled gardens designed by Carl R. Frye (n.d.) providing each house with privacy.[174]

The neighborhood, consciously evoking the "atmosphere of an old French village," is entered from East Broad Street, Columbus's principal artery, under a bridge linking two houses. High garden walls on the east and west boundaries combine with the native woods at the north and the entry gate and flanking entrance houses on the south to define the enclave, forming what the developers described as "a community within itself." The development was intended—and largely succeeded—to be perceived "as a whole before erecting any part," with strict emphasis on architectural conformity. The first eleven houses built were conceived as a unit, but with enough variety in detail to establish individuality. A hundred or so feet inside the gate, the road splits at a Y-shaped intersection forming a small village square with a fountain. The east branch of the street system, a dead end, did not conclude in a cul-de-sac or a circle in order to "discourage Sunday afternoon traffic."[175]

Among Eastern cities, Brooklyn, New York, which after 1898 became a borough of the consolidated metropolis of Greater New York, has the greatest concentration of garden enclaves modeled along the lines of the private place, beginning with **Tennis Court** (1886), a neighborhood of frame houses in the Flatbush section developed by Richard Ficken (1840?–1907).[176] Located on a site bordered by Albermarle Road, Church and Ocean Avenues, and East Eighteenth and East Nineteenth Streets, Ficken's development was the beginning of a movement by Brooklyn real estate developers to establish specific neighborhoods, where the construction of houses could be carefully controlled. Ficken divided the property into 50-foot-wide lots, encouraged owners to site their houses behind lawns, and required that the houses cost a minimum of $6,000. He reinforced the sense of his development's identity by constructing brick gateposts at its entrance off Ocean Avenue and designing a garden and fountain at the junction of East Nineteenth Street. Tennis Court included the grounds of the Knickerbocker Field Club, established in 1889 in a small facility that quickly proved inadequate and was replaced by an elegant, gambrel-roofed, clapboard and shingle clubhouse (1892) at 114 East Eighteenth Street, designed by the English-born Parfitt Brothers—at the time Walter (1845–1924) and Albert (1863–1926) Parfitt.[177] In 1893 the *Brooklyn Daily Eagle* described the clubhouse as "an old-time family mansion, cozy but substantial," going on to praise the contrast between the yellow and white color scheme and the surrounding greenery.[178] The clubhouse was surrounded by comfortable wooden houses such as the one designed by E. G. W. Dietrich (1857–1924) and A. M. Stuckert (n.d.) for W. A. Porter (1887), a tightly massed version of the Shingle Style.[179]

Prospect Park South was Brooklyn's most important planned enclave, helping establish Flatbush as a particularly desirable residential district.[180] Begun in 1899 on 60 acres of former farmland lying between Prospect Park and the historic center of Flatbush village at Church and Flatbush Avenues, Prospect Park South was developed by Dean Alvord (1856–1941), who

Chatham Fields

1. Promotional brochure. RBA1 (1914)

2. Aerial view. GE (2012)

2

Trier Center Neighborhood

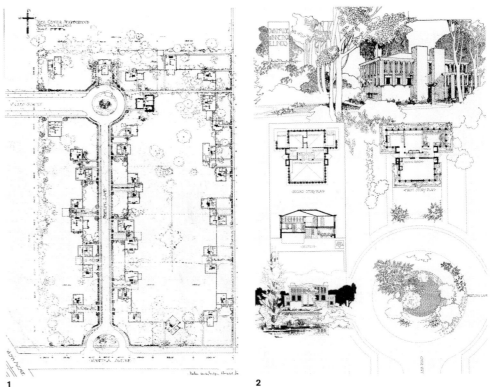

1

2

3

1. Plan, Walter Burley Griffin. WA13 (1913)

2. Plan and rendering of Griffin residence. WA13 (1913)

3. Model. WA13 (1913)

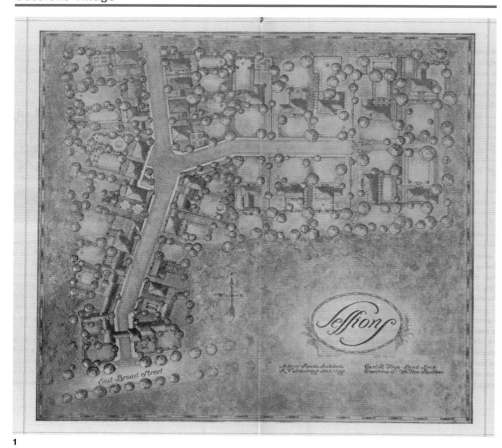

1. Plan from promotional brochure, Miller & Reeves and Carl R. Frye, 1927. OHS1 (1927)

2, 3. Typical views. Loversidge. RDL (2011)

employed the Scottish-born landscape designer John Aitkin (n.d.) and the architect John J. Petit (1870–1923), partner in the firm of Kirby, Petit & Green, to plat eleven blocks as a densely built-up "Suburban Residence Park"—"A rural park within the limitations of the conventional city block and city street . . . [and] produce an ensemble without discord and . . . [with a] feeling of harmony throughout."[181] Crowned by planters, brick gateposts at each point of entrance contained a "PPS" logo in cast stone. Although the lots were smaller than those in many of the St. Louis private places, Alvord conveyed a sense of spaciousness by requiring that houses be set back 30 feet from the street, by insisting on 8-foot-wide curb plantings between the sidewalk and the road, and by providing planting strips in the center of Albermarle and Buckingham Roads. Two kinds of trees were planted, quick-growing but short-lived Carolina poplars, and slow-maturing, long-lived Norway maples. Houses, mostly designed by Petit, were stylistically eclectic and included a remarkable three-story Japanese-style villa.

Alvord went on to reprise Prospect Park South in the Gulf Coast town of Clearwater, Florida, in 1912, where, working with his brother Donald (n.d.), he purchased 70 acres and developed **Harbor Oaks** (1914–37), an enclave of three north–south streets and five east–west streets, including a divided boulevard, Bay Avenue, bound by Druid Road, South Fort Harrison Avenue, Lotus Path, and Clearwater Harbor.[182] With underground utilities, electric streetlights, deed restrictions that called for two-story houses on 60-by-130-foot lots, and paved and curbed streets planted with oak and palm trees, Harbor Oaks attracted a number of prominent northerners who built seasonal retreats there, including Charles Ebbett, owner of the Brooklyn Dodgers, and Donald Roebling, of the bridge-building family, who invented an amphibious tank that he developed and tested on his Harbor Oaks property. Included among the Mediterranean-, Greek Revival–, Mission-, and Dutch Colonial–style residences were bungalows suited to the Florida climate.

Prospect Park South influenced a number of subsequent Brooklyn enclaves, which, though not as elaborately planned, further helped to establish Flatbush as a desirable gardenesque residential area. **Ditmas Park** and Ditmas Park West were developed after 1902 by Lewis H. Pounds (1860–1947) on a large property stretching from Ocean Avenue to Coney Island Avenue between Newkirk and Ditmas Avenues and Dorchester Road.[183] Pounds set out to give his developments a "distinctly suburban effect," with setback controls and ample planting along the streets and on the individual lots.[184] Convinced that he had a moral responsibility to properly lay out his development, Pounds also selected appropriate residents who could cooperate in the improvement of their property. The houses in Ditmas Park were more modest than those of Prospect Park South, but several were designed by the architect Arlington Isham (1868–1911) and his partner Harry Grattan (b. 1865), whose

Tennis Court

1. Knickerbocker Field Club, Parfitt Brothers, 1892. BHS (1905)

2. Typical street. CRS

Prospect Park South

1. Dean Alvord house, John J. Petit, 1902. CU (1902)

2. Japanese-style house, John J. Petit, 1902. CU (1902)

3. Albermarle Road. VPF (c. 1908)

4. East 16th Street. RAMSA (2012)

5. Church Avenue gatepost. RAMSA (2012)

cluster of thirteen bungalows, built in 1899 on East 16th Street, north and south of Ditmas Road, were fine representations of a type that Gustav Stickley (1858–1942) was beginning to proselytize in his magazine *The Craftsman*. Ditmas Park also included large houses along Ocean Avenue and a group of buildings for the Flatbush Congregational Church that included a remarkably inventive seven-sided Shingle Style rectory built in 1899 by the firm of Henry D. Whitfield (1876–1949) and Beverly S. King (1879–1935) and a redbrick and limestone Georgian church designed eleven years later by the firm of Francis R. Allen (1843–1931) and Charles Collens (1873–1956) in association with Louis Jallade (1876–1957).

Ditmas Park was followed in 1905 by **Fiske Terrace**, another development for middle-class families, with central garden malls on major streets as well as brick gateposts and bronze plaques at their entrances.[185] Unlike Prospect Park South, Fiske Terrace, occupying 30 acres between Ocean Avenue, Avenue H, the Brighton Beach Railroad tracks, and Glenwood Road (formerly Avenue G), did not emphasize uniquely designed houses. The developer, the T. B. Ackerson Construction Company, featured a few designs by architects, including Isham and John Slee (1875–1947).

Private places can also be found in Southern cities. **Laburnum Park**, two miles northwest of downtown

1. Aerial view. GE (2010)

2. Advertising display. Burgert. TCPL (1919)

3. Magnolia Drive, looking toward Gulf. Burgert. TCPL (1921)

4. Typical street. Burgert. TCPL (1924)

5. Gatepost. Burgert. TCPL (1924)

Richmond, Virginia, with which it was connected by two streetcar lines, was conceived in 1912 by the heirs of Joseph Bryan (1845–1908), who had built a country house in the 1880s named Laburnum after the original house on the property. Occupying over 100 acres bound by Laburnum Avenue, Brook Road, Westwood Avenue, and Hermitage Road, Laburnum Park was laid out as a three-by-three grid of 80-foot-wide tree-lined boulevards edged by tiled drainage ditches and divided by 20-foot-wide planted medians featuring ornamental wooden fences. Development took a few years to get under way and was then slowed down by shortages of labor and materials during World War I. By 1919, 68 of Laburnum Park's 175 available half-acre lots, measuring 100 by 230 feet, were sold, but many remained undeveloped.

To drum up new interest in the project, in 1919 architect Charles Morrison Robinson (1867–1932) and landscape architect Charles Freeman Gillette (1886–1969), both based in Richmond, were hired to design Laburnum Court, a single block within the Laburnum Park development that was anomalously built according to a cooperative ownership model.[186] Bound by Gloucester and Chatham Roads and Westwood and Palmyra Avenues, Laburnum Court featured twenty-four single-family houses designed by Robinson arranged around an interior court that was the collective property of the residents who, rather than purchase individual residences, bought shares in the Laburnum Court Corporation. The western edge of the block included a community garage, a central heating plant with a second-story community room, and a residence for maids and a "furnace man." The houses were similar in plan but featured five styles of exterior elevations varying from Mediterranean and Tudor Revival to Dutch Colonial and Craftsman, with stucco, brick, and wood siding. The remainder of Laburnum Park was built out during the 1920s and 1930s both by the original developers and independent builders.

New Orleans followed St. Louis's lead with twelve suburban-scale private place–type enclaves realized between 1891 and World War I.[187] Of these, only a few reflected the sophistication of the St. Louis models. The first, **Rosa Park** (1891), developed by John M. Bonner and Durant da Ponte (who named the enclave for his second wife, Rosa Solomon da Ponte), echoed St. Louis's Benton Place, filling the block bound by Nashville and St. Charles Avenues, St. Patrick and State Streets.[188] The heart of the plan was a 100-foot-wide

1. Newkirk Avenue. VPF (c. 1908)

2. East 19th Street. RAMSA (2012)

3. Flatbush Congregational Church. Rectory, right, Whitfield & King, 1899, church, left, Allen & Collens in association with Louis Jallade, 1910. RAMSA. (2012)

Fiske Terrace

1. Typical street. CRS (c. 1905)

2. Glenwood Road. RAMSA (2012)

landscaped boulevard, entered from St. Charles Avenue, New Orleans's most fashionable residential street. More ambitious than Rosa Park, **Audubon Place** (1894), 6900 St. Charles Avenue, laid out by George H. Grandjean (1846–1900), a Swiss-born civil engineer, for a St. Louis syndicate and George Blackwelder, a Fort Worth developer, set twenty-eight lots behind two entrance lodges supporting an iron arch designed by Thomas Sully (1855–1939) that incorporated the development's name.[189] Audubon Place Block No. 2, extending the development from Freret to Willow Street, was laid out by Grandjean in 1896, providing for 114 30-foot-wide lots and two larger corner lots. Financial problems prevented the expanded development from going forward immediately

and the design was modified. Eventually, after about fifteen or twenty houses were built, Tulane University incorporated Block No. 2 into its campus.

Richmond Place (1905) is less park-like than the Audubon enclaves, but it is nonetheless clearly identified by the brick and stucco gateposts designed by its planners, Charles Allen Favrot (1866–1939) and Louis Adolphe Livaudais (1871–1932), to flank the Loyola Avenue entrance.[190] **Everett Place** (1906), centered on a landscaped boulevard, was entered past more elaborate Craftsman-style gateposts.[191] **Audubon Boulevard** (1915) extended the concept to great length but with some sacrifice to intimacy, perhaps a reflection of the impact of automobiles.[192]

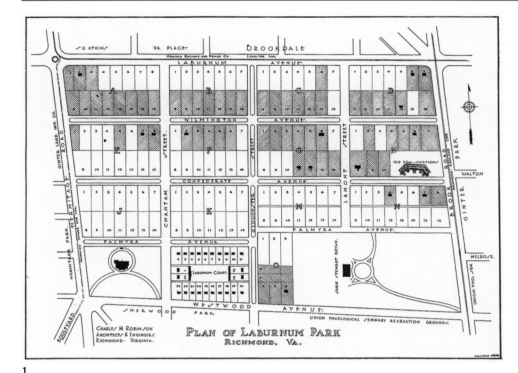

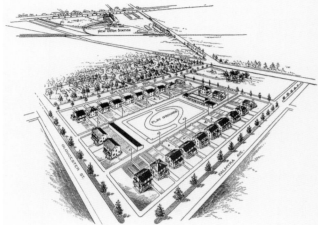

1. Laburnum Park, plan, Charles Morrison Robinson. LAB (1919)

2. Laburnum Court, aerial perspective. LAB (1919)

3. Laburnum Court, house designs, Charles Morrison Robinson. LAB (1919)

4. Laburnum Park, Palmyra Street. Taylor. KT (2012)

5. Laburnum Court, block interior showing community garage in distance. Taylor. KT (2012)

Glen Iris Park (1902), the first subdivision in Birmingham, Alabama, to be designed by a professional landscape architect, was a private place initiated in 1898 when Robert Jemison Sr. (1853–1926) hired Samuel Parsons Jr. (1844–1923) to subdivide a rectangular parcel of 30 rolling acres set amid "heavily forested wilderness"[193] one mile south of the city center to serve as "a home place for himself and a few congenial friends."[194] Jemison, president of the Birmingham Railway and Electric Company, extended streetcar service to within two blocks of the property. The enclave consisted of just one road, its entrance flanked by low stone walls and stone lampposts. Within, Parsons placed twenty lots around a broad central lawn ringed by a driveway, shaded by trees, and intended to accommodate a fish pond and fountain, which were not realized. Jemison's own Greek Revival–style house (1902), designed by Thomas Ustick

Walter III (1864–1931), commanded a double lot on axis with the entry. By 1929, eighteen houses set back at least 100 feet from the road were built and occupied by attorneys, doctors, and bankers, all of whom were Jemison's friends or relatives.

Westmoreland (1902) was the first planned residential enclave within Houston, Texas, enjoying new prosperity as a result of oil discovery and the establishment of a deepwater port.[195] Located on 44 acres one-and-a-half miles south of downtown at the terminus of the trolley line, it was not only named for its predecessor in St. Louis but was also laid out by that development's planner, Julius Pitzman, who placed ceremonial entrance gates at its boundaries. The plan was conventionally gridded and, because the covenants permitted multifamily as well as single-family dwellings, the development never achieved anything near the level of rusticity of its St.

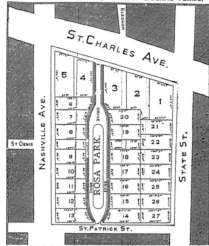

1. Advertisement from the *Daily Picayune*, 1891. TDP91

2. Rosa Park. LSM (c. 1890s)

3–5. Rosa Park. Lamb. DL (2012)

Audubon Place

1. Entrance. LOC1 (1903)

2. Audubon Place. LOC2 (c. 1905)

3. Audubon Place. Barnett. LOCP (1910)

4. Audubon Place. Garvin. AG (1998)

5. Entrance. Garvin. AG (1998)

Richmond Place

1. Richmond Place. Lamb. DL (2012)

1

Everett Place

1

1. Everett Place. PSS (c. 1910)

2, 3. Everett Place. Lamb. DL (2012)

2

3

Louis namesake. In 1908, Westmoreland was advertised as "a home to homeseekers desiring to be rid of the noise, dust, and heat of the city . . . Westmoreland boasts that she has no unsightly corner groceries and noisy street cars within her gates . . . However it is very convenient to have them just outside the gates."[196]

As laid out by civil engineer A. J. Wise (n.d.), **Courtlandt Place** (1906), developed on 15.47 acres north of Westmoreland, was also closely based on ideas initiated in St. Louis, with twenty-six lots flanking a 110-foot-wide block-long landscaped boulevard entered between colossal piers on the east and west.[197] The crescent-shaped east gate (1912), incorporating two stone piers topped by lantern globes with four shorter piers framing the sidewalks, was designed by William Ward Watkin (1886–1952) and landscape consultant Arthur Seiders (n.d.). Many of the houses, served by rear alleys, were designed by distinguished architects, including the New York firm of Whitney Warren (1864–1943) and Charles D. Wetmore (1867–1941) and the Houston architects Birdsall P. Briscoe (1876–1971) and John F. Staub (1892–1981).

Shadyside, also in Houston, was begun in February 1916 by Joseph S. Cullinan (1860–1937), founder of Texaco, on 38 acres of land providing for twenty-four houses near Rice Institute's new campus.[198] Intended by Cullinan as an enclave "for a few congenial friends and neighbors," Shadyside was laid out by George Kessler working with Herbert A. Kipp (1884–1968?), a Houston civil engineer.[199] Kessler and Cullinan had met on a train, and Cullinan, interested in Kessler's ideas, brought him to Houston to work on the design of Hermann Park, which sat across South Main Street, Shadyside's southeastern boundary, as well as the development of Main Street as a grand boulevard, and the residential neighborhood of which Shadyside was intended to be a significant part. According to architectural historian Christopher Gray, Cullinan, who was aware of the private places in St. Louis and who hired St. Louis architect James P. Jamieson to design his own house, took a strong personal interest in Shadyside's design, which consisted of only two streets, the curving Remington Lane and the straight Longfellow Lane. Here, as at Forest Park Addition in St. Louis and Forest Hills Gardens in New York, the development took advantage of a bordering, expansive public greensward.

Shadow Lawn, developed by John H. Crooker, a native of New Orleans, followed in 1921–23, laid out by engineer J. S. Boyles (n.d.) on an adjacent site to the north of Shadyside entered off Bissonnet Street from the north and Mount Vernon Street from the east.[200] The enclave's stately houses, designed by prominent Houston architects, including William Ward Watkin, John Staub, and J. W. Northrop Jr. (1886–1968), were more densely situated than at Shadyside, with four house lots originally platted within the central Shadow Lawn Circle and an additional eleven placed around it, leading owners to combine properties so that, as built, just two houses were located within the circle and nine outside.

Audubon Boulevard

Glen Iris Park

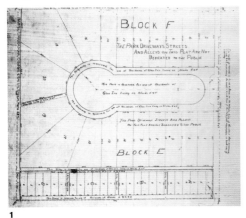

In 1922, William Ward Watkin planned and landscaped the 160-acre **Southampton** neighborhood, north and west of Rice Institute.[201] The well-located site had remained vacant because of a railroad spur that proved difficult to remove. The developer, E. H. Fleming & Company, wanted Southampton to be affordable for Rice's middle-income faculty members. Selecting English street names, Watkin fanned the streets out on either side of Sunset Boulevard, the enclave's east–west spine that featured a narrow median planted with a single line

of live oaks. Watkin also lined the north side of Rice Boulevard with oaks matching those that the university planted to the south.

The following year Watkin planned the smaller but more affluent **Broadacres** (1923), a decidedly lush 34-acre enclave conceived by two lawyers, Capt. James A. Baker (1821–1897) and his son James A. Baker Jr. (1857–1941).[202] Planned for twenty-five house sites, Broadacres was organized around North, West, and South Boulevards, connected in a horseshoe-like configuration to

Westmoreland

1. Entrance. CCF (c. 1909)

2, 3. Westmoreland Street.
Williams. SWLD (2012)

Courtlandt Place

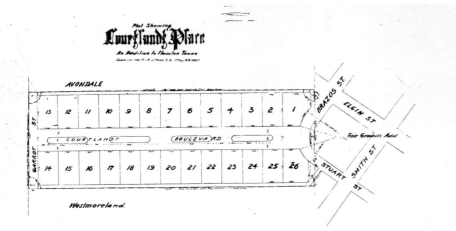

1. Plat map, A. J. Wise,
1907. HMRC

2. West entrance.
HMRC (c. 1910)

3–5. Courtlandt Place.
Williams. SWLD (2012)

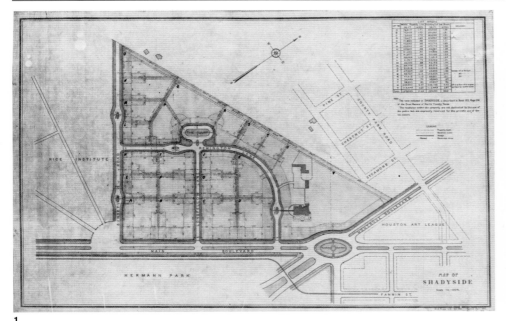

1

2

3

4

1. Plan, George Kessler and Herbert A. Kipp, 1916. HMRC (1918)

2. Gatepost. Williams. SWLD (2012)

3, 4. Typical streets. Williams. SWLD (2012)

Shadow Lawn

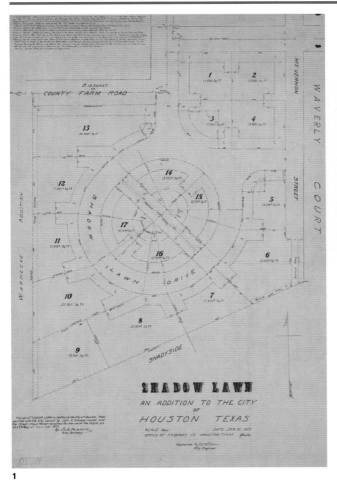

1

2

1. Plat map, J. S. Boyles, 1922. UHL

2. Shadow Lawn Circle. Williams. SWLD (2012)

1. Sales brochure, bird's-eye view. HMRC (c. 1923)

2. Aerial view. GE (2003)

3. Typical street. Williams. SWLD (2012)

4. Sales brochure. HMRC (c. 1923)

form a continuous landscaped boulevard opening to the city at four places. Staggered rows of live oaks, six across, were planted along the boulevards and their broad medians to transform the barren prairie site into a park-like setting shaded by a thick canopy of leaves. As Stephen Fox writes, "Watkin had the streets graded low, so that, from the boulevards, house sites appear to occupy raised terraces. All sidewalks in the neighborhood were paved with red brick in a herringbone pattern. Pairs of brick piers at the four points of entry identified Broadacres as a private place."[203] Again, property owners called on prominent Houstonians to design their houses, including Staub, Watkin, and Briscoe.

Just beyond Houston's city limits, **Braeswood** (1926) was the last of the exclusive suburban enclaves to be built along the Main Street axis.[204] The 456-acre neighborhood was developed by George F. Howard and planned by the firm of Sidney J. Hare (1860–1938) and S. Herbert Hare (1888–1960) from Kansas City. The Depression curtailed development, but about half of Braeswood was realized. Hare & Hare's plan included a significant boulevard intended to combine MacGregor Park with Westwood along the banks of Brays Bayou, but only a portion was completed.

In Fort Worth, **Ryan Place** (1911), built by the developer John C. Ryan (1865–1928) according to a landscape plan by George Kessler, was an upper-class enclave connected to downtown by streetcar lines.[205] Intended to attract oil industry executives, its entrances at each end of the main street, Elizabeth Boulevard, a seven-block-long, 95-foot-wide tree-lined boulevard with marble street curb signs named for the developer's wife, were marked by elaborate gateposts designed by the firm of Marshall R. Sanguinet (1859–1936) and Carl G. Staats (1871–1928). Encompassing 26 acres, Ryan Place was Fort Worth's first restricted development, with houses required to be set back 35 feet from the property line and built of masonry.

Beginning in 1905, in nearby Dallas, Robert S. Munger (1854–1923), an inventor and manufacturer before becoming a real estate developer, undertook to build an exclusive residential enclave, **Munger Place**, consisting of 300 acres of former East Dallas pastureland.[206] Munger's cotton business had brought him to reside temporarily in Birmingham, Alabama, where he was inspired by restricted residential developments such as Glen Iris Park. Munger Place was Dallas's first housing development to feature restrictive covenants governing

Broadacres

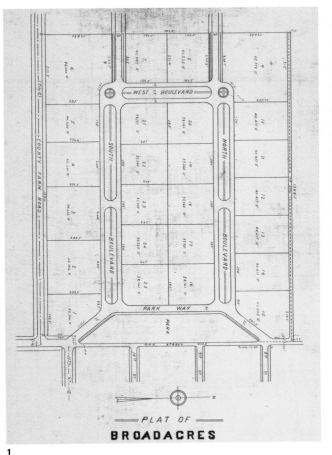

1. Plat map, William Ward Watkin, 1923. HMRC

2. Typical street. Williams. SWLD (2012)

Braeswood

1. Plan, Hare & Hare, 1927. HMRC

2. Aerial view. GE (2004)

Ryan Place

1

Munger Place

1

2

3

minimum lot sizes, setbacks, unobstructed front yards, and the like. Yards were raised one to four feet above the street to aid drainage and all utilities were placed in 15- to 40-foot-wide rear alleys along with stables. Stone entrance gates along Gaston and Swiss Avenues and Junius Street marked the most important entrances to the enclave. Like those at Ryan Place in Fort Worth, the gates were deemed traffic hazards in the 1950s and 1960s and were demolished. The 100-foot-wide Munger Boulevard, the principal street, featured 40-foot-wide private parks down its center. Swiss Avenue, 130 feet wide, was also a planted boulevard with a 40-foot-wide median. With large lot sizes and high minimum construction costs, Swiss Avenue emerged as the most exclusive section of Munger Place.

THE GARDEN VILLAGE: RAILROAD SUBURBS

Glendale (1851), Ohio, is arguably the first American garden village.[207] Lying about ten miles north of Cincinnati, Glendale, which preceded Llewellyn Park by two years, is notably distinct from it. While Llewellyn Park was intended as an idealistic community of like-minded individuals, but with no pretensions to village life, Glendale was a commercial development, a commuter village with the characteristics of a town, including a business district and a station on the newly opened Cincinnati, Hamilton, and Dayton Railroad. The train trip to downtown Cincinnati took forty-five minutes.

Glendale began to take form in 1851 when George Crawford (b. 1805) and Henry Clark (1789–1879) assembled 600 acres of land, and when later in the same year a group of investors formed a joint stock company with the purpose of developing a suburb on 200 acres of the rolling site, crossed by two brooks. Reflecting the ideas of Andrew Jackson Downing, Robert C. Phillips (n.d.), a civil engineer, planned the new village with 60-foot-wide looping avenues and irregularly shaped lots interspersed by a lake and three small parks—in reality, fenced-off areas left in their original natural condition—crisscrossed with pedestrian paths. Only 80-foot-wide Sharon Avenue followed a straight east–west line through the village. Amid the typical rectangularity of Midwest land platting, the plan was a marvel.

By 1870, Glendale had developed sufficiently for Sidney D. Maxwell, in his book describing the various suburbs of Cincinnati, to write that the village "should rather be considered as a whole than in detail. There are no palatial mansions, no extensive lawns, no long, sweeping graveled drives, such as the visitor sees in some other suburbs. It is rather a collection of beautiful homes, with ample grounds and profuse shrubbery, approached by circuitous avenues . . . Glendale is laid out irregularly. Whichever way the stranger takes, he is constantly impressed with the thought that he has made a mistake, and whatever point he attains is certain to be some one unlooked for."[208] Most important of all, as Maxwell

VIEW OF GLENDALE,

1

noted: "The great advantage about Glendale is, that it is a complete community. Too far removed from the city to depend upon it for general society or amusement, it becomes a society itself, bound together as well by common necessity and the intimate friendships that frequent intercourse fosters, as by common effort to supply the want of entertainment and amusement which absence from the city occasions."[209]

Also anticipating Llewellyn Park by two years, **Evergreen Hamlet** (1851), Ross Township, six miles north of Pittsburgh, was conceived as a garden village by a local lawyer, William Shinn (1809–1865), who joined with a group of other affluent citizens to develop 85 acres a short carriage ride away from the nearest railroad station.[210] Laid out by Heastings & Preiser, a local firm of surveyors who situated the building lots along the principal street, Rock Ridge Avenue, reserving the rest of the land for public purposes, Evergreen Hamlet was a tiny village providing accommodation for sixteen families, each in a house on one acre, as well as a schoolhouse, ice house, and spring house, and a 40-acre farm intended to serve the needs of the residents, with the rest to be sold commercially. The sixteen houses were grouped together with "footways" between them, fostering "friendly and frequent intercourse."[211] The Hamlet's

first board-and-batten cottages were occupied in 1852. The suburb was sized according to the founders' belief that it represented all "that is required for the support of a suitable school, and form a sufficient neighborhood, to exclude all fear of that loneliness which so many persons dread in country life."[212]

The original development agreement for Evergreen Hamlet lasted until 1866, a year after Shinn's death, by which time only four houses had been built. But the physical shape of the community endured, as did the intention for it of its founder: "To secure the advantages and comforts of the country at a moderate cost, without doing violence to the social habits incident to city life . . . to combine some of the benefits of country and city life; and at the same time, avoid some of the inconveniences and disadvantages of both."[213] Evergreen Hamlet, despite its minute size, cannot be overlooked. As John Archer has written, "Here an ironic combination of late-Jeffersonian yeoman farmer ideology together with the practical realities of commuting to jobs in a capitalist workplace resulted in a remarkable quasi-communitarian, quasi-suburban experiment." As Archer continues: "The founders of Evergreen Hamlet, unlike those of most other contemporary developments, sought to address more openly the contradictions of living in a bourgeois mercantile

1. Bird's-eye view. CMC (c.1860)

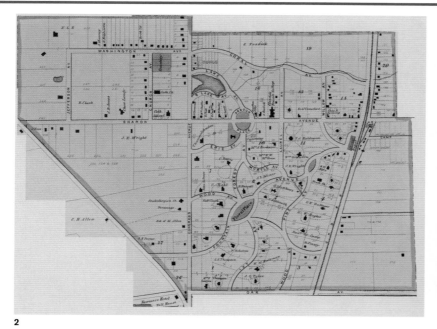

2. Plan, Robert C. Phillips, 1851.
VG (1869)

3. Fountain Avenue. Garvin.
AG (1996)

4. Fountain Avenue. VG (1917)

Evergreen Hamlet

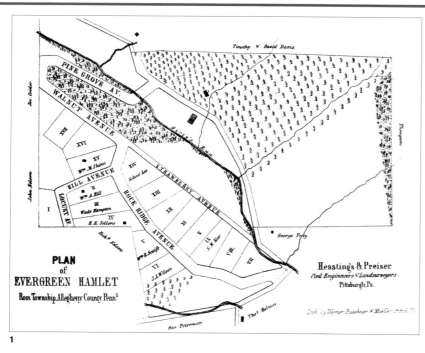

1. Plan, Heastings & Preiser, 1851.
CEH

2. View showing school and
typical house. PITT (c. 1850s)

economy. Perhaps the greatest effort in this direction was the communal ownership of the home economy."[214]

Riverside (1869), Illinois, the first comprehensively planned garden village, was conceived by Frederick Law Olmsted as a place where "urban and rural advantages are agreeably combined" to provide for the "counter-tide of migration" from city to the urban periphery that the introduction in the 1860s of reliable, regular passenger railroad transportation made possible.[215] Emery E. Childs

(1832–1886) and the Riverside Improvement Company commissioned Olmsted and his partner, architect Calvert Vaux, to plan "at once an elegant drive, a handsome park, and a delightful suburban city" on a 1,600-acre site on the Des Plaines River, nine miles west of Chicago's central business district.[216] Childs and his designers were convinced that an ideal suburb offered not only the pleasures of rural retreat combined with the convenience of all the latest advances in public utilities and transportation but

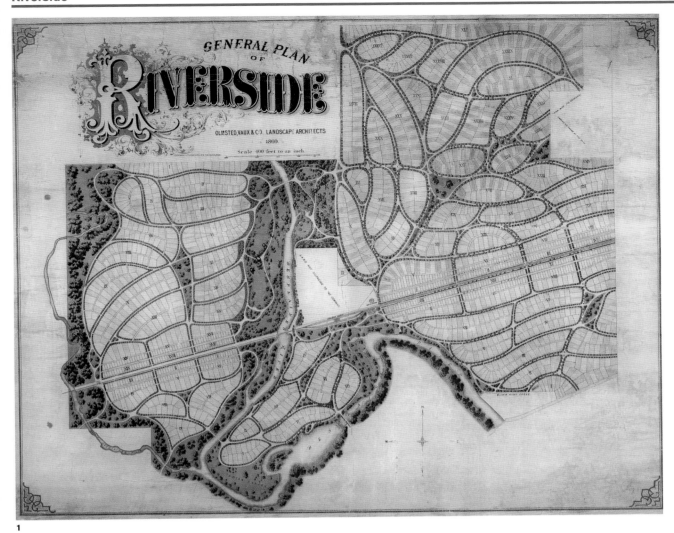

1

most significantly the conviviality to which city dwellers had become accustomed: "Messrs. Olmsted, Vaux & Co., the designers and constructors of the Central Park of New York, Prospect Park, Brooklyn, and many of the finest Villa residences and private grounds on the Hudson, have accordingly been engaged, with a large staff of engineers and other assistants . . . in the preparation designed to provide whatever, in their judgment, should be required, without restriction as to necessary expense, to make Riverside, in all respects, a MODEL SUBURBAN NEIGHBORHOOD. The Company believe that when their plans are carried out, Riverside will combine the conveniences peculiar to the finest modern towns, with the domestic advantages of the most charming country, in a degree never before realized."[217]

Riverside was to house 10,000, a goal only reached in the post–World War II era. Although it now seems a marvel of village-scale living amid abundant nature, prior to development, much of Riverside's site was largely flat, featureless farmland, leading an observer to note in 1869 that the site presented "a plentiful lack of improvements, and an overwhelming generosity of raw prairie wind and waste prairie land which were anything but inviting."[218] To turn prairie into paradise, Olmsted arranged for the planting of 32,000 deciduous trees,

7,000 conifers, and 47,000 shrubs—as John Coolidge pointed out, these were roughly four trees and five shrubs for each of the maximum number of inhabitants.

Olmsted was explicit in his reasons for taking on the Riverside commission: "Owing partly to the low, flat, miry, and forlorn character of the greater part of the country immediately about Chicago, and the bleak surface, arid soil, and exposure of the remainder to occasional harsh and frigid gusts of wind off the lake, and partly to the fact that the rapidity with which the town is being enlarged, causes all the available environs to be laid out with a view to a future demand for town purposes, and with no regard to the satisfaction of rural tastes, the city, as yet, has no true suburbs or quarters in which urban and rural advantages are agreeably combined with any prospect of long continuance." Significantly, Olmsted's work on Central Park, combined with his readings in the literature of English picturesque landscape by Uvedale Price (1747–1829), William Gilpin (1762–1843), and others, and his visit to Birkenhead Park (see p. 32) in 1850, convinced him that the suburb was the "most attractive, the most refined, the most soundly wholesome" form of domestic life.[219]

Olmsted recognized that urbanization was a condition of modern life, and though he appreciated its many

2

3

4

5

benefits, he disliked the overcrowding of contemporary cities and especially the relentless rule of straight streets lined with rowhouses. For him, the suburb was not, as Robert Fishman has observed, "an ebbing of the nineteenth century flood of urbanization" but, as Olmsted put it, "a higher rise of the same flood," without "a sacrifice of urban conveniences" but with those conveniences in combination "with the special charms and substantial advantages of rural conditions of life."[220] The Riverside commission came at a perfect time for Olmsted; by experience and inclination he was prepared for the challenge. As Fishman writes: "His plan represents both a summation of previous Anglo-American suburban design and a highly personal . . . vision of a community in harmony with nature. If there is a single plan that expresses the idea of a bourgeois utopia, it is Olmsted's Riverside."[221]

It is not insignificant to note that Ebenezer Howard (1850–1928), at the century's end the founder of the Garden City movement, was living in Chicago from 1872 to 1876 when the development of Riverside was very much at the front of public attention. One marvels at how close to Olmsted's vision of the unity of suburb and city is Howard's argument that "neither the Town magnet nor the Country magnet represents the full plan of nature. Human society and the beauty of nature are meant to be enjoyed together. The two magnets must be made one."[222]

Riverside's site straddled the right-of-way of the Chicago, Burlington and Quincy Railroad—its Riverside station, opened in 1864, was the first stop out of Chicago,

thereby guaranteeing residents rapid transit to the city. Olmsted's plan paralleled the railroad right-of-way with streets, each separated from the tracks by one block and each lined with small lots intended for the shops and cheaper housing that would be needed to accommodate the work force required to build and maintain the new suburban village. Thus, as David Schuyler has pointed out, "Olmsted's prototype for the suburban community envisioned the same degree of inclusiveness he hoped his parks would provide for the people of the city," as made clear in his essay "Public Parks and the Enlargement of Towns," in which he wrote that "all classes [are] largely represented, with a common purpose, not at all intellectual, competitive with none, disposing to jealousy and spiritual or intellectual pride toward none, each individual adding by his mere presence to the pleasure of all others, all helping to the greater happiness of each. You may thus often see vast numbers of persons brought closely together, poor and rich, young and old, Jew and Gentile."[223]

Away from this trackside linear core, in a brilliantly pragmatic move—one that became a standard feature of suburban planning—a gently curving grid provided both easily divisible real estate and the illusion of a natural settlement pattern extending from village center to open country. Olmsted thought that the gridiron plan, though sensible from the point of view of real estate development, was "too stiff and formal for such adornment and rusticity as should be conceived in a model suburb."[224] By gently curving his streets, he compensated

6

7

8

9

6. Typical residence. RAMSA
(c. 1985)

7. Railroad depot and water
tower. RAMSA (c. 1985)

8. Nutall Road, adjacent to the
Long Common. RHM

9. Scottswood Drive. Garvin.
AG (2004)

for the site's flatness with vistas. Equally important, he believed that his sinuous grid would contrast with the "ordinary directness" of typical city streets and "suggest and imply leisure, contemplativeness, and happy tranquility."[225] At Riverside, the looping geometry of the roads and Olmsted's avoidance of right-angle intersections created triangular parks serving as neighborhood foci that were to be furnished with "croquet or ball grounds, sheltered seats and drinking fountains, or some other object which would be of general interest or convenience to passers-by."[226] Such devices had previously appeared in Robert C. Phillips's plan for Glendale, but in a rigid rather than natural way. Olmsted made the street pattern seem effortless and inevitable.

Olmsted's plan for Riverside turned the site's principal deficit into an incomparable advantage, transforming the floodplains of the Des Plaines River into parkland. Although the plan was a distinct product of the site's topography and its location on both sides of an established railroad line, it was also the outgrowth, as David Schuyler has pointed out, of ideas Olmsted had previously explored in 1860 when, with Vaux, he was consultant to a commission responsible for planning the north end of Manhattan above 155th Street, and in 1866, when he undertook to plan the grounds of the College of California at Berkeley, where in addition to issues of topography and climate, he sought to establish, as Schuyler has written, "a clear line of demarcation between public spaces within the community—roadsides, parks and communal facilities—and the private

domestic landscape."[227] Olmsted, as Schuyler points out, had proposed a parkway linking his Berkeley neighborhood to Oakland's ferry, and he would recommend in the same year a network of parkways as part of his plan for Brooklyn's Prospect Park. Riverside was a bold breakthrough, going beyond these precedents to constitute Olmsted's first comprehensive statement about the suburb as a planned garden village in which "urban and rural advantages are agreeably combined."[228]

Riverside was a more significant contribution to metropolitan urbanism than any of the garden suburbs that went before it. In its scope and ambition, it had only Nash's Regent's Development (see p. 23) as a rival. For Olmsted, Riverside was a suburban garden village, but it was not a place in opposition to the metropolitan city. Olmsted did not see the garden suburb as a rejection of city life: he fully appreciated the economic, educational and cultural opportunities that it provided. To hammer that point home he called for a landscaped roadway connecting Riverside to Chicago, with separate lanes for pleasure and commercial vehicles. The road, which he called the "park way," a term he may have picked up from Llewellyn Park, was to be lined with villas. Olmsted's parkway—which was to be between 200 and 600 feet in width—was to be more than just a commuter's alternative to the railroad. It was to be a European-style promenade—a Champs Élysées at regional scale—the lack of which he felt detracted from urban life in the United States. In this way he may also have been influenced by the plan, prepared by Arthur Gilman

(1821–1882) with advice from architect George Snell (1820–1893) and the landscape gardening partnership of Horace William Shaler Cleveland and Robert Morris Copeland (1830–1874), for Commonwealth Avenue in Boston's Back Bay, a 200-foot-wide boulevard with dual carriageways divided by 100-foot-wide landscaped malls.[229] Olmsted had previously proposed parkways to the park commissions in Brooklyn and Buffalo, so that his Riverside parkway only seemed to reinforce his sense of suburbs as intimately part of metropolitan cities. The parkway was never built, but he would realize his idea to an extent in the Midway, designed in 1871, which formed part of his plan for the Chicago Park system. As Witold Rybczynski has written, Olmsted "understood that a potential drawback to suburban living was isolation. Later planners conceived suburbs as a means of escaping the city. Olmsted did not see it this way. The parkway was an essential link. For him the 'metropolitan condition' included cities and suburbs."[230]

Another key aspect of Olmsted's plan for Riverside was the establishment of a town center located at the railway station. In this, Riverside marked a significant advance in town making over its predecessors. A Swiss chalet–inspired hotel designed by William Le Baron Jenney was built in 1870 close to the railroad station, the first instance of what would become a recurring marketing pattern for garden suburb development. Exaggeratedly touted by the developers as "the most complete and comfortable hotel in the United States," it was intended to introduce urbanites to the new suburb.[231] Later on it became a gathering place for the fledgling community.

Olmsted was not especially interested in civic or commercial architecture. As John Coolidge has observed, he "was so entirely concerned with domesticity and outdoor recreation that he gave almost no thought to anything else. Only utilitarian buildings appear on the plan—no public library or town hall."[232] Consequently, although a variety of buildings were realized at the town center, the turreted water tower by Jenney (1870), a work of infrastructural necessity, became the symbol of the community. Jenney, who early on took up residence in Riverside, not only designed the hotel and water tower but also the refectory, a clublike restaurant and playhouse overlooking the Des Plaines River, as well as several chalet-style houses. Frederick Clarke Withers (1828–1901), who frequently partnered with Vaux, designed the Arcade Building (1871), the town's first shopping center. Withers also designed Riverside's first church (1869), sited in the woods away from the village center. Originally conceived as a nondenominational chapel, it soon became the Riverside Presbyterian Church.

Landscape rather than houses was primary in Olmsted's thinking, and he did not include any stylistic stipulations in his plan. However, certain environmental and economic controls were established to ensure that the town's residential neighborhoods would have the appearance of affluent spaciousness and visual coherence. To achieve this sense of enhanced rurality it was stipulated that houses were to be set at least 30 feet from private property lines; that building lots were to be at least 100 feet wide and about 200 feet deep; and that no fences be permitted in front yards. Intending Riverside to become a middle-class haven where the businessman and his clerk could live in close proximity, Olmsted required that the houses cost at least $3,000 and be owner-occupied.

Riverside's progress was stifled by a cloud of financial malfeasance: one of the partners in the Riverside Improvement Company, who was also city treasurer of Chicago, was accused of misappropriating municipal funds. But the most significant impediment to growth was the effect of the Panic of 1873, leading to the development company's bankruptcy. Once the economy rebounded, the village began to develop in earnest, with William Le Baron Jenney and his partners in charge of the detailed work. From this time forward, the size of the houses and their cost considerably exceeded Olmsted's wishes. The median price for a house in Riverside in 2011 was $373,500.

Seven hundred of Riverside's 1,600 acres were to be devoted to open space, including roads, some of which were depressed slightly below natural grade to minimize their visual intrusion, a kind of inverse use of the earth berms Paxton employed at Birkenhead Park to vary the flat topography. "Sinking the streets," as Walter Creese has pointed out, allowed Olmsted "to keep the basic earth plane moving. He wanted the pedestrian to enjoy the 'range' of vistas up to a quarter of a mile in some spots."[233] In addition to the road network, the plethora of small parks and playgrounds—seventy in number—and ornamental greenswards, including the nucleus of the plan, Long Common, are notable, connecting Riverside's plan not only to that of Llewellyn Park but also to Paxton's Birkenhead.[234] As a result of his visit to England, Olmsted commented on "the vast increase in valuable sites for dwellings near the public parks," a conviction that he may also have developed as a result of Alphonse Pallu's Le Vésinet (see p. 43), which he may have seen on his trip to Paris in 1859.[235]

Not a "new town" or a "garden city," Riverside, unsupported by its own economy, is a garden village which, though rooted in the values of the past, could never have existed before the age of fast transportation in particular and mechanization as a whole. It was the first complete integration of suburban arcadianism with the urban economy—an integration that Birkenhead Park, Le Vésinet, and Llewellyn Park had been moving toward. Riverside was an idealized alternative to conventional city living, a suburb of a city, not cut off from it. Embracing within its own boundaries a reasonably full articulation of community life, Riverside was not autonomous and separated from the larger world as were the model villages that Fourier and other utopists had proposed (see p. 204). Providing the template for a metropolitan suburbanism that would be a crucial but dependent aspect of inner-city urbanism for at least seventy-five subsequent years, Riverside is, as its designers and developers wanted it to be: "not the country, pure and simple; the country of kerosene lamps. But it is the country with the discomforts eliminated; the country plus city convenience . . . It is the golden mean between the two kinds of life."[236]

Following quickly on the heels of Riverside, Olmsted and Vaux's unrealized design for **Tarrytown Heights** and East Tarrytown Heights (1871) was intended for an irregularly shaped, three-mile-long, 653-acre parcel in Westchester County, roughly 30 miles north of New York City.[237] The plan provided building sites of five acres each on average in topographically challenging countryside stretching from the Hudson River to the Saw Mill River valley, a site that a promotional brochure hailed without exaggeration for its "natural rural and sylvan charms . . . channels of air from the ocean . . . and elevation affording fine prospects."[238]

Bisected by the New York, Boston and Northern Railroad line that Olmsted hoped would provide two stations serving as the nuclei of estate workers' villages within the development, Tarrytown Heights was to be sparsely populated, with 226 villas. The project reflects Olmsted's darkening view of city life. Its promotional brochure, "A Report on a New Suburban District," warns that New York City's older suburbs, such as those in the Annexed District, were being engulfed by a rapidly expanding city bringing with it boardinghouses and tenements, and the presumably undesirable social classes that went with them.

In the Chicago area, Riverside had as its principal rival **Lake Forest**, about twenty-eight miles north of the city, which was founded in 1856 by several wealthy Chicagoans connected with Presbyterian College (now Lake Forest College) and originally intended as a home for the school and as a resort.[239] The plan of the village dates from 1857, when Almerin Hotchkiss (1816–1903), a St. Louis planner and landscape architect, who was chosen based on Olmsted's suggestion, prepared a design for the 1,300-acre site in which curving roads followed the challenging landscape of ravines and rolling hills on a bluff overlooking Lake Michigan, giving rise to a plan that thwarts the needs of the casual visitor, who is likely to get hopelessly lost in its mazelike pattern.[240] A visitor in 1869 observed that the "design . . . everywhere manifest, is to aid Nature by Art and not to bully her, which a great many men in Western towns seem to have aimed to do and succeeded in accomplishing . . . Winding graveled walks, smooth green lawns, rustic bridges—spanning ravines; . . . and grand old trees present a scene the eye is never weary of."[241]

While the foundation stone of the suburb was a college, as was typical with many American suburbs, Lake Forest's appeal to the affluent began in earnest with the introduction of golf to America in the late nineteenth century. Chicagoans of means began to establish estates there, working with local as well as New York architects to design large houses. However, the most interesting feature of Lake Forest as a garden village was not realized until 1916, when Market Square, designed by the

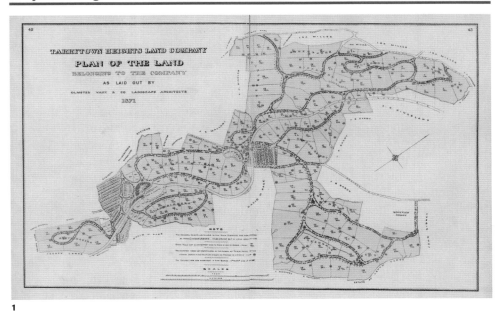

1

Chicago architect Howard Van Doren Shaw, helped establish as the heart of the Lake Forest Improvement plan a community focus—a charming, intimately scaled group of buildings surrounding a park, which replaced a ragtag collection of commercial buildings that had grown up around the railroad station. Money to execute what was in effect an "urban renewal" project *avant la lettre* was obtained from village residents who saw the value in replacing fifteen or so failing shops with twenty-eight stores, twenty-four apartments, twelve offices, a YWCA occupying the ground floor of the building at the west end of the square, and the entirety of a 50-by-94-foot building behind it devoted to a men's club and gymnasiums. Two other sites were left open with the expectation of a public library and another civic building. As the architect Peter B. Wight (1839–1925) put it in *Western Architect* in 1917: "So far as we know this is the first time in America that the *center of a town* has been taken and replanned and rebuilt, not as an altruistic or charitable undertaking, but in order to produce good practical as well as aesthetic effects."[242]

Lake Forest would inspire the development of a number of other nearby planned commuter villages, including **Highland Park** (1872), in Lake County, five miles south of Lake Forest and twenty-three miles north of Chicago.[243] Highland Park's development can be traced to 1854 when Walter Gurnee (1813–1903), president of the Chicago and Northwestern Railroad and a former Chicago mayor who had bought up large tracts of land a year before, established a train station. As such Highland Park actually precedes Lake Forest, although it did not take off as a development until ten years after its neighbor, when in 1867 the Highland Park Building Company was formed, purchasing 1,200 acres of Gurnee's land and engaging William M. R. French to work with landscape architect Horace William Shaler Cleveland—the landscape historian John Brinckerhoff Jackson regarded Cleveland as "undoubtedly the leading

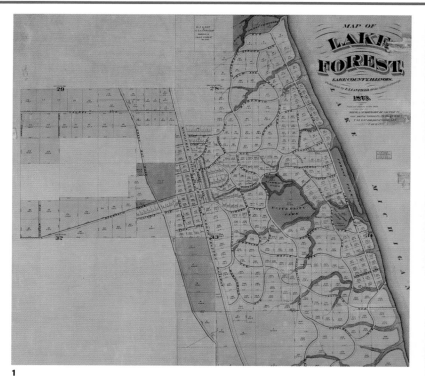

1. Plan, Almerin Hotchkiss, 1857. CHM (1873)

2. Deerpath Avenue. Childs. LCDM

3. Typical street. RAMSA (2012)

4. Western Avenue, with Market Square in distance. AF17 (1917)

5. Plan of Market Square, Howard Van Doren Shaw, 1916. LFC

6. Market Square. Garvin. AG (2005)

7. Railroad depot, with Market Square in distance. Garvin. AG (2005)

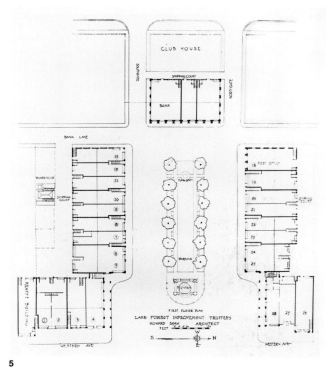

landscape architect of the region"—to plat the acreage along the choice Lake Michigan frontage from Walker Avenue to Beech Street.[244] French and Cleveland's plan called for large home sites along intricately curved streets laid out between the train tracks and Lake Michigan, with smaller houses to be located to the west where a business district was to be developed around the station, from which, sloping down to a lakefront park, a broad boulevard was intended. Incorporated as a city in 1869, by 1876 Highland Park was home to 1,076 residents, but the Panic of 1873 terminated the Building Company's operation.

Surprisingly, Cleveland's important and influential book, *Landscape Architecture, As Applied to the Wants of the West* (1873), which discusses the spread of railroad suburbs, does not specifically mention Highland Park, although the town exemplified his mentor A. J. Downing's ideal of picturesque landscape so much that it was advertised as a "vast natural park."[245] This characterization was not far from the truth, given that the deep ravines opening to Lake Michigan were preserved in their wild state, with some designated for public purposes but the majority retained as the backyards of contiguous house lots. "In effect," as Daniel J. Nadenicek and Lance M. Neckar have written, "the ravines [were] naturalized commons" that would form "a connective public realm" shared by individual homeowners.[246]

By the 1870s garden villages were undertaken along railroad lines leading from most Northern cities. **Irvington**, Indiana, seven miles east of Indianapolis, was developed beginning in 1870 by Jacob Julian, a banker, and Sylvester Johnson, a county auditor. Its design, by local civil engineer Robert Howard (n.d.), featuring 109 lots on nearly 400 acres adjacent to the railroad, was directly influenced by Glendale, Ohio, where Julian's daughter attended college and about which she "wrote glowingly" in letters home.[247] Covenants restricted "vicious or offensive" structures as well as alcohol. By 1873 Irvington had prospered to the extent that North Western Christian University (later Butler University) located its campus there and an addition to Irvington was built to the south along similar lines as the original development.

Ridley Park (1872), ten miles southwest of Philadelphia, was developed by Isaac Hinkley, president of the Philadelphia, Wilmington & Baltimore Railroad, and his partners who had in 1870 begun to buy up farms along the path of the Darby Improvement, a newly planned railroad line.[248] Ridley Park was laid out by Robert Morris Copeland, who had recently planned Oak Bluffs on Martha's Vineyard and was asked both to select the site and to design the new suburb, choosing a 600-acre elevated parcel stretching along both sides of the projected rail line with distant views of the Delaware River. Copeland's eclectic design called for a complex network of straight and winding 40-foot-wide, sidewalk-lined streets interspersed by all manner of open space and parkland as well as two large lakes created by damming streams that crossed the land. In all, a third of the acreage was devoted to parks and public rights-of-way. Ridley Park's founders hoped to attract members of both the upper middle and middle classes. The suburb's 900 lots varied widely in size so that "the millionaire may plant his villa, and the honest mechanic his pretty cottage . . . and both will breathe the same pure air, enjoy the same scenery, and derive the same political and domestic benefits, and have the same opportunity to rear their families in freedom and health."[249] The distribution of parcels reflected the developer's social utopianism: "Small lots for those whose means permit only a small expenditure, are grouped in the vicinity of the public grounds, so that the largest number of persons can enjoy them; whilst larger lots and more distant from the centre can be bought by men who are disposed to create all the beauty around their homes which they may desire."[250] As landscape planner Randall Arendt has noted, Ridley Park demonstrated how the same design principles at Riverside and Llewellyn Park "could be successfully applied at building densities that were considerably higher and therefore more challenging."[251]

Ridley Park was to be a complete village, with space set aside for a village hall, churches, schools, stores, lumber and coal yards, and a 15-acre cemetery. Two

Highland Park

1. Plan, William M. R. French and H. W. S. Cleveland, 1867. CHM (1872)

Irvington

1. Plat map, Robert Howard, 1870. IHS

2. Irvington Circle. IHS (1912)

3. Typical street. Roberts. BR (2012)

1. Plan, Robert Morris
Copeland, 1872. NYPLM

2. House on West Ridley Avenue.
RAMSA (2009)

3. West Hinckley Avenue.
RAMSA (2009)

4. Ridley Park Lake. RAMSA
(2009)

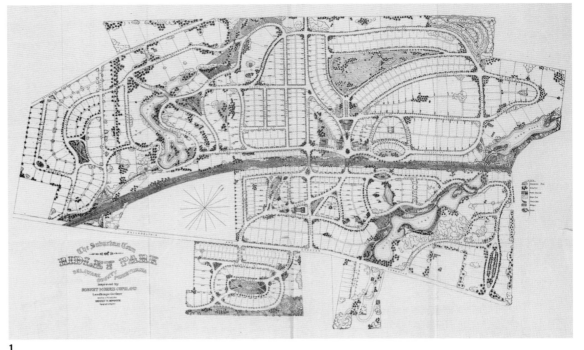

railroad stations designed by Copeland protégé Theophilus P. Chandler Jr. (1845–1928) served the community. The convenience of the railroad was touted in the suburb's promotional literature, where comparisons were drawn between its short twenty- to twenty-five-minute commute to Philadelphia and that of in-city suburban neighborhoods such as Germantown, which could only be reached by "long lines of horse cars."[252] Nonetheless, Ridley Park's isolation initially made it a hard sell, and those contemplating a house there were offered a discount on the transportation of building materials by rail as well as a year's worth of train travel for every thousand dollars spent on their house.

When on October 19, 1872, members of the Philadelphia press traveled to Ridley Park aboard a special train on the new Darby Improvement, the town had gotten off to an auspicious start, with a hotel completed, the Little Crum Creek dammed to create a 20-acre half-mile-long lake, and two miles of the street system finished as well as several houses. The journalists were so enraptured after listening to Copeland's speech that they bid him farewell with "three hearty cheers."[253] One observer, writing in *Lippincott's Magazine*, lauded Copeland's ability to "compose his picture, arranging the groves and lakes in

the most beautiful sequence, leaving sites for fine houses in the manner of pedestals for beautiful statues, and shading with discreet and natural veils the more utilitarian and prosaic features of the scene."[254] Looking back from almost one hundred years later, the historian John Reps was not taken with Copeland's work, writing that it possessed "a mechanical quality resulting from mere imitation of the superficial features of the romantic plan without real comprehension of the over-all effect that was essential."[255] Superficial or not, only a small portion of the plan survived the Panic of 1873 and Copeland's death the following year from an infection resulting from a broken arm sustained at Ridley Park. The site was subsequently subdivided into rectangular blocks, its open spaces vastly diminished.

Short Hills (1877), New Jersey, unlike Llewellyn Park, was planned as a village. But like Llewellyn Park, it was the product of a single entrepreneurial vision, that of Stewart Hartshorn (1840–1937), whose boyhood dream was to found an ideal community.[256] Short Hills was to be a personal obsession of the founder who controlled its destiny for most of his long life. By 1871 Hartshorn had prospered sufficiently in the window-shade business to move to the New Jersey countryside, first settling in Springfield, where he began to plan his "ideal suburban village." Three years later, he moved with his family to Short Hills, only six miles from Llewellyn Park, and began his town by purchasing 13 acres of land not too far from the Morris & Essex Railroad station in Millburn, a commuter village that had been established in 1857. Continuing to acquire land until he eventually owned almost 1,600 acres, Hartshorn personally laid out what was originally called the village of Short Hills Park.

Hartshorn's plan was in a way an antiplan, allowing Short Hills Park to evolve episodically over the years as a pleasant village spilling out into the countryside to meet the need for more houses. As John Archer has written,

> Unlike countless British and American counterparts, Hartshorn chose not to plat his land in advance but rather to individualize each plot for every purchaser. He would meet with prospective parties individually and if he then approved of them, would work with them in arranging a parcel . . . that would suit their interests. This process naturally suited Hartshorn's overall interest as well, in that he exercised full control not only over the planning and aesthetic design of the community, often with impressive results, but also over the social composition of the community. And to the extent that the residents' interests and tastes all mirrored Hartshorn's, the community naturally became a site for mutual confirmation and reinforcement of those tastes.[257]

At Short Hills Park the streets were graded and curved to complement the site's undulating topography. The irregularly shaped building lots were large, varying from one to five acres. Hartshorn, who built houses to rent and sold properties to buyers who would build their own in about equal proportion, picked his neighbors carefully. He wanted nature-loving people to live in his community, believing that such people had taste and initiative. But to assure that their taste and initiative jibed with his own, he reserved the right to review all plans even after the land was sold. Hartshorn's requirements included the stipulation that no two houses be alike. The suburb grew slowly, reaching thirty-three houses in 1885, and by the time of Hartshorn's death in 1937, at the age of ninety-seven, Short Hills Park had only 150 houses.

Hartshorn started his development in earnest in July 1879, when he built a small, clapboard-sheathed railroad station for Short Hills Park, giving his new suburb an identity independent from Millburn's. For a nearby site, he commissioned the fledgling architectural firm of Charles Follen McKim (1847–1909), William Rutherford Mead (1846–1928), and Stanford White (1853–1906) to design the community's social center, first called the Casino (1879–80), but soon known as the Music Hall, a building condemned for its lightheartedness by the critic Montgomery Schuyler. While he did not endorse the casino's design, Schuyler, perhaps inadvertently, did

identify the key characteristic of Hartshorn's vision for the architecture of Short Hills, and perhaps of the best suburban architecture as a whole: "It is an example of that kind of design in which the 'effect' precedes the cause, and which must continually be compromising itself, no matter how cleverly it is done, when it comes to be adjusted to the actual requirements of a building instead of being developed out of those requirements, so that the impression it ultimately leaves is not so much architectural as scenic."[258]

Schuyler's reservations notwithstanding, the Music Hall, until it burned down in 1978, was a compelling community symbol, as appropriate an emblem of the sporting and socializing weekends of this commuters' paradise as the Newport Casino (1880), by the same architects, was of summertime resort life. Though the Music Hall represented the most significant work of architecture in Short Hills, a number of the houses are also notable. In mid-1879 Hartshorn hired McKim, Mead & White to design a $5,000 model house, which, like the Music Hall, would serve as an advertisement for the community close to the new passenger depot and visible from passing trains. The many-gabled house, with bargeboards and half-timbering, seemed quaintly out-of-date, a late recollection of cottages promoted a generation earlier by Andrew Jackson Downing, and in no way as stylistically sophisticated as the Music Hall.

Ultimately, Short Hills Park would become more interesting for its various houses in a variety of architectural styles—Shingle Style, Colonial, and English Queen Anne, among others—than for its street plan, though as a result of Hartshorn's obsessive control, the town is also an excellent example of how the sensitive siting of houses can make a significant difference. Hartshorn approved of houses picturesquely set on knolls, and forbid any outbuildings or fences that would mar the view. (He provided a community stable, as well as a sewage and water system to preclude the need for outbuildings.) Firms like the partnership of Hugh Lamb (1848–1903) and Lorenzo Wheeler (1854–1899), and its successor firm of Lamb and Charles Alonzo Rich (1855–1943), designed houses that gave Short Hills Park its early reputation for innovative and individualistic domestic architecture. Later, after the century's turn, Short Hills' collection of architects seemed to reflect an ambition to transfer England to America. At Short Hills there are a number of very fine English-inspired houses by the partnership of Lewis Colt Albro (1876–1924) and Harrie T. Lindeberg (1879–1959); there is also the only American building by the English Arts and Crafts architect M. H. Baillie Scott, whose work is closely associated with the English garden suburb movement.[259] Baillie Scott's The Close (1913) was designed for Henry Binse, who provided the initial idea that the house be built around a courtyard to evoke an English inn. (Construction was supervised by Harold Tatton [1879–1965] of McKim, Mead & White.) The design excelled as a naturalistic work of architecture, using chestnut trees felled on the site for the nine-inch-thick framing. This is particularly ironic, in that Baillie

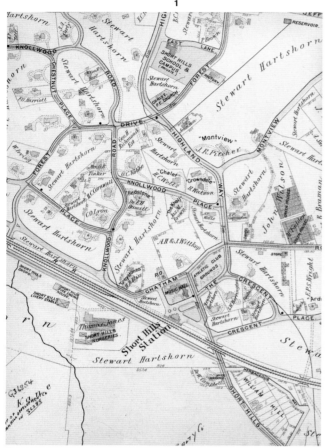

Scott was only able to "fake" traditional half-timbering in his English houses due to the scarcity of mature lumber in England, but in America he could literally build a house from the raw materials of the site itself just as had been the case in medieval England. Will Bradley (1868–1962), the illustrator, also lived in Short Hills Park in a particularly inventive stucco Arts and Crafts cottage of his own design.[260]

By 1884, when a history of Essex County was published, Short Hills was an established success:

> [It] has been brought into existence as the solution of a long baffling problem of how to make beautiful and healthy suburban homes. Mr. Hartshorn has made such homes, with all the happiness and comfort which they imply . . . and his enterprise in this direction . . . is perhaps the most practically successful one which has been undertaken in this country and it may be added that its result is at least as fair to the aesthetic eye as to the examination of the utilitarian. Mr. Hartshorn entered on his work with a love for it . . . His conception of what a town should be was thoroughly formed . . . There was never a rude clearing of the land. The noblest trees were left about the sites of future homes, and thus the place was given the appearance of a great park, by which term, indeed, Short Hills is better described than by any other.[261]

Hartshorn's control extended to all aspects of the village, including its only store. There were no saloons or factories to compromise his arcadia, leading the *American Architect and Building News* to describe it as "the original and only garden wherein Mother Eve and Father Adam built their home and commenced housekeeping."[262] In

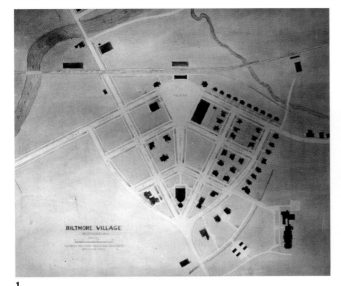

1. Plan, Frederick Law Olmsted, 1889. FLO (c. 1900)

2. Biltmore Village. LOCP (1889)

3. All Souls Crescent. TBC (1906)

4. All Souls Church, Richard Morris Hunt, 1895. LOCP (c. 1902)

5. Light standard and signage. RAMSA (2010)

6. Boston Way and All Souls Crescent. RAMSA (2010)

7. Typical street. FLO (c. 1900)

his survey of New York's suburbs, Montgomery Schuyler assessed Short Hills Park with knowing sarcasm: "A very pleasant place Short Hills must have been even before it occurred to an enterprising merchant of New York to buy it and convert it into an artistic and unique suburb . . . Short Hills," Schuyler continued, "is scene-painters' architecture in an opera village, as it were, where the houses have no further function than to look pretty and to possess 'practical' doors out of which you momentarily expect a chorus of happy villagers to emerge with a view to dancing on the sward. We see at Short Hills what the satirist meant when he declared that American humor never found full expression except in architecture." Nonetheless, Schuyler grudgingly concluded: "You certainly derive a distinct impression that all these places must be inhabited by very nice people, which is not a bad impression for a collection of country houses to make. And you must be of an unthankful spirit if when you leave Short Hills you do not invoke blessings upon its proprietor for having afforded you so much entertainment by building you this unique and delightful suburb."[263]

Biltmore Village, Asheville, North Carolina, planned in conjunction with George Vanderbilt's Biltmore Estate (1889–95) to house its workers and provide the amenities of a town, was begun in 1889 when Vanderbilt purchased the small railroad settlement of Best (aka Asheville Junction), relocated its residents, and called upon Frederick Law Olmsted and the architects Richard Morris Hunt (1827–1895) and Richard Sharp Smith (1852–1924) to reinvent it as a manorial village.[264] Olmsted prepared the fan-shaped street plan with a central axis that connected Hunt's Romanesque Revival All Souls Church (1895), the centerpiece of the village and its tallest structure, with a diamond-shaped public plaza, the forecourt of a railroad depot also designed by Hunt, anticipating the plan of Forest Hills Gardens by Frederick Law Olmsted Jr. A parish house and an estate office rounded out the architect's work in the village, with many of the remaining structures designed by Smith, including a post office, hospital, twenty-four pebbledash cottages built between 1898 and 1901, and the Biltmore Village Commercial Buildings, a mixed-use structure containing stores and apartments. The overall Tudor vocabulary of half-timbering, brick, and tile, evoking an old-fashioned English village, was juxtaposed with modern elements such as macadamized roads, streetlights, electricity to each house, and granite-curbed brick sidewalks lined with parking strips. By the early 1900s, when the village was an established suburb for Asheville, to which it was connected both by train and streetcar, Budgett Meakin (1866–1906), a widely traveled English writer and lecturer who wrote extensively on Morocco, where he had been the editor of an English language newspaper, before turning his attention to social reform and issues of labor and industrial housing, described it as "compact, as if it were in a garden formed in the leveled floor of a valley . . . [combining] the advantages of town and country . . . Lawns run down on all sides to the red-brick pathways, flanked by shrubs against the pebbled houses . . . No effect could be more easy or pleasing. Artistic, old-style, wrought-iron standards at the street-corners bear fifty-candlepower incandescent lights in suitable lanterns, with the names of the streets below in tasteful lettering."[265]

In April 1893, the *New York Times* dramatically reported that "the doom of **Katonah** is sealed" and that the "picturesque" Westchester County village thirty miles northeast of Bronxville would soon "be barely more than a memory conjured up in the mind" because, in order to accommodate New York City's increasing demands for water, the town would have to be completely cleared and flooded to make way for the expansion of the Croton Watershed and the creation of the Muscoot Reservoir and new Croton Dam.[266] Originally known as Whitlockville, the town's name was changed to Katonah in honor of a local Indian chief in 1852, five years after the tracks of the New York and Harlem Railroad first reached the community. Although Katonah grew haphazardly, with light manufacturing along the banks of the Croton and Cross Rivers, the residents were active in seeking civic enhancements, creating in 1878 the Katonah Village Improvement Society, which planted trees, installed kerosene street lamps and wooden sidewalks, and built a library and reading room. When the New York State Commission of Public Works mandated the evacuation of Katonah, the well-organized community created the Katonah Land Company, a syndicate that purchased 37 acres of farmland on high ground one-half mile south of the original settlement and in 1894 hired landscape architects B. S. (n.d.) and G. S. (n.d.) Olmstead (no relation to Frederick Law Olmsted) to create a plan for the new village, quickly dubbed New Katonah. The main focus of the plan was to separate residential and commercial uses, with the broad tree-lined Bedford Road intended for houses and Katonah Avenue, parallel to Bedford Road, to contain two- and three-story commercial structures.

The geometric plan—uncharacteristic of most suburban villages—also called for modest green spaces, and both Bedford Road and the Park Way featured central grassy sections dividing traffic and planted with trees. The syndicate took the opportunity of a fresh start to restrict certain businesses from the hamlet, including breweries, slaughterhouses, and tanneries. In addition, various deed restrictions were enacted, including the provision that no structure could be built for less than $2,500.

Instead of constructing completely new buildings, fifty-five structures, including houses, barns, and stores, were pulled by horses along soaped timber tracks to the new town before the Inundation, as it was known. New Katonah was officially dedicated before the move was complete on April 5, 1897, the day that the first railroad cars stopped at the new station. By the early 1900s, the new village was largely in place.

Nearby, **Lawrence Farms** (1929), New York, 40 miles from Grand Central Terminal, proposed by landowner and developer Dudley B. Lawrence (1879–1970), of the Bronxville family (see p. 310), for 1,000 acres lying between Mt. Kisco and Chappaqua, was the last suburban village principally conceived in terms of rail-based commuting.[267] The plan, devised by architect Penrose V. Stout (1887–1934) working in consultation with Thomas Adams (1871–1940) of the Regional Plan of New York, reserved 90 acres for a village, with the rest to be developed with country estates and preserved open spaces. The village had a grand, 120-foot-wide central boulevard, wide enough to be landscaped by a double row of shade trees and to handle surface car parking, connecting the railroad station with the open country. Plans for the village included a central town square surrounded by shops, a town hall, churches, and a theater. According to Lawrence, the project was undertaken to bring the benefits of zoned development to the country before suburban sprawl overtook it. As he put it in an interview in 1929: "Protected country life is a very definite thing, which is coming in this country, but which has not existed hitherto. While our countryside still remained fairly open, people failed to realize that they would ultimately need protection from unsightly surroundings and noisy or disturbing neighbors."[268]

Although the economic depression forced Lawrence to dramatically scale back his plans, especially for Stout and Adams's ambitious village, he was able to develop some of the property, constructing the Lawrence Farms Golf Club in 1930 and a modest enclave of six similarly sized single-family houses, each on an acre of land on Colony Row, just east of Bedford Road, for which Lawrence selected six "special architects" to design the houses in order "to attract attention" for the project.[269] Completed in 1933, the coordinated group of houses, each an interpretation of an early American style, were designed by Stout, Walker & Gillette, Dwight James Baum, Morris & O'Connor, Office of John Russell Pope, and Delano & Aldrich.

Although the embedded urban garden village is typically a phenomenon of the streetcar era, two

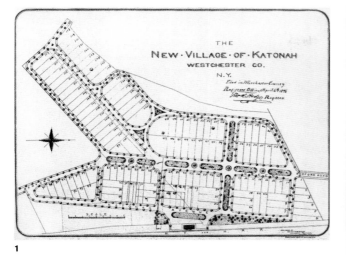

1

2

3

4

critically important examples—Chestnut Hill, Pennsylvania, and Forest Hills Gardens, New York—belong to the railroad era. From the point of typological clarity, **Chestnut Hill** (1854), Philadelphia, is a muddle, but it is of exceptional interest as the largest garden suburb to be developed within the political boundaries of a major city.[270] Chestnut Hill is a diffuse settlement comprising a collection of distinct enclaves each with some focal element, but overall lacking a commercial and civic center. Begun as a summer resort, Chestnut Hill evolved into a commuter paradise after 1884, when Henry Howard Houston (1820–1895), a powerful executive of the Pennsylvania Railroad, saw to it that the area was connected to the center of Philadelphia by a special branch line, known officially as the Philadelphia, Germantown, and Chestnut Hill Railroad. Houston had assembled approximately 3,000 acres of land nestled between the historic settlement of Germantown and the forested valleys of the Wissahickon River that Houston and his daughter, Gertrude (1868–1961), would subsequently donate to the city of Philadelphia to become part of Fairmount Park.

Houston had no clear vision of Chestnut Hill as a singular planning entity, relying instead on the existing village of Germantown to provide local shopping and other essential services, but building social centers around which residential development would naturally take place, such as the Wissahickon Inn (1884), located convenient to the station. While only about eight miles

from the center of Philadelphia, the inn functioned as a summer resort for families who still maintained houses in town, and in the off-seasons served as an introduction to the possibilities of year-round suburban life. Houston also built an English Gothic–style church, St. Martin-in-the-Fields (1888). Both inn and church were designed by his preferred architects, brothers George Watson Hewitt (1841–1916) and William D. Hewitt (1848–1924). To provide a social focus, Houston donated land to the Philadelphia Cricket Club, which built a Queen Anne–style clubhouse (1884), also designed by the Hewitt brothers. The building was lost to fire in 1908 and replaced by a Georgian-style redbrick structure (1910) designed by George T. Pearson (1849–1920).[271] Houston also transformed an old mill dam and pond into Lake Surprise, located just below the inn, and established an arboretum at St. Martin's Green.

Houston's principal activity as a developer was the construction of large houses for himself and several of his children as well as sixty of the seventy-nine houses that constituted what would come to be called Wissahickon Heights by the time of his death in 1895. Houston set the lot sizes, keeping them small to discourage further subdivision in the future, and controlled street and yard setbacks as well as the number of outbuildings permitted. The blocks of his land plan were irregular, in keeping with the topography and a desire to retain a rural character. The almost exclusive use of

1. Plan, B. S. and G. S. Olmstead, 1896. WCA

2. Aerial view. GE (2004)

3. Houses on Bedford Road. WCHS

4. Methodist Church, George Kramer, 1901, on Bedford Road. CRS

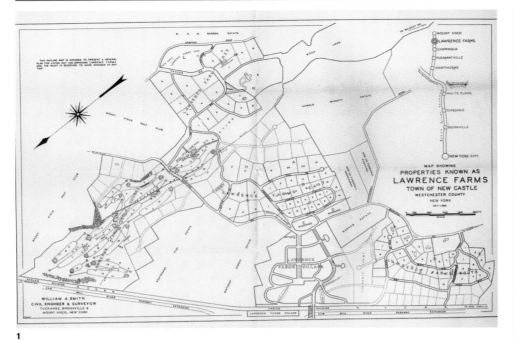

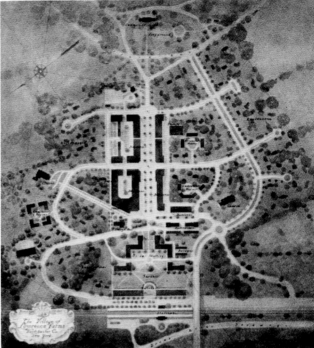

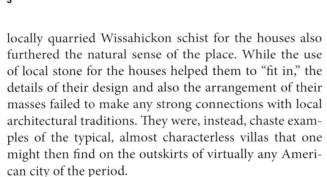

1. Plan, Penrose V. Stout and Thomas W. Adams, 1929. WCHS

2. Detail of village plan, Penrose V. Stout and Thomas W. Adams, 1929. RPA

3. House, Walker & Gillette. WCHS (c. 1933)

4. House, Penrose V. Stout. WCHS (c. 1933)

locally quarried Wissahickon schist for the houses also furthered the natural sense of the place. While the use of local stone for the houses helped them to "fit in," the details of their design and also the arrangement of their masses failed to make any strong connections with local architectural traditions. They were, instead, chaste examples of the typical, almost characterless villas that one might then find on the outskirts of virtually any American city of the period.

Preferring to lease his properties, Houston sold only a few. Upon his death, he willed his interests to his daughter, who was married to Dr. George Woodward (1863–1952). Today, the family-run firm, George Woodward, Inc., still owns many of the houses in Chestnut Hill and maintains deed restrictions to control development on property it sells. The Woodwards, possessing a far more carefully thought-through vision for the development's future than Houston, transformed Wissahickon Heights into what is now known as Chestnut Hill, developing it in keeping with the Anglophile tastes of many upper-class Philadelphians at the turn of the century. But their engagement with English building culture not only led them to admire the Cotswold country villages then coming into favor among architects, artists, and other tastemakers, but also to become experts in

the reform-minded English housing and town planning movement, with George Woodward becoming an important advocate and major participant in the garden suburb and city planning movement in the United States in the years leading up to World War I. As a result, Chestnut Hill became a testing ground for some of the most interesting American versions of English garden suburb planning, as best exemplified by the work of the partnership of Barry Parker (1867–1947) and Raymond Unwin.

Woodward was particularly interested in English experiments with group and semidetached housing, commissioning for Chestnut Hill a number of important projects—enclaves within the village, as it were—from leading Philadelphia architects.[272] What had begun as a vaguely defined Anglophilia on the part of Houston, in the hands of the Woodwards became a comprehensive artistic and social program, leading them to drop the Amerindian place name for the Wissahickon Heights section and train station that lay at the heart of the development and replace it with the very English St. Martin's, the place name of the church Houston had built, St. Martin-in-the-Fields.[273]

Under George Woodward's management, Chestnut Hill was more socially diverse than most garden suburbs of its time. While he was never interested in housing the

1. Map. JAJ (2002)

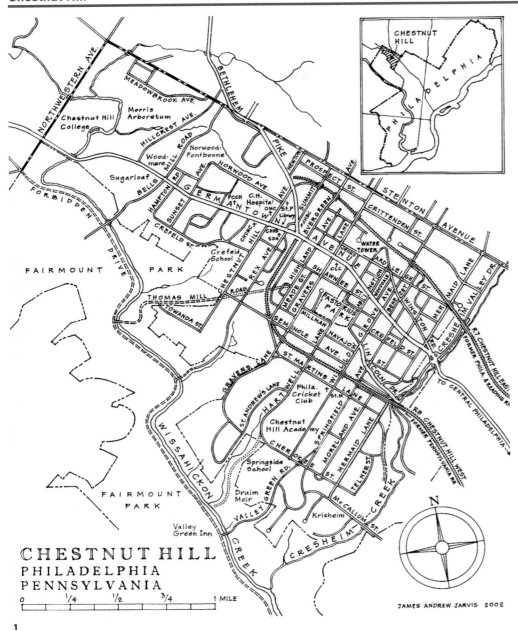

CHESTNUT HILL
PHILADELPHIA
PENNSYLVANIA

0   ¼   ½   ¾   1 MILE

JAMES ANDREW JARVIS 2002

1

poor in Chestnut Hill, and for a long time maintained a no-Jews-allowed policy, Woodward, like his father-in-law before him, was committed to building a variety of housing types to accommodate households and incomes representing a wide spectrum of the middle class. Houston had been content to play a passive role and simply take his architects' advice about design, but the Woodwards were very involved in the planning and design of the houses and took pride in their ability to have individual architects work together toward a shared social and aesthetic goal.

In 1904 the Woodwards commissioned their first houses in Chestnut Hill, four sets of double or paired houses on West Springfield Avenue, replacing some inadequate structures near Germantown Avenue. Between 1910 and 1912 Woodward and Samuel F. Houston (1867–1952), his brother-in-law, commissioned Edmund B. Gilchrist (1885–1953) to undertake a more ambitious project: a number of small houses for very

tight lots, most of which reflected an approach derived from the work of the English architect C. F. A. Voysey.[274] Later, Gilchrist was also to design for Woodward in a Cotswold-inspired mode using local stone that would become the local vernacular.

Around 1910 Woodward began to experiment with the kind of group house developments that were becoming the stock-in-trade of English garden suburb development. His earliest project along these lines, on Benezet Street, was intended to demonstrate that relatively high-density townhouses could combine a sense of overall stylistic cohesion without undue sacrifice to individuality—a very important point given the uniformity of rowhouses in Philadelphia, to which they would most likely be compared. The Benezet Street group was conceived as a totality, with houses at the ends framing the composition. It featured a variety of accommodations, including single-, double-, and quadruple-unit models. Adapting the twin or semidetached villa idea typical of

2

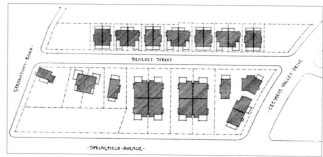

3

4

5

the kind that John Nash introduced in the Park Villages (see p. 26), Woodward, working with H. Louis Duhring (1874–1953), of Duhring, Okie & Ziegler, devised a quadruple-house type for the south side of the street (1910–12), with duplex units that were entered at the side rather than the front.[275] Set on deep lots, they effectively did away with rear yards: the "rear" units actually faced the parallel street, Springfield Avenue. On the other side of Benezet Street, on shallower lots, were twin houses, which used a wide palette of materials, including local stone, stucco, and brick.[276] Duhring designed a number of other developments for Woodward, including quadruple houses on Nippon Street, twin houses on Charlton Street, as well as Winston Court (1926), a group of apartments on Germantown Avenue.[277]

Between 1913 and 1917 Woodward developed a 13.5-acre district alternately called St. Martin's Green and the Pastorius Park development, consisting of twenty-one buildings for a total of forty house units.[278] The construction of Pastorius Park, which came at the expense of a number of preexisting houses deemed undesirable, provided needed public open space for Chestnut Hill residents living on the east side of the railroad tracks. The park was planned by Duhring, who left most of the site's natural features intact, but three separate architects worked on the houses that faced it, each agreeing to submit his designs to the other two as well as to Woodward for criticism. The architects and their client met together weekly.

Woodward commissioned Gilchrist to design a group of six rental houses on Willow Grove Avenue known as Linden Court, finished in 1915.[279] The redbrick Georgian design was a departure from the Chestnut Hill stone vernacular, and the project was later renamed Brick Court. The six-house group was praised by Harold D. Eberlein in *Architectural Forum*, who noted that Gilchrist's departure from the standard rowhouse "struck an entirely new note in the American practice of designing small contiguous dwellings." The cluster plan, according to Eberlein, permitted six houses "where under conventional conditions only four, or at the most, five houses could have been placed. Over and above that it is an achievement worthy of emulation to create a group in which every feature of the site and of the buildings is made to count for its utmost practicality and artistic value . . . a group whose occupants, whether they realize it or not, are evidently responsive to the architectural appeal to their imagination."[280] Gilchrist also designed a freestanding stucco and brick house at the corner of Willow Grove Avenue and Crefeld Street, which served as a link between the Linden group and the adjoining neighborhood.

Gilchrist designed another part of the St. Martin's Green development, a group of stone houses on Navajo Street.[281] These were designed as part of a larger group that consisted of Duhring, Okie & Ziegler's Quarter Circle Group,[282] dubbed the Half Moon Houses, and the three-house quadrangle designed by Robert Rodes

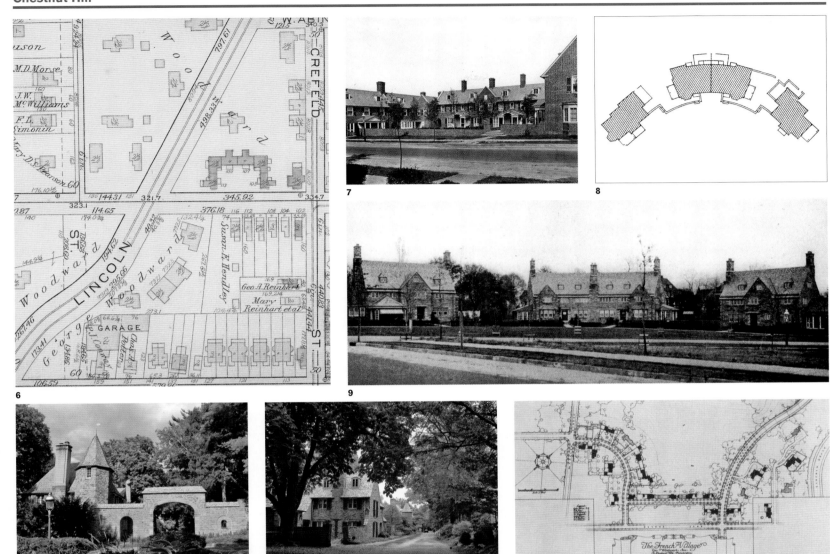

McGoodwin (1886–1967), both on Lincoln Drive.[283] The semicircular arrangement of the Half Moon Houses, arrived at to accommodate an oddly sized parcel of land, recalls the Paragon at Blackheath (see p. 19). McGoodwin was also to pursue the Cotswold-inspired vernacular for many individual Chestnut Hill house clients during the 1920s.[284]

Perhaps the most remarkable of the coordinated house groupings at Chestnut Hill is the French Village, designed for Woodward between 1919 and 1928 by McGoodwin.[285] Two "gatehouses" at Allens Lane—in reality small dwellings—flank one of the main entrances, not only announcing the French Village but also serving as a gateway to the entire Chestnut Hill development. Like most of the houses at St. Martin's Green, the French Village was built of local stone but in a freely interpreted version of Norman architecture with which Woodward had been impressed as a result of a trip to France in 1923. Mellor, Meigs & Howe's French-inspired work for individual clients in Chestnut Hill may also have played a part in shifting the direction of Woodward's taste.[286]

Walled in stone, with a placard that remonstrated "Defense d'Afficher," the French Village consisted of twenty-one lots fronting on Elbow Lane, Gate Lane, and Emlen Street. McGoodwin was commissioned to draw up the master plan and design eight of the houses; subsequently, he designed others for private clients to create sixteen houses in all.[287] Had McGoodwin's design for a set of shops at Mermaid Plaza been built, the French Village might have truly functioned as a focal village within sprawling Chestnut Hill; his Recreation Center (1930) on Hartwell Lane, housing an auditorium, gymnasium, and clubhouse, did provide a measure of civic identity.[288]

Despite the lack of a more compelling focus, Chestnut Hill, by virtue of its consistently held interpretations of Cotswold and French Norman architecture realized in local stone and its creative exploration of the possibilities of clustered housing, succeeds as a synthesis of form and content in the service of a sophisticated planning agenda. Yet some historians, such as Robert Fishman, see Chestnut Hill in darker terms: "the dream of the classic late nineteenth-century railroad suburb: an exclusive world of prosperity, beauty, health, and family life, a

6. Site plan, showing Linden Court and Quarter Circle Group. CHHS (1923)

7. Linden Court, Edmund B. Gilchrist, 1915. AF 17 (c. 1917)

8. Site plan, Quarter Circle Group, Duhring, Okie & Ziegler, 1917. AF 18

9. Quarter Circle Group. AF 18 (c. 1918)

10, 11. French Village, Robert Rodes McGoodwin, 1919–28. RAMSA (2007)

12. Site plan, French Village. RRM

grassy retreat at the city's edge where white, Protestant 'Americans' could preserve their identity and continue to dominate the turbulent industrial metropolis."[289] Though that may be the case, ambitions were for something quite a bit more egalitarian: Chestnut Hill is a veritable encyclopedia of multifamily suburban houses not found elsewhere in the United States. With some justification, it can be said to rival Forest Hills Gardens as the American Hampstead Garden Suburb.

Forest Hills Gardens (1909) is arguably America's most fully realized urban garden village.[290] Early in 1909 the Russell Sage Foundation purchased 142 acres (eventually increased to 175) of open land in the Forest Hills section of the borough of Queens, New York, nine miles east of Pennsylvania Station in Manhattan via the newly electrified main line of the Long Island Rail Road. The opening of the Steinway Tunnels in 1907, the Queensboro Bridge in 1909, and Pennsylvania Station in 1910 had combined to focus the attention of New York's development community on the potential of Queens to meet the newly consolidated city's need for affordable housing, and the project was intended to set an example for the still-rural borough's future growth. The Sage Foundation hired the Olmsted Brothers as planners and Grosvenor Atterbury (1869–1956) as architect for their model suburb.

Although Lewis Mumford rather antagonistically, and definitely mistakenly, stated that Forest Hills Gardens failed because "Atterbury designed . . . for industrial workers in the fashion that he did for the upper middle classes," in fact there was never any intention of developing a workers' village.[291] Forest Hills Gardens was aimed at those on the lower and middle rungs of the managerial class. Atterbury was aware of the possible confusion that the seeming schizophrenia of enlightened planning for the middle class might bring with it. "It is unfortunate," he wrote in 1912, "that the somewhat misleading word 'model' must be applied to such an eminently practical scheme as the development of the Russell Sage Foundation, for the reason that there is a subtle odium which attaches to 'model' things of almost any kind, even when they are neither charitable nor philanthropic—a slightly sanctimonious atmosphere that is debilitating rather than stimulative of success."[292] Never affordable even to middle management, Forest Hills Gardens soon became home to the upper middle class, which it continues to attract.

The Forest Hills Gardens promoters intended it to be a "model town" that would also succeed as a "business" proposition, like Hampstead Garden Suburb, combining enlightened planning and social ideals, and like Hampstead Garden Suburb, realizing a profit, though in point of fact it was sponsored by a foundation. As with Hampstead Garden Suburb, Forest Hills Gardens enjoyed a prime location close to the center of the city and in close proximity to major parkland. In both cases, the original intentions were not quite fulfilled. The strategic location resulted in a high initial land cost, encouraging comparatively high-density development.

In the early stages, the use of a system of prefabricated concrete construction developed by Atterbury, whose contributions in this area are largely overlooked, also contributed to high development costs.[293]

Frederick Law Olmsted Jr.'s plan, organized along a continuous line of movement from the railroad station to the 500 acres of Forest Park, constituted a metaphoric journey from city to country, not unlike that of Nash's Regent's Development in London a century before. At Forest Hills Gardens, the metaphor was much clearer than that of its contemporary, Parker and Unwin's Hampstead Garden Suburb. Though in many respects the most English of American garden suburbs, Forest Hills Gardens also reflected American civic-mindedness by incorporating an emphasis on monumental urban planning and collective public space—in the form of Station Square and the broad boulevard of the Greenway leading from it—that had gained momentum after the 1893 World's Columbian Exposition in Chicago.

The relationship of Olmsted's street system to that of the greater city was a key factor in Forest Hills Gardens' success. The automobile was barely more than a rich man's plaything in 1907 when the planning was begun, but by 1916, as Charles C. May put it, when the community was already well established, the demands it placed on the plan had "multiplied amazingly." Nonetheless, Forest Hills Gardens met the motor car's challenge, according to May, because of its "system of main traffic arteries, independent of the short residential streets," and the "articulation of this system with the natural lines of travel to and from the boroughs of the Greater City."[294]

The orchestration of street types—the boulevard-like Greenway, the culs-de-sac, as well as the local streets—was instrumental in creating a sense of community. As Olmsted wrote: "Probably one of the most notable characteristics of Forest Hills Gardens will be the cozy, domestic character of these local streets, where the monotony of endless straight, wind-swept thoroughfares which represent the New York conception of streets will give place to short, quiet, self-contained and garden-like neighborhoods, each having its own distinct character."[295] Clarence Perry (1872–1944), an early resident and an employee of the Sage Foundation, was so impressed with the social structure fostered by the town plan that he used the Gardens as the basis for his highly influential planning strategy, the "neighborhood unit."[296]

In its effort to at once be a model community and a practical business proposition, Forest Hills Gardens represented a more complex kind of suburbanism than ever before attempted. Atterbury, working with other architects, provided a wide variety of housing types, from the hotel, apartments, and shops at Station Square to grouped houses as well as semidetached and single-family dwellings. A number of housing groups were clustered around shared garden spaces in a bold and largely successful assault against the American tradition of ornamental but useless front yards.

Anticipating its eventual engulfment by the expanding city, Olmsted and Atterbury treated the garden

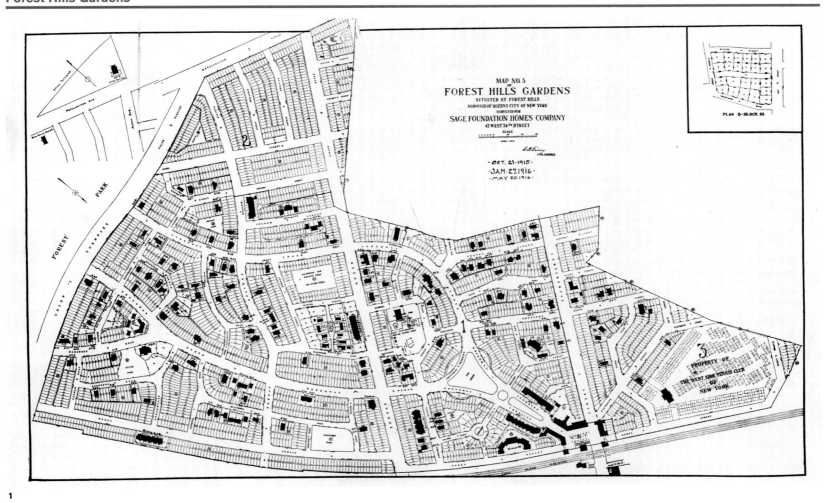

1

1. Plan showing development up to 1916. A16

suburb as a self-contained village, using a potentially blighting feature, the railroad embankment that runs along its most exposed flank, as an asset, handling it as a defensive earthwork berm and lining it with apartment and group houses that formed three sides of courtyards bound on the fourth by a peripheral street, Burns Street, and the embankment itself. Forest Park established a clear boundary on the south edge of the village. But absent either an embankment or a park on its other sides, the village edges abutting adjoining properties were less clearly demarked, although the landscaping, street design, and distinctive architecture went a long way to defining even these loose boundaries.

Station Square was established as the gateway to the community. A notably coherent urban set piece, it consisted of a brick-paved plaza dominated by the tower of the Forest Hills Inn, bordered on one side by the embankment of the railroad and its station, designed by Atterbury, and on the other three by a continuously arcaded building, also designed by Atterbury, containing apartments and shops spanning the two principal streets leading from it into the residential neighborhoods. Station Square reminded the architectural journalist Samuel Howe "of a college or cathedral city."[297] With the restaurants and meeting rooms of the Forest Hills Inn, Station Square quickly became the focus of community life, serving as the setting for public events.

Despite a compact site, the overall layout of Forest Hills Gardens, while it hardly achieves the naturalism of Riverside, nonetheless convincingly evokes a rural village. In the prospectus of 1911, the sponsors stated that "fantastically crooked layouts have been abandoned for the cozy, domestic character of local streets, not perfectly straight for too long, but gently curving to avoid monotony."[298] The village became more rural as the distance from the square increased, further reinforcing the impression of a journey from town to open country, in this case Forest Park. This was in effect the principal open space and its equivalent to the Heath at Hampstead Garden Suburb though technically not part of the development.

Honoring Frederick Law Olmsted's belief in the value of small neighborhood parks, the Olmsted Brothers aerated the plan with a number of green spaces, including the three-and-a-half-acre Greenway that extended the civicism of Station Square into the suburb's residential heart, as well as the one-and-a-half-acre Hawthorne Park for quiet recreation, and a one-acre natural hollow, Olivia Park, named to honor Olivia Sage. The Olmsted Brothers also provided for "enclosed private parks" located in the center of some blocks, where they could be shared by those living in the surrounding houses. These were intended for the use of small children and were deliberately designed to discourage active sports and the

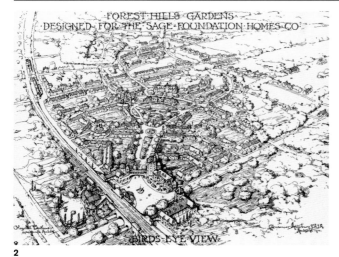

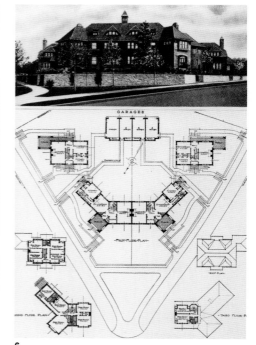

2. Bird's-eye view. BP11 (1911)

3. Greenway Terrace from tower of the Forest Hills Inn. FHG (1913)

4. Houses, Grosvenor Atterbury, Greenway Terrace. FLO (1914)

5. Village green looking toward the Forest Hills Inn. FLO (1914)

6. Group XII, Grosvenor Atterbury, 1912, Greenway North and Markwood Road. A16

7. Station Square. RAMSA (2012)

8. Greenway looking toward the Forest Hills Inn. RAMSA (c. 1980)

9. Burns Street group, Grosvenor Atterbury, 1913, employing prefabricated panels. RAMSA (2012)

10. Greenway. RAMSA (2012)

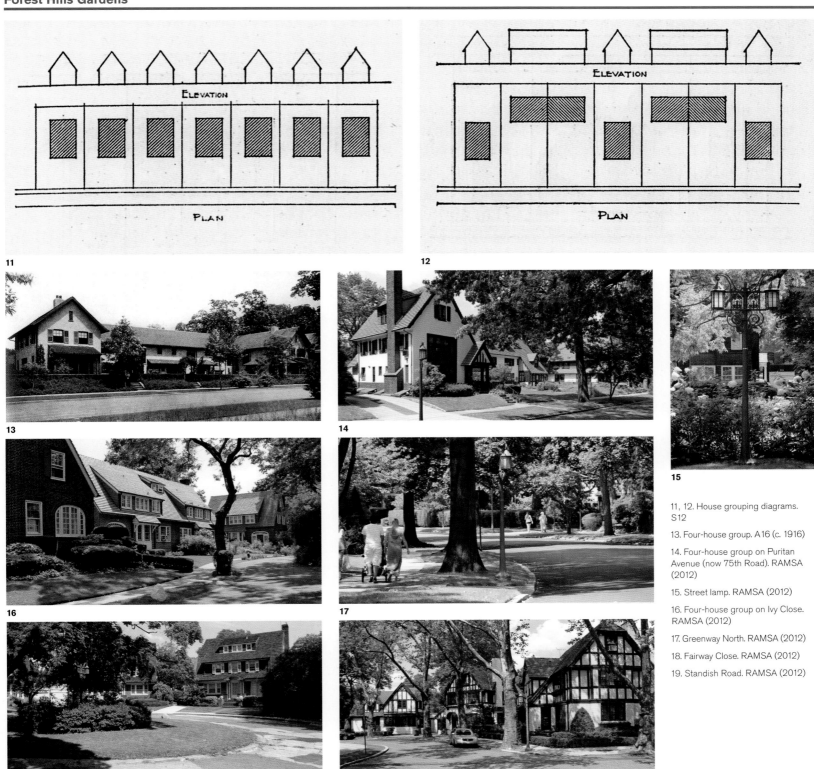

11, 12. House grouping diagrams. S12

13. Four-house group. A16 (c. 1916)

14. Four-house group on Puritan Avenue (now 75th Road). RAMSA (2012)

15. Street lamp. RAMSA (2012)

16. Four-house group on Ivy Close. RAMSA (2012)

17. Greenway North. RAMSA (2012)

18. Fairway Close. RAMSA (2012)

19. Standish Road. RAMSA (2012)

intrusion of "loafers." To capture this space, surrounding lots were shallow, but their smaller size was to be offset by increased value owing to the proximity of the collective midblock greens. In order to achieve these special enclaves, the Olmsted plan called for far more in the way of attached rows of houses than was typical of American practice, leading Atterbury to observe that "the apparently anomalous fact remains that a supposedly model town is being built largely of contiguous houses in more or less continuous rows directly adjoining plowed fields."[299]

Atterbury was responsible for some of the loveliest buildings in the Gardens. His Station Square group, including the tower of the Forest Hills Inn, melds English planning with German medieval architecture, testifying to the influence of Parker and Unwin's work and their admiration for such German towns as Rothenberg. Station Square was matched by Atterbury's group houses along Greenway Terrace, as well as his Burns Street group, which used a crescent plan to provide a courtyard facing the railroad embankment.

To fend off the potential threat of a perceived over-density, Atterbury, assisted by John Almy Tompkins 2nd (1871–1941) and Stowe Phelps (1869–1952), undertook inventive experiments with coordinated housing groups, demonstrating how even the individual cottage on its own lot could be arranged to create shared open space, so that, as a later observer, John Stilgoe, has pointed out, the "pairing of two single-family houses with one two-family 'double' house radically shifted traditional arrangements of front and back yards" and in a single blow, virtually abolished outdoor privacy.[300] Atterbury's Group XII, at the fork between Greenway North and Markwood Road, had four houses, two of which were combined into a semidetached unit. His design skillfully adapted the axial composition principles of the City Beautiful to the suburban milieu, simultaneously culminating the axis of Greenway North and providing an interior space that made a virtue of the site's awkward geometry.

Property deeds strictly limited future construction and ensured that houses and gardens would be properly maintained for the overall benefit of the community. Though most of the land was sold as undeveloped lots, the Sage Foundation provided the first one hundred buyers of single house lots with preapproved plans not only in order to stimulate but also "to maintain a high standard of design and construction in the buildings erected."[301] An architectural review process was initiated under the direction of Atterbury and Robert Tappan (1884–1961), his successor as consulting architect, to ensure the continued development of a cohesive building fabric that, together with the town plan, established a convincing sense of place in what amounted to a semi-self-sufficient suburban village embedded within the rapidly expanding and largely unplanned outlying neighborhoods of the greater city.

Almost from the first, visitors marveled at the beauty of the place. Forest Hills Gardens, unlike so many of its predecessors whose early days were patchy at best, was realized quickly, with the greatest investment made early on in the set pieces of Station Square and the Greenway, leading John Stilgoe to observe that "without realizing it," the early visitors like Samuel Howe "wandered into the first deliberately photogenic residential development built in the United States. Forest Hills was not pretty as a picture . . . It *was* the picture," a veritable painting in brick, stucco, tile, decorative ironwork, and landscape.[302]

Because of its unique combination of city planning and architecture, Forest Hills Gardens is the preeminent American expression of the garden suburb ideal. It represents both a pinnacle and an end of a particular kind of suburb that the railroad made possible, with a single point of connection to the central city. But by virtue of being embedded in a rapidly developing section of a major city, it also demonstrates how careful planning can enhance a sense of ruralesque identity within the metropolitan city's sprawling urbanism.

THE GARDEN VILLAGE: STREETCAR SUBURBS

With the introduction of electric-powered streetcars in 1887, suburban-style neighborhoods began to proliferate within the confines of cities, frequently catering to a working-class rather than managerial-class tenantry.[303] Many of the streetcar suburbs were not planned as distinct entities, but rather as extensions of established local street patterns, with little in the way of distinctive architecture. However, some streetcar suburbs were also arcadian in character, planned to meet the growing taste for country living, both among the working classes and those of greater financial means. For example, **Roland Park**, named after Roland Thornberry, a seventeenth-century English landholder of Baltimore County, is an upper-middle-class suburban village at the edge of Baltimore, Maryland, and one of the most important garden villages of the streetcar era.[304] Originally intended only for single-family residences, Roland Park later came to include clustered house groups and apartment houses. Its row of shops (1896) is considered by some to be the first example of the modern shopping center. Roland Park is particularly important as a model for later developments, especially the Country Club District in Kansas City, Missouri, whose developer, J. C. Nichols, after visiting it in 1912, wrote to Edward H. Bouton (1858–1941), a partner in the Roland Park Company and its general manager from 1903 until his retirement in 1935, that "when people ask me how I enjoyed my trip and what I saw, I tell them I saw Roland Park; and I feel there is not much need of describing anything I saw elsewhere."[305]

In 1891 an English syndicate invested in two tracts of land comprising 550 acres about four miles north of Baltimore, forming the Roland Park Company to develop the site that included several country estates. The English withdrew their support in 1903, and from then on Bouton was in charge, although his influence had been central to the suburb's development since at least 1893, when he founded the Lake Roland Elevated Railroad, an electric streetcar line that carried residents on a thirty-minute trip to Baltimore City Hall every four minutes, twenty-four hours a day. To accommodate the streetcar, Bouton called for the transformation of Roland Avenue, the north–south street bisecting the suburb, from a narrow country road into a spinelike 120-foot-wide landscaped boulevard divided by a spacious center island.

The first portion of Roland Park to be developed, a 150-acre tract east of Roland Avenue and north of Cold Spring Lane, was laid out in 1891 by twenty-nine-year-old George Kessler, a German engineer who briefly worked in Frederick Law Olmsted Sr.'s office and, in 1892, began work on the design of the Kansas City Boulevard system.[306] Kessler exaggerated the features of the heavily wooded site in order to enhance the suburb's rural image, allowing streets to follow the gently sloping topography of the land, locating houses and rustic

1

pathways around existing trees. The second phase of development, comprising 300 acres west of Roland Avenue, was laid out in 1897–98 by the Olmsted Brothers, led by Frederick Law Olmsted Jr. This section, opened in 1901, occupied significantly steeper terrain resulting in an even more curvilinear street pattern and greater variation in the size and shape of lots. Throughout, streets ranged from 40 to 60 feet in width, and 20-foot service alleys extended in the midblocks, frequently used as pedestrian pathways. A 12-foot-wide strip of land separating the building lots from the roadways accommodated a three-and-a-half- to five-foot-wide sidewalk and a grassy tree-planted verge.

The early houses of the 1890s were chiefly the work of the firm of James B. N. Wyatt (1847–1926) and William G. Nolting (1866–1940), who built in the same comfortable Shingle Style found all along the Eastern Seaboard. Both Wyatt and Nolting, whose work also included the design of the shopping center, took up residence in Roland Park. Eventually more than 1,000 houses were built, most of them planned for individual clients by more than 100 architects, testament to the compatibility of comprehensive planning and private building.

Strict covenants were incorporated into each property deed. Initially regarded as an inhibitor to sales, the covenants were eventually credited with the suburb's great popularity and in later phases were touted in promotional campaigns. By governing setbacks, landscaping standards, and minimum prices for the houses, the strictures ensured the community's character as a country village despite its close proximity to Baltimore. Standards were set for the size of houses permitted and, beginning with the second phase, required their designs to be reviewed by the company architect, Edward L. Palmer Jr., who also built extensively in Roland Park. Only one house was allowed on each lot, and private stables were not permitted—a shared facility for boarding horses, carriages, and coachman's quarters was built by the company. Buyers also agreed to contribute to the cost of maintaining streets, lighting and sewer systems, garbage collection, and other common services. In addition, as Waldon Fawcett observed in 1903: "Saloons and shops are effectively banned from the community, and in order to maintain the strictly suburban character of the park, the various stores which serve the residents are located together in one block, which is set back to the building line of the residences, and is robbed of all suggestion of the commonplace, owing to the judicious employment of the picturesque Flemish architecture."[307] One hundred and fifty acres along Falls Road were set aside for an eighteen-hole golf course belonging to the Baltimore Country Club.[308]

2. Plan of second phase of Roland Park, Olmsted Brothers, 1897–98. FLO (1901)

3. Group houses, Edward L. Palmer Jr., 1909, University Parkway. FLO (c. 1912)

4. Typical street. RAMSA (2008)

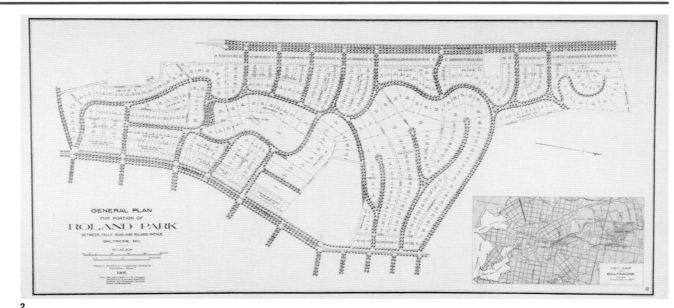

2

3

4

Edward Palmer's work included several house developments involving group planning and collective construction, such as those on University Parkway (1909), among the most interesting works of the Roland Park Company, built using poured-in-place concrete construction. With landscape architect James Gilbert Langdon (1866–1950), Palmer also designed the single-block Edgevale Park (1911), bound by Edgevale Road, Englewood Road, and Falls Road Terrace, a group of twelve Voyseyesque detached and semidetached houses encircling a private greensward.[309] As a partner in the firm of Palmer, Willis & Lamdin, he also designed the Roland Park Apartments (c. 1926), one of several apartment houses constructed in the suburb during the 1920s.[310]

The popularity of Roland Park led to its expansion. Beginning in 1911 an adjoining 210-acre tract to the southeast was developed as the Guilford district, laid out by the Olmsted firm with Palmer designing semidetached and group houses of considerable sophistication, most notably those at Bretton Place and York Road, where three groups of twelve houses in all were placed among grass courtyards around a Y-shaped intersection.[311] The first lots in Guilford were sold in 1913, at which point the district had the strictest regulations of any subdivision in the United States, including newly added covenants governing side and rear as well as front setbacks. The covenants also excluded blacks from living in the development.

In 1924, Bouton and the Roland Park Company undertook the Homeland section on a 390-acre tract abutting Roland Park to the northeast.[312] Also laid out by the Olmsted Brothers, the Homeland grid of gently curving streets accommodated lots of varying shape and size, ranging from 60 by 150 feet to 135 by 207 feet. The last major development of the Roland Park Company was the Northwood section, begun in 1929, intended for middle-class home buyers and planned by company architect John A. Ahlers (1895–1983), who also designed a majority of its houses.[313] The Depression curtailed development, however, and the plan was not realized.

5

6

7

9

8

10

11

5, 6. Typical views. RAMSA (2008)

7. Roland Park shopping center, Wyatt & Nolting, 1896. Munro. DM (2010)

8. Study for Edgevale Park, Edward L. Palmer Jr. 1911. NYPL

9. Edgevale Park. Munro. DM (2010)

10. Homeland, typical street. Garvin. AG (1997)

11. Homeland Lake. Garvin. AG (1996)

Chevy Chase (1890), Maryland, outside Washington, D.C., was planned as an upmarket streetcar suburb.[314] The brainchild of Francis Newlands, an attorney and heir by marriage to a fortune made from mining the Comstock Lode, Chevy Chase was part of a grand strategy to capitalize on Washington's growth. Chevy Chase was initially undertaken in 1887, when Newlands began to quietly amass some 1,713 acres five miles northwest of the D.C. border, a location he selected because of its adjacency to the National Zoological Park (founded in 1889) and Rock Creek Park (founded in 1890), the presence of which would increase the value of his property by taking 2,000 acres of developable land off the market. When word of his land purchases got out in 1890, Newlands formed the Chevy Chase Land Company to "establish a suburban town, connect it with Washington by a railroad line which will furnish quick transit, and then let the improvement in value at both ends build up the immediate property."[315] Newlands connected his site to the city by completing an extension to Washington's

Connecticut Avenue, and building the Rock Creek Railway, a streetcar line, down its middle, ensuring ridership even before the construction of houses began by also providing transportation for visitors to the zoo and park.

To plat the first area, known as Section 2 (Section 1 was developed as the Chevy Chase Club, a country club), Newlands turned to Nathan F. Barrett, who prepared a straightforward gridiron plan. Apparently disappointed, Newlands asked Frederick Law Olmsted Sr. to work with Barrett on revising the design. Olmsted declined, writing: "Mr. Barrett must have long ago settled down upon a general theory of design as the basis of the plan he has furnished you, and in a great degree his mind must now be made up as to what is best."[316] Olmsted offered to consider the commission if Barrett were to withdraw completely, but Barrett stayed on. By the time his plan was filed in 1892, the grid had been overlaid with curving boulevards lined with double rows of trees and interspersed with small parks, resulting in a hybrid of

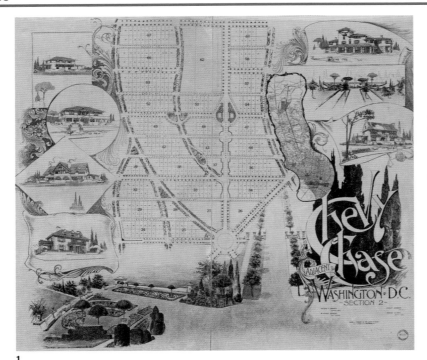

1. Plan of Section 2, Nathan F. Barrett, 1892. LOCG

2. Chevy Chase Circle. EW (1893)

3. Connecticut Avenue showing Chevy Chase Club trolley. CCHS

4. Sales plat of Section 4, David J. Howell, 1909. CCHS

5. East Lenox Street. CCHS (1904)

6. Section 4 from Rosemary Circle Water Tower, with Rosemary Street on left and Elm Street on right. Truax. CCHS (1927)

axial formality and picturesque informality such as he had explored in his plan for Rochelle Park (see p. 55). Barrett's collaborators were E. C. Reynolds (n.d.), a civil engineer, and the Philadelphia architect Lindley Johnson (1854–1937), who designed the first model cottages but was succeeded as company architect in 1893 by Leon E. Dessez (1858–1918). Section 2 was bisected longitudinally by the 130-foot-wide, landscaped Connecticut Avenue, which was diverted from its northwestern trajectory from Washington to turn due north at Chevy Chase Circle, a *rond-point* located at the District line,

where the plan provided for two 100-foot-wide curving roads, Magnolia Parkway and Laurel Parkway, crossed by parallel, 60- and 100-foot-wide east–west streets. Ninety-six acres were devoted to house sites averaging 60 by 125 feet, and 59 acres were occupied by rights-of-way and parkland.

Restrictive covenants banned commercial uses from Chevy Chase, established minimum house costs, and mandated that houses be set back a minimum of 25 feet from the front lot line. Rowhouses were not permitted and although semidetached houses were allowed,

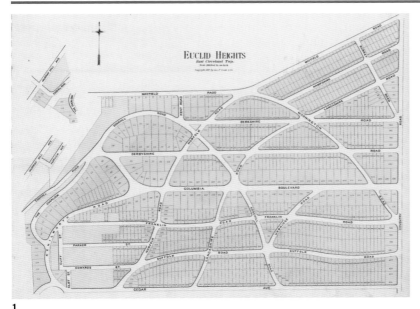

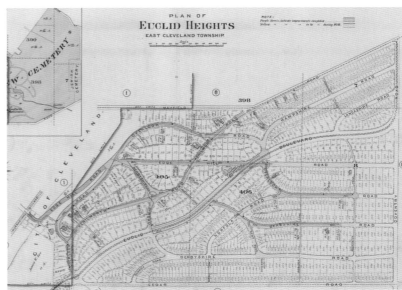

1

2

3

4

1. Plan, Ernest W. Bowditch, 1892. CPL

2. Plan, Ernest W. Bowditch, 1898. CPL

3. Euclid Heights Boulevard. CSU (c. 1912)

4. Aerial view. GE (2006)

none were built. The Land Company provided water and sewer systems along with other services and maintained roads and public areas. The second subdivision, Section 3 (1907), occupying flat land east of Connecticut Avenue between Bradley Lane and Taylor Street, was planned with a combination of narrower gridded and angled streets. Section 4, which opened in 1909, west of Connecticut Avenue in steep hilly terrain crossed by streams, led David J. Howell (n.d.), an engineer, to modify the otherwise rigid plan with meandering parks and indirect roads, such as the tree-lined Meadow Lane that followed the route of a stream along the edge of a reservoir. Section 4 also benefited from its location between the Chevy Chase Club and the Columbia Country Club, a second club opened in 1911.

In 1907, Chevy Chase, D.C., a five-block area within the District of Columbia, was laid out with smaller lots, shallower front setbacks, and midblock service alleys. It was followed in 1910 by Chevy Chase Heights, across Connecticut Avenue to the west, consisting of sixteen rectangular blocks cut through by the sinuous Reno Road. The Chevy Chase Land Company continued to open subdivisions through the teens and into the 1920s, although most of the new areas—particularly those built after Newlands's death in 1917—were not imaginatively designed.[317]

In 1892, for Patrick Calhoun (1856–1943), an attorney who represented railroad companies and later became a prominent railroad and streetcar builder, Ernest W. Bowditch planned the suburban village of **Euclid Heights**, just east of the Cleveland, Ohio, city limits.[318] Two years earlier, during a visit to Cleveland's Lake View Cemetery (1869), Calhoun had taken an interest in adjacent land to the south and soon amassed 300 acres naturally bordered on the west by bluffs overlooking the city. The site lay close to the system of parks (1894) that Bowditch was then designing for Cleveland and to which Calhoun, along with John D. Rockefeller, Jr. (1874–1960), whose father's summer home, Forest Hill, was nearby, would donate considerable land. Bowditch's plan called for east-west streets crossed by gently warped north-south drives. The eastern edge of the development was platted with smaller lots for families of modest means, while the choice western lots were intended to lure Cleveland's social elite from nearby Euclid Avenue. Euclid Heights' first resident was the architect Alfred Hoyt Granger (1867–1939), who completed his own house in 1895 on The Overlook, a street running along the bluffs that would develop into a wealthy enclave.[319] Granger designed several other Euclid Heights residences, some in partnership with Frank Meade (1867–1947).[320]

In the mid-1890s, after additional parcels were acquired, Bowditch prepared a new plan to guide the suburb's overall development. The design differed in detail but was similar in spirit, now cut through by Euclid Heights Boulevard, accommodating a streetcar line. Over 50,000 poplar, maple, and oak trees were planted to reforest the land that had previously been stripped of its timber. Restrictive covenants called for single-family houses limited in height to three stories and set back from the street between 25 and 40 feet, with minimum construction costs based on the location of the house. The establishment of the Euclid Golf Club in 1901 helped attract residents to the slowly growing village, which by 1914 had only 102 houses dotting its 841 sites.

Significantly, many of the more affluent garden villages of the streetcar era were realized in less established cities on large tracts of land within or just beyond the city limits. For example, **Inman Park** (1887), arguably the first garden suburb planned with the streetcar in mind, occupied a high plateau two miles east of Atlanta's downtown.[321] Conceived by Joel Hurt (1850–1926), a civil engineer deeply impressed by Riverside, Inman Park was planned by landscape architect Joseph Forsyth Johnson (1840–1906), who established a lush residential development, importing from coastal Georgia live oak trees hitherto believed not to be hardy in Atlanta. To serve the 138-acre site (51 acres were added in 1891), Hurt planned and engineered Atlanta's first electric trolley line, which began operating in 1889, running along Edgewood Avenue, a broad boulevard he built to connect the new neighborhood with the city's downtown business district.

Named for Samuel M. Inman (1843–1915), Hurt's business associate and close friend, the suburb was ringed by a 20-foot-wide landscape buffer to protect it from encroachment (regrettably, with time's passage, the buffer disappeared). The lots were large—typically 100 feet wide and 200 to 300 feet deep. Except for Waverly Way and Druid Circle, the streets were straight or only gently curved but arranged to discourage through traffic. The plan called for two large central parks, one called the Mesa and the other Springvale Park, a 10-acre oasis with a spring-fed lake. Additionally, other open spaces were provided so that 49 of the development's 130 lots fronted directly on parkland. As Hurt turned his attention to other projects in the mid-1890s, the company that took over subdivided a good number of Inman Park's open spaces into house lots.

Druid Hills (1892–1905), the second of Atlanta's streetcar arcadias, and the one with the greatest scope and significance, was also conceived by Joel Hurt, who provided trolley service from downtown Atlanta along Ponce de Leon Avenue.[322] The development consisted of 1,500 acres roughly three miles northeast of Atlanta's downtown, extending toward the adjacent city of Decatur. As initially planned in 1893, Druid Hills was the last of Olmsted Sr.'s suburban projects. But after his death in 1903, it became one of the first significant undertakings

of the successor firm, Olmsted Brothers, which reconceived the project, as Dana F. White has written, to reflect "new stages in urban transportation and city building," anticipating and even embracing the automobile as the principal mode of suburban travel.[323] Nonetheless, Olmsted Sr.'s initial concept of Druid Hills prevailed, although it has until recently been largely invisible in the Olmsted canon, overwhelmed by the better-documented and thirty-years-older railroad-dependent Riverside, and Boston's "Emerald Necklace" of parks and parkways. However, as Darlene E. Roth points out, Druid Hills deserves to be taken seriously precisely because it afforded Olmsted the chance to combine the key missing feature of Riverside—the parkway connecting the suburb and the city center—with landscape elements associated with the Emerald Necklace in an "ideal residential setting. The result is that Druid Hills represents the fullest realization of Olmsted's ideal suburban development."[324]

Druid Hills was approximately the size of Riverside. Hurt, whose principal business was trolley car lines, fought a legal battle against the Georgia, Carolina and Northern Railroad's proposal to build a commuter line through the proposed development, significantly enlisting the senior Olmsted's support in opposition to the railroad's plans. As a result, the railroad located its tracks east of the property. Olmsted Sr., no doubt reflecting his client's interests, deemed an electric trolley line to be better, but advocated that its right-of-way be located adjacent to rather than in the middle of the proposed parkway, an expensive solution in Hurt's view, requiring the use of more choice land.

The plan of 1905, based on Olmsted Sr.'s initial design, was developed by John Olmsted and Solon Z. Ruff (n.d.). At Riverside the curving streets were intended to vary the flat prairie topography; at Druid Hills their purpose was to minimize the impact of rolling topography on infrastructure costs. Six parks were located along Ponce de Leon Avenue's two-mile length, each with its own distinct character and each, as Roth puts it, "related to the residential lots, making . . . [the parks] more than recreation areas, but also places to view from the houses themselves." At many locations, the parks appear to be extensions of private lawns and gardens, an arrangement that is markedly different from Riverside's pocket parks, which were developed as islands surrounded by streets. At Druid Hills, as Roth notes, "walkways and lanes connect the houses to the parks and cut across the longer streets to make free pedestrian passage possible."[325] Ponce de Leon Avenue was the address reserved for the biggest houses, but along its way the openings of the cross streets led the eye deep into the woodlands where the smaller houses were situated. Two lakes were planned, surrounded by roads in similar fashion to the drives and ribbon green spaces of Riverside.

Although Olmsted used the term "subdivision," Riverside was a garden village. By contrast, Druid Hills was a subdivision in the modern sense of the word, without a civic or business center. While it is perhaps overreaching to suggest that at Druid Hills Olmsted anticipated the large-scale centerless suburban development that automobile travel would make possible after World War II, he certainly made clear that his plan marked a significant departure from the Riverside model, stating that Druid Hills is "being rapidly accelerated by various recent improvements in means of communication, such as electric streetcars, electric lighting, the telegraph and telephone,"[326] and thereby leading Roth to claim that

> *in making the transition from "suburban village," as exemplified by Riverside, to the "centerless suburb" of Druid Hills, Olmsted introduced a suburban form which would become ubiquitous across the American landscape in the twentieth century. Indeed, the centerless suburb is now so common a phenomenon that, to the uninformed observer, the significance of Druid Hills is unapparent. But seen against the backdrop of suburban development in the United States, Druid Hills emerges as the prototype for early-twentieth-century suburbanization, in the same way that Riverside is prototypical for nineteenth-century suburbanization.*

Whether or not Olmsted anticipated the automobile, his provisions of turnouts, separate entry roads for residents, and circular carriage drives at each house, as Roth points out, "*looks* like an early automobile suburb."[327] When Hurt encountered financial problems in 1908, he sold the property to the Druid Hills Company, controlled by Asa Candler (1851–1929), a Coca-Cola Company magnate, which continued its development but failed to realize certain key features such as broadened creeks nourished by hillside parklands, and transformed the unexcavated lake sites into building sites and the Druid Hills golf course.

Atlanta's third garden village, **Ansley Park**, lies firmly within the city's borders. A 275-acre subdivision with curving, parkway-like streets two-and-a-half miles north of Five Points in downtown, it was developed in four stages between 1904 and 1913 according to Solon Z. Ruff's plans.[328] Ruff had the requirements of automobiles as much in mind as he did streetcars. Ansley Park benefited from its proximity to Piedmont Park, the city's premier public open space, lying to its east, and Edwin P. Ansley (1865–1923), the developer, instructed Ruff to integrate the streets as much as possible with the road system the Olmsted Brothers were concurrently devising for it. Ruff also provided for Winn and McClatchy Parks within the village.

The **West End** of Winston (now Winston-Salem), North Carolina, was that state's first gardenesque streetcar suburb.[329] Begun in 1890 by the West End Hotel & Land Co., a consortium of fifty-nine prominent citizens including tobacco baron R. J. Reynolds (1850–1918), tobacco-turned-underwear magnate P. H. Hanes (1845–1925), and tobacco executive James A. Gray (1889–1952), the West End, occupying 180 acres west of downtown, was initially home to the 300-foot-long, 100-room

Inman Park

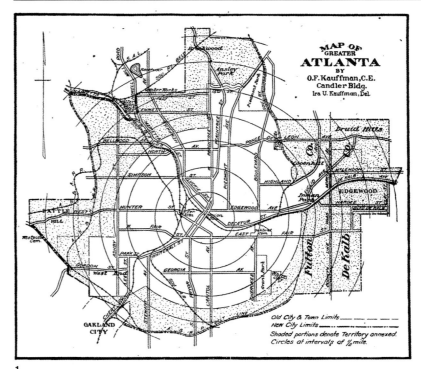

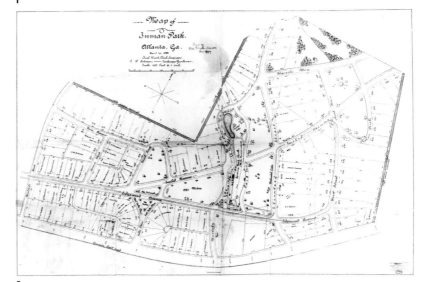

1. Map of Greater Atlanta showing location of Inman Park, Druid Hills, and Ansley Park. AC (1908)

2. Plan, Joseph Forsyth Johnson, 1891. KRC

3. Edgewood Avenue. KRC (1900)

4. Edgewood Avenue shortly after the streetcar began operating. KRC (c.1889)

5. Typical street. Adkisson. DA (2012)

1. Plan, Olmsted Brothers, 1905. FLO

2. Plan for subdivision of western portion of Druid Hills, Olmsted Brothers, 1905. FLO

3. Typical cross sections of parkway and 50-foot road. FLO (1902)

4. Ponce de Leon Avenue. Garvin. AG (2005)

5. Ponce de Leon Avenue, with trolley. KRC (1940)

6. Typical street. Adkisson. DA (2012)

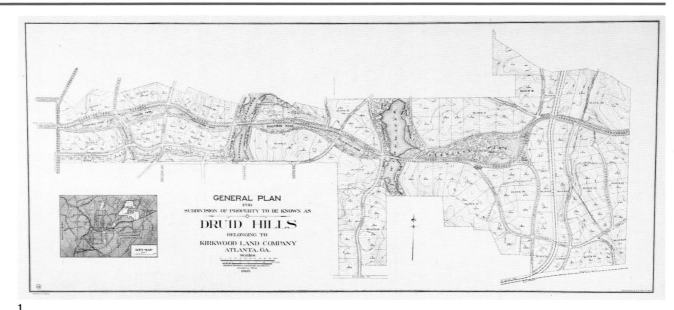

1

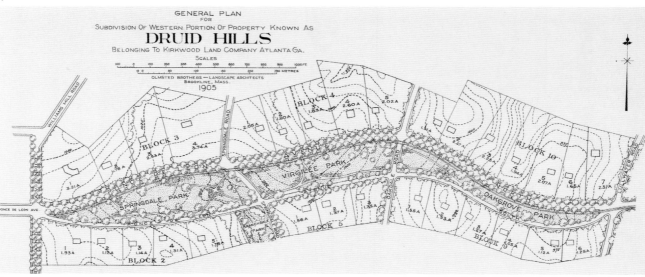

2

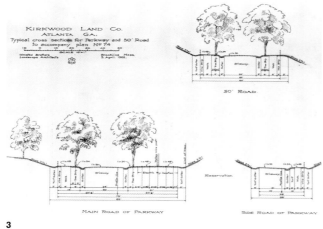

3

4

5

6

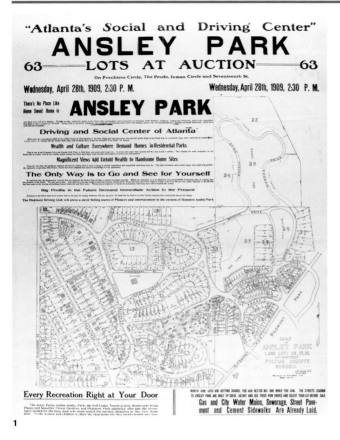

1. Auction notice, showing 1908 plat map. KRC (1909)

2. Aerial view. GE (2010)

3. Typical street. Adkisson. DA (2012)

wood-shingled Zinzendorf Hotel (Wheelwright & Haven, 1892), built on a hilltop in the middle of the site. To connect the hotel with downtown, the developers provided an electric trolley line, one of the first built by Thomas Edison's apprentice, Frank Sprague. When the hotel burned down in 1892, just six months after its completion, the decision was made not to rebuild it but to capitalize on the presence of the streetcar and focus on subdividing the surrounding land.

Jacob Lott Ludlow (1862–1930), who earned his master's degree in civil engineering in 1890 while serving as Winston's first city engineer, platted the network of curving streets that skirted the West End's ravines and creeks to allow for their retention as open space. West Fourth and West Fifth Streets briefly continued the city's grid for a half-block into the development, but the remainder of the looping drives stood in stark contrast to the abutting street pattern. Ludlow incorporated several parks, including the bowl-shaped Grace Court, near the center of the plan, and Springs Park, created from a wooded ravine. Land along Peters Creek was also preserved to become Hanes Park in 1919. Stone retaining walls helped keep hills intact, and many houses were set back on multitiered terraced front lawns. The bulk of residential construction occurred between 1900 and 1929, giving rise to an eclectic mix of architectural styles. Some of the original residents moved to Washington Park (1892), an enclave to the south of Winston-Salem developed by the same company and also laid out by Ludlow but as a more conventional grid reached by streetcar.

Bridging the streetcar and automobile eras, **Belle Meade Park** (1909–30), Nashville, Tennessee's "first successful example of romantic planning being applied to a neighborhood," occupies the former Belle Meade Plantation, famous for its thoroughbred nursery, located six miles southwest of the city center.[330] The Belle Meade Land Company, headed by officials of the Illinois Central Railroad, acquired the plantation in 1906 and hired the Chicago office of landscape architect Ossian Cole Simonds to subdivide the land into suburban lots. Simonds's plan (1909) envisioned a development of generously sized parcels, curving tree-lined streets, small parklets dispersed among the houses and at intersections, and an extensive landscaping program that would bring greenery back to the largely deforested plantation. Simonds also included restrictive covenants governing building setbacks, minimum house prices, allowable types of fences (low and covered by plantings), and land use, permitting only residences, churches, and schools for females.

Construction of an initial section, Deer Park, commenced in 1909 with forty-six lots ranging in size from two to 20 acres placed along four miles of streets laid out according to existing informal pathways. In the following year, the property changed ownership, settling in the hands of two developers who continued to work with Simonds: the Bransford Realty Group, led by realtor Johnson Bransford, took over Deer Park and built two additional enclaves in 1914 and 1915; and the Belle Meade Company, led after 1916 by Luke Lea, founder and publisher of *The Nashville Tennessean* and a United

1. Bird's-eye view with West
End and Zinzendorf Hotel
in foreground. LOCG (1891)

2. Aerial view. GE (2008)

3. West End Boulevard.
RAMSA (2012)

4. Plat map, Jacob Lott
Ludlow, 1890. FCR

States senator (1911–17), controlled 1,879 acres that, with the exception of a hiatus during World War I, would be steadily developed up until 1930 as a series of enclaves.

It was Lea who in 1910 persuaded the Nashville Street Railway and Light Company to extend its West End line four miles to the Belle Meade property, agreeing to underwrite the cost of the streetcar and two flanking 25-foot-wide roadbeds that would form the new Belle Meade Boulevard. The line was completed in 1913, bringing the suburb to within forty minutes of downtown and attracting a number of residents to the Belle Meade Boulevard sites. It failed to populate the curving side streets, however, where some were discouraged by the prospect, as historian John Joseph Ellis put it, of "walking from the trolley stops to houses over sometimes muddy ground, no sidewalks having been planned."[331]

To help attract prospective buyers, Lea suggested the establishment of a zoological park at the southern terminus of Belle Meade Boulevard, perhaps consciously emulating a similar arrangement in Chevy Chase, but the idea never materialized and in 1927 Lea instead donated the 868-acre tract to become Percy Warner Park, a valuable amenity for the suburb. More crucial to the project's success, Lea donated a central 144.5-acre site to the Nashville Golf and Country Club, which agreed to relocate to Belle Meade Park, completing a clubhouse in 1916 and an eighteen-hole course in 1922. The golf course proved popular among Nashville's wealthier residents, some of whom, as Ellis points out, also made up the city's dedicated community of automobile enthusiasts that had formed the Nashville Auto Club in 1910, maintained a lodge near Belle Meade, and possessed the wealth to commute to and from the city by automobile. "Ironically," Ellis writes, "although Belle Meade was a product of the streetcar era, in the long run only the automobile could ensure the area's appeal and the low density desired by its landscape architects."[332]

In 1915, Johnson Bransford, who owned adjacent land to the north of the golf course, built the Belle Meade Golf Links subdivision, placing 161 lots on a roughly triangular 43-acre tree-ringed site.[333] Most of the lots were 60 feet wide, with houses set uniformly back from the oak- and elm-lined streets. As planned by Simonds, the enclave included three parks—one open to all residents and two just to those living on neighboring lots. Restrictive covenants helped shelter the neighborhood from commercial development.

Lea's Belle Meade Company developed more lavish enclaves, including Lynwood Park (1913), Forrest Park (1914), Royal Oaks (1915), Berkeley Hills (1925), and Highlands of Belle Meade (1928–30), all providing, to varying degrees, large lots for stately residences—many by prominent architects—along quiet streets and occasional culs-de-sac. Belle Meade Park was incorporated in 1938, at which point it became known simply as Belle Meade.

Myers Park (1911), North Carolina, one-and-a-half miles southeast of Charlotte's center, was the first important town planning project undertaken by John Nolen.[334] Nolen, who graduated from the University of Pennsylvania's Wharton School of Finance and Economics in 1893, worked for a decade as secretary of the American Society for the Extension of University Teaching before enrolling in 1903 at the Harvard School of Landscape Architecture, founded three years earlier under the direction of Frederick Law Omlsted Jr. as the nation's first such program. After graduating from Harvard in 1905, Nolen set up offices in Cambridge, embarking on a prolific and influential career that would include the design of city plans at almost every conceivable scale including garden suburbs, garden cities, resort suburbs, and industrial villages. Myers Park was a real estate development of George Stephens (1873–1946), whose father-in-law, John Springs "Jack" Myers (1847–1925), owned a 1,200-acre farm on a three-mile-long property that varied in width from a few hundred feet to a mile, terminating in the full width of the ridge between Sugar and Briar Creeks. Stephens retained Nolen, who had previously designed Charlotte's Independence Park (1903) as well as the smaller Piedmont Park (1905), one of the city's earliest subdivisions, a triangular area now part of the Elizabeth neighborhood. Closer to Charlotte, off Queens Road, the principal street connecting the small city with its suburbs, Nolen also designed Hermitage Court (1911). Working together, Stephens, Nolen, and Nolen's assistant, Earle Draper, who eventually settled in Charlotte, transformed the site of Myers Park, an almost treeless farm, into a high-end garden village.

Myers Park was intended to attract Charlotte's most affluent citizens, but Nolen included a variety of lot sizes so that Amherst and Colonial Avenues are lined with modest bungalows. The plan placed all residents within walking distance of a streetcar line that looped through the neighborhood along Queens Road but with a "combination gate and waiting station (1912) of singular beauty and lithic solidity" built at its intersection with East Fourth Street.[335] A second waiting station was built at Hermitage Road shortly afterward. The plan also located a small neighborhood shopping center on a triangular block at the intersection of Queens and Providence Roads, but only one store was built, and in the 1920s the site became home to the Myers Park

Belle Meade Park

1

Presbyterian Church. Perhaps Nolen's and Stephens's most significant decision, growing from a belief that the new suburb needed gravitas, was to persuade the Presbyterian College for Women to move from downtown to a site provided without charge where, renamed Queens College, it became Myers Park's centerpiece.

Rejecting Charlotte's "unnatural checkerboard streets on an undulating surface," Nolen laid down a network of avenues that hewed to the contours of the gently rolling site, arguing that "not every street is a carrier of traffic; some merely lead to the home." Intending residents to enjoy "a sense of seclusion together with the means for easy and convenient access to the broad world," Queens Road and its streetcar line formed what was in effect a giant cul-de-sac, preventing outsiders from passing through the suburb.[336] Nolen provided detailed specifications for each of the five types of streets he proposed, from the 100-foot-wide boulevard with streetcar medians to the 80-foot-wide main road, 60-foot-wide residence roads, 50-foot-wide minor roads, and 40-foot-wide roads fronting park areas with sidewalks and planting space located on only one side and the carriageway limited to 20 feet in width. Various green spaces for recreation were provided, including an innovative midblock children's play area that was subsequently abandoned, and a "greenway" following the banks of a branch of Sugar Creek, only a small portion of which was executed despite Nolen's hope to see it extended to all parts of Charlotte. Earle Draper revised Nolen's plan in 1921, "smoothing out the street curves," according to Charles Warren, "and redividing some blocks to provide more lots," changes reflecting "the fact that the trolley loop was being superseded by the automobile; Draper's

1. Aerial view of Belle Meade Golf Links subdivision, Ossian Cole Simonds, 1915. NPL (c. 1922)

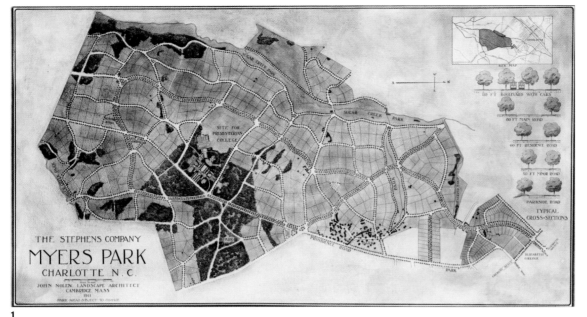

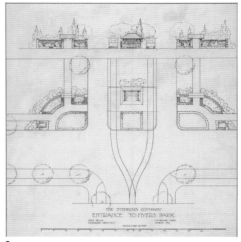

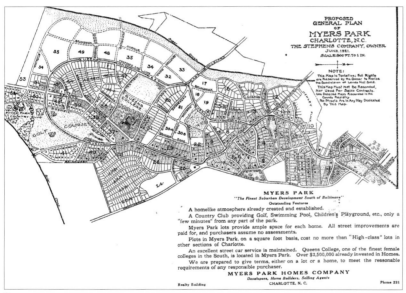

1. Plan, John Nolen, 1911. COR

2. Design for entrance gates and trolley waiting station, John Nolen, 1912. COR

3. Revised plan, Earle S. Draper, 1921. MPF

4. Queens Road. Garvin. AG (2001)

5. Typical street. COR (c. 1929)

6. Entrance gate. PLC (c. 1912)

7. Entrance to Hermitage Court. PLC (c. 1915)

smooth curves accommodate the car's greater speed, but his design lacks the finer-scale topographic sensitivity of Nolen's original plan."[337] Trolley service would continue until 1938.

Los Angeles, California, gave rise beyond its inland downtown core to a pattern of low-density suburbanism so that, in 1925, the city was lampooned by the tart-tongued H. L. Mencken as "nineteen suburbs in search of a metropolis," and later derided by another

wicked wit, Dorothy Parker, who, upping the ante, quipped that Los Angeles was seventy-two suburbs in search of a city.[338] Lying ten miles west of downtown Los Angeles, **Beverly Hills** (1906) was the city's first planned suburb, quickly rivaling Hancock Park, a neighborhood much closer to downtown, as a preferred upper-class residence location. Current opinion notwithstanding, Beverly Hills was not developed to meet the challenge of the automobile but was in fact conceived to take advantage of the network of streetcar-like interurban railroads that served the Los Angeles basin.[339] As Reyner Banham points out in his *Los Angeles: The Architecture of the Four Ecologies* (1971), a book as important to understanding Los Angeles as Steen Eiler Rasmussen's *London: The Unique City* (1937) is to appreciating the British capital, it was the extensive coverage of the old Southern Pacific and later Pacific Electric systems—the two companies would combine in the "Great Merger" of 1911—that made possible the sprawling form of modern Los Angeles.[340]

Beverly Hills, an independent city, occupies the roughly six-square-mile site of the early nineteenth-century Mexican land grant Rancho Rodeo de las Aguas, the "gathering of waters," so named for streams that collected at the base of Coldwater and Benedict Canyons in the rainy season. Before Beverly Hills was founded there were several attempts to develop the 3,200-acre tract, including Edward Preuss's effort in 1868 to establish Santa Maria, a colony for German immigrant farmers. Preuss's plan to subdivide the property into five-acre lots fell victim to a historic drought and the land reverted to scattered attempts at cattle and sheep ranching as well as a largely unsuccessful effort by wildcatters to discover oil to be used as fuel for lamps. A land boom in the 1880s spurred by the construction of the Southern Pacific's interurban rail line connecting the inland city of Los Angeles and the city of Santa Monica facing the Pacific Ocean included a right-of-way through the site, convincing landowning farmers Charles Denker and Henry Hammel to plan a residential subdivision in 1887. But Denker and Hammel's scheme for a North African–themed village to be called Morocco was abandoned a year later. For the remainder of the century the tract was primarily used for farming, growing lima beans, wheat, and walnut trees.

In 1900 a renewed hunt for oil brought additional speculators to the area. The Amalgamated Oil Company, a syndicate that included Henry E. Huntington (1850–1927), Charles A. Canfield (1848–1913), and Burton M. Green (1868–1965), purchased the Denker and Hammel ranch and began drilling, to their disappointment finding only water, itself a valuable commodity in the desert-like area but not nearly as desirable as oil. Instead of selling the property, the group, led by Green, decided in 1906 to reorganize as the Rodeo Land and Water Company, proposing a new residential subdivision called Beverly Hills, a name coined by Green and his wife who were inspired by Beverly Farms, Massachusetts, an exclusive resort suburb about twenty miles north of Boston that Green had visited in his youth. According to Brendan Gill, "despite so many failed attempts in the past," Green believed that money could be made "not by the usual hit-or-miss development of an ordinary subdivision but by the founding of a town designed as a whole and down to the smallest details according to strict aesthetic and economic standards—a town that would be the embodiment of the increasingly sophisticated dreams of an increasingly wealthy middle class."[341]

To plan his development Green hired New York landscape architect Wilbur D. Cook Jr. (1869–1938), who had previously worked in the offices of Frederick Law Olmsted and the Olmsted Brothers and who would go on to form the firm of Cook, Hall & Cornell, designing other subdivisions such as Highland Park in Dallas. Working with the Northwestern- and MIT-trained, Los Angeles architect Myron Hunt (1868–1952), Cook devised a scheme for gently "curving streets instead of the ordinary, checker-board subdivision which up to that time had been the accepted method in subdividing land in and around Los Angeles."[342] Ranging from 60 to 110 feet wide, the streets were unusual for their long blocks that reduced the number of streets and intersections and cut down on the cost of road construction.

The plan focused on the Pacific Electric system's Santa Monica line, running down the principal east–west artery, Santa Monica Boulevard, a double-carriageway landscaped boulevard that they took advantage of to ensure a wide fire break between the new suburb's business district on the south and the residential area to the north. A second east–west street—Sunset Boulevard—intended to be served by a streetcar line, separated the gently sloping portions of the residential area extending south of it to Santa Monica Boulevard from the larger lots in the hills and canyons to the north. Though the streetcar line was never built, the central landscaped median intended for its tracks was retained for use as a bridle path. To publicize Beverly Hills' official opening on October 22, 1906, Green took out a full-page advertisement in the *Los Angeles Times*, touting the development's natural beauty as well as its convenience. Despite the provision of interurban rail service along Santa Monica Boulevard, the future hegemony of the automobile was anticipated in a drawing of a car racing along a road bordered by mountains.

The first three streets to be constructed (1907)—Rodeo, Beverly, and Cañon Drives—were bordered by palm trees, acacias, and Arizona pepper trees picked out by horticulturist John J. Reeves (d. 1939), setting a pattern for distinctive tree selections for each of the city's streets. Although the first house, for businessman Henry C. Clark (1859–1928), was completed the same year, the financial panic of 1907–8 stymied progress and few houses were built, although MIT-trained, Pasadena-based architects Charles Sumner Greene (1868–1957) and Henry Mather Greene (1870–1954) designed a house in 1909 for car dealer Earl C. Anthony (1880–1961) on Bedford Drive north of Sunset Boulevard. By 1911, only six houses had been completed in Beverly Hills.

To spur development, Burton Green took a cue from previous planned suburbs and built a hotel to entice visitors, who in turn might be inspired to purchase a lot and build a house. Located on a 10-acre site on Sunset Boulevard at the base of the Santa Monica Mountains, the 300-room Beverly Hills Hotel (1912) was designed in what David Gebhard and Robert Winter have described as "a rather complicated version of the Mission style" by Elmer Grey (1872–1963), a Chicago-born architect

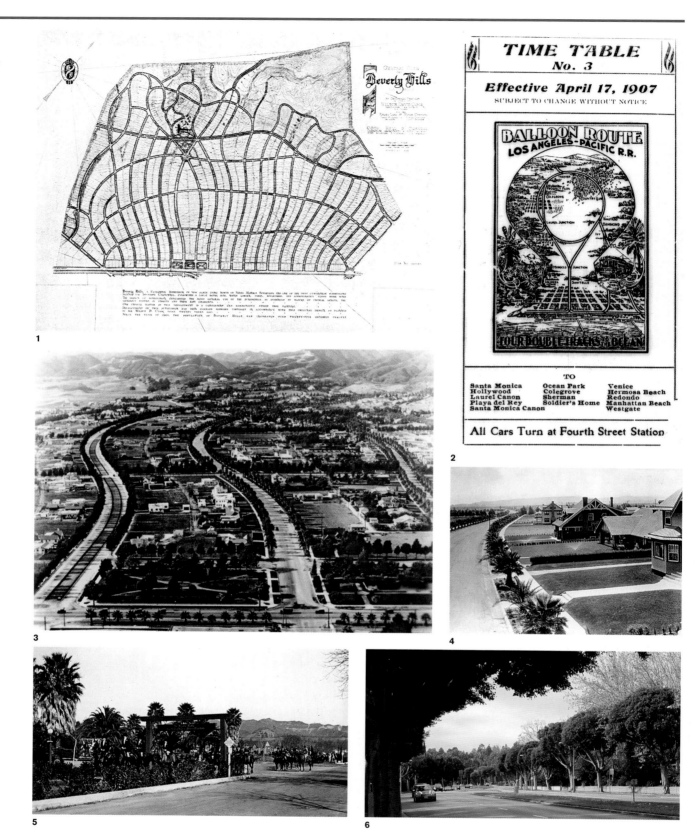

who received his architectural training while working between 1887 and 1899 at the Milwaukee firm of George B. Ferry (1851–1918) and Alfred C. Clas (1859-1942).[343] It was an immediate success and became the focal point of the community, also serving as a church, a theater, and a meeting place. Other improvements accompanied the construction of the hotel, including a one-car horse-drawn-trolley line running down the center of Rodeo Drive. Nicknamed the "dinky," it connected the hotel with the Pacific Electric station at Santa Monica Boulevard and Cañon Drive. Across from the Beverly Hills Hotel, Wilbur Cook planned Sunset Park, a triangular-shaped parcel complete with fountain and reflecting pool, while at the trolley's other depot he planned a second, three-block-long, 100-foot-wide greensward paralleling the northern edge of Santa Monica Boulevard

from Rodeo to Crescent Drives, including an ornamental arched sign in front of a vine-covered wall announcing the entrance to Beverly Hills. In addition, on a 100-acre site at the intersection of Wilshire and Santa Monica Boulevards, a nursery was established to provide trees and shrubs for the neighborhood's parks and streets, a resource also made available to residents in order to encourage them to landscape their private lots.

Two years after the January 1914 opening of the Beverly Hills Hotel, the population of the subdivision reached 550, surpassing by fifty the threshold necessary to declare it an independent city within the confines of Los Angeles County. The residents at the time were predominantly lawyers, doctors, oilmen, and retirees from colder climes, but it was not until 1919, when the immensely popular screen actors Mary Pickford and Douglas Fairbanks moved there, that Beverly Hills began to acquire the cachet it now enjoys. The newly married couple hired Hollywood set designer Max E. Parker (1882–1964) to transform a former hunting lodge located on an 11.5-acre site on Summit Drive into a twenty-two-room Tudor mansion (1920; additions, Wallace Neff, 1928–41) quickly dubbed Pickfair by the press. Their decision led to a parade of other movie stars moving to the community, joined by industry executives. By 1926 the population of Beverly Hills had grown to 12,000 and the suburban city was thriving, with a sophisticated shopping district and a second high-end hotel. Soon a civic center would follow, consisting of a Spanish Renaissance–style City Hall (William J. Gage, 1932) and a U.S. Post Office (Ralph C. Flewelling, 1934).

The success of Beverly Hills attracted the attention of John S. Armstrong (1850–1908) and his sons-in-law, Hugh E. Prather (1879–1959) and Edgar Flippen (1876–1958), who controlled 1,326 acres along Turtle Creek, four miles north of downtown Dallas, Texas, even more than Los Angeles, a city with no distinct natural boundaries.[344] Armstrong, Prather, and Flippen turned to Beverly Hills' planner, Wilbur D. Cook Jr., to design the first four phases of their development, **Highland Park** (1907–24). A fifth installment and the contiguous Highland Park West (1923) was laid out by George Kessler, whose master plan for Dallas (1911) included Turtle Creek Parkway, an important link between the city's downtown and its northern outskirts.

The idea for Highland Park can be traced to 1889 when J. T. Trezevant (1842–1931) and Henry Exall (1848–1913) visited Philadelphia to sell 1,200 acres of North Dallas property. Encountering Fairmount Park, they were inspired to advocate the development of the area's single natural feature of consequence, Turtle Creek, as a parkway and greenbelt. Had the Panic of 1893 not interrupted their plans, which were realized only to the extent that gravel roads were laid and a dam built across Turtle Creek to create Exall Lake, Highland Park would have been developed with the name Philadelphia Place. Interest in the project resumed in earnest in 1906 when Armstrong, a successful developer, bought the property. Following Armstrong's death two years later, Prather and Flippen continued his work, and in 1908 his widow donated 100 acres of land for the establishment of Southern Methodist University, providing an important focus

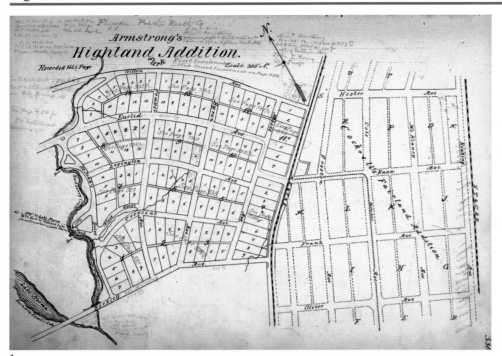

1

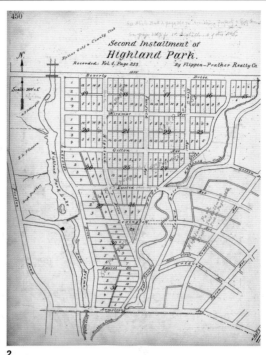

2

1. Plan, Wilbur D. Cook Jr.,
first installment of Highland Park
("Armstrong's Highland Park
Addition"). DPL (c. 1910)

2. Plan, Wilbur D. Cook Jr., second
installment of Highland Park
("Lakeside Addition"). DPL
(c. 1910)

3. Plan, Wilbur D. Cook Jr., third
installment of Highland Park.
DPL (c. 1910)

4. Article by Hugh E. Prather in
April 1925 issue of *Golf Illustrated*.
GI

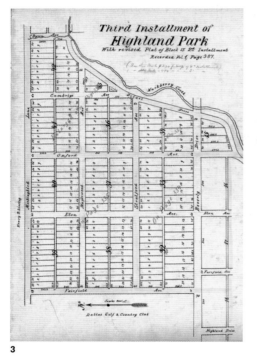

3

4

for the new development that became an independent city in 1913.

Cook was selected to design Highland Park after Armstrong and Prather visited him in California. He made only one site visit and within six months' time prepared the plan that was carried out under the supervision of Dallas engineer Nils Werenskiold (1860–1929). Cook was directed by his clients to set aside 20 percent of the first section for parks. The initial 92-acre installment, begun in 1907, lay east of St. John's Drive and south of Gillon Avenue. The second installment, the Lakeside Addition (1910), included the construction of a streetcar line that connected Highland Park to the Knox Street Station downtown. The third and fourth installments were completed in 1912 and were, according to Cheryl Lynn Caldwell Ferguson in her exhaustive study of Highland Park, "less picturesque and platted using a more orthogonal plan to market smaller lots to a lesser well-to-do clientele."[345]

Typically, Highland Park's street plan formed a gridiron, seldom interrupted except by the natural topography of Turtle and Hackberry Creeks or by pre-existing through streets. In the neighborhoods east of Preston Road, the lots were usually narrow and deep, served by 14-foot-wide back alleys for cartage and power lines. Along with the single-family houses, the development also included a golf course and country club (1910–12) that Hugh Prather believed was a critical

5

6

7

8

9

component of the project: "The situation was such that it was absolutely necessary to possess some unusual advantage over other developments to attract the better class of people we desired as buyers and builders within our development . . . If I was asked to name the most helpful element in the sale of residential property, I would unhesitatingly answer: 'A country club.'"[346]

In 1917, Kessler, together with Lee M. Jenney (1882–1968) of Cleveland, designed the fifth installment known as the Highland Park Acreage Addition, leading across Turtle Creek as a grand southern entrance to the now independent city. Kessler also began his design of Highland Park West, west of Preston Road, in 1917, but following his death in 1924, that plan was carried out by Sidney J. Hare and S. Herbert Hare.

In 1931, Highland Park Village opened, a shopping center that went a significant step beyond Country Club Plaza in accommodating the automobile to retail development.[347] Flippen and Prather engaged Hare & Hare to plan for the Village on a 10-acre site in their second installment at the southwest corner of Mockingbird Lane and Preston Road. The architectural design in the Spanish Colonial style was the work of James Cheek of the firm Fooshee & Cheek, who was probably influenced by the Malaga Cove Plaza development at Palos

Verdes (see p. 297), although, together with Prather, Cheek traveled widely in search of inspiration, including Seville and Barcelona, where they probably visited the Pueblo Español (1929), with its spatially seductive sequence of reproduced historic village centers. Like Pueblo Español, which was built for an international exposition but retained as a tourist attraction afterward, Highland Park Village faced inward—the first shopping village ever to do so. The plan, locating the cars along interior parking streets facing the stores, may have also been inspired by Snider Plaza, University Park, Dallas, a nearby small but at the time largely unrealized shopping center, as well as by typical small Texas towns featuring courthouses at their centers and an outer ring of commercial buildings with ground-floor retail separated by a street, allowing for car parking. Highland Park Village provided parking for 700 cars as well as a filling station and 1,350-seat theater (1935). Some early visitors accessed the facility on horseback from nearby bridle trails.

By the new century's second decade, the issue of housing reform as a key to good city planning had taken preeminence over the design of monumental civic structures characteristic of the City Beautiful movement. On December 21, 1912, only three years after Daniel

5. Aerial view of Highland Park Village. SCDO (c. 1950)

6. Highland Park Village. Garvin. AG (1998)

7, 8. Typical streets. Garvin. AG (1998)

9. Park. Clique. SC (2012)

Burnham (1846–1912) released his grandly monumental plan for Chicago, the City Club of Chicago, a nine-year-old progressive civic organization, announced plans for the **City Residential Land Development Competition**, which called for the development of a typical but hypothetical quarter section of land on the outskirts of the city.[348] The goal of the competition, whose program was prepared by the Illinois chapter of the American Institute of Architects, was "to extend information and awaken public interest concerning the possibility of developing residential neighborhoods in the unbuilt portions of Chicago and to encourage landowners and capitalists to promote social welfare by developing ideal suburbs."[349] The competition was one part of a broader program sponsored by the City Club that also included lectures and exhibitions examining the history of housing in Chicago as well as current slum conditions in the city. *American City* magazine had high hopes for the contest, believing that "the ideas submitted would be applicable to many growing cities."[350]

The 160-acre undivided square site called for in the competition was conceived as lying southwest of Chicago's central business district, about eight miles away, and served by streetcar lines on two sides. The treeless, building-free flat site was assumed to be surrounded by the city's prevailing grid pattern of streets with industrial plants between one-half and four miles away, and in that and other respects suggested a garden enclave embedded in the city's fabric. Although primarily residential, it can also be seen as a prototypical garden village because the program called for a mix of uses, including commercial buildings, a social center, schools, and churches, as well as a mix of incomes, with the majority of the housing geared toward the working class.

Thirty-nine schemes were submitted by the March 3, 1913, deadline, with twenty-one coming from the Chicago area and the remaining from thirteen American cities and one from Sweden.[351] The entries mostly came from architects, engineers, and landscape architects, but a high school teacher and a doctor also submitted designs. On March 17, a jury composed of architects George W. Maher (1864–1926) and A. F. Woltersdorf (1870–1948), engineer and town planner John W. Alvord (1861–1943), landscape architect Jens Jensen, and John C. Kennedy (1884–1966), former secretary of the housing committee of the Chicago Association of Commerce, picked three winners. Acting as consultant to the jury was Edward H. Bouton, general manager of Roland Park. Despite their selections, the premiated schemes have largely been overshadowed in subsequent critical discussions of the competition by other proposals, particularly the entries from William Drummond (1876–1946) and from Frank Lloyd Wright, who entered the competition under the condition that his design not be considered for a prize.

Chicago architect Wilhelm Bernhard (b. 1885?), who had worked for Wright as a draftsman, was awarded first prize with a scheme calling for civic and commercial buildings surrounding a central square entered on axis under a 34-foot-wide archway. Bernhard proposed two main 60-foot-wide thoroughfares, with less important streets to be 40 feet wide. The main streets were arranged on a gentle curve in order, in Bernhard's words, "to discourage their use as through streets and, from an esthetic viewpoint, to avoid the monotony of straight street lines so predominating in this country." Houses on 40- and 80-foot-wide lots accommodating 1,280 families would also be grouped to avoid monotony, with some set back and others brought forward, and "wherever possible there has been provision made for a private park in every block."[352] The design was reminiscent of the recent Olmsted and Atterbury plan for Forest Hills Gardens, a distinction also shared by the second-place winner, landscape architect Arthur C. Comey (1886–1954), of Cambridge, Massachusetts, who had worked for the Olmsted Brothers. Albert Kelsey, in his review of the entries, published three years after the competition in a book that featured twenty-six of the submissions, deemed Comey's scheme "simple and sensible. It has one advantage over the first prize design in its application to officially projected gridiron plans; and that is, that it provides for the diagonal circulation (if only in one direction) our cities so generally need. The scheme is economical and compact. The social center is distinctly good. But his division of private parcels of property into fairly long, narrow lots, abutting upon other fairly long and narrow lots is poor, as it provides many uninviting back-yard vistas."[353] The one foreign entry garnered third prize. Albert Lilienberg (1879–1967), head of city planning in Gothenburg, Sweden, and his wife, Ingrid (n.d.), proposed a Beaux-Arts-inspired axial plan featuring a wall of buildings on the perimeter of the site in an attempt to block out the noise and grime of the surrounding city. The four corners of the site were marked by prominent entranceways that each led via diagonal streets to a central square of public buildings and recreation space.

The proposal of Chicago architect William Drummond, a grid seemingly scaled to the limitless expanse of the prairie, generated much more interest than the winning schemes. Drummond, a disciple of Frank Lloyd Wright who worked in his office for ten years after a brief stint with Louis Sullivan, declared that "the whole city be divided into areas approximately such as the quarter-section," although he was not sure if the competition's site was the ideal size. Drummond called these sections "neighborhood units"—a term that Clarence Perry would promote in the 1920s based on his experiences as a resident of Forest Hills Gardens—noting that "the unit is intended to comprise an area which will permanently exist as a neighborhood or primary social circle. Each unit has its intellectual, recreational, and civic requirements featured in the institute which is located approximately at its center and its local business requirements featured at its corners."[354] Assessing the competition in 1981, historian David P. Handlin wrote that "Drummond's plan stands out from other schemes . . . not only because of the intensity of his idealistic vision

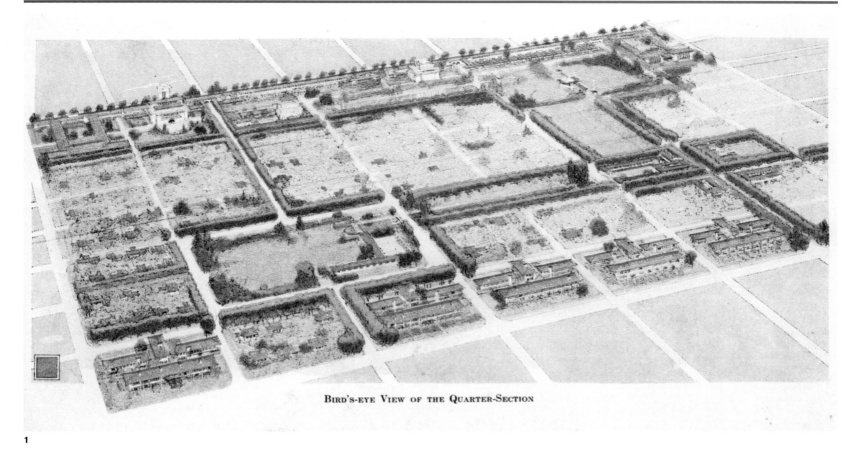

BIRD'S-EYE VIEW OF THE QUARTER-SECTION

1

of what a community could be, but also because he made a unique interpretation of its physical form. Instead of creating an introverted community by laying out curved streets or running diagonals to the center, Drummond tried to find a system of streets and landscaping that was compatible with the flat prairie." Drummond also anticipated future development, believing that once the "nucleus" of his neighborhood unit plan was built any new growth could follow the existing pattern. As Handlin observes, "When everyone else was trying to find ways to control urban growth and to fix a final urban form, Drummond seemed to intimate that the inexorable forces of the modern city could themselves be used as the basis not only for a new type of community, but also for a new pattern of urban architecture."[355]

Other nonpremiated entries included one by New York landscape architect Robert A. Pope, whose design grouped modest Colonial-style cottages around communal parks; in addition to curving streets, the scheme included a broad diagonal boulevard leading from commercial buildings at the southwest corner of the site to the gymnasium and athletic fields. Chicago engineers Riddle & Riddle produced a formal Beaux-Arts scheme that owed its inspiration to the municipal center in Daniel Burnham's Chicago plan. Walter Burley Griffin participated in the competition somewhat surreptitiously as adviser to Edgar H. Lawrence (n.d.), who worked in his office. Wilbert Hasbrouck has described their plan as "an extraordinary octagon-in-a-square design,"[356] and Gwendolyn Wright has compared it to

that of a "miniature city, with formal gardens and public plazas regularly placed at the intersections of major avenues. He [Griffin] eased the overall sense of a large capital city by providing narrow curved streets between the avenues and the largest amount of open space—parks and playgrounds and rows of tree-lined streets with wide sidewalks—of any of the competitors."[357]

Like William Drummond's plan, Frank Lloyd Wright's entry attempted to connect the new enclave to the surrounding city, accepting both the regularity of the grid and the indeterminacy of the prairie. According to Brendan Gill, Wright objected to the idea of the competition because he believed "that a jury by its nature is bound to award the prize to the least controversial—and therefore the least interesting—entry."[358] Wright's scheme represented a reworking and dramatic expansion of his quadruple-block plan of 1900, a design that rejected the traditional straight rows of typical subdivisions and instead called for groupings of four houses, each house occupying a corner lot on small square blocks to maximize privacy and improve views.

For the 1913 competition, Wright divided the quarter section into sixty-four square blocks, including public, commercial, cultural, and religious buildings in the plan, all linked together and to the housing by a number of public parks. Wright included apartment buildings geared to the working class, placing them in less desirable locations at the periphery of the site. As Robert McCarter has noted, the plan was "highly symmetrical and repetitive, yet Wright carefully designed an

1. Entry by Frank Lloyd Wright. CRLD

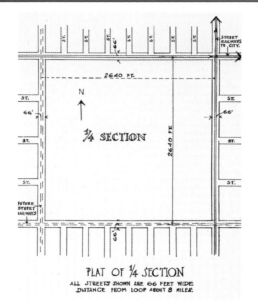

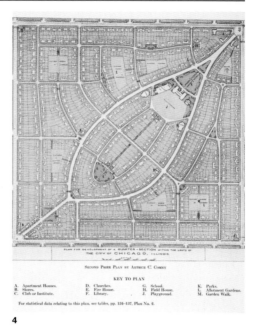

2

3

4

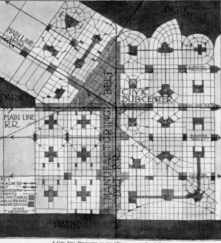

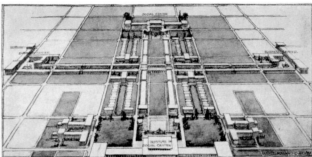

BIRD'S-EYE VIEW OF TWO ADJOINING UNITS
Showing in the "Nucleus" a portion of the area developed with a formal arrangement of certain buildings and grounds, the blocks adjoining being for individual residence.

7

5

6

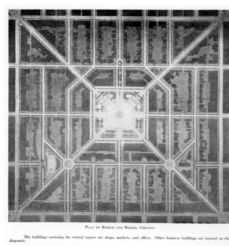

PLAN BY RIDDLE AND RIDDLE, CHICAGO

The buildings enclosing the central square are shops, markets, and offices. Other business buildings are located on the diagonals.
For statistical data relating to this plan see tables pp. 134-137, Plan No. 4.

8

2. Plan of typical quarter-section for 1913 competition. CRLD

3. First-place entry by Wilhelm Bernhard. Bird's-eye view and plan. CRLD

4. Second-place entry by Arthur C. Comey. Plan. CRLD

5. Third-place entry by Albert and Ingrid Lilienberg. Plan. CRLD

6, 7. Entry by William Drummond. Plan and bird's-eye view showing two adjoining neighborhood units. CRLD

8. Entry by Riddle & Riddle. Plan. CRLD

9, 10. Entry by Robert A. Pope. Bird's-eye view and plan. CRLD

BIRD'S-EYE VIEW OF PART OF THE QUARTER-SECTION

9

PLAN BY ROBERT ANDERSON POPE
KEY TO PLAN
1. Church.   2. Athletic Field.   3. Gymnasium.   4. School Sites.   5. Stores.
For statistical data relating to this plan see tables pp. 134–137, Plan No. 10.

10

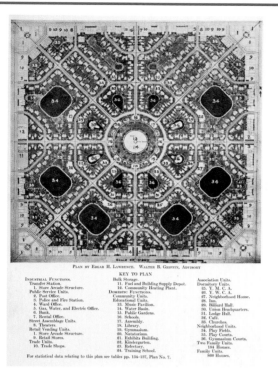

PLAN BY EDGAR H. LAWRENCE.   WALTER B. GRIFFIN, ADVISORY.
KEY TO PLAN

INDUSTRIAL FUNCTIONS.
  Transfer Station.
  1. Store Arcade Structure.
Public Service Units.
  2. Post Office.
  3. Police and Fire Station.
  4. Ward Office.
  5. Gas, Water, and Electric Office.
  6. Bank.
  7. Rental Office.
Street Assemblage Units.
  8. Theaters.
  9. Retail Stores.
Retail Vending Units.
  1. Store Arcade Structure.
Trade Units.
  10. Trade Shops.

Bulk Storage.
  11. Fuel and Building Supply Depot.
Domestic Functions.
  12. Community Heating Plant.
Community Units.
Educational Units.
  13. Music Pavilion.
  14. Water Basin.
  15. Public Gardens.
  16. Schools.
  17. Assembly.
  18. Library.
  19. Gymnasium.
  20. Natatorium.
  21. Exhibits Building.
  22. Kindergarten.
  23. Refectory.
  24. Training School.

Association Units.
  25. Y. M. C. A.
  26. Y. W. C. A.
  27. Neighborhood House.
  28. Inn.
  29. Billiard Hall.
  30. Union Headquarters.
  31. Lodge Hall.
  32. Café.
  33. Churches.
Neighborhood Units.
  34. Play Fields.
  35. Play Courts.
  36. Gymnasium Courts.
Two Family Units.
  184 Houses.
Family Units.
  860 Houses.

For statistical data relating to this plan see tables pp. 134–137, Plan No. 7.

11

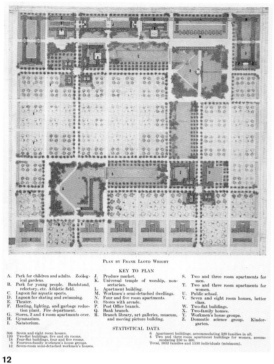

PLAN BY FRANK LLOYD WRIGHT
KEY TO PLAN

A. Park for children and adults. Zoological gardens.
B. Park for young people. Bandstand, refectory, etc. Athletic field.
C. Lagoon for aquatic sports.
D. Lagoon for skating and swimming.
E. Theater.
F. Heating, lighting, and garbage reduction plant. Fire department.
G. Stores, 3 and 4 room apartments over.
H. Gymnasium.
I. Natatorium.

J. Produce market.
K. Universal temple of worship, non-sectarian.
L. Apartment building.
M. Workmen's semi-detached dwellings.
N. Four and five room apartments.
O. Stores with arcade.
P. Post Office branch.
Q. Bank branch.
R. Branch library, art galleries, museum, and moving picture building.

S. Two and three room apartments for men.
T. Two and three room apartments for women.
U. Public school.
V. Seven and eight room houses, better class.
X. Two-flat buildings.
Y. Two-family houses.
Y. Workmen's house groups.
Z. Domestic science group. Kindergarten.

STATISTICAL DATA
  304 Seven and eight room houses.
  126 Two-flat buildings, five and six rooms.
  18 Four-flat buildings, four and five rooms.
  6 Fourteen-family workmen's house groups.
  0 Seven-room semi-detached workmen's houses.

  6 Apartment buildings, accommodating 320 families in all.
  2 Two and three room apartment buildings for women, accommodating 250 to 300.
  Total, 1023 families and 1330 individuals (minimum).

12

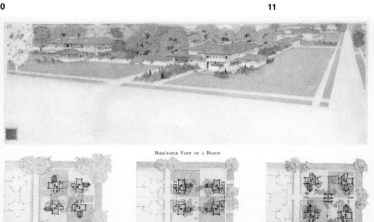

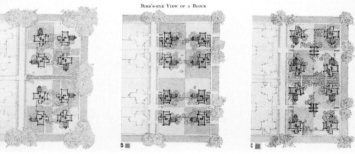

BIRD'S-EYE VIEW OF A BLOCK

A   B   C

13

14

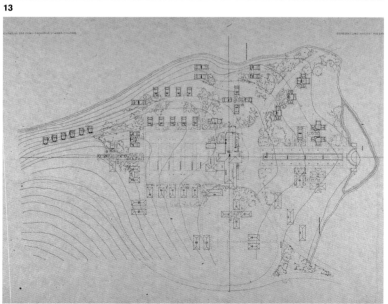

15

16

11. Entry by Edgar H. Lawrence, in consultation with Walter Burley Griffin. Plan. CRLD

12, 13. Entry by Frank Lloyd Wright. Plan; bird's-eye view of one block and three alternative block arrangements. CRLD

14, 15. Como Orchards. Frank Lloyd Wright, 1909. Perspective and plan. UU

16. Bitter Root. Frank Lloyd Wright, 1909. Plan. FLW

asymmetrical, pinwheel-based series of primary boulevards centered in two corners by large parks, which take up four blocks each, set diagonally across the quarter from one another, and centered in the other two corners by courtyard apartment buildings set in a pinwheel configuration around the street intersection." Observing that the "balance between the public and private spaces is carefully developed," McCarter has characterized the scheme as "a city-in-miniature."[359] In addition to drawing on his quadruple-block plan, Wright also incorporated aspects of his two recent town planning projects in the Bitter Root Valley of Montana: Como Orchards (1909), also known as University Heights, a partially realized summer retreat intended for 160 university professors to be housed in fifty-three cottages along with a central clubhouse; and an axial plan (1909–10) for the new town of Bitter Root that did not move forward.[360] Wright's 1913 proposal would prove important for the next development of the suburb, that in which the automobile became the dominant means of transportation, an issue he tackled directly twenty-two years later with his design for Broadacre City (see p. 941).

Spanning the streetcar and automobile eras, **Wyomissing Park** (1917–21), a garden village first planned by Werner Hegemann and Elbert Peets, with the assistance of Joseph Hudnut, and later reenvisioned by John Nolen, was situated west of Reading, Pennsylvania, a small, booming industrial city that was having trouble coping with its explosive growth.[361] Though neither plan was fully realized, Nolen's contribution, according to Charles Warren, promised "one of North America's most elegantly planned suburbs" featuring "some of Nolen's most beautifully designed residential streets."[362] Nolen's involvement in Reading first began in 1909 when he was asked to prepare a comprehensive plan. But his report, issued in 1910, recommending an increase in playground space, improved housing, smoke abatement, new parks, additional bridges over the Schuylkill River, the acquisition of outlying lands, and a "belt boulevard" around the city, fell victim to political wrangling and was voted down.[363]

In 1913, three supporters of Nolen's plan, the textile magnates Ferdinand Thun (1866–1949), Henry Janssen (1866–1948), and Gustav Oberlaender (1867–1936), formed the Wyomissing Development Company and began three years of preparatory work leading to the selection of Hegemann and Peets in 1917 to plan a "Modern Garden Suburb" on a 500-acre site across the Schuylkill River from Reading, expressing their hope that "the public will appreciate how closely the efforts made by the company towards the creation of a truly modern residential park are in harmony with the best city planning thought as recorded, for instance, in the memorable report on Greater Reading written . . . by Dr. John Nolen."[364]

Retaining the site's natural features, which included the winding Wyomissing Creek and its surrounding meadows, Hegemann, who was cited as author of the plan's text, and Peets and Hudnut, who were credited

with the drawings, called for housing for a mix of social classes as well as community features, including a horseshoe-shaped business center with shops and a theater, twelve plazas, courts, and squares, and parks and playgrounds. The intention, according to the planners, was to design "a living organism reflecting in prismatic variety the surrounding topographical conditions . . . accentuating certain features of the topography . . . which, with thoughtless planning, are often submerged in an unbending system of straight streets or, more recently, in an altogether characterless adaptation of wildly winding streets to every whimsicality of the contours."[365]

The plan abounded in group houses, many with rear alleys providing access to garages, anticipating, as Christine Crasemann Collins has written, "that the industrial workers would own cars,"[366] although streetcar service was provided on Shillington Boulevard and the one- to three-mile distance to downtown Reading was touted in promotional literature as being "largely within walking distance from the heart of the City."[367] In conscious emulation of Forest Hills Gardens, Hegemann and Peets combined "fine framed-in squares" enclosed by rowhouses with "the open charms of parklike districts in detached country house style . . . thus securing an alternation of open and closed textures, of garden city and city square. By this procedure the moderately priced row house becomes an element of as great artistic importance as the effective setting of the millionaire's residence; the beauty of the one is increased by the other."[368] Single-family houses were to be separated by no less than 30 feet to avoid the "unpleasant effect of crowding," and in the western reaches of the community four- and five-acre lots and larger were planned and landscaped in a manner that would allow for future subdivision.[369] The scheme preserved large amounts of the site's beautiful landscape, threading the community with a network of open spaces, and transforming a former agricultural dump into an active recreation area. The brochure promoting the subdivision, proclaiming "the Re-Democratization of American Country Life," drew attention to a nine-hole golf course in the valley of the creek, while noting that "since the introduction of the automobile the idea of country life has gradually abandoned walking and driving or riding horses. The rapid development of the game of golf is becoming one of the victorious substitutes."[370] Unlike in Hegemann and Peets's Washington Highlands (see p. 82), the parks and recreational spaces were to be open to all, not only residents. By 1917 four of the housing groups were laid out and built more or less according to plan: Hamilton Place, Trebor Place, Cherry Gardens (now Cherry Drive), and Holland Square, the latter two enclosing greens, but the plan was subsequently shelved.

In 1923, Wyomissing Development hired John Nolen to resuscitate the project that now focused on recently acquired land to the south, a 265-acre former nursery. Portions of the original had been given over to several large estates as well as the Reading Hospital and the Reading Public Museum, for which Nolen prepared

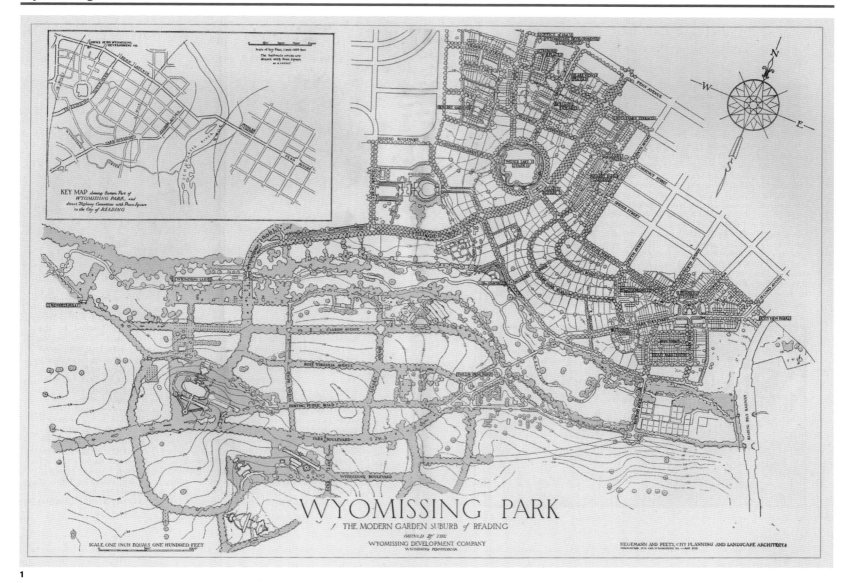

1. Plan, Hegemann and Peets, 1919. COR

landscape plans.[371] In addition to laying out Parkside Drive North and Parkside Drive South along parkland bordering the Wyomissing Creek valley, connecting the grounds of the hospital and museum with Wyomissing Boulevard, Nolen covered the former nursery with a series of wide, gently curving, tree-lined residential streets accommodating large house lots, hoping to make the development seem less like a typical subdivision and more like a "residential park wherein homes may be built." Nolen provided "neighborly lanes cut through the blocks, allowing fine walks and short cuts for pedestrians, away from the automobile traffic of the street," stressing that "the plan of Wyomissing Park is one of the first to call for proper provision for the pedestrian. Now that automobiles put such intensive use on the road itself, it is altogether fitting that walks and paths and lanes should have special attention as a part of the recreation scheme. Few people walk today," wrote Nolen, "and one reason is that attractive promenades and footpaths are not provided."[372] Although the Wyomissing Development Company and other developers carried out most of the Nolen plan, a particularly

appealing residential area around the circular Weiser Lake was not realized.

Hegemann and Peets also laid out **Lake Forest** (1916), in Wisconsin's capital city, Madison, proposing three preliminary studies for an 840-acre community on the southern shore of Lake Wingra.[373] Each of the three schemes offered "straight shot" views of George B. Post's State Capitol building (1904) to the northeast and incorporated variously shaped lagoons set among a formal arrangement of streets that, as Christiane Crasemann Collins has noted, "reflect the influence of Washington, D.C., perhaps derived from Peets's study of L'Enfant's plan."[374] The selected scheme's circular civic center was to be ringed by a tall pergola intended to ensure a unified appearance as buildings were gradually built behind it. The site's marshy conditions led to financial challenges that the developer could not overcome.

The evolution of the **Country Club District** of Kansas City, Missouri, the largest and one of the most carefully conceived garden villages, began in the first decade of the twentieth century and continually developed until the late 1930s.[375] Although the streetcar provided the

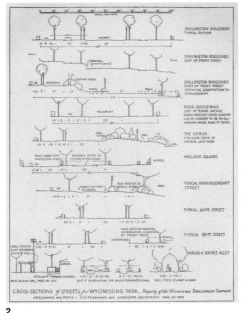

2

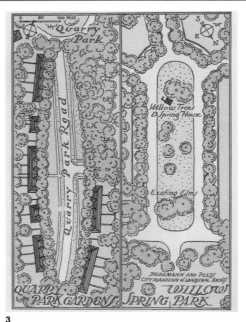

3

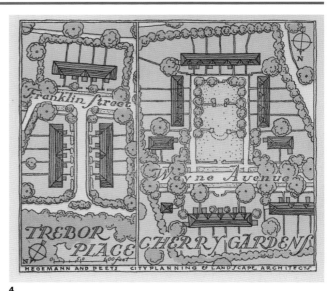

4

5

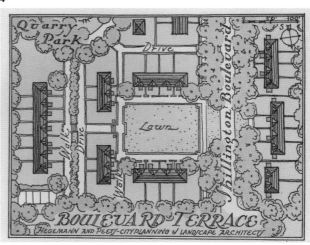

6

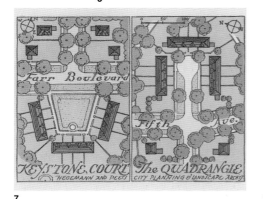

7

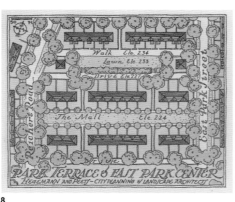

8

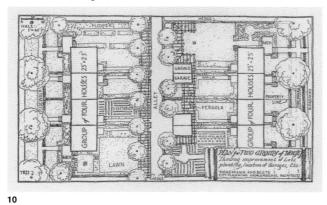

10

9

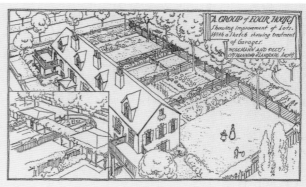

11

2–11. Plans and renderings from the Hegemann and Peets 1919 plan for Wyomissing Park. COR

12

13

14

15

16

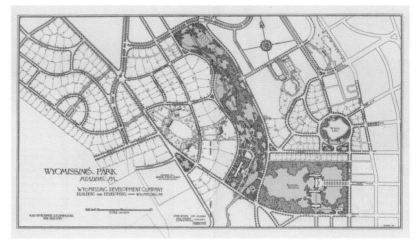

17

18

19

12–14. Plans and renderings from the Hegemann and Peets 1919 plan for Wyomissing Park. COR

15. Trebor Place. RAMSA (2011)

16. Holland Square. RAMSA (2011)

17. Plan, John Nolen, 1927. COR

18–20. Typical streets in John Nolen-designed section. RAMSA (2011)

20

1. Aerial perspective. UWM (c. 1917)

2. Sketches of public buildings, Hegemann and Peets, 1920. COR

3. Study of Civic Center, Hegemann and Peets, 1920. COR

4. Preliminary studies, Hegemann and Peets, 1916. COR

1

2

3

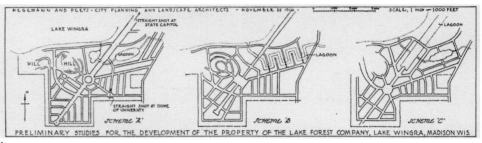

4

initial impetus for the development, it was as an automobile suburb that the Country Club District made its greatest contribution, embodying the shift from garden village before World War II to postwar subdivision. Located on the south side of the city, three miles from downtown, and extending west into Kansas City, Kansas, the Country Club District was begun in 1906 when Jesse Clyde Nichols purchased an almost worthless 10-acre tract of land one mile beyond the end of streetcar service. The tract had been abandoned after the collapse of Kansas City's real estate boom of the 1880s. Within thirty years, Nichols's development, which derived its name because the original parcel bordered the Kansas City Country Club, encompassed over 10 square miles of land and housed 60,000 people—10,000 in apartments—becoming what Robert Fishman has described as "an ideal suburban refuge, a protected environment of privilege . . . [adapting] the forms of the late-nineteenth-century railroad and streetcar suburb to the needs and the social structure of the automobile age."[376]

J. C. Nichols was introduced to enlightened land planning while a graduate student at Harvard, studying with the economist O. M. W. Sprague (1873–1953). Nichols possessed an unusually strong appreciation for land development not only as a business but also as an art form and would become the leading advocate for the recognition of the property developer as a professional held to similar ethical standards as the architect and landscape architect, spearheading the establishment of the Urban Land Institute in 1936. Nichols's vision was matched by that of the planner George Kessler, designer of the system of landscaped boulevards that give Kansas City its distinctive character, whom he retained to help

with the plan and, after Kessler moved to St. Louis in 1911, by his disciples, Sidney J. and his son, S. Herbert, Hare, who had studied under Frederick Law Olmsted Jr. at Harvard and worked with his former teacher on the planned extensions to Roland Park. Hare & Hare were Nichols's landscape architects until the onset of the Great Depression in the 1930s when work on the suburb was virtually halted. Nichols also claimed to have been influenced by what he saw on a bicycle tour of European garden villages and suburbs that he undertook in 1900.

Purposely choosing land outside the city's transportation system and thus inexpensive enough to allow him to provide generously sized lots and parks, Nichols quickly increased the property's market appeal by arranging to have an old freight line converted for use as an extension to the streetcar line. Alert to the dramatic increase in automobile ownership around the outbreak of World War I, Nichols situated a high-class shopping center, Country Club Plaza (1922), within easy reach of the city's expanding boulevard system, so that it would serve as a connective knuckle between his residential development, the existing streetcar suburbs of Kansas City, and the city's downtown.

Prior to Nichols's development, a number of modest suburban enclaves had been undertaken on Kansas City's south side, including Janssen Place, Hyde Park, and the Rockhill District (see p. 103). These were connected by trolley to downtown. In 1910, Nichols, perhaps anticipating the extended geographical reach that the automobile would make possible, began to expand his initial holdings by gaining control of the 400-acre historic Ward Farm. It was at this point that he retained Kessler to plan a new subdivision intended

1

to be called Sunset Hill, although the name Ward Farm would ultimately prevail. Guided by Kessler, Ward Farm emerged as much more than a typical subdivision, with a plan of long east–west oriented blocks that Nichols believed provided better solar and wind orientation to houses and escaped the north–south flow of traffic from the suburb to downtown. The plan for Ward Farm also allowed for large lots, some with 200 feet of street frontage. As part of his arrangement with the Ward family, a second trolley, the Sunset Hill line, was extended from Forty-seventh to Fifty-sixth Street. At this time Nichols began to work with Kansas City officials to connect his Ward Farm holdings with the existing Kessler-designed boulevard system. Even before his development of Country Club Plaza and the residential neighborhoods

that lay to its south, Nichols, grasping the new scale made possible by the automobile, developed Mission Hills (1913–14), across the state line in Kansas City, Kansas, which arguably was the first suburb exclusively dependent on the automobile for access. With five-acre parcels promoted as being only an eighteen-minute drive to downtown Kansas City, Missouri, Mission Hills had even longer east–west blocks that hugged the topography with gentle curves.

Ward Parkway, laid out by Kessler, was the backbone of the Country Club District. Few houses faced it in keeping with Nichols's belief that houses should not line high-traffic streets; but to live just to one side or other of the parkway was to enjoy a smart address as Evan Connell made clear in his 1959 novel of Kansas

2. Aerial view of Country Club Plaza. MVSC (c. 1930)

3. Ward Parkway. MVSC (1932)

4. House near intersection of West 52nd and Wyandotte Streets. MVSC (1922)

5. Advertising sign at Brookside Boulevard and 52nd Street. SHSM

6. Huntington Road and Brookside Boulevard. SHSM (1913)

7. Ward Parkway from Fifty-fifth Street showing Sunset Hill streetcar. SHSM (1915)

8. Mission Hills. Garvin. AG (2011)

9 The Walnuts apartment building. Garvin. AG (2011)

10. Prairie Village. Garvin. AG (2011)

11. Ward Parkway, with fountain in distance. Garvin. AG (2011)

12. Ward Parkway. Garvin. AG (1994)

2

3

4

5

6

7

8

9

10

11

12

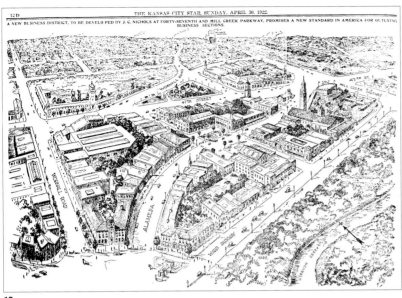

13

14

15

16

17

18

19

20

13. Rendering by Edward Buehler Delk of original Country Club Plaza plan, 1922. SHSM

14. Country Club Plaza, at intersection of Mill Creek Parkway and 47th Street. MVSC (c. 1945–50)

15. Country Club Plaza parking garage. MVSC (c. 1947)

16. Brookside Shopping Center. SHSM (c. 1920)

17. Parking lot in Country Club Plaza, south of Alameda Road. SHSM (1930)

18. Standard Oil Company filling station at 62nd Terrace and Brookside Boulevard. SHSM

19. Shopping center at entrance to Westwood Hills. SHSM (1925)

20. Country Club Plaza. Garvin. AG (2011)

City upper-middle-class life, *Mrs. Bridge*, in which Mr. Bridge, rapidly rising in the legal profession, was able to move with his family "to a large home just off Ward Parkway several years sooner than they had expected."[377]

In planning the district, which would eventually accommodate 6,000 houses, Nichols and his staff eschewed right-angle intersections and gridiron streets, preserved existing trees, and endeavored to respect the natural topography. Early on in the development, he offered relatively small lots, similar to those in most streetcar suburbs, but as the use of the automobile proliferated, his suburb spread out and lot sizes grew commensurately. Nonetheless, given the extensive number of apartment houses surrounding the Country Club shopping plaza and the smaller lot sizes in some of the earlier developments, the Country Club District, like Shaker Heights, Ohio, became home to a reasonably diverse population.

While there were no stylistic restrictions placed on the individual architects, there were many land-use restrictions, ranging from regulations governing front-yard setbacks to a requirement for foundation planting. It is important to note that the restrictions and mandates at the Country Club District were intended for perpetuity. Those at Roland Park, which influenced Nichols's thinking, were modified by Edward H. Bouton, to a twenty-five-year duration. According to the developer, no planner could claim to be "wise enough for eternity."[378]

Realizing that unless he controlled much more land his development would be swallowed up in the inevitable sprawl of cities, Nichols continued to acquire property until America entered World War I. But it was not until 1922, when he had already developed about 2,000 acres, that Nichols's vision for an entire district began to take shape, with land set aside for schools, churches, and parks. By 1939 there were four golf courses, eleven churches, and fifteen schools.

The provision of parkland was more ingenious than generous; frequently the parks were little more than pocket-size. According to Nichols, triangular parks at street intersections, presumably modeled on those at Riverside, "give refinement of character to street entrances" and "overcome the effect of ugly barren wide stretches of pavement in front of homes."[379] Wherever possible, a "rural feeling" was preserved or enhanced. Fords rather than bridges were used where roads crossed streambeds; both sides of streambeds were landscaped to form parkways. Even more notably, as Robert and Brad Pearson, Nichols's biographers, point out, "In a very real sense, the golf courses in the Country Club District . . . served as parks, and . . . [as] barriers protecting the district from commercial intrusion or undesirable development beyond its borders."[380] Not every feature of the Nichols park plan worked. Almost without exception, he wrote in 1939, all attempts at establishing "little parks or playgrounds in the interior of residential blocks . . . proved unsuccessful," encouraging "neighborhood quarrels" that were hard to police and resisted by childless residents who resented the noise. Efforts to vary tree species in an attempt to suggest informality was also not a success: "It does not create an orderly appearance in the street."[381]

The Country Club District is not pedestrian friendly. Aspects of the plan, in particular the long blocks that provided better orientation of houses and reduced street traffic, discourage walking. To remedy this, Nichols included midblock pedestrian ways that were "improved with sidewalks, otherwise in scarce supply in the district, especially in the most affluent neighborhoods." Additionally, Nichols introduced jogs in roads, rotary intersections, and other strategies to deliberately calm traffic. Early on he "abandoned providing alleys in our residential sections. We feel they become the source of disorder and uncleanliness . . . and are very offensive to the use of the garden side of the home."[382]

Reflecting on his accomplishments, Nichols wrote in 1939 that "there is no greater crime in city planning than to have all of your streets of the same size, the same distance apart, or having all of your lots and blocks of the same size." From the beginning, Nichols had argued for

wider lots to give more open space between homes. As the old idea that the porch had to be on the front of the house gradually gave way, and we started placing the porch on the side, we made every effort to encourage the greater lot width. As the horse and buggy days passed and with it the stable and manure pile, we vigorously advocated the placing of the porch on the garden side of the home for the more intensive use of the rear lawn for living purposes. As the garage took the place of the barn, we advocated its incorporation as part of the house, resulting in the house becoming wider in the front and requiring greater lot widths. We find that today even in our smaller lot subdivisions a 70- or 75-foot lot does not give much more open space between houses than the old 50-foot lot did with the narrow front of the house to the street and the porch on the front.[383]

Country Club Plaza shopping center is generally regarded as Nichols's greatest innovation—the first "downtown" created with the automobile in mind. The Plaza was originally designed under the direction of Philadelphia architect Edward Buehler Delk (1885–1956), but the bulk of the work was supervised from 1925 to 1974 by Edward W. Tanner (1896–1974). Nichols was an active design participant as well, traveling with his wife to "Italy to study hillside villas, Spain for architectural style, France for the uniform building heights of Paris, Germany for streets planned in relation to building density and the most efficient traffic movement, and England for its thorough planned 'new towns.'"[384] Nichols was especially impressed with what he saw in Spain—the mix of plazas and towers and tiled roofs characteristic of city and villa architecture. Once it came down to actually designing the Plaza's buildings, it is most likely that Nichols and his architects were also capitalizing on the historic Hispanic connections of the

Southwest and were inspired by the example of Addison Mizner's work at Palm Beach (see p. 333). In any case, the copy of the Giralda tower in Seville, the fountains, and extensive use of brightly colored tiles worked astonishingly well, at least until the cars grew too numerous and the "parking stations" gave way to parking decks. Despite the changes, Country Club Plaza has remained an exceptionally pleasant and convenient shopping area.

To assure sufficient local trade for the shopping district and to support restaurants in the evenings, Nichols surrounded Country Club Plaza with 160 multiple dwellings at densities varying from double- and triple-decker walk-ups to ten- and twelve-story blocks of flats. The best of the apartment towers were beautifully massed, and their motor courts with ornamental gateways and illuminated lanterns of wrought iron, combined with penthouse rooftop turrets and towers concealing mechanical equipment, created just enough sense of skyscraper style to imbue the shopping district with a real sense of downtown.

Even before he undertook Country Club Plaza, beginning in 1907 Nichols embarked on the first of a number of neighborhood shopping centers. Early on he addressed the needs of motorists, with four artistically conceived filling stations (1914–17). Nichols retained John Nolen to help with the planning and design of the Tudoresque Brookside Shops (1920) at Sixty-third Street and Brookside Boulevard, a neighborhood center located at a remote corner of the development that included a combined police and fire station and, on the second story, professional offices. The design, as Robert and Brad Pearson point out, "obviously reflected the appearance of villages J. C. [Nichols] had observed in England and the Roland Park shops."[385] Seven neighborhood centers were built by 1939, with each center designed in an architecturally distinctive style complementing the residential surroundings.

Nichols was a synthesizer and an innovator, with a tremendous working knowledge of urban and suburban precedent. He absorbed the lessons of Riverside and Roland Park, and with the advice of Kessler and Hare & Hare, he orchestrated his sprawling residential district into a series of quiet country villages, adapting to changing conditions as his project evolved, so that what began as a streetcar suburb of the late nineteenth century became the exemplar par excellence of upper-middle-class automobile suburbia in the 1920s and then, with the recovery of the economy in the late 1940s, met the needs of a less affluent middle class with mass-produced, mass-marketed houses that nonetheless enjoyed the benefits of sound land planning.

In many ways, the development of **Shaker Heights**, Ohio, parallels that of the Country Club District.[386] But the connection of Shaker Heights to its host city is much more sharply defined, and both mass transit and private automobiles were taken into consideration at the outset of development. Like the County Club District, Shaker Heights begins where the city leaves off, the point of transition being Market Square where shops are grouped around the first stop on the Shaker Heights Rapid Transit line leading from the center of Cleveland. The Shaker Rapid, as the train is known, not only provides residents with their own exclusive link to the city's downtown but also with streetcar-like service within the suburb itself. Sprawling though Shaker Heights is, it is but a part of an even larger planned suburbia, including Beachwood and Pepper Pike, so that it becomes in effect a suburb with its own suburbs.

Oris P. (1879–1936) and Mantis J. (1881–1935) Van Sweringen, brothers who were self-made entrepreneurs, envisioned Shaker Heights as one of the largest planned suburbs ever, including country estates, parks, country clubs, denser single-family-house sections, and villages. The plan was laid out by the F. A. Pease Engineering Company whose serviceable pattern of roads sympathized with the rolling topography of the site, adapting the principles of Olmsted's Riverside plan to the bolder scale and expanded reach of the automobile. The Van Sweringen brothers—typically referred to as the Vans—acquired their first piece of farmland in Shaker Heights (population 250) in the early 1900s. By 1912 their holdings had grown sufficiently to justify incorporating Shaker Heights as an independent village, with brother Oris as trustee. The Vans realized, however, that they needed a direct rapid-transit link to downtown Cleveland, eight miles to the west. In 1920 the Cleveland Interurban Railroad began operation, with trains running from downtown Cleveland to Shaker Heights in fifteen minutes.[387] The Shaker Rapid, departing from Public Square in downtown Cleveland, made its first stop at Shaker Square, just west of Shaker Heights proper, where the line divided into two branches, providing service to most areas in Shaker Heights. Because the Cleveland leg of the Shaker Rapid ran for miles along the right-of-way of an existing railroad, the Nickel Plate Road, the Vans were forced to buy all 513 miles of the line.

With the establishment of the Rapid, Shaker Heights boomed. Two principal boulevards, South Moreland and Shaker, curve out toward the east from Shaker Square. In addition to the two natural lakes and two man-made ones, extensive tree planting was introduced to further foster the area's scenic appeal, while the long, narrow valley that ran down the site was developed as the Shaker Heights Country Club, one of four ultimately established in the suburb. School and church sites were provided by the Vans, and plans were made for the even more rural developments of Beachwood and Pepper Pike, where small country estates could be enjoyed with urban conveniences, including an extension of the Rapid and a limited access highway connecting back to downtown Cleveland.

The focus of the expansive village was Shaker Square (1929), consisting of twelve commercial buildings designed by Philip L. Small (1890–1963) and Charles Bacon Rowley (1890–1984). Its success fostered the development of elegant blocks of flats at its immediate edges,

1. Plan, F. A. Pease Engineering Company, 1919. SHS

2. Advertisement. CSU (1929)

3. Shaker Rapid, Coventry Station. CSU

4. Shaker Square, Philip L. Small and Charles Bacon Rowley, 1929. Garvin. AG (1999)

5. View across Green Lake. Spencer. WC (2008)

6. Typical street. RAMSA (c. 1980)

7. Aerial view of Shaker Square. SHS (c. 1950)

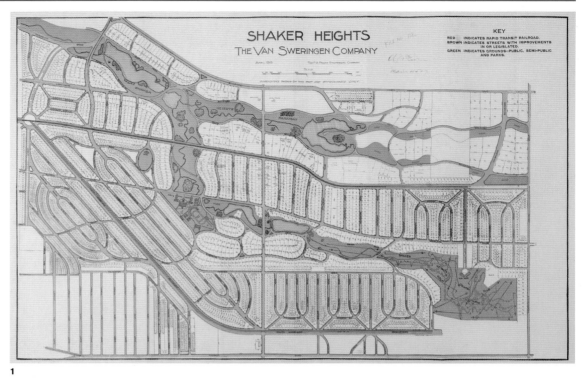

such as the Tudor-style Moreland Courts designed by Small with Alfred Harris (1860?–1943).[388] Shaker Square, which was actually across the village line in Cleveland, was the commercial gateway to the Vans' earthly paradise, where rental residences and commerce—which they felt did not harmonize with substantial private homes, churches, schools, and country clubs—were clustered, forming a transition from city to suburban living.

Deed restrictions for the single-family house lots were imposed by the Van Sweringens, based on those first drawn up in 1900 by an earlier syndicate that had hoped to develop the land, and were then revised and expanded by the Vans in 1927. A single architectural vocabulary was eschewed in favor of a broad range of traditional styles, but the synthesis of planning and architecture convincingly adapted the traditional village feeling to a new scale. Virtually every fashionable traditional style of the 1920s can be found.[389] The Vans built several houses to sell, using Bloodgood Tuttle (1880–1936) as their architect, but by and large, individual owners contracted for their own houses.

In an earlier era, at Riverside and Chestnut Hill, a resort hotel had served as the lure for the rich and socially prominent. For the upmarket Beachwood and Pepper Pike areas, several country clubs were built to perform a similar function. The Depression not only ruined the Van Sweringens but also slowed development of these two new neighborhoods. However, with the street plans and country clubs set in place, the outer edges of Shaker Heights were fully prepared to take off in the post–World War II development boom.

Near Shaker Heights and developed at about the same time was the far less ambitious **Forest Hill** (1930), lying six miles east of Cleveland's Public Square and occupying 400 acres of the larger estate that John D. Rockefeller Sr. (1839–1937) began to acquire in the 1870s.[390] The Rockefeller mansion, built as a summer home for the family, was destroyed by fire in 1917, by which time its owner had improved 700 acres of property with two lakes, an icehouse, a horse track, bridle trails, footpaths, and a nine-hole golf course. After the fire, Rockefeller never returned to Forest Hill, and the land was held by the family as the city grew around it. In 1923, John D. Rockefeller Jr. purchased the property from his father and donated portions for a hospital, school, and Masonic temple. Two years later, he announced that his Abeyton Realty Corporation would build a model community of 1,000 houses on the estate's former farm and grazing lands east of Lee Boulevard as a for-profit venture. Andrew J. Thomas (1875–1966), who had designed luxury, middle-income, and working-class multifamily housing in New York for the Rockefellers as well as some multifamily housing at Radburn (see p. 275), was given complete control over the subdivision's plan, architecture, and infrastructure.

Significantly, the site was not served by public transportation. In contrast to the straight, parallel Brewster and Glynn Roads running along its northern boundary, Thomas planned a patchwork of concentric arcing streets following the contours of two overlapping, curved Y-shaped intersections. Houses were executed in the French Norman style, sheathed in wavy-edged cedar siding, hand-split shakes, oak half-timbering with brick nogging, local Ohio sandstone, and soft red and pinkish tan bricks developed specially for the project. Steeply pitched roofs were of either shingle tile or polychromatic slate, graduated in size and thickness, and given intentional irregularities to appear as if they had been repaired over time. Thomas prepared nine distinct seven- and eight-room house designs, situating the residences in mirror-image pairs at the edges of the blocks to enclose common interior green spaces. Coupled driveways, separated by thin strips of grass, led behind the houses to broad paved areas which allowed for maneuverability in and out of basement-level two-car garages, keeping cars out of sight. Only the corner houses featured attached garages. Promotional materials touted the subdivision's underground gas and water mains, phone lines, and electric transformers, avoiding what C. Matlack Price considered one of the "outstanding blemishes of the average American suburb—overhead wires."[391] Houses, set back from the street behind curving front walks, were delivered fully landscaped, with corner and foundation plantings and flowering fruit trees in the front yards. Hundreds of oak and elm trees were planted throughout the development.

Residents were promised exclusive membership in a country club located across Lee Road, where the Rockefeller homestead had formerly stood and where Rockefeller's personal golf course was redesigned and enlarged by Donald Ross (1872–1948) in 1931. Thomas also designed a mixed-use building, the Heights Rockefeller Building (1931), on the northeast corner of Mayfield and Lee Roads, in the same Norman vocabulary as the residences, providing retail space for small stores, a second-floor bank occupying a grand 50-by-100-foot vaulted and chandeliered room, and a wing of three- to five-room apartments.

The promising plan fell victim to its timing and overall concept. It was submitted for public approvals in August 1929, just before the stock market crash, and was formally announced to the public in September 1930, after fifteen houses—known locally as "Rockefellers"—had been built in a line along Brewster Road. Over the next few years an additional sixty-six houses were completed, but the Depression took its toll. In 1931 *Fortune* magazine, in part taking revenge on the city of Cleveland in which its publisher, Henry Luce, had spent an unhappy year in the early 1920s when his and Briton Hadden's fledgling *Time* magazine was forced to relocate there to avoid the high costs of New York, reported that of the eighty-one houses built, only five were sold:

> *Forest Hill is not a success [and] threatens to be a most resounding failure . . . not because it was carelessly undertaken, not because it is badly planned, but because it is a New York project located in Cleveland . . . [Mr. Rockefeller]*

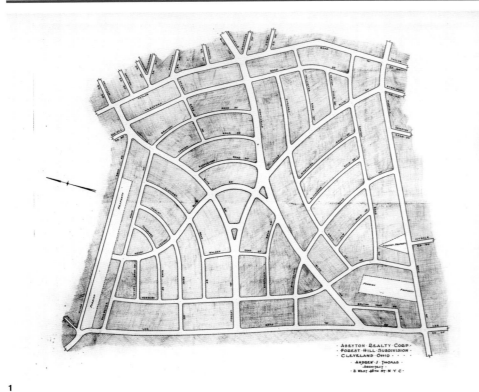

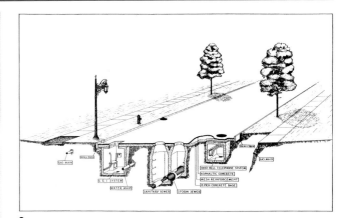

1. Plan, Andrew J. Thomas, 1930. RAC

2. Cutaway diagram showing underground utilities, 1931. FHHO

3. "Rockefellers." FHHO (2006)

4. Heights Rockefeller Building, Andrew J. Thomas, 1931. RAC

5–7. Typical houses and streets. RAC

forgot that real-estate values are higher in crowded land-hungry New York than they are in expansive Cleveland. He forgot that while a young executive would have to go far afield to find an apartment of any size in Manhattan for $3,000 a year (the equivalent in rent of a $30,000 house), there are plenty of well-located apartments in Cleveland for that rent. He forgot that a $30,000 house is a necessity in suburban New York but a luxury in Cleveland . . . With real-estate values sinking fast under the waters of the current depression, Mr. Rockefeller's houses seemed all the more definitely in the upper register . . . Thus has one of the deepest of Rockefeller plans gone wrong, and all because Mr. Rockefeller and the people of Cleveland place different values on $30,000.[392]

Asking prices for the unsold houses were soon cut in half and those that did not sell were leased.

The *Fortune* editors suggested that the architectural character of Forest Hill—thought to be one of its great assets—was in fact a deficit:

[Clevelanders] expected a great deal more than Mr. Rockefeller had arranged to give. They particularly disliked the fact that all the houses were variations on five or six basic designs, the variations often consisting in little more than the switching of a dining room and living room. They disliked the small space between the houses, though lawns 75 by 140 feet would be considered ample in most New York suburbs. Clevelanders argue that if they are to put all that money in a house, they want to be at least certain of not mistaking it for the one next door some dark night . . . Inevitably [Clevelanders compared] the grass plots of Forest Hill with the broad stretches of Shaker lawns, the monotony of Mr. Rockefeller's Norman architecture with the harmonious variations of the individually built houses in Shaker Heights. And they compare the accessibility of Shaker, which can be reached by rapid transit from Public Square in thirty minutes, with the practical impossibility of reaching Forest Hill except by automobile. The nearest street-car line is a mile away and takes forty-five minutes to get into the city . . . [Rockefeller's] aim, reasonable enough on paper, was to bridge in the gap between Shaker and Cleveland's $10,000 ready-built houses. But instead of filling a gap, he seems to have fallen between two stools.[393]

Responding to slow sales, Rockefeller explored other strategies, including the construction in 1936 of five experimental prefabricated "steel homes" by the Arcy Corporation on Monticello Boulevard between Burlington Road and Newbury Drive. In 1937, 200 lots were put on the market in the southern portion of the subdivision,

but Thomas's French Norman vocabulary was discarded to make way for more popular Colonial-style houses offering upgraded conveniences like air-conditioning and electric appliances as well as two-car garages facing the street. In 1938, Rockefeller donated the country club's 266 acres to the cities of East Cleveland and Cleveland Heights for the creation of Forest Hill Park, designed by Albert D. Taylor (1883–1951). Development stalled once again during World War II, and in 1948, although the streets had been entirely laid out and lined with trees, most of the site remained vacant, with 650 open lots and only about 200 houses built. It wasn't until the 1950s boom that the remainder of the neighborhood was built out, largely owing to the purchase of the land in 1949 by Toledo-based developer George A. Roose, who within seven years sold most of the remaining parcels to assorted developers building primarily ranch houses.

THE GARDEN VILLAGE: AUTOMOBILE SUBURBS

In the post–World War II era, the enhanced mobility made possible by the automobile quickly put to rest the garden village idea, eliminating single points of entry around which components of a village could be naturally grouped and giving rise to the sprawling subdivision. But in the years between the two world wars, a number of automobile-dependent garden villages were initiated, constituting a coda to a seventy-five-year tradition.

During the interwar period, the so-called New South proved to be fertile ground for enlightened garden village planning, with many examples illustrating the transition from the streetcar to the private automobile. Unlike Atlanta, Georgia, which had to rebuild itself after the Civil War, Birmingham, Alabama, was a New Southern city, founded after the war in 1871, and by 1900, owing to the regional presence of rich mineral deposits allowing for robust steel production, firmly established as the South's industrial powerhouse. As the city expanded south and east to reach the foothills of Red Mountain, the common practice of laying out gridded subdivisions along streetcar routes became less feasible, leading developers to adopt naturalistic planning techniques to meet the challenges of hilly terrain traversed by private automobiles. Birmingham's suburbs, even more than Atlanta's, reflect the transition from the compact organization demanded by a railroad or streetcar to a more sprawling pattern that reflected the scale of the automobile. Nonetheless, Birmingham's pocket arcadias have been admired from their earliest days, so that, in 1909, S. Mays Ball could observe in *House and Garden* that "about three hundred to five hundred feet above the city are these foothills upon which live all the people of the city who can afford to get out of the grime and dirt of a steel, iron and coal metropolis, such as Birmingham, 'The Magic City,' has become . . . Those who have only heard of Birmingham

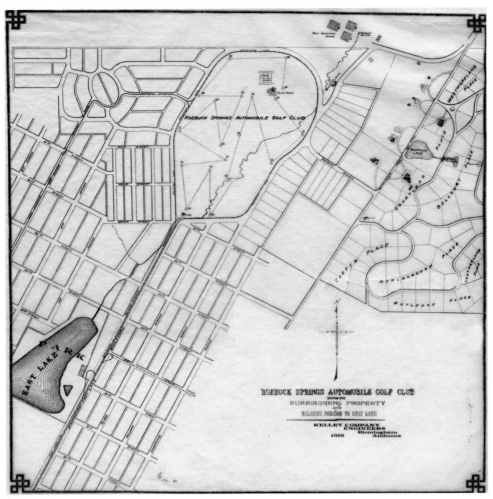

1. Plan, Scott, Tedd, and Tom Joy, 1910 showing Roebuck Springs on right. BPLA

2–4. Typical streets. Adkisson. DA (2012)

as the 'Pittsburgh of the South' have no idea of the beautiful residence section just outside the city:—it is a revelation when first seen."[394]

According to historian Marjorie Longenecker White, **Roebuck Springs** (1910), a subdivision adjoining the Roebuck Springs golf club eleven miles east of the city center, developed by the East Lake Land Company and designed by the architects and civil engineers Scott (1880?–1942), Tedd (1878–1943), and Tom (1875–1944) Joy with curvilinear roads on 140 acres previously considered undevelopable because of a 200-foot rise in elevation, "set several precedents for land planning in the Birmingham area." Roebuck Springs was situated on "mountainous slopes . . . reached by narrow roads contoured to the topography . . . English landscape traditions and nomenclature provided the physical and psychological planning model . . . And, its development was associated with the game of golf . . . [featuring] Birmingham's first 'designed' 18-hole golf course and club grounds."[395] The grounds, designed by Birmingham landscape architect George H. Miller (1856–1927), included an automobile "pleasure drive," a rare amenity to motorists accustomed to the city's unpaved streets.

One of the most prolific Birmingham developers, Robert Jemison Jr. (1878–1974), who founded the Jemison Realty Company in 1903, built conventional districts

like East Lake (1906) and Ensley Highlands (1907), where the grid was "accepted with difficulty," leading to "roller coaster roads," according to Longenecker White, before shifting gears for the development of a series of arcadian neighborhoods that bled into one another as they rose up and over Red Mountain.[396] Jemison hired Samuel Parsons Jr. to design **Mountain Terrace** (1906), covering 40 acres adjacent to Lakeview Park and its golf course and linked to downtown Birmingham two miles to the northwest by streetcar.[397] With roads laid out to retain the site's rock formations, trees, and vegetation, promotional literature boasted that Mountain Terrace "happily avoided [the] endless repetition of city lawns, the effect of 'sameness' and monotony which disfigures so many residential properties from an artistic view point."[398] The three main "driveways"— Crescent, Glenview, and Cliff Roads—where houses commanded sweeping views of the city, became Birmingham's most prestigious addresses. In 1917, Warren H. Manning (1860–1938) designed Forest Park, a 300-acre eastern addition to Mountain Terrace, adhering to similar design principles.[399]

George H. Miller's design for the 40-acre **Valley View** (1911), also developed by Jemison Jr., limited houses to only one side of the road to provide long views not only from the home sites but from automobiles traveling

Mountain Terrace

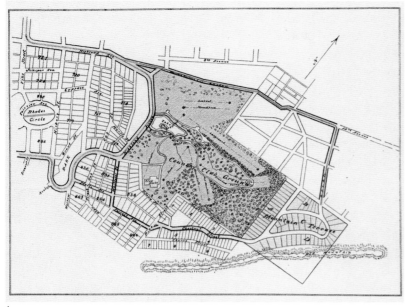

1. Plan, Samuel Parsons Jr., 1906. BPLA

2. Bird's-eye view. BPLA

3. Typical street. Adkisson. DA (2012)

4. Cliff Road. BPLA (c. 1913)

5. Entrance to Mountain Terrace. BPLA

Valley View

1, 2. Typical streets. Adkisson. DA (2012)

along the looping Cliff and Altamont Roads, conceived as scenic drives along the narrow Red Mountain ridge.[400] During the 1920s, Jemison Jr. continued to focus on the development of the ridge, building **Redmont Park** (1924–26), consisting of five contiguous subdivisions on 150 acres, planned by the Birmingham landscape architect William H. Kessler (1880–1966), who situated 257 house sites averaging one-half acre along culs-de-sac and winding drives.[401] **Mountain Brook Estates**, on over 2,500 acres, was far more expansive.[402] Planned in 1926 by Kessler, with Manning serving as design consultant, Mountain Brook was designed with landscaped

roadways winding through preserved natural features. It included the 450-acre Birmingham Country Club, several schools, and 27 miles of bridle paths affiliated with the Mountain Brook Riding Academy. It also had its own town center, Mountain Brook Village, a series of Tudor Revival commercial buildings designed by the firm of Miller & Martin around a five-way elliptical intersection located on the development's western edge.

Windsor Farms (1924), Virginia, four miles west of downtown Richmond, was a collaboration between John Nolen and a local engineer, Allen Saville (n.d.), working for the former farm property's owner, T. C. Williams

Redmont Park

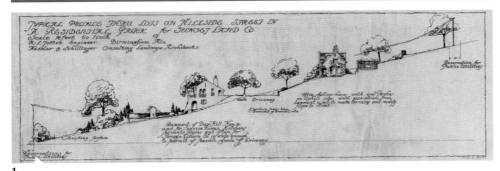

1

1. Redmont Park, profile of lots on a hillside street. BPLA

2. Redmont Park. Adkisson. DA (2012)

2

Mountain Brook Estates

1

1. Bird's-eye view. BPLA (1929)

2. Bird's-eye view of proposed development of Mountain Brook Village, Miller & Martin. BPLA (1927)

3. Mountain Brook Village. Adkisson. DA (2012)

4. Mountain Brook Estates. Adkisson. DA (2012)

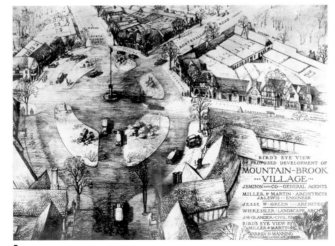

2

3

4

Jr., whose idea it was to re-create an English village.[403] While the impression is less that of a town than an estate park, principally because of its low density, especially along the James River bluffs where affluent gentry built large houses, several designed by William Lawrence Bottomley (1883–1951), the development does have a strong plan focused on a village green where a few public buildings were located. The plan's combination of diagonal and concentric avenues, intended to discourage automobile through traffic, makes it difficult to navigate even for residents.

In an echo of the story of Katonah, New York, Lawrence V. Sheridan (1887–1972) prepared a plan for the relocated town of **Columbus**, Kentucky, at the urging of the American Red Cross after flooding in 1927 devastated the earlier settlement on the banks of the Mississippi River.[404] The town had a rich Civil War–era history, but since 1900, when it counted 1,235 residents, its population had steadily declined. The new town, set atop 150-foot-high bluffs to the east, was planned for 500, its 80 acres dotted with 116 houses on irregularly shaped lots along curving tree-lined streets. Hoover Parkway, the principal approach road, flanked by a pair of filling stations and a church and a school, passed between two commercial buildings framing a village center and into the residential neighborhood, where it forked around a large park. As designed by Foltz, Osler & Thompson, the planned commercial buildings were to be realizable in stages but were nonetheless too ambitious for the small town, calling for more than twenty stores in addition to a post office, bank, movie theater, barbershop, restaurant, and drugstore as well as a community center and municipal and private offices. House lots were generously sized and featured frontages ranging between 65 and 110 feet, leading the Indianapolis-based Sheridan, a civil engineer and landscape architect, to state: "Crowding, often present even in small communities, cannot exist in Columbus."[405] Indeed, crowding would never be an issue; the town's population continued to decrease, and after some streets were laid out and the school and church built, residential development occurred only on a piecemeal basis.

In its sprawling configuration and complete dependence on automobiles, **River Oaks** (1923), Houston, has very little of the sense of community focus that characterizes typical garden villages. Nonetheless, its plan and development controls demand that it not be overlooked in this discussion. Begun as Country Club Estates, a 180-acre residential subdivision next to the newly founded River Oaks Country Club, it evolved into a 1,100-acre enclave within the sprawling city of Houston when two brothers, Will (1875–1930) and Mike (1885–1941) Hogg, and their friend Hugh Potter (1888–1968), envisioned an ideal community that would be a model of land use for a booming city without any land-use zoning. "What City Planning [had traditionally] accomplished by operation of law throughout the whole city," Potter noted, "the modern developer accomplishes by private contract." Potter asserted that the residential developer "is really planning your cities today, and especially so in Houston because it is unzoned."[406] For Will Hogg, River Oaks was part of a civic-minded campaign that included the reorganization of the City Planning Commission, the creation of an urban park system and a civic center, and the founding of the Forum of Civics, a public group devoted to city beautification and urban improvement.

River Oaks is set between Memorial Park, the Buffalo Bayou, and the buffer formed by the River Oaks Country Club. Though largely a gridiron in plan, a number of modest interventions—cul-de-sac developments, gently curving boulevards, planted esplanades, and small parks with lavish planting—succeed in conveying an overall impression of informality and ruralesque spaciousness quite apart from the typical Houston subdivision. The plan was influenced by Roland Park, Palos Verdes, Shaker Heights, and Highland Park, but most especially by J. C. Nichols's Country Club District. Herbert A. Kipp (1884–1968), who had laid out the original River Oaks Country Club Estates and went on to become the development's consulting engineer, was initially assisted by Hare & Hare, who, taking cues from George Kessler's plan for Turtle Creek Parkway in Dallas, were at work designing a two-and-a-half mile linear park and parkway along Buffalo Bayou that linked Houston's downtown with Memorial Park and with which River Oaks would be smoothly integrated.

Like that of the Country Club District, the plan for River Oaks includes shopping centers, sites for six schools and a church, and lot sizes stratified to include a reasonably wide spectrum of homeowners from the middle and upper classes, with lots as small as a quarter of an acre placed at the development's edges and others as large as four acres bordering the country club. In the early years, the developers built a number of model houses, many designed by John Staub, an MIT-trained architect from New York, who had come to Houston in 1921 to supervise the work of his employer Harrie T. Lindeberg. Staub also designed gateposts at the development's entrances and, over the years, many houses in River Oaks for prominent Houston families.

The development required deep front setback lines and, with some exceptions, two-story construction, so that the streets had a strange sense of spatial definition that was uncharacteristic of typical Houston subdivisions. In addition, efforts were made to introduce topographical variety. Front lawns were terraced up from the sidewalk and ravines and bayous were transformed into features, among them Troon Falls and the River Oaks Rock Garden, both created in 1927. Other small open spaces were incorporated into the various subdivisions, most taking the form of midstreet greenswards.

As Houston grew up around it, River Oaks became notable as a "suburb inside the city."[407] As Will and Mike Hogg noted in 1925, "We have convinced ourselves that in a comparatively few years residential Houston will have grown around River Oaks and be beautified by it."[408] Barry J. Kaplan and Charles Orson Cook have observed

Windsor Farms

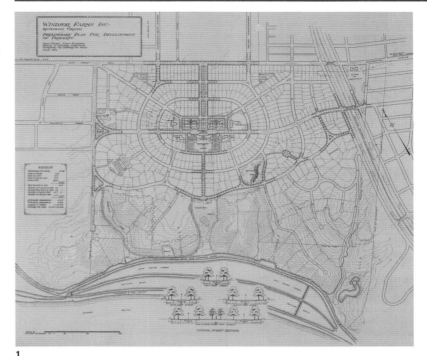

1

2

1. Plan, John Nolen, 1924. COR

2. Aerial view. LVR (c. 1925)

Columbus

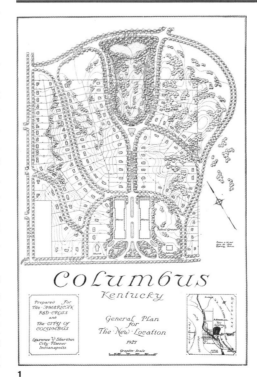

1

1. Plan, Lawrence V. Sheridan, 1927. AR28

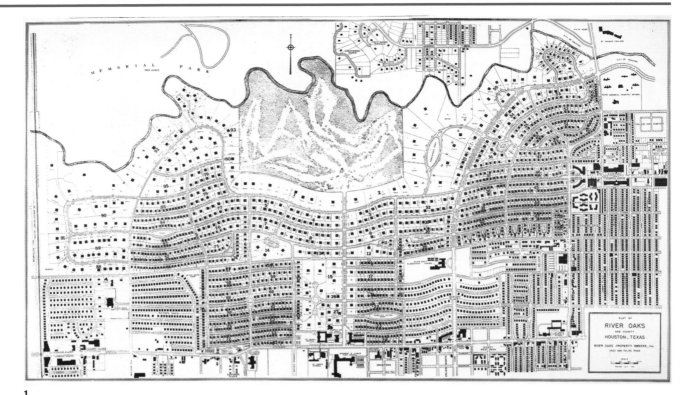

1

2

that "the assumption of the founders that River Oaks would be annexed to the city was consistent with the view that River Oaks was a civic improvement. Unlike similar developments in other cities that remained politically autonomous—Shaker Heights in Cleveland or Highland Park in Dallas for example—River Oaks operated independently for only the first three years of its existence. Moreover, evidence indicates that Hogg intended that River Oaks be the model for surrounding residential areas."[409]

With the construction of a small shopping center (1927) at River Oaks Boulevard and Westheimer Road, River Oaks began to develop a sense of centeredness, but it was not until 1936–37, when the River Oaks Community Center (Oliver C. Winston [1905–1992] with Stayton Nunn [1899–1985] and Milton B. McGinty [1905–2000]), a large shopping center at the West Gray–South Shepherd intersection, was constructed, along with the ten-building River Oaks Gardens, an apartment group south of the community center, that the sprawling suburb began to develop a public identity.

River Oaks has been studied in detail by a number of scholars, but its physical attributes and their meaning in the culture of Houston's rapid urbanization have nowhere been better explained than by Stephen Fox. According to Fox, the developers

compensated for [its] problematic location west of downtown Houston (rather than south of downtown, where Broadacres, Shadyside, and Courtlandt Place lay) by projecting a vision of community intended to set it apart from these small elite neighborhoods [see p. 112]. Through community planning, landscape design, architecture, and—most unusually in the context of earlier elite neighborhoods—advertising imagery, the River Oaks Corporation represented River Oaks not simply as a neighborhood but as a way of life. Mythic imagery was consciously and repeatedly used to construct community identity that emphasized civic idealism, elite status, and suburban exclusivity.[410]

3

4

5

6

Fox goes on to describe the plan:

> The site plan of Country Club Estates and the subsequent phases of River Oaks contributed to its aura of distinction. Kipp's plans spatially distinguished River Oaks from Broadacres, Shadyside, and Courtlandt Place by representing it as the country place alternative to what were antithetically constructed as city neighborhoods. Kipp's plan for Country Club Estates, designed to be free-standing, was based on a curving grid of east–west streets (which he named for famous golf clubs), which gave almost all the house sites a north–south orientation and thwarted the endless vista effect that straight, urban streets produced in the coastal flatlands.[411]

Most important, as Fox points out, the plan constructed

> urban space as suburban scenery, indeed overlaying a new dynamic on the city—a continuous drive that minimally intersected with the existing street network to facilitate rapid mobility through a landscaped setting not previously urbanized because it had been treated as a problematic edge . . . Allen Parkway introduced to Houston the modern experience of moving freely through the city at the speed of machines rather than constraining machines to operate at the tempo of the nineteenth-century city . . . River Oaks belonged to Houston of the future rather than Houston of the past. Systematically integrated into the new Houston, River Oaks comprised a "utopian fragment" constructing enlightened suburban modernity in the chaotically mixed field of the early-twentieth-century American city.[412]

Westwood Village (1929), Los Angeles, was an automobile-oriented village-like development that by virtue of a strong commercial nucleus and the presence of an important institution, the University of California, took

1. Aerial view. SCWH (c. 1937)

2. Westwood Boulevard.
SCWH (c. 1937)

3. Broxton Avenue. Garvin.
AG (1998)

on greater significance than might have been expected.[413] Located on a 3,300-acre tract bound on its east and west, respectively, by the independent cities of Beverly Hills and Santa Monica, the site was acquired in 1919 by department store magnate Arthur Letts (1862–1923), who gave his son-in-law, Harold Janss (1889–1972), responsibility for its development. Janss, with his father, Peter (1858–1926), and brother, Edwin (1882–1959), operated one of the largest residential real estate development companies in Southern California. In 1922, taking advantage of the westward expansion of the city of Los Angeles, the Janss family began building subdivisions on the Westwood land, although, as Richard Longstreth has noted, "no comprehensive plan was prepared, nor was the final product envisioned as a distinct community . . . Indeed, there was little cohesiveness to the whole. The acreage instead became a mosaic of residential areas encompassing a cross section of the income groups then in the western half of the metropolis."[414]

The seeming randomness of the early neighborhood planning notwithstanding, from the start a commercial district was intended, although an initial attempt in 1922 to establish one along Santa Monica Boulevard failed in part because the presence of the right-of-way of the interurban "red cars" proved both a physical and psychological barrier for motorists. Janss then turned his attention to the area north of Wilshire Boulevard, which

had no rail line but was the principal automobile route from downtown to the Pacific Ocean. Wilshire proved a far better location for the new commercial center, named Westwood Village, planned as the gateway to the new campus of the University of California, Los Angeles, located on 384 acres donated by the Janss family, thereby trumping efforts by the developers of Palos Verdes to bring the university to their site (see p. 297). Westwood Village was promoted as "The Town for the Gown."[415]

If Janss eschewed comprehensive planning in the residential portions of Westwood, he embraced it in its commercial heart, hiring the St. Louis–based city planner Harland Bartholomew (1889–1989) to orchestrate the design. Working with L. Deming Tilton (1890–1949), a former employee who had relocated to Santa Barbara, Bartholomew consulted closely with Gordon Whitnall (1888–1977), director of the Los Angeles City Planning Department, during a nearly three-year-long planning process that included a study of comparable shopping centers around the country.

With varying degrees of success, Bartholomew struggled to plan Westwood Village as both a pedestrian- and automobile-friendly environment. In an effort to discourage traffic congestion, he situated the village several blocks north of Wilshire Boulevard and oriented it along and around Westwood Boulevard, a north–south spine that terminated at the UCLA campus. There was no clearly identifiable center, "no plaza, no green, no singular focal point of any kind," as Longstreth has observed, a strategy intended to ease traffic flow and maximize "property values throughout the complex by having all frontage seem desirable to merchants and customers alike."[416]

Bartholomew did not plat specific lots. Janss, who carefully selected the merchants—at first discouraging competition by allowing only one store each per type of goods sold—worked with individual businesses to determine the size and location of their sites, often keeping adjacent lots free for expansion. While the goal was to eventually accommodate hundreds of businesses, only thirty-four were in place when the village opened in 1929, reflecting Janss's strategy of incremental development that would allow him to adapt to changing market conditions.

According to Longstreth, Janss decided early on that the district should have "an exceptional character. The ensemble would suggest a 'village,' not a city; it would be cohesive and meet an unusually high architectural standard. Buildings would in effect form a commercial campus that would complement the university's and be commensurate in quality of expression."[417] To help ensure this, a Board of Architectural Supervisors was required to approve all designs. Buildings, primarily of stucco and brick with red-tile roofs, were to be at least 17 feet tall but not more than two or three stories. Variety in massing and detail was encouraged. Shops featured large display windows to make goods clearly visible from passing cars. Janss made significant investments in the streetscape, paying careful attention to signage and street furniture and installing multicolored sidewalks and a palm- and oleander-planted median down the center of Westwood Boulevard. Perhaps the most significant identifying features of the village were the whimsical towers and spires placed at key locations ostensibly to help orient shoppers and announce certain types of businesses like gas stations, movie theaters, and banks, but also to introduce a sense of civicism to the otherwise wholly commercial venture. Among the more prominent towers was that of the Fox Westwood Village Theater (P. O. Lewis, 1931), terminating an axial view on the northwest corner of Broxton and Weyburn Avenues.

Working with the firm of David Clark Allison (1881–1962) and James Edward Allison (1870–1955) and with Gordon Kaufmann (1888–1949), the Janss Investment Corporation developed the first two sections of Westwood Village to suggest a streetscape built up over time, an idea, Longstreth suggests, that was inspired by a recent civic improvement campaign for downtown Santa Barbara following the 1923 earthquake. Most notable was Allison & Allison's octagonal Janss Corporation Sales Office (1929) at the intersection of Westwood Boulevard and Broxton and Kinross Avenues, with its polychromatic tiled dome set above a deeply recessed arched entrance.

Despite the fact that its formative years occurred during the Depression, Westwood Village was re-soundingly successful, owing in large measure to the phenomenal growth of Los Angeles as a whole. To compete with shopping districts in Beverly Hills and nearer downtown on Wilshire Boulevard's Miracle Mile, Janss introduced entertainment venues such as a bowling alley and movie theaters that gave Westwood Village more universal appeal. By the spring of 1939, Westwood Village could count 452 businesses employing 1,700 people. In 1941, the WPA guide to Los Angeles described Westwood Boulevard, "lined with tall palms and green parkways," as the main thoroughfare of "a community resplendent with high-towered filling stations, new, dazzling-white shops under red-tile roofs, and many patios with fountains."[418] Eventually, after the Janss family ceased ownership in the 1950s and architectural review ended, the district's cohesiveness began to erode, furthered by UCLA's construction of overscaled buildings on land at the edge of the village.

Longstreth has noted the similarities between Westwood Village and J. C. Nichols's Country Club Plaza in Kansas City, which he suggests served as a model and was likely a part of the survey undertaken by Bartholomew and his team in 1927: "The similarities between the Plaza and Westwood Village were too numerous, and the differences between them and all other examples of the period too great, for coincidence to explain the relationship." Each was conceived as a "very large, integrated business development created as part of a much larger network of comprehensively planned residential subdivisions for the well-to-do."[419] Neither had a strongly articulated center and both were planned to facilitate traffic flow and allow for incremental growth. In each case a Spanish architectural style was adopted and a height limit was set, broken only by strategically located towers. Moreover, Nichols maintained a greater degree of control over the design, construction, maintenance, and management of his project than did Janss. Nichols called for multiple tenants to share large buildings so that spaces could be flexible over time, while Janss treated each tenant and building individually. Whereas Nichols imagined Country Club Plaza as a complement to downtown Kansas City, Janss envisioned Westwood Village as an alternative to downtown Los Angeles, recruiting established local businesses as well as national chains to open branches in his development.

Significantly, the developers took different strategies toward parking. While Nichols planned streets wide enough for diagonal parking and conspicuously placed free "parking stations" between and behind the stores, Janss provided employee parking behind the stores so that customers would not have to compete for street parking, a strategy that failed when employees resisted using their allotted spaces. Lots and garages were added to the village over time but were typically small and haphazardly located. By 1949, Stanley L. McMichael, in his survey of American real estate subdivisions, could comment that Westwood Village, "an excellent off-highway business center . . . is a delightful place in which to shop, if you can find a parking space."[420]

URBAN SUBURBIA

The urban suburb was one further category of garden suburb that emerged in the early twentieth century in an ambitious attempt to meet the explosive population pressures of growing cities. Combining some sense of life in nature with the relatively high-density multiple dwelling, the urban suburb was typically realized on inner-city sites like so many of the private places. Its multistory multiple dwellings, frequently called garden apartments, rising no more than six stories, were set in greenery that often included decorative lawns as well as areas for active recreation. **Jackson Heights**, Queens, New York, the first urban suburb, introduced a higher density to the typical garden enclave or village. As such it could be seen as a response to its near neighbor Forest Hills Gardens (see p. 140). While Forest Hills Gardens is ruralesque in plan and conceived of as a totality in the tradition of the garden suburb planned for the outer ring of the metropolis, Jackson Heights is episodic in conception and absolutely rooted in the city's grid, creating its distinctiveness much as the private places of St. Louis had fifty years earlier. Begun in 1909, when real estate developer Edward A. MacDougall (1874–1944), president of the Queensboro Corporation, purchased 350 acres of undeveloped farmland and fields in northwest Queens, in the Trains Meadow section of Newtown, Jackson Heights was from the first conceived as a relatively dense housing enclave for middle- and upper-middle-income residents.[421] Nonetheless, despite the density, MacDougall was intent on conveying a gardenesque atmosphere.

Development activity in the still-rural borough was on the rise due to the opening of the Steinway Tunnels, Queensboro Bridge, and Pennsylvania Station, which provided easy rail and automobile connections to Manhattan. Roughly bound by Ninety-second and Seventieth Streets on the east and west, Jackson Avenue (renamed Northern Boulevard) and Roosevelt Avenue on the north and south, MacDougall named the tract Jackson Heights after John Jackson, president of the Hunters Point and Flushing Turnpike Company, which built the trolley line that ran along the road that bore his name. The fact that the site rose 65 feet above the surrounding farmland led MacDougall, a savvy real estate promoter, to attach the word "heights" to Jackson's name.

Jackson Heights was to be a gridded garden suburb densely developed with apartment houses as well as attached and single-family houses. MacDougall, after convincing the city to demap Trains Meadow Road, proceeded to pave streets and sidewalks and construct two dozen two-story rowhouses (1911) designed by Charles Peck (n.d.) along Eighty-second and Eighty-third Streets just north of Roosevelt Avenue, ordinary buildings similar to those MacDougall had built in the nearby communities of Woodside and Elmhurst. But in 1914, after a visit to Europe, MacDougall decided to change the direction of his development efforts, drawing inspiration from the growing garden suburb movement and from the expansive courtyard apartment houses being built in Berlin. MacDougall, who now determined to develop his buildings on a cooperative as opposed to rental basis, dramatically accelerated the pace of construction after 1917, when the extension along Roosevelt Avenue of the Corona elevated subway line connected Jackson Heights with Grand Central Terminal in a swift twenty minutes.

Although MacDougall would employ several different architects to realize Jackson Heights, it was the self-taught architect Andrew J. Thomas who was chiefly responsible for its special character, establishing a key principle in the design of the urban multiple dwelling—that the unit of planning should be the entire city block and not just the individual building. Precedents for this in New York can be traced as far back as the Tower and Home Buildings (William Field & Son, 1879) in Brooklyn, but Thomas took the idea much further, insisting that no more than 50 percent of the land be built upon, as opposed to the 70 percent permitted by law, and in his work in Jackson Heights in the late teens and early twenties the density levels sometimes were significantly lower, with buildings covering only 25 percent of the site.[422] As John Taylor Boyd Jr. noted, "the use of the block as a unit . . . reached its fullest development" at Jackson Heights "because the developers . . . owned a large tract of land which they were willing to develop over the period of years as an investment. Providing community amenities as well as housing accommodation, this little-known development is a sub-city within the city."[423]

By taking the city block as the unit of development, Thomas established at Jackson Heights a new urban-suburban multiple-dwelling type, the "garden apartment," a term he is generally credited with inventing, in which the courtyard, now the center of the entire block, was treated as a continuous landscaped green space that established what the historian Richard Plunz has described as "the illusion, if not the reality, of the house in a garden."[424] Thomas also separated the individual apartment houses from the sidewalks with narrow planting strips and from each other with planted side alleys, furthering the illusion of *rus in urbe* while allowing at least two exposures in each apartment and introducing into the multiple dwelling a sense of individuality hitherto almost exclusively associated with the single-family house.

Thomas's eclectic mix of essentially vernacular ornamental details, based for the most part on those used in Italian villas and Spanish farmhouses, particularized each building without compromising the status of the block as the development unit. Typical of his innovative work at Jackson Heights was the four-story, Spanish Renaissance–style Operation No. 8 (1919), 37-39 Eighty-fourth Street, later known as Linden Court, which prophetically included a garage for tenants' cars, and the Italianate Towers Apartments (1924), Eighty and Eighty-first Streets between Thirty-fourth and Jackson Avenues, where he made it possible to introduce additional apartments at the basement level by sinking the 80-foot-wide, 550-foot-long landscaped rear courtyard.

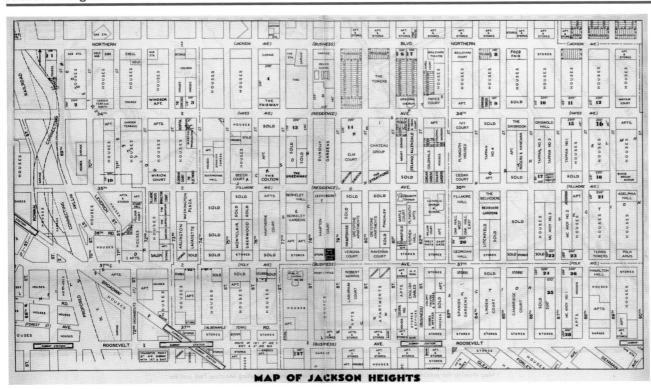

1

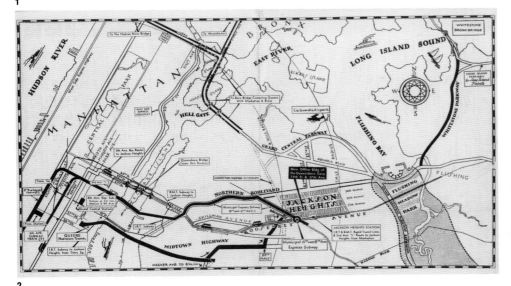

2

1. Map. DK (c. 1950)

2. Locator map. DK

3. The Chateau and The Towers apartment buildings, Andrew J. Thomas, 1924. MCNY

4. The Chateau. OMH (1928)

5. Plan, Operation No. 8, Andrew J. Thomas, 1919. AR20

6. Courtyard, The Towers. RAMSA (2012)

3

4

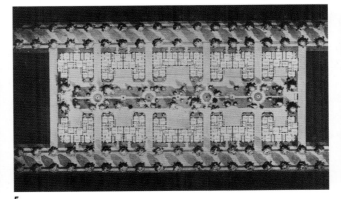

5

6

1. Block plan showing interior garden courts, Clarence S. Stein and Henry Wright, 1924. CHC

2. Plan for block of apartments and one- and two-family houses, 1924. COR

3. Aerial view. BETT (1929)

4. Typical courtyard. NYPL (c. 1930)

5. Gosman Avenue. NYPL (c. 1930)

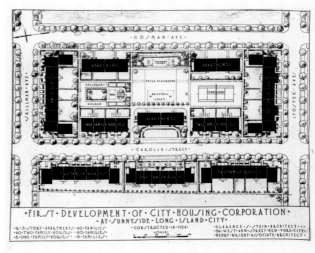

MacDougall promoted Jackson Heights with a sophisticated campaign that included mass advertising and fifteen-minute radio commercials. By 1925, after five years of construction yielded eight block-long garden apartment complexes, the Queensboro Corporation could boast that Jackson Heights was the largest community in the world of cooperatively owned garden apartment homes under a single management. In 1924 single-family houses were added to the mix; dubbed English Garden Homes, many were designed by Robert Tappan, who had succeeded Grosvenor Atterbury as consulting architect at Forest Hills Gardens. MacDougall also promised residents houses in the "restricted

garden residential section of New York City"—a not so subtle suggestion that Jews, Catholics, and blacks need not apply.[425] In addition to the housing, Jackson Heights included a coherently designed shopping center on Eighty-second Street, a twelve-hole golf course, thirty tennis courts, a motion picture theater, a community clubhouse named the Casino, and churches built on land donated by the developer.

In 1924, two miles west of Jackson Heights and therefore that much closer to midtown Manhattan, the City Housing Corporation began the development of **Sunnyside Gardens**, which embedded low-cost dwellings and garden suburb character within the city's

6

7

8

9

6–8. Typical views. RAMSA (2012)

9. Phipps Garden Apartments, Isadore Rosenfield, 1931. MCNY

grid.[426] Like Jackson Heights, Sunnyside Gardens also embraced the block as the unit of development rather than the house. Led by real estate developer and philanthropist Alexander M. Bing (1879–1959), who along with his brother Leo had made a fortune building high-end apartment houses in Manhattan, the goal of the City Housing Corporation, a limited-dividend company whose members were culled from the ranks of the Regional Plan Association of America (RPAA), was to provide well-designed homes for low-income workers in a felicitous setting. Dedicated to the ideals of "health, open space, greenery, and idyllic community living for all," Bing also pledged to provide a 6 percent return on investors' capital.[427] The City Housing Corporation purchased 77 undeveloped acres roughly bound by Forty-third (Laurel Hill) and Forty-ninth (Heiser) Streets, Skillman and Barnett Avenues, from the Long Island Rail Road, whose Sunnyside Yards were just north of the site. The sixteen-block area was served by the elevated Corona line, providing access to Grand Central Terminal in about fifteen minutes.

Architects Clarence S. Stein (1882–1959) and Henry Wright, founding members of the RPAA in 1923, were hired to plan the new community of 1,200 families. Wright had begun his career as a planner laying out

private places near St. Louis. Stein, working in the office of Bertram Grosvenor Goodhue (1869–1924), had been in charge of plans for the new city of Tyrone, New Mexico (see p. 849). Stein saw the cooperative development as a reaction against the poor conditions and ill-conceived planning of recently built, nearby housing, which he characterized as "endless rows of cramped shoddy wooden houses and garages [that] covered the land and destroyed natural green spaces." Reflecting on Sunnyside Gardens in his book *Toward New Towns for America* (1957) and with the experience of Radburn, another City Housing Corporation project, behind him, Stein noted that "the ultimate aim of the City Housing Corporation was to build a garden city" and that the "knowledge and experience gained at Sunnyside was intended to serve that objective." Stein observed that "most earlier well-intentioned American attempts at community housing for low-income workers had been tempted, by planners' delight in spacious elaboration, into becoming middle-class suburbs. Wright and I were determined to simplify and even squeeze our house plans so as to make them available at as low a price as possible. Economical spaciousness we hoped for as a result of judicious group planning."[428]

Although Stein and Wright had prepared studies proving the "unnecessary costliness of developments based on the typical gridiron layout," they were forced to work within the confines of such a grid because the Sunnyside area had already been laid out in blocks that were 190 to 200 feet wide and 600 to 900 feet long. Their plan ingeniously grouped 600 one-, two-, and three-family two-story rowhouses and nine apartment houses around an exceptionally generous amount of open space, much of it conceived as interior garden courts, with the buildings covering only 28 percent of the site. The open space consisted of private, 30-foot-deep rear gardens as well as 60-foot-wide shared central greenswards. The long blocks were broken up by east–west paths lined by London plane trees that connected adjacent streets and intersected with north–south paths granting access to the communal areas. Stein emphasized that the abundant amount of open space was hardly profligate, citing the example of Raymond Unwin and "his revolutionary pamphlet 'Nothing Gained by Overcrowding,'" which "had adequately proved that large open spaces could be preserved in block centers at practically no additional cost per lot, and with far less investment of capital or labor."[429]

Marjorie Sewell Cautley (1891–1954), placed in charge of the landscaping, enclosed the garden courts with modest hedges that marked the private areas behind each house while still promoting community hospitality and interaction in shared central malls. Cautley was also responsible for the design of the three-and-a-half-acre community park (1926) at the northeastern portion of the site. Although Stein and Wright devised the Sunnyside Gardens plan, they left most of the detailed architectural design to Frederick L. Ackerman (1878–1950), whose modest, even ugly buildings of the first wave of development were soon joined by more intentionally charming designs featuring imaginative brickwork. Stein did, however, design the public garage, as well as Wilson Court (1928), a group of eight four-story apartment houses, 43-02 to 43-38 Forty-seventh Street.

Lewis Mumford, another influential member of the RPAA who lived in Sunnyside Gardens from 1925 to 1936, first in an apartment house at 41-12 Forty-eighth Street and later in a rowhouse at 40-02 Forty-fourth Street, was an active booster, writing often about the development. Mumford and the architects were close friends, and his observations were quoted in pamphlets promoting the project (the stretch of Skillman Avenue running through the neighborhood was later given the honorary name Lewis Mumford Way). He was even able to find virtue in the bland aesthetics: that "no one of the . . . houses has any remarkable individuality" was something he regarded as a healthy abstemiousness, demonstrating

> how, with standardized plans and a few simple types of buildings, a whole may be built up which is much more sound and aesthetically satisfying than any amount of stylistic individuality and fake picturesqueness . . . The critic of architecture, who has looked eagerly for some attempt to

> use modern methods and materials in domestic building, and who perpetually is put off by the association of domesticity with archaeology, or, what is just as bad, the habit of giving new forms the flavor of hospital wards and barracks, will find more promise in Messrs. Stein and Wright's work at Sunnyside than in half the shady triumphs which are hailed as the beginning of a new epoch in architecture . . . Those who think we shall never have a good all-round architecture—as distinct from a handful of show-buildings—until the architect can design his single units with reference to the community as a whole will find a thrill of promise in Sunnyside.[430]

But housing reformer Louis H. Pink (1882–1955) was not so sure, writing in 1928 that Sunnyside Gardens had "none of the artistry" of John Nolen's Mariemont (see p. 266) or nearby Forest Hills Gardens. "It had no Grosvenor Atterbury to ensure architectural beauty. . . It lacks grace and charm. The flat roof predominates. There is little variety. The buildings are square boxes relieved only by good proportion. But for the tree and shrub planting and occasional window boxes and awnings, Sunnyside would be somber as well as plain." Still, Pink emphasized, "what it lacks in art it makes up in intelligence."[431] In 1931, three years after the completion of the low-rise portions of Sunnyside Gardens, a measure of Pink's concerns were addressed with the completion of the Phipps Garden Apartments, the aesthetic jewel of the complex, located on a vacant two-block site in the northeast corner of the development and sponsored by the Society of Phipps Houses, a model tenement group that purchased the property from the City Housing Corporation.[432] As designed by Isadore Rosenfield (1893–1980) of Clarence Stein's office, the four- and six-story brick buildings were organized around a large landscaped courtyard and geared toward the middle class, bringing a higher level of density along with greater architectural distinction.

Clarence Stein and Henry Wright's **Chatham Village** (1931), Pittsburgh, was conceived as "a modern community of garden homes" by its sponsors, the Buhl Foundation, a Pittsburgh-based charitable trust founded in 1928 after the death of Henry Buhl Jr. (1848–1927), owner of Boggs and Buhl, a prominent department store on the city's North Side, who set aside funds for the organization dedicated to improving conditions in Pennsylvania's Allegheny County.[433] Led by Charles F. Lewis (1890–1962), former chief editorial writer for the *Pittsburgh Sun*, the Buhl Foundation was organized as a limited-dividend company, but the group's philanthropic reach extended beyond model housing to include the support of cultural and educational institutions.[434]

Chatham Village was intended for about 200 low- to moderate-income families to be accommodated in clustered groups of rowhouses on a challenging 45-acre hillside site located in the Mount Washington section of Pittsburgh, across the Monongahela River and about one-and-a-half miles southwest of downtown's Golden

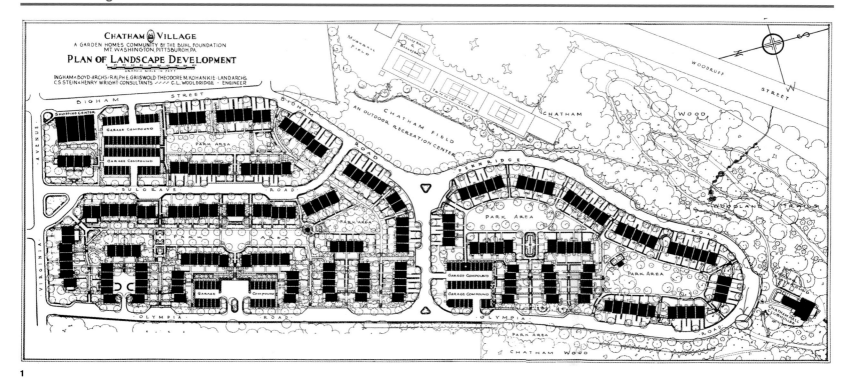

1

1. Plan, Clarence S. Stein and Henry Wright, 1931. SJH

Triangle business district. The site, the mid-nineteenth-century former Thomas Bigham estate, roughly bound by Virginia Avenue on the north, Woodruff Street on the east, Saw Mill Run Boulevard on the south, and the nine-acre Olympia Park on the west, was considered a good choice because of its commuting convenience to downtown by automobile, surrounding stable neighborhoods of single-family houses, and high elevation that was relatively smoke-free, then an important consideration in the Steel City.

Although Stein and Wright were initially committed to providing housing for clerical workers and others of modest means, Charles Lewis and the Buhl Foundation, alarmed by the ongoing economic tumult and concerned about the success of their first major venture, decided instead to target a professional class of workers and to rent rather than sell the dwelling units, seeking out "sound, middle class . . . folks who had achieved financial stability and who now wanted the social stability of just such a neighborhood of homes for their youngsters and themselves."[435] Or, as C. V. Starrett characterized this group of desired tenants: "white collar people with good taste."[436] Still, Lewis, who consulted on the tenant makeup of Chatham Village with City Housing Corporation administrator and Radburn veteran Herbert Emmerich (1897–1970), retained the naive and unrealized hope that lower-income workers would take over the vacated houses of middle-class Pittsburgh residents who moved into Chatham Village.

In light of their work at Radburn, Stein and Wright sought to provide Chatham Village with the density of an urban enclave while accommodating the project to the requirements of the automobile. Some off-street parking was provided in open lots, but the majority of

cars were stored in closed garages either grouped in isolated compounds or tucked below the houses. As at Radburn the houses turned their backs on the vehicular streets, but the internal walkways and greenswards were more intimately scaled, and the project as a whole benefited from the greater density of buildings to landscape that conveys a distinctly urban impression, but with a convincing enclave-like intimacy. Stein and Wright laid out the curvilinear streets to follow the topography of the hillside site and, unlike at Sunnyside Gardens and Radburn but closer to Garden City principles, were able to provide a 25-acre greenbelt that, along with the public park, protected the planned community on all but its northern border.

The principal development unit was the rowhouse grouped in rows of eight, although there were also smaller buildings, including semidetached two-unit houses. For the project, Stein and Wright served as consulting architects to the firm of Charles T. Ingham (1876–1960) and William Boyd (1882–1947) who were responsible for the design of the 197 Georgian-style red-brick houses, 129 completed in 1931–32, and 68, including larger four-bedroom units, built in 1935–36. Ingham & Boyd, who also designed other Buhl Foundation–sponsored projects in Pittsburgh, including the 1939 Institute of Popular Science and Planetarium, proved adept at introducing some variety in the similarly styled houses, randomly alternating hipped and gabled slate roofs. The Pittsburgh-based firm also designed two one-story Georgian-style commercial buildings at the northwest and southwest corners of Bigham Street and Virginia Avenue, six modest gardener's toolsheds scattered like follies throughout the site, and in 1936 renovated the Thomas Bigham house (1849) to serve as a community

2. Aerial perspective. SJH
(c. 1931)

3. Drawing of houses by
Ingham & Boyd. SJH (c. 1931)

2

3

center. Landscape architects Ralph E. Griswold (1907–1993) and Theodore Kohankie (1904–1992) added more than 500 trees, 4,000 shrubs, three miles of hedges, and 10 acres of lawns as part of the extensive greenbelt that was largely composed of virgin woodland.

Chatham Village was both an immediate and ongoing financial success, providing the Buhl Foundation with stable annual returns of over 4 percent and enjoying an extremely low turnover and vacancy rate, a not surprising development considering the affluence of the tenants. Catherine Bauer Wurster (1905–1964), a leading housing expert, deemed the project an artistic success as well, describing the neighborhood in 1934 as "probably the best example of modern planned housing in the country."[437] A quarter-century later, Lewis Mumford reiterated Wurster's endorsement, writing that "where the pressure of population remains high, the best way of meeting it is by reorganizing both city and suburb into more organic neighborhood units, such as that of Chatham Village . . . which combine compactness and urbanity with both domestic open spaces and local park areas. Since Chatham Village remains one of the high points in site planning and architectural layout of the last generation,

its failure to excite even local imitation remains inexplicable."[438] However, Jane Jacobs (1916–2006), in her 1961 polemic, *The Death and Life of Great American Cities*, offered a dissenting view that reflected her disdain for all garden enclaves and for suburbia in general. Criticizing the plan's "inevitable insularity," Jacobs concluded that "there is no public life here, in any city sense. There are differing degrees of extended private life."[439]

Stein's next New York City project, in the borough of the Bronx, was **Hillside Homes** (1932–35), consisting exclusively of multistory apartment buildings.[440] Starting out as merely "an architect's abstract conception without site, client, local precedent, or financing," Hillside Homes was to be "a self-contained residential neighborhood for desirable community living in apartments" that would be available at far lower rents than those charged at the Phipps Garden Apartments in Sunnyside Gardens.[441] The project got under way after Nathan Straus Jr. (1889–1961), who later served as head of the U.S. Housing Authority, sold a 26-acre site he owned in the northeast Bronx to the limited-dividend Hillside Housing Corporation, which financed the acquisition with the help of the federal government's newly created Public Works

4. Aerial view. SJH (c. 1931)

5. Internal walkways. SJH (c. 1931)

6, 7. Typical rowhouses and greensward. RAMSA (c. 1984)

8. Typical street. Garvin. AG (2012)

Administration (PWA). The size of the site and the lack of a strongly defined context propelled Stein toward a solution in which the unit of planning was no longer the city block but the superblock. But, as a result of a perhaps happy accident of bureaucratic recalcitrance—the city refused to close certain mapped but unbuilt streets—Stein was forced to maintain the traditional relationship between building and street.

At Hillside Homes, Stein distributed 1,400 apartments across five blocks. Because the site was ample and the population density relatively low, Stein was able to include generously proportioned courtyards, with some large enough to be used for active sports. Despite the project's expansiveness, the continuous wall of buildings and the splendidly framed gateways that connected one courtyard to another contributed a sense of security throughout the project. Stein was able to take advantage of the sloping site to provide a number of grade-level apartments suitable for the elderly, with private gardens abutting the interior courts. Virtually unornamented brick walls, punctuated by metal casement sash, achieved for Hillside Homes an almost perfect neutrality of expression, an astylar modernity that as accurately

reflected Stein's lack of concern for hothouse aesthetics as it documented the lull between two rushing stylistic currents, the traditional and the Modernist. Considered by some critics as Stein's masterpiece, Hillside Homes culminated the evolution of the courtyard type, at the same time introducing the looser site planning and idealized superblocking that would come to dominate post–World War II planning. Lewis Mumford found Hillside Homes "by far the most imposing and successful piece of domestic building" in New York, although he shared Stein's view that the existing street pattern was "obsolete and obstructive."[442]

The federal government expanded its role in the housing market beyond the work that the PWA inaugurated at Hillside Homes with the formation of the Federal Housing Administration (FHA), a product of the National Housing Act of 1934 that was created to stimulate the construction industry by insuring loans, a necessity in light of the banking system's collapse.[443] Inspired by the garden suburb model, **Colonial Village** (1935), Arlington, Virginia, was the first FHA project to move forward.[444] Located on a 55-acre site about two miles southwest of Georgetown, the project was built

1. Plan, Clarence S. Stein, 1932. COR

2. Aerial view. COR

3. Patio. COR (1935)

4. Entryway. RAMSA (1977)

5. Interior courtyard and passageway. Gottscho-Schleisner. MCNY (1935)

by local developer Gustave Ring (1910–1983), working in partnership with the New York Life Insurance Company and the FHA. Washington-based architect Harvey H. Warwick (1893–1972) prepared the plan for Colonial Village, to be realized in four stages.

Warwick's low-density plan grouped apartment houses around variously sized open courtyards, staggering the buildings to avoid monotony as well as provide light and ventilation. The 245 buildings accommodating 1,189 three- to five-room apartments occupied only 18 percent of the site, with a generous greenbelt located in roughly the center of the parcel and a smaller greenbelt placed along the western boundary. Pedestrian and automobile traffic was segregated. Warwick was responsible for the design of the Colonial Revival–style two-story redbrick apartment houses in the first three phases, completing 233 units by 1937. The development was an immediate success, and more than 15,000 applicants tried to secure apartments in Colonial Village, the large number credited in part to the modest rental price of the units as well as to the publicity surrounding the project. In 1940 Ring completed Colonial Village's fourth phase, consisting of twelve stylistically similar apartment buildings designed by Francis L. Koenig (1910–1993), but this last stage of development was not associated with the FHA insurance program.

Buckingham Village, a second FHA project in Arlington, was the last work of Henry Wright, with construction beginning a year after his death in 1937.[445] Intended for the middle class, Buckingham Village was developed by the Committee for Economic Recovery, a group of prominent businessmen led by Allie S. Freed (1891–1938). Wright's low-density plan for 100 acres of former farmland, prepared in collaboration with long-time associates Allan Kamstra (1896–1964) and Albert Lueders (n.d.), was intended to provide 2,000 dwelling units, with the buildings to occupy only 20 percent of the site. The project was also to include a community center, shops, a theater, and a school. Laura Bobeczko and Richard Longstreth describe the plan, which separated pedestrian and automobile traffic, as a "denser and more tightly structured arrangement than at Colonial Village."[446] Oscar Fisher, writing in *Architectural Record* in 1938, noted that "heavy traffic is shunted around the community. Local traffic is slowed down by means of narrow angular streets. This is accomplished without recourse to costly curved roads or the now popular cul-de-sac streets. Parking bays in the streets provide an innovation which preserves the full street width for traffic and an orderliness not otherwise possible. The parking bays grew out of the need to provide for the Washingtonians' habit of parking outdoors rather than in garages."[447]

Only a 25-acre portion bound by North Glebe Road, Fifth Street North, North Oxford Street, and Second Street North was built according to Wright's plan. This first phase consisted of fifty-two two-story Colonial Revival–style apartment buildings placed in straight rows or grouped in a U-shaped arrangement around

Colonial Village

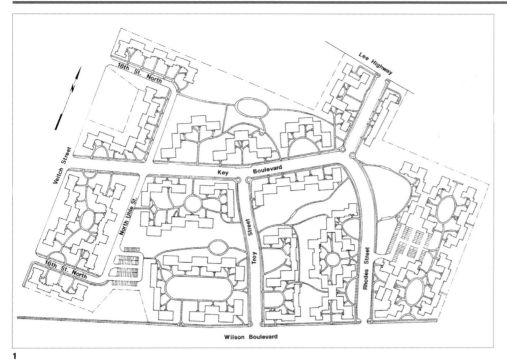

1. Plan, Harvey H. Warwick, 1935. NGAL (1985)

2. Apartment houses and pedestrian path. LOCP (c. 1950)

3. Apartment houses. Arl. FL (2008)

2

3

Buckingham Village

1

1. Aerial view. GE (2011)

2, 3. Apartment houses and landscaped courtyards. LOCP (c. 1937)

2

3

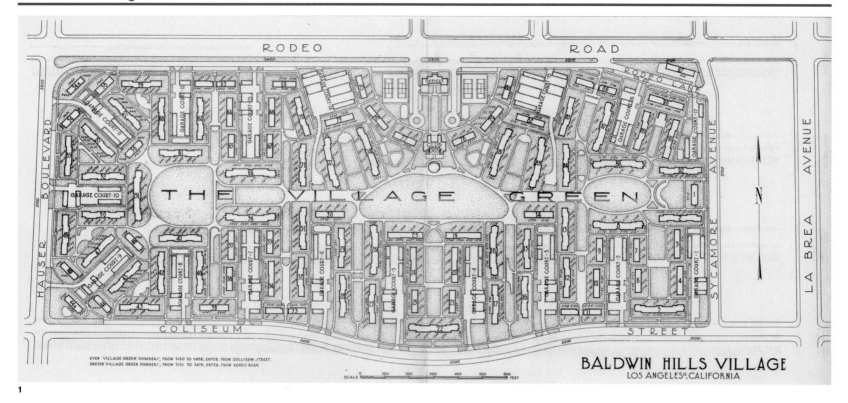

1

1. Plan, Clarence S. Stein,
1941. COR

landscaped courtyards. In a nod to the Modernist move-ment, Wright also included a three-story flat-roofed brick apartment building with balconies. Kamstra and Lueders oversaw additional development at Bucking-ham until 1953, adding stylistically similar two-story apartment buildings as well as semidetached units and a denser arrangement of three-story apartment buildings on a 38-acre site.

Clarence Stein considered his design for **Baldwin Hills Village** (1941), Los Angeles, the "complete and most characteristic expression" of the Radburn idea.[448] It is ironic that it was built in a city Stein acknowledged as particularly challenging because of the dominance of the automobile. The elements of Radburn adopted at Bald-win Hills Village—the superblock, complete separation of pedestrian and automobile, and the use of a park to focus the community away from the street—were inher-ently alien to the general uniformity of the surrounding city fabric with its established neighborhoods of grid-ded blocks lined with mostly small single-family houses and its new subdivisions of looping roads. The 80-acre, 1,100-by-2,750-foot site accommodating 627 families was developed with about eight apartments per acre, and only 15 percent of the site was covered by buildings, including garages. Fourteen percent of the budget was spent on landscaping, but only at the expense of the no-frills architecture designed by the well-known designer of luxury houses, Reginald D. Johnson (1882–1952), in association with Lewis Wilson (1900–1957), Edwin Mer-rill (n.d.), and Robert Alexander (1907–1992).

The surrounding subdivisions, mocked by one Baldwin Hills Village supporter for their "'unimagi-native" front-yard, side-yard concept, were built with freestanding houses at roughly half the density of Bald-win Hills Village, raising the question of whether or not the development was a suitable experiment for Los Angeles.[449] But Stein's surprisingly "symmetrical and balanced" plan, as George C. Randall has noted, with "spaces [that] tend to flow in and out while at the same time narrowing and expanding," yielded an "ordered" village "without being pompous or repetitive." Ran-dall also believed that the garden courts were "a notable improvement on Radburn's narrow pathways that led to a central park. The pedestrian greenways insure privacy while interconnecting the community. No cross-streets cut the block apart."[450]

Fresh Meadows, Queens, New York, is a hybrid case: an enclave within the city planned to function as a village. Despite being embedded in the city's grid, Fresh Meadows was laid out almost as if on a sprawling site in open country. The large area bound by Kissena Park Corridor, Cunningham Park, Union Turnpike, and Flushing Meadows-Corona Park included a 50-acre tract that had been planned in 1905 as a development called Utopia, a "Jewish colony" intended for residents relo-cated from Manhattan's Lower East Side.[451] The streets of Utopia, which lay between what became 164th Street and Fresh Meadow Lane, Horace Harding Boulevard and Jewell Avenue, were intended to be named after streets on the Lower East Side, like Ludlow, Hester, and Divi-sion. The scheme failed, however, and the land was sold in 1911. The area began to take on an affluent character at that time, and a country club was established to its east, at Fresh Meadows. In 1946 the club relocated and sold the land to the New York Life Insurance Company, which built an innovative housing project there over the

2. Aerial view. GE (2006)

3. Pedestrian path. Lowe. COR

4. Apartment houses and landscaped courtyard. RAMSA (1984)

5. Apartment houses. Wilson. COR

next three years, designed by Voorhees, Walker, Foley & Smith.[452] An attempt to synthesize the garden suburb tradition with the vertical garden city idea of Le Corbusier (1887–1965), Fresh Meadows, realized on a 170-acre site roughly bound by 186th and 197th Streets, Horace Harding Boulevard, and Seventy-third Avenue, was New York Life's deliberate answer to its rival Metropolitan Life's developments in Los Angeles (Parklabrea)[453] and San Francisco (Parkmerced)[454]—where pre–World War II plans for two-story garden apartment enclaves were, in the aftermath of the war, compromised by the seemingly random introduction of high-rise towers—and to Metropolitan Life's Parkchester[455] in the Bronx and Stuyvesant Town[456] in Manhattan, which were super-urban in density. Fresh Meadows was distinctly suburban in scale and density: if it had been built at the density of Stuyvesant Town, Fresh Meadows would have housed 75,000 people instead of the 11,000 who were accommodated.

The principal feature of the design was the sprawling, spacious site plan, in which buildings covered less than 15 percent of the site. As Otto L. Nelson, New York Life's vice president, explained, the development was intended to function "not merely as 'housing' but as a complete residential community for a healthful and pleasant life for the whole family—particularly the family with children."[457] The site plan faintly echoed the organizing ideas of its relatively nearby, rail-focused predecessor, Forest Hills Gardens, but in a way that more directly responded to the automobile, with Forest Hills Gardens' Station Square echoed in a shopping center and green marking the principal entrance at Horace Harding Boulevard, a main thoroughfare targeted for rebuilding as an expressway. Just beyond the green, along 188th

Street, the principal north–south spine, stood two apartment towers, vertical elements equivalent to the hotel at Forest Hills Gardens' Station Square, except that here they were isolated in a sea of green and not linked to lower buildings to form a cloister.

While an echo of the strongly articulated streetscape at Forest Hills Gardens could be felt in the occasional ovals and miniparks that interrupted the flow of the principal streets in Fresh Meadows, there was none of the earlier development's hierarchy of street patterns or its sense of a sequence of movement through the project area. Gone were the street pictures of Forest Hills Gardens and the metaphorical journey from city to country that they enabled. Gone, in fact, was the sense of village; Fresh Meadows instead suggested a landscaped park with buildings scattered in it. Fresh Meadows had almost no discernable governing geometry; its site plan not only lacked geometric rigor, but it failed to embrace the deterministic planning of Radburn. At Fresh Meadows, the intention was to bring the car to the door but to maintain private open space by grouping the units in quadrangles—"a series of enclaves," as Martin Meyerson wrote, "that create a sense of small social groups within the larger one" and provide "communal space for all age-groups."[458] The principal landscape feature was a 20-acre central open area, which had been the immediate setting for the clubhouse of the golf course. The apartment towers, the nursery, and, oddly, a garage were the only buildings permitted to encroach on this space.

The contracts for construction of the 3,200-unit housing estate were let in 1946, before the architects, assisted by New York Life's in-house architect, G. Harmon Gurney (1896–1985), had completed the plans.

1. Plan, Voorhees, Walker, Foley & Smith, 1946. ADA

2. Diagrams showing, from top to bottom, green spaces, circulation patterns, garage locations, recreation spaces, and commercial areas. ADA

3. Aerial view. NYSA (1951)

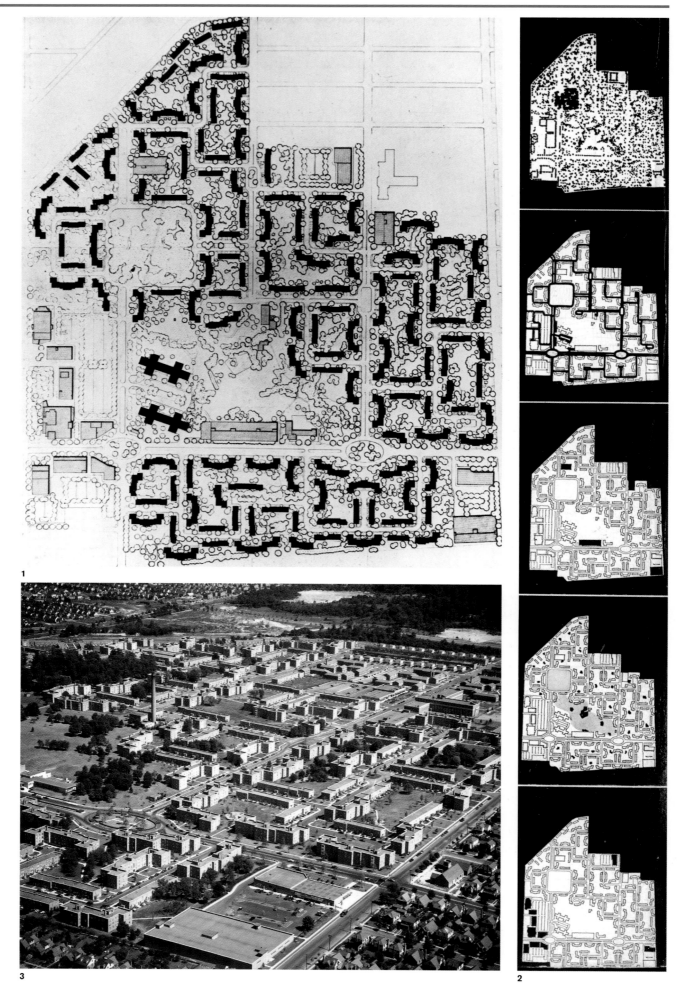

1

3

2

4

5

6

Fresh Meadows' two thirteen-story towers housed a total of 600 families amid the mixture of seventy-two two-story and sixty-eight three-story buildings housing the remainder of the residents. In addition to the village center, two neighborhood shopping centers as well as a community center were provided to meet the needs of the population. Off-street spaces for 1,000 cars were provided in central garages.

Fresh Meadows was more notable for its generous greenery than for the design of its redbrick, flat-roofed, lightly detailed buildings, which did not hold up to close scrutiny on an individual basis. As *Architectural Record* put it: "The buildings do not assert their smartness in the current vocabulary; neither do they hum softly in the sweetness of yesterday. They do not impress one with the gadgetry of sun control or factory assembly. Their effect, aesthetically, is a great, timeless unobtrusiveness."[459]

Lewis Mumford disagreed with the *Record*'s editors. Mumford had high praise for the development, whose design he said was pervaded by "order and comeliness and charm." He explained: "The community as a whole is probably the best-looking piece of architecture in the metropolitan area, for it presents a series of architectural compositions, executed with a varied play of light and shade, of masses and volumes, and of color, that have all but disappeared from the urban architect's repertoire." He also extolled the project's low density—seventeen units to the acre—and its extraordinary amount of open space: "Apart from those two dominating thirteen-story apartment houses, the human scale (one- to three-story buildings) has everywhere been maintained, and the aesthetic qualities are balanced by human qualities."[460]

For Mumford, Fresh Meadows was the culmination of a sequence of projects that began with Sunnyside Gardens and continued outside of New York with Radburn, the Greenbelt towns (see p. 283), and Baldwin Hills Village. But his assessment was based more on "quality of life" issues than on physical planning. "In general," he wrote, "the field has been divided between the conscious and unconscious disciples of Le Corbusier, who believes that even a village should be a skyscraper on stilts, and the disciples of Frank Lloyd Wright, who believes that cities should be abolished and that everyone should have at least an acre of land to live on. Neither school is producing the sort of city we all seem to have forgotten, the city in which it is a pleasure and a convenience to live."[461] Fresh Meadows, according to Mumford, was "the only large-scale project I know of that rivals Baldwin Hills Village . . . and it is the only one in this part of the country, except Greenbelt, in Maryland, that presents a detailed view of what the residential neighborhoods of our cities would be like if they were planned not merely with a view to creating a safe, long-term investment but also to promote the comfort, the joy, and the equability of their inhabitants."[462] For Mumford, Fresh Meadows was a superscaled garden enclave, a bridge between city and country, and a viable model for the redevelopment of outlying urban areas: "Fresh Meadows is a distinctly urban section, part and parcel of a big city. And because its density of population . . . is almost the minimum that can be expected in a city, it sets a basic pattern for the ideal reconstruction of the outer metropolitan area: a vision of harmony, order, and joy. Fresh Meadows is not a temporary refuge from overcrowding; it exemplifies the sort of city planning and building that would decrease the need for rural hideouts and escapist bungalow colonies."[463]

Mumford's enthusiasm notwithstanding, the bland architecture and loose open space robbed Fresh Meadows of the vitality that came with previous compact garden suburbs like Forest Hills Gardens or Jackson Heights. Situated at a tipping point, Fresh Meadows, it can be argued, had as much to do with postwar sprawl as with the garden suburb tradition.

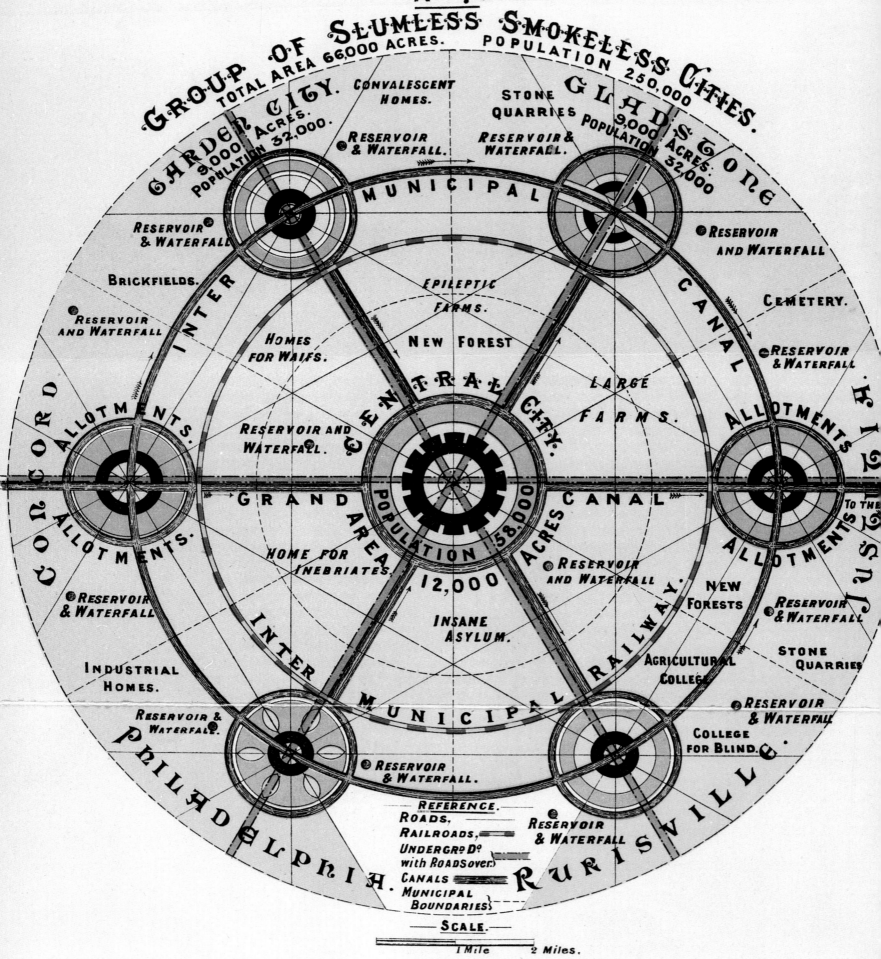

CHAPTER THREE

The Garden City in Europe and America 1869–1940

The garden city is an independent entity near a metropolis but with its own industry, government, and, of course, residential neighborhoods. Although garden cities were established in England and the United States before 1900 (for example, Port Sunlight), it was not until Ebenezer Howard codified the Garden City as an idea and an ideal that the term began to be widely used and frequently misused to describe what were in fact garden suburbs—i.e. garden villages having the components of a town but with no significant industry, and garden enclaves, which are purely residential. Garden suburbs, in short, were conceived as parts or dependencies of large cities; garden cities were intended to be largely self-sufficient.

The Garden City movement coalesced in 1898, when Howard, an unassuming career stenographer and avocational inventor, published *To-morrow: A Peaceful Path to Real Reform*, proposing an ideal city, Garden City, as a "master key" capable of solving the problems of industrialized society.[1] Howard envisioned a prototypical city that was limited in population, surrounded by a protected rural belt, relatively self-sufficient, with a mix of agriculture and industry providing local jobs for residents, and most important but also most often forgotten, cooperatively owned by its residents, a component that would prove difficult to achieve in reality. Howard proposed Garden City as a way to stem the migration of the population from the country to the city, a phenomenon that was leaving rural areas depressed and cities overcrowded with a poor, and poorly housed, working class.

Envisioning town and country as magnets to which people, like needles, were drawn, Howard felt the solution was not to improve conditions in one or the other but to create a third magnet "of yet greater power"—Town-Country, or Garden City—that offered the benefits of both and the problems of neither, an alternative "in which all the advantages of the most energetic and active town life, with all the beauty and delight of the country, may be secured in perfect combination; and the certainty of being able to live this life will be the magnet which will produce the effect for which we are all striving—the spontaneous movement of the people from our crowded cities to the bosom of our kindly mother earth, at once the source of life, of happiness, of wealth, and of power . . . Town and country *must be married*," Howard wrote, "and out of this joyous union will spring a new hope, a new life, a new civilization."[2]

Surprising even its author, the book sold well, and the movement was begun. In 1899, the Garden City Association was founded to promote Howard's idea, and in 1902, by which time the association counted 1,300 members, *To-morrow* was republished in a slightly abridged edition as *Garden Cities of To-morrow*. The same year, the Garden City Pioneer Company was established to look for a site upon which to demonstrate Howard's concept, leading to the development of Letchworth, or as it was initially known, First Garden City. By 1914, *To-morrow* had been widely translated and Garden City associations were active in eleven countries. The very term "garden

Diagram from *To-Morrow: A Peaceful Path to Real Reform*, Ebenezer Howard, 1898. FGC

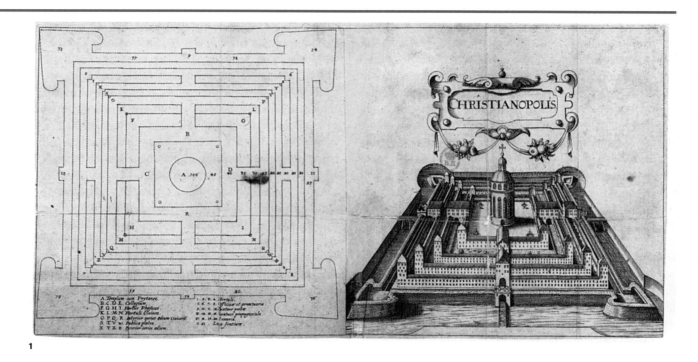

1

city" had come to obtain such wide currency by this time and to be used so indiscriminately to describe virtually any type of arcadian suburb that Howard was moved in 1910 to write to the editor of *Builder* magazine in an attempt to clarify the terminology:

> A "garden city" is a self-contained town—industrial, agricultural, residential—planned as a whole, and occupying land sufficient to provide garden-surrounded homes for at least 30,000 persons, as well as a wide belt of open fields. It combines the advantages of town and country, and prepares the way for a national movement stemming the tide of the population now leaving the countryside and sweeping into our overcrowded cities.
>
> A "garden suburb" provides that the normal growth of existing cities shall be on healthy lines; and when such cities are not already too large such suburbs are most useful, and even in the case of overgrown London they may be, though, on the other hand, they tend to drive the country yet further afield, and do not deal with the root evil—rural depopulation.
>
> "Garden villages," such as Bournville and Port Sunlight, are garden cities in miniature, but depend upon some neighboring city for water, light, and drainage; have not the valuable provision of a protective belt, and are usually the centre of one great industry only.[3]

But Lewis Mumford, one of Howard's key disciples, was to clarify the concept more definitively: "The Garden City, as Howard defined it, is not a suburb but the antithesis of a suburb: not a more rural retreat, but a more integrated foundation for an effective urban life."[4] Garden cities, including those that preceded Howard's specific vision and those that were influenced by his example, may represent a place to escape the city but not a repudiation of the city. Equally important, garden cities embrace and accommodate a diversity of social classes, from the middle-class residents of Letchworth and Welwyn, to the factory workers of Port Sunlight and Pullman.

UTOPIAN PRECEDENTS

The paradoxical concept of a "garden city," although most closely associated with the movement spawned by Howard, was part of an ongoing search in the nineteenth century and even before by reformers, industrialists, and speculators alike who began to devise alternatives to increasingly filthy and overcrowded cities. Underlying its call for a new type of city was the vision of a vastly reworked ideal society, placing Garden City both in the long tradition of "utopias"—a word coined by Thomas More (1478–1535) for the title of his 1516 book—and in the realm of practical urban planning. Lewis Mumford has pointed to Leonardo da Vinci's proposal of the early 1490s to expand Milan with a series of ten satellite cities, each limited in population, as a precedent of Garden City.[5] The earliest utopian scheme to which conceptual threads of Garden City can be traced is that of Johann Valentin Andreae (1586–1654), a prominent German Lutheran theologian who in 1619 published *The Description of a Christian Republic*, in which the narrator finds himself shipwrecked on an island where, after passing a moral examination, he is granted entry into the walled utopia of **Christianopolis**.[6] Presented toward the end of the Reformation's religious violence, Andreae's vision was for a peaceful Christian civilization guided by rectitude, communality, education, and justice, with no need for private property, currency, luxurious material items, or prisons, and where residents would have "very few working hours" because there would be no idle leisure class relying on the labor of others.[7]

As a part of his treatise, Andreae included a plan and rendering of Christianopolis showing a square city in which four concentric bands of buildings alternated with open spaces inside a battered fortification wall measuring 700 feet on each side. At the center stood a circular, 100-foot-diameter, 70-foot-high tower containing a church and council chamber. A college, with educational, cultural, and scientific wings, occupied the innermost buildings, surrounded by two rings of three-story apartment buildings and an outer ring of businesses, warehouses, slaughterhouses, and the like, each side of the square dedicated to a different purpose. The degree to which Andreae's plan was influential on Howard is not known, but Lewis Mumford commented in 1922 that Andreae's zoning "anticipated the best practice that has been worked out today, after a century of disorderly building."[8] Notwithstanding the clarity and innovation of Andreae's plan, Patrick Abercrombie (1879–1957), the English town planner best known for his Greater London Plan (1944) and who, through the writings of Mumford, would have a profound influence on American housing practice in the 1920s, criticized "the typical Renaissance absence of any idea of growth . . . The city is described as a finite community complete at the moment of visiting. There is no feeling of a living organism. Nor are we told that the surplus population migrates elsewhere to form colonies or sister towns according to our garden city principle."[9]

With the emergence of industrialization in the early nineteenth century, and the accompanying population shifts from rural to urban areas, the idea of utopia was reborn with a new sense of urgency. As planning historian E. A. Gutkind has written:

The utopias of the 19th century were fundamentally different from those of the preceding periods. True, their avowed aim was the improvement of the living conditions of mankind, and in a general though rather ambiguous manner, they invoked moral principles as the justification of their ideas. But the gap between utopian dreams and feasible social reforms was narrowing . . . The utopians of the 19th century were blatantly materialistic, trying to be as pragmatic as possible, so much so, that one is almost inclined to attribute to them a shrewd sense of opportunism in the hope that their schemes would be taken more seriously if they adapted their ideas to "what might be possible" and relegated idealistic dreaming to the role of a skeleton in the cupboard.[10]

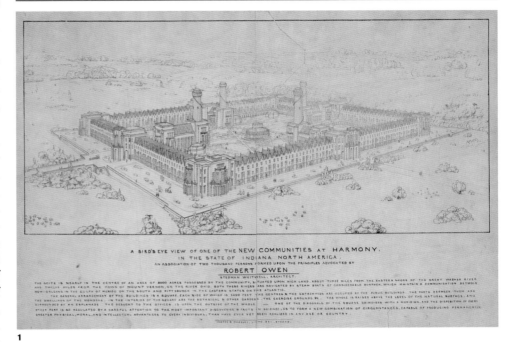

1

The Welshman Robert Owen (1771–1858), whose tangible success with instituting labor reforms in his New Lanark, Scotland, textile mills spurred him to take his ideas further, proposed prototypical "Agricultural and Manufacturing Villages of Unity and Mutual Cooperation," (see p. 699) one of which he attempted to realize at **New Harmony**, Indiana. Had it been a success, New Harmony would have housed a population of 1,200 in a single, rectangular, courtyard-enclosing megastructure, with stables and industrial mills placed in the nearby countryside that was otherwise devoted to farmland.[11] Unquestionably, as the editors of *The Garden City*, the journal of the Garden City Association that began publication in 1904, made clear, Owen's project, despite its failure, was an important step toward Howard's idea. Nonetheless, the editors objected to Owen's willingness to consider "high dwellings necessary, even on the prairie lands of America." They also objected to the proposed structure designed by Stedman Whitwell (1784–1840), a pupil of John Soane's, which "looks like a large prison or asylum on the outside, with a sort of graveyard in the interior, and is conspicuous for the absence of beauty in its architecture."[12]

Robert Owen's French contemporary François Marie Charles Fourier (1772–1837) also gave architectural expression to a utopia, in his case a proposal, published in 1829, calling for communities known as phalanxes, in which 5,000 acres of agricultural land would surround a so-called **phalanstère**, a sprawling, three-winged building modeled on the royal palace at Versailles, intended to house 1,620 people (two examples each of the 810 types of human nature Fourier had identified) as well as most components of a complete city.[13] The phalanxes were to be cooperatively owned, allowing citizens to share in profits. Fourier fantastically expected the world's population to eventually reside in two million phalanxes, but as

1. Bird's-eye view, Stedman Whitwell, 1825. LOCP

1. Depiction of a *phalanstère* by
Jules Arnoult based on Fourier's
ideas. CFVW (1840s)

2. *La Phalange*, volume 1,
showing Victor Considerant's
design for a *phalanstère*.
CFVW (1836)

1

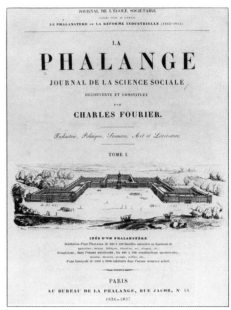

2

Familistère

1

2

3

4

1. Panorama showing
Familistère on left.
CFG (1864)

2. Schools and theater. Velvet.
WC (2010)

3. Engraving. CFG (1871)

4. Central pavilion. Velvet. WC
(2010)

E. A. Gutkind has written, he "was not a paper idealist. He was convinced that his Ideal City was an eminently practical possibility that could and would become a realistic fact. His program was aimed at the abolition of the wage earner, who would be transformed into a property owner on the joint-stock principle, with the cooperation of capital and labor, thus making one and the same person producer and consumer, debtor and creditor."[14]

Fourier never found a sponsor to implement his plan, but his ideas were widely embraced, particularly in the United States, where twenty or more phalanxes were attempted by followers, largely due to the efforts of Albert Brisbane (1809–1890), who translated and popularized Fourier's writings while eliminating some of their more eccentric aspects.[15] None of the American phalanxes can be considered a success—most were plagued by financial problems and infighting—but several scraped by for more than a few years, including the North American Phalanx, near Red Bank, New Jersey (1843–55), with its community of one hundred that favorably impressed Frederick Law Olmsted, and the Wisconsin Phalanx (1844–50), counting 180 members.[16]

The failed community of La Réunion (1853–69), in Dallas, Texas, the overly ambitious project of Victor

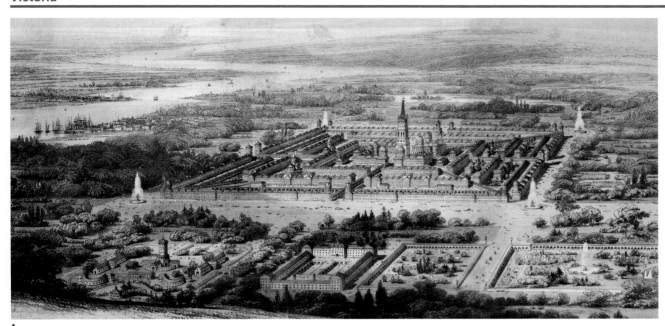

1

Considerant (1808–1893), Fourier's most committed disciple, marked the last gasp of American Fourierism.[17] Among La Réunion's financial backers was Jean-Baptiste Andrè Godin (1817–1888), a French entrepreneur and industrialist who invented a popular cast-iron stove and, after witnessing the failure of so many American phalanxes, decided to adapt the form to house employees of his ironworks in the northern French town of Guise, envisioning "an entire city for the workers," as he wrote in 1853, "in which true comfort could be offered to them, in contrast to the state in which they are living at the present time."[18] In 1859, Godin began work on an 18-acre site divided in two by the River Oise, with the factory located east of the river and the town on the west, dominated by what Godin termed the **Familistère** (1859–80), the name being a portmanteau of *famille* and *phalanstère*. Also known as the Social Palace, the Familistère consisted of three four-story rectangular buildings connected at their corners by galleries. Like Fourier, Godin modeled the form on the palace of Versailles, reflecting his belief that "since it is impossible to make a palace of the cottage or hovel of every working family, we have aimed to place the worker's dwelling in a palace."[19] But Godin's structure was only a fraction of the size of the *phalanstère* and was reserved solely for residential use, with separate buildings provided for schools, stores, a theater, library, printing office, baths, and a laundry as well as nurseries and advanced childcare facilities, constituting, all in all, a village that was developed over twenty years and lasted as a cooperative until 1968.

In 1849, James Silk Buckingham (1786–1855), a widely traveled English journalist, publisher, and Member of Parliament (1832–37) who, while living for four years (1837–41) in the United States, was taken with the communal lifestyle he observed in the Rappite village of Economy, Pennsylvania, and the German Separatist

settlement of Zoar, Ohio, published *National Evils and Practical Remedies, with the Plan of a Model Town*, a book in which he not only railed against society's ills but put forth, in two hundred pages of text accompanied by two engravings, his vision for a complete, self-sufficient ideal city.[20] Buckingham's town of **Victoria**, named to honor the Queen and also to commemorate "a great moral 'victory' over many of the evils that now afflict society," was to be home to no more than 10,000 residents living within a one-mile-square, 620-acre community surrounded by a 10,000-acre agricultural belt.[21] Ebenezer Howard identified the unrealized scheme as one of three specific forerunners of his Garden City—the others were ideas on organized population migration, put forward by Edward Gibbon Wakefield (1796–1862) and Alfred Marshall (1842–1924), and land nationalization, advocated by Thomas Spence (1750–1814) and Herbert Spencer (1820–1903)—though he claimed not to have seen it until after having developed Garden City's basic principles.

Buckingham, a disciple of Robert Owen who also intended his scheme to be the prototype for many more such cities, called for the formation of a Model-Town Association to develop and retain ownership of Victoria's land, houses, factories, and materials. Every resident would be required to own shares in the association. The hypothetical site was located on a navigable river, not far from the coast. The plan was made up of concentric squares cut through by eight 80-foot-wide radial avenues, closely resembling Christianopolis and also recalling the geometry of Owen's Village of Unity and Mutual Cooperation. Like Christianopolis, the center of Victoria was to be dedicated to academic and public buildings around which the city's concentric square bands would alternate between residences, streets, parks, gardens, public buildings, and glass-covered arcades accommodating workshops and stores. A public park was to sit just outside of town. Residents were to be bound by a strict social code that, if broken, would lead to their expulsion.

Although the project never went forward, many of its ideas endured. The editors of *The Garden City* considered Victoria to be "probably the first proposal made in English history for creating an entirely new city from the beginning." The editors went on to say that while standards of hygiene and architecture along with population limits had been "present in the minds of all who have conceived the idea of building a model city," with "Buckingham's proposal to have a permanent belt of agricultural land round the town, and to form his factories in a ring on the outer edge of the town area, we cannot but be struck with the extraordinary similarity between his scheme and that outlined by Ebenezer Howard in 'Tomorrow.'"[22]

As Howard explained: "Though in outward form Buckingham's scheme and my own present the same feature of a model town set in a large agricultural estate, so that industrial and farming pursuits might be carried on in a healthy, natural way, yet the inner life of the two communities would be entirely different—the inhabitants of Garden City enjoying the fullest rights of free association, and exhibiting the most varied forms of individual and co-operative work and endeavor, the members of Buckingham's city being held together by the bonds of a rigid cast-iron organization, from which there could be no escape but by leaving the association, or breaking it up into various sections."[23]

The editors of *The Garden City*, devoutly attached to the low densities that had come to define garden city development, took issue with Victoria's density, arguing that, given the presence of an agricultural belt, the population could have been spread over twice the area, thereby "housing the people in small two storey dwellings, and providing broad tree-planted avenues with wide margins of grass along each side," rather than expensive 100-foot-wide paved streets lined by terraces.[24] Patrick Abercrombie, however, noted that not only had Buckingham devoted equal acreage to streets and houses—almost 180 acres to each—but he far exceeded modern standards of green space that would have called for 50 to 62 acres as opposed to Buckingham's 160 acres (not including 20 acres of indoor recreational space). "Generally speaking," wrote Abercrombie, "when it is considered that certain of the inhabitants would work in the fields and in detached factories, the space allowed inside the town is too lavish, at any rate as regards working areas; the town, indeed would appear barely inhabited."[25]

Overall, Abercrombie and his peers were most impressed by the very breadth and detail of Buckingham's plan for Victoria—"neither a glorified building estate, nor the appendage of a factory, but an honest attempt to visualize a reasonable state of civic existence as a whole."[26] Writing in 1922, Lewis Mumford applauded that, with "definite plans and specifications, accompanied by drawings . . . this is surely one of the first attempts

to put a problem in social engineering on a basis from which an engineer or an architect could work."[27] As John Nelson Tarn later concluded, Victoria may be most significant for its integration of country and town, its alternating terraces and green spaces giving rise to "a garden city which was urban in concept—a contradiction in terms according to the subsequent definition of a modern garden suburb."[28] In contrast to Victoria, utopias

which came later in the century were essentially rural, or semi-rural at best . . . This urban tradition in a sense was the legacy of the eighteenth century, although horribly debased and plagiarized; an aristocratic and essentially English tradition, humbled and interpreted for the myriad masses, continuing to be popular because the terrace was the cheapest way to build houses. The tradition died during the nineteenth century, slowly and imperceptibly; first the aristocracy lost faith in the town, were attracted to villa-dom and then the lure of suburbia percolated downwards until in the twentieth century the concept of the closely built town was replaced by a new and anti-urban attitude to housing, for every class.[29]

Buckingham's Victoria impressed at least one other utopian whose scheme can be seen as a stepping-stone to the Garden City. In 1854, Robert Pemberton (1788–1879), about whom little is known—he is thought to have been a philanthropist who resided in London and Paris—published *The Happy Colony*, his proposal to build ten 20,000-acre model "garden cities" in New Zealand, choosing that distant country because of the ease with which land could be acquired.[30] The first so-called **Happy Colony** was to be named Queen Victoria Town. The two drawings in which Pemberton presented the scheme showed a circular town, about a mile in diameter, "taking the form of belts or rings, which will become larger as they recede from the center." Pemberton explained the geometry by arguing, with some exaggeration, that "all the grand forms in nature are round—the sun, moon, stars, planets, our world, the human form, animals, trees, and perhaps, everything in the animate creation." Pragmatically, he acknowledged the circle's advantages to traffic planning: "Right angles are opposed to the harmony of motion, and in a town there must be motion; therefore, the best method for the free circulation of man and beast must be adopted. You must make up your minds," he declared, "to abandon the system of the old countries in everything relating to the bad formation of towns as well as the bad formation of minds; and discard, and for ever renounce all crooked lanes, angles, narrow streets, filthy alleys, and nasty courts and *impattes*." In the Happy Colony, all streets would be "wide, spacious, and planted with ornamental trees."[31]

Recalling the plan for Chaux (see p. 727) by Claude-Nicolas Ledoux (1736–1806), the center of Happy Colony was to feature a 50-acre circle outlined by four curving, classical-style pavilions functioning together as

1

2

a Natural University. Pemberton consolidated manu-facturing buildings in the second ring from the center, reserving the outer rings for houses and gardens and the outermost ring for a park measuring three miles in circumference. Circular tree-lined streets continued to ripple out through the farms and orchards of the sur-rounding landscape. Circulation to and from the center was provided by eight radial avenues. Taken together, the ten interconnected colonies anticipated Howard's Gar-den City diagram.

Howard's **Garden City** idea synthesized elements of these proposals with a pragmatic sensibility steeped in the late nineteenth century's atmosphere of social reform. In his introduction to the 1946 edition of *Garden Cities of To-morrow*, Mumford underscored the signifi-cance of Howard's proposal: "At the beginning of the twentieth century two great new inventions took form before our eyes: the aeroplane and the Garden City, both harbingers of a new age: the first gave man wings and the second promised him a better dwelling-place when he came down to earth." Yet Mumford had to acknowl-edge an unfortunate reality, that while "*Garden Cities of To-morrow* has done more than any other single book to guide the modern town planning movement and to alter its objectives . . . it has met the traditional misfortune of the classic: it is denounced by those who have plainly never read it and it is sometimes accepted by those who have not fully understood it." [32]

Ironically, the book that would have such a conse-quential impact on town planning did not include a specific urban plan or architectural designs. Howard was not a designer. He was a stenographer, a man of words, concerned more with social matters than physical planning. His book *To-morrow: A Peaceful Path to Real*

Reform described Garden City in 176 pages of text and seven drawings that he clearly marked "Diagram Only," leaving it to others to translate his ideas into built form.

Howard envisioned groups of complementary 6,000-acre garden cities that would be linked by railroad to form Social Cities, "slumless smokeless cities" occu-pying about 66,000 acres. When a garden city reached its population limit, which Howard set at 32,000, a new one would be built, leapfrogging over the protective belt. Most important, all land was to be collectively owned by a garden city's residents and held in a trust admin-istered by "four gentleman of responsible position and of undoubted probity and honour." [33] The municipality would derive its income solely from rent. Because garden cities were to be built from the ground up, undeveloped agricultural sites could be acquired at depressed prices. As the cities grew, property values would naturally rise and rents could be increased, allowing the municipality not only to pay off debt and provide standard services but also to fund pensions, health insurance, and other welfare programs. The scheme took direct aim at land-lords profiting from the "unearned increment"—the increased rent that could be charged without making any improvement to a property.

In delivering his proposal, Howard took care to avoid the kind of fervor of most previous utopistic resettlement schemes—religious, paternalistic, or oth-erwise—that might alienate either side of the political spectrum. His measured, rational prose had "nothing of the cocksureness of propaganda," as Garden City cham-pion C. B. Purdom (1883–1965) put it: "It was difficult not to agree with him." [34] Howard adopted the same tone in promotional lectures and articles: "Reading and listening to Howard," historian Standish Meacham observed, "one

1. Plan, Robert Pemberton, 1854. LOCP

2. Bird's-eye view (detail), Robert Pemberton, 1854. ATL

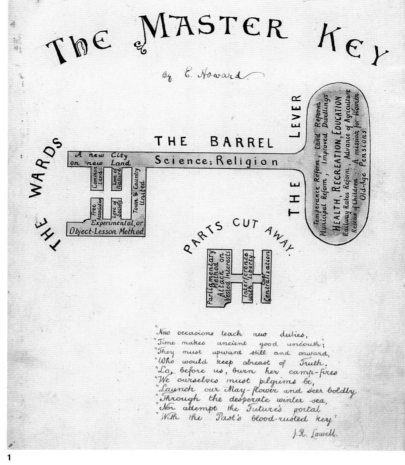

1

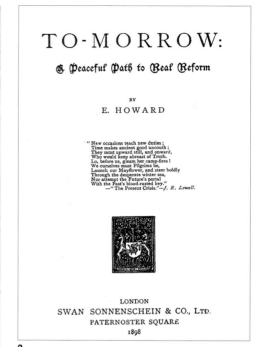

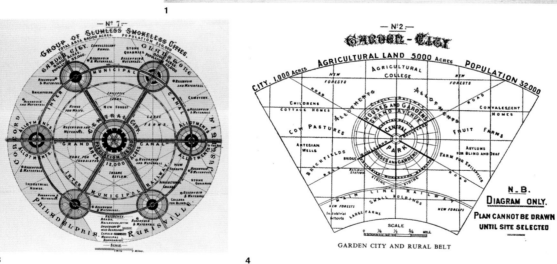

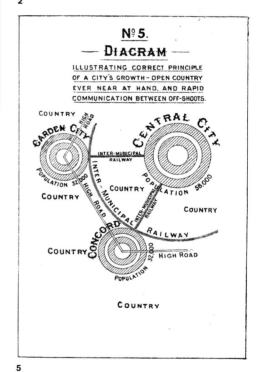

3

GARDEN CITY AND RURAL BELT

4

5

could forget that his proposal had to do with a major reorganization of society and assume, rather, that his goals merely coincided with those of others bent on the remaking of community in a less cosmic fashion."[35]

Many of the key ideas in *To-morrow* were popular contemporary themes, a fact Howard acknowledged in a chapter entitled "A Unique Combination of Proposals," writing, "I have taken a leaf out of the books of each type of reformer and bound them together by a thread of practicability."[36] Yet Garden City was uniquely colored by Howard's background. One of nine children born to lower-middle-class London shopkeepers, Howard was sent to boarding school at the age of four.

He spent his childhood in small country towns, leading some to suggest that his love of nature and embrace of communality was instilled at an early age.[37] At fifteen, Howard began a string of office jobs, clerking for stockbrokers and merchants and teaching himself the shorthand notational system introduced by Englishman Isaac Pitman in 1837 in which characters represented sounds rather than letters, a skill that would become his lifelong occupation.

On the advice of an uncle, in 1871 Howard and two friends moved to America to become farmers, settling in Nebraska where each worked 160 acres of land. Howard decided that farming was not his calling and in

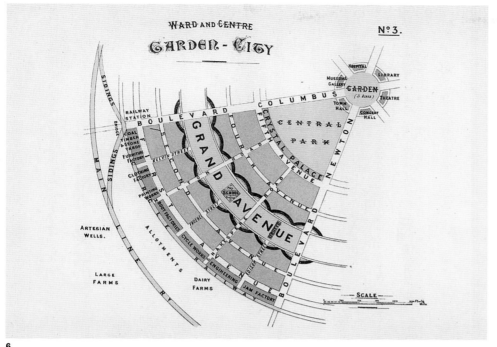

6

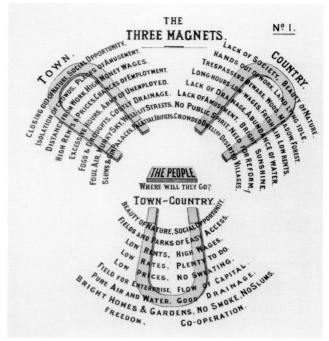

7

8

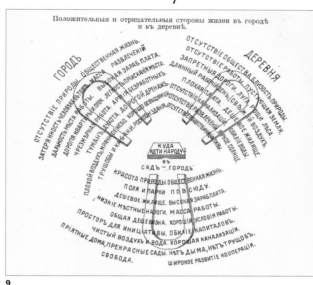

9

6. Diagram No. 3 from *To-morrow: A Peaceful Path to Real Reform*, Ebenezer Howard, 1898. FGC

7. Diagram No. 1 from *To-morrow: A Peaceful Path to Real Reform*, Ebenezer Howard, 1898. FGC

8. The Three Magnets, French translation of *Garden Cities of To-morrow*. HALS

9. The Three Magnets, Russian translation, 1911, from P. G. Mizuev, *Garden Cities and Housing Questions in England*, 1916. HALS

10. The Three Magnets, Japanese translation, 1907, of *Garden Cities of To-morrow*. HALS

11. The Three Magnets, Dutch translation from J. Bruinwold Riedel, *Tuinsteden*, 1906. JBR

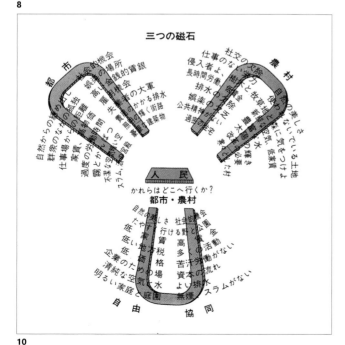

10

11

1872 moved to Chicago to resume work as a stenographer. During four years in Chicago, Howard's interest in social issues blossomed. He experienced the city at an extraordinary time, a moment of vast urban reconstruction following the Great Fire of 1871. Although Howard never acknowledged a connection, he must have known that Chicago was called "The Garden City" up until the fire. He may also have been aware of A. T. Stewart's recent Garden City (see p. 241), on Long Island, and was almost certainly aware of Olmsted's Riverside (see p. 122), which, intimately connected to Chicago by railroad, was prominently advertised as a community of country amenities with access to the city. That Howard never acknowledged a familiarity with Riverside may be because, as Walter Creese has suggested, after the fire, when the suburb was inundated with refugees and workmen, "fever and ague broke out, giving it a reputation for unhealthiness."[38]

Howard the inventor also emerged in Chicago. He began experimenting with mechanical objects such as watches and guns and soon honed in on typewriters, working with the Remington company in an effort to invent a shorthand machine. Howard approached the city with the same tinkerer's mind, later describing Garden City as the "greatest labour-saving invention yet discovered."[39] Toward the end of his time in Chicago, Howard read *Hygeia, or the City of Health* (1875), a pamphlet by British doctor Benjamin Ward Richardson (1828–1896), which proposed cities of low population density, high standards of housing and sanitation, abundant park space, and an underground railway, all elements that would crop up in Garden City.[40] As Lewis Mumford has noted, during his time in America, Howard also "had before him the constant spectacle of new communities being laid out every year on new land, and he was impressed by the possibility of a fresh start."[41]

Howard returned to England in 1876 and took up work as a Parliamentary reporter, a job that kept him in touch with the issues of the day. He joined a debating society, became involved with various reform groups, and through extensive reading, began to pick out the elements that would help him to define his idea. In addition to James Silk Buckingham, he specifically acknowledged Edward Gibbon Wakefield, who proposed to establish colonies in Australia and New Zealand in which all social classes were represented rather than just the lower rungs, and economist Alfred Marshall, who applied Wakefield's idea to England, calling for the planned migration of people and industry from overcrowded London to independent urban colonies. Howard almost directly borrowed the ideas of eighteenth-century utopian Thomas Spence that land should be nationalized, residents should pay rent to corporations of which they were owners, and rent payments should provide a municipality's income.

In 1888, Howard was spurred to action after reading *Looking Backward, 2000–1887*, by the American author Edward Bellamy (1850–1898), which imagined a classless, cooperative industrial society in the year 2000 devoid of poverty, crime, greed, pollution, and corruption. The book was a bestseller, read by hundreds of thousands, and Howard not only arranged for its publication in England but also cofounded a society to promote Bellamy's ideas, later writing that he was "fairly carried away by the eloquence and evidently strong convictions of the author . . . I realized, as never before, the splendid possibilities of a new civilization based on service to the community and not on self-interest, at present the dominant motive. Then I determined to take such a part as I could, however small it might be, in helping to bring a new civilization into being."[42] As Frederic J. Osborn has observed, Bellamy's "two basic assumptions—that technological advance could emancipate men from degrading toil, and that men are inherently cooperative and equalitarian—were the essence of Howard's own optimistic outlook, in which there was no proletarian resentment or class-bitterness, and not a trace of nostalgic anti-urbanism, anti-industrialism, or back-to-the-land-ism."[43] However, Howard took exception to certain of Bellamy's ideas, particularly, as Peter Hall notes, Bellamy's "centralized socialist management and his insistence on the subordination of the individual to the group, which he saw as authoritarian."[44]

By 1892, Howard had worked out the essential elements of Garden City, or as he initially called it, Rurisville, circulating the scheme among colleagues until 1898, when a financial gift from a friend allowed for the publication of *To-morrow*. In the more commonly known edition of 1902, four of the seven diagrams were omitted, most notably the Social City drawing that, with six interconnected Garden Cities surrounding a central city, was the only one to convey the full scope of the plan.

Ostensibly a diagram, Howard depicted Garden City as a circle, while making clear that each city would be "of different design from the others."[45] Nonetheless, Howard's diagram could—and indeed would—be read as the basis of a specific plan as well as the representation of a set of principles. Howard called for a 6,000-acre site, with 1,000 acres devoted to a city of 32,000 people and 5,000 acres reserved as a rural belt that provided not only agricultural land but also recreational space, a setting for various institutions, and housing for another 2,000. Making a strong statement against congestion, Howard placed a five-and-a-half-acre park at the city center, encircled by a ring of public buildings and a larger 145-acre "central park" that was in turn ringed by a glass-covered shopping arcade and winter garden known as the Crystal Palace, referencing, at least in name, Joseph Paxton's structure from the Great Exhibition of 1851 but also reflecting the 100-year-old tradition of shopping galleries in Paris and London and even Providence, Rhode Island, and Cleveland, Ohio, as well as the glass-covered shopping street proposed by James Buckingham for his ideal city of Victoria.

Beyond the Crystal Palace lay the residential areas, where 5,500 detached and group houses of "the most varied architecture and design that ingenuity and individuality can suggest," some sharing "common gardens and co-operative kitchens," were to be placed along concentric streets and radial avenues of varying width.[46] The average lot size was 20 by 130 feet, resulting in an overall density of about twenty houses—or between seventy and ninety-five people—per acre. Howard expected the municipality to play a limited role in construction, with building societies and cooperatives taking the lead. The circular 420-foot-wide Grand Avenue provided a broad swath of parkland and sites for schools and churches. Six 120-foot-wide tree-lined radial boulevards divided the plan into wards, each with its own schools and stores, allowing construction to occur in phases and anticipating the concept of the neighborhood unit. The city's outer edge was given over to "factories, warehouses, dairies, markets, coal yards, timber yards, etc., all fronting on the circle railway, which encompasses the whole town, and which has sidings connecting it with a main line of railway which passes through the estate."[47]

When *To-morrow* appeared, according to Frederic J. Osborn, "it seems to have struck the conservative-minded as merely fantastic, and idealists of the political Left as disrespectful to their over-simplified panaceas."[48] *The Times* (London) reported on the plan in 1898, admiring its overall direction and the tidiness with which Howard had worked out the "details of administration taxation, etc.," but ultimately dismissing it: "the only difficulty is to create it; but that is a small matter to Utopians."[49] The *Fabian News*, a leading Socialist journal, was even more negative, attacking it for ignoring the reform of existing conditions that they advocated:

> [These] plans would have been in time if they had been submitted to the Romans when they conquered Britain. They set about laying-out cities, and our forefathers have dwelt in them to this day. Now Mr. Howard proposes to pull them all down and substitute garden cities, each duly built according to pretty coloured plans, nicely designed with a ruler and compass. The author has read many learned and interesting writers, and the extracts he makes from their books are like plums in the unpalatable dough of his Utopian scheming. We have got to make the best of our existing cities, and proposals for building new ones are about as useful as would be arrangements for protection against visits from Mr. Wells' Martians.[50]

First Garden City, soon known as Letchworth, would illustrate the kind of physical environment that could be achieved in response to Howard's ideas. But the compromised nature of the town also demonstrated the virtually insurmountable economic challenges that Howard's ideas of cooperative ownership posed, giving rise to a relaxation of ideals. Standish Meacham points out that in 1907, when the Garden City Association changed its name to the Garden Cities and Town Planning Association, it was an acknowledgment of "the degree to which the bold vision of *To-morrow: A Peaceful Path to Real Reform* had been occluded by reformers' willingness

to work for more readily achievable half-measures."[51] Recognizing the unlikelihood of realizing pure Garden Cities, Raymond Unwin urged cities struggling with expansion to begin buying land on their outskirts for low-density development, offering up a rendering in 1912 depicting "The Garden City Principle applied to Suburbs."[52] Builders and architects began to trade on the Garden City's reputation: "Men having sub-standard goods to offer will put the popular label thereon," Osborn wrote, "and in time the odium attaching to the substitute will diminish the prestige of the label, and therefore of the original goods. That has happened to the Garden City."[53] It was not long, according to C. B. Purdom, before "the claim that a housing estate or a building development was 'laid out on garden city lines' was considered sufficient to justify its description as a garden city."[54]

As the twentieth century wore on and suburban planning degenerated from garden villages into sprawling subdivisions, while traditional cities were increasingly being abandoned, champions of urban life such as Jane Jacobs, with great vehemence and less than full understanding, began to criticize Howard anew: "His prescription for saving the people was to do the city in . . . His aim was the creation of self-sufficient small towns, really very nice towns if you were docile and had no plans of your own and did not mind spending your life among others with no plans of their own." As with "all Utopias the right to have plans of any significance belonged only to the planners in charge."[55] Jacobs's mistaken assertion that Howard "simply wrote off the intricate, many-faceted, cultural life of the metropolis"[56] was directly countered by Mumford, who, seven years later, insisted that "Howard was no small-town isolationist. Not for a moment did he suppose that a single community of thirty-two thousand people could satisfy all modern man's social and cultural needs, or provide a sufficient variety of economic opportunities. Nor did he underestimate the special advantages of large numbers and plentiful capital resources, though he suspected that the great metropolis exacted too high a price for supplying them."[57]

More than a century after Howard first published his plan, the Garden City idea has been given new currency in the form of the New Urbanism. Planning historian Robert Fishman has called Howard "the oldest and wisest of the New Urbanists . . . The Garden City is the locus classicus of the New Urbanist ideal for the planned community that combines work and residence, housing for a wide range of incomes, and a town center with well-defined civic space—all at a walking scale, with easy access to parkland."[58]

THE GARDEN CITY AND THE GARDEN SUBURB: GRAMMAR AND VOCABULARY

Given that Howard was not a designer, it fell to others to give the Garden City its architectural grammar and vocabulary, a task most notably fulfilled by architects

Barry Parker and Raymond Unwin.[59] Parker and especially Unwin, who was also a formidable historian, statistician, and theorist, gave credibility to "Ebenezer the Garden City Geyser," as George Bernard Shaw managed to both affectionately and dismissively dub his friend, "the Geyser being a mere spring of benevolent mud."[60] Unwin, as Mumford writes, "had both literary facility and the cultural background that Howard lacked," and as a result "his vision of the new town carried greater authority."[61]

Barry Parker and Raymond Unwin, half-cousins who became brothers-in-law in 1893 when Unwin married Parker's sister, Ethel, were raised in middle-class households in England's industrial north. Unwin, the son of a businessman, had studied at Balliol College, Oxford, but decided against a scholarship in divinity in order to undertake an engineering apprenticeship at the Staveley Coal and Iron Works, where the harsh conditions of working-class life left a strong impression. Parker, son of a bank manager, apprenticed in architecture and entered into practice in 1894, with three large houses for his father among his earliest commissions. Parker and Unwin established their partnership in 1896, with the understanding, as Unwin wrote, of "he doing the artistic part and me the practical."[62] The partnership lasted until 1914, when Unwin began working for the government, continuing until his retirement in 1928, after which he remained active as an adviser and lecturer. Parker remained in practice, designing houses and town plans that included garden suburbs in São Paulo, Brazil (see p. 635), among others, and serving as adviser for the garden city of Wythenshawe (see p. 239).

Committed to the Arts and Crafts movement, Parker and Unwin were part of the generation of British domestic architects that included M. H. Baillie Scott and Edwin Lutyens (1869–1944). Embracing the ideals of authenticity, quality, and craftsmanship, they balanced a romantic view of village and rural life with a solid appreciation of the problems that industrialization posed to cities. Unwin was strongly influenced by the socialist thinking of John Ruskin (1819–1900), William Morris (1834–1896), and Edward Carpenter (1844–1929), the latter two of whom he knew personally. He became secretary of the Manchester branch of Morris's Socialist League in 1886 and maintained a career-long commitment to the concept of "Beauty"—that it was, in Morris's words, "no mere accident of human life which people can take or leave as they choose, but a positive necessity of life, if we are to live as Nature meant us to—that is, unless we are content to be less than men."[63] Unwin believed that the ideal of beauty extended beyond individual buildings to urban life in its entirety, that "to the architect town planning specially appeals as an opportunity for finding a beautiful form of expression for the life of the community."[64]

In practice, Parker focused on the houses and Unwin the town plans. Their early work included modest cottages—John Astley has noted that "Unwin's slogan 'Art and simplicity' reminds us that many of those who commissioned the work of these designers were Quakers."[65] In their scheme (c. 1898) for a Cooperative Village,

Parker and Unwin showed an emerging interest in site planning, experimenting with houses grouped around shared quadrangles and greens such as would become a hallmark of their work.[66] They were particularly critical of the so-called "bye-law streets" that, created out of the Public Health Act of 1875, had markedly improved working-class housing by raising standards of sanitation and hygiene and eliminating back-to-back houses by requiring open air on two sides of a house, but at the same time resulted in a bleak urbanism of straight streets, block after block of identical rowhouses, and little or no gardens or public space.[67]

In 1901, Parker and Unwin published **The Art of Building a Home**, a collection of essays and lectures suggesting, among other domestic conveniences, common facilities so that "instead of thirty or forty housewives preparing thirty or forty little scrap dinners, heating a like number of ovens, boiling thrice the number of pans and cleaning them all up again, two or three of them retained as cooks by the little settlement would do the whole, and could give better and cheaper meals into the bargain."[68] These ideas had been part of previous plans for housing reform, ranging from the phalanxes of Fourier to the early apartment houses of New York.[69]

In 1902, Unwin, the more prolific writer of the two, published the Fabian tract **Cottage Plans and Common Sense**, continuing his campaign against bye-law housing by presenting standards for light and air, privacy and comfort. After hearing Unwin speak at the 1901 Garden City Association Conference in Bournville, the Quaker chocolate manufacturer Joseph Rowntree (1836–1925) gave Parker and Unwin their first important planning commission for the town of New Earswick (1902) (see p. 228). In 1903, Parker and Unwin were invited to submit plans for First Garden City (Letchworth) (see p. 230). The same year they participated in an exhibition for the Northern Art Workers Guild with a proposal for **Cottages Near a Town** which filled a 30-acre site with housing in which back alleys and monotonous rows were replaced by a checkerboard arrangement of rowhouses stepped forward and back from the street on thin blocks or surrounding internal greens on larger blocks. Their involvement with Hampstead Garden Suburb (see p. 350), beginning in 1905, firmly established their reputation as the preferred architects–town planners of the Garden City movement.

Unwin published his definitive text, **Town Planning in Practice**, in 1909, setting his ideas in a broad historical context and spelling out basic principles of site planning and density. The book was inspired by the introduction of the bill that would become the Housing and Town Planning Act of 1909, empowering municipalities to prepare town plans for peripheral districts. Walter Creese has articulated some of the underlying principles of Parker and Unwin's work: "The village as an animate symbol," "the necessity for understanding the past," "the Middle Ages as the historic standard," "the indispensability of beauty," and "twelve houses to the acre,"[70] the last becoming the worldwide

HE ART OF
BUILDING
A HOME.

A Collection of Lectures and
Illustrations by Barry Parker
and Raymond Unwin.

Longmans, Green & Co.,
39, Paternoster Row, Lon-
don, New York, & Bombay,
1901.   *Second Edition.*

1

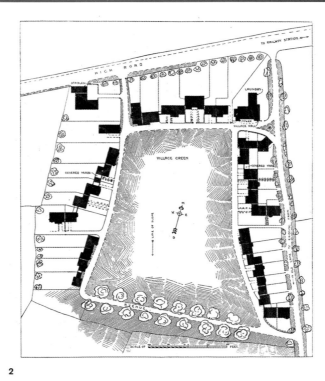

2

Fabian Tract No. 109.

COTTAGE PLANS

AND

COMMON SENSE

By RAYMOND UNWIN.

WITH ILLUSTRATIONS BY BARRY PARKER AND RAYMOND UNWIN.

PUBLISHED AND SOLD BY

THE FABIAN SOCIETY.

PRICE ONE PENNY.

LONDON:
THE FABIAN SOCIETY, 3 CLEMENT'S INN, STRAND, W.C.
MARCH 1902.

1

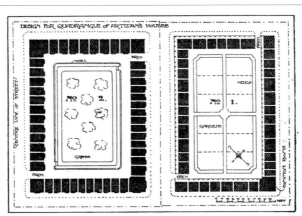

PLATE I.

PLATE II.
View in Quadrangle No. 1, Plate I. Showing Common Room at the angle.

2

1. Title page. CPCS (1902)

2. Plans and view of a quadrangle
of artisans' houses. CPCS (1902)

1. Plan of cottages near a town, prepared for an exhibit at the Northern Art Workers Guild, Manchester, Barry Parker and Raymond Unwin, Architects, 1903. TPP

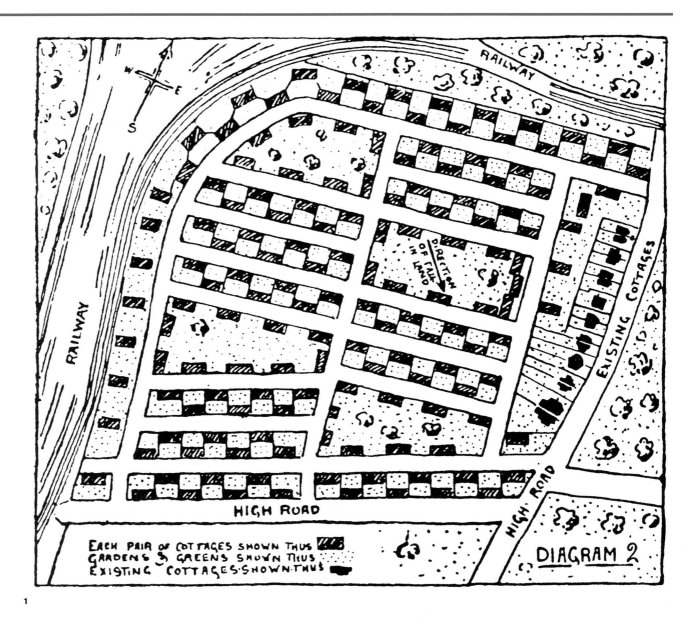

1

accepted standard for suburban density. Unwin did not endorse such dogma, arguing that there was nothing "magical or sacrosanct in the number twelve,"[71] but that trial and error had "proved to be about the right number to give gardens of sufficient size of commercial value to the tenants—large enough, that is, to be worth cultivating seriously for the sake of the profits, and not too large to be worked by an ordinary labourer and his family."[72]

While Barry Parker explained the importance of understanding the past—"The greatest geniuses have never attempted to evolve something new. Their contribution has been the improvement and carrying further of traditional methods"[73]—Creese points out that Parker and Unwin's dedication to the "rambling layout of medieval German hill towns was even in some degree at war with Howard's rational clarifications and forward-looking proposals."[74] As Lewis Mumford observed, Parker and Unwin "did not fully share Howard's old-fashioned delight in Victorian invention and mechanical progress: for they were under the corrective humanizing influence of William Morris, and were more interested

in recapturing the genial older traditions of domestic architecture than in finding a fresh, striking image for a new kind of city as a whole."[75]

Using photographs and drawings by members of the Parker and Unwin staff, most notably Charles Paget Wade (1883–1956), *Town Planning in Practice* instructed on the design of "boundaries and approaches," "centers and enclosed spaces," the placement of public buildings, and the importance of sight lines and street pictures that allowed one to feel drawn in and engaged with the streetscape. Unwin argued that a site's natural features should determine the formality or informality of a town plan and promoted, as Creese describes, "a graded network of major and minor, paved and unpaved, wide and narrow streets that led to the invention both of the cul-de-sac and the secondary and service roads: as one comes closer to the Unwin and Parker homes, as in Hampstead, one is always slowed down by narrower and shorter roads. It brings a respect of approach to the domicile."[76]

In his 1912 pamphlet, ***Nothing Gained by Overcrowding***, Unwin provided an economic analysis to

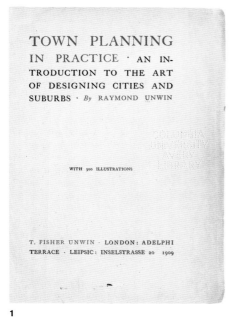

1

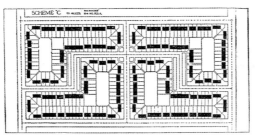

2

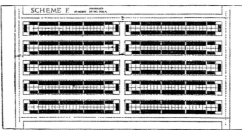

3

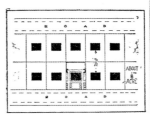

4

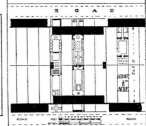

5

6

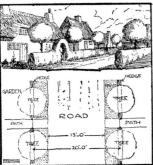

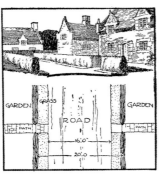

7

1. Title page. TPP (1909)

2. Diagrams comparing the layout of a 20-acre site with 12.4 houses per acre and 25 houses per acre. Unwin argued that landowners could benefit from developing twice the land at half the density. TPP (1909)

3. Diagrams comparing the placement of houses on ⅛-acre plots. Unwin argued that square plots provided less practical gardens than long, narrow plots and that the grouping of houses provided better street pictures. TPP (1909)

4. "Plan and sketch of street showing on one side the uninteresting vanishing perspective of the unbroken building line, and on the other the more picturesque result of breaks." TPP (1909)

5. "An imaginary irregular town." TPP (1909)

6, 7. "Examples of lighter building roads and drives as used at Earswick, Letchworth, and Hampstead." TPP (1909)

8, 9. Diagrams showing right-angled (left) and three-way (right) street crossings that provide for traffic circulation, closed street pictures, and small "places." TPP (1909)

10. Sketch of a road junction similar to that shown in 9D. TPP (1909)

11. Plan of a curved road with buildings designed to frame and terminate street pictures. TPP (1909)

12. "Plan of road junction with four buildings set diagonally," one of several diagrams Unwin suggested as an improvement to typical bye-law corner treatment. TPP (1909)

13, 14. Plan and sketch of a curved road with buildings designed to be square with each other. TPP (1909)

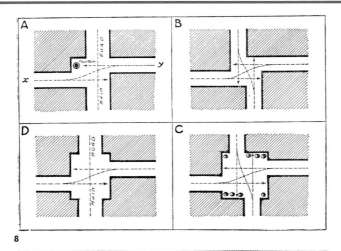

8

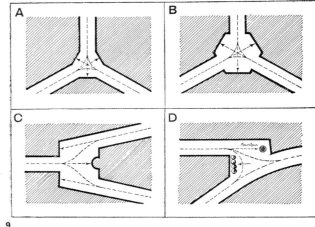

9

10

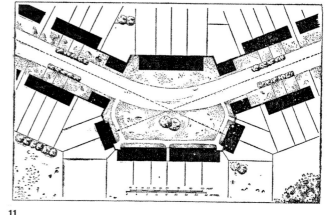

11

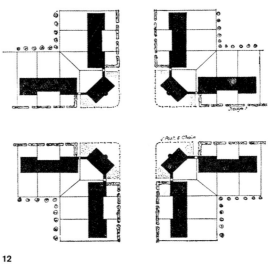

12

13

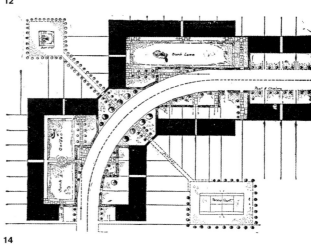

14

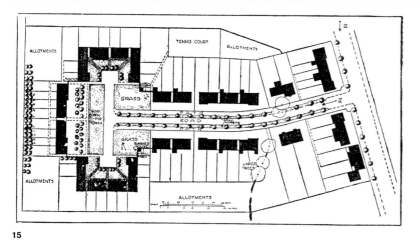

15

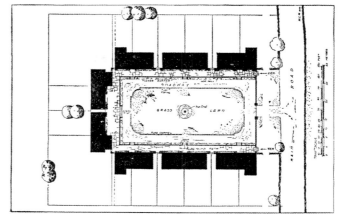

16

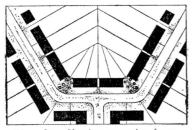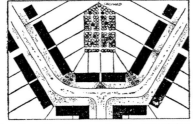

Illus. 282.—*Showing converging fences.*   Illus. 283.—*Showing an orchard in place of these.*

17

15. Plan for the development of land at a great depth from the main road. TPP (1909)

16. "Pairs of houses arranged around a green." TPP (1909)

17. Alternate plans for fenced yards with and without orchard. TPP (1909)

Nothing Gained by Overcrowding

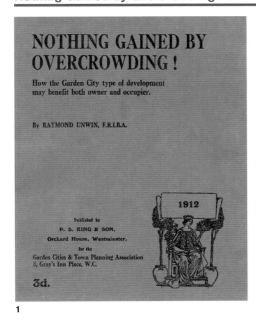

1

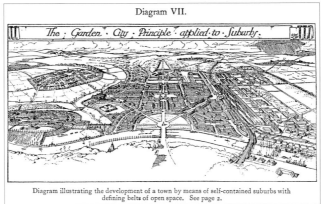

2

3

4

1. Cover. NGBO (1912)

2. Diagram I: Two Systems of Development Contrasted. NGBO (1912)

3. Diagram VII: The Garden City Principle applied to Suburbs. NGBO (1912)

4. A comparison of back gardens as developed under Garden City and bye-law (bottom) methods. NGBO (1912)

prove the claim of the title and included diagrams, now classic, that compared tracts of typical bye-law housing with his own designs for low-density perimeter houses replacing streets and alleys with parks and playgrounds similar to the superblocks of Port Sunlight. These proposals would have a particular impact on American practice, as exemplified by the use of the superblock by Clarence Stein and Henry Wright at Sunnyside (see p. 190) and Radburn (see p. 275).

Unwin also helped define the responsibilities of the town planner at a time when the profession was still young, stressing the importance of preliminary site surveys that studied existing industry, utilities, historic places, public buildings, traffic flow, movement of commuters in and out of the city, local building traditions and materials, and regional species of trees and vegetation. "Any other characteristics which go to make up the individuality,—economic, historic and artistic,—of the town should be very carefully noted with a view to preserving and fostering such individuality," observed the editors of *The Craftsman* magazine after the publication of *Town Planning in Practice*.[77] The design of a town plan, Unwin insisted, must begin on-site:

> *The picture will grow in the designer's mind as the various needs are considered and met; and all the while he is thinking out the main points of his problem he will be finding spots of natural beauty to be preserved, trees to be guarded from destruction, distant views from the town and views into it of the fine buildings he hopes some day to see rise on their allotted sites, to be kept open. There will be steep places to be avoided or overcome, the cost of roads always to be remembered, and a due relation to be maintained between this and the building areas opened up. But, while the problem seems to become more and more complicated, it is really solving itself; for every fresh need and every circumstance considered is a new formative agency, determining for the designer the lines of his plan; and his chief aim at first must be to determine and keep clearly before him the right proportional importance of each, and to give it due expression, and only when, on the ground, all these formative influences have been balanced, can the designer safely commence to draw out his design.*[78]

THE GARDEN CITY IN ENGLAND

Begun in 1888, **Port Sunlight** was founded by W. H. Lever (1851–1925), one of the original Lever Brothers, English soap manufacturers.[79] Named for their Sunlight brand of soap, the town initially occupied a 56-acre site on a branch of the River Mersey, with 24 acres devoted to a new factory and the rest to the village. Over the following twenty years Port Sunlight, five miles from

Birkenhead (see p. 32)—where presumably Lever had visited Paxton's suburban villa park, though he never made reference to it—and seven miles across the River Mersey from Liverpool, was expanded on filled land to stretch nearly a mile long by almost half that wide, covering 221 acres, approximately 130 of which were devoted to the village, and the rest to the factories.

The site was awkward, cut through by three muddy ravines formed by the tidal wash of Bromborough Pool, an inlet of the Mersey. In this respect it was somewhat similar to Olmsted's Riverside, with its floodplains. The ravines were altered over time, with the southernmost drained and landscaped to become the Dell, around which the earliest blocks of housing were located. The other ravines were earmarked for housing blocks during a 1910 competition for the town's completion, but the housing was only partially realized and the ravines were filled and retained as recreational areas.

The authorship of the original plan for Port Sunlight is unclear. It would appear that Lever, an architect manqué, played the decisive role in its formulation, but it may be that William Owen (1846–1910), a local architect, drew the plan on the basis of Lever's ideas. Owen certainly designed the factory and the first group of twenty-eight dwellings (1889–90) as well as an entrance lodge. The oldest part of the village is the most picturesque, with cottages looking inward to the Dell and outward toward the factory to the south and the railway embankment that formed the site's western boundary. The embankment was parallel to Greendale Road, where houses fronted the railroad tracks for the greater part of a mile, creating a positive impression for travelers. Around the Dell, superblocks of housing enclosing small service alleys attempted to reflect the site's contours, but as Edward Hubbard and Michael Shippobottom have noted, "the very size of the superblocks minimized the irregularities of plan resulting from the curving roads" outlining the Dell.[80] Many public buildings were constructed during the early years, including Gladstone Hall (William Owen, 1891), built as a community center, the Schools (Douglas & Fordham, 1894–96), the Bridge Inn (Grayson & Ould, 1900), and shops. The style of this "neat and cheerful little village," as George Augustus Sala wrote in the *Illustrated London News* in 1890, was "old English; and in process of time as the village develops it will be pleasantly demonstrated that it is quite practical to erect a large number of industrial buildings without such habitations being hideous in design and grimy in aspect."[81]

Later developments at Port Sunlight reflect the academic planning principles of the City Beautiful movement. The 1910 competition to expand the village, open to students at the Liverpool School of Architecture and its Department of Civic Design, was won by Ernest Prestwich (1889–1977), a third-year student in the architecture school whose formal scheme contrasted with the more picturesque original plan. As developed and executed by the landscape architect Thomas Mawson

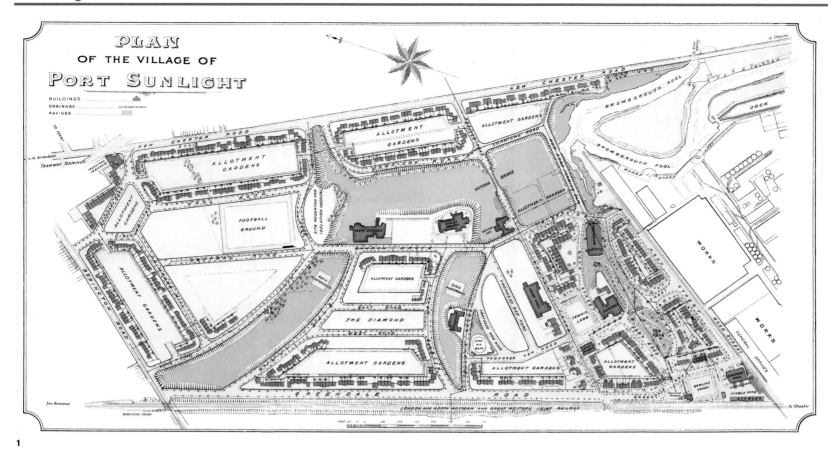

1

1. Plan, 1888. WHL

(1861–1933) and architect James Lomax-Simpson (1882–1977), Prestwich's scheme exhibited the growing importance for English architects of the American City Beautiful movement, and coincided with Lever's evolving tastes, which were influenced by his visit to Chicago in 1892, when the World's Fair buildings were under construction. This visit may have been the genesis of the large superblocks and landscaped malls that Mawson developed from Prestwich's classicizing plan, wherein the Diamond, originally planned as a rectangular open space, was expanded to form an 1,800-foot-long-by-195-foot-wide mall that would eventually give up some of its length to Lomax-Simpson's classical-style Lady Lever Art Gallery (1922), constructed at its north end. The Causeway, a central boulevard running east–west and more or less occupying the footprint of one of the filled ravines, intersected the Diamond to open the village to the railroad on the west and allowed long views of W. & S. Owen's Christ Church (1904) on the east.

Unlike the high naturalism of the Dell development, the rest of Port Sunlight was more conventional in its use of large, regular blocks of 50 to 100 houses surrounding allotment gardens, an arrangement that dramatically reduced the amount of roadway construction, and resulted in a very low density of five to eight houses per acre. Between 80 and 100 feet separated the housing terraces, guaranteeing sunny interiors. The streets were significantly wider than was typical, with 24-foot-wide carriageways, 8- to 12-foot-wide pavements and 18- to 30-foot-wide front gardens on each side

maintained by the company's gardeners to provide a uniform high-quality public realm.

Many architects participated in the design of the housing, including Lomax-Simpson, Ernest George (1839–1922), and Maurice B. Adams, resulting in a stylistic eclecticism within the boundaries of English traditions from the Tudors to the Georges, that, as Walter Creese observed, was part of the larger tradition that "began in Bedford Park [see p. 37], [but] grows almost rampant in Port Sunlight and Bournville. The only other possible way to explain Port Sunlight visually is as a kind of last, ruddy glow of High Victorianism, with all its little dignities and affectations, its prosperity and expansiveness. This eclecticism of forms, styles, and surfaces was to swell until, as W. L. George put it, each street exhibited its own 'local nationality.'"[82]

Port Sunlight represents the first effective large-scale integration of nineteenth-century social reform with picturesque town design. For the first time, the utilitarianism of social-minded town planning, with rows of narrow houses on straight bye-law streets, gave way to a new sensibility of the garden village. Creese has written that the planning strategies employed were consistent and impressive:

In angling [the houses] at the street corners and forming rudimentary U-shaped courts out of the larger combinations, Lever's architects effectively forecast certain devices to be incorporated in the garden cities. The most important advance was

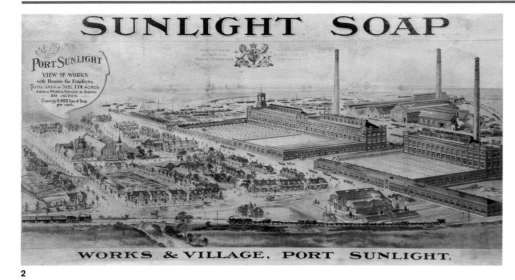

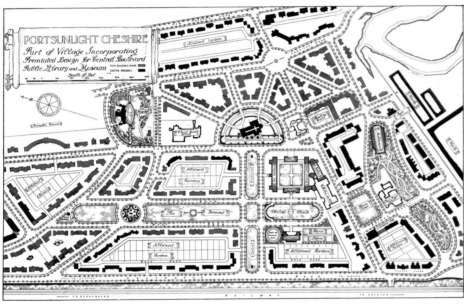

2. Bird's-eye view. UNI (c. 1900)

3. Aerial view. GE (2008)

4. Plan, Ernest Prestwich with Thomas Mawson and James Lomax-Simpson, 1910. THM

5. Bird's-eye view of Prestwich plan showing the Causeway, 1910. THM

6. Bath Street. WHL (c. 1905)

7. The Bridge Inn, Victoria Bridge, and Christ Church. WHL (c. 1905)

8. Corner panorama. JC (1905)

9

10

9. Cottages facing the railway. THM (c. 1910)

10. Post office. WHL (c. 1905)

11. Gladstone Hall. IAO06

12. Bowling Green. IAO06

13. Park Road. UNI (c. 1913)

14. The Lyceum and Park Road houses. Scales. LS (2007)

15. Primrose Hill. Benkid. WC (2009)

16. The Dell. Scales. LS (2007)

17. War Memorial and Lady Lever Art Gallery. Scales. LS (2007)

11

12

13

14

15

16

17

in the use of the houses on both sides of the road to characterize and punctuate the space between, rather than simply to limit it. At Port Sunlight they were so designed that little or no distinction could be perceived among the individual houses of each group externally. What it amounted to visually was a street of mansions in which the volumes held up remarkably well, a need increasingly felt as the thoroughfares grew wider under the pressure of circulatory reform . . . The superhouse equated with the superblock at last. The Shavian country house had become the multiplex.[83]

Lever was a master of publicity for his company and for his model town. Word of Port Sunlight's innovations soon spread in England and elsewhere. In his book *Das englische Haus* (1904–5), Hermann Muthesius wrote that, "If one wishes to obtain a quick and accurate appreciation of the achievement of contemporary English house-building, there is hardly a more comfortable means than by undertaking a journey to the factory village of Port Sunlight near Liverpool." At Port Sunlight, "the gates of a new world were first opened; in place of the dismal appearance of utilitarian buildings we were shown a new vision; in place of the misery associated with the barren rows of workers' terraces we find joyfulness and homeliness."[84]

"In one sense," Muthesius continued,

Port Sunlight may be regarded as the present-day outcome of Norman Shaw's pioneering work at Bedford Park thirty years ago for it is a solution of the problem of the small house and a grouping together of houses to form a residential area in a way that is modern and satisfies all practical and artistic requirements. In both places the architects drew upon early vernacular architecture . . . In both instances the layout of the streets was not merely planned on the drawing-board but was closely harmonized with the terrain . . . It was in the ground-plan, at Port Sunlight as at Bedford Park, that the real innovation lay, because it was here that the economic conditions of the time set the guide-lines. In this respect the houses at Port Sunlight did for the workman's house what those at Bedford Park had done for the lower middle-class home; they provided an ideal combination of comfort, ease and artistic quality with the economic possibilities appropriate to their status.[85]

James Cornes, in his book *Modern Housing in Town and Country* (1905), made the essential point that although only 3,000 people lived in Port Sunlight, it presented "the character of a town, on account of its manifold features of social life. It is, indeed, a small garden city."[86]

Port Sunlight is not only an enduring icon of enlightened industrial village design but of suburban planning for all classes. As Creese has written:

Places like Port Sunlight and Bournville, and Bedford Park before and Letchworth and Hampstead after them, were made important in history by the manner in which they adapted the achievements of the contemporary English domestic school of architects, the best in the world at the time, to the earlier concern for the housing of the working classes. The conviction that the surroundings of the lower classes deserved any aesthetic treatment at all was revolutionary. But the new realization expressed through the incorporation of the Beaux-Arts viewpoint was that the model communities had begun to attain such a size that it was more fitting to regard them as complete towns than as overgrown residential districts. Up to that time they were virtually without centers in respect to planning. Again this represented a kind of logical progression, for where Lever's architect had first hollowed out the individual blocks for gardens, they now hollowed out the whole settlement for axial malls.[87]

Port Sunlight does not scream out "workers' housing." In fact, as Gillian Darley has written, "Port Sunlight, together with New Earswick, represented the breaking down of distinctions between housing for workers, and housing for others. Excellent housing of the highest available standards had been the privilege of the few—Lever's efforts were instrumental in extending this privilege to the many." Port Sunlight had a powerful effect on American practice, but Darley, reflecting an insufficient grasp of the American scene and perhaps a prejudice against American capitalism, is only partially correct when, in *Villages of Vision*, her history of the garden suburb, she writes that in America, "the fact remained that the influence that Bournville and Port Sunlight exerted . . . was not in the area of industrial housing, but in that of suburban development. The social message had little meaning in a country where the rich very rarely considered crossing the divide to assist those who had failed to match their own achievement."[88] Stephen Bayley far more cogently explains Port Sunlight's seeming lack of influence. "Perhaps it is just because of Port Sunlight's visual and conceptual perfection," Bayley has written, "that it has been slightly less influential than it deserves to have been."[89]

In the 1920s Lever expanded the village to the east, developing the Bromborough and Woodhead Estates, where he experimented with new housing patterns. At Edgeworth Estate, another of his 1920s expansions, he went so far as to allow the tenants to erect their own houses, subject to approval by the company architect.

Bournville is one of three well-planned "chocolate towns"—the other two being Hershey, Pennsylvania (see p. 251), and Jules Saulnier's Menier development at Noisiel-sur-Marne in France (see p. 731). George Cadbury (1839–1922), the Quaker pacifist and cocoa and chocolate baron, and Lever had much in common, both in their business positions and their social attitudes, so it is not

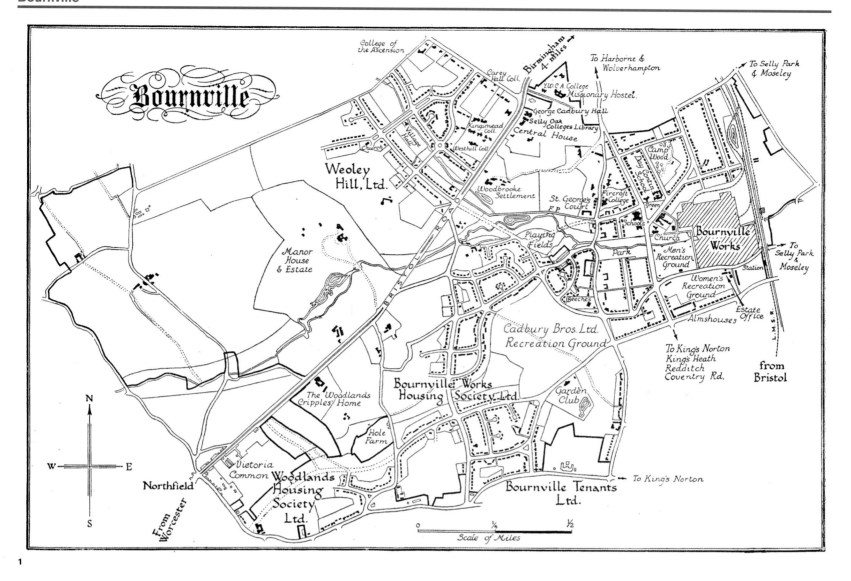

1

1. Map. BVTB (c. 1927)

surprising that Cadbury's village of Bournville is in many ways similar to Lever's earlier Port Sunlight. Bournville, four miles southwest of central Birmingham, was started in 1879 but it was not until 1895 that Cadbury formed the Bournville Estate and began the development of a model village that soon grew to the size of a large garden suburb, managed after 1900, when there were 313 houses, by a charitable trust.[90] The estate tripled in size during the interwar years and eventually grew to more than 1,000 acres accommodating 7,600 houses. Echoing the pattern at Port Sunlight, Bournville's development followed upon the construction of a new factory in 1879, along with sixteen houses for foremen designed in a Gothic style by George H. Gadd (n.d.), on a site connected to the city center by railroad. The new factory was set in spacious grounds, leading the company to later proclaim it "a factory in a garden."[91]

Cadbury's earnest pronouncements had a tone similar to the writings of Lever:

The Founder is desirous of alleviating the evils which arise from the insanitary and insufficient accommodation supplied to large numbers of the working classes, and of securing to workers in factories some of the advantages of the outdoor village life, with opportunities for the natural and healthful occupation of cultivating the soil. The object is declared to be the amelioration of the condition of the working-class and labouring population in and around Birmingham, and elsewhere in Great Britain, by the provision of improved dwellings, with gardens and open spaces to be enjoyed therewith.[92]

Perhaps the main difference between Bournville and Port Sunlight was Cadbury's emphasis on the garden. While Lever went so far at Port Sunlight as to commandeer the cottages' front gardens as public space so that they would be maintained to proper standards, Cadbury never tired of talking of the economic and therapeutic value of the workers cultivating their own gardens, and he specified more restrictive covenants for those gardens. No house could cover more than 25 percent of its lot, and front, side, and rear gardens were necessarily maintained to company standards. Bournville differs from Port Sunlight in another significant way. It was

2. The Triangle. CRS

3. Linden Road houses, William Alexander Harvey, c. 1895. HAG03

4. Stores with dwellings above. HAG03

5. Typical street. AHG06

6. Weoley Hill and Witherford Way. RIBAP (1926)

2

3

4

5

6

not built to solely meet the housing needs of Cadbury's workers; therefore, unlike Port Sunlight, it was not heavily subsidized, which explains why the architecture of both its houses and public buildings is plainer than at Port Sunlight.

A. P. Walker (n.d.), a surveyor, produced the first sketch plan for Bournville in 1894, but this was soon revised to include a central village green with shopping and institutional buildings from which wound informally planted roads. Local bye-laws required 42- or 45-foot-wide roads, compromising the intention to shape an intimately scaled village. Walker designed the first houses and continued to be involved in the project until the early 1900s, but William Alexander Harvey (1874–1951) served as estate architect from 1895 until 1904, when he went into private practice, though he remained as a consultant to the trust. It was Harvey's hand that guided the estate, along with his successor, Henry Bedford Tylor (1871–1915), estate architect from 1904 until 1911, and later, S. A. Wilmot (n.d.). Harvey, like very many other architects of his day specializing in residential design, also engaged in garden village planning. At Bournville, he assembled compact cottages into groups without sacrificing a sense of individuality.

Bournville had a density of seven to eight houses per acre. In addition to the generous open land around each house—the semidetached houses were wider than at Port Sunlight owing to the bigger lots and gardens— the village plan included a rich collection of public open spaces including the Green, the Triangle, Camp Wood, with its stand of old trees, and the Park along the Bourn

Brook. The Cadbury factory also had extensive sports grounds, but their use was restricted to factory workers. At Bournville, the backs of houses along Elm Road were specially designed to present an attractive view to railroad passengers, an idea borrowed from Port Sunlight and later espoused by Barry Parker and Raymond Unwin. Numerous public buildings, including schools and shops, were built.

According to John Nelson Tarn, Bournville's

layout was much less pretentious than that of Port Sunlight, and in character it was more typical of a suburban estate, except that the area of housing and private gardens was broken up by public open space, including a park, a recreation ground and a wood. There was no attempt to group the housing around them in a systematic way as at Port Sunlight, and no attempt to achieve organization and coherence. Despite the purposeful way the estate was developed, the early stages do not suggest that there was a real grasp of planning and its implications. By contrast with Port Sunlight there were, of course, fewer public buildings, and in this the village was more typical of the garden city of the future than was Port Sunlight. Before the first world war, the Meeting House, School and Ruskin Hall provided the nucleus of the community centre, and there were of course some shops, but there was no lavish provision of public amenities.[93]

7

8

9

10

11

12

The first areas to be developed at Bournville remain close to the old rectilinear block and corridor street plan, brought out from the city like the Dell area at Port Sunlight. As Bournville continued to expand, however, it evolved from a discrete model village to a collection of separate but interconnected neighborhoods.[94] In 1914 Unwin was asked to submit plans for Weoley Hill, a section of the expanded town north of Bristol Road, but did not bring them to completion, and S. A. Wilmot carried out a different scheme. Weoley Hill, developed in 1914, is far more site sensitive, adjusted, as Creese puts it, "with finesse to the slope of the ground and includes cul-de-sacs, hollow superblocks with a cricket field, woods, bowling green, and park within them, and a road system that takes account not only of the rise and fall of the land and of ancient trees but also of the difference in function between major and minor roads."[95]

Bournville was widely documented in the press and in books, but its greatest impact on future development came as a result of its hosting the Garden City Association's first conference in 1901 (Port Sunlight hosted the following year's meeting), which gave promoters of the First Garden City, Letchworth, as well as Seebohm Rowntree (1871–1954), son of Joseph Rowntree (1836–1925), founder of New Earswick, a chance to see the village and to meet Unwin, who also attended the conference. Through this conference, Bournville may also have come to the attention of the Krupp interests, leading to Margarethenhöhe (1909), frequently characterized as the German Bournville (see p. 749). In 1906 Ebenezer Howard paid tribute to Bournville: "A garden village has been built, a garden city is but a step beyond."[96] Nonetheless, from the conceptual point of view, the early part of Bournville, which was what

1. Plan, Barry Parker and Raymond Unwin, Architects. TPP (1907)

2. Plan, Barry Parker, 1937. TPR37

3. Aerial view of eastern section. JRF (1920)

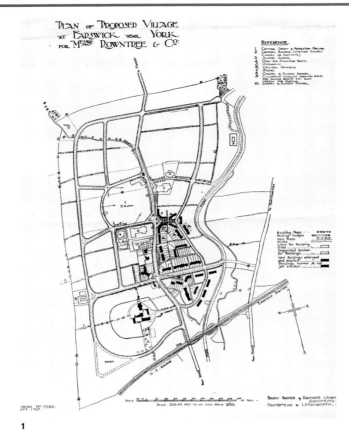

1

2

3

visitors to the conference saw in 1901, offered no real advance over Port Sunlight. As Tarn has written, "There was little attempt at first at organized planning, in the sophisticated way that Leverhulme practiced it; Cadbury tried deliberately to foster anti-urban irregularity." But, Tarn continues, "After 1907 more attention was paid to creating a coherent development and to the consideration of housing as part of a street once more," so that Bournville's success made it "the practical precursor of the garden suburb of almost any town, anywhere, in the twentieth century."[97] According to Stephen Bayley: "Bournville's contribution to the garden city idea and to the developing notions of suburban consciousness was not the invention of any fine architectural feature but rather the innovation in street planning with the twenty-foot setback which both added visual interest to the scene, gave room for the front gardens which Cadbury demanded and created a progeny of imitators which are still alive today. In fact, the layout of the individual streets at Bournville can fairly be said to be among the first settings where the English suburban scene was created."[98]

New Earswick (1902), three-and-a-half miles northeast of York, occupying a flat, approximately 130-acre site bisected by the winding north–south Haxby Road, with the meandering River Foss on the east, forms a link between the emerging tradition of industrial workers' villages and the more holistic approach of the Garden City as Howard imagined it.[99] New Earswick was developed by a local industrialist, Joseph Rowntree, who purchased the property in 1901 for his own account, not

that of his firm, processors of cocoa. Establishing a trust, Rowntree did not intend his village to be exclusively populated with his company's employees. His objective was less the creation of a town than the provision of good housing, "artistic in appearance, sanitary, and thoroughly well built" for people of modest means.[100] Given York's modest housing needs, New Earswick was likely to remain small. While its social and financial details were modeled on Bournville, the new village's overall effect was more like Port Sunlight, which was also built on a flat site.

In their planning and especially in the building design of the earliest section of New Earswick, Parker and Unwin were strongly influenced by the distinguished residential architect C. F. A. Voysey. This was in a way quite ironic, given that Voysey was dismissive about both the garden city and suburb, which he regarded as affronts to individualism. (Voysey seems to have swallowed his principles when he undertook to design a group of workers' houses and an Institute for Whitwood Colliery [1904–5], near Leeds, developed by Henry Briggs, whose son, A. Currer, was the client for Voysey's most important house, Broadleys.[101]) Parker became the sole consulting architect in 1919, to be followed in 1946 by Louis de Soissons (1890–1962), better known as planner and chief architect of Welwyn Garden City (see p. 236).

As Michael G. Day has pointed out, the principal characteristic of New Earswick's plan is "its carefully considered informality."[102] In the first half of New Earswick's development, east of Haxby Road, staggered rows

4

5

6

7

8

9

10

4. Houses. GBL (c. 1903)

5. Chestnut Grove. JRF (1915–20)

6. Poplar Grove. JRF (1908)

7. Chestnut Grove. Sunderland. MSP (2010)

8. Cul-de-sac, Rowan Avenue. Mead. CME (2010)

9. Lime Tree Avenue crescent. Mead. CME (2010)

10. Whitwood Terrace housing and the Miner's Welfare Institute, near Leeds, C. F. A. Voysey, c. 1905. RIBAD

of two-, four-, and six-unit houses were arranged "to avoid producing the spotty restless effect in the village which would result from using pairs only."[103] Nonetheless, this portion, consisting of 150 dwellings on 28 acres, was a bit formless compared to the second half of the development, west of Haxby Road, where Parker and Unwin employed culs-de-sac to overcome irregular sites and to permit the development of deep lots known as "back land" sites. Stephen Bayley points out that "Unwin's planning is characterized . . . by cul-de-sacs which force a new attitude to the placing of houses in relation to the streets and immediately create a sense of intimacy and

community."[104] In 1907, echoing Whitwood's Institute, a community center, Folk Hall, was built. New Earswick also featured an "open air" school. "Overall," as Mervyn Miller and A. Stuart Gray have written, "the informal 'villagey' character, with softly curving roads and short terraces, brought into view in a picturesque sequential street picture," constituted the basis of Letchworth.[105]

Michael Harrison has observed that Bournville and New Earswick "share certain visual and physical characteristics. Both have informal layouts, with linear parkways laid out alongside the streams that run though the estates. A considerable amount of land is given up

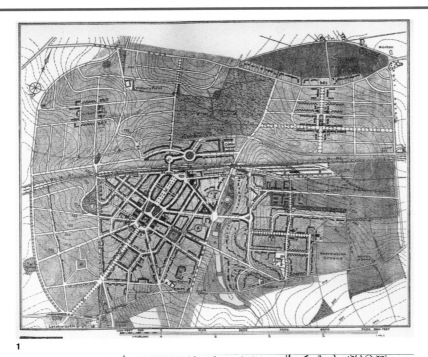

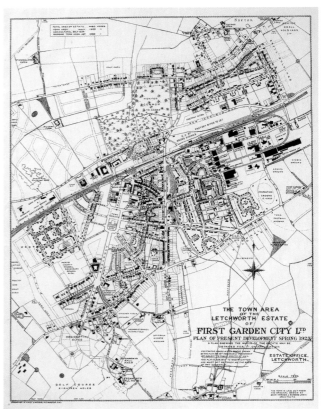

1. Plan, Barry Parker and Raymond Unwin, Architects, 1903. SB05

2. Plan of development to 1925. FGC

3. Plan, Halsey Ricardo and W. R. Lethaby, 1903. FGC

4. Aerial view. EHC (2009)

in both to recreation grounds and open spaces . . . Gardens were a significant feature . . . and the size of those gardens was determined, on both estates, by calculating 'the amount of land a man could easily and profitably work by spade cultivation in his leisure time.' Housing densities were also low at New Earswick because they followed the Bournville lead in allowing only a quarter of any building plot to be occupied by the dwelling."[106]

Letchworth (1903), or as it was initially called, First Garden City, marks the first mature expression in physical terms of Ebenezer Howard's ideas for rationally planned satellite garden cities.[107] Intended for 30,000 residents on a site of 6,000 acres, Letchworth was realized on a smaller property, with 1,250 acres devoted to development and 2,500 additional acres serving as a greenbelt. It was to provide, on average, five houses or twenty-four

people per acre. Despite its compromised size, the intention of its developers, who initially included W. H. Lever and Edward Cadbury (1873–1948), was to create a self-sufficient independent city. However, almost from the start, Letchworth functioned as a commuter suburb serving London, thirty-four miles by rail from King's Cross.

Letchworth was organized as a private, limited-dividend company dedicated to community benefit. Consequently, in contrast to prior developer- or industrialist-sponsored planned suburbs, Letchworth's evolution was significantly retarded by lack of funds. Cash-flow problems aside, Barry Parker and Raymond Unwin, Letchworth's planners, were faced with a daunting challenge. As Nikolaus Pevsner put it, their job was to "make an organism" out of Howard's diagram.[108] Not only vernacular villages but also grand urban ensembles were

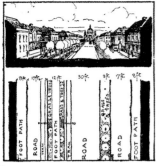
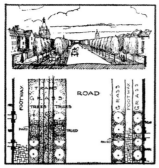

5

7

6

8

9

10

looked to for inspiration. The residential neighborhoods have about them the informality of medieval villages in England and, especially, in Germany—Rothenberg was a particular favorite. But just as much, if not even more, the layout of the town's center was guided by the plan (1666) by Christopher Wren (1632–1723) for the rebuilding of London. Samuel Swift, an early observer, had it right when he characterized the overall plan of Letchworth as "a compromise between the French *rond point* system, where all streets radiate from a single pivot, and the recent German method of bringing convergent streets together in a series of separate or preliminary intersections to avoid confusion of traffic at the principal junction."[109] The seeming split between the formal heart of Letchworth's plan and the naturalistic character of the neighborhoods created what early-twentieth-century

observers tended to deem a regrettable schism. But this no longer seems quite the case, and the strategy was certainly a cornerstone of Parker and Unwin's planning philosophy. Rather, Letchworth can be said to exhibit a healthy tension between opposing compositional modes.

The absence of funds in Letchworth's early years not only slowed the growth of the residential neighborhoods but also the development of the public buildings along the main street, The Broadway, which connects the railroad station and its adjacent shopping area with the civic buildings around the landscaped Central Square. It is with the Central Square, whose design was not fully conceptualized until 1912, that Parker and Unwin turned most directly to English precedent, admitting to the free adaptation of "Wren and other masters . . . to illustrate the layout."[110] Clearly, one of their other sources was the

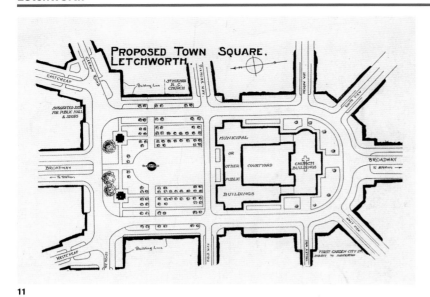

11

12

13

14

16

15

17

11. Plan, Central Square, Barry
Parker and Raymond Unwin,
Architects, 1912. FGC

12. Bird's-eye view, Central
Square. FGC

13. Plan, Cheap Cottages Exhibition,
1905. FGC

14. Cheap Cottages Exhibition. FGC

15. St. Edmundsbury Weaving Works,
Barry Parker and Raymond Unwin,
Architects, 1908. FGC

16. The Fairway, Norton
Common. FGC

17. Rushby Mead. FGC

classicizing work of Edwin Lutyens, especially his work on the monumental core at Hampstead Garden Suburb. But beyond specific stylistic influences lies a more profound structural underlining to the plan as a whole, which derives in large measure from the Viennese architect and city planner Camillo Sitte (1843–1903), even though Unwin claimed to have planned Letchworth before encountering Sitte's book *Die Städtebau nach seinen künstlerischen Grundsätzen*, which was originally published in 1889.[111] Unwin did not read German, but he did read French so he could have familiarized himself with Sitte's ideas in 1902 when the book was translated into French. (It was not brought out in English until 1945.)

The design deficiencies of The Broadway, a 100-foot-wide boulevard with space reserved in the central mall for a never-realized tram, especially the less than robust architecture along it and at Central Square, have prevented many observers from appreciating Letchworth as a whole. As a result of the separation of the shopping area from the Central Square, Letchworth's commercial heart has been generally regarded as lacking in vitality. But the shopping area, consisting mostly of two- and three-story buildings with ground-floor shops and apartments above, stretching from Station Place east along Station Road and Leys Avenue, is in fact quite lively. A through-block glazed galleria, The Arcade (Bennett and Bidwell, 1922–23), connects the two shopping streets and is a welcome surprise. The Broadway made one important but little-known contribution to British planning history: at Sollershot Circus (1910) it was the site of England's first roundabout.

Pevsner acknowledged the liveliness of the business district but seemed to imply that it was almost accidental to the plan.[112] Such was not the case. Unwin deliberately separated the business center from the civic center, in part a reflection of London's traditional urbanism, where the big squares like Belgrave or Grosvenor are quiet backwaters and the hustle-bustle of commerce is elsewhere, and in part the influence of the ideas of the American City Beautiful movement.

Fearing that the houses constructed in Letchworth would largely be "builder designed," Unwin drew up bye-laws to control the aesthetics of the city, published in 1904 as a booklet, *General Suggestions and Instructions Regulating Buildings other than Factories in the Garden City Estate*. But as it turned out, the most powerful influence on the town's aesthetics was the considerable number of houses Parker and Unwin designed during the early years of its development and the fact that Parker remained in place as a consultant to First Garden City Ltd. until 1943 (Unwin moved to Hampstead Garden Suburb in 1906.) The partners' considerable visual authority over the city's appearance is especially noticeable in the residential neighborhoods south of the railroad tracks, where a combination of straight and gently curving streets were lined with a rich mix of detached and grouped houses and where culs-de-sac and closes added a density and variety reflecting Unwin's belief

that "the six to ten foot gaps so common between villas are of little service, but if the villas were united into groups of four or six, and a gap of some thirty feet then left between the groups, this would be a pleasing break, and might afford a view of garden, country, or building beyond, that would add interest to the street."[113]

In addition to Parker, other notable architects who built at Letchworth included M. H. Baillie Scott, Geoffry Lucas (1872–1947), and Halsey Ricardo (1854–1928). Ricardo, in collaboration with W. R. Lethaby (1857–1931), was involved with First Garden City from the outset when he entered the competition for the town plan; Geoffry Lucas, working with Sidney Cranfield (1870–1961), also competed. The Lethaby-Ricardo plan also called for a central square from which diagonal streets radiated.

Parker and Unwin's combination of curved and straight roads in the residential neighborhoods, devised to preserve trees, would become a hallmark of garden suburb planning, as would their strategy of grouping houses around shared open spaces in the manner of the traditional English close. Westholm Green (Parker and Unwin, 1906), growing out of Unwin's diagram published in *The Art of Building a Home* and their work at New Earswick, the first close to be realized at Letchworth, consisted of a village green surrounded by groups of houses.[114] Westholm Green was aimed to meet the needs of workers, while more middle-class folk were accommodated at Eastholm Green (1906), which reflected their previous work at Station Road, New Earswick, with grouped two-, four-, and five-unit cottages set around an open green overlooking Norton Common. Westholm's houses were located on both sides of Norton Way, Letchworth's principal north–south street, so that its green functioned as a very public feature of the plan.

Pixmore Hill (1907–11) was the most holistic of Parker and Unwin's Letchworth groupings, a neighborhood unit that included five greens, allotment gardens, an outdoor bowling green, and a community institute, now serving as the Hillshott School. The 16.35-acre site accommodated 164 houses, mostly organized in four-house groups, creating a density of ten houses per acre. A lanelike central street ran in three separate legs through the site, its configuration similar to the one Frank Lloyd Wright adopted for his entry to the City Residential Land Development Competition (1913) (see p. 162).

Parker and Unwin's house designs transformed relatively standard plans—Mervyn Miller has described them as "a kit of parts"—into specific compositions "capable of almost infinite variety of assembly to fit particular site conditions and orientation." Birds Hill (1906), one of their best groupings, on a commanding site adjoining one intended for factories and workshops, presented, as Miller observes, "the opportunity to develop an effective sequence of street pictures," such as Sitte advocated. Rushby Mead, developed for the Howard Cottage Society, was planned by Unwin but realized (1911–12) by several architects, including Robert Bennett (1878–1956) and Wilson Bidwell (1877–1944). Miller correctly deems Unwin's plan for the group "a masterpiece of informal design, through which he reworked his early admiration of village groupings in terms of his more recently acquired analytical approach."[115] Included in the plan was Rushby Walk, a cul-de-sac along which were built two rows of houses by Parker and Unwin as well as two by C. M. Crickmer (1879–1971). Norton Way South (Parker and Unwin, 1903–10), with many houses designed for Ebenezer Howard's own portfolio, was also excellent.

Although modest cottages were included in the residential neighborhoods south of the railroad, Letchworth's greatest concentration of small houses is to be found north of the railroad where the Cheap Cottages Exhibition (1905) took place, organized by J. St. Loe Strachey, editor of *The Spectator* and owner of *The County Gentleman and Land & Water* magazine.[116] Parker and Unwin, skeptical about the Cheap Cottages Exhibition, warned against "the fatal mistake of regarding the price as the fixed element. It is most necessary to remember that the problem before us is: 'How cheaply can we build a good cottage?' Not 'How good a cottage can we build for £150.'"[117]

Despite misgivings, the partners participated in the exhibition, but their contributions did not dominate the scene. Instead, it was the highly individual houses by various architects that stood out in sharp contrast to the orchestrated coherence of the typical Parker and Unwin neighborhoods. Some would say the contrast resulted in cacophony and was an empty formalist exercise. However, many of the architects and builders made use of innovative construction techniques, including metal framing, prefabricated partitions, and cast-in-place concrete block wall systems, sometimes in support of traditional stylistic detailing, but sometimes in a search for new forms of expression. One hundred and twenty-five "cheap cottages" were erected, and the exhibition attracted 60,000 visitors. The small size of the cottages and the attempts at stylistic innovation were widely commented on in Britain and America, and the goal of the exhibition to produce innovative affordable housing—originally intended for agricultural workers but quickly heralded as industrial workers' cottages—was widely applauded, although one notable observer, C. B. Purdom, writing in 1913, noted that it "set a rage for cheapness from which Garden City has hardly yet recovered. It gave the place a name for cranky buildings."[118] A second exhibition, held in 1907 under the auspices of the National Housing Reform Council, did not attract as much attention.

Most of Letchworth is decidedly family-oriented. However, Howard, who strongly believed in cooperative housing for working professionals, especially unmarried men and women, promoted the construction of Homesgarth (H. Clapham Lander, 1911) on a four-acre site, consisting of thirty-two service flats in two-story blocks grouped around an implied quadrangle and a three-story community building including a residents' club with central kitchen and community dining hall. Homesgarth in part reflected Howard's own needs—he had moved to Letchworth in 1904. Soon, after the death of his first wife and a failed second marriage, he found himself once again a bachelor who like other "numerous folk of the middle class . . . have had a hard struggle for existence on a meager income . . . [and] require domestic help, but can very ill afford it."[119]

Letchworth is ringed by a greenbelt, but Norton Common is the city's focal open space, consisting of 60 acres of woodland and meadow on part of what had been common land awarded to Norton villagers at the time of the enclosure in 1798 but had subsequently reverted to private owners. Crisscrossed by paths, the Common constitutes for pedestrians and cyclists the principal connection of the northern neighborhoods to the railroad station and village shopping. Additionally, small parks are interspersed in the plan, most notably the highly formal Central Square and the more informal Howard Park along Norton Way.

Industry on the whole shunned Letchworth, except for one notable business housed in a remarkable structure: the Spirella Building (1912–22) by Cecil Hignett (1879–1960), located near the town center, just north of the railroad station, and waggishly referred to as "Castle Corset." Spirella, a powerful exemplar of Howard's ethos, a "factory in a garden," manufactured a widely known brand of corsetry that replaced whalebones with metal stays—the patented system was American in origin and the Spirella Company was American owned. Additionally, there was a cottage-industry-like tapestry workshop (1908) designed by Parker and Unwin on the corner of Birds Hill and Pixmore Avenue.

In the post–World War II era, Letchworth was subjected to dismissive criticism. But as its centennial approached, Letchworth's positive points began to be appreciated again. It had become a fine place to live, even though it failed to meet its founders' hopes for a Garden City. In 2003, architecture and culture critic Jonathan Meades's essay "Paradox of the Picturesque" made the point that

> to prefix city or village with garden was not unprecedented . . . Nonetheless, in its drawing together of these characteristics, and in the extent of its social and architectural ambitions, Letchworth was—and remains—remarkable. It is a fusion of conflicting traditions . . . Had Letchworth been built a decade earlier, its anti-urbanism would have been manifest only in its isolated, muddy site near Hitchin. Its buildings would probably not have been cottages. They would have lacked the whimsy and prettiness which render so many of them beguiling. As it was, its timing could not have been happier: it is a made place constructed at the very apogee of English domestic architectural design. There is a whiff of the maypole about the town. It does not take much of an imaginative leap to conjure up a coast of naked dew bathers, toga'd theosophists, vegetarians, rational dressers and teetotalers (no license to sell alcohol was applied for until the 1960s—and that after a referendum).[120]

18

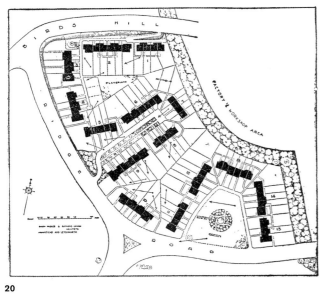

20

22

24

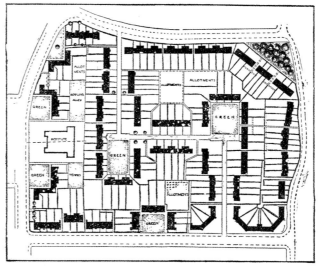

19

21

23

25

18. Rushby Walk. RAMSA (2007)

19. Plan, Pixmore Hill. FGC

20. Plan, Birds Hill Estate. FGC

21. Ridge Road horseshoe, Birds Hill Estate. RAMSA (2007)

22. Eastholm Green. CRS (1907)

23. Westholm Green. RAMSA (2007)

24. Meadow Way Green. RAMSA (2007)

25. Spirella Building, Cecil Hignett, 1912–22. RAMSA (2007)

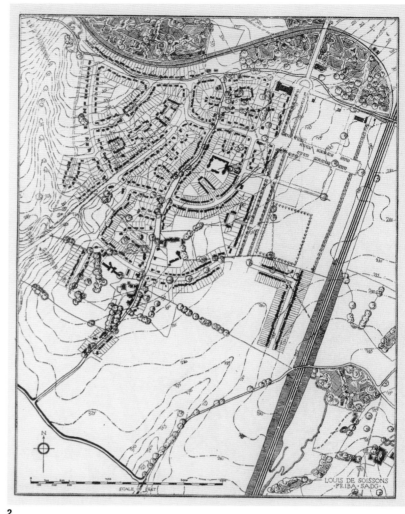

1. Plan, Louis de Soissons, 1920. LDS

2. Plan of development to 1924. CBP

Welwyn Garden City (1920), twenty-one miles from King's Cross, London, in effect Second Garden City, was established as an entirely new town on 2,378 rural acres.[121] It was realized at a time of drastically diminished resources compared to the golden affluence of the Edwardian era that characterized the early years of Letchworth's development, but nonetheless very quickly took on a sense of completeness, the lack of which long dogged Letchworth's reputation. Ebenezer Howard located the site for Welwyn in 1919, and arranged for the financing and establishment of the Second Garden City Company, appointing as chairman a well-known surveyor, Theodore G. Chambers (1871–1957). A preliminary town plan was hastily drafted by the architect C. M. Crickmer before responsibility was turned over to Louis de Soissons, a comparatively inexperienced Canadian-born graduate of the École des Beaux-Arts who served as Welwyn's planner and resident architect from 1919 until his death. As developed by the Second Garden City Company (reorganized and renamed Welwyn Garden City Ltd. in 1920) under the guidance of Howard and Chambers, the town grew slowly but steadily, reaching a population of about 18,000 people in 1948, well below the target of 50,000 initially intended by de Soissons.

While Letchworth and Hampstead Garden Suburb combined cottage-y neighborhoods with Georgian formality in their central squares, Welwyn was designed by de Soissons and Arthur W. Kenyon (1885–1969) as a Georgian town peppered by occasional enclaves of Arts and Crafts–inspired cottage groups, usually the work of other architects. Located even closer to London than Letchworth, Welwyn nonetheless succeeded to a greater extent in establishing itself as an independent entity, becoming a minor industrial center. It was home in 1925 to the American-affiliated Shredded Wheat Company, housed in de Soisson's straightforwardly gridded reinforced-concrete-framed factory set in the industrial quarter on the east side of the railroad tracks and, in 1936–39, to a branch of Hoffman-La Roche, the Swiss pharmaceuticals company, occupying a widely admired early English example of continental Modernism designed by the Swiss architect Otto R. Salvisberg (1882–1940).[122]

De Soissons developed his scheme in response to criticism leveled against Letchworth. In contrast to Letchworth, Welwyn's commercial center opens directly from the railroad station, combining shops with apartments in one- to three-story buildings arranged along Howardsgate, a 400-yard-long, 200-foot-wide

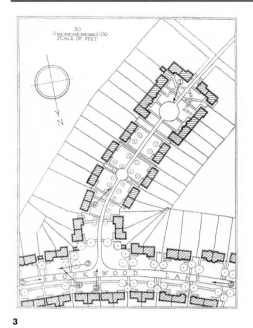

3

4

5

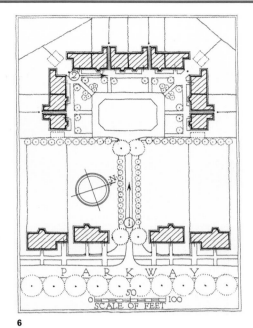

6

7

8

3. Plan, Dellcott Close. LDS (1927)

4. Dellcott Close. LDS (1927)

5. Parkway Close. RAMSA (2007)

6. Plan, Parkway Close. LDS (1927)

7. Aerial view showing Shredded Wheat factory beyond Howardsgate. EHAC (1928)

8. Aerial view. EHC (2009)

9. Plan, Handside Green. LDS (1927)

10. Handside Green. LDS (1927)

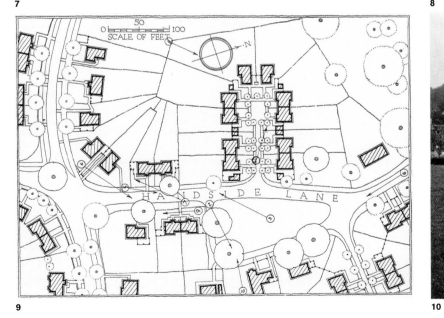

9

10

11

12

11. Howardsgate. RAMSA (2007)

12. Howardsgate shops. RAMSA (2007)

13. Lytton Gardens. RAMSA (2007)

13

landscaped boulevard that leads west from the railroad station to the 3,280-foot-long Parkway, a broad 200-foot-wide boulevard terminating at its north end in a semicircular exedra called the Campus, intended as home to important public buildings.

The layout of Welwyn's residential neighborhoods follows Unwin's prescriptions, with curving roads introduced to save existing trees and respect existing topography. Single and paired houses line streets punctuated by residential greenswards and rowhouse groups mixed with intimate midblock closes at the ends of culs-de-sac. De Soissons initially called for the "American practice" of continuous open front lawns, resisting, for the most part, residents' demand for the more typically English "front gardens" separated by hedges or fences.

One of de Soissons's earliest housing groups (1921) combined single and paired gambrel-roofed, two-story houses arranged with some facing the streets directly, some facing shared greens, and others in a cul-de-sac, all gathered around a small park, Handside Green. Other groups, such as Dellcott Close, by C. Murray Hennell (1883–1929) and Charles Holloway James (1893–1953), followed de Soissons's aesthetic lead.

Despite the goal of mixing up the social classes, Welwyn Garden City Ltd. located the middle- and upper-class houses near the commercial center on the west, while the working-class houses were built to the east of the railroad, beyond the industrial zone, tending, as Tony Rook has written, to make the working class feel that "they were 'on the wrong side of the tracks.'"[123] The sense of physical and social division was further exacerbated by the fact that the railroad insisted on a one-eighth-mile-wide swath of undevelopable land on either side of its right-of-way. Moreover, the main line of the railroad could be crossed in only three places.

Notwithstanding its elegant plan and architecture, Welwyn garnered comparatively little attention in the British architectural press in its early days. In the post–World War II era, it came to be better appreciated by English critics, so that in his 1951 guide to Hertfordshire, Nikolaus Pevsner, generally not a fan of historicist design, deemed the design of Welwyn's houses "a quiet comfortable Neo-Georgian, no longer olde-worldy," but also decried it as vapid.[124] Critics aside, Welwyn has proved very popular as a place to live, perhaps because as Clough Williams-Ellis put it, Second Garden City is a "paragon of a place . . . unique—or almost unique— . . . a by-word and a wonder . . . comely and spacious, prosperous and healthy."[125] According to Stanley Buder, "The building of Welwyn Garden City offered no serious challenge to the appeal of suburbia. Indeed, many who lived there thought of the community as a commuting suburb of London rather than as the intended experiment in metropolitan growth and regional planning. If Letchworth had appeared ahead of its time, Welwyn Garden City had not." But, as Buder also notes, the public at large deemed it "a handsome town whose aesthetic order contrasted greatly with the usual suburban hodgepodge."[126]

1

Although not much emulated in England, Welwyn was studied by American housing experts such as Clarence Stein and Henry Wright, who absorbed many of its lessons into their work at Sunnyside and Radburn. **Wythenshawe** (1931–41), intended as Manchester's Garden City, on the other hand seemed to take its cues from American practice.[127] Initiated under Barry Parker's direction, Wythenshawe was the first example in Britain of a municipally owned satellite suburb, with a target population of 100,000. The 5,567-acre estate, including a 1,000-acre green reserve to separate it from Manchester, and another 1,000 acres of open space within the satellite town, according to Clare Hartwell, Matthew Hyde, and Nikolaus Pevsner, "is hard to get to grips with, having no natural center, few landmarks, and no topography to speak of. Even residents get lost in the endless maddeningly curving residential roads."[128]

Roughly 54 percent of the site (3,030 acres) was assigned to residential purposes, with 28,000 houses planned; 550 acres were given to nonresidential buildings. The scattered centers were considered as "neighborhood units," but the idea that these might function as more-or-less self-contained village entities was seriously compromised by the merchant-influenced decision to locate shopping at secondary crossroads with approximately three-quarters of a mile between each.

With Parker's enthusiastic support, Wythenshawe's design was strongly influenced by American planning, with two limited-access landscaped parkways that, at their crossing, featured a cloverleaf intersection. Shopping, schools, and recreational grounds were dispersed, with only one significant attempt at defining a center where a railroad station led north to the 250-acre Wythenshawe Park and south past a primary school to

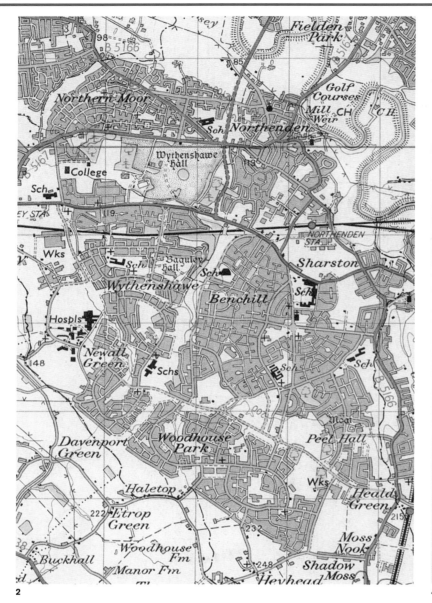

2

3

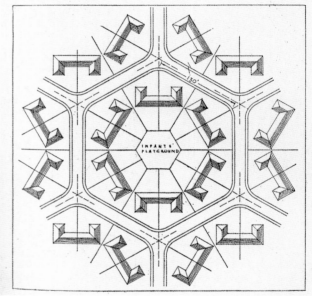

4

2. Ordnance Survey map. OS (1961)

3. Calder Avenue hexagon. GE (2003)

4. Diagram illustrating the application of a hexagonal layout to a site for small houses in blocks of four, Barry Parker. TPR37

the Town Square. Given that these elements were disconnected from the nearby parkways, they seemed more like leftovers from an earlier planning model than potential generators of community life.

For Walter Creese, Parker's enthusiasm for the American parkway type, which he introduced to Britain at Wythenshawe, was ironic, tending "to become autodidactic, evolving its own rules and environment out of key" with the rest of the plan.[129] This became especially evident after World War II, when Princess Parkway was extended beyond Wythenshawe, flooding the development with through traffic. To Parker, writing in 1945, it was "the most perfect example of a garden city," basing his claim, as Creese has stated, "on the fact that the increment on the land as a result of its development would return to the municipality, fulfilling Howard's hope in a way that Letchworth had so far been unable to do."[130] But this judgment was strategic in outlook and not concerned with the quality of the place. Despite fine examples of collective architecture echoing Parker and Unwin's pre–World War I work—such as Chamberlain

House (G. Topham Forrest, 1931–39), providing single-person flats, Mitchell Gardens (Leonard Heywood, 1938), a twenty-four-house development for older people, and groups of mansarded, Dutch-inspired cottages (1930–39) designed by Parker himself—the housing stock in general lacked distinction.

At Wythenshawe, Parker was also influenced by the Canadian planner Noulan Cauchon (1872–1935) who advocated the hexagon as opposed to the rectangle as the basis of residential street planning, making possible a 10 percent reduction in house length, thereby saving on street length per house and creating safer and fewer road intersections. Parker employed Cauchon hexagons in laying out the Roundwood estate in the Northenden section of Wythenshawe, widely agreed to be the most confusing district in the suburb.

The incorporation of American planning ideas, especially from Radburn, and the effort to balance the neighborhood unit with the demands of the motor age, marks Wythenshawe as an end point to the long cycle of the Garden City movement and not a new stage

5

6

5. Brownley Road. MAN (1934)

6. Chamberlain House, G. Topham Forrest, 1931–39. MAN (1955)

7. Mitchell Gardens, Leonard Heywood, 1938. MAN (1955)

8. Princess Parkway and Wythenshawe Road roundabout. MAN (1934)

9. Aerial view of Sharston School and neighborhood. MAN (1937)

10. Cottages, Barry Parker, 1931–39. TCP33

11. Roughey Gardens. Mike. PAN (2008)

12. Meliden Crescent. Mike. PAN (2008)

7

8

9

10

11

12

going forward. As Creese writes: "The functionalism of postwar automotive technology and the functionalism of the environment, on which Parker and Unwin had labored for decades, seem about to meet and merge at Wythenshawe. Everything appears to have reached a fitting conclusion until one reads a final sentence by Parker" that reveals the degree to which he has become "imbued with enthusiasm for the parkway." Parker writes: "In these roads there must be separate 'carriageways,' one for mechanically propelled vehicles, and another for horse-drawn vehicles . . . and bicycles, and separate tracts will perhaps be provided for trams." But, as Creese points out, this statement, made in 1929, "has something anachronistic about it . . . The form seems correct, but the content too late . . . Parker and Unwin never stopped thinking, but the conditions never stopped changing either. Despite the municipal sponsorship, the flaw of Wythenshawe was essentially that of Letchworth. It took overlong to build. Theory, uninhibited and international as it now was, never quite caught up to changing technology."[131]

THE GARDEN CITY IN AMERICA

The first attempt to plan a for-profit garden city–type development took place in America with the 1827 proposal for the city of **Hygeia**, a "rural town" intended for a site in Kentucky on a bend in the Ohio River across from Cincinnati.[132] The project was put forward by an English developer, William Bullock, and designed by an English architect, J. B. (John Buonarotti) Papworth (1775–1847), whose plan incorporated parks, allotment gardens, and promenades into a geometrically ordered center surrounded by residential streets that seemed to curve in response to the terrain. Were it not to have failed for lack of funding, Hygeia would have accommodated a mix of social classes in detached villas set on large lots, semidetached houses, and rowhouses placed around London-inspired residential squares, and provided shops, a chapel, theater, community building, and museum.

The first planned development to adopt the name **Garden City** (1869) was located in New York in a part of Queens County on Long Island that would later split off

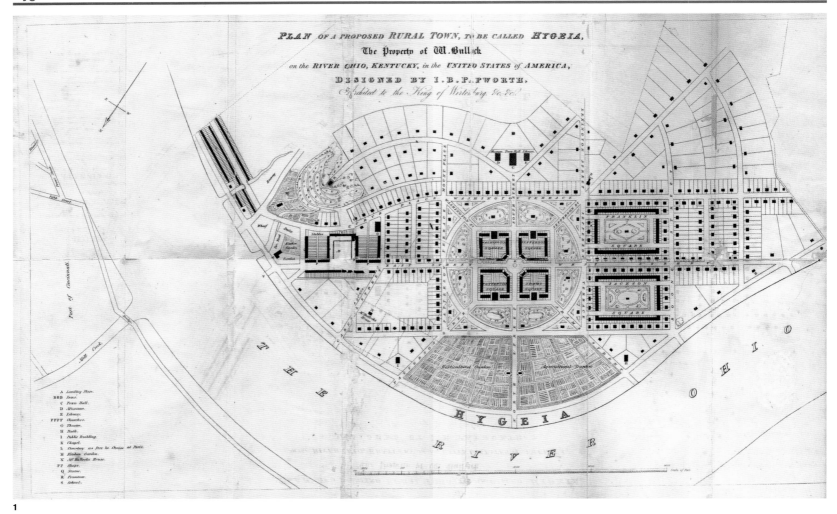

1. Plan, J. B. Papworth, 1827. FHS

to become a new county, Nassau.[133] Also initially called Hygeia—reflecting the motivation for the community's founding, to provide a more healthful place to live than the city—Garden City was the brainchild of A. T. Stewart (1803–1876), the pioneering department store magnate, who was not intent on creating an estate park for like-minded people, but on developing, owning, and managing over a long period of time a large residential area that would in effect be a small suburban city. In this Stewart may have overreached the market or confounded the expectations of would-be residents. In any case, his plan stumbled in the economic chaos of the early 1870s, leading Kenneth Jackson, in his *Crabgrass Frontier*, to describe Garden City as "the most ambitiously planned suburb of the nineteenth century, as well as the most conspicuous failure."[134] In 1879, a reporter identified only as "M," but perhaps Montgomery Schuyler, writing in the Boston-based journal *American Architect and Building News*, grasped the fact that many of the basic ideas that Howard would later adopt were present in Stewart's blueprint for development: "It is a suburb, a sanitarium, and a cathedral town, all made at once and all made to order," promising "an economic and an architectural interest, in addition to its sanitary interest."[135] Ironically, much of Garden City's interest lies in the possibility that Howard took its name for his own idealized town plan.

Garden City occupied a basically uncongenial site: the almost treeless, 7,000-acre Hempstead Plain, between Mineola and Hempstead. The site would in 1873 be served by a Long Island Rail Road branch connecting it directly to Long Island City, where ferry service was provided to New York City (Manhattan Island). Perhaps Stewart's decision to buy the land was inspired by his favorite architect, John Kellum (1809–1871), who came from Hempstead. Eventually Stewart added 3,000 more acres to his holdings, intending, according to the *New York Herald*, to "build a city to be rented by men of moderate means, who prefer to hire houses rather than invest in real estate the capital they need in their business."[136] Stewart had in mind a town of 10,000 houses "for clerks and . . . businessmen, and it is known that he intended that not one single house should be sold in Garden City. It is conjectured that he desired to bequeath to the world a city that should own itself—a city whose every inhabitant should pay house-rent to the city treasury direct—a city that should ultimately become so wealthy that it might support schools and encourage art." Stewart died in 1876, before much development had taken place, leading the *New York Herald* to predict that there "is little doubt that the executors of [Stewart's] great trust will eventually sell homes in Garden City as a means of attracting a class that will be

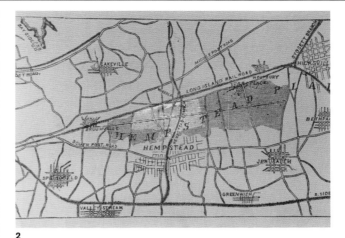

1. Map. NYPLMD (1891)

2. Map showing extent of A. T. Stewart's 1869 purchase in dark shading. JEKP

3. An "Apostle" house, John Kellum, 1872. JEKP (1877)

4. Franklin Court, Ford, Butler & Oliver, 1910. Korten. NCP (1910)

5. Garden City Hotel, John Kellum, 1874. JEKP

6. Panoramic view showing two "Apostle" houses. JEKP (1878)

welcomed there," presumably a polite way of saying people with money.[137]

As laid out on a grid containing twenty-seven miles of roadway, Garden City departs from the arcadianism of typical planned suburbs. Kellum's gridded plan, only occasionally relieved by diagonal avenues, provided for block sizes far larger than the typical 200-by-800-foot block in New York City. Not only larger than those of the Manhattan grid, Kellum's block sizes varied from 1,000 to 1,500 feet in length, each being about 500 feet wide. Similarly, Garden City's streets were broader than those typical in New York City, with 50 feet of roadway and an additional 30 feet reserved for sidewalks and grassy verges. The typical building lot was about one-and-a-half acres, also very generous, certainly compared with the typical 25-by-100-foot lot of New York, making clear that this was intended as a suburban city for the affluent. The plan was aerated with a number of parks varying from 50 to 150 acres each.

At the center, a simple brick railroad station and a manager's office as well as a row of shops faced a "square and almost flat treeless park, traversed by rectilinear roads, and decorated by two fountains kept diligently at play."[138] A four-story, twenty-five-room hotel (1874) designed by Kellum was set in its own 23-acre park facing the square, constructed so that, as Stewart put it, prospective residents could be well-housed "while looking at the houses that I offer for rent."[139] Ten large houses were constructed around the hotel to set the tone for the new development's architecture. Quickly dubbed "the Apostles," the houses were soon followed by smaller brick and frame houses sometimes called "the Disciples." Stewart himself lived in the hotel, which the *New York Herald* labeled a "phenomenal country-house"; after his death, his "sumptuous room" was "sacredly kept" by his widow.[140] Although Garden City was planned as a large town, not much thought seemed to be given to providing any significant commercial activity. With only a few shops near the railroad station, as a shopkeeper put it, "the gentlemen, they go into New York every morning, and the ladies,—well, the ladies go in too."[141]

When first announced, Stewart's plan was favorably received. In 1869 *Harper's Weekly* rejoiced: "This design is so gigantic that it throws into the shade every attempt of the kind hitherto made . . . Hempstead Plains, hitherto a desert, will be made to blossom as the rose; it will be the most beautiful suburb in the vicinity of New York. God speed the undertaking!"[142] But the following year the *New York World* was not so sure: Stewart's "purchase of Hempstead Plains, simply because it was the cheapest large property near New York, is certainly against the judgment of real estate operators. He is attempting a daring experiment, nothing less than a community which should have churches, schools, water, gas and all the appliances of municipal life, without a single other person having interest in a foot of the whole domain. He proposes to be landlord, mayor, alderman, in fact the whole municipality."[143]

By 1879 the development consisted of about sixty houses, some brick, some wood, but all, according to "M," "suburban villas of the deepest dye, and apparently designed out of the Practical Builder's Assistant."[144] Some of the early houses were designed by Kellum, but his death in 1871 left the town artistically rudderless. Eighteen cottages were built on Franklin Avenue in 1872 to house families of the skilled workmen, many of them recent immigrants from Poland. A central waterworks (1876) was constructed, featuring a great well, 50 feet in diameter and 40 feet deep.

With the national economy's recovery in the 1880s, Garden City at last began to prosper. But even as late as 1885, it was still debunked as "Stewart's Folly," with only 550 residents. Montgomery Schuyler, in his 1884 survey of New York's suburbs, was almost completely negative in his assessment:

When the late A. T. Stewart [ventured beyond his area of expertise] his excursions were apt to be as unsuccessful as his exertions in his own line were uniformly successful. Garden City was one of the boldest of these excursions and one is not surprised to hear that as an investment it has not been profitable. The site has nothing to recommend it except salubrity, nor indeed anything to explain its selection. The village simply occurs on the great Long Island plain in the same fortuitous way in which villages crop out on the Western prairies, with nothing to indicate why it should be here rather than elsewhere . . . Neither the hotel nor any of the houses has the slightest interest as a visual object . . . Though the cathedral be the architectural lion not only of Garden City but of all Long Island, it does not remove one's wonder at the patient suburban people who can endure to live in a place where there is nothing else to look at.[145]

Stewart's idea did not seem to include much in the way of manufacturing, but by the turn of the century, Garden City began to attract industry, bringing its functional composition closer in line with Howard's Garden City idea. In 1910 the publishers Doubleday, Page and Doran purchased 40 acres to build a printing plant, christened the Country Life Press, which was designed by Henry Kirby (1853–1915) and John J. Petit to resemble Hampton Court in England. The arrival of industry increased the demand for modest houses, resulting in the construction of a number of interesting groupings based on English garden suburb precedents. Most notable of these is Franklin Court (Ford, Butler & Oliver, 1910), a combination of two-family and group cottages on a triangular lot with an interior common playground and, at the apex, a set-aside parcel for car parking.[146] In addition, the Garden City Company built for rental twenty-five seven-room workmen's cottages as well as a tenement building that provided lower-priced apartments.

Garden City was also able to take advantage of the growing popularity of the automobile when it became the gateway to the Long Island Motor Parkway, a toll road intended for pleasure driving built by William K. Vanderbilt Jr. in 1909–11 and generally regarded as the first-ever limited-access highway. Perhaps in anticipation of Vanderbilt's project, a large tract of the original Stewart holdings was sold in 1907 to a separate company that developed what is now known as Garden City Estates. The new community was organized by Cyril E. Marshall (1878–1933) and Charles Leavitt Jr. (1871–1928) along lines similar to Garden City, but in order to distinguish the new development from Stewart's, and possibly to take into account the fluidity of automobile travel, curvilinear streets were introduced into the gridiron plan and Nassau Boulevard was planted with a central mall, a feature later repeated at an even bolder scale on Stewart Avenue.

Pullman (1880–86), Illinois, outside Chicago, was the vision of George M. Pullman (1831–1897), whose "palace cars" had revolutionized rail travel. Though not especially gardenesque, the community did embody many of the principles of Howard's ideal.[147] Pullman's reputation

1. Plan, Solon S. Beman and Nathan F. Barrett, 1880. AR18 (1918)

1

has been severely compromised by the labor policies of its founder. But it is more than worthy of consideration not only as the embodiment of Garden City ideals but also as the most ambitious planned industrial village of the nineteenth century and arguably America's first new industrial village to be both conceived of and realized as a unified whole. Just as Garden City, Long Island, signaled an expansion of scale from "suburb" to "suburban city," Pullman represented a giant step forward in size and complexity from Lowell, Massachusetts, and other New England industrial villages (see p. 797) and was the first American undertaking to rival its British contemporaries, Port Sunlight (1888) and Bournville (1895).

Pullman was designed by the twenty-seven-year-old architect Solon Spencer Beman (1853–1914) and the landscape designer Nathan F. Barrett, taking to a significantly high level the collaboration between an architect and a landscape designer for the purpose of establishing a new community. Beman, an alumnus of the Richard Upjohn and Son office in New York, had been sharing space with Barrett, who introduced the young architect to George Pullman. Barrett was working on the landscape of Pullman's summer home in Elberon, New Jersey. Pullman was impressed and offered Beman the commission to design his new factory on the south side of Chicago. Only later, over a two-year period, did the idea of building an integrated industrial village begin to take shape, and Beman's scope of work was expanded to include the design of the entire enterprise. Richard T. Ely noted in *Harper's Magazine* in 1885: "This is probably the first time a single architect has ever constructed a whole town systematically upon scientific principles."[148] As a Pullman Palace Car Company brochure distributed in

1893 stated, "The story of Pullman naturally divides itself into three parts—the building of the car, the building of the operating system, and the building of the town."[149] Moreover, as John W. Reps has pointed out, Pullman "stands out as a company town project . . . [because] the developers . . . produced a three-dimensional plan in which the design of individual buildings received as much attention as the layout of streets, parks, and building sites . . . Pullman thus constitutes a valuable reference point in American planning—an example of a complete town, conceived and built as a unit, and under the direction of a team of designers who presumably embodied in the plan the most up-to-date theories and practices of town design."[150]

Reasonably independent yet a satellite to Chicago, Pullman was geographically suburban, but it was not a bedroom village like Riverside; it was a full-fledged town with its own balanced ecology of manufacture, agriculture, commerce, and community. As such, it could very well be considered a model for Howard's Garden City diagram, something that is tempting to assume, except that Howard lived in Chicago from 1872 to 1876, before Pullman was planned. Yet Howard may have known about it, given Ely's extensive 1885 article in *Harper's Magazine*. Nonetheless, there is no specific evidence of Pullman having had an impact on Howard's thinking.

Pullman grew up out of George Pullman's simultaneously idealistic and opportunistic belief that a well-designed industrial complex was not necessarily incompatible with a suitable environment for family life and that the benefits accruing from such an arrangement would benefit owner and wage earner alike. Pullman kept ownership of all housing, commercial, and

2. View from Arcade showing Hotel Florence, center, and works in distance. Johnson. RBA2 (c. 1885)

3. View from Arcade showing park and works. Johnson. RBA2 (c. 1885)

4. View from Arcade showing Arcade Row houses (right), Greenstone Church (center), and first Market Hall (left). Johnson. RBA3 (c. 1885)

5. Workers' houses. LOC3 (1901)

6. Houses on Pullman Avenue. RBA7 (c. 1885)

7. Typical street. RAMSA (1984)

8. Executive houses. RAMSA (1984)

9. Hotel Florence, Solon S. Beman, 1881. Henschen. FL (2012)

2

3

4

5

6

7

8

9

industrial buildings, as well as the parks and the church.

Pullman was built on a portion of a 4,000-acre site thirteen miles south of Chicago's center along the right-of-way of the Illinois Central Railroad, lying between 103rd and 116th Streets. The site was bound on one side by Lake Calumet and on the other by the railroad. Beman and Barrett's scheme employed a gridiron plan for the residential areas north and south of the Pullman factory. Additional land was set aside to buffer the community and allow for future growth. Pullman was a model community not only as a result of its provision for adequate housing and cultural and recreational amenities, but also because of its sophisticated infrastructure. Most notable were the separate storm and sewage systems that carried

the rainwater from roofs and streets through cobble-stone gutters to Lake Calumet, while sending sewage in glazed pipes to a 300,000-gallon reservoir where, as part of a complex process, it was fermented, the unpolluted effluent recycled, and the remainder used as fertilizer for nearby farms owned by Pullman. Power for the factory and the town was supplied by the 700-ton Corliss engine that had powered the 1876 Centennial Exposition in Philadelphia.

The town's rapid growth was astounding. By 1882 the south section, which was the larger of the two residential districts planned, was fully occupied and work began north of the factory where 600 units were built in a fourteen-block area from 104th to 108th Streets that came to

10

12

13

11

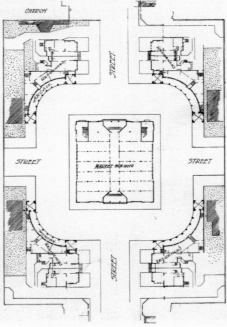

14

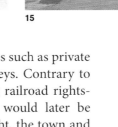

15

be called North Pullman. The residents in North Pullman were generally unskilled and the houses were less elaborate than in the original development. Moreover, no shops or community facilities were provided, forcing residents, as Stanley Buder points out, to walk ten or twenty minutes to the Arcade.[151] By September 1884, all in all, Pullman consisted of over 1,400 dwellings housing approximately 8,500 people.

Pullman was notable for pioneering applications of mass-production techniques to housing development. The housing was solid, if somewhat dour in its appearance, with a variety of types provided to meet the needs of a diverse community of workers. The workers' housing was admirably constructed with slate roofs and brick trimmed in stone and provided amenities such as private backyards connected to rear service alleys. Contrary to most residential construction adjoining railroad rights-of-way, and initiating a strategy that would later be employed at Bournville and Port Sunlight, the town and the factory were planned as a unit and intended, as Ely pointed out, to present an attractive appearance to passengers on the Illinois Central Railroad, which serviced one of Pullman's two train stations.

Pullman established as a development principle that sound housing was fundamental to the well-being and productivity of each and every worker. Decent accommodations were provided at moderate rents for workers at all pay levels, from freestanding houses to rowhouses to two- and three-room tenements. By varying roofs and the way in which standardized windows, doors, and trim were composed on different buildings, visual monotony was avoided. Consistency, however, was maintained by the repeated use of brick as a building material and the use of standardized building elements.

A large hotel, the Florence, was built at right angles to the manufacturing plant, across from the railroad station, together forming a picture when seen across a naturalistically landscaped park designed by Barrett, who also relieved the town's strict geometry of streets and residential rows with informal planting. Nearby, the Arcade, modeled on the Reynolds Arcade (1828) in Rochester, New York, which Beman had researched in 1881, was a mixed-use facility crisscrossed by a 90-foot-long, north–south, glass-roofed interior passageway on two floors, combining commerce with culture. It included a 5,000-book library, offices, meeting rooms, a bank, and a theater that was said to be the finest in the Chicago area at the time of its completion. A Market Hall, reflecting the redbrick Queen Anne character of virtually all of Beman's work at Pullman, supplemented the dry goods shopping facilities in the Arcade with stalls for vegetable and meat sellers and, on the second floor, a public hall. The building stood in the center of a square until it burned down in 1892, ten years after its completion; its replacement was grander still, reflecting the classicism then being introduced to Chicago at the World's Columbian Exposition of 1893, the square ringed by four two-story arcaded structures, all finished in limestone and the light-colored yellow brick that the new classicists preferred. As Robert M. Lillibridge pointed out in his pioneering reassessment of Pullman's architecture and urbanism: "The market square as finally developed proved to be one of Beman's most successful architectural efforts . . . [and] as a unit . . . set a new standard for the urban square as conceived in America."[152]

George Pullman's paternalism was grudgingly tolerated by workers, but when the Depression of the 1890s came and the company laid off workers and simultaneously increased rents, all hell broke loose. Pullman, failing to recognize the significance of the ensuing strike by the workers, ignored the advice of the eminently pragmatic Republican politician Mark Hanna, who told him to "arbitrate, arbitrate, arbitrate." Hanna wrote him off, saying that "a man who won't meet his own men halfway is a God-damn fool."[153] The strike culminated in violence in 1894, bringing the National Guard, armed with Gatling guns, into the town. Although the strikers ultimately capitulated, they had succeeded in attracting national attention and the support of the pioneer labor leaders Eugene V. Debs and Samuel Gompers. Pullman and his town, once lionized as progressive, now symbolized corporate feudalism. Within four years, the Illinois Supreme Court upheld the workers' demand that Pullman sell them their houses. When he died, Pullman had become so hated as a symbol of capitalist abuse that his family feared for his mortal remains and had his coffin

bound in steel and embedded in asphalt.

Ely was highly skeptical of George Pullman's paternalism almost a full decade before the strike. But he was enthusiastic about Beman and Barrett's work:

> *The streets cross each other at right angles, yet here again skill has avoided the frightful monotony of New York . . . A public square, arcade, hotel, market, or some large building is often set across a street so ingeniously as to break the regular line, yet without inconvenience to traffic. Then at the termination of long streets a pleasing view greets and relieves the eye—a bit of water, a stretch of meadow, a clump of trees, or even one of the large but neat workshops. All this grows upon the visitor day by day. No other feature of Pullman can receive praise needing so little qualification as its architecture.*[154]

Although it is appropriate to situate Pullman in the tradition of planned American industrial villages, it is likely that George Pullman had in mind the example of European developments in enlightened paternalism, possibly those of the Krupp Works in Essen, Germany (see p. 741), but more likely, that of Sir Titus Salt's Saltaire (1850–76) (see p. 703). This connection was first proposed by the French economist Paul de Rousiers in his book *American Life* (1892).[155] Thomas J. Schlereth, Beman's biographer, has drawn attention to the likelihood of Pullman's having visited Saltaire in 1873 and Thomas Grant, a close personal friend of Pullman's who was a student of British and American industrial towns, also said that Beman had explicitly employed Saltaire as a prototype. As Schlereth points out, several parallels exist between Saltaire and Pullman: "Both plans were the work of trained architects . . . working with industrialists who had achieved recognition because of technological innovation. Both town plans called for a location outside an existing city . . . for two reasons: to avoid the municipality's taxes, building code restrictions, and congestion and to be able to place the factory/residential complex in a pastoral setting . . . Both town plans called for residential, commercial and recreational land usage; both were built primarily in a single building material . . . both strove for a harmonious architectural vocabulary . . . "[156]

The bitter aftertaste of the strike stigmatized the town for generations to come. The housing deteriorated; the Arcade was torn down in 1926. By the 1960s, with passenger railroading in deep decline, the long-neglected town was threatened with demolition. Yet the fundamental humanity of Pullman's vision endured. Town residents—now homeowners—stuck it out and preservationists began to lobby on its behalf. More than one hundred years after its construction, Pullman is being gentrified as an affordable suburb. A new middle class that punches computer keys in Chicago offices instead of rivets in Pullman's factories is bringing it back to life. However, the remarkable balance of workplace and dwelling that was Pullman's original goal and

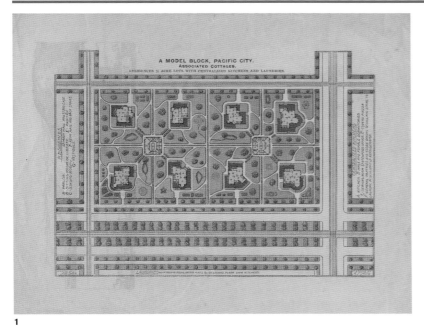

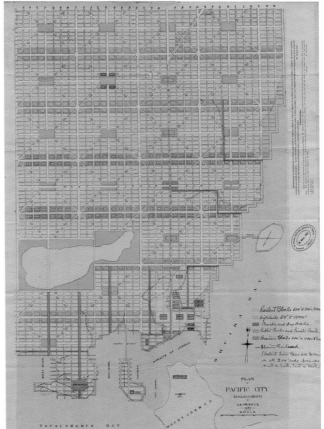

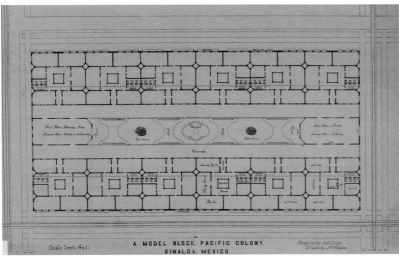

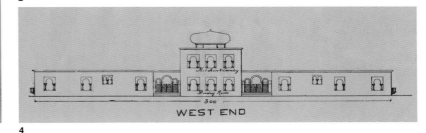

achievement has been lost, as the majority of its citizens commute to their jobs by train or freeway.

The vicissitudes of its role in the history of labor notwithstanding, as John Reps has written, Pullman "was a remarkable achievement. Not since Williamsburg had an entire town been designed with equal attention to the ground plan and to the buildings that would form the third dimension. Beman and Barrett succeeded in creating in their two town squares real civic design. Despite the relatively small size of the town, the whole effect remained distinctly urban in character. The designers must be given full credit, but George Pullman deserves equal praise for his vision of what a model industrial town might be."[157]

Pullman is more industrial village than garden city. **Pacific City** (1886) more convincingly stakes its claim as America's first garden city.[158] Although not located in the United States but on Mexico's Topolobampo Bay, across the Gulf of California from the tip of the Baja Peninsula and about midway between San Diego and Mexico City, Pacific City was an American proposition, a heavily promoted but unsuccessful attempt to establish, as its

founder, Albert Kimsey Owen (1847–1916), put it, "the first city in which will be town and country combined."[159] Owen, of no relation to Robert Owen, was a Pennsylvania Quaker who studied civil engineering before moving to Colorado in 1871 to work on the expansion of the Denver and Rio Grande Railroad into Mexico. The following year, during an eleven-month survey of Mexico, Owen came upon the sparsely populated but well-located Topolobampo Bay, deeming it "the best, the most picturesque and most desirable harbor on the Pacific and Gulf Coast of northwestern Mexico" and vowing to "get a railroad at Topolobampo within less than one year . . . It will control the winter traffic, passenger and freight between the United States and China."[160]

During the next ten years, Owen, facing one obstacle after another in realizing the railroad, shifted his focus toward Pacific City, which he intended to operate as a cooperative community based on his own brand of "integral cooperation." Owen set up a joint stock company that attracted some 2,500 investors, including Horace Greeley and Marie Howland, the latter of whom

1. Plan for a model block of eight detached cottages with cooperative housekeeping buildings shared by four families, Albert Kimsey Owen, 1885. MSCL

2. Plan, Albert Kimsey Owen, 1889. MSCL

3. Plan for a model block with one-story courtyard houses and central two-story kitchen, dining room, laundry, parlor, and library, Albert Kimsey Owen, 1885. MSCL

4. Studies of Moorish ornamentation for a courtyard housing model block, 1885. MSCL

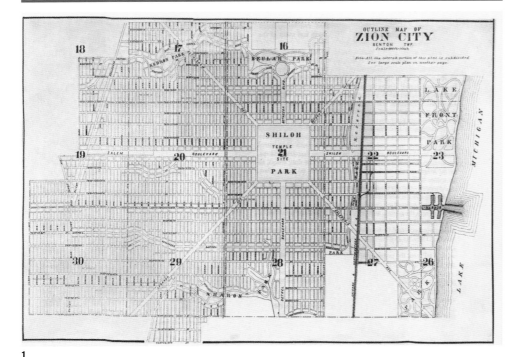

1. Map. REPS (1907)

2. Elisha Avenue. CRS

had lived in Godin's Familistère in 1864 and wrote a popular feminist romance, *Papa's Own Girl* (1874), colored by her experiences there.

Owen envisioned a city of 500,000 on the 29-square-mile site, resulting in an overall density of twenty-six people per acre. The plan, prepared by Owen in collaboration with the Philadelphia architectural and civil engineering firm of John Jerome Deery (d. 1919) and James S. Keerl (n.d.), called for a conventional grid with six-lane-wide principal streets able to accommodate electric streetcars, bicycles, and horse-drawn carriages. A network of diagonal streets was overlaid to create a diaper pattern that for Stanley Buder evoked "L'Enfant's plan of Washington, D.C., although much more mechanical."[161] Park blocks were placed at regular intervals, recalling the plan of Philadelphia. Cooperative stores, factories, libraries, and theaters were, as Dolores

Hayden has noted, "all suggestive of an endless supply of communal and private resources, and leisure to enjoy them."[162] At Marie Howland's request, Owen included not only detached houses on landscaped lots, but also courtyard apartment hotels based on the Familistère, and rowhouses that were placed in groups of between twelve and forty-eight to enclose gardens and communal buildings containing a parlor, library, kitchen, dining room, and laundry facility. Similar communal facilities were provided for each group of four detached houses.

The first colonists arrived in mid-1886. Promised a job, a house, an economy based on the exchange of labor and services, and a life free of lawyers, advertising, prostitution, taverns, and taxes, they found instead a desolate, barely farmable site with poor supplies of fresh water and rampant malaria. Many returned to the United States while others chose to live in shacks and tents on better land thirty miles inland. By 1890, about 200 residents remained. Owen was able to drum up support from various investors until 1893, when, after attempting to sell the colony, he withdrew. It was virtually abandoned by 1894. Nonetheless, according to Hayden, Owen's plans were "influential in both the United States and England, where they were studied by Ebenezer Howard . . . The ambiance is as suburban as Howard's Letchworth." The plan, Hayden concluded, "makes the transition from early nineteenth-century concepts of a single phalanstery housing an entire community to late nineteenth-century notions of mass housing consisting of complementary urban and suburban building types bordering endless similar streets."[163]

In 1900, the Rev. John Alexander Dowie (1847–1907), a faith healer and founder of the Christian Catholic Apostolic Church, announced his acquisition of 6,500 acres—10 square miles—of gently sloping farmland on the Lake Michigan shore 40 miles north of Chicago and three miles from the Wisconsin border, where he intended to build **Zion City,** a theocratic utopia and church headquarters from which, as John Reps has written, "the whole world would be converted."[164] While at first Zion City seems a far cry from the secular Garden City ideals of Ebenezer Howard, it bears inclusion in this survey by virtue of its physical plan, its program, and, most important, its holistic concept of work and dwelling. Although Dowie is said to have conceived the initial layout, Burton J. Ashley (1857–1921), an experienced civil engineer who signed on as Zion City's resident engineer after crediting Dowie with healing him and his daughter, was the designer of record. The plan focused on a central 200-acre square, Shiloh Park, the intended location of a temple. A 300-foot-wide boulevard extended from each side of the square and a narrower diagonal avenue from each corner. Most of the site was blanketed by a grid of 66- to 150-foot-wide streets interrupted by curving drives that followed the courses of existing streams. Six parks were also included, two of which, featuring naturalistic plans, were to be located on the lakeshore, north and south of a harbor.

Although an easy commute by railroad to downtown

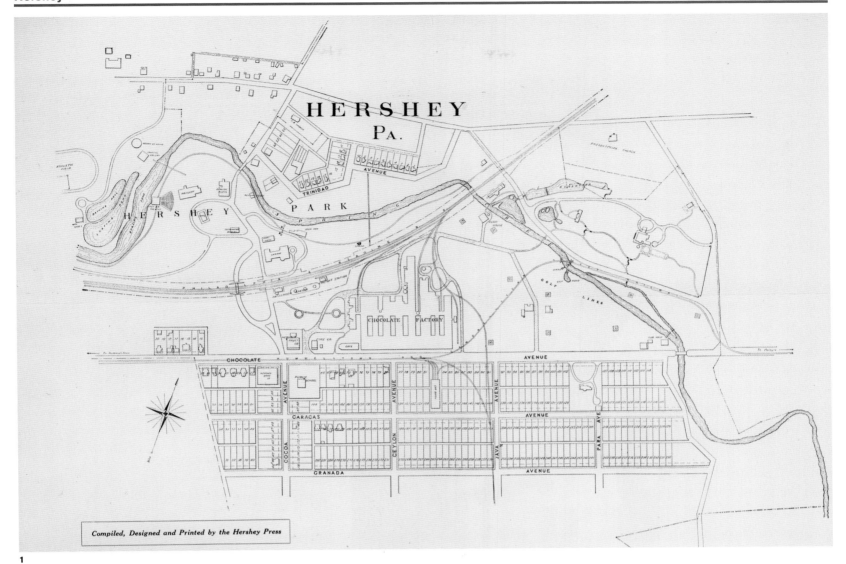

HERSHEY Pa.

Compiled, Designed and Printed by the Hershey Press

1

1. Plan, Henry H. Heer, 1903. HCA (1909)

Chicago, Zion City was intended to be self-sufficient. A successful laceworks and a brick factory were established, employing many early residents, and as of 1903, 180 acres of farmland were being cultivated. Recalling the harsh paternalism of some nineteenth-century English industrial villages, Dowie's Zion was to include, as one contemporary observer put it, "no saloons, no harlots' dens, no tobacco shops, no theatres, no gambling halls, no opium joints, no drug stores, no secret lodges, no pig markets, no surgeons' offices, no labor unions, no oyster traffic."[165] Leases were set to expire in the year 3000 but could be termiated if any covenant was broken. Defying many observers' expectations, when sales commenced in 1901, Zion City got off to a strong start. By 1905 it counted a population of 6,000, and it continued to thrive under new leadership after Dowie died in 1907. In 1933, however, the land company went bankrupt. The waterfront parks and harbor were never built, but much of the rest of the plan was implemented, and Zion City, as Reps has written, evolved into "a relatively normal suburban community whose residents have little knowledge of its unique history."[166]

Hershey, Pennsylvania, founded in 1903 by Milton S. Hershey (1857–1945), joins Bournville in England (see p. 224) and the Menier company's development at Noisiel-sur-Marne in France (see p. 731) as one of the three planned "chocolate towns."[167] Raised in the rural farm community of Derry Church in central Pennsylvania's Lebanon Valley, fifteen miles east of Harrisburg, Hershey left school after the fourth grade, apprenticing with a candy manufacturer in nearby Lancaster before striking out on his own in 1876 when he opened a confectionery in Philadelphia to take advantage of the crowds at the Centennial Exposition. The business ended in bankruptcy, a fate that befell subsequent ventures over the next decade in Denver, New Orleans, and New York City. In the late 1880s Hershey finally found great success by returning to his roots, starting the Lancaster Caramel Company, which prospered. In 1893 he attended the World's Columbian Exposition in Chicago, where he became fascinated with a German chocolate-making machine on exhibit, purchasing the equipment on the spot and shipping it back East. Reps speculates that Hershey also visited Pullman on the trip, "and the idea of combining his proposed chocolate plant with a new town for its employees must have

2. Chocolate Avenue. HCA
(c. 1913)

3. Hershey chocolate factory
and office. HCA (c. 1920)

4. Trinidad Avenue houses, William
Henry Lebkicher, c. 1904. HCA
(c. 1910)

5. Java Avenue houses, C. Emlen
Urban, c. 1906. HCA (c. 1913)

6. Trinidad Avenue. Heisey.
HCA (1991)

7. Hershey Park. HCA (1918)

2

3

4

5

6

7

seemed logical."[168]

In 1900 Hershey sold the caramel enterprise to concentrate exclusively on his chocolate factory and on a model town, intending to build on 1,200 acres of cornfields and pastures just south of his hometown. The site, with ready access to ample supplies of fresh water and milk, was located near the tracks of the Philadelphia & Reading Railroad, facilitating the importation of cocoa beans and sugar via ports in Philadelphia and New York as well as the shipment of the finished product. After convincing the railroad to build a new station in Derry Church (the town changed its name to Hershey in 1906), Hershey began planning what he called his "industrial utopia."[169]

Hershey worked closely with engineer Henry H. Heer (n.d.), who laid out the streets in a rectilinear grid, although in subsequent stages of development curving streets were employed in residential areas. The factory was sited north of the railroad tracks, with the residential and commercials areas to the south within walking

distance. Chocolate Avenue, a broad, east–west boulevard, was the main thoroughfare, home to the town's most imposing public buildings. To continue the theme, another major street was named Cocoa Avenue and several others were named after cocoa-producing regions, including Areba, Granada, Java, and Caracas. The utilitarian plan was relieved by an extensive planting scheme devised by landscape architect Oglesby Paul (1876–1939), who not only lined residential streets with an abundance of shade trees but also landscaped the areas surrounding the ivy-covered factory complex to provide workers with an attractive environment.

The majority of the housing consisted of spacious single-family dwellings on 50-by-150-foot lots. Hershey initially turned to family friend and architect manqué William Henry Lebkicher (1845–1929), but his efforts on Trinidad Avenue just north of the railroad tracks were derided by Hershey as "slave quarters" for their dull uniformity.[170] For the remainder of the houses south of the railroad, Hershey hired experienced Lancaster-based architect C. Emlen Urban (1863–1939), who produced designs more to Hershey's liking, including a charming development on Java Avenue. By 1906 Urban had completed sixty houses.

Perhaps chastened by the example of Pullman, Hershey did not allow his paternalism to degenerate into a harsh authoritarianism, instead offering houses for sale as well as rent and allowing company workers to purchase unimproved lots to build their own houses. He did put in place a series of restrictive covenants, prohibiting fences, pigpens, and chicken coops. Hershey was so pleased with Urban's houses that he commissioned him to design many of the town's buildings, including the vast limestone factory (1905) boasting six acres of floor space.

Hershey supplied an impressive array of public services, building an extensive trolley network that not only provided inexpensive transportation for commuting workers but also allowed town residents to conveniently travel outside the village to neighboring communities. Along Chocolate Avenue, where the streetcar line ran, Hershey built a three-story brick department store, a two-story white marble bank, and the Spanish-style white stucco Cocoa Inn, all designed by Urban. Hershey also provided the funds for the building and upkeep of a library, school, hospital, five churches, and an orphanage.

Hershey set aside 150 acres north of the factory for a park, an amenity that brought unimagined dividends. Initially designed by Oglesby Paul to serve as picnic grounds for company workers, Hershey Park quickly grew in both size and scope to include a children's playground, swimming pool, bowling alley, bandshell for concerts, a zoo, and a carousel. It also began to attract visitors from outside the village who arrived by trolley and train and later by automobile, becoming a tourist destination with an annual attendance of over 100,000 people by 1915, at which time tours of the chocolate factory itself were added to the mix of amusements. The town of Hershey continued to prosper even during the Depression, when a major building campaign culminated in the construction of the 241-room, Mediterranean-style Hotel Hershey (Paul D. Witmer, 1933).

University City, Missouri, was the vision of Edward Gardner Lewis (1869–1950), a gifted entrepreneur and an indicted but never convicted defrauder who, after arriving in St. Louis as a peddler of mosquito repellents, made a fortune publishing magazines directed mainly toward women.[171] Lewis's first foray into real estate development came when his business empire, based in downtown St. Louis, required expansion, leading him to decide "that I would buy outright a suitable piece of property, establish a new plant and beautify the surroundings." Observing that St. Louis's westward pattern of growth away from the Mississippi River seemed to occur "from high ground to high ground, from hill to hill," with the hollows filling up later, Lewis singled out a stretch of vacant land on either side of Delmar Boulevard, the main artery leading from downtown.[172] In 1902, emboldened by the recent announcement that a campus for the newly founded Washington University

would be built nearby and that the neighboring Forest Park was to be the location of the 1904 World's Fair, he purchased 85 acres: "My tract is thus the centre of a complete little district in between Forest Park and Washington University on the south and the far less demandable land on the north, like a cork in the neck of a bottle."[173]

Lewis set about planning a "model city which should be a real 'City Beautiful'" with residential subdivisions around a campus-like civic and business center, University City Plaza, housing his magazine offices and printing plant as well as the People's University, a correspondence school.[174] Although some of the core buildings were not built, including versions of the Taj Mahal and the Parthenon, Lewis's penchant for the theatrical was expressed in the 135-foot-tall octagonal Woman's Magazine Building (Herbert C. Chivers, 1903) from the top of which a searchlight—reportedly the world's most powerful—served as a beacon at night to attract visitors (and potential customers) from the fair. The Egyptian Building (Ralph Chesley Ott, 1905), modeled on the Temple of Karnak, was also built, but the streetcar line that was planned to run through its base was never realized. The Studio Building (Eames & Young), completed in 1909, served as the Art Institute of the People's University. Lewis also provided a dramatic entrance to University City along Delmar Boulevard, where the Lion Gates (Eames & Young, 1903–9), a pair of 40-foot-tall pylons, supported eight-ton lion and tiger sculptures by George J. Zolnay (1863–1949).

Lewis developed only one of seven planned subdivisions in University City before departing for California in 1912 to work on his next real estate venture, Atascadero. University Heights Subdivision #1, platted in 1902 by Ernest Bowditch and landscape engineer H. Buckingham (n.d.), looped curving streets named after universities on an undulating site with 258 houses spread across ten blocks, with the most expensive houses perched on the highest sites. Many of the houses, set back uniformly on 30-foot lawns, were built on speculation by the University Heights Realty and Development Co. between 1906 and 1907, and by 1910, University Heights had undergone three expansions to cover 400 acres stretching one mile by three-quarters of a mile. The developers called for 1,000 maple trees to line the streets, each at least six inches in diameter so that shade would be provided during the first season, requiring the "city and suburbs" to be "ransacked for the trees."[175] Lewis allowed for the provision of community facilities in three designated districts for schools, houses of worship, and commercial and retail use. Initial plans for the area west of Subdivision #1 featured an hourglass-like street configuration, but the land was built out more conventionally by other developers.

University City continued to develop after Lewis's departure for California. In 1923, Julius Pitzman's firm, now led by his son Frederick (1889–1951), broke up the prevailing street plan of long parallel blocks with a naturalistic design for the University Hills subdivision,

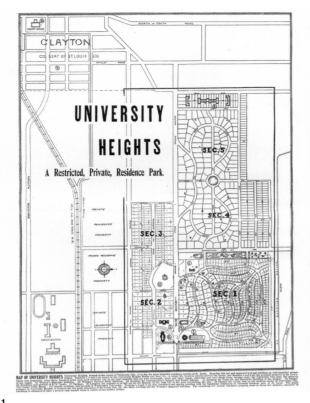

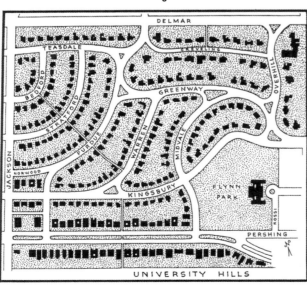

1. Map of University Heights, showing University City Plaza in bottom center. UCPL (1908)

2. Model of University City Plaza, UCPL (1910)

3. Delmar Boulevard, showing Woman's Magazine Building, Herbert C. Chivers, 1903, Lion Gates, Eames & Young and George J. Zolnay, 1903–09, and Egyptian Building, Ralph Chesley Ott, 1905. UCPL (c. 1909)

4. Advertisement for University Heights from *The Republic*, May 17, 1908. LOCCA

5. University Heights from the Woman's Magazine Building. UCPL (c. 1908)

6. University Heights. Naffziger. CN (2012)

7. Plan of University Hills, Frederick Pitzman, 1923. Baer. HSUC (c. 2000)

8, 9. University Hills. Naffziger. CN (2012).

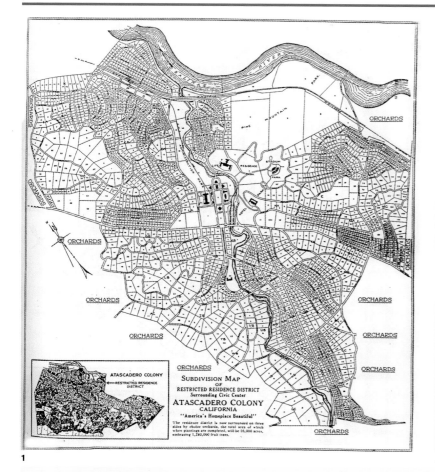

1. Plan, Walter D. Bliss and William B. Faville, 1913. CAHS

2. Painting of civic center by Jack Smith. CAHS (c. 1915)

3. Civic center. CAHS (late 1920s)

4. Typical street. CAHS (1917)

bound by Delmar Boulevard and Jackson, Pershing, and Wellesley Avenues, containing 184 houses, a school, and a church on 96 acres developed by Cyrus Crane Willmore (1889–1949). Entrance gates marked the neighborhood's threshold.

Meanwhile, Edward Gardner Lewis was realizing what was to be his masterwork, and certainly one of the few truly serious attempts to realize a garden city on American soil: **Atascadero** (1913), California, 120 miles north of Santa Barbara, located on a 23,000-acre, 40-square-mile property. Lewis clearly connected Atascadero to Garden City ideals when he proclaimed its motto to be: "All the advantages of country life with city conveniences."[176] In laying out the development, San Francisco architects Walter D. Bliss (1872–1956) and William B. Faville (1866–1947) combined Beaux-Arts formality and picturesque naturalism. A monumental

civic center organized around an axial mall was surrounded by a business district including commercial buildings, low-scale industrial buildings, and parks, beyond which residential neighborhoods were placed among curvilinear streets winding through a natural setting. To the south, east, and west of this central garden city (the north boundary was the Salinas River) were self-contained farms and expansive orchards. A university was also planned. While not all of the civic center buildings were realized and comparatively few houses were built, the structure of the plan was in large measure realized and remains in place to this day.

In 1911, responding to the rapid growth of Los Angeles, businessman Jared Sidney Torrance (1853–1921) purchased 2,800 acres of the former Rancho Dominguez, fifteen miles southwest of downtown, and launched plans to develop the namesake industrial city of **Torrance**.[177]

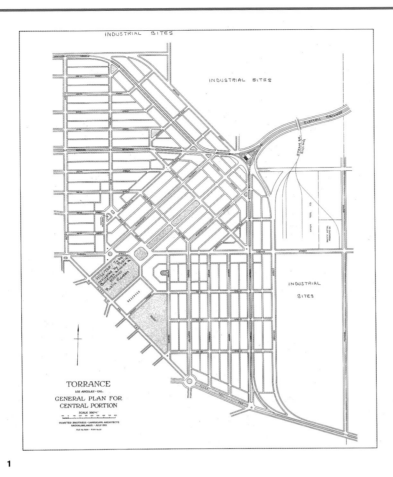

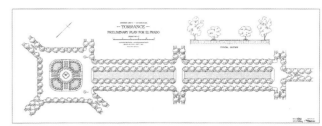

1. Plan of central portion, Olmsted Brothers, 1912. FLO

2. Preliminary plan for El Prado, Olmsted Brothers, 1912. FLO

3. Station and apartment houses. THS (1913)

4. Typical street showing house by Irving Gill on right. SUN13 (1913)

Rather than establish a single-industry town, Torrance, a member of more than 140 corporate boards, marketed the development to companies in Los Angeles and beyond, touting low land costs, residential neighborhoods for workers, a business district, and community facilities, including schools and hospitals. Coming in the midst of major labor disputes in Los Angeles, the plan was quick to gain support among anti-union companies, including the Llewellyn Iron Works, the Union Tool Company, and the Pacific Electric Railway, which in 1912, partnering with Torrance's development group, the Dominguez Land Company, agreed to move from downtown Los Angeles.

Olmsted Brothers prepared plans for the flat site that was soon expanded to cover 3,530 acres, 750 of which were reserved for the town. Frederick Law Olmsted Jr. successfully lobbied to have Irving Gill (1870–1936) retained as chief architect, although plans had been solicited from Gill's staunch critic, Elmer Grey (1872–1963), as well as from Sumner P. Hunt (1865–1938), Parker Wright (1873–1952), and R. D. Farquhar (1872–1967). Olmsted and Gill had recently collaborated on the design of San Diego's Panama-California Exposition of 1915, but neither had much success there: Gill left the design staff after seeing his contribution vastly compromised at the hands of Bertram Grosvenor Goodhue, while Olmsted resigned to protest a change in the fair's site.

Olmsted divided Torrance into civic, commercial, industrial, and residential zones planned for a population of 10,000. A central spine, El Prado Avenue, pointed northeast toward distant Mt. Saint Antonio and incorporated the two-and-a-half-block-long El Prado Park, connecting the residential area on the southwest, centered around a town square and a site reserved for a city hall, with the business district on the northeast that provided a buffer between the living and industrial zones. The axis of El Prado Avenue continued through the business district to terminate in Gill's Pacific Electric Station (1913–14), providing interurban trolley service to downtown Los Angeles. Beyond the depot lay the factory sites, located in the northeast to allow prevailing winds to carry smoke and dust away from town. Olmsted designed the residential neighborhoods on a modified grid plan incorporating parks, *rond-points*, and radial avenues, as well as several crooked streets conforming to irregularities in the site, but his design was soon rejected by the developers' engineers, who called for a more regular grid, leading Olmsted to withdraw from the project in 1912, stating that his scheme was "more or less butchered by the local people."[178] Left intact, however, was Olmsted's general layout of zones placed around the central El Prado Avenue and its grassy park. The town hall site remained undeveloped until 1917, when it was given over for the construction of a high school.

Relocating from San Diego to work on the project, Gill, who had evolved a minimalistic interpretation of the Mission style in his individual houses, multifamily

5

6

7

8

housing, and public buildings, was "ready for a major work," according to historian Esther McCoy, having matured as a planner "to the point where he was perfectly capable of unifying a city."[179] As Margaret Crawford notes, however, Gill's stylistic unification of industrial, civic, and residential buildings at Torrance helped subvert what remained of Olmsted's site plan that "had clearly separated the industrial area from the commercial district . . . while Gill's undifferentiated application of a stark and symbolically functional aesthetic reunited the town areas, accentuating the town's industrial purpose."[180]

A number of Gill's designs were completed in Torrance between 1913 and 1914, beginning with a reinforced-concrete railroad viaduct for freight cars supported by six arches of varying width allowing automobiles, trolleys, and pedestrians to pass beneath. Situated at the site's eastern edge, architectural historian Thomas S. Hines has observed that the viaduct, "as a modernist version of a triumphal arch . . . became the symbolic city gate."[181] Gill's Pacific Electric Station, a low-slung, hollow tile block and stucco-clad building with a recessed entry with four unfluted Doric columns *in antis*, interpreted Mission-style train stations but in a very abstract way, rising to a domed double-height waiting room. South of the depot, Gill completed two bare-bones three-story hotels, roughly triangular in plan, with first-floor retail space. Slightly less austere were two additional hotels, the Murray and El Roi Tan,

situated on El Prado Avenue along with the Bank of Torrance, a smaller iteration of the depot.

Although Gill prepared designs for an extensive industrial district, including a five-acre complex of domed and sawtooth-roofed colonnaded factories for the W. C. Hendrie Rubber Company, only the modest Fuller Shoe Manufacturing Company, Salm Manufacturing Company, and Rubbercraft Corporation factories were built, the last fronted by stylized Dutch gables harkening back to Gill's Wheaton House (1908) in San Diego.[182] The architect's two-room schoolhouse was covered by a pitched roof that gave it the domestic look of a bungalow.

Gill's plan to group hundreds of semidetached cottages around gardens and common courts was rejected by the developers who asked for a conventional arrangement of single-family houses that they deemed more marketable. Gill's L-shaped four-room model houses, featuring skylit bathrooms and hallways and garden walls shielding side entrances from the street, were praised by some but ardently opposed by labor unions, which probably correctly feared that the elimination of baseboards, beams, moldings, and virtually all other ornamentation would eliminate the need for skilled craftsmen. Only ten were built before the designs were scrapped in favor of more familiar California bungalows that appealed both to the unions and the working-class home buyers, who seemed to prefer their warmth and individuality. The preference also affected Gill's executed

1. Plan, Walter Burley Griffin, 1913–15. MOSS

2. Locator map. MOSS (c. 1915)

3. Aerial perspective. MOSS (c. 1915)

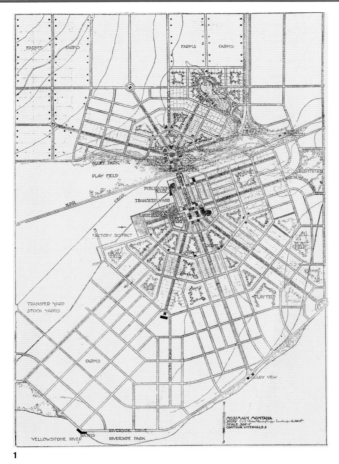

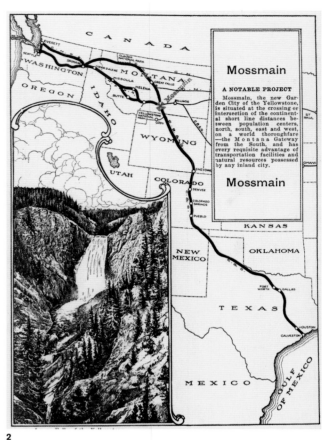

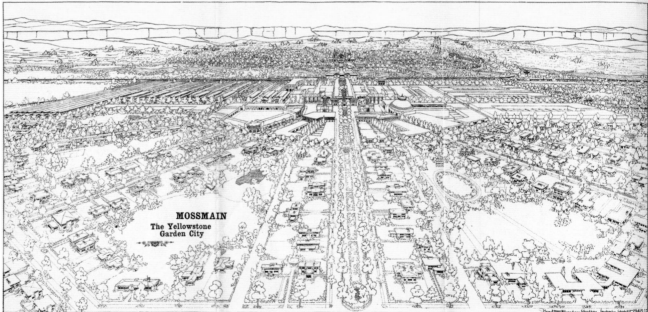

houses, which were decorated and augmented over time until their original forms were unrecognizable, a fate that a decade later would befall Le Corbusier's similar experiment at Pessac, France (see p. 482). After stumbling during the 1913 recession and World War I, Torrance flourished during the 1920s, in part because of the discovery of a nearby oil field. By 1939 the city had been enlarged by six additions and was home to almost sixty manufacturing plants sprawling across a 12,000-acre industrial district around the original core, now known as Old Torrance.

Mossmain (1913–15), Montana, fifteen miles west–southwest of Billings at the junction of the Great Northern, Northern Pacific, and Burlington Railroads, was Walter Burley Griffin's last American planning project, touted in promotional literature as the "first garden city in America" and "the new Garden City of the Yellowstone."[183] The town was named for its sponsor, Preston B.

Moss (1863–1947), a Billings businessman who also edited a journal, *The Scientific Farmer*, promoting agricultural investment in the state. Although it never proceeded past the planning stage, Mossmain, with an anticipated population of 25,000 to be spread across 5,000 acres, was an ambitious attempt to carry out a Garden City modeled directly on its English precedents, specifically Letchworth, which, according to Mossmain's promoters, "with such modifications as change in local conditions demand has been adopted as the Yellowstone Garden City Plan."[184]

Mossmain's plan, divided at its center by the east–west railroad right-of-way, featured a series of concentric octagonal boulevards cut through by radial avenues. The civic center, including a city hall and municipal market intended to sell the products of local farms, was located south of the tracks, while a social center with schools, clubs, and churches was placed across the tracks to the north, leading Mark L. Peisch to note that "accepting a railroad junction of three transcontinental railways as a planning core . . . was hardly in keeping with the ideas of the garden city movement."[185]

Closer to the Garden City model were the residential neighborhoods around the core, where blocks of houses enclosed open spaces and playing fields. Griffin replaced the group dwellings of Letchworth with detached single-family houses and eliminated Parker and Unwin's mix of curved and straight streets in favor of regular geometries, so that while Mossmain's overall plan may resemble the town center portion of Letchworth, it is tied more to Griffin's own brand of town planning as seen in the suburban areas of Canberra and the plans for Leeton and Griffith in Australia (see p. 646). Beyond the center was a buffer of five- and ten-acre farms. A factory district was included to the west and space for an institution reserved to the east. The plan failed in 1918 when its backers lost interest.

Occupying 13,929 acres, **Longview**, Washington, begun in 1922, and perhaps the largest industrial city ever to have been developed according to a master plan, was the project of Robert Alexander Long (1850–1934), head of the Kansas City–based Long-Bell Lumber Company, which, having depleted its resources in Louisiana, Texas, and Mississippi, moved operations to the West Coast, purchasing more than 200,000 acres in California, Washington, and Oregon.[186] The site, located fifty miles inland from the Pacific Ocean at the confluence of the Cowlitz River, which formed its eastern border, and the Columbia River, which formed the southern and southwestern borders, was a floodplain requiring the construction of fourteen miles of dikes.

Long envisioned the construction of a model city for 15,000 inhabitants, hoping to attract a nonunion workforce in an area that was notably rife with labor disputes. Having never attempted such a project, Long consulted his hometown friend, Jesse Clyde Nichols, developer of Kansas City's Country Club District (see p. 167), who, after visiting the site, convinced Long instead to plan a city of 50,000 that would also cater to outside industries. Nichols, no stranger to large-scale

plans, brought great enthusiasm to the project, which was touted as the country's largest planned city since Washington, D.C., proclaiming: "Measured in the scope of national importance, in gigantic financing, in human vision, human courage, human daring and adventure into an almost entirely new field of American endeavor—the Highest Peak, towering above all the structures we have surveyed, is the building of the wonder-city, Longview, Washington."[187]

Although Nichols would not agree to develop the town, he signed on as a consultant, assembling for Longview the same team responsible for the Country Club District: the father-and-son landscape architecture and planning firm of Hare & Hare and George E. Kessler, who served as planning consultant until his death in 1923. To help generate profits, Nichols recommended a Seattle-based real estate developer, B. Letcher Lambuth (1890–1974), who suggested that a grid be employed to maximize corner lots and to allow an easier pricing structure.

As advised by Nichols, Hare & Hare and Kessler divided Longview into distinct zones, separating a central business district from heavy and light industrial areas and calling for seven distinct residential additions, each governed by a different set of restrictions dictating minimum construction costs, setbacks, building materials, and the like. Aside from a district reserved for apartment buildings, this was to be a city of single-family houses. According to Nichols, zoning was "not completely understood by the officials of this company. So I went to considerable length in explaining to them how many communities throughout the United States were placing themselves under zoning; how the supreme courts of the largest states had upheld zoning laws and that it was economical in the long run to zone. And I made the suggestion that if a community could adopt zoning after it was already built, with great hardship to people whose property was affected, it certainly would be profitable for us to do it here when we could begin with a clean slate."[188] To counteract what Hare & Hare termed the "inside out" pattern of urban growth, in which industrial and commercial areas inevitably encroached on residential zones, the planners established "nuclei,"[189] outlining "a center of development for each class of use, with reserve space for expansion adjacent to each center."[190]

With the Cowlitz and Columbia riverfronts necessarily given over to industrial plants, an inland business district formed the core of the plan, anchored by the six-acre, rectangular Jefferson Park (now R. A. Long Park), from the corners of which radial avenues cut through a surrounding grid. To avoid awkward intersections, the grid was modified to cross the radials at right angles. The southeasterly radial was cut short so as not to interfere with railroad tracks accessing the light-industrial district. From the east side of the park a divided boulevard, Broadway, extended for ten blocks through a commercial district centered around its intersection with Commerce Street, to terminate in a railroad depot. On the west

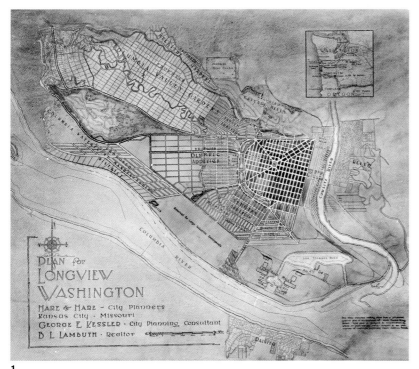

1. Plan, George E. Kessler and Hare & Hare, 1923. HHCR

2. Aerial view. COWL

3. Lake Sacajawea Park. COWL

4. Jefferson Square and Broadway from Monticello Hotel. HHCR

5. Lake Sacajawea Park with residential neighborhood in distance. COWL

6. Typical street. COWL

edge of the park, the town's first building, the six-story Hotel Monticello, was completed in 1923. Past the hotel, a neighborhood of high-priced homes extended to the west and south toward the city's largest open space, the 100-acre, crescent-shaped Lake Sacajawea Park, where a former slough was dredged and reshaped into a procession of five linked lakes. Lining the park were schools, churches, a hospital, and a YMCA.

Beyond Lake Sacajawea Park, the Sunset, Olympic, and St. Helens Additions fanned out as colliding residential gridirons, each with an average lot size of 50 by 120 feet but subject to different restrictions. North of the business district, hills gave rise to the only curvilinear subdivision, Hillside Acres, where the topography combined with the site's adjacency to Longview Country Club—and its nine-hole golf course—to create the most desirable section where minimum construction costs were set at the highest level. The fertile land that stretched for two or three miles west of the city to the 560-foot-high Mount Solo was divided into lots of three-quarters to five acres, forming a kind of agricultural belt, while a naturalistic cemetery was laid out on the far side of the mountain.

Hare & Hare platted wide streets to accommodate automobiles, allowing 120 feet for major boulevards, 50 and 60 feet for residential streets, and 80 to 100 feet in the business area. Streetcar lines were not built, but the company provided bus service. The planners were careful to provide "alternate routes and by-passes" for cars, "so that while traffic is invited to the central business district, it is not forced through it."[191] According to Leland Roth, this qualified Longview as "perhaps the only industrial town of its period planned with consideration of the impact of the private automobile."[192]

By 1927 five large dormitories for single men and a tight grid of small houses in the St. Helens Addition were built near the factories and railroad tracks to the south. But further residential development did not proceed as planned because even in the most inexpensive districts, minimum housing costs were higher than workers could afford, leading employees to settle in the neighboring towns of Kelso, Washington, and Rainier, Oregon, or, in the case of at least 500 workers, to live in tents or cars on the outskirts of town, constituting such a blight that the company established a temporary district of two-room, 10-by-24-foot mobile homes south of the business core on land reserved for upper-middle-class houses but now known as "Skidville" for the skids upon which the houses were placed. As historian Abraham Ott has noted, Long and his associates "failed to take into account the actual situation of the workers that they were planning to house. Inherently built into the city, in the form of dedicatory statements, architecture, advertisements, and landscaping, was an assumption that Longview would attract the best workers in the industry and provide for them a wholesome home. This, as well as the opulence exuded by structures like the hotel, was also meant to attract businesses and entrepreneurs who would be attracted to the stable labor force. Unfortunately,

few members of the labor force had enough money in their bank account to buy anything, much less a home."[193]

Longview's failure to develop highlighted the shortcomings of the "nucleus" strategy. For decades, the various small cores were separated by what seemed like vast, vacant expanses. As early as 1923, Wesley Vandercook, Long-Bell's chief engineer, who oversaw the project, had become unsure of the plan's validity, arguing that the residential and commercial districts were too large and "might be about right for a city of several million people."[194] After visiting Longview in 1927, Geddes Smith, an editor of *The Survey*, noted:

A pre-planned city must of course anchor its business section and its civic center and other focal points and, I suppose, it must then wait patiently for the interstices to fill up, but I began to wonder about pre-planning of this sort when I walked or was driven over blocks and blocks of paved but empty streets in Longview. Here stood the hotel, far from the railroad. There beside it, the public library, far from most of its readers. At the center of town, the shops, far from the customers. A town doesn't grow that way left to itself. Is there no middle course between the wasteful process of spreading, tearing down and spreading again, that most cities go through (but which is at least organic and natural) and this business of condemning your early settlers to live for years in the stark, gaping skeleton of a city?[195]

Longview fell far short of its goal to house 50,000 people by 1930. In 1932, its population of 12,000 occupied 2,700 houses and apartment buildings. Eventually the plan filled out, aided after a lull during the Depression by more than thirty additional industries that established plants along the rivers during World War II. By 2000 the population had reached nearly 35,000.

In 1928, as part of the effort to build Boulder Dam, to be located on the Colorado River at the Nevada-Arizona border and intended to provide irrigation water as well as produce hydroelectric power and control flooding, the United States Department of the Interior authorized the Bureau of Reclamation to plan a new city to house the workers who would construct the dam. The agency had concluded that Las Vegas, thirty-three miles to the northwest, was too far away to efficiently house the thousands of workers needed for the massive undertaking, the largest engineering project on the continent since the Panama Canal.[196] Walker Young (1885–1982), an engineer with the bureau, selected the site for **Boulder City** (1930), an elevated parcel six-and-a-half miles from the proposed dam that would overlook the 220-square-mile lake which would be created. Young also chose the city's planner, Dutch-born landscape architect Saco Rienk DeBoer, at the time Denver's official landscape architect as well as the designer of that city's Park Lane Square enclave

1. Plan, Saco Rienk DeBoer, 1930. RES

2. Aerial view. USNA (1932)

3. View from water tank. USNA (1932)

4. Commercial development, Nevada Highway and Avenue B. USNA (1932)

5. Houses, Utah Street. USNA (1932)

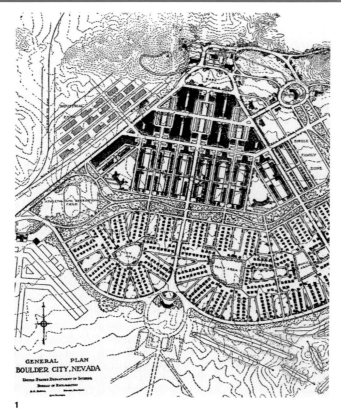

1

2

3

4

5

(see p. 68). Planned to house approximately 5,000 people during construction, Boulder City was intended to serve a permanent population of 2,000.

DeBoer bisected the triangular parcel with a wide north–south boulevard that extended throughout the site, connecting park space at both ends. DeBoer described the plan of the "model town" as consisting of a "large V, with main traffic lines along each side and a third one through the middle. These three major streets all center in the apex of the V which is the main entrance of a government office building. Two other buildings for government use form, with the first one, a small civic center group with an open park on the side of the city. In this way the government buildings are the focus point of the city which will lie fanlike to the south of the building group."[197] This gridded civic section, featuring arcaded buildings to shelter pedestrians from the desert sun, was also planned to include stores, churches, and schools, as well as an area of single-family houses. The strictly residential southern portion of the site, with single- and multifamily brick and stucco houses grouped around parks and playgrounds, was to be separated from the commercial and civic district by a greenbelt. DeBoer located industrial facilities in the northwest corner and planned for the construction of an airport and golf course.

The Depression quickly put an end to DeBoer's ambitious plans. As he explained, "There was no control over the location of business houses. The contractors built store buildings and dormitories in a separate part of the city, and by having practically a monopoly on retail business created a business district away from the center of the city. This has made the growth of the city's business district impossible. With the heart of the plan taken out there was only the street skeleton left without any coordination or reason . . . Much was expected of the architectural control embodied in the plans as approved by the Department. Due to the unhappy building of another business district, so far architectural control has amounted to very little."[198] Still, a portion of the civic district was laid out as originally planned. The residential portion and its accompanying greenbelt, however, remained completely unrealized, replaced by a ragtag collection of temporary dwellings nicknamed "dingbat houses" for the poor quality of their construction.

Construction of Boulder City began in 1931, and

within a year its population reached the 5,000 residents originally envisioned. Construction on the dam, also begun in 1931, was completed four years later; the structure was renamed to honor President Herbert Hoover in 1947. Even after the completion of the dam, Boulder City continued to prosper economically, if not aesthetically, remaining under the control of the federal government until 1960, when it was incorporated as an independent city within the state of Nevada.

North Charleston (1913), South Carolina, undertaken by a group of local businessmen not "as a utopian experiment by starry-eyed dreamers" but as "a business venture intended to turn a handsome profit," was another effort to create a self-sustaining suburban city loosely modeled on Howard's Garden City concept.[199] About seven miles up the Cooper River from Charleston, adjacent to a United States Navy Yard and in proximity to existing factories, North Charleston's radial plan was prepared by William Bell Marquis (1887–1978), a Harvard-trained landscape architect. As an employee of the Augusta, Georgia–based P. J. Berckmans Co., owner of Fruitland Nursery, one of the largest nurseries in the United States, which had branched out into the field of landscape architecture in the early 1900s, Marquis was among the first professionally trained landscape architects to live and work in the South. His plan, covering 1,000 acres (with 4,000 adjacent acres reserved for agriculture) and intended to accommodate a population of 30,000, sprawled outward from Park Circle along axial avenues and informal winding boulevards. Factory sites were placed away from the center, adjacent to rail lines, while schools and a variety of parks were distributed throughout. Space was also set aside for a commercial center. Despite some alterations and, as Dean Sinclair has noted, "the abandonment of many of the more innovative features of the layout such as the large public plaza," the overall street plan can be discerned in the present city.[200]

Erwin (1916), Tennessee, sponsored by the Holston Corporation, parent company of the Carolina, Clinchfield and Ohio Railway, had a relatively complex history leading to its planning as an important exemplar of the Garden City ideal, balancing industrial employment with diverse residential neighborhoods.[201] The company, which had moved its headquarters to the northeast Tennessee town in 1908, asked Grosvenor Atterbury, codesigner of Forest Hills Gardens (see p. 140), to plan a subdivision intended to provide housing for the growing number of railway workers living in the area. Erwin, set in a valley surrounded on three sides by the Blue Ridge Mountains, had a population of 3,000 when Atterbury first visited in 1916, observing the existing settlement of ragtag buildings laid out in a standard grid along unpaved streets. Under Atterbury's leadership, Erwin's future evolved, leading to a plan for a city that would number between 30,000 and 40,000 people.

Atterbury's comprehensive scheme, to be realized in three stages, featured tree-lined streets that connected to the existing town grid. He gathered the principal

1. Plan, William Bell Marquis, 1913. PALD

2. Aerial view. GE (2010)

existing connector roads into a broad, north–south boulevard located roughly at the center of the site and culminating in a circular green intended to be surrounded with houses. He provided only plots for housing, with the expectation that all other needs would be met by Erwin's existing facilities and institutions. Veteran housing reformer Lawrence Veiller (1872–1959) praised Atterbury for his disciplined use of curving streets: "The tendency in many of the new developments is to over-exaggerate and misplace the curvilinear element, forgetting that where the radius is short, as is necessarily the case in short streets, the lotting problem, and consequently the building problem, is enormously complicated and considerably increased in cost by irregular and curved plots. On the other hand where, as in this case, the curves are confined to the larger thoroughfares, which have greater sweeps, with correspondingly greater curves, this practical objection in the lotting and building is largely avoided."[202]

Atterbury initially platted "Section A," the area closest to the existing community. As at Indian Hill (see p. 827), he failed in his efforts to convince the

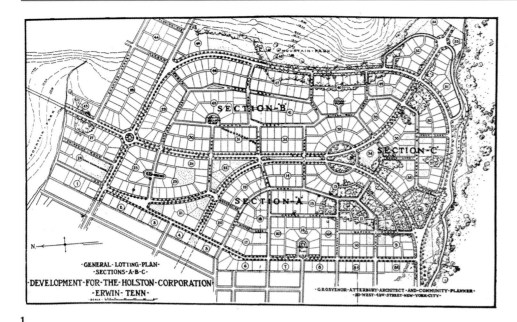

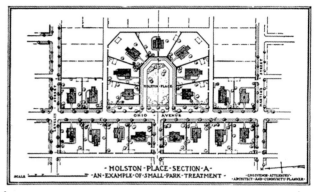

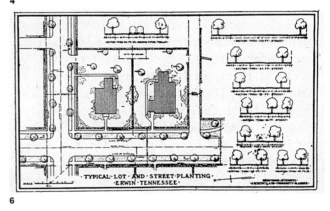

1. Plan, Grosvenor Atterbury, 1916. HFW

2. Aerial view, Holston Place. GE (2012)

3. Rendering of four-house group. HFW

4. Plan, Holston Place. HFW

5. Houses, Grosvenor Atterbury, 1916–17. UCHS

6. Plan, typical lot and street planting. HFW

developer to build substantial numbers of semide-tached dwellings. Between 1916 and 1917 forty-five Atterbury-designed single-family one- and two-story stucco- or shingle-clad houses were completed in what Veiller considered a "very attractive little settlement."[203] Holston Place, the development's finest ensemble, featured seven houses grouped around a landscaped green. Despite the Holston Corporation's stated intentions to expand Erwin into a major city, the railroad's declining fortunes brought the project to a hasty close, with progress limited to the very modest collection of rental houses.

In addition to garden villages and enclaves, resort suburbs, and industrial villages, John Nolen designed garden cities, of which **Kingsport**, Tennessee, can be

claimed as the closest the United States came to realizing Howard's ideal.[204] Kingsport began with a comparatively small land area of 260 acres that would soon grow to 1,100 acres and a planned population of 10,000. Located in the remote northeastern corner of an unpopulous state, 400 miles from Washington, D.C., and 300 miles from Atlanta, Georgia, Kingsport was for some "the last and most sophisticated of the nineteenth century railroad towns."[205] But a strong case can be made, based on Nolen's plan, the decision to wrap the town in a permanent greenbelt, the consecration of parts of the town to major industries like the Federal Dyestuff and Chemical Corporation and Corning Glass Works, and the architectural embellishment of civic, commercial, and residential districts, that Kingsport has all the physical

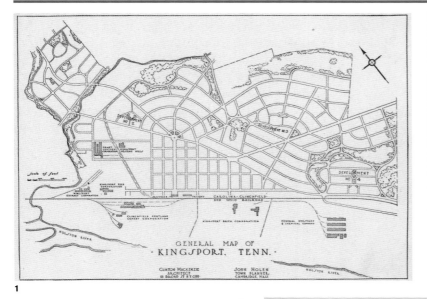

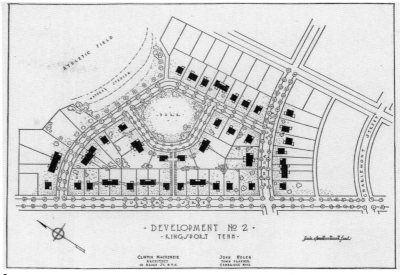

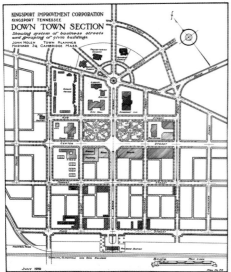

1. Plan, John Nolen, 1919. COR

2. Plan, detail of Development No. 2, 1919. COR

3. Plan, detail of downtown section, 1919. COR

4. View along Broad Street showing train station. COR (c. 1920s)

5. East Main Street. COR (c. 1920s)

6. White City houses, Clinton Mackenzie, c. 1920. COR

7. Shelby Street houses, Clinton Mackenzie, c. 1920. COR

8. Development No. 2 (the Fifties) houses, Clinton Mackenzie, c. 1920. Wurts. COR

9. Church Circle and Broad Street. Garvin. AG (1995)

characteristics and functional components of Howard's Garden City ideal. Architect Clinton Mackenzie (1872–1940), who was deeply involved in Kingsport's planning and architecture, implicitly made the case for it as a Garden City when he wrote that it "is the first attempt in this country to build a fully rounded city out of whole cloth. We have numerous examples of individual industrial towns, but none deliberately planned and laid out in advance to accommodate diversified industries, with provisions made for the education, recreation, and social life of a population not then in existence. The amazing success accomplished at Kingsport has opened up a new vista in industrial city planning."[206]

Planning began in 1906 when the heads of the Carolina, Clinchfield and Ohio Railroad, a new line constructed to tap into the area's abundant natural resources, including coal, realized that they needed a manufacturing town along its route to generate additional revenue through increased passenger and freight usage. But Kingsport only began to take significant shape when Nolen was brought on board, joining with Mackenzie and the railroad representative, J. Fred Johnson (1874–1944), to give the enterprise definitive form.

The new town was situated in what Nolen described as "a wide and winding valley of remarkable natural beauty, coursed by the Holston River."[207] When Nolen first visited in 1916, as Charles Warren tells us, "Kingsport was just an unpaved street grid dotted with tents and utilitarian frame buildings."[208] Nolen drew a preliminary plan for the town in 1916 and a more comprehensive plan three years later that addressed the expansion of the overall land area. Prepared with the assistance of Earle S. Draper, the plan comprised three functional districts. The industrial district, consisting of two separate areas at the west and south edges of the town, had been put in place before Nolen took over as planner. Taking the industrial sites as given, Nolen's plan located what John Hancock has described as "a thumb-shaped business-civic center of 110 acres on the left-central side of town."[209] A broad landscaped boulevard, Broad Street, ran up the center of the district from the railroad station to the civic center perched on a knoll where four churches, an inn, a city hall, a post office, and a library were planned, and most soon afterward realized. From here, four major streets led to the principal residential areas, while an east–west arterial street led to the two industrial centers and the state highways.

Howard Long, in his somewhat promotional 1928 book on Kingsport, writes that "the business section, including 17 streets, is situated in almost the exact geographic center of the city. The stranger, alighting from the train at the railroad station, finds, in the first place, this station surrounded by a spacious park . . . He steps out, then, into a broad Parisian boulevard" that leads to the civic center. "The cumulative effect is inspiring and delightful."[210] Keller Easterling notes that given the location of industry just south of the business district between the railroad and the Holston River, "the City Beautiful axial view from Church Circle ironically

affords the best view of smoke stacks and factories."[211]

Small parks helped define the residential neighborhoods located on the higher ground, yet within a five-minute drive from downtown. Enclaves of architecturally coherent development gave each neighborhood a defined identity. Clinton Mackenzie designed some of these on his own or parceled them out to a roster of other well-known architects. Development No. 2, known as the Fifties, was designed by Mackenzie in the English Tudor style. Warren found his grasp of the style "tentative" and the development of single-family houses "defeated by the difficult terrain." Development No. 3 was called White City because of what Warren described as Mackenzie's intricately planned, "deceptively simple" white painted clapboard houses surrounding a lozenge-shaped hilltop park.[212] Above the Fifties and White City the network of radial roads led to the choicest ridgetop sites, where larger houses were located, especially along Watauga Street. Down the hill, an area known as Little White City was given over to small houses designed by Mackenzie and Evarts Tracy (1868–1922).

As was typical of his other Southern developments, Nolen was required to provide segregated housing for African Americans. According to Mackenzie, his and Nolen's 1,000-person "Negro Village," which they refused to set amid the industrial area but insisted be relocated on high ground between a stand of oak trees and a creek, "was the first time that an attempt has been made to build a negro village of a high order with their own schools, churches, stores, lodges, etc., providing the same grade of housing and general development as it furnished the white population of the same economic condition."[213] Moreover, Nolen argued that it was "worthwhile to get out of the habit of calling it the Negro Village, and give it some name that our colored friends would like . . . We ought to try to please them."[214] Unfortunately, Nolen's plan did not come to fruition. Once he was no longer on the scene after 1922, the fine site he had selected was sold to speculators, who put up inferior houses.

After Nolen's separation from the project, his former assistant, Earle S. Draper, took over, planning the Fairacres section in the northeast hills. Here can be said to have begun the suburbanization of Nolen's city. As Easterling describes Fairacres: "There is little street hierarchy though there are some specialized streets and cul de sacs. Rather most streets are designed as secondary streets to serve large lots that together attempt to create the illusion of a prestigious private enclave in the country, though it is just minutes from the city center."[215]

With John Nolen's **Mariemont**, pronounced "Marrymont," the garden suburb took on the scale and, to a considerable extent, the ambitions of the Garden City type.[216] Located ten miles east of Cincinnati, the nation's third most congested city, Mariemont was first conceived before America's entrance into World War I but only begun in 1921. Mariemont adopted the planning and architectural styles of previous garden cities but with a significant difference. It replaced the railroad with the automobile as the primary mode of transportation

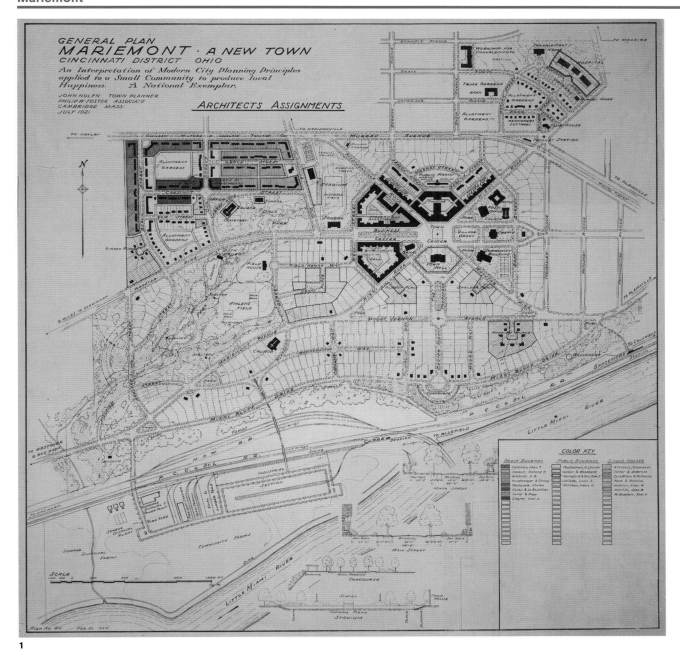

1

between the suburb and the central city. In the words of a promotional publication of 1925, the new development was intended to illustrate "how well *people of moderate means* can live near great cities." Not planned as either a philanthropic or paternalistic enterprise, Mariemont was conceived as "an ordinary real estate development on normal American lines, except that everything has been scientifically planned in advance and that the owner limits profits and will share the town's success with those who live in it." As such, Mariemont, envisioned as "A National Exemplar," was not to be "an experiment, but the application of the town-planning principles, adapted to American methods, that were used in such success-ful 'garden cities' as Port Sunlight and Letchworth in England. It should be explained, though, that these were essentially attempts to counteract the disastrously rapid growth of large cities . . . Mariemont was not so intended, and does not have to combat those conditions.

Its projectors believe in a Greater Cincinnati, being con-vinced that the tendency toward life in cities still persists in the United States. Mariemont, therefore, is simply another jewel suburb in the crown of the 'Queen of the West,'" as Cincinnati was known. [217]

The developer, Mary M. Emery (1844–1927), intended Mariemont as a community for industrial and white-collar workers. The members of the Emery fam-ily were leading real estate developers in Cincinnati and the name of the town was taken from the family's sum-mer estate in Newport, Rhode Island. Mary Emery was influenced by the economic predictions of Roger W. Bab-son of the Babson Institute in Wellesley, Massachusetts, who believed that wage earners "during the last period of prosperity [had] spent their money for motor cars" and would "in the next period of prosperity . . . buy country homes." [218] To help realize her ideas, she relied on Charles J. Livingood (1866–1952), a knowledgeable expert in city

2. Aerial view. MP (1929)

3. Sheldon Close houses, Grosvenor Atterbury, 1925. COR

4. Apartment building, Murray Avenue and Beech Street, Clinton Mackenzie, 1924. COR

5. Chestnut Street houses, Ripley & LeBoutillier, 1925. COR

6. Theater and retail area, Wooster Pike. Garvin. AG (2005)

7. Advertisement. MP (1930)

8. Mariemont Inn, Zettel & Rapp, 1925. Mydans. LOCPF (1926)

9. Honeymoon cottage, Maple Street, Edmund B. Gilchrist, 1925. COR (1925)

10. Albert Place houses, Robert Rodes McGoodwin, 1924. MP (1925)

11. Murray Avenue houses, Edmund B. Gilchrist, 1925. MP

12. Chestnut Street houses, Richard H. Dana Jr., 1924. MP (1925)

13. Dale Park, apartment buildings with ground-level shops, Ripley & LeBoutillier, 1925. MP (1926)

2

3

4

5

6

8

9

7

10

11

12

13

planning who brought in John Nolen to design the project. As Livingood told Nolen in 1927, he had been selected because of "the good impression you made at various conventions where I watched you closely. I selected you because of your sanity and strong character."[219]

Mariemont occupies a high bluff commanding the Little Miami River Valley, with 250 acres in the town itself and another 115 acres devoted to a hospital group, an industrial area located near the railroad, and other uses. Seven hundred house lots were provided in the initial plan, and a population of 5,000 was anticipated. Nolen's plan, executed in association with Philip W. Foster (b. 1884), included six sizes of hierarchically arranged streets, from 100-foot-wide business streets to 40-foot-wide minor residential streets. Wooster Pike, as Charles Warren points out, "widens by small increments in its transit across the site until the planted esplanade separating its traffic lanes becomes a forested park . . . The north–south axis of this central street pattern connects the town center through a series of progressively narrower streets to a dramatic termination at an exedra with commanding views across the verdant river valley." Together, as Warren notes, the opposing "axial sequences rely more on tree trunks and canopies than on architecture to establish spatial order. Both also express quite literally the notion of the American garden city as a mediation between city and country."[220] Diagonal roads leading from the square were to be lined by shops and apartments, with the less intensively, more naturalistically planned neighborhoods set beyond. The city hall was placed to one side of an octagonal central square, which culminated the axis of Wooster Pike, leading east from Cincinnati. The retail center was scaled to serve citizens of the new town as well as those in surrounding developments—an unusual instance in which local and regional considerations were both addressed. The plan also included an inn, a golf course, a hospital, and an industrial park. All in all, half of the town's 365 acres were in residential lots, 25 percent in streets and greenswards, 10 percent in business or civic lots, and the rest in parks and permanent open spaces.

Nolen's plan included a lagoon for boating in summer and skating in winter (these were badly damaged in floods in the 1930s and never restored) and a sophisticated infrastructure that included steam heat piped to all houses from a central power source, and paved streets with sidewalks. But by the late 1920s it had become clear that too much money had been invested in infrastructure before houses were developed for sale. Even before the stock market crash of 1929 curtailed the town's development, many houses were sold below cost to improve the project's cash flow.

Emery was so convinced about the future role of the automobile that, though the town was located on the main line of the Pennsylvania Railroad as it ran into Cincinnati, no provision was made for a passenger station. There was, however, an interurban railway (electric trolley) incorporated into the original plan, connecting "wage earner" rental housing in the Dale Park section with nearby industry. Dale Park, intended for blue-collar

14. Denny Place houses, Howe & Manning, 1924. RAMSA (c. 1980)

15. Albert Place houses, Robert Rodes McGoodwin, 1924. RAMSA (c. 1980)

16. Oak Street houses, Charles W. Short Jr., 1924. RAMSA (c. 1980)

17. Lane I showing Dale Park school, Fechheimer, Ihorst & McCoy, 1925, in distance. RAMSA (c. 1981)

workers, was "separated from the others by Dogwood Park . . . and the schoolyards, which were strung along a ravine that deepens as it traverses southwest across the site."[221] Thus the Dale Park neighborhood was not only physically distanced from its middle-class counterparts but also intended as a somewhat self-contained entity with its own neighborhood commercial center. The physical features of the street plan further served to isolate Dale Park from Mariemont's town center.

The civic center was only partially realized—and derided by Werner Hegemann, who agreed with comments made at the 1923 Town Planning Exhibition in Gothenburg, Sweden, that the "ill-fated disjointed 'Platz' surrounded by public buildings represents an ugly intersection."[222] But twenty-six architects, many of national stature, were involved in the development of the residential neighborhoods, with initial attention paid to the Dale Park neighborhood of modest rental houses arranged in groups, followed by "The 'Places' or Groups of Single Houses"—five in all—such as Denny Place and Albert Place, intended to seed the higher-end neighborhoods with "standards of excellence up to which individual home builders must measure, and to which all may aspire. In this way, the buyer of the lot will know in advance the character of his neighborhood."[223]

While Memorial Church (1923), designed by Louis Jallade, was the village's most substantial building, it was the stylistically and typologically varied housing that contributed to the distinct, inventive street pictures that are Mariemont's hallmark. According to Warren, "Though Nolen suggested a list of architects to work on the buildings, Livingood had some ideas of his own, and evidently he enjoyed dispensing commissions to distinguished practitioners. Selections were carefully made so that each architect had control of a coherent group, and so that jarring juxtapositions of style would be avoided. Wanting the architecture to grow out of his designs, Nolen provided a color-coded plan to show Livingood how to group the commissions, emphasizing building pairs at street intersections and careful placement of buildings at vista terminations."[224]

Construction of the houses began in 1924 with a complex of group houses designed by Richard H. Dana Jr. (1879–1933) incorporating a Georgian-style brick farmhouse already on the site. Other notable architects invited to design parts of the town included Hubert G. Ripley (1869–1942) and Addison B. LeBoutillier (1872–1951), responsible for apartments and shops in Dale Park, as well as houses on Chestnut Street; Charles F. Cellarius (1891–1973), designer of group housing on Beech Street; and Clinton Mackenzie, architect of an apartment house as well as seventeen group houses. Grosvenor Atterbury was responsible for Sheldon Close; Wilson Eyre (1858–1944) and John G. McIlvaine (1880–1939) worked on Hopkins Place; and Lois L. Howe (1864–1964) and Eleanor Manning (1884–1973), one of the nation's few female-led firms, were designers of the limestone houses facing Denny Place.

Edmund B. Gilchrist and Robert Rodes McGoodwin brought to Mariemont the experiences they had garnered working for George Woodward at Chestnut Hill (see p. 135). According to McGoodwin, the group of twelve six-room whitewashed single and double houses on Albert Place was the result of Mrs. Emery's wish "to build a village which would solve the housing problem for people of *very moderate means*."[225] McGoodwin's design, inspired in part by the work of C. F. A. Voysey and M. H. Baillie Scott, was culminated by a double house on axis with Albert Place, itself a landscaped cul-de-sac. Relying on simple construction and fenestration and the elimination of superfluous detail, McGoodwin hoped that landscape would provide the necessary softening touches. Gilchrist's group of thirty-nine houses of varying size was one of the largest in the village. The two- and three-story brick Georgian rowhouses were drier in their details than McGoodwin's, but nonetheless composed to form a lively streetscape. The principal feature of Gilchrist's group was the so-called "honeymoon cottage" arching over the east end of Maple Street. All in all, Gilchrist's group exemplified the virtues, as Lewis Mumford noted in 1928, "of simple and inexpensive materials . . . used with great directness."[226] As the promoters intended, Mariemont was a successful community with its own identity closely linked to that of Cincinnati; it was not "a 'Toy Town,' set prim and precise as a child's plaything, nor on the other hand a pretentious 'Subdivision' marked only by elaborate gateways at the head of a 'Floral Garden.'"[227]

Penderlea (1921), forty miles north of Wilmington, North Carolina, in the southeastern corner of the state, was initially conceived as a "Farm City" to be located on 10,000 acres convenient to the Atlantic Coast Line Railroad, where it could take advantage of access to Eastern markets twenty-four to thirty-six hours away.[228] The concept, sponsored by the private Farm Cities Corporation of America, was almost utopian and in many ways European: a small city for farmers to live in so that they could tend their crops yet enjoy the stimulation of communal life, an idea "conceptualized," as Charles Warren has written, by Hugh S. MacRae (1865–1951), an idealistic banker and land developer based in Wilmington who was interested in finding a way to solve "the twin ills of urban congestion and rural depopulation with a combination of modern agricultural methods, communal cooperation, and education."[229] MacRae, joining with a group of fifty-one conservationists and city planners including Thomas Adams, Raymond Unwin, Gifford Pinchot (1865–1946), Elwood Mead (1858–1936), and F. H. Newell (1862–1932) to form a limited-dividend company with the intention of raising capital to develop Farm Cities across the rural United States, embarked on Penderlea as a prototype, choosing John Nolen, another original member of the Farm Cities Corporation of America, as its town planner.

Nolen and his associate Philip W. Foster sketched a plan accommodating 313 families on two- to 40-acre farms. Typical of his work, Nolen's scheme combined a monumental center for a community building, library and museum, school, inn, and village green, with a central axis lined by commercial buildings concluding in boat and bath houses facing a pond, and a radial plan of residential streets extending into the landscape and connecting with the train station. Sites nearest the center were for the smallest farms, with the larger plots located farther from the core. At the edge, woodland was to be held in reserve and land set aside for public pastures, a "training farm," four five-acre parks, and a country club. Nolen had high hopes for what he believed was one of his most important projects to date, stating, "It is not chewing gum or safety razors or new automobile accessories . . . that our civilization needs, it is food and homes and recreation, and do you know of any enterprise that

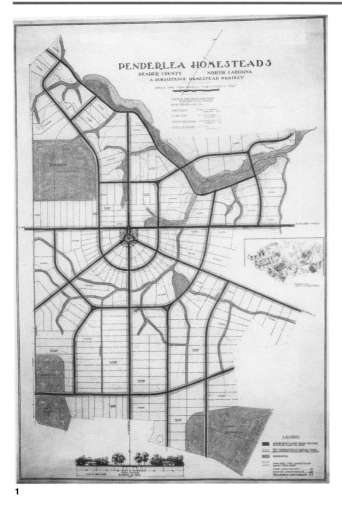

1. Plan, John Nolen, 1933. COR

2. Farmhouse. Mydans. LOCPF (1936)

3. Farmhouse and tobacco fields. Mydans. LOCPF (1936)

1

2

3

strikes at the heart of food and homes and wealth and the soundness of our civilization like the solving of the problems of the country combined with the satisfaction which people now crave and which is made quite evident that they feel can be found only in the city? So we have this device—invention—whatever I may call it, of the 'Farm City.'"[230]

Penderlea did not go forward in the 1920s when the South experienced a severe agricultural depression, but MacRae revived the plan in 1933 when he proposed it to the newly created Subsistence Homesteads Division of the U.S. Department of the Interior. MacRae agreed to sell 4,700 acres of the original site to the federal government at a deep discount, and Penderlea Homesteads Farms became the first of 152 homestead projects developed as part of President Roosevelt's New Deal program. MacRae, who was initially placed in charge of building the town, had Nolen rework his scheme for the smaller site, still intended for 313 families who would now occupy 5- to 20-acre farms. After 1,500 acres had been cleared and ten houses completed, MacRae was removed from the project as the federal agency asserted its authority. The plan was reworked again, with half of the planned houses eliminated and the farm plots increased to 20 acres.

By May 1935, 142 four- to six-room one-story houses were completed in Penderlea, simple wood-sided structures with screened porches to which no architect's name is attached. Nolen's civic center was also partially realized in the form of a thirty-one-room, multipurpose building housing a general store, school, library, health clinic, administrative offices, and an auditorium. In 1936 the Department of Agriculture's Resettlement Division assumed control of the project, purchasing 6,000 adjacent acres and proposing an additional 158 houses, only fifty of which were built. Two years later, the federal government expanded Penderlea's original mission beyond agriculture, constructing a large hosiery mill that would soon be spinning nylon for parachutes as part of the war effort. After World War II, the government ended the pioneering cooperative venture, selling off the farms and mill to private interests. Ninety-nine of the original houses, or about half those built, remain in the still-rural farm community.

Venice (1925), "The City by the Gulf," John Nolen's most important project in Florida, was to be uniquely a tropical garden city.[231] Located south of Sarasota on the site of a long-established small settlement originally called Horse & Chaise, Venice took its Italian-inspired name after 1888, when a post office was established, and only began to come to life after 1910 when Chicago's Palmer family started assembling acreage, convincing the Seaboard Air Line Railway to extend its line south from Sarasota. In 1915 Bertha Honoré Palmer (1849–1918) hired Charles Leavitt Jr., a New York–based

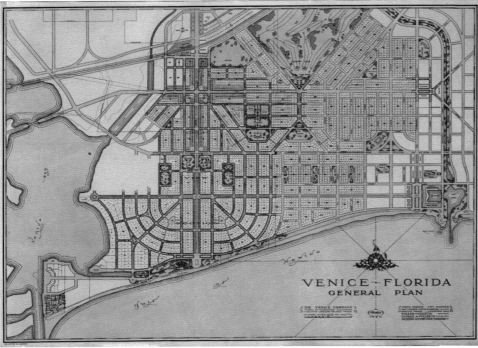

1

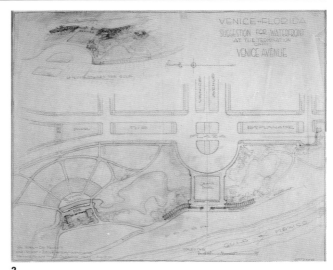

2

4

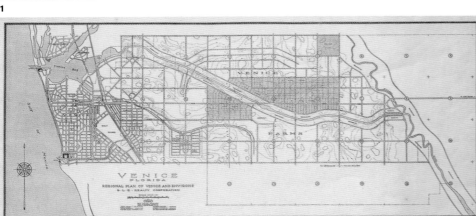

3

1. Plan, John Nolen, 1926. VA

2. Waterfront plan, Venice Avenue, John Nolen, 1926. COR

3. Regional plan of Venice and environs showing Venice Farms area, John Nolen, 1926. COR

4. Aerial view. JBrown. COR

5. Landscaped median, Venice Avenue. VA (2008)

6. Aerial view, business district. HSmith. VA (c. 1930)

7. Armada Road. Ebyabe. WC (2010)

8. Train station. VA (c. 2008)

5

6

7

8

9

10

landscape architect and civil engineer, to quickly develop a plan for a resort hotel, civic center, golf course, yacht club, school, church, stores, canals, and parks. Leavitt's plan was rejected as too ambitious and Palmer set out to develop a small "close to nature" community in its place.

World War I interrupted progress. In 1917, a 112-acre waterfront parcel belonging to the Palmers was purchased by Dr. Fred Albee (1876–1945), a well-known orthopedic surgeon practicing in New York City who had developed a number of important surgical tools that made him wealthy. Albee built his own house and the Pollyanna Inn resort before acquiring 1,468 acres— virtually all of the City of Venice—from the Palmers in 1924, by which time he owned about 30 miles of waterfront land facing the Gulf of Mexico and Venice (Roberts) Bay.

Albee hired Nolen, who with staff member, Hale J. Walker (1891–1967), proposed a town that would combine plants for processing citrus crops and some light industry with houses, retail buildings, and extensive recreational facilities. To raise quick cash for his development, Albee sold part of his holdings and concentrated on Venice Beach, releasing a new Nolen plan in January 1925. However, sensing weakness in the Florida land market, Albee put the property up for sale, receiving a dozen offers, including one from a major trade union, the Brotherhood of Locomotive Engineers, which took over the development, initially as a quick fix to a financial shortfall, but then changing course as a long-term investment.

George T. Webb was the union executive who led the project, taking on responsibility as president of the Venice Company. To get the job done, Webb retained the George A. Fuller Construction Company, a national firm that had previously built a Brotherhood building in Cleveland, and the New York architectural firm of A. Stewart Walker (1906–1945) and Leon N. Gillette (1878–1945) to serve as supervising architects. Later, a young landscape architect named Prentiss French (1894–1991) came on board to help bring Nolen's plan to life.

Nolen's plan, developed with Philip W. Foster and Justin R. Hartzog (1892–1963) of his office, called for the relocation of the Seaboard rail line one quarter of a mile east of the city and for the straightening of the Tamiami Trail, the principal highway linking Tampa to Miami. Extending from the train station west to the beach where radial streets created the town's most distinctive neighborhood, the plan's principal feature was Venice Avenue, a broad boulevard, 200 feet wide in the residential district, 120 feet wide in the business section, with an 80-foot-wide bridle path down its middle. Elsewhere, most of the land was gridded into rectangular blocks, but the judicious use of diagonals and a scattering of small parks and a golf course helped to foster neighborhood identity.

As Bruce Stephenson has described the plan: "Greenbelts protected important natural features, and parkways extended from the hinterlands into Venice's downtown. A greenbelt bounded the town to the east and south, while Venice Bay marked the northern edge and the Gulf of Mexico lay to the west . . . The civic center not only defined the town center but also stood midway between the commercial core and Venice's most sublime natural feature: the Gulf of Mexico."[232] Nolen put it succinctly: "Nature led the way" and the plan "followed her way."[233]

One neighborhood of the town, the Edgewood section, east of the railroad tracks—on the "wrong side of the tracks" as it were—was planned with small houses intended for union members. As well there were a number of two-story apartment houses built in the Armada Road "Multi-Family District" that would meet the needs of those unable to purchase and maintain their own homes. Walker & Gillette required North Italian–inspired buildings—essentially Mediterranean Revival—calling for tiled sloping roofs, stucco exterior walls, and colorful awnings. The firm's resident architect, Howard S. Patterson (1890–1958), had to approve all plans. Additionally, the Hotel Venice (1926), a three-story, 100-room facility designed by Walker & Gillette, provided accommodation for potential town residents as well as offices for the Brotherhood. The hotel quickly proved inadequate to demand, and a similar facility, Hotel Park View, was rushed to completion, quickly followed by a third, the San Marco Hotel, which opened in December 1926. A number of smaller hotels were also built, but Nolen's plan for resort hotels at Casey Pass (Venice Inlet) and Rocky Point was not realized.

Nolen developed a series of deed restrictions governing land use, density, and, characteristic of the time, race. Nonetheless, he regarded Venice as one of the best exemplars of his belief in the incorporation of democratic principles in town planning: "Provision should be made in cities and in the country for all classes, especially for labor. The Venice, Florida, development, is one of the best from this point of view."[234] Nolen's unrealized plan for Harlem Village, intended for "colored" farm labor, east of the Edgewood neighborhood, echoed, as Jean-François Lejeune points out, the Emergency Fleet Corporation's housing program (see p. 861) with accommodations for about 3,500 residents, and it was "harmoniously designed with a village square shaped by stores and a school, and four church sites terminating vistas."[235] The provision of church sites in Harlem Village is particularly notable, given that the plan for Venice itself made no specific provision for religious structures. Harlem Village, moreover, was to be a suburb of Venice, itself a suburb of Northern cities. In this Nolen was following Olmsted's basic strategy for suburban development, as at Riverside (see p. 122). That is to say, as Bruce Stephenson has pointed out, Nolen "followed the same model he used in St. Petersburg, [Florida], connecting African American neighborhoods to the larger community with parkways. In cities separated by race, interconnected parkways offered the hope of uniting diverse people through 'nature' and, Nolen wrote, to 'the brotherhood of man.'"[236]

Nolen expected Venice to grow over time, eventually accommodating 10,000 people in an economically balanced community combining industry and resort facilities. He concentrated the business district near the intersection of Venice Avenue and The Rialto, the town's

stretch of the Tamiami Trail. Farther east, next to the relocated Seaboard tracks, Nolen provided for an industrial park. By the end of 1926, 3,000 people were living in Venice, with over 185 buildings either completed or under construction. In 1926 the Brotherhood acquired an additional 20,000 acres, bringing their total holdings to 53,000 acres, or about 83 square miles. Despite the fact that Florida had been opened up to the middle class as a result of better highways, Nolen made no specific provisions for car parking in the business district.

Venice is an unclear paradigm: at varying times due to changing ownership, the town was to function as a resort suburb and as an independent self-sustaining city serving an agricultural community. But, because of Nolen's "Venice Farms Plan" for land due east of the railroad, his intention to create a balanced regional economy clearly exemplified his determination to establish a garden city. By 1929, the collapse in Florida real estate and then in the economy as a whole had left the town with unoccupied houses and empty hotels. Even more significantly, the Brotherhood of Locomotive Engineers, in severe financial trouble as a result of bad investments, was facing a flood of lawsuits that dragged Venice down even further, until it became little more than a ghost town, with only 300 residents in 1930. The town slowly began to revive in 1932 when the Kentucky Military Institute arrived to establish its winter headquarters, and during World War II, when military bases brought jobs. After the war, the Nolen plan was compromised by new subdivisions and the failure to realize his vision for the beachfront, where he had imagined a boardwalk, an outdoor music theater, and a monumental plaza at the end of Venice Avenue. By 1980, more than 12,000 people lived in Venice, topping Nolen's original estimates for the town. Despite the many compromises, the Nolen plan still holds sway as a result of the deed and general land restrictions he put in place, leading Lejeune to write that "the historical significance of the Venice Regional Plan should be recognized for its full value: a national experiment in regional planning."[237] And, according to Stephenson, Venice "stands as the most complete example of the garden city in Florida."[238]

Clewiston (1924), Florida, was planned by Nolen for a 2,500-acre inland site on the southeast coast of Lake Okeechobee, far from the state's two resort-oriented coasts.[239] The land, which included a preexisting village of seventy-five people, had been purchased in 1920 by Philadelphia investors John and Marion O'Brien and Tampa banker Alonzo Clewis, who sought to establish an agricultural center that would also be home to light manufacturing and, because of the lake, would attract tourism. Nolen's plan for a town of 10,000 featured diagonal avenues leading through a neighborhood of radial streets from the lake, which was kept in public ownership, to various neighborhoods. The plan was regional in its ambitions, including twenty to twenty-eight farm sites, an airport, as well as hotels, a golf course, a marina, and an industrial park. A "Negro" section was planned for the western edge of the community, separated from

1. Plan, John Nolen, 1925. COR

2. Aerial view. CM (c. 1940)

3. Typical street. CM (c. 1940)

4. Royal Palm Avenue and Circle Drive. Ebyabe. WC (2010)

the town center by industrial and business districts. A regional canal that later became part of the Intracoastal Waterway supplemented a newly built rail line connected to the Atlantic Coast line at Moore Haven, as well as highways, enabling Clewiston to prosper and grow, especially as Florida's sugarcane industry expanded after World War II. Nolen planned extensions in 1929 and 1936, although the 2000 population was only 6,460.

Radburn (1928), New Jersey, is notably the most comprehensive attempt to realize a garden city for the automobile age.[240] At the same time, it took advantage of existing rail connections to New York City, locating the town's shopping village at the railroad station. Clarence Stein and Henry Wright were Radburn's planners, working under the sponsorship of Alexander Bing's City Housing Corporation. Radburn's plan was prepared in collaboration with Herbert Emmerich, a City Housing Corporation administrator who in December 1927 sketched on the back of an envelope a town plan featuring shared parkland and houses tightly grouped around

culs-de-sac. As planners and sponsors, they saw the new town as an opportunity to build upon the lessons learned at Sunnyside Gardens in Queens, New York (see p. 190). Situated about twenty miles northwest of New York City, Radburn's two-square-mile site was located along the right-of-way of the Erie Railroad within the boundaries of Fair Lawn, a rural community with large areas of undeveloped farmland. Originally intended as a self-contained entity of 25,000 moderate-income residents, Radburn was designed, in Stein's words, "to answer the enigma 'How to live with the auto,' or, if you will, 'How to live in spite of it.'" Stein and Wright proposed "a radical revision of relation of houses, roads, paths, gardens, parks, blocks, and local neighborhoods." Their plan featured five major components that Stein outlined in his 1957 book, *Toward New Towns for America*: "the superblock in place of the characteristic narrow, rectangular block"; "specialized roads planned and built for one use instead of for all uses"; "complete separation of pedestrian and automobile, or as complete separation as

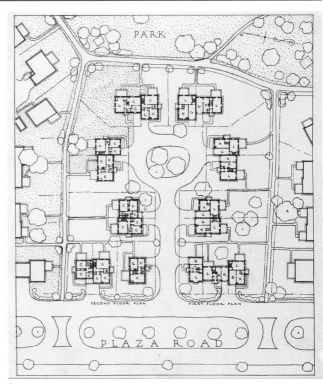

1. Partial plan, Clarence S. Stein and Henry Wright, 1929. TNT

2. Plan, Burnham Place cul-de-sac. COR

3. Aerial view. COR (1929)

possible"; "houses turned around," with "living and sleeping rooms facing toward gardens and parks" and "service rooms toward access roads"; and the "park as backbone of the neighborhood [with] large open areas in the center of superblocks, joined together as a continuous park."[241] Radburn, promoted as the "town for the motor age," was to be more than the next step after Sunnyside—it was to be the next step of the Garden City type. As Geddes Smith described it after the plan was first published: "A town where roads and parks fit together like the fingers of your right and left hands. A town in which children need never dodge motor-trucks on their way to school. A *new* town—newer than the garden cities, and the first major innovation in town-planning since they were built."[242] To prepare for their self-imposed challenge, Stein and Wright went to England "on a special investigation to study superblocks with culs-de-sac," visiting Letchworth, Hampstead Garden Suburb, and Welwyn.[243]

As developed, Radburn's superblocks, ranging in size from 35 to 40 acres, were surrounded by streets accommodating automobile traffic off of which were located 20-foot-wide, 275-foot-long cul-de-sac streets serving between ten and eighteen houses arranged in a roughly U-shaped pattern, leaving the interiors of the superblocks free for development as three- to seven-acre finger-like extensions of a greenbelt-like park system, landscaped by Sunnyside Gardens collaborator Marjorie Sewell Cautley. The parks were not only intended to provide recreation space but also pedestrian circulation routes through the town with the expectation that residents would use them as they visited each other—the front doors of the houses faced the parks—but also as they traveled to the village community centers on foot or by bicycle. The pedestrian paths, carrying pedestrians and cyclists, were grade separated from the roads, thereby avoiding virtually all conflict between, on the one hand, pedestrians and cyclists, and automobiles on the other.

The principal unit of housing designed by Stein and

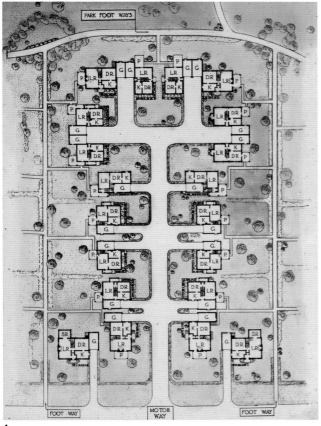

4

5

6

7

8

9

10

11

4. Plan of typical "lane." COR
(c. 1929)

5. Houses and inner park.
RASmith. LOCP (c. 1929)

6. Gas station. RAC

7. Underpass. RAC

8. Plaza Building, Frederick L.
Ackerman, 1929. RAC

9. Croquet game on greensward.
RAC

10. Rear view of houses and
attached garages along cul-de-sac.
A29 (1929)

11. Radburn Terrace Apartments,
Clarence S. Stein and Charles
Butler, 1933, rendering by J. Floyd
Yewell. COR (1933)

12–15. Typical views.
RAMSA (2008)

Wright, assisted by Frederick L. Ackerman, was a Colonial-style, two-story, single-family freestanding house on a 30-by-100-foot site, with its own garage, opening off a cul-de-sac. The decision to place the "front" doors on the greensward and the "back" doors next to the garages on the culs-de-sac proved a mistake, with the doors facing the culs-de-sac taking on both "formal" and "service" functions, a flaw recognized as early as 1937 by landscape architect Elbert Peets. A portion of the town center was realized at the railroad station, where the four-story Collegiate Gothic Abbott Court Apartments (1929), designed by Andrew J. Thomas, was located at the edge of a commercial district that also included a similarly styled shopping center, the Plaza Building (1929), designed by Frederick L. Ackerman, with apartments above the stores, topped by a clock tower. In an attempt to fulfill Garden City principles calling for a fully functioning, self-sufficient community, Stein and Wright set aside 127 acres for an industrial district where, as a first step, the American Radiator Company and the Central Supply Company, another plumbing concern, each built modest warehouses.[244]

The *New York Times* regularly reported on the planning and initial construction of Radburn. In January 1928, when the project was first announced, the editors, characterizing it as "the first deliberate attempt to harmonize the rights of the pedestrian and the motorist," stated that the ultimate success of Radburn depended on the ability of its sponsors to create "a self-contained community with its own industries," as opposed to just another "dormitory suburb" of New York. "In this sense Radburn would be a pioneer of the 'new city' to which many minds have been turning as a cure for the congestion of centralized industry. It is a step toward decentralization made possible, in the first instance, by development in the distribution of electric power for manufacturing purposes. If

the buildings of Radburn succeed in creating model factories as well as model homes and schools, they will really have entered upon a new field. That this is a much more difficult problem than building 'dormitories' for New York City's shop and office workers is obvious."[245]

The cautious hopes of the *Times* editors, not to mention housing advocates from around the world, were abruptly and permanently dashed by the stock market crash of 1929, which occurred five months after the first residents moved into Radburn in May 1929. The Depression that followed at first slowed and then virtually halted construction, so that only one superblock as well as a portion of a second, located on 149 acres near the railroad station, were completed as planned. In 1933, despite plans by Stein and Charles Butler (1871–1953) for the mid-rise Radburn Terrace Apartments complex, only twelve new houses were built, and the following year the City Housing Corporation declared bankruptcy. All told, the realized section of Radburn includes 430 single-family houses, 44 two-family houses, 90 rowhouses, a 92-unit apartment complex, and 23 acres of parkland.

With only about one quarter of the original vision realized, it was never possible to take full measure of Stein and Wright's plan. Even Lewis Mumford, a member with Stein and Wright of the Regional Plan Association of America, was of two minds about Radburn, lauding it extravagantly as "the first major departure in city planning since Venice [Italy],"[246] then going on to express reservations about its architecture, writing that no matter how "admirable" the layout, "no candid critic can pretend that the individual one-family houses are particularly triumphant examples of modern architecture."[247]

In 1964 Harvard architecture student Alden Christie, who had grown up in Radburn, rendered a far harsher judgment, noting that "neighboring . . .

cul-de-sac complexes have no social connections. Interests are turned inward. The kitchen becomes an inelegant focal point for all outside activity, which consists of 'across the pavement' contacts . . . The children play more in the lanes than in the parks. That special care is exercised in Radburn to separate the pedestrian from the automobile—underpass, overpass, internal pathways—is quite paradoxical, since the automobile becomes, in fact, a member of the family." Christie also took issue with what was generally regarded as among the most positive features of the plan—the quality and amount of open space:

> *The layout of dwellings in the superblocks creates a network of intensively developed spaces which abruptly evaporates into a shapeless common, too vaguely defined to suggest an extension or expansion of private yards, too wide to command a directional tendency toward a focal point, too sparsely landscaped to invite refuge from the tight complex of houses . . . The dwelling complexes surrounding the open green in effect are drawn away from it. The automobile has been made such a dominant feature of the Radburn scheme that life is more oriented toward the peripheral access road, the source of the automobile, than toward the common green (that hence is not a common).*[248]

Daniel Schaffer, in his 1982 history of Radburn, offered a more measured assessment, observing that "Radburn's [original] sections remain an unique alternative to conventional suburban development," but also pointing out that the daring and innovative "Radburn idea" did not foster the social goals advocated by the suburb's developers, concluding that "the communal atmosphere the designers hoped to generate in Radburn was subject to forces far more powerful than the physical environment, and Radburn is far from a communal village. The community's unique physical environment has not made its families substantially different from other contemporary suburban families. Indeed, a sociologist would be hard-pressed to distinguish the values, behavior patterns, and lifestyles of Radburnites from those of residents living in the conventional suburban landscape."[249]

In a critique delivered on the occasion of the planned community's fiftieth anniversary, Paul Goldberger placed the design at the crossroads of two "Utopian dreams—that people would give up some of their private suburban land in exchange for much larger, shared open space, and that a way would be found to control the automobile. The years since have shown, sadly, that the faith Radburn's makers had in these dreams was largely misplaced. Few later suburbs followed Radburn's ideas, and today Radburn appears like an earnest and naïve experiment." But, he continued, "it is the touchstone of all progressive community design in the United States, the place to which idealistic planners refer when they

Valley Stream

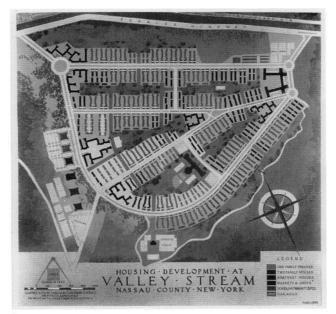

1. Plan, Clarence S. Stein, 1933. COR

2. Service and garden court study showing proposed planting. COR

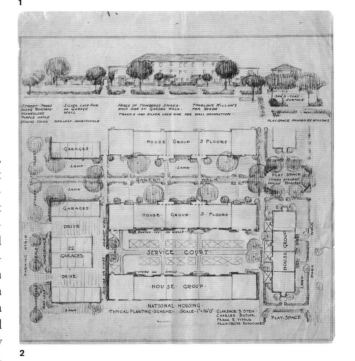

want to show that an idea can be made real."[250]

In 1933 Clarence Stein revisited the Radburn idea with his unrealized proposal for a flat, 350-acre site formerly home to an airfield in **Valley Stream**, Long Island, just outside New York City's border.[251] The project, planned to accommodate 18,000 residents, was part of an effort by the largely idle construction industry in concert with the federal government to stimulate the Depression-era economy and provide employment as well as modest rental housing. As Stein noted, "We architects wanted to carry the Radburn Idea further—to see complete, modern integrated communities planned, built and operated . . . The town plan followed the Radburn pattern with superblocks, underpasses, central parks, and an even more complete separation of pedestrian and auto." Valley Stream's plan called for 4,500 two- and three-story

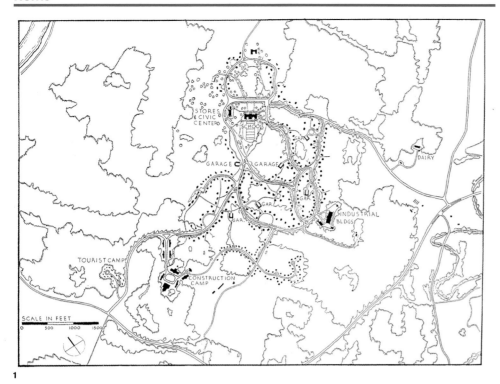

1. Plan, Tracy B. Augur and Carroll
A. Towne, 1933–35. TVA (c. 1935)

2. Plan, detail of town center.
TVA

3. West Norris Road. TVA (1939)

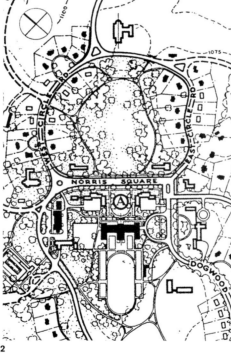

rowhouses, developed at a density of thirteen dwellings per acre, along with a modest greenbelt home to athletic fields and a central seven-acre site for a school and playgrounds. The airfield's hangars were to be converted into garages and market buildings. Stein believed that the Valley Stream proposal, "even though it was only a project . . . formed an important step toward the development of the Greenbelt Towns." Stein blamed the project's failure on the fact that "a large government is slow of action and its machinery complicated."[252] The Valley Stream site was conventionally developed in the 1930s and 1940s as Green Acres by Irwin S. Chanin (1891–1988), who built a large shopping mall in addition to about 800 detached single-family houses.

During the Depression years of the 1930s, the federal government undertook a series of garden cities beginning with **Norris** (1933–35), Tennessee, built to house workers on the Norris Dam (1936).[253] Norris was the first and most significant planning project of the Tennessee Valley Authority (TVA), the agency established in 1933 to revitalize an impoverished 45,000-square-mile rural and farming region spread across seven states. Combining key physical elements of the Radburn plan with the social ideals of the Garden City movement, Norris was designed to demonstrate "what the Garden Cities of England have demonstrated, that the diversified employment opportunities and social advantages of urban life can be enjoyed in a rural setting, and that the small town, properly planned internally as well as in its relation to the country about it, can offer most, if not all, of the benefits that come from life in big cities—without its disadvantages."[254] As developed, Norris marks a decisive transition between the careful orchestration of Garden City design and the seeming unboundedness of the sprawling subdivision.

Named for Nebraska Senator George Norris, a key figure in the establishment of the Tennessee Valley Authority, the town was more directly linked to the vision of Arthur E. Morgan (1878–1975), a former hydraulics engineer and president of Antioch College (1920–36) who, as TVA chairman, imagined not just a temporary encampment for dam workers but also a permanent town that would subsist after the dam's completion as a mixed agricultural and industrial community complementing the Knoxville metropolitan area, a principle in keeping with the authority's emphasis on regional planning. Earle S. Draper, since 1933 the director of the TVA's Division of Land Planning and Housing, oversaw the project, enlisting Tracy B. Augur (1896–1974), a Harvard-educated city planner and like Draper an alumnus of John Nolen's office, to prepare the plan with the assistance of landscape architect Carroll A. Towne (1901–1991). The architectural work, while overseen by TVA chief architect Roland A. Wank (1898–1970), was handled by a team led by the young Robert Cerny (1908–1985), a 1933 graduate of Harvard's architecture school.

The site for Norris, four miles southeast of the dam and 23 miles north of Knoxville, consisted of 2,500 rugged, undeveloped acres forming a high plateau

4. Typical street. TVA (1935)

5. Town Center. TVA (c. 1939)

6. Underpass. Poynter. NYT (2008)

surrounded by steep ravines and wooded hills. Combined with additional lands that the authority purchased between the town site and the dam, the property totaled 4,200 acres, allowing for the inclusion of the first fully realized greenbelt in an American planned town. Norris's planners decided against a railroad connection to Knoxville, gearing the village toward the automobile. A two-lane construction road between the dam and the village was transformed into a twenty-one-mile freeway that linked up with two highways near Knoxville. Eliminated from the freeway's 250-foot right-of-way were, as Draper wrote, "the signboards, hot-dog stands, shacks, and all the other roadside clutter so destructive to the natural beauty of any section."[255]

The town was intended to accommodate between 1,000 and 1,500 families for a total population of about 5,000. Because of the immediate need to house dam workers, a group of dormitories and a mess hall were built while designs for the village were still being prepared. In fact, the plan was still very much in flux when construction of the village proper began. The level area in the middle of the site was reserved for the town center—Norris's only formally composed group of buildings, presided over by a combined elementary and high school that doubled as a community center. The school, set back on a landscaped court framed by stores and town offices, pointed northeast toward Norris Square, a widened street lined by additional public buildings, beyond which lay a large oval commons edged by houses and intended to be anchored on the far end by a church that was never built. To the south of the school were 14 acres of athletic fields and parkland around which the bulk of the residential development was concentrated. During the dam's construction, community life had focused on the dormitory complex in the southwest where almost 1,000 workers lived, but by the time of the dam's completion, funding for the town center had dried up and it remained only partially realized, accommodating the school, a grocery store, and town and post offices.

The residential streets were deliberately narrow and lined not by curbs but by gutters fashioned from local stone. As dictated by the topography, many streets followed gullies, allowing houses to occupy higher ground on either side, while culs-de-sac branched off to hilltops. Looping roads formed a series of loosely defined superblocks with houses dotting the edges and open spaces cleared in the middle. As at Draper's earlier Chicopee (see p. 858), group garages were provided on block interiors but were infrequently used. House lots, averaging 60 by 100 feet (downsized from a planned 75 by 200 feet), were staked out to preserve existing trees and maximize views, resulting in a high degree of informality. Lot lines were unmarked by hedges or fences, and the traditional intimacy of the garden village was sacrificed to a looser form of rurality so that, as William H. Jordy has written, "When the foliage was full, it was often possible to avoid seeing adjacent houses at all . . . That part of Norris completed by the TVA now seems settled into its wood, each property blending unidiosyncratically into the next."[256]

With no standard setbacks, the houses appeared to float in the landscape. As Jordy observed, "Although most of the rows . . . adhere at least loosely to the road there are noticeable divergences . . . Some occur as minor incidents, where three or four houses cluster to form mini-courts, or, more frequently curve to form mini-crescents. More venturesome are deeper scallops of the residential loops, where the road hews to its gully while the line of houses curves away in a rough semicircle, up a hill and back down, before rejoining the road."[257] In an attempt to counteract the sprawling informality, a network of footpaths, taking the place of conventional sidewalks, connected the houses with the town center. As at Radburn, the planners separated automobile and pedestrian traffic, employing underpasses to minimize grade crossings of roads. This "loose interplay of road, sidewalk, and house," according to Jordy, "is among the most delightful and original aspects of the town."[258]

Robert Cerny and his team designed thirty-five distinct house plans based on careful study of the vernacular, yielding what Norman T. Newton described as a "completely native look."[259] At first the houses were clad with brick, clapboard, and native cedar shake and each dwelling was provided with a porch, but as budgets shrank, later phases introduced cinder-block construction. In all, about 290 houses were built in two initial phases between 1933 and 1935. Together with some apartments, ten semidetached houses, and a few nearby converted farmhouses, Norris peaked in its early years at a population of 350 families.

Cooperative facilities were located between the village and the greenbelt, including a dairy farm, a poultry farm, and four-acre garden plots provided for individual households. The site reserved for a light-industrial complex was never fully developed, although a ceramics lab was established and later taken over by the TVA for internal research purposes. A tourist camp was also included in the plan, reflecting a strong belief that the village would become as much of an attraction as the dam.

Upon completion of the dam in 1936, many workers left Norris, but enough of a population remained for the town to survive. In 1948, Norris was auctioned off by the federal government to a Philadelphia investment group that resold properties to individual residents. A growing population of professionals led to the village's emergence as a white-collar Knoxville suburb, but the absence of controls allowed owners to add dormers, porticoes, and additional rooms, as well as individual garages, compromising the original character of the architecture. Eventually, much of the greenbelt was also sold off. Despite these disappointing developments, Norris managed to retain a high level of its integrity and was listed on the National Register of Historic Places in 1975.

Given the prominence of the TVA's work and the expertise brought to bear on Norris's plan (Draper later acknowledged that both the Olmsted office and Henry V. Hubbard [1875–1947] had served in advisory capacities), critical reaction to Norris was muted. Jordy attributes this in part to the fact that the "Clarence Stein/Henry Wright/Lewis Mumford clique of progressives"—the Regional Planning Association of America—had, despite Roosevelt's familiarity with the group and its work, been snubbed by the Tennessee Valley Authority in favor of Draper and his colleagues, who were thought to be more in touch with Southern culture, leading Mumford to later state that "the things I had worked for during the twenties came to a head in Washington and in the Tennessee Valley, without myself or any of my colleagues

being given a chance to work in any of the strategic positions: while other, less capable people fumbled and muffed the opportunities which they were only partly prepared to handle."[260]

According to Earle Draper Jr., the planner's son and an architect in his own right, Raymond Unwin came away from his visit to Norris believing it to be "the most successful American planned town embodying English garden city principles."[261] But others felt that given the project's rural location, small size, limited funding, and hasty planning, it could never live up to its high ideals. While the TVA, as Walter Creese has written, may have believed that "the precise model mattered less than the symbolic implication," the disparity between the two posed problems for "American experts [who] could not easily describe what they were seeing, due to the fact that the cue-giving English Garden City motifs of the cul-de-sac, superblock, and greenbelt originally had been developed for relationships larger in scale." Norris's density of 2.7 families per acre starkly illustrated that it was "a large model interpreted in a small way."[262]

Arthur Comey and Max Wehrly, in their 1936 study of planned communities, found Norris to have "perhaps the most natural and informal appearance" of any of the communities they had visited, a credit to the designers' ability not to "superimpose any development upon the community in the form of design or use of materials which was not wholly natural and fitting." Addressing criticisms that "the plan lacks composition," Comey and Wehrly defended the strategy: "Any composition which would have resulted from the introduction of strong formal relationships is happily absent, and in its place a more subtle form of unity has been obtained based on functional and topographic relation."[263] Norman T. Newton, who praised Norris "as an outstanding contribution to the American community planning story," felt that its concurrent design and construction rendered "the technical excellence of the planning all the more astonishing. Perhaps the need for quick decisions contributed somehow to the casual charm that critical visitors have noted at Norris ever since the little town was finished."[264]

Norris may best be understood as a rural version of Radburn. As Newton writes, "the rugged topography precluded adoption of the 'Radburn idea' in its complete form," but the important elements were in place: "dead-end streets were used to serve groups of houses, in most of the large blocks there is a central core of undeveloped open space, and garage compounds within the blocks take the place of individual garages, with cars otherwise restricted to the streets."[265] Radburn and Norris were both conceived in terms of the automobile, meeting its demands with mixed success. "Although Radburn was heralded at the time of its design as a town 'planned for the motor age,'" Jordy writes, "it really represented an enlargement of the city block to accommodate the scale permitted by the automobile . . . If Radburn was the prototype of an automobile town in a densely populated area, Norris was its equivalent in the countryside, which was perhaps the more natural habitat of the 'motor age.'"[266] Yet Jordy identified "no absolute differences between Radburn and Norris, only predilections toward contrasting modes of operation in planning. Radburn was the partial realization of a theoretical scheme, Norris the result of enlightened coping (and groping) with a specific and changing situation." Established under nearly opposite conditions, neither town could achieve its planners' vision:

> Radburn was conceived in the plush economic circumstances of the late 1920s, financed by a limited-dividend private corporation, and intended for middle-income suburban living within the metropolitan area of New York . . . Even though Norris developed a suburban character similar to Radburn's it began with a different perspective, including an almost exaggerated austerity. No one could accuse Radburn or any of Stein's other projects of anything but sobriety in concentrating on essentials, but Norris outdid them . . . In truth, there was a 'country' quality to the improvisational, commonsense response to problems at Norris . . . Norris was begun under great political pressure in a backwoods environment; it is difficult to see how it could have developed otherwise.[267]

The Greenbelt towns, consisting of Greenbelt (1937), Maryland, Greenhills (1938), Ohio, and Greendale (1938), Wisconsin—a fourth town, Greenbrook (1935), New Jersey, was not realized[268]—were built by the Suburban Resettlement Division of the federal government's Resettlement Administration, headed by Rexford Guy Tugwell (1891–1979), a New Dealer who fervently believed in the ideas of Ebenezer Howard and Clarence Stein. Charged with helping clear inner-city slum sites by moving residents to new suburban villages protected by encircling greenbelts, in 1935 the Resettlement Administration initiated the development of the Greenbelt towns, together representing, according to Stein, "the first experiments in the combined development of the three basic ideas of the modern community: the Garden City, the Radburn Idea, and the Neighborhood Unit."[269]

As planned in 1935 by Hale Walker, **Greenbelt**, Maryland, set on 3,600 acres and ultimately intended to house 5,000 families in what was then an easy twenty-five-minute drive from Washington, D.C., incorporated many of the planning tropes of Radburn, particularly the use of the superblock and the separation of pedestrian and vehicular circulation systems, though it did not carry forward that community's density or its architectural style.[270] Instead the design team of Reginald D. Johnson and the partnership of Douglas D. Ellington (1886–1960) and Reginald J. Wadsworth (n.d.) adopted a stripped classicism for the shopping center and an almost featureless minimalism for the group houses that, clad with white-painted stucco on cinder block or painted brick veneer, combined trends in European Modernist housing estate design with hints of American Georgian detailing.

The developed areas were confined to 750 acres

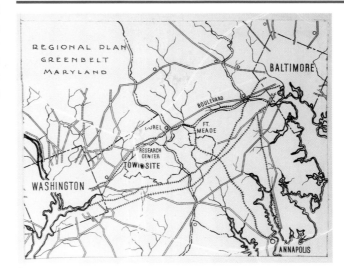

1

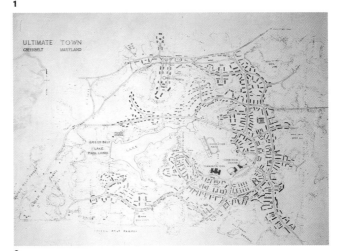

2

3

4

1. Locator map. LOCPF (1936)
2. Plan, Hale Walker, 1935. LOCPF
3. Aerial view. LOCPF (1936)
4. Aerial view. LOCPF (1939)

5. Typical rowhouses.
Rothstein. LOCPF (1936)

6. Underpass and apartment
buildings. Wolcott. LOCPF (1938)

7. Shopping center. Wolcott. LOCPF
(1938)

8. Pedestrian paths. Bossi.
WC (2008)

5

6

7

8

of the total site, with 217 acres devoted to the town, 250 acres for parks, and 107 acres for allotment gardens. The rest of the land was kept as a buffer, and a 500-acre swath was reserved for future expansion. The horse-shoe-shaped town plan, following the ridge of a plateau, encircled a village green where shops and community facilities, including an inn, were proposed. A continuous loop road was crossed by radial streets leading from the center to arterials. Pedestrian paths also led from the center, helping to break up the large, approximately 15-acre superblocks, with underpasses provided to cross busy streets. Of the 885 dwelling units, 574 were in grouped row units and 306 were apartments. Five freestanding houses were also built as experiments in plywood construction. With no rail connection to Washington, express bus service was inaugurated during rush hours, when the trip was scheduled for about thirty-five minutes.

Greenbelt was intensely scrutinized by the press and was the subject of numerous reports and studies. For Lewis Mumford, it was "a new type of city," differing "radically from both the metropolitan and suburban patterns lingering from the past." But it did not go far enough for him: "We have to go one step beyond . . . in the planning for the future," providing industry as part of the whole, "if we are to banish the waste and fatigue and inanity of long-distance commutation."[271] After World War II, Greenbelt, which had been built as a community for renters, was turned into a cooperative with much of the excess land gradually sold off to developers taking advantage of interstate highways planned to criss-cross the site.

Greenhills, on a gently rolling 5,930-acre woodland site five miles north of Cincinnati, was planned by Justin R. Hartzog and William A. Strong (n.d.) working with Roland A. Wank and G. Frank Cordner (n.d.).[272] The first stage saw 676 units built, distributed between apartments, rowhouses, and twenty-four single-family detached dwellings. Much less like Radburn and Greenbelt, Greenhills marks a decisive step away from the pedestrian-dominated village idea and toward an automobile-dominated pattern of land subdivision. Bisected by a main highway, Greenhills was nestled into the topography so that, as Paul Conkin has described it, "although there were several superblocks with cul-de-sacs and central park areas, much of the town consisted of single, fingerlike cul-de-sacs or small circular drives, both surrounded by natural scenery."[273] Unlike Radburn's tightly configured culs-de-sac, those at Greenhills were generously sized with a broad common or greensward at the turnaround. As a result, the town was less compact than Greenbelt and therefore less pedestrian friendly.

Greendale, on 3,410 acres three miles southwest of Milwaukee, was planned by Jacob Crane (1892–1988) and Elbert Peets, working with architects Harry H. Bentley (n.d.) and Walter G. Thomas (d. 1969).[274] Of the three Greenbelt towns, Greendale is the most distinctly embedded in the Garden City tradition, effectively balancing tightly defined urbanity with open landscape and eschewing the abstract geometry of the Greenbelt and Greenhills site plans. Greendale was designed as a critical response to what Peets took to be the failure of Radburn's plan of culs-de-sac and linked open spaces. As Peets wrote in 1937, "it is overdoing it to let the motor

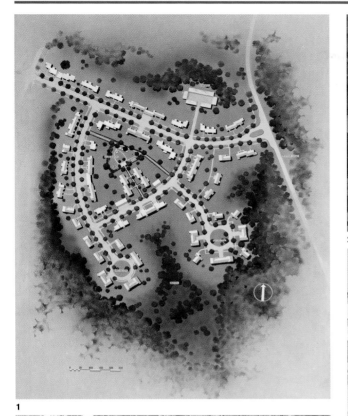

1

2

3

4

1. Model of block plan, Justin
R. Hartzog and William A. Strong,
1936. LOCPF

2. Aerial rendering. LOCPF
(c. 1936)

3. Typical street. Vachon. LOCPF
(1938)

4. Typical street. Garvin. AG (2004)

Greendale

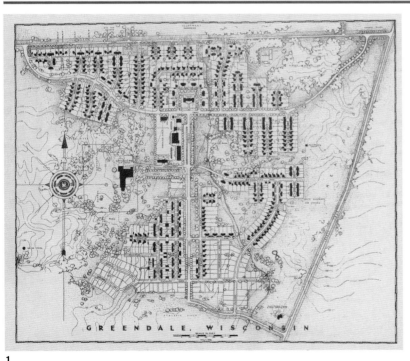

1

2

1. Plan, Jacob Crane and Elbert
Peets, 1938. COR

2. Plan of town center. JSL
(c. 1938)

3. Plan, cul-de-sac with grouped houses. LOCPF

4. Plan, cul-de-sac with single houses. LOCPF

3

Cul-de-sac with Grouped Houses
plan showing roadway and planting.
scale: 1"=20'

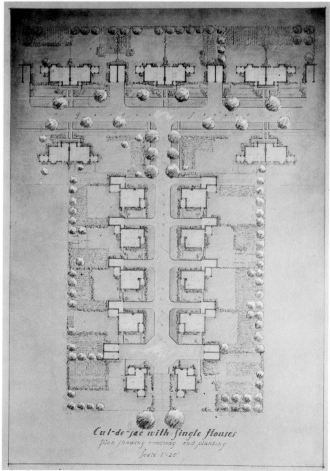

4

Cul-de-sac with single Houses
plan showing roadway and planting
scale 1"=20'

age deprive us of personal relationship with the 'ancient mother.' The Greendale plan started with the premise that every house should have its patch of ground, with a fence around it." Peets described in detail the design of the town's residential streets:

> *The special way of putting together street, house, and lot that distinguishes the Greendale street . . . appears most novel to those whose knowledge of town planning history is least. The type of house it implies is much like the side-garden house of our colonial towns, a house built on the street and along one side of the lot, with a garden between it and the neighbor. Even more it resembles the ancient and universal arrangement of the houses in farm villages, where one does not enter the house directly from the street but through a court around which the buildings are grouped . . . This plan conceives of the house, the car, and the garden as together comprising the "home." It was worked out as a correlation of the house with the community and the world on one side and the privately held bit of land that is the garden on the other. The motorcar is the link between the house and the world: the court brings the car into the home complex—one can go from the car to the house as directly and with almost as perfect privacy as one goes from room to room in the house . . . This Greendale type of house and lot planning brings the residence street back into civic art— it rescues the street from the street trees and the front lawns. The street becomes a defined channel of space, as it was in the old town plans . . . And it is not quite an accident that in its skeleton organization the plan of Greendale is much like the plan of Williamsburg.*[275]

As well, Greendale's architecture is more distinctly attached to Anglo-American suburban precedent than the relatively featureless buildings of Greenbelt and Greenhills, despite Peets's assertion that it "was to be a workingmen's town; in actuality and appearance it must be direct, simple, and practical, free of snobbishness, not afraid of standardization."[276] This can be seen both in the specifics of style—with a preponderance of gabled roofs— but even more so in the careful calibration of mostly single-family houses, garages, and gardens that convey a distinct feeling of traditional residential streets as opposed to the loosely placed siedlung-like rows of Greenbelt and Greenhills. At its opening in 1938, half of Greendale's 572 units, accommodated in 366 buildings, were in single-family houses; the rest, in social group houses.

Significantly, in 1949, as the federal government was setting out to sell the Greenbelt towns, Peets prepared plans for anticipated new development, covering almost five square miles. Peets called for the preservation of open space as well as street patterns that would be more or less adopted by private sector developers, but also studied refining the original house, garage, garden, and

5

6

7

8

9

10

11

5. Plan for future development, Elbert Peets, 1950. PDS

6. Bird's-eye view of Apple Court. JSL (c. 1938)

7. Typical street. LOCPF (1939)

8. Pedestrian path and houses. LOCPF (1939)

9. Berry Court. Garvin. AG (2012)

10. Retail stretch of Broad Street showing Village Hall in distance. Garvin. AG (2012)

11. Pedestrian path and houses. Garvin. AG (2004)

lot arrangements, which can be seen as crucial linkages between the more or less moribund garden suburb tradition and its revival in the 1970s.

Although Peets planned Greendale as a critique of Radburn, he did retain Radburn's "basic principle of differentiating the street system into three classes of traffic—regional, village, and residential—while terminating most of the latter on cul-de-sacs (or courts as they were termed at Greendale)."[277] In their history of Greendale, Joseph A. Eden and Arnold R. Alanen write that Peets departed from "a suburban cliché of sinuous streets," laying out Broad Street, the main thoroughfare, to present "a long vista into a public area of shops, a community building, and at the apex, a village hall styled as an unabashed borrowing from Colonial Williamsburg. As

if to place the Greendale plan within a historical context of civic planning, Peets incorporated themes from colonial townscapes, midwestern county seats, European Renaissance cities, and the work of Camillo Sitte . . . The typical Greendale street, Peets felt, evoked feelings of belonging within those who lived along it; the street became, in Peets's opinion, 'a defined channel of space as in the old town plans.'"[278] This distinct urbanity was obvious even to the casual visitor. For example, in 1958, James Dahir reported that "a newcomer" to the village "expressed her surprised pleasure at seeing a friendly town with a European village air so close to Milwaukee," leading Dahir to observe that "a good community in which you can walk to work and to shops, have good neighbors, and a modern home, has an air of unreality about it in the America of the second half of the 20th century."[279]

THE GARDEN CITY IN FRANCE

In 1898, the year Howard published *To-morrow: A Peaceful Path to Real Reform*, Tony Garnier (1869–1948), then a student at the École des Beaux-Arts, began designing his **Cité Industrielle** (1898–1917), initiated as a student project but continuing on for many years as an ongoing critique of the vernacular-dependent sentimentality of its English prototype.[280] Garnier began his architectural training in 1886, studying for three years at the École des Beaux-Arts in his hometown of Lyons before advancing to the École in Paris, where he remained through the 1890s. After several failed efforts, Garnier won the coveted Prix de Rome in 1899. During his four years at the Villa Medici, he defied his instructors by neglecting to comply with what he considered to be an irrelevant curriculum based on the examination and proposed reconstruction of ancient monuments. Instead, he spent the bulk of his time developing the Cité Industrielle, submitting general plans to the École in 1901 and exhibiting the final design in 1904. The scheme would remain essentially intact—although Garnier continued to adjust it—until 1917, when it was published as a series of 164 plates accompanied by a short introductory text.

The Cité Industrielle, envisioned for a population of 35,000 but designed to allow for easy expansion, attempted to synthesize advances in building technology—especially the use of reinforced concrete—with socialist ideologies. In its planning, the Cité, picking up on Howard's diagrammatic approach, anticipated modern zoning through the designation of separate districts for industry, town, and hospitals, each of which was to be buffered by a greenbelt. Although the breadth and detail of Garnier's plan indicates a strong realism, the architect's socialist zeal places the Cité within the narrative of nineteenth-century utopian thought as first translated into architectural terms by Charles Fourier. Not only did Garnier toe the socialist line by calling for the elimination of private property and for the public administration of utilities and services, including the distribution of medicine and the operation of slaughterhouses, mills, shops, bakeries, and dairies, he also excluded churches, legal courts, jails, and a police force, believing that in socialist society there would be no cause for crime.

The hypothetical site, located at the convergence of a river and a tributary, with a low plain rising in plateaus to mountains in the north, was characteristic of the region around Lyons. Garnier believed that new cities should be sited wherever they could draw on natural resources, an energy supply, and transportation. "In our case, it is the strength of a tributary that is the reason," he stated. "There are also mines in the region, but perhaps further away."[281] The tributary would be dammed to provide hydroelectric power while the mines would provide the Cité with an industrial base along with silk manufacturing.

Garnier used changes in the topography to buffer one zone from the other, situating industry along the river, the town on a high plateau to the north, and a hospital complex still higher in the mountains where it would be sheltered from cold winds. He placed railroad tracks between the factories and town, locating the main railway station where it would be convenient to each district, in a mixed-use sector adjacent to an imagined old village in the northeast. The grounds of an old hilltop chateau would be converted into one of several public parks. Agricultural land was to surround the Cité, dotted with mills and small factories.

Garnier platted the town as an elongated grid centered on an east–west spine originating at the main railroad station, the ordered geometry of the plan revealing his debt to Beaux-Arts training. North–south streets were 66 feet wide while east–west streets were either 62 feet wide with trees along the south side or 43 feet wide with no street trees. The center of the town was given over to a "vast space reserved for public buildings" that Garnier organized into administrative, cultural, and recreational clusters.[282] The administrative complex was anchored by a lozenge-shaped assembly building that was something of a technical and ideological showpiece, with deep cantilevers that seemed, according to Nikolaus Pevsner, "hardly possible at such an early date," implying "an understanding of the possibilities of reinforced concrete which was still rare by 1904."[283] Above the entrance, much as Ledoux had inscribed passages upon the House of Union at Chaux (see p. 727), Garnier placed two quotations from Emile Zola's novel *Travail* (1901), "the literary counterpart of the Cité Industrielle," as Dora Wiebenson has observed, which was "almost solely based on the early socialist Utopian doctrines of Fourier."[284] Other components of the city center included parks and plazas, a botanical museum, a local history museum, an exhibition hall, a library, a theater, an amphitheater, a hotel, a restaurant, a gymnasium, a stadium, and an indoor swimming pool.

In the residential neighborhoods, Garnier placed single-family detached and semidetached houses on rectangular, 492-by-98-foot blocks divided into 49-by-49-foot lots, mandating that more than half of each lot remain open as a "public garden for pedestrians." Setting the stage for the continuous field of Modernist urbanism, the arrangement, Garnier wrote, "allows circulation through town in any direction independent of the street which one needs no longer follow; the land of the town as a whole is like a large park, with no enclosing wall to limit the grounds."[285] Nonetheless, as Reyner Banham observed, the houses, "though freely sited—more or less—are squared up to the road grid. The pattern, indeed, is like Camillo Sitte with the serpentinings taken out."[286] Anticipating Clarence Perry's neighborhood unit concept of 1929, Garnier inserted primary schools evenly among the blocks.

The town's east–west orientation was geared toward maximum sunlight exposure, while the banishment of courtyards and narrow light wells allowed "every space,

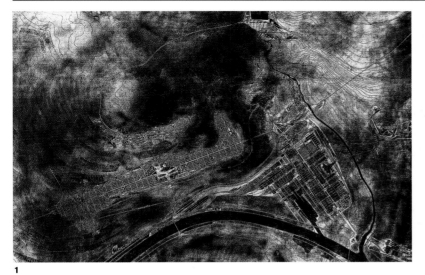

1. Plan, Tony Garnier, 1904, from *Une cité industrielle*. FML (1917)

2. Aerial perspective of public services from *Une cité industrielle*. FML (1917)

3–7. Perspective of streets in residential neighborhoods from *Une cité industrielle*. FML (1917)

no matter how small," to be "lighted and ventilated from outside."[287] Interiors were to feature smooth surfaces and rounded corners. Architecturally, Garnier's reinforced-concrete houses, limited in height to two stories, were free of ornament and covered by flat roofs that frequently doubled as terraces to evoke "above all else," as Kenneth Frampton put it, "the vision of a Mediterranean socialist arcadia."[288]

Le Corbusier was among the architects to be most influenced by the Cité Industrielle. He visited Garnier's Lyons studio in 1908 and reproduced a plan and two renderings of the Cité's residential district in *Vers Une Architecture* (1923), highlighting the ability of pedestrians to circulate independent of the street grid and celebrating the city's park-like environment, but adding: "One can criticize Garnier for one thing: placing such

low-density quarters in the heart of the city."[289] Much as Ledoux's Chaux had sought, according to Ruth Eaton, "to glorify every rung of the social ladder without displacing it,"[290] Le Corbusier recognized that Garnier, through the implementation of a "unitary code" that "distributes the same set of essential volumes through all parts of the city and determines the spaces in ways consistent with needs of a practical order and with the promptings of a poetic sense that is the architect's own," as well as through the "happy invention of a system of lot division," had allowed "even the quarters of workers' housing [to] take on a high architectural significance. Such are the consequences of a plan."[291]

Notwithstanding Garnier's influence on Le Corbusier, Kenneth Frampton notes that the Cité's broader impact was muted because it was never "tested or

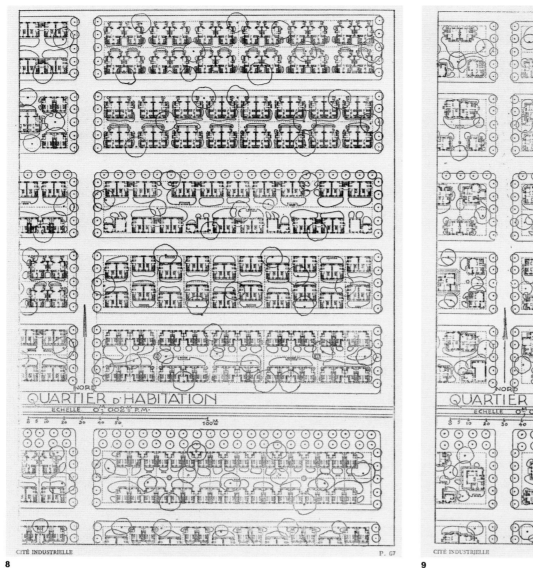

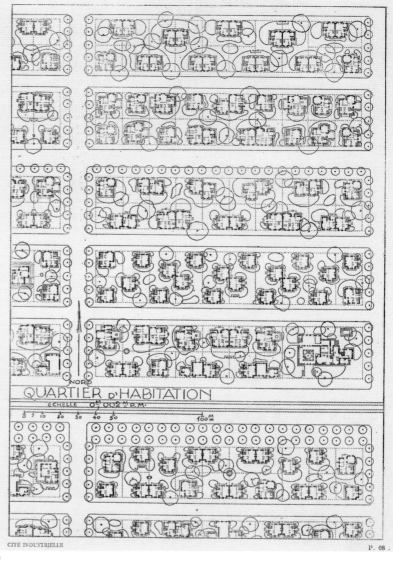

8

9

8, 9. Plans of residential neighborhoods from *Une cité industrielle*. FML (1917)

extensively published. Unlike Ebenezer Howard's garden city model . . . which was realized as a developmental strategy at Letchworth," the Cité Industrielle "could hardly be referred to as a proven model. These two alternatives could not in fact have been more opposed, for where Garnier's Cité was inherently expandable and graced with a certain autonomy due to its base in heavy industry, Howard's Rurisville was limited in size and economically dependent, with its base in light industry and small-scale agriculture."[292]

Although largely ignored by the press, the Cité's 1904 unveiling did receive a favorable review in a Lyons journal that encouraged Garnier to return to his hometown, where during the next forty years, the architect undertook a string of projects at the behest of a progressive socialist mayor, Édouard Herriot (1872–1957), who, as Dora Wiebenson states, "wished to transform Lyon into an actual version of Garnier's projected city."[293] Garnier was put in charge of the *Grand Travaux* in Lyons, ultimately realizing a municipal abattoir, dairy, stadium, market hall, hospital, and the Quartier États-Unis, a residential district of mid-rise apartment buildings lining a three-mile-long boulevard, built between 1928 and 1935.[294]

THE GARDEN CITY IN GERMANY

Hellerau (1906), generally regarded as Germany's first and only Garden City, was realized four miles outside of Dresden, to which it was connected by a tram.[295] Intended for 8,000 residents occupying 2,000 houses, Hellerau, as an early commentator, Ewart G. Culpin, put it, was "a combination of Letchworth and Hampstead, having the former's factory sites but without its belt of agricultural land."[296] The town plan and design of many of the houses were the work of Richard Riemerschmid (1868–1957), although other architects designed buildings, most notably Hermann Muthesius, Theodor Fischer (1862–1938), Georg Metzendorf (1874–1934), Heinrich Tessenow (1876–1950), and Kurt Frick (1884–1963).

The elevated 400-acre site, known as Dresden Heath, was bounded by pine woods, with the plan's loose grid of streets conforming to its moderate slope.

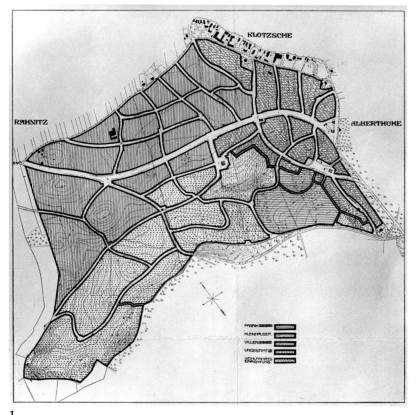

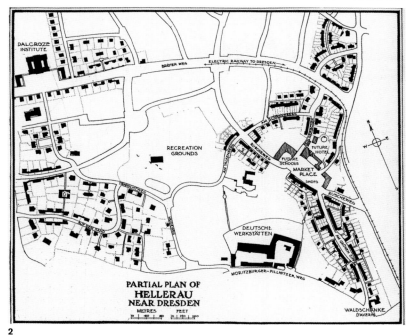

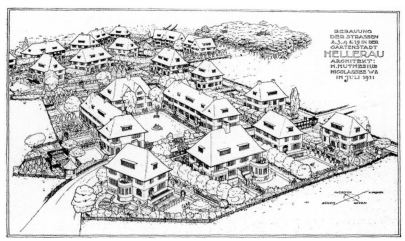

1. Land use plan, Richard Riemerschmid, 1907. FM

2. Partial plan, 1907. AR14

3. Bird's-eye view of proposed houses, Hermann Muthesius, 1911. AR14

4. Factory, Deutsche Werkstätten für Handwerkskunst, Richard Riemerschmid, 1909–11. FM

5. Tram along Breiter Weg. CRS

6. Festspielhaus, Heinrich
Tessenow, 1910–11. FM (c. 1913)

7. Am Talkenberg. FM (c. 1909)

8. Am Grünen Zipfel. FM (c. 1909)

6

7

8

Hellerau's principal factory was designed by Riemerschmid, housing the arts and crafts workshops of the Deutsche Werkstätten für Handwerkskunst (German Workshops for Handcrafted Art), Germany's largest interior decoration firm, owned by Karl Schmidt (1856–1934), the town's developer. Riemerschmid's factory was entered under an arch guarded by "a quaint hut resembling the porter's lodge of a grand estate," as historian Maiken Umbach has observed. "In terms of layout, the entire factory was closely modeled on the traditional tripartite structure of a Baroque castle or country villa. Read in conjunction with the village laid out around the factory, with curving little streets all oriented towards this central building, it invariably reminded the visitor of a small Saxon residential town, complete with the princely residence at its heart."[297]

In addition to the craft workshop, Hellerau was

home to Tessenow's building for the "School for Harmony," a progressive physical culture institute founded by Professor Émile Jaques-Dalcroze (1865–1950) and relocated from Switzerland. Tessenow's severely classical Festspielhaus (festival theater) constituted the town's most important building, attached by covered passageways to student cottages, all together forming a monumental open court. Jaques-Dalcroze was a Swiss-born music teacher influenced by the Swiss theater set designer Adolphe Apia (1862–1928) whose method focused on rhythmic gymnastics. Tessenow's design for the Festspielhaus was seen as a defiant challenge to the suburb's Heimatstil (home-style vernacular) and, as a result, the building was not constructed in the market square as originally proposed but at the northwest edge of the village. Startling as the Dalcroze Institute building was, it was in its way no more so than the very

9

10

11

12

9. Marketplace. PV (2007)

10. View along Heideweg showing Festspielhaus in distance. RAMSA (2007)

11. Am Dorffrieden. RAMSA (2007)

12. Am Grünen Zipfel. RAMSA (2008)

13. Am Sonnenhang. RAMSA (2008)

14. View along Schmaler Weg showing elementary school, Kurt Frick, 1914. RAMSA (2008)

15. Heideweg. RAMSA (2008)

13

14

15

modest workers' houses Tessenow realized in Hellerau which eschewed the numerous details of typical Arts and Crafts villas in favor of a severity of expression that, when newly completed and before garden features could take root, were said to exhibit "the stink of poverty."[298] On the other hand, Tessenow's single-family houses were set back from the road, suggesting Goethe's house in the park at Weimar, "the primordial house of German culture."[299]

Am Grünen Zipfel ("At the Green Coat-Tail" Street [also translated as "The Green Point" by John V. Maciuika]), east of the factory, hewed to the landscape's sloping contours, lined with groups of houses forming courtyards and midblock pathways like those in medieval German towns.[300] To further the impression of growth over time, street widths were irregular and buildings featured setbacks and projections to form plaza-like eddies of outdoor space. Am Grünen Zipfel's completion in time for a presentation at the Berlin planning exhibition of 1910 ensured Hellerau's position as a foundation stone in Germany's garden suburb movement. After a visit in 1912, Hermann Muthesius extolled it as a perfect blend of artistic principles and social reform.[301]

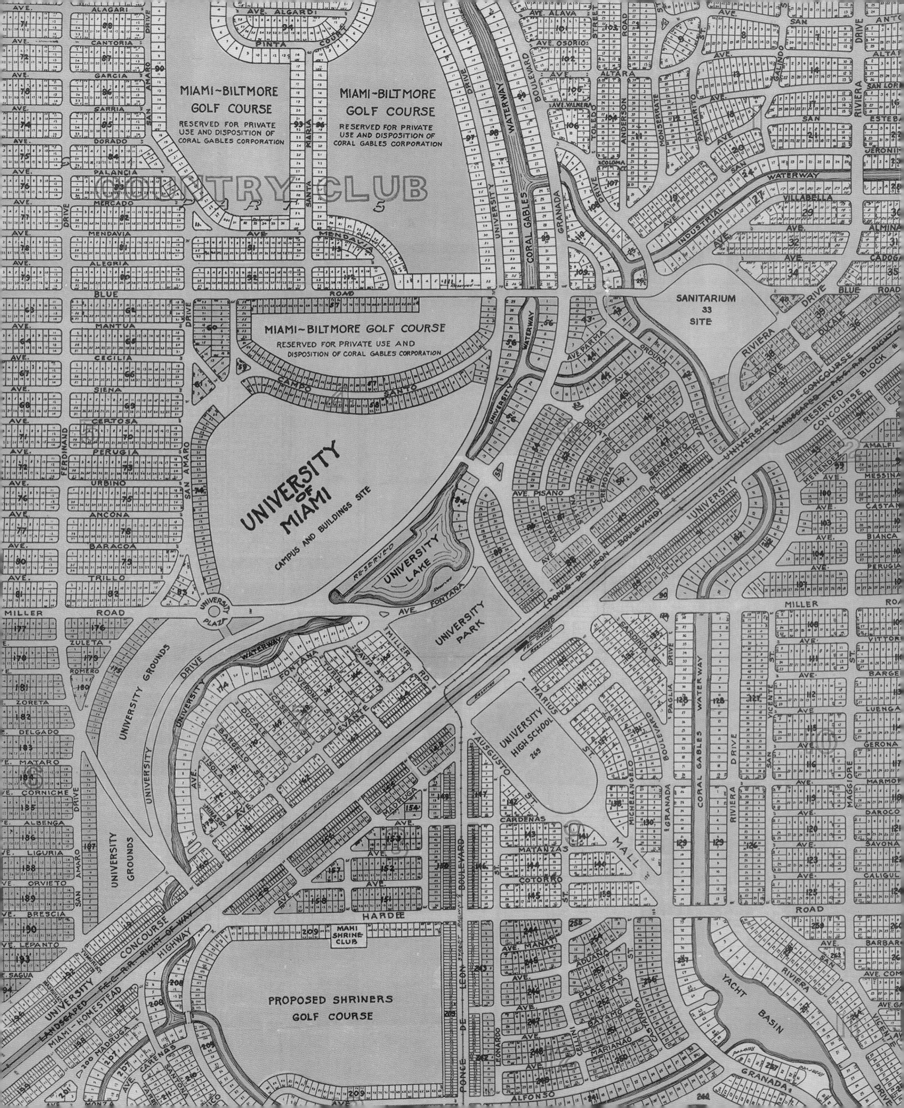

CHAPTER FOUR

The Resort Garden Suburb in America 1866–1930

From its outset the garden suburb tradition has been bound up with resorts for seasonal leisure. In England, Leamington Spa (see p. 28) and Brighton and Hove (see p. 27) were home to garden villages. But in no country has the resort garden suburb been so widely embraced as in the United States, perhaps because it is on holiday that Americans release their collective architectural libido and relax in nature. Fast trains and then automobiles combined with increasingly sophisticated electronic communication to foster mobility among the monied classes, enabling them to live away from their home cities for extended periods of time. The garden suburb proved an ideal setting for their leisure.

As travel times sped up in the late nineteenth and early twentieth centuries, many of the first resort suburbs evolved into commuter suburbs. Such was the case of **Tuxedo Park** (1885), the brainchild of tobacco heir Pierre Lorillard (1833–1901).[1] The earliest exemplar of the purposely planned American resort suburb, Tuxedo Park began as a club for 200 families wishing to escape the city into the deep countryside. While Llewellyn Park (see p. 48) in nearby New Jersey surely provided Tuxedo Park's planners with a model—both share the concept of a gated residence park in which the scenery and not the architecture is paramount, and each was conceived to accommodate a carefully selected community of residents with shared values—Llewellyn Park was a commuter suburb from the start, while Tuxedo Park began as a resort, one whose plan and architecture would respect the land and character of the site. Tuxedo Park was in many ways like an English country estate on a colossal scale—a fenced-in property that at its peak consisted of over 7,000 acres.

Inside the gates, Tuxedo Park adopted the English ideal of an institutionalized communal life attached to the land, in which the country club and its clubhouse stood in for the lord of the manor and his "power-house." In its early years, Tuxedo Park was relatively democratic, with the small-scale cottages—Lorillard called them "boxes"—harmonized with the surrounding landscape.[2] Lorillard obtained control over his family's 4,552-acre property in the Ramapo Mountains in 1885 and with the assistance of James Smith Haring (n.d.), a civil engineer, Ernest W. Bowditch, a Boston landscape architect, and the architect Bruce Price (1845–1903), laid out a 32-mile network of looping roads that hugged the rugged contours and maximized natural vistas, including views of Tuxedo Lake. An association was formed to conserve and control Tuxedo Park's physical and social fabric. Samuel Swift, the author of a pioneering series on American suburbs that appeared in the early issues of *House and Garden*, observed that "in laying out and improving the Park, Mr. Lorillard and his aides sought rather to take advantage of the natural beauty of the landscape than to turn this wild region into a cultivated garden . . . No main axes . . . are to be found . . . The vistas are purely natural . . . The single exception is furnished by the principal gate, just north of the village . . . Here Bruce

Coral Gables, Riviera section plan, Frank Button, 1925. HM

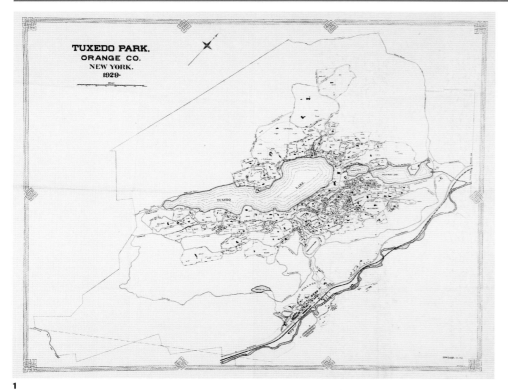

1. Plan, James Smith Haring, Ernest W. Bowditch, and Bruce Price, 1885. TPL (1929)

2. East Lake Road. EM92 (c. 1891)

3. Tower Hill. HG05 (c. 1905)

4. Main entrance with gatehouse and keep, Bruce Price, 1886. EM92 (c. 1891)

5. Tower Hill. EM92 (c. 1891)

Price constructed a stone lodge and keep which, viewed from the road or train, offered an admirable entrance, suggesting faithfully the character of the Park, as the prelude to an opera hints at what is to come."[3] Price is said to have described the lodge and gatehouse as looking "like a frontispiece to an English novel."[4]

Lorillard may have wanted to escape the snobbish formal life of Newport, where the list of the socially acceptable "400" drawn up by Ward McAllister (1827–1895) held sway, but Tuxedo Park soon became part of fashionable society. The rustic clubhouse, which stood in for the manor house of this mythical estate, included an octagonal ballroom that soon became the setting for the annual New Debutantes' Ball of New York society. Even the place name, Tuxedo, a corrupted Amerindian word that evoked the unsullied forest, came to be linked with the social whirl when Lorillard's son Griswold initiated a trend of wearing dinner jackets without tails.

Outside the gates, Lorillard established a workers' village for the 200 families of artisans and merchants

necessary to maintain the preserve and its life (1,800 had worked to prepare the development for its 1886 opening). The *Real Estate Record and Builders' Guide* observed in 1886 that the workers' village, designed by Price, the official architect of the Tuxedo Park Association, to be harmonious with the Park's architecture, "makes a pretty sight from the railroad . . . Immediately in the rear of the station now underway is the row of stores, which, with bay windows, piazzas and small window panes, enters into the reigning architectural harmony."[5]

By 1900, when the fashion for English-style country living began to become popular among New York's upper classes, Tuxedo Park, with its proximity to New York's downtown business district—an hour or so away by railroad and ferry—began to function as a commuter suburb. As such, the character of its architecture changed radically, with the cottages giving way to a dazzling array of extravagant mansions designed by some of the leading firms of the day, including McKim, Mead & White, Walker & Gillette, and Warren & Wetmore,

6

7

8

6. Gatehouse. RAMSA (1997)

7. Railroad station. RAMSA (1984)

8. Hedera house, Bruce Price, 1887. Garvin. AG (1992)

who met their clients' ambitions with year-round residences that, though conforming to the original planning scheme, abandoned the simplicity of the founder's vision in favor of a cacophony of styles.

Though much admired, Tuxedo Park, like Llewellyn Park before it, had no immediate impact on the planned suburban tradition. No comparably scaled, individually controlled resort suburb like it was undertaken until 1914 when **Palos Verdes Estates**, one of the most important planned suburbs of the first half of the twentieth century, was conceived as a winter resort, although it did not really succeed until it was repositioned as a commuter suburb in 1923.[6] Palos Verdes Estates is situated twenty miles south of downtown Los Angeles overlooking the Pacific Ocean from what was then a rugged treeless headland. After two separate owners were forced to foreclose on the property in less than a year, in 1913 a California bank sold the majority of the parcel to the New York banker Frank A. Vanderlip (1864–1937), who planned to develop the 16,000-acre, 25-square-mile site as a "millionaire's colony" like Tuxedo Park but in a milder climate. The site reminded Vanderlip of the Sorrentine Peninsula and Amalfi Drive in Italy and initially he imagined an Italian village populated by craftsmen and a large country house inspired by the Villa Papa Giulia of Pope Julius III. But for Vanderlip, "The most exciting part . . . was that this gorgeous scene was not a piece of Italy at all but was here in America, an unspoiled sheet of paper to be written on with loving care."[7]

To plan the property, Vanderlip hired the Olmsted Brothers, who beginning in 1913 had served as landscape architects for his 147-acre country estate, Beechwood, in

Scarborough-on-the-Hudson, New York.[8] He also retained Howard Van Doren Shaw, the Chicago architect who had planned the Market Square at Lake Forest (see p. 127), and Myron Hunt, the Northwestern- and MIT-trained architect now resident in Pasadena, as consulting architects. Ambitious plans were prepared for large estates centered around different clubs and three model villages that the *Boston Evening Transcript* wrote would have "all the charm of some places that so delight tourists traveling in certain rural districts of Germany and England."[9] The scheme called for a "Palos Verdes Country Club" on the bluff above Portuguese Bend, with 150 guest rooms as well as extensive social facilities including a 60-by-120-foot swimming pool, golf links, tennis courts, and polo grounds. A yacht club was also planned. Even though the principal idea was for a resort playground catering to Eastern sunseekers, the plan for the Estates from the first also recognized the need for a connection to downtown Los Angeles to be provided by means of Pacific Electric cars running in the median of a scenic boulevard, Palos Verdes Drive.

Vanderlip built himself a house in Palos Verdes in 1916, but it stood for seven years as the only evidence of his project. World War I prevented the resort from developing, and by the time the armistice came members of the syndicate had lost interest and Vanderlip had come to the realization that California, unlike Florida, was too far from the cold cities in the East and Midwest from which he hoped to draw his clientele. In 1921, an experienced real estate promoter named Edward Gardner Lewis, developer of University City (see p. 253) in St. Louis and Atascadero (see p. 255), California, heard of Vanderlip's problems and took an option on the property.

Lewis, part genius, part con man, had a different idea for Palos Verdes, proposing a city of 200,000 to be built as part of an involved profit-sharing plan that was radical for its day. Adding city planner Charles H. Cheney (1884–1943) to the design team of Hunt and Frederick Law Olmsted Jr., Lewis now proposed two Beaux-Arts-inspired civic centers surrounded by naturalistic residential areas. But when Lewis ran into his own difficulties, Vanderlip reacquired control of 3,200 acres of the original parcel and, building upon progress already made under Lewis's stewardship, started an intensive development and promotional campaign for a pared-down scheme by Olmsted, Cheney, and Hunt, with the development reemerging in 1923 as what Cheney was convinced would be "the best protected and most comprehensively planned residential suburb in the United States." The vast size of the site—a 16,000-acre build-out was still contemplated—led the planners to "group residence and shopping districts into convenient community units—the store centers being approximately two miles apart" and "to make exceptional provision for open spaces and recreation. Every mile across the property, about ten acres have been set aside for an elementary school-playground-park unit; every two miles, twenty-five acres for a junior high school and children's ball fields; every three miles, forty acres for a senior high school and community playground."[10]

Olmsted and Cheney proposed five districts: Malaga Cove, near Redondo; Valmonte, on the interior where its location on high ground commanded broad views; Miraleste, a "high class, restricted neighborhood" overlooking San Pedro and Los Angeles Harbor; Lunada Bay, a three-mile-long development along the coast; and Margate, north of Lunada Bay on the coast.[11] Three main roads entered from the north and from the east and a broad circuit road wound along the site's perimeter. With a few wide streets to handle through traffic, the plan, according to Olmsted, left "the great majority of local residence streets indirect, comparatively free of traffic, quiet, and safe for children."[12] Protective restrictions were drawn up, reserving half of the entire site for parklands and public rights-of-way, including the entirety of the twelve-mile coastline as well as a protective buffer along the inland boundary. Ninety percent of the remaining land was reserved for single-family houses. Group houses and garden apartments were allowed in the vicinity of the commercial centers.

As a crucial innovation, a permanent Art Jury was assembled to govern all matters aesthetic, requiring, as Hunt, who chaired the first jury, put it, "that nothing be built, and that no color be put on or changed, until approved in writing . . . The arrangement is such that the majority of the jury must always be selected from men nominated by the national organizations representing the architects and the national organizations representing the city planners . . . This arrangement was deliberately made in order to insure against the possibility of any clique getting the control of the jury at any time in the distant future."[13] The original jury consisted of Cheney, the architects David Clark Allison, Robert D. Farquhar, John Galen Howard, and Myron Hunt, the landscape architect James F. Dawson of the Olmsted firm, and Jay Lawyer, general manager of the project.

Initially, the community was zoned according to three stylistic "types": Type I was to be the Mediterranean, or "Latin type"; Type II was to be English Colonial or Georgian; Type III was to be Elizabethan, Norman French, or Flemish. But by 1929 the Art Jury had expressed a clear preference for what they termed the "California Style," consisting of houses rendered in light painted plaster, stucco, or adobe with low-pitched red-tile roofs. As Hunt wrote,

The time is now ripe for us in California to recognize that we have arrived at a distinctive style of architecture which is our own, and which is a real expression of our culture and civilization. Whether it has been arrived at through the rich Colonial heritage of the Spanish fathers who used forms that they knew and loved from their earlier days on the Mediterranean, or through the fortunate blending of the New England Colonial with the Spanish Colonial at Monterey which gave us the pleasant galleried type of house with its tile, shake or shingle roof, or through our better trained architects of recent years who have wider knowledge and understanding of the architecture that preceded us, all that we have done here is, after all, of a new time, in a new spirit, and the product of our western thought and progress in expression.[14]

The maximum degree of architectural control was reserved for the lots bordering the commercial plazas, the principal public spaces, which were inspired by the centers at Lake Forest, Roland Park (see p. 144), and the Country Club District of Kansas City (see p. 167). That the plazas would be realized over time was taken into consideration. As Olmsted wrote, "a complete preliminary architectural design was made for each plaza, and purchasers of the several lots are permitted to build only in accordance with this design, or such harmonious modification of the design *as a whole* as may be approved at the time when final plans of the successive buildings are prepared to meet the detailed requirements of individual owners. Furthermore," Olmsted continued, "the Project retains the right to complete the Plaza facade, with its arcade across the front of any lot that may be left vacant and to assess the cost of such construction on the lot owner."[15] Neither the design by Kirtland Cutter (1860–1939) for Lunada Bay Plaza (1924) nor that by Marston & Mayberry for Valmonte Plaza (1930) was realized, but Malaga Cove Plaza (Webber, Staunton & Spaulding), begun in 1925, was developed as originally planned, with its open space surrounded by arcaded commercial buildings. Nearby, a public library (Myron Hunt and H. C. Chambers, 1930) furthered the sense of civicism.

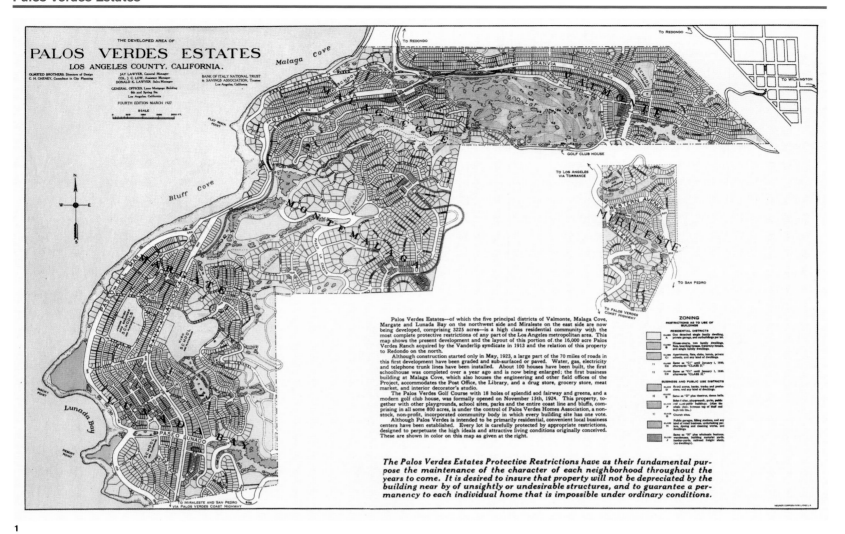

1

1. Plan, Olmsted Brothers and Charles H. Cheney. 1923. FLO (1927)

In contrast to Tuxedo Park or even Kansas City's Country Club District and Coral Gables (see p. 337), Florida, which are similar to Palos Verdes in many respects, Palos Verdes had no major entrance gateway. Olmsted, arguing that nature in its abundance was all that was needed to provide the requisite visual separation from the encroaching metropolis, advised "against a large plaza or any other marked demonstration at the property line where it would be liable to be spoiled by developments in contact with it outside the property. I think the most effective treatment at the entrance will be to plunge directly into the wood of Eucalyptus through an opening as narrow as would be practicable and dignified . . . and after passing through this sylvan gateway for a considerable distance, then widen out into an impressive demonstration where the view of the valley and hills and sea can burst upon one."[16] To ensure nature's abundant presence, Olmsted supervised the planting of hundreds of thousands of trees.

In 1924 houses began to appear, including one Olmsted commissioned from Hunt for himself on a hill overlooking the Pacific. But he was one of the few Easterners attracted by the development, choosing to live there year-round. Sales were helped along by an intense promotional push that included the construction of La Venta Inn (Walter S. Davis and C. E. Howard, 1924), a romantic hilltop hostelry built to welcome prospective buyers. Kirtland Cutter would prove a master of Palos Verdes's California-style houses, designing sixteen of them, including one for Adrian E. Cameron, which the Art Jury deemed "Best House of 1924," and the Schellenburg-Gilmore house, which it selected in 1929 as one of the "ten most notable buildings in Palos Verdes."[17]

As part of the overall plan established by Lewis, 1,000 acres were set aside for a university campus. In 1925, when a southern branch of the University of California was being contemplated, the Palos Verdes site was offered along with other inducements such as the construction of model grammar and high schools. But the University Regents chose Los Angeles instead, lured by Edwin Janss Sr. and his plans for Westwood Village (see p. 185).[18] By the mid-1920s it was clear that streetcar ridership was declining and that the ailing Pacific Electric Railway would not be able to build and operate the Palos Verdes extension, so that the resort-turned-suburb joined the rest of Los Angeles in what would soon be almost complete auto-dependence.

Despite the promotional rhetoric that accompanied the development in the 1920s, Palos Verdes Estates was not intended as either a "New City" or a Garden City,

2

3

4

5

6

2. Valmonte Plaza. PVLD (c. 1923)

3. Pacific Coast Yacht Club. PVLD
(c. 1923)

4. Sales brochure, Lunada Bay
Plaza. PVLD (c. 1923)

5. Malaga Cove. PVLD (1929)

6 Frederick Law Olmsted Jr. house,
Myron Hunt, 1925. PVLD (1925)

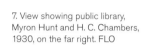

7

8

9

10

11

12

13

7. View showing public library, Myron Hunt and H. C. Chambers, 1930, on the far right. FLO

8. La Venta Inn, Walter S. Davis and C. E. Howard, 1924. PVLD (1925)

9. Street sign. PVLD (1925)

10. Via Anita, Valmonte. Megowan. MM (c. 2009)

11. Malaga Cove Plaza. RAMSA (1978)

12. Malaga Cove. Megowan. MM (c. 2009)

13. Malaga Cove Plaza. RAMSA (1978)

but according to Olmsted, an exceptionally extensive garden suburb "predominantly for fairly prosperous people wanting detached houses and a garden setting but unwilling to burden themselves with the care of extensive grounds."[19] In essence, as Cheney wrote, this "largest piece of city planning by private enterprise ever undertaken in this country for permanent development" was to be "a Model Residential Suburb" planned along the lines that Frederick Law Olmsted Sr. had first developed in his ill-fated proposal for Berkeley, California, fifty years before.[20]

There was a significant difference between Olmsted Sr.'s view of the suburb as part of the city and that of the Palos Verdes promoters. They presented it as a "community, compact and secluded which has succeeded in shutting out all din and confusion of metropolitan life."[21] In its evolution Palos Verdes has been, in fact, something of a hybrid: both a Los Angeles suburb and a resort. No one made this clearer than Olmsted Jr., who in 1927 wrote that "the community, or series of communities, was conceived not as self-sufficient and self-supporting like the English Garden Cities, but as in part suburban, for people working in Los Angeles . . . In large part also it would be an independent residential community for people not tied to the necessity of daily work in any city."[22]

As resort suburb or commuter retreat, the importance of Palos Verdes Estates cannot be overestimated, despite

1. Plan, Olmsted Brothers, 1929.
FLO

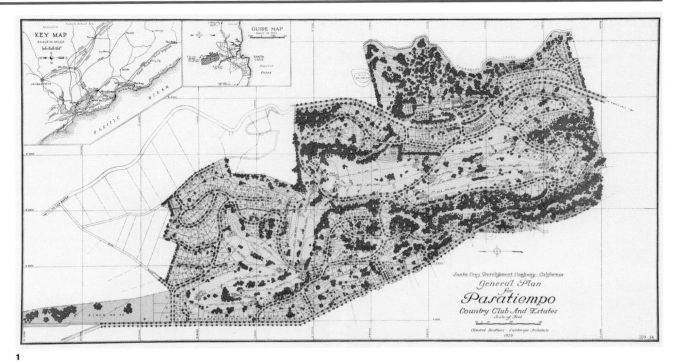

1

the fact that it has received comparatively little attention from historians. Perhaps its significance was best articulated by Fukuo Akimoto, who has written that "in the 1920s, Palos Verdes Estates was ahead of all other garden suburbs because it was developed as the largest new town to be constructed under a single general plan."[23] Palos Verdes was hard hit by the Depression, but it recovered afterward and has thrived since. The Vanderlip family continued to develop the land until they sold the remainder of it to the Great Lakes Carbon Corporation in 1957.

Designed by the Olmsted Brothers, the 600-acre compound of the **Pasatiempo Country Club and Estates** (1929), Santa Cruz, California, a residential golf club situated on the sunny side of Monterey Bay, was the first Tuxedo Park–like development conceived for the automobile age.[24] Like Tuxedo Park, Pasatiempo was the brainchild of a single, conservation-minded developer, the famous golfer Marion Hollins (1892–1944), who worked closely with the architect William Wilson Wurster (1895–1973) and landscape architect Thomas Church (1902–1978) to develop a private community with simple houses based on Monterey's vernacular buildings. As Daniel Gregory has written, Hollins was a "visionary who wished to preserve the beauty of the land she was developing. No tree could be removed without her personal permission. She established small parks along creek beds and in the heavily forested sections. With Wurster, Church, and her business manager, she drew up a list of restrictions" to ensure the preservation of the site's natural character.[25] In addition to an eighteen-hole golf course, the plan included nine miles of roads, a clubhouse, tennis courts, park areas, and six miles of bridle paths.

The idea that lay behind Tuxedo Park, that of a like-minded group of people living simply in a planned arcadia, also lay behind a number of resorts initially conceived as summer religious retreats. Probably the most elaborate of these, **Oak Bluffs** (1830s–80), a summer settlement on Martha's Vineyard, an island four miles off the Massachusetts coast, grew out of a desire to bring together a congenial and essentially middle-class group interested in the life of the spirit, catering to families intent on morally uplifting seaside holidays.[26] Incorporating the most extensive, interesting, and best preserved of the perhaps hundreds of campgrounds built by Methodists in the mid-nineteenth century as religious retreats, Oak Bluffs evolved out of three component parts: Wesleyan Grove, Vineyard Highlands, and Oak Bluffs, whose development began in earnest in 1866 on a site just south of the thirty-year-older Wesleyan Grove campground, which was becoming overcrowded. The Grove's original configuration of nine tents arranged in a semicircle around a shed and a preacher's stand had grown to an elaborate tent city focused on a big top capable of accommodating 2,000 worshipers that one nineteenth-century observer described as "sweet disorder," with the rows of cottages lying "in unintelligible radiation from some imaginary center or huddled together according to some undiscovered law of affinity."[27]

Post–Civil War prosperity swelled the Wesleyan Grove crowds, bringing at least as many sun worshipers as religious revivalists. The annual meetings had grown to the extent that in 1866 camp directors considered buying the land between the camp and the beach but did not act on their instincts, believing the acquisition to be too profane. As they deliberated, a group of local businessmen and retired sea captains bought the parcel and hired Robert Morris Copeland, a self-described "landscape artist" from Boston, to lay out a permanent village that would link the tent city and the sea. Copeland had

2

3

2. Mackenzie house, William Wilson Wurster, c. 1931, located along golf course's 6th fairway. Graham. LHS

3. Gatehouse. Graham. LHS (1936)

been a partner of the landscape architect Horace W. S. Cleveland before the latter left Boston to establish an independent practice in Chicago.

Over the course of five years, Copeland, no doubt influenced by Andrew Jackson Downing and Frederick Law Olmsted, prepared three plans for the site. The first, dating from 1866, was similar to the plan of the Wesleyan Grove campground, with 75 acres of naturalistically curving roads contained by a loop road appropriately named The Circuit. Scattered throughout were to have been twelve parks of about an acre each, some located on block interiors. In the second plan, from 1867, many of the smaller parks were eliminated and the seven-acre semicircular Ocean Park, bordered by a broad crescent of closely spaced houses, was proposed to replace 131 staked lots near the ocean. The decision to include a large oceanfront park is said to have been made not by Copeland but by the developers, who felt it would be a good use of land with poor drainage, would provide a firebreak, and lend "magnitude" to the development.[28] The third plan was prepared in 1870–71 after an additional 45 acres were acquired to the southwest, where long rectangular blocks were separated by linear parks.

Architectural historian Ellen Weiss observes that the plan of Oak Bluffs, "with its loose counterpoint of curves and countercurves," was "patterned as if the topography was rough, which it was not, or as if the style was derived from embroidery-like patterns endemic to the Victorian age."[29] Weiss notes that Erastus P. Carpenter (1822–1902), who led the development team, was also the president of a corporation which had commissioned the picturesque Rock Hill Cemetery (H. F. Walling, 1851) for the town of Foxboro, Massachusetts, pointing to the likelihood that the Oak Bluffs design was a hybrid of the romantic plans of rural cemeteries and the "mazy" plan of the

Wesleyan Grove camp.[30] The result, for Weiss, was "not great design. The joinery between the different sections of the community is not smooth, and the loss in orientation which the traveler sometimes experiences often seems more accidental than intended."[31]

Meanwhile, Wesleyan Grove campground was redeveloped in gradual steps with one-and-a-half-story-high, 14-foot-wide houses that were versions of the original tents, situated to be clearly subordinate to the central tabernacle, which was rebuilt in cast iron in 1879. The Methodists went further than the Oak Bluffs developers in sponsoring the imaginative carpenter-builders to produce elaborate fantasies with their jigsaw ornamentation. Wary of the encroachment of secular Oak Bluffs, in 1868 close associates of the Wesleyan Grove community purchased 55 acres to its north and hired civil engineer Charles Talbot (n.d.) to lay out Vineyard Highlands, reserving a central open circle for camp meetings. According to Henry Beetle Hough, who chronicled the history of Martha's Vineyard in 1936, "If Mr. Copeland, in laying out Oak Bluffs, had eschewed the straight line as if it were a deadly peril, Mr. Talbot, in laying out the Highlands, had gone him one better. The early plans of the Highlands resemble nothing so much as the whorls of an unsteady thumb print . . . largely because provision had been made for a large circle, copied after the Wesleyan Grove circle . . . The first plan prepared in the summer of 1869 was not wholly satisfactory, and Mr. Talbot made another, more inclusive than the first and differing from it materially. Both plans, however, were utilized, and both were made of record, with the result that an unborn generation was to suffer not a little confusion and inconvenience."[32]

In 1880 the three prospering communities of Wesleyan Grove, Oak Bluffs, and Vineyard Highlands were

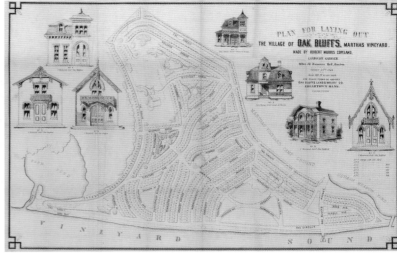

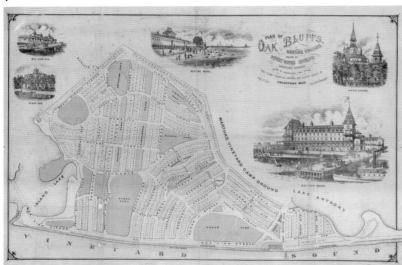

1. Wesleyan Grove. CRS (1845)

2. Plan, Robert Morris Copeland, 1866. MVM

3. Plan, Robert Morris Copeland, 1871. MVM

4. Cottage City, bird's-eye view. LOCG (1890)

5. Ocean Park and bandstand. CRS

6–8. Typical views. RAMSA (1984)

incorporated as the town of Cottage City, renamed Oak Bluffs in 1907. By then Oak Bluffs had become an American version of the great English resorts of Brighton and Hove with freestanding cottages instead of continuous rows of terraced housing and a 125-room hotel, a Unitarian chapel, and an arcaded shopping center, all designed by S. F. Pratt (1824–1920).

In 1872, Copeland prepared designs of two additional resort suburbs for the developer Erastus P. Carpenter: Dering Harbor on Shelter Island, New York, and **Katama**, on a 200-acre site about eight miles south of Oak Bluffs, which was to feature a large central park with housing blocks and a wide range of smaller parks arranged around it so that a majority of the cottages would face green space, with wedge-shaped parks situated at the perimeter to maximize views of the bay.[33] Ellen Weiss deemed Copeland's plan for the unrealized Katama, "with its graceful oppositions of long swinging arcs of roads and the counterpoint rhythm of short streets and slivers of parks fanning out towards the sea," to be "more coherent and lyrical" than that for Oak Bluffs.[34] A hotel was built in 1872, but the Panic of 1873 put an end to the Copeland plan. Copeland's 200-acre **Dering Harbor** proved more enduring. Also known as Shelter Island Park, it never achieved its intended size, but many of its "winding streets with colorful Indian names" were built around the prestigious Manhanset House hotel (1873), designed by S. F. Pratt, and quite a few houses were constructed before the economic crash took its toll.[35] Across Dering Harbor, Copeland prepared a similar plan in 1872 for **Shelter Island Heights**, a 300-acre Methodist camp-meeting developed by a group of Brooklyn clergymen and laymen.[36] By the late 1880s about one hundred cottages had been completed in Shelter Island Heights, along with the 150-room Prospect House hotel (1873).

As the religious fervor that accompanied the "Second Great Awakening" (1800–30s) waned in the post–Civil War years, many revivalist campgrounds such as Wesleyan Grove evolved into resorts like Oak Bluffs, representing a new type based on what might be called "recreational spiritualism." Vacation days were no longer devoted almost exclusively to long hours of organized church worship but also began to include a mix of games and especially culture in the form of readings, lectures, and concerts. The pioneer in this new type of resort was the Chautauqua Institution, founded by Methodists as the Chautauqua Assembly Ground, located on a lakefront site near Jamestown, in the southwestern part of New York State.[37] The Chautauqua Institution, consisting of an inn and various outbuildings to accommodate guests and provide settings for lectures, musical events, and religious services, was laid out on a conventional gridded pattern. However, across the lake, a Baptist version, **Point Chautauqua** (1875), had a more interesting plan devised by Frederick Law Olmsted, who in 1868 was invited to develop a master park plan for Buffalo, New York, seventy miles away.[38] Critical of Chautauqua's gridded plan, Olmsted instead proposed contour-hugging curving streets that afforded lot owners views of the lake.

Katama

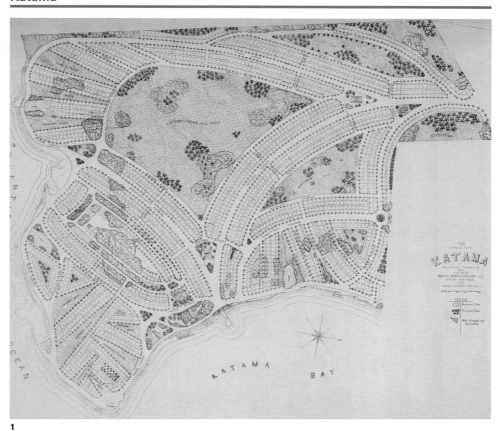

1

The plan of Point Chautauqua had its precedents in Olmsted's Riverside (see p. 122), his unrealized proposal (1873) for Tacoma, Washington, and Parkside, designed as part of the Buffalo park system (see p. 55).[39] Like Tacoma, Point Chautauqua's 100-acre site sloped down to the water. As a result, Olmsted came to the project with a freshly prepared strategy, enabling him to quickly produce, as reported in the *Jamestown Journal*, a plan that called for "winding avenues twenty-six feet wide, enclosing four hundred and sixty-five lots, of one-eighth of an acre each."[40] On the waterside of Lake Avenue, land was set aside for The Strand, an open public recreational area only interrupted by two docks for lake steamers. House sites were located on the steep hillside where the slope was as much as 12 feet in every 100. Olmsted kept the roads to a comfortable 1 to 20 slope, with long narrow curving blocks. Earth ditches along street edges channeled storm water into the lake. To meet the needs of the religious community, the design provided for two assembly areas—an enclosed Tabernacle and an open-air Pavilion—situated on the flattest portions of the site in Corinthian Grove Park. Below the forested Corinthian Grove lay the more open Ashmore Park, at the foot of which a lot was set aside for a hotel and refectory. When the much larger than originally intended Grand Hotel was constructed in 1878, it was built within Ashmore Park but, as Edgar C. Conklin points out, "The substantial increase" in its size "and its relocation to a park area originally intended for the tents of families attending revival meetings, suggests the beginnings of a shift in purpose for Point Chautauqua. It is noteworthy that the open-air meeting place—called the 'meeting ground' on Olmsted's plan and 'the Pavilion' on the Association

1. Plan, Robert Morris Copeland, 1872. MVM

1. Map. ASC (1909)

2. Manhanset House hotel, S. F. Pratt, 1873. LOC4 (1905)

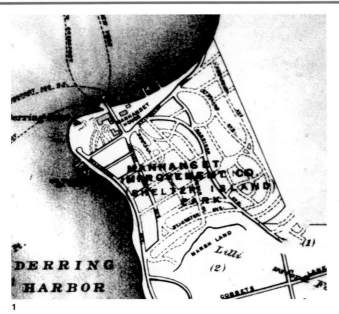

Shelter Island Heights

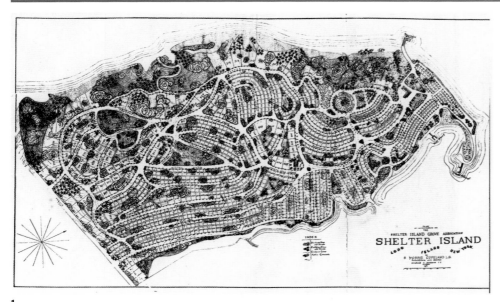

1. Plan, Robert Morris Copeland, 1872. SIHS

2. Prospect House hotel. LOC5 (c. 1900)

3. Cottages and pedestrian path along the water. LOC6 (c. 1905)

maps—which was to have been located in the Corinthian Grove, was apparently never built."[41]

With revivalism on the wane and with the Chautauqua Institution setting a standard for summertime cultural destination resorts, in 1885 the Point Chautauqua Association began to reorient its operations, supplanting its religious programs with cultural ones, rechristening the Tabernacle as the Temple of Music. Soon, as Conklin notes, "a roller-skating rink, bowling alley, and billiard room were added to the Tabernacle grounds. The division of labor between Point Chautauqua and its rival on the other side of the lake was thus complete: henceforth Dr. Vincent's Chautauqua was the center for religion and education; Point Chautauqua, the pleasure resort."[42]

In 1883 Olmsted prepared a preliminary subdivision plan for **Cushing's Island**, located in Casco Bay, a short ferry ride from Portland, Maine.[43] The island had served as a summer resort since 1859, when Lemuel Cushing built the 150-room Ottawa House hotel. After Cushing's death, his son Francis assumed control of the island, hiring Olmsted to prepare a plan for fifty house lots along with recreational facilities and an expansion of the hotel. Olmsted's report, completed just a week after his visit to the island, called for "few improvements," according to architectural historian Elizabeth Igleheart. "Instead the intent was to enhance the natural scenery, mainly by providing access to the desirable features: walks, vistas and beaches."[44] In order to preserve the island's natural beauty, Olmsted proposed that houses be set back at

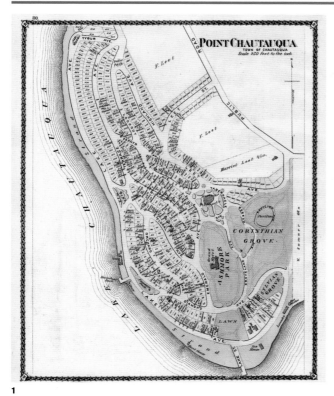

1. Map. FWB (1881)

2. Aerial view. GE (2009)

3. View from steamboat. FHC (c. 1895)

4. Grand Hotel. FHC

5. Tabernacle. FHC (c. 1890)

6. Cottage. FHC (c. 1895)

7. House, Emerald Avenue. Pug. WC (2012)

least 30 feet from the road and be no more than two stories in height, with the lower story built of local stone. He also suggested that at least 50 percent of the site be held as common property. Olmsted's plan called for a 70-foot-wide tree-lined road leading from the ferry dock to Ottawa House, while other streets were to be 40 feet wide. Although most of the recommendations in Olmsted's study were not carried out, his idea that a significant amount of land be kept common property was adopted, and Cushing's Island retained its scenic character during the modest development that did occur over the next two decades. Between 1884 and 1910, one hundred rooms were added to the hotel and twenty Shingle Style cottages were completed, the majority the work of John Calvin Stevens (1855–1940).

Farther up the Maine coast, a group of wealthy investors joined together as the Gouldsboro Land Improvement Company to develop **Grindstone Neck** (1890), occupying a small peninsula jutting into Frenchman's Bay at Winter Harbor, as a summer resort planned by Nathan F. Barrett.[45] At its peak there were perhaps forty summer cottages, although the site had the capacity for much more development. Barrett's plan called for a main street—he referred to it as a plaza—running the length of the peninsula at its crest. A network of diagonal streets was to connect with elliptical streets projected, in Barrett's words, "upon the first terrace below the plaza, so as to give the effect of encircling the plaza with a road . . . The severity of the geometric plat I should retain only as to the upper terrace, and the lower terraces and the eastern and southern borders of the Neck, I should plot after a less severe and more picturesque or rustic style. The advantages of such a plan as the foregoing would be that by adopting some general harmonious design for the cottages of the upper terrace, a most imposing general effect of *mass* would be produced, and the cottages would present, when viewed from either the harbor or the Frenchman's Bay side, the appearance of a very unusual summer settlement, the unique character of which would afford the best possible advertisement of the place . . . By my plan," Barrett continued, "the two well known styles in the art of landscape, the severe or

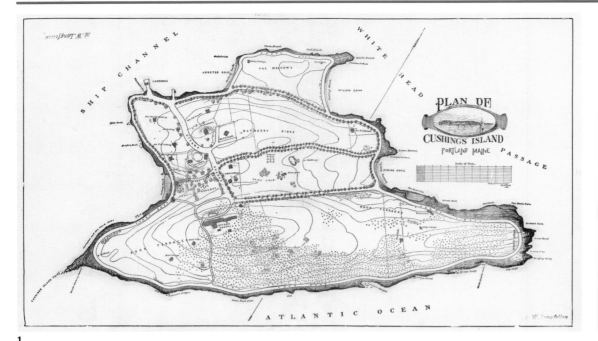

1

2

1. Plan. MMN (1888)

2. Portland Harbor from Cushing's Island. LOC7 (1905)

3. Charles M. Hays cottage, John Calvin Stevens, 1910. MHPC

4. Houses from water. Haley. FL (2010)

3

4

artificial, and the rough weird and picturesque would be combined, and the unusual natural topography availed of to the best advantage."[46]

Barrett's plan called for about 200 lots, with some land reserved for the benefit of all. The early houses were mostly in the Shingle Style, with Lindley Johnson, the company architect, designing twenty of them and Wilson Eyre completing two houses. Stables and carriage houses were confined to separate areas as were sites for entertainment facilities, including a 200-room inn built at the center of one of the ovals. A ferry terminal, yacht club, casino, and swimming pool occupied shorefront sites. Barrett's separation of private houses from shared facilities, as Allan Smallbridge has written, fostered exclusivity, giving "the cottagers a chance to create their own means of recreation and diversion, to live among the people they chose to be with, to dictate who was acceptable and who was not."[47]

Olmsted was to design one more resort suburb, **Sudbrook Park**, Maryland, which he laid out in 1889 working with John Charles Olmsted.[48] Located on 204 acres ten miles northwest of Baltimore, Sudbrook was first intended as a commuter suburb, so its location on the extension of the Western Maryland Railroad seemed

ideal to its Philadelphia and Boston investors incorporated as the Sudbrook Company. The site was part of the 800-acre estate of James Howard McHenry (1820–1888), who, in 1876, had himself unsuccessfully attempted to retain Olmsted to design a suburban village.

Sudbrook failed to attract year-round commuters, so that its early success came as a summer resort after the completion of the railroad station, nine cottages, and the Woodland Inn, all designed by Boston architects Cabot, Everett & Mead. Resort or commuter village notwithstanding, Sudbrook was not intended to be self-sufficient. The Olmsted plan was based on the availability of shops and other conveniences in the nearby town of Pikesville, so the development can be said to have been a suburb of both a city and a village. Sudbrook only began to attract full-time residents around 1900 when Baltimoreans started to realize that the ten-mile train journey could easily be managed on a daily basis.

Olmsted's plan for Sudbrook called for curvilinear streets providing house lots that were at least an acre in size, except in an area along the railroad tracks where, as at Riverside, he platted more modest plots for small houses. The plan provided for both a pedestrian and carriage bridge across the railroad tracks with five roads

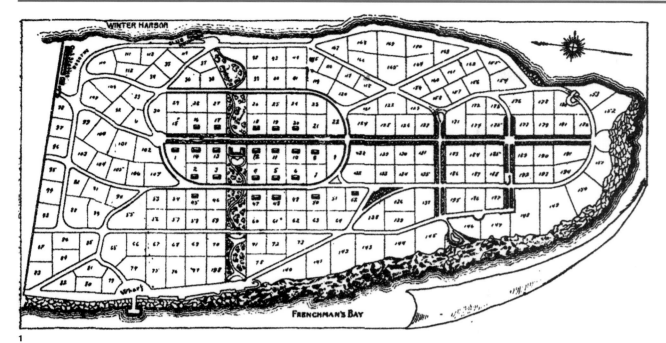

1

1. Plan, Nathan F. Barrett, 1890. WHHS

2. House, Lindley Johnson, c. 1892. Emerson. BE (2012)

3. Bird's-eye view showing Grindstone Inn, Lindley Johnson, 1892, in center. CRS

4. Typical houses. CRS

5. Laura McCrea house, Wilson Eyre, c. 1892. Emerson. BE (2012)

2

3

4

5

fanning out from the station into the development. As at Riverside, the roads were set slightly below natural grade to minimize their visual intrusion on the landscape. Six-foot-wide gravel walkways were included in keeping with Olmsted's belief that sidewalks were desirable to foster community. Triangles of open space were located around Sudbrook Station, but the 8.5-acre Cliveden Green, intended to be the principal public green space, was eventually divided into lots and developed.

At Sudbrook, Olmsted went beyond the limited number of controls he had called for at Riverside, recommending sixteen restrictions intended to remain in effect for thirty years, including a ban on any manufacturing in the town; no subdivision of lots to under one acre, except for those near the railroad station; prohibition of fences and hedges over four feet high; and mandatory 40-foot setbacks of houses from the edge of the roadway and 10 feet from the sides of the lots. The houses themselves were to be "distinctly in a rural and not an urban style."[49] Each resident also had to commit to connect to the town's shared water, gas, and electric systems. As John Olmsted put it in a letter of 1889, such restrictions were considered "a part of a plan for a suburb as truly as certain lines on paper."[50]

The Sudbrook Company ceased operations in 1910, after some thirty-five houses had been completed.

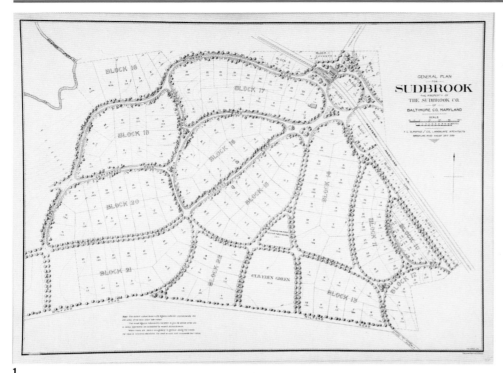

1. Plan, Frederick Law Olmsted, 1889. FLO

2. Bridge spanning Western Maryland Railroad tracks. BCPL

3. Cottage #1, Cabot, Everett & Mead, 1890. BCPL

4. Woodland Inn, Cabot, Everett & Mead, 1890. BCPL

5, 6. Typical streets. Garvin. AG (1997)

Another dozen more were built according to the Olmsted plan over the next decade before the Woodland Inn burned in 1926. The Depression halted further development and when construction resumed with hundreds of new brick houses in a boom after World War II, adherence to Olmsted's plan and restrictions was no longer in evidence. Still, as Melanie Anson has observed, "Although the new development altered aspects of Olmsted's design, the artful skill of Olmsted's planning principles was powerful enough to mold the diverse parts into a unified whole."[51] After visiting Sudbrook in the 1990s, Alexander Garvin wrote that "the plan limits the number of houses within each resident's angle of vision (thereby increasing the feeling of privacy) and heightens the sensation of nature by screening out surrounding structures. The resulting design makes each house seem to be an inevitable part of a 'natural' landscape."[52]

Lawrence Park, New York, was another suburb that began life as a resort but soon evolved into a commuters' arcadia. Located in Westchester County, four miles northeast of Park Hill (see p. 58) and just fifteen miles from Grand Central Terminal, Lawrence Park, begun in 1892, in time came to be subsumed as a neighborhood in what would become a larger-scale suburban town,

Bronxville, which enjoys the reputation, as Victor Mays puts it, of being "a suburb endlessly copied and never matched."[53] Lawrence Park and Bronxville were developed by William Van Duzer Lawrence (1842–1927), a chemical manufacturer and financier who made a fortune marketing a patent medicine called Pain Killer, a remedy quite possibly enhanced with opium and alcohol. Lawrence first visited the area in 1888 and two years later purchased Prescott Farm, a hillside tract of about 86 acres, with the idea of developing a summer resort convenient to the city, catering to renters or home buyers in the arts. The poet and critic E. C. Stedman (1833–1908) and the painters William Henry Howe (1846–1929) and Will Low (1853–1932) were early residents.

Lawrence took credit for the street plan, claiming to use the natural paths of cattle as the basis for his layout. Later, he had the streets paved in brick or cobblestone, beveling the brick edges to provide traction for the horses. The winding, hilly roads rendered the character of the development informal with many rock outcroppings. No significant dedicated open space was provided, but small bits of greenery marked intersections. Most lots were within easy walking distance to the railroad station. The entrances to the development

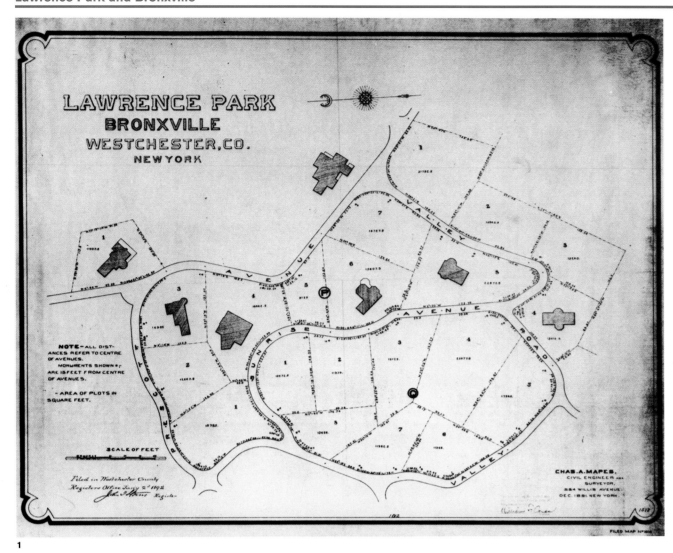

1

were marked by stone gates, and the houses were closely spaced. Lawrence selected the house sites based on the best views and sunlight. As a consequence, the typical pattern of deep, narrow, regularly shaped lots then characteristic of most suburban neighborhoods gave way to more organic platting resulting in oddly shaped but essentially squarish lots.

Alice Wellington Rollins (1845–1897), an author, was a Lawrence Park resident when, in 1895, she wrote *The Story of Lawrence Park*, a sales brochure that was instrumental in attracting other people in the arts to the village. Three years later Lawrence Park and its surroundings were incorporated into the village of Bronxville. Theodore Tuttle, writing in 1904, noted: "There are no smart traps wheeling obtrusively at the depot, or vistas through tree-lined roads, or hedge-bordered lawns with vari-colored floral designs and artificial fountains. All is simplicity here." Surveying the domestic architecture, Tuttle concluded: "The Park may indeed be termed [a] colony. The houses of artists and men of letters, as well as architects . . . are here . . . It may . . . be said that there is a prevailing type of dwelling, the English timber frame house, though the so-called free Colonial, the Norman French and the shingle cottages are represented."[54]

To design the houses, Lawrence hired William A. Bates (1853–1922), who came from Monroe, Michigan, where Lawrence had spent most of his childhood and where their families were friends. At first alone, but beginning around 1910 in collaboration with Kenneth G. How (1883–1950), Bates designed many of the single-family houses as well as the majority of the other types of accommodation built by the Lawrence family in Lawrence Park as well as in greater Bronxville, thereby establishing a remarkably coherent architectural character for the suburb.

Bates & How, who proved themselves not only imaginative designers but also expert technicians, were able to shepherd Bronxville's development from a resort village of single-family houses into a commuter suburb with a sophisticated mix of housing types, including medium-density group- and garden-type apartments.[55] As Lawrence Park was evolving, Lawrence grew more ambitious, with the idea of a sophisticated village structure taking form that would include the Casino, a stone and shingle structure to house family guests and provide a social center for the community, as well as a sports field and two tennis courts. In 1897 the Hotel Gramatan, designed by Bates, opened, but it burned two years later

and it was not replaced until 1905 when a more elaborate structure was completed, also designed by Bates.[56] Bates, in association with Alfred E. Barlow (1855–1926), also designed the Lawrence Arcade (1903), a many-gabled stone and stucco complex of stores and offices replete with a delightful clocktower. The new Gramatan, sited on Sunset Hill overlooking the railroad station, was connected to the Arcade at Pondfield Road next to the mid-nineteenth-century station, which would be rebuilt in 1916 in the Mission style.

After 1900, cement-clad buildings, deemed more fire-resistant than houses of shingle and stone, began to become Bronxville's characteristic vernacular. The rebuilt Hotel Gramatan, which introduced the town to many people on a day's or weekend's outing from New York City, and often encouraged them to settle there

permanently, was also realized in cement, leading its designers to adopt a Mission-style vernacular with a domed bell tower, scroll gables, and red-tile roofs reminiscent of the Mission Inn at Riverside, California. To Frederick Partington, writing in 1906, the new Gramatan seemed "out of expression" with the character of Lawrence Park, but he tried to justify its exotic appearance by claiming that its "shaded courts and heavy walls . . . [suggest] coolnesss, the best of all things for the tired New Yorker." In the end, however, he had to admit that "it harmonizes in no way with the simple and peaceful architecture of the park houses, all of which are in marvelous keeping with the surroundings. The . . . [hotel] is fortunately well covered with trees and shrubs, and the larger spaces of the great white hotel are effectively screened."[57]

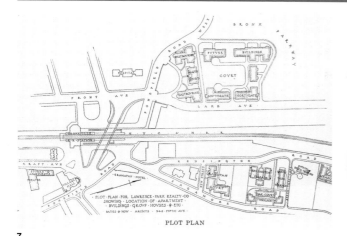

7

8

9

10

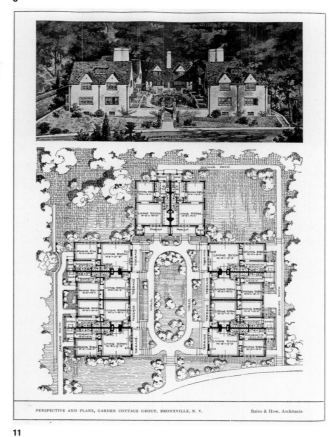

11

PERSPECTIVE AND PLANS, GARDEN COTTAGE GROUP, BRONXVILLE, N. Y.   Bates & How, Architects

7. Village of Bronxville, plan showing apartment buildings and group houses by Bates & How, 1916. AA16

8. Lawrence Arcade, William A. Bates and Alfred E. Barlow, 1903, and Gramatan Hotel, William A. Bates, 1905. ARB13 (c. 1913)

9. Lawrence Arcade from the train station. RAMSA (2012)

10. Kensington Terrace, Bates & How, 1915. RAMSA (2012)

11. Kensington Terrace, perspective and plans. A15

After Lawrence Park's craggy landscape was almost completely built out with shingle and stone cottages, Bronxville itself remained Lawrence's principal canvas, though with less picturesque possibilities. In 1909, west of the railroad tracks, he commissioned Bates to design the Studio Arcade, a three-story, block-long, mixed-use complex that included six ground-level shops topped by ten apartments with 14-foot ceilings intended for artists. On other properties abutting the tracks, Lawrence developed rental apartments at various scales, from large apartment houses to terrace houses and group houses, most designed in an English style of country village architecture, thereby sharing the nostalgia for the preindustrial vernacular with similar contemporary developments at Letchworth (see p. 230), Hampstead Garden Suburb (see p. 350), Roland Park (see p. 144), and Chestnut Hill (see p. 135). In the process he transformed Bronxville into one of the most important exemplars of garden suburb ideals, if not land platting, in the United States. The superior organization and expression of the modest but comfortable group houses such as Kensington Terrace, Oak Court Terrace Cottages, and Beech Tree Terrace, designed by Bates & How and all realized between 1915 and 1917, ensured that Bronxville would complement the ruralesque Lawrence Park, while taking on the physical appearance and social vitality of a village. Alger Court (1914), Bronxville's first apartment house, a multi-unit, five-story walk-up complex facing Pondfield Road from the west side of the New York Central railroad tracks, was a more ambitious undertaking.[58] The somewhat stiffly composed Tudor-style buildings provided balconies and staff rooms and three exposures in each apartment.

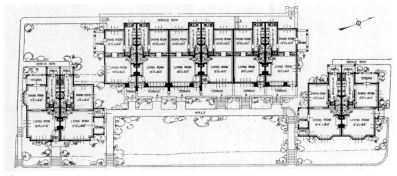

12

13

12. Plans, Oak Court Terrace Cottages, Bates & How, 1917. A17

13. Oak Court Terrace Cottages. RAMSA (2012)

14. Beech Tree Lane and Sagamore Road apartments, Bates & How, 1920. A21

15. Normandy Houses, R. H. Scannell, 1930. AR31

14

15

Kenneth How was an articulate exponent of the group house type and one of its most knowledgeable American theorists. In his essay, "Housing Problems in Small Suburban Developments," he wrote that one's "individuality is as easily retained in [the] block system as in the isolated dwelling, but with so many added advantages both in decreased care and expense and from the resultant cheaper rentals," owing to the lower construction costs. "It has been found that there should not be more than six houses in one block. It is difficult to treat without monotony a building of this type and length and to segregate the families as the tendency of the housing scheme is too much in the other direction. The two and four family houses are probably the better size, insuring privacy, light and ventilation. They also work out much better architecturally."[59] The first of these was Kensington Terrace, two four-unit group houses and one double house, surrounding three sides of a landscaped courtyard off Kensington Road.[60] Tightly planned, and with no provision for parking, its charming stucco-sheathed Arts and Crafts villas provided childless families with a kind of accommodation lacking in most American suburban communities. The same planning strategies were repeated by Bates & How in the Oak Court Terrace Cottages, located around the corner facing Sagamore Road, where two double houses flanked a six-unit group to form a broad, shallow court parallel to the road.[61]

Bates & How also designed Gramatan Court (1914), intended to sympathize in style with the Spanish Mission vocabulary of the nearby Hotel Gramatan.[62] Consisting of two four-story buildings, sheathed in white stucco and roofed in red tile, Gramatan Court's large apartments included bowed balconies and shaded loggias. By the 1920s, the scale of Bronxville's garden or terrace apartment groups became larger almost in direct proportion to a diminution of architectural detail. Bates & How's four-story apartments at the corner of Beech Tree Lane and Sagamore Road (1920) featured smaller rooms and a much simplified, battlemented expression that took advantage of a steeply sloping site to enliven the rooftop silhouette.[63] Bolton Gardens (1920), by the same firm, contained thirty-three stucco-sheathed townhouse units, whose gabled profile and half-timbering gave them a strongly English, Arts and Crafts appearance.[64] As a sign of the times, Bolton Gardens provided separate garage structures with capacity for one car per unit.

Bates died in 1922, leaving the path clear for Penrose V. Stout and Lewis Bowman (1890–1971) to become Bronxville's leading architects. Stout also had the advantage of being married to a Lawrence.[65] His Merestone Terrace (1924), another townhouse-like apartment building, held on to detailing that distinguished the prewar work with stone-clad bases supporting shingled and half-timbered superstructures, and intricately composed tower-like corner units.[66] By the time of the stock market crash in 1929, Bronxville's development was largely complete. One last notable project, Normandy Houses (1930) by R. H. Scannell (1894–1985), revealed the Lawrence family's continued preference for coordinated planning.[67] A cluster of French Norman–style double and four-unit houses on a tight site off Gramatan Avenue, each house was provided with a private garage, with the site plan permitting thirteen of the houses to share a common service cul-de-sac in the manner of Radburn (see p. 275), although each house maintained a distinct front entrance facing a public street.

16

17

18

19

20

Pinehurst (1895), located in Moore County in south central North Carolina, was the first in a series of suburban-style resorts planned to cater to the desire of Northerners to escape the winter's cold.[68] The brainchild of James Walker Tufts (1835–1902), a retired Boston businessman who made his fortune with the American Soda Fountain Company and who set out to establish a winter colony for patients recovering from tuberculosis, Pinehurst is located amid 5,500 acres of desolate sand hills acquired at a little over one dollar an acre. According to Tufts's grandson, the soil was rumored to be so poor that "it was said to be necessary to bury a person with commercial fertilizer in order to afford some prospect of his rising on the day of judgement."[69] Tufts retained Olmsted, Olmsted & Eliot to lay out the town with landscape architect Warren H. Manning, at that time planting superintendent for the firm, also working on the project. With the exception of Manning, who provided some on-site supervision before going out on his own, no one else from the Olmsted office visited the site but instead worked from topographical maps to develop the plan.

Pinehurst was conceived as an idealized version of a typical New England village with a community green at the center of the site but, unlike its New England precedents, with winding streets. Although the curving streets were 60 feet wide, the roadways were only 16 feet wide, leaving 22 feet on each side as public rights-of-way, including planted areas and a five-foot-wide sidewalk made of sand and clay. To transform the barren site into something approaching the verdant New England precedent, more than 200,000 plants, a quarter of them imported from France, were planted. As the

landscape grew in, the impression was that each house was "set in its own private forest."[70]

Tufts built a seven-mile-long electric railway to connect the resort with Seaboard Air Line Railroad's station at the nearby village of Southern Pines. He also put up a small hotel, the three-story Holly Inn, opened on New Year's Eve in 1895. Other early structures, including a store, several boardinghouses, and about sixteen small cottages, were soon joined by the Casino, the village's social center with a large dining room, a ladies' parlor, a small library, a billiards room for men, a post office, and a Town Hall, seating 250 people, used for religious services, lectures, and recitals. Tufts aggressively promoted his village, especially among physicians, extolling the virtue of the dry, moderate winter climate, the aroma of the pine forests, and the "bright, cheery village, artistically laid out," which he felt would suit "a refined and intelligent class of people . . . whether of large or small means."[71] But, once he realized that tuberculosis was contagious, Tufts switched direction and began to position his dream suburb as a winter resort.

Like most suburbs, Pinehurst was not to be a place of employment except by local workers engaged in construction and management. Moreover, as Richard J. Moss has written, "The village was to be an exhibit, a re-creation of a vanishing reality," with Tufts "in firm control of the illusion."[72] The resort began to blossom when golf was introduced in 1898 with a nine-hole course laid out on 60 acres south of the village green, the work of fledgling designer Dr. D. LeRoy Culver (1862–1943). The course was doubled in size the next year by golf instructor John Dunn Tucker, the same year that the clubhouse opened. With the arrival in 1900 of the Scottish golfer

16. Bolton Gardens, Bates & How, 1920. RAMSA (2012)

17. Bolton Gardens. RAMSA (2012)

18. Merestone Terrace, Penrose V. Stout, 1924. RAMSA (2012)

19. Beech Tree Terrace, Bates & How, c. 1917. RAMSA (2012)

20. Gramatan Court, Bates & How, 1914. RAMSA (2012)

1. Plan, Olmsted, Olmsted & Eliot, 1895. FLO

2. Advertisement, *Scribner's Magazine*, January 1911. S11

3. Typical street. CRS

4. Holly Inn, 1895. Garvin. AG (1990)

5. Maple Road. Garvin. AG (1990)

6. Typical street. CRS

7. Carolina Inn, 1901. Garvin. AG (1990)

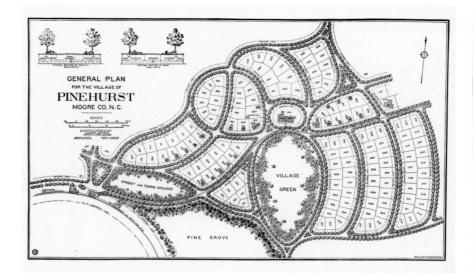

and golf-course designer Donald Ross, Pinehurst began to develop as one of the world's most famous golfing centers, setting the tone for an infinite number of golf-based resorts and suburbs alike. Ross would remain in residence at Pinehurst until his death.

As Tufts's initial conception of a kind of village-scale sanitarium gave way to that of a golf resort, the Holly Inn proved too small and in 1901 was joined by the more luxurious Carolina Inn. By that year, in addition to the boardinghouses, there were also about fifty cottages "for persons wishing to live in a quiet home-like way."[73] In 1903, in order to free up cash, Tufts's son Leonard (1870–1945) began to sell house lots, imposing strict design controls. Pinehurst continued to be run by the Tufts family until 1971. It remained a village until 1980, when it

was officially incorporated as a municipality with a population of 1,746 residents.

In 1897, William Greene Raoul (1843–1913), a railroad executive from Georgia, and his tubercular son, Thomas Wadley Raoul (1876–1953), undertook to build the resort suburb of **Albemarle Park** on 35 acres of steeply sloping terrain one mile northeast of Asheville, North Carolina, to which it was connected by a trolley line.[74] In addition to private residences, Albemarle Park included a large hotel, the Manor (1899; expanded 1903 and 1914), a clubhouse (1902), and a collection of rental cottages, which were provided with housekeeping and other services so that "all the conveniences of city life are available . . . and yet all the discomforts are lacking."[75] The developers were encouraged by the

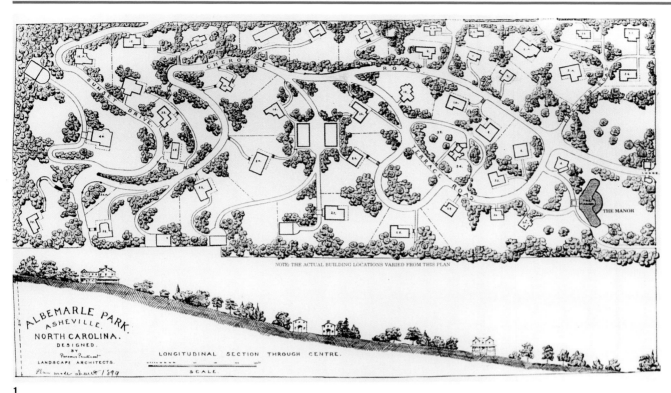

1

2

3

4

5

6

7

1. Plan and longitudinal section, Samuel Parsons Jr. and George F. Pentecost Jr., c. 1899. APMG

2. Overall view showing the Manor, cottages, and gatehouse designed by Bradford Lee Gilbert. RFP (c. 1905)

3. The Manor, Bradford Lee Gilbert, 1899. CRS

4. Gatehouse, Bradford Lee Gilbert, 1897. RAMSA (2010)

5–7. Typical views. RAMSA (2010)

1. Plan, Chauncey Beadle, 1927. TBF

2. Locator map. TBF

3. Biltmore Forest Country Club, Edward L. Palmer Jr., 1922. EMBC

4. Street lamp and shelter. Anoldent. FL (2009)

5. House. Anoldent. FL (2009)

construction of George W. Vanderbilt's Biltmore (Richard Morris Hunt, 1889–95). Seeking to promote Asheville as a desirable seasonal retreat for Northerners as well as the wealthy Southerners who had long enjoyed it, they set out to "establish a sort of Country Club such as those to be found at various places in the North, where patrons may always be assured of finding a refined and congenial gathering of friends."[76] William Raoul hired Bradford Lee Gilbert (1853–1911), the New York architect specializing in railroad structures, with whom he had previously collaborated, to design the Manor and most of the houses, and Gilbert in turn recommended that Samuel Parsons Jr. and his partner George F. Pentecost Jr. (n.d.) prepare an overall plan for the exceptionally challenging site, which featured a 310-foot rise in elevation at a more than 20 percent grade.

According to Parsons, who described the project in his book, *How to Plan the Home Grounds* (1901), the site "had fine views, and not much else that fitted it for a residence park." In preparing the layout, Parsons "respected and enhanced" the half-wooded site and its topography, closely collaborating with Gilbert in platting one-half- to three-acre house lots, then laying out the tightly winding, almost switchback drives required to access them.[77] In many cases, flights of steps were needed to reach houses where carriages could not be led. The first structure to be completed was Gilbert's

stone and wood Tudor Revival gatehouse (1897), straddling the entrance road with an archway and doubling as a sales office. Just beyond the lodge, three acres were reserved for the Manor and clubhouse and provided one of the few open stretches of grass turf—various ivies were employed as ground cover elsewhere on the site. Between 1898 and 1913 more than twenty houses were built, although after Gilbert's death in 1911 the quality of design deteriorated. Initially intended for seasonal use, Albemarle Park became a year-round community.

In 1920, Thomas Raoul sold the property to focus on the development of **Biltmore Forest**, located on a 1,500-acre site seven miles south of Albemarle Park that he had purchased from George Vanderbilt's widow, Edith Stuyvesant Dresser (1873–1958), and planned as a "community where persons of moderate means could build homes that would embody on a smaller scale the same ideals that had actuated Mr. Vanderbilt."[78] Chauncey Beadle (1866–1950), Biltmore Estate's full-time landscape architect, laid out the new residential area. The Biltmore Forest Country Club, with a golf course designed by Donald Ross, was the principal attraction of the new community. Although intended for those of "moderate means," the suburb's residents comprised Asheville's business and civic leaders, not to mention Mrs. Vanderbilt herself, whose house, The Frith, was completed in 1925 by Palm Beach–based

architect Bruce P. Kitchell (1872–1942) and landscaped by Fletcher Steele (1885–1971).

Bayberry Point (1897), facing Great South Bay near West Islip on Long Island, 50 miles east of New York City, was developed on 125 acres of land by Henry O. Havemeyer (1847–1907), founder of the American Sugar Refining Company, and his brother-in-law, Samuel T. Peters (1854–1921), who imagined a "modern Venice" with a 100-foot-wide man-made canal providing twelve villas direct water access to the bay.[79] To plan the subdivision and design the houses, Havemeyer commissioned Grosvenor Atterbury in consultation with Louis Comfort Tiffany (1848–1933), a close friend of Havemeyer's who had designed the interiors of his New York house at 1 East Sixty-sixth Street (Charles C. Haight, 1889–90).[80] James Pooton Jr., writing in the *New York Times* in 1897, predicted that "Bayberry Point will become a Tuxedo of the seaside."[81] By 1901 ten Moorish-inspired stucco houses located on one-and-a-half-acre lots had been completed. As Peter Pennoyer and Anne Walker have written:

For the ten houses comprising the artistic ensemble, Atterbury developed four well-organized compact plans and oriented them differently to create variety. Shockingly stark in their architectural expression, especially when compared to similar summer colonies of the period, the low-lying flat-roofed stucco cottages were well suited to their seaside location with an abundance of porches, piazzas, trellises, and outdoor stairs . . . Although strikingly different from any of Atterbury's other commissions, Bayberry Point still displayed the architect's ability to forge a dialogue between the cottages' broad massing and light stucco walls and the landscape's flat contours and sandy terrain. While smaller in scope than his planning commissions to come, it presented Atterbury with the opportunity to contemplate relationships between dwellings and to generate picturesque variety through modest means and materials and limited plan templates.[82]

On Long Island's north shore, **Belle Terre** (1904), dubbed "the Tuxedo of Long Island" by *Country Life in America*, was poised on the bluffs above Port Jefferson Harbor, enjoying five miles of Long Island Sound waterfront.[83] The Port Jefferson railroad station was about one mile away. Built by a company of investors led by Dean Alvord, developer of Prospect Park South, in Brooklyn (see p. 107), Belle Terre was originally intended as a 1,320-acre setting for large estates accessed by 40 miles of roads with 400 acres of meadowland reserved for active recreation, including golf and polo. Prospective land

1. Bird's-eye view. ABN09

2. Aerial view. GE (2007)

3. Bridge and house, Grosvenor Atterbury, c. 1901. AR10

4. House, Grosvenor Atterbury, c. 1901. ABN09

1. Map. NYPLMD (1917)

2. Pergola, Kirby, Petit & Green, 1906. Greene. LOCP

3. Bungalow, Aymar Embury II, c. 1910. HS

4. House, Frederick J. Sterner, c. 1910. BR10

5. Gatehouse, Kirby, Petit & Green, c. 1905. Doug. FL (2007)

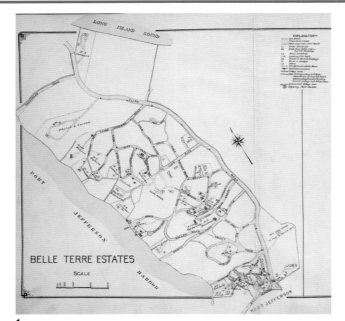

1

2

3

4

5

buyers were invited to ride from New York on a private railroad car, courtesy of Alvord's friend, Ralph Peters, then president of the Long Island Rail Road. Alvord paid for the replacement of the old Port Jefferson station with a white-columned classical pavilion designed by Kirby, Petit & Green and built the one-mile-long road that led from the station to the development, where a mini-château served as a gatehouse. Most of the land was perched high above the harbor, with a pair of classical pergolas dramatically sited to command the view. A rambling clubhouse by Kirby, Petit & Green (1906) was also realized in the development's first years, but by 1910 Alvord had to reposition his project as a middle- and upper-middle-class commuter suburb, with the plan now calling for housing types ranging from bungalows on half-acre and one-acre wooded sites—designed by Kirby, Petit & Green, Aymar Embury II (1880–1966), and Frederick J. Sterner (1862–1931), among others—to one- to two-acre country estates in the "Devonshire" subdivision to estate properties of 5 to 25 acres.

Although the railroad was crucial to Belle Terre, the developers were quick to see the potential of the automobile, boasting in 1910 that "the building of the Long Island Motor Parkway will . . . materially shorten the time between Belle Terre and the City . . . The main features of the Estates, such as the Club House, the Pergolas, and Golf Links, may be visited by automobile, while the woodland drives are reserved for carriages and equestrians. A commodious garage is a feature that will appeal to the owners of motor cars."[84] Despite all efforts, Belle Terre failed to catch on and went into receivership in 1913.

Shoreby Hill (1896), located on the island of Jamestown, Rhode Island, is a resort enclave at the edge of a small village.[85] Developed by Ephron Catlin (n.d.) and James Taussig (1827–1916), two well-connected St. Louis businessmen, for families from that city, its concept was that of the Private Places (see p. 90) back home. In fact, five of the street names were the same as those used in St. Louis. Located on what for two centuries had been the Greene Farm, just north of Narragansett Avenue, Jamestown's main street, the Shoreby Hill enclave was laid out by Ernest W. Bowditch, who had helped plan Tuxedo Park, and the extensive plantings were supervised by his brother, the landscapist James H. Bowditch (n.d.). Like many of St. Louis's Private Places, Shoreby Hill's privacy is guarded by little more than gateposts marking the entrances to its streets—though, as Elizabeth M. Delude points out, the entrance was placed on a secondary

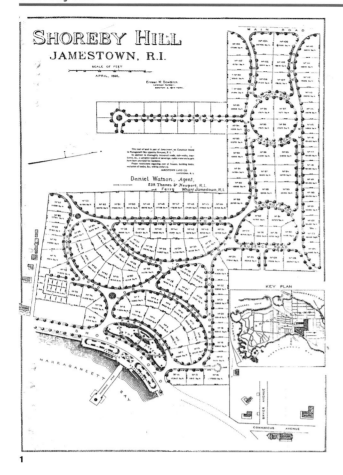

street, Conanicus Avenue, and not on the main street, Narragansett Avenue, to help ensure a sense of privacy.

Bowditch planned for a 128-lot development, though many lots were combined by early purchasers. His layout called for the looping roads of the typical suburb on the downslope toward the sea. But the seeming naturalism of the plan was in fact imposed on the topography, as Charles Savage has observed, to enhance the long slope of the land on the lower portion of the development. At the rear of the oddly shaped site, Bowditch introduced the axial formality of straight streets interrupted by a broad *rond-point* that may have been inspired by the World's Columbian Exposition, but this part of the development was not carried out according to plan. A crescent-shaped green facing Conanicus Avenue, the shore road, was originally intended for thirteen house lots. However, in a gesture echoing one that took place at Oak Bluffs, it was probably bought up by early residents to protect their water view, thereby creating the enclave's only community green space.

Venice (1905), California, was developed by Abbot Kinney (1850–1920), a successful businessman in the tobacco industry.[86] Born in Brookside, New Jersey, and raised in Washington, D.C., Kinney came to California in 1880. After developing with partners the resort known as Ocean Park, just south of Santa Monica, he undertook one of his own on 120 acres of sand dunes and marshland to its south, with the intention of building an American Venice. A dual concept guided planning: Venice was to

at once be a culture-focused suburban village connected by interurban trolley to downtown Los Angeles twenty miles away as well as a resort. As Kevin Starr has written in *Inventing the Dream: California Through the Progressive Era*, Venice "expressed the most dramatic version possible of Southern California's Mediterranean metaphor. Venice combined elements of do-goodism and old-fashioned real estate speculation . . . a residential community and a fantasy resort, the first of many theme developments in Southern California, culminating in Disneyland."[87] At first Kinney called his new town St. Marks but soon changed its name to Venice-of-America.

Once Kinney persuaded Henry Huntington to extend his Los Angeles Pacific Railway to the new suburb, he moved forward with his plans, beginning with the construction of a network of pedestrian-only streets, and a system of canals—eventually to total seven miles— as well as a 1,600-foot-long ocean pier on which, among other things, he built a 2,500-seat auditorium. The pier and its buildings were badly damaged in a storm in March 1905 but rebuilt in time for the town's official opening on July 4 of the same year. Windward Avenue, the principal street, connected the ocean pier with the Grand Canal. Here Kinney constructed a three-story Venetian-style arcaded hotel designed by Norman F. Marsh (1871–1955) and Clarence H. Russell (1874–1942), who are also credited with the layout of the canals. Kinney built a miniature railway to serve the new suburb and connect it with Ocean Park, its neighbor to the

1. Plan, Ernest W. Bowditch, 1896. JHS

2. Aerial view. GE (2010)

3. Gateposts and houses, Conanicus Avenue. JHS (c. 1900)

4. Gateposts and houses, Conanicus Avenue. JHS (2012)

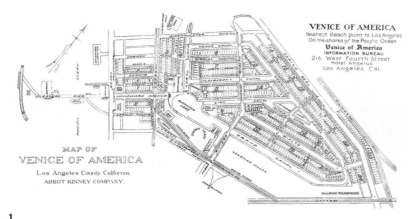

1. Map. LOCP (1905)

2. Aerial view. LAPL (1928)

3. Windward Avenue. SCWH

4. Villa City. USC

5. Overall view. USC

6. Gondola on Aldebaran Canal. LAPC (c. 1909)

7. Houses along Grand Canal. Angeles. WC (2008)

north. He also imported a fleet of gondolas staffed by Italian gondoliers who toured passengers and prospective buyers through the town.

To get things going, in what was perhaps a conscious recall of the origins of earlier planned resort suburbs like Oak Bluffs, Kinney built Villa City, a neighborhood of 300 canvas-covered furnished cottages with their own electricity and cooking facilities. A lending library was built to serve the tent residents—Kinney, a highly educated and well-read man, was intent on bringing culture to all. Popular tastes quickly squashed Kinney's vision of a cultural center, and the pier as well as the downtown business district soon evolved into a Coney Island–like amusement center replete with the Ferris wheel from the Chicago World's Fair, which he bought and re-erected on the pier. By 1912, as Kevin Starr points out, the failure of the canals to function properly was evident, their poor water circulation rendering them "stagnant and slimy."[88] With Kinney's death and Venice's subsequent annexation into Los Angeles,

the explicit provision of Kinney's will that the canals be maintained forever was thrown out. By 1927 most were filled in to create streets deemed essential to meet the proliferating demands of the automobile.

Further south and somewhat inland, **Rancho Santa Fe** (1923), 25 miles north of San Diego, on what had been a 9,000-acre Spanish land grant, was initially developed by the Santa Fe Railroad as a eucalyptus grove for use as railroad ties.[89] The eucalyptus project was an economic failure but an environmental success: when the railroad abandoned its experiment it was left with a plot of land covered by three million aromatic trees. Hoping to recoup some of their losses, railroad officials, led by W. E. Hodges (1860–1942), decided in 1922 to divide the land into a resort village of "gentleman ranchos," likely to be owned by affluent retired or semiretired people. To develop a plan as "eminently practical as it was realistic," the Santa Fe Land Improvement Company hired the San Diego firm of Richard Requa (1881–1941) and Herbert Jackson (1867–1948), who placed Lilian Rice (1889–1938)

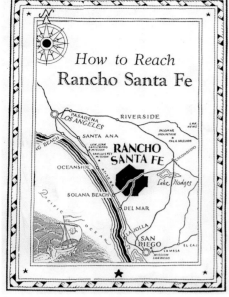

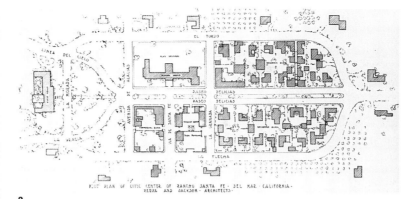

1. Locator map. RSFHS (c. 1923)

2. Civic Center plan, Lilian Rice, 1923. RSFHS

3. Aerial view. RSFHS (1928)

4. Santa Fe Land Improvement Company headquarters. RSFHS (1923)

5. Paseo Delicias. RSFHS (1925)

6. Typical houses. RSFHS

7. Gas station. RSFHS (c. 1923)

8. Guest house for prospective investors. RSFHS (1923)

9. Paseo Delicias. RAMSA (c. 1983)

10,11. Typical views. RAMSA (c. 1983)

in charge of the project.[90] Rice moved to Rancho Santa Fe, where she later established her own office.

Designing in the Spanish Colonial style, Rice established a formal city center in the midst of a loose pattern of curving streets that mirrored the contours of the rolling countryside. The heart of the town plan was the Paseo Delicias, a landscaped boulevard terminated at one end by the La Morada guest house, which she designed as well as some of the stores and houses. The overall effect of the development was controlled by the informal Spanish Colonial vocabulary as specified by Charles H. Cheney, who in 1928 was asked to develop a set of covenants that included an Art Jury like the one he had instituted at Palos Verdes Estates.

In 1925, after several failed attempts beginning in the 1880s, another California resort suburb, **Hope Ranch Park**, was developed on 2,000 oceanfront acres two miles from Santa Barbara.[91] The development honored

Hope Ranch Park

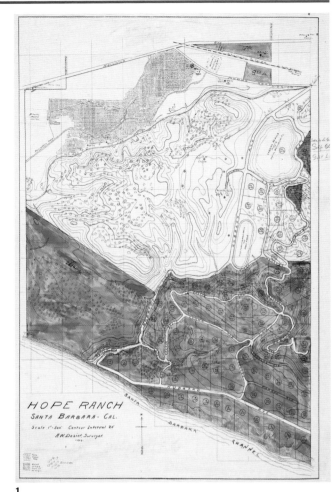

1

2

3

Thomas Hope (1820–1876), an Irish immigrant who acquired 4,000 acres in 1861 but died fifteen years later shortly after completing a house for his family. Hope's will divided the land between his widow and six children. In 1887 the "Big Four" owners of the Southern Pacific Railroad, through their holding company, the Pacific Improvement Company, purchased the widow's half, built railroad tracks to the site, and began laying out roads to prepare for the construction of a tourist hotel surrounded by large estates. By 1899 new leadership had scuttled plans for the hotel but, with a residential area still planned, constructed a 3,000-foot-long water tunnel and irrigation system and in 1904 hired John McLaren, landscape architect of Northern California's Burlingame Park, and a local nurseryman, Francesco Franceschi (1843–1924), to plant 360 palm trees. By 1908, the company was ready to market the land according to a subdivision plan by surveyor A. W. Dozier (n.d.) in which the central Las Palmas Drive extended from the mountains toward the ocean with winding roads branching off through the hills on either side.

Despite its proximity to Santa Barbara and a railroad station, sales were few, and for many years Hope Ranch served as a popular day-trip destination and as a venue for sporting and recreational events focused around the Potter Country Club (later the La Cumbre Golf and Country Club), founded in 1908, surrounding Laguna Blanca, a natural lake. In 1919, New York developer G. Maurice Heckscher (1886–1967) attempted to advance the project but gave up four years later, optioning the eastern half to another developer, who placed hundreds of 50-foot-wide lots facing the ocean and Las Palmas Drive, where only eighty-nine had been in the Dozier plan. This endeavor also failed after a land auction went unattended.

In 1925, Harold S. Chase (1890–1970), a realtor who had been involved in the project during the Pacific Improvement Company days, finally struck the right chord, helped by the growing popularity of the automobile, which brought Santa Barbara to within a twelve-minute drive. Initially investing in only the eastern portion of the site but soon taking on the entire 2,000 acres, Chase's plan for Hope Ranch Park retained Dozier's streets and called for spacious lots of two to fifty acres. At once, Chase began to upgrade the site with an improved water supply, tennis courts, a gun club, a private beach with a bathhouse, a riding club with 30 miles of bridle paths, as well as a reforestation program that planted 50,000 trees and shrubs, later adding another 50,000 lemon trees. Over the next twenty years, nearly 100 houses were built (almost 700 were built by 2009), oriented to maximize views of the foothills and the sea and governed by covenants regarding size and design. The preservation of views was of paramount importance, dictating the allowable height of plantings and the placement of telephone lines, which were buried where poles were inappropriate. A design review board ruled on aesthetic matters and, as a private unincorporated suburb, a homeowners' association was formed to oversee police

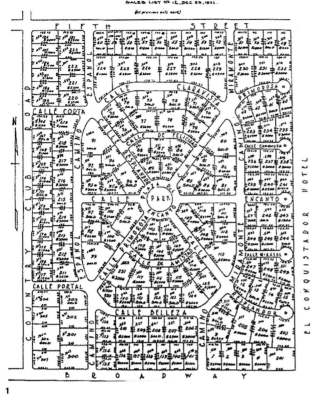

1

2

3

4

5

and fire patrols and the maintenance of roads, beaches, and picnic grounds.

While Southern California and South Florida were the two leading destinations for sun-seeking vacationers and retirees between the two world wars, the Arizona desert also proved attractive, encouraging the development of a number of garden suburb resorts. A popular destination for "health seekers" after World War I, the city of Tucson grew dramatically when the gridded plan that had been established in 1872 pushed outward across the flat Tucson Basin toward the city's surrounding mountains. During the late 1920s real estate developers began to differentiate projects aimed at the affluent by abandoning the grid and its middle-class associations. Development of the neighboring enclaves of **El Encanto Estates** and **Colonia Solana**, both begun in 1928 in the desert east of the city limits, were characterized by irregular street plans, varied lot sizes and shapes, and extensive landscaping, all controlled by deed restrictions. The 123-acre El Encanto Estates, bordered by East

Broadway, North Country Club Road, East Fifth Street, and North Jones Boulevard, was a nearly symmetrical radial plan whose central circle, enclosing a .74-acre park landscaped with native plantings, was connected by six diagonal avenues to an outer circle and a series of culs-de-sac.[92] The subdivision was developed by W. E. Guerin (1871–1960) and laid out by the Los Angeles–based Engineering Service Corporation, which had also planned Hollywoodland, California (see p. 78). Merritt H. Starkweather (1891–1972), a prominent local architect, reviewed all designs on behalf of the developer to ensure that they were, as the deed restrictions mandated, "of Moroccan, Spanish, Italian, Mexican, Indian or Early Californian architecture."[93] Starkweather was also responsible for sixteen of the houses as well as the landscape plan calling for a variety of nonnative species, including palm trees lining the roads.

Just south of El Encanto Estates, Colonia Solana, developed by Harry E. Bryant as a desert community, was the last-known and possibly only surviving work

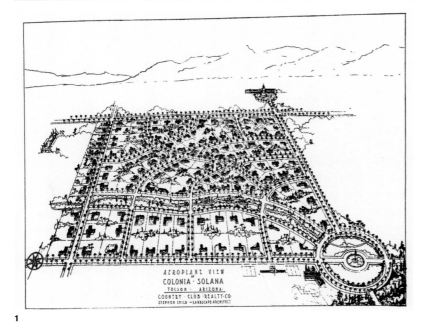

1

2

1. Bird's-eye view. LA28 (1928)

2. Typical view. AHS (c. 1930s)

3. Via Guadalupe. Clinco. DC (2012)

4. Via Golondrina. Clinco. DC (2012)

3

4

of the landscape architect Stephen Child (1866–1936), whose goal was "to make the 'Colony' interesting and beautiful,—different from what had been done heretofore hereabout."[94] The result, according to Virginia and Lee McAlester, was "an exquisite . . . neighborhood in which you feel as if you have driven directly into the surrounding desert and stumbled upon a few scattered houses."[95] While located in the heart of Tucson, the quarter-section site—160 acres measuring one-half-mile square—was buffered on the east and south by an existing country club and a planned public park. Covered in sagebrush and other desert plants, the land was almost featureless except for an arroyo that meandered diagonally through its southern half and two minor "washes," each of which could have "been easily filled up and ignored," as Child put it. Instead they were emphasized, with the largest of the three becoming the "keynote" of the 250-foot-wide Parkway, consisting of a 150-foot-wide linear park planted with a higher concentration of native vegetation than would occur naturally, and two flanking 50-foot swaths accommodating footpaths, planting strips, and roads. "Those who live alongside this Parkway," wrote Child, "will have in front of their doors the desert beauty many now ride miles to see only to find it scattered about, more or less

detached."[96] The Parkway sustained a population of rabbits, quail, squirrels, and hummingbirds that produced the effect of "exploring a life-size terrarium in the middle of the city."[97]

In all, Child reserved 9.4 acres for parks and open space and provided 123 house lots, each about an acre in size, along narrow, 16-foot-wide roads that were paved in concrete and did not feature curbs but were separated from front yards by a line of rocks. Wherever roads crossed the Parkway, culverts were avoided in favor of "Arizona dips," gentle depressions graded so there would be "no uncomfortable jounce, but rather the very agreeable sensation one has when riding the surf at Waikiki."[98] A large traffic circle with a monument, intended for the site's southeast corner, was never realized. In 1932 local architect Roy Place (1887–1950) enclosed the 65-foot-tall, 50,000-gallon water tower at the northeast corner of the subdivision in a Spanish Colonial Revival skin, creating a prominent landmark intended to draw attention to the project and stimulate house sales.

A third development undertaken in 1928 catalyzed the redirection of Tucson's expansion from its westward trajectory, toward the Tucson Mountains, northward to the foothills of the Santa Catalina Mountains, where developer John W. Murphey (1898–1977)

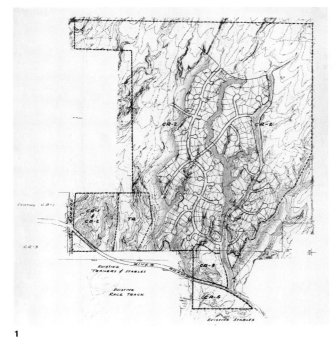

1. Map. AHS (c. 1964)

2, 3. Houses, Josias Joesler. AHS (c. 1930s)

4. Typical street. Clinco. DC (2012)

5. St. Philip's in the Hills Church, Josias Joesler, 1936. Clinco. DC (2012)

purchased 7,000 acres and persuaded the Swiss-born Los Angeles–based architect Josias Joesler (1895–1956) not only to plan the **Catalina Foothills Estates** but also design more than 400 of its houses.[99] Aimed at attracting wealthy Easterners, the subdivision, four miles north of the city limits, stretching along both sides of Campbell Avenue, from River Road on the south to Skyline Drive on the north, was governed by familiar covenants mandating minimum construction costs and materials. But it was the protection of views, the large multi-acre lots, and the stipulation that no vegetation be removed unless for construction purposes, that established the development's desirability. As a gateway to the estates, Murphey built St. Philip's Plaza, a stylized Mexican village comprising restaurants, offices, and Joesler's Spanish Colonial Revival St. Philip's in the Hills Church (1936), around a public park. The project's success led to emulation, but the developers who followed Murphey's lead in the foothills built at significantly higher densities, and over time even the large lots within Murphey's original development were extensively subdivided.

In quick succession in the 1920s the Olmsted Brothers planned four resort communities centered around the development of golf courses. Henry V. Hubbard explained the appeal of such an arrangement in *Landscape Architecture* in 1927: "If you are planning a particularly select land subdivision or residential area you usually organize a club to take care of the question of membership and land ownership. Since your land is probably farm land or even wild land, and you mean to preserve for the lot purchasers at least some of the present space and openness, you naturally organize a country club and set aside a portion of the area for its use. And the use which is now by all odds the most attractive, the least necessarily destructive of natural beauty, the most adaptable to topography, the easiest to adjust to the adjacent roads and house-lots, is the golf course."[100] The Olmsteds began with **Gibson Island** (1922), Maryland, located in the Chesapeake Bay and connected to the mainland by a single-road causeway.[101] The 1,000-acre island, 25 miles southeast of Baltimore and 45 miles northeast of Washington, D.C., was developed by Baltimore Judge W. Stuart Symington Jr. (1871–1926) and his brother Thomas (1869?–1931) who intended to build a summer resort for wealthy area residents. The Symingtons purchased the undeveloped, heavily wooded, hilly parcel from three farmers and hired the Olmsted firm based on the recommendation of Edward H. Bouton of Roland Park. The Olmsted plan, which placed the golf course at the northern end of the site, and most

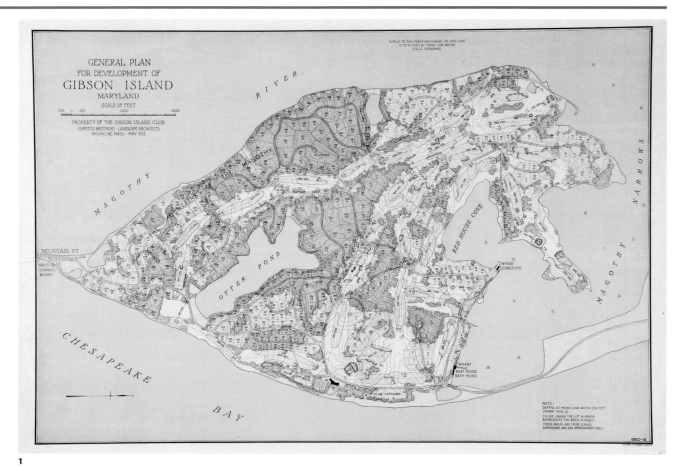

1

2

3

of the house lots on the western and southern coasts, was primarily focused on the retention of the island's natural beauty, with two-thirds of the site reserved for recreation, open space, and a hardwood forest.

Although a golf course designed by Charles Mac-Donald (1855–1939), a modest clubhouse, a marina, and forty houses were quickly realized, development activity, which first slowed after Stuart Symington's death in 1926, was brought to a halt by the Depression. When building began again in the 1930s, Gibson Island, no longer under the control of the Symington family, was reorganized as the Gibson Island Corporation, a cooperative with all homeowners having a say in community affairs. It was also no longer exclusively home to summer visitors, with a growing number of families living on the island year-round. H. Clay Primrose (1892–1951), who replaced the Olmsteds as landscape architect, also advocated

retaining a significant amount of undeveloped land as common property, advice that was generally followed although the Gibson Island Corporation did reduce the golf course to nine holes to free up more building lots. The corporation also built a stone gatehouse guarded twenty-four hours a day, restricting access to homeowners and their guests. After a third round of luxury residential construction in the 1980s, Gibson Island numbered some 200 houses, still retaining both its exclusive character as well as its scenic beauty.

The Olmsteds' equally ambitious plans for **Yeamans Hall Club** (1925), South Carolina, were also only partially realized.[102] Developed by a group of Northern investors led by Edward S. Harkness (1874–1940) and Starling W. Childs (1870–1946), who wanted to build a wintertime retreat, Yeamans Hall was located on a 1,000-acre former plantation ten miles north of Charleston. The Olmsteds'

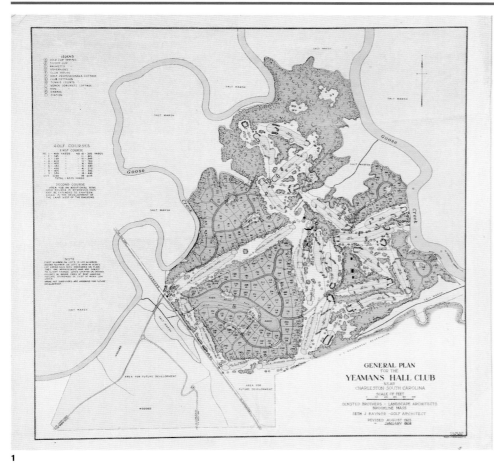

1

2

1. Plan, Olmsted Brothers, 1925. FLO (1928)

2. Entrance gate. CCaldwell. CC (2010)

3. Clubhouse, James Gamble Rogers, 1927. YHC

4. Starling Childs house, Grosvenor Atterbury, 1928. CCaldwell. CC (2010)

3

4

original scheme called for two golf courses, a clubhouse that could accommodate 200 guests, and 200 privately owned cottages connected by looping roads. Frederick Law Olmsted Jr. was enthusiastic about the site's possibilities, writing that "what I saw was sufficient in extent and in quality to afford the basis of an admirable winter resort development. Its peculiar advantages, apart from climate and transportation facilities, consist of its topography and its vegetation. The form of the ground is diversified and picturesquely undulating." Olmsted was also enthusiastic about the "live oaks, of which a sufficient number are so exceptionally large and magnificent as to give the landscape great distinction."[103] Unfortunately, the Depression stopped development after the completion of an eighteen-hole golf course, designed by Seth Raynor (1874–1926), and thirty-five cottages, thirteen the work of James Gamble Rogers (1867–1947),

who was also an investor in the development. Aaron Betsky describes Rogers's houses as "simple wood buildings, painted white and extended into the landscape through the extensive use of porches and telescoping side wings." Rogers was also responsible for the design of the two-story clubhouse that, according to Betsky, "bears a passing resemblance in its massing to some of the houses Rogers designed for the country around New York."[104] Grosvenor Atterbury designed Starling Childs's stucco and frame house (1928), "inspired by the original planters' estates in the region."[105]

The Olmsted Brothers also drew up plans for Boston developer Ferris W. Norris's **Oyster Harbors** (1925), an extensive residential subdivision intended to surround a golf course facing Cotuit Bay on Cape Cod.[106] Although Norris was unable to proceed with plans for the houses, he did complete a golf course designed by

Oyster Harbors

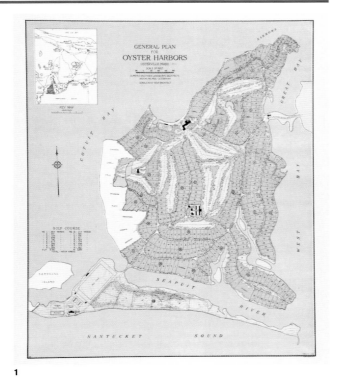

1

Fishers Island Club

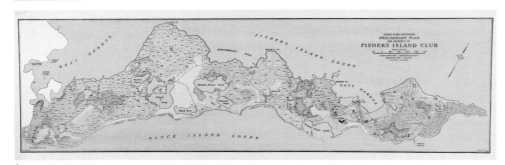

1

2

3

4

5

Donald Ross. The Olmsteds again collaborated with Seth Raynor on the design of one of his last golf courses for the **Fishers Island Club** (1926), located on the east end of Fishers Island, New York, a nine-mile-long, one-mile-wide island in Long Island Sound, two miles off the coast of Connecticut and nine miles from the tip of Long Island.[107] Developed by brothers Alfred L. and Henry L. Ferguson, plans for the golf course also included a large stone clubhouse designed by Charles R. Wait (d. 1973). The Olmsted plan, which identified 398 potential house lots on the 1,800-acre site, was generally adhered to over the years and in 1958 it was officially adopted by the Southold Town Board. In its 1994 *Fishers Island Growth Plan*, the Town Board noted that houses had been built on 176 of the lots identified in the Olmsted plan. Of the remaining 222 plots, only 31 were deemed not suitable for building.

While Carl G. Fisher (1874–1939), a Midwestern industrialist, is best known for his pioneering development of the conventionally platted city of Miami Beach, he also developed the more sophisticated, suburban-scaled resort village of **Montauk Beach** (1926), New York, on 10,000 acres at the eastern tip of Long Island.[108] After Fisher purchased the land, he released ambitious plans calling for thirty miles of new roads, three golf courses, a gambling casino, a yacht club, bathing pavilions, two polo fields, an automobile racetrack, three hotels, apartment houses, and at least forty large single-family houses. Although Fisher's hope to realize the "Miami Beach of the North" fell victim to the collapse in Florida real estate values and the stock market crash, some portions were realized, including a workers' village intended for the laborers needed to construct the resort, designed by Robert Tappan, an architect with extensive experience in Forest Hills Gardens. The village translated into wood-frame construction ideas about unit and modular construction that had been explored earlier in concrete at Forest Hills Gardens by Grosvenor Atterbury. Also completed at Montauk Beach was an eighteen-hole golf course, a seven-story office building (1926) serving as company headquarters, and Schultze & Weaver's 200-room, H-shaped, Tudor-style Montauk Manor (1927), a hotel built on a bluff overlooking Fort Pond.

Arcady (1929), proposed by John T. Woodside (1864–1946), a textile executive from Greenville, for a 16,000-acre, forested oceanfront site near Myrtle Beach, South Carolina, was conceived as a long-distance commuters' retreat, "a national playground where the leaders of contemporary life may sustain their capacity for work by bringing to its utmost the art of rest and recreation."[109] Arguably the last great resort scaled to railroad travel, Arcady, in recognition of the increasing amount of leisure time available to affluent Americans, was to be accessible to New Yorkers for long weekends in a climate with mild temperatures for at least nine months a year. Designed by Raymond Hood (1881–1934) with his partners Frederick A. Godley (1886–1961) and J. André Fouilhoux (1880–1945), it was to be a resort for the new executive and managerial class. At the time of Arcady's

Montauk Beach

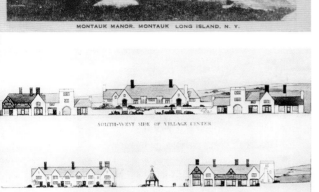

1. Montauk Manor, Schultze & Weaver, 1927. CRS

2. Montauk Improvement Company office building, 1926. CRS

3. Plan for workers' village, Robert Tappan, 1926. AA26

4, 5. Workers' village, proposed village center and houses. AA26

6, 7. Workers' village, single- and two-family houses. AA26

Arcady

1. Plan, Hood, Godley, and Fouilhoux, 1929. ARC

2. Clubhouse, aquatint by Donald Douglas. ARC (1929)

3. Perspective drawing of clubhouse. ARC (1929)

4. Beach clubhouse. ARC (1929)

CORAL GABLES
Miami Riviera
40 Miles of Water Front
GEORGE E. MERRICK

announcement at a Manhattan press conference in early 1929, Woodside was just finishing up work on the Ocean Front Hotel and Ocean Front Golf Course and Country Club, which Arcady members were to use until their own course and clubhouse were completed. But cost overruns at the hotel and the effects of the Depression doomed Woodside's plans for the resort.

FLORIDA: A NATIONAL WINTER SUBURB

In the 1920s, Florida was unquestionably the scene of some of the most significant garden city and garden suburb planning in the United States. Ironically, this flowering of inspired land development went hand in hand with some of the wildest real estate speculation ever witnessed in America or, for that matter, anywhere. First made a United States territory in 1821 and a state in 1845, Florida remained an agricultural backwater until the 1880s, when rail connections to populous Northern cities both in the East and the Midwest helped unlock its potential as a winter resort. Key to this was Henry Flagler (1830–1913), who consolidated various independent carriers to form the Florida East Coast Railway, connecting Northern and Midwestern cities to Jacksonville, Florida, then on to St. Augustine in 1883, and down the coast reaching Palm Beach in 1894 and Miami in 1896.[110] At first Florida was the playground of the very rich, but with the spread of wealth into the middle class, especially after World War I, it attracted a broad clientele who got there not only by train but also by automobile, causing whole new towns to be invented seemingly overnight to meet the demands of Northerners for a place in the sun.

With much of its land mass literally scooped up from the sea by Carl G. Fisher, who cut down the mangrove trees to two feet above ground, leaving the stumps in place, and pumped sand from the bottom of Biscayne Bay to a height of two feet to create new land, Miami Beach was the best known of the new resort city-suburbs but not necessarily the best planned. Other Florida resort communities were much more significant from the point of view of planning, especially those laid out by John Nolen, two of which, Venice (see p. 271) and Clewiston (see p. 274), were conceived at the scale, complexity, and degree of self-sufficiency to be considered garden cities.

Most of the other new Florida resort communities were not quite so self-sufficient. They usually had their own governments and year-round residents to provide necessary services; otherwise they were dependent on the comings and goings of sun-seeking visitors, so that they were in effect suburbs of New York, Chicago, and other Northern cities. This led the architectural and political commentator Herbert Croly, writing during the land boom of the mid-1920s, to observe that while the usual pattern of such booms appealed

to a local clientele [and took place] in the neighborhood of rapidly growing cities . . . in the case of Florida, the speculation pervades a large part of an entire state and it appeals to a clientele which lives all over the country. It is based on the assumption that millions of American citizens who live and work in the cities of the north and the west will buy a building lot in Florida, erect a bungalow and live there for a part of the winter. Enough land has already been cleared and subdivided into building lots to accommodate about 6,000,000 new residents; and the manufacture of this popular commodity goes merrily on. They are creating in Florida a really national suburb and winter resort. It is intended not for exceptionally wealthy people but for the average small town American who in the past has considered himself unable to afford such luxury.[111]

Palm Beach was the first and the most famous of Florida's resort suburbs but, from the point of view of planning, it was by no means the most significant, nor was it aimed at the middle class. Though a winter suburb of Northern cities, Palm Beach was also, ironically, a suburb of West Palm Beach, the town across Lake Worth—in effect the local stretch of the Intracoastal Waterway—to which it banished most of its routine businesses and workers, a situation that conjures up the worst possible image of suburbia as elitist and exclusionary.

Palm Beach began to develop as a resort in 1894, as a result of Flagler's construction of the Royal Poinciana Hotel to promote passenger travel on his Florida East Coast Railway line.[112] In its early years, visitors to Palm Beach largely confined themselves to hotels, and the town remained hardly more than a rude frontier town fortuitously located by the sea. But in 1917 Paris E. Singer (1868–1932), an heir to the sewing machine fortune, visited it accompanied by the flamboyant architect Addison Mizner (1872–1933) and dramatically changed the character of the place. World War I had effectively stopped trans-Atlantic travel, and Singer, deciding to develop Palm Beach as a wintertime equivalent to the resorts he had customarily enjoyed on the French Riviera, inaugurated a ten-year transformation of the swampy, overgrown island into a lushly planted residential community by constructing a small but intensely developed downtown area of exclusive shops, theaters, and clubs.

The architecture Singer and Mizner found at Palm Beach was an adaptation of the Shingle Style typical of Northeastern seaside resorts that Mizner felt "didn't register" in subtropical Florida.[113] Struck by the similarity of the winter climate to that of spring in Andalusia in Spain, as well as that of Central America, where he had traveled extensively, and stoked by Singer's wartime nostalgia for the inaccessible resorts in the South of France, Mizner devised a remarkable architectural and urban synthesis that soon came to represent Florida architecture in the popular imagination. Mizner's highly eclectic stylistic blend of architectural elements from the Mediterranean proved to be the perfect vocabulary to establish a sense of place. His was a romantic

1. Royal Poinciana Hotel, Carrère & Hastings, 1894. SAF (1896)

2. Via Parigi, Worth Avenue, Addison Mizner, 1923. SAF (c. 1928)

3. Aerial, view, Everglades Club, Addison Mizner, 1918. Seldomridge. LOCP (1921)

4. House, 780 South Ocean Boulevard, Addison Mizner, 1926. Boucher. LOCP (1972)

1

2

3

4

style that worked well on the smaller scale of the individual house as well as club and commercial buildings, where its loose rules of composition allowed numerous, intimate indoor and outdoor rooms blending building and garden, street and plaza, as never before in post–Colonial America. While the architecture of the Mediterranean coasts in Spain, France, and Morocco were important sources of inspiration, Venice and its Lido no doubt provided an equally important frame of reference. Mizner may also have known about the other Venice, the one in California that Marsh & Russell planned and designed for Abbot Kinney in the first years of the century.

To begin with, Singer and Mizner built what would become the Everglades Club but started out as a hospital in order to permit its construction during wartime.[114] The club's design fulfilled Mizner's avowed ideal of architectural romance, a building as he stated, "based on Romanesque ruins that had been rebuilt by triumphant Saracens, added to by a variety of conquerors bringing in new styles from the Gothic to the Baroque; and picturesquely cracked up by everything from battering rams to artillery duels between Wellington and Napoleon's marshals."[115] But, romance aside, once the war was over, its shaded loggias opening on to fountained patios proved exactly right for Florida, and the club's success led to

numerous house commissions. In addition, Mizner was able to inspire other architects, including Howard Major (1883–1974), Marion Syms Wyeth (1889–1982), and Maurice T. Fatio (1897–1943), to work with the themes he established so that by the late 1920s the residential neighborhoods of Palm Beach were filled with an array of excellently conceived houses.

But it is not the Everglades Club or the individual houses that give Palm Beach its particular distinction as a resort suburb; rather, it is the mixed-use commercial center that Singer developed and Mizner designed across Worth Avenue from the club. With its arcaded shops along the avenue and narrow, twisting, shop-lined pedestrian streets cut through the block—Mizner called them "Vias," one named the Via Parigi to honor the owner and one the Via Mizner to honor the architect—this complex of shops with flats and small offices above gave the town a distinct, atmospherically suggestive and commercially viable focus that was perfectly calibrated to the needs of customers who could park their automobiles at the edges and stroll along what Christina Orr has described as "the first pedestrian-only environment to be developed as a defense against the noise and general intrusiveness of the automobile."[116] The intelligence of the plan was recognized from the start. As John Taylor Boyd observed in 1930, "The genius of the Vias is that they not only

5

6

7

8

9

10

create intimacy but also generate movement. The visitor is immediately at ease and no matter how frantic upon entrance to a Via he slackens his pace and begins to stroll at leisure. The Vias and the shops within the cloistered arcade of Worth Avenue seem separate from the rest of Palm Beach. They become their own village. The buildings are tall, then low; with intricate stonework, then utterly plain; and all seem compressed and condensed."[117] Mizner's Worth Avenue development inspired another mixed-use development, sadly only partially realized. Called Barrio De Los Palmeras—"Neighborhood of the Palms"—it was commissioned around 1925 by Singer and planned by the New York architects C. Howard Crane (1885–1952), Kenneth Franzheim (1891–1959), and Charles H. Bettis (1891–1960), who proposed to flank a new building for the American Society of Arts and Letters with two groups of shops and small apartments.[118]

In 1925, just before the bottom fell out of the Florida boom, Mizner, perhaps inspired by George E. Merrick's success at Coral Gables, embarked on planning and developing an entirely new town about 25 miles south of Palm Beach that he named **Boca Raton**—in Spanish the name means "rat's mouth"—conceiving it as a super-suburb on 1,600 acres of land reaching back two miles from the oceanfront into the Everglades.[119] Most of the planning, left in the hands of engineer Karl Riddle

(n.d.), conformed to the typical Southern Florida pattern of squared blocks containing 25- and 35-foot-wide lots. These were grouped into neighborhoods given names like Old Floresta and Spanish Village, each presumably to have been developed with some suggestion of a distinct architectural character. But the plan also had its innovative aspects, including the decision to transform the land farthest from the ocean, typically regarded as the least valuable, into a highly desirable subdivision called Ritz-Carlton Park, with Olmsted-like winding streets lined by generous lots backing up to a golf course.

To begin his town, Mizner concentrated his attention on the 160-foot-wide, two-and-a-half-mile-long Camino Real. The east–west boulevard was to extend west from a beach-front Ritz-Carlton hotel, cross the Intracoastal Waterway on a Mizner-designed Venetian bridge replete with a tower apartment for the bridge keeper, and pass through a golf course before becoming an arcaded shopping and business street with a central canal modeled on the Botafago of Rio de Janeiro, where several electric gondolas, imported from Italy, would ply. Farther west, Camino Real was to open to a large plaza at the Seaboard Railway tracks, where a new "Addison Station" would be built. Crossing the tracks, it would continue to the middle of Ritz-Carlton Park. Boca Raton's projected facilities were to include an airport as well as golf

5. Patio Marguery. RAMSA (1984)

6. Courtyard off Worth Avenue. RAMSA (1984)

7. Worth Avenue. RAMSA (1984)

8. Villa Mizner, Addison Mizner, 1924. RAMSA (1984)

9. Via Mizner, Addison Mizner, 1923. RAMSA (c. 1977)

10. Barrio De Los Palmeras, C. Howard Crane, Kenneth Franzheim, and Charles H. Bettis, c. 1925. TA26

Boca Raton

1. Perspective of plan by Addison Mizner and Karl Riddle. BRHS (1927)

2. Cloister Inn. Addison Mizner, 1926. SAF

3. Administration Building, Addison Mizner, 1926. Ebyabe. WC (2010)

4. Boca Raton Realty Company office, Ocean Drive. Fishbaugh. SAF (1925)

5. City Hall, Addison Mizner, 1926. Ebyabe. WC (2010)

6. House, 801 Hibiscus Street, Old Floresta, Addison Mizner, 1926. Ebyabe. WC (2010)

1

2

3

4

5

6

Coconut Grove

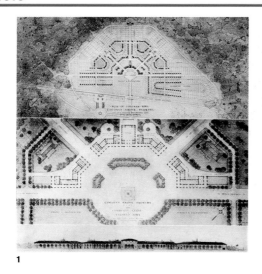

1

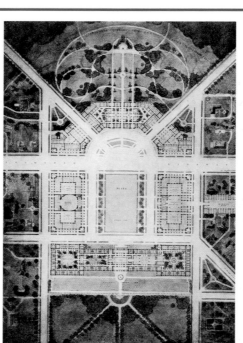

2

3

1. Plan, colored town, top; plan and elevation, community center, bottom. John Irwin Bright, 1919. JAIA21

2. Plan, civic center. JAIA21

3. Model, municipal group. JAIA21

CORAL GABLES--MIAMI'S MASTER SUBURB

1. Plan, northern section, Frank Button, 1922. AMP

1

courses, a polo field, a yacht basin, and a floating cabaret. It would also have a church dedicated to the developer's mother. Although Mizner claimed that his resort suburb would be "the world's most architecturally beautiful playground," Boca Raton would also provide a subdivision for workers and an industrial district.[120]

When initially marketed, Boca Raton produced pandemonium in the realty offices. On the record-breaking opening day, two million dollars worth of lots were sold. But uncontrolled hucksterism and the devastating hurricane of 1926 brought Florida's real estate boom to an abrupt end, dashing any hope of completing Mizner's scheme. Fragments of the plan were realized, but very little of importance except for the Cloister Inn, which opened in February 1926. Also completed were a portion of El Camino Real, some of the houses designed by Mizner in the Old Floresta and Spanish Village subdivisions, and the development company's Administration Building, which Mizner modeled after El Greco's house in Toledo. The Boca Raton City Hall was completed toward the end of 1926, but Mizner's original scheme was significantly diminished in size because the town, counting on real estate tax revenue to pay for infrastructure,

could not afford to construct it as proposed. Today, Mizner's Boca Raton is more illusion than reality. "Monumental in scale and magnificent in concept," as Donald Curl has written, "the vastness of the . . . enterprise doomed it to failure from the beginning."[121]

City-like in scale, but with no provision for industry except for craft workshops, **Coral Gables** (1921), planned as a resort, deserves consideration as one of the world's preeminent garden villages.[122] Like Palos Verdes, Coral Gables has until recently been largely ignored by historians who seem unable to take it seriously as urbanism, perhaps because it is a South Florida resort. An independent city, Coral Gables now functions as a suburb of Miami, but at the time of its founding it was conceived as a wintertime suburb for Northern businessmen who might settle their families there for months at a time while they shuttled back and forth using trains or automobiles.

The son of a rich orange grower who built a luxurious family homestead that he called Coral Gables, George E. Merrick (1886–1942) was said to have dreamt of building "Castles in Spain" on the agricultural land he inherited on his father's death in 1911. Dreams aside,

2

3

4

5

6

8

9

2. Plan, Riviera section, Frank Button, 1925. HM

3. City Hall, Harold Steward and Phineas Paist, 1928. RAMSA (c. 1996)

4. Douglas Gate, Phineas Paist and Denman Fink, 1925–27. Fishbaugh. SAF (1927)

5. Colonnade Building, Phineas Paist, Paul Chalfin, and Walter De Garmo, 1925–26, and trolley. SAF

6. Prado Entrance, Phineas Paist and Denman Fink, 1927. Fishbaugh. SAF

7. Granada Entrance, Phineas Paist and Denman Fink, 1922. Fishbaugh. SAF (1923)

8. Miami-Biltmore Hotel, Schultze & Weaver, 1925, and golf course. Fishbaugh. SAF (1926)

9. Paul Whiteman and band, Venetian Pool, Phineas Paist, 1924. SAF (1925)

10

11

12

13

10. George E. Merrick house, South Greenway Drive. Fishbaugh. SAF (1925)

11. Dutch South African Village, Le Jeune Road, Marion Syms Wyeth, 1925–26. SAF (1926)

12. French City Village, Hardee Road, Mott B. Schmidt, 1925–26. SAF (1927)

13. Colonial Village, Santa Maria Street, Coulton and John Skinner, 1925–26. SAF (1926)

14. Chinese Village, Maggiore Street, Henry Killam Murphy, 1925–26. SAF (1927)

15. Dutch South African Village. RAMSA (1984)

16. French City Village. RAMSA (1999)

17. Chinese Village. RAMSA (1984)

18. Venetian Pool. RAMSA (1984)

19. Commercial entrance, Phineas Paist and Denman Fink, 1924. RAMSA (1984)

20. Canal. Ebyabe. WC (2011)

21. Typical street. Averette. WC (2010)

14

15

16

17

18

19

20

21

Merrick may have been inspired to develop the land by the unrealized plan designed by Philadelphia architect John Irwin Bright (1869–1940) for a monumental civic center and "colored town" for **Coconut Grove** (1919), a small village lying between Merrick's orange groves and Miami.[123] Bright, in turn, appears to have been influenced by the geometric formality of Yorkship Village in Camden, New Jersey (see p. 863).

When Merrick's early education as a lawyer was interrupted by his father's death, he joined his mother in Florida and became active in local real estate, increasing his holdings from the original 160 agricultural acres that he inherited to 3,000 acres by the time Coral Gables opened for business in 1921. Eventually, the city would encompass 10,000 acres, or 16 square miles. To plan his resort city, Merrick turned to Frank Button (1866–1938), who had come from the Chicago area to help with the design of Vizcaya, the James Deering estate, in Miami.[124]

The plan for Coral Gables was in many respects straightforward, with a grid of streets defining rectangular blocks running east–west. The suburb was crossed by a major east–west boulevard known as Coral Way and Granada Boulevard running north–south. But the plan was lifted from the conventional by occasional diagonal avenues that sliced through its northern section, by 40 miles of canals looped through it in the Riviera section to the south, by elaborately landscaped plazas placed where the diagonals crossed major streets, and by dramatic gateways that marked the principal entrances to the city along its periphery. According to Button, "On all the principal boulevards at Coral Gables have been laid out delightful parks, plazas and rest spots, one-half to five acres in area, that break the vistas of the avenues and provide the most charming possibilities for landscape work of the most effective kind . . . Whenever possible fruit trees in parkways between sidewalks and streets have been preserved . . . Large plots have been set aside in prominent locations for churches, schools, library and other community centers . . . Winding boulevards encircle the entire tract, diagonal streets make every part accessible."[125]

In place of the Green or Common of Colonial New England, or the central park of the nineteenth-century city, the plan for Coral Gables provided large open areas of green in the form of two golf courses, "only dubiously public," according to Vincent Scully, but nonetheless a valuable visual asset for all to enjoy, given that at many places the public roads edged the greens.[126] Crucial to Merrick's vision of a resort suburb was the overall landscape design, which he entrusted to Button. Although Merrick's original land holdings were cultivated as orchards, the majority of Coral Gables lay on land consisting of pines and scrub palmetto requiring the planting of over 50,000 trees before 1924.

The town grew rapidly, benefiting from the boom in Florida real estate that took place between 1920 and 1925. The first phase of development was located in the city's northwest corner, where the Granada Golf and Country Club's golf course provided the principal interruption to the plan's regularity. Coral Way, which bisected this section was home to the city's shopping district and City Hall. The second stage, known as the Riviera section, began to be developed in 1925 just as the real estate market was softening. It contained an area reserved for the new University of Miami, which Merrick proposed to finance as the city's centerpiece. This section also contained golf courses, the Miami-Biltmore Hotel, a church, and some other civic structures. The third section, the so-called Cocoplum (later Biscayne) section, extended the city south to the shores of Biscayne Bay. The crash of Florida real estate in 1925 denied this section its realization.

Trolley service between Miami and Coral Gables was inaugurated in 1925; a station on the Florida East Coast Railway planned for a location opposite the University of Miami was not built. Merrick did, however, complete miles of canals which he stocked with gondolas—the canals allowed him to advertise "more than 40 miles of waterfront"—and he did transform an abandoned limestone quarry into a spectacular public swimming hole known as "The Venetian Pool," where, on a floating raft, the portly band leader Paul Whiteman, resplendent in a swimming suit and hat, conducted his jazz orchestra. In between sets, William Jennings Bryan led "the largest outdoor bible class in the world," peppered with pitches for the development itself: "You can think about the future of Coral Gables—and before you go to bed tonight, you will be ashamed of your modesty."[127]

Largely unrealized was the wall Merrick intended to enclose his development in emulation of a medieval town, although he did build a number of elaborate entrance gates that helped define the boundaries. Even more than the canals, the entrance gates are the city's most distinct feature, giving it definition that ensures its status as an oasis amid metropolitan Miami's surrounding sprawl. Only four entrances of the seven planned were built, all designed by Phineas Paist (1875–1937), Merrick's principal architectural adviser who was born, raised, and educated in Philadelphia, and Denman Fink (1881–1956), Merrick's uncle and a successful illustrator for magazines. The Granada Entrance (1922) and the Commercial Entrance (1924), both built of rough-cut oolitic limestone, were hundreds of feet long, suggesting the bounding wall Merrick hoped for, but their mass was softened by wooden pergolas and trellises. The Douglas Gate (1925–27), with stucco walls and oolitic stone trim, was the most programmatic of the gates, suggesting Station Square at Forest Hills Gardens, with a tower, gateway, entrance hall, ballroom, and two wings of shops and apartments, all part of an incompletely realized village square, La Puerta del Sol. The Prado Entrance (1927) was the most monumental, with pylons surrounding an ellipse that contained a stepped fountain and reflecting pool, appropriately leading to the grandest residential boulevard, the Country Club Prado.

Paist's contributions were critical. Drawing on his knowledge of Philadelphia, he modeled Coral Gables

City Hall on the Merchants' Exchange Building (William Strickland, 1834), and adopted strategies to identify villages within the development similar to those employed by George Woodward in Chestnut Hill (see p. 135): "use of indigenous materials; the employment of accomplished architects; the use of gates as symbolic points of entry; and the seminal idea that individual houses can maintain their own identity, while still contributing to their collective character as an ensemble."[128] While there is no record of Merrick taking an interest in Chestnut Hill, he did acknowledge Shaker Heights (see p. 175), with its controls for architectural style and building materials and colors, as a source of inspiration.[129] Denman Fink and his cousin H. George Fink (1890–1975) helped coordinate the work of the many staff architects employed at Coral Gables, including Martin L. Hampton (1890–1950), Walter C. DeGarmo (1876–1964), and L. D. Brumm (n.d.). Paist, who like Button had come to South Florida in 1916 at the invitation of Paul Chalfin (1874–1959), one of the designers of Deering's Villa Vizcaya, would be crucial to the town's overall success. Named by Merrick "Supervisor of Color" and later "Supervising Architect," Paist "set up the review process that required a high standard of design for all buildings constructed within the city."[130]

Typically, the houses in Coral Gables were in the Spanish or Mediterranean style, and many were designed by H. George Fink. Embedded in the overall neighborhood matrix, however, were "theme" villages intended to mitigate against the sameness and newness of an instantly conceived real estate development and to satisfy the taste for the exotic that many of Florida's visitors seemed to crave. Had all the villages been realized, they would have peppered the town with clustered housing in the following styles: Florida Pioneer; Venetian Country; French Country House; Mexican Pioneer or Hacienda; Dutch African Pioneer; Dutch East Indian Pioneer; Spanish Pioneer or Mission; Venetian Town or Canal Houses; Persian Canal Houses; Persian Village; Neopolitan Baroque; African Bazaar; Tangier Village; Chinese Compound; and even Colonial American. Fifteen of these villages, containing over 1,000 houses, were planned in 1925 when land was deeded to developers who retained seven Miami architects and five New York architects. Only seven themed villages with a mere eighty houses were constructed: the French City, French Normandy, French Country, Chinese, Colonial, Italian, and Dutch South African villages.[131] Each of these, by virtue of style and composition, provides an oasis of urban collectivity in a sea of suburban individuality. The French City Village, designed by the young architect Mott B. Schmidt (1889–1977), typically specializing in Georgian-style work, was a remarkable example of the potential for high-density development using single-family villa-like houses and walled gardens. The French Normandy Village, designed by John (1893–1972) and Coulton (1891–1963) Skinner, consisting of eleven townhouses, half-timbered, stucco-clad, and roofed by flat shingles, in a style based on French and English fifteenth-century

precedent, was less tightly organized. Even looser was the French Country Village, consisting of discrete, rustic "châteaux" designed by Philip L. Goodwin (1885–1958), who combined seemingly ad hoc planning and materials with a spare arrangement of classical details. The Chinese Village, by Henry Killam Murphy (1877–1954), a New York– and New Haven–based architect with considerable direct experience building in China, comprised eight two-story "oriental" houses, with flared roofs, carved balconies, and latticework windows; the details were rendered in vivid reds, yellows, blues, and greens.[132] Like Schmidt's French Village, the Chinese Village was densely planned yet with enough green space between houses to ensure privacy. In 1929, Murphy, serving as chief architectural adviser for the plan of the capital city of Nanjing, China, proposed a more fully developed version of the Chinese village, designing a prototypical garden suburb for wealthy families and government officials in which villas with Chinese architectural features would sit on individual lots along curving streets around a central park—but the design was never implemented.[133] In the Colonial Village, the houses designed by John and Coulton Skinner faced the street with two-story-high, facade-long porches, not unlike Mount Vernon's. The Italian Village, designed by Frank Wyatt Woods (1881–1951) in the midst of a typical neighborhood of Spanish Mediterranean houses, consisted of five stucco-clad villas. Perhaps the most charming village, Marion Syms Wyeth's Dutch South African Village used scrolled chimneys and steeply pitched pediments as stylistic identifiers, while garden walls linked four of the five houses into a compound. Remarkably, these isolated, exaggerated concentrations of stylistic quotation, which might seem to threaten the suburb's coherence, have proved themselves essential to the identity of Coral Gables.

The plan also provided for schools, including a campus for the University of Miami with a monumental building designed by Phineas Paist and commissioned by Merrick. The collapse of the Florida real estate market put an end to Merrick's largesse, and the new building was not completed until 1950, when Paist's unfinished concrete-and-steel structure was adapted to accommodate a Modernist design by Robert M. Little (1902?–1999). The town also included the Coral Gables Inn (1924), and a hotel, the Miami-Biltmore, along with its thirty-six-hole golf course, which was opened in 1925.[134] Designed by the hotel architects Schultze & Weaver, the Biltmore dominated Coral Gables' prime residential neighborhoods from its strategic site between the waterfront and a golf course ringed with single-family houses—in its way a hybrid recalling the Regent's Development of villas-in-the-park and the terraces that defined its edges (see p. 23). Next door to it Merrick provided an indoor sports center known as the Coliseum.

The Coral Gables City Hall (Harold Steward and Phineas Paist, 1928) terminated the principal access street from Miami (Twenty-second Street), which Merrick redesigned as a grand boulevard, Coral Way, lined with rows of arcaded shops intended to stretch from the Douglas Gate. Coral Way was also home to the monumental Spanish Baroque Colonnade Building (1926), which may have been designed by Paul Chalfin and Walter DeGarmo, although Paist is the architect of record. Inside, a principal room crowned by a shallow oval dome provided the most impressive interior in the town.

In 1925, the state granted Coral Gables a charter of incorporation, but by that time the land boom was almost over, though the sound thinking behind the plan assured the lasting success of Merrick's dream community. While Merrick initially described Coral Gables as a suburb, by 1927 he and Denman Fink were calling it a "city-region . . . a place developed to the highest degree for people to live in, more or less as a city is. So when we combine the idea of 'region' which means country, and 'city,' which is where men live, we get a better thing by calling it a 'city-region.'"[135] Coral Gables was, as Vincent Scully has put it, "a contradiction in terms"—a city that is suburban and dependent on automobiles, although it was initially connected to Miami by streetcar. But Scully also points out that, despite Merrick's failure to build the boundary walls he initially proposed, Coral Gables "is a walled garden, a *paradeisos*, fortified against chaos" with a tight grid to "hold the edges of its fabric dense and steady to a certain depth, within which some of the freedoms of the Romantic Garden, the curving avenues, the golf courses, the canals, progressively open up and free the urban structure."[136]

While no other Florida resort suburb measures up to Coral Gables in terms of urbanism, others are well worth consideration, including **Hollywood**, developed by Joseph Wesley Young Jr. (1882–1934), from Long Beach, California, who relocated to Indianapolis, Indiana— Carl Fisher's home city—during World War I where he greatly prospered, before visiting South Florida in 1920 and purchasing a square mile of farmland ten miles north of Miami Beach with the idea of establishing a resort town.[137] The following year, working first with his company engineer George Schmidt and then with Indianapolis architects Preston C. Rubush (1867–1947) and Edgar O. Hunter (1873–1949), Young planned Hollywood, a gridded city bisected by a 100-foot-wide boulevard extending westward from the Intracoastal Waterway to the Everglades and, inspired by classical French garden planning and Daniel Burnham's 1909 proposal for the Chicago lakefront, penetrated by identical, precisely defined, keyhole-shaped lakes acting as turning basins for private yachts cruising the Intracoastal Waterway. The town was bisected by the north–south route of the Federal Highway, the East Coast's principal road, and by the main line of the Florida East Coast Railway, for which Young built a station in 1924. In some respects, the plan anticipated Mizner's at Boca Raton. Running east–west, a grand boulevard, named Hollywood Boulevard, was intersected by three 10-acre circles of land, one intended as parkland, another as the site of the city hall, and the third as the site of a military academy, before terminating in the west at Riverside, a radial-plan neighborhood where Young intended to maximize the value of his property with a hotel.

Young's strategy was precisely worked out:

Here will be a wide boulevard extending from the ocean westward to the edge of the Everglades. Here, one on each side of the boulevard and opening into Intracoastal canal, we'll create two lakes, each with a turning basin for yachts. The materials dredged from the lakes will be the fill to elevate the lowland occupied by mangrove swamps. Here, centrally located on the plan, will be the business section. We must plan large park areas and locations for schools and churches. A golf course would be both convenient and beautiful, just here, and there must be a large clubhouse or community building. This will be a city for everyone—from the opulent at the top of the industrial and society ladders to the most humble of working people.[138]

Young adopted an early form of zoning, arranging Hollywood into various districts, including a centrally located business district. Central Hollywood was begun in 1921, with the first building, significantly a company garage, completed in 1922, designed by Rubush & Hunter, as was the Hollywood (later Park View) Hotel and the Hollywood Beach Hotel, both of which soon followed, and designs for twenty-four different houses for prospective buyers to choose from. All buildings were to be in the Spanish style, but the interpretation of that style tended to that of the California Mission variety, which the developer knew from his time in San Diego. A nine-hole golf course was soon to come as sand dunes were leveled to make way for choice ocean-facing houses—an environmentally disastrous decision that would make the town vulnerable to flooding.

In 1923, faced with the reality of Florida's segregation laws, Young purchased more land, on high ground, to develop Liberia, a new town for African-Americans, consisting of forty square blocks around a circular park. Young regarded Coral Gables as his principal competition. In 1923, he hired Martin Hampton, architect of the Country Club of Coral Gables as well as various projects for Carl Fisher, developer of Miami Beach, to design the Hollywood Golf and Country Club. Hampton would also design a number of other buildings for the town.

Opa-locka (1925), located midway between Miami and Fort Lauderdale, was developed by Glenn Curtiss (1878–1930), the pioneering aviator, as a resort suburb, the design of which more than that of any other bordered on fantasy.[139] According to Catherine Lynn, whose essay "Dream and Substance: Araby and the Planning of Opa-locka" was the first serious study of the town, Opa-locka followed on Curtiss's two previous efforts to develop Miami suburbs that had both proved disappointments: **Hialeah** (1921) and Country Club Estates (1924). Hialeah, developed with James H. Bright (1866–1959), sprawled out of control amid the Florida boom and is best known for its racetrack (1925); Country Club

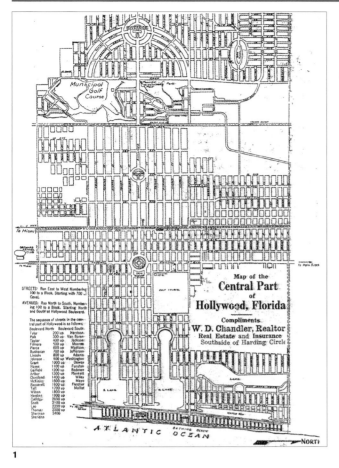

1. Plan, George Schmidt and Rubush & Hunter, 1921. HOLL (c. 1930s)

2. Hollywood Hotel, Rubush & Hunter, 1923. Fishbaugh. SAF

3. Jackson Street. HOLL (1924)

4. Aerial view. Elliott. HOLL (1924)

5. Aerial view. HOLL (c. 1950s)

Hialeah

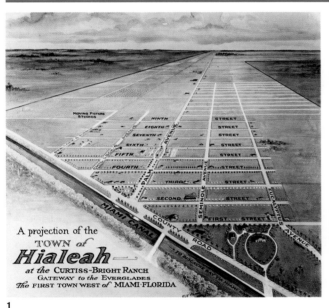

Estates, renamed **Miami Springs** in 1930, was also undertaken with Bright.[140] Miami Springs had much stronger development controls and an architectural theme, the Spanish Pueblo, but failed to establish its own distinct identity in the marketplace. The high points of Miami Springs were Curtiss's own house, a house he built for his mother, and the Pueblo Hotel (1926), converted three years later into the Miami Battle Creek Sanitarium by cereal inventor and physician John Harvey Kellogg. In

1925, Curtiss undertook Opa-locka, the name being a shortened version of the Seminole name for the area. All three developments were realized on portions of the 125,000 acres known as the Curtiss-Bright ranch.

The seemingly whimsical and certainly fantastical decision to adopt an *Arabian Nights* theme for Opa-locka is alternately attributed to the developer, to one of the town's first home buyers, and to the New York architect Curtiss hired in 1925, Bernhardt E. Muller (1878–1964),

1. Advertisement. SAF (1922)

2. Real estate office, right; welcome sign, Seminole Indian Jack Tigertail, left. SAF (1922)

3. County Road and Palm Avenue. Fishbaugh. SAF (1921)

4. Eucalyptus Avenue. Fishbaugh. SAF (1924)

5. Tour buses with prospective home buyers. Fishbaugh. SAF (1921)

Miami Springs

1. Bridge over Miami Canal connecting Hialeah and Miami Springs. Fishbaugh. SAF (1926)

2. Entry gates, Glenn Curtiss house, Martin L. Hampton, 1926. Fishbaugh. SAF (1926)

3. Pueblo Hotel, 1926. SAF

4. Entry gates, Glenn Curtiss house. Ebyabe. WC (2011)

5. Lua Curtiss house, Martin L. Hampton, c. 1926. Ebyabe. WC (2011)

1

2

3

4

5

Opa-locka

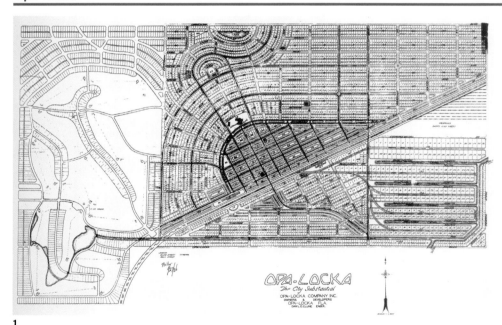

1

2

3

1. Plan, Clinton Mackenzie, c. 1926. UML

2. Early rendering for Administration Building, Bernhardt E. Muller, 1925. UML

3. Administration Building, Bernhardt E. Muller, 1926. SAF

4. Administration Building. Ebyabe. WC (2010)

5. Hurt Building, Bernhardt E. Muller, 1926. Ebyabe. WC (2010)

6. House, Sharar Avenue. Ebyabe. WC (2010)

4

5

6

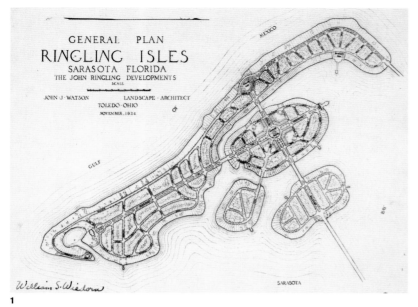

1

2

3

who according to his account, proposed to "lay the city out on the basis of the stories [from the *Arabian Nights*], using a story for each of the most important buildings, naming the streets accordingly."[141] Given the evidence of Muller's previous late-medieval, Cotswold-inspired work, typically in the New York suburbs, and in spite of Muller's explanation of how he gave expression to the theme, the *Arabian Nights* idea seems likely not to have been his.[142] A more plausible story has it that Muller proposed a medieval English village, with a castle at its center to serve as the city hall and streets lined with thatched-roof and half-timber houses, but that Curtiss had second thoughts and sent him a copy of the book *One Thousand and One Tales From the Arabian Nights*.

Opa-locka was planned by Clinton Mackenzie, also a New Yorker, who had considerable previous experience in garden suburb planning and architecture, including at Amatol, New Jersey (see p. 890), which he planned for the United States Ordnance Department, as well as his collaboration with John Nolen at Kingsport, Tennessee (see p. 264). Mackenzie's plan placed a grid of streets at right angles to the tracks of the Seaboard Air Line Railway that slashed diagonally through the site. Farther out, to the northwest, a radial plan was employed, while near the golf course that was to provide the town's largest open space, Mackenzie adopted a curving pattern of streets.

Like Merrick at Coral Gables, which was clearly a precedent for this project, Curtiss saw that a binding architectural theme was crucial to establishing an identity for his new town and, as Lynn points out, the eroticism of the *Arabian Nights* theme, which was enjoying great popularity via the movies, was deemed a marketing advantage. In an ad for the new town, the copy ran: "Of course you have seen Douglas Fairbanks' 'Thief of Baghdad,' with its wealth of Oriental picturesqueness reminding one indeed, of the famous illustrations to the Arabian Nights."[143] Curtiss's city had

a hotel, zoo park, golf course, archery club, swimming pool, airport, and a train station. All in all, eighty-six themed buildings were realized by Muller, including the administration building, now City Hall.

Florida's Gulf Coast developed more slowly than that of its Atlantic Coast. In 1924 John Ringling (1866–1936), co-owner of the Ringling Brothers and Barnum & Bailey Circus, announced ambitious plans for **Ringling Isles**, a resort development consisting of hotels, casinos, bathing pavilions, and fine residences to be located on St. Armands, Bird, Coon, Otter, and Lido Keys, uninhabited barrier islands off the coast of Sarasota, as well as on 2,000 acres at the southern tip of Longboat Key.[144] Ringling, who had been wintering in Sarasota since 1912, teamed with local developer Owen Burns (1869–1937) for the project, together building a 1.35-mile-long, 26-foot-wide causeway connecting the mainland with St. Armands Key, hitherto accessible only by boat. Intended for the most luxurious houses, St. Armands Key was the centerpiece of the plan, designed by Ohio landscape architect John J. Watson (1876–1950), who divided the oval-shaped island with two landscaped boulevards meeting at a circular park.

Although Ringling was able to boost the local economy by making Sarasota the winter home of his circus, progress at Ringling Isles was limited to the laying out of St. Armands Key and the building of a bathhouse on Lido Key. The collapse in Florida real estate values and subsequent Depression doomed the project. In the early 1930s the causeway was closed because of rotting timber planks and St. Armands Key became something of a wasteland, with overgrown grass and deteriorating Italian and Spanish pink and white marble statuary that Ringling had purchased to surround the central circular park. Development at Ringling Isles did not resume in earnest until the early 1950s.

John Nolen maintained an active practice in Florida throughout the 1920s boom, setting up a satellite office

1. Plan, John J. Watson, 1924. SAA

2. Aerial view. SAF (1971)

3. St. Armands Circle. RAMSA (2012)

1. Preliminary study, John Nolen, 1925. COR

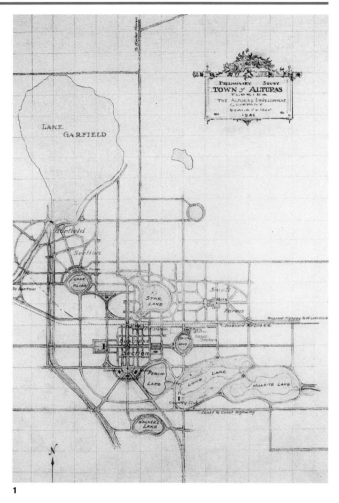

1

Belleair

1. Plan, John Nolen, 1924. COR

2. Bird's-eye view. COR

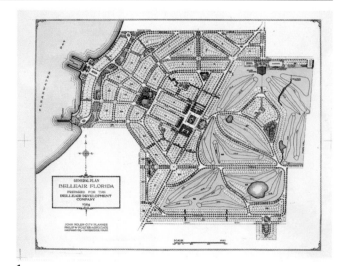

1

2

in Jacksonville. His most important Florida projects were the garden cities of Venice and Clewiston. He also produced preliminary plans for three subdivisions that were not completed, **Alturas** (1925), Tamiami City (1925), and Canal Point (1929).[145] In addition he prepared plans for West Palm Beach (1922), Sarasota (1925), Clearwater (1925), and St. Petersburg (1925).[146] Nolen, working with associate Philip W. Foster, also prepared a plan for the town of **Belleair** (1924) for Dean Alvord, developer of Prospect Park South in Brooklyn (see p. 107).[147] Belleair was to take advantage of the land between the Belleview Hotel (Michael J. Miller and Francis J. Kennard, 1897) and the coast, where Nolen proposed a yacht basin and club, pier, and pavilion facing Clearwater Bay. The loose grid of the street plan, interspersed with a number of small parks and a small commercial center, had a meandering linear park separating the development along the bluff from that along the coast, where the choicest residential sites were to be found. Although Nolen's basic street plan was carried out, the collapse of the Florida real estate market prevented any significant progress and substantial development did not begin in Belleair until after World War II. In addition to his plan for St. Petersburg, Nolen also designed **Maximo Estates** (1925), an unrealized subdivision of that city which Thomas E. Low described as "a prime example of a well-laid-out town with all the attributes of the neighborhood unit, incorporating physical forms of the waterfront and bay," with the waterfront property largely retained for public use.[148]

Although intended for year-round commuters, **San Jose**, a 1,000-acre development four-and-a-half miles from downtown Jacksonville, rounds out the story of Nolen's work in Florida. In 1925 planning was initiated by Nolen under the leadership of a local businessman, Charles W. Strickland, whose vision included two hotels, a golf course and country club, a 100-foot-wide esplanade along the St. Johns River, a yacht club, parks, a swimming pool, and a shopping center.[149] San Jose was focused on waterfront sports and a golf course designed by Donald Ross. The Jacksonville-based architectural firm of William Mulford Marsh (1889–1946) and Harold Frederick Saxelbye (1885–1964) was retained to design several of the important buildings as well as many of its houses. The suburb was entered at two points, guarded by gate towers designed by Marsh & Saxelbye, proclaiming, as the *Times-Union* put it in 1925, "in symbolic fashion the wonders within."[150] The San Jose Hotel opened in 1926. Quickly falling victim to the faltering Florida real estate market, the hotel was eventually incorporated into the campus of the Bolles School, a military academy. By 1926, only thirty-one houses were undertaken, many only partially finished. In addition, a few nonresidential buildings were completed, including Marsh & Saxelbye's Administration Building (1925), the San Jose Country Club (1925), designed by the firm of Victor Earl Mark (1876–1948) and Leeroy Sheftall (1887–1963), a shopping center, and a gas station, the latter a vivid reminder that the new suburb was completely dependent on the automobile.

Maximo Estates

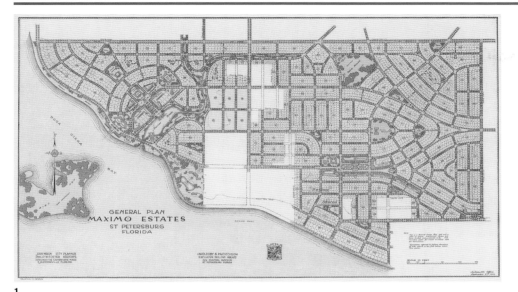

1. Plan, John Nolen, 1925. COR

San Jose

1

2

3

4

7

6

8

1. Plan, John Nolen, 1925. COR

2. Aerial view. GE (2010)

3. Typical houses, c. 1925. COR

4. Shopping center, c. 1925. COR

5. Entry gate, Marsh & Saxelbye, 1925. Ebyabe. WC (2011)

6. Administration Building (Episcopal church since 1941), Marsh & Saxelbye, 1925. Ebyabe. WC (2011)

7. House, 3703 Via de la Reina, Marsh & Saxelbye, 1925. Ebyabe. WC (2011)

8. House, 3609 Via de la Reina, Marsh & Saxelbye, 1925. Ebyabe. WC (2011)

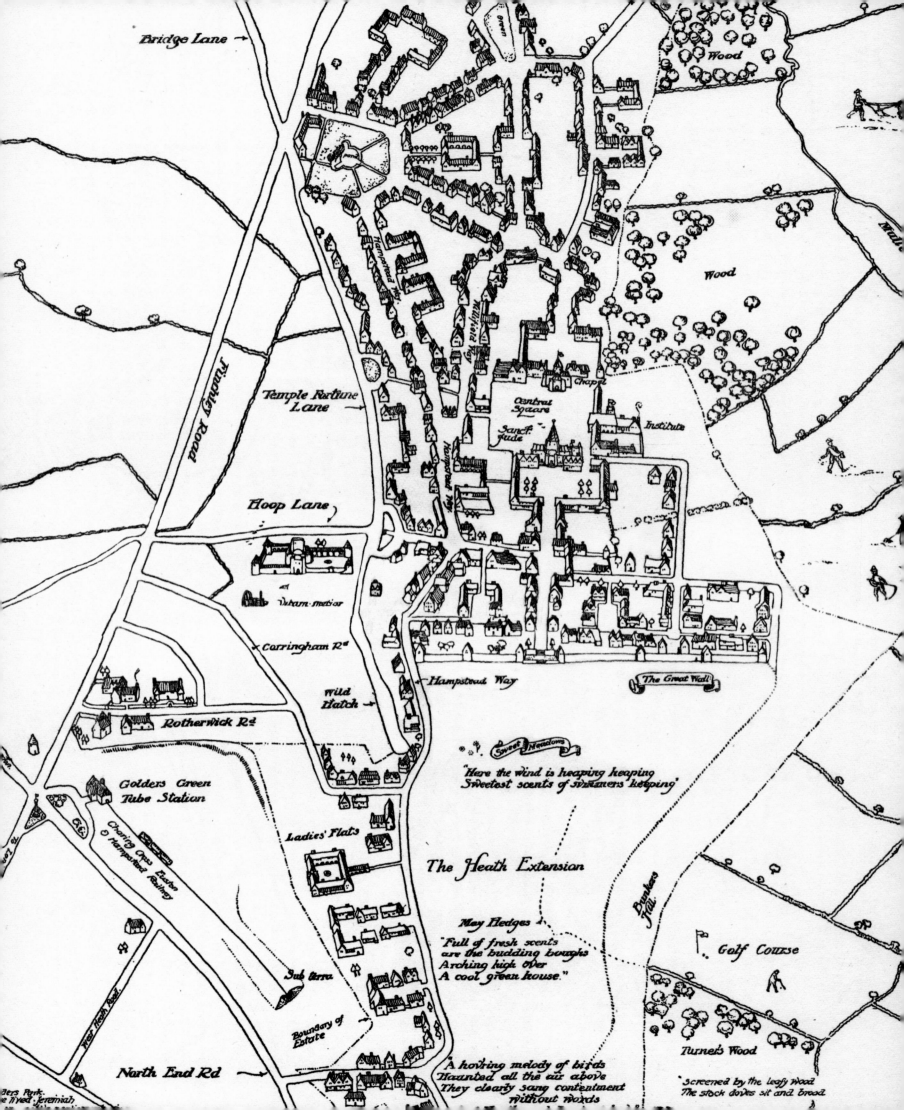

Bridge Lane →

Wood

Wood

Finchley Road

Hampstead Way

Temple Fortune Lane

Chapel

Central Square

Sanct. Jude

Institute

Hoop Lane

Wolcam station

Carringham Rd

Wild Hatch →

Hampstead Way

The Great Wall

Rotherwick Rd

Sweet Meadows

"Here the wind is heaping heaping
Sweetest scents of summers keeping"

Golders Green
Tube Station

Ladies' Flats

The Heath Extension

Charing Cross Euston
Hampstead Railway

May Hedges

"Full of fresh scents
are the budding boughs
Arching high over
A cool green house."

Bunkers Hill

Golf Course

Sub terra

Boundary of
Estate

Turner's Wood

North End Rd →

"A hov'ring melody of birds
Haunted all the air above
They clearly sang contentment
without words"

"Screened by the leafy Wood
The stock doves sit and brood"

CHAPTER FIVE

The Garden Suburb in England, Wales, Scotland, and Ireland 1900–1940

While it is difficult to accept the claim of the noted planner and planning historian Sir Peter Hall that **Brentham** (1901–15), at the northern edge of Ealing, and not Bedford Park (see p. 37), was England's first garden suburb, it is clear that it is one of the earliest of the great outpourings of the type that occurred after 1900.[1] Undertaken by London's first copartnership of building workers, construction of Brentham began on a 32-acre property in 1901–2. At first, nine conventional terrace houses were built. But in 1906, after 28 additional acres were acquired, the Ealing Tenants Limited, encouraged by Henry Vivian (1868–1930), a Liberal MP, invited Barry Parker and Raymond Unwin to develop a more ambitious plan. With New Earswick (see p. 228) and Letchworth (see p. 230) behind them, and having recently begun work at Hampstead (see p. 350), Parker and Unwin produced a plan with a central cooperative Institute from which a radial arrangement of streets formed superblocks with allotment gardens at their cores. The Brent River's floodplain provided a major recreational area behind the Institute. Roads lined with four- and six-unit group houses were fitted to the gently sloping land. A key to the plan was the limited number of access points, ensuring that Brentham would maintain its distinct identity as surrounding areas developed. Brentham Way, the main avenue running straight through the suburb, was originally planned by Unwin to include public buildings and shops at the T-shaped intersections that fall near its midpoint. By 1908, however, with competition from commercial developments just outside the estate, shops were excluded from the plan, diminishing the street's importance and compromising Brentham's integrity as a holistic community.

By 1913 Brentham contained 510 houses with a population of about 2,000, and by World War I 620 houses had been completed in the suburb, with a variety of winding roads, culs-de-sac, staggered frontages, angled street intersections, and vernacular-based houses, devices which became the standard repertoire of garden suburb design.[2] Parker and Unwin designed a few of Brentham's houses, including 1-7 Winscombe Crescent (1908) and 2 Brentham Way (1909). But most of the houses were the work of Frederic Cavendish Pearson (1882–1963), who built there from 1907 to 1911, and George Lister Sutcliffe (1864–1915), who replaced him as architect in 1911 and continued in that position until his death four years later. Only twenty-four years old when he began to work at Brentham, Pearson was completely in tune with the planning strategy, so that his houses, with their sweeping roofs, tapered buttresses, and oriel windows beautifully combine to create the "street pictures" Unwin desired. Sometimes, however, the pressures of the site and the desire to create memorable street pictures got the better of the young architect, as in butterfly-shaped blocks in Brunswick and Ludlow Roads where the plans suffered, resulting in overly complex layouts that included diamond-shaped living rooms. Sutcliffe's houses were more restrained, but he seemed to grasp Unwin's planning

Hampstead Garden Suburb, plan drawn by Charles Paget Wade, 1909. TPMA

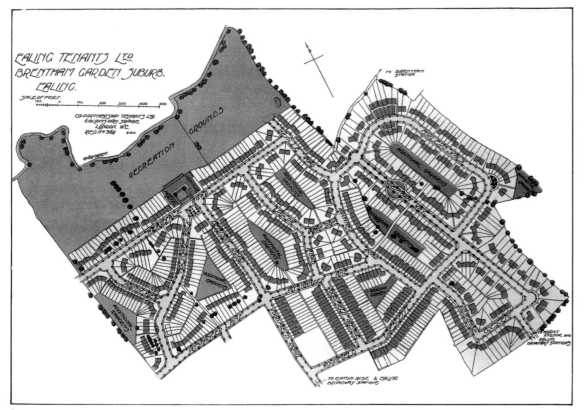

1. Plan, Barry Parker and Raymond Unwin, Architects, 1906. BSA (1911)

2. First houses, c. 1902. BSA

3. 2 Brentham Way, right, Barry Parker and Raymond Unwin, Architects, 1909, and 4–6 Brentham Way, G. L. Sutcliffe, 1911. BSA (1911)

4. Holyoake Walk and Meadvale Road. BSA (c. 1913)

5. Ludlow Road. BSA (1910)

6. Institute, G. L. Sutcliffe, 1911. BSA (1911)

intentions even better than his predecessor, mastering the staggered placement of houses to produce picturesque vistas, frequently combining group houses with setbacks and projections to vary the streetscape along longer roads, and on shorter, winding roads, to preserve landscape features. Hedge-lined footpaths led to allotment gardens, providing additional circulation routes through the entire village. Sutcliffe's Holyoake House (1912), Holyoake Walk, contained twenty-four small flats for single and elderly people. He was also responsible for the Institute (1911), Meadvale Road, which the Pevsner guide describes as a "bold, rather Germanic-looking red brick corner tower with pyramid roof."[3] Brentham's most prominent building, the Institute resembles the Club House on Willifield Green at Hampstead Garden Suburb, a building destroyed by German bombing in 1940.

Paralleling the development of Brentham, the **Webb Estate** (1901–20) (originally the Garden First Estate), between Croydon and Purley, was not part of the social reform tradition of Howard, Parker, and Unwin, but instead a late English example of the paternalistic land developer tradition that can be said to have culminated in Bedford Park.[4] Far more gardenesque than Bedford Park, the Webb Estate is an upmarket 260-acre neighborhood of about 230 houses set along elaborately landscaped roads. The development's plan and some of the house designs are attributed to William Webb (1862–1930), a businessman and horticulturalist in nearby Deal, who labeled his approach the "Garden First" system: "The name Garden First means that the garden shall . . . be carried out before any buildings are erected . . . the house is but the complement of the garden in a general survey of the estate."[5] Webb also built a model village, Upper Woodcote Village, for those working on the property, where, facing a green, he located the Lord Roberts Teetotal Pub and Village Store and a village blacksmith.

The garden suburb achieved its English apogee with **Hampstead Garden Suburb** (1907), demonstrating, as Walter L. Creese has written, "that the suburb was a legitimate invention of the age . . . only wanting the master touch to give it true form."[6] Not to be confused with

7

8

9

10

11

7. Brentham Way. RAMSA (2009)

8. Butterfly-plan house on corner of Brunswick and Neville Roads. RAMSA (2009)

9. Holyoake House, G. L. Sutcliffe, 1912. RAMSA (2009)

10. Typical street. RAMSA (2009)

11. Footpath, Meadvale Road. RAMSA (2009)

the historic village of Hampstead, about two miles away, Hampstead Garden Suburb is a wholly new development that commands our respect as planning and as architecture and to a considerable extent as enlightened social engineering: it is a glorious composition of buildings, streets, and landscape and a crucial landmark in the history of modern urbanism.

Hampstead Garden Suburb was developed as the result of the initiative of Henrietta Barnett (1851–1936), working with her husband, Rev. Samuel Augustus Barnett (1844–1913), whose parish lay in London's East End, the city's most overcrowded slum district. To escape the pressures of their work, the Barnetts owned a weekend cottage on the fringes of Hampstead Heath, in what was still relatively open country though surprisingly close to the city. When the Barnetts learned in 1896 that the American investor Charles T. Yerkes proposed to build the first true—that is completely tunneled—underground north from Charing Cross with a station at Golders Green Crossroads, and that Wyldes Farm, a 323-acre property owned by Eton College, was being put in play as a development site, they became concerned for the fate of their bucolic neighborhood. Mrs. Barnett immediately launched a campaign to preserve 80 acres of the college property for use as open space extending Hampstead Heath and then dedicated herself to the development of Hampstead Garden Suburb.

Barnett's intention was to create on the remaining 243 acres of the Wyldes Farm "A Garden Suburb for the Working Classes," as she stated in a 1903 letter published in the *Hampstead and Highgate Express*. In the letter she was quite specific on one key point of social and physical planning: "The conditions of building are those which ensure the establishment of not a 'Garden City' but a 'Garden Suburb,' in which every house, however humble, will be productive as well as pleasurable. The plan however, will necessitate the provision of some shops, and some houses of a larger size and more extensive gardens."[7]

Mrs. Barnett had a clear and remarkably holistic vision for the Garden Suburb: "We wish, in the first place, to have pretty and wholesome dwellings with gardens and open spaces at hand where working men and clerks may live who are engaged in London . . . We wish, in the next place, to have an orderly and well designed plan of the Estate, so that each house may be placed with a regard to every other house . . . We wish to make the life of the Hampstead Suburb a life in which men shall have understanding of each other, in which the poor shall teach the rich, and in which the rich shall, let us hope, in some ways, teach the poor, and minister to them."[8] The new tube railway opened on June 22, 1907, approximately seven weeks after ground was broken for Hampstead Garden Suburb on May 2, at which time Parker and Unwin had already been working on the development for almost three years. The garden suburb was developed by the Hampstead Garden Suburb Trust, a newly formed limited-profit company chaired by Alfred Lyttleton (1857–1913).

Hampstead Garden Suburb, at once a work of aesthetic synthesis and of typological innovation, was consciously conceived with the examples of both

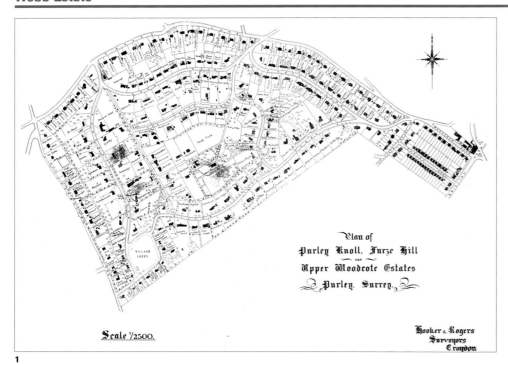

1. Plan, William Webb. c. 1901. WEL (1934)

2. Furze Lane. CLSLA (c. 1910)

3. Upper Woodcote Village. CLSLA (c. 1908)

4. Typical street. Kereshun. AK (2011)

5. Lord Roberts Teetotal Pub and Village Store. EMunro. FL (2008)

Bedford Park and Letchworth in mind. The planning of its residential neighborhoods, the work of Parker and Unwin, like those at Letchworth, evokes traditional English and Northern European villages and, as at Letchworth, the principal Central Square reflects the legacy of Wren. Hampstead Garden Suburb's formal antecedents also include American influences, reflecting small town and suburban American townscapes where no walls front streets or separate properties. While Letchworth's Central Square was linked to the business district, at Hampstead Garden Suburb, the Central Square, the work of Edwin Lutyens, is not located near the business district, which lay largely outside the suburb on Finchley Road. In this, the Central Square reflects the thinking of the American City Beautiful movement, which called for the development of civic centers apart from commercial districts. More American Beaux-Arts than English village, Central Square is a place apart, intentionally off the beaten track. As a result, like many American civic centers of the 1890s and early 1900s, it is grand but virtually lifeless.

While Hampstead's contemporary German counterpart, Margaretenhöhe (see p. 749), is underscaled, Hampstead Garden Suburb is bold, with a robust vocab-ulary of spatial and architectural elements. Despite the narrow streets arranged to sort out traffic, to minimize hazards for pedestrians, and to work in combination with the topography and the architecture to establish the street pictures Parker and Unwin deemed essential to good town planning, Hampstead Garden Suburb is in no way twee. Mindful of the devastation that increasing through traffic was already wreaking upon historic English towns, Unwin made no provision for on-site car parking, and planned Hampstead's road network to resist through traffic: "The idea that a town consists of streets is very much to be avoided. Streets are not a virtue in themselves. In fact, the less area given over to streets, the more chance one has of planning a nice town. To be obsessed with the idea of planning for traffic is a mistake. One rather plans to avoid all needless traffic as far as possible."[9] The village plan, as Walter Creese has written, is subtly hierarchical: "The proportions of circulation at Hampstead dwindle and descend from roads and streets to the lane and way, then to the pedestrian close and walk, and finally to mere paths. At the same time, the road was not permitted to pick up spatial momentum. Unwin set about recapturing the medieval implication of mystery, safety and enclosure within the

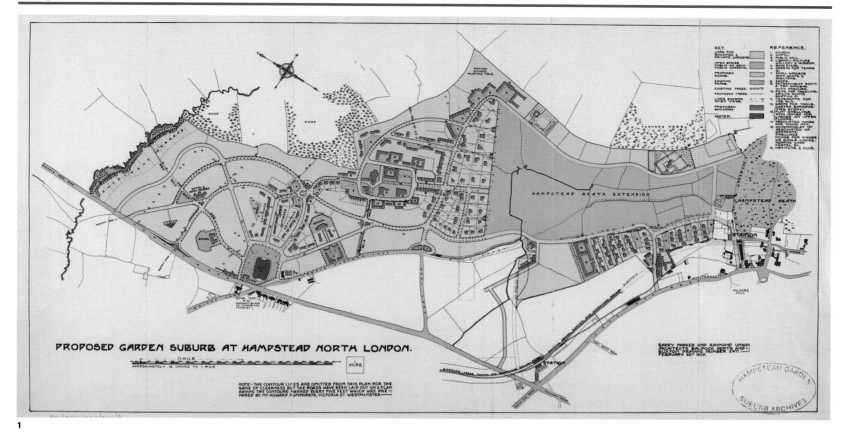

1

1. Plan, Barry Parker and Raymond Unwin, Architects, 1905. LMA

settlement."[10] Unwin's plan was, as Danish architect-urbanist Steen Eiler Rasmussen put it, "like a tree with branches, an organic pattern channelling traffic down to the smallest leaves of the plant."[11]

Unwin's use of cul-de-sac roads was in its way a throwback to medieval practice that had been legislated out of existence by industrial-era reformers wishing to rid cities like London of the inner courts and hidden yards of tenement developments. To be able to introduce culs-de-sac, as well as such other design features as mandated 60-foot-wide separation of buildings facing each other across streets and mandated 10-foot front yard setbacks, the development required an act of Parliament, "The Hampstead Garden Suburb Act" (1906), to overcome well-intentioned but fundamentally antipicturesque bye-laws.

At Hampstead a number of new housing types were introduced, or at least adapted, to the suburban situation. Most notable is the quadrangle, the collective planning of which recalls collegiate precedent, but had been recently adapted by Lutyens in his Surrey houses. In fact, one of the earliest and loveliest of Hampstead's quadrangles, called "The Orchard," designed by Parker and Unwin in 1909, bears considerable similarity to Lutyens's house (1897) of the same name.

Hampstead's development density was very low, with eight houses per acre. But, as Geoffrey Lee pointed out in 1974, at this density the entire population of England could be housed within a thirty-five-mile radius of Charing Cross railroad station. One exception to the eight-per-acre rule was in the Artisans' Quarter, where

it was increased to ten per acre to meet Mrs. Barnett's request for a neighborhood for the industrial classes. The Artisans' Quarter was developed on 70 acres to form what was, as Mervyn Miller has written, "probably Unwin's masterpiece of site layout and housing design," benefiting from "the collaboration of a number of his best assistants, among them Charles Paget Wade, Samuel Pointon Taylor [1884–1958], and Frank Bromhead [1881–1972]." Miller describes the Artisans' Quarter as a neighborhood with

> groupings, particularly in Asmuns Place . . . arranged to encourage neighborliness. At its head, this cul-de-sac featured a bowling green and two small children's play areas, complete with playhouses. In the backland there were allotments, while along the frontages of the roads, the building lines were used to create sub-groupings and avoid the visual monotony of the corridor street, which was anathema to Unwin. A primary school lay on the northern fringe of the area and also served a second phase of Hampstead Tenants housing construction further north to Addison Way. The Club House [Parker and Unwin, 1909] lay at a strategic position where the Artisans' Quarter met middle-class development: it was intended to foster the breaking down of class barriers. Circulation through the area was assisted by footpaths independent of the street network, a particular feature of the second phase of development along Addison Way and Hogarth Hill.[12]

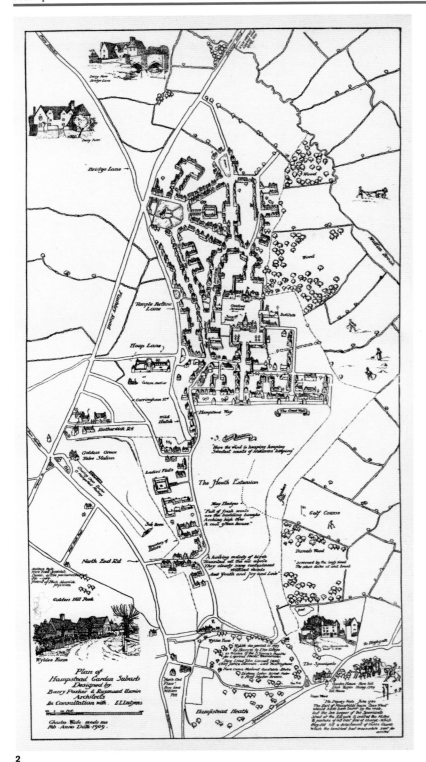

2

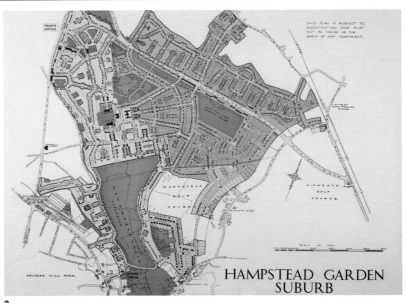

3

4

5

2. Plan drawn by Charles Paget
Wade, 1909. TPMA

3. Plan. LMA (1937)

4. Asmuns Place. LMA

5. View across Willifield Green to
the Club House. HGS (c.1938)

6. Artisans' Flats, Addison Way.
HGS (c. 1938)

6

7

8

10

9

7. Waterlow Court, M. H. Baillie
Scott, 1911. RAMSA (2007)

8, 9. Rendering and photograph of
the Great Wall. TPMA

10. Temple Fortune House and
Arcade, A. J. Penty, 1909. RIBAP
(1979)

To subsidize the Artisans' Quarter neighborhood, Barnett's intention was to lease large properties—one-, two-, and three-acre lots—facing the Heath Extension. Mrs. Barnett, as Creese put it, "wanted the whole rainbow of existence plainly visible."[13] She also planned for the specific needs of the elderly, single working women, and the blind. Parker and Unwin's The Orchard catered to the elderly with a low second story to ease stair climbs; Waterlow Court (1911) designed for working women by M. H. Baillie Scott, was much grander, a celebration of female emancipation comparable to a collegiate quadrangle; the quad for the blind was never realized.

Hampstead Garden Suburb abounded in memorable features. Along the extensive boundary with the Hampstead Heath Extension, every effort was made to avoid "that irregular fringe of half-developed suburb and half-spoilt country which forms such a hideous and depressing girdle around modern growing towns," resulting in the 787-foot-long, brown-brick so-called Great Wall built to define the north end of the Heath Extension and provide a uniform view from the suburb across the parkland.[14] Punctuated by occasional viewing platforms, the Great Wall was interrupted at its midpoint to form a spacious plaza at the end of Meadway. Unwin had observed that "in the old towns which we admire . . . we notice that the country comes up clean and fresh right to the point where the town proper begins . . . In

the oldest cities we sometimes find a wall within the country coming up right to the gates, which adds to the effect."[15]

The Great Wall was Hampstead Garden Suburb's most distinct boundary marker. Another, the dramatically massed Temple Fortune House and Arcade House, containing shops and flats, was designed by A. J. Penty (1875–1937) to face Finchley Road at one of the few points where the garden suburb directly confronted the expanding city. Because no such other strong gateway markers were realized, the differences between the ordered suburb and the chaos of uncontrolled development around it was not as vividly articulated as it might have been. One proposal for a gateway development that went unrealized was Wellgarth gate, a split crescent of four highly abstract flat-roofed houses designed by Edgar Wood (1860–1935) that would have marked the approach to the Heath at the garden suburb's south corner near Golders Green.

Unwin, smarting over the seeming misstep of the Cheap Cottages Exhibition at Letchworth, insisted on high-quality construction and the virtual suppression of compositional individuality. Eave lines and roof pitches were kept virtually uniform. Colors were muted, and houses were grouped in pairs, or fours, or even longer rows, along streets and notably around open courtyards or greens. Particular attention was paid to the arrangement of buildings at street intersections, so that positive

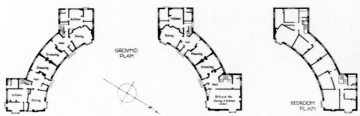

11

12

11. Wellgarth gate, Edgar Wood, 1909. TPMA

12. Baillie Scott corner, Meadway and Hampstead Way. TPMA (1909)

13. Quadrangle, Hampstead Way. RAMSA

14. Temple Fortune Lane. RAMSA (2003)

15. House on Hampstead Way facing the Heath Extension. RAMSA (2007)

16. Houses on Hampstead Way, Barry Parker and Raymond Unwin, Architects, c. 1908. RAMSA (2003)

13

14

15

16

spaces were established throughout the suburb's plan. Streets were never overly long and were very often terminated by the gable of a house set on axis. Midblock culs-de-sac grouped houses around greenswards large enough for the lawn-tennis courts that were provided. Everywhere, the idea of the street picture was adhered to, perhaps most dramatically at the so-called Baillie Scott corner, southeast of Meadway and Hampstead Way, one of the most memorable bits in the suburb and a fairly explicit representation of Camillo Sitte's influence on the garden suburb plan.[16]

Top architectural talent helped flesh out Unwin's plan, providing a varied streetscape despite the imposition of design controls. Unwin appreciated the need to

have first-class architecture: "The Town Planner may lay out . . . the main thoroughfares and *places* of the town. The site planner may follow with the best designs for arranging the plots, the building lines and the positions of the buildings, but the aim of both is almost sure to be frustrated by . . . those who follow. The design may be good, but for the want of any co-ordination the result will be little more than an unharmonious jumble." As Unwin continued, describing his goals for the suburb: "It is hoped that the general introduction of town planning . . . [will] turn the attention of architects to the consideration of the total effect of streets and districts, will encourage them to regard the individual building . . . as a unit in a larger picture . . . In this way there may grow

17. Bigwood Road. RAMSA (2003)

18. Multiple Houses for Plot 400,
M. H. Baillie Scott, 1908. BA08

19. Plan, Rossall Beach Estate,
Edwin Lutyens, 1901. ASGB

20. Aerial view of Central Square.
HGS (c. 1938)

21. Heath Gate toward Central
Square. HGS (c. 1938)

17

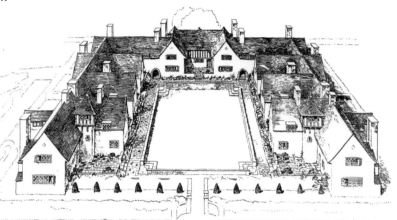

18

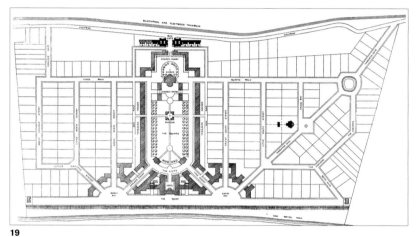

19

20

21

up among architects the habit of co-operation, the habit of regarding the setting of their buildings more than has been customary in recent years."[17]

Unwin remained Architect to the Garden Suburb until 1914, when he was replaced by John C. S. Soutar (1881–1957). In addition to his own architectural contributions in partnership with Barry Parker, and those of Lutyens and M. H. Baillie Scott, other notable architects, such as E. Guy Dawber (1861–1938), W. Curtis Green (1875–1960), and C. Harrison Townsend (1851–1928), built at Hampstead Garden Suburb. Sadly, Baillie Scott's most inventive proposal—perhaps the most inventive of his entire career—was not realized. This was the Multiple Houses for Plot 400, a quadrangle

covering a full acre that J. D. Kornwolf claimed "would have been a veritable museum of the Arts and Crafts achievement in architecture."[18]

The decisive contribution of Edwin Lutyens to the plan was the transformation of Parker and Unwin's loose, agglomerative concept of the Central Square into a temenos-like place of precise geometry. Lutyens, who had designed Grey Walls (1900) in Scotland for Alfred Lyttleton, was probably introduced to the project by his former client. The vastness of the Central Square is tempered by Lutyens's pictorial invention, the two churches, the Institute, and the surrounding precinct of houses, only a few of which the architect designed, although his intentions were more or less honored by others who completed this

22

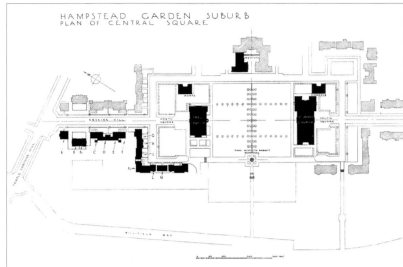

23

24

25

22. St. Jude's Church showing
The Free Church, left, and Vicarage,
right, all by Edwin Lutyens. LW

23. Plan, Central Square, Edwin
Lutyens, 1908. ASGB

24. Institute. RAMSA (2003)

25. Aerial view. EHC (2009)

aspect of the project. Taken together, the houses and the Institute introduce a welcome formality. While the concept reflects American civic centers, the architecture grows out of Lutyens's respect for the achievements of Christopher Wren and, Christopher Hussey suggests, the drawings of Georgian houses made by Randolph Caldecott (1846–1886) for various children's books.[19] Although almost exclusively known for country house design, Lutyens had at least one previous experience in town design: an unrealized proposal (1901) for the Rossall Beach Estate, Lancashire, an 88-acre development to have been situated between a tramway line and 875 yards of seaside frontage. According to Hussey, that project was intended for holiday homes for Manchester residents and even some permanent houses on an eighth- to a quarter-acre lots. A. S. G. Butler has noted that the Rossall Beach development, sometimes called Cleveleys, was to have "all the amenities of a small town, with communal gardens, a church, a club and—later on—a hotel."[20] Its church in the center, its flanking terrace houses, and its geometrically intricate beachside developments flanking the hotel set the stage for Lutyens's work at Hampstead.

Mervyn Miller documents the evolution of the Central Square from Parker and Unwin's initial sketch to Lutyens's revised and executed version with its Institute,

on one edge, and two churches in the center of the greensward, closing the vistas up Erskine Hill and Highgate Road. Lutyens's redbrick William and Mary–style terrace houses, originally intended to connect with the churches, were complexly planned to help define the square and form inner courtyards of their own. Unfortunately, Henrietta Barnett and Lutyens regularly clashed. Although he admired Mrs. Barnett as a social idealist, Lutyens did not think she had much appreciation for town or building design. He described her in a letter to the architect Herbert Baker (1862–1946) as "a nice woman but proud of being a philistine—has no idea much beyond a window box full of geraniums, calceolarias and lobelias, over which you can see a goose on a green."[21] Dame Barnett engineered Lutyens's dismissal from the project, so that the houses around the Central Square were not completed according to design and the Institute is only partially his work, although the two churches are among his masterpieces.

Nothing could be more distinct than the contrast between Parker and Unwin's neighborhoods and the Central Square. Robert Kornfeld Jr. noted:

An aerial photograph of Hampstead Garden Suburb dramatizes the contrast . . . The symmetrical

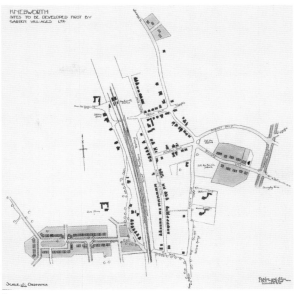

figure of Central Square with its appended fan of residential streets stands out as an object embedded in the relaxed fabric of Unwin's streets. Lutyens's open, figural space for the civic and religious buildings is well set off surrounded as it is by a luxurious, leafy matrix. Central Square, despite being the civic, cultural and religious center, remains serene because it is not crossed by major circulation axes and is not connected to a commercial center. This characteristic is intended because, aside from the civic fashions of the day, the suburb is considered differently than a Garden City; Hampstead is not self-contained entirely, or self-supporting, because it is also a part of London. The civic center is really more atmospheric than functional. The main commercial center, at Finchley Road and Hampstead Way is busier and more extroverted, on the edge of town, a threshold formed by a pair of German-inspired, arcaded shop buildings with residences above designed by Parker and Unwin. Oddly, the East Finchley Station of the railroad and the Golders Green tube station, whose existence made the suburb possible, have a seemingly random relation to the scheme. The stations are not

much inconvenience, however, and building a plan around feeding the train to London would have been self-defeating.[22]

By 1912 Hampstead Garden Suburb housed over 5,000 people, and an additional 400 acres were acquired for a "New Suburb" planned by Unwin largely lying to the north and east of the original development, connected to it by principal roads radiating from the Central Square across the valley. Realized mostly after World War I, the new development, as Mervyn Miller put it, has a more stereotyped character, with detached and semidetached houses in sharp contrast to "the carefully composed groupings of the 'Old Suburb.'"[23]

Unlike Letchworth, which largely failed to impress critics, from the first Hampstead Garden Suburb was widely appreciated. For example, R. Randal Phillips, an American author who visited it in 1910, wrote in *The Brickbuilder* that "some people have started with an undefined prejudice against this place . . . arising from the remembrance of work which a certain class of big-tie and homespun architects have done elsewhere in the country, with the fostering approval of a band of supporters. Let it be said at once there is always a taint of crank about these zealots."[24] Steen Eiler Rasmussen, assessing

1. Plan, Thomas Adams and Edwin Lutyens, 1909. TPR10

2. Plan, Pepler & Allen, 1911. KHA

3. Stockens Green and Wadnall Way. Fleck. KHA (2012)

Hampstead at the time of its fiftieth anniversary in 1957, put Parker and Unwin's achievement wonderfully in the context of twentieth-century planning as a whole: "Some town planners (usually Germans) have interpreted town planning as the art of creating enclosed spaces. And others—as Le Corbusier—have reacted against this theory and maintained that we must recapture the open horizon: the town should be transferred into a green landscape with enormous trees and tall buildings dotted around here and there. I shall always remember that afternoon with Unwin in Hampstead, that day in the quiet study and in the large Heath, as a lesson in better understanding: man must have both, the enclosed wall and the open space."[25]

In 1908, the second Earl of Lytton (1876–1947), concerned about the haphazard and "ordinary" pattern of residential development currently under way at roughly the center of his ancestral 5,000-acre estate at **Knebworth,** Hertfordshire, commissioned Thomas Adams, in consultation with Edwin Lutyens, Lytton's brother-in-law, to prepare a plan for an 800-acre village to be centered around Knebworth's Great Northern Railway station, twenty-five miles north of King's Cross London.[26] The site, about one-and-a-half miles east of the Lytton family mansion and its extensive gardens, was bisected by the north–south path of the railroad, creating a natural division for the plan, intended to be developed at a density of eight dwellings per acre accommodating 6,400 detached, semidetached, and terraced houses, or about 30,000 residents. In addition to the Lytton family properties and the scattering of houses built east of the train station, the site also included golf links in its northern reaches west of the railroad, laid out by gifted player and prolific course designer Willie Park Jr. (1864–1925) along with an "indifferently neo-Georgian" clubhouse (1908) designed by Lutyens.[27]

Lord Lytton established the nonprofit Garden Villages, Ltd., to administer the development of Knebworth Garden Village, intended to serve a rich mix of social classes, not only "providing admirable sites for residences for the rich," but also "adequate provision for cottages for the poor." Lytton also envisioned a modest industrial component, although one that was "artistically designed and free from smoke or nuisance . . . It is not proposed to make Knebworth a factory town, but it is recognized that it will be necessary to provide sites for industrial concerns and workshops for the supply of the needs of the community."[28] The majority of working residents, however, were expected to make the daily thirty-five-minute rail commute to London.

Adams and Lutyens's plan, completed by September 1909, placed the civic center and most desirable residential areas west of the railroad, where the undulating landscape was more picturesque. The centerpiece of this half of the site was a proposed 100-foot-wide boulevard, to be lined by important public buildings as well as some stores, that would lead to a church located at the village's highest point. Short diagonal streets connected this tree-lined thoroughfare to the train station

and a second group of civic buildings. The largest houses were intended for plots near the golf course to the north, while a market square was to be located south of the civic center. Adams selected the firm of George L. Pepler (1882–1959) and Ernest G. Allen (1881–1964) to carry out the plan and design most of the buildings, subject to Lutyens's approval.

The main business district, as well as the small industrial component, was to be located east of the railroad tracks, where there would be less architectural oversight over the more modest houses. For this area, Adams and Lutyens proposed to replace the "narrow, tortuous, and uneven" North Road leading to London with a new 80-foot-wide boulevard, allowing the old street to "become a picturesque residential road, upon which the houses can face without being covered with dust," as Patrick Abercrombie noted in *Town Planning Review* in 1910. "This new main road forms the chief feature of the plan on this side, having at one point on its course an oblong village square, on which will be placed the principal inns, shops, etc."[29]

According to historian Michael Simpson, "The bulk of the planning was done by Adams, Lutyens acting as a consultant. The layout was more formal than his other designs, essentially a series of rectangles divided by diagonals [with] ample open spaces . . . On hilly ground the road paid court to the contours in gentle curves."[30] Unfortunately, only a small portion of the plan was realized before the war interrupted construction. At Stockens Green, a long landscaped rectangle west of the railway, Pepler & Allen completed 250 semidetached houses and short terraces accommodating 1,250 people, set behind front lawns and including rear allotment gardens. A number of large detached houses were also completed along Deards End Lane, including two by Lutyens, in close proximity to the golf course.[31] In addition to the houses, Lutyens also designed a church, St. Martin's (1915), but it was located east of the railroad tracks and without the benefit of the broad ceremonial approach originally envisioned.[32] After the war, Garden Villages, Ltd., hired brothers Archibald Stuart Soutar (1879–1951) and John C. S. Soutar to design additional houses for the middle class at Knebworth Garden Village, but Lord Lytton soon lost interest in the project, moving to India in 1920 to serve as undersecretary of state, and Adams and Lutyens's ambitious plan was dropped.

Hampstead unleashed what might be described as a golden age of English garden suburb design, inspiring developers, including property owners, enlightened capitalists, aristocratic land owners, and public agencies such as the London County Council (see p. 382) to propose garden suburbs intended to cater to the needs of both the middle and working classes. In 1907 John Sutton Nettlefold (1866–1930), a prominent Birmingham industrialist and politician turned housing advocate, established the Harborne Tenants Limited, a housing association organized as a copartnership, in order to develop a low-density garden suburb outside of Birmingham on a "thoroughly business-like footing and in

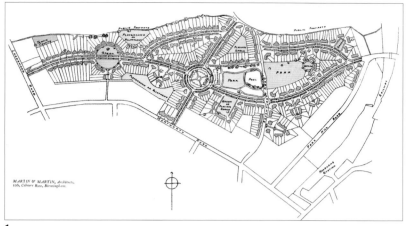

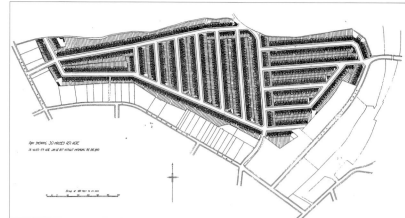

1

2

Tennis Courts, The Circle, Harborne, Bhm. 17.

3

4

5

6

7

1. Plan, Frederick William Martin, c. 1907. JSN

2. Plan if developed at thirty houses per acre. MPRA (c. 1908)

3. East Pathway. MPRA (1908)

4. Tennis club. MPRA

5. Shops, The Circle. MPRA

6. Park Edge. Sutton. MPRA (2009)

7. Rear of houses facing The Circle, viewed from park adjacent to Moor Pool. Shops are visible in background left. Sutton. MPRA (2009)

no way as a charity," with surplus profits from rents to be distributed to investors and the subdivision's tenants.[33] Nettlefold, who had been appointed the first chairman of the Birmingham Housing Committee in 1901 and five years later authored a report on slum conditions that called for the establishment of garden suburbs, selected the 54-acre site in Harborne for the proposed suburb, which became known as the **Moor Pool Estate.** The site, served by the Harborne Railway, a short branch line providing service to Birmingham, was a long and narrow tract three miles southwest of the city center whose most prominent feature, the Moor Pool, gave the development its name. Under Nettlefold's direction, the Harborne Tenants Limited commissioned architect Frederick William Martin (1859–1917) to plan the estate as well as design its first buildings, mandating a ratio of about nine dwellings per acre as opposed to the forty to fifty houses per acre typically found in Birmingham.

The focal point of Martin's plan was The Circle, a central *rond-point* with streets branching off to all four compass points that was home to three shops, a

clubhouse, a community hall, tennis courts, and a bowling green. Houses were arranged in rows of two, four, six, and eight dwellings, each featuring private rear gardens separated by beech hedges. The curving carriageways were only 16 feet wide, with five-foot planted verges on each side, allowing enough room for houses to be set back behind front yards. Southeast of The Circle, three rows of houses were arranged around a cul-de-sac. A 10-acre public park was located next to the Moor Pool, supplemented by several playgrounds placed throughout the hilly site.

The Moor Pool Estate was built as planned, with 494 brick-and-stucco houses completed between 1908 and 1911. Raymond Unwin was sufficiently impressed with the effort to feature the layout in a planning exhibition held by the Royal Institute of British Architects in 1910. Nettlefold was also pleased with the results, especially the fact that the project was profitable after its first year of operation. Writing in 1914, he cited the example of the Moor Pool Estate in his defense of the garden suburb's practicality: "Can garden suburb development

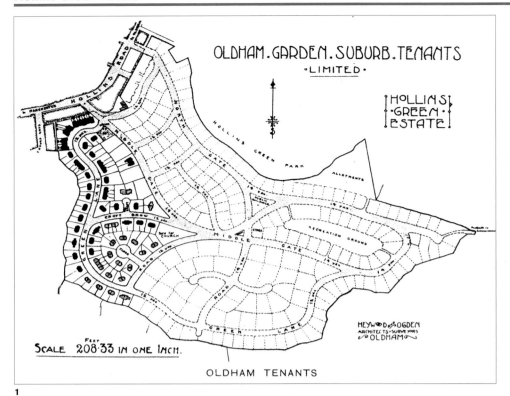

1. Plan, Heywood & Ogden, 1909. TPR10

2. Rising Lane. OLSA

3, 4. Green Lane. OLSA

5. The Croft. Mellor. GJM (2012)

be made to pay? It not only can be made to pay, it has been made to pay . . . This being the case, it is most earnestly to be hoped that the general public will no longer allow themselves to be misled by the pretences and fairy tales of the landjobbers' party, but will insist" on the building of garden suburbs which provide "better housing at reasonable rents."[34]

Nikolaus Pevsner and Alexandra Wedgewood praised the suburb as "an important and early example of the work of a co-partnership . . . The housing is as enterprising as any in the country and strongly influenced by Unwin."[35] In December 2009, Mervyn Miller, in a report commissioned by the Moor Pool Residents' Association, wrote that "Moor Pool originally represented, and still reflects, best practice in Garden City style housing and development. It has a coherent plan, within a boundary which gives it identity and integrity, and the feeling of a self-contained neighborhood."[36]

Philanthropists Mary Higgs (1854–1937) and Sarah Lees (1842–1935), both early members of the Garden City Association, established the Beautiful Oldham Society in 1902 in order to "create gardens and improve open spaces in deprived areas" of Oldham, a textile

manufacturing town of 150,000 residents located seven miles northeast of Manchester.[37] Five years later, Higgs and Lees would extend their efforts on behalf of the town's welfare, establishing the Oldham Tenants Society for the purpose of developing a garden suburb on a copartnership basis. The society purchased a 52-acre tract "within a penny tram ride of the center" of Oldham and commissioned the local firm of James Herbert Heywood (1861–1939) and George Ogden (1862–1920) to prepare the plan for the **Hollins Green Estate** (1909), also known as Oldham Garden Suburb, and design its first houses.[38]

Although intended to include about 700 houses, developed at a density of fourteen dwellings per acre, less than a third of the site was built according to Heywood & Ogden's original plan, despite praise from *Town Planning Review*.[39] Located at the southwest corner of the site, Heywood & Ogden's contribution was composed primarily of semidetached Arts and Crafts houses set behind modest front lawns and with rear allotment gardens. By 1914 156 houses had been completed in the exclusively residential subdivision, with the Oldham Tenants Society producing its own bricks on site. After

Grapenhall Estate

1. Plan, A. & J. Soutar, 1907. TPR10

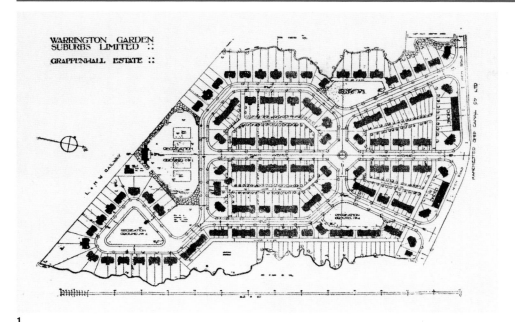

1

Great Sankey Estate

2

1

1. Plan, A. & J. Soutar, 1907. TPR10

2. Cottages, J. E. Wright, 1907. WL

the war, development continued but with smaller houses and with less open space than originally envisioned.

Two suburbs planned for Liverpool, in Warrington—A. & J. Soutar's **Grappenhall Estate** (1907) and **Great Sankey Estate** (1907), with, respectively, only twelve and twenty-four houses realized by 1914—can be labeled failures.[40] But nearby, **Wavertree** (begun in 1910 as Liverpool Garden Suburb) proved successful with its "simple leafy layout and low, rough-cast cottages" yielding an "understated" effect.[41] Unwin planned the first part of Wavertree, west of Wavertree Nook Road, including the houses, and G. L. Sutcliffe planned the second, begun in 1913–15, by which time 360 of the intended 1,800 houses were realized, most designed by Sutcliffe. Fieldway Green (1913) lies at the heart of Sutcliffe's portion, a close of over thirty attached houses forming a quadrangle. Significantly, Wavertree was not

built in relationship to a railroad that would provide passenger service for commuters to Liverpool but to Queens Drive (opened 1910), designed by Liverpool's city engineer, John A. Brodie (1858–1934), as a boulevard-like ring road intended to have tram service, which never materialized.

Alkrington (1902–14), on a 700-acre site between Manchester and the industrial town of Middleton, was planned for middle-class families by Thomas Adams.[42] When Adams was appointed to the Local Government Board, he was succeeded by Pepler & Allen. Alkrington's plan, with its strong, essentially radial street geometry, was a far cry from the naturalism of Letchworth, although the park-like arrangement of the suburb's west end was an exception. Adams anticipated a long-term build-out of fifty years. In reality, the development was interrupted by World War I with little

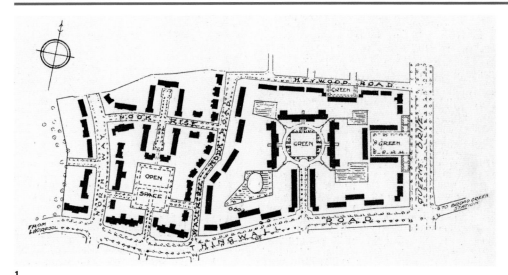

1. Plan, Raymond Unwin, 1910, and G. L. Sutcliffe, 1912. TB12

2. Fieldway Green. TWS (1913)

3. Nook Rise. TWS (1911)

4. Nook Road. TWS (1911)

5. Fieldway Green. Scales. LS (2011)

except a stretch of the boulevard-like Mainway leading to an unrealized town center of shops and civic buildings realized as intended.

Sir Richard Paget (1832–1908), a wealthy landowner and former Member of Parliament, announced his intentions in 1907 to develop **Fallings Park Garden Suburb** on 400 "picturesque, elevated, well-wooded and well-drained" acres two miles northeast of Wolverhampton, a West Midlands town seventeen miles northwest of Birmingham.[43] *The Garden City*, the official publication of the Garden City Association, greeted the project, to be designed by Thomas Adams in association with the firm of Detmar Jellings Blow (1867–1939) and Fernand Billerey (1878–1951), with enthusiasm, even though it did "not fulfill the requirements" of the organization, "as the estate is owned by a private landowner and not by a public company with a restricted dividend. But, whatever arguments may be used in favour of public ownership, it must be agreed on all sides that so long as land remains private property any efforts which may be made by the landowner to secure the development of his property on right principles deserves support from the Association."[44] Conditions in the depressed industrial town of Wolverhampton were particularly bad with a recent

municipal survey indicating that two-thirds of the housing stock was considered unsanitary. Thomas Adams noted that "some of the slums are worse than any I have seen in London, but owing to the low rents overcrowding does not seem so great . . . The creation of Garden Suburbs in pleasant, aristocratic surroundings is much easier; but with all the laudable effort that is given to the work, it scarcely touches the real problem."[45]

Fallings Park was located one-and-a-half miles northeast of the Wolverhampton station of the London and North-Western Railway as well as served by a tram line. Paget, with the assistance of Wolverhampton's municipal government, intended to extend the tram line into the new suburb's northern reaches but also planned to include bus service until the extension was completed. In addition, several businesses and industrial facilities were located within walking distance of the proposed suburb.

Adams and Blow & Billerey's plan was intended to serve an eventual population of 20,000, with a density of between twelve and fourteen houses to the acre, including detached and semidetached houses as well as short terraces. Substantial space was set aside for parks, playgrounds, and allotment gardens, with the main

Alkrington

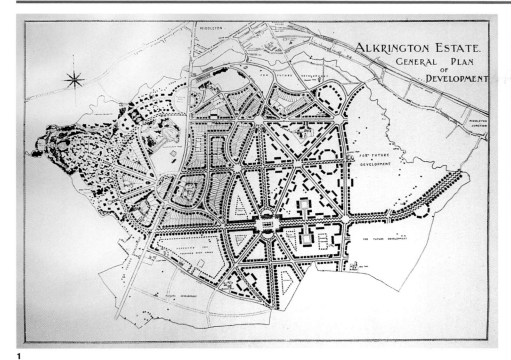

1. Plan, Thomas Adams, 1902. EGC

2. Aerial view. EHAC (1925)

Fallings Park Garden Suburb

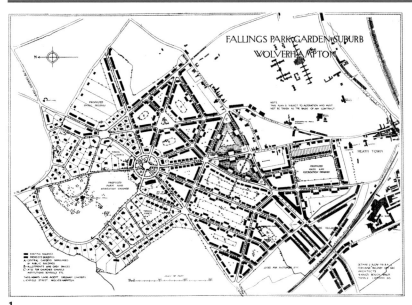

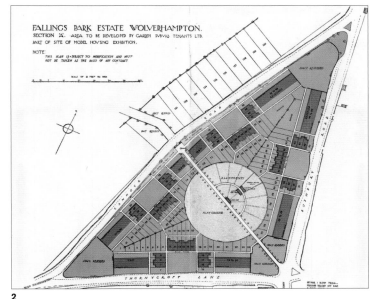

1. Plan, Thomas Adams and Blow & Billerey, 1907. JSN

2. Plan of "Section A," where construction began in 1907. WALS (1908)

3. Aerial view. EHAC (1927)

4. Quadrangle, Thornycroft Lane. WALS (1910)

5. Quadrangle, Cannock Road. Cadman. FL (2008)

1. Plan, Thomas Adams, 1909.
BRO

2. Drawing by Samuel Loxton.
BRRL

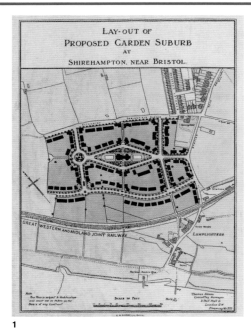

1

2

40-foot-wide roads lined by trees. Michael Simpson, Adams's biographer, assigned primary credit for the plan to Detmar Blow, a disciple of John Ruskin, writing that "from a central hub, Blow proposed radials leading to four subsidiary foci. The roads were generally straight, punctuated by frequent set-backs of houses fronted by greens . . . It was an effective if somewhat pedestrian and stilted design."[46] In addition to the housing and recreational space, land was set aside for a church and school.

Construction began in 1907 at the southern end of the site near the tram line on a triangular seven-acre parcel bound by Cannock, Victoria, and Bushbury Roads. Blow and Fernand Billerey, a French-born architect trained at the École des Beaux-Arts, designed the majority of the first houses, grouped around a central playground and shared garden space. C. M. Crickmer and the firm of Pepler & Allen designed additional houses, a little more than half of which were developed by Paget and the Fallings Park Garden Suburb Tenants' Society, with the remainder built by individuals who purchased lots but had to submit their plans to the society for approval. In order to promote the project, as well as the Garden City movement as a whole, a Model Housing Exhibition was held in September 1908, with Pepler & Allen winning gold medals for two houses.

Seventy-five houses were completed at Fallings Park before construction stopped in 1909, a year after Paget's death. In addition to losing its patron, Michael Simpson has noted that progress was also "killed off by the local slackness of trade and the persistence of the national building depression," concluding that Fallings Park "thus achieved little."[47] After World War I, Pepler & Allen were placed in charge of future planning at Fallings Park as well as given responsibility for the design of many of its houses. Nikolaus Pevsner has described their revised plan as "formal, with a central circle surrounded by an almond shape, two ovals north and south of it, and

radiating streets. It looks ornamental on paper but is not noticed visually as one walks around. Moreover, the architecture is not at all enterprising. Small public buildings face the central circle."[48]

Occupying 26.5 acres on the western edge of Bristol, **Shirehampton Garden Suburb** (1909) was another work of Thomas Adams's, with Frank Bromhead providing the architecture.[49] The site was adjacent to the Shirehampton station of the Avonmouth branch railway providing easy service to Bristol. Land next to the railroad was set aside for industrial purposes, and the suburb was considered to be the potential nucleus of more extensive development in the future. Adams's strict geometric plan, calling for mostly semidetached houses, 280 in all, or short terrace groups, had at its heart a diamond arrangement of streets bounding a site intended for a church and tennis courts. Despite dreams of expansion, only forty-four houses were built.

Gidea Park (1910), Essex, also known as the Romford Garden Suburb, lay thirteen-and-a-half miles from Liverpool Street Station.[50] Initiated by Sir Herbert Raphael (1859–1924) in conscious emulation of Hampstead Garden Suburb, Gidea Park is less interesting as a village than as a collection of stylish, if modest, houses. It began with an exhibition of 159 small houses designed by different architects employing Arts and Crafts and neo-Georgian vocabularies, including M. H. Baillie Scott, Clough Williams-Ellis (1885–1978), Parker and Unwin, and C. R. Ashbee (1863–1942). Gidea Park is an early example of an English garden suburb developed in conjunction with a golf course. The 90-acre Romford Golf Course, founded by Raphael in 1894, bounds the development on the east, and the 15-acre Raphael Park, donated by the developer in 1902, forms the border on the west. The value of the golf course to the plan was acknowledged early on. As R. Randal Phillips noted in 1913: "The roads have been so laid out that there is a long frontage for houses looking

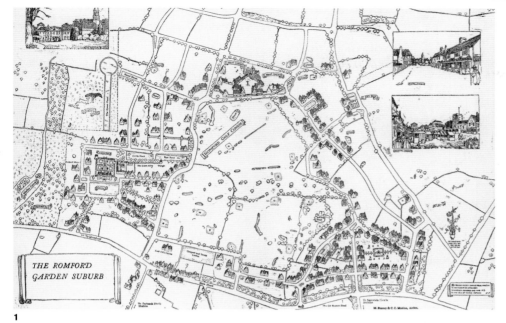

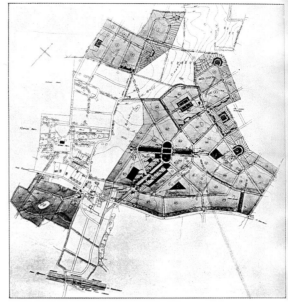

1. Plan, Michael Bunney and C. C. Makins, drawn by Charles Paget Wade, 1909. TPMA

2. Plan, W. Garnett Gibson and Reginald Dann, 1911. TPR11

3. "Group of three cottages designed to turn the corner," Barry Parker and Raymond Unwin, Architects, 1910. TPMA

4. Reed Pond Walk. BR13 (1913)

5. Meadway and Parkway. Kereshun. AK (2011)

6. Typical street. Kereshun. AK (2011)

onto this delightful space, and similarly, on the opposite side, the roads are disposed as to give the utmost benefit to the houses that face Raphael Park."[51]

Gidea Park was originally laid out on 440 acres by Michael Bunney (1873–1926) and C. C. Makins (1876–1963), whose scheme of 1909 was rendered "in a very primitive style," as John East put it, by Charles Paget Wade, an assistant to Parker and Unwin.[52] The development did not proceed according to the Bunney and Makins plan, and in 1911, after the cottage exhibition, Wade made a second rendering of the estate that reflected it as-built, leading some to believe that Parker and Unwin, who designed two of its houses, were also responsible for

the layout, which featured gently curved roads to retain trees and worked with other natural features of the site.

Initially, Edwin Lutyens was asked to prepare designs for the land east of the golf course, but the decision was then made to hold a competition for that area's development. A plan submitted by W. Garnett Gibson (n.d.) and Reginald Dann (1883–1939) received first place, but the project never went forward. Their scheme, according to Bridget Cherry and her Pevsner guide colleagues, "made much of a series of formal squares and avenues and placed the church in an axial arrangement with Gidea Hall," a late-medieval mansion vastly rebuilt in the eighteenth century.[53]

1. Plan, A. & J. Soutar, 1910. LBH

2. Green Walk. LBH

3. Cottage designs for typical street. TPR13

4, 5. Typical streets. Kereshun. AK (2011)

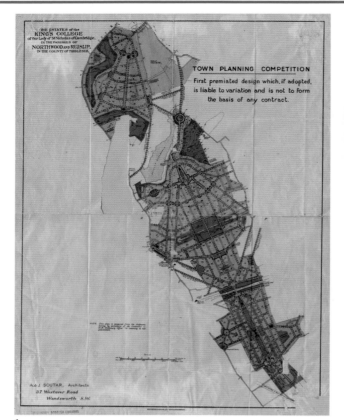

1

2

Types of Cottages suggested for the Ruislip Manor Cottage Society

3

4

5

Shortly after Gidea Park began, another 60 acres were acquired to the south of Main Road, providing access to the newly opened Great Eastern Railway station at Squirrels' Heath, which was built at the developer's request. A commercial building, Balgores Square (c. 1912), designed by Fair & Myer, was never fully carried out. Despite Gidea Park's interest as a collection of distinctive houses by leading architects, the competition between them struck at least one participant, M. H. Baillie Scott, negatively: "Art is underlined everywhere and each of these miniature bijou residences seem to pose and smirk in the conscious appreciation of its own artistic qualities."[54]

In 1910, the first important town planning competition under the Housing and Town Planning Act of 1909 was held to determine the plan of **Ruislip Manor**, near Harrow, a 1,300-acre wooded tract of land twelve miles from London.[55] The land, stretching four miles in length, was served by five railway stations from which passengers could reach the city within eighteen to forty minutes. Sixty-two architects entered the competition, judged by Sir Aston Webb (1849–1930) and Raymond

Unwin, and the totality of the work reveals the prevailing high degree of sophistication in garden suburb planning. Archibald Stuart Soutar and John C. S. Soutar, who succeeded Unwin as town architect of Hampstead, won first place with a scheme intended to house 40,000 people. The Soutars' mostly gridded plan, cut through with diagonal streets, was organized to facilitate access to the principal railroad stations. A town square, included in the portion of the garden suburb nearest historic Ruislip Village, and a marketplace near the rail station at its southern tip, were to accommodate shops. The estate adjoined Northwood Golf Course and two wooded areas that were to be retained along with the Ruislip Reservoir water basin, dividing the site into north and south sections.

The editors of the *Architectural Review*, writing in 1911, were dubious about the benefit of the competition, noting that while the entries "indicated that many architects are giving close study to town planning," it was "noticeable that only two or three engineers and surveyors submitted designs . . . One would have thought that better results would have been obtained by paying a thoroughly qualified group of designers (including an architect, engineer, and surveyor) to prepare a plan." The *Review* bemoaned the fact that in the majority of the schemes, the "number of public buildings proposed is totally inadequate, and this notwithstanding that one of their aims should have been to give dignity to their plan on the one hand, and a suitable setting for public buildings on the other." Overall, the *Review* observed, "One of the features of the competition is the triumph of what a contemporary calls the 'pretty pattern' plan," of which A. & J. Soutar's winning entry, "more or less modeled on" L'Enfant's plan for Washington (1791), with "mixed rectangular and radial roads," was a representative example. Moreover, the *Review*'s editors continued, "competitors who appeared to be influenced by modern garden-city planning as practiced so excellently at Hampstead do not seem to have been considered of much account. Does this indicate that there is already a reaction against the pretty narrow culs-de-sac of the Garden Suburb? It is hoped that the aim after aesthetic effect will not go so far as to drive us back to the stereotyped methods which have too long been encouraged by the Model By-laws [of the Public Health Act of 1875]."[56]

The Soutar plan was adopted, allowing for 7,642 houses, many of them designed by A. S. Soutar after World War I but still exhibiting what Clarence Stein described as "the old traditions" of the Garden City movement.[57] The Soutar scheme, developed by the Ruislip Manor Cottage Society, should not be confused with the 186-acre area to the south now known as Ruislip Manor, a speculative development of modest homes built by George Ball between 1933 and 1939.

In 1912, Frederic Cavendish Pearson abandoned his post at Brentham to take on the master planning and architectural design at **Sutton Garden Suburb**, in southeast London, developed under the initiative of Thomas Wall II (1846–1930), a sausage magnate and philanthropist.[58] Only three streets of the roughly 75-acre development intended to house 1,000 families were realized, but they reveal Pearson's understanding of the lessons of Hampstead Garden Suburb. A woodland area lies near the heart of the Sutton site, where an institute was to have commanded a recreation ground. Peripheral entrances and edges were marked by housing crescents and other special geometries, while most of the internal streets were to be lined with houses, many intended to be realized in pairs. Inside the large blocks there were to be closes surrounding generous greens as well as allotment gardens.

In 1907 London department store magnate William Whiteley (1831–1907) was shot to death by a man purporting to be his illegitimate son. In his will, Whiteley had set aside one million pounds, an enormous sum at the time, for the establishment of a self-sufficient village "to house the elderly poor."[59] The bequest was quite specific, stating that the philanthropic venture was intended for single or married women and men, the former at least sixty years of age and the latter sixty-five or over, with prescribed limited incomes, and "of good

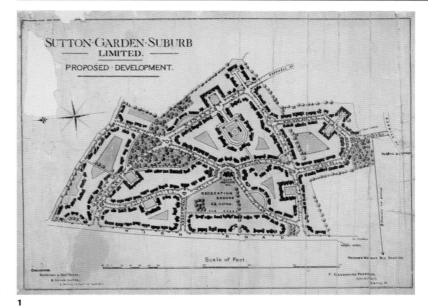

1

2

3

4

5

6

1. Plan, Frederic Cavendish Pearson, 1912. SLSA

2. Block plan. SLSA

3. Hawthorn Close. SLSA

4. Meadow Close. SLSA

5. Horseshoe Green. Kereshun. AK (2011)

6. Oak Close. Kereshun. AK (2011)

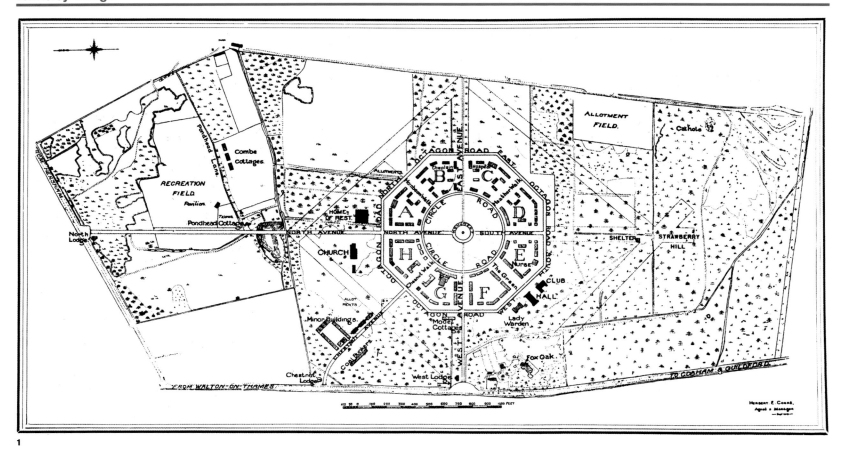

1. Plan, R. Frank Atkinson, 1912.
ARB24 (c. 1924)

character and sound mind, not affected by any contagious or infectious diseases, and never having been convicted of any criminal offense."[60] The entrepreneur also delineated his wishes for the site—to "be in as bright, cheerful and healthy spot as possible"—as well as the development's buildings, which were to be "of good and substantial character and of a plain and useful design and shall be well lighted, ventilated and drained and so placed as to be protected as far as possible from the north and east winds."[61]

The estate's trustees established Whiteley Homes to administer the project and selected Walter Cave (1863–1939) to act as architectural consultant. In 1911, a picturesque, well-wooded, 225-acre rectangular site was purchased for **Whiteley Village**, three miles south of Walton-on-Thames, Surrey, and about twenty-three miles southwest of London. On Cave's recommendation, a limited competition was held in 1912 to select a planner, with R. Frank Atkinson (1869–1923), best known for his collaboration with Daniel H. Burnham on London's Selfridges department store (1907), beating five other entries.

Atkinson's unusual and formal plan, intended for 500 residents, was focused around a 23-acre octagonal village in roughly the middle of the site that included at its center a circular green with a monument to Whiteley designed by sculptor George Frampton (1860–1928). In addition to Cave and Atkinson, additional architects were selected to contribute to the village's residential, civic, and commercial architecture, including Ernest George, Aston Webb, Mervyn Macartney (1853–1932), Reginald

Blomfield (1856–1942), Ernest Newton (1856–1922), and Walter J. Tapper (1861–1935). The majority of buildings were placed in the eight parcels formed by Octagon Road, although a church, a "home of rest" for residents in need of medical attention, and housing for staff members were situated outside the development's core, along with allotment gardens and recreational facilities.

Whiteley Village's cornerstone was laid on July 21, 1914, but England's entry into the war two weeks later, on August 4, put the project on hold. Construction soon resumed and the first residents were able to move in in 1917, and by 1921 the project was substantially complete, with 240 cottages for single men and women and 48 houses for married couples. In addition to the one- and two-story semidetached and terraced redbrick dwellings, each with its own garden, the development included a village hall, shops, post office, library, church, hospital, communal kitchen, three bowling greens, and a cricket ground. All of the buildings shared a similar Arts and Crafts vocabulary except for Walter Tapper's Gothic church. The village provided regular bus service to Walton-on-Thames where residents could catch direct trains to London.

R. Randal Phillips, writing in 1922 in the pages of the American magazine *Architectural Forum*, observed that "all too often houses are spoilt by restrictions in cost, and this results in poor building. In Whiteley Village the very opposite is true, for here the best materials have been used in the very best way. There is nothing shoddy anywhere. The houses are meant to last, and

2. Aerial view. SG (1921)

3. View across green toward village hall. SG (1921)

4. Typical view. SG (1921)

5. Circle Road. SG (1921)

6. Shelter. ARB24 (1924)

7. View across green toward village hall. MRWV (2005)

8. Cottages. MRWV (2005)

they look like it."[62] Two years later, Maurice Webb wrote in London-based *Architectural Review*: "A collection of houses is a soulless thing without its church, its shops, its club, and its village hall, where the inhabitants can meet and talk and pray and sing together. Each of and all these buildings must belong to the village and must be intimate to it. They are so here: the village is complete."[63] In her history of English villages, Gillian Darley noted that Whiteley Village "continues successfully today . . . The human scale of the buildings emphasizes the individual's place in the life of the community whilst the overall planning reinforces the visual unity of the village. It is an extremely attractive example of architectural form and function happily integrated."[64]

Some of the most interesting of the post-Hampstead garden suburbs were pocket-size, little more than enclaves that have become oases amid the less-enlightened development that has grown up around them. In spirit, if not necessarily in specific design, these garden enclaves are in the tradition of Nash's Blaise Hamlet (see p. 21) and Regent's Park villages (see p. 23). **Rookfield Estate** (c. 1901–15), immediately to the west of Alexandra Park in north London, was planned by the builder W. J. Collins (1856–1939), who also designed

Rookfield Estate

1. Aerial view. GE (2010)

2. Rookfield Avenue. Kereshun. AK (2011)

3. Rookfield Close. Kereshun. AK (2011)

4. Rear gardens. Kereshun. AK (2011)

1

2

3

4

Finchley Garden Village

1. Aerial view. GE (2010)

2. Village Road. FS

3. Green. RAMSA (2007)

4. Green, showing monument to Frank E. Stratton. RAMSA (2007)

1

2

3

4

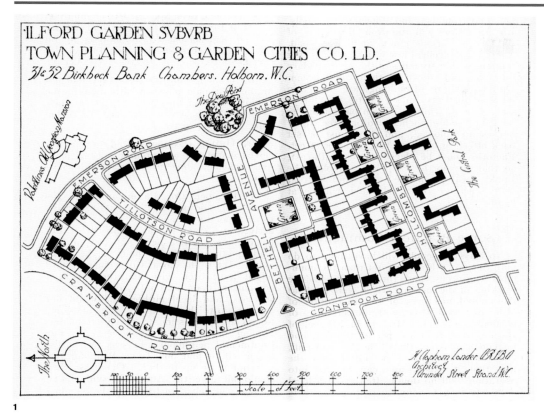

1

1. Plan, H. Clapham Lander, 1909. GCTP10

2. Holcombe Road. Kereshun. AK (2011)

3. Emerson Road. Kereshun. AK (2011)

2

3

the early houses.[65] Later on, Collins's two architect sons, Herbert (1885–1975) and William (d. 1977), introduced a higher level of house design, with two groups of houses, Cranmore Way and Rookfield Close, echoing in detail some of the best work at Hampstead Garden Suburb while opening onto street-facing greens in the manner advocated by Parker and Unwin.

Finchley Garden Village (1909–14), in north London, a 24-acre enclave with a simple plan grouping cottage-style houses around a green, was designed by Frank E. Stratton (d. 1922), who is memorialized by a lantern-surmounted monument prominently sited on the green that straddles Village Road at the bottom of Hendon Avenue.[66] One of the most idyllic of the garden enclaves, Finchley Garden Village consists mostly of two-family houses, with those facing the green only accessible by footpaths. To the west, Windsor Open Space buffers many back gardens and further enhances the illusion of a preexisting country village surrounded by a burgeoning metropolis.

In 1909 the Garden City and Town Planning Association (the new name of the Garden City Association), became aware of a 40-acre parcel in northeast London in Ilford that was up for sale, attracting the attention of several developers.[67] The picturesque site, formerly a part of the Valentines Estate with its late-seventeenth-century mansion, 125 acres of which had been turned into a public park in 1898, was located on the park's western border about a mile north of the Ilford Railway Station and nine miles northeast of Charing Cross. The association, seeking to "preserve [the site] from the ravages of the ordinary builder," was able to purchase the property with the aid of banker, politician, and area resident Sir John Bethell (1861–1945), who stipulated that any profits generated by the subdivision had to be used for the improvement of "public objects in the district."[68]

H. Clapham Lander (1868–1955) was responsible for **Ilford Garden Suburb**'s plan, dividing the site bordered on three sides by Valentines Park into two building parcels bisected by Bethell Avenue, named

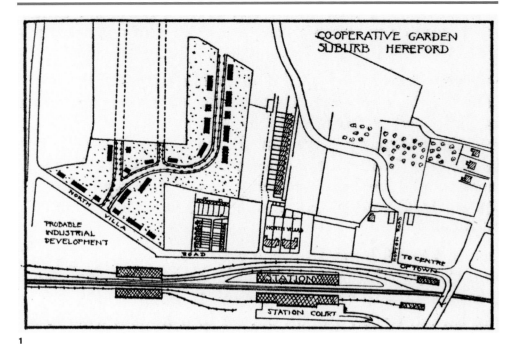

1

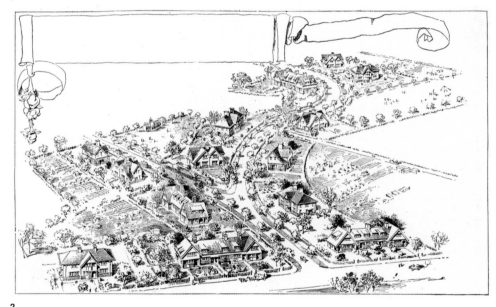

2

1. Plan, Arthur R. Groome and
Edward J. Bettington, 1909.
TPR13

2. Bird's-eye view. TPR10 (1909)

3. Barr's Court Road and Bulmer
Avenue. TPR13 (c. 1913)

3

for the development's benefactor and home to a central public green. Lander placed semidetached houses and terraces of up to six houses along curving streets, staggering their placement for interest, and grouped longer terraces around landscaped greens. C. M. Crickmer's seventy houses were completed by 1911, their "double 'M' gables" reminding Mervyn Miller of work at Hampstead Garden Suburb.[69]

Hereford Garden Suburb (1909), a cooperative venture sponsored by the local town council, was undertaken as part of a slum clearance project in the West Midlands town of Hereford, a trading center sixteen miles east of the Welsh border that served the needs of the primarily agricultural county of Herefordshire.[70] In 1908 the Hereford Town Council identified 156 unsanitary dwellings in the center of town that were deemed beyond repair. Due to a severe housing shortage, however, the municipality was unable to tear them down until suitable replacements could be built. To remedy the situation, the council purchased nine-and-a-half unimproved acres about a mile northeast of Hereford's center and just north of the town's railroad station for the purpose of building a modest garden suburb. As Patrick Abercrombie reported, "It was not intended that the very poor should migrate to this garden suburb . . . but it was hoped that the houses vacated by the better class moving [to the new housing] might provide accommodation for the occupants of the condemned houses."[71]

The Hereford Co-operative Housing Limited, the housing association created to administer the project, leased the site from the town for eighty years and hired the local firm of Arthur R. Groome (1873–1945) and Edward J. Bettington (n.d.) to plan the subdivision and design the housing. Groome & Bettington's plan, developed at a density of nine dwellings per acre, featured semidetached houses as well as terraces of three and five houses set back behind front yards along roads "laid out in picturesque curves," as Abercrombie wrote.[72] One-and-a-half acres were reserved for open space, with each of the house groups including generous rear allotment gardens. The project was built as planned, with eighty-six brick-and-stucco houses completed by 1911.

Ewart G. Culpin explained the significance of Hereford Garden Suburb, writing in 1913 that it "possesses a great distinction over most Garden Village schemes, in that it is the first community of its kind in England to be called into being through the assistance of a municipality."[73] A year later, J. S. Nettlefold, a housing advocate responsible for the development of the Moor Pool Estate, praised the cooperative as "one of the best examples, if not the very best example, in this country of garden suburb development on economical town planning lines. It may be much smaller than some of the other and better known ventures, but it is the most complete and best adapted to the needs of the case."[74]

Burnage Garden Village (1910), five miles from the center of Manchester, a small enclave of 136 houses—mostly semidetached—set on an 11-acre site, was

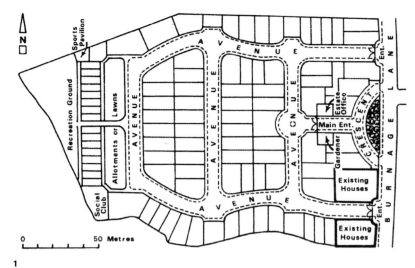

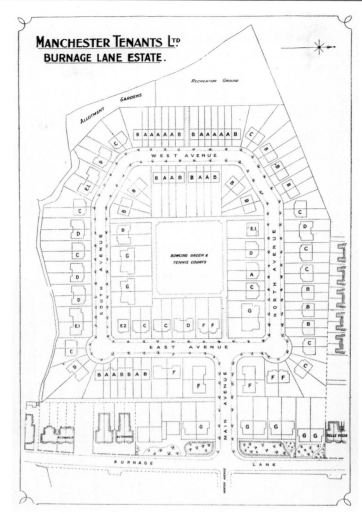

1. Proposed plan, J. Horner Hargreaves, 1907. TPR76

2. Main Avenue. CRS (1912)

3. Plan, J. Horner Hargreaves in consultation with C. G. Agate, F. B. Dunkerley, and Raymond Unwin, 1910. TPR10

4. Green and houses. MTL (2012)

planned by J. Horner Hargreaves (n.d.) in consultation with C. G. Agate (n.d.), F. B. Dunkerley (1869–1951), and Raymond Unwin.[75] Significantly, though two train stations were nearby, the railroads serving them were not interested in local traffic and no tram lines were built either, so that unlike most garden suburbs of the period, Burnage was not served by public transportation. Hargreaves's first plan (1907), with three north–south avenues, and a grassy crescent leading to the main entrance set between the estate office and a gardener's cottage, included two rows of cheap cottages at the far end of the property. Once Hargreaves teamed with the consultants, a new plan was developed, with the

principal feature being a large open space, home to two tennis courts, a bowling green, and a small clubhouse. Although these opened to the back of a ring of houses, they were accessible to the suburb as a whole via footpaths. Nonetheless, Patrick Abercrombie took a dim view of the results: "The estate is laid out simply with no attempt at creating a centre of local life; it is frankly a group of houses situated in a suburb of Manchester, forming part of the general life of the district."[76]

Chorltonville (1911–13), in south Manchester, a 36-acre garden enclave of winding streets and Tudorbethan "black and white" mostly semidetached villas, offered an even more "overtly pretty" effect than

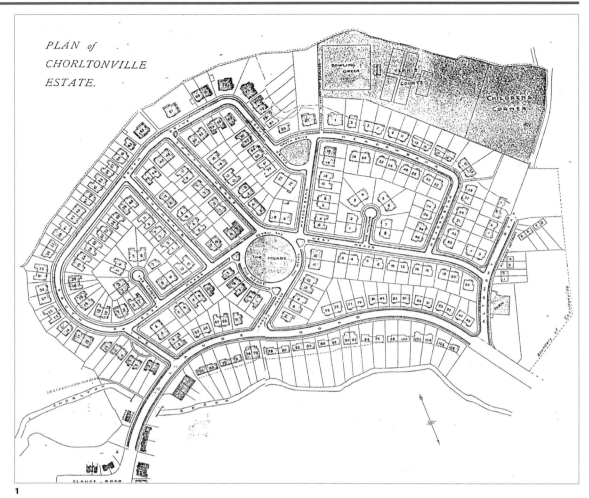

1

2

3

Burnage.[77] Albert Cuneo (n.d.), a young local architect, was put in charge of the work. The wide looping roads are flanked by generous seven-foot-wide grassy verges on either side. Despite its small size, the developer's ambitions were large: "to solve the housing problem of a great city."[78]

In 1912 a small group of middle-class residents from Droylsden, about four miles east of Manchester's city center, banded together as the Fairfield Tenants' Association in order to build **Fairfield Housing Estate** on 22 slightly hilly acres owned by the Moravian Church and located just south of the church's cemetery.[79] In 1784 the church had built the Fairfield Moravian Settlement, a group of houses, civic buildings, and church facilities. The church granted a 999-year lease to the cooperative, some of whose members belonged to the Moravian Church, on the condition that it build houses that would respect the well-preserved buildings of the Moravian Settlement. The Fairfield Tenants' Association commissioned the Manchester firm of Edgar Wood and J. Henry Sellers (1861–1954) to prepare the plan and design the houses for this exclusively residential development. Writing in 1954, architectural historian John H. G. Archer noted that the pair's "work is little known, which is hardly surprising, because most of it is situated in the smaller textile towns of Lancashire and Yorkshire, like Middleton, Oldham and Huddersfield, and is found in the secluded residential parts once inhabited by wealthy cotton spinners and wood merchants."[80]

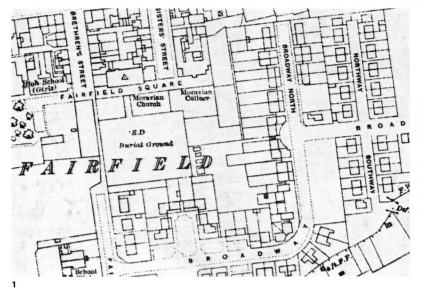

1. Ordnance Survey map. TLSAC (1933)

2. Aerial view. GE (2009)

3. Typical houses. TLSAC (1913–20)

4. Houses near the village green. Boardman. DBO (2000)

5, 6. Broadway. LSmith. TMBC (2009)

Although the plan's provenance is murky, Wood is generally given more credit for the layout and Sellers considered largely responsible for the design of the detached, semidetached, and terraced houses, thirty-three of which were completed in 1913 and 1914 and an additional eight built after the war in 1920. Wood placed the houses, with staggered setbacks and rear gardens, along both sides of a gently rising J-shaped street with wide planted verges. A village green, surrounded on three sides by terraced units, sat at roughly the center of the site.

Archer praised "this harmonious group" of houses that "was sensitively laid out with planting and changes of level and direction . . . The environment created is enjoyable and human and it clearly demonstrates the immense importance of layout."[81] The Pevsner team

share the sentiment, writing that "everything is subtle and restrained . . . The homes seem at first to be the standard Neo-Georgian semi-detacheds coming into fashion just before the First World War, but then one notices such features as the severely cubic shape of the projecting part of each house. In fact they vary in detail and in form, with detached, semi-detached and terraced housing, doubtless a nod to the houses of the Moravian settlement." Pevsner and his colleagues go on to draw attention to the section "where the street turns to the north, and becomes Broadway North, [where] the corner is taken by a sudden, deep, concave expanse of brickwork with chimneys on each side and pairs of inwardly curved windows—the only big architectural statement. The walk back is rewarding for all the details

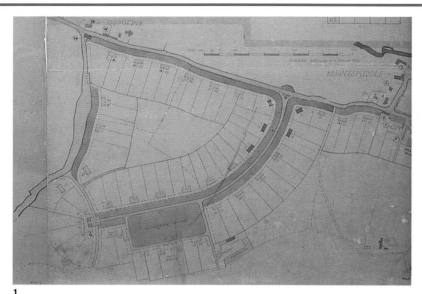

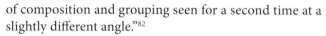

1. Plan, Halsey Ricardo and Macdonald Gill, 1914. DBF

2. Perspective of proposed building works, Macdonald Gill, 1917. AJ

3. The Ring. AJ (1919)

4. Houses under construction. AJ (1919)

5, 6. Typical views. Walker. CW (2007)

of composition and grouping seen for a second time at a slightly different angle."[82]

Briantspuddle (1914), Dorset, designed by Halsey Ricardo (1854–1928) and Macdonald Gill (1884–1947), has about it the charm and whimsy of Nash's Blaise Hamlet but at a larger scale.[83] The village was developed by Ernest Debenham (1865–1952), the department store heir, who had assembled large tracts of land in the area. Ricardo had also designed Debenham's London house (1906).[84] Debenham's intention was to create a self-sufficient agricultural enterprise, at the core of which a workers' village with twelve highly picturesque cottages was initially built to set a high standard for what was to come. Progress was delayed by the war and construction did not begin in earnest until 1919. By 1929 forty cottages had been built and eight more were under way. The principal agricultural activity was a dairy farm providing stalls for one hundred cows.

The Pevsner guide to Dorset finds "much to delight and amuse at Briantspuddle . . . a village of dumpy white-walled cottages with thatched roofs." The high point was The Ring, "a linked group, two-storeyed with a one-storeyed center, round an oval green planted with walnut trees. The rather studied symmetry and the self-conscious brick-trimmed turrets with their caps of thatch, if typical of the 1920s, are just what is needed in the way of personal expression."[85] Interestingly, the cottage walls were made of concrete block, using the local gravel.

In 1917 architect F. C. Eden (1864–1944) designed **Ardeley**, "a Blaise Castle Revived, though without the capriciousness of the original."[86] Located in Hertfordshire, forty miles north of London, Ardeley, which was also similar to Briantspuddle but smaller, was built by local developer John Howard Carter. Eden, who would leave architecture to concentrate on the design of

1. Aerial view. GE (2009)

2. Green, showing village hall on right. Houghton. JH (2001)

Holly Lodge Estate

1. Aerial view. GE (2010)

2. Makepeace Avenue. GH (2012)

church fittings and stained glass, placed cottages and a village hall around a green, with a hexagonal brick-and-tile well house in the center. As Gillian Darley has written, "Here no details were skimped to produce a satisfactory link with the traditional villages of the area, for Hertfordshire was falling victim to the grasping fingers of London and needed to reassert its regional identity before it was too late."[87]

Another interesting garden suburb enclave, containing sixty small units arranged in thirty-one buildings, **Holly Lodge Estate** (begun in 1923), north London, in Highgate, east of Hampstead Heath, was situated on the grounds of a demolished early-nineteenth-century villa, landscaped (1825) by J. B. Papworth, that partially remains as a private park. The plan is of no particular significance, but the introduction among the villa-type houses of half-timbered four- to five-story blocks of flats intended for "lady workers," who were provided with a restaurant and social center, is noteworthy. The architect and builder was Abraham Davis (1857–1924). The Pevsner guide deems the houses "weird."[88]

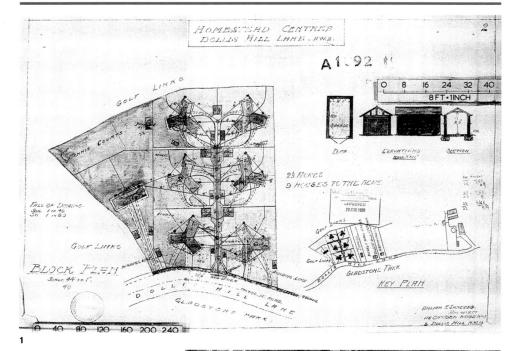

1

1. Plan, William E. Sanders, 1926.
BRENT

2. Aerial view. GE (2003)

3, 4. Typical views. Kereshun. AK
(2011)

2

3

4

As designed by William E. Sanders (n.d.), the twenty-house **Homestead Park** (1926), Brent, was a highly unusual arrangement of Y-shaped house clusters with shared service cores situated along a single narrow street leading from Gladstone Park at Dollis Lane.[89] Although the Y-shaped clusters conveyed the impression of far more open space than was actually the case, they subverted the function of the street much as the tower-in-the-park superblocks were to do in post–World War II housing estates. The Pevsner guide lauded the plan as an embodiment of "a progressive idea expressed in entirely traditional picturesque form."[90]

Typically, garden enclaves were ruralesque, with curving roads and vernacular-inspired cottage-like houses. But the 45-acre **Kennington Estate** (1913), in South London, designed by Stanley Davenport Adshead (1868–1946) and Stanley Ramsey (1882–1968) and developed by the Duchy of Cornwall, was far more urban in plan and architecture.[91] With its Georgian Regency-style rowhouses and cottages, Kennington was more like a late-eighteenth-century development focused around a square than a garden suburb. Nonetheless, by virtue of its low density and its remarkable planning and building design, this enclave very much deserves representation here. The estate included both workmen's and middle-class flats, two-story cottages, a crèche for babies, a church, and a quadrangle of housing for the elderly.

The simplicity of the Kennington Estate's town plan and architecture reflected Adshead's admiration for the classicizing work of American architects such as McKim, Mead & White that was introduced to him by Charles Reilly (1874–1948), the architecture educator, who visited the United States for the first time in 1909 with the express purpose of studying American town planning.[92] Nonetheless, as realized, the Kennington Estate seems distinctly English, and remarkably at home in its neighborhood, carrying through existing streets while at the same time creating its own sense of place, focused on Courtenay Square, a green space bordered by simple, very modest-size, two-story, cast-stone-trimmed brick rowhouses graced by elegant front porches shading paired entry doors. Ironically, the estate was a slum clearance project that replaced a neighborhood of dilapidated houses dating from the late eighteenth and early nineteenth centuries which provided the inspiration for their replacements.

The importance of the Kennington Estate to the evolution of the garden suburb type cannot be overestimated. Its influence was especially felt in America, not only in the quiet redbrick architecture adopted by Frederick L. Ackerman, Clarence Stein, and Henry Wright at Sunnyside (see p. 190) but more importantly in that development's urbanism, whereby a sense of a special enclave in the city is created, one with the scale and ambience of a suburb, yet one which never loses sight of the essential structure and character of the surrounding urban fabric. Patrick Abercrombie assessed Kennington's importance as a "modern town quarter" in 1917:

1. Aerial view of Courtenay Square. GE (2003)

2. Courtenay Square. HWTJ (c. 1917)

3. Old Tenants' Hostel quadrangle. HWTJ (c. 1917)

4. Grocer's shop at the corner of Old Tenants' Hostel. HWTJ (c. 1917)

5. Kennington Lane and Courtenay Street. HWTJ (c. 1917)

6. Courtenay Square. RAMSA (1985)

7. Sancroft Street and Courtenay Street. RAMSA (2003)

8. Cardigan Street. RAMSA (1985)

*The importance and significance of the Kenning-
ton estate is thus two-fold; it is the first example
of urban housing carried out on town-planning
lines and conceived in no apologetic mood, as
though it were a makeshift caused by the difficulty of carrying people out to the suburbs. No,
this is frankly a group of town houses for town
dwellers and sets up a standard of its own, quite
distinct from that of the suburb. The extent of the
area dealt with and the radical re-arrangement
in the proportion of built-on land to open space
which is being effected in the site planning, lift
this work above the piecemeal rebuilding of street
blocks which is always taking place to a great or
less extent. The other reason of its importance is,
that it is artistically sound: that this should be
achieved at the outset is indeed fortunate. We
know how usual is the early fumbling of a new
departure—The Garden Suburb is only now
beginning to find its permanent idiom after endless experiments. At Kennington a satisfactory
result has been obtained by the close study of a
local tradition and usage which, carefully modified to suit modern requirements, was admirably
adapted to its present purpose.*[93]

LONDON COUNTY COUNCIL

Although private entrepreneurs endeavored to sponsor planned suburban villages and enclaves for workers
during the years leading up to World War I, most of
these failed to materialize for lack of sufficient capital.
As if to fill this breach, the London County Council
(LCC), which since its founding in 1889 as the principal
administrative body for the county of London had been
exclusively building high-density inner-city flat houses
for the working classes, began to meet their needs with
a series of garden suburbs that brought, as Susan Beattie has written, "the working class cottage within the
same architectural context as the country house of the
private patron: to establish the right of Council tenants
to that flattering sense of identity and pride in unique-
ness which the privileged expected to derive from their
architectural environment."[94]

Totterdown Fields Estate (1902–11), near Toot-
ing Common, Wandsworth, about five miles south of
central London, was the first of the London County
Council's cottage estates.[95] Designed by W. E. Riley
(1852–1937) with the assistance of E. Stone Collins
(1874–1942), Totterdown provided 1,261 houses on 39
acres of land. The gridded plan of streets, yielding 31.81
houses to the acre, was not particularly garden-like, but
the design of the very small houses, grouped in rows of
twelve units, was inventive, with elegantly executed Arts
and Crafts details that gave residents some sense of the
country house idea.

White Hart Lane Estate (1903–20s), Tottenham,
now also known as Tower Gardens, followed soon after.[96]

Planned to house 33,000 people on 177 acres, the initial
portion (1903–13), developed north of Lordship Lane and
the Lordship Recreational Ground, had a village green,
Tower Garden, surrounded by a grid of streets lined with
rows of picturesque, two-story terraced cottages featuring slate-hung and tile-hung gables, hip roofs, and bay
windows. A far cry from the dense flats the LCC was
building in the inner city, the houses, with a density of
25.05 cottages to the acre, were nonetheless intended
for the same working-class occupancy. But when they
proved difficult to rent, in part because of their physical remoteness from jobs and established communities,
the LCC introduced accommodations intended for
a more middle-class clientele, such as the Georgian-
inspired layout around Waltheof Gardens (1920–23), a
broad, spinelike greensward north of Risley Avenue off
of which diagonal streets radiate to form a more affluent
and distinctly gardenesque neighborhood bound to the
north by The Roundway, a spacious, planted boulevard
intended as part of a regional bypass. In addition, the
Topham Square flats (1924) off Risley Avenue, terraces
along Lordship Lane (1925–26), and cottages around
Flexmere Road, north of The Roundway, also catered to
greater affluence.

Norbury (1905–21), following Totterdown Fields
and the first phase of White Hart Lane, also had a gridded plan yielding twenty-nine Arts and Crafts–inspired
houses per acre.[97] Designed by LCC architects George
Weald (b. 1874), P. F. Binnie (1873–1945), J. R. Stark
(n.d.), and J. S. Brooks (n.d.), the estate was realized in
two parts: Norton Gardens, for Susan Beattie, "the architectural as well as geographical climax of the scheme,"
completed in 1909–14 at the top of the hill; and the
remainder, completed in 1919–21, on the hillside below,
where the influence of the picturesquely massed Hampstead Garden Suburb is more keenly felt, especially in
the hillside quadrangle straddling both sides of Isham
Road, echoing M. H. Baillie Scott's unrealized quadrangle design of 1908.[98]

One of the most attractive and extensive of the London County Council's cottage estates, the 54-acre **Old
Oak Estate** (1911–14), around the East Acton station of
what is now the Underground's Central Line, has as its
improbable neighbor the Wormwood Scrubs prison.[99]
Old Oak was the first garden suburb to benefit from the
Housing and Town Planning Act of 1909, which essentially institutionalized the principles incorporated in a
special Act of Parliament in 1906 that enabled Unwin to
lay out Hampstead Garden Suburb free from restrictive
bye-laws and opened up the way for the introduction of
closes, greens, squares, and culs-de-sac as elements of
large-scale estate plans.

The railroad cuts Old Oak into two unequal areas.
The first phase, west of the railroad, consists of 14
acres containing five shops and 319 modest two-story
redbrick cottages and cottage flats providing for 2,231
persons. Archibald Stuart Soutar was the lead architect,
with F. J. Lucas (n.d.) and J. M. Corment (n.d.) also contributing. The second phase, consisting of a larger plot

Totterdown Fields Estate

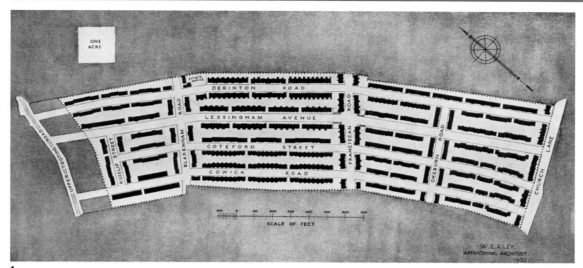

1

2

3

1. Plan, W. E. Riley with E. Stone Collins, 1902. LCC37

2. Okeburn Road North. HAM1 (1903)

3. Typical street. LMA (1910)

White Hart Lane Estate

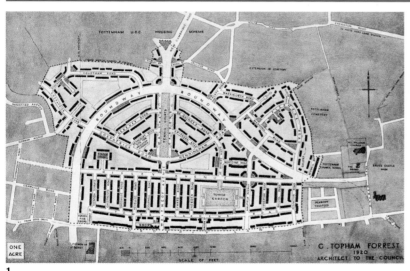

1

3

2

4

5

1. Plan, 1920. LCC37

2. Tower Garden East Terrace. LCC37

3. Flexmere Road and Marshall Road. LMA (1928)

4. Morteyne Road and De Quincey Road. RAMSA (2007)

5. Waltheof Gardens. RAMSA (2007)

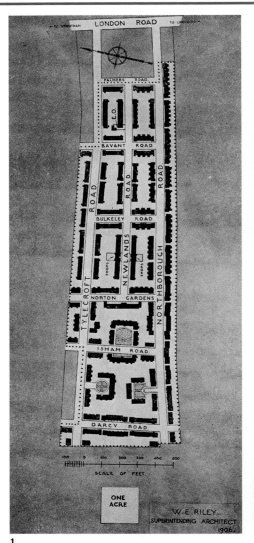

of land (developed 1919–21) to the northeast, nearer the prison, contains two shops, a school, and 721 cottages intended for 5,330 persons. Susan Beattie writes that Soutar's work at the western section of Old Oak provides "dramatic evidence of the homage . . . [being paid] to Hampstead Garden Suburb—homage not only to the Suburb as it was carried out but to the fantasy that lay behind it, the fairy-tale village tenderly portrayed in the illustrations to *Town Planning and Modern Architecture at the Hampstead Garden Suburb*. The deep quadrangles and closes, angle blocks and terraces unfolding along the line of a curving street or deliberately diverging from it show a scrupulous regard for the composite 'picture' to which they contribute, as if the housing branch [of the LCC] had set out to prove the strength of the book's central arguments."[100]

South of Western Avenue, later widened into the Westway, the **Wormholt Estate** (1919–27), built for the borough of Hammersmith, follows similar principles, with H. T. Hare (1860–1921) taking the lead and J. Ernest Franck (d. 1970), M. J. Dawson (1875–1943), and P. Streatfield (n.d.) each responsible for a section.[101] By 1926, 600 houses had been built on the 50 acres between Old Oak Common Lane, Steventon

Road, and Bloemfontein Road, where, reflecting the "homes for heroes" campaign to provide for returning war veterans, a high level of design was achieved with pan-tile-roofed Georgian-inspired brick houses, many grouped away from the street around greens, of which Viola Square, designed by H. T. Hare and B. Lisle (n.d.), is an excellent example. A charmingly eccentric branch library (Hampton C. Lucas, 1930) and a generously proportioned school dramatically enlivened the neighborhood's architecture.

In contrast to the cottagey informality of the Old Oak Estate and the slightly more formal Wormholt Estate, the **Cleverly Estate** (1928), designed by Victor Wilkins (1878–1972), lying directly south of Wormholt along Sawley Road, was developed by the Peabody Trust, historically the developer of high-quality inner-city working-class housing.[102] Cleverly was dramatic to the point of monumentality, with expressive Wren-aissance-Georgian-style buildings that broke with the Peabody tradition of Queen Anne–style tenements. Red brick with stone trim makes for an impressive contrast with neighboring buildings, reflecting the impact of the Lutyens housing at Hampstead Garden Suburb on the profession. Three-story-high apartment blocks at the

Old Oak Estate

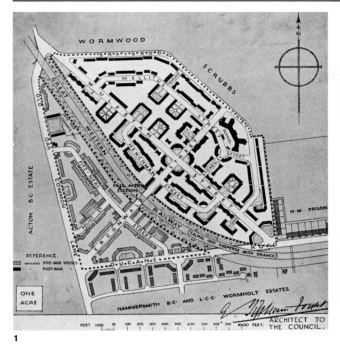

1

2

3

4

5

6

1. Plan, Archibald Stuart Soutar with F. J. Lucas and J. M. Corment, 1920. LCC37

2. Erconwald Street. LMA

3. Henchman Street. RAMSA (2007)

4. Fitzneal Street from Du Cane Road. LMA

5. Fitzneal Street. LMA

6. Du Cane Road. RAMSA (2007)

Wormholt Estate

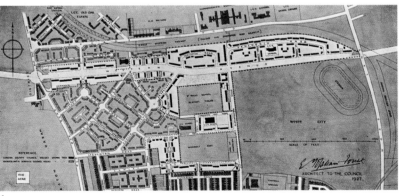

1

2

3

4

1. Plan, H. T. Hare with J. Ernest Franck, M. J. Dawson, and P. Streatfield, 1927. LCC37

2. Tamarisk Square. RAMSA (2007)

3. Hilary Road. RAMSA (2007)

4. Wormholt Library, Hampton C. Lucas, 1930. RAMSA (2007)

Cleverly Estate

1. Aerial view. GE (2010)

2. Steventon Road. RAMSA (2007)

3. Interior courtyard. RAMSA (2007)

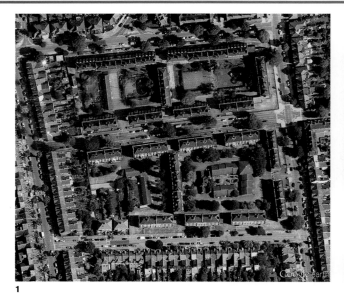

Roehampton Estate

1. Plan, G. Topham Forrest, 1921. LCC37

2. Pleasance Road. LMA (1924)

3. The Pleasance. LMA (1922)

4. Typical street. Kereshun. AK (2011)

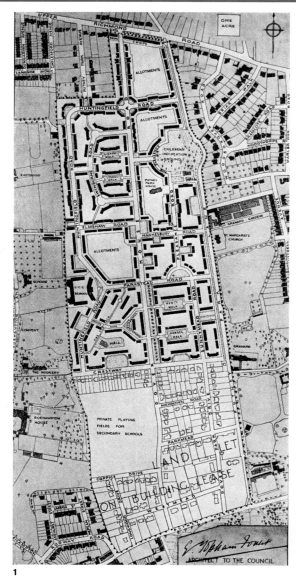

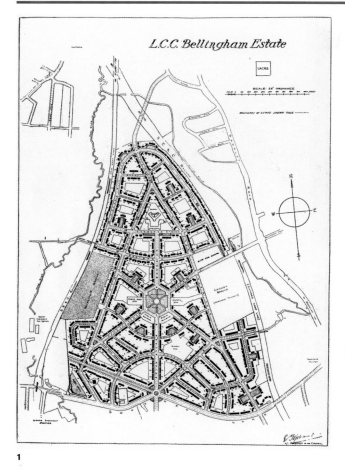

1. Plan, G. Topham Forrest, 1921. AJ23

2. Aerial view. EHAC (1999)

3. Typical street. Kereshun. AK (2011)

1

3

northern edge of the estate along Steventon Road are punctuated by monumental column-framed arches leading to inner courtyards large enough to contain tennis courts and playgrounds. The entrances to the separate blocks of flats open up from the inner courtyards.

Many workers' villages built to meet the needs of World War I were located in or near London. The pressures to get the villages in place quickly and cheaply did not seem to diminish the artistic quality of the product. In fact, it can be argued that the opposite was true. As Susan Beattie observed, in the wartime work, "new qualities began to emerge both in the articulation of facades and in terrace lay-out. The detailing of porches is richer and more decisive, the character of each group of cottages more distinct. There is an increasingly committed use of features recommended by Parker and Unwin . . . Slowly, almost stealthily, with each attempt at a bolder articulation of facade and terrace, the Housing branch moved closer to the ideal set forth in *Cottage Plans and Common Sense*."[103]

Although a few privately sponsored post–World War I industrial villages were built (see p. 716), it was the London County Council that bore the brunt of meeting the needs of London's ill-housed working classes. G. Topham Forrest (1872–1945) was the LCC's chief architect in the 1920s and 1930s. Forrest's 1,118-house, 146-acre **Roehampton Estate** (1920–27) carries forward the Parker and Unwin manner, with copses and setback groups and a reasonable variety of houses in brick and roughcast.[104]

The *Architects' Journal* deemed Roehampton and Bellingham to be "two of the L.C.C.'s most important housing estates." Roehampton, it reported, "is one of the most charming of the municipal housing estates in the country. The combination of the different colored materials in the houses, the grouping of the blocks, the width of the roads, and the sense of openness about the estate, give in the result all that is looked for in the lay-out of a garden city."[105] The Wren-inspired brick architecture was counterpointed with some use of wood, the value of which for housing impressed Forrest on a visit to the United States. In 1972, when Paul Davies visited Roehampton, by then commonly known as the Dover House Estate, he admired its "houses . . . laid out on a gentle domestic theme, set back from small front gardens among trees, in closes and cul-de-sacs," and observed that "although the gardens and old-style houses with pitched roofs" gave it "something of a suburban air, the enclosed vistas and grouping of houses are more typical of a garden city."[106]

The much larger **Bellingham Estate** (1921–23), on the still agricultural edge of Lewisham in south London, also laid out by G. Topham Forrest, contained 2,674 red-brick cottage-type houses on a 250-acre site (175 acres were devoted to housing).[107] Although the houses were nearly identical, the formal arrangement of the estate plan, with six roads converging on a hexagonal green, yielded a very strong sense of place. Two years later, in 1923, the even larger, nearby 522-acre **Downham Estate** (1923–30), again by Forrest, provided 6,021 houses for

1. Plan, G. Topham Forrest, 1923. LCC37

2. Aerial view. EHAC (1929)

3. Typical street. Kereshun. AK (2011)

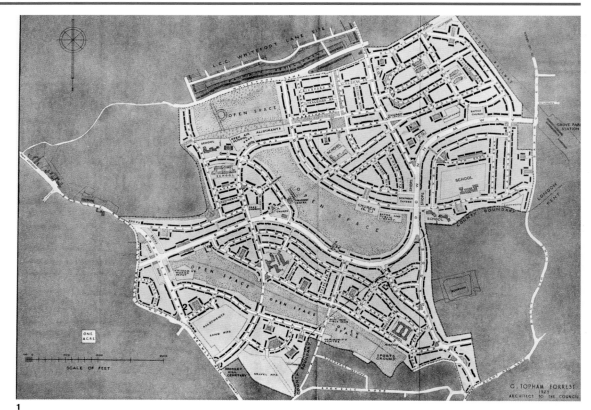

1

2

3

skilled and semiskilled blue-collar workers, laid out along winding roads that made for a more diffuse and typically suburban environment, although the provision of significant greenswards aerated the plan, and the provision of civic and commercial areas gave it more of a sense of community.[108]

St. Helier Estate (1925–36), also master planned by Forrest, was a still larger development—the largest south of the Thames and the second largest overall in the LCC portfolio.[109] St. Helier was set in 825 acres of farmland, with 120 acres retained as open space. The plan of roads was set out to preserve as many existing trees and natural features as possible. Intended to be more self-sufficient than most LCC garden suburbs, St. Helier included eighteen schools, seven churches, two pubs, a 200-seat movie theater, and sixty shops to serve the 9,000 families, or 40,000 people, living in houses and flats.

The **Watling Estate** (1925–31), Burnt Oak, consisting of 3,600 homes and 400 flats on approximately 387

acres of former farmland, was among the largest working-class garden suburbs realized, with 11,500 residents, although the density was comparatively low—10.7 units per acre, with 41 acres of parkland.[110] Located in north London, quite close to the Burnt Oak tube station of the recently extended Northern line, the development was also designed by Forrest, with subtle groupings of house rows and a rich play of materials and details recalling Frank Baines's Well Hall Estate (see p. 713) but with a bolder and clearer if less picturesque plan that at first glance seems almost commonplace. However, closer inspection reveals a subtle orchestration of landscaped vistas, with architecturally defined street intersections— typically angled buildings at corners—and culs-de-sac, set-back group houses facing closes, and broad greenswards called "groves" that help create the kinds of street pictures highly prized by Unwin.

Despite its working-class character, Watling Estate has something of the character of Hampstead Garden

St. Helier Estate

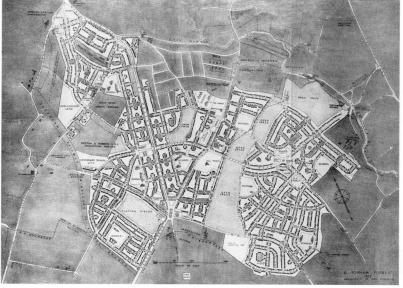

1

2

4

3

1. Plan, G. Topham Forrest, 1925.
LCC37

2. Shops. LMA (1931)

3. Typical street. Kereshun. AK
(2011)

4. Darley Gardens. Kereshun. AK
(2011)

Watling Estate

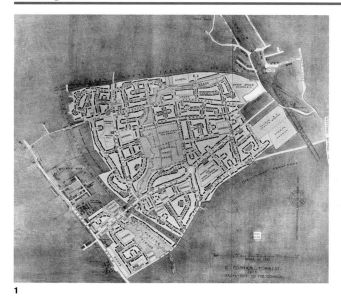

1

Blundell Road, Burnt Oak.

2

1. Plan, G. Topham Forrest, 1925.
LCC37

2. Blundell Road. BIB (1930)

3. Watling Avenue shops. BIB
(1948)

4, 5. Typical views. RAMSA (2007)

3

4

5

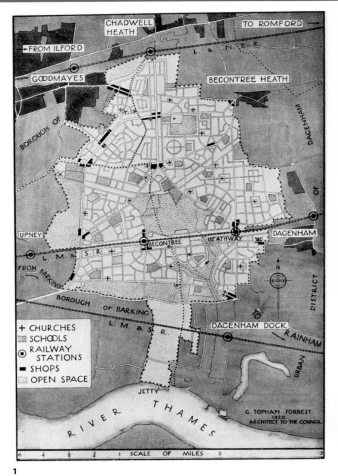

1

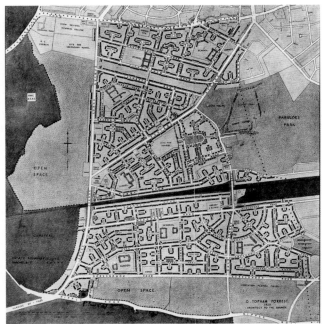

2

3

4

5

Suburb but much looser and with less refined architecture. Watling Avenue is the spine, off of which the various streets, many of them undulating, take advantage of the gently sloping topography and existing mature trees. Watling Park, Silkstream Park, and The Meads break the plan into manageable neighborhoods. Three sites were reserved for schools, which were soon constructed, including Woodcroft Junior and Infants School (1928–30), designed by H. A. Welch (1883–1953) on Goldbeaters Grove between Abbots Road and Watling Avenue. Some shopping was developed at the west end of Watling Avenue, where other shops off the property clustered around the tube station.

Though the aesthetics of the suburb were "olde English Village," the politics of the residents were not. Residents of neighboring housing estates referred to Watling as "Little Moscow." Interestingly, the development was at first not a social success. As was the case with White Hart Lane, its remote location—though within greater London—and its suburban character proved alienating to many prospective residents who were reluctant to relocate there from inner-city neighborhoods.

Becontree (1920–29), in the east London Borough of Barking and Dagenham, was the largest of all LCC housing estates, with a population of over 100,000.[111] The speed of its completion was astonishing, with

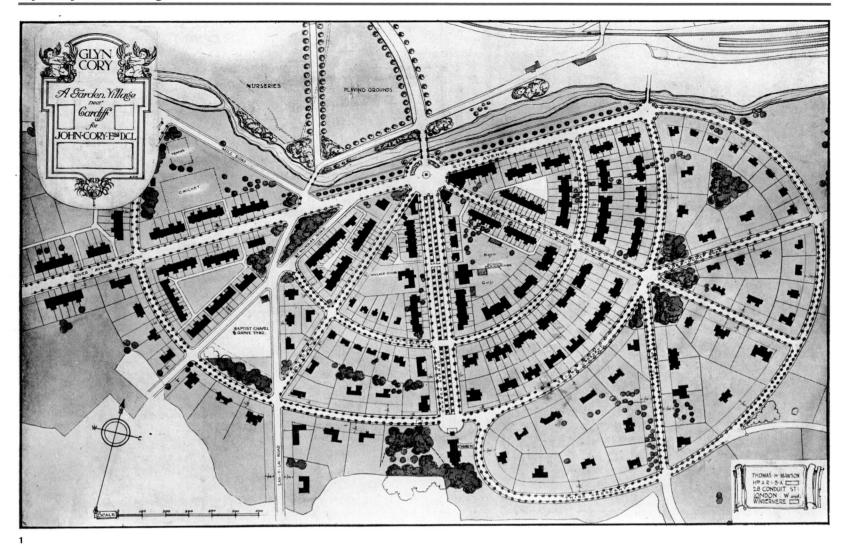

1

1. Plan, Thomas Mawson, 1907.
THM

2,000 to 4,000 houses realized per year between 1922 and 1929. Forrest was the principal designer, arranging the new suburb along Valence Avenue, a north–south spine, and retaining the historic Valence Mansion. On either side of the spine, winding roads contained terrace cottages and the occasional pub "in a genteel Neo-Georgian taste ('not conducive to inebriety')."[112] For Pevsner, Becontree, despite the occasional pub, was "a dormitory, not a town."[113]

WALES

The Garden City and garden suburb movement quickly spread beyond England to the rest of the United Kingdom. In Wales, the typical heady mix of idealism and paternalism could be seen at **Glyn Cory Garden Village**, conceived by coal magnates John (1828–1910) and Reginald (1871–1934) Cory in 1906 to provide for 1,400 houses on 300 acres of sloping land that rises 260 feet to form a natural amphitheater.[114] The site lay seven miles west of Cardiff in the coal-mining county of Glamorgan. The initial plan by landscape architect Thomas Mawson reserved part of the site for a golf course and 60 acres for

allotments and small holdings. Mawson's plan respected the site's contours with three concentric crescents intersected by a 100-foot-wide boulevard-like central avenue leading up from the Peterson train station to a church. A village club and a school were to face each other across the avenue, near its midpoint. Housing densities were to be concentrated in the low portions of the site, with villas located on the upland. Designs were prepared for a full range of houses as well as the club and school.

Mawson's plan was revised by Thomas Adams, who moved the housing to higher ground in order to avoid flooding from the Ely River, and shortened the avenue. Though the project got off to a vigorous start, with the construction of roads and a new bridge over the river, by 1914 only twenty houses had been constructed. The suburb's failure was attributed by some to the grand manner of the plan, but more likely it was the combination of the war and competition from other suburbs nearer to Cardiff that did it in.

Rhiwbina Garden Village, planned by Raymond Unwin in 1912, was one such competitor, located three-and-a-half miles northwest of Cardiff.[115] Only ten minutes by train from the center of the city, Rhiwbina, situated on 110 acres at the base of wooded hills,

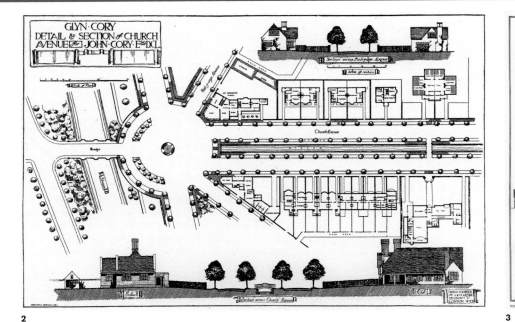

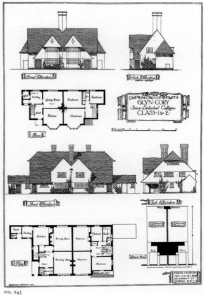

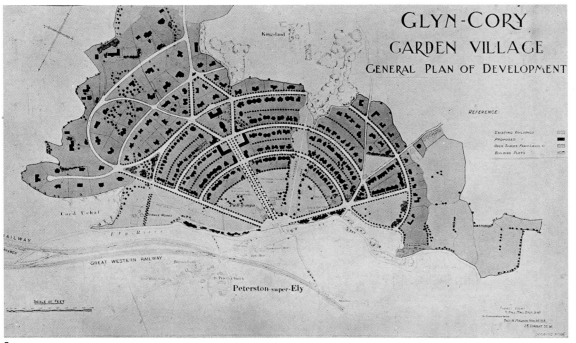

2. Detail and section of Church Avenue, Thomas Mawson, 1907. THM

3. Plans and elevations of semidetached cottages, Thomas Mawson, 1907. THM

4. Perspective, Thomas Mawson, 1907. THM

5. Plan, Thomas Adams, c. 1909. TPR10

6. Cory Crescent. McGahey. PMG (2012)

7. Cory Crescent. PMG (c. 1910)

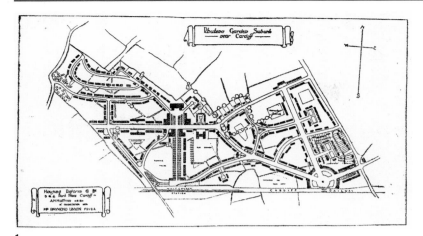

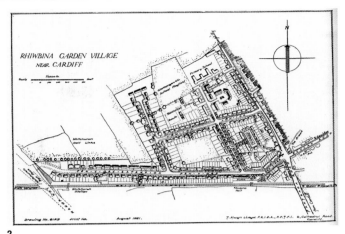

1

2

3

4

1. Plan, Raymond Unwin, 1912. GCTP13

2. Plan, T. Alwyn Lloyd. TPR52 (1951)

3, 4. Pen-y-Dre. TPR52

5. Rhiwbina Tea Gardens, T. Alwyn Lloyd, 1916. ABJ16

6. Pen-y-Dre. Grayson. GEO (2010)

5

6

was intended for both a middle- and working-class population. An early project of the Welsh Town Planning and Housing Trust, Ltd., established in 1912 as a public utility company limiting its dividends to 5 percent and dedicated to the "acquisition, laying-out and control of buildings estates in Wales . . . along garden village lines," Rhiwbina sat on land leased by the trust to the newly created Cardiff Worker's Co-operative Garden Village Society, which oversaw the project.[116] In addition to addressing the general housing shortage of rapidly expanding Cardiff, the garden suburb was also envisioned as a healthy antidote to the overcrowded city, which was experiencing a disturbing surge of tuberculosis cases.

Rhiwbina lay north of the Cardiff Railway tracks. Unwin's plan called for two main roads radiating from the two railroad stations, Rhiwbina Halt and

Whitchurch Station. A. H. Mottram (1886–1953), who worked in Parker and Unwin's office on Hampstead Garden Suburb, was responsible for the first phase, consisting of seventy roughcast houses, some of which were set behind hedges on tree-lined streets while semidetached pairs were also grouped around oblong greens. The plan left space for shopping near Rhiwbina Halt and included a recreation ground with eight tennis courts, a bowling green, and a croquet lawn, as well as an institute with a capacity of 300 for concerts and community meetings. Writing in 1913, after thirty-four houses had been completed, Ewart G. Culpin praised Unwin's plan for its "vistas, closes, and other features . . . similar to the best characters of the Hampstead Garden Suburb," but with "rather more spaciousness, and a feature is being made of enclosed children's playgrounds at the backs of gardens in each block of houses."[117] Over

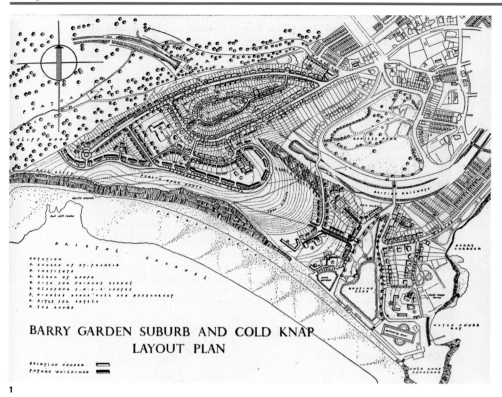

BARRY GARDEN SUBURB AND COLD KNAP
LAYOUT PLAN

1. Plan, Raymond Unwin and
T. Alwyn Lloyd, c. 1914. TPR52
(1951)

2. Aerial view. TC (1930)

3. Cold Knap. TC

4. Tan-y-Fron. TC

5. Porth-y-Castell. TC

the next decade a total of 300 houses were completed, with H. Avray Tipping (1855–1933) designing a later group of brown brick houses near the railway. Cardiff-based T. Alwyn Lloyd (1882–1960), who also worked for Unwin at Hampstead and became chief architect of the Welsh Town Planning and Housing Trust, was responsible for additional groups of houses as well as his own freestanding house and the Rhiwbina Tea Gardens, a concrete structure with a pyramidal blue-slate roof that accommodated a shop on the ground floor and four bedrooms above.

Barry Garden Suburb (1914–17), located on 175 acres in the seaside town of Barry, ten miles southwest of Cardiff, marked a second collaboration between Unwin and Lloyd and the Welsh Town Planning and Housing Trust.[118] Barry was both an industrial town as well as a popular summer vacation destination for miners from South Wales, which Lloyd and Unwin took into consideration, providing easy access to the water and pebble beach for residents and the significant numbers of expected

holidaymakers. The suburb was planned in two distinct sections with the majority of housing concentrated on the upper, or Castle Farm, part of the site, high above the Bristol Channel. This commanding, cliff-top site was bound by two parks, Porthkerry Park and Romilly Park, whose existing recreational facilities permitted Lloyd to provide less open space than at Rhiwbina. Planned for up to 400 houses, a total of 232 were erected in semidetached pairs and short rows, most with white walls, slate roofs, and bay windows. This part of town also included a church, an institute, and a group of shops. Lloyd turned the existing footpath at the top of the cliff overlooking the beach and Bristol Channel into a 150-foot-wide boulevard. The so-called Cold Knap, or lower section of Barry Garden Suburb, was planned for the needs of visitors as well as residents and included public gardens, a seawater swimming pool, a dance hall, restaurants and shops, small hotels, and the "Glan-y-Mor," a group of buildings suitable for hosting conferences. In an early recognition of the potential impact of the automobile, the Cold Knap

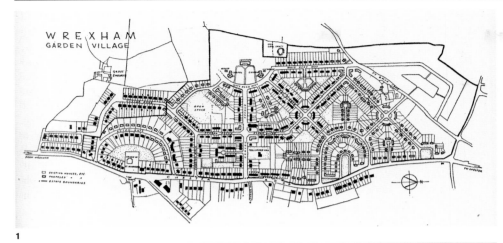

area also included a car park. In a departure from previous practice, the Welsh Town Planning and Housing Trust, in addition to leasing land for ninety-nine years to the local housing society, offered direct leases to builders and individuals, although the trust retained the right to approve their designs.

On almost 200 acres outside Wrexham, the largest town in North Wales, **Wrexham Garden Village** was another effort of the Welsh Town Planning and Housing Trust, undertaken to alleviate a severe housing shortage brought about by the rapidly expanding Gresford Colliery.[119] For this suburb, the trust turned in 1913 to G. L. Sutcliffe, who had designed houses at Parker and Unwin's Brentham as well as planned the second part of Liverpool Garden Suburb after Unwin's example. Sutcliffe's axial plan, which included recreation grounds, allotment gardens, and a school, called for a density not to exceed twelve dwellings per acre and sited houses along tree-lined roads of varying width, around greens, and in crescents. Provision was made for a church and an institute, but these did not move forward. Before his death, Sutcliffe designed forty-four brick-and-roughcast houses. T. Alwyn Lloyd then stepped in and by 1917 completed another 200 houses grouped in pairs and short rows and designed in the same rustic vernacular style. Less than a mile south of Wrexham Garden Village, Patrick Abercrombie was commissioned in 1918 by the local Borough Council to design a housing estate on 60 acres.

1. Plan, G. L. Sutcliffe, c. 1913. TPR52 (1951)

2. Aerial view. GE (2005)

3. Wat's Dyke Way. WXAS

4. Ael-y-Bryn. WXAS

5. Wat's Dyke Way. TPR52

6. Acton Gate. TPR52 (1915)

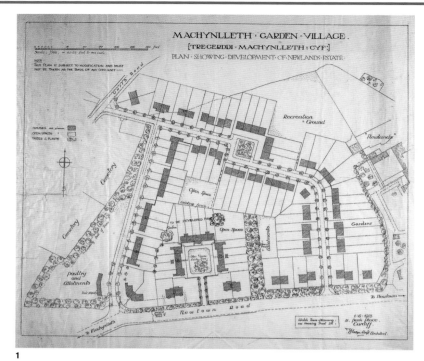

Llanidloes

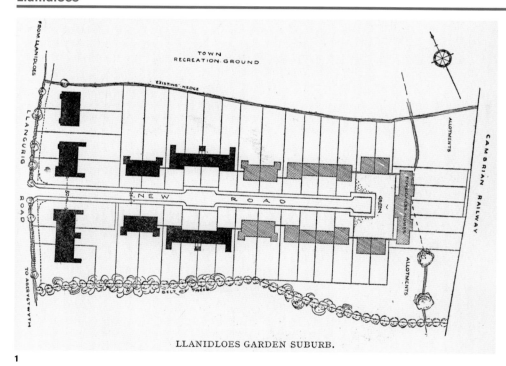

Ambitious plans that would have included a circus were quickly abandoned, although Abercrombie did complete a number of two-story neo-Georgian houses facing Rhosnessney Lane.

The trust experimented with the idea of bringing modest garden suburbs—little more than enclaves—to the more rural, agricultural regions of Wales, and T. Alwyn Lloyd was responsible for the design of two of them located about twenty miles apart in the county of Powys.[120] **Machynlleth** (1913) consists of nineteen gabled houses grouped in a quadrangle around a "large clump of trees" that "was made a feature in the layout" in order, in Lloyd's words, "to give local Welsh character to it."[121] **Llanidloes** (1914) also contains nineteen roughcast houses arrayed in a straightforward manner on a site adjoining a public recreation ground. Lloyd included a third story in some of the houses in deference to buildings in the older parts of town where the third story was used to accommodate home handlooms for workers in the woolen industry.

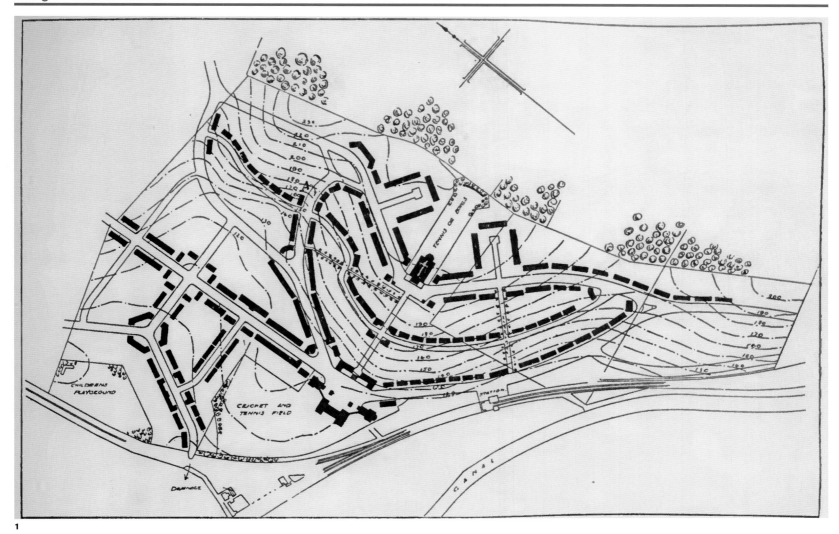

1

1. Plan, Raymond Unwin, 1912.
EGC

SCOTLAND

Inspired by a speech titled "A Garden Suburb for Glasgow," delivered in December 1910 by English politician T. R. Marr, who had written a book six years earlier documenting poor housing conditions in Manchester and Salford, a group of Glasgow's most prominent residents banded together with the goal of creating Scotland's first garden suburb.[122] Led by Sir John Stirling Maxwell, a philanthropist and Member of Parliament who would later go on to establish the National Trust of Scotland, the Glasgow Garden Suburb Tenants Ltd. was officially registered in 1912. The suburb's prospectus noted that the town "will be for all classes, but particularly the working classes," with special attention paid to postal workers.[123] After rejecting sites in Cathcart and Giffnock, the group chose 200 acres in the Westerton section of Bearsden, six miles northwest of central Glasgow, after the North British Railway Company agreed to build a new station there. Unwin was hired to prepare the plan and the Glasgow-based architect John A. W. Grant (1885–1959) was commissioned to design the anticipated 300 houses for **Glasgow Garden Suburb.**

The garden suburb movement had yet to catch on in Scotland, although the need for affordable, quality housing was urgent in heavily industrial Glasgow, where "factories and forges belched black smoke unceasingly into the atmosphere."[124] As the promoters of the project noted: "Glasgow has been accurately described as four square miles of stone and lime. This deplorable state of affairs is not confined to the heart of the City, but has been carried into nearly all our suburbs" where "up go great barrack-like shoddy tenements which in a very short time become dismal, monotonous rows . . . as inimical to life and light as the older buildings in the most densely populated" areas in the central city. "Scotland is far behind England in the matter of housing. During the past ten years, our friends across the border have witnessed the rise of Garden Cities, Model Village Communities, and Garden Suburbs, as wonderful as they have been successful."[125] Maureen Whitelaw, in her history of Westerton, posited an explanation for this failure, writing that "land was at a premium so the Garden Suburb movement which was becoming popular in England was not in favour here because of its need for greater areas of land."[126]

In 1912 the Glasgow Garden Suburb Tenants Ltd. secured necessary funding after an act of Parliament declared that housing societies could borrow up to two-thirds the value of the houses erected. The promoters

2. Ordnance Survey map. OS (1933)

3, 4. Typical views. EDLCT

5. Village Hall. EDLCT

6–8. Typical views. EDC (2010)

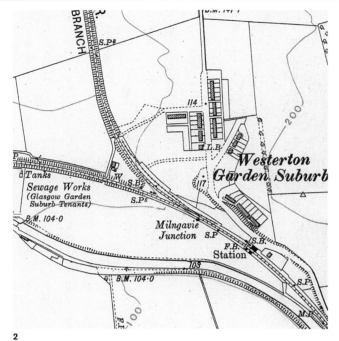

2

3

4

5

6

8

7

of Glasgow Garden Suburb, also known as Westerton Garden Suburb, stated that although the project was not intended "for their own gain, but for the public good," they still believed that the "housing problem can only be solved on a sound commercial basis." Planned as a cooperative venture, prospective tenants would purchase five shares at a value of £10 each, although they could pay the £50 in installments if they could not afford a lump sum payment. The tenant would be paid a dividend from the housing society, which kept the funds and used them for necessary repairs. When tenants left the suburb they could either retain their investment or take the accrued capital.

Unwin's plan (1912) took into consideration the hope that the 300 proposed houses were only the first phase of a larger enterprise. The steeply contoured rural site consisted of former farmland that abutted a golf course and a navigable canal. According to Unwin, "the lay-out of the land . . . is influenced by one or two considerations. The fixed position of the railway station, immediately at the foot of a very steep incline, prevented any road leading off at right angles to the station; and the general slopes, with the importance of securing ready access from the station to the land to the north of the suburb which will some day be developed if the suburb proves successful, determined that the main road from the station must skirt the steep hill and gradually rise up to the top of the ridge at the extreme north-east corner of the plan." Unwin placed playing fields on level ground near the railway and "where the main road from the station is able to diverge in different directions a small square is planned with a steep path leading up to some public building, perhaps a church or chapel on the crest of the hill, which would form a splendid landmark for the surrounding district."[127] Public buildings would be situated west of the square while shops and other businesses would go on the east side.

The first forty-five houses designed by John A. W. Grant, completed in May 1913, were built on relatively flat ground near the railroad station on Maxwell and Stirling Avenues. Unwin called for about half of the proposed houses to be grouped in rows of eight. The plan also included blocks of semidetached dwellings as well as terraced groups of three, four, five, and six houses. The English cottage–style two-story roughcast houses featured steeply pitched slate roofs, many with dormers, as well as glazed redbrick chimney stacks and decorative half-timbering on some of the gables. Set behind privet hedges, the three-, four-, and five-bedroom houses included narrow back lanes and roughcast garden walls. Grant was soon joined at Glasgow Garden Suburb by architect Albert Victor Gardner (1884–1944).

Eighty-four houses were completed before World War I put a halt to progress in 1915. The only public building to be realized was the Village Hall (1914), which was forced to serve multiple roles as an elementary school, church, and community meeting house. A recreation ground with tennis courts and a bowling green was included but only one store was built, with housing above for the shopkeeper. By the time development began again at Glasgow Garden Suburb two decades later, in 1935, Unwin's plan had been abandoned and Grant's architectural services were no longer sought.

IRELAND

The attempt to promote the Garden City movement in Ireland in the first decade of the twentieth century was largely met with indifference, if not outright hostility. As architect and historian Murray Fraser has written, "Until 1911 there had been no real Irish town planning movement, only a few isolated supporters. This is not surprising, given that Ireland was hardly fertile ground for those advocating garden cities or garden suburbs. Ireland's slow industrial growth compared with Britain, and its predominantly agricultural economy, meant that it had neither the proliferation of ugly manufacturing towns nor the tradition of intellectual critiques of industrial urbanization that had prompted the communitarian ideals of Ebenezer Howard and Raymond Unwin."[128] Still, there was a serious housing problem at the time, especially in Dublin, where a growing number of substandard dwelling units was accompanied by severe overcrowding. But Dublin's local town council, known officially as the Dublin Corporation but more popularly as The Corpo, refused to consider a solution grounded in Garden City principles. When the idea of building garden cities was brought to The Corpo's attention in 1910, John Clancy, the group's counsel, stated, "We want no garden city—give us working class dwellings,"[129] leading historian F. H. A. Aalen to observe that in Ireland, "Town planning was not to interfere with the solution of the housing problem!"[130]

In the 1910s, however, "there was a determined attempt, involving many of the leading British exponents of town planning, to introduce garden suburb ideals to Ireland," as Fraser has noted.[131] In November 1913 the Irish Local Government Board asked Scottish biologist and town planner Patrick Geddes (1854–1932) to offer his thoughts on how best to improve the housing situation. In his testimony before the Dublin Housing Inquiry, Geddes criticized the policy of high-density tenement development adopted by the Dublin Corporation, instead proposing the development of low-density garden suburbs on relatively cheap land outside the city center, stating, "I plead for the utilization of such splendid examples as Hampstead and Letchworth."[132] Five months later, in April 1914, the Irish branch of the Housing and Town Planning Association invited Raymond Unwin (who would terminate his partnership with Barry Parker the following month) to speak at Trinity College in Dublin, where his lecture was titled "How Town Planning May Solve the Housing Problem."[133] In August, after a spring and summer filled with additional lectures, exhibitions, newspaper articles, and editorials devoted to the housing problem, the Dublin Corporation, at the urging of the Citizens' Housing League,

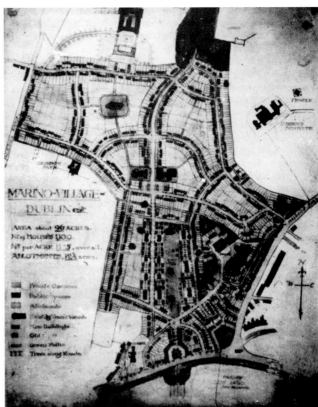

1. Aerial rendering, Raymond Unwin and Patrick Geddes, 1914. DCA

2. Plan, Raymond Unwin and Patrick Geddes, 1914. DCA

hired Geddes and Unwin to "formulate such recommendations, alternatives, suggestions or new plans in connection" with the redevelopment of the city.[134] Although Geddes and Unwin would spend the majority of their time and energy focused on Dublin's core, they did prepare a preliminary proposal for **Marino Village**, a garden suburb outside the city center, hastily completed before the end of 1914.

For their proposed garden suburb, Geddes and Unwin selected a 96-acre site three miles northeast of Dublin's center, convenient to a tram line. The largely unimproved parcel was home to Marino, the former estate of James Cauleild (1728–1799), the 1st Earl of Charlemont, who commissioned William Chambers to design the Marino Casino (1775), a local landmark that remained well preserved into the twentieth century.[135] Geddes and Unwin described the site as "every way suitable for the erection of a Garden Village, one indeed second to none in Dublin, perhaps anywhere . . . on grounds of accessibility, economy and beauty alike."[136]

The centerpiece of Geddes and Unwin's unrealized plan, prepared in collaboration with Geddes's son-in-law, architect F. C. Mears (1880–1953), was an 800-foot-long, 130-foot-wide public green. Mervyn Miller, who credits Unwin as primary author of the layout, believed that it represented an expansion of "the concept of a village green with Beaux Arts grandeur to result in a 'peoples Versailles.'"[137] The plan called for 1,100 detached, semi-detached, and terraced one- and two-story houses for workers, developed at a density of 11.5 dwellings per

acre, with private rear and front gardens for each house in addition to 12.5 acres reserved for public open space. No retail facilities were included but the plan featured a school, a recreational hall, and public baths, as well as the retention of the Marino Casino for community use.

Mervyn Miller has praised Marino's "little-known layout,"[138] with its

> *two types of roadway . . . —'green paths' which really represented a kind of proto-Radburn traffic-free pedestrian network, and the 'traffic roads' themselves which were varied in width according to anticipated loading and many of which were shown tree lined . . . Unwin took a central point on the Fairview Road frontage to create a 'gateway' into the suburb following the precedent of Hampstead . . . The line of this was projected northwards into the Marino land to create one of the major axes of the layout. A modified grid layout can be discerned in much of the remainder of the site . . . incorporating natural features wherever possible, but conforming overall to Unwin's general theory of housing layout in* Nothing Gained by Overcrowding.

But, as Miller writes, "it is difficult to evaluate Unwin's scheme for Marino with any degree of certainty due to the small amount of evidence which has survived, and the tentative nature of his proposals." Had the project moved forward "the result would have been a striking landmark in the canon of his major achievements, and

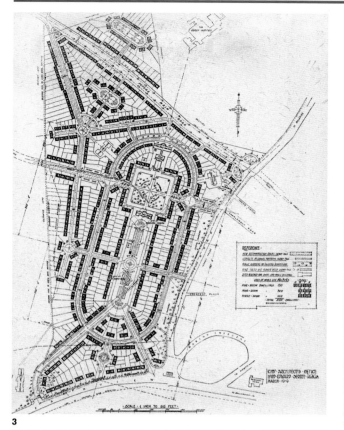

3

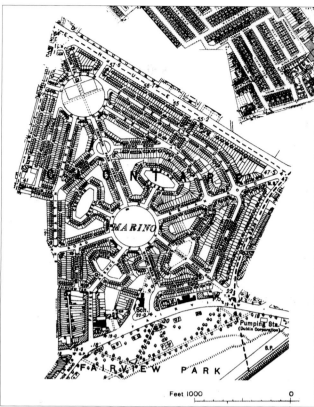

4

3. Plan, Horace O'Rourke, 1919. TB20

4. Plan, Horace O'Rourke, 1923. DCA (1927)

5. Typical street. Shiels. PS (2012)

6. St. Aidan's Park Road. Shiels. PS (2012)

7. Marino Park Avenue. Shiels. PS (2012)

5

6

7

a landmark in the evolution of Irish housing and town planning policy and practice."[139]

After the war, interest in the Marino project resurfaced, this time with the Dublin Corporation retaining Horace O'Rourke (1880–1963), assistant city architect of Dublin, to develop a new plan (1919), although his superior, C. J. MacCarthy (1858–1947), city architect since 1893, is sometimes credited as well.[140] Working with a reduced site of 50 acres, O'Rourke retained the prominent central public green, now surrounded by an oval-shaped, tree-lined street. North and south of the oval, two triangular shaped parcels grouped houses around landscaped greens. Developed at a density of twelve houses per acre, O'Rourke's scheme included 600 semidetached and terraced houses, along with some centrally located shops and community buildings. Miller has written that O'Rourke's "plan as a whole appeared much more rigid and formal than Unwin's, which strove to balance the grand-scale features with the opportunity to develop more intimate scale street pictures and spatial enclosures. The overall influence of the Unwin plan is still, however, readily apparent."[141] Despite the support of the Dublin Corporation, the scheme, which would have also resulted in the demolition of the Marino Casino, fell victim to Ireland's political turmoil, which led, in 1922, to the nation's independence from the United Kingdom, except for six northern counties.

In 1923 O'Rourke, who became city architect the previous year, completely reworked his earlier layout for an enlarged site that now encompassed 126 acres.[142] The third plan proved the charm for the Marino development. The heart of the "highly symmetrical" plan was a large circular green, Marino Park, with radiating avenues branching off in all directions and connecting to the remainder of the development, composed of curving and straight streets lined by semidetached houses and terraced groups in rows of three to eight houses.[143] Close to Marino Park, four sets of houses were grouped

1. Plan, Thomas Joseph Byrne, 1915. DCA

2–4. Typical streets. Shiels. PS (2012)

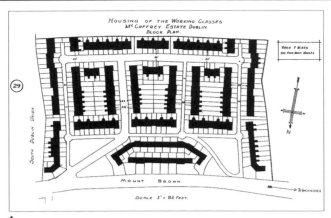

1

2

3

4

around lozenge-shaped greens. Construction began in 1924 and the following year 4,400 applications were received for the 243 completed working-class dwellings, many designed by local architect F. C. Hicks (1870–1965). By the end of the decade the Marino Estate numbered 1,283 houses.

The Dublin Corporation was responsible for several additional housing estates influenced by Geddes and Unwin's advocacy as well as by their unrealized Marino scheme. In 1915 the corporation hired Dublin architect Thomas Joseph Byrne (1876–1939) to plan the **McCaffrey Estate**, located on a flat seven-acre site about a mile west of the city center.[144] Byrne arranged the 202 working-class cottages in terraces at a density of twenty-nine dwellings to the acre, "substantially higher than the Unwinian stricture of 12 dwellings to the acre, but . . . well below the norm for Dublin Corporation schemes," according to Murray Fraser, who was impressed with both the "symmetrical" plan providing two triangular public green spaces and with the houses, which were completed by 1918: "Byrne's distinctive Arts and Crafts approach can be seen at the McCaffrey Estate in the picturesque, Neo-Vernacular terraces built in yellow stock bricks, and adorned with complex, stepped rooflines punctuated by hips and gables. The elevational treatment was evocative of the 'street picture' diagrams in Unwin's *Town Planning in Practice* (1909), and hence followed both pre-war LCC estates and the picturesque strain of munitions housing epitomized by the Well Hall Estate."[145]

The Dublin Corporation's **Fairbrothers' Fields Estate** was a significantly larger undertaking, located on 22 acres of farmland about a mile south of Dublin's center.[146] The project was initially planned in 1913 for 800 houses arranged in a grid, but C. J. MacCarthy, influenced by Geddes and Unwin, decided to rework his scheme (1918) with the help of O'Rourke, reducing the number of houses to 413 and adopting "a lay-out more nearly approaching the treatment recommended by the advocates of the garden suburb" with "bye-law roads intersecting at right angles . . . replaced by roads laid out 'in a more pleasing manner with grass verges and trees' and the houses 'spaced out with a view to securing greater variety of effect without involving extra cost.'"[147] Murray Fraser, who credits O'Rourke with the design, has written that the revised scheme for Fairbrothers' Fields, which was largely realized as planned, "represented the first use in Ireland of Unwinian set-backs and cul-de-sacs in order to break up the scale and monotony of the large site blocks." Fraser also notes that the plan "was published in the London-based *Architect*, the first Irish housing project to receive such an accolade."[148] The three- to five-room cottages were arranged in pairs and terraces of up to twelve dwellings, with rear allotment gardens provided for each house and several public green spaces placed throughout the development.

In 1927, the Dublin Corporation developed a working-class suburb in **Drumcondra**, three miles north of central Dublin.[149] O'Rourke was responsible for the

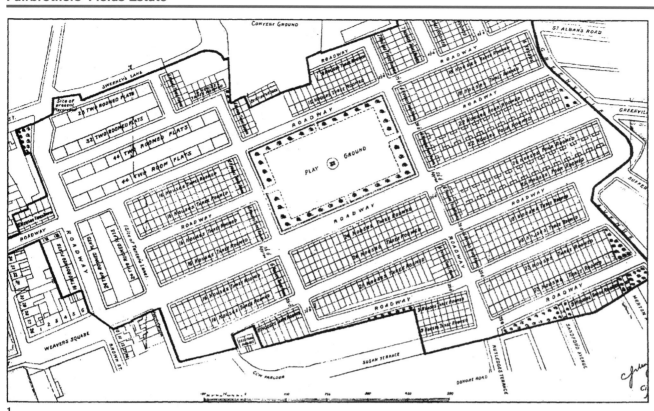

1. Plan, C. J. MacCarthy, 1913. DCA

2. Plan, C. J. MacCarthy and Horace O'Rourke, 1918. DCA

3. Elevations and plans, 1918. DCA

4, 5. Typical views. Shiels. PS (2012)

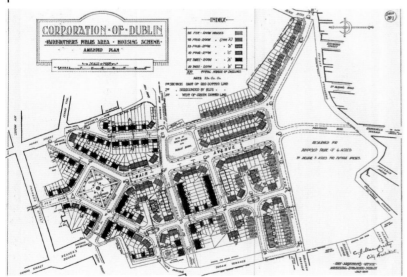

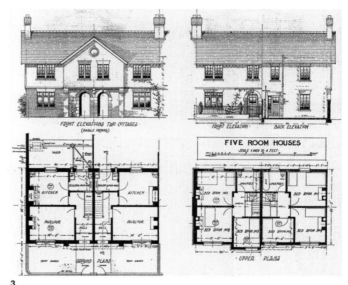

1. Ordnance Survey map. OSI (1938)

2. Aerial view. GE (2008)

3. Walsh Road. Shiels. PS (2012)

4. Ferguson Road. Shiels. PS (2012)

5. Windele Road. Shiels. PS (2012)

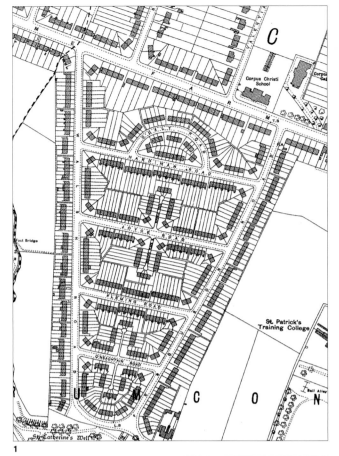

development's V-shaped plan, located on a 32-acre site bordered by the playing fields of St. Patrick's Training College to the east and by a landfill to the west that was converted into a park in the 1930s. The Drumcondra plan, primarily composed of terraced units but with some semidetached houses, featured four east–west streets creating five blocks, four of which were further divided by central north–south culs-de-sac. The perimeter streets were lined with the longest terraces. Some variety was achieved in the development's 534 houses by varying setback distances and many of the corner units were placed at an angle. Historian Ruth McManus was most impressed with the "layout of four small culs-de-sac off O'Neachtain and Joyce Roads. The arrangement of the houses in these cases is strikingly similar to that employed in the London County Council schemes such as Becontree."[150]

O'Rourke was responsible for one additional working-class garden suburb developed by the Dublin

Corporation in **Donnycarney** (1929), located on a 31-acre site three-and-a-half miles northeast of the city center and just north of the Marino Estate.[151] O'Rourke's plan for 421 semidetached and terraced two-story, three-bedroom houses, with front and rear gardens, was less picturesque than his previous efforts for the corporation, with a more gridded layout featuring long rows on straight streets. Although some houses were located along culs-de-sac, corner house groups were often placed at an angle, and a large *rond-point* was located at the intersection of Elm and Oak Roads. The housing estate also included a large playground, a church, and a school.

In addition to the work of the Dublin Corporation, another publicly sponsored housing initiative was begun in 1919 when the Irish Land (Provision for Sailors and Soldiers) Bill, inspired by the English Homes for Heroes campaign, granted the Irish Local Government Board broad powers of land acquisition in order

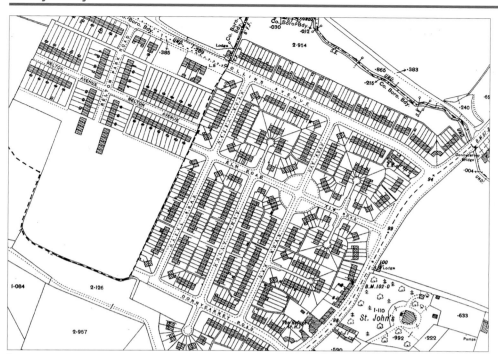

1. Ordnance Survey map. DCA (1936)

2–4. Typical streets. Shiels. PS (2012)

to build "cottages in Ireland, with or without plots or gardens, for ex-servicemen."[152] With offices in Dublin, Belfast, and London, and funding from the British Treasury, the Local Government Board was expected to work with municipal governments as well as private developers in constructing modestly sized housing developments, primarily to be located near the country's most populous cities, but with some units planned for the countryside as well. The effort was not only intended to provide much-needed housing but also to offset widespread unemployment, with demobilized servicemen expected to work on the construction of the new projects. After Irish independence in 1922, the project continued with the establishment of the Irish Sailors' and Soldiers' Land Trust, administered by a five-member board, three picked by British authorities and one each selected by the Irish Free State and the government of Northern Ireland.

The largest project developed for "Irish heroes" was designed along garden suburb lines by F. C. Mears for a 60-acre site that became **Killester Garden Suburb** (1920), about four miles northeast of central Dublin.[153] Mears had been recommended to the Local Government Board by engineer Frederick Purser Griffith (1877?–1939), an influential member of the Dublin Citizens' Housing League, who persuaded philanthropist Lady Aberdeen (1857–1939) to provide additional funding for the project. Griffith also served as the engineer, with Mears responsible for the houses in addition to the plan. The picturesque, well-treed site, originally assembled in 1916 by the Dublin Relief Committee for use as a training facility for market gardening, was largely undeveloped, with the tracks of the Great Northern Railway cutting through the parcel near its southern border (a new station on the line was opened to serve Killester in 1923).

1. Plan, F. C. Mears, 1920. ISSLT
2. Bungalows. TNA1 (1920s)
3. Green. Shiels. PS (2012)
4. The Demesne. Shiels. PS (2012)

1

2

3

4

Mears's plan for 247 houses was developed at an extremely low density of about four dwellings per acre, with generous amounts of space reserved for private gardens and communal open spaces in the form of rectangular greens and irregularly shaped parcels where existing trees were retained. Mears grouped the housing in three separate areas—Abbeyfield, Middle Third, and Demesne—connected by curving streets with grass verges. The housing was essentially segregated by military rank, with the smallest houses for privates located in Abbeyfield, and the officers placed in the largest houses south of the railroad tracks in Demesne. The single-story precast-concrete bungalows, with both front and rear gardens, hip roofs, and prominent chimney stacks, were primarily arranged in pairs with only thirty-two detached units. Describing Killester as the "most interesting" of the "homes for Irish heroes," F. H. A. Aalen has posited that the development "may have first popularized the bungalow as a working-class house style in Ireland."[154] A church was built in 1926 and a school followed two years later. According to a letter written by Lady Aberdeen to Mears, Patrick Abercrombie was "delighted" with the suburb.[155] The

project also had its fair share of detractors, including those who believed that the garden suburb approach was too expensive to repeat throughout the rest of the country, especially for projects developed without the beneficence of someone like Lady Aberdeen. The naysayers held sway with the Irish Sailors' and Soldiers' Land Trust, which eschewed the garden suburb model for future developments, although the trust was able to build about 4,000 much-needed dwelling units by the end of the 1930s.

Mount Merrion Park was a prominent garden suburb developed solely by private interests working without government support, a rarity for Ireland.[156] In 1925, developer T. J. Wilson began building bungalows on a 300-acre parcel he had recently purchased in Mount Merrion, four miles south of Dublin's city center. Three years later, after limited success and only a few houses completed, Wilson's company, Mount Merrion Estates, was taken over by a much larger concern, the Housing Corporation of Great Britain, which commissioned a plan for the picturesque hilly site, the author of which remains unknown. The southwest corner of the site was reserved for a golf course, with the semidetached

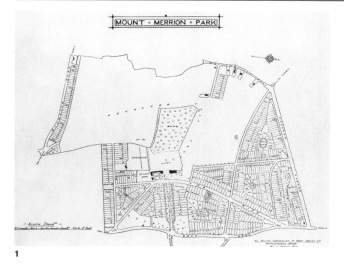

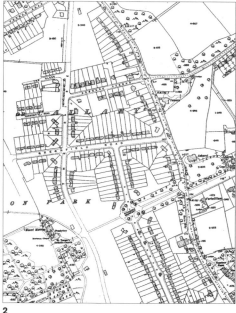

1. Plan, 1928. IAA

2. Ordnance Survey map. OSI (1939)

3–5. Typical views. Shiels. PS (2012)

and detached houses placed along curving and straight streets and several culs-de-sac. Although the company sponsored a competition for model houses of four different sizes that attracted sixty-two entries and mention in the *Irish Times*, interest in the project waned as the economy turned downward. The Housing Corporation of Great Britain was able to lay out a number of the major streets but the construction of houses did not proceed, and the site remained home only to the five bungalows built by Wilson.

In 1933 developer John Kenny, head of Irish Homes Limited, purchased 200 acres of the site for the purpose of building 1,500 houses for the middle and upper-middle classes, expected to commute to the city center by bus.[157] Kenny hired Rupert Jones (n.d.) to rework the plan for Mount Merrion Park, concentrating first on the northern triangular parcel bound by Stillorgan Road, The Rise, and Trees Road, where the architect inserted a prominent *rond-point* along Sycamore Road. Jones's low-density scheme placed the semidetached and detached houses behind "low white-capped brick walls" and front gardens and each dwelling featured a generous rear garden.[158] Kenny built houses on a

speculative basis but also sold plots to individuals and other builders. In either case, Jones was the architect of the majority of houses built in the first phase of development as well as the designer of the shopping complex completed in 1936.

Kenny was unable to build additional houses at Mount Merrion Park, but the garden suburb continued to be filled out, with a modest amount of development realized in the 1940s and more substantial progress occurring in the 1950s. McManus has pointed out the importance of the development in Irish town-planning history: "Kenny's development at Mount Merrion shows some of the changes experienced by the house-building industry in the 1930s. In particular, it was one of the earliest speculative schemes to apply the principles of modern town planning and which fully advertised the fact. However, within Kenny's overall plan, there were many different builders engaged in house-building on the estate. Thus, the piecemeal nature of development, involving various builders, was being focused through the intervention of a developer with an overall plan. The estate also shows the newly important role of the architect, whose name is now mentioned in advertisements."[159]

CHAPTER SIX

The Garden Suburb in Europe 1900–1940

GERMANY

The Garden City movement came to Germany in 1902 with the formation of the Deutsche Gartenstadtgesellschaft or DGG (German Garden City Association), the first of its kind to be founded outside England. According to architect and historian Jean-François Lejeune, the DGG was "marked by a profound dichotomy that made it at once more utopian and more realistic than its English original source. It was not only a breeding ground for socialist, cooperative, and reformist ideals, but also for nationalist, capitalist, and idealized vernacular values."[1] With the exception of Hellerau (see p. 290), the German Garden City movement, nomenclature notwithstanding, was preoccupied primarily with garden suburbs. The DGG's pragmatic side, as Lejeune has written, was "adapted briskly to the national reality and oriented towards the concept of environmental reform rather than Howard's new socioeconomic foundations. From the start the Germans included the possibility of expanding the field of application of garden city principles to the improvement of . . . suburban conditions."[2]

The DGG was closely allied to the Werkbund, founded in 1907 by the architect Hermann Muthesius, who had lived in England from 1896 to 1903 when he was attached to the German Embassy with the specific responsibility of studying contemporary English domestic architecture, and the pastor and politician Friedrich Naumann (1860–1919) with the idea of fostering collaboration between artisans, artists, and industrialists.[3] Many of the most important architects associated with the Werkbund were also closely tied to the German Garden City movement, including Theodor Fischer, Richard Riemerschmid, Fritz Schumacher (1869–1947), Georg Metzendorf, and Heinrich Tessenow.

Germany was especially receptive to the Garden City movement where, as Lejeune writes, "the particular cultural conditions of encounter between Howard's theories, the rampant nationalism, the Werkbund's ideology, and the lessons of Sitte produced a particular type of urban foundation, a genuine revival of the traditional German city as esthetic and sociological archetype. Thus it was in Germany that the Garden City acquired its most urban character."[4] This may be attributed in part, as Patrick Abercrombie has pointed out, "to the high price of land in Germany [where] much less open space is left to the individual houses."[5]

Lejeune has distilled the "clear and unique set of urban principles" that governed the planning of all German garden suburbs, no matter their stylistic differences, enumerating them as follows:

One: "The spatial definition of the streets relied primarily on buildings, their architecture and height, the repetition and rhythm of elements such as gables, chimneys, staircases, entrance doors, etc. In contrast and in accordance with

Falkenberg, Bruno Taut, 1913–14. Bernoully. MB (2009)

Römerstrasse

1. Plan, Wilhelm Holch, 1907. TPR10

2. Starengasse. SU

3. Ziegelgasse. Gräfe. UG (2012)

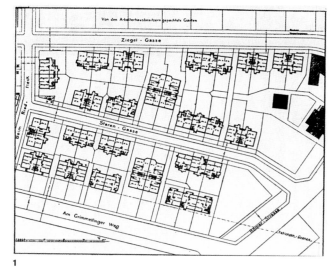

Kohleninsel

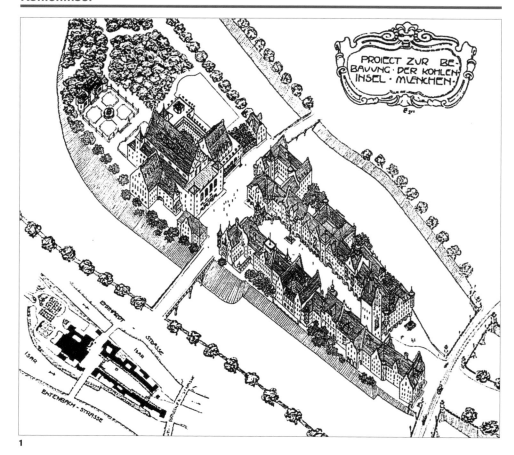

1. Bird's-eye view and site plan, Theodor Fischer, 1902. DK02

Sitte, street trees were rare and used only in specific circumstances and for specific spatial effects . . . Most streets were narrow with no or very small setbacks (often paved or defined as courts) even within entirely residential areas. Asymmetrical street sections were usual."

Two: "Housing types were few and strongly standardized, both dimensionally and materially; most houses formed long rows, were attached in groups of two or more, or organized around courtyards. These typologies were directly linked to Paul Mebes in his best-seller Um 1800 and in Paul Schultze-Naumberg's ten documentary volumes titled Kulturarbeiten."

Three: "Market squares and other public spaces followed the medieval repertory, while some—for instance of circular form—borrowed to [sic] the Baroque models. Main entrances were treated as urban gates, while town walls were often simulated with long, uninterrupted rows of houses along the edges of the district."

Four: "Narrow and deep allotment gardens at the back of houses created a strong rural image and provided substantial support to the family; thus blocks were not continuously built and frequent openings allowed a varied and always changing perception of both worlds: town and countryside."[6]

The earliest German examples of garden suburb design were primarily industrial villages, including such notable developments as the Krupp colonies (see p. 741) and Gronauerwald (see p. 735). The **Römerstrasse** development (1907), an early garden suburb design not associated with industry, was located in the historic walled city of Ulm on the Danube River in Baden-Württemberg.[7] In 1890, in anticipation of the removal of the town's fortifications, Ulm's mayor, Dr. Heinrich von Wagner, instituted a continuous program of suburban land acquisition. By 1909, 200 acres had been acquired, the value of which skyrocketed when Ulm's wall was demolished so that the sale of 65 of these acres provided sufficient capital to develop the suburb with an English-inspired group of forty-eight cottages for workers arranged in blocks of two, three, and four units designed by Wilhelm Holch (b. 1855), city architect, whose plan, according to Thomas Adams, reflected "the characteristics that distinguish" Olmsted's for Riverside.[8]

Theodor Fischer was the designer of the influential industrial village of Gmindersdorf (1903–15) (see p. 737), which represented his second attempt at village design. In 1899–1902, on the **Kohleninsel** (coal island) in Munich, he prepared an unrealized plan for a Bavarian-type village to serve as a museum, focused on a colonnaded square overlooked by a tower.[9] Fischer had better success in Munich about a decade later with two developments in Laim, a primarily residential district in

Siedlung Stadlohner Strasse

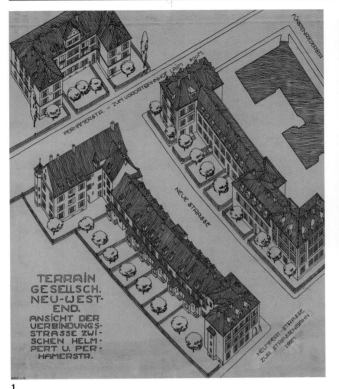

1. Bird's-eye view. ATU (c. 1909)

2. Stadlohner Strasse. Varzi. AV (2012)

Kleinhaussiedlung Laim

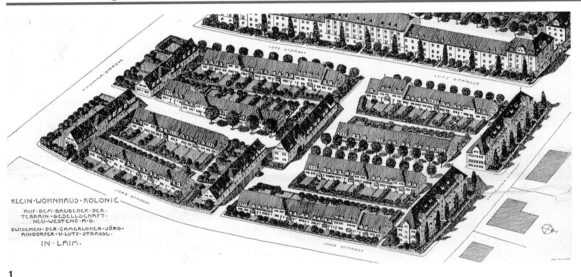

the western part of the city. His modestly sized **Siedlung** (settlement) **Stadlohner Strasse** (1909–11), built for local developers Terrain Neuwestend, consisted of twenty terraced houses and apartments set behind small gardens on either side of Stadlohner Strasse, with a three-story U-shaped apartment house with large garden court closing the composition to the north across Perhamer Strasse.[10] About a half mile to the south, Fischer was only able to complete half of his plan for **Kleinhaussiedlung Laim** (1910–11), resulting in four rows of between nine and twelve terraced houses with 100-square-meter gardens, a generous size for this part of Munich, where the architect also built a detached single-family house for himself.[11] The project included a community center with shops and a restaurant at what

would have been the middle of the site if the southern half had been built.

In 1910 the municipal government of Mannheim established the Gartenvorstadt-Genossenschaft (Garden Suburb Cooperative) to build housing for both workers and the middle class that would help relieve a serious shortage of available units for the rapidly industrializing city of about 200,000 residents.[12] The cooperative selected a triangular-shaped 49-acre site four miles north of the city in the Waldhof district that was less than half a mile from a railroad line and an existing station. The local firm of Hermann Esch (1879–1956) and Arno Anke (1879–1968) won a competition for both the plan of **Gartenstadt Waldhof** and the design of its 400 two- and three-story houses.

1. Bird's-eye view. ATU

2. Houses, Theodor Fischer, c. 1911. FM

3. Gunzenlehstrasse. Varzi. AV (2012)

Gartentstadt Waldhof

1. Plan, Esch & Anke, 1911. DKD17
2. Typical street. DKD17 (c. 1917)
3. Westring. Egermann. HE (2012)

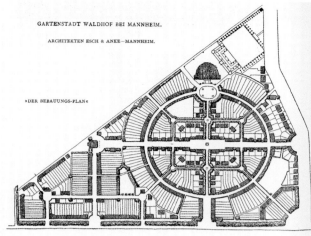

GARTENSTADT WALDHOF BEI MANNHEIM.

ARCHITEKTEN ESCH & ANKE—MANNHEIM.

»DER BEBAUUNGS-PLAN«

VERGLEICHE HIERZU DAS AUF SEITE 311 ABGEBILDETE MODELL DER GARTENSTADT WALDHOF.

1

2

3

Gartenstadt Munich-Perlach

1. Plan, Hans Eduard von Berlepsch-Valendas, 1910. HEBV

2. Market square, central section, 1910. HEBV

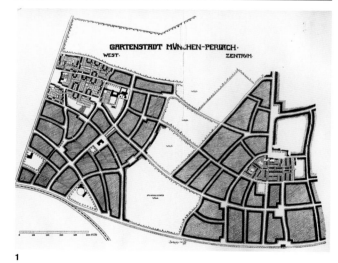

GARTENSTADT MÜNCHEN-PERLACH. WEST. ZENTRVM.

1

GARTENSTADT MÜNCHEN-PERLACH. CENTRVM. SÜDL·WESTL·TEIL DES MARKTPLATZES

2

The most interesting part of Esch & Anke's plan (1911) was a circular road lined on both sides with row-houses and bisected by north–south and east–west streets, also lined on both sides with terraced units and semidetached and detached houses. Inside the circle, a square of streets featured *rond-points* at all four corners, connecting to radiating avenues that led to other sections of the housing estate. Within the circle and at the very heart of this portion of the plan, Esch & Anke proposed a modest town square. Outside the circle, the remainder of the development was conventionally planned with long, straight rows but also with groups surrounding court-yards as well as semidetached and detached houses. All of the dwellings were to feature rear gardens.

Gartentstadt Waldhof began construction in 1912, and by 1914, 174 dwelling units with gardens were completed. Esch & Anke's ambitious plan would fall victim to the war, however, and only a portion of the circular arrangement at the western end was realized before construction was halted. Between 1919 and 1925 Esch & Anke completed an additional 195 houses at the housing estate along with a community house at Freyaplatz, but plans for completing the circle were never revived.

Zurich–born and –educated painter and architect Hans Eduard von Berlepsch-Valendas (1849–1921) pub-lished ambitious plans for **Gartenstadt Munich-Perlach** (1910), envisioning a community of 31,000 residents on a 410-acre site four miles south of the city along the Iser River, connected to the Bavarian capital by an exist-ing railroad line and located within the 15,000 acres of the Perlach Forest.[13] Berlepsch-Valendas divided the site into two roughly equal portions, the west and cen-tral settlements, separated from each other by a dense forest that would be retained but connected by an exten-sion of the railroad with a loop line running along the site's southern border. The painter-architect, who also intended to include an eastern section, only produced detailed plans for a small percentage of the site, with the western settlement intended as home to three- and four-story apartment houses grouped along three sides of a landscaped court, and the central section intended for two-story single-family houses arranged in rows, with each section including substantial market squares, public parks, schools, churches, and areas for indus-trial development. Inspired by the English Garden City movement, Berlepsch-Valendas had drafted the plans for Gartenstadt Munich-Perlach on his own. With no insti-tutional or commercial support, his grand scheme was not implemented.

In 1912, in Altglienicke, on the southwestern side of Berlin's Treptow-Köpenick district, Hermann Muth-esius was called in by the Landwohnstätten, a local building society devoted to providing "healthy and prac-tical housing for families and individuals with lower incomes," to rework the plan for **Preussensiedlung**, begun the previous year by architects Max Bel (n.d.) and Franz Clement (n.d.) who had completed four semide-tached houses on Germanen Strasse.[14] Muthesius, in a letter to the society, noted that his new plan would place

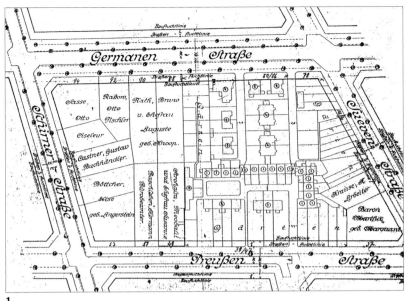

1. Plan, Hermann Muthesius, 1912. MT

2, 3. Typical views. TERR

"a greater emphasis . . . on the more recent principles of the garden city concept," calling for a six-unit building on Sueven Strasse, terrace houses near Bel & Clement's Germanen Strasse work and along Preussen Strasse, as well as a group of houses built around a courtyard.[15] In addition, the development would include a clubhouse and laundry. Muthesius was only able to complete the courtyard housing, described by Annette Ciré as "a kind of inversion of a block perimeter development, as the entrances to the houses are facing the narrow courtyard, while the perimeter is enclosed by a circle of private gardens." In terms of the architecture, Ciré writes that Muthesius appears "to have been guided by the question of how many gables and cross gables a housing terrace could accommodate, as the gables of different height and width seem to have been the dominating design element applied to the otherwise unadorned houses . . . Together with the characteristic chimneys they are strongly reminiscent of English garden city houses."[16]

Falkenberg (1913–14), about a half mile east of Preussensiedlung in Brandenburg, a garden village intended to house about 7,000 residents in 1,500 apartments on approximately 185 acres, was only partially realized in the Akazienhof (acacia court) area with 80 single-family and ten multifamily houses designed by Bruno Taut (1880–1938), the village's master planner.[17] Taut, who had worked for Theodor Fischer before opening his own office in Berlin in 1910, had recently visited English garden suburbs at the suggestion of Muthesius. In addition to Taut's delightfully detailed, pastel-painted houses, the development includes a single house by Heinrich Tessenow. Mixing various housing types was Taut's way to vary the social mix: "A lively neighborhood exists, which cancels out differences and creates social values."[18] Initially, residents, used to Berlin's drab gray, were uncomfortable with the color scheme—pink, olive-green, golden brown, and blue—of what came to be known as the "paint box estate," and "repeatedly

declared," as Taut recalled, "that the architect deserved to be locked up."[19]

The overall plan for Falkenberg, commissioned by the Ansiedlungsverein Gross-Berlin (Greater Berlin Housing Association), founded in 1908, incorporated a rich mix of planning tropes, including a grand boulevard and a crescent intended to crown the downward slope of a public park, a device based on an earlier plan by Hans Bernoulli (1876–1959) that Taut would later develop at Britz (see p. 440). Basing a proposed market square on a village square in Brandenburg, Taut called for a wide, linear platz faced by shops, at one end of which, forming "a civic complex," there would be a school. The plan's "main thoroughfares, twelve to fifteen metres in width," were to "delineate a number of blocks . . . not arranged on garden-city lines" but to create north–south–oriented interior recreational courts keeping 15 percent of the city in green open space. "Within the blocks . . . paved residential streets, five or six metres wide," were arranged so "that they should all interconnect, in order to help people find their way through the area."[20] Though Falkenberg was planned with Garden City aspirations, as Vittorio Magnago Lampugnani points out, from the point of view of "Howard's theories, [it] was too close to Berlin to avoid being swallowed up by it. With its 1,500 planned homes for 7,000 people it was too small to be able to support the industry it needed to be economically autonomous. It had no agricultural green belt to supply it with food and protect it."[21]

Taut was also the planner and architect of **Gartenstadt Reform** (1912–15), a village largely home to factory workers about 100 miles southwest of Berlin in Magdeburg, the capital of Saxony-Anholt.[22] Taut's plan arranged two-story terraced houses in straight rows, except for a slightly curving group of twelve at the western edge of the site on Fliederweg (Lilac Road), a far less complex plan than his mixed-use scheme for Falkenberg. However, as at Falkenberg, the houses were animated

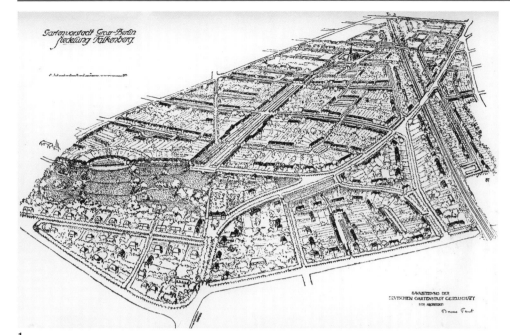

1. Aerial rendering, Bruno Taut,
c. 1913. BTS

2. Courtyard. MB22

3, 4. Typical views. Bernoully. MB
(2009)

Gartenstadt Reform

1. Plan, Bruno Taut, c. 1912. MAG

2. Maienhof. Eddy. WC (2010)

3. Bunter Weg. Kochi. WC (2004)

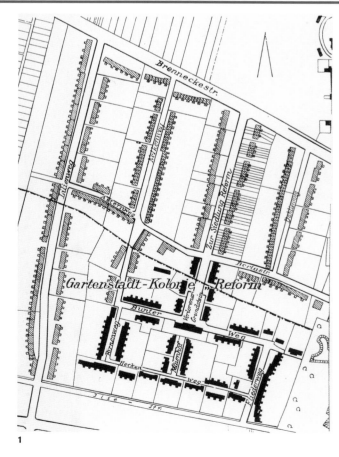

by brightly colored stucco facades, with entrance doors varying in color. By 1918, more than 100 houses had been completed on the 30-acre site, with plans for additional dwellings in the works. Taut, whose 1919 book **Die Stadtkrone** featured designs for a utopian city that was in essence a garden city, served as Magdeburg's city architect from 1921–23.[23] After he ended his involvement with Gartenstadt Reform, the village continued to grow throughout the 1920s and early 1930s, with another 240 houses completed by a number of different architects, including Carl Krayl (1890–1947).

In 1912, after local government officials in Berlin-Zehlendorf altered the building code to encourage terraced housing in an area more typically home to detached villas, the Government Employees' Housing Association hired architects Paul Mebes (1872–1938) and his partner and brother-in-law Paul Emmerich (1876–1958) to plan **Gartenstadt Zehlendorf** (1913) on a plot of land southwest of Zehlendorf's center bound by Camphaussenstrasse on the east, Dallwitzstrasse on the south, Radtkestrasse on the west, and Berlepschstrasse on the north.[24] Within a year's time they had completed ninety-two two-and-a-half-story, single-family houses in eleven terraced rows of between three and twelve houses. Annette Ciré writes that "each building seems to differ from the others . . . [with] the only consistent elements . . . the gutter height and the roof shape, along with the unified vocabulary of the period 'around 1800,' which Mebes advocated in his influential book of the same title. With their triangular gables, projecting walls and oriel towers these Zehlendorf houses emulate the classicist townhouses with their unobtrusive and relatively austere design—perfectly in keeping with the tastes of the civil service residents."[25] Mebes and Emmerich completed similarly designed additions in 1921 and 1923 while a third, complementary phase in 1930 was planned by Franz Tonndorf (n.d.).

Siedlung Gablenz (1913), located two miles southeast of Chemnitz's city center, was the work of a trio of local architects, Erwin Schäller (n.d.), Bruno Kalitzky (n.d.), and Curt Henning (n.d.), who collaborated on both the plan and the buildings.[26] Intended for laborers and low-paid white-collar workers, the project was sponsored by the Allgemeine Baugenossenschaft, Chemnitz's most prominent housing association. The residential development of terraced three-story Heimatstil (regional style) buildings featured abundant greenery in the form of large rear allotment gardens and landscaped squares. The dominant feature of the design was the wall-like row of buildings lining both sides of the curving path of Geibelstrasse, the suburb's main thoroughfare with a landscaped median that marked the eastern boundary of the site and helped to provide a measure of privacy for the siedlung and its gardens. Construction began in 1914, but the war halted development after the completion of only eighteen houses. Building resumed one year after the end of the war, and by 1930, the estate numbered 189 houses.

Am Sommerberg–Am Winterberg (1914), named for the development's two main streets and designed

Die Stadtkrone

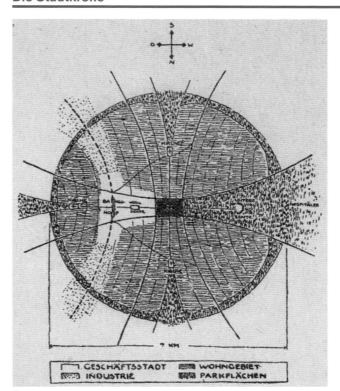

1. Plan, Bruno Taut, 1919. BTDS

1

Gartenstadt Zehlendorf

1. Plan, Paul Mebes and Paul Emmerich, 1913. LB

2. Camphausenstrasse. BAR15 (c. 1915)

1

2

1. Plan, Erwin Schäller, Bruno
Kalitzky, and Curt Henning, 1913.
CAWG

2. Geibelstrasse. CAWG (1938)

3. Overall view. CAWG

1

2

3

Am Sommerberg–Am Winterberg

1. Plan, Karl Pohl, 1914. SDO
(1921)

2. Am Sommerberg. Kleemann.
SDO (2012)

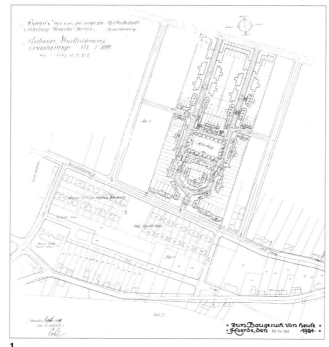

1

2

by Karl Pohl (1881–1947), was located six miles southeast of the city center of Dortmund in the Ruhr area of North Rhine-Westphalia.[27] The garden suburb, intended primarily for factory workers, occupied a long and narrow 15-acre site with the main entrance located at Steinkühlerweg on the southern border, which quickly branched off into two parallel roads (Am Sommerberg and Am Winterberg) lined with terraced groups of two to four houses. In the northern half of the site, the largest group of houses surrounded a courtyard, while the large central plaza, suggestive of a market square, served as a public park surrounded by additional housing, with no commercial or civic buildings included. Over a six-year period Pohl completed a total of 185 dwellings.

Paul Schmitthenner (1884–1972), whose most significant planning activity at the time of World War I centered on the design of industrial villages for the defense industry, most notably his influential Staaken project (see p. 756), also designed **Villenkolonie Carlowitz** (1911–13), a development of semidetached and detached houses located two miles north of Breslau (now Wroclaw, Poland).[28] After completing thirty-three houses at Carlowitz, located on tree-lined streets and often set back behind walled front gardens, Schmitthenner quarreled with the private development company, Eigenheim Baugesellschaft für Deutschland, and left for Berlin to work on Staaken. Schmitthenner's **Ooswinkel** (1918), near Baden Baden, a venture promoted by psychoanalyst and housing reformer George Groddeck (1866–1934), was not completed to the original plans, with 160 houses built by 1924.[29] In addition to the houses, the plan

Villenkolonie Carlowitz

1

2

Ooswinkel

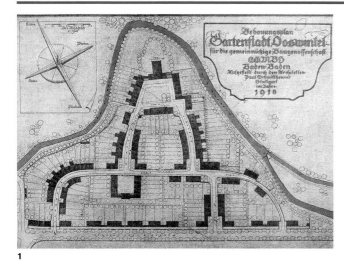

1

2

3

Kolonie Askania

1

included a small square with a hotel, shops, and a community building that remained unrealized.

About a mile and a half west of the center of Dessau, Saxony-Anhalt, architect Theodor Overhoff (1880–1963) designed **Kolonie Askania** (1913), a modest, exclusively residential development consisting of thirty-seven houses on a rectangular site.[30] Five years later, on a site directly adjacent to the south, Overhoff would design a much more significant development, **Siedlung Hohe Lache** (1918). Working with landscape architect Leberecht Migge (1881–1935), who designed ten model gardens in support of his theories of existence management enabling newly urbanized residents to grow their own food, Hohe Lache, completed over an eight-year period, was, as Lejeune writes, "another astonishing Siedlung, a genuine and abstract encounter between the 'urban' and the 'rural,' between pure urban forms as fragments and the cultivated garden as potent symbol of the self-sufficiency goals of the workers' housing movement." The plan was based on "a series of urban moments: the U-shaped entrance plaza, the Lindenplatz defined by four long buildings with arcaded ground floors, the 'street of gables,' the elliptical square (unbuilt), and the spectacular *Achteck*, a totally enclosed octagon with two symmetrical gates, whose 'metaphysical' quality was best observed from a Junkers plane or along the 'medieval' sequence of access from the adjacent streets to its center."[31]

Although formally dazzling, Achteck, the great hexagonal square, was "not a true town center," as Jeannette Redensek points out, since it lacked "the magnetic attractions of commerce, trade and culture," which were located on streets throughout the garden village. Nonetheless, as Redensek writes, "the plaza provided a powerful graphic symbol of Hohe Lache as a cohesive community, a power that was most apparent in aerial views, a fact proudly noted through the 1920s by the settlement's designers, and a need neatly serviced by flyovers of Junker airplanes manufactured in factories at Dessau. From the ground, Hohe Lache exuded the ambiance of a small town idyll, suspended between baroque prosperity and bourgeois decorum. From the air it became the symbol of the power of modern planning to generate new communities."[32]

1. Plan, Theodor Overhoff, 1918. WID

2. Garden plan, Leberecht Migge, c. 1918. DBK

3. Aerial view. Dogs. WRD (2005)

4. Achtek. WID (c. 1928)

5. Aerial view of Hohe Lache showing Kolonie Askania in upper right corner. NRW (1924)

6. An der Hohen Lache. Dogs. WRD (2012)

7. Typical view. Dogs. WRD (2012)

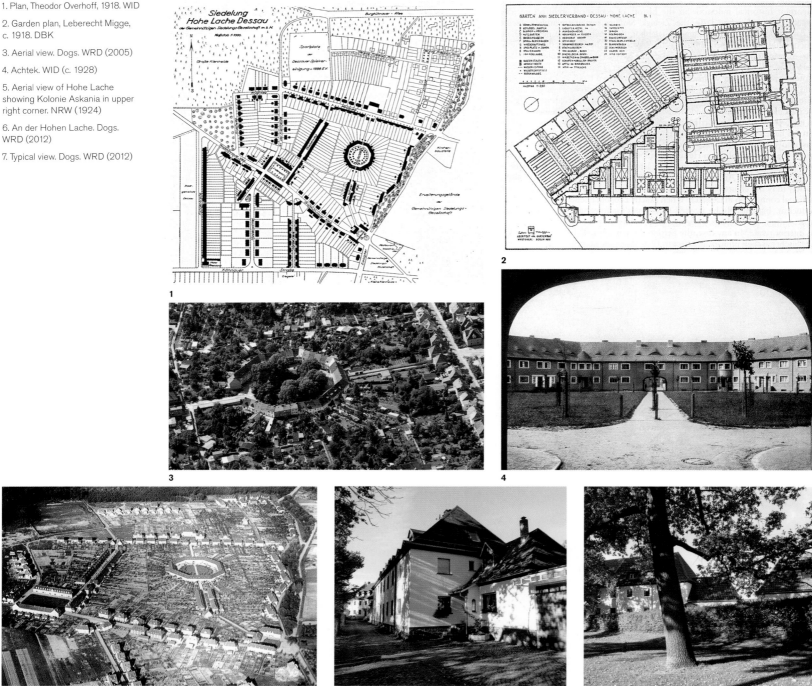

Leberecht Migge, best known for the gardens and landscaping he created for housing estates designed by such architects as Martin Wagner (1885–1957), Bruno Taut, and Ernst May (1886–1970), was an outspoken advocate of the role that gardens could provide for a settlement's self-sufficiency, delivered in the form of articles, books, lectures, as well as the establishment of a school, Siedler-Schule Worpswede, to teach these principles. In 1920, at the request of Emil Lueken, mayor of Kiel, a port city in the northern German state of Schleswig-Holstein, Migge was commissioned to plan **Siedlung Hof Hammer**, intended as a self-sufficient development on 470 acres located four miles southwest of the city center.[33] The municipally sponsored project was planned for two groups: unemployed shipyard workers, who would be given large gardens intended to help with the goal of self-sufficiency, as well as workers commuting to Kiel who would be expected to cultivate smaller gardens. The 100 "full-time" gardeners were to occupy 153 acres, while the remaining 1,000 families were to be located on 131 acres. Not surprisingly, Migge paid primary attention to Hof Hammer's gardens, including rear allotments equipped with dry toilets designed by the landscape architect to allow for the efficient collection of human waste for use as the development's primary fertilizer, a key requirement of his garden philosophy. Migge's plan also included picturesque birch-lined paths, a nursery, a public park,

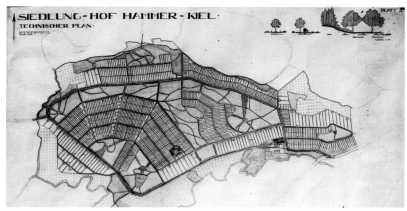

1. Plan, Leberecht Migge, 1920. SK

2. Typical street. SK

3. Speckenbeker Weg. Petersen. FL (2012)

4. Speckenbeker Weg. SK

Siedlung Grünberg

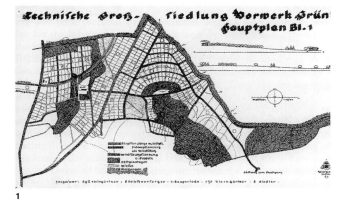

1. Plan, Leberecht Migge, 1922. DBK

playgrounds, a school, and two waste-aging facilities known as dung factories or compost parks.

Willy Hahn (1887–1930), who also collaborated with Migge on a largely unrealized city plan for Kiel, was responsible for Hof Hammer's traditionally styled two-story houses, arranged in short terraces but also including semidetached and detached units. About fifty houses were completed when the first phase of construction ended in 1927. The goal of self-sufficiency, however, proved too ambitious. As Migge's biographer David H. Haney has noted, Willy Hahn blamed the failure on the residents,

> who did not understand the difference between 'have' and 'do.' Rather than taking the necessary initiative, settlers simply looked to the city to provide for them. His comments were probably somewhat biased and unfair, since while many residents of the Hof Hammer Siedlung continued to support themselves through normal jobs in the city rather than exclusively through their own garden produce, historical photographs show that the community did contain many well-tended gardens. The degree of participation and labor required of the citizens to realize Migge and Hahn's self-sufficient urban dream was never attained. The call for inner-city residents to carry their own waste to collection centers was simply not realistic. Migge's concepts of urban agriculture and waste management were well received, but distribution methods requiring less intensive mass participation would be needed to realize them.[34]

Migge was already at work on a city plan for Grünberg (now Zielona Góra, Poland), a moderately sized industrial city primarily home to wool mills, when the mayor, Albert Finke, asked him to prepare a plan (1922) for a self-sufficient siedlung to be located on 215 acres just south of the city center.[35] Migge's plan, which closely resembled his scheme for Hof Hammer, included a substantial number of "garden colonies," separate communal gardens intended to supplement the allotments behind each house. Although some of the garden colonies were realized, the residential portion of **Siedlung Grünberg** never really got off the ground and only about a dozen houses were completed by 1925.

In March 1913, in response to a growing housing shortage caused by Cologne's rapid industrialization, Mayor Konrad Adenauer (1876–1967), who was later appointed first chancellor (1949–63) of West Germany, established a nonprofit housing corporation, the Gemeinnützige Aktiengesellschaft für Wohnungsbau (GAG), to develop affordable housing outside the central city. GAG, the first housing cooperative established in Cologne, was under the control of the municipal

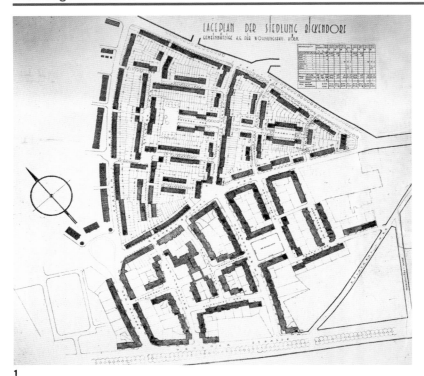

1. Plan, Caspar Maria Grod and Wilhelm Riphahn, 1914–18, top; plan for Bickendorf II, Grod and Riphahn, 1922, bottom. ABR (1925)

2. Aerial view of Bickendorf, top, and Bickendorf II, bottom. Schmölz. ABR (1926)

3. Weissdornweg. Schmölz. ABR (1925)

4. Am Rosengarten. ABR (2008)

5. Apartment buildings and St. Dreikönigen Church, Bickendorf II. Mantz. ABR (1925)

government, but several philanthropic businessmen were also investors in the association. GAG hired different architects and planners for its developments, although one practitioner, Wilhelm Riphahn (1889–1963), dominated the scene, planning several housing estates along garden suburb lines.

Siedlung Bickendorf (1914), located on a 27-acre triangular site three-and-a-half miles northwest of central Cologne, was GAG's first built project.[36] Essen-based architect Caspar Maria Grod (1878–1931) won a competition for the commission with a plan titled "Licht, Luft und Bäume" (light, air, and trees), a phrase that soon became GAG's official motto. Grod lined the three perimeter streets with two-story rowhouses that were staggered to avoid monotony. Additional rows clustered

around landscaped courtyards and detached single-family houses were placed behind the perimeter rows. Grod was able to complete eighty dwelling units before the war interrupted construction.

In 1918, Wilhelm Riphahn, who had worked in Bruno Taut's office before starting his own practice in 1913 in Cologne, joined Grod when building resumed at Bickendorf. Riphahn revised the plan, eliminating the detached houses and increasing the height of some of the buildings but still retaining the same village-like feel. Grod and Riphahn's Heimatstil houses, accommodating 578 modestly sized dwelling units, each featured rear gardens ranging in size from 50 to 150 square meters. The character of the estate, completed by 1920, was further enhanced by narrow curving streets and numerous

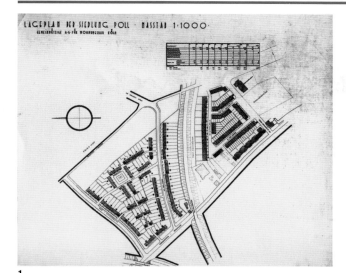

1. Plan of first section, Emil Mewes, 1919, left, showing 1924 addition on right. ABR (1924)

2. Efeuplatz. Schmölz. ABR (1925)

3. Immergrünweg. ABR (2010)

4. An den Maien. Mantz. ABR (1927)

arched openings leading to courtyards. In addition to the housing, the estate included several shops.

In 1922 Grod and Riphahn began work on an expansion of Siedlung Bickendorf on a vacant site directly to the south bound by Grüner Brunnenweg, Häuschensweg, Venloer Strasse, and Akazienweg.[37] Bickendorf II (1923–38), composed of three- and four-story apartment buildings grouped around large landscaped courtyards as well as in long rows, represented a striking stylistic break with their previous effort, abandoning the village-like atmosphere for a denser development that ultimately accommodated 1,121 apartments. The architects were able to introduce some elements of interest by varying the treatment of corner buildings, staggering the placement of some of the apartment houses, and implementing a color scheme of yellow, green, and red accents devised by Constructivist artists Heinrich Hoerle (1895–1936) and Franz Wilhelm Seiwert (1894–1933). The housing estate also included a church as well as several one-story shops with rounded storefronts and projecting flat roofs.

Milchmädchen (milkmaid) **Siedlung** was developed by GAG between 1919 and 1921, continuing the village-like feel and Heimatstil architecture established in the housing corporation's first project at Bickendorf.[38] Milchmädchen was located on a wedge-shaped site formed by the path of two railroad lines, three miles southeast of Cologne's center in the Poll quarter east of the Rhine. The plan, by architect Emil Mewes (1885–1949),

consisted of 114 single-family houses with rear allotment gardens primarily arranged in rows but with some semidetached units. The perimeter of the site was lined with two-story houses, shielding additional east–west and north–south rows. The focal point of the village was the Efeuplatz, where three rows surrounded a courtyard containing a bronze sculpture of a milkmaid. Perhaps the most picturesque grouping was along the southern border at An den Maien, a curving street that followed the path of the railway line. Mewes was also responsible for the design of the houses, along with Adolf Haug (n.d.) and Heinrich Reinhard (1868–1947). Three years after the completion of the housing estate, additional, similarly styled rows composed of two- and three-story houses were constructed south of the railroad.

Siedlung Iddelsfeld (1920), more commonly known as Märchen (fairy tale) Siedlung, went even further than Milchmädchen in trying to evoke an earlier, simpler time, with streets named for such Brothers Grimm characters as Sleeping Beauty, Snow White, and Rapunzel.[39] The low-density plan with abundant garden space, allowing for the keeping of small animals as well as vegetable gardening, was devised by Fritz Kreiss (n.d.), an employee of GAG, for an irregular site five miles northeast of central Cologne but convenient to a railway line. Kreiss's plan placed the larger, two-story, two-family houses in long north–south rows while grouping one-and-a-half-story houses around courtyards. The romantic scheme, which included narrow curving

Siedlung Iddelsfeld

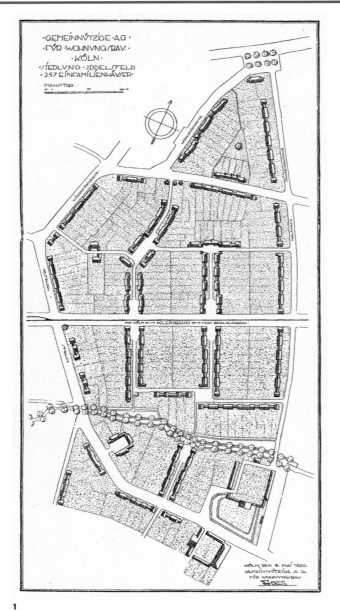

1

2

3

4

Siedlung Iddelsfelder Strasse

1

streets without sidewalks, evoked a medieval village. Along Märchenstrasse, the main street, the rows were set back behind sidewalks and front gardens. Architect Manfred Faber (1879–1944) was responsible for almost all of the 181 houses, with the most traditional designs reserved for the courtyard groups. Wilhelm Riphahn was responsible for a few houses, including a detached villa for GAG's director. The housing estate, with its generous planting scheme, was completed by 1929. Directly southwest of Siedlung Iddelsfeld, the partnership of Fritz August Breuhaus (1883–1960) and Jakob Dondorff (b. 1881) designed **Siedlung Iddelsfelder Strasse** (1920), a modest settlement built by the Baugenossenschaft Kölner Kriegerheimstätten, a housing association set up to aid veterans.[40] The semidetached and detached houses were located along two streets and faced a small triangular green.

Wilhelm Riphahn designed two housing estates for GAG on either side of Cologne's Nordfriedhof (north cemetery), located in the Mauenheim district three-and-a-half miles north of the city center. He began at the western end with **Siedlung Am Nordfriedhof** (1921–28), which occupied a long, irregularly shaped parcel between the cemetery and a railway line.[41] Responsible for both the plan as well as the houses, Riphahn bisected the site with the 100-foot-wide, north–south Kempener Strasse, lined by rows of houses. West of this main thoroughfare, the one-and-a-half- to three-story houses were primarily arranged in long, staggered rows, while the eastern portion of the site featured houses grouped around landscaped courtyards. Many of the houses featured both front and rear gardens. Also east of Kempener Strasse was a market square, home to twenty stores, a restaurant, a bakery, and a tavern. Siedlung Am Nordfriedhof included a school as well. Initially planned for 1,000 families, only 676 dwelling units were completed at the housing estate.

East of the cemetery, Riphahn's **Grüner Hof** (green court) (1922–24) was a much denser arrangement of three- and four-story apartment houses accommodating 676 dwelling units.[42] The central, rectangular portion of the estate consisted of an enormous landscaped courtyard surrounded by apartment houses with loggias facing the green, which was embellished with several sculptures and a sundial. Additional, north–south apartment house rows were located on either side of the main courtyard group, along with a few stores and offices for the cooperative. For the courtyard houses and offices, Riphahn adopted a more stripped-down design vocabulary.

Riphahn embraced a more minimalist aesthetic, along with simpler, denser plans, for **Blauer Hof** (blue court) (1926–27) and **Weisse Stadt** (white city) (1929–32), two projects developed by GAG that still showed the influence of the garden suburb movement, although to a much lesser extent. The adjacent housing estates were located on the 40-acre site of a former beech forest two-and-a-half miles northeast of central Cologne in the Buchforst district, convenient to a railway line. Riphahn's plan for Blauer Hof, designed in collaboration with Caspar Maria Grod, accommodated 427 apartments in thirty-seven four-story apartment buildings arranged in two courtyard-bounding groups.[43] The southern group was triangular in shape, with a closed courtyard. The larger, roughly square group was open to the south, with a central break in the buildings allowing access to the courtyard. The primarily flat-roofed apartment buildings featured loggias overlooking the courtyard while corner buildings received special treatment, equipped with balconies and ground-level stores. The color scheme that gave the estate its name was designed by Heinrich Hoerle.

Riphahn's Weisse Stadt, also designed in association with Grod, was located on a triangular site southeast of Blauer Hof bound by Heidelberger Strasse, Kopernikusstrasse, and Waldecker Strasse.[44] The housing estate's scheme of straight rows of five-story, flat-roofed apartment buildings was clearly influenced by the Zeilenbau planning strategies adopted by Ernst May for some of his

Siedlung Am Nordfriedhof

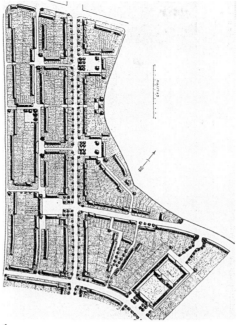

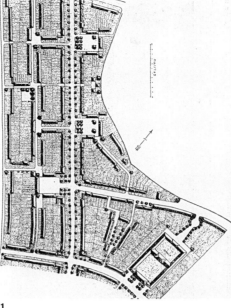

1. Plan, Wilhelm Riphahn, 1921. WID

2. Aerial view. ABR (1925)

3. Kriemhildplatz. Schmölz. ABR (1922)

4. Nibelungenplatz. ABR (2009)

Grüner Hof

1. Aerial view. RB

2. Courtyard. ABR (2008)

Blauer Hof

1. Dortmunder Strasse and Kasseler Strasse. ABR (2009)

2. Dortmunder Strasse and Kasseler Strasse. ABR (1929)

Weisse Stadt

1. Plan of Weisse Stadt, Caspar Maria Grod and Wilhelm Riphahn, 1929, upper right; plan of Blauer Hof, Grod and Riphahn, 1926, lower left. ABR

2. Eulerstrasse. Mantz. ABR

3. Aerial view. ABR (2008)

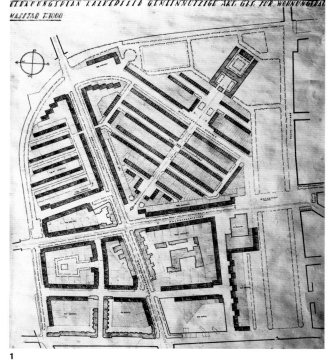

Neue Frankurt projects (see p. 448). Weisse Stadt accommodated 578 modestly sized apartments with balconies along with several ground-level shops, a school, a community center, and a church.

Düsseldorf, like Cologne, its historic rival located twenty-one miles to the southeast, was also in the throes of a severe housing shortage in the years leading up to World War I. After the war, when construction could begin in earnest, the municipality of Düsseldorf responded to the challenge by primarily constructing apartment buildings and multistory apartment-block complexes, frequently grouped around landscaped courtyards. Known since the early eighteenth century as the "garden city" for its extensive array of parks, Düsseldorf also became home to relatively low-density housing estates inspired by the garden suburb tradition. **Musterbausiedlung** (prototype settlement) **Am Nordfriedhof** (at the north cemetery) was developed in 1919–20 by the city in an attempt not only to respond to the housing deficit but also to address the postwar shortage of building materials.[45] The siedlung, located two miles north of the city center in the Derendorf district, was intended to be built as quickly and cheaply as possible while still providing attractive dwellings for the anticipated population of civil servants. No planner's name is attached to the project, but the twenty-five two- and four-family two- and three-story stucco-clad houses with hipped or gabled roofs were designed by such local architects as Josef Kleesattel (1852–1926), Eduard Lyonel Wehner (1879–1952), and Carl Krieger (1867–1957). The siedlung, located on a wedge-shaped site crossed by two north–south streets and one central east–west street, was composed of narrow, curving roads. The heart of the plan consisted of a small courtyard with a central tree at the intersection of Am Adershof and Am Tannenwäldchen, around which several houses were grouped. The most appealing houses were located along Am Tannenwäldchen, including the development's only half-timbered structure, as well as two facing pairs that featured open arcades at their bases. All of the houses included rear gardens. The overall effect of the development was quite charming, despite the extensive use of concrete construction necessitated by the scarcity of bricks. In 1931 and 1935 larger apartment houses were built by the city along the perimeter of the site.

The city of Düsseldorf followed up Musterbausiedlung Am Nordfriedhof with **Siedlung Heimgarten** (1920), a larger settlement geared toward a less affluent tenantry.[46] Located in the Lierenfeld district on an isolated site surrounded by scattered factories and farms, Siedlung Heimgarten lacked a direct transit connection to the city center located about four miles to the northwest. Both the plan and the buildings for the municipally sponsored project remain uncredited. Siedlung Heimgarten was entered at its southern end through a relatively narrow, one-story opening in a four-story concave building straddling Heimgarten, the main street. This gatehouse-like building featured ground-level stores topped by apartments. Past the

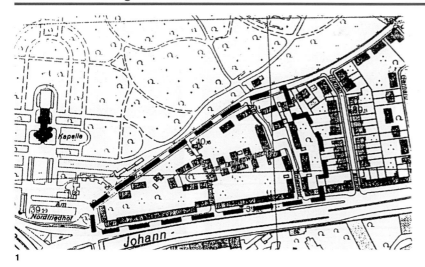

1

1. Plan. SLD

2. Am Tannenwäldchen. Wiegels.
WC (2011)

Siedlung Heimgarten

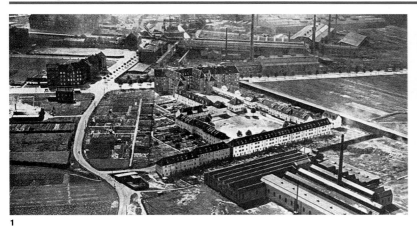

1

2

1. Aerial view. SLD (c. 1925)

2. Heimgarten. Gehrmann. WC
(2008)

sheltered entrance, Heimgarten was divided by a landscaped median, with two-story terraced rows lining both sides of the street and an additional house located at the head of the median. The rowhouses each featured rear gardens and were staggered to avoid monotony. At the northern end of the site, Heimgarten, lined by additional rows of staggered, two-story terraces, wrapped around all four sides of a large square park and playground. The abundant greenery, combined with the sense of closure established by the discreet entrance and the wall of rowhouses, convincingly created the feel of a village.

On a rectangular site near Musterbausiedlung Am Nordfriedhof that was directly north of the cemetery, city architect Ernst Schubert (n.d.) designed **Siedlung Unterrath** (1925), accommodating 643 families in a combination of detached and semidetached houses as well as terraced units.[47] The most attractive part of the settlement was the earliest part built at the southern end, where Schubert arranged primarily detached and semidetached traditionally styled brick and stucco two-story houses with steeply pitched roofs along narrow curving streets, avoiding monotony by turning some of the houses so that their gable ends did not face the street. In addition to allotment gardens, Schubert provided greenery and open space by including several landscaped

squares as well as a park located between Efeuweg and Dünenweg. The two- and three-story terraces built at the northern end of the site, completed by 1931, were not as well detailed but included a group of houses placed around a large landscaped *rond-point*.

Reichsheimstätten-Siedlung Unter den Eichen (under the oaks) (1929), located in the Gerresheim district four-and-a-half miles east of central Düsseldorf, was planned by architect and critic Heinrich de Fries (1887–1938), who managed to retain some elements of the garden suburb tradition in a city-sponsored settlement composed of minimally detailed, flat-roofed, two-story stucco-and-brick terraces, designed in collaboration with local architect Gustav August Munzer (1887–1973).[48] De Fries's plan consisted of one gently curving street, Am Zollhaus, with long terraced rowhouses located on the south side of the street. On the other side of Am Zollhaus, seven shorter terraces were arranged at right angles to the street. Each house featured an allotment garden large enough for the keeping of small animals. Pedestrian paths between the rows led to the gardens, and a communal greenspace was located in the middle of the block on the south side of the street. After the completion of de Fries's Unter den Eichen, the trend to ever-larger developments with stripped-down aesthetics accelerated. For example, in 1930 the

Siedlung Unterrath

1. Plan, Ernst Schubert, 1925. WID
2. Aerial view. WID (c. 1928)
3. Typical street. WID (c. 1928)

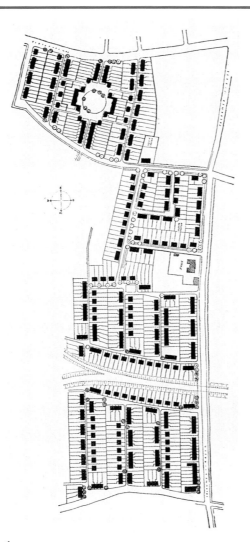

1

2

3

Reichsheimstätten-Siedlung Unter den Eichen

1

2

3

1. Aerial view. GE (2012)
2. Am Zollhaus. ABR (1941)
3. Am Zollhaus. ABR (2011)

municipality of Düsseldorf sponsored the construction of **Siedlung Flinger Broich**, which accommodated over 1,000 families in small apartments on a site three miles east of the city center.[49] Planned by the local firm of Hanns Bökels (1891–1965) and Otto Biskaborn (1890–1978), the siedlung primarily consisted of parallel north–south rows of four-story flat-roofed apartment buildings clad in stucco with brick and glass block details. Despite the severity of the similarly designed cubic buildings from a number of different architects, including Bökels & Biskaborn, Carl Krieger, and Fritz Hofmeister (1869–1941), the plan included a generous amount of open space and greenery in the form of gardens and landscaped medians.

In 1936, as a rebuke to the proliferation of large, multistory Modernist housing estates, the National Socialist government sponsored two low-rise, low-density siedlungen in Düsseldorf, built as part of an exhibition titled "Reichsausstellung Schaffendes Volk" (The Reich's Exhibition of a Productive People).[50] The main focus of the propagandistic exhibition, which opened the following year to millions of visitors, was the construction of a public park on 90 acres of largely undeveloped land along the Rhine in the Stockum district three-and-a-half miles north of the city center. Willi Tapp (1887–1958), director of Düsseldorf's Parks Department, was responsible for the design of the formal and elaborate Nordpark, which required the planting of hundreds of trees and included a 550-foot-long pool with fountains, sculpture, and geometric flowerbeds. In the northeast and southeast corners of the park, space was set aside for two housing estates designed by Peter Grund (1892–1966). **W. Gustloff Siedlung**, now known as Siedlung Nordpark and located in the northern parcel, consisted of fourteen detached houses grouped around a central squarish green to appear as if they had been built over time. The two-story, whitewashed brick, Heimatstil single-family houses featured steeply pitched roofs. Grund's scheme for **Schlageter Siedlung** (now Siedlung Golzheim) was more elaborate, calling for neat rows of ninety-six houses set along curving streets. The single-family detached houses shared a similar architectural vocabulary to Grund's other housing estate but were larger, set back behind modest front gardens and also including rear gardens. A central community green with fountain helped to establish Schlageter Siedlung's village-like character.

In 1910, in order to address a severe shortage of available dwelling units in the northern German city of Hamburg, the Deutsche Gartenstadtgesellschaft helped set up a local chapter to build Hamburg's first garden suburb on a 38-acre site four miles northeast of the central city in the Wandsbek district.[51] The housing cooperative established to build the settlement, Gartenstadt-Gesellschaft Wandsbek, commissioned Hamburg architect Paul A. R. Frank (1878–1951) to prepare the plan as well as design the first buildings, intended primarily for workers and low-level civil servants. Frank's loosely gridded plan for the rectangular

Siedlung Flinger Broich

1

2

1. Typical street. SLD

2. Aerial view. GE (2007)

W. Gustloff Siedlung

1

1. Houses, Peter Grund, 1937. SLD

parcel arranged semidetached units and terraces on either side of Gartenstadtweg, the main north–south boulevard that was also home to the development's modest commercial component.

Between 1911 and the beginning of the war, Frank completed 188 dwelling units at **Gartenstadt Wandsbek**, including seventy-six semidetached houses and thirty-six houses grouped in four terraces. The stylistically similar two-story houses, some arranged with staggered setback distances, featured modest front lawns and rear gardens. This first stage of development also included eight stores. In 1913, the city's streetcar line was extended to reach the settlement.

1. Bird's-eye view. SLD (1937)

2. Houses, Peter Grund, 1937, showing train for exhibition-goers. LVRZ (1937)

3. Typical street. LVRZ (1955)

1. Map. SCH (c. 2005)

2. Gardens, Berner Strasse. BHAM

3. Lesserstrasse and Tilsiter Strasse. Staro. WC (2006)

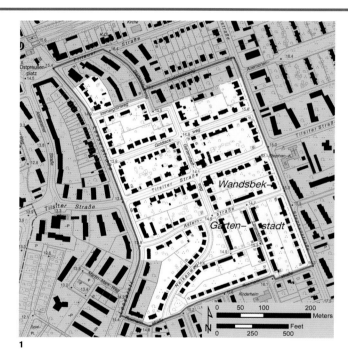

Denser development resumed after the war, and in three separate building campaigns between 1920 and 1939 an additional 282 houses were built.

Siedlung Steenkamp (1914–26), located five-and-a-half miles northwest of central Hamburg on a 96-acre site in the city of Altona, which would not be incorporated into Hamburg until 1937, began construction just before the beginning of the war.[52] The project, developed by a nonprofit housing association with the assistance of Altona's municipal government, was initially intended for military personnel and workers but was instead occupied by the middle class. The first phase of development was overseen by local architects Fritz Neugebauer (n.d.) and Kurt F. Schmidt (n.d.), who were able to establish a village-like feel despite the size of the project with a plan that featured narrow curving streets and landscaped squares. The vernacular two-story houses, fifty-three of which were completed by 1915, were arranged in terraces and included rear allotment gardens, some large enough to enable the keeping of small animals. A central landscaped green served as the community focus. Gustav Oelsner (1879–1956) and Friedrich Ostermeyer (1884–1963) were largely responsible for Steenkamp's stylistically similar postwar development, which ultimately numbered 670 single-family terraced and semidetached houses, 92 apartments, and a residence for single women. At the eastern border of the site along Ebertallee, a generous landscaped median was planted with trees. Siedlung Steenkamp also included nineteen stores, a youth center, and a meeting house.

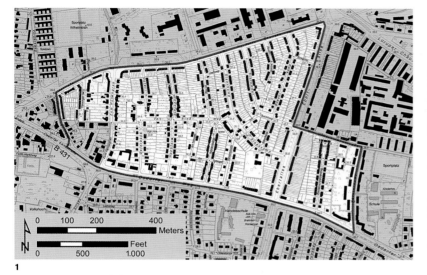

1. Map. SCH (c. 2005)
2. Typical street. BHAM
3. Aerial view. ABR (2006)
4. Gardens. BHAM

Siedlung Langenhorn (1919), sponsored by Hamburg's municipal government, was primarily intended for returning veterans and their families.[53] The housing estate was located on a rectangular, 200-acre site nine miles north of central Hamburg but adjacent to a train line along its western border. Fritz Schumacher, who served as Hamburg's City Architect and Chief Planner between 1909 and 1933 and whose prolific efforts transformed the face of the city, was responsible for both the plan and the buildings at Siedlung Langenhorn, which was later renamed in honor of the architect.[54]

Schumacher bisected the site with the slightly curving north–south path of Tangstedter Landstrasse, the development's main thoroughfare. Immenhöven, a wide strip of green planted with a double row of trees, ran east–west through the tract at roughly its midpoint. Schumacher's spacious plan accommodated about two-thirds of the intended 800 houses in north–south terraced units, although there were also several courtyard-bounding groups. The remainder of the houses were semidetached and detached two-story houses. All of the houses featured substantial rear allotment gardens, some as large as 650 square meters, allowing for the keeping of small animals in addition to fruit and vegetable cultivation.

By 1922, 650 dwelling units, or about 80 percent of the number originally envisioned, were completed at

Siedlung Langenhorn. Because of a shortage of building materials, the brick that Schumacher would have preferred was unavailable, leading to experiments in concrete and clay construction that led to later complications and extensive rebuilding. Schumacher also completed a school at the southeast corner of the site and a row of shops along Timmerloh, but a planned central community center was shelved due to budgetary constraints.

Schumacher's **Siedlung Dulsberg-Gelände** (1919) was located in an industrial district of Hamburg five miles northeast of the city center but directly linked to it by tram.[55] Intended for the laboring classes and low-paid white-collar workers, the development was financed by the municipal government of Hamburg. Schumacher bisected the site with a 200-foot-wide east–west landscaped strip, arranging courtyard-bounding three- and four-story redbrick apartment buildings on either side of the greenery. The courtyards were either fully enclosed or open at the middle or the end. The most interesting group of houses occupied a V-shaped parcel bound by Lothringer Strasse, Dulsberg-Nord, Nordschleswiger Strasse, and Alter Teichweg, where Schumacher placed progressively larger courtyard groups, culminating in the final three, which each occupied a full block. In addition to the houses, Schumacher also designed an elementary school at the western border of the site along Krausestrasse. Between 1927 and

Siedlung Langenhorn

1. Plan, Fritz Schumacher, 1919. WID

2. Harnacksweg. BHAM

3. Immenhöven. BHAM

4. Gardens. WID (c. 1928)

1

2

3

4

Siedlung Dulsberg-Gelände

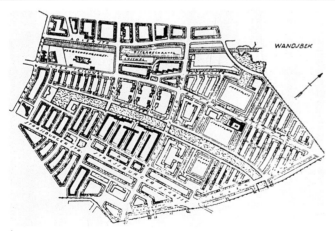

1

2

1. Plan, Fritz Schumacher, 1919, also showing later addition, 1927–31, south of landscaped strip. BHAM

2. Swimming area in landscaped strip between Dulsberg-Nord and Dulsberg-Süd. BHAM (c. 1930)

3. Elementary school, Fritz Schumacher, 1922. BHAM

4. Aerial view. ABR (2004)

3

4

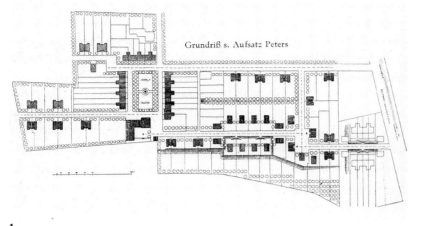

Grundriß s. Aufsatz Peters

1

2

3

4

1931 Paul A. R. Frank, who had designed Hamburg's Gartenstadt Wandsbek, added apartment buildings south of the green strip that broke with the courtyard model. These four-story linear buildings, separated by landscaping, featured exterior corridors, rounded corners at the ends, and ground-level shops.

After the end of World War I, Hannover's municipal government, responding to a housing shortage, announced plans for workers' housing on the site of an abandoned brick factory in the district of Laatzen, about six miles southeast of the central city and just west of a railroad line.[56] Architect Paul Wolf (1879–1957), planning and building director of the Hannover City Council, was selected to design both the plan and the buildings for **Siedlung Laatzen** (1919), producing a low-density scheme of 108 houses with generous rear allotment gardens. The focal point of the plan was the rectangular landscaped green at Am Lindenplatz, surrounded by terraced units and a community building containing a cooperative store and a restaurant. The remainder of the generously spaced two- and three-story brick houses, whose design was inspired by North German vernacular architecture, were detached or semidetached. Siedlung Laatzen was completed as planned by the beginning of 1921.

Hannover's municipal government also sponsored **Gartenstadt Kleefeld** (clover field) (1927–30), a middle-class housing estate located three miles east of the city's center on a 74-acre site surrounded by woods on all sides except for the railway line marking its northern border.[57] Karl Elkart (1880–1959), appointed Hannover's city architect in 1925, devised the plan for the long and

relatively narrow parcel, accommodating 600 single-family houses along with a central town square, home to a large playground, a school, and several stores. The houses, the majority of which featured both front and rear gardens, were arranged around courtyards in pairs or terraces of four to six houses. The building groups were not completely closed, with the spaces between rows spanned by arches that provided access to the courtyards. Additional landscaping was provided along Wallmodenstrasse, the development's central east–west thoroughfare, where Elkart placed a linear strip of greenery planted with a double row of trees.

The local firm of Alexander Kölliker (b. 1883) and Adolf Springer (1886–1978), working with architect Wilhelm Fricke (n.d.), won a competition to design Kleefeld's two-story brick houses. They were able to complete 140 dwelling units by 1930 before construction was halted due to the poor economy. Sympathetic additions were added in the mid-1930s as well as after the war, so the overall feel of Gartenstadt Kleefeld remains close to Elkart's original vision.

In 1922, the Beamten-Wohnungsverein, a nonprofit housing association composed of civil servants from Potsdam, purchased a 74-acre site in the Teltower Vorstadt, a primarily agricultural district about two miles southeast of the central city, in order to build a housing estate for its members.[58] The plan of 148 terraced, semidetached, and detached buildings accommodating 510 dwelling units may have been the work of City Gardener Hans Kölle (1880–1950), who was at least responsible for the landscaping scheme. The plan was composed of three streets, with the longest rows

1. Plan, Paul Wolf, 1919. WID

2–4. Typical streets. WID (c. 1928)

1. Plan, Karl Elkart, 1927. NBH

2. Wallmodenstrasse. Voltmer. RV (2012)

3. Senator-Bauer-Strasse. Voltmer. RV (2012)

LAGEPLAN DER GARTENSTADT KLEEFELD.

1

2

3

placed at the northern border, primarily in straight lines but also in one group that surrounded three sides of an open landscaped courtyard. The most picturesque group of houses was placed along the curving path of Am Brunnen (at the fountain), named for the triangular plaza at its eastern end that also gave the estate its name. At several key intersections the houses were arranged to create the feel of a small square. The majority of the two- and three-story houses, designed by such local architects as Reinhold Mohr (1882–1978), Heinrich Dreves (n.d.), and Hans Hermann (n.d.), featured both front and rear gardens. The first phase of construction at **Siedlung Am Brunnen** ended in 1930, but additional houses designed by Heinrich Laurenz Dietz (1888–1942) were added in 1937–39 and, in 1958, the estate was expanded to the south with the extension of Kunersdorfer Strasse.

Gartenstadt Habichtshöhe (1924), a housing estate for 650 lower-middle- and middle-class families located on former farmland two-and-a-half miles southwest of central Münster, a city of around 100,000 residents in North Rhine-Westphalia, was developed by the Westphalian Housing Association, a nonprofit organization.[59] The housing cooperative selected architect Gustav Wolf (1887–1963) to plan the exclusively

residential project as well as design the first buildings for what would become Münster's largest planned housing development.

According to Sylvaine Hänsel and Stefan Rethfeld, Wolf's plan (1925) "adapted ideas" from the "England garden city movement," but the design of the buildings was strictly inspired by local German precedent.[60] The highlight of the scheme was the Grüner Grund, a 1,300-foot-long open green bordered by trees that bisected the site. Widest at its southern border, where it stretched for nearly 330 feet, the public space narrowed as it reached the northern end of the site, where two gatehouse-like projections marked the formal entrance. In the center of the Grüner Grund, sculptor Albert Mazzotti (1882–1951) designed a fountain decorated with a hawk placed atop a tall narrow pedestal.

Semidetached and terraced houses, each with a rear garden, bordered the green as well as both sides of the estate's two main north–south streets, with the largest paired units located along the site's eastern edge. Additional houses were located southwest of the green, and rows of terraces were placed along the curving path of Sentmaringer Weg at the northern end of the site. Wolf remained at Gartenstadt Habichtshöhe until 1927, when he was replaced by architect Eugen Lauffer (n.d.), who

Siedlung Am Brunnen

1

2

1. Aerial view. GE (2009)

2. Fountain with houses along Am Brunnen. Knuth. WC (2008)

Gartenstadt Habichtshöhe

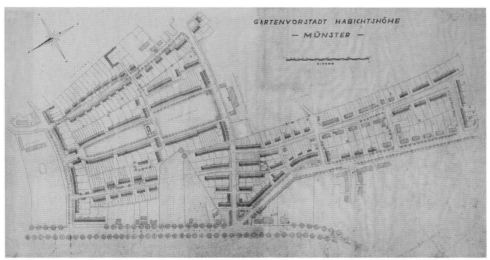

1

2

3

1. Plan, Gustav Wolf, 1925. LNW

2. Aerial view. SSM

3. Grüner Grund. SSM

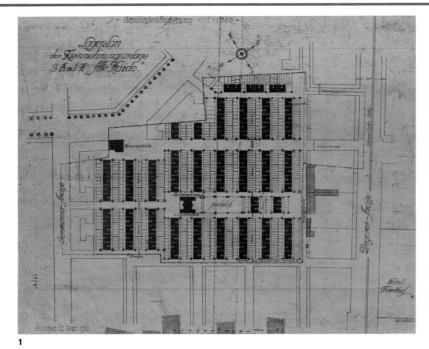

oversaw the completion of the development as originally planned over the next four years.

Vittorio Magnago Lampugnani credits Theodor Fischer's **Alte Heide** (1918), Munich-Nordschwabing, as the unsung prototype for the Modernist siedlungen that would later follow, writing that "orthodox historiography has never acknowledged" this fact, "perhaps because Fischer did not belong to the Martin Wagner, Walter Gropius [1883–1969] or Taut generation and was skeptical of their modernism."[61] The first major housing project to move forward in Munich after the end of World War I, Alte Heide (old heath) was sponsored by a nonprofit housing association composed of the city's leading industrial concerns, including locomotive manufacturers Maffei and Krauss & Company, engine maker BMW, and the German Railway, and intended for factory workers and their families. Located on a flat, 16-acre site three-and-a-half miles north of the city center, Fischer's plan called for sixteen north–south rows of three-story apartment buildings placed at right angles to the subdivision's streets, a "strict system of parallel rows, long before this kind of layout was proposed in Berlin, Dessau-Törten or Karlsruhe-Dammerstock as the urban form of the future."[62] Three shorter east–west rows were located at the northern border of the site.

Fischer, sensitive to the objections that might be raised to his straightforward plan and similarly designed buildings, wrote in 1919 that "some may well fear the aesthetic consequences of this [identical units] . . . It does indeed involve renouncing some of the joys of creating new things—a renunciation that only the architect subjectively suffers momentarily, but that, objectively, makes nothing worse and perhaps makes some things better. For a long time to come, the trend toward standardization in mass production can only be welcomed, in order that we might escape from the excesses of diversity corrupted by individualism. The small home, as soon as it appears in terraces, groups or blocks of rented flats, is certainly nothing but a mass product."[63]

All told, 786 two-room, 60-square-meter apartments were accommodated on the site, allowing Fischer to achieve the "special compactness" that had eluded him at Gmindersdorf (see p. 737).[64] Spacious, private gardens separated the housing rows, which featured staggered entrances so that no two directly faced each other. The school occupied roughly the center of the site along Alte Heide, which was divided into two parts. A clubhouse was also housed in a freestanding building but the other community facilities, including shops, restaurants, and a fire station, were incorporated within the terraced buildings. Construction began in 1919 and was largely complete by 1924, although Fischer's work continued until 1927. Between 1928 and 1930, additional apartment buildings were designed by other architects along the site's periphery.

Siedlung Lindenhof, designed by Martin Wagner, was located in the southern portion of Berlin's Tempelhof-Schöneberg district, which until 1920 was the independent city of Schöneberg, where the architect, a Werkbund member who had been a draftsman in Muthesius's office, was appointed city planner in 1918.[65] Wagner convinced the local city council to form a public benefit corporation to sponsor the project, intended for workers and their families as well as single male workers. Working with landscape architect Leberecht Migge, Wagner took full advantage of the picturesque site, home to two ponds and a grove of linden trees and bounded by cemeteries on the south and east and by railroad tracks to the west. Wagner's plan, similar in many ways to Schmitthenner's scheme for Staaken, arranged 492 two-story terraced houses in either long perimeter rows or along both sides of a curving road

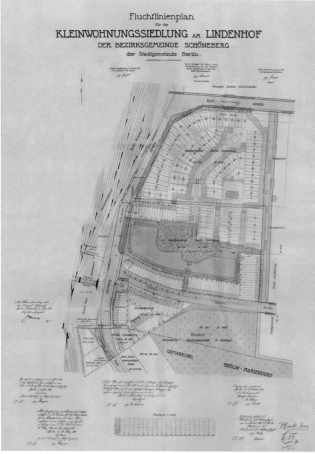

1

2

3

4

5

6

1. Plan, Martin Wagner, 1921. LB

2. Aerial view. WID (c. 1928)

3. Ledigenheim, Bruno Taut, c. 1921. MWA

4. View from Ledigenheim of houses. Köster. AKA

5. Pond. Kühne. PAN (2010)

6. Addition, Heinz Lassen, 1930. BBG (1930)

that led to the village square, surrounded by shops, restaurants, a school, and a day-care center.

Wagner was responsible for the design of the buildings, except for Taut's monumentally scaled Ledigenheim (bachelors' flat) in the northeast corner of the site, a 112-room building including shops, a restaurant, and community meeting hall that was intended to discourage the socially disruptive practice of single men subletting rooms in dwellings occupied by families. In addition to the significant amount of public open space, Migge included allotment gardens behind the terraced houses.

Lampugnani sees the strong influence of Schmitthenner's work at Lindenhof, writing that "the idea of the estate as a fortress surrounded by walls of houses" came from him, adding that "the composition of the streets and squares corresponds" to the plan for Staaken, "which was not far away [fourteen miles to the northwest] and had just been completed . . . Wagner's estate, however, has a sense of uniformity which Schmitthenner's consciously avoids and there is much less of an overall picturesque atmosphere." Lampugnani notes that at Lindenhof, Wagner "anticipates some of the most important principles of the estates built by the advocates of *Neues Bauen*: the green center as the architectural and social focal point; the low, uninterrupted perimeter development as the basic element of the modern village; the large distance between the blocks of flats amply provided with loggias and balconies in order to ensure sufficient sunlight and good ventilation; finally the uniform architecture of all the apartment buildings,

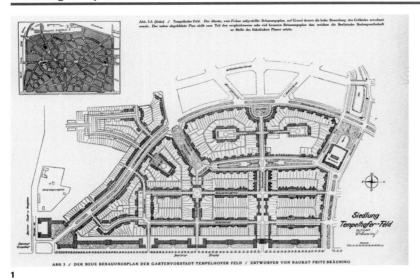

1

2

1. Plan, Fritz Bräuning, 1920. WM24

2. Aerial view. WID (c. 1928)

3. Typical street. WID (c. 1928)

4. Adolf-Scheidt-Platz. Sekamor. WC (2012)

3

4

intended to demonstrate the equality of the inhabitants, idealistically called members of a 'New Community.'"[66]

In 1930 architect and politician Heinz Lassen (1864–1953) designed an addition to Lindenhof in the northwest corner of the site, completing 500 apartments in three- and four-story buildings that in their severe minimalism broke with Wagner's stylistic direction. Allied bombing during World War II destroyed nearly 80 percent of Lindenhof, about half of which was rebuilt in 1953–54 under the direction of architects Franz Heinrich Sobotka (1907–1988) and Gustav Müller (1906–1987). "It is an interesting footnote," observes historian Ronald Wiedenhoeft, "that the Lindenhof design had gone so far in correcting the overcrowding of typical workers' housing that the site density of this project was later considered to be excessively low. During rebuilding in the 1950s, additional housing was added to bring the density up to contemporary standards for urban areas."[67]

Siedlung Tempelhofer Feld (1920–28), Tempelhof-Schöneberg, was planned by Fritz Bräuning (1879–1951) for a flat 360-acre site one-and-a-half miles northeast of Lindenhof, bordered on its east by a military parade ground that was converted into an airport in 1923.[68] The local government, which had been trying to develop the municipally owned land since 1910, established a nonprofit company to build 2,000 houses for middle-income veterans. Bräuning's plan of one- to three-family

detached and terraced houses placed taller buildings along the perimeter, creating a "higher-density band around a low-density core."[69] The main entrance to the village, at the southeastern corner of the site, was through two-story-high arched openings in a five-story cupola-topped apartment building straddling Manfred-von-Richthofen-Strasse, the principal thoroughfare with landscaped median that followed a gentle curve throughout the site, lined on both sides by houses. Named for a prominent aviator and hero of World War I, the so-called "Red Baron," Manfred-von-Richthofen-Strasse led to the plan's centerpiece, a crescent of houses surrounding a formal plaza that was bisected by an east–west road connecting to other north–south streets. Ronald Wiedenhoeft praised the plan for its "emphasis on curving streets, closed vistas, and the creation of intimately scaled squares," adding that "great care was taken to limit through traffic to a minimum."[70]

About half of the houses planned for Siedlung Tempelhofer Feld were completed, the vast majority by Bräuning who orchestrated a variety of Biedermeier-inspired one-and-a-half- and two-and-a-half-story units to form Unwinesque street pictures. The depth of the front gardens varied, and generous rear gardens were provided for each dwelling. Bräuning was also the architect of a round domed church (1928) in the northwest corner of the site, as well as a large U-shaped school

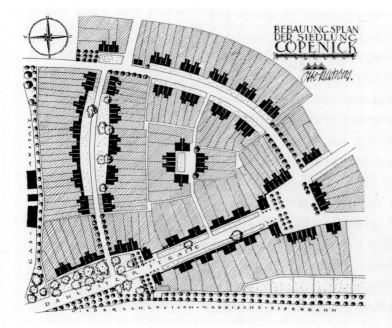

1. Plan, Otto R. Salvisberg, 1919. ORS

2, 3. Typical streets. ORS (c. 1927)

4. Semidetached house. RAMSA (2008)

(1928) located west of the crescent. Berlin architect Eduard Jobst Siedler (1880–1949) designed the four- and five-story apartment buildings (1925–28) along the site's eastern border that helped shield the village from the adjacent airport.

In a wooded area of Berlin's Köpenick district, in the southeastern part of the city, Otto R. Salvisberg designed **Siedlung Elsengrund** (1919–21), an exclusively residential suburb consisting of 153 semidetached and terraced houses.[71] Salvisberg's pie-slice-shaped plan was formed by the intersection of the three bounding streets lined on both sides by houses, including gently curving streets marking the western and northern edges. Dahlwitzer Strasse (later Stellingdamm), the southern border, led diagonally to a squarish plaza at the eastern end that served as the main entrance. Lindenhof, another curving north–south street, was home to four semidetached houses surrounding a courtyard. In roughly the center of the site, Salvisberg retained a number of the original pine trees but cleared space for allotment gardens. The principal charm of the development was the effect created by staggering the placement of the hip-roofed two- and three-story houses, many with decorative door surrounds. Later in the decade, Salvisberg designed complementary if less picturesque additions to the north and east, completing 400 dwellings by 1929.

Siedlung an der Lentzeallee (1920–21), Wilmersdorf, Berlin, designed by Heinrich Schweitzer (1871–1953), also evoked prewar work both in plan and architecture, constituting a U-shaped arrangement of two-story shingle-and-brick terraced houses with eyebrow dormers surrounding a large courtyard divided into allotment gardens.[72] At the southern border along Lentzeallee, the row of houses, intended for government bureaucrats working for the finance ministry, was bisected by a path leading to the gardens. Three-story half-timbered buildings with ground-level shops topped by apartments marked the end of each row. At the rear of each dwelling, a single-story shed was included for keeping small animals.

Similar in spirit but larger in scale, Paul Mebes and Paul Emmerich's **Siedlung Am Heidehof** (1923–24), Zehlendorf, Berlin, accommodated 147 brick houses in

1. Aerial view. GE (2010)

2. Lentzeallee and Zoppoter Strasse. BBG (1930)

1

2

long terraces surrounded by generous garden spaces.[73] Located one-and-a-half miles northwest of the firm's Gartenstadt Zehlendorf realized a decade earlier, Am Heidehof, like Lentzeallee, was built for government employees. At the center of the site, the village square was wrapped on three sides by a continuous row of houses. At the southern edge, a long row set back from the street was bracketed at each end by shorter rows closer to the street. The overall effect of the plan and the vernacular architecture was distinctly rural, yielding a cozy domesticity no doubt appealing to the civil servants expected to live there.

Bruno Taut's **Siedlung Schillerpark** (1924), Wedding, the architect's first housing estate undertaken in Berlin during the Weimar years, marked a decisive break in German garden suburb development and design, described by Ronald Wiedenhoeft as "one of the first settlements directly linked to the socialist labor unions and the first to have a strikingly non-traditional appearance."[74] The project also represented the beginning of a remarkably productive period for Taut, who built over 10,000 dwelling units in Berlin between 1924 and 1932. Plans for a residential development on the 11-acre site were originally announced in 1914 when the adjacent, 72-acre public Schillerpark was opened, but the start of the war shelved the proposal for the next decade until it

was taken up by two nonprofit groups, the Berlin Savings and Building Association and GEHAG (Gemeinnützige Heimstätten-, Spar- und Bau-Aktiengesellschaft).

Taut's plan employed the traditional technique of perimeter house rows surrounding a landscaped courtyard, but he opened the rows up at the corners, allowing access to the interior courtyards, where entrances to the stair towers were located. In the northern half of the site, the only part of the plan to be completed to Taut's original intentions, the rows were not strictly parallel, with the eastern group placed at an angle. The two southern blocks also featured courtyard-bounding buildings, with elaborate arrangements of trees planned for the green spaces, including an unrealized pair of crescents on either side of a north–south row of houses in the center of the courtyard. Oxforder Strasse, with its double row of trees, served as the village's principal thoroughfare, leading to an entrance to Schillerpark to the west and to a church to the east.

Most significantly, at Schillerpark, Taut abandoned any overt reference to the *völkisch* (folkloric) village vernacular of individual houses in favor of three-story rows of flat-roofed brick houses with loggias and balconies that owed their inspiration to Dutch precedent, primarily that of the Amsterdam School. As Rosemarie Haag Bletter points out, "Taut was fully aware of Dutch

Siedlung Am Heidehof

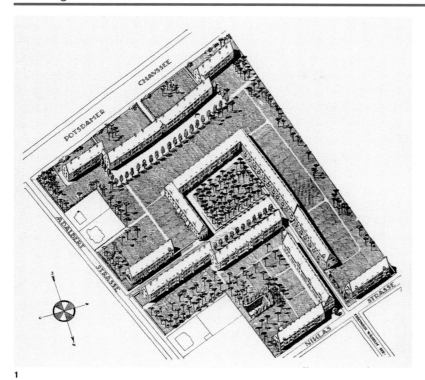

1

2

3

1. Bird's-eye view. JSHK

2. Am Heidehof. JSHK (c. 1926)

3. Am Heidehof. Schröder. HESC (2009)

Siedlung Schillerpark

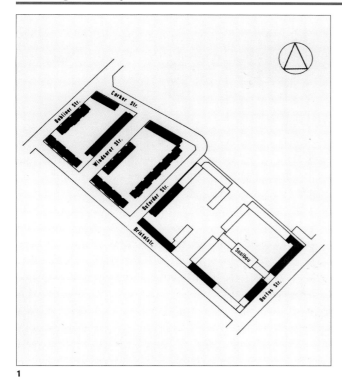

1

2

3

1. Plan, Bruno Taut, 1924. BTS

2. Windsorer Strasse. Köster. BTS (c. 1928)

3. Bristolstrasse and Windsorer Strasse. Bernoully. MB (2009)

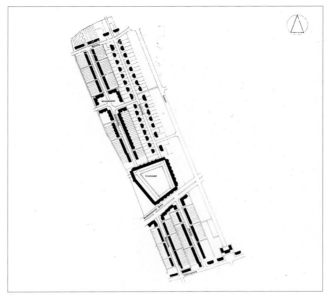

advances in housing and housing legislation. Taut had . . . attended a city planning congress of the International Garden City Association in Amsterdam . . . [visiting] Oud's Tusschendijken housing in Rotterdam and the Hook of Holland estate."[75] Complementing the abstraction of the massing and details, and in a break with his work at Falkenberg and Magdeburg, Taut abandoned applied color, relying instead on the contrast between the dark-redbrick and the light-colored-stucco sections decorated with strips of raised brick.

Between 1924 and 1930 Taut completed 303 one-and-a-half- to four-and-a-half-room apartments at Siedlung Schillerpark, accommodating a laundry, a kindergarten, and a cooperative grocery in the terraces. Economic turmoil at the end of the decade prevented the completion of the southern half of the site, where Taut was confined to five perimeter rows. During World War II, a number of buildings were damaged by Allied bombing, but Taut's younger brother Max (1884–1967) rebuilt them in 1951, thirteen years after Bruno's death. In 1954 Hans Hoffmann (1904–1975) added several buildings to the southern half of the site, including three parallel rows in the space Taut had reserved for landscaped courtyards.

In 1924 the nonprofit housing cooperative **Freie Scholle** (free soil) commissioned Taut to design a new working-class village directly to the west of seventy-one semidetached houses that architect and social reformer

Gustav Lilienthal (1849–1933) had built in still-rural Berlin-Tegel between 1895 and 1910 for the organization he had founded.[76] Except for a group of thirty-two semidetached two-story houses with pitched roofs along both sides of Schollenweg, the remainder of Taut's work, consisting of rows of flat-roofed three-story houses, many with brightly colored stucco facades and balconies, stood in stark contrast to Lilienthal's traditionally styled houses. The trapezoidal arrangement of houses surrounding a large landscaped courtyard at Schollenhof was the centerpiece of the development, admired by Jean-François Lejeune, who wrote that "Taut used shifts of axis and distorted symmetries to create genuine public spaces like . . . the enclosed square at Freie Scholle."[77] In two phases between 1924 and 1931 Taut completed close to 800 dwelling units.

Taut, who had earlier collaborated with architect Martin Wagner and landscape architect Leberecht Migge at Siedlung Lindenhof, again teamed with the pair on the design of **Hufeisensiedlung** (Horseshoe Estate) (1925), named for the U-shaped arrangement of apartment houses surrounding an existing pond that defined "a great, large form that symbolizes the communal thinking of the entire housing estate."[78] Located on a 92-acre site in the southeastern part of Berlin in Britz, Hufeisensiedlung, the first housing estate in Germany to number over 1,000 dwelling units, was developed by the housing

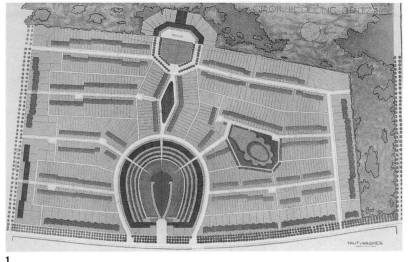

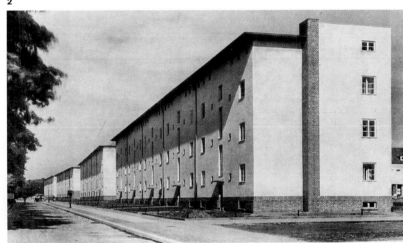

1. Plan, Bruno Taut and Martin Wagner, 1925. DWO26

2. Aerial view. BTS (c. 1930)

3. Horseshoe. BTS (c. 1930)

4. Parchimer Allee. WID (c. 1928)

5. Lowise-Reuter-Ring and Hüsung. Voigt. WC (2010)

6. Liningstrasse. Bernoully. MB (2009)

cooperative GEHAG, which had named Taut its chief architect following his work at Schillerpark.

The enormous horseshoe, composed of twenty-five three-story, flat-roofed terraced buildings with recessed balconies, served as the focal point for the community, accommodating a central laundry, a café, a restaurant, and offices for the cooperative in addition to the apartments. Architectural historian Jeannette Redensek writes that "the use of the half arc building form as symbol and condenser of community life had its historical sources, such as the primitive *Runddorf*, a settlement typology that was well known to Taut. The half arc also recalled the medieval town center, the crescent at Bath, and Theodor Fischer's plan for the workers' colony of Gmindersdorf. It was a planning form that Taut had been experimenting with since the earliest years of his professional career. But the horseshoe-shaped plan was also a brilliant intuition into the graphic signature of the modern site plan and the symbolic power of biologistic form."[79]

In addition to the horseshoe, Taut and Wagner positioned long rows of three-story apartment houses at the perimeter of the site along the northern, southern, and eastern borders. Of particular interest were the houses lining the western side of Fritz-Reuter-Allee, nicknamed the "Red Front" for the politically charged bright red paint job. The remainder of the development consisted of two-story single-family terraced houses with pitched roofs and generous rear gardens arranged primarily in north–south rows, some of which connected to the road that looped around the horseshoe. Directly west of the horseshoe's midpoint, angled terraces created a diamond-shaped green space bordered on either side by roads leading to a proposed pentagonal public park and arc-shaped school. The park and school remained unrealized. To further avoid monotony, Taut and Wagner included curved streets and staggered setback distances.

Lampugnani notes that Taut had used similar planning devices at Falkenberg, where the rows are also "repeatedly interrupted, twisted off axis, slightly bent or curved, opened up onto courts. The streets [at Britz] sometimes taper to create false perspectives, are sometimes almost imperceptibly concave, sometimes enclosed by projecting buildings at the end of a development and sometimes closed off visually by a slab placed across the axis. On the facades of the buildings rendering is always combined with brickwork and abundant use is made of color which Taut loved so much. However," Lampugnani concluded, "Taut and Wagner never used ways of creating lively variety of this kind to accentuate an individual building. They are always intended to give a coherent character to the estate."[80]

Taut, who is generally given more credit than Wagner for the Hufeisensiedlung design, had high hopes for the project. Reflecting the widely held belief among architectural Modernists in the social efficacy of the new language of architecture, Taut saw his work at the housing estate as a potential force for moral good by improving the living conditions of the working-class families expected to live there. As he wrote in 1929, "the people who use a house like this for whatever purpose will be led by the very way the house is to a better way of behaving to each other, to better relations with each other. Architecture thus becomes the creator of social forms."[81] Unfortunately, despite trying to save costs by standardizing construction practices and limiting the houses to only four basic plans, by the time the 1,027 dwelling units were completed by 1931—427 in single-family houses and 600 in apartments—they were too expensive for the intended blue-collar workers and were instead occupied by civil servants and other professionals.

A year after beginning work at Hufeisensiedlung, Taut was again commissioned by GEHAG to plan Waldsiedlung Zehlendorf (1926), the "forest" settlement, an even larger housing estate proposed for 87 heavily wooded acres just south of the Grunewald forest in the southwestern part of Berlin.[82] The development, more commonly known as **Onkel Toms Hütte**—a nickname derived from a popular local tavern whose owner, Thomas, no doubt inspired by Harriet Beecher Stowe's antislavery novel of 1852, had placed several huts known as Tom's Cabins in his beer garden beginning in 1885—was controversial from the start because of its size, location, and architecture. Intended to accommodate close to 2,000 working-class families, Onkel Toms Hütte was hardly welcomed in the area, described by historian Nike Bätzner as "the most popular and expensive garden district in all of Berlin. Inevitably, this kind of large-scale project raised a heated political and architectural controversy."[83] Taut's proposal represented his most advanced statement of Modernist Neues Bauen principles to date with its emphasis on the collective good as opposed to the suburb's traditional embrace of the individual family, a direction in keeping with the Socialist ideals of the developers.

Taut, who collaborated with Otto R. Salvisberg and Hugo Häring (1882–1958) on the buildings and Leberecht Migge on the landscaping, was responsible for the plan, dividing the site with two principal streets, Riemeisterstrasse, running north–south, and the east–west boulevard, Argentinische Allee. Fundamental to the success of the venture was the extension of the Dahlem U-Bahn line to the site, with a new station designed by Salvisberg and engineer Alfred Grenander (1863–1931) at the western edge. But the U-Bahn's open-cut right-of-way had an equally significant impact on the plan, dividing the site roughly in half and combining with the principal streets to define small neighborhoods. Taut's first decision was to retain as many mature pine and beech trees as possible, setting the tone for the development where more than 70 percent of the site was either open, wooded, or preserved for gardens. The commercial core, consisting of shops, restaurants, and a cinema, was clustered around the station.

The first part of Onkel Toms Hütte to move forward occurred south of the U-Bahn station, on a rectangular parcel bound by Wilskistrasse, Riemeisterstrasse, Im Gestell, and Waldhütepfad, where Taut placed four rows of flat-roofed houses, broken at the corners, around the development's largest courtyard. The centerpiece of the plan was the so-called "Peitschenknall," or crack of the whip, an unbroken row of three-story flat-roofed apartment houses stretching in a slight curve for over 1,300 feet along Argentinische Allee, parallel to the U-Bahn's open cut. Rosemarie Haag Bletter writes that this group shows "Taut's knack for humanizing long rows of apartment houses . . . Because it is convex, all of it is never visible at one time. Portions of the building unfold gradually. The length of this unit is further broken by the varied colors of stairwells."[84] Opposite this row, on the north side of Argentinische Allee, Taut paired short rows of three three-story apartment houses perpendicular to the street, each sharing a common entrance courtyard.

Salvisberg was responsible for the long, primarily north–south terraces of single-family houses with rear gardens at the southwestern part of the site, while Häring designed similar flat-roofed rows at the southeast corner. The A-shaped group of rowhouses north of the U-Bahn station, the last to be completed, was the work of Taut, who collaborated with Häring on the

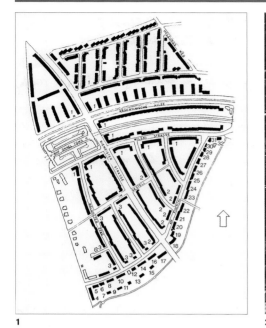

1. Plan, Bruno Taut, 1926. BTS

2. Aerial view. BTS (c. 1931)

3. Wilskistrasse. BTS (c. 1931)

4. Am Lappjagen. Leersum. FL (2012)

5. Argentinische Allee. Leersum. FL (2012)

northern ensemble of terraces east of Riemeisterstrasse, notable for the staggered sets of three to four houses placed at an angle to Am Hegewinkel. Although Taut used color throughout the estate, it was this five-block group that received the most dramatic treatment, with the brightest yellows and greens employed, in combination with light blue and dark red, earning Waldsiedlung Zehlendorf the moniker of the "parrot colony," reminiscent of the nickname—the "paint box estate"—given to Falkenberg. Bletter notes that while "Taut still uses vivid Expressionist color . . . it is used here not just as a synaesthetic device, but in a rational urbanistic sense: it is employed to enhance architectural forms and occasionally even to counteract unpleasant density. Color is used both psychologically and pragmatically: it elicits a sensory response, to be sure, but at the same time it helps to create, as in the Zehlendorf row houses, the illusion of intimate scale."[85] All told, 1,915 dwelling units were completed at Onkel Toms Hütte, 1,100 in apartments and the remainder in rowhouses.

In 1928, with about half of the estate complete, another nonprofit housing corporation, GAGFAH, issued a provocative challenge to Taut's Modernist scheme, contending that as the cottage quality gave way to the communality of continuous, abstractly massed and detailed rows, the inherent symbolic essence of the suburb as a celebration of the family was lost. GAGFAH commissioned Heinrich Tessenow to oversee the construction of a group of houses embracing *völkisch* themes on a rectangular site directly south of Onkel Toms Hütte between the south side of **Am Fischtal** and Fischtalpark. The model development, planned for the occasion of the group's tenth anniversary, consisted of 120 middle-income dwelling units in detached and terraced single-family and double houses as well as small apartment buildings "arrayed along the length of . . . Am Fischtal, resembling in their disposition the plan of a traditional Strassendorf."[86] Designed by a group of seventeen architects that included Tessenow, Hans Poelzig (1869–1936), Fritz Schopohl (1879–1948), and Paul Schmitthenner, the stucco houses each featured 45-degree pitched roofs in stark contrast to the sea of flat-roofed houses located just to the north, sparking what came to be known as the "war of the roofs."

Taut's next large-scale housing estate for GEHAG, **Wohnstadt Carl Legien** (1928), named for a leading trade union official, occupied a relatively expensive, 21-acre inner-city site completely unlike that of Onkel Toms Hütte, necessitating a far denser plan consisting exclusively of four- and five-story apartment houses.[87] Located northeast of Berlin's city center in the densely

Am Fischtal

1. Plan, Heinrich Tessenow, 1928. LB

2. View showing Am Fischtal, right, and Onkel Toms Hütte, left. FM (c. 1930)

3. Apartment building, Heinrich Tessenow, 1928. HTS (c. 2007)

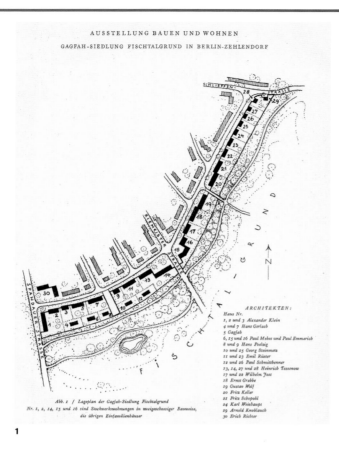

AUSSTELLUNG BAUEN UND WOHNEN

GAGFAH-SIEDLUNG FISCHTALGRUND IN BERLIN-ZEHLENDORF

ARCHITEKTEN:

Haus Nr.
1, 2 und 3 Alexander Klein
4 und 7 Hans Gerlach
5 Gagfah
6, 15 und 16 Paul Mebes und Paul Emmerich
8 und 9 Hans Poelzig
10 und 25 Georg Steinmetz
11 und 23 Emil Rüster
12 und 26 Paul Schmitthenner
13, 14, 27 und 28 Heinrich Tessenow
17 und 22 Wilhelm Jost
18 Ernst Grabbe
19 Gustav Wolf
20 Fritz Keller
21 Fritz Schopohl
24 Karl Weishaupt
29 Arnold Knoblauch
30 Erich Richter

Abb. 1 / Lageplan der Gagfah-Siedlung Fischtalgrund
Nr. 1, 2, 14, 15 und 16 sind Stockwerkswohnungen in weizgeschossiger Bauweise, die übrigen Einfamilienhäuser

Wohnstadt Carl Legien

1. Aerial view. BTS (c. 1930)

2. Erich-Weinert-Strasse. Köster. AKA (c. 1930)

3. Courtyard. Köster. AKA (c. 1930)

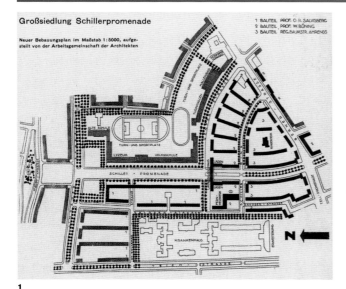

1. Plan, Otto R. Salvisberg, 1929. B30

2. Aroser Allee. Martens. LB (1943)

3. View over rooftops. NMS (c. 1931)

4. Aerial view. Roletschek. ROL (2009)

populated tenement house district of Prenzlauer Berg, Carl Legien was designed by Taut in collaboration with architect Franz Hillinger (1895–1973); they were greatly influenced by the courtyard-bounding apartment blocks of J. J. P. Oud's Tussendijken Workers' Housing (1920–21), Rotterdam, leading to the development's nickname of "Flemish Town." Leberecht Migge was again placed in charge of the landscaping.

At Carl Legien, Taut and his colleagues walked a fine line between suburban and urban scale and character. Taut and Hillinger's plan divided the site into six deep rectangular blocks bisected by Carmen-Sylva-Strasse (now Erich-Weinert-Strasse), the main east–west thoroughfare with landscaped median. U-shaped groups of flat-roofed apartment houses surrounding landscaped courtyards opened to this wide road, except at the northeast corner where the group was closed by a one-story commercial building. Continuous loggias faced the courtyards, while some apartments featured balconies, which were curved at the corners. In a two-year construction period, 1,149 one-and-a-half- to four-and-a-half-room apartments were completed, with close to 80 percent just two rooms, occupied primarily by trade-union workers, although close to one-third of the approximately 4,000 residents were civil servants. In addition to the apartments, Carl Legien also included shops, a restaurant, café, and common laundry with child-care facilities. Plans for an additional 400

apartments for a site just to the north were dropped as the economy collapsed.

In 1928 the Berlin municipal government set aside funds to build urgently needed housing for at least 2,000 families, resulting in the construction of two large-scale estates, Gross-Siedlung Reinickendorf and Gross-Siedlung Siemensstadt, built to house workers for the Siemens industrial complex (see p. 761). City architect Martin Wagner selected the design teams, choosing Otto R. Salvisberg as chief architect for Gross-Siedlung Reinickendorf (1929), assisted by architects Bruno Ahrends (1878–1948) and Wilhelm Büning (1881–1958) and landscape architect Ludwig Lesser (1869–1957).[88] Located on 35 acres in the northwestern part of the city just south of the Reinickendorf village green, the development of three- to five-story flat-roofed apartment houses quickly became known as **Die Weisse Stadt**, the white city, for the uniform color of its stuccoed facades, although all of the architects provided colorful accents on doors, window frames, roof overhangs, and drainpipes.

Salvisberg, responsible for the plan, was limited in his options by several largely undeveloped streets originally laid out in 1906. Adopting a north–south orientation centered around Aroser Allee, the main thoroughfare with landscaped median, he basically divided the site into separate parcels for each of the architects. Ahrends was responsible for both the triangular-shaped

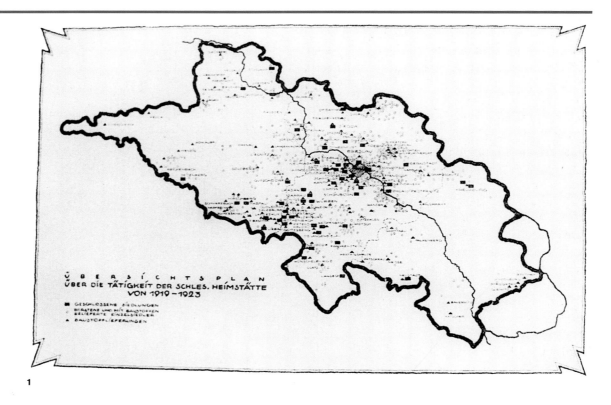

1

row of broken terraces located between Emmentaier Strasse and Schillerring and the long rows surrounding a courtyard just to the west on the other side of Aroser Allee. In the middle of the fan-shaped group, Ahrends included a kindergarten and children's home among the greenery. Büning designed the north–south terraces separated by landscaped courtyards that opened toward Schillerring but were closed by short rows at the northern border along Genfer Strasse. Büning also was the architect of the southernmost group of houses that formed a parallelogram around a courtyard.

Salvisberg designed the long U-shaped row at the northwest corner of the site between Aroser Allee and Romanshorner Weg as well as the White City's most notable building from both an aesthetic and technical point of view, an apartment house that bridged Aroser Allee. "In a dramatic visual statement of the machine-age esthetic," writes Ronald Wiedenhoeft, "Salvisberg created a hovering horizontal band of gallery-access housing (*Laubenganghaus*) raised on *pilotis* above the flow of traffic. This building was one of the few applications in Berlin of the exterior access system and was also unusual in its use of a reinforced concrete frame construction and in the provision of a large roof-terrace for sunbathing."[89] With large central clocks on both the north and south facades, the building served as the symbolic heart of the community, taking on the traditional role of the local church or town hall.

Between 1929 and 1931, 1,268 apartments, 80 percent of which were two-and-a-half rooms or less, were completed at Gross-Siedlung Reinickendorf, which also featured an unusually large nonresidential component scattered across the site, with twenty-four shops, two community laundries, extensive sports facilities, and

a hospital joining the school and orphanage. A solitary power plant provided heat and hot water for the entire estate. Wiedenhoeft observes that "the simple geometry of forms and the white rendering of flat surfaces gave the development a strikingly modern appearance," concluding that "the entire complex of The White City was calculated to express a new way of life, a new social order, a touch of the Fourierist Utopia."[90]

In 1925 Ernst May was appointed head of the departments of city planning and housing in his native Frankfurt. May, who had worked in Raymond Unwin's office (1910–12) before studying with Theodor Fischer at Munich's Technische Hochschule (1912–13), had just completed a six-year term (1919–25) running the building department of the Schlesische Landgesellschaft (Silesian Land Company) in Breslau (now Wrocklaw, Poland), a nonprofit housing association under the control of the government-sponsored Schlesische Heimstätte (Silesian Rural Settlement Authority).[91] Established to help relieve a severe housing shortage caused by a flood of refugees by encouraging the development of rural areas and the creation of farm communities, the goal of the **Schlesische Heimstätte** was to provide "the less prosperous members of the population with healthy and practically furnished homes at low prices," with each family to receive its "own house with garden plot."[92] Despite the pedigree of his experience with Unwin and Fischer, May, according to historian Beate Störtkuhl, was considered a surprising choice for the leadership role as "he had virtually no independent projects to his name apart from the design of military cemeteries during his army service."[93] May was also appointed editor of *Das Schlesische Heim*, a monthly magazine intended to document the work of the housing association, a promotional venture that the architect would repeat with his editorship of *Das Neue Frankfurt*.

May's most ambitious project for the Schlesische Heimstätte was **Siedlung Goldschmieden** (1920), a self-sufficient community planned for 750 families on an 865-acre estate eight miles northwest of Breslau.[94] For this project, as for all his work for the settlement authority, May was committed to adapt "the architecture to its setting in each case," stylistically guided by the vernacular farm buildings found in Silesia's Sudeten Mountains.[95] May's plan for Goldschmieden was focused around a central, rectangular civic and commercial core composed of a town hall, *Volkshaus* (community building), shops, and a school. Semidetached and terraced houses were placed on both sides of gently curving streets that connected back to the town center. May also planned for a number of villas to "encourage social diversification." According to Störtkuhl, he "broadened the intersections to form little squares in order to create the impression of a town that had grown organically," concluding that May's scheme represented an attempt "to transfer the English model of the garden city to Silesia."[96] The estate's existing manor house was to become a hotel and its grounds turned into a public park. Unfortunately, less than 13 percent of Siedlung Goldschmieden was realized, with only ninety-four houses built in the northwest corner of the large site.

May had even less success with the 500-family settlement he planned in 1923 as part of the expansion of the city of **Leobschütz** (now Glubczyce) near the Czech border.[97] May's scheme included two familiar elements, a central community green surrounded by civic and commercial buildings and rows of detached and semi-detached houses lining both sides of gently curving streets. At the southern end of the site May included a more interesting arrangement where, as Störtkuhl has noted, the architect "used a gentle rise above a stream to arrange the houses like a city wall along the road which curves in a quarter circle, interrupting them with protruding 'bastions' in the shape of 'courtyards,' which he was fond of using as a feature of his town planning."[98] This element of the plan remained unrealized, and in fact only a few of Leobschütz's streets were laid out according to May's direction.

The majority of May's settlement work for the Schlesische Heimstätte was on a smaller scale, including three subdivisions planned in 1919, each consisting of houses grouped around a communal green: **Kleinsiedlung Frankenstein**, composed of twenty-seven semidetached and detached houses; **Siedlung Gottesberg**, with fifty-one terraced units; and **Siedlung Hirschberg**, consisting of eleven semidetached houses.[99] **Kleinsiedlung Ober-Salzbrunn** (1920), located in a mining district fifty miles southwest of Breslau, was only partially realized, with the two areas of houses grouped around courtyards lost to cost-cutting measures, resulting in a row of forty-five terraced, semidetached, and detached houses lining both sides of the settlement's one street.[100] The 120 dwelling units planned for **Siedlung Klettendorf**

Siedlung Goldschmieden

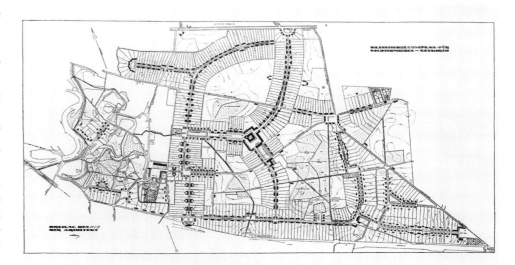

1

2

1. Plan, Ernst May, 1920. DSH20

2. Typical street. Lanowiecki. MLA (2010)

Leobschütz

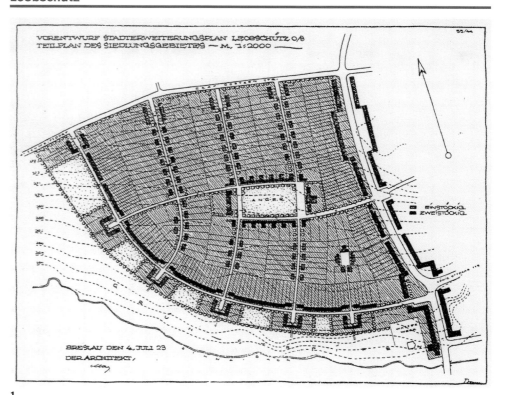

1

1. Plan, Ernst May, 1923. DSH23

Kleinsiedlung Frankenstein

1. Plan, Ernst May, 1919. DSH20

2. Typical street. Lanowiecki. MLA (2012)

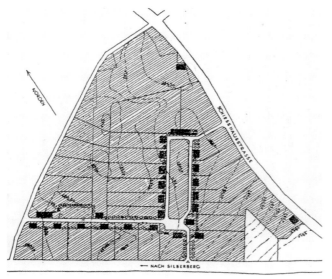

1

2

Siedlung Gottesberg

1. Plan, Ernst May, 1919. DSH20

2. Typical street. Lanowiecki. MLA (2012)

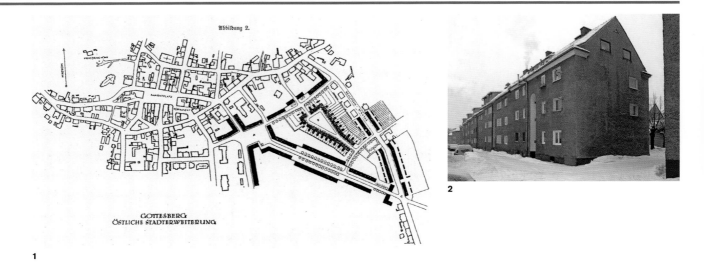

1

2

(1922), located on a triangular site three-and-a-half miles west of Breslau, were also scaled back for economic reasons, resulting in the completion of only five four-family houses, although each featured generous 700-square-meter gardens for vegetable cultivation as well as the keeping of small animals.[101] Four miles south of Breslau in the town of **Oltaschin**, May designed a subdivision (1920–25) on a seven-acre site consisting of a village green and sixteen semidetached houses and four detached houses, occupied by farmers who helped build the development.[102] **Siedlung Neustadt** (1920–23), built for the staff and families of the border police who patrolled the nearby Czech border, was originally planned to include seventy houses but only a small percentage was completed, including five semidetached units and nine small detached houses.[103]

In order to save both time and money, May created sixteen standardized house models, initially identified by number but later named for prominent figures in Silesian culture such as writer Gustav Freytag. May was still able to impart a measure of individuality to the standardized vernacular designs with Störtkuhl noting the influence of Unwin and Fischer: "May produced aesthetically attractive pictures of the Siedlungen, which were intended to convey to the residents a feeling of comfort and homeliness despite the material shortages. Carefully espaliered fruit trees, window shutters and transom windows as well as the prominent dormer windows of the standard houses all contributed to the impression."[104]

May's tenure at the Schlesische Heimstätte, which also included city-planning work and the building of temporary housing for refugees, ended in 1925, when he left Breslau for **Frankfurt**, abandoning his commitment to designs derived from vernacular precedent. But, as Störtkuhl has observed, "The transformation from the typical rural style of the Schlesische Heimstätte to the New Building was by no means as sudden as a superficial glance may suggest."[105] In his last years in Breslau, May attempted but failed to include Modernist designs to the mix of vernacular houses, and in the 1924 expansion of Siedlung Klettendorf he was able to include a flat-roofed store building.

Between 1925 and 1930 May, who was granted broad powers to commandeer and clear land in order

Siedlung Hirschberg

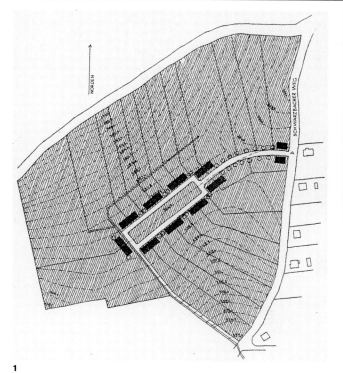

1

2

1. Plan, Ernst May, 1919. DSH20

2. Typical street. Lanowiecki. MLA (2010)

Kleinsiedlung Ober-Salzbrunn

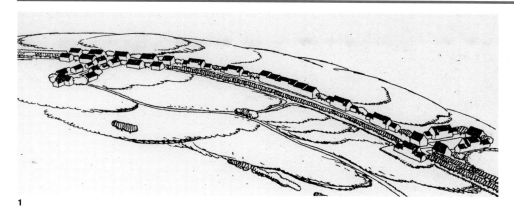

1

2

1. Bird's-eye view. DSH20 (1920)

2. Rear view of houses. DSH20 (1920)

Siedlung Klettendorf

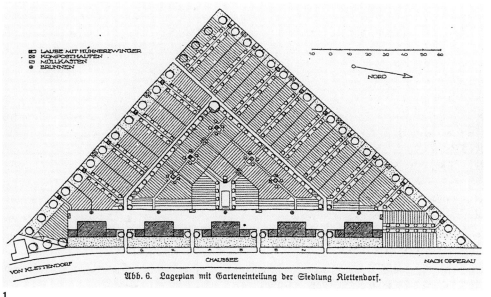

Abb. 6. Lageplan mit Garteneinteilung der Siedlung Klettendorf.

1

2

1. Plan, Ernst May, 1922. DSH22

2. Typical houses. Lanowiecki. MLA (2010)

Oltaschin

1. Bird's-eye view. DSH22 (1922)

2. Typical street. Lanowiecki. MLA (2010)

1

2

Siedlung Neustadt

1. Plan, Ernst May, 1920. DSH20

2. Typical street. DSH23 (1923)

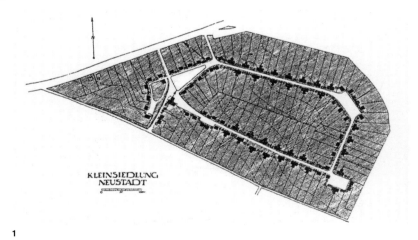

KLEINSIEDLUNG
NEUSTADT

1

2

Frankfurt

1. Land use plan showing existing buildings, industrial areas, open areas, built garden suburbs, and planned garden suburbs. DNF30 (1930)

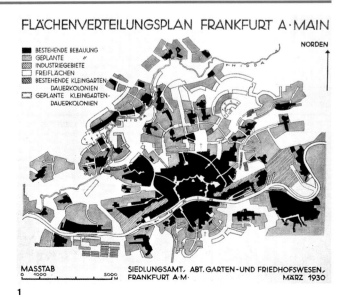

1

to build new housing to address Frankfurt's acute shortage, designed and oversaw the construction of more than 15,000 dwelling units, or roughly one new house or apartment for every eleventh Frankfurter.[106] In collaboration with a number of different architects, May arranged twenty-three separate siedlungen of varying quality—as the economy worsened, the buildings and plans became increasingly simplified—in a ring around the central city, "with a large green belt separating the older parts from the new developments. His overall plan," according to architectural historian Hilde Heynen, "was designed according to the principle of the *Trabantenstadt* [satellite cities], May's interpretation of the Howard and Unwin principle of the garden city. Unlike the English examples, however, which tended to be situated at quite a distance from the existing city, May's satellites are integrated into the Frankfurt urban

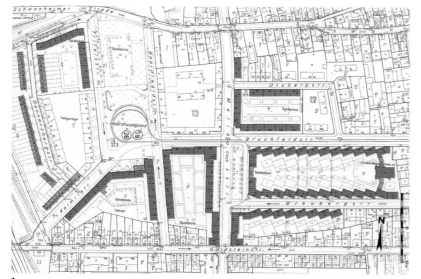

1

2

1. Plan, Ernst May and Herbert Boehm, 1926. DWD (c. 1988)

2. Courtyard. Collischonn. HMF (1935)

3. Rooftop terraces. Wolff. HMF (1927)

4. Breubergstrasse. Jünger. DJ (2006)

3

4

complex. The city of Frankfurt remains as a whole, with the green belt acting as a complex of 'city parks' rather than as a non-urban area situated between the nucleus of the city and the *Trabanten*."[107]

At Frankfurt, May's political goals and new aesthetic intersected. As historian Barbara Miller Lane writes, "minimalism in housing was not just a response to economic necessity, but was also an act of faith" for May,[108] a point the architect made clear in 1926 in the first issue of *Das Neue Frankfurt*, a monthly publication intended to promote the massive housing project to a wide audience:

> *Architecture has left behind it the path of decadent imitation and now recognizes the laws of form appropriate to our time . . . The altered spiritual attitude of mankind has resulted in a new dwelling form . . . [in] the crystal clear, often intentionally humble, spatial arrangements of modern architecture . . . Our co-workers in Frankfurt have drawn together in a philosophy of building . . . [intended] to provide housing for the masses . . . They seek . . . architectural and planning goals that grow out of our own era. They know that the forms of Frankfurt's housing not only succeed in embodying a new style, but also*

> *that their labors are essential as milestones on the road toward an architecture which is specifically expressive of the twentieth century.*[109]

May began his Frankfurt work with **Siedlung Bruchfeldstrasse** (1926–27), located southwest of the city center in the district of Niederrad.[110] Planned in collaboration with architect Herbert Boehm (1894–1954) and landscape architect Max Bromme (1878–1974), May was forced to accommodate 643 dwelling units in apartment buildings and terraced single-family houses on streets that had largely been laid out in advance. The development also included a prominent community center, the only one to be realized by May, although he expressed a desire to include such facilities in other Frankfurt housing estates. Siedlung Bruchfeldstrasse was quickly nicknamed "Zickzackhausen," or zigzag houses, after the project's most compelling component, staggered rows of three-story apartment buildings surrounding a generous landscaped courtyard, designed by May in collaboration with Carl Hermann Rudloff (1890–1949), who adopted a tripartite color scheme, with a gray concrete base, white-painted middle section, and a band of dark red running beneath the projecting cornice. May maintained that the rationale behind the sawtooth plan was strictly practical,

1. Plan, Ernst May and Herbert Boehm, 1926–27. DBA28

2. Aerial view. Hansa. HMF (1937)

3. Ortenberger Strasse. EMG (c. 1928)

4. Wittelsbacherallee. Heegmann. WC (2009)

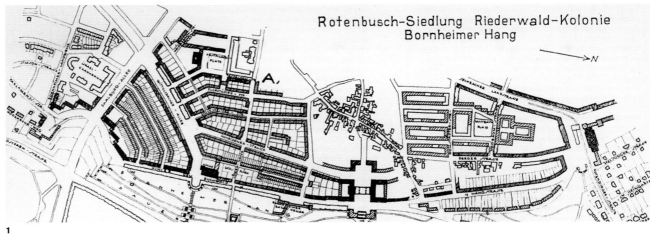

Rotenbusch-Siedlung Riederwald-Kolonie
Bornheimer Hang

improving solar orientation and ventilation, although he did not repeat the arrangement anywhere else in the city. The courtyard, filled with allotment gardens, was entered via a central gate at the western end.

In addition to the zigzag group, Siedlung Bruchfeldstrasse also included more conventionally arrayed rows of apartment buildings, the most notable of which featured a tower-like building designed by Ferdinand Kramer (1898–1985) at the southeast corner of Haardtwaldplatz, with a ground-floor library and top-level duplex apartment with striking angular double-height window, home to the local symphony conductor. At the western edge of the site near the railway line along Donnersbergstrasse, May and Boehm positioned forty-nine three-story single-family terraced houses with rear gardens. Each dwelling unit in the complex was equipped with a so-called "Frankfurt kitchen," a mass-produced, prefabricated kitchen designed by Margarete Schütte-Lihotzky (1897–2000), who was said to have been inspired by railroad dining cars. Separated from the living room by a sliding door, the 6.25-by-11-foot kitchens, with their built-in furniture and abundance of labor- and space-saving devices, were considered quite revolutionary, and more than 10,000 were installed in Neue Frankfurt. Although intended for the working class, rents at the siedlung proved too high, representing about one-half of an average worker's monthly wage, and most of the 2,500 tenants were civil servants and other white-collar professionals and their families.

Siedlung Bornheimer Hang (1926–30), located northeast of the city center, was built by the same design team as Siedlung Bruchfeldstrasse, with May joining Boehm for the planning and Rudloff for the buildings, and with Bromme serving as landscape architect.[111] The largest of the Frankfurt siedlungen, accommodating 1,540 working-class families primarily in two- and three-room flats along with sixty-three single-family houses, the development was arranged on either side of Wittelsbacherallee, the wide, curving main street with a tram line and double row of plane trees. The first part of the scheme to move forward occurred west of Wittelsbacherallee, where May encountered an existing street pattern as well as building regulations that required pitched roofs, the only use of that traditional building form at Frankfurt; otherwise, the rows of three- and four-story apartment buildings conformed to Neue Frankfurt standards, with flat unornamented facades and horizontal strip windows. The most interesting part of the development, west of Wittelsbacherallee, featured rows of four-story flat-roofed apartment houses enclosing a large courtyard. Amid the courtyard's greenery there were short east–west terraces of single-family houses. In addition to the housing, the complex included a central heating plant and a laundry in a building straddling Ortenberger Strasse, eight shops at Pestalozziplatz, as well as additional shops at the major corners of Wittelsbacherallee and Inheidener Strasse.

Siedlung Römerstadt (1927–29), located on the site of a first-century Roman town in the Nidda Valley northwest of the city's center, was "the most famous and convincing example of May's city planning," according to Hilde Heynen, "a very successful combination of

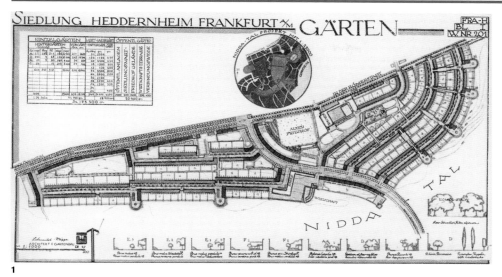

1. Plan, Ernst May, Herbert Boehm, and Wolfgang Bangert, 1927. GS28

2. Aerial view. EMG (1928)

3. Typical street. Wolff. HMF (1930)

4. Hadrianstrasse. EMG (c. 1928)

5. Typical street. Rödel. FM (1995)

organic design principles, which bear the imprint of the garden city tradition, with the sensation of simultaneity and movement created by the dynamism of a new, modern architectural idiom."[112] Planned in collaboration with Boehm and Wolfgang Bangert (1901–1973), the siedlung occupied a long and narrow site between the through-road In Der Römerstadt and the Nida River, with east–west streets on either side of Rosa-Luxemburg-Strasse, the north–south access road that bisected the site. Close to one-half of the 1,220 dwelling units were two-story single-family terraced houses, a much higher percentage than was typical at other Neue Frankfurt settlements, with the remainder of the residences in two-family houses and three- and four-story apartment buildings. The buildings were primarily designed by May and Rudloff but architects Martin Elsäesser (1884–1957), Karl Blattner (1881–1951), and Franz Schuster (1892–1972) also contributed. Leberecht Migge was responsible for the extensive gardens and landscaping.

In large part the plan was a response to the topography of the site. As Heynen has written,

The basic idea behind Römerstadt was to make good use of the qualities of the landscape: the development follows the contours of the hillside in the form of terraces while it is related to the valley of the Nidda by viewpoints on the bastions that punctuate the [three-meter] retaining wall

1. Plan, Ernst May, Herbert Boehm, and Wolfgang Bangert, 1927. DWD (c. 1988)

2. Aerial view. HMF (1936)

3. Olbrichstrasse. Weiss. HMF (1936)

4. Rear gardens. RAMSA (2008)

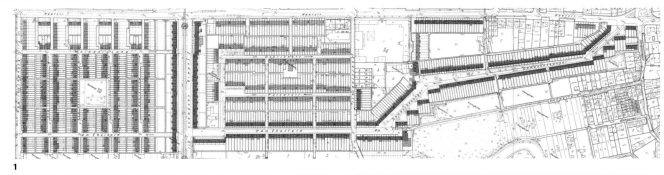

between the Siedlung and the valley. There is an obvious hierarchy with a main street (the Hadrianstrasse), residential streets, and paths inside the blocks, a hierarchy that the architecture accentuates . . . The blocks, however, are no longer closed like the nineteenth-century type. By staggering the long straight streets at the height of the bastions, long monotonous sightlines are avoided. All of these elements bear the clear imprint of Unwin's design principles.

Heynen goes on to note that May went beyond Unwin's example to add "a number of important new features: the brilliant interplay of curved and rectangular shapes, both in the layout of the streets and in the relating architectural elements: rounded ends for the buildings at the height of the bastions in the western part . . . right-angled ends for the buildings in the corresponding eastern part; rounded ends, rounded windows, and quarter-circle transitions to overcome the differences in height in the northern block of the Hadrianstrasse."[113]

In 1934, housing advocate Catherine Bauer wrote that Siedlung Römerstadt, "its handsome curved white rows silhouetted against the Taunus Mountains, and facing Frankfurt across the wide permanent 'green belt'

of the Nidda Valley, is in many respects the partial fruit of experiments at Letchworth and Welwyn in England, at Breslau, at Stuttgart, and on the Hook of Holland."[114] Four years later, Bauer's mentor and paramour Lewis Mumford offered unequivocal praise, describing Römerstadt as "an urban nucleus that meets the need for concentration (social advantage), for openness (hygienic and biological advantage), and for collective order and beauty: an environment in which the varied needs of the individual and the common life are effectively reconciled."[115]

Beginning with **Siedlung Praunheim** (1927–30), also located in the Nidda Valley about one-half mile west of Römerstadt, May and his associates increasingly abandoned Garden City principles in favor of Zeilenbau planning strategies. These called for long parallel north–south rows of houses, organized without regard to topography and placed at right angles to the principal roads and open at the ends, an arrangement largely dictated by the circulation of light and air.[116] This turn toward environmental determinism and away from community-fostering spatial hierarchies marks the beginning of the critical break with garden suburb planning that would play out in Europe and America in the years leading up to World War II.

At Praunheim, May worked with Herbert Boehm and Wolfgang Bangert on the plan, building the siedlung in three stages. The first phase, at the eastern end of the site, consisted of 164 two- and three-story one-family houses arranged in long, staggered rows along the curving angular path of Damaschke Anger, with rear gardens designed by Leberecht Migge and Max Bromme. This section, with buildings designed by May and Hermann Rudloff, also included nine apartments placed above three stores and a restaurant.

For Praunheim's second phase, located on a square site directly to the west bound by Heerstrasse, Eberstadtstrasse, Am Ebelfeld, and Ludwig-Landmann-Strasse, May arranged primarily straight rows of 442 two- and three-story one-family houses in an east–west direction, with the rows on the north sides of Olbrichstrasse and Pützerstrasse staggered at both their ends. These east–west terraces, designed by May in collaboration with Rudloff, Eugen Kaufmann (1894–1984), and Anton Brenner (1896–1957), featured an extensive use of prefabricated construction materials. A north–south row of four-story apartment buildings housing 123 families closed the group at the western border along Ludwig-Landmann-Strasse. In addition to a central laundry designed by Max Cetto (1903–1980) in the middle of Olbrichstrasse, the second phase included two stores topped by four apartments.

The largest and last phase of Praunheim, accommodating 699 dwelling units primarily in two-story one-family houses arranged in rigid north–south rows and with identical floor plans, was located farther to the west on a site that featured a large central playground. As historian John Robert Mullin put it, "The subtle integration of land contours and structures that marked Römerstadt did not occur at Praunheim."[117] Here, because of deteriorating economic conditions, May relied to an even greater extent on standardized, mass-produced precast-concrete panels. In partial relief to the severe plan, at the northern end of the site shorter rows of houses were grouped around landscaped courtyards open to the west. In addition to the housing, which also featured a row of three-story apartment houses with balconies along the western side of Ludwig-Landmann-Strasse, eight shops and a central power plant and laundry were included. As with the other segments, Migge and Bromme provided extensive gardens between the terraces.

Susan Rose Henderson has summarized Praunheim's three stages of construction: "Moving from east to west through the settlement one retraces the basic history of Weimar housing: from the early Sittesque segment, with its varied street patterns and house types, to an area of greater monotony and constraint, the results of mass production and techniques of economy, and, finally, to an area of oppressive rigidity and uniformity, impelled by increasing economies and an advancing cult of science."[118]

Siedlung Westhausen (1929–31), May's last Neue Frankfurt project before his departure in 1930 to build linear cities in Stalin's Soviet Russia, was also his most

1

1. Aerial view. HMF (1930)

literal statement of Zeilenbau principles.[119] Located on a Nidda Valley site south of Praunheim, from which it was separated by a cemetery, Westhausen, planned by May in collaboration with Boehm and Bangert, accommodated 1,116 dwelling units primarily in uniform rows of two-story, two-family north–south terraces arranged perpendicular to the long through streets, with pedestrian paths connecting the dwellings. The only variation in the rows of seven houses, designed by May and Kaufmann, was at the northern edge, where a double house was slightly staggered off line. At the eastern border, east–west rows of four-story apartment houses with balconies, designed by May, Ferdinand Kramer, and Eugen Blanck (1901–80), provided 216 three-room flats. Migge designed the gardens placed between each row of houses and apartments. As at the later stages of Praunheim, the architects relied on prefabricated concrete slabs to keep construction costs down.

Perhaps most striking of all was the plan's lack of center or community focus, created neither by architecture nor landscape, resulting in a completely nonhierarchical arrangement of straight streets on a rectangular site. Abandoning virtually all characteristics of Unwinesque hierarchies, May's Zeilenbau scheme seemed completely rational, even scientific. As John Robert Mullin has pointed out, its "courtyards were open-ended and therefore were reached by the free flow of air. Vehicular traffic was prohibited from permeating the project area and was forced to stay on the perimeter. This resulted in cleaner air, a quieter environment, safer pedestrian movement, and a financial savings due to the need for less pavement."[120]

Though there was much to admire in the spare design, and in particular the logical handling of the open spaces, there was no escaping the fact that some might find the project's minimalism, with its "degree-zero" approach, alienating and formulaic. No matter how commendable the intention to meet the material needs of the least well-off class, it is hard to quarrel with

1. Plan, Walter Gropius, 1926. BAB

2. Aerial view. SDR (1929)

3. Konsum Building, Walter Gropius, 1928. HAM (c. 1928)

4. Typical street. RAMSA (2008)

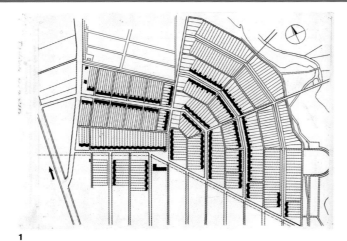

1

2

3

4

Jean-François Lejeune's terse assessment of the devolution of May's Neue Frankfurt work, "from the spatial inventions of the Siedlungen Bornheimer Hang, Römerstadt, and Bruchfeld-strasse to the inhuman rigidity of Praunheim and Westhausen."[121]

In 1926, a year after the Bauhaus moved from Weimar to Dessau, founding director Walter Gropius was commissioned by the city of Dessau to build a housing estate for low-income workers in order to address a severe shortage of available units.[122] Located on a semirural site about four miles south of the Bauhaus school building (Walter Gropius, 1925–26) on the outskirts but connected to the central city by tram, **Siedlung Törten** was financed by the Reichsforschungsgesellschaft für Wirtschaftlichkeit im Bau- und Wohnungswesen (National Research Institute for Economic Efficiency in Construction and Housing) in partnership with the municipal government. In a somewhat unusual move, all of the residences were to be offered exclusively for sale, as opposed to the typical practice, especially for working-class dwellings, of renting them.

Gropius's plan called for 316 dwelling units to be accommodated in rows of four to twelve single-family houses, with rear gardens of between 350 and 400 square meters, to be used for fruit and vegetable cultivation as well as for keeping small animals. The plan consisted of various segments, the largest of which, inspired by Howard's Garden City diagram, was a fan-shaped section

composed of three curving concentric streets lined on both sides by two-story, flat-roofed, cube-shaped houses with horizontal strip windows. To help break up the monotony of the long rows of sparely detailed houses, several of the sections featured staggered setback distances. By virtue of its purpose, central location, and commanding height, Gropius's Konsum Building, comprising a five-story apartment tower with communal rooftop terrace and the siedlung's sole commercial facility, served as the estate's main focus.

Like May, Gropius also relied on prefabricated building parts to keep construction costs down. But Gropius would go further in his attempt to mechanize the building process. As designer and historian Chup Friemert writes:

Walter Gropius made Törten into a testing ground for new methods of organization and planning in the development of estates and the utilization of new materials and machines. His stock of machinery included cement mixers, slag breakers, special tables for producing the roof beams, hollow block pressing machines, rotating tower cranes and a field train . . . For Gropius there was no difference between the mass production of houses and mass production in industry: he designed the construction site for the estate as a street transformed into a conveyor belt. The

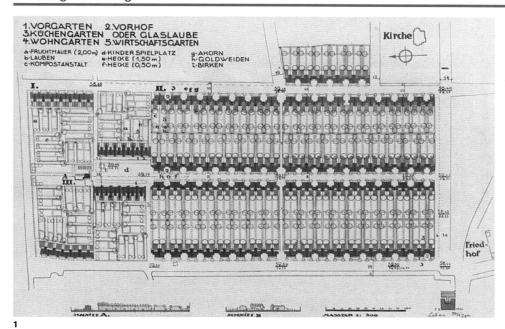

1. Landscape plan, Leberecht
Migge, 1926. GS28

2. Typical street. Kuras. CK (2011)

3. Rear gardens. GS28 (c. 1928)

4. Bird's-eye view. SW27

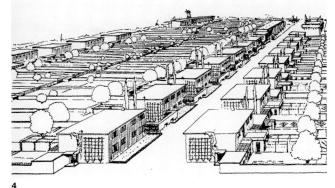

*materials enter the system at one end and com-
plete terraced houses come out at the other . . .
And, just like in a factory, the workers were paid
piece wages and only used for one specific task.*[123]

All of the planned houses and the Konsum Building were completed in three phrases between 1926 and
1928. An attempt to market Bauhaus-made furnishings
for the new houses fell flat, as a model house equipped
with pieces designed by Marcel Breuer (1902–1981) failed
to attract much interest. This was hardly the only setback as design and construction flaws quickly surfaced,
leading to the 1928 decision to ask Hannes Meyer (1889–
1954), who had assumed directorship of the Bauhaus
after Gropius's resignation earlier in the year, to oversee
the southern extension of the estate and to design some
additional housing.

After visiting the housing estate in 1927, Swedish
architect Sven Markelius (1889–1972) wrote that "this
whole building project's organizational plan, thoroughly
conceived in detail prior to building, is perhaps the
most interesting and most exemplary thing about this
housing design." Markelius concluded that the "Dessau-
Törten housing area seems to me to point to new and
proper avenues for modern housing production. The

possibility to make, for broad sectors of the population,
technically sound, well planned and—not least importantly—sufficiently spacious dwellings is worth the most
serious endeavors."[124] But the efficiencies in construction
produced a Pyrrhic victory, as the tedious repetition of
the plan and house designs came at the expense of the
street pictures advocated by Unwin. Not all would agree;
Jean-François Lejeune has praised "its ingenious urban
design," especially "its concentric, fan-shaped network of
streets [and] the pedestrian paths meandering through
the blocks," as well as "the Sittesque method of setting
back or pushing forward houses to mark street entrances
and other spatial moments, and especially, the . . .
mixed-use cooperative building."[125]

Leberecht Migge and architect Leopold Fischer
(1901–1975), a disciple of Adolf Loos (1870–1933), collaborated on the design of **Siedlung Knarrberg** (1926),
also known as Siedlung Ziebigk, located in Dessau on
a 40-acre site four miles north of Siedlung Törten.[126]
Overshadowed by Gropius's far more prominent development, Migge and Fischer's exclusively residential
project was sponsored by the Anhalt Settlers' Union, a
cooperative building society that intended to provide
dwellings for workers and lower-level civil servants
as well as the middle class. The plan consisted of four

SIEDLUNG AM WEISSENHOF

1. J. FRANK, WIEN
2. J. J. P. OUD, ROTTERDAM
3. M. STAM, ROTTERDAM
4. LE CORBUSIER, GENF-PARIS
5. P. BEHRENS, BERLIN
6. R. DÖCKER, STUTTGART
7. W. GROPIUS, DESSAU
8. L. HILBERSEIMER, BERLIN
9. MIES VAN DER ROHE, BERLIN
10. H. POELZIG, BERLIN
11. A. RADING, BRESLAU
12. H. SCHAROUN, BRESLAU
13. A. G. SCHNECK, STUTTGART
14. B. TAUT, BERLIN

1

2

3

4

5

1. Model. SS (1927)

2. Aerial view. FM

3. Rathenaustrasse. BPK (c. 1932)

4. Single and double houses, Le Corbusier, 1927. UDC

5. Apartment house, Ludwig Mies van der Rohe, 1927. Praefcke. WC (2007)

parallel rows of 182 houses, although the end units were set back. Each house featured 400-square-meter gardens. Fischer's two-story flat-roofed houses, described by Lejeune as "starkly Loosian but traditionally built volumes," were completed by 1928 and included five different sizes to accommodate Knarrberg's economically diverse tenantry.[127]

The twenty-one flat-roofed residential buildings of **Siedlung Weissenhof**, constructed as part of the Deutscher Werkbund's 1927 exhibition in Stuttgart and designed by sixteen different architects including J. J. P. Oud (1890–1963), Walter Gropius, Le Corbusier, Bruno Taut, and Ludwig Mies van der Rohe (1886–1969), have earned a special place in the history of twentieth-century architecture, but the site plan by Mies, who also served as the project's director, has been undervalued.[128] The permanent housing exhibition, financed by the city of Stuttgart and erected in just five months, was intended to showcase new methods of building, with "the leading representatives of the modern movement" asked to "take their own approach to the problem of the modern dwelling," as Mies noted in the preface to the exhibition catalogue.[129]

The siedlung was located about two miles north of the city center. In devising the plan, Mies was assisted by Richard Döcker (1894–1968), who also designed two buildings at the estate. Weissenhof's plan, providing sixty dwelling units in detached and terraced houses and apartment buildings, was ingeniously adapted to its hilly site, suggesting, especially in Mies's initial plaster model, a Mediterranean hill town, with the most prominent sites reserved for Le Corbusier's single and double

houses as well as Mies's own centrally located four-story apartment block.

More than half a million people visited the Deutscher Werkbund's exhibition, which also elicited a vocal, negative reaction among many critics and architects, including Paul Schmitthenner, who issued a rebuke in the form of a housing estate, **Siedlung Kochenhof** (1927), which he designed employing *völkisch* themes as opposed to the cubistic abstractions used by all of the Weissenhof architects.[130] Also known as the "wood estate" because of its sponsorship by an association promoting wood as a building material, progress at Kochenhof, located about a half-mile southwest of Weissenhof, was stymied by the economic depression. When the project was resurrected in the early 1930s, it had a new sponsor, prominent Nazi theorist Alfred Rosenberg's Kampfbund für deutsche Kultur, an organization established to rally support for the National Socialist cause. Schmitthenner, in collaboration with Heinz Wetzel (1882–1945), revised the plan for Siedlung Kochenhof (1933), providing twenty-five detached two- and three-story single- and multifamily houses with steeply pitched roofs arranged in irregular rows with substantial rear gardens. Schmitthenner designed three of the houses at Kochenhof, with the remaining undertaken by Paul Bonatz (1877–1956) and others. At the village's opening, the magazine *Bauzeitung* painted an idyllic picture of the Heimatstil development:

In the Am Kochenhof housing project, a true children's paradise has been created in the spirit of the poetics of the village and the countryside: small gardens, small courtyards, small passageways,

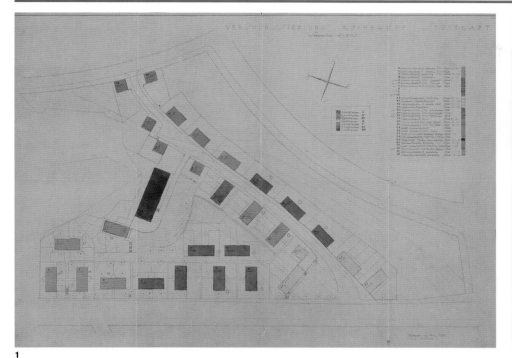

1. Plan, Paul Schmitthenner, 1928. SS

2. Aerial view. ATU (c. 1933)

3. Hermann-Pleuer-Strasse. ATU (c. 1933)

4. Hermann-Pleuer-Strasse. WC (2006)

5. Rear gardens. ATU (c. 1933)

and small squares, in which children rejoice in harmless games, where the leisure of the old is to enjoy the happiness of the young. Romanticism was long deemed outmoded. Yet it is the inevitable outcome as long as one allows all those small coincidences, which disrupt every regularity here and there, to be seen rather than covered up, as long as we embrace them as a welcome ingredient that enriches and enlivens the whole, and that deserves our special care and attention.[131]

In 1933, Italian-born German architect Guido Harbers (1897–1977), head of the Department of Housing and Human Settlement, convinced officials of the new National Socialist government to sponsor the construction of a model housing estate on former farmland three miles southeast of Munich's center, convenient to a tram line and adjacent to a prominent local landmark, the fifteenth-century St. Mary's Church, topped by a late-eighteenth-century onion dome.[132] Harbers, who had studied at Munich's Technische Hochschule

with Theodor Fischer as well as served as editor of the magazine *Baukunst*, was a longtime member of the Nazi party married to the daughter of a high official. Harbers was inspired by the example of Siedlung Weissenhof but wanted instead to promote Heimatstil architecture as well as garden suburb ideals. Munich's municipal government agreed to pay for the cost of **Mustersiedlung** (model settlement) **Ramersdorf**, with the houses to be sold to skilled workmen and middle-class civil servants and businessmen.

Harbers's low-density plan (1934) for the wedge-shaped site included generous amounts of public green space and curving streets lined with 153 detached single-family houses, 10 semidetached and 30 terraced units. Each of the houses featured a rear garden, and plot sizes for the single-family houses ranged from 47 by 87 feet to 60 by 150 feet. No commercial facilities were included but space was reserved for a church. The editors of London-based *Architect and Building News* were impressed with the layout. Writing in 1935, the year that construction concluded, they noted that "the houses lie each to one side

1

2

3

4

1. Plan, Guido Harbers, 1934. BAU34

2. Bernauer Strasse. SM

3, 4. Krottenmühlstrasse. Varzi. AV (2012)

of its plot to obtain maximum use of the garden space. Each house has a carefully arranged aspect and plan with relation to the sun; where the plot runs east and west, the house is at the east side of it; where it runs north and south, the house is at the north end. There is a paved sun-terrace for every house."[133] Seventeen different architects were responsible for the white-stucco-clad brick houses with red-tile gabled roofs, realized in thirty-four different configurations. Harbers, who designed thirty of them in addition to the church, was joined by such practitioners as Theo Pabst (1905–1979), Sep Ruf (1908–1982), Friedrich Haindl (1910–2002), and Hanna Löv (1901–1989).

Harbers's scheme for Mustersiedlung Ramersdorf was intended as a rebuke to Siedlung Neu-Ramersdorf (Oscar Delisle, Bernhard Ingwersen, and Richard Berndl, 1928–30), a dense development of courtyard-bounding buildings accommodating over 1,300 apartments and forty-nine stores that was built by the Weimar government on a site less than half a mile away. As *Architect and Building News* noted: Mustersiedlung Ramersdorf "is particularly interesting as demonstrating the complete change in housing that the Nazis have brought about. They look with disfavor on blocks of flats, which they associate with Marxist policy. The people must get in touch with the land once more, and each family have its own house and garden; there must be no hint of anything communal in domestic life. In striking contrast to the abundance of buildings for collective use in the housing schemes built by the late Social Demo-cratic Governments, particularly in Vienna, the only public building here is a church."[134]

Mustersiedlung Ramersdorf was completed as originally planned but failed to impress influential

government officials and, as Winfried Nerdinger has written, "the project was not a propaganda success."[135] The individuality of the houses as well as their place-ment along curving roads resulted in a development "that differed noticeably from the uniform simplicity of other Reichskleinsiedlungen [small settlements of the Reich]. For precisely this reason, many Nazi politicians rejected the 'exemplary settlement.' They argued that it was unsuitable to serve as a model for future housing in the 'national community.'"[136]

Gartenstadt Alsterdorf (1935–38), located five miles north of central Hamburg, was a more typical example of the Nazi era's Heimatstil housing estates.[137] The 50-acre city-owned site, formerly home to farms and pasture-land, was just north of a rail line. The development was designed by six different architects in two phases, with Walter Holst (n.d.) credited with the plan of the first stage that set the tone for subsequent development. The pre-dominantly detached single-family houses were located on narrow streets, occupying modest 500-square-meter plots. Though designed by different architects, includ-ing Willy Eggers (n.d.) and Emil Mewes, architect of the "milkmaid" siedlung in Cologne, the two-story houses, set back behind hedges and front lawns, were quite simi-lar, with each required to be clad in red brick and with all gable ends facing the street. The focus of community life was the row of thirteen shops located at the center of the development at the intersection of Heilholtkamp and Frühlingsgarten, home to small stores, including a phar-macy, a butcher, a grocery store, a bakery, a tobacconist, and a florist. By 1938, after a second phase of develop-ment with slightly larger houses, Gartenstadt Alsterdorf numbered 282 single-family houses.

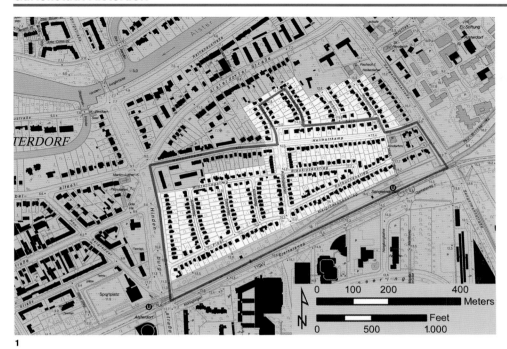

1. Map. SCH (c. 2005)
2. Typical street. BHAM
3. Shops. BHAM

FRANCE

Although the French Garden City Association, founded in 1903, was the second to be established outside of England, trailing Germany by one year, enthusiasm for Howard's ideas was rarely translated into built form until after the bombings of World War I destroyed 625 French towns and 450,000 buildings, leaving the country in need of more than 600,000 new dwellings. The lag is attributable in part to the fact that the new movement was initially embraced not by architects and planners but rather social reformers and politicians who, as planning historian Jean-Pierre Gaudin has written, "seemed to be less concerned with the ways and means of garden city planning than with the ideal of a new polity model, of a *cité* understood as a community pattern and citizen matrix. It was these aspects of the garden city idea, the parts that were most rapidly jettisoned elsewhere, that most excited French interest."[138]

Howard's emphasis on social reform, cooperation, and culling the best aspects of city and country positioned the Garden City, according to Gaudin, as the "natural heir to the paternalistic experiments of the nineteenth century," with their emphasis on "family values and morality . . . public hygiene and health

. . . Howard was refreshing an indigenous French tradition of local utopian socialist and anarchist thought." But the idea went further, as Gaudin notes, offering a way to carry "bourgeois reformism beyond the limitations of industrial philanthropy without seriously threatening middle-class sensibilities."[139]

The Garden City Association had its roots in the Musée Social, a group of politicians, civil servants, and industrialists who banded together in 1894 to promote workers' welfare and whose members—several would join the association—saw "the garden city's emphasis on low-density housing for factory workers" as a way of retaining "many of the advantages of rural life within an industrial setting."[140] Paul-Henri d'Estournelles de Constant (1852–1924), a member of parliament and peace advocate who would win the Nobel peace prize in 1909, served as the Garden City Association's president. Other notable members included the social economists Charles Rist (1874–1955) and Charles Gide (1847–1932). Gide, having written a study on nineteenth-century cooperative communities as well as a biography of Charles Fourier, considered the Garden City to be the most viable proposal for a cooperative society.

Georges Benoît-Lévy (1880–1971), a lawyer and former student of Gide's, served as the association's

1–12. Locator map and plans for
garden villages of the Chemin de
Fer du Nord. ANMT (c. 1923)

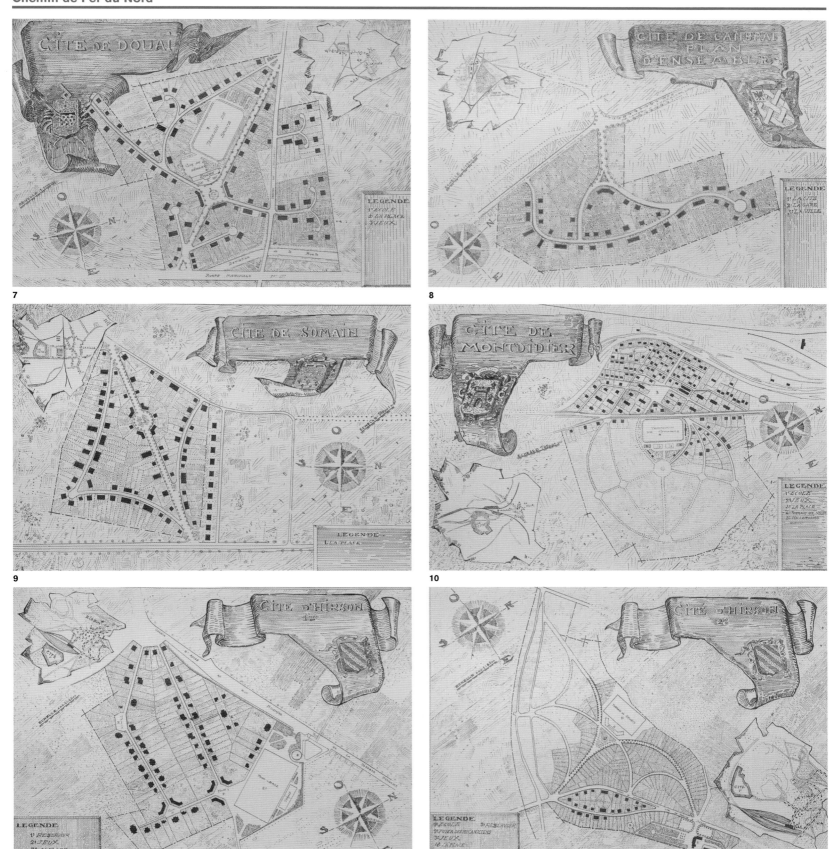

7

8

9

10

11

12

secretary and treasurer and quickly became its public face. With funding from the Musée Social, he attended the first International Garden City Congress in 1904, visited Letchworth, lived for six months in Port Sunlight and Bournville, and published two of the earliest studies of the garden city: *La Cité Jardin* (1904) and *Les Cités Jardins d'Amérique* (1905), the latter of which hinted at Benoît-Lévy's increasingly loose definition of the subject, including, for instance, discussions of public parks in existing cities. Although his efforts were crucial in bringing attention to the movement on an international level—he was particularly influential in Belgium— Benoît-Lévy's enthusiasm undermined his advocacy. His reports on the Garden City Association's progress, which "he forwarded with frequency to Britain for publication in the Garden City movement's journal," were, as historian Stanley Buder notes, "highly unreliable."[141] In addition, according to planning historian Anthony Sutcliffe, "the garden city was sold short by Benoît-Lévy's extraordinarily insensitive choice of the translation 'cité-jardin'—'cité' might have seemed an inspiringly poetic synonym for 'ville' but in general usage it had come to mean an estate of workers' dwellings, and some of the grimmest blocks of flats to be found in France bore the name of 'cité.'"[142] On the other hand, Sutcliffe points out, "Benoît-Lévy's failure to capture the French urban reform movement was partly due to a deep-seated French resistance to the British suburban ideal," as articulated in French journals such as *La Construction Moderne*, which remained "faithful to the Parisian upper-class ideal of ultra-urbanity" and "constantly derided Benoît-Lévy and the garden city idea" with a "sardonic, defensive and basically ignorant attitude [that] greatly attenuated the impact of the British example in France."[143] Benoît-Lévy's decision to merge the French Garden City Association with the linear city concept of Arturo Soria y Mata (1844–1920), renaming the group the French Garden and Linear Cities Association, overlooked "the clear antithesis of the two concepts," as Buder put it. But "for over a half century, Benoît-Lévy irrelevantly plodded on."[144]

Railroad Workers' Villages

The devastation of World War I was particularly severe in northern France, where the **Chemin de Fer du Nord** (Northern Railway), "at the time of the armistice a mere skeleton of its former self," as one observer put it, lost 1,452 miles of track and hundreds of stations, bridges, and tunnels as well as at least six complete towns and twenty-eight villages that lay along the line. Under the guidance of head civil engineers Raoul Dautry (1880–1951) and Paul-Emile Javary (1866–1945), the company undertook a massive rebuilding campaign. Adopting the garden village as a model for new workers' villages, the Chemin de Fer du Nord became "the real animator of the garden city movement in France," completing 8,700 houses by 1922 (the number grew to 11,141 by 1926) in Tergnier, Lille-Délivrance, Lens-Méricourt, Aulnoye,

Laon, Hirson, Longeaue, Arras, Bethune, Dunkirque, Valenciennes, and other villages, many of which were only to be destroyed again during World War II.[145]

Each settlement was designed according to its specific site and purpose, but certain components were common to all, including primary and technical schools, cooperative stores, medical facilities, meeting halls, and public baths as well as modern infrastructure such as sewer and electrical systems. Most of the villages—along with others built during the same period but outside the purview of the Chemin de Fer du Nord—featured an *école menagère* or *école maternelle*, where mothers were taught parenting skills, girls were given instruction in domestic arts such as sewing and cooking, and nurseries and children's health-care centers were provided in an effort to reverse the country's declining birthrate and rising infant mortality rate. Each community sat cheek by jowl with its rail yard, but orchards, nurseries, or parks were often provided as buffers. Most of the plans also incorporated landscaped plazas focused on decorative fountains or old wells.

The villages, initially intended for low-level workers and their families, soon attracted managers and officers whose large houses, with dining rooms, drawing rooms, dressing rooms, and bathrooms, stood apart from the common one-story workers' dwelling that featured three bedrooms, a kitchen, and a living room. Additional types of workers' houses included rows of two or more houses designed by an assortment of architects whose standardized types were adapted for different villages. Among the architects were Ernest Bertrand (n.d.), Charles Patris (n.d.), and the firm of Molinié, Nicod & Ponthier.

To help trim costs, the houses were constructed of blocks of slag and cinder, readily available industrial by-products, and occasionally covered in painted cement. Brick was used in limited quantities. Despite the inherent modernity of the materials used, both houses and public buildings adopted "the distinctly traditional aesthetic of each province," helping the railroad company, as Gwendolyn Wright has observed, to "present a benign portrait of their relations" with workers.[146] "In all our work," stated an official, "we have avoided the old blunder of building long rows of houses all alike. Even in our temporary groups of wooden barracks, necessarily similar, we tried to vary the planting and colors to avoid monotony."[147] The company was also careful to avoid paternalism, placing only three representatives on the village council whose other councilors were elected by fifty-family groups.

According to Benoît-Lévy, **Tergnier** (1919–23) was the "most beautiful" of the railroad villages, "with its fine plazas, public parks, lawns and playgrounds, its splendid educational centre, and its delightful cottages."[148] A railroad junction and administrative headquarters, Tergnier had boasted a prewar population of 10,000 but was left after the armistice "the most deplorable wreck of a town imaginable."[149] The rebuilt village officially opened on July 10, 1921 and by the following year counted nearly 1,500 houses accommodating 7,000 people.

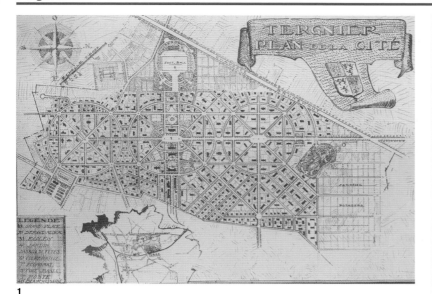

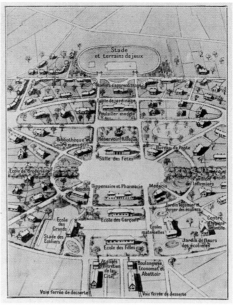

1. Plan, Raoul Dautry, 1919. ANMT (c. 1923)

2. Perspective plan showing part of the village devoted to public buildings. SSDJ

3. Typical street. RMN (c. 1919)

4. Buttes Chaumont. SNCF (c. 1923)

As planned by Raoul Dautry, the 271-acre site, on the west side of the rail yard, included eighteen miles of streets forming a complex if not overwrought network of superimposed geometries. Three loop roads—an oval flanked by two circles—circumscribed the district's principal neighborhoods and were overlaid by grids of varying orientation to create a plethora of block sizes and shapes and a profusion of intersections, with those at the junction of six or seven streets treated as *rond-points*. An axial tree-lined boulevard connected the open plazas at the middle of each neighborhood, the central of which served as a civic center ringed by a community hall, post office, doctor's house, two schools, and a bathhouse. An *école maternelle*, a medical center, a 240-bed hotel, and office buildings extended east toward the rail yard while athletic fields and a gymnasium were placed at the western edge of the site. A naturalistic park with a man-made lake was located in the north adjacent to public gardens.

The predominant dwelling type in Tergnier was a two-story quadruple house—the units were placed side-to-side and back-to-back—set deep within the block at the intersection of four individual lots, an arrangement that made the diminutive one-twentieth-of-an-acre (2,178 square feet) lots seem larger. The absence of a defined street wall helped to create the impression of individual villas set within an open landscape, a feeling also enhanced, as Bryant Hall wrote in 1922, by "the entire absence of walls, hedges or trellises between lots, boundaries being marked by attractive open fences of reinforced concrete posts joined by lines of wiring or by wire netting."[150] Although small, the lots allowed room for vegetable gardens and fruit trees provided by the company. Tergnier was completely destroyed during World War II. Urbain Cassan (1890–1979) guided the town's postwar reconstruction, replacing most but not all of the old geometries with an open plan of long terraces differentiated architecturally from one neighborhood to the next.[151]

Lille-Délivrance and Lens-Méricourt came next in terms of size and scope. Both were largely built in six months. **Lille-Délivrance** (1921), a northwestern suburb of Lille, the north's largest industrial city, was laid out on 165 acres by École des Beaux-Arts studio master Gustav Umbdenstock (1866–1940) for a population of 8,150 residing in 830 houses.[152] The plan was looser than that of Tergnier, organized by three landscaped *rond-points*, each with a plaza in the center, the westernmost accommodating one of the village's two *écoles maternelles*. The straight and gently curving streets that extended tentacle-like from each circle gave shape to large blocks featuring vernacular-style, detached, two-, three-, and four-family houses around the perimeter. Culs-de-sac allowed for development on the block interior. The streets were narrow with the exception of two main intersecting boulevards that were lined by chestnut

1. Plan, Gustav Umbdenstock. ANMT (1921)

2. Boutiques designed by Gustav Umbdenstock. SNCF (c. 1923)

3. Rue Jules Goury. ACL (2012)

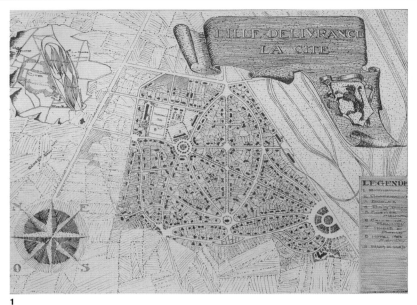

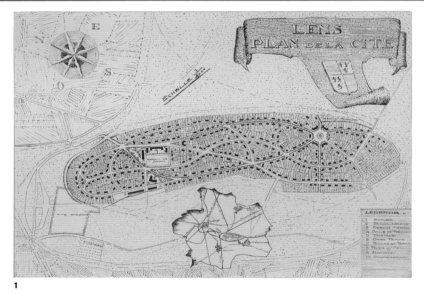

and acacia trees, sidewalks, and flowerbeds. Many of the streets converged in a semicircular park across from the rail yard, providing residents with a direct route to work. Umbdenstock designed several individual houses in Lille-Délivrance, including ones for the doctor and district chief, while Ernest Bertrand contributed designs for public buildings such as the school and medical center. The village also featured athletic facilities, public baths, administrative offices, stores, a 156-bed hotel, and a recreation hall.

Lens-Méricourt (1922), a railroad-owned coal-mining community, featured an Olmstedian plan that, with the exception of a *rond-point*, consisted entirely of long, softly curving streets accommodating 800 houses designed by Louis Süe (1875–1968).[153] In addition to the usual community facilities, the village included public gardens and a prominently sited primary school for girls with a steeply pitched pyramidal roof rising to a clock tower cupola.

In **Aulnoye**, the Chemin de Fer du Nord built three separate neighborhoods southeast of the railroad tracks, each likely intended for a different class of worker, with houses and lots varying in size from one to the next.[154] Almost every intersection was opened up as a plaza. A school, a 204-bed hotel, and other public buildings were included. The village of **Laon,** bounded by the rail yard to the south and farmland all around, was principally composed of six straight and slightly curved residential streets that funneled workers south to a plaza, with an adjacent sports field and a nearby *école maternelle*.[155] Schools were placed in the residential section to the north, where single-family detached houses were rhythmically paired along narrow streets, sharing the blocks with multifamily houses. **Valenciennes** combined aspects of Tergnier and Lille-Délivrance, with a semicircular plaza facing the rail yard, a *rond-point*, and a mix of detached, semidetached, and quadruple houses sited to resemble villas in an open landscape.[156]

Aulnoye

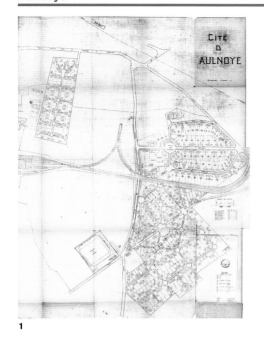

1

16. – AULNOYE. – La Cité – Rue de Bellevue et l'École des Garçons.

2

1. Plan, 1925. SNCF

2. Rue Belleville showing boys' school, right. CRS (c. 1926)

Laon

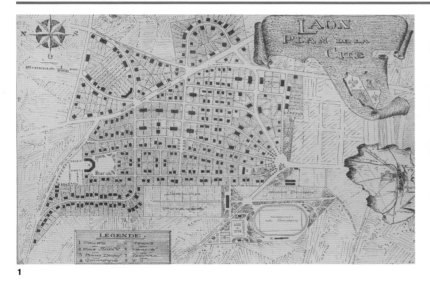

1

2

1. Plan. ANMT (c. 1923)

2. Aerial view. ECTM (2012)

Valenciennes

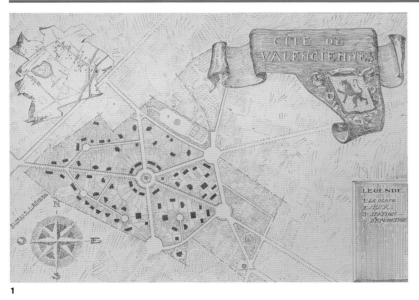

1

2

1. Plan. ANMT (c. 1923)

2. Aerial view. TIW (1924)

1. Plan, Jean Walter, 1913. AED14

2. View toward château. AED14

3. Le Grand Étang (the big pond). RAMSA (2012)

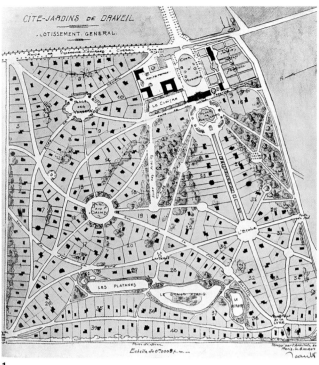

1

2

3

Paris-Banlieue

The close of the war found Paris in need of approximately 100,000 dwellings within a ten-mile radius. Although Le Vésinet (1858) (see p. 43) had been a pioneering suburban village, most subsequent suburban development was chaotic, with land speculators subdividing old farms, hundreds of acres in size, and hastily marketing lots to poor purchasers while failing to provide promised infrastructure, resulting in a landscape of shanties.[157] By World War I, private development had consumed nearly 7,500 acres around the city, a number that continued to grow during the interwar period.

Few English-inspired planned garden suburbs stand out from the early 1900s. The most notable example, **Cité-Jardin de Draveil**, located about fifteen miles south of Paris, was undertaken by a cooperative housing society to provide affordable houses for workers in a "garden city" environment.[158] Initiated in 1909 and officially opened after fifty houses were completed in 1912, Draveil was situated on a beautiful, 111-acre site, the fenced-in grounds of an early-eighteenth-century château replete with formal gardens, rolling woodlands, waterfalls, streams, and ponds. Far from any factories, the suburb was a fifteen-minute walk to a railroad station and a twenty-minute ride to the city. As low-cost dwellings (*habitations à bon marché*), the houses were eligible to receive government subsidies under an 1894 law. Architect Jean Walter (1883–1957) prepared the site plan, taking care to preserve natural features and vegetation. Walter kept the château and its immediate environs intact, including a boulevard extending axially from its western flank, while tracing a new network of gently curving streets meeting in *places* and *rond-points* across

the rest of the site. The houses enjoyed relatively large lots made possible by the low land costs. In all, Walter devoted 42 acres to communally owned parks and public spaces. He also led a panel that reviewed designs for the 322 houses that had to fall within minimum and maximum size limits, some of the more than 100 strictures governing land use, building height, setbacks, fences, outbuildings, street furniture, and the like. The château was adapted for use as a communal center with a library, recreational halls, a restaurant, offices, stores, and, in later years, a theater. Construction was largely complete by the 1930s and both Walter's plan and the housing association remain.

In 1910, landscape architect Édouard Redont (1862–1942) planned the garden suburb of **Petit-Groslay** on a 123.5-acre site northeast of Paris along the Paris-Soissons railroad line.[159] Redont's formal layout of tree-lined boulevards extending from a central oval park toward peripheral *rond-points* was to be the setting of detached and semidetached villas with individual gardens. Redont took advantage of a stream to create a pond, placing athletic fields in the northeast. Before substantial work could begin, however, the project was taken over by a railroad company headquartered nearby. As built, Petit-Groslay closely reflected Redont's street plan, but the workers' houses were built at a much higher density than originally intended. Rail yards have since truncated the district.

Unable to rely on the private sector to address the housing shortage, in 1912 the French government initiated a program to buy land around Paris for the construction of more than a dozen cités-jardins, garden city-inspired districts ranging from small ruralesque enclaves to quasi-urban neighborhoods, seven of which

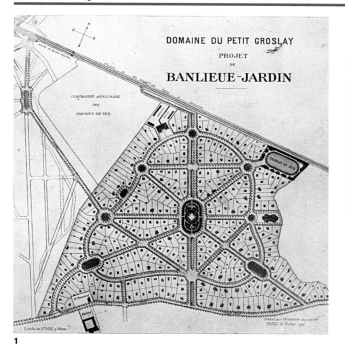

1. Plan, Édouard Redont, 1911. GBL

2. Typical houses. SSDB

Offices publics des habitations à Bon Marché

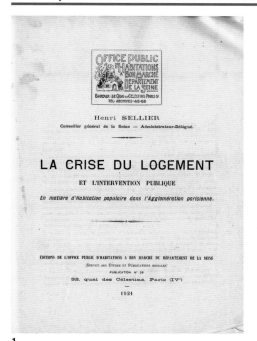

1   2   3

each contained over 1,000 dwellings.[160] By the 1930s, the French program had brought to fruit 17,000 units of housing. To administer development on a national basis, regional **Offices publics des habitations à Bon Marché** (Offices for Public Low Cost Housing) were formed. Development in the Department of the Seine, which included the area around Paris but not the city itself, was overseen by the Conseil Général de la Seine. Land purchases began in 1916, and by the time construction commenced in 1921, having waited for costs to fall from their wartime highs, the council had accumulated 600 acres within a six-mile radius of central Paris.

Henri Sellier (1883–1943), a Social Democrat and member of the International Garden Cities and Town Planning Association, was the council's first manager and the driving force behind the effort to build, as he put it,

groups of houses fitted to relieve the congestion of the City of Paris and its suburbs, to serve as an example to the owners of building sites who have during the past thirty years literally exploited the area and to show how, while keeping in sight the normal economic and moral conditions of urban life, it is possible to supply the working population, manual and intellectual, with dwellings presenting the maximum of material comfort, hygienic conditions of a kind to eliminate the inconveniences of the great towns, and methods

1. *La crise du logement*, title page. LCDL (1921)

2. Study models for garden suburb development, André-Louis Arfvidson, Joseph Bassompierre, and Paul de Rutté, 1921. LCDL

3. Locator map showing Parisian cités-jardins. LCDL (1921)

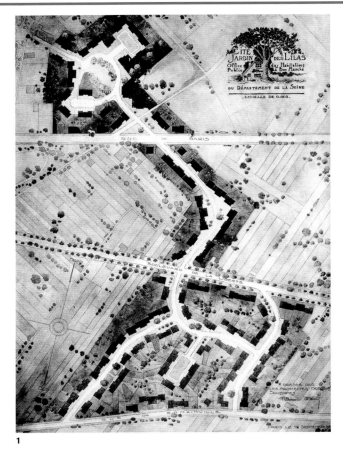

1

2

3

of aesthetic lay-out contrasting markedly with the hideousness of the systems hitherto in force.[161]

Although a Garden City devotee, Sellier had a clear enough understanding of Howard's vision to state that "the objective is not the real garden city but new districts planned in order to fight high population density."[162] As G. Montagu Harris reported in 1919, when the planning effort was under way, Sellier "quotes constantly and at length from Mr. Raymond Unwin's book on Town-Planning in Practice and expresses the intention of the Office to be guided by Mr. Unwin's advice."[163] The first Parisian cités-jardins, including Les Lilas, Drancy, Dugny, Arcueil, Nanterre, and Gennevilliers, were designed under Sellier's guidance by an assortment of architects whose accurate adaptations of Unwin's ideas revealed both a close reading of *Town Planning in Practice* and a careful study of existing models such as Letchworth and Hampstead Garden Suburb. Each of the cités-jardins incorporated varied street pictures, closed visual axes, street hierarchies, the special treatment of intersections, and vernacular-inspired detached, semidetached, and rowhouses stepped back and forth from the street and grouped to enclose quadrangles and courtyards.

Cité-Jardin Joseph-Dépinay aux Lilas, typically called **Les Lilas** (1921–23), three-and-a-half miles east of Paris, occupied an irregularly shaped 15-acre site divided into northern and southern sections by two existing thoroughfares.[164] Architects Paul Pelletier (1884–1958)

and Arthur-Pierre Teisseire (1885–1943) planned the village and designed its 197 buildings accommodating 212 residences, most of which took the form of detached and semidetached single-family houses in addition to a few short rows. A second phase (1930–31) added 100 units in three-story apartment buildings. The enclave was solely residential, drawing on nearby public amenities. The naturalistic plan, with a curving road linking the two sections, included a landscaped park in the center of the hillier, more forested northern neighborhood. Front gardens were for the most part eliminated to provide continuous green strips along the street, while each house had its own rear yard with formal landscaped areas and vegetable gardens. Intended to last for only fifteen years, the houses were not demolished until the early 1970s. The apartment buildings remain and were rehabilitated in 1980.

Cité-Jardin de Drancy (1921–31), occupying 13 acres seven miles northeast of the city, was designed by Joseph Bassompierre-Sewrin (1871–1950) and Paul de Rutté (1871–1943) to house railroad workers in 214 units built in three phases, the first two of which were aesthetically similar and completed in 1922.[165] Lying to the north and south of Rue de la République, the houses were placed in rows of up to six units that angled and bent to frame parks and street-facing courtyards and to allow for the retention of existing trees. The use of only three standardized house types that employed brick, stucco, tile roofs, and concrete lintels was disguised by variations in fenestration and orientation. Front yards were about

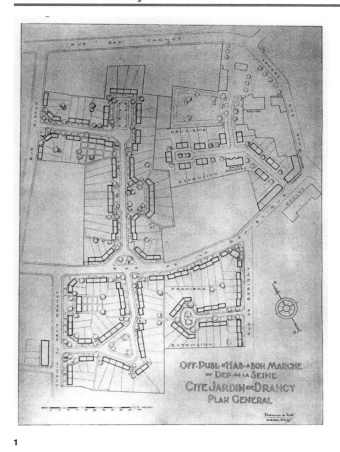

1

2

3

4

1. Plan, Joseph Bassompierre and Paul de Rutté, 1921. SSDO

2. Bird's-eye view of northern section. HBM

3. Typical street. SSDI (c. 1922)

4. Cité Paul Bert. CVD (c. 2010)

15 feet deep and treated as continuous strips while individual gardens were allotted in the rear. In the 1929–30 expansion known as Cité Paul Bert, the same architects, working in partnership with Paul Sirvin (1891–1977), abandoned the village-y architecture for flat-roofed, two-story semidetached houses with roof terraces placed along an elbow-shaped cul-de-sac entered through an arched gateway. A bathhouse was provided in the new section but a planned school, church, park, and town hall were never realized. The village was partially demolished in 1986. A number of brick-and-stucco houses remain intact but the open spaces have been either given over to car parking or left unmaintained. The Cité Paul Bert is in better condition.

Bassompierre, de Rutté, and Sirvin also laid out **Cité-Jardin de Dugny** in the northeastern suburbs, placing 200 houses on a roughly square, 22-acre site and installing thirty-eight apartments into a former school.[166] The plan discouraged through traffic by bringing three entrance roads together in a small central square. Narrow lanes branched off to most of the houses, reflecting Henri Sellier's belief that minimal space should be given over to streets, which were expensive to maintain. The many private and shared green spaces included a pond, individual rear gardens delineated by hedges and fences, and a thickly wooded park situated at the center of a large block but accessible to all via pedestrian paths. The mix of detached, semidetached, and rowhouses were alternately set flush to the street, stepped back incrementally on common greens,

or grouped around quiet closes and crescents. A second phase carried out in 1932–33 by architects Eugène Gonnot (1879–1944) and Georges Albenque (1877–1963) added apartments around the western entry. The district was destroyed by bombing during World War II.

On the southern outskirts of Paris, **Cité-Jardin d'Arcueil-Cachan Aqueduc** (1923), named for a high aqueduct along the edge of the 24-acre site, was designed by Maurice Payret-Dortail (1874–1929) to contain 230 houses in addition to a school, cooperative grocery store, community hall with movie theater, and recreational fields created by filling in a quarry that divided the site into eastern and western halves.[167] The high ground on the east was laid out with narrow culs-de-sac and closes branching off of a single 26-foot-wide spine that shifted its axis at a central square. The lower section on the west featured curving streets responding to the hilly topography, with houses oriented to maximize sunlight exposure for individual gardens separated from one another by latticework and from the street by whitewashed concrete fences. Only 43 of the original 228 houses survived demolition during the 1980s, but the street plan is still discernable.

In his plan for **Cité-Jardin de Nanterre** (1923), located seven miles west of Paris, André Berry (1869–1960) placed ninety-two detached, semidetached, and rowhouses along a crooked orthogonal spine that opened up to tree-dotted greens.[168] Thirty-eight additional units were provided in two apartment buildings flanking the southern entrance. The neighborhood was largely

Cité-Jardin de Dugny

1. Plan, Bassompierre, de Rutté, and Sirvin. HBM (1921)

2. Bird's-eye view. HBM (1921)

3. Elevation, Rue de la Pièce d'Eau. HBM (1921)

4. Typical street. CRS (c. 1922)

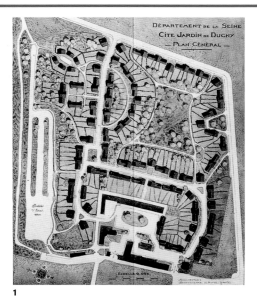

Cité-Jardin d'Arcueil-Cachan Aqueduc

1. Plan, Maurice Payret-Dortail, 1920. LCDL

2. Impasse Arago and Impasse Jacquart. ADVM

3. Former cooperative grocery store showing aqueduct in background. RAMSA (2012)

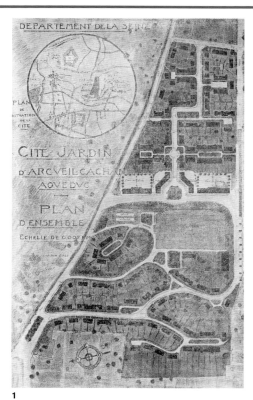

demolished in the 1950s. **Cité-Jardin de Gennevilliers** (1923–24), occupying 20 acres northwest of the city, was designed by Jean Hébrard (1878–1960) and Félix Dumail (1883–1955) to feature a crescent-shaped street inscribed within a long rectangular block.[169] The 250 semidetached houses and rowhouses constituted an almost textbook application of Unwinesque groupings. With the exception of a triangular park at the south end of the crescent, the green spaces have been taken over for automobile parking. Dumail designed an extension, built between 1930 and 1934, adding 100 apartments in five-story balconied buildings.

While many of the Parisian cités-jardins were modified by the addition of apartment buildings in the early 1930s, Stains and Suresnes, carried out on much larger sites and offering a wider range of amenities, innovatively combined single-family houses and mid-rise apartment blocks from the earliest stages of planning. **Cité-Jardin de Stains** (1921–33), accommodating 7,000 low-wage workers and their families on a flat, 67-acre site in Paris's industrial northeastern suburbs, included 472 single-family houses and 1,176 apartments in four- and five-story blocks.[170] The site was adjacent to the village of Stains, occupying the grounds of a château that had been destroyed in 1870. Architects Eugène Gonnot and Georges Albenque incorporated two roads leading south from the old village into their plan of broad avenues which, embellished by trees and planted medians, radiated from a central square to be crossed midway by a three-quarter-circle loop road that broke the site up into large blocks. The square provided an open plaza, bathhouse, and community center while schools, shops, a medical center, nursery, and men's and women's dormitories were located nearby.

The village's two distinct sections were characterized not by major differences in the site plan but by building type. In the west, Gonnot and Albenque called for two-story vernacular-style brick-and-pebbledash rowhouses of varying length to be angled around intersections and grouped in quintessentially Unwinesque fashion around closes and greens on the block interior. In the east, exposed concrete-frame-with-white-brick-infill apartment buildings stepped back and forth from the avenues on street-facing greens, making room on the block interiors for allotment gardens and narrow lanes lined by rowhouses. Aside from the town square that was reconfigured in the 1930s to replace the bathhouse and community center with a combination theater/apartment building, the district's original plan survives.

Cité-Jardin de Suresnes (1921–39), planned by Alexandre Maistrasse (1860–1951), was the most urban of the Parisian garden villages, built on a 59-acre site six miles west of Paris at the southwest corner of Suresnes, to which its street system was connected.[171] The plan was initially English in character, calling for the partial use of gabled terraces, particularly in the south where they would help transition from a high-density core of apartment buildings to lines of semidetached cottages on individual gardens that opened up to the expansive

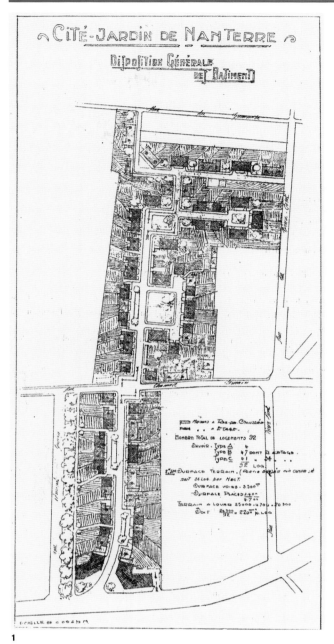

1. Plan, André Berry, 1921. LCDL

2. Typical street. CRS (c. 1935)

Cité-Jardin de Gennevilliers

1. Plan, Jean Hébrard and Félix Dumail, 1921. SIAF

2. Aerial view. Comellec. VDG (2011)

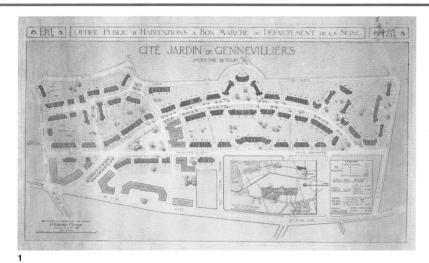

1

2

Cité-Jardin de Stains

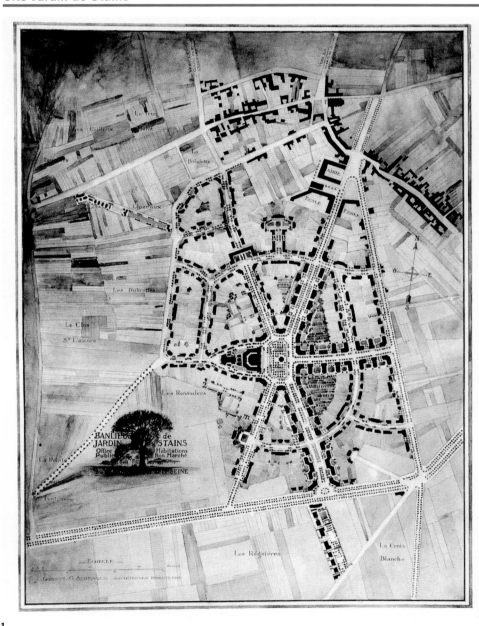

1

2

3

4

1. Plan, Eugène Gonnot and Georges Albenque, 1921. HBM

2. Avenue Solon. CRS (c. 1925)

3. Avenue Paty. CRS (c. 1925–30)

4. Rue Lebrun. RAMSA (2012)

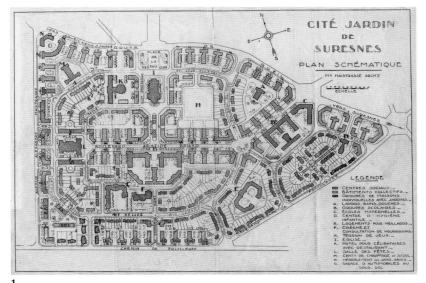

greenery of Saint-Cloud racetrack. As constructed, most of the planned cottages gave way to apartment buildings that conveyed a sense of Parisian urbanism, although the courtyards typical of those in the capital were here much more generously proportioned, allowing for communal gardens.

The plan followed Unwinesque principles of street pictures, with carefully planned corners at intersections and streets terminated by important buildings. A school and church closed either end of an axis crossing the central boulevard, which itself led from a *rond-point* to a theater square ringed by shops, although most commercial shopping remained outside the principal entrance to the cité. Departing from the English model, its accommodation of 8,000 to 10,000 people in 2,500 dwelling units, representing a density of about 42 units per acre, far exceeded the 12 units per acre prescribed by Unwin. Both the size of the mostly five-story apartment houses and their style of design, perhaps best described as Art Deco classicism, were also far from Parker and Unwin's tastes. Many community facilities called for in the original plan were successfully realized—some located on the block interiors—however most of the small cottages planned for the southern edge were scrapped in favor of the T-shaped apartment buildings typical in the rest of the cité.

Suresnes, marking a significant departure from English precedent in its increased population density

and decreased emphasis on ruralesque environmentalism, had a significant impact on American practice in the 1920s and 1930s, helping housing reform–minded architects, especially in New York City, to combine the quadrangular block with the communal green courtyard in response to requirements for high-density accommodation. For example, although Springsteen & Goldhammer's Grand Street Houses (1930) were detailed in the manner of Dutch Amsterdam School work, the organization of the complex closely resembled typical blocks at Suresnes.[172]

The 1930s witnessed the construction of the largest Parisian cités-jardins but also the loss of the garden suburb as a model. As Gaudin has written, the two largest cités-jardins, La Butte Rouge, in Châtenay-Malabry, and Le Plessis-Robinson, "dramatically diluted the Unwin-style informality in the Arts and Crafts tradition with more formalist designs that derived from the Beaux Arts approach, while also incorporating elements of Modernism."[173] The two adjacent districts occupied a varied site of plateaus, valleys, and hillsides surrounded by forests seven miles southwest of Paris. The area had been the subject of a 1919 competition intended to generate ideas for an independent garden city.[174] Chosen from sixty submissions, the winning entry, by Paul de Rutté, Paul Sirvin, Maurice Payret-Dortail, and Joseph Bassompierre-Sewrin, proposed to accommodate 100,000 residents in 22,000 houses spread across 3,700 acres at

1. Plan, Alexandre Maistrasse. MUS (1933)

2. Typical street. RAMSA (2007)

3. Detached house with roof terrace and gardens. MUS (1921–23)

4. Place Stalingrad. RAMSA (2007)

5. Boulevard Aristide Briand, looking toward Théâtre de Suresnes. RAMSA (2007)

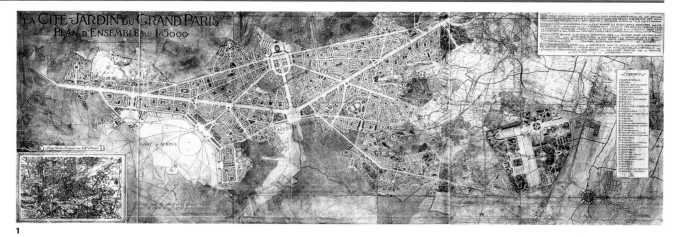

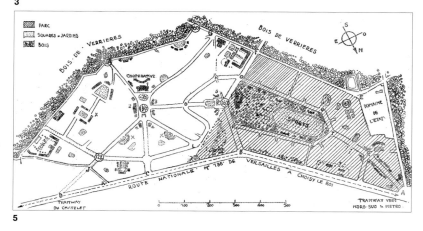

a density of about fourteen houses per acre. The scheme placed Unwinesque residential neighborhoods within a Hausmannian plan that brought three monumental boulevards together in a *centre social* adjacent to a railroad station. Ambitious in scope but never intended to be built—entrants were asked to ignore municipal boundaries—the scheme also included an airport, a university, an industrial zone, cemeteries, and parks. As a result of their winning entry, however, Bassompiere, de Rutté, and Sirvin were asked to design **Châtenay-Malabry** in collaboration with André-Louis Arfvidson (1870–1935), while Payret-Dortail was hired to design Le Plessis-Robinson.

In each of these projects, planned beginning in the early 1920s but not developed in earnest until 1931, the architects first prepared schematic designs identifying the location of parks, squares, public buildings, and major streets. As originally envisioned, Malabry ("Châtenay" was added to the name later), covering 182 acres, was to include two-, four-, and six-unit rowhouses in a plan that combined radial boulevards emanating from a central square on half of the site and a central park surrounded by Unwin-inspired quadrangles on the other half.[175] The architects also allowed a hilly area in the south to help shape a series of curving streets. By the time new legislation jump-started the development in 1928, revisions had already begun that would eliminate virtually all of the plan's irregularities, replacing the small houses first with longer rows and finally with apartment buildings that by World War II held 1,573 units, with 2,000 more added between 1949 and 1965. Despite the changes in building type, aspects of the original street plan survived, reflecting the efforts of collaborating landscape architect André Riousse

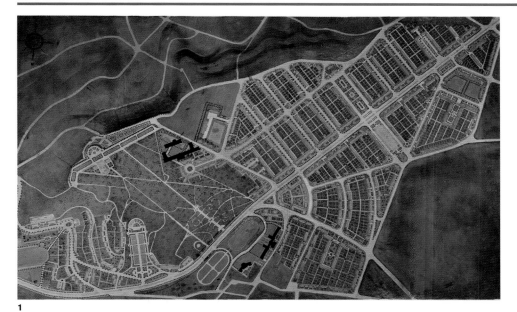

1. Plan, Maurice Payret-Dortail. AMPR (1933)

2. Cité des Lunettes. AMPR (c. 1930)

3. View from gardens off of Rue Fernande Fourcade. RAMSA (2008)

1

2

3

(1895–1952), whose work was critical to the preservation of the site's topographical attributes.

Le Plessis-Robinson's site included the former grounds of a château that Payret-Dortail retained as a 52-acre park that separated the plan into two sections. The larger piece, a 182-acre plateau in the southwest, was given over to four- and five-story apartment buildings arranged along a main spine crossed by perpendicular side streets, while a rugged 22-acre site in the northeast, nestled into the edge of the park, was built out according to a naturalistic street plan in 1925 to become Cité des Lunettes, an enclave of 217 two-story flat-roofed single-family houses, each with its own garden, in rows of varying length, as well as athletic fields and park space.[176] The Cité des Lunettes benefitted from the relative proximity—just over half a mile—of a station on the Sceaux Line, which provided easy access to the Latin Quarter and attracted a population of working-class artists, artisans, and intellectuals. However a planned extension of the railroad to the plateau site was never completed—the railroad company argued that the population was too small (ironically, a function of poor transportation)—and by 1939 many of the units remained vacant. To compensate, a special bus route was established from the Porte d'Orléans and taxis were instructed to offer reduced fares. Residency picked up after the war and Le Plessis-Robinson eventually provided 1,200 dwellings for a population of 5,000.

Provincial Garden Suburbs

Garden villages also found sponsors in provincial French cities. **Chemin Vert** (1920–24), on the southeastern outskirts of Reims, was a project of the Foyer Rémois, a philanthropic society founded by Georges Charbonneaux and fellow Reims industrialists in 1912 to improve the city's stock of workers' housing.[177] Inspired by England's model industrial villages, which Charbonneaux had visited with members of the Reims city council, the Foyer Rémois undertook two small residential projects before the war halted its plans for three more substantial villages. Resuming its efforts within a year of the armistice, with Reims still in ruins, the Foyer expanded its scope with Chemin Vert, calling for 617 houses and public buildings on a flat, 111-acre farmland site separated from the city center, about a half-hour's walk away, by an industrial zone but otherwise surrounded by open fields. To avoid further congestion at

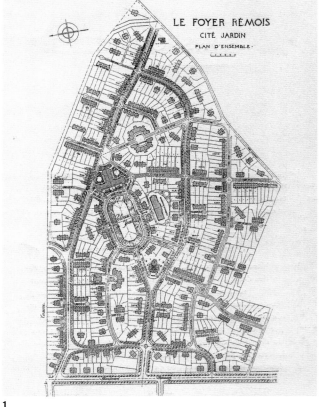

1

2

3

4

5

the city's main train station, which was already struggling to handle materials needed for reconstruction, the Foyer Rémois built its own rail line to transport building supplies from the town of Bazancourt, about 12.5 miles away. Upon the village's completion, the railroad was adapted for local use.

As planned by Jean-Marcel Auburtin (1872–1926), Chemin Vert was centered around a large, racetrack-shaped civic plaza anchored on the east end by a community hall containing a town hall, library, meeting rooms and classrooms, a 500-seat auditorium for concerts, movies, and theatrical productions, and bathhouse facilities. Semidetached houses ringed the remainder of the plaza with public amenities such as two blocks of shops, a church, and an *école menagère* with a nursery, kindergarten, and health clinic, located just beyond. The Foyer Rémois's goal of increasing the birthrate and providing a healthy environment for children seemed to pay off. By 1926, the population of 3,700

included 2,200 children. Ironically, primary schools were not included in the village.

Auburtin designed fourteen dwelling types, including two- and four-family semidetached houses and four-, six-, and ten-unit rows, scattering the different types evenly throughout the village. The houses were covered in roughcast and provided with individual 3,200-square-foot gardens that were intended to offer the men a constructive pastime. The plan combined continuous, but not straight, tree-lined main streets, with short, curving, and crooked secondary streets. There was no apparent pattern in the siting of the residential buildings. Houses were set back at varying depths, sometimes placed at 45-degree angles on important intersections, and rowhouses were aligned both parallel and perpendicular to the street.

Writing in 1934, Pierre Vago (1910–2002), the editor of France's Modernist-leaning periodical *L'Architecture d'Aujourd'hui*, voiced dissatisfaction with Chemin Vert's regionalist architecture, finding that despite a

1. "Legende," plan by Karl Bonatz, Georg Martin, and Karl Wolf, 1909. DS11

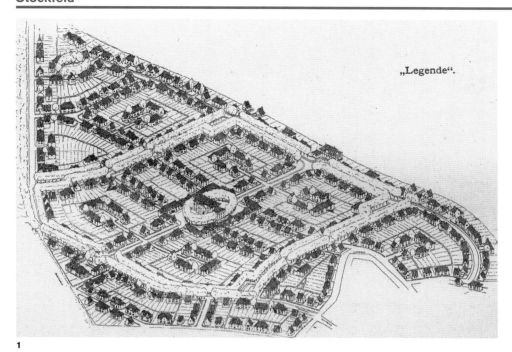

„Legende".

1

"well-thought out" and "well-envisioned" plan, the village was "artificial" in character: "Here, one senses the architect who, with his diploma and in a large office in Paris, outlines plans for a city that he would like to create in the image of so many beloved corners of his country that are dear to his heart . . . One feels it is too much or not enough. The houses are very simple, but not quite simple enough. In spite of everything, one feels the constant sensation of searching." Noting the rather jumbled plan, Vago would have "preferred more straightforwardness in the parti." Yet, he continued: "What we must remember in all this is the clarity, focus, and, we might almost say, the feeling of health that emerges. From this point of view, and it is essential, the subdivision of Chemin Vert can serve as a lesson and model."[178] Much of the development survives, as does the Foyer Rémois, and has been renovated in recent years.

Two notable garden villages were built in the Alsatian capital of Strasbourg. The first, **Stockfeld**, was initiated in 1909 during the period of German rule that lasted from 1870 until 1918. The second, Les Jardins Ungemach, was built in the early 1920s with profits made during World War I. Developed by the Gemeinnützige Baugenossenschaft, a cooperative housing society made up of politicians and local businessmen, Stockfeld, occupying a 59-acre farmland site bordered on the east and west by forests, in the Neuhof district about four miles south of the city, was among the early continental garden villages to be specifically modeled on English examples, conceived just three years after Hellerau (see p. 290).[179] The project supplied housing for 455 low-income families who had been displaced in 1907 by the *Grande Percée*, a controversial slum clearance program in which 135 apartment buildings were demolished in the congested city center—the current path of Rue du 22 Novembre—to introduce light and air.

Stockfeld's town plan was determined by a 1909 competition open only to Alsace-based architects, twenty-four of whom submitted entries. Architects were asked to incorporate identifiable garden village elements, including hierarchically arranged streets and open spaces as well as multiple housing types, stores, restaurants, a community center, and a route designated for a tram line. The two submissions that were most favored by the housing cooperative—though not popular with the jury—addressed regionalist concerns about the impact of industrialization on the countryside by evoking the feel of traditional Alsatian villages. The plan by Karl Bonatz (1882–1951), Georg Martin (n.d.), and Karl Wolf (n.d.), entitled "*Legende*," placed alternating detached and semidetached houses around the perimeter of large square blocks and in courtyard-enclosing groups on the block interior. The same team submitted another design, "*Drei*," the most geometrically ordered entry, in which three parallel axes were punctuated by squares and public buildings and lined by houses around greens in direct emulation of those at Hampstead.

The winning scheme, proposed by Strasbourg architect Edouard Schimpf (1877–1916), was entitled "Howard" in tribute to Ebenezer Howard. It featured a rationally organized center giving way to informal elements on the periphery. Schimpf made room for the tram by widening an existing road along the eastern edge of the site to become a 60-foot-wide landscaped boulevard bordered on one side by rowhouses. The town's principal axis originated in the east, where it framed views of an existing house at the edge of the forest, and extended west into the center of the village to arrive at a paved plaza framed on three sides by a school building, post office, and shops. Secondary streets crossed the axis at right angles but then curved or angled to intersect in Sitte-esque squares. Schimpf

2. "Drei," plan by Karl Bonatz, Georg Martin, and Karl Wolf, 1909. DS11

3. "Howard," plan by Edouard Schimpf, 1909. DS11

4. Perspective of design by Edouard Schimpf, c. 1910. BNUS (1910)

5. Typical street. ADS (c. 1910)

6. Typical house. Zvardon. RA (2004)

7. Aerial view of Rue de Grives. Zvardon. RA (2009)

8. Aerial view. Zvardon. RA (2009)

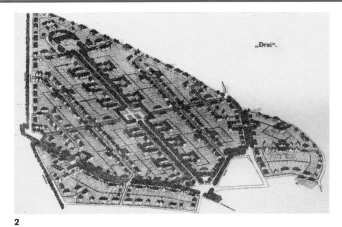

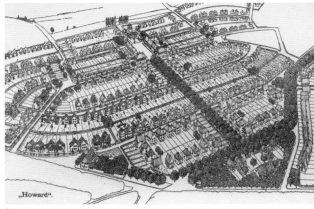

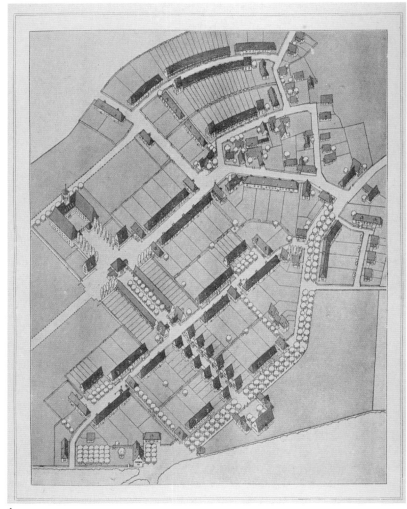

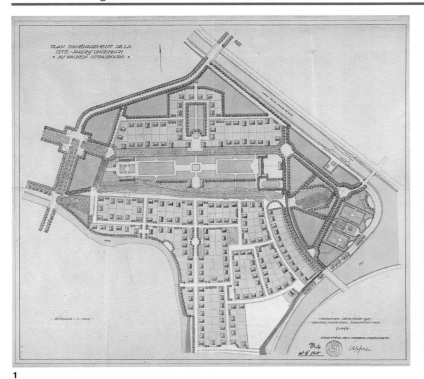

1. Plan, Paul de Rutté and Jean Sorg, 1923. ADS

2. Aerial view. Zvardon. RA (c. 2009)

3. Typical street. Zvardon. RA (2010)

4. Place des Acacias. JV (1931)

1

3

4

threaded a network of six-foot-wide pedestrian paths throughout the village, originating in small parks and leading through the block interiors. Although the program called for only one type of three-room house, Schimpf proposed various types of detached, semidetached, quadruple, and rowhouses, mostly set back on shallow decorative front gardens and provided with deep rear gardens for cultivating vegetables.

As construction got under way, Schimpf adjusted the plan to introduce more rowhouses and apartment buildings, including long two- and three-story crescents lining Rue de Grives. Progress proceeded apace, with 363 houses completed between July and December 1910. In 1911 Schimpf resigned and a local architect, Ernst Zimmerlé (n.d.), took over, keeping the bones of the original plan but notably breaking apart the village center so that the stores, school, and public buildings were no longer placed around the central plaza. In all, more than 400 units of housing were built on roughly 29 acres. The architecture was based on the Alsatian vernacular, combining steep-pitched flared gable roofs with half-timbering; yellow, pink, red, and green stucco walls; awnings; shutters; dormers; and turrets. The population grew slowly at first but the completion of the tram in 1912

gave the village a boost, and by 1913 Stockfeld counted 2,200 residents. The village remains largely intact.

Les Jardins Ungemach (1923), by all appearances a well-planned if fairly typical garden village, was dubiously conceived and promoted as "the World's First Eugenic Garden City," the vision of Alfred Dachert, who recounted in a 1931 issue of *The Eugenics Review* his desire to "make the city a means for perfecting the human race."[180] Dachert's "eugenic experiment," seemingly quite different from the ones soon to be carried out under the Third Reich, was intended to help reverse the declining French birthrate by providing, as a commemorative plaque would later state, for "healthy young married couples wishing to start families and raise children under sound conditions of hygiene and morality."[181] As such, his motives were not unlike those of the Foyer Rémois, which built Chemin Vert in Reims, and other contemporary French efforts intended to rebuild the population after the devastating losses in World War I.

The village was named for Leon Ungemach (1844–1928), a candy manufacturer-turned-politician whose foreign investments during the war earned him a fortune that, after the armistice, was deemed to have been gained through profiteering. As an alternative to confiscation,

Dachert, who was an upper-level manager working for Ungemach, successfully lobbied to have the money put toward affordable housing for large families. A foundation was created to administer the project, and in 1920 the city of Strasbourg, with Ungemach as mayor, donated a 30-acre site on the northern outskirts, stipulating that the land and houses be turned over to the city after thirty years.

For Dachert, the project melded his two long-held passions: eugenics and the Garden City, the latter of which he became familiar with through business trips to "all the garden cities which had been built in England and France,"[182] resulting in the impression that "England's Garden Cities became residences for old maids, for pensioners past the age of reproduction. The eugenical element was lacking in their otherwise marvelous planning."[183] Dachert observed the same phenomena in Stockfeld, determining that the garden village "did not assist, as it should, the progress of the human species," and that the residents "had been chosen by the purest chance."[184]

The Ungemach foundation held a design competition in 1921, selecting the Paris-based architect Paul de Rutté, of the firm of Bassompiere, de Rutté, and Sirvin, to work with the fourth-place entrant, Strasbourg architect Jean Sorg (n.d.). Their plan called for 155 single-family detached houses designed to recall a small Alsatian town as it would have appeared in 1830. The architects prepared twenty-seven house variations, all built of brick and covered in cream and pink stucco with tile roofs. Each house sat on an individual garden delineated by hedges. Although the streets were of uniform width, curves and crooks gave way to varied views, and small parks and courts, some incorporating existing trees, were dispersed throughout. Pinwheel-shaped intersections came directly from Unwin and several house types were specially designed to close street vistas.

Designed to ease the work of busy housewives who could not afford a servant, running water was provided in every bedroom and the houses were limited to one story (with cellar and attic) to eliminate trips up and down the stairs. To foster a child-friendly environment, an *école maternelle* and playground were within easy and safe walking distance. The overall density was about twenty-four people per acre. Two large parks bordered the village on the east and the north. A plan to extend the neighborhood beyond the northern park was not realized.

With rents 25 percent below those in the Strasbourg slums, the 140 houses of Les Jardins Ungemach met with an overwhelming demand that allowed Dachert to select residents according to his eugenic method, which focused on youth, fitness, and a desire to have at least four children—and two within five years. Envisioning the houses as "hospitals," Dachert expected that families would outgrow the houses and make room for new couples, while on the same token, nine couples who failed to procreate were asked to leave during the project's first seven years. In 1950, Strasbourg took ownership of the village according to the initial agreement. The park that buffered the neighborhood on the north was used as an exhibition area and eventually given over to buildings, while the park on the east became home to the futuristic headquarters of the European Parliament (1990), adding an otherworldly backdrop to the well-maintained garden village.

The Modernist Swiss architect-urbanist Charles-Édouard Jeanneret-Gris (after 1920, resident in France, where he adopted the name Le Corbusier), was influenced early on by the garden city, contributing two notable plans for developments intended for relatively remote French localities. In 1917, three years after he proposed Cité-Jardin aux Crétets (see p. 571) for his hometown of La Chaux-de-Fonds, Switzerland, Jeanneret was asked to design a garden enclave for workers of Duverdrey and Bloquel, clockmakers, in the small town of **Saint-Nicolas-d'Aliermont,** near Dieppe, Normandy.[185] In place of the curving streets he had proposed in Switzerland, Jeanneret, guided by the 7.5-acre site's elongated trapezoidal shape, positioned forty-three houses on either side of a single 18-foot-wide spine, "almost like a miniature Champs-Elysées," as H. Allan Brooks described it, lined by sidewalks, planting strips, and trees.[186] At one end of the axis, Jeanneret placed an indented entrance court featuring a small reflecting pool and several shops. At the other end, where he closed the street vista with the long facade of a semidetached house, Jeanneret provided a courtyard-like playground, from the corner of which a narrow service road continued to the far side of the site.

In early studies, Jeanneret envisioned terraces up to eight houses long and shorter rows linked together by garden walls. In the final plan, he broke the masses down, calling for five detached houses for foremen, fourteen semidetached houses, two three-unit rowhouses, and one four-unit rowhouse. With a few exceptions, the houses ran parallel to the site's boundaries. In order to maximize sunlight exposure for the individual gardens, Jeanneret pulled the houses to the edges of their sites, with those on the north side of the street set back on deep front yards and those to the south placed closer to the street to open up rear yards.

Despite Jeanneret's commitment to standardized and industrial building processes, the client would not indulge his recommendation of a Swiss system of hollow concrete blocks that, fabricated on-site, would have required the purchase of two machines requiring five skilled operators. The client called for brick instead. In addition, Jeanneret was asked to work in the architectural style of the region, leading to his studied designs for one-and-a-half story gabled and dormered cottages with deep-set windows and brick stringcourses and dentils that gave, according to Brooks, "both unity and dignity" to the "small yet well-proportioned designs."[187] Only one semidetached house was built in 1917 before rising costs led to the project's abandonment.[188]

Few of the compromises that Jeanneret had to make at Saint-Nicolas-d'Aliermont were at play in his next significant workers' village, the Quartiers Modernes Frugès (1925–27), in **Pessac**, Bordeaux, where his client, sugar

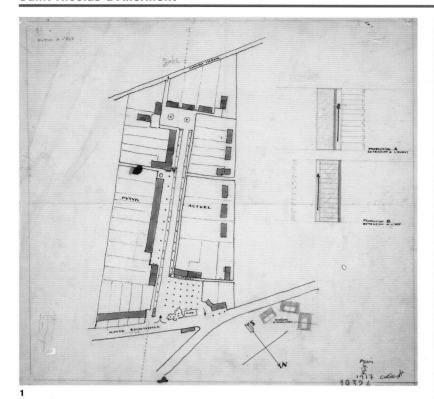

1

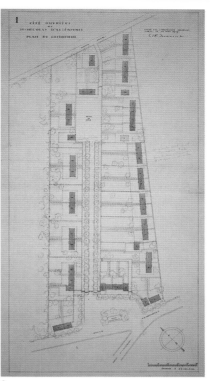

2

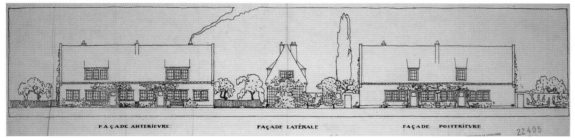

3

4

1. Early plan, Charles-Édouard Jeanneret-Gris (Le Corbusier), 1917. FLC

2. Plan, 1917. FLC

3. House elevations. FLC

4. Semidetached house. FLC

manufacturer Henri Frugès, having encountered his ideas in a French journal, wrote to the architect, now renamed Le Corbusier: "I authorize you to realize your theories in practice, even in their most extreme consequences . . . Pessac will be a laboratory."[189] Although the project may be best known for its polarizing effect on those who labeled it a success or failure based largely on their reaction to alterations that residents made to the houses over time, Pessac has been less closely scrutinized for its site planning, which lies somewhere between garden city humanism and machine age placelessness.

As a kind of testing ground for Pessac, Frugès asked Le Corbusier to design a small workers' enclave to support a new sawmill in **Lège** (1923).[190] Working with his engineer cousin, Pierre Jeanneret (1896–1967), the architect placed six detached single-family houses and a twenty-three-bed dormitory around the edges of a triangular site to embrace a courtyard planted with plane trees and featuring a wall for the racquetball-like sport of *pelote basque*. The project, in which prototypical houses were treated as freestanding sculptural objects placed at unorthodox angles to the street, highlighted serious shortcomings in the construction process, in which cement was sprayed onto wooden formwork.

At Pessac, Le Corbusier was faced with a much larger, irregularly shaped site—a meadow bordered by pine trees and the diagonal path of a railroad line—that was intended to accommodate 130 houses, only fifty-one of which were completed before financial problems, construction setbacks, and community hostility killed the plan in 1930. The built portion was to have been approached by a tree-lined axis recalling that at Saint Nicolas-d'Aliermont but at a greater scale, extending from a monumental entrance court framed by six-story apartment blocks, through two sections of housing to reach a village square dotted with trees, bound by shops, a café, and apartments, and including a *pelote basque* court.

As built, the Quartiers Modernes Frugès consisted of three blocks, the largest of which, a broad trapezoid, included a single-family house type in different configurations, most notably in so-called "staggered" five- and six-unit rowhouses with second-story terraces placed alternately in the front and rear to create a solid-void pattern in both plan and elevation. Each house had an individual garden. Le Corbusier also set two detached houses on the block interior to define street-facing gardens, as well as a pair of Z-shaped houses formed by

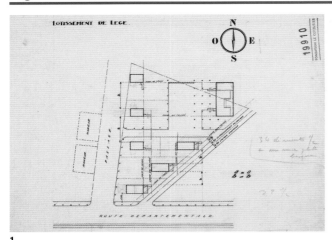

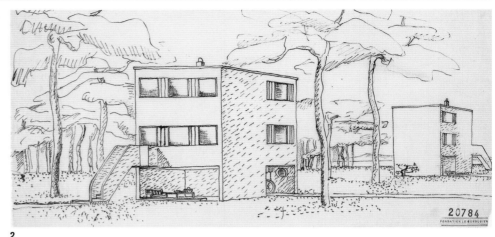

1. Plan, Le Corbusier, 1924. FLC

2. Sketch, Le Corbusier, 1924. FLC

3. Overall view. FLC (c. 1923)

4. Renovated houses with new surfacing material. Blanc. FL (2012)

three of the standardized units. Across the street, which was to be lined on one side with poplar trees spaced every five meters, the same module that guided the architecture, Le Corbusier placed three-story *grattes ciels*, or "skyscrapers," back-to-back houses with two floors and a roof terrace elevated on pilotis to allow for a partially enclosed ground floor. By placing the semidetached houses perpendicular to the street, Le Corbusier required residents of the rear units to enter their houses by crossing the gardens of the front units, blurring the distinction between public and private space. The absence of a well-defined street wall and the openness of the ground floors also served to break down the traditional division of street, house, and garden. The third block, a secluded rectangular parcel lying along a dead-end street, featured a line of seven two-story houses linked by full-height, shallow-barrel-vaulted concrete roofs that the British garden suburb historian Mervyn Miller suggests were inspired by Parker and Unwin's Hampstead houses in Reynolds Close and Heath Close.[191] As noted in the Fondation Le Corbusier's guide to the Quartiers, the site plan, "through its complexity, diversity, quality of urban spaces and introduction of hierarchy . . . fits neatly into the conceptual tradition of garden cities, a link that is accentuated by the treatment accorded in the scheme to exterior spaces, pavements, greenery and enclosure of separate plots. Nonetheless . . . discontinuities, elimination of certain front-back hierarchies and design concepts such as the 'skyscrapers' and 'staggered'

constructions, as well as the free-standing dwellings . . . conceived as individual sculptured objects hinted toward Le Corbusier's emerging planning mode."[192]

As work commenced at Pessac, lessons learned from the failure of the Lège housing resulted in changes to the design, drastically increasing construction costs. The project also suffered from the failure to secure proper planning permits, which kept the city from building road and water connections, leaving the houses empty for years. When the first buildings took form, the architecture was derisively compared to Frugès sugar cubes and to the houses of North African villages. Once they began to move in, residents quickly altered the dwellings, adding gabled tile roofs, enclosing ground floors and roof terraces, and eliminating strip windows in favor of traditionally proportioned, shuttered windows. While many of the changes occurred as residents repaired leaking roofs and rusted windows, others seemed to reflect the new owners' rejection of Le Corbusier's aesthetic vision. Critics of the project, egged on by Le Corbusier's early proclamation that inhabitants should "adapt their mentalities" to the houses, quickly latched on to the modifications as an illustration of Modernism's failure to adequately address psychological needs, something even Le Corbusier had to eventually acknowledge, remarking: "It is always life that is right, the architect who is wrong."[193]

Henry-Russell Hitchcock, writing in 1929, was among the first to note that Pessac was "a serious disappointment to all who had taken Le Corbusier seriously

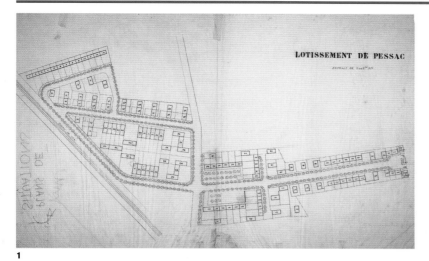

1

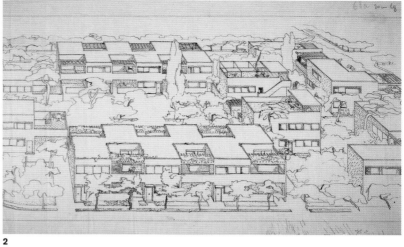

2

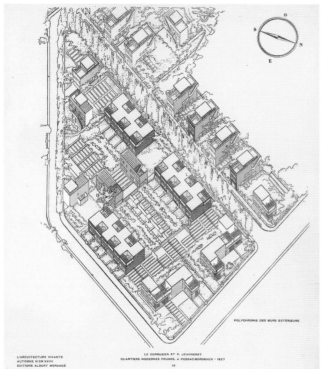

3

4

5

1. Plan, Le Corbusier, 1924. FLC

2. Bird's-eye view. FLC (c. 1924)

3. Bird's-eye view. FLC (1927)

4. Rue Le Corbusier. FLC (c. 1924)

5. Altered rowhouse. Doyle. MD (2008)

6. Rue des Arcades. FLC

7. Rue Le Corbusier. Koslowski. FLC (1995)

7

6

as a sociologist. Effective it admittedly was, but practical not at all, even in very elementary matters." Conceding that Le Corbusier "avoided monotony in the grouping and related the buildings pleasantly to the gardens in which they stood," Hitchcock took the architect to task for having "done too much work for millionaires and artists ready and able to afford the expenses of aesthetic research to be able to carry out in actuality the practical principles of his earlier housing-schemes. Considering the fact that so large a part of the site was given over to gardens it was senseless extravagance to devote nearly half the cubic content of the houses to the luxury of open entrances and terraces." Hitchcock reserved some praise for Le Corbusier's experimental use of standardized materials and for not going to the "extremes of practical expression to which German admirers of the *machine à habiter* were going," yet concluded that "as the first executed housing-scheme of the New Pioneers in France it certainly has done much more harm than good to the development of modern housing there."[194]

Public perception of Pessac evolved over time. In 1972, Philippe Boudon undertook a case study that attempted, through interviews and analysis, to shed light on the reasons behind the residents' changes. Often misinterpreted as a detractor, Boudon felt that the houses' adaptability was an asset: "The modifications carried out by the occupants constitute a positive and not a negative consequence of Le Corbusier's original conception. Pessac could only be regarded a failure if it had failed to satisfy the needs of the occupants. In point of fact, however, it not only allowed the occupants sufficient latitude to satisfy their needs, but by doing so it also helped them to realize what those needs were."[195]

Ada Louise Huxtable agreed, pointing out almost a decade later that the houses "were not commissioned by those who were to live in them, and they are not, like Frank Lloyd Wright houses, objects of curatorial pride, or a responsibility that has led some owners to breakdown, divorce or flight. Pessac was built as experimental 'workers' housing; there was no personal contract between occupant-patron and famous architect in which the owners' tastes, and even lives, are subordinate to the maintenance of a work of art, in which any change is a violation." After visiting the enclave, Huxtable came away full of admiration for Le Corbusier's work: "The scale and relationship of the houses to each other and to the gardens was excellent. The shapes and proportions of the buildings were unusually strong and good. There was a feeling of a cohesive whole. Even with the loss of key elements of the Corbusian style . . . the settlement retained an impressive and recognizable integrity. Pessac was a very pleasant place to be . . . housing on a small, intimate scale . . . truly designed in the measure of man."[196] In 1973, a Le Corbusier enthusiast moved into one of the houses and restored it to its original condition, setting into motion broader efforts that have led to the entire site's designation as a national monument and the restoration of many houses to their original condition and coloration.

Resort Suburbs in Northern France and Belgium

French seaside resorts offered another setting for garden village planning. The coast of France's Nord-Pas-de-Calais region, on the English Channel, featuring sandy beaches interspersed with steep cliffs and estuaries, became home to a string of planned resorts in the early twentieth century, when promoters seeking to cast the area as a luxurious destination dubbed it La Côte d'Opale.[197] Only five hours from London and three hours from Paris, the resorts of La Côte d'Opale were developed to cater to both French and English patrons, the latter made to feel at home by amenities such as golf links and cricket fields.

Wissant, the northernmost of the villages, eleven miles from Calais and across the English Channel from Dover, had been a popular retreat since the late nineteenth century, particularly among artists.[198] In 1903, Émile Ségard, a wool trader who owned two villas in Wissant, purchased 56 beachfront acres and hired architect Jean-Baptiste Maillard (1858–1929) to subdivide the land as a quiet destination for families. Maillard centered the plan on a circular avenue at the heart of an inland district of spacious sites for villas, each of which was subject to design controls. On either side of the circle, angled streets led toward open squares provided between rectangular blocks along the beach. The waterfront was given over to densely subdivided orthogonal blocks accommodating apartments, stores, and restaurants while also sheltering the inland houses from ocean winds and spray. A hotel was completed in 1904 along with infrastructural components, but sales were slow, hampered initially by the inaccessibility of the site, which was not served by a nearby railroad station, and then by World War I, when the town was home to Belgian, French, and British troops. Work resumed in earnest in 1922, but Raoul Brygoo (n.d.), who succeeded Maillard as architect, serving from 1925 to 1930, softened the distinction between the compact seafront and sparse inland residential streets. The German occupation of Wissant during World War II took a severe toll on the original buildings, although some remain.

The chain of resort villages continued south past Ambleteuse and Wimereux, both of which developed according to plans that were not particularly notable, and on to **Le Touquet Paris-Plage**, which enjoyed a beautiful site of beaches and dunes as well as inland forests planted by the landowner, Alphonse-Jean-Baptiste Daloz, in the mid-nineteenth century to help stabilize the storm-battered landscape.[199] In 1880, Daloz leveled a portion of the seafront and hired Raymond Lens (1807–1887), a surveyor, to plan Paris-Plage. Lens's design, completed in 1882, packed development into a dense and surprisingly urban grid, positioned to stay parallel to the coastline.

In 1894, Sir John Robinson Whitley (1843–1922), an English businessman, proposed a luxurious resort for the land all around Paris-Plage, retaining Charles Garnier

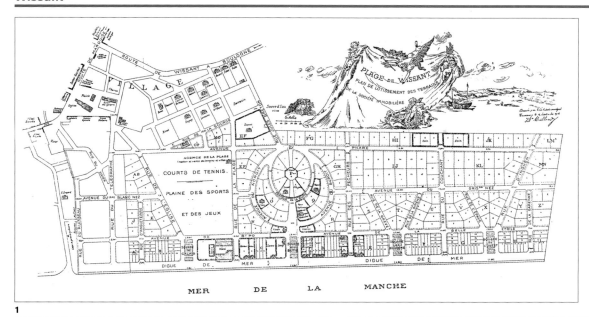

1. Plan, Jean-Baptiste Maillard, 1903. CPG

2. Aerial view. CPG

3. Place du Contour de la Butte. Bouvet. RNPC (2010)

(1825–1898), famous not only for the Paris Opera but also for the casino at Monte Carlo, to work with English architect Thomas W. Cutler (1841?–1909) on a scheme that Whitley promoted as the "Monterey, Newpoart [sic] and Tuxedo of Europe."[200] Visitors to the resort, named Mayville, to honor princess May de Teck, wife of the Duke of York, would typically arrive by train, traveling through a forest dotted with facilities for tennis, cricket, polo, and horseracing, to disembark in a central square framed by the train station and two churches. From the square, an axial shopping street led to a beachfront casino. The axis continued into the ocean in the form of a pier. The plan, blanketing the coast to the north and south with winding streets and grand villas, was not approved. Whitley regrouped, forming a development syndicate that in 1902 extended Paris-Plage to the east according to plans by architect Joseph-Louis Sanguet (1855–1914), who retained sections of the forest and called for contour-hugging naturalistic streets that accommodated a mammoth casino and several hotels in addition to villas. The project attracted a mainly English clientele.

Whitley came even closer to his initial vision for Mayville on a site twelve miles to the north, where in 1905 he purchased nearly 1,000 acres from five separate landowners and built **Hardelot** for both English and

French vacationers, "a sort of half-way rendezvous, or meeting-place, for the two allied peoples where they can meet on the common ground of holiday pleasure, and thus learn to know each other better," as one observer put it. At Hardelot, "an Englishman leaving London at 10 a.m. can lunch with a friend from Paris, teach him how to play golf, then dine à la Française, and be back in town an hour before midnight, after enjoying a complete change in every respect, with a couple of breezy trips across the Channel into the bargain."[201] Aside from Jules Verne's Phineas Fogg, it is doubtful that any other Englishman could have kept up with this regimen.

Lillois architect Louis Cordonnier (1854–1940), working with surveyor Henri Triffault (n.d.), planned Hardelot as an adaptation of Garnier and Cutler's design for Mayville but also, as Richard Klein has noted in his history of the village, as a resort version of Letchworth.[202] The planners retained Hardelot Castle and designated the surrounding forests as hunting grounds. An axial entry sequence brought visitors through the forest, past a golf course, and through wooded villa sites to a church square buffered from the sea by a kidney-shaped residential block. Six tennis courts occupied a central beachfront site, flanked by a roughly symmetrical series of blocks. Whitley ceded the land to the Société

THE FUTURE MAYVILLE.

1

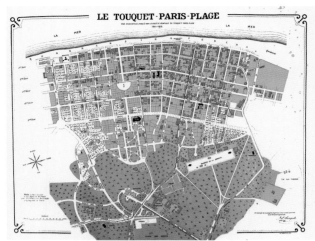

2

1. Bird's-eye view of proposed Mayville, drawn by Thomas W. Cutler, 1894. PDC

2. Plan, Joseph-Louis Sanguet. SATP (1911–12)

3. Gardens, Paris-Plage. CPB (1910)

4. Aerial view. IGN49 (1949)

3

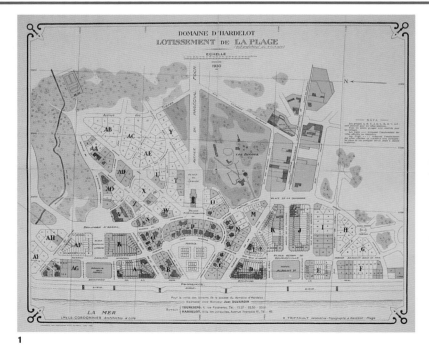

4

Hardelot

1

1. Plan, Louis Cordonnier and Henri Triffault. PDC1 (1930)

2. Tennis courts. CRS (c. 1925)

3. Le Bon Gîte and Avenue Guy Barbe Blanche. Thru. FL (2011)

2

3

Hardelot, which set about building roads and infrastructure as well as amenities such as golf links, tennis courts, hotels, and a church. The project was a success, counting about 100 completed villas by 1912.

The last of the Côte d'Opale resorts to get under way, **Stella-Plage**, bound by Le Touquet Paris-Plage on the north and Merlimont on the south, was developed by two Parisians, Edmond Labrasse and Victor Poulain, who in 1914 purchased 867 acres and commissioned architect Charles Plumet (1861–1928) to prepare a master plan.[203] Construction waited until after the war, picking up in 1922 with the completion of a railroad station on the Berck–Le Touquet line and a nearby casino. Plumet organized the resort into a "summer" village on the sea and a "winter" village adjacent to the train station. A broad park separating the two subdivisions was to contain pine trees in order to buffer the winter village, known as Les Pelouses, from the cold ocean breezes. Les Pelouses was built first, laid out with picturesquely curving residential streets wrapping around a Parc des Sports, and marketed not so much as a seaside paradise but as an urbane cultural center offering casino gaming, theatrical productions, movies, and hunting.

The oceanfront district was quite different in character, its radial plan based on the seaside resort of Cabourg, laid out in 1854–55 by Paul Leroux (n.d.).[204] Like Cabourg, Stella-Plage was focused on a casino placed one block back from the beach in the semicircular Place de l'Etoile, from which nine avenues extended outward to intersect with concentric cross streets at circular and rectangular *places*. The wide streets, lined by lawns but not sidewalks, catered to automobile transportation, while a tram was installed to carry residents to and from the beach. The project proved popular, so much so that the park separating the two villages gave way early on to construction. Architect Lucien Dufour (n.d.) designed many houses during the interwar period, but World War II witnessed massive destruction in Stella-Plage, leaving relatively few of these intact.

The nearby resorts of Belgium also enjoyed the patronage of British vacationers. **Knokke**, forty miles from the French border, received its first speculative development proposal in 1887, when the Brussels-based architect Jean Baes (1848–1914) laid out an elaborate, sprawling villa park organized around a central avenue leading toward a beachfront lighthouse and a pier, although a lack of financial means reduced the plan to a sober, linear subdivision around what is now Lippenslaan.[205] The extension of a coastal tram to Knokke during the 1890s reinforced its popularity, as did the completion of several hotels and a golf course that catered to an English clientele. In 1900, the Société Anonyme de Duinbergen hired German town planner Joseph Stübben (1845–1936) to design Duinbergen on a dune site to the west with curving residential streets and an organically shaped central park leading to a beachfront hotel and commercial district. In 1908 Stübben was asked to design Het Zoute on the opposite side of Knokke, extending the resort to the east with a villa district of

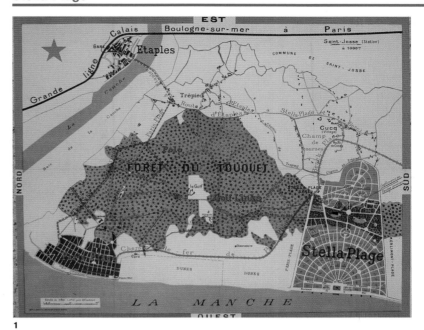

1

2

1. Plan showing Stella-Plage, Charles Plumet, 1914, right, and Paris-Plage, left. PDC2 (c. 1922)

2. Villa designed by Lucien Dufour. CRS (c. 1935)

3. Plan of Cabourg, Paul Leroux, 1855. DAC

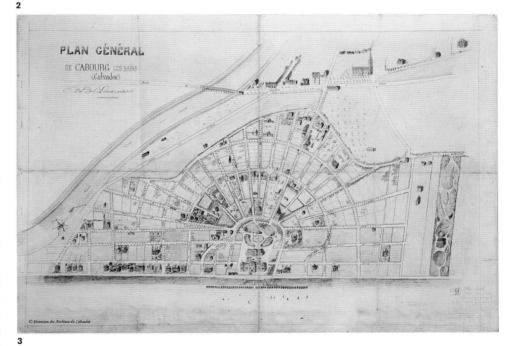

3

Knokke

1. Bird's-eye view and plan of Knokke, Jean Baes, c. 1887. MZR

2. Aerial view of Knokke, showing Het Zoute, left, Lippenslaan, left center, Albert Plage, right center, and Duinbergen, right. GE (2009)

3. Plan of Duinbergen, Joseph Stübben, 1900. MZR

4. Hôtel du Chalet, Duinbergen. GUL

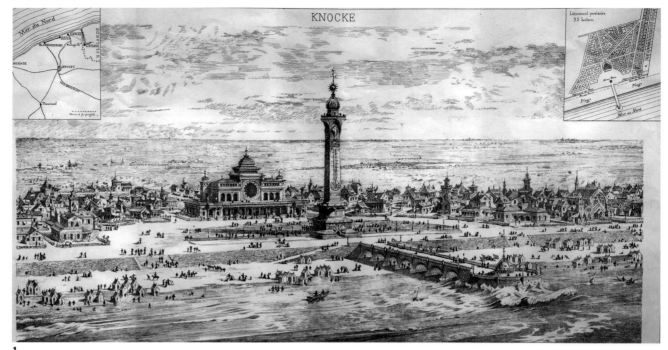

1

2

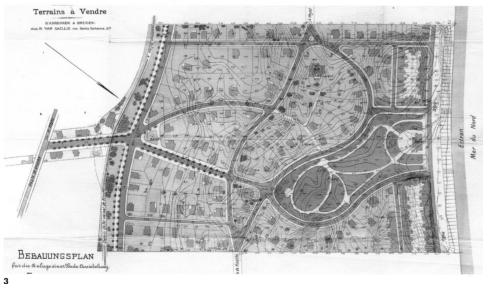

3

4

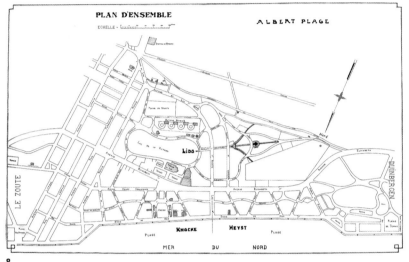

gently curved streets, narrow lanes, and culs-de-sac as well as two golf courses. Other plans were halted by the war, but development picked up again in 1922 on available land between Knokke and Duinbergen, where the district known as Albert-Plage featured a park and a man-made lake amid curving streets. A waterfront section featured straight streets angling toward the beach and cut through by an undulating crossroad. Knokke continued to grow during the interwar period with a casino, carousel, posh villas, and hotels.

Resort Suburbs at La Côte Basque

The area around France's border with Spain, La Côte Basque, was another popular seaside destination and the setting of two planned resorts from the 1920s. **Hossegor**, a quiet retreat thirty-five miles from the border, had been the subject of failed development schemes in 1906 and 1911 before a young but experienced resort developer, Alfred Eluère (1893–1985), in partnership with financier Aimé Meunier-Godin, began, in 1923, to purchase more than 360 acres stretching inland from the beach.[206] The site was divided into eastern and western halves by a lake running parallel to the coastline and a canal linking the lake to the ocean. The subdivision plan called for curving, Olmsted-inspired streets meeting in Y-shaped

intersections, *places*, and *rond-points*, as well as some built-up orthogonal intersections, an arrangement that maximized the amount of saleable land while avoiding uniform blocks and lots. Culs-de-sac and winding roads allowed access to topographically rugged parts of the site. In 1924 a bridge was completed across the canal—a crucial element that had been lacking in the earlier plans. More than 150 houses were built by 1930, many designed in the Basque vernacular by Henri Godbarge (1872–1946) and the brothers Louis (1876–1940) and Benjamin (1885–1959) Gomez, who were also responsible for most of the buildings in the oceanfront Quartier de la Dune.

The only significant green space was an inland golf course overlooked by more than sixty lots placed around its edges and along the Avenue du Golf, which was threaded through the greens. In light of the absence of public parks, strictures were put in place to retain natural elements in the residential areas, limiting to a certain extent the deforestation of the lots and mandating that houses be set behind front gardens. Minimum construction costs were also set and architectural guidelines established. As Hossegor's popularity increased, helped by the construction of hotels, a racetrack, marina, and beachfront casino, other developers extended the resort to the north along the coast and to the east side of the lake with subdivisions that followed the spirit of the original plan.

5. Aerial view of Het Zoute. MZR (1910s)

6. Fochlaan, Het Zoute. MZR (1922)

7. Typical street, Het Zoute. RAMSA (2003)

8. Plan of Albert Plage. MZR

1

2

3

Three villages sat around the Bay of Chingoudy on the border between France and Spain: Hendaye on the French side and Irun and Fontarabie on the Spanish side. **Hendaye** became a popular resort after the arrival of the railway in 1860.[207] In 1871 a group of businessmen hired engineer Léopold Dupuy (n.d.) to plan for the extension of the railroad to the beach, where a station would join a hotel, casino, café, market, and hot and cold baths. A nearby plaza, bound by mixed-use buildings, was to be surrounded by streets of detached villas set back on individual lots. Although the plan, revised in 1878, did not go forward, the mixed-use plaza appeared in each subsequent proposal, eventually making its way into reality. Dupuy revisited the scheme again in 1881, now working in collaboration with Parisian architect Le Roy de Bonneville (n.d.), on behalf of a building society. The plan eliminated the train station in favor of a tram line, broke up the cluster of resort facilities so that they now lined the beachfront, reinforced the plaza to become an eight-way intersection, the Place du Commerce, and most significantly, called for the enlargement of a sandbar into a peninsula between the sea and the bay to provide more developable land. The tip of the peninsula was to feature an arena and restaurant, with a waterfront promenade wrapping from the ocean to the bay side. In 1882, V. Erhard (n.d.), an engineer, retooled the design of the peninsula so the concave side would face the bay.

Despite the flurry of plans, by 1900 Hendaye was still a small resort of scattered villas, a Moorish-style hotel, and a beachfront casino. In 1906, architect-developer Henry Martinet (1867–1936) proposed a more pragmatic scheme, the inspiration for which he credited to his visits to English garden cities. Martinet made the Place du Commerce into a circle and introduced separate market

and church squares, more direct routes to the beach, and a larger peninsula that could accommodate twice as many lots, overlaying the land with a loose street grid cut through by gently curving avenues radiating from an elliptical public garden. Aside from Martinet's beachfront Hôtel Eskualduna (1912), the plan showed little progress until 1923, when the architect was at the helm of a new building society that set about developing transportation links between Hendaye and other towns in the region and connected the three sections of Hendaye—the beach, town, and station/border crossing—with widened roads and tram lines. The site required extensive work, including dredging the bay, raising the level of the beach, and building dikes and dams, all of which increased the amount of developable land.

Martinet imagined Hendaye as an alternative to the chaos and noise of nearby Biarritz, a calm and elegant resort tailored to families and sports lovers, featuring hunting and fishing, exotic plant species, and Spanish-influenced architecture. The physical environment was to be controlled by architectural and planning guidelines. Martinet called upon Beaux-Arts-trained architect Edmond Durandeau (1878–1960) to design many of the houses. The plan was partially implemented before the building society went bust in 1929. The peninsula was never fully completed—a sizable portion gave way to a marina, and the tip, known as Sokoburu, was not developed until the 1990s.[208]

Across the Bay of Chingoudy, a peninsula in **Fontarabie** was the subject of a 1914 plan by José Ángel Fernández de Casadevante (1881–1939), who echoed Martinet's plan of Hendaye-Plage in his scheme of radial avenues connecting circular plazas and a waterfront esplanade, but the plan fell victim to economic problems and civil war, and the site, having lost some appeal in the

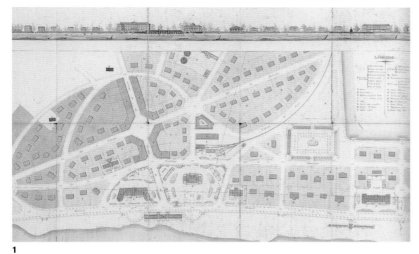

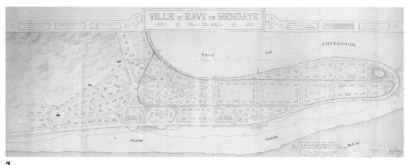

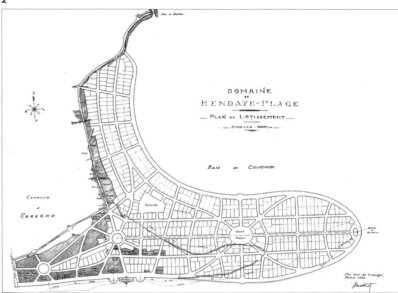

1. Plan, Léopold Dupuy, 1878. CUL

2. Plan, Léopold Dupuy, 1881. CUL

3. Plan, V. Erhard, 1882. CUL

4. Plan, Henry Martinet, 1906. IFA

5. Aerial view. IGN38 (1938)

6. Villas. CRS (1927)

7. Typical houses. CPT (c. 1930)

8. Boulevard showing tram. CPT

Fontarabie

1. Plan, José Ángel Fernández de Casadevante, 1914. CUL

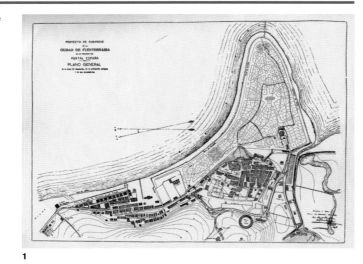

Cité-Jardin d'Anaka

1. Plan, F. Mondrilla, 1926. AMI1

2. Aerial view. PE (1959)

3. Typical street. AMI2

PLANO GENERAL
DE LOS TERRENOS CON LAS CALLES, PLAZAS, PARCELAS
Y EMPLAZAMIENTO DE LAS CASAS.

1960s with the construction of an adjacent airstrip, was built up in the 1980s.[209] In the adjacent village of Irún, a garden enclave—**Cité-Jardin d'Anaka**—was laid out in 1926 by F. Mondrilla (n.d.) on behalf of a cooperative society, providing 130 affordable one- and two-story houses designed by Teodoro de Anasagasti (1880–1938) spaced evenly along curving streets lined by sidewalks and trees.[210] Construction began in 1928 and the enclave remains intact.

BELGIUM

Garden village planning came slowly to Belgium, with no projects undertaken before World War I. Early attempts to import English planning models, such as the Association des Cités-Jardins de Belgique's 1904 proposal for a garden city to serve the coal industry in the Campine region, failed.[211] In 1913, Charles Didier, secretary of the Belgian Garden City Association, bemoaned "our lack of success in Belgium," blaming "conditions as to land tenure, etc." that "really in a measure make the Garden City unrealizable."[212] Things changed in the wake of the devastation wrought by the war. The need for large-scale reconstruction created the impetus to make real progress, and at least twenty-five garden villages and enclaves were under construction by 1925, many of which, both public and private, in an effort to meet the needs of the poorer classes, were subsidized by the Société Nationale des Habitations à Bon Marché, a government housing agency patterned on that in France.[213] The suspension of subsidies in the mid-1920s resulted not only in projects being halted before completion, but also in the effective termination of the Garden City movement in Belgium.

Some Belgian garden suburbs eschewed the naturalistic arrangements typical of prewar English and German examples in favor of a regularity of streets and a crisp, cubic articulation of building mass, reflecting a new Modernist stylistic sensibility. However, this Modernism paralleled and sometimes coexisted with a more traditional vernacularism so that, as Gabriele Tagliaventi has pointed out, many of the garden villages also reflected the *beguinages* built in Belgium and the Netherlands beginning in the Middle Ages, groups of houses surrounding a public green space and church forming self-sufficient communities enclosed by walls within the greater city. According to Tagliaventi, the last *beguinage* to be built, **Sint Amandsberg** (1872), in Ghent, designed by Arthur Verhaegen (1847–1917), accommodating eighty houses, fourteen convents, a church, chapel, and hospital on 20 acres, was "one of the main examples of romantic town planning of medieval inspiration, along with Howard's garden city and Parker and Unwin's projects."[214] Marcel Smets, in his study of interwar city building in Belgium, has emphasized the transitional character of many of the new garden villages "in which elements from a new age (the social one-family home) were incorporated into a design still largely inspired by the previous century."[215]

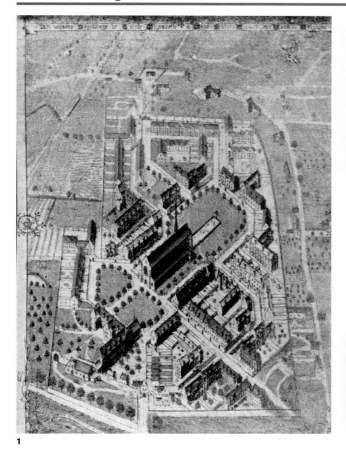

1. Axonometric. GUL

2. Typical street. CRS

3. Sint Beggaplein. Limo. WC (2008)

1

2

3

Brussels

Brussels was the center of planning activity. By the late 1920s, it was dotted with garden villages and enclaves that, unlike English, American, and, to a lesser extent, German examples, which were typically undertaken without recourse to a larger strategy of development of the cities they were dependent upon, did relate to an ideal metropolitan plan, as depicted in the 1924 **hub-and-spoke diagram** by Raphaël Verwilghen (1885–1963). As Louis Van der Swaelmen (1883–1929), the landscape architect who planned many of the new garden suburbs and who called himself, alternately, architect-urbanist and *paysagiste*, wrote, this "creates a true garden-periphery with the nodes connected together by tree-lined avenues and large landscaped open spaces forming a true park system."[216]

Three of the garden suburbs, in the Anderlecht section of southwest Brussels, were planned before the war to provide relocation housing for inner-city working-class citizens forced out of their neighborhoods by infrastructural work. Planning for **Cité la Roue**—in English, "City of the Wheel," said to be named in memory of an old wheel of torment—was begun in 1910, but after the interruption of the war, work was carried forward between 1920 and 1928.[217] Planned by Van der Swaelmen and a group of architects working under the direction of Jean-Jules Eggericx (1884–1963), the suburb, with a number of landscaped squares in the English manner, provided for 688 families housed in almost sixty different

Hub-and-spoke diagram

LA CITE. DECEMBRE 1924.

/CHEMA THEORIQUE DE LA REPARTITION RATIONNELLE DE/ MOYEN/ DE TRAN/PORT DAN/ L'HYPOTHÈSE DU PLAN REGIONAL
VILLE-MERE; VILLAGES ET VILLES SATELLITES

1

1. Diagram, Raphaël Verwilghen, 1924. LC24

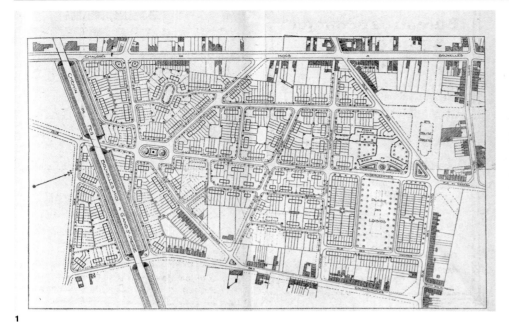

1. Plan, Louis Van der Swaelmen, 1920. HBM23

2. Place Ernest S'Jonghers. CRS

3 . Plaine des Loisirs. Ben. WC (2006)

4. Pedestrian path. Ben. WC (2006)

house models. **Bon Air** (1922–31), the second of Anderlecht's garden suburbs, was set at the city's edge, adjacent to agricultural fields, organized on a somewhat irregularly platted diagonal street grid focused, at its center, upon a large green faced by a school.[218] **La Cité de Moortebeek** (1922–32), the third of the Anderlecht suburbs, had a less interesting plan by Jean-François Hoeben (1896–1969) calling for a regular grid of streets on 20 acres cut across by a diagonal boulevard.[219] But, as if to compensate for the layout, the 456 dwellings, typically disposed in three- and four-family units, were richly embellished by the architects, Rene Bragard (1892–1971?), who designed most of the houses south of Boulevard Shakespeare, Joseph Diongre (1878–1963), who worked north of the boulevard, and Achille (n.d.) and Josse Mouton (n.d.). Diongre also designed **Cité Diongre** (1923–25), considered, with some exaggeration, by Maurizio Cohen in his comprehensive overview to be "probably the finest 'Regionalist' garden city" in Brussels, a "deliberately picturesque" gathering of 140 units on a former country estate.[220]

Many of the garden suburbs of Brussels were built on small sites but with varying densities, ranging from the almost rural feel of **Tuinbouw** (1922), in the Evere district, occupying a triangular parcel organized by Jean-Jules Eggericx to include an internal loop road

lined by semidetached houses on large, lushly planted gardens that set the enclave apart from its higher-density surroundings,[221] to **Het Heideken** (1920–23), one of the most urban of the Brussels garden suburbs, designed by Jules Ghobert (1881–1978) with 164 dwellings in long rows of street-defining structures happily relieved by a rich mix of architectural details and a plan that is penetrated by pedestrian paths leading to an internal square.[222] **Cité du Transvaal** (1919–21), also known as Cité van Lindt, was one of the city's smallest enclaves, occupying only 10 acres planned by Rene Bragard, Jean De Ligne (1890–1985), and the firm of E. Van der Slagmolen (n.d.) and P. Verbist (n.d.) to house eighty-nine families in four- and five-family blocks around a small recreational green.[223]

Forest-Vert (1922–27), designed by H. Van Monfort (n.d.) with 504 dwellings, two-thirds of which were allocated to working-class families and the remaining one-third reserved for middle-class and office workers, contained a rich variety of housing typologies, including five-story apartment houses, though only two blocks remain,[224] while **Cité Wannecouter** (1921–22), a pocket-size garden enclave on either side of Rue Gustave Demanet, wraps forty-four dwellings around two midblock landscaped courts accessed beneath arches.[225]

Bon Air

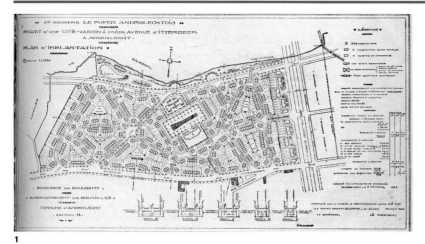

1

2

3

4

1. Plan, 1922. HBM23

2. Green and school. CRS

3, 4. Typical streets. Ben.
WC (2006)

La Cité de Moortebeek

1

2

3

4

1. Plan, Jean-François Hoeben,
1922. CUL

2, 3. Typical streets. Ben.
WC (2006)

4. Aerial view. GE (2004)

Cité Diongre

1

2

1. Aerial view. GE (2004)

2. Rue Joseph Diongre. Patart.
ETU (2001)

1

2

1

2

3

Zaventen (1921–23), twice the size of Wannecouter, shares some of its characteristics but, owing to budget problems, its houses, by Jean De Ligne, J. Allard (n.d.), J. Mouton, and Van Der Slagmolen and Verbist, are less well detailed.[226] Other small but noteworthy garden enclaves include **Cité Verregat** (1921–26) by Henri Derée (1888–1974),[227] **Cité Heymbosch** (1921–28) by H. Dammon (n.d.),[228] and **Cité des Hougnes** (1921–25), in Verviers, little more than a single street artfully jogged at its midpoint by its designer Carlos Thirion (n.d.) to suggest a village square.[229]

About four miles south of central Brussels, near Uccle, **Cité Homborch** (1928–30), consisting of 108 mostly one- and two-family dwellings, was arranged according to an interesting plan of Y-shaped streets connecting a semicircular road on the north with a gently

curved street to the south. Designed by Fernand Bodson (1877–1966), Homborch has, as Burniat, Puttemans, and Vandenbreeden write in their guide to Brussels's Modernist architecture, "all the landscape characteristics of the beautiful Brussels garden city estates: lots of public open spaces, picturesquely varied groups of buildings, pedestrian footpaths, and, in the center of the estate, the impressive church square and shopping center."[230]

Le Logis-Floréal (1922–30), located in Watermael-Boitsfort, about three miles southeast of the city center, was the most important garden village not only in Brussels but in all of Belgium. Consisting of two separate housing cooperatives linked together by plan and architectural expression, one promoted by a group of bank workers and the other by print workers, the village was planned by Van der Swaelmen and implemented

Cité du Transvaal

1. Aerial view. GE (2009)

2. Rue Henri Ver Eycken. WC (2008)

Forest-Vert

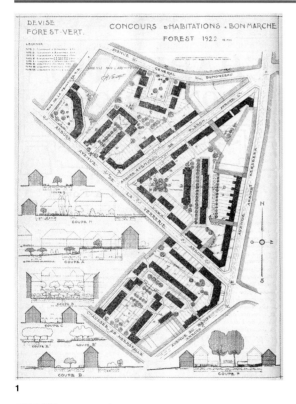

1. Plan, H. Van Monfort, 1922. HBM23

2. Rendering, intersection of Avenues de Fléron and de la Verrerie. GUL (1923)

3. Avenue de Fléron. CRS

Cité Wannecouter

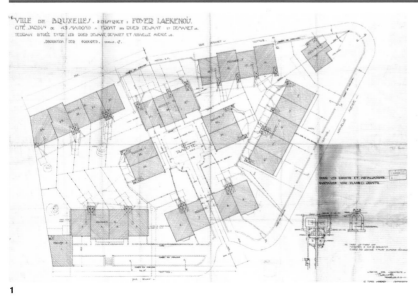

1. Plan, 1921. AVB

2. Aerial view. GE (2012)

Zaventen

1. Plan, Jean De Ligne, 1921. AAM

2. Typical street. AAM (c. 1927)

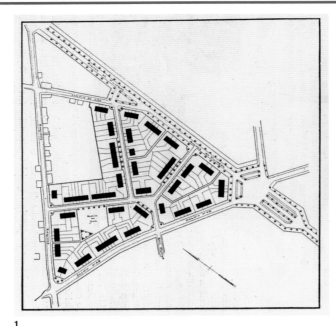

1

2

Cité Verregat

1. Plan, Henri Derée, c. 1921. AAM

2. Typical street. AAM (1920s)

1

2

Cité Heymbosch

1

2

1. Aerial view. GE (2004)

2. Avenue du Heymbosch.
CRS (1920s)

Cité des Hougnes

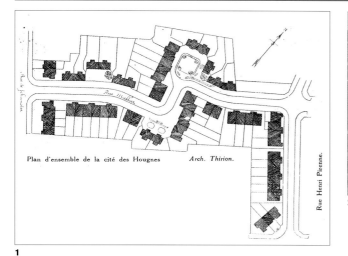

1

Plan d'ensemble de la cité des Hougnes   Arch. Thirion.

Rue Henri Pirenne.

2

553. Verviers — Nouveau Quartier des Hougnes
Place Léopold Mallar

1. Plan, Carlos Thirion. HBM25 (1925)

2. Place Léopold Mallar. MDV (c. 1925)

Cité Homborch

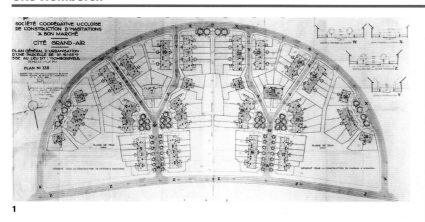

1

2

1. Plan, Fernand Bodson, 1929. AAM

2. Typical street. AAM

by Jean-Jules Eggericx, who designed a majority of the buildings, along with J. Mouton, and the firm of Lucien François (1894–1983) and Raymond Moenaert (1882–1977).[231] Floréal's plan and most of the architecture is distinctly English in inspiration. However, the so-called "Horseshoe Building" (Le Fer-à-Cheval) (Jean-Jules Eggericx, 1925–28), containing community services and bachelor flats and taking the form of a nine-story tower flanked by three- and four-story wings embracing a landscaped forecourt, has decided connections to Amsterdam School Modernism. Another mixed-use building, but technically a part of Le Logis, was added in 1928–30 at the junction between the two housing estates: Van der Swaelmen's Trois Tilleuls, containing flats, shops, an auditorium, and a polyclinic.

While Unwin's street pictures and hierarchies formed the basis of many Belgian garden suburbs, at Le Logis-Floréal, it was the rolling topography that set the planning agenda and led to the formation of linked areas that Van der Swaelmen referred to by shape: the Triangle, Square, Horseshoe, Trapezoid, and Funnel. The care taken with landscape, street furniture, and signage, and the careful attention to the extensive system of pedestrian paths, make Le Logis-Floréal a rival to Hampstead Garden Suburb and Forest Hills Gardens.

Served by a subway, the suburb did not initially include garages, but these were provided later. Helen Meller, in her book *European Cities, 1890–1930s*, regards Le Logis-Floréal as "the nearest thing to a garden city to be found in the inter-war period in Western Europe,"[232] qualifying the claim to recognize, as Van der Swaelmen noted at the outset of the project, that "here, and all over Belgium, we have never managed to create a garden-city in the full sense; but we have managed the methodical enlargement of the city, an organic planning, in the form of the garden-suburb. Here garden-city should be taken to mean a low-density housing estate in a garden setting."[233]

La Cité Moderne (1922–25), designed by architect Victor Bourgeois (1897–1962) and Van der Swaelmen, located in the Berchem-Sainte-Agathe section of Brussels, west of the Basilique Nationale de Sacré-Cœur, is perhaps the first example of the confrontation between Unwinesque density and street-planning principles and Modernist aesthetics, reflecting the use of the ash-concrete system of prefabrication initiated at Zelzate (see p. 768). The design of the houses was possibly influenced by Tony Garnier's project for La Cité Industrielle (see p. 288), but in more likelihood by early Neoplasticist work in Holland by J. J. P. Oud and Jan Wils (1891–1972), which Bourgeois had visited.[234] By introducing

1. Plan, Louis van der Swaelmen, 1922. AAM

2. Pedestrian path. AAM

3. Pedestrian path. Ben. WC (2006)

4. Bosduiflaan from Le Fer-à-Cheval. AAM

5. Place du Tarin. RAMSA (c. 2005)

6. Rue du Coucou. RAMSA (c. 2005)

7. Rue des Scilles. Ben. WC (2006)

8. Le Fer-à-Cheval, Jean-Jules Eggericx, 1925–28. Ben. WC (2006)

9. Rue du Friquet. Ben. WC (2006)

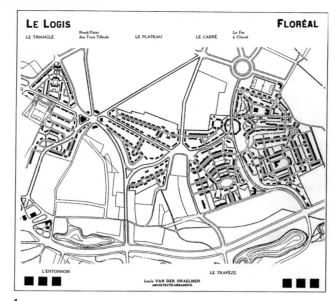

1

2

3

4

5

6

7

8

9

1

2

3

4

1. Plan, Victor Bourgeois and Louis Van der Swaelmen, 1922. AAM

2. Houses, Victor Bourgeois. GUL (1924)

3. View during construction. AAM (1920s)

4. Place des Coopérateurs. AAM (1920s)

5. Typical street. RAMSA (c. 2000)

6. Place des Coopérateurs. RAMSA (c. 2000)

7. Pathway between rear gardens. RAMSA (c. 2000)

5

6

7

a cubistic architectural language, the garden suburb type was transformed, displacing the sense of individual dwelling in favor of an expression of the collective. The development of 370 dwellings, out of 500 initially planned, was originally occupied by government bureaucrats. The plan provided a picturesquely modified grid of streets leading to a central spine intersected by the civic focal point of Place des Coopérateurs. As realized, La Cité Moderne was only half the size originally intended by the tenants' cooperative that had been established by Bourgeois's poet brother, Pierre, and the writer Georg Rens. Plans were curtailed when the government's subsidy program was suspended out of fear that La Cité Moderne and the other new garden suburbs would give rise to a political "red belt" such as those arising around Paris and Vienna.

Only three small shops were built in the diminished commercial center.

Incomplete though it is, **Kapelleveld** (1923–26), on about 100 acres in St. Lambrechts-Woluwe, an eastern suburb of Brussels, forms what Geert Bekaert has described as "one of the most fascinating experiments in modernist garden suburbs," exhibiting a "fruitful" tension "between the cubist approach of someone like [Huib] Hoste and the combined forms of someone like [Antoine] Pompe, in which tradition and renewal go hand in hand."[235] The suburb, comprising 440 dwellings on a gently rolling site, was planned by Van der Swaelmen assisted by Jean-François Hoeben, Huib Hoste (1881–1957), Antoine Pompe (1873–1980), and Paul Rubbers (1900–1985), combining traditional-style houses by Hoeben, Rubbers, and Pompe, with Cubist designs by Hoste.

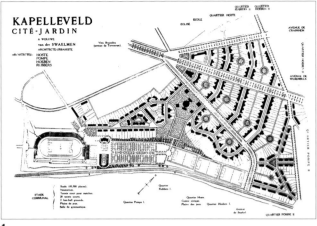

1. Plan, Louis Van der Swaelmen, 1922–26. AAM

2. Houses designed by Huib Hoste. AAM

3. Design for six-house group, Paul Rubbers. HBM24

4. Design for four-house group, Antoine Pompe. HBM24

5. Design for four-house group, Paul Rubbers. HBM24

6. Korenbloemplein, showing houses by Antoine Pompe. RAMSA (c. 2000)

7. Avenue de la Semoy, showing houses by Huib Hoste. Ben. WC (2011)

8. Avenue de la Spirale, showing houses by Jean-François Hoeben. Ben. WC (2011)

For Marcel Smets, the stylistic mix is a bit jarring, with Hoste's industrialized units looking "like 20th-century prototypes that have landed in a late 19th-century landscape." But the close marriage of the town plan to the topography overcomes the stylistic disconnect, with "identifiable fragments, arranged around commonly shared inner courts at the back of the private gardens," and a clear hierarchy of streets consisting "of relatively short, broken, or curved pieces that lead to closed vistas and articulate enclosed domains" enhanced by Van der Swaelmen's lush plantings.[236] The placement of the residential streets perpendicular to the busy boulevards crisscrossing the site enhance the sense of community, as do the network of pedestrian paths and small plazas located between the gardens. Under pressure from the local mayor, the density was kept very low with only twelve units per hectare or roughly five houses per acre. Extensive playing fields were located along Kapelleveld's southern edge where they buffered the negative impact of a regional rail line. Medium-height tower apartment buildings with ground-floor shops were designed by Hoste to serve as a transition between the low-density housing and the sports ground, but they were not built.

Provincial Suburbs

Notable garden suburbs were built in Belgium's secondary cities as well. **Moretusburg** (1921), Hoboken, located in an industrial section of Antwerp and designed by M. Van Rompaey (n.d.), was described in 1922 by the French garden city advocate Georges Benoît-Lévy as a "delightful creation," with semidetached and group houses of up to nine units set back modestly from the sidewalk to give definition to the street while opening up block interiors for gardens.[237] The irregular pattern of straight and gently curved tree-lined streets, focused around a church and square, provided additional blocks for recreational use. **Unitas** (1923–28), in Deurne, Antwerp, an elongated perimeter block scheme designed by Eduard Van Steenbergen (1889–1952), confronted the adjoining Boekenbergpark with a virtually unbroken wall of traditional gable- and hip-roofed group houses detailed to reflect Modernist design trends, but all in all anticipating many of the suburban semidetached houses that would characterize London's Metroland in the 1930s.[238]

In the war-damaged West Flanders city of Menen, work began in 1922 on the adjacent garden villages of **Ons Dorp** and **Ezelbrugwijk**.[239] The latter, with 224 vernacular-inspired workers' houses designed by Richard Acke (1873–1934) and Jean-Jules Eggericx, was laid out according to a plan by Raphaël Verwilghen, who employed closed street vistas, crooked roads opening up to small plazas, and hierarchical street types that included a broad tree-lined boulevard terminating on axis with a public square and school. Semidetached and three-unit houses predominated but two six- and eight-unit rows were placed on the long edges of a rectangular plaza. Adjacent to the north, Ons Dorp contained fifty mirror-image semidetached and multiple-unit brick houses built from four distinct types designed by Menen architect Gaston Boghemans (1891–1984).

Acke was also responsible for the plan of **Kalfvaart** (1920), in Ypres, West Flanders, as well as the village's 100 houses that he placed in long street-defining rows allowing for deep rear gardens.[240] Four short rows framed a quiet plaza in the middle of the site, but a planned market square did not materialize after the public and commercial buildings at its edges were canceled. **Ligy** (1921), a garden village on the eastern edge of Ypres, featured 140 brick, stucco, and half-timbered gable- and gambrel-roofed houses on a site bordered on the west by a cemetery and the east by agricultural land.[241] Raphaël Verwilghen's plan, prepared with H. De Bruyne (n.d.) and including a large central green, consisted of a half-octagon road accommodating double, triple, and quadruple houses arranged in the Unwinesque tradition to provide parks along the street and to frame small courtyards.

Moretusburg

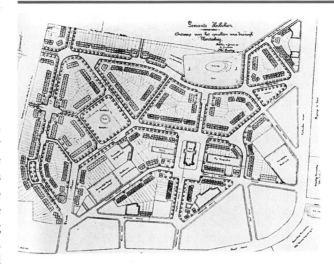

1

2

Unitas

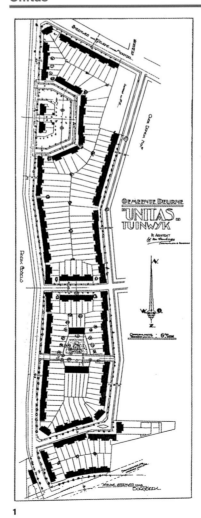

1

2

3

Ons Dorp and Ezelbrugwijk

1. Plan, Raphaël Verwilghen, 1922. KUL

2. Typical street. CRS

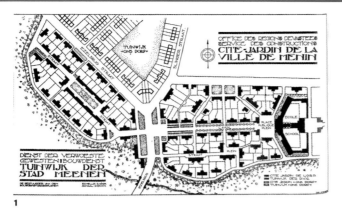

1

2

Kalfvaart

1. Plan, Richard Acke, 1920. IEPA

2. Aerial view. IEPF (1950s)

3. Vrijheidstraat. Opsommer. IEP (2012)

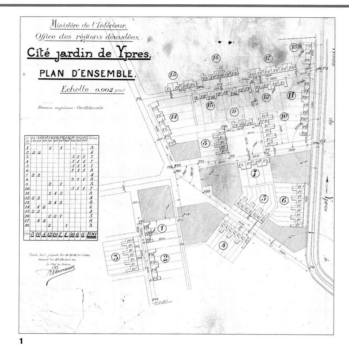

1

2

3

Ligy

1. Plan, Raphaël Verwilghen, 1921. KUL

2. Typical street. Opsommer. IEP (2012)

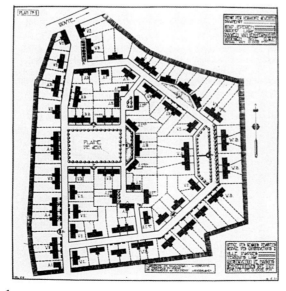

1

2

1

THE NETHERLANDS

The Garden City idea was introduced to the Netherlands by J. Bruinwold Riedel, secretary of the Maatschappij tot Nut van 't Algemeen, a public welfare group, whose book *Tuinsteden* (1906) combined a synopsis of Ebenezer Howard's *Garden Cities of To-morrow*—including the first translations of Howard's "The Three Magnets," "Garden City," and "Garden City Center" diagrams—with Riedel's firsthand accounts of English examples such as Letchworth and Port Sunlight, as well as discussions of leading figures in the field, including Germany's Theodor Fischer and France's Georges Benoît-Lévy.[242] Riedel published his book just as municipalities were starting to cope with the country's relatively late industrialization, contemplating coordinated expansion plans as a way of combating the rampant speculative development that was leading to poorly planned, overcrowded, and unhealthy urban areas.

Riedel concluded his study by proposing the establishment of a garden city eighteen miles east of Amsterdam in **Het Gooi**, a naturally beautiful region that was under pressure of development without any plan in place. The proposal failed to gain traction but was revived in 1923 by S. R. De Miranda (1875–1942), a Socialist alderman, whose official 200-page study, released in 1929—the only Dutch scheme to approach the scale and scope of Howard's idea—included a diagrammatic plan by K. P. C. de Bazel (1869–1923) that echoed the architect's 1905 proposal for a World Capital Foundation of Internationalism outside of The Hague (see p. 514).[243] Despite the support of influential groups and individuals, the plan, slated for a 2,471-acre tract, 40 to 50 percent of which would be preserved as parks and open spaces, was rejected partly because the population limit of 50,000 was not adequate to address Amsterdam's housing shortage and partly because Het Gooi had by then become highly valued as a nature reserve, but most important, because it was already moot when it was released—Amsterdam had embarked on a General Expansion Plan (1926) that did not include a garden city in its scope.

Despite early enthusiasm for the garden city and garden suburb planning—at a 1906 meeting of the Union of Dutch Teachers, Henri Polak, a Social Democrat on the Amsterdam city council, portrayed garden villages as "broad curving lanes with large trees [and] individual houses surrounded by large gardens: here's a marvelous glimpse of Utopia"—even less ambitious efforts were difficult to get off the ground.[244] In 1913 R. de Clercq, secretary of the Dutch Garden City Association, reported being unable to "give very good news of the movement in Holland. We have tried several times to start a society for actual work, but although we have got a few people together, we have not been able to go further. It seems that Holland is not yet ready for the movement, the reason being perhaps that we have here only a few big towns and hundreds of small towns and thousands of villages, with cheap houses and gardens, while the rich people have their country seats quite close to the great towns."[245]

Nonetheless, Garden City planning principles eventually caught on, seeing widespread implementation in the late 1910s and 1920s, even if, as in the case of Germany's embrace of the movement, the Dutch examples, "apart from their abundant greenery and village atmosphere . . . scarcely lived up to Howard's description of the garden city," as Hans Ibelings notes. "They were not complete towns but mere suburbs, they were located not outside but inside or adjacent to the city, and they were not concentrically laid out."[246]

The passage of the National Housing Act in 1902 enabled the construction of a majority of the Dutch garden suburbs by providing loans to local governments and housing associations that were in turn expected to set, by example, higher standards of housing. In 1906, fourteen housing associations existed, but by 1920, after rising prices during World War I had virtually halted the private development of low-cost housing, 743 housing associations were active, a number that grew to 1,341 by 1922.[247] In addition to providing subsidies, a key piece of the legislation required each town or city with a population greater than 10,000—or that had grown over 20 percent during the previous five years—to prepare and adopt an extension plan every ten years.

In the forty years after its passage, the Housing Act provided subsidies for 20 percent of all residential complexes realized. The percentage was especially high during the teens and twenties, when garden suburbs were most popular. Significantly, as Nancy Stieber has written, prior to the Housing Act, architects viewed housing as a "problem in hygienic construction . . . The most pressing question was how to build healthful and cheap dwellings." But in the two decades after the legislation, she points out, "architects redefined not only their aesthetic treatment of housing, but also the criteria of architectural competence. The opportunities opened to architects by the Housing Act resulted in far reaching changes both in the field's professional organization and its disciplinary focus. Housing was the activity through which the Dutch architectural profession modernized."[248] Significantly, as Daniele Baroni notes, because of the ability of housing associations to build at a large scale with funds from the Housing Act, "architects—especially during the First World War period—were able to do entire residential estates, each one conceived as a whole."[249]

Villa Parks

As in England and America, the roots of Dutch suburbia can be traced to the ability of the wealthy to easily escape the city center by railroad. During the nineteenth century, villa parks designed in the romantic English landscape style began to spring up in rural areas, on open sites close to the city, and on former country estates outside of the major cities. **Kenaupark**, Haarlem, is an early example, laid out in 1868 by Jan David Zocher Jr. (1791–1870) on a 15-acre site northwest of the city center and a short walk to a railroad station.[250] News of the site's impending development led builders to construct housing around its edges, including a domineering but stately terrace of nine townhouses on the eastern border and three detached and two semidetached villas on the north. Zocher incorporated these projects into his plan that, calling for a park surrounded by houses, resembled a miniature Birkenhead or Prince's Park (see p. 32). Zocher added two semidetached and ten detached villas, four of which were set on individual parcels within the park itself. In 1873, Zocher's son, Louis Paul Zocher (1820–1915), laid out **Florapark** on the southern outskirts of Haarlem, dividing a triangular 15-acre former meadow site into four rounded blocks, the northern of which was kept open as a landscaped park and the other three built out with fifty-six detached and semidetached villas and terraces, some of the latter arranged in a formal gateway-like group in the south opposite an elliptical lawn and a now-demolished hospital.[251]

In 1881, the prominent landscape architects Hendrik Copijn (1842–1923) and Leonard Springer (1855–1940) submitted designs to a private developer for a villa park, later named **Wilhelminapark** in honor of the Dutch queen, in Zeist, an eastern suburb of Utrecht.[252] Copijn's plan placed sixty-eight houses on large, irregularly shaped lots, with meandering streets on either side of a divided boulevard grandly linking two picturesque parks. Springer chose to work on a smaller portion of the site, surrounding a central park with thirty houses on modest lots of less than one-half acre each. Both designers enlarged an existing pond and landscaped the area around it as a park. As Constance Moes points out, Copijn placed a majority of the houses on streets connecting the parks while Springer positioned the houses around—and thus seemingly within—the park itself. As a result, Springer's design had the feel of a park that made room for houses rather than a residential area incorporating parkland.[253] Copijn's design was selected on the basis that it could accommodate roughly twice as many houses as Springer's. Construction began in 1881 but sales were slow. The northern of the two parks was not realized and many of the sites were built out between 1885 and 1900 at a higher density than originally intended.

Springer was one of Holland's most prolific and highly regarded landscape architects. His work included the villa park of Zuiderhoutpark (1900) in Haarlem, later the site of Tuinwijk Zuid (see p. 531); an unrealized resort enclave, **Bergen aan Zee** (1907), where he devoted almost as much space to parkland as to houses;[254]

Kenaupark

1

2

3

4

1. Bird's-eye view, 1867. NHA

2. Aerial view. GE (2007)

3. View across park. NHA (1905)

4. Entrance at Rozenstraat. NHA

Florapark

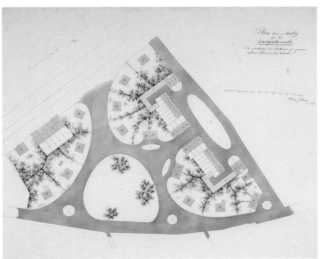

1

3

2

4

1. Plan, Louis Paul Zocher, 1873. NHA

2. Florapark. NHA (1904)

3. Florapark. Onna. NVO (2012)

4. Florapark. NHA

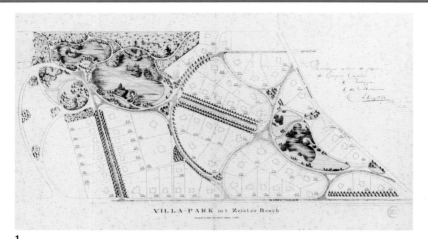

1

1. Plan, Hendrik Copijn, 1881. WUR

2. View across pond. Kreupeling. PAN (2010)

3. Plan, Leonard Springer, 1881. WUR

2

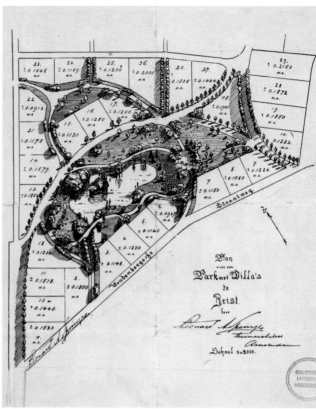

3

Bergen aan Zee

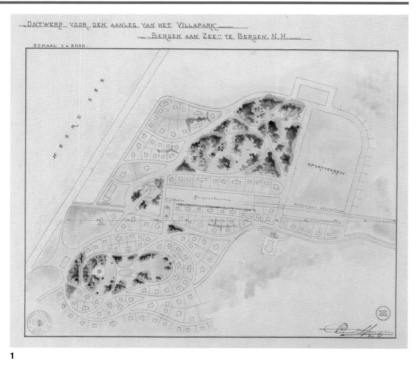

1

1. Plan, Leonard Springer, 1907. WUR

Zwaluwenberg (c. 1905), another unrealized design that placed forty-three villas on a former estate located between Utrecht and Hilversum;[255] and an unrealized villa park in **Oud-Bussum** (1903), where he screened houses from one another with mature-growth trees along the side and rear lot lines but also, to satisfy Hilversum's wealthy citizens looking for a rural retreat, provided wooded parks threaded through with paths and interspersed by lakes.[256]

Nimrodpark (1899), designed by the garden architects A. P. Smits (n.d.) and O. Schultz (n.d.), was another retreat for Hilversum's upper class.[257] The exceptionally wooded neighborhood on the northwestern outskirts of the city combined free-form and axial tree-lined streets around a landscaped green. Existing trees were used to screen properties from one another. In 1904, Hendrik Copijn designed **Diergaardepark** on an adjacent site to the south, with only twenty-six lots (many were later subdivided) along radial streets extending from a thickly wooded circular park.[258] Roughly a quarter of the site was reserved as recreational grounds bordered by winding pathways, although the area was partially developed in the 1960s with a college. **Villapark Overbeek** (1901) is another notable example, located in the town of Velp, northeast of Arnhem, where landscape architect Hugo A. C. Poortman (1858–1953), working with architect W. Honig (n.d.), who was also one of the developers and designed a number of the early houses, placed wooded lots along five curving streets organized around a network of streams and ponds that were connected by a waterfall, made possible by excavating the moat of the former estate.[259]

Zwaluwenberg

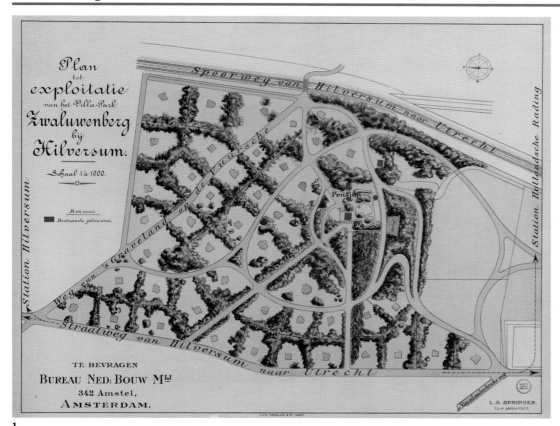

1. Plan, Leonard Springer, c. 1905.
WUR

Oud-Bussum

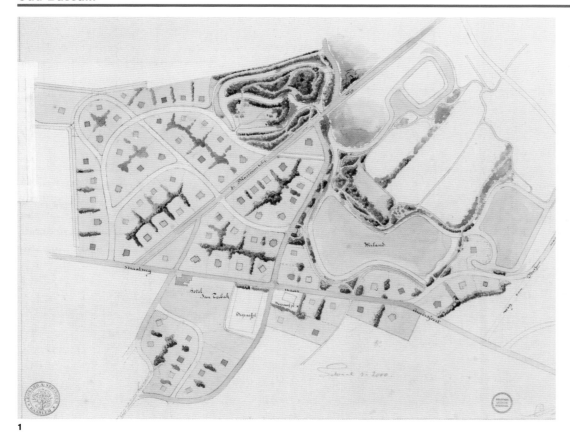

1. Plan, Leonard Springer, 1902.
WUR

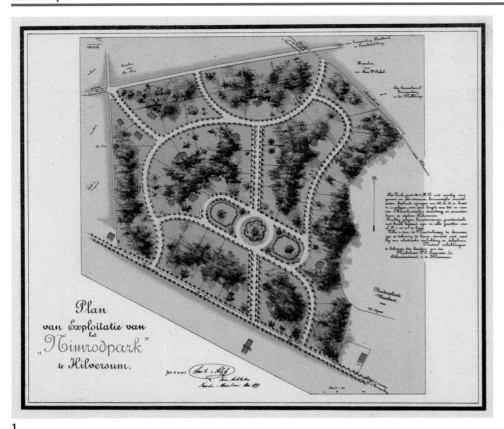

1

1. Plan, A. P. Smits and O. Schulz, 1899. WUR

2, 3. Typical streets. Onna. NVO (2012)

2

3

Diergaardepark

1

1. Typical street. Onna. NVO (2012)

Although it belongs to a later era, **Park Meerwijk** (1916–18), thirty miles north of Amsterdam in the seaside municipality of Bergen, represents the villa park's stylistic peak, a "rustic Weissenhof Siedlung," (see p. 458) as Dennis J. De Witt and Elizabeth R. De Witt have winkingly characterized it.[260] An enclave of six detached, four semidetached, and two triple houses, as well as a small summer cottage and gatehouse set amid lushly planted gardens on a single trapezoidal block traversed by a stream, Meerwijk included the work of Amsterdam School architects Jan Frederik (Fritz) Staal (1879–1940), who coordinated the project, Pieter Lodewijk Kramer (1881–1961), Cornelis Jonke Blaauw (1885–1947), Guillaume Frédéric La Croix (1877–1923), and Margaret Kropholler (1891–1966), Holland's first female architect. Developed as a speculative venture by Arnold M. A. Heystee, a tile manufacturer, Park Meerwijk represents the only collection of rural freestanding houses to be built by Amsterdam School architects, who were more typically engaged in the design of urban housing blocks. At Park Meerwijk they employed timber, brick, tile, and thatch in a freewheeling burst of Expressionism but one strongly recollecting the plan and villa design of John Nash's Blaise Hamlet (see p. 21), with houses that stand out individually yet hold together as a group.

Villapark Overbeek

1. Plan, Hugo A. C. Poortman, 1901. WUR

2–4. Typical views. Onna. NVO (2012)

Park Meerwijk

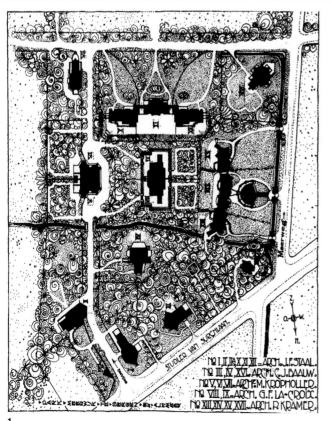

1. Plan, 1918. WUR

2–4. Typical views. Onna. NVO (2013)

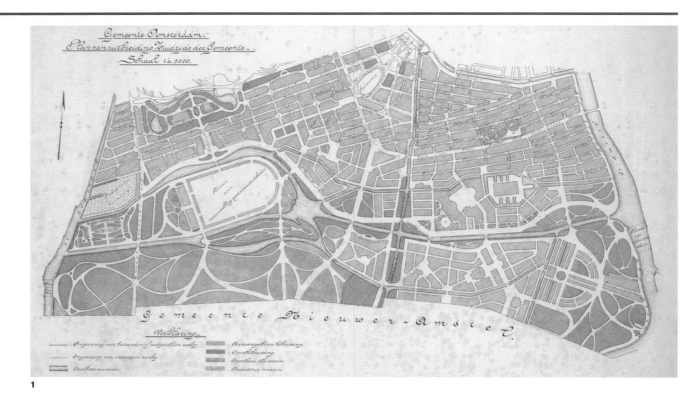

1

Rotterdam

Private developers and industrialists were relatively quick to find merit in garden suburb planning, but it was with reluctance that municipalities allowed aesthetics to join economy, hygiene, and functionality as a priority in laying out new areas. Amsterdam became the first major Dutch city to wrest planning out of the technical hands of the civil engineer when in 1899 Hendrik Petrus Berlage (1856–1934) was commissioned to design a southern extension known as **Plan-Zuid**.[261] The decision came after a wave of new districts had come under attack for their bleakness, the most egregious of which, the Pijp, a triangular area with long narrow streets designed by city engineer J. G. van Niftrik (1833–1910) on the southern outskirts of the city, was described in 1897 as "the ultimate expression of *la vie grise*, the negation of all except empty boredom, a monument to laissez-faire and private enterprise, and also to the taste of the politicians."[262]

Berlage, whose impact on Dutch architecture cannot be overstated, was also the most influential voice in town planning, a studious observer and active lecturer who argued in 1914 after more than a decade of advocacy that "if one wishes that the plan satisfy all practical requirements with mathematical accuracy, then an engineer should make the plan; if, on the other hand, one wishes that the plan be a work of art, that is, that all the parts be composed into a whole not only scientifically but also aesthetically and practically, then an architect should do it."[263] Completed in 1900, approved in 1905, and ratified in 1906, Berlage's Plan-Zuid was part medieval townscape and part English romantic park, overtly picturesque and abundantly green, but ultimately too expensive to be built.

Berlage's work on Plan-Zuid captured the attention of **The Hague**, where officials hired him to improve upon a 1903 plan by I. A. Lindo (n.d.), the public works director whose scheme was rejected in 1907.[264] Rather than take over completely, Berlage collaborated with Lindo on the revision, prepared between 1907 and 1911, that featured not only tweaked details but also bold new gestures such as the addition of monumental plazas and squares, a large park in the southwest, and what Sergio Polano characterized as "a well-conceived chain of partial plans . . . a continuous band of neighborhoods" that circled the city while leaving space, particularly in the north, for interstitial parks.[265] On a site in the northeast, Berlage resuscitated architect K. P. C. de Bazel's 1905 **World Capital Foundation of Internationalism** scheme, reinterpreting it as a self-sustained garden city buffered by parks and agricultural land.[266] The radial plan featured relatively dense inner blocks giving way to neighborhoods of detached villas comfortably placed along curving streets. While that portion of the plan was never executed, other aspects of Berlage's design were followed as The Hague developed into the 1940s.

The closest Berlage came to realizing a garden village was not in Amsterdam but in Rotterdam, where **Vreewijk Garden Village**, the first large-scale implementation of Garden City ideas in Holland, was built in phases between 1916 and 1942 to include 5,700 rowhouses spread across 420 acres.[267] The development, according to Donald Grinberg, which was among the "most successful syntheses of the Housing Act, the Dutch garden city movement, and architectural design sensitivity . . . both influenced the development of Modernist housing in Holland and eventually suggested grounds for its rejection."[268]

The Hague

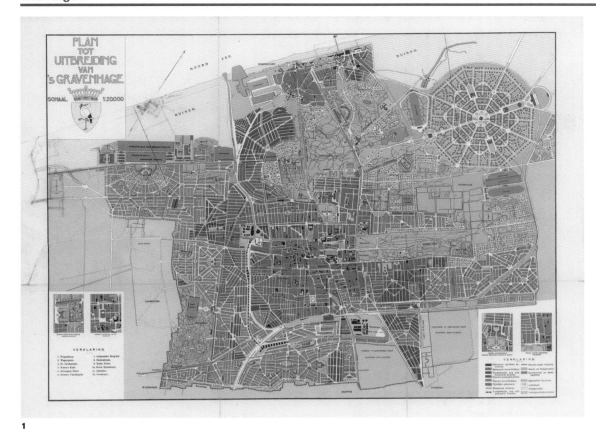

1. Plan, Hendrik Petrus Berlage
and I. A. Lindo, 1907–11. NAI

1

World Capital Foundation of Internationalism

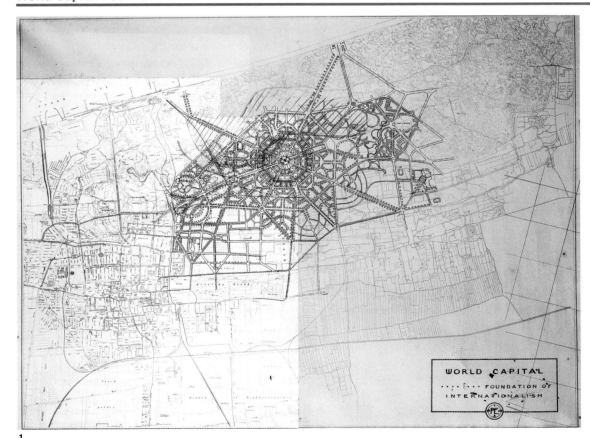

1. Plan, K. P. C. de Bazel, 1905. NAI

1

The garden village concept came to Rotterdam after officials within the Department of Public Works, inspired by English examples, looked to the type as "the most ideal solution for the working-class districts of the future" and began to promote their construction on the river Maas's rural left bank.[269] The idea was embraced by Karel Paul van der Mandele (1880–1975), a banker who in 1913 enlisted a group of similar-minded businessmen to establish NV Eerste Rotterdamse Tuindorp (First Rotterdam Garden Village, Ltd.), intending to provide housing for the "less prosperous social class."[270] As realized, Vreewijk would acquire a population of middle-class workers, such as office clerks, council officials, and teachers, as well as manual laborers who were screened for eligibility.

Development of the site began in the east, on a roughly square shaped area divided into quarters by two 55-meter-wide thoroughfares: Lange Geer, with a central canal running north–south, and Groene Zoom, a partially divided boulevard running east–west. Berlage laid out the northwest quadrant in 1913, but by the time the plan was approved in 1916, obligations to another client had forced him to hand the project down to architect Marinus Jan Granpré Molière (1883–1972), who revised Berlage's work and designed the remainder of Vreewijk in partnership with landscape architect Pieter Verhagen (1882–1950) and architect A. J. Th. Kok (1874?–1941). Architects J. H. De Roos (1875–1942) and W. F. Overeijnder (1875–1941) designed the houses east of Meiendaal.

Working on a 39.5-acre, kite-shaped tract, Berlage, displaying "more than just sympathy for the garden city ideas," devoted roughly 20 percent of the site to public green space and called for a density of sixteen houses per acre, resulting in an openness that, with the exception of Heijplaat (see p. 771), was unknown in Rotterdam.[271] Berlage transformed existing drainage ditches into canals, one of which he flanked with streets and landscaped verges to become a principal boulevard, the 45-meter-wide Lede, running diagonally northeast–southwest across the site. A second boulevard, the 22-meter-wide Dreef, crossed the Lede at its midpoint, forming a main intersection where Berlage placed the Brink, or village green, designed as Willemijn Wilms Floet has noted, as a "Berlagian fork," with "two small squares and a gateway building, arranged along a diagonal axis of symmetry."[272] The presence of a community center on the Brink provided a civic focus, but there was no commercial center in Vreewijk. Instead, shops were placed in the ends of rowhouses throughout the neighborhood. A post office, a hotel, a restaurant, and athletic fields were also included, but Vreewijk was primarily residential, eventually feeding off of adjacent areas for commercial and public amenities.

Despite an almost complete avoidance of curves, Berlage introduced variety through carefully studied, asymmetrical street profiles, jogged roads creating closed vistas, plantings that varied from block to block, and the occasional insertion of aberrant house types.

The street plan was vaguely oriented along north–south lines to maximize sunlight exposure, and front gardens were only included on streets where plants would prosper, recognizing, as Edith Elmer Wood put it, that "no garden at all looks better than one which is ragged."[273] Rear yards were provided for each house, backing up to common courtyards threaded through with a complete network of footpaths.

Granpré Molière's plans for the remainder of Vreewijk were less nuanced, calling for elongated north–south rectangular blocks rarely interrupted by cross streets. To cut housing costs, the use of standardized middle units was maximized, with rows reaching 240 meters in length, occasionally broken and set back and forth from the street to allow footpaths into the block interiors that, because the corners of the blocks were left open, were more easily identified as public space. Over time, material shortages and reduced budgets led to the inclusion of tall, habitable roofs that were pitched steeply enough to essentially replace the brick of the second story with roof tiles, which were not only cheaper but, owing to their lightness in weight, also allowed for less expensive foundations. Granpré Molière himself bemoaned the fact that the architecture was "rather shabby, even if 'bedecked with nature's mantle.'"[274]

Vreewijk made a strong impression, attracting, as Mieke Dings has noted, "designers and policymakers from all over the country [who] came . . . to see this example of a successful urban extension."[275] Despite the modernity inherent in the standardized construction, floor plans, and building materials, the traditional architecture divided the Dutch avant-garde. Jan Duiker (1890–1935) admired the "spacious dwellings, landscaping, and open site planning," but Johannes Bernardus van Loghem (1881–1940), designer of Tuinwijk Zuid, called the houses *boerenwoning architecture*—peasant architecture," and Mart Stam (1899–1986) took issue with the pitched roofs: "If the minimal dwelling has no attic . . . so much the better. The people will not cling to everything: neither Grandmama's furniture nor memories of youth."[276] Stylistic quibbles notwithstanding, Vreewijk's role as the first garden village within the boundaries of a major Dutch city was significant. "It was primarily through this urban design," according to Mieke Dings, "that Howard's model came to the attention of Dutch municipal leaders, enriching the Dutch debate over urban design and over the status of designers within the municipality."[277]

Hilversum

No Dutch city became more closely associated with the work of its municipal architect than Hilversum, where between 1916 and 1952 Willem Marinus Dudok (1884–1974) designed twenty-five municipal housing complexes in addition to numerous public buildings, including the Raadhuis (Town Hall) (1924–30), his best-known work.[278] Serving as director of public works between 1915

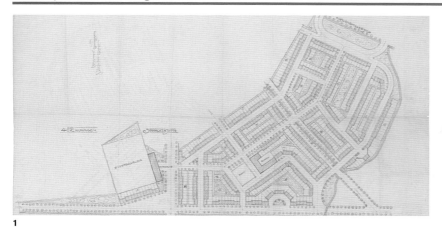

1

2

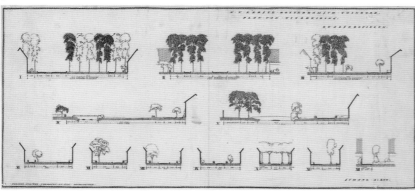

3

4

5

6

1. Plan, Hendrik Petrus Berlage, 1913–16. NAI

2. Plan, Granpré Molière, Verhagen & Kok, 1916–19. NAI

3. Street profiles, 1916–19. NAI

4. Communal yard with playground. ACA (1913–22)

5. Typical street. ACA (1913–22)

6. Brink. ACA (1913–22)

7. Gateway to the Brink. ACA (1913–22)

8, 9. Typical streets. Onna. NVO (2012)

7

8

9

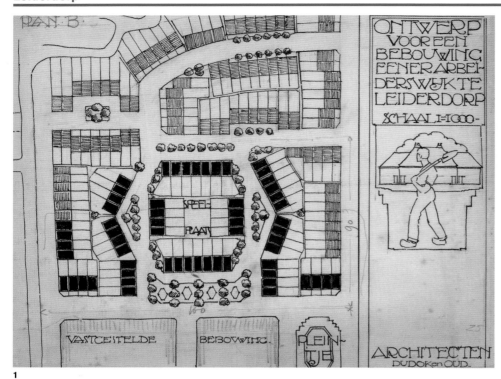

1. Plan, Willem Marinus Dudok and J. J. P. Oud, 1913. NAI

2. Typical view. NAI (c. 1915)

and 1927 and city architect from 1928 until 1954, Dudok was also responsible for nearly every aspect of the public realm including transportation infrastructure, parks and gardens, fire safety, sewers, and telephone, electric, gas, and water utilities.

Located fewer than twenty miles southeast of Amsterdam and twelve miles from Utrecht, Hilversum developed an urgent need for housing during the first decades of the twentieth century, when the former market town boomed as a commuter suburb of Amsterdam, a popular tourist destination, and the center of Holland's broadcasting industry. Although the municipally sponsored projects were built primarily for working-class families, Hilversum, as Joseph Buch has written, was "fertile ground for architecture, similar to Wright's Oak Park—a growing population with above-average income and education, who were looking for town amenities amid country serenity."[279]

After beginning his career as an engineer in the military, Dudok assumed a two-year post as assistant director of public works in Leiden, during which time he collaborated with J. J. P. Oud on the design of a small neighborhood in **Leiderdorp** (1914–16) built for the Dorpsbelant Housing Association.[280] It was the first significant town planning project for both architects and they turned to Raymond Unwin's *Town Planning in Practice* for guidance, producing a design that, although "more Spartan," has been characterized as "one of the most authentic examples of English (Parker & Unwin) garden city-inspired housing in the Netherlands," with twenty-three houses in rows of up to seven units, as well as a mixed-use building facing a public square.[281] Red-tile roofs enlivened by cupolas, chimneys, and dormer windows complemented a landscape plan that provided

street trees as well as small street-facing parks. The neighborhood was razed in 1978.

When Dudok took office in Hilversum, the city had acquired a "star-like aspect" in which development occurred in nodes along main routes to and from the center. "From the very start," Dudok stated in 1934, "I have aimed at concentration . . . and have strongly opposed ribbon development which extends the town and robs it of its unity, so destroying both town and country. Building was first begun in parts either neglected or casually left open; the star-like development had to make way for the central growth of a flower."[282] A strong proponent of preserving agricultural land beyond the city's boundaries, Dudok successfully advocated for the establishment of a 3,800-acre greenbelt by the neighboring city of Amsterdam so that, combined with swaths of woodlands purchased by Hilversum, the provincial town, as Dudok noted, was "almost entirely enclosed by a natural reserve, in the same manner as a medieval town was hemmed in by its fortifications."[283]

In designing the housing complexes, Dudok sought to combine "two values, town and country, entirely different, but complementing each other so beautifully, in the same way that in an harmonious building the vertical element can resonate with the horizontal."[284] Although no two were alike, the projects shared certain characteristics, typically including public buildings such as primary schools (he designed nineteen in Hilversum), bathhouses, libraries, or abattoirs, designed in a sophisticated manner that combined De Stijl aesthetics and local brickwork. The housing he designed, however, "was generally rather plain, in the simplified traditional style in common use throughout the country," as Joseph Buch has observed.[285] Despite its vernacular roots, Dudok's housing in the teens

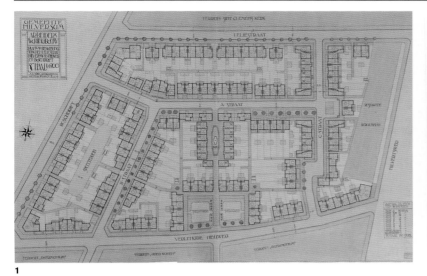

1. Plan, Willem Marinus Dudok, 1916. SGV1

2. Aerial view showing 1st, 2nd, 5th, and 7th Municipal Housing Complexes. GE (2007)

3. 141 and 143 Papaverstraat. SGV0 (1918)

4. Papaverstraat. SGV0 (1918)

and twenties was finely detailed, innovative, and thoughtfully conceived, but by the 1930s, dwindling resources led to simplifications, a condition that further degenerated in the post–World War II era when relatively prosaic rows of multistory apartment buildings prevailed.

In the **First Municipal Housing Complex** (1915–19), bound by Bosdrift, Leliestraat, Hilvertsweg, and Neuweg, Dudok placed 180 dwellings around a public library that doubled as a gatehouse, set back on a landscaped court (now partially lost to automobile parking) at the southern edge of the site. The reading room sat above an arched passageway leading north into the quiet neighborhood while a second portal provided access from Leliestraat in the north. Although diverse in their massing and expression, the houses were built from standardized types and used inexpensive materials—brick, which had yet to see the drastic price increases that came with World War I, combined with white and yellow stucco, and tile roofs—making them affordable to the lower class. The alternation of types, varied groupings, staggered alignments, and differences in detail and roof profiles gave each street its own identity. Dudok generally kept the rowhouses close to the streets, stepping them back and forth modestly to allow for rear yards backing up to pedestrian pathways and courts.

Adjacent to the south, the **Second Municipal Housing Complex** (1918–20) comprised three east–west oriented blocks with more than a dozen groups of houses in which a wider range of types accommodated higher-income residents. Dudok focused the complex around the Geraniumschool (1917–18) whose splayed west-facing wings embraced a landscaped court and whose prominent tower served as a landmark visible from surrounding areas. To the east of the First and Second complexes, the **Fifth Municipal Housing Complex** (1920–22) added a commercial component, with a cluster of shops at the intersection of Neuweg and Hilvertsweg near the northern entrance to a series of intimately scaled Sitte-esque streets bordered by erratically angled and setback houses, all centered around the Oranjeschool, whose pinwheel-like wings defined playgrounds and parks. The Seventh Municipal Housing Complex (1922–23) extended the Fifth to the east along Fuchsiastraat, consisting of twenty-one houses built according to three types.

Taken together, these initial developments, with a density of about twenty-four houses per acre, exemplified, according to Herman van Bergeijk, Dudok's view of the town "as consisting of different 'rooms.' Visual key points not only had to reinforce the orientation towards the neighborhood, but also that within it. A school was therefore soon fitted with a tower, and from afar could be taken for a church. Staggered building lines, bends in streets and an articulated design of the built block

5. Anemonestraat. SGV0 (1920)

6. First design of the street walls. SGV1 (1916)

7. Library and gatehouse building. Onna. NVO (2012)

8, 9. Typical houses. Onna. NVO (2012)

5

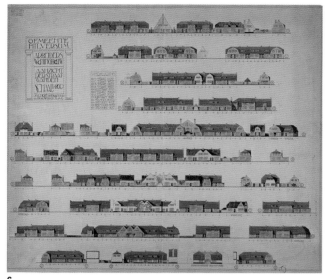

6

7

8

9

Second Municipal Housing Complex

1. Typical view. SGV0 (1917)

2. Geraniumschool. Onna. NVO (2012)

1

2

helped to give the neighborhood a distinct recognizability . . . Public greenery, low walls and flowerpots were standard elements in designing the neighborhood."[286]

The **Third Municipal Housing Complex** (1919–20), at Huygenstraat, built across the railroad tracks that separated Hilversum's southern and eastern outskirts, was a compact development comprised of a single T-shaped building in which a public bathhouse formed the hinge between two wings containing eleven houses. A courtyard provided public open space, but the houses also featured private gardens. With a passage through its base

and a prominent chimney, the bathhouse served as a focal point in the neighborhood but was closed down in 1970 and the complex was later demolished.

In the **Fourth Municipal Housing Complex** (1920–21), occupying a north-pointing triangular site, Dudok first began to differentiate the public buildings from the housing, exploring the functionalist language that would reach full bloom in his Raadhuis design. At the north end of the site, within a park at the acute angled intersection of Hilvertsweg and Bosdrift, Dudok's flat-roofed, cubistic, brown-brick bathhouse, with a tall chimney

Fifth Municipal Housing Complex

1

1. Plan, Willem Marinus Dudok, 1921. SGV1

2. Lupinestraat. Deul. SGV0 (1921)

3. Typical street. Onna. NVO (2012)

2

3

Third Municipal Housing Complex

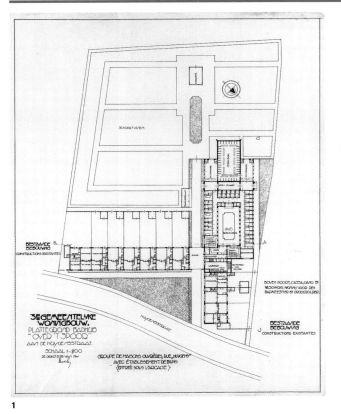

1

2

1. Plan, Willem Marinus Dudok, 1921. SGV1

2. Bathhouse, Huygensstraat. SGV0 (c. 1922)

at the center of a symmetrical facade, had a decidedly industrial look that was accentuated by its juxtaposition with the traditional housing block across the street. The Bavinckschool (1922) shared a similar aesthetic, bordering the site on the south. Vernacular-style rowhouses edged the east and west sides, with small sheds in the rear gardens lining a quiet pathway between the bathhouse and school.

In the **Sixth Municipal Housing Complex** (1921–23), geared toward lower-income working-class families, Dudok wrapped forty-two modest, attached single-story houses around a landscaped square, Edisonplein, that was accessible only through a break in the houses in the west and a portal in the base of a two-story section in the east. By providing the cloistered courtyard and adding green, red, orange, and white accents to the houses, Dudok hoped to eliminate the "stamp of inferiority" typical of working-class neighborhoods. Two-story blocks alternated with one-story rows beyond the inner ring so that as Herman van Bergeijk has observed, "viewed from the square, the roofs of the higher housing complexes to the rear are

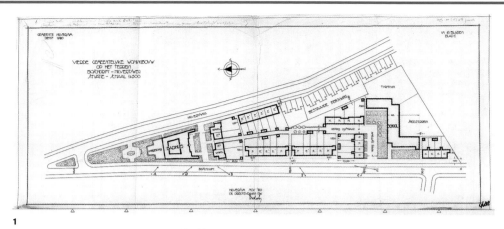

1

2

3

4

5

1. Plan, Willem Marinus Dudok, 1921. SGV1

2. Bathhouse, left, and houses. SGV0 (1921)

3. Rear pathway. Onna. NVO (2012)

4. Houses on Bosdrift. Onna. NVO (2012)

5. View of bathhouse through archway. Onna. NVO (2012)

conspicuous, which gives the whole a pleasing effect in plastic aesthetic terms."[287]

The **Tenth Municipal Housing Complex** (1927–28) was the first of a series in which a reduced budget called for greater standardization of house types and less emphasis on nuanced site planning. Here, Dudok lined the houses up in long rows arranged parallel to the street. Stripped of ornament, it became more difficult to discern individual residences, while the facades, with ground-floor windows grouped horizontally and ribbon windows introduced just beneath the eaves or in some cases above them as continuous dormers, were interrupted only by pairs of tall rectangular brick slabs demarcating the pedestrian passageways. Two blocks to the north, in the **Thirteenth Municipal Housing Complex** (1929–30), the rows grew even longer but featured more traditional round archways. In the **Fourteenth Municipal Housing Complex** (1929), directly west of the Edisonplein, the product was further diminished, with unadorned rectangular portals leading through the buildings. Despite the comparatively bleak housing, Dudok's layout of the tree-lined Edisonstraat, leading past a pair of gatehouse-like rows on the west

to the Edisonplein entrance on the east, was intimately scaled, with trees, hedges, and small gardens providing a sense of seclusion that was also present in the **Eleventh Municipal Housing Complex** (1927–28), where Duivenstraat, a single, angled street cutting the corner between Minckelerstraat and Valkstraat incorporated a grassy median overlooked by two rows of one-story houses bookended by two-story gabled blocks of brick and wood.

As municipal work slowed down during the 1930s and Dudok spent more time on private commissions, the garden village aspect of Hilversum's housing complexes was virtually eliminated, although the **Eighteenth Municipal Complex** (1931–35), oriented counter to the surrounding blocks, was notable for its two parallel two-story rows, punctuated by the occasional three-story house, combining with shorter end rows to enclose common space on the block interior.

The evolution of Dudok's garden village work from vernacularism to functionalism was as much a matter of aesthetics as economics. But as early as 1923, the noted American housing specialist Edith Elmer Wood, perhaps anticipating the spreading popularity of functionalism

Sixth Municipal Housing Complex

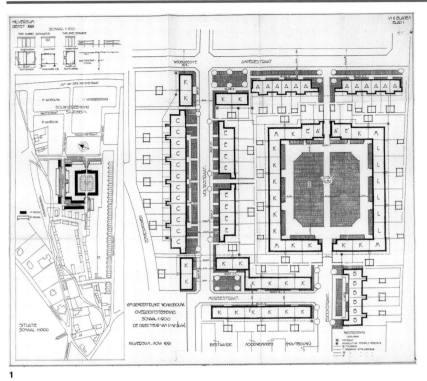

1

2

3

1. Plan, Willem Marinus Dudok, 1921. SGV1

2. Aerial view. GE (2007)

3. Edisonplein. SGV0 (1922)

Tenth Municipal Housing Complex

1

2

1. Merelstraat. Deul. SGV0 (1928)

2. Houses. Onna. NVO (2012)

Thirteenth Municipal Housing Complex

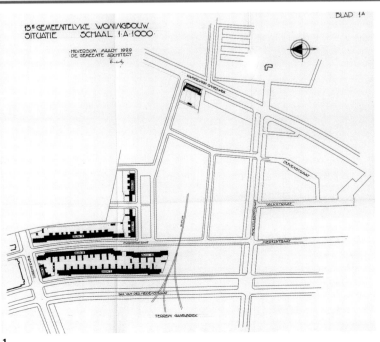

1

2

1. Plan, Willem Marinus Dudok, 1929. SGV1

2. Jan van der Heijdenstraat. Deul. SGV0 (1929)

Fourteenth Municipal Housing Complex

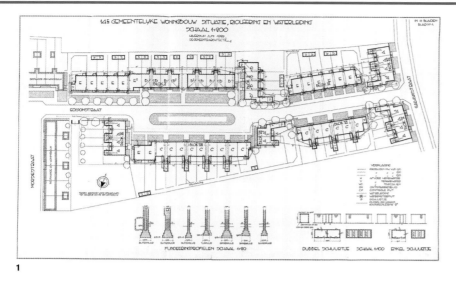

1

2

1. Plan, Willem Marinus Dudok,
1930. SGV1

2. Edisonstraat. Onna. NVO (2012)

Eleventh Municipal Housing Complex

1. Plan, Willem Marinus Dudok,
1927. SGV1

2. Duivenstraat. Onna. NVO (2012)

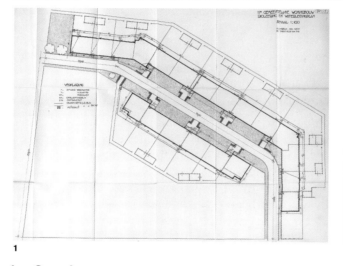

1

2

Eighteenth Municipal Housing Complex

1. Dudokplein. Onna. NVO (2012)
2. Aerial view. GE (2007)

1

2

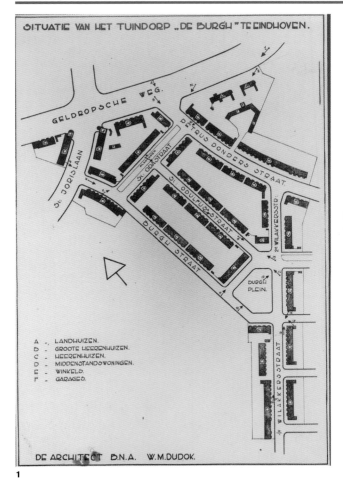

1. Plan, Willem Marinus Dudok, 1938. NAI

2. Typical view. NAI (c. 1938)

3–5. Typical views. Onna. NVO (2007)

but certainly aware of the banality of market-driven housing in the United States, voiced her preference for Dudok's traditional houses, writing that the cottages were "thoroughly and essentially Dutch—and that is why I like them so much. They preserve the red tile roofs of Holland and the traditional aspect of a Dutch cottage, than which no more peaceful, homelike, wholesome type exists. Why should a country blessed with red tile roofs want to trade them off for our ugly flat roofs? . . . Wherever one goes in the Hilversum Garden Suburb," Wood observed, "there are vistas, interesting both in form and color,—a great deal of variety with complete, essential unity of style and purpose. All this has been brought about by the use of very simple and inexpensive means. The varying angles of the roofs, the heights and widths of chimneys, the sizes and groupings of windows, the shapes of the window panes, the treatment of front doors, the occasional use of a low brick wall on the boundary line,—these and a hundred other details have been employed to bring about the desired effects."[288]

Dudok's most characteristic garden suburb—**De Burgh Garden City** (1937–38)—is not in Hilversum but in Eindhoven, in the southern part of Holland.[289] With its plan of straight, crooked, and softly arcing streets terminating in closed vistas and making room for a secluded green, De Burgh Garden City accommodated 265 one- to three-story houses in long rows broken up by an occasional extra story and terminated by rotated end units. Dudok left the corners of the blocks open. The whitewashed brick houses with red-tile gable and saltbox roofs recalled Oud's Oud-Mathenesse (see p. 777) and earned the district the same nickname, "White Village." Dudok set the houses back behind hedge-lined gardens and included a wide planting strip on the north side of Sint Odastraat. Automobile garages were also provided on some block interiors, and while shops were integrated into the plan—one of which seemed a direct homage to the curving storefronts in Oud's Hoek of Holland (see p. 778)—other public amenities were within walking distance. Occupying a middle ground between the traditional and modern, De Burgh was the last convincing prewar Dutch garden village.

Amsterdam

Despite the seemingly innumerable housing developments contributing to Amsterdam's expansion in the early part of the century, examples of garden villages are rare. **Watergraafsmeer Garden Village** (1923–27), like its Belgian contemporary Kapelleveld, had a double personality, with 1,000 traditional style houses adjacent to 900 experimental concrete dwellings making up the district known as **Betondorp** (the "concrete village").[290] Betondorp signified the first large-scale use of concrete for

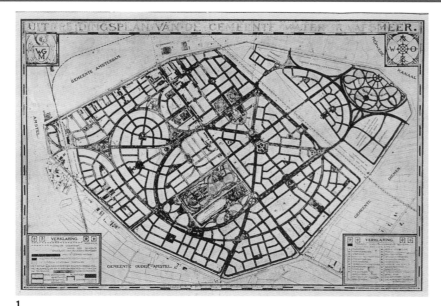

1. Unrealized master plan by Pieter Vorkink and J. Ph. Wormser, 1906–7. NAI

2. Plan, Jan Gratama and G. Versteeg, 1918. NAI

3. Design for a workers' garden village, J. F. Repko, 1915. PRIJ

4. Houses designed by W. Greve. ACA (1925)

5. Brink. ACA

6. Houses on corner of Weidestraat and Gaffelstraat in Watergraafsmeer, Jan Gratama and G. Versteeg, 1921. ACA

7. Houses on Schovenstraat, J. B. van Loghem, 1925. ACA (c. 1925)

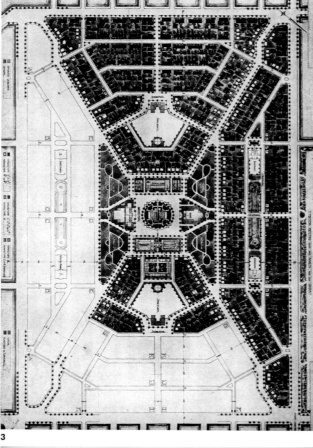

8

9

8. Brink. Onna. NVO (2012)

9. Houses on Veeteeltstraat, D. Greiner. Bakker. WC (2011)

10. Corner of Duivendrechtselaan and Graanstraat, showing houses and shops by W. Greve, 1923–25. Onna. NVO (2012)

11. Harkstraat, Watergraafsmeer. RAMSA (2012)

12. Aerial view. GE (2004)

10

11

12

residential construction in the Netherlands. The material had previously been used in factories and engineering works, but it was usually replaced by plaster-covered brick when specified for houses.

Watergraafsmeer, a thirty-minute tram ride southeast of central Amsterdam, was annexed by the city in 1921 after roughly two decades of resistance that included the preparation of a master plan in 1906 intended to assert the municipality's independence. The unrealized plan, by architects Pieter Vorkink (1878–1960) and J. Ph. Wormser (1878–1935), envisioned a population of 250,000 and incorporated parks and gardens, cultural institutions, churches, schools, hotels, and a hospital, as well as an industrial district and workers' village located in the north across the railroad tracks connecting Amsterdam with Hilversum.

In 1917, Arie Keppler (1876–1941), the ambitious director of Amsterdam's municipal housing department, oversaw the purchase of part of the Watergraafsmeer site and the following year retained Jan Gratama (1877–1947) and G. Versteeg (n.d.) to lay out a working-class village. The team based their design on geometries that had been established in the earlier plan, specifically the inclusion of a central Brink, or village

green, surrounded by radial streets extending through residential areas that included culs-de-sac, squares, and gardens. The layout also resembled the competition-winning design (1915) by J. F. Repko (1883–1955) for a workers' garden village that Berlage included in his second Plan-Zuid.

Eschewing Amsterdam's typical street-defining perimeter block, Gratama and Versteeg, as Helen Searing has noted, called for "straight or picturesquely curved or staggered rows" of between two and twenty units "that do not meet at the corners, so that the definition between public and private areas is less strict than in the case of the perimeter block, resulting in a much lower density development than in other districts of Amsterdam."[291] The rows were to be set back from the sidewalk on gardens and include additional private gardens off of rear kitchens.

Work began on the traditional section to the northeast of the Brink in 1921, and 300 brick and steep-pitched tile-roofed houses, designed by Gratama and Versteeg and sponsored by the Eigen Haard and Algemene Woninbouw Vereeniging housing associations, were completed within a year. In addition to the houses, stores were provided along two streets. However, as work continued, Keppler, a "card-carrying paternalistic" Socialist faced with a severe housing shortage, rising brick prices, and a surfeit of unemployed unskilled laborers, determined that switching to concrete for the rest of the village could, as Marieke Kuipers put it, "kill three birds with one stone: break the monopoly of the brick manufacturers, tackle the housing crisis, and ultimately help the unemployed find work."[292]

In 1922, after embarking on a study trip to England where he turned up more examples of steel than concrete construction but was nonetheless emboldened, as P. K. A. Pennink writes, by "an atmosphere in which experimenting with untraditional building methods was not shunned and . . . in which the idea of garden cities was in anything but ailing condition," Keppler issued a request for proposals for Betondorp's 300 single-family and 600 two-family houses.[293] To choose among the more than fifty submissions and to administer the implementation of the plan, he assembled a panel consisting of Jan Frederik Staal, Berend Tobias Boeyinga (1886–1969), and Pieter Vorkink, all members of the Club of Amsterdam Housing Architects. Vorkink was also an author of the 1906 plan.

Seven contractors were chosen to build houses designed by nine architects: Dirk Roosenburg (1887–1962), J. B. van Loghem, Dick Greiner (1891–1964), Jan Gratama, J. Hulsbosch (n.d.), W. Greve Jr. (n.d.), Herman Frederik Mertens (1885–1964), J. H. Mulder (1900–1988), and H. W. Valk (1886–1973). Ten building systems were employed, based on the three principal methods of concrete construction—concrete block, poured, and prefabricated. A fourth process was used on four houses in which concrete was sprayed onto steel frames and mesh to form exterior surfaces.

The house plans were subject to strict guidelines that dictated the dimensions and layout, mandating, for example, the location of living rooms in the front, kitchens in the rear, and the provision of a water closet but no shower, leaving the architects to do most of their heavy creative lifting in the massing and exterior finishes. Although varied widely in detail, the houses were almost entirely two-story, cubic volumes with smooth surfaces and flat roofs, "sober, abstract designs," according to Erik Mattie, occasionally dressed up with ornamental panels and tile work.[294]

J. B. van Loghem and Dick Greiner's work was widely hailed as the most interesting. Greiner, "more than any other individual involved in designing for the garden suburb," according to Searing, "seems to have transcended the financial restrictions and difficulties of the experimental medium to achieve an architecture comparable to the best brick housing erected by his fellow members of the Amsterdam School . . . The hauntingly memorable character" of his houses on Zaiersweg and parts of Veeteeltstraat and Graanstraat, employing one of the more sophisticated construction systems in which concrete panels were poured on site and then hoisted into place, featured protruding polygonal living rooms and horizontal striations on the facades.[295] Van Loghem's houses along Schovenstraat and Graanstraat were also a cut above the norm, with black varnish bands and decorative panels above the grouped doorways that have unfortunately been replaced by lesser designs. On the corners of Onderlangs and Schovenstraat and Duivendrechtselaan and Graanstraat, W. Greve placed cubistic three-story striated volumes forming a distinctive gateway to the van Loghem houses.

The Brink was the last component to be built, with construction beginning in 1925 after 800 concrete houses had been finished. The double symmetry of Gratama's plan was difficult to detect at street level as a result of the lushly planted green but more so the varied massing of the surrounding buildings that, as designed by Greiner, "not only gave an urbane focus to the entire garden suburb but deftly harmonized its disparate parts," according to Searing.[296] Included around the Brink were houses and apartments, a community center with residences for senior citizens, shops, offices, a café, storage spaces, a public reading room, two meeting halls for community activities, and parking lots and bike sheds. Initial plans to include bachelors' residences, a bathhouse, and a Montessori school proved too expensive. Churches—and pubs—were prohibited from the village, so Greiner provided an iconic secular spire, a clock tower on the Brink-Veeteeltstraat. The ban on churches was lifted after World War II.

As planning for the Brink began, debate broke out as to whether to revert to brick construction. Advocates for brick had a clear aesthetic preference for the material that was aided by its falling price, but their claims of rampant failure of concrete in the houses proved to be overblown. Ultimately the Korrelbeton system of poured concrete was chosen. Yet after several of the Brink's buildings had gone up, Greiner himself voiced some concern: "The dull grey color of the facades forces us to paint the window-frames and doors in strong, bright colors . . . It goes almost without saying that we count on the planting of a considerable amount of greenery, which would certainly be suitable here."[297] The strategy worked wonders not only on the Brink but throughout the residential streets.

Eventually the untested nature of the concrete revealed itself. After World War II, many houses had to be sheathed in wood or tar paper, particularly those made of concrete block. Some were lost, including houses by W. Greve, torn down in the 1950s. Renovations on the entire village began in the 1970s. In the end, as Searing has noted, Betondorp was a "vivid representative of the aggressive housing policy pursued by the municipality of Amsterdam" during the 1920s. "In particular, it fulfills the Social Democratic goal of offering the workers an alternative to the densely populated inner city, in the form of low-rise housing in an open landscape where they could share the middle-class idyll of living close to nature."[298]

Outside of Betondorp, garden village planning in Amsterdam occurred mostly in a series of neighborhoods built during the 1920s in Amsterdam North,

Tuindorp Oostzaan

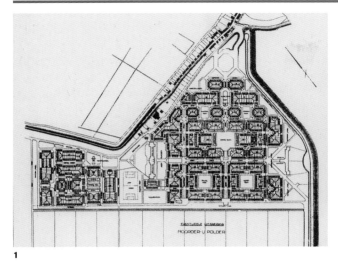

1

2

3

4

1. Plan, B. T. Boeyinga and J. H.
Mulder, 1920. ACA

2. Rear gardens. ACA (1921)

3. Central square. Onna. NVO
(2012)

4. View through portal. Onna. NVO
(2012)

Buiksloterham

1

2

1. Aerial view. GE (2004)

2. Typical street. RAMSA (2012)

across the river IJ from the city center where a three-story height limit was established in the late 1910s. **Tuindorp** (garden village) **Oostzaan** (1919–30), built by the Municipal Housing Authority on a distant north-western site, featured an orthogonal plan by B. T. Boeyinga and J. H. Mulder that accommodated 1,300 brick rowhouses along narrow residential streets, a central village square lined by arcaded shops, numerous smaller squares and playgrounds, schools, shops, a library, and public baths.[299] Painted wood was used to brighten up the buildings around the main square as well as the pedestrian and automobile passage-ways dispersed throughout the district. The village was expanded to the south in the 1930s. **Buiksloterham** was another development built by the housing authority,

which retained a private architect, J. E. van der Pek (n.d.), to lay out and design 560 houses for people displaced by slum clearance programs.[300] Prepared in 1916 and built in 1921, the plan featured an axial tree-lined boulevard, short curved terraces, and long rowhouses that despite the inclusion of yellow brick courses and the periodic insertion of parks and playgrounds, made for a somewhat monotonous streetscape.

The most interesting of the Amsterdam North garden villages was **Nieuwendam I** (1924–27), planned by Boeyinga to include 1,000 houses designed by four architects—Jan Boterenbrood (1886–1932), J. H. Mulder, J. Roodenburgh (1886–1972), and J. Zietsma (1893–1962)—each working in his own designated section.[301] Around the central Purmerplein, an octagonal public

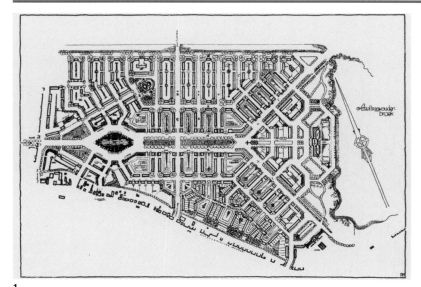

1. Plan, B. T. Boeyinga, 1920. ACA

2. Edammerstraat, showing houses by J. Roodenburgh. ACA (1935)

3. Ilpendammerstraat, showing houses by J. Boterenbrood. ACA (1935)

4. Purmerplein. ACA (1928)

5. Pathway between houses on Blokkerstraat and Wijdenesserstraat. ACA (c. 1926)

6. Purmerplein. Onna. NVO (2012)

7. Gateway building on Purmerweg, B. T. Boeyinga. Onna. NVO (2012)

1

square, Boeyinga designed distinctive three-story mixed-use buildings that featured tall roofs, half-octagonal ends, and ground-floor shops shaded by flat, cantilevered canopies. Boeyinga also designed the stores and apartments along Purmerweg, the district's main axis, a broad tree-lined divided boulevard, employing white-, green-, and black-painted wooden bands to mark passageways leading to intimately scaled residential streets beyond. Public buildings were also provided. The district's abundant greenery helped disguise the overall geometry of the plan, as did the diversity of house groupings, roof profiles, materials, and colors employed by the different architects.

Haarlem

In Haarlem, the two-block **Tuinwijk Zuid** (1919–22) enclave, designed by J. B. van Loghem, stood in stark contrast to its surrounding neighborhood, the well-to-do Zuiderhoutpark, designed by Leonard Springer in 1900 in the romantic style of an English park.[302] Working on an almost ideal site bound on the east by a broad tranquil canal and on the west by Haarlemerhoutpark,

a public park, Springer laid out gently curving tree-lined streets accommodating a mix of detached, semidetached, and rowhouses on generously sized lots, including one block in the north where nine detached residences were placed around a stream-fed pond. Among the houses were several designed by van Loghem, including the architect's own residence. When in 1919 van Loghem was asked to rework a central portion of Zuiderhoutpark as Tuinwijk Zuid, he projected a very different vision of middle-class living. Instead of stylistically diverse, individually built houses on private, wooded lots, van Loghem called for attached dwellings with continuous facades enclosing shared open spaces.

Using some of the existing infrastructure, van Loghem altered Springer's plan by creating two superblocks to accommodate eighty-six, eight- to twelve-room single-family rowhouses in two groups—one U-shaped and the other L-shaped (the open sides made room for existing houses)—defining courtyard gardens entered through arched passageways on the east and west. The passages were aligned from block to block to provide continuous paths. The western block also featured a community center.

2. House in Zuiderhoutpark, "De Steenhaag," designed by J. B. van Loghem, 1912. Onna. NVO (2012)

3. Tuinwijk Zuid, aerial view. GE (2007)

4. Zonnelaan. NAI (c. 1923)

5–7. Typical views. Onna. NVO (2012)

Although the rows were unbroken, van Loghem's two- and three-story red-brown-brick facades were textured and architecturally complex, with oriel windows, second-story balconies, round archways, dark red and yellow painted wood trim, tall chimneys, and roof terraces shaded by wooden pergolas. With virtually no ornament, "the plainness" of the brick contrasted "with dense planting for an effect of great richness," according to Joseph Buch.[303] Each house had a private rear garden overlooking the public space, with the transition between the two handled as a slight change in level, achieving, as Donald Grinberg notes, a "much more effective symbiosis . . . between the two realms" that eliminated "the arbitrariness of the fences between the private gardens and the communal gardens in Oud's Rotterdam blocks."[304] Sinking foundations plagued Tuinwijk

Zuid from the start and the village barely escaped the wrecker's ball in 1925, 1938, and 1962. Owing to residents' advocacy, it received national monument status in 1978, and a restoration during the early 1990s kept true to the original designs.

Van Loghem's other notable town planning projects include a partially completed scheme for the **Huis ter Cleef** Housing Association (1917) in Haarlem in which he placed double lines of two- and three-story flat-roofed brick rowhouses featuring pergolas and hedge-lined front yards around two gardens with additional small house groups at the center.[305] In his design (1921–22) for the **Rosehaghe** Housing Association, also in Haarlem, van Loghem provided relief from the surrounding gridiron with a tight but comfortable arrangement of 130 workers' houses, three shops, and a community center in

1. Kleverlaan. Onna. NVO (2012)

2. Aerial view. GE (2007)

1. Aerial view. GE (2007)

2. Typical street. NAI (1921–22)

3. Hoofmanstraat. Onna. NVO (2012)

4. Brouwerskade. Onna. NVO (2012)

irregular rows that "left little space for courts and strips of green," according to Paul Groenendijk and Piet Vollard, but nonetheless introducing a healthy amount of greenery—street trees and hedge-lined front gardens—to the streetscape of "anything but rural" redbrick houses in which Modernist corner windows were mixed with Italianate cornices.[306]

The Polder and the Rise of Functionalism

Beginning in 1923, the Dutch government steadily cut back housing subsidies, reducing the work of housing associations so that the proportion of subsidized dwellings sank from 26.4 percent in 1924 to 14.4 percent in 1929 and 7.6 percent in 1935.[307] Despite the poor economy of the 1930s, private developers continued to build working-class and to a greater extent middle-class housing in which the characteristic garden village townscape eroded as Functionalists, influenced by German Zeilenbau planning, developed the *Strokenbouw* model of long, parallel, slightly off-axis north–south rows in an open landscape of *kijk tuinen* (gardens to be viewed).[308] High-rise construction was also increasingly proposed.

The tug of war between those representing the Dutch arm of Modernism known as Nieuwe Bouwen, and the traditionalist Delft School led by Marinus Jan Granpré Molière, can be seen in the development of **Wieringermeer** in North Holland, an expansive, flat polder that was drained in 1930 for the construction of three villages—Middenmeer, Wieringerwerf,

1. Plan. Marinus Jan Granpré
Molière. CRAAT (1955)

2. Aerial view. GE (2004)

3, 4. Farmhouse sketches. WUR
(c. 1937)

5. Plan of Middenmeer, Granpré
Molière, 1931–32. NAI

6. Aerial view of Middenmeer.
CRAA (1934)

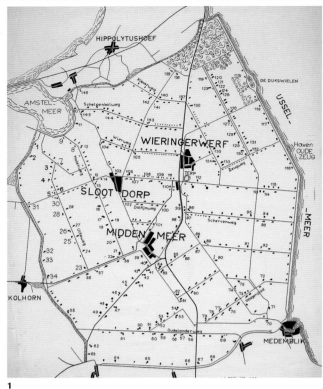

1

2

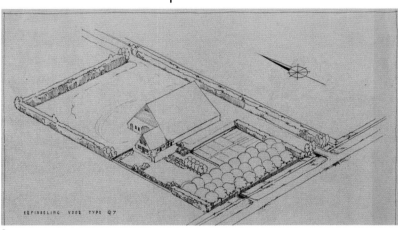

3

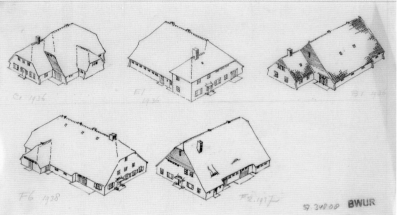

4

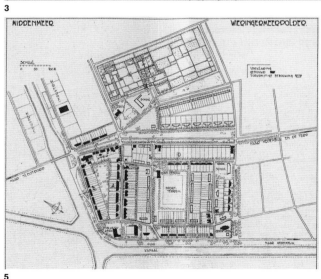

5

6

7

8

7. Slootdorp, aerial view. GE (2004)

8. Torenstraat, Middenmeer. CRAA (1934)

9. Torenstraat, Middenmeer. CRAA (1939)

10. Slootdorp. CRAA (1932)

11. Washday on Meeuwstraat, Wieringerwerf. CRAA (1939)

9

10

11

and Slootdorp—separated by agricultural land made up of 50-acre farms. The result, according to Bernard Colenbrander, was "a man-made landscape of the most modern kind, on an unprecedented scale."[309] Granpré Molière planned the villages beginning in 1927, collaborating with J. F. Ligtenberg (n.d.) and landscape architect J. T. P. Bijhouwer (1898–1974), who was responsible for the landscape design of both the villages and of the expansive polder, specifying street trees, low protective plantings and groups of trees around the farmhouses. The clients, a governmental, private, and church partnership, mandated that only single-family homes with pitched roofs be built. Johannes Fake Berghoef (1903–1994) designed the red-and-brown brick semidetached and rowhouses that featured individual rear gardens and, on some blocks, surrounded interior parks. Middenmeer, designed in 1931–32 and built largely between 1933 and 1941 with construction extending into the postwar period, was at the heart of Wieringermeer, with shops, schools, churches, and a café set among tree-lined streets. In each village, sports

fields were provided, and tapered linear parks formed central public spaces.

In 1933, when four Nieuwe Bouwen architects visited the polder, they criticized the "deliberate romanticism"[310] of the villages, particularly, according to Colenbrander, "the small blocks" that "were not all systematically aligned and in some cases . . . even seemed to have been arranged with a certain arbitrariness." The visiting architects preferred to interpret the site "literally as a blank page, an expression of boundless freedom, whereas Molière considered it as a merely illusory emptiness which was linked to established culture in many different ways."[311] The Nieuwe Bouwen architects took careful aim at the houses, claiming that they were grouped "timidly head-to-head" like sheep and that they failed to address "modern cultural life with greater light and openness, more happiness and awareness, less small-mindedness, pettiness or faint-hearted individualism." The attacks, as Colenbrander notes, were a "fine example of 'projection', as though the foursome imagined themselves having to go and live in the houses . . . But that was not so. The

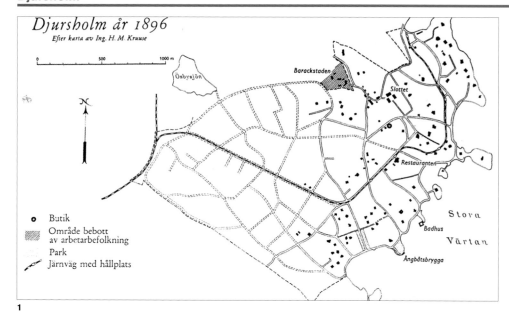

Djursholm år 1896
Efter karta av Ing. H. M. Kruuse

o   Butik
▨   Område bebott
     av arbetarbefolkning
     Park
⤙   Järnväg med hållplats

1

1. Plan showing development up to
1896. SLMA

2. Auravägen. CRS (c. 1942)

houses were not built for cosmopolitan urbanites but
for people who came from far and wide in the existing
countryside who surely would have felt little want of 'a
stimulus to a more modern cultural life with greater light
and openness'."[312] The district, widely visited by planners
and the public alike, continued to be built out during the
postwar years according to the original plans.

SWEDEN

Sweden was the first of the Scandinavian countries to
assimilate the planning ideas of Camillo Sitte, Ebenezer Howard, and Parker and Unwin, paving the way for
Finland, Norway, and Denmark to follow. While each
country adapted the models to its own conditions, each
also followed a more or less similar pattern: the National
Romantic movement of the late nineteenth century set
the stage for an appreciation of Sitte, establishing the
validity of artistic planning and setting into motion
the transference of town planning responsibilities from
the civil engineer to the architect. As architect Gustav
Linden (1879–1964) wrote in 1924, "Reacting against
the schematic gridiron plans of the former period, the
new movement was at first characterized by a strong
tendency towards the picturesque and the irregular.
Straight streets were banished and crooked ones became
the rule." During the first decades of the new century,
Sitte gave way to the Garden City model as introduced
by way of English and German examples that became
frequent travel destinations for Scandinavian architects,
so that, as Linden put it, "the straight traffic street won
back her supremacy" as architects called for "order and
clearness and for the most suitable use of the different
sections of the available area."[313] Garden villages and suburbs enjoyed popularity during the late 1910s and 1920s,
acquiring a distinct regional character through the use
of local vernacular, or so-called Nordic classicism, but

by the end of the 1920s, stylistic Functionalism combined with so-called rational planning entered the scene.

Sitte's powerful influence in Sweden is attributable in part, as Eva Eriksson has noted, to the fact that
Swedes learned German as their first foreign language
and were able to read *Der Städtebau* (1889) in its original form.[314] (The first translation was a French edition
published in 1902.) In 1897, Swedish architect Fredrick
Sundbärg (1860–1913), railing against the gridded plans
of the civil engineer in the journal, *Ord och Bild*, created
a ripple effect as he introduced Sitte's alternative vision
to his Nordic colleagues. Sweden's passage of the Town
Plan and Lot Division Act in 1907 aided planning progress, not only giving municipalities the power to draw lot
lines on private land—and thus providing a legal framework to solve the disputes that hampered many planning
efforts—but also including zoning restrictions that governed both land use and building design.

Sweden's main hub of Sitte-esque and garden
suburb planning was Stockholm. As industrialization
arrived, the city followed a familiar course of suburban
expansion, with the wealthiest residents taking advantage of new railroad lines to flee the crowded center and
live in English-inspired villa parks. **Djursholm** (1889),
six miles northeast of the city, was among the earliest, accessible by a railroad completed in 1890 and an
electric tram line in 1895.[315] **Saltsjöbaden** (1891), ten
miles southeast of the city, was initially conceived as
a Baltic seaside resort by a prominent financier, Knut
A. Wallenberg, who in 1893 built a railroad to the hilly
farmland site and developed two hotels while parceling out the surrounding land to individual buyers.[316]
Störangen, another early suburb, dating from 1904,
founded by a group of middle-class civil servants
for their own residence and for those to whom they
granted membership, predominantly artists and intellectuals, was built along the railroad line connecting
Saltsjöbaden to Stockholm, in the Nacka district, with

Saltsjöbaden

Störangen

lots varying in size and shape to accommodate individual architect-designed houses.[317]

In 1904, as its city center became increasingly crowded and private suburban development catering to the affluent began to consume outlying land, the city of Stockholm undertook a campaign to buy cheap land—primarily large country estates—on the western and southern outskirts in order to secure sites for affordable housing. By the mid-1930s, Stockholm had amassed 21,000 acres between two-and-a-half and eight-and-a-half miles from the city center. According to a government publication, "the form of dwelling for which it was chiefly considered the sites should be made available" was the "single family house and the type of planning was the *garden city*."[318] Intending to limit land speculation and retain control over the new districts, in 1908 Stockholm established the "Own Home" program, a sixty-year leasehold system based on Howard's communal ownership model in which the city would build streets, utilities, and public services such as transportation, and lease lots to residents, who, benefiting from favorable building terms, would be responsible for the construction of their houses.

The first of the municipal garden villages, **Enskede**, was planned in 1907 by Per Olof Hallman (1869–1941) in collaboration with Herman Ygberg (1844–1917) on a triangular 140-acre site, part of a larger 1,500-acre tract roughly four miles south of the city that could be reached in fifteen minutes by way of a new tram line.[319] Hallman's plan for the hilly and somewhat rocky terrain mixed straight, gently curving, and jagged medieval-inspired residential streets ranging in width from 16 to 32 feet, retaining a central hilltop as a park. Two 60-foot-wide roads provided indirect routes across the village, while Hallman blocked out major encircling traffic arteries with a perimeter of three-story mixed-use buildings. Pedestrian paths and stairways kept foot traffic away from the streets.

Hallman included detached and semidetached houses in the plan but devoted most of the area to blocks of rowhouses with individual rear gardens backing up to alleys and shared courts. Public buildings were distributed among the houses but linked to one another by parks and visual axes. A school occupied the largest site, with a church, a parish hall, and stores placed around a nearby triangular green adjacent to a larger park and playground. A community hall, a library, and a small amusement park rounded out the public amenities. The plan was published in the German periodical *Der Städtebau* and caught the attention of Raymond Unwin, who congratulated Hallman on the design.

In 1908, the city jumpstarted development by building six rowhouses designed by Victor Bodin (1860–1937)

Enskede

1. Map of Stockholm showing municipal land reserves on southern and western outskirts. CPHV (1938)

2. Church. CRS (1930–50)

3. Plan, Per Olof Hallman, 1907. DS08

4. Aerial View. SLMX (1991)

5. Margaretavägen. CRS (1920s)

6. School. CRS (c. 1939)

7. Rowhouses on Margaretavägen, Victor Bodin, 1909. Jord. WC (2009)

8. Typical house. Arild. WC (2012)

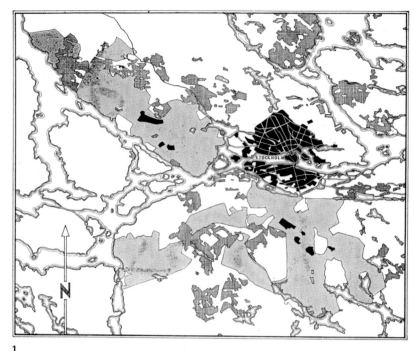

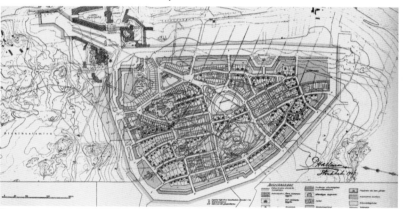

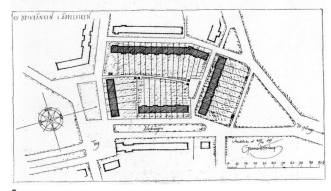

1. Aerial view. GE (2008)

2. Alviksvägen and Äppelvikstorget, showing Drivbänken block, left. CRS (c. 1930)

3. Stavgårdsgatan. CRS (c. 1931)

4. Drivbänken block. Wernström. PAN (2007)

5. Drivbänken block, plan and elevation, Gunnar Wetterling, 1919. HQS

along Margaretavägen, some of the first examples of terraced housing in Sweden. As the private sector took over, however, Swedes showed their distaste for row-house living by abandoning the type in favor of detached and semidetached houses to which they were more accustomed. Soon enough, middle-class families were attracted to Enskede's garden village atmosphere and the goals of the Own Home program were undermined in a process that would be repeated in other districts until the city devised a new program in 1926.

The middle-class houses of Enskede, some built according to seven standardized house plans but many others designed as large villas by individual architects, were located more or less according to Hallman's street plan and lot divisions but placed scattershot on their sites—set perpendicular and parallel to the street and varying widely in their setbacks—creating, according to Heleni Porfyriou, "a sense of anarchy in the outlook of the suburb, thus strongly contradicting the intention of Hallman's plan to create an overall effect of a restful village atmosphere."[320] Completed in 1914, Enskede failed as a working-class district—it was described in a 1921

government report as an "ugly example to be carefully avoided"—but is today considered to be one of Sweden's finest garden villages.[321]

Stockholm's next two municipal garden suburbs were built in the western parish of Bromma, where the city owned 3,350 acres. The waterside village of **Äppelviken** was planned in 1910 by former competitors and now collaborators Nils Gellerstedt (1875–1961) and Per Hallman, whose design was further developed by municipal architects.[322] High land costs led the city to gear the project toward the middle class from the start. With curving streets that gave shape to large, irregular blocks, the plan accommodated a variety of house types, including residential buildings with commercial first floors along the main roads and single- and multifamily houses and rowhouses that, though designed by different architects, still maintained a consistency in character. Construction began in 1914, and by 1920, 167 buildings—mostly larger than average one-family five-room-with-kitchen houses—had been built to accommodate 1,900 people. Along Äppelviken's main street, Alviksvägen, where a tram line was located, the

1. Plan, Albert Lilienberg, 1908. GS (1932)

2. Kolonigatan. GSGK (1930–45)

3. Furuplatsen. Thulin. GSM

4. Typical street. WC (2010)

1

2

3

4

Drivbänken block (1919) by Gunnar Wetterling (1891–1967) stands out as an interesting, roughly rectangular grouping of four terraces of varying length, angled to meet the surrounding streets, containing a total of forty-three units. The northernmost group was set back behind deep front gardens while the other three featured rear gardens that, though private, were heavily planted and backed up to a hedge-lined pedestrian pathway, contributing a park-like atmosphere to the public realm.

Ulvsunda (1914–15), the second of Bromma's garden villages, designed around a lake by Gustaf Larson (1884–1962), was the last of Stockholm's municipal efforts before the war brought a temporary halt to the Own Home program.[323] In 1920, Ulvsunda contained only thirty-six houses. Much of the area was eventually dedicated to industrial uses.

The Own Home program reached beyond Stockholm, most notably to Gothenburg, where the **Landala Egnahem** garden enclave provided dwellings for 105 working-class families in 63 detached and semidetached houses.[324] Landala was the first in a string of closely watched and highly regarded planning projects designed by Albert Lilienberg, Gothenburg's municipal engineer from 1907 to 1927 and subsequently, between 1927 and 1944 the head of Stockholm's town planning department. Lilienberg's planning activity was not limited to Sweden. In 1913, his was the only foreign entry—and the third-prize winner—in the City Club of Chicago's competition for the design of a suburban quarter section (see p. 162).

As planned in 1908, just months after construction began in Enskede, Landala featured a mix of curving and short, straight streets that conformed to the shape and topography of the site. Lilienberg provided a woodland buffer on the west, south, and east sides, incorporated two landscaped squares into the plan, and provided each house with its own garden to create a verdant atmosphere. He also dictated the placement of the houses on their sites. Architect Carl Westman (1866–1936) won a competition to design the dark-brown-painted wooden-sided dwellings with stone foundation walls, and red-tiled gable and gambrel roofs. The even spacing of the houses and the use of stone retaining walls and low, brown picket fences contributed to a consistent streetscape. Within a few years the enclave attracted middle-class residents, leading to the construction of eight larger houses in two terraces (1922) designed by Malte Erichs (1888–1966) on the north and east sides of the more idyllic southern square. Despite the construction of massive courtyard apartment blocks to the north, Landala's garden suburb character has been well preserved.

Christinedal-Bagargården

1

2

1. Plan, Albert Lilienberg, 1908. RSG

2. Model. ICTP (c. 1908)

Kungsladugård

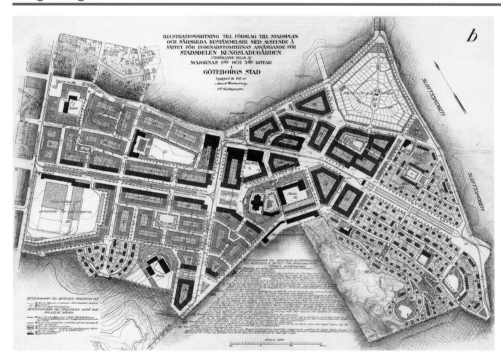

1

2

1. Plan, Albert Lilienberg, 1915. RSG

2. Aerial view. GE (2008)

Lilienberg's earlier, unrealized design for the working-class Gothenburg district of **Christinedal-Bagargården** (1908) garnered more attention—it was published in *Der Städtebau* in 1910—and elevated his status as a planner to that of his former employer, Per Hallman.[325] More programmatically complex than Landala, encompassing a full range of village amenities, Christinedal-Bagargården also occupied a more interesting site, with a central plateau surrounded by lowlands. Evoking the image of a medieval city wall, Lilienberg encircled the plateau with an undulating wall of

four-story apartment buildings. Within, he proposed to flank an axial procession of civic and public buildings with long blocks of curving terraces, furthering the medieval feel by including a few towers and spires. Beyond a buffer of woodlands that nearly surrounded the plateau, Lilienberg called for a ring of detached and semidetached houses with gardens as well as community facilities such as athletic fields, a market square, and schools.

In the **Kungsladugård** section of western Gothenburg, planned in 1915 and developed in stages through the 1920s, Lilienberg drew on both Sitte and Unwin in a

Änggården

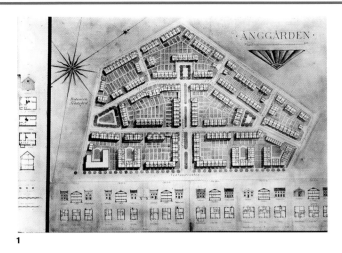

1

2

Enskededalen

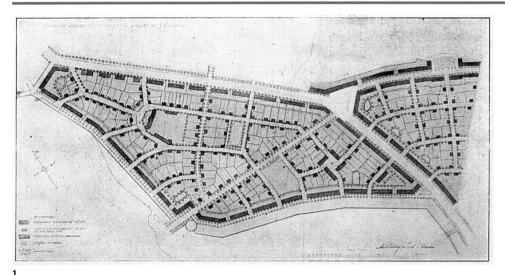

1

2

3

4

plan that attempted, according to Eva Eriksson, to distinguish "between public buildings, monumentally laid-out main thoroughfares and intimate housing quarters with varied perspectives of courtyards and streets."[326]

In the **Änggården** district (1908), on an isolated Gothenberg site bounded on two sides by a botanical garden and on the third by a busy thoroughfare, Lilienberg eliminated detached houses entirely, calling primarily for two-story terraces of up to seven and eight units as well as a handful of semidetached houses, overcoming the skepticism toward rowhouses that Hallman had experienced in Enskede.[327] Lilienberg prepared

at least a dozen Nordic classical designs for the two-, three-, and four-bay-wide, brightly painted wooden rowhouses set back from the street on small gardens and provided with long, narrow rear yards. The plan's interior road echoed the site's pentagonal shape. A planted boulevard ran on axis from the entrance to a small park, one of three that included a playground within a ring of trees.

Enskededalen, a Stockholm suburb planned by Axel Dahlberg (1882–1963) in 1919 with construction continuing until 1930, also harkened back to the traditional small Swedish village of wooden houses, "recreating," according to Heleni Porfyriou, "its coherent urban scene and architectural elegance."[328] Like its western neighbor, Enskede, Enskededalen was planned with a ring of apartment buildings intended to shelter the core. The simple and consistent, detached and semidetached houses, many of which were designed by Gustaf E. Pettersson (1887–1925) with pitched and gambrel roofs and standardized windows, lined the streets in a staggered arrangement, entered at the side and accessed through gateways in tall wooden fences that shielded the block interior from both street noise and the public eye. Planting strips provided space for street trees along major roads, and several blocks were reserved as parks. Dahlberg paid careful attention to closing street views. In the southeast, for example, where he broadened an intersection to form a fountained square, Dahlberg called for a pinwheel arrangement in which the axes of the four streets entering the square were closed by two-story rowhouse facades, a classic Unwin technique that Dahlberg may also have borrowed from the 1917 plan by S. E. Lundqvist (n.d.) for the **Röda Stan** (Red Town) quarter in Norrköping, where at a slightly larger scale, the scheme of four rectangular blocks around a central park and playground accommodated about eighty units in thirty-five red-painted-with-white-trim wooden workers' houses built by the municipality.[329] Röda Stan included three house types: single-family detached houses, one-and-a-half-story semidetached houses, and two-story four-family houses.

Gustav Linden was another architect who designed districts of vernacular-style housing artistically grouped according to garden suburb principles. His 1920 plan for a workers' village in **Åtvidaberg** was carefully keyed to its site, with houses placed around hilltop courtyards and lined up along hillsides above winding streets.[330] The very low building density allowed ample space for private gardens and communal areas. Aside from portions of the street plan, the scheme was never realized. A similar fate befell Linden's 1920 design for **Norra Lund**, an industrial village in Norrköping that specified rowhouses along broad avenues connecting three village greens and small, linked workers' dwellings along narrow residential streets in a plan that was punctuated frequently with parks and plazas.[331]

In 1926, Stockholm, having made additional suburban land purchases and responding to the fact that the Own Home developments attracted wealthy residents instead of the working-class families for whom they were intended, established the so-called "small cottage" program under the City Small Homes Bureau.[332] To minimize residents' need for capital, the program asked owners and their families to construct their own houses, allowing labor to count for 10 percent of the cost and offering mortgages for the remaining 90 percent. The city provided standardized building materials and professional instruction as well as electrical and plumbing subcontractors. The program was a success. By 1939, 3,500 one- and two-story houses had been built to accommodate 12,500 people.

The first phase of the program included 200 small, detached four-room workers' cottages in Olovslund,

Röda Stan

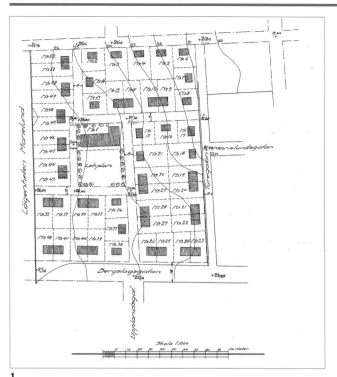

1. Plan, S. E. Lundqvist, 1917. CAN

1

Åtvidaberg

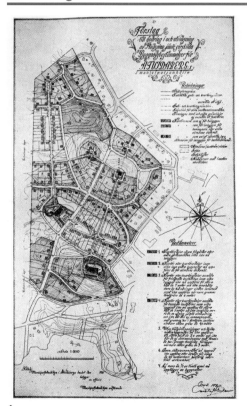

1. Plan, Gustav Linden, 1920. ICTP

2. Model Cabezos. ARKM (c. 1920)

1

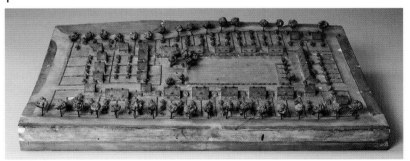

2

Norra Lund

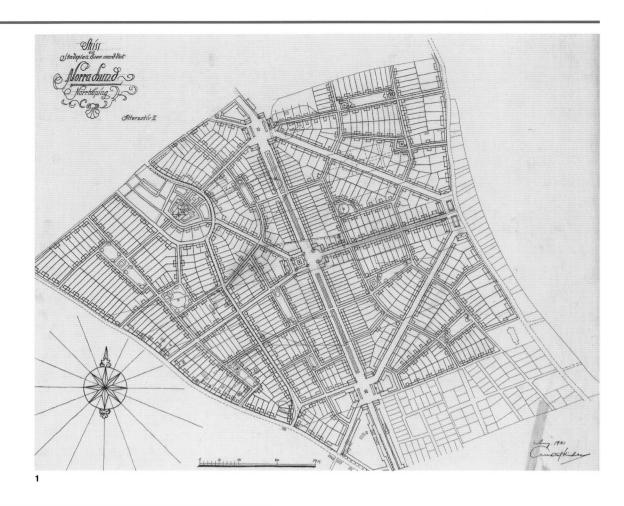

1

Olovslund

1

Pungpinan

1

west of Äppelviken, and Pungpinan, in Skarpnäck, near Enskede.[333] **Olovslund** (1927–40) was laid out around a central park with a pond. The lots were leased to owners who constructed two-story, two-bedroom, gambrel-roof houses that have been enlarged over the years. The same houses were built in a more orthogonal street plan in **Pungpinan** (1927). Nearby, **Tallkrogen**, built over ten years beginning in 1933, was designed by architects within the City Small Homes Bureau who attempted to enliven the flat and featureless site with a racetrack-shaped loop road within which curving streets filled one end, a park the other, and rectangular blocks occupied the middle.[334] To the north, **Enskede Gård** occupied an equally unremarkable site with rectangular residential blocks on either side of a tapered park commanded on its southern end by a public school. The small one-story houses were designed by Edvin Engström (1890–1971).

Planned by Albert Lilienberg and Thure Bergentz (1892–1965), the **Norra Ängby** (1931–38) and **Södra Ängby** (1933–40) sections of western Bromma followed, the former featuring more than 1,200 board-and-batten houses built from at least ten types along narrow streets and tree-lined avenues, with squares providing a village feel; and the latter, occupying a wooded and hilly site, featuring 525 houses mostly designed by Engström along curving and straight streets that incorporated generous amounts of parkland, including rugged woods retained on the block interiors.[335] "Probably the largest and most unified district of functionalist villas in

Tallkrogen

1. Aerial view. SLML (c. 2000)

1

Enskede Gård

1. Aerial view. GE (2010)

1

Norra Ängby

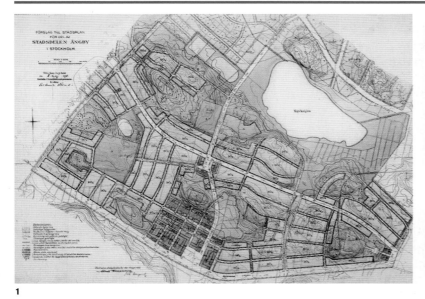

1

2

3

1. Plan, Albert Lilienberg and Thure Bergentz, 1931. SCPD

2. Typical street. Ellgaard. WC (2008)

3. Aerial view. Augustsson. SNHB (2010)

1. Typical street. Ellgaard. WC (2008)

2. Aerial view. Norrman. SNHB (1992)

3. Börjesonsvägen I, Edvin Engström, c. 1938. STS (1938)

4. Plan, Albert Lilienberg and Thure Bergentz. Ellgaard. WC (2008)

the world," according to Olof Hultin, Södra Ängby, referred to as Stockholm's "last garden suburb," began construction in 1938, by which time Sweden had entered a new phase of housing dominated by narrow three-story apartment buildings known as *lamellas*.[336] Hints of the new open planning could be seen in Södra Ängby, where in an effort to create a park-like feel, it was prohibited to install fences or hedges along the lot lines.

FINLAND

As the largely agricultural country of Finland began to industrialize during the early twentieth century, its cities, including the capital of Helsinki, on the Gulf of Finland, were generally spared the intense overcrowding and poverty that inspired urban reformers in other industrializing countries. As a result, the young architects who introduced international planning principles into Finnish practice were driven less by social than by aesthetic considerations.

Lars Sonck (1870–1956) was the most prominent Finnish advocate of artistic planning. Inspired by Camillo Sitte's ideas, which he first encountered in Fredrik Sundbärg's 1897 article in *Ord och Bild*, Sonck published an influential and incendiary essay entitled "Modern Vandalism: The Town Plan of Helsinki" in 1898 in the Finnish journals *Finsk Tidskrift* and *Teknikern*. Sonck examined Helsinki through a Sittean lens, criticizing what he felt was a lifeless urbanism of streets and squares as exemplified by the "mechanical authoritarian town planning of the 19th century [that] had managed to produce only boring city landscapes."[337] Launching an attack against the engineers responsible for districts such as Kallio and Katajanokka where grids had recently been laid down with little regard for topography, Sonck advocated design competitions for Helsinki's undeveloped Eira and Töölö districts.[338] The competition for Töölö, according to Mikael Sundman, "launched a new phase in Finnish urban planning" that allowed "the international currents . . . to acquire their Finnish interpretation."[339]

The **Töölö** site, located on the west side of the peninsula, had resisted development because of its rocky terrain. The competition drew eleven entries, from which the jury, resisting the advice of its invited foreign expert, Swedish architect Per Hallman, selected

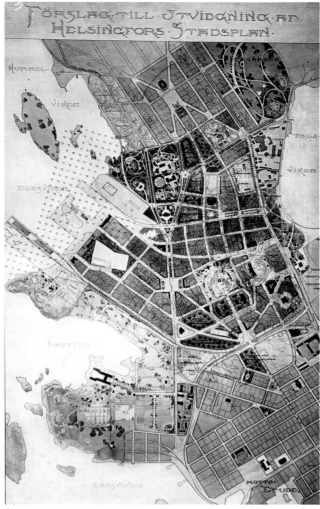

1

2

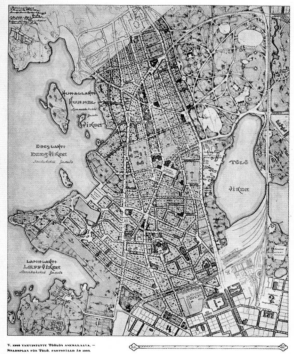

4

3

1. First prize-winning competition entry, Gustaf Nyström and Herman Norrmén, 1899. HELS

2. Second prize-winning competition entry, Lars Sonck, 1899. HELS

3. Collaborative design, Gustaf Nyström and Lars Sonck, 1902. HELS

4. Final plan, Gustaf Nyström and Lars Sonck, 1906. HELS

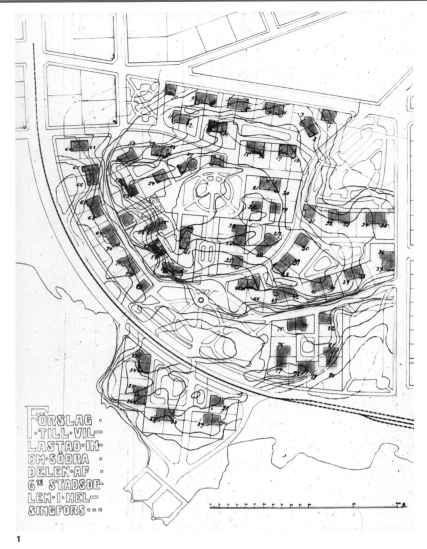

1. Plan, Lars Sonck, Bertel Jung, and Armas Lindgren, 1905. MFA

2. Aerial view. Rauhamaa. HCM

3. Typical houses. Suomi. HH (2005)

a scheme by architect Gustaf Nyström (1856–1917) and city engineer Herman Norrmén (n.d.), whose plan addressed some of the issues raised by Sonck in "Modern Vandalism" but was still conventional by international standards, with large residential blocks organized within a framework of broad radiating boulevards designed to facilitate traffic flow. In the debate surrounding the competition, the entry came to represent an "engineer's" plan.

Sonck won second prize and collaborated on the third-place entry with Bertel Jung (1872–1946) and Valter Thomé (1874–1918). In his own submission, Sonck called for comparatively small blocks shaped by short streets that carried the eye toward carefully sited public buildings and parks. He located a church on the site's highest point, one in a series of public buildings and squares that formed the heart of the plan. In the residential areas, he made the lots wider than they were deep, a Sittean rule, and placed public gardens on the block interior. Along the water, where Nyström proposed buildings, Sonck called for a park. The third-place entry shared elements with both plans but featured the highest proportion of public to residential sites and proposed a distinctly nostalgic townscape.

The judges, dissatisfied with aspects of each scheme, called for a second stage in which the teams were encouraged to borrow freely from one another, eventually leading to a reluctant collaboration between Nyström and Sonck. Their plan was approved in 1903 and adopted in 1906. According to Riitta Nikula, the outcome was "a compromise in which Sonck's wild visions were visible only in the curving routes of certain streets and in a few minor points of detail,"[340] a view echoed by Arvi Ilonen, who has written that the final plan "relinquishes the surprises and small scale of the Sittean urban ideal."[341] The plan was abandoned in 1916.

The second district for which Sonck had advocated a planning competition was **Eira**, on the southwestern tip of the Helsinki peninsula. Sonck envisioned a villa park on a site that was formerly slated for industrial development. A competition failed to occur, and in 1905, with the land still dormant, Sonck collaborated with Bertel Jung and Armas Lindgren (1874–1929) on an unsolicited proposal that they hoped would attract a developer.[342] The scheme was geared toward the wealthy, providing eighty-seven parcels for detached and semidetached houses along gently curving streets that maximized views of the harbor. Sonck placed

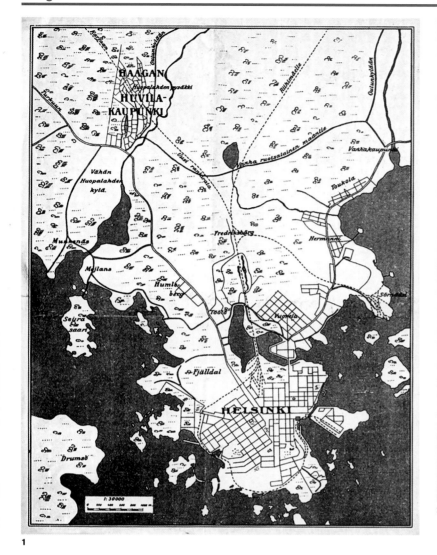

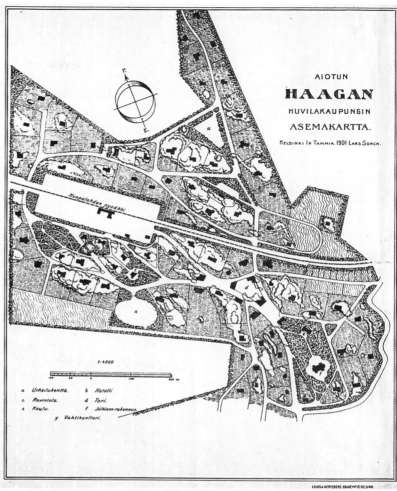

1, 2. Locater map and plan, Lars Sonck, 1901. HELS

parks at the northeast and southeast entrances and an open square in the center, on the highest topographical point, connected by a broad lawn to a picturesquely planned waterfront park. The architects established maximum cornice heights and drew up a building code that would regulate the design of facades, landscaping, walls, and gardens. The scheme was rejected but municipal engineers used it as the basis for their official plan of 1908. Construction occurred primarily between 1910 and 1914, resulting in a visual consistency among the houses, many of which were designed by Selim A. Lindqvist (1867–1939).

Speculators found a way around the two-story limit by building habitable ground floors and attics so that what were intended as one- and two-family houses were in effect realized as small apartment buildings— what Riitta Nikula has called "tenements in disguise."[343] According to Mikael Sundman, "the discrepancy was only too obvious between the reality and the vision of an 'English' type of building which Sonck had launched in 1898 as his ideal for this area."[344] In 1915 the architect and architectural theorist Gustaf Strengell (1878–1937) called Eira an "utter failure," although today it is one of Helsinki's most desirable neighborhoods.[345]

As large, central sites like Töölö and Eira disappeared, developers looked further afield, aided by the construction of new railroads and the introduction of electric tram service in 1900. By 1906 a spate of "garden suburb" companies had formed. Speculative in nature, they were typically made up of liberal-minded middle-class bankers, senators, and intellectuals and not infrequently architects and engineers. The companies, twenty-one of which were active around the city between 1895 and 1930, prepared site plans, built roads, infrastructure, and transportation lines, and provided building materials and labor to individuals who purchased lots.[346]

Sonck was engaged on both the design and development sides. By the early 1900s, according to Asko Salokorpi, his name "was almost a household word among building companies."[347] In 1901 Sonck laid out **Haaga** on the northwestern outskirts of Helsinki for the M. G. Stenius Company, which would later commission Eliel Saarinen (1873–1950) to include the same area in the much larger Munkkiniemi-Haaga plan.[348] Straddling a coastal rail line, Sonck's design provided for seventy-six houses, a school, hotel, restaurant, caretaker's cottage, and civic building along freeform streets that followed

1. Plan, Lars Sonck, 1902. MFA

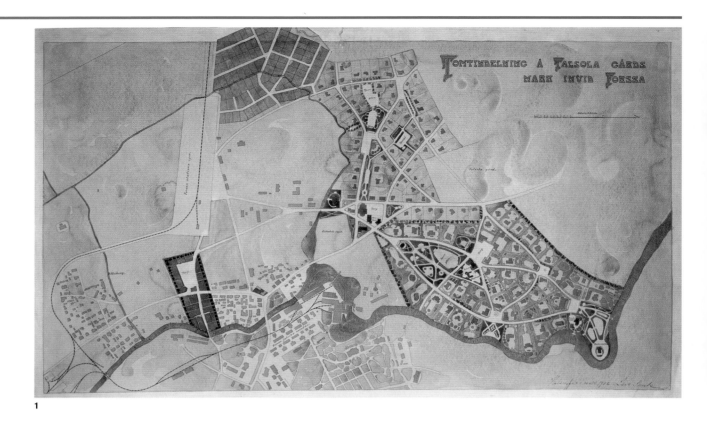

1

1. Plan, Lars Sonck, 1908. GKA

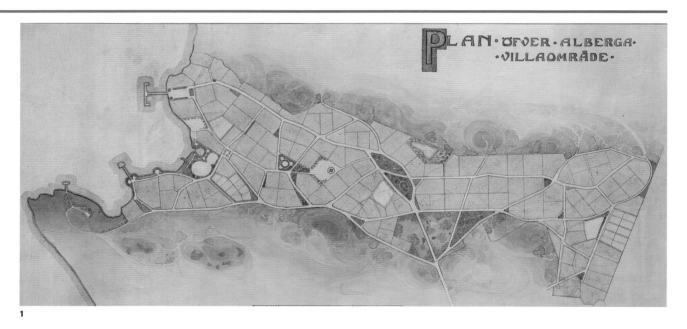

1

the site's contours and reserved large hilltop sites for houses. The plan was not realized.

In 1902, Sonck prepared a picturesque layout for an unrealized villa park in the **Talsola Manor** area of Forssa, a city about seventy miles northwest of Helsinki, and in 1908 he designed a villa park around the former **Alberga** mansion in the city of Espoo adjacent to Helsinki, platting lots for individual houses along irregularly shaped streets interspersed by parks of varying type and size.[349] Sonck also included villa districts in his second-place entry for the Kuopio (1900) competition; in his winning competition entry for the Pyynikki Ridge and **Ratina** (1902) areas of Tampere;

and a competition entry for the town plan of **Vaskiluoto** (1903), Vaasa.

In 1907, two years after Sonck, Jung, and Lindgren proposed their plan for Eira, the trio, joined by architects Oskar Bomanson (1869–1939) and Karl Lindahl (1874–1930) and a group of engineers and businessmen, formed the AB Brändö Villastad company and purchased **Kulosaari** (Brändö, in Swedish), a 250-acre island off the eastern coast of Helsinki where they planned and built an administratively independent upscale suburb.[350] Sonck drew the initial plan of gently curving, terrain-hugging streets that provided villa sites near the water and converged on the high ground in the center where public buildings were positioned to serve as landmarks for surrounding areas and to visually terminate axes such as that leading from a ferry landing on the west. From the top of the hill, which, as Mikael Sundman notes, was left open in accordance with Sitte's rule of "keeping the middle empty," one could enjoy views down three main streets toward historical monuments on nearby islands.[351]

Initial sales were slow, particularly of the upland parcels. Sonck revised the plan in 1909, redrawing the center to include smaller, more densely arranged lots around tightly framed squares that added, as Sundman put it, "a medieval touch—which had been wholly absent from the former plan."[352] In 1916 a bridge was built to connect the island to the Helsinki peninsula. The following year, Bertel Jung drafted a new design calling for a significantly higher density in the center, where tall apartment buildings, perimeter blocks, and rowhouses—previously unknown in Finland—were arranged in a geometrically structured, classicized layout that would also be abandoned as the center gave way to scattered mid-rise apartment houses. Over the years, the project proved an economic success and most of the early wooden houses were replaced. The area around Kluuvi Bay in the southwest remains closest to the original plan, with detached houses, a small park, a hotel (now an office building), and a pair of rowhouses, Ribbingshof (1917), designed by Armas Lindgren and Bertel Liljeqvist (1885–1954) as the country's first examples of the type.

Eliel Saarinen followed Lars Sonck as Finland's leading urban planner. In 1910, Saarinen began work on the 2,127-acre **Munkkiniemi-Haaga** district two-and-a-half miles northwest of the city center, a tract of forest and farmland owned by the M. G. Stenius Company, of which Saarinen was a shareholder and board member.[353] As Riitta Nikula has written, the idea to develop what was in essence an independent city of 170,000 residents—equal in size to the projected population of inner Helsinki—Munkkiniemi-Haaga represented "a utopian effort to produce an urban environment of high aesthetic quality on the one hand" and "on the other . . . one of the gigantic financial speculations typical of the prewar era."[354]

Saarinen spent five years developing the scheme, during which time he traveled widely and worked on a series of comparable projects, including master plans for Budapest (1911), Canberra (1912) (see p. 646), and the Estonian city of Tallinn (1912). In 1921, Saarinen described the philosophy that had guided his planning work: "Carefully planned monumentality and picturesque intimacy should be used to render the modern city attractive."[355]

The Munkkiniemi-Haaga plan, published in 1915 as a richly illustrated book, was Finland's first complete town-planning document, serving as a textbook for Finnish designers until after World War II. Saarinen included designs for every street and square and elevations and floor plans for an array of civic and residential buildings, including eleven rowhouse variations geared toward different social classes. The plan featured an

Ratina

1. Plan, Lars Sonck, 1902. NAF

Vaskiluoto

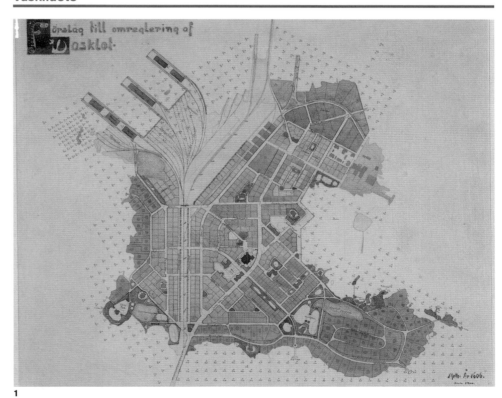

1. Plan, Lars Sonck, 1903. MFA

analysis of the legal and organizational factors required in its implementation as well as an historical chapter written by Gustaf Strengell that recounted Howard's Garden City idea and surveyed important English examples such as Port Sunlight, Bournville, Letchworth, and Hampstead. Saarinen's wife, Loja (1879–1968), built an impressive 1:1000-scale, 8-by-16-foot model to help convey the site's topography and its proposed skyline of more than forty towers rising above a 75-foot maximum cornice line.

1. Plan, Lars Sonck, 1907. MFA

2. Revised plan, Lars Sonck, 1909. HELS

3. Revised plan, Bertel Jung, 1917. HELS

4. Rendering of Ribbingshof rowhouses, Armas Lindgren and B. Liljequist, 1917. HELS

5. Aerial view, showing Wihuri Company Building (originally a seaside hotel), Lars Sonck, 1917, in center, and Ribbingshof rowhouses in left distance. Veljekset. HCM (1930s)

6. Aerial view. Migro. WC (2009)

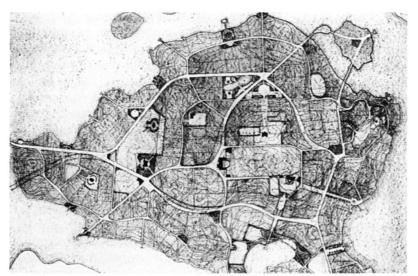

The plan, encompassing Munkkiniemi in the southwest extending to the bay, and Haaga in the northeast across a railroad line, was, as Sundman put it, a synthesis of "garden city and big city planning."[356] Munkkiniemi was to be predominantly urban, with a consistent fabric of six- and seven-story courtyard-enclosing apartment buildings set within a framework of broad boulevards converging in star- and Y-shaped intersections. Roughly ten civic centers were placed throughout, varying in character from informal Sitte-esque squares to symmetrical plazas terminating monumental axes.

To the south, a neighborhood of three- and four-story townhouses that included Unwin-inspired U-shaped quadrangles transitioned to a waterfront district of detached upper-middle-class villas along curving streets. Saarinen limited the villas to two-and-a-half stories and called for compact lots that owners could maintain without hiring outside help. A similar density was to characterize Haaga, where a semicircular park was bordered by concentric streets of middle-class villas comparable to those in Letchworth but occupying larger lots with space for vegetable gardens. Townhouses were placed along avenues radiating from the park. Saarinen

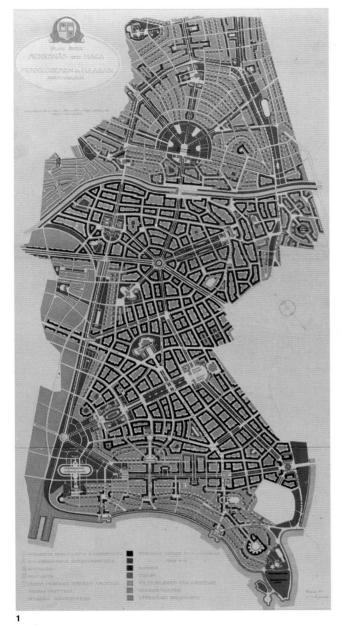

1. Plan, Eliel Saarinen, 1915. HCPD

2. Aerial rendering of preliminary plan, 1911. ESP

3. Model built by Loja Saarinen, 1912–15. PENC

4. Plan, detail. HCM

housed workers in the northwest, adjacent to industrial sites, specifying one-story rowhouses with individual gardens that matched the 20-by-130-foot dimensions recommended by Howard.

Saarinen prioritized traffic circulation, with streets varying from 20-foot-wide residential drives to 145-foot-wide thoroughfares that carried automobiles—he was the first to propose motorways in Finland—trams, and non-motorized traffic in dedicated lanes. The plan was less forward-looking in regard to open space, with only 37 percent of the site devoted to planted areas, predominantly linear parks that defined district boundaries and buffered residential from industrial zones. To critics, the paucity of more substantial parks highlighted the fact that the scheme was developed for a private land speculator.

Saarinen's plan did not survive the economic and political instability brought on by the civil war that followed Finland's declaration of independence from

Russia in 1917. Only two buildings were built: a boardinghouse, now used as an educational facility, and a small block of rowhouses in Hollantilaisentie. Fragments of the street pattern were also implemented, including portions of the waterfront villa district and a part of the principal boulevard, Munkkiniemen puistotie, that, with four rows of trees and a tram line, hinted at the scheme's high civic aspirations.

In 1918, Julius Tallberg (1857–1921), a politician and businessman who held a significant stake in the Munkkiniemi-Haaga project, commissioned Saarinen to prepare a master plan for the Greater Helsinki region, expanding upon ideas that the architect had sketched out in an appendix to the earlier plan.[357] As Riitta Nikula has observed, the **Pro-Helsingfors** plan (1918), prepared during the chaos of civil war—Saarinen drafted the design in his Hvitträsk studio while Bertel Jung wrote the text in his Kulosaari villa—"can be thought of as a newly independent state's optimistic

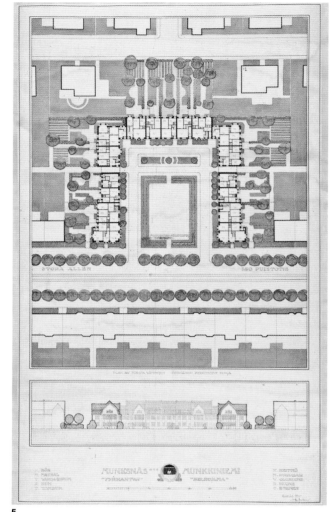

5

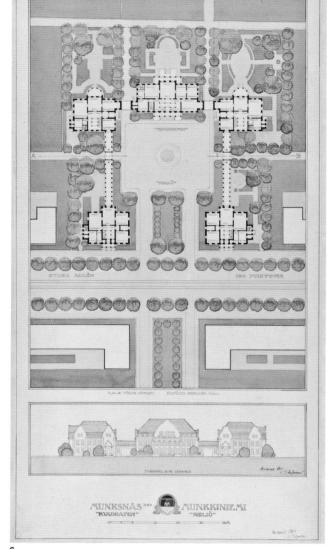

6

7

8

vision of the future, based on forecasts of stupendous growth."[358] Anticipating a population of 700,000, Saarinen's plan guided development well beyond Helsinki's boundaries while significantly restructuring the city center to accommodate more people. The latter hinged on abandoning Saarinen's recently completed main railway station (1904–19), considered to be a masterpiece, in order to build a new station at the heart of a business district about two miles to the north in Pasila, a shift that would bring greater value to the Munkkiniemi-Haaga site. To link the new and historic centers,

Saarinen called for a 295-foot-wide multilevel landscaped boulevard, Royal (or King's) Avenue, that would carry automobiles, trams, and railroad tunnels beneath a planted concourse.

Saarinen, influenced by Ebenezer Howard, proposed one of the most significant early examples of regional planning, calling for a chain of eight to ten satellite towns to the northwest and northeast of the city, each with a population of 10,000 to 12,500. The suburbs were to be linked to one another and to Helsinki by railroad and tram and would be surrounded by parks, agricultural

Munkkiniemi-Haaga

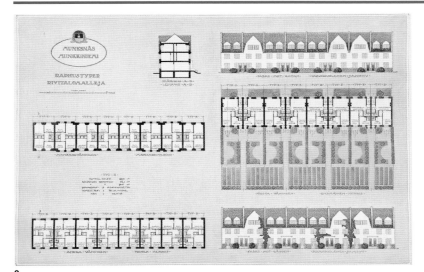

9

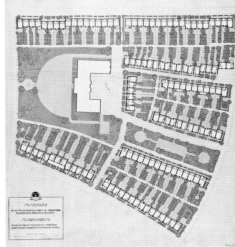

10

9. Model terrace house, plan and elevation. HCM

10. Residential area for working people, site plan. HCM

11. Aerial rendering of apartment house block. HCPD

12. Rowhouses on Hollantilaisentie, Eliel Saarinen, 1920. Eino. HCM

11

12

Pro-Helsingfors

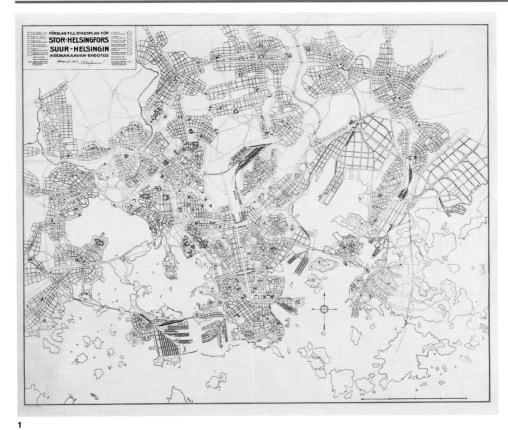

1

2

1. Plan, Eliel Saarinen, 1918. HCM

2. Aerial perspective down King's Avenue, 1917. ESP

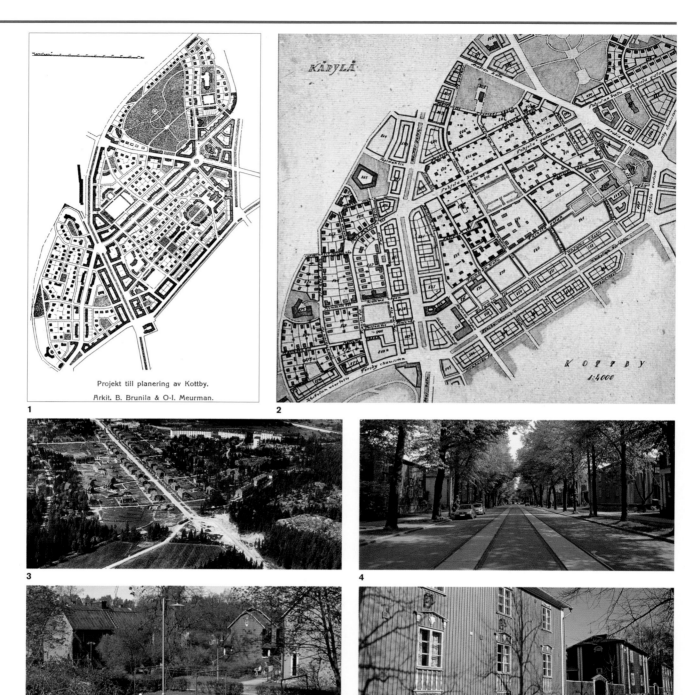

1. Plan, Birger Brunila and Otto-Iivari Meurman, 1917. MFA

2. Plan incorporating houses by Martti Välikangas, 1921. HELS

3. Aerial view. Nisonen. HCM

4. Typical street. Kantokari. PAN (2012)

5. Block interior. Suomi. HH (2005)

6. Pohjolankatu. Tuntematon. HCM (1970s)

Projekt till planering av Kottby.
Arkit. B. Brunila & O-I. Meurman.

land, forests, and waterways that also extended as green-belts into the city. Each of the towns, which Saarinen described as "daughters" around the mother city, was to include a civic center surrounded by terraced housing and villas.[359] Saarinen compared the plan to Helsinki's existing arrangement of residential districts around a dense core: "Only the scale will be altered in order to accommodate the wider perspective. Commuter journeys will lengthen with the enlarged scale but there will be a corresponding increase in speeds: the speed of the horse and cab will give way to that of motorized transport."[360] Saarinen would later term the concept "organic decentralization."[361] Contrary to Howard's intention, which Heleni Porfyriou

claimed, "was progressively to replace all existing urban development with the creation of a system of garden cities, Saarinen aimed simply to avoid disorganized future expansion by introducing a decentralized planning form based on satellite towns—which nothing, of course, could prevent from becoming dormitory communities."[362] In 1919 Saarinen suggested that a coalition of private, state, and city interests be created to carry out the plan but efforts ceased after Tallberg's death in 1921.

The construction of **Käpylä,** also known as Puu-Käpylä, in Helsinki, was a notable exception to the 1920s planning lull.[363] Carried out in three phases between 1920 and 1925 on a city-owned site three miles northeast

1. Plan, Otto-Iivari Meurman,
1921. MFA

1

of the city center, Käpylä was Finland's first publicly sponsored effort to build affordable workers' houses in a park-like setting. The district included 165 standardized multifamily houses spread across a loose grid of fifteen large but not identical blocks laid out in 1917 by Birger Brunila (1882–1979), who had succeeded Bertel Jung as Helsinki's town planner, and Otto-Iivari Meurman (1890–1994). Meurman had been an assistant in Saarinen's office during the preparation of the Munkkiniemi-Haaga plan, and the initial design of Käpylä, which was never implemented in full, closely resembled Saarinen's townscape of radial boulevards, parks, and mixed building types.

As built, Käpylä's distinctive combination of Nordic classicism and garden village communality is attributable to architect Martti Välikangas (1893–1973), who at age twenty-six both designed the houses as his first independent commission and situated them in Brunila and Meurman's plan. Inspired by Finland's traditional farmhouses and red-and-ocher-colored industrial buildings as well as the Swedish small house movement and his travels in Italy, Välikangas called for two types of two-story four-unit wooden houses painted in warm, muted colors, topped by shallow pitched roofs, and sparingly ornamented with garlands, medallions, pilasters, keystones, and festoons. The third phase of construction introduced one- and three-story houses.

Välikangas linked the houses with wooden plank fences and arcades and kept them close to the street in order to maximize internal space for gardens and communal buildings. The garden plots were designed by Elisabeth Koch (1891–1982), Helsinki's City Garden adviser, who also coached residents on how to grow vegetables. Pathways provided separate circulation for foot traffic. A central block was reserved for athletic fields and playgrounds, and a rocky section in the north was kept open as a park with an observation tower.

In later years, apartment blocks were built around the edges of the district, but efforts in the 1960s to redevelop the core in a similar fashion were unsuccessful. As Roger Connah has written, Käpylä is "an antidote to the diagrammatic, utopian nightmares pre-scripted by Functionalism and followed by many Finnish architects in competitions throughout the 1920s . . . Softening the neo-classical influence, the asymmetric formality of the rectangular blocks merged the idea of a modern open plan, light and planting with the beginning of Functional regularity. Architecturally and socially, the area has remained exemplary."[364]

After working on the Käpylä plan, Meurman became town-planning architect (1918–37) in the eastern city of Viipuri (now part of Russia), where large portions of the housing stock had been destroyed during the civil war. To create affordable housing for workers, Meurman advanced the *omakoti* idea of small single- or two-family vernacular–inspired wooden dwellings surrounded by gardens and built by occupants from standardized plans and building materials. In 1921, Meurman planned **Kelkkala** on Viipuri's southeastern outskirts, staggering houses along the street and on the block interior where they enjoyed individual gardens and in some cases enclosed courtyards.[365] The houses were built by their

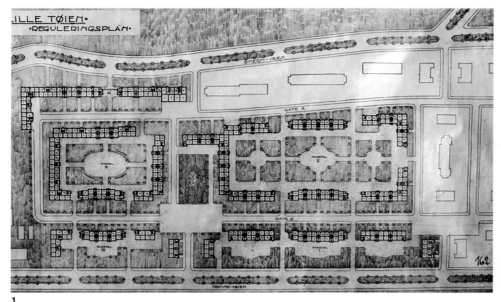

1. Plan, Magnus Poulsson. OSLO (c. 1917)

2. Ansgar Sørlies at intersection of Kaare Røddes Plass. OSLO (1920s)

3. View across Ansgar Sørlies showing stores in distance. OSLO (1920s)

4. Overall view. Yosh. WC (2008)

residents according to designs by municipal architects Elli Ruuth (1893–1975) and Clara Meuschen (b. 1890) and were subject to rules governing colors as well as lot landscaping and fences, although the strictures were frequently disobeyed.

NORWAY

Garden village planning took hold in Norway just before the outbreak of World War I, when the need to improve working-class housing became an issue of national importance. In the absence of private development, municipalities took up the construction of new districts, especially around the capital city of Oslo, holding competitions to select town plans. Sweden was looked to as a model. Its leading planners, Per Hallman and Albert Lilienberg, were frequently asked to judge the competitions, with awards initially going to Swedish entries but soon enough to Norwegian architects who, as Heleni Porfyriou has noted, did not strictly follow the Swedish example: "Contrary to Stockholm's garden suburb developments on municipally owned land, characterized by low-density planning with single-family houses, the garden suburbs of Oslo had a distinctive urban character, due not only to their design but also to their building densities."[366]

One such neighborhood, **Lille Tøyen** (1917), designed by Magnus Poulsson (1881–1958) on a rectangular site in northeast Oslo, featured a perimeter of two-and-a-half- and three-and-a-half-story brick and tile-roofed rowhouses set back on deep gardens to buffer the site from the surrounding urbanism.[367] Within, two more groups embraced grassy courtyards and playgrounds and four stores were provided on a plaza inside the northern entrance.

Norway's most significant garden village—and a worthy example of the type by international standards—was **Ullevål Haveby** (1913–26) in Oslo's Nordre Aker borough.[368] The development, occupying a city-owned site, was built by the municipality and sold in 1918 at about half the cost of construction to an "Open Co-operative Savings and Building Society," which administered the property. Norwegian architect Oscar Hoff (1875–1942) won the 1913 competition for the plan of the village, and between 1915 and 1922, Adolf Jensen (1879–1959) and Harald Hals (1876–1959), Oslo's municipal housing director (1918–20), designed the buildings, with the bulk of construction occurring between 1918 and 1926.

Intended for a population of 5,000, Ullevål Haveby included 116 buildings containing 654 dwellings. At its core, a formally planned town center featured a nearly symmetrical arrangement of two-and-a-half-story

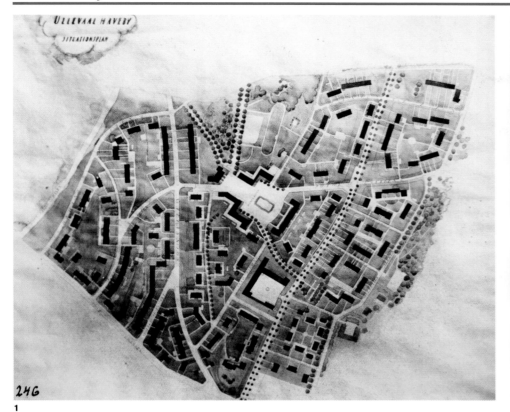

1

4

5

6

7

1. Plan, Oscar Hoff, 1913. OSLO

2. Overall view. OSLO (c. 1925–30)

3. Town center. OSLO (c. 1925–30)

4–7. Typical views. Holzheimer. NH. (2012)

redbrick, mixed-use buildings around a reflecting pool. A school was placed diagonally to the south. The remainder of the hilly site featured contour-hugging residential streets. As Christian Norberg-Schulz has written, the mix of picturesque and formal planning was intended to contrast "the private-domestic from the public-universal . . . The result is undoubtedly successful."[369] In addition to detached and semidetached dwellings, Ullevål featured rowhouses of varying length, often linked by archways and curved or angled in response to the street. Some groups commanded hilltop sites while others were set back so deeply within lushly planted gardens as to be virtually hidden from view. Drawing inspiration from England, the architects clad the houses in stucco and

wood and introduced variety and texture through the use of quoins, latticework, balconies, porches, and dormers. Spaces were provided for playgrounds, athletic fields, and parks that were outfitted with benches and made use of existing trees. Residential gardens were bordered by hedges and picket fences and pedestrian paths were threaded throughout the village. Despite the fact that the modest-size dwellings were built for working-class families, the overall quality of Ullevål attracted the middle class.

Harald Hals and Adolf Jensen also designed the five-block Oslo neighborhood of **Lindern** (c. 1919), where they linked two- and three-story perimeter apartment buildings around interior parks and playgrounds,[370]

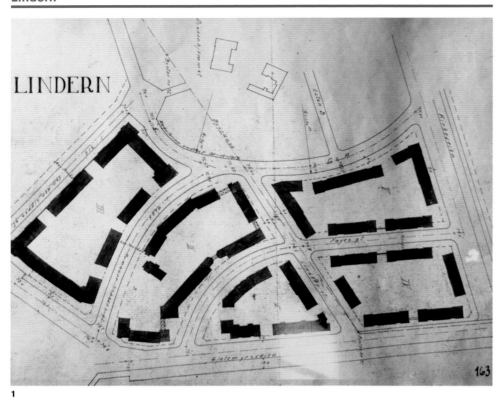

1

1. Plan, Harald Hals and Adolf Jensen, c. 1919. OSLO

2. Courtyard. OSLO (1920s)

2

while Oscar Hoff laid out the Olso district of **Ekeburg** (c. 1919), southeast of the city center, for a population of 15,000, calling for an orthogonal street plan focused around a public square within a loop road, beyond which a less formal street plan took over.[371] Hoff planned a mix of housing types and an array of public buildings, parks, and athletic grounds as well as several street profiles, but the proposal was only fractionally implemented.

In the 1920s, Sverre Pedersen (1882–1971) emerged as Norway's leading planner. Based in the city of Trondheim, in 1920 he became the country's first professor of town planning and would exert a strong influence over the profession through a string of competition-winning plans for cities across the country.[372] While Pedersen had taken a sabbatical in 1908 to work in Per Hallman's office in Sweden, he was not as interested in Camillo Sitte's ideas as Hallman or his Scandinavian colleagues, later commenting: "Many plans of suburbs suffer from a want of lucidity, simplicity and power, in spite of their

technical perfection. They may have picturesque details but are lacking totality."[373] Pedersen believed that "the Norwegian town planning movement, while it tries to keep in contact with the general European movement, must find its own ways to solve the peculiar problems set by the conditions of the country."[374] He found particular value in those English precedents that took the natural landscape into consideration. "Hampstead Garden Suburb," he wrote, "is one of the schemes where I think the chief characteristics of the site are brought out and harmoniously completed by the buildings . . . One almost everywhere realizes the formation of the land. From several points there are excellent, conscientiously planned outlooks to the surrounding landscape."[375]

Pedersen's plans, closely tailored to natural features, characteristically juxtaposed geometrically ordered public areas with naturalistically planned residential neighborhoods. Aiming to "follow the advice of Ebenezer Howard to combine the advantages of living in the city and in the country," Pedersen favored simple, uniform wooden houses spaced at even intervals "to preserve a certain effect of unity . . . Nature will care for the picturesque." Believing that the Garden City prescription of twelve dwellings per acre was "a somewhat close grouping" for Norwegian sensibilities, Pedersen called for unusually low housing densities: "We Norwegians . . . will never develop to common town people to whom the street and the square are the main interest."[376]

Werner Hegemann included several of Pedersen's plans—including those for Hamar, Lillehammer, Tromsø, Fredriksstad, Namsos, and Narvik—in his 1938 study of city planning and housing in order to illustrate that "breadth and formality in group planning are not incompatible with irregular topography and accordance to the street pattern of an existing city; and that an intimate human scale and economical simplicity in buildings can both be achieved without sacrifice of dignity and spaciousness."[377]

Pedersen's early plans were in keeping with international trends. He designed two garden suburbs in Trondheim, his peninsular native city whose expansion had been the subject of a 1910 competition in which the winning entries were combined to outline a series of garden suburbs along local railway stops, all within a designated agricultural belt.[378] His plan for the small, municipally developed neighborhood of **Lillegaarden** (1916) placed detached, semidetached, and four-unit rows of concrete housing along irregular blocks formed by gently curving landscaped streets. Squares were incorporated on the block interiors and each house was given its own garden. The plan was partially followed. In **Rosenborg** (1918–21), Pedersen planned half of the district with closed perimeter blocks and the other half with simple, architecturally consistent semidetached wooden houses, many of which still remain.

Working at a larger scale, Pedersen's competition-winning designs for the waterfront cities of Mo i Rana (1921) and Hamar (1921) introduced strong axes to frame views of surrounding mountains and fjords.

Ekeburg

1. Plan, Oscar Hoff, c. 1919. ICTP

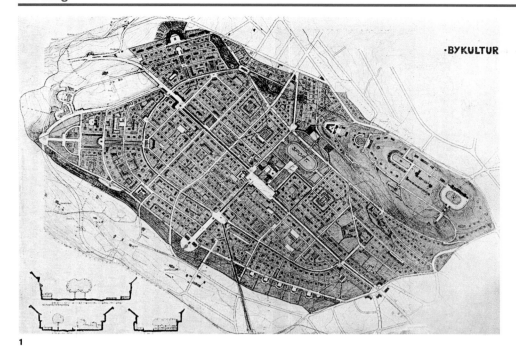

1

Lillegaarden

1. Model, 1916. ICTP

2. Typical houses. TCA (c. 1918)

1

2

Rosenborg

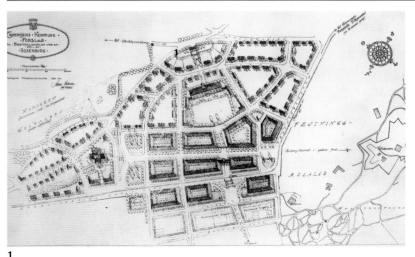

1

2

1. Plan, Sverre Pedersen, 1919. TCA

2. Henrik Mathiesens vei. TCA (1920)

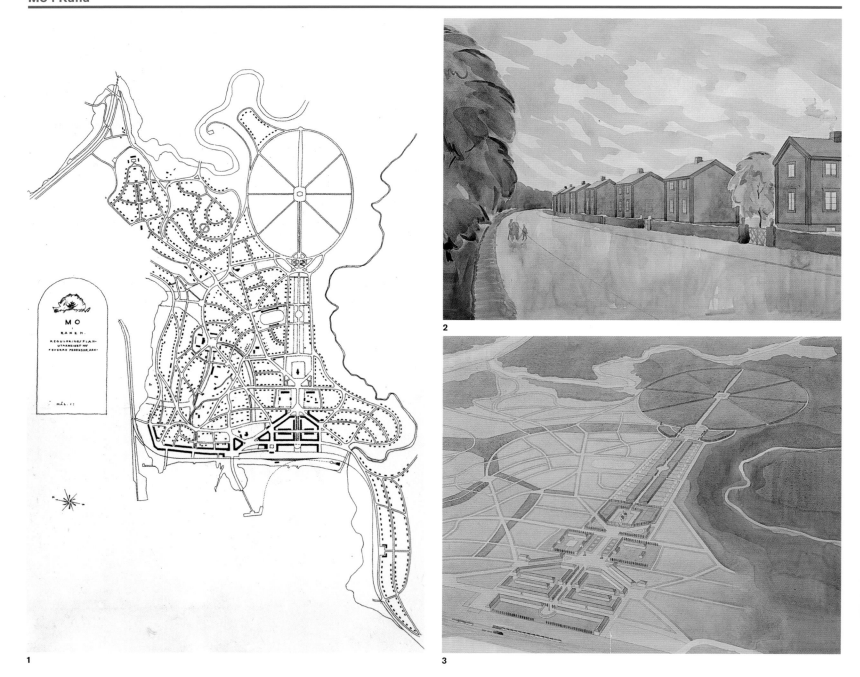

1

2

3

1. Plan, Sverre Pedersen, 1921.
NTNU

2. Perspective rendering of
Boliggate. NTNU (1923)

3. Aerial perspective. NTNU (1923)

In **Mo i Rana**, a mining community, he situated a lacy network of residential streets adjacent to a spinelike tapered park connecting public buildings on the water-front to a preexisting elliptical "town forest" in the north: "Seen from the fjord from a distance," he wrote, "the park strip looks like an immense green column in the middle of the housing area . . . A powerful con-trast between housing areas and open spaces arises in this way."[379] In **Hamar**, Pedersen expanded a gridded harbor-front industrial town with an elaborate net-work of boulevards linking public buildings, plazas, and parks and leading through residential areas that ranged in form from axial processions to picturesque tangles while keeping to Pedersen's belief in simple, evenly spaced wooden houses.[380] The plan's three principal axes pointed north to a town forest modeled on the one in Mo i Rana.

Pedersen's plan for the northern island city of **Tromsø** (1920) also prioritized views of the surrounding landscape and called for a series of organizing axes, one of which, a linear park oriented to run perpendicularly down a hillside, was bordered by straight- and crescent-shaped rowhouses, featured cascading gardens, and was punctuated by monuments and plazas.[381] In **Bodö** (1921), another northern city, Pedersen called for broad swaths of parkland to emanate like "beams" from a cir-cular park surrounding the old town, widening as they extended outward to buffer suburban areas from one another.[382] For the remote peninsular iron-exporting city of **Narvik**, Pedersen's 1925 plan, recalling his ear-lier designs, surrounded a gridded industrial district with sinuous, low-density streets of detached houses interspersed by parks and public buildings, a format that he echoed in his 1926 plan for **Lillehammer**.[383] In

Hamar

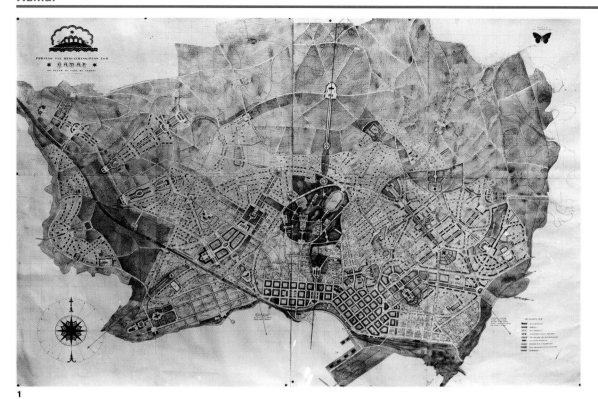

1

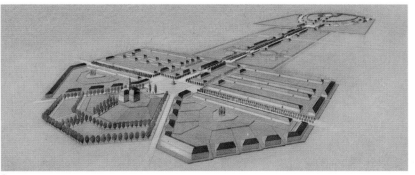

2

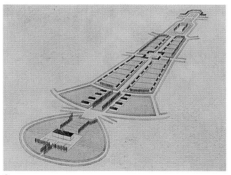

3

1. Plan, Sverre Pedersen, 1921.
NTNU

2. Perspective of residential area
southwest of Prestrud Gård. NTNU
(1921)

3. Perspective of eastern axis.
NTNU (1921)

Tromsø

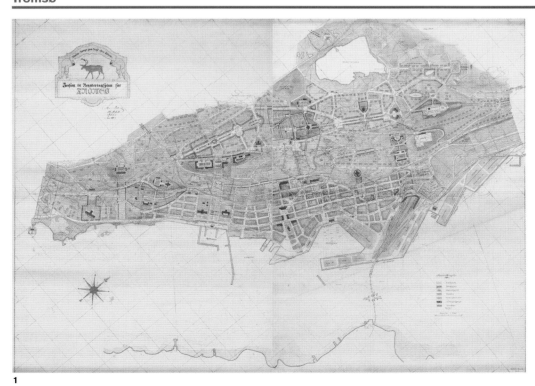

1

2

1. Plan, Sverre Pedersen, 1918.
NTNU

2. Perspective of linear park with
formal arrangement of housing
groups. NTNU (c. 1918)

Bodö

1. Aerial perspective. NTNU
(c. 1921)

1

Narvik

1. Plan, Sverre Pedersen,
1925. NTNU

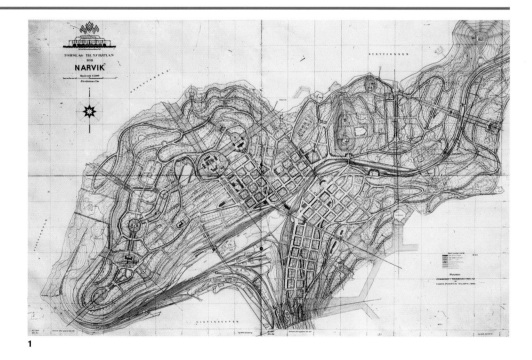

1

Lillehammer

1. Plan showing proposed park
belts, Sverre Pedersen,
1926. NTNU

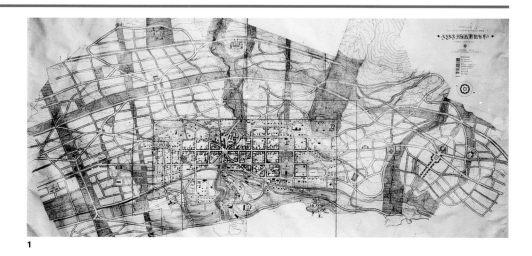

1

his design for **Fredrikstad** garden suburb (1928), Pedersen wrapped an entirely new district around the town's historic fortification walls, employing a framework of terrace-lined radial boulevards and axes giving way to secondary streets lined by small, evenly spaced houses with individual gardens.[384]

DENMARK

In Denmark, garden village planning was adopted in an effort to improve the aesthetics of both the chaotically developing countryside—558 new railway villages were established between 1860 and 1930 along 870 miles of track—as well as the expanding capital of Copenhagen.[385] In 1908, seven years after Copenhagen tripled its size through annexation, Carl Strintz (n.d.), a German civil engineer, won a competition to design the new areas with a Sitte-inspired proposal locating squares and parks in an intricate street system, only traces of which are now discernable.[386] According to Bo Larsson and Ole Thomassen, most of the premiated submissions "showed a clear reaction against dense, high-rise urban development" in favor of "the garden-suburb concept" in which limited areas of multistory housing were designed with green spaces on the block interior, separate zones were included for industry, and street hierarchies were introduced.[387]

In 1908, the Association of Academic Architects established a "design assistance service" to help improve the quality of housing across the country, much of which was self-built and located in the new railroad villages that were essentially unplanned, guided only by strictures that limited building height and guarded against the spread of fire. For a small fee, the design service would provide plans for new dwellings or help improve existing ones. In 1909, on the occasion of the National Exhibition in Århus, the Association of Academic Architects waged a "battle against ugliness," building **Stationsbyen,** a full-scale model railway village laid out by Hack Kampmann (1856–1920) with a multitude of architects contributing houses and public buildings that celebrated craftsmanship and vernacular traditions rather than classicism and industrial building methods.[388] The same ideals led to the establishment in 1915 of the Society for Better Building Practices (Bedre Byggeskik), which focused on the design of both self-built and housing-association-sponsored single-family houses but also promoted garden village planning as introduced through the ideas of Sitte, Howard, and Parker and Unwin.[389]

Copenhagen's first garden village, **Grøndalsvænge** (1911–28), on the city's northwestern outskirts in Nørrebro, was planned by Poul Holsøe (1873–1966), an active member of the Society for Better Building Practices and head of the design assistance bureau, and Jesper Tvede (1879–1934).[390] The project was built on a city-owned site by the Danish Garden House Society, a housing association formed in 1912 by F. C. Boldsen, a lawyer and Ebenezer Howard devotee. Its members, primarily laborers, city workers, and artisans, could rely on leasing

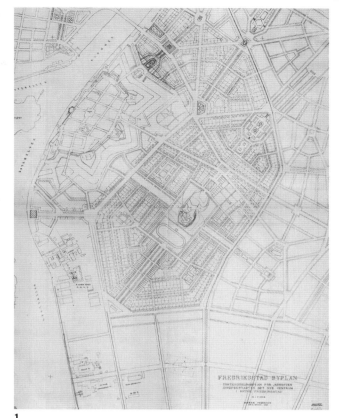

1

the affordable houses for life and could pass the leases on to their children. As completed in 1928, the district, situated on a flat site divided into northern and southern sections by a broad tree-lined thoroughfare, included 339 dwellings in the form of two-story, one- and two-family, redbrick and stucco houses topped by clipped-gable red-tile roofs. Each house had its own small garden bordered by hedge or picket fence. Rear yards backed up to one another, leaving no room for common space on the block interior. However, two quiet squares were provided as well as a modest village green in the south where the planners located five or six stores. The streets were 27 feet wide, lined by sidewalks, and gently curved.

Remarking on Grøndalsvænge in the late 1950s, the functionalist-leaning architect and historian Steen Eiler Rasmussen noted that "the people in the neat little houses behind the white fences are highly respectable. The social standing of the residents has steadily risen and to-day most of the houses are occupied by members of the lower middle-class. The buildings are in good repair and the gardens neatly kept."[391] "Unusually," as Christopher Woodward observed in the late 1990s, "the landscaping seems never to have matured, and the roads are not curved enough, suggesting that the models were insufficiently understood."[392]

In 1913, Charles I. Schou (1884–1973), a Danish architect who had visited Letchworth and subscribed to Camillo Sitte's periodical, *Der Städtebau,* planned the garden suburb of **Vigerslev** in southwest Copenhagen, the first Danish plan to introduce clear street hierarchies.[393] Schou lined the major roads and intersections

Stationsbyen

1. Plan, Hack Kampmann, 1909.
TEK09

2, 3. Typical views. TEK09

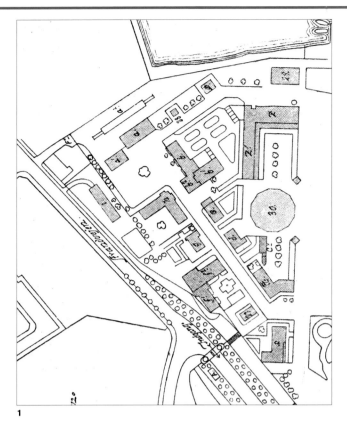

Grøndalsvænge

1. Plan, Poul Holsøe and Jesper
Tvede. KKS (1954)

2. Overall view. Andersen. LAR
(2011)

3. Typical street. Konoy. LAR (2011)

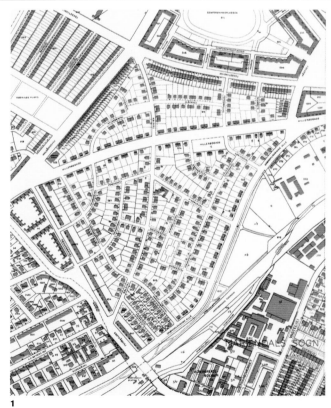

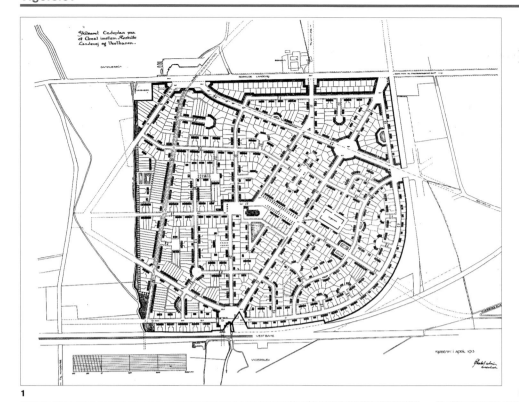

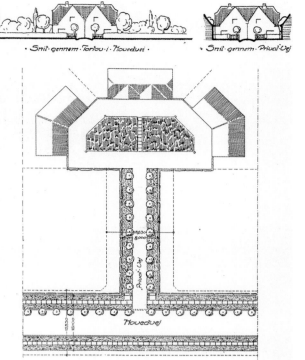

1

2

3

4

with apartment blocks and called for semidetached houses in the rest of the district, laying out curving, angled, and crooked streets as well as a number of culs-de-sac and dead-ends that allowed for the development of the block interiors. As built, detached houses far outnumbered semidetached houses. A church square provided the anchor for a town center that was eventually developed more densely than planned, with several apartment buildings benefiting from a series of landscaped gardens. Smaller squares and parks were distributed throughout.

In Copenhagen's Bavnevangens Haveby (1923), or as it would become known, **Den Engelske Haveby** (English Garden City), in the Brønshøj district, occupying a compact site crossed by a curving main street, Bavnevangen, from which four dead-end streets extended to the east and west, architect Niels Gotenburg (1878–1964) designed a roughly mirror-image arrangement of

one-and-a-half-story semidetached houses linked to one another by gateways to create a serpentine form whose unbroken facade gave privacy to rear gardens.[394] A gap in the houses was provided in the east to allow pedestrian access to an adjacent park.

In the city of Odense, architect Anton Rosen (1859–1928) laid out **Gerthasminde** garden village (1912–17) on the grounds of a centrally located former nursery whose owner decided to subdivide the land as the city developed around it.[395] Rosen, having taken the owner's son, N. P. E. Rasmussen (1870–1953), on a tour of planned villages in England and Germany, modeled his design on Georg Metzendorf's Margarethenhöhe (see p. 749) and Theodor Fischer's Gmindersdorf (see p. 737), although the influence was felt less in the planning of the compact neighborhood than in the architecture of the fifty or so tightly grouped houses that were set back on small front gardens. Construction commenced

1. Plan, Charles I. Schou, 1913. TEK14

2. Plan of houses grouped around a close. TEK14

3, 4. Typical streets. Lindgreen. HOL (2012)

Den Engelske Haveby

1. Aerial view. GE (2005)

2. Bavnevangen. Sommer. GES (2012)

1

2

Gerthasminde

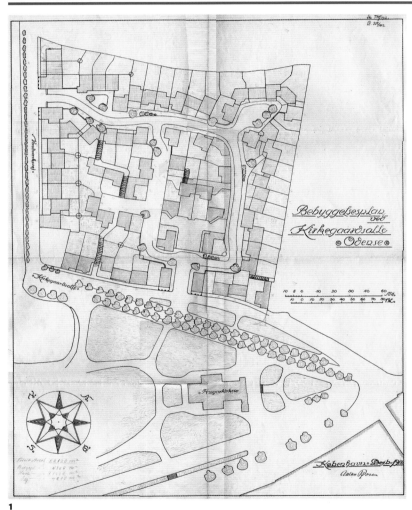

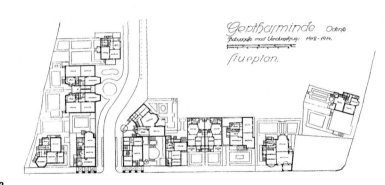

1

3

1. Plan, Anton Rosen, 1912. OCA

2. Elevation and plan of houses on Vandværksvej, Anton Rosen, 1912–14. ARA

3. Typical houses. ICTP (c. 1918)

4. Typical street. Thøgersen. OCA (2011)

5. Houses on Vandværksvej. Thøgersen. OCA (2012)

4

5

in 1912 on a staggered line of detached, coarsely plastered villas along the site's western edge, two of which, boldly colored red, flanked the entrance with arcaded bases. As time went on, however, Rosen's sophisticated, sculptural houses gave way to fairly pedestrian interpretations of his work designed by Rasmussen. The site also received higher-density housing, particularly in 1925 when two parallel terraces of ten and eleven dwellings were completed in the center of the plan, and again in the mid-1930s, when much larger apartment buildings bucked the scale.

After World War I, Steen Eiler Rasmussen emerged as a prominent voice in Danish planning. In the 1919 competition to design **Hirtshals** garden city, one of two new harbor cities planned for the western coast of Jutland, twenty-one-year-old Rasmussen, partnered with Knud H. Christiansen (1896–1970), put forth a proposal that showed the strong influence of Unwin, particularly in the resemblance, as Heleni Porfyriou has noted, to Unwin's perspective drawing, "The Garden City Principle applied to Suburbs," published in *Nothing Gained by Overcrowding* (1912).[396] Rasmussen's plan, extending inland from a semicircular harbor, envisioned a rectangular market square from which boulevards radiated outward to frame industrial and residential districts, the latter consisting of terrace-lined superblocks within which detached houses were placed along a secondary street system. The plan also called for a prominently sited church, school, town hall, shopping district, and cemetery. The design was revised several times and only partially realized.

Rasmussen and Christiansen won another planning competition in 1919 for the small town of **Ringsted**, where a tract of church-owned land had recently become available between the town center and a new railway station.[397] The plan combined closed perimeter blocks in the center with curving streets of villas in the periphery. The plan was slow to be realized and was finished in altered form in the 1960s.

SWITZERLAND

In 1907, the same year that a German translation of Howard's *Garden Cities of To-morrow* was first published in Zurich, members of that city's town council traveled to London for a housing conference that included a tour of Letchworth. Although Zurich did not suffer from the kinds of deteriorating housing conditions or severe shortages of available dwelling units found in the rapidly industrializing cities of England and Germany, interest in the Garden City movement continued to grow, highlighted by a January 1908 exhibition at the Kunstgewerbemuseum (Museum of Decorative Arts) titled "Die Gartenstadt-Bewegung" (The Garden City Movement). In April 1908, with the help of Zurich's municipal government, a housing cooperative was established to develop the garden suburb of **Kolonie Bergheim** (mountain home).[398]

Hirtshals

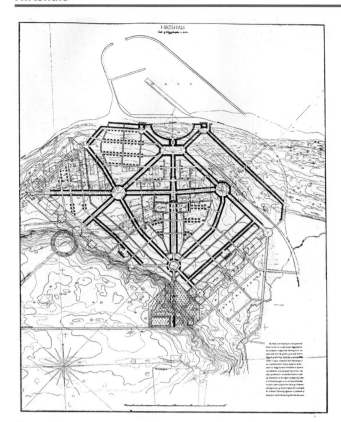

1. Plan, Steen Eiler Rasmussen and Knud H. Christiansen, 1919. ICTP

Ringsted

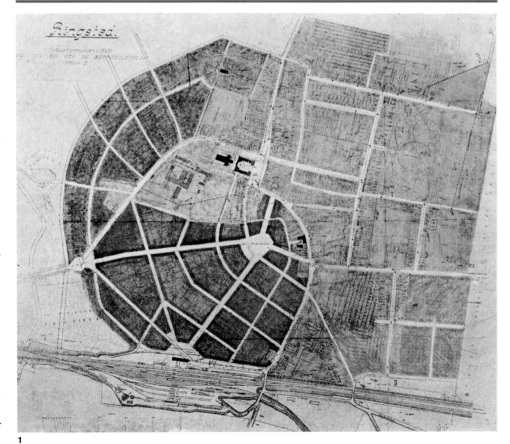

1. Plan, Steen Eiler Rasmussen and Knud H. Christiansen, 1919. TEK19

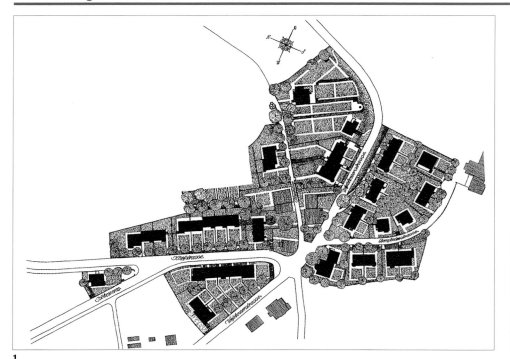

1. Plan, Gebrüder Pfister, 1908, right, also showing plan for Gartenstadt Im Kapf, Gebrüder Pfister, 1910. GAP

2, 3. Typical views. SCB10 (c. 1910)

4. Watercolor. GAP

Intended for the middle class, Kolonie Bergheim was located on a very hilly, two-and-a-quarter-acre site three miles southeast of central Zurich in the Hirslanden quarter, convenient to an existing tram line and surrounded by forests on its southern and eastern borders. The cooperative hired Otto (1880–1959) and Werner (1884–1950) Pfister, brothers who had just returned to their native city after several years of working in Germany, to plan the exclusively residential development as well as design its houses. Gebrüder (Brothers) Pfister organized the fourteen single-family and four two-family houses along curving streets that followed the topography of the site, creating a loose arrangement meant to evoke a village that had grown over time. The two- and three-story houses, designed as variations on Zurich's traditional gabled houses, were oriented toward the south or southeast and planned to maximize lake and mountain views. The Pfister brothers included three detached units, twelve houses grouped in pairs, and one row of three houses. All of the dwellings featured rear gardens. By the end of 1909, all of the eighteen planned houses were completed and occupied.

Gebrüder Pfister also designed **Gartenstadt Im Kapf** (1910), another cooperative located on an adjacent, five-acre irregularly shaped site north of Bergheim.[399] Here the majority of the fifty-two houses were arranged in straight or staggered rows although the development included both detached and semidetached houses, adopting the same basic design vocabulary used at Kolonie Bergheim for houses that featured even larger gardens. The first phase of construction at Gartenstadt Im Kapf was completed by the end of 1911, but plans to expand the suburb were interrupted by the war and never revived, although the Pfister brothers continued to design villas for private clients in the immediate vicinity.

Outside central Zurich, Karl Moser (1860–1939) designed several workers' villages influenced by the Garden City movement (see p. 789). **Siedlung Riedtli** (1912), located in Zurich's Oberstrass quarter about two miles north of the central city, was another prewar settlement whose architecture was inspired by vernacular precedent.[400] Designed by City Architect Friedrich Fissler (1875–1964) for a roughly triangular nine-acre site, Riedtli was intended for higher-paid workers and the middle class. Over a seven-year period Fissler completed twenty-eight terraced groups yielding 288 apartments. To avoid monotony, the three- and four-story buildings were staggered in their placement and each featured a slightly different architectural expression on their facades.

Gartenstadt Im Kapf

1. Kapfstrasse. Honegger. MHZ (2012)

2. Gardens. Honegger. MHZ (2012)

Siedlung Riedtli

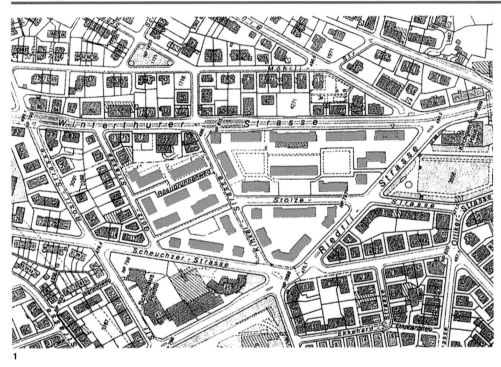

1. Map. SZ (2006)

2. Typical street. Wolf. SZ (1913)

3. Typical houses. SZ (2006)

Switzerland's two most important garden suburb plans directly inspired by English and German tradition were, ironically, produced by native-born architects now best known for their rejection of historical precedent, Le Corbusier and Hannes Meyer. In May 1914 Charles-Édouard Jeanneret-Gris (later Le Corbusier) prepared plans for a garden suburb in his home town of La Chaux-de-Fonds, located high in the Jura mountains in northwestern Switzerland's canton of Neuchâtel, three miles from the French border.[401] Real estate developer Arnold Beck had purchased a large sloping parcel on the south side of the watchmaking town earlier in the year, commissioning Jeanneret to not only prepare the plan for **Cité-Jardin aux Crétets** but also to design all of the 120 intended houses.

Jeanneret's proposal for Cité-Jardin aux Crétets, with its detached houses and terraces deployed along curving streets bisected by a tree-lined boulevard leading to a U-shaped group of houses, was undoubtedly influenced by Tessenow's Hellerau (see p. 290), which the young architect was quite familiar with after visits to his brother Albert, who was studying there at Émile Jaques-Dalcroze's School for Harmony. H. Allen Brooks, besides relating the proposal to Hellerau, points out that by following "the contour of the land while using curving streets of different widths with closed vistas at the ends," Jeanneret was clearly influenced by Unwin and Hampstead Garden Suburb (see p. 350). "What was different," Brooks goes on to write, "is that he located the houses only on the up-hill sides of the streets, thus providing each with long views across the town to the Pouillerel mountains beyond," perhaps reflecting "John Wood's planning at Bath, England, where the Royal Crescent [see p. 19] occupied but one side of its sloping site," and in so doing providing "an early instance of Jeanneret's attraction to eighteenth-century planning

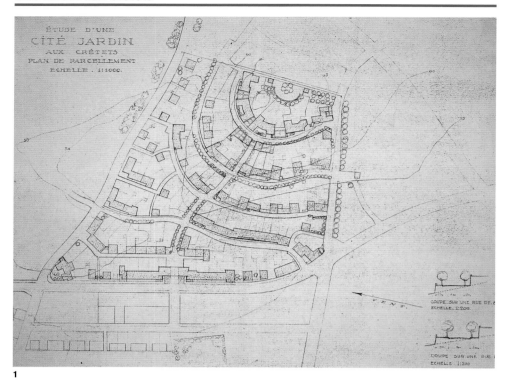

1

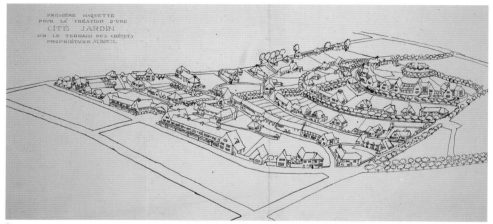

2

1. Plan, Charles-Édouard Jeanneret-Gris (Le Corbusier), 1914. FLC

2. Bird's-eye view. FLC (1914)

ideals" that would become obvious in his mature work as Le Corbusier.[402]

Jeanneret was promised 5 percent of the selling price of each completed house. But the project was first thwarted by the inability to receive a variance from the local government to allow for the use of curved streets in the otherwise gridded town and then by the outbreak of World War I, leading to the collapse of the watchmaking industry. Three years later, Jeanneret would attempt a second garden suburb for workers in Saint-Nicolas-d'Aliermont, France (see p. 482).

In 1919 Basel-native Hannes Meyer was commissioned by the nonprofit Swiss Co-operative Union to prepare plans for its first suburban housing estate, **Siedlung Freidorf** (free village), located on an unimproved 21-acre site in Muttenz, about four miles southeast of Basel.[403] Meyer, a member of the housing cooperative, had studied the planned towns of Bath, Bournville, Port Sunlight, and Letchworth in an extended visit to England in 1912–13 and had just finished a two-year

stint (1916–18) working under Georg Metzendorf at the Krupp colony of Margarethenhöhe in Essen, Germany. Intended for workers and low-level white-collar employees, Siedlung Freidorf was directly connected to Basel by a tram line built between 1919 and 1921.

Meyer's plan for the triangular-shaped parcel consisted of 150 single-family houses placed in straight rows of two to fourteen dwellings, set back behind modest front lawns. Narrow but deep allotment gardens separated the rows at the rear. At the southern end of the site five rows of houses were grouped around a landscaped cul-de-sac while the northern tip featured an eight-house row set at an angle. In addition to the private allotment gardens, three large communal gardens were included. All told, open space represented about 62 percent of the site. To shelter the development, its three bounding streets were lined with a belt of cherry and walnut trees. In addition, as Meyer explained, "the entire estate is monastically girded by a garden wall which is pierced here and there by narrow gates, affording a glimpse of the interior, and runs like a stone bond of friendship from gable to gable, covered with clematis, hops and brambles."[404]

A dominating Co-operative Hall (1922–24) was placed at roughly the center of the site at the parcel's highest point, just north of a formal landscaped green surrounded by trees and featuring a fountain and obelisk. Topped by a clock tower, the community building included a school, library, restaurant, café, cooperative store, gymnasium, bowling alley, banquet and meeting rooms, and a chapel. Meyer, who lived in Siedlung Freidorf from 1921 to 1926, also served as head of its building commission during his residency, conducting annual inspections of each house. The development had an impact beyond Switzerland's border, influencing the design of Hugo Mayer's Siedlung Rosenhügel in Vienna (see p. 584).

In the late 1920s Meyer, who served as second director of the Bauhaus (1928–30), embraced Communism and along with it a vocabulary of deterministic functionalism that deliberately emphasized class solidarity over individualism. In 1933, while working in Soviet Russia, he explained the evolution of Freidorf's design: "At the age of 27, when I was engaged on large-scale housing schemes for a big German industrial concern [Krupp], I used my free time to draw all Palladio's plans on thirty standard sheets of paper . . . in a common scale. This work on Palladio prompted me to design my first housing scheme, the Freidorf estate . . . on the modular system of an architectural order. By means of this system all the external spaces (squares, streets, gardens) and all public internal spaces (school, restaurant, shop, meeting rooms) were laid out in an artistic pattern which would be perceived by those living there as the spatial harmony of proportion."[405] But what would become the extreme communitarianism of his work beginning in the late 1920s can be said to have been anticipated by Meyer's decision to paint all of Freidorf's 110 four-room, 30 five-room, and 10 six-room

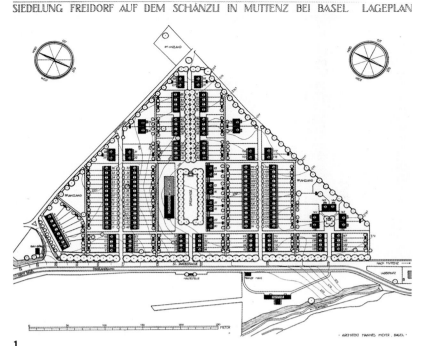

SIEDELUNG FREIDORF AUF DEM SCHÄNZLI IN MUTTENZ BEI BASEL   LAGEPLAN

traditionally styled two-story houses the same "dull red." According to the architect, "houses painted in different colors would have evoked the differences and distinctions of lower-middle-class life and suggested different dates of construction. Hence the color is simply an expression of concord, and unity of architecture is partnered by unity of color."[406]

In 1920, the newly established Société Coopérative d'Habitation of Lausanne acquired a sixty-year lease from the municipal government on an irregular three-acre site one mile west of Lausanne's center for the purpose of building a garden suburb to address the city's growing postwar housing shortage.[407] The nonprofit housing cooperative hired the local firm of Frédéric Gilliard (1884–1967) and Frédéric Godet (1885–1937) to plan **Cité-Jardin de Prélaz** as well as design its exclusively residential buildings. Gilliard & Godet's scheme consisted of east–west terraces of two-story single-family houses with rear gardens, three rows of eight dwellings and one terrace of ten houses, located along gently curving streets on either side of a central landscaped public green and a three-story apartment house surrounded by allotment gardens. A larger, three-story apartment building, also bounded by allotment gardens, was situated at the southern border of the site, also home at its western end to a

small triangular green with trees and benches. By 1922 thirty-four houses and twenty-six apartments had been completed at Prélaz, a picturesque development that is largely intact and well preserved to this day although, as architectural historian Christa Zeller has noted, "The gardens have been partially overrun by parking shelters and spaces."[408]

Geneva's Société Coopérative d'Habitation was also founded in 1920.[409] The nonprofit group was headed by architect Camille Martin (1877–1928), who commissioned Arnold Hoechel (1889–1974) of the Geneva-based firm of Aubert (Paul Aubert, 1872–1972) & Hoechel to prepare plans for **Cité-Jardin d'Aïre**. Located on a triangular, 20-acre site one-and-a-half miles northwest of central Geneva, Hoechel's plan called for ninety single-family houses arranged primarily in rows of four to fourteen dwellings but with some detached and semidetached units. The strictly residential development did include a community focus in the form of a rectangular plaza bordered by north–south rows of houses in roughly the center of the site just north of Avenue d'Aïre. Long and narrow rear allotment gardens were provided for each house.

By 1926 all of Cité-Jardin d'Aïre's traditionally styled two-story houses along tree-lined streets were completed

1. Plan, Hannes Meyer, 1919. SF

2. Aerial view. SF (c. 1925)

3. Typical street. SF (c. 1922)

4, 5. Typical views. JWeiss. SKB (2012)

Cité-Jardin de Prélaz

1. Plan, Gilliard & Godet, 1921. AVL

2. Overall view. SCHL

3. Aerial view. SCHL (2010)

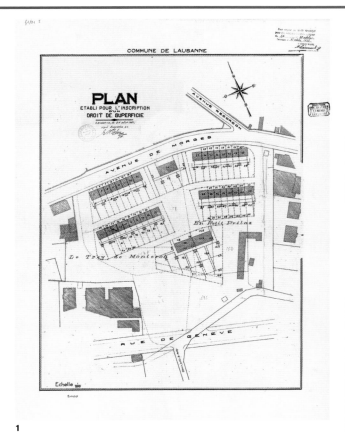

1

2

3

Cité-Jardin d'Aïre

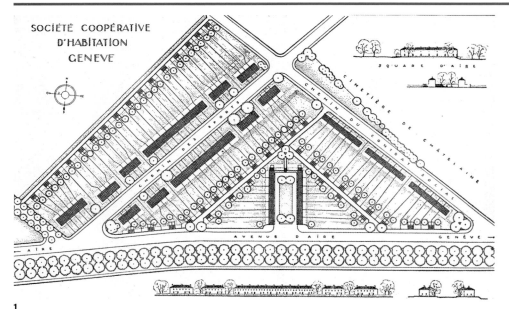

1

1. Plan, Arnold Hoechel, 1922. WM24

2. Rear gardens. CIG (c. 1923)

3. Chemin de l'Essor. Rogg. YOR (2010)

2

3

Siedlung Hirzbrunnen

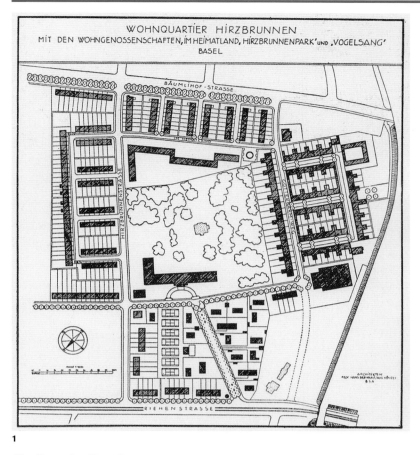

1

2

3

1. Plan, Hans Bernoulli, 1924, also showing plan for Siedlung Im Vogelsang, Hans Bernoulli, 1924, right. GTA

2. Typical street. GTA

3. Hirzbrunnenschanze. JWeiss. SKB (2012)

Siedlung Im Vogelsang

1

2

and sold, although in an unusual arrangement, the gardens were leased by the cooperative on an annual basis. Two years later the firm of Frédéric de Morsier (1861–1931) and Charles Weibel (1866–1942) added forty additional houses south and west of the original development along Avenue d'Aïre and Avenue Henri-Bordier. Dubbed Cité-Jardin Nouvel-Aïre, these rowhouses were similar to Hoechel's earlier efforts. Beginning in the 1950s the majority of Cité-Jardin d'Aïre was demolished and replaced with denser development although the house rows along Chemin de l'Essor remain largely intact as well as part of the 1928 addition.

Hans Bernoulli was responsible for the design of two nearby developments in his native Basel: **Siedlung Hirzbrunnen** (1924–28) and **Siedlung Im Vogelsang** (1924–26), located on either side of the St. Clara Hospital complex about two miles east of the city center.[410] Served by two tram lines and sponsored by the same nonprofit housing cooperative, both developments consisted exclusively of rowhouses with rear allotment gardens intended for workers. Designed in collaboration with August Küntzel (1888–1965), Han von der Mühl (1887–1953), and Paul Oberrauch (1890–1954), Siedlung Hirzbrunnen was the larger estate, although

1. Eugen Wullschleger-Strasse. GTA

2. Eugen Wullschleger-Strasse and Paracelsusstrasse. JWeiss. SKB (2012)

Siedlung Hardturmstrasse

1. Overall view. GTA (c. 1926)

2. Hardturmstrasse. GTA

1

2

Siedlung Unterer Deutweg

1

2

1. Aerial view. GE (2008)

2. Weberstrasse. Bächinger. WG (2008)

the one-and-a-half- and two-story stucco houses painted in a variety of colors with gabled dormers created a more village-like atmosphere than the more severe brick rows enclosing courtyards at Im Vogelsang, a collaboration of Bernoulli and Küntzel. In addition to the houses, several schools and cooperative shops were shared by the two siedlungen.

Bernoulli was also active in Zurich after the end of World War I when the city experienced a serious housing shortage. His **Siedlung Hardturmstrasse** (1924), located two miles northeast of the city's center, was intended for lower-middle-class civil servants and developed by the architect with the assistance of the Zurich City Council.[411] The housing estate occupied a long and narrow site between a tram line and the Limmat River. Bernoulli arranged single-family terraced houses on six parallel north–south culs-de-sac. The three western rows were U-shaped, closed at their northern border by a three-house row while the other groups of houses were closed by a wall or a one-story storage building. All of the two-story houses faced a courtyard planted with trees that was open to the south.

The plan of back-to-back rear allotment gardens created a spacious feel.

Siedlung Hardturmstrasse's ninety-nine houses were completed and sold in two phases between 1924 and 1929, with the U-shaped groups built first. Bernoulli received a rare honor when the development's tram station was later named for him. Christa Zeller has noted that the architect's scheme was unusual for Switzerland, providing "a viable alternative to multi-story construction . . . This principle, which is prevalent in English garden cities, of small terraced houses arranged along courtyard-like culs-de-sac set at right angles to the main road, has never really been accepted in Switzerland."[412]

Bernoulli, working in collaboration with architect Adolf Kellermüller (1895–1981), designed two additional housing estates along garden suburb lines in Winterthur, a city about sixteen miles northeast of the center of Zurich. **Siedlung Unterer Deutweg** (1923–25), also known as Siedlung Weberstrasse and intended for the working class, was developed by Heimstätten-Genossenschaft Winterthur, a nonprofit housing cooperative administered by the municipal government.[413] Bernoulli

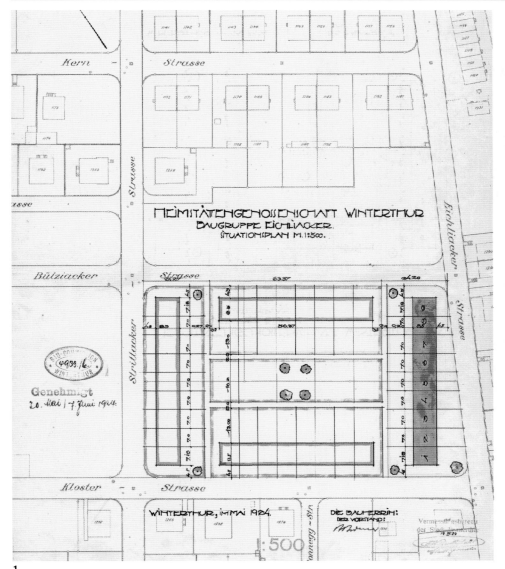

1. Plan, Hans Bernoulli and Adolf Kellermüller, 1924. SW

2. Typical view. WB (1930s)

3. Typical street. Bächinger. WG (2008)

and Kellermüller divided Unterer Deutweg's squarish site in two, bisected by the north–south path of Weberstrasse. In the western portion of the site, terraces bracketed the eastern and southern borders of a large, landscaped public green. The eastern parcel constituted a denser, gridded nine-block arrangement of rowhouses and semidetached units. The sixty-four one-and-a-half- to two-and-a-half-story single-family houses, the majority with both front and rear gardens, featured habitable attics and basements.

Bernoulli and Kellermüller's **Siedlung Eichliacker** (1924), located two miles west of Unterer Deutweg on a rectangular site, was also intended for workers and sponsored by Heimstätten-Genossenschaft Winterthur.[414] The architects arranged terraces of single-family houses around three sides of a landscaped community green. The northern border of the housing estate featured a centrally located kindergarten, flanked by additional green spaces. The twenty-five one-and-a-half-story houses—rows of eight on the eastern and western borders and a row of nine at the southern end—included both front and rear gardens. By 1927,

Eichliacker was completed as planned, although the kindergarten and its neighboring lawns were subsequently replaced by additional rowhouses.

Kellermüller, whose practice was based in Winterthur, collaborated with other architects on the design of additional municipally sponsored workers' estates outside Winterthur's center. **Siedlung Selbsthilfe** (self-help) (1925–29), planned by Kellermüller and Winterthur native Franz Scheibler (1898–1960), featured an unusual financial arrangement in which prospective residents could gain equity in the cooperative in exchange for helping in the construction of the housing estate.[415] Selbsthilfe shared its rectangular site with a factory located in the southeast corner. Kellermüller and Scheibler's plan consisted exclusively of uniform terraces located on straight, tree-lined streets, not only eschewing the naturalistic site planning of the typical garden suburb but also the vernacular-derived domestic architecture. In the portion of the site next to the factory, the terraces were all oriented east–west, with one six-house group, four seven-house rows, and two terraces of ten dwellings. The remainder of the estate north of Eigenheimweg was organized as eight

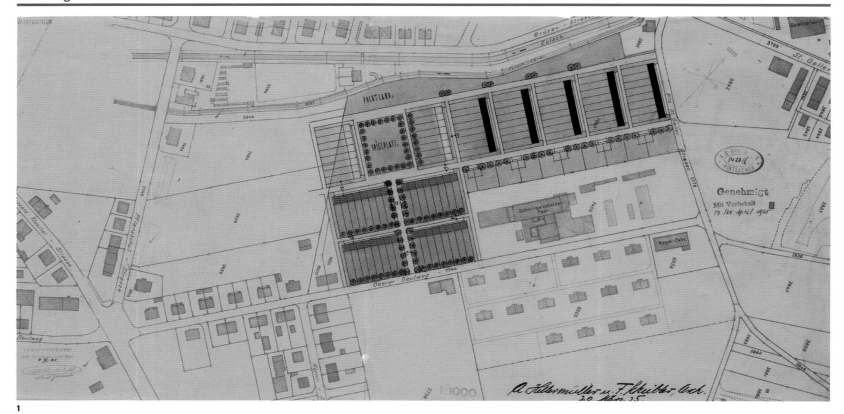

1

1. Plan, Adolf Kellermüller and Franz Scheibler, 1925. SW

2. Overall view. WB (1930)

3. Typical street. Bächinger. WG (2012)

2

3

parallel north–south rows of eight houses each. This portion also included a large public green and community house, home to meeting rooms, shops, and a kindergarten. All of the two-and-a-half-story single-family houses featured long and narrow rear allotment gardens.

Kellermüller partnered with Zurich-based architect Hans Hofmann (1897–1957) on the design of **Siedlung Stadtrain** (1928), located about a half mile northeast of Selbsthilfe on a similar rectangular site.[416] Intended for workers, the project was sponsored by Heimstätten-Genossenschaft Winterthur. Kellermüller and Hofmann's plan was dominated by long, north–south rows of single-family houses arranged with back-to-back gardens, a cost-saving measure recalling Bernoulli's scheme for Siedlung Hardturmstrasse that allowed two terraces to be served by a single road. North and south of the cubic, two-story, flat-roofed, stucco rowhouses the architects placed two- to four-story apartment buildings. A school and large playground were located at the southeast corner of the site. Construction began in 1928 and lasted until 1943,

with the apartment houses, several with ground-level shops, growing larger in size as time passed. All told, Stadtrain provided 377 dwelling units.

Closer to the center of Zurich, the firm of Karl Kündig (1883–1969) and Heinrich Oetiker (1886–1968) designed two housing estates sponsored by Zurich's City Council and intended for workers and low-level civil servants. **Siedlung Erismannhof** (1926) was located on a rectangular, three-acre site just west of a tram line that was occupied by two buildings at its northern border, which the architects let stand.[417] For this courtyard-bounding complex, Kündig & Oetiker lined the perimeter north–south streets with five-story apartment houses separated at their midpoints to allow access to the large courtyard via one-story, flat-arched entrance gates. The five-story apartment houses at the southern border were set back from the street, allowing additional access to the courtyard at the corners. The courtyard included a shared, landscaped green and a kindergarten. By 1928, seventeen brick buildings accommodating 169 apartments were completed at Erismannhof.

Siedlung Stadtrain

1. Aerial view. WB (1938)

2. Typical rowhouses. WB (1930s)

3. Typical street. Bächinger. WG (2012)

Siedlung Erismannhof

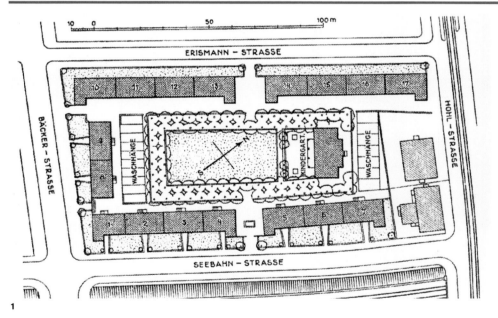

1. Plan, Kündig & Oetiker, 1926. SZ

2. Aerial view. SZ

Kündig & Oetiker's **Siedlung Utohof** (1927) was a more interesting, less dense development located on a squarish site about two miles south of Erismannhof and three miles southwest of central Zurich.[418] Utohof's eighty-three two-story single-family houses with gardens were arranged in terraces of three to eight houses, along with two semidetached units. The site was bisected by an east–west road leading from the main entrance to a kindergarten located between two house rows at the site's western border. This street also led to a long and narrow north–south public green located at roughly the center of the site. The casual arrangement of both east–west and north–south rows, some placed at an angle and set back from the development's narrow streets, created a village-like feel that strongly contrasted with Erismannhof's urban ambience.

In 1929, two years after the Deutscher Werkbund sponsored the construction of Siedlung Weissenhof for its exhibition in Stuttgart (see p. 458), the Swiss branch of the organization developed **Siedlung Neubühl**, a larger permanent housing exhibition of Modernist buildings that, like Mies's scheme for Weissenhof, was located on a hilly site and featured a plan influenced by the garden suburb movement.[419] Siedlung Neubühl was intended

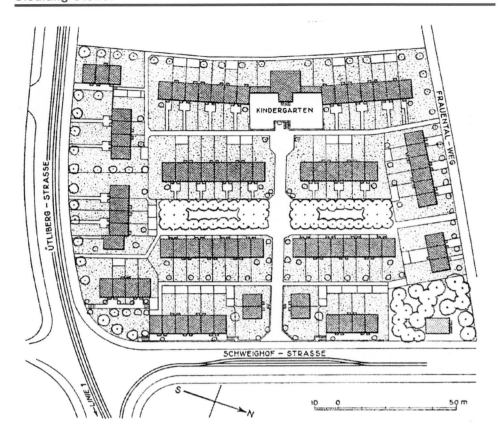

1

2

1. Plan, Kündig & Oetiker, 1927.
SCB30

2. Typical view. Linck. SZ

from the outset for the middle class due to the high cost of the land, a 10-acre parcel on the western bank of Lake Zurich in the Wollishofen quarter about three miles south of the city center. Seven members of the Schweizerischer Werkbund were responsible for the plan and its buildings, including Paul Artaria (1892–1959), Emil Roth (1893–1980), Hans Schmidt (1893–1972), Werner Max Moser (1896–1970), the son of Karl Moser, Carl Hubacher (1897–1990), Rudolf Steiger (1900–1982), and Max Ernst Haefeli (1901–1976)—although Steiger is generally given primary credit for the plan, having sketched a preliminary scheme in November 1928.

The plan consisted of four- to nine-unit terraces accommodating 105 two-story single-family houses as well as ninety apartments located in nine three-story buildings. Steiger and his collaborators were able to inject some variety in the scheme of spare flat-roofed houses placed perpendicular to the straight and curved streets by taking advantage of the varied topography to arrange them in a tiered pattern. All of the dwellings faced south to maximize lake and mountain views, and generous rear gardens were provided for each of the single-family units. In addition to the houses, the estate included a kindergarten, gymnasium, artist studios, café, garages, and shops.

Siedlung Neubühl was not completely finished until April 1932, but the exhibition celebrating its construction was held in September 1931, attracting 12,000 visitors. In his history of modern architecture, Leonardo Benevolo offered high praise for the housing estate, writing that "the ground plan was relatively simple while the types of buildings were designed with great care; the perfection of the details gave the dwellings intimacy and precision, and the repetition of the types did not produce monotony, since it was quite plainly made up for by the high standard of finish in each one."[420]

Architect and Socialist politician Maurice Braillard (1879–1965) prepared the plan for another Modernist housing estate, **Vieusseux Garden City** (1930), located two miles northwest of Geneva's center.[421] Braillard's plan for the wedge-shaped site was heavily influenced by Walter Gropius's Siedlung Törten (see p. 456) as well as Ernst May's Neue Frankfurt work (see p. 448), with north-south rows of three-story apartment buildings arranged along three gently curving streets divided by tree-lined streets. The main thoroughfare bisecting the site led from a modest landscaped plaza at the eastern end to the civic components at the western border, consisting of a community center, school, and day-care center. The apartment houses were the work of a number of architects, including Louis Vincent (n.d.), Jean-Jacques Honegger (1903–1985), Max Baumgartner (1894–1953), and Frèdèric Mezger (n.d.), who designed the Modernist flat-roofed, balcony-access home for the elderly.

The Garden City movement continued to influence Swiss development into the 1940s. **Siedlung Bethlehemacker**, located on a wedge-shaped site three miles west of Bern's city center, was conceived in 1944 as a low-income cooperative for woodworkers

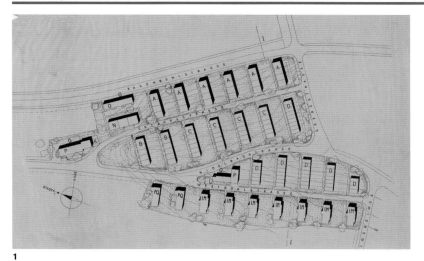

1

2

1. Plan, 1929. GTA

2. Aerial view. GTA (c. 1932)

3. Houses and rear gardens. GTA (c. 1932)

4. Ostbühlstrasse. Paebi. WC (2007)

3

4

Vieusseux Garden City

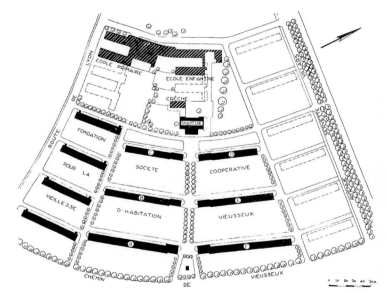

1

2

1. Plan, Maurice Braillard, 1930. FBA

2. Aerial view. CIG (1933)

3. Typical view. CIG (1933)

3

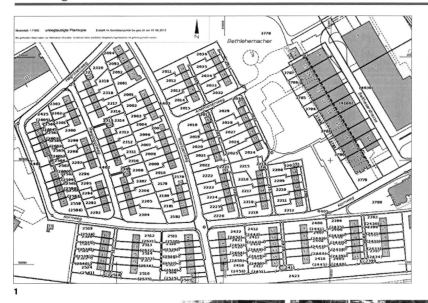

1. Plan, Hans and Gret Reinhard, 1944. HGRA (2012)

2. Rear gardens. HGRA (1947)

3. Aerial view. HGRA (2010)

4. Aerial view. HGRA (1947)

and carpenters.[422] The nonprofit cooperative hired the husband-and-wife team of Hans (1915–2003) and Gret (1917–2002) Reinhard to prepare the plan as well as design all of the buildings, a project not completed until 1948. The Reinhards' plan consisted of 143 single-family houses arranged primarily in terraces of four or five dwellings along slightly curving streets. The houses were set back behind modest front lawns and featured substantial rear gardens for fruit and vegetable cultivation. The two-story vernacular wood houses were basic fare, appropriate for their intended tenantry, who were also largely responsible for the construction of the housing estate. Christa Zeller has praised Siedlung Bethlehemacker, writing that "the architecture is impressive by virtue of its straight-lined simplicity and careful details."[423]

AUSTRIA

Pre–World War I Austria, unlike Germany, did not readily or enthusiastically embrace the Garden City movement.[424] In the capital city of Vienna in the last decades of the nineteenth century and the first of the twentieth, a large number of single-family houses

were built outside the inner ring, but these were privately developed without the benefit of any coordinated planning, resulting in "schematic, chessboard-like development without consideration of the nature of the terrain," as architectural historian Dietmar Steiner put it. "The aim was to create as many sites as possible with a minimum amount of green space."[425]

It was not until the end of the war that a confluence of events conspired to change Vienna's development pattern. Of primary importance was an acute housing and food shortage in the city, where more than 10,000 people, many recent refugees, were either homeless or living in substandard temporary accommodations. A Siedlerbewegung (settlers' movement) soon emerged, with surrounding fields and woods occupied by families who built shacks and planted vegetable gardens. There was also a dramatic change in the government, with the Social Democrats assuming power in 1919 and pledging to address the housing problem, establishing a Siedlungsamt (settlement office) headed by Hans Kampffmeyer (1876–1932), a founding member of the German Garden City Society. Kampffmeyer explained how the activity of the settlers launched Vienna's garden suburb movement: "It was therefore quite obvious that the allotment gardeners, who were suffering from the

1. Plan, Hugo Mayer, c. 1918.
HGDK

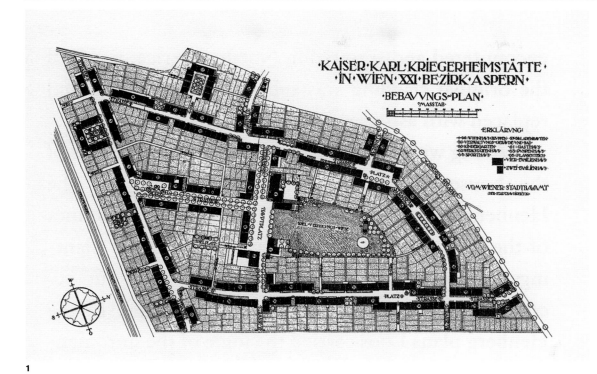

1

housing shortage, were to make the demand that public money from the state or the councils should no longer be spent on the reconstruction of tenement blocks, but instead on single family houses in the garden colonies. This is how the first housing estate co-operatives grew up from the circle of allotment gardeners."[426] Adolf Loos was appointed chief architect (1920–22) of the Siedlungsamt, reviewing proposals and providing advice to Kampffmeyer, but individual architects remained free to come up with their own plans and house designs for municipally sponsored projects.

Several newly created nonprofit housing associations generally aligned with a trade or industry joined the Socialist government of what came to be known as Rote Wien (Red Vienna) in promoting garden suburb construction, but the movement, dominated by a small number of architects, proved short-lived. A return to prosperity in the mid-1920s and concomitant sharp rise in the demand for housing led the Social Democratic government, which remained in power until 1934, to begin a five-year program to add 5,000 dwelling units in 1923, a number that would rise to 25,000 within two years, necessitating the rejection of low-density, semirural development, including projects where plans had already been produced, in favor of increasingly massive multistory urban apartment complexes. Between 1919 and 1934, only 11 percent of the municipally sponsored development consisted of low-rise suburban estates, constituting for many garden suburb enthusiasts, such as Werner Hegemann, a "missed opportunity."[427]

Hugo Mayer (1883–1930) was among the most active designers of Viennese garden villages until his death at age forty-seven of purulent tonsillitis. Employed since 1907 as a staff architect at Vienna's municipal construction office, which sent him in 1912 to study garden suburbs in England, Mayer's first siedlung design, **Kaiser Karl-Kriegerheimstätte** (c. 1918), intended for war widows and discharged soldiers, remained unrealized.[428] To be located in semirural Aspern in Vienna's Floridsdorf (XXI) district, the plan evoked prewar German garden villages with rows of two-story two- and four-family houses, some grouped around landscaped courtyards and set among squares, parks, and allotment gardens. Mayer had better luck with a similar scheme prepared for war workers' housing on the 25-acre site of the Schmelz military parade ground, about five miles west of the city center in the Fünfhaus (XV) district.[429] Initially intended to provide 1,000 units in 150 two-story rowhouses, plans for **Siedlung Schmelz** (1919) were scaled back after the end of the war, resulting in a less dense program with buildings occupying only 25 percent of the elevated, flat site, providing a stark contrast to the neighborhood's collection of tightly packed working-class tenements.

Mayer divided the rectangular site into four blocks, placing rows of two- and three-story multifamily houses on the perimeter, shielding generous allotment gardens behind. The design of the gardens at Schmelz, like those at almost every Viennese siedlung that followed, was strongly influenced by the work of the prolific German landscape architect Leberecht Migge. The curving north–south path of Mareschgasse, the main street lined on both sides by terraced houses and commercial structures, bisected the site and led to Mareschplatz, the town square. In her survey of Viennese housing, Eve Blau has found the design "firmly within the prewar tradition of German *Siedlung* and garden city design" but also saw the influence of such wartime work as Paul Schmitthenner's

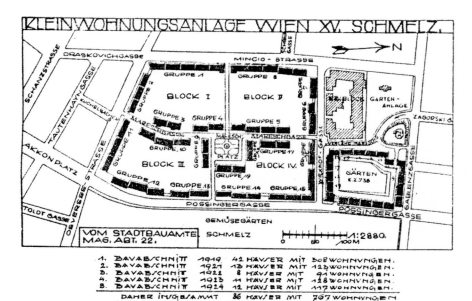

1. Plan, Hugo Mayer, 1924. ZOI

2. Wickhoffgasse and Mareschgasse. Gerlach. VGA (c. 1924)

3. Gardens. WM

4. Mareschplatz. Gugerell. WC (2010)

Staaken (see p. 756) in Berlin, "widely published at the time." In describing Siedlung Schmelz, Blau has written that "the picturesque sightlines and preindustrial village imagery evoke the *Kleinstadt* idyll that was so much a part of prewar *Siedlung* ideology. But the relationship between dwelling and garden, and the emphasis on food cultivation and subsistence gardening, places it within the typology of postwar *Gardensiedlung*."[430]

Siedlung Schmelz, the first municipal housing project to move forward in Vienna after the war, was built in several stages, with Mayer designing all of the buildings. Forty-two two- and three-story Biedermeier-style houses accommodating 308 households were completed by the end of 1920, accompanied by fourteen shops. The initial units were constructed from hollow cement blocks and received a minimum of ornament, but as the economy improved the houses did as well, becoming larger in the process, rising to four and even five stories. By 1924, the village numbered eighty-three houses along with twenty-two stores, an infirmary, central laundry, bathhouses, and a small lecture hall.

Mayer followed his work at Schmelz with **Siedlung Rosenhügel** (rose hill) (1921), located six miles southwest of the city center in the Hetzendorf (XII) district.[431] The project was the first venture of the Altmannsdorf-Hetzendorf Association, a nonprofit housing cooperative composed primarily of railroad workers. Mayer's V-shaped plan, inspired by Hannes Meyer's Siedlung Freidorf in Basel completed two years earlier, called for rows of two-story Heimatstil houses lining the perimeter of the site, which was divided by six east–west roads lined on both sides by similar rows of houses. As at Schmelz, substantial allotment gardens were placed behind the houses. Mayer had high hopes for the development, describing it as

a city within the metropolis, having an economic, social, and cultural life of its own; a place of progress and of a higher conduct of life. The co-operative house should stand on the highest spot of the site, right in the middle of an expansive green, as a center of cultural life. Assembly and lecture halls, a library and a reading room, and offices are to be accommodated here. The market square with the co-operative shop, the workshop, artisans' houses and the co-operative nursery are to concentrate the economical life at the center of the settlement . . . Each block is to contain a playground, two larger playgrounds are planned in conjunction with ponds, which do not only serve to collect waste water, but also to allow for the rearing of fish and ducks.[432]

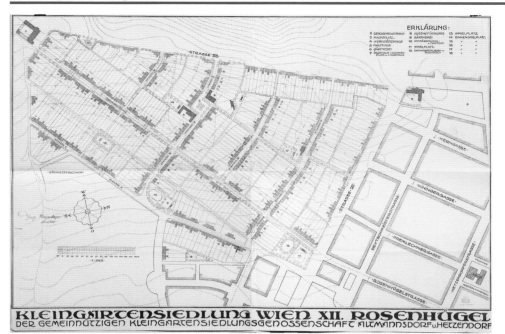

1. Plan, Hugo Mayer, 1921. WM

2. Dorfmeistergasse. SRV

3. Semidetached house. Jahn. VS (2011)

4. Commercial area. SRV

5. Typical street. Jahn. VS (2011)

1

2

3

4

5

Unfortunately, the strong demand for houses forced the elimination of the market square, playgrounds, and ponds, and the 400-square-meter gardens envisioned by Mayer were reduced by half to allow for more residences. A second stage of development, overseen by architect Emil Krause (1873–1937), cut the size of some gardens by half again to 100 square meters. Even with the reduced size of the gardens, Siedlung Rosenhügel, with several landscaped squares placed throughout the site, still provided a large measure of open space to accompany the 559 houses, social center, school, restaurants, and several shops completed by 1926.

Siedlung Heuberg (1921) was a collaboration between Mayer and Adolf Loos, although Mayer is generally credited with the plan.[433] Located on a steeply sloping site overlooking the Wienerwald (Vienna Woods) in the Hernals (XVII) district five miles northwest of the city center, Heuberg, intended primarily for workers in the building trades who would be required to help construct the estate, was cosponsored by the city and a nonprofit housing cooperative. Mayer's plan arranged terraces of single-family houses on both sides

of Röntgengasse, the east–west main street. At the eastern end of the site, the curving paths of Röntgengasse and Schrammeigasse created a roundish parcel wide enough to accommodate several rows of houses and a community center equipped with stores, a kindergarten, café, and meeting hall. Additional terraces were placed north and south of Röntgengasse, with each house featuring a modest front garden and a deep rear allotment garden. Loos's contribution appears to have been limited to the overall stylistic direction of the houses, although only eight of the 168 dwellings completed by 1924 can be definitively attributed to him. The two-story cubic houses, with flat gravel roofs and shingle siding, provided a stark contrast to the traditionally styled buildings at Schmelz and Rosenhügel. Loos's row along Plachygasse, just north of Röntgengasse, was built according to a new structural system that the architect had patented in 1921 known as the *Haus mit einer Mauer* (house with one wall), where "the foundations of the two external walls are dispensed with," as Loos stated. "This is done by suspending them from, rather than basing them on, the foundation that supports them."[434]

Siedlung Heuberg

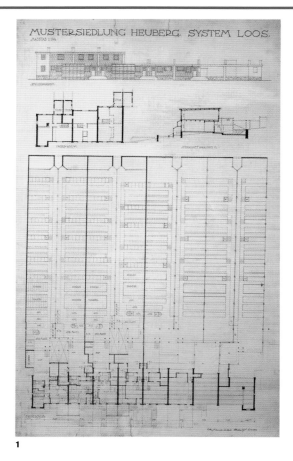

1

2

3

Gartenstadt Friedenstadt

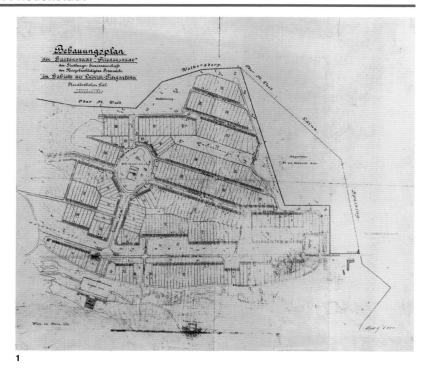

1

1. Plan, Adolf Loos, 1921. ALB

In 1921, on his own, Loos prepared a plan for **Gartenstadt Friedenstadt** that was quickly rejected by the sponsoring nonprofit housing association.[435] Intended for a 74-acre site in the Lainzer Tiergarten donated by Vienna's municipal government, the plan was, in Loos's own words, "intentionally unpicturesque." Blau has written that the Czech-born, Vienna-based architect "retained the preexisting broad, straight, brick-paved allée that connected two ponds at the summit and base of a hill on the site. At the elevated end Loos placed a tower, at the lower end a community center and school buildings. The principal residential streets of the *Siedlung* were sited on axis with these monuments and perpendicular to the allée, with the houses set back from the street, interspersed among the trees." The developers objected to the principal features of the design, including the north–south orientation of the dwellings, the straight streets, and the deep allotment gardens. The site was later developed in a "piecemeal and uncoordinated" manner, although Loos did complete one row of eight houses.[436]

Josef Frank (1885–1967), best remembered for his furniture and textile designs, was another important designer of siedlungen in Vienna until the Jewish architect emigrated to Sweden in 1933 after the German elections, "fearful that the growing tide of Nazism would soon spill over into Austria."[437] At the conclusion of World War I, Frank, sympathetic to the goals of the settlement movement and lacking work in the depressed economy, proposed a city-financed model

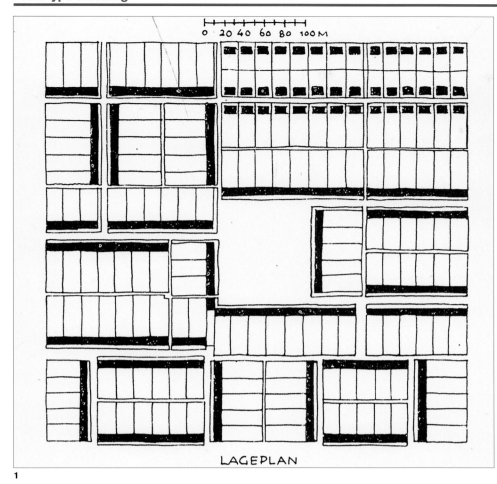

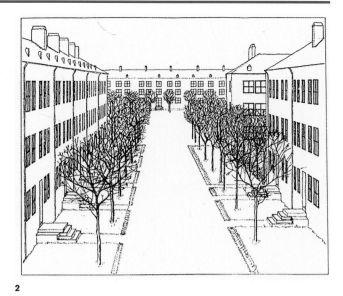

1. Plan, Josef Frank, 1919. DA 19
2. Perspective. DA 19 (1919)

siedlung composed of prefabricated poured-concrete buildings designed in collaboration with engineers Hugo Fuchs (n.d.) and Franz Zettinig (n.d.).[438] The plan for the **prototype siedlung**, published in *Der Architect* early in 1919 and intended for a flat site at the city's edge, called for an irregular grid of 15-meter-wide streets with a large square placed at the center of the site, where a tram or underground station was to be located, providing transportation to the central city and surrounding factories. Frank arranged straight rows of three-story, six-family minimally detailed apartment buildings perpendicular or parallel to each other. The rows were slightly set back behind a small strip of green planted with trees with long, narrow allotment gardens placed at the rear, accessed by two-meter-wide paths. At the northeast corner of the prototypical site, Frank included rows of two-story detached houses with rear gardens.

Although Frank was unable to realize his model workers' village, the plan did influence his **Siedlung Hoffingergasse** (1921), the second project sponsored by the Altmannsdorf-Hetzendorf Association, the nonprofit housing cooperative responsible for Siedlung Rosenhügel.[439] Located six miles southwest of Vienna's city center and two miles west of Rosenhügel, Siedlung Hoffingergasse occupied a squarish site of open fields that had been taken over by settlers who put up makeshift dwellings and planted extensive vegetable gardens. The housing cooperative instructed Frank to preserve as many of the

gardens as possible, resulting in a low-density plan with buildings occupying only about 10 percent of the site.

The long and narrow rear allotment gardens, averaging about 400 square meters, were the most important element of the design, with the rowhouses pushed forward to the street's edge in order to make as much room as possible for cultivation. Christopher Long, Frank's biographer, has noted that Hoffingergasse's plan "deviated from the standard planning ideas of the time. Rather than arranging the houses in north–south rows, as Loos suggested, or east–west, as was the common practice in Germany, Frank oriented most of the houses at a roughly forty-five degree angle so that the rows ran northeast–southwest. This ensured not only that all of the gardens would receive sufficient light, but also that the facades would not be exposed to the prevailing north wind. In contrast to most of the other *Siedlungen* constructed in Vienna in the early 1920s, Frank's site plan also avoided traditional monumental axes or symmetry, producing an antipicturesque and matter-of-fact effect."[440] Eve Blau has added that "the rows of houses slide past each other in alignment with the existing streets and grid of paths and lanes established by the allotment gardens to give the *Siedlung* the quality of seeming incomplete and open-ended, a fragment of the larger shifting grid of the city itself."[441]

Between 1921 and 1924 Frank completed 284 two-story three-bedroom single-family rowhouses at

1. Plan, Josef Frank, 1921. DNW26

2. Overall view showing gardens. WM

3. Typical street. WM

4. Typical street. Jahn. VS (2011)

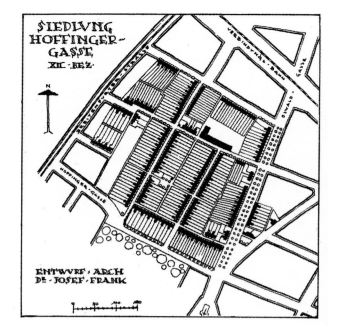

Siedlung Hoffingergasse, designed in collaboration with Erich Faber (n.d.), an architect on staff at the Viennese municipal building office. The simple, stucco-clad houses with pitched roofs were largely unornamented but featured wall trellises for the training of vines and roses, a feature Frank most likely borrowed from Heinrich Tessenow. Balconies were added to the end units. Frank also included a community building, day-care center, cooperative store, and several playgrounds in the siedlung. Political philosopher and housing advocate Otto Neurath wrote in 1923 that the houses displayed "an expression of frugality, but also an expression of a feeling of equality . . . Each individual house is not an object of design, but rather the entire collection of houses. The individual house is like a brick in a building."[442] Many early residents, who were required to spend at least 2,000 hours in helping to build the community, saw it differently. Objecting to the extreme similarity of the designs, they quickly added *völkisch* touches to personalize their homes.

At the same time Frank was working on Hoffingergasse, he received commissions for five additional siedlungen, all located outside of Vienna and all unfortunately unrealized. In the spring of 1921, Frank released plans for a workers' village to be located on a triangular site in the farming town of Traiskirchen, twenty miles south of Vienna and noted for its vineyards.[443] Frank arranged long rows of two-story houses primarily in an east–west direction, behind which were long and narrow allotment gardens. A main square in roughly the center of the site was placed near a planned community garden, kindergarten, and hospital. In the northern corner of the site was a large sports field with swimming pool and bath, while two playgrounds were to occupy rectangular sites. What separated the plan of **Siedlung Traiskirchen** from Frank's typical efforts was a new attention to landscaping that went beyond the allotment gardens and connecting pedestrian paths to include double rows of trees bordering the site on all three sides as well as a nursery. Rows of trees were also to be placed along the village's main thorough-fares. Christopher Long has found the plan to be "more refined" than that of Hoffingergasse, but when it failed to move forward, Frank produced a slimmed-down version that eliminated the trees, nursery, and play-grounds, a scheme that also never progressed beyond the planning stages.[444]

In 1922–23 Frank produced slight variations on the Siedlung Hoffingergasse model for the Viennese suburbs of Rodaun, Stockerau, and **St. Veit an der Triesting**.[445] Of note was the unusual harp-shaped plan of St. Veit an der Triesting and the introduction of flat roofs in some of the houses at Rodaun. **Siedlung Klosterneuburg**, intended for a site eight miles north of the city center, was the most ambitious and stylistically modern of the unrealized siedlungen.[446] Frank's denser plan of terraced flat-roofed houses included the typical long and narrow allotment gardens but also featured a prominent civic focus in the form of a wide Haupt Platz (main square) that bisected the site, home to a two-story concrete-and-brick community center topped by a clock.

Siedlung Flötzersteig (1921), the work of Franz Kaym (1891–1949) and Alfons Hetmanek (1890–1962), was located on a semirural site in Vienna's Penzig (XIV) district, six miles west of the city center.[447] The project, sponsored by the nonprofit housing cooperative Gemeinnützige Bau- und Wohnungsgenossenschaft and intended primarily for white-collar workers, was large by Viennese standards, comprising 549 dwelling units in a combination of detached, semidetached, and rowhouses realized in two separate building campaigns that lasted until the end of the decade.

The plan, by Kaym and Hetmanek, who had both studied between 1910 and 1913 at Vienna's Academy of Fine Arts under Otto Wagner (1841–1918), responded to the demands of the steeply sloping, irregularly shaped site with curving streets that divided the various groups of buildings arrayed on either side of Flötzersteig Strasse, the main artery. The plan, as well as the Voysey-esque two-story single- and multifamily houses, was clearly influenced by Parker and Unwin and the English garden suburb movement, but Blau has noted that "the broad encompassing roofs with gable ends facing the street also reflect Kaym and Hetmanek's Wagner School origins and their own engagement with the simple geometries of alpine vernacular building in Upper Austria."[448] At the southern end of the site, two groups of perimeter terraces sheltered interior houses, while the northern half of the site featured rows that mostly followed the topography of the site. Some of the houses were set behind modest front lawns, and each included a rear allotment garden averaging 350 square meters. The picturesque arrangement of houses was joined by landscaped squares, several stores, and a community center.

Kaym and Hetmanek adopted a more formal plan for their next project, **Siedlung Weissenböck** (1922), located in Vienna's Simmering (XI) district, six miles southeast of the city center.[449] Initially sponsored by the Altmanns-dorf-Hetzendorf Association and intended primarily

Siedlung Traiskirchen

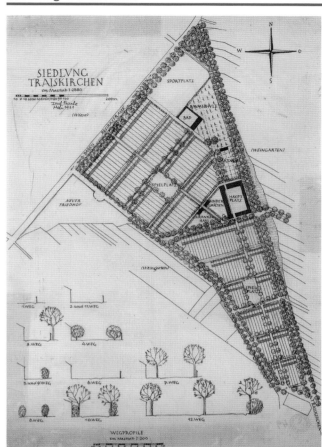

1. Plan and street profiles, Josef Frank, 1921. ALB

St. Veit an der Triesting

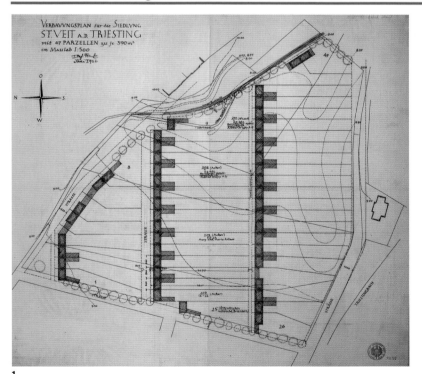

1. Plan, Josef Frank, 1922. UAK

Siedlung Klosterneuburg

1. Plan, Josef Frank, 1922. ALB
2. Perspective. ALB (1923)

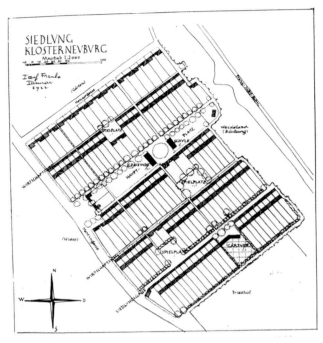

1

2

Siedlung Flötzersteig

1. Plan, Franz Kaym and Alfons Hetmanek, 1921. WM26
2. Aerial view. MB34 (c. 1934)
3. Typical street. MB34 (c. 1934)
4. Gardens. WM
5. Typical view. Bürgmann. PB (2009)

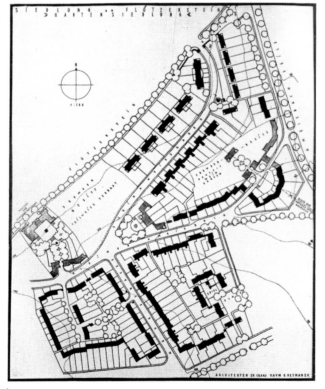

1

2

3

4

5

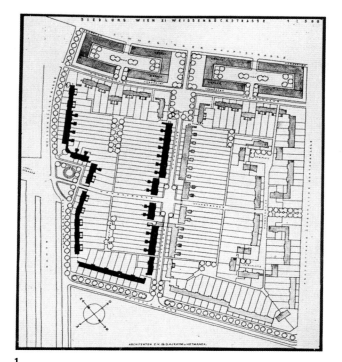

1

2

3

4

1. Plan, Franz Kaym and Alfons Hetmanek, 1922. WM26

2. Houses from first stage of development, 1922–23. WM

3. Houses from second stage of development, 1927–28. Invis. WC (2007)

4. Houses from second stage of development, 1927–28. WM

for workers at a nearby gasworks, the architects' original plan for the rectangular site called for terraced housing on two adjacent parcels bisected by a north–south street with a central square created by the crossing of an east–west through street. Two groups of courtyard-bounding rowhouses, with central openings along both their north and south sides, were intended to close the development's northern border. The nonprofit housing cooperative was unable to finance the project, however, and Vienna's municipal construction office took over the exclusively residential development, retaining Kaym and Hetmanek and reducing the site to just its western component.

Kaym and Hetmanek lined the perimeter of the site, except along the northernmost block, with terraces of two-story single-family houses, mostly in straight rows but a few that were staggered, and others which followed the path of the irregularly shaped parcel. Set back behind 30- to 90-square-meter front gardens, the design of the seventy-six houses with steeply pitched roofs and

paired gables, like those at Siedlung Flötzersteig, owed their inspiration to the English Arts and Crafts movement and featured 350-square-meter rear allotment gardens. Artmanngasse was the only street that passed through the wall of buildings. A central internal path connected the long and narrow gardens. In 1927, four years after the completion of the perimeter group, Kaym and Hetmanek designed an unusual arrangement for the northern block, geared to a more affluent tenantry and consisting of two rows of four-family villa-like houses arranged around a central landscaped square. Completed the following year, the houses accommodated fifty-six families with gardens between 50 and 100 square meters.

Heinrich Schlöss (1886–1964) and Karl Ehn (1884–1957), both on the staff of Vienna's municipal construction office, collaborated on the plan for **Siedlung Hermeswiese** (1923), although they each designed separate groups of rowhouses for the site in the Hietzing

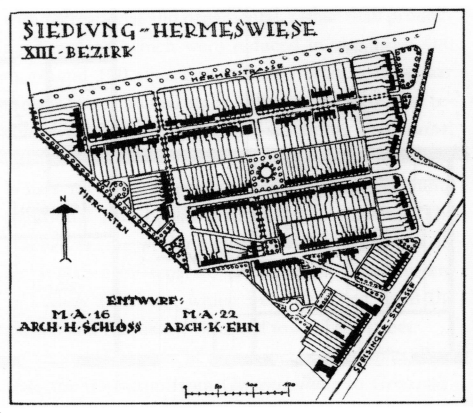

1. Plan, Heinrich Schlöss and Karl Ehn, 1923. DNW26

2. Aerial view. BON (1935)

3. Entrance at Lynkeusgasse. VGA (1925)

4. Houses, Karl Ehn, c. 1924, Lynkeusgasse. VGA (1925)

5. Lynkeusgasse. Haeferl. WC (2011)

(XIII) district.[450] The project was jointly sponsored by the city and the nonprofit Altmannsdorf-Hetzendorf Association and intended for workers at a nearby municipal electric works. Ehn, who had also studied with Otto Wagner and is best known for his Karl Marx Hof (1927–30), the most monumental of Vienna's apartment complexes, was responsible for the most interesting group of houses at the northern end of the site along both sides of Lynkeusgasse.[451] The siedlung was entered at the eastern end of the site through a broad arch that recalled Georg Metzendorf's gateway to Margarethenhöhe, outside Essen, as well as Mayer's Schmelz and Paul Schmitthenner's Staaken. Ehn arranged the terraces of ninety-five two-story single-family houses primarily in a straight row, although a few groups were set back to provide variety. The design of the brick and stucco houses, with fenced-in front gardens and large rear allotment gardens, like those of Kaym and Hetmanek, was firmly

situated in the English Arts and Craft movement.

Schlöss's parcel for Hermeswiese, also known as Siedlung Lainz-Speising, was located south of Ehn's group and separated from it by a central landscaped square. The 180 two-story single-family houses, primarily along both sides of Dvorakgasse, were designed in a similar vein in collaboration with Emil Krause, who had worked on the second stage of development at Siedlung Rosenhügel. Like Ehn, Schlöss and Krause also included a building that spanned the main entrance at Paoliweg. In 1928, Ehn oversaw the expansion of Siedlung Hermeswiese south of Lainz-Speising, including two U-shaped groups at both ends of Neukommweg.

Siedlung Am Wasserturm (at the water tower) (1923–24), designed by Franz Schuster and Franz Schacherl (1895–1943), was an early project of the Gemeinwirtschaftlichen Siedlungs- und Baustoffanstalt (GESIBA), an influential nonprofit housing

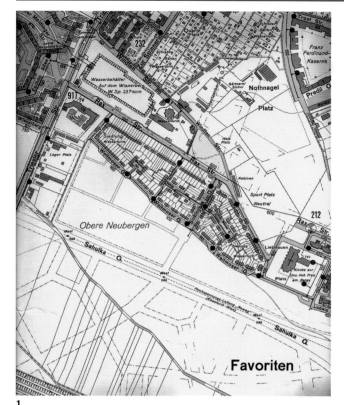

1. Map. BF (1977)

2. Rear gardens. WM

3. Rear gardens. FG

4. Raxstrasse. Buchhändler. WC (2010)

5. Rear gardens. WM

association founded in 1921 and partially financed by Vienna's municipal government.[452] Located on a long and narrow, irregular, lozenge-shaped site in the Favoriten (X) district four miles south of the city center, the exclusively residential housing estate was intended for the middle class. Schuster & Schacherl's plan called for rows of two to seven two-story single-family houses lining the perimeter of the site, which was cut through by two north–south through streets. Houses were also located behind the wall of buildings along both sides of two internal streets running down the center of the eastern half of the site. The perimeter was broken as well at Weigandhof, a short street surrounded by three houses set back from Weitmosergasse, the southern border of the site. The rear gardens behind each row were less rigidly arranged than was typical at Viennese siedlungen with their elongated allotment gardens.

Both the plan and the design of the 188 three-bedroom houses displayed the strong influence of Heinrich Tessenow, who had been Schuster's teacher at Vienna's Kunstgewerbeschule as well as his employer between 1916 and 1922.[453] Blau makes the point that Tessenow's impact "is unmistakable in the balanced massing of the plain stucco-faced facades, the cubic proportions of the blocks, and especially the hipped roofs under which the units are variously grouped. Rather than being a fragment of a larger urban grid, the *Siedlung* is self-contained and oriented inward to the gardens and cul-de-sacs at its center." In keeping with Am Wasserturm's white-collar aspirations, Blau has noted that "the image . . . is of bourgeois gentility rather than proletarian subsistence."[454]

Schuster & Schacherl, whose practice lasted until 1927, when Schuster moved to Frankfurt to work with Ernst May, also designed **Siedlung Neustrassäcker** (1924–26), located in the northeast part

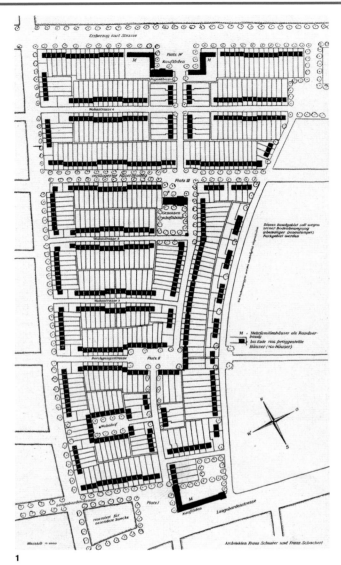

1

2

3

4

of Vienna in the Donaustadt (XXII) district east of the Danube.[455] The 332-dwelling estate was sponsored by the nonprofit Aus Eigner Kraft cooperative and intended for a less affluent tenantry than Am Wasserturm. Schuster & Schacherl's plan lined the perimeter of the trapezoidal site with terraces of two-story single-family houses as they had previously done, but the interior of the parcel, which widened toward the north, was far more intensively developed with long east–west and north–south rows. To avoid monotony the central units in the east–west rows were set back, while the longest north–south row was placed on a curving street. Houses were also grouped around landscaped courtyards. Narrow 120- to 150-square-meter allotment gardens were placed behind each row and several landscaped squares and playgrounds were placed throughout the site. Although the design of the houses closely resembled the firm's previous effort, the effect was less charming, the result of a more formal plan and the length of the terraces.

Siedlung Am Freihof (1923), designed by Karl Schartelmüller (1884–1947) for Vienna's city government and intended for municipal employees, was by far the city's largest garden suburb at 1,014 dwelling units, 678 of which were in single-family houses.[456] Located five miles northeast of the city center and east of the Danube in the Kagran area of the Donaustadt district, the mixed-use development occupied a 126-acre site roughly bound by Am Freihof to the north, Siebenbürgerstrasse to the east, Kagraner Anger to the south, and Komzakgasse to the west. Schartelmüller's plan included both long east–west and north–south terraces along with several courtyard-bounding groups, some located on culs-de-sac while others provided through-street passages beneath arches. The most interesting group of rowhouses was a V-shaped section formed by the curving path of Polletstrasse. Each of the dwellings included rear gardens of between 200 and 300 square meters.

A main square at roughly the center of Siedlung Am Freihof was created by the intersection of Strassmeyergasse and Steigenteschgasse, the two main through streets, with many of the public facilities, including shops, restaurants, a school, youth center, and community center, placed around it. Playgrounds were scattered throughout the site and a large sports field was located at the southwest corner. In addition to the plan, Schartelmüller was responsible for the design of all of the

1. Plan, Karl Schartelmüller, 1923. DNW26

2. Polletstrasse. BON (1933)

3. Typical view. WM

4. Polletstrasse. Jumb. PAN (2009)

two- and three-story houses. Completed over a four-year period, the stucco houses with pitched roofs were somewhat plain but praised by architectural historian Dietmar Steiner for their "Expressionist detailing."[457] In 1938–39 Schartelmüller, who remained under government employ after the Anschluss, when Austria was annexed by Nazi Germany, expanded the siedlung.

Schartelmüller was also the planner and architect of one of Vienna's last significant garden estates, **Siedlung Lockerwiese** (1928), located on a gently sloping site in the Hietzing (XIII) district and developed by the city in conjunction with the nonprofit housing cooperative GESIBA, which had earlier sponsored Siedlung Am Wasserturm.[458] Although smaller than Am Freihof at 643 dwelling units, Lockerwiese was still large by Viennese standards, composed primarily of two-story terraced single-family houses but with a U-shaped four-story apartment complex at roughly the center of the site spanning Faistauergasse, the main thoroughfare with landscaped median. August Sarnitz has described the project as "a rather belated attempt by a civil architect to revive the housing estate model. The Lockerwiese estate is not of the self-supporting type (where residents grow their own vegetables, etc.) favored by earlier complexes." Except for the increased density and scale, the plan for Lockerwiese resembled Schartelmüller's earlier project, with curving streets connecting various groups of buildings enclosing allotment gardens. But the cubic, spare buildings at Lockerwiese were more Modernist in style and the gardens much smaller, averaging just 70 square meters. However, as Sarnitz has written, "the stripped-down massing, at

a closer look, reveals succinct and subtle details."[459] In addition to the houses, the siedlung included shops, a library, and a community center located near the central apartment component.

Clearly influenced by the numerous large apartment blocks being built in Vienna, Lockerwiese illustrates, as Dietmar Steiner has written, "an 'objective' reconciliation of elements from the super-blocks with housing estate construction,"[460] while Catherine Cook, in her brief guide to Vienna, has noted that the "curved roadways ... give softness and variety to what ... threatens to have super-block rather than cottage scale."[461] As at Am Freihof, Schartemüller expanded Lockerwiese in 1938–39, designing 131 additional single-family houses.

The prolific siedlung designer Josef Frank was granted one final opportunity to design a low-rise suburban estate when he was asked in 1930 to oversee the Austrian Werkbund's housing exhibition in Vienna, timed to correspond with that summer's Werkbund Congress but delayed because of financial difficulties until 1932.[462] Frank had been the only Austrian selected by Mies to participate in the Deutsche Werkbund's 1927 exhibition in Stuttgart (see p. 458), but his double house proved controversial, with interiors criticized by some Modernists as "almost provocatively conservative" and derided as "Frank's bordello."[463] Intent on avoiding the stridently Modernist tone of Weissenhof, Frank selected thirty-one architects more in keeping with his less doctrinaire views, primarily from Austria and including Josef Hoffmann (1870–1956), Adolf Loos, Oskar Strnad (1879–1935), Oskar Wlach (1881–1963), and Margarete Schütte-Lihotzky. Hugo Häring was the

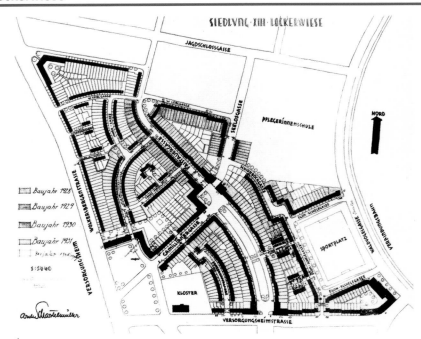

1. Plan, Karl Schartelmüller, 1928. BON (1939)

2. Aerial view. BON (1932)

3. Typical street. BON (1930)

4. Typical street. VGA (1939)

5. Versorgungsheimstrasse. BON (1930)

only German asked to participate. The only surprising choice was that of Austrian-born Modernist Richard Neutra (1892–1970), then living in the United States. Limiting the program to detached, semidetached, and terraced one- to three-story single-family houses, Frank saw the model estate not only as an alternative to Weissenhof but also as a protest against the monumental apartment complexes proliferating in Vienna, even though he had been actively involved in their construction as a matter of professional necessity.[464] As Christopher Long has put it, Vienna's **Werkbund Siedlung** "represented one final attempt on Frank's part to respond to the Vienna municipal building program, to demonstrate in concrete terms alternatives to the high-density housing blocks and reawaken interest in the *Siedlung* movement."[465]

The Werkbund Siedlung occupied a triangular, somewhat hilly and marshy parcel on the western outskirts of Vienna in the Hietzing district. Frank arranged seventy houses in an informal, seemingly random manner, connected by the curving path of the one internal street that wound its way through the site. The freestanding, semidetached, and short terraces were oriented in every direction and featured rear gardens. In the introduction

to the exhibition's catalogue, Frank stated that his aim was to create a housing estate that would seem to have "grown up over time."[466] To soften the severity of the flat-roofed buildings, Hungarian artist Laszló Gábor (1895–1938) devised a color scheme of yellow, blue, green, pink, and off-white, that, according to Long, "not only achieved the amiable appearance and sense of delight and novelty that Frank intended, but . . . also emphasized the modest, villagelike scale of the plan."[467]

The Werkbund Siedlung was, as Blau has succinctly observed, "the last gasp of the settlement movement."[468] Despite the fact that over 100,000 people visited between June and August 1932, the siedlung was regarded by many as a disappointment, assailed by Modernists for its "unscientific" site plan and criticized by more traditionally minded observers for the austerity of its cubic stucco-clad buildings. House sales were disappointing as well, with only fifteen dwellings purchased, although this lack of success can perhaps best be attributed to the deteriorating economy as opposed to popular displeasure with the estate and its buildings. More important, certainly to Frank, was the exhibition's failure to revive Austria's siedlung movement, with its commitment to low-density developments.

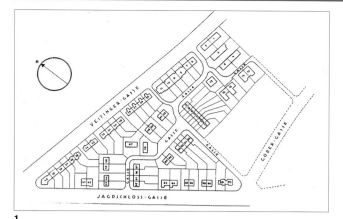

1. Plan, Josef Frank, 1932. DIW

2. Aerial view. BON (1932)

3. Veitingergasse. VGA (1932)

4. Houses, Oskar Wlach, 1932, Veitingergasse. Heard. WC (2006)

ITALY

The Garden City movement spread to Italy in 1908 when Luigi Buffoli (1850–1914), founder and director of the powerful Unione Cooperativa, established in 1886 as a retail cooperative specializing in the clothing industry but quickly growing to include such other businesses as hotels, restaurants, printing, and banking, announced plans to build **Città Giardino** (garden city) **Milanino**, intended for 12,000 residents drawn predominantly but not exclusively from the cooperative's ranks.[469] Inspired by the example of Letchworth (see p. 230), Buffoli acquired a 321-acre site about four miles north of central Milan in the municipality of Cusano that was convenient to an existing tram line. In addition to its business interests, the private cooperative also exhibited a commitment to social issues, building public baths and schools.

The Milan-based firm of Giuseppe Mentasti (1875–1958?) and Stefano Lissoni (1878–1939) was commissioned to draw up the plan (1909) for Milanino as well as design most of its first houses as well as its civic and commercial buildings. Their plan called for a 200-foot-wide north–south thoroughfare with landscaped median bisecting the site. Surrounding streets were arranged in an elliptical pattern. A semicircle at the south end and a *rond-point* near the north end anchored the suburb's main street, named after Buffoli following his death in 1914, although only the semicircle at the southern end was completed. Mentasti and Lissoni divided the site into 2,000 lots intended for villas with

gardens, placing few restrictions on their development except for setback requirements and a height limit of three stories. Several large parks were included in the plan, with building limited to about 40 percent of the heavily treed site.

Between 1909 and 1914 about 100 detached villas were completed in Milanino, along with a tram station, community center, general store, theater, elementary school, church, old-age home, sports field, and headquarters for the Unione Cooperativa. After Buffoli's death, progress was initially stymied by a lack of leadership and later halted by the beginning of the war. In 1919 construction resumed, with one- and two-family terraced houses joining the stylistically eclectic collection of villas. In 1923, a year after Mussolini and the Fascists took control of the government, the Unione Cooperativa was disbanded.

Carlo Santi, writing in 1984, described Milanino's fate after the Unione Cooperativa ended its involvement, noting that the suburb

no longer propelled by the ideals that had inspired its conception, continued growing over the years, with varying degrees of respect for its starting rules. However, the township is still one of the most interesting episodes in Italian town-planning, on account of the spirit in which it was constituted, the lack of speculative intent behind it, the awareness of a free association seeking community integration for family life, the urban vision of the town and its surroundings,

1. Plan, Giuseppe Mentasti and Stefano Lissoni, 1911. AM

2. Viale Luigi Buffoli. AM (1923)

3. Tram station. AM

4. Villa Nagas. AM (1923)

5. Viale dei Tigli. AM (1912)

6, 7. Typical streets. Lovene. AM (2008)

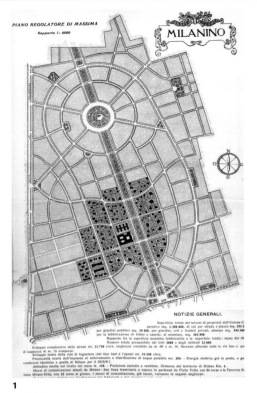

1

2

3

4

6

5

7

in contrast with Milan's development, and the strength of the urban plan which expressed all this and which still stands out clearly amidst the chaos of the Milan area.[470]

Reporting on a conference honoring the suburb's centennial in 2009, by which time its population had reached over 19,000, or about 60 percent more than originally contemplated, John Haywood compared Milanino to Hampstead Garden Suburb (see p. 350):

Milanino shares many of the principles and ideas of the [Hampstead Garden] Suburb . . . The layout . . . was carefully planned using the ideas from Ebenezer Howard's 'Garden Cities of Tomorrow,' adapted by Luigi Buffoli to ensure that overall densities were kept low and buildings were restricted in height and kept back from the edges of plots to enhance the feeling of space . . . and to provide release from the congestion and overcrowding of Milan . . . Travelling from

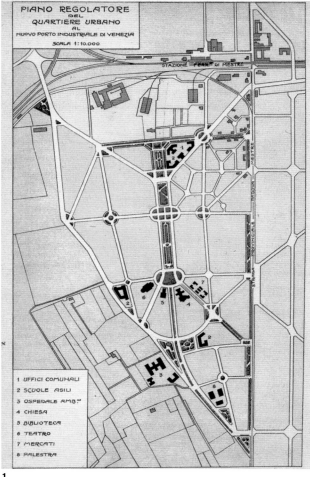

1. Plan, Pietro Emilio Emmer, 1921. SAR

2. Aerial view after bombing by British Royal Air Force. AN (1945)

3. Aerial view. Giacomelli. CDV (1925)

4. Via Nicolo Vergottini and Via Antonio Canetti. Bombieri. CDV (2012)

5. Via Giuseppe Zambelli and Via Demetrio Mircovich. Bombieri. CDV (2012)

the high densities and high rises of Milan, upon entering Milanino the difference is immediately obvious, much like walking into the Suburb from Finchley Road. The sense of space and abundant trees and other soft landscaping provides a peaceful and pleasant surrounding. The architecture of Milanino is not as coherent as the Suburb but there are several examples of exceptional design with elaborate stucco decoration, fine wood carving and intricate metalwork designs.[471]

Plans for a residential subdivision to accompany the creation of a new industrial port on the mainland side of the Venetian lagoon just south of the town of Mestre were first announced in 1917, but the start of construction was delayed until the end of the war.[472] The driving force behind **Città Giardino Marghera** was industrialist and politician Count Giuseppe Volpi (1877–1947), president of the Società per il Porto Industriale di Venezia, created by the municipal government and granted broad powers to build and connect critical infrastructure as well as reclaim land needed for both the port and the residential component. Intended primarily for the chemical and petroleum industries, the Porto Marghera was deemed critical for the future of Venice, as architectural historian Deborah Howard has noted: "Without the major new source of income created by the industrialization of the lagoon, Venice would probably have become a ghost town."[473]

The plan for the almost 500-acre area was placed in the hands of two engineers, with Enrico Coen-Cagli (n.d.) in charge of the industrial district and Pietro Emilio Emmer (n.d.) designing the 150-acre residential component directly west of the port. Emmer's plan featured a wide north–south thoroughfare with generous landscaped median that was linked by radiating streets to several piazzas, primarily in the form of *rond-points*, scattered throughout the site. Major and minor streets were lined with trees and small landscaped sections marked many intersections. Plots of land were sold to plant managers and executives who commissioned spacious villas, while workers' housing in semidetached and terraced units and apartment buildings was built by the nonprofit Istituto Autonomo per le Case Popolari di Venezia as well as by private developers.

Porto Marghera grew rapidly, and by 1925 the harbor was home to thirty-three companies and more than 3,400 employees. The residential district was affected by the continued growth of the port and the original idea of an airy, bucolic garden city was compromised by the increased population density caused by the demand for new housing and the environmental impact of the industrial facilities. As Deborah Howard recently put it: "As well as bringing prosperity . . . this development . . . led to severe problems of air and water pollution, while the need to admit giant oil tankers has inhibited plans for flood-prevention schemes at the entrances to the lagoon."[474]

In 1920, the Istituto per le Case Popolari (ICP; Institute for Social Housing), founded in 1903 by the Roman municipal government "with the aim of creating hygienic and comfortable houses for craftsmen and laborers," commissioned architect, urban planner, and architectural historian Gustavo Giovannoni (1873–1947) to prepare plans for two housing estates outside Rome's city center: **Aniene** and Garbatella.[475] The intended working-class tenantry was the group most severely affected by the post–World War I housing shortage in which more than 15 percent of the Roman population was forced to live in shantytowns. Giovannoni's plans for Aniene and Garbatella, similar in design but varying greatly in scale, were heavily influenced by the example of Ebenezer Howard and the English Garden City movement. According to architect and historian Christopher Woodward, the two schemes of "rustic"– and "medieval"–style low-rise houses "arranged along picturesquely winding roads" were also influenced by a 1916 book written by Marcello Piacentini (1881–1960), *Sulla conservazione della bellezza di Roma e sullo sviluppo della Città moderna* (The preservation of the beauty of Rome and the development of the modern city), which "argued against the grandiose" for new Roman development and "for the 'contextual' and picturesque."[476] Piacentini's forty-six-page treatise had been promoted by the powerful Associazione artistica fra i cultri di architettura (Artistic Association for the Patronage of Architecture), founded in 1875 and dedicated to the preservation of Rome's historic monuments as well as the planning of the evolving city.

Città Giardino Aniene was located on a hilly, 1,730-acre parcel five miles northeast of the city center along the Aniene River in the Monte Sacro area.[477] Access to the site, which the municipal government quickly improved with sewers, water, electricity, and gas, was primarily along Via Nomentana, and the stretch from the heart of Rome to Aniene was widened to accommodate trolley service. Via Nomentana led to the main entrance at the southern end of the site but skirted the estate itself. The ICP instructed Giovannoni to preserve the historic Ponte Nomentano (bridge, 552; tower, 1455) and to save as many of the mature pine trees as possible. A new bridge, Ponte Tazio (1922), was built nearby to handle the increased traffic.

Giovannoni's plan for Aniene distributed close to 700 two- and three-story single- and multifamily houses with rear gardens along a maze of narrow tree-lined interconnected curving streets that wound their way through the large site. Although the project was intended for the working class, Giovannoni included a number of larger villas for the middle class in order to promote "fusion between classes," an additional goal of the nonprofit developers.[478] The focal point of the plan was Piazza Sempione at the southern end of the site, marking the entrance to the community and surrounded by a school, church, post office, cinema, shops, and a public park. Located on axis with the principal approach along Via Nomentana, Piazza Sempione, "irregular in form and lined by picturesque rustic buildings by [Innocenzo] Sabbatini [1891–1983], was," according to architectural historian Richard Etlin, "conceived as a quiet oasis, 'clearly distinct from the movement of trams and other vehicles, similar to the old piazzas of small Italian cities, cozy and closed in, defended from the winds and lined with the most noteworthy buildings.'" Describing the entire plan, Etlin added that the garden suburb "was organized as a cluster of small neighborhoods with a smaller square on each of the seven hills . . . At Aniene Giovannoni applied the principles of hierarchical street design . . . in which the secondary and tertiary roads would take on a quiet, residential aspect. As the report [1920] by the Ufficio Municipale del Lavoro [Municipal Bureau of Labor] described them, these streets had 'movement and a varied character' corresponding to 'this picturesque aesthetic that is now coming to dominate modern planning, not only in outlying zones, but even in the downtown urban center.'"[479]

In keeping with the ICP dictum that "a beautiful house does not only mean an expensive house," Aniene's houses, many designed by Giovannoni and Sabbatini, "were constructed at low cost but not at the expense of the quality of construction, inhabitants' living standards or attention to architectural detail," as architectural historian Antonella De Michelis has written. "These criteria produced a unique style called the Barocchetto in which craftsmanship transformed low-cost materials such as local volcanic tufa, brick and concrete into ornamental design features . . . This eclectic and historicizing style drew its motifs from the minor architecture of Rome . . . from the Medieval, Renaissance and Baroque periods. This style communicated a Roman identity that was not imperial and did not possess the grandeur of the neo-classical

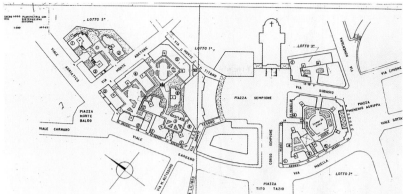

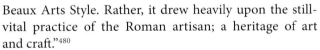

1. Detail of plan, Gustavo Giovannoni, 1920. AU (1947)

2. Plan, Piazza Sempione. AU (1985)

3. Piazza Sempione. Lalupa. WC (2009)

4. Via Cimone, with Piazza Sempione in distance. AU (1920s)

5. Viale Gottardo. AU (1920s)

Beaux Arts Style. Rather, it drew heavily upon the still-vital practice of the Roman artisan; a heritage of art and craft."[480]

Twenty years after the completion of the relatively low-density development, the increased demand for housing resulted in the replacement of Aniene's houses with larger-scale multifamily houses and apartment buildings, a trend that would continue until the only enduring feature of the original plan was Piazza Sempione and its surrounding buildings by Sabbatini. As architectural historian Diane Ghirardo put it, "demographic pressure eventually transformed" Aniene into a "fully urbanized" area, "and the dream of a house and garden remained out of reach of ever larger numbers of residents."[481]

Giovannoni's second project for the Istituto per le Case Popolari, the garden suburb of **Garbatella**, was located on a much smaller, nine-acre site four miles south of Rome's city center in the Ostiense district.[482] Designed in collaboration with engineer Massimo Piacentini (1898–1974) (not to be confused with Marcello Piacentini), the plan divided the hilly site into separate *lotti* (lots) connected by relatively wide thoroughfares,

with buildings arranged around formal piazzas. The houses were primarily placed on narrower, curving streets in order "to provide 'a varied and picturesque ensemble from different points of view' that would explicitly avoid the 'monotonous aspect of the unending lines of hundreds of small houses of the same type' that could be found in some of the English garden suburbs," as Richard Etlin put it.[483] Plans for this largely undeveloped part of Ostiense, home to a few historic structures deemed worthy of preservation but mostly occupied by vineyards and sheep pastures, dated back to 1910 when municipal authorities tried and failed to develop the area as an industrial maritime district. Intended primarily for railway and dock workers, Garbatella was to include a new wharf that would link the area with the ancient Roman port of Ostia, but plans for the harbor facilities did not move forward.

On February 18, 1920, King Vittorio Emanuele III laid the cornerstone for Garbatella's first section, located closest to existing transportation as well as the proposed dock. Giovannoni and Piacentini divided the site into five *lotti* surrounding Piazza Benedetto Brin, located on axis with the main approach road and accessed via

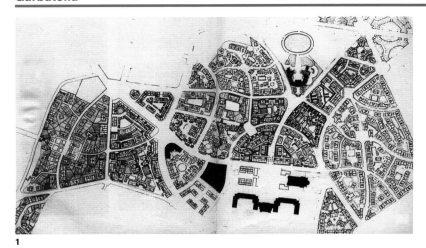

1. Plan, Gustavo Giovannoni and Massimo Piacentini, 1920. ATER

2. Stairway entrance to Piazza Benedetto Brin. AD22 (c. 1922)

3. Via Alberto Guglielmotti. AD22 (c. 1922)

4. Piazza Benedetto Brin. RAMSA (2010)

5. Typical street. RAMSA (2010)

a broad flight of stairs. The houses, designed by Giovannoni and Innocenzo Sabbatini in the same Barocchetto style the pair had employed at Aniene, consisted of two basic types: two-story detached, semidetached, and terraced single-family villas with rear kitchen gardens, and larger apartment buildings surrounding landscaped courtyards known as *palazzina*. As Antonella De Michelis has written, "The early design of the Garbatella faithfully adhered to key Garden City principles. The peripheral location was chosen because of its depressed commercial value; its plan clearly reflected the site's topography and its proximity to both the railway line and Via Ostiense [which] was vital in connecting Garbatella with Rome, the 'Central City,' and to the off-shoot cities of Ostia Nuova and Montesacro. However, while planners Giovannoni and Piacentini fully embraced the ideals of the town-country—'the beauty of nature, social opportunity, easy access to fields and parks . . . pure air and water, good drainage, bright homes and gardens'—they did not rigidly apply [Ebenezer] Howard's theories. Instead, the Garbatella was an interpretation of the English model in a Roman context."[484] By 1922 the area around Piazza Benedetto Brin numbered forty-four residential buildings and thirty-seven commercial and civic structures.

Although subsequent additions to Garbatella did not completely abandon the Garden City ideals displayed at the initial development, the demand for a larger number of dwellings than originally anticipated, created by a surging population, forced the ICP to significantly increase the density and scale of future construction, altering the overall character of the suburb. Single-family villas were simplified in design and arranged in longer terraces, and the *palazzina* grew dramatically to superblock size. This less-picturesque, monumental character was in keeping with the wishes of the new Fascist government and Benito Mussolini's desire for the rebirth of Imperial Rome. Giovannoni continued to design buildings at Garbatella, joined by a number of other architects, including Pietro Aschieri (1889–1952), Plinio Marconi (1893–1974), and Mario De Renzi (1897–1967). Sabbatini, appointed head of the ICP design office in 1927, was responsible for some of the most prominent apartment blocks as well as bachelor hotels, the public baths, and a combined cinema and concert hall. Garbatella was developed over a twenty-year period and its population grew from about 3,000 in the early 1920s to close to 30,000 by 1940.

In December 1928 Mussolini, in his sixth year as head of the government, announced plans to reclaim the malaria-ridden marshes of the Agro Pontino in order to construct new towns and *borghi* (rural villages) primarily dedicated to agricultural pursuits.[485] The 310 square miles of the Pontine marshes, bordered by the Mediterranean Sea to the west and the Alban Hills to the east, began about thirty miles south of Rome, connected to the city by Via Appia, a military road originally built in 312 B.C. Largely deemed uninhabitable, the thirty-mile-long stretch of land, both above and below sea level, had a population in 1928 of only 1,637 who lived in shanties and mostly tended sheep. So virulent were the frequent malaria outbreaks that, according to the Department of Health, 80 percent of visitors to the marshes during the high season would contract the disease after spending only one night. In the popular imagination, the area in the province of Lazio was home to vagrants and dangerous thieves.

In 1929 "Mussolini's Law"—which pledged to "redeem the earth; and with the earth, man; and with men, the race"—was passed by the Italian parliament.[486] The following year work began on reclaiming the marshland in order to build five new towns completed between 1932 and 1939: Littoria, Sabaudia, Pontinia, Aprilia, and Pomezia. Mussolini, whose ultimate goal was to promote ruralization, was also committed to resettling up to 80,000 people from economically depressed regions as well as providing work for the vast number of unemployed. At its peak, more than 124,000 workers were engaged in the so-called "battle of the swamps," digging 10,300 miles of canals and trenches, building sand dunes, draining and filling low-level areas, and placing dikes along the banks of dredged rivers.

The Opera Nazionale Comabattenti (ONC; National Veterans Organization), founded in 1917 to help decommissioned soldiers, was placed in charge of the project. The ONC had recently joined with the Fascists as well as redirected its emphasis to focus on veterans who wished to work on or own farms. As historian Wolfgang Schivelbusch has observed, "From its very inception, the project was promoted as the fulfillment of earlier governments' promises to soldiers that they would be given a piece of land when they returned from the field of battle. That is why the national veterans' organization was put in charge of the project and why it officially owned the property concerned. The ONC coordinated and paid for land reclamation; built the houses, *borghi*, and cities; and selected the settlers. It also watched over, directed, and controlled their lives, with a discipline similar to that in a military camp."[487]

Mussolini saw the five new towns as a powerful propaganda tool. Failure to reclaim the Pontine marshes was historic and legendary and if Mussolini could succeed in their rapid redevelopment—he boasted that each town could be built in a year—the victory would be enormous. Schivelbusch has pointed out that "since the fall of the Roman Empire, various papal and secular authorities had tried to reclaim it without success," rendering the "project . . . a symbol of Italian incompetence."[488] First tackled by Julius Caesar, and studied by Leonardo da Vinci, who prepared an abandoned reclamation scheme for Pope Leo X in 1513, the problems of the marshes had been addressed in more than fifty laws passed and ignored in the years since Italian unification in 1870.

The first and largest of the new towns to be built was **Littoria** (1932), named for the lictoral fasces adopted as a Fascist symbol.[489] Located roughly in the center of the Agro Pontino, Littoria (renamed Latina in 1946 in an effort to obscure its origins) was planned as the capital of the reclaimed province, intended for an initial population of 6,000 culled from the northeastern regions of the Veneto and Friuli but projected by Mussolini to grow to between 40,000 and 50,000 residents. In April 1932 the Opera Nazionale Comabattenti selected Roman architect Oriolo Frezzotti (1888–1965) to prepare the plan as well as design Littoria's first buildings. A ground-breaking ceremony attended by Mussolini took place in June, and within six months enough of the town had been completed to allow Il Duce to preside over its official inauguration on December 18, 1932, when he declared: "Today is a great day for the revolution of the Black Shirts, it is a happy day for the Agro Pontino, a glorious day in the history of the Nation. What was in vain attempted during twenty-five centuries, today we have translated into a living reality."[490]

Frezzotti's formal radial plan of eight major streets connecting ring roads to a central piazza resembled "an irregular spider's-web," in the words of Wesley Dougill, writing in *Town Planning Review* in 1936.[491] Recalling the "imperial grandeur of ancient Roman prototypes" in the layout of its streets and piazza, Littoria's plan was more immediately influenced by the work and writings of Giovannoni, planner of Aniene and Garbatella, whose 1931 book *Vecchie città ed edilizia nuova* (Old Cities and New Buildings), praising radial-concentric plans, was extremely influential in Roman architectural circles.[492]

Architectural historian Diane Ghirardo has observed that Littoria, "perhaps because it had been designated provincial capital," had "a more grandiose . . . and urban character" than the other Pontine towns that quickly followed. She described the plan, writing that "the central rectangular piazza, with the Municipio [town hall] and the offices of the ONC prominently lining it, gives onto four stellar avenues at the corners, with the religious center at the terminus of the north–south axis. Two orthogonal thoroughfares, broken by the central green piazza, serve as implied cross-axes in this modified radial plan, and a set of secondary roads are laid out on a grid further traversed by a series of encircling roads (*annulari*), the largest one terminating to the west with a sports facility and a low-income housing district. In a pattern repeated in all but one of the Agro Pontino New Towns, the final *annulare* closes off the city both visually and physically from the countryside."[493]

In addition to the influences from ancient Rome and Giovannoni, Ghirardo pointed out that Littoria's plan, though more modest because it was a provincial as opposed to a national capital, also bore a resemblance to Walter Burley Griffin's 1912 scheme for Canberra, Australia (see p. 646) and "may well derive from Unwin's *Town Planning in Practice* (1909), certainly well known in Italy by the 1930s. The proposal adopted in Littoria avoids the monotony of the endless grid and follows, in Unwin's explanation, a traditional irregularly radiating system of streets and cross streets."[494]

In his 1936 review of Littoria, Wesley Dougill doubted "whether the completed town will prove successful from

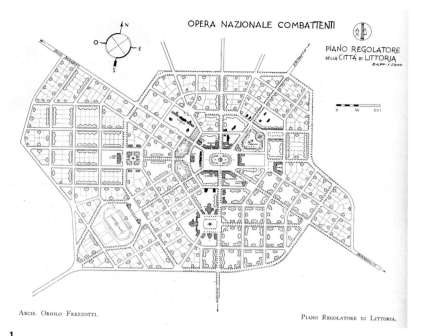

1. Plan, Oriolo Frezzotti, 1932. AD33

2. Town Hall, Oriolo Frezzotti, 1932. AAF (c. 1932)

3. Typical apartment houses. LI (1936)

4. Piazza XXIII Marzo. AAF (1935)

5, 6. Typical views. RAMSA (2008)

an aesthetic point of view. The central Place [piazza], which is now built, leaves a good deal to be desired. This is due in the main to the numerous wide roads entering it, six of them at the angles, where strength is specially desirable. These entering roads destroy all sense of enclosure and definition in the Place, and in effect considerably increase the size of the latter which in itself is too large when related to the height and character of the buildings forming the Place walls."[495] In a 1936 interview about new Italian architecture, Le Corbusier was

far more dismissive, but probably for different reasons, stating "Littoria? Don't even mention it!"[496]

The architectural highlight and dominating structure of Littoria was Frezzotti's two-story town hall topped by a clock tower, a suitably grand and imposing setting for community events and speeches by Mussolini. Other buildings surrounding the central plaza and just beyond its periphery included offices for the Opera Nazionale Comabattenti, stores, a hotel, cinema, church, hospital, schools, militia barracks, Fascist party headquarters,

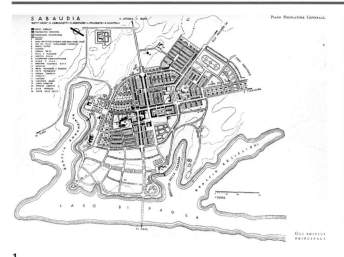

1. Plan, Gino Cancellotti, Alfredo Scalpelli, Luigi Piccinato, and Eugenio Montuori, 1933. AD34

2. Aerial view. AAF (1939)

3. Piazza della Rivoluzione. LI (1934)

4. Piazza Regina Margherita. AAF (1935)

5. Via Oddone from Piazza Regina Margherita. RAMSA (2008)

6. Corso Principe di Piemonte. RAMSA (2008)

and two buildings designed by Angiolo Mazzoni (1894–1979)—a post office with shorter clock tower and a railroad station. The housing stock was composed primarily of apartment blocks, but modest single-family houses and larger palazzi were also included. Rome-based architect Giuseppe Nicolosi (1901–1981) designed a 542-unit low-income apartment complex (1936) sponsored by the Istituto per le Case Popolari. Littoria grew rapidly, as Mussolini had predicted, and by 1941 its population was close to 20,000.

Sabaudia (1933), named for the Royal House of Savoy, was the second of the Agro Pontino towns to be completed and the southernmost of the quintet, located on a 148-acre coastal site surrounded on three sides by Lake Paola.[497] The Opera Nazionale Comabattenti organized a competition to pick the town planner, appointing Giovannoni as head of the selection jury and limiting the entrants to registered Italian architects and engineers. The competition brief, released on April 25, 1933, specified a town of 5,000, requiring that each entry "must provide all the necessary public services for the efficient functioning of the new agricultural center, and must include all the typical institutions of the Fascist Regime (which must be constructed before other buildings)."[498] Fourteen entries were received by the deadline only one month later, with the jury announcing the three winners in two weeks' time. Oriolo Frezzotti, planner of Littoria, received third prize with a scheme that divided the site into several discrete centers separated by building type and function, connected by straight and angular wide thoroughfares. The second-place entry, designed by Angelo Vicario (n.d.), was, according to a reporter for the Fascist party newspaper, "inspired by the criterion to give Sabaudia a large panoramic square opening up towards the Lago de Paola . . . genuinely Italian, and quadrangular, with buildings bordering on three sides of the square, and one open towards the solemn [Mount] Circeo."[499] As a reward for their second- and third-place finishes, Vicario and Frezzotti were granted several commissions for buildings at Sabaudia.

The winning scheme was the work of four Roman architects, Gino Cancellotti (1896–1987), Alfredo Scalpelli (1898–1966), Luigi Piccinato (1899–1983), and Eugenio Montuori (1907–1982), all members of the progressive Gruppo Urbanisiti Romani (GUR). Organized as the Gruppo del Quattro and led by Piccinato, they were also responsible for the design of most of the Rationalist-style buildings at Sabaudia. Their plan, which was largely realized in just 253 days by a crew of 6,000 laborers working day and night, was defined by two central piazzas, the main one devoted to civic functions and a smaller one focused around various religious buildings. Beyond the piazzas were the residential areas as well as several large public parks, with a loop road encircling the main area of development and a generous green belt surrounding the town. Two main roads led to the town center at Piazza della Rivoluzione, one heading south from Rome and Littoria and a second connecting to Terracina, thirteen miles to the east. The L-shaped Piazza della Rivoluzione was surrounded by the two-story town hall, with a 140-foot-high slender travertine tower and prominent second-story balcony used by Mussolini for speeches; the Fascist party headquarters; a combination cinema, restaurant, and retail building; a hotel; and an apartment house. Just to the north, the rectangular Piazza Regina Margherita was home to a church with a bell tower, baptistery, rectory, convent, and nursery.

Architect Marcello Piacentini, in a positive assessment of Sabaudia published in the June 1934 issue of *Architettura*, praised the Piazza Regina Margherita, writing that

> the arrangement of the church square has been influenced by the spatial ambience of our typical medieval 'piazze'; the atmosphere is created by a purity and lightness of elements, characteristically Mediterranean in their spiritual intensity and poetic intimacy. The few, simple volumes are harmoniously distributed according to a conventional theme, but in their geometric clarity they express the desire for a return to a more serene and simple way of life and faith. The freestanding masses of the baptistery and the church, within the piazza, create a series of attractive views and spatial effects surrounded by the more regular minor buildings which enclose the open space. The proportions of these buildings and their balanced relation to the larger urban structure recreate the simplicity and intimacy of the traditional village environment.[500]

In her dissertation on Sabaudia, Hanne Storm Ofteland observed that "the streets and buildings in Sabaudia are laid out in a grid around these two main squares. However, the town plan has been given an asymmetrical, rhomboidal shape, extended by a rectangular core in the east. This lines the periphery of the grid system with curved, organic roads tying in the landscape. The town plan was rather easy to expand, if necessary." Ofteland added that the "architects were very concerned with the aesthetic aspects of Sabaudia: Many streets end or make a bend in front of some landmark building, such as is the case with the town hall, the church, or the Balilla building [Fascist Youth League headquarters designed by Frezzotti] . . . The different vistas through porticoes, of walls and pilasters in red brick, dark and lighter travertine, peperino stone, red and yellow stucco bordering on each other, in different geometric constellations, always with the blue sky right over your head, green trees and lawns and maybe a glimpse of glittering sea, make for a very pleasant environment." Ofteland concluded that "the integration of the town with the surrounding landscape is well considered, harmonizing ocean and wilderness and fields and parks with the town."[501]

Sabaudia's housing stock, for the most part designed by the Gruppo del Quattro, included eight different types of two- and three-story stucco apartment houses, many clustered around landscaped courtyards and some with ground-level shops. The Gruppo del Quattro also provided six different types of semidetached two-story yellow and red stucco houses with gardens, while Angelo Vicario designed many of the more spacious two-story villas. Although the original plan called for terraced rows, these remained unrealized. Referring to the housing as well as to the rest of Sabaudia's flat-roofed buildings, Terry Kirk described their style as "severe and unadorned," representing "the first large-scale expression of functionalist modernism in Italy. Even the church's flanks look like grain silos."[502]

French architect and urban planner Gaston Bardet (1907–1989) visited Littoria and Sabaudia in 1934, preferring the latter for its "'stable serenity' . . . although one gets the impression, at times, of 'strolling through a Hollywood set,' waiting for 'a signal that will suddenly flood the scene with a horde of extras.'"[503] Contemporary observer Richard Burdett also addressed the ceremonial aspect of the design, writing that "the dominant position of the Fascist institutions and the provision of a

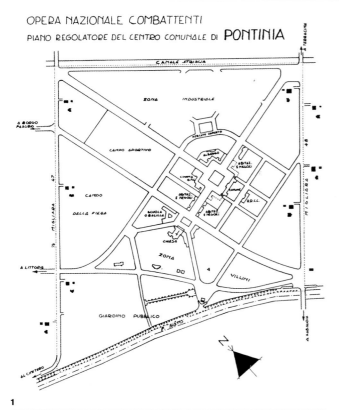

OPERA NAZIONALE COMBATTENTI

PIANO REGOLATORE DEL CENTRO COMUNALE DI **PONTINIA**

1

2

3

4

5

1. Plan, Alfredo Pappalardo and Oriolo Frezzotti, 1934. RA34

2. Piazza 28 Ottobre. LI (1935)

3. Chiesa di Sant'Anna, Oriolo Frezzotti, 1935. LI (1942)

4. Piazza 28 Ottobre. LI (1942)

5. Via Cesare Battisti. RAMSA (2008)

piazza for political rallies clearly reflect the Fascist spatial rhetoric" but added that Sabaudia avoids the "cold and calculated stage-like scenarios of grandiose Fascist schemes."[504] Manfredo Tafuri and Francesco Dal Co, pointing out that the "scheme was not unmindful of the usual emphasis on monumentality," also drew attention to its roots in "the garden city tradition and also . . . the German urbanistic models with which Piccinato was very familiar," having studied town planning at Munich's Technische Universität.[505]

Under pressure to rapidly build the next new town, **Pontinia** (1934), the Opera Nazionale Comabattenti eschewed a competition, earning the enmity of many Roman architects, especially those associated with the Rationalists.[506] The ONC also resisted the advances of Le Corbusier, who would later go on to severely criticize Littoria. The job instead was handed to little-known

engineer Alfredo Pappalardo (n.d.), an employee of the ONC's technical division. Oriolo Frezzotti, planner of Littoria, was hired to assist Pappalardo as well as design most of Pontinia's principal buildings. Located eleven miles northeast of Sabaudia, Pontinia, the smallest of the Agro Pontino towns, was officially announced on December 19, 1934, and within a year's time, on December 18, 1935, the majority of the town, intended for 3,000 residents, was substantially complete for its inauguration.

Pappalardo and Frezzotti's plan was centered on the nine blocks laid out around the principal square, Piazza 28 Ottobre, the administrative and civic center. "As in the case with Sabaudia," Ofteland has pointed out, "a short broad avenue leading west connects the main square with another somewhat smaller square upon which the church is placed at the furthermost end of the axis. Even though somewhat more symmetrical, Pontinia's

1. Plan, Concezio Petrucci, 1936.
AD38

2. Aerial view. TCI (c. 1938)

3. Town Hall, center, and Casa del
Fascio, right. TCI (c. 1938)

4. Via Degli Aranci. TCI (c. 1938)

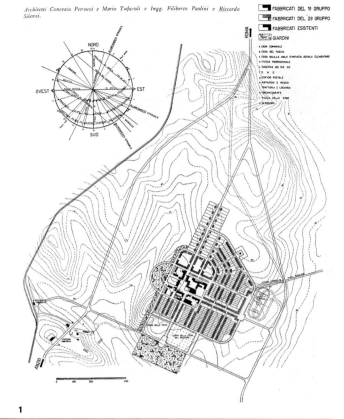

Architetti Concezio Petrucci e Mario Tufaroli e Ingg. Filiberto Paolini e Riccardo Silenzi.

1

2

3

4

layout resembles that of Sabaudia, as to the place and divisions of different zones in town."[507] Pontinia's housing consisted of two-story apartment houses, some with street-level stores, along with semidetached houses and a small number of villas, largely designed in a style that matched the institutional buildings.

Pontinia, in contrast to the national and international attention received by Littoria and Sabaudia, has escaped widespread and detailed scrutiny. It was, however, roundly criticized by Rationalist leader Giuseppe Pagano (1896–1945), who stated that the town provided an illustration of "how not to draw up a plan and how not to build."[508]

The ONC returned to a competitive process to select the designer of **Aprilia** (1936–37), awarding the commission to a team headed by architect Concezio Petrucci (1902–1946) and including architect Mario Tufaroli (n.d.) and engineers Emanuele Filiberto Paolini (n.d.) and Riccardo Silenzi (n.d.).[509] Although the seventeen received entries were supposed to have been submitted anonymously, recent scholarship has uncovered a letter written by the winners to the jury that not only reveals their names but asks for "special attention."[510] Given a "romantic name . . . evoking spring and fertility," Aprilia was located thirty miles south of Rome and about seven miles east of the Mediterranean.[511] Founded on April 25, 1936, and inaugurated on October 2, 1937, Aprilia, intended for an initial population of around 3,000, took longer to complete than the three previous towns due to economic sanctions imposed on Italy by the League of Nations after the 1935 invasion of Abyssinia (Ethiopia).

Petrucci and his team's "compact" plan placed the residential component consisting of rows of apartment houses, semidetached houses, and villas on straight and curved streets beyond the boundaries of the civic and commercial core.[512] Ellen Ruth Shapiro has observed that "the town center, like that of Sabaudia and the other new towns, is imbued with a poetic melancholy reminiscent of some cityscapes by De Chirico."[513] Ghirardo has drawn attention to Aprilia's similarity to previous Pontine towns, writing that "once again the town is conceived as a closed corporate entity, roughly rectangular with curving roads at the corners. The institutional center, slightly displaced to the west, places the Casa del Fascio and the church in direct confrontation with one another, perhaps in ironic acknowledgment of their historical confrontation and their parallel hierarchical structures."[514] However, architectural historian Henry Millon has taken issue with the view that Aprilia shared its basic plan and design with Sabaudia and the other Pontine towns, writing that it was

quite rural in character by comparison. The rustic quality is achieved not only by the use of hipped tile roofs (as opposed to the flat roofs of Sabaudia and Pontinia) and arcuated loggias and windows (where strict trabeated loggias were used in all three previous towns) but also

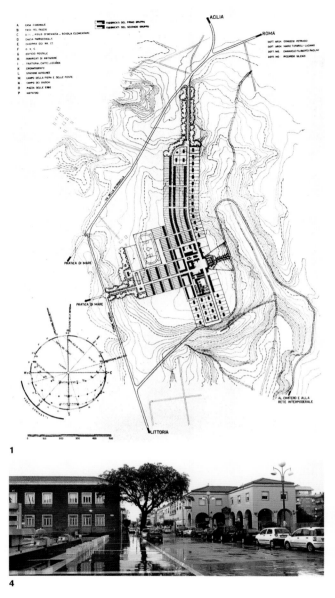

1. Plan, Concezio Petrucci, 1938. AD38

2. Overall view. LI (1942)

3. Piazza dell'Impero. LI (1942)

4. Piazza dell'Impero. RAMSA (2008)

5. Chiesa di San Benedetto and Casa del Fascio. LI (1942)

the size of the public open spaces. In Aprilia…the main square with its casa (not palazzo) comunale, Fascist party headquarters, the military police headquarters, office of the ONC and parish church all fronting on it is . . . one quarter the size of that in Sabaudia.

Millon attributes "some of the reasons for the rustic, indigenous character" to "Italian economic and political theory of the period," adding that "this change parallels . . . an alteration in official policy that can be traced in Italian architectural publications."[515] Historian Federico Caprotti described this shift "from a dalliance with modernism in the 1920s and early 1930s to a return to neo-classicism in parallel with a re-entrenchment of the regime as it drew closer to Germany and shut itself off from the world after the mid-1930s."[516] Alfredo Giarratani, writing in 1936 in the Milan-based journal *Quadrante*, captured the controversy surrounding this transition with his criticism of Aprilia "as a mean polemic against modernity."[517]

Pomezia (1938–39), the last of the five new towns to be completed, was planned by Aprilia's designers, Concezio Petrucci, Mario Tufaroli, Emanuele Filiberto Paolini, and Riccardo Silenzi, who were selected in a competition.[518] The team was again led by Petrucci, who was responsible for the design of the principal buildings. Located twenty miles south of Rome, Pomezia's site was technically a part of the Agro Romano, but the town, developed and administered by the Opera Nazionale Comabattenti, is considered part of Mussolini's ambitions to reclaim the Pontine marshes. Similar to the previous towns, Pomezia's plan, intended to accommodate 3,000 residents, was focused on piazzas serving civic, religious, and commercial functions, but differed in its long and narrow, less concentrated layout.

During World War II, the Agro Pontino, due to its strategic seaside landing location relatively close to Rome, was the scene of heavy fighting and extensive Allied bombing, especially during the 1944 Battle of Anzio, a city about midway between Pomezia and Sabaudia. Aprilia, which was almost completely demolished, along with Pomezia, suffered the most damage, with Littoria also subject to significant aerial bombing. Sabaudia and, especially, Pontinia, were the least affected. Rebuilding after the war, combined with the replacement of much of the housing with denser development, increased the population of the five towns. "Because of the taint of Fascism," Ghirardo has observed, "these towns were poorly maintained through the 1970s; only as their fifty-year anniversaries approached did the communities undertake to spruce up the buildings."[519]

SPAIN

Although **Park Güell**, Spain's only project directly inspired by the Garden City movement, was a failure as a private residential development, the unorthodox scheme by Antoni Gaudí (1852–1926) ultimately found great success as a public amenity in the form of an enormously popular municipally sponsored park. In 1900 Catalan textile magnate Eusebi Güell (1846–1918) commissioned Gaudí, a close friend who had designed several buildings for the industrialist over the previous two decades, to prepare a plan for a subdivision to be located outside of Barcelona.[520] Güell, a frequent visitor to England "whose connections with the design-conscious British textile industry brought him into contact with the ideas then being advanced in progressive English design circles," was influenced by Ebenezer Howard but Güell's planned community was intended solely for the wealthy with no anticipation of self-sufficiency, as it included no significant commercial or industrial component.[521] The 37-acre site, purchased in 1899 and mostly vacant except for a large nineteenth-century farmhouse, was located about two miles north of the city center at the top of Montaña Pelada, enjoying a commanding view of Barcelona and the Mediterranean.

Strongly influenced by the demands of the challenging topography with its dramatic and sudden changes in elevation, as well as the desire to retain most of the parcel's original trees, Gaudí divided the parcel into sixty triangular plots that measured between one-third and one-half of an acre, although it was assumed that some land purchasers, who would then build their own detached villas, might combine more than one lot. The circulation system connecting the house sites was composed of five- and 10-meter-wide roads whose looping routes, following the dictates of the topography, resulted in a "meandering" plan that "looked like a compacted spring," according to Gaudí biographer Gijs Van Hensbergen.[522] Gaudí worked with architect Joan Rubió (1870–1952) on the design of these roads, many carried on viaducts held aloft by distinctive, tree-like stone columns, "at times inclined," supporting "Catalan brick vaults covered with rough stones. The idea," as architect and historian Arleen Pabon-Charneco wrote, "was to integrate as much as possible the architectural elements with nature as existing on the site grounds." In addition to supplying "structural support requiring a minimum of earth movements in the rugged terrain," the viaducts provided covered pedestrian passageways across large portions of the site.[523]

Gaudí surrounded Park Güell with a two-and-a-half-meter-high rubblework wall, while further protecting the site with a gated entrance flanked by two elaborately fanciful gatehouses that "look as though they might have been taken straight out of the tales of the Brothers Grimm," one serving as a porter's lodge and the other providing space for the garden suburb's administrative and service needs.[524] The theatricality of the entrance sequence continued just inside the entrance gate, where a monumental staircase embellished with three fountains depicting serpents, dragons, and symbols of Catalan nationalism led to a large two-level plaza that was to serve as the residential community's civic focus. The lower level of the plaza, intended as the site for a weekly market, a common feature of Spanish villages, was composed of eighty-six 20-foot-high Doric columns, "some of them leaning like mighty trees bent by the weight of time."[525] Dennis and Elizabeth De Witt observed that the "subtly Moorish mood of this hypostyle hall springs from its not-quite-Greek, mosque-like column grid, while the pragmatic slight buttressing angle at which its outermost columns incline is also symbolic of the ethical and genetic bonds which Gaudí, as a disciple of Viollet-le-Duc [1814–1879], would have felt linked the Greeks to the 'Goths.'"[526] The roof of the covered marketplace constituted Park Güell's main square, described by Gaudí as the "Greek Theater" and most notable for the long serpentine bench winding its way along the piazza's perimeter, designed by Gaudí and architect Josep Maria Jujol (1879–1949) and decorated with broken ceramic tiles. At the summit of the site Gaudí intended to build a chapel but this building remained unrealized, replaced by a prominent calvary.

In 1902 construction began on Park Güell's first house (1904), a model home designed by Gaudí assistant Francesc Berenguer i Mestres (1866–1914) that was intended to promote the project and provide a prototype for future construction. The following year Don Martín Trías Domènech, a longtime friend of Eusebi Güell's, purchased two lots and commissioned architect Juli Batllevell (1864–1928), another assistant to Gaudí, to build a house (1906) for his extended family. To guard against inappropriate development, Güell and Gaudí imposed several building restrictions, primarily setback requirements intended to preserve views. In addition, Güell detailed a long list of prohibited activities, essentially guaranteeing an exclusively residential community by banning the practice of any "industry, trade or profession."[527]

Construction on the infrastructure and plaza continued until 1914 but no other houses were built as the gated suburb was unable to attract additional residents, a failure generally attributed to the high cost of the land as well as the relative inaccessibility of the site which lacked a direct transit link to Barcelona's city center. In 1906 Güell and his family moved to Park Güell, renovating

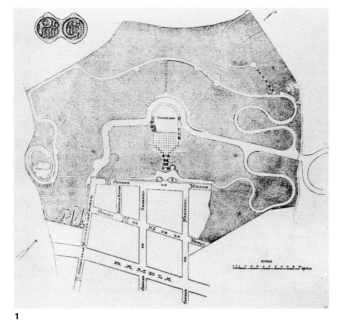

the original farmhouse. That same year, at Güell's urging, Gaudí also took up residence in the park, purchasing the model house where he lived until 1925. Faced with such disappointing land sales, Güell, as early as 1907, raised the possibility of selling the site to the city and converting it into a public park, an objective achieved by his heirs and Barcelona's city council in 1925 after seven years of negotiations.

HUNGARY

In 1908 Hungarian prime minister Sándor Wekerle (1848–1921), acting on the advice of architect Róbert Fleischl (1864–1926), president of the Union of Hungarian Architects and Engineers, pledged government support for the creation of the country's first garden suburb to be based on the English model.[528] The development was intended for a location outside of Budapest, which had recently experienced a surge in population from the countryside, resulting in the construction of large apartment blocks unpopular alike with long-time residents, who regretted

the increased density, as well as with recent arrivals, who missed their former rural surroundings. Budapest mayor István Bárczy (1866–1943) announced a competition (1908) for the plan of a municipally financed, self-sufficient suburb, intended for up to 20,000 moderate- and middle-income residents drawn primarily from the ranks of the civil service, selecting a flat, square 416-acre site six miles southeast of the central city in the Kispest district, bound by Endre Ady, Rákóczi, Nagykőrösi, and Határ Roads. Administered by Fleischl and open only to Hungarians, the planning contest for what soon came to be known as the **Wekerle Estate** attracted sixty entries and was won by architect Antal Palóczi (1849–1927). A second competition, devoted exclusively to the design direction of the housing, was won by Fleischl.

Palóczi's plan featured a maze of picturesque, curving streets creating irregular building plots. Surrounded by a broad loop road, the plan included a diagonal street bisecting the site that led to a central rectangular green intended as the civic and commercial focus of the suburb. Less than a year after selecting Palóczi's scheme, the Finance Ministry, the government

1. Plan, Antoni Gaudí, c. 1902. CG

2. Overall view. CRS

3. Gatehouses. Gagnon. BG (2009)

4. Market Hall and Greek Theater. Canaan. WC (2008)

5. Pedestrian passageway. Böhringer. WC (2008)

6. Staircase and plaza. RAMSA (2011)

1. Competition-winning plan, Antal Palóczi, 1908. GN

2. Revised plan, Ottmár Győri, 1909. GN

3. Central square. CRS

4. Aerial view. GN

1

2

3

4

agency placed in charge of the project, decided that it was too complex to be completed in the three years they had allotted for it. In 1909 engineer Ottmár Győri (1867–1946), an employee of the Finance Ministry, substantially reworked the plan, simplifying the design with a geometric scheme of gridded blocks surrounding an enlarged central square, again intended as the community's focal point. Two 85-foot-wide diagonal roads leading to the square divided the site into four triangular building parcels, each intended for 5,000 residents and each to have its own schools, shops, and other community facilities. An octagonal ring road enclosed the square, connecting to the suburb's other symmetrical streets. Győri provided landscaped triangular parcels to mark important intersections, instituted an extensive tree-planting program for both major and minor streets, and supplied each household with two peach tree saplings.

Anxious to get started on the project, the municipality began construction of the housing in 1909, even before the design of the central square had been finalized. A number of architects, including original plan competition winner Antal Palóczi, Aladár Árkay

(1868–1932), and István Bierbauer (1861–1939), designed one- and two-story semidetached and terraced multifamily houses, many with modest front lawns and all with rear gardens. A small number of villa-like detached houses were also included. All of the houses followed the basic direction indicated by Róbert Fleischl's prize-winning scheme, which called for designs evoking the vernacular architecture of rural Hungary, often including fanciful ornamental wood detailing on the exteriors. Fleischl also designed a number of houses.

Ottmár Győri proved unable to come up with a satisfactory design for the monumental square, where each side measured about 200 meters. In 1912, in an invited competition, Károly Kós (1883–1977) bested five other entries with a scheme that enclosed the square with rows of buildings on all four sides, shielding a large public park accessed via decorative gates located under broad arches cut into the midway point of each row. Kós recommended that different architects design the surrounding buildings to provide a welcome variety, but he set their general architectural direction, choosing a style influenced by the vernacular architecture of his native Transylvania, then under the control of the Hungarian

5. Central square row, Károly Kós,
c. 1913. Betts. HBE (2011)

6, 7. Typical streets. Betts. HBE
(2011)

5

6

7

government. Kós, who designed the row along the eastern edge of the square, which was later named for him, also picked the architects for the park-bounding buildings, selecting other members of the so-called "Young Ones" (*A Fiatalok*), including Dezső Zrumeczky (1883–1917), Zoltán Tornallyay (1882–1946), and Dénes Györgyi (1886–1961). The three-story apartment houses built around the square included street-level shops and were joined by a church, a post office, and an 800-seat cinema, then one of the largest in Budapest.

Between 1909 and 1926, with a pause in construction during World War I, 1,007 dwellings were completed in the Wekerle Estate, accommodating 4,412 families. In addition to the commercial and civic buildings located in the center, the suburb included nursery and elementary schools, sports facilities, and common laundries and bathhouses for each of the four residential sections. A tram intended to directly connect to Budapest remained unrealized, and the estate was forced to rely on bus service. Although originally intended for government workers, about 25 percent of the houses were rented by laborers and white-collar workers employed by the private sector.

The Wekerle Estate has been lauded by British architect and critic Edwin Heathcote as "one of the most successful schemes to be based on the garden-city ideal . . . Planned as an affordable and pleasant environment for commuting workers, the scheme remains a verdant oasis of calm among the barren concrete estates of the 1960s and 1970s." Heathcote especially admired Kós's design of the central square, where "the notion of a medieval city is evoked by the huge arches which lead to the avenues beyond," adding praise for the "monumental national romanticism enriched with folk detailing; the result is one of the finest achievements of the national romantic movement." Heathcote concluded that "the estate has managed to avoid the didactic paternalism of many English garden cities and has grown into a real community with all the necessary amenities, including shops and schools."[529] Mervyn Miller, also favorably impressed by the Wekerle Estate, noted its debt to English precedent, writing that "the design was by a group of architects who were steeled in both arts and crafts architecture and the revival of local Transylvanian tradition, what might be called 'Parker and Unwin with paprika,'" adding that Kós's sketches for the

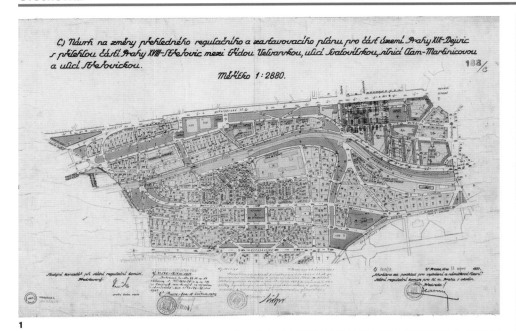

1. Plan, Jaroslav Vondrák and Jan Šenkýř, 1919. CDAP (1937)

2. Lomaná Street. CDAP (1957)

3–5. Typical views. Schankler. AS (2011)

project "could almost have come from Unwin's book *Town Planning in Practice*."[530]

CZECHOSLOVAKIA

Although the Czech translation of Howard's *Garden Cities of To-morrow* (1902), prepared in 1919, was not published until 1924, interest in the Garden City idea surfaced much earlier in what in 1918 became Czechoslovakia, in large part due to its proximity to Germany but also because of the movement's promotion by Czech architects.[531] Czechoslovakia's most important Garden City advocate was Jan Kotěra (1873–1923), an active practitioner who was also an influential professor at the Prague Academy of Fine Arts. Kotěra, who traveled to England in 1905 to study garden suburbs firsthand, urged his students to "open the windows toward Europe."[532] In 1909 Kotěra prepared the plan for a workers' village inspired by garden suburb precedent on a site forty miles northwest of Prague (see p. 793).

In 1912, a year after the Karlsruhe branch of the Deutsche Gartenstadt Gesellschaft organized an exhibition about garden cities and Hermann Muthesius delivered a lecture in Prague on town planning, a group of local architects and government officials banded together to form a committee to promote and build garden suburbs in Prague.[533] Progress, however, was delayed until the end of World War I, when the Building Cooperative of Public Servants organized a competition to build the garden suburb of **Ořechovka** (1919), located on farmland and vineyards in the Střešovice neighborhood, three miles northwest of Prague's city center. Jaroslav Vondrák (1881–1937), a pupil and disciple of Kotěra's, partnered with Jan Šenkýř (n.d.) to best thirty-seven other entries with a plan influenced by English precedent that featured a prominent civic core. Although heavily subsidized by the state through the Ministry of Public Works and originally intended to ease a severe shortage of workers' housing brought about by the postwar influx of Czechs from the surrounding countryside, Ořechovka instead became home to upper-level civil

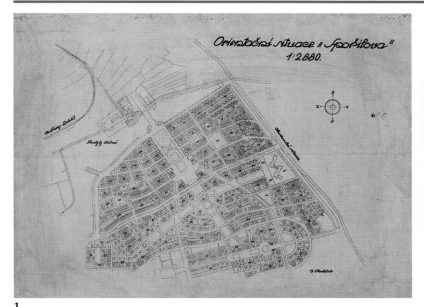

1. Plan, Josef Barek, 1924. ACP

2. Hlavní Street. CDAP (1957)

3. Roztylské náměstí. CDAP (1957)

4. Typical street. Schankler. AS (2011)

servants, businessmen, successful artists and writers, and university professors.

The centerpiece of Vondrák and Šenkýř's plan was Macharovo náměstí (square), a large rectangular plot that contained a public park and, at its northern end, a civic and commercial center home to a town hall, shops, restaurants, and a cinema. The housing was located in a network of streets surrounding the town square, with "the grid structure softened by some curved roads and housing blocks placed at corner angles to the street plan," as architectural historian Jane Pavitt has written.[534] Vondrák was primarily responsible for the semidetached and terraced houses produced in twenty-nine different styles, while leading Prague architects, such as Pavel Janák (1881–1956), Jindřich Freiwald (1890–1945), and Ladislav Machoň (1888–1973), were hired by individual lot owners to design substantial villas. All of the houses included generous rear gardens, and the intersections of many of the picturesque streets featured triangular landscaped parcels.

The majority of Ořechovka, consisting of the civic and commercial component as well as 197 houses, was completed by 1925, although construction, primarily in the form of villas, continued for another five years. Pavitt has described the subdivision as "the Bedford Park or Hampstead Garden Suburb of Prague," which "acquired a similar reputation for its liberal and intellectual middle-class community. It was a garden city

in style rather than in philosophy," planned "to be an idyllic alternative to the modern city."[535] The strong English sensibility of the affluent garden suburb was evident from the design of the brick and stucco semidetached and terraced houses, with half-timbering, gables, pitched roofs, and dormers.

The Ministry of Public Works, in collaboration with a newly created nonprofit housing association as well as the Vinohraská Savings Bank, also sponsored the development of **Spořilov** (1924), Prague, a much larger, denser garden suburb that nonetheless featured an abundance of greenery in the form of public parks, landscaped medians, private gardens, and an extensive tree-planting program.[536] Located on 200 acres purchased from the city as well as from some private landholders, predominantly farmers, the slightly hilly site was located in the Záběhlice district, six miles southeast of the city center but directly connected to it via a tram line completed in 1929. Intended for low- and mid-level civil servants, and quickly nicknamed "clerks town," Spořilov was planned by Josef Barek (b. 1882), a professor of engineering at Czech Technical University in Prague.

Barek's scheme clustered housing for approximately 1,000 families around a town square located roughly in the center of the site with a long and narrow park leading to a church perched at the top of a hill. The town square also included an administrative building, a cinema, shops, restaurants, and a school. At the southeast

1

2

3

4

corner of the site Barek included a second, smaller civic area that featured a linear park. Local architects Karel Polívka (1894–1970) and Vlastimil Brožek (1900–1974) were responsible for all of the 1,092 detached, semi-detached, and two- and three-story terraced houses (1925–30), many constructed on-site of concrete block and prefabricated materials.

Zahradní Město (1928), literally translated as "garden city," was also located in Prague's Záběhlice district, about two-and-a-half miles northeast of Spořilov.[537] Like Spořilov, it was sponsored by the Czech government for low- and mid-level civil servants. The plan, designed by architect Alex Hanuš (n.d.), featured a gridded town square lined by civic and commercial buildings as well as by two- and three-story apartment houses. Home to a large public park, the town square was adjacent to curving streets occupied by 740 semidetached and terraced houses as well as villas, all equipped with gardens and designed by a variety of local architects. Writing about both Spořilov and Zahradní Město, Pavitt has noted: "Such projects provided a workable and economically viable solution to problems of sanitation and mass construction. However, as they lacked a didactically Modernist image they received scant attention from the press and later, from historians. They were popular with both the state and with commerce as they stressed a traditional social structure, with much-vaunted characteristics of domesticity and 'family values.' As construction continued on both these sites in the late 1920s

and early 1930s, it is possible to see the 'Unwinesque' style of the cottages give way to a Modernist language, as flat roofs, sun terraces with steel railings and porthole windows are incorporated."[538]

POLAND

In 1909, the Warsaw Hygienic Society established the Warsaw Garden Cities Association, appointing Dr. Władysław Dobrzyński (1855–1931) as its president and pledging to "spread the beautiful idea of [Ebenezer] Howard among our population."[539] The association sent Dobrzyński on a tour of English and German suburbs, produced pamphlets and reports, and sponsored lectures. In the summer of 1911, when it numbered 120 members, the organization held an exhibition touting the movement that drew over 25,000 visitors. That same year the group identified a 210-acre site four miles north of Warsaw's city center along the Vistula as an excellent location to build its first garden city, noting, "the ground is sandy, high-lying, undulating, surrounded by forests with a wide horizon, reminding one of Hampstead."[540] But plans for the project did not progress, hampered by a lack of funds and the start of World War I.

Another proposal stymied by the war did, however, eventually move forward, resulting in the construction of **Miasto-Ogród Podkowa Leśna** (Garden City Horseshoe Grove) (1925), the first and only Polish development

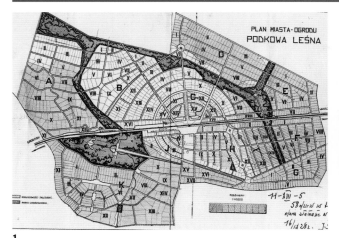

1. Plan, Antoni Jawornicki, 1925. PL

2. Casino, Juliusz Dzierżanowski, 1928. PL

3. Blonska Street. PL (2008)

4. Villa Krzyzewski, Stanisław Futasewicz, 1930. Maziarski. PL (2004)

directly inspired by Howard's example, although no industrial component was ever contemplated for the project nor was self-sufficiency stated as a goal.[541] In 1913 industrialist Stanisław Wilhelm Lilpop (1863–1930), acting on the advice of architect Tadeusz Tołwiński (1887–1951), announced his intention to build a residential estate on 522 heavily wooded acres in his family's possession since 1861, about 16 miles southwest of Warsaw. The first glimmer of progress occurred in 1922, when Lilpop joined with other businessmen to found Elektryczne Koleje Dojazdowe (Electric Commuter Rail), with the intention of constructing an electric train line to directly connect his parcel to Warsaw. Three years later Lilpop established a limited-dividend company to build the suburb, retaining 40 percent of the shares for himself with the remainder divided between a Warsaw bank and a local power company. Also in 1925 Warsaw-based architect and urban planner Antoni Jawornicki (1886–1950) was hired to prepare a plan.

Jawornicki's scheme for Podkowa Leśna, clearly influenced by Howard's Garden City diagram, called for concentric rings of semicircular streets located at the center of the site, just north of the railroad tracks bisecting the parcel. This horseshoe-shaped section was divided by diagonal north–south streets leading to the remainder of the development surrounded on three sides by a greenbelt, including a 35-acre public park designed by landscape architect Leon Danielewicz (1878–1970) at the western edge just south of the railroad. Jawornicki

was instructed to retain as many of the site's natural features as possible, as well as some of the original wooden summer cottages dating back to the 1870s. In keeping with the emphasis on nature, all of the streets were named after flowers, trees, birds, and other animals native to the location.

In 1926 the company began selling generously sized lots for private house development, marketing the project to affluent Varsovians and attracting a cultured, artistic crowd. The following year saw the construction of the first houses as well as the opening of the commuter railroad and a new station located at roughly the center of Podkowa Leśna. By 1930 thirty-nine wooden and fifty-nine masonry single-family houses were completed, the majority designed as traditional Polish manor houses by such architects as Stanisław Futasewicz (d. 1937) and Stanisław Gądzikiewicz (1879–1962). An exception to the vernacular-based designs was an International Style house designed by Maksymilian Goldberg (1895–1942) for the writer Irena Krzywicka on Sasnowa (Pine) Street. In addition to several shops and restaurants, the development also included a Roman Catholic church (1932) by Bruno Zborowski (1888–1983). Juliusz Dzierżanowski (1874–1943) was the designer of the suburb's social center and architectural highlight, the turreted Casino (1928), a sports facility with café and community meeting rooms located in the public park. In 1934 Podkowa Leśna was officially declared an independent town in Poland's Helenów district.

THE FEDERAL CAPITAL

OF

AUSTRALIA

Scale 400 Feet to an inch

GOVERNMENT

FACTORIES

GAS WORKS 35

PLAY GROUNDS

GARDEN CITY

RESIDENCE QUARTER

GOLF

CEMETERY

EXHIBITION PARC

CONCORDIA PLACE

CENTRAL MARKET

SOUTH PLACE

ASTRONOMICAL OBSERVATION

COLD STORAGE

RAILWAY MARSHALLING YARDS

ENUMERATION of the PUBLIC BUILDINGS

POLITICAL AND ADMINISTRATIVE QUARTER

1. Houses of Parliament of the City
2. Residence of Governor General
3. " " The Prime Minister
4.
5. Department of the eight Ministry
6. Courts of Justice
7. Criminal and Police Courts
8. State House
9. Triumph Arch
10. Mint
11. Printing Office
12. City Hall and Annexes
13. Chamber of Commerce
14. Social Museum

BUSINESS QUARTER

15. Central Railway Station
16. General Post Office
17. Telephon and Telegraph Offices
18. Stock Exchange
19. National Bank
20. Savings Bank
21. Central Market

PLACES of PUBLIC WORSHIP

22. Cathedral
23. Seminary
24. Church Museum
25. Bishop
26. Church and Chapels
27. Masonnic Temple

INDUSTRIAL QUARTER

28. People's Palace
29. Theatal Cinema
30. Markets
31. Town Hall
32. Technical Colleges
33. Government Factories
34. Central Power Station
35. Gas Works
36. Railway Marshalling Yards

RESIDENTIAL QUARTER

37. In Town   38. Out of Doors

UNIVERSITY QUARTER

39. Medecin
40. Fine Arts
41. Theology
42. Law

SPORTS and PLAY GROUNDS

EXHIBITION PARK

OUT of DOORS ETABLISSEMENTS

42. Military Barracks
43. Hospitals (Lunatic asylum &c)

PLACES of GENERAL INTEREST

44. Opera-House and Concert Hall
45. Library
46. Museum of Fine Arts
47. Public Baths
48. Gymnasium
49. Schools

CHAPTER SEVEN

The Globalization of the Garden City and the Garden Suburb 1900–1940

While the Garden City movement and the development of the garden suburb are predominantly associated with England, the United States, and the major western European countries, the fact of the matter is that the movement has spread throughout the world, often a product of colonial expansion.

CANADA

In Canada, as in the United States, the earliest planned suburbs appeared in the mid-nineteenth century in the form of arcadian enclaves on the outskirts of major cities. **Rosedale** (1854), developed by Edgar John Jarvis (1835–1907) on a heavily wooded 120-acre parcel a little over a mile north of Toronto, was most likely Canada's first.[1] Like its American contemporary counterpart Llewellyn Park, Rosedale enjoyed a "picturesque ravine-cut site" that surveyor John Stoughton Dennis (1820–1885) subdivided into sixty-two lots, with meandering streets following the topography to preserve three ravines as common parkland.[2] Jarvis built several houses, including one for his own use, as well as two bridges crossing the southern ravine before progress was halted by a faltering economy, not to pick up again in earnest until the last two decades of the nineteenth century, when Rosedale was characterized by *American Architect and Building News* as Toronto's "most beautiful suburb, from a picturesque point-of-view."[3]

Unlike Llewellyn Park, Rosedale was not gated, but two miles to the west, the similarly picturesque if considerably smaller **Wychwood Park** (1888) began to take form in 1874, when Marmaduke Matthews (1837–1913), an English-born landscape painter, purchased a 10-acre site northwest of the intersection of Davenport Road and Bathurst Street and built a hilltop house that he named Wychwood in honor of a forest near his English hometown.[4] Three years later, Alexander Jardine (n.d.), a baking-soda manufacturer, built a house on an adjacent 12 acres, and in 1888, Jardine and Matthews, who had been appointed official artist of the Canadian Pacific Railway, filed a plan to subdivide the combined 22-acre property in order to create a cooperative artists' colony. The plan outlined seventeen lots around an internal loop road with gated entrances in the south and in the northwest. Within the loop, roughly half the land would be developed while the other half, cut through by a ravine and by Taddle Creek, was set aside as communal parkland. Later Taddle Creek would be dammed to create a pond. In 1891 Jardine and Matthews revised the plan to accommodate thirty-eight parcels ranging from quite small peripheral lots to generously sized house sites near the center. The new plan carried deed restrictions permitting only detached houses, setting minimum construction costs, and establishing a board of trustees.

In 1906, George Reid, a muralist, built the first house in the Wychwood Park suburb, followed the next year by houses that English-born architect Eden

Canberra, third-place competition entry by Alfred Agache, 1912. NAA

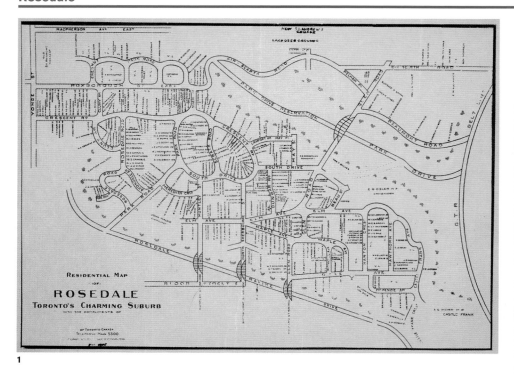

1. Map. CTPL (1905)

2. Chestnut Park Road, viewed from Roxborough Street East. CTA1 (1919)

3. South Glen Road bridge. CTPL2 (1885–95)

Wychwood Park

1. Plan, Marmaduke Matthews and Alexander Jardine. CTPL (1900)

2. Typical street. O'Brien. POB (2010)

3. 7 Wychwood Park, Eden Smith, 1910. O'Brien. POB (2010)

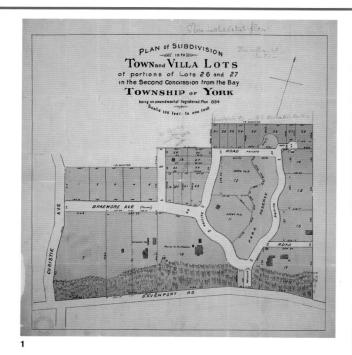

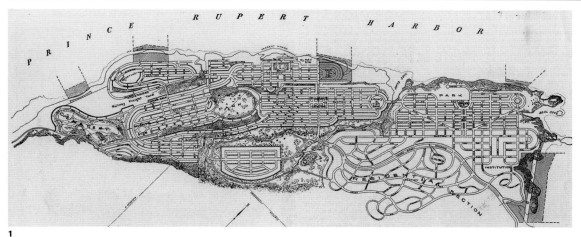

1. Plan, Franklin Brett and George Duffield Hall, 1909. AR09

2. Aerial view of courthouse and grounds. CPR (c. 2007)

3. Aerial view. CPR (c. 2007)

Smith (1859–1949), Canada's principal exponent of the Arts and Crafts movement, designed for himself and for his neighbors. The finest houses were built prior to 1917, although work continued during the inter-war years and into the postwar era. Toronto annexed Wychwood Park in 1909, but the enclave continues to be privately managed and maintained. In 1986 it was designated a Heritage Conservation District because of its "park-like ambience," the "manner in which the houses are situated in relation to the mature trees and natural land contours," and the "open space around the houses."[5] In addition to establishing architectural and landscape guidelines, the conservation plan warned against improving the roads, which did not meet municipal standards but were an "essential part of the visual, social and circulation character of the park . . . It is therefore important to refrain from adding street signs, white lines or a one-way street system."[6]

Suburban town planning picked up considerably after the turn of the century, flourishing between about 1906 and 1912, with many of the new developments carried out by railroad companies as they made their way across the continent. In 1905, the Grand Trunk Pacific Railway selected **Prince Rupert**, British Columbia, as its western terminus, setting into motion plans for a city of more than 10,000 residents that would also become a major center of international trade, providing a strategic, convenient gateway to Japan and the Far East.[7] The site comprised 2,000 acres on the northwestern shore of

the virtually untouched, 28-square-mile Kaien Island, 550 miles north of Vancouver and 40 miles from the Alaska border. The island, situated a short distance off the coast, was dominated by the central, 2,300-foot-high Mount Hays. Combined with a 10,000-acre grant from the government, which would share ownership of Prince Rupert, the railway held 24,000 acres, allowing plenty of room for growth.

To plan the new town, the company turned to Boston landscape architects Franklin Brett (n.d.), a former employee of Frederick Law Olmsted, and George Duffield Hall (1877–1961), who had studied with John Charles Olmsted. Construction began soon after Brett and Hall first visited the site in 1908. The designers called for nine "sections," or zones, devoted to industrial, commercial, residential, and other uses, employing natural ravines, creeks, and valleys as buffers and parks.

Describing the design strategy in 1909, Hall warned against formal rigidity: "The desire to make a show plan on paper, with enforced symmetry in design, has frequently led to great disappointment in result, and the practical landscape architect realizes fully that theory on paper must generally concede to the vagaries of nature." The "first great aim," Hall explained, was "to decide on a skeleton system of fundamental roads . . . so as to tie the whole development together."[8]

The planners specified 94-foot-wide arterial roads, 72-foot-wide business roads, and 56-foot-wide side streets, the last "a width which the designers consider

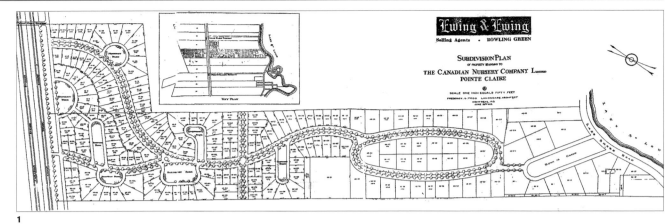

1

2

3

4

ample for streets not destined to become accumulative for through traffic."[9]

Each section's plan was tailored to its function, with the commercial district, for instance, laid out with rectilinear streets on two of the site's only flat areas. The residential section, by contrast, featured an organic street pattern in which the most expensive houses were set among meandering roads leading up the slopes of the mountain. Throughout the plan, Hall noted, "park reservations, squares, playgrounds and public building sites have been carefully considered, and so located as to enhance the effectiveness of main avenues, by giving definite terminal features, by planning for architectural factors at salient points along their course, and by providing for suitable civic centres or squares where important thoroughfares intersect."[10]

Raymond Unwin was sufficiently impressed to illustrate the plan in his 1909 volume, *Town Planning in Practice*. Unfortunately, in 1912, after significant progress had been made, the project suffered a major blow when its chief advocate, Charles Hays, president of the railway, went down on the *Titanic*. Hays's successor did not share his vision. Among the more elaborate components never to be realized were a steamship terminal, train station, and hotel complex designed by British-born Canadian émigré architect Francis Mawson Rattenbury (1867–1935). Less dazzling elements were also diminished. Architectural historian Harold Kalman notes that while Prince Rupert was built "according to the essentials of

the Brett and Hall plan and, despite some deviations, the designers' intentions remain clearly legible,"[11] axial boulevards intended to terminate in grand vistas suffered not only from a lack of development along their edges but also from "the insubstantiality of the buildings that were erected."[12]

Prince Rupert was one of the many Canadian town plans to be carried out by disciples of Frederick Law Olmsted. In addition to his son, Frederick Law Olmsted Jr., and nephew and stepson, John Charles Olmsted, who, practicing as the Olmsted Brothers, received several Canadian commissions, Olmsted's protégés included Rickson Outhet (1872–1951), Canada's first native-born landscape architect, and the American Frederick G. Todd (1876–1948), a New Hampshire-born landscape architect who had worked for Olmsted, Olmsted & Eliot between 1896 and 1900, helping to implement the plan for Mount Royal Park (1874), in Montreal, before establishing one of Canada's most prominent landscape architecture firms.

In 1905, Todd designed **Bowling Green**, fifteen miles west of downtown Montreal, on the north shore of Lake St. Louis, for a developer who initially intended it as a summer community but later marketed it for year-round living. Working on a flat site of former farmland accessed by stations on the Canadian Pacific Railway (CPR) and Grand Trunk Pacific Railway, Todd introduced variation to the plain, rectangular parcel by way of a longitudinal meandering drive that branched off into culs-de-sac and

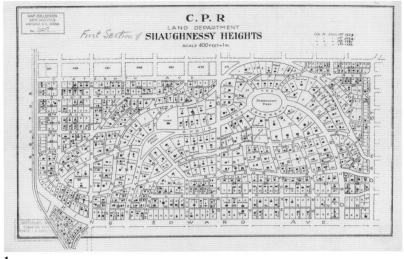

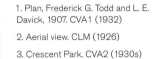

1. Plan, Frederick G. Todd and L. E. Davick, 1907. CVA1 (1932)

2. Aerial view. CLM (1926)

3. Crescent Park. CVA2 (1930s)

4. 3338 The Crescent, 1912. CVA3 (1910s)

5. Typical street. Cuan. CUA (2012)

courts and separated into two as it approached the lakefront, embracing a grassy park.

Todd's 1907 plan for **Shaughnessy Heights**, Vancouver, built by the Canadian Pacific Railway, the city's largest landowner and the driving force behind its early development, offered a rare respite from the city's prevailing grid.[13] Named for railway president Sir Thomas Shaughnessy, the enclave occupied 250 acres bound by Oak Street on the east, King Edward Avenue on the south, a trolley line on the west (now Arbutus Street), and a curving northern border that reached Fifteenth Avenue. The site was divided into eastern and western halves by a major thoroughfare, Granville Street.

Todd collaborated with Danish engineer L. E. Davick (n.d.) on the plan, integrating open spaces into a hybrid of orthogonal streets on the level land and curvilinear streets meeting in Y-shaped intersections in the hillier areas. In the northeast, the circular Shaughnessy Park acted as a hub for five boulevards, one of which, Angus Boulevard, included a landscaped median that briefly widened into a crescent-shaped park in the west. Todd's landscape plan called for diverse tree species to be placed along the streets between the curb and sidewalk. To entice purchasers, the CPR sponsored a nearby golf course as well as tennis and lawn-bowling clubs. House lots, between one-fifth and one-and-a-half acres, protected by restrictive covenants, attracted an affluent clientele who later added strictures mandating single-family construction and banning the further subdivision of lots. The Depression took a toll on Shaughnessy Heights, where the prevalence of repossessed houses earned it the nickname "Mortgage Heights." For years, the restrictive covenants were not enforced and houses were broken up into apartments. When the neighborhood eventually regained its prestige, relaxed rules permitted multifamily housing.

Todd's most ambitious scheme was for **Mount Royal**, a northwestern suburb of Montreal built by the Canadian Northern Railway to help offset the cost of a three-mile-long tunnel it was digging through the 763-foot-high Mount Royal to provide a route to the city center.[14] Plans to develop the rectangular, roughly 1,450-acre parcel took shape in 1911, shortly after Frederick Law Olmsted Jr. and the British housing reformer and copartnership advocate Henry Vivian separately visited Montreal to deliver influential lectures on town planning, with Vivian showing images of Letchworth, Hampstead, Port Sunlight, and Bournville. Hoping to capitalize on the resulting wave of public enthusiasm, the railroad company touted Mount Royal alternately as a Garden City, Garden Suburb, and ambitiously a "Model City."

As built, it fell short of all three designations. But Mount Royal was not without merit. The design synthesized Beaux-Arts axiality and naturalistic informality, featuring a tight gridiron of streets overlaid by two intersecting 80-foot-wide diagonal boulevards that provided quick access to a central railroad station. The site presented one major challenge that Todd's design did

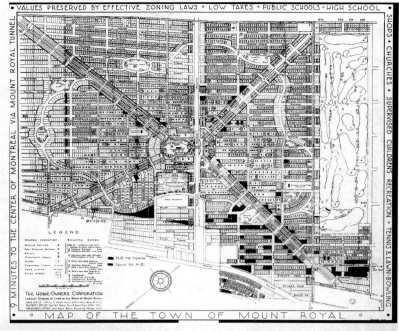

1. Plan, Frederick G. Todd, c. 1911. TMRA (1938)

2. Aerial view of town center. TMRA (c. 1942)

3. Typical street. TMRA

4. Aerial view. TMRA (1964)

5. Typical house. CLP (1995)

not quite overcome: the railroad cut that bisected the neighborhood from south to north. Todd positioned a town square, with public buildings and a park, around the train station on the west side of the cut, but about one-third of the town center extended awkwardly to the other side of the tracks, connected by a too-narrow bridge. (A second bridge was later built.) Institutional and commercial buildings created a civic center around the square, and the diagonal boulevards were zoned to accommodate apartment buildings. The rest of Mount Royal was reserved for a lower-density fabric of detached and semidetached houses on lots measuring a comfortable 50 by 100 or 110 feet, with mandated 15-foot building setbacks. Todd's most enlightened move was a meandering loop road—about a half mile from the center—linking thirteen variously shaped parks that he referred to as "small squares and breathing places."[15] In addition, following Raymond Unwin's example at Letchworth, Todd modified the grid so that it crossed the diagonal boulevards in right-angled intersections. Nonetheless, as writer John Sewell has noted, the "road system seems not fully integrated: the curves interrupt

the grid, as do the diagonals, but seem an add-on or an after-thought."[16]

Development was almost nonexistent until the completion of the tunnel in 1918, at which point Mount Royal's population catapulted from 100 to 2,000 by the mid-1920s. Initially, the houses echoed the architectural vocabularies of Letchworth and Hampstead. But "this early architectural landscape is deceptive," according to planning historian Larry McCann: "Besides its imitative looks—its Garden City and Garden Suburb appearance—Mount Royal's early domestic landscape shares little else with the idealistic housing reforms that so strongly influence the built environment of early twentieth-century suburban England."[17]

In 1912 the Canadian Pacific Railway hired Todd to design **Leaside**, four miles north of Toronto, where it joined nearby Rosedale and Wychwood Park.[18] Todd's plan for the 1,025-acre site was looser and more successful than at Mount Royal, combining serpentine boulevards, concentric arcing streets, and conventionally gridded streets with a curving transverse drive where he situated administrative buildings, offices, and shops. In

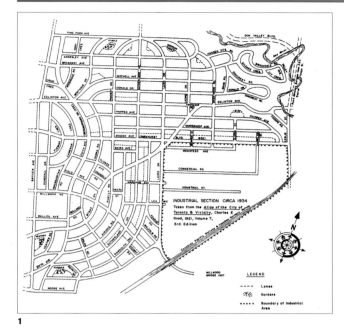

1

2

3

1. Plan, Frederick G. Todd, 1912. MTRL (c. 1930s)

2, 3. Typical views. McCann. CLM (1993)

the northeast, the plan gave way to a free-form layout reflecting the path of the Don River. Common gardens were included on some block interiors as well as rear lanes that were later eliminated. The southeast portion of the site was industrial, accommodating a munitions plant and a pilot-training facility, from which the neighborhood drew residents. World War I stalled development, with only sixty-eight houses built by 1929, but the enclave expanded heavily during the 1930s when the completion of a viaduct allowed easier passage across the Don River valley to Toronto. The rapid construction of 2,000 uniformly setback houses created coherent tree-lined streetscapes that matured by the 1990s to provide what John Sewell called "a wonderfully leafy experience."[19]

One mile northwest, the garden enclave of **Lawrence Park** (1909) was developed by Wilfred Dinnick, a real estate and railroad executive and president of the Dovercourt Land Building & Savings Company, and designed by Walter S. Brook (n.d.), a British engineer who incorporated crescents, circles, and diagonals into a rather stiff arrangement that Sewell has deemed "tentative."[20] Brook's plan retained a stream and its surrounding ravine, harkening back to Rosedale and Wychwood Park but by that time a rarity among subdivisions in which watercourses were typically covered over. Toronto architects William Craven Vaux Chadwick (1868–1941) and Samuel Beckett (1869–1917) provided model house plans to purchasers who could also submit their own architects' designs for approval, at least until World War I interrupted development. Lots were sold off in 1919, but construction continued in fits

and starts, and much of the area was not built out until the 1980s, when affluent residents crowded the typically 50-foot-wide lots with much larger houses than those originally envisioned.

Frederick Todd also played a role in the design of **Tuxedo Park** (1910), a Winnipeg neighborhood that had little but its name in common with the New York suburb from which developer Frederick W. Heubach (1859–1914) sought to borrow cachet.[21] Situated on 148 acres, at first glance Tuxedo Park seems a fairly standard subdivision. However its plan was developed with careful consideration, beginning with a 1905 design by Rickson Outhet that was revised in 1907 by Todd and again in 1910 by the Olmsted Brothers, who had been asked to coordinate an international design competition when the site was expanded but were subsequently hired for the job. Outhet's initial design overlaid a grid plan with diagonal landscaped boulevards able to accommodate streetcars and bridle paths, while peripheral "speedways" for horses and automobiles kept fast moving traffic out of the two residential sections centered around an oval athletic field and a diamond-shaped golf links. As completed, the plan was a softer, modified grid featuring straight north–south and gently arcing east–west streets interrupted by a diagonal boulevard that created a series of plazas as it cut across the site from southwest to northeast. Long rectangular blocks featured rear service alleys, allowing utilities to be buried, and 50-by-130-foot lots, of which houses were allowed to cover a maximum of 40 percent. While the role of each designer in the final plan remains unclear, the Olmsteds' chief contribution

1. Advertisement showing plan, Walter S. Brook, 1910. CTPL

2. Advertisement. CLM (c. 1910)

3. Path through ravine. DFP (c. 1910)

4. Typical street. DFP (c. 1910)

5. Early view of streets. DFP (1911–13)

6. St. Edmunds Drive and Weybourne Crescent. Aquitaine. WC (2009)

7. Houses on Lawrence Crescent. McCann. CLM (c. 2000)

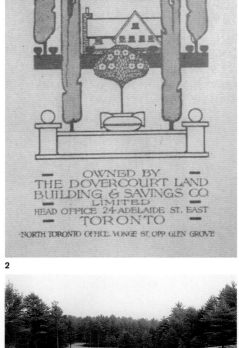

seems to have been the expansion of Outhet's small athletic oval into a 3,000-by-400-foot open space that, for "advertising purposes," the developer named Olmsted Park, although not all of its amenities, planned to include bridal paths, drives, a wading pool, playgrounds, and flower beds, were realized.[22]

Tuxedo Park's real promise lay in the integration of three public and institutional entities: a campus for the University of Manitoba in the west, a linear campus for the Manitoba Government Agricultural College that formed the entire eastern border, and the 400-acre Assiniboine Park which, along with the Assiniboine River, formed the northern border. Unfortunately, the Agricultural College soon relocated because there was no room to expand in Tuxedo Park, and the University of Manitoba chose another location entirely, leaving its site to be developed as a golf course. Lacking the institutional components and hemmed in by industrial development to the south, Tuxedo Park suffered. Up until World War I, development was limited to a ten-block patch in

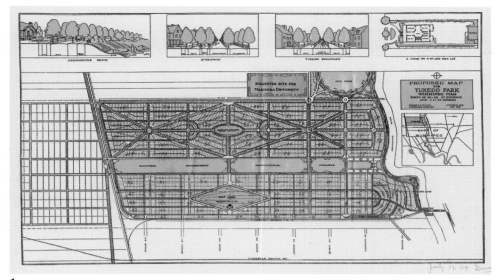

1. Plan, Rickson Outhet, 1905. FLO

2. Plan, Olmsted Brothers, 1910. UMAS

3 Aerial view. GE (2005)

4. Typical street. McCann. CLM (c. 1995)

the north that despite a rectilinear plan matured into a beautiful district of tree-shaded streets. The heart of the enclave remained undeveloped until the 1950s, after which most of the original plan was abandoned.

Although their input was muted in Tuxedo Park, the Olmsted Brothers succeeded with a number of independent commissions in Canada. Working for the Canadian Pacific Railway, the firm planned the Calgary suburbs of **Sunalta** (1909–10) and **South Mount Royal** (1910–11), with John Charles Olmsted leading the effort in both cases, calling for curvilinear streets and integrated parks that—especially in the lushly planted, tree-shaded South Mount Royal, one of Calgary's most desirable neighborhoods—starkly contrasted with the city's prevailing grid.[23] John Charles Olmsted also designed the wealthy enclave of **Uplands** (1908), in Oak Bay, British Columbia, working on a 465-acre site on the eastern tip of Vancouver Island with three miles of Inner Harbor frontage.[24] Previously occupied by a farm and slaughterhouse, the land had been purchased a year earlier by the Winnipeg development firm of Oldfield, Kirby & Gardner in an effort to capitalize on the construction of a streetcar line connecting with Victoria, two miles to the west. Olmsted visited the site six times, impressed by its beautiful, tree-dotted hills descending in benches toward the harbor and commanding

distant views of Mount Baker and the Cascades. He organized the enclave around Midland Way, a divided boulevard connecting two traffic circles, lining the axis with quarter-acre residential lots and covering the rest of the land with curving streets that formed irregularly shaped blocks with lots of up to 3.5 acres. Utilities were buried, allowing for an uncluttered streetscape in which sidewalks, placed along only one side of the road, were illuminated by ornamental cast-iron light standards. Gateposts marked the development's principal entrances, and characteristically Olmstedian triangular parks filled in the spaces at irregular intersections.

Uplands was subject to municipal restrictions banning commercial uses and setting minimum construction costs and building setbacks. In the project's early years, house plans had to pass muster with the developers' consulting architect, Francis Mawson Rattenbury. Olmsted's recommendation that the enclave include a club led to the establishment in 1912 of the Royal Victoria Yacht Club, giving the project added appeal. Despite heavy marketing between 1912 and 1914, only 83 of the 424 lots were sold—and only nine houses built. After World War I, momentum proved hard to regain, with only 34 houses built by 1930 and 235 by 1945. In order to settle back taxes, in 1946 the developers turned over 65 acres in the southeast to become Uplands

1. Plan, John Charles Olmsted. GAI (1913)

2. Typical street. McCann. CLM

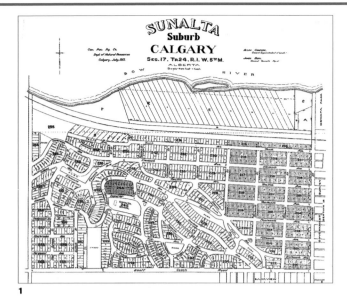

South Mount Royal

1. Plan, John Charles Olmsted. GAI (1913)

2, 3. Typical streets. McCann. CLM (c. 2000)

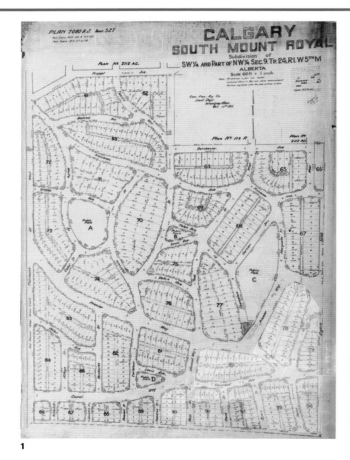

Park, a rugged landscape that remains essentially in its natural state. "While this maneuver may have kept the Company afloat," Martin Segger and Douglas Franklin wrote in their 1979 architectural history of Victoria, "it seems difficult to justify the open space in terms of necessity, since the development is itself generous with park amenities at everyone's front door. It also had the effect of slicing through the symmetry of the Olmsted plan, choking the style of the area in the southern sector. As a consequence, the grand Edwardian axial set-piece, Midland Avenue, has never been executed."[25]

Back on the mainland, in Vancouver, the Olmsted Brothers carried out a series of subdivisions for British Pacific Properties, a partnership between the Dublin-based Guinness family and a consortium of British investors that had acquired 4,000 acres in West Vancouver's North Shore area for the development of contiguous suburbs that they would link to the city, six miles away, by constructing the Lions Gate Bridge over Burrard Inlet. The initial subdivision, **Capilano Estates** (1931), occupied a 1,100-acre tract rising at a 15 percent grade up the south-facing slope of Hollyburn Mountain.[26] Olmsted

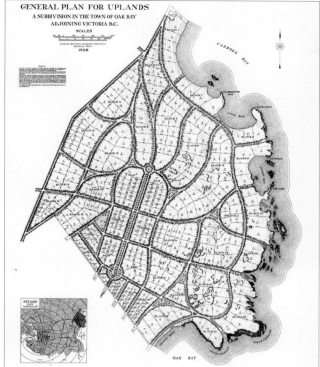

1. Plan, John Charles Olmsted, 1908. FLO

2. Bird's-eye view. CLM

3–5. Typical views. McCann. CLM (2012)

partner James Frederick Dawson led the design effort, calling for an organic street pattern that made the most of the hillside, employing switchbacks and culs-de-sac to access 416 two-and-a-half- to four-and-a-half-acre sites with sweeping views of Mount Baker and Vancouver. Access was gained from the south by way of a 1,500-foot-long tree-lined divided boulevard leading to an unrealized entrance plaza and shops. The plan provided 97 acres of business lots, an eighteen-hole golf course, polo grounds and stables, 51 acres of parks, 10 acres reserved for schools, and seven miles of bridle paths. Major streets were 80 feet wide, secondary streets were 60 and 70 feet wide, and short spurs that led to difficult sites were 40 feet wide. Construction successfully spanned the Depression and continues in phases today.

Farther north, in the fairly remote reaches of central British Columbia but situated along the Grand Trunk Pacific Railway, in 1914 Walter Burley Griffin,

shortly after moving to Australia, collaborated with partner Barry Byrne on the garden village of **Vanderhoof**. The scheme both modified the town's existing grid plan, which had been implemented to maximize salable lots despite the site's irregular topography, and laid out a new, adjacent residential district with an Olmsted-esque network of streets bounding organically shaped blocks where detached houses sat around internal reserves.[27] Griffin proposed to distribute governmental and public buildings, including a library, churches, community houses, and primary and high schools, among three new cores—a municipal center in each of the sections and a more substantial civic center straddling the two. According to Griffin, by placing these centers "so that they could be reached directly by a system of radiating streets following the ravines," many of the existing "cross streets became entirely unnecessary, easy gradients were obtained everywhere, the depths of the

Capilano Estates

1. Plan, Olmsted Brothers, 1931.
CVA4

2. Aerial view of Vancouver
showing location of Capilano
Estates in the distance. CVA
(1931)

3. Rendering of entrance plaza.
CLM

4. Taylor Way. CLM

5. Typical street. McCann. CLM
(1998)

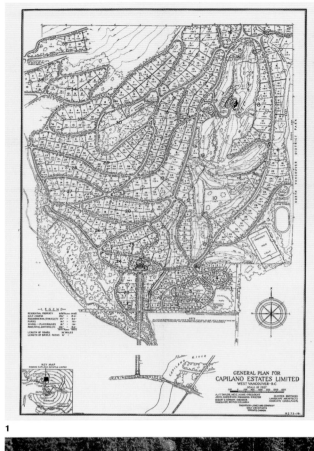

1

2

3

4

5

Vanderhoof

1. Plan, Walter Burley Griffin and
Barry Byrne, 1914. CHM

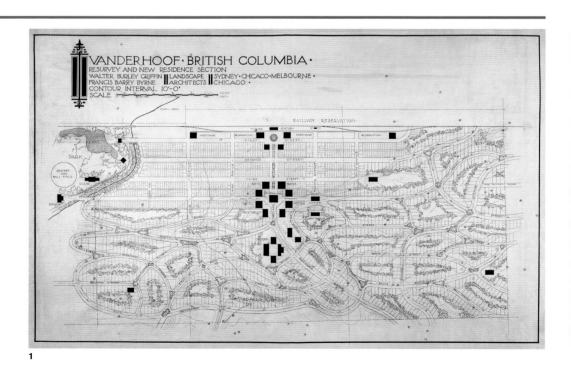

1

blocks were increased till almost without exception all the blocks had interior parks, while at the same time the private allotments were increased from 130 feet to 150 feet in depth, and when the count of lots was made there were still as many as before."[28] Byrne laid out a picturesque park to the west of the village. The town plan was never implemented.

Beginning in 1912, a successful Canadian lecture tour brought a spate of commissions to the English landscape architect and town planner Thomas Mawson ranging in scale from private residential gardens to campus and city plans. Owing largely to the onset of World War I, few of the projects would be realized. In 1912, Mawson planned two garden suburbs, the James Estate and Meadlands, on coastal sites on Vancouver Island for the B. C. Electric Railway Company, which intended them as suburbs of Victoria. **Meadlands,** with a beachfront site suggesting "a resort rather than a suburb," according to garden historian Janet Waymark, juxtaposed a neighborhood of freeform streets conforming to hilly terrain with a roughly symmetrical district on a flat site enlivened by a U-shaped street plan cut through by a broad arcing mall.[29] The unrealized plan included hierarchical streets, circular and triangular parklets, and detached houses.

Mawson's design of the **Borden Park Estate** (1914) was more ambitious in scope, calling for a resort garden village on the shores of Lake Deschenes, near Ottawa, where the developer, the Great Eastern Realty Company, marketed the never-built project to wealthy buyers who could enjoy a new golf course and country club, tennis courts, and a marina.[30] The 600-acre site was accessible by an existing tram but a new electric railway was also planned and the site was near the transcontinental railroad. In addition, Mawson called for an automobile drive leading to Ottawa. More complex than the typical garden village, Borden Park was to feature a manufacturing zone with workers' houses near the railway, a business district with stores, hotels, and a second class of housing near the tram, and first-class houses along radiating streets between the harbor and a semicircular block accommodating a hotel and clubhouse facing the golf course. The layout recalled Raymond Unwin's diagram, "The Garden City Principle Applied to Suburbs," (see p. 219) but turned 180 degrees to face inland instead of the harbor.

In his planning work for **Regina** (1913–15), Saskatchewan, Mawson designed an upper-class garden suburb adjacent to the lieutenant governor's residence and a model workmen's village near a manufacturing zone, both shaped by concentric semicircular streets. Mawson's broader vision for Regina, complete with protective greenswards, parks, a civic center, zoning laws, and City Beautiful–inspired boulevards, was intended to create the "Garden City of the Prairies," but never moved forward.[31] As part of his urban plan for Calgary, begun in 1913 and released as *Calgary: Past, Present and Future* in 1914, Mawson suggested two workers' garden suburbs: **Manchester** and **Connaught,** each closely hewing to the English model with, in the former, detached and semidetached houses and three-,

Meadlands

1. Plan, Thomas Mawson, 1912. CVA

Borden Park Estate

1. Bird's-eye view. CCA (c. 1914)

Regina

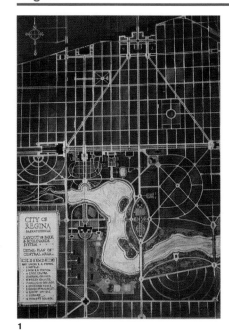

1. Plan, Thomas Mawson, 1913–15. JWTM

Manchester

1. Plan, Thomas Mawson, 1914.
MAW

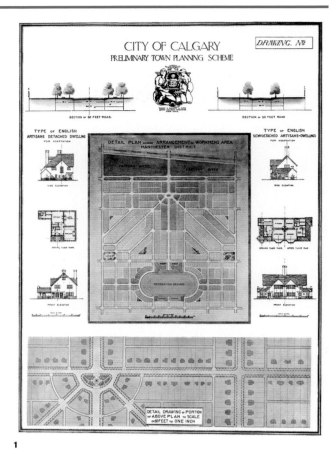

1

Connaught

1. Plan, Thomas Mawson, 1914. MAW

1

five-, and seven-unit rowhouses on 1,200 narrow lots in a symmetrical 220-acre plan of diagonal and rectilinear 50- and 80-foot-wide tree-lined streets extending from a factory site toward an oval recreation ground and, in Connaught, a topographically determined mix of straight and freely curving streets giving shape to large blocks of detached and semidetached houses and rowhouses enclosing allotment gardens.[32] Both plans incorporated parks and green buffers. Connaught, covering 80 acres, featured a church as "a dominant note in the composition" as well as a block containing a school and its attendant playgrounds, a museum, gallery, and workmen's club.[33] The plan was prohibitively expensive for the city's struggling economy. It was released in April 1914 but as Max Foran has written, "In the next six months . . . slipped into obscurity . . . It seems fairly certain that city officials took the easiest way out and allowed the report to die while paying lip service to its utility as a guide to future development."[34]

After the war, Mawson's sometime collaborator Thomas Adams emerged as both the chief advocate for and designer of garden suburbs in Canada, working in both the public and private sectors. Born in Scotland, Adams helped pioneer the Garden City idea in England, serving as secretary of the Garden City Association (1901–6) and first president of the Town Planning Institute (1913–14) before relocating to Canada in 1914, where, in practice for ten years, he acted as town-planning adviser to the Commission of Conservation and as president of the Town Planning Institute of Canada before reestablishing a practice in London in 1922 and relocating to the United States the following year to focus on the preparation of the Regional Plan of New York, published in 1929. In 1918, Adams helped formulate the Federal Housing Scheme, legislation that paved the way for Canada's first federally financed housing, intended to provide dwellings for the working class and for returning soldiers and to stimulate activity in the construction industry by providing low-interest loans to developers and municipalities.

Adams planned the first of the program's initiatives, the enclave of **Lindenlea** (1918–24), located roughly two miles northeast of downtown Ottawa.[35] Lindenlea was also the capital city's first planned community and its developer, the Ottawa Housing Commission, promoted it as a model for other municipalities to follow, hoping it would demonstrate not only the physical principles of garden suburb planning but also the social benefits, with Adams advocating that it be managed like a British copartnership. That model, however, "questionable in the cultural context of Canada's *laissez faire* political economy," as Larry McCann has written, never took hold.[36]

At Lindenlea, Adams incorporated as many garden suburb elements as possible into the small, square-shaped, 22-acre site bound by Maple Lane, Lambton Road, Rideau Terrace, and Springfield Road, including culs-de-sac, crescents, and courtyards. He devoted 10 percent of the site to public spaces such as parks, playgrounds, tennis courts, and a wading pool. His plan of diagonal and curving roads discouraged

Lindenlea

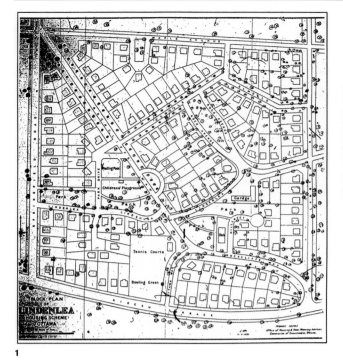

1

2

1. Plan, Thomas Adams, 1921. JSSC

2. Typical street. Wisniowski. HW (2012)

Richmond

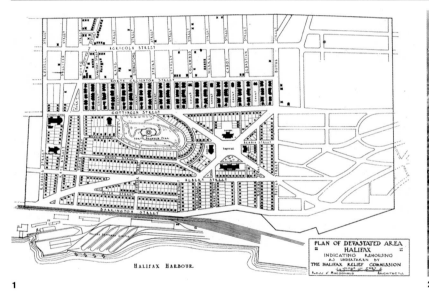

1

2

1. Plan showing Hydrostone District, top, Thomas Adams and Ross & MacDonald, 1918. NSA

2. Aerial view of Hydrostone District. NSA (c. 1921)

through traffic and created closed visual axes. The scheme also reserved a site for an institute and a community parking garage that was never widely used and was later demolished. The initial plan would have mixed single-family and group houses designed by Adams's assistant, English-trained architect W. D. Cromarty (n.d.), but the group houses were rejected. Instead, 168 lots accommodated individual two-story dwellings clad primarily in brick and stucco, indicating, as Jill Delaney has noted, that Lindenlea, while intended for low-income residents, was "carefully modeled after the current middle-class preferences" and, as a result, was beyond the reach of the working class for whom it was intended.[37] Making matters worse, the architectural quality was poor, and Adams, according to planning historian Michael Simpson, was "unfairly made the

scapegoat."[38] In 1920 he withdrew from the project, bemoaning that "as a town planning project, Lindenlea was a complete success" but was reduced by others to "an ordinary real estate development."[39]

Adams's next Canadian plan was for the working-class industrial neighborhood of **Richmond,** Halifax, bordering Halifax Harbor, where on December 6, 1917, the Halifax Explosion, resulting from the collision of a Norwegian vessel loaded with relief supplies and a French munitions ship, leveled 325 acres, killing and injuring more than 10,000.[40] At the behest of the Halifax Relief Commission, Adams arrived on-site eight days after the explosion. He retained some surviving portions of the historic street pattern, but otherwise undertook what Michael Simpson called "a technical exercise in the destruction of the standard grid," inserting diagonal

1. Aerial view. GE (2001)
2. Aerial view. FICA (1932)
3. Aerial view. FICA (1936)
4. Aerial view. FICA (1943)

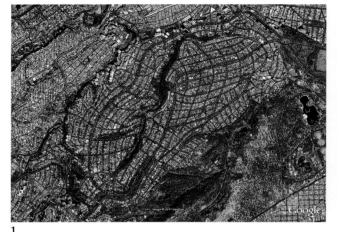

and curving streets, alternating between east–west- and north–south-oriented rectangular blocks, providing open spaces, and establishing firm building lines.[41] In the center of the site, Adams reserved the hill around Fort Needham as a public park. To the northwest, he placed public buildings around a town square at the intersection of two 80-foot-wide diagonal boulevards.

Richmond's most distinguished section was the half-mile-long 23-acre Hydrostone District (1918–20), built on the upland, between North Creighton and Gottingen Streets, where ten rectangular blocks of rowhouses alternated with broad landscaped malls. The MIT- and École des Beaux-Arts-trained architect George Allen Ross (1879–1946), of the Montreal firm of Ross & MacDonald, designed the 326 dwelling units, specifying, in light of the site's catastrophic history, a fireproof patented concrete block called Hydro-stone, which gave the district its name. Ross prepared seven distinct house types. Duplexes were placed at the ends of each block and four- and six-unit rows in between, separated by rear alleys. A commercial group of sixteen stores and offices was placed across from a commons on Young Street. The Hydro-stone was covered in half-timbering and stucco and combined with a variety of roof styles to create what Harold Kalman has called "an attractive, yet unpretentious, neighborhood—a combination of good planning and good architecture—with a decidedly Old English

flavour."[42] Unfortunately, even the group houses were beyond the means of those who had previously lived in the area and were now forced to relocate. After years of high vacancy rates, the houses were sold off beginning in the 1940s, at which point the district came into its own as a desirable enclave.

MEXICO

Chapultepec Heights (1922), now known as Lomas de Chapultepec, a northwestern suburb of Mexico City, was built by a consortium of American developers. Landscape architect George Kessler worked with Mexican architect José Luis Cuevas Pietrasanta (1881–1952) on the layout of a nearly 2,000-acre site, a beautiful plateau with a mountain backdrop and, as a 1923 guidebook described it, dramatic views of "a charming, semi-medieval castle, palms and snow-clad volcanoes, city spires and country shrines, and one of the finest forest reserves on the continent."[43]

In contrast to the streetcar suburbs being developed south of Mexico City, Chapultepec Heights was geared toward the automobile. The enclave was a fifteen-minute drive from the city by way of a new boulevard, today the Paseo de la Reforma, that passed through the adjacent Chapultepec Park to arrive at an "automobile promenade"

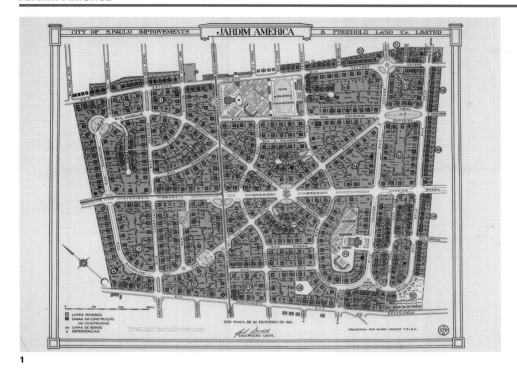

1

at the entrance to the Heights. A deep, wooded ravine cut diagonally across the site, creating a park-like setting for those houses facing it. On each side, a 135-foot-wide boulevard led through narrower residential streets arranged to form warped grids of varying orientation, laid out according to the topography. Many of the streets had landscaped medians. An early observer remarked on Chapultepec's "broad walks flanked by flowering trees and shrubs, plazas, parks, glorietas [roundabouts], bridal-paths, golf-links, children's playgrounds, tennis-courts, fields for baseball, football and polo, and attractive club houses."[44] The layout distinctly resembled Wilbur Cook's plan of Beverly Hills (see p. 156), a similarity that may not have been accidental. As historian Carol McMichael Reese has written, "Not only the emphasis on the automobile in Chapultupec Heights, but also the relationship between house styles there and in contemporary Los Angeles signaled the growing presence of North American suburban residential imagery in Mexico City—a presence that commentators ascribed to the increasing influence of Hollywood films."[45]

Bungalows were built initially, then more lavish residences whose occupants, including prominent diplomats, government officials, wealthy Americans, and aristocrats, gave the enclave its nickname, "paradise of the potentates," a cachet that has not faded.[46] Chapultepec Heights remains, according to historian John M. Hart, "the most distinguished housing subdivision in the nation."[47] Perhaps the only subdivision to rival Chapultepec Heights was the 1,250-acre Jardines del Pedregal ("El Pedregal"; 1945–52), south of Mexico City, comprising 1,200 building lots, the design, development, and marketing of which were personally overseen by Modernist architect Luis Barragán (1902–1988) in the immediate aftermath of World War II.[48]

BRAZIL

Roughly two years before their partnership ended in 1914, Raymond Unwin and Barry Parker were commissioned to design **Jardim América**, a garden enclave in São Paulo, Brazil, for the City of São Paulo Improvements and Freehold Land Company Limited (now Companhia City de Desenvolvimento), a development concern founded in 1911 with 29,652 acres of land on the city's southern and western outskirts, about equal in size to one-third of the developed area of São Paulo.[49] Although the company was incorporated in England, it was led by French architect Joseph Bouvard (1840–1920); Edouard Fontaine de Laveleye, a French banker who provided much of the principal financing; a Brazilian utilities company that also crucially owned a tram line; and an assortment of other banks and individual investors.

Unwin prepared the initial site plan for Jardim América, but Parker, who lived in São Paulo between 1917 and 1919, was responsible for subsequent revisions leading to the final design. The roughly 260-acre rectangular site had previously been platted as a gridiron in keeping with the surrounding city plan but overlaid by diagonal boulevards intersecting in a central plaza of parks and public buildings. Now working with a strictly residential program, Parker retained the diagonal streets, reducing and reconfiguring the plaza as a *rond-point*, and kept many of the connections to the surrounding grid, but otherwise called for a mix of curved and angled streets that shaped large, irregular blocks upon which 669 detached houses surrounded internal landscaped courtyards. A system of pedestrian paths connected one internal reserve with the next, creating a semipublic network of open spaces. A broad boulevard with a grassy median traversed the enclave, while

2. Plan, Raymond Unwin, c. 1915. SWJA

3. Plan, Barry Parker and Raymond Unwin, Architects, c. 1917. CIA

4. Aerial view. CIA (1977)

5. Aerial view with hand drawing. CIA

6. Typical street. CIA (1950)

7. Typical street. CIA (2006)

8. Typical street. Dias. DIAS (2012)

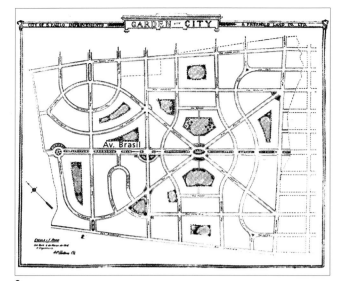

2

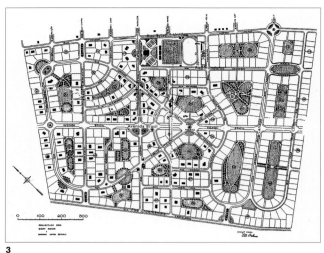

3

4

5

6

7

8

somewhat narrower residential streets included sidewalks and planting strips.

Construction, occurring principally between 1915 and 1929, was subject to rules governing setbacks and to a certain extent architectural design. The enclave proved popular, attracting wealthy residents seeking in part to move away from the waves of immigrants flocking to the central city. As it developed, however, Parker's plan was gradually corrupted, most notably in the co-opting of the internal reserves for construction beginning as early as the 1930s. Owners erected high boundary walls to the detriment of the streetscape, and the residential zoning was loosened to allow commerce. In 1986, Jardim América was listed by CONDEPHAAT (Council for the Defense of Historical, Artistic and Cultural Assets), a São Paulo state agency, and remains one of the city's most desirable addresses, starkly contrasting with the high-rise urbanism to the north.

Parker went on to design four more São Paulo garden suburbs for the same company: the upper-class districts of **Anhangabaú** (1917) and **Pacaembú** (1925) and the contiguous middle-class suburbs of **Alto da Lapa** (1921) and **Bela Aliança** (1921), which featured curvilinear street plans with free-form residential blocks evoking the work of Olmsted as much as any of Parker and Unwin's English projects. Parker continued to call for internal reserves, an uncommon element in Brazil that met with mixed success, and he also began to use both traffic rotaries and the tapered ends of residential blocks as a form of park space.

As historian Margareth da Silva Pereira has written, after Parker introduced the garden suburb to São Paulo, "the form of the city began to present a configuration very common in certain North American cities where the urban image resulted much more from the green suburban residential areas than from the 'historic city.'"[50] Not all of the "garden neighborhoods" that came to characterize São Paulo lived up to Parker's examples. Jardim Paulista and Jardim Paulistano, to name but two, were nothing more than relatively low-density grids trading on the name "Jardim." Among the more convincing efforts was **Jardim Europa** (1924), built on a contiguous site to Jardim América according to a plan by Hipólito Gustavo Pujol Jr. (1880–1952), who called for an elegant plan of symmetrical gently curving streets and a more generous allocation of park space but smaller residential lots.[51]

Although Parker first introduced the garden suburb to Brazil, it was native civil engineer Jorge de Macedo Vieira (1894–1978) who became the idea's chief disseminator, planning almost three dozen garden enclaves, villages, and resorts between the 1920s and 1950s in São Paulo, Rio de Janeiro, and beyond.[52] Macedo Vieira learned directly from Parker, having worked for the architect after graduating from the University of São Paulo's Polytechnic School in 1917. Parker's influence, along with that of Unwin, Olmsted, and Sitte, can be seen in Macedo Vieira's designs well into the 1950s, by which time most planners had turned toward the open-field discontinuities of Modernist urbanism.

Anhangabaú

1. Avenida 9 de Julho. CIA (1950)

Pacaembú

1. Aerial view. CIA (1936)

Alto da Lapa and Bela Aliança

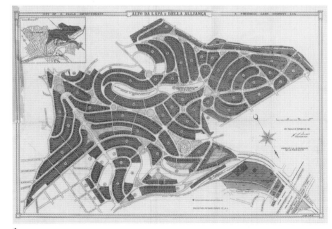

1. Plan, Barry Parker, 1921. CIA (1955)

2. Aerial view. CIA

3. Typical street. CIA (2009)

2
3

Jardim Europa

1. Plan, Hipólito Gustavo Pujol Jr., 1924. BLDT

2. Overall view. Indech. WC (2006)

3. View across park. Azambuja. PAN (2009)

4. Typical house. Ornb. PAN (2011)

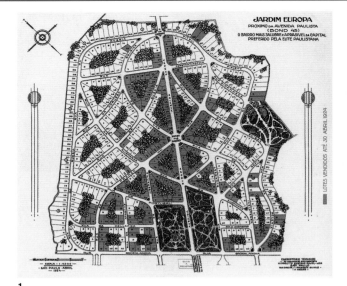

Jardim Japão

1. Plan, Jorge de Macedo Vieira, 1922. AJMV (c. 1937)

Macedo Vieira's first substantial subdivision was **Jardim Japão** (1922), occupying a 260-acre tract in northeast São Paulo.[53] The plan featured many of the elements that would become Macedo Vieira's hallmarks, including an organic street pattern partially derived from the course of a stream, landscaped rotaries linked to one another by streets to form minor axes, and a mix of formal and free-form parks. Construction began in the 1930s, but by the end of the decade, the individual residential lots, initially featuring up to 100 feet of street frontage, were already being subdivided to make room for two or three houses, resulting in a densely built-up community made more so in recent years by the introduction of high-rise apartment towers. **Vila Maria** (1923), contiguous to the northwest of Jardim Japão, occupied 321 acres that Macedo Vieira laid out with winding roads, parks, and generously sized parcels that were also subdivided in the late 1940s so that today the district retains its picturesque street plan but is relatively urban in feel, with a continuous street wall, no front or side yards, and minimal landscaping.[54] Macedo Vieira's layout (1924) for a 30-acre section of São Paulo's Ipiranga district was similarly curvilinear and interspersed with parks as well as some culs-de-sac.[55]

Chácara da Mooca (1923–41), covering 642 acres on the industrial eastern outskirts of São Paulo, consisted

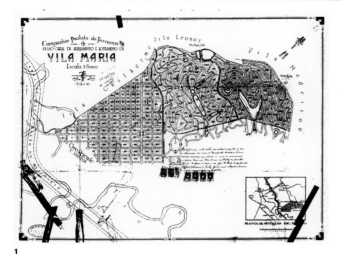

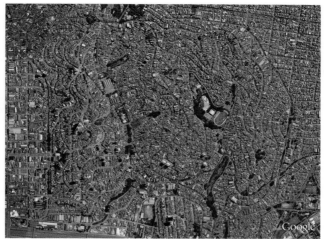

1. Plan, Jorge de Macedo Vieira. AJMV (c. 1922)

2. Aerial view showing Jardim Japão, top, and Vila Maria, bottom. GE (2010)

3. Typical street. Santos. PAN (2010)

4. Park. Santos. PAN (2011)

Chácara da Mooca

of a manufacturing zone in the west along a railroad line, and a residential section in the east, where Macedo Vieira mixed straight, angled, and curved streets to create a variety of block sizes, some of which were intended to have internal reserves that were never realized.[56] **Vila Nova Manchester** (1923), also in east São Paulo, was built on a 319-acre site whose flat topography allowed for a rational geometric plan in which four semicircular neighborhoods surrounded a central diamond-shaped park.[57] Working on another flat site in northeastern São Paulo, Macedo Vieira's 102-acre **Parque Edu Chaves** (1926) was almost entirely given over to a circular composition made up of nearly forty blocks surrounding a landscaped plaza now occupied by a church.[58] The plan called for street trees and a buffer of parks and athletic fields in the east.

Located on Rio de Janeiro's Governor's Island, **Jardim Guanabara** (1925) presented Macedo Vieira with a dramatic 741-acre waterfront site with exceptionally hilly terrain that dictated a sinuous street plan virtually devoid of right angles.[59] The planner took the unusual step of reserving those sites with the best views not for residential lots but for parks and plazas that would be accessible to the district's 20,000 residents. In one location, however, the linking together of four or five such plazas caused traffic confusion. Initial development

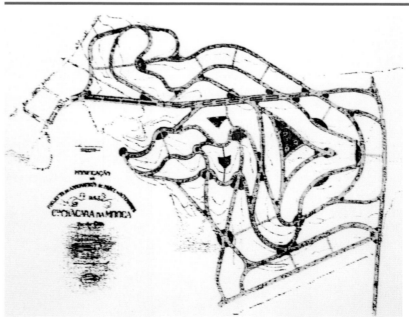

1

1. Plan, detail, Jorge de Macedo Vieira. AJMV (c. 1923)

Vila Nova Manchester

1. Plan, detail, Jorge de Macedo
Vieira, 1923. AJMV

2. Aerial view. GE (2009)

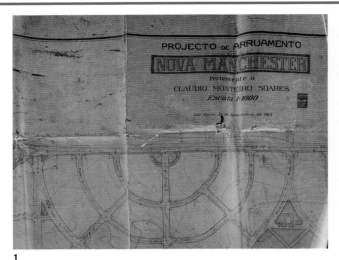

1

2

Parque Edu Chaves

1. Plan, Jorge de Macedo Vieira,
1926. AJMV

2. Aerial view. GE (2008)

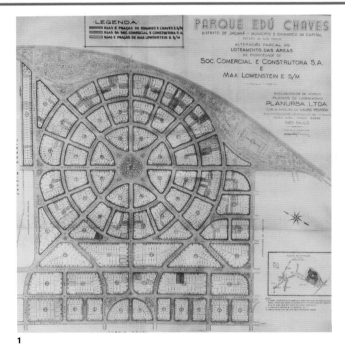

1

2

Jardim Guanabara

1. Plan, Jorge de Macedo Vieira,
1925. AJMV

2. Aerial view. AJMV

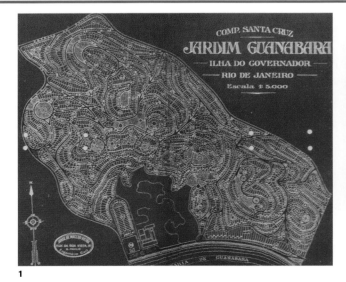

1

2

was completed in 1931, but over the years, many of the best views were blocked by new construction. The same developers commissioned Macedo Vieira to lay out **Vila Isabel** (1931) on a roughly 740-acre site in the mountain town of Campos do Jordão, about 100 miles northeast of São Paulo. Hills naturally divided the site into three sections, two of which featured large lots along snaking roads and the third more densely platted.[60] Macedo Vieira retained the land around several streams to create linear parks.

Cidade Mãe do Céu (1937) was another of Macedo Vieria's São Paulo subdivisions whose curvilinear plan starkly contrasted with the adjacent grid.[61] Unfortunately, the original vision of tree-lined streets and comfortably sized lots beginning at 2,000 square feet gave way to more crowded conditions. In 1938, Macedo Vieira laid out **Jardim de Saúde** on a 333-acre site in south São Paulo bisected by a broad north–south thoroughfare.[62] The neighborhood of straight, curved, and semicircular streets and a partial buffer of parkland could be entered from the east by way of a broad boulevard with a landscaped median leading to a central park. The enclave is now protected against the high-rise construction that has transformed nearby areas.

Among the best preserved of Macedo Vieira's garden suburbs is the health resort of **Aguas de São Pedro** (1939), roughly eighty miles northwest of São Paulo at the site of hot springs discovered in 1930 during oil exploration. A development company gained control of the site and the surrounding farms and ranches and hired Macedo Vieira to prepare a plan that retained one-third of the land as parks while creating separate zones in the developed area for residential, commercial, agricultural, and industrial use. Because its remote location required a local source of food, the developers included cattle, dairy, and vegetable farms as well as an aviary and apiary. Industrial uses grew dramatically as the resort began to bottle and sell its water. A greenbelt surrounded the development but its soil, having cultivated coffee plants year after year, was depleted, making reforestation efforts more difficult. Soil had to be imported for the thousands of eucalyptus, acacia, palm, and other tree species planted throughout. The residential areas, designed for a population of 10,000, were laid out with curving streets and roundabouts. The low portions of the site were cleared to facilitate drainage and to provide an internal greensward. Lots went on sale in 1940, the same year the first of several grand hotels opened. Aguas de São Pedro retains much of its original density and character.

Macedo Vieira's post–World War II site planning incorporated the key characteristics of his earlier work. Notable garden suburbs from the period include **Vila Nova Campinos** (1945), a suburb of Campinos, and Vila Medeiros (1947), **Vila Campesina** (1947), **Vila Formosa** (1947), and **Jardim Rolinópolis** (1949), in São Paulo, the last occupying a 60-acre site whose rugged topography led to the establishment of a central park and the laying out of flanking residential neighborhoods with winding

Vila Isabel

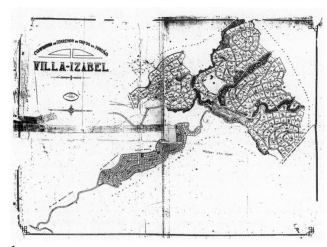

1

1. Plan, Jorge de Macedo Vieira, 1931. AJMV

Cidade Mãe do Céu

1

1. Bird's-eye view. AJMV (1937)
2. Overall view. Igor. WC (2010)
3. Park. Ortlieb. PAN (2011)

2

3

Jardim de Saúde

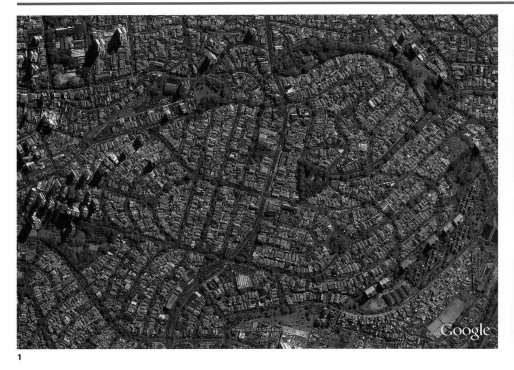

1

1. Aerial view. GE (2009)

2. Typical street. Jackson. PAN
(2010)

3. Typical street. Jackson. PAN
(2009)

2

3

Aguas de São Pedro

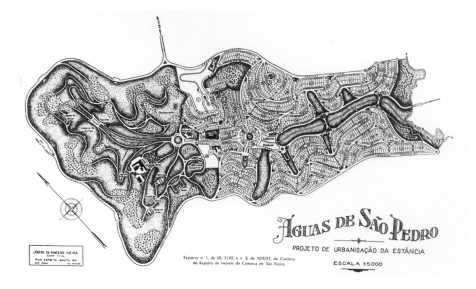

1

1. Plan, Jorge de Macedo Vieira,
c. 1939. AJMV

2. Aerial view. GE (2007)

3. Rua Principal. Guerra. WC
(2010)

2

3

streets, switchbacks, and pedestrian stairways.[63] The planner's culminating design, coming closer in scope to the Garden City model than any of his previous subdivisions, was for the city of **Maringá** (1945–47), located in the southern Brazilian state of Paraná, where in the late 1920s, a London-based company acquired three million acres of fertile, forested land from the state government and, establishing a land development subsidiary and a railroad subsidiary, initiated a colonization plan in which Ebenezer Howard's ideas played "a central role," according to historian Renato Rego, calling for "a cluster of independent, equivalent, and regularly spaced new towns, connected by a railway line."[64] Maringá was one of four major cities to be located roughly sixty miles apart, the others being Londrina (1932), named to honor London, Cianorte (1953–55), and Umuarama (1955).

After the war, Brazilian investors took over from the British, altering the plan but keeping the overall strategy of constructing self-sufficient satellite cities along the rail line. Maringá, intended for a population of 200,000, included distinct zones for industrial, civic, and recreational purposes as well as for working-class and middle-class residences. Macedo Vieira's plan combined gridded sections oriented according to the topography with radial neighborhoods and organically curving streets, resulting in a mix of City Beautiful monumentality and loose informality. The design included an agricultural greenbelt as well as internal greenswards, one covered by a thickly wooded forest and another later built out with a zoo, lake, and Japanese garden. The city was beautified with 160,000 trees grown in a dedicated nursery that also served broader reforestation efforts in the surrounding landscape. Today, the central city is densely developed with high-rise buildings while the residential neighborhoods retain their low-scale suburban character.

Other notable Brazilian garden suburbs include **Interlagos** (1939), in south São Paulo, named for its position between two reservoirs that resembled the location of Switzerland's Interlaken. Interlagos was built by a London-based developer and laid out by Alfred Agache (1875–1915), the French architect who had won third prize in the Canberra competition (see p. 646) and had recently prepared a Beaux-Arts master plan for Rio de Janeiro (1930). Francis Violich, in his 1944 study of Latin American urbanism, called Interlagos "a remarkably well done job of modern subdivision planning," observing that the developer "has built a splendid divided highway through the open country to the edge of Lake Guarapiranga, and has under construction beside the lake a satellite garden city . . . The first unit for some six thousand people is now complete with streets, parks, beach, and boating facilities."[65] Today, Interlagos is an upper-class district best known for its racetrack (1939), home to the Brazilian Grand Prix.

Violich also singled out Rio de Janeiro's Cidade Jardim Hygienopolis, describing it as "a complete garden-city subdivision, well-planned, with contour streets, cul-de-sac dead-ends, playgrounds, school-sites, and

Vila Nova Campinos

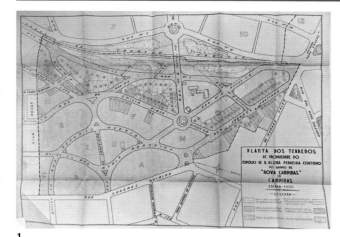

1. Plan, Jorge de Macedo Vieira, 1945. AJMV

Vila Campesina

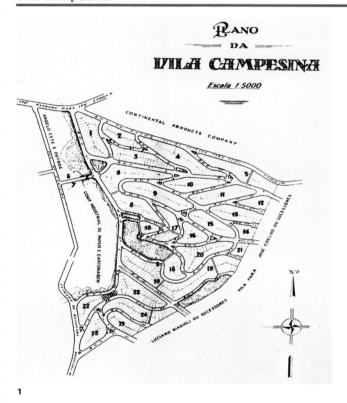

1. Plan, Jorge de Macedo Vieira, 1947. AJMV

Vila Formosa

1. Plan, Jorge de Macedo Vieira, 1947. AJMV

1. Plan, Jorge de Macedo Vieira, 1949. AJMV

2. Aerial view. GE (2009)

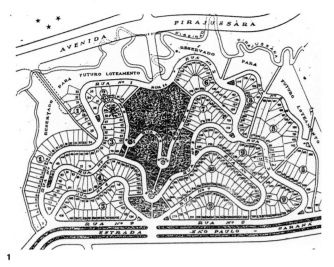

1

2

Maringá

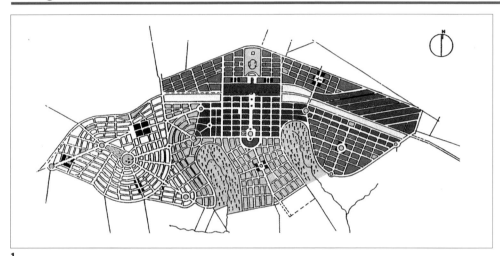

1

2

1. Plan, Jorge de Macedo Vieira, c. 1947. ACB

2. Aerial view. PMM (2007)

3. Aerial view. GE (2005)

4. Avenida Cerro Azul. Marcotti. PAN (2009)

3

4

shopping centers laid out along the lines of Radburn, New Jersey."[66] The district was planned by Washington Azevedo (n.d.), a Brazilian architect who studied planning at Harvard. Another Harvard-educated Brazilian civil engineer, Lincoln Continentino (1900–1976), working for a steel company, designed the industrial garden village of **Monlevade** (1934), looking to the work of Thomas Adams, John Nolen, Raymond Unwin, and Alfred Agache for inspiration, as well as American garden suburbs that he considered to be "beautiful, comfortable, cheerful, healthy."[67] The design was chosen in a competition that drew thirteen entries, including a

Modernist scheme by architect Lucio Costa (1902–1998), who would go on to plan the new capital city, Brasilia, in 1957. The program called for schools, stores, a theater, church, parks, and a sports arena. The site was divided in half by a railroad line, on either side of which Continentino laid out residential neighborhoods around public squares, one of which, elliptical in shape, served as the focus of a civic center. Continentino allowed the tree-lined streets to curve with the terrain and employed hierarchical 20-foot-wide residential and 30-foot-wide arterial streets, providing a separate system of four-foot-wide pathways for pedestrians. The simple workers'

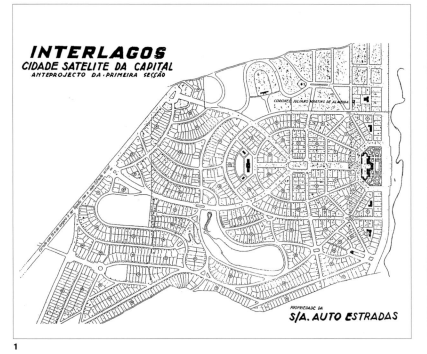

1

2

3

1. Plan, Alfred Agache. GUAR
(c. 1939)

2. Aerial view. Urban. GUAR
(c. 2000)

3. Typical street. Minho. PAN
(2009)

Monlevade

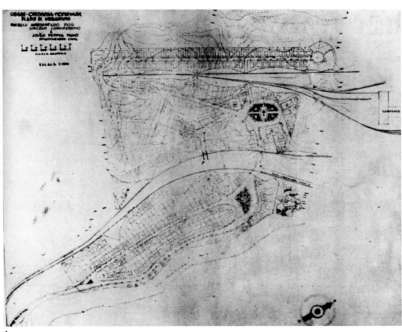

1

2

1. Plan, Lincoln Continentino,
c. 1934. ETSAV

2. Typical street. OSL

3. Hotel and casino. OSL

3

houses were oriented to maximize sunlight exposure and minimize dust and smoke from the factories. Houses sat on individual lots that were about 40 feet wide. Restrictions were put in place to ensure front setbacks and minimum distances between houses.

AUSTRALIA

The most important event in twentieth-century Australian town planning was the development of **Canberra** (1912), the country's new capital, intended to initially house 25,000 persons and grow to an eventual population of 100,000.[68] Despite its monumental ambitions, Canberra was the principal stimulus for Australia's embrace of the garden suburb. Canberra was planned by the American architect Walter Burley Griffin, assisted by his partner and wife, Marion Mahony Griffin (1871–1961), whose proposal triumphed over 136 others, including Eliel Saarinen and Alfred Agache, in an international competition that was disapproved by the Royal Institute of British Architects and by the American Institute of Architects, effectively discouraging many of the world's leading architect-planners from participating.

Prior to the competition, Sir John Sulman (1849–1934), an architect who served as president of the Town Planning Association of New South Wales (1913–25) and chairman of the Federal Capital Advisory Committee (1921–24), laid the groundwork for the new city, advocating a number of fundamental ideas: the preference for single-family houses and the rejection of terraced housing; the abolition of back lanes and front fences; the use of rounded street intersections; and extensive tree planting along with generous provisions for parks and playgrounds. But there was also a feeling that, as William Hardy Wilson argued, "bigger thought" than "present garden suburb ideas" was needed to create "the ideal city."[69]

The beautiful site lay in the valley of the Molonglo River, at the foot of the Australian Alps, 312 miles northeast of Melbourne and 148 miles southwest of Sydney. Griffin's design, like that for the contemporaneous New Delhi (see p. 661), reflected the two principal strands of planning thought in the early 1900s: the monumentality of the City Beautiful movement, and the landscape and social engineering of the Garden City movement. The impact of City Beautiful thinking can be seen in the powerful axes focused on the relationship between man-made landmarks, especially the key government buildings like the Parliament, and nature, especially the views to be obtained from the site across the Molonglo River toward Mt. Ainslie. The Garden City aspects are reflected in the diagrammatic separation of residential, industrial, and civic areas, and in the use of parks to screen residential neighborhoods from highways and other uses deemed incompatible to quiet domesticity at the suburban scale, features that had previously been explored by Griffin in his American work.

Saarinen's second-place competition plan was also strongly geometric, but instead of Griffin's dependence on a series of concentric figures, the Finnish architect-planner proposed grids of radially arranged streets defining neighborhoods, each with a distinct character. The French architect Alfred Agache, founder in 1911 of the Société Française d'Urbanistes, earned third place in the competition, following Beaux-Arts principles—and by extension the City Beautiful movement—with a gridded plan cut through by bold diagonals on either side of a central ceremonial axis. Of the three plans, Agache's seemed to many the more distinctly urban. Though it was, as planning historian Robert Freestone has written, a "version of the city beautiful, a sort of provincial Paris with novel features like an 'aerostatic station,'" Agache's submission also "recorded the most literal influence of garden city thought," reflecting his association with the French reform group Musée Social, and, as Freestone writes, "in line with the Musée concept of 'social hygiene' . . . [included] a cité jardin described as a 'workman's city with pretty villas nicely distributed amongst the gardens . . . fulfilling almost exactly the conditions desired by the British socialist Howard.'"[70]

The plan of the Swede Nils Gellerstedt, although not premiated, impressed the editors of *Der Städtebau*, the influential German magazine of town planning, coming, as Mark L. Peisch has pointed out, closer to Camillo Sitte's ideas than did the others. Gellerstedt's plan notably lacked a main axis, did not rework the river, used a gridiron plan for the commercial, industrial, and military sectors of the city, and embraced the civic center with a boulevard not unlike Vienna's Ringstrasse, beyond which he placed the residential neighborhood that could therefore grow outward from the core over time. As proposed by Gellerstedt, the residential neighborhoods were to be threaded through by irregular streets offering strong street pictures in the best manner of Unwin.

Griffin's plan was criticized by Garden City advocates who resented the supervening geometry of the monumental core. The editors of *Town Planning Review* took objection to what they saw as Griffin's decision "to devote the whole of a lay-out to a geometrical formalistic treatment," going on to protest that the plan was not for "a town divided by a noble river" but one that was "severed in half by a series of artificial lagoons . . . All this glorification should have been reserved and intensified in some large park, whose entrance was adjacent to, but which did not separate, the closely associated components of the city."[71] In other words, even those who advocated the Garden City felt that Canberra was too spread out and disjointed to achieve any real urbanity. Moreover, they were unhappy with the plan's failure to provide for a greenbelt to define the edges. Although Canberra's residential street plan was conceived to discourage through traffic, from the point of view of Garden City theorists, its "checkerboard" of streets lacked the interest of the more complex networks of Letchworth.

The negative assessment of the Canberra plan was taken up by William Davidge (1879–1961), a British

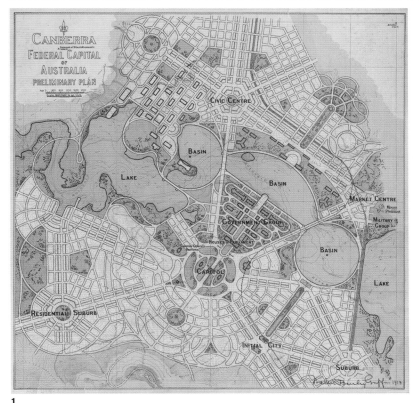

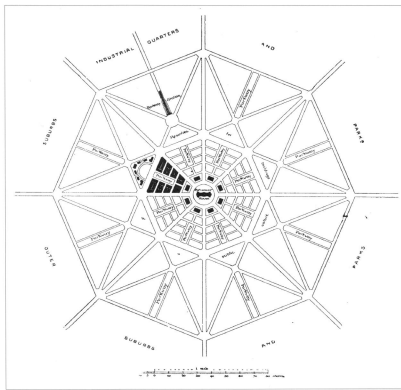

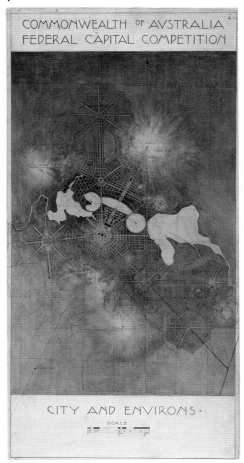

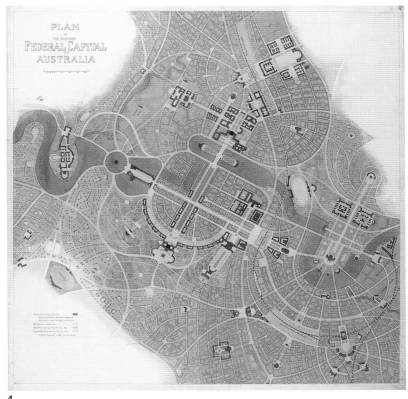

1. Preliminary plan, Walter Burley Griffin, 1913. NLA53

2. Diagram for a federal capital, Sir John Sulman, c. 1911. SUL

3. First-place competition entry by Walter Burley Griffin, plan drawn by Marion Mahony Griffin, 1912. NAA

4, 5. Second-place competition entry by Eliel Saarinen. Plan and perspective, 1912. NAA

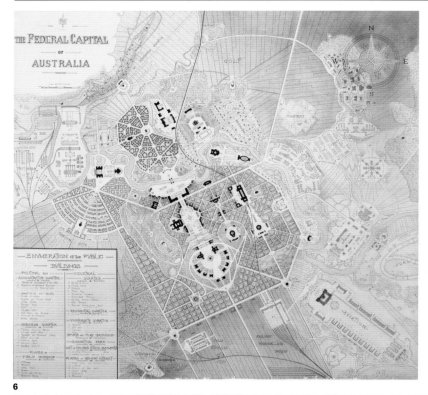

6

7

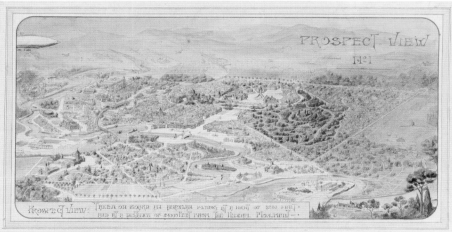

8

9

6. Third-place competition entry by
Alfred Agache. Plan, 1912. NAA

7. Competition entry, Nils Otto
Gellerstedt, 1912. NAA

8. Third-place competition entry
by Alfred Agache, prospect view,
1912. NAA

9. Aerial view. NLA14 (c. 1930)

10. Commonwealth Avenue, Albert
Hall, and Hotel Canberra. NAA
(1929)

11. View from Mount Ainslie of
axis from Australian War Memorial
to Parliament House. Peta. WC
(2005)

10

11

architect, civil engineer, and surveyor who argued that it "violated garden city thought on two grounds. First there was no evidence of town planning on garden city lines," lacking Letchworth's charming irregular streets, its "distances filled in with some architectural creation on which the eye could rest," and its "roads laid out to follow the contours of the country." Additionally, there was no agricultural belt: "The vision of these unending circuses and star points . . . spreading in the future far away into the distant suburbs, awake one to the octopus-like growth of every one of our great cities and the necessity for girdling them round with an open belt of country to give some little breathing space to the workers and travelers ere they plunge from one seething pot of a town into the seething cauldron of the next."[72]

Benjamin Higgins, writing in 1915 in the *Journal of the Royal Architectural Institute of Canada*, also decried Canberra, identifying as shortcomings the principal features of its plan: "the emphasis on open space, especially parks, gardens, lakes and boulevards; and its sharp functional divisions. Canberra is unquestionably a beautiful little town; but it must be the most inconvenient little town in the world . . . Griffin and his followers set out to make Canberra a beautiful garden city. Few would deny that they have made Canberra a beautiful garden; but it is a garden without a city."[73]

Canberra's plan, with its strict zoning by uses, would prove premonitory of later developments, particularly in the United States, where it has been argued that it was the precursor of the neighborhood unit plan that Clarence Perry articulated in the 1920s and which would be at the center of late garden suburb and garden city planning. In 1913, Griffin wrote that "the segregated sections, formed and separated by the general traffic lines, furnish not only suitable individual home sites, but comprise social units for that larger family—the neighborhood group, with one handy district school or more for the children, and with local playground, game fields, church, club, and social amenities accessible without crossing traffic tracks, or encountering the disturbing elements of temptations of business streets, since these family activities may best be directed internally toward the geographical centers of their groups for their special congregation."[74]

To Peter Hall, the urban historian, Griffin's argument

sounds almost like a pre-Radburn Radburn. The original diagram shows the units as hexagons, a device Parker used later in his Radburn layouts at Wythenshawe. And, in the neighborhoods of the 1980s, that is how it has emerged: a morning jogger may emerge from the front door, go from path via linear park to a vast central space of playing fields, making a circuit of a mile or more without ever seeing traffic. These neighborhoods, and the new towns that are supplementing them farther out, are strung like beads on the strings of the traffic roads which pass between and around them. So Canberra achieves the difficult feat of being one of the last Cities Beautiful, and also the

world's biggest Garden City. It is even, in its way, one of the few extant realizations of Howard's polycentric social city: no small achievement for a city that for a long time never looked like growing up. Thus, unlike a number of other examples of the City Beautiful genre, it manages to be rather likeable.[75]

As Canberra slowly grew, it was continually criticized in the international debate over urban morphology, so that forty years after the competition, the New Zealand architect and town planner A. J. Brown, writing in *Town Planning Review*, could complain that Canberra "is an overgrown garden city, with the emphasis on the garden, and with isolated architectural incidents which are too distant from one another to give any cohesion to the plan."[76]

Griffin's success in the Canberra competition catapulted him to prominence in Australia, where, as urban planner and historian Peter Harrison has observed, he was "the only man . . . with accomplishments as a town planner."[77] In 1914, Griffin was hired to design the two new towns of Leeton and Griffith, forty miles apart in the Murrumbidgee Irrigation Area, New South Wales, the largest government-sponsored irrigation scheme in the world when it was initiated in 1906 to transform semi-arid plains, described ninety years earlier as "uninhabitable and useless to civilized man," into workable farmland.[78] The towns were to serve as commercial and government centers for the remote district located 350 miles west of Sydney and 280 miles north of Melbourne, and to meet the demand for housing created after new railroads and a government-sponsored advertising campaign attracted a surge of farmers.

In his plan for **Griffith**, Griffin reiterated themes he had established at Canberra, locating government buildings on a grand circle at the highest topographical point, where they would terminate vistas from radial avenues that extended outward through a series of concentric octagonal boulevards.[79] Commercial areas were to be distributed around the circle and a wide, tree-lined boulevard was to lead one-half mile northeast to a horseshoe-shaped site reserved for an academy. An irrigation channel traced a prominent path through the town, feeding water gardens and forming an arc around the main circle. Residential neighborhoods, designed on the Trier Center model (see p. 105), spread out from the center before giving way to agricultural land.

The scale of the new suburb proved overambitious. Planned for 30,000 residents, it took more than fifty years for Griffith's population to reach just 11,000. The street plan was largely implemented, but a proposal to elevate streets and plazas above surface-level railroad tracks was not. The business district did not develop in its intended location because at the initial auction for commercial lots, those parcels nearest the train station were priced lower than those around the circle, leading to the development of a main street parallel to the tracks. The great moments of civic grandeur never arrived, with the government

1. Plan, Walter Burley Griffin, 1914.
NLA17

2. Aerial perspective. NLA75
(c. 1915)

3. Aerial view. GE (2003)

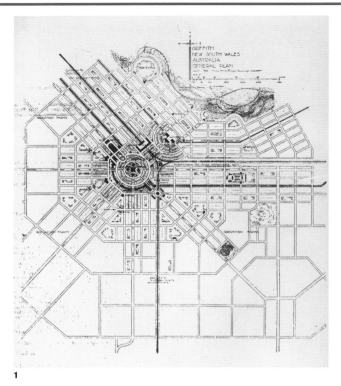

1

2

3

Leeton

1. Plan, Walter Burley Griffin, 1914.
NLA23

2. Leeton War Memorial. Bidgee.
FL (2010)

3. Typical cottage. Bidgee. FL
(2010)

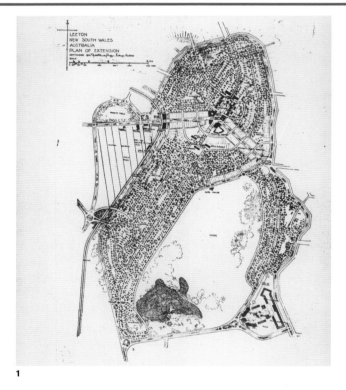

1

2

3

buildings constructed in Leeton, which had begun development slightly earlier. In their place, a technical college anticlimactically occupied Griffith's premier site and the area reserved for the academy received a hospital. As Peter Harrison has noted, "As in so many of his projects, [Griffin] assumed far more than could reasonably be expected, with a result in this case that his plan conferred scant benefit on the development of the town."[80]

Leeton, according to Freestone, was "the better demonstration of garden city design, with Griffin drawing more on his residential land planning concepts."[81] The town had begun to develop before Griffin became involved, with the main road already in place as well as an irrigation canal that Griffin adopted as the town's northern border and whose irregular curve helped relieve the plan of geometric rigidity. A rectangular plaza near the junction of three main boulevards was to be lushly landscaped, adorned with fountains, and lined with public buildings. As built, according to Harrison, it failed "to measure up to the vision," although Griffin's hope for the plaza's "'refreshing shaded promenades, fountains, pool, and music' have at least been partly fulfilled."[82] The residential areas, planned to accommodate 7,000, were to consist of single-family and group houses set among a pleasant mix of straight and curving streets landscaped with native plantings, but these areas were not built according to Griffin's plan. In addition to recreational areas intended for within the residential blocks, Griffin provided a 300-acre park that occupied nearly as much land as the rest of the town and eventually came to accommodate a racetrack and golf course. According to Harrison, Griffin's "proposals for land use, recreation areas and residential planning were far in advance of anything previously attempted in Australia and, given the difference in requirements, at least as skillful as the designs for the Garden City of Letchworth."[83] Harrison found Leeton and Griffith to be "examples of Griffin's planning at its best and worst. Leeton is a successful fulfillment of the modest requirements of a small town; Griffith, a pretentious essay so unrelated to reasonable needs and expectations that his plan has proved more of an embarrassment than an advantage."[84]

Griffin's design for a third city in New South Wales, **Port Stephens** (1918), was not built because its fate was tied to an unrealized port it was intended to serve.[85] Griffin's plan would have reserved the edges of the peninsular site as waterfront parks, with residential development organized around an internal spine linking civic, commercial, and administrative buildings as well as parks and playgrounds. Two railroad stations were planned for the city, which also included an industrial district. Some progress was made on implementing the street plan before development was permanently halted.

Griffin's strictly residential enclaves were more successful, beginning with the adjacent **Summit** (1914) and **Glenard** (1916) estates at Mount Eagle (now part of Eaglemont). Built on former farmland in Heidelberg, Victoria, a northeastern suburb of Melbourne, each marked a departure in Australia from the standard gridded subdivision.[86] Griffin's layout consisted of curving hillside roads affording each house with a view, with internal parks placed at the heart of each block and pedestrian paths offering separate circulation for foot traffic.

Also in Victoria, Griffin planned the **Croydon Hills Estate** (1921), also known as the Blue Mountain Subdivision, on an irregular pentagonal site divided by the southwest–northeast path of a railroad line and water pipeline.[87] Griffin placed a railroad station at the heart of a shop-lined concourse west of the tracks and provided space on the larger residential blocks for internal greens that could be accessed by the public via footpaths. Many of the houses faced parks, one of which, now known as Yarraduct Place, was also a utility easement. Only development to the south and east of the rail line adhered to Griffin's plan. The railroad station and shopping concourse were never built.

At the **Ranelagh Estate** (1924), in Mount Eliza, a coastal resort suburb about thirty miles south of Melbourne, Victoria, Griffin, working with his wife, Marion

Port Stephens

1. Plan, Walter Burley Griffin, 1918. NLA85

1

Summit and Glenard

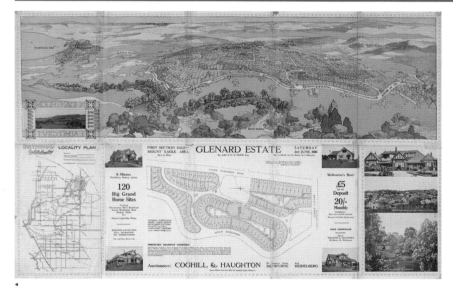

1

1. Sales brochure. NLA41 (1916)

2. Typical street. Ottre. WC (2009)

2

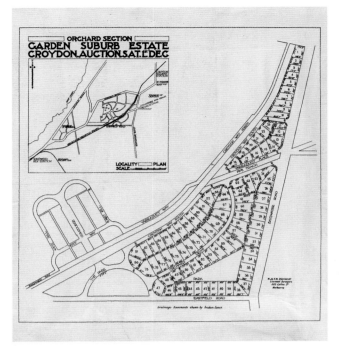

1

2

3

1. Plan, Walter Burley Griffin, 1921.
SLV (1923)

2, 3. Orchard Section auction
announcement. NLA37 (1923)

Mahony, and town planner and surveyor Saxil Tuxen (1885–1975), placed long, gently arcing streets lengthwise across the narrow site, retaining indigenous plantings in thirteen reserves, one of which was located along a cliff overlooking Port Phillip Bay and included a clubhouse and facilities for boating and tennis.[88] Griffin also added new plantings to the site, such as along Wimbledon Avenue, where Monterey cypresses and tuarts form a continuous canopy. The plan called for 795 lots but purchasers were encouraged to combine parcels, with 400 being the target number of houses. All owners were members of the Ranelagh Club, responsible for the maintenance of parks and public spaces. The site's old homestead was retained as a guest house, first for owners of parcels in the estate and later for the general public.

Griffin's culminating planning project was for the enclave of **Castlecrag**, four miles north of Sydney on a 640-acre site including three promontories and five miles of rocky shoreline on Middle Harbour.[89] Griffin had a considerable stake in the project. He purchased the land in 1919 and established a development company over which he retained a controlling number of shares, selling others to employees, friends, and clients. As his own client, Griffin was able to fully indulge himself. He oversaw all design work and administered the restrictive covenants to ensure that "the buildings must be subordinate to the landscape."[90] The initial development area of 90 acres included a system of twenty-eight reserves and parks—including the entirety of the waterfront—connected by pathways. He employed narrow 20-foot-wide roads and culs-de-sac (in contrast to the 66-foot roadways of the surrounding street system), and disallowed fences. Houses were oriented toward internal reserves, which could range from natural rock formations to tennis courts, or views of the harbor, allowing residents to

enjoy the vistas as they walked from the driveway to a side or front entry. Lots were small, averaging 40 by 120 feet, and the houses were diminutive, mostly geared toward childless couples.

Castlecrag was the nearest Griffin came to realizing a utopia. According to Donald Leslie Johnson, Castlecrag "was not only an experiment in suburban development, it was an experiment in community living. But a country club it was not. The philosophy and political thoughts of Walter and Marion Griffin were dominant factors in life at Castlecrag. There was a community social centre . . . [and] a neighborhood circle which met every month and in which everyone participated . . . The houses were to be private, personal places in specific proximity to the total community and related to every facet of the environment. It was a special community by the sea for people devoted to understanding and enjoying what they believed was a natural relationship with the land."[91] Griffin offered free lots to those who would hire him to design their house, and he typically presented other purchasers with unsolicited and often eccentric plans for their lots, discouraging some from settling there. Progress was slow, stunted by delays in the construction of a bridge spanning Sydney Harbor and then by the Depression. Out of roughly 340 houses, Griffin designed only sixteen, five of which were demonstration houses built in the project's first years. Griffin laid out two similar northerly expansions to the initial development, Covecrag and Castlecove, but they were not realized.

Griffin's Australian peers also adopted the garden suburb model with mixed success. Initiated in the same year as the Canberra competition, **Dacey Garden Suburb** (1912), also known as Daceyville, was Australia's first attempt to develop a garden city based on English

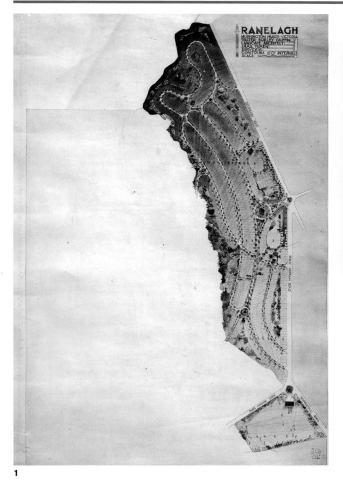

1. Plan, Walter Burley Griffin, 1924.
NLA39

2. Ranelagh beach. Rose. SLV
(1920–54)

models.[92] Named for John Rowland Dacey (1854–1912), a politician who had advocated model garden suburbs, the state-sponsored project was intended to house a mix of social classes in a self-sufficient neighborhood complete with residential, commercial, and industrial sectors as well as schools, churches, and other public and administrative facilities. The density was earmarked at twelve houses per acre but was later lowered to seven.

The approximately 270-acre swampy and sandy site, roughly seven miles southeast of central Sydney, to which it was connected by an electric tram (1913), was the subject of three plans between 1911 and 1917. The first, prepared by the Public Works Department, was a somewhat chaotic composition of rectangular blocks of varying size and orientation, with tree-lined streets and rear alleys that by that time were deemed unenlightened in planning circles. In 1912, planners John Sulman and J. F. Hennessy (1853–1924) prepared a new design that regularized the layout, covering a reduced 336-acre, roughly triangular site, with rectangular blocks flanking a central spine leading from a village center with schools, offices, shops, a post office, library, police station, and a 32-acre park to an area of hotels and shops. The residential areas were punctuated by church sites, internal reserves and playgrounds, and midblock pedestrian paths. With 1,437 houses planned, by 1914, 100 mostly semidetached houses were completed in straight rows, such as along Boussole Road, where deep rear gardens were eventually

built upon with a third row of houses. Over time, the provision of street trees and a ban on front fences helped soften the monotony of the streetscape. However, the Garden City movement officially rejected the plan. Ewart G. Culpin, secretary of the Garden Cities and Town Planning Association, illustrated the scheme in his 1913 survey of the movement's progress, writing: "not only is the lay out open to serious objection, both on the practical and aesthetic sides, but the roads are planned absurdly wide—all 66 feet, in accordance with legislative requirements—and practically the only feature common to Garden Suburbs is that the area is pre-planned!"[93]

In 1917, architect William H. Foggitt (n.d.) prepared a new layout for Dacey devoid of right angles and featuring larger, organically shaped blocks with curved edges and rounded corners. The result was perhaps overly complicated but provided a balance of direct and indirect routes through the neighborhood that now centered on an oval garden surrounded by civic buildings. The plan, covering a smaller site of 273 acres, allowed for more park space, including the Recreation Oval and internal reserves, but decreased lot sizes while increasing the number of houses. Construction got off to a good start, and by 1920 roughly 300 houses were up. Unfortunately progress died out in about 1924, owing to changing priorities on the part of the government. Completed houses included competition winning designs by architect S. G. Thorp (n.d.) and by the Housing Board that ranged from

1. Plan of Parapet subdivision, Walter Burley Griffin, 1921. NLA29

2. Plan of houses on Edinburgh Road, Walter Burley Griffin, 1922. NLA55

3. Houses in the Parapet subdivision. NLA15 (c. 1922)

4–6. Typical streets. Knight. PK (2007)

7. Topographic model. NLA82 (c. 1921)

8. Houses under construction. NLA54 (c. 1922)

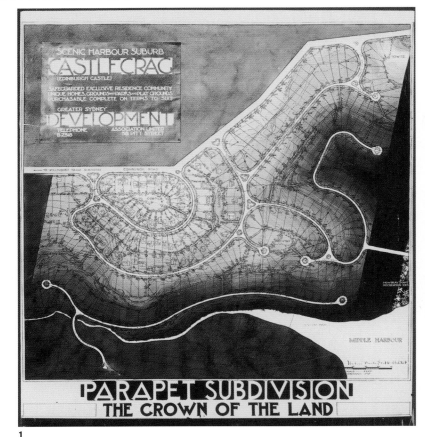

1

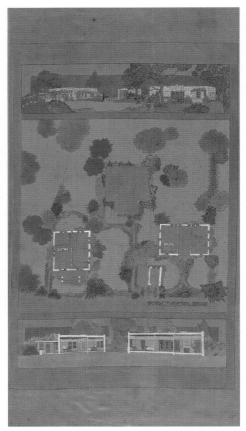

2

3

4

5

6

7

8

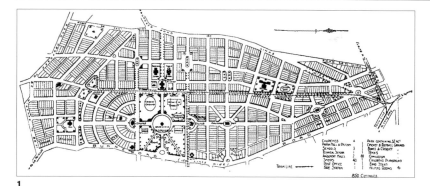

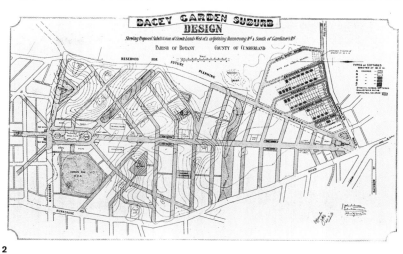

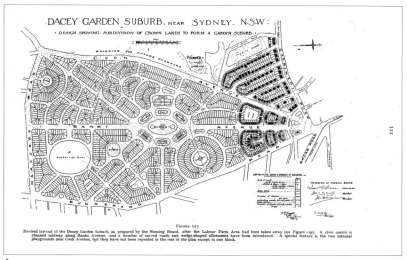

1. Plan, 1911. PK

2. Plan, John Sulman and J. F. Hennessey, 1912. SUL

3. Aerial view. GE (2009)

4. Plan, William H. Foggitt, 1917. SUL

5, 6. Typical streets. Knight. PK (2007)

bungalows to English cottages, almost universally built of brick. Industry never came to Dacey, but among the many community facilities were an arts school, community hall, shopping center, church, police station, infant health center, kindergarten, and public school. Later, unbuilt sections of the site were given over to athletic fields and golf links. By the 1980s the neighborhood had fallen on hard times, but efforts at revitalization soon began, and Dacey was listed on Australia's Register of the National Estate in 1991.

Described by Donald Langmead as "South Australia's *real* paradigm of the Garden City Movement,"

Mitcham Garden Suburb (1917), in the southern outskirts of Adelaide, designed by Charles Reade (1880–1933) and since 1921 known as **Colonel Light Gardens** to honor the surveyor responsible for Adelaide's town plan, was an exceptionally ambitious, almost utopian vision of community design.[94] Reade was Australia's principal garden suburb proponent, a New Zealand journalist who had traveled to London in 1905 and soon began writing about industrial living and working conditions, leading to his active involvement in the Garden Cities and Town Planning Association, culminating in a 1914 Australasian lecture tour with William Davidge to promote the idea.

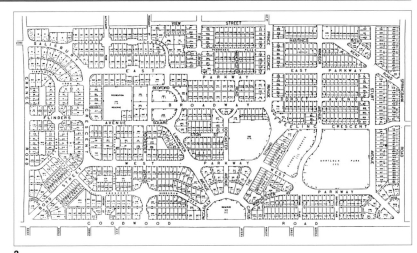

1

2

3

4

1. Bird's-eye view of plan by Charles Reade. PK (1917)

2. Plan, Walter Scott Griffiths, c. 1924. PK

3. Extending the tram line down Goodwood Road. PK (1927)

4. Salisbury Crescent and West Parkway. PK (c. 1930)

5. Types of streets. PDSA (1918)

6. Broadway. Knight. PK (2008)

7. Salisbury Crescent and East Parkway. Knight. PK (2008)

8. Intersection of West Parkway, Windsor Avenue, and Winchester Avenue. Knight. PK (2008)

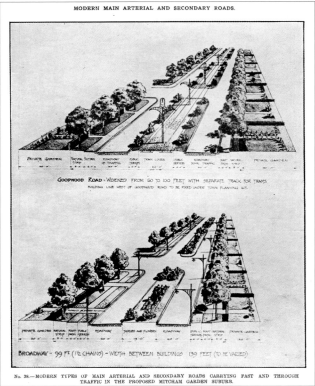

5

6

7

8

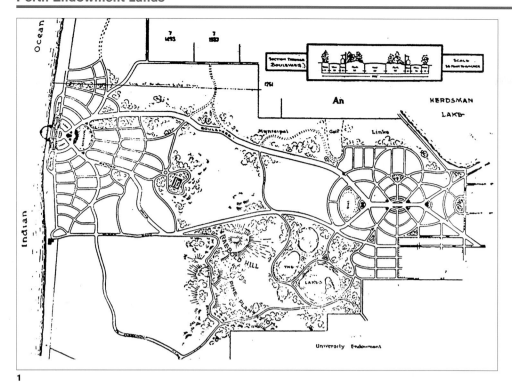

1. Plan, Percy Hope and Carl Klem, 1925. PK

1

Reade's bungalow garden suburb was developed on the 300-acre Grange Farm, acquired with public funds in 1915. Located at the city's edge, it was accessed by an extension of a tram line that would terminate at the main entrance. The plan provided for virtually all aspects of community life except industrial employment. Departing from the site's rectangular geometry, the arrangement of streets was complex, with diagonals leading into the residential area from two peripheral commercial centers, one of which, The Strand, sat at the principal entrance, Picadilly Circus, a semicircular park bordered by an administrative center with a town hall, theater, school, and fire station, among other facilities. An internal loop road—the broadest of three street types ranging in width from 42 to 99 feet—was also included to relieve residential areas of through traffic. Reade's plan was influenced by that of Hampstead Garden Suburb, as historian Christine Garnaut has noted, carefully pointing out similarities in entrance sequence, terminal vistas, the use of culs-de sac, and open spaces.[95] Reade took environmental factors into consideration, addressing prevailing north–south winds, placing an ornamental pond at the site's low point in the southwest to exploit the site's natural drainage, and making use of existing roads and trees.

A network of 16-foot-wide rear "utility ways" contained easements for sewers, water, and electricity while providing off-street circulation for pedestrians. The plan was characterized by curves regularly interrupting the grid of mostly rectangular residential blocks to provide vistas of key buildings and open spaces, which were generously distributed throughout and ranged from athletic fields to playgrounds, internal reserves, and grass lawns. Strict controls of house placement varied the streetscape—houses were set back and forth on the blocks, typically mirroring the placement of those on the opposite side of the street. The exclusive use of detached single-family houses, however, catering to Australian tastes, ruled out many of Unwin's defining site-planning techniques.

Reade left the project in 1920, at which point surveyor Charles Davenport Harris (n.d.) further refined the design. When the first lots were offered for sale in 1922, applications trickled in, in part because infrastructure was not yet in place. In 1924, the passage of the government sponsored Thousand Homes Scheme provided a great stimulus for the suburb's development, with 695 houses constructed by 1926, 300 of which were located in a western extension area laid out by government town planner Walter Scott Griffiths (1864–1929). At the same time, Griffiths modified the plan of the original site to accept higher densities, especially in the south, where he standardized the blocks into what was essentially a gridiron with significantly smaller lots and fewer open spaces, witnessing the loss of the internal recreation areas and the planned pond in its setting of formal gardens. Moreover, the altered plan compromised the social mixing of classes that Reade had intended. Nonetheless, Colonel Light Gardens developed as a stable community and remains one of Australia's most intact garden suburbs. It was added to Australia's Register of the National Estate in 1999 and designated a State Heritage Area in 2000.

Despite a multitude of other proposed garden cities and suburbs, only a fraction ever made it off the drawing board.[96] Among those realized was a design by surveyors Percy Hope (1883–1952) and Carl Klem (1885–1979) for the so-called **Perth Endowment Lands** (1925), in which 3,500 city-owned acres between downtown Perth

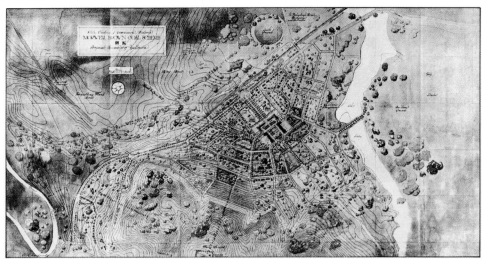

1

2

1. Plan, Alan La Gerche, 1921. SEC

2. Aerial view. SLV (1929)

3. Typical houses. HERM (c. 1948)

4. General store, town center. SLV
(c. 1922)

3

4

and the coast were laid out as two distinct villages—the oceanfront City Beach and the inland Floreat Park—separated by a greenbelt.[97] The municipally funded and administered project, first conceived in 1902 with Letchworth in mind as a model, was intended to demonstrate, as Christine Garnaut has written, "how the garden city idea of satellite suburbs and reserved open space could be used to shape and control the expansion of metropolitan Perth."[98] Although the naturalistic plan of City Beach and the more geometrically ordered plan of Floreat Park, with overlapping circular streets, were not implemented as first drawn, the intervening open space remains intact as a forest and golf course.

In Australia, as in Europe and America, the garden suburb served as a development model for industrial villages, the most interesting of which, **Yallourn** (1920), located in Latrobe Valley, about ninety miles east of Melbourne, was built by the State Electricity Commission of Victoria (SEC) to house workers and related personnel at a new brown-coal mine intended to ease the region's reliance on coal from New South Wales.[99] Yallourn, according to Robert Freestone, although "overshadowed by the national capital . . . was Australia's first fully-fledged garden town."[100] Alan La Gerche (1878–1949), a Public Works Department architect who became the SEC's chief architect, prepared several site plans beginning in 1920, using Unwin's *Town Planning in Practice* as a "major guide."[101] The final scheme, completed in 1921 in collaboration with consulting planner

Arthur Stephenson (1890–1967), called, as Freestone writes, for a "compact, self-contained garden town of predominantly single family dwellings at a density of about five to the acre" that avoided "a grand manner Canberra-style scheme requiring decades to realize" and also eliminated "potentially troublesome details like internal reserves and culs-de-sac."[102] Although the SEC chairman who oversaw the project espoused the idea of homeownership, it was ruled out due to the company's need to control the town's fate. In fact, Yallourn was entirely demolished by 1981 to allow the mining of the land beneath it.

Planned for a population of 3,000, the vaguely fan-shaped, semihexagonal town, separated by a greenbelt and railroad line from the mines, retained the native vegetation except where it was to be cleared for construction. At the heart was a Letchworth-inspired town center, with a public square, shops, and civic buildings connected to the railroad station by a 132-foot-wide tree-lined mall, the axis of which extended through the town as The Broadway, referring to that at Letchworth. Streets ranged in width from 32 to 50 feet and were lined by trees and planting strips. Although the planners took wind direction into consideration, they appear to have miscalculated, for coal dust so frequently covered the houses that darker paint colors were specified to hide the dirt.

Between 1921 and 1930, about 500 houses were built, accommodating 2,000 people. The town featured a hotel, general store, post office, fire station, bank, schools, churches, and a hospital as well as public gardens, athletic facilities, and tennis courts. On one hand, the company's ownership of the town and the continued involvement of La Gerche maintained a consistency and quality of character. At the same time, life in Yallourn featured the familiar compromises of a company town. As a government report put it in 1944, "the townsman enjoys all that the heart of man may desire—except freedom, fresh air and independence. He lives his life on a great many days in a fine rain of abrasive coal particles and breathes with them, perforce, the nauseating stench . . . Be he never so provident, he can not acquire a home or an equity in a home. He has no authoritative voice in the management of the town because there is no democratic local government."[103] Pressures to mine the town site had cropped up as early as 1928, when the developable area was cut in half. By the 1970s, despite protests, the land under the town was deemed more valuable than the town itself, and soon Yallourn was gone, its houses demolished or relocated.

Other notable industrial villages were planned but never built. In 1918, the Hydro-Electric Power and Metallurgical Company commissioned Melbourne architect Marcus Barlow (1890–1955) to design **Electrona**, in Tasmania.[104] Barlow placed winding residential roads outside of a semicircular town center adjacent to the factory, calling for a shop-lined boulevard leading through the town to the factory gates. A significant amount of land was given over to parks, playgrounds, and gardens, as well as a large lake, and sizable sites were reserved far from the factory for managers and company officers. The plan failed because of lackluster growth at the industrial plant.

In 1925, Cadbury, the chocolate maker and builder of Bournville (see p. 224), established a plant in Australia and contemplated the construction of workers' housing at **Claremont**, north of Hobart, Tasmania, on a promontory on the Derwent River.[105] The plans drawn up by Charles Reade and his successor, William Earle (n.d.), proved well beyond the expectations of the Cadbury family, who had a much smaller community in mind. Rooted in the garden suburb tradition, Reade and Earle's plan preserved the shoreline as public park space and surrounded the factory with single-family houses on individual lots arranged along formal tree-lined axes terminating in *rond-points* and public buildings. Only a fraction of the plan, including roughly a dozen houses and assorted public facilities, was implemented.

NEW ZEALAND

New Zealand's "temporary enthusiasm" for the garden suburb, witnessing only a few attempts at its realization, had a "faddish quality to it," as historian Ben Schrader has written, leaving no lasting impression on the country's suburban landscape.[106] Garden suburbs were promoted in the 1900s as a means of improving slums by returning urban dwellers to the countryside, an

Electrona

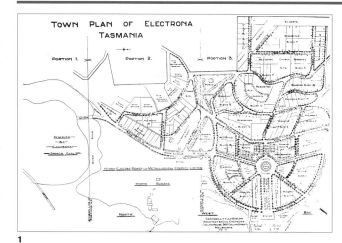

1. Plan, Marcus Barlow, 1918. PK

Claremont

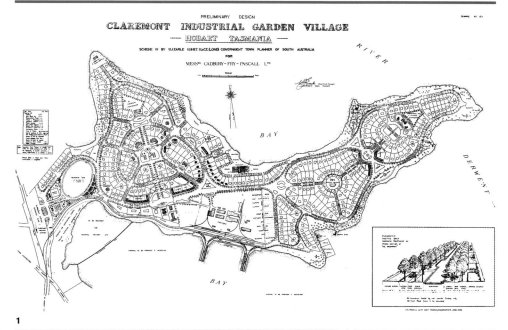

1

2

1. Plan, Charles Reade and William Earle, 1921. PK

2. Bournville Crescent. TAHO (c. 1921)

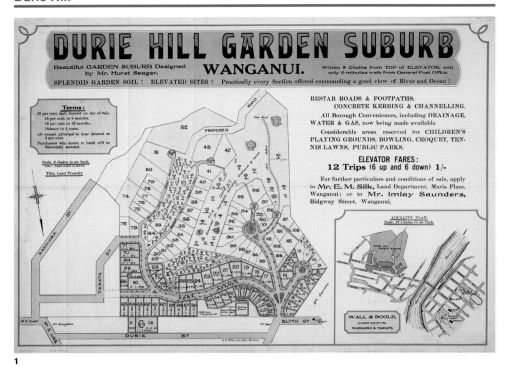

1

1. Sales brochure. ATL (c. 1920)

2. Cul-de-sac. ATL1 (1919)

3. Aerial view. GE (2005)

2

3

Samuel Hurst Seager's Proposal

1. "Principles of Garden Cities and Villages on which Repatriation Schemes Should be Based," 1919. ATL2

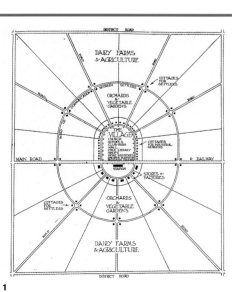

1

argument that traded on the prevailing middle-class distaste for cities in general and a belief that cities fostered unproductive members of society, given the country's agrarian and rural character. In reality, New Zealand's slums were not nearly as bad as garden suburb advocates made them out to be, and their argument fell on deaf ears. The garden suburb idea was revived after World War I as a solution for resettling returning servicemen. However, when New Zealand held its first town planning conference in 1919, participants seemed unimpressed by the garden city, to which a day of the conference was devoted. In two competitions held during the conference—one for a "Garden City" of 1,000 houses and 4,000 people and the other for a garden suburb of 100 houses and 400 people—no one entered the garden city competition and only a few competed in the garden suburb contest. By the mid-1920s, it had become difficult, as Schrader notes, for Howard and Unwin's disciples "to convince the New Zealand public that their product was significantly better or different from what they already possessed, or aspired to possess. As far as most New Zealanders were concerned the nation's existing suburban landscape already gave them the best of 'town and country.'"[107]

Durie Hill, in the North Island city of Wanganui, was the first modest attempt to realize a garden suburb.[108] Located on a hilltop across the Wanganui River from the city, the 62-acre site, recently made accessible by the Durie Hill Elevator (1919), carrying passengers on a five-minute ride from the base to the top of the hill, was laid out in 1920 by London-born New Zealand-based architect Samuel Hurst Seager (1855–1933), the Garden City movement's primary exponent in New Zealand. Seager had drawn some attention at the 1919 town planning conference with his **proposal** (1917) for a prototypical garden village vaguely modeled on Howard's diagram, in which an oval-shaped town center with a church, schools, clubhouse, library, shops, and parks was ringed by workers' cottages and factories that were in turn surrounded by orchards, vegetable gardens, and larger farms beyond.[109] Radial avenues extended from the center, but the plan was contained within orthogonal roads that acknowledged New Zealand's typical rural road system.

At Durie Hill, Seagar, working for a private development syndicate, kept streets as narrow as possible, calling mainly for culs-de-sac twisting along the site's ridges, separated by finger-like reserves of open space of dubious value, with much of the land consisting of gullies that were undevelopable and unusable even for the recreational and gardening purposes intended. Sites were also reserved for a church and community center, a bowling green, tennis courts, playgrounds, and a croquet lawn, as well as allotment gardens, an unfamiliar concept in New Zealand that did not catch on. Despite considerable promotion, Durie Hill did not succeed as a garden suburb. The elevator proved inconvenient and car and bus access was difficult, although automobiles eventually made their impact, resulting, for instance, in the widening of the residential paths, East Way and West Way, into

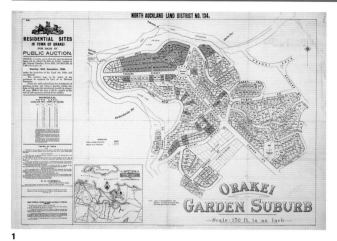

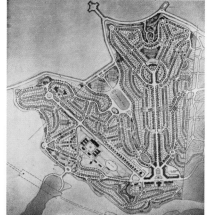

1. Auction announcement. ATL (1929)

2. Plan, Reginald B. Hammond, 1925. ATL

3. Aerial view of Paratai Drive. ATL3 (1948)

4. Aerial view. GE (2004)

paved streets. Parcels were sold without restrictions, and Durie Hill became a solidly middle-class neighborhood without an identifiable character. As Schrader writes: "Only a curvilinear street plan, reserves, bowling green and church were established and survive today as a legacy to Seager's original vision."[110]

Prospects for a successful garden suburb seemed better when, in 1925, the New Zealand government sponsored the **Orakei Garden Suburb** competition for a 631-acre site in Auckland, adjacent to existing suburbs and overlooking Waitemata Harbor, specifying that submissions include contour-hugging streets, pedestrian paths, sites for a university and other civic institutions, and a perimeter esplanade.[111] Of the forty-two entries, the winning plan by New Zealand architect and surveyor Reginald Hammond (1894–1970) was the only one to approach the quality of contemporary European designs, reflecting Hammond's training in town planning at University College in London, an education that earned him the distinction of being New Zealand's first professionally trained town planner.

Hammond's design was organized around two splayed axes that extended along the site's ridges from an inland civic center toward the water. Winding, tree-lined residential streets filled out the plan, providing 1,400 lots ranging in size from one-third to one-fifth of an acre. The houses were rather unimaginatively lined up side-by-side along the streets, only occasionally stepped back,

placed in groups, or angled to meet corners. Culs-de-sac were employed to reach the interiors of large blocks. Hammond devoted 40 acres to the university and punctuated the plan with public buildings and a variety of parks and recreational spaces, including a 15-acre sports center on low land fronting the bay.

The plan was only partially implemented. Hammond left the project to help draft New Zealand's 1926 Town Planning Act. Development began along the cliffs, where lots were auctioned off starting in 1928, although roughly half of the purchasers defaulted in the next few years. Dramatic views of the harbor eventually made those sites, particularly along the cliff-front Paritai Drive, the most desirable and expensive in Auckland, but much of the rest of the land was developed in stages between the 1930s and 1960s without recognition of the original design. Plans for the university, civic center, and most parks were ignored, and Orakei, despite considerable development, did not receive a shopping district until the 1990s.

INDIA

The new capital city of the British Raj in India, **New Delhi** (1912–31), was, as Robert Grant Irving has written, "a contradiction in terms, both Garden City and City Beautiful, *rus in urbe*. Air and light and greenery

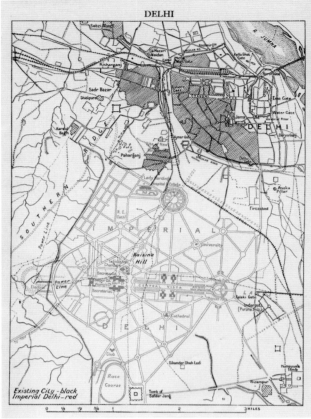

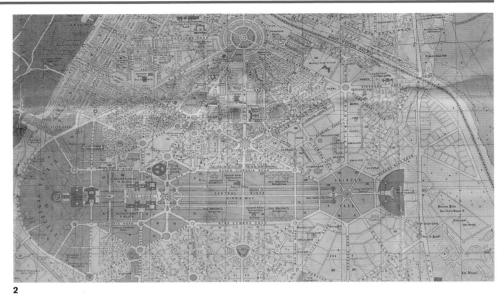

1. Map of Edwin Lutyens's projected Imperial Delhi. WC (1910–12)

2. Plan, Edwin Lutyens. ID (1931)

3. Aerial view of Secretariat buildings showing "Schedule B" in left distance. CSAS

4. Aerial view. CSAS

. . . abounded, and town and country were interwoven."[112] New Delhi may have been a new capital city, but without the full mixture of uses that one associates with a city, and with its low density, low scale, and extensive greenery, it was also like a suburb—which was the case, given that it was in actuality an appendage to the historic city of Delhi, or Old Delhi, to the north.

The Delhi Town Planning Committee, charged in 1911 with the design of the new city, consisted of Edwin Lutyens, who had been nominated by the Royal Institute of British Architects; John A. Brodie, borough engineer of Liverpool, who represented the local government board; and Captain George Swinton (1859–1937), chairman-elect of the London County Council, who stated, "I have been an earnest student of the Garden City and Town Planning Movement. I hope that in the new Delhi we shall be able to show how the ideas which Mr.

Howard first put forward . . . can be brought in to assist this first Capital created in our time . . . No new city should be permissible in these days to which the word 'garden' can't be applied."[113] Henry Vaughan Lanchester (1863–1953), editor of *Builder* magazine and a planner and architect with experience working in India, was appointed a temporary consultant to the committee. Lanchester favored a garden-esque approach, but he also advocated the incorporation of aspects of local culture into the plan. However, Lutyens, who one might have assumed from his work at Hampstead Garden Suburb and other projects in England would resist a strictly Garden City approach, was intent on seeing to it that New Delhi took its place in the great tradition of monumental world capitals. As a result, New Delhi is a hybrid.

Two sites were considered for the new city-suburb and eleven plans prepared before a final design for the

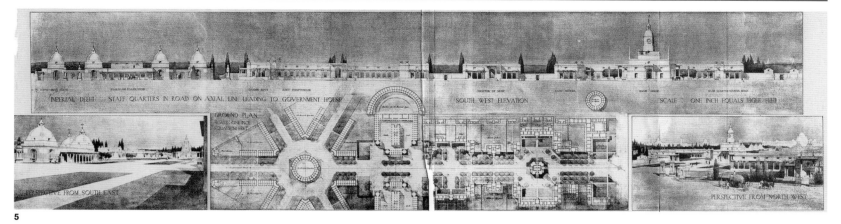

5

6

7

8

9

10

5. Elevations, plans, and perspectives of "Schedule B." TA22 (1922)

6. Aerial view of Connaught Place. CSAS (1930s)

7. Connaught Place. Vasenka. FL (2012)

8. Ashoka Road. Ayumi. FL (2010)

9. Bungalow, King Edward Road. CSAS (1938)

10. Typical street. RAMSA (2011)

roughly 10-square-mile capital, located on an elevated site and intended to house about 65,000 people, was settled upon. While some natural features of the site, such as Raisina Hill, where the governmental complex was located, and the Jumna River, on the east, were taken advantage of in planning, the layout was largely abstract, with a bold geometry of diagonal avenues radiating from key monuments and centers of activities but cut through at its heart by a broad mall, King's Way, as in Pierre L'Enfant's plan for Washington, D.C. (1791)—especially as it was redrawn by the McMillan Commission in 1902.

Allan Greenberg has analyzed the plan: "New Delhi is formed by the superimposition of two different geometric systems. One, a narrow rectangular grid, is monumental and relates to the major scale of the region and the governmental buildings. It forms the main axis of the city. The other, a hexagonal system, is local, devoted to the residential city. The outer limits of the symmetrical plan are defined by the two overlapping major hexagons."[114]

As a plan, New Delhi is nothing short of enigmatic, eliciting all sorts of interpretations by scholars and critics. In its monumental aspects, New Delhi's predecessors include Versailles and Wren's plan for the rebuilding of London. But in many other respects it was a decidedly modern construct, as Irving has pointed out, with buildings "arranged in a discontinuous pattern, zoned according to function as Ebenezer Howard would have wished; housing was separated from recreation and business."[115] Wolfgang Sonne has placed the monumental qualities of its layout within the context of the then prevalent "international classic trend," which influenced "not only academic designs" but *also bore fruit in the practice of town planning. In the first decade of the twentieth century, civic centres were realized in existing cities—for example in Cardiff by Lanchester & Lodge—and in newly planned garden cities, such as Hampstead Garden Suburb by Edwin Lutyens. In other instances, formal comprehensive planning overpowered existing picturesque developments—as was the case in the plan by Ernest Prestwich, Thomas Mawson and Robert Atkinson for Port Sunlight in 1910, which simply superimposed the cruciform axes from Washington onto an English company town—or resulted in rigorous comprehensive plans—for example A. and J. Soutar's plan for Ruislip Manor from 1910, whose street grid can be taken as an immediate forerunner of New Delhi.[116]*

Allan Greenberg has emphasized New Delhi's place in the context of the Garden City movement as a whole: "Lutyens' interest in the idea of a qualified monumentality is bound up with his decision to build a garden city at New Delhi rather than a Beaux-Arts capital."[117] The hybrid of formal and informal planning, Greenberg continues, "is precisely the incongruity that appealed to Unwin, and to Lutyens. It is therefore not surprising to find that the main characteristics of the plan of Letchworth—the grand approach that bisects the symmetrical plan and connects the centre to the regional transportation route, the 'monumental' centre and 'rural' city, the variety of vistas, and the interpenetration of the landscape and city—were used by Lutyens as the basis for his plan of New Delhi." Greenberg argues that the

double-faceted aspect of New Delhi has not been recognized. While it is an imperial fiat-city . . . its distinguishing features root it in the new town movement that began at Saltaire and Letchworth. Unwin's 'via latior' also attempted to resolve in terms of town planning the precise problem that Lutyens set himself in both his house architecture and his garden layouts. This juxtaposition of the monumental and the picturesque (in the Reptonian sense of the word), the formal and the natural, and their paradoxical resolution all have roots in the English landscape tradition. They are old ideas that had been used in English architecture and town planning in the work of the Elizabethan and Baroque architects as well as the Adam brothers, the Woods at Bath, and Sir John Soane.[118]

While contemporary observers tend to regard as notable New Delhi's hybrid blend—or is it a juxtaposition?—of monumental groupings in a garden city, in 1932 Thomas Sharp, the planner and planning writer critical of the Garden City movement, contemptuously described "little dwellings crouching separately under trees on either side of a great space." In fact, New Delhi was for a long time seen as a failure, in effect because it was inherently suburban. As Sharp put it: "We want something to reflect our achievement, our great overtopping of nature: something that is a worthy symbol of civilization . . . That we can only get through pure medium, the town. Town-country, garden-city will never give it. Only sheer, triumphant, unadulterated urbanity will."[119]

A vivid expression of New Delhi's hybridity can be seen in what was known in the plan as "Schedule B," the viceregal staff quarters. Surrounding the capital group, the staff quarters formed a residential village suitably deferential to the monumentality of the buildings it supported. Lutyens's development of the grouping—as well as the radial and diagonal avenues to the north and southwest of the Viceroy's House—was not simply, as Irving has put it, "a formal and symbolic microcosm of the garden city," but specifically a full elaboration of Lutyens's Erskine Hill complex in Hampstead Garden Suburb.[120] Here, as Irving has written, two villages echo "both the form and intent of the garden city capital in the precise geometries of their interwoven radial and grid plans," with "predominant quadrangular groupings" interspersed with "other basic geometric forms—circuses, crescents, and wedge-shaped designs."[121]

Although a center of government, provision was also made for commercial activity as well as the city's eventual physical expansion, acknowledging "hygiene and traffic circulation as priority considerations."[122] The new city's commercial center, the circular Connaught Place, situated where the major north–south axis of the monumental city, the Queen's Way, intersects the northernmost of the plan's bounding hexagons, near the Old City, was realized in 1931 to the designs of Robert Tor Russel (1888–1972), who based his work on that of W. H. Nicholls (1875–1949). For the circus-like Connaught Place, Russel adopted as models the Royal Circus at Bath and Park Place in London, designing a virtually continuous row of two-story-high stucco-clad arcaded buildings punctuated by Palladian archways. The low height of the Connaught buildings failed to effectively define the lushly planted, broad park at the center of the circle, while the wide avenues crisscrossing the park interrupted the easy flow of pedestrians attempting to circumnavigate it under the shopping arcades along its edge.

A key to New Delhi's livability and a vivid expression of the Garden City thinking that lay behind its planning was Lutyens's decision to plant umbrella-like evergreen Jamun trees along the monumental streets, and a wide variety of other trees, many of them flowering, which all in all do so much to ameliorate the city's heat. Lutyens's plan was "remarkable," as Patwant Singh has observed, "for the generous green spaces . . . and their integration with the parks developed around monuments. What emerged was one of the world's outstanding garden-cities, not only on account of its refined emphasis on elegance and civic grace, but also because in practical terms its greening reduced temperatures during the hot, dust-laden summer months of northern India. New

Delhi's unique green character was augmented still further by placing official residences—or bungalows—in rolling lawns and gardens."[123]

Robert Byron, observing New Delhi from the vantage point of the Viceroy's House at the time of the city's official inauguration in 1931, wrote that "on all sides radiate the avenues of the new city, lined with bungalows in spacious woody gardens, and carved into merry-go-rounds at points of intersection . . . The English Quarter presents the aspect of a forest. Each house is set in a compound of two to three acres, whose trees have matured in ten years and become enormous in twenty. At one or two points only are the buildings beginning to congregate in close formation."[124] So evocative of the garden city were these neighborhoods flanking the King's Way that, as Andreas Volwahsen writes, New Delhi is "the largest of all garden cities . . . not built in England, but in the India of the Raj."[125]

ZAMBIA

In 1930, British town planner and Garden City advocate Stanley Davenport Adshead was commissioned to select a site and prepare plans for **Lusaka**, the new capital city of the British colonial government in Northern Rhodesia (now Zambia).[126] The government had determined a year earlier that the current capital, Livingstone, in the Zambezi valley near the territory's southern border, was no longer suitable and that a location closer to the emerging Copperbelt in the north was necessary. As an added benefit, the new site—1,000 feet higher in elevation than Livingstone—provided cooler temperatures. Adshead, working closely with a water engineering firm, chose Lusaka from eight proposed locations. Unlike New Delhi, its peer colonial capital built twenty years earlier adjacent to the historic city of Delhi, Lusaka, established in 1905 as a railroad siding, was at the time only a small European-founded town with a modest African population. The principal settlement, later known as Old Town, was laid out as a grid west of the railroad tracks along the Great North Road (now Cairo Road). The remainder of Lusaka consisted of working farms on both sides of the railroad, several of which had been subdivided for residential use.

As presented in 1931, Adshead's plan took advantage of a four-mile-long-by-one-mile-wide ridge roughly two miles east of Old Town, a partially wooded, relatively breezy and cool site deemed suitable for sewerage. Covering roughly nine square miles and accommodating a population of 8,000 Europeans, an African police force of 1,000, and 4,000 African residents who were expected mostly to be domestic servants and their families, the resulting density was quite low even by Garden City standards. In addition to residential districts, Adshead was tasked with providing a government center, commercial districts, schools, native and European hospitals, a cathedral, library, market hall, movie house, trade school, light industry including a printing plant,

an abattoir, a site for a university, an airport, and a new clubhouse for an existing golf course.

Like New Delhi and Canberra, Lusaka was part City Beautiful and part Garden City, combining axial boulevards connecting major public squares and grand *rond-points* with leafy, less formal residential neighborhoods. Zoning restrictions separated commercial, civic, residential, recreational, and manufacturing uses. The government buildings, spread across the ridge and connected by the 400-foot-wide Independence Avenue, were spaced at such broad intervals that the Government House—the governor's residence that also hosted state and social affairs—was almost two miles from the monumental plaza housing the government offices. Another broad avenue, 120 feet wide, connecting the government center to the railroad station, had at its midpoint a planned-but-never-built commercial district intended to shift commerce away from Old Town. Other axial boulevards terminated in sites for the cathedral, hospital, hotel, and market square. Typical streets were to be 60 or 90 feet wide and lined by double rows of trees planted in a variety of species including Mediterranean cypresses intended to "make the capital more and more reminiscent of Italy as the years go by."[127] A nursery was established for the purpose, also providing seedlings for residents' gardens free of charge.

Lusaka was racially segregated. Europeans resided on the choice land to the east and southeast of the government center as well as to the north, where it extended west to the edges of Old Town and was divided into three socioeconomic zones. The first zone featured one-and-a-half- to two-acre lots, followed by a zone of one-acre lots and an unrealized zone of .2-acre lots on the flatter land by the railroad tracks, the last still yielding a density of just five houses per acre. Regulations governed lot subdivision, maximum lot coverage, and setbacks, including minimum ten-foot side setbacks. Africans, residing more or less out of sight in Native Compounds on the fringes to the south and west of the center, were viewed as temporary residents—domestic servants who would leave Lusaka when their term of service was over. Servants working in the Government House lived closer to the center in the Governor's Village along with the native staff of the nearby hospital. In the compounds, which also contained bazaars, saloons, and entertainment halls, quasi-communal kitchens served groups of four huts, each circular hut occupying one quarter of a square parcel and the kitchen building, located at the intersection of the lots, partitioned into four separate rooms. In Lusaka, the vernacular hut was altered to feature burnt brick rather than mud construction, concrete rather than clay floors, and introduce small windows high on the walls to provide light and ventilation, though thatch was still used as roofing.

Single-family detached houses were predominant. Among the few apartment buildings were those built on Birdcage Walk in what John Collins, an architect who served for three years (1965–68) as a city engineer in Lusaka and in 1969 wrote a definitive critique of the

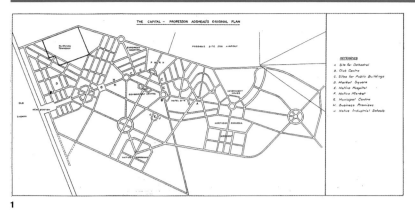

1

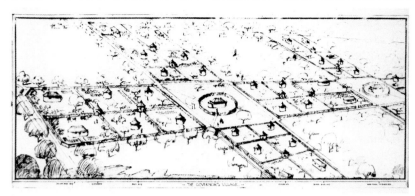

2

3

4

5

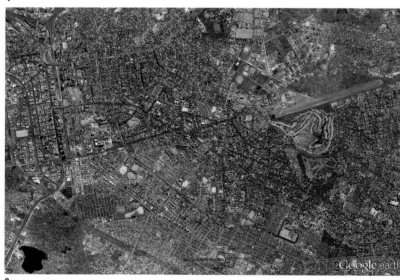

6

1. Plan, Stanley Davenport
Adshead, 1931. ZUS

2. Governor's Village, 1931. KBL

3. Staff flats, J. A. Hoogterp, 1931.
KBL

4. Staff house, J. A. Hoogterp,
1931. KBL

5. Aerial view of Native Compound.
GE (2004)

6. Aerial view. GE (2009)

7. Typical street. Rese. PAN (2012)

7

city's development, has described as a "singularly ugly red-brick-institutional style of architecture, which no doubt, and not unreasonably contributed to the general prejudice in favour of detached houses." Terraces and rowhouses were just as rare and were treated as "if they were merely an unusually large house, which must therefore have the same relationship to street and plot boundaries as would a house. Their architectural potential for creating different urban forms—the square, the crescent, the pedestrian lane—is consequently seldom realized or permitted."[128] J. A. Hoogterp (1892–1972), a Nairobi-based South African-born architect of Dutch descent, designed most of the government buildings and also improved the standards of European housing from the somewhat shoddy bungalows that had been built by the Public Works Department.

Adshead's plan failed for a number of reasons, beginning with the planner's initial misstep: "It is wise to err on the side of being too widely spaced rather than to have the buildings conveniently near with a possibility of being overcrowded in the future."[129] A publication celebrating the city's official dedication in 1935 stated that the strategy, "particularly on a site which is quite unoccupied and where land is inexpensive, is clearly the more sound. Initial expenditure will be heavier, but the preservation in the future of the original carefully conceived plan of the city is assured."[130]

Unfortunately, because of a bureaucratic oversight the plan for Lusaka was deemed illegal according to Northern Rhodesia's Town Planning Ordinance of 1929. A non-statutory development plan was relied upon, using leases (most of the land was government-owned) and other methods to control development as much as possible, although as a 1949 report to the Executive Council noted, "the non-statutory development plans . . . are too easily amended," resulting in "individual proposals being considered and approved without reference to the effect upon the general planning of the town." Adshead had been retained as a consultant, leaving the plan's detailed development and implementation to a succession of government planners and administrators who were not as well versed in the Garden City idea. Without statutory controls and under inconsistent leadership, Adshead's plan was steadily eroded. Areas reserved for one function were given up for other uses. Privately owned land was not subject to planning controls and was typically built out with low-density subdivisions bearing little relation to their surroundings or the vision of the master plan. Almost immediately the target population grew but instead of increasing density and thereby filling in the empty stretches that separated built-up areas, each successive change favored greater sprawl, reflecting the notion that land was plentiful in Africa, and, as Collins has noted, the planners' belief "that a city of garden suburbs could become a Garden City." By 1969 Collins could observe that "Adshead's grandest conception—the 400 ft wide avenue . . . along the ridge is now a relatively minor link-road between three garden suburbs." Many of the parks and open spaces, he continued, were simply wasteful, "serving little purpose in a city where there is no visual justification for spatial contrast or 'lungs,' because all buildings are set in so much space."[131]

It wasn't until 1952 that Lusaka received its first statutory plan. By then the damage was largely done. Old Town had emerged as the central business district, cut off from the rest of Lusaka by the railroad tracks that could only be crossed via two increasingly congested roads. Efforts to relocate commerce to the east side of the tracks failed after business owners asked for financial compensation to move. The sprawling infrastructure that had been accepted as a greater initial expenditure also proved burdensome to maintain and made it prohibitively expensive to provide basic services—roads, electricity, sewerage—to the non-central areas that Africans were forced to settle in when they flocked to the capital after independence was declared in 1964. Perhaps, as Collins writes, the Garden City idea was simply an inappropriate strategy given the task: "There is clearly no connection between a brief of this sort and the aims of the Garden City Movement, nor is there any reason to suppose that Adshead thought that there was. There was [sic] no philanthropic motives, no industrial squalor to escape from, no desire to improve the lot of manual workers or provide them with rapid transport, and certainly no intention of producing a balanced community. Adshead's thinking was nevertheless garden city thinking."[132]

SOUTH AFRICA

Pinelands (1921), seven miles east of Cape Town, represents "the first authentic attempt at providing a proper town plan for a parcel of land in South Africa."[133] It also holds the less glowing distinction of being among the country's first racially segregated housing developments, built exclusively for whites. The garden village was conceived and substantially funded by Richard Stuttaford (1870–1945), a Cape Town department store magnate and city councilor. He was moved to action by his concern for the unhealthy living conditions of the poor, particularly in the wake of the deadly 1918 influenza epidemic, though counterintuitively, Stuttaford built Pinelands for the middle class.

Stuttaford's decade-long interest in the Garden City concept led him on a 1917 pilgrimage to Letchworth, where he met Ebenezer Howard. Returning to South Africa, Stuttaford organized a Garden Cities Trust, to which he persuaded the government to donate a 988-acre site, part of an 1884 forestry experiment that had left it half covered by pine trees. Like many international "garden cities," Pinelands was not the genuine article. There was no population limit or greenbelt, it was not cooperatively owned, and it lacked an industrial sector or any major source of local jobs. Although the Garden Cities Trust intended to use income from commercial rents for the construction of parks and recreational spaces, residential sites were to be sold, not rented. As historian John Muller has written, Pinelands "was

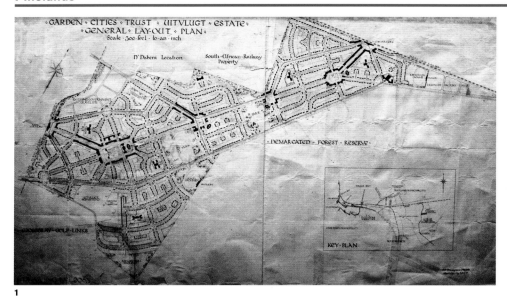

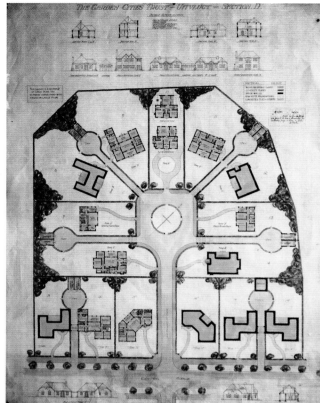

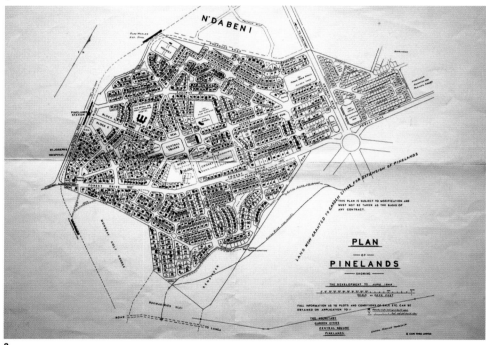

1. Plan, A. J. Thompson, 1921. WCAR

2. Houses in Section D, John Lyon and W. A. R. Fallon, 1921. WCAR

3. Plan showing development to 1943. WCAR

4. Type A house, Eagle, Pilkington & McQueen, 1921. WCAR

conceptually and essentially a housing scheme; a scheme that was to display greater allegiance to Unwin's planning prowess than Howard's social percipience."[134]

Architect John Perry (n.d.) won the competition to plan the village, but his scheme was discarded after being sent to Raymond Unwin for feedback. In place of Perry, the trust hired A. J. (Albert John) Thompson (1878–1940), an Unwin protégé who had worked on Letchworth and Hampstead and later, in practice with C. Murray Hennell and Charles Holloway James, designed Swanpool Garden Suburb (see p. 717). Using Perry's plan as a starting point, Thompson prepared his design while in England and then revised it after arriving on-site in 1920, taking into closer consideration the parcel's mountain views, vegetation, and a 40-foot change in elevation.

The site was reached by a railroad line leading from Cape Town and an existing street that traversed it. Drawing on Letchworth, Thompson called for a rectangular civic center from which radiating boulevards extended toward planned new railroad stations (five stations would serve Pinelands by the 1950s) and led to *rondpoints* or into residential neighborhoods. Thompson ringed the civic center's open park with an administration building, community center, churches, police station, and other facilities, although for many years, the community's only shop was a cooperative store.

The hierarchical street network included arterial boundary roads, wide internal boulevards with landscaped medians, and 18.5-foot-wide residential lanes lined by planting strips and narrow sidewalks. Early designs made use of short culs-de-sac extending into the superblocks, but most were later eliminated. Despite the absence of grouped houses—the neighborhood featured only detached houses with individual gardens—Thompson inserted several residential closes that approximated Unwin's quadrangles, linking houses together with

5, 6. Typical streets. Niven. HN (2012)

7. Civic center. Niven. HN (2012)

8. Meadway. Niven. HN (2012)

5

6

7

8

garden walls and paired garages. The initial plan also featured several large parks that functioned as internal greenbelts, but these never made it to the final design. Instead, the 18 percent of the site that Thompson reserved for open space took the form of small neighborhood greens, playgrounds, and athletic fields. Street names such as Welwyn Avenue, Wythenshawe Avenue, Letchworth Road, and Hampstead Heath Street made explicit the plan's progenitors.

Construction began in 1921. Restrictions mandated thatched roofs on the first houses, such as those along the Mead and Meadway that now comprise a historic district, but were soon loosened to allow most kinds of construction. Most houses were built by individual owners benefitting from government loans. Thompson left the project in 1924 when he relocated to Nigeria. J. W. P. Logan (n.d.), a land surveyor, took over, altering the plan significantly. By 1935, about 520 houses had been built. In the immediate aftermath of World War II, a construction boom calling for the expansion of the site saw to the rapid development of about 450 acres, with 1,600 houses built by the 1950s.

EGYPT

In 1905 Belgian industrialist Baron Édouard Empain (1852–1929) purchased about 6,200 acres of desert six miles northeast of Cairo for the purpose of building a new city to be planned along lines inspired by the English Garden City movement.[135] Working in partnership with Boghos Nubar (1851–1930), son of a former Egyptian prime minister, Empain, an amateur Egyptologist, was able to buy the land from the government at the symbolic price of one Egyptian pound per acre. The

following year Empain and Nubar established two limited-dividend companies: one to construct and manage the new town and the other to build an electric tram line to connect it to central Cairo's existing tram network, which Empain had been largely responsible for since winning the contract for its construction in 1894. Empain named the development **Heliopolis**, or sun city, in the belief that the site encompassed the location of the ancient city of Heliopolis dating from Egypt's Predynastic Period, before 3,100 B.C. As the *American Review of Reviews* reported in 1913: "Baron Empain, having discovered that the air of ancient Heliopolis was unusually pure, especially when compared with the dust-choked atmosphere of Cairo, that it had an unusual supply of pure water, that the view was excellent, and believing that the historic associations would add charm to the place as a residential center, conceived the scheme of transforming this patch of desert into a modern town."[136] Belgian archaeologists later discovered that the ancient city was in fact located about six miles northwest of Empain's site, but the atmospheric name was retained.

The plan of Heliopolis is generally credited as the product of a collaboration between Empain, who trained as an engineer and worked briefly as a draftsman, and British town planner Reginald Oakes (1847–1927). The original idea (1906) was to create two "oases" separated by a kilometer of desert, one a main development for the middle and upper classes and the other a secondary enclave for the workers who would serve them and the town. This plan was dropped in favor of the single scheme (1907) that went forward, which catered predominantly to foreign businessmen, diplomats based in Cairo, and upscale Egyptians, with some workers' housing to be provided in apartment buildings and small houses. Although Cairo's business district could

1. Plan, Édouard Empain and Reginald Oakes, 1907. HSO

2. Map. NW (1952)

3. Palace Hotel, Ernest Jaspar, 1910. CRS

4. Boulevard Abbas and Boulevard Ismail. AJDC (1920s)

be reached by tram in just twenty minutes, Heliopolis's extensive and varied building program, which in addition to housing and civic and commercial areas included an unusual recreational component, was intended to foster its independence from the Egyptian capital.

As architect and historian Khaled Adham has pointed out, the plan for Heliopolis, especially its town center, owed a great deal to Ebenezer Howard as well as to Parker and Unwin's plan for Letchworth: "For instance, an echo of Parker and Unwin's geometrical formality, which they emulated from Howard's diagrams, was retained around the main square of Heliopolis, where later the main cathedral was located. In addition, the area of Heliopolis, its capacity of inhabitants, and the selection of its location far from Cairo may have been influenced" by Howard's belief that a self-sufficient development could best provide relief from "the urban ills of cities." Adham has also noted that "while Heliopolis may have had formal planning similarities with the Garden City," the for-profit real

estate venture "did not share Howard's goals and socio-political intentions."[137]

A gridded town square, with wide radiating boulevards leading to the residential sections of the suburb, included an impressive array of public and commercial buildings designed in a style that fused Moorish facades, Arabic cross sections, and European floor plans. In addition to the tram station and railway headquarters, this area included arcaded buildings with ground-level stores and restaurants topped by apartments for upper-level government bureaucrats, several schools, and, most prominently, the 400-room Palace Hotel designed by Belgian architect Ernest Jaspar (1876–1940). Houses of worship serving the Muslim, Jewish, Anglican, Coptic Orthodox, and Greek Orthodox communities were built in the civic area, but Empain, a Catholic, saved the most prominent site in the center for the Roman Catholic basilica designed by French architect Alexandre Marcel (1860–1928) as a quarter-size version of Istanbul's Hagia Sophia. H. G.

5. Basilica Square. AJDC (1920s)

6. Avenue des Pyramides. AJDC (1930s)

7. Boulevard Ismail. AJDC (2006)

8. Empain villa, Alexandre Marcel, 1911. Jasmine. WC (2006)

Hunting, writing in 1909, was most impressed by the 120-foot-wide, 2,400-foot-long Avenue des Pyramides, the town's "beautiful" main thoroughfare, "lined with handsome trees [that] runs in the direction of the pyramids from that of Cairo . . . On each side of it face seven squares of buildings and there are four squares laid out in the flower-beds only, along the center of the city."[138] Empain and Oakes also included several public parks placed throughout the site.

In addition to the apartments in the town center, the housing stock, located on an extension of the gridded layout, was composed of detached villas with gardens, apartment buildings, and modest workers' houses. Although the villas were built by individual lot buyers, they were stylistically similar, sharing the basic architectural vocabulary of the commercial and civic buildings. Empain broke with the model for his own massive villa, designed by Alexandre Marcel to resemble a Hindu palace, with Cambodian craftsmen brought in to help with the construction.

Heliopolis featured a large number of recreational facilities, including a cricket field, a polo ground, a golf course, a sporting club, a casino, a race track known as the Hippodrome, and Luna Park, the continent's first Western-style amusement park. As Khaled Adham has observed, "By 1915, the entertainment and leisure spaces, the essential components of Howard's third magnet, comprised 25 per cent of the total built area . . . It could be said that prior to the introduction of entertainment activities and commercialized leisure in Heliopolis there was no public entertainment zone in the whole of Cairo. In fact, following the opening of the Heliopolis palace hotel, the fast metro tram, and the various entertainment places, Heliopolis became the entertainment hub of Cairo."[139]

Heliopolis was successful from the start, with 238 of the planned 400 villas completed or under construction by 1910. In 1913, Sydney A. Clark, writing in the pages of *Suburban Life* magazine, observed that

> *everything in Heliopolis was planned and executed with an eye to the future, with an eye to permanence, and to artistic beauty and sanitation, money being apparently a point of small importance . . . It seems almost paradoxical to associate with dirty, picturesque Egypt the thought of broad avenues actually as clean and well kept as the streets of Germany's capital, yet the paradox has become an actual fact in Heliopolis . . . Doubtless the phenomenal success of Heliopolis depends largely upon the sagacity and foresight of the founders, who acted on the principle that a suburb, spacious and clean and healthy, near a city where these qualities were unknown, would prove an irresistible attraction and, in the end, a paying business proposition.*

1. Plan, José Lamba, 1906. MVC

2. Aerial view. GE (2004)

3. Villa Harari. FBAH (1921)

4. Typical street. Dobrowolski. AJDC (2012)

5. Typical street. Volait. MVC (2012)

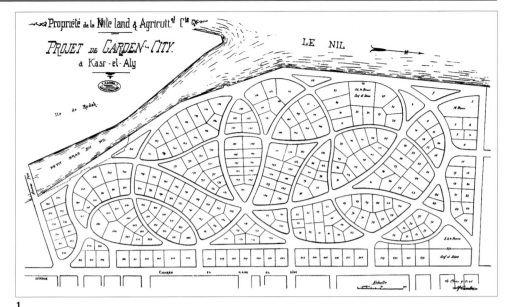

1

2

3

4

5

Clark concluded that "nine years ago there was nothing but a barren, sandy waste where there is now the civilization of the city, tempered by the quiet restfulness of the suburb, and guarded by those whose first aim it is to make and keep their new creation a model of beauty in all that the word implies."[140]

In 1928 Heliopolis's population reached 24,000 residents, a figure that would more than double after the end of World War II, when a good percentage of the park space was lost to housing. By the mid-1950s the northern march of Cairo's development had reached Heliopolis, and the suburb, though it was able to retain its distinct identity, became a part of the city. Many of the large villas

have since been replaced by apartment houses and office buildings, but some still remain, including Empain's Hindu palace and the Palace Hotel, which was converted into Egypt's presidential palace in the 1980s. In 2005, the year of its centennial, writer Andrew Beattie described Heliopolis in his cultural history of Cairo: "The main streets, below the elegant neo-Islamic facades, are lined with nightclubs and cinemas, burger joints and fashionable boutiques. For this is now Masr el-Gadida, or New Cairo. The community is wealthy and still includes large numbers of foreigners."[141]

The upper-class residential subdivision of **Garden City** (1906) was located closer to the heart of Cairo on a

50-acre site on the east bank of the Nile about a mile south of the city center.[142] The swampy site, home to a soon-to-be demolished eighteenth-century palace built by Ibrahim Pasha and located just south of the British Embassy (1893), was purchased in 1904 by three developers, Frantz Sofio, Charles Bacos, and George Maksud, organized as the Nile Land & Agriculture Company. The private development of detached single-family villas was intended for diplomats and successful expatriate businessmen as well as some wealthy natives. José Lamba (d. 1914), a French engineer, was commissioned to prepare the plan, with all of the houses to be independently built by purchasers of lots.

Lamba's plan, highly distinct from Cairo's prevailing grid, was a maze of looping streets that produced 273 irregular building parcels. The maximum height of a house was set at four stories, or 50 feet, and each was to include a walled garden. Historian Samir Raafat has described the confusing scheme of interconnected, swirling streets as "the work of an Art Nouveau dabbler who preferred compasses to rulers, hence the absence of straight lines. Lamba laid out a series of narrow winding roads outlining ill-defined triangles and curvy rectangles. Three times out of four you end up where you started . . . Equally perplexing, for anyone without a sense of whimsy, Lamba chose a giant fish as the centerpiece for his Neptunian maze; its head, which stands in as the neighborhood's only public garden, pointing toward the Nile."[143]

The Nile Land & Agriculture Company went bankrupt in 1907, but Lamba's plan continued to hold sway. Forty, mostly two-story villas were completed before the beginning of World War I, along with two schools and a small club with tennis courts. When development resumed after the war it was far more dense, with apartment buildings and commercial structures joining the mix, a trend that would only continue as Garden City became home to banks, embassies, hotels, restaurants, and, in 1957, to Cairo's first skyscraper, the thirty-story Belmont Building, designed by Antoine Selim Nahas (1901–1966). Still, the area retained its identity as an upscale leafy enclave for Cairo's elite. In fact, after a visit in 1998, Toronto architect Paul Reuber described what he believed were the positive attributes of the passage of time and increased density, writing that "it is this faded elegance and extreme intensification that, in my opinion, give Cairo's Garden City such an urbane air, ironically achieved by the elimination of most of its original gardens, side yards and setbacks. Its Art Nouveau streets still slither around and about this inhabited reef with the agility of water snakes. And those hopelessly confusing intersections have produced a spectacular inventory of habitable ship prows, which both command and provide a virile array of architectural vistas. Could the evolution of Cairo's Garden City be a ray of hope for the geometry of garden cities everywhere?"[144]

Maadi (1906), located on a 450-acre site seven-and-a-half miles south of Cairo, was a third garden suburb inspired by English precedent that was intended

Maadi

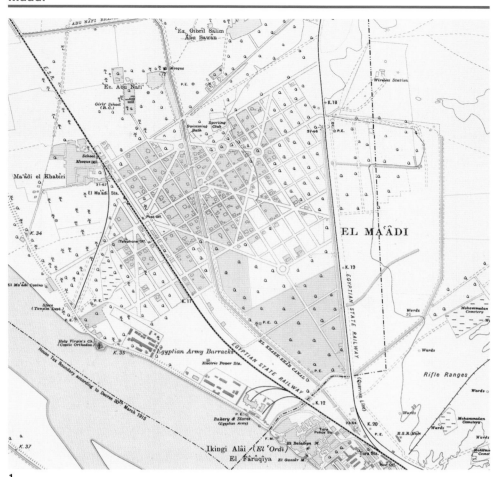

1. Map. NW (1934)

2–4. Typical streets. Dobrowolski. AJDC (2012)

1. Plan, Wilhelm Stiassny, 1909. TAY

2. Bird's-eye view. TAY (1909)

3. Herzl Street with Hebrew school,
Joseph Barsky, 1909, in distance.
EIM

4, 5. Rothschild Boulevard. EIM

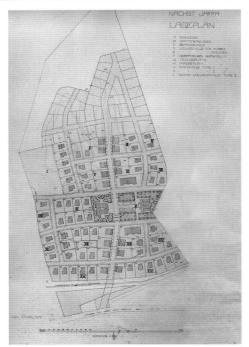

1

2

3

4

5

primarily for wealthy expatriates.[145] The project was privately developed by the Egyptian Delta Land and Investment Company for a site along the east bank of the Nile that was adjacent to a railway line running from Cairo to the city of Helwan, located twelve miles south of Maadi. Like Heliopolis, Maadi's plan was a variation on Cairo's traditional gridded arrangement, in this case crisscrossed by wide radiating avenues with *rond-points*. Civil engineer Alexander James Adams (1867–1921), a retired Canadian military officer and managing director of the development company, was responsible for the plan of tree-lined streets, divided into quarter-acre lots accommodating detached villas with gardens, although it was assumed that individuals would purchase multiple adjacent lots for the construction of particularly large houses. All house plans were required to be submitted to Delta Land for approval, and several restrictions were instituted. Houses, limited in height to 50 feet, could occupy no more than half of their lots, while garden fences could not exceed six-and-a-half feet. Commercial construction, consisting mostly of modest retail shops,

was confined to prescribed areas. Adams's plan also anticipated the addition of schools and religious facilities for the Christian, Jewish, and Muslim populations.

Maadi's first houses were completed by the middle of 1908, followed by a new railroad station the following year. By 1911, thirty-two houses had been built, a number that would rise to 128 by 1925. Paralleling the experience of Heliopolis and Garden City, subsequent development has included multistory apartment houses and commercial buildings; like them, Maadi has managed to retain its standing as an exclusive residential district.

PALESTINE

In 1906 sixty-six Jewish families living in Jaffa, home to a population of 23,000 Muslims, 7,000 Jews, and 5,000 Christians, banded together to form **Ahuzat Bayit** (homestead), a housing cooperative intent on developing a garden suburb based on the English model.[146] The group, led by Russian-born jeweler Akiva Aryeh

Weiss (1868–1947), an amateur student of urban planning and architecture, was composed primarily of recent immigrants from Eastern Europe, secular Zionists who had settled in the port city instead of Jerusalem, which tended to attract religious pilgrims. The members of Ahuzat Bayit were motivated by two factors: the desire to leave overcrowded Jaffa with its unsanitary housing stock of small dilapidated dwellings on narrow streets, and the wish to establish an exclusively Jewish enclave in keeping with their ideological tenets. In March 1908, with the financial help of the Jewish National Fund, founded seven years earlier to purchase and develop land in Palestine, the housing cooperative was able to acquire 21 acres of barren sandy soil for their garden suburb. The site was a little more than a mile northeast of the heart of Jaffa, a distance close enough to allow for daily commutation to work but one that the historian Yossi Katz has described as sufficient to "protect the Jews from the problems of overpopulation . . . [and] provide a place in which they could gather and nurture their national values by speaking Hebrew, opening Jewish educational and cultural institutions in Hebrew, evolving national public life and independent national community life. This could be achieved only if the Zionist-nationalist community would be geographically separated from Jaffa."[147]

Austrian architect Wilhelm Stiassny (1842–1910), best known for prominent synagogues in Vienna and Prague, designed the plan in 1909; the following year, Ahuzat Bayit's name was changed to Tel Aviv (Hill of Spring), referring not only to a Babylonian town mentioned in the Old Testament but also to the title selected by Nahum Sokolow for his Hebrew translation of Theodor Herzl's *Altneuland* (Old New Land) (1902), a utopian novel describing the formation of a Jewish state in the Holy Land. Stiassny, who visited the site before returning to Vienna to prepare the plan, arranged the roughly rectangular parcel into a loose grid formed by the north–south path of the development's main 16-meter-wide boulevard crossed by four narrower east–west streets. The site was divided into sixty-six irregular plots measuring no less than 570 square meters, intended exclusively for detached single-family houses with gardens. The focal point of the community was the centrally located Hebrew school. The housing cooperative banned stores, factories, and all businesses from the proposed suburb, relying on nearby Jaffa for all commercial needs. Stiassny also included large areas for public parks and communal gardens, with the buildings expected to occupy 30 percent of the site.

The foundation stone was laid on April 11, 1909, and by the end of the year fifty stylistically similar one- and two-story red-tile-roofed houses had been completed, independently commissioned by well-to-do and middle-class members of Ahuzat Bayit who were assigned lots by lottery. The Hebrew school (1909), later named for Herzl, was the work of Russian-born architect Joseph Barsky (d. 1943), a recent immigrant who mixed the Art Nouveau with Arabic detailing in designing a dominating

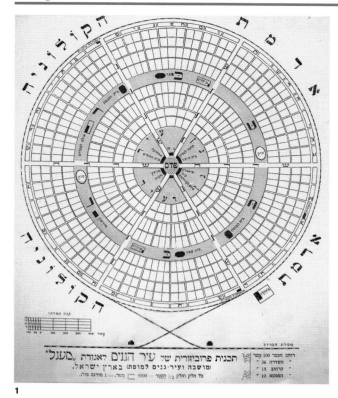

Ma'agal

1. Plan, 1917. YKLB

1

structure that became the focus of community life. With its wide paved roads, street lighting, up-to-date sewage system, and water piped to individual houses and gardens, the settlement provided a striking contrast to Jaffa.

Successful from the start, the suburb immediately began to expand, and although the housing stock remained primarily composed of detached single-family houses with gardens, subsequent building was not governed by an overall plan, with houses sprouting in all directions from the original development. By 1914 Tel Aviv numbered 204 houses on a site that had grown almost sevenfold to encompass 141 acres. Development, which slowed considerably after the outbreak of World War I, was abruptly halted in 1917 when the Ottoman government temporarily evacuated the suburb. After the British took control of Palestine the following year, the Jewish population returned to Tel Aviv, and the suburb's expansion resumed, again without the benefit of a plan.

In 1917, a group of recent immigrants from Warsaw known as **Ma'agal** (circle) attempted to build a garden city outside of Tel Aviv that was a more literal reflection of Ebenezer Howard's ideas.[148] The plan that they released, prepared by an anonymous member of the group, was essentially a knockoff of Howard's diagram No. 2 of the ideal garden city illustrated in *Garden Cities of To-Morrow*. The circular scheme, complete with a central public park, house plots with gardens, wide radiating boulevards, and greenbelts, departed from Howard's model with its inclusion of Jewish institutions such as a *mikveh* (ritual bath) and synagogue. Although some funds were raised for the purchase of a site east of Tel Aviv, the overly ambitious undertaking never progressed beyond the planning stages.

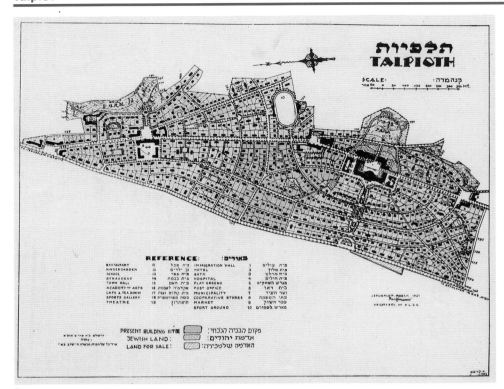

1. Plan, Richard Kaufmann, 1921. CZA

2, 3. Typical streets. CZA

4. Houses. LOCPM (1920s)

5. Ein Gedi Street. RAMSA (2011)

In British Mandate Palestine, several garden suburbs were planned outside the center of Jerusalem in the early 1920s, all the work of German-born architect and town planner Richard Kaufmann (1887–1958), who had studied with Theodor Fischer at Munich's Technische Hochschule and worked under Georg Metzendorf at the Krupp colony of Margarethenhöhe (see p. 749) before emigrating to Palestine in 1920. Kaufmann, who became the most prolific architect of his generation in Palestine, designing more than 400 public and private buildings in addition to his town planning efforts, began his work in Jerusalem in 1921 with his partially realized plan for **Talpiot**, located two miles south of the city center.[149] The garden suburb, named for a verse from the Song of Songs, was privately developed by the Anglo-Palestine Bank, which had purchased the hilly, 148-acre site before World War I. Kaufmann's plan of curving tree-lined streets was divided into 800 plots, intended exclusively for detached single-family houses with gardens to be occupied by bank employees as well as other middle- and upper-middle-class families. In addition to the houses, Kaufmann's ambitious scheme included an array of civic and cultural buildings to be located at the parcel's highest elevation. The plan also featured several public parks and a sports stadium. Construction began in 1922, but only thirty houses were completed before the British authorities temporarily took over the land for an airstrip. Building soon resumed in Talpiot but not according to the original plan.

Kaufmann had more success with his plan for **Rehavia** (1922), an upscale garden suburb built by the private Palestine Land Development Company on 30 acres about a mile north of Jerusalem's center purchased from the Greek Orthodox Church.[150] Kaufmann's plan for 140 dwellings, primarily detached single-family houses with gardens but a few semidetached units as well, was bisected by a tree-lined north–south boulevard open only to pedestrian traffic. The suburb's narrow, curving streets were designed to further discourage through traffic, with the small amount of commercial space relegated to the periphery of the site. Public buildings and a Hebrew school were grouped together at the northern border. A brochure published by the developers described Rehavia as a "Garden-City.

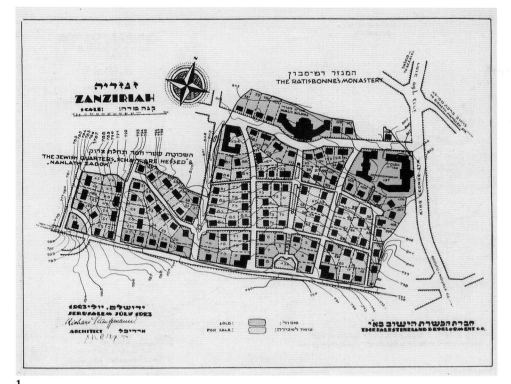

Of every plot, at least 2/3 must be sacrificed for gardens and fresh air, and between every two houses a good space must be allowed. Rehavia commands a beautiful view of the mountains of Jerusalem and Moab. The special advantage possessed by the Quarter, that of being a garden-city in close proximity to the town, attracts wide circles of people bound by their occupation to the city, who desire to live surrounded by gardens and plenty of fresh air."[151] Rehavia prospered and was completed as planned by 1928, leading to an expansion to the south that added another 180 houses. Kaufmann was responsible for the design of many of the International Style houses, commissioned primarily by immigrants from Germany, leading to the sobriquet "a Prussian island in an Oriental sea."

Kaufmann's **Beit HaKerem** (house of the vineyard) (1922), located on a 70-acre site three-and-a-half miles northwest of Jerusalem's Old City, was a more modest private development, geared primarily to teachers and mid-level civil servants.[152] Beit HaKerem was the least gridded of Kaufmann's Jerusalem suburbs, a collection of curving tree-lined streets that followed the topography of

the hilly site, crossed by a wide diagonal pedestrian boulevard slightly south of the parcel's midpoint. Kaufmann's low-density plan divided the site into 148 single-family plots measuring between 1,000 and 1,500 square meters, allowing room for generous gardens. Due to its relatively isolated location, surrounded by Arab villages, bus service was provided to the city center and Kaufmann set aside space for a cooperative market, elementary school and kindergarten, synagogue, sports field, and an electric-power station. A teacher-training school was located on four acres at the northern end of the site, surrounded by additional houses. By 1924, seventy mostly single-story detached stone houses with gardens had been completed at Beit HaKerem, many the work of architect Yehoshua Salant (1890–1980). The development continued to expand throughout the British Mandate and after the 1948 declaration of statehood.

Kaufmann's town planning work extended beyond Jerusalem. His circular plan for **Nahalal** (1921), a *moshav* (cooperative agricultural settlement) located in the northern part of Palestine, twenty miles southeast of Haifa, was influenced not only by Howard's Garden City

1. Plan, Richard Kaufmann, 1923. CZA

2–4. Typical streets. CZA

5. Abarbanel Street. RAMSA (2011)

6. Alharizi Street. RAMSA (2011)

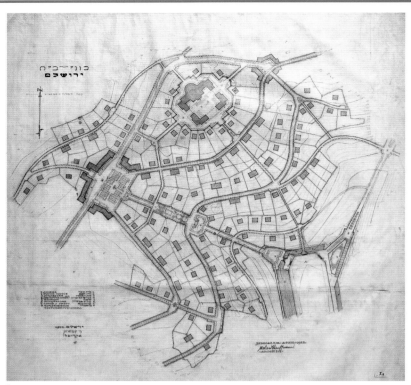

1. Plan, Richard Kaufmann, 1922. CZA

2, 3. Typical views. CZA

4. HeHaluts Street. RAMSA (2011)

5. Pedestrian path. RAMSA (2011)

diagram but also by the utopian city illustrated by Bruno Taut in his 1919 book *Die Stadtkrone* (see p. 415).[153] A *moshav* differed from a kibbutz in that it kept the traditional family structure intact, shunning communal dining and separate sleeping arrangements for children. The site, purchased by the Jewish National Fund, occupied a total of 2,000 acres, divided into eighty 25-acre parcels. Kaufmann's plan of concentric circles located the public buildings in the center, including a school, administrative offices, cooperative store, and a building housing cultural facilities. Single-family houses for Nahalal's eighty families were placed just beyond the civic area, followed first by farm buildings and finally by gardens and the agricultural fields.

Historian S. Ilan Troen has noted that the plan, which would influence future *moshavim*, "offered security advantages even as it limited the size of the village . . . Buildings, principally the cowsheds that were shared by two neighbors, are erected parallel to the ring road and serve as a protective barrier. Moreover, bunkers are located but a few paces from the cowsheds. In effect these

form an outer wall. The community is thus concentrated together at the hub in a manifestly defensive position, with the fields radiating out from the protected core . . . Kaufmann's plan was 'closed.' The design explicitly limited the opportunities for expansion, in keeping with the thinking of contemporary European planners, particularly proponents of Ebenezer Howard's garden city concept. Additional population would have to be accommodated in other controlled communities."[154]

In 1923, German architect Erich Mendelsohn (1887–1953) was commissioned by Berlin builder Adolf Sommerfeld (1886–1964) to design a garden suburb outside Haifa on **Mount Carmel**.[155] Sommerfeld, who had hired Walter Gropius to design his house (1920–21) in Berlin, popularly known as "the log house," had recently purchased the site on the south slope of the mountain. Mendelsohn was visiting Palestine at the invitation of engineer and businessman Pinhas Rutenberg (1879–1942), who hired the architect to design an electric-power station in Haifa, a project (1923) that never progressed beyond the planning stages. The same fate befell

Nahalal

1. Plan, Richard Kaufmann, 1922. CZA

2. Aerial view. DCI (1956)

3. Typical street. RAMSA (2011)

4. Typical view. CZA

Mount Carmel

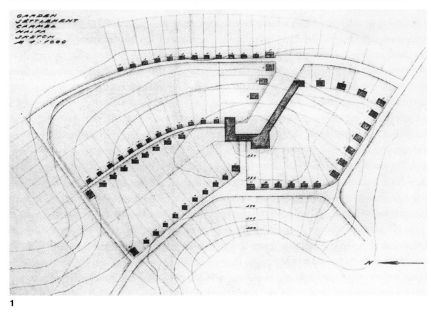

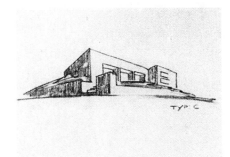

1. Plan, Erich Mendelsohn, 1923. MEND

2. Prototypical houses. MEND

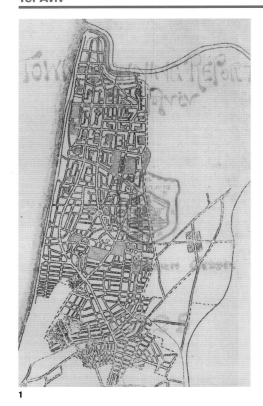

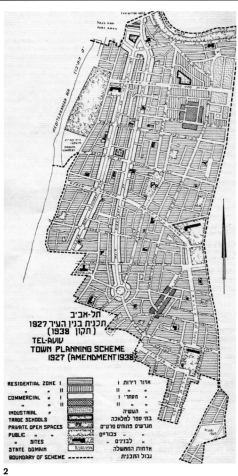

1. Plan, Patrick Geddes, 1925. TAY

2. Revised plan, 1938. TAY

3. Aerial view. LOCPM (1932)

4. Dizengoff Circle. LOCPM (c. 1937)

5. Rothschild Boulevard. RAMSA (2011)

6. Dvora Baron Garden. RAMSA (2011)

Sommerfeld's proposed garden suburb as well as a commercial center for Haifa (1923) that Mendelsohn designed in collaboration with Richard Neutra.

Mendelsohn's plan called for sixty-five detached single-family houses with gardens on three gently curving streets that were to be grouped around the centrally located civic and commercial area. The architect also prepared prototypical houses for the suburb, International Style designs in keeping with his work in Europe. After arguments with Sommerfeld, Mendelsohn resigned the commission in January 1924, and the developer dropped plans for the settlement. After fleeing Nazi Germany in 1933, Mendelsohn settled in Palestine from 1934 to 1941, designing some of the country's most prominent public buildings and distinguished private residences.[156]

Unchecked growth in Tel Aviv in the first years of the British Mandate led to calls for the introduction of a plan to guide future growth.[157] Although still considered a suburb of Jaffa, **Tel Aviv** had obtained a measure of municipal independence in 1921 with the establishment of its first town council. In 1925, with a population of 34,000, Meir Dizengoff, head of the town council and one of the suburb's original founders, commissioned Scottish biologist and town planner Patrick Geddes to prepare Tel Aviv's plan. Geddes had visited Palestine in 1919 when, at the behest of the British Zionist Organization, he had designed, in collaboration with his son-in-law F. C. Mears, an unrealized master plan for Hebrew University on Mount Scopus in Jerusalem.[158]

Geddes produced not only a plan for the long and narrow, 1,648-acre site but also, according to architect and historian Neal I. Payton, a "far-reaching sixty-two-page treatise" consisting of "recommendations, history, flights of poetic license, romantic diatribes addressing such things as the connection of roads, railway, port, open space, parks, public buildings, commercial zones, general building questions, and other odds and ends that he was moved to discuss." Payton continues, "The diagrammatic plan itself consisted of two major north–south streets running parallel to the Mediterranean . . . as well as three lesser north–south streets. Running east–west were a series of parallel streets creating a more or less rectilinear grid of very large blocks. One of Geddes's important contributions centered on his adaptation of these 'super blocks' which were already well-used to this date, and justified, theoretically, by Unwin in 1912 in his pamphlet: *Nothing Gained by Overcrowding*. By including secondary streets within this version, Geddes departed from the model as it was typically used."[159] Inside each block a collection of short and narrow streets known as "home ways" surrounded a modest, centrally located public park.

Geddes did not specify the types of houses to be built in the garden city of Tel Aviv, but envisioned that the majority would be detached single-family houses with both front and rear gardens. Commercial and civic facilities were to be placed throughout the site. Geddes, who spent two months in Tel Aviv and an additional five back in Edinburgh working on the project, was in correspondence with Lewis Mumford at the time and the two discussed the project. Mumford, who described himself as "a disciple of Patrick Geddes," in turn solicited the advice of Clarence Stein, who recommended the introduction of culs-de-sac in the plan, an idea that Geddes rejected.[160]

Geddes's plan was quickly adopted by the Tel Aviv town council, but the rapid, dramatic influx of new immigrants resulted in a much denser development composed primarily of multistory apartment buildings, the majority designed by European-born architects working under the influence of the Neue Sachlichkeit. By 1934, the same year that Tel Aviv was declared an independent city, its population reached 80,000 residents, a number that would nearly double to 150,000 only three years later, leading to a reworking of the Geddes plan in 1938, six years after his death.

GREECE

The first attempt in Greece to build a town inspired by the Garden City movement was born of crisis.[161] Between 1916 and the end of World War I, the occupying Bulgarian army leveled 170 villages in Eastern Macedonia in northern Greece. After the war, Greece's ruling Liberal Party placed the Ministry of Communications, headed by sociologist Alexandros Papanastasiou (1876–1936), in charge of their reconstruction. In February 1919 Papanastasiou, a housing advocate who had studied and lived in Berlin and London for seven years, selected British town planner John William Mawson (1886–1966), son of prominent landscape architect Thomas Mawson, who had worked in Greece, to oversee the newly created Service for Reconstruction. Mawson's ambitious mandate was to quickly rebuild between 130 and 150 towns, construct over 12,000 houses, and, at the same time, "create something in Macedonia to which the whole world will look with admiration."[162] With the help of his father, he recruited European architects to prepare the town plans, expecting that more than 500 architects, civil engineers, and construction workers would ultimately be employed by the Service for Reconstruction.

In a flurry of activity between 1919 and 1920, several town plans were produced. English architect Harold Fletcher Trew (1888–1968) prepared similar schemes for **Lakkovikia, New Doiran**, and **Karadza Kadi**, each featuring central civic and commercial areas surrounded by single-family houses with gardens located on interconnected curving streets cut by wide boulevards extending through the site. Each of the three plans included parks and landscaped parcels placed throughout the site. The compact plan for **Koumli** by Scottish architect Morrison Hendry (1893–1952) closely resembled Trew's scheme for Karadza Kadi. British architect Piet de Jong (1887–1967) and French architect Ernest Hébrard (1875–1933) collaborated on the more formal plan for **Jumaya**, employing a denser, gridded arrangement that for the most part eschewed curved streets. The defeat of the Liberal Party by the People's Party in the December 1920 elections abruptly put an end to the progressive program before any towns could be realized.

In her assessment of the schemes produced under Mawson's direction, architectural historian Kiki Kafkoula has written that "the plans of the villages are testimony of a garden-city approach to town design, with their layout, the elaboration of the open spaces, the tree planting, and the public utility services."[163] Although designed by different architects, "there is an overall unifying element: the careful consideration of the central areas, which are designed and landscaped with the greatest care, with sites reserved for school, church, town hall, shops and public gardens." Kafkoula also pointed out that this approach represented a decisive break with Greek town-planning tradition: "The street plans that were produced reflect a knowledge of layout standards, making a sharp contrast with the contemporary Greek plans of the time. Although connections with European planning thought were firmly rooted, they had not resulted in any updating of professional training. Drawing up plans 'on garden city' lines was not included in the curriculum of the newly founded School of Architecture."[164] Mawson and his team of architects left Greece after 1920, but in the early 1930s, with the Liberal Party once again in control of the government, some elements of de Jong and Hébrard's plan for Jumaya (now known as Heracleia) were used in its reconstruction, including the adoption of the detached single-family house with garden as the principal building type.

Lakkovikia

1. Plan, Harold Fletcher Trew,
1919–20. KK

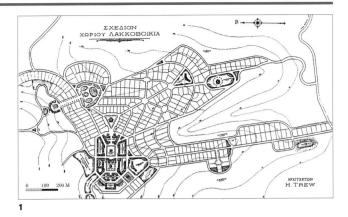

1

New Doiran

1. Plan, Harold Fletcher Trew,
1919–20. KK

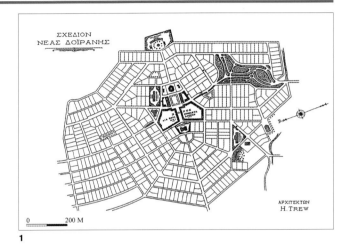

1

Karadza Kadi

1. Plan, Harold Fletcher Trew,
1919–20. KK

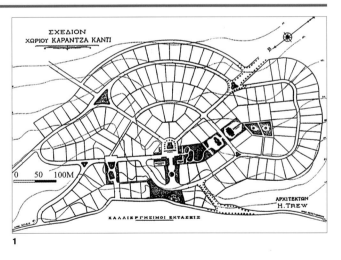

1

The next attempt to develop planned garden suburbs, precipitated by a major shift in population, was more successful.[165] Until the catastrophic effects of the Greco-Turkish War (1919–22), in which a decisive Turkish victory resulted in a flood of more than one million refugees pouring into the country, Greek cities, including the capital, Athens, though they had their fair share of dilapidated and substandard housing units, were not particularly overcrowded. But after the Turkish conflict, which coincided with the return of many ethnic Greeks from Bulgaria, Yugoslavia, and Russia, the increased population density of Greek cities became a serious

problem. In 1923, in an attempt to address the issue, a group based in Athens was established to promote the construction of Agropoles (Garden Cities). That same year the Greek legislature passed a law encouraging the formation of housing cooperatives by making it easier for such groups to purchase land and obtain loans.

Although the garden suburbs that were built were geared almost exclusively to the middle and upper classes, the Greek government, through its Ministry of Social Welfare, was able to complete one project intended for homeless refugees.[166] **New Philadelphia** (1923), located five miles north of Athens, was designed by an anonymous engineer on the ministry's staff and featured a plan composed of a large elliptical section with a circular plaza at its center from which radiating boulevards led to gridded parcels. The majority of the housing for the suburb's 1,800 families consisted of two-story, four-family houses with rear allotment gardens for the ground-floor tenants.

Psychiko (1923), located three miles northeast of Athens, was developed by the Kekrops Company, a private real estate firm with large holdings in the area, in partnership with several local banks, and was intended from the outset for the upper middle class and wealthy.[167] D. Diamandidis (1871–1926), an engineer who was the director of Kekrops, selected architect Alexandros Nikoloudis (1874–1944), who had studied at the École des Beaux-Arts in Paris, to prepare the plan for the 230-acre site.

Nikoloudis's plan, according to architectural historian Dimitri Philippides, consisted of five squares connected "through a network of straight and curved streets, a popular scheme in Europe at the time but unknown in Greece."[168] At the heart of the plan a large hippodrome-like pattern of streets was bisected by a wide, tree-lined north–south boulevard that terminated in landscaped *rond-points* from which streets radiated, in some cases leading to other grassy circles and dividing parts of the site into pie-shaped sections connected by curving streets. Nikoloudis carved out about 1,000 lots intended exclusively for detached single-family houses with gardens, each occupying a minimum of 550 square meters, or about eight houses per acre, but with many significantly larger plots intended for substantial villas.

Although primarily residential, Psychiko was also planned to allow for several commercial and civic facilities to be scattered throughout the site, including a church, two schools, stores, restaurants, a hotel, and a casino with an open-air dance hall. Nikoloudis set aside a generous 75 acres for parks and recreational space, leading Philippides to speculate that the developers seem "to have been eager to imitate the rich pine-tree covered summer resorts such as Kifissia, further away from Athens."[169] Located beyond the reaches of Athens' electric tram network, Psychiko was linked to the city center by bus.

The Kekrops Company sold plots to individuals who would build their own houses, placing few restrictions on their design but setting height limits of three stories. By 1927, 150 lots had been sold but the pace of construction was slow and the population only numbered 390 in 1928. The houses, chiefly built of stone from a local quarry owned by the real estate company, were designed in a wide variety of styles, including Modernist villas beginning in the mid-1930s. Although the hotel was not built, the suburb did include several stores, a café, a church, and two prestigious private schools that helped to cement its high-end reputation. The casino was also completed, only to be demolished during World War II. Psychiko, which grew to 2,377 residents by 1940, was developed more intensively after the war.

New Psychiko (1929), located on a 93-acre parcel directly southeast of Psychiko, was intended for a less affluent population, primarily middle-class civil servants and military personnel who banded together, with the help of the municipal government, to form a cooperative to develop the site, formerly occupied by farms and woods.[170] The plan, by an unidentified civil engineer, was primarily arranged in an irregular grid but also included, at the southern end of the site, a landscaped *rond-point* with radiating streets, one of which connected to Psychiko's main boulevard. Dimitri Philippides deemed this feature "a half-hearted attempt to imitate [the] street pattern" of its tonier neighbor.[171]

The Co-operative of Civil Employees and Army Officers sold individual, modestly sized plots at New Psychiko, but most residents were unable to afford the expense of an architect so "civil engineers, contractors, or even the owners themselves undertook construction" of the one- and two-story single-family houses. As Philippides has pointed out, "Visually this architecture contrasts sharply with that found" in Psychiko; "on the other hand, it is typical of the majority of the housing in Athens."[172] New Psychiko also included a town square composed of stores, restaurants, and a church located near the *rond-point*, but because the development lacked strict building regulations additional commercial facilities and even light industry were scattered throughout the site.

Philothei (1931), a cooperative housing development sponsored by the National Bank of Greece and intended for its employees, was located directly north of Psychiko on a somewhat hilly 284-acre site.[173] Konstantinos Zoumboulidis (n.d.), a bank employee who had studied architecture at the School of Fine Arts in Constantinople and the Technische Universität Berlin, prepared a plan that in many ways resembled Nikoloudis's scheme for Psychiko, with generous amounts of park space, curving tree-lined streets, landscaped *rond-points*, and large single-family house lots that on average measured 1,500 square meters, with a minimum of 550 square meters. The plan's modest, nonresidential component included two small food markets, a few shops, a church, an elementary school, a gym, and a theater.

As Kafkoula has pointed out, the "architectural identity of Philothei was given special character. Greek architects were invited to participate in a kind of competition, which produced the models for the houses to be built. In the words of the competition text, the future

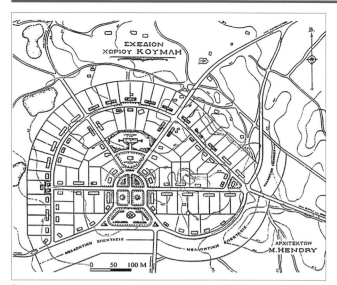

1. Plan, Morrison Hendry, 1919–20. KK

Jumaya

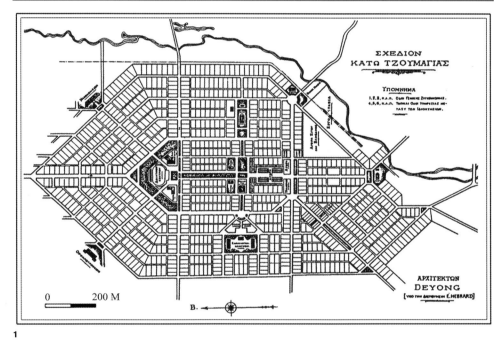

1

2

1. Plan, Piet de Jong and Ernest Hébrard, 1919–20. KK

2. Houses, early 1930s. Kafkoula. KK (c. 1993)

1. Plan, 1923. KK

2. Aerial view. KK (1932)

3. Typical street. Kafkoula. KK (1991)

Psychiko

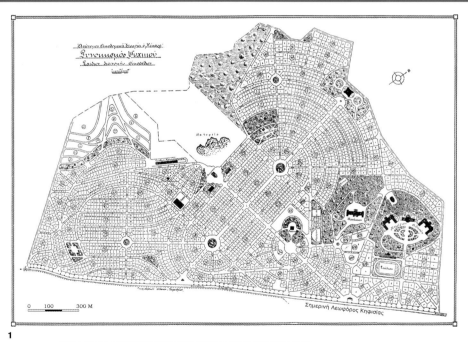

1. Plan, Alexandros Nikoloudis, 1923. KK

2. Typical villa. Kafkoula. KK (1996)

3, 4. Typical streets. Yerolymbos. YY (2012)

New Psychiko

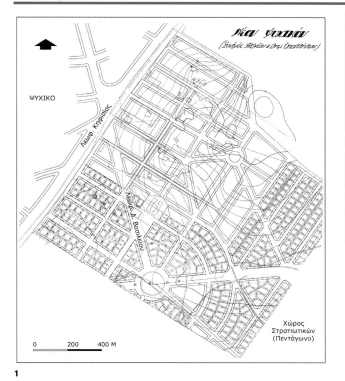

1

2

1. Plan, 1929. KK

2. Aerial view. GE (2007)

Philothei

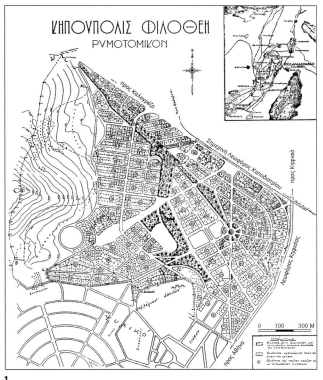

1

2

3

1. Plan, Konstantinos Zoumboulidis, 1931. KK

2, 3. Typical streets. HBAA

4–6. Typical streets. Yerolymbos. YY (2012)

4

5

6

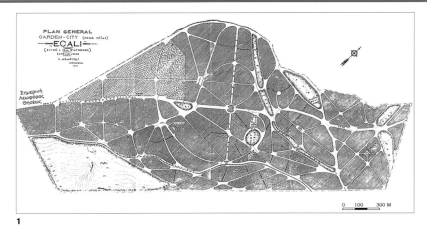

1

2

3

4

houses should 'avoid useless ornament' and opt for 'the serene and plastic expression of volumes, the austere lines, the simple and quiet architectural forms of the country, so as to avoid the exposition of architectural rhythms that are in disharmony with the local character and the grace, the balance, the transparency, and the nobleness of the Attican landscape.'" A jury selected forty-one house models designed by such Athens-based architects as Panos Tzelepis (1894–1978), Georges Kontoleon (1896–1952), and Kimon Laskaris (1905–1978). The approved styles ranged "from simple bungalows echoing island villages or two-story vernacular houses of the Greek highlands to urban houses on the lines of the modern movement."[174] Members would be given the opportunity to choose both a house model and plot of land. After first completing the necessary infrastructure and planting 70,000 trees and bushes, 247 houses were built between 1933 and 1935. Development slowed after that point, in large part due to the high cost of the house lots, but after the war, when the cooperative was expanded to include newspaper employees, another 100 houses were completed.

Ekali (1922), Athens's northernmost planned garden suburb, was located on a rural, wooded 240-acre site at the foot of Pentelli Mountain, eight miles northeast of Philothei and fourteen miles from the city center.[175] Like Psychiko, Ekali was developed by a private real estate company intent on building detached, single-family houses for the upper middle class and wealthy.

The picturesque site was selected by the civil engineer responsible for the plan, Spilios T. Agapitos (1877–1943), who had represented Greece at the Fourth International Conference of the International Federation for Housing and Planning held in London in 1920, seven years after the organization's founding by Ebenezer Howard. Agapitos's plan was more casual and less geometric than the schemes for Psychiko, New Psychiko, and Philothei, with a loose arrangement of curving streets that followed the topography of the site. Landscaped *rond-points* were distributed throughout the site, with the central one home to a modest civic and commercial area composed of a food market, two restaurants, a hotel, a police station, an elementary school, and a church. Agapitos included several parks and left untouched an adjacent 62-acre forest.

House lots in Ekali were large, with a minimum established of 1,000 square meters, or about double the size of the smallest plots at Psychiko and Philothei. The developers built a few houses on a speculative basis but the majority of lots were sold unimproved, with buyers commissioning their own houses from such local architects as Andreas Kriezis (1880–1967), who also designed a substantial villa for his own use. Ekali developed slowly, a pace attributed to its distance from central Athens and the high price of lots. In 1928 the suburb numbered 206 residents, growing to a population of 708 by 1940. Nikos Vatopoulos has praised Ekali's "inward-looking layout" and its "small round squares, into which run peaceful, shady roads bearing the names of gods,

1

2

mountains and plants," resulting in a town "which combined a romantic natural environment with suburban architecture."[176]

Ilioupoli (1925), a privately developed garden suburb intended for the middle class, was built seven miles southeast of downtown Athens on a tract formerly occupied by farms.[177] The distinctive plan by architect Aristomenis Valvis (n.d.) was dominated by four round landscaped plazas of varying sizes that were surrounded by civic and commercial facilities and rings of single-family houses. Placed in close proximity to each other, these plazas were connected by radiating boulevards. On the eastern and western ends of the site, Valvis replaced the circular forms with a gridded arrangement. A greenbelt surrounded the site on all but its western side, and parks and recreational areas were scattered throughout the suburb.

RUSSIA

In Russia, the first development inspired by Howard and the Garden City movement was **Kaiserwald** (forest park) **Garden Suburb** (1902), located about four miles north of Riga, Latvia, under Russian control since the early eighteenth century, a political reality that would remain in place until Latvian independence in 1918.[178] Riga, the third largest city in the Russian empire after Moscow and St. Petersburg, was home to a large number of Baltic Germans who constituted the civic, commercial, and cultural elite, with German the official administrative language of the capital city until 1891 when Tsar Alexander III instituted a policy of Russification in the Baltic provinces. The driving force behind the project was Riga mayor George Armitstead (1847–1912)—his grandfather was from Yorkshire, England, and his mother was Russian—who established the Riga Building Society, a nonprofit housing association that partnered with the

municipal government to finance and build the suburb, initially intended to house workers and their families but quickly reimagined due to economic considerations as a leafy subdivision for the German-speaking middle and upper-middle classes.

Adolf Agte (1850–1906), chief engineer of Riga, selected Kaiserwald Garden Suburb's 100-acre site overlooking Lake Kisezers in the middle of a 2,500-acre pine forest that formed a natural greenbelt. Agte also oversaw the extension of the Electric Tramcar Company's line to the northern border of the site, resulting in a twenty-six-minute commute to the city center. Landscape architect Georg Kuphalt (1853–1938), director of Riga's parks, drew up the plan, dividing the site into one-half-acre lots on average, primarily intended for detached single-family houses. Kuphalt's network of curving, picturesque streets followed the contours of the site. In addition to the vast forest surrounding the site, Kuphalt included several public parks within the subdivision's borders, as well as a 40-acre Zoological Garden (1912), the first in the Baltic provinces, and a recreational facility and a sanatorium along the shores of the lake. A modest civic and commercial center was located near the tram station.

The Riga Building Society sold plots to individuals and by 1910 eighty-three villas had been completed. The majority were designed by three local architects, Rudolf Dohnberg (1864–1918), August Witte (1876–1969), and Oskar Bars (1848–1913), in a Gothic Revival style inspired, according to historian Irene Bakule, by Andrew Jackson Downing's 1842 pattern book, *Cottage Residences*.[179] Along Stockholm Street, Riga-based architect Gerhard von Tiesenhausen (1878–1917) designed twenty semidetached two-family houses (1911) for lower-middle-class families. Successful from the start, Kaiserwald Garden Suburb was expanded after 1911, with twenty-five additional villas completed before the start of the war on a gridded parcel laid out by Berlin architect and town planner Hermann Jansen (1869–1945).

1. Plan, Aristomenis Valvis, 1925. PT

2. Aerial view. KK

1

2

3

4

5

1. Bird's-eye view. GCTP22

2. Villa Wasa. MNA

3, 4. Typical streets. Kublins. IK (2012)

5. Tram. CRS

Stanley Buder has taken note of Kaiserwald Garden Suburb's unusual pedigree: "Occupied by middle-class Germans, it presented the remarkable sight of an English-appearing community whose residents spoke German while living in Latvia under Russian rule."[180] According to historian S. Frederick Starr, "Embodying garden city notions on density, building regulations, and parks, and replacing the 'corridor street' with gently curving avenues, this village was at the same time lacking in both the social facilities and the productive function which lay at the heart of Howard's scheme."[181] A third, complementary wave of building took place between 1928 and 1932 in what was now known as Mežaparks (forest park), the Latvian name for the suburb coined after independence. After World War II, when the Russians again took control of Latvia, the Soviet government confiscated the suburb's privately owned villas, allowing the majority of them to deteriorate through neglect although some have recently been restored.

In the heart of Russia, the first public discussion of Ebenezer Howard and the Garden City movement took place in 1904 when *Zodchii* (The Architect), a journal sponsored by the St. Petersburg Society of Architects, published the article "Goroda sady" (garden cities).[182] Two years later, after the Revolution of 1905 led to the seating of the first Duma (parliament), legislation was introduced, but ultimately not passed, that would have provided state support for workers' villages to be built

outside the overcrowded cities of Moscow and St. Petersburg. In 1908 St. Petersburg architect M. G. Dikanskii (n.d.) provided the first detailed examination of Howard's ideas and how they might apply to Russia, praising the Englishman for his "non utopian" approach: "Howard does not make the usual mistake . . . of assuming life can be stopped, crystallized, where in reality it turns in perpetual movement, always gradually modifying established relationships, especially through the latest exceptional successes of technology."[183] Dikanskii concluded that Russia would greatly benefit from "a planning policy based on low density, cooperative settlement."[184]

In 1909, a group of thirty Russians joined a tour of English suburbs led by the German Garden City Association. Inspired by the visit, St. Petersburg lawyer Dmitrii Protopopov (1864?–1918) founded the journal *Gorodskoe Delo* (The Urban Question), Russia's first magazine to focus on town planning issues. As Protopopov wrote in its pages in 1909: "It is not just for fresh air and greenery that people want to move to garden cities. They want more: a more integrated, friendly, straightforward life, less conflict, more institutions for the common good, new legal and economic forms."[185] A second St. Petersburg lawyer, Alexander Bloch (1868?–1955), also drew inspiration from the same tour of British suburbs. In 1911 Bloch completed the first translation of Howard's *Garden Cities of To-morrow* into Russian. Howard wrote an introduction to the edition, optimistically predicting

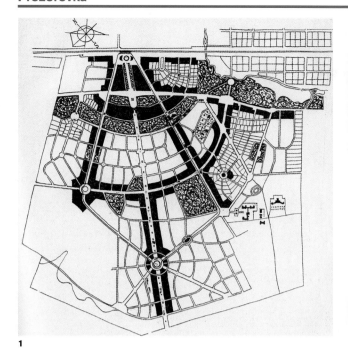

1. Plan, Vladimir Semionov, 1912. KUS

2. Cottage. Skvortsov. SKV (2012)

3. Civic area showing hospital on right. Skvortsov. SKV (2012)

that "Russia with its vast space of scarcely populated land will long serve as the arena of a series of truly brilliant experiments in the field of systematic town planning."[186] That same year the Imperial Academy of Fine Arts in St. Petersburg created the country's first professorship in town planning, and in 1913 Protopopov and Bloch joined forces to form the Russian Garden City Society.

Perhaps the most influential voice to promote the Garden City idea in Russia belonged to architect and engineer Vladimir Semionov (1874–1960). Semionov lived in England from 1908 to 1912 where he was introduced to Howard in 1909 and also worked briefly for Raymond Unwin. Upon his return to St. Petersburg, he published *Blagoustroistvo Gorodov* (The Planning of Towns), which architect and historian Catherine Cooke has described as "the canonical work of Russian and early Soviet town planning . . . a shattering indictment of the primitiveness and anarchy of urban development in Russia, where booming industrialization was creating hundreds of new towns 'planned' only by land surveyors."[187] Like Howard, Semionov was confident about the possibility of building garden cities in Russia.

Semionov was given an opportunity to translate his ideas into practice when he was commissioned to prepare the plan for **Prozorovka** (1912–13), a garden city twenty-five miles southeast of Moscow, a somewhat surprising location given that the most vocal advocates of the movement were based in St. Petersburg.[188] The development was the brainchild of Nikolai von Meck (1863–1929), owner of the Moscow-Kazan Railway Company, who extended his railroad line to the heavily wooded, 1,700-acre site surrounded by farmland. Von Meck hired British engineers for the expansion and, as a result, trains passed each other on the right according to English practice. Prozorovka was intended primarily but not exclusively for railroad employees.

Semionov's radial plan, with a prominent civic and commercial center, numerous parks, and a greenbelt, was clearly indebted to Howard's example, although at no time was an industrial component contemplated, a decision heavily criticized by members of the Russian Garden City Society who feared that without an economic base of its own, the town would be "kept in bondage" by the railroad company and too dependent on Moscow's influence.[189] Still, the plan itself was warmly embraced by some Garden City advocates, with M. G. Dikanskii praising it as an example of "the best modern town planning principles."[190]

Cooke has described the ambitious scope of Semionov's plan, prepared in collaboration with Armenian architect Aleksandr I. Tamanov (1878–1936): "There was a 'ventilation' system of green spaces linked to green belts and the town's own agricultural surroundings. The plan was designed for expansion. There was a four-level hierarchy of different sized circulation routes, designed to give all housing areas an equal accessibility to a wholly exceptional range of community facilities."[191] These civic and commercial facilities, primarily located along and near the broad tree-lined thoroughfare that bisected the site, were to include a town hall with a theater, a public library, a hospital, a church, a bank, restaurants, and stores. Public baths and communal laundries, along with three kindergartens, three elementary schools, and separate high schools for boys and girls were to be placed throughout the site. In order to facilitate travel between the many public services, an intra-town tram line, which would also connect to the commuter railroad station, was planned for roughly the center of the site. In addition to the 420-acre greenbelt and 131 acres of landscaped space within the town, recreational facilities were to be located along a lake as well as along the shores of the Moscow River.

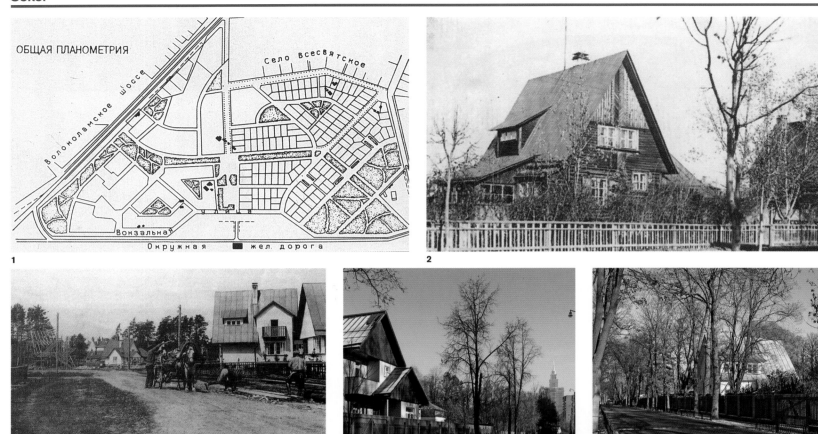

1. Plan, Nikolai Markovnikov, 1923. SDC

2. Typical house. SDC

3. Surikova Street. SDC (1928)

4, 5. Typical streets. Koltsov. EK (2008)

Semionov allotted 827 acres for the housing, dividing the site into large plots that on average measured about half an acre. The one-, two-, and four-family houses, primarily one- and two-story vernacular cottages located along curving, interconnected tree-lined streets, were to feature private allotment gardens for each tenant, with the houses to remain the property of the railroad company. Stanley Buder has described the scheme as an attempt to combine "Unwin's principles of street planning with traditional wooden cottage housing."[192]

Despite the sponsorship of the Moscow-Kazan Railway Company, progress at Prozorovka was partially stymied by state authorities. As Protopopov and Bloch reported to the readers of the London-based journal *Garden Cities and Town Planning* in July 1914, one month after the assassination of Archduke Franz Ferdinand of Austria and one month before the beginning of the war: "Strange as it may seem, the Government views the idea of a garden city with suspicion. For instance, the project of a garden city for the employees of the Moscow-Kazan Railway . . . for which the railway had contributed 6,000,000 roubles and the realization of which had already begun, was buried in the Government offices."[193]

The burdens of the war, followed by the chaos surrounding the Bolshevik Revolution in 1917, only served to further impede the realization of Semionov's plans. Several elements, however, were completed, including the "very broad ornamental" main thoroughfare, as Etienne De Groër noted in 1922, as well as the tram

network and a few of the planned areas of housing.[194] Only a modest amount of the civic component was completed. Post-Revolution development at Prozorovka, now known as Kratovo, did not follow the original plan.

In 1918, after falling out of favor with the new regime, the Russian Garden City Society disbanded. There were still optimists who believed that the Socialist state might provide the perfect proving ground for Howard's ideas. In 1922, the society was resurrected, this time with the support of the government and with a base of operations in Moscow instead of St. Petersburg. According to historian Timothy J. Colton, there was quickly "talk of a dozen or more garden towns around Moscow," but only one project, **Sokol** (1923), was able to move forward, a meager success rate that he attributed to a lack of support from the ideological and cultural elite: "The garden city fell between stools. It did not suit the politically engaged intellectuals who befriended avant-garde policies. To their way of thinking, sodalities of prim, picket-fenced, single-family English cottages were either boring or morally dubious."[195]

Located seven miles northwest of Moscow, Sokol was sponsored by the municipal government and intended for mid- and upper-level civil servants expected to commute to the city center via an existing tram line.[196] Nikolai Markovnikov (1869–1942), who had recently overseen the renovation of the Kremlin, was responsible for the plan as well as the design of the housing. Inspired by English garden suburb design,

1. Aerial view. GE (2009)

2. Hudec residence, 57 Columbia Road, László Hudec, 1933. UVL (c. 1935)

3, 4. Typical views. Best. AB (2007)

Markovnikov laid out the 148-acre site with curving tree-lined streets and generous amounts of green space, including public parks, planted medians, and triangular landscaped parcels marking many street intersections. Sokol was planned exclusively for detached, single-family houses with gardens, with lots that measured between 6,500 and 8,600 square feet.

Sokol was initially beset by construction delays and cost overruns, but by 1929 100 one- and two-story cottages, the majority set behind picket fences, had been completed, designed in a variety of rural vernacular styles. In addition to the anticipated government workers, the picturesque suburb attracted artists and academics. Contemporary critical reaction was decidedly negative, led by those who believed that the low-density project represented an inefficient use of government resources. As planning historian Helen Meller has pointed out, Sokol "had been designed on such a scale of lavishness that there was no likelihood that a programme of garden cities in a similar style could follow . . . The costs of the infrastructure of low-rise building, especially roads with wide verges as demonstrated by the Sokol experiment . . . gave victory" to the proponents of high-density, high-rise residential development. Subsequent construction in and around Moscow was therefore dominated by large-scale apartment blocks and by the end of the 1920s, "Howard's ideas were castigated as hopelessly bourgeois" by a majority of the planners, architects, and government officials who determined housing policy.[197]

CHINA

Columbia Circle (1928–30), a unique example of the garden enclave type in Shanghai, China, was designed by a Hungarian architect, László Hudec (1893–1958), a member of the Royal Institute of Hungarian Architects who, while serving during World War I as a lieutenant in the Austro-Hungarian army, escaped Siberian captivity in 1918 by jumping from a train during a prison camp transfer, eventually finding his way to China where he was able to resume work as an architect.[198] Columbia Circle was developed by the Asia Realty Company, whose founder, a Californian named Frank Jay Raven (1875–1943), had a rather colorful history of his own, having moved to Shanghai in 1904 to work as a civil engineer in the Public Works Department, where he stayed on only long enough to learn the location of planned new roads before resigning to use the information for a fledgling real estate development venture. The somewhat duplicitous nature of Raven's early dealings would persist as his real estate and banking activities expanded, eventually unraveling and landing him in prison for embezzlement in 1935. Hudec was hired to design Columbia Circle by Hugo Sandor, general manager of the Asia Realty Company and a fellow Hungarian. The enclave was originally situated on Shanghai's western outskirts but is now embedded within the city's dense urbanism west of the intersection of Fanyulu and Xinhualu. Hudec's plan placed seventy detached single-family houses along a U-shaped road

1. Plan, Ernest Hébrard, 1923.
ILL23

2. Langbian Palace Hotel. CRS

3. Typical view. CRS (c. 1930)

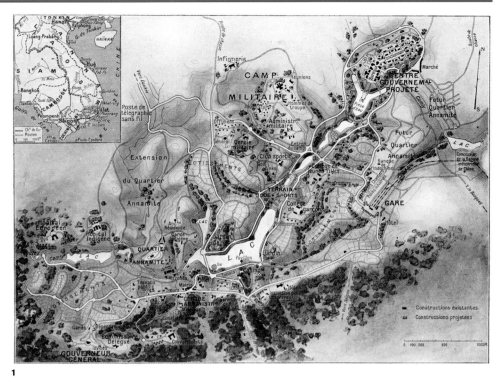

and a single cul-de-sac leading to the block interior. The enclave was marketed to foreigners as an "estate designed for garden homes," built "with a full appreciation of the business man's need for quiet after a day spent amidst the work and worry of money getting."[199] Hudec designed thirteen house variations based on English, American, Italian, and Spanish architectural styles. Many of the houses remain, despite having been subdivided to accommodate multiple units. The site's suburban character has been encroached upon by mid-rise apartment buildings and nearby industrial and high-rise development.

VIETNAM

Of the numerous urban planning projects carried out by the French during the period of colonial rule in Vietnam,

the garden suburb made only a brief appearance in plans for the summer capital of **Dalat** (1923), a so-called "hill station," or *station d'altitude*, in the southern Central Highlands where, like similar villages established by the British in India, colonists could enjoy a cool, healthy retreat during the hot summer months.[200] Intended to be equal parts government center and resort, Dalat occupied a beautiful plateau in the Truong Son Mountains, 300 kilometers north of Saigon (now Ho Chi Minh City), first encountered by the French in 1893, who admired its dramatic views, winding ridges, hills, basins, and stretches of flat land perfectly suited to building. Initial efforts to establish the site as a sanatorium crawled along, in part because access was so difficult but also because the governor-general in charge of the project was recalled to France in 1901. Plans soon followed for a military camp, but the sketchy layout, drawn by military surveyor Paul

4. Aerial view. URB35 (c. 1935)

5, 6. Tran Hung Dao Street. Selwyn.
WC (2011)

4

5   6

Champoudry (n.d.) in 1905, was only partially adhered
to and development remained sporadic and unregulated. Things changed with the construction of new roads
to the site in the 1910s. By the close of World War I, the
outpost's popularity among Western, Vietnamese, and
Chinese tourists inspired the French government, "convinced that Dalat was destined to continue its growth,"[201]
to ask French architect Ernest Hébrard to take control of
the town's physical development and plan for its transformation into what historian Eric T. Jennings has called a
"sheltered French micro-universe."[202]

Hébrard completed his plan in 1923. Because earlier development had been so haphazard, according to
Robert R. Reed, he "enjoyed an almost free rein in com-
posing a scheme that conformed to the terrain, blended
with the framework of natural vegetation, fostered
orderly expansion through effective zoning and allowed

for appropriate growth without destroying Dalat's
natural beauty."[203] For Gwendolyn Wright, however,
Hébrard's design fell short in crucial ways: "The surveying he requested proved to be of poor quality, and since
he never seems to have visited the site himself," working from previous surveys, "Hébrard failed to take into
account many of the splendid panoramic views."[204]

Hébrard provided separate zones for a military
camp, medical complex, an administrative center with
religious, educational, and commercial buildings, and
a tourist district with a golf course, tennis courts, and
athletic fields, as well as a zoo, theater, casino, hotel, and
parks that added to the recreational possibilities. Footpaths, bridle trails, and hunting roads wove through
preserved sections of forest and an artificial lake occupied a central position. Schools and churches were
provided for longer-term residents. The concept of an

exclusive resort for the French was intrinsic. Industry and commerce were kept to a minimum and the housing was segregated, placing residences for the French on ridges and hilltops and for the Vietnamese in the lowlands, where houses were nonetheless grouped in picturesque clusters, sparing the Europeans "any evidence of poverty or industry."[205] Design guidelines controlled building height, construction materials, and lot sizes.

Although Hébrard's design was in step with contemporary international planning trends, according to Wright, it did not necessarily sit well with colonists, who resented "its insistence on zoning and design guidelines, curtailing the absolute freedom many Frenchmen believed to be their right, especially in the colonies. Only from Paris would he hear praise, and this precisely because of the progressive demands for such controls."[206] Development was slow during the 1920s and plans for the government buildings were scrapped. After the completion of the railroad in the early 1930s, however, Dalat flourished, following a 1932 plan by Louis-Georges Pineau (1898–1987), a consulting architect and planner for the Indochina government who retained the basic spirit of Hébrard's design. By 1949, more than 1,000 houses had been built in evocation of the countryside of southern France. By the 1980s the population had topped 100,000.

JAPAN

In 1918 Eiichi Shibusawa (1840–1931), a prominent Tokyo-based industrialist credited with bringing Western-style capitalism to Japan with the founding of the Tokyo Stock Exchange and the introduction of double-entry bookkeeping, established the Garden City Company (Denentoshi Kabushiki-gaisha), intended to create a residential development based on the English model and the writings of Ebenezer Howard.[207] Shibusawa's interest in the Garden City movement, inspired and cultivated by frequent visits to Europe, was shared by others in Japan, especially after a 1907 article in Tokyo's leading newspaper extolled the movement as a way to relieve overcrowding in the city where the population had more than tripled in the past thirty years. That same year the Local Government Bureau of the Home Ministry published *Garden City* (*Denen Toshi*), a book about the subject that included Howard's diagrams from *Garden Cities of To-morrow*.

Shibusawa and his partners at the Garden City Company, culled from the ranks of leading Japanese businessmen, purchased 325 acres of undeveloped farmland along the Tama River about seven-and-a-half miles southwest of central Tokyo to build **Denenchōfu** (garden suburb). Although inspired by Howard's ideals, and believing that the undertaking should be considered an act of philanthropy, Shibusawa had no intention of creating a self-sufficient communal development with a significant industrial and commercial component that would be populated by a range of classes. Instead, he imagined a leafy garden suburb composed of middle- and upper-middle-class commuters who would purchase lots and build their own houses.

Shibusawa's first move was to secure permission to build a rail connection from downtown Tokyo to the site. He then sent his son Hideo (1892–1984) on a seven-month tour of European and American projects for inspiration. In 1919 Hideo reported on his disappointment with Letchworth (see p. 230): "Broad front yards on both sides of the streets were covered with dead leaves. It was a lonely place where I would not dare to live."[208] He was more impressed with St. Francis Wood (see p. 74), an upscale development of detached houses in San Francisco, where the "ruggedness of the wilderness with big trees and many flowers as well as a concentric road pattern like the one around the Arch of Triumph in Paris" appealed to him. He also praised the curvilinear streets, writing that "a street with a curve has no perspectival vanishing point, and consequently engenders a sense of curiosity and embrace's one's dreams."[209]

Acting on the recommendation of Hideo Shibusawa, Kintaro Yabe (n.d.), an architect on the Home Ministry's staff, was hired to prepare Denenchōfu's plan. Yabe's scheme (1920) of connecting ring and radial roads represented a radical departure from Japanese tradition, as architectural historian Ken Tadashi Oshima has pointed out: "The geometric clarity of Denenchōfu's radial plan was unprecedented in residential neighborhoods in Japan . . . Nonlinear streets did previously exist in Japan . . . but their layout primarily followed natural contours rather than geometric patterns."[210] The focus of the plan was the railway station and its modest plaza, with the housing located west of the railroad tracks where rings of semicircular streets were cut through by wider diagonal avenues. Irregular house lots averaging about 1,000 square meters, a generous amount for the area around Tokyo, were placed on streets planted with gingko trees. A few shops and restaurants, along with a semicircular pool and bench, were positioned next to the railroad station, but the majority of the civic and commercial section was located east of the railroad tracks. One-half mile southwest of the plaza, Yabe designed a Roman Catholic church and school. A large, heavily wooded public park with a pond was built at the southwest corner of the site next to the banks of the Tama River. The farms otherwise surrounding the site provided a second, quasi-greenbelt until they were extensively developed with housing following the end of World War II.

Historian Jordan Sand has noted the "distinctive" resemblance of Yabe's plan to "Howard's hypothetical map . . . Three broad boulevards radiate from the center, intersecting five semi-circular avenues. Secondary radials project from the second ring out to the fifth. All of this appears to replicate Howard's schema. Although the Japanese garden city possessed none of the social aims and few of the functional features of the English program, it resembled the original diagram more closely than did any of the new towns Howard's vision had

田園都市多摩川
經營地平面圖

1. Plan, Kintaro Yabe, 1920. DEN

2. Aerial view. DEN (1934)

3. Railway station and plaza. DEN (1934)

4. Half-timbered house. DEN (c. 1930)

5. House. Sorensen. SOR (2011)

parented in England and elsewhere."[211] Philip Pregill and Nancy Volkman have posited another influence, describing Denenchōfu's plan as "very close" to John Nolen's scheme for Kingsport, Tennessee (see p. 264).[212]

Construction at Denenchōfu began in 1920 and within three years the streets were laid out and the Meguro-Kamata Electric Railway was able to provide direct service to central Tokyo in about an hour from Kintaro Yabe's new station, planned "to look like a Western-style house with a mansard roof," a design "expressive of the Western-inspired plan."[213] The sale of lots was promoted by a campaign that referred to its ideological origins and Ebenezer Howard's desire to humanely house factory workers but added that this development "has in sight a residential area for members of the intellectual class commuting to the great factory called Tokyo . . . As a result, we were naturally compelled to build a smart suburban residential neighborhood with a high standard of living."[214] In order to control development, the Garden City Company instituted a number of specific requirements regarding building-to-lot ratios, setback distances, and minimum construction costs but also included such vague rules as prohibiting any house "which disturbs its neighbors" and mandating that fences and walls must be "refined and elegant."[215]

Initial attempts to sell plots were disappointing, but the Great Kantō Earthquake of September 1, 1923, which killed over 100,000 people, leveled nearly half of central Tokyo, and destroyed 20 percent of the housing stock, but left Denenchōfu virtually untouched, spurred a boom that lasted until 1928, by which time all of the original 500 house lots had been purchased. The privately commissioned single-family houses with gardens were built in a wide variety of styles, including traditional Japanese designs, Swiss cottages, Edwardian villas, and flat-roofed Modernist houses.

Denenchōfu prospered dramatically, so much so that it quickly shed its middle-class roots to become an affluent garden suburb not unlike St. Francis Wood. Ken Tadashi Oshima has written that Denenchōfu's "completion affirmed the possibility of modernizing and Westernizing the chaotic Japanese townscape. Now one could escape the hustle and bustle of the city and retreat to the solitude of a garden within a small self-contained universe. While Denenchōfu's plan and streetscape had a distinctly European flavor, the project was a Japanese interpretation rather than a foreign one imposed on Japan. Consequently Denenchōfu became extremely popular and eventually gained the reputation of being the premier suburb of Japan."[216]

Despite Denenchōfu's success, as well as a continued demand for spacious detached single-family houses with gardens, no other planned developments adhering to Garden City ideals were built outside of central Tokyo, a situation primarily attributed to the inability of any developer to acquire enough land. As Hideaki Ishikawa (1893–1955), an engineer and planner working for the Home Ministry, noted in a 1930 report titled "Feasibility of the Garden City in Japan," land prices were simply too high to permit the purchase of enough adjacent lots needed for a coordinated town plan.[217] Even the sponsors of Denenchōfu, intended from the outset for prosperous commuters, had always thought of their project as a philanthropic venture whose land costs and infrastructure improvements could not be economically justified. The suburbs that did proliferate outside Tokyo, according to historian André Sorensen, suffered greatly because they lacked the type of planning controls instituted at Denenchōfu, "and the lack of such protections for residential areas became one of the most distinctive characteristics of Japanese suburban development in the post-war [World War I] period."[218]

Osaka, Japan's second largest city, like Tokyo, also witnessed the growth of suburbs to relieve overcrowding, primarily located along extensions of the railroad lines leading to the central city. The housing situation in Osaka, the country's most industrialized city, was rather bleak with an estimated shortage of more than 20,000 dwelling units in 1921, and the condition of much of the housing stock, composed of overcrowded tenements, was deemed "a serious threat to the health, morals, and public discipline of city dwellers."[219] Osaka's new suburbs were primarily sponsored by the Minō Electric Railway Company, which either built new housing or sold plots of land to individuals or developers, allowing the residential developments to grow on a piecemeal basis with little or no thought given to an overall planning strategy.

One notable exception was **Senriyama** (1922), a planned garden suburb located about eight miles north of Osaka.[220] The housing estate, intended for factory workers and low-level clerks, was developed by the Osaka Housing Management Corporation (Osaka Jutaku Keiei Kabushikigaisha), a limited-dividend company founded in 1920 by Hajime Seki (1873–1935), an economist and planner who at the time was also deputy mayor of Osaka, a position he held until 1924, when he became mayor. Limiting shareholder profits to 6 percent, the housing corporation developed the project in partnership with the city of Osaka, the Home Ministry, the Minō Electric Railway Company, as well as several prominent Osaka-based businessmen.

Seki's plan for Senriyama, like that for Denenchōfu, was centered around the railroad station and adjacent public plaza. A wide boulevard with landscaped rondpoint led from the station to the irregularly shaped residential parcels organized as modified grids. Seki divided the site into lots that on average measured 330 square meters, about one-third the size of those in Denenchōfu, but reserved large areas of the hilly site for public parks, playgrounds, and athletic fields. Seki rejected calls for multistory apartment houses, believing that the building type was fundamentally flawed, forcing children to play indoors and discouraging "social harmony" (shakaiteki chowa). "I asked a friend who recently returned from America about the advantages of apartment living," Seki wrote in 1923. "He said they have all

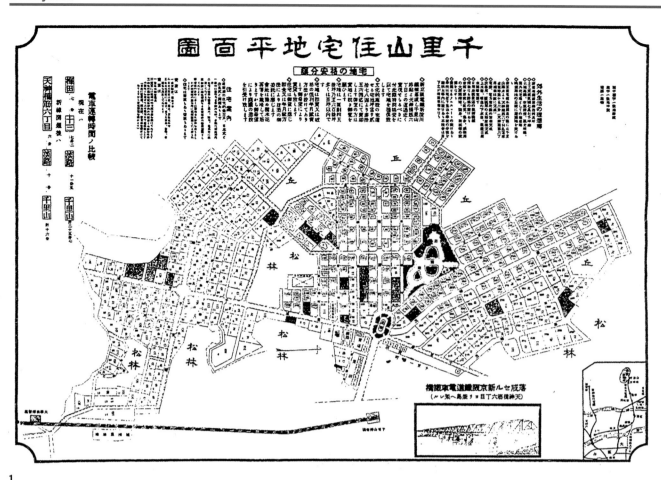

the [necessary] facilities, but that it is difficult to rid oneself of a certain feeling of fatigue. As a result, many [residents] feel the need to escape and go off to the country on weekends."[221] Senriyama was instead developed exclusively with "small houses" (*kojutaku*) with modest gardens. Stores, restaurants, and other commercial and civic facilities were clustered around the railroad station.

Senriyama was successfully marketed by an advertising campaign that urged "unfortunate Osaka citizens" to flee "this smoke-darkened metropolis."[222] By 1924, 438 two-story single-family houses had been completed and rented to workers and their families. Four years later the Osaka Housing Management Corporation disbanded, and the suburb was taken over by the New Keihan Railway Company, which promptly discarded Seki's social vision, developing the parkland with housing and replacing many of the houses with apartment buildings.

CHAPTER EIGHT

The Industrial Garden Village in Europe 1774–1940

The rise of industrialization in late eighteenth-century Europe brought dramatic changes to living patterns, causing vast migrations of agricultural workers to cities that were unable to keep up with the demands for decent housing and sanitation. In an ironic twist, as industrialization attracted rural people to urban centers where jobs were to be had, causing the cities to explode in size, the development of railroads, a principal exemplar of the industrial age, provided a way for the cities to expand into the surrounding countryside, giving rise to the possibilities of suburban living, first for the very rich but soon enough for the working classes. But even before the phenomenon of suburban development took root at the edges of the big cities, formerly agricultural towns situated at significant railroad intersections or near fast-moving rivers that could supply power to mill machinery gave birth to a host of deliberately planned new towns intended for workers, setting in place the idea of the workers' garden village that would become, beginning in the later nineteenth century and extending until World War II, a significant phenomenon of enlightened urbanism. As evolved, the industrial garden village puts the lie to the claim that the garden suburb is an exclusive phenomenon of bourgeois life.

The industrial garden village has close connections to the utopistic ambitions of Robert Owen's New Lanark, on the River Clyde, near Glasgow, Scotland. Though more "a social experiment than an architectural conception," New Lanark was the first utopistic new town to be realized in the industrial age.[1] Owen was a self-made textile entrepreneur who, purchasing the New Lanark mill, established in 1785, from his father-in-law, David Dale, significantly improved the lot of his factory workers through social and educational reforms beginning in the late 1790s and continuing into the new century. Owen's dream of a model industrial society was widely disseminated, making a strong impact through the publication of his book, *A New Vision of Society* (1813), and his *Report to the Committee for the Relief of the Manufacturing Poor* (1817), proposing the construction of industrial villages housing between 500 and 1,500 people on 1,235-acre sites surrounded by 1,000 to 1,500 acres of agricultural land. To illustrate his ideas, Owen prepared a perspective drawing of a monastery-like structure that was more a diagram than a design, consisting of a four-square range of houses bounding a central open space containing the village's communal facilities—one building for cooking and eating and two others for lecture halls, libraries, a nursery, and schools. While Owen's so-called **Agricultural and Manufacturing Villages of Unity and Mutual Cooperation** were not realized, the example of his success at New Lanark and his arguments on behalf of decentralized manufacturing were not lost on the business community, which accepted his claims that well-housed workers were more productive. A number of disciples tried to realize Owen's ideas in the United States, most notably at New Harmony, Indiana (see p. 205), but these experiments failed.

1. Bird's-eye view. (1818)

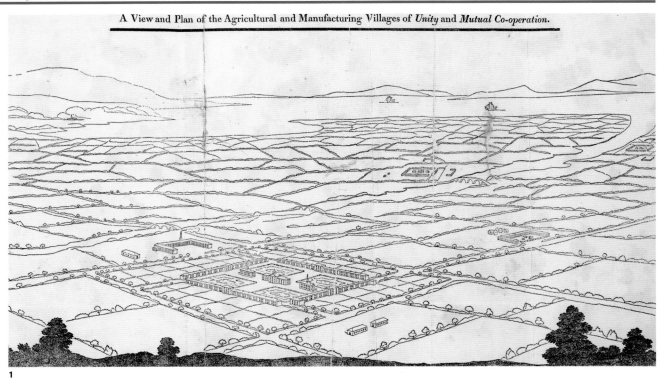

A View and Plan of the Agricultural and Manufacturing Villages of *Unity* and *Mutual Co-operation.*

1

Cromford

1. Aerial view. Bird. GEO (2008)

1

Belper

1. Long Row. AFC

LONG ROW, BELPER.

1

ENGLAND

Early industrial villages realized in Great Britain included **Cromford** (1771), Derbyshire, where Richard Arkwright and Jedediah Strutt built a public house, market buildings, and terraced houses for workers at the first successful water-powered cotton-spinning mill; **Belper** (1776), also a cotton town in Derbyshire, founded by Strutt, consisting of a gridded arrangement of back-to-back housing terraces and small blocks of four semidetached interlocking houses interspersed by gardens; and **Milford** (1780) and **Derby** (1786), additional model mill towns built by Strutt and his son, William.[2] Nikolaus Pevsner has written that these "communities ... were the earliest form of the factory-based community, which, together with the pit villages of the coalfields, are still the most emotive symbols of the social effects of industrialization." The dwellings therein, he continues, "are more than the industrial form of the tied cottage; they represent an enlightened, if self-interested approach to the need to provide adequate planned housing as an inducement for potential employees. These early terraces were superior to contemporary agricultural dwellings and set a standard for industrial housing rarely surpassed by [eighteenth-century] housing of similar type."[3]

    Goole (1823), created by the Aire & Calder Navigation Company as part of its effort to modernize the Knottingly-Goole Canal, was neither a social experiment nor an act of industrial philanthropy but, as J. D. Porteous has written, "an early example of what has become known in modern America as 'the company town.'"[4] Goole offered important lessons for the future, including a clear plan of arcaded buildings facing three sides of an open square, the fourth side of which opened to the ship docks. Only the eastern portion of the plan was realized, with streets put in place, followed by the construction of an inn, then redbrick houses, eventually resulting in what Porteous describes as "a singular port town, with over 250 building structures [and] each street and quarter . . . planned to perform some specified function."[5] Also notable among early examples is **Bessbrook** (1846), not in England but in Ireland, where John Grubb Richardson developed a mill town that included space for two village greens, playing fields, and allotment gardens as well as schools, shops, and buildings for worship, leading an 1852 visitor to describe it as "a most happy, prosperous place with its immense linen factory, beautiful schools, model houses for workmen, and lovely landscape, valley and waters."[6]

As railroad lines crisscrossed England, new towns grew up at points of intersection in what had been open country. Of these, a number were conceived as model towns, most notably Wolverton (1838), Crewe (1840), and New Swindon (c. 1842). **Wolverton**, built on an open site near the medieval village of old Wolverton and the Grand Union Canal, was the project of the London & Birmingham Railway, which by 1841 had realized 165 railway workers' cottages as well as nine shops, a market square, a library, a school, and 120 allotment gardens. Six classes of accommodation were provided, the majority in two-story redbrick rowhouses arrayed in conformity with a gridiron street pattern. Some houses were built on three sides of a quadrangle, the fourth side of which contained the engine shed and workshops.[7]

The plan of **Crewe** was the work of Joseph Locke (1805–1860), a railway engineer, and John Cunningham (1799–1873), an architect from Liverpool, who in 1842 was put in charge of the buildings that soon consisted of a mix of villa-style lodges for the officers, Gothic-style houses for lesser executives, detached mansions for the engineers (four families to a mansion, but with separate gardens and entrances), and workers' cottages.[8] Largely demolished in the late 1960s, Crewe was, for its day, a model of urban civility, with wide streets, gardens, public baths, a church, and solid if stolid houses.

New Swindon, like Wolverton, was built on an undeveloped site next to an historic town—Old Swindon. Far more attractive than Crewe, it has been attributed to the architect Sir Matthew Digby Wyatt (1820–1877), though there is no real evidence to substantiate the claim, and engineer Isaac K. Brunel (1806–1859), who was probably responsible for the straight, wide streets along which sat attractive low cottages built from local stone, most featuring diagonal chimney stacks suggestive of Elizabethan manor houses and set behind small gardens.[9] Other architects soon took over, but the cottages were superior to anything else built for workers at the time, even if somewhat compromised by exceptionally narrow back alleys and poor sanitation in the early years. With blocks of shops constituting a focus at the town's center, New Swindon presented an exceptionally dignified urbanity.

Barrow-in-Furness (1847), initially developed as a railway town but later growing prosperous as the result

Milford

1. Overall view. PPC (c. 1910)

Derby

1. Mile Ash Lane. JSutton. GEO (2004)

Goole

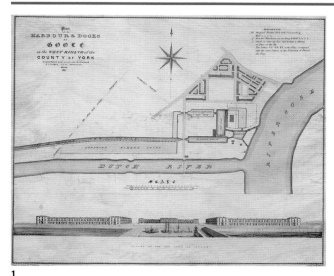

1. Plan of the harbor and docks, with elevation of part of the town, 1825. TNA2

2. Aerial view. GM (1930s)

2

1. Ordnance Survey map. OSNI

2. View from bowling green of College Square East. Beck. VB (c. 2009)

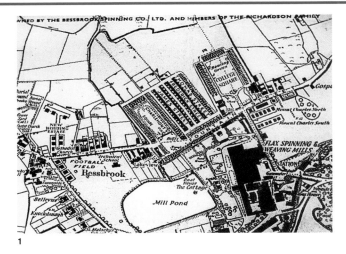

1. Map. BODR (c. 1847)

2. Creed Street before demolition. Jack. HJES (1962)

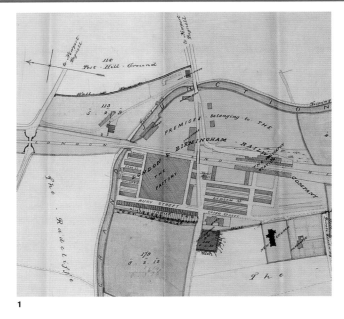

of nearby ironfields, was first planned perfunctorily by James Ramsden (1822–1896), a railway engineer who would serve five terms as the town's mayor, but reimagined in 1865 to constitute what Pevsner praised as one of the few nineteenth-century planned towns in England: "The plan, God knows, is not imaginative," he wrote, "but the wide, tree-lined streets . . . convey a sense of space and ease which even the casual visitor is likely to comment on."[10]

Copley (1847–53), the first of the model villages to be built in the wool and worsted manufacturing centers of Yorkshire's West Riding, was developed on 20 acres by the firm of James Akroyd & Son, with 112 model houses intended "to be secure against the sudden withdrawal of workpeople."[11] Organized in three long rows, the terraces, with facades conceived in what Edward Akroyd (1810–1887), who inherited the business from his father and was responsible for the construction of Copley and other model villages, called "a picturesque outline in the modified old English style," were modest in the extreme and their back-to-back arrangement was considered unenlightened by contemporaries.[12] Nonetheless, Copley

reflected an intention to develop a sense of community, with allotment gardens provided along with a recreation area, four shops, and a school with its own playing field.

Copley also marked a shift in the architectural expression of working-class housing. Stephen Bayley has observed that the cottages, laid out in "parallel, rigidly formal corridors running along the line of the new railway with open country forming a bizarre counterfoil at the ends of each street," constituted a stylistic departure from "the earlier drying houses (which had themselves become residential dwellings at some time before 1849)" and

were simply unstyled Pennine cottages built in short rows; solidly and unostentatiously made in vernacular style typical of that area, they contrasted markedly with the cardboard Gothic effect which Akroyd so evidently admired and wanted for his new development. In his opinion this modified old English style, as he called it, was in harmony with many of the existing local dwellings. It also, of course, had all the associations of

1. Overall view. NRM (1895)

2. Railway superintendent's house. NRM (1877)

3. Dorfold Street. JTurner. GEO (2009)

4. Church Street. CRO (1962)

New Swindon

1. Bird's-eye view of Swindon Works and Railway Village, 1846. GWR11

2. Overall view. Lover. FSRM (2006)

'village' which Akroyd wished to nurture . . . In 1849 it would have been quite possible for Akroyd to specify an Italianate style for his model dwellings because the battle between the two was far from settled; Salt had chosen a bastardized Italianate style for Saltaire but this was not influential. From this time on the accepted stylistic expression for the model estate, the garden suburb and the garden city was the vernacular.[13]

Saltaire (1850–76), the second of the West Riding industrial villages and the brainchild of Sir Titus Salt

(1803–1876), a successful industrialist whose fortune was made in the wool trade, was a town of 25 acres, housing, at forty dwellings per acre, about 4,500 people on the River Aire, three miles from Bradford.[14] An additional 10 acres were devoted to mills and 14 acres to a public open space, People's Park (also known as Saltaire Park).

A key monument in the evolution of the garden city and garden suburb, Saltaire marks a bold advance over Copley. Located at the edge of the Yorkshire Moors, near Bradford's traditional recreation area, Shipley Glen, Saltaire was deliberately conceived as an escape from the inner city. In 1850, Salt decided to relocate his mills

Barrow-in-Furness

1. Partial plan, 1856. CALS
2. Plan, 1867. CALS
3. Abbey Road. CCC (c. 1898)

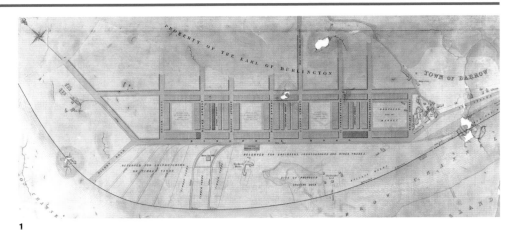

1

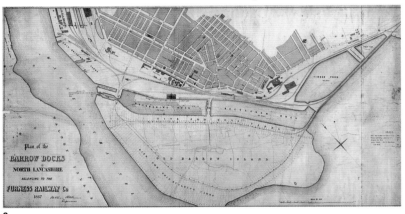

2

3

Copley

1. Bird's-eye view. HWC (1866)
2. Typical street. Green. FL (2008)
3. Rear alley. Bolton. HB (2006)
4. Shop on Mill Street. Bolton. HB (2006)

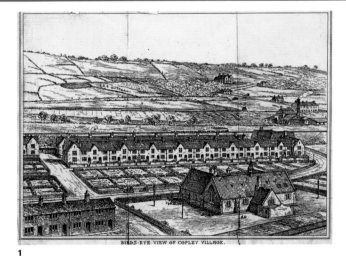

BIRDS-EYE VIEW OF COPLEY VILLAGE.

1

2

3

4

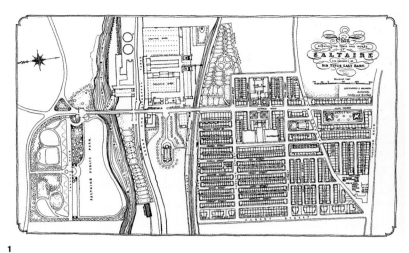

1. Plan, Henry Francis Lockwood and William Mawson, c. 1851. TPR60

2. Almshouses, Lockwood & Mawson, 1868. BLS (1950)

3. Congregational Church, Lockwood & Mawson, 1859. BLS

4. Saltaire Grammar School, Lockwood & Mawson, 1868. Whale. GEO (2008)

5. Bridge leading to People's Park showing mill tower in distance. Green. FL (2011)

6. Typical street. Green. FL (2011)

7. Shops on Victoria Road. Andrew. PAN (2011)

8. Titus Street. Eccles. GEO (2012)

out of polluted central Bradford, retaining Lockwood & Mawson, a local partnership of Henry Francis Lockwood (1811–1878) and William Mawson (1828–1889), to first build a factory (1853) and then houses, which were constructed between 1853 and 1863, as well as various social-service facilities.

Intended as a self-sufficient village, Saltaire contained about 850 houses situated within a gridiron plan of stone-paved streets allowing for rows of cottages—sixteen to the row—each with a small backyard typically accommodating a coal and ash pit and lavatory, opening to a seven-foot-wide service alley. The monotony of rows was avoided by careful massing and the mixture of two-, three-, and four-bedroom units as well as the introduction of three-story houses in the middle or at the ends of the terraces, reflecting the accommodation of both workers and managers, and individuals and families. Greenery was sparingly introduced into the town fabric, confined to 40- and 60-foot setbacks in front of the school (1868) and institute (1871), and the Alexandra Quadrangle, bordered by a group of forty-five almshouses (1868) built for aged and retired workers.

Though the town was densely populated and had very little garden space for the residents, the construction of a bridge leading to People's Park (1871) on the far side of the railway, canal, and river, and the location of nearby open country, went a long way toward alleviating the sense of overcrowding. In fact, as Walter Creese has written, Saltaire's density provides comfort to "those who regard the planning of the garden city and new town as too loose and undisciplined, too low in density, and lacking in urbanity."[15]

The architectural expression of Saltaire's houses and factory is Venetian-Gothic, which, though at first glance appears somewhat exotic, on further reflection, seems appropriate to the quintessentially urban plan. The town's most notable buildings were the Congregational Church (1859), a severe classical composition, and the almshouses. Saltaire's village imagery—but not its rigid plan—provides an early indication in England of the garden suburb pattern that would be widely adopted in the early twentieth century. The town was begun well after the completion of Lowell, Massachusetts (see p. 797), which may have influenced Salt.[16] But the industrialist was more likely influenced by Benjamin Disraeli's novels, *Coningsby* (1844), and especially *Sybil* (1845), in which the construction of a model village for 2,000 people is described in some detail as part of the book's argument in favor of establishing closer relationships between employers and employees in rapidly industrializing England. Salt was also undoubtedly influenced, according to historian Ian Campbell Bradley, by the working-class housing reform efforts of Lord Shaftesbury's Society for Improving the Condition of the Labouring Classes, as well as by the Great Exhibition of 1851, where Prince Albert's model cottages were exhibited, though Salt's "model village stands out both in its scale and its scope."[17]

As A. E. J. Morris has written,

The main significance of Salt's work is not in the way the mill, streets, houses and public buildings were laid out. It is in the decision to move industry and its work-force out from cramped, inefficient, unhealthy (and deteriorating) locations in Bradford to a new site in the countryside. Salt was not an originator in this respect—new industrial villages had been established near sources of power and raw materials from the commencement of the Industrial Revolution, and other industrialists, including Messrs. Richardson at Bessbrook in Ireland (1846) had earlier made similar moves. Saltaire however was widely publicized at a time when influential consciences were slowly realizing that all was not well with the state of the nation. Although of only limited physical planning importance Saltaire provided vastly improved living conditions and obviously influenced the Cadburys and Levers in founding Bournville and Port Sunlight respectively. In turn the latter served as primary influences on Ebenezer Howard's Garden City philosophy.[18]

Nonetheless, picturesque-minded observers writing during the early twentieth century when the Garden City and garden suburb movement was at its peak, tended to fault Saltaire for being "very uninteresting and featureless," a sentiment Creese echoes, observing that "the absence of street incidents is . . . striking upon entering Saltaire. It has a tidy, fixed, and diagrammatic quality that somehow recalls James Silk Buckingham's Victoria city project of 1849 [see p. 207]."[19] But as J. M. Richards has written: "The model world Sir Titus Salt imagined and, for the time being created . . . must have come as close to an industrial Utopia in its day as the unquestioning Victorian acceptance of arbitrary social and economic distinctions could have allowed."[20] In more recent times, as high-density village planning has gained in influence, Saltaire has gradually begun to be appreciated, so that in 1972 James Stevens Curl could write that "Salt and his architects succeeded in creating an aesthetically effective industrial town, large enough to provide communal and other facilities, but not likely to be strangled by excessive growth. Bradford is today practically joined to Saltaire, but the latter preserves its identity and individual character."[21]

Price's Village (also known as Bromborough Pool), following Saltaire by two years, on the Cheshire side of the River Mersey across from Liverpool, was, like Saltaire, built to form a community, in this case combining workers' housing with a new factory for Price's Patent Candle Company.[22] It was notable for the emphasis placed on gardens by the founders, the Wilson family. The factory and village occupied a 42-acre site, and by 1858 there were seventy-six houses, a school, a cricket pitch and pavilion, and a bowling green. The village

1. Map. UNI (c. 1900)

2. Village Hall and gardens. UNI (c. 1890)

3. Typical street. UNI

4. South View. Scales. LS (2012)

continued to grow over the next fifty years, so that there were eventually 142 houses occupied by 728 people. The simple village plan, laid out by London architect Julian Hill (n.d.), consisted of parallel streets, with the first houses realized in short terraces and the later ones in pairs. In his monographic study of the village, Alan Watson locates Price's Village as an important step toward the Garden City movement. "In an informal sense," he writes, "it was a 'garden village.'" While Saltaire "was given a park," tenants at Price's Village "were given the chance to cultivate allotments. Both private gardens and public ones play a part in a garden village." Watson also notes that the "village aided the Garden City movement in a more specific way. It proved that industry and its labor force could settle away from the large cities and do so with no loss of industrial efficiency and a great gain in social happiness . . . Finally, the village made a success of its rural isolation, not because of its buildings but because these were used to help construct a community."[23]

John Nelson Tarn is even more specific in his advocacy of the importance of Price's Village:

Bromborough's place in the history of the model community should be recognized more widely than it is today, for, although a small village at first, it was in reality the first garden village, with its open spaces, its gardens and planting. In these respects it was far in advance of anything built at that time. Only in the simple unaffected layout of the streets and the vernacular quality of the architecture does Bromborough suggest its early date. In the concept of space and density it was a forerunner of the garden city as expounded by Ebenezer Howard, and for its place in the history of this movement as well as its place in the history of enlightened factory management it merits our attention today.[24]

The third of the West Riding industrial villages, **Akroydon** (c. 1859), near Halifax, West Yorkshire, was developed by Edward Akroyd in association with his Haley Hill Mills.[25] Akroydon comes ten years after Akroyd and his brother built model houses for the workmen of their Copley Mills. Considerably more ambitious in conception than Copley, however, Akroydon is notable for its high level of architecture, initiated by George Gilbert Scott (1811–1878), who established the character of the buildings, but taken over by a local architect, W. H. Crossland (1835–1908), Scott's former pupil.

Set on a sloping site at the edge of the Hebble Valley, Akroydon, even more than Copley, self-consciously reflected its developer's intention "of keeping up the old English notion of a village," replete with squire, parson, tenant-farmers, and workers.[26] A scheme (1862) for a crowded village with a small central square containing a reading room and clock tower and allotment gardens on the periphery was adopted, but as the town evolved, some blocks of houses were omitted, although the idea of mixed house types for

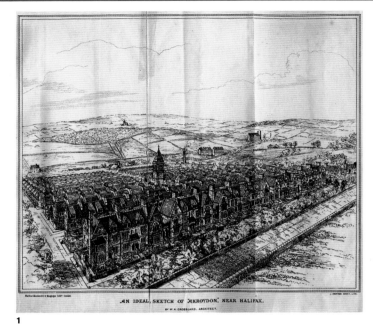

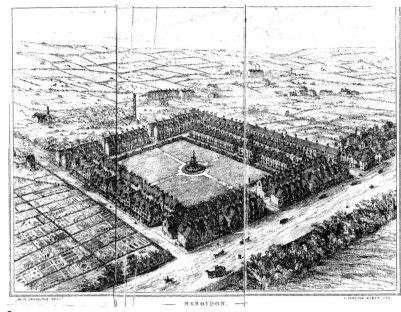

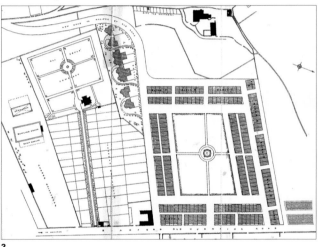

1. Bird's-eye view, 1862. AKR

2. Bird's-eye view, 1866. HWC

3. Plan, 1866. HWC

4, 5. Typical views. Green. FL (2008)

various classes was retained and the central square was enlarged, as reflected in a revised scheme published in 1866. The clock tower and library were not built. Of 350 houses initially projected, only ninety were realized. Although the Owenesque medieval close was abandoned, the Gothic style was retained "because it is the original of the parish of Halifax . . . Intuitively this taste of our forefathers pleases the fancy, strengthens house and home attachment, entwines the present with the memory of the past."[27] Where Saltaire's Italianate architecture, and indeed its gridded plan, broke with local precedent, Akroyd's Gothic reflected his desire, as Walter Creese has written, "to heal the breach in feeling between the ancient village and the new industrial age." Nonetheless, Creese goes on to point out, Akroyd could no more revive the medieval picturesque than Salt could implant the Italian Renaissance in the Bradford mills: both were visions from books, "a product off the drawing board, set down in a very literal environment."[28]

Interestingly, as Akroyd reported, "the public battled stoutly against the Gothic for some time; although they liked the look of it, they considered it antiquated,

inconvenient, wanting in light, and not adapted to modern requirements. The dormer windows were supposed to resemble the style of almshouses, and the independent workmen who formed the building association positively refused to accept this feature of the Gothic, which to their minds was degrading. This point I was obliged to concede."[29] Stephen Bayley goes on to observe:

Thus Copley and Akroydon model villages were medievalist in appearance and Saltaire is exceptional in England of a non-native style being chosen for a housing experiment. Generally, the Italian renaissance style was not considered suitable because the associations of medievalism were always more appropriate to the ideal of a planned community than was an exotic style; therefore, while the crudity of vision and planning in the south Yorkshire model villages have little in common with the sophistication of conception and appearance of the garden city proper they are noteworthy as forerunners in that the planners

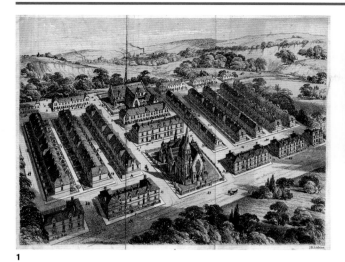

1

2

and architects sensed that a revival of medieval architectural forms was the proper expression of the ideal planned community.[30]

The deliberate use of established architectural imagery at Copley, Saltaire, and Akrodyon set in place a crucial theme in the Garden City movement. At Copley, and much more so at Akroydon, the seeds for the future were sown, not as the result of a willy-nilly aestheticism but as a definite conviction that the old English village was a desirable social anchor amid the turmoil of rapid industrialization.

Coming two years after Akroydon, and inspired by it, Halifax mill-owner Sir Francis T. Crossley's **West Hill Park Estate** (1863–68), Halifax, was laid out by the Manchester firm of Henry John Paull (d. 1888) and Oliver Ayliffe (n.d.), whose design, selected in a competition, placed rectangular blocks of rowhouses between streets and back alleys. As Creese has suggested, the layout was more subtle than its predecessors, "with a better feeling for the site and for the house, with its individual front garden."[31] In contrast to Akroydon's formalistic plan for a hillside square, West Hill situated its Gothic-style houses following the site's topography. The houses addressed the needs of four different categories of tenants, with some of the more elaborate residences situated to visually terminate the service alleys so that, as Creese observes, "the gardens and walks, but not the service roads, would be visible from the major streets."[32] John Nelson Tarn notes that with each house treated to its own garden, "like so much of the model housing as it moved towards the middle class," West Hill "is nearly indistinguishable from the work of the speculative developer except for its higher standard of building and layout."[33] Crossley had recently developed a large open space called People's Park (1857) in an attempt, as he put it, "to arrange art and nature that they should be within the walk of every working man in Halifax; that he shall go and take his stroll there after he has done his hard day's toil, and be able to get home again without being tired."[34] The 12.5-acre People's Park, laid out by Joseph Paxton and Edward

Milner (1819–1884), adjoined Crossley's mansion, Belle Vue, as well as almshouses he had built in 1855.

In 1888, around the time when plans for Port Sunlight were getting started, Sir William Hartley of the Hartley's Jams and Marmalades company, was inspired to hold a competition for a five-acre project at **Aintree**, north of Liverpool, with the firm of William Sugden (1821?–1892) and his son, William Larner Sugden (1850–1901) selected to design a superblock surrounding a bowling green, described by Budgett Meakin in 1905 as "a square of neat cottages with small gardens in front, facing four roads, and surrounding an open garden and playground square."[35] The plan was said to have been inspired by the railroad village at Crewe.

Toward the end of the century, as coal mining picked up in remote central England, "with every new colliery that was opened, it was necessary for the owners to provide housing for the workers," a majority of which consisted of "groups of a few hundred houses, or less, huddled close to the pit head . . . usually laid out in double rows with privies, refuse heaps and coal sheds between. The houses were commonly of the two-up, two-down variety, and were built to a minimum standard with no effort to 'improve' the aspect or appearance of the property."[36] Some industrialists, however, sought to provide better housing. At the behest of its director and chairman, Emerson Bainbridge, the Bolsover Colliery Company, operating in the Chesterfield coalfield, undertook two model villages, **New Bolsover** (1891) and Creswell (1896), located about six miles apart. Like many such endeavors, Bainbridge's combined philanthropy—providing significantly better housing and a host of community amenities—with the belief that workers would be morally improved by living in an environment where "these things should exist successfully—the absence of drunkenness, the absence of gambling and the absence of bad language."[37] The company's managing director, J. P. Houfton, called on his architect brother Percy B. Houfton (d. 1926) to design the new villages, each of which had public buildings as well as common green spaces, allotment

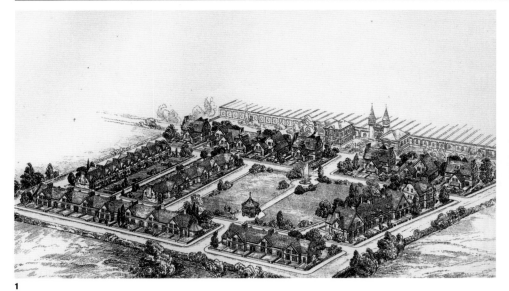

1

2

1. Bird's-eye view, 1888. TB88

2. Houses on Spice Street. Scales. LS (2012)

3, 4. Typical streets. CNH

3

4

gardens, and recreational fields such as bowling greens and cricket pitches.

Development of New Bolsover started a year after the coal company established a mine in the near vicinity of Bolsover Castle, a hilltop manse that would soon look out on a landscape of "torn-open ground, long flags of smoke from chimneys, soot and mist."[38] Working on a gently sloping site to the west of the castle grounds, Houfton designed New Bolsover as a quadrangle, with three sides occupied by double rows of houses separated by a service road, and the fourth side left open with the exception of a combination school and town hall, now demolished, at the midpoint. The Nottingham firm of Arthur William Brewill (1861–1923) and Basil E. Baily (1869–1942) designed the school and most likely the cooperative store and clubhouse that flanked the village's northern entrance. The plan's 194 dwellings were accommodated in two-story redbrick seven- and eight-unit-long rowhouses. The inner ring faced onto a central green and the outer row looked to surrounding allotment gardens, with the backs of the houses facing an internal street that featured a tram line connecting with the colliery to allow for the transport of workers and the easy delivery and removal of coal, ash, and refuse.

An orphanage and church were also included, the latter demolished in 1987. The community also featured twelve villas for company officials occupying six semidetached houses a short distance to the north.

Creswell offered the same basic components but with a more imaginative plan in which a double row of 281 redbrick houses, now in shorter groups containing no more than six units, formed an elongated octagon enclosing a sprawling central lawn outfitted with a bandstand and children's playground.[39] A tram was again included between the rows, while a school, a cooperative store, and a clubhouse were placed just beyond the outer houses at the midpoint of the octagon's long south side. Writing in 1934, the housing expert Catherine Bauer called Creswell "still one of the best pieces of community planning in England. The houses are grouped around a . . . common and, about thirty years before Radburn, they face inward on the gardens and the footpath is separated from the street."[40]

The plan of the next model coal-mining village, **Woodlands** (1907), shows a dramatic step forward, reflecting the impact during the intervening years of Port Sunlight (1888) and Bournville (1895) as well as Parker and Unwin's New Earswick (1902), key industrial

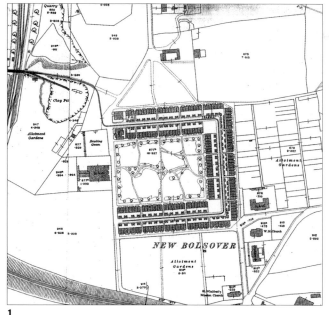

1. Ordnance Survey map. DLSL (1918)

2. Aerial view. Tunnard. BT (2012)

3. View across green of school. PPC (c. 1908)

4. Houses showing Bolsover Castle in background. UOL (2007)

villages that are discussed in the context of Ebenezer Howard's emerging Garden City idea (see p. 203). Woodlands, built for the Brodsworth Main Colliery in the Doncaster coalfield in Yorkshire's West Riding, was referred to at the time, though somewhat exaggeratedly, as a "serious rival" to Letchworth, Bournville, and Port Sunlight.[41] The mining company's director, Arthur B. Markham, had been involved in the development of New Bolsover, which, according to Martin Gaskell, he viewed as "an example of the benefits and possibilities of village development on enlightened lines."[42] Perhaps because of Markham's interest in New Bolsover, despite a design competition for Woodlands that was won by A. & J. Soutar, Percy B. Houfton was retained as planner and also as the designer of fifty-three houses built between 1907 and 1915.

Occupying a 127-acre site directly on top of the mine, the new village was named for an adjoining private residence known as "the Woodlands" that was converted into a Workmen's Club set in a 21-acre recreation ground. A 4.5-acre lake and 10-acre plantation were also kept for recreational purposes. The plan, giving rise to 653 houses, consisted of two residential areas separated by a district of public buildings placed around two landscaped plazas. To the south, the initial residential area, known as the Park, adjacent to the Woodlands estate, comprised 121 cottages placed around a single loop road at a density of five to the acre. The houses, built in one year's time, looked onto a communal 24-acre green but also featured individual gardens delineated by hedges. Many were set back 25 to 30 feet from the street and arranged in groups around closes. According to Gaskell, this section was "the most satisfactory," its houses resembling those designed by C. F. A. Voysey for the Whitwood Colliery (see p. 228): "The resemblance to Voysey's style," wrote Gaskell, "with its emphasis on the detailing of gables and the width of porches, doorways and windows, gave a steady rhythm and tranquility to this part of the village."[43]

The so-called Field Area, north of the public buildings, comprised 532 houses built in fifteen months, a hurried pace made necessary by the rapid growth of the mining operations but that degraded the quality of construction. Here the plan was more complex, with a 120-foot-wide central avenue lined by wide grass verges and a quadruple row of trees forking into two 50-foot-wide diagonal boulevards that intersected with a curving loop road to form ten superblocks. The houses, in rows

1. Ordnance Survey map. DLSL (1916)

2. Aerial view. Tunnard. BT (2012)

3. Typical view. PPC (c. 1900)

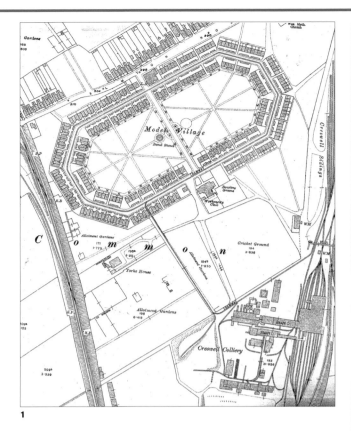

of varying length, faced outward, turning their backs on expansive internal greens that could be reached from the sidewalk by footpaths.

Reaction to Woodlands was mixed. Ebenezer Howard was enthusiastic, not only because the village was realized by a private company but also because its design was "simply a wonderful advance—not a step forward, but a great leap."[44] Patrick Abercrombie, however, writing in 1911, felt the community fell short in several ways despite cottages that were "as satisfactory as any," in terms of design—and even exceptional in plan—but "quite marred by the bad materials."[45] Abercrombie took particular issue with Houfton's decision to turn the houses away from the internal reserves, leaving the rear facades "entirely open, more so even than the front. A narrow paved way runs along, and on this facing the back door of each cottage is placed the dustbin—there is no privacy and no screens for those little untidinesses which are very apt to appear near the back door; there is a tendency for these little untidinesses to get scattered on the whole enclosed green, which presents a certain dirty, squalid appearance. Instead of a garden at the back, or allotments in close proximity, these must be far away, and the house, except for a little show garden in front is situated in a kind of public desert."[46]

Comparing Woodlands to its near contemporary, Hull Garden Village, Abercrombie wrote that while "on paper the plan of Woodlands appears far more

interesting, at any rate in the more formal part, than that of Hull . . . in execution, owing perhaps to the dust and dirt of the colliery and a sort of general feeling of shabbiness, the general impression of the Woodlands village is far inferior to that of Hull, which represents the last word in neatness and thoroughness."[47] Even Houfton found fault in his design, later acknowledging that the excessive width of the streets was perhaps an overreaction to cramped urban streets, resulting in long, broad vistas that he at times neglected to visually terminate: "A wide street," wrote Houfton, "with a view to the open country, has a windswept appearance, and fails to give that sense of shelter which the clustering homes of a village should suggest."[48]

Hull Garden Village (1907–13; 1923–24) was designed by Percy T. Runton (1874–1947) and William E. Barry (1868?–1924), who were given full responsibility for the town plan and for the housing, including almshouses, for James Reckitt's factory workers.[49] Like George Cadbury and Joseph Rowntree, Reckitt (1833–1924), a Quaker industrialist famous for Robin Starch and Reckitt's Blue laundry products, was an idealist imbued with garden suburb values: "It seems to me the time has come . . . to establish a Garden Village, within a reasonable distance of our Works, so that those who are wishful [of it] might have the opportunity of living in a better house, with a garden, for the same rent that they now pay for a house in Hull—with the advantages of

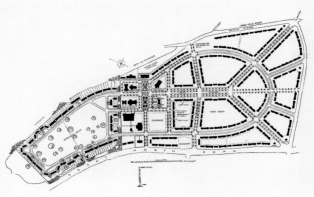

1. Plan, Percy B. Houfton, 1907. GSTP

2. Aerial view. GE (2008)

3. The Park. WLC

4. Typical view. UOM

5. Typical houses. WLC

6. Overall view of Field Area. Gardner. ASCW (2010)

fresher air, and such Clubs, and out-door amusements, as are usually found in rural surroundings."[50] Reckitt purchased the 130-acre Holderness House estate and by July 1908 the garden village was officially opened, with over 500 houses completed by the middle of 1913. Runton and Barry's plan had two foci: the oval, a large green; and the shopping center, with twelve streets laid out in an irregular mix of straight runs and curves. The oval was home to the village hall and the clubhouse, the latter with its own triangular green at the back intended as a children's playground. The shopping center consisted of a two-story building wrapping three sides of an open courtyard with a classical colonnade sheltering shoppers from the weather on all three sides and providing balcony access to second-story flats.

Hull Garden Village's public architecture has been characterized as "polite" in contrast to the vernacular-influenced Voyseyesque residential architecture that ranged from individually designed "first class" houses facing the oval to the more modest houses which were almost as big but had fewer amenities, including no indoor bathrooms. With the passage of time, back roads or alleys, initially intended for garden carts, were adapted to provide access to subsequently constructed garages. Nonetheless, there was a lack of spaciousness owing to narrow streets, and the house designs did not achieve the "picturesqueness" of Port Sunlight or the "originality" of New Earswick, perhaps because Runton and Barry were "good provincial architects but no more than that."[51] Though the garden village lay within Hull's boundaries and was accessible to the city center by electric tram, it was intended to be "beautifully open," with "a thoroughly rural feeling."[52]

Well Hall Estate (1915), Eltham, located on a 96-acre rolling site and consisting of 1,298 houses, including 212 flats, was England's first wartime workers' garden village

1. Plan, Percy T. Runton and William E. Barry, 1907. TPR10

2. Aerial view. CRS (c. 1920)

3. The Oval. CWH (c. 1907)

4. Juliet Reckitt Havens, Laburnum Avenue. Houlton. CWH (2004)

5. Shopping center. Houlton. CWH (2004)

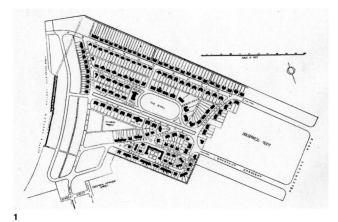

1

2

3

4

5

but was preceded by similar efforts of the London County Council to house industrial workers and other wage earners on suburban-type housing estates (see p. 382). Intended for senior and skilled workers at the nearby Woolwich Arsenal, Well Hall Estate was built by the Office of Works, originally established in 1378 to supervise the construction of royal residences but converted into a municipal government agency in 1851.[53] Designed by Frank Baines (1877–1933), principal architect of the Office of Works and a former pupil of C. R. Ashbee, Well Hall Estate was "intended from the start as a showpiece solution" to the World War I housing emergency.[54] G. E. Phillips (n.d.), an Office of Works architect who assisted Baines, noted that the garden suburb was intended to look "as if it had grown and not merely been dropped there."[55] Situated east and west of Well Hall Road, between Shooters Hill Road and Rochester Way, in east London, the plan of the portion east of Well Hall Road was particularly interesting, with long, relatively straight streets crisscrossed by short, block-long connecting lanes and, at its center, Lovelace Green, on axis with a principal walkway connecting to Well Hall Road through the gateway arch of a butterfly-shaped apartment house.

To cope with wartime shortages, in the design of the houses Baines used a wide variety of available materials, combining them to brilliant picturesque effect: timber-framing, tile-hanging, slate-hanging, stone, brick, and

rendered stucco were all employed in varied designs that abounded in period detail to evoke an "old English Village," inspiring Ewart G. Culpin, secretary of the Garden Cities and Town Planning Association, to somewhat hyperbolically proclaim that Well Hall was "easily the first thing in cottage plans and elevations for the whole world."[56] Culpin had far less glowing reviews for the "social side of the scheme," condemning "the Well Hall scheme for its entire lack of social and other amenities, despite its architectural achievements, and with all my enthusiasm for aesthetic treatment I consider that scheme will never be a success until these glaring defects are remedied."[57]

Baines followed the Well Hall Estate with another government-sponsored development for munitions workers, **Roe Green Village** (1916–20), sometimes known as Roe Green Garden Hamlet, a 250-dwelling-unit garden suburb laid out around a village green on a 23-acre site in the north London Borough of Brent, eight miles from Charing Cross.[58] As Mark Swenarton has observed, the "scheme continued the 'virtuoso-picturesque' mode" established at Well Hall, "albeit in a rather more restrained manner."[59] Forty percent of the units were flats arranged in two-story blocks that resembled ordinary cottages. Located on a slight hill just 600 yards off the "somewhat dreary line of the Edgeware Road," the hamlet was entered from Stag Lane past a pair of village

Well Hall Estate

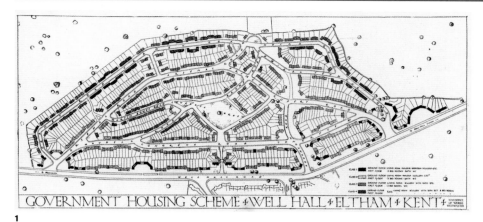

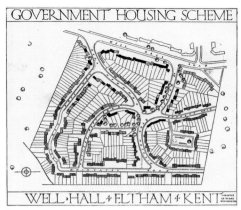

1

2

3

4

5

6

1. Plan of eastern section, Frank Baines, 1915. HWTJ

2. Plan of western section, Frank Baines, 1915. HWTJ

3. Butterfly-plan house with pathway to Lovelace Green. HWTJ

4. Arsenal Road. LMA (1925)

5. Well Hall Road. PBird. BIRD (2010)

6. Typical houses. PBird. BIRD (2010)

Roe Green Village

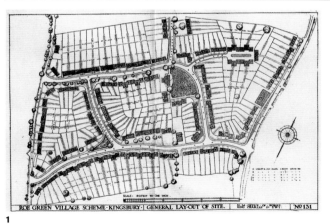

1

2

3

4

1. Plan, Frank Baines, 1916. AAAR

2. Cottages and gardens. JGA

3. Shops on Goldsmith Lane. BRENT (1971)

4. Goldsmith Lane. RGV

Crayford

1. Plan, J. Gordon Allen, 1915.
TB19

2. Crayford Way near western
entrance. JGA

3. Rendering of staff houses. RIBA

4. Farm Place. JGA

Dormanstown

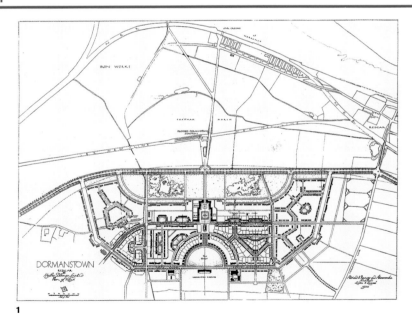

1. Plan, Adshead & Ramsey and
Abercrombie, Architects, 1916–20.
SHC

2. Houses bordering village green.
AF19 (c. 1919)

3. Houses. SHC

shops on Goldsmith Lane.[60] While the common green was provided as a community focus, the extensive back gardens accessible to all by way of footpaths provided an exceptional sense of spaciousness.

Crayford (1915–16), housing workers in the Vickers-Maxim munitions factory, was parallel in conception and design with the Well Hall Estate, but without the deliberate intricacy of its street plan and variety of its building forms.[61] As designed by J. Gordon Allen (1885–1964), the plan of long streets was pleasantly punctuated by a number of closes and considerable greenery in the

form of rear allotment gardens, a village green, and a sports ground. Over 600 houses were built to very strict construction budgets, mostly in groups of two and four.

While most of the wartime garden villages were undertaken by the public sector, some private companies continued in the tradition of late-nineteenth-century paternalistic capitalism. **Dormanstown** (1916–20), near York, was developed as a self-contained workers' village by the steel company Dorman Long on an 850-acre, flat, marshy, windswept coastal site.[62] Designed by Adshead & Ramsey and Patrick Abercrombie, the village sat

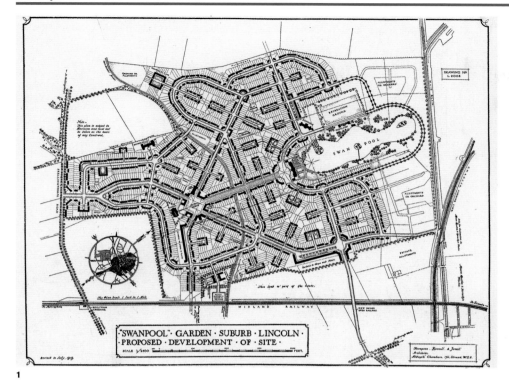

1

2

3

along a railway line where a new station was proposed, with a strong axis connected to a central square and a semicircular crescent green bound on the far side by recreation grounds and a community clubhouse. A permanently deeded greensward separated the town from the industrial works. Schools were located at the east and west ends of the village. Provision was also made for a market square to the north of the crescent, dominated by one of five planned churches. To Simon Pepper and Mark Swenarton, who have studied Dormanstown in detail, what "distinguishes" the village "from the best-known pre-war schemes—Hampstead Garden Suburb, Bournville, Port Sunlight—is the formality of the design . . . At Hampstead the intention had been to recreate the old English village. At Dormanstown we have a Georgian 'New Town.'"[63] The Baroque-inspired plan was geometrically sophisticated, consisting of two concentric circles with crescents, culs-de-sac, and closes used to fill in the details. When completed in 1920, 342 families were housed. The redbrick Georgian-style houses were organized in pairs and groups of varying lengths of up to ten units. Single-family houses, also included in the plan, were grouped around small closes opening to the street. Some houses were rendered in white stucco, taking the architectural story forward into the Regency period. Significantly, as Pepper and Swenarton have made clear, the simple houses were highly advanced in their construction, with the first 300 units (1917–18) combining load-bearing brickwork with steel joists and precast-concrete slabs. Among other innovations, the post–World War I houses employed lightweight steel frames bolted together on-site.

Swanpool (1919), Lincoln, built by the engineering company Ruston & Hornsby to house its employees, was designed by the partnership of Albert John Thompson, C. Murray Hennell, and Charles Holloway James, all alumni of the Parker and Unwin firm, with cottage-style houses recollective of Letchworth's.[64] The 370-acre estate had as its principal feature a large lake, known as the Swan Pool, reserved for recreational purposes, with the land surrounding it devoted to tennis courts, a bowling green, and parks. Originally, 2,000 houses were planned, but by 1920 only 113 were built and the company's declining business prevented a full build-out. The brick-trimmed, roughcast, steep-pitched cottages were organized as rows of ten units but with many smaller corner groups fitted to the intricate road geometries that were intended to form strong gateways at the periphery and to focus on important public buildings. The long axis of Swan Pool was extended to become the principal axis of the village, leading across the plan to a central square bordered by churches and an institute. The planners made maximal use of culs-de-sac that allowed development to reach into the superblocks where private gardens were intended to be complemented by tennis courts, orchards, allotments, and bowling greens.

The prolonged hostilities of World War I halted most development of any kind in the United Kingdom. In the early 1920s, however, construction, especially for returning military and workers in general, picked up as part of a massive effort called "Homes for Heroes."[65] **The Grove** (1921–30), Teddington, was developed by St. Helen's Housing Company, a subsidiary of the Royal Dutch Shell Company, to provide rental housing to company employees.[66] Messrs. Joseph, London-based architects, were responsible for the plan that was originally intended to cover the complete site of Teddington Grove, containing an eighteenth-century house designed

1. Plan, Thompson, Hennell, & James, Architects, 1919. AF 19

2. Houses at main entrance to estate. SHC

3. Hartsholme Drive. LINC (1992)

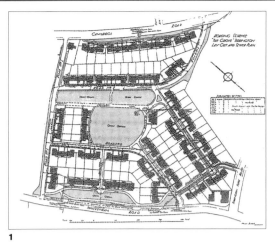

1. Plan, Messrs. Joseph, 1921. RLS

2. Grove Terrace. Avery. TTA (2012)

2

1

Acton

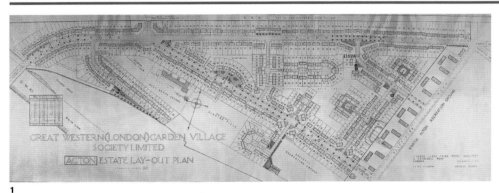

1

2

1. Plan, T. Alwyn Lloyd. (1937) LMA

2. Norman Way. RAMSA (2009)

Fairholme Estate

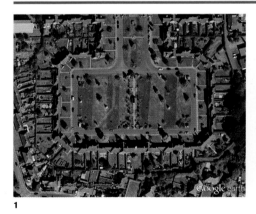

1

2

3

1. Aerial view. GE (2003)

2. Community hall. Cadman. FL (2008)

3. Houses. Cadman. FL (2008)

by William Chambers for Moses Franks but demolished in 1920. Only fifty-two houses, organized in groups of two, three, and four, were built by 1925, facing Cambridge Road, Grove Terrace, and The Grove. Many of the site's trees and stone walls were retained, so that the effect is of a peaceful garden enclave arranged around a bowling green. The house designs strike observers as more continental than English in inspiration, probably a reflection of the sponsor's preference.

Acton (1923–25), one of the last garden villages for industrial workers realized by a private company, was set in the Great Western Railway's extensive recreational grounds. The plan focused on the West Acton station, which was subsequently incorporated into the Underground. Designed by T. Alwyn Lloyd, a former assistant to Raymond Unwin, the scheme, setting "attractively simple paired cottages . . . behind low privet hedges," was relieved "by angling corner houses and by a few groups with gables instead of hipped roofs."[67]

Another late manifestation of the privately funded workers' village was a low-rent philanthropic venture, T. Cecil Howitt's **Fairholme Estate** (1934), a tiny gem consisting of seventy-two, one- and two-story brick houses placed around a grassy quadrangle.[68] Grouped together, the houses were linked by large semicircular arches that served as porches while also providing access to rear gardens. A beautifully detailed community hall lies opposite the entrance of the close-like estate.

WALES

Harbour Village (1902–8), Goodwick, Pembrokeshire, among the first of the Welsh industrial villages to reflect the twentieth century's enlightened planning ideals, was built for employees of the Great Western Railway on a picturesque clifftop site where company engineer G. L. Gibson (n.d.) made the most of breathtaking views over Fishguard Harbor, calling for a single, crooked street to be lined by 112 roughcast houses built in terraces from thirteen distinct designs.[69] Decidedly more picturesque, the **Elan Valley Estate Village** (1906–9), built for maintenance workers of the Elan dam and reservoir, which supplied water to Birmingham, England, lacked a village center but featured a nearby school as a focus for the idyllic layout of paired cottages placed along a single road.[70] Designed by the Birmingham-based firm of Herbert Buckland (1869–1951) and Edward Haywood-Farmer (1871–1917), the cottages, built from local stone in the Arts and Crafts style, were set upon spacious, verdant lots.

Although only half-realized, **Sealand Garden Suburb** (1910), in Queensferry, Clwyd, housing employees of the John Summers & Co. steel company, more directly reflected the tenets of garden suburb planning, with an Unwinesque street plan that minimized through traffic, angled houses back from the intersections, featured closed street vistas—although a club that was intended to terminate the main axis was never built—and placed gabled terraces at the perimeter of large blocks to allow room for internal reserves.[71]

Fforestfach Miners' Village (1910), in northwest Swansea, South Wales, was another partially realized garden village, designed by London-based George Pepler and Ernest Allen to house coal miners.[72] Occupying just eight acres but planned to allow for easy expansion, Fforestfach featured a single crescent-shaped, 60-foot-wide street, Llwyn Derw, made up of a 24-foot-wide roadway, 10-foot-wide planting strips, and 8-foot-wide sidewalks, from which extended culs-de-sac and short spurs. Space was provided for a bowling green, allotment gardens, and playgrounds, but development was halted after only eight of the intended 100 dwellings, to have been situated in groups of two, three, and four units, were built. Also housing coal miners, **Fernhill Garden Village** (1913), in Abercwmboi, Glamorgan, built by the Aberaman Housing Society, a local branch of Welsh Garden Cities Limited, was given "quite a spacious layout" by W. Beddoe Rees (1877–1931), who additionally designed the 190 semidetached and row-houses clad in red brick and pebbledash with front

Harbour Village

1. Overall view. Chroustchoff. GEO (2007)

Elan Valley Estate Village

1. Aerial view. CRS

2. Cottages, Herbert Buckland and Edward Haywood-Farmer. AHMW (2012)

gables and bracketed porch hoods. The houses, climbing the hillside in roughly parallel terraces, enjoyed distant views over the rooftops below.[73] A triangular green at the entrance provided a civic gesture.

The most ambitious of the Welsh coal-mining villages, **Oakdale** (1913), roughly twenty miles north of Cardiff, housing workers in the Oakdale colliery of the Tredegar Iron and Coal Company, was the work of local architect A. F. Webb (n.d.), the brother-in-law of the company's managing director, who prevailed in a 1910 competition to both plan the village and design its 660 houses and public buildings.[74] Working on a gently sloping hillside surrounded by green fields, Webb's roughly symmetrical, teardrop-shaped layout was bisected by a longitudinal spine that in its upper half featured a landscaped central mall bordered by shops

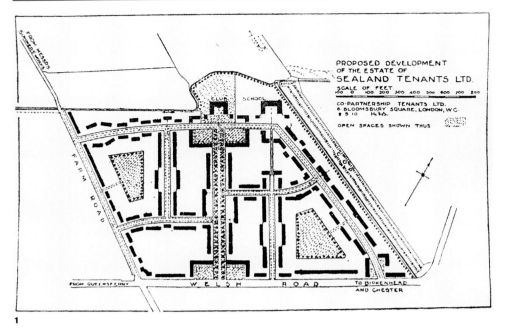

1

1. Plan. EGC (c. 1913)

2. Farm Road. FRO (c. 1912)

3. Bridge View and Sealand Avenue.
Turner. GEO (2009)

2

3

Fforestfach Miners' Village

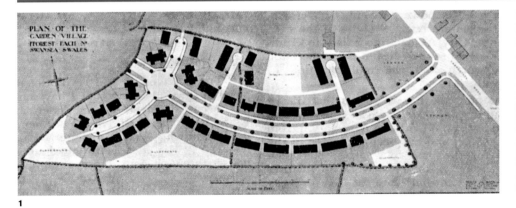

1

1. Plan, Pepler & Allen, 1910.
GCTP10

2. Elevation. HWTJ (c. 1917)

3. Llwyn Derw. Steel. AST (2012)

4. Llwyn Derw. CAM (1940s)

2

3

4

and public buildings, including an institute and hotel. The axis narrowed as it led downhill, splitting into a Y at the location of a small church. Two avenues crossed the axis, running parallel to one another in the town center before curving in opposite directions as they extended outward. As John Newman observed in his 2002 guidebook to Gwent and Monmouthshire, Webb's design, "expansive and highly formalized," marked a "radical departure" from the area's "traditional ribbons of valley-bottom terraces."[75] Both the housing, consisting predominantly of multi-unit rows, each with a front and rear garden, and featuring a "mixture of facing materials, red brick and pebbledash, and some pretty details, especially doorhoods," as well as the village's "most memorable feature, the symmetrical overall plan," were "probably derived from Letchworth."[76] Despite the loss of the institute, which was moved to another location in 1989, Oakdale remains largely intact.

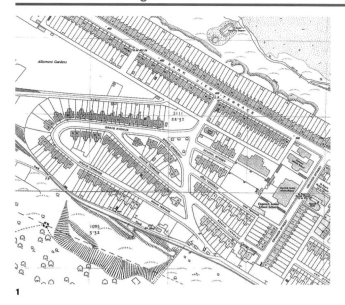

1

2

1. Ordnance Survey map. AL (1957)

2. Graig Avenue. SGraham. AL (2013)

Oakdale

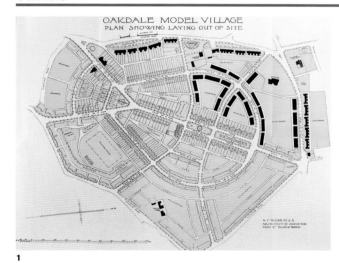

1

2

3

4

1. Plan, A. F. Webb, 1913. GA

2. Aerial view. AHMW (2006)

3. Central Avenue with church in distance. RI

4. West End Terrace. RI

During World War I, the Ebbw Vale Steel, Iron and Coal Company hired Walter Rosser (n.d.) to plan the so-called enclave of **Garden Suburbs** (c. 1918–22), in Pontywaun, Risca, eight miles northwest of New-port, comprising about sixty units of semidetached and rowhouses for managers and officers of three different collieries. Rosser laid out two curving hillside streets, at the intersection of which he set four quadruple houses back at a 45-degree angle, leading John Newman to deem

the design "a convincing demonstration for the Parker & Unwin garden suburb style" realized in "exposed sand-stone and rendered walls, grey slated and red tiled roofs, gables and hips, canted bays and bows."[77] The enclave's preindustrial charm was mirrored in another of Rosser's designs, that of **Victoria** (1918), Ebbw Vale, now known simply, if exaggeratedly, as Garden City. Here Rosser cre-ated "the impression of a compact hillside village rather than anything suburban."[78] Located in the hills above

Garden Suburbs

1

Victoria

1

2

3

the Prince of Wales Colliery, Victoria featured rendered houses with gables, dormers, and red-tile roofs along with canted houses at the main intersection, comprising "altogether quite an artful performance."[79] In both enclaves, Rosser augmented the Arts and Crafts architecture with well-crafted stone retaining walls and steps.

Burry Port Garden Suburb (1915–17), located on the southwest coast of Wales overlooking the Irish Sea, was a wartime effort of the Welsh Town Planning and Housing Trust.[80] As designed by T. Alwyn Lloyd, who also served as an editor at *Garden Cities and Town Planning* magazine, it was commissioned by the government to provide 300 houses for munitions workers in nearby Pembrey. Not surprisingly, due to wartime needs, the design of the two-story roughcast houses with low-pitched, slate-covered roofs was kept relatively simple, but some variety was achieved in the plan by including quadrangle groups and open greens and setting back building lines. Construction did not begin on the first 104 houses until 1917, and these were not completed until 1920. Ultimately, 204 houses were built, occupied by colliers, iron and tinplate workers, and railwaymen.

In 1916, just outside the historic port city of Chepstow, located at the confluence of the Wye and Severn Rivers in the southeast corner of Wales near the English border, the growing demands of the wartime economy convinced two local shipbuilding concerns to build a significant garden suburb to house a varied class of employees, including laborers, skilled tradesman, clerical workers, and managers.[81] **Hardwick Village** (1916–19), also referred to locally as "Garden City"—the approach to the town was via Garden City Way—was planned by Dunn, Watson & Curtis Green on a 28-acre valley site bounded by Chepstow's late-thirteenth-century Port Wall. According to partners William Dunn (1959–1934) and William Curtis Green (1875–1960)—Robert Watson (1865–1916) died as work began on the project—the hilly site precluded the possibility of "any grandiose axial plan," and the 24-foot-wide side streets that opened off the central road, 36-foot-wide Hardwick Avenue, followed "the natural contours of the land. It was only by following these contours, more or less, that reasonable gradients could be obtained."[82] The suburb was planned at a density of ten houses per acre and included three open spaces: a village green at the center of the site; a space for bowling greens and tennis courts at the fairly level area near the Port Wall; and a large general recreation ground near the railroad tracks.

Dunn, Watson & Curtis Green were also responsible for the design of the 236 three- and four-bedroom houses completed at Hardwick Village. Instead of the blue Welsh slate roofs typical of trust-sponsored projects, the roofs at Hardwick were covered in sand-faced tile of various colors and were complemented by redbrick chimney stacks. More significant, the houses were constructed of concrete block, an unusual choice necessitated by inadequate supplies of bricks due to wartime demand. The 32-inch-long, 9-inch-high, 4-inch-thick blocks were made on-site of sand and local stone chippings. H. J. Birnstingl,

Burry Port Garden Suburb

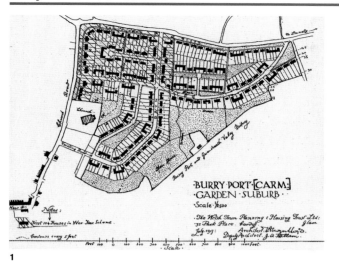

1. Plan, T. Alwyn Lloyd, 1917. AJ20

2. Chivers Corner. CRS (1926)

Hardwick Village

1. Plan, Dunn, Watson & Curtis Green, 1918. RIBA18

2. Typical houses. JGA (c. 1919)

3. Severn Crescent. Sharville. RS (2007)

4. Portwall Road. Sharville. RS (2008)

writing in the American periodical *Architectural Forum* in 1920, stated that this was "the first instance" in the United Kingdom "where this material has been so extensively used for small buildings." Birnstingl pointed to "the variety of treatment that it is possible to obtain" using concrete blocks. "The significance of this fact would not require such insistent emphasis in America where the possibilities of concrete have for some time been fully recognized, but in England it is to many almost in the nature of a revelation that this material is capable of yielding such varied and pleasing results."[83] The backs of the houses faced service lanes for the removal of trash, to accommodate coal deliveries, and to "give access to the back doors, by which the working man enters after the day's work." According to the architects, these back lanes,

placed at right angles to the streets, featured "dead ends . . . as it was believed that lanes with through-ways were open to objection, in that they facilitated thieving and other improper use of the lanes."[84]

In his guidebook to Wales's Monmouthshire county, published in 1995, John Newman suggested that the "concrete blockwork" at Hardwick Village "was deliberately chosen for walling as an expression of modernity," although there is no evidence of anything other than fiscally driven constructional expediency. On surer ground, Newman also argued that the town's plan was "clearly much indebted to the Parker & Unwin garden suburb model," writing that the houses "are grouped in terraces of four, with pairs in specially favoured situations, as along Port Wall Road, the topmost of the north

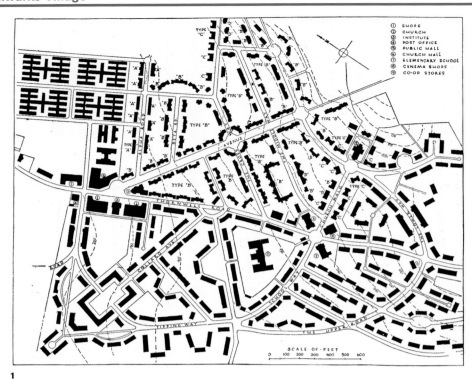

① SHOPS
② CHURCH
③ INSTITUTE
④ POST OFFICE
⑤ PUBLIC HALL
⑥ CHURCH HALL
⑦ ELEMENTARY SCHOOL
⑧ CINEMA SHOPS
⑨ CO-OP STORES

1

2

3

1. Plan, Henry E. Farmer and H. Avray Tipping, c. 1920. AF20

2. Typical houses. AF20 (c. 1920)

3. Camp Road. Sharville. RS (2008)

roads, and forming open-ended courts along Hardwick Avenue. Each group is symmetrical, but play is made with pairs of gables set close together or far apart, cat-slide roofs and end projections, to provide constant variety. Originally all this was enhanced by substantial but elegantly detailed timberwork, in window frames and doorway canopies, but all too much has given way to metal or PVC replacement."[85]

Hardwick Village was not sufficient to satisfy the demand for new housing, and after the British Admiralty took control of the Chepstow shipyards in 1918 plans for a second garden suburb were announced.[86] Laid out by Admiralty architect Henry E. Farmer (b. 1865), in consultation with H. Avray Tipping, who had designed houses at Rhiwbina Garden Village (see p. 391), **Bulwarks Village** was a denser, 1,150-dwelling development of stylistically similar concrete houses connected to Hardwick Village by paths through existing woods.

SCOTLAND

In 1915 the Ministry of Munitions announced plans to build a massive explosives factory near the small town of Gretna, in the southwestern part of Scotland on the English border.[87] Originally, the 15,000 workers were to be housed in temporary wooden huts, but the ministry quickly reversed course and decided to build permanent housing in **Gretna** and **Eastriggs**, another modest town four-and-a-half miles to the west. Raymond Unwin, who was in charge of the housing branch of the Department of Explosives Supply, was responsible for the plan, while the housing was under the direction of C. M. Crickmer, who led

a team that included Geoffry Lucas and C. E. Simmons (1879–1952). Crickmer was also the designer of houses in Letchworth and prepared an early plan for Welwyn. In addition to the housing and the munitions plant, which at its peak would produce 800 tons of Cordite each week, more than all the other factories in the United Kingdom put together, the plan called for shops, schools, cinemas, recreation halls, an institute, and separate churches for Presbyterians, Episcopalians, and Catholics. The extensive undertaking, spread out on over fifteen square miles, was the largest built by the government since Well Hall Estate and required the construction of the development's own narrow-gauge railway network with 125 miles of track.

Unwin's axial plan for Gretna (1915–18) was dominated by Central Avenue, a broad boulevard aligned with the tower of the Gretna Green Church (1790) in the historic village. Lined with shops and public buildings, Central Avenue also served as the main approach from the railroad station. As Mervyn Miller observed, "a more spacious place was envisaged at the junction of Annan Road and Central Avenue, with enclosure across the minor axis after the manner of the junction of Heathgate and Meadway at Hampstead Garden Suburb." Unwin "balanced formal and informal elements" in the northern part of the plan, where "linked housing groups and greens opened off the curving Victory Avenue, which led from Annan Road to a more formally composed place in front of the Roman Catholic Church." The township of Eastriggs (1916–18), located on former farmland, was smaller and, in his book on Unwin, Miller found the plan, which "preserved an existing tree-lined avenue," to be "more fragmented than Gretna and there were fewer communal buildings."[88]

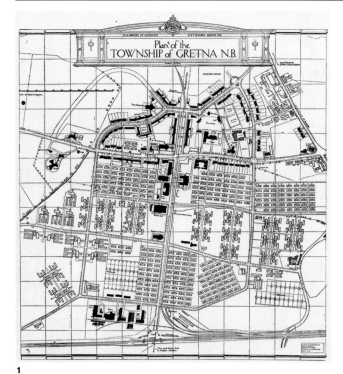

1

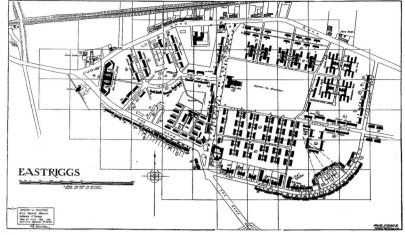

2

3

4

5

6

8

7

1. Plan, Gretna, Raymond Unwin, 1918. ACR18

2. Plan, Eastriggs, Raymond Unwin, 1917. JAIA17

3. Victory Avenue, Gretna. JGA (c. 1915)

4. The Rand, Eastriggs. LWCF (c. 1916)

5. Central Avenue, Gretna. HS (2012)

6. Victory Avenue showing Catholic Church, C. E. Simmons, c. 1915, in distance, Gretna. RCA

7. Canberra Road, Gretna. RCA (1996)

8. Shops on Central Avenue, Gretna. Dixon. GEO (2010)

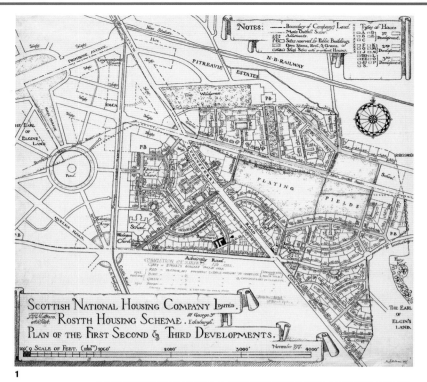

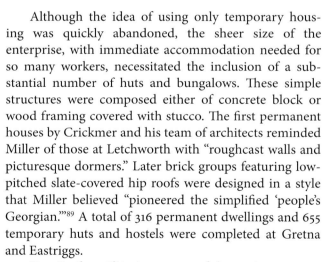

1. Plan, A. H. Mottram, 1917. RIAS

2. Queensferry Road and Aberlour Street. CFS (1950s)

3. King's Place. MR

4. Queensferry Road. MR

5. Backmarch Crescent. Rogers. MR (2009)

Although the idea of using only temporary housing was quickly abandoned, the sheer size of the enterprise, with immediate accommodation needed for so many workers, necessitated the inclusion of a substantial number of huts and bungalows. These simple structures were composed either of concrete block or wood framing covered with stucco. The first permanent houses by Crickmer and his team of architects reminded Miller of those at Letchworth with "roughcast walls and picturesque dormers." Later brick groups featuring low-pitched slate-covered hip roofs were designed in a style that Miller believed "pioneered the simplified 'people's Georgian.'"[89] A total of 316 permanent dwellings and 655 temporary huts and hostels were completed at Gretna and Eastriggs.

Despite the utilitarian nature of the project, or perhaps because of it, Robert Lorimer (1864–1929), one of Scotland's most distinguished architects, praised Gretna, writing that "here all is plain, practical, straightforward, of pleasant and reasonable proportion, and mercifully devoid of ornament or prettiness. A satisfying feeling of variety is achieved, not so much in an artificial attempt to get variety in the individual houses as by a happy scheme of plan and by the retention, wherever possible, of trees that existed on the site, and by seizing on any

feature or contour that suggested a reasonable motive." Lorimer singled out for special mention C. E. Simmons's Roman Catholic Church, describing it as "a fresh and expressive piece of architecture [that] illustrates how, if a man has a feeling for rhythm and proportion and fitness, and is able to handle his materials, quite excellent results can be achieved by the knowing use of ordinary brick and plain white plaster."[90] The production of Cordite was halted in 1919, and the houses at Gretna and Eastriggs were sold to private citizens beginning in the late 1920s.

Second to Gretna-Eastriggs, Scotland's most ambitious wartime garden village, **Rosyth**, was begun in 1915 by the Admiralty in order to house workers at the Rosyth Docks, a naval shipyard being built on the shores of the Firth of Forth, one mile south of the center of Dunfermline near the northern terminus of the Forth Bridge.[91] England's Garden City Association had vociferously advocated for the development of an auxiliary garden city since the docks construction project had first been announced in 1903.[92] Unwin prepared a master plan that was developed in detail by architect A. H. Mottram, a former employee of Parker and Unwin who now served as architect for the Scottish National Housing Company, the entity created to develop Rosyth.

Between 1915 and 1918, Mottram designed more than 1,400 houses based on Unwin's initial scheme. As John Gifford wrote in his 2003 architectural guidebook to Fife, Rosyth was "generously laid out and well provided with trees and churches, but lacking a clear centre."[93] The housing comprised terraces of varying length set behind individual front gardens along a mix of straight and curving roads bordered by grass verges and trees. King's Place served as a central spine, terminated at one end by a school, while Queensferry Road, with a broad land-scaped planting strip on one side, formed the principal residential axis from which culs-de-sac and short spurs branched off. The village featured numerous secluded closes. Houses along certain streets backed up to open spaces that included playing fields and parks, one of which was labeled The Wilderness. Sites were also pro-vided for churches, an institute, a YMCA, a theater, and shops, the last grouped around the confluence of major diagonal axes.

The first houses were completed at the time of the dockyard opening in 1916. When Mottram left for military service in 1918–19, Edinburgh-based archi-tects Alfred Greig (n.d.) and Walter Fairbairn (b. 1877) stepped in to design 150 houses, with Mottram resum-ing his work after the war and designing an additional 100 houses, a Masonic lodge, and a church. In 1925, development was halted with the closure of the ship-yard. World War II brought the docks back to life, but new construction, beginning in 1939 and continuing steadily through the century, did not follow Unwin and Mottram's plan.

Unwin also oversaw the design of **Mancot Village** (1916), in Queensferry, Clwyd, providing dwellings for munitions workers in stripped-down two-story red-brick semidetached and rowhouses with hipped roofs, occasional arched doorways, and protruding bays.[94] The houses featured individual front and rear gardens, with some grouped around closes. The plan also included hostels, a church, and a hospital. The neighborhood, comprising Hawarden Way, Crossways, and Mancot Way, was visually coherent in a way that later extensions to the village did not replicate.

FRANCE

Claude-Nicolas Ledoux's design for the ideal city of **Chaux**, prepared in the last decades of the eighteenth century both before and after the French Revolution, is the first significant planned village in France to be built around a modern industrial entity.[95] In 1774, Ledoux, a fashionable architect who had been appointed an inspector responsible for overseeing salt production in three regions of eastern France, was placed in charge of designing a new saltworks, the *Saline Royale*, near the Forest of Chaux, in Arc-et-Senans, near Besançon. Years earlier Ledoux had outspokenly criticized the haphaz-ard arrangement of France's principal saltworks and its attendant town. In his initial plan for the *Saline Royale*,

Mancot Village

1. Typical rowhouse and gardens. JGA (c. 1918)

prepared before a site had been finalized, Ledoux called for a single, square building containing the full compo-nents of a village, including not only the saltworks but also workers' quarters, a director's residence, a store, workshops, and a chapel. The fortresslike structure, enclosing a 470-foot-square courtyard for wood stor-age, was surrounded by a 20-foot-wide ring of gardens and a boundary wall. Louis XV rejected the plan in part because it did little to prevent the spread of fire but also, as Ruth Eaton has noted, "on account of its unprec-edented architectural grandeur, shocking to a king who was used to seeing columns employed for palaces and temples but not for factories."[96]

Ledoux's second scheme, prepared after a pictur-esque site had been selected in the Loüe Valley, was no less ornate, calling for individual pavilions arranged in a closed half circle: "What before had been a single fac-tory building," according to Anthony Vidler, "Ledoux now broke up into elements of a small town, planned . . . to take advantage of breezes from different direc-tions, which would at once disperse the smoke and noxious fumes from the evaporation process and render the inhabitants healthier."[97] Along the diameter, Ledoux flanked a director's house that also included offices, accounting rooms, a courtroom, laboratory, and chapel, with the factory sheds, allowing for easy surveillance of the workers. The arc of the semicircle was formed by five curving pavilions, four of which, nearly identical in design, accommodated 200 workers and their families grouped according to trade. The central building served as a gatehouse and included guards' quarters, a prison, and bakery. Vegetable gardens were provided between the houses and a wall that wrapped the entire complex. Construction began in 1775 and was completed in 1778.

As built, however, the saltworks represented only a piece of what Ledoux envisioned as a grand indus-trial and agricultural utopia. Ledoux intended that the saltworks would become the core of a new city, its plan mirrored to complete the circle. A wall would enclose the complex and would in turn be ringed by concen-tric landscaped boulevards lined by terraced houses and outbuildings to become, as Vidler put it, a "town whose center, so to speak, is inaccessible."[98] Ledoux would soon eliminate the boundary wall, allowing the village to spill

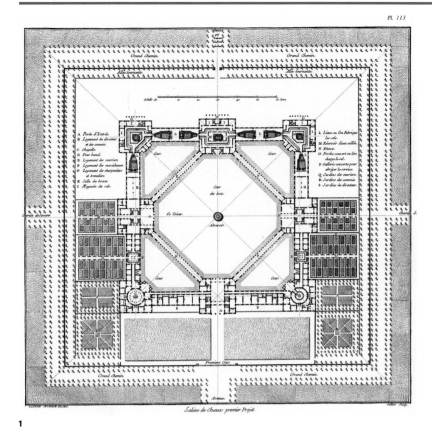

1

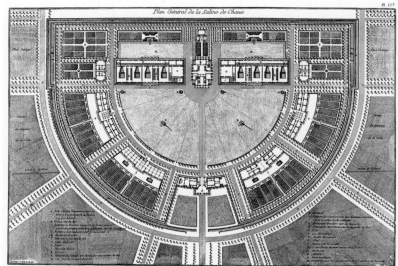

3

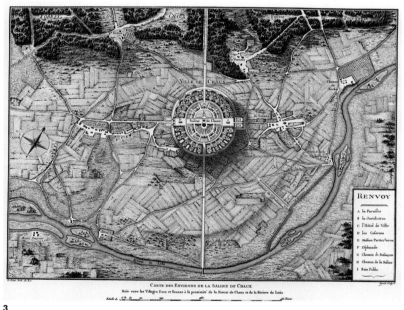

2

4

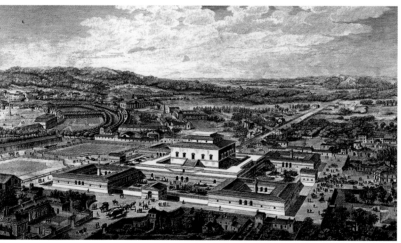

5

1. Initial plan, Claude-Nicolas
Ledoux, 1773–74. CNL

2. Plan, Claude-Nicolas Ledoux,
1774–78. CNL

3. Plan showing location of
the Saline de Chaux, c. 1795.
CNL

4. Bird's-eye view, 1795–1802.
CNL

5. Bird's-eye view of Market,
after 1784. CNL

6 **7**

into the surrounding landscape. In place of the terraces, Ledoux encircled the saltworks with freestanding public buildings, such as a church, a market hall, a town hall, a stock exchange, and a bathhouse. For the hills and forests beyond, he designed workshops and houses for coopers, sawyers, woodcutters, milliners, and other rural tradesmen, as well as merchants, stockbrokers, and academics, proposing, as Eaton has written, "monumental structures for the most humble dwellings as for the most prestigious."[99] Imprisoned in the wake of the Revolution, Ledoux turned his attention toward institutions with a moral bent as he invented new building types such as a *Pacifère*, a kind of legal court where mediation would be used to resolve conflicts; a Panaretheon and House of Union, both dedicated to moral enlightenment, and the latter decorated with inscriptions promoting fraternity; and quite dubiously, the Oikema, or Temple Dedicated to Love, which was in fact a brothel intended to educate children about vice. Other among the architect's designs included foundries, schools, warehouses, farm buildings, a hospice, and a hunting lodge.

The austere and often simple architecture would have been just as appropriate, as Vidler observed, in an urban setting as in rural Chaux. In that regard, Ledoux's vision offered a sharp contrast to the associative rustic architecture that characterized the picturesquely designed hamlets (*hameaux*) that were popular at the time, perhaps the most famous example being Marie Antoinette's **Hameau de la Reine** (1783–88) at Versailles, designed by Richard Mique (1728–1794) and Hubert Robert (1733–1808) in a rustic style which belied the luxurious appointments within.[100]

The *cités ouvrières*, or workers' housing estates, of nineteenth-century France were on par with those of England and Germany. In 1846 J. A. Scrive, a textile manufacturer, built one of the first *cités ouvrières* in **Marquette**, near Lille.[101] The roughly symmetrical plan by architect C. Tierce (n.d.) featured a central church

square from which long rectangular blocks angled outward. Tierce may also have designed the semidetached and quadruple houses that were provided with individual gardens and rented to employees, marking a notable increase in standards from the typical workers' dwelling. The quadruple houses—each unit occupying a quarter of the plan—were placed in single rows down the center of the block. Although freestanding when built, the houses, roughly half of which remain, are now connected by single-story garage and entrance additions. The neighborhood was situated between the factory and an administrative complex, and workers enjoyed a company-built dining hall, bathhouse, and recreational building set within an adjacent park.

In 1852, Louis-Napoléon passed a housing act that provided funding for additional *cités ouvrières*, although the overall results "were not especially encouraging," according to the American housing expert Edith Elmer Wood.[102] Among the successes was an estate begun in 1853 in the eastern industrial town of **Mulhouse** by the Société des cités ouvrières de Mulhouse, a housing association led by local industrialist Jean Dollfuss.[103] The plan was similar in some ways to Marquette, with rectangular blocks accommodating one- and two-story quadruple houses and rowhouses, each with its own garden, but the project differed substantially in that it allowed workers to purchase their homes in affordable annual payments over about thirteen years. Émile Muller (1823–1889), a civil engineer-turned-housing reformer, designed the houses that would influence many industrial villages to follow, and prepared the town plan, using the government funds to provide landscaping and to build streets, sidewalks, a water system, bathhouse, bakery, and restaurant. Beginning with 100 houses completed in 1854, the project grew in phases to include nearly 1,250 houses by the turn of the century, most of which have been altered beyond recognition, although remnants can be found among the streets that remain largely as planned.

6. Aerial view. Joly. CRT (2006)

7. Director's house, Claude-Nicolas Ledoux, 1775–78. Süssbrich. WC (2007)

Hameau de la Reine

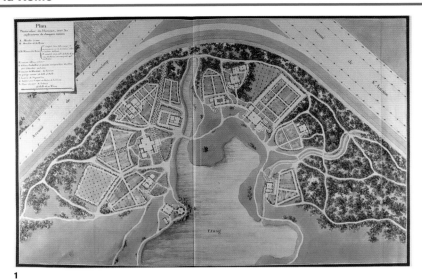

1

2

1. Plan, Richard Mique and Hubert Robert, 1786. BEM

2. Typical view. Dalbéra. FL (2012)

3, 4. Typical views. RAMSA (2004)

3

4

Marquette

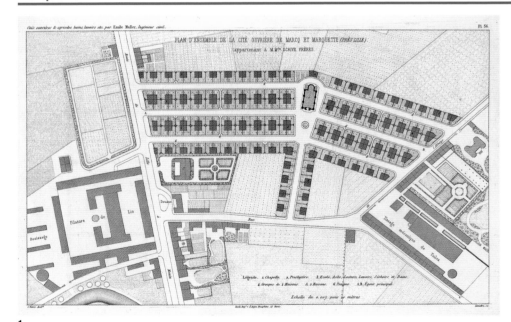

1

2

1. Plan, C. Tierce, 1846. NYPL

2. Entrance. AMMB

3. Aerial view. SPVM (2010)

3

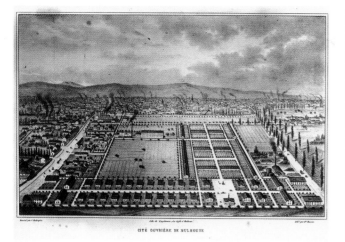

CITÉ OUVRIÈRE DE MULHOUSE

Cités ouvrières de Mulhouse. — Pavillon pour quatre ménages (*). — Dessin de Lancelot, d'après une photographie.

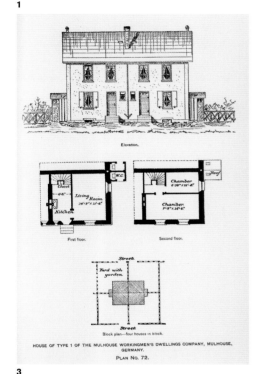

Elevation.

First floor.   Second floor.

Block plan.—four houses in block.

HOUSE OF TYPE 1 OF THE MULHOUSE WORKINGMEN'S DWELLINGS COMPANY, MULHOUSE, GERMANY.
PLAN NO. 72.

1. Aerial perspective. RA (1853)

2. Quadruple house, Émile Muller, c. 1853. MUL

3. Elevation and plans of quadruple house. HWP

4. Overall view. Wioland. RA (1905)

5. Rue Madeleine and Rue Gustave Doré. Patart. ETU (2004)

Built in the 1870s, the Menier Chocolate Company's village of **Noisiel-sur-Marne**, fifteen miles east of Paris, "epitomized the *ville industrielle*," according to John S. Garner, "in that it combined the planning and paternal aspects" of its predecessors "with an unusual commitment to architecture."[104] In 1825, Jean-Antoine Brutus Menier (1795–1853), who first hit upon the idea of marketing chocolate as a confectionary item in bars wrapped in paper, purchased land for a new factory on the southern banks of the Marne, just east of the hamlet of Noisiel. The existing town comprised little more than a single road, some farms, and the expansive Parc de Noisiel, which would remain as a green space. Between 1850 and 1875, as the chocolate business boomed, the Menier company expanded its factory and built a supporting village according to a master plan by Bonneau (n.d.), who had designed the Menier family's Noisiel château, and his assistant and successor Jules Saulnier (1817–1881), who was commissioned to design the new

factory complex in 1864 that would include Noisiel's best-known building—the structurally innovative (Sigfried Giedion identified it as "the first building of true skeleton type") and architecturally distinguished iron-frame, brick-and-tile-infill turbine building (1871–72), straddling the Marne.[105]

The workers' village, also believed to have been designed by Saulnier, was laid out on a sloping, partially wooded, roughly 75-acre site southeast of the factory, from which it was buffered by the Menier château, with its picturesque gardens, and a large tract of privately held land. The plan, featuring gaslit 32-foot-wide streets bordered by sidewalks and poplar trees, consisted of rectangular north–south blocks crossed by a broad promenade that functioned as a village square, with a school prominently terminating the east side, and the west side left open to views of a church and cemetery in the near distance. Also bordering the square were stores, meeting halls, a concert hall, library, and a dining hall

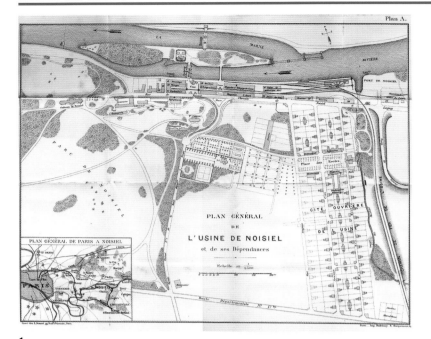

1. Plan, Bonneau and Jules Saulnier. MDN (1889)

2. Aerial view. MDN1 (1954)

3, 4. Typical streets. MDN (c. 1900)

5. Rue Jean Jaurès and Rue Henri Menier. Myra. WC (2012)

6. Turbine building, Jules Saulnier, 1871–72. Myra. WC (2012)

where workers could buy or prepare meals. Saulnier provided a picturesque park to the east of the village across a small creek.

The two-story predominantly semidetached houses—larger and admitting more light and air than those in Mulhouse and Marquette—shared generously sized, 100-by-100-foot lots delineated by brick and iron fences. Placed flush against the sidewalk, the houses were entered from the side, allowing for rear gardens, in each of which the company planted twelve fruit trees. Saulnier staggered the houses along the street so that those on one side overlooked gardens across the way. The blocks were deep enough to accommodate

quadruple houses on the interior. Detached houses were also included, facing intersections with chamfered corners and finialed gables. The simple but sound brown-brick, red-tile-roofed houses were rented to employees at affordable rates—roughly one-twelfth the wage of the head of household—giving the company a modest 3 percent return.

Construction of the *cite ouvrière* began in the early 1870s and continued in phases until 1896, by which time 156 houses accommodated 600 of the factory's 1,500 employees, the remainder of whom lived in dormitories or off-site. Menier was eventually acquired by Nestlé, which has restored the village and factory.

Germany's first workers' colonies, typically known as *arbeiterkolonies*, began to appear in the mid-nineteenth century as mining and textile companies took steps to provide higher standards of accommodation in an effort to attract and retain workers. The series of colonies built by Krupp, the steel and armaments manufacturer, during the late nineteenth and early twentieth centuries are the best-known examples in Germany, but these are paralleled by numerous other efforts. Much of the activity from an early date took place in the Ruhr region of North Rhine-Westphalia, the center of the country's coal-mining and iron and steel industries.

The Ruhr's first company-built housing was begun in 1844 in **Eisenheim**, Oberhausen, by the Jacobi, Haniel & Huyssen mining company, later to become Gutehoffnungshütte (Ironworks of Good Hope). The colony began with seven individual "masters' houses," two townhouses, and a semidetached house for upper-level ironworkers who commuted to the factory one half-hour's walk away.[106] The settlement would develop in phases until 1903, when it included fifty-one mostly miners' houses that emulated the quadruple house type pioneered in Mulhouse, France. At Eisenheim, where they were introduced in 1865, the houses were placed close to the street in order to reserve the interiors of the three blocks for gardens. Despite some destruction during World War II and later threats of demolition, much of the settlement remains intact.

Stahlhausen (1868), west of the Ruhr city of Bochum, was the first colony to be built by the Bochumer Verein, a giant mining conglomerate that required housing for workers at a new steel factory.[107] Architects Oscar Spetzler (b. 1841) and A. Sartorius (n.d.) also based their quadruple houses on those of Mulhouse, allowing each unit to have its own garden and a shed for keeping pigs and hens, with 40 additional acres provided for allotment gardens. The provision of what were essentially small farms for the miners, a type known as *Bergmannskotten* (miners' cottages), or simply *kotten*, with space to grow vegetables and keep livestock, would persist as a prevalent feature of many German colonies, forming a bridge, as historian Cedric Bolz has written, from the "agrarian to industrial eras."[108] Beginning with eight brick houses in 1868, by 1905 Stahlhausen included more than ninety buildings containing about 460 units of housing that an English delegation, visiting in 1906, deemed "quite up to the standard of workmen's requirements," and "in regard to some of their sanitary arrangements . . . highly creditable. There is plenty of air and plenty of room. The houses stand apart and there is no overcrowding."[109]

In 1864 Ferdinand Heye (1838–1889) established a glass factory in the city of Gerresheim, five miles east of Düsseldorf.[110] Heye soon began to provide free housing to his workers in one-story brick rowhouses with rear gardens located next to the glassworks. By 1880 the **Glashüttensiedlung** (glass works settlement) numbered

1

2

3

1. Plan. SRW (1903)
2. Typical street. SRW
3. Houses. LVRI

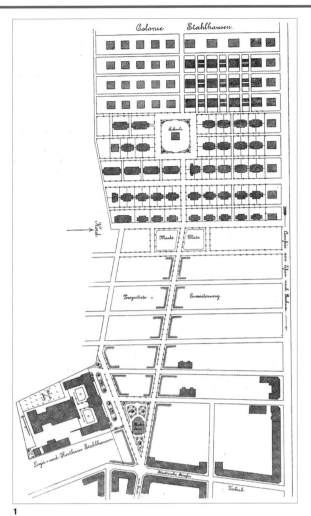

1. Plan. ZB

2. Typical street. SBPI

3. Overall view. SBPI (1910)

4. Gardens. SBPI

5. Baarestrasse. Cschirp. WC (2009)

some 204 dwelling units, grouped around four court-yards. Heye's beneficence extended beyond free housing for his workers (maintained by the company till 1918) to include eight-hour workdays, medical care, pensions, the establishment of a school on donated land, and the sponsorship of athletic clubs and a library. For workers employed on the night shift, Heye provided window-less rooms for daytime rest. In 1906, three years before Gerresheim was incorporated into the city of Düssel-dorf, the architect W. Jacobi (n.d.) provided additional housing for higher-level workers and managers. Meis-tersiedlung, located about one-half mile southwest of

the original settlment, consisted of two-story brick row-houses with rear gardens wrapping all four sides of one squarish block.

Spindlersfeld (1873), on the southeastern outskirts of Berlin, along the river Spree, housed workers of the W. Spindler dye works in four three-story houses, each able to accommodate twelve to fourteen people placed amid gardens along a single street. Significantly, the company also sponsored social welfare programs and built amenities, including a bathhouse, kindergarten, schools, a library, a recreation house, and a 25-acre park.[111] In **Wildau,** twenty miles southeast of Berlin, the

1

2

3

4

1. Typical houses. SLD (1900)

2. Typical houses. ABR (2008)

3. Meistersiedlung houses, W. Jacobi, c. 1906. SLD (c. 1920)

4. Meistersiedlung houses. Gehrmann. WC (2008)

Spindlersfeld

1

2

1. Mentzelstrasse. HG06 (c. 1906)

2. Recreation house. HG06 (c. 1906)

Schwartzkopff Company, makers of locomotives, built a workers' colony (1897) containing sixty-one four-unit houses, thirteen double houses for higher-level employees, stores, a casino and clubhouse, and a schoolhouse and gymnasium.[112] Construction began in 1906 on a second phase of thirty-five houses. Balconies, variations in building massing, and ornamentation disguised the nearly identical house plans, working with street trees and landscaping to add texture to the rectilinear streets.

Gartensiedlung Gronauerwald (1900–1906), developed by paper manufacturer Richard Zanders (1860–1906) on 30 heavily wooded acres on the outskirts of Bergisch-Gladbach, a town of 15,000 ten miles northeast of Cologne in North Rhine-Westphalia, was one of Germany's earliest exemplars of garden village design.[113]

The plan, by landscape architect Albert Brodersen (1857–1930), provided generously spaced house plots (on average 50-by-100 feet) on either side of a 50-foot-wide thoroughfare that diagonally bisected the site and led to a plaza at the northwest corner surrounded by houses with shops on the ground floor. North of the main street, in roughly the center of the site, along An der Eiche, a crescent of shops was topped by apartments. The seventy-two one-and-a-half- to two-story detached and semidetached cottages, half-timbered or with buff- or yellow-tinted plaster facades and red-tile roofs, were largely the work of architect Ludwig Bopp (1869–1930), who had designed Zanders's house in Bergisch-Gladbach. In 1911, Ewart G. Culpin praised Gronauerwald as "a very picturesque estate . . . Although not comparable

Wildau

1. Four-family house. HG06 (c. 1906)

2. Aerial view. OSG (2010)

3. Gardens. OSG (2010)

4. Aerial view. OSG (2010)

1

2

3

4

Gartensiedlung Gronauerwald

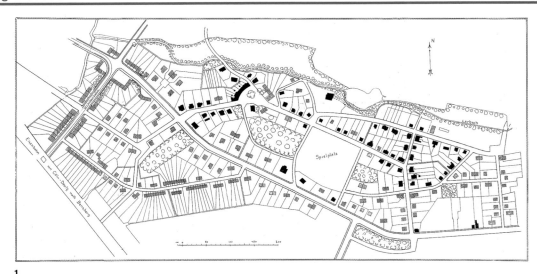

1

2

1. Plan, Albert Brodersen, c. 1900. SBG

2. An der Eiche. Wihl. SBG (c. 1960)

3. An der Eiche. Roscher. SBG (1919)

4. Houses, Ludwig Bopp. SBG (1909)

3

4

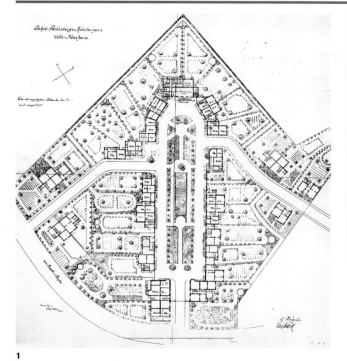

1

2

1. Plan, Hans Verbeek and Balduin Schilling, 1907. RB

2. Pallenbergheim. ABR (2008)

from an architectural point of view to Bournville or Port Sunlight, the village is an enormous improvement upon the usual German type, and there is an evident trend towards a better condition of things, physically and artistically. What one, perhaps, misses most is any concentrated idea of making the central square a focus-point."[114] In 1913 Zanders's widow established a nonprofit society to administer the development, which, by 1930, had grown to include over 400 houses on about 100 acres.

Siedlung Pallenberg (1905–7), located four miles north of central Cologne, was the brainchild of furniture manufacturer Jacob Pallenberg, who, perhaps following the example of Krupp's Altenhof estate (see p. 745), wanted to build affordable housing for a number of his retired employees.[115] Hans Verbeek (1873–1954) and Balduin Schilling (1868–1929) designed the twenty-three single-family houses with individual gardens and prepared the low-density plan that loosely focused on a landscaped green. The arched entrance to the village was flanked by two apartment houses, intended to serve single residents of each sex. The estate also included a community house containing a library and public baths. The extensive landscaping scheme by Fritz Enke (1861–1931) contributed to the rural, village-like feel.

Theodor Fischer's **Gmindersdorf** (1903–15), outside Reutlingen in Baden-Württenberg, built for workers of the Ulrich Gminder textile mill, was a 33-acre garden village composed of 115 houses and a marketplace.[116] Fischer softened the rigidity of his orthogonal plan, as Vittorio Magnago Lampugnani has written, with "gentle curves and strategically placed irregularities."[117] Fischer only partially succeeded in fulfilling his intention of bounding the streets with continuous terraced houses as his client requested folkloric freestanding buildings,

about fifty of which were realized in blocks of four flats each. However, the architect–urban designer had his way in one section, where Biedermeier-style terraced houses, arranged in a crescent with, at its center, a village hall in the form of a large country house, faced a formal park and was buffered at the rear by back buildings and a small greenbelt. Semidetached houses in groups filled most of the village's other blocks, and a main street, now named for the architect, linked the crescent, a market square, and the Gminder cotton works. Though little remembered today, Gmindersdorf was exhibited at the influential Universal City Planning Exhibition in Berlin in 1910, the first such exhibition ever held devoted exclusively to the topic.

Fischer's ambitious plans to expand the village of **Limburger Hof** (1911–13) were also only partly realized.[118] Located in the city of Ludwigshafen, Rheinland-Pfalz, on the Rhine River opposite Mannheim in the southwestern part of the country, the industrial area was home since 1865 to Germany's largest chemical company, BASF (Badische Anilin- und Soda-Fabrik), which had built around the turn of the century long straight rows of barracks-like brick houses accommodating close to 3,700 people in 660 dwellings. Fischer's fan-shaped expansion plan of straight and curved streets included a significant amount of park space along with a church, school, nursing home, and terraced houses. The recreational and community facilities were never built, and Fischer's architectural contribution was limited to seventeen groups of houses yielding ninety-eight dwelling units.

Gartenstadt Marga (1906–14), Brieske, Senfentberg, claimed by some to be Germany's first garden city, was built to house coal miners, factory workers, and company executives of the town's leading industrial concern, Bergbau-Actiengesellschaft, an undertaking deemed

1. Plan, Theodor Fischer, c. 1903. CHB

2. Bird's-eye view of crescent. ATU

3. Typical houses. ATU

4. Blockäckerstrasse. HDG (c. 1905)

5. Zaisentalstrasse. Vux. WC (2011)

6. Aerial view. RBG (c. 2010)

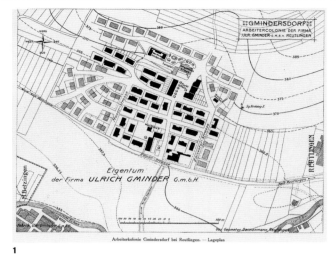

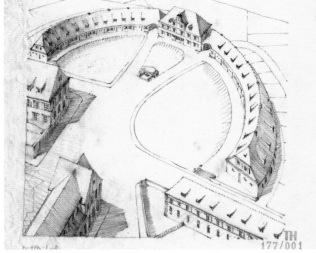

"highly ambitious" as the area was considered the "dust bowl" of lower Brandenburg and thus "correspondingly sparsely populated."[119] Dresden-based architect Georg von Mayenburg (1870–1930) was responsible for both the plan and most of the buildings, including a significant civic component that accompanied the housing. At the center of Mayenburg's circular plan was a rectangular market square from which tree-lined streets radiated, leading to a greenbelt with allotment gardens separating the village from the industrial areas. Mayenburg's delightful collection of buildings included a meeting hall, an inn, a school, shops, and a church surrounding the square, as well as seventy-eight houses in fifteen different vernacular styles, including English country cottages and half-timbered designs inspired by examples from rural Saxony, many set behind modest front lawns.

Mayenburg was also responsible for the plan and houses of **Kolonie Zschornewitz** (1915), Saxony-Anhalt, "built in the awesome shadow of the largest AEG powerhouse in Central Germany" and admired for its "garden city layout and 'heimatschutz' square and streets."[120] Over the course of seven years, Mayenburg completed about 200 mostly two-story Biedermeier-style houses whose placement along charming, curving streets stood in stark contrast to the looming industrial structures. The centerpiece of the estate was a cupola-topped community building with arched openings at its base.

The **Teutoburgia Estate** (1909–23), Herne, built by the Bochumer Verein for both upper- and lower-level

Limburger Hof

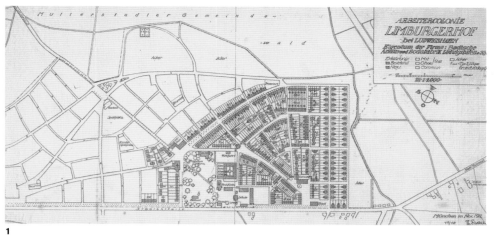

1. Plan, Theodor Fischer, 1911. ATU

2. Rendering. ATU (c. 1911)

3. Typical houses. ATU

4. Knietschstrasse. AGL (2007)

Gartenstadt Marga

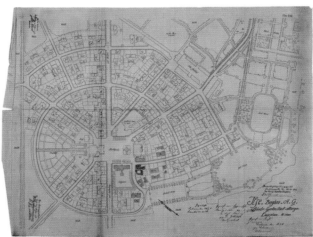

1. Plan, Georg von Mayenburg, 1911. BL

2. Bird's-eye view. BL

3. Market square. BL

4. View showing church tower in distance. Drews. RDD (2007)

5. Typical street. Drews. RDD (2007)

Kolonie Zschornewitz

1. Houses with powerhouse in background. FM (c. 1920)

2. Typical street. Antony. WC (2005)

3. Community building. Horn. MH (2011)

4. Community building. CRS (1920s)

1

2

3

4

Teutoburgia Estate

1

1. Aerial view. GE (2006)

2, 3. Typical views. Arnold. WC (2007)

4. Schreberstrasse. Icema. PAN (2012)

3

2

4

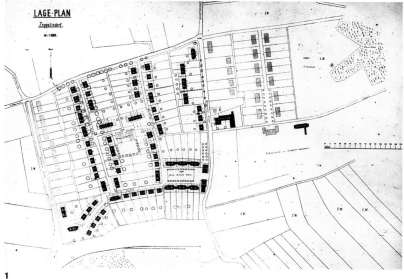

workers at a new colliery, included 459 housing units in 136 buildings designed by company architect Otto Berndt (n.d.), who prepared four prototype vernacular designs, with steep roofs and half-timbering combined with brick and plaster, used in twenty-one configurations ranging from detached houses to rambling terraces.[121] Berndt's site plan covered 53 acres with curving streets branching off of an entrance boulevard with a landscaped median that led to the colliery gates.

Zeppelindorf (1913–17), in the south German town of Friedrichshafen, was designed by Stuttgart-based architects Paul Bonatz and Friedrich Eugen Scholer (1874–1949) to house workers of the airship company Zeppelin-Wohlfahrt GmbH.[122] Bonatz had recently designed a house (1910) for the company's director, Alfred Colsman. Working on a roughly rectangular, 25-acre site north of the factory and about a mile from the city center, Bonatz, showing the influence of his former employer, Theodor Fischer, with whom he had worked on the design of Gmindersdorf, called for six types of predominantly one-and-a-half-story houses with low-eaved hip roofs, dormers, and bay windows, which he placed along a subtly curving hierarchical street network. Each of the thirty-one detached, thirty-one semidetached, and four-unit terraced houses that were realized included a front and rear garden. In total, less than 10 percent of the site was built upon.

Konig-Wilhelm Platz, a village green, was situated not at the center of the plan, which Bonatz reserved for a Kinderheim (orphanage), but at the eastern edge, where a tavern and a shop formed an entrance gateway, leaving the Hindenburgstrasse, an arcing diagonal road in the southwest, to serve as the link between the village and the works.

In addition to planting fruit trees in residents' gardens, the company, against Bonatz's advice, encouraged workers to keep cattle in sheds adjacent to the houses. This and other "differences in opinion with regard to hygiene and expediency," led Bonatz to distance himself from the project, which was ultimately supervised by his former colleague Paul Zeller (n.d.). World War I halted development before Zeppelindorf was completed, and World War II witnessed the destruction of portions of the village, but later reconstruction preserved the original street plan and architectural character.

The Krupp Colonies

The planned workers' colonies built by Krupp beginning in 1863 and continuing for more than fifty years illustrate the evolution of model workmens' colonies from hastily constructed barracks to enlightened garden villages. Most of the Krupp settlements were built

1. Plan, Paul Bonatz and Friedrich Eugen Scholer, c. 1917. ALZ

2. Aerial view. ALZ

3. Houses on Konig-Wilhelm Platz. CHB (c. 1918)

4. Houses on Konig-Wilhelm Platz. Currlin. CUR (2009)

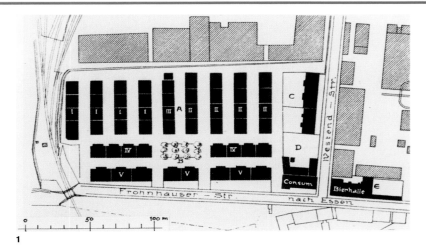

1. Plan showing Alt-Westend, top, and Neu-Westend, bottom, c. 1871. WGK

2. Neu-Westend. HAK (1875)

in and around Essen, the "Pittsburgh of Germany," as American journals called it, a city which was, in its way, one large industrial village, with a medieval core surrounded by coal mines, iron and steel works, and pockets of housing. Essen's development was intertwined with the explosive growth of the Krupp enterprise, especially during the period after the wars of 1859 to 1862, when, as planning historian Ursula Petz has noted, "Krupp is Essen and . . . the city of Essen is synonymous with Krupp."[123] In 1850, the population of Essen was 9,000 and Krupp, founded forty years earlier as the Friedrich Krupp Cast Steel Works, counted 100 employees. By 1906, Krupp employed 35,000 of Essen's 240,000 residents. By the close of World War I, Krupp, having constructed more than 12,000 units of housing, was Germany's largest private sector housing provider. As Catherine Bauer observed in her 1934 book, *Modern Housing*, in which she claimed that "there is little housing in all Europe which is physically better than that of the Krupps," the company "had three acknowledged purposes: to attract the best workers and keep them efficient, to inspire 'filial loyalty,' and to insure that Essen itself should be a wholesome, attractive, and modern city. As for the last purpose, they succeeded quite remarkably. Their own large-scale construction served to heighten competition, lower speculative land-prices, and raise the standards of purely commercial building. Their favorable attitude toward city and regional planning makes the Ruhr district today one of the most advanced and orderly regions in the world in this respect. Anyone who will compare Essen with its American counterpart, Pittsburgh, cannot sneer too hastily at the paternal 'enlightenment' of the Krupps."[124]

The Krupp colonies can be divided into two phases, the first overseen by Alfred Krupp (1812–1887), son of the company's founder, between 1863 and 1873, and the second by Alfred's son, Friedrich "Fritz" Alfred Krupp (1854–1902), who, beginning in the early 1890s after his father's death, undertook an ambitious series of colonies that both influenced and reflected international trends in town planning.[125] As a publication issued by Krupp on the occasion of its centennial in 1910 stated, "If we wish

to draw a comparison between the work of the two men in this field, we may say, that the father completed the foundations and the rough walls of the building, while the son finished the house and made it pleasant to dwell in."[126] As Budgett Meakin put it in 1905, the Krupp colonies exhibited "the gradual development of the ideal garden cottage from the most unsatisfactory beginnings,"[127] illustrating what Cedric Bolz has more recently described as a "conscious shift towards building quaint single-family 'cottage' style homes situated along curved streets and lined with greenery."[128]

Completed in 1863, the first Krupp colony, **Alt-Westend**, amounted to little more than nine rows of "ungainly" two-story barracks clad in corrugated iron containing 144 two-room lodgings built in three months' time on a superblock adjacent to the Essen works.[129] The same year, Alfred Krupp, "aware that this first venture into the housing sector left much to be desired," established a division of housing and planning to be led by Gustav Kraemer (d. 1890), a former state planner.[130] Kraemer's maiden effort, **Neu-Westend** (1871), carried out after a nearly decade-long lull in construction, added five buildings to Alt-Westend as well as a beer hall and company store. Aside from slightly larger units and a small central square, however, the colony offered little in the way of improved conditions.[131] **Nordhof** (1871) and **Schederhof** (1872), north and south of the works, respectively, provided similarly prosaic barracks grouped together on large blocks, but Schederhof, the only Krupp colony to be designed by company architect Julius Rasch (1830–1887), marked a notable improvement in the communal environment, including amenities such as a park with a music pavilion, allotment gardens, stores, a beer hall, schools, and a market square, all helping to offset the bleak residential scene of 772 dwelling units in which, as an observer put it in 1886, "gloomier, more forlorn-looking streets could hardly be imagined than are made by the rows of these houses, all in dark, smoky brick, no yards, no trees, no sidewalks even, no grass plots, nothing but these gloomy three-story structures, reaching from street to street, and as repulsive as a prison or a tobacco factory."[132]

Nordhof

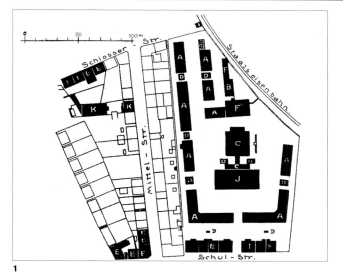

1

2

1. Plan, c. 1871. WGK

2. Typical view. HAK (1900)

Schederhof

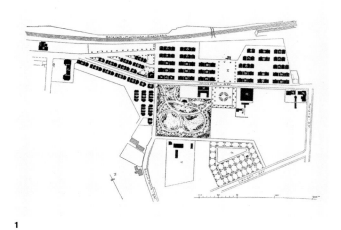

1

2

1. Plan, Julius Rasch, 1872. FDE

2. Barracks. MFV (c. 1905)

Baumhof (also known as Drei Linden), built in two stages in 1872 and 1890, represented "the first step towards the ideal."[133] It was established at a farther distance—about three-quarters of a mile—from the works, in the fields south of Essen where land costs were low enough to allow for a more dispersed layout in which the superblocks of earlier colonies were replaced by smaller blocks and the barracks were broken up into slightly more picturesque two-story multifamily brick houses with brick stringcourses, arched windows, and bracketed gables, each set within its own garden and embellished with loggias and balconies. The houses accommodated three, four, or eight families each to provide a total of 154 units, although conditions were hardly luxurious. Describing Baumhof's quadruple-house type, John S. Garner observed: "The small apartments and poor ventilation offer small improvement over the row houses at Copley [see p. 702]."[134] Despite gardens that provided residents with social spaces and free-time activities, the community lacked a full range of social institutions.

Cronenberg (1873), west of the works in Essen, was more ambitious in size and scope, housing by 1905 a population of 8,000 workers and their families in 1,572 dwellings.[135] Here, smaller blocks were again employed,

but the overall size of the colony resulted in a sprawling grid of unadorned brick and quarry-stone three- and four-story semidetached and terraced houses, the bleakness of which was only relieved by street trees and small allotment gardens surrounding the houses, as well as diminutive 30-square-foot gardens for drying clothes and a central two-and-a-half-acre park that helped give the "colony a rural character," according to William Mayner, writing in *House & Garden* in 1906, by which time the colony's street trees had begun to mature.[136] Cronenberg also included community facilities, such as a market square with music pavilion, a library, meeting hall, beer hall, and a co-op store adjacent to the park in the center of the plan. An elementary school was established to also serve residents of nearby Krupp settlements. Despite the amenities, C. H. Blackall (1857–1942), a Boston-based, Beaux-Arts-trained American architect who was also a prolific architectural writer, commenting in 1886, wished for something more: "As to the houses themselves, they are well built and kept in good order and answer every purpose of housing the people, but they are far from pleasant in appearance. They are plain, inexpensive barracks—hardly more; and no one could possibly conjure a home out of the forlorn,

Baumhof

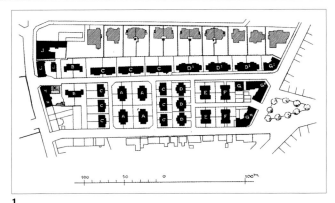

1

2

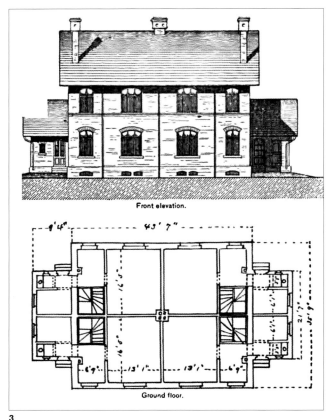

Front elevation.

Ground floor.

3

Cronenberg

1

2

dull red structures which repeat themselves block after block with such monotonous sameness . . . It costs so little more to make the houses attractive that one cannot help wishing for a little less comfort, perhaps, and more individuality."[137] Cronenberg was demolished in 1933 to make way for a factory expansion.

While recognizing that these early Essen colonies deserved "high praise" and that "not every wealthy manufacture would do what Herr Krupp has done, even were the necessity great," Blackall found more to admire in France's Mulhouse and in Italy's Schio (see p. 786):

Signor Rossi's colony in the latter city is certainly by far the most pleasing in appearance, and much more is done there to thoroughly educate the workmen and give them comfortable surroundings, than in either Essen or Mülhausen. But at Mülhausen each man is his own master, and the conditions of sale and ownership of property tend to develop individuality and self-reliance, which while perhaps inexpedient under all conditions, certainly work very successfully among the Alsatians. Considered simply as working-men's colonies, Herr Krupp's establishments are by all odds least satisfactory . . . It is doubtful if any one would take a special pride in announcing himself as a resident of the Schederhof Colony, for instance, and we can hardly believe that any son of Herr Krupp would be contented to build him a house and live right in the midst of the workmen, as Signor Rossi's son has done at Schio. Herr Krupp has simply recognized the absolute necessity of providing for his workmen, who but for his care, would be undoubtedly a hundredfold worse off than they are.[138]

The colonies built after 1890 under the direction of Friedrich Alfred Krupp were to demonstrate that "the principle of sensible and artistic town-planning" could assert "itself side by side with the demands of domestic architecture."[139] With Gustav Kraemer's death in 1890, Robert Schmohl (1855–1944) took over as head of Krupp's planning and housing division, a position he would hold for more than thirty years, during which time he was responsible for nearly all of the new colonies. Schmohl, hailing from a family of master builders in Isny, trained in Stuttgart before becoming a railway architect and later a municipal architect for the city, a job he held at the time of his recommendation for the position at Krupp. In 1896, Schmohl made a study trip to England. He was also an early member of the Deutscher Werkbund.

Schmohl's first colony, **Altenhof**, begun in 1893, built for retired or disabled Krupp employees, widows, and widowers who could live the remainder of their days rent-free, ushered in the new era.[140] With no need to be near the works, Altenhof was laid out by Schmohl on a former farm south of Essen to feature one- and two-story half-timber-and-stucco houses with porches and half-hip roofs sitting comfortably among flower gardens on irregular blocks shaped by a mix of curving and straight, wide tree-lined streets. Compared with the earlier colonies, Altenhof was "almost exaggeratedly idyllic," according to Theodore Böll: "The loyalty of [Krupp's] 'folk' was rewarded with houses as small as toys though certainly functional, surrounded by little gardens in a green area with quiet streets."[141] Traffic islands were planted as small greens and an exceptional amount of land—roughly 50 acres—was given over to the Kruppscher Waldpark, a wooded park with a valley that separated the 186 houses in the western half of the colony, known as Altenhof I (1893–99), from the later-built eastern half, Altenhof II (1907–13), where gabled one- and one-and-a-half-story terraces with simplified rendered facades followed the contours of the hilly site, set back on shallow gardens behind picket fences. By 1912, 450 dwellings were completed.

According to William Schuchardt, writing in 1914, "In the individual beauty of the houses, as well as in charm and location and parking, Altenhof is quite the equal of the other later colonies" where "the influence of the revived interest in town planning is very apparent. The streets, open spaces, the vistas, and planting have been most carefully considered and architecturally, complete harmony has been established in spite of very considerable diversity."[142] Stephen Child echoed the impression in 1922, calling Altenhof "by far the most beautiful of all the Krupp colonies," with "picturesque, winding, tree-shaded, narrow streets, bordered almost exclusively with detached houses, some of the most attractive cottage architecture the writer has ever seen anywhere."[143] To serve residents with limited mobility, Altenhof included two churches and other social and recreational institutions. The eastern portion of the estate remains, but the western half was demolished and the park built over with a highway.

Schmohl's next colony, **Alfredshof** (1894), located south of Essen on a site in the open country about a half-hour's walk from the works, was deemed by Budgett Meakin to be one "of the half-dozen models of the world."[144] In his design of Alfredshof, Schmohl, preserving some of the site's natural features, called for a central rectangular market place from the corners of which diagonal roads radiated out through a regular street grid. Each of the 232 single-, two-, three-, and four-family houses was surrounded by a garden, through which each unit was entered. Single-family houses contained five rooms—three downstairs and two upstairs—and multifamily groups were slightly smaller, with three or four rooms to each house. Architecturally, the houses were a cut above their Krupp predecessors, picturesquely rendered in half-timber and brightly colored stucco and brick, with bay windows and balconies and colorful hip and half-hip roofs adding charm to the streetscape.

Only the southern half of Alfredshof was completed by 1899, when complications with mines below the site halted construction. Work resumed in 1907, but rising land values and a strong housing demand led to the abandonment of the original plan in favor of a denser arrangement of apartment buildings in keeping with the pattern of urbanism that had grown around the colony. In addition to the northern section, redesigned around a large park connected to the town center by a tree-lined boulevard, Schmohl's plan guided the development of an expansive area to the southeast of the original development with three- and four-story terraces rather intricately sited to provide formal axes allowing long vistas across courtyards and plazas, lawns and playgrounds, through archways, and across streets.[145] Apartment houses were placed along the block perimeters and additional housing terraces and allotment gardens were built within the blocks. Writing in 1922, Werner Hegemann and Elbert Peets found some of the architectural elements, such as the archways, to be "not quite beyond question" but deemed the expanded town "an unusually successful effort to apply

1. Plan, Robert Schmohl. CHB
(c. 1907)

2. Typical street. CHB (c. 1918)

3. Waldpark. CRS

4. Overall view. HAK (c. 1906)

5. Typical street. CRS

6. Typical street. FDE (1907)

7. House in Altenhof I. Kung. WC
(2007)

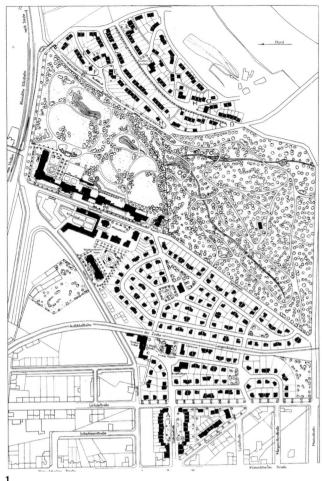

1

2

3

4

5

6

7

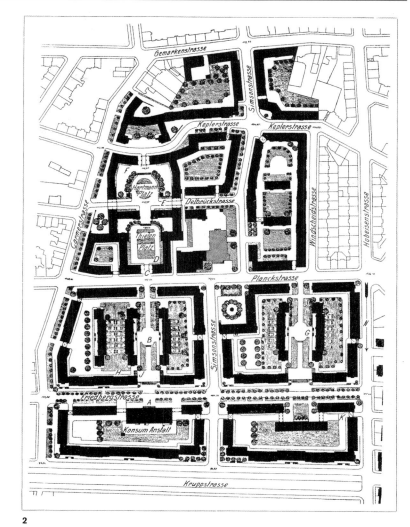

1. Plan of first section, Robert Schmohl, 1894. WGK

2. Plan of second section, Robert Schmohl, c. 1907. WM20

3. View of first section. HAK (c. 1905)

4. Friedbergstrasse axis in second section. WMB20 (c. 1920)

the principles of formal gardening to a compact group of inexpensive houses."[146]

Friedrichshof, built between 1899 and 1906 on a constricted site close to the Essen works, was by necessity a compact arrangement of three-story apartment blocks framing planted courtyards and playgrounds to contain dwellings for about 523 families.[147] Schmohl placed smaller two-family houses informally around a traffic semicircle at the entrance to the colony. Schmohl's

Margarethenhof (1903–27), outside of Düsseldorf, called for a mix of semidetached houses and rows of up to nine units, many forming courtyard-enclosing groups. The residential blocks, surrounding a single main intersection, were cut through by crooked, tree-lined lanes and foothpaths leading to interior allotments.[148]

The last two colonies to be designed by Schmohl (he would serve in an advisory capacity on some later plans), Dahlhauser Heide (1906–15) and Emscher-Lippe

Friedrichshof

1. Plan, Robert Schmohl, 1899.
WGK

2. Bird's-eye view. WGK (c. 1899)

3. Entrance to colony. HG06
(c. 1906)

4. Courtyard. HAK (c. 1905)

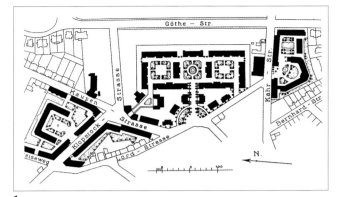

1

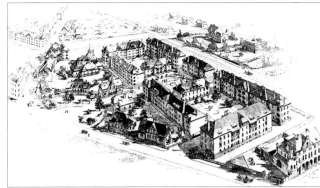

2

3

4

Margarethenhof

1

2

1. Plan, Robert Schmohl, 1903.
GCTP11

2. Typical view. HAK (c. 1912)

(1907–11), housed workers at the newly acquired Hannover and Hannibal mines about twenty-five miles north of Essen, near Bochum. Krupp had built pockets of housing in the area, including the small **Kolonie Hannover** (1874–90), with its identical back-to-back wooden houses aligned in straight rows amid gardens, but needed substantial new construction to attract its needed workforce.[149] Working on a 99-acre site north of the Hannover mine, Schmohl planned **Dahlhauser Heide** around a central park, the grounds of a former manor house, allowing the surrounding streets to

follow the site's contours, leaving behind "any vestiges of the rigid grid patterns of the earliest colonies."[150] Public buildings, placed sequentially across the plan, included two stores, a beer hall, two kindergartens, two schools, and an assembly hall with seats for 800, billiard and reading rooms, and a bowling alley. By 1915, 725 houses had been built from 45 distinct types. Schmohl's Heimatstil designs called for low, deep eaves and occasional half-timbering, evoking vernacular Westphalian farmhouses and barns. Most of the houses were semi-detached and were connected by single-story sheds able to house small livestock, so that together the houses formed continuous rows stepping back and forth from the street and at intersections to frame closes and create "a meaningful variety of urban places."[151] In both Dahlhauser Heide and Emscher-Lippe, the company employed the traditional *kotten* type of miner's house, providing livestock sheds and generously sized gardens for vegetable cultivation that could afford residents a second source of income.

Emscher-Lippe was similarly conceived, its curving streets incorporating existing roads and woodland features as well as an old farmhouse that Schmohl retained as a focal point in the new village and an inspiration for the design of the 1,038 dwelling units, only about fifty of which were for officials and the rest, for miners, predominantly taking the form of semidetached houses connected by livestock sheds.[152] Schmohl also placed quadrangles within the larger blocks. The colony was bordered on the east and south by a forest.

The crowning achievement of the Krupp housing initiatives, and the first to display the full impact of the Garden City movement, **Margarethenhöhe** (1909–38), built on the southwestern outskirts of Essen, 1.86 miles from the city's main train station on a plateau surrounded by wooded ravines, comprised 123.5 acres of developed land surrounded on three sides by 123.5 acres of protected forest.[153] Georg Metzendorf, an architect from Darmstadt who had designed an award-winning workers' house in that city in 1908 but who had no experience in town planning, was hired to design Margarethenhöhe on the recommendation of Schmohl, who was thirty years his senior. Metzendorf served as town architect from 1909 until 1934. It is likely that Robert Schmidt (1869–1934), Essen's municipal architect whose signature appears alongside Metzendorf's on early plans for Margarethenhöhe, contributed significantly to the layout.

Unlike previous Krupp colonies, Margarethenhöhe was not developed by Krupp but by the Margarethe-Krupp Trust, established in 1906 by Friedrich Alfred Krupp's widow, Margarethe, on the occasion of her daughter's marriage. Also, unlike the earlier colonies, residency in Margarethenhöhe, projected for a population of 15,000 to 18,000 (though it would not reach that figure—only 5,300 people lived there by the end of the 1930s), was not limited to Krupp employees. However, in 1915 about 45 percent of the town's 1,300 residents worked for Krupp.

Entered across a 580-foot-long sandstone bridge spanning a valley, traffic to Margarethenhöhe was diverted to the right and left—Sommerburgstrasse, to the right, carried streetcars along a curving path that brought to mind the footprint of a medieval fortification wall. On axis with the bridge, the village's ceremonial entrance, consisting of a pair of narrow switchback roads flanking a broad stairway, carried residents up through an archway cut through the base of an apartment building. Entering the village via the arch, the axial arrival sequence opened to a village-like informality as the medieval-inspired, slightly crooked Steile

Kolonie Hannover

1. Aerial view. SB (1965)

Dahlhauser Heide

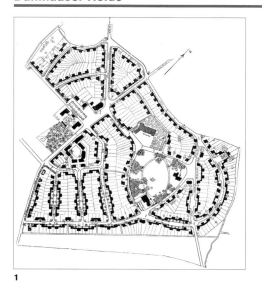

1. Plan, Robert Schmohl, 1906. GCTP11

2. Aerial view. SB (2003)

3. Typical house. SB (2002)

4. Sechs-Brüder-Strasse. Rasi. WC (2004)

2

3

4

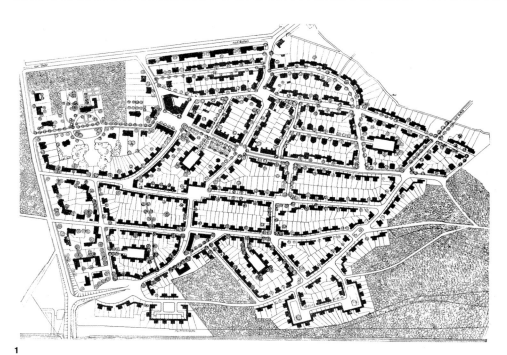

1. Plan, Robert Schmohl, 1907. GCTP11

2. Typical street. CHB

3. Typical street. Icema. PAN (2012)

4. Typical street. CHB

5. Typical street. Icema. PAN (2012)

Strasse, Margarethenhöhe's main residential street, led to a market square, the primary public space and focus of community life, bordered on two sides by the rather imposing facades of a co-op store and inn, before continuing on to the site of a church. Along Steile Strasse, Metzendorf turned the gables of the houses toward the street to create "a charming old-world appearance," as an early observer wrote, comparing the effect to Bournville.[154] Here as elsewhere in Margarethenhöhe, the gardens provided for each household, ranging in size from 750 to 3,230 square feet, were not placed in front of the houses, where they were too often perceived as "but places for poor floral display," but behind the houses, where, separated by low fences, they provided expansive views across open green space.[155]

Metzendorf, echoing Parker and Unwin, drew particular inspiration from medieval German villages, seeking to conjure the image of a walled city in which multistory tenements served as a surrogate for the fortification wall. Although he preferred straight streets, Metzendorf allowed the roads to conform to natural contours, thereby reducing the amount of earth-moving required. In areas of flat topography, where straight streets were the economical solution, Metzendorf manipulated street walls and building massing and terminated vistas to create varied, romantic street pictures. As the American planner Earle S. Draper observed in 1931, Metzendorf was able to avoid those monumental vistas that had become so typical of American practice: "The whole development is encouraging to those who may feel that formality in town planning is sometimes carried too far."[156]

Aesthetically, Metzendorf was able to establish consistency while avoiding monotony. He employed a limited palette of materials—stucco, slate, and tile for building exteriors and rough stone for foundations and walls—but juxtaposed them to great effect. Stucco was applied with varying degrees of roughness and in gray, yellow, and soft pink hues. Only one door size and four window sizes were used, but the shapes and arrangement of dormers and gables, the placement of windows, the variety of fences, gates, porches, stairs, and other

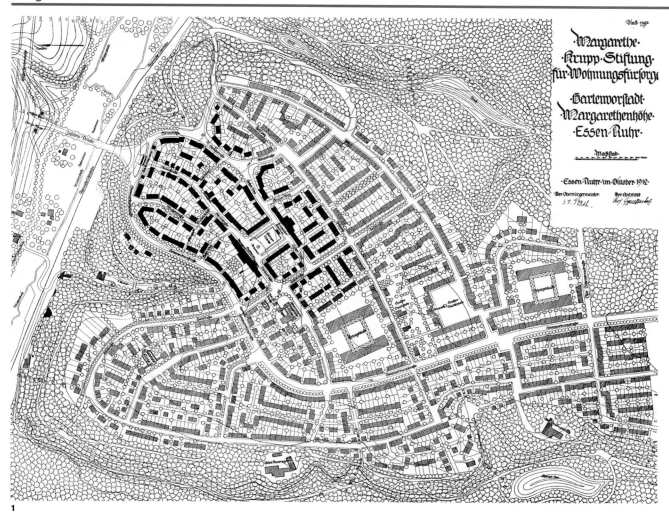

1. Plan, Georg Metzendorf, 1912.
ARB 15

1

embellishments, such as latticework around doorways, added visual complexity. As well, numerous dwelling types were employed, ranging from semidetached houses to three-, four-, and five-family rows and twelve-house terraces. "Great as this diversity is," wrote Elsa Rehmann in 1914, "it is dominated by the harmony of the whole . . . there exists a consistent style of architecture throughout the town," achieved "through practically the same means as those used in the development of the old towns, namely uniformity of material and harmony of house forms." The idea of putting the design work in the hands of a single architect, so that the "practical elements of town planning" could achieve "artistic unity," represented "a new thought in the garden city movement," and an arguable success over Letchworth, where architectural cohesiveness was guided by bye-laws but with mixed results.[157]

The influence of Raymond Unwin and Camillo Sitte on Metzendorf's design was everywhere to be seen: in the diversion of traffic from the town center; in the combination of curved, crooked, and straight roads; in the placement of group houses around common greens such as at Robert Schmohl-Platz; in the treatment of corners, where houses were angled or set back to allow more light and air and to provide better sight lines for traffic safety; and in the careful formulation of street pictures.

Metzendorf's placement of schools within housing blocks reduced the amount of road construction, allowed children to avoid crossing streets, and positioned the schools for community and after-hours use.

Because it was administered by trust and open to the general population, some dubbed Margarethenhöhe the German Bournville.[158] "Physically," however, as planner and planning historian Peter Hall has written, Margarethenhöhe "is a transplanted New Earswick [see p. 228]. Its architect . . . faithfully followed the Unwin-Parker tradition to create a magic little town, separated from the city by a wooded mini-green belt, its entrance gateway, its central market square, its medieval-looking inn, its narrow curving streets from which all through traffic is excluded. Thus, ironically, it out-Unwins Unwin." Referring to one of Unwin's favored models of urbanity, Hall continues, "it really does look like a twentieth century Rothenburg. Perhaps it took a German architect, working in a German environment with a top German planner—Metzendorf worked hand in hand with Essen's municipal architect Robert Schmidt—to achieve what Unwin so zealously strived for."[159]

Margarethenhöhe was Metzendorf's masterpiece, but the architect designed another notable garden village, the contemporaneous **Hüttenau** (1909–17), in Hattingen-Welper, five miles south of Bochum, where

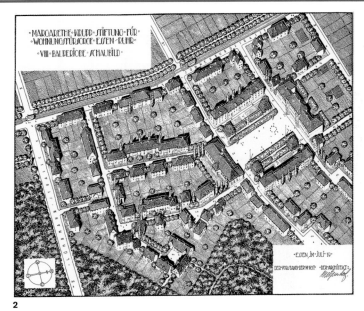

2

3

2. Axonometric view showing market square, 1919. METZ

3. Aerial view. GE (2006)

4. View across bridge. METZ (c. 1920)

5. View from bridge showing entrance to Steile Strasse. Eckhardt. PAN (2006)

6. Steile Strasse through entrance portal. GCTP11 (c. 1911)

7. Steile Strasse. HAK (c. 1912)

8. Houses on Steile Strasse. METZ (c. 1920)

9. Rear gardens. METZ (c. 1920)

4

5

6

7

8

9

Margarethenhöhe

10

11

10. Market square. RAMSA (1977)

11, 12. Typical streets. RAMSA (1977)

13. Waldlehne. Halama. WC (2011)

12

13

Hüttenau

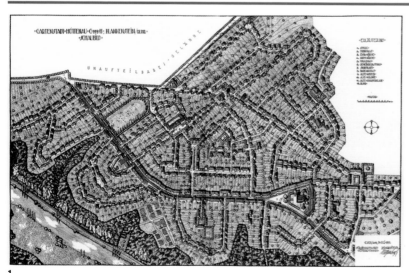

1

2

3

4

1. Axonometric plan, Georg Metzendorf, 1919. METZ

2. Rear gardens of houses facing Ringstrasse. FM

3. Ringstrasse. FM

4. Typical street. CHB

1. Plan, Theodor Suhnel, 1920. TS

2. Aerial view. GE (2006)

3, 4. Typical streets. TS (1920s)

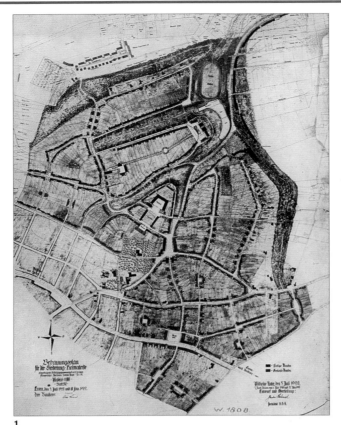

1

2

3

4

a less geographically constricted site allowed him to spread the plan out, supplanting the rather dense fabric of Margarethenhöhe with a rural spaciousness characterized by gardens and greenery.[160] The village, comprising nearly 400 houses, was built by the German Garden City Association but largely sponsored by two local companies that would supply many of the residents. The site was cut through by an east–west road connecting the towns of Welper and Blankenstein that Metzendorf chose as the location of a tram line, lining the thoroughfare with housing terraces. To the north, looping residential streets backed up to a forest that buffered the colony from a railroad line. The southern section was a patchwork of irregular blocks with perimeter rowhouses and interior quadrangles accessed by narrow roads. Each house had its own garden and barn. With the exception of some more elaborate houses for foremen and managers, the typical steep-pitched

tile-roof house was sparsely ornamented, with a smooth gray plaster exterior above a brick or stone base and uniform rectangular door and window openings with occasional bays and arches. Yet Metzendorf achieved a remarkably varied streetscape, alternating house types and the orientation of gables, bending roads and terminating street vistas, carving out intimate courtyards and creating plazas at street intersections, and making judicious use of street trees. A planned market square was not realized, but a church square provided a civic node between the northern and southern sections. Construction was largely complete by 1917, when the village, with a school, a church, and a bachelor's residence, counted 389 dwellings in 381 buildings.

The last Krupp colony to embrace garden village planning before changing economic conditions necessitated a shift to apartment houses was **Heimaterde** (native soil) (1916–28), located halfway between Essen

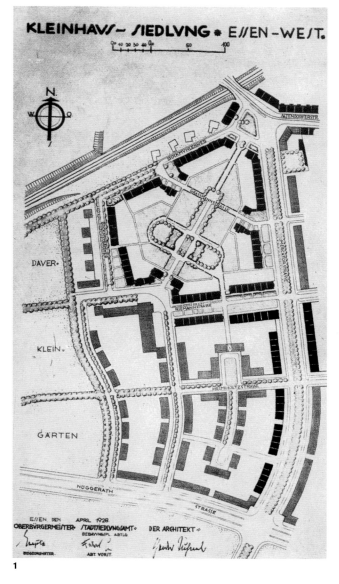

1. Plan, Theodor Suhnel, 1918. NWTS (1928)

2. Aerial view. WEN (1927)

3, 4. Typical views. WEN (2012)

and the city of Mülheim to the southwest, undertaken after World War I to provide detached, semidetached, and terraced houses for "deserving workers," as Cedric Bolz has put it, particularly "returning veterans and large families who . . . were in most desperate need of being re-rooted in the German soil." Mülheim architect Theodor Suhnel (1886–1965) designed the village in a stripped-down mode devoid of ornament, placing emphasis on the attributes of the 865-acre, hilly and ravine-crossed site: "Suhnel's creativity was to be channeled into bringing out the natural beauty of the land. In his opinion, it was neither the time nor place to be overly concerned about architectural aesthetics."[161] Mud and clay were chosen as initial building materials but were deemed unsatisfactory and replaced by brick in later phases. Intended to "reintroduce elements of rural self-sufficiency back into the industrial heartland," residents were encouraged to take up farming and raise livestock in a full embrace of the *kotten* house type. As in Dahlhauser Heide and Emscher-Lippe, a farmhouse was preserved on the site, but it did not serve as an architectural inspiration for Suhnel's houses. "In

striking this balance between natural beauty and austere architectural functionalism," writes Bolz, "this project differed considerably from anything the Krupp Housing office had previously undertaken."[162] Between 1918 and 1928, 323 dwellings were built, including 173 single-family and 75 two-family houses. The settlement was expanded up until 1941 and, after sustaining heavy damage during World War II, was rebuilt with the addition of a school, church, and new housing.

At the same that he was at work on Heimaterde, Suhnel was also responsible for the design of **Kleinhaussiedlung Essen-West** (1918–28), located less than four kilometers to the northeast.[163] Intended for workers, but not exclusively Krupp employees, the project was sponsored by a housing association led by local politician Heinrich Hirtsiefer (1876–1941), a leader in the Catholic labor movement who had first worked as a locksmith for Krupp before heading a union of Krupp metal workers. Initially conceived in 1914, the project was delayed by the war and the original idea of including only detached single-family houses was dropped in favor of a denser arrangement of terraced units in response

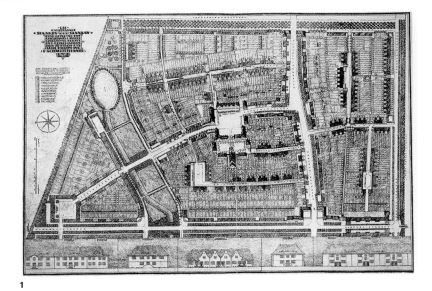

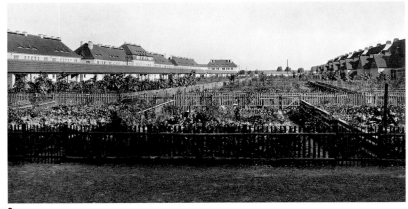

1. Plan, Paul Schmitthenner, c. 1914. ATU

2. Aerial view. ATU (c. 1917)

3. Gardens. ATU (c. 1917)

4. Zwischen den Giebeln. DGS (1917)

5. Am Langen Weg. ATU (c. 1917)

to the city's housing shortage. Still, Suhnel was able to provide a generous amount of open space. The most interesting part of the plan was completed first in the northern part of the site where Suhnel arranged a diamond-shaped pattern of two- and three-story roughcast houses around a large landscaped green that also served as a public park for the surrounding area. The remainder of the site was primarily fitted out with north–south and east–west rows along curving streets, some set behind front gardens and all featuring rear gardens, although Suhnel also included a group of houses around three

sides of a landscaped court. By the time of its completion, Kleinhaussiedlung Essen-West, later renamed in honor of Hirtsiefer, accommodated 600 families in five different types of one-, two-, and three-family houses.

After Krupp

The 100-acre garden village of **Staaken** (1914–17), accommodating 800 households in one-, two-, and four-family houses, a department store, two schools,

6

7

8

9

10

a church, and a market square, was built to meet the housing needs of employees of the state-owned munitions factory a little over three miles away at Spandau, on the western outskirts of Berlin.[164] Paul Schmitthenner was commissioned as part of the war effort to plan and design Staaken along with two other garden villages, Plaue in Brandenburg and Forstfeld in Kassel. Staaken was intended by the state to serve as a model *siedlung* establishing guidelines for the future, as Jean-François Lejeune points out, not only architecturally and urbanistically but also with regard to housing construction standards and financing methods. In this respect, it parallels wartime efforts in the United Kingdom by the London County Council or the numerous but largely unrealized projects in the United States sponsored by the United States Housing Corporation and the Emergency Fleet Corporation. As Annette Ciré writes, Staaken "comes closer to being a true garden city than any other housing colony in Berlin, because it is not just a residential project but a self-sufficient community with school, church, shops and restaurant."[165]

Though Staaken's architecture reflects Schmitthenner's interest in *völkisch* (folkloric) themes, his planning is distinctly rational, despite some attention to the street-picture approach derived from Sitte and Parker and Unwin. Lejeune describes its "strong geometric diagram and parti" as "somewhat abstract in its collage of juxtaposed urban elements sacrificing the organic quality of the traditional medieval plan to a more functional approach."[166] Making the most of a flat, featureless site lying between two railway lines, Staaken is entered past ceremonial gate lodges leading to two arterial streets. The plan of long blocks of rowhouses is peppered with picturesque squares such as the arcaded Market Square, with its combined shops and residences modeled after those in Potsdam's eighteenth-century Holland Quarter, and adjoining it, the quiet Kirchplatz (church square), the two separated from each other by a school. As Ciré writes, the village "appears less like a typical suburb and more like a small town," representing "a major step in the development from the small-house colonies of the Wilhelminian era to the housing estates of the Weimar period. World War I may have been a major break in terms of politics and social structure, but as far as the planning of housing projects was concerned, it caused only a minor delay in a development that followed its inevitable course."[167]

Amazingly, Schmitthenner designed all the buildings, realizing 80 percent of what was originally intended, with impressive results that in no way seem overdetermined. Following the care taken with the design of Hellerau's group houses, Staaken's five building types were individualized with a variety of facade, dormer, and roof types, combined with prefabricated doors and windows to achieve impressive economies in construction. Most of the houses were for single families but connected by walls and various other devices to suggest, as Vittorio Magnago Lampugnani has observed, an "inhabited town wall" that "at least symbolically" protects residents "from the supposedly 'hostile' outside world," giving rise not to an "experimental estate for the New Community but to a reproduction of a small bourgeois German town for the lower middle classes, whose careful camouflage . . . served as a higher seal of quality for the inhabitants."[168]

Staaken's place in the history of the garden suburb has been compromised by Paul Schmitthenner's fall from grace as the result of his ideas about the *Volk* (people/nation) being taken up by National Socialists in the 1920s and 1930s.[169] But, as architectural historian Wolfgang Sonne has pointed out, "traces of nationalist ideology and hostility towards the metropolis" should not be too glibly connected to National Socialism's anti-Semitism but seen more as a reflection of a fear of Communism. For example, Sonne points out, in the preface to a 1917 publication on Staaken, Franz Oppenheimer, a Jewish physician-turned-sociologist and liberal economist, wrote that "'the metropolis is heavily dangerous in regard to politics. It is everywhere the place of the most avant-gardist radicalism.'"[170]

Plaue Garden City (1915–17), a half-mile north of the town of Plaue, fifty miles west of Berlin along the Havel River, was a garden village designed by Schmitthenner for workers at the Royal Prussian Powder factory.[171] The plan for the site, intended for 300 houses—212 were built—was divided by a main road widened to form a central square lined with large houses. The charming architecture, based on *völkisch* and Biedermeier precedents, provides strong definition to the squares and streets, some of which were preexisting, as were the site's mature trees. At the village edges, the houses established a sense of walled enclosure for the suburb as a whole. **Forstfeld** (1915–17), near Kassel, the third of Schmitthenner's wartime garden village plans following Staaken and Plaue, was intended for 595 families but was only partially realized on an 18-acre rectangular site.[172] A central market square was served by three stores, the cooperative's administration building, and an inn.

Siedlung Piesteritz (1916–18), Lutherstadt Wittenberg, planned by Otto R. Salvisberg, is, according to Lejeune, "one of the most accomplished garden cities of the period."[173] It was developed to house war workers under the direction of Walther Rathenau (1867–1922), a leading industrialist and advocate of German modernization. Piesteritz, in essence a *Randbebauung*, or superblock, was "designed like a Sittesque little town, complete with its streets, public buildings, and squares, and fully surrounded by a continuous wall of apartment houses, accessible through limited entries." As Lejeune writes, Piesteritz's suburban adaptation of the *Randbebauung* concept "was a masterpiece: the 470 houses, town hall, school, churches, and gatehouses," all designed by Salvisberg, constituting "a small town," the plan of which synthesized medieval and Baroque features, with three "interconnected squares and the entry sequence from the main gate houses" forming what Harald Kegler described as a "small town utopia" in which "all parts tell, in a certain way, a social story."[174] Piesteritz was intended to accommodate all categories of plant workers, so that individual dwelling units ranged from 50 to 160 square meters in size and each one contained a bathroom, an inside toilet, and a garden intended for families to grow their own food. A department store was included in the plan.

Seven miles southeast of central Cologne, **Siedlung Gremberghoven** (1919), built for railway administrators and workers, was designed by architect Martin Kiessling (1879–1944), an employee of the state railway system, for an irregularly shaped site just east of the railroad and within walking distance of a repair depot and the railway line's headquarters.[175] Kiessling's plan combined courtyard-bounding groups along with perimeter rows that were arranged in a gentle curve, creating an almost oval-shaped space occupied by additional rows as well as semidetached and detached single-family houses. All of the houses featured substantial rear gardens. By 1922, 167 houses were completed, accommodating 206 dwelling units. During World War II, Siedlung Gremberghoven, a ripe target due to its proximity to important railroad facilities, was severely damaged by Allied bombing and later rebuilt at a much higher density, although many original buildings still remain.

In 1926 a nonprofit housing cooperative established for the benefit of railroad employees announced plans to build a garden suburb for 200 workers and their families on an 18-acre site one-and-a-half miles southwest of Gotha, a city of 40,000 in the central German state of Thüringen.[176] The unimproved rectangular parcel

Plaue Garden City

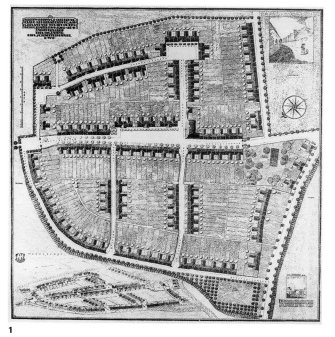

Forstfeld

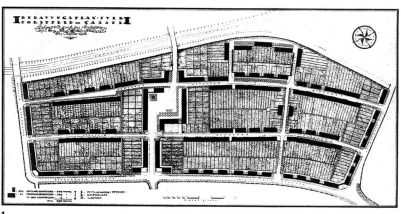

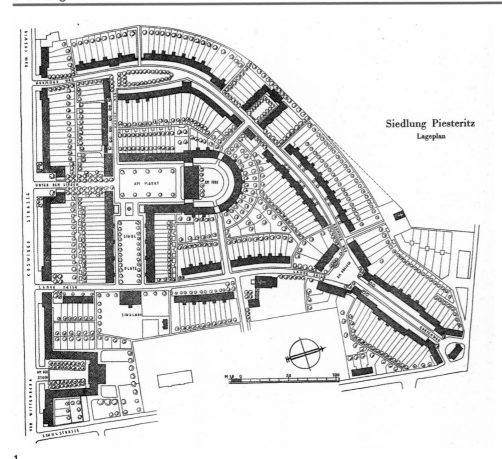

1

1. Plan, Otto R. Salvisberg, c. 1916.
JBBG

2. Aerial view. Titze. LFD (1998)

3. Unter den Linden. KB (c. 1930)

4. Krummer Weg. KB (c. 1930)

5. Stiller Winkel. KB (c. 1930)

6. Gartenweg. KB (c. 1930)

7. Am Tore. Weihmann. FW (2010)

4

5

6

7

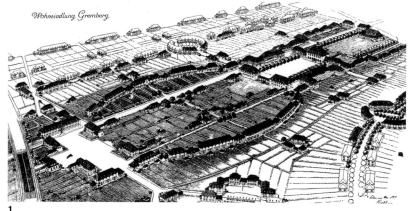

was just south of the railroad tracks and within walking distance of the railway's repair depot. Local architects Richard Neuland (1884–1958) and Bruno Tamme (1883–1964) were hired to prepare the plan for **Siedlung Am Schmalen Rain** as well as design its buildings.

Neuland and Tamme's scheme featured rows of two- and three-story houses lining the perimeter of the site. At the southern end, the terraces were slightly staggered, shielding two rows of north–south houses behind, while at the northern portion of the site the houses were arranged in a semicircle fronting a green. The middle of the site was reserved for the large town hall flanked by two rectangular greens. On either side of the town hall east–west rows closed the development's two building parcels, anchored by four three-story gatehouse-like apartment buildings straddling the development's north–south streets with V-shaped arches that matched the V-shaped gable roofs.

Between 1927 and 1928, 202 dwelling units were completed at Am Schmalen Rain, along with the town hall accommodating civic facilities, stores, and a restaurant. Neuland and Tamme were responsible for different parts of the estate, but all of the ninety-six houses were traditional in style, primarily inspired by Hellerau. Many of the buildings were also painted in bright shades of red, green, blue, and yellow. During the economic hardships of the 1930s, several of the houses were subdivided, raising the number of dwelling units to 269. The housing estate remains intact to this day, and a rehabilitation program begun in the late 1990s has restored much of the original color scheme.

Hans Hertlein (1881–1963), architect of many of the factories in the massive complex known as Siemensstadt, built for engineering and manufacturing conglomerate Siemens in northwest Berlin's Spandau district, also designed a residential component for the company, **Siedlung Siemensstadt** (1922–28), accommodating workers and their families in 900 apartments arranged primarily in long rows of two- to four-story buildings.[177] Hertlein's decision to line the perimeter of the rectangular site with tall buildings helped shelter the development from the surrounding industrial plants. Landscape architect Leberecht Migge was responsible for the abundant greenery, including allotment gardens as well as grassy courts bordered by trees. Ronald Wiedenhoeft has pointed out the "Sittesque qualities of Rapsstrasse," the curving north–south main road bisecting the site, "with houses moved forward or backward or off axis to contract, expand and articulate spaces."[178] The architectural highlight was a four-story building topped by a clocktower that straddled the northern end of Rapsstrasse, leading via an arched opening to the landscaped court of a U-shaped apartment building across Harriesstrasse.

Martin Wagner, city planner of Berlin, selected Hans Scharoun (1893–1972) as the planner of **Gross-Siedlung Siemensstadt** (1929), built in part to house Siemens workers on a 48-acre site bisected by the curving path of the elevated S-Bahn and just southeast of Hertlein's

1. Bird's-eye view. RB (1919)

2. Frankenplatz. Koerber. RB

3. Hohenstaufenstrasse. Koerber. RB

4. Hohenstaufenstrasse. Heinrich. WC (2007)

1. Bird's-eye view. WID (c. 1928)

2. Overall view. WID (c. 1928)

3. Am Schmalen Rain. Sander. WC (2010)

4. Geschwister-Scholl-Platz. Metilsteiner. WC (2011)

Siedlung Siemensstadt.[179] Wagner selected five architects to join Scharoun on the design of the buildings: Hugo Häring, Walter Gropius, Otto Bartning (1883–1959), Fred Forbat (1897–1972), and Paul Rudolf Henning (1886–1986). All six were members of Der Ring, a progressive group of architects founded in 1926 that also included Bruno and Max Taut, Ludwig Mies van der Rohe, Erich Mendelsohn, as well as Martin Wagner.[180] As at Die Weisse Stadt (see p. 445), Scharoun's plan for Ringsiedlung, the popular nickname for the project, was primarily driven by the need to provide separate building parcels for each architect. Gone is any sense of a vernacular village; gone are the street pictures of Parker and Unwin and Metzendorf. In their place is a rigidly functionalist, solar-oriented north–south orientation for rows of three- to five-story flat-roofed apartment houses that provided 1,370 dwelling units. This had the effect of eliminating the street as the focus of communal life—given that to ensure perfect orientation in each dwelling unit, front doors were always placed so that the back of one row faced the front of the next. At Gross-Siedlung Siemensstadt, the essence of the garden village type was decisively abandoned in favor of a determinist planning approach based almost exclusively on solar conditions and also a devaluation of individual expression in favor of the collective. The estate included no single-family terraces or private gardens, with the prolific Leberecht Migge designing the green spaces between the rows. In addition to the housing, the complex included a central laundry and power station, seventeen stores, restaurants, and a school.

Although the scheme emphasized the urban collective over the ruralistic individual, the generous amount of greenery conveyed a suburban character. Architect and historian Peter Blundell Jones has characterized the plan as "atypical of that schematic period—in being highly site specific," with "special care" taken "to preserve mature trees, and to work with the high railway embankment cutting through the site."[181] Scharoun's rows of four-story, nautical-inspired buildings, the most vivacious in the development, included sail-like metal sheets wrapping around curved balconies and rounded roof terraces, while Gropius's long north–south row on the west side of Jungfernheide Weg was more diagrammatic. Bartning's curving east–west terraces, constituting the project's longest continuous row, stretching for over 1,100 feet, shielded the eastern part of the development from the railway. Just to the north, Häring's parallel rows separated by landscaped courtyards were the least severe of all, with kidney-shaped masonry balconies and wide horizontal bands of brownish-yellow brick placed at the top of the four-story buildings.

In their 1987 survey of European modern architecture, Dennis and Elizabeth De Witt point out, mixing irony and sarcasm, that Gross-Siedlung Siemensstadt, though "the most famous and influential of all . . . German siedlungen that set the standard for housing in interwar Europe . . . does not truly represent the type. It is not sufficiently earnest or scientific: its buildings are not all parallel, all identical, all pure white. It is, in fact, not sufficiently boring. Gropius is too elegant here.

Siedlung Siemensstadt

1

2

3

4

1. Rapsstrasse. SCA (c. 1930)

2. Courtyard. SCA (c. 1930)

3. Rapsstrasse. SCA (c. 1930)

4. Rapsstrasse. Antony. WC (2008)

Gross-Siedlung Siemensstadt

1

2

3

4

5

1. Plan, Hans Scharoun, 1929, center, showing plan of Siedlung Siemensstadt, Hans Hertlein, 1922, top. LB

2. Housing by Hans Scharoun. LBE (c. 1929)

3. Housing by Walter Gropius. B30 (c. 1930)

4. Housing by Otto Bartning. Antony. WC (2008)

5. Housing by Hugo Häring. Antony. WC (2008)

SIEDLUNG MASCHERODER HOLZ

1

2

4

3

Häring is too folksy. As for Scharoun—his willful manipulation of balconies and other elements must once have seemed scandalous!"[182]

The "street pictures" and individuality of house design abandoned at Gross-Siedlung Siemensstadt were revived in several industrial villages built after the National Socialists came to power. **Siedlung Mascheroder Holz** (1936–39) was developed by the government-run Deutsche Arbeitsfront (German Labor Front) on a rural site surrounded by forests one mile north of the village of Mascherode and about four miles southeast of Brunswick, Lower Saxony, an important center for the defense industry.[183] The development, intended for military personnel as well as civilian war workers, was planned to accommodate close to 6,000 people. Architect Julius Schulte-Frohlinde (1894–1968), head of the Schönheit der Arbeit (Beauty of Work), a subsidiary of the Deutsche Arbeitsfront, was responsible for the plan, which deviated from the customary practice of providing mostly single-family detached houses in estates sponsored by the National Socialist government,

an adjustment necessitated by the need to house a great many people, resulting in the inclusion of substantial numbers of semidetached units and terraces.

The focal point of Schulte-Frohlinde's plan was the L-shaped marketplace, designed by Rudolf Rogler (n.d.), that sat at roughly the center of the irregularly shaped site, accommodating a market, a town hall seating 600, and Nazi party offices. Each of the traditionally styled one- and two-story houses featured rear allotment gardens with the longest terraces placed near the town center. In addition to the housing and the community and government facilities, the estate included several stores, a kindergarten, an elementary school, and playground and park space. Winfried Nerdinger and Cornelius Tafel have praised the development as "the largest coherent housing complex from the period of National Socialism . . . In spite of the standardized method of construction and the similar floor plans, the image of a traditional, village-like housing estate is produced by means of the curving streets and a green belt that has the appearance of a village green."[184]

In 1940–42, Heinrich Tessenow attempted to build a Heimatstil siedlung in **Mosigkau**, a district of Dessau six miles southwest of the city center.[185] Intended for workers at the nearby Junkers & Company airplane factory, Tessenow was recommended for the job by his one-time pupil and assistant, Albert Speer (1905–1981), at the time chief architect of the Third Reich. The plan called for 800 detached and terraced single- and two-family houses arranged in nine rectangular blocks along with a school and community center located in a dominating tower-like structure. Although the plan remained unrealized, it has recently attracted the attention of Andrés Duany, who deemed it "probably the most accomplished new town designed by Heinrich Tessenow." Duany observes: "At first sight it appears to be a simple network of long blocks, but it is very sophisticated in its details. The streets all have slight curvatures and deflections so that the vistas vary continually."[186]

BELGIUM

Belgium's first significant planned workers' village, **Grand-Hornu** (1819–32), near Mons, Wallonia, a product of the country's active coal-mining industry, was undertaken by Henri de Gorge (1774–1832), a French industrialist who owned several collieries in the Borinage region near the French border.[187] De Gorge built Grand-Hornu directly over one of his mines, hoping that the village's "previously unheard-of comfort" would attract a stable population of 2,500 miners and their families, about 500 of whom would relocate from France.[188]

Bruno Renard (1781–1861), a Belgian architect who had recently returned from Paris having studied under architects Charles Perciér (1764–1838) and Pierre-François-Léonard Fontaine (1762–1853), planned the village and designed its stripped-down neoclassical buildings. The layout was roughly rectangular, measuring approximately 1,640 by 1,310 feet, with the edges of the village defined by straight, continuous terraces of two-story single-family houses lining 40-foot-wide streets, with chamfered facades at the street intersections. Construction began in 1819, with about 425 houses eventually built, each with six rooms and its own garden. At the center of the plan, an elliptical building containing workshops, offices, stables, stores, and foundries enclosed a grassy park, recalling the geometries of Ledoux's *Saline Royale* at Chaux. The ends of the ellipse were open arcades, used for storing materials. Both the houses and workshop buildings were constructed in brick covered in yellowish stucco. In addition to the central park, another park, Place Verte, containing a bandstand, was provided across from the de Gorge residence. The village also included baths, meeting rooms, a school, a hospital, a dance hall, a church, and a town hall. As Phillipe Vandermaelen observed in 1833, "everything has been admirably arranged, both for walking and for relaxation."[189] De Gorge died of cholera in 1832 but members of his family took over the mining operation, which

Mosigkau

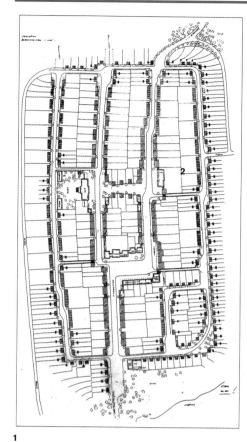

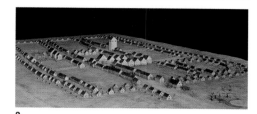

1. Plan, Heinrich Tessenow, 1940. HTS

2. Model. HTS (1942)

Grand-Hornu

1. Watercolor by M. V. Rose. GHI (1900)

2. Aerial view. GHI (2007)

3. Typical houses. GHI (2010)

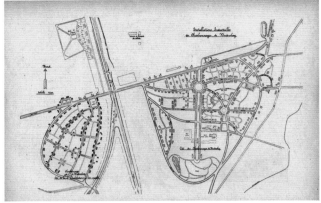

1

2

3

4

5

6

continued to function along with the town until 1954. After a period of decline and decay, Grand-Hornu was revived in the 1990s, with portions of the structure renovated to house a contemporary art museum.

In the twentieth century, Belgian mining villages in the Limburg region began to reflect the principles of the Garden City and garden suburb movement. **Winterslag** (1910–25), about sixty miles east of Brussels, in Genk, planned before World War I but realized after, was designed by Adrien Blomme (1878–1940) as a 700-acre garden village accommodating 2,000 houses at the rate of eight to the net acre.[190] Intended to be surrounded by a greenbelt, the village plan, providing accommodations for both miners and supervisory personnel, consisted of principal avenues meeting at *rond-points* and gently curving residential streets lined with English-inspired, red-tile-roofed, whitewashed roughcast rowhouses of various sizes and individual villas. The central north–south spine, Margarethalaan, featuring a broad grassy

mall, was anchored on the south by a church square and other public buildings. The village expanded to the west during the early 1920s, with smaller and less ornate houses built along two looping roads encircling a modified grid of streets around a church square. **Waterschei** (1922–58), another mining village three miles to the northeast, was planned before the war by the André Dumont company, but the construction of houses, beginning in 1914, was halted and not resumed until the early 1920s. At that time, the original gridded layout was replaced by a teardrop-shaped plan of tree- and sidewalk-lined streets by Gaston Voutquenne (1882–1940) providing more than 400 one- to five-family houses for workers and company officers as well as a variety of shared and private open spaces, athletic fields, a church, town hall, public square, and schools.[191]

Eisden, Massmechelen, nine miles east of Genk on the Dutch border, is another notable mining village in the Limburg region, begun in 1908 as a series of houses for

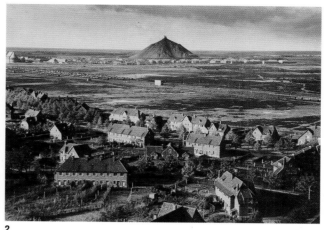

1. Aerial view. GE (2007)

2. Overall view showing slag heap in background. Kadar. ASG (c. 1940)

3. Typical street. Kadar. ASG (c. 1940)

4. Square des Eglantines. ASG

5, 6. Typical streets. Onna. NVO (2012)

Charbonnages André Dumont, Siège de Waterschei.
Square des Eglantines.

the newly acquired mine's manager, director, and engineers, but picking up in earnest after the war according to a plan by L. Jamine (n.d.), a local architect, who organized the village around two major axes that crossed at a central square anchored by a church and a boys' school.[192] Unfortunately, public buildings planned for the north and west sides of the square, including a restaurant and post office, were never built, depriving the space of defined boundaries. The village's predominantly semidetached two-story brick-and-half-timber houses, asymmetrically massed to resemble larger villas, were placed on hedge-lined lots, each a minimum of 7,000 square feet, along a mix of wide boulevards and gently curving streets meeting in informal intersections occasionally incorporating small parks. The overall density was a sparse three-and-a-half houses per acre. The mining company provided each garden with fruit trees, rose bushes, and vines and required residents to cultivate flower and vegetable gardens. The village was situated southwest of the mine to minimize the impact

of pollution. Significant expansion during the 1930s added more than 1,000 houses, four boardinghouses, and apartment buildings.

In the mining town of Beringen, fourteen miles northwest of Genk, construction also began in 1908 on two- and four-family engineers' and executives' houses designed by Antoine Huybrighs (n.d.) with painted concrete block, decorative brick bands and quoins, and ornamented gables in reference to the architecture of the northern French commune of Anzin. Between 1919 and 1926, the early houses were joined by a garden village known as **Beverlo**, built on a triangular site bound by Stationkaai, Laan op Vurten, and Leysestraat.[193] The plan incorporated squares and greens into a network of gently curving roads converging in a *rond-point*. A large semicircular site was reserved in the southwest for a school. Four architects—Huybrighs, Boulanger (n.d.), L. Geukens (n.d.), and G. Nijs (n.d.)—prepared nine distinct house types. Following the construction of the garden

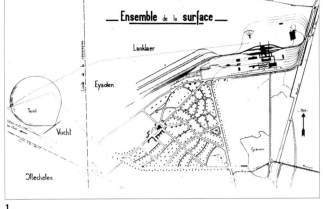

1

2

3

4

5

6

village, a series of elegant enclaves were built west of Koolmijnlaan, beginning in 1927 with Kioskplein, where Adrien Blomme spaced large houses for mine directors and engineers at regular intervals around a landscaped square with a kiosk, connecting the houses with low garden walls with arched entryways. Adjacent to the north, Eeuwfeestplein was added in 1930 with a similar arrangement of houses around a triangular tree-lined park, this time providing for lower-level workers and including a boardinghouse for unmarried men.

Klein Rusland (Little Russia) (1921–23), in Zelzate, north of Ghent, notable as much for the Modernist architectural expression of its buildings by Huib Hoste as for its plan by Louis Van der Swaelmen, was intended to provide housing for 300 families in what was to have been the first phase of a linear city extending along the Gent-Terneuzen Canal, serving workers in a parallel industrial zone lying between the canal and the railroad.[194] The design called for tree-lined streets and boulevards to converge in a central square, with detached, semidetached, and terraced houses placed at low densities on the surrounding blocks, which each featured a mix of private gardens and communal internal reserves. Closes and short culs-de-sac were also incorporated. Despite visions for a linear city, only 168 houses were built, as well as a shopping area and a community meeting hall.

The buildings were initially realized in brick, but Hoste, faced with material shortages and a lack of qualified construction workers, soon turned to a system using ash-concrete, an industrial waste material, for most of the development, abandoning gabled roofs for a cubical, flat-roofed configuration. The system Hoste adopted was an early form of prefabrication, consisting of pouring uncompressed concrete between formwork in which

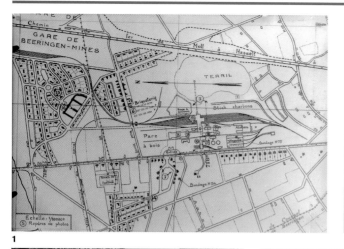

1. Plan. RH (1930–39)

2. Four-family house designed by Boulanger. RH (1923)

3. Eeuwfeestplein showing boardinghouse (1930), center. Onna. NVO (2012)

4. Kioskplein. Onna. NVO (2012)

Klein Rusland

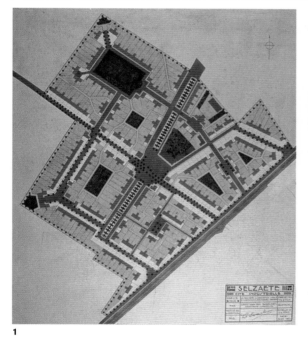

1. Plan, Louis Van der Swaelmen, 1921. CUL

2. Men pouring concrete. KUL (1920s)

3. Overall view. KUL (1920s)

4. Central square. Vandevorst. FH (2012)

doors and window openings had been previously cut out. While the system was justified on the basis of expediency, Marcel Smets suggests that this was "perhaps only an excuse to conceal the need for a new esthetic outlook. And yet, on comparing the first (brick) and the ensuing (ash-concrete) houses at Zelzate, one gets the impression that Hoste arrived at his design by way of the material used, and not the other way around."[195] Because of moisture issues, the ash-concrete houses were resurfaced in brick in the 1950s.

NETHERLANDS

Although conceived for the wealthy, the villa park was adopted by early Dutch industrialists as a suitable model for workers' villages. **Agneta Park** (1883), on the northwest outskirts of Delft, was the first such development in the Netherlands, built by Jacques C. van Marken (1845–1906) to house employees of his adjacent Netherlands Yeast and Spirit Factory.[196] Dutch landscape architect Louis Paul Zocher (1820–1915) focused the 11-acre

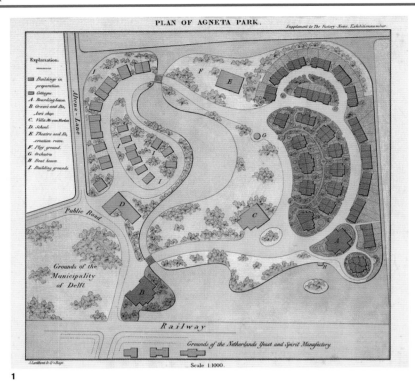

1

2

3

4

1. Plan, Louis Paul Zocher, 1884. DLF

2. View across pond. Onna. NVO (2012)

3. View showing bandstand, left, houses on Zocherweg, center, and J. C. van Marken residence (Eugen Heinrich Gugel), right. DLF1 (1900)

4. Frederik Matthesstraat. Onna. NVO (2012)

village, "possibly the most striking example of the picturesque" among all European workers' villages, around a stream-fed lake that wound its way across the center and then up the eastern edge of the site to provide a buffer against the neighboring railroad tracks and factory.[197] Reserving the area around the lake for recreational use, Zocher grouped the houses along winding roads to the north and south. Van Marken and his family resided in a large central villa designed by Eugen Heinrich Gugel (1832–1905) that set the architectural tone for the seventy-eight dwellings designed by Gugel's assistant, F. M. L. Kerkhoff (1858–1909) in emulation of the quadruple houses built for workers in Mulhouse, France. The grouping of multiple units under one roof—semidetached houses and six-unit rows were also included, as well as a boardinghouse—allowed the modest residences to read as substantial villas placed together "in an idyllic pastoral setting."[198] Van Marken's paternalistic tendencies were enough to keep some workers from residing in the community, but those who did so enjoyed a range of amenities including a recreation hall with a theater capable of seating 1,200, a library, a bowling alley, a bakery, a school, and food and clothing stores. Van Marken intended for full ownership of Agneta Park, established as a cooperative, to eventually be transferred to the workers. The village was expanded to the

southwest between 1925 and 1928 according to plans by Jan Gratama, who added 156 rowhouses in an orthogonal plan around a rectangular lake.

Agneta Park inspired another workers' village, **Snouck van Loosen Park**, in Enkhuizen, laid out and designed in 1897 on five acres by C. B. Posthumus Meyes (1858–1922) with a similar architectural vocabulary applied to the fifty villa-like houses rented to workers who, according to the will of Margaretha Snouck van Loosen (1807–1885), were forbidden to participate in drunkenness, fornication, or other vices and could not own chickens, dogs, or cats. Set behind an iron archway supported by stone columns, the enclave featured gravel lanes winding through a lush landscape of hedges, flowers, streams, and ponds.[199] The six house types included detached, semidetached, quadruple, and rowhouses. A superintendent's house was also built. The enclave was purchased by the municipality in 1977 and sensitively renovated during the 1980s.

Holland's first deliberately conceived garden village, **Het Lansink** ('t Lansink) (1911), Hengelo, was undertaken by a group of businessmen led by C. F. Stork (1865–1934) to house workers, officers, and directors of the Stork Company but was not limited to company employees.[200] After attending a local health inspector's lecture on workers' housing in which the link between

1. Aerial view. GE (2008)

2. Entrance. ZE

3. Overall view. ZE

4. Typical view. Schiphouwer. PAN (2008)

housing, health, and productivity was highlighted, Stork was inspired to tour Bournville and Port Sunlight. Two years later he hired Karel Joan Muller (1857–1942) to lay out 't Lansink's 30-acre site with a network of straight and gently curving, 10- to 13-meter-wide streets mostly oriented to run north–south, allowing sunlight to reach the fronts and backs of the houses. Closely adhering to Unwin's recently published *Town Planning in Practice* (1909), Muller called for closed street vistas, the diagonal orientation of houses at intersections, for example at the junction of Ketelstraat and Weversweg, and the grouping of houses around greens. A town square with built-up corners provided a place for public buildings, including a shopping arcade, a community center, and a coffeehouse. The village also featured a school, hotel, and tennis courts. Working with landscape architect Pieter Wattez (1871–1953), Muller added a variety of new trees to the many retained on the site. Leonard Springer was another collaborator, designing the houses' front gardens. Sand was excavated from the southern end of the property to level the northern development area, leaving a large pit that continually filled with water, prompting residents to call for its permanent transformation into a pond.

A. K. Beudt (1855–1934) designed 't Lansink's 300 stylistically diverse traditional brick, stucco, and half-timbered tile-roofed rental houses that alternated between semidetached, three-, four-, and six-unit rows to provide different types for various income groups. One of the workers' groups was modeled on traditional Dutch *hofjes*, U-shaped almshouses embracing a courtyard. Block and lot sizes varied widely and houses

stepped back and forth from the street so that rear gardens ranged from 15 to 29 meters deep. Pedestrian footpaths were threaded through block interiors. Beginning in the north, construction occurred in three phases between 1910 and 1929. After World War II, the village was extended south of the pond, with architect H. B. van Broekhuizen (1889–1948) overseeing the completion of Muller's plan.

The next industrial garden village, **Heijplaat,** begun in 1913 using funds from the 1902 Housing Act, was undertaken by the Rotterdamsche Droogdok Maatschappij (Rotterdam Dry Dock Company), one of the largest shipbuilders in the country, to provide housing for skilled workers on a roughly 17-acre peninsular site between the Waalhaven and Heysehaven basins, across the River Maas from Rotterdam's center.[201] Its planner, Herman Ambrosius Jan Baanders (1876–1953), provided space for 400 brick houses as well as a host of community facilities that were all "within the context of the company's moralistic paternalism," as Donald Grinberg has written.[202] During the first phase of construction that lasted until 1918, two churches, two schools, a community center with shops, a library, a bathhouse, a firehouse, and a café and theater located in an after-work center were constructed. A village square with a bronze fountain provided a civic focus and an archway spanning Vestastraat added a familiar element of Dutch villages, with bachelors' apartments located above and a restaurant next door. Although its density of about seventeen houses per acre was more than twice that of 't Lansink, "the underlying town-planning

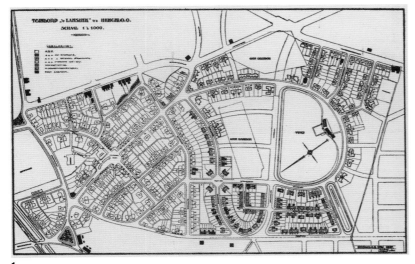

1

2

3

4

5

1. Plan, Karel Joan Muller, 1911. NAI (1927)

2. Storkstraat. MAR

3. *Hofje*-like group on Lansinkweg. MAR (1919)

4. Ketelstraat and Weversweg. Onna. NVO (2012)

5. Storkplein. Onna. NVO (2012)

principles are essentially the same," as Rg. Hofstee has observed.[203] Later phases extended the village to the south and during the 1950s, to the southwest. Heijplaat was threatened with demolition during the 1980s, but protestors were able to win its protection.

Tuindorp Elinkwijk (1914–17), Zuilen, in north-western Utrecht, was another project by 't Lansink's planner, Karel Muller, built by a housing association to provide accommodations for skilled railway workers of the Werkspoor company, many of whom were being relocated from Amsterdam.[204] Muller prioritized north–south streets that would allow maximum sunlight into the living rooms. Street hierarchies called for 40-foot-wide main roads and 32-foot-wide secondary roads. The 208 dwellings, a mix of semidetached and terraced houses with green- and white-painted wood and plaster facades and pitched tile roofs, included a group that turned the neighborhood's southwestern corner where, set back on a small park, it featured an arched gateway in its base through which workers could access a footpath leading to the factory. At the district's southeast corner, Muller angled two houses back on their sites to mark the entrance to Bessemerlaan, a curving perimeter road that was the backbone of the plan. From Bessemerlaan, streets crooked and curved toward a central square that was intended to be ringed by stores. These were instead realized just outside of the site, along its eastern boundary,

Amsterdamsestraatweg, which could also serve lower-level workers in the Lessepsbuurt district across the street. The intended store buildings were converted into two-story houses and the central square became a playground with an adjacent community center.

Philipsdorp (1910–16), Eindhoven, was undertaken after the Philips corporation, having historically relied on private-sector housing, learned that the municipality had failed to develop an extension plan, forcing the company to build on its own. Using funds from the 1902 Housing Act, Philips began in 1910 with the construction adjacent to its factory complex of three blocks of rowhouses laid out by Anton Philips's father-in-law, G. J. de Jongh (1845–1917), who was retiring as Rotterdam's director of public works. The project included 200 houses built from three types designed by Eindhoven's municipal architect Louis Kooken (1867–1940) and an additional three variations by company architect C. Smit (n.d.).[205] In 1916, when the company was ready to expand Philipsdorp to the southeast, it hired the well-known architect K. P. C. de Bazel to take on what was an unusually modest task compared to the country houses and public buildings that occupied most of his time.

Working with J. W. Hanrath (1867–1932) and de Jongh, de Bazel, according to Vladimir Stissi, avoided "streets with rows of more or less identical little houses," in favor of "terraced housing designed as a unified

Heijplaat

1

2

3

4

5

Tuindorp Elinkwijk

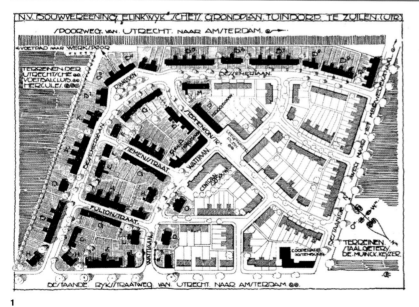

1

2

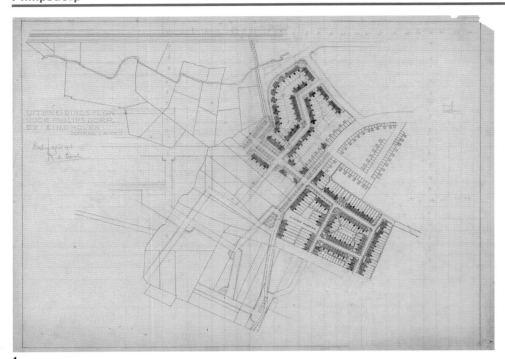

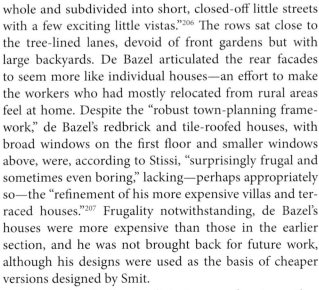

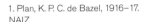

1. Plan, K. P. C. de Bazel, 1916–17. NAIZ

2. Wingerdlaan, in the K. P. C. de Bazel-designed section. NAIZ (c. 1918)

3. Overall view. Onna. NVO (2005)

4. Typical street in section planned by G. J. de Jongh. Onna. NVO (c. 2010)

5. Overall view showing backs of houses. Onna. NVO (2005)

whole and subdivided into short, closed-off little streets with a few exciting little vistas."[206] The rows sat close to the tree-lined lanes, devoid of front gardens but with large backyards. De Bazel articulated the rear facades to seem more like individual houses—an effort to make the workers who had mostly relocated from rural areas feel at home. Despite the "robust town-planning framework," de Bazel's redbrick and tile-roofed houses, with broad windows on the first floor and smaller windows above, were, according to Stissi, "surprisingly frugal and sometimes even boring," lacking—perhaps appropriately so—the "refinement of his more expensive villas and terraced houses."[207] Frugality notwithstanding, de Bazel's houses were more expensive than those in the earlier section, and he was not brought back for future work, although his designs were used as the basis of cheaper versions designed by Smit.

Hollanderwijk (1914–15), in Leeuwarden, is another workers' community with garden village elements,

designed by Willem Cornelis de Groot (1853–1939) on a roughly triangular site accommodating 177 houses at a high density of about 27.5 units per acre in three arcing terraces and ten parallel rows cut through by a serpentine transverse street that opened up to a grassy square in the center.[208] The district also contained two stores and a workshop.

Heveadorp (1916–18) was a small workers' village designed by J. Rothuizen (1888–1979) to not only accommodate current workers but also attract new workers to the Hevea rubber factory in the remote municipality of Renkum, Gelderland.[209] The 120 thatch-roofed rowhouses were built on rectangular blocks on a wooded slope according to only two distinct types, but they varied considerably in detail. Twenty-three houses for higher-level employees were located closer to the factory. Portions of the village were destroyed during World War II, but the remaining sections were rehabilitated in the 1970s.

In 1919, Philippus Jacob Hamers (1882–1966) turned to the villa park model in the garden village he designed for state railway workers on the grounds of a former estate in **Haren**, Groningen.[210] Asked to lay out only a small enclave, Hamers instead produced plans for a complete village with 224 houses, a bathhouse, school, and stores, although the stores were never built. Hamers scattered thatch-roofed detached, semidetached, and rowhouses of up to six units on small freeform blocks shaped by curving streets. Residential lots, bound by hedges and fences, averaged 2,150 square feet. With no standard house setbacks or alignment and a density of roughly eight dwellings per acre, the village retained a naturalistic informality. An existing pond was retained on the site, along with native vegetation that Hamers complemented with new trees and plantings. The village was built in three phases in 1919, 1921, and 1925, eventually accommodating 150 houses. H. A. Pothoven (n.d.) designed the third phase in the northwest at about twice the density of the earlier sections. Only a small portion of the village remains. In Deventer, a small city roughly 60 miles east of Amsterdam, architect W. P. C. Knuttel (1886–1974) designed the compact garden village of **Knutteldorp** (1919–24) for a private association, placing 334 dwellings on a 15-acre triangular site located between two growing industrial areas whose lower-level workers it would house.[211] Knuttel focused the plan toward the center of the site. Rowhouses and a prominent gateway building around the perimeter sheltered Knutteldorp's internal network of tree-lined streets that focused on three interconnected squares at the center of the plan, linked at their corners by gateway buildings. The central square was bordered by ten shops that added to other amenities, such as a meeting house and bathhouse. A site for a school was provided in the north, near a fourth square, but the school was never built and the property was developed with housing. Knuttel designed the houses, each with a rear garden, to be architecturally consistent yet individualized. He also designed the village's street furniture. The density was about 22 houses per acre. With the exception of the main gateway building in the southwest, the village has been entirely rebuilt, although the original street plan remains intact.

Perhaps the largest and best-executed of the Dutch industrial garden villages was **Pathmos**, in the textile manufacturing center of Enschede, built in two phases between 1914 and 1928 according to designs by W. K. de Wijs (1884–1964) in collaboration with the director of Public Works, Anton Helmich Op ten Noort (1881–1975).[212] The first phase of 974 two-story houses was completed by 1922 and remains intact, while the second phase of 226 apartments, built in the northwest, was demolished and replaced in recent years.

De Wijs's plan, focused around the central Thomas Ainsworth Park, was separated into eastern and western halves by the serpentine Pathmossingel, a divided boulevard with a landscaped median. The residential neighborhoods, integrating shops, schools, a community center, and public baths, were made up of short,

Hollanderwijk

1. Aerial view. CFH
2. Typical view. CFH (1921)

Heveadorp

1. Houses. Eskens. ESK (2010)

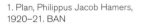

1. Plan, Philippus Jacob Hamers, 1920–21. BAN

2. Typical house showing school in background. NAI22

3. Typical house. NAI26 (1920)

crooked streets punctuated by plazas, squares, and *rond-points*. The combination of a part-Unwin part-Sitte plan with a high degree of architectural diversity stemming from eighty-nine distinct house designs based on nine types, made no two streets alike. Moreover, de Wijs employed a traditional palette of red brick and red-tile roofs in a majority of the district but used white painted brick and white stucco at key intersections and public squares to great aesthetic effect. Near the southeastern entrance, a circular plaza was defined by concave stucco facades and triple-arch passageways. On the larger blocks, rows stepped back and forth from the street to disguise their length, while elsewhere U-shaped groups were set back on grassy lawns in the tradition of the *hofje*.

In 1917, J. J. P. Oud, on the recommendation of his friend, H. P. Berlage, was placed in charge of municipal housing at the Rotterdam Gemeentelijke Woningdienst (Municipal Housing Authority), where, serving until 1933, he "repeatedly had to compromise between his 'ideal' designs and the harsh realities of bureaucratic life," according to Gunther Stamm.[213] Oud was born in the small town of Purmerend, north of Amsterdam, and designed his first house at the age of sixteen while studying decorative arts. After two years as a draughtsman in the architectural office of Joseph Cuypers (1861–1949) and Jan Stuyt (1868–1934), Oud briefly audited classes at the University of Technology at Delft and then in 1911 went to Munich for a few months to work for Theodor

Fischer, who became a strong influence. He began his career with a series of commissions for small houses and shops. His first town-planning project was the garden village he designed in Leiderdorp (1914) (see p. 518) in collaboration with W. M. Dudok.

When he took his post in Rotterdam, the twenty-eight-year-old Oud, closely affiliated with the De Stijl group (he was not an official founder but contributed to its eponymous publication until he distanced himself from the movement in 1920), had evolved a view of town planning in which, as Bernard Colenbrander has noted, "the idyll of the garden city was replaced by a truly urban concept, with the different components fitting exactly one inside the other."[214] Oud's focus was on a streetscape dominated by communal housing blocks built from standardized components and modern materials with a minimum of ornament and within which, as he put it, "dwellings will accommodate themselves to a rhythmical interplay of mass and plane."[215]

Once in Rotterdam, Oud was left to cope with a vast shortage of housing combined with a "political debate about the desirability of and need for municipal housing," as Ed Taverne, Cor Wagenaar, and Martien de Vletter have written. "Initially, Oud must have imagined that his slightly exalted, aesthetic ideas concerning standardization, the monumental townscape and construction technology were perfectly in keeping with the day-to-day practice of municipal housing policy," but "the fragile position of designers of municipal social

Knutteldorp

Pathmos

housing became apparent in 1921 and again in 1923," when there was a "realignment of political power at the local level" while "at the national level, the existing funding models were abandoned. Partly as a result of these developments, Oud found his activities at the Woningdienst severely curtailed" and increasingly dogged by political and bureaucratic resistance.[216]

In 1922, Oud designed **Oud-Mathenesse**, a village of working-class houses also known as Witte Dorp (1922–24), the White Village, west of downtown Rotterdam.[217] He had been eyeing the site since 1919, when in collaboration with T. K. van Lohuizen (1890–1956), a research engineer, he conceived it as part of a much larger district of 30,000 inhabitants that included fifteen schools, churches, shops, a library, bathhouse, and offices. State funds for the project dried up, but the Rotterdam city council decided to develop a fragment of the site with semipermanent housing.

Oud planned the village and designed the 343 predominantly one-and-a-half-story single-family houses that were scheduled to be torn down after twenty-five years to make way for a park. He also designed eight shops with apartments above and a firehouse with offices above. The plan conformed to the site's rigid triangular boundaries, with rows of dwellings laid out parallel to the edges but intersected by perpendicular rows leading

1. Central square showing shops, left, and administration building, center. NAIO (1924)

2. Typical street. RAMSA (c. 1978)

3. Site plan and house elevations and plans, J. J. P. Oud, 1922. NAIO

4. Aerial view. NAIO (c. 1926)

1

2

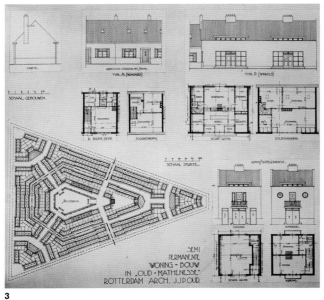

3

4

from the corners to a central square planted with poplar and willow trees. The mixed short and long rows stepping back and forth from the street, some kinked at the ends and others framing gardens and courts, gave Witte Dorp a village-like character of closed vistas and spatial irregularity that disguised the fact that 331 of the dwellings were identical, with only minor differences in the front doors and windows. Punctuating the vistas were freestanding, folly-like administration and transformer houses.

The buildings were placed on concrete slabs set directly on the soil. Yellow brick plinths supported wood-frame construction and the houses were faced in white rendered plaster, earning the White City its moniker despite the presence of steep-pitched red-tile roofs (a requirement placed upon Oud) as well as a De Stijl palette of blue front doors and yellow door frames, gutters, and canopies. The shop buildings were slightly different, with plinths of gray facing brick and terrazzo tile, yellow framed storefront windows, and long, low dormer windows. As Henry-Russell Hitchock observed, "With these smooth, white, amply fenestrated walls above bases of yellowish brick and beneath roofs of red tiles, this is an architecture that Vermeer might have painted."[218]

Construction got under way in 1923 and was completed in 1924 on the village that was received as "one of Rotterdam's most popular and most maligned residential districts," according to Taverne, Wagenaar, and de Vletter, but nonetheless "an urban neighborhood of remarkable intimacy; a neighborhood with a village-like atmosphere that had not been achieved by pseudo-villagey means."[219] The plan "might almost have been excerpted" from Berlage's second Plan-Zuid: "The chief points of similarity are the severely geometrical street plan, the various short axes that come together at the (social) hub of the neighborhood, the playground, and the introverted townscape . . . Every 'hiccup' in the street plan—a narrowing or widening of the access roads, a bend—had immediate repercussions in the architecture of the walls and was translated into a steeply pitched roof or a change in the facade. In the Witte Dorp the focus was firmly on the streetscape as a whole and it was onto the streets that the living rooms faced. The inner courts here played hardly any role as a communal area."[220] Although it long outlasted its intended life span, the village was demolished in 1985 and rebuilt with houses (1992) by P. de Ley (b. 1943), who preserved the central park space but replaced the ringed streets with short parallel rows.

Oud's next important housing estate was in the portside village of **Hoek van Holland** (1924–27), about

1

2

1. Shops and recessed gateway. Dukker. RCE (1998)

2. Rear facades. RAMSA (1977)

twenty miles west of Rotterdam and two miles from the sea.[221] The project, located at 2e Scheepvaartstraat, with forty-one dwellings placed in two symmetrical two-story rows linked by a recessed gateway building, was more important as a work of architecture than planning but established ideas that would carry through to Oud's next estate, De Kiefhoek, and earned the architect international renown. When the site was annexed by Rotterdam in 1914, it was envisioned as an upscale seaside resort. However, its location on an estuary of the Nieuwe Waterweg attracted dock-related industries faster than pleasure seekers and by the early 1920s workers' housing had become the priority. Despite the drying up of state funds for the purpose, the Rotterdam city council decided to sponsor the project in 1923.

Oud worked hard on the striking design and once built he publicized it tirelessly on the international scene. The curving shops at the end of each row became the project's defining feature. The buildings were designed to emphasize horizontality, expressed in bands, with a 16-inch gray painted plaster plinth set beneath a yellow brick base rising to windowsill height and the remainder of the facade—from the windowsills to the continuous projecting balconies and up to the roofline—covered in beige plaster so that, as Taverne, Wagenaar, and de Vletter note, in the Hoek van Holland housing, "a process that had seen the individual dwelling gradually absorbed into a new entity, that of the block, reached its logical conclusion."[222] The rear facade was more varied, with a rhythmic expression of narrow and wide, protruding and receding bays. Units had private rear gardens, shaped in plan as interlocking Ts separated by low walls from a public park beyond. Although the overall impression was of a white building, a De Stijl color scheme was again at play, with blue doors and fences, red lampposts, red- and white-striped blinds, and yellow brick walls enclosing the front gardens.

In recognition of its waterside location, Oud intended for Hoek van Holland to evoke both city and country: "the horizontality of the building," he wrote, "with its long, unbroken line, with its open-work fencing and its broad windows, alludes to the need for vastness and boundlessness (the advantages of the countryside); the tautness and smoothness of the exterior, the perfectionism of the details—simplicity in particular demands the greatest care—bespeak the refinement that distinguishes the city from the village. The light, bleached colour takes its cue from the dune landscape, while the front gardens, in their somewhat rigid demarcation, represent the less welcoming aspect of the city."[223]

In his design of **De Kiefhoek** (1925–29), Oud adapted the architectural language of the Hoek van Holland houses to the scale of a village covering 10 acres.[224] The project responded to a shortage of housing for large, low-income families displaced by slum clearance programs undertaken as part of the National Housing Act. The site, located south of the river Maas and just north of Vreewijk Garden Village (see p. 514), had been cleared as part of the slum clearance initiative. In 1923 architect R. J. Hoogeveen (1879–1960) prepared a plan for its development, outlining a cloistered garden village of 358 standardized dwellings in long, snaking rows on nine blocks that made room for an array of open spaces, including squares, interior courts, private gardens, playgrounds, and pedestrian paths. Thirteen shops were distributed throughout the village, near the entrances, around squares, and at corners. A prominent site was reserved in the northeast for a church.

However promising, the Hoogeveen plan did not go forward. When Oud began to reimagine the site, he may not have had "much freedom with respect to the lot division," according to an official at the housing agency, but he severely altered the site plan into a more regular grid accommodating 291 dwellings, two stores, two playgrounds, a public garden, a church, two warehouses, and a water boiling plant.[225]

Only families with eight or more children were permitted to reside in De Kiefhoek. To keep costs down, Oud called for simple, standardized two-story rowhouses ending in blank walls. Flat roofs allowed for full-height bedrooms on the second floors. He initially specified concrete construction—prefabricated slabs for

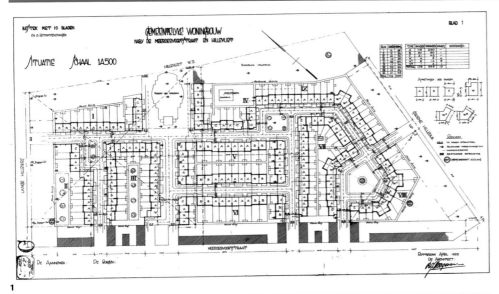

1

2

3

4

1. Early plan, R. J. Hoogeveen, 1923. DKR

2. Aerial view. NAIO (c. 1930)

3. Looking down Heer Arnoldstraat. Onna. NVO (2012)

4. Church, J. J. P. Oud, 1929. Onna. NVO (2012)

the exterior and poured-concrete party walls—but brick was found to be cheaper and so the buildings were covered in white plaster and again enlivened by the use of primary colors. Banded ribbon windows at the ground and second levels accentuated the low horizontality of the facades. Oud adapted the Hoek van Holland's rounded storefronts to the constraints of the site and budget, using curves on the acute angled corners of two perimeter blocks in the south, where they provided a strong visual marker just within the main entrance. Concrete canopies remained, but the dramatic glazing was replaced by recessed chamfers. Elsewhere in the district, Oud referred to the curves by designing small second-story balconies that punctuated the ends of rows.

Oud left the corners of each block open to allow access to the block's interior, indicating his fixation, as Martien de Vletter put it, "on the effect of contrast between the enclosed interior courtyards and the open, long perspective of the street. The many sketches for corner solutions and perspectives demonstrate how to deliberately compose a town- or villagescape."[226] In De Kiefhoek, unlike Hoek van Holland but similar to J. B. van Loghem's Tuinwijk Zuid, Oud gave similar expression to the front and rear facades, although the effort was later undermined by residents who individualized their backyards. Oud's Protestant church was completed

in 1929 at the northeastern entrance to De Kiefhoek, where its crisp, white rectangular form—built with a concrete frame supporting stucco-covered brick—stood in stark contrast to the surrounding fabric of redbrick houses. De Kiefhoek's last house was completed in 1930.

According to de Vletter, De Kiefhoek allowed Oud to unite "a modern urban character and a rural character . . . The urban and modern is emphasized by the compact density, the standardized house types, the flat roofs and the grand town planning gestures—certainly when compared to the neighboring Tuindorp Vreewijk garden suburb . . . The rural was encapsulated in the ground-hugging construction and the open spaces."[227] The neighborhood was entirely reconstructed in the 1990s. In the initial phase of reconstruction, significant changes were made to the houses both inside and out, but public outcry led to a more respectful approach for most of the village, with internal reconfigurations, such as the combination of units, undertaken in such a way as to be barely noticeable from the outside.

SWEDEN

Kiruna (1899), Sweden's northernmost city and Scandinavia's first planned industrial city, built to support

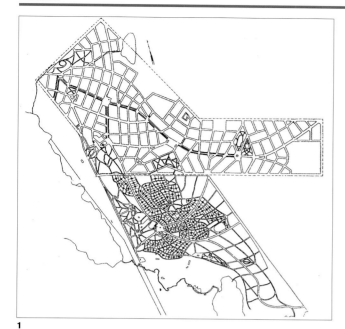

1

2

4

3

1. Plan, Per Hallman and Gustaf Wickman, 1900. LAS

2. Houses designed by Gustaf Wickman. Lundberg. RIKS (2006)

3. Overall view. RIKS (1920–49)

4. Kiruna church, Gustaf Wickman, 1909–12, with mine in background. RIKS (1920–49)

iron mining, was also the first of many Scandinavian towns to be deliberately planned along Sitte-esque lines.[228] Designed by Per Hallman, who was soon to become the country's preeminent planner, and Gustaf Wickman (1858–1916), a prominent Swedish architect known especially for his banks, the development of Kiruna, conceived almost a decade after iron deposits began attracting settlers in earnest to the remote, snowy region, coincided with the government's construction of a railroad, the so-called Ore Line, completed in 1902, connecting major ports in Sweden and Norway. The decision to undertake a planned community was made by Hjalmar Lundbohm (1855–1926), a geologist and the managing director of the mining company LKAB, who hoped to prevent the proliferation of shanties that plagued other mining towns. Kiruna was placed on a hilltop site where temperatures would be milder during the winter months than in the low marshlands. Its streets were oriented to help block cold winds. Hallman and Wickman divided the site into northern and southern sections, the former with large blocks and wide, angled streets intersecting in Sittean squares, and the latter featuring a more organic, curvilinear plan of narrower streets that, as Mats Ahnlund and Lasse Brunnström have pointed out, seem more inspired by Olmsted than Sitte.

The plan was approved in 1900 and Kiruna grew quickly, counting 7,500 residents by 1910. Wickman designed a majority of the buildings, including a residence for Lundbohm, two-story semidetached workers' houses, detached houses for engineers, and a range of stylistically varied but mostly vernacular-based public buildings that included schools, offices, public baths, a fire station, a hospital, a post office, a bank, and a hotel. Wickman's red-painted church (1909–12), occupying the town's highest point, became a landmark of Swedish architecture. The multifamily workers' dwellings, designed to resemble individual houses, were painted in bright colors that differed from street to street. The mining company held art exhibitions, lectures, and concerts and employed children during the summer months to maintain parks and public spaces. In 1907 an electric tram was completed to carry residents around town and to transport workers to and from the mine.

The harsh climate did not allow for the intended street trees or waterways, and the plan was only partially followed as Kiruna grew during the post–World War II period. The transition to underground mining in the 1960s led to surface cracks in the town above and began to force the abandonment of built-up sections, a process that is expected to continue into the 2030s, by which time most of the city—including the railway station,

Nyvång

Eneborg

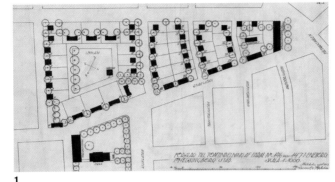

Pålsjö

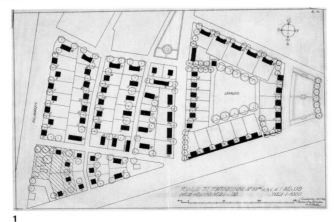

city hall, fire station, schools, historic neighborhoods, and the Kiruna church—will have been undermined. Although the historic buildings are to be relocated and others demolished, the sense of town that is the most important part of the story will be lost.

Following the example of Kiruna, industrial villages played an important role in Sweden's emerging garden village movement. **Nyvång** (1910–13), also known as Ormastorp, in Helsingborg, was a coal-mining village built by the company Skånska Kolbrytnings, whose leadership, believing that improved living conditions would foster more productive workers, purchased 50 acres near its new mine shaft and in 1910 asked town engineer Sigfrid Ewald (1877–1949) to plan, as Janne Ahlin has put it, "a self-sufficient garden community patterned after English examples, with a school, stores, a library and a church."[229] Ewald in turn asked Sigurd Lewerentz (1885–1975) and Torsten Stubelius (1883–1963) to assist on the plan and design prototypical two- and three-family workers' houses as well as single-family houses for managers, each of which was to have a hedge-lined garden with eight fruit trees provided by the company. To accommodate workers on the night shift, the architects provided some houses with upper floors suited to daytime sleeping. The dwellings were intended to feature roughcast plaster exteriors with painted trim, but most were not realized according to Lewerentz and Stubelius's designs. The buildings, closely based on the architects' sketches, were fleshed out by company architect Martin Cronsiö (n.d.). The town remains largely intact.

Lewerentz & Stubelius planned two additional industrial villages in Helsingborg, both in collaboration with Ewald: **Pålsjö** (1912), in the north, and **Eneborg** (1912), in the south.[230] Though intended to house workers of specific factories, the plans were financed by the government's Own Home program (see p. 537). Stubelius had identified the sites in 1907, before joining with Lewerentz, but developed the plans after their partnership commenced in 1911. The architects proposed fifteen types of housing for the sites, some based on vernacular forms and most constituting single-family detached houses, though examples of semidetached and three- and four-family rows were also included. In Eneborg, the roughly triangular site was divided into four blocks, the largest of which incorporated a central playground. The sparsely detailed redbrick and white-trimmed, red-tile-roofed houses featured gardens of varying size, with trees placed in between or in front of the houses depending upon their setbacks. Only twelve of the planned buildings—two twelve-family, two six-family, three four-family, and five single-family houses—were realized, built in 1917–18 according to designs by Lewerentz. The housing showed the influence of Richard Riemerschmid's work at Hellerau (see p. 290), a project that Lewerentz had assisted on for several months in 1909 and 1910. The unexecuted plan for Pålsjö was similar but covered a slightly larger site and devoted two blocks to parks. The houses were oriented both parallel and perpendicular to the street and stepped back and forth from the lot line.

In 1911, Lewerentz & Stubelius designed a small colony for workers at a pulp-mill factory in the town of **Karlshäll**, outside of Luleå.[231] Their plan for the sloping, windy site consisted primarily of a single road that shifted its axis at a central square around which playgrounds, a well, and other communal facilities were placed in addition to houses, one of which was set at an angle to help block winds. Thirty, two- and three-family dwellings were intended to be realized in phases, but only six were ever built (two remain) as well as a washhouse. Each house had an individual garden and outhouse.

Lewerentz & Stubelius's unrealized design for a workers' colony in **Forsbacka** (1914) was particularly promising, calling for about eighty houses set on individual lots on a wooded, riverfront site organized around two internal roads whose shape followed the terrain.[232] The architects placed small squares at intervals along the road and provided a larger, tapering tree-lined square that widened toward views of the river. One group of houses surrounded a quiet courtyard on a peninsular portion of the site. Public amenities including a swimming pool and a marina were provided along the water. Three types of houses were designed, each of wooden construction on stone bases.

The city of **Porjus**, in northern Sweden, was planned to support a state-owned hydroelectric plant on the Lule River supplying power for the mines in Kiruna and for the Ore Line railroad.[233] The plan was prepared in 1917 after a shantytown had been built on adjacent private lands and as rising coal prices during World War I brought new emphasis to hydroelectric power. Knut Plahn (n.d.), an engineer in the State Power Board's construction department, prepared the layout, linking an industrial district in the northeast with the power plant by a 92-foot-wide powerline right-of-way that doubled as a buffer between the workers' village and a commercial district around a railroad station near the river. The workers were to reside in detached houses with individual gardens placed along tree-lined streets, and a central site was reserved for a park, athletic grounds, and public buildings. After extensive infrastructural work was completed, including the laying of roads, water and sewage systems, and electrical lines, declining economic conditions forced the closure of the factories in 1920–21 and Porjus "never recovered from the blow."[234]

Bergslagsbyn (1915–20), built in the Dalecarlia region of central Sweden as a model community for employees of the Domnarvet Ironworks, is notable for being the first of the new Swedish villages to meld modest, vernacular-inspired wooden houses of uniform design with garden village site planning.[235] Osvald Almqvist (1884–1950) laid out the development, working from an earlier plan by Per Hallman. Guided by the site's gently rolling topography and the angles produced by two crisscrossing railroad lines, Almqvist's layout, divided by a wide north–south thoroughfare, called for an irregular patchwork of short residential streets and dead ends. In an unusual arrangement, deep lots accommodated two- and four-family workers' houses

Karlshäll

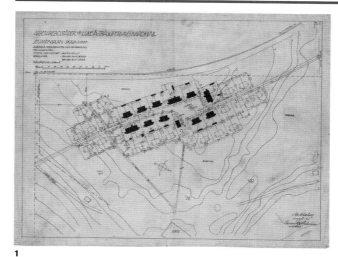

1. Plan, Sigurd Lewerentz and Torsten Stubelius, 1911. ARKM

2. Overall view. Tegström. LUL (1920s)

Forsbacka

1. Model. ARKM (1914)

Porjus

1. Plan, Knut Plahn, 1917. GARN

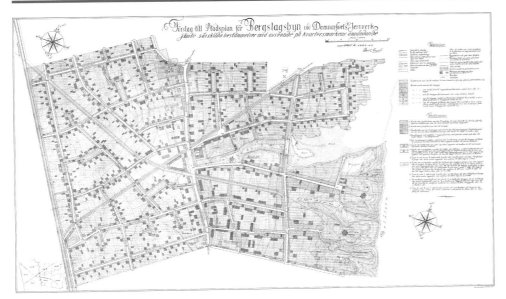

1

1. Plan, Osvald Almqvist, 1920. BK

2, 3. Typical streets. Ludvigsson. (2012)

4. Typical street. Eklund. WC (2009)

2

4

3

Mänttä

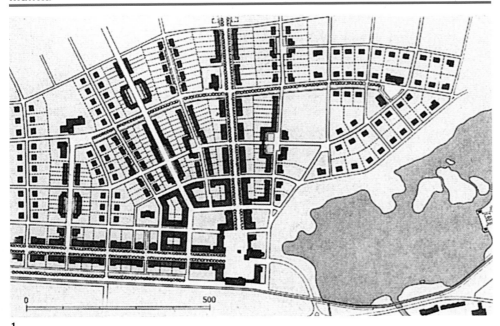

1

1. Plan, Eliel Saarinen and W. G. Palmqvist, 1920. ESP

along the street, and detached and semidetached houses, probably for higher-ranking employees, behind, creating a small courtyard that gave way to individual and communal gardens farther back on the site. In several locations, Almqvist placed dwellings around long rectangular landscaped lawns extending perpendicularly from the street. With the exception of a house for the company's president, Almqvist's red-painted wooden clipped-gable houses with individual porches were mainly limited to two types in order to produce a uniform and orderly streetscape that conjured "a Swedish village-like atmosphere, even though these buildings were in fact manufactured in a rational way with a high degree of standardization."[236] Almqvist provided two public gathering places in the form of grassy squares outfitted with maypoles and playgrounds.

FINLAND

In Finland, Eliel Saarinen designed two small mill communities before relocating to the United States in 1923. He collaborated with W. G. Palmqvist (1882–1964) on the design of the **Mänttä** mill town (1920) in western

Finland's Vilppula, placing detached, semidetached, and rowhouses along angled streets that converged in a village square bordered by apartment houses, a community center, market place, and church.[237] The longer rowhouses were set back to enclose street-facing courts, and each house was given its own garden regardless of its lot size. The partially executed scheme was replaced by a new design in 1950. In 1921, Saarinen drafted the plan of **Kangas Pappersbruk** in the Jyväskylä district of central Finland, working from an earlier plan by Palmqvist and Hilding Ekelund (1893–1984).[238] The unbuilt scheme, intended to bring order and density to a haphazard arrangement of millworkers' houses, introduced public squares and an irregular street plan accommodating detached and semidetached houses on individual lots. Saarinen reinforced an existing street in the south with rowhouses and a church square.

In 1922, Otto Meurman, serving as Viipuri's town-planning architect, laid out the village of **Havi** for soap and candle factory workers on a site just beyond the city's northern fortifications.[239] The plan included 190 residential lots for detached and terraced houses. Aiming to establish "a garden city character," Meurman allowed streets to follow the site's contours, created closed street vistas, and provided front gardens and courtyards that linked up with other planted areas.[240] By 1930, the district housed 1,387 residents. Meurman also included garden village elements in several remote industrial communities of the 1920s, but the notion of a significant garden city–inspired project would not resurface in Finland until Meurman began planning the sprawling Helsinki suburb of Tapiola in 1945.

NORWAY

One notable Norwegian industrial garden village, **Rjukan,** possibly "the most elaborately designed company town in Scandinavia," according to Mats Ahnlund and Lasse Brunnström, was comparable in scope to Sweden's Kiruna.[241] Situated on a narrow valley site in Vestfjorddalen, a popular tourist destination since the nineteenth century, Rjukan was established in 1908 by the Norsk Hydro company to derive electricity from the 340-foot Rjukanfossen waterfall. The electricity was used to harvest nitrogen from the atmosphere in the same process that gave rise to the town of Muscle Shoals, Alabama, and other ordnance towns built in the United States during World War I (see p. 886).

As laid out by company engineers, Rjukan was inspired by the Krupp housing estates in Essen, which Sam Eyde (1866–1940), Norsk Hydro's lead engineer, had observed firsthand while studying and working in Germany between 1886 and 1898. In addition to in-house staff, the company called upon a number of prominent young architects, including Thorvald Astrup, B. Keyser-Frølich, Joh. E. Nielsen, Bjarne Blom, Harald Aars, Helge E. Blix, H. Monrad Hansen, Magnus Poulsson, and Ove Bang, to design Rjukan's public buildings

Kangas Pappersbruk

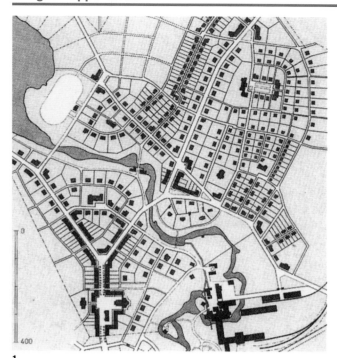

1. Plan, Eliel Saarinen, 1921. ESP

Havi

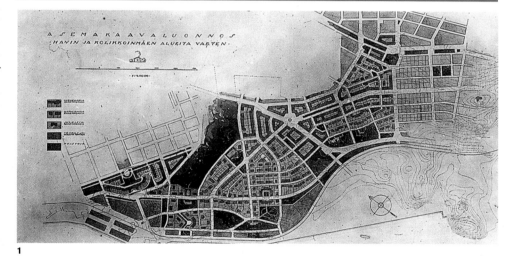

1

1. Plan, Otto Meurman, 1922. MFA

2. Typical view. MFA

2

1

2

3

and dwellings, the latter consisting mainly of detached houses with front gardens placed around the block perimeter. With almost no exception, the architects employed vernacular styles.

The plan clearly reflected prevailing social hierarchies. Houses for workingmen were located close to the factory, with those for higher-level employees placed on south-facing slopes where they could enjoy sunlight for a greater part of the year. The largest houses were placed on spacious sites along Villa Road. The company built stores, schools, a post office, a public bath, a library, an athletic club, a fire station, and a hospital and set aside space for parks. The architects were put to work on the design of infrastructural components, such as bridges, as well as kiosks, bus stops, benches, streetlights, and bathrooms. In 1912, during a second stage of residential construction, Magnus Poulsson won a competition to design small wood and brick houses that would be owned by the workers. The town was largely completed by 1920, with 1,200 units of company-built housing realized from more than fifty different types.

ITALY

Italy's earliest planned workers' subdivisions were built by entrepreneurs seeking to house employees convenient to their factories. The industrial village at **Schio** (1872) was the creation of wool manufacturer and politician Alessandro Rossi (1819–1898), the "first Italian to deal with the problem of housing for his own employees in an organized way," as historian Bernardetta Ricatti has put it.[242] Located in the Veneto region seventeen miles northeast of Vicenza and surrounded by Mount Pasubio and the Little Dolomites, the town of Schio began manufacturing wool in the twelfth century but only acquired its moniker of "little Manchester" after Rossi took control of his father's mills in 1849 and built a massive five-story factory (1862) designed by Belgian architect Auguste Vivroux (1824–1899), greatly improving both the quantity and quality of his wool production. Rossi built workers' housing in the 1860s near Vivroux's Fabrica Alta in the form of so-called *palazzoni*, "a synthesis between a large tenement house and a block of flats, clearly inspired by the French and English example," as Ricatti has noted, but in 1872 he hired Venice-based architect Antonio Caregaro Negrin (1821–1898) to prepare plans for a self-sufficient village to house about 1,000 residents on a 40-acre site between the mills and the Leogra River.[243]

Caregaro Negrin's initial gridded plan of rectilinear streets was rejected by Rossi, who envisioned a more naturalistic scheme with houses "built in alternating irregular groups" so as to avoid a "barrack-like appearance," all with the goal of helping to "amalgamate the social classes."[244] The second, approved plan consisted of detached, semidetached, and terraced houses on curving streets with new trees planted every 26 feet. On major

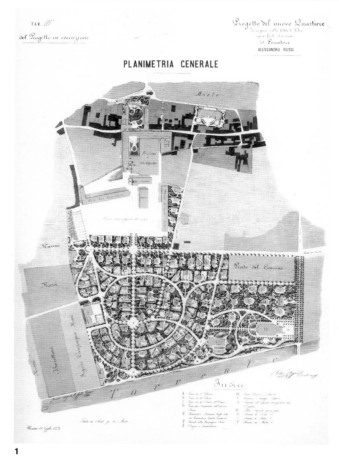

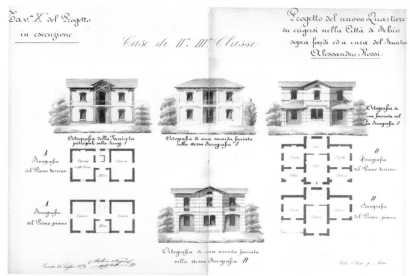

cross streets trees were planted every 33 feet, while various town squares had trees every 20 feet. The houses, on average, featured 50-foot-long vegetable gardens, protected by three-foot-high iron fences. Caregaro Negrin designed most of the houses, with managers located in the larger villas along Via Petro Maraschin and workers in the semidetached and terraced units. A separate section of semidetached houses was provided for pensioners. Houses were offered for rent or sale, but buyers had to agree to make no substantial changes to their properties for at least fifteen years.

Rossi instituted a comprehensive social program, directing Caregaro Negrin to build nursery and elementary schools, an agricultural college, a theater, and a community center. Caregaro Negrin also designed a church, a railway station, as well as several town squares decorated by sculpture, the most prominent being Giulio Monteverde's *Monument to the Weaver* (1879), located near the entrance to the mill but moved in 1945 to Piazza Alessandro Rossi in the northeast part of the village. Caregaro Negrin, who is better known as a garden designer, also included several public parks.

In 1882, a survey of European cotton and woolen mills prepared by the United States State Department praised the village at Schio for both its factories and housing. The village grew rapidly, reaching over 1,500 residents by 1890, but new development reverted to a gridded pattern, an ironic reversal considering Rossi's rejection of Caregaro Negrin's original scheme. Still, the

industrial village continued to impress visitors. Horatio Forbes Brown, writing in a history and travel guide of the region published in 1905, praised a trip to Schio as one "full of interest, partly for the sake of its natural beauty, and partly because of the social experiment which is in operation there . . . One cannot help being struck by the comfort and content of the population, their cheerful looks, their *esprit de corps*, their pride in Schio, and their evident sense of being properly based in the world. The mills themselves stand in large garden-like grounds, with plenty of space on all sides and are kept in perfect order and cleanliness . . . The company has laid out a town of new houses, each with a plot of land attached, large in proportion to the size of the house."[245]

Crespi d'Adda (1890), a second industrial village centered around a textile factory, was developed by Cristoforo Benigno Crespi (1833–1920) on 210 acres in the town of Capriate San Gervasio in the Lombardy region, twenty-eight miles northeast of Milan.[246] Crespi commissioned Milan-based architect Ernesto Pirovano (1866–1934) to prepare the plan as well as design the initial buildings. The cotton mill, on the western edge of the site, was built on the banks of the Adda River, separated from the housing by Corso Alessandro Manzoni, the village's main north–south tree-lined thoroughfare. The fifty semidetached workers' houses were arranged in neat parallel rows and each featured a modest lawn and kitchen garden. Larger villas located south of the workers' dwellings were built for the factory

1. Plan, Antonio Caregaro Negrin, 1872. CFS

2. Elevations and plans. CFS (1872)

3. Pensioners' houses. CFS

4. Typical street. CFS

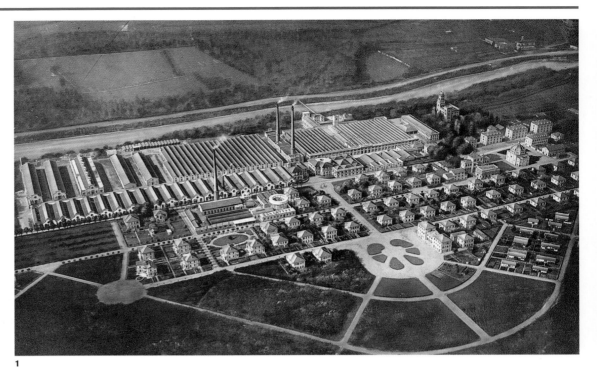

managers, while Pirovano designed a neo-Gothic castle for the Crespi family. The residential area was bisected by a short, east–west road leading from the factory entrance to Piazzale Vittorio Veneto, the town square. A fan-shaped arrangement of two semicircular streets enclosing a park concluded the development to the east. In addition to the houses, Crespi d'Adda also included a school, community center, theater, hotel, sports facility, grocery and clothing shop, health clinic, public washhouse, and church. South of the factory and the houses along Corso Alessandro Manzoni was a cemetery and elaborate mausoleum designed by Gaetano Moretti (1860–1938) in 1896.

Developed by Carlo Giovanni Napoleone Leumann (1841–1930), an Italian-Swiss textile manufacturer, **Leumann Village** (1898–1911) was designed by Turin-based architect Pietro Fenoglio (1865–1927), who abandoned his practice in 1912 in favor of a career as a financier of large engineering projects in Italy and abroad.[247] The village adjoined the Leumann cotton mills, which were first established in 1875 on what would eventually grow to become a 15-acre site along Corso Francia seven miles west of Turin's city center in the municipality of Collegno, near two canals and a railroad. By constructing his own self-sufficient village, as Alberto Abriani has written in his history of Leumann Village, the progressive industrialist made "a conscious attempt . . . at urbanism" by creating a place that "could develop without affecting the city."[248]

The factory compound was entered through chalet-like twin gatehouses (c. 1875), reflecting not only the owner's Swiss origins but also the influence of Viollet-le-Duc. The gates suggested a country estate rather than an industrial complex. By the time the village itself began to take shape, the plan and stylistic imagery became more distinctly urban. A simple grid of streets and lanes was laid out on either side of the 600-loom, 1,500-worker cotton mill. More interesting were the varied types of

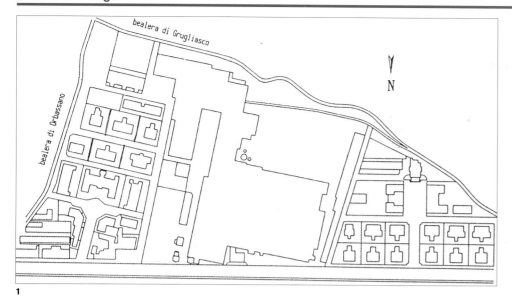

1. Plan, Pietro Fenoglio, c. 1898. AASL

2. Gatehouses. AASL (2006)

3, 4. Houses. AASL (c. 1900)

5. Corso Francia. RAMSA (2007)

houses, also designed by Fenoglio, many in the Stile Floreale, an Italian version of Art Nouveau, intended to meet the needs and pocketbooks of office staff, foremen, as well as ordinary factory workers. The house designs with their private gardens, as Abriani noted, "took the form of a country cottage in town; detached, semi-detached, or terrace houses built for workers, with productive vegetable patches [which were] supposed to feed the family and therefore keep wages down, while living in one's house and garden was expected to foster a healthy moral life and create a sense of property, stabilizing labor and dispersing too great a massing of workers so as to avoid outbursts of social conflict."[249]

The village, numbering about 550 residents by 1911, also contained a train station, a post office, a public washhouse, a girls' dormitory, a gymnasium, and a small hotel presumably for factory visitors. A Roman Catholic church, Santa Elisabetta, also designed by Fenoglio, was located at the end of the village's only significant public space, flanked by the workers' social club with a cooperative shop and a combination nursery and elementary school.

SWITZERLAND

In 1909, influenced by the garden suburbs being built outside Zurich for the middle class (see p. 569), as well as by examples in Germany and England, Karl Moser, the prominent Swiss architect best known for his

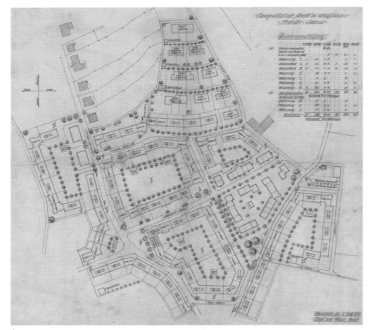

1. Plan, Curjel & Moser, 1910. GTA

2. Model. GTA (1909)

3. Gardens. Linck. GTA (1911)

4. Stahlwerkstrasse. Linck. GTA (1911)

institutional and ecclesiastical commissions, prepared a plan to house 300 iron and steel workers and their families on a site convenient to the Georg Fischer plant in the city of **Schaffhausen,** thirty-two miles north of Zurich.[250] Designed in collaboration with Robert Curjel (1859–1925), his partner since 1888, the plan, intended for a high, flat site less than a mile west of the city center, called for terraced units grouped around courtyards and gardens. Only a small percentage of the scheme moved forward, however, the most prominent part being a U-shaped arrangement of ten three-story gabled houses (1911) shielding modest gardens and providing thirty-six three- to five-room apartments.

Curjel & Moser had greater success with a more modest settlement planned in 1911 for the workers and administrators of Maggi AG, an industrial food company that began manufacturing bouillon cubes for widespread distribution in 1908.[251] Curjel & Moser's plan for a slightly hilly site in **Kemptthal,** twelve miles northeast of Zurich, mixed detached and semidetached houses, placed along curving streets, with a central group of terraced units arranged around a green. After four years of

construction, seventy dwelling units were completed in houses that closely resembled the firm's previous vernacular work at Schaffhausen. A planned school and bakery remained unrealized.

In 1915 Moser ended his partnership with Curjel, accepting a professorship at the Swiss Federal Institute of Technology Zurich (ETH Zurich); two years later, on his own, he prepared a plan to house workers of the Von Roll iron and steel factory in **Gerlafingen,** sixty miles southwest of Zurich and twenty-two miles north of Berne.[252] Moser's ambitious plan for the fan-shaped site was bisected by a chestnut-tree-lined north–south boulevard, home to a large square park, with shorter east–west, slightly curving streets on either side, lined by semidetached and detached houses. In the southern portion of the site, terraced units were oriented north–south and east–west and also arranged in a U-shaped pattern around a green. By 1920 Moser was only able to complete two terraced north–south rows accommodating fifty-one apartments as well as a school for young children. Moser's settlement (1918) for employees of the Bally shoe factory in **Schönenwerd,** thirty-seven miles

Kemptthal

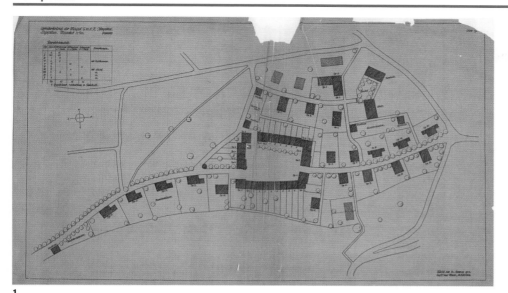

1. Plan, Curjel & Moser, 1912. GTA
2. Aerial view. ETH (1963)
3. Floraweg. Tokapi. PAN (2007)

2

3

Gerlafingen

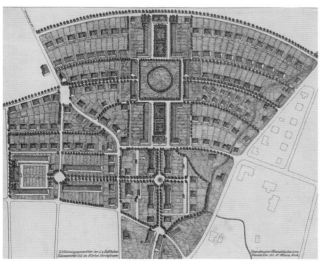

1

1. Plan, Karl Moser, 1917. GTA
2. Model. GTA (1918)
3. School, garden facade. GTA (1919)
4. Mühlackerstrasse. Strahm. MOG (2013)

2

3

4

1. Plan, Karl Moser, 1918. GTA
2. Houses. GTA (1919)

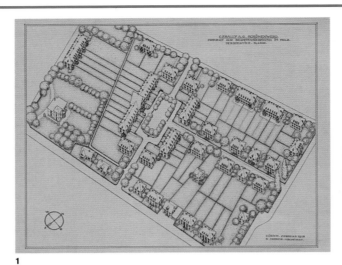

1

2

Dorfsiedlung Geissenstein

1. Plan, Möri & Krebs, 1910. GEIS
2. Overall view. SSL (c. 1920)
3. Typical street. GEIS
4, 5. Typical views. RAMSA (2011)

1

2

3

4

5

west of Zurich, calling for a village-like arrangement of traditionally styled detached, semidetached, and terraced houses with large rear gardens, met a similar fate, and only a single row of two-story houses with hip roofs was completed.[253]

Moser headed the jury that selected the architects for **Dorfsiedlung Geissenstein** in Lucerne, picking the firm of Alfred Möri (1880–1936) and Karl-Friedrich Krebs (1880–1910).[254] Krebs, who had worked in the

Curjel & Moser office for three years, died a year before construction began in 1911 on the housing cooperative built for railway workers. Located one-and-a-half miles south of the city center on an irregularly shaped hilly site formed by curving streets, Dorfsiedlung Geissenstein accommodated 300 families in 173 detached, semidetached, and terraced houses that each featured generous rear gardens and stylistically recalled Moser's settlement work.

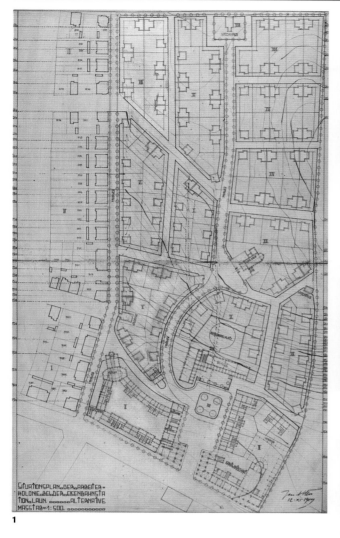

1

2

3

4

1. Plan, Jan Kotěra, 1909. NTM

2. Typical street. NTM

3, 4. Typical streets. Schankler. AS (2011)

CZECHOSLOVAKIA

In 1909 Jan Kotěra, a Prague-based architect as well as a prominent professor at the Prague Academy of Fine Arts, designed the country's first development inspired by the English garden suburb model as well as by examples in Germany when he was commissioned by the Prague-Duchcov Railway to design a workers' village in **Louny**, Bohemia, forty miles northwest of Prague.[255] The undeveloped site was located one-and-a-half miles from the center of Louny, just south of the company's railway repair yards and the main artery leading east to the village of Černčice.

The focus of Kotěra's plan was a town square surrounded by arcaded buildings shielding a public park with playground and fountain. The plan called for a town hall, restaurants, shops, a social club, a communal laundry, and public baths to be located around the square, while a school and church were to be placed nearby on the surrounding hillsides. The housing, as historian Pavel Šopák has observed, was "arranged . . . around three separate axes and connected via transverse or diagonal paths, while a long street oriented from north to south, curving around the houses and widening into a promenade of avenues lined with trees, became the main communication axis of the entire project."[256] The residential area was composed predominantly of two-story terraced units, but Kotěra included detached villas as well, although the architect was not convinced they were suitable for a workers' village, writing: "Although the ideal of family life will always be an independent dwelling, surrounded by a sufficient amount of free space, whether it be a garden or field . . . we must ask ourselves whether this type of architecture is appropriate for the working classes, and whether the price of land would allow this to come about."[257] Between 1909 and 1913 fifty-one freestanding, semidetached, and terraced brick and stucco houses were completed at Louny, and an additional dozen terraced houses were built in 1919–20, but except for the laundry and playground, the civic and commercial components remained unrealized.

Czechoslovakia's largest, most important development inspired by the Garden City movement was the

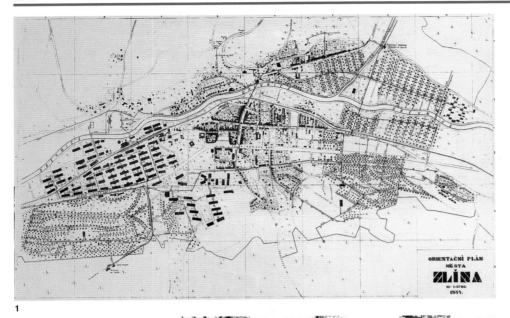

1. Plan, František Lydie Gahura, 1934. RGFA

2. Overall view. RGFA (1930s)

3. Residential section. RGFA (1940)

4. Houses. RGFA (1932)

2

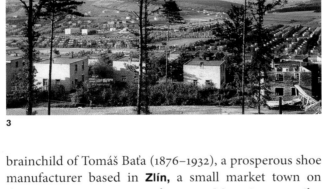

3

4

brainchild of Tomáš Baťa (1876–1932), a prosperous shoe manufacturer based in **Zlín,** a small market town on the Dřevnice River in southeastern Moravia, 100 miles southeast of Prague.[258] At the end of World War I, Baťa visited Henry Ford's River Rouge automobile plant in Dearborn, Michigan, to study its innovative, internationally recognized assembly-line techniques. Baťa, who had previously visited the United States in 1904, a decade after founding his own company, to observe shoe factories in Lynn, Massachusetts, was impressed with Ford's industrial efficiency but strongly objected to "company policy toward its workers" as well as the living conditions of the average employee and his family.[259] He returned home with the intention of combining Ford's production methods with the ideas of Ebenezer Howard and the English Garden City movement, which he had become acquainted with from trips to England and as the result of the advocacy of Jan Kotěra, designer of his villa (1911) in Zlín as well as the workers' village at Louny. The paternalistic entrepreneur, who "held himself responsible not only for the training of his skilled employees, but also for their moral and educational welfare, and that of their families,"[260] believed that "people with dirty character cannot do clean work . . . It would not be difficult to create a town with 50,000 people huddled in barracks or tenement houses without caring as to how their wives and children are living and what opportunities for earning they have in the town . . . Our aim is to build a garden town, full of sunshine, water and green grass—a

clean town with the highest of wages, prosperous crafts and businesses, a town with the best of schools."[261]

To design his garden city, Baťa logically turned to Kotěra, who began preparing sketches in 1918 calling for rows of single-family detached houses within walking distance of the factory buildings but separated from them by parkland. Although a few houses were built and the industrial facilities expanded, progress on a comprehensive town plan was not made until 1923, after the postwar economy had improved and Baťa was elected mayor of Zlín, granting him the kind of authority needed to make large-scale changes in the town. That same year Raymond Unwin traveled to Prague to receive an honorary degree as well as to lecture on town planning. Also in 1923 Kotěra died and was replaced by František Lydie Gahura (1891–1958), a Zlín native who had studied under Kotěra in Prague and who would guide the development of Zlín for the next fifteen years, even after the death of Tomáš Baťa in a plane crash in 1932.

The heart of Gahura's plan was the reworked industrial component, consisting of similarly designed modular reinforced-concrete buildings, some of which were massive multistory facilities connected by wide pedestrian paths and in many cases by aerial conveyer belts. A greenbelt surrounded the town, while landscaped strips separated the factories from the residential areas located on the surrounding hillsides but within walking distance of work. The large civic and commercial core was placed in roughly the center of

5

6

7

the site, just east of the manufactories, although some schools and smalls shops were mixed in with the housing. In addition to a prominent community center that was home to restaurants, public meeting rooms, and administrative offices, the civic center included a town square and marketplace, a 300-room hotel, a 2,580-seat theater, a hospital, three department stores, churches, and recreational facilities.

The housing, designed to give "physical expression" to Tomáš Baťa's motto, "work collectively, live individually," consisted of detached and semidetached houses, each equipped with an allotment garden.[262] Gahura designed many of the square two-story brick houses, first with hip roofs and, after 1927, with flat roofs. The houses were primarily arranged in long rows along straight and curving streets, creating "a neat geometrical pattern against the hillsides," as Jean-Louis Cohen has written, going on to characterize the town and its plan as "remarkable for its aim, scope and the quality of its achievements."[263] Dormitory facilities for unmarried male and female workers were placed away from the "family" sections and closer to the civic center.

Zlín prospered dramatically, growing from a population of 4,678 in 1921 to 37,342 by 1937. Even after Tomáš Baťa's death and his replacement by his stepbrother Jan, the Baťa Shoe empire continued to expand in Zlín as well as around the world, with new factories in Switzerland, France, the Netherlands, England, Canada, and India. In several instances, these factories were accompanied by housing built by the company, but these new developments never achieved the size or the level of coordinated planning realized at Zlín. In 1935, Le Corbusier was invited to be one of the judges at a competition for new housing at Zlín. Impressed by the garden city, which he deemed "the most interesting construction of an industrial city in Europe," Le Corbusier advocated for its expansion, proposing a version of his linear city plan with high-rise apartment blocks that was rejected for betraying the company's ethos and Tomáš Baťa's emphasis on the individual.[264]

Zlín's growth along the lines outlined in Gahura's plan was abruptly halted by Germany's annexation of Czechoslovakia in 1938, but the family-run company was able to reorganize itself in Ontario, Canada, where Baťa's son Thomas established the town of Batawa, built on the model of Zlín but at a vastly smaller scale.[265] After World War II and the nationalization of the shoe company's operations in Czechoslovakia, the original character of Zlín was compromised by the construction of large multistory apartment houses, as Le Corbusier had earlier proposed. Alternately described by Tomáš Baťa as a "town among gardens" or a "factory within a garden," Zlín, according to planning historian Helen Meller, writing in 2001, nonetheless "remains an example of what Ebenezer Howard's Garden City looks like in modern form . . . a small but living example of the power of Howard's ideas in Europe and how they were modernized and brought up to date for a future age."[266]

5. Aerial view. RGFA (1930s)

6, 7. Typical views. Dezidor. WC (2011)

The Industrial Garden Village in the United States, Canada, and Mexico 1822–1940

Following on the heels of English industrialists' early efforts to ameliorate workers' housing conditions, American industrialists began to take similar steps. In 1822 the treasurer of the Boston Manufacturing Company, Kirk Boott (1790–1837), reflecting principles evolved by the company's founder, Francis Cabot Lowell (1775–1817), planned and developed a community for textile workers at **Lowell**, Massachusetts.[1] Lowell had introduced the power loom, causing the textile business to boom. As a result, he and his fellow mill owners were confronted with severe labor shortages. Lowell realized that young unmarried women, then living on farms, could perform the work previously undertaken exclusively by men and boys if it was possible to overcome the resistance of their families. To do so, Lowell and other mill owners initially built convent-like boardinghouses run by matrons of impeccable reputation, imposing strict standards of behavior, including compulsory Bible classes and church attendance. But the rapid growth of the mills meant that more than sleeping facilities were needed for their enterprises to succeed. Lowell realized that, as John Reps has written, "the industrial plant could no longer exist apart from the community and that it was now a responsibility of industries to create the towns in which they would be located."[2] But it was not until the Boston Manufacturing Company's original plant became too small and the company purchased a new site on the Merrimack River that Lowell's ideas were tested in actual practice with a campus-like factory

complex surrounded by a long grid of streets containing houses and community buildings.

Lowell, as Francesco Dal Co has argued, was not an organically evolved mixed-use town, although some existing roads were incorporated into the street system, nor was it an ideal town based on shared utopistic values, but a town conceived directly in support of "the productive requirements of the industrial plants," with "no other motivation for its development than to be an appendage to the manufacturing system."[3] The clarity of Lowell and Boott's plan and of the powerful redbrick and granite architecture attracted and impressed many visitors, one of whom, Michael Chevalier, observed in 1839: "The town of Lowell . . . is a pile of huge factories, each five, six, or seven stories high, and capped with a little white belfry . . . By the side of these larger structures rise numerous little wooden houses painted white, with green blinds, very neat, very snug, very nicely carpeted, and with a few small trees around them, or brick houses in the English style . . . Here are all edifices of a flourishing town in the Old World, except the prisons, hospitals, and theatres."[4]

The Lowell idea was carried much further in **Manchester**, New Hampshire, planned in 1838 by a company engineer, Ezekiel A. Straw (1818–1882), who later became governor (1872–74) of the state. Between the 1830s and World War I, the Amoskeag Millyard, a mile-long, quarter-mile-wide industrial village, consisting of rows of redbrick factory buildings along the Merrimack River and two parallel canals as well as workers'

Marktown. Schalliol. DSCH (2012)

1. View across Merrimack River. ATHM (1834)

2. Plan, Kirk Boott. CLH (1832)

3. Dutton Street. ATHM (1849)

1

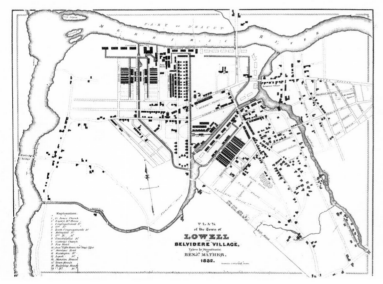

2

3

housing, brought together, as architectural historian Randolph Langenbach has written, "the simplicity and classical unity of the New England colonial town with the dynamic intensity of the modern industrial city, combining in its fabric the pastoral dignity of great barns with the urban density of a European marketplace."[5] The canals not only provided power for the mills but also were treated by the corporation as tree-lined borders between the factories and the houses. A British visitor in 1902 compared the entire grouping with the "ancient colleges" of Oxford and Cambridge.[6]

The newly realized complex turned Derryfield, a hamlet of 125 inhabitants, into a village of 10,000

workers renamed in honor of England's industrial powerhouse. Like Lowell, Manchester embodied a utilitarian urbanism, "providing," as Langenbach has written, "for the complete life of the millworkers within a closed and carefully set-up community."[7] As the village evolved, the housing district was interspersed with public parks and squares, an innovation in industrial village planning.

Although its development did not follow a set plan, **South Manchester**, Connecticut, home to the Cheney Brothers Manufacturing Company, was, according to historian John S. Garner, "the first company town to place equal emphasis on producing a good environment while manufacturing a good product. The landscape of

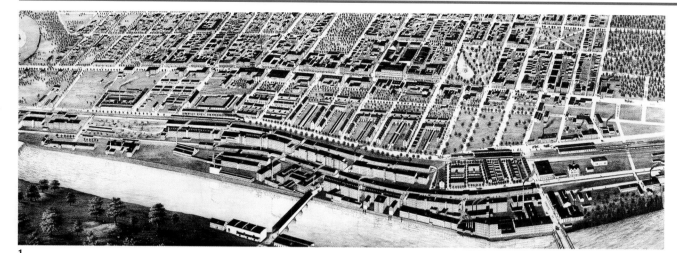

1

1. Bird's-eye view. LOCPH (1876)

2. Houses between Middle and Market Streets. LOCPH1 (c. 1890)

3. Green, between West Merrimack and Middle Streets, converted to parking. LOCP (c. 1935)

2

3

South Manchester

1

2

1. Bird's-eye view. LOCG (1880)

2. View across park of houses on Linden Street. TCHS (1890–1909)

Fairbanks Village

1. Bird's-eye view. LOCP (1884)

Whitinsville

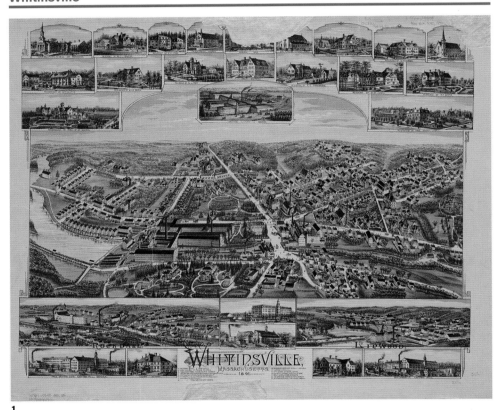

1

1. Bird's-eye view. BPL (1891)
2. Forest Street. HAM2 (c. 1903)

2

South Manchester was a garden in comparison to the back-lot appearance usually described in factory towns."[8] Beginning with the construction of a silk factory in 1838 and continuing in earnest through the second half of the nineteenth century, the site was developed with 200 single and double houses surrounded by individual gardens and loosely grouped around Cheney Hall, a library and lyceum. As it developed, portions of the site were kept as open space, including a natural forest threaded through with pathways. By 1905, according to English writer and lecturer Budgett Meakin, the community, spread across more than a thousand acres, was for the most part "too scattered to convey much idea of a village."[9] The continued maintenance and improvement of the landscape is attributable in part to the fact that fourteen Cheney families resided among the workers: "We have nothing to show," they stated. "We are not philanthropists: this is our home, and we like it to look nice, that's all."[10]

Industrial villages continued to be realized in New England throughout the nineteenth century. **Fairbanks Village,** in St. Johnsbury, Vermont, first established with a gristmill in 1815, prospered after 1831, when the Fairbanks family invented a platform scale that was almost universally adopted by industry.[11] In 1875, the factory was expanded, and Lambert Packard (1832–1906), a Vermont architect and landscape designer, designed seventy double houses along streets that conformed to the topography of the valley. At the same time, the company transformed the banks of the Passumpsic River into parkland and began to build cultural institutions that included an academy, library, museum, and art gallery.

Good housing was an important factor in attracting workers to remote areas where industry located to take advantage of water power. **Whitinsville**, Massachusetts, with about 500 uniform, detached white clapboard houses built along tree-lined streets for employees of the Whitin Machine Works, made an impression on Grosvenor Atterbury, who, calling it "a picture of considerable architectural harmony and charm," found inspiration for his design of Indian Hill (see p. 827).[12] By contrast, the forty houses that constituted **Oakgrove,** built by the Willimantic Linen Company in Willimantic, Connecticut, in 1865, were different in architectural treatment, leading Meakin to describe the community in 1905 as "varied and picturesque."[13] Also notable as architecture was the group of shingled two-and-a-half-story gable- and gambrel-roofed houses designed by John Calvin Stevens in 1886 for the S. D. Warren Company in **Westbrook**, Maine, about seven miles northwest of Portland.[14]

At first glance, **Wilmerding** (1889), Pennsylvania, fourteen miles east of Pittsburgh, in the Turtle Creek Valley, a model community for workers of the Westinghouse Air-Brake Company, seems similar to Pullman (see p. 244).[15] Its sponsor, George Westinghouse Jr. (1846–1914), was, like George Pullman, a railroad tycoon who, in 1867, at only twenty-one years old, conceived of the air brake, revolutionizing railroad safety. Two years later he formed the Westinghouse Air-Brake Company, one of the several transformative companies to be founded by Westinghouse, a brilliant inventor. Westinghouse took great interest in workers' welfare. Unlike Pullman and other industrialists who viewed industrial villages from a "pragmatic business viewpoint," Westinghouse, as his biographer Quentin Skrabec Jr., writes, viewed "the phenomenon as part of a capitalistic Christian imperative . . . Westinghouse viewed business and workplace fairness as integrated, not motivational."[16]

After purchasing a 307-acre site in order to build a new plant situated between Turtle Creek and the tracks of the Pennsylvania Railroad, with residential neighborhoods to the north and south, Westinghouse established the East Pittsburgh Improvement Company to develop the property, retaining an engineer, W. W. Fortune (d. 1923), to plat the triangular southern site. Fortune's fan-shaped street plan, fitted to the contours of its valley setting, with streets converging to a point in the south, had Westinghouse Avenue as a central spine, leading north to a village green. To the east and west, houses were built on terraces up the hillside until it became too steep for development. Westinghouse purchased 150 of the first lots and built two-and-a-half-story frame hip-, gable-, and pyramidal-roofed houses for his employees, with full verandas. Individual purchasers also built houses and by 1890 the section was fully realized. The second phase of development occurred north of the creek, where between 1898 and 1900 semidetached and terraced houses were constructed by Westinghouse along Air Brake and Middle Avenues, long parallel streets built into the hill. Little construction occurred after 1900 and the town of 6,000 or so persons prospered but did not evolve.

In 1890 the Niagara Falls Power Company set aside 368 acres of land two-and-a-half miles from the city of Niagara Falls, New York, for an industrial park and workers' housing to be built in anticipation of an influx of employees and industries associated with the construction of America's first water-powered electrical generating plant.[17] Engineer and financier Edward Dean Adams (1846–1931), president of the Cataract Construction Company, a subsidiary of the Niagara Falls Power Company, selected the name **Echota,** a Cherokee word meaning "town of refuge," for the new industrial village. Civil engineers John Bogart (1836–1920) and J. J. Fanning (n.d.), assisted by W. A. Brackenridge (n.d.) and Albert H. Porter (n.d.), were responsible for platting the 84-acre oblong parcel intended for the workers' housing. The flat site, located on high ground about half a mile from the Niagara River, was bound on the north and east by property lines, on the west by a small stream, and on the south by the straight line of the Niagara Junction Railway, which connected to both the Erie Railway and the New York Central Railroad. Difficult subsoil conditions caused problems in the design of sanitary facilities, leading to the installation of an extensive drainage system that also allowed for the planting of substantial trees, including evergreens, Norway maples, and elms. Bogart and Fanning's modified gridiron

Oakgrove

1. Bird's-eye view. LOCG (1909)

2. Typical street. MFV (c. 1905)

Westbrook

1. Cottage Place houses, John Calvin Stevens, 1886. Cheek. RC (c. 1976)

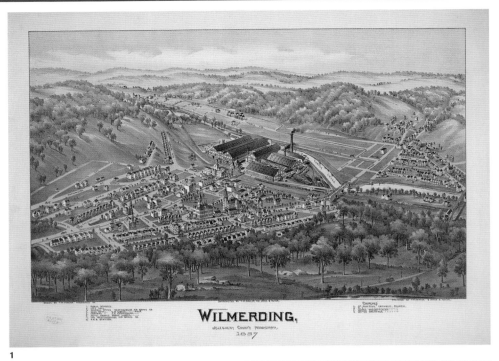

WILMERDING,

ALLEGHENY COUNTY PENNSYLVANIA,
1887

1

2

3

plan, oriented predominantly toward the railroad line, featured 50-foot-wide tree-lined streets with 25-foot roadways. The plan accommodated the 66-foot-wide Sugar Street, which already ran through the site.

Of far more interest than Echota's simple plan is the architecture of the industrial buildings and housing designed by Stanford White of McKim, Mead & White, who was selected by Adams as a result of their previously successful collaboration on the interiors of his New York City residence in the Villard Houses (1882–85) on Madison Avenue as well as on a summer home, Rohallion (1888), in Rumson, New Jersey.[18] White was charged not only with the design of Echota's houses but also its industrial structures, which, according to Leland Roth, took the form of "simple, bold, yet restrained" buildings realized in masonry partly "to resist the incessant vibration" but also to "express symbolically the brute power of nature being harnessed, all the more so because nothing of this would be immediately visible—there would be no great turning wheels or sliding pistons, only the whirl of the generators and the hum of transformers."[19] By contrast, White's modest, yet thoughtful, wood-frame

workers' houses attempted to establish an arcadian character for the town. Sheathed in clapboard and shingles, the houses were set back 20 feet on lots that were on average 115 feet deep, allowing for an ample sense of greenery along the streets as well as backyards large enough for private gardens. Employing the Niagara Falls Power Company's colors, they were painted yellow with white trim. White provided a variety of house types, including detached single-family houses, side-by-side duplexes, and three- and four-unit rowhouses. On Sugar Street, he located a larger facility that included bachelors' apartments on the upper floors, a ground-level general store, and an assembly hall for community events.

By 1894 Echota was home to 112 families living in sixty-seven dwellings. And on November 15, 1896, street lamps in Buffalo, twenty miles to the southeast, were lit by electricity powered by the new plant. Echota continued to prosper, and by 1918 the houses in the village were no longer operated on a rental basis but owned by the workers, fulfilling Adams's initial wishes. John Bogart was proud of his efforts, writing in 1895 that "a district, not fit for comfortable residence, has been transformed

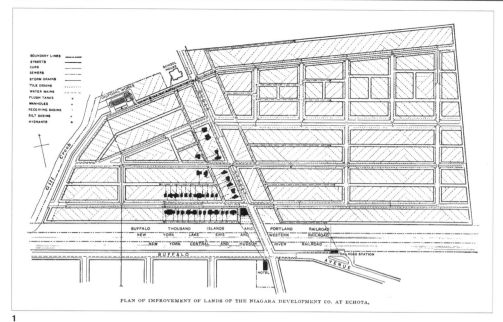

PLAN OF IMPROVEMENT OF LANDS OF THE NIAGARA DEVELOPMENT CO. AT ECHOTA.

1

2

3

4

into an ideal, healthful village . . . An unattractive expanse of poor meadowland has become a model town, with inviting residences at very moderate expense for the families of all who may have to do with the busy industries called into action by the wonderful power drawn from the Falls."[20] Not all observers shared Bogart's enthusiasm. Charles Mulford Robinson (1869–1917), in an early article in his career as town planning consultant and proselytizer, claimed that White's houses exhibited "a pretense of the familiar suburban straining for art and variety."[21] But Meakin was kinder, characterizing Echota as "a small but tasteful experiment in industrial housing" where a "great variety has been secured in the designs."[22] Recently, historian Margaret Crawford has written rather peevishly that "the houses were small but carefully planned, with particular attention paid to cross-ventilation and interior circulation. However, once built, their architectural variety could not counteract the monotony of the engineers' gridiron planning. Lined up in rows, and set back uniformly from the road, the houses reproduced the repetitious order that had become a hallmark of the company town."[23]

At the same time that Stanford White was working at Niagara Falls, he was also designing similar facilities, albeit on a much smaller scale, for the **Roanoke Rapids** Power Company in North Carolina, near the Virginia border.[24] Again it was a personal connection that involved him in the enterprise: New Yorker John Armstrong Chanler (1862–1935), the leading investor in the company and a member of the Astor family, was a friend. As at Niagara Falls, White worked within the confines of a regular gridiron plan devised by unnamed company engineers. In 1895 White designed a spinning mill, a modest Queen Anne–style Baptist church, and fifty single-family and duplex houses, "known locally," according to Leland Roth, "as the 'turtle-top' houses, no doubt because their broad gables resembled sheltering carapaces."[25] White received no fee, billing only for the time of his draftsmen. But his connection to the project also included a role in the company's management. For a short time he held Chanler's power of attorney and served as interim president of the mill. Apparently Chanler's fascination with the psychic world resulted in a stay at the Bloomingdale Insane Asylum, requiring

1. Plan, John Bogart and J. J. Fanning, c. 1891. CM17

2. B Street houses, McKim, Mead & White. NG (1907)

3. Power plant, McKim, Mead & White. LOCP (1941)

4. Typical street. Garvin. AG (2009)

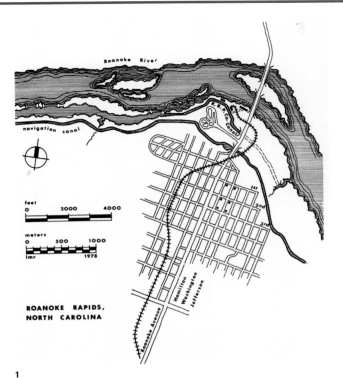

1

2

White to step in and help out his friend. Chanler, of this world or not, was pleased with White's work, writing to White's partner, Charles Follen McKim in 1895 that Roanoke Rapids "does McKim, Mead & White distinctly proud. It is the handsomest mill of this type I've ever seen, here or abroad, and excites admiration from the untutored natives."[26]

With the founding of **Leclaire**, Illinois, in 1890, the evolution of American industrial garden village planning takes a dramatic turn from a fundamental utilitarianism toward a deliberate embrace of aesthetic considerations. Norwegian-born but Missouri-raised industrialist Nelson O. Nelson (1844–1922), after serving as a clerk for the Union Army in the Civil War, established the N. O. Nelson Manufacturing Company, a wholesaler and later producer of plumbing equipment and other goods, acquiring 125 acres of gently rolling Illinois farmland 18 miles northeast of St. Louis, Missouri.[27] Nelson set out to build a factory complex and town, which he named after Edme-Jean Leclaire (1801–1872), the French founder of a large house-painting company who as part of a broader program of workers' benefits implemented a pioneering profit-sharing system in 1842.[28] After touring planned European villages, including Godin's Familistère at Guise (see p. 207), Nelson started a profit-sharing program in 1886, making his one of the first American companies to do so. Initially Nelson paid year-end dividends in cash, but after establishing the town of Leclaire, he issued dividends in the form of company stock, a shift that would in time transfer ownership of the entire business to its employees. In later years, Nelson was to become an advocate of Ebenezer Howard's Garden City concept, serving as a director of the Garden Cities Association of America after its founding in 1906.

Nelson retained the St. Louis architect E. A. Cameron (b. 1861) to design Leclaire's redbrick factory complex in which one-story buildings were separated from each other by grass lawns on a 15-acre tract at the northern end of the site. But he turned to Julius Pitzman to lay out the residential district that distinguishes Leclaire as America's first industrial village to break free of the grid for aesthetic purposes. Pitzman, planner of many of the Private Places of St. Louis (see p. 92), called for 100-by-150-foot lots on tree-lined streets with houses set back 30 feet to ensure continuous front yards. The effect was initially park-like but was compromised by later additions that reverted to a gridiron plan with distinctly smaller lots.

The factory complex was screened from the houses by a line of 30-foot-high Osage orange trees and by a six-acre village green providing picnic areas and playing fields with bleachers for 1,000 spectators. A seven-acre man-made lake was added to the residential area, outfitted for recreational use, and kept free of contaminants. The company maintained public gardens and greenhouses, offering free flowers and plants as an incentive for residents to cultivate their own gardens. In addition to a town hall, schools, and a library, Nelson provided a clubhouse (1890) where workers could take advantage of a bowling alley and billiards tables. Nelson named Leclaire's streets for figures he admired, among them Ruskin, Longfellow, Jefferson, Emerson, and Edward Everett Hale, the Unitarian minister and philanthropist, who upon visiting the town found "a pretty cluster of pretty houses, shaded with young trees."[29]

By 1894, Leclaire boasted 130 residents living in twenty-six four-, six-, and eight-room houses, some built by individual owners while others were designed by

Cameron and built by the company, which either rented or sold them to workers as well as to families unaffiliated with the factory, at 5 percent above cost. Until 1910, Nelson resided in a modest two-story house at the south end of the village, stating that "there is no master, in even the remotest sense. The design was to make favourable conditions for work, intelligence, recreation and duty. We have not aimed to make it large or extraordinary."[30]

Although Leclaire was small, more a company village than a town, it was widely scrutinized, particularly in the immediate wake of the Pullman strike. On July 29, 1894, Nellie Bly (1864–1922), the pioneering female journalist who would also become a leading industrialist, operating her own factories producing steel barrels, after visiting the "model town" of Leclaire, reported in *The World* that it compared favorably to the troubled Pullman.[31] From her initial approach by train, Bly was pleased by the lack of pretense: "In Pullman the fine buildings and the park face the railroad and hide the poverty flats and the squalor from view. At Leclaire the backs of the houses were towards the tracks. They looked very simple and country-like, but prosperous and clean. That impressed me most." Visiting the light- and air-filled factories outfitted with fire sprinklers, heating systems, and electric fans, she remembered "the pens I have seen in New York and elsewhere, where slaves, male and female, labor in ill-lighted, badly ventilated, foul-smelling firetraps, and I had an irresistible longing to say to them: 'I know a place where to labor is a pleasure, not an agonizing slave task.'" She continued, "A high green hedge with a dividing driveway separated the factories of Leclaire from the home part. I thought if there was nothing else to recommend Leclaire the beautifully constructed factories would, but when I was once within the green hedge I began to realize the beauty of the town. If one expects to find grandeur in Leclaire one will be disappointed. The town is simple and pretty and it wears splendidly. The longer I was in Leclaire the better I liked it. The longer I was in Pullman the less I liked it . . . In Leclaire," Bly concluded, "the more I searched for faults the more I became impressed with the perfection of the place. The streets are not laid out like a checkerboard, with barracks of brick tenements filling every square, as at Pullman, but wind this way and that in pleasing and artistic irregularity. The only brick employed in Leclaire are the factory buildings. All the houses are frame, as country houses should be . . . There are no double houses for two or more families in Leclaire, there are no blocks of tenements with from six to a dozen people in two rooms as at Pullman. Every house in Leclaire is individual, and only one family lives in a house. Along the winding roads I saw the two-storied frame houses, prettily painted, set in wide green lots that were only broken by pretty flower beds or growing trees."[32] Bly's article prompted at least 600 readers to write letters asking to join the community. By 1910, the population reached 700 and Leclaire counted 150 houses. In 1934 it was annexed by neighboring Edwardsville, ending its autonomy.

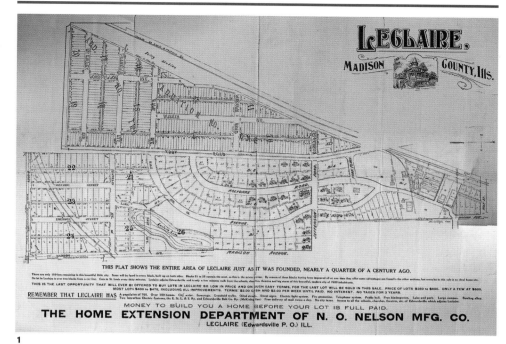

1. Advertisement showing plan, Julius Pitzman. MCHS (c. 1915)

2. Nellie Bly article, *The World* (July 29, 1894). TW94

3. Hale Avenue and Jefferson Road. CFL

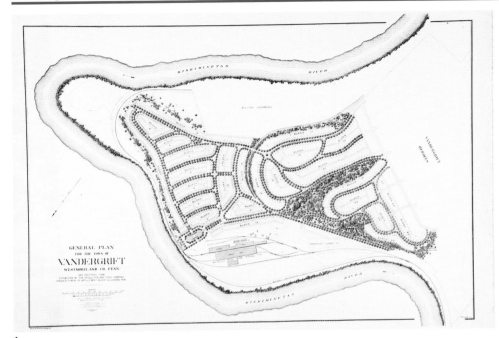

1. Plan, Olmsted, Olmsted & Eliot, 1897. FLO

2. Aerial view. GE (2006)

3. Typical street. FLO (1910)

4. Village green and casino. CRS (c. 1913)

5. Typical street. Garvin. AG (1970)

Vandergrift (1895), Pennsylvania, one mile north of the town of Apollo and forty miles northeast of Pittsburgh, was built by the Apollo Iron and Steel Company during its transition from iron to steel production.[33] Named for Jacob Jay Vandergrift (1827–1899), an oil magnate and Apollo board member, responsibility for Vandergrift lay with George Gibson McMurtry (1838–1915), the company's president, whose interest in the planning of industrial villages took him on a tour of the Krupp estates in Essen, Germany, and other examples of the type in England, France, and Russia. To plan the 640-acre Vandergrift, located on a promontory formed by a hairpin bend of the Kiskiminetas River, McMurtry and his colleagues, wanting "something better than the best,"[34] turned to the firm of Olmsted, Olmsted & Eliot in April 1895, just as Frederick Law Olmsted Sr.'s declining health demanded that he cede design responsibilities to his stepson and nephew, John

Charles Olmsted, despite the senior Olmsted's assertion that the project was "the sort of work that I would like best, as being more comprehensive and more fully touching social problems on a large scale than others coming to us."[35] Collaborating with partner Charles Eliot (1859–1897), John Olmsted propelled the model of the industrial village well beyond that of Leclaire toward an aesthetic naturalism that hitherto had only been typically realized in developments for the affluent, such as Llewellyn Park (see p. 48), Riverside (see p. 122), and Tuxedo Park (see p. 295).

However ambitious the developers were for the new town, the fact of the matter was that the decision to build Vandergrift came as the result of a strike and lockout at Apollo's plant in 1893–94—paralleling that at Pullman—which resulted in the permanent rejection of unionized labor. This prompted the company to start fresh in a new location where, McMurtry hoped, improved living and working conditions would result in a more productive and loyal workforce. The Pullman strike cautioned against excessive company involvement in workers' lives, and McMurtry shied away from any practice that might be construed as "playing providence."[36] Whereas Pullman had incited unrest in part by charging workers fixed rents while lowering their wages, Apollo would provide Vandergrift's infrastructure—streets, sewers, water supply, and electric, gas, and telephone lines—and then sell lots to workers who would finance the construction of their own homes. Anne E. Mosher, in her 2004 study of Vandergrift, *Capital's Utopia*, writes that this strategy "offered several advantages. First, by owning residential property, workers built equity, took pride in, and were uplifted by their homes. Second, by making fixed investments in housing, workers made financial and emotional commitments to the town in which they lived and to the jobs they held. Third, by participating in company real-estate ventures, workers assumed from their employers the responsibility for maintaining housing and infrastructure."[37]

McMurtry determined that the best location for the factory was on the flattest portion of the land, 80 acres at the site's northern edge adjacent to the river and the railroad tracks. From here, the site sloped gently upward as it extended south and west. Olmsted and Eliot placed a railroad station next to the factory, and a broad, rectangular village green leading from the station to a casino (1900), with a library, theater, and borough offices that provided a civic focus for a commercial district that included hotels, stores, and an office building. The axial village green recalled Olmsted Sr.'s recent plan for Biltmore Village (see p. 133), where a plaza and boulevard connected the train station and a monumentally sited church. Vandergrift's residential neighborhood fanned out to the southeast as a series of long blocks framed by concentric, arcing streets and divided longitudinally by service alleys. House lots were generously sized with 50-foot-wide street frontages. Covenants called for one single-family house per lot. A line of houses also curved around the perimeter of the neighborhood. The path of an out-of-use rail line provided a western border, beyond which land was reserved for a future phase of residential development.

Ground was broken in 1895, but differences between McMurtry and Olmsted soon arose, at first concerning seemingly mundane issues such as street names and plant species but then, owing to the influence of budget-minded board members and shareholders, affecting all aspects of the site plan to the extent that within the year John Olmsted deemed the project a "considerable disappointment."[38] The first major blow came at the expense of the village green. McMurtry had asked that the train station be relocated to better accommodate factory requirements, and as a result, the green was sharply reduced in size and reoriented so that it terminated adjacent to, rather than in the heart of, the business district. More damaging still was Apollo's insistence that in order to recoup its investment while making parcels affordable to workers, lot widths be halved, leading Olmsted to regret that "much rurality must go . . . a large part of the value of our plan was destroyed by reducing lots from fifty to twenty-five feet frontage."[39]

Finally, none of Olmsted's twenty-nine proposed restrictive covenants was implemented, replaced by a single ban on the manufacture or sale of liquor (possession and consumption was permitted). According to Mosher, McMurtry and his colleagues believed that the covenants, which would have mandated, for instance, minimum construction costs, setbacks, and building materials, bore a New England and upper-middle-class bias that was "impractical and inappropriate for a western Pennsylvania steel town."[40] When initial sales proved strong (only Apollo workers were eligible during the first week), McMurtry's colleagues, frustrated that more lots weren't available, came to resent the Olmsted plan even more, asking for an explanation of the advantages gained "to us from the town having been laid out on the curved plan instead of the square plan usually followed in this part of the country."[41] To meet the demand for more housing, the company built the gridded thirteen-block Vandergrift Heights subdivision on a plot outside the Olmsted plan's boundaries.

When in 1896 Olmsted and Eliot submitted their final plan reflecting these many changes, they insisted on omitting Vandergrift Heights out of concern that it be associated with them and also, according to Mosher, "that on the final copy of the plan, in a space that had to be filled, they be allowed to use a portion of their original design . . . [where] Olmsted drew in what he and Eliot had really wanted for both settlements: large residential lots sitting astride streets that meandered gracefully across the map as well as a ravine serving as the convenient path for a parkway and place where steelworkers could convene with nature."[42] But this was a symbolic gesture—the Olmsted plan was scrapped when that area was built out in the 1900s and 1920s. "In the end," as Mosher writes, "the enthusiasm that John Olmsted once had for the project waned so much that he did not want his family name to be linked with it."[43]

All in all, according to John Reps, the plan showed "little of the genius that marked the best residential plans of the elder Olmsted. Although the streets are well adapted to the hilly site, the plan as a drawing is much more impressive than when applied to the ground. The town has no central focus, no group of buildings that marks the center. Nor are the curving streets particularly well suited for business use, however admirable they may be for residential purposes . . . the results must be catalogued among the small number of inferior designs associated with the name of Olmsted."[44] But if Vandergrift was a failure for the designers it was not necessarily so for the steel company that had by 1900 attracted a population of 4,300 skilled nonunion workers who were apparently content with their environment. Some saw benefit in the lack of restrictions, including one observer who wrote in *The Craftsman* in 1910: "Vandergrift is today an unusually beautiful and interesting town. The houses are not built in blocks or after one prevailing style, but are as individual as the tastes of their owners, so that the place looks more like a thriving Western town built by well-to-do people in varied walks of life, than like a community made up of the employees of one large manufacturing concern."[45] The 1916 visit of Ida Tarbell, the pioneering muckraker journalist, worried members of the town council, but they were relieved when, in the following year, she wrote that Vandergrift "is probably the most successful workingman's town in the country, at least one of the five or six most successful . . . It would be difficult in the United States today to find a prettier town, greener, trimmer, cleaner and more influential than this town of Vandergrift, owned outright by men who daily carry a dinner pail . . . Mr. McMurtry believed that men, given an opportunity to live in a clean, healthy, beautiful town which gradually they could own and govern, would become a permanent group of citizens working together like other citizen bodies. And this has happened."[46]

Without restrictive covenants, some purchasers banded together to establish their own building codes, calling for 20-foot front setbacks along certain streets. But many others established boardinghouses, built alley-facing structures, erected fences, and further subdivided parcels to the extent that a 1936 study found "1 to 3 feet of side yard, in many cases without enough room for access, painting, or repairs."[47] Planned green spaces were also lost or compromised, including the village green, which by the 1930s was paved over and used as a parking lot. With no form of zoning, the business district bled into areas intended in the Olmsted plan to be residential.

In 1904, having outgrown its mill in Trenton, New Jersey, John A. Roebling's Sons Company, builder of the Brooklyn Bridge (1869–83) as well as a number of other significant spans, announced plans for a new facility to manufacture steel cables, purchasing 250 acres of farmland in Kinkora, ten miles south of Trenton, a site located along a bend in the Delaware River that was also convenient to an existing station of the Camden and Amboy Railroad.[48] The Roebling family were motivated by pragmatism when they undertook to build the residential portion of the village, which became known as **Roebling**. As Washington A. Roebling (1837–1926), the eldest of the three sons of John A. Roebling (1806–1869), pointed out, the "most troublesome feature of Kinkora . . . was the utter lack of houses where the working men could live. This could only be overcome by building an entire town, a so-called Model Town." Roebling further stated on one occasion that "we certainly are not posing as idealists or reformers,"[49] and on another that "the man who owns a town often wishes he had never been born," going on to complain about the need to provide even the most basic of services, such as water, gas, and sewers.[50]

Charles Roebling (1849–1918), the youngest of John Roebling's three sons, was placed in charge of planning the new town (1905), which he platted in a standard grid with most of the 530 houses placed on 30-by-100-foot

lots along 80-foot-wide streets lined with newly planted maple and London plane trees. Solidly built, redbrick and slate-roof single-family houses were set back from the street behind sidewalks and modest front yards. Ten-foot-wide rear alleys accommodated delivery wagons and facilitated trash collection. Entry-level employees lived closest to the factory in two-story rowhouses, while bachelors took up residence in boardinghouses. On Riverside Avenue, the managerial class inhabited more spacious eleven-room Colonial- and Tudor-style dwellings. Both Main Street and Fifth Avenue were 100 feet wide, with planted medians; a bank and general store marked their intersection, which also featured a grassy circle, home to a prominent water tower. Land adjacent to the river not needed for the factory was set aside for a park.

John A. Roebling's Sons Company owned and controlled virtually every aspect of town life. Housing was only offered on a rental basis to mill workers who were required to sign leases that gave the company the option of eviction with only one week's notice. And if any doubt remained, concrete posts placed at each street corner indicated that the land was "private property." Nonetheless the Roeblings managed to hold paternalism to a minimum. For example, the taverns so often prohibited in company towns were permitted, even welcomed, in Roebling. As Washington Roebling quipped, "There is no use trying to make a mollycoddle out of a mill man."[51]

Despite repeated statements that they were only interested in the most utilitarian of designs, the Roeblings built a town of considerable charm, with broad streets, neat rows of well-built houses, and thoughtful landscaping, leading David McCullough, in the epilogue to his history of the Brooklyn Bridge, to write, with perhaps a bit of overstatement, that Roebling "turned out to be one of the best-planned industrial towns ever built in America, a model in every respect, as company towns went."[52]

Gary, Indiana, begun in 1906 by the United States Steel Corporation to support its new steel mills on the shores of Lake Michigan, like Pullman and Roebling, does not easily fit into the conventional model of the industrial garden village.[53] Though its gridiron planning is like that of Pullman, located only about twenty miles away, Gary was conceived in deliberate reaction to Pullman. Named for Elbert H. Gary (1846–1927), a prominent Illinois lawyer who in 1901 oversaw the consolidation of dozens of companies into U.S. Steel, America's first billion-dollar corporation, and became its first chairman, Gary sprung up almost overnight, expanding from an 800-acre planned subdivision to a sprawling 11-square-mile industrial city with a population of 16,000 in 1910 and 50,000 by 1914.[54] The location east of Chicago benefited from excellent rail access to the iron ore and limestone of Minnesota, as well as the coal deposits of Pennsylvania and West Virginia, but the site's swamplands and sand dunes required massive amounts of infrastructure, including the rerouting of the Grand Calumet River.

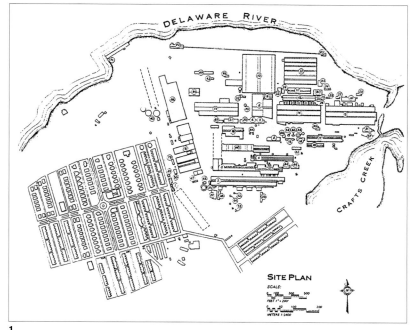

Seeking to avoid an extended role in the town's affairs, U.S. Steel built only an initial section, turning over later additions to outside interests. The original town site, the so-called First Subdivision, was platted by Arthur P. Melton (1875–1932), a company engineer who called for an unrelenting grid providing 4,000 residential lots between the Wabash Railroad tracks on the south, Fourth Avenue on the north, and Tennessee Avenue and Fillmore Street on the east and west. Two parks were provided, one occupying a four-block and one a two-block area. A business and commercial district including hotels, stores, restaurants, a theater, and banks was centered at the intersection of Fifth Avenue and Broadway, the two principal thoroughfares, which both accommodated streetcar lines. Company officers donated land for civic facilities such as libraries, schools, and churches, but the buildings themselves were to be funded privately and, though situated on combined or corner sites, did little to relieve the monotony of the street grid. As a result, according to Reps, "the Gary plat closely resembles the typical speculative plat of the nineteenth-century town boomers, most of which showed sites reserved for similar uses."[55]

However, certain features differentiated Gary from the norm. According to James B. Lane's 1978 history, *City of the Century*, the development was initially modeled—at least in administration if not plan—on Vandergrift, "where most steelworkers owned their homes, took pride in civic activities, and seemed less interested in strikes than had been the case at Pullman." However, Vandergrift's "small largely native-born population made too rigid a duplication impossible."[56] Gary's workforce, consisting almost exclusively of unskilled laborers, many from Southern and Eastern Europe, was not expected to placidly comply with restrictions on their behavior, nor was U.S. Steel interested in playing an overt role in workers' lives. Within the First Subdivision, standards were set for residential design and construction, including minimum construction costs, building materials, and setbacks. Houses were to be completed within eighteen months of lot purchase, effectively excluding all but the highest paid supervisors,

1. Plan, Charles Roebling, 1905. RM

2. Fifth Avenue. RM (c. 1909)

3. Fifth Avenue. RAMSA (2011)

4. Sixth Avenue. RAMSA (2011)

5. Third Avenue. RAMSA (2011)

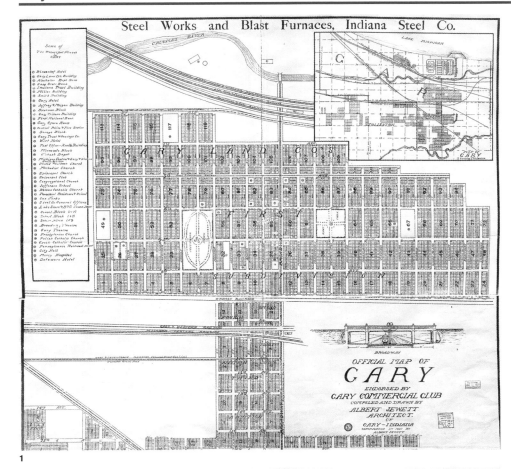

1. Plan, Arthur P. Melton, 1907. GPL

2. Jackson Street. CRA (1908)

3. House, Dean & Dean, Ambridge Avenue. CRA (1915)

4. Typical houses built by Gary Land Co. CRA (1922)

5. Typical street. CRA (1924)

foremen, and skilled laborers. When sales got off to a slow start, the company reluctantly began building some of the housing, including prototype quasi–Prairie Style houses with wide eaves, broad gables, and low-pitched roofs designed by the Chicago firm of George Robinson Dean (1864–1919) and Arthur Randall Dean (1869–1949), which were well received.

But as the steel mills went into production and Gary's population boomed, a stark contrast emerged between the well-maintained First Subdivision and outlying areas where the company actively promoted speculative housing for low-wage workers, particularly in an area south of the Wabash railroad tracks known as "the Patch," where slum conditions prevailed and workers resided in makeshift shacks or boardinghouses at best. By 1910, as Margaret Crawford has written, "private developers seeking quick profits, aided by the town's elected politicians, who allowed virtually unregulated

growth, had turned the town into a dreary and chaotic industrial city."[57] Arthur Comey and Max Wehrly, in their 1936 study of planned communities, declared that Gary, "which may be considered as a planned town, served its best purpose . . . by providing a complete example of what not to do in future developments."[58]

U.S. Steel had come to a similar conclusion. In 1910, even as Gary was still taking form, the company adopted a different approach for the development of **Fairfield** (originally Corey), Alabama, eight miles southwest of downtown Birmingham in an area busily harvesting its rich deposits of coal, iron ore, and limestone.[59] U.S. Steel had recently acquired the Tennessee Coal, Iron & Railroad Company. Inheriting two factories in the area, it planned to build a third for the American Steel and Wire Co. on contiguous land. To house an anticipated workforce of 5,000, U.S. Steel asked the prominent Birmingham developer Robert Jemison Jr. to develop a

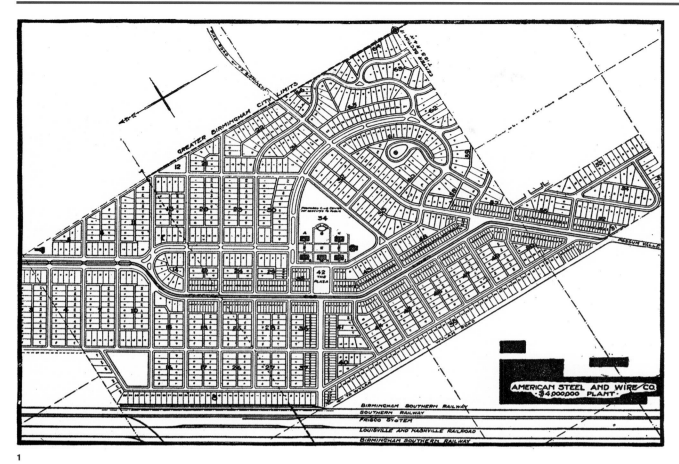

1

256-acre site of cotton fields and wooded slopes just west of the mills.

Jemison toured European industrial villages as well as domestic examples, including Pullman, Vandergrift, Roebling, and Gary, before hiring the Boston-based landscape architect George H. Miller to lay out Fairfield and architects William T. Warren (1877–1962) and William Leslie Welton (1874–1934) to design its housing as well as its civic and business buildings. Both Warren and Welton had worked in the New York office of McKim, Mead & White before establishing a short-lived partnership in Birmingham.

The implementation of a professionally prepared master plan at Fairfield reflected, according to Margaret Crawford, the "major transfer of power within the giant steel corporation" that occurred when Judge Gary, as he was known, became chairman, signaling "a victory over the old-line ironmasters, unrelenting in their dealings with labor, who controlled the company's local subsidiaries. Gary's supporters were financiers who, more conscious of public opinion, favored industrial welfare rather than coercion in dealing with workers."[60] U.S. Steel, along with its peers in the industry, had come under fire by labor unions and reformers, and efforts to polish the company image contributed not only to Fairfield's planning but also to its rechristening in 1913, several years after former U.S. Steel president William Ellis Corey (1866–1934), for whom the town was first named, had become embroiled in a divorce scandal that

received national attention.[61] The new name circuitously honored the company's current president, James A. Farrell, who resided in Fairfield, Connecticut.

In contrast to the centerless urbanism of Gary, Miller's plan for Fairfield called for a strongly defined 18-acre core with a formally planned civic center flanked on one side by a park, with residential tracts beyond, and on the other side by a plaza leading to a commercial district. Warren and Welton's civic center group, including five buildings accommodating a city hall, a library, YMCA, a public bath, and a school, was arranged as a quadrangle not unlike those McKim, Mead & White had frequently employed in their civic and educational master planning, with a porticoed and domed city hall occupying a central position. Southeast of the civic center, a park provided woodlands, tennis courts, playgrounds, and athletic fields, as well as a wading pool and running track. Northwest of the civic center, a 247-by-150-foot fountained plaza, on axis with city hall and lined with business blocks, extended to Gary Avenue, the main business street. Cranford Street continued the plaza's axis across Gary Avenue, reaching the town's train station and an entrance to the factory complex.

Although Miller had envisioned a naturalistic plan for the residential neighborhoods, Jemison asked that he work with an earlier land survey that divided the site into 40-acre rectangles. Miller complied, covering most of the site in short blocks divided by service alleys. He had also planned to include group houses but was

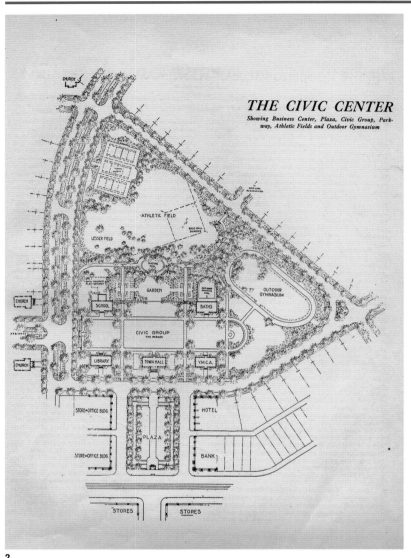

THE CIVIC CENTER

Showing Business Center, Plaza, Civic Group, Parkway, Athletic Fields and Outdoor Gymnasium

3

4

2. Plan, civic center. BPLA (1911)

3. Bird's-eye view of civic center. BPLA

4. Business area, showing plaza and bank, left, and stores, right. BPLA (1911)

dissuaded by their cost, the difficulty of maintaining common yards and gardens, and the extra time required for construction. Even more important, Miller wrote, "That which might be gained by the group plan would have been either entirely esthetic, and this at the sacrifice of much of the backyard space, or would have set an example which through unskilled designing might result in the building of unattractive rows."[62]

Miller divided the blocks into 926 50-by-125-foot lots, calling for detached single-family Craftsman-style bungalows with occasional double-family duplexes added along the major roads.[63] The Craftsman style lent itself to variation in form and decoration and was seen as a tonic for workers who spent their days in the factory. Houses were situated in one of four zoned subdivisions, each with a different minimum construction cost. Ninety percent of the houses were within a two-minute walk of parkland. Jemison built the first houses in each of the residential zones to establish a standard of construction and landscaping. Residential roads were 50 or 60 feet wide and houses were set back 20 feet on average to provide front and rear yards for which Miller prepared numerous landscape plans. In addition to formal and vegetable gardens,

private yards featured chicken coops and livestock pens so as not to saddle public parks with these functions. In the southern portion of the site, hillier terrain gave Miller the opportunity to break from the grid with a network of contour-hugging streets lined with large, irregularly shaped lots reserved for more expensive houses. At the center of this upscale section, a park, Overlook Place, commanded sweeping views of the town and factory site.

Fairfield's principal approach was an existing road leading south from Birmingham that Miller broadened into a 140-foot-wide boulevard as it entered town. At a knoll, the road briefly disrupted the grid forking into two branches: the northern arm became the 100-foot-wide Gary Avenue, the main business street, while the southern arm, known as the Parkway, a 100-foot-wide divided boulevard with a lushly landscaped median and pedestrian pathway, led to the civic center and then turned in a sweeping curve toward Overlook Place.

Construction began in March 1910, but completion was delayed by the slow progress on the American Steel and Wire Co. mill, which did not open until 1914, when the town's population had reached only 1,200. More than twenty miles of guttered and curbed streets

5

6

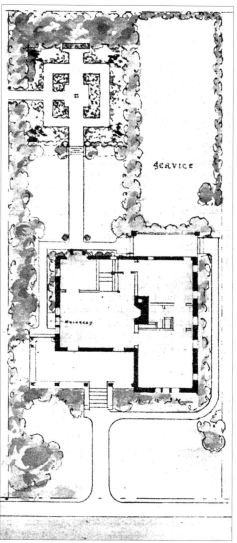

7

5. Parkway. BPLA (1913)

6. Backyard. BPLA (1913)

7. Study of the arrangement of "outdoor rooms," Miller's term for front yards and backyards and service areas surrounding housing. BPLA (1911)

8. Various bungalow types and view of entrance. HFW (c. 1919)

9. Forty-third Street. JLowe. LOCP (1993)

8

9

were installed as well as many of the gates, street furniture, fountains, flagpoles, and pavilions that Warren and Welton had designed. Over 100,000 trees and shrubs were planted and a city nursery provided residents free plants for their private gardens. In addition to the early houses built by Jemison, U.S. Steel built more than 100 houses for superintendents and skilled workers who could obtain low-interest financing from the company. By the time of Fairfield's incorporation in 1918, portions of the business group facing the plaza had been built, including a bank, hotel, stores, and restaurants. But the town's most promising component, the civic center, was never realized, its space given over instead to athletic fields. Two of its intended landmarks—the post office and city hall—were completed in less than ceremonial locations in 1936 and 1945, respectively, with funds from the Works Progress Administration. Much of the area reserved for Overlook Place was later developed with housing, although a park remains at the top of the hill.

Always intended for high-wage earners, by the 1930s Fairfield was a segregated community, with whites living in the original portion and blacks, who constituted a majority of the plants' workforce, occupying unzoned, gridded additions to the north and south. As Margaret Crawford has noted: "Residential zoning, a concept borrowed from expensive suburban developments, was intended to protect the workers' property values, but in the context of the company town, took on less positive connotations."[64]

Observing Fairfield in 1936, Comey and Wehrly, imbued with the utilitarian functionalism of the Depression era, found portions to "present a well-kept appearance which is heightened by the maturity of the trees and yard plantings" but were disappointed by the "uneconomical . . . area devoted to the streets . . . due to the use of exceedingly short blocks, the disposition of the business district, the occurrence of double frontage lots and excess street fronts in certain sections, and the wide rights-of-way devoted to parkway."[65] They also found fault in the three-quarters-of-a-mile-long business district that they believed was excessive given the town's population and its location relative to the factories, resulting in "short residential blocks between the two, which are depreciated on one side by the backs of the stores and on the other by the steel plant, and which, having but little of their area left not so affected, are obviously undesirable as residences and form the only decadent area within the limits of the original plan."[66]

Crawford, writing in the 1990s, deplored Fairfield's stylistically diverse architecture and its mixture of formal and informal site planning: "The town's most popular elements, its Craftsman bungalows and lavish plantings, were suitable only for domestic purposes and could not be adapted to the scale of comprehensive planning. Thus, neither Fairfield's architecture nor planning could provide the town with a unified identity."[67]

George H. Miller also prepared the town plan for **Kaulton**, Alabama, built in 1912 by the Kaul Lumber Company on the southwestern outskirts of Tuscaloosa.[68]

The idea of a permanent lumber town was unusual—typically, most were envisioned as temporary, with the expectation that once local resources were exhausted, both mill and settlement would be vacated. Although they estimated that their timber holdings would last for only twenty-five years, Kaulton's founders intended the town to remain, leading them to locate the plant near Tuscaloosa, fifteen to twenty miles north of the remote timberlands that were beyond the reach of rail or river.

For the 101-acre town site, Miller prepared a fan-shaped plan of circumferential unpaved roads around a central park accommodating a tree-ringed oval athletic field, playgrounds, and a wading pool. Across from the park, a road led south to the 100-acre mill complex, passing between a symmetrical company store and combination office building/YMCA. A school, a church, and a hotel rounded out the town center. Fifty-five detached single-family wooden houses designed by William Leslie Welton were built by the company and rented to workers. The majority were nondescript, but some attractive Craftsman bungalows were provided for superintendents. A 29-acre "negro village" with sixty-seven houses and a separate YMCA was also constructed between the town center and the mill. Although the small school, hotel, office building, and company store were built, the town's infrastructure, including sewer and water systems, was underdeveloped. By 1931, the lumber supply was exhausted and the mill closed. While the company had seen "the possibility . . . of Tuscaloosa's growing and establishing new industries and the need for new residential sections, which might eventually take in our town," the Depression dashed those hopes and Kaulton fell into disrepair. Writing in 1936, Comey and Wehrly found that the "portion of the town which was developed was . . . substantially and attractively built,"[69] but John Reps, in what may be regarded as a lapse of judgment, later determined the plan to be "considerably superior to the buildings" which were "of poor design and cheaply constructed."[70]

Between 1913 and 1922, U.S. Steel developed the town of **Morgan Park** in northeast Minnesota's Iron Range, altering the pattern it had established at Gary and Fairfield by renting rather than selling houses to employees and by seeking to provide for all levels of its workforce instead of only the most highly paid.[71] Named for J. P. Morgan, the steel company's chief financier, Morgan Park, ten miles from the business center of Duluth, on the western shore of Spirit Lake, a tributary of Lake Superior, was built to house 500 families. Residents would be drawn from a newly built Minnesota Steel factory to the south of the town and from nearby facilities for Universal Portland Cement and the Duluth, Missabe and Northern Railroad, all U.S. Steel subsidiaries.

Several ravines were filled in to level the 190-acre brush-covered site that occupied a 40-foot plateau surrounded by woodlands. Preliminary plans by the Minneapolis-based landscape architects Anthony Morell (1875–1924), who was French born and educated, and Arthur Nichols (1880–1970), an American trained at

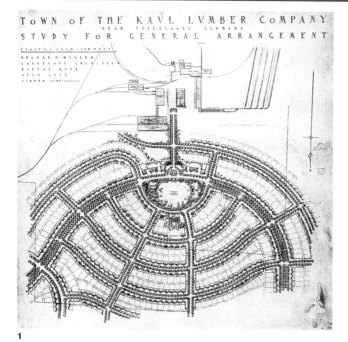

1

2

3

5

4

1. Plan, George H. Miller, 1912. BPLA

2. Clubhouse. BPLA (c. 1912)

3. Town center, with company store on left and office building/YMCA on right. BPLA (c. 1912)

4. Typical street. HFW (c. 1919)

5. "Negro village." HFW (c. 1919)

MIT, called for curving residential streets and a geometrical civic center composed of diagonal boulevards defining contiguous triangular blocks. Simplified over the following years, Morell and Nichols's plan emerged as a less rigorous modified grid within a boundary road that curved to meet topographical conditions.

The town was bisected by the 80-foot-wide 88th Avenue West (originally Fourth Street), a north–south thoroughfare accommodating two streetcar lines on a grassy median and serving as the main entry road leading south from Duluth through Morgan Park to the factory site. High-wage earners were housed to the east of 88th Avenue and low-wage earners to the west. A small commercial district was situated along the avenue to the north and a civic core established to the south where a cross axis was formed by the alignment of a clubhouse, set back on eight acres to the east, and a school, occupying a 10-acre block to the west. Wherever possible, Morell and Nichols retained existing plantings while adding 1,500 trees and 5,000 shrubs, grouping particular species together to individualize streets. Park

benches and drinking fountains adorned some intersections and nine playgrounds were inserted throughout the plan.

Morgan Park's principal distinction lay in its houses and public buildings, which were built almost exclusively of concrete block, often left exposed but occasionally covered with stucco. The still-experimental material was chosen "with the view of providing dwellings that are attractive, practically fireproof, durable, comfortable and involving a minimum maintenance and depreciation cost."[72] Concrete was pervasive in Morgan Park, used for floors and walls within the houses and as paving for streets and sidewalks. Chicago architects George Robinson Dean and Arthur Randall Dean, with the assistance of their chief draftsman H. F. Robinson (1883–1959), a former Frank Lloyd Wright employee who had also worked for Walter Burley Griffin and Marion Mahony, were responsible for most of the public and residential buildings, preparing dozens of plans for single-, two-, and four-family houses as well as rowhouses and boardinghouses.

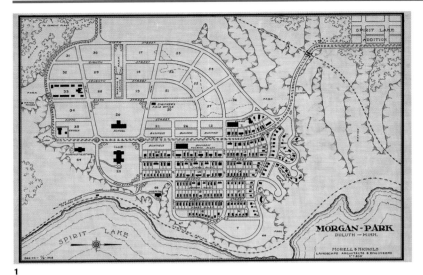

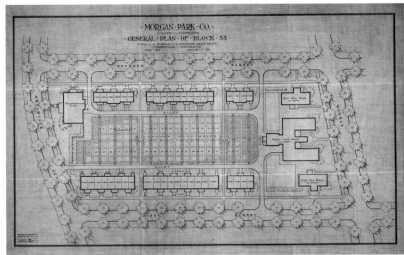

1. Plan, Morell & Nichols, 1918. UM

2. Plan of Block 33. UM (1917)

3. Streetcar waiting station. NEMHC (c. 1921)

4. Eighty-eighth Avenue, showing Lake View Building on left and steel plant in distance. NEMHC (1920)

The first 349 single- and multifamily houses were completed in 1915 to the east of 88th Avenue West, aligned parallel and perpendicular to a four-by-four grid of streets. Multiple roof styles and porch shapes softened the boxy effect of the concrete-block construction. In 1917, forty-six houses for supervisors, managers, and salaried workers were completed at the northern edge of the town according to twelve prototypical plans. Thirty of the houses enjoyed irregularly shaped lots along curving roads and culs-de-sac that benefited from lake views and a wooded setting.

Housing for low-wage earners was first provided in 1916 on Block 33, bound by Hilton and Idaho Streets and 90th and 91st Avenue West. In addition to three boardinghouses and a community center containing a nurse's office, children's playrooms, lounges, and meeting rooms, the block accommodated short groups of rowhouses containing four to ten units each. Backyard garden plots were provided for each household. In 1920, two adjacent blocks were developed according to the Block 33 model but incorporating single-family and semidetached houses. After 1922, by which time 510 residential units had been created in 246 buildings, no new residential construction occurred in Morgan Park until the 1950s, when additional

blocks in the western neighborhood were developed with modest single-family houses.

In addition to their residential work, Dean and Dean designed the two-story, hip-roofed, concrete-block Lake View Building (1916), a business block accommodating a company store, offices, a bank, and a barber shop; and the Good Fellowship Clubhouse (1918), a stucco-covered concrete-block and red-tile-roofed community center providing meeting rooms, bowling alleys, a swimming pool, a gymnasium, a tennis court, and an auditorium/movie theater. The firm also designed a four-story hospital (1916), distinguished by two solariums on the second and third floors of the south facade and Minnesota Steel's administration building (1915), located near the factory entrance. Morgan Park's school, designed by the Duluth firm of Clyde W. Kelly (1880–1927) and Owen J. Williams (1853–1926), was dedicated in early 1917, and two churches were built in the residential areas.

Having flourished during the 1920s, Morgan Park began to lose its vitality in 1930 when the Depression halted industrial operations. Nonetheless, in 1936, when Comey and Wehrly surveyed the town, the population was 2,000 and the physical plant still conveyed an air

5

6

7

8

5. Overall view showing Block 33 on right. NEMHC (c. 1922)

6. Rear garden. NEMHC (c. 1922)

7. Arbor Street and Eighty-seventh Avenue West. NEMHC (1920)

8. Block 33. AA18 (c. 1918)

of well-being: "Considering the age of the greater part of Morgan Park," they wrote, "its present appearance is especially good. The use of concrete blocks in housing has been intelligent and gives the community a harmonious although somewhat drab appearance. They have, however, stood up better than the stucco houses . . . The planting and landscaping have matured and are highly effective, although somewhat heavy in places. The individual lots are consistently well maintained, and together with the street plantings relieve the drabness of the grey concrete."[73]

Neponset Garden Village (1913), outside East Walpole, Massachusetts, seventeen miles southwest of Boston, was one of fifty projects undertaken by John Nolen for Charles S. Bird Jr. (1883–1980), a local industrialist and Walpole's largest employer, who was intensely interested in liberal politics and planning.[74] Nolen's work for Bird ranged from playgrounds to regional plans. The site, close to Bird's paper mill, was next to East Walpole's train station and was also served by a trolley. Nolen provided four zones: one next to the railroad station intended for shops and apartments; the second, surrounding the civic center, reserved for the best class of houses. Two other areas were for less

expensive houses. Land was also left open for small farms or allotment gardens.

Neponset was based on English and German precedents. It was intended to be financed as a copartnership "managed and conducted by the residents in the village for their own benefit."[75] The 150-acre subdivision, with its open space reserves as well as land set aside for recreation and gardening, was organized as a loose grid of streets defining large squarish blocks. A north–south main street was to run through the middle, dividing at the center to bound a village green. While the plan was typical of contemporary English garden enclaves, the houses shown in the perspective drawings were distinctly American Colonial in style, similar, as Crawford suggests, to what was to be found in nearby textile towns like Whitinsville and Hopedale.

In 1915 Bird hired the architecture firm of Horace B. Mann and Perry R. MacNeille, who also worked with Nolen at Kistler, to carry Neponset Garden Village forward. Their analysis of Nolen's work led to the rejection of copartnership financing, substituting more typical ownership and rental practices. They also suggested a program of social engineering that would include the construction of a model house to be inhabited on an

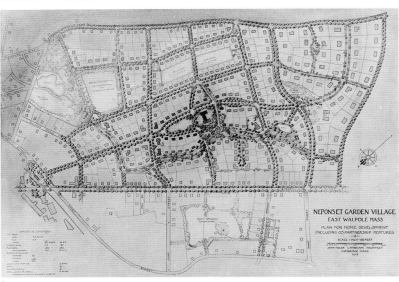

1. Bird's-eye view. COR (1914)

2. Plan, John Nolen, 1913. COR

ongoing basis by a female social worker who would, among other assignments, organize company-subsidized entertainments for the workers, such as "afternoon teas and little luncheon parties."[76] Neponset Garden Village was not built, a victim of the weak, post–World War I economy and the death in the influenza epidemic of 1918 of Bird's eldest son, Francis William III, who was memorialized when the family gave the site over for use as a public park.

Nolen had better luck with **Westerly Gardens** (1912–14), Bound Brook, New Jersey, a modest subdivision for forty-nine employees of paper manufacturer George La Monte & Son, which was completed as planned on five acres bound by West Second Street, Romney Road, and Talmadge and La Monte Avenues.[77] Nolen placed twenty-one multifamily houses at various setback distances along straight, tree-lined streets, breaking up the long site at its midpoint with an east–west lane. No designer's name accompanied the hollow-tile, stucco-clad two-and-a-half-story houses "of modern plan but commonplace architecture," according to *Architectural Review*.[78]

The years leading up to the entry of the United States into World War I saw a proliferation of new industrial garden villages, as new and established manufacturing businesses geared up to meet the rising demand for goods to be sold to England and France and eventually to supply the American war effort. Also in New Jersey, Nolen's plan for **Allwood** (1916), two-and-a-half miles west of Passaic, went unrealized, with the exception of a handful of houses by Henry Killam Murphy and Richard H. Dana Jr.[79] Allwood stands out from the majority of American industrial garden villages planned around the time of World War I in that it was not conceived as an appendage to an existing industrial plant but, like Port Sunlight and Bournville, which were visited as part of the planning, was to be the setting for relocated facilities of its sponsor, Brighton Mills, manufacturers of cotton and special fabrics. The plan was the particular project of William L. Lyall, the firm's president and treasurer, who

reluctantly abandoned it when building costs spiraled upward after the war. The square, 300-acre site lay along Bloomfield Avenue, an important arterial served by a bus line connecting it with Paterson, eight miles away. A broad entrance plaza was proposed for the midpoint of the Bloomfield Avenue frontage. The area for the factory was situated to the northeast, where it would have access to a rail freight line. Playing fields were to buffer the factory from the residential neighborhoods, which were to provide 1,000 units in group and paired houses.

Kistler (1915), Pennsylvania, one-and-a-half miles from Mount Union, was planned by Nolen for a 60-acre site with houses designed by Mann & MacNeille.[80] Built for workers of the Mount Union Refractories Company, which had opened its nearby brickworks in 1912, the plans originally called for 220 houses, only half of which were built. The triangular site lay between the Juniata River and the high embankment of the Harrisburg-Altoona branch of the Pennsylvania Railroad. In contrast to the region's grim coal-mining towns, Kistler was located on a beautiful site that Nolen capitalized upon, turning the sloping embankment and the flood-prone riverbanks into parkland, and devising a loose plan that would result in a somewhat scattered townscape when the company ceased to build the town out after World War I.

Nolen proposed a railroad station and a block of shops, neither of which was constructed. A community building was also not built, but existing farm structures were adapted to civic functions instead. In addition to the green spaces on the town's periphery, two parks were embedded in the plan, one a sports field facing the Juniata River, the other, Nolen Park, at the triangular confluence of two neighborhoods. Juniata Park was a third open space, occupying a steep stretch of land near the town's geographical center. Nolen regarded Kistler Green, intended to face the new railroad station, as "the central point of the plan." Nonetheless, he admitted that "the design has really no definite axis . . . but is rather

Westerly Gardens

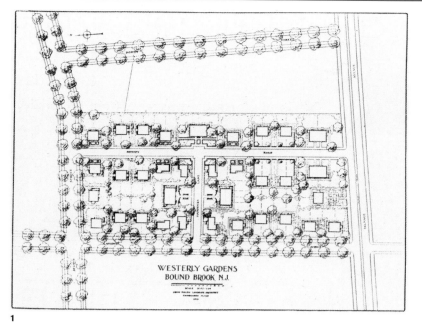

1. Plan, John Nolen, 1912. ARB17

2. New Hampshire Lane. ARB17 (c. 1917)

Allwood

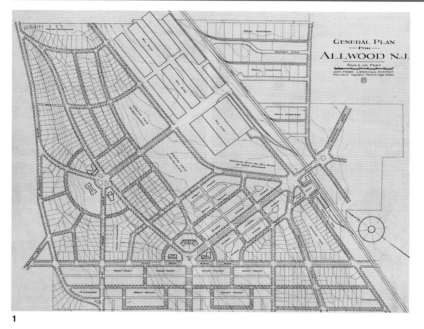

1. Plan, John Nolen, 1916. COR

2. Typical houses. ARB18 (c. 1918)

a centralization of the community life than a concentration at any particular point."[81]

Kistler, as Crawford emphasizes, "was one of the few towns explicitly designed for unskilled workers."[82] Great pains were taken so that the variously sized houses, which were rented to unskilled as well as skilled factory workers, were given the same design attention. According to Nolen, "The population being so largely foreign in its make-up, there is distinct necessity for a lead to be given in the direction of Americanism. This is done in a much better way than by exhortation—by the provision of something tangible, in the form of good living conditions, which more nearly expresses the ideals of this country."[83] To further Nolen's Americanization plan, the "artistic" houses featured highly evocative, regional names such as Vermont Farmhouse and Georgian

Cottage, although there was also a Norman Cottage. Perry MacNeille was impressed with the positive reception of his firm's work by the residents: "Rest for the mind and soul, not just for the body should become the principal aim in designing workingmen's houses . . . It is often claimed that these effects are produced only among educated and refined people but that the common working man is insensible to them . . . This has not been found to be the case. An artistic house in a picturesque village makes a pleasanter home to return to, is more restful, more inspiring and increases the family pride."[84]

Loveland Farms (1917–18), just outside the city limits of Youngstown, Ohio, was planned by Nolen for the Buckeye Land Company, a subsidiary of the Youngstown Sheet and Tube Company, one of the nation's largest steel producers.[85] The subdivision, to be composed exclusively

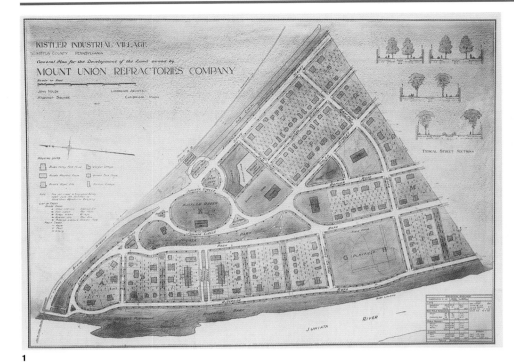

1

2

1. Plan, John Nolen, 1916. COR

2. State Street. COR (1926)

3. Birch Street. JLowe. LOCP (1990)

4. Cedar Street. Ames. LOCP (1990)

3

4

Loveland Farms

1. Plan, John Nolen, 1917. AA18

2. Rendering and plans of Franklin Circle. AA18

3. Typical street. OHS

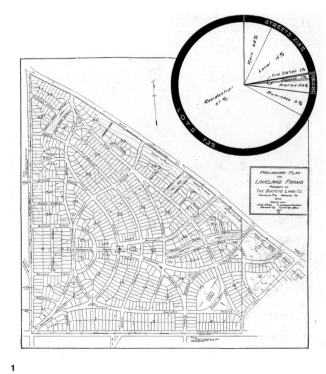

1

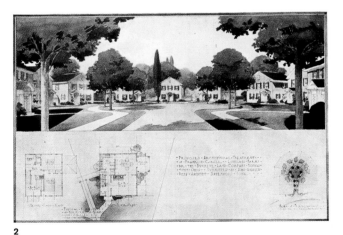

2

3

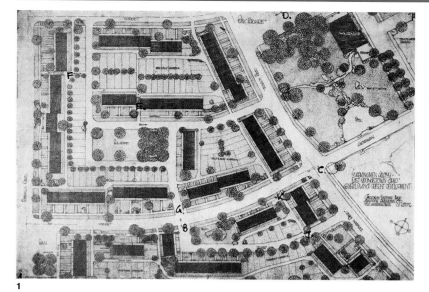

of detached single-family houses, was intended for skilled workmen and management. Nolen's plan, only a portion of which was realized, responded to the challenges of the hilly 220-acre site that could not economically accommodate the kind of rectilinear grid that was typical of the surrounding area. According to Morris Knowles, the engineer for the project, 67 percent of the 40-, 50-, and 60-foot-wide streets were arranged in roughly concentric arcs following the topography of the rugged triangular site located just south of the factory complex and bound by four existing streets: Loveland Road, Midlothian Boulevard, and Oakland and Poland Avenues.

Nolen divided 156 acres of the site into 838 generously sized residential lots, with frontages of at least 42 feet and with many houses placed on culs-de-sac. Unusual for Nolen was the small amount of open space in the plan, with only 5.2 percent of the site reserved for parks, as compared with 29.7 percent at Kistler or 19 percent at Overlook Colony; defending this decision, Nolen noted that many playgrounds were located nearby. Loveland Farms was almost exclusively residential but did include a school, a church, and a fire station, as well as an unrealized civic center, Ohio Square, in roughly the center of the site, planned for public and business buildings and a green. Less than a third of Nolen's original

plan was realized, with 275 two- and two-and-a-half-story wood-frame houses, designed by John Andrew Ross (1887–1966) in sixteen different variations of the same basic theme, completed by 1919.

Youngstown Sheet and Tube also sponsored through its Buckeye Land Company the development of the **Blackburn Plat** (1917–18), a denser enclave of semidetached and rowhouses geared toward lower-paid factory workers.[86] The company was not only responding to a shortage of workers' houses estimated at 5,000 units but was also motivated by a belief that improved living conditions for its employees could lessen labor tensions in Youngstown, where a bitter and violent steel-plant strike in 1916 had led to the burning of several blocks of the city. Franz J. Herding (1887–1968), of the St. Louis–based architectural and engineering firm Conzelman-Herding-Boyd, was responsible for both the layout of the 40-acre hillside site as well as the design of its buildings. As at Loveland Farms, located about three miles away on the other side of the steel mill, ambitious plans for a civic center remained unrealized. The most interesting feature of Herding's plan was the decision to group many of the reinforced-concrete houses around generous landscaped courts that could also be accessed from the street through arched entrances. The 16-foot-wide one-family,

1. Plan, Franz J. Herding, 1918. AA18

2. Entrance to courtyard. OHS

3. Typical houses. AA18 (c. 1918)

4. Aerial view. GE (2012)

1. Plan, John Nolen, 1917. COR

2. West Court and Third Streets.
COR (c. 1922)

3–5. Typical streets. RAMSA
(2007)

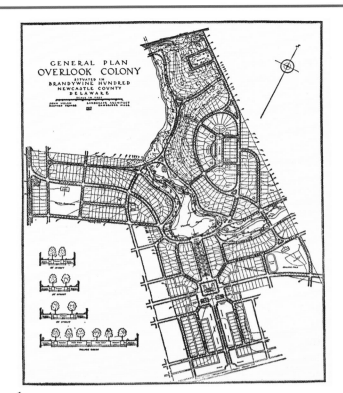

1

2

3

4

5

22-foot-wide two-family, and 42-foot-wide three-family three- and four-room houses were kept deliberately small to discourage renters from taking on boarders. The inclusion of deep porches, touches like shutters, and the planting did little to relieve the monotony of the long rows of almost identical two-story buildings placed along 40- and 50-foot-wide streets. By the time construction ended in 1922, the Blackburn Plat consisted of 281 dwellings, four company stores, and modest park and playground spaces.

In addition to his government-sponsored work for the Emergency Fleet Corporation at Union Park Gardens, Wilmington, Delaware (see p. 873), Nolen also planned a nearby, privately developed industrial village, **Overlook Colony** (1917–20), nine miles to the northeast in the town of Claymont along the Delaware River.[87] The General Chemical Corporation financed the village, intending ultimately to house 5,000 people on a

240-acre tract convenient to its factory in Claymont. Overlook Colony's oddly configured, three-pronged property, with a narrow frontage on the Wilmington Post Road, presented Nolen with both a challenge and an opportunity. To counteract the site's "artificial and indecisive boundaries," as Charles C. May described them in *Architectural Forum*, Nolen developed a plan that would face as few houses as possible away from the village. Between the bifurcated arms of the Y-shaped site, lay a stream that Nolen, as at Union Park Gardens, turned to advantage, damming its flow to form a village pond in a linear park. May was impressed with the plan, describing it as "exceptionally interesting and successful . . . The three isolated arms of land have been brought into a unified and coherent scheme by carefully located arteries of travel and the development of the central depression into a parked space to be enjoyed by all members of the community."[88]

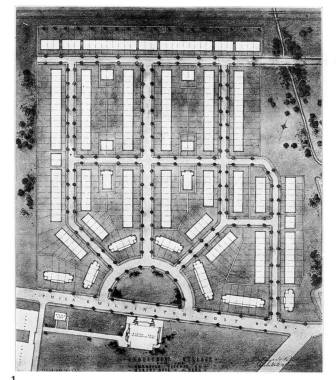

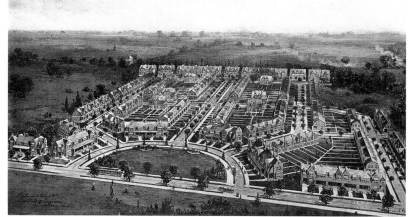

1. Plan, Ballinger & Perrot, 1912. BP

2. Bird's-eye view. EGP (1912)

3. Typical houses. BP (c. 1919)

4–6. Typical streets. RAMSA (2009)

Although General Chemical originally intended to build a mix of housing types, including detached single-family houses for managers and higher-paid employees, the completed housing at Overlook Colony comprised 196 dwellings grouped in rows ranging from four to thirty-nine houses. H. Errol Coffin (1891–1969), of the New York firm of Coffin and Coffin (Kenneth F. Coffin, 1896–1968), designed the handsome two-story four- to seven-room slate-roofed houses clad in stucco and clapboard. In addition to the rowhouses, Coffin also designed a community garage, a boardinghouse, and a community building featuring an auditorium and a superintendent's apartment.

Close to Overlook Colony, on a site located near the Delaware River between Wilmington, Delaware, ten miles to the southwest, and Chester, Pennsylvania, five miles to the northeast, **Marcus Hook** (1912–15), Pennsylvania, was a 20-acre industrial village sponsored by the American Viscose Company, a textile manufacturer.[89] The factory had begun operations in 1910 when Samuel Salvage first imported British technology to manufacture "artificial silk," or rayon as it was named in 1924, founding the company as a subsidiary of the English firm Samuel Courtauld and Company. The Philadelphia-based architectural and engineering firm of Walter F. Ballinger (1867–1925) and Emile G. Perrot (1872–1954) was responsible for both the town's plan and the design of its buildings. Viscose Village, as the enclave was commonly called, consisted of 261 dwellings, two boardinghouses, a general store, and a community center, leading Perrot, its designer, to describe it as "more of a housing development than a village, although we tried to instill into the plan certain fundamental features which underlie industrial developments on a large scale."[90] A subsequent plan (1913) by Perrot for an additional 122 houses on a triangular parcel to the northeast of the village was not executed.

1. Double houses on Dutcher Street, fronting Hopedale Pond. ATHM (1914)

2. Bird's-eye view. LOCG (1899)

3. Aerial view of Bancroft Park. GE (2010)

4. Bancroft Park. ATHM (c. 1898)

In preparing to undertake the project, Perrot spent the greater part of a year studying workingmen's houses in the United States and England, paying special attention to Cadbury's Bournville. On his overseas trip, Perrot also toured Bedford Park, Letchworth, and Hampstead Garden Suburb, and met with Thomas Adams and Raymond Unwin. Reflecting on the differences between various types of planned garden villages, Perrot wrote that "unlike the model suburb, which aims to remove itself far from the din of the factory or city noise, the Industrial Village becomes an adjunct to the plant, and it is the proximity to it that makes the problem more difficult of solution."[91]

Perrot's plan provided for a semicircular landscaped plaza in the center of the site's southern border, from which radiated three roads leading to a more regular neighborhood of rectangular blocks divided into lots that on average measured 20 feet wide and 70 feet deep. The juxtaposition of radial and rectilinear geometries created interesting vistas. Most streets were 70 feet wide, except for the 100-foot-wide central boulevard, Maple Street. Facing the plaza was a village hall intended to form the social center for the community, with rooms for dining and recreation as well as a roof garden. Though the plaza itself was uninspired, the diverse streetscape comprised twenty different designs for the mostly duplex redbrick rowhouses that were based on

local vernacular precedent, with slate roofs, shingle, clapboard, and textured stucco walls, and well-detailed porches and chimney and gable ends. The most impressive houses were situated facing the plaza, with more modest houses behind.

The industrial village of **Hopedale**, Massachusetts, thirty miles southwest of Boston, in many ways marking the culmination of the nineteenth-century tradition of industrial village planning on the part of private enterprise, grew over time from a small Christian Socialist commune founded in 1841 into what by 1900 was the largest producer of textile machinery in the United States.[92] Hopedale was originally established by the Reverend Adin Ballou (1803–1890) and thirty of his followers who practiced agriculture and light industry on 258 acres along the Mill River. Within a few years, the town had attracted 300 more residents, including the brothers George (1817–1887) and Ebenezer (1813–1887) Draper, who as producers of textile manufacturing equipment operated Hopedale's only robust enterprise. When in 1856 the Drapers decided no longer to sustain the rest of the town with the profits from their company, they withdrew their stock in the utopian commune, which could not survive without their support, and over the next half-century transformed Hopedale into a booming single-enterprise manufacturing center while carefully maintaining the natural beauty of its setting,

5

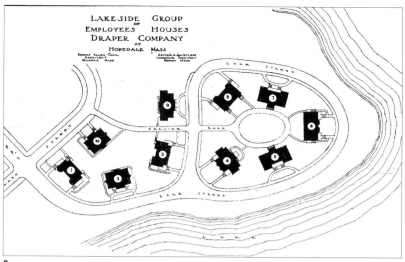

6

7

8

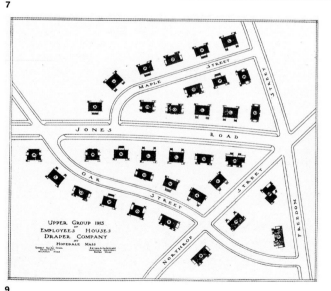

9

10

5. Bancroft Park. RAMSA (2012)

6. Plan of Lake Point, Arthur A. Shurtleff, 1910. AR16

7. Overall view of Lake Point. AR16 (c. 1915)

8. Lake Street. RAMSA (2012)

9. Plan of Upper Jones Road Group, Arthur A. Shurtleff, 1913. AR16

10. Maple Street and Jones Road. ATHM (1914)

11. Northrop and Oak Streets. RAMSA (2012)

11

leading Budgett Meakin to write in 1905 that among model villages, Hopedale was "America's best."[93]

For thirty years after the Drapers took control, Hopedale's growth mirrored that of a typical mill village, with an orthogonal street system spreading out from a central factory and mill complex. But the company's housing, which it built and maintained ownership of while renting units to workers, was of higher quality than most of its peers. With the exception of three boardinghouses near the factory providing accommodations for single men, houses were almost exclusively of the semidetached variety. Between the 1860s and 1890s, roughly eight types, ranging from one-and-a-half to two-and-a-half stories, were built to the northeast, northwest, and west of the plant, where infrastructural improvements and the laying out of new streets was handled by local civil engineers. In 1886, when Hopedale was incorporated as a town, the Drapers, expecting a period of strong growth but also wanting to safeguard the character of its valley site (3,547 acres had been acquired over time), called on Warren H. Manning, a landscape designer employed by Frederick Law Olmsted, to undertake a series of landscape plans that began with the grounds of a high school, the private gardens of one of the company's officers, and a cemetery, but grew to include the establishment of more than 1,000 acres of parkland around Mill Pond, created by damming the Mill River.

In 1896, Manning laid out Hopedale's Bancroft Park, comprising thirty two-and-a-half-story semidetached houses placed on either side of an oval road looping around a knoll to the west of the factory, which was screened from view by a berm. Completed in 1903, the symmetrical cypress-shingle-clad houses were designed according to eleven distinct plans by Robert Allen Cook (1872–1949), Edwin J. Lewis Jr. (1859–1937), J. Williams Beal (1855–1919), and the partnerships of Robert Swain Peabody (1845–1917) and John Goddard Stearns Jr. (1843–1917) and C. Howard Walker (1857–1936) and Thomas Rogers Kimball (1862–1934). The houses were widely recognized for their quality, garnering a silver medal at the Paris Exposition Universelle in 1900, a gold medal at the 1904 St. Louis World's Fair, and gold medals at the expositions in Liège in 1905 and Milan in 1906.

The Boston landscape architect and town planner Arthur A. Shurtleff (1870–1957)—Shurtleff changed his name to Shurcliff in 1930—was asked to plan Hopedale's next group of thirty-one double houses, known as Lake Point (c. 1910), along Progress, Soward, and Lake Streets, the latter occupying a promontory to the north of the factory jutting out into Mill Pond. Shurtleff took advantage of the waterfront setting, arranging the houses (all but one were adapted from the Bancroft Park designs) around a circle, with the fronts facing the pond and the backs on a cul-de-sac-like service road in some respects anticipating the arrangement of Radburn, New Jersey, almost thirty years later (see p. 275). Shurtleff consciously rejected

the old-fashioned way of placing such houses, [which was] to back them upon the water and

to face them upon an interior road. Everyone is familiar with the results of this program—in a perfectly automatic way rubbish, ash dumps, hen-yards, clotheslines, and privies make their appearance along the edge of the water shores which are naturally attractive, [but] become unnaturally ugly and a source of disease . . . If a marginal road is arranged immediately adjoining the shore line, and houses are made to face the water, automatic protection of the shore results. The dumping of rubbish, and in general the mis-use of the shores, is fended off. If unsightly conditions prevail about the houses, they are confined to the houses and especially to the rear premises. In these districts, disorder and confusion can be combated and corrected, whereas it cannot be coped with on the shores of streams and ponds without the greatest difficulty.[94]

Shurtleff's work in Hopedale continued through 1914 as he laid out Jones, Oak, and Maple Streets in the hills east of the town where difficult terrain required houses to rest on steep inclines. Both the so-called Upper Jones Road Group, consisting of thirty-four double houses, and Lower Jones Road Group, with twenty-four double houses, featured adaptations of the Bancroft Park and Lake Point houses as well as newly introduced designs. Lower Jones Road was the last double-house development to be undertaken in the village.

As John Garner noted in his study of nineteenth-century New England company towns, Manning and Shurtleff's mandate in each project was that "houses be located near to the shop and that they be arranged in a density to accommodate employment. Yet the site could not be overbuilt, which would cause congestion, especially in relation to trafficways leading to the factories. At the same time, workers should not be made to walk out of their way purely for the sake of aesthetic considerations." The goal was "maximum land use for housing with a minimum amount of street paving and complete separation of operations for living and working."[95]

After 1916 physical changes within Hopedale were few. The town held on to its village-like atmosphere by banning fences and for many years disallowing even street signs or house numbers in order to minimize manmade visual intrusions. Full-time grounds and building maintenance crews worked to keep gardens and lawns well tended and houses painted inside and out. Crucially, the Drapers also limited development within Hopedale's boundaries. A trolley connected Hopedale with Worcester, about fifteen miles away, in 1889, and another reached Milford, two miles away, in 1897, allowing many workers to live outside the town limits in housing that the company occasionally built, such as Manning's Prospect Heights (1903–13) neighborhood in Milford, where higher-density multifamily rowhouses containing four to six apartments were arranged in culs-de-sac.

Writing in 1936, Comey and Wehrly singled out Hopedale for its "charm and beauty which were found

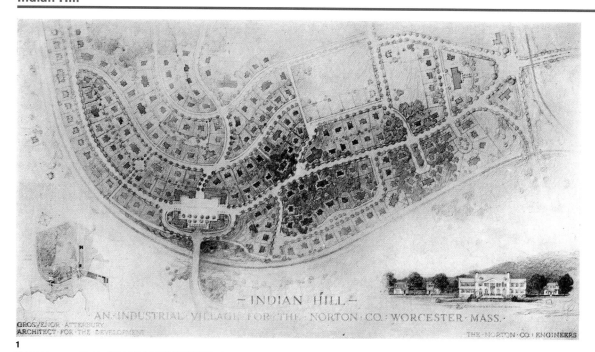

1. Plan, Grosvenor Atterbury, 1915.
APT

2. Nashoba Place. NCA (1918)

3. Nashoba Place and Indian Hill
Road. RAMSA (2011)

in only a few of the other communities visited, such as Forest Hills Gardens, Indian Hill, and Chicopee. This is partly due to its maturity and fully as much to the careful maintenance of the town, its open spaces, and the harmony of most of the housing, which is not beautiful individually but, taken together, presents a highly successful effect, in no way to be associated with the appearance of the ordinary mill village." Progress—particularly the presence of the automobile—had taken its toll, though as the authors noted: "Telephone poles and wires have been allowed on some of the streets . . . and the garage groups, although hidden from view, could be decidedly improved in appearance and maintenance more in character with the rest of the community. In general, however, Hopedale has maintained the excellent character and individuality which gave it the reputation of a model industrial town."[96]

In 1913 the Norton Company, based in Worcester, Massachusetts, purchased 116 acres just west of its 26-acre factory complex in order to build housing for its growing workforce in a community that became known as **Indian Hill**.[97] The prosperous business, founded in 1885 by mechanical engineer Charles

Hotchkiss Norton (1851–1942), was the nation's leading provider of precision-made mass-produced grinding wheels used to build and maintain industrial machinery. The company also hoped that the establishment of a model workers' village would lesson labor unrest in the industrial city forty-five miles west of Boston as well expand an already extensive and innovative program of employee benefits that included a company hospital, education scholarships for employees and their children, and a pension plan. Two years after purchasing the land, Norton's directors hired Grosvenor Atterbury as both town planner of Indian Hill and architect of its first houses, choosing him based on his recent work at Forest Hills Gardens.

Atterbury took full advantage of the site, located on a ridge and commanding views of Indian Lake, a pristine body of water a mile and a half in length and three-quarters of a mile wide. The site was separated from the lake to the south and the factory to the east by the tracks of the Boston and Maine Railroad. Atterbury selected 30 acres at the southeastern corner of the property to begin the development, dividing it into 150 plots with the expectation that thirty houses would be built annually for the next five years. His plan featured long east–west streets that followed the topography of the hilly site, breaking them up with midblock pedestrian footpaths leading to modest landscaped parks in the interior of the blocks. Atterbury proposed a formal entrance at the southern end of the site, with a broad road bridging the railroad tracks and continuing directly to the proposed community center, consisting of a collection of buildings providing for all of Indian Hill's needs, with stores, churches, a school, and a large auditorium for public events. A second entrance via an elevated footbridge connected the factory to the town. No provision was made for public transportation within the development itself.

Atterbury's initial proposal to include substantial numbers of semidetached houses at Indian Hill was rejected by Norton, which preferred freestanding single-family dwellings intended for foremen and their superiors. The five- to seven-room, gable- or gambrel-roofed, wood-frame Colonial-style two-story houses, set back from tree-lined streets, were finished in a variety of materials, including stucco, shingles, and clapboard. To add visual interest, many houses were set perpendicular to the street. The first thirty houses were completed by the summer of 1915, with an additional twenty-eight finished the following year; Norton financed their purchase at cost, requiring a 10 percent down payment. Charles May, writing in *Architectural Record* in 1917, was impressed with Atterbury's houses, calling out for particular attention the ones on Nashoba Place, one of Indian Hill's culs-de-sac, noting that the street "already has some of that quality which, a few years ago, one sought vainly in this country and found only by traveling to England or Germany."[98]

Despite the comparatively modest scope of the development, Indian Hill attracted a fair amount of attention, including a 1916 visit by former president Theodore Roosevelt (1858–1919) who planted a Pin oak and pronounced the houses "good enough for any good American to live in."[99] Ida Tarbell declared Indian Hills "the most suggestive and promising" of recent industrial villages. "It is planned for utility, economy and beauty," she wrote in a 1917 book titled *New Ideals in Business*. "It will be the most attractive town of its kind in the United States if it is carried out as begun."[100]

The remaining ninety-two lots were not built out according to Atterbury's design. In 1917, citing rising labor and material costs, Norton put plans for the subdivision on hold, so that Atterbury's elaborate entrance sequence and extensive commercial center were not realized and the community consisted solely of the fifty-eight completed houses. Soon after, America's entry into the war brought a surge of new business for the Norton Company, which again contacted Atterbury. To satisfy this new demand for housing, Atterbury proposed apartment houses built using his innovative Nailcrete system of precast-concrete panels. The company rejected this idea and instead built Norton Village without Atterbury's consultation, an undistinguished development of

ninety-four five-room houses laid out in a gridiron pattern just north of Indian Hill.

Billerica Garden Suburb (1914), in North Billerica, Massachusetts, a farming and manufacturing town twenty-one miles northwest of Boston and four miles south of Lowell, was an attempt to build an industrial garden suburb based directly on the English model.[101] It was the first attempt to do so with public assistance in the form of a limited-dividend corporation, undertaken by the Massachusetts Homestead Commission, which had been established in 1911 to help provide improved housing for workingmen. Although not officially affiliated with an industrial site, Billerica was situated in proximity to the recently opened Boston and Maine Railroad repair shops in hopes that it could house some of their 1,200 employees—expected soon to reach 2,000 to 3,000—who were offered free train service to and from the suburb.

The 56-acre site, bordered on the east by the railroad right-of-way and on the south and west by a bend in the Concord River, adjoining an existing village center with schools and other public buildings, was planned by the landscape architect Arthur C. Comey and Warren H. Manning, who was based in North Billerica. The low-density scheme called for five or six families per acre and a carefully orchestrated plan of gently curved streets. The debt to English garden suburb precedents was acknowledged in the choice of street names, which included Letchworth and Hampstead Avenues and Brentham and Port Sunlight Roads. The initial plan called for a town center set around an elliptical lawn near the train station, but this promising civic space was probably too ambitious given Billerica's size and was not realized. Tree-lined streets spread across the rest of the site, which was divided into purchase, rental, and copartnership zones; intended to offer flexibility to workers who might have to relocate, the copartnerships proved difficult to achieve. Development was slow overall because the Boston and Maine Railroad changed the location of its shops. "The novelty of the project," according to Margaret Crawford, made it difficult to find investors, and the Massachusetts Homestead Commission was abolished in 1919, illustrating "the difficulties of using the limited dividend system to finance suburban settlements that working-class families could afford. Even by limiting profits, new settlements providing low-cost housing for workers could not be built within existing housing markets."[102] However, Billerica eventually matured into a leafy neighborhood of about 300 small houses, though revisions to the plan eliminated interior allotments and playgrounds.

In 1919 William Madison Wood (1858–1926), founder and president of the American Woolen Company, announced his intentions to build **Shawsheen Village** (1919–24), a self-sufficient "model industrial community" that would include housing for mid-level office workers and executives along with industrial, administrative, civic, retail, and recreational facilities on a 1,500-acre tract in Andover, Massachusetts, twenty-five

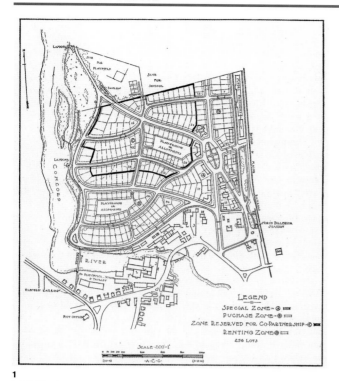

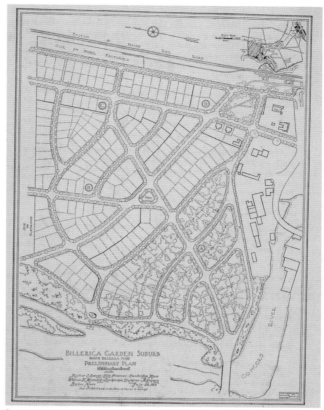

1. Initial plan, Arthur C. Comey and Warren H. Manning, c. 1913. LA14

2. Plan, Arthur C. Comey and Warren H. Manning, 1914. HAM3

3. Hampstead Avenue. RAMSA (2011)

4. Ilford Road and Mason Avenue. RAMSA (2011)

miles north of Boston.[103] The site, which Wood had gradually acquired over the past dozen years, was convenient to mills he operated in Lawrence and was partly occupied by Frye Village, a sleepy mill town established in 1718 that was now home to about 100 wood-frame houses, a three-room schoolhouse, and several mills along the banks of the Shawsheen River. Although the textile magnate commissioned several Boston firms to design the town's buildings, Wood himself, with the advice of civil engineer John Franklin (n.d.), is credited with the plan of Shawsheen Village, representing a comparatively late example of the paternalistic company town, albeit one intended exclusively for white-collar workers and their families.

Wood ordered the demolition of Frye Village's mill facilities but kept and renovated twenty-five nineteenth-century houses, moving some to the central town square. New housing was separated in two distinct areas, with upper management, who were required to move to the village, occupying two- and two-and-a-half-story red-brick dwellings located on a site west of the town square and north of Haverhill Street. The houses in "Brick Shawsheen" were laid out in neat rows behind modest front lawns. "White Shawsheen," intended for managers, wool buyers, and other office workers, occupied a larger gridded parcel south of the town square bound by York Street, Burnham Road, and the tracks of the Boston and Maine Railroad. These wood-frame houses, a few designed for two families, were all painted white with green shutters. Additional housing for clerical workers was provided west of the railroad in smaller gridded rows north and south of Haverhill Street. The firms of John Adden (n.d.) and Wint Parker (1873–1955), James E. Allen (n.d.), Clifford Allbright (1883–1961), and Hubert G. Ripley (1869–1942) and Addison B. LeBoutillier (1872–1951) were responsible for the 251 houses completed by 1924, each a variation of the Colonial Revival style as mandated by Wood, who also lived in the village,

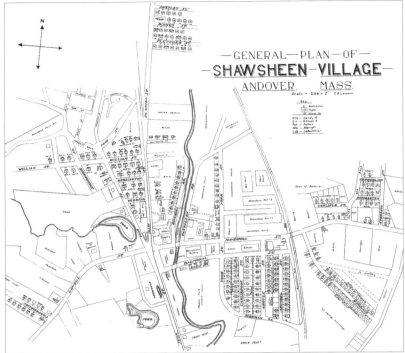

1. Plan, William Madison Wood and John Franklin, c. 1922. AH

2. Aerial view. ATHM (1938)

3. View toward Balmoral Spa, Adden & Parker, 1921. RAMSA (2012)

4. White Shawsheen. ATHM (c. 1920s)

5. White Shawsheen. RAMSA (2012)

6. Brick Shawsheen. RAMSA (2012)

occupying a mid-nineteenth-century house on 70 acres at the southern end of the site.

The extensive commercial and civic district in the center of the village was the work of the same group of architects, who designed Tudor- and Georgian-style buildings in contrast to the residential sections. In addition to a post office, town hall, and elementary school, the civic district contained two communal garages, a dormitory for single female workers, a bank, retail shops, and a company restaurant. Adden & Parker designed the imposing four-story brick-and-limestone

company headquarters. Wood did not overlook the recreational needs of his employees, constructing for their exclusive use tennis courts, a swimming pool, a bowling green, athletic fields, and a golf course one mile west of the town. The architectural highlight was Adden & Parker's three-story redbrick Georgian-style Balmoral Spa, which hosted community dances and theatrical events in its large second-story auditorium.

The mill complex, located west of the railroad and north of Haverhill Street, exerted a commanding presence over the village, with its pair of five-story

850,000-square-foot mills, five-story power plant, and ten-story warehouse capable of storing forty million pounds of wool. To accommodate the 2,600 mill workers, who largely commuted from Lawrence via a new station on the Boston and Maine line, Wood built a one-and-a-half-story cafeteria building that included six bowling lanes in the basement.

By 1924 Shawsheen Village, as originally envisioned by Wood, was largely complete. Two years later, despondent over his failing health and the recent death of his eldest son in a car accident, Wood took his own life. The village he created continued to prosper, even after American Woolen closed its mills in 1953, by which time the houses were primarily in the hands of owners unaffiliated with the company. Despite the loss of original buildings, unsympathetic renovations, and new construction, Shawsheen Village retains a good measure of its original character.

The Peabody Coal Company's town of **Kincaid** (1913), Illinois, twenty-five miles southwest of Springfield on a rolling site overlooking the South Fork of the Sangamon River, was, according to John Reps, "perhaps the most curious of the company town plans," with a "pattern of sinuous loops and curves superficially similar to those of the elder Olmsted but lacking his skill and feeling for the land."[104] As designed by engineers John W. Alvord and Charles B. Burdick (1874–1955) in collaboration with landscape architect Ossian Cole Simonds, the plan, which was not executed as intended, devoted an unusual amount of land to open space and natural reserves, including a broad oval meadow, two circular blocks of public gardens, various small parks, a central park, playgrounds located on block interiors, a lake, and three lagoons. Chicago architect George W. Maher designed both the public buildings and the housing, consisting of single-family bungalows, for which he produced more than two dozen plans.

In 1911 the Pittsburgh Crucible Steel Company acquired the five-year-old settlement of **Midland**, Pennsylvania, thirty-seven miles northwest of Pittsburgh, comprising a steel plant and an adjacent town of unpaved gridded streets on a plateau 40 feet above the Ohio River, establishing the Midland Improvement Company to upgrade and expand the 600-acre community onto an additional 600 acres.[105] Plans were prepared in 1913 by architect Albert H. Spahr (1873–1966), formerly of the Boston firm of Peabody & Stearns, who added new residential neighborhoods, schools, public facilities, and open spaces including a centrally located six-acre teardrop-shaped park.

According to Spahr, various residential zones were created to segregate "as completely as possible, the negro help from the other foreign elements, such as the Slavs and Italians, while another section provides for the American laboring class, and a fourth division, to be located on the heights at the back, will provide for the more skilled workmen, the foremen, the superintendents, and officials of the company."[106] The American workers resided in a section known as "Toyland," where

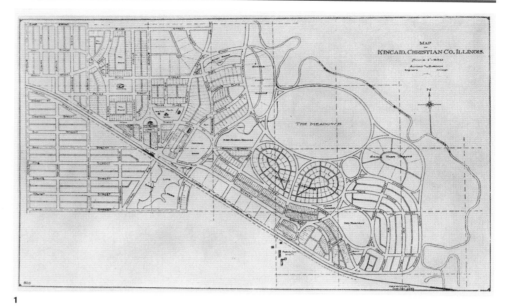

hundreds of single-, two-, and three-family houses built of hollow terracotta block covered in pebbledash and topped by green slate roofs were compared at the time to the housing of the Krupp colonies in Essen, Germany, bearing a particular resemblance to Altenhof and Alfredshof (see p. 745), where single- and semidetached houses prevailed, though Spahr's interpretation of Robert Schmohl's work from fifteen years earlier was less ornate. Houses were offered for rent or sale and restrictions were placed on setbacks, minimum construction costs, and materials. The typical streetscape featured a mix of house styles, while at least one block, bound by Ohio and Virginia Avenues and Seventh and Eighth Streets, accommodated several types, with each long side featuring a triple house flanked by pairs of semidetached houses and a single-family house on each corner.[107]

For foreign mechanics, Midland built experimental poured-concrete houses according to a system invented and heavily promoted by Thomas Edison (1847–1931), whose efforts to see such structures built cheaply and

1. Plan, John W. Alvord, Charles B. Burdick, and Ossian Cole Simonds, c. 1915. AC15

2. Four-room bungalows designed by George W. Maher. AC15 (c. 1914)

3. Five-room bungalows designed by George W. Maher. AC15 (c. 1914)

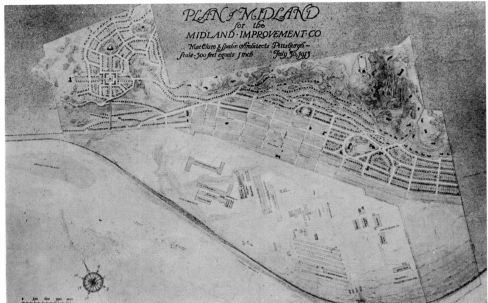

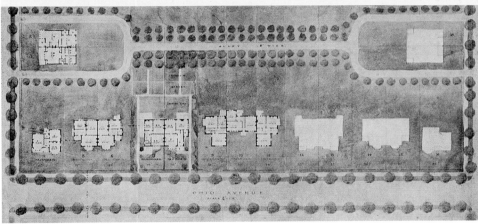

1. Plan, Albert H. Spahr, 1913.
ARB16

2. "Toyland" houses. ARB16
(c. 1916)

3. Elevation and plan of Ohio
Avenue, between Seventh and
Eighth Streets. ARB16 (1913)

4. Eighth Street and Ohio Avenue.
MHP (c. 1916)

5. View showing Edison's poured-
concrete houses on left. MHP
(c. 1913)

6. Typical house. Tilove. GT (2011)

7. Eighth Street and Ohio Avenue.
Tilove. GT (2011)

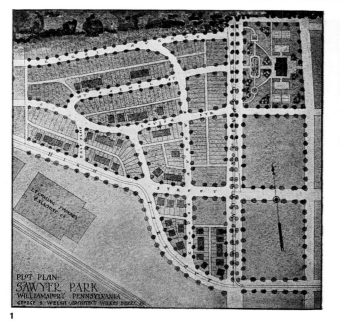

1. Plan, George S. and Lewis E. Welsh, 1918. AR18

2. Aerial view. GE (2005)

3. Bird's-eye view. AA18

4. Rendering of houses. AR18

quickly throughout the country were largely unsuccessful in part because the process called for expensive and extremely heavy iron molds but also because the finished houses did not hold up as well as Edison had hoped.[108] Midland's Edison houses, according to J. E. Wright, of the Pittsburgh Industrial Development Commission, "while not beautiful," were "clean-cut, solid structures."[109]

Skilled mill operators were accommodated in frame and stucco dwellings. Even though more than 1,000 residential units were built at Midland, the plan was not fully implemented. The most expensive houses, intended to comfortably dot the foothills to the north, were not built, nor was the western half of the town, reserved for foreign and black workers, where irregularly shaped residential blocks were to have been placed around a central square from which axial boulevards would lead to public buildings.

Sawyer Park, deemed an "unusually attractive garden suburb" by Edith Elmer Wood, was initiated in 1917 when the local board of trade established the Williamsport Improvement Corporation to develop a 36-acre site on the western outskirts of the city of Williamsport,

Pennsylvania, but within a one-mile radius of fourteen industrial plants employing 5,000 workers.[110] Billed as a "straight business proposition designed to meet an acute local situation which threatened the industrial growth and prosperity of the city through lack of housing facilities," the project quickly garnered the support of 887 individual investors who agreed to limit their dividends to 6 percent.[111] The Dodson Realty Corporation, of Bethlehem, Pennsylvania, was contracted to build the development and its infrastructure, working with the Wilkes Barre, Pennsylvania, firm of George S. (n.d.) and Lewis E. (b. 1888) Welsh, who prepared the town plan and architectural designs. The same team was currently at work on the Elmwood Park neighborhood in Bethlehem (see p. 902).

Sawyer Park's plan dedicated 16 acres to residential lots, roughly six acres to schools and recreational space, seven acres to factories, just over six acres to streets, and one-and-a-half acres to sidewalks and alleys. The site was connected to downtown Williamsport by two trolley lines and benefited from nearby public schools, churches, and stores. A block of shops and apartments, a movie theater, and club rooms were planned as a buffer from factories to the south, and a site on the east was reserved for a school. Houses were spread across twenty-five blocks of irregular size and shape bound on the east by the 80-foot-wide Wildwood Boulevard, where a double row of trees screened the trolley from view, and on the south by the curving 60-foot-wide Park Avenue, which accommodated the second trolley line. All other streets were 40 feet wide, lined by trees, and shaped according to the site's contours, with a series of parallel streets forming terraces of housing that climbed a hillside in the north, suggesting to Lawrence Veiller, "in their general appearance those attractive crescent terraces of Bath, England."[112]

Sawyer Park's 300 residential units consisted entirely of semidetached, four-, and six-family stucco-on-hollow-tile houses, leading Veiller to herald the development as an antidote to what he perceived as an American distaste for group houses due to their association with the "long rows of hideous small dwellings of Philadelphia, or of the equally hideous rows of tall New York tenements, or of New York's earlier brownstone fronts . . . So strong throughout the country has been the feeling that the detached house is the only type of house for an American, that with considerable difficulty has a hearing been had for the claims of the group house, notwithstanding its successful use in Great Britain and on the Continent for many generations." Detached dwellings, he noted, could be equally monotonous "if they are all alike and do not possess beauty of design or line."[113]

The four types of houses, with six distinct floor plans rendered in twelve styles, were angled on their sites to maximize exposure to sunlight and take advantage of distant views. Gables, dormers, a variety of window types and sizes, and porches helped produce a textured streetscape. Veiller found the dwellings "attractive in design, picturesque, quaint and with great charm" while still well-suited to their purpose: "They are essentially workingmen's houses and have been built at a cost that makes their purchase well within the means of the skilled worker for whom they have been designed." He particularly appreciated the handling of the porches, which showed "great skill. As a rule, the average piazza demanded by American custom destroys the architectural style of the building, but the architects in this case have with very great skill provided the necessary porches without in any way detracting from the appearance of the building. So, on the contrary, they have made the front porch add to the architectural design of the structure."[114]

On the whole, Veiller greeted Sawyer Park—neither "an employers' enterprise; nor . . . a land speculation scheme"—as an illustration of what could be achieved "in the smaller cities of America and also with comparatively small parcels of land." He praised the development as "architecturally the best thing in industrial housing that has thus far been done in this country" and "the nearest approach that this country has to the best English Garden Village developments."[115] Veiller did, however, identify one critical shortcoming: the decision to sell rather than rent the houses, noting, "When houses are sold, control is surrendered." Without restrictive covenants, workers would apply their own erratic standards of upkeep. "Under such conditions the Garden Village loses its character; while it still remains a village, the garden vanishes."[116] Veiller's prediction appears to have been accurate. By 1936, Arthur Comey and Max Wehrly noted that "Sawyer Park has been so transformed in the last few years as to lose its individuality and has become merely a part of Williamsport."[117]

Marktown, Indiana, featured a promising but only fractionally realized plan by Chicago architect Howard Van Doren Shaw, who also designed its houses and public buildings.[118] The town was developed in 1917 by Clayton Mark (1858–1936), an industrialist whose company, Mark Manufacturing, producers of well-drilling bits and metal pipe, was building a factory near the southern shore of Lake Michigan. Mark was well acquainted with Shaw's work: the two were neighbors in Lake Forest, Illinois, where Shaw had designed Mark's residence (1913) and where he had recently completed the highly regarded Market Square (see p. 127).[119] Shaw's triangular plan for Marktown, a grid rotated 45 degrees from a principal east–west axis, was anchored by a Market Square–inspired sunken plaza set on axis with a railroad station to the east and bordered on the north and south by symmetrical buildings intended to provide more than thirty shops as well as a bank, movie theater, and post office occupying separate buildings. As at Lake Forest, there were second-floor apartments. Shaw reserved a triangular site near the square for a school and provided a large rectangular park with a man-made lake.

Intended to house 8,000 workers on its 190-acre site, Marktown's progress was halted during World War I when the government commandeered the steel mill to produce armor plating. Roughly 40 acres were developed—just four of thirty-two planned sections. In addition to three commercial buildings, ninety-seven single, double, and quadruple workers' houses were built along with three supervisors' houses and one of two planned boardinghouses providing forty rooms. The market square was completed but demolished in 1936 to improve traffic flow.

Shaw, accustomed to designing country and suburban houses for the upper classes, brought a measure of elegance to Marktown's modest two-story Tudor- and Arts and Crafts–inspired cottages. Built of hollow terracotta block, the houses were finished in tinted stucco and vibrantly colored trim. Shaw's own Lake Forest residence, Ragdale (1898), informed the design of Marktown's quadruple houses, which were topped by symmetrical stuccoed gables.[120] By alternating hip roofs and yard- and street-facing gable and double-gable roofs, Shaw devised eleven distinct house exteriors from about six plans. While the streets were exceptionally narrow—only 32 feet separated one facade from another—Shaw opened up the plan by staggering the houses on their lots to allow through-block views. A space of forty feet was provided between most of the houses, which were

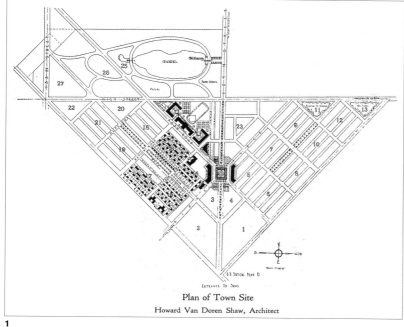

Plan of Town Site
Howard Van Doren Shaw, Architect

1

2

3

4

5

1. Plan, Howard Van Doren Shaw, 1918. ARB18

2. Aerial view. Schalliol. DSCH (2012)

3, 4. Typical views. HFW (c. 1919)

5. Market square. LFC

tied together visually by three-foot-high walls. The over-all effect, according to Ralph F. Warner, writing in 1918, was "very similar to the streets of English villages, or the old continental towns such as Prague. The architect has thus avoided a feature unfortunately characteristic of many of our American town-planning developments, where small . . . houses are on broad streets wide enough for the Chicago Loop District, with an unescapable loss in proportion and scale."[121] Only the supervisors' houses were provided with detached garages. Other residents could rent space in a central garage, but ultimately a pattern was established in which cars were parked on sidewalks and pedestrians walked in the streets. In 1923, Mark Manufacturing sold the steel mill and town site to the Youngstown Sheet and Tube Co., which in turn divested itself of the property during World War II.

Kohler (1915), Wisconsin, was built by the well-known plumbing manufacturers on a rolling farmland site on the Sheboygan River, four miles west of Lake Michigan.[122] Although the company first built a factory

there in 1899, it was not until several years later, after forty houses had been built by employees, that Walter Jodok Kohler (1875–1940), son of the company's founder and later governor of Wisconsin (1929–31), decided to establish a model village that would guide future development. Accompanied by architect Richard Philipp (1874–1959), a partner in the Milwaukee firm of Brust & Philipp, Kohler set out on a tour of the garden cities of America and Europe, including Letchworth and Port Sunlight in England and the Krupp estates in Essen, Germany, where he was impressed by what he saw but reluctant to maintain ownership over workers' houses. On a later visit to Welwyn, Kohler consulted with Ebenezer Howard.

In 1913, the Village of Kohler was incorporated, encompassing almost 3,000 acres, including the factory, town site, and a 500-acre buffer used for farming. Two years later, planning of the model village began when Walter Kohler asked Werner Hegemann to collaborate with Brust & Philipp and a Sheboygan civil engineer, J. Donohue (n.d.), on the design. Because the

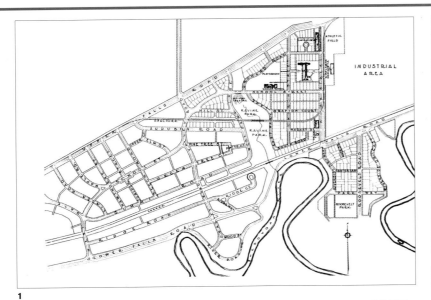

1. Plan. KC (1925)

2. Lincoln Circle. KC (c. 1915)

3. Two-family house. KC

4. American Club, Brust & Philipp, 1917. KC

5. Workers' houses. KC

6. Commercial row topped by apartments. KC

German-born Hegemann was not a planner but a planning historian and housing expert, he requested that Elbert Peets, a landscape architect currently residing in Cambridge, Massachusetts, assist him, initiating a long and fruitful collaboration between the two. Hegemann found the site to be "full of delightful gifts of nature, rolling land, fine trees, a most surprising wide stream, high ravines, wide, perfectly framed views; in short, an ideal location for a garden city."[123] Presented in 1916, the town plan sought to preserve and enhance these conditions, taking advantage of a natural ravine to introduce a continuous park running through the center of the site from the winding Sheboygan River on the south to a school set amid expansive grounds on the north. The industrial area lay to the northeast of two major roads, the north–south High Street and the east–west Lower Falls Road. Upper Falls Road formed the town's northern border. Hegemann and Peets widened High Street, the main approach to the factory, to accommodate streetcars and lined it with trees and planting strips. Development was to begin in the areas directly west and south of the plant known as West I and South I. The former, between the factory and Ravine Park, included housing along a rectangular system of shaded streets as well as commercial and institutional buildings. The most unusual of these was the three-story American Club (1917) on the west side of High Street, a residence for more than 100 single men maintained by the company that included a dining hall, a reading room, a bowling alley, and billiard tables. The name also described the building's secondary purpose of Americanizing its primarily European-born residents through classes and the establishment of an environment that created a "distinctively American" way of life within.[124] To the north, a two-and-a-half-story redbrick commercial and apartment building designed in the free Elizabethan mode with street-facing gables and arched storefront windows included space for a post office and recreation hall. In South I, bending streets matched the course of the Sheboygan River and flanked a tree-lined divided boulevard leading south to a park.

Brust & Philipp's single and double houses were built by the Kohler Improvement Company, a nonprofit development company that sold land and houses at cost. Residential lots were between 50 and 62 feet wide and 90 and 160 feet deep. According to Hegemann, "The houses should not, by exigencies of economy, be packed together in the streets like dead flowers in a book, but shall be grouped opening up to the sun like living flowers and leaves of a tree in free nature."[125] He arranged houses in informal groups of three and four, stepping back and forth from the street to enclose and define playgrounds and yards. Each group was given certain shared characteristics—rooflines, landscaping, and materials—but variation was introduced among individual houses. Lincoln Circle, a cul-de-sac north of the American Club, was a more formal arrangement that, according to Margaret Crawford, "virtually duplicated" Grosvenor Atterbury's Nashoba Place at Indian Hill.[126] Extensive landscaping included hedges, street trees, and foundation plantings. Vines covered many houses as well as the walls that screened the factory from the town, evoking, for James C. Young, writing in the *New York Times* in 1930, the feel of a university: "Perhaps it will be fitting to say that Kohler is just that—a kind of university of industry."[127]

By the end of 1916, relations between Hegemann and Kohler had soured. According to Christiane Crasemann Collins, Hegemann's biographer, Kohler felt his planner had become distracted by other projects, including Washington Highlands (see p. 82) and Lake Forest (see p. 167), both in Wisconsin. Progress on West I was slow to start because, as Kohler saw it, too much design work was being devoted to the parks, and, more damning, Hegemann had spent an inordinate amount of time learning drafting skills from Peets. For his part, Hegemann may have been frustrated by certain changes, such as decreased street widths, called for by Kohler, who exerted strong control over the design. As well, Philipp's houses were turning out to be more expensive than anticipated. Kohler and Hegemann considered using prefabrication to lower costs but were unable to find a solution that did not result in "a battery of monotonous rows of houses," as Kohler put it.[128] When Hegemann chided Kohler for passing on the costs of planning to the workers through the purchase price of lots and houses, suggesting that Kohler should absorb the costs himself, Kohler responded in an unsent letter that it was outside of Hegemann's area of expertise to comment on the matter and that Hegemann "did not possess a consistent attitude when evaluating economics and paternalism within America."[129]

By January 1917 Hegemann and Peets were off the project, although by the mid-1920s, Philipp and Donohue had guided West I and South I to completion according to their plan. When further expansion was contemplated, Kohler hired the Olmsted Brothers, led by partner Henry V. Hubbard, to design the West II and West III neighborhoods. From that point on, Kohler and his successors discounted Hegemann and Peets's role in the project, never again using their names in company publications or documentation and instead attributing the plan to the Olmsted firm. The residential area of West II, west of Ravine Park, was built in the late 1920s with eclectically styled English cottage, American Colonial, and bungalow houses set among a softer network of streets, including a Y-shaped configuration whose splayed arms embraced a small park. Progress on West III was curtailed by the Depression and by two labor strikes, one of which lasted from 1954 to 1960. Work began again in 1962 but only vaguely followed the 1920s Olmsted plan that had featured a mix of curving and gridded streets centered around a small rectangular plaza at the intersection of two main streets. Modifications called for larger lots, resulting in a density of 1.59 houses per acre as compared to 3.45 in the earlier sections. Houses were no longer built by the Kohler Improvement Company but by outside developers or individual purchasers who were required to submit their plans for approval by the architectural firm of Perkins & Will. As a result, the character of the West III neighborhood adheres more to the centerless postwar, automobile-oriented suburb of single-family homes set back on large private lots, than to the tight, focused Garden City principles that governed the town's early development.

Goodyear Heights (1913) was developed by Frank A. Seiberling (1859–1955), founder and president of the Goodyear Tire & Rubber Company, based in Akron, Ohio, who realized that the booming city's severe housing shortage was harming his business by creating an unstable and transient workforce. The company, which began life producing bicycle and carriage tires and rubber pads for horseshoes, was established in 1898 in the gritty industrial city thirty-five miles south of Cleveland.[130] Seiberling named his company after Charles Goodyear (1800–1860), the inventor of vulcanized rubber, but some have speculated that he was also attracted to the name because it sounded similar to B. F. Goodrich, a rival Akron rubber manufacturer founded three decades earlier. Seiberling's proposal that Goodyear build a substantial amount of workers' housing was rejected as too risky by a majority of the company's board of directors, forcing the wealthy entrepreneur and part-time inventor (he patented an automatic twine binder while working for his father) to proceed on his

1. Plan, Warren H. Manning, 1913. ARB17

2. Aerial view. UA (1925)

3. Typical street. UA (1915)

4. Typical houses. Ford. APD (c. 2002)

5. Typical street showing bus provided by developer. UA (1918)

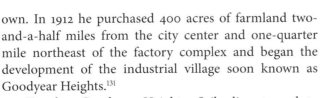

own. In 1912 he purchased 400 acres of farmland two-and-a-half miles from the city center and one-quarter mile northeast of the factory complex and began the development of the industrial village soon known as Goodyear Heights.[131]

To plan Goodyear Heights, Seiberling turned to Warren H. Manning, who was working on the landscape design of his 1,000-acre west Akron estate, Stan Hywet (1911–15), which included a Tudor Revival mansion designed by Charles S. Schneider (1874–1932), at the time the largest private house in Ohio.[132] Goodyear Heights was within walking distance of the factory, separated from it by the tracks of the Akron & Chicago

Junction Railroad. Manning initially platted 100 acres into 436 lots, with the remainder of the holdings kept in reserve for future development. Manning laid out curving 50- and 60-foot-wide streets that followed the hills of the site. To imbue a sense of individuality, different species of shade trees were planted on adjacent blocks, with each street also given, in Manning's words, "a distinctive floral character."[133] In addition to the extensive planting program, which included an abundance of fruit trees, Manning also set aside 28 acres for public parks. Goodyear Avenue, the village's main street, was a 70-foot-wide diagonal boulevard that bisected the site and led directly from the factory to the town square, home to a modest collection of commercial and public buildings. Manning intended for an electric trolley to run down the middle of Goodyear Avenue, but the streetcar line was never completed and Goodyear Heights instead became a pioneer in providing bus service, creating an extensive transportation network that left no resident more than two blocks from a bus stop.

The firm of Mann & MacNeille designed the two- and two-and-a-half-story single-family houses, producing ten different five- and six-room models. The dark-redbrick or stucco-clad wood-frame houses, set back from the street behind sidewalks and modest front yards, sat on lots that were 50 feet wide and between 110 and 125 feet deep. Corner houses were set back an additional 10 feet from the street line to provide visual interest. Unimproved lots were also available for sale, but every house design required the approval of the Goodyear Heights Realty Company, the entity Seiberling set up to administer the village's development. In order to make the houses affordable for Goodyear workers, Seiberling financed fifteen-year mortgages with no down payment required. He also provided a unique incentive to remain with the company, offering the houses to workers at cost plus a 25 percent premium, an added charge that would be refunded after five years if they remained in Goodyear's employ. People outside the company fold could also purchase houses or lots, but since they were not covered by the refund policy few takers emerged.

Goodyear Heights was both an economic and social success, with the first 250 houses, completed by August 1916, quickly sold. The solidly built dwellings, praised by Edith Elmer Wood as "very attractive," represented a significant improvement in the lives of their new owners, many of whom had lived in a grim section of east Akron known as Cinder World.[134] The industrial village attracted the attention of the editors of the *New York Times*, who wrote in 1916 that "most of the commonplace features of allotment development have been eliminated. There are no rows of houses all alike. Each is a real home, with architectural individuality." The *Times* editors further noted that "the tract is one of the show places of the city, and its fame has spread so that manufacturers from many parts of the country have made detailed inquiries, with a view to the possibility of adopting in whole or part, similar housing plans."[135]

In 1917, four years after the development began, Goodyear Heights was dramatically expanded to include the 300 remaining acres of Seiberling's original purchase.[136] This time, the Goodyear company, now convinced of the merits of building workers' housing, relieved Seiberling of the responsibility for developing the property on his own. Manning was again responsible for the plan, extending Goodyear Avenue through the site and laying out 50- and 60-foot-wide streets in a more traditional gridiron pattern, realizing 1,500 50-by-115-foot lots. George H. Schwan (1874–1929) replaced Mann & MacNeille as architect of the houses, designing a similar array of brick and stucco single-family dwellings.

Fairlawn Heights

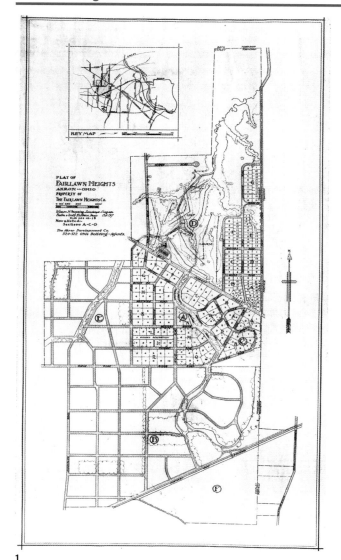

1. Plan, Warren H. Manning, 1917. ISUL

1

Seiberling and Manning collaborated on one additional project in Akron: **Fairlawn Heights** (1917), a subdivision that landscape historian Robin Karson recently described as "a wealthy man's Goodyear Heights."[137] Located on over 1,000 acres in the western part of the city, less than five miles from Seiberling's Stan Hywet estate, Fairlawn Heights, with its generous lots on curving streets and its golf course and country club, was geared to Goodyear executives and other wealthy area residents, ultimately becoming the most exclusive neighborhood in the so-called "Rubber Capital of the World."

In 1915 Harvey Firestone (1868–1938), owner of the eponymous rubber manufactory founded fifteen years earlier, followed Seiberling's lead, purchasing 800 acres in south Akron one mile from his factory in order to build workers' housing.[138] Firestone borrowed an additional idea from Seiberling, selecting as planner of **Firestone Park** (1916) Alling S. DeForest (1875–1957), the landscape architect of his personal estate, Harbel Manor (1912). DeForest, who briefly worked in the office of Olmsted, Olmsted & Eliot, platted 400 acres of the flat site, creating 600 45-by-120-foot lots on 60-foot-wide tree-lined streets, many of them gently curved. Before

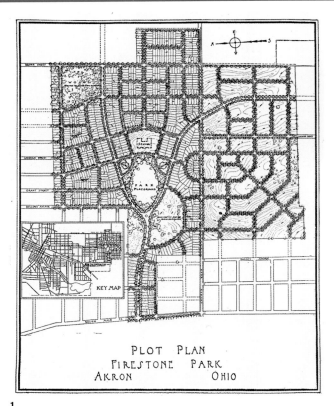

1

2

3

1. Plan, Alling S. DeForest, 1916. A19

2. Typical houses. A19 (c. 1919)

3. Firestone Boulevard. HFW (c. 1919)

branching off into two 80-foot-wide segments, Firestone Boulevard, the subdivision's main 110-foot-wide thoroughfare, led from the manufacturing complex to a 16-acre public park near the center of the site, shaped to resemble the company's shield emblem, a conceit requested by Firestone. A large public school stood directly north of the park, while the modest commercial core was placed at its southern border. Comey and Wehrly found that "the arrangement of the central portion of the [Firestone Park] plan and its parkway approach are considerably better than similar arrangements" at Goodyear Heights.[139] But the writers were less impressed with the six- to eight-room single-family houses designed by John F. Suppes (1878–1972).

In 1917 Fairbanks, Morse & Co., manufacturers of internal combustion engines and steam pumps, purchased 53 acres north of its factory complex in Beloit, Wisconsin, in order to build housing to accommodate new workers hired to meet wartime demands for its products.[140] The company had a long tradition of looking after its employees, dating back to its founding in the early nineteenth century in St. Johnsbury, Vermont, when the fledgling business built Fairbanks Village. To design the Wisconsin industrial village, **Eclipse Park**, located seventy-five miles southwest of Milwaukee and one hundred miles northwest of Chicago, Fairbanks, Morse hired Rochester-based landscape architect William Pitkin Jr. and the prominent New York firm of George B. Post & Sons, then headed by William S. Post (1866–1940) following the death of his father in 1913. The firm was well known in Wisconsin for the design of the State Capitol (1906–17) in Madison.[141]

Pitkin and the Post firm's plan, intended to locate 360 single-family houses within a fifteen-minute walk of the factory as well as a substantial town center, rejected the surrounding grid for a curvilinear treatment "conforming to the lines of least resistance in the easiest and most natural grades," as William Comstock wrote in 1919.[142] Bound by Henry Avenue to the north, Park Avenue to the east, the factory to the south, and River Road overlooking the Rock River to the west, the plan's most prominent feature was Morse Avenue, an 80-foot-wide main thoroughfare that cut through on a diagonal and was originally intended to include an extension of a single-track belt-driven trolley connected to Beloit's business district one-and-a-half miles to the south. At the town's formal entrance in the southeastern corner of the site, the architects proposed a 260-foot-wide-by-150-foot-deep plaza containing a 145-by-115-foot park with a fountain. The plaza, planned to include an arched entrance to the factory 200 yards to the southwest, was to be surrounded on three sides by two-story arcaded buildings, home to stores, a motion-picture theater, and community facilities with offices and apartments located above. Schools and churches were planned for major intersections along Morse Avenue, and a heavily wooded six-acre parcel enjoying 370 feet of frontage on the Rock River in the southwest corner of the site was to be set aside for a public park.

Fifty-foot-wide residential streets, designed to discourage through traffic, were bound by lots that ranged from 40 by 80 feet for the smallest four-room houses to 75 by 110 feet for the largest, eight-room dwellings. The freestanding single-family houses, geared to skilled

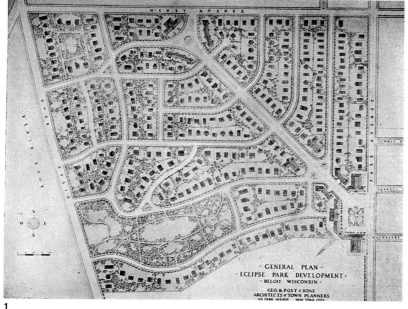

GROUPING OF HOUSES ON A TYPICAL STREET

3

4

1. Plan, William Pitkin Jr. and George B. Post & Sons, 1917. AA18

2. Aerial view. GE (2011)

3. Elevation and plan of typical group of houses. AA18 (1917)

4. Pine Street. BEL (1999)

Fairbanks Flats

1

2

1. Overall view. MPR (1938)

2. Apartment building. Preuschl. MPR (2008)

workers and management, who would receive company-sponsored mortgages after making 10 percent down payments, were typically designed in the Colonial style and sheathed in shingles or clapboard, although a number of stucco-clad Mission-style models with deep porches and steeply sloping roofs were also provided. The houses were set back between 20 and 28 feet from the sidewalk and included side yards of at least 15 feet. To add variety to the streetscape, buyers could choose from among eight different types of shutters, seven chimney caps, and five window flower boxes. All told, buildings were planned to occupy 12.5 percent of the site, with a density of about seven families per acre. Lawrence Veiller

had high hopes for Eclipse Park, writing in early 1918: "This development is one which marks real progress in the housing of America's working people. While it cannot compare in beauty with the best developments of England, it gives promise of being one of the most artistic and attractive thus far evolved in this country."[143]

Construction began in the northeast corner of the site, with eighty houses on five streets completed by the summer of 1918. On the opposite side of Rock River, along Birch Avenue and Carpenter Street, the company built a small enclave for skilled and unskilled African-American workers dubbed **Fairbanks Flats** (1917), consisting of four barracks-like, two-story, flat-roofed

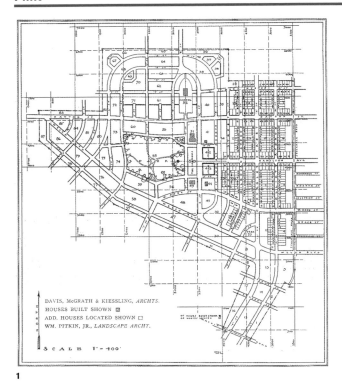

1. Plan, William Pitkin Jr., 1917.
AA18

2. Typical houses. HFW (c. 1919)

concrete-block apartment buildings.[144] The end of World War I drastically decreased the demand for Fairbanks, Morse's machinery, dooming the ambitious plans for Eclipse Park. No additional houses were completed; the trolley line was never constructed down the center of Morse Avenue; and the entirety of the community center remained unrealized. Despite its incomplete state, historian John S. Garner described Eclipse Park as "perhaps the finest industrial housing estate constructed" in the United States during the World War I era.[145]

William Pitkin Jr. also prepared the town plan (1917) for a development located just outside the city limits of **Flint**, Michigan, home to manufacturing plants for Buick and Chevrolet as well as other businesses associated with the automobile industry.[146] Sixty-five miles northwest of Detroit, Flint was in the midst of a population boom, growing from 13,000 residents in 1900 to more than 90,000 by 1916, resulting in a severe housing shortage; its board of trade, composed of leading businessmen and civic leaders, decided to form the nonprofit Civic Building Company to address the problem and develop housing that would be sold at cost. The group purchased 400 acres of former farmland about two miles from most of Flint's factories and roughly bound by Welch and Brownell Boulevards, Trumbull Avenue, and Dupont and Dartmouth Streets, commissioning a plan from Pitkin and hiring the New York firm of Herbert E. Davis (1870–1947), Dudley McGrath (1871–1922), and Calvin Kiessling (1874–1956) to design the new development's buildings.

Pitkin designed the enclave to easily connect to Flint's surrounding grid, including an extension of the city's streetcar line, dividing the relatively flat site into 1,500 residential lots that were on average 50 feet wide and 100 feet deep. Pitkin's use of curving streets helped to avoid monotony, as did the strategy of staggered house placement, with selected groups of houses set back 30 feet from the lot line while the remainder on the same block enjoyed only 20-foot setbacks. Two blocks were set aside for retail buildings while an assembly hall, churches, schools, firehouse, and library were placed around a village green located directly east of 22 wooded acres reserved for a public park.

Davis, McGrath & Kiessling produced twenty-nine different designs for Flint's five- to eight-room one-and-a-half- and two-story wood-frame houses sheathed in clapboard or shingles. Herbert Davis, while noting the emphasis placed on designing models that could be quickly and inexpensively produced, described his firm's freestanding single-family houses as resembling the "old New England village type, with the simplest possible roof lines, close eaves, small-paned windows, and blinds. Simple lattice work is introduced here and there to relieve the bald spots, and flower-boxes are used under windows and on the sides of the porches to provide other simple additional elements of individuality."[147] Construction began in the spring of 1917, and 133 houses were completed by the time material shortages brought about by the war halted the project in 1918. Fortunately, development resumed after the armistice, when the Civic Building Company sold the site in 1919 to General Motors, founded in 1908 and headquartered in Flint until the mid-1920s. Retaining the basic features of Pitkin's plan, including the park, village green, and extension of the streetcar line, over the next several years, the car company completed 950 single-family houses on the site, the vast majority built to Davis, McGrath & Kiessling's original plans.

In 1918, inspired by the Civic Building Company's subdivision in Flint, Henry Ford (1863–1947) proposed

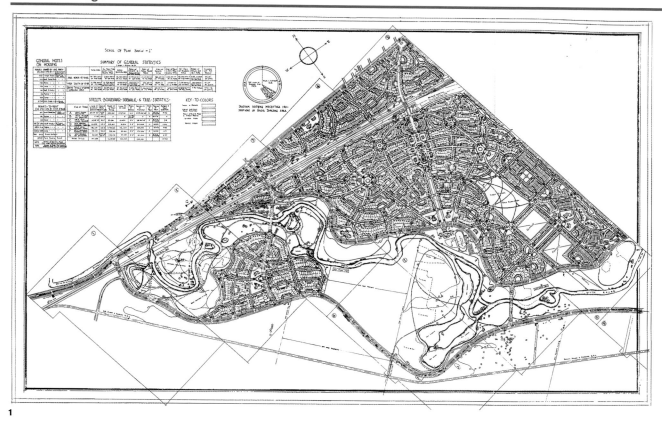

1. Plan, Leonard B. Willeke, c. 1919. TWB

to build a large industrial village to accommodate a growing workforce at his Fordson Tractor Plant established three years earlier in Dearborn, Michigan.[148] In addition to the manufacture of tractors, Ford wanted to expand the industrial facilities at Dearborn to include automobile production as well as an iron and steel plant. Located just west of the factory, the triangular, 2,700-acre site intended for the town of **Fordson Village** was roughly bound by Michigan Avenue to the north, the Rouge River to the south and west, and Greenfield Road to the east. Ford had purchased the somewhat hilly parcel from the Detroit Zoological Society, which instead built its home along Woodward Avenue in Detroit, twelve miles to the northeast. Ford, well known for his dedication to efficiency and frugality, initially suggested that Fordson's housing be mass-produced in the poured concrete system patented by his close friend Thomas Edison. Fearing the aesthetic consequences of such a development, Ford's son, Edsel (1893–1943), intervened, convincing his father to hire architect Leonard B. Willeke to both plan the community and design its residential and public buildings. Willeke, who earlier in his career had served as chief designer in the firm of Rudolph Tietig (1877–1958) and Walter H. Lee (1877–1952) in his native Cincinnati, had designed an addition (1916–17) to Edsel's private residence as well as worked on renovations to Henry Ford's estate, Fair Lane. In addition to his work for the Fords, Willeke had another connection to the automobile industry, designing the Essex Phaeton (1919) for the Hudson Motor Company of Detroit, a budget model for the upscale manufacturer intended to compete with cars from Ford and Chevrolet.

Willeke platted about 63 percent of the available site, or 1,700 acres intended for 3,700 families. The architect had long been interested in industrial villages, dating back to his student days at the École des Beaux-Arts in Paris, when in the spring of 1910 he visited the Krupp workers' colonies in Essen, George Cadbury's Bournville, and Hampstead Garden Suburb. In addition, soon after Willeke was hired to design Fordson Village, Edsel Ford sent Willeke to study John Nolen's Loveland Farms, whereupon Willeke prepared a chart of contemporary industrial developments for Edsel's review; the one-page document included a list of twenty-five towns (Indian Hill, Eclipse Park, Kistler, for example), listing the acreage, number of houses and their exterior treatment, as well as the kind of plan ("curved streets," "mostly gridiron plan," "quite irregular but curved").

Fordson Village's plan of curving residential streets that followed the topography of the site also included a substantial civic and commercial core located at the proposed formal entrance to the town reached via a broad tree-lined boulevard running south from Michigan Avenue. The plan of the town center and its most prominent feature, an arcaded building topped by a clock tower surrounded by stores, a bank, a bus station, a modest park, and a Ford automobile showroom and garage, appears to have been based on Station Square at Forest Hills Gardens. Throughout the development, numerous roundabouts were planned to ease traffic congestion, and a trolley line was intended for the center of Michigan Avenue.

Willeke provided for a variety of different housing types, proposing a mix of 1,700 single-family homes,

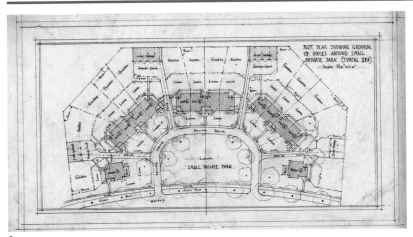

2

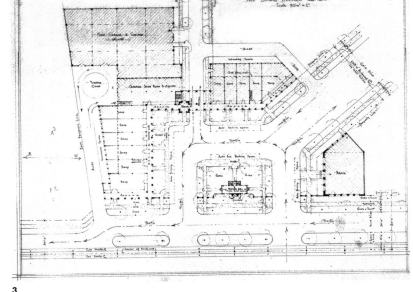

3

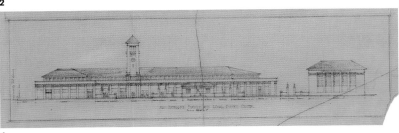

4

2. Plan of houses grouped around a private park. BHL (c. 1919)

3. Plan of main entrance and town center. BHL (c. 1919)

4. Elevation of buildings in town center. BHL (c. 1919)

758 double homes, and 1,232 four-family homes, supplemented by a number of boardinghouses and workingmen's hotels for unmarried employees. In a feature reminiscent of English precedent as well as that of Forest Hills Gardens, some of the houses were to be grouped around modest private parks. Willeke also planned to include a substantial amount of public park space, devoting 52 acres for recreational areas while retaining a large virgin timber reserve; a "railroad park" was to border both sides of the Michigan Central Railroad's tracks running through the site, providing a buffer for the surrounding residential development. According to Thomas W. Brunk, Willeke's biographer, the architect believed

that the most successful housing projects were those which incorporated traditional building designs. He therefore adapted English vernacular architecture to fit American taste by designing varied buildings with roughcast plaster or half-timbered walls, prominent roof lines, picturesque dormer groups, tall shafted chimneys with brick caps, and colorful tile roofs. Even though Willeke incorporated elements of the past, his designs have a geometrically severe expression which was more appropriate for this modern industrial village than the romantic eclecticism expressed in the earlier workers' housing built at Port Sunlight and Letchworth, England.[149]

The proposed town plan was completed by February 1919 but progress was stymied by the postwar tightening of credit and an influenza outbreak. Throughout the entire process, Henry Ford insisted on absolute secrecy,

fearing price gouging by building-supply companies, and the project was never publicly connected with Ford during planning. Danish-born sculptor Alfred Nygard (1870–1941) produced a wax model of the town center as well as models of the various housing types, and by October 1919 a few of the streets south of the railroad tracks were laid out. In 1920, however, the ambitious plans for Fordson Village were permanently dropped by Henry Ford, who believed them too elaborate. In 1939 a small portion of the proposed Fordson Village site, a 132-acre parcel in the northeast corner, was developed by the Ford Foundation, the private charitable institution established by Henry and Edsel Ford in 1936.[150] Called **Springwells Park**, it was an enclave of single-family houses and apartments whose plan of curving streets, culs-de-sac, and ample park space, devised by Ford engineer Ralph Taylor (n.d.), clearly drew inspiration from Willeke's original scheme.

The failure of Fordson Village to move forward exacerbated the demand for housing for Ford employees, with many workers burdened by long commutes by streetcar from Detroit. To remedy the situation, Henry Ford tried his hand at residential development a second time, establishing the Dearborn Realty and Construction Company to build **Ford Homes** (1919–21), a modest enclave of workers' houses more in keeping with the entrepreneur's cheese-paring approach.[151] Located four-and-a-half miles from the tractor plant, Ford Homes occupied a ten-block tract bound by the tracks of the Michigan Central Railroad and Lapham, Monroe, and Nowlin Streets, which had been laid out in 1891 in a standard grid of 60-foot-wide streets, resulting in 312 lots that on average measured 50 feet wide and 125 feet deep. Of more interest than the plan was the assembly-line-like method of construction inspired by Henry Ford's experience with the Model T, with different crews responsible for each stage of the house-building process.

Architect Albert Wood (1886–1973), a Ford employee, produced six different designs for the single-family, three-bedroom, two-story Colonial-style houses sheathed in brick, clapboard siding, and shingles. Within the confines of the grid, Wood broke up the monotony by staggering setback distances, setting houses either 24 or 32 feet from the lot line, varying the placement of porches and front doors, and distributing all the house designs throughout the site, with no matching models next to each other. As Kathryn Eckert succinctly put it in her survey of Michigan buildings, "Wood achieved unity without uniformity."[152] By 1921, 250 houses had been completed as well as an elementary school at the southwest corner of Beech and Lapham Streets. A linear park intended to shield Ford Homes from the railroad tracks at the site's northern border remained unrealized. The houses were sold to Ford employees at cost, but Henry Ford kept some measure of control, retaining the right to repurchase any house within the first seven years of ownership if the buyer and his family were deemed "undesirable."

In addition to Michigan's industrial villages associated with the automobile industry, the Solvay Process Company, a chemical manufacturer, developed **Jefferson Rouge** (1917–18), a strictly residential enclave along the Rouge River for workers at its adjacent coke-oven plant located two miles from downtown Detroit.[153] Mann & MacNeille, who had recently designed the buildings for two prominent industrial villages, Goodyear Heights and Kistler, were responsible for both the town plan and the design of the 186 completed dwellings. Leonard Willeke, in his survey of workers' housing undertaken in preparation for his Fordson Village design, described Jefferson Rouge's plan as "irregular," with "part curved, part straight streets."[154] The most interesting feature of the plan was the grouping of the two-, three-, four-, and six-family Colonial-style brick and stucco houses around generous interior landscaped courts. Two boardinghouses were incorporated in the development, which included no detached houses. After the Solvay plant closed in the 1960s, Jefferson Rouge was demolished and its streets demapped.

In 1906 the new owners of the Arizona and Calumet Mining Company commissioned landscape architect Warren H. Manning to lay out **Warren,** a model village on the site of the former Warren Ranch, located eight miles north of the Mexican border and four miles southeast of the bustling and overcrowded mining town of Bisbee, Arizona, founded in 1877 and notorious for its main street, Brewery Gulch, home to dance halls, saloons, and brothels open twenty-four hours a day.[155] Intended to provide a healthy environment for its employees consisting of Mexican miners and American technical experts and managers, the new village of Warren was to be a self-sufficient community, with a

Springwells Park

1. Plan, Ralph Taylor, 1939. SPA

Ford Homes

1. Park Street. HF (1919)

2. Nona Street. Massey. JCM (2011)

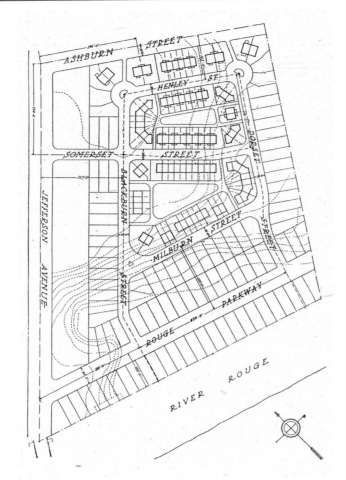

1

2

To design the public and commercial buildings as well as the housing, Manning selected two architects who had studied at the École des Beaux-Arts, George A. Applegarth (1875–1972), a California native then practicing in New York, and Huger Elliott (1877–1948), a Tennessee-born architect then teaching at the University of Pennsylvania, who proposed Spanish Mediterranean–style buildings for the plaza, including an arcaded complex containing the railroad station and the post office, both topped by towers. The plaza was also to include a hotel, theaters, and shops. Spanish Mediterranean precedent was also adopted for the individual houses, which ranged from small flat-roofed cottages for the miners to more elaborate villas for the American workers. The architects proposed several design directives as well, mandating uniform cornice heights proportionate to the width of the streets, a cream color for exterior walls, and reddish-brown tile roofs. As an additional measure, they called for the creation of an art commission to review all building plans for the community.

A short-lived but dramatic drop in copper prices in 1907 put the elaborate plans on hold, but Huger Elliott, in a somewhat bitter-toned article published in September 1908 in the *Architectural Review* (Boston), noted that even before the economic crisis surfaced there were strong objections to the architectural direction and controls he and Applegarth had proposed. Elliott, blaming unsophisticated Americans, sarcastically noted that "every American has an inalienable right to build as d—d ugly as he pleases," adding that "no one is willing to give up somewhat of his desires for the good of the community as a whole . . . Our people are not yet far enough advanced in the way of culture to realize the absolute necessity of some kind of uniformity, some suggestion of symmetry." Applegarth and Elliott were unable to complete a single building in Warren after construction resumed in 1908. As Elliott observed at the conclusion of his piece, "the West lost a chance to point the country toward The City Beautiful."[156] Nonetheless, Warren did prosper and grow using Manning's plan, with construction consisting primarily of modest-size bungalows, many designed by El Paso–based Henry Trost (1860–1933), as well as a forty-one-room mansion for the general manager of the mine company at the northern end of The Vista. By 1930, when Warren reached its peak, it was home to 532 buildings and 3,000 people.

A year after Manning planned Warren, he was asked to lay out another mining village, **Gwinn** (1907), Michigan, prepared for the Cleveland-Cliffs Iron Mining Co., whose president, William Gwinn Mather (1857–1951), would commission a total of sixty projects from the landscape architect, including the grounds of his Charles Platt–designed house, also called Gwinn, outside of Cleveland.[157] The 440-acre village, in a remote area of northern Michigan, at a fork in the Escanaba River and bordered on the south and east by railroad lines, was a patchwork of grids laid out around irregularly shaped "reservations" where the site's natural features were

substantial civic and commercial component to accompany the housing.

After a February 1906 visit to the flat mountain-rimmed desert site, Manning, mindful of the constant danger of flash floods, produced a fan-shaped plan of radial streets emanating from an oblong plaza with semicircular ends intended as the town's civic and commercial focus located at the southern portion of the site. The most interesting feature of the plan was The Vista, a central six-block-long tapered linear park landscaped with grasses and flowers. Housing for Mexican miners was to be separated from that for American workers, and that for top executives was placed at the northern end with the most scenic views. Within a year of the plan's completion, many of Warren's main features were realized, including an electric trolley line that connected it to Bisbee as well as to the mining town of Lowell, two miles to the north.

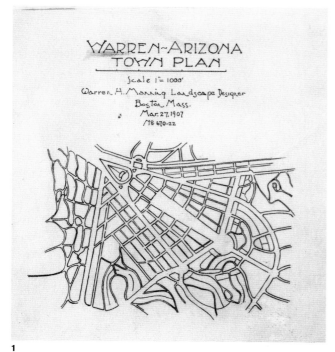

1

2

3

4

1. Plan, Warren H. Manning, 1907. ISUL

2. Aerial view. GE (2004)

3. Bird's-eye view of The Vista and town center. ARB08 (1907)

4. Bird's-eye view. ARB08 (1907)

5. Worker's cottage. ARB08 (1907)

6. Executive's villa. ARB08 (1907)

7. The Vista. Walton. AW (2012)

8. Bungalows, Vista Street. RBH

5

6

7

8

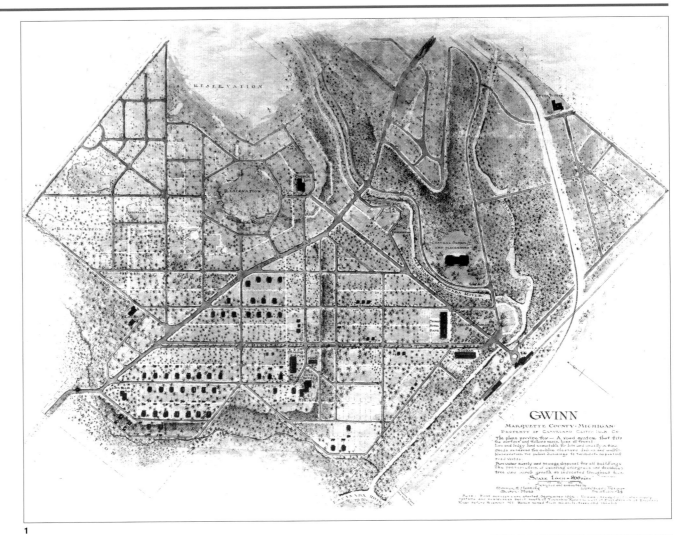

1

2

3

retained. Throughout the village, Manning called for thousands of trees and shrubs to be transplanted from the surrounding forest, which was kept as a protective greenbelt. The introduction of abundant greenery was viewed as a salve for the mine workers, who spent so much time underground. Long, diagonal roads were cut across the plan to create vistas terminated by public buildings, with one road leading from the railroad depot to one of the town's four churches. Manning also situated a school, stores, a bank, and a hotel around a village common. Both the predominantly redbrick commercial buildings and the houses were designed by the English-born Michigan architect Demetrius Frederick

Charlton (1856–1941). House lots measured 50 by 150 feet. To get things started, the company built fifty-five two-family saltbox houses for low-wage earners and eighteen single-family houses for managers and supervisors, using a variety of plans and paint colors to relieve visual monotony. By 1923, upper-echelon workers had built eighty-two more houses but only half of the residential area was built out and the town, projected for a population of 5,000, only reached 1,000.

The company instituted strict rules against gambling, alcohol, and "immoral" activities, and carefully screened those seeking to establish businesses within its borders, leading one group of rejected applicants to found the

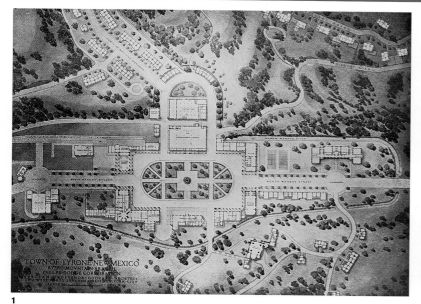

1. Plan, Bertram Grosvenor Goodhue, 1915. AR18

2. Bird's-eye view of plaza. AR18 (c. 1915)

3. Railway station. AR18 (c. 1918)

4, 5. Semidetached houses for American workers. AF18 (c. 1918)

6. Typical houses for American workers. AR18 (c. 1918)

7. Sketch by James Perry Wilson of proposed house for American worker. AF18

neighboring town of New Swanzy, where a plenitude of saloons earned it a reputation as Gwinn's "alter ego."[158] The Depression took a toll on mining activities and after a strike in 1946, the Gwinn mines were sealed and all company-owned properties were sold. After a period of decline, the establishment of the K. I. Sawyer Air Force base in 1956 brought vitality back to Gwinn until the base's closure in the 1990s. According to planning historians Arnold R. Alanen and Lynn Bjorkman, writing in 1998, "Postwar Gwinn, which displays curvilinear, suburban-like streets and groupings of single-story ranch houses poised on individual lots, stands in marked contrast to early Gwinn, with its duplexes and compact,

orthogonal road system. Over time, several early commercial and institutional buildings have been removed, and a significant portion of the architectural unity and character originally embodied in many of the remaining buildings has been destroyed or modified significantly." But some features remain: "The 'commons' continues to function as the community's primary public space, and Manning's insistence that everyone be 'within ten minutes of extensive wild wood and river reservation,' is as true today as it was almost a century ago."[159]

Manning's scheme for Warren clearly influenced the planning of **Tyrone** (1914–18), New Mexico, designed by Bertram Grosvenor Goodhue for the Phelps Dodge

Corporation, the world's leading producer of copper.[160] Surrounded by the Burro Mountains in the southwestern part of the state, sixty miles from Mexico, Tyrone was conceived as a self-sufficient model mining town on a relatively isolated site twelve miles east of Silver City. The area's low-grade ore had only been sporadically mined since the turn of the twentieth century. But in 1914, encouraged by the dramatic rise in copper prices caused by the outbreak of war in Europe, and mindful of the company's severe labor problems at its Arizona mines, Phelps Dodge purchased all of the area's mining rights and completed a forty-eight-mile spur line (1914) that connected the site to the El Paso and Southwestern Railroad.

Goodhue, whose ambitious plans for Tyrone were only partially realized, was selected by Walter Douglas (1871–1946), president of Phelps Dodge, largely on the strength of the Spanish Colonial–style buildings he had designed for the Panama-California Exposition (1915) in San Diego.[161] To prepare for the Tyrone job, the prominent New York architect (who had a winter retreat in Montecito, California) and Douglas traveled throughout New Mexico in the executive's private rail car, seeking inspiration for the new industrial village. For this commission, one of his first as an independent practitioner since dissolving the twenty-year partnership of Cram, Goodhue & Ferguson, Goodhue embraced a style that represented a stripped-down version of his San Diego work. Although Goodhue was inspired by Native American adobe buildings in the region, as Richard Oliver, his biographer, suggests, the work of pioneering Modernist Irving Gill, which Goodhue greatly admired on visits to California, also served as an important inspiration for Tyrone. As Oliver observed, the "strength of Goodhue's design was its arrangement into the image of an idealized Mexican town, with all the small-scale urbanity that image evokes."[162] On one of these train trips, Goodhue selected the site for Tyrone's town center, a narrow picturesque valley next to the railroad spur's terminus and about one-and-a-quarter miles southeast of the mines.

Goodhue's scheme had as its principal feature a monumental core of arcaded buildings surrounding a 140-by-250-foot central landscaped plaza with fountain and bandstand. The plaza could be reached from either the east or west via 60-foot-wide tree-lined streets that each featured prominent circular plazas. The first buildings completed around the plaza included the railway station, with its open-air arcaded waiting room and post office; a large company department store dubbed the "Wanamaker's of the desert," with an equally large warehouse behind; a building that housed privately owned shops, a bank, and a 5,000-volume library; and the company headquarters. Only the headquarters building lacked an arcade; set back slightly from the plaza, it occupied the place of honor usually reserved for a town hall.

Except for the heavy cornices and moldings of the department store and company office, the buildings were designed, in Goodhue's own words, "without an ounce of ornament anywhere, nothing but plaster walls with

tile or flat parapeted roofs."[163] As Oliver explains, the architect began with the Spanish-inspired style of the Panama-California Exposition buildings and "moved decisively toward greater simplicity," relying in large measure on "composition of volume" and color for variety and interest, with each of the buildings tinted a different shade (pearl white for the department store; pink for the railroad station and post office; and purple for the store and bank building, for example), a "subtle kaleidoscope of color," as Oliver wrote, that "was particularly suited to the soft nuances of Western sunlight, which Goodhue found so different from the brilliant skies of the East."[164] In addition to the buildings directly surrounding the plaza, a 500-student schoolhouse and hospital were built, but the medical facility, said to be the best equipped between Kansas City and San Francisco, was the work of company engineers, not Goodhue.

Goodhue also proposed additional shops, a hotel, a theater, and a large clubhouse with extensive recreational facilities, which were not realized. Perhaps not surprisingly, given his experience as one of America's leading church architects, Goodhue pulled out all the stops in his proposed Roman Catholic Church with dome and tower, modeled after his California Building at the San Diego exhibition and planned for a hillside site north of the plaza. But by the time construction of the first phase of building drew to a close in 1917, the material shortages brought about by America's entry into the war halted progress on the project.

Goodhue was also responsible for the design of the housing for American and Mexican workers, built as separate neighborhoods. The single-family dwellings for the Americans, mostly foremen and technical experts, were located on a ridge southwest of the plaza and reached by a winding 20-foot-wide road. The three- to six-room hollow-clay-tile houses featured deep porches and stucco exteriors tinted in shades of brown, cream, pale green, or salmon. The most interesting were two-story structures placed on hilly sites, accommodating one family on each level. At first the houses were built with flat roofs but after complaints about leaks, the designs featured pitched roofs covered in red clay tile. *Architectural Forum* was impressed with the results, writing in 1918 that "the particular charm of these houses is their suitability to the country in which they are located. Their broad stucco surfaces, on which there is a refreshing absence of effort to secure even planes and rigid angles, are extremely restful in the brilliant light. The simple exterior details and arched openings furnish strong shadows, giving the necessary points of accent."[165]

The two-, three-, and six-family flat-roofed row-houses Goodhue designed for the Mexican miners were located southeast of the plaza along two sides of a 30-foot-wide road. Although the houses did not include indoor plumbing, substituted cement floors for hard pine, and received untinted concrete exteriors, they represented a significant improvement over the standard fare typically provided to immigrant laborers. Between 1914 and 1918 Phelps Dodge completed 67 single-family houses for American workers and 124 dwellings for the miners. Still, the Goodhue-designed housing accommodated only a small percentage of Tyrone's growing population, which numbered over 4,000 in 1920. To house the overflow, Phelps Dodge rented unimproved lots to workers who had to be content with pitching a tent or erecting the simplest of houses.

Unfortunately, the postwar period was not accompanied by the resumption of work on Goodhue's master plan. Copper prices dropped as dramatically as they had risen during hostilities and Phelps Dodge decided to concentrate on mining higher-grade ore. In April 1921 the company announced the close of operations at Tyrone, and within weeks the population of the town was reduced to 700 people; by the next year, it stood at fifty residents. Despite periodic rumors of renewed activity, in August 1928 Phelps Dodge removed the mine's pumps, flooding the facilities and thereby effectively ending chances for resuming underground mining. Although Goodhue traveled at least twice a year to inspect Tyrone during its construction, he entrusted a talented assistant, Clarence Stein, from his New York office, with site supervision. And it was through Stein's later work that Goodhue's project would have a lasting influence, especially at Radburn (see p. 275).

Tyrone became something of a romantic ghost town after the mine closed. It was for a time home to the Ranchos Los Pinos guesthouse, and the occasional artist and writer would move into one or another of the vacant and deteriorating houses. Over the years the workers' houses, the warehouse, and the school were torn down, while the railroad station, department store, and headquarters building were fenced off behind barbed wire. In September 1966 Tyrone's fate was permanently sealed when Phelps Dodge announced that it would reopen the operation as an open-pit mine where the town stood. Between 1967 and 1969 the remaining houses and public buildings were demolished, leaving only the 100,000-gallon water tank.

In 1916, inspired by Tyrone's example, John Campbell Greenway (1872–1926), a personal friend of Walter Douglas and the owner of the New Cornelia copper mine in **Ajo**, Arizona, decided to build his own model village to accommodate a growing workforce.[166] Located forty miles north of the Mexican border, the area around Ajo, which had been irregularly and unprofitably mined since the middle of the nineteenth century, was hamstrung by a lack of water and transportation facilities. An isolated village of adobe shacks had grown up in connection with mining operations. The name Ajo—the word means garlic in Spanish but also is used as a popular Mexican curse—led some to believe that the town was named less for the area's wild garlic plants and more for the site's harsh conditions in the middle of the Sonoran Desert. Ajo's fortunes began to turn around after Greenway, a Yale-educated engineer who served with Theodore Roosevelt's Rough Riders in the Spanish-American War, tapped an abundant water source in an ancient lava flow six miles north of the town, building a deep well and the

necessary infrastructure to deliver more than five million gallons of water to the site each day. He also arranged for the construction of the Tucson, Cornelia and Gila Bend Railroad, whose completion in 1916 linked Ajo to Tucson 130 miles to the east. Although Goodhue expressed interest in planning the town and its buildings, Greenway turned to architects he was familiar with from his time managing mines in northern Minnesota, the short-lived Minneapolis-based firm of William M. Kenyon (1884–1940) and Maurice R. Maine (1881–1950).

Kenyon and Maine's plan divided the site into three separate and unequal sections: the largest area was intended for the town center and residences for American workers; south of this section and separated from it by modest hills was the simply gridded Mexican town site; and adjacent to the miners' housing was a still smaller area for the native Papago Indians. The focal point of the Anglo section was Ajo's town center and its ample palm- and oleander-lined plaza with bandstand. The arcaded railroad station, designed in a pared-down version of the Spanish Colonial style, stood directly east of the plaza. Similarly styled buildings linked by arcades faced the plaza on both its north and south sides, home to a company store, restaurant, separate vaudeville and motion-picture theaters, and additional stores. West of the plaza, a broad boulevard led directly to the schoolhouse, located on axis with the railroad station's tower. Architectural historian David Gebhard, who described the shape of the American town site as that of a "winged bird," believed the "most potent single direct source" for the architecture surrounding the plaza to have been the work of Goodhue, "especially Tyrone, though when one compares Tyrone with Ajo it becomes apparent that Goodhue's design was in a far richer version of the traditional (Spanish) and more inventive."[167]

Kenyon and Maine produced fifteen different designs for the four- to five-room single-family pastel-colored, stucco-clad, hollow-clay-tile houses intended for purchase by American skilled workers and supervisors, which, to Margaret Crawford, were "cruder versions of Goodhue's designs for Tyrone, with literal ornament derived from Spanish and Pueblo styles—wrought iron, mission gables, and wooden vegas—applied to simple cubic forms."[168] The flat-roofed multifamily houses for Mexican miners lacked indoor plumbing and could only be rented. For the Papago Indians, the company provided no housing, renting unimproved lots on gridded, unpaved streets.

By the time the first wave of building was completed in 1918, the population of Ajo topped 5,000. In addition to the housing and the public buildings around the plaza, a hospital and administrative office were built outside the town center. Two of the most interesting buildings in Ajo were built after Kenyon and Maine left Arizona. In 1923 Greenway's wife, Isabella, hired a longtime friend, nationally known, California-based architect George Washington Smith (1876–1930), to design a house as well as a church. An acknowledged master of

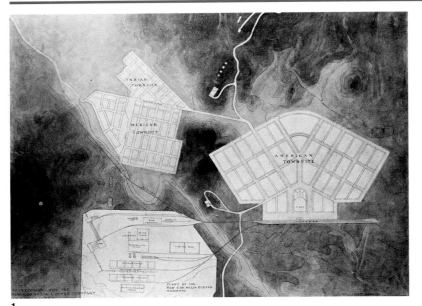

1

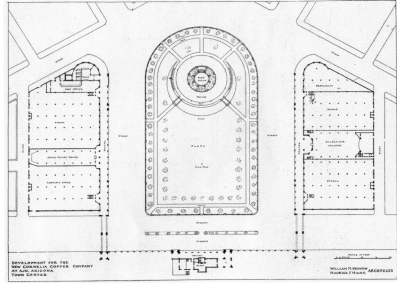

2

1. Plan, William M. Kenyon and Maurice R. Maine, 1916. A19

2. Plan of town center. A19

3, 4. Typical houses for American workers. A19 (c. 1918)

5. Hospital and houses for American workers. A19 (c. 1918)

6. Plaza. A19 (c. 1918)

7. View from plaza showing Church of the Immaculate Conception, George Washington Smith, 1924–26, right, Federated Protestant Church, Leslie J. Mahoney, 1927, left, and school, Leslie J. Mahoney, 1919–26, in distance. Boozer. FL (2007)

8. Greenway house, George Washington Smith, 1924–26. Perry. ACC (2008)

3

4

5

6

7

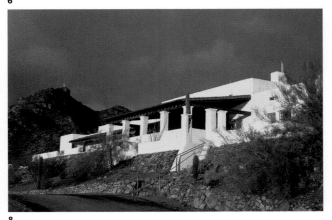

8

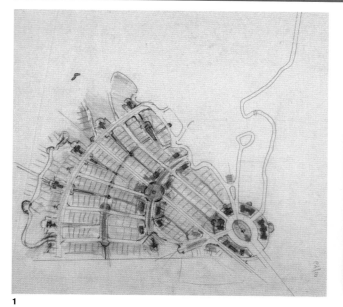

1. Study, Bernard Maybeck, 1913–15. BMC

2. Hotel. Cardwell. KCC (1973)

3. Plan, Bernard Maybeck, 1913–15. BMC

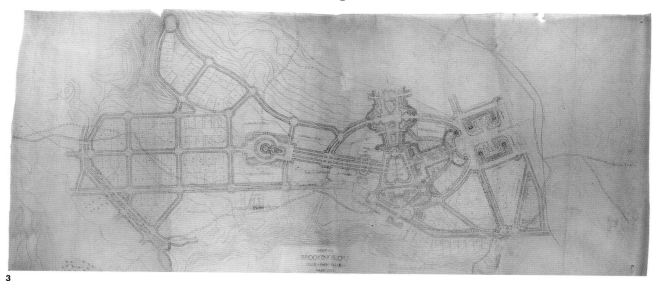

the Spanish Colonial style, Smith provided a low-slung adobe hacienda (1924–26) located on a hill overlooking the town. His inventive Church of the Immaculate Conception (1924–26), placed on a wedge-shaped site west of the plaza, featured a wood-frame dome originally intended to be covered in multicolored tiles until budget constraints intervened. A year after its completion, the Roman Catholic church was joined across the street by a Protestant adobe chapel designed by Leslie J. Mahoney (1892–1985). Unlike Tyrone, Ajo managed to survive and prosper. In 1931, five years after Greenway's death, the mining operations and the town were purchased by Phelps Dodge, which did not neglect its upkeep. As Gebhard noted in 1986, "the character of the town as a planned garden city persists."[169]

The 1913 design for the lumber town of **Brookings**, Oregon, by Bernard Maybeck (1862–1957) represents one of the San Francisco architect's few forays into town planning.[170] He had recently entered the competition to design the Australian capital of Canberra, but it was his scheme for the Palace of Fine Arts at San Francisco's

Panama-Pacific Exposition (1915) that probably brought him to the attention of J. E. Brookings (1846–1929), a mill owner who was expanding from Oakland, California, to southern Oregon's coastal timberlands. Initially asked to design workers' houses and a few community buildings, Maybeck convinced Brookings that a master plan was in order for the village whose population was expected to reach 2,500. The site, perched above a bay on the Pacific Ocean near the mouth of the Chetco River, included a gently sloping plateau between the ocean bluffs and mountains. Maybeck retained steeper hillsides as parkland and situated public spaces around wooded knolls. Though isolated, the area was scheduled to receive a branch line of the North-Western Pacific Railway.

In a series of detailed studies, Maybeck, a graduate of the École des Beaux-Arts, called for a monumental procession of formal squares and parks leading axially from the site's highest point, reserved for a trapezoidal civic center based on Michelangelo's Campidoglio in Rome, southeast through an elliptical park at the heart of a residential district, and on to a circular terrace commanding

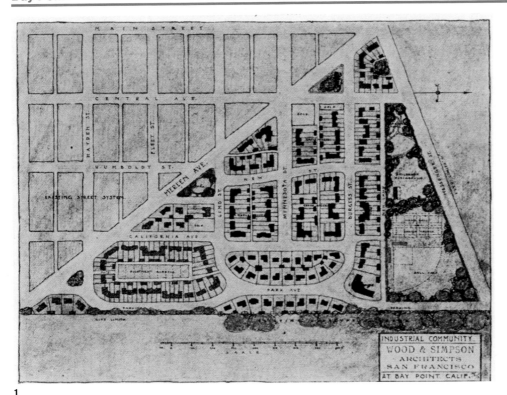

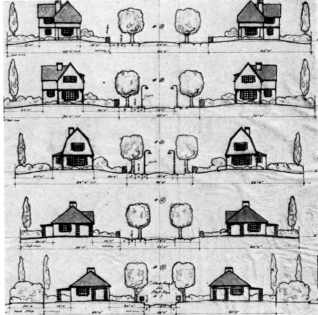

1. Plan, Wood & Simpson, 1918.
ARB18

2. Typical street sections. ARB18
(1918)

3. Semidetached house. ARB18
(1918)

dramatic views down the coast. A secondary axis led northeast from the civic center along an elaborately landscaped boulevard to another residential neighborhood combining curving and rectilinear streets. Maybeck softened the gridded areas by treating each intersection as a circle. Because foot traffic would predominate, a separate network of pedestrian paths, including a highly ornate stair, was provided to connect the residential blocks with the civic center as well as a commercial district that buffered the village from the mill.

Maybeck's planning stretched out for years, requiring the interim construction of modest houses and temporary community buildings, including a store, mess hall, company offices, and hotel. By the time plans were completed in 1922, the town had developed around a simplified central circle with four radial avenues. The mill's unexpected closure in 1925 led to the project's demise. Unrelated to the mill's failure, the planned extension of the North-Western Pacific Railway never occurred while U.S. Highway 101, which Maybeck had intended to skirt the town, was instead built through its heart, obscuring the realized portion of the plan that was later largely obliterated by industrial redevelopment. Some early cottages remain, reflecting two or three of more than fifteen distinct house types that Maybeck prepared. With unpainted cedar-shake cladding and hip roofs, the cottages, lining

unpaved roads, for a time gave the impression of a seaside resort. Maybeck also prepared designs for double houses as well as groups situated around garden courts, but these were never built. Ironically, the temporary hotel "more properly described as a dormitory for mill hands than a hostelry of elegance"—according to Maybeck's biographer Kenneth H. Cardwell—remains.[171]

In 1917 the Pacific Electro Metals Company, a newly established manufacturer, opened a smelting plant on Suison Bay at **Bay Point**, California, thirty-six miles northeast of San Francisco.[172] With housing scarce, the company asked Beckman & Linden, the engineering firm responsible for the factory design, to plan a workers' village and design its buildings. The engineers demurred, believing the job was outside their expertise, and instead recommended the San Francisco–based firm of Hart Wood (1880–1957) and Horace G. Simpson (1881–1955). The fledgling industrial concern, mindful of cash flow, reluctantly agreed and directed the architects to find a suitable location for a subdivision intended for about 200 workers and their families. Wood & Simpson selected a triangular parcel just south of the tracks of the Bay Point & Clayton Railroad and two miles north of the Emergency Fleet Corporation–sponsored town of Clyde, a site that Ralph F. Warner, writing in *Architectural Review*, believed was the best possible choice:

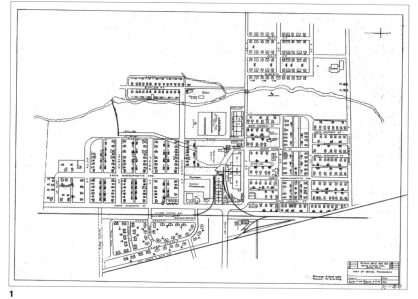

"Setting against the hill, the little town of Bay Point slopes gently down toward the bay. Although practically devoid of foliage as a whole, there are wooded areas at two opposite corners of the town. To serve as a background, as well as to obtain shelter from the wind, which blows constantly, the site was selected near one of these groves of trees on the edge of the town."[173]

Wood & Simpson's "artistic and informal" grouping of semidetached and detached houses broke with Bay Point's prevailing grid.[174] By closing the vistas of Lind, Minnesota, and Burgess Streets with an elliptical grouping of houses on Park Avenue, which faced the most built-up section of Bay Point, the plan convincingly created the feel of a place apart, an ambience furthered by the large, trapezoidal park located at the northern end of the site, designed to provide a buffer from the railroad and factory beyond. The largest group of houses was to be built around an allotment garden, and the plan also featured several additional small triangular parks. The one- and two-story four- to seven-room stucco, clapboard, and shingle cottages were basic fare, but Wood & Simpson avoided monotony and achieved a certain measure of charm by the judicious mixing of roof types, including gambrel, hip, and gable examples.

In June 1919, with fifty houses completed, Pacific Electro Metals was forced to close the factory, a victim of a severe drop in the chrome and manganese market. No additional houses were completed according to the original plan. A two-story Tudor-style clubhouse designed by Hart Wood, who later became one of Hawaii's leading architects, also remained unrealized. In 1969, after a protracted battle between the federal government and local residents, the Bay Point subdivision and 600 surrounding houses were demolished to make way for an expansion of the Port Chicago Naval Station.

Having first established a foothold in the South during the 1840s, textile manufacturing began to migrate to the region from New England in earnest during the late 1880s, attracted by cheap land and power, low taxes, proximity to raw materials, and, most important, an abundance of inexpensive labor. The vast majority of the mills, located in remote locations, built their own villages, leading planning historian Dean Sinclair to describe the textile village as "the predominant planned urban form of the post-Reconstruction South."[175]

Often overlooked, **Bemis**, Tennessee, was begun in 1900, thirty-five years after Judson Moss Bemis (1833–1926), founder of the Bemis Brothers Bag Company, first determined that in order to ensure a dependable supply of cotton for his bag factories located in various cities, the company needed to build and operate its own cotton mill.[176] The impetus to build a model

1. Plan. BEHI (1966)

2. Overall view, Bicycle Hill. BEHI (1907)

3. Overall view. BEHI (1907)

4, 5. Typical views. JJackson. JJ (2012)

workers' village came from Bemis's son, Albert Farwell Bemis (1870–1936), who upon graduating from the Massachusetts Institute of Technology in 1893 with a degree in civil engineering went to work in the company's Boston office, heading the Engineering Division in charge of plant construction. The younger Bemis's increasing involvement in the family business—he took over as president in 1909, remaining in that position until 1925—was paralleled by his growing activity in the field of housing. In 1916, he was asked to serve on the Council of National Defense, a Presidential advisory commission charged with the oversight of domestic war emergency activities that included the establishment of the United States Housing Corporation (USHC). In 1918, Bemis formed The Housing Company, a design-build firm that he staffed with former MIT classmates and Boston colleagues. One of their first projects was workers' housing in Bemis, Tennessee, but the company's focus would shift to the development of modular housing systems. In addition to supporting the research of others, Bemis coauthored with John Ely Burchard a three-volume study, *The Evolving House*, published between 1933 and his death in 1936.[177]

Bemis, Tennessee's 300-acre site, three miles south of Jackson on either side of Cane Creek, was chosen for its proximity to raw materials, rail lines, and an ample labor supply. Anxious to attract development, Madison County donated the land to the Jackson Fibre Company, a Bemis subsidiary, for the purpose. As built over a twenty-six-year period, each of the village's five residential neighborhoods, surrounding a central mill complex, was "distinctive in its architectural and environmental character to an extraordinary degree, reflecting the conscious effort of the community's planners to avoid the unending regularity and inhumanity of the stereotypical mill village," as John Linn Hopkins wrote in his nomination of Bemis to the National Register of Historic Places.[178] Over time, the village also gained a full complement of community and public facilities around the mill including an administration building that doubled as a city hall and hospital, an auditorium, laundry, YMCA, stores, and schools. A six-hole golf course was installed at the site's western edge, and two ponds adjacent to the factory afforded fire protection. After 1910, a portion of one pond was used as a swimming pool with a bathhouse but was later filled in for the construction of a warehouse.

The first three neighborhoods, frequently referred to as "Old Bemis," built in tandem with the factory between 1900 and 1905, were planned by Albert Bemis working with Charles A. Tripp (1870–1930), an MIT classmate, and the engineering firm of Lockwood, Green and Company. North of the mill, Old Bemis comprised fourteen rectangular blocks containing roughly seventy gable-fronted houses set back on wide, paved, tree-lined streets and serviced by unpaved rear alleys carrying many of the utilities. Some variation was provided by orienting three central blocks on an east–west axis in opposition to the neighboring north–south blocks. Car-barns—small garages with outhouses—were clustered together at the rear lot lines. Comfortably sized yards provided ample space for gardens, but the company also offered larger garden plots and cattle pens near the mill.

The second residential section, New Bemis, also known as Bicycle Hill, was built for upper management on the site's highest ground to the south of the mill. With rectangular blocks flanking South Massachusetts Avenue, the neighborhood had a similar feel to Old Bemis, but each street featured a grassy median planted with ornamental shrubs and trees that have since been stripped away. The third area of housing included twenty-seven residences and a school for black employees lining Congo Street (later renamed Butler Street). Although segregated, the area featured similar landscape characteristics, including street trees, planting strips, and large yards. While their authorship is uncertain, more than thirty distinct house types were included in the first phase, primarily shotgun, double-shotgun, L-plan, hall-and-parlor, and cubical cottages that "appear to be directly derived from types considered traditional to the Southern region," according to Hopkins, though certain features, such as high roof pitches and gambrel and jerkinhead roofs, "suggest the hand of a non-local designer."[179]

After World War I, development in Bemis reflected the examples provided by the Emergency Fleet Corporation and the United States Housing Corporation. The Silver Circle addition, built in 1920–22, included fifteen duplex and twenty-four single-family houses planned and designed by The Housing Company's consulting architect, Arthur Shurtleff, whose recent work included the USHC projects in Bridgeport and, a half-dozen years earlier, the Lake Point group in Hopedale, Massachusetts, which similarly marked a new pattern in that mill village's residential development. Located east of the mill, beyond the tracks of the Illinois Central Gulf Railroad, Silver Circle had previously been platted as a grid, but the construction of a second railroad line through the site, decreasing its size by two-thirds and giving it a more challenging triangular shape, prompted Shurtleff's plan combining angled and gently curving streets. Houses along the tree-lined Young, Judson, Heron, and Farwell Streets were set back 30 feet from the curb and driveways were provided in pairs. A majority of the site was given over to a central, oval-shaped block in which rear alleys were eliminated in favor of backyards that, according to Hopkins, produced "something of a communal open space, shared by all houses lining the exterior perimeter," a feature that remained even after the residences were sold to employees in 1965.[180]

The development of Silver Circle was accompanied by an overall upgrading of the town also carried out by The Housing Company, including improved sewer and water systems and indoor plumbing for all existing houses. Andrew H. Hepburn (1880–1967), who had collaborated with Shurtleff in Bridgeport, designed a new civic center northeast of the plant with a central grassy commons faced by a new auditorium (1922), administration building (1920), and unbuilt hotel. The last phase of residential development, West Bemis, built in 1926, reverted to a simple grid, presumably because of its level, featureless site. With automobile use on the rise, rear alleys were again eliminated and shared driveways were provided. Tennessee architect Reuben A. Heavner (b. 1875) designed the more than sixty duplex and single-family houses.

By the mid-1960s construction to the east and north of Bemis meant that "the town no longer has complete exposure to open countryside." Nonetheless, James A. Spencer, a Tennessee urban planner, could report that it had not been "radically altered since the mid-twenties" and "the internal physical character of the town has changed little." Spencer identified Bemis as Tennessee's "oldest 'new town,'" noting,

> [It] is obvious that Bemis was built for the pedestrian. Few residences are more than half a mile from the centrally located community facilities and mill. Sidewalks were built on both sides of every street at the time of initial construction, or soon thereafter . . . Age has not damaged the appearance of the town. The buildings reflect a policy of careful maintenance. The lawns are neatly clipped and vegetation, including beautiful trees which line the streets, is impressive. Well developed groupings of shrubbery are located at strategic intersections and in grass medians of the streets. A sense of order is evident in the town. Each residential area has its own style and texture. The repetition of building designs and materials give a sense of harmony, yet there is sufficient variety in the treatment of facades and in building sizes to avoid monotony. It is worthy of note that there are no fences in the residential areas . . . The rear yards have a character somewhat akin to common open spaces found in modern subdivision designs. Bemis presents an impressive contrast to the chaotic development which many communities have experienced since the turn of the century. It provides a pleasing environment and the town functions well in the twentieth century.[181]

Earle S. Draper, born in Falmouth, Massachusetts, the grandson of a cotton mill owner and a relative of the Draper family associated with Hopedale, revolutionized the standards of Southern textile village planning. After graduating with a degree in landscape architecture from Massachusetts Agricultural College (later University of Massachusetts) in 1915, Draper began his career in the Cambridge, Massachusetts, office of John Nolen, who within three months asked him to relocate to Charlotte, North Carolina, to develop the design of Myers Park (see p. 155) and Kingsport, Tennessee (see p. 264). In 1917 Draper took up residence in Myers Park and opened his own office in Charlotte, establishing what is believed to be the first professional city-planning firm in the Southeast. Draper's neighbors included prominent textile families who turned to him hoping, as Margaret Crawford has written, that his "planning expertise could produce a new type of mill village, one that would reconcile their economic aims with growing local criticism of village conditions and the continuing restlessness of the mill workers."[182]

Between 1917 and 1933, with satellite branches in Atlanta, Washington, D.C., and New York, Draper designed more than 100 suburbs and 150 mill villages across the South, as well as college campuses, private estates, parks, and cemeteries. As the South's foremost expert on industrial village design, the high demand for his work allowed him to turn away commissions that did not meet his minimum requirements for roads, utilities, and sanitary conditions. While Draper's work for Nolen embraced Beaux-Arts planning principles, his own designs hewed closer to Olmsted's naturalism: "I was of the old school, the Olmsted school," he later explained, "that said that the best and finest use of the land is the most important thing and that all developments should be keyed to the land itself."[183] He was also a student of the Garden City movement, both from a formal and theoretical standpoint, hoping—albeit with a good measure of skepticism—that workers might one day "carry on themselves, take over the government of the villages, and gradually develop into proprietors themselves."[184] To help assimilate textile workers, who were typically drawn from an uneducated rural population, Draper endeavored to introduce, Crawford suggests, "a microcosm of the Piedmont landscape in every village."[185] Draper wrote of the workers: "Usually intensely individualistic, they retain the love of their mountain cottage, and dislike living under any conditions which do not give them the right to live in a single-family home and control the plot of ground about them . . . To bring such people into a mill village of a fairly attractive type is like advancing them one or more generations in the standard of living."[186]

Draper's textile village work ran the gamut from small improvements of existing settlements to the planning and development of new mill towns. In 1917, he added on to the village of **Erlanger Mills**, in Lexington, North Carolina, where fabric was made for the BVD brand of underwear.[187] Draper expanded a four-year-old gridded neighborhood with fourteen irregular blocks to provide space for over 100 shingled bungalows that were designed under his supervision by the Greenville, South Carolina–based J. E. Sirrine & Co., one of the South's major textile-mill engineering firms. Two semicircular roads—Rainbow Street (later First Rainbow Street) and Snow Street (later Second Rainbow Street)—closed the northern end of the grid. Draper proposed a community center on axis with Broad Street, a north–south spine with a wide grassy median, but it was not built, nor was a pond and a network of curving residential streets that he envisioned to the west of the grid. The houses were held by the company until 1953, when they were sold to individual owners.

At **Laurens Cotton Mills**, in Laurens, South Carolina, the mill buildings were retained but old shacks were

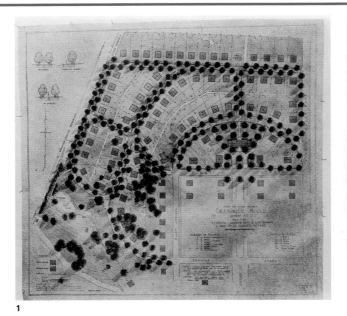

demolished, and a new street pattern, heavily planted with trees and incorporating a variety of small parks and an existing lake, was established. In 1918, Draper planned **Pacolet Mills Village**, South Carolina, a new residential village replacing an earlier settlement that had been destroyed by a flood.[188] Here, without the constraints of an existing road network, Draper was able to implement more of the fundamental components of his design philosophy, distancing and visually screening the new neighborhoods from the existing mill and surrounding the village with a greenbelt. North and east of the mill on either side of the Pacolet River, two residential hillside sites were planned to take advantage of river views, with Draper making extensive use of local stone for retaining walls, steps, and terraces. He also included a scenic overlook above the dam, with a series of steps and landings leading down to the riverbank, and a network of open spaces incorporating an amphitheater set within a secluded two-level park. In addition, the town included two churches, a mill office, and a company store.

The houses were not the typical vernacular frame dwellings of most mill villages but Craftsman-style single- and two-family bungalows designed by J. Frank Collins (1883–1969), a North Carolina native who prepared five distinct types with several variations of each. As described in a 1927 article in *Nation's Health*, a visitor to Pacolet Mills Village "might believe he was in a suburb of a modern American city to judge from the appearance of the streets, homes, and surrounding yards."[189] The housing was sold in 1955 and the mill was shut down in 1983, its buildings demolished. However, the village remains and was designated a National Register Historic District in 2007.

Chicopee (1925), Georgia, was Draper's most successful textile village, and his last.[190] Located about four miles south of Gainesville, Georgia, and fifty miles northeast of Atlanta, it was built by the Chicopee Manufacturing Corporation, a subsidiary of the Johnson & Johnson Company, to produce surgical and sanitary dressings. The mill was to supplement production at the company's plant in Chicopee Falls, Massachusetts, for which the new town was named. Chicopee most fully captured Draper's principles in a set of near-perfect circumstances. The generously funded project benefited from Johnson & Johnson's concern for the welfare of its workers. Given the nature of the goods being produced, the company had an interest in maintaining a sanitary, healthy, and stable environment. As Draper wrote: "The general plan represents a solution of a problem which comes as near being ideal in the relation of the street circulation to the mill and town center, satisfactory adjustment of the block and lot plan to the topography, and the provision for open areas, as I have ever seen worked out . . . The improvements to be carried out from this plan, when completed, will make it the best example of the well built, completely developed textile community in the South."[191]

Laurens Cotton Mills

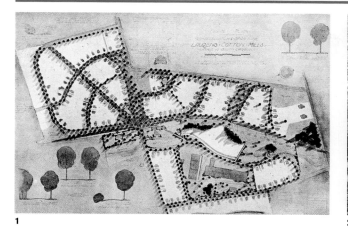

Pacolet Mills Village

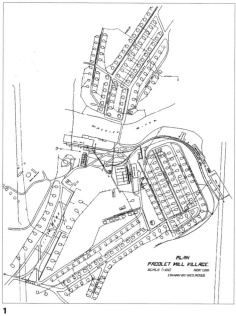

Draper began design work on Chicopee in 1925 and construction got under way in 1927, giving him enough time to shape nearly every aspect of the town, beginning with the selection of the site, which represented a significant departure from standard practice. While plant engineers typically chose flat, easily cleared tracts, Draper, seeking to connect the workers with their mountain roots, chose a heavily wooded, topographically varied, 4,000-acre site, persuading Johnson & Johnson to use only 250 acres for the town and several hundred more for the mill while reserving most of the rest as a partly forested and partly agricultural greenbelt surrounding virtually the entire settlement.

The site was strategically located near the main line of the Southern Railway, which formed its northern boundary. It was bisected longitudinally by the Atlanta Highway leading through Gainesville to Atlanta, a thoroughfare that Draper adopted as a dividing line, placing the mill to its west and the village to its east. At Chicopee, for the first time in a Southern textile village, the

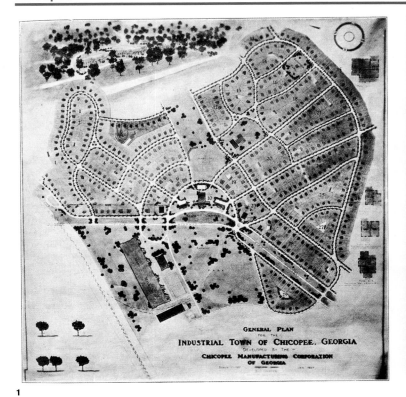

1

2

1. Plan, Earle S. Draper, 1927. LA27

2. Aerial view. ENSC

3, 4. Typical streets. Adkisson. DA
(2012)

3

4

mill was not the focal point. Instead, it was set back from the highway on a high knoll that helped screen it from view. As landscape architect and historian Norman T. Newton has observed, "The factory setting was visually peaceful, consisting chiefly of green lawn and trees—a refreshing scene that characterized other Johnson & Johnson installations in later years."[192] Moreover, according to Margaret Crawford, the physical marginalization of the mill made it no longer seem like "a necessary condition for the village's existence."[193]

Taking the place of the mill in the heart of the village was a town center featuring a community building, stores, and churches on a semicircular block east of the highway. Draper was finally able to employ a radial street system, "theoretically ideal," because it allowed for direct access between the center and the residential neighborhoods, "although rarely ever practical, on account of topographic features, existing streets or highways, railroad, etc."[194]

Fanning east from the center, the plan included two residential neighborhoods to the north and south of a large park that connected with the perimeter greenbelt and accommodated athletic fields, picnic areas, and pathways. A school occupied an adjacent park-like block to the south and additional open spaces were worked into the residential areas. According to Crawford, "the town center's intersection with the belt of recreation space and parkland formed the conceptual and aesthetic lynchpin of . . . the plan, suggesting that the village had an existence independent of the mill and encouraging a community identity separate from the workplace."[195] Comparing Chicopee's "combination of a formal center with informal housing areas" to Indian Hill and Tyrone, Crawford states "Chicopee's center lacks the sense of enclosure . . . to convey urbanity. Instead, Draper emphasized the openness of the site, setting the village in the center of a large area of open parkland."[196]

Draper provided roughly 500 residential lots to accommodate a population of 2,000. Individual parcels varied in size and shape but averaged 65 by 130 feet, allowing for private rear gardens and wide side yards. Houses featured uniform front setbacks of 40 feet. The streets were 44 feet wide with 20-foot-wide paved roadways. Trees were planted in thick rows to provide shaded sidewalks. To accommodate automobiles, which were increasingly available even to lower-paid mill workers, Draper discreetly placed group garages on the block interiors. To mitigate the effect of automobile traffic along the main highway, he provided a wide right-of-way and parallel local roads accessing the town center and residential streets. Draper also suggested that communal livestock pens be provided but, mindful of the importance of cleanliness, the company decided instead to operate a model dairy farm and provide free milk to households. Power lines and utilities were placed underground, while the street inclines were engineered, along with gutters and storm drains, to confront the drainage challenges presented by the red clay soil.

After ten years, 217 houses were built. Although J. E. Sirrine & Co. prepared the architectural designs, Draper exerted a strong influence over the thirty-one distinct types of primarily four-room, but also three-, five-, six-, and seven-room, low-slung, single-family bungalows atypically clad in brick veneer rather than wood, with stuccoed gables, varied roof styles, and front and back porches. Norman T. Newton called the dwellings "unpretentious . . . structures in neat and pleasantly kept grounds."[197] The bungalow type, according to Crawford, had larger social implications for Southern mill workers: they "removed much of the stigma attached to easily identifiable mill houses, suggesting equality between mill workers and their urban neighbors."[198] Black workers at the company's plant were not provided for in Chicopee, but left to commute from Gainesville or elsewhere.

Early concerns, as Newton has written, that the "highly individualistic Georgia hill folk would not take kindly to the new living conditions offered, that there would be a feverishly rapid labor turnover, and that accordingly this would never be a settled community with a stable work force," were shown to be off mark: "Again the power of design had proved itself in the quiet contentment of this tree-shaded industrial town."[199] Comey and Wehrly called Chicopee the "best, although not the largest, of the mill villages" that they visited in the South.

Important features of Draper's plan were not realized, including the schoolhouse and the town center, though both sites were "maintained in open well-kept lawns." As well, some residential sections remained undeveloped but were given to employees for use as garden plots. Nonetheless, Comey and Wehrly reported that development "closely followed the original plan" and that "even in its immature state, Chicopee has a charm which is the result of good planning and landscape treatment. The houses are not architecturally beautiful but enough variation has been introduced into

HOUSING
THE SHIPBUILDERS

Constructed During the War
Under the Direction of

UNITED STATES SHIPPING BOARD
EMERGENCY FLEET CORPORATION
PASSENGER TRANSPORTATION AND
HOUSING DIVISION

PHILADELPHIA, PA.
MCMXX

1

their exterior lines to add interest; and this, together with the plantings, which are still small, the well-aligned streets and the large areas of well-maintained lawn give a charm and character to the town which should increase with maturity." As for the buffer, Comey and Wehrly saw the proof of its effectiveness in "the poor development which has taken place where it is lacking, at the point immediately adjacent to the railroad right-of-way" in the northwest, "and continuing sporadically to Gainesville."[200] Thirty years later, planning historian Mel Scott considered Chicopee to be "among the outstanding industrial towns of the period."[201]

A BOLD EXPERIMENT: INDUSTRIAL VILLAGES FOR VICTORY, 1917–20

Emergency Fleet Corporation

On April 17, 1917, eleven days after America's entry into World War I, President Woodrow Wilson (1856–1924) signed legislation creating the Emergency Fleet Corporation (EFC), a federal agency charged with addressing the nation's shortage of military and passenger vessels, a "ship famine" deemed so severe that it imperiled the country's chances of victory.[202] Administratively, the EFC was a component of the United States Shipping Board, established one year earlier to regulate the shipping industry as well as support the development of the merchant marine. Responding to the demand, major shipbuilders complained to the government that they were hampered in their efforts to increase production because of a transient and unstable workforce, a situation exacerbated, if not created, by a lack of adequate housing. As Sylvester Baxter wrote in *Architectural Record*: "A chief impediment in the work was the impossibility of securing workers in sufficient numbers and quality. The labor-turnover was enormous; the prodigious losses in time, money and energy from this source were fairly incalculable. The great want of homes for the workers near their work was at the root of the problem."[203]

It was not only the shortage of housing for shipyard workers but also the dismal quality of what did exist that increased the problem of attracting and retaining qualified workers. The editors of the *Journal of the American Institute of Architects* described the era's typical shipyard housing: "Beds worked three shifts, and several beds were crowded into a room. Men lived in tents and cooked their food in holes in the earth."[204] With speculative builders unwilling or unable to meet the housing demand, stymied not only by the sheer number of new units required but also by rapidly rising costs and material shortages, the EFC stepped in and created the Division of Housing and Passenger Transportation to develop workers' villages in forty-seven different cities, a bold initiative that was also highly controversial given the many members of Congress who did not believe in the federal government's involvement in providing housing of any kind beyond cantonment facilities for the army. Along with concurrent programs to provide war workers' housing from the Ordnance Department and the newly created United States Housing Corporation, a division of the Labor Department, the EFC proposal not only represented the nation's first foray into public housing, but also, in the eyes of many—especially considering the left-leaning politics of the Garden City movement in England—the thin edge of the Socialists' sword.

Led by A. Merritt Taylor (1874–1937), former Transit Commissioner of Philadelphia, the EFC was granted broad powers to accomplish its goals, including the right to seize private property, whether occupied or not, and commandeer any transportation facility; the agency also had a direct line of access to the War Industries Board, the authority in charge of allocating scarce building materials. According to the *New York Times*, there was "practically no limitation on the extent to which the Fleet Corporation may go in order to provide comfortable homes for the employees at reasonable prices."[205] Taylor selected architects Frederick L. Ackerman and Robert D. Kohn (1870–1953) to head the Fleet Corporation's housing division and oversee the planning and design of the new towns. Ackerman, who had been sent by the American Institute of Architects to study workers' housing in England in the spring of 1917, strongly advocated a community-building approach, with the construction of permanent,

substantial houses accompanied by the provision of significant civic components, a position that put him at odds with some members of the EFC as well as others in the federal government who believed that the priority should be in erecting adequate dwellings as quickly as possible. Ackerman argued that "the scale of the operation requires the use of such a vast amount of material and so many elements of a permanent character, such as streets, public utilities, etc., which must be provided in any case, that it would be sheer madness to attempt to solve this problem by the erection of temporary barracks; madness, because it would end in an utter waste of housing—and we shall need a vast number of new homes when our armies return from France; madness, because experience has already shown us that temporary accommodations will not bring to the shipyard the skilled mechanic with a family."[206]

The EFC sent out questionnaires to shipbuilding yards to gauge housing needs, following up the surveys with field investigations. Although towns were planned for sites across the country, including in Ohio, Wisconsin, and California, given that the war was being fought in Europe, the majority of the new towns were intended for the East Coast, with a particular concentration around the Delaware Valley. Financed by a $75 million appropriation from Congress granted in March 1918, the EFC's preferred method of development was to fund newly created realty companies composed of shipyard owners, who often provided the land for the project, and other local businessmen. The EFC maintained complete control of the projects, including the determination of fair rental prices. The EFC also used its substantial powers to help ensure the success of the new housing in other ways, encouraging worker stability by mandating uniform wages for all shipyards and granting blanket deferments to those who remained on the job.

Within a few months of receiving its appropriation, the EFC had made substantial progress on the building of twenty-seven communities. But the rapid pace of construction was interrupted by the surprisingly quick end to hostilities with the signing of the armistice on November 11, 1918, in a railway carriage in Compiègne Forest in northern France, leaving the government in a predicament about its next step. Should the EFC continue construction on all planned projects or only those near completion? Or should all work be halted entirely? And what should happen to the housing already completed? President Wilson weighed in, writing in a letter to the chairman of the Shipping Board that "it would seem a distinct loss to allow the sale of these properties without imposing such restrictions and safeguards as will preserve the ideal industrial living conditions which we have sought to establish." Wilson, who was disposed toward completing projects already under way, directed the agency to investigate "how far practical and beneficial restrictions could be imposed to prevent these very modern and ideal communities from being lost as examples of what the homes of industrial workers ought to be."[207]

Raising the specter of creeping Socialism, loud voices in Congress demanded that the federal government immediately cease constructing housing, believed by some to be excessively generous to workers, and to quickly sell those units already completed. With the emergency over, they reasoned, the EFC should end its involvement in the private sector. Electus D. Litchfield (1872–1952), architect of perhaps the finest of the new industrial villages, Yorkship Village, countered this argument by stating that "these workmen's towns . . . are a God-given opportunity for combating Bolshevism. How can a man be discontented when his Government is mobilizing the best talent in the country to provide for his comfort."[208] In the end, congressional leaders carried the day and the EFC, as well as the United States Housing Corporation (the Ordnance Department's housing arm had earlier been taken over by the Housing Corporation), were ordered out of the housing business. In December 1918, one month after the end of the war, Congress required that all work stop on developments less than 75 percent complete and seven months later all finished dwellings were put up for sale for either individual or group purchase. All told, 8,644 single-family houses, 849 apartments, 94 dormitories, 8 hotels, and 6 boardinghouses were completed in twenty-seven towns, accommodating 28,064 shipyard workers and their families for a total of 55,308 people. As Robert Kohn succinctly put it in May 1919: "It may be said, fairly enough, that as a civic problem the war has put housing 'on the map' in this country."[209] By the mid-1920s most of the houses had been sold at a substantial loss, although the inflated costs of building during the war was a contributing factor to their seeming economic failure.

In his 1941 study of the EFC housing developments, John L. Tierney (1892–1972), a Federal Housing Administrative executive, took pains to applaud the high quality of design achieved at many of the villages, regretting the abrupt dissolution of the pioneering program, and concluding that its "commendable accomplishments were forgotten."[210] Half a century later, historian Kristin Szylvian also lavished praise on the planning and architecture of particular villages while pointing out the EFC's failure to usher in a new era of political activism and social responsibility: "What is clear is that although an increase in state and local government involvement in housing did occur on some fronts, the goals of industrial housing reformers remained unrealized. Not until the onset of the Great Depression and the creation of the New Deal by President Franklin D. Roosevelt would reformers receive a second opportunity to join forces with the federal government in promoting housing reform for working people."[211]

Despite its short life, the EFC housing program marks a milestone in the history of American town planning, introducing on a large scale and to a class hitherto largely excluded from it many of the best practices of the garden suburb and garden city. Ackerman and Kohn, assisted by Henry Wright and Philadelphia engineer B. A. Haldeman (1867–1955), selected prominent architects and planners to design the new villages, closely supervising their planning and construction but imposing no specific stylistic direction, although encouraging the various architects to look to local traditions for inspiration. As a result, the EFC program produced plans for, and realized significant parts of, some of the most successful workers' housing ever realized in the United States, and comparable to the best then available in England and Germany. The program thereby demonstrated the value of the garden village idea and its potential to benefit not only the upper middle classes fleeing the industrialized inner city but also those, as it were, left behind.

As early as May 1919, planner and landscape architect Karl B. Lohmann (1887–1963) assessed the impact of the recently halted program, writing in the pages of *The American City* that "it has been a huge undertaking and one that will have an incalculable influence for years to come on the growing communities of this country . . . In general it has given an impetus to sensible thinking and has removed forever in this country the customary premium on slipshod, hit-or-miss practices in the laying out of cities."[212] In his 1950 eulogy for Ackerman, published in the *Journal of the American Institute of Architects*, Lewis Mumford credited him with "the remarkable quality of the work that the Shipping Board so promptly turned out," adding that "without his work on the Shipping Board, it is safe to say that the housing and planning movement would have lost some of the main footings for the work done in the twenties and still more in the thirties," citing as an example, "Sunnyside Gardens [see p. 190], that experimental project . . . which grew so directly out of Government war housing."[213]

Francesco Dal Co, writing in 1973, though disappointed that the efforts of the EFC "produced only a model, extremely rich in potential but deficient in immediate results," nonetheless recognized that "the experiences of the war years eventually proved invaluable during another period of emergency, after 1929 and during the New Deal. Moreover, the 'war villages' may be considered an embryonic expression of that mixed economy about which certain reformers would construct an original theory and form new proposals, which would ultimately be put into operation in the 1930s, even if only partially."[214]

The most highly regarded of the EFC undertakings, **Yorkship Village** (1918), now known as Fairview in honor of a subsidiary of the New York Shipbuilding Company, the Fairview Realty Company, was organized to house workers at its Camden, New Jersey, shipyard.[215] The architect and planner was Electus D. Litchfield, a lifelong New Yorker, working with his associate, Pliny Rogers (1882–1930). Litchfield drew inspiration from French academic as well as English garden suburb planning, combining formal axes with closed street views, grouped houses, common open spaces, and a protective greenbelt.

The site, located one mile southeast of the shipyard, consisting of 225 acres of gently undulating, irregularly shaped farmland on the southern outskirts of Camden, was cut off from downtown and from neighboring

1. Plan, Electus D. Litchfield, 1918.
EFC

2. Aerial view. GE (2010)

3. Apartment house. EFC (c. 1919)

4, 5. Elevation sketches of house
groups. AA18

6. Overall view during construction.
NYSC (1918)

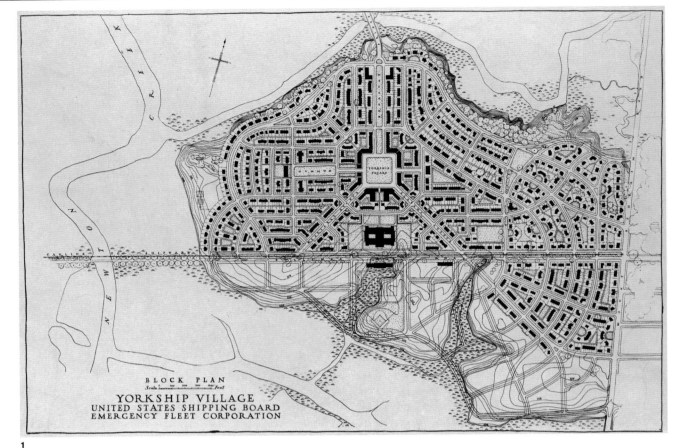

1

2

3

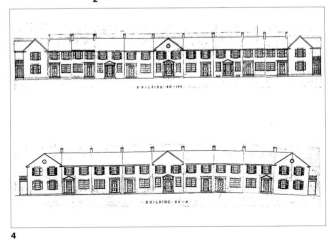

4

5

6

7

8

7, 8. Typical views. RAMSA (2007)

9. Rendering of Yorkship Square. JAIA18

10. Yorkship Square. RAMSA (2007)

11. Rendering of three-house group. HB18

12. Three-house group on Octagon Road. RAMSA (2007)

9

10

11

12

Gloucester by Newton Creek and the marshlands that formed its northern, western, and southern borders. Mt. Ephraim Pike, a north–south road connecting to Camden, formed the site's eastern boundary. The entire plot had space for 2,400 residential lots. The initial phase of construction, on 90 acres, called for the development of 907 houses, 821 of which were grouped in rows of three, four, five, and up to eleven units. A second phase of construction soon followed on 60 acres to the east, providing more than 100 detached, semidetached, and rowhouses in a variety of groupings along concentric curving streets.

At the heart of the town, Yorkship (originally Albemarle) Square, a 320-foot-square village green from which all of the principal streets, pedestrian paths, and public spaces radiated, was to be the focus of community life. Its

northwest and northeast corners were lined by two- and three-story L-shaped mixed-use blocks, with apartments located over stores, while the south side was to accommodate a community center with club rooms, movie theaters, and office space. A centrally located school occupied a large site to the south of the community center, within walking distance of any part of the village.

Workers could commute to the shipyard via a streetcar line on Collings Road, an east–west street tracing the southern edge of the plan, but the town's formal entrance was the 124-foot-wide Yorkship Avenue (originally Broadway), which brought pedestrians and automobiles in from the north, across Newton Creek, and terminated in Yorkship Square. From the west side of the square, a 125-foot-wide-by-450-foot-long axial landscaped common led to sites reserved for a civic building and two churches. Diagonal avenues extended from the square's southwest and southeast corners through an octagonal ring road to connect with Collings Road. The remaining streets, reserved for housing, were typically 50 feet wide with 18-foot-wide roadbeds. Curving streets were introduced toward the site's perimeter, where they followed the contours of Newton Creek, whose wooded banks were preserved as parkland.

The residential lots were small, ranging between 12 and 18 feet in width for units in the middle of a group and wider for those on the end. The sixty-three semi-detached houses realized in the first phase sat on 35-foot-wide lots, while the twenty-three detached houses enjoyed more generous 60-foot-wide parcels. The inclusion of 12-foot rear alleys limited the depth of the lots to about 70 feet, which was typical in the Philadelphia area. The 22-to-28-foot-deep houses set back 15 feet from the street left only 30 feet for rear yards. The size was no accident, as Litchfield explained: "The back yard is ever a presumptive point of untidiness and squalor" and was "therefore kept at the minimum with space only sufficient to provide adequately for drying the weekly wash."[216] Unfortunately, later residents crowded the backyards with garages.

Considering the speed at which the project had to be realized, the architectural quality was remarkably high. The buildings were executed in a comfortable Georgian Colonial style, inspired, according to Litchfield, by nearby examples in New Jersey and Pennsylvania as well as his own collection of more than 7,400 photographs of Colonial buildings.[217] The predominantly two- and three-story group houses, no more than two rooms deep in order to provide good light and ventilation, were arranged according to a process best described by the architect: "I hit upon the idea of having small-scale drawings made on slices of cardboard for different portions of a house—one for the middle, one for the right corner, one for the left, &c. By combining these slips like children's picture blocks so as to form a whole group-house, we obtained a surprising variety of combinations. As soon as particularly attractive combinations were made I had them photographed, and it is these selected combinations which will appear again and again at York-ship."[218] In all, there were 243 separate groups composed of 27 distinct house types arranged in 70 combinations. Included among the designs were units with 45-degree angles in plan, allowing the rows to turn corners. These were used with particularly strong effect at the intersections of Alabama and Kearsarge Avenues with Octagon Road, where three-family roughly crescent-shaped compositions were set back on each of the four corners.

The houses were well detailed, incorporating wooden shutters, porches, mullioned windows, and decorative moldings that made the village appear, as an early observer wrote, "like a beautiful old New England town instead of a put-up-while-you-wait industrial village."[219] The aged effect was enhanced by the use of transplanted mature trees, hedges, and bushes rather than nursery stock. Brick, the principal building material, was supplied from nine different manufacturers, each providing a slightly different shade of red "so there is no fear that the aspect of the village will be monotonous."[220] The order placed for eleven million bricks was claimed to have been the largest ever made. Only a few houses were of stucco on hollow terracotta block and one or two were of wood-frame construction. Single-pitch, gable, hip, flat, and combined gable and pitch roofs added variety, while changes in brick bonding patterns and color helped further individualize the designs. "Here is a little house in red brick with a green slate gable," Litchfield explained. "That house there in stucco with the red composition roof is just like it, although you would never notice the similarity. Here is the same plan again as part of a double house and there it appears at each end of a row of five. And there it is with a different porch and roof angle . . . I am painting some of the brick houses and using colored stuccos and I have seven different roofing materials to work with."[221]

Construction proceeded at breakneck pace. According to a July 14, 1918, report in the New York Times, one group of five houses was completed from foundation to roof in thirty-six hours.[222] Within eighteen months, approximately 1,400 houses were built on 179 acres as well as four apartment buildings, a hotel, school, gymnasium, garage, and more than a dozen stores. Absent from the mix was the community center that Litchfield had deemed "the one building which should have first been erected," bemoaning in late 1919 that "plans have been prepared, estimates have been obtained, and the money is available."[223] But his appeal for its construction fell on deaf ears and the site remained vacant along with various residential sites south of Collings Road and commercial sites near the north end of Yorkship Avenue, south of Collings Road, and in other peripheral areas, compromising the initial intention to realize a self-sufficient community.

When the federal government abandoned the EFC housing program, the town was prepared for auction in December 1921, with Litchfield shifting his energies from advocating for the plan's full build-out to ensuring that its integrity as a village be maintained, either through sale in its entirety to the shipbuilding company, which could operate it as a company town, or to a copartnership of residents, which he preferred. To that end he collaborated with planner Thomas Adams and tax expert Lawson Purdy on the preparation of a copartnership plan by which a Yorkship Village Company would be established to "operate it for, and sell it to, its inhabitants—not piecemeal, but as a whole."[224] But his efforts did not receive the necessary support, and during a three-day auction, said to be the largest real estate auction ever held in the United States, Yorkship Village's 1,574 houses were sold to individual bidders.

The town's zoning remained intact after the sale, with deed restrictions limiting the location of new commercial buildings to certain sites. But, according to Comey and Wehrly, who included Yorkship Village in their 1936 survey of planned communities, *herein lies the greatest failure in the well-conceived and executed scheme . . . No restrictions were imposed that subsequent development on vacant sites should be in keeping with the character already established. Had these vacant areas occurred only at the periphery, the subsequent results would not have been quite so disastrous . . . It may be a platitude to state that the more distinctive and unique the layout and architecture of a community, the less is required to throw the whole composition off balance, thus obtaining not only a less pleasing result by the introduction of incongruous elements but an actual shock and disappointment to the observer when the promise of a culminating feature or a harmonious pattern is suddenly dissipated. This is forcibly illustrated by such structures as have been subsequently "dumped" on the vacant areas at Yorkship Village. It brings home with renewed force the great desirability of a continuing agency to function not only during the formative stage of a development but defensively and in adaptation during the subsequent periods of its life.*

Noting in their report that a lack of maintenance had taken a toll on the houses, particularly evident in the "sagging and rotting conditions of many of the stoops" and in other wooden details such as the "delicately designed . . . cornices and porticos" that had likely never been repainted, Comey and Wehrly went on to criticize the village's almost fifty parks and open spaces, which were small and scattered and occupied only about 35 acres.[225] While some of the various triangular and semicircular parks may have helped, as Dal Co has written, "to resolve the more complex intersections of the street system,"[226] Comey and Wehrly found the green space, "varying in size from that of a front yard to that of the school grounds," to be "not functionally arranged for any use" and quite often "used for some unintended purpose" such as car parking.[227] Despite these shortcomings, Comey and Wehrly could not help but view the village as a cut above the norm: "Yorkship is a good place to observe what a well-designed community might have looked like with proper care. It has a charm which the general lack of maintenance of homes and yards and the intrusion of architectural monstrosities have not entirely destroyed."[228]

These charms became even more apparent as the century progressed. Despite periods of decline and neglect, the community fared well when compared to its surroundings, leading architectural historian Michael H. Lang to write in 1999 that Yorkship Village's "most notable success has been its ability, for the most part, to successfully resist being affected by the decline of Camden and the availability of nearby affordable suburban housing. While some small sections have managed to hold their value, most of Camden's other neighborhoods have experienced a severe decline in home values . . . In contrast, Yorkship Village has consistently experienced

an appreciating market for its housing units and the highest resale level in the city." Less disturbed by architectural intrusions than Comey and Wehrly, Lang concluded: "While there has been some encroachment, and some inappropriate infill development, Yorkship Village appears today much the same as when it was built; a bucolic country village in the city."[229]

The EFC also funded two shipbuilding communities in nearby Chester, Pennsylvania, fifteen miles southwest of Philadelphia, both on relatively small, expensive sites adjoining developed neighborhoods. **Buckman Village**, built for the Chester Shipbuilding Company, was planned by Philadelphia architect G. Edwin Brumbaugh (1890–1983) working with the Philadelphia firm of Edward Paul Simon (1875–1949) and David B. Bassett (n.d.), who designed the houses.[230] Unlike most EFC projects, Buckman Village was largely complete by the time the armistice was signed. Its 38-acre site, between Ninth and Thirteenth Streets, Clover and Meadow Lanes, was acquired from the Buckman family, who had built a country house there in 1902 before rapid industrial growth transformed the local landscape. The Buckman residence, at the southern edge of the property, was retained as a community center.

Brumbaugh's modified grid plan, adapted to meet the site's contours and connect to surrounding streets, featured elongated north–south blocks with rear alleys lined by 278 two-story, four- to six-room houses grouped in asymmetrical rows of between two and eight units each that stepped back and forth from the street to "simulate a more slowly developed community."[231] Twenty-three four-unit apartment houses were also built, placed at the southern end of town near a trolley stop at the intersection of Ninth Street and Keystone Road. Stores, a park, and a small commons were also grouped in the area to give the neighborhood a civic focus. A second trolley stop was provided farther west on Ninth Street to serve residents of the Buckman Inn, a 152-room redbrick, porticoed boardinghouse with a large dining room and recreational facilities.

Simon & Bassett's house types recognized "the delightful old farm and village groups which have survived from the days of the colonies in every eastern community . . . Rambling, picturesque, and of necessity, simple in detail, they have withstood neglect and changing 'styles,' and alone, of all our architecture, are beautiful in their decay."[232] Realized in combinations of brick, stucco, and clapboard and covered by gambrel, gable, and double-gable black Pennsylvania slate roofs (the first choice of green Vermont slate was ruled out because of a shortage of freight cars), the houses have survived subsequent vicissitudes with considerable success, although the neighborhood's original charm, as George Gove observed in 1920, owing to a sense "that Buckman has been occupied for a long time," has given way to ill-considered additions and renovations that began soon after the properties were auctioned off on March 18, 1922, with special provision allowing occupants to buy the units in which they resided.[233]

1. Plan, G. Edwin Brumbaugh, c. 1918. EFC

2. Keystone Road, showing stores and commons, center. EFC (c. 1919)

3. Typical street. AF20 (c. 1920)

4–7. Typical views. RAMSA (2009)

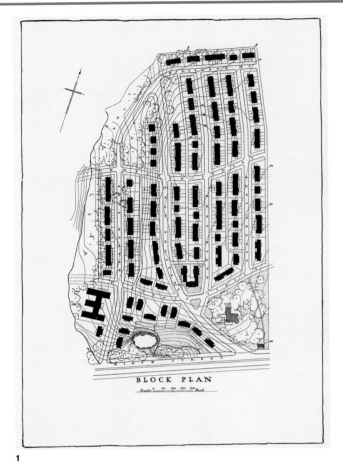

Two-and-a-half miles northeast of Buckman Village, architect Ernest Flagg (1857–1947) designed an EFC project calling for 650 houses for workers of the Sun Shipbuilding Company.[234] According to his biographer Mardges Bacon, Flagg, a steadfast Republican, was opposed to the idea of government-financed housing, but as an architectural innovator, he welcomed the opportunity to apply at village scale some of the ideas about small houses that he had begun to test on his Dongan Hills, Staten Island, estate, which Frederick Ackerman visited, coming away "convinced that the design and methods of construction of these houses, complete with their patented wall partitions and other Flagg-invented details, could be adapted to wartime housing."[235]

Flagg's Chester site was divided in half by railroad tracks but instead of designing a single community, as Bissell & Sinkler unsuccessfully attempted at Noreg Village (see p. 874), he designed the separate neighborhoods of **Sun Hill** on the north and **Sun Village** on the south. In each case, there was not much opportunity for town planning. "The problem at Chester," Flagg stated, "was complicated owing to the former housing operation of the ship-building company. Two or three hundred houses of the Philadelphia type had already been built

Sun Village

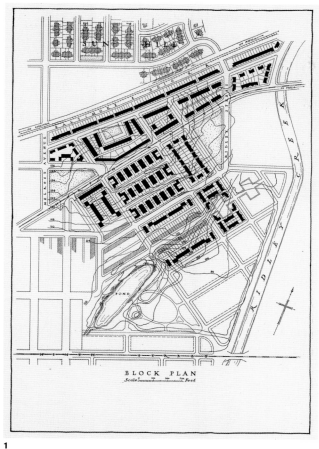

1

2

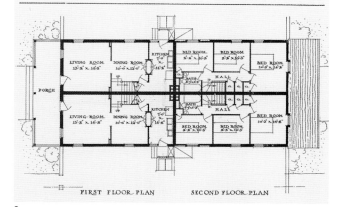

3

4

5

1. Plan, Ernest Flagg, c. 1918, showing partial plan of Sun Hill, top. EFC.

2. Photograph and plans of four-family houses designed by Ernest Flagg. EFC (1920)

3. Rendering of houses around courtyard, Ernest Flagg. A18

4. Courtyard, Taylor Street. RAMSA (2009)

5. Pathway between four-family houses. RAMSA (2009)

Sun Hill

1

2

1, 2. Typical streets. RAMSA (2009)

on a part of the site; some of these were located almost in the heart of the plot. Thus the street layout, and to a certain extent the character of the future development, was already determined and had to be accepted."[236]

Flagg prepared more than a dozen house types for Sun Village, including semidetached, four-family, and longer multifamily rows as well as apartments and mixed-use buildings combining first-floor stores and second-floor residences. Brick was the principal building material but stucco was also incorporated. Flagg felt strongly that through streets should be avoided to allow children to play safely by their houses. But with the street grid already established, the architect was forced to reduce the size of yards, "necessary for clothes drying and for the use of very small children," to the "least practicable dimensions and utilize the space thus saved for the formation of squares, courts, and other places where children might play in comparative safety." On one block, bound by Vauclain, Curry, Terrill, and Remington Streets, Flagg created a central courtyard embraced by mirror-image group houses consisting of a four-family house flanked by adroitly massed tower-like L-shaped arms. Inevitably, the courtyard was later taken over for parking. Flagg covered three blocks of Sun Village with unusual quadruple houses in which two side-by-side houses facing one street were placed back to back with two houses facing the parallel street, recalling Frank Lloyd Wright's 1913 experiments with the type. The arrangement eliminated rear yards and alleys. The houses, with side-facing flared gable roofs, front porches, and Flagg's characteristic ridge-dormer windows, were unique among the EFC towns. Elsewhere, Flagg, trying to "steer a middle course between too great concentration on the one hand and what seemed extravagance on the other," provided more conventional rows staggered back and forth from the street.[237]

Sun Village was completed largely as planned, but tensions between Flagg and the Shipping Board arose when the architect rejected the use of specified standard details and insisted on using ones of his own derivation, including ridge-dormer windows and fireproof partitions. As Bacon noted, "When his first houses were completed" in 1918, "they were officially condemned and the Board terminated its contract with Flagg."[238] After the armistice, the government completed the project with the assistance of its in-house design department and Bissell & Sinkler, who placed redbrick multifamily groups on the modified gridiron blocks of Sun Hill.

Westinghouse Village (1918), planned on a gently sloping 90-acre tract of open country in Essington, Pennsylvania, three miles north of Chester and eight miles southwest of downtown Philadelphia, originally undertaken as a corporate project of the Westinghouse Electric & Manufacturing Company to house workers at a new turbine plant on the west bank of the Delaware River, was to include 1,100 houses for a population of 6,000 as well as a full complement of commercial, public, and civic buildings.[239] After America entered the war, however, rising prices made private financing undesirable and the company sought funds from the EFC, which paid for a section of 200 houses, the only portion of the village to be realized.

The town planner and architect was Clarence Wilson Brazer (1880–1956), a Philadelphia-born, New York–based architect who enjoyed a subsequent career as a preeminent philatelist. Brazer's symmetrical plan consisted of rectangular superblocks flanking a central, north-pointing triangle that was divided longitudinally by a 150-foot-wide parkway incorporating medians and *rond-points* and punctuated along its length by schools, civic buildings, and churches. A wooded section at the center was partially retained as a lush setting for two crescents of single- and double-family houses intended for Westinghouse executives. Powhatan Street, the plan's southern border, accommodated a trolley line and was bordered by three-story commercial blocks providing two upper floors of apartments that served as a buffer between the two-story residences of the village to the north and the factory complex and railroad to the south. As built, the residential neighborhood, known as the South Philadelphia Houses, located in the southwest quadrant of the plan, consisted of staggered groups of two-, four-, six-, and eight-unit, brick and stucco, slate-roofed Georgian and Dutch Colonial Revival houses. The units averaged six rooms and featured front porches. Angled groups were placed at intersections and along the midblocks to create grassy street-facing courts. While rear service alleys were placed close to the houses, the blocks were large enough to also include gardens and common open spaces that were later eliminated with the construction of central alleys allowing access to individual garages.

With a peak population of 3,778, **Harriman,** twenty miles northeast of Philadelphia, in Bristol, Pennsylvania, was the largest single EFC project to be realized, incorporating 320 houses, 278 apartments, and 22 dormitories in addition to a 500-room hotel, a 40-bed hospital, and its own police and fire squads.[240] It was built to house employees of the Merchant Shipbuilding Corporation, a company founded in early 1917 by twenty-five-year-old W. Averill Harriman (1891–1986), a future investment banker, U.S. secretary of commerce (1946–48), and governor of New York (1955–58), who had inherited a fortune from his railroad-magnate father, Edward Henry Harriman (1848–1909). Young Harriman purchased the Standard Cast Iron Pipe & Foundry Company and transformed its facilities for shipbuilding purposes, soon receiving the EFC's largest single order to date, calling for the construction of forty steel cargo vessels within eighteen months.

At once, thousands of workers descended upon Bristol, a seventeenth-century port town on the west bank of the Delaware River that had emerged as a small but active milling and manufacturing center during the nineteenth century. Six rows of existing barracks, built around 1907, provided temporary housing while preparations were made to blanket the surrounding area with similar barracks. When those plans were submitted for

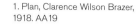

1. Plan, Clarence Wilson Brazer, 1918. AA19

2. Saude Avenue and Seneca Street. RAMSA (2009)

3. Rear alley. RAMSA (2009)

4, 5. House groups on Jansen Avenue. RAMSA (2009)

6. Saude Avenue. RAMSA (2009)

approval, however, Perry R. MacNeille, director of the housing division of the Ordnance Department, who was called upon for advice, was asked, with his partner, Horace B. Mann, to design a more complete and permanent community that included housing for every level of employee, whether, as an early observer put it, "he was a married man with a large family or a married man with a small family, a forlorn bachelor, a highly paid executive or the very humblest of workers."[241]

Somewhat hyperbolically considered by C. Stanley Taylor to be "America's Greatest Single Industrial Housing Development," Harriman, occupying a 17-acre site bound by the shipyard to the north and east, the Pennsylvania Railroad right-of-way to the west, and Bristol to the south, was divided into a gridiron mostly contained within an elongated oval ring road.[242] Two diagonal streets interrupted the pattern to accommodate the old barracks and an existing building intended to become a YMCA but used as a restaurant instead. A central spine, Wilson Avenue, named for the current U.S. president, ran the length of the site, facilitating movement to and from the shipyard. In the middle of the plan, a school, a park, playgrounds, churches, and civic buildings formed a cross axis and firebreak while establishing distinct

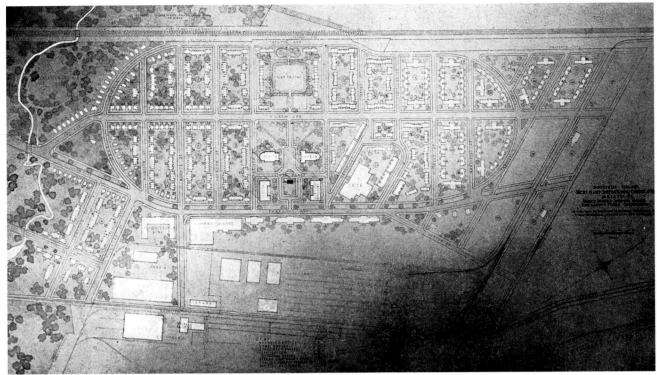

1

2

3

4

5

6

northern and southern districts separating common laborers from skilled workers and managers. Although the village provided for all classes, social stratification was deliberately built into the plan, with the lowest wage earners residing closest to the factory in order "to avoid the passing through of the better section of the village by laborers going to and returning from work . . . First, the single common laborer, nearest the plant and occupying the least expensive quarters; next the married common laborers in attractive apartment groups, offering economy in accordance with income; next the mechanics in individual houses, but built in group form to attain economy, and finally the high grade apartments and individual houses for foremen and superintendents, whose income is larger."[243]

Mann & MacNeille's preliminary residential designs were developed in detail by New York architect Carroll Henry Pratt (1874–1958), then in charge of the Merchant Shipbuilding Corporation's drafting staff. Ranging from dormitories and boardinghouses to single- and two-family houses and three-, four-, six-, seven-, eight-, and sixteen-unit rows, the stylistically diverse designs combined stucco, brick, clapboard, and wood-shingle cladding with gambrel, hip, clipped-gambrel, street- and yard-facing gable roofs to give "the completed street an appearance not unlike that of a high-class suburban development," as William Phillips Comstock, editor of *Architecture and Building* magazine, wrote.[244] The neighborhoods for single workmen were of particular interest, with twenty-unit dormitories on the side streets and sixty-unit houses on the block ends enclosing common open spaces. Though identical in plan, three different facade treatments were applied to the smaller dormitories that each comprised two five-bedroom wings (two men to a room) linked by a common bathroom accessible from the outside, allowing workmen to wash off before entering the house. The bedrooms were situated around a living room that—or so it was hoped—offered the men an alternative gathering place to the saloon. The sixty-unit dormitories featured residential wings entered from the side, flanking a central dining room and kitchen entered from the street. The housing for married couples was also of note, with single-story apartments placed within two-story blocks that gave each unit a private balcony or terrace and its own entrance so that separate households need not share corridors. Additional social amenities included eighteen stores and the Merchant Restaurant, covering almost an acre of land and capable of serving 12,000 meals each day. A sprawling administration building contained company offices.

Operations continued after the signing of the armistice, but by February 1921 the EFC and the Merchant Shipbuilding Corporation decided to close the shipyard. A December 1921 auction saw many of the houses purchased by residents and investors, but most of the boardinghouses and public buildings, including the Spanish Colonial Revival Victory Hotel and the Merchant Restaurant, were demolished, their sites subdivided and redeveloped with detached houses.

Union Park Gardens, at the western edge of Wilmington, Delaware, was commissioned by the Liberty Land Company, a limited-dividend company working in partnership with the EFC.[245] The 50-acre farmland site, a ten-minute streetcar ride from the shipyards and Wilmington's downtown, abutted existing parkland. John Nolen's plan directly linked streets with those already in place in the city, although the plan, which was only partially carried out, was more ruralesque in an oddly formal way than strictly urban, extending Grant Avenue, a gently curving boulevard linking Wilmington's parks, as Valley Creek Parkway, breaking through the city's street grid with a broad, meandering greensward down the center of which ran a local brook with a spillway dam and pool. The various landscape features associated with the creek went unrealized and eventually the creek bed was filled in and covered with lawn. Emile Perrot of Ballinger & Perrot, the architects charged with the design of the redbrick Colonial-style

row and group houses, praised the "charming effect" of Nolen's "varied vistas" that "materially add to the intrinsic value of the property."[246]

For William E. Groben (1883–1961), an architect who worked on the project, the plan included "all the essentials of a thoroughly organized garden suburb."[247] In addition to the 399 group houses and 104 semidetached houses, land was set aside for a school and for baseball and tennis, as well as for allotment gardens. A community building was to face a block of shops across Lancaster Avenue at Grant Avenue marking the village gateway. The community building and shops were never constructed. An innovative communal garage was the one public facility that was realized.

Also not realized were the service alleys called for in the original plan. Groben felt that the front area service ways were one of the most important contributions of Nolen's "extremely ingenious and practical plan," notably increasing the amount of land available for rear gardens, but Nolen eliminated them to save money and because he believed that the new system of "cash and carry" stores drastically reduced the amount of vehicles needed to service each house.[248]

Twenty house types were provided and they were carefully distributed on the site so that, according to Nolen, "group-houses have been located as near as possible to the transportation lines, and the semidetached houses are in locations farther away—an arrangement which gives the lesser-paid workman living in a group-house (minus an automobile) the just claim to transit facilities."[249] Complementing Nolen's plan, Ballinger & Perrot's rationally planned house designs introduced "stylistic diversity that stretched local traditions" with a rich palette of features including detailed porches, dormers, and gable ends, a mix of brick and stucco, clapboard and shingles with slate roofs, full basements, and well-detailed interiors.[250]

Margaret Crawford points out that Union Park Gardens, "one of the most sophisticated plans executed by Nolen," was "clearly influenced by Forest Hills Gardens [and] balanced geometry and nature . . . Like Forest Hills Gardens, the settlement moved sequentially from the urban square on the east of the site to terminate in a wooded park at the western boundary."[251] Charles Warren, in his study of Nolen's work, writes that the development, with its "departure from both the rigid street pattern and the relentless mid-Atlantic row houses of the adjacent area," stands out. "Nolen's design allowed the taut geometry of the city to relax into the easier, topographically determined curve of the park. This subtle shift from straight to curved streets formed a graceful transition from the geometric, urban order to the irregular forms of the woodland park beyond; it was a clever bit of composition that allowed Union Park Gardens to stand alone as a neighborhood enclave while integrating the surrounding area into an artful urban sequence. Housing density also becomes sparser and more irregularly planned as the parkway blends into the park, enhancing, quite explicitly, the transition from the city to the country."[252]

1. Plan, John Nolen, 1918. COR
2. Panoramic view. COR (1918)
3–6. Typical views. RAMSA (2007)

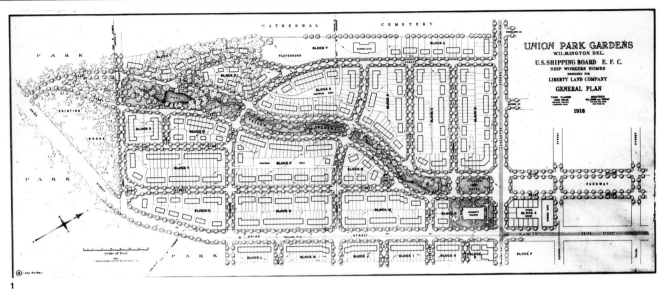

1

2

3

4

5

6

Despite its state of incompletion—the lack of shops and community facilities was sorely felt—Union Park Gardens succeeded as a stable neighborhood, maintaining, even in the Depression, a high level of homeownership, making it one of the most convincing demonstrations of the enduring appeal for industrial workers of high-quality suburban villages convenient to factories and downtown.

Wilmington was also the proposed site of **Cleland Heights**, a collaboration between the EFC and the limited-dividend Liberty Housing Company that did not

get beyond the planning stages.[253] To have been located a little more than a mile south of Union Park Gardens, as planned by Wilmington-based architect John Dockery Thompson Jr. (1872–1924), it would have accommodated 800 families in various housing types. The ambitious if stiff plan also included a civic center, stores, and a new railroad station.

The plan of **Noreg Village** (now known as Brooklawn), in Gloucester, New Jersey, four miles southwest of Yorkship Village, designed by the Philadelphia firm of seasoned architects but less-experienced town planners,

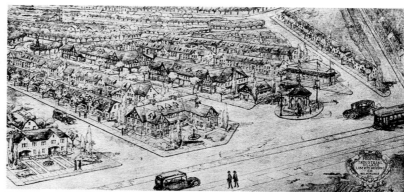

1. Plan, John Dockery Thompson Jr., 1918. A18

2. Aerial perspective. A18 (1918)

Elliston Perot Bissell (1872–1944) and John F. Sinkler (1875–1959), to house workers at the Pusey & Jones shipyard, was plagued by site-related problems. The 200-acre flat farmland site, similar in some ways to that of Yorkship Village, differed in one significant respect: it was bisected by the West Jersey and Seashore Railroad and by the Woodbury and Gloucester Turnpike. The planners seemed to ignore this inherent intrusion, so that the sense of a village gave way to two distinct neighborhoods lacking a shared center.[254]

Bissell and Sinkler's formal layout of *rond-points* and plazas connected by diagonal boulevards giving form to blocks of irregular shape and size was criticized as early as May 1919 by Karl B. Lohmann, who noted that "the effort to introduce variety and irregularity has been carried to such an extent that in the opinion of many it is overdone."[255] The architects' attempt to link public buildings and schools on one side of the tracks with a town center of commercial and civic buildings on the other would be criticized by Comey and Wehrly: "The railroad right-of-way, in addition to cutting the town in half as to use, is partially elevated, which makes the separation visually complete . . . At the town center, the strong connection between the two parts of the town which might be expected from looking at the plan is, in fact, provided for only by an inadequate pedestrian underpass."[256] The only automobile crossing occurred at the southern edge of the plan, leaving residential areas in the north virtually isolated.

Noreg incorporated 449 dwelling units spread equally between detached, semidetached, and group houses finished mainly in stucco applied to wood frame and hollow tile and either placed along the street to provide common spaces on the block interior or set back in groups to frame street-facing courts. As Comey and Wehrly pointed out, "the most objectionable feature," the complex geometry of the various blocks, "created a very uneven allotment of alley frontage to the lots, and in many cases no alley frontage at all," requiring services such as garbage removal to be duplicated on the street. The alleys, which in some cases were dead ends with insufficient space to turn a car around, became less and less efficient as they were crowded with garages that proved "difficult to relate to the alley because of the eccentric lot lines."[257] Additionally, Comey and Wehrly felt that the group houses, "in spite of the strong architectural attempt," were "unsatisfactory, visually as well as functionally," especially where the "attempt to end street vistas with two houses placed at 45 degrees in the middle of a block not only fails to make a group but leaves a void on the axis, and the resulting diagonal lines of the house mass produce an unpleasant and awkward effect."[258]

While a good part of Noreg was carried out to completion, the southwestern 50 acres were deemed unsuitable for development because the land was too close in elevation to the river. This area included the southern half of the town center, leaving the planned public space malformed and bordered by only one block of stores. Moreover, as built, Noreg Village provided just 14 acres of open space. While Newton Creek formed a significant buffer of parkland at Yorkship Village, Timber Creek at Noreg Village was hardly an amenity, with untreated sewage from Philadelphia, Camden, and other northern areas creating "an extremely polluted and odorous condition."[259]

Noreg was sold during a nonstop twelve-hour auction in 1923 and the following year the Pusey & Jones shipyard closed. The village, incorporated as Brooklawn, soon began to fall into disrepair as the Shipping Board, which held the mortgages on most of the houses, could not collect taxes on about half of them. In 1931, with $48 in the treasury, a last-minute sale of government-owned properties staved off total collapse. Conditions were slow to improve, so that by the time Comey and Wehrly issued their report in 1936, many of the houses were uninhabitable. Additional housing was built later but, for better or worse, not according to the original plan.

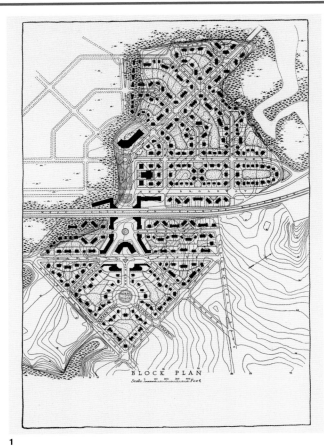

1

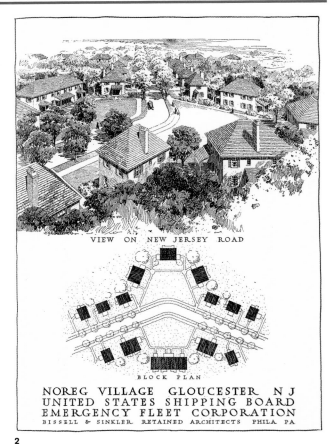

VIEW ON NEW JERSEY ROAD

BLOCK PLAN

NOREG VILLAGE GLOUCESTER N J
UNITED STATES SHIPPING BOARD
EMERGENCY FLEET CORPORATION
BISSELL & SINKLER RETAINED ARCHITECTS PHILA PA

2

3

4

5

6

While the greatest concentration of EFC villages was realized in the vicinity of Philadelphia, a number of interesting examples were also developed at less important port locations. **Atlantic Heights**, in Portsmouth, New Hampshire, was designed by the Boston-based firm of Walter H. Kilham and James C. Hopkins.[260] Robert Kohn, who had invited Kilham to join him at the EFC, knew the architect from their mutual involvement with housing reformer Lawrence Veiller's National Housing Association. Although Kilham rejected the offer to join the EFC administrative staff, he was pleased to accept the Portsmouth commission in April 1918, and, working in great haste, within three weeks prepared a plan so that construction could begin on May 20, with the first houses ready for occupancy before the end of the summer.

The 64-acre site, about two miles northwest of downtown Portsmouth, was bound by the Piscataqua

BLOCK PLAN

1

1. Plan, Walter H. Kilham and William Roger Greeley, 1918. EFC

2, 3. Typical streets. PA (1919)

4. Raleigh Way. HALC (2012)

River to the north, the shipyards of the Atlantic Corporation to the east, the tracks of the Boston and Maine Railroad to the south, and open land to the west. The plan, designed by Kilham working with William Roger Greeley (1881–1966) of his office, navigated the hilly, rocky site with a network of 40-foot-wide streets. Only one street, 50-foot-wide Kearsarge Way, led via an overpass spanning the railroad tracks out of the relatively isolated site to Portsmouth's town center. A triangular common was located near the overpass where Kilham hoped to include a prominent town hall topped by a clock tower, but the only buildings built at the green were a group of five stores. Park and playground space was reserved along the riverfront.

The *Portsmouth Daily Chronicle* noted that the architects "have followed as far as possible the colonial lines of the city, many of the houses having reproductions on a smaller scale of some of the best of the colonial doorways."[261] A majority of the 278 redbrick one-and-a-half-story houses were semidetached and contained only four rooms, with a small number of five-, six-, and seven-room models grouped in rows or sited individually. To add variety to the streetscape, Kilham and Hopkins produced six different house designs, topped by gambrel or pitched roofs with slate, stucco, or shingle dormers, distributing them throughout the site so that no two streets were alike. To house 400 single men, the architects designed eight two-story stucco-clad dormitories for a site near the shipyard. An 800-seat communal cafeteria in the shipyard never opened for its intended

purpose but was used as a recreation center; a school planned for Saratoga Street remained unrealized.

After the war the neat rows of houses, with modest front and back yards, were put up for auction. With most workers unable to afford them, the houses were sold in 1925 to a small group of landlords who neglected their maintenance. The dormitories were demolished by the 1930s, but many of the houses ultimately found more appreciative owners who restored them, helping to preserve the working-class enclave's cohesiveness.

In **Bath**, Maine, Boston architect R. Clipston Sturgis (1860–1951), who also designed distinguished housing for the USHC in Bridgeport, Connecticut, was responsible for 109 detached and semidetached houses, some of the latter also divided up as dormitories and grouped, along with a dining hall and "lounging rooms," around an open green on Oliver Circle.[262] To the west, residential blocks featured alternating house types set back varying degrees from the street and arranged to create closed street vistas. Sturgis's five-room redbrick semidetached houses were only one room deep, resembling multi-unit rows with steep pitched roofs punctuated by six dormer windows.

While every shipbuilding community struggled to provide workers' housing, the situation was particularly dire in Newport News, Virginia, where, taking advantage of a strategically located port, the army also established embarkation and aviation camps and other facilities that put further pressure on the available housing stock. Faced with accommodating a workforce that had nearly

1. Bird's-eye view and block plan of dormitories. EFC (c. 1919)

2. Oliver Circle. Bartlett. PAN (2013)

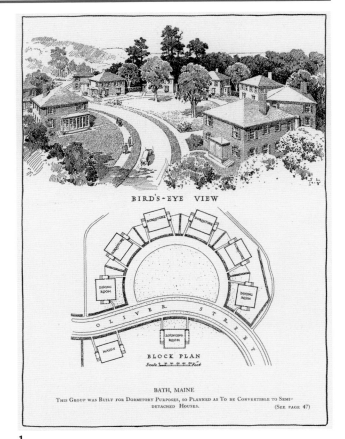

BIRD'S-EYE VIEW

BLOCK PLAN
Scale ⌐ ⌐ ⌐ ⌐ ⌐ Feet

BATH, MAINE
THIS GROUP WAS BUILT FOR DORMITORY PURPOSES, SO PLANNED AS TO BE CONVERTIBLE TO SEMI-
DETACHED HOUSES.   (SEE PAGE 47)

1

2

Kimball, had recently published *An Introduction to the Study of Landscape Design* (1917), the first standard text on the practice of landscape architecture.[265] Joseph D. Leland III (1885–1968) was initially retained as architect but left after preliminary planning was completed to become assistant director of the Housing Bureau of the Department of Labor. He was replaced by Francis Y. Joannes (1876–1952).

The flat, thickly wooded rectangular site, between the James River on the west and the Chesapeake & Ohio Railroad tracks on the east, was selected because of the ease with which it could be cleared and its ability to be linked to the shipyard by an extension of the Newport News streetcar line. One hundred acres were scheduled for immediate development and the other 100 acres left open for future expansion. Hubbard adopted the existing Warwick County Road, which cut a roughly north–south path across the site, as a dividing line, placing stores, apartments, public squares, and playing fields to the east and a quiet grid of residential streets containing 473 primarily detached and semidetached houses to the west. The county road, accommodating the streetcar, was lined by rowhouses for lower-paid workers. A station square was to be bordered by two business blocks and a community garage, but because of the popularity of the trolley, neither the stores nor the railroad station itself was realized. Hilton Square, a village green faced by two churches, a village hall, and additional shops, sat along Warwick County Road at its intersection with Main Street, a parkway extending west through the residential neighborhood to conclude in a combination school and community center set within a riverfront park. Two additional churches flanked Main Street opposite the school.

With the exception of a cul-de-sac and a horseshoe-shaped block providing larger lots along the river for those who could afford to buy land and build their own houses, residential lots were 25 and 40 feet wide. The elimination of rear alleys allowed a depth of between 118 and 130 feet, providing ample room for backyards. While streets were a generous 50 and 100 feet wide, automobile traffic was discouraged by the provision of narrow roadbeds spanning only 20 or 24 feet, affording room for broad planting strips. To soften the linearity of the grid, the planning team stepped the houses back from the street in the middle of each block. In some locations, the roadway was split to create a median, providing, as one observer put it, "little neighborhood open spaces for interest and additional feeling of room."[266] Attention was also paid to the appearance of block interiors, where small outbuildings for tools, wood, and coal were clustered together, according to Joannes, "to avoid the dotting of the landscape with what might appear to be small dog-houses."[267]

Joannes prepared fourteen variations of one-and-a-half- and two-and-a-half-story houses, mostly in the Jacobethan, Dutch, and Georgian Colonial styles with steep-pitched, multi-gabled gray slate roofs and a combination of six-over-six sash and six-paned casement

doubled to 14,000, in October 1917, the Newport News Shipbuilding and Drydock Company, anticipating that government funding for housing would soon come through, took an option on 200 acres on the east bank of the James River, two miles north of its shipyard, and initiated plans to develop **Hilton Village**.[263] On January 9, 1918, Homer L. Ferguson, president of the company, testified at a Senate inquiry that the "the influx of army men into Newport News, taking up all the available houses," had forced his own workers to be "herded into shacks and anything else we can find."[264] Ferguson's testimony struck the right chord. Two days later, after reviewing preliminary plans, the Shipping Board approved $1.2 million in funding for the town, and site work began in April.

On the recommendation of Frederick Law Olmsted Jr., Henry V. Hubbard, a former Olmsted Brothers partner now with the firm of Pray, Hubbard, and White, was hired as town planner. Hubbard, together with Theodora

1. Plan, Henry V. Hubbard, 1918. AA18

2. Aerial view. NNPL (c. 1919)

3. Warwick Road. NNPL (c. 1919)

4, 5. Typical streets. Massey. JCM (2010)

windows. With supplies of lumber nearby, frame construction was employed throughout, and stucco, clapboard, and wood shingle used as cladding. Recessed and protruding porches and bay windows added texture, especially to the rowhouses along the county road, which were up to ten bays wide.

To make sure the housing would be affordable, Joannes studied the shipbuilders' wages to determine an acceptable level of rent—considered to be 20 percent of an adult male worker's wages—using this figure to come up with the maximum house cost that would allow for a 10 percent return on the investment. A survey was also undertaken of workers and their wives, finding a distinct preference for single-family houses, although Joannes introduced two-family units "to avoid the 'pill box' effect

of a large group of small houses."[268] Many of the double houses, with individual units placed side by side or back to back, were later converted to single-family use.

The first families took up residence in September 1918 and unlike many of its companion towns, construction continued at Hilton Village after the signing of the armistice. By the end of 1919 much of the town had been built, giving the overall impression, as Comey and Wehrly later noted, "of housing a relatively higher income group than is actually the case."[269] Unfortunately, Hubbard and Joannes's plans for closing the axis of Main Street were, according to Comey and Wehrly, "disappointing, not through faulty layout but because the buildings originally designed were not erected. The present school of red brick and uncertain design terminates

1. Plan, Edward L. Palmer Jr., c. 1918. EFC

2. Typical street. EFC (c. 1919)

3. Semidetached house. EFC (c. 1919)

4. Dundalk Shopping Center. Crews. FL (2010)

5. Portship Road. Crews. FL (2010)

1

2

3

4

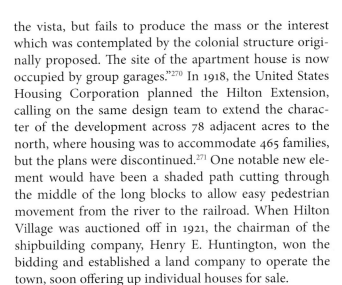

5

the vista, but fails to produce the mass or the interest which was contemplated by the colonial structure originally proposed. The site of the apartment house is now occupied by group garages."[270] In 1918, the United States Housing Corporation planned the Hilton Extension, calling on the same design team to extend the character of the development across 78 adjacent acres to the north, where housing was to accommodate 465 families, but the plans were discontinued.[271] One notable new element would have been a shaded path cutting through the middle of the long blocks to allow easy pedestrian movement from the river to the railroad. When Hilton Village was auctioned off in 1921, the chairman of the shipbuilding company, Henry E. Huntington, won the bidding and established a land company to operate the town, soon offering up individual houses for sale.

Dundalk, Maryland, nine miles southeast of Baltimore, was built to house workers of the Bethlehem Steel Company's Sparrow's Point industrial complex

containing both a shipyard and a steel mill.[272] The 86-acre undeveloped site was convenient to both the Sparrow's Point Branch of the Pennsylvania Railroad and an electric trolley line providing a ten-minute commute to the shipyard two miles to the southeast. The EFC discarded its preferred development technique of financing a newly created real estate company and instead hired the developers of Roland Park (see p. 144) to work with the government agency in planning the new industrial village. Edward H. Bouton, president of the Roland Park Company, oversaw the effort, bringing with him the architect Edward L. Palmer Jr., who built extensively in Roland Park, to plan Dundalk and its buildings, leading the new village to be widely proclaimed a "working man's Roland Park."[273]

As planned, Dundalk consisted of two adjacent parcels separated by Dundalk Avenue, a wide north–south boulevard with median strip. To the east lay the 70-acre Old Dundalk section, the more substantial and

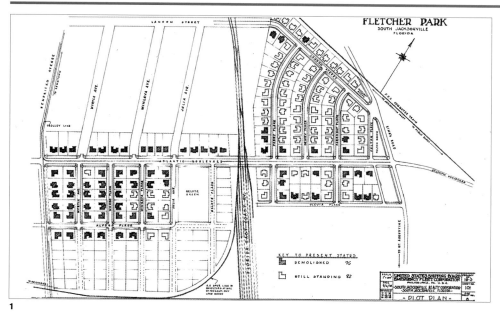

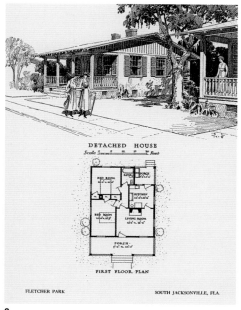

distinguished component of the design with ample park space and a well-defined commercial center. For Old Dundalk, Palmer produced nine different designs for the five- and six-room terraced, semidetached, and detached stucco-clad Arts and Crafts–inspired houses with pitched roofs and dormers. The 16-acre St. Helena section west of Dundalk Avenue featured a more regimented gridiron plan with long rows of four-room, two-story houses set back behind modest front lawns on lots that were on average 26 feet wide and between 90 and 150 feet deep.

By the time the EFC was ordered out of the housing business by Congress, 296 houses had been completed in St. Helena along with a communal one-story cafeteria and an electrical powerhouse. In keeping with standard procedure, the EFC placed the houses up for immediate sale. Old Dundalk (now commonly referred to simply as Dundalk) fared better than many of the other new villages: the Roland Park Company and Palmer maintained

their association with the village, which continued to grow under their supervision, so that by the mid-1920s, 529 houses had been completed as well as the Dundalk Shopping Center, loosely based on Wyatt & Nolting's Roland Park Shopping Center. In their 1997 guide to Baltimore area architecture, John Dorsey and James Dilts observed that although "less expensive than their Roland Park predecessors," Palmer's Dundalk houses "make a harmonious group on their intimate streets . . . Few urban areas in the county have [its] cozy, small town ambiance."[274]

The EFC's southernmost project, **Fletcher Park**, in South Jacksonville, Florida, housing workers of the Merrill-Stevens shipyard, was designed by Henry John Klutho (1873–1964), an Illinois-born architect who had settled in New York before moving to Jacksonville in 1901, shortly after the city was ravaged by fire.[275] Strongly influenced by Frank Lloyd Wright, whom he met in 1905, Klutho rose to prominence in Jacksonville designing

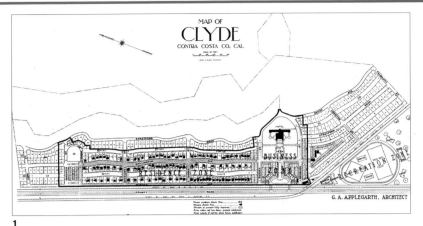

1. Plan, George A. Applegarth, 1919. BRV19

2. Aerial view. GE (2011)

3, 4. Typical houses, George A. Applegarth, 1919. BRV19

5. Hotel, George A. Applegarth, 1919. BRV19

Prairie Style public and private buildings. Fletcher Park, occupying a 48-acre site less than a half mile from the shipyard and connected by trolley to downtown Jacksonville, consisted of a gridded section west of the Florida East Coast Railway tracks and a neighborhood of concentric curving streets to the east. Klutho designed 165 single-family, one- and two-story wood, shingle, and stucco cottages, 158 of which were ultimately realized from four basic designs. In these, Klutho adjusted the Prairie Style to suit north Florida's mild climate, with low-slung roofs and deep eaves carried on cantilevered two-by-four beams. Site work began in July 1918, and the first house was completed on October 28, two weeks before the armistice was signed. Two boardinghouses, five stores, and recreational facilities were planned but not built.

The EFC's only West Coast development, **Clyde**, California, named for the Scottish river famed for its world-class shipbuilding facilities, occupied a 100-acre site adjacent to the tracks of the Bay Point & Clayton Railroad, two miles south of the Pacific Coast Shipbuilding Company's yards on Suisun Bay and thirty-four miles northeast of San Francisco.[276] The EFC selected Bernard Maybeck as supervising architect for the project, but the bulk of the work on the town's plan as well as the design of its buildings was undertaken by George A. Applegarth, a former student of Maybeck's at Berkeley who also attended the École des Beaux-Arts at the urging of his teacher.

Maybeck's contribution to the plan consisted primarily of his suggestion to modify Applegarth's strictly rectilinear gridiron by gently curving the enclave's streets to follow the topography. Applegarth also acceded to Maybeck's request to vary the setback distances of the three- to eight-room single-family houses located on 50- and 60-foot-wide lots. The focus of community life was Applegarth's large and elaborate stucco-clad hotel whose Spanish-inspired design clearly reflected Maybeck's influence. In addition to providing housing for 176 single men, the hotel had extensive public spaces, including a communal dining hall that could seat 300 and accommodate a motion-picture screen as well as a basement-level seventeen-lane bowling alley. The hotel was surrounded by ample park space, but an intended business district remained unrealized, although a modest schoolhouse was built.

Of the 200 planned houses, Applegarth, working with architect Edward W. Cannon (d. 1942), completed 103 before construction was halted with the cessation of hostilities. Harris Allen, writing in *Building Review* in October 1919, was impressed that the "compact and well planned" houses had "been kept simple, with much of the 'California' feeling, suggestive partly of Italian, partly of Spanish origin, with a few cottages of a modified English type, so unobtrusive as to fit quietly into the ensemble."[277] Artists Maurice Del Mue (1875–1955) and Harold von Schmidt (1893–1982) created a color scheme for the entire community, selecting colors that complemented the brownish hills surrounding the site but brightening the palette with such touches as orange-trimmed green flower boxes and blue corbels.

A few of the EFC projects were realized at some remove from major ports. In partnership with Thomas Desmond (1887–1972), owner of the Newburgh Shipyards, the EFC sponsored the development of Colonial Terraces, **Newburgh**, New York, a picturesque enclave of 127 houses built to accommodate the rising number of shipyard workers in the Hudson River town 60

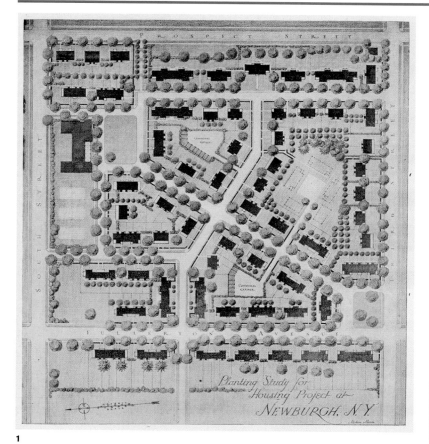

1. Plan, Henry Wright, c. 1919. EFC
2. Aerial view. GE (2007)
3. Norton Street. RAMSA (2011)
4. Wilson Street. RAMSA (2011)
5. Typical house. RAMSA (2011)

miles north of New York City.[278] Henry Wright, working under Frederick L. Ackerman and Robert D. Kohn in the housing division of the EFC, collaborated with the Boston-based firm of Peabody & Stearns, whose founding principals had died in 1917, and New York architect Charles H. Sparry (n.d.) to produce a plan notable for its irregular street layout and generous spacing of two-story, brick and shingle, Colonial-style, semidetached and rowhouses. Tree-lined Bush Avenue diagonally bisected the site, leading from the town square at the village's southwest corner to another park located at the northeast corner. In addition to the five- and six-room houses, a group of stores topped by apartments was located near the main entrance at Fullerton and Bush Avenues.

The English-born architect Alfred C. Bossom designed a modest development for workers employed at the Bayles Shipyard in **Port Jefferson,** Long Island, New York. Bossom's work for the EFC consisted of a row of nine five- to seven-room detached houses "carried out in a character similar to the old Long Island fishing villages with the long shingles and low eaves," according to the architect.[279] Intended for supervisory personnel, the two-story shingle and clapboard houses were located near the shipyard on a curving stretch of Liberty Avenue. Bossom was also responsible for temporary dormitory facilities built to house 400 workers in eight stucco-clad buildings arranged in a V-shaped pattern with a large cafeteria and recreation building located at the base.

Groton Park, on a sloping site east of the Thames River, in Groton, Connecticut, included ninety-two houses designed by New York architect Eugene J. Lang (1879–1952) on a modified grid platted by the EFC's design staff.[280] Lang's work included dormitories, boardinghouses, detached houses, and at least six types of semidetached houses uniformly set back and aligned parallel to the street. A village green was sited on a

1. Houses, Alfred C. Bossom, 1918.
AA19

1

Groton Park

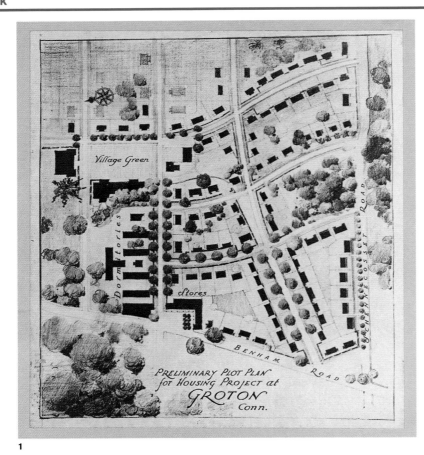

1

2

3

1. Plan, 1918. HAM4

2, 3. Typical streets. RAMSA (2013)

plateau in the north and bordered by a school, community building, and church, with stores and a theater nearby, all accessible to different levels of employees of the Groton Iron Works. Authorized in August 1918 and begun in September, only some of the housing was completed before the project was halted in November.

The Great Lakes provided another location for shipbuilding. **Wyandotte**, Michigan, featured an enclave of seventy-nine houses designed by the EFC's Branch of Design for employees of the Detroit Shipbuilding Co.[281] Work was begun on September 1, 1918, just two months before the signing of the armistice. The one- and two-story cottages with small trellised porches were set back from the street to add variety to the streetscape and to preserve existing trees, although street trees were also planted. Many of the houses faced a central rectangular green and a tree-lined pedestrian path provided a short-cut through the neighborhood.

Wyandotte

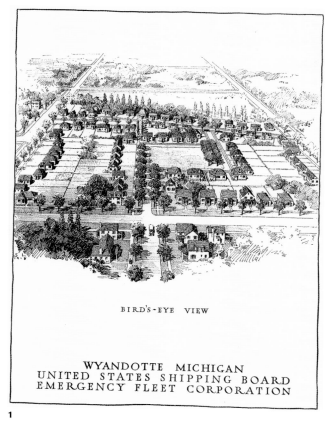

BIRD'S-EYE VIEW

WYANDOTTE MICHIGAN
UNITED STATES SHIPPING BOARD
EMERGENCY FLEET CORPORATION

1

2

3

1. Bird's-eye view. USSB (c. 1918)

2. Spruce Street. Luttermoser. LUTT (2012)

3. Rendering of detached house. EFC (c. 1919)

Manitowoc

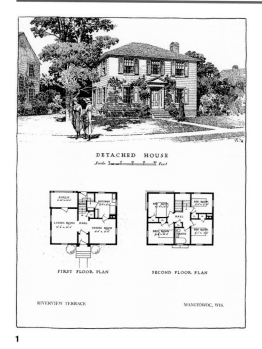

DETACHED HOUSE
Scale

FIRST FLOOR PLAN   SECOND FLOOR PLAN

RIVERVIEW TERRACE   MANITOWOC, WIS.

1

2

1. Rendering and plan of detached house, Earl Franklin Miller, c. 1918. EFC

2. Aerial view. GE (2011)

In **Manitowoc**, Wisconsin, local architect Earl Franklin Miller (n.d.) designed 100 two-story Colonial-style houses with clapboard siding, painted trim, and hip and gambrel roofs as well as a dormitory for 300 unmarried workers of the Manitowoc Shipbuilding Co. along a grid of streets bound on the north, west, and east by the meandering Riverview Terrace, where larger houses for senior workers were placed opposite a buffer of woods.[282]

In **Lorain,** Ohio, about twenty-five miles west of Cleveland on the Lake Erie shore, Cleveland architect Abram Garfield (1872–1958), son of United States president James A. Garfield, designed 232 houses and two apartment buildings on 44 acres for employees of the American Shipbuilding Co.[283] The houses varied in type, including detached and semidetached houses and six-family rowhouses. Garfield also designed a combination store and apartment block.

1

2

Ordnance Towns

Of the many challenges faced by the U.S. Army's Ordnance Department upon entering the war in April 1917, perhaps the most vexing and immediate was the production of nitric acid, the principal ingredient in high explosives. The United States had previously manufactured the substance in small amounts for fertilizer but had imported larger quantities from Chile, whose saltpeter beds provided an ample source. Concerns about the ability to secure sea routes during the war led the U.S. to undertake its own mammoth plants for harvesting nitrates from the air, a process that required vast amounts of electricity best provided by water power, leading the government to make available for the purpose inland waterways located sufficiently far from the coast to protect against attack. The nitrate and affiliated munitions plants that were built within a span of eight or nine months—often nearing but not quite reaching completion by the signing of the armistice—constitute some of the largest construction projects in the nation's history, commonly compared at the time with the building of the Panama Canal many times over. To house the tens of thousands of workers at the new plants, the Ordnance Department's Industrial Division established a housing branch headed by the New York architect and town planner Perry R. MacNeille.

The village of **Perry Point**, Maryland, about halfway between Philadelphia and Baltimore and connected by railroad and turnpike to the nearby town of Perryville, supported a new ammonium-nitrate plant built by the Atlas Powder Company, the largest prewar producer of the substance.[284] Eight thousand workers began construction on the Perry Point plant in February 1918, and

by early May it was recognized that the expected workforce of 1,000 engineers, chemists, superintendents, foremen, and mechanics would need permanent, quality housing. MacNeille was asked to assess the situation, and then, with his partner Horace B. Mann, to serve as architect and town planner for a village of 400 houses and associated community facilities. Mann & MacNeille's architectural designs were further developed by the F. T. Ley Company, general contractor, and W. E. Stevens (n.d.), a local architect working for the powder company.

The 500-acre site, a level plateau at the mouth of the Susquehanna River, facing Chesapeake Bay, included a natural buffer of dense woods separating the town from the factory to the north. Mann & MacNeille called for an elongated street plan hugging the river, whose banks were landscaped and opened up as a park. An antebellum farmhouse in the middle of the site was kept as a residence for the plant's general manager while its grounds were retained as open space, also providing a central location for a school and effectively dividing the plan into eastern and western neighborhoods.

Mann & MacNeille adopted the Colonial style for the houses and public buildings in order to avoid "fantastic and picturesque types of design, which although novel and appealing at first sight do not prove permanently satisfying nor economical in construction and maintenance."[285] Work began west of the park, where 187 two-story frame houses covered in white-painted white pine siding with green shutters and lattice, gray cedar-shingle roofs, and white chimneys, occupied 50-by-100-foot lots set on large blocks. The neighborhood was organized around a spine leading from the village's main entrance, a *rond-point* ringed by stores, a movie theater, and a church, through a

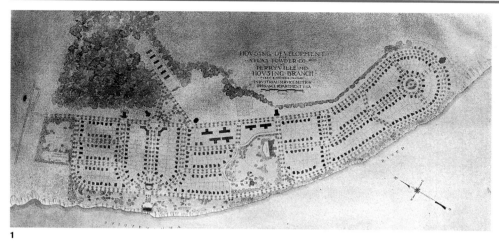

horseshoe-shaped residential block toward the water, where it culminated in a two-story balconied and cupolaed community clubhouse providing a lounge, library, billiard room, kitchen, and a 41-by-50-foot second-floor auditorium opening onto a broad balcony overlooking the river.

Six forty-six-room boardinghouses were also completed, but work on the eastern neighborhood of 200 single-family houses similarly placed along comfortable tree-lined streets was canceled at the end of the war and the land was eventually used as a golf course. The built portion of the community later served as a rehabilitation center for soldiers, a supply depot, and a psychiatric hospital.

The villages of Sheffield and Muscle Shoals, Alabama, were built to house workers of United States Nitrate Plants No. 1 and No. 2, respectively, together representing the largest ammonium-nitrate plants in the world, situated on the southern banks of the Tennessee River, where construction began in 1918 on the Muscle Shoals (later Wilson) Dam. As designed by Mann & MacNeille, the industrial village of **Sheffield**, built by the Air Nitrates Corporation of New York on behalf of the federal government, was located about a mile southwest of Nitrate Plant No. 1 and almost two miles from the existing town of Sheffield, to which it was connected by streetcar.[286] The site was a wedge-shaped plateau bordered on the west and south by a stream and on the east by railroad tracks. The elevation of the land not only

safeguarded the village against the flooding of the Tennessee River, but, as an early observer noted, "it is safe to predict that the scenic effects during spring freshets, when the town becomes flood bound on two sides, will be one of the features of life in the community."[287]

Mann & MacNeille called for a bell-shaped plan of informally curving tree-lined streets adapted to the site's topography but allowing for formal parks, parade grounds, and drill grounds that served the part-civilian, part-military population. A school, hotel, and two churches occupied central sites, while a hospital, barracks, and community garage were placed at the periphery, the latter provided to allow "a great gain for the appearance of the neighborhood at only the slightest sacrifice in accessibility."[288] Although the intention was to rely on the town of Sheffield for most commercial needs, Mann & MacNeille echoed their plan for Perry Point, Maryland, by bringing traffic into the village through a *rond-point* ringed by shops providing basic services such as a newsstand, barber shop, and cigar store. Houses were separated into zones for civilian and military personnel, with further hierarchies based on military rank. The double-winged commandant's house—the only two-story house in the village, with a guest suite on the first floor—occupied two central acres at the site's highest topographical point, flanked by four majors' houses. The low cost of land allowed for large lots of varying size and shape, averaging 50 by 100 feet, while narrow roadbeds of 20 and 24 feet were bordered by wide planting strips.

1. Plan, Horace B. Mann and Perry R. MacNeille, 1918. AA18

2. Theater. LOCP (1918)

3–5. Typical views. RAMSA (2009)

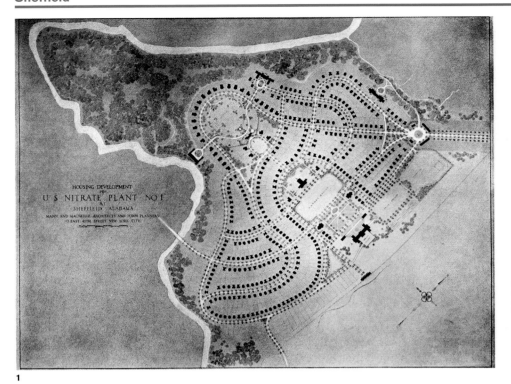

1

2

3

1. Plan, Horace B. Mann and Perry R. MacNeille, 1918. AF18

2. Aerial view. CRS

3. View of houses across park. Chamberlain. OC (2008)

Red-tile-roofed, Mediterranean-style dwellings, acknowledging the warm Alabama climate, were clad in stucco applied to hollow tile block. Fireplaces provided the only source of heat during the winter. Of the 400 houses originally planned according to seven distinct designs, only eighty-five were built, including many of the officers' houses and all four majors' houses. The commandant's house was unrealized. At the edge of the neighborhood, a barracks, "more like a college dormitory," as Charles C. May noted in 1918, accommodated a civilian guard with "a combination of hotel and club life that would be hard to match outside a government plant."[289] Because the guard operated in three shifts, the building was divided into three discrete sections so shift changes wouldn't disturb off-duty workers. Although Sheffield was not completed in its entirety, many of the houses remain, as do the school and barracks.

East of Sheffield, the industrial village of **Muscle Shoals** housed workers of the American Cyanamid Company's United States Nitrate Plant No. 2, a monumental operation encompassing 2,428 buildings under 78 acres of roof spread across four square miles.[290] The affiliated residential district was laid out by the New York firm of Charles Ewing (1872–1954) and Jerome Ripley Allen (1871–1928), the latter having served during the war as architect for the navy's Bureau of Yards and Docks. Ewing & Allen called for 1,500 modest but charming one- and two-story cottages ranging from three to six rooms, "equally divided between white and colored sections," as Ralph F. Warner observed in *Architectural Review* in 1919, noting: "A small valley not suitable for building afforded a peculiarly happy means" for separating the two areas.[291] The neighborhoods, each occupying a conventional street grid, were intended to converge in an oval town center that was not built according to plan.

To keep costs down, Ewing & Allen specified only two or three window, door, and shutter sizes as well as simple, uniform hardware, lighting fixtures, and plumbing materials for both the public and private buildings, introducing variety by reversing the house plans, changing porch locations, and alternating between stucco and shingle cladding. In addition, twenty-eight different color combinations were devised, each calling for eight tints to be used on a single house's walls, trim, shutters, doors, roof, window sash, and porch floor and ceiling. Construction on the plant and town began in February 1918 but was halted with the signing of the armistice. In all, 186 houses were completed in the area for white workers and 263 houses in the "colored" section, as well as ten one-story apartment houses. The nitrate plant was not completed in time to contribute to the war effort.

Located sixteen miles northwest of Charleston, West Virginia, the industrial city of **Nitro** was another "Alladin-like" undertaking that within ten months' time transformed a 1,900-acre farmland valley into the second-largest smokeless powder plant in the world.[292] Named for nitrocellulose, a delicate explosive (the name "Redwop," "powder" spelled backward, was also considered), Nitro encompassed the DuPont Engineering Company's U.S. Government Explosives Plant "C" as well as a town for 20,000 inhabitants. The Chicago firm of Graham, Anderson, Probst & White served as design engineers for the factory and town. The site, benefiting from the region's rich supplies of coal, natural gas, and petroleum, ran for three miles along the eastern banks of the Kanawha River. The main line of the Kanawha and Michigan Railway

Muscle Shoals

1. Bird's-eye view. ARB19 (1919)

Nitro

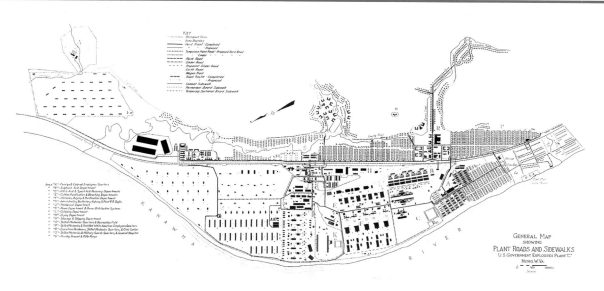

1. Plan of plant and town, Graham, Anderson, Probst & White, c. 1917. WVSA

2. Aerial view. GE (2012)

3. Typical street. WVSA (1918)

4. Executives' houses on Twenty-first Street. Hubacher. WVSA (c. 1918)

divided the land longitudinally, providing a suitable boundary between the factory to the west and the town that was laid out as a grid of three north–south avenues crossed by fifty-seven numbered streets.

Workers lived in separate sections distributed according to race, nationality, and skill level, and with the exception of sixty-two one- and two-story multigabled executives' houses along Twenty-first Street, reaching east into the foothills, Nitro's 1,724 houses consisted of nearly identical one-story, four-, five-, and six-room gabled rectangular boxes aligned parallel to the street. All featured small front porches and vertical, brown creosote-stained siding. To speed construction, the frames were prefabricated by the Minter Homes Division of the Huntington Lumber and Supply Co., eighty-five miles by rail from Nitro, and designed to each fit on a single boxcar. Assembled by workers on site, the houses were also designed to be portable so that with the close of the war they could be shipped to other locations. Construction of the town began in February 1918 and was completed on July 9, forty-five days ahead of schedule. A record sixty houses were completed on a single day in May.

Although Nitro quickly sprouted a full range of public facilities, including clubhouses, YMCAs and YWCAs, movie theaters, stores, hotels, a 14-acre hospital complex, schools, a police station, and a bank, little to no land was reserved within the town for parks, and living conditions were cramped, with, for example, 250 four-room houses accommodating 2,000 black workers, 100 four-room bungalows built for 685 foreign workers, 100 six-room houses for 800 foremen, and 250 four-room bungalows housing 1,500 skilled mechanics.

Only one shipment of powder had been made when the signing of the armistice brought all operations to a halt. Within a week, half the population had left to seek work elsewhere. The end of the war also led to the demise of some plans that would have benefited the town, including the construction of a highway and streetcar connecting it to Charleston, a railroad bridge across the Kanawha, and 117 more executive houses in the foothills, as well as a dozen nearby real estate developments. In late 1919, Nitro—the entire town and 737 manufacturing plants—was sold by the U.S. government to a group of businessmen organized as the Charleston Industrial Corporation, who paid $8.5 million, a fraction of the $70 million it cost to build, and began marketing Nitro across the nation to attract manufacturers. But, as Work Projects Administration writers described it in 1941, "the mushroom city of 1918 slowly shriveled in size and importance. Most of the factory buildings were scrapped; many of the houses were sold to coal companies and shipped down the river on barges without being dismembered."[293] Other houses remain in altered form on the blocks bound by Twenty-third and Fortieth Streets, First and Second Avenues. The executive houses on Twenty-first Street have also survived remarkably intact. Over time, Nitro was revived as an industrial center, attracting chemical plants that earned

the Kanawha Valley the nickname "The Chemical Capital of the World."

In December 1917, the Atlantic Loading Company was founded by a consortium of businessmen to build a plant in which the explosive ingredients manufactured at places like Nitro and Perry Point would be loaded into shells of various sizes, ranging from hand grenades and 75-mm projectiles to 10-inch drop bombs.[294] The plant and its affiliated town, **Amatol,** New Jersey, named for the mixture of 80 percent ammonium nitrate and 20 percent TNT that the Ordnance Department employed as its principal explosive, was located four miles south of Hammonton, about halfway between Philadelphia and Atlantic City. Set amid 6,000 acres of New Jersey's densely wooded and swampy pine barrens, Amatol's 350-acre town site, planned for a population of 25,000, was safely distanced two miles northeast of the 2,550-acre plant.

Clinton Mackenzie, a New York architect who had recently collaborated with John Nolen on the design of Kingsport, Tennessee (see p. 264), prepared the town plan and designed the uniformly steel-framed, stucco-on-metal-lath buildings that could "be wrecked and readily converted into a large variety of manufacturing buildings," as company literature put it: "This steel construction was adopted because of the salvage value of the material."[295] Intended to be temporary, Mackenzie noted that the housing "presented no unusual features except in detail construction," and he illustrated only a few of the auxiliary buildings in his 1920 book, *Industrial Housing.*[296]

Mackenzie's town plan, combining formal and naturalistic elements, adhered to Garden City planning principles, with an overall density of about twelve houses per acre and the various dormitories, single- and multifamily dwellings, and barracks staggered back and forth from the street and placed in courtyard-enclosing groups. Although basic, Mackenzie livened up the houses with trellised arches, shutters, and enclosed porches. Blocks varied in size and shape and parks were scattered throughout, including a central 800-foot-long oval. Automobiles were brought in from the west along J Street, a broad avenue leading to Liberty Court, "the keynote of the complete scheme," where a 950-seat vaudeville and movie theater commanded a shop-lined mall.[297] To the north, Lincoln Square served as a civic hub with mess halls, offices, and administrative buildings surrounding a plaza, from the southwest and southeast corners of which extended radial avenues. Workers traveled via railroad from Lincoln Square to the plant.

Construction began on March 4, 1918, less than twenty-four hours after the site was chosen, and the first shell was loaded on August 3. When operations were halted after the signing of the armistice, a town for 10,000 had been built, numbering 465 buildings that included 11 single-family houses, 33 multiple houses, 227 workmen's houses, and more than 100 dormitories, as well as four YMCAs, a post office, school, hospital, office building, 16 recreation centers, 21 stores, 18 mess halls, and a theater. As planned, most of the buildings were

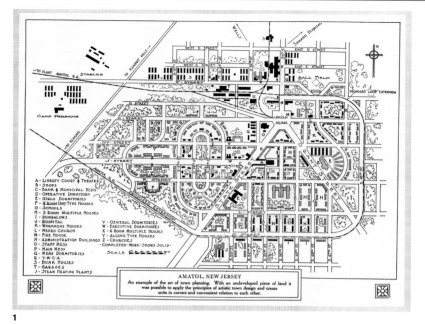

1

2

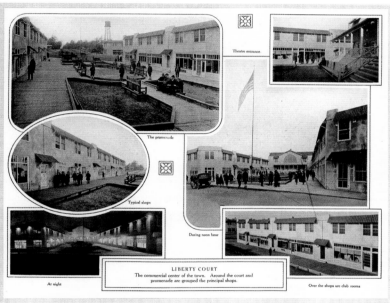

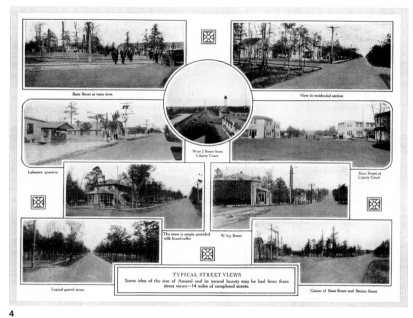

3

4

1. Plan, Clinton Mackenzie, 1918. AMAT

2. Typical houses. AMAT (1918)

3. Liberty Court. AMAT (1918)

4. Typical streets. AMAT (1918)

dismantled for scrap and the machinery was auctioned off. In 1926, a portion of the site was reincarnated as the immensely popular Atlantic City Speedway, a wooden automobile racetrack capable of handling speeds of up to 160 mph and providing parking for 60,000 cars, but only lasting a short time. With the exception of an administration building that was reused for the New Jersey State Police, Amatol is an overgrown ruin.

United States Housing Corporation

Similar in makeup and purpose to the Emergency Fleet Corporation, the United States Housing Corporation, headed by civil engineer and prominent New York builder Otto M. Eidlitz (1860–1928), began its work later than the EFC and was therefore even more seriously affected by the quick end to the war. The USHC's original program called for the construction of eighty-three subdivisions serving munitions plants and other factories converted to war production, accommodating roughly 25,000 families, or 125,000 people, in houses and 24,000 single men and women in dormitories. After the signing of the armistice, fifty-four projects were completely dropped and another seventeen reduced in scope. All told, 5,899 houses and dormitory space for 8,109 people were completed. Like the EFC, the USHC called upon the nation's top architects, planners, and landscape architects, making an effort to employ local firms whenever possible. Despite the fact that so much of the work was not completed, the USHC produced a remarkable record of its operations, a surprisingly objective two-volume report published in 1919 that exhaustively analyzed the agency's built and unbuilt projects.[298] As John Taylor Boyd Jr. wrote in *Architectural Record*, the release of the USHC report "must be considered an event in the

1. Title page. USHC (1919)

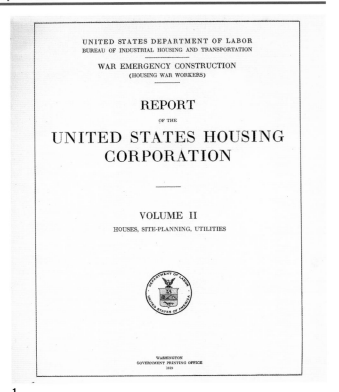

UNITED STATES DEPARTMENT OF LABOR
BUREAU OF INDUSTRIAL HOUSING AND TRANSPORTATION

WAR EMERGENCY CONSTRUCTION
(HOUSING WAR WORKERS)

REPORT
OF THE
UNITED STATES HOUSING
CORPORATION

VOLUME II
HOUSES, SITE-PLANNING, UTILITIES

WASHINGTON
GOVERNMENT PRINTING OFFICE
1919

1

literature of architecture. It will be welcomed by a much wider circle than our profession—by town planners, engineers, manufacturers, labor interests and agencies devoted to social betterment, philanthropy and civic improvement." The USHC report stood in stark contrast to one issued by the Emergency Fleet Corporation, which as Boyd noted, "we may infinitely regret . . . is so much less complete," including "only here and there part of a site plan" and offering "no explanations of policy, of organization employed in the program, of technical details used, or any of that so generous admitting of mistakes that is found in . . . the Housing Corporation report." Taking the long view, Boyd declared that "the significance of the war industrial housing lies in the future. We are interested in it as architecture, not for archaeology. If rightly taken, it could inspire a great movement, of benefit not simply for the professions concerned, but for American civilization."[299]

Boyd's view was not shared by all. In 1919 the work of the USHC was the subject of a series of hearings before a Subcommittee of the United States Senate's Committee on Public Buildings and Grounds during which every detail of the initiative was scrutinized—from the selection of architects to the amount paid for land and the types of materials used.[300] Criticism of the program came from private real estate developers who believed that the government was taking work from them and overcomplicating the process to an unpatriotic extent but also from within the ranks of the USHC itself, as articulated by William E. Shannon, who, as both a prominent Washington realtor and manager of the Real Estate and Commandeering Division of the USHC, responsible for acquiring sites, had disagreed strongly with its planning

and architectural arm. Shannon confronted the Convention of the National Association of Real Estate Boards in 1919 with a negative assessment that reflected the rapidly escalating xenophobia of the postwar era:

The personnel of the United States Housing Corporation was as high as in any bureau of the Government. It was composed of men who were successful leaders in their respective businesses and professions, but, with exceptions, amateurs in the business of industrial housing. They were in the main full of theoretical European ideas, always looking to England and Germany for example and not realizing or appreciating the fact that the American-born industrial worker resented being patronized by his employer or subsidized by his Government . . . A home and its construction and purchase is inherently a local proposition and can best be handled from beginning to end by the local people . . . The street layout of the English "village beautiful" for this country is . . . all wrong. Their design is to have many blocked streets for the purpose of seclusion, and those that are open must be as crooked as possible, even where the topographical features of the land do not demand it. This ancient and un-American scheme was very much favored by a group of landscape gardeners of the bureau who renamed themselves "town planners," which the architects of the bureau resented, and renamed themselves "architects and town planners." These so-called "town planners" from the appearance of their town designs must have secured their experience in this work from old books on landscape architecture published by the monks. Their plans were mostly of the de Medici period, when towns were built for defense, when streets were on angles and curves so they could be defended with the weapons of the day from the rush of invading hordes. They did not appreciate that Benjamin Franklin [sic] planned a town in this country not designed for defense, but with straight, broad streets, so that God could purify every corner with his sun and fresh air; and they did not seem to know that later came the great French engineer—L'Enfant—who, assisted by Washington and Jefferson, improved the plan of Philadelphia in the design of the Nation's Capital by putting in diagonal avenues. From that date to this America has broken away from the European idea of town planning, and I think it is safe to say we are not going back to it. I mention these things to show that we have little to learn from England, or Italy, and nothing to learn from Germany as to housing conditions in this country.[301]

While Shannon's diatribe can be dismissed as real estate bluster, or worse, as a sign of the provincialism that would grip American political life for at least two

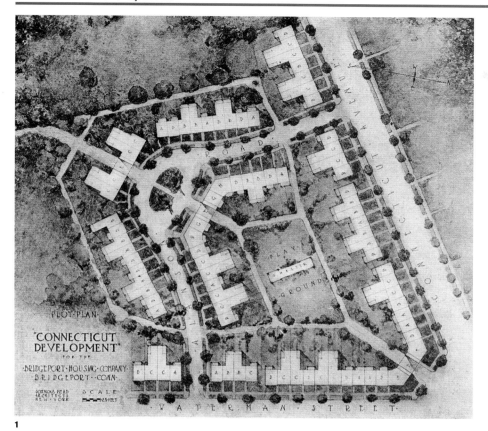

1. Plan, Marcia Mead, 1917–18.
AA18

2. Kitchen court and gardens.
AA18 (c. 1918)

decades, it nonetheless cannot be ignored as a symptom of the qualitative decline of standards that would characterize suburban development between the two world wars and their virtual abandonment in the 1940s through the 1970s. As a result of such resistance to ideas, especially foreign ideas, just as the industrial village movement reached a pinnacle of sophisticated design and social idealism, it was largely ignored.

The EFC's industrial villages represent a highpoint of accomplishment, but those of the USHC are in many cases of equal importance. For example, five planned subdivisions scattered throughout Bridgeport, Connecticut, are a worthy complement to the EFC's Yorkship Village.[302] Viewed as a group, the Bridgeport projects are quite impressive, achieving a high level of design, while one of the subdivisions, Seaside Village, can be considered exceptional, representing one of the most accomplished examples of workers' housing built during the period.

Even before America's entry into the war, Bridgeport, a well-diversified industrial center specializing in machine manufacture and metalworking, located on the Long Island Sound sixty miles northeast of New York City, was experiencing a severe housing shortage as the population of workers boomed to accommodate factories supplying material to the war effort in Europe. In 1915 housing was so scarce that some workers purchased train tickets "simply to enjoy the privilege of sleeping on a railroad station bench."[303] Adding tension to the situation was labor unrest, with more than 30,000 workers, ranging from employees of munitions plants and corset manufacturers to school teachers, going out

on strike in 1915 to demand better conditions, including improved housing, leading Mayor Clifford B. Wilson and the Bridgeport Chamber of Commerce to hire John Nolen to study the problem. Nolen returned with a comprehensive plan for the city that recommended the decentralization of industry and residents, with skilled workers accommodated in single-family detached houses in the outlying sections of the city, semiskilled workers housed in apartment groups that would form small "industrial villages," and single men and women placed in boardinghouses near factory sites.[304] In addition, Nolen suggested the creation of a new agency to oversee the housing effort.

In late 1915 Mayor Wilson, with the support of twelve of Bridgeport's leading manufacturers and three of the city's public utilities, heeded Nolen's advice and created the Bridgeport Housing Corporation. Led by Boston engineer William H. Ham (n.d.), who believed that "the home of the workingman is the balance wheel of democracy," the group immediately set to work surveying the city for possible development sites.[305] A first effort—to build housing in concert with the Remington Arms Company—was not successful, but the munitions manufacturer was encouraged to build on its own, completing housing (1916–17) for 700 employees near its factory, including straight rows of two- and three-story semidetached brick houses and a twelve-family apartment house designed by Alfred C. Bossom, as well as two- and four-family houses and three girls' dormitories designed by the firm of Philip Hiss (1857–1940) and H. Hobart Weeks (1867–1950).[306] The development was uninspired.

1. Key map showing USHC
subdivisions. USHC (1918)

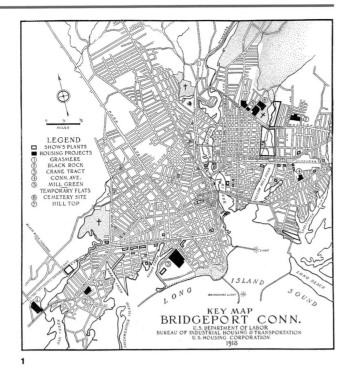

1

Black Rock

1. Plan, Arthur A. Shurtleff, 1918.
USHC

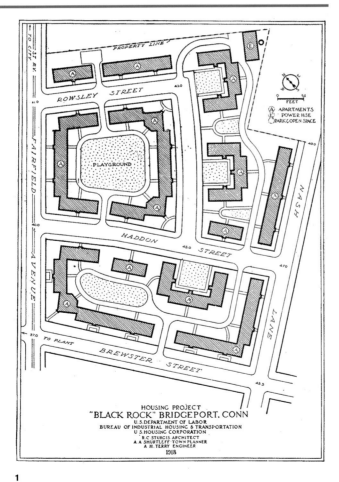

1

The Bridgeport Housing Corporation had better luck with its next venture, the so-called **Connecticut Development** (1917–18), or Connecticut Village, designed by New York architect Marcia Mead (1879–1967), who with her partner Anna Pendleton Schenck (1874–1915) had won first prize in the Chicago City Club's Neighborhood Center Competition of 1915.[307] Located in a densely settled section of the city near manufacturing plants on a site bound by Connecticut Avenue, Waterman Street, and curving Alonson Road, the enclave, now known as Gateway Village, consisted of eighty-seven blandly detailed brick rowhouses with slate roofs grouped around a generous shared interior court. Mead alternated four different types of house plans, including two-, three-, and four-room flats and five-room houses. It was an artistic and social success. Nonetheless, America's deeper involvement in the war brought with it material shortages and goods and transportation rationing, rendering the Bridgeport Housing Corporation inadequate to take on the larger projects required, leading them to be taken over by the USHC. The first step was to hire a new design team to manage all of the planned projects, selecting Boston-based architect R. Clipston Sturgis who brought with him landscape architect Arthur A. Shurtleff, planner of the industrial village of Hopedale, Massachusetts.

Sturgis and Shurtleff examined twenty **Bridgeport** sites in detail and selected seven: Black Rock, Connecticut Avenue, Crane Tract, Grasmere, Mill Green, and two sites for temporary housing near Mill Green that remained unrealized due to the quick end of the war. Although all were chosen to bring the greatest number of workers within walking distance of their plants, economic returns were kept in mind, and the cost of land in the long-established, heavily developed city, higher than in most other USHC cities, produced a higher density than was usual in the wartime housing program. One advantage of building in Bridgeport was the wide availability of commercial resources and public services, such as schools, allowing the architects to concentrate solely on providing housing in the villages.

The Black Rock and Connecticut Avenue tracts were the most densely developed subdivisions, consisting exclusively of apartment houses. Roughly bound by Fairfield Avenue, Nash Lane, and Brewster and Rowsley Streets, the seven-acre **Black Rock** site, two-and-a-half miles from the center of the city and adjacent to the Bullard Machine Tool plant, included a large number of mature shade trees that Sturgis and Shurtleff incorporated into their plan to great effect.[308] Sturgis's thirty-three, three-story, six-family, two-room-deep brick apartment houses were designed in a restrained neo-Georgian style with a sparing use of cast-stone details and three-story wooden porches located at the rear of the buildings. The principal set of apartment houses was grouped around a large, shared planted courtyard accessible by a service road, reminiscent of the college quadrangles that had recently been built at many American universities. Other apartment houses were sited in rows or placed in

2. Pathway winding through housing blocks. USHC (c. 1919)

3. Rowsley Street. AR24 (c. 1919)

4–7. Typical views. RAMSA (2007)

a U-shaped arrangement around a wide court open to the street. There were only three different apartment plans repeated throughout the subdivision, with the majority containing four rooms. Five-room units were placed facing Fairfield Avenue, a major thoroughfare that was home to a trolley line. Sturgis also included a small number of three-room corner apartments that, according to Frank Chouteau Brown, broke "up the angularity of the block corners, particularly in the rectangular 'courtyard' plans, thus introducing a pleasing element of irregularity into the hardest and most irreconcilably rectilinear of the architectural forms adopted for the whole project . . . This recessed or 'set-back' corner also increases the range of visibility at the intersecting streets."[309]

The apartments represented a significant improvement over the typical fare in Bridgeport, which usually had at least one room facing a shaft, small court, or side yard, whereas all of the rooms at Black Rock enjoyed direct outside lighting and ventilation. In his 1925 survey of American apartment houses published in the

1. Plan, Arthur A. Shurtleff, 1918.
USHC

2. Courtyard. AR24 (c. 1919)

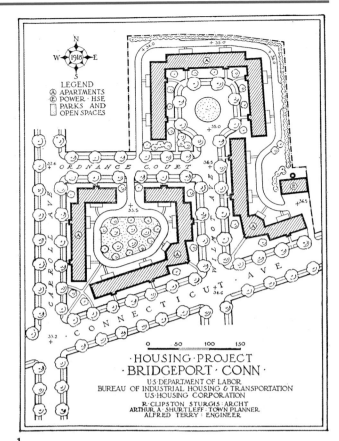

1

2

Journal of the Royal Institute of British Architects, English architect William T. Benslyn (1885–1947) praised Black Rock as "an excellent example of an apartment housing scheme which combines good design of the apartments themselves with a well thought out development of the land on which they are built. There is ample sunshine, light and air everywhere, and where trees occurred they have been carefully preserved . . . Economy has been studied throughout, but there is no unpleasant effect of standardization, the elevations are greatly helped by the use of classical detail for the entrance porches."[310]

Sturgis and Shurtleff's **Connecticut Avenue** subdivision was a smaller, similarly dense, less picturesque enclave of three-story, two-room-deep apartment houses located in the eastern part of the city on a three-acre parcel just north of the intersection of Wilmot and Connecticut Avenues, four blocks west of Marcia Mead's

Connecticut Village.[311] Here, the architects, regrettably unencumbered by existing trees or other natural features on the vacant, flat site bordered on its north by an ordnance plant, grouped the eighteen brick buildings housing 108 families in three different configurations: a roughly L-shaped block at the southeast portion of the site; a quadrangle enclosing a shared, irregularly shaped courtyard at the southwestern corner; and a U-shaped arrangement of six buildings facing Wilmot Avenue which concluded in a large circle, "terminating an agreeable vista of dignified architecture," as Sylvester Baxter wrote in *Architectural Record* in 1919.[312] Sturgis employed the same spare neo-Georgian vocabulary he had used on the Black Rock tract but added an occasional bay window and provided for larger five-room units. Shurtleff instituted a comprehensive planting program to help relieve the featureless site.

The Mill Green and Grasmere subdivisions were developed at a more suburban scale. Located on 20 acres in the northeastern part of the city roughly bound by Boston Avenue and East Main, Essex, Plymouth, and Colony Streets, **Mill Green**, within walking distance of several factories, fronted the Old Mill Green, a long, narrow common parallel to the historic Boston Post Road, on its southern border.[313] Sturgis and Shurtleff provided a mix of detached and semidetached single- and two-family houses and rowhouses located on three irregularly shaped adjacent parcels. The plan of two of the sections, the Mill Green and Judson (Mill Green Extension) plots, was largely determined by the site's picturesque natural features, which were incorporated into the scheme, including numerous mature trees, wild shrubbery, rock outcroppings, and large ledges. East of Asylum Street, the so-called Cemetery Extension, located on a flat vacant site, featured a more regular grid. The best of the groupings was at the Judson site, where buildings surrounded three sides of a deep, planted court open to Boston Avenue and the Old Mill Green. Sturgis's one-and-a-half- and two-story four- to six-room neo-Georgian brick houses, with slate roofs, modest front yards, and rear gardens, were placed on irregular plots that on average measured 90 feet deep, while the rowhouses occupied 50-foot-deep lots. The architects, with the luxury of a large, comparatively inexpensive site, achieved a density of ten families per acre, as opposed to the thirty-one families per acre at Black Rock.

Frederick Law Olmsted Jr., the manager of the Town Planning Division of the USHC, took special note of Mill Green in an article chronicling his work at the government agency, writing that he was impressed with the village's "irregular" plan "offering some very interesting compositions." He also liked the individual buildings, writing that "the skillfully straightforward architecture of these buildings, all of simple outline, with plain brick walls and uncomplicated slate roofs, produces some of the most attractive results to be found in any of the projects of the Housing Corporation."[314]

Grasmere, located on a 10-acre site just beyond the western border of Bridgeport in the town of Fairfield,

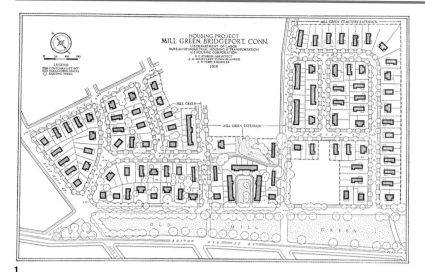

1. Plan, Arthur A. Shurtleff, 1918. USHC

2. Typical street. USHC (1918)

3, 4. Typical views. RAMSA (c. 1980)

was less successful, owing mostly to the fact that the level tract was already platted in a standard grid and several of the lots developed with houses.[315] Sturgis and Shurtleff added semidetached single- and two-family houses and rowhouses to the existing mix in the hope that the new buildings would improve the overall look of the neighborhood. But as the USHC noted in its report, the opposite turned out to be the case: "Owing to the disharmony between our brick houses and the previous wooden ones . . . it is less attractive than before we built and probably less agreeable than it would have been if its blanks had been filled up by wooden houses of inferior architecture but not so contentious with their neighbors." Even where the architects had a freer hand in shaping the plan, as along unimproved and vacant Roanoke Avenue, they faltered, "overdoing the desirable variation of setback," and enlarging "the front yards too much at the expense of the back." The USHC report also criticized the individual buildings, designed by Sturgis in association with Skinner & Walker, a local Bridgeport firm, observing that "a noticeable feature of some of the houses at Grasmere is the unsymmetrical spacing of windows in elevations otherwise symmetrical," adding that the porches were "almost too small for comfort" with "details . . . somewhat too delicate in design."[316]

The largest and most accomplished of the Bridgeport subdivisions was the Crane Tract, soon known as

Seaside Village, ironically intended for the least-skilled workers, developed with the smallest houses, and purposely planned with reduced standards intended to keep the middle class from annexing the conveniently located housing after the war (a goal that was not realized).[317] Located on a flat, rectangular 25-acre site adjacent to the plant of the R. T. Crane Company, manufacturers of metal products, Sturgis and Shurtleff's plan, designed in association with Boston architect Andrew H. Hepburn, benefited from a delay in the schedule, allowing the architects to study the houses in model form, with the result, according to Sylvester Baxter, that "the plan well illustrates the possibilities and advantages of a nonrectangular development in economizing ground space and street construction and equipment with due regard to convenience of movement and the maximum benefit from sunlight and air, together with the housing of a population as large as such a tract can hold without congestion."[318] The only downside to the delay in beginning construction was the abrupt end of the war, which prevented the full implementation of the plan, leaving unrealized the section between Burnham and Atlantic Streets west of Forest Street. As a result, Seaside Village ultimately accommodated 257 families instead of the intended 377 households.

The rows of single- and two-family neo-Georgian brick houses at Seaside Village were arranged in

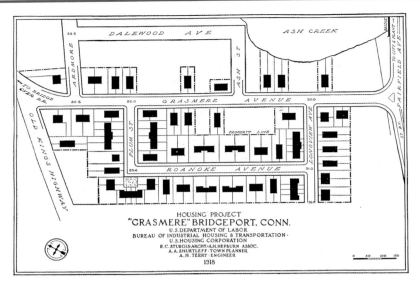

1. Plan, Arthur A. Shurtleff, 1918. USHC

2–5. Typical views. RAMSA (2007)

groups designed according to street layout and other considerations. The carefully detailed massing of the one-and-a-half- and two-story houses, their architectural treatment, and their placement along the picturesque streets recalled an old New England village where outbuildings and extensions were added over time to the original houses. But the irregularities in plan were not arbitrary. Some were caused, as at Black Rock, by the location of existing trees. Other features, such as the several courts, stemmed from a desire to have as few houses as possible front on South Avenue, a heavily traveled road leading directly to the Crane factory. The resulting green spaces were often used as playgrounds by neighborhood children. A larger, triangular green at roughly the center of the site served as a quasi-town square, hosting community events.

Both Seaside Village's plan and its houses were widely praised in the USHC's report: "In the grouping of the houses into rows and into linked-up building masses so irregular that they can hardly be called rows, and in the grouping of these rows and building masses themselves into larger compositions; in the deflections of angle, in the relation of the road and sidewalk lines to the building masses, and apparently in the placing of the trees, an artistically dangerous and difficult thing has been done with notable artistic success. From almost any point of view within the development the houses look well." Though small and spartan—the houses were built

with no source of heat except for the kitchen stoves—the report declared them "pleasant to the eye, being of a soft red tone and they appeal to good taste because of their simple long lines, and the delicate moldings of doorways and cornices and their general proportions. There is a distinct similarity in the houses, yet nowhere is the view of any row monotonous."[319]

In 1993, seventy-five years after its construction, Mark Alden Branch, writing in *Progressive Architecture*, attributed Seaside Village's continued status as a stable community in an otherwise run-down section of Bridgeport—it was nicknamed "the oasis" by local police—to its plan of "curving, tree-lined streets" and architecture of "houselike Georgian buildings . . . Physically, Seaside Village has aged well," Branch added. "With its brick facades, slate roofs, and large trees, it looks as good as any number of upper-middle-class suburbs of the day, even though there are subtle signs that it was built hastily and cheaply."[320]

Vincent Scully, who praised all of the Bridgeport subdivisions, singled out Seaside Village for special attention, writing that "the one that was intended for the lowest-paid workers in the factories is the most beautiful of them all . . . It was designed . . . by some of the best architects in the United States . . . The image of the single-family house is present everywhere, though subdivided in various ways to meet the narrow budget. But the identity is always there, the good door, the bay window.

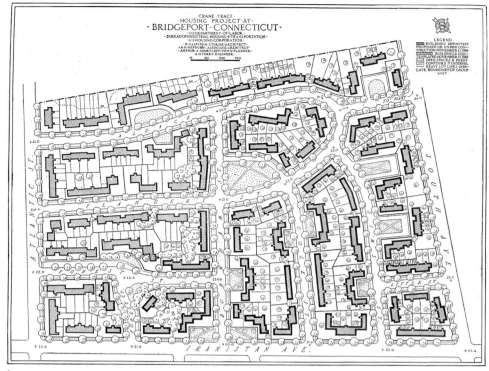

1. Plan, Arthur A. Shurtleff, 1918. USHC

2. Rear yards. USHC (c. 1919)

3–7. Typical views. RAMSA (2007)

Directly after the war, a congressional investigation concluded that the federal government should get out of the housing field, calling it too 'socialistic' and, it said, 'un-American,' and it specifically chided the architects" of Seaside Village for "'undue elegance in design.'"[321]

All told, in less than a year's time, the USHC completed five distinct subdivisions in Bridgeport accommodating 889 families, a remarkable achievement considering the high level of design. The supply of substantial new houses no doubt helped the industrial city fulfill its wartime obligations, with Bridgeport manufacturing two-thirds of all small arms and ammunition shipped to the Allies from the United States. Referring to all of the USHC projects built in Bridgeport, Sylvester Baxter declared them "a model of their kind; an invaluable asset to the community, enhancing the beauty of the city and setting so high a standard of convenience, comfort and taste as inevitably to encourage a demand among working-people of this class that will hereafter not be easily satisfied with anything less than 'something just as good' in the truest sense of the term. Such leaven can hardly fail to work. And what a contrast to the jerrybuilt

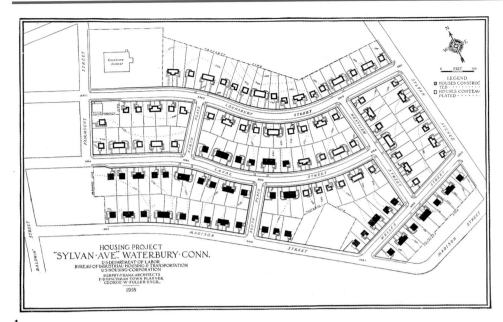

1. Plan, Frederick B. Hinchman, 1918. USHC

2. Madison Street. Harris. LOCP (c. 1918)

3. Laval Street. RAMSA (2013)

4. Rear gardens. Harris. LOCP (c. 1918)

wooden three-deckers and two-flatters, in which workers are so often deluded into investing their good savings, are these substantially handsome and dignified apartments and equally substantial individual dwellings, enduringly built, beautifully cosy and garden-embowered!"[322] Thomas Adams, writing a dozen years later in a 1931 Regional Plan of New York publication, seconded the notion with the assertion that "it is doubtful if any large housing project has proved such a valuable object lesson in good housing as that carried out at Bridgeport."[323]

Waterbury, Connecticut, located thirty miles northeast of Bridgeport in the Naugatuck River Valley and surrounded by high hills, nicknamed the "brass city," was since the mid-nineteenth century an important industrial center known for its metal-manufacturing mills and watch and clock factories. Between July 1917 and June 1918 Waterbury's population grew by 32 percent, to 115,000 residents, prompting the USHC to hire landscape architect Frederick B. Hinchman (1871–1951) and the New York and New Haven firm of Henry Killam Murphy and Richard Henry Dana Jr. to prepare plans for two sites in the city.[324]

Except for a modest trolley line, Waterbury lacked significant public transportation, leading the architects to select sites within walking distance of the industrial plants. To serve workers at the Chase Metals Works located in the northern part of the city, 11 acres were donated by the company. But before Hinchman and Murphy & Dana prepared any detailed plans for the subdivision, intended to provide housing for seventy families in forty-seven detached and twenty-two semi-detached houses and one apartment unit, the project was abandoned as the USHC decided to concentrate its energies and resources on a more centrally located 18-acre parcel convenient to existing schools, a fire station, as well as a public park. This steep and rocky tract, the so-called Sylvan Avenue site, adjacent to the Scovill Manufacturing Company and within walking distance of the American Brass Company, was intended to accommodate 135 families in sixty-eight detached and sixty-six semidetached houses, along with one household to be located in an apartment over a store building.

Hinchman and Murphy & Dana's plan of topographically responsive curving streets divided the property into lots that on average measured 100 feet deep, with detached houses separated from each other by 20 to 25 feet and semidetached houses featuring side yards of 25 to 35 feet, a typical configuration for Waterbury. No two pairs of semidetached houses were placed next to each other, and the most common grouping

1. Plan, Charles N. Lowrie, 1918. USHC

2. Lincoln Oval. USHC (1919)

3. Lincoln Oval. RAMSA (2013)

4. Colver Street. RAMSA (2013)

consisted of a pair of semidetached houses flanked on each side by a detached house. The houses in these groups were set back the same distance from the street, as opposed to many USHC projects where the central building was set back much farther. In its report, the USHC approved of this approach, writing that "the effect produced here by placing the front walls all on the same line, and relying for the effect of projection and recession upon the positions and forms of the porches and of the roof lines, is pleasanter from the artistic standpoint, and as a commercial proposition avoids the objection which some purchasers have to a house set further back than its neighbors."[325]

Murphy & Dana's two-and-a-half-story, stucco-clad five- and six-room houses were similar in design, but architectural historian Talbot Hamlin, in his 1926 book, *The American Spirit in Architecture*, praised their ingenuity in giving a sense of variety to what were "only two plans . . . by reversing, turning, and combining these, and by careful use of inexpensive materials."[326] The handsome houses, deemed by the USHC "among the best work done for the corporation," had steeply sloping shingle-clad roofs that swept down to serve as the covers of the projecting porches, giving "to the houses the comparatively low appearance so much to be desired in houses of small plan area." Although intended to save money, the decision to exclude window trim was commended by the USHC because it made "the windows appear larger in scale."[327] Similarly, *Architectural Review* pointed out that the economizing measure of dipping the blinds in a creosote stain instead of painting them "produced a very attractive effect."[328] All told, due to

the quick end to the war, only twenty-nine detached and twenty-six semidetached houses were completed at Waterbury's Sylvan Avenue site, or roughly 40 percent of the number initially planned.

Two additional industrial cities in Connecticut, New London and Groton (also home to an EFC project), separated from each other by the Thames River, were also experiencing housing shortages due to an influx of wartime workers. So severe was the shortage in **New London**, whose population had more than doubled between 1910 and 1918, that rampant rent gouging had attracted the attention of the Department of Labor, which dispatched agents from the War Labor Policies Board to review the situation. Appeals to the patriotism of local landlords had little effect and attempts to ease the housing shortage by running additional trains to New London from Saybrook only brought modest relief. To solve the problem, the USHC commissioned the firm of Francis L. V. Hoppin (1867–1941) and Terence A. Koen (1858–1923) along with landscape architect Charles N. Lowrie (1869–1940), town planner of the USHC developments in New Brunswick, New Jersey, and Alton, Illinois, to plan subdivisions.[329]

The architects examined sixteen sites before selecting a 20-acre parcel in New London and a 3-acre tract in Groton. The New London site was located in the western part of the city, less than a mile from City Hall, convenient to a trolley line, and within a half mile of schools, churches, stores, playgrounds, and recreational facilities. Bound by Jefferson Avenue to the north, West Pleasant Street to the east, Colman Street to the south, and Fuller Street to the west, the well-served location allowed the design team to concentrate on the subdivision's exclusively residential character, consisting of fifteen detached and 148 semidetached houses intended for skilled mechanics and their families. As at Waterbury, a store building topped by an apartment was planned but not realized.

The plan consisted of a modified grid with mostly straight streets but none running over 500 feet in length, "thus maintaining a good scale for the street vistas of a strictly residential district," according to the USHC's report. Lowrie provided 25- to 30-foot-wide lots for the semidetached houses, while the small number of detached houses enjoyed more generous 40- to 50-foot-wide lots; side yards measured between 16 and 25 feet and most lots had a depth of 110 feet. The rows of houses featured staggered setbacks that the USHC report considered "greater than necessary, or even desirable, and do not sufficiently take into account the forms of the porches and house roofs, and the size of the porches." The entrance sequence to the subdivision, beginning at the intersection of Jefferson and Lincoln Avenues, was attractive and well planned: the continuation of Lincoln Avenue, which included a landscaped median, led to an oval green. While the USHC noted that "the grouping of houses around the oval is pleasant," it felt that it "would have been still more effective if the houses, especially those next to Lincoln Avenue and Colver Street, had been advanced nearer to the oval, reducing the spaces between the corners of the houses framing the oval and emphasizing the curve which they define."[330]

Despite the abrupt end to hostilities, 71 percent of the New London project—12 detached and 104 semidetached houses—was built, a comparatively high percentage of completion for the USHC. The smaller Groton site, already platted, was of much less interest, consisting of seven detached and eighteen semidetached houses of the same design as the New London buildings, laid out along two straight streets.

Bethlehem, Pennsylvania, founded as a Moravian settlement in 1741, boomed during World War I when the Bethlehem Steel Co. began supplying arms to the European allies. Between the outbreak of war in 1914 and the entry of the United States in 1917, Bethlehem Steel's workforce grew from 11,000 to 28,000. The company's 10-mile-long works dominated the south side of the Lehigh River while the north side contained Bethlehem's Moravian core and outlying residential districts, many of which were being built by private developers who responded to wartime demand by purchasing blocks of the street grid and building semidetached and rowhouses with no consistency in size or style. Bethlehem's first planned residential neighborhood was built in 1917, when the Pittsburgh-based developers Wood and Hawthorne undertook **Elmwood Park** on a 27-acre, L-shaped site owned by Weston Dodson & Company, a realty corporation that marketed the housing to Bethlehem Steel workers.[331]

Although it was not a USHC project, Elmwood Park served as a precedent for Pembroke Village, a neighboring USHC development built in 1918. Roughly bound by Pembroke Road and Broad, Wood, and Elm Streets, Elmwood Park was planned by landscape architect Ruth Bramley Dean (1889–1932), working with Wilkes Barre architect George S. Welsh, who designed the houses. Welsh was also currently at work on the garden village of Sawyer Park, in Williamsport, Pennsylvania, built by the same developer, and Dean was completing her book *The Livable House: Its Garden* (1917).[332]

In an effort to capture "some of the artless charm of old villages which have grown up naturally," Dean eschewed the "so-called checkerboard plan, with its monotonous straight streets crossing each other at regular intervals" and focused the neighborhood inward on an elongated north–south oval. From the south side of the oval, roads led diagonally southeast toward the steel mill and southwest toward Bethlehem's business district. "Almost everyone recognizes the complete ugliness of the illimitable street down which one gazes to nothing," Dean wrote, "and admits the delightfulness of what is known as the closed vista, the street whose end is blocked by a pleasing building . . . The number of direct cross streets on the Bethlehem plan was cut to a minimum, and in two or three places the streets curved moderately in order to introduce the pleasing informal spirit that belongs to the winding road." Dean's landscape design specified street trees, hedges, stone walkways, and foundation plantings, while "the inevitable triangles and other awkwardly shaped pieces of land of which there are always a resultant few" were used "as sites for group houses or stores or community buildings of one sort or another which will undoubtedly come when the settlement is a little older."[333]

Sixteen of the planned 27 acres were developed, with 2 acres given over to parks, 3.5 acres to streets and rear alleys, and the remaining 10.5 acres parceled into 235 house lots that were 22 by 80 feet on average, producing a density of about 20 houses per acre. A majority of the 160 detached, semidetached, and rowhouses that were only 14 or 16 feet wide and 32 to 38 feet deep, were situated to form two concentric ovals, with just 8 to 10 feet separating houses from one another. The houses were consistent in scale, construction, and style and were placed on or within 10 feet of the sidewalk, creating a village-like atmosphere. Welsh included two-story corner-hugging "butterfly units" in which the central of three contiguous houses faced an intersection diagonally and the two flanking units paralleled the streets.

Welsh attempted to strike a balance between Bethlehem's historic Colonial architecture and local preferences for more contemporary styles. But his efforts were not always appreciated: "One prospective buyer looked at the colonial cottage offered him for sale and objected, 'But I don't want that kind of a house; that's the same sort of houses they were building fifty years ago,'" leading Welsh to find it "rather discouraging, from the architect's point of view, to note the details with which the purchasers find fault. Small paned windows constitutes one of them." Moreover, Colonial houses did not

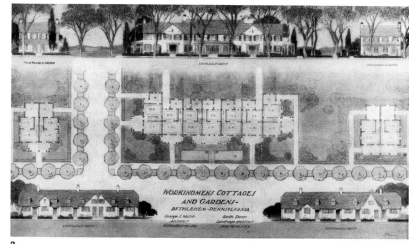

1. Plan, Ruth Bramley Dean, 1917. A17

2. Elevations and plans of workingmen's cottages and gardens, George S. Welsh, 1917. A17

3. East Garrison Street. RAMSA (2011)

4. Dodson Place, a rear alley cul-de-sac. RAMSA (2011)

5. Goepp Circle. RAMSA (2011)

6. Hawthorne Road. RAMSA (2011)

typically have front porches, "another item for which there is an inevitable demand; every architect knows that he can make a small house fairly attractive if he is not burdened by the necessity of porches—but the fate of the house minus a piazza is sealed—from the workingman's point of view it has no place in which to smoke one's evening pipe in solid coatless ease, and no vantage point from which to observe the doings of one's neighbors."[334] Elmwood Park was designated a National Register Historic District in 1988, by which time the report's authors warned that its "planned unity" was "declining" as owners individualized their houses by enclosing porches, replacing columns, removing slate roofs, and using various types and colors of siding. Nonetheless, they reported, "roughly 60 percent of original dormers, porches, windows and surfaces remain."[335]

While Bethlehem Steel could rely to a certain extent on private development to house the bulk of its workforce, in order to ensure decent accommodations for machinists and other skilled employees, in 1917 it formed a company to purchase land and develop 1,000 houses on the north side of the Lehigh River, one-and-a-half miles from the steelworks and only a couple of hundred feet northeast of Elmwood Park. But the project, which would have extended the city's gridiron across the site, was canceled for a lack of funds until 1918, when the USHC recognized Bethlehem Steel's housing shortage and provided financing for 2,000 dwellings. After looking fruitlessly for a site on the south side of the river nearer the works, the original gently sloping 170-acre tract was chosen and the landscape architect Thomas Warren Sears (1880–1966), of Philadelphia, prepared a new scheme for **Pembroke Village**.[336] At the time, Sears was also planning temporary quarters for troops in South Carolina and Michigan as well as the USHC's Penrose Avenue development in Philadelphia.

1. Plan, Thomas W. Sears, 1918.
USHC

2. Proposed commercial building,
Zantzinger, Borie & Medary, 1918.
USHC

3. Media Street. RAMSA (2011)

4. Arcadia Street. RAMSA (2011)

5. East Washington Avenue.
RAMSA (2011)

1

2

3

4

5

Sears widened Newton Avenue, running diagonally across the site, to accommodate a streetcar, and placed a civic center at its right-angled intersection with Washington Avenue, which continued circumferentially around Bethlehem. Residential streets formed concentric arcs surrounding the core and were cut through by gently curving transverse roads. A former quarry and knoll in the center of the property was retained as a park with a school located diagonally across the street. A second school, additional stores, and a library were slated for the site's northeast border to serve later phases of development.

Milton Bennett Medary Jr. (1874–1929), chairman of the USHC and a partner in the Philadelphia firm of Zantzinger, Borie & Medary, designed the houses and public buildings in a Colonial mode that the USHC's report described as "somewhat Dutch in character . . . conforming to local traditions and the preferences of the workers."[337] Difficulties in transporting materials to the

site led to the use of locally available brick, cement, and slate. After visiting neighboring Elmwood Park, Medary identified a local preference for six- and eight-room houses with porches and habitable attics that could be rented to boarders. Only 10 percent of the houses were built with attic rooms but all of the roofs were pitched at 45 degrees to provide a consistent streetscape. Nine rowhouse plans were prepared, the most common containing four and six houses. The groups were uniformly set back from the street on lots that either backed up to one another or enclosed temporary playgrounds—"blockways" as they were termed—that could be converted to rear alleys when necessary. The USHC's report detected an "uneasiness in composition" that could have been relieved by "a variety in grouping rather than by a variety in type of houses."[338]

The town center offered particular promise, with its four corners anchored by three-story combination store and apartment blocks, two of which featured angled corner facades dominated by overscaled archways. Renderings depicted one of the buildings in the rain, highlighting a sheltered vestibule that led to a movie theater. A firehouse and belfry were included in the companion block. Sears enhanced the village square with an oval commons pointing northeast on Newton Avenue, flanking it with double and triple houses and two apartment buildings. Unfortunately, the public buildings were not realized.

When the armistice was signed, only about an eighth of the Pembroke Village plan had been implemented. Although Bethlehem's mayor, city council, chamber of commerce, and other local officials made a strong push for completing the scheme, local developers opposed it and Bethlehem Steel, with a declining postwar workforce, was indifferent. The USHC officially scrapped the project on December 28, 1918, with more than 100 houses frozen in mid-construction. When the properties were sold off, individual buyers were provided with copies of Medary's designs and in some cases followed them, although as architectural historian Nicholas Adams has noted, with so many houses "roughly approximating Medary's plans, it is hard to estimate the full number that reflect his ideas."[339] In 1987, sixty-three of the single and multifamily dwellings that retained "good integrity" were designated a National Register Historic District.[340] Observing Pembroke Village at around the same time, Adams wrote: "Looking along one of the completed streets, today, we see that the rows are jogged (house to house and row to row) to give as little impression of symmetry as possible. There is nothing of the conventional contractor's terrace in the arrangement . . . Today a few blocks retain something of the character of the original World War I workers suburb, but they bleed off almost immediately to the bungalows of the 1940's and the fast-food chains and muffler shops of the contemporary American strip that has now engulfed much of the area."[341]

In addition to Pembroke Village, Thomas W. Sears planned the USHC's **Penrose Avenue** site in Philadelphia, slated for a triangular 94-acre parcel in a relatively undeveloped area near the Philadelphia Navy Yard bound by Penrose Avenue on the south and east, Twenty-eighth Street on the west, and Hartranft Street on the north, intended to accommodate 1,105 families in a mix of rowhouses, apartments, and semidetached houses. In the middle of the site, Sears outlined a commercial center that recalled his proposal for Pembroke Village, with almost identically planned store and theater blocks turning the northwest and northeast corners of the principal intersection and the south side opened up as a semicircle bordered by apartment buildings set back behind wedge-shaped parks. A streetcar line was to connect the town center with Philadelphia to the north and the navy yard to the southeast. Two large sites were set aside for schools—one in the center and one at the periphery to serve later expansions—and two prominent corners reserved for churches.

Sears's plan for the residential areas called for diversely shaped and sized residential blocks, some

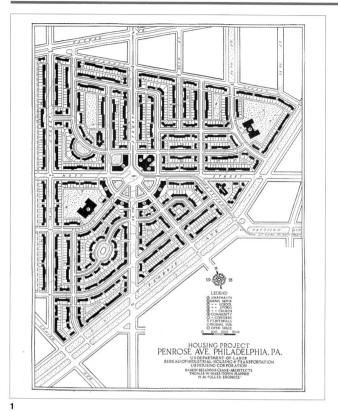

1. Plan, Thomas W. Sears, 1918. USHC

1

enclosing internal playgrounds and others shaped around crescents and ovals intended to become "the nuclei for different local arrangements."[342] Rowhouses, the predominant dwelling type, ranging from three to eleven units in length and designed by the Philadelphia firm of John Hall Rankin (1868–1952), Thomas Moore Kellogg (1862–1935), and Edward Andrew Crane (1867–1935), were staggered back and forth from the street and serviced by rear alleys. The project was discontinued before construction began.

At **Erie**, Pennsylvania, a long-established, well-diversified industrial center concentrating on munitions manufacture in response to the war, the population of workers nearly tripled, leading the USHC to step in with a plan for 1,500 houses distributed on three separate sites.[343] Initially the New York firm of Goldwyn Starrett (1876–1918) and Joseph Van Vleck Jr. (1876–1948) was retained to design the housing, but after Starrett's death the job went to Albert H. Spahr, architect of the recently completed industrial village of Midland, outside of Pittsburgh, who was joined by landscape architect Charles Downing Lay (1877–1956), who served as town planner.

On a level, 27-acre site near the General Electric plant, bound by two major thoroughfares on its north and south—East Lake Road and East Tenth Street, respectively—Lay planned the so-called East Site to include a near-equal mix of detached and semidetached single-family houses, along with a number of rowhouses and thirty-eight units of apartments, to house 223 skilled workmen and their families. Unfortunately, the most interesting part of the plan featuring rows of houses

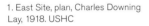

1. East Site, plan, Charles Downing Lay, 1918. USHC

2. East Site, typical street. USHC (1918)

3. West Site, plan, Charles Downing Lay, 1918. USHC

4. East Site, Euclid Avenue. Wieczorek. WIE (2013)

5. West Site, typical houses. USHC (1918)

6. West Site, houses. Wieczorek. WIE (2013)

along curved streets bordered by parks remained unrealized, with most of the construction confined to the gridded streets at the north end of the site. In contrast to the majority of USHC projects, which predominantly featured wood-frame houses clad in stucco, shingles, and clapboard, most of Spahr's houses were built of brick, owing to Erie's status as a leading center of brick production. The USHC report praised the Colonial-style slate-roofed houses, writing that "to these materials [brick and slate] one may attribute part of the good effect of this project—the color, the appearance of stability, and the lack of newness; but more important than any of these desirable qualities is the beauty of the design of each individual building. The houses have been excellently placed in relation to one another along the streets."[344]

Lay's plan for the 72-acre West Site called for a denser mix of 200 rowhouses, 172 semidetached and 95 detached houses, and 32 apartment-house units intended for workers of the American Brake Shoe & Foundry and Erie Forge Companies. A new east–west thoroughfare, Twelfth Street, bisected the site. A commercial component was planned for just north of Twelfth Street, while to the south room was set aside for a church, school, and community building. South of Woodland Drive, a large tract with a ravine and a dense grouping of trees was kept undeveloped to serve as a park. Spahr and Lay had better luck at the West Site, completing more than half of the proposed dwellings, including 161 of the 200 planned rowhouses. The civic buildings south of Twelfth Street were not built, but eight stores were completed to the north between Lincoln and Argonne Avenues. Although the design of the individual houses remained the same as at the East Site, the editors of the USHC report found the West Site's longer, four- and six-house groups less attractive. To supplement the housing built by the USHC, the American Brake Shoe & Foundry Company sponsored its own development (1918–19) of six- and nine-family three-story brick apartment houses and two-family houses placed on a regular grid and designed by Albert F. Edwards (1882–1968).[345] Lay picked a more picturesque, 115-acre parcel in the south central part of Erie as the third site, but the quick end to the war took plans for the 825-family South Site off the table before any detailed design work could be completed. All told, 315 dwellings were built by the USHC in Erie's two projects, about one-fifth of the amount originally planned.

Charles Downing Lay prepared a second plan for the USHC, designing an industrial village in **Butler**, Pennsylvania, thirty miles northeast of Pittsburgh and home to Spang & Company, metal manufacturers, and the Standard Steel Car Company, which built railway cars.[346] Lay's promising but unrealized plan of curving tree-lined streets followed the topography of the 22-acre hillside site in the southern part of the city. The sudden end to hostilities scuttled plans for the exclusively residential project, and no designs were released for the 29 detached and 138 semidetached single-family houses to be designed by Harvard-trained, Pittsburgh-based architect Edward B. Lee (1876–1956). The tract was ultimately developed as a regular grid of detached, single-family houses.

To ease the shortage of workers' housing in **Niagara Falls**, New York, estimated at 2,000 units, the USHC turned to planner John Nolen and the Chicago firm of George Robinson Dean and Arthur Randall Dean to provide accommodations for 401 families.[347] Nolen, one of the few planners who worked for both the USHC and the Emergency Fleet Corporation, was a logical choice for the project, having just completed a study (1917) of the city that concluded that "while the tourist interests of Niagara Falls should be more carefully served, the industrial interests are of even greater consideration."[348] Nolen's report also suggested the inclusion of additional park space and the construction of a civic center and railroad station. For the war workers' housing, the planner selected three sites within city limits, only one of which managed to move forward.

Located in roughly the center of Niagara Falls about one mile northwest of the industrial village of Echota, Site B, within walking distance of a plant producing iron alloys essential for the manufacture of guns, was a 22-acre flat tract surrounded by rowhouses. Working within the confines of an already gridded street plan, Nolen proposed 150 rowhouses, 46 semidetached, and 4 detached houses laid out in simple rows with only minor setback variations, reserving, as his major intervention, the interiors of two large allotment gardens between Twenty-fourth and Twenty-fifth Streets, Orleans and Ferry Avenues, to serve as playgrounds after the war.

Butler

1. Plan, Charles Downing Lay, 1918. USHC

Niagara Falls

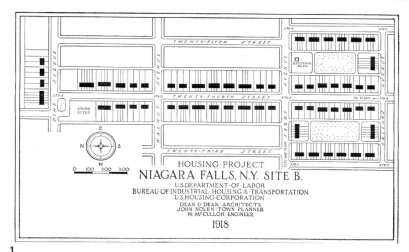

1. Site B, plan, John Nolen, 1918. USHC

2. Aerial view. GE (2011)

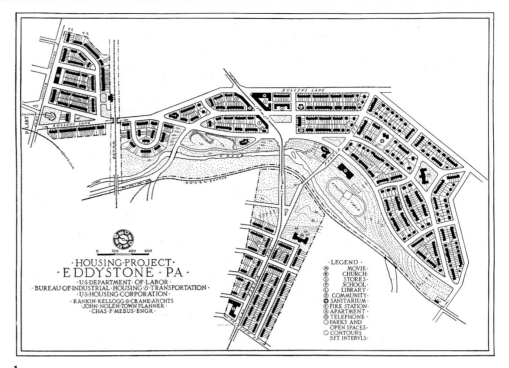

1

2

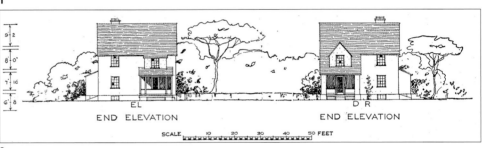

3

A landscaped square and store grouping proposed for the south side of Twenty-fourth Street at Pine Avenue remained unrealized. Dean & Dean's two- and three-story four- to six-room clapboard houses, intended for semiskilled workers, featured prominent, steeply sloping roofs covering the entrance porches. As completed by the end of 1919, the Niagara Falls development at Site B numbered 196 units, with only the detached, single-family houses dropped from the plan.

Nolen prepared plans for two additional USHC subdivisions located within a few miles of Chester, Pennsylvania, both of which remained unrealized. His proposal for **Eddystone** (1918) occupied a 167-acre site convenient to the Midvale Steel & Ordnance Company and the Eddystone Rifle Plant and was intended to accommodate 1,128 families in 922 rowhouses, 70 apartment-house units, and two detached and 134 semidetached houses.[349] Temporary dormitory space for 608 single men was to be provided in buildings along Eddystone Avenue. Nolen's plan called for the development of the long and narrow Crum Creek valley, too steep for residential development, as a public park crossed by bridges, with a commercial and community center located at the central bridgehead. The firm of Rankin, Kellogg & Crane designed the four- and five-room

stucco-and-terracotta-block houses intended to be placed in rows as long as seventeen houses.

Nolen's **Ridley Park** subdivision, one of the program's most interesting projects, remained on paper.[350] Located on a 54-acre parcel about two miles from the closest industrial facilities but served by a trolley line, the development was planned for 565 skilled workers and their families to be accommodated in 483 rowhouses, 60 semidetached houses, and 22 apartment-house units. The main entrance at the intersection of Chester Turnpike and Dianthus Avenue, flanked by groups of stores, led directly to the development's heart, a town green surrounded by housing as well as stores and a theater. The design of the brick rowhouses and clapboard semidetached houses was the work of Philadelphia architect Edgar V. Seeler (1867–1929).

The USHC selected landscape architect Charles N. Lowrie and the firm of S. B. Parkman Trowbridge (1862–1925) and Goodhue Livingston (1867–1951) to plan an industrial village for skilled workmen and their families in the central New Jersey town of **New Brunswick**, thirty miles southwest of New York City.[351] Home to the Wright-Martin Aircraft Corporation, the USHC initially tried to improve the area's overcrowded housing situation by increasing the number of

Ridley Park

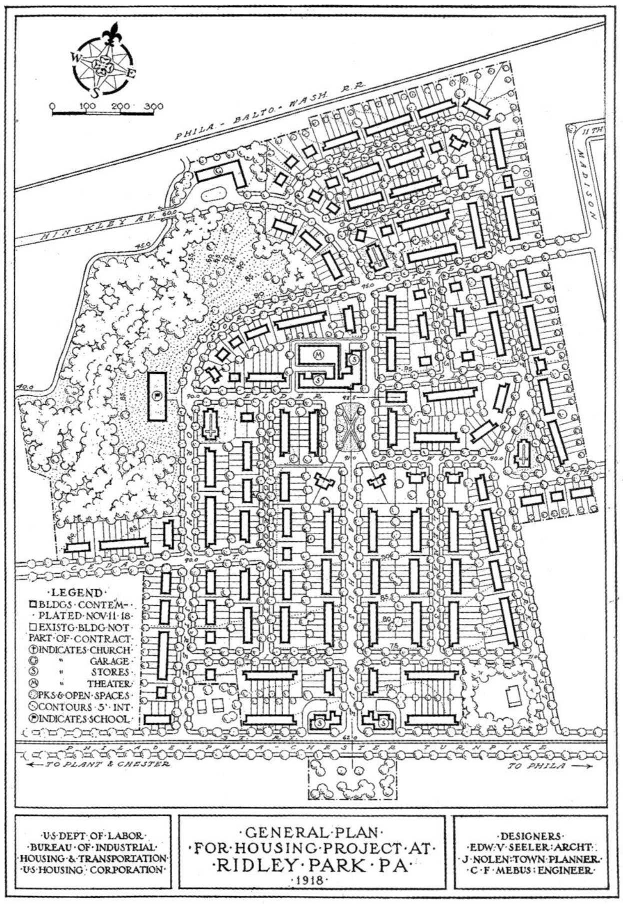

1

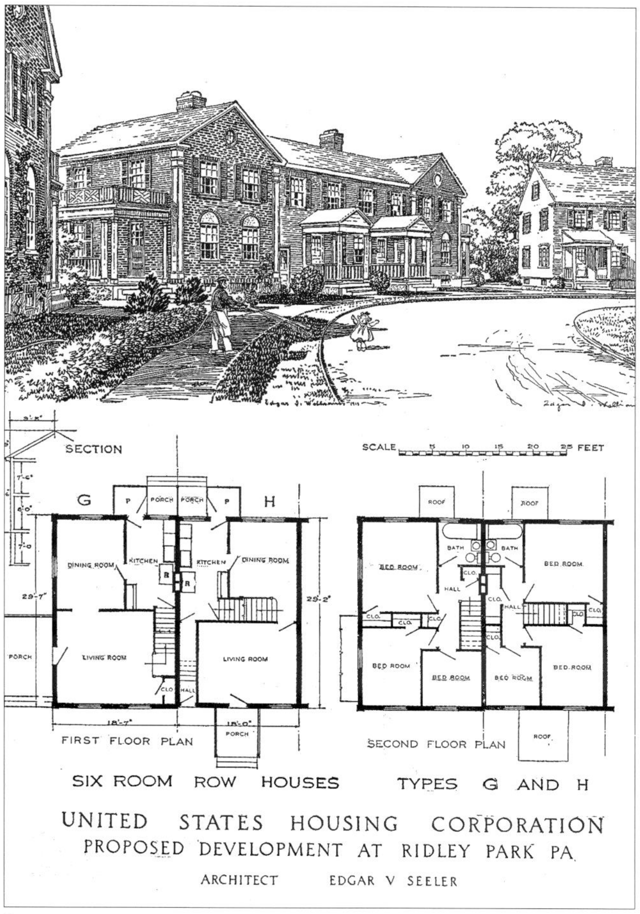

2

1. Plan, John Nolen, 1918. USHC

2. Rendering and plans of houses designed by Edgar V. Seeler, 1918. USHC

New Brunswick

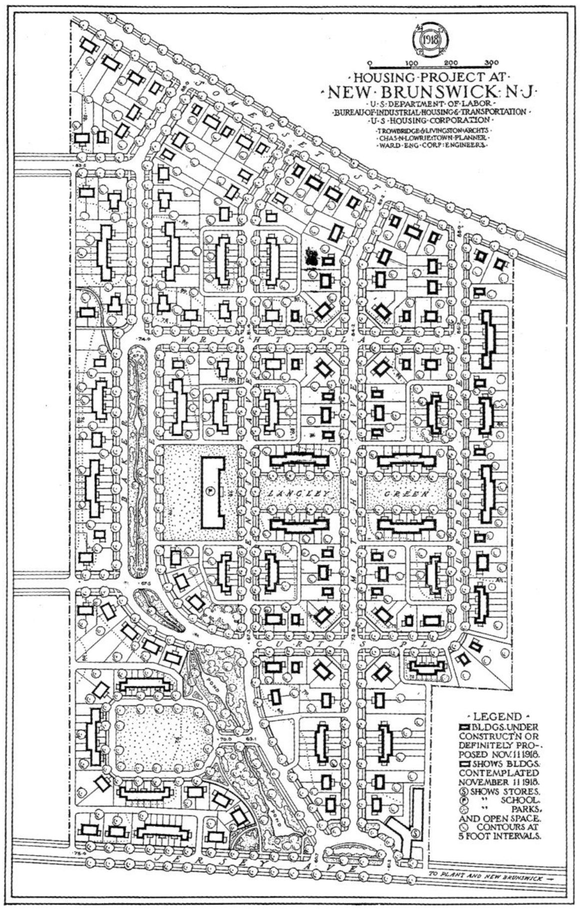

1

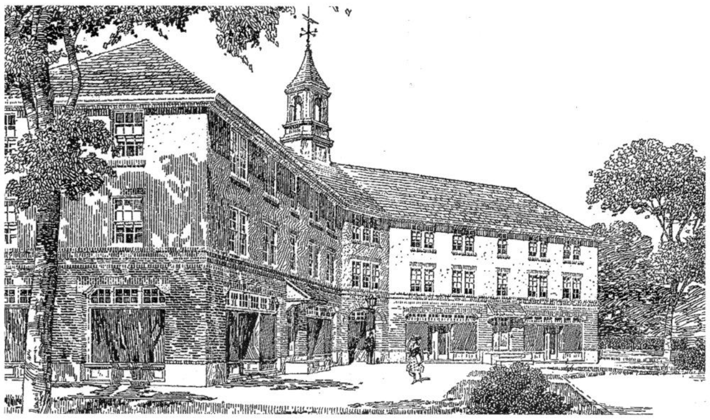

2

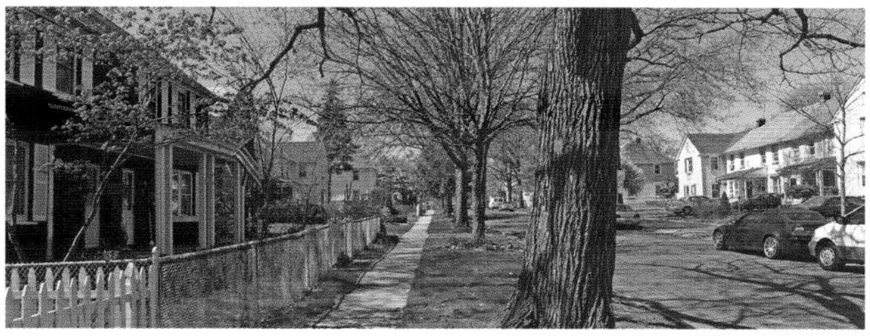

3

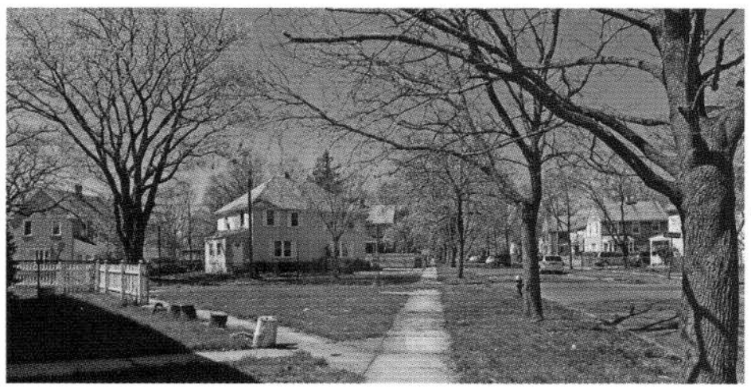

4

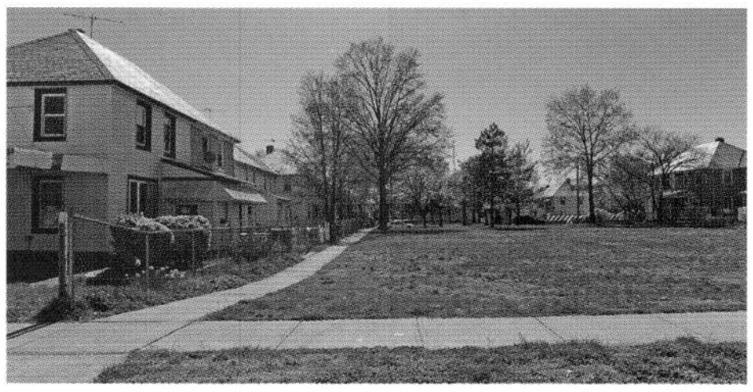

5

1. Plan, Charles N. Lowrie, 1918. USHC

2. Proposed commercial building, S. B. Parkman Trowbridge and Goodhue Livingston, 1918. USHC

3. Mitchell Avenue. RAMSA (2012)

4. Mitchell Avenue and Curtis Place. RAMSA (2012)

5. Green between Mitchell and Lufberry Avenues. RAMSA (2012)

Pennsylvania Railroad trains that served New Brunswick as well as building a footbridge over the railroad tracks at Sandford Street leading directly to the manufactory. These efforts proved inadequate and the government agency authorized the construction of houses to accommodate 397 households. A 43-acre site in the southwestern part of the city just north of the factory and railroad right-of-way, bound by Lufberry Avenue on the east, Baker Avenue on the west, and two major thoroughfares on its north and south, Somerset Street (also known as Lincoln Highway) and Jersey Avenue, was selected, which the *Architectural Forum* described as "an almost ideal location" where "the natural surfaces of the ground are gently rolling, with a general inclination toward the south, except for a well defined valley through which a small stream runs westward from Jersey Avenue, forming a natural watershed" that eliminated the need for extensive and expensive storm sewers.[352] Lowrie, a founding member of the Society of Landscape Architects, planned the 60-foot-wide, tree-lined streets to facilitate easy access to the plant located just beyond Jersey Avenue, where the formal entrance to the village was established with a landscaped island that branched off into the subdivision's two main streets, Mitchell and Quentin Avenues. Lowrie's plan consisted primarily of a regular grid at the center of the site that was "successfully modified in several ways for reasons of economy as well as attractiveness," with "curves introduced at intervals where topography gives reason, so as to obviate a stiff and formal treatment."[353]

The plan was intended to accommodate nine families per acre in 41 detached and 150 semidetached houses as well as 206 rowhouses along with an elementary school and a modest commercial component. Unfortunately, the most promising portion of the plan consisting of groups of houses along the gently curving stretch of Baker Avenue with its landscaped median remained unrealized. Also failing to move forward was a large playground at the southwest corner of the site and the grade school in roughly the center, although the open Langley Green to its east was retained. Trowbridge & Livingston designed a three-story cupola-topped building just east of the Jersey Avenue entrance intended to house small apartments, stores, recreational facilities, and a motion-picture theater, but plans for the handsome structure were also dropped.

In order to quickly address the housing shortage, the USHC first instructed the architects to design temporary dormitory facilities for 200 women and 100 men at the southern end of the site. By the time the armistice was signed, the dormitories were about 70 percent complete but the USHC ordered that work stop on them immediately. The 150 carpenters employed at the subdivision dismantled the partially completed buildings and were then dispatched to work on the permanent houses, reusing the materials from the demolished dormitories. All told, about one half of the proposed housing was completed by the end of 1919, accommodating 192 families in twenty-eight detached and sixty-eight semidetached houses as well as ninety-six rowhouses. Trowbridge & Livingston's two-story four- to six-room Colonial-style houses featured hollow tile walls clad in stucco and green slate roofs, with the largest houses placed on higher ground near Somerset Street and smaller rowhouses grouped around Langley Green. *Architectural Forum* liked the "extremely simple" houses, noting that "the only purely decorative elements are brick lintels and sills at the first-story windows."[354]

The USHC took issue with some elements of the New Brunswick subdivision, writing in its report that "in execution the framing of the outside of the bend of Lufberry Avenue is not as successful in closing the two vistas of this street as the plan suggests, because the spaces between buildings occupied by the two alley entrances are too wide and two detached buildings on the bend between these openings have their gable ends toward the street. If they had been turned with the length of the houses and of their roof ridges following the street curve, the effect of the entire street would have been greatly enhanced, the more so because the vista down the street from the northwest comes through the gap to an ugly factory in the distance." The editors of the report did not entirely place the blame for this miscue on the architects, noting that "it is such refinements as these, important in their total effect, that the designers of all our projects were precluded from making by the pressure of speed in getting out the plans. They can seldom be recognized in advance on plan without time for staking and revision on the ground."[355] Overall, however, the USHC report was favorably disposed to the development, calling out for particular praise the diagonal placement of the corner houses at the intersections of Mitchell Avenue with Curtis and Wright Places.

In addition to New Brunswick and New London, Charles N. Lowrie planned three unrealized USHC projects for workers of the Western Cartridge Co. in the southern Illinois city of **Alton**, just north of St. Louis, Missouri, on the Mississippi River.[356] Lowrie, working with the St. Louis architectural firm of John Lawrence Mauran (1866–1933), Ernest John Russell (1870–1956), and William DeForest Crowell (1880–1967), provided a mix of detached, semidetached, row, and apartment houses providing space for 200 families. In addition, room for 485 workers was supplied in twenty-one dormitories that could each be converted to four six-room houses. Lowrie placed a traffic circle at the western edge of the site, ringing an open plaza with public buildings and combination store and apartment blocks. To the west, a park stretched to the edge of the site while radial streets extended in the other directions to cut through a geometrical plan of octagonal ring roads. A main axis, the Mall, connected the plaza with an athletic field, beyond which a footbridge carried workers over the tracks of the Chicago & Alton Railroad. Two roads paralleling the Mall to the north and south would, according to the USHC report, accommodate the bulk of the "hurried foot traffic" although the Mall, with its planted median, would serve as the "backbone of the scheme and would be a good promenade."[357]

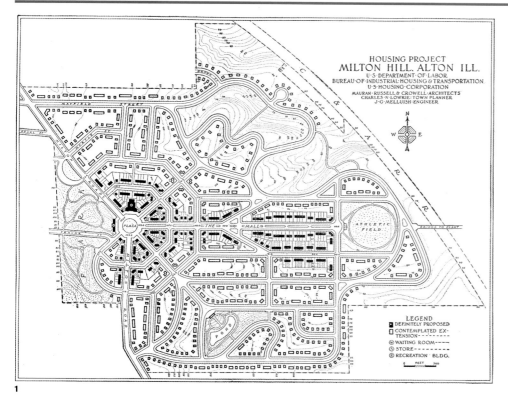

1

2

1. Plan, Charles N. Lowrie, 1918.
USHC

2. Rendering of proposed
semidetached house designed by
Mauran, Russell & Crowell,
1918. USHC

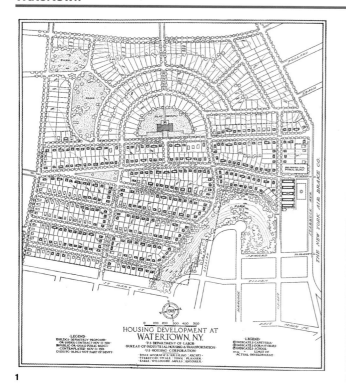

1

2

3

1. Site plan, Ferruccio Vitale, 1918.
USHC

2, 3. Renderings of houses
designed by Davis, McGrath &
Kiessling, 1918. USHC

The formal geometries of the plan's center gave way to curving residential streets and irregular blocks in the north and south where the topography changed. The houses were given a "more or less English character" with special attention being paid to large casement windows that alleviated the need for sliding windows that would have required metal "essential to important war industries."[358] Some houses were angled to face the corner at 45 degrees. The project was discontinued at the war's end.

Watertown, New York, a remote city of 40,000 on the Black River, near Lake Ontario, was home to the New York Air Brake Co. whose production of shells for Allied forces increased markedly with the United States' entry into the war.[359] The USHC planned a town for the company's foremen and skilled workmen on a gently rolling 48-acre site in the northeast of the city and just west of the plant. The location was served by a streetcar line and benefited from a nearby school, churches,

1. Plan, Ferruccio Vitale, 1918.
USHC

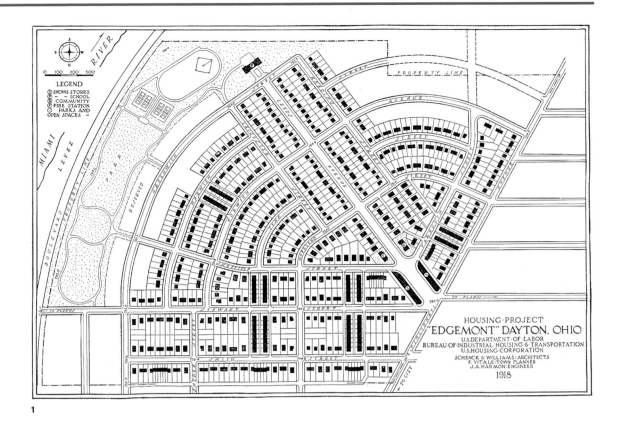

1

and stores. Utilities and streets were already in place in southern portions of the site and some houses were already built, creating an added challenge for landscape architect Ferruccio Vitale (1875–1933), who had to work with officially approved but conflicting plans in order to illustrate "how an existing haphazard street system can be related to a larger district."[360] Vitale's most notable change concerned a series of streets that, as platted, ignored the site's topography to climb and descend a tall hill, requiring a rise in grade of 14 to 17 percent and a subsequent decline of 9 percent. Vitale decided instead to cut the streets short, leaving the hill open as a park, and in so doing increased the value of the lots along the shortened streets, "thus offering a striking instance of the economic advantages of a street layout adapted to topography as against conventional hit-or-miss rectangular platting on hilly ground."[361]

Katherine Street, an east–west axis made wide enough for a streetcar line, separated the existing gridiron in the south with Vitale's semicircular plan in the north, where a school was centrally located and two parks were provided in the northwest. The residential lots were typically 100 feet deep by 40 or 50 feet wide—for semidetached and detached houses, respectively—and called for at least 16 feet between houses. Each lot was to be lined by hedges, and many featured apple trees, shrubs, and vines. Although 300 houses were envisioned, only the southern half of the village was built, providing for 115 families in 85 detached and 15 pairs of semidetached houses. The New York firm of Davis, McGrath & Kiessling prepared fourteen different exteriors, employing varying widths of gray-, white-, and cream-painted clapboarding, silver- and gray-stained shingle, and a mix of roof styles to create "a simple cottage type of design in complete accord with the older farm and village houses of the vicinity."[362]

According to the USHC report, the "grouping of the houses, in connection with their excellent design, affords probably the most agreeable solution to be found among the executed projects of the corporation of the difficult problem of small detached houses with a limited number of semidetached. They are frequently arranged in symmetrical groups of three, four, or more, some without variation in setback and others with the central portion of the group moderately recessed. In very few instances is the variation in setback overdone . . . The houses have been designed about as well as houses of this type and material could be. It would be difficult to pick serious flaws."[363]

Vitale also planned two unrealized USHC projects in **Dayton,** Ohio, the first a three-acre parcel to be developed with ten semidetached, two-flat houses and the second, the Edgemont Tract, comprising 108 acres in southern Dayton within walking distance of two plants and connected by streetcar to other parts of the city.[364] The sloping Edgemont site included a developable highland that descended to a levee in the southeast, with the Miami River beyond.

The towns of Cradock and Truxtun, in the Hampton Roads district around Norfolk and Portsmouth, Virginia, were built to house white and "colored" workers, respectively, of the nearby naval shipyards. **Cradock,** with a more elaborate plan, larger houses on more spacious lots, and a wider range of amenities, was the largest

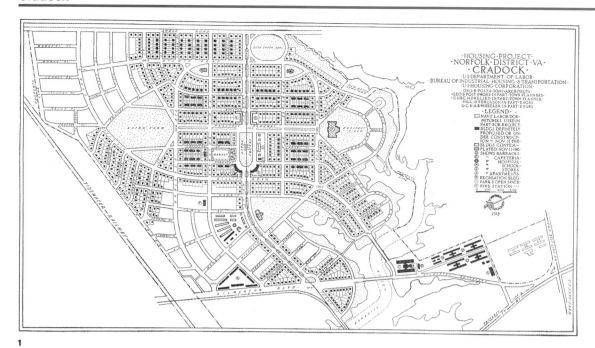

1

1. Plan, George B. Post & Sons and Harlan P. Kelsey, 1918. USHC

2. Cottage. USHC (1919)

3. Typical street during construction. NACP (c. 1918)

2

3

of the USHC's projects to begin construction.[365] Located three-and-a-half miles south of Portsmouth's center, Cradock's flat 310-acre site was buffered by Paradise Creek on the north and east, the Virginia Railroad's 300-foot right-of-way on the south, and Shell Road (George Washington Highway) on the west, beyond which lay a large farm. The Portsmouth Navy Yard was a short distance to the northeast.

The town, named for British Rear Admiral Christopher G. F. W. Cradock (1862–1914), whose fleet was sunk by the Germans off the coast of Chile in 1914, was designed by the New York firm of George B. Post & Sons under the direction of James Otis Post (1874–1951), who also served as a consultant to the chief engineer of the army, overseeing the construction of cantonments. The Post firm had recently engaged in the design of Eclipse Park in Beloit, Wisconsin. Landscape architect Harlan P. Kelsey (1872–1958) and A. C. Manning (n.d.) collaborated on a town plan that was to provide for a population of 6,175, including 1,235 families and 2,000 male workers housed in barracks.

Post's layout, with a core of rectangular blocks giving way to curved streets at the periphery, placed two open spaces—a school with its recreational grounds, and Afton Park, featuring a stand of mature trees—at either end of Prospect Parkway, a north–south divided boulevard lined by houses. A cross axis formed by a second anchor-shaped street configuration included a main spine, Afton Parkway, accommodating a streetcar line. At its intersection with Prospect Parkway, Afton Parkway opened up to the central Afton Square, a village green bordered by shops and a movie theater on one end and the town hall, fire house, and library on the other. The alphabetically arranged streets, named for navy admirals, were lined by carefully chosen trees that prospered because of the high water table. Post's Colonial-style wood-frame houses, with some bungalow and English Cottage examples mixed in, were of fifty different designs derived from forty plans.

Construction began in July 1918 but was halted at the signing of the armistice, at which point light, water, and gas were cut off and the town was nearly abandoned. The

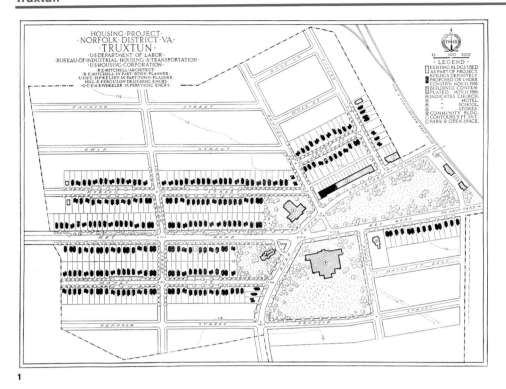

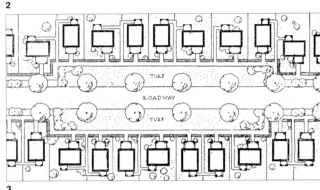

1. Plan, Harlan P. Kelsey, 1918. USHC

2. Typical street. COM (c. 1919)

3. Typical street setback. USHC

original phase of development provided for 759 families, and in 1920 the houses were sold by the government. Of the sixty planned business lots around Afton Square, only twelve were developed with handsome commercial blocks featuring second-floor apartments. None of the parkland was developed.

The overall quality of the housing was high. In 1919, the *New York Times* found that "while the entire project presents a general impression of uniformity there are no tiresome rows of houses built on the same pattern."[366] By 1936, when Comey and Wehrly visited Cradock, it had a population of 3,500 and had emerged from its "transition period . . . [as] the best residential section in the Portsmouth district."[367] Comey and Wehrly found the well-kept yards and "consistently well-maintained dwellings" to be "relatively large, of excellent design and good construction," and observed that "the variety of the original designs gives an individuality to each home which has been heightened through private ownership over a period of years, without destroying the harmonious effect as a whole. The inhabitants have perhaps unconsciously realized the charm to be obtained by continuing to paint their houses white, selecting various conservative tones for reroofing which largely remove the criticism made of the monotony of the original grey. They have maintained the hedges which separate the lots and add greatly to the interest of the street."[368]

But Comey and Wehrly echoed the criticisms of the USHC report, identifying a lack of "satisfactory terminations for many of the street vistas" and finding that "the regularly repeated arrangements of the houses in consecutive blocks" produced "a series of unintentional vistas across blocks," although this effect was later softened with the maturation of plantings and the construction of garages and other outbuildings.[369] George B. Post & Sons' second planned community for the USHC, Glenwood, northeast of Norfolk, was canceled before it could begin. The plan had called for a mix of detached, semidetached, and group houses on a 79-acre site incorporating a town square, park, and community center in a Y-shaped street pattern.[370]

Truxtun, Virginia, was the first USHC project designed specifically for black workers, occupying a 43-acre cornfield site less than a half mile from the Norfolk Naval Shipyard.[371] Named for American naval officer Thomas Truxtun (1755–1822), the town was planned by Harlan P. Kelsey, who placed a triangular park, church, community house, and school at the intersection of two existing roads, Deep Creek Boulevard, the main road leading to Portsmouth, and Key Road (later Portsmouth Boulevard). Around this principal civic and commercial intersection, Kelsey aligned rectangular residential blocks in an east–west orientation to allow exposure to the wind, "a very important matter in the climate of Portsmouth."[372]

As designed by Norfolk architect Rossel Edward Mitchell (d. 1959), Truxton's Craftsman-style houses included fifty semidetached dwellings on 40-by-100-foot lots and 200 detached five-room houses on 28-by-100-foot lots. The single-family houses, spaced only 11 feet from one another, were virtually identical in plan but rendered in four different elevations. "Viewing the houses along the streets," the USHC reported in 1919, "they present a very interesting appearance though possibly a little unrestful because of the variety of the roof lines . . . The colors selected for the finish of these houses are in the main satisfactory though possibly a little dark in shade, but in their entirety they look well,

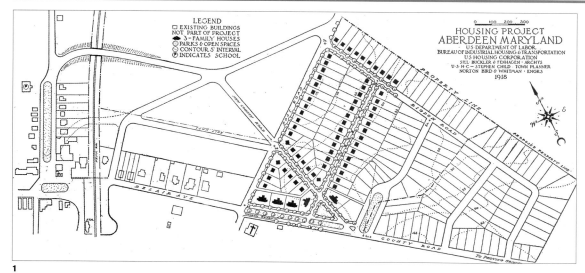

1

2

being relieved by reason of the few houses which have been painted white and by the white of the blinds and porches." Although of a much higher quality than most housing provided for black workers in other industrial villages, the Truxtun residences did not provide hot water, an omission that the USHC later found to be "specially . . . questionable."[373] The original portions of Truxton retain much of their character and only a few houses have been lost.

Landscape architect Stephen Child designed four USHC projects, three of which were planned in connection with proving grounds for explosives and weaponry. Child's enclave in the small village of **Aberdeen**, Maryland, population 600, was affiliated with a 35,000-acre proving ground on Chesapeake Bay, thirty miles northeast of Baltimore.[374] While military personnel could be accommodated on-site, civilian workers who had been commuting by train from Baltimore needed nearby housing, leading the USHC to undertake a neighborhood for sixty-eight families on a 26.5-acre site of rolling cornfields three miles from the military facility to which it would be connected by train. The location, bordered on the west by Post Road, connecting Baltimore with Philadelphia, and on the south by a county road leading to the proving ground, benefited from nearby stores and a school. Child's modified grid eliminated rear alleys on the irregularly shaped blocks and discouraged through traffic. Child widened a portion of the county road to accommodate Church Green, a 30-foot-wide grass median that, with the exception of a small open triangle, was the only park space provided.

The Baltimore firm of Howard Sill (1865–1927), Riggin Buckler (1883–1955), and G. Corner Fenhagen (1884–1955) prepared three types of houses, including a so-called convertible type that could serve as a boardinghouse and, with the removal of temporary partition walls and the addition of kitchen and bathroom fixtures, be easily converted into a three-family rowhouse. The type was also employed in the USHC's Alton, Ilion, and Indianapolis projects. The other two housing types were both single-family detached dwellings with gambrel, gable, and hip roofs. In all, sixty-five individual and five convertible houses were built. Three of the latter formed a row across from Church Green, leading the USHC to note that if the "central structure . . . had been set back 2 feet . . . a far more agreeable arrangement" would have resulted, "breaking the monotony of the present straight line."[375]

Child was given more latitude in designing a village in **Indianhead,** Maryland, a peninsula twenty-five miles south of Washington, D.C., at the junction of the Mattawoman Creek and the Potomac River.[376] The site, serving two navy facilities—a smokeless powder plant and a proving ground—consisted of 180 level, partly wooded acres perched 100 feet above the river, whose steep wooded banks formed the western limit of development and would be retained as parkland. Near the site was what the USHC termed a "straggling village of about 40 houses" and beyond that were miles of farmland.[377]

At the southern end of the property, a complex of dormitories and apartments had already been built along a rectilinear street pattern that would be left in place and built out with additional dormitories capable of housing 1,400 individuals, as well as apartments for forty-four families. Locating the center of the village at the juncture of the old and new developments, Child placed a post office and fire station at the head of a rectangular, 700-foot-long-by-125-foot-wide village green that stretched northward to a school and its attendant playing fields.

The long sides of the village green were fronted by hedge-lined house lots and, between the green and the river bluffs, Child laid out looping streets to form four residential blocks. The lots became larger and more irregularly shaped as they approached the river, and two of the blocks enclosed internal playgrounds. The 50-foot-wide streets featured 18-foot roadbeds, with the rest devoted to sidewalks and planting strips accommodating street trees at 40-foot intervals. To the south of the residential blocks, the commandant's residence occupied a hilltop site overlooking the river.

1. Plan, Stephen Child, 1918. USHC

2, 3. Renderings of houses designed by Howard Sill, Riggin Buckler, and G. Corner Fenhagen, 1918. USHC

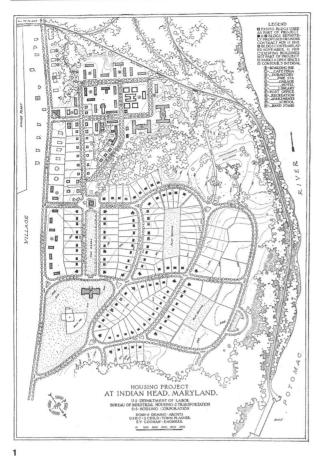

1

2

3

4

1. Plan, Stephen Child, 1918. USHC

2. Typical houses. Arm. FL (1921)

3. Overall view showing post office, left, and village green leading to school in distance. Arm. FL (1921)

4. School. Arm. FL (1921)

The plan called for 146 detached houses designed by Edward Wilton Donn Jr. (1868–1953) and William I. Deming (1871–1939), of Washington, D.C., who also designed the community buildings. Although the entire site would eventually be developed, the only part of the original scheme to be realized, in addition to three temporary dormitories, was forty-five detached six-room dwellings based on two plans and four exterior treatments, all painted white with wood-shingle and asphalt-shingle roofs. The houses were differentiated mainly by the location of the porches and the color of the shutters, leading the USHC report to find "too much similarity" in comparison to "other projects, where more varieties of exterior designs have been used," highlighting "with certainty how much better the project would look if some of the houses were of a more distinctly different type—if, for instance, a gambrel-roofed house had been introduced at certain points."[378] The project also suffered from the replacement of Donn & Deming's designs for the school and post office with "cheaper" plans by the Bureau of Yards and Docks: "As the village green was designed with these two buildings as first planned particularly in view, there is a material loss in effect."[379]

Twenty miles south of Indianhead, in **Dahlgren**, Virginia, at the junction of the Machodoc Creek and the Potomac River, the navy built a gun-proving facility on several hundred acres of lowland.[380] The development of a 166.5-acre village far enough away from the grounds to remain safe in case of an accident was planned by

the USHC, with the navy intending to finance the project in stages. Notably, the only access to the site was by water. A dock was built on the southern shore and the material dredged during its construction was used to fill in four narrow marshes that extended inland from the Potomac. The remoteness of the site required the construction of all utilities and roads as well as a wide range of community facilities. Child focused the plan on Dock Square, the "starting point of all traffic from the water."[381] From there, a road and railroad line led east to the proving ground. To the west, Sampson Row, a rectangular green, formed the heart of the village, bordered by stores, a movie theater, post office, fire station, and bandstand as well as, on the south, a three-acre waterfront park accommodating a headquarters building. A larger rectangular commons extended north from Dock Square, its west side lined by four apartments and dormitories, known as Colonnade Row, toward a formal, diagonally oriented, roughly 2,500-foot-long-by-400-foot-wide parade ground ringed by a double row of trees and terminated on the north by a brick barracks and on the south by the Potomac. A less formal park sat next to the Parade Ground and incorporated a school, library, church, and athletic fields.

In a similar arrangement to Indianhead's, the commandant's house occupied a four-acre promontory along the river, to the north of which officers' houses, also designed by Donn & Deming, occupied two culs-de-sac whose shape conformed to the curving shoreline. The lots were between 75 and 100 feet wide and 150 to 250 feet deep, with the largest parcels situated closest to the river. Houses were set back 35 feet from the street and sited to maximize views. Despite the luxury of space, forty of the seventy-eight houses were to be semidetached. Pedestrian paths were threaded throughout the village, including along the water's edge. The project was not developed according to the original plan.

The USHC's 17-acre enclave in **Ilion**, New York, twelve miles east of Utica, serving the Remington Arms Union Metallic Cartridge Company, was less notable for Stephen Child's gridded street plan than for its well-designed but unrealized houses by the New York firm of A. Stewart Walker and Leon N. Gillette.[382] The site, located three-quarters of a mile west of the works on high, level ground, benefited from the presence of local stores and schools. Except for a 20-by-900-foot median added to one of the avenues (the only portion of the project to be completed before its cancellation), no park space was provided. The rectangular residential lots were to be occupied by ninety detached and forty semidetached houses, which Walker & Gillette alternated with one another for variety. The architects prepared eleven different single-family models, cladding them in stucco or wide clapboard and carefully studying the impact of projecting porches on the streetscape. In addition, eight convertible houses, to be used initially as dormitories for 168 female workers, were planned on corner sites so that service vehicles could access the back of the houses from the side street.

The 876-acre Mare Island Navy Yard, located twenty-five miles northeast of San Francisco on San Pablo Bay, was the Pacific Coast's oldest such facility, established in 1854, and also one of its busiest during World War I, responsible for the construction of destroyers and battleships. The huge influx of wartime workers to the yard quickly overwhelmed the island's existing housing stock as well as available units in the nearby city of **Vallejo**, accessible by ferry across the Mare Island Strait. Vallejo was at the time of the war largely dependent on the navy yard for its prosperity, although the city also featured a large flour mill. Even before the war, there were legitimate complaints about its scarce supply of quality housing. After first rejecting as impractical the hiring of workers who would be expected to make the lengthy, daily commute from San Francisco by ferry, the USHC was given the task of providing affordable housing convenient to the yard.[383]

The USHC commissioned San Francisco–based architect George W. Kelham (1871–1936) and landscape architect Percy R. Jones (1875–1962), a twenty-five-year veteran of the Olmsted office, to plan accommodations for 400 single men and 419 skilled workers and their families. With only scattered, expensive lots available in the central parts of Vallejo, Kelham and Jones selected two relatively isolated sites on the city's northern outskirts, about two miles from existing developments but close to the planned causeway intended to connect Vallejo with Mare Island, a bridge ultimately completed

Dahlgren

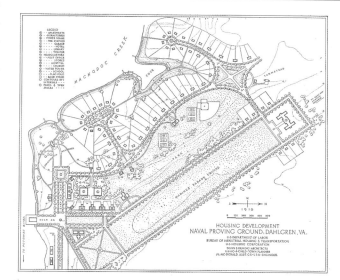

1. Plan, Stephen Child, 1918. USHC

Ilion

1. Plan, Stephen Child, 1918. USHC

2. Rendering of houses designed by A. Stewart Walker and Leon N. Gillette, 1918. USHC

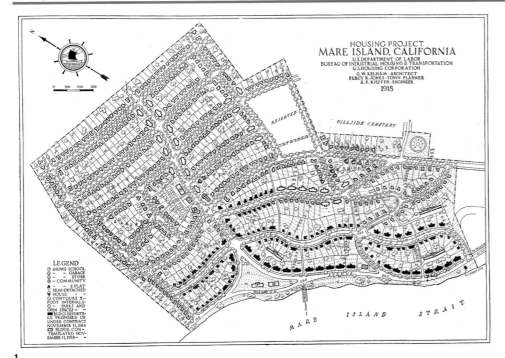

1. Plan, Percy R. Jones, 1918. USHC

2. Typical house, George W. Kelham, 1918. USHC

3, 4. Typical streets. Harris. LOCP

5. Typical house. Ben-Joseph. WC (2011)

two years after the signing of the armistice. On a seven-acre parcel bound by Stockton Street, and Wilson, Yolo, and Santa Rosa Avenues, the architects laid out a straightforward arrangement of ten forty-room dormitories lining both sides of a street that included a landscaped traffic circle and led to the somewhat grand, two-story cafeteria building with a tripartite entrance arch. Attesting to the high quality of their design, the dormitories were not immediately dismantled at the war's end as was typical of USHC projects, but instead continued to provide housing for naval yard workers for more than a decade.

Less than half a mile north of the dormitory complex was the picturesque 110-acre undeveloped tract selected for the houses, a steeply sloping site enjoying views of Marin County's Mount Tamalpais. Kelham and Jones initially planned the 55 acres closest to the water, reserving the second half of the site for future expansion. The placement of the proposed buildings—thirty-six semidetached and 231 detached houses, along with semi-detached two-flat apartment houses accommodating 152 families—was largely determined by the site's challenging topography. Entered off Wilson Avenue, the subdivision's main arterial street was Daniels Avenue, which branched off into curving 24-foot-wide streets divided into lots that on average measured 40-by-100 feet for the detached houses, although some of the single-family houses on the steepest sites featured plots that were 150 feet deep. The semidetached houses enjoyed frontages of between 35 and 40 feet while the apartment houses were placed on 80-by-100-foot lots. Three-and-a-half- to five-foot-wide cement sidewalks were provided, some raised as high as 10 feet above the street because of the hilly site, where houses ranged in elevation from 20 to 120 feet above sea level.

The large triangular space at the subdivision's main entrance at the intersection of Wilson and Daniels Avenues was intended for a school, community hall, and public park. Although an informal park was created, the two buildings were not built. Additional park space was provided west of Wilson Avenue on the long and narrow strip of land overlooking the water, as well as at the corner of Benson Avenue and West Baxter Street, which was too steep for residential development. In addition to the parks, more attention was paid to the landscape than was typical for a USHC project, with extensive tree and

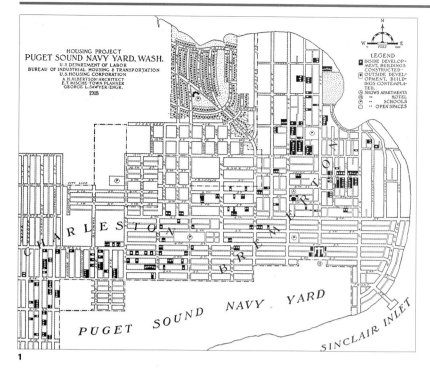

shrubbery planting undertaken by Jones's assistant, horticulturalist and landscape architect Emanuel T. Mische, who worked with Jones in the Olmsted office before entering private practice in Portland, Oregon. A group of stores planned for the intersection of Wilson and Benson Avenues also remained unrealized.

One unusual amenity that was completed as planned also proved highly controversial: the provision of neighborhood group garages built into the hillside at two locations, a feature designed "to take advantage of the steep slope in the considerable area between parallel streets," according to Comey and Wehrly.[384] In highly partisan congressional hearings conducted in 1919 concerning the federal government's role in providing public housing, the garages in Vallejo were criticized as an example of the excessively generous nature of the USHC projects.[385] Because of the site's relative isolation, beyond the reach of local utility companies, extensive infrastructure improvements were required, realized by underground conduits, making it the only USHC project beside the one realized in Bath, Maine, to avoid overhead wires. In addition, a new pier was constructed roughly in the center of the site to accommodate ferry service to Mare Island.

Kelham's two- and two-and-a-half-story woodframe houses were clad in shingles, stucco, or clapboard, with shingle roofs, white trim, light green blinds, and gray chimneys. The architect was able to complete 54 percent of the original plan before construction was halted, providing a comparatively rich mix of variously sized accommodations, including seventeen six-room, thirty-two five-room, and thirty-four four-room detached houses, along with twenty-four semidetached five-room houses. The subdivision also included 120 three- and four-room apartments in semidetached

buildings. Ironically, although the war workers' housing was constructed in part because it was determined that naval yard employees would be unable to commute from San Francisco, a majority of the construction workers who built the project did just that.

In its report, the USHC praised Kelham and Jones's efforts, writing that "the project in its entirety is, because of its situation and topography, one of the most picturesque of the Corporation's developments. The successful result is due to the correct conception of the kinds of houses suitable for the site and to skillful adjustment of the streets and house locations to the steep and rolling hillside . . . The houses are so designed and placed that they look well individually and collectively whether viewed from front or rear, and the rears are distinctly visible from many points of view."[386] Comey and Wehrly concurred, observing that "most streets were arranged in tiers along the hillsides and allowed the houses facing them to obtain morning and afternoon sun, with either the front or rear porches or rooms commanding excellent views of the mountains in Marin County across the upper waters of San Pablo Bay."[387] Unfortunately, the majority of houses built after the end of World War I within the boundaries of the Vallejo development were not the equal of those sponsored by the USHC.

The USHC was also responsible for the development of a subdivision for wartime workers employed at the Puget Sound Navy Yard in **Bremerton**, Washington, the only other West Coast project sponsored by the agency.[388] Bremerton, whose economy was almost entirely dependent on the navy yard, was experiencing a housing shortage due to the influx of workers at the shipyard, which had expanded its operations to include the construction of submarines in addition to

1. Plan, Emanuel T. Mische, 1918. USHC

2. Typical houses. Harris. LOCP (c. 1919)

3. Cogean Avenue. Harris. LOCP (c. 1919)

minesweepers, subchasers, tugboats, and ammunition ships, as well as the manufacture of munitions. The importation of workers from Seattle was rejected, not only because the ferry ride at over an hour was deemed too long but also because Seattle was in the middle of its own housing shortage. The USHC was called upon to provide new housing, hiring Emanuel T. Mische, who had worked on the landscape scheme at Vallejo, as town planner, and Columbia-educated Seattle-based architect Abraham H. Albertson (1872–1964) as designer of the proposed buildings.

Mische and Albertson initially selected a picturesque, vacant, 63-acre parcel in the northwestern part of the city, intending to provide a dense grouping of 286 detached single-family houses. But this so-called "outside development" was quickly abandoned because the unimproved tract would require substantial and time-consuming infrastructure improvements, and the speedy erection of affordable housing was deemed the top priority. Instead, the architects were forced to build houses on small, scattered, unoccupied sites throughout the city as well as in the neighboring community of Charleston, in areas already equipped with utilities. This "inside development" was planned for 295 families to be located in single-family houses as well as apartments.

To provide immediate relief, Albertson first designed a buff- and redbrick 360-room hotel located adjacent to the navy yard on Park Avenue between Third and Fourth Streets. It included basement-level recreational facilities and a 750-seat cafeteria directly accessible by shipyard workers via a tunnel beneath Third Street. Albertson's U-shaped three-story brick apartment house, located four blocks north of the navy yard on Warren Avenue and Seventh Street, featured a large, grassy court open to the street and included forty-five two-, three-, and four-room units. The 250 proposed single-family detached houses, all located within walking distance of the shipyard, were modest one-and-a-half- to two-story wood-frame structures clad in shingles or clapboard and with shingle roofs. Albertson was able to provide nine distinct three- to five-room models.

All of the apartment-house units were completed and only five of the houses were dropped from the original plan, yielding accommodations for a total of 290 families. Because of the scattered sites, the houses often stood by themselves or were grouped in irregular clusters of between two and eight buildings, although one grouping numbered twenty houses. Referring to this challenging situation, the USHC report noted that the new houses were "mixed in with houses quite different in design and character. There is, therefore, no designed harmony in the general aspect of the community. Among the corporation's houses themselves, there is a unity of expression which makes it possible to single them out and yet they are not so radically different as to look out of place." Although the editors of the report criticized some details of the houses, finding the columns supporting the large porch roofs too "delicate," overall they deemed the houses "excellent" and "refined,"

adding that "nowhere among the corporation's developments have bungalows been designed better."[389]

Among the USHC projects were numerous modest-size residential enclaves with little or no civic or commercial component. In the case of **Armor Park**, built in conjunction with the United States Naval Ordnance Plant in South Charleston, West Virginia, a small industrial city on the southern banks of the Kanawha River whose population quadrupled in size between 1900 and 1918, by which point it had reached 40,000, community amenities were originally planned, but, as an observer explained, "because of the limited appropriation" the "public and semi-public buildings were the ones which had to go."[390] Armor Park's houses were intended to attract skilled laborers being recruited from Philadelphia, Pittsburgh, and Cincinnati who, as married or older men, were exempt from the draft. The 16-acre site, a scenic, level tract 45 feet above the river, was a seven-minute walk from the plant and adjoined a 17-acre tract to the south reserved for parks and playgrounds.

New York landscape architect James Leal Greenleaf (1857–1933) arranged the streets to provide easy access to a trolley line on Eighth Avenue, the southern boundary, while leaving vistas open to the north toward the view over the Kanawha River that "was worth preserving and enhancing."[391] The streets, one of which curved to match Eighth Avenue, were 20 and 24 feet wide and lined by 3-foot sidewalks and 6-foot-wide planting strips accommodating 220 plane trees. Greenleaf also partially leveled a gulley that cut diagonally across the site.

The New York firm of Frederick A. Godley, Fitch H. Haskell (1883–1962), and Henry R. Sedgwick (1881–1946) designed the forty-five single-family and forty semidetached stucco-on-terracotta-block houses. In keeping with local custom, some of the four-, five-, and eight-room residences provided separate quarters for lodgers. Houses were sited to allow space for residents to install driveways and rear garages; some of the lots were lined by hedges in an effort to break up the streetscape and discourage people from shortcutting through yards. However, as the USHC noted in its 1919 report, hedges were used sparingly to avoid giving "the development in the eyes of the prospective householders a cut and dried and paternalistic appearance, especially to be avoided in this case where at best some dissatisfaction might arise from the necessarily permanent governmental land ownership."[392] The development was realized in full but did not survive the 1990s, when it was razed to make way for a shopping mall.

Hammond, one of the sprawling northern Indiana steel towns that included Gary and East Chicago, hosted a small USHC neighborhood built for workers of the Standard Steel Car Co., whose location on the western fringes of the city left it poorly supplied by transportation.[393] The company's limited experience in building houses included two- and three-story wooden tenements for its foreign-born common laborers who, according to the USHC, "were quite willing and even preferred to live in the cheaper type of buildings, such as barracks

Armor Park

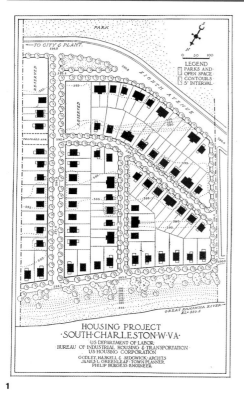

1

2

3

1. Plan, James Leal Greenleaf, 1918. USHC

2. Perspective. AA19

3. Rear of houses on "Street No. 5." AA19

Hammond

1

2

or tar-paper covered shacks of their own construction."[394] But major wartime contracts from the Ordnance Department for shrapnel and 9-inch guns necessitated more substantial housing for skilled workers. Although the USHC first acted to improve transportation for commuters to the plant, it also recognized the need for local housing and assisted in the development of a wedge-shaped, 19.5-acre tract of gently rolling land that the steel company had already begun to develop to the north of the earlier tenements and adjacent to the works. By the time the USHC entered the picture, a hotel had been constructed on a central block and a modified grid of streets laid out around it. The New York firm of Mann & MacNeille was brought on to divide the blocks into residential lots, and Joseph C. Llewellyn (1855–1932), a Chicago architect, was asked to design the houses. Stores were located one-half mile away in a nearby town.

In order to meet the challenging schedule, Llewellyn eliminated concrete, stucco, and tile, which required agreeable weather and time to dry, and instead used locally available brick and gray-stained white pine clapboarding applied to wood-frame construction. In all, 174 families were accommodated in 69 detached, 32 semidetached, and 52 four-family rowhouses as well as 11 boardinghouses that were aligned in a crescent across from the hotel. The residential lots averaged 40 by 100 feet and rear alleys were not provided. The USHC's report found little to criticize in the overall layout: "The plan types are quite sufficient in number to give interest, and the exteriors are harmonious, the grouping giving variety without any feeling of unrest." But it regretted that "the first impression one gets" is the neighborhood's "sombreness, due to the fact that all the wood-covered houses are stained gray instead of being painted in the colors generally applied to clapboards. All the roofs, too, are of one color—green—this covering being asphalt shingles. There are a few red brick houses, but even these as well as the white trim of the houses do not greatly improve the dullness of the effect as a whole. A great improvement would result if color were introduced."[395]

1. Bird's-eye view. A19 (1918)

2. Aerial view. GE (2005)

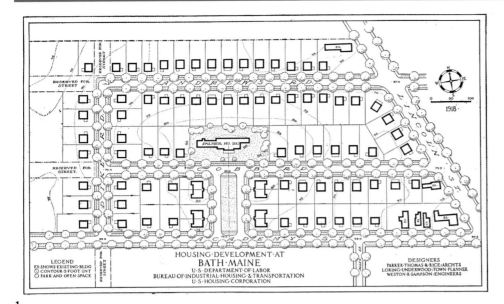

1

2

3

4

5

1. Plan, Loring Underwood, 1918. USHC

2. Rendering of view across green toward Palmer house. AR19

3.. Cobb Road. Bartlett. PAN (2013)

4. Types of houses. AR19

5. Plant Street. Bartlett. PAN (2013)

The USHC development for employees of the Bath Iron Works, builders of navy torpedo-boat destroyers, in **Bath**, Maine, was similar in some respects to Hammond, with a regular arrangement of streets around a central block accommodating the existing Palmer farmhouse, which was intended for reuse as a community center.[396] The site's eastern border, Lincoln Street, led past nearby stores for three-quarters of a mile to the iron works. Only nine of the site's 24 acres were initially developed to house ninety families in seventy-four detached and four semidetached two-flat dwellings. The remainder of the ledged and wooded land was kept in its natural state pending the need for further development.

Loring Underwood (1874–1930) provided the town plan and the architectural firm of J. Harleston Parker (1873–1930), Douglas H. Thomas (1872–1915), and Arthur Wallace Rice (1869–1938) designed the housing. Underwood situated five rows of houses along two new east–west streets paralleling the existing Academy Street, the site's southern boundary, that, with the other rectilinear borders, "practically dictated" the straightforward plan, according to the USHC report.[397] An axial green, Flaherty Park, in later years used for automobile parking, led south from the Palmer house's high portico and was flanked by the semidetached houses. Although

the principal residential streets were long and straight, the midblock houses were set back to provide visual relief. Moreover, as the USHC reported, each street "is in appearance divided into two units by the high points in their profiles," although the authors were bothered by the fact that the summit of the hill did not align with the most deeply setback houses.[398]

Parker, Thomas & Rice's simple, Colonial-style, clapboarded and asphalt-shingle-roofed houses, adorned with front porches and trellises, were deemed "excellent" in the USHC report that went on to state that the project would "bear comparison with those of any of the other developments," offering evidence "that the designers were thoroughly conversant with what is called 'colonial' architecture." The semidetached groups facing the green were even "more interesting in architectural appearance than the other houses . . . well planned and nicely designed, and, though they differ in style from the old Palmer house . . . they are not too inconsistent with its design."[399]

Landscape architect Alling S. DeForest, of Rochester, New York, and architect George H. Schwan, of Pittsburgh, collaborated on two USHC projects twenty miles from one another near the Pennsylvania-Ohio border. **Niles**, in Ohio, was partially realized, while

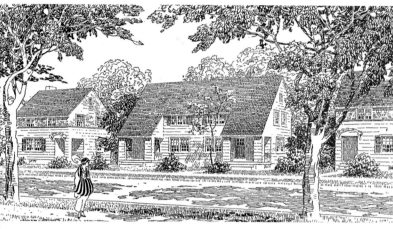

1. Plan. Alling S. DeForest, 1918. USHC

2. Aerial view. GE (2006)

3. Rendering of houses designed by George H. Schwan, 1918. USHC

4. House on Washington Avenue. Wyle. HMW (2008)

Sharon, Pennsylvania, was discontinued. Both designers had recently carried out work in Akron, where DeForest planned Firestone Park and Schwan designed workers' houses for the second phase of development in Goodyear Heights.

Niles, in an industrial region along the Mahoning River, was poorly served by transportation, a condition that the USHC initially remedied by chartering special rail cars to Warren, Ohio, where housing was more plentiful.[400] DeForest's site plan connected to the surrounding street grid but made adjustments within, placing a curved fork on Lafayette Street to preserve a stand of trees and, in the western half of the neighborhood, using a 45-degree diagonal grid to meet Vienna Avenue at a right angle. In this section, the development featured 130-foot-deep lots and eschewed rear alleys, allowing lots to either back up to one another or, in the case of one irregularly shaped block, to incorporate an internal playground. The eastern half of the site followed Niles's established pattern with 180-foot-deep lots allowing houses to be set back far enough to keep existing trees in the front. Rear alleys were included on these exceptionally deep blocks, even though they invited, as the USHC later warned, "the evil of alley dwellings," which were sure to be built unless "controlled by arbitrary restrictions on the part of the Housing Corporation or by drastic municipal regulations."[401] In the end, individual owners built garages and small back buildings along the alleys. Schwan's houses, a mix of four-, five-, and six-room bungalows varying only slightly in design, were clapboarded and covered by asphalt-shingle roofs. Porches were "the sole ornament," as the USHC curtly reported, and the construction quality was subpar.[402] Seventy-five detached houses were completed out of the 108 planned.

Sharon, one of a half-dozen towns forming an industrial district in the Shenango Valley of western Pennsylvania, hosted a 48-acre USHC enclave planned by DeForest to accommodate 215 families in 199 detached and eight pairs of semidetached houses.[403] To provide desperately needed housing for workmen at Sharon's industries, clustered in the lowlands by the Shenango River, the USHC chose an upland site in the eastern reaches of the city with utilities nearby and surrounding land available for expansion. The proximity of schools, churches, stores, and other community facilities allowed the enclave to be almost entirely residential.

The land, a short distance east of the plant, sloped gently down to Pine Run, a creek whose winding path formed the site's northern boundary. DeForest's street

Sharon

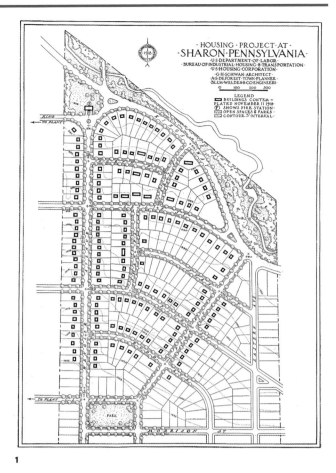

1. Plan, Alling S. DeForest, 1918.
USHC

Alliance

1. Plan, Alling S. DeForest, 1918.
USHC

2. Aerial view. GE (2006)

3. House employing oversize brick.
USHC (1918)

plan arose "almost inevitably, since it was plainly desirable to have streets parallel to the east and west boundaries of the property, [cross] streets running generally along the hillside, a curved road leaving a reasonable park area along Pine Run, and a general system so that there should be direct routes to the plant."[404] Through traffic was discouraged along the tree-lined streets, one of which cut diagonally across the neighborhood to connect a rectangular park in the southwest with the linear park along Pine Run. Houses stepped back and forth from the street, usually in reverse of the typical pattern, with those on the midblock closer to the sidewalk than those on the corner. Although the project was canceled after the signing of the armistice, the street plan was implemented and continues to set the neighborhood apart from its surroundings.

Alling S. DeForest planned another USHC enclave in the eastern central Ohio city of **Alliance**, about forty miles southwest of Niles, collaborating with the prominent Cleveland architectural firm of Frank R. Walker (1877–1949) and Harry E. Weeks (1871–1935).[405] Two sites were chosen for development—one in the northwest comprising nine acres of previously platted streets that didn't go forward, and the other in the southeast, occupying 62 acres of level land just beyond the limits of the built city. The southeast site had been partially developed according to a gridiron plan, but DeForest made some important changes, most notably cutting a square out of one of the blocks by inserting the L-shaped Grace Street to create "a secluded group of dwellings." In its report, the USHC questioned whether "the picturesque possibilities of the elbow street" were "sufficiently well realized to justify" the loss of one residential lot that could have otherwise been included. The arrangement of the four houses on Grace Street's northwest corner was also poorly handled, according to the report: "They would have looked better and probably had a higher value if they had not been set back so far and if the side spaces between them had been less than elsewhere instead of more." Moreover, the report noted that the houses closing Grace Street's vistas were not quite on axis because of an unwillingness to alter the lot sizes, a rigidity which also resulted in long "transverse lanes or accidental vistas between buildings extending across several blocks," a common complaint of the USHC that was typically remedied as landscaping matured.[406]

With an absence of nearby stores, DeForest placed a retail building on Morgan Avenue, a central street that concluded at its south end in a naturalistic park. Equivalent in size to about four of the neighborhood's blocks, the park was large by USHC standards but its size was justified by Alliance's overall deficit of green space, its location across the street from a planned school, and perhaps more directly, by the low cost of land and its elevation below the level of the sewer system. Eighty-nine of the 129 planned houses were completed according to six designs that were adjusted here and there with an extra room or variation in exterior treatment. The houses were clad in brick, shingle,

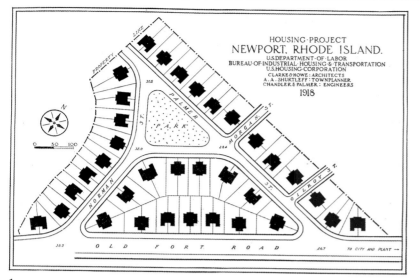

1

2

1. Plan, Arthur A. Shurtleff, 1918.
USHC

2. Aerial view. GE (2010)

and clapboard, but to the chagrin of the USHC, each was "exactly like its next-door neighbor in design as well as in color. The brick houses are in one row; the shingle houses in another; the clapboard houses in still another," but all, according to the USHC, contributing to "a monotony of appearance." A special oversize, hollow-face brick was employed to great effect, however, "very good in color" and "capable of being laid quickly."[407]

The USHC commissioned landscape architect Arthur A. Shurtleff, town planner of the agency's development in Bridgeport, Connecticut, and the Providence-based firm of Prescott O. Clarke (1858–1935) and Wallis E. Howe (1868–1960) to provide housing in **Newport**, Rhode Island, for sixty-eight skilled mechanics employed at the torpedo manufacturing plant on Goat Island at the mouth of Newport Harbor, the city's only major industrial facility, on a seven-acre triangular parcel served by a trolley line one block away.[408] Shurtleff's plan grouped semidetached houses in three separate sections created by the curving path of Norman Street, which branched off in two directions around a triangular park. According to the USHC report, Clarke & Howe's four- to six-room Colonial-style shingle houses, separated by privet hedges in keeping with local custom, fit in comfortably "with the old houses which abound in and near the city and the refined details of porches and other millwork contributes much to the appearance of the development." By the end of 1919, forty-eight semidetached houses were completed before construction was halted. Overall, the USHC report declared that "the general appearance of the project is decidedly good," and despite the nearly uniform architectural treatment of the buildings, there was no "unpleasant feeling of monotony." They reserved their criticism for the "injudicious . . . turning of the four pairs of semi-detached houses at the corners of Morgan Street and Gilroy Street to face on those streets, instead of on Palmer Street . . . The houses would be worth more facing toward the rest of the development and the park, and they stand, as

placed, at a slight but unpleasant angle with the general line of Palmer Street."[409]

Increased activity at the **Portsmouth**, New Hampshire, navy yard resulted in a housing shortage only partially relieved by the EFC's Atlantic Heights development and the USHC's renovation of two hotels in Kittery, Maine, providing rooms for 150 single workers. Consequently, the USHC commissioned landscape architect William H. Punchard (n.d.) and the Boston-based firm of Francis R. Allen and Charles Collens to provide additional housing for sixty-four skilled workers and their families on a 21-acre site in Kittery, convenient to the yard as well as schools, stores, and a trolley line.[410] A survey of workers indicated a preference for single-family detached houses on half-acre lots, but the architects determined that such an arrangement was too expensive and instead proposed a mix of forty-eight semidetached and sixteen detached houses generously spaced on curving, tree-lined streets, a proposal that was still less dense than the typical USHC project.

The USHC report found Punchard's street plan, largely determined by the site's topography and utility needs, "interesting . . . with its two 'dead ends,' the streets being placed on the tops of the low ridges. There is the minimum of grading for both streets and lots, a particularly important consideration on account of the underlying ledge."[411] The two-story, shingle and clapboard five- and six-room houses proposed by Allen & Collens were largely patterned after local farmhouses. The abrupt end to the war cancelled plans for the subdivision.

Quincy, Massachusetts, located 10 miles southeast of Boston, was primarily a residential suburb of 50,000 at the start of World War I, with only a modest amount of industrial activity, including granite quarrying that first began in the early part of the nineteenth century and shipbuilding at the Fore River Shipyard, established in 1901.[412] In 1913 Bethlehem Steel acquired the yard, and the number of employees quickly quadrupled after America's entry into the war, leaving Quincy with

Portsmouth

1. Plan, William H. Punchard, 1918. USHC

2. Rendering of houses designed by Charles Collens, 1918. USHC

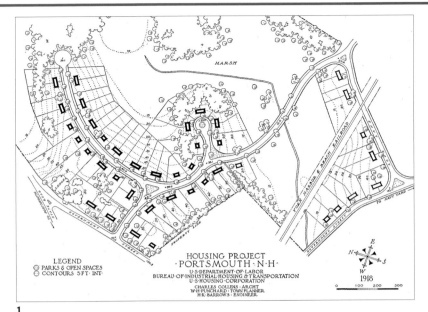

Quincy

1. Plan showing Arnold Street, River Street, and Baker Yacht Basin tracts and dormitory site, James E. McLaughlin and Herbert J. Kellaway, 1918. USHC

2. Commonwealth Avenue and Ruggles Street, Arnold Street tract. RAMSA (2011)

3. Avalon Street, Baker Yacht Basin tract. RAMSA (2011)

4. Perspective of houses on Avalon Avenue, Baker Yacht Basin tract, James E. McLaughlin, 1918. AR19

5. Whiton Avenue, Baker Yacht Basin tract. NACP (c. 1919)

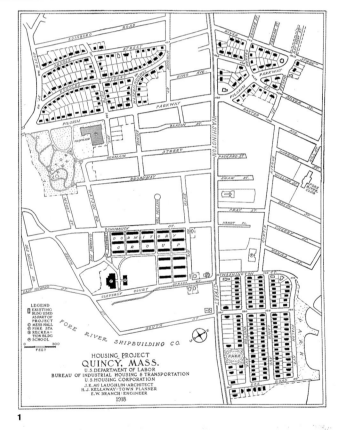

a severe housing shortage inadequately addressed by overcrowded boardinghouses operating beds on a three-shift basis to accommodate round-the-clock operations at the works. Surprisingly, the USHC, and not the EFC, was called in to study the situation. The USHC initially tried to solve the problem by improving access to the shipyard, widening Washington Street, and installing a double-track trolley line as well as sponsoring a jitney bus line to connect the yard with other parts of Quincy as well as surrounding towns. These measures proved inadequate and the USHC began to plan for new workers' housing, hiring architect James E. McLaughlin (1873–1966) and landscape architect Herbert J. Kellaway (1867–1947), both based in Boston, who selected four development sites within walking distance of the shipyard in the Quincy Point neighborhood, otherwise home to single-family detached wood-frame houses on modest lots. As *Architectural Review* noted, "the problem which confronted the town-planner at Quincy differed materially from many of the [government-sponsored] projects which thus far have attracted so much public notice. This was not a case where a new town-site was to be developed from the raw. There was no large open tract that could be converted into a new village. The best that could be done therefore was to take over such open areas as had not been developed beyond a few lines of speculative street stakes and a 'For Sale' sign or two."[413]

Farthest from the shipyard in the western part of Quincy Point, McLaughlin, best known for his design of Fenway Park (1912), and Kellaway, who worked in the Olmsted office before setting out on his own in 1906, laid out two subdivisions for skilled workers and their families. Bound by Edinboro Road, Pilgrim Parkway, Murdock and South Streets, the 18-acre Arnold Street tract featured rows of 127 detached and semidetached houses placed on lots that on average measured 90 feet deep. The architects widened Pilgrim Parkway to 110 feet and portions of Ruggles Street and Fifth and Commonwealth Avenues were gently curved to follow the topography of the site. Although the USHC report praised the "very pleasant" effect along Ruggles Street, other sections of the Arnold Street tract were deemed less successful, as along Pilgrim Parkway where the setbacks were "overdone" and especially the "arrangement of houses on the south side of Commonwealth Avenue en echelon instead of parallel with the street," which the report declared "distinctly unpleasant in appearance."[414] On a hilly site just east of Pilgrim Parkway, Kellaway designed the optimistically named Victory Park, but a large school proposed just to the north remained unrealized. McLaughlin and Kellaway extended Pilgrim Parkway in a curve to the north to create the second subdivision for skilled workers, a smaller enclave of fifty-nine detached and semidetached houses located on a nine-acre irregularly shaped parcel known as the River Street tract.

Quincy's largest subdivision, the 22-acre Baker Yacht Basin tract, was planned for unskilled workers on a site overlooking the water just north of the shipyard.

In order to keep costs down, the site was developed at almost twice the density of the other Quincy projects. To offset the effects of the regular gridiron plan, two parks were placed on sites that previously served as unofficial town dumps: the modestly sized Whiton Park and the shorefront Town River Park enjoying 600 feet of frontage along the bay. The results along Avalon Avenue, where the two-family houses faced the park and water beyond, were particularly successful.

Temporary housing for 925 single men was provided in straight rows of twenty-one identical 100-foot-long dormitories located on a 13-acre site just west of Cleverly Court. Though basic fare, the dormitories represented a significant improvement over accommodations in Quincy's typical boardinghouses, with the *Boston Daily Globe* noting at their opening that each 82-square-foot room was "furnished already by the Government with a neat bed, a bureau, a writing table and chair, all in the attractive mission style."[415] Also located on the site was a communal mess hall capable of serving 2,000 meals per day as well as a recreation building outfitted with billiard tables, a player piano, and a canteen. After the war, as planned, the dormitories were demolished.

Despite the sudden end to the war, enough progress had been made at Quincy's three permanent subdivisions to allow construction to continue until all were completed as originally planned, a rarity in the USHC program. All told, 256 houses accommodating 422 families, or 2,120 people, were built in Quincy. A majority of the ninety detached single-family houses contained five rooms, although there were both six- and eight-room models; the fifty-seven semidetached houses featured either five or six rooms; and the 109 two-family dwellings had four or five rooms. McLaughlin produced twelve different designs for the Colonial-style brick and wood-frame houses clad in shingles or clapboard "so that when they are finished they will not look like a string of sausages." According to the architect, "There is a variety of design, both inside and out." In the same interview in the *Boston Daily Globe*, McLaughlin stated that the houses had been designed in consultation with future residents. The workers "told us their ideas and then we interviewed their wives on the subject, getting their ideas also. As a rule, the men said that they didn't need a dining-room, as they invariably ate in the kitchen, and for that reason they wanted a sort of a combination living room; but every woman we talked to put her foot down on that plan. They all wanted a good-sized kitchen and a dining-room to use Sundays or when company came. Of course, the women had their way."[416]

Sylvester Baxter, writing in *Architectural Record* in 1919, favorably assessed all of the permanent USHC projects at Quincy Point, asserting that "these three developments fit harmoniously in with the built-up sections in the midst of which they are placed—all being typical of a prosperous middle-class population, pleasantly housed . . . There is no hint in any of these cheery, new streets of the dull monotony that characterizes the average locality where the cheap contractor has cast his

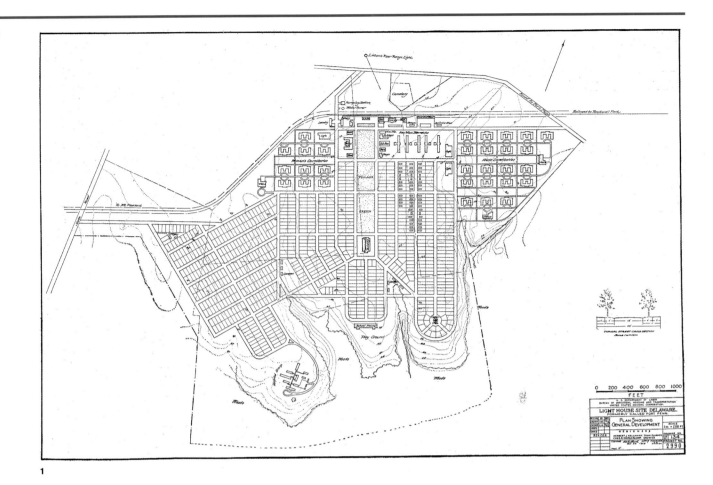

1

blight upon the scene. Neither is there any suggestion of the uneasy striving for originality, where each house seems to be crying out: 'Here I am! Just look at me!'"[417] Also writing in 1919, the editors of *Architectural Review* agreed: "While a very few types of plans have been used yet a great variety of appearance has been obtained by the use of varying types of roofs, porches and other external features, such as clapboards here and shingles there, with some few brick houses. Green blinds, with red or green asphalt shingle roofs, have been used to give the necessary contrasts of color. Simplicity of line and decoration has been the keynote of the designs and they have been modeled very appropriately, after those fascinating relics of the Old Colony which one sees in the villages of Norfolk and Portsmouth counties."[418]

In 1995, architecture critic Robert Campbell, in an article titled "Forgotten Utopias," observed that the USHC developments in Quincy had weathered the years well, particularly the Arnold Street tract "and especially the S-curved street called Ruggles. When you look up Ruggles . . . you feel the essence of these early planned communities. The houses are of only two or three standard types, and they're built conventionally, of wood frame and clapboard. But there's an indefinable generosity of spirit at work . . . You sense that this is a case where the hand of Big Brother—the United States Housing Corp., as it happens—was entirely beneficent. The shipworkers and their successors, grateful for the neighborhood, grabbed hold and made it their own."[419]

Herbert J. Kellaway prepared an additional USHC town plan to serve workers of a new bomb plant to be built outside of **Port Penn**, Delaware, twenty-four miles south of Wilmington.[420] The project faced delays after Kellaway's first two site choices were rejected, one for being too close to the proposed factory and the other for being too far away. Kellaway's third choice, the 372-acre Light House site, was accepted on October 21, 1918, and the hastily prepared plan, calling for 100 detached six- and eight-room houses for managers, 500 five- and six-room bungalows for married workers, and dormitory space for 3,000 single men and women, was completed on November 11, the day the armistice was signed. The USHC stopped work on the factory, and Kellaway's gridiron plan, with a large village green and dense groupings of dormitories, was also abandoned.

The New Orleans firm of Charles Allen Favrot and Louis Adolphe Livaudais provided architectural and town-planning services for two distinctive USHC garden villages, both of which were discontinued at the signing of the armistice. The first, planned for workers of the Navy Aeronautic Station on Pensacola Bay, Florida, six-and-a-half miles south of **Pensacola**, called for 135 single-family bungalows and one dormitory on 35 sandy acres one-half mile north of the naval station.[421] The triangular site was bound on the east by a steep bank leading down to the railroad connecting Pensacola to the naval base, and on the west by a county road intended to carry a streetcar line. Land was available for expansion to the north. The street pattern responded to the site's shape, with three avenues converging in the south and funneling into a pedestrian path that provided a quick route through a valley to the base. The middle avenue, Park Road, extended north to the heart of the neighborhood, where the plan opened up with two churches and a school situated in a park. Station Road crossed the neighborhood in the middle, connecting a proposed passenger rail station on the east with the automobile entrance on the west that featured two store blocks and a community center framing a small park.

Residential blocks were formed by concentric arcing streets that, because scant automobile traffic was expected, were given narrow roadways and geared toward service vehicles. In an unusual move anticipating Radburn, the planners turned the houses away from the street to face wide, planted greenways that combined with tree-lined sidewalks to supply shaded pathways throughout the town. Work commenced in late September 1918, just as the influenza epidemic broke out, delaying progress for one month—or long enough for the war to draw to a close and the project to be canceled.

Favrot & Livaudais's proposal for **New Orleans**, Louisiana, was of similar size and scope, planned to accommodate 209 families in detached bungalows spread across a flat, 42-acre site south of the New Orleans Naval Station, about four miles from New Orleans's business district, in the suburb of Algiers.[422] The plan's teardrop-shaped street pattern featured two house-lined loop roads inscribed within the site's rectilinear borders. In the Olmsted tradition, the "leftover" spaces created by the combination of curved and straight features were treated as small parks. Certain lots were left open along the boundaries to allow for their paving as streets should expansion be necessary. Traffic was brought in from the northwest, through a cluster of three store buildings opening up to a triangular green and a community center that anchored one end of the central oval, the opposite end of which accommodated a school. Two sites were also reserved for churches. Although the tree-lined streets and generous green spaces showed promise, particularly as the core of a larger residential area that might someday be built, the project was discontinued while still in the design stage.

Favrot & Livaudais were involved with one additional USHC project, a 31-acre neighborhood in **Charleston**, South Carolina, planned by Canadian architect Rickson Outhet, a USHC staff member and former Olmsted employee.[423] The site, six miles north of downtown Charleston, was near a concentration of military facilities whose workers either lived in speculatively developed private housing that was of poor construction or commuted by overloaded railroad or trolley from the city. Responding to a need for good local housing—and expecting continued postwar demand for such a product—the city of Charleston transferred a wooded, gently rolling site adjacent to the Charleston Navy Yard to the USHC for one-tenth of its market value. Water lines, electricity, and sewers were already nearby, making the

Pensacola

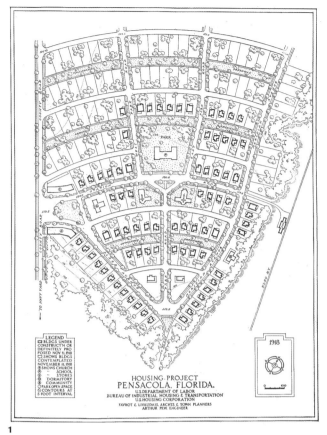

1. Plan, Charles Allen Favrot and Louis Adolphe Livaudais, 1918. USHC

New Orleans

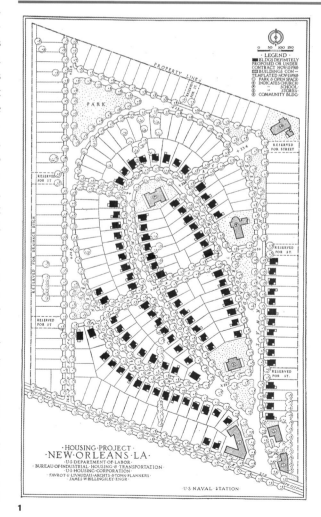

1. Plan, Charles Allen Favrot and Louis Adolphe Livaudais, 1918. USHC

1. Plan, Rickson Outhet, 1918.
USHC

1

1. Plan, James F. Dawson, 1918.
USHC

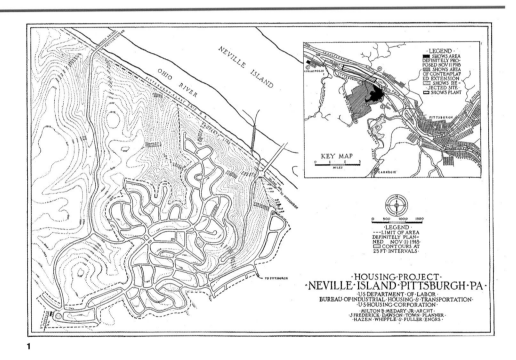

1

property prime for development, although there was an absence of schools, churches, and other amenities.

Outhet's triangular plan was organized around a park-lined central spine, which led south from a railroad station, shops, and a dormitory set on an open square, past houses and two churches to a central park accommodating a community building. At each of the intersections along the spine, known as Park Row, the corners were angled "for greater amplitude and interest," according to the planners, while on the side streets, houses stepped back midblock to "form groups surrounding a little quiet open space." Preserving trees was a priority, with "the scheme being to fill in the open spaces among existing trees and produce ultimately the effect of houses standing in an open woodland."[424] Favrot & Livaudais proposed single-family bungalows suited to the warm climate and local preferences. Work

was soon to begin when the end of the war led to the project's cancellation.

Landscape architect James F. Dawson, who in 1904 became Olmsted Brothers' first associate partner and remained with the firm for the rest of his career, is credited individually with the design of the USHC's **Neville Island** project, located on the south bank of the Ohio River across from its six-mile-long, one-third- to one-half-mile-wide namesake island, two miles west of Pittsburgh, Pennsylvania.[425] The plan represented one of the only USHC designs to eschew formal geometries in favor of a naturalistic pattern of curving streets and culs-de-sac. Frederick Law Olmsted Jr., who as manager of the USHC Town Planning Department ostensibly oversaw all of the bureau's work, was attached by name only to the Neville Island proposal, serving as district town planner. Intended to house the families of

Staten Island

1. Rendering of houses designed by Delano & Aldrich, 1918. USHC

2. Rendering of apartment house designed by Delano & Aldrich, 1918. USHC

Perth Amboy

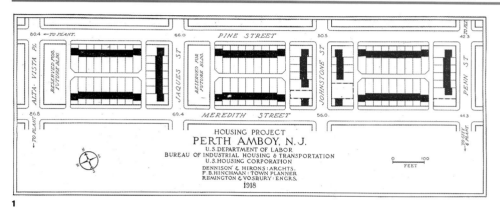

1. Plan, Frederick B. Hinchman, 1918. USHC

2. Rendering of houses designed by Dennison & Hirons, 1918. USHC

2,000 workers at a planned U.S. Steel gun foundry and shell-finishing plant, Neville Island was envisioned as a permanent town with an eventual population of 100,000. The site occupied one-and-a-half miles of riverfront, encompassing a 500-acre rolling plateau perched 450 feet above steep bluffs and slopes, making it "a beautiful tract from the aesthetic standpoint" for "an ideal city of homes."[426]

An existing bridge over the Ohio River (two more were planned) provided the main approach, with traffic brought uphill via a series of curves and switchbacks, into a town center occupying the highest topographical point, and on to a proposed railroad station in the southwest. With the exception of the town center's store-lined village green, open space was provided on land too steep for development, some of which was threaded through with pedestrian paths. The plan was designed to minimize street and lot grading. According to the USHC report, "The topographic conditions were so severe that no regularity or apparent design of street layout on plan was practicable or reasonable. The kind of aesthetic excellence to be sought was plainly that of picturesqueness, of unexpectedness, of careful and interesting adaptation of means to ends in a multitude of individual cases."[427] The development would have required extensive infrastructural work including all utilities and roads, a water works and sewer system, and all means of transportation to the site. The team of designers had been dispatched to the site for extensive study when the armistice "suddenly ended the whole venture in midcourse."[428]

The USHC failed in its sole attempt to build workers' housing in New York City.[429] The proposed subdivision, comprising a thirty-six-unit apartment house and seventy-eight two-family houses, was planned for 10 level acres in the Mariner's Harbor section of **Staten Island**. Landscape architect Arthur F. Brinckerhoff (1880–1959) was responsible for the regular gridiron plan, and the firm of William Adams Delano (1874–1960) and Chester Holmes Aldrich (1871–1940) designed the four-story, H-shaped Georgian-style brick apartment house and the stucco-clad six-room houses. Five different designs for the semidetached houses were prepared, earning the approval of the editors of the USHC report, who wrote that one "characteristic of the design is the general incorporation of the porches in the body of the house, thus magnifying the impression of size of the house while simplifying the mass." The editors also praised the "high roofs, long gable lines, and the total elimination of flat roofs," adding that "the consistent similarity of roof line gives harmonious simplicity of grouping."[430]

The USHC was also unable to complete workers' housing intended for a seven-acre site in **Perth Amboy**, New Jersey, a heavily industrialized city in close proximity to fifteen major manufactories, separated from Staten Island by the Arthur Kill.[431] Frederick B. Hinchman, town planner of the USHC development in Waterbury, Connecticut, devised the regular gridiron plan intended to accommodate 152 unskilled workers in long rows of two-flat houses, with four detached two-flat houses included for foremen. Hinchman's plan featured three pairs of rowhouses with the end units

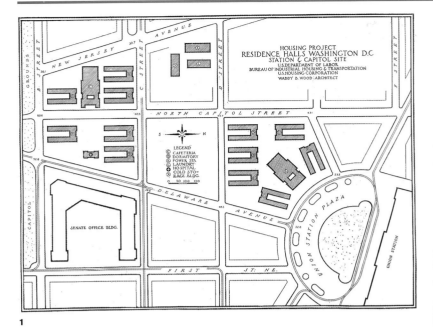

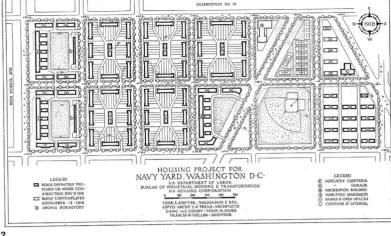

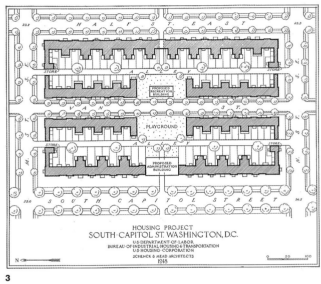

1. Plan, Union Station Plaza site, Waddy B. Wood, 1918. USHC

2. Plan, navy yard site, Arthur C. Comey, 1918. USHC

3. Plan, South Capitol Street site, Marcia Mead, 1918. USHC

4. Dormitories, Union Station Plaza site, Waddy B. Wood, 1918. USHC

5. Proposed houses, South Capitol Street site, Marcia Mead, 1918. USHC

slightly set back; four additional north–south rows completed the scheme. The New York firm of Ethan A. Dennison (1881–1954) and Frederick C. Hirons (1882–1942) were responsible for the two-story, four-room, stucco-clad houses criticized in the USHC report for their cost-driven severity.

Although **Washington, D.C.**, was home to only one substantial manufacturing plant, the Steel & Ordnance Company on Portland Street, south of the Anacostia River, the city, according to the USHC report, still "suffered more than did most of the industrial towns by overcrowding during the war" because of the enormous increase in the number of civilian government employees.[432] The shortage extended beyond housing to include a lack of office space, with the USHC forced to occupy three upper floors in a garage building taken over by the federal government. The majority of housing planned for Washington, and the only component realized, took the form of temporary dormitories proposed for sites throughout the city.[433]

On a largely undeveloped 17-acre site facing Union Station Plaza, Washington-based architect Waddy B. Wood (1869–1944) provided dormitory space for 1,944 single women in a dense development of twelve three-story, terracotta-block buildings arranged in two groups around large cafeterias as well as a power station and a two-story cupola-topped administration and recreation building. *Architecture* magazine was impressed with the "simple colonial designs" intended to "give the impression of an American city in crown colony days."[434] In 1930 the Union Station Plaza dormitories were demolished, replaced by a park and an underground parking garage for the Senate Office Building.[435]

On a 56-acre site in the southeast part of the city about a mile from the navy yard, Arthur C. Comey prepared plans for a subdivision intended to house 582 families in a near-equal mix of rowhouses and apartment-house units. Although the twelve-block site was largely vacant, the gridded street plan was already established, leaving Comey with the opportunity to propose only modest interventions, including the creation of two triangular parks formed by the diagonal path of Massachusetts and Potomac Avenues as well as a large full-block ball field. Comey took advantage of the large site, generously spacing the proposed three-story brick apartment buildings designed by the firm of Edward Palmer York (1865–1928) and Philip Sawyer (1868–1949) as well as the two-and-a-half-story six-room rowhouses designed by Clarke Waggaman (1877–1919) and George Ray (1887–1959). Although the permanent housing was not built, Waggaman & Ray completed nineteen dormitories accommodating 540 single men in uniform 8-by-11-foot rooms. The dormitories, located in straight rows at the southern end of the site nearest the navy yard, were razed in 1930.

Marcia Mead designed the most promising proposal for permanent housing on a seven-acre site bound by N and M Streets, South Capitol and Half Streets.[436] Mead was responsible for both the subdivision's gridded plan and the design of the proposed rowhouses and apartment buildings intended to accommodate 201 families. Mead broke up the dense development of long rows with pathways at the center of the site that led to a shared interior playground as well as to administration and recreational buildings. The USHC report praised the design of the handsome, two-story three- to six-room houses whose "facades are exceptionally well designed and show a pleasant variety in elevation gained by the change in roof balustrade, porches, and doorways." Although planned for white wartime employees of the expanded federal bureaucracy, after the end of hostilities the development was intended to be inhabited primarily by African-Americans owing to its location in what was otherwise a "solidly built area of Negro homes."[437] Mead's project, like several others envisioned for Washington that did not progress to the planning stages, was dropped after the signing of the armistice.

CANADA

Canada's so-called "resource towns" provided fertile ground for garden village planning, with two industries in particular rising above the common practice of building temporary settlements for their workers in favor of ambitious examples: the pulp and paper industry, which blossomed amid Canada's vast forests, and the aluminum industry, whose considerable power consumption was easily met by hydroelectric plants being realized to take advantage of Canada's abundant waterways.

Grand Falls (1907–11), Newfoundland, described by planner Jeffrey P. Ward as "the first fully realized garden city experiment in Canada," did not quite live up to Ebenezer Howard's ideals, although it did have direct ties to the English movement.[438] The project was initiated by Alfred Harmsworth (1865–1922), the Irish-born, English-raised and -educated publisher of the *Daily Mail* newspaper, who supported Howard's efforts through a mix of coverage and free advertising and also contributed financially to Letchworth. In 1905, Harmsworth, seeking to secure a non-European supply of newsprint and drawn to Newfoundland by the completion of a railroad opening up the interior, established the Anglo Newfoundland Development Company and commissioned a now-unknown firm to draw plans for a paper mill to be located on a bend in the Exploits River, with a commercial and administrative district adjacent to the east, leading to two residential neighborhoods and a racetrack in the northeast. One of the neighborhoods was laid out as a grid within a circular loop road. The other featured a looser configuration of contour-hugging streets.

Development occurred principally between 1906 and 1912, resuming after World War I to witness the eventual construction of 485 detached Arts and Crafts–style wooden workers' houses set amid front and rear gardens and about fifty additional buildings, such as a hospital, schools, churches, and stables. Yet Grand Falls never reached the size that Harmsworth hoped for it, in part because of a strict policy that granted residence only to millworkers, effectively shunning outsiders, who instead settled in neighboring Grand Falls Station. As a result, despite having a modest downtown, with a "company club, haberdashery, restaurant and blacksmith," according to Jeffrey Ward, "the real economy lay across the tracks, four miles away."[439] Grand Falls became independent in 1961 when the company sold a controlling share of its stock.

Témiscaming, Quebec, can more rightfully be designated Canada's first industrial garden village.[440] It was built in 1917 by the Riordan Pulp and Paper Company to house employees of a plant that would supply 60 percent of the world's viscose pulp, used to make artificial silk, among other products. Initially named Kipawa after one of the company's chief products, the village was intended for a population of 3,000, all of whom, with the exception of postal workers, worked at the paper mill. The site, on Lake Témiscaming, was virgin forest that would require total transformation.

The company had high ambitions, hiring Thomas Adams, the Scottish planner then practicing in Canada, to design a roughly 400-acre village (part of the company's 8,000-acre holdings) to the north of the mill. The land was extremely hilly, with only two level areas that Adams devoted to a central square and a peripheral village green. Once cleared of trees, the site was dotted with huge boulders, some of which Adams retained and others of which he broke up to become house foundations or to be used in a popular company-built rock garden.

After an initial study determined that a province-mandated grid plan would result in streets with an 18 percent gradient, a topographically sensitive plan was adopted calling for 5 or 6 percent grades with some as steep as 14 percent, prompting Comey and Wehrly to point out in their 1936 examination of North American planned communities: "Thus an unfavorable site from the point of view of relatively level building land assumed a decidedly interesting and varied as well as economical layout."[441]

1. Plan, 1911. PC05

2. Overall view of town from the mill. QEL (pre-1949)

3. Typical street. Lane. RSL (2013)

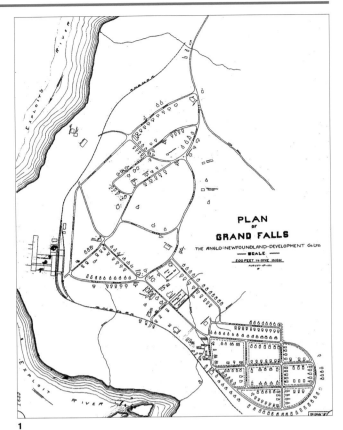

1

2

3

Adams centered the roughly triangular plan on a public square containing a church, a hospital, a school, and a convent. Separate neighborhoods were provided for workers and managers. The streets—40, 50, or 60 feet wide depending on their function—were lined by sidewalks, with a system of footpaths and stairways also helping pedestrians to negotiate the challenging terrain. The plan featured numerous parks and playgrounds. Adams made the irregular residential blocks

large enough for the houses, primarily rows of between three and six units, to be set back on common gardens, with no delineation of individual lots. Rear service lanes formed loop roads within the blocks, enclosing allotment gardens and playgrounds that kept children within sight of the house. The company built a movie theater, sports fields, tennis courts, a ski jump, golf course, hockey rink, and pool. Because the nearest farms were forty miles away and accessible only by rail, the company also established its own farm and dairy. Both houses and public buildings were designed by Montreal architects George Allen Ross and Robert Henry Macdonald (1875–1942).

In an unanticipated change, after the plan was completed, the paper company decided to run an eight-foot-diameter aboveground water pipeline through the town, leading to major adjustments that included a linear park around the pipeline and bridges to carry streets over it. The town was officially established in 1919, and by 1936, 317 houses were completed, with different types for company officials, mechanics, mechanics' helpers, and laborers. The original aim to build multifamily houses was mostly abandoned, however, and ultimately about half of the dwellings were semidetached, just 2 percent were multifamily, and the remainder were detached. Despite the absence of individual lots, residents took it upon themselves to enhance the land around their rented houses, so that by 1934 the town manager could report: "Today the centre of the town may be viewed as one garden; but investigation shows that it is made up of the individual gardens of the various householders, so harmoniously blended, however, that it is impossible to realize that the whole is the product of individual effort."[442]

In 1923, Adams, now splitting his time between Canada, London, and the United States, was commissioned to lay out another Canadian industrial village, **Corner Brook**, on Newfoundland's remote western shore.[443] Corner Brook was an unusual project built under the sponsorship of the government by a British engineering and manufacturing firm which had founded a pulp and paper mill on the Humber River. The 200-acre town site lay amid high wooded hills a short distance southeast of the mill. According to Adams, because an "ideal site was not available immediately adjacent to the mills . . . the choice was made of a beautiful and undulating but difficult site stretching into three valleys and occupying a fairly convenient position . . . Forest-clad hills, the rocky knolls, and streams entered into the attractive setting."[444] Reserving 75 acres for parks and playgrounds, some of which occupied sites too rugged for development, Adams let the topography organize the plan: "The main business street," he wrote, "was laid out along a narrow plateau on the edge of the principal valley with a square at each end, one forming the focal point connecting residential areas, and the other occupying a strategic position at the entrance of the town and at the intersection of an existing main road connecting with the adjacent villages and towns."[445]

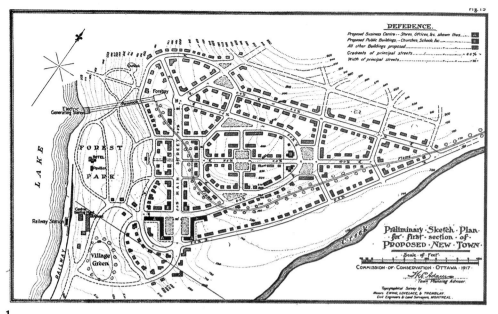

Corner Brook provided housing only for skilled workers and managers, leaving lower-level employees to fend for themselves outside of town. Architect Andrew Randall Cobb (1876–1943), a Brooklyn native educated at MIT and the École des Beaux-Arts who settled in Halifax in 1909 to become the city's first professionally trained architect, designed Corner Brook's 180 houses and civic buildings, including a hotel perched on a hill between the mill and town, two schools, a hospital, a fire station, a police station, a custom house, a bank, a general store, and a Salvation Army church. Cobb adopted the Craftsman style for most of the two-story houses, calling for shingled exterior walls, steep pitched roofs, dormers, front porches, and verandas. He designed dozens of variations on seven basic house types. Most were detached, although a few semidetached models were built as well as larger Classical Revival– and Tudor-style residences for upper management. Construction proved more costly than anticipated and the plan was only partially realized. Portions of the layout are still discernable, and original houses can be found along verdant, hilly streets, but much of the integrated park space has been taken over by automobile parking.

Kapuskasing, among the northernmost towns in Ontario to be accessible by road, lay seventy miles west of Cochrane on the route of the Canadian National Transcontinental Railway.[446] Planned in 1921 by the Toronto- and Buffalo-based landscape architect Alfred V. Hall (n.d.), who had worked in the office of Warren Manning, and his partner, William E. Harries (1886–1972), Kapuskasing was built by the government, which dubbed it the "model town of the north."[447] The village was intended at first to house workers of the Spruce Falls Power and Paper Company, a subsidiary of the Kimberly-Clark corporation, but over time to also accommodate employees of other industries—part of a government effort to minimize the village's dependence on a single company.

Hall's design of the 221-acre site, located at a bend in the Kapuskasing River, hinged on the construction of a bridge leading from a planned railroad station to the south, on the opposite side of the river, into the town center, where the entrance road forked at a village green to become the basis of a fan-shaped street plan extending north to a curving boundary road. Businesses around the village green were to form one of two

1. Plan, Thomas Adams, 1917. RPD

2. Fountain and houses. SHG (1930–59)

3. Gordon Avenue. SHG (1930–59)

4. Thorne Avenue showing pipeline in distance. SHG (1930–59)

5. Overall view. SHG (1930–59)

6. Rock garden. SHG (1930–59)

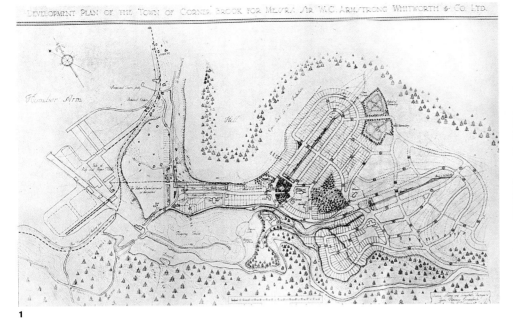

1

2

1. Plan, Thomas Adams, 1923.
RATP

2. Aerial view of upper town site
showing North Street, East Valley
Road, Central Street, and Reid
Street. CBMA (1934)

3. Glynmill Inn, Andrew Randall
Cobb, 1923. CRS

4. Central Street. Coyne. MC
(2010)

3

4

planned commercial areas, the other located in the east-ern part of the town around an oversized traffic circle that broke up an otherwise gridded street system.

Planning for a population of 2,500, Hall carved out 818 residential lots and thirty-two business lots, reserving 1,853 acres around the village as a greenbelt that could also provide space for expansion. The tree-lined streets, between 66 and 100 feet wide, occupied a substantial 33 percent of the site. By comparison, 12 percent of the site, or 26 acres, was given over to parks and playgrounds, including land along the river that was deemed too low-lying to be developed. Amenities included schools, churches, hospitals, athletic fields, and a community hall with a library, movie theater, and gymnasium. James Govan (1882–1963), an archi-tect working for the provincial government, designed the initial 504 houses, which were mostly detached resi-dences but included a few examples of semidetached and terraced houses.

A change in government proved detrimental to development, eliminating the bridge and relocating the railroad station. As a result, according to Comey and Wehrly, writing in 1936, "the entire plan was thrown out of balance . . . The failure to provide the bridge to the railroad station as originally planned has reversed the area intended for business from the central to the subordinate section of the plan, the main entrance being through the 'back door,' so to speak. This rever-sal has further been fixed by the location of permanent public structures, several of which are poorly related to their sites."[448] Nonetheless, as John Sewell observed in 1993, Kapuskasing retained the feel of a garden suburb: "The curvilinear street pattern, the handsome lot sizes, the greenbelt edging the river, and the careful attempt to create pleasing vistas are notable. The form of larger buildings (such as the hotel and the residences for single men) seems to be taken from Letchworth, or any other English town spawned by the Garden City movement: large sloping roofs which, though shingled, have the feel of being thatched; small windows, signaling the mod-est means of the inhabitants; and the carefully arranged lawns and gardens."[449]

In 1926, Leonard E. Schlemm (1879?–1942), a Montreal-based town planner and landscape architect, designed **Pine Falls**, Manitoba, for the newly formed Manitoba Paper Company.[450] In plan, the village, eighty-two miles northeast of Winnipeg and situated on the heavily wooded southern shore of the Winnipeg River, resembled "the back of a terrapin," according to J. P. Mertz (n.d.), a town planner who assisted on the design, with a tapered circular form consisting of concentric residential streets surrounding an oblong village green.[451]

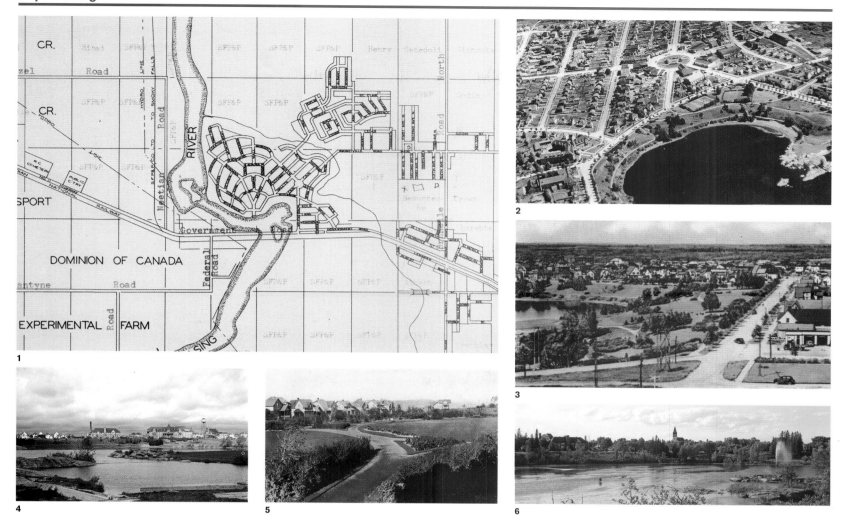

The village and the paper mill, a short distance away, were linked by a 40-foot-wide road that, as it crossed the central green widthwise, broadened into a divided boulevard with a 15-foot-wide planted median, separating the green into two sections, the larger of which included a grass lawn, tennis courts, bowling green, and playground, and the smaller, semicircular in shape, containing shops, an inn, and a community center.

According to Mertz, the "dominating idea in the design and the setting of the dwellings was to adopt the English type of cottage to local conditions and group the various types in pleasing perspective."[452] Thirty-foot-wide residential streets accommodated thirty types of workers' houses that were alternated to create a varied streetscape. The houses were faced in roughcast stucco and many incorporated ersatz but somewhat charming half-timbering. Rear alleys were absent but service strips behind the houses allowed for the burial of utility lines. The lots were 55 and 60 feet wide and 110 feet deep on average, allowing the houses to be set back 35 feet from the sidewalk. The planners included conveniently located group garages and small service buildings on each block where lawn mowers and garden equipment could be stored. After significant progress, the Depression halted development of the town, and the paper company was in receivership by 1936.

Arvida, Quebec, about 150 miles north of Quebec City in the Saguenay industrial region, was an ambitious undertaking by the Aluminum Company of America (Alcoa).[453] The area had recently seen the development of a massive hydroelectric plant by Canadian paper and pulp magnate William Price and American industrialist James Buchanan Duke. In 1926, Alcoa, attracted by the power supply as well as rail connections and a deep-water port that could accommodate the importation of materials from British Guyana, Greenland, and New Mexico and the export of aluminum, acquired nearly 6,000 acres from sixty farmers and hired New York architects Harry Beardslee Brainerd (1887–1977) and Hjalmar E. Skougor (n.d.), also an engineer, to plan an industrial city capable of housing between 30,000 and 40,000 people.

The site, cut through by north–south ravines, sloped downward from a road on the south to a bluff overlooking a river on the north, with terraces between the bluff and the river scheduled for substantial development. The plant and the railroad station occupied a central position around which Brainerd plotted locations for a business district and discrete residential neighborhoods that would each have schools and stores and be buffered and interspersed by parks. Once these areas were determined, Brainerd platted streets that

1. Plan, Alfred V. Hall, 1921. ONT (1964)

2, 3. Overall views. CAL

4. View across Kapuskasing River of civic center. Powley. ONT (1941)

5. Houses around a park. CAL

6. View across Kapuskasing River. Pen. WC (2009)

Pine Falls

1. Aerial view. Reichert. CRS

Arvida

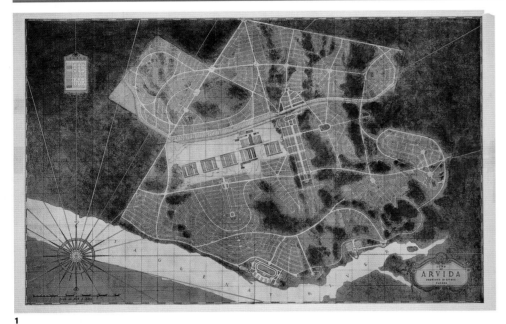

1

2

3

4

5

1. Plan, Harry Beardslee Brainerd, and
Hjalmar E. Skougor, 1926. VDS

2. Typical street. SHDS

3. Stores on Rue Mellon. SHDS

4. Overall view. SHDS

5. Typical houses. Col. FL (2011)

ranged in width from 50 feet for residential areas to 106 feet for highways.

Brainerd's plan combined Beaux-Arts formality, as seen in the layout of the business district, where a principal axis, terminated by public spaces and buildings on either end, was crossed by a secondary axis leading from the industrial plant to a monumental cathedral, with informal neighborhoods of contour-hugging streets, on the narrowest of which houses were set back 25 feet on generously sized 50-by-100-foot lots. Sidewalks were placed snug against the curb, with street trees lined up in the front yards. Because utility lines were buried behind the houses, the neighborhoods remained visually uncluttered, illuminated at night by streetlights.

Construction began in 1926 on an initial section near the plant. Progress was encouraging, with 270 houses for workers, foremen, and superintendents completed in 165 days according to an assembly-line-like process, an impressive rate given the 148 distinct house types. The houses were of frame construction, one-and-a-half stories tall, and clad in wood, stone, and stucco, incorporating aluminum for roofs, insulation, flashing, and windowsills. Workers' and managers' houses were not visibly different, though the latter featured better systems and amenities such as central heating.

In 1928, Alcoa, in danger of being designated a monopoly, spun off its Canadian operations to form the Aluminum Company of Canada, which soon, feeling the impact of the Depression and several failed experimental production methods at the plant, halted development of Arvida. After a period of declining population, business picked up with World War II. Between 1939 and 1950, the population quintupled, with urban growth expanding in tandem although according to new plans, leading historian Lucie K. Morisset to curiously claim that "it would have been considered absurd in 1950 to follow 30-year-old architectural plans. Nevertheless, the grandeur of its original plan and the first steps taken to realize the vision had set in motion the initiative for the completed city."[454]

MEXICO

In 1921, the American Smelting & Refining Co. hired Hjalmar E. Skougor to design the industrial garden village of **Rosita** (now called Nueva Rosita), Mexico, in the northeastern state of Coahuila, 185 miles southwest of San Antonio and about 70 miles from the Texas border, to house workers at a recently purchased coal mine that was in dire need of modernization.[455] Skougor's plan for Rosita, located 2,000 feet east of the mine on a gently sloping site stretching toward a rugged mesa, was to house the workforce of 31 Americans and 1,173 Mexican workers and their families.

Skougor called for a road to lead east from the mine site into the heart of the town, terminating at the corner of a village square whose diagonal orientation established the plan's overall geometry in which two neighborhoods for Mexican workers extended to the

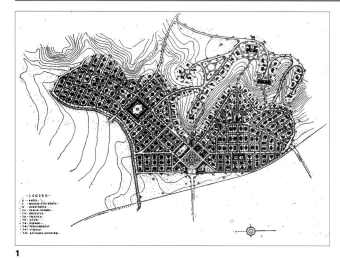

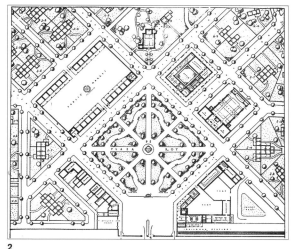

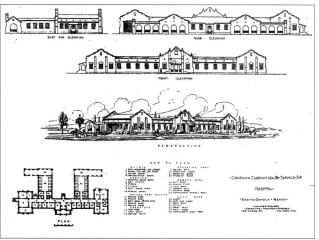

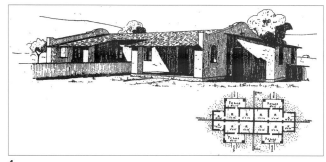

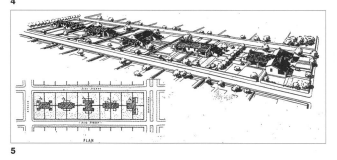

1. Plan, Hjalmar E. Skougor, 1921. CA21

2. Plaza de Roy, plan. CA21

3. Proposed hospital. CA21

4. Quadruple house for miners and laborers. CA21

5. Block of twenty houses for miners and laborers in groups of four. CA21

northeast and southeast as a mix of straight and curved streets. The landscaped town square featured a fountain and bandstand, considered to be traditional elements of Mexican village life. Public buildings bordered the square, including a church, an open-air market, a block of shops with apartments above, a 500-seat theater, a club containing a bowling alley, pool room, barber shop, assembly rooms, and baths, and a mixed-use community building providing a railroad station, restaurant, post office, and administrative offices. A public school for 1,500 children was located in the northeastern residential area. With the exception of the plant manager, who resided near the town square, the remainder of the American staff lived on spacious lots atop the mesa to the east, where a hospital and hotel were also situated to take advantage of thirty-mile views.

In addition to the plan, Skougor designed Rosita's houses and public buildings in a Mexican Colonial mode that made use of adobe and plaster walls and wood-shingle roofs. The numerous house types included detached residences for upper management, semidetached houses for Mexican mechanics with families, and quadruple houses for married native workers. All houses were one story. The quadruple houses, of which Skougor designed seven variations, were predominant and included only two rooms and a kitchen as well as a porch, where it was expected that families would spend much of their leisure time. Each house had a 50-by-50-foot yard enclosed by a low adobe wall, affording some privacy and enough space for gardening, although separate allotments were also available. The houses did not have bathrooms. Instead, twenty-one comfort stations were scattered across the plan. Skougor eliminated rear alleys and backyards, setting the quadruple houses that numbered between one and five per block, back from the street on the spot where the four individual lots intersected, much in the manner of the workers' villages of nineteenth-century France and Germany. The first wave of construction was completed in 1925, but the town quickly outgrew its plan, expanding into the surrounding landscape, so that by 1936 the population was 14,000, more than twice that initially envisioned. Portions of the original plan, including the town square, remain intact.

The Fall and Rise of the Garden Suburb

In 1941, when the U.S. Bureau of Public Roads prepared for World War II by undertaking a survey of the nation's daily commutation patterns, it found that 2,100 communities with populations ranging from 2,500 to 50,000 had dispensed with or had developed without mass transportation systems and were almost exclusively dependent on the private automobile for travel both within their own boundaries and to the downtown business districts of their host cities.[1] As a result, by the post–World War II era, the development of compact garden suburbs gave way to sprawling tract developments. Even in places where the car was not so ubiquitous, other new phenomena—the cinema, radio, telephone, and television—reduced dependency on city centers. But the automobile was the most catalytic: new suburban developments no longer had to be located adjacent to railroad stations or along trolley lines, and houses no longer needed to be within walking distance of public transportation, eliminating the raison d'etre of focal village centers.

In the years between the two world wars, a few American planners, most notably John Nolen at Mariemont (see p. 266), Ohio, and Henry Wright and Clarence Stein at Radburn (see p. 275), New Jersey, realizing that the automobile severely challenged the future of the garden suburb, had shown how the type could be adapted to it. However, two other influential architect-planners, who were in most ways diametrically opposed to each other's ideas but shared a passion for the automobile and its consequent decentralizing effect on cities, the Swiss-French Le Corbusier and the American Frank Lloyd Wright, each in his own way embraced the garden city and garden suburb but not the inherent humanity of village scale. Le Corbusier argued that his megalomaniacal proposal to reconstruct the center of Paris, the **Plan Voisin** (1925), would result in a "vertical garden city" of office towers set in vast greenery bound by perimeter housing blocks, while **Broadacre City** (1934), which Vincent Scully has suggested was Wright's answer to Le Corbusier's Paris plan, was in many ways the apotheosis of decentralization, a garden suburb at continental scale, destroying virtually all sense of town.[2]

Wright actively worked on Broadacre City from the 1930s to the end of his life in 1959, but he achieved the greatest publicity for it in 1935 when a model representing an area of four square miles, designed to house and provide work places for 1,400 families, was exhibited at Rockefeller Center in New York. Donald Leslie Johnson has shown how very close Wright's proposal was to Ebenezer Howard's Garden City "Ward and Centre" diagram as well as to the Soviet theorist N. A. Milyutin's proposal of the early 1930s for a linear city.[3] Not a city away from the city, as Ebenezer Howard proposed, or a suburb existing in natural symbiosis with the city, as Frederick Law Olmsted had advocated, Broadacre City was a super suburb incorporating the philosophical premises of the former and the formal principles of the latter. "Let the auto take the city to the country,"

Seaside. Brooke. SBS (1993)

1. Bird's-eye view, Le Corbusier, 1925. FLC

1

Wright wrote somewhat cryptically.[4] In Olgivanna Lloyd Wright's biography, Wright is quoted as saying that "what we need is the wedding of the city and the country. I designed Broadacre City on that idea," arguing in contradiction to so much garden suburb planning over the previous one hundred years, that Broadacre City would "have all the advantages of the city, without the city . . . [that] you cannot take the country into the city; the city has to go to the country."[5]

Broadacre City is contradictorily an attempt to establish a highly dispersed yet somehow—at least in Wright's mind—urban conurbation using landscape techniques. As Diane R. Blum wrote in a student paper in the late 1970s, "Essentially, Broadacre City is not really a city as we know it. Rather it is a spreading out of the suburbs across the countryside and a conception of the city as landscaping."[6] While it is difficult to assess to what extent Broadacre City's planning ideals influenced the development of the automobile suburbs of the post–World War II era, it is evident that far more than John Nolen, Henry Wright, or Clarence Stein, Frank Lloyd Wright understood the planning potential of the automobile. His proposal envisioning a national grid of broad arterial highways with as many as twelve lanes and an elevated monorail along which would be located supermarkets and hotels, with small factories of the artisan type (often with dwellings upstairs) set just beyond, was a highly aestheticized prophesy of postwar sprawl. Borrowing from Clarence Perry's concept of the neighborhood unit, Wright proposed that schools focus clusters of dwellings, the nearest his plan came to providing a place for communal gathering. As in Le Corbusier's Plan Voisin, there would be tall buildings, though nowhere as massive as in the French proposal. Wright's towers would "stand free in natural parks" as cooperative apartment houses of eighteen stories, modeled on those he had proposed in 1929 for New York.[7] These towers would be built to satisfy the needs of unreconstructed urban cliff-dwellers, some "with their

children who have grown so accustomed to apartment life under serviced conditions that they would be unable or unwilling (it is the same thing) to establish themselves in the country otherwise."[8] In the detailed model Wright prepared of one sector of his proposed "city," an "automobile objective," a spiral ramp, leads to an overlook atop a hill from which the entire region can be observed.

While the direct impact of Wright on suburban planning is difficult to document, it cannot be denied. Futurama, designed by Norman Bel Geddes (1893–1958) and exhibited in the General Motors Pavilion at the New York World's Fair of 1939–40, where it was visited by 25 million people, combined Wright's planning ideas with Le Corbusier's shiny architectural Modernism to make the new sprawling suburb seem more urban than it could ever be.[9]

By the time of Wright's death, with Broadacre City's prophecy of decentralization all too much a reality, planner Carl Feiss (1907–1997) wrote that "Broadacre City is the subdivision plat for a middle-class suburb in Utopia,"[10] while the historian Robert Fishman, in his book *Urban Utopias in the Twentieth Century*, contrasting Howard's Garden City with Wright's Broadacre City, observed that

Neither shape nor scale appear recognizably urban: one "city" might sprawl over 100 square miles without any recognizable center. Yet Wright insisted that he was presenting a coherent planned community. He based his claim on the new sense of time and space he was introducing . . . When Howard fixed the size of the Garden City, he was thinking in terms of pedestrians (or perhaps bicyclists). The 30,000 inhabitants of the Garden City could walk across the city in fifteen minutes or less. The motorized citizen of Broadacres could make a similar claim: traveling at 60 miles per hour he too could reach any of his 30,000 neighbors in fifteen minutes. However, the "open plan" of Broadacre City was a genuine departure from the neat concentric circles of the Garden City. Although Howard spoke of the "marriage of town and country," he sharply distinguished the two realms in his plan. He wished to preserve within the confines of the city a genuine urban life. Wright's hopes for Broadacre City were the exact opposite. His fundamental tenet was that there must be no more distinction between urban and rural life-styles. Therefore, there must no longer be a physical separation between urban and rural areas. Broadacre City was planned to ensure this.[11]

Broadacre City represents Wright's profound understanding of the changing American landscape. He believed in the sprawling suburb and considered himself its chief architect. There is a story that Wright took the Finnish architect Alvar Aalto (1898–1976) around Boston to show him the American suburban landscape. Wright majestically gestured to the surrounding scene and said, "'None of this could've been accomplished without me.' And Aalto, telling the story later, commented on suburbia: 'You know, I couldn't see it.'"[12]

With the resumption of development after World War II, legitimized by the example of Broadacre City, planners caved in to the nation's love affair with the car and with the open road and sacrificed all sense of the suburb as a village of pedestrian-friendly streets to a far more developer-friendly model of large-scale land subdivision that amounted to little more than a near totalizing usurpation of countryside outside and between cities by low-density housing interrupted by strips of commercial development along local and regional roads that quickly proved inadequate to the traffic they were forced to bear.

While Wright's Broadacre City can be cited as the conceptual template for postwar suburban sprawl, many other reasons can be cited to explain how the United States and to a considerable extent the rest of the Western capitalist nations were propelled to virtually abandon the very essence of what city and village life had historically been for centuries and to destroy the glorious metropolitanism of the nineteenth and early twentieth centuries that had balanced intense central city development and low-density suburban villages and preserved the countryside in its natural state as was advocated by Ebenezer Howard and realized in such cities as Chicago with its linked parks and even more significantly the forest preserve that marks its peripheral borders.

From a social point of view, the post–World War II appeal of sprawling suburbia and its concomitant rejection of urban life is understandable if one considers that after fifteen years of economic depression and world war cities were overcrowded and run-down. In the United States, millions of middle-class Americans, deprived of adequate housing, eagerly left dense conditions in cities for large, affordable new houses on the fringes, their house purchases eased for them by government-backed mortgages and their auto journeys to jobs vastly aided

Broadacre City

1. Model, 1934 –35. Weidemann. FLW

2. Concept sketch. FLW

3. Plan, Frank Lloyd Wright, 1940. FLW

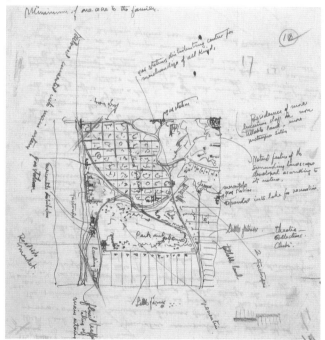

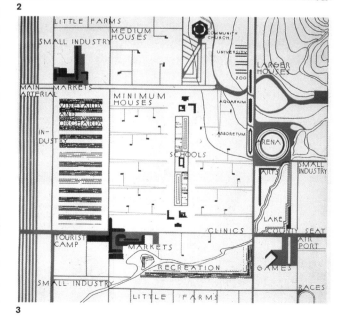

1. Aerial view. APL (1958)

2. Royal Street. RAMSA (c. 1970)

by the construction of superhighways under the Federal Highway Act of 1956. Within ten years of war's end, the nation had transformed itself into a "patchwork of low density settlements that became known as suburban sprawl."[13] Suburban sprawl was not a simple matter of environmental choice, as many of its apologists tend to suggest, but, as Charles Siegel emphasizes in his book *Unplanning*, basing his observations on Herbert Gans's social survey of Levittown, Pennsylvania, a product of necessity, or at least expedience: "There is no reason to think that they wanted houses . . . designed according to the planners' principles, rather than similar houses in neighborhoods designed like old-fashioned streetcar suburbs . . . During the prosperous postwar period, many people were able to buy their own homes for the first time, so there certainly was demand for more private houses. But there is no reason to think that people wanted to move to the land of cul-de-sacs, strip malls, and total automobile dependency. This sprawl exists not because of consumer choice but because of planning by local zoning boards and the Federal Housing Authority."[14]

Sprawling tract developments were accompanied by a virtual collapse in design standards for the single-family house as our best architects abandoned house design in traditional styles to the ordinary practitioner and to the speculative builder whose work, unsupported by high-style artistic models, was generally dismal. As a result the level of prevailing speculative residential development sank to an appallingly low level. Even the comparatively enlightened "cluster" and "townhouse village" developments, where the quality of the site planning was reasonably acceptable, usually lacked the architectural elements needed to establish an identifiable sense of place.

As the suburbs sprawled, the inner cities collapsed, with only the poor and some high-minded high-income optimists remaining in them to occupy the crumbling legacy of traditional architecture and urbanism. Regrettably, in a misguided effort to help cities survive, as Vincent Scully pointed out in his 1966 analysis of the situation as it affected his native city of New Haven,

Connecticut, architects and urbanists at the same time allowed cities to be "redeveloped" in emulation of the suburbs, with limited-access highways, parking garages, and enclosed malls.[15] Gradually, faced with the devastation this mass migration to the periphery left in its wake—devastation to both the historic cities and the open countryside—architects and urbanists eventually began to take action, protesting new highways and advocating preservation of inner-city buildings and neighborhoods and garden suburbs as well. But by the time their protests were heard a great deal of environmental damage had been done.

The youth-led countercultural revolution of the late 1960s, and the harsh realities of the early 1970s—stalemate in Vietnam, stagnating economy, and gasoline shortages leading to concern for the planet's future—led many to reconsider prevailing social values and in so doing not only to question sprawl but also to rediscover both the typologies of the traditional town and the garden suburb. Slowly, young architects, influenced by Herbert Gans and other sociologists, as well as by Vincent Scully, engaged in a larger reassessment of Modernism and began to argue that garden suburbs were models for future planning which were not only practical but also popular, that the single-family house could be part of inner-city urbanism as it had been for one hundred and fifty years. Soon enough, the tide of public opinion began to turn, measured in many ways, not the least of which was real estate values; for example, it was the village-like Roland Park that was preferred in Maryland and not the sprawling "new town" of Columbia. Gradually, many began to rediscover not only the garden suburb's potential for better use of land on the periphery of cities but also, and perhaps more significantly, its potential for rebuilding burnt-out neighborhoods on the sites of failed mass-scale social housing projects in a way that could address the needs of the working poor as well as the middle class.

Ironically, it was not a suburban housing development but an uninhabited themed amusement park, **Disneyland,** opened in 1955 in Anaheim, California, that more than any other single development drew attention to the enduring human values of traditional urbanism.[16] The brainchild of entertainment visionary Walt Disney (1901–1966), Disneyland was a modern city in miniature, a kind of garden village with a downtown business district leading from a "station square" along a tightly defined commercial Main Street to neighborhoods—Adventureland, Tomorrowland, and Frontierland. After the city of Burbank, California, rejected a request to build near the Disney film studio on an 11-acre site, Disney hired the Stanford Research Institute in 1953 to find a suitable location. The think tank suggested Anaheim, twenty-seven miles southeast of Los Angeles, an area destined to become a center of sprawling Orange County, and Disney purchased 160 acres of the city's orange groves for the project. Construction began in May 1954 and fourteen months later, on July 17, 1955, Disneyland opened. Within seven weeks more than one million people had visited the village-like development, which, ironically, quickly became the de facto urban center for the entire county.

Disneyland's success with the public was surprising enough. Even more so was how seriously Disneyland was taken as a development model. In 1963, in his keynote speech at Harvard's Urban Design Conference, James Rouse (1914–1996), the developer of the garden city–inspired but sprawling Columbia, Maryland, stated that

I hold a view that may be somewhat shocking to an audience as sophisticated as this: that the greatest piece of urban design in the United States today is Disneyland. If you think about Disneyland and think of its performance in relationship to its purpose, its meaning to people—more than that, its meaning to the process of development—you will find it the outstanding piece of urban design in the United States. It took an area of activity—the amusement park—and lifted it to a standard so high in its performance, in its respect for people, in its functioning for people, that it really does become a brand new thing. It fulfills all the functions it set out to accomplish unselfconsciously, usefully, and profitably to its owners and developers. I find more to learn in the standards that have been set and in the goals that have been achieved in the development of Disneyland than in any other piece of physical development in the country.[17]

Soon enough, the lessons of Disneyland were brought to the attention of the architectural profession by the architect Charles W. Moore (1925–1993), who recognized that, though it was a place with only visitors and no residents, Disneyland had revived the time-honored typology of a defined paradise of buildings and landscape set apart from yet embedded within a larger metropolitan conurbation—a gated garden suburb if you will, although Moore did not describe it as such. Writing in 1965, Moore pointed out that

Disneyland . . . engaged in replacing many of those elements of the public realm which have vanished in the featureless private floating world of southern California . . . Curiously, for a public place, Disneyland is not free. You buy tickets at the gate. But then, Versailles cost someone a great deal of money, too. Now, as then, you have to pay for the public life. Disneyland, it appears, is enormously important and successful just because it recreates all the chances to respond to a public environment. It allows play-acting, both to be watched and to be participated in, in a public sphere . . . In an unchartable sea of suburbia, Disney has created a place, indeed a whole public world, full of sequential occurrences, of big and little drama, of hierarchies of importance and excitement, with opportunities to respond at the speed of rocketing bobsleds . . . or of horse-drawn street cars.[18]

Robert A. M. Stern (b. 1939), influenced by Moore's observations and concerned about the celebration of sprawl in the academy, especially by Robert Venturi (b. 1925) and Denise Scott Brown (b. 1931) with their enthusiasm for the desert city of Las Vegas, Nevada, and their embrace of sprawl development in their project for California City (1971), called upon architects to examine without prejudice the varieties of suburban types that existed but were mostly neglected and return to the model of garden suburbs that had been disdained as bourgeois by architects and intellectuals alike but enthusiastically embraced by the public as a whole.[19] Going further, Stern began to urge architects, planners, sociologists, economists, and political strategists to consider the burnt-out wastelands of older cities—typically vast areas of largely abandoned land constituting what he called the middle city that lay between inner cities and peripheral suburban development—as fertile territory for new garden suburbs, believing that the tradition of freestanding houses within walking distance of village centers and rapid transit stations was a viable development model for urban renewal that could replace the failed, socially stratified high-rise Le Corbusier-inspired vertical garden city utopias exemplified by St. Louis, Missouri's Pruitt-Igoe housing project (Hellmuth, Yamasaki & Leinweber, 1955; demolished in 1972), the sprawling autopia of Frank Lloyd Wright's Broadacre City, as exemplified by the Levittowns of New York, New Jersey, and Pennsylvania, and the high-density low-rise Modernist-style housing enclaves such as **Marcus Garvey Village** (1976) being advocated by Kenneth Frampton (b. 1930) and others associated with the Institute for Architecture and Urban Studies in New York.[20]

The middle cities, Stern argued, offered the possibility of building new garden suburbs—not in the remote reaches of the outer city and beyond, but near the center. There they had the capacity to rebuild communities for the disenfranchised working classes and especially the poor on land with no evident higher use but already

1. Typical block, Kenneth Frampton, Arthur Baker and Peter Wolf; Theodore Liebman, Anthony Pangaro and J. Michael Kirkland; and David Todd & Associates, 1976. Liebman. TL

2. Mews. Liebman. TL (1975)

served by infrastructure: networks of roads, utilities, and rapid transit whose existence would greatly offset development costs while providing access to employment opportunities that automobile-dependent sprawling suburbia denied them. Such areas, having experienced massive population decline as the middle and lower middle classes fled beyond the city limits, were left with only the very poor occupying a building stock that was rapidly deteriorating as landlords, frequently unable to meet tax obligations, abandoned properties. In many neighborhoods, all the existing building stock had been destroyed. As neighborhoods crumbled, tax revenues spiraled downward, forcing municipal governments to maintain infrastructure and public services without being able to generate tax revenue, threatening the future of these cities with virtual extinction. New York's near bankruptcy in 1975 can in large part be attributed to this situation. The contemporary state of Detroit, Michigan, is perhaps the most extreme example of this.

In 1976, Stern, attempting to physically express a way out of the cycle of decay and abandonment, developed **Subway Suburb**.[21] The immediate trigger for the project was the invitation of Peter Eisenman (b. 1932) to participate in the United States' contribution to the architectural component of the 1976 Biennale held in Venice, Italy. Stern, hoping to provide a unifying theme among the participating American architects, suggested that of the suburb, while undertaking Subway Suburb as a speculative proposal to transform a decrepit site in Brownsville, Brooklyn, into a leafy oasis, a garden suburb not unlike such predecessor exemplars as Prospect Park South (see p. 107) or Ditmas Park (see p. 108) in Brooklyn's Flatbush section. The specific site was selected because it lay immediately south of Marcus Garvey Village, designed, as previously noted, as a Modernist-style low-rise, high-density alternative to the tower-in-the-park public housing of the post–World War II era—but also a social failure. Stern, for a bit of ironic effect, included the Marcus Garvey Village site as part of Subway Suburb.

Watercolor renderings depicting skyscrapers on the horizon behind villa homes suggested that Subway Suburb was to be very much a part of the city—it was, for the most part, to follow the existing street and utility grids. Crucially, an elevated subway line traversed the site, placing houses within a few blocks of a subway stop where retail and other commercial uses would be located.

Although village-like in character, Subway Suburb called for a reasonably high density, achieved through the introduction of semidetached houses and the placement of the neighborhood's smaller detached houses close to one another. To relieve the numbing repetition of the area's unbroken street grid, in a manner echoing many of the private places of St. Louis (see p. 90) as well as Hilton Village in Newport News, Virginia (see p. 878) not to mention English precedents dating back to the Paragon at Blackheath (see p. 19) and Nash's Park Villages (see p. 26), a variation of the traditional boulevard was introduced, with roadways interrupted by oval-shaped midblock parks lined by one- and two-family houses, the latter taking on the appearance of single large villas. The gridded streetscape would also be enlivened with houses on corners built on a grander scale to take advantage of two street fronts and create gateways to individual blocks, while the streets of villas and parklets alternated with traditional streets of modest cottages to create visual variety and provide for the possibility of catering to different tastes and budgets. Stern lined alternate streets with detached single-family vernacular-style gambrel-roofed cottages evocative of those common around the turn of the twentieth century. John Calvin Stevens's 1886 development of workers' cottages in Westbrook (see p. 800), Maine, was a distinct precedent for the design of houses set behind substantial front yards to mark out clearly definable turf to be maintained by the homeowners for the benefit of the community. Although the suburb was intended to be oriented to public transit, each house featured a garage placed to the side, designed to be part of the streetscape as symbolic recognition that car ownership was a fundamental hallmark of status. Moreover, given changing patterns of production that resulted from thirty years of sprawl development, not all jobs could be reached by public transportation.

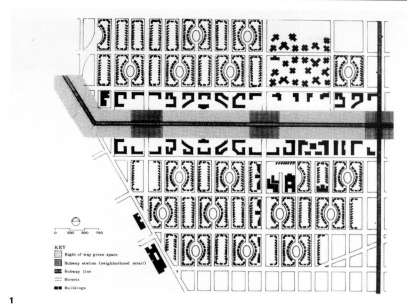

1

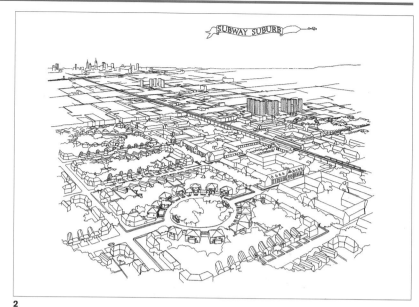

2

1. Brownsville site plan, Robert A. M. Stern Architects, 1976. RAMSA

2. Bird's-eye view. RAMSA

3. Plan, elevation, and site plan. RAMSA

4. Typical house elevation. RAMSA

5. Entrance to courtyard. RAMSA

6. Plan and axonometric drawing of houses. RAMSA

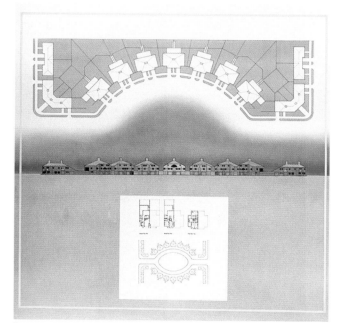

3

4

5

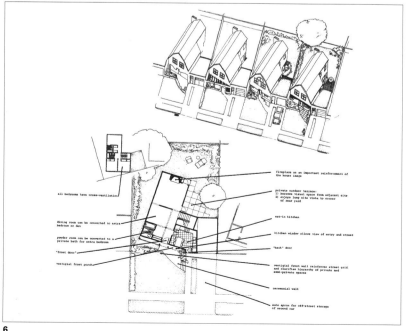

6

1. Plan, Harry Weese & Associates, 1976. PA76

2. Aerial view. NRHA (1988)

3. West Olney Road. NRHA (1991)

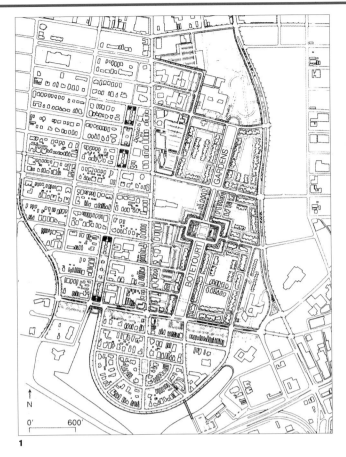

The garden suburb, as exemplified by Subway Suburb, was pitched to the person without much means for whom a house and a lot and being able to grow a little something in a yard that also allowed for a secure children's play area, was significant as was the ability of the homeowner to tinker with the house and expand it according to need, something that could not be done in the towers of typical public housing.

Subway Suburb was not about edge city, or the open country, or sprawl. It addressed a fundamental misconception of the garden suburb type. It recognized that long-familiar garden suburbs such as those at Hampstead Garden Suburb in London or Forest Hills Gardens in Queens, New York, were built within the confines of the city and could not be understood apart from the cities that formed their larger setting. Subway Suburb was not about the flight from the inner city to the rural fringes that characterized the post–World War II scene. Quite the opposite, it called for the introduction of the garden suburb type into those areas of the central cities where the prevailing mode of redevelopment—the disconnected vertical garden cities of towers in the park—had clearly failed. Subway Suburb was an attempt to take back the garden suburb movement from the Modernists who had so transformed it that it was no longer recognizable or meaningful.

Vincent Scully and Walter Creese took note of Subway Suburb. Creese, pioneering scholar of the garden city and garden suburb, found "many American memories reflected" in it, "even of the Lawn of the University of Virginia; but in addition to the recollection of the English superblock, the refashioned cul-de-sacs and the double, or semi-detached, houses reinvoke the garden city images the most."[22] Subway Suburb also influenced a number of subsequent developments. As Jonathan Barnett observed, its principles were closely incorporated at **Ghent Square**, a neighborhood in Norfolk, Virginia, located at the edge of a large city (albeit one much smaller than New York), where new yet traditional single-family houses were built for middle-income residents surrounding a small square according to a master plan developed by Harry Weese [1915–1998] & Associates of Chicago, with controls designed to evoke the aesthetic of traditional towns in America and abroad.[23]

In the mid-1980s, a version of Subway Suburb was given a chance in New York when the New York State Urban Development Corporation targeted Charlotte Street in the Bronx for revitalization. The site, a veritable national poster child for the collapse of urban neighborhoods, had been the subject of study for Stern's students at Yale and Columbia in 1978 who were asked to devise an "In-City Suburb" (Columbia) and an "Urban Suburb" (Yale) in which they looked to pre–World War I English and American prototypes to guide site planning, street configurations, and architectural style.[24] Calling their project **Charlotte Gardens**, the Urban Development Corporation tried to evoke the garden suburb tradition, yet ended up placing on the site some eighty-nine prefabricated, one-and-a-half-story ranch-style houses designed with little regard for the surrounding context

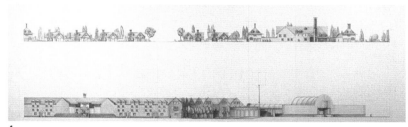

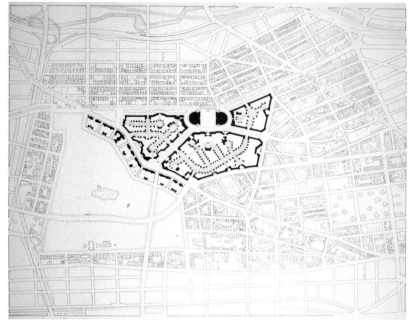

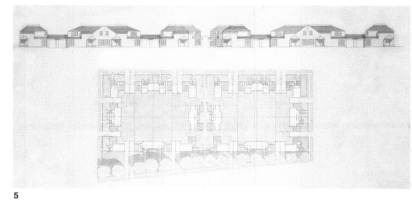

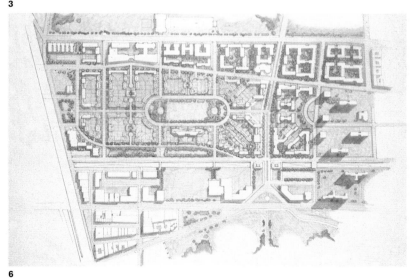

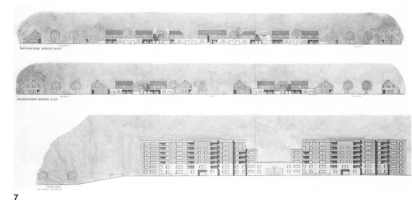

1. Charlotte Street. Vergara. CV (1981)

2. Charlotte Street and Wilkins Avenue. Vergara. CV (1989)

3. Urban Suburb, site plan, Gavin Macrae-Gibson, 1978. GMG

4. Urban Suburb, elevations, Gavin Macrae-Gibson, 1978. GMG

5. In-City Suburb, plan and elevation, Henry Jessup, 1978. HJ

6. In-City Suburb, site plan, Henry Jessup, 1978. HJ

7. In-City Suburb, elevations, Roger Seifter, 1978. RAMSA

Henry Horner Homes

1. Henry Horner Homes, Skidmore, Owings & Merrill, 1957. DWilson. FL (2002)

2. Plan, Skidmore, Owings & Merrill, 1957, drawn by Calthorpe Associates, 1993. TRC

3. Plan, Calthorpe Associates, 1993. TRC

4. West Randolph Street. DWilson. FL (2002)

1

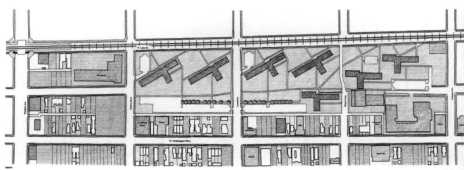

2

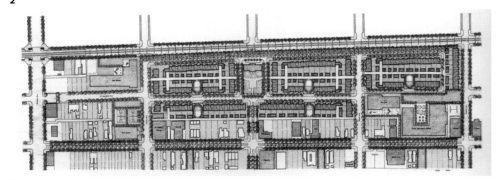

3

4

not to mention the historic elements that defined the suburban villages of the past, leading Vincent Scully to observe that the "few single-family houses . . . may be seen as a spinoff from Stern's project, but they have not been able to touch the needs of those whom President Reagan has referred to as 'the truly needy.'"[25] No one would mistake Charlotte Gardens for a suburban-type garden suburb—the architecture was banal, the landscape almost nonexistent, and there was no communal open space. Moreover, the failure to recognize the fundamental misfit between a metropolitan street grid and a typically stretched out ranch house was ludicrous. Nonetheless, Charlotte Gardens represented a sincere effort to rebuild abandoned metropolitan neighborhoods as distinct neighborhood enclaves. Charlotte Gardens proved crucial in turning around the fortunes of the South Bronx as a whole and validated what Subway Suburb had proposed: it was practical and theoretical; it addressed the urgent need to rebuild the city at the scale of the individual family in a community; and though it evoked arcadian values, it also embraced the reality of the city.

The success of Charlotte Gardens led to the Hope VI program of the 1990s.[26] Spearheaded by Henry G. Cisneros (b. 1947), secretary of the Federal Housing and Urban Development Administration (HUD) from 1993 to 1997, with the guidance of Peter Calthorpe (b. 1949), Hope VI brought many of the planning principles of the garden enclave to bear on some of the thorniest problems of inner-city redevelopment, carrying the ideas of Subway Suburb much further. Under HOPE VI, planners and architects redeveloped inner- and middle-city housing projects into village-scale but fundamentally urban neighborhoods, demonstrating that the garden suburb constituted a viable prototype for community development that could meet both quotidian requirements and the hopes and dreams of a virtually disenfranchised urban population. Typically, Hope VI projects replaced superblocks with tower-in-the-park developments or European siedlung-inspired high-density low-rise projects of the Marcus Garvey type with a mix of traditional low-rise row housing types arranged along through street networks interspersed by clearly defined public squares. Calthorpe was responsible for the planning of some of the most successful Hope VI projects, including **Henry Horner Homes** (1995), Chicago, Churchill Homes (1995), Holyoke, Massachusetts, and Curtis Park (1999), Denver. Also of note was **Monterey Place** (2002), New Haven, a 600-unit development designed by Fletcher Thompson in association with landscape architects Blades & Goven that replaced the notorious Elm Haven (1939) public housing project.

Seaside (1980), a coastal resort community on the Florida panhandle, the pioneering exemplar of what would become known as New Urbanism, was the first significant manifestation of the garden suburb, or to be more precise, the resort garden suburb, to be realized since the 1920s.[27] Developed by Robert S. Davis (b. 1943) on an 80-acre parcel of Gulf of Mexico beachfront originally intended by his mercantile family

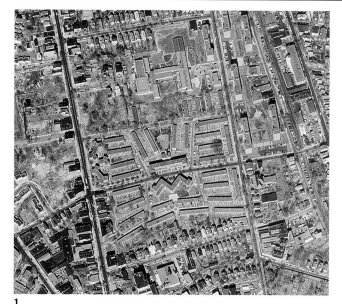

1. Aerial view of Elm Haven. CTIA (1965)

2. Aerial view. BGO (c. 1995)

3, 4. Typical views. DSU (c. 1995)

to serve as a vacation retreat for company workers, Seaside was the first important planning project for the architect-planners Andrés Duany and Elizabeth Plater-Zyberk who brought in Leon Krier (b. 1946), the Luxembourgian architect-planner.

The approach Davis and his planners took at Seaside was unconventional, and given then prevailing planning theory, unorthodox in the extreme. The land would have been easy to sell as a single parcel to a large-scale resort developer. Instead, Davis, a product of the 1960s environmental movement (as well as a graduate of the Harvard Business School), envisioned something more important: "To construct a demonstrable and overdue antidote to the well-intentioned idea that took hold at the beginning of this century, the idea that social ills could be ameliorated by the separation of housing from workplaces. Certainly the desirability of living at some distance from steel mills or slaughterhouses was obvious. But this idea, like many, was distorted into the current practice of rigidly separating all land uses from each other and, thus, requiring that we spend inordinate portions of each day encapsulated in automobiles, leaving behind, at the end of the day, lifeless downtown areas. More importantly, civic intimacy was vanishing."[28]

When Davis began his development, the Florida panhandle, known rather disdainfully as the "Redneck Riviera," primarily featured banal single- and multi-family housing clusters spreading out from Panama City, the resort area's center. Davis was not interested in creating more of the same; he insisted that Seaside demonstrate that the pattern of traditional towns could form the basis for profitable development even in the late twentieth century. Duany and Plater-Zyberk, at the time working as part of the Miami-based architecture firm Arquitectonica, which they had helped to found, were not the first to work on Seaside: Robert Altman (b. 1947), a Florida architect, had devised an earlier scheme (1978) for Davis with winding roads and a small golf course. But when Davis turned to Duany and Plater-Zyberk, former students of Vincent Scully, the project was reimagined. Together with Davis, the two architect-planners toured many of the region's best-planned towns, including those of John Nolen and of the Chautauqua Revival such as Defuniak Springs, Mississippi. In addition, a charette was conducted to solicit feedback and Leon Krier was asked to make design recommendations. Krier was enthusiastic to do so, because, he said, 80 acres was just large enough to sustain a vibrant community while remaining small enough so that the beach,

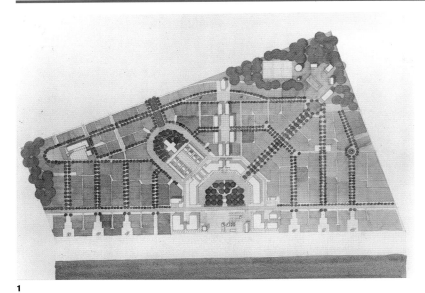

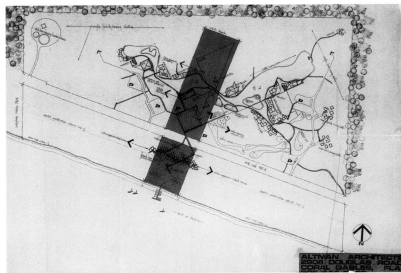

1

2

1. Plan, Duany Plater-Zyberk & Company, 1980. DPZ

2. Plan, Robert Altman, 1978. ALT

3. Aerial view. MacLean. ASM (1994)

4. House designed by Leon Krier, Tupelo Street. Brooke. SBS (1989)

3

4

retail locations, and public centers would be within a comfortable, quarter-mile, roughly five-minute walk of most houses.

Davis undertook Seaside's development a single neighborhood at a time. Recognizing that the location was generally regarded as a risky investment, he arranged to build houses that could be rented to holidaymakers—in effect the rented houses were "horizontal hotels," a version of the strategy used at Riverside and other early garden suburbs. Once the renters experienced Seaside's modest vernacular architecture and intimate scale, not to mention the glories of its beach, many chose to purchase lots and build. By the early 1990s, Davis had no need to worry about attracting visitors to his town: it had grown to such an extent and had garnered so much attention in the media that it came to represent the very epitome of what American small towns had once been and could be again. That Davis's interpretation of the American village as a planned garden suburb proved to be one many Americans shared was not lost on Hollywood filmmakers, who set *The Truman Show*, a 1998 film about a man whose seemingly perfect life is entirely scripted for television, in Seaside.

Seaside's roots are firmly in the garden suburb tradition. It is especially true to the work of John Nolen, such as Venice, Florida (see p. 271), but also surprisingly close to Edwin Lutyens's Rossall Beach Estate (see p. 358). Eschewing repetitive block and lot patterns, the Seaside plan is undergirded by diagonal main arteries to ensure that no block extends for too long and that there can be flexibility so that lots can be reconfigured as the market demands, thus creating an "organic" process of growth over time. While families tend to use the beach in isolated groups, the semi-octagonal town square, wrapped with stores and restaurants at ground level and apartments or offices above, is the focus of community life. It is also the point from which two main boulevards radiate out into the village. With the exception of those streets, Duany and Plater-Zyberk planned relatively narrow, two-way, 20-foot-wide roads paved in rose-colored brick. The roads are narrow to slow traffic but just wide enough to allow street parking on their verges. Most importantly, they encourage walking, as does one of Krier's most significant contributions to Seaside's plan, a network of sand-and-shell footpaths lined by picket fences that cut through the middle of most blocks, affording pedestrians alternate routes around town. The Seaside streets reinvent Parker and Unwin's street-as-picture concept, each terminating at the beach where individually designed shade pavilions conclude vistas and seem to bring the presence of the water closer to landside neighborhoods. The landscaping by

5. Odessa Street. Brooke. SBS (1993)

6. Ruskin Square. Brooke. SBS (1999)

7. Typical street. DPZ (2005)

8. Footpath. Joevare. FL (2010)

9. Town square. Joevare. FL (2010)

5

6

7

8

9

Douglas Duany (b. 1953) plays an important part in the town's appearance: lawns are forbidden in favor of native plantings, which, together with the pastel of the houses, wooden porches, and picket fences, combine to convey a remarkable informality and a clear sense of the local.

When it was new, Seaside was a tiny enclave in an empty landscape crying out for future development. Davis counted on the extensive wooded holdings to protect his village from inappropriate development on the periphery. The woodlands, however, were not in public hands, belonging instead to the St. Joe Corporation. Fortunately, Peter Rummell (b. 1946), newly appointed chairman and CEO of St. Joe, fresh from his experience in guiding the development of Celebration, chose to capitalize on Seaside's success and develop a larger town, **WaterColor** (1997), planned by Cooper, Robertson & Partners, that sympathetically connects with Seaside.

Seaside's orderly street pattern is enlivened by houses and buildings that are mostly straightforward versions of Florida vernacular cottages but also include individualistic, even idiosyncratic, examples by high-profile architects that nonetheless follow stringent design guidelines developed by Duany and Plater-Zyberk. Although Seaside was subject to few government-imposed codes, the developers established their own—depicted on a widely disseminated poster—specifying a range of dimensions, styles, color, and form for every detail of housebuilding.

As in the case of Forest Hills Gardens and other precedent garden suburbs, Seaside has a town architect who sees to it that all building plans conform to its codes. Davis often retained promising young talents to serve one-year terms as town architect. Leon Krier, notoriously shy of building, realized his first independent work in a house for himself at Seaside; other young architects given opportunities to build there include Steven Holl (b. 1947), Robert Orr (b. 1947), John Massengale (b. 1951), Deborah Berke (b. 1954), Alexander Gorlin (b. 1955), and Melanie Taylor (b. 1957). Berke and Holl, the first to build facing the town square, eschewed Seaside's typical Southern vernacular by employing a more abstract Modernism—signaling that the code was not strictly tied to issues of style. Although the town is made up of freestanding single-family houses, Ruskin Square, one of the diagonals leading from the center, is lined with stylistically surprising townhouses.

Amid the intense press coverage of Seaside, some have criticized the town precisely for its financial success, arguing that it has become merely a collection of over-detailed second homes for the rich, "a completely artificial place inhabited only by yuppies, with none of the nitty-gritty problems of a real town with a diverse population, real economic concerns, and a history."[29] But Seaside should be seen in the broader context of the garden suburb tradition. It is a resort suburb where many visitors become residents and many more, experiencing on vacation the kind of community life it supports, take its example back home and demand an alternative to sprawling subdivisions. In fact, Seaside has proven to be one of the most influential planned communities of the twentieth century. Interestingly,

1. Aerial view. MacLean. ASM
(2010)

1

and significantly, Seaside's influence has not only been on other resort developments but has become the basis for year-round suburban villages such as Duany and Plater-Zyberk's Kentlands (1988).[30] It has also inspired many ill-considered initiatives promoted by developers who have seized on the "look" of Seaside and the New Urbanist Traditional Town movement it inspired, without adopting its ambitions to the social integration of community. Such is the case of New Daleville, Pennsylvania, documented by Witold Rybczynski in his book *Last Harvest*.[31]

In 1988, HRH Prince Charles (b. 1948), The Prince of Wales, in his capacity as head of the Duchy of Cornwall, set out to develop **Poundbury**, a mixed-use extension to Dorchester, on 390 acres about one mile west of the historic city center.[32] Prince Charles, who would articulate his views about architecture and planning in his book, *A Vision of Britain*, commissioned Seaside veteran Leon Krier to prepare the master plan for "a form of urban development which," in Krier's words,

> *rather than segregating urban uses as has been the trend for many decades, instead integrates all essential community needs and activities within . . . four urban communities, of 500–800 households each . . . none of which exceed 100 acres. Each of these districts is conceived of as a traditional Dorset town or village with a traditional street pattern and common, traditional building types and materials. Each section of development will be self-sufficient in education, employment, shopping, leisure. Those who seek employment will be able to find residential accommodation within ten minutes walking distance. Regular markets will be held within each district and most shopping needs satisfied without using the car.*[33]

Specific architects were commissioned to design Poundbury's prominent public and residential buildings in order to establish a "high standard" of design but otherwise plots were sold to individuals and developers who would be guided by a "simple" design code, prepared with the help of Andrés Duany, to "give 'key building lines and general proportions of the houses and acceptable local materials,'" while also encouraging "a creative response from designers rather than [inhibiting] individual initiative."[34] The plan called for phased development lasting about twenty-five years, resulting in a total of 2,500 dwellings, including both market-rate and subsidized housing, with the 20 percent of low-income units indistinguishable and intermingled with the other residences.

Dan Cruickshank, writing in the British magazine *Architects' Journal* in June 1989, a week after Krier's plan was presented to local planning officials and Dorchester residents, praised it as "the most daring urban project this decade . . . [and] the culmination of [Krier's] thinking on both the rejuvenation of old cities and on the ideal form new urban communities should take. The proposal is also an attempt to achieve that most difficult of things—a planned and controlled development that possesses some of the essential characteristics of the organic, traditional town."[35] The economic downturn of the late 1980s and early 1990s delayed progress until October 1993, when construction began on Poundbury's first phase, Middle Farm, located on an 18.5-acre parcel. Composed of curving, narrow streets intended to promote "traffic calming," and developed at a density of sixteen units per acre, Middle Farm was centered on Pummery Square, home to a dominant structure designed by John Simpson (b. 1954) modeled after the market hall at Tetbury (1655). Other buildings at Pummery Square included ground-level stores, a pub, a café,

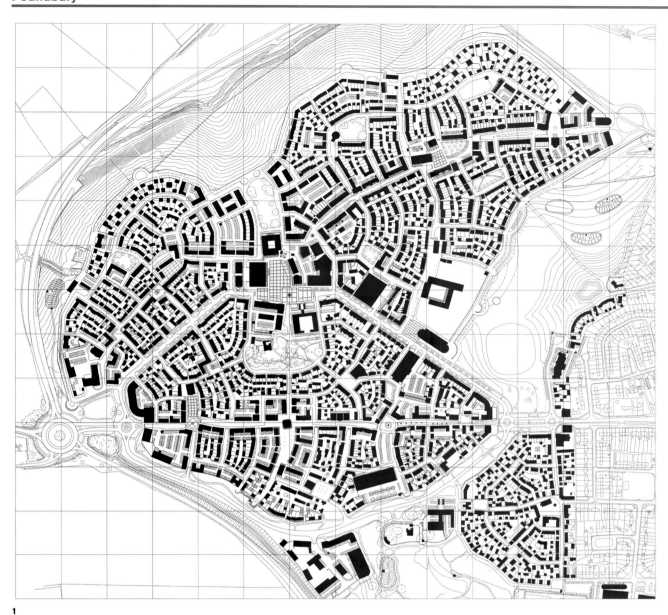

1

and a medical clinic topped by apartments. Krier's proposed tower for the town square remains unrealized, as do offices and light industrial workshops designed by Demetri Porphyrios (b. 1949). The housing, stylistically inspired by the Dorset vernacular, includes a mix of detached and semidetached houses as well as terraces and apartments, including a twenty-nine-unit building intended for the elderly. By 2010 the town numbered 931 dwellings accommodating a population of 1,820, with about 25 percent of the units subsidized for low-income residents. In addition, more than 1,100 people worked in the town's factories and retail operations.

A common criticism of Poundbury centers around the belief that it is a toy town representing "the apotheosis of retrograde aesthetics."[36] Critics dismissively note that some "visitors have stopped residents to ask if 'it's open,' as if Poundbury were a theme park."[37] Writer Stephen Bayley went further, denouncing the development as "a retirement community of the mind, a shabbily executed artistic dead end."[38] But Prince Charles defended

his project against the attacks, stating that "far from being 'old fashioned,' Poundbury has merely tried to revisit those timeless principles that are best able to create a real sense of community."[39] Most significantly, Poundbury enjoys the widespread support of its residents.

Mervyn Miller has identified Poundbury's historic roots in the garden suburb tradition: "One needs only to open the pages of Unwin's book *Town Planning in Practice* to find sketches, particularly those by Charles Paget Wade . . . from which the theme for the Poundbury idea might have come." To Miller, whose historical writing concentrates on the garden suburb tradition, Poundbury "is an indication that the theories of town planning, embracing urban design and the garden city, as they emerged in the pre-First World War period, may still have lessons for us today."[40]

Celebration (1996), Florida, developed by the Walt Disney Company and largely completed by 2006, is the most ambitious realization to date of the principles of the Traditional Town movement. Described

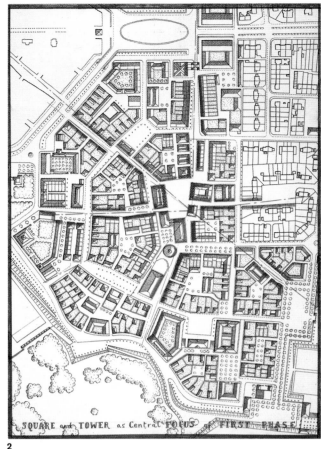

2

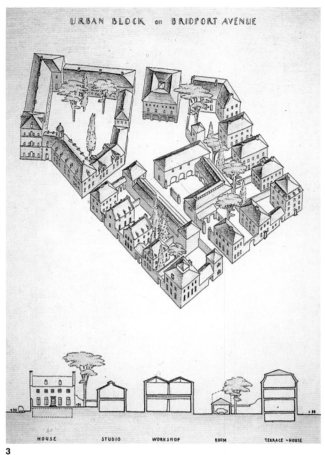

3

4

5

6

7

8

9

10

11

12

by Andrés Duany as "one of the most intricate and accomplished examples of urban development since the 1930s," with a "diversity of housing built in close proximity" that "breaks new ground with its inclusion of rental apartments and rowhouses seamlessly integrated with single-family houses and mansions," the planning of Celebration is based on a careful consideration of American precedent, including Seaside.[41] Celebration's corporate origins lie in quite the opposite direction from that of its immediate model, the unfulfilled promise of Walt Disney to build the "town of tomorrow" as part of the 28,000 Central Florida acres he assembled in 1966 to create Walt Disney World just outside of Orlando. With the success of Disneyland behind him, Disney had begun to think of himself as much as an urban planner as an entertainer, and so, in conceiving his superscale Florida development, though he began with the core theme park, the Magic Kingdom (1971), which was very similar to Disneyland, he devoted considerable attention to what he called **EPCOT**, an acronym for Experimental Prototype Community of Tomorrow, a utopian, decidedly futuristic city designed on a radial plan not unlike the diagram devised by Ebenezer Howard in 1898.

Disney described his vision shortly before his death: "It will be a planned, controlled community; a showcase for American industry and research, schools, cultural and educational opportunities. In EPCOT there will be no slum areas because we won't let them develop. There will be no landowners and therefore no voting control. People will rent houses instead of buying them, and at modest rentals. There will be no retirees, because everyone will be employed according to their ability. One of our requirements is that the people who live in EPCOT must keep it alive."[42]

Walt Disney died in December 1966 and the EPCOT that was built (1982) is very different from what he had proposed: a nonresidential, permanent version of a world's fair. But Disney's bold plans were never quite forgotten, and by the late 1980s, Disney CEO Michael Eisner (b. 1942), seeking a use for some 10,000 acres of Orlando property the company did not need for themed attractions, had the idea of building a new town.

In 1987, Disney invited three architectural firms to prepare planning proposals: Gwathmey Siegel & Associates, Duany Plater-Zyberk & Company, and Robert A. M. Stern Architects, along with one landscape firm, Edward D. Stone Jr. and Associates. Three more competitions were held as ongoing negotiations with Florida government officials led to dramatic reductions in the land available for development. Included in these later competitions were the architecture firms of Skidmore, Owings & Merrill, Charles Moore, and Jaquelin T. Robertson (b. 1933) of Cooper, Robertson & Partners. In the end, a consensus for the design was reached and Robert A. M. Stern Architects was chosen to complete the master plan in partnership with Cooper, Robertson & Partners. Their plan was definitely not futuristic but was, instead, based on careful analyses of traditional American towns, including East Hampton, New York, and Southern towns such as Charleston and Beaufort, South Carolina, as well as the tradition of the garden suburb. Michael Bierut (b. 1957) of Pentagram was placed in charge of the town's graphic design program including street signage and specially fabricated manhole covers.

1. Walt Disney standing in front of
EPCOT plan. DIS (1965)

1

In large part defined by the ecological makeup of the relatively flat, 10,000-acre former pastureland interspersed by protected vegetation and wetlands, Celebration's plan provides for a 4,700-acre greenbelt surrounding the approximately 4,900 acres deemed suitable for development. The first phase, construction on which began in 1994 and was for the most part completed in 1996, included the downtown business district and a 100-acre golf course threaded through the town in park-like fashion reminiscent of the golf courses at Coral Gables (see p. 337). Overall build-out of the town was virtually complete by 2005, with 9,000 residents living on 5,000 acres that also included a regional hospital and about one million square feet of office space. Celebration is a rare case of a large planned garden suburb comparable in scope to the Country Club District of Kansas City (see p. 167).

Bound by the golf course and the designated wetlands, Celebration Village, the heart of the new town and its architectural centerpiece, accommodates families in a mix of apartments, townhouses, and single-family dwellings, all within a short walk of an 18-acre mixed-use downtown, complete with buildings for retail, office, and civic uses abutting a small lake. Celebration Village features buildings designed by prominent architects, including a town hall by Philip Johnson (1906–2005), a movie theater by Cesar Pelli (b. 1926), a post office by Michael Graves (b. 1934), a Preview Center incorporating Celebration's tallest tower by Charles Moore, and a bank by Robert Venturi and Denise Scott Brown. Cooper, Robertson & Partners and Robert A. M. Stern

Architects were responsible for the design of eleven other downtown buildings, intended to provide the background texture while also serving the important purpose of accommodating local and regionally based stores on ground floors and offices and rental apartments on upper floors. Adjacent to the center is a 36-acre educational complex combining a grade and high school with a teaching academy run by Stetson University.

Celebration comprises a number of distinct enclaves ranging from the pedestrian-oriented Celebration Village to relatively remote clusters of houses deep in the woods. Celebration Village is the most diverse and physically sophisticated, with a hierarchically organized warped grid plan of wide, landscaped boulevards, narrow streets and alleys, and a necklace-like sequence of parks. In the residential neighborhoods, rear alleys with backyard parking are provided to separate parked automobiles from the streetscape, while in or near downtown, many streets provide parallel parking, augmented by parking lots in the center of the blocks. Andrés Duany has observed that Celebration's "plan makes several improvements to new urbanist models such as Seaside . . . For example, true alleys were provided to accommodate the parking . . . In addition, the privacy of the backyards was carefully secured by the design of the units, while in Seaside outdoor privacy is neglected. Also, Celebration has a set of controls that discourages the purchase of houses by individuals who would use them as vacation houses, which can undermine the underlying reality of a community."[43]

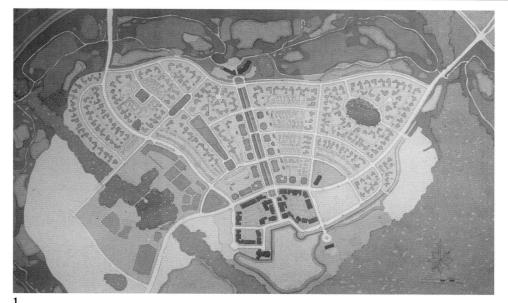

1
2

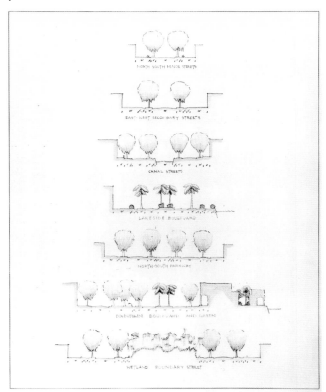

4

3
5

The massing, site placement, and style of Celebration's architecture is carefully coded. The *Celebration Pattern Book*, developed by the planners in association with Ray Gindroz (b. 1940) of Pittsburgh-based Urban Design Associates, consists of three sections: Community Patterns, Architectural Patterns, and Landscape Patterns, providing developers and individual homebuilders with clear guidelines defining the relationship of the houses to the street, the neighborhood, and each other.

Six traditional styles of architecture, each with strong associations to Southern towns, are enumerated in the *Pattern Book*, and a kit of parts for each style is illustrated to facilitate flexibility in the design of the houses. Plans for every house are submitted to the

Celebration architectural review manager to ensure compliance with the *Pattern Book*. Except in the case of high-end single-family houses, residential construction was undertaken by national and regional homebuilders who, though conforming to Disney's aesthetic standards on the outside of their buildings, would not configure their interiors accordingly, which led architecture critic Reed Kroloff to comment that "Celebration houses are the usual developer bait-and-switch that substitutes undifferentiated volume for architectural integrity. Even the more modest houses nearly burst at the eaves from the vaulting excess of space stuffed inside them."[44] Houses vary in size, allowing for the town to include families of various income levels, and also allowing for

1. Plan of Celebration Village, Robert A. M. Stern Architects with Cooper, Robertson & Partners, 1994. RAMSA

2. Aerial view. SAP (1991)

3. Typical street sections. RAMSA (1987)

4. Celebration Village. Ha'Eri. WC (2002)

5. Café with residences above. Aaron. PAO (1996)

6. Town Hall, Philip Johnson, 1996, left, and United States Post Office, Michael Graves, 1996, right. Aaron. PAO (1996)

7. Main street with market. Shlabotnik. FL (2007)

8. Light standard and signage, Michael Bierut. Aaron. PAO (1996)

9. Veranda Place. Aaron. PAO (1996)

10. Townhouses on Campus Street. Aaron. PAO (1996)

11. Canal. CEL (2006)

the streetscape to take on a natural appearance. Home-owners are provided with enough flexibility to allow for individualistic architectural expression.

Disney's strong brand made the development popular from the beginning. The rapid home sales were in large part driven by people who were curious about what a "Disney" town would be like. Disney's masterful market-ers helped this effort along, but it was also the company's financial clout that allowed Celebration to take root, with Disney taking on responsibilities normally expected of tax-supported government agencies. The costs of Cel-ebration were huge, and largely up-front. In addition to providing roads, utilities, and other infrastructure, Disney devoted tremendous resources to building a town center long before there would be enough residents to support its stores. As at Seaside, where Robert Davis inherited his tract, Celebration, with land acquired by Disney thirty years before, was a largely unique phenomenon and not one that other developers needing to carry land acquisi-tion costs could easily replicate.

Eisner, who understood that Celebration could play an important part in helping to spread the gospel of New Urbanism and Traditional Town planning, saw the proj-ect as hugely important, telling a group of executives at one point, "This is a design contribution to Ameri-can Architecture that the Disney Company is making. We've got to do it in a fashion that brings honor to the company. Don't just make it a real-estate subdivision. Anybody can do a subdivision. The Disney Company will not do real-estate subdivisions."[45]

Not everyone welcomed Celebration. Critics were particularly concerned about the relationship between Disney and its residents, with some describing the town as a "private government" and even a kind of secession-ist entity. Ada Louise Huxtable bemoaned Celebration's traditional appearance but admired the plan's execu-tion, calling the town, "an example of the wrong thing being done right. Enormously and alarmingly right."[46] Others complained about the level of design control, many of them ignorant of precedents such as Forest

Hills Gardens, suggesting that this was something new and faintly fascistic.

It is true that Celebration is not the radically futuristic development that Walt Disney had proposed. But Celebration did impress many as a bold new direction, including Vincent Scully, who stated that "Celebration is the most important thing happening in architecture. It marks a return of community."[47]

By the early 1990s, with Seaside, Poundbury, and Celebration in various stages of development and a growing number of similar-minded communities underway, a movement had firmly taken root. In 1993, a group of sympathetic architects and planners inaugurated the Congress for the New Urbanism (CNU) with a conference planned by Duany and Plater-Zyberk. Follow-up congresses organized by Elizabeth Moule (b. 1960), Stefanos Polyzoides (b. 1946), Peter Calthorpe, and Daniel Solomon (b. 1939)—the six official founders of the New Urbanism—culminated in the ratification of a manifesto, the Charter of the New Urbanism, at the fourth congress held in Charleston, South Carolina, in 1996. Originally conceived as a sort of "'ten commandments' for better planning,"[48] the Charter was developed into a set of twenty-seven guiding principles, nine in each of three categories addressing different scales: "The Region: Metropolis, City, and Town"; "The Neighborhood, the District, and the Corridor"; and "The Block, the Street, and the Building." The Charter's introduction recognizes that "physical solutions by themselves will not solve social and economic problems, but neither can economic vitality, community stability, and environmental health be sustained without a coherent and supportive physical framework." The introduction goes on to state in broad strokes the goals of the movement: "We advocate the restructuring of public policy and development practices to support the following principles: neighborhoods should be diverse in use and population; communities should be designed for the pedestrian and transit as well as the car; cities and towns should be shaped by physically defined and universally accessible public spaces and community institutions; urban places should be framed by architecture and landscape design that celebrate local history, climate, ecology, and building practice."[49]

Ironically, the idea for the establishment of a formal organization with a written set of principles was based, according to Duany, on a suggestion from Krier that "We must refound the Congrés Internationaux d'Architecture Moderne," known as CIAM, which between 1928 and 1959 codified and disseminated the ideals of Modernist architecture and urbanism—the very principles that the New Urbanists were seeking to supersede. "What he meant," Duany stated, "was that CIAM was the last organization that effectively and comprehensively changed the way we design the world . . . The fact that the Congress for the New Urbanism goes by the initials CNU has something to do with the prior success of CIAM—as does the fact that our meetings are called 'congresses' and have been numbered with Roman numerals as CNU I, II, III, IV, and so on. The conscious choices reflect the effectiveness of that earlier effort . . . The Charter of the New Urbanism itself—the very fact that we developed a statement, both symbolic and functional, to inform everyone where we stand—also builds on our recognition of the effectiveness of CIAM's charter."[50]

———

We stand at a crossroads with regard to the future of cities. Modernists, especially those in the academy who have reinvented themselves as landscape urbanists, see the future form of the city as, in essence, sprawling developments of varying densities situated in ecological parks connected by a network of high-speed roadways—in effect updated versions of Le Corbusier's Ville Radieuse and Frank Lloyd Wright's Broadacre City.[51] They dismiss advocates of the Traditional Town and its garden suburb tradition as nostalgia-driven fantasists unwilling to embrace modern technologies of construction and communication. This is ridiculous. Unless architects and planners address the human need for walkable neighborhoods, easy public transportation, and diminished use of the automobile, we will abandon the very essence of what is meant by "community." The experience of the last two hundred years, the lessons of Nash, Olmsted, Parker and Unwin, Nolen, and so very many others, need to be embraced. Our thinking needs to be freed from the biases and orthodoxies of anti-contextual, anti-historical Modernism that have encouraged us to see old cities and old buildings—not to mention established construction traditions and recognizable forms—as virtually worthless and certainly wrong to emulate. Designers and intellectuals need also to shake themselves free of their indiscriminate dismissal of the suburb. They need to separate the good from the bad, the planned garden suburb from the sprawling subdivision. Suburbs will not go away, nor should they. Planned as part of the metropolitan city, the garden suburb is the best template yet devised to achieve a habitable earthly paradise.

At the core of modern town planning lies a tragically interrupted 150-year-old tradition, that of the garden suburb. The idea of the garden suburb, and its worldwide realization as seen by the examples in this book, deserves a fresh look by planners and architects. Our cities need to be orchestrated to address the contradictory social and economic conditions that define modern democratic life. The garden suburb does not try to escape urban problems but to help address them. If one looks beyond the shaded streets and appealing house types, one sees that these developments embodied complex social relationships. Planned suburban towns were the products of developers and architects acting to enable modern people to enjoy a fulfilled life that would meet both their material and their spiritual needs, that would foster a new kind of metropolitan community with plans broad enough to permit both the intensity of the inner city and the passivity of nature. Without both, cities as we know them will cease to exist. The garden suburb may well hold the key to the future of our cities.

NOTES

Foreword

1 Frederick Law Olmsted, "Preliminary Report upon the Proposed Suburban Village at Riverside, near Chicago," (1868), in S. B. Sutton, ed., *Civil American Cities: A Selection of Frederick Law Olmsted's Writings on City Landscapes* (Cambridge, Mass.: MIT Press, 1971), 294–95, also quoted in Dana F. White, ed., *Olmsted South: Old South Critic/New South Planner* (Westport, Conn.: Greenwood Press, 1979), 196 (n.4). This introduction incorporates ideas first advanced by the author in "The Suburban Alternative for the 'Middle City,'" *Architectural Record* 164 (August 1978): 93–100, and in collaboration with John M. Massengale, *The Anglo-American Suburb* (London: Architectural Design, 1981), and in the author's *Pride of Place: Building the American Dream* (Boston: Houghton Mifflin; New York: American Heritage, 1986) and "Garden City Suburbs," *Wharton Real Estate Review* 11 (Fall 2007): 84–93.

2 For example, see Robert Fishman, *Bourgeois Utopias: The Rise and Fall of Suburbia* (New York: Basic Books, 1987); Robert M. Fogelson, *Bourgeois Nightmares: Suburbia, 1870–1930* (New Haven, Conn.: Yale University Press, 2005).

3 Lewis Mumford, *The City in History* (New York: Harcourt, 1961), 497. Also see Lewis Mumford, "The Garden City Idea and Modern Planning," introductory essay in Ebenezer Howard, *Garden Cities of To-morrow* (1898), ed. F. J. Osborn (London: Faber and Faber, 1945; Cambridge, Mass.: MIT Press, 1965), 29–40.

4 See Walter L. Creese, *The Search for Environment*, expanded edition (New Haven, Conn.: Yale University Press, 1966; Baltimore and London: Johns Hopkins University Press, 1992); Gillian Darley, *Villages of Vision* (London: Architectural Press, 1975); John R. Stilgoe, *Borderland: Origins of the American Suburb, 1820–1939* (New Haven, Conn.: Yale University Press, 1988); Stanley Buder, *Visionaries and Planners: The Garden City Movement and the Modern Community* (New York: Oxford University Press, 1990); Mervyn Miller, *Raymond Unwin: Garden Cities and Town Planning* (Leicester: Leicester University Press, 1992); Stephen V. Ward, ed., *The Garden City: Past, Present and Future* (London: E & FN Spon, 1992); Gabriele Tagliaventi, ed., *Garden City: A Century of Theories, Models, Experiences* (Rome: Gangemi Editore, 1994); Jean-François Lejeune, "The Grid, the Park, and the Model-T—Searching for Paradise: Garden Cities in Florida," in Tagliaventi, ed., *Garden City*, 220–65; Margaret Crawford, *Building the Workingman's Paradise: The Design of American Company Towns* (London: Verso, 1995); Andres Duany, Elizabeth Plater-Zyberk, and Jeff Speck, *Suburban Nation: The Rise of Sprawl and the Decline of the American Dream* (New York: North Point Press, 2000); Andrés Duany, Elizabeth Plater-Zyberk, and Robert Alminana, *The New Civic Art: Elements of Town Planning* (New York: Rizzoli International Publications, 2003); John Archer, *Architecture and Suburbia: From English Villa to American Dream House, 1690–2000* (Minneapolis: University of Minnesota Press, 2005); Mervyn Miller, *Hampstead Garden Suburb: Arts and Crafts Utopia?* (Chichester, Sussex: Phillimore, 2006).

5 T. J. Jackson Lears, *No Place of Grace: Antimodernism and the Transformation of American Culture, 1880–1920* (New York: Pantheon, 1981; reissued by University of Chicago Press, 1994), ch. 2.

6 The "suburban" potential of such sites was first identified in Stern, "The Suburban Alternative for the 'Middle City'": 93–100.

Chapter 1

1 *Oxford English Dictionary* (New York: Oxford University Press, 1971), 71.

2 Gillian Darley, *Villages of Vision* (London: Architectural Press, 1975), 10. Also see Thomas Sharp, *The Anatomy of the Village* (Harmondsworth, Middlesex, Eng.: Penguin Books, 1946).

3 John Jewell, *The Tourist's Companion or the History and Antiquities of Harewood* (Leeds: B. Dewhirst, 1819), n.p. Also see Sydney D. Kitson, "Carr of York," *Journal of the Royal Institute of British Architects* 17 (January 22, 1910): 241–66; W. A. Eden, "Harewood Village: an Eighteenth Century 'Housing Scheme,'" *Town Planning Review* 13 (May 1929): 181–84, plates 46–47; Thomas Sharp, *The Anatomy of the Village* (Harmondsworth, Middlesex, Eng.: Penguin Books, 1946), 25; Peter Leach and Nikolaus Pevsner, *Yorkshire West Riding: Leeds, Bradford and the North* (1959; New Haven, Conn., and London: Yale University Press, 2009), 44, 305; Gillian Darley, *Villages of Vision* (London: Architectural Press, 1975), 10–11; Richard Muir, *The English Village* (New York and London: Thames and Hudson, 1980), 121, 123.

4 Sharp, *The Anatomy of the Village*, 25.

5 Gillian Darley, *Villages of Vision* (London: Architectural Press, 1975), 11, 12. Also see Thomas Sharp, *The Anatomy of the Village* (Harmondsworth, Middlesex, Eng.: Penguin Books, 1946), 28, 29–30; Nikolaus Pevsner, *Cumberland and Westmorland* (1967; New Haven, Conn., and London: Yale University Press, 2002), 274; David King, *The Complete Works of Robert and James Adam* (1991; Oxford, England: Architectural Press in association with the University of Stirling, 2001), 380, 383–85.

6 Richard Warner, *Tour through the Northern Counties* (1802), quoted in Darley, *Villages of Vision*, 11.

7 S. D. Adshead, "Milton Abbas: an Eighteenth Century Village of Standard Cottages," *Town Planning Review* 7 (October 1916): 41–42, plates 14–16; Thomas Sharp, *The Anatomy of the Village* (Harmondsworth, Middlesex, Eng.: Penguin Books, 1946), 22, 23; Arthur Oswald, "Market Town into Model Village," *Country Life* 29 (September 1966): 762–66; John Newman and Nikolaus Pevsner, *Dorset* (Middlesex, England: Penguin Books, 1972), 31, 61, 293–94; Gillian Darley, *Villages of Vision* (London: Architectural Press, 1975), 3, 11–13; *Home Sweet Home: Housing Designed by the London County Council and Greater London Council Architects, 1888–1975* (London: Academy Editions, 1976), 14–15; Richard Muir, *The English Village* (New York and London: Thames and Hudson, 1980), 116; Thomas Hinde, *Capability Brown: The Story of a Master Gardener* (New York: W. W. Norton & Company, 1987), 155–57, 168–69; Clive Aslet, *Villages of Britain: The Five Hundred Villages That Made the Countryside* (London: Bloomsbury, 2010), 191–92.

8 Gillian Darley and Arthur Oswald believe that the village resembles Chambers' plan as he described it in a 1773 letter while Thomas Hinde finds it "probable" that Brown's plan was used. See Darley, *Villages of Vision*, 11–12; Oswald, "Market Town into Model Village": 764–65; Hinde, *Capability Brown*, 156.

9 Sharp, *The Anatomy of the Village*, 22.

10 Charlotte Frances Barrett, ed., *Diary and letters of Madam d'Arbley* (1842–46; 1891 edition, III), 358, quoted in Hinde, *Capability Brown*, 157 and Darley, *Villages of Vision*, 12–13.

11 Darley, *Villages of Vision*, 14. Also see Nikolaus Pevsner and David Lloyd, *Hampshire and the Isle of Wight* (New Haven, Conn., and London: Yale University Press, 2002), 202; Michael Bullen, John Crook, Rodney Hubbuck, and Nikolaus Pevsner, *Hampshire: Winchester and the North* (New Haven, Conn., and London: Yale University Press, 2010), 248, fig. 92.

12 John Summerson, *Georgian London*, rev. ed. (London: Barrie & Jenkins, 1945, 1988), 276; *Nairn's London* (Harmondsworth: Penguin Books, 1966), 184; Bridget Cherry and Nikolaus Pevsner, *The Buildings of England: London 2, South* (1983; London: Penguin Books, 1999), 53, 92, 423–24; W. Bonit, *Michael Searles: A Georgian Architect and Surveyor* (London: Society of Architectural Historians of Great Britain, 1987), 14–15, 36–46, 53; James Stevens Curl, *Georgian Architecture* (Newtown Abbot: David & Charles, 1993), 184; *London Suburbs* (London: Merrell Holberton, 1999), 49; Oliver Bradbury, "Paragon Buildings, Cheltenham," *Georgian Group Journal* 10 (2000): 141–49.

13 John Archer, *Architecture and Suburbia: From English Villa to American Dream House, 1690–2000* (Minneapolis: University of Minnesota Press, 2005), 209–10, 212. Also see Agnese Ghini, "The Piazza as a Garden: Bath," in Gabriele Tagliaventi, ed., *Garden City* (Rome: Gangemi Editore, 1994), 140–47; Gabriele Tagliaventi, "The Garden City's Archetype," in Taglieventi, ed., *Garden City*, 132; Michael Forsyth, *Bath* (New Haven, Conn., and London: Yale University Press, 2003), 20–21, 146–51; Kirsten Elliott and Neill Menneer, *Bath* (London: Frances Lincoln, 2004), 110–35.

14 Andrew Saint, "Introduction: The Quality of the London Suburb," in *London Suburbs*, 15.

15 Summerson, *Georgian London*, 159–61. Also see Florence M. Gladstone, *Notting Hill in Bygone Days*, new edition (1924; London: Anne Bingley, 1969), 239–40; Peter Dickinson and Stephen Gardiner, "St. John's Wood," *Architectural Review* 105 (June 1949): 273–86; Stella Margetson, "A Wood with a Regency Look; 600 Years of St. John's Wood," *Country Life* 152 (November 16, 1972): 1266–68; F. M. L. Thompson, *Hampstead: Building a Borough, 1650–1964* (London and Boston: Routledge & Kegan Paul, 1972), 64–67, 82; F. M. L. Thompson, "Introduction: The Rise of Suburbia," in F. M. L. Thompson, ed., *The Rise of Suburbia* (Leicester: Leicester University Press; New York: St. Martin's Press, 1982), 8, 9, 15; Robert Fishman, *Bourgeois Utopias: The Rise and Fall of Suburbia* (New York: Basic Books, 1987), 64; "Hampstead: St. John's Wood," *A History of the County of Middlesex: Volume 9: Hampstead, Paddington* (1989), 60–63, in http://www.british-history.ac.uk/report/aspx?compid=22639; Bridget Cherry and Nikolaus Pevsner, *London 3: North West* (London: Penguin Books, 1999), 40, 593; *London Suburbs*, 234; J. W. R. Whitehand and C. M. H. Carr, *Twentieth-Century Suburbs: a Morphological Approach* (London: Routledge, 2001), 3; Richard Russell Lawrence, *The Book of the Edwardian & Interwar House* (London: Aurum Press, 2009), 27; Mireille Galinou, *Cottages and Villas: The Birth of the Garden Suburb* (New Haven, Conn., and London: Yale University Press, 2010), esp. ch. 2.

16 Hermann Pückler-Muskau, *Tour in England, Ireland, and France* (Philadelphia: Carey, Lea & Blanchard, 1833), 463–64; George Godwin, "Letter," *The Civil Engineer and Architect's Journal* 2 (November 1839): 428; John Summerson, "Blaise Hamlet: An Early Nineteenth Century Essay in the Revival of the Picturesque Cottage," *Country Life* 86 (October 1939): 396–97; Terence Davis, *The Architecture of John Nash* (London: Studio, 1960), 70, 72, figs. 106–19; Gillian Darley, *Villages of Vision* (London: Architectural Press, 1975), 26–36; Gillian Darley, "Blaise Hamlet and the Picturesque: The Making of a Model Village," *Country Life* 158 (November 6, 1975): 1080–82; Nigel Temple, "In Search of the Picturesque," *Architectural Review* 60 (August 1978): 96–100; Nigel Temple, *John Nash and the Village Picturesque* (Gloucester: Alan Sutton, 1979), 1–9, 72–79, plates 32–51; William Tickell, "Cottage Charisma," *Period Homes* (July 1988): 6; Michael Mansbridge, *John Nash: A Complete Catalogue* (New York: Rizzoli International Publications, 1991), 170–72; Michael Southworth and Eran Ben-Joseph, *Streets and the Shaping of Towns and Cities* (Washington: Island Press, 2003), 30; Andrew Foyle, *Bristol* (New Haven, Conn., and London: Yale University Press, 2004), 288–90; Clive Aslet, *Villages of Britain: The Five Hundred Villages That Made the Countryside* (London: Bloomsbury, 2010), 302.

17 Godwin, "Letter," *The Civil Engineer and Architect's Journal*: 428. For a discussion of associationism, see George L. Hersey, "Associationism and Sensibility in Eighteenth Century Architecture," *Eighteenth Century Studies* 4 (1970): 71–89.

18 "A Panoramic View of Regent's Park," *Architectural Review* 62 (December 1927): 213–15; Steen Eiler Rasmussen, *London: The Unique City* (Cambridge, Mass.: MIT Press, 1934; first English edition, 1937), 271–91; John Summerson, *Georgian London* (London: Barrie & Jenkins, 1945, 1988), 162–80; Davis, *The Architecture of John Nash*, 70–71, plans 1–2, figs. 92–97; John Summerson, "Introduction," in Davis, *The Architecture of John Nash*, 9–18; Edmund Bacon, *Design of Cities* (New York: Viking, 1967); F. M. L. Thompson, *Hampstead: Building a Borough, 1650–1964* (London and Boston: Routledge & Kegan Paul, 1972), 64–68; Terence Davis, *John Nash: The Prince Regent's Architect* (Newton Abbot: David & Charles, 1973), 63–82; *John Summerson, The Life and Work of John Nash* (Cambridge, Mass.: MIT Press, 1980), 28–29; F. M. L. Thompson, "Introduction: The Rise of Suburbia," in F. M. L. Thompson, ed., *The Rise of Suburbia* (Leicester: Leicester University Press; New York: St. Martin's Press, 1982), 15; Fishman, *Bourgeois Utopias*, 65–72; Mansbridge, *John Nash*, 158–61, 174–76, 183–84, 217, 220–29, 234–43, 248–84, 288–89, 292, 300, 303; Geoffrey Tyack, *Sir James Pennethorne and Making of Victorian London* (Cambridge: Cambridge University Press, 1992), 24–29; Geoffrey Tyack, "John Nash and the Park Village," *Georgian Group Journal* 3 (1993): 68–74; Bridget Cherry and Nikolaus Pevsner, *London 3: North West* (London: Penguin Books, 1999), 41–42, 616–29; Southworth and Ben-Joseph, *Streets and the Shaping of Towns and Cities*, 29–34; Archer, *Architecture and Suburbia*, 212–13; J. Mordaunt Crook, "John Nash and the Genesis of Regent's Park," in Geoffrey Tyack, ed., *John Nash: Architect of the Picturesque* (Swindon: English Heritage, 2013), 75–100.

19 Rasmussen, *London: The Unique City*, 277–78.
20 Tyack, "John Nash and the Park Village": 68.
21 J. M. Richards, *The Castles on the Ground* (London: Architectural Press, 1946; London: J. Murray, 1973), 19, 21.
22 Florence M. Gladstone, *Notting Hill in Bygone Days* (London: T. Fisher Unwin, 1924; London: Anne Bingley, 1969), 236–40; E. Maxwell Fry, "Slum and the Land," *Architects' Journal* 78 (October 26, 1933): 550–51; Henry-Russell Hitchcock, *Early Victorian Architecture in Britain* (New Haven, Conn.: Yale University Press, 1954; New York: Da Capo Press, 1972), 442–45; James Stevens Curl, "A Story of Mixed Fortunes: The Ladbroke Estate Development," *Country Life* 158 (November 13, 1975): 1278–80; Bridget Cherry and Nikolaus Pevsner, *London 3: North West* (London: Penguin Books, 1999), 42, 449, 524–26; Andrew Saint, "Introduction: The Quality of the London Suburb," in *London Suburbs*, 16; James Steven Curl, *Victorian Architecture: Diversity & Invention* (Reading, England: Spire Books, 2007), 515–21. Also see "The Ladbroke Estate," www.british-history.ac.uk.
23 Nicholas Antram and Richard Morrice, *Brighton and Hove* (New Haven, Conn., and London: Yale University Press, 2008), 10. Also see Antony Dale, *Fashionable Brighton, 1820–1860* (London: Country Life Limited, 1947), 38–40; Ian Nairn and Nikolaus Pevsner, *Sussex* (London: Penguin Books, 1965; New Haven, Conn., and London: Yale University Press, 2003), 62–65, 426, 445–55; Antram and Morrice, *Brighton and Hove*, esp. pp. 10–14, 91, 113–41, 143–54, 168–78, 184–85.
24 David Verey and Alan Brooks, *Gloucestershire. 2, The Vale and the Forest of Dean* (New Haven, Conn., and London: Yale University Press, 1976), 94, 279–80; Dr. Steven Blake, *Pittville 1824–1860—A Scene of Gorgeous Magnificence* (Cheltenham: Cheltenham Art Gallery and Museums, 1988); Archer, *Architecture and Suburbia*, 212–15; Stephen Morris, *Cheltenham* (London: Frances Lincoln Limited, 2009), 29, 33, 102–9.
25 John Archer, "Country and City in the American Romantic Suburb," *Journal of the Society of Architectural Historians* 42 (May 1983): 139–56. Also see Mansbridge, *John Nash: A Complete Catalogue*, 290–91; Phyllis Hembry, *British Spas from 1815 to the Present* (London: Athlone Press, 1997), 21–22.
26 Archer, *Architecture and Suburbia*, 215–16. Also see Christopher Hussey, "Calverley Park, Tunbridge Wells—II," *Country Life* 145 (May 8, 1969): 1166–69; Terence Davis, *Tunbridge Wells: The Gentle Aspect* (London: Phillimore, 1976), 46–63; Philip Miller, "Calverley Estate di Decimus Burton," *Casabella* (December 1985): 44–53; Charles C. Savage, *Architecture of the Private Streets of St. Louis* (Columbia: University of Missouri Press, 1987), 7, 33, 35; Phyllis Hembry, *British Spas from 1815 to the Present: a Social History* (London: Athlone Press, 1997), 107–9; "Calverley Park Area," in Tony Fullwood, *Royal Tunbridge Wells and Rusthall Conservation Areas Appraisal* (Royal Tunbridge Wells: Tunbridge Wells Borough Council, November 2000), 47–52; John Newman, *West Kent and the Weald* (New Haven, Conn., and London: Yale University Press, 2002), 104–5, 110.
27 Clare Hartwell, Matthew Hyde and Nikolaus Pevsner, *Lancashire: Manchester and the South-East* (1969; New Haven, Conn., and London: Yale University Press, 2004), 51, 477–78. Also see Maurice Spiers, *Victoria Park Manchester: A Nineteenth-Century Suburb in Its Social and Administrative Context* (Manchester: Chetham Society, 1976), esp. pp. 1–20; Fishman, *Bourgeois Utopias*, 91–96.
28 Fishman, *Bourgeois Utopias*, 94–95. Also see Richard Cobden, "Incorporate Your Borough," in *Cobden as a Citizen*, ed. William E. A. Axon (London: Unwin, 1907), 31.
29 Eric Hardwicke Rideout, *The Growth of Wirral* (Liverpool: E. A. Bryant, 1927), 86–90; Archer, "Country and City in the American Romantic Suburb": 143, 146. Also see *Manchester As it Is* (1839), 182; Nikolaus Pevsner and Edward Hubbard, *Cheshire* (1971; New Haven, Conn., and London: Yale University Press, 2003), 103; John R. Stilgoe, *Borderland: Origins of the American Suburb, 1820–1939* (New Haven, Conn.: Yale University Press, 1988), 49–52.
30 Archer, "Country and City in the American Romantic Suburb": 143.
31 Nathaniel Hawthorne, *English Note-Books* (1853–1858), quoted in Stilgoe, *Borderland*, 49.
32 "European Parks," *The Horticulturist and Journal of Rural Art and Rural Taste* 15 (1860): 531; Archer, "Country and City in the American Romantic Suburb": 146–47; Tyack, *Sir James Pennethorne and Making of Victorian London*, 95; Joseph Sharples, *Liverpool* (New Haven, Conn., and London: Yale University Press, 2004), 24, 276–81; Archer, *Architecture and Suburbia*, 218; Kate Colquhoun, *The Busiest Man In England: A Life of Joseph Paxton, Gardener, Architect & Victorian Visionary* (Boston: David R. Godine, 2006), 108–12.
33 Colquhoun, *The Busiest Man In England*, 109, 112.
34 Frederick Law Olmsted, "The People's Park at Birkenhead, near Liverpool, by W., Staten Island, New York," *The Horticulturalist* 6 (May 1851), reprinted in Robert Twombly, ed., *Frederick Law Olmsted: Essential Texts* (New York: W. W. Norton, 2010), 39–48; "European Parks," *The Horticulturist and Journal of Rural Art and Rural Taste* 15 (1860): 531; Henry Kelsall Aspinall, *Birkenhead and Its Surroundings* (Liverpool: Liverpool Booksellers' Co., 1903), 169–73; Christopher Tunnard, "The Romantic Suburb in America," *Magazine of Art* 40 (May 1947): 184–87; Walter L. Creese, *The Search for Environment*, expanded edition (New Haven, Conn.: Yale University Press, 1966; Baltimore and London: Johns Hopkins University Press, 1992), 46; Nikolaus Pevsner and Edward Hubbard, *The Buildings of England: Cheshire* (Middlesex, England and Baltimore: Penguin Books, 1971), 91–93; Penny Beckett and Paul Dempster, "Birkenhead Park," *Landscape Design* 185 (November 1989): 24–27; George Chadwick, "Paxton's Design Principles for Birkenhead Park," *Landscape Design* 188 (March 1990): 16–17; Roy Rosenzweig and Elizabeth Blackmar, *The Park and the People: A History of Central Park* (Ithaca and London: Cornell University Press, 1992), 107; Carol Grove, "Aesthetics, Horticulture and the Gardenesque: Victorian Sensibilities at Tower Grove Park" (Ph.D. diss., University of Missouri-Columbia, 1998): 114–19, fig. 73; Kate Colquhoun, *A Thing in Disguise: The Visionary Life of Joseph Paxton* (London: Harper Perennial, 2003), 119–21, 135–36; Kate Colquhoun, "The Man Who Gave Parks to the People," *Country Life* 197 (June 12, 2003): 112–13; Archer, *Architecture and Suburbia*, 218; Colquhoun, *The Busiest Man in England*, 113–15, 129–31.
35 Pevsner and Hubbard, *The Buildings of England: Cheshire*, 92.
36 Quoted in Colquhoun, *The Busiest Man in England*, 130.
37 Frederick Law Olmsted, *Walks and Talks of an American Farmer in England* (New York: G. P. Putnam, 1852), quoted in Colquhoun, *The Busiest Man in England*, 130.
38 Nikolaus Pevsner, *The Buildings of England: Derbyshire*, revised by Elizabeth Williamson (London: Penguin Books, 1953, 2000), 115–16; Colquhoun, *The Busiest Man in England*, 197; *Buxton Conservation Area Character Appraisal* (High Peak, England: High Peak Borough Council, 2007), 88–95.
39 *Buxton Conservation Area Character Appraisal*, 91.
40 Nikolaus Pevsner, *The Buildings of England: Suffolk* (1961; revised by Enid Radcliffe, New Haven, Conn., and London: Yale University Press, 2002), 59, 423. Also see Richard Muir, *The English Village* (New York and London: Thames and Hudson, 1980), 121–23; Gillian Darley, *Villages of Vision* (London: Architectural Press, 1975), 29–30.
41 Samuel Palmer, *St. Pancras* (London: Samuel Palmer and Field & Tuer, 1870), 137–39; Charles G. Harper, *Rural Nooks Round London (Middlesex and Surrey)* (London: Chapman & Hall, 1907), 28–29; Christopher McIntosh, "Victorian Fantasy in Highgate," *Country Life* 144 (December 5, 1968): 1491–93; Darley, *Villages of Vision*, 30, plates 9, 10; *London Suburbs*, 186; Bridget Cherry and Nikolaus Pevsner, *The Buildings of England: London 4, North* (New York: Penguin Books, 1999), 36, 415, plate 56.
42 Harper, *Rural Nooks Round London (Middlesex and Surrey)*, 28–29.
43 Miles Rathmell, "Park Town, Oxford: An Example of Urban Planning," *Town Planning Review* 18 (July 1938): 48–50, figs. 1–4; David A. Hinton, "An Early Garden Suburb," *Country Life* 156 (September 26, 1974): 844–46; S. Morley, "A Neo-Georgian Oasis," letter to the editor, *Country Life* 156 (November 7, 1974): 1371; Tanis Hinchcliffe, *North Oxford* (New Haven, Conn., and London: Yale University Press, 1992), esp. ch. 4; Jennifer Sherwood and Nikolaus Pevsner, *The Buildings of England: Oxfordshire* (1974; New Haven, Conn., and London: Yale University Press, 2002), 57, 317–22.
44 Archer, *Architecture and Suburbia*, 217–22. Also see Alan Charles Bell Urwin, *Twickenham Parke* (Twickenham: Alan C.B. Urwin, 1965), esp. pp. 116–22.
45 Archer, *Architecture and Suburbia*, 217–22.
46 Archer, *Architecture and Suburbia*, 220.
47 T. Affleck Greeves, "The Making of a Community: Bedford Park, Chiswick—II," *Country Life* 142 (December 14, 1967): 1600–2. Also see "Bedford Park," *Building News* 32 (1877): 26, 77, 134, plate; "The Famous Bedford Park," *American Architect and Building News* 10 (August 13, 1881): 70; Hermann Muthesius, *The English House* (1904–5; New York: Rizzoli International Publications, 1987), 30–32, 124, 148; Steen Eiler Rasmussen, *London: The Unique City* (Cambridge, Mass.: MIT Press, 1934; first English edition, 1937), 266–70; Nikolaus Pevsner, *Pioneers of Modern Design* (London: Penguin Books, 1960), 106; "The Enchanted Circle: Phyllis Austin," *Architectural Review* 133 (March 1963): 205–7; Walter L. Creese, *The Search for Environment*, expanded edition (New Haven, Conn.: Yale University Press, 1966; Baltimore and London: Johns Hopkins University Press, 1992), 87–107; Ian Fletcher, "Bedford Park: Aesthete's Elysium?" in Ian Fletcher, ed., *Romantic Mythologies* (London: Routledge & K. Paul, 1967), 169–207; T. Affleck Greeves, "London's First Garden Suburb: Bedford Park, Chiswick—I," *Country Life* 142 (December 7, 1967): 1524, 1526, 1529; "Bedford Park: The First Garden Suburb," *European Heritage* 1 (1975): 42–44; T. Affleck Greeves, *Bedford Park: The First Garden Suburb* (London: Anne Bingley, 1975); T. Affleck Greeves, "London's First Garden Suburb: 100 Years of Bedford Park," *Country Life* 158 (November 27, 1975): 1446–48; Andrew Saint, *Richard Norman Shaw* (New Haven, Conn.: Yale University Press, 1976), 201–10; Margaret Jones Bolsterli, *The Early Community of Bedford Park* (Athens: Ohio University Press, 1977); Mark Girouard, *Sweetness and Light* (Oxford: Clarendon Press, 1977), 160–76; Susan Beattie, *A Revolution in London Housing: LCC Housing Architects & Their Work, 1893–1914* (London: Greater London Council; Architectural Press, 1980), 85, 89; Mary Belle Lawson Pendleton, "Bedford Park: An Introduction to Further Study" (Ph.D. diss., Northwestern University, 1981); Robert A. M. Stern with John Massengale, *The Anglo-American Suburb* (London: Architectural Design, 1981), 27–29; Mervyn Miller and A. Stuart Gray, *Hampstead Garden Suburb* (Chichester: Phillimore, 1992), 9–11; Bridget Cherry and Nikolaus Pevsner, *London 3: North West* (London: Penguin Books, 1999), 406–12; Standish Meacham, *Regaining Paradise: Englishness and the Early Garden City Movement* (New Haven, Conn., and London: Yale University Press, 1999), 156; Susie Basson, "Infinite Variety in Brick and Stucco: 1840–1914," in *London Suburbs* (London: Merrell Holberton, 1999), 85–92, 190; Saint, "Introduction," in *London Suburbs*, 17–19; Norbert Schoenauer, *6,000 Years of Housing*, rev. and expanded edition (New York: W. W. Norton, 2000), 309–11; Southworth and Ben-Joseph, *Streets and the Shaping of Towns and Cities*, 47–50; Richard Russell Lawrence, *The Book of the Edwardian & Interwar House* (London: Aurum Press, 2009), 21–22. Also see "A Short History of Bedford Park," www.bedfordpark.org.
48 Saint, "Introduction," in *London Suburbs*, 17.
49 Girouard, *Sweetness and Light*, 160.
50 Cherry and Pevsner, *London 3: North West*, 407.
51 Creese, *The Search for Environment*, 89–90, 105.
52 *The Pioneer* (March 22, 1881), quoted in Creese, *The Search for Environment* (1992), 89.
53 Creese, *The Search for Environment*, 89.
54 Girouard, *Sweetness and Light*, 166.
55 Girouard, *Sweetness and Light*, 166.
56 Saint, *Richard Norman Shaw*, 202.
57 Muthesius, *The English House*, 30–31.
58 Fletcher, "Bedford Park: Aesthete's Elysium?" in Fletcher, ed., *Romantic Mythologies*, 173.
59 "The Shaftesbury Park Estate," *The Sunday Magazine* (1874): 211; Henry Fawcett, *Manual of Political Economy* (London: Macmillan and Co., 1874), 278–79; Frederick Clifford, *The Agricultural Lock-Out of 1874* (Edinburgh and London: William Blackwood and Sons, 1875), 213–20; William Spencer Clarke, *The Suburban Homes of London: A Residential Guide* (London: Chatto and Windus, 1881), 320–21; Henry S. Simmonds, *All About Battersea* (London: Ashfield, Printer, 1882), 141–43; John Nelson Tarn, "Some Pioneer Suburban Housing Estates," *Architectural Review* 143 (May 1968): 367–70; John Nelson Tarn, *Working-Class Housing in 19th-Century Britain* (London: Lund Humphries for the Architectural Association, 1971), 12, 21; Susan Beattie, *A Revolution in London Housing: LCC Architects and Their Work* (London: Architectural Press, 1980), 85–86; Bridget Cherry and Nikolaus Pevsner, *The Buildings of England: London 2, South* (1983; London: Penguin Books, 1999), 75, 678; *London Suburbs*, 76–77,

232; Richard Russell Lawrence, *The Book of the Edwardian & Interwar House* (London: Aurum Press, 2009), 37.

60 Quoted in John Burnett, *A Social History of Housing, 1815–1985* (London and New York: Methuen, 1986), 85. Also see Tarn, "Some Pioneer Suburban Housing Estates": 367–70; Tarn, *Working-Class Housing in 19th-Century Britain*, 12, 49, 82; Donald J. Olsen, "Victorian London: Specialization, Segregation, and Privacy," *Victorian Studies* 17 (March 1974): 265–78; Bridget Cherry and Nikolaus Pevsner, *London 3: North West* (London: Penguin Books, 1999), 698–99; *London Suburbs*, 78–79; *Queens Park Estate Area Conservation Area* (May 2004); Gill Davies, *One Thousand Buildings of London* (New York: Black Dog & Leventhal Publishers, 2006), 397; Lawrence, *The Book of the Edwardian & Interwar House*, 78–79. Also see "Queen's Park," www.british-history.ac.uk.

61 Cherry and Pevsner, *London 3: North West*, 698.

62 Tarn, "Some Pioneer Suburban Housing Estates": 369.

63 Tarn, "Some Pioneer Suburban Housing Estates": 367–70; Nikolaus Pevsner and Bridget Cherry, *The Buildings of England: London 4: North* (1951; New Haven, Conn. and London: Yale University Press, 1998), 41, 594; John Nelson Tarn, *Working-Class Housing in 19th-Century Britain* (London: Lund Humphries for the Architectural Association, 1971), 12, 19, 49, 92; *London Suburbs*, 200.

64 Tarn, "Some Pioneer Suburban Housing Estates": 369.

65 Theodore Turak, "Riverside: Roots in France," *Inland Architect* 25 (November 1981): 12–19. Also see Sophie Cueille, *Maisons-Laffitte: Parc, Paysage et Villégiature, 1630–1930* (Paris: APPIF, 1999).

66 Georges Poisson, *La Curieuse Histoire du Vésinet* (Le Vésinet: Ville du Vésinet, 1975); Gérard Bauer, Gildas Baudez, Jean-Michel Roux, *Banlieues de charme ou l'art des quartiers-jardins* (Aix-en-Provence: Pandora editions, 1980), 38–57; Turak, "Riverside: Roots in France": 12–19; *Le Vésinet, Modéle Francais d'Urbanisme Paysager, 1858–1930* (Le Vésinet: Ministére de la culture et de la communication inventaire générale des monuments et des richesses artistiques de la france, 1989); Barry Bergdoll, *European Architecture, 1750–1890* (Oxford and New York: Oxford University Press, 2000), 264–65.

67 Quoted in Turak, "Riverside: Roots in France": 13.

68 Quoted in Turak, "Riverside: Roots in France": 14.

Chapter 2

1 James Richardson, "The New Homes of New York: A Study of Flats," *Scribner's Monthly* 8 (May 1874): 63–76.

2 "A Revolution in Living," editorial, *New York Times* (June 3, 1878): 4.

3 Raymond Westbrook, "Open Letters from New York," *Atlantic Monthly* 41 (January 1878): 91–99.

4 For a discussion of commuting times, see F. A. Wright, "Suburban Houses of New York, Part I," *Building* 4 (February 20, 1886): 87; F. A. Wright, "Suburban Houses of New York, Part II," *Building* 4 (April 10, 1886): 172; "Suburban New York—I," *Real Estate Record and Builders' Guide* 40 (July 19, 1890): 73–76.

5 "The Problem of Living in New York," *Harper's New Monthly Magazine* 65 (November 1882): 918–24.

6 Westbrook, "Open Letters from New York": 93.

7 "Landscape-Gardening," *The Crayon* 4 (August 1857): 248; Henry Winthrop Sargent, *Supplement to Andrew Jackson Downing, A Treatise on the Theory and Practice of Landscape Gardening, Adapted to North America;...With Remarks on Rural Architecture, 6th ed.* (New York, 1859), 567–73; "Llewellyn Park," *Demorest's New York Illustrated News* 2 (May 12, 1860): 5; "Country Seats and Parks," *Demorest's New York Illustrated News* 2 (May 19, 1860): 20, 32; "Country Seats and Parks," *Demorest's New Illustrated News* 2 (June 23, 1860): 100–101, 106; "Literature: The May Festival in Llewellyn Park," *Demorest's New York Illustrated News* 2 (June 23, 1860): 107; Theodore Tilton, "Llewellyn Park," *Independent* (May 26, 1864), reprinted in *New York Times* (April 23, 1865): 5; *Newark Daily Advertiser* (May 11, 1866), Newark Public Library Clipping Files; Llewellyn Park: Country Homes for City People (Orange), undated promotional leaflet, ca. 1870; "Llewellyn Park," *Every Saturday* 3 (September 2, 1871): 227; Samuel Swift, "Llewellyn Park, West Orange, Essex Co., New Jersey: The First American Suburban Community," *House and Garden* 3 (June 1903): 327–35; Christopher Tunnard, "The Romantic Suburb in America," *Magazine of Art* 40 (May 1947): 184–87; Christopher Tunnard and Henry Hope Reed, *American Skyline* (New York: New American Library, 1953), 115; Richard Guy Wilson, "Charles F. McKim and the Development of the American Renaissance: A Study in Architecture and Culture" (Ph.D. diss., University of Michigan, 1972): 6; Jane B. Davies, "Llewellyn Park in West Orange, New Jersey," *Antiques* 107 (January 1975): 142–58; Wayne Andrews, *American Gothic: Its Origins, Its Trials, Its Triumphs* (New York: Random House, 1975), 43, 49; John Donoghue, "Alexander Jackson Davis, Romantic Architect, 1803–1892" (Ph. D. diss., New York University, 1977): ch. 8; Michael Robinson, "The Suburban Ideal: 19th-Century Planned Communities," *Historic Preservation* 30 (April–June 1978): 24–29; Deborah S. Gardner, "The Architecture of Commercial Capitalism: John Kellum and the Development of New York, 1840–1875" (Ph.D. diss., Columbia University, 1979): 275–77, fig. 112; Leland M. Roth, *A Concise History of American Architecture* (New York: Harper & Row, 1979), 102–7; Richard Guy Wilson, "Idealism and the Origin of the First American Suburb: Llewellyn Park, New Jersey," *American Art Journal* 11 (October 1979): 79–90; Stern with Massengale, *The Anglo-American Suburb*, 21; John Archer, "Country and City in the American Romantic Suburb," *Journal of the Society of Architectural Historians* 42 (May 1983): 139–56; Kenneth T. Jackson, *Crabgrass Frontier: The Suburbanization of the United States* (New York: Oxford University Press, 1985), 76–79, 84–86; Clay Lancaster, *The American Bungalow: 1880–1930* (New York: Abbeville Press, 1985), 66–67, 84; David Schuyler, *The New Urban Landscape* (Baltimore and London: Johns Hopkins University Press, 1986), 156–59; Robert A. M. Stern with Thomas Mellins and Raymond Gastil, *Pride of Place: Building the American Dream* (Boston: Houghton Mifflin; New York: American Heritage, 1986), 129, 132–33, 144–45; Susan Henderson, "Llewellyn Park, Suburban Idyll," *Journal of Garden History* 7 (No. 3, 1987): 221–43; John R. Stilgoe, *Borderland: Origins of the American Suburb, 1820–1939* (New Haven, Conn., and London: Yale University Press, 1988), 52–55; Richard Plunz, *A History of Housing in New York City* (New York: Columbia University Press, 1990), 9–10; Christian Zapatka, *The American Landscape* (New York: Princeton Architectural Press, 1995), 79; Melanie D. Anson, *Olmsted's Sudbrook: The Making of a Community* (Baltimore: Sudbrook Park, Inc., 1997), 7, 11, 26, 175 (n.28); Philip Pregill and Nancy Volkman, *Landscapes in History: Design and Planning in the Eastern and Western Traditions* (New York: John Wiley, 1999), 532–34; Robert A. M. Stern, Thomas Mellins, and David Fishman, *New York 1880: Architecture and Urbanism in the Gilded Age* (New York: Monacelli Press, 1999), 1008–16; Leland M. Roth, *American Architecture: A History* (Boulder, Co.: Icon Editions/Westview Press, 2001), 199–202; Alexander Garvin, *The American City: What Works, What Doesn't, 2nd ed.* (New York: McGraw-Hill, 2002), 319; Dolores Hayden, *Building Suburbia: Green Fields and Urban Growth, 1820–2000* (New York: Pantheon Books, 2003), 54–61; Thaïsa Way, *Unbounded Practice: Women and Landscape Architecture in the Early Twentieth Century* (Charlottesville and London: University of Virginia Press, 2009), 225–26; Tom Martinson, *The Atlas of American Architecture: 2000 Years of Architecture, City Planning, Landscape Architecture and Civil Engineering* (New York: Rizzoli International Publications, 2009), 365–66.

8 Alexis de Tocqueville, *Democracy in America*, vol. 1 (1834) and vol. 2 (1840), trans. and ed. by Harvey C. Mansfield and Delba Winthrop (Chicago and London: University of Chicago Press, 2000), 482.

9 *Llewellyn Park: Country Homes for City People* (Orange), undated promotional leaflet. Also see advertisements in the *Orange Journal*, May 16, 1857, to November 28, 1863, and March 24 to April 14, 1866.

10 For a discussion of the Cottage Style and Stick Style, see Vincent Scully, *The Shingle Style and The Stick Style: Architectural Theory and Design from Downing to the Origins of Wright* (New Haven, Conn.: Yale University Press, 1955; rev. ed. 1971), xxxix–lix, 1–18.

11 Roger Hale Newton, *Town & Davis Architects* (New York: Columbia University Press, 1942), 59–60, 95–96, 123–33, figs. 1, 5–7; Brooks Mather Kelley, *New Haven Heritage: An Area of Historic Houses on Hillhouse Avenue and Trumbull Street* (New Haven, Conn.: New Haven Preservation Trust, 1974), 9–54; Elizabeth Mills Brown, *New Haven: A Guide to Architecture and Urban Design* (New Haven, Conn., and London: Yale University Press, 1976), 35–36, 134–43; David N. Fixler, "The Development of Hillhouse Avenue: Prologue to an Interpretive Color Study Master Plan," (May 1992, unpublished paper for Perry Dean Rogers & Partners, Architects); Vincent Scully, "Yale in New Haven: An Introduction," in Vincent Scully et al., *Yale in New Haven: Architecture & Urbanism* (New Haven, Conn.: Yale University, 2004), 16.

12 Scully, "Yale in New Haven: An Introduction," in Scully et al., *Yale in New Haven: Architecture & Urbanism*, 16.

13 Tilton, "Llewellyn Park," *Independent*, reprinted in *New York Times*: 5.

14 Frederick Law Olmsted, letter to Edward Everett Hale (October 21, 1869), quoted in Anson, *Olmsted's Sudbrook: The Making of a Community*, 11.

15 Letter of Edward D. Page, March 24, 1916, quoted in Wilson, "Idealism and the Origin of the First American Suburb, Llewellyn Park, New Jersey": 85.

16 "Landscape-Gardening," *The Crayon*: 248.

17 Tilton, "Llewellyn Park," *Independent*, reprinted in *New York Times*: 5.

18 John Dorsey and James D. Dilts, *A Guide to Baltimore Architecture*, 3rd ed. (Centreville, Md.: Tidewater Publishers, 1997), 23–24, 374–76; Charles Belfoure, "On Dixon's Hill, a Suburban Village Inside the City Limits," (April 9, 2000), www.baltimoresun.com; "Mt. Washington," www.ci.baltimore/md.us/government/historic/districts; Eric L. Holcomb, *The City as Suburb: A History of Northeast Baltimore Since 1660*, updated edition (Chicago: The Center of America Places at Columbia College, 2008), xix–xx.

19 "House at Winchester, Mass. Mr. George D. Rand, Architect," *American Architect and Building News* 2 (June 23, 1877): 197–98; Kevin Stevens, *Winchester, Massachusetts: The Architectural Heritage of a Victorian Town* (Winchester, Mass.: The Winchester Historical Society, 1988), 54–59; Maureen Meister, "Rangeley: A Romantic Residential Park in Winchester, Massachusetts," *Antiques* 152 (August 1997): 188–97; Maureen Meister, "Rangeley," in Keith N. Morgan, ed., *Buildings of Massachusetts: Metropolitan Boston* (Charlottesville and London: University of Virginia Press and the Society of Architectural Historians, 2009), 415.

20 H.W.S. Cleveland, *A Few Hints on Landscape Gardening in the West* (Chicago: Hazlitt and Reed, 1871), 10–11; Newton Bateman and Paul Selby, eds., *Historical Encyclopedia of Illinois and History of Du Page County, Volume II* (Chicago: Munsell Publishing Company, 1913), 674–78; Virginia Luckhardt, "Horace William Shaler Cleveland: An Overview of the Life and Work of an Early American Landscape Architect, 1814–1900" (Master's thesis, University of Wisconsin-Madison, 1983): 45–48; Philip Pregill and Nancy Volkman, *Landscapes in History: Design and Planning in the Eastern and Western Traditions* (New York: John Wiley, 1999), 533; Historic Certification Consultants, *Architectural Resources in the Robbins Survey Area, Hinsdale, Illinois: A Summary and Inventory* (Chicago: Historic Certification Consultants, 2002); Ann Durkin Keating, *Chicagoland: City and Suburbs in the Railroad Age* (Chicago: University of Chicago Press, 2005), 104–8.

21 H.W.S. Cleveland, *A Few Hints on Landscape Gardening in the West* (Chicago: Hazlitt and Reed, 1871), 10–11, quoted in Luckhardt, "Horace William Shaler Cleveland: An Overview of the Life and Work of an Early American Landscape Architect, 1814–1900": 47–48.

22 William Robbins, quoted in Luckhardt, "Horace William Shaler Cleveland: An Overview of the Life and Work of an Early American Landscape Architect, 1814–1900": 47–48.

23 Cleveland, *A Few Hints on Landscape Gardening in the West*, 13; Luckhardt, "Horace William Shaler Cleveland: An Overview of the Life and Work of an Early American Landscape Architect, 1814–1900": 55–57.

24 Luckhardt, "Horace William Shaler Cleveland: An Overview of the Life and Work of an Early American Landscape Architect, 1814–1900": 58–59, 61–65.

25 Luckhardt, "Horace William Shaler Cleveland: An Overview of the Life and Work of an Early American Landscape Architect, 1814–1900": 61.

26 Quoted in Camille LeFevre, "St. Anthony Park," *Architecture Minnesota* 21 (March/April 1995): 44–47. Also see "St. Anthony Park, St. Paul," *Northwest Magazine* 4 (April 1886): 29; Warren Upham, *Minnesota Geographic Names: Their Origin and Significance* (St. Paul: Minnesota Historical Society, 1920), 631–33; David Gebhard and Tom

Martinson, *A Guide to the Architecture of Minnesota* (Minneapolis: University of Minnesota Press, 1977), 89–90; Virginia Brainard Kunz, *St. Paul: Saga of an American City* (Woodland Hills, Calif.: Windsor Publications, 1977), 65; Luckhardt, "Horace William Shaler Cleveland: An Overview of the Life and Work of an Early American Landscape Architect, 1814–1900": 122–24; Judith A. Martin and David A. Lanegran, *Where We Live: The Residential Districts of Minneapolis and Saint Paul* (Minneapolis: University of Minneapolis Press in association with the Center for Urban and Regional Affairs, 1983), 42–44; Camille LeFevre, "St. Anthony Park," *Architecture Minnesota* 21 (March/April 1995): 44–47; Larry Millett, *AIA Guide to the Twin Cities* (St. Paul, Minn.: Minnesota Historical Society Press, 2007), 570–75; David Lanegran, "Four Nineteenth Century Residential Districts," in http://www.macalester.edu/geography/mage/curriculum/goMN/ tc_geog/4_19th_century_residential_districts.pdf.

27 Luckhardt, "Horace William Shaler Cleveland: An Overview of the Life and Work of an Early American Landscape Architect, 1814–1900": 159–61; Millett, *AIA Guide to the Twin Cities*, 235–37.

28 David Gebhard and Tom Martinson, *A Guide to the Architecture of Minnesota* (Minneapolis: University of Minnesota Press, 1977), 93. For Warrendale, see "Warrendale," *Northwest Magazine* 4 (April 1886): 34; Millett, *AIA Guide to the Twin Cities*, 520. For Prospect Park, see Martin and Lanegran, *Where We Live: The Residential Districts of Minneapolis and Saint Paul*, 44–45; Millett, *AIA Guide to the Twin Cities*, 140–43. For Macalester Park, see Gebhard and Martinson, *A Guide to the Architecture of Minnesota*, 108; Kunz, *St. Paul: Saga of an American City*, 65; Millett, *AIA Guide to the Twin Cities*, 543.

29 David Schuyler, "Introduction," in Jacob Weidenmann, *Victorian Landscape Gardening, a Facsimile of Jacob Weidenmann's Beautifying Country Homes* (1870; Watkins Glen, New York: Athenaeum Library of Nineteenth Century America, 1978), n.p.; Robert R. Harvey, "Documenting a Victorian Landscape in the Midwest," *Bulletin of the Association for Preservation Technology* 9 (No. 3, 1977): 73–99; "Terrace Hill," *National Register of Historic Places Registration Form* (2003): 30; Philip Pregill and Nancy Volkman, *Landscapes in History: Design and Planning in the Eastern and Western Traditions* (New York: John Wiley, 1999), 537; Rudy J. Favretti, *Jacob Weidenmann: Pioneer Landscape Architect* (Hartford, Conn.: Cedar Hill Cemetery Foundation in cooperation with Wesleyan University Press, 2007), 119, 121, 123.

30 Jacob Weidenmann, quoted in Schuyler, "Introduction," in Weidenmann, *Victorian Landscape Gardening*, n.p.

31 Francis R. Kowsky et al., *Buffalo Architecture: A Guide* (Cambridge, Mass.: MIT Press, 1981), 189–90; Francis R. Kowsky, "Municipal Parks and City Planning: Frederick Law Olmsted's Buffalo Park and Parkway System," *Journal of the Society of Architectural Historians* XLVI (March 1987): 49–64; Francis R. Kowsky, ed., *The Best Planned City: The Olmsted Legacy in Buffalo* (Buffalo: Buffalo State College Foundation, 1991), 12, 37; Scott A. Carson, "Frederick Law Olmsted and the Buffalo Park and Parkway Systems" (Master's thesis, State University of New York, College of Environmental Science and Forestry, Syracuse, 1993): 122–27; Gianni Pettena, *Olmsted: l'origine del parco urbano e del parco natural contemporaneo* (Florence: Centro Di, 1996), 197; http://www.parksidebuffalo.org/about.html.

32 Frederick Law Olmsted, quoted in Carson, "Frederick Law Olmsted and the Buffalo Park and Parkway Systems": 126.

33 Kowsky et al., *Buffalo Architecture: A Guide*, 189.

34 Wanderer, "New Rochelle," *Real Estate Record and Builders' Guide* 40 (December 17, 1887): 1582; "Rochelle Park," *New York Daily Graphic* (May 14, 1887): 612; "Proposed House at Rochelle Park, New Rochelle, N.Y. George Martin Huss, Architect, N.Y.," *Architecture and Building* 12 (March 1, 1890): plate; "Suburban New York. IV. New Rochelle," *Real Estate Record and Builders' Guide* 46 (August 30, 1890): 271–74; Samuel Swift, "Community Life at Rochelle Park, American Suburban Communities IV," *House and Garden* 4 (May 1904): 235–43; "Study of a New York Suburb, New Rochelle," *Architectural Record* 25 (April 1909): 235–48; Richard Schermerhorn Jr., "Nathan Franklin Barrett, Landscape Architect," *Landscape Architecture* 10 (April 1920): 108–13; Herbert B. Nichols, *Historic New Rochelle* (New Rochelle, N.Y.: Board of Education, 1938); David Finn, *New Rochelle: Portrait of a City*, with an intro. by Ruth Kitchen (New York: Abbeville, 1981); Stern with Massengale, *The Anglo-American Suburb*, 30, 95; Marilyn E. Weigold, ed., *Westchester County: The Past Hundred Years* (Valhalla, N.Y.: Westchester County Historical Society, 1984); Stern, Mellins, and Fishman, *New York 1880*, 969–73; Charles A. Birnbaum and Robin Karson, eds., *Pioneers of American Landscape Design* (New York: McGraw-Hill, 2000), 12–13; Dolores Hayden, *Building Suburbia: Green Fields and Urban Growth, 1820–2000* (New York: Pantheon Books, 2003), 65; Gray Williams, "Westchester County: Historic Suburban Neighborhoods," in Roger Panetta, ed., *Westchester: The American Suburb* (New York: Fordham University Press; Yonkers, N.Y.: Hudson River Museum, 2006), 184–87. For a description of New Rochelle prior to the Civil War, see Robert Bolton, *Guide to New Rochelle and Its Vicinity* (New Rochelle, N.Y.: A. Hanford, 1842).

35 Albert Fein, ed., *Landscape Into Cityscape: Frederick Law Olmsted's Plans for a Greater New York City* (New York: Van Nostrand Reinhold, 1967), fig. x; Christian Zapatka, *The American Landscape* (New York: Princeton Architectural Press, 1995), 78; David Schuyler, "Weidenmann, Jacob," in Charles A. Birnbaum and Robin Karson, eds., *Pioneers of American Landscape Design* (New York: McGraw-Hill, 2000), 440; Rudy J. Favretti, *Jacob Weidenmann: Pioneer Landscape Architect* (Hartford, Conn.: Cedar Hill Cemetery Foundation, 2007), 22–25.

36 Swift, "Community Life at Rochelle Park, American Suburban Communities IV": 235.

37 Anonymous (Montgomery Schuyler?), "Study of a New York Suburb, New Rochelle," *Architectural Record* 25 (April 1909): 235–48.

38 Swift, "Community Life at Rochelle Park, American Suburban Communities IV": 236.

39 "Rochelle Park," *New York Daily Graphic*: 612.

40 Wanderer, "New Rochelle": 1582.

41 "Rochelle Park," *New York Daily Graphic*: 612.

42 Williams, "Westchester County: Historic Suburban Neighborhoods," in Panetta, ed., *Westchester: The American Suburb*, 186.

43 Charles Elmer Allison, *The History of Yonkers* (New York: W. B. Ketcham, 1896; Harrison, N.Y.: Harbor Hill Books, 1984), 229; "The Incline Elevator at Park Hill, N.Y.," *Scientific*

American Building Edition 153 (July 1898): 9, 16; "'Rock Villas,'" *Scientific American Building Edition* 153 (July 1898): 12, 15; "Hotel Destroyed by Fire," *New York Times* (April 1, 1901): 1; Yonkers Board of Trade, *Yonkers Illustrated* (Yonkers, N.Y., 1902), 99; "A Residence at Park Hill, N.Y.," *Scientific American Building Monthly* 197 (March 1902): 45, 56; *Park Hill-on-the-Hudson* (New York: American Real Estate Company, 1903); *Park Hill: An Idyll of the Hudson* (New York: American Real Estate Company, 1903); "House of Jules Breuchaud, Esq., Park Hill, N.Y.," *American Architect and Building News* 86 (November 1904): 63, plate 1508; "Bungalow Idea Popular," *New York Times* (July 26, 1908), C: 4; John H. Whitaker, Jr., "Country Living in Westchester," *Country Life in America* 15 (March 1909): 431–34; "New Dwelling at Park Hill," *New York Times* (December 19, 1909): 21; "Park Hill, a New and Delightful Suburb That Is Being Built on a Plateau Overlooking the Hudson," *Craftsman* 17 (February 1910): 572–76; *Park Hill Homes* (New York: American Real Estate Company, 1912); Fremont Rider, ed., *Rider's New York City and Vicinity, including Newark, Yonkers, and Jersey City* (New York: Henry Holt and Company, 1916), 394; Frank E. Sanchis, *American Architecture: Westchester County, New York: Colonial to Contemporary* (Croton-on-Hudson, N.Y.: North River Press, 1977), 117; Joseph Giovannini, "Park Hill on the Hudson, an Early Planned Community," *New York Times* (January 3, 1985), C: 1, 6; Joseph P. Griffith, "If You're Thinking of Living In: Park Hill," *New York Times* (January 12, 1992), IX: 5; Philip Pregill and Nancy Volkman, *Landscapes in History: Design and Planning in the Eastern and Western Traditions* (New York: John Wiley, 1999), 537; Andrew S. Dolkart, *Park Hill Historic District Application* (New York: Park Hill Residents' Association, 2002); Robert Estony, "Remembering the Yonkers Railroad," *The Yonkers Historian* 12 (Winter 2003): 4–5; Marc Ferris, "At Loggerheads Over Landmarks," *New York Times* (September 12, 2004), XIV: 5; Gray Williams, "Westchester County: Historic Suburban Neighborhoods," in Roger Panetta, ed., *Westchester: The American Suburb* (New York: Fordham University Press; Yonkers, N.Y.: Hudson River Museum, 2006), 191–95; Frank E. Sanchis, "The Suburban House," in Panetta, ed., *Westchester: The American Suburb*, 232–33.

44 *Fieldston, Riverdale-on-Hudson, Upper New York City*, promotional brochure (New York: Delafield Estate, Inc, 1911); "Country Clubs and Good Roads Important Factors in Stimulating Growth of Suburban Communities," *New York Times* (September 7, 1913), X: 13; Edward C. Delafield, "A Fashionable Suburban Section," *Real Estate Record and Builders' Guide* 92 (November 22, 1913): 940; Robert A. M. Stern, Gregory Gilmartin and John Montague Massengale, *New York 1900: Metropolitan Architecture and Urbanism 1890–1915* (New York: Rizzoli International Publications, 1983), 432–33; "Fieldston Building Plots in Demand as Villa Sites," *New York Times* (October 14, 1923), XI: 1; "Syndicate Forming to Buy Fieldston," *New York Times* (December 2, 1923), X: 2; "Group Buys Fieldston," *New York Times* (May 2, 1924): 35; Anthony Robins, "Visible City," *Metropolis* 4 (December 1984): 36–39; Robert A. M. Stern, Gregory Gilmartin, and Thomas Mellins, assisted by David Fishman and Raymond W. Gastil, *New York 1930: Architecture and Urbanism Between the Two World Wars* (New York: Rizzoli International Publications, 1987), 500–503; Bernard L. Stein, "Fieldston: A Suburb in the City," *Riverdale Press* (December 3, 1998): cover, D: 7–8, 11–12, 15–16, 19–20, 22–23; Barbaralee Diamonstein-Spielvogel, *Landmarks of New York* (New York: Monacelli Press, 2005), 609; New York City Landmarks Preservation Commission, *Fieldston Historic District Designation Report Volume 1* (January 10, 2006).

45 Barbaralee Diamonstein-Spielvogel, *Landmarks of New York* (New York: Monacelli Press, 2005), 609.

46 For Baum's work in Fieldston, see Dwight James Baum, "Making Old Homes New," *Architecture* 38 (December 1918): 333–41; "Portfolio of Current Architecture," *Architectural Record* 35 (May 1914): 455–62; Carleton Van Valkenburg, "An Interesting Group of Houses," *American Homes and Gardens* 11 (October 1914): 331–35; "House of Dwight James Baum, Riverdale, N. Y., Mr. Dwight James Baum, Architect," *American Architect* 57 (June 2, 1915): plate; William Morrison, ed., *The Work of Dwight James Baum*, rev. ed. (New York: W. Helburn, 1927; New York: Acanthus Press, 2008), 44–47, 50–52, 96–109, 115, 120–21, 147–49, 156–57, 159, 162–63, 166–71, 176–79, 224. For the country club, see "Country Club, Fieldston, New York, Dwight James Baum, New York, Architect," *Architect* 3 (October 1924), plates x–xii.

47 Delafield, "A Fashionable Suburban Section": 940. For Mann & MacNeille's Fieldston work, see "Portfolio of Current Architecture," *Architectural Record* 35 (May 1914): 455–56, 459.

48 Cynthia Zaitzevsky, "Frederick Law Olmsted in Brookline," *Proceedings of the Brookline Historical Society* (Fall 1977): 42–65, also in www.highstreethill.org/history/olmsted. html; Cynthia Zaitzevsky, *Frederick Law Olmsted and the Boston Park System* (Cambridge, Mass., and London: Belknap Press of Harvard University Press, 1982), 115–17; William S. Worley, *J. C. Nichols and the Shaping of Kansas City* (Columbia and London: University of Missouri Press, 1990), 140; Arleyn A. Levee, "The Olmsted Brothers' Residential Communities: Preview of a Legacy," in Charles A. Birnbaum, ed., *The Landscape Universe: Historic Designed Landscapes in Context* (Bronx: Catalog of Landscape Records in the United States at Wave Hill, 1993), 28; Charles E. Beveridge and Paul Rocheleau, *Frederick Law Olmsted: Designing the American Landscape* (New York: Rizzoli International Publications, 1995), 124; Gianni Pettena, *Olmsted: l'origine del parco urbano e del parco naturale contemporaneo* (Florence: Centro Di, 1996), 199; Greer Hardwicke and Roger Reed, *Images of America: Brookline* (Charleston, S.C.: Arcadia Publishing, 1998), 77; Alexander Garvin, *The American City: What Works, What Doesn't*, 2nd ed. (New York: McGraw-Hill, 2002), 320–22, 338; Dolores Hayden, *Building Suburbia: Green Fields and Urban Growth, 1820–2000* (New York: Pantheon Books, 2003), 65; Linda Olson Pehlke, "Places: Past and Present: Fisher Hill," *Our Town Brookline* (2005), also in www.brooklinehistoricalsociety.org. Also see Brookline Preservation Commission, "Fisher Hill," www. brooklinehistoricalsociety.org.

49 Jacob Pierce, quoted in Brookline Preservation Commission, "Fisher Hill," www. brooklinehistoricalsociety.org.

50 Pehlke, "Places: Past and Present: Fisher Hill," *Our Town Brookline* (2005), also in www.brooklinehistoricalsociety.org.

51 Garvin, *The American City: What Works, What Doesn't*, 321.

52 Zaitzevsky, "Frederick Law Olmsted in Brookline": 42–65; Zaitzevsky, *Frederick Law Olmsted and the Boston Park System*, 115; Hardwicke and Reed, *Images of America: Brookline*, 51; Linda Olson Pehlke, "Pill Hill & the Point," *Our Town Brookline* (2005), also in www.brooklinehistorical society.org. Also see http://www.highstreethill.org/tours/

pillhill.html.
53 Quoted in Hardwicke and Reed, *Images of America: Brookline*, 51.
54 Zaitzevsky, "Frederick Law Olmsted in Brookline": 42–65; Zaitzevsky, *Frederick Law Olmsted and the Boston Park System*, 115–16.
55 Bradford Kingman, *History of Norfolk County, Massachusetts* (Philadelphia: J.W. Lewis & Co., 1892), 785–86, 790; Thomas C. Quinn, ed., *Massachusetts of Today* (Boston: Colonial Publishing Co., 1892), 36; Edwin Bacon, *Boston: A Guidebook* (Boston: Ginn & Co., 1903), 114; Zaitzevsky, "Frederick Law Olmsted in Brookline": 42–65; Zaitzevsky, *Frederick Law Olmsted and the Boston Park System*, 115; Hardwicke and Reed, *Images of America: Brookline*, 69. Also see http://www.town.brookline.ma.us/neighborhoods/PDFs/ahnh.pdf; http://www.town ofbrooklinemass.com/neighborhoods/PDFs/AHNAannualmtg2003.pdf.
56 Ernest W. Bowditch, unpublished memoirs (c. 1917), quoted in Zaitzevsky, "Frederick Law Olmsted in Brookline": 42–65.
57 Zaitzevsky, "Frederick Law Olmsted in Brookline": 42–65.
58 Kevin D. Murphy, "Ernest W. Bowditch and the Practice of Landscape Architecture," *Essex Institute Historical Collections* 125 (April 1989): 162–76; Karen Hamley O'Donnell, "Ernest W. Bowditch," in Charles A. Birnbaum and Robin Karson, eds., *Pioneers of American Landscape Design* (New York: McGraw-Hill, 2000), 32–35.
59 M. F. Sweetser, *King's Handbook of Newton, Massachusetts* (Boston: Moses King Corp., 1889), 244; "Free Excursions for Newton Terraces, Newton," advertisement, *Boston Daily Globe* (May 8, 1897): 2; Jeffrey Karl Ochsner, "Architecture for the Boston & Albany Railroad: 1881–1894," *Journal of the Society of Architectural Historians* 47 (June 1988): 109–31; Murphy, "Ernest W. Bowditch and the Practice of Landscape Architecture": 169–72; O'Donnell, "Ernest W. Bowditch," in Birnbaum and Karson, eds., *Pioneers of American Landscape Design*, 34.
60 "Two Groups of Houses Built for the Boston Dwelling Housing Company, Kilham & Hopkins, Architects," *Brickbuilder* 22 (April 1913): 93–96; "Woodbourne—A Residential Settlement Near Boston, Mass.," *Western Architect* 27 (July 1918): 55–57, plates 7–11; Richard Heath, "Design for Pleasant Living: The Work of the Olmsteds Are Still With Us," *The Post* (Boston) (May 31, 1978): 23–24; Richard M. Candee and Greer Hardwicke, "Early Twentieth-Century Reform Housing by Kilham and Hopkins, Architects of Boston," *Winterthur Portfolio* 22 (Spring 1987): 47–80; Robert Campbell, "Forgotten Utopias," *Boston Globe Sunday Magazine* (May 21, 1995): 18.
61 Campbell, "Forgotten Utopias": 18.
62 Heath, "Design for Pleasant Living": 24.
63 I. T. Frary, "Suburban Landscape Planning in Cleveland," *Architectural Record* 43 (April 1918): 371–84; Blythe Gehring, *Vignettes of Clifton Park* (self-published, 1970); Kara Cathleen Hamley, "Cleveland's Park Allotment: Euclid Heights, Cleveland Heights, Ohio, and Its Designer, Ernest W. Bowditch" (Master's thesis, Cornell University, 1996): 67–72.
64 Frary, "Suburban Landscape Planning in Cleveland": 375.
65 Thomas J. Noel and Barbara S. Norgren, *Denver: The City Beautiful and Its Architects, 1893–1941* (Denver: Historic Denver, Inc., 1987), 60–61; Denver Landmark Preservation Commission & Planning and Development Office, *Design Guidelines for Country Club Historic District* (Denver: City and County of Denver, May 1995); Thomas J. Noel, *Denver Landmarks & Historic Districts: A Pictorial Guide* (Niwot: University Press of Colorado, 1996), 76–77; Thomas J. Noel, *Buildings of Colorado* (New York: Oxford University Press, 1997), 85–86, 89; Virginia and Lee McAlester, *A Field Guide to America's Historic Neighborhoods and Museum Houses: The Western States* (New York: Alfred A. Knopf, 1998), 309–10; Alice Millett Bakemeier, *Country Club Heritage: A History and Guide to a Denver Neighborhood* (Denver: Heritage Press, 2000), passim; Don Etter, "S. R. DeBoer," in Charles A. Birnbaum and Robin Karson, *Pioneers of American Landscape Design* (New York: McGraw-Hill, 2000), 85–88.
66 William S. Ladd, quoted in Arnold M. Berke, "Subtracting from the Addition?" *Preservation News* (September 1984): 7, 10. Also see *Ladd's Addition Historic District, National Register of Historic Places Registration Form* (Washington, D.C.: National Park Service, 1988); Kathleen McCormick, "Coming Up Roses," *Historic Preservation* 44 (November/December 1992): 68–71; Philip Langdon, *A Better Place to Live: Reshaping the American Suburb* (Amherst: University of Massachusetts Press, 1994), 81–82; Randall Arendt, *Crossroads, Hamlet, Village, Town: Design Characteristics of Traditional Neighborhoods, Old and New (Revised Edition)* (Chicago: American Planning Association, Planning Advisory Service, 2004), 20–21; Kiril Stanilov and Brenda Case Scheer, eds., *Suburban Form: An International Perspective* (New York and London: Routledge, 2004), 231–35; Bart King, *An Architectural Guidebook to Portland* (Corvallis: Oregon State University Press, 2007), 230–31; Lawrence Kreisman and Glenn Mason, *The Arts and Crafts Movement in the Pacific Northwest* (Portland, Ore.: Timber Press, 2007), 125–26.
67 "A Suburban Development, Laurelhurst, Portland, Oregon," *American Architect* 113 (June 5, 1918): 764; Virginia and Lee McAlester, *A Field Guide to America's Historic Neighborhoods and Museum Houses: The Western States* (New York: Alfred A. Knopf, 1998), 522–23; Kiril Stanilov and Brenda Case Scheer, eds., *Suburban Form: An International Perspective* (New York and London: Routledge, 2004), 231–35; Lawrence Kreisman and Glenn Mason, *The Arts and Crafts Movement in the Pacific Northwest* (Portland, Ore.: Timber Press, 2007), 125–26.
68 Paul C. Murphy, *Laurelhurst and Its Park* (Portland, Ore.: Paul C. Murphy, 1916), 19–20, quoted in Kreisman and Mason, *The Arts and Crafts Movement in the Pacific Northwest*, 174; Arthur C. Comey and Max S. Wehrly, "A Study of Planned Communities" (Department of Regional Planning of Harvard University, November 1936): 411–12; Kimberly K. Lakin, "Ellis F. Lawrence: Residential Designs," in Michael Shellenbarger, ed., *Harmony in Diversity: The Architecture and Teaching of Ellis F. Lawrence* (Eugene: University of Oregon, 1989), 41–42.
69 Dwight James Baum, "Architecture in the Northwest Shows a True Modern Spirit," *American Architect* 136 (September 1929): 211–17; Board of Park Commissioners, *Park Playgrounds and Boulevards of Seattle, Washington* (Seattle: Pacific Press, 1909), 27–28; Sally B. Woodbridge and Roger Montgomery, *A Guide to Architecture in Washington State: An Environmental Perspective* (Seattle: University of Washington Press, 1980), 184–88; David A. Rash, "Edward Otto Schwagerl," in Jeffrey Karl Ochsner, ed., *Shaping Seattle Architecture* (Seattle: University of Washington Press, 1994), 52–57; Walt Crowley, *National Trust Guide: Seattle* (New York: Wiley, 1998), 222–24; Virginia and Lee McAlester, *A Field Guide to America's Historic Neighborhoods and Museum Houses: The Western States* (New York: Alfred A. Knopf, 1998), 674–75; Caroline Tobin, *Mount Baker: Historic Context Statement* (Seattle: Department of Neighborhoods, May 2004); Lawrence Kreisman, *The Arts and Crafts Movement in the Pacific Northwest* (Portland, Ore.: Timber Press, 2007), 124–25.
70 Rash, "Edward Otto Schwagerl," in Ochsner, ed., *Shaping Seattle Architecture*, 55.
71 Roger Sale, *Seattle: Past to Present* (Seattle and London: University of Washington Press, 1976), 81–82; Sally B. Woodbridge and Roger Montgomery, *A Guide to Architecture in Washington State: An Environmental Perspective* (Seattle: University of Washington Press, 1980), 35, 48–49; Arleyn A. Levee, "The Olmsted Brothers' Residential Communities: A Preview of a Career Legacy," in Charles A. Birnbaum, ed., *The Landscape Universe: Historic Designated Districts in Context* (Bronx: Wave Hill, 1993), 41–43; Jane Holtz Kay, *Asphalt Nation: How the Automobile Took Over America, and How We Can Take It Back* (New York: Crown, 1997), 182; Beth Dodrill, "Olmsted Designed Estate Gardens of the Pacific Northwest," (April 2003), www.historicseattle.org; Charles Mudede, "A Tale of Two Gated Communities: An African Memoir," www.radicalurbantheory.com.
72 Vernon Macan and Clyde D. Pike, *Broadmoor: Restricted Residential Park with Golf Course* (Seattle: Puget Mill Company, 1924); "Golf Courses in Subdivisions," *National Real Estate Journal* 28 (August 23, 1926): 52–53; *Broadmoor: "The Country Club Within the City," a Restricted Residential Park with Its Own Private Golf Course* (Seattle: Puget Mill Company, c. 1927); Dwight James Baum, "Architecture in the Northwest Shows a True Modern Spirit," *American Architect* 136 (September 1929): 211–17; Hector A. Escobosa, *Seattle Story* (Seattle: F. McCaffrey, 1948), 102–3; Sally B. Woodbridge and Roger Montgomery, *A Guide to Architecture in Washington State* (Seattle and London: University of Washington Press, 1980), 174–75; William S. Worley, *J. C. Nichols and the Shaping of Kansas City* (Columbia and London: University of Missouri Press, 1990), 271; Roger Sale, *Seeing Seattle* (Seattle: University of Washington Press, 1994), 162; Walt Crowley, *National Trust Guide: Seattle* (New York: Wiley, 1998), 156, 158; BOLA Architecture + Planning and Karen Kiest/Landscape Architects, *Washington Park Arboretum Historic Review* (Seattle: Seattle Parks and Recreation, 2003), 34–35; Charles Mudede, "A Tale of Two Gated Communities: An African Memoir," www.radicalurbantheory.com; "Broadmoor," www.seattletimes.nwsource.com.
73 *Broadmoor: "The Country Club Within the City," a Restricted Residential Park with Its Own Private Golf Course.*
74 Baum, "Architecture in the Northwest Shows a True Modern Spirit": 216.
75 Mudede, "A Tale of Two Gated Communities: An African Memoir," www. radicalurbantheory.com.
76 *Character of Improvements at Ingleside Terraces*, brochure (San Francisco: Urban Realty Improvement Company, 1913); "Recent Municipal Activities in San Francisco," *Pacific Municipalities* 29 (October 1915): 439; Betty Carman, "Some Notes on the History of Ingleside Terraces," (1968), www.itha.org/history/history.html; Sally B. Woodbridge and John M. Woodbridge, *Architecture: San Francisco: The Guide* (San Francisco: San Francisco Chapter of the American Institute of Architects, 1982), 175; Mel Scott, *The San Francisco Bay Area: A Metropolis in Perspective*, 2nd ed.(Berkeley: University of California Press, 1985), 168; Virginia and Lee McAlester, *A Field Guide to America's Historic Neighborhoods and Museum Houses: The Western States* (New York: Alfred A. Knopf, 1998), 234–35; Scott Ostler, "A Lap Around an Old Track," *San Francisco Chronicle* (August 28, 2000), A: 2; Sam Whiting, "Ingleside Terrace Giant Sundial," *San Francisco Chronicle* (April 14, 2002), CM: 6; Patrick McGrew, "Ingleside Terraces," (2004), www.mtdavidson.org; Dave Weinstein, "Joseph A. Leonard: Suburbs in the City," *San Francisco Chronicle* (April 10, 2004), F: 1; Jacqueline Proctor, *Images of America: San Francisco's West of Twin Peaks* (Charleston, S.C.: Arcadia Publishing, 2006), 7–8, 18, 24, 26–31; Sally B. Woodbridge, *San Francisco in Maps & Views* (New York: Rizzoli International Publications, 2006), 126; Jacqueline Proctor, *Bay Area Beauty: The Artistry of Harold G. Stoner, Architect* (privately published, 2010), 54–56; Woody LaBounty, *Ingleside Terraces: San Francisco Racetrack to Residence Park* (San Francisco: Outside Lands Media, 2012).
77 Quoted in Carman, "Some Notes on the History of Ingleside Terraces," (1968), www.itha.org/history/history.html.
78 Quoted in Weinstein, "Joseph A. Leonard: Suburbs in the City": 1.
79 Werner Hegemann and Elbert Peets, *The American Vitruvius: An Architects' Handbook of Civic Art* (1922; New York: Benjamin Blom, 1972), 272; Werner Hegemann, *Amerikanische Architektur & Stadtbaukunst* (Berlin: E. Wasmuth, 1925), 115–16; Arthur C. Comey and Max S. Wehrly, "A Study of Planned Communities" (Department of Regional Planning of Harvard University, November 1936): 436–37; Woobridge and Woodbridge, *Architecture: San Francisco: The Guide*, 170–71; David Gebhard et al., *Architecture in San Francisco and Northern California* (Salt Lake City: Peregrine Smith, 1985), 111–12; Scott, *The San Francisco Bay Area: A Metropolis In Perspective*, 167–68; Sally Woodbridge and John Woodbridge, *San Francisco Architecture* (San Francisco: Chronicle Books, 1992), 384–85; Ken Tadashi Oshima, "Denenchofu," *Journal of the Society of Architectural Historians* 55 (June 1996): 144; Virginia and Lee McAlester, *A Field Guide to America's Historic Neighborhoods and Museum Houses: The Western States* (New York: Alfred A. Knopf, 1998), 234–35; Peter Booth Wiley, *National Trust Guide—San Francisco: America's Guide for Architecture and History Travelers* (New York: John Wiley & Sons, 2000), 172–73; Carolyn S. Loeb, *Entrepreneurial Vernacular: Developers' Subdivisions in the 1920s* (Baltimore and London: Johns Hopkins University Press, 2001), 94, 95; Woodbridge, *San Francisco in Maps & Views*, 126; Fukuo Akimoto, "California Garden Suburbs: St. Francis Wood and Palos Verdes Estates," *Journal of Urban Design* 12 (February 2007): 43–72; Jacqueline Proctor, *Bay Area Beauty: The Artistry of Harold G. Stoner, Architect* (privately published, 2010), 34, 76, 96, 109, 147; Richard Brandi, *San Francisco's St. Francis Wood* (San Francisco: Outside Lands Media, 2012).
80 Duncan McDuffie, to the St. Francis Homeowners' Association, transcript of address, December 11, 1932, as quoted in http://www.outsidelands.org/mcduffie.php. Duncan-McDuffie Papers, Bancroft Library, University of California, Berkeley.
81 Duncan McDuffie, quoted in Akimoto, "California Garden Suburbs: St. Francis Wood

and Palos Verdes Estates": 46.
82 Werner Hegemann, quoted in Duncan McDuffie, to the St. Francis Homeowners' Association, transcript of address, December 11, 1932, as quoted in http://www.outsidelands.org/mcduffie.php. Duncan-McDuffie Papers, Bancroft Library, University of California, Berkeley.
83 Quoted in www.westwoodpark.com/history.htm. Also see "Why I Chose Westwood Park for My Bungalows," advertisement, *San Francisco Chronicle* (June 5, 1920): 6; F. J. Glunk, "Westwood Park and Westwood Highlands," *Home Designer and Garden Beautiful* 8 (March 1925): 194–96, 203; Lawrence Kinnard, *History of the Greater San Francisco Bay Region*, vol. 2 (New York: Lewis Historical Publishing, 1966), 215; Woodbridge and Woodbridge: *Architecture: San Francisco: The Guide*, 173; Scott, *The San Francisco Bay Area: A Metropolis in Perspective*, 167; John Punter, *Design Guidelines in American Cities* (Liverpool: Liverpool University Press, 1999), 136–40; Carolyn S. Loeb, *Entrepreneurial Vernacular: Developers' Subdivisions in the 1920s* (Baltimore and London: Johns Hopkins University Press, 2001), 94, 96, 99; Nanette Asimov, "Westwood Park," *San Francisco Chronicle* (July 6, 2001), WB: 1; Dave Weinstein, "Ida McCain: Builder of Bungalows," *San Francisco Chronicle* (October 9, 2004), F: 1; Proctor, *Images of America: San Francisco's West of Twin Peaks*, 7–8, 19, 26, 34–35, 57, 84; Woodbridge, *San Francisco in Maps & Views*, 126; Sarah Allaback, *The First American Women Architects* (Urbana and Chicago: University of Illinois Press, 2008), 133–35.
84 "Why I Chose Westwood Park for My Bungalows": 6, quoted in Allaback, *The First American Women Architects*, 134.
85 Glunk, "Westwood Park and Westwood Highlands": 194–96, 203; Loeb, *Entrepreneurial Vernacular: Developers' Subdivisions in the 1920s*, 13–14, 88–139, 187–91; Alison K. Hoagland, "Entrepreneurial Vernacular," book review, *Journal of the Society of Architectural Historians* 62 (March 2003): 148–50; Sam Whiting, "The Secretive Subdivision," *San Francisco Chronicle* (September 5, 2004), CM: 6; Proctor, *Images of America: San Francisco's West of Twin Peaks*, 7–8, 26, 53–54. Also see "Westwood Highlands," www.mtdavidson.org
86 Quoted in Elizabeth Jo Lampl and Kimberly Prothro Williams, *Chevy Chase: A Home Suburb for the Nation's Capital* (Crownsville: Maryland Historic Trust Press, 1998), 94. Also see Alvin D. Hyman, "The Peninsula," in *The Suburbs of San Francisco* (San Francisco: Chronicle Books, 1969), 81–82; Richard Longstreth, *On the Edge of the World* (New York: Architectural History Foundation; Cambridge, Mass.: MIT Press, 1983), 148–50; Kevin Starr, *Inventing the Dream: California Through the Progressive Era* (New York and Oxford: Oxford University Press, 1985), 188–89; Gary Brechin, *Imperial San Francisco: Urban Power, Earthly Ruin* (Berkeley: University of California Press, 1999), 85, 90, 94–96.
87 "Glimpse of First Unit of New Hollywood Tract," *Los Angeles Times* (April 1, 1923), V: 5; "Hollywoodland to Have Bridle Paths," *Los Angeles Times* (July 22, 1923), V: 14; "Sales Records High at Tract in Foothills," *Los Angeles Times* (September 23, 1923), V: 8; "Bonds Assure New Highway," *Los Angeles Times* (October 14, 1923), V: 2; "Hillside Tract Sets New Pace," *Los Angeles Times* (July 13, 1924), D: 6; "Reforestation Planned," *Los Angeles Times* (December 14, 1924), E: 5; "Stores Structure Completed," *Los Angeles Times* (April 19, 1925), F: 8; "Tract's Success Seen in Its Homes," *Los Angeles Times* (September 5, 1926), E: 3; Bruce T. Torrence, *Hollywood: The First 100 Years* (Hollywood: Hollywood Chamber of Commerce and Fiske Enterprises, 1979), 130, 133–34; Greg Williams, *The Story of Hollywoodland* (North Hollywood, Calif.: Papavasilopoulos Press, 1992), passim; Virginia and Lee McAlester, *A Field Guide to America's Historic Neighborhoods and Museum Houses: The Western States* (New York: Alfred A. Knopf, 1998), 85, 87; Charles Moore, Peter Becker, and Regula Campbell, *The City Observed: Los Angeles: A Guide to Its Architecture and Landscapes* (Santa Monica: Hennessey & Ingalls, 1998), 249–50; David Gebhard and Robert Winter, *An Architectural Guidebook to Los Angeles* (Salt Lake City: Gibbs Smith, 2003), 182.
88 "Fix Sales Date of Tract," *Los Angeles Times* (April 25, 1926), E: 6; "Huntington Palisades to Be Developed for Beach Homes by Santa Monica Concern," *Los Angeles Times* (May 2, 1926), E: 4; "Delegates Visit New Palisades Subdivision," *Los Angeles Times* (June 13, 1926), E: 11; "Call Bids on Improvements: Huntington Palisades Is to Spend Million," *Los Angeles Times* (June 20, 1926), F: 7; "Cement Work Begins in Tract," *Los Angeles Times* (September 5, 1926), E: 5; "Huntington Palisades Lots Carry Rights to Frontage on Ocean," *Los Angeles Times* (September 26, 1926), E: 10; Santa Monica Land and Water Company, *Huntington Palisades, on Santa Monica Bay: Buy Now at Opening Prices*, promotional brochure (1927); "Palisades Celebrates Year Mark," *Los Angeles Times* (May 22, 1927), E: 7; "Beach Acreage Reaches Goal," *Los Angeles Times* (June 6, 1929), E: 5; "Residence of Mrs. W.S. Parry, Huntington Palisades—Gable and Wyant, Architects," *Architectural Digest* 8 (No. 1, 1931): 82–85; "Residence of Mr. and Mrs. W.H. Theobald, Huntington Palisades—Paul R. Williams, Architect," *Architectural Digest* 8 (No. 3, 1931): 86; Robert M. Fogelson, *The Fragmented Metropolis: Los Angeles 1850–1930* (Cambridge, Mass.: Harvard University Press, 1967), 155–57; David Gebhard and Robert Winter, *A Guide to Architecture in Los Angeles & Southern California* (Santa Barbara and Salt Lake City: Peregrine Smith, 1977), 46–47; Robert Fishman, *Bourgeois Utopias: The Rise and Fall of Suburbia* (New York: Basic Books, 1987), 168; Kevin Starr, *Material Dreams: Southern California Through the 1920s* (New York: Oxford University Press, 1990), 84; Karen E. Hudson, *Paul R. Williams: A Legacy of Style* (New York: Rizzoli International Publications, 1993), 231; David Gebhard and Robert Winter, *An Architectural Guidebook to Los Angeles* (Salt Lake City: Gibbs Smith, 2003), 43, 46; Libby Motika, "Huntington Palisades: An Irresistible Suburb," *Palisadian-Post* (March 11, 2004), www.palisadepost.com; Mary Trahan, "10 Great Neighborhoods: Huntington Palisades," *Los Angeles Magazine* 49 (December 2004): 86–87; Robert Fogelson, *Bourgeois Nightmares, Suburbia, 1870–1930* (New Haven, Conn., and London: Yale University Press, 2005), 147; Jan Loomis, *Images of America: Pacific Palisades* (Charleston, S.C.: Arcadia Publishing, 2009), 7–8, 15–17, 30–32, 46–51, 72–77, 125.
89 "Huntington Palisades," advertisement, *Los Angeles Times* (May 9, 1926), E: 7.
90 Fogelson, *The Fragmented Metropolis: Los Angeles 1850–1930*, 155.
91 Starr, *Material Dreams: Southern California Through the 1920s*, 84.
92 "The Right Spirit Displayed in Griffin's Planning," *Western Architect* 20 (August 1913): 66.
93 "Emory Hills," *Western Architect* 20 (August 1913): 72–73. Also see James Birrell, *Walter Burley Griffin* (St. Lucia, Brisbane: University of Queensland Press, 1964), 61–62, 66; Albert J. Drap Jr. and Thomas A. Heinz, "Walter Burley Griffin: Comprehensive Subdivision Planning in the Midwest," (May 25, 1972): n.p.; Donald Leslie Johnson, *The Architecture of Walter Burley Griffin* (Melbourne: Macmillan Company of Australia, 1977), 30; Peter Harrison, *Walter Burley Griffin: Landscape Architect* (Canberra: National Library of Australia, 1995), 52.
94 "Emory Hills": 72–73.
95 "Emory Hills": 73.
96 "Ridge Quadrangles," *Western Architect* 20 (August 1913): 71–72; Mark L. Peisch, "The Chicago School and Walter Burley Griffin, 1893–1914" (Ph.D. diss., Columbia University, 1959): 137; James Birrell, *Walter Burley Griffin* (St. Lucia, Brisbane: University of Queensland Press, 1964), 61–62; Mark L. Peisch, *The Chicago School of Architecture: Early Followers of Sullivan and Wright* (London: Phaidon Press, 1964), 102, 104; Albert J. Drap Jr. and Thomas A. Heinz, "Walter Burley Griffin: Comprehensive Subdivision Planning in the Midwest," (May 25, 1972): n.p.; Donald Leslie Johnson, *The Architecture of Walter Burley Griffin* (Melbourne: Macmillan Company of Australia, 1977), 28; Peter Harrison, *Walter Burley Griffin: Landscape Architect* (Canberra: National Library of Australia, 1995), 52.
97 "Clark's Resubdivision of Addition to Grinnell, Iowa. Town Extension," *Western Architect* 20 (August 1913): 73–75; James Birrell, *Walter Burley Griffin* (St. Lucia, Brisbane: University of Queensland Press, 1964), 61, 62, 63, 66, 67; Donald Leslie Johnson, *The Architecture of Walter Burley Griffin* (Melbourne: Macmillan Company of Australia, 1977), 28, 30; Peter Harrison, *Walter Burley Griffin: Landscape Architect* (Canberra: National Library of Australia, 1995), 52; Andrés Duany, Elizabeth Plater-Zyberk, and Robert Alminana, *The New Civic Art: Elements of Town Planning* (New York: Rizzoli International Publications, 2003), 308.
98 Duany, Plater-Zyberk, and Alminana, *The New Civic Art: Elements of Town Planning*, 308.
99 "Rock Crest and Rock Glen. Domestic Community Development, Mason City, Iowa," *Western Architect* 20 (August 1913): 75–76; Mark L. Peisch, "The Chicago School and Walter Burley Griffin, 1893–1914" (Ph.D. diss., Columbia University, 1959): 130–34; James Birrell, *Walter Burley Griffin* (St. Lucia, Brisbane: University of Queensland Press, 1964), 42, 44, 53; Mark L. Peisch, *The Chicago School of Architecture: Early Followers of Sullivan and Wright* (London: Phaidon Press, 1964), 83, 96–97, 99, 114, 128, figs. 23–25; Robert E. McCoy, "Rock Crest/Rock Glen: Prairie School Planning in Iowa," *Prairie School Review* 5 (Third Quarter, 1968): 5–40; Albert J. Drap Jr. and Thomas A. Heinz, "Walter Burley Griffin: Comprehensive Subdivision Planning in the Midwest," (May 25, 1972), n.p.; *Mason City, Iowa: an Architectural Heritage* (Mason City: Klipto Printing, 1977); Donald Leslie Johnson, *The Architecture of Walter Burley Griffin* (Melbourne: Macmillan Company of Australia, 1977), 28; Wesley I. Shank, *The Iowa Catalog, Historic American Buildings Survey* (Iowa City: University of Iowa Press, 1979), 71, 76, 108; Robert McCoy, "Concrete and Nature: A Mason City Dream," *Iowa Architect* 36 (March–April 1988): 34–37; David Gebhard and Geral Mansheim, *Buildings of Iowa* (New York: Oxford University Press, 1993), 410–17; Peter Harrison, *Walter Burley Griffin: Landscape Architect* (Canberra: National Library of Australia, 1995), 53–54; Christopher Vernon, "'Expressing Natural Conditions with Maximum Possibility': the American Landscape Art (1901–c.1912) of Walter Burley Griffin, part two," *Landscape Australia* 17 (August 1995): 146–52, 214–16; Mati Maldre and Paul Kruty, *Walter Burley Griffin in America* (Urbana and Chicago: University of Illinois Press, 1996), 116–44, 182–73; Donald Dunbar, "Of Social Concern: Towns and Buildings for Ordinary Australians," in Jeff Turnbull and Peter Y. Navaretti, eds., *The Griffins in Australia and India* (Melbourne: The Miegunyah Press, 1998), 28, 103; Christopher Vernon, "The Landscape Art of Walter Burley Griffin," in Anne Watson, ed., *Beyond Architecture, Marion Mahony and Walter Burley Griffin* (Sydney: Powerhouse, 1998), 91–93; Tom Martinson, *The Atlas of American Architecture: 2000 Years of Architecture, City Planning, Landscape Architecture and Civil Engineering* (New York: Rizzoli International Publications, 2009), 368, 440.
100 Vernon, "'Expressing Natural Conditions with Maximum Possibility': the American Landscape Art (1901–c.1912) of Walter Burley Griffin, part two": 152.
101 Griffin, "Rock Crest and Rock Glen": 76.
102 Richter, Dick & Reuteman, *Washington Highlands* (Milwaukee: Richter, Dick & Reuteman, c. 1915); Werner Hegemann and Elbert Peets, *The American Vitruvius: an Architects' Handbook of Civic Art* (1922; New York: Benjamin Blom Inc., 1972), 280; *International Cities and Town Planning Exhibition. English Catalogue. Jubilee Exhibition, Gothenburg, Sweden, 1923* (Göteborg, Wezäta, W. Zachrissons boktyrckeri a.-b., 1923), 376–77; Werner Hegemann, *Amerikanische Architektur & Stadtbaukunst* (Berlin: E. Wasmuth, 1925), 125; Caroline Shillaber, "Elbert Peets, Champion of the Civic Form," *Landscape Architecture* 72 (November 1982): 55–56; Jill Pearlman, "Joseph Hudnut's Other Modernism at the 'Harvard Bauhaus,'" *Journal of the Society of Architectural Historians* 56 (December 1997): 454; Arnold A. Alanen, "Elbert Peets: History as Precedent in Midwestern Landscape Design," in William H. Tishler, ed., *Midwestern Landscape Architecture* (Urbana and Chicago: University of Illinois Press, 2000), 199–202; Jill Pearlman, "Joseph Hudnut and the Unlikely Beginnings of Post-Modern Urbanism at the Harvard Bauhaus," *Planning Perspectives* 15 (2000): 211; Wauwatosa Historical Society, *Wauwatosa* (Charleston, S.C.: Arcadia, 2004), 113; Christiane Crasemann Collins, *Werner Hegemann and the Search for Universal Urbanism* (New York: W. W. Norton & Co., 2005), 125–30; Christiane Crasemann Collins, "Camillo Sitte across the Atlantic: Raymond Unwin, John Nolen, and Werner Hegemann," in Charles C. Bohl and Jean-François Lejeune, eds., *Sitte, Hegemann and the Metropolis: Modern Civic Art and International Exchanges* (London and New York: Routledge, 2009), 184–85; "The Washington Homes Association," in http://washingtonhighlands.org; "Washington Highlands Historic District," in http://www.wisconsinhistory.org/hp/register/viewSummary.asp?refnum'89002121.
103 Richter, Dick & Reuteman, *Washington Highlands*, 4.
104 Richter, Dick & Reuteman, *Washington Highlands*, 5.
105 Richter, Dick & Reuteman, *Washington Highlands*, 8–9.
106 *International Cities and Town Planning Exhibition. English Catalogue. Jubilee Exhibition, Gothenburg, Sweden, 1923*, 377–78.
107 Hegemann and Peets, *The American Vitruvius: an Architects' Handbook of Civic Art*, 280; *International Cities and Town Planning Exhibition. English Catalogue. Jubilee Exhibition,*

Gothenburg, Sweden, 1923, 377; Hegemann, *Amerikanische Architektur & Stadtbaukunst*, 125; Collins, *Werner Hegemann and the Search for Universal Urbanism*, 128–30.

108 E.I. duPont de Nemours & Company, *Wawaset: A Residential Development*, brochure (March 1918); Anna T. Lincoln, *Wilmington, Delaware: Three Centuries Under Four Flags, 1609–1937* (Rutland, Vt.: Tuttle Publishing Co., 1937), 221; National Register of Historic Places, *Wawaset Park Historic District Survey* (Washington, D.C.: United States Department of the Interior, National Park Service, 1985); David Allan Hamer, *History in Urban Places: The Historic Districts of the United States* (Columbus: Ohio State University Press, 1998), 69.

109 John Nolen, "Housing Project at Olean, N.Y.," *Engineering News-Record* 86 (January 18, 1921): 80; Alfred C. Bossom, "The Housing Development at Olean, N.Y.," *Architecture* 44 (August 1921): 249–53; E. W. Fitzgerald, "What a Housing Corporation Has Accomplished," *American City* 29 (August 1923): 114–15; *Supplementary Report of the Urbanism Committee to the National Resources Committee* (Washington, D.C.: U. S. Government Printing Office, 1939), 146, 151; Dennis Sharp, *Alfred C. Bossom's American Architecture, 1903–1926* (London: Book Art, 1984), 49–50.

110 Nolen, "Housing Project at Olean, N.Y.": 80.

111 Sinclair Lewis, *Babbitt* (New York: Harcourt, Brace & Company, 1922), 52.

112 Kathryn Bishop Eckert, *Buildings of Michigan* (New York: Oxford University Press, 1993), 100; Eric J. Hill and John Gallagher, *AIA Detroit: The American Institute of Architects Guide to Detroit Architecture* (Detroit: Wayne State University Press, 2003), 208–11; Robert E. Grese, "Ossian Cole Simonds," in Charles A. Birnbaum and Robin Karson, eds., *Pioneers of American Landscape Design* (New York: McGraw Hill, 2000), 366.

113 Joseph G. Butler Jr., *History of Youngstown and the Mahoning Valley, Ohio*, vol. 2 (Chicago and New York: American Historical Society, 1921), 25; "Golf Courses in Subdivisions," *National Real Estate Journal* 28 (August 23, 1926): 52–53; William S. Worley, *J. C. Nichols and the Shaping of Kansas City* (Columbia and London: University of Missouri Press, 1990), 271. Also see www.warren.org.

114 Butler, *History of Youngstown and the Mahoning Valley, Ohio*, 25.

115 Thomas W. Brunk, *Leonard B. Willeke: Excellence in Architecture and Design* (Detroit: University of Detroit Press, 1986), 156, 159–60.

116 Coy T. Phillips, "City Pattern of Durham, N.C.," *Economic Geography* 23 (October 1947): 233–47; Jean Bradley Anderson, *Durham County: A History of Durham County, North Carolina* (Durham: Duke University Press, 1990), 343–44; Catherine W. Bishir and Michael T. Southern, *A Guide to the Historic Architecture of Piedmont, North Carolina* (Chapel Hill and London: University of North Carolina Press, 2003), 207–8; National Register of Historic Places, *Forest Hills Historic District Survey* (Washington, D.C.: United States Department of the Interior, National Park Service, 2005). Also see www.preservationdurham.org.

117 Bishir and Southern, *A Guide to the Historic Architecture of Piedmont, North Carolina*, 207.

118 Arleyn Levee, "Whiting, Edward Clark," in Charles Birnbaum and Robin Karson, eds., *Pioneers of American Landscape Design* (New York: McGraw Hill, 2000), 452; Andrés Duany, Elizabeth Plater-Zyberk, and Robert Alminana, *The New Civic Art: Elements of Town Planning* (New York: Rizzoli International Publications, 2003), 33. For the Stokes house, see "'Khakum Wood' Estate: Mr. I. N. Phelps Stokes, Greenwich, Conn.," *Architect* (New York) 1 (February 1924): 109–15; "The Oldest House in America: 'Khakum Wood,' the I.N. Phelps Stokes Estate in Greenwich, Conn.: This Old English Home was Transported from Suffolk England," *Country Life* 45 (April 1924): 63–66; The Junior League of Greenwich, *The Great Estates: Greenwich, Connecticut, 1880–1930* (Canaan, N.H.: Phoenix Publishing, 1986), 110–13.

119 Duany, Plater-Zyberk, and Alminana, *New Civic Art*, 33.

120 Nancy Haston Foster and Ben Fairbank Jr., *San Antonio: An Indispensable Guide to One of Texas' Favorite Cities* (Austin: Texas Monthly Press, 1983), 48–49; Char Miller and Heywood T. Sanders, "Olmos Park and the Creation of a Suburban Bastion, 1927–39," in Char Miller and Heywood T. Sanders, eds., *Urban Texas: Politics and Development* (College Station: Texas A & M University Press, 1990), 113–27; Virginia and Lee McAlester, *A Field Guide to America's Historic Neighborhoods and Museum Houses: The Western States* (New York: Alfred A. Knopf, 1998), 632.

121 Foster and Fairbank Jr., *San Antonio: An Indispensable Guide to One of Texas' Favorite Cities*, 47–48; Chris Carson and William McDonald, eds., *A Guide to San Antonio Architecture* (San Antonio: San Antonio Chapter of the American Institute of Architects, 1986), 9; *Golden Anniversary, Alamo Heights, Texas, 1922–1972* (Alamo Heights, 1972); Paris Permenter and John Bigley, *Insider's Guide to San Antonio* (Guilford, Conn.: Globe Pequot, 2006), 257; *Handbook of Texas Online*, s.v. "Alamo Heights, Texas," http://www.tshaonline.org/handbook/online/articles/AA/hfa2.html.

122 Foster and Fairbank Jr., *San Antonio: An Indispensable Guide to One of Texas' Favorite Cities*, 49; *Handbook of Texas Online*, s.v. "Terrell Hills, Texas," http:www.tshaonline.org/handbook/online/articles/TT/hgt5.html.

123 Quoted in Miller and Sanders, "Olmos Park and the Creation of a Suburban Bastion, 1927–39": 126.

124 O. H. Koch, "'Built-in Playgrounds,'" *City Planning* 4 (January 1928): 39–43, partially reprinted in *Garden Cities & Town Planning* 18 (March 1928): 69; "Greenway Parks," *National Real Estate Journal* 29 (April 2, 1928): 60–63; Clarence A. Perry, "The Neighborhood Unit: A Scheme of Arrangement for the Family Life Community," *Regional Survey of New York and Its Environs*, vol. 7 (New York: Regional Plan of New York and Its Environs, 1929), 68; Arthur C. Comey and Max S. Wehrly, "A Study of Planned Communities" (Department of Regional Planning of Harvard University, November 1936): 410; O. H. Koch, "Land Subdivision for City Purposes," *Bulletin of the Agricultural and Mechanical College of Texas* 12 (January 1, 1941): 54–62; Dallas Chapter, American Institute of Architects, *The Prairie's Yield: Forces Shaping Dallas Architecture from 1840–1962* (New York: Reinhold, 1962), 36; Loraine F. Goodman, *Greenway Parks: A Special Place* (Dallas: privately printed, 1980); Muriel Quest McCarthy, *David R. Williams: Pioneer Architect* (Dallas: Southern Methodist University Press, 1984), 28–31; Richard B. Peiser and Gregory M. Schwann, "The Private Value of Public Open Space Within

Subdivisions," *Journal of Architectural and Planning Research* 10 (Summer 1993): 91–104; Larry Paul Fuller, ed., *The American Institute of Architects Guide to Dallas Architecture* (New York: McGraw-Hill, 1999), 132–33; Nancy Myers, "A Neighborhood Serene," *Dallas Home Design* (January–February 2006): 46–53; Virginia Savage McAlester, Willis Cecil Winters, and Prudence Mackintosh, *Great American Suburbs: The Homes of the Park Cities, Dallas* (New York and London: Abbeville Press, 2008), 149, 198, 333, 347, 373; www.greenwayparks.com.

125 For Aguila Colony, see McCarthy, *David R. Williams: Pioneer Architect*, 23–24, 30.

126 Charles C. Savage, *Architecture of the Private Streets of St. Louis: The Architects and the Houses They Designed* (Columbia: University of Missouri Press, 1987), 3. Also see S. L. Sherer, "The Places of St. Louis, a Form of the Suburban Community Peculiar to the World's Fair City," *House and Garden* 5 (April 1904): 187–91; Norman J. Johnston, "St. Louis and the Private Residential Street," *Journal of the American Institute of Planners* 28 (August 1962): 187–93; Elinor Martineau Coyle, *Saint Louis; Portrait of a River City* (St. Louis: Folkestone Press, 1966), 90–93; Robert L. Vickery, Jr., *Anthrophysical Form: Two Families and Their Neighborhood Environments* (Charlottesville: University Press of Virginia, 1972); Robert A. M. Stern with Thomas Mellins and Raymond Gastil, *Pride of Place: Building the American Dream* (Boston: Houghton Mifflin; New York: American Heritage, 1986), 139, 142; Angela Miller, "Book Review," *Journal of the Society of Architectural Historians* 48 (March 1989): 93–94; Mark A. Hewitt, "Architecture of the Private Streets of St. Louis: The Architects and the Houses They Designed," book review, *Journal of Southern History* 55 (May 1989) 346–48; David T. Beito and Bruce Smith, "The Formation of Urban Infrastructure Through Nongovernmental Planning: The Private Places of St. Louis, 1869–1920," in *Journal of Urban History* 16 (May 1990): 263–303; Alexander Garvin, *The American City: What Works, What Doesn't* (New York: McGraw Hill, 1996), 256–58.

127 Garvin, *The American City: What Works, What Doesn't*, 257.

128 James Neal Primm, "Foreword," in Julius K. Hunter, *Westmoreland and Portland Places: The History and Architecture of America's Premier Private Streets, 1888–1988* (Columbia: University of Missouri Press, 1988), 9.

129 Sherer, "The Places of St. Louis, a Form of the Suburban Community Peculiar to the World's Fair City": 187–91.

130 Garvin, *The American City: What Works, What Doesn't*, 257.

131 Stern, *Pride of Place: Building the American Dream*, 139; Savage, *Architecture of the Private Streets of St. Louis: The Architects and the Houses They Designed*, 13–17; Beito and Smith, "The Formation of Urban Infrastructure Through Nongovernmental Planning: The Private Places of St. Louis, 1869–1920": 264; Mary Bartley, *St. Louis Lost* (St. Louis: Virginia Publishing, 1994), 22–29; "History—Lucas Place," in http://stlouis.missouri.org/501c/chm/lucas.htm.

132 Savage, *Architecture of the Private Streets of St. Louis: The Architects and the Houses They Designed*, 15.

133 Stern, *Pride of Place: Building the American Dream*, 139; Savage, *Architecture of the Private Streets of St. Louis: The Architects and the Houses They Designed*, 18–21; Beito and Smith, "The Formation of Urban Infrastructure Through Nongovernmental Planning: The Private Places of St. Louis, 1869–1920": 265–66.

134 "West Entrance to Vandeventer Place," *American Architect and Building News* 50 (December 21, 1895): 139, plate; Savage, *Architecture of the Private Streets of St. Louis: The Architects and the Houses They Designed*, 22–32; Beito and Smith, "The Formation of Urban Infrastructure Through Nongovernmental Planning: The Private Places of St. Louis, 1869–1920": 265–69; Bartley, *St. Louis Lost*, 107–18; Charles Savage, "Vandeventer Place, St. Louis, Missouri," in Jan Cigliano and Sarah Bradford Landau, eds., *The Grand American Avenue* (San Francisco: Pomegranate Artbooks, 1994), 230–57.

135 Savage, *Architecture of the Private Streets of St. Louis: The Architects and the Houses They Designed*, 22.

136 Mariana Griswold Van Rensselaer, *Henry Hobson Richardson and His Works* (Boston: Houghton Mifflin, 1888; New York: Dover, 1969), 108, 140.

137 Savage, *Architecture of the Private Streets of St. Louis: The Architects and the Houses They Designed*, 32.

138 Savage, *Architecture of the Private Streets of St. Louis: The Architects and the Houses They Designed*, 42.

139 Savage, *Architecture of the Private Streets of St. Louis: The Architects and the Houses They Designed*, 33–35.

140 Savage, *Architecture of the Private Streets of St. Louis: The Architects and the Houses They Designed*, 36–37, 38–39.

141 Advertisement, *Spectator* 370 (October 15, 1887): 123, quoted in Savage, *Architecture of the Private Streets of St. Louis: The Architects and the Houses They Designed*, 38. Also see *West Cabanne Place Historic District, National Register of Historic Places Inventory—Nomination Form* (Washington, D.C.: National Park Service, 1979).

142 Savage, *Architecture of the Private Streets of St. Louis: The Architects and the Houses They Designed*, 42–67; Hunter, *Westmoreland and Portland Places*; Bartley, *St. Louis Lost*, 128–42.

143 Savage, *Architecture of the Private Streets of St. Louis: The Architects and the Houses They Designed*, 42.

144 Carolyn Hewes Toft and Jane Molloy Porter, *Compton Heights: A History and Architectural Guide* (St. Louis: Landmarks Association of St. Louis, 1984); Savage, *Architecture of the Private Streets of St. Louis: The Architects and the Houses They Designed*, 68–74; Bartley, *St. Louis Lost*, 83–85; Philip Pregill and Nancy Volkman, *Landscapes in History: Design and Planning in the Eastern and Western Traditions* (New York: John Wiley, 1999), 537.

145 Savage, *Architecture of the Private Streets of St. Louis: The Architects and the Houses They Designed*, 68.

146 Savage, *Architecture of the Private Streets of St. Louis: The Architects and the Houses They Designed*, 75–76.

147 Savage, *Architecture of the Private Streets of St. Louis: The Architects and the Houses They Designed*, 77–81.

148 "East Entrance to Westmoreland Place," *American Architect and Building News* 50 (December 21, 1895): 139, plate; Savage, *Architecture of the Private Streets of St. Louis: The Architects and the Houses They Designed*, 90–104; Allen Freeman, "Teutonic Timepiece,"

Historic Preservation 45 (May/June 1993): 40–41; Bartley, *St. Louis Lost*, 142–46.

149 Eileen Manning Michels calls into question Ellis's contribution to the design of the Washington Terrace gatehouse, calling the attribution "ambiguous, at best" and positing that an unsigned rendering generally attributed to Ellis was "arguably . . . a pastiche of Ellis's previously published renderings put together by someone else in his orbit who was working for [George] Mann." See Eileen Manning Michels, *Reconfiguring Harvey Ellis* (Edina, Minn.: Beaver's Pond Press, 2004), 207. Ellis did sign renderings of two notably astylar unbuilt gatehouses (1893) proposed for Bell Place. See "Perspective Studies by Harvey Ellis of Entrance to Private Streets, St. Louis, Mo., George R. Mann, Architect," *Architectural Review* 15 (December 1908): 180; Michels, *Reconfiguring Harvey Ellis*, 200–202.

150 For Windermere Place, see Savage, *Architecture of the Private Streets of St. Louis: The Architects and the Houses They Designed*, 105–7. For Hortense Place, see Savage, *Architecture of the Private Streets of St. Louis: The Architects and the Houses They Designed*, 108–11. For Lenox Place, see Savage, *Architecture of the Private Streets of St. Louis: The Architects and the Houses They Designed*, 112. For Beverly Place, see Savage, *Architecture of the Private Streets of St. Louis: The Architects and the Houses They Designed*, 113–15. For Parkview, see Savage, *Architecture of the Private Streets of St. Louis: The Architects and the Houses They Designed*, 116–18; Bartley, *St. Louis Lost*, 85.

151 David E. Tarn, "Co-operative Group Planning: A Suburban Development, Henry Wright, Architect & Landscape Architect," *Architectural Record* 34 (November 1913): 467–75; Henry Wright, "The Autobiography of Another Idea," *Western Architect* 39 (September 1930): 137–41, 153; Henry N. Wright, "Radburn Revisited," *Architectural Forum* 135 (July–August 1971): 52–57; *Brentmoor Park, Brentmoor and Forest Ridge, National Register of Historic Places Inventory—Nomination Form* (Washington, D.C.: National Park Service, 1982); Savage, *Architecture of the Private Streets of St. Louis: The Architects and the Houses They Designed*, 11; Cydney Millstein, "Henry Wright," in Charles A. Birnbaum and Robin Karson, eds., *Pioneers of American Landscape Design* (New York: McGraw-Hill, 2000), 461–64; Eileen Ostermeier, "Brentmoor Park & Delmar Garden: Henry Wright in St. Louis," *Society of Architectural Historians Missouri Valley Chapter Newsletter* IX (Winter 2003): 1–2. For Henry Wright, see Henry S. Churchill, "Henry Wright, 1878–1936," *Journal of the American Institute of Planners* 26 (November 1960): 293–301; Alan Mather, "Henry Wright," *Pencil Points* 21 (January 1940): 3–14; Millstein, "Henry Wright," in Birnbaum and Karson, eds., *Pioneers of American Landscape Design*, 461–64.

152 For Henry Wright, see Henry S. Churchill, "Henry Wright, 1878–1936," *Journal of the American Institute of Planners* 26 (November 1960): 293–301; Alan Mather, "Henry Wright," *Pencil Points* 21 (January 1940): 3–14; Millstein, "Henry Wright," in Birnbaum and Karson, eds., *Pioneers of American Landscape Design*, 461–64.

153 *Brentmoor Park, Brentmoor and Forest Ridge, National Register of Historic Places Inventory—Nomination Form*, 6.

154 David E. Tarn, "Co-operative Group Planning: A Suburban Development, Henry Wright, Architect & Landscape Architect," *Architectural Record* 34 (November 1913): 467–75.

155 "Carrswold Historic District, National Register of Historic Places Inventory—Nomination Form," (United States Department of the Interior, May 1982); Frank Peters and George McCue, *A Guide to the Architecture of St. Louis* (Columbia: University of Missouri Press, 1989), 130–31.

156 Edward A. Leary, *Indianapolis: The Story of a City* (Indianapolis and New York: Bobbs-Merrill, 1971), 117–18; Wesley I. Shank, *Woodruff Place, Historic American Buildings Survey, HABS No. IND-67* (1977); Woodruff Place Civic League and Neighborhood Volunteers and Staff of the Indianapolis Historic Preservation Commission, *Woodruff Place Historic Area Preservation Plan* (September 2001); Janet Schmidt, Robert W. Smith, and Dorothy A. Nicholson, *Woodruff Place, Indianapolis, Indiana, Visual Collection, Ca. 1875–1980* (Indianapolis: Indiana Historical Society, 2007).

157 Shank, *Woodruff Place, Historic American Buildings Survey, HABS No. IND-67*, 3.

158 Bert Joseph Griswold, *The Pictorial History of Fort Wayne, Indiana: Volume 2* (Chicago: Robert O. Law Co., 1917), 120–21; Ralph Violette, *Fort Wayne, Indiana* (Charleston, S. C.: Arcadia Publishing, 1999), 65; *Forest Park Boulevard Historic District, National Register of Historic Places Registration Form* (Washington, D. C.: National Park Service, 2006); Angela M. Quinn, *Indiana's Historic Suburban Developments: A Hoosier Heritage of Community Design* (Fort Wayne: ARCH, 2010), 40–41, 42.

159 Francis H. Bulot, "Developing a Restricted Home Community," *American City* 15 (July 1916): 533–35; John R. Stilgoe, *Borderland: Origins of the American Suburb, 1820–1939* (New Haven, Conn., and London: Yale University Press, 1988), 223–24; Angela M. Quinn, *Indiana's Historic Suburban Developments: A Hoosier Heritage of Community Design* (Fort Wayne: ARCH, 2010), 41, 43, 44, 45; "Shawnee Place Historic District," in http://www.cityoffortwayne.org/index.php?option=com_content&task=view&id=111&Itemid=254.

160 Walter B. Stevens, *Centennial History of Missouri (The Center State) One Hundred Years in the Union, 1820–1921* (St. Louis: S. J. Clarke, 1921), 900–901; William H. Wilson, *The City Beautiful Movement in Kansas City* (Columbia: University of Missouri Press, 1964), 43, 130.

161 William H. Wilson, *The City Beautiful Movement in Kansas City* (Columbia: University of Missouri Press, 1964), 44, 130; *Historic Kansas City Architecture* (Kansas City: Landmarks Commission of Kansas City, Missouri, 1975), n.p.; Landmarks Commission, Kansas City, Mo., *Kansas City: A Place in Time* (1977); William S. Worley, *J. C. Nichols and the Shaping of Kansas City: Innovation in Planned Residential Communities* (Columbia: University of Missouri Press, 1990), 57–59; "Kansas City's Historic Hyde Park/Janssen Place Historic District, National & Kansas City Register of Historic Places," in http://www.hydeparkkansascity.retrosites.com/index.php?option=com_content&task=view&id=141&Itemid=40.

162 William H. Wilson, *The City Beautiful Movement in Kansas City* (Columbia: University of Missouri Press, 1964), 18–19, 130; *Rockhill Neighborhood, National Register of Historic Places Inventory—Nomination Form* (Washington D.C.: National Park Service, 1975); Anne Sutton Canfield, *Kansas City: A Place in Time* (Kansas City: Landmarks Commission of Kansas City, Missouri, 1977), 208; William S. Worley, *J. C. Nichols and the Shaping of Kansas City* (Columbia and London: University of Missouri Press, 1990),

60–62, 67, 82, 94, 97–98, 163, 248, 290; *American Institute of Architects Guide to Kansas City Architecture & Public Art* (Kansas City: American Institute of Architects/Kansas City, 2000), 35.

163 Worley, *J. C. Nichols and the Shaping of Kansas City*, 93–94.

164 http://www.historicbostonedison.org.

165 *Chatham Fields, Gem of the South Side*, pamphlet (Chicago: Wm. E. Harmon & Co., c. 1915); Joan E. Draper, *Edward H. Bennett, Architect and City Planner, 1874–1954* (Chicago: Art Institute, 1982); Robert Bruegmann, "Built Environment of the Chicago Region," in Ann Durkin Keating, ed., *Chicago Neighborhoods and Suburbs: A Historical Guide* (Chicago: University of Chicago Press, 2008), 123, 124.

166 Bruegmann, "Built Environment of the Chicago Region," in Keating, *Chicago Neighborhoods and Suburbs*, 123.

167 "Trier Center Neighborhood, Winnetka, Ill.," *Western Architect* 20 (August 1913): 67–70; Mark L. Peisch, "The Chicago School and Walter Burley Griffin, 1893–1914" (Ph.D. diss., Columbia University, 1959): 134–37; James Birrell, *Walter Burley Griffin* (St. Lucia, Brisbane: University of Queensland Press, 1964), 42, 44, 57–58, 61; Mark L. Peisch, *The Chicago School of Architecture: Early Followers of Sullivan and Wright* (London: Phaidon Press, 1964), 99, 101, 110, 114, 142, fig. 27; Sally Anderson Chappell, "Barry Byrne, Architect: His Formative Years," *Prairie School Review* 3 (Fourth Quarter, 1966): 14; Albert J. Drap Jr. and Thomas A. Heinz, "Walter Burley Griffin: Comprehensive Subdivision Planning in the Midwest," (May 25, 1972): n.p.; Donald Leslie Johnson, *The Architecture of Walter Burley Griffin* (Melbourne: Macmillan Company of Australia, 1977), 28; Peter Harrison, *Walter Burley Griffin: Landscape Architect* (Canberra: National Library of Australia, 1995), 52–53; Donald Dunbar, "Of Social Concern: Towns and Buildings for Ordinary Australians," in Jeff Turnbull and Peter Y. Navaretti, eds., *The Griffins in Australia and India* (Melbourne: The Miegunyah Press, 1998), 28.

168 "Trier Center Neighborhood, Winnetka, Ill.": 67.

169 Peisch, "The Chicago School and Walter Burley Griffin, 1893–1914": 135.

170 "Trier Center Neighborhood, Winnetka, Ill.": 69–70.

171 "Trier Center Neighborhood, Winnetka, Ill.": 67.

172 "Trier Center Neighborhood, Winnetka, Ill.": 68, 70.

173 Johnson, *The Architecture of Walter Burley Griffin*, 28.

174 *Sessions Village: The Development of an Ideal* (Columbus, Ohio: Converse & Fulton, 1927); Bill Arter, *Columbus Vignettes, Vol. 2* (Columbus, Ohio: Nida-Eckstein Printing, 1967), 43; Jane Ware, *Building Ohio: A Traveler's Guide to Ohio's Urban Architecture* (Wilmington, Ohio: Orange Frazer, 2001), 222–23; Jeffrey T. Darbee and Nancy A. Recchie, *AIA Guide to Columbus* (Athens: Ohio University Press, 2008), 240–41.

175 *Sessions Village: The Development of an Ideal*, n.p.

176 Edmund Drew Fisher, *Flatbush, Past and Present* (Brooklyn: Flatbush Trust Co., 1902), 47, 84; Andrew Scott Dolkart, *Suburbanization of Flatbush* (Preservation thesis, Columbia University, January 1977); Landmarks Preservation Commission of the City of New York, LP-0989 (July 11 1978), 2; Stern, Mellins, and Fishman, *New York 1880*, 940, 941.

177 Fisher, *Flatbush, Past and Present*, 84; Landmarks Preservation Commission of the City of New York, LP-0988 (July 11, 1978); Norval White and Elliot Willensky, *AIA Guide to New York City* (San Diego: Harcourt Brace Jovanovich, 1988), 698; Christopher Gray, "Fire-Damaged Flatbush Landmark May Be Razed," *New York Times* (April 3, 1988), X: 8; Barbaralee Diamonstein, *The Landmarks of New York II* (New York: Harry N. Abrams, 1993), 214.

178 *Brooklyn Daily Eagle*, quoted in Gray, "Fire-Damaged Flatbush Landmark May Be Razed": 8.

179 "House at Flatbush, L.I. for W. A. Porter," *Building* 6 (April 16, 1887): 145, plate.

180 Herbert F. Gunnison, *Flatbush of To-Day* (Brooklyn, 1908), 37. Also see "Prospect Park South," *Architects and Builders Magazine* 3 (January 1902): 134–40; Henry Harrison Lewis, "Building Towns to Order," *World's Work* 6 (May 1903): 3438–44; Dolkart, *Suburbanization of Flatbush*; Marcia Chambers, "Metropolitan Baedeker, Flatbush," *New York Times* (May 7, 1978), C: 4; Marge Blaine and Roberta Intrater, "The Grandeur That Is Flatbush," *New York* 14 (August 14, 1978): 42–46; Landmarks Preservation Commission of the City of New York, *Prospect Park South Historic District Designation Report* (New York, 1979); Paul Goldberger, "To Utopia by Bus and Subway," *New York Times* (April 17, 1981), C: 1, 24; Stern, Gilmartin, and Massengale, *New York 1900*, 424–25; Andrew S. Dolkart, *This is Brooklyn: A Guide to the Borough's Historic Districts and Landmarks* (Brooklyn: Fund for the Borough of Brooklyn, 1990), 68–70; Alexander Garvin, *The American City: What Works, What Doesn't*, 2nd ed. (New York: McGraw Hill, 2002), 310. Petit & Green's Japanese house, with its garden by Chogoro Sugai, color scheme and decorations by Shunsi Ishikawa was offered for sale at $26,500 by Alvord in an advertisement in *Country Life in America* 4 (July 1903): 169.

181 Quoted in Dolkart, *This is Brooklyn*, 68–69.

182 "Pavement Construction in Clearwater, Florida," *Good Roads* VII (March 7, 1914): 145–49; *Harbor Oaks Residential District, National Register of Historic Places Historic District Designation Report* (Washington, D.C.: National Park Service, 1988); Diane Steinle, "Historic Status Is Key to Preserving Harbor Oaks," *St. Petersburg Times* (July 31, 1988): 1, 3; Lisa Coleman, *Clearwater* (Charleston, S.C.: Arcadia, 2002), 22.

183 Dolkart, *Suburbanization of Flatbush*, 40–45; Landmarks Preservation Commission of the City of New York, *Ditmas Park Historic District Designation Report* (New York, 1981); Stern, Gilmartin, and Massengale, *New York 1900*, 425; Dolkart, *This is Brooklyn: A Guide to the Borough's Historic Districts and Landmarks*, 64–66; Barbaralee Diamonstein-Spielvogel, *The Landmarks of New York* (New York: Monacelli Press, 2005), 589.

184 Lewis Pounds, quoted in Gunnison, *Flatbush of To-day*, 93.

185 Dolkart, *Suburbanization of Flatbush*, 45–47; Stern, Gilmartin, and Massengale, *New York 1900*, 425; Landmarks Preservation Commission of the City of New York, *Fiske Terrace-Midwood Park Historic District Designation Report* (New York, 2008).

186 *Laburnum Park*, promotional brochure (Richmond, Va.: Laburnum Corporation, 1919); Sarah Driggs, "Laburnum Court," *Ginter Park Residents Association Newsletter*

(June 1999); *Laburnum Park Historic District, National Register of Historic Places Registration Form* (Washington, D.C.: National Park Service, 2001); Richard Guy Wilson, ed., *Buildings of Virginia: Tidewater and Piedmont* (New York: Oxford University Press, 2002), 284; *Laburnum Park Historic District, National Register of Historic Places Registration Form (2006 Amendment)* (Washington D.C.: National Park Service, 2006).

187 Rosa Park (1891), Audubon Place (1894), Richmond Place (1905), Everett Place (1906), Audubon Boulevard (1909), Dunleith Court (1910), State Street Drive (1914), Vincennes Place (1915), Newcomb Boulevard (1917), Wirth Place (1919), Trianon Plaza (1925), Versailles Boulevard (1925).

188 Susan Lauxman Kirk and Helen Michel Smith, *The Architecture of St. Charles Avenue* (Gretna, La.: Pelican, 1977), 52, 53; Robert J. Cangelosi, "Residential Parks," in Friends of the Cabildo, *New Orleans Architecture, Volume VIII: The University Section* (Gretna, La.: Pelican, 1997), 65–66, 69–72.

189 *The WPA Guide to New Orleans* (Boston: Houghton Mifflin, 1938; New York: Pantheon, 1983), 222–23; Susan Lauxman Kirk and Helen Michel Smith, *The Architecture of St. Charles Avenue* (Gretna, La.: Pelican, 1977), 66–67; Christopher Gray, "Audubon Place," *House & Garden* 155 (June 1983): 62, 64; Carolyn Kolb, *The Dolphin Guide to New Orleans* rev. ed. (1972; Garden City, N.Y.: Dolphin, 1984), 115; Roulhac Toledano, *The National Trust Guide to New Orleans* (New York: John Wiley & Sons, 1996), 176; Robert J. Cangelosi, "Residential Parks," in Friends of the Cabildo, *New Orleans Architecture, Volume VIII: The University Section* (Gretna, La.: Pelican, 1997), 68, 72–77; Karen Kingsley, *Buildings of Louisiana* (New York: Oxford University Press, 2003), 131; Dorian Hastings, "Early Neighborhood Development in New Orleans, Neither New South Nor Old" (Ph.D. diss.: University of New Orleans, 2004): 205–7.

190 Robert J. Cangelosi, "Residential Parks," in Friends of the Cabildo, *New Orleans Architecture, Volume VIII: The University Section* (Gretna, La.: Pelican, 1997), 77–80.

191 Robert J. Cangelosi, "Residential Parks," in Friends of the Cabildo, *New Orleans Architecture, Volume VIII: The University Section* (Gretna, La.: Pelican, 1997), 80–81.

192 Robert J. Cangelosi, "Residential Parks," in Friends of the Cabildo, *New Orleans Architecture, Volume VIII: The University Section* (Gretna, La.: Pelican, 1997), 82–84.

193 Marjorie Longenecker White, "Glen Iris Park and the Residence of Robert Jemison, Sr.," *Journal of the Birmingham Historical Society* 6 (July 1979): 6.

194 Philip A. Morris and Marjorie Longenecker White, eds., *Designs on Birmingham: A Landscape History of a Southern City and Its Suburbs* (Birmingham, Ala.: Birmingham Historical Society, 1989), 13. Also see S. Mays Ball, "The Suburbs Beautiful," *House and Garden* 15 (May 1909): 166–71; White, "Glen Iris Park and the Residence of Robert Jemison, Sr.": 4–13; "The Birmingham Public Library," *Newsletter/The Catalog of Landscape Records in the United States* 9 (Fall 1997/Winter 1998): 1–2; Philip Pregill and Nancy Volkman, *Landscapes in History: Design and Planning the Eastern and Western Traditions* (New York: John Wiley, 1999), 532.

195 W. G. Love, "Suburbs of Houston," in Mrs. Henry Fall, *The Key to the City of Houston* (Houston: State Printing Company, 1908); Dorothy Knox Howe Houghton, Barrie M. Scardino, Sadie Gwin Blackburn, and Katherine S. Howe, *Houston's Forgotten Heritage: Landscape, Houses, Interiors, 1824–1914* (Houston: Rice University Press, 1991; College Station: Texas A&M University Press, 1998), 46–47, 50, 99; Cheryl Lynn Caldwell Ferguson, "Upscale Suburban Architecture and Development in Dallas and Houston, Texas, 1890–1930" (Ph.D. diss.: University of Delaware, 2004): 355–56.

196 Love, "Suburbs of Houston," in Fall, *The Key to the City of Houston*, as quoted in Ferguson, "Upscale Suburban Architecture and Development in Dallas and Houston, Texas, 1890–1930": 356.

197 Howard Barnstone, *The Architecture of John F. Staub, Houston and the South* (Austin: University of Texas, 1979), 5; *Houston Architectural Survey, Volume Six: Supplement* (Houston: Southwest Center for Urban Research, 1981), 1363–71; Stephen Fox, "Courtlandt Place on Tour," *Texas Architect* 32 (November 1982): 62–63; Houghton et al., *Houston's Forgotten Heritage*, 46–47, 101, 162, 279, 319; Stephen Fox, *Houston Architectural Guide*, 2nd ed. (Houston: American Institute of Architects/Houston Chapter and Herring Press, 1999), 70–71; Cheryl Lynn Caldwell Ferguson, "Upscale Suburban Architecture and Development in Dallas and Houston, Texas, 1890–1930" (Ph.D. diss.: University of Delaware, 2004): 356–57.

198 Barnstone, *The Architecture of John F. Staub, Houston and the South*, 5; *Houston Architectural Survey, Volume Five* (Houston: Southwest Center for Urban Research, 1980), 1126–38; Christopher Gray, "All the Best Places/Shadyside," *House & Garden* 155 (August 1983): 46–47, 50; Sadie Gwin Blackburn, "The Evolution of the Houston Landscape," in Houghton, et. al., *Houston's Forgotten Heritage*, 58, 191; Marguerite Johnston, *Houston, the Unknown City, 1836–1946* (College Station: Texas A & M University, 1991), 228–29; Patrick J. Nicholson, *William Ward Watkin and the Rice Institute* (Houston: Gulf Publishing Company, 1991), 177–80; H. T. Lindeberg, *Domestic Architecture of H. T. Lindeberg* (New York: Acanthus, 1996), XIII: 134–35; Stephen Fox, *Houston Architectural Guide*, 2nd ed. (Houston: American Institute of Architects/Houston Chapter and Herring Press, 1999), 90–92; Stephen Fox, *Rice University* (New York: Princeton Architectural Press, 2001), 192–95; Ferguson, "Upscale Suburban Architecture and Development in Dallas and Houston, Texas, 1890–1930": 360–61.

199 Joseph S. Cullinan, quoted in Gray, "All the Best Places/Shadyside": 46.

200 Barnstone, *The Architecture of John F. Staub, Houston and the South*, 7; *Houston Architectural Survey, Volume Five* (Houston: Southwest Center for Urban Research, 1980), 1113–15; Marguerite Johnston, *Houston, the Unknown City, 1836–1946* (College Station: Texas A & M University, 1991), 230; Stephen Fox, *Houston Architectural Guide*, 2nd ed. (Houston: American Institute of Architects/Houston Chapter and Herring Press, 1999), 94–95.

201 Patrick J. Nicholson, *William Ward Watkin and the Rice Institute* (Houston: Gulf Publishing Company, 1991), 179; Stephen Fox, *Houston Architectural Guide*, 2nd ed. (Houston: American Institute of Architects/Houston Chapter and Herring Press, 1999), 102–3; Stephen Fox, *Rice University* (New York: Princeton Architectural Press, 2001), 208–9; Stephen Fox, "Watkin, William Ward," in http://www.tsha.utexas.edu/handbook/online/articles/ww/fwa91.htm.

202 Barnstone, *The Architecture of John F. Staub, Houston and the South*, 7; "Broadacres

Historic District," *Houston Architectural Survey, Volume Six: Supplement* (Houston: Southwest Center for Urban Research, 1981), 1335–59; Marguerite Johnston, *Houston, the Unknown City, 1836–1946* (College Station: Texas A & M University, 1991), 230–31; Patrick J. Nicholson, *William Ward Watkin and the Rice Institute* (Houston: Gulf Publishing Company, 1991), 180–81; Stephen Fox, *Houston Architectural Guide*, 2nd ed. (Houston: American Institute of Architects/Houston Chapter and Herring Press, 1999), 95–97; Ferguson, "Upscale Suburban Architecture and Development in Dallas and Houston, Texas, 1890–1930": 361–62; Stephen Fox, *The Country Houses of John F. Staub* (College Station: Texas A&M University Press, 2007), 16–66.

203 Fox, *The Country Houses of John F. Staub*, 19–20.

204 Peter D. Waldman, "Braeswood: On the Last Neighborhood in Houston," *Cite* (Winter 1986): 12; Stephen Fox, "Braeswood: an Architectural Tour," *Cite* (Winter 1986): 12–13.

205 *Elizabeth Boulevard Historic District, National Register of Historic Places Inventory—Registration Form* (Washington, D.C.: National Park Service, 1979); *Tarrant County Historic Resources Survey: Phase III, Fort Worth's Southside* (Fort Worth: Historic Preservation Council for Tarrant County, 1986), 3–4, 5, 7, 11; Carol Roark, *Fort Worth's Legendary Landmarks* (Ft. Worth: Texas Christian University Press, 1995), 104–5; Carol Roark, *Fort Worth Then & Now* (Fort Worth: Texas Christian University Press, 2001), 68–69; Cheryl Lynn Caldwell Ferguson, "Upscale Suburban Architecture and Development in Dallas and Houston, Texas, 1890–1930" (Ph.D. diss.: University of Delaware, 2004): 441.

206 *Swiss Avenue Historic District, National Register Historic District Designation Report* (Washington, D.C.: National Park Service, 1974); *Munger Place Historic District, National Register Historic District Designation Report* (Washington, D.C.: National Park Service, 1978); R. Lawrence Good, "Neighborhoods," in *Dallasights: An Anthology of Architecture and Open Spaces* (Dallas: American Institute of Architects Dallas Chapter, 1978), 124–25; William L. McDonald, *Dallas: a Photographic Chronicle Rediscovered: Of Urban Expansion, 1870–1925* (Dallas: Dallas Historical Society, 1978), 155, 161–66; Douglas Newby and Jim Bratton, *A Guide to the Older Neighborhoods of Dallas* (Dallas: Historic Preservation League, Inc., 1986), 22–29; Virginia and Lee McAlester, *A Field Guide to America's Historic Neighborhoods and Museum Houses: The Western States* (New York: Alfred A. Knopf, 1998), 570–72; Cheryl Lynn Caldwell Ferguson, "Upscale Suburban Architecture and Development in Dallas and Houston, Texas, 1890–1930" (Ph.D. diss.: University of Delaware, 2004): 76–139.

207 Sidney D. Maxwell, *The Suburbs of Cincinnati: Sketches, Historical and Descriptive* (Cincinnati: Geo. E. Stevens & Co., 1870), 76–99; Harland Bartholomew & Associates, *The Village Plan, Glendale, Ohio* (Glendale: Prepared for the Village Planning Commission, 1944); Angeline Loveland Faran, *Glendale, Ohio, 1855–1955* (Cincinnati, Ohio: McDonald Printing Company, 1955); John Archer, "Country and City in the American Romantic Suburb," *Journal of the Society of Architectural Historians* 42 (May 1983): 139–56; Spiro Kostof, *America By Design* (New York: Oxford University Press, 1987), 27–28; John Clubbe, *Cincinnati Observed: Architecture and History* (Columbus: Ohio State University Press, 1992), 432–47; Alexandra M. Buckley, "Glendale Ohio: A Study of Early Suburban Development in America" (Master's thesis, University of Oregon, March 1993); Philip Pregill and Nancy Volkman, *Landscapes in History: Design and Planning in the Eastern and Western Traditions* (New York: John Wiley, 1999), 532–33; Leland M. Roth, *American Architecture: A History* (Boulder, CO: Icon Editions/Westview Press, 2001), 199–200, 202; Susan L. Klaus, *A Modern Arcadia: Frederick Law Olmsted Jr. and the Plan for Forest Hills Gardens* (Amherst and Boston: University of Massachusetts Press in association with Library of American Landscape History, 2002), 58; Jon A. Peterson, *The Birth of City Planning in the United States, 1840–1917* (Baltimore and London: Johns Hopkins University Press, 2003), 24.

208 Maxwell, *The Suburbs of Cincinnati*, 77–78.

209 Maxwell, *The Suburbs of Cincinnati*, 99.

210 Charles C. Arensberg, "Evergreen Hamlet," *Western Pennsylvania Historical Magazine* 38 (Fall–Winter 1955): 117–33; Stefan Lorant, *Pittsburgh: The Story of an American City* (Garden City, N.Y.: Doubleday, 1964), 106–7; Edgar Kaufmann Jr., ed., *The Rise of an American Architecture* (New York: Praeger in association with the Metropolitan Museum of Art, 1970), 230; Edgar Kaufmann Jr., "Environment Is an Art," *Metropolitan Museum of Art Bulletin* 28 (April 1970): 321–30; Charles C. Arensberg, "Evergreen Hamlet: Another Utopia," *Carnegie Magazine* 46 (May 1972): 207–13; Jane B. Davies, "Llewellyn Park in West Orange, New Jersey," *Antiques* 107 (January 1975): 142–58; John Archer, "Country and City in the American Romantic Suburb," *Journal of the Society of Architectural Historians* 42 (May 1983): 139–56; David Schuyler, *The New Urban Landscape* (Baltimore and London: Johns Hopkins University Press, 1986), 156–57; Philip Pregill and Nancy Volkman, *Landscapes in History: Design and Planning in the Eastern and Western Traditions* (New York: John Wiley, 1999), 532; John Archer, *Architecture and Suburbia: From English Villa to American Dream House, 1690–2000* (Minneapolis: University of Minnesota Press, 2005), 224–25.

211 *The Constitution of Evergreen Hamlet* (c. 1851), 2, quoted in Archer, *Architecture and Suburbia*, 225.

212 Quoted in Lorant, *Pittsburgh: The Story of an American City*, 107.

213 Quoted in Arensberg, "Evergreen Hamlet": 208, 213.

214 Archer, *Architecture and Suburbia*, 224.

215 Frederick Law Olmsted, quoted in David Schuyler, "Frederick Law Olmsted's Riverside," *Planning History Present* 7 (No. 2, 1993): 1–5. Also see Olmsted, Vaux & Co., *Preliminary Report Upon the Proposed Suburban Village at Riverside, Near Chicago* (1868), reprinted in S. B. Sutton, ed., *Civilizing American Cities: A Selection of Frederick Law Olmsted's Writings on City Landscapes* (Cambridge, Mass., and London: MIT Press, 1979), 292–305, and David Schuyler and Jane Turner Censer, eds., *The Years of Olmsted, Vaux & Company, 1865–1874*, vol. 6 (Baltimore and London: Johns Hopkins University Press, 1992), 273–90; Olmsted, Vaux & Co., "Notes on Tree Grouping at Riverside (ca. 1868)," in Schuyler and Censer, eds., *The Years of Olmsted, Vaux & Company, 1865–1874*, vol. 6, 303–4; Frederick Law Olmsted, letter to Leverett W. Murray, April 24, 1869, in Schuyler and Censer, eds., *The Years of Olmsted, Vaux & Company, 1865–1874*, vol. 6, 343–46; "Riverside," *American Builder* 2 (December 1869): 228–29; Riverside

Improvement Company, *Riverside in 1871* (Chicago: D. & C. H. Blakely, Printers, 1871); Everett Chamberlin, *Chicago and Its Suburbs* (Chicago: T. A. Hungerford & Co., 1874), 415–16; A. T. Andreas, *History of Cook County, Illinois: From the Earliest Period to the Present Time* (Chicago: A. T. Andreas, Publisher, 1884), 876–77; *Picturesque Riverside* (Chicago: J. W. Taylor, ca. 1887); "Riverside, Illinois: A Residential Neighborhood Designed Over Sixty Years Ago," *Landscape Architecture* 21 (July 1931): 257–91; Howard K. Menhinick, "Riverside Sixty Years Later," *Landscape Architecture* 22 (January 1932): 109–17; Thomas Adams, *The Design of Residential Areas* (Cambridge, Mass.: Harvard University Pres, 1934), 237–40; Herbert J. Bassman, ed., *Riverside: Then and Now* (Riverside, Ill.: Riverside News, 1936; Chicago: University of Chicago Press, 1958), 116–19; Mrs. E. O. C. Hoefer, "A Model Suburb Is Born," in Bassman, ed., *Riverside: Then and Now*, 72–105; James Dahir, *Communities for Better Living* (New York: Harper & Brothers, 1950), 177–78; Leonard K. Eaton, "The American Suburb: Dream and Nightmare," *Landscape* 13 (Winter 1963–64): 12–16; John W. Reps, *The Making of Urban America* (Princeton, N.J.: Princeton University Press, 1965), 347–48; Walter L. Creese, *The Search for Environment*, exp. ed. (Baltimore and London: Johns Hopkins University Press, 1966, 1992), 153–57; Julius Gy. Fabos, Gordon T. Milde, and V. Michael Weinmayr, *Frederick Law Olmsted, Sr.: Founder of American Landscape Architecture in America* (Amherst: University of Massachusetts Press, 1968), 47–55; H. Mayer and R. C. Wade, *Chicago: Growth of a Metropolis* (Chicago: University of Chicago Press, 1969), 184; *Riverside: A Village in a Park* (Riverside, Ill.: Frederick Law Olmsted Society of Riverside, 1970); Christopher Tunnard, *The City of Man*, 2nd ed. (New York: Charles Scribner's Sons, 1970), 192–93, 202–3; Norman T. Newton, *Design on the Land: The Development of Landscape Architecture* (Cambridge, Mass., and London: Harvard University Press, 1971), 464–69; Albert Fein, *Frederick Law Olmsted and the American Environmental Tradition* (New York: George Braziller, 1972), 33–35, fig. 21; Victoria Post Ranney, *Olmsted in Chicago* (Chicago: R. R. Donnelley, 1972), 4, 10–15; Laura Wood Roper, *FLO: A Biography of Frederick Law Olmsted* (Baltimore and London: Johns Hopkins University Press, 1973), 322–24; Robert W. Heidrich, "'A Village in a Park': Riverside, Illinois," *Historic Preservation* 25 (April–June 1973): 28–33; Perry Duis, *Chicago: Creating New Traditions* (Chicago: Chicago Historical Society, 1976), 40–41; Gunther Barth, *City People* (New York: Oxford University Press, 1980), 40–41; Gérard Bauer, Gildas Baudez, and Jean-Michel Roux, *Banlieues de charme* (Aix-en-Provence: Pandora Editions, 1980), 17–38; Carl Abbott, "'Necessary Adjuncts to Its Growth:' The Railroad Suburbs of Chicago, 1854–1875," *Journal of the Illinois State Historical Society* 73 (Summer 1980): 117–31; Stern with Massengale, *The Anglo-American Suburb*, 24; Theodore Turak, "Riverside: Roots in France," *Inland Architect* 25 (November 1981): 12–19; Cynthia Zaitzevsky, *Frederick Law Olmsted and the Boston Park System* (Cambridge, Mass.: Harvard University Press, 1982), 28–29; Walter L. Creese, *The Crowning of the American Landscape* (Princeton, N.J.: Princeton University Press, 1985), 221–40; Kenneth T. Jackson, *Crabgrass Frontier: The Suburbanization of the United States* (New York: Oxford University Press, 1985), 79–81, 84–86; John Coolidge, "American Architecture: The Search for Tradition," in David G. De Long, Helen Searing, and Robert A.M. Stern, eds., *American Architecture: Innovation and Tradition* (New York: Rizzoli International Publications, 1986), 171–83; David Schuyler, *The New Urban Landscape* (Baltimore and London: Johns Hopkins University Press, 1986), 162–66; Robert A. M. Stern, *Pride of Place: Building the American Dream* (Boston: Houghton Mifflin; New York: American Heritage, 1986), 133–34, 142, 146; Robert Fishman, *Bourgeois Utopias: The Rise and Fall of Suburbia* (New York: Basic Books, 1987), 126–33; John Zukowsky, "Introduction," in John Zukowsky, ed., *Chicago Architecture, 1872–1922: Birth of a Metropolis* (Munich: Prestel Verlag, 1987), 22; "Riverside," *Abitare* (July–August 1987): 196–203, 321; Malcolm Cairns and Gary Kesler, "Protecting a Prototype," *Landscape Architecture* 77 (July/August 1987): 62–65, 100; Michael H. Ebner, *Creating Chicago's North Shore: A Suburban History* (Chicago and London: University of Chicago Press, 1988), 42, 45; John R. Stilgoe, *Borderland: Origins of the American Suburb, 1820–1939* (New Haven, Conn., and London: Yale University Press, 1988), 258–59; Dana F. White, "Frederick Law Olmsted, the Placemaker," in Daniel Schaffer, ed., *Two Centuries of American Planning* (Baltimore: Johns Hopkins University Press, 1988), 97–98; William S. Worley, *J. C. Nichols and the Shaping of Kansas City* (Columbia and London: University of Missouri Press, 1990), 26–29; Schuyler and Censer, eds., *The Years of Olmsted, Vaux & Company, 1865–1874*, vol. 6, 29–32; Alexandra M. Buckley, "Glendale Ohio: A Study of Early Suburban Development in America" (Master's thesis, University of Oregon, March 1993), 89–94; Arleyn A. Levee, "The Olmsted Brothers' Residential Communities: A Preview of a Career Legacy," in Charles A. Birnbaum, ed., *The Landscape Universe: Historic Designated Districts in Context* (Bronx: Wave Hill, 1993), 28–45; William Alex, *Calvert Vaux: Architect and Planner* (New York: Ink, Inc., 1994), 21–22, 162–63; Charles E. Beveridge and Paul Rocheleau, *Frederick Law Olmsted: Designing the American Landscape*, rev. ed. (New York: Rizzoli International Publications, 1995, 1998), 102–6; Lee Hall, *Olmsted's America: An 'Unpractical' Man and His Vision of Civilization* (Boston: Little, Brown & Co., 1995), 164–66; Francis R. Kowsky, *Country, Park and City: The Architecture and Life of Calvert Vaux* (New York: Oxford University Press, 1998), 102, 200, 227, 292; Philip Pregill and Nancy Volkman, *Landscapes in History: Design and Planning in the Eastern and Western Traditions* (New York: John Wiley, 1999), 535–36; Witold Rybczynski, *A Clearing in the Distance: Frederick Law Olmsted and America in the Nineteenth Century* (New York: Scribner, 1999), 290–302; Robert A. M. Stern, "In Praise of Invented Towns," Seaside Prize Acceptance Speech, Seaside, Florida, May 15, 1999, in Cynthia Davidson, ed., *Tradition and Invention in Architecture: Conversations and Essays Robert A. M. Stern* (New Haven and London: Yale University Press, 2011), 39–46; Elmer W. Johnson, *Chicago Metropolis 2020* (Chicago and London: University of Chicago Press, 2001), 132; Peter Hall, *Cities of Tomorrow: An Intellectual History of Urban Planning and Design in the Twentieth Century*, 3rd ed. (Oxford and Malden, Mass.: Blackwell Publishers, 2002), 376–79; Susan L. Klaus, *A Modern Arcadia: Frederick Law Olmsted Jr. and the Plan for Forest Hills Gardens* (Amherst: University of Massachusetts Press, 2002), 57–59, 112–13; Andrés Duany, Elizabeth Plater-Zyberk, and Robert Alminana, *The New Civic Art: Elements of Town Planning* (New York: Rizzoli International Publications, 2003), 93; Dolores Hayden, *Building Suburbia: Green Fields and Urban Growth, 1820–2000* (New York: Pantheon Books, 2003), 61–66; Ann Durkin Keating, *Chicagoland: City and Suburbs*

in the Railroad Age (Chicago and London: University of Chicago Press, 2005), 93–96, 148–53; Frank Edgerton Martin, "Rethinking Riverside," *Landscape Architecture* 95 (October 2005): 44–55; Thaïsa Way, *Unbounded Practice: Women and Landscape Architecture in the Early Twentieth Century* (Charlottesville and London: University of Virginia Press, 2009), 226; Tom Martinson, *The Atlas of American Architecture: 2000 Years of Architecture, City Planning, Landscape Architecture, and Civil Engineering* (New York: Rizzoli International Publications, 2009), 366–67.

216 Quoted in Mayer and Wade, *Chicago: Growth of a Metropolis*, 184.

217 *Prospectus of the Riverside Improvement Enterprise* (n.p., n.d.), in the Laura Wood Roper Files, Washington, D.C.; *Riverside Directory* (1869), quoted in Mayer and Wade, *Chicago: Growth of a Metropolis*, 183–86.

218 Quoted in Mayer and Wade, *Chicago: Growth of a Metropolis*, 184.

219 Olmsted, Vaux & Company, *Preliminary Report Upon the Proposed Suburban Village at Riverside, Near Chicago* (New York, 1868), quoted in Sutton, ed., *Civilizing American Cities: A Selection of Frederick Law Olmsted's Writings on City Landscapes*, 292, 295.

220 Fishman, *Bourgeois Utopias*, 128. Also see Olmsted, Vaux & Company, *Preliminary Report Upon the Proposed Suburban Village at Riverside, Near Chicago* (New York, 1868), quoted in Sutton, ed., *Civilizing American Cities: A Selection of Frederick Law Olmsted's Writings on City Landscapes*, 295.

221 Fishman, *Bourgeois Utopias*, 129.

222 Ebenezer Howard, *Garden Cities of To-morrow* (London: S. Sonnenschein & Co., 1902; Cambridge, Mass.: MIT Press, 1965), 48.

223 Frederick Law Olmsted, "Public Parks and the Enlargement of Towns," *Journal of Social Science* 3 (1871): 18, quoted in Schuyler, "Frederick Law Olmsted's Riverside": 3.

224 Olmsted, Vaux & Company, *Preliminary Report Upon the Proposed Suburban Village at Riverside, Near Chicago* (New York, 1868): 17.

225 "Riverside, Illinois: A Residential Neighborhood Designed Over Sixty Years Ago": 268–69.

226 Frederick Law Olmsted, quoted in Beveridge and Rocheleau, *Frederick Law Olmsted: Designing the American Landscape*, 104.

227 Schuyler, "Frederick Law Olmsted's Riverside": 2. For Olmsted's Berkeley neighborhood, also see Michael Southworth and Eran Ben-Joseph, *Streets and the Shaping of Towns and Cities* (New York: McGraw-Hill, 1997), 30–31.

228 Olmsted, Vaux & Company, quoted in Schuyler, "Frederick Law Olmsted's Riverside": 2.

229 For Commonwealth Avenue, see Bainbridge Bunting, "The Plan of the Back Bay Area in Boston," *Journal of the Society of Architectural Historians* 13 (May 1954): 19–24; Bainbridge Bunting, *Houses of Boston's Back Bay: An Architectural History, 1840–1917* (Cambridge, Mass., and London: Belknap Press of Harvard University Press, 1967), 374, 378, 397; Cynthia Zaitzevsky, *Frederick Law Olmsted and the Boston Park System* (Cambridge, Mass., and London: Belknap Press of Harvard University Press, 1982), 110; Susan and Michael Southworth, *AIA Guide to Boston*, 2nd ed. (1984; Guilford, Conn.: Globe Pequot Press, 1992), 213.

230 Rybczynski, *A Clearing in the Distance: Frederick Law Olmsted and America in the Nineteenth Century*, 292.

231 Coolidge, "American Architecture: The Search for Tradition," in De Long, Searing, and Stern, eds., *American Architecture: Innovation and Tradition*, 177.

232 Coolidge, "American Architecture: The Search for Tradition," in De Long, Searing, and Stern, eds., *American Architecture: Innovation and Tradition*, 176.

233 Creese, *The Crowning of the American Landscape*, 227.

234 Olmsted, *Walks and Talks of an American Farmer in England*, 52, quoted in Coolidge, "American Architecture: The Search for Tradition," in De Long, Searing, and Stern, eds., *American Architecture: Innovation and Tradition*, 175.

235 S. B. Sutton, ed., *Civilizing American Cities: A Selection of Frederick Law Olmsted's Writings on City Landscapes* (Cambridge, Mass.: MIT Press, 1971), 52, quoted in Coolidge, "American Architecture: The Search for Tradition," in De Long, Searing, and Stern, eds., *American Architecture: Innovation and Tradition*, 175.

236 Riverside Improvement Company, *Riverside in 1871*, quoted in Buckley, "Glendale, Ohio: A Study of Early Suburban Development in America": 94 (n.159).

237 Olmsted and Vaux, *Tarrytown Heights Land Company; Description of the Lands of the Company, Report of Messrs. Olmstead[sic], Vaux & Co., Landscape Architects* (New York, 1872); J. B. Beers & Co., *Country Atlas of Westchester, New York* (New York, 1872); "Prospectus of the New Suburban District of Tarrytown Heights (February 1872)," in David Schuyler and Jane Turner Censer, eds., *The Papers of Frederick Law Olmsted, Volume VI: The Years of Olmsted, Vaux & Company, 1865–1874* (Baltimore and London: Johns Hopkins University Press, 1992), 503–22; John Reps, *The Making of Urban America* (Princeton: Princeton University Press, 1965), 348; Albert Fein, *Frederick Law Olmsted and the American Environmental Tradition* (New York: George Braziller, 1972), 34; Laura Wood Roper, *F.L.O.: A Biography of Frederick Law Olmsted* (Baltimore and London: Johns Hopkins University Press, 1973), 326; Charles E. Beveridge and Paul Rocheleau, *Frederick Law Olmsted: Designing the American Landscape* (New York: Rizzoli International Publications, 1995), 106; Witold Rybczynski, *A Clearing in the Distance: Frederick Law Olmsted and American in the Nineteenth Century* (New York: Scribner, 1999), 316; Roger Panetta, "Westchester, the American Suburb: a New Narrative," in Roger Panetta, ed., *Westchester: The American Suburb* (New York: Fordham University Press; Yonkers: Hudson River Museum, 2006), 28, 30.

238 Quoted in Panetta, "Westchester, the American Suburb: a New Narrative": 30 (n.31).

239 A.H.G., "Lake Forest, the Beautiful Suburb of Chicago, American Suburban Communities V," *House and Garden* 5 (June 1904): 265–75; "Market Square Group, Lake Forest, Ill.," *Architectural Forum* 27 (October 1917): 113, plates 65–68; Peter B. Wight, "The New Market Square at Lake Forest," *Western Architect* 26 (October 1917): 27–30, plates 1–15; Jacques Gréber, *L'Architecture Aux États-Unis* 1 (Paris: Payat & Cie, 1920), vol. 1: 109–10; Werner Hegemann and Elbert Peets, *The American Vitruvius: An Architect's Handbook of Civic Art* (New York: Architectural Book Publishing, 1922), 279; Christopher Tunnard and Henry Hope Reed, *American Skyline* (New York: New American Library, 1953), 167; *Lake Forest, Illinois: History and Reminiscences, 1861–1961* (Lake Forest: Lake Forest Rotary, 1963); H. Mayer and R. C. Wade, *Chicago: Growth of a Metropolis* (Chicago: University of Chicago

Press, 1969), 84–89; Carl Abbott, "'Necessary Adjuncts to Its Growth:' The Railroad Suburbs of Chicago, 1854–1875," *Journal of the Illinois State Historical Society* 73 (Summer 1980): 117–31; Michael H. Ebner, "'In the Suburbs of Toun': Chicago's North Shore to 1871," *Chicago History* 11 (Summer 1982): 66–77; Susan Dart, *Market Square, Lake Forest, Illinois* (Lake Forest: Lake Forest-Lake Bluff Historical Society, 1984); Kenneth T. Jackson, *Crabgrass Frontier: The Suburbanization of the United States* (New York: Oxford University Press, 1985), 93–94; Michael H. Ebner, *Creating Chicago's North Shore: A Suburban History* (Chicago and London: University of Chicago Press, 1988), passim; William S. Worley, *J. C. Nichols and the Shaping of Kansas City* (Columbia and London: University of Missouri Press, 1990), 24–26; "Renovation of Market Square, Lake Forest, Illinois, Office of John Vinci, Architect," *Architectural Record* 181 (March 1993): 86–87; Richard Longstreth, *City Center to Regional Mall: Architecture, the Automobile, and Retailing in Los Angeles, 1920–1950* (Cambridge, MA: MIT Press, 1997), 150–52; Virginia A. Greene, *The Architecture of Howard Van Doren Shaw* (Chicago: Chicago Review Press, 1998), 27–28, 84–85; Philip Pregill and Nancy Volkman, *Landscapes in History: Design and Planning in the Eastern and Western Traditions* (New York: John Wiley, 1999), 534–35; Leland M. Roth, *American Architecture: A History* (Boulder, Co.: Icon Editions/Westview Press, 2001), 200; Andrés Duany, Elizabeth Plater-Zyberk, and Robert Alminana, *The New Civic Art: Elements of Town Planning* (New York: Rizzoli International Publications, 2003), 253; Dolores Hayden, *Building Suburbia: Green Fields and Urban Growth, 1820–2000* (New York: Pantheon Books, 2003), 68; Ann Durkin Keating, *Chicagoland: City and Suburbs in the Railroad Age* (Chicago and London: University of Chicago Press, 2005), 100, 102–3; Tom Martinson, *The Atlas of American Architecture: 2000 Years of Architecture, City Planning, Landscape Architecture and Civil Engineering* (New York: Rizzoli International Publications, 2009), 292.

240 Traditionally attributed to Jedediah Hotchkiss (1828–1899), recent scholarship suggests that it was Almerin who was the planner. See Pregill and Volkman, *Landscapes in History: Design and Planning in the Eastern and Western Traditions*, 542 (n.17).

241 Unnamed visitor, *Waukegan Gazette* (September 18, 1869), quoted in Ebner, "'In the Suburbs of Toun': Chicago's North Shore to 1871": 74.

242 Wight, "The New Market Square at Lake Forest": 29.

243 H. Mayer and R. C. Wade, *Chicago: Growth of a Metropolis* (Chicago: University of Chicago Press, 1969), 334–36; *Highland Park: By Foot or Frame* (Highland Park: Highland Park Landmark Preservation Committee, 1980), passim; Philip Berger, ed., *Highland Park: American Suburb At Its Best* (Highland Park: Highland Park Landmark Preservation Committee, 1982), passim; Michael H. Ebner, "'In the Suburbs of Toun': Chicago's North Shore to 1871," *Chicago History* 11 (Summer 1982): 66–77; Virginia Luckhardt, "Horace William Shaler Cleveland: An Overview of the Life and Work of an Early American Landscape Architect, 1814–1900" (Master's thesis, University of Wisconsin-Madison, 1983): 49; Kenneth T. Jackson, *Crabgrass Frontier: The Suburbanization of the United States* (New York: Oxford University Press, 1985), 92–93; Michael H. Ebner, *Creating Chicago's North Shore: A Suburban History* (Chicago and London: University of Chicago Press, 1988), passim; Philip Pregill and Nancy Volkman, *Landscapes in History: Design and Planning in the Eastern and Western Traditions* (New York: John Wiley, 1999), 537–38; William H. Tishler, ed., *Midwestern Landscape Architecture* (Urbana and Chicago: University of Illinois Press, 2000), 34; Daniel J. Nadenicek and Lance M. Neckar, "Introduction," in H.W.S. Cleveland, *Landscape Architecture, As Applied to the Wants of the West* (Chicago: Jansen, McClurg & Co., 1873; Amherst and Boston: University of Massachusetts Press in association with the Library of American Landscape History, 2002), xxvii–xxxii.

244 John Brinckerhoff Jackson, *American Space: The Centennial Years, 1865–1876* (New York: W. W. Norton & Co., 1972), 74.

245 H.W.S. Cleveland, *Landscape Architecture, As Applied to the Wants of the West* (Chicago: Jansen, McClurg & Co., 1873; Amherst and Boston: University of Massachusetts Press in association with the Library of American Landscape History, 2002). Also see Advertisement published in Nadenicek and Neckar, "Introduction," in Cleveland, *Landscape Architecture, As Applied to the Wants of the West*, xxxii.

246 Nadenicek and Neckar, "Introduction," in Cleveland, *Landscape Architecture, As Applied to the Wants of the West*, xxx.

247 Quoted in Irvington Historical Society, "A Brief History of Irvington," in http://society.historicirvington.com/a_brief_history_of_irvington.htm. Also see Edward A. Leary, *Indianapolis: The Story of a City* (Indianapolis: Bobbs-Merrill Company, 1971), 117; Sheryl D. Vanderstel, "Irvington," in David J. Bodenhamer and Robert G. Barrows, eds., *The Encyclopedia of Indianapolis* (Bloomington and Indianapolis: Indiana University Press, 1994), 134, 831–32; Angela M. Quinn, *Indiana's Historic Suburban Developments: A Hoosier Heritage of Community Design* (Fort Wayne: ARCH, 2010), 11, 12, 13, 14.

248 *Plan of the Town of Ridley Park, Delaware County, Pennsylvania, With Description, Views in the Environs, Maps, &c* (Philadelphia: Wm. Butt & Co., 1872); "Through William Penn's 'Low Counties,'" *Lippincott's Magazine of Popular Literature and Science* (September 1872): 249–61; "Details, Crum Lynne Station, Philadelphia, Wilmington and Baltimore R.R.," *Architectural Sketchbook* 1 (January 1874): plate 28; "Obituary/Robert Morris Copeland," *The Gardener's Monthly and Horticulturalist Advertiser* 16 (May 1874): 146–47; "A Fine Park," *The Horticulturalist, and Journal of Rural Art and Rural Taste* 29 (July 1874): 222; "Stores at Ridley Park, Delaware County, PA, Theophilus Chandler Jr.," *American Architect and Building News* 1 (August 5, 1876): plate following p. 252; "Design for a Country House at Ridley Park, PA, Rankin & Kellogg, Archts.," *American Architect and Building News* 44 (June 23, 1894): plate following page 140; John W. Jordan, ed., *A History of Delaware County Pennsylvania and Its People, Volume 1* (New York: Lewis Historical Publishing Company, 1914), 319; John W. Reps, *The Making of Urban America* (Princeton: Princeton University Press, 1965), 348; Daniel Joseph Nadenicek, William H. Tishler, and Lance M. Neckar, "Robert Morris Copeland," in Charles Birnbaum and Robin Karson, eds., *Pioneers of American Landscape Design* (New York: McGraw Hill, 2000), 68–70; Randall Arendt, *Crossroads, Hamlet, Village, Town: Design Characteristics of Traditional Neighborhoods, Old and New (Revised Edition)* (Chicago: American Planning Association, Planning Advisory Service, 1999), 26–28.

249 Quoted in *Plan of the Town of Ridley Park*, 23.

250 *Plan of the Town of Ridley Park*, 5–6.

251 Arendt, *Crossroads, Hamlet, Village, Town*, 27.

252 *Plan of the Town of Ridley Park*, 8.

253 Quoted in *Plan of the Town of Ridley Park*, 19.

254 "Through William Penn's 'Low Counties'": 257.

255 Reps, *The Making of Urban America*, 348.

256 William T. Comstock, *Modern Architectural Designs and Details* (New York: William T. Comstock, 1881), reprinted as *Victorian Architectural Plans and Details* (New York: Dover, 1987), plate 45; "Cottage for A. B. Rich, D.D., Short Hills Park, N.J. Messers. Lamb & Rich, Architects, New York, N.Y.," *American Architect and Building News* 11 (January 7, 1882): 6, plate; "Redstone, Short Hills, N.J. Messrs. Lamb & Rich, Architects, New York, N.Y.," *American Architect and Building News* 12 (September 2, 1882): 110, plate; G. W. Sheldon, *Artistic Houses: Being a Series of Interior Views of a Number of the Most Beautiful and Celebrated Homes in the United States, with a Description of the Art Treasures Contained Therein*, 2 vols. (New York: D. Appleton, 1883–84; New York: Benjamin Blom, 1971), vol. 2, part 1: 76–78, vol. 2, part 2: 187–88; G. W. Sheldon, ed., *Artistic Country-Seats*, 2 vols. (New York: D. Appleton, 1886; New York: Da Capo Press, 1979), vol. 1: 114–18, vol. 2: 132–35; M. G. Van Rensselaer, "Recent Architecture in America—II," *Century* 28 (July 1884): 323–34; Montgomery Schuyler, "Some Suburbs of New York I— New Jersey," *Lippincott's Magazine* 8 (July 1884): 9–23; "An American Park," *American Architect and Building News* 16 (July 12, 1884): 15–16, 19, plates; "House at Short Hills, N.J., for Mr. A. Stewart, Jr. and Other Sketches," *Building* 7 (July 16, 1887): 21, plates; "Notice," *Building* 8 (February 23, 1888): 29; Bruce Price, "The Suburban House," *Scribner's Magazine* 8 (July 1890): 3–19; Cora L. Hartshorn, "A Little History of the Short Hills Section of Millburn Township, N.J., Developed by Stewart Hartshorn," manuscript dated July 31, 1946, Millburn Public Library; Vincent Scully, *The Shingle Style and the Stick Style* (New Haven, Conn.: Yale University Press, 1955), 133; Marian Keefe Meisner, "A History of Millburn Township, N.J.," manuscript dated 1957, Millburn Public Library; *Millburn: 1857–1957* (Millburn, N.J.: Millburn Centennial Committee, 1957); Leland M. Roth, *A Monograph of the Work of McKim, Mead & White 1879–1915* (New York: Benjamin Blom, 1973), 22–24; Leland M. Roth, "The Urban Architecture of McKim, Mead and White, 1870–1910" (Ph.D. diss., Yale University, 1973): 333, 336–37; Leland M. Roth, *The Architecture of McKim, Mead & White, 1870–1920: A Building List* (New York and London: Garland, 1978), 14, 143, fig. 37; Millburn-Short Hills Historical Society with David Gibson Associates, *Historic Structures Survey: Township of Millburn* (Millburn, N.J., 1979); David Gibson and the Millburn-Short Hills Historical Society, "Survey for the National Register," manuscript dated 1980; Anne Klemme, ed., *Sticks, Shingles and Stones: The History and Architecture of Stewart Hartshorn's Ideal Community at Short Hills, New Jersey, 1878–1937* (Millburn, N.J.: Millburn-Short Hills Historical Society, 1980); Robert Philip Griter, "The New Jersey Commissions of McKim, Mead & White, 1874–1916" (Master's thesis, Columbia University, 1981): 153–54; Stern with Massengale, *The Anglo-American Suburb*, 26; E. Richard McKinstry, book review, *Journal of the Society of Architectural Historians* 40 (December 1981): 344–46; Leland M. Roth, *McKim, Mead & White, Architects* (New York: Harper & Row, 1983), 67–68; Mary Corbin Sies, "American Country House Architecture in Context: The Suburban Ideal of Living in the East and Midwest, 1877–1917" (Ph.D. diss., University of Michigan, 1987): 206–71; Jerry Cheslow, "If You're Thinking of Living In: Millburn," *New York Times* (April 5, 1992), X: 7; Philip Pregill and Nancy Volkman, *Landscapes in History: Design and Planning in the Eastern and Western Traditions* (New York: John Wiley, 1999), 537; Stern, Mellins, and Fishman, *New York 1880*, 1016–25; John Archer, *Architecture and Suburbia: From English Villa to American Dream House, 1690–2000* (Minneapolis and London: University of Minnesota Press, 2005), 226–27, 245.

257 Archer, *Architecture and Suburbia*, 226–27.

258 Schuyler, "Some Suburbs of New York I—New Jersey": 21–23.

259 "American Country Houses, The Close: Residence of Henry Binsse, Esq. at Short Hills, N.J.," *Country Life in America* 39 (February 1921): 68–69; James D. Kornwolf, *M.H.Baillie Scott and the Arts & Crafts Movement: Pioneers of Modern Design* (Baltimore: Johns Hopkins University Press, 1972), 434–35, 546–47. The Close is the only positively identified Baillie Scott work in America, however, Kornwolf notes documentary evidence of others. See Kornwolf, *M.H. Baillie Scott and the Arts & Crafts Movement*, 537, 546–47.

260 Harold Donaldson Eberlein, "A Family Built House," *American Homes and Gardens* 11 (July 1914): 218–23.

261 *The History of Essex County* (1884), quoted in Klemme, ed., *Sticks, Shingles and Stones*, 2–3.

262 "An American Park": 15.

263 Schuyler, "Some Suburbs of New York I— New Jersey": 21–23.

264 Thomas Adams, *Outline of Town and City Planning, a Review of Past Efforts and Modern Aims* (New York: Russell Sage, 1936), 178; *Supplementary Report of the Urbanism Committee to the National Resources Committee* (Washington, D.C.: U. S. Government Printing Office, 1939), 499–500; Catherine W. Bishir, *North Carolina Architecture* (Chapel Hill: University of North Carolina Press, 1990), 359–61; John M. Bryan, *Biltmore Estate: The Most Distinguished Private Place* (New York: Rizzoli International Publications, 1994), 90, 143, 148; Catherine W. Bishir, Michael T. Southern, and Jennifer F. Martin, *A Guide to the Historic Architecture of Western North Carolina* (Chapel Hill and London: University of North Carolina Press, 1999), 292–93; Ellen Erwin Rickman, *Biltmore Estate* (Charleston, S.C.: Arcadia, 2005), 63–70; Bill Alexander, *Around Biltmore Village* (Charleston, S.C.: Arcadia, 2008), passim.

265 Budgett Meakin, quoted in *Supplementary Report of the Urbanism Committee to the National Resources Committee*, 499. For Budgett Meakin, see "Budgett Meakin Dead," *New York Times* (June 28, 1906): 7; S. E. Fryer, "Meakin, James Edward Budgett," in Sir Sidney Lee, ed., *Dictionary of National Biography: Second Supplement, Volume 2* (New York: Macmillan; London: Smith, Elder, 1912), 598–99.

266 "Destruction to Katonah," *New York Times* (April 8, 1893): 1–2. Also see "Cleaning Up the Watershed," *New York Times* (June 8, 1893): 12; "'Katonah's Wood': House of Clarence Whitman, Esq., Katonah, N.Y., Lamb and Rich," *American Architect and Building News* 51 (January 18, 1896): 35, plate 1047; "Westchester County," *New York Times* (January 22, 1896): 8; "Moving Houses and Bodies," *New York Times* (August 7, 1899): 1; Frances Riker Duncombe, *Katonah, the History of a New York Village and Its People* (Katonah,

N.Y.: Katonah Village Improvement Society, 1961); Frank E. Sanchis, *American Architecture: Westchester County, New York: Colonial to Contemporary* (Croton-on-Hudson, N.Y.: North River Press, 1977), 324, 471–72, 492; Gary Kriss, "Katonah Debates Plans In Its Historic District," *New York Times* (January 6, 1985), XXII: 1, 23; Tessa Melvin, "If You're Thinking of Living In/Katonah," *New York Times* (July 24, 1994), IX: 5; Anne C. Fullam, "Antique Train Rides Offered to Celebrate Village's Move," *New York Times* (January 26, 1997), XIII: 17; Penny Singer, "Katonah to Observe 100 Years of Rebirth," *New York Times* (March 30, 1997), XIII: 6; Gray Williams, "Westchester County: Historic Suburban Neighborhoods," in Roger Panetta, ed., *Westchester: The American Suburb* (New York: Fordham University Press; Yonkers, N.Y.: Hudson River Museum, 2006), 195–200. Also see www.katonahlibrary.org; www.katonahchamber.org.

267 "Demand for Suburban Homes Is Bright Realty Feature," *New York Times* (June 30, 1929), XI: 2; "Lawrence Farms Divided," *New York Times* (August 4, 1929): 14; "Model Westchester Village to Retain Rural Charm," *New York Times* (October 13, 1929), XII: 2; "Architectural News in Photographs," *Architecture* 60 (December 1929): 334; Ralph Pierson, "Town Planning for Country Life Protection," *American City* 42 (January 1930): 134–35; "Building a Village," *New York Times* (August 31, 1930), XI: 2; Thomas Adams, *Regional Plan of New York and Its Environs, vol. 2: The Building of the City* (New York: Regional Plan of New York and Its Environs, 1931), 571–73; "Colonial Row," *Octagon* 5 (January 1933): 50; "Plan New Home Group," *New York Times* (May 21, 1933), X: 4; "Lawrence Farms," *Architectural Forum* 59 (July 1933): 82–83; "Buys New Lawrence Farms Home," *New York Times* (August 6, 1933), XI: 1; "A Real Country Home," advertisement, *New York Times* (August 13, 1933), X: 9; Thomas Adams, *The Design of Residential Areas* (Cambridge, Mass.: Harvard University Press, 1934), 73–74, 259–60, plate 11; "Six Small Houses," *American Architect* 144 (March 1934): 49–55; "Lawrence Farms," *Architectural Forum* 62 (May 1935): 468–69.

268 Dudley B. Lawrence, quoted in "Model Westchester Village to Maintain Rural Charm": 2.

269 Dudley B. Lawrence, quoted in "Lawrence Farms," *Architectural Forum*: 83.

270 For an extensive architectural history of Chestnut Hill, see Willard S. Detweiler, Jr., Inc., *Chestnut Hill: An Architectural History* (Philadelphia: Chestnut Hill Historical Society, 1969). Also see Rev. S. F. Hotchkin, *Ancient and Modern Germantown, Mount Airy and Chestnut Hill* (Philadelphia: P. W. Ziegler & Co., 1889); George Woodward, *The Memoirs of a Mediocre Man* (Philadelphia: Harris & Partridge, 1935), 102–9; Horace Mather Lippincott, *A Narrative of Chestnut Hill, Philadelphia with Some Account of Springfield, Whitemarsh and Cheltenham Townships in Montgomery County, Pennsylvania* (Jenkintown, Pa.: Old York Road Publishing Co., 1948); Edward Teitelman and Richard Longstreth, *Architecture in Philadelphia: A Guide* (Cambridge, Mass.: MIT Press, 1974), 240–53; Richard J. Webster, *Philadelphia Preserved* (Philadelphia: Temple University Press, 1976), 254–55; Stern with Massengale, *The Anglo-American Suburb*, 22; Robert Fishman, *Bourgeois Utopias: The Rise and Fall of Suburbia* (New York: Basic Books, 1987), 142–45; Mary Corbin Sies, "American Country House Architecture in Context: The Suburban Ideal of Living in the East and Midwest, 1877–1917" (Ph.D. diss., University of Michigan, 1987): 272–361; David R. Contosta, "Suburban Quasi Government in Chestnut Hill, Philadelphia," *Pennsylvania Magazine of History and Biography* 116 (July 1992): 259–93; David R. Contosta, *Suburb in the City: Chestnut Hill, Philadelphia, 1850–1990* (Columbus, Oh.: Ohio State University Press, 1992); Witold Rybczynski, *City Life: Urban Expectations in a New World* (New York: Scribner, 1995), 187–89; Mary Corbin Sies, "Paradise Retained: An Analysis of Persistence in Planned, Exclusive Suburbs, 1880–1980," *Planning Perspectives* 12 (1997): 165–91; David R. Contosta, "Chestnut Hill, Pennsylvania," in Neil Larry Shumsky, ed., *Encyclopedia of Urban America: The Cities and Suburbs, Volume 1, A–L* (Santa Barbara, CA: ABC-CLIO, 1998), 145; Alexander Garvin, *The American City: What Works, What Doesn't*, 2nd ed. (New York: McGraw-Hill, 2002), 381–82; Thomas H. Keels and Elizabeth Farmer Jarvis, *Images of America: Chestnut Hill* (Charleston, S.C.: Arcadia Publishing, 2002); Dolores Hayden, *Building Suburbia: Green Fields and Urban Growth, 1820–2000* (New York: Pantheon Books, 2003), 69.

271 "Death in Cricket Club Fire," *New York Times* (September 9, 1908): 1.

272 For a full discussion of Woodward's patronage, see Cynthia Ann MacLeod, "Arts and Crafts Architecture in Suburban Philadelphia Sponsored by Dr. George Woodward" (Master's thesis, University of Virginia, May 1979). Also see George Woodward, *Proceedings of the National Housing Conference* (1911): 65; George Woodward, *Proceedings of the National Housing Conference* (1912): 31; George Woodward, "Perfect Plan of Renting Houses," *Proceedings of the National Housing Conference* (1920): 121–42, 173, 300–301.

273 MacLeod, "Arts and Crafts Architecture in Suburban Philadelphia Sponsored by Dr. George Woodward": 39.

274 "Some Preliminary Sketches and 'Office Studies' by Edmund B. Gilchrist, Architect," *Architectural Review* 6 (June 1918): 83–87, plate 65.

275 "A Practical Housing Development: The Evolution of the 'Quadruple House' Idea," *Architectural Record* 34 (July 1913): 46–55; George Woodward, "Another Aspect of the Quadruple House," *Architectural Record* 34 (July 1913): 51–55; C. Matlack Price, "Architecture and the Housing Problem," *Architectural Record* 34 (September 1913): 240–47; Harold D. Eberlein, "Pastorius Park and Its Residential Development," *Architectural Record* 39 (January 1916): 24–39; MacLeod, "Arts and Crafts Architecture in Suburban Philadelphia Sponsored by Dr. George Woodward": 43–47; Contosta, *Suburb in the City*, 105–8.

276 MacLeod, "Arts and Crafts Architecture in Suburban Philadelphia Sponsored by Dr. George Woodward": 48; Contosta, *Suburb in the City*, 108.

277 MacLeod, "Arts and Crafts Architecture in Suburban Philadelphia Sponsored by Dr. George Woodward": 49–51; Contosta, *Suburb in the City*, 107. Duhring's Roanoke Court (1931), similar to Winston Court, returned to the Elizabethan Arts and Crafts vernacular of his earliest work in Chestnut Hill. See "Roanoke Court," *Architecture* 68 (October 1933): 223–26.

278 Eberlein, "Pastorius Park and Its Residential Development": 26–37; C. A. Ziegler, "Developing a Suburban Community," *American Architect* 112 (August 1, 1917): 77–81, plates 51–55. Also see "House on Lincoln Drive, St. Martin's, Philadelphia, Edmund B. Gilchrist, Architect," *Architectural Record* 53 (May 1923): 411–12; "House on Crefeldt [*sic*]

Street, St. Martin's, Philadelphia, Edmund B. Gilchrist, Architect," *Architectural Record* 53 (May 1923): 413–15; "Group of Houses, Dr. George Woodward, St. Martin's, Philadelphia, E. B. Gilchrist, Architect," *The Architect* 5 (January 1926): plate; MacLeod, "Arts and Crafts Architecture in Suburban Philadelphia Sponsored by Dr. George Woodward": 59–70; Contosta, *Suburb in the City*, 108–11.

279 Harold D. Eberlein, "Linden Court, St. Martin's, Philadelphia," *Architectural Forum* 27 (July 1917): 19–22, plates 9–15; "House at Linden Court, St. Martin's, Pa.," *Architectural Forum* 27 (September 1917): plates 74–76; Werner Hegemann and Elbert Peets, *The American Vitruvius: An Architect's Handbook of Civic Art* (New York: Architectural Book Publishing, 1922), 278–79. Linden Court probably influenced the design of Mellor, Meigs & Howe's Germantown Avenue development. See "Group of Four Houses at Chestnut Hill, Philadelphia, Pa.," *American Architect* 126 (October 22, 1924): plates 141–43; Robert A. M. Stern, *George Howe: Toward a Modern American Architecture* (New Haven, Conn.: Yale University Press, 1975), 44, figs. 20–21; MacLeod, "Arts and Crafts Architecture in Suburban Philadelphia Sponsored by Dr. George Woodward": 51–58.

280 Eberlein, "Linden Court, St. Martin's, Philadelphia": 22.

281 Harold D. Eberlein, "A Group of Stone Houses at St. Martin's Green, Philadelphia," *Architectural Forum* 28 (May 1918): 181–86, plates 53–54; Charles Z. Klauder, "A Group of Stone Houses at St. Martin's Green, Philadelphia," *Architectural Forum* 28 (May 1918): 187–88, plates 61–64; Harold D. Eberlein, "Modern Cotswold at St. Martin's, Pa.: A Group of Suburban Houses by Duhring, Okie & Ziegler, Architects," *Architectural Forum* 33 (July 1920): 7–16.

282 Eberlein, "A Group of Stone Houses at St. Martin's Green, Philadelphia": 181–86, plates 49–52; Contosta, *Suburb in the City*, 110.

283 American Institute of Architects, Philadelphia Chapter, and the T-Square Club, "'Cotswold Court,' St. Martin's Philadelphia," *The Year Book of the Twenty-second Annual Architectural Exhibition* (Philadelphia, 1916), unnumbered plate; Charles Z. Klauder, "A Group of Houses on Willow Grove Avenue, St. Martin's, Philadelphia," *Architectural Forum* 28 (May 1918): 187–88, plates 61–64; Hegemann and Peets, *The American Vitruvius*, 272; *Monograph of the Work of Robert Rodes McGoodwin, 1910–1940* (Philadelphia: William F. Fell, 1942), plates 29–32. For the Tohopeka project of 1938, a later unrelated coordinated grouping of double houses designed by McGoodwin for Mrs. Samuel F. Houston, George Woodward's sister-in-law, see *Monograph of the Work of Robert Rodes McGoodwin, 1910–1940*, plate 116.

284 See "Publisher's Department," *Architectural Review* 6 (June 1918): xi, plates 65–66; "House, Mr. Persifor Frazer, Chestnut Hill, Philadelphia," *The Architect* 3 (December 1924): plate 60; "House, Mr. W. Griffin Gribbel, Chestnut Hill, Philadelphia," *The Architect* 3 (December 1924): plate 65; *Monograph of the Work of Robert Rodes McGoodwin, 1910–1940*, plates 33–49, 62–64, 85–89, 139, 145–47.

285 *Yearbook of the 32nd Annual Architectural Exhibition of the Philadelphia T-Square Club* (Philadelphia: A. H. Sickley, 1929); "A French Village, Chestnut Hill, Pa.," *American Architect* 135 (April 20, 1929): 499–509; *Monograph of the Work of Robert Rodes McGoodwin, 1910–1940*, plates 65–84; Contosta, *Suburb in the City*, 111–12.

286 Stern, *George Howe*, 44–45, figs. 22–25.

287 J. P. Button's, Conyers Button's, R. Dilworth's, W. P. Newhall's, P. B. Lee's, and Herbert S. Welsh's houses were part of the French Village. See *Monograph of the Work of Robert Rodes McGoodwin, 1910–1940*, plates 66–69, 72–73, 78–84. Also see "House of J. P. Button, Chestnut Hill, Pa.," *American Architect* 135 (April 5, 1929): 501–3; "House of Conyers Button, Chestnut Hill, Pa.," *American Architect* 135 (April 5, 1929): 504–5.

288 *Monograph of the Work of Robert Rodes McGoodwin, 1910–1940*, plates 127–28.

289 Robert Fishman, "Suburb in the City: Chestnut Hill, Philadelphia, 1850–1990," book review, *Journal of American History* 81 (March 1995): 1722–24.

290 "Group of Inexpensive Homes at Forest Hills," *American Homes and Gardens* 7 (June 1909): 244–47; John A. Walters, "A Model Town in America, Development of a Suburban Town After the Ideals of Architect, Landscape Architect and the Sage Foundation," *Arts and Decoration* 1 (January 1911): 118–20; John A. Walters, "A Model Town in America," *Arts and Decoration* 2 (January 1911): 118–20; Grosvenor Atterbury et al., "Forest Hills Gardens," *The Survey* 25 (January 7, 1911): 563–68; Edward Hale Brush, "A Garden City for the Man of Moderate Means," *Craftsman* 19 (February 1911): 445–51; Louis Graves, "A 'Model Village' Run on Business Principles," *Building Progress* 1 (July 1911): 209–15; Grosvenor Atterbury, "Model Towns in America," *Scribner's* 52 (July 1912): frontispiece, 20–35; Samuel Howe, "A Forerunner of the Future Suburb," *Arts and Decoration* 2 (October 1912): 414, 419–22; Samuel Howe, "Forest Hills Gardens," *American Architect* 102 (October 30, 1912): 153–58, plates; "The Sage Foundation at Forest Hills," *American Architect* 102 (October 30, 1912): 159–61; "Forest Hills Gardens, Long Island: An Example of Collective Planning, Development and Control," *Brickbuilder* 21 (December 1912): 317–18, plates 155–64; W. F. Anderson, "Forest Hills Gardens—Building Construction," *Brickbuilder* 21 (December 1912): 319–20; *Forest Hills Gardens*, 2nd edition (New York: Russell Sage Foundation, 1913); Aymar Embury II, "Co-Operative Building," *House Beautiful* 33 (March 1913): 116–18; Samuel Howe, "Town Planning on a Large Scale," *House Beautiful* 36 (October 1914): 129–36; Samuel Howe, *American Country Houses of To-Day* (New York: Architectural Book Publishing Co., 1915), 405–15; Mary Eastwood Knevels, "What the Suburban Dweller May Learn from a Model Town," *American Homes and Gardens* 12 (February 1915): 39–45; "The Architect's Scrap Book—Houses at Forest Hills, Long Island," *Architecture* 32 (August 1915): 210–12, and (September 1915): 234–36; Nelson P. Lewis, *The Planning of the Modern City* (New York: John Wiley & Sons, 1916), 309–12, 316–19, plate 86; "Recent Houses at Forest Hills Gardens, Long Island, from the Work of Grosvenor Atterbury, Architect, and Eugene Schoen, Architect," *Brickbuilder* 25 (June 1916): 139–42; "Two Houses Designed by Albro & Lindeberg, Architects, at Forest Hills Gardens in Long Island, N.Y.," *Brickbuilder* 25 (June 1916): 149–50; Charles C. May, "Forest Hills Gardens from the Town Planning Viewpoint," *Architecture* 34 (August 1916): 161–72, plates CXIX–CXXVII; Grosvenor Atterbury, "How to Get Low Cost Houses," *American Architect* 110 (November 22, 1916): 317–21; "Mr. Atterbury's Solution of the Housing Problem," *American Architect* 110 (November 22, 1916): 323–26; "Two Modern Apartments for City and Country," *Architecture* 38 (October 1918): 286–89, plate CLXX; "Garden Cities," *Encyclopedia*

Americana 12 (New York: Encyclopedia Americana Corp., 1919), 284–85; "The Church in the Gardens at Forest Hills, N.Y.," *Architectural Review* 9 (August 1919): 37–40, plate XXIV; "House at Forest Hills Gardens," *Architectural Forum* 31 (November 1919): plate 74; "Portrait of Grosvenor Atterbury," *Country Life* 107 (October 1920): 947–52; Charles S. Keefe, ed., *The American House* (New York: U.P.C. Book Company, 1924), 19, plates 129–32; Henry Isham Hazelton, *The Boroughs of Brooklyn and Queens, Counties of Nassau and Suffolk, Long Island, New York, 1609–1924*, vol. 2 (New York and Chicago: Lewis Historical Publishing Company, 1925), 1006–11; "Arbor Close, Forest Hills, L.I., Robert Tappan, Forest Hills, Architect," *Architect* 6 (August 1926): plates CXXI–CXXIV; Werner Hegemann, *Amerikanische Architektur & Stadtbaukunst* (Berlin: Ernst Wasmuth, 1927), 53, 117; Frank Chouteau Brown, "Some Recent Apartment Buildings," *Architectural Record* 63 (March 1928): 193–272; "The Forest Hills Gardens Development," *Regional Survey of New York and Its Environs*, vol. 7 (New York: Regional Plan of New York and Its Environs, 1929), 132–40; Lewis Mumford, "Mass-Production and the Modern House," *Architectural Record* 67 (January 1930): 13–20, and (February 1930): 110–16; Grosvenor Atterbury, *The Economic Production of Workingmen's Homes* (New York: Russell Sage Foundation, 1930); Grosvenor Atterbury, "Bricks without Brains: A Challenge to Science and the Factory-Made House," *Architecture* 73 (April 1936): 193–96; Arthur C. Comey and Max S. Wehrly, "Planned Communities," (November 1936) in *Supplementary Report of the Urbanism Committee to the National Resources Committee* (Washington, D.C.: U. S. Government Printing Office, 1939), vol. 2: 104–9, 112, 146; "A Problem of Resources in Planning," *Architectural Record* 95 (January 1944): 87–92; Christopher Tunnard, "The Romantic Suburb in America," *Magazine of Art* 40 (May 1947): 184–87; James Dahir, *Communities for Better Living* (New York: Harper & Brothers, 1950), 181–84; Norman T. Newton, *Design on the Land: The Development of Landscape Architecture* (Cambridge, Mass., and London: Belknap Press of Harvard University Press, 1971), 474–78; Francesco Dal Co, "From Parks to the Region: Progressive Ideology and the Reform of the American City," in Giorgio Ciucci et al., *The American City: From the Civil War to the New Deal* (Cambridge, Mass.: MIT Press, 1979), 143–291; David P. Handlin, *The American Home: Architecture and Society, 1815–1915* (Boston: Little, Brown and Co., 1979), 285–88; Carl W. Condit, *The Port of New York* (Chicago: University of Chicago Press, 1981), 272; Stern with Massengale, *The Anglo-American Suburb*, 32–34; Paul Goldberger, "To Utopia By Bus and Subway," *New York Times* (April 17, 1981), C: 1, 24; Stern, Gilmartin, and Massengale, *New York 1900*, 428–30; Claudia Henao, "History and Development of Forest Hills Gardens, Forest Hills, New York" (Master's thesis, Columbia University, 1984); Elaine D. Engst and H. Thomas Hickerson, *Urban America: Documenting the Planners*, exhibition catalogue (Ithaca, N.Y.: Department of Manuscripts and University Archives, Cornell University Libraries, 1985), 1, 3–5; John R. Stilgoe, *Borderland: Origins of the American Suburb, 1820–1939* (New Haven, Conn.: Yale University Press, 1988), 225–38; Daniel Levy, "Miniature Metropolis," *Metropolis* 8 (September 1988): 100–103; Jeffrey A. Kroessler, "Building Queens: The Urbanization of New York's Largest Borough" (Ph.D. diss., City University of New York, 1991): 352–56; Vincent F. Seyfried and William Asadorian, *Old Queens, N.Y. in Early Photographs* (New York: Dover, 1991), 158–62; Margaret Crawford, *Building the Workingman's Paradise: The Design of American Company Towns* (London and New York: Verso, 1995), 75–76; John Rather, "An 'English Village' Where Tudors Reign," *New York Times* (October 29, 1995), IX: 5; Evie T. Joselow, "Designed for Profit, Not Charity: A Different Look at Forest Hills Gardens, Queens," *Colloqui* 13 (Spring 1998): 43–52; Alexander Garvin, *The American City: What Works, What Doesn't*, 2nd ed. (New York: McGraw-Hill, 2002), 324; Susan L. Klaus, *A Modern Arcadia: Frederick Law Olmsted Jr. and the Plan for Forest Hills Gardens* (Amherst and Boston: University of Massachusetts Press, 2002); Mary Corbin Sies, book review, *Journal of the Society of Architectural Historians* 62 (December 2003): 533–35; Jon A. Peterson, book review, *Studies in the History of Gardens and Designed Landscapes* 24 (January–March 2004): 91–92; Robert M. Fogelson, *Bourgeois Nightmares: Suburbia, 1870–1930* (New Haven, Conn., and London: Yale University Press, 2005), 129–30; Claudia Gryvatz Copquin, *The Neighborhoods of Queens* (New Haven, Conn., and London: Yale University Press, 2007), 68–71; Peter Pennoyer and Anne Walker, *The Architecture of Grosvenor Atterbury*, foreword by Robert A. M. Stern (New York: W. W. Norton, 2008), 53–54, 148–81, 185, 263; Tom Martinson, *The Atlas of American Architecture: 2000 Years of Architecture, City Planning, Landscape Architecture and Civil Engineering* (New York: Rizzoli International Publications, 2009), 368.

291 Mumford, "Mass-Production and the Modern House" (January 1930): 13–20, and (February 1930): 110–16.

292 Grosvenor Atterbury, quoted in "Forest Hills Gardens, Long Island": 317–18.

293 "Studies in Economic Construction: An Outline of Research Work in Building Construction Being Done by Grosvenor Atterbury, F.A.I.A., with Particular Reference to the Use of Concrete in Model Dwellings," *Cement Age* 11 (December 1910): 315–25; Grosvenor Atterbury, "How To Get Low Cost Houses: The Real Housing Problem and the Art of Construction," *American Architect* 110 (November 22, 1916): 317–21, 323–26; R. Clipston Sturgis, "How to Get Low-Cost Houses," *AIA Journal* 4 (December 1916): 495–96; Atterbury, *The Economic Production of Workingmen's Homes*; Pennoyer and Walker, *The Architecture of Grosvenor Atterbury*, 252–59. Barry Bergdoll, in his 2008 exhibition at the Museum of Modern Art, takes note of Atterbury's contribution to the field of prefabrication, see Barry Bergdoll, "Home Delivery: Viscidities of a Modernist Dream From Taylorized Serial Production to Digital Customization," in Barry Bergdoll and Peter Christensen, *Home Delivery: Fabricating the Modern Dwelling* (Basel: Birkhauser, 2008), 16.

294 May, "Forest Hills Gardens from the Town Planning Viewpoint": 161–63, 167, 169–71.

295 Frederick Law Olmsted Jr., quoted in Lewis, *The Planning of the Modern City*, 312.

296 Clarence A. Perry, "The Neighborhood Unit: A Scheme of Arrangement for the Family Life Community," *Regional Survey of New York and Its Environs*, vol. 7 (New York: Regional Plan of New York and Its Environs, 1929); Clarence A. Perry, "Planning a Neighborhood Unit, Principles Which Would Give Added Character, Convenience and Safety to Outlying Sections of Cities," *American City* 41 (September 1929): 124–27; Mel C. Scott, *American City Planning Since 1890* (Berkeley: University of California Press, 1969), 90–91.

297 Howe, "Forest Hills Gardens": 153–58.

298 Quoted in Tunnard, "The Romantic Suburb in America": 317–18.

299 Grosvenor Atterbury, quoted in "Forest Hills Gardens, Long Island: An Example of Collective Planning, Development and Control": 317.

300 Stilgoe, *Borderland: Origins of the American Suburb, 1820–1939*, 228, 230.

301 Stilgoe, *Borderland: Origins of the American Suburb, 1820–1939*, 228, 230.

302 Stilgoe, *Borderland: Origins of the American Suburb, 1820–1939*, 228, 232.

303 See John A. Miller, *Fares, Please! From Horse-Cars to Streamliners* (New York and London: D. Appleton-Century Company, 1941), 54–67; Harold C. Passer, "Frank Julian Sprague, Father of Electric Traction, 1857–1934," in William Miller, ed., *Men in Business: Essays in the History of Entrepreneurship* (Cambridge, Mass.: Harvard University Press, 1952), 212–37; George W. Hilton and John F. Due, *The Electric Interurban Railways in America* (Stanford, Calif.: Stanford University Press, 1960), 3–44; Sam Bass Warner, *Streetcar Suburbs: The Process of Growth in Boston (1870–1900)*, 2nd ed. (Cambridge, Mass: Harvard University Press, 1962, 1978); Kenneth T. Jackson, *Crabgrass Frontier: The Suburbanization of the United States* (New York: Oxford University Press, 1985), 107–15; David E. Nye, *Electrifying America: Social Meanings of a New Technology, 1880–1940* (Cambridge, Mass.: MIT Press, 1990), 8–12, 85–97, 133–37.

304 "Wyatt & Nolting, Architects," *Architecture and Building* 26 (May 8, 1897): n.p.; Waldon Fawcett, "Roland Park, Baltimore County, Maryland, a Representative American Suburb," *House and Garden* 3 (April 1903): 175–96; E. Otis Williams, "Roland Park: The Homebuilders' Suburb of New Baltimore," *Indoors and Out* 3 (March 1907): 259–67; E. Otis Williams, "Roland Park: The Homebuilders' Suburb of New Baltimore," *Indoors and Out* 4 (April 1907): 23–31; Roland Park Company, *A Book of Pictures in Roland Park, Baltimore, Maryland, March and June 1911* (Roland Park, Md.: Norman T. A. Munder & Co., 1911); Thomas Adams, "An American Garden Suburb: Roland Park, Baltimore," *Architectural Review* 30 (November 1911): 288–93; Arthur B. Cranford, "A Suburb Conforming to Architectural Standards: Roland Park, Baltimore, Maryland," *Brickbuilder* 23 (August 1914), 191–94, plates 113–28; Samuel Howe, *American Country Houses of To-Day* (New York: Architectural Book Publishing Co., 1915), 404, 416–19; Roy G. Pratt, "A Joint-Ownership Apartment-House in Baltimore, Maryland," *Architecture* 45 (May 1922): 170–71; Roy G. Pratt, "Design for Tenant-Ownership Apartment-House, Guilford, Baltimore, MD.," *Architecture* 42 (January 1923): 3–4; "Roland Park Apartments, Baltimore, Md, Palmer, Willis & Lamdin, Architects," *American Architect* 129 (June 20, 1926), plate 143; James Dahir, *Communities for Better Living* (New York: Harper & Brothers, 1950), 178–79; John W. Reps, *The Making of Urban America: A History of City Planning in the United States* (Princeton: Princeton University Press, 1965), 348; Harry G. Schalck, "Mini-Revisionism in City Planning History: The Planners of Roland Park," *Journal of the Society of Architectural Historians* 29 (December 1970): 347–49; Harry Schalck, "Planning Roland Park, 1891–1918," *Journal of the Society of Architectural Historians* 35 (December 1976): 288; Stern with Massengale, *The Anglo-American Suburb*, 39; Elaine D. Engst and H. Thomas Hickerson, *Urban America: Documenting the Planners*, exhibition catalogue (Ithaca, N.Y.: Department of Manuscripts and University Archives, Cornell University Libraries, 1985), 3; Kenneth T. Jackson, *Crabgrass Frontier* (New York: Oxford University Press, 1985), 258; John R. Stilgoe, *Borderland: Origins of the American Suburb, 1820–1939* (New Haven, Conn., and London: Yale University Press, 1988), 258–59; William S. Worley, *J. C. Nichols and the Shaping of Kansas City* (Columbia and London: University of Missouri Press, 1990), 28–36, 141–43; Arleyn A. Levee, "The Olmsted Brothers' Residential Communities: A Preview of a Career Legacy," in Charles A. Birnbaum, ed., *The Landscape Universe: Historic Designed Landscapes in Context* (Bronx: Catalog of Landscape Records in the United States at Wave Hill, 1993), 39–40; Michael Watkins, ed., *A Guidebook to Old and New Urbanism in the Baltimore/Washington Region* (San Francisco: Congress for the New Urbanism, 1993), 104; Christian Zapatka, *The American Landscape* (New York: Princeton Architectural Press, 1995), 79–81; John Dorsey and James D. Dilts, *A Guide to Baltimore Architecture*, 3rd ed. (Centreville, Md.: Tidewater, 1997), 24–28, 364–68; Richard Longstreth, *City Center to Regional Mall: Architecture, the Automobile, and Retailing in Los Angeles, 1920–1950* (Cambridge, Mass.: MIT Press, 1997), 147–48; Sherry H. Olson, *Baltimore: The Building of an American City, Revised and Expanded Bicentennial Edition* (Baltimore and London: Johns Hopkins University Press, 1997), 213, 257; Susan L. Klaus, *A Modern Arcadia: Frederick Law Olmsted Jr. and the Plan for Forest Hills Gardens* (Amherst and Boston: University of Massachusetts Press in association with Library of American Landscape History, 2002), 68, 114; Mary Ellen Hayward and Frank R. Shivers Jr., eds., *The Architecture of Baltimore: An Illustrated History* (Baltimore and London: The Johns Hopkins University Press, 2004), 229–32, 245–47; Robert M. Fogelson, *Bourgeois Nightmares: Suburbia, 1870–1930* (New Haven, Conn.: Yale University Press, 2005), 59–66.

305 Letter, J. C. Nichols to Edward H. Bouton, December 12, 1912, cited in Fogelson, *Bourgeois Nightmares: Suburbia, 1870–1930*, 63.

306 Schalck, "Mini-Revisionism in City Planning, the Planners of Roland Park": 347–49.

307 Fawcett, "Roland Park, Baltimore County, Maryland, a Representative American Suburb": 190.

308 The Country Club relocated in the 1960s and seventy-two acres of its land were developed by the Rouse Company as the Village of Cross Keys (1964).

309 Roland Park Company, *A Book of Pictures in Roland Park, Baltimore, Maryland*, n.p.; *Edgevale Park* (Baltimore: The Roland Park Company, 1913); Hayward and Shivers, Jr., *The Architecture of Baltimore: An Illustrated History*, 246–47; Zapatka, *The American Landscape*, 80.

310 Pratt, "A Joint-Ownership Apartment-House in Baltimore, Maryland": 170–71; Pratt, "Design for Tenant-Ownership Apartment-House, Guilford, Baltimore, MD.": 3–4; "Roland Park Apartments, Baltimore, Md., Palmer, Willis & Lamdin, Architects": pl. 143.

311 "Edward L. Palmer, Jr., Architect," *Brickbuilder* 24 (September 1915): 223–27, plates 124–33; "Guilford and York Courts," in Watkins, ed., *A Guidebook to Old and New Urbanism in the Baltimore/Washington Region*, 66; Dorsey and Dilts, *A Guide to Baltimore Architecture*, 367–68; Hayward and Shivers Jr., eds., *The Architecture of Baltimore: An Illustrated History*, 245–46.

312 "Homeland, Roland Park, Baltimore, Md., Roland Park Company," *Architectural Forum* 62 (May 1935): 466–67; Watkins, ed., *A Guidebook to Old and New Urbanism in* the Baltimore/Washington Region, 72; Dorsey and Dilts, A Guide to Baltimore Architecture, 367–68; Hayward and Shivers Jr., eds., The Architecture of Baltimore: An Illustrated History, 245–46.

313 Dorsey and Dilts, A Guide to Baltimore Architecture, 369.

314 Richard Schermerhon, Jr., "Nathan Franklin Barrett Landscape Architect," Landscape Architecture 10 (April 1920): 110; Mary Roselle George, "Developer Influence in the Suburbanization of Washington, D.C.: Francis Newlands and Chevy Chase" (Master's thesis, University of Maryland, 1989); Michael Watkins, ed., A Guidebook to Old and New Urbanism in the Baltimore/Washington Region (San Francisco: Congress for the New Urbanism, 1993), 47; Elizabeth Jo Lampl and Kimberly Prothro Williams, Chevy Chase: A Home Suburb for the Nation's Capital (Crownsville, Maryland: Maryland Historic Trust Press, 1998), passim; Roderick S. French, "Chevy Chase," in Neil Larry Shumsky, ed., Encyclopedia of Urban America: The Cities and Suburbs, Volume 1, A-L (Santa Barbara: ABC-CLIO), 146–47; Andrea Oppenheimer Dean, "Sleuthing Olmsted," Preservation 51 (January/February 1999): 58–65; Judith Helm Robinson and Stephanie S. Foell, "Barrett, Nathan Franklin," in Charles A. Birnbaum and Robin Karson, eds,. Pioneers of American Landscape Design (New York: McGraw-Hill, 2000), 11, 13; Mary Corbin Sies, "Chevy Chase: A Home Suburb for the Nation's Captial," book review, Journal of the Society of Architectural Historians 59 (December 2000), 549–52; Dolores Hayden, Building Suburbia: Green Fields and Urban Growth, 1820–2000 (New York: Pantheon Books, 2003), 73.

315 Francis Griffith Newlands, quoted in Lampl and Williams, Chevy Chase: A Home Suburb for the Nation's Capital, 154 (n.1).

316 Frederick Law Olmsted to Francis Griffith Newlands, December 10, 1891, Olmsted Associates Records, Library of Congress, Manuscript Division, quoted in Lampl and Williams, Chevy Chase: A Home Suburb for the Nation's Capital, 45.

317 See Lampl and Williams, Chevy Chase: A Home Suburb for the Nation's Capital, esp. chapter 7.

318 I. T. Frary, "Suburban Landscape Planning in Cleveland," Architectural Record 43 (April 1918): 371–84; Murphy, "Ernest W. Bowditch and the Practice of Landscape Architecture": 168; William C. Barrow, "The Euclid Heights Allotment: A Palimpsest of the Nineteenth Century Search for Real Estate Value in Cleveland's East End" (Master's thesis, Cleveland State University, June 1992); Kara Cathleen Hamley, "Cleveland's Park Allotment: Euclid Heights, Cleveland Heights, Ohio, and Its Designer, Ernest W. Bowditch" (Master's thesis, Cornell University, 1996); Marian J. Morton, "The Suburban Ideal and Suburban Realities: Cleveland Heights, Ohio, 1860–2001," Journal of Urban History 28 (September 2002): 671–98; Kara Hamley O'Donnell, "Patrick Calhoun and the Birth of Cleveland Heights," in http://www.chhistory.org/people.php.

319 When Granger departed Cleveland to become the architect for the Northwestern Railroad in 1897, his Euclid Heights home, "Uplands," was purchased by Homer H. Johnson, father of Philip Johnson.

320 For other residences by Granger, see "'Lowe Ridge,' Euclid Heights," Inland Architect and News Record 28 (January 1897): plate following p. 64; "Residence of P. Calhoun, Cleveland, Ohio," Inland Architect and News Record 30 (September 1897): plate following p. 19; "Residence of Dr. W.R. Lincoln, Cleveland, Ohio," Inland Architect and News Record 30 (September 1897): plate following p.19.

321 Sarah Simms Edge, Joel Hurt and the Development of Atlanta (Atlanta: Atlanta Historical Society, 1955), 101–39; Howard L. Preston, Automobile Age Atlanta: The Making of a Southern Metropolis, 1900–1935 (Athens, Ga.: University of Georgia Press, 1979), 47; Eileen Segrest, "Inman Park: A Case Study in Neighborhood Revitalization," Georgia Historical Quarterly 63 (Spring 1979): 109–17; Rick Beard, "Hurt's Deserted Village: Atlanta's Inman Park, 1885–1911," in Dana F. White and Victor A. Kramer, eds., Olmsted South: Old South Critic/New South Planner (Westport, Conn.: Greenwood Press, 1979), 195–221; Rick Beard, "From Suburb to Defended Neighborhood: Change in Atlanta's Inman Park and Ansley Park, 1890–1980" (Ph.D. diss., Emory University, 1981): esp. chs. 2, 4; Don H. Doyle, New Men, New Cities, New South: Atlanta, Nashville, Charleston, Mobile, 1860–1910 (Chapel Hill: University of North Carolina Press, 1990), 195–96; Isabelle Gournay, AIA Guide to the Architecture of Atlanta (Athens, Ga.: University of Georgia Press, 1993), 185–93; Robert Isbell, Atlanta: A City of Neighborhoods (Columbia: University of South Carolina Press, 1994), 50–53; Don O'Briant, Atlanta (Baton Rouge and London: Louisiana State University Press, 1994), 92–93; Christine V. Marr and Sharon Foster Jones, Inman Park (Columbia, S.C.: Arcadia, 2008), esp. ch. 1.

322 Sarah Simms Edge, Joel Hurt and the Development of Atlanta (Atlanta: Atlanta Historical Society, 1955), 277–85; Elizabeth Stevenson, Park Maker: A Life of Frederick Law Olmsted (New York: Macmillan Publishing; London: Collier Macmillan, 1977), 406–7; Elizabeth A. Lyon, "Frederick Law Olmsted and Joel Hurt: Planning for Atlanta," in Dana F. White and Victor A. Kramer, eds., Olmsted South: Old South Critic/New South Planner (Westport, Conn.: Greenwood Press, 1979), 165–82, 186; Rick Beard, "From Suburb to Defended Neighborhood: Change in Atlanta's Inman Park and Ansley Park, 1890–1980" (Ph.D. diss., Emory University, 1981): 32–36; Isabelle Gournay, AIA Guide to the Architecture of Atlanta (Athens, Ga.: University of Georgia Press, 1993), 207–16; Dana F. White, "Foreword," National Association for Olmsted Parks Workbook 4 (1993): 2; Darlene R. Roth, "Frederick Law Olmsted's First and Last Suburbs: Riverside and Druid Hills," National Association for Olmsted Parks Workbook 4 (1993): 3–11; Robert Isbell, Atlanta: A City of Neighborhoods (Columbia: University of South Carolina Press, 1994), 38–41; Charles E. Beveridge and Paul Rocheleau, Frederick Law Olmsted: Designing the American Landscape (New York: Rizzoli International Publications, 1995), 125; Gianni Pettena, Olmsted: L'origine del parco urbano e del parco naturale contemporaneo (Florence: Centro Di, 1996), 150–51, 205; Christian Zapatka, The American Landscape (New York: Princeton Architectural Press, 1996), 81–82; Witold Rybczynski, A Clearing in the Distance: Frederick Law Olmsted and America in the Nineteenth Century (New York: Scribner, 1999), 400–401; Alexander Garvin, The American City: What Works, What Doesn't, 2nd ed. (New York: McGraw-Hill, 2002), 321–24; Dolores Hayden, Building Suburbia: Green Fields and Urban Growth, 1820–2000 (New York: Pantheon Books, 2003), 65; National Park Service, "Druid Hills Historic District," http://www.cr.nps.gov/nr/travel/atlanta/dru.htm.

323 White, "Foreword": 2.

324 Roth, "Frederick Law Olmsted's First and Last Suburbs: Riverside and Druid Hills": 3.

325 Roth, "Frederick Law Olmsted's First and Last Suburbs: Riverside and Druid Hills": 6–7.

326 Frederick Law Olmsted, letter to Joel Hurt, quoted in Roth, "Frederick Law Olmsted's First and Last Suburbs: Riverside and Druid Hills": 10–11.

327 Roth, "Frederick Law Olmsted's First and Last Suburbs: Riverside and Druid Hills": 11.

328 Allan Rogers, "Famous Land Lot 105 Comes Again to Fore," Atlanta Constitution (October 8, 1905), E: 2; "Edwin P. Ansley Scores Great Realty Success," Atlanta Constitution (October 20, 1905): 2; "Ansley Park an Ideal Recreation Center," Atlanta Constitution (May 6, 1906), C: 8; "Ansley Park's Future, as Seen By Mr. Anlsey," Atlanta Constitution (September 23, 1906), B: 4; "The Real Builders of Atlanta—Edwin P. Ansley," Atlanta Constitution (October 20, 1907), B: 3; Irma Dooly, "An Object Lesson in Civic Beauty," Atlanta Constitution (June 7, 1908), D: 9; "Ansley Park Will Have Splendid Car Service," Atlanta Constitution (February 7, 1909), B: 7; Howard L. Preston, Automobile Age Atlanta: The Making of a Southern Metropolis, 1900–1935 (Athens: University of Georgia Press, 1979), 76, 84–87; Dana F. White and Victor A. Kramer, eds., Olmsted South: Old South Critic/New South Planner (Westport, Conn.: Greenwood Press, 1979), 186–87; Rick Beard, "From Suburb to Defended Neighborhood: Change in Atlanta's Inman Park and Ansley Park, 1890–1980" (Ph.D. diss., Emory University, 1981): 109–90; Isabelle Gournay, AIA Guide to the Architecture of Atlanta (Athens and London: University of Georgia Press, 1993), 137–46; Don O'Briant, Atlanta: Photographs by David King Gleason (Baton Rouge and London: Louisiana State University Press, 1994), 54–55; Robert Isbell, Atlanta: A City of Neighborhoods (Columbia: University of South Carolina Press, 1994), 22–25.

329 Davyd Foard Hood, "Winston-Salem's Suburbs: West End to Reynolds Park," in Catherine W. Bishir and Lawrence S. Earley, eds., Early Twentieth-Century Suburbs in North Carolina (Raleigh: Archaeology and Historic Preservation Section, Division of Archives and History, North Carolina Dept. of Cultural Resources, 1985), 60–62; Frank V. Tursi, Winston-Salem: a History (Winston-Salem, N.C.: John F. Blair Publisher, 1994), 132; Catherine W. Bishir and Michael T. Southern, A Guide to the Historic Architecture of Piedmont North Carolina (Chapel Hill and London: University of North Carolina Press, 2003), 390–91; J. Eric Elliott, Winston-Salem's Historic West End (Charleston, S.C.: Arcadia, 2004); Michael Bricker, Winston-Salem: a Twin-City History (Charleston, S.C.: History Press, 2008), 136–39.

330 John Joseph Ellis, "Belle Meade: Development of a Southern Upper-Class Suburb, 1905–1938" (Master's thesis, Vanderbilt University, August 1984): 17. Also see "Make Town Lots of Belle Meade," Atlanta Constitution (February 25, 1906), C: 1; William Waller, Nashville 1900 to 1910 (Nashville: Vanderbilt University Press, 1972), 17–22, 318; Eleanor Graham, ed., Nashville: A Short History and Selected Buildings (Nashville: Historical Commission of Metropolitan Nashville-Davidson County, 1974), 183, 193; Don H. Doyle, Nashville in the New South, 1880–1930 (Knoxville: University of Tennessee Press, 1985), 97–98; Ridley Wills II, The History of Belle Meade: Mansion, Plantation, and Stud (Nashville: Vanderbilt University Press, 1991), 285–86, 292–97; Mary Louise Lea Tidwell, Luke Lea of Tennessee (Bowling Green, OH: Bowling Green State University Popular Press, 1993), 25–26, 60–61, 76–77; Christine Kreyling et al., Classical Nashville: Athens of the South (Nashville and London: Vanderbilt University Press, 1996), 113–14; Cindy Stooksbury Guier and Jackie Sheckler Finch, Insiders Guide to Nashville (Guilford, Conn.: Globe Pequot, 2007), 320.

331 Ellis, "Belle Meade: Development of a Southern Upper-Class Suburb, 1905–1938": 20.

332 Ellis, "Belle Meade: Development of a Southern Upper-Class Suburb, 1905–1938": 20

333 Belle Meade Links Triangle Conservation Zoning District, Handbook and Design Guidelines, ftp://ftp.nashville.gov/web/mhc/design_guidelines_Belle_Meade_Links.pdf, accessed August 28, 2008; "Belle Meade Links: History," in http://web.mac.com/kirk.manz/iWeb/BLMTA/Welcome.html, accessed June 13, 2011.

334 "Finishing a Concrete Pavement in Myers Park, Charlotte, N.C.," Engineering News-Record 76 (October 26, 1916): 803; Earle S. Draper, "Successful Methods of Transplanting Big Tree," Baltimore Sun (February 15, 1920), B: 13; Guy Wilfred Hayler, "Myers Park, Near Charlotte, N.C.," American Review of Reviews 62 (December 1920): 637; John Nolen, New Towns for Old (Boston: Marshall Jones, 1927; Amherst and Boston: University of Massachusetts Press, 2005), 100–110; Arthur C. Comey and Max S. Wehrly, "A Study of Planned Communities" (Department of Regional Planning of Harvard University, November 1936): 413–14; John Loretz Hancock, "John Nolen and the American City Planning Movement: A History of Culture Change and Community Response, 1900–1940" (Ph.D. diss., University of Pennsylvania, 1964): 258, plate 7; Margaret Crawford, Building the Workingman's Paradise: The Design of American Company Towns (London and New York: Verso, 1995), 179–80; Christopher Silver, "John Nolen: Planner for the New South," Journal of Planning Education and Research 15 (Winter 1996): 77–88; Charles D. Warren, "Introduction," in Nolen, New Towns for Old (2005), lxxxvii–xcii; Thomas W. Hanchett, "Myers Park: Charlotte's Finest Planned Suburb," www.cmhpf.org; Jack McNeary, "Original Tree Planting Machine," www.mpha.com; Dan L. Morrill, "Myers Park: Charlotte's Most Elegant Streetcar Suburb," www.mpha.com; Dan L. Morrill and Nancy B. Thomas, "The New South Neighborhoods: Myers Park," www.cmhpf.org. Also see John Nolen, A Good Home for Every Wage-Earner, pamphlet (Cambridge, Mass.: 1917); John Nolen, The Industrial Village (New York: National Housing Association, 1918); John Nolen, "American Small Towns," Town Planning Review (July 1934): 16–24.

335 Charlotte Observer (August 29, 1912), quoted in Morrill, "The Trolley," www.mpha.com.

336 Nolen, New Towns for Old, 101, 103.

337 Warren, "Introduction," in Nolen, New Towns for Old, xc.

338 H. L. Mencken, Americana (1925), quoted in John Gunther, Inside U.S.A., rev. ed. (New York: Harper, 1951), 51. For the Dorothy Parker quip, see Leslie Frewin, The Late Mrs. Dorothy Parker (New York: Macmillan, 1986), 114.

339 "Beverly Hills," Los Angeles Times (October 21, 1906), V: 1; "Beverly Hills: 'Between the City and the Sea,'" advertisement, Los Angeles Times (October 21, 1906), II: 20; "Beverly Hills: Park Effects in Homesite," Los Angeles Times (August 16, 1907), III: 7; "Mansions and Bungalows Rise at Call of the High and Airy Foothills," Los Angeles Times (September 20, 1907), III: 1; George D. Hall, "Beverly Hills, California: A Subdivision that Grew into a City," *American Landscape Architect* 3 (August 1930): 21–26; Pierce E. Benedict and Don Kennedy, *History of Beverly Hills* (Beverly Hills: A.H. Cawston-H. M. Meier, 1934); Writers' Program of the Work Projects Administration in Southern California, *Los Angeles: A Guide to the City and Its Environs* (New York: Hastings House, 1941), 198–204; Reyner Banham, *Los Angeles: The Architecture of the Four Ecologies* (New York: Harper and Row, 1971), 76–84; Fred E. Basten, *Beverly Hills: Portrait of a Fabled City* (Los Angeles: Douglas-West Publishers, 1975), 26–33, 42–55; David Gebhard and Robert Winter, *A Guide to Architecture in Los Angeles and Southern California* (Santa Barbara, Calif.: Peregrine Smith, 1977), 120–30; Brendan Gill, *The Dream Come True: Great Houses of Los Angeles* (New York: Lippincott & Crowell, 1980), 12, 17–18, 21, 42–43; Michelle Behey, "Beverly Hills: Despite All the Wealth and Opulence, This Community Has Some Familiar Problems," *American Preservation* 3 (January–February 1980): 47–57; Brendan Gill, "Reflections: The Horizontal City," *New Yorker* 56 (September 15, 1980): 109–14, 116–24, 126–30, 132–36, 138–42, 144, 146; Stern with Massengale, *The Anglo-American Suburb*, 78–79; Kevin Starr, *Inventing the Dream: California Through the Progressive Era* (New York: Oxford University Press, 1985), 186, 334–38; Robert Fishman, *Bourgeois Utopias: The Rise and Fall of Suburbia* (New York: Basic Books, 1987), 167–72; Genevieve Davis, *Beverly Hills: An Illustrated History* (Northridge, Calif.: Windsor, 1988), 45–53; Christopher Gray, "The Galloping Growth of Rodeo Drive," *Avenue* (March 1988): 138–43; Philip Pregill and Nancy Volkman, *Landscapes in History: Design and Planning the Western Tradition* (New York: Van Nostrand Reinhold, 1993), 547–48; Virginia and Lee McAlester, *A Field Guide to America's Historic Neighborhoods and Museum Houses: The Western States* (New York: Alfred A. Knopf, 1998), 76–81, 575; Charles Moore, Peter Becker, and Regula Campbell, *The City Observed: Los Angeles: A Guide to Its Architecture* (Santa Monica: Hennessey & Ingalls, 1998), 197–99, 212–14; Janet L. Abu-Linghod, *New York, Chicago, Los Angeles: America's Global Cities* (Minneapolis: University of Minnesota Press, 1999), 156; David Weddle, *Among the Mansions of Eden: Tales of Love, Lust, and Land in Beverly Hills* (New York: William Morrow, 2003), 16–21, 138, 161; Alexander Garvin, *The American City: What Works, What Doesn't*, 2nd ed. (New York: McGraw-Hill, 2002), 382–84; David Gebhard and Robert Winter, *An Architectural Guide to Los Angeles*, rev. ed. (Salt Lake City: Gibbs Smith, 2003), 151–56; Andrés Duany, Elizabeth Plater-Zyberk, and Robert Alminana, *The New Civic Art: Elements of Town Planning* (New York: Rizzoli International Publications, 2003), 97; Cheryl Lynn Caldwell Ferguson, "Upscale Suburban Architecture and Development in Dallas and Houston, Texas, 1890–1930" (Ph.D. diss., University of Delaware, 2004): 49–61, 512–28; Marc Wanamaker, *Early Beverly Hills* (Charleston, S.C.: Arcadia, 2005), 37–44, 57; Robert Winter and Alexander Vertikoff, *The Architecture of Entertainment: LA in the Twenties* (Salt Lake City: Gibbs Smith, 2006), 54–57; Sam Watters, *Houses of Los Angeles: 1885–1919* (New York: Acanthus Press, 2007), vol. 1: 23–24, vol. 2: 26–39; Jeffrey Hyland, *The Legendary Estates of Beverly Hills* (New York: Rizzoli International Publications, 2008), esp. pp. 8–15; Tom Martinson, *The Atlas of American Architecture: 2000 Years of Architecture, City Planning, Landscape Architecture and Civil Engineering* (New York: Rizzoli International Publications, 2009), 367.

340 Banham, *Los Angeles: The Architecture of the Four Ecologies*, 77–78.

341 Gill, *The Dream Come True: Great Houses of Los Angeles*, 17.

342 Hall, "Beverly Hills, California: A Subdivision that Grew into a City": 21.

343 Gebhard and Winter, *A Guide to Architecture in Los Angeles and Southern California*, 123.

344 "Highland Park: 'The Residence Show Ground of Texas,'" advertisement, *Dallas Morning News* (June 20, 1909): 22; "Highland Park Has Extensive Program," *Dallas Morning News* (November 20, 1921): 15; "Highland Park Adding Area to Beauty Spot," *Dallas Morning News* (August 2, 1922): 13; Hugh E. Prather, "A Beautiful Suburb Created Through a Golf Club," *Golf Illustrated* (April 1925): 16; "Highland Park," *Dallas Morning News* (May 8, 1928): 13; "Highland Park: A Beauty Spot of Southwest: Dallas Suburban Town Realizes Ideal of Early Builder," *Dallas Morning News* (May 8, 1928): 21; "Flippen-Prather's Central Section of Highland Park West," advertisement, *Dallas Morning News* (May 8, 1928): 24; "Fine Residence City Is Formed Out of Prairie," *Dallas Morning News* (October 1, 1935): 12; *The Prairie's Yield: Forces Shaping Dallas Architecture from 1840–1962* (New York: Reinhold, 1962), 25–26; A. C. Greene, *Dallas: The Deciding Years: A Historical Portrait* (Austin: Encino, 1973), 39, 175; *Dallasights: An Anthology of Architecture and Open Spaces* (Dallas: American Institute of Architects Dallas Chapter, 1978), 126–27; William L. McDonald, *Dallas Rediscovered: A Photographic Chronicle of Urban Expansion 1870–1925* (Dallas: Dallas Historical Society, 1978), 202–5, 209; Bill Blodgett, "Highland Park Village: A Bit of Barcelona," *Texas Architect* 30 (November–December 1980): 68–70; Diane Galloway and Kathy Matthews, *The Park Cities: A Walker's Guide & Brief History* (Dallas: Southern Methodist University Press, 1988), 6–15, 28–37, 52–55, 66–87, 90–97; *The WPA Dallas Guide and History: Written and Compiled from 1936 to 1942 by the Workers of the Writers' Program of the Work Projects Administration in the City of Dallas* (Denton: University of North Texas Press, 1992), 201; Patricia Evridge Hill, *Dallas: The Making of a Modern City* (Austin: University of Texas Press, 1996), 7–8; Virginia and Lee McAlester, *A Field Guide to America's Historic Neighborhoods and Museum Houses: The Western States* (New York: Alfred A. Knopf, 1998), 574–77; Larry Paul Fuller, ed., *The American Institute of Architects Guide to Dallas Architecture* (New York: McGraw-Hill, 1999), 118–25; Cheryl Caldwell Ferguson, "River Oaks: 1920s Suburban Planning and Development in Houston," *Southwestern Historical Quarterly* 104 (October 2000): 201 (n.18); Andrés Duany, Elizabeth Plater-Zyberk, and Robert Alminana, *The New Civic Art: Elements of Town Planning* (New York: Rizzoli International Publications, 2003), 255; Cheryl Lynn Caldwell Ferguson, "Upscale Suburban Architecture and Development in Dallas and Houston, Texas, 1890–1930" (Ph.D. diss.: University of Delaware, 2004): esp. chapters 4, 5, and 6; Virginia Savage McAlester, "Part One: History and Development," in Virginia Savage McAlester, Willis Cecil Winters, and Prudence Mackintosh, *Great American Suburbs: The Homes of the Park Cities, Dallas* (New York and London: Abbeville Press, 2008), esp. pp. 27–109. Also see "Highland Park, Texas," http://www.tshaonline.org/handbook/online/articles/HH/hfh3.html.

345 Ferguson, "Upscale Suburban Architecture and Development in Dallas and Houston, Texas, 1890–1930": 163.

346 Prather, "A Beautiful Suburb Created Through a Golf Club": 16, quoted in McAlester, "Part One: History and Development," in McAlester, Winters, and Mackintosh, *Great American Suburbs: The Homes of the Park Cities, Dallas*, 51–52.

347 "A Model Shopping Village in Texas, Fooshee and Cheek, Architects," *Architectural Record* 70 (September 1931): 197–98; Blodgett, "Highland Park Village: A Bit of Barcelona": 68–70; Anita Toews, "Spanish Colonial Revival Architecture in Dallas: The Work of Fooshee and Cheek," *Perspective* 13 (1984): 9–15; *A Guide to the Older Neighborhoods of Dallas* (Dallas: Historic Preservation League, 1986), 86–87; Lawrence W. Speck, *Landmarks of Texas Architecture* (Austin: University of Texas Press, 1986), 62–65; Galloway and Matthews, *The Park Cities: A Walker's Guide & Brief History*, 98–107; Keller Easterling, *American Town Plans: A Comparative Time Line* (New York: Princeton Architectural Press, 1993), 80; Jay C. Henry, *Architecture in Texas, 1895–1945* (Austin: University of Texas Press, 1993), 188–90; Lisa C. Maxwell, "Highland Park Village," in *The New Handbook of Texas*, vol. 3 (Austin: Texas State Historical Association, 1996), 602–3; Fuller, ed., *The American Institute of Architects Guide to Dallas Architecture*, 125; "Highland Park Shopping Village," *National Register of Historic Places Nomination* (2000); Alexander Garvin, *The American City: What Works, What Doesn't*, 2nd ed. (New York: McGraw-Hill, 2002), 123; Andrés Duany, Elizabeth Plater-Zyberk, and Robert Alminana, *The New Civic Art: Elements of Town Planning* (New York: Rizzoli International Publications, 2003), 255; Ferguson, "Upscale Suburban Architecture and Development in Dallas and Houston, Texas, 1890–1930": 342–46; McAlester, "Part One: History and Development," in McAlester, Winters, and Mackintosh, *Great American Suburbs: The Homes of the Park Cities, Dallas*, 172–75. Also see "Highland Park Shopping Village," http://tps.cr.nps.gov.

348 "Ideal Chicago Wanted Here; City Club Offers Reward," *Chicago Daily Tribune* (December 23, 1912): 1. Also see G. E. Hooker, "Program of a Competition for the Procuring of a Scheme of Development for a Quarter-Section of Land with the Limit of the City of Chicago, Illinois," *Architecture* 27 (January 1913): 18–19; "City Club Housing Show Will Be Opened March 17," *Chicago Daily Tribune* (March 14, 1913): 13; "Pick Winners of Housing Prizes," *Chicago Daily Tribune* (March 23, 1913): 124; "Prize-Winning Plans for Laying Out a Quarter-Section of Urban Land," *American City* 8 (April 1913): 421–23; "City Club Competition," *Western Architect* 21 (April 1913): 39–41; John Ihlder, "Chicago City Club's Housing Exhibition," *National Municipal Review* 2 (1913): 497–99; Graham Romeyn Taylor, *Satellite Cities: A Study of Industrial Suburbs* (New York: D. Appleton, 1915), 275–76; John Nolen, ed., *City Planning* (New York: D. Appleton and Co., 1916), 40, plate; Alfred B. Yeomans, ed., *City Residential Land Development: Studies in Planning: Competitive Plans for Subdividing a Typical Quarter Section of Land in the Outskirts of Chicago* (Chicago: University of Chicago Press, 1916); Robert Craik McLean, "City Residential Land Development," *Western Architect* 25 (January 1917): 6–8, plates; Fiske Kimball, "The Social Center," *Architectural Record* 46 (July 1919): 29–46; Werner Hegemann, *Amerikanische Architektur & Stadtbaukunst* (Berlin: E. Wasmuth, 1925), 121; Lewis Mumford, *The Urban Prospect* (New York: Harcourt, Brace & World, 1968), 65; Robert C. Twombly, "Undoing the City: Frank Lloyd Wright's Planned Communities," *American Quarterly* 24 (October 1972): 538–49; Paul D. Spreiregen, *Design Competitions* (New York: McGraw-Hill, 1979), 81–82, 91–94; Gwendolyn Wright, *Moralism and the Model Home* (Chicago and London: University of Chicago Press, 1980), 280–90; David P. Handlin, "The Context of the Modern City," *Harvard Architecture Review* 2 (Spring 1981): 78–89; Stern with Massengale, *The Anglo-American Suburb*, 10–11; David Van Zanten, "Walter Burley Griffin's Design for Canberra, the Capital of Australia," in John Zukowsky, ed., *Chicago Architecture, 1872–1922: Birth of a Metropolis* (Munich: Prestel-Verlag, 1987), 319–43; Charles R. Wolfe, "Streets Regulating Neighborhood Form," in Anne Vernez Mondon, ed., *Public Streets for Public Use* (New York: Van Nostrand Reinhold, 1987), 116–18; Stanley Buder, *Visionaries & Planners: The Garden City Movement and the Modern Community* (New York: Oxford University Press, 1990), 160–61; Donald Leslie Johnson, *Frank Lloyd Wright Versus America: The 1930s* (Cambridge, Mass.: MIT Press, 1990), 147–48; Robert E. Grese, *Jens Jensen: Maker of Natural Parks and Gardens* (Baltimore: Johns Hopkins University Press, 1992), 93; Bruce Brooks Pfeiffer, ed., *Frank Lloyd Wright Collected Writings, vol. 1: 1894–1930* (New York: Rizzoli International Publications, in association with the Frank Lloyd Wright Foundation, 1992), 139–43; Anthony Alofsin, *Frank Lloyd Wright: The Lost Years, 1910–1922: A Study of Influence* (Chicago: University of Chicago Press, 1993), 72; Cynthia L. Girling and Kenneth I. Helphand, *Yard, Street, Park: The Design of Suburban Open Space* (New York: Wiley, 1994), 71; Robert McCarter, *Frank Lloyd Wright* (London: Phaidon, 1997), 239–40; Brendan Gill, *Many Masks: A Life of Frank Lloyd Wright* (New York: Da Capo Press, 1998), 422–23; David G. De Long, "Frank Lloyd Wright and the Evolution of the Living City," in David G. De Long, ed., *Frank Lloyd Wright and the Living City* (Milan: Skira, 1998), 9–21; J. Michael Desmond, "Buildings for Communal Dwelling," in De Long, ed., *Frank Lloyd Wright and the Living City*, 237–38, 248; Charles E. Aguar and Berdeana Aguar, *Wrightscapes: Frank Lloyd Wright's Landscape Designs* (New York: McGraw-Hill, 2002), 162–65; Donald Leslie Johnson, "Origin of the Neighborhood Unit," *Planning Perspectives* 17 (2002): 227–45; Donald Leslie Johnson, "Frank Lloyd Wright's Community Planning," *Journal of Planning History* 3 (February 2004): 3–28; Evan Ben-Joseph, *The Code of the City: Standards and the Hidden Language of Place-Making* (Cambridge, Mass.: MIT Press, 2005), 61–64; Emily Talen, *New Urbanism and American Planning: The Conflict of Cultures* (New York: Routledge, 2005), 180, 196–97; Wilbert R. Hasbrouck, *The Chicago Architectural Club: Prelude to the Modern* (New York: Monacelli Press, 2005), 404–7; Pamela Hill, "Marion Mahoney Griffin: The Chicago Years," in Charles Waldheim and Katerina Rüedi Ray, eds., *Chicago Architecture: Histories, Revisions, Alternatives* (Chicago: University of Chicago Press, 2005), 154–55.

349 Quoted in "Pick Winners of Housing Prizes": 124.

350 "Prize-Winning Plans for Laying Out a Quarter-Section of Urban Land": 421.

351 The list of entrants includes Wilhelm Bernhard, Arthur C. Comey, Albert and Ingrid Lilienberg, H.A. Anderson and Victor Reecer, Louis H. Boynton, Brazer & Robb, G. C. Cone, William Drummond, H.J. Fixmer, Edmund Grover, W.B. Hartigan, Herbert E. Hudson, Robert Kingery, Edgar H. Lawrence, Marcia Mead, Morell & Nichols, Robert A. Pope, Charles H. Ramsdell, Riddle and Riddle, William H. Schuchardt, Albert Sturr, A.C. Tenney, Charles A. Tirrell, Phelps Wyman, Alfred B. Yeomans, A. Booth, John I. Door, Byron

H. Jillson, Percy T. Johnstone, C. Hamilton Keeber, J. Hal Lynch, Charles Mayo, Edgar W. Norton, Alfred J. Roewade, Henry T. Snyder, Leo Strelka, and Frank Lloyd Wright.

352 Quoted in Yeomans, ed., *City Residential Land Development*, 14.

353 Albert Kelsey, "Aesthetic Review of the Plans," in Yeomans, ed., *City Residential Land Development*, 109.

354 Quoted in Yeomans, ed., *City Residential Land Development*, 39.

355 Handlin, "The Context of the Modern City": 87.

356 Hasbrouck, *The Chicago Architectural Club: Prelude to the Modern*, 406.

357 Wright, *Moralism and the Model Home*, 284.

358 Gill, *Many Masks: A Life of Frank Lloyd Wright*, 423.

359 McCarter, *Frank Lloyd Wright*, 239.

360 For Como Orchards, see Henry-Russell Hitchcock, *In the Nature of Materials, 1887–1941: The Buildings of Frank Lloyd Wright* (New York: Duell, Sloan and Pearce, 1942), 55, fig. 167; Grant Carpenter Manson, *Frank Lloyd Wright to 1910: The First Golden Age* (New York: Van Nostrand Reinhold, 1958), 205–7; James Birrell, *Walter Burley Griffin* (St. Lucia, Brisbane: University of Queensland Press, 1964), 42, 44; Twombly, "Undoing the City: Frank Lloyd Wright's Planned Communities": 538–49; Delton Ludwig, "Frank Lloyd Wright in the Bitter Root Valley of Montana," *Frank Lloyd Wright Newsletter* 5 (1982): 6–15; Grant Hildebrand and Thomas Bosworth, "The Last Cottage of Wright's Como Orchards Complex," *Journal of the Society of Architectural Historians* 41 (December 1982): 325–27; Donald Leslie Johnson, "Frank Lloyd Wright's Architectural Projects in the Bitter Root Valley, 1909–1910," *Montana: The Magazine of Western History* 37 (1987): 12–15; Bruce Brooks Pfeiffer, *Frank Lloyd Wright Monograph, vol. 3: 1907–1913* (Tokyo: ADA Edita, 1987), 92–99; Johnson, *Frank Lloyd Wright Versus America: The 1930s*, 18, 148–49, 168; William Allin Storer, *The Frank Lloyd Wright Companion* (Chicago and London: University of Chicago Press, 1993), S; 144; McCarter, *Frank Lloyd Wright*, 237–39; De Long, "Frank Lloyd Wright and the Evolution of the Living City," in De Long, ed., *Frank Lloyd Wright and the Living City*, 18; Desmond, "Buildings for Communal Dwelling," in De Long, ed., *Frank Lloyd Wright and the Living City*, 149–51; Dixie Legler, *Frank Lloyd Wright: The Western Work* (San Francisco: Chronicle Books, 1999), 14–17; Aguar and Aguar, *Wrightscapes: Frank Lloyd Wright's Landscape Designs*, 133–35; Johnson, "Frank Lloyd Wright's Community Planning": 3–28. For the Bitter Root town plan, see Hitchcock, *In the Nature of Materials, 1887–1941: The Buildings of Frank Lloyd Wright*, 55; Ludwig, "Frank Lloyd Wright in the Bitter Root Valley of Montana": 6–15; Johnson, "Frank Lloyd Wright's Architectural Projects in the Bitter Root Valley, 1909–1910": 12–15; Pfeiffer, *Frank Lloyd Wright Monograph, vol. 3: 1907–1913*, 94–99; Johnson, *Frank Lloyd Wright Versus America: The 1930s*, 141–49; Storer, *The Frank Lloyd Wright Companion*, S; 145; McCarter, *Frank Lloyd Wright*, 237–39; Legler, *Frank Lloyd Wright: The Western Work*, 16; Aguar and Aguar, *Wrightscapes: Frank Lloyd Wright's Landscape Designs*, 135–38; Johnson, "Frank Lloyd Wright's Community Planning": 3–28.

361 Hegemann and Peets, *Wyomissing Park; the Modern Garden Suburb of Reading, Pennsylvania* (Wyomissing, Pa., 1919); Werner Hegemann and Elbert Peets, *The American Vitruvius: an Architects' Handbook of Civic Art* (1922; New York: Benjamin Blom, 1972), 281–83; *International Cities and Town Planning Exhibition. English Catalogue. Jubilee Exhibition, Gothenburg, Sweden, 1923* (Göteborg, Wezäta, W. Zachrissons boktyrckeri a.-b., 1923), 377; Werner Hegemann, *Amerikanische Architektur & Stadtbaukunst* (Berlin: E. Wasmuth, 1925), 116–17, 128–33; Caroline Shillaber, "Elbert Peets, Champion of the Civic Form," *Landscape Architecture* 72 (November 1982): 56; Jill Pearlman, "Joseph Hudnut's Other Modernism at the 'Harvard Bauhaus,'" *Journal of the Society of Architectural Historians* 56 (December 1997): 454; Arnold R. Alanen, "Elbert Peets," in Charles A. Birnbaum and Robin Karson, eds., *Pioneers of American Landscape Design* (New York: McGraw-Hill, 2000), 293, 295; Jill Pearlman, "Joseph Hudnut and the Unlikely Beginnings of Post-Modern Urbanism at the Harvard Bauhaus," *Planning Perspectives* 15 (2000): 211, 214; Randall Arendt, *Crossroads, Hamlet, Village, Town: Design Characteristics of Traditional Neighborhoods, Old and New (Revised Edition)* (Chicago: American Planning Association/Planning Advisory Service, 2004), 32–34; Christiane Crasemann Collins, *Werner Hegemann and the Search for Universal Urbanism* (New York: W. W. Norton & Co., 2005), 133–38; George H. Edmonds, *Wyomissing, an American Dream: Enterprise Shaping Community* (Pennsylvania: GHE Books, 2006), esp. ch. 11; Christiane Crasemann Collins, "Camillo Sitte across the Atlantic: Raymond Unwin, John Nolen, and Werner Hegemann," in Charles C. Bohl and Jean-François Lejeune, eds., *Sitte, Hegemann and the Metropolis: Modern Civic Art and International Exchanges* (London and New York: Routledge, 2009), 185.

362 Charles D. Warren, "Introduction," in John Nolen, *New Towns for Old* (1927; Amherst, Mass.: University of Massachusetts Press, 2005), xliii.

363 John Nolen, *Replanning Reading: An Industrial City of a Hundred Thousand* (Boston: Geo.H. Ellis Co., 1910); John Loretz Hancock, "John Nolen and the American City Planning Movement: a History of Culture Change and Community Response, 1900–1940" (Ph.D. diss., University of Pennsylvania, 1964): 305–49.

364 Quoted in Edmonds, *Wyomissing, an American Dream: Enterprise Shaping Community*, 75.

365 Hegemann and Peets, *Wyomissing Park; the Modern Garden Suburb of Reading, Pennsylvania*, 8.

366 Collins, *Werner Hegemann and the Search for Universal Urbanism*, 137.

367 Hegemann and Peets, *Wyomissing Park; the Modern Garden Suburb of Reading, Pennsylvania*, 7.

368 Hegemann and Peets, *Wyomissing Park; the Modern Garden Suburb of Reading, Pennsylvania*, 10.

369 Hegemann and Peets, *Wyomissing Park; the Modern Garden Suburb of Reading, Pennsylvania*, 23.

370 Hegemann and Peets, *Wyomissing Park; the Modern Garden Suburb of Reading, Pennsylvania*, 36.

371 John Nolen, *Wyomissing Park, Reading, Pennsylvania* (Wyomissing, Pa.: Wyomissing Development Co., n.d.); Charles D. Warren, "Introduction," in John Nolen, *New Towns for Old* (1927; Amherst, Mass.: University of Massachusetts Press, 2005), xliii; Nolen, *New Towns for Old*, 167, 194–95, 197–98.

372 Nolen, *Wyomissing Park, Reading, Pennsylvania*, n.p.

373 Werner Hegemann and Elbert Peets, *The American Vitruvius: an Architects' Handbook of Civic Art* (1922; New York: Benjamin Blom, 1972), 283; *International Cities and Town Planning Exhibition. English Catalogue. Jubilee Exhibition, Gothenburg, Sweden, 1923* (Göteborg, Wezäta, W. Zachrissons boktyrckeri a.-b., 1923), 377; Werner Hegemann, *Amerikanische Architektur & Stadtbaukunst* (Berlin: E. Wasmuth, 1925), 126–27; Caroline Shillaber, "Elbert Peets, Champion of the Civic Form," *Landscape Architecture* 72 (November 1982): 56; Arnold A. Alanen, "Elbert Peets: History as Precedent in Midwestern Landscape Design," in William H. Tishler, ed., *Midwestern Landscape Architecture* (Urbana and Chicago: University of Illinois Press, 2000), 196–99; Christiane Crasemann Collins, *Werner Hegemann and the Search for Universal Urbanism* (New York: W. W. Norton & Co., 2005), 130–31.

374 Collins, *Werner Hegemann and the Search for Universal Urbanism*, 130.

375 Ben J. Lubschez, "The Influence of Park and Boulevard Development on Domestic Architecture," *Journal of the American Institute of Architects* 1 (October 1913): 441–42; J. C. Nichols, "City Planning," *National Real Estate Journal* (May 15, 1916): 277–85; J. C. Nichols, "City Planning and Real Estate Development," *Landscape Architecture* 7 (October 1916): 27–35; J. C. Nichols, "Suburban Subdivisions with Community Features," *American City* 31 (October 1924): 335–38; J. C. Nichols, "A Developer's View of Deed Restrictions," *Journal of Land & Public Utility Economics* 5 (May 1929): 132–42; J. C. Nichols, "Developing Outlying Shopping Centers," *American City* 41 (July 1929): 98–101; "Inexpensive Small Houses," *Architectural Forum* 56 (March 1932): 307; "'Colonial Village' Development in Kansas City, Mo.," *Architectural Record* 73 (March 1933): 191–95; "J. C. Nichols Builds Again," *Architectural Forum* 60 (October 1934): 302–6; "Portrait of a Salesman: Jesse Clyde Nichols," *National Real Estate Journal* 40 (February 1939): 19–23, 76; "Famous Objects of Art in the Country Club District," *National Real Estate Journal* 40 (February 1939): 24–25; J. C. Nichols, "The Lessons of a Lifetime of Land Developing," *National Real Estate Journal* 40 (February 1939): 26–33, 88–91; "Restrictions Create Values in Country Club District," *National Real Estate Journal* 40 (February 1939): 37–39, 47; "Houses Designed and Built by J. C. Nichols Companies," *National Real Estate Journal* 40 (February 1939): 42–43, 46–47; "Home Owners' Associations Protect Country Club District Values," *National Real Estate Journal* 40 (February 1939): 74–75; Ward Allan Howe, "Model Home Community in Kansas City Finding Answer to the Traffic Problem," *New York Times* (August 22, 1948): 1, 5; William H. Wilson, *The City Beautiful Movement in Kansas City* (Columbia: University of Missouri Press, 1964), 130–35; Sam Bass Warner, *The Urban Wilderness: A History of the American City* (New York: Harper & Row, 1972), 210, figs. 105–9; "The Country Club District: Metropolitan Kansas City's Major Residential Area Developed by J. C. Nichols Company," promotional brochure (May 1978); "The Outdoor Art of the Country Club District," promotional brochure (May 1978); Stern with Massengale, *The Anglo-American Suburb*, 76–77; Charles N. Glaab and A. Theodore Brown, *A History of Urban America*, 3rd rev. ed. (New York: Macmillan, 1983), 291–94; Kenneth Jackson, *Crabgrass Frontier: The Suburbanization of the United States* (New York: Oxford University Press, 1985), 177–78, 258–59; Richard Longstreth, "J. C. Nichols, the Country Club Plaza, and Notions of Modernity," *Harvard Architecture Review* 5 (1986): 120–35; William S. Worley, *J. C. Nichols and the Shaping of Kansas City* (Columbia and London: University of Missouri Press, 1990); Robert Fishman, "William S. Worley: J. C. Nichols and the Shaping of Kansas City," book review, *American Historical Review* 96 (December 1991): 1632; Charles N. Glaab, "J.C. Nichols and the Shaping of Kansas City," book review, *Journal of Southern History* 58 (August 1992): 566–68; Robert Pearson and Brad Pearson, *The J. C. Nichols Chronicle: The Authorized Story of the Man, His Company, and His Legacy, 1880–1994* (Lawrence, Kans.: Country Club Plaza Press, 1994); William S. Worley, "Ward Parkway: Kansas City, Missouri," in Jan Cigliano and Sarah Bradford Landau, eds., *The Grand American Avenue, 1850–1920* (San Francisco: Pomegranate Artbooks, 1994), 281–305; Richard Longstreth, *City Center to Regional Mall: Architecture, the Automobile, and Retailing in Los Angeles, 1920–1950* (Cambridge, Mass.: MIT Press, 1997), 171–74; William S. Worley, *The Plaza, First and Always* (Lenexa, Kans.: Addax Publishing Group, 1997), 16–50; Andrés Duany, Elizabeth Plater-Zyberk, and Robert Alminana, *The New Civic Art: Elements of Town Planning* (New York: Rizzoli International Publications, 2003), 253; Dolores Hayden, *Building Suburbia: Green Fields and Urban Growth, 1820–2000* (New York: Pantheon Books, 2003), 68–69; Tom Martinson, *The Atlas of American Architecture: 2000 Years of Architecture, City Planning, Landscape Architecture and Civil Engineering* (New York: Rizzoli International Publications, 2009), 292, 368. Also see undated speech (KC106) by Nichols, "Country Club Plaza," in the Western Historical Manuscript Collection, Kansas City, Missouri.

376 Fishman, "William S. Worley: J. C. Nichols and the Shaping of Kansas City": 1632.

377 Evan S. Connell, *Mrs. Bridge: A Novel* (New York: Viking Press, 1959; Washington, D.C.: Shoemaker & Hoard, 2005), 5, quoted in Worley, "Ward Parkway: Kansas City, Missouri," in Cigliano and Landau, eds., *The Grand American Avenue, 1850–1920*, 286.

378 Edward H. Bouton, quoted in Pearson and Brad Pearson, *The J.C. Nichols Chronicle: The Authorized Story of the Man, His Company, and His Legacy, 1880–1994*, 57.

379 Nichols, "The Lessons of a Lifetime of Land Developing": 29.

380 Pearson and Pearson, *The J. C. Nichols Chronicle: The Authorized Story of the Man, His Company, and His Legacy, 1880–1994*, 51.

381 Nichols, "The Lessons of a Lifetime of Land Developing": 29–32.

382 Nichols, "The Lessons of a Lifetime of Land Developing": 29–32.

383 Nichols, "The Lessons of a Lifetime of Land Developing": 32–33.

384 Pearson and Pearson, *The J. C. Nichols Chronicle: The Authorized Story of the Man, His Company, and His Legacy, 1880–1994*, 92.

385 Pearson and Pearson, *The J.C. Nichols Chronicle: The Authorized Story of the Man, His Company, and His Legacy, 1880–1994*, 66.

386 *Shaker Heights: Ideal Home Sites* (Cleveland: O.C. Ringle & Co., 1905); *Shaker Heights Village Told in Illustrations* (Cleveland: Shaker Heights Improvement Co., 1914); "Shaker Heights Country Club," *National Architect* 6 (December 1915): plate 65; I.T. Frary, "Suburban Landscape Planning in Cleveland," *Architectural Record* 43 (April 1918): 370–84; *The Heritage of the Shakers* (Cleveland: The Van Sweringen Company, 1923); F.A. Cushing

Smith, "The Glory of Shaker Village," *American Landscape Architect* 1 (July 1929): 21–35; "The City Hall of Shaker Heights, Ohio," *Through the Ages* 9 (March 1932): 41–42; *Let's Dream of a New Joy in Living* (Cleveland: The Van Sweringen Company, 1947); *The Shaker Heights Subdivision of Shaker Heights* (Cleveland: Shaker Heights Improvement Co., 1948); William Ganson Rose, *Cleveland: The Makings of a City* (Cleveland: World Publishing Co., 1950), 1093; Christopher Tunnard and Henry Hope Reed, *American Skyline: The Growth and Form of Our Cities and Towns* (New York: New American Library, 1956), 168–69; Cleveland Chapter of the A.I.A., *Cleveland Architecture, 1796–1958* (New York: Reinhold, 1958), 34; Joseph G. Blake, "The Van Sweringen Developments in Cleveland" (Senior thesis, History Department, University of Notre Dame, 1968); Stewart Finck and Victor Ptak, *Some Sites and Homes in Shaker Heights That Might Merit Description*, unpublished manuscript (May–June 1974); Ian S. Haberman, *The Van Sweringens of Cleveland: The Biography of an Empire* (Cleveland: Western Reserve Historical Society, 1979); Patricia J. Forgac, "The Physical Development of Shaker Heights" (Master's thesis, Kent State University, 1981); Eric Johannesen, *Cleveland Architecture, 1876–1976* (Cleveland: Western Reserve Historical Society, 1981), 131–33; Stern with Massengale, *The Ango-American Suburb*, 45; Kenneth T. Jackson, *Crabgrass Frontier: The Suburbanization of the United States* (New York: Oxford University Press, 1985), 152, 169; John R. Stilgoe, *Borderland: Origins of the American Suburb, 1820–1939* (New Haven, Conn.: Yale University Press, 1988), 239–51; James Toman, *The Shaker Heights Rapid Transit* (Glendale, Calif.: Interurban Press, 1990); Jane Wood, "Shaker Heights, Then and Now," *Urban Land* 55 (April 1996): 26–28; Virginia P. Dawson, *Hands on the Past: Celebrating the First 50 Years of the Shaker Historical Society* (Shaker Heights, Ohio: Shaker Heights Historical Society, 1997); Cynthia Mills Richter, "Integrating the Suburban Dream: Shaker Heights, Ohio" (Ph.D. diss., University of Minnesota, 1999); Alexander Garvin, *The American City: What Works, What Doesn't*, 2nd ed. (New York: McGraw-Hill, 2002), 390–91, 420; Herbert H. Harwood, *Invisible Giants: The Empires of Cleveland's Van Sweringen Brothers* (Bloomington and Indianapolis: Indiana University Press, 2003); Bruce T. Marshall, *Images of America: Shaker Heights* (Charleston, S.C.: Arcadia Publishing, 2006); Tom Martinson, *The Atlas of American Architecture: 2000 Years of Architecture, City Planning, Landscape Architecture and Civil Engineering* (New York: Rizzoli International Publications, 2009), 367.

387 Geoffrey Baker and Bruno Funaro, *Shopping Centers: Design and Operation* (New York: Reinhold, 1951), 6.

388 "Moreland Courts," *Interest* 2 (August 1922): 10.

389 "Several Houses in Cleveland, Ohio, by Meade and Hamilton, Architects," *American Architect* 123 (April 11, 1923): plates; "Residence of J.B. Crouse, Cleveland," *American Architect* 123 (April 11, 1923): 16; "House of R.B. Moser, Shaker Heights," *American Architect* 128 (December 5, 1925): 503–5; "House of John A. Guyer, Shaker Heights, Cleveland, Ohio," *American Architect* 128 (December 20, 1925): 550; "House of C.A. Thompson," *American Architect* 129 (January 20, 1926): 209–10; "House of Ralph H. Comey, Shaker Heights, Cleveland, Ohio," *American Architect* 129 (January 20, 1926): 211–12; "House at Cleveland, Ohio: Architect, Chester N. Lowe," *American Architect* 130 (December 5, 1926): plates 307–8; "House in Shaker Heights," *American Architect* 132 (October 5, 1927): 477; "Two Houses in Cleveland, Ohio," *American Architect* 134 (September 5, 1928): 343; "Colonial for Cleveland: Residence of Melville J.M. Cox, Shaker Heights, Ohio," *House and Garden* 58 (November 1930): 90; "House of Dr. J.R. Driver, Shaker Heights, Cleveland, Ohio," *House Beautiful* 69 (May 1931): 492–93; "House of Mrs. Nelson Rogers, Shaker Heights, Cleveland, Ohio," *House Beautiful* 70 (September 1931): 222–23; "Residence of Patrick Butler, at Shaker Heights," *House and Garden* 61 (January 1932): 52–53; "House of Mr. and Mrs. Lawrence McDonough, Shaker Heights, Ohio," *American Architect* 145 (December 1934): 45; "Residence of H.M. Rosencrans, Shaker Heights, Ohio," *House and Garden* 70 (September 1936): 113; "Residences, Shaker Heights, Cleveland, Ohio," *Architectural Forum* 65 (October 1936): 389.

390 "Rockefeller Building 81 Houses in Cleveland," *Business Week* (October 1, 1930): 17; Arthur C. Holden, "Realty Developments and the Architect," *Architectural Record* 69 (April 1931): 346–52; "Mr. Rockefeller Returns to Cleveland," *Fortune* 4 (July 1931): 30–31, 78; Arthur H. Dreher, "Forest Hill–A Modern Suburban Development," *American Landscape Architect* 5 (July 1931): 8–13; Matlack Price, "Forest Hill, Cleveland, Ohio," *Architecture* 65 (March 1932): 125–36; "How to Mix Houses of Varying Heights in Subdivision Planning," *American Builder* 75 (November 1953): 204–6; Grace Goulder, *John D. Rockefeller: The Cleveland Years* (Cleveland: Western Reserve Historical Society, 1972), 229–32; David D. Van Tassel and John J. Grabowski, eds., *The Encyclopedia of Cleveland History* (Bloomington: Indiana University Press, 1987), 417; Joseph W. Ernst, ed., *"Dear Father"/"Dear Son": Correspondence of John D. Rockefeller and John D. Rockefeller, Jr.* (New York: Fordham University Press in cooperation with Rockefeller Archive Center, 1994), 183–84, 212–13; Sharon E. Gregor, *Forest Hill: The Rockefeller Estate* (Charleston, S.C.: Arcadia, 2006), 57–95. For Thomas's work for Rockefeller in New York, see Stern, Gilmartin, and Mellins, *New York 1930*, 419–21.

391 Price, "Forest Hill, Cleveland, Ohio": 129.

392 "Mr. Rockefeller Returns to Cleveland": 31. For the story of Time's move to Cleveland, see Isaiah Wilner, *The Man That Time Forgot: A Tale of Genius, Betrayal, and the Creation of Time Magazine* (New York: HarperCollins, 2006), 155–57.

393 "Mr. Rockefeller Returns to Cleveland": 31, 78.

394 S. Mays Ball, "The Suburbs Beautiful," *House & Garden* 15 (November 1909): 166–71.

395 Marjorie Longenecker White, "The Grid and the Garden," in Philip A. Morris and Marjorie Longenecker White, eds., *Designs on Birmingham: A Landscape History of a Southern City and Its Suburbs* (Birmingham, Ala.: Birmingham Historical Society, 1989), 22. Also see "Biographies of Early Planners," in Morris and White, eds., *Designs on Birmingham*, 68–69.

396 White, "The Grid and the Garden," in Morris and White, eds., *Designs on Birmingham*, 12.

397 *Mountain Terrace: The Residence Park of Birmingham* (Birmingham: The Jemison Real Estate & Insurance Co., c.1906); Samuel Parsons, *Landscape Gardening Studies* (New York: John Lane Company, 1910), 32–36; Carl Martin Hames, *Hill Ferguson: His Life and Works* (Tuscaloosa: University of Alabama Press, 1978), 35–36; Philip A. Morris and Marjorie Longenecker White, eds., *Designs on Birmingham: A Landscape History*

of a Southern City and Its Suburbs (Birmingham, Ala.: Birmingham Historical Society, 1989), 13–15.

398 Quoted in *Mountain Terrace: The Residence Park of Birmingham*, 12.

399 White, "The Grid and the Garden," in Morris and White, eds., *Designs on Birmingham: A Landscape History of a Southern City and Its Suburbs* (Birmingham, Ala.: Birmingham Historical Society, 1989), 15.

400 Marjorie Longenecker White, "The Grid and the Garden," in Philip A. Morris and Marjorie Longenecker White, eds., *Designs on Birmingham: A Landscape History of a Southern City and Its Suburbs* (Birmingham, Ala.: Birmingham Historical Society, 1989), 22–23.

401 Marjorie Longenecker White, "The Grid and the Garden," in Philip A. Morris and Marjorie Longenecker White, eds., *Designs on Birmingham: A Landscape History of a Southern City and Its Suburbs* (Birmingham, Ala.: Birmingham Historical Society, 1989), 23–24.

402 "Builders of Birmingham—Jemison & Company," *Birmingham* II (September 1926): 4–6; "Subdividing the U.S., 1935–36," *Architectural Forum* 65 (October 1936): 388; Carl Martin Hames, *Hill Ferguson: His Life and Works* (Tuscaloosa: University of Alabama Press, 1978), 55–59; Marjorie Longenecker White, "The Grid and the Garden," in Philip A. Morris and Marjorie Longenecker White, eds., *Designs on Birmingham: A Landscape History of a Southern City and Its Suburbs* (Birmingham, Ala.: Birmingham Historical Society, 1989), 25–27; Philip A. Morris, "Village Idiom," *Landscape Architecture* 87 (February 1997): 34–41; Robert Fogelson, *Bourgeois Nightmares, Suburbia, 1870–1930* (New Haven, Conn., and London: Yale University Press, 2005), 76.

403 William B. O'Neal and Christopher Weeks, *The Work of William Lawrence Bottomley in Richmond* (Charlottesville: University Press of Virginia, 1985), 103–7; Marcus Binney, "An English Garden Suburb on the James," *Country Life* 177 (April 4, 1985): 912–14; Richard Guy Wilson, ed., *Buildings of Virginia: Tidewater and Piedmont* (New York: Oxford University Press, 2002), 273–78.

404 Lawrence V. Sheridan, "Columbus, Kentucky," *Architectural Record* 63 (March 1928): 280–84; *Supplementary Report of the Urbanism Committee to the National Resources Committee* (Washington, D.C.: U. S. Government Printing Office, 1939), 112, 119, 127, 128, 450.

405 Sheridan, "Columbus, Kentucky": 283.

406 Hugh Potter, quoted in Barry J. Kaplan and Charles Orson Cook, "River Oaks: A Planned Elite Community," *East Texas Historical Journal* 15 (February 1977): 29–37. Also see Will and Mike Hogg, *Our Story of River Oaks* (Houston: Country Club Estates, 1925); Will and Mike Hogg, *Our Story of River Oaks, Chapter II* (Houston: Country Club Estates, 1926); "Homes Are Still Being Sold," *Architectural Forum* 59 (July 1933): 82–83; "River Oaks," *Architectural Forum* 62 (May 1935): 472–73; "Living in the Suburbs," *Architectural Forum* 114 (January 1961): 71–74; *Houston: An Architectural Guide* (Houston: American Institute of Architects, Houston Chapter, 1972), 85–86; Wendy Haskell Meyer, "River Oaks: Still the 'Satin Slipper Suburb,'" *Houston Home & Garden* 2 (August 1976): 42–45, 48, 134–35; Stephen Fox, *River Oaks: A Tour of Its Architecture* (Houston: American Institute of Architects, Houston Chapter, 1978); Howard Barnstone, *The Architecture of John F. Staub: Houston and the South* (Austin: University of Texas Press, 1979), 7–11; "River Oaks Subdivision," *Houston Architectural Survey, Volume 3* (Houston: Southwest Center for Urban Research, 1980), 498–507; Stern with Massengale, *The Anglo-American Suburb*, 83; William S. Worley, *J. C. Nichols and the Shaping of Kansas City* (Columbia and London: University of Missouri Press, 1990), 175–77; Marguerite Johnston, *Houston, the Unknown City, 1836–1946* (College Station: Texas A & M University, 1991), 227–37; Richard Longstreth, "River Oaks Shopping Center," *Cite* 36 (Winter 1996): 8–13; Cheryl Caldwell Ferguson, "River Oaks: 1920s Suburban Planning and Development in Houston," *Southwestern Historical Quarterly* 104 (October 2000): 191–228; Cheryl Lynn Caldwell Ferguson, "Upscale Suburban Architecture and Development in Dallas and Houston, Texas, 1890–1930" (Ph.D. diss., University of Delaware, 2004): 349–429; Stephen Fox, *The Country Houses of John F. Staub* (College Station: Texas A&M University Press, 2007), 68–112.

407 "Living in the Suburbs": 72.

408 Will and Mike Hogg, *Our Story of River Oaks*, 1, also quoted in Ferguson, "River Oaks: 1920s Suburban Planning and Development in Houston": 208.

409 Kaplan and Cook, "River Oaks: A Planned Elite Community": 10.

410 Fox, *The Country Houses of John F. Staub*, 68.

411 Fox, *The Country Houses of John F. Staub*, 70.

412 Fox, *The Country Houses of John F. Staub*, 70, 73.

413 WPA Writers' Program of the Work Projects Administration in Southern California, *Los Angeles: A Guide to the City and Its Environs* (New York: Hastings House, 1941), 204; Stanley L. McMichael, *Real Estate Subdivisions* (New York: Prentice-Hall, 1949), 61–62, 116, 249; WPA Writers' Program of the Work Projects Administration in Southern California, *Los Angeles: a Guide to the City and Its Environs*, 2nd ed., completely rev. (New York: Hastings House, 1951), 208; David Gebhard and Harriette Von Breton, *L.A. in the Thirties: 1931–1941* (Layton, Utah: Peregrine Smith, 1975), 17; Charles Moore, Peter Becker, and Regula Campbell, *The City Observed: Los Angeles* (New York: Random House, 1984), 206–9; Jan Cigliano and Sarah Bradford Landau, eds., *The Grand American Avenue, 1850–1920* (San Francisco: Pomegranate Artbooks; Washington, D.C.: Octagon, 1994), 325–26; Richard Longstreth, *City Center to Regional Mall: Architecture, the Automobile, and Retailing in Los Angeles, 1920–1950* (Cambridge, Mass.: MIT Press, 1997), 159–75; Douglas S. Brown, "The Renaissance of Westwood Village," *Urban Land* 57 (February 1998): 22–25; Andrés Duany, Elizabeth Plater-Zyberk, and Robert Alminana, *The New Civic Art: Elements of Town Planning* (New York: Rizzoli International Publications, 2003), 252; Sally Sims Stokes, "In a Climate Like Ours: The California Campuses of Allison & Allison," *California History* 84 (Fall 2007): 51–52.

414 Longstreth, *City Center to Regional Mall*, 160.

415 Quoted in Sally Sims Stokes, "In a Climate Like Ours: The California Campuses of Allison & Allison," *California History* 84 (Fall 2007): 52.

416 Longstreth, *City Center to Regional Mall*, 165.

417 Longstreth, *City Center to Regional Mall*, 166.

418 *Los Angeles: A Guide to the City and Its Environs*, 204.

419 Longstreth, *City Center to Regional Mall*, 171.

420 McMichael, *Real Estate Subdivisions*, 62.

421 "New Queensboro Apartment Houses," *New York Times* (April 9, 1916): 27; "Apartment

Building at Jackson Heights," *Real Estate Record and Builders' Guide* 100 (July 7, 1917): 6, 11–12; "Million Dollar Apartment House Development for Queens," *New York Times* (May 25, 1919): 112; "New Garden Apartments, Queens County, New York City: A Group of Buildings Now Under Construction Showing Economy of Plan and New Principles of Land Development," *Architectural Forum* 30 (June 1919): 187–91; "Apartment Houses at Jackson Heights, N.Y.," *Architectural Forum* 33 (July 1920): 29–30; John Taylor Boyd, Jr., "Garden Apartments in Cities," *Architectural Record* 48 (July 1920): 53–74, and (August 1920): 121–35; "Garden Apartment Buildings for the Queensboro Corp., Jackson Heights, Queens, New York," *Architecture* 42 (September 1920): plates 129–31; "Revolutionizing the Apartment House," *House Beautiful* 49 (March 1921): 186–87; "Two Types (4 and 5 Rooms) for Apartment-House Group, Borough of Queens, N.Y.," *Architecture* 43 (June 1921): plate 82; "New Jackson Heights Apartment Will Cost $5,000,000," *Real Estate Record and Builders' Guide* 109 (March 11, 1922): 300; Frank Chouteau Brown, "Tendencies in Apartment House Design, Part XI: The Unit Apartment Building and Its Grouping," *Architectural Record* 51 (May 1922): 434–46; "The Button-Control Elevator in a New Type of Moderate-Price Apartment Buildings at Jackson Heights, New York City," *Architectural Record* 51 (June 1922): 486–90; "Jackson Heights Visit," *New York Times* (July 30, 1922): 104; "Apartment Houses for the Queensboro Corporation," *Journal of the American Institute of Architects* 10 (October 1922): 324–25; C. Stanley Taylor, "Recent Progress in Developing Co-Operative Apartment Buildings," *Architectural Forum* 37 (November 1922): 219–24; "Hawthorne Court: Jackson Heights Apartments," *American Architect* 122 (November 1922): 464–66; "Recent Progress in Developing Co-operative Apartment Buildings," *Architectural Forum* 37 (November 1922): 219–24; "The Chateau Apartments, Jackson Heights, N.Y.," *Architecture and Building* 55 (February 1923): plates 22–26; "Cambridge Court, Jackson Heights, Queens, Long Island," *Architecture* 48 (September 1923): 309–10; "Chateau Apartments, Jackson Heights, Queens, Long Island," *Architecture* 48 (September 1923): 311–14; "We Need More of Them," editorial, *Architecture* 48 (October 1923): 335; "Garden Apartments, Jackson Heights, N.Y.," *American Architect* 125 (February 13, 1924): 178; "The Garden Homes at Jackson Heights, Long Island," *Architecture and Building* 56 (June 1924): 53–56, plates 123–24; "The Towers, Jackson Heights, L.I.," *Architect* 2 (July 1924): plates 87–88; "The Evolution and Development of Jackson Heights," *Architectural Forum* 41 (August 1924): 61–66; *Investment Features of Cooperative Apartment Ownership at Jackson Heights*, promotional brochure (New York: Queensboro Corporation, 1925); William T. Benslyn, "Recent Developments in Apartment Housing in America," *Journal of the Royal Institute of British Architects* 32 (June 27, 1925): 504–7; A. E. MacDougall, "New Features in Apartment House Building," *Architectural Forum* 43 (September 1925): 153–60; R.W. Sexton, ed., *American Apartment Houses of Today* (New York: Architectural Book Publishing Co., 1926), 87–88, plates 10, 18, 31; "Towers Apartment Wins Queens Prize," *New York Times* (January 30, 1926), X: 2; "Entrance Detail, the Towers Apartments, Jackson Heights, N.Y.," *American Architect* 129 (June 1926): plate 146; Margaret J. Sylvester, "Garden Apartments," *House Beautiful* 66 (November 1929): 582–83, 622; Federal Writers' Project of the Works Progress Administration, *The WPA Guide to New York City* (New York: Random House, 1939; New York: Pantheon Books, 1982), 566–67; Richard Plunz, "Institutionalization of Housing Form in New York City, 1920–1950," in Richard Plunz, ed., *Housing Form and Public Policy in the United States* (New York: Praeger, 1980), 158–64; Robert A. M. Stern, "With Rhetoric: The New York Apartment House," *Via* 4 (1980): 78–111; Michael Winkleman, "The Visible City," *Metropolis* 1 (March 1982): 23–25; Richard Plunz and Marta Gutman, "The New York Ring," *Eupalino* 1 (Winter 1983/1984): 32–47; Stern, Gilmartin, and Mellins, *New York 1930*, 477–85; Daniel Karatzas, *Jackson Heights: A Garden in the City*, with an intro. by Robert A. M. Stern (Jackson Heights, N.Y.: Jackson Heights Beautification Group, 1990); Richard Plunz, *A History of Housing in New York City* (New York: Columbia University Press, 1990), 130–31, 138–47; Jeffrey Kroessler, "Building Queens: The Urbanization of New York's Largest Borough" (Ph.D. diss., City University of New York, 1991): 352–53, 356–59; Vincent F. Seyfried and William Asadorian, *Old Queens, N.Y. in Early Photographs* (New York: Dover Publications, 1991), 168–72; Robert A. M. Stern and Thomas Mellins, "1920/1929 Housing America," *Architectural Record* 179 (July 1991): 158–61, reprinted in Cynthia Davidson, ed., *Tradition and Invention: Essays on Architecture, Robert A. M. Stern* (New Haven, Conn., and London: Yale University Press, 2011), 16–22; Landmarks Preservation Commission of the City of New York, *Jackson Heights Historic District Designation Report* (New York, 1993); Vincent Seyfried, "Jackson Heights," in Kenneth T. Jackson, ed., *The Encyclopedia of New York City* (New Haven, Conn., and London: Yale University Press; New York: New-York Historical Society, 1995), 607; *Historic Jackson Heights Visitors Guide* (Jackson Heights, N.Y.: Jackson Heights Beautification Group, 1996); Norval White and Elliot Willensky, *AIA Guide to New York City*, 4th ed. (New York: Crown Publishers, 2000), 823–85; Andrew S. Dolkart and Matthew A. Postal, *Guide to New York City Landmarks*, 3rd ed. (Hoboken, N.J.: Wiley, 2004), 279–81; Claudia Gryvatz Copquin, *The Neighborhoods of Queens* (New Haven, Conn., and London: Yale University Press, 2007), 94–99; Matthew Gordon Lasner, *High Life: Condo Living in the Suburban Century* (New Haven, Conn., and London: Yale University Press, 2012), 66–72.

422 For the Tower and Home Buildings, see Stern, Mellins, and Fishman, *New York 1880*, 878–83.

423 Boyd, "Garden Apartments in Cities" (August 1920): 121–35.

424 Plunz, "Institutionalization of Housing Form in New York City, 1920–1950," in Plunz, ed., *Housing Form and Public Policy in the United States*, 158.

425 *Homes & Gardens. Jackson Heights. The Restricted Garden Residential Section of New York City*, undated promotional brochure, Wurts Collection, Museum of the City of New York.

426 "Model Community Buyers Moving In," *New York Times* (September 7, 1924), X: 1; "Housing for Wage Earners," *New York Times* (November 16, 1924), XX: 7; Lewis Mumford, "Houses—Sunnyside Up," *The Nation* 120 (February 4, 1925): 115–16; Clarence S. Stein, "A New Venture in Housing," *American City* 32 (March 1925): 277–81; Bruce Bliven, "Houses of Tomorrow," *New Republic* 42 (March 4, 1925): 34–37; "Sunnyside Homes," *New York Times* (April 19, 1925), XII: 2; Richard T. Ely, "The City Housing Corporation and 'Sunnyside,'" *Journal of Land & Public Utility Economics* 2 (April 1926): 172–82; Herbert Emmerich, "Experience with Open Spaces and Community Recreation in a New Subdivision," *American City* 36 (February 1927): 159–62; Louis H. Pink, *The New Day in Housing* (New York: John Day Co., 1928), 86–89; City Housing Corporation, *Sunnyside and the Housing Problem* (New York, ca. 1928); Herbert Emmerich, "The Problem of Low-Priced Cooperative Apartments: An Experiment at Sunnyside Gardens," *Journal of Land & Public Utility Economics* 4 (August 1928): 225–34; City Housing Corporation, *Sunnyside Gardens: A Home Community* (Long Island City, N.Y., ca. 1929); "Garage, Sunnyside Gardens, Long Island," *Architectural Record* 65 (March 1929): 248; "Wilson Court, Sunnyside Gardens," *Architectural Record* 65 (March 1929): 246–47; Alexander M. Bing, "Minimum Costs for Low-Rental Apartments," *Journal of Land & Public Utility Economics* 5 (May 1929): 113–24; Alexander M. Bing, "American Garden Colonies," *Housing and Building* (May–June 1930): 99–113; C. Theodore Larson, "Play Areas for Apartment Houses," *Architectural Record* 69 (March 1931): 225–33; Rosalind Tough, "Production Costs of Urban Land in Sunnyside, Long Island," *Journal of Land & Public Utility Economics* 8 (February 1932): 43–54, (May 1932): 164–74; "Sunnyside, Queens, New York," *Architectural Forum* 56 (March 1932): 250–52; Charles S. Ascher, "The Enforcement of Deed Restrictions," *City Planning* 8 (October 1932): 193–202; Henry Wright, "The Architect and Small House Costs," *Architectural Record* 72 (December 1932): 389–94; Henry Wright, *Rehousing Urban America* (New York: Columbia University Press, 1935), 29–42; "Rolling Their Own Relief," *Survey* 71 (February 1935): 51; Lewis Mumford, *The Culture of Cities* (New York: Harcourt, Brace, 1938), 484; Federal Writers' Project of the Works Progress Administration, *The WPA Guide to New York City* (New York: Random House, 1939; New York: Pantheon Books, 1982), 578–79; Lewis Mumford, *City Development: Studies in Disintegration and Renewal* (New York: Harcourt, Brace, 1945), 74; Lewis Mumford, *Green Memories: The Story of Geddes Mumford* (New York: Harcourt, Brace, 1949), 30–31; Clarence S. Stein, *Toward New Towns for America* (New York: Reinhold, 1957), 21–35; Lewis Mumford, *The Urban Prospect* (New York: Harcourt, Brace & World, 1968), 75; Norman T. Newton, *Design on the Land: The Development of Landscape Architecture* (Cambridge, Mass., and London: Belknap Press of Harvard University Press, 1971), 489–90; Ada Louise Huxtable, "Clarence Stein—The Champion of the Neighborhood," *New York Times* (January 16, 1977): 23, 28; Robert A. M. Stern, "With Rhetoric: The New York Apartment House," *Via* 4 (1980): 78–111; Stern with Massengale, *The Anglo-American Suburb*, 46; Paul Goldberger, "To Utopia by Bus and Subway," *New York Times* (April 17, 1981), C: 1, 24; Franklin J. Havelick and Michael Kwartler, "Sunnyside Gardens: Whose Land Is It Anyway?" *New York Affairs* 7 (1982): 65–80; Martin Filler, "Planning for a Better World: The Lasting Legacy of Clarence Stein," *Architectural Record* 170 (August 1982): 122–27; Stern, Gilmartin, and Mellins, *New York 1930*, 487–92; Marcus W. Brauchli, "If You're Thinking of Living in Sunnyside," *New York Times* (July 3, 1983), X: 7; Tom Robbins, "The Democratic Vision of Sunnyside Gardens," *City Limits* 10 (March 1985): 16–19; Nina Rappaport, "Sunnyside Gardens, a Walking Tour," *Sites* 16–17 (1986): 81–89; "Sunnyside Gardens Renewed," *Progressive Architecture* 67 (November 1986): 47; Richard Plunz, *A History of Housing in New York City* (New York: Columbia University Press, 1990), 168–73; Nina Rappaport with Steven Saltzman, "Sunnyside Gardens," *Metropolis* 20 (June 1991): 15–19; Robert A. M. Stern and Thomas Mellins, "1920/1929 Housing America," *Architectural Record* 179 (July 1991): 158–61, in Cynthia Davidson, ed., *Tradition and Invention: Essays on Architecture, Robert A. M. Stern* (New Haven, Conn., and London.: Yale University Press, 2011), 16–22; Norimitsu Onishi, "Sunnyside Gardens/Long Island City," *New York Times* (October 2, 1994), XIII: 10; Patricia A. Doyal, "Sunnyside Gardens," in Kenneth T. Jackson, ed., *The Encyclopedia of New York City* (New Haven, Conn., and London: Yale University Press; New York: New-York Historical Society, 1995), 1143; Frank G. Novak, ed., *Lewis Mumford and Patrick Geddes: The Correspondence* (New York: Routledge, 1995), 228–29, 269–71; Norval White and Elliot Willensky, *AIA Guide to New York City*, 4th ed. (New York: Crown Publishers, 2000), 810–11; James Trager, *The New York Chronology* (New York: Harper Resource, 2003), 409; Claudia Gryvatz Copquin, *The Neighborhoods of Queens* (New Haven, Conn., and London: Yale University Press, 2007), 196–98; Landmarks Preservation Commission of the City of New York, *Sunnyside Gardens Historic District Designation Report* (New York, 2007); Thaïsa Way, *Unbounded Practice: Women and Landscape Architecture in the Early Twentieth Century* (Charlottesville and London: University of Virginia Press, 2009), 229, 236, 239–40, 243, 252; Cynthia Zaitzevsky, *Long Island Landscapes and the Women Who Designed Them* (New York: W. W. Norton & Company and Society for the Preservation of Long Island Antiquities, 2009), 210–15; Matthew Gordon Lasner, *High Life: Condo Living in the Suburban Century* (New Haven, Conn., and London: Yale University Press, 2012), 110–12.

427 Quoted in Trager, *The New York Chronology*, 409.

428 Stein, *Toward New Towns for America*, 21–22.

429 Stein, *Toward New Towns for America*, 21–22.

430 Mumford, "Houses—Sunnyside Up": 115–16.

431 Pink, *The New Day in Housing*, 86.

432 "Garden Apartments," editorial, *Architect* 14 (June 1930): 242–43; Isadore Rosenfield, "Phipps Garden Apartments," *Architectural Forum* 56 (February 1932): 110–18, 183–87; "The Phipps Garden Apartments," *Architectural Forum* 56 (February 1932): 119–24; "Phipps Garden Apartments," *Architectural Record* 71 (March 1932): 201–7; Stein, *Toward New Towns for America*, 87–92, 109–13; Stern, "With Rhetoric": 99; Stern, Gilmartin, and Mellins, *New York 1930*, 487–89, 492; Plunz, *A History of Housing in New York City*, 160–61, 173; White and Willensky, *AIA Guide to New York City*, 4th ed., 812; *Sunnyside Gardens Historic District*, 34–37, 87, 145–61.

433 "Chatham Village: A Modern Community of Garden Homes Combining Architectural Charm with Security and Cultural Living," *The Foundation* (Pittsburgh: Buhl Foundation, January 1932). Also see Frederick Bigger, "More Limited Dividend Housing," *Octagon* 3 (October 1931): 3–7; Charles F. Lewis, "A Moderate Rental Housing Project in Pittsburgh," *Architectural Record* 70 (October 1931): 217–34; "Foundation Alters Homes Sale Plan," *New York Times* (November 7, 1931): 18; "Buhl Plan to Give 300 Families Home," *Washington Post* (November 8, 1931), R: 2; Charles F. Lewis, "A Community Built on Facts," *Architectural Forum* 56 (March 1932): 254–58; Henry Wright, "Housing—Why, When, and How? V. The Case for Group Housing: Chatham Village," *Architecture* 68 (August 1933): 99–103; Clarence S. Stein, "New Towns for the Needs of a New Age," *New York Times* (October 8, 1933),

VI: 6–7, 13; Thomas Adams, *The Design of Residential Areas* (Cambridge, Mass.: Harvard University Press, 1934), 258–59; Catherine Bauer Wurster, *Modern Housing* (Boston and New York: Houghton Mifflin, 1934), 152, 239; R. L. Duffus, "What Modern Housing Means and Why It Is Delayed," book review, *New York Times* (December 23, 1934), V: 3; Henry Wright, *Rehousing Urban America* (New York: Columbia University Press, 1935), 46–50; "Chatham Village, Second Unit," *American Architect* 150 (February 1937): 63–66; "Reviews Career of Home Project," *New York Times* (October 3, 1937): 68; C. V. Starrett, "Housing That Pays," *Survey Graphic* 27 (January 1938): 24; Albert Mayer, "What Retards Housing? How Can It Go Ahead?" *New York Times* (May 15, 1938): 7, 21–22; Arthur C. Comey and Max S. Wehrly, "Planned Communities," (November 1936) in *Supplementary Report of the Urbanism Committee to the National Resources Committee* (Washington, D.C.: U. S. Government Printing Office, 1939), vol. 2: 101–3, 126–27, 136; Alan Mather, "Henry Wright," *Pencil Points* 21 (January 1940): 10–11, 13; *Chatham Village News* 14 (June 11, 1945): 1; Clarence S. Stein, "Chatham Village, Pittsburgh," *Town Planning Review* 20 (October 1949): 252–58, plates 46–48; *Chatham Village, Pittsburgh* (Pittsburgh: Chatham Village Incorporated, June 30, 1956); Clarence S. Stein, *Toward New Towns for America* (Cambridge, Mass., and London: MIT Press, 1957), 74–85; "Chatham Village Revisited," *Architectural Forum* 112 (May 1960): 118–21; Jane Jacobs, *The Death and Life of Great American Cities* (New York: Random House, 1961), 64–65, 73, 80, 84; Lewis Mumford, *The City in History: Its Origins, Its Transformations, and Its Prospects* (New York: Harcourt, Brace & World, 1961), plate 43; Martin Meyerson, *Face of the Metropolis* (New York: Random House, 1963), 138–40; James D. Van Trump and Arthur P. Ziegler Jr., *Landmark Architecture of Allegheny County, Pennsylvania* (Pittsburgh: Pittsburgh History & Landmarks Foundation, 1967), 156–57; Roy Lubove, *Twentieth-Century Pittsburgh* (New York: John Wiley & Sons, 1969), 70–82; Norman T. Newton, *Design on the Land* (Cambridge, Mass., and London: Belknap Press of Harvard University Press, 1971), 496–500; Arthur B. Gallion and Simon Eisner, *The Urban Pattern* (New York: D. Van Nostrand Company, 1975), 146; *Chatham Village: A Timeless Community*, promotional brochure (Pittsburgh: Chatham Village Homes, 1976); Ada Louise Huxtable, "Clarence Stein—The Champion of the Neighborhood," *New York Times* (January 16, 1977): 23, 28; Richard Pommer, "The Architecture of Urban Housing in the United States during the Early 1930s," *Journal of the Society of Architectural Historians* 37 (December 1978): 239; Giorgio Ciucci, Francesco Dal Co, Mario Manieri-Elia, and Manfredo Tafuri, *The American City: From the Civil War to the New Deal* (Cambridge, Mass.: MIT Press, 1979), 242–43; Leland M. Roth, *A Concise History of American Architecture* (New York: Harper & Row, 1979), 268; Daniel Schaffer, *Garden Cities for America: The Radburn Experience* (Philadelphia: Temple University Press, 1982), 222–23; Martin Filler, "Planning for a Better World: The Lasting Legacy of Clarence Stein," *Architectural Record* 170 (August 1982): 122–27; Franklin Toker, *Pittsburgh: An Urban Portrait* (University Park and London: Pennsylvania State University Press, 1986), 138–39; Richard Cleary, "Edgar J. Kaufmann, Frank Lloyd Wright and the 'Pittsburgh Point Park Coney Island in Automobile Scale,'" *Journal of the Society of Architectural Historians* 52 (June 1993): 141 (n.8); Randall Arendt, *Rural by Design: Maintaining Small Town Character* (Chicago: Planners Press, 1994), 161, 359; Peter Walker and Melanie Simo, *Invisible Gardens: The Search for Modernism in the American Landscape* (Cambridge, Mass., and London: MIT Press, 1994), 49–51; Edward K. Spann, *Designing Modern America: The Regional Plan Association of America and Its Members* (Columbus: Ohio State University Press, 1996), 183; David Vater, "Chatham Village Historic District," *National Register of Historic Places Registration* (1996), VII: 1–4; Walter Kidney, *Landmark Architecture: Pittsburgh and Allegheny County* (Pittsburgh: Pittsburgh History & Landmarks Foundation, 1997), 113, 136, 302; Kenneth Kolson, *Big Plans: The Allure and Folly of Urban Design* (Baltimore and London: Johns Hopkins University Press, 2001), 107–9; Leland M. Roth, *American Architecture: A History* (Boulder: Icon Editions/Westview Press, 2001), 400–401; Randall M. Miller and William Pencak, eds., *Pennsylvania: A History of the Commonwealth* (University Park: Pennsylvania State University Press, 2002), 297; Malcolm Gladwell, "Designs for Working," in Rob Cross, Andrew Parker, and Lisa Sasson, eds., *Networks in the Knowledge Economy* (New York: Oxford University Press, 2003), 188–89; "National Historic Landmark," *Planning* 71 (June 2005): 47; Jane Roy Brown, "Four for the Record: Landscapes Are Among Newly Designated Historic Landmarks," *Landscape Architecture* 95 (August 2005): 20, 22; John F. Bauman and Edward K. Muller, *Before Renaissance: Planning in Pittsburgh, 1889–1943* (Pittsburgh: University of Pittsburgh Press, 2006), 203–4; Franklin Toker, *Buildings of Pittsburgh* (Chicago: Society of Architectural Historians; Charlottesville and London: University of Virginia Press, 2007), 66; Paul Farmer, "Chatham Village Turns 75," *Planning* 73 (June 2007): 6; Angelique Bamberg, *Chatham Village: Pittsburgh's Garden City* (Pittsburgh: University of Pittsburgh Press, 2011).

434 See Donald Lisio, "Investing in Pittsburgh's Progress: The History of the Buhl Foundation" (Ph.D. diss., University of Wisconsin, 1964).

435 *Chatham Village News*, quoted in Lubove, *Twentieth-Century Pittsburgh*, 81.

436 Starrett, "Housing That Pays": 24.

437 Wurster, *Modern Housing*, 239.

438 Mumford, *The City in History*, plate 43.

439 Jacobs, *The Death and Life of Great American Cities*, 64.

440 Stein, *Toward New Towns for America*, 92–107; Stern, Gilmartin, and Mellins, assisted by Fishman and Gastil, *New York 1930*, 491–92, 494; Richard Plunz, *A History of Housing in New York City* (New York: Columbia University Press, 1990), 212–13; William P. Macht, "Solution File: Blighted Icon Reborn," *Urban Land* 60 (July 2001): 28–29; Thaïsa Way, *Unbounded Practice: Women and Landscape Architecture in the Early Twentieth Century* (Charlottesville and London: University of Virginia Press, 2009), 229, 240, 243–45, 248.

441 Stein, *Toward New Towns for America*, 93.

442 Lewis Mumford, "The Sky Line: The New Housing," *New Yorker* 11 (December 7, 1935): 134–36.

443 William E. Leuchtenburg, *The FDR Years: On Roosevelt and His Legacy* (New York: Columbia University Press, 1995), 248–49; Laura Bobeczko and Richard Longstreth, "Housing Reform Meets the Marketplace," in Richard Longstreth, ed., *Housing Washington: Two Centuries of Residential Development and Planning in the National Capitol Area* (Chicago: Center for American Places at Columbia College Chicago, 2010), 159–67.

444 "Air Conditioning for Homes," *Architectural Forum* 63 (August 1935): 136–39; Gustave Ring, "The FHA Plan Applied to a Large-Scale Development," *Real Estate Record* 140 (August 21, 1937): 8–13; "1937 Building for Arlington Near 7 Millions," *Washington Post* (December 28, 1937): 12; "The Federal Housing Administration," *Federal Architect* 9 (October 1938): 36–37; Sandra G. Boodman, "First FHA Garden Apartments, Colonial Village, May Be Sold," *Washington Post* (October 6, 1977), Virginia weekly: 1, 7; Erin Marcus, "Colonial Village: Quiet and Diverse," *Washington Post* (January 18, 1992), E: 1, 6–7; Gail Baker, "Garden Apartments: Three Preservation Case Studies in Virginia," *CRM Bulletin* 22 (No. 5, 1999): 23–25; Richard Guy Wilson, ed., *Buildings of Virginia; Tidewater and Piedmont* (New York: Oxford University Press, 2002), 53–54; Bobeczko and Longstreth, "Housing Reform Meets the Marketplace," in Longstreth, ed., *Housing Washington*, 167–72; Matthew Gordon Lasner, *High Life: Condo Living in the Suburban Century* (New Haven, Conn., and London: Yale University Press, 2012), 120–21.

445 "1937 Building for Arlington Near 7 Millions": 12; Oscar Fisher, "Buckingham: Housing Laboratory," *Architectural Record* 83 (January 1938): 68–82; Lee E. Cooper, "New Ideas Used for Model Housing," *New York Times* (January 9, 1938), XII: 1–2; Clarence Arthur Perry, *Housing for the Machine Age* (New York: Russell Sage Foundation, 1939), 44–48; "Buckingham Historic District," *National Register of Historic Places* (1998); Baker, "Garden Apartments: Three Preservation Case Studies in Virginia": 23–25; Wilson, ed., *Buildings of Virginia; Tidewater and Piedmont*, 51; Emily Talen, *New Urbanism and American Planning: The Conflict of Cultures* (New York: Routledge, 2005), 192; Bobeczko and Longstreth, "Housing Reform Meets the Marketplace," in Longstreth, ed., *Housing Washington*, 174–77.

446 Bobeczko and Longstreth, "Housing Reform Meets the Marketplace," in Longstreth, ed., *Housing Washington*, 176.

447 Fisher, "Buckingham: Housing Laboratory": 70.

448 Clarence S. Stein, *Toward New Towns for America*, 3rd ed. (Cambridge, Mass.: MIT Press, 1966), 188–216. Also see Charles C. Cohan, "Nation's Greatest Housing Project Announced for City," *Los Angeles Times* (September 29, 1939): 1, 3; "How Huge Housing Project Will Appear," *Los Angeles Times* (October 8, 1939), E: 1, 3; Charles C. Cohan, "Bird's-Eye View of Huge Housing Development," *Los Angeles Times* (March 30, 1941): 9; "Community of Living Units in the West," *California Arts and Architecture* 59 (January 1942): 32–33; Lewis Mumford, "Baldwin Hills Village," *Pencil Points* 25 (September 1944): 44–45; Catherine Bauer, "Description and Appraisal . . . Baldwin Hills Village," *Pencil Points* 25 (September 1944): 46–60; Martin Meyerson, *Face of the Metropolis* (New York: Random House, 1963), 141–43; Richard D. Berry, "Baldwin Hills Village—Design or Accident," *Arts & Architecture* 81 (October 1964): 18–21, 32–35; Vincent Scully, *American Architecture and Urbanism* (New York: Praeger, 1969), 164–65; Norman T. Newton, *Design on the Land: The Development of Landscape Architecture* (Cambridge, Mass., and London: Belknap Press of Harvard University Press, 1971), 507–13; "A Peaceful Retreat in the Automobile Age," *Journal of the American Institute of Architects* 58 (July 1972): 26–27; Arthur B. Gallion and Simon Eisner, *The Urban Pattern: City Planning and Design*, 3rd ed. (New York: D. Van Nostrand Co., 1975), 156; Stern with Massengale, *The Anglo-American Suburb*, 87; Martin Filler, "Planning for a Better World: The Lasting Legacy of Clarence Stein," *Architectural Record* 170 (August 1982): 122–27; "Baldwin Hills Village," *National Register of Historic Places* (1993); Gregory C. Randall, *America's Original GI Town: Park Forest, Illinois* (Baltimore and London: Johns Hopkins University Press, 2000), 79–82; David Gebhard and Robert Winter, *An Architectural Guidebook to Los Angeles* (Salt Lake City: Gibbs Smith, 2003), 120; Tom Martinson, *The Atlas of American Architecture: 2000 Years of Architecture, City Planning, Landscape Architecture and Civil Engineering* (New York: Rizzoli International Publications, 2009), 370.

449 Berry, "Baldwin Hills Village, Design or Accident": 18–21, 32–35.

450 Randall, *America's Original GI Town: Park Forest, Illinois*, 80–81.

451 "A Hebrew Utopia," *New York Times* (June 7, 1905): 16.

452 "Builders Acquire Queens Golf Club for Home Center," *New York Times* (February 3, 1946), VIII: 1; "N.Y. Life Acquires Large Housing Site," *New York Times* (March 23, 1946): 28; "Housing Project," *Architectural Record* 100 (August 1946): 18, 134; "New Suites Open at Fresh Meadow," *New York Times* (September 2, 1947): 36; "Housing Development Opened in Queens," *New York Times* (September 3, 1947): 28; "Housing Project to Have New Store," *New York Times* (September 14, 1947): 53; "Fresh Meadow Gets Six-Acre Tree Grove," *New York Times* (November 16, 1947), VIII: 1; James Dahir, "Fresh Meadows—New York Life's Big Rental Development in the Borough of Queens, N.Y.," *American City* 63 (July 1948): 80–82; "N.Y. Life's Colony with 3,000 Suites Is 50% Completed," *New York Times* (August 29, 1948), VIII: 1; Kathryn Close, "New Homes with Insurance Dollars," *Survey Graphic* 37 (November 1948): 450–54, 487–88; Otto L. Nelson, "Fresh Meadows: An Equity Investment by a Life Insurance Company," *Journal of the American Institute of Architects* 10 (December 1948): 254–61; "First Units Open in Shopping Area Near Apartments," *New York Times* (February 13, 1949), VIII: 1, 4; "Store Is Opening in Queens Tuesday," *New York Times* (May 22, 1949): 35; Lewis Mumford, "The Sky Line: From Utopia Parkway Turn East," *New Yorker* 25 (October 22, 1949): 102–6, reprinted in Lewis Mumford, *From the Ground Up* (New York: Harcourt, Brace and Company, 1956), 3–10; Lewis Mumford, "The Sky Line: The Great Good Place," *New Yorker* 25 (November 12, 1949): 73–78, reprinted as "Fresh Meadows, Fresh Plans," in Mumford, *From the Ground Up*, 11–19; "Fresh Meadows," *Architectural Record* 106 (December 1949): 85–97; New York Life Insurance Company, *Fresh Meadows, a Residential Community* (Flushing, NY: New York Life Insurance Company, 1950); "Fresh Meadows, Queens, New York City," *L'Architecture d'Aujourd'hui* 20 (September 1950): 48–51; Talbot F. Hamlin, ed., *Forms and Functions of Twentieth-Century Architecture*, vol. 3 (New York: Columbia University Press, 1952), 188, 190, 195; Voorhees, Walker, Smith, Smith & Haines, *75th Anniversary* (New York, May 1960), 39, 53; Martin Meyerson, *Face of the Metropolis* (New York: Random House, 1963), 144–47; Paul Goldberger, "To Utopia by Bus and Subway," *New York Times* (April 17, 1981), C: 1, 24; Richard Plunz, *A History of Housing in New York City* (New York: Columbia University Press, 1990), 282–84; Stern, Mellins, and Fishman, *New York 1960*, 1002–5; Blanche M. G. Linden, "Stein, Clarence S. (1882–1975)," in Neil Larry Shumsky, *Encyclopedia of Urban America: The Cities and Suburbs, Volume 1, A–L* (Santa Barbara, Calif.: ABC-CLIO, 1998), 743–44.

453 For Parklabrea, see Louis I. Dublin, *A Family of Thirty Million: The Story of the Metropolitan Life Insurance Company* (New York: Metropolitan Life Insurance Company, 1943), 353–54; "At Parklabrea," *Los Angeles Times* (October 3, 1943): 6; "Parklabrea Apartments," *Architect and Engineer* 156 (February 1944): 19–22; "Parklabrea, Los Angeles," *Architectural Record* 99 (May 1946): 88–90; "$30,000,000 Apartment Project to Start Soon," *Los Angeles Times* (March 31, 1948): 1, 2; "Metropolitan Starts Housing on Coast," *New York Times* (April 2, 1948): 39; "Apartment Buildings Rising at Parklabrea," *Los Angeles Times* (January 3, 1949), G: 10; Howard Whitman, "At Last, Houses that Fit People," *Collier's* (March 12, 1949): 24, 52, 53; "Great Development Program Furthered at Parklabrea," *Los Angeles Times* (July 4, 1949): 8; "18 Apartment Buildings Grow at Parklabrea," *Los Angeles Times* (October 2, 1949), E: 1; "Huge Apartment Center to Be Ready Next Year," *Los Angeles Times* (April 13, 1950): 2; "Parklabrea," (New York: Metropolitan Life Insurance Company Archives, n.d.); "Parklabrea—Los Angeles," (New York: Metropolitan Life Insurance Company Archives, n.d.).

454 For Parkmerced, see Louis I. Dublin, *A Family of Thirty Million: The Story of the Metropolitan Life Insurance Company* (New York: Metropolitan Life Insurance Company, 1943), 353–54; "Parkchester II & III," *Architectural Forum* 74 (February 1941): 2; "Parkmerced Housing Project," *Architect and Engineer* 154 (September 1943): 43; "Parkmerced: San Francisco's First All-Rental Community Housing Project," *Architect and Engineer* 158–159 (September 1944): 15–22; "High Standards, Low Rents, Parkmerced, San Francisco," *Architectural Record* 101 (March 1947): 90–91; "Parkmerced Housing Project," *Arts & Architecture* 67 (April 1950): 39–41; David V. Griffin, "Parkmerced," *Preservation* 60 (May/June 2008): 94; Steve "Woody" LaBounty, "Parkmerced," in http://www.outsidelands.org/parkmerced.php accessed 12/8/08; Inge S. Horton, "Parkmerced," document prepared for DoCoMoMo U.S. Northern California Chapter (2002), accessed at http://www.parkmercedresidents.org/docomomofichepg001.html.

455 For Parkchester, see Stern, Gilmartin, and Mellins, *New York 1930*, 496–500; Stern, Mellins, and Fishman, *New York 1960*, 963–64.

456 For Stuyvesant Town, see Stern, Mellins, and Fishman, *New York 1960*, 278–83.

457 Nelson, "Fresh Meadows: An Equity Investment by a Life Insurance Company": 254–61.

458 Meyerson, *Face of the Metropolis*, 146.

459 "Fresh Meadows," *Architectural Record*: 85–97.

460 Mumford, "The Sky Line: From Utopia Parkway Turn East," in Mumford, *From the Ground Up*, 5.

461 Mumford, "The Sky Line: The Great Good Place," reprinted as "Fresh Meadows, Fresh Plans," in Mumford, *From the Ground Up*, 11.

462 Mumford, "The Sky Line: From Utopia Parkway Turn East," in Mumford, *From the Ground Up*, 3–4.

463 Mumford, "The Sky Line: The Great Good Place," reprinted as "Fresh Meadows, Fresh Plans," in Mumford, *From the Ground Up*, 12.

Chapter 3

1 Ebenezer Howard, *To-morrow: a Peaceful Path to Real Reform* (London: S. Sonnenschein, 1898; London and New York: Routledge, 2003); Ebenezer Howard, *Garden Cities of To-morrow* (London: S. Sonnenschein, 1902; London: Faber and Faber, 1946; Cambridge, Mass.: MIT Press, 1965); Jessie Kingsley Curtis, "Book Reviews/'Garden Cities of To-morrow,'" *The Craftsman* 6 (June 1904): 317–18; Georges Benoît-Lévy, "The Garden City," *The Craftsman* 7 (December 1904): 284–93; G. Montagu Harris, *The Garden City Movement* (London: Garden City Association, 1906); Ebenezer Howard, "Garden Cities, Suburbs, and Villages," letter to the editor, *Builder* 98 (June 11, 1910): 665; Ewart G. Culpin, *The Garden City Movement Up-to-Date* (London: Garden Cities and Town Planning Association, 1913); A. T. Edwards, "A Criticism of the Garden City Movement," *Town Planning Review* 4 (July 1913): 150–57; Julian Julian, *An Introduction to Town Planning* (London: Charles Griffin & Co., 1914), 128–30; Lawrence Veiller, "Are Great Cities a Menace? The Garden City as a Way Out," *Architectural Record* 51 (February 1922): 175–84; Dugald Macfadyen, *Sir Ebenezer Howard and the Town Planning Movement* (Manchester: University Press, 1933); Lewis Mumford, *The Culture of Cities* (New York: Harcourt, Brace & Co., 1938), 394–400; Lewis Mumford, "The Garden City Idea and Modern Planning," introductory essay in Ebenezer Howard, *Garden Cities of To-morrow* (1898), ed. F.J. Osborn (London: Faber and Faber, 1945; Cambridge, Mass.: MIT Press, 1965), 29–40; F. J. Osborn, "Preface," in Ebenezer Howard, *Garden Cities of To-morrow* (1898), ed. F.J. Osborn (London: Faber and Faber, 1945; Cambridge, Mass.: MIT Press, 1965), 9–28; W. A. Eden, "Ebenezer Howard and the Garden City Movement," *Town Planning Review* 19 (Summer 1947): 123–43; C. B. Purdom, *The Building of Satellite Towns*, rev. ed. (London: J. M. Dent & Sons, 1949), 3–48; F. J. Osborn, "Sir Ebenezer Howard: The Evolution of His Ideas," *Town Planning Review* 21 (October 1950): 221–35; Jane Jacobs, *The Death and Life of Great American Cities* (New York: Random House, 1961; New York: Vintage Books, 1992), 17–20; Lewis Mumford, *The City in History* (New York: Harcourt, 1961), 515–24; Lewis Mumford, "Beginnings of Urban Integration," *Architectural Record* 133 (January 1963): 119–26, reprinted in Lewis Mumford, *The Urban Prospect* (New York: Harcourt, Brace & World, 1968), 142–52; Walter L. Creese, *The Search for Environment*, exp. ed. (New Haven, Conn.: Yale University Press, 1966; Baltimore and London: Johns Hopkins University Press, 1992), 144–57; Waclaw Ostrowski, *Contemporary Town Planning, From the Origins to the Athens Charter* (The Hague: International Federation for Housing and Planning, 1970), 33–43; John Moss-Eccardt, *Ebenezer Howard, an Illustrated Life of Sir Ebenezer Howard, 1850–1928* (Aylesbury, Bucks: Shire, 1973); Enid Gauldie, *Cruel Habitations: A History of Working-Class Housing, 1780–1918* (London: Allen & Unwin, 1974), 194–95; Stephen Bayley, *Unit 23: The Garden City/Unit 24: Conclusion, The Open University, Arts: A Third Level Course* (Milton Keynes: The Open University Press, 1975), 24–28; Gillian Darley, *Villages of Vision* (London: Architectural Press, 1975), 91–92; Robert Fishman, *Urban Utopias in the Twentieth Century: Ebenezer Howard, Frank Lloyd Wright, and Le Corbusier* (New York: Basic Books, 1977; Cambridge, Mass., and London: MIT Press, 1982), 3–20, 23–88; Carol A. Christensen, *The American Garden City and the New Towns Movement* (Ann Arbor, Mich.: UMI Research Press, 1986), 45–54; Robert Beevers, *The Garden City Utopia: A Critical Biography of Ebenezer Howard* (Basingstoke, Hampshire: Macmillan Press, 1988); Robert Beevers, "Ebenezer Howard: The Man and His Message," in *Garden Cities and New Towns: Five Lectures* (Hertford: Hertfordshire Publications, 1990), 12–37; Stanley Buder, *Visionaries and Planners: The Garden City Movement and the Modern Community* (New York: Oxford University Press, 1990), passim; Frederick H. A. Aalen, "English Origins," in Stephen V. Ward, ed., *The Garden City: Past, Present and Future* (London: E & FN Spon, 1992), 28–51; Dennis Hardy, "The Garden City Campaign: An Overview," in Stephen V. Ward, ed., *The Garden City: Past, Present and Future* (London: E & FN Spon, 1992), 187–209; Stephen V. Ward, "The Garden City Introduced," in Stephen V. Ward, ed., *The Garden City: Past, Present and Future* (London: E & FN Spon, 1992), 1–27; Paolo Bertozzi and Agnese Ghini, "The Classic Garden-City," in Gabriele Tagliaventi, ed., *Garden City* (Rome: Gangemi Editore, 1994), 169–91; Peter Hall and Colin Ward, *Sociable Cities: The Legacy of Ebenezer Howard* (Chichester, England: John Wiley & Sons, 1998); Daniel W. Hollis III, *The ABC-CLIO World History Companion to Utopian Movements* (Santa Barbara, Calif.: ABC-CLIO, 1998), 88–90; Robert Fishman, "Howard and the Garden," *Journal of the American Planning Association* 64 (Spring 1998): 127–28; Evan D. Richert, "Ebenezer Howard and the Garden City," *Journal of the American Planning Association* 64 (Spring 1998): 125–27; Stephen V. Ward, "The Vision Beyond Planning," *Journal of the American Planning Association* 64 (Spring 1998): 128–29; Standish Meacham, *Regaining Paradise: Englishness and the Early Garden City Movement* (New Haven and London: Yale University Press, 1999), esp. ch. 3; Richard C. S. Trahair, *Utopias and Utopians: an Historical Dictionary* (Westport, Conn.: Greenwood Press, 1999), 189–90; Peter Hall, *Cities of Tomorrow: An Intellectual History of Urban Planning and Design in the Twentieth Century*, 3rd ed. (Oxford and Malden, Mass.: Blackwell Publishers, 2002), 88–97; David Schuyler, "Introduction," in Kermit C. Parsons and David Schuyler, eds., *From Garden City to Green City: The Legacy of Ebenezer Howard* (Baltimore and London: Johns Hopkins University Press, 2002), 1–13; Stephen V. Ward, "Ebenezer Howard: His Life and Times," in Parsons and Schuyler, eds., *From Garden City to Green City*, 14–37; Pierre Clavel, "Ebenezer Howard and Patrick Geddes: Two Approaches to City Development," in Parsons and Schuyler, eds., *From Garden City to Green City*, 38–57; Mervyn Miller, "Garden Cities and Suburbs: At Home and Abroad," *Journal of Planning History* 1 (February 2002): 6–28; John Astley, *Access to Eden: The Rise and Fall of Public Sector Housing Ideals in Britain* (London: Information Architects, 2010), 77–96; Vittorio Magnago Lampugnani, *Die Stadt im 20. Jahrhundert* (Berlin: Verlag Klaus Wagenbach, 2010), 10, 24–28; Charles Siegel, *Unplanning: Livable Cities and Political Choices* (Berkeley, Calif.: Preservation Institute, 2010), 17–18.

2 Howard, *Garden Cities of To-morrow*, 45–46, 48.

3 Howard, "Garden Cities, Suburbs, and Villages": 665.

4 Mumford, "The Garden City Idea and Modern Planning," in Howard, *Gardens Cities of Tomorrow*, 34–35.

5 Mumford, "The Garden City Idea and Modern Planning," in Howard, *Garden Cities of To-Morrow*, 29.

6 Johann Valentin Andreae, *Reipublicae Christianopolitanae descriptio* (Strasbourg: Héritiers de Lazare Zetzher, 1619); Johann Valentin Andreae, *Christianopolis: an ideal state of the seventeenth century; translated from the Latin of Johann Valentin Andreae with an historical introduction by Felix Emil Held* (New York: Oxford University Press, 1916); Patrick Abercrombie, "Ideal Cities No. 1: Christianopolis," *Town Planning Review* 8 (April 1920): 99–104; Lewis Mumford, *The Story of Utopias* (New York: Boni and Liveright, 1922), ch. 4; Gerald Burke, *Towns in the Making* (London: Edward Arnold, 1971), 139; John Rockey, "From Vision to Reality: Victorian Ideal Cities and Model Towns in the Genesis of Ebenezer Howard's Garden City," *Town Planning Review* 54 (January 1983): 83–105; Roland Schaer, Gregory Claeys, and Lyman Tower Sargent, eds., *Utopia: the Search for the Ideal Society in the Western World* (New York: New York Public Library/Oxford University Press, 2000), 108–10.

7 J. V. Andreae, quoted in Abercrombie, "Ideal Cities No. 1: Christianopolis": 103.

8 Mumford, *The Story of Utopias*, 85.

9 Abercrombie, "Ideal Cities No. 1: Christianopolis": 103–4.

10 E. A. Gutkind, *International History of City Development, Volume VI: Urban Development in Western Europe: the Netherlands and Great Britain* (New York: The Free Press; London: Collier-Macmillan, 1971), 278–79.

11 "Model Towns and Communities: Plato's Republic," *The Garden City* 1 (February 1906): 16–18; E. A. Gutkind, *International History of City Development, Volume VI: Urban Development in Western Europe: The Netherlands and Great Britain* (New York: Free Press; London: Collier-Macmillan, 1971), 281–82, 478–79; Norman T. Newton, *Design on the Land: The Development of Landscape Architecture* (Cambridge, Mass., and London: Belknap Press of Harvard University Press, 1971), 448; Gillian Darley, *Villages of Vision* (London: Architectural Press, 1975), 82; Ion Tod and Michael Wheeler, *Utopia* (New York: Harmony Books, 1978), 81–86; Donald F. Carmony and Josephine M. Elliott, "New Harmony, Indiana: Robert Owen's Seedbed for Utopia," *Indiana Magazine of History* 76 (September 1980): 161–261; Richard C. S. Trahair, *Utopias and Utopians: An Historical Dictionary* (Westport, Conn.: Greenwood Press, 1999), 281; Leland M. Roth, *American Architecture: A History* (Boulder, Colo.: Icon Editions/Westview Press, 2001), 202–3; Ruth Eaton, *Ideal Cities: Utopianism and the (Un)Built Environment* (New York: Thames & Hudson, 2002), 128–29; Robert P. Sutton, *Heartland Utopias* (DeKalb, Ill.: Northern Illinois University Press, 2009), ch. 2.

12 "Model Towns and Communities: Plato's Republic": 17–18.

13 Lewis Mumford, *The Story of Utopias* (New York: Boni and Liveright, 1922), 117–23; Dora Wiebenson, "Utopian Aspects of Tony Garnier's Cité Industrielle," *Journal of the Society of Architectural Historians* 19 (March 1960): 16–24; Jonathan Beecher, *Charles Fourier: The Visionary and His World* (Berkeley: University of California Press, 1986), esp. ch. 12; Daniel W. Hollis III, *The ABC-CLIO World History Companion to Utopian Movements* (Santa Barbara, Calif.: ABC-CLIO, 1998), 257; Roland Schaer, Gregory Claeys, and Lyman Tower Sargent, eds., *Utopia: the Search for the Ideal Society in the Western World* (New York: New York Public Library/Oxford University Press, 2000), 209, 213, 222; Ruth Eaton,

Ideal Cities: Utopianism and the (Un)Built Environment (New York: Thames & Hudson, 2002), 127–28; Robert P. Sutton, *Heartland Utopias* (DeKalb, Ill.: Northern Illinois University Press, 2009), 70–88.

14 E. A. Gutkind, *International History of City Development, Volume V: Urban Development in Western Europe: France and Belgium* (New York: Free Press; London: Collier-Macmillan, 1970), 101.

15 For the American phalanxes, see Robert P. Sutton, *Heartland Utopias* (DeKalb, Ill.: Northern Illinois University Press, 2009), 70–88. Also see Daniel W. Hollis III, *The ABC-CLIO World History Companion to Utopian Movements* (Santa Barbara, Cal.: ABC-CLIO, 1998), 258; Richard C. S. Trahair, *Utopias and Utopians: An Historical Dictionary* (Westport, Conn.: Greenwood Press, 1999), 140, 290.

16 Frederick Law Olmsted, "The Phalanstery and the Phalansterians. By An Outsider," *New York Daily Tribune* (July 29, 1852), reprinted in Robert Twombly, ed., *Frederick Law Olmsted: Essential Texts* (New York: W.W. Norton, 2010), 49–57.

17 George Henry Santerre, *White Cliffs of Dallas; the Story of La Réunion, the Old French Colony* (Dallas: Book Craft, 1955); James Pratt, "La Réunion: The Fourierist Last Hurrah," *Arts + Architecture* 2 (1983): 30–33; Richard C. S. Trahair, *Utopias and Utopians: An Historical Dictionary* (Westport, Conn.: Greenwood Press, 1999), 337–38.

18 Jean-Baptiste André Godin, quoted in "Le Familistère Illustré," *Werk* 56 (December 1969): 822. Also see James Hole, *The Homes of the Working Classes* (London: Longmans, Green & Co., 1866), 166–72; "The Social Palace at Guise," *Harper's New Monthly Magazine* 44 (April 1872): 701–16; "The Familistère at Guise, France," *Harper's New Monthly Magazine* 71 (November 1885): 912–18; E. R. L. Gould, *The Housing of the Working People* (Washington, D.C.: Government Printing Office, 1895), 274–75, plans 38A, 38B; "Le Familistère Illustré," *Werk* 56 (December 1969): 817–22, 865–66; Stephen Bayley, *The Garden City* (Milton Keynes: Open University Press, 1975); Leo Balmer, "Cooperation Between Capital and Labour," *Lotus International* 12 (September 1976): 58–71; Annick Brauman, "Le Familistère de Guise," *Monuments Historiques* (March 1977): 64–68; Robert Alan Mandel, "Andre Godin and the Familistère de Guise, 1817–1888: A Study of Industrial Paternalism and Social Reform" (Ph.D. diss, University of Toronto, 1978); *Jean-Baptiste Andre Godin, 1817–1888: The Familistère at Guise or the Equivalents of Wealth*, second edition (Bruxelles, Belgium: Archives d'architecture Moderne, 1980); Josée Doyère, "A été classé dernièrement parmi les monuments historiques Le Familistère de Guise (Aisne)," *Sites et Monuments* 139 (1992): 13–16; Ruth Eaton, *Ideal Cities: Utopianism and the (Un) built Environment* (New York and London: Thames & Hudson, 2002), 125, 132–33; Denis Picard, "Une Utopie Habitable," *Connaissance de Arts* 596 (July–August 2002): 86–93; Rudolf Stumberger, "Familistère Godin in Guise," *Bauwelt* 95 (July 23, 2004): 12–25, 26–31.

19 Jean-Baptiste André Godin, *Solutions Sociales* (1871), quoted in Eaton, *Ideal Cities*, 132.

20 James S. Buckingham, *National Evils and Practical Remedies with the Plan of a Model Town* (London: Peter Jackson, Late Fisher & Co., 1849); Ebenezer Howard, *Garden Cities of To-Morrow* (London: S. Sonnenschein, 1902; Cambridge, Mass.: MIT Press, 1965), 119, 125–27; "Model Towns and Communities," *The Garden City* 1 (March 1906): 33–34; "Model Towns and Communities: Buckingham's Model Town," *The Garden City* 1 (April 1906): 56–58; Patrick Abercrombie, "Ideal Cities: No. 2—Victoria," *Town Planning Review* 9 (March 1921): 15–20; Lewis Mumford, *The Story of Utopias* (New York: Boni and Liveright, 1922), 124–29; Catherine Bauer, *Modern Housing* (Boston and New York: Houghton Mifflin, 1934), 74–76; Lewis Mumford, *The Culture of Cities* (New York: Harcourt, Brace & Co., 1938), 394; W. Ashworth, "British Industrial Villages in the Nineteenth Century," *Economic History Review* 3 (1951): 379; Colin and Rose Bell, *City Fathers: Town Planning in Britain from Roman Times to 1900* (New York: Frederick A. Praeger, 1969), 196–97; Gerald Burke, *Towns in the Making* (London: Edward Arnold, 1971), 138–40; E. A. Gutkind, *International History of City Development, Volume VI: Urban Development in Western Europe: The Netherlands and Great Britain* (New York: Free Press; London: Collier-Macmillan, 1971), 283, 480–84; Norman T. Newton, *Design on the Land: The Development of Landscape Architecture* (Cambridge, Mass., and London: Belknap Press of Harvard University Press, 1971), 448–49; John Nelson Tarn, *Working-Class Housing in 19th-century Britain* (London: Lund Humphries for the Architectural Association, 1971), 31–32; Stanley Pierson, "The Way Out," in H. J. and Michael Wolff, eds., *The Victorian City: Images and Realities, Volume II* (London and Boston: Routledge & Kegan Paul, 1973), 881–82; John Nelson Tarn, *Five Per Cent Philanthropy: An Account of Housing in Urban Areas between 1840 and 1914* (London: Cambridge University Press, 1973), 150–52; Gordon E. Cherry, *The Evolution of British Town Planning* (New York: John Wiley & Sons, 1974), 18; Arthur Gallion and Simon Eisner, *The Urban Pattern: City Planning and Design, Third Edition* (New York: D. Van Nostrand Company, 1975), 76; John Rockey, "From Vision to Reality: Victorian Ideal Cities and Model Towns in the Genesis of Ebenezer Howard's Garden City," *Town Planning Review* 54 (January 1983): 83–105; Richard C. S. Trahair, *Utopias and Utopians: An Historical Dictionary* (Westport, Conn.: Greenwood Press, 1999), 51–52; Chris Coates, *Utopia Britannica, Volume 1: British Utopian Experiments: 1325 to 1945* (London: Diggers & Dreamers, 2001), 195–97; Ruth Eaton, *Ideal Cities: Utopianism and the (Un)Built Environment* (New York: Thames & Hudson, 2002), 145, 147; John W. Reps, "Plan of the Model Town, James S. Buckingham," in http://www.library.cornell.edu/Reps/Docs/buckham.htm.

21 Buckingham, *National Evils and Practical Remedies*, 142.

22 "Model Towns and Communities": 33–34.

23 Howard, *Garden Cities of To-Morrow*, 126–27.

24 "Model Towns and Communities: Buckingham's Model Town": 58.

25 Abercrombie, "Ideal Cities: No. 2—Victoria": 19.

26 Abercrombie, "Ideal Cities, No. 2—Victoria": 15.

27 Mumford, *The Story of Utopias*, 128.

28 Tarn, *Working-Class Housing in 19th-Century Britain*, 31.

29 Tarn, *Five Per Cent Philanthropy*, 150, 152–53.

30 Robert Pemberton, *The Happy Colony* (London: Saunders and Otley, 1854); Gerald Burke, *Towns in the Making* (London: Edward Arnold, 1971), 139; E. A. Gutkind, *International History of City Development, Volume VI: Urban Development in Western Europe: The Netherlands and Great Britain* (New York: Free Press; London: Collier-Macmillan, 1971), 283–85; John Nelson Tarn, *Five Per Cent Philanthropy: An Account of Housing in Urban Areas between 1840 and 1914* (London: Cambridge University Press, 1973), 152; John Rockey, "From Vision to Reality: Victorian Ideal Cities and Model Towns in the Genesis of Ebenezer Howard's Garden City," *Town Planning Review* 54 (January 1983): 83–105; Daniel W. Hollis III, *The ABC-CLIO World History Companion to Utopian Movements* (Santa Barbara, Calif.: ABC-CLIO, 1998), 88–89; Ruth Eaton, *Ideal Cities: Utopianism and the (Un)Built Environment* (New York: Thames & Hudson, 2002), 145, 147; John W. Reps, "Queen Victoria Town," in http://www.library.cornell.edu/Reps/DOCS/pemberto.htm.

31 Pemberton, *The Happy Colony*, quoted in Reps, "Queen Victoria Town."

32 Mumford, "The Garden City Idea and Modern Planning," in Howard, *Garden Cities of To-morrow*, 29.

33 Howard, *Garden Cities of To-morrow*, 50.

34 Purdom, *The Building of Satellite Towns*, 29.

35 Meacham, *Regaining Paradise*, 57.

36 Howard, *Garden Cities of To-morrow*, 131.

37 Moss-Eccardt, *Ebenezer Howard, an Illustrated Life of Sir Ebenezer Howard, 1850–1928*, 6.

38 Creese, *The Search for Environment*, 155.

39 Ebenezer Howard, quoted in Meacham, *Regaining Paradise*, 51.

40 Benjamin Ward Richardson, *Hygeia, or the City of Health* (London: Macmillan and Co., 1876).

41 Mumford, "The Garden City Idea and Modern Planning," in Howard, *Garden Cities of To-morrow*, 30.

42 Ebenezer Howard, quoted in Moss-Eccardt, *Ebenezer Howard, an Illustrated Life of Sir Ebenezer Howard, 1850–1928*, 14.

43 Osborn, "Preface," in Howard, *Garden Cities of To-morrow*, 20.

44 Hall, *Cities of Tomorrow*, 92.

45 Howard, *Garden Cities of To-morrow*, 139.

46 Howard, *Gardens Cities of Tomorrow*, 54.

47 Howard, *Gardens Cities of Tomorrow*, 55.

48 Osborn, "Preface," in Howard, *Gardens Cities of Tomorrow*, 11.

49 *The Times* (October 18, 1898): 13d, as quoted in Bayley, *Unit 23: The Garden City/Unit 24: Conclusion*, 28.

50 *Fabian News* (December 1898): 39, as quoted in Bayley, *Unit 23: The Garden City/Unit 24: Conclusion*, 28. The reference is to H. G. Wells' novel *The War of the Worlds* (1898).

51 Meacham, *Regaining Paradise*, 61.

52 Unwin, *Nothing Gained by Overcrowding!*, 19.

53 Osborn, "Preface," in Howard, *Gardens Cities of Tomorrow*, 28.

54 Purdom, *The Building of Satellite Towns*, 23.

55 Jacobs, *The Death and Life of Great American Cities*, 17.

56 Jacobs, *The Death and Life of Great American Cities*, 19.

57 Mumford, "Beginnings of Urban Integration," reprinted in Mumford, *The Urban Prospect*, 147.

58 Fishman, "Howard and the Garden": 127, 128.

59 Barry Parker and Raymond Unwin, *The Art of Building a Home* (New York: Longmans, Green & Co., 1901); Raymond Unwin, *Cottage Plans and Common Sense* (London: The Fabian Society, 1902); Raymond Unwin, *Town Planning in Practice: An Introduction to the Art of Designing Cities and Suburbs* (London: T. Fisher Unwin, 1909; New York: Princeton Architectural Press, 1994); "Town Planning in Theory and in Practice: The Work of Raymond Unwin," *The Craftsman* 17 (January 1910): 391–401; Raymond Unwin, *Nothing Gained by Overcrowding! How the Garden City type of Development May Benefit Both Owner and Occupier* (London: Garden Cities and Town Planning Association, 1912); Walter L. Creese, *The Search for Environment*, exp. ed. (New Haven, Conn.: Yale University Press, 1966; Baltimore and London: Johns Hopkins University Press, 1992), 158–90; Lewis Mumford, "Beginnings of Urban Integration," *Architectural Record* 133 (January 1963): 119–26, reprinted in Lewis Mumford, *The Urban Prospect* (New York: Harcourt, Brace & World, 1968), 149–51; Stephen Bayley, *Unit 23: The Garden City/Unit 24: Conclusion, The Open University, Arts: A Third Level Course* (Milton Keynes: The Open University Press, 1975), 28–30; Gillian Darley, *Villages of Vision* (London: Architectural Press, 1975), 91–98; *Barry Parker & Raymond Unwin, Architects* (London: Architectural Association, 1980); Frank Jackson, *Sir Raymond Unwin: Architect, Planner and Visionary* (London: A. Zwemmer, 1985); Rupert Hebblethwaite, "Housing Programme in Sheffield before 1914," *Architectural History* 30 (1987): 143–79; Stanley Buder, *Visionaries and Planners: The Garden City Movement and the Modern Community* (New York: Oxford University Press, 1990), 85–89; Mervyn Miller, *Raymond Unwin: Garden Cities and Town Planning* (Leicester: Leicester University Press, 1992); Walter L. Creese, "An Extended Planning Progression from the Late Nineteenth to Early Twentieth Century," in Raymond Unwin, *Town Planning in Practice: An Introduction to the Art of Designing Cities and Suburbs* (1909; New York: Princeton Architectural Press, 1994), v–xxvi; Standish Meacham, *Regaining Paradise: Englishness and the Early Garden City Movement* (New Haven, Conn., and London: Yale University Press, 1999), 70–94; Peter Hall, *Cities of Tomorrow: An Intellectual History of Urban Planning and Design in the Twentieth Century*, 3rd ed. (Oxford and Malden, Mass.: Blackwell Publishers, 2002), 97–109; Mervyn Miller, "The Origins of the Garden City Residential Neighborhood," in Kermit C. Parsons and David Schuyler, eds., *From Garden City to Green City: The Legacy of Ebenezer Howard* (Baltimore and London: Johns Hopkins University Press, 2002), 99–130; Mervyn Miller, *Hampstead Garden Suburb: Arts and Crafts Utopia?* (Chichester, Sussex: Phillimore, 2006), 44–49; John Astley, *Access to Eden: The Rise and Fall of Public Sector Housing Ideals in Britain* (London: Information Architects, 2010), 109–17.

60 George Bernard Shaw, quoted in Robert Beevers, *The Garden City Utopia: A Critical Biography of Ebenezer Howard* (Basingstoke, Hampshire: Macmillan Press, 1988), 70.

61 Mumford, "Beginnings of Urban Integration," reprinted in Mumford, *The Urban Prospect*, 149.

62 Raymond Unwin, letter to Ethel Parker (August 9, 1891), quoted in Miller, *Hampstead Garden Suburb: Arts and Crafts Utopia?*, 45.

63 William Morris, quoted in Unwin, *Town Planning in Practice*, 9.

64 Unwin, "Introduction to the Second Edition," in Unwin, *Town Planning in Practice*, xiv.

65 Astley, *Access to Eden*, 111.
66 For Co-operative Village project, see Nicholas Taylor, "The Houses of Parker and Unwin," in *Barry Parker & Raymond Unwin, Architects*, 22, 23, 24.
67 Stephen Bayley, *Unit 23: The Garden City/Unit 24: Conclusion* (Milton Keynes: The Open University Press, 1975), 20.
68 Parker and Unwin, *The Art of Building a Home*, 104–5, as quoted in Meacham, *Regaining Paradise*, 92.
69 Stern, Mellins, and Fishman, *New York 1880*, 495–514.
70 Creese, "An Extended Planning Progression," in Unwin, *Town Planning in Practice*, xii–xiv.
71 Barry Parker, "The Life and Work of Sir Raymond Unwin," *Town Planning Journal* (July–August 1940): 160, as quoted in Bayley, *Unit 23: The Garden City/Unit 24: Conclusion*, 29.
72 Unwin, *Town Planning in Practice*, 320.
73 Barry Parker, *A Lecture on Art in Industry* (Letchworth: Letchworth Printers, 1925), 5–6, quoted in Creese, "An Extended Planning Progression," in Unwin, *Town Planning in Practice*, xii.
74 Lewis Mumford, "The Garden City Idea and Modern Planning," introductory essay in Ebenezer Howard, *Garden Cities of To-morrow* (1898), ed. F.J. Osborn (London: Faber and Faber, 1945; Cambridge, Mass.: MIT Press, 1965), 32.
75 Mumford, *The Urban Prospect*, 148–49.
76 Creese, "An Extended Planning Progression," in Unwin, *Town Planning in Practice*, xxii.
77 "Town Planning in Theory and in Practice: The Work of Raymond Unwin": 397.
78 Unwin, *Town Planning in Practice*, 150, 153, also quoted in "Town Planning in Theory and in Practice: The Work of Raymond Unwin": 398–99.
79 Octavius Grant Wood, "English Homes for Workingmen," *Inland Architect and News Record* 29 (March 1897): 12–14, plates; G. L. Morris, "Evolution of Village Architecture in England," *International Studio* 1 (May 1897): 177–84; "Port Sunlight," *Architecture and Building* 30 (February 4, 1899): 35–37; George Howard Barton, "Port Sunlight: A Model English Village," *Architectural Review* 6 (May 1899): 62–66; "Group of Cottages, Port Sunlight, Cheshire," *Architect and Contract Reporter* 62 (September 29, 1899): 201, plate after p.184; "Proposed Village Church, Port Sunlight, Cheshire," *Builder* 83 (September 13, 1902): plate after p. 240; Georges Benoît-Lévy, *La Cité-Jardin* (Paris: Editions des Cités-Jardins de France, 1904), 15–102; Hermann Muthesius, *The English House, Volume I: Development*, trans. by Janet Seligman, (1904; London: Frances Lincoln, 2007), 199–201; "Workmen's Model Cottages, Port Sunlight, England," *American Architect* 83 (March 19, 1904): n.p.; James Cornes, *Modern Housing in Town and Country* (London: B. T. Batsford, 1905), 76–79; W. H. Lever, *The Buildings Erected at Port Sunlight and Thornton Hough: Paper Read by W. H. Lever, at a Meeting of the Architectural Association, London, March 21st, 1902* (1905); Budgett Meakin, *Model Factories and Villages: Ideal Conditions of Labour and Housing* (London: T. Fisher Unwin, 1905), 426–32; W. H. Williams, "Port Sunlight," *The Garden City* 1 (March 1906): 43–44; J. G. H. Northcroft, *Indoors and Out* 2 (April 1906): 1–8; "Cottages at Port Sunlight, England," *Brickbuilder* 15 (April 1906): plates 49–50; J. G. H. Northcroft, *Indoors and Out* 2 (May 1906): 65–69; "Port Sunlight," *The Garden City* 1 (January 1907): 257–58; Mabel Tuke Priestman, "Port Sunlight: A Significant English Experiment in Village Building," *American Homes and Gardens* 4 (October 1907): 395–400; "Port Sunlight," *The Garden City* 2 (January 1908): 495; "Modern English Churches. No. 1, Christ Church, Port Sunlight, William and Segar Owen, Architects," *Architectural Review* 15 (October 1908): 153, plates 68–69, 75; W. L. George, *Labour and Housing at Port Sunlight* (London: Alston Rivers, 1909); "Port Sunlight," *Garden Cities and Town Planning* 4 (May 1909): 197; Frederick Law Olmsted, "Through American Spectacles: an Expert's View of English 'Garden City' Schemes," *Garden Cities and Town Planning* 4 (May 1909): 198–200; Patrick Abercrombie, "Modern Town Planning in England: A Comparative Review of 'Garden City' Schemes in England," *Town Planning Review* 1 (April 1910): 33–35, plates 8–9; E. W. Beeson, *Port Sunlight: The Model Village of England* (New York: Architectural Book Publishing Company, 1911); Thomas H. Mawson, *Civic Art: Studies in Town Planning, Parks, Boulevards, and Open Spaces* (London. B. T. Batsford, 1911), 279–87; Patrick Abercrombie, "A Tour of the Garden Cities," *Town Planning Review* 2 (October 1911), 230–33; Ewart G. Culpin, *The Garden City Movement Up-to-Date* (London: Garden Cities and Town Planning Association, 1913), 41; Perry R. MacNeille, *The Industrial Village* (New York: Standard Buildings, 1913), 2–9; Wm. H. Schuchardt, "The Fibre of the Nation. Part I," *American Architect* 103 (March 12, 1913): 137–42, 144; Henry R. Aldridge, *The Case for Town Planning* (London: National Housing and Town Planning Council, c.1915), 399–402; T. Raffles Davison, *Port Sunlight: A Record of Its Artistic and Pictorial Aspect* (London: B. T. Batsford, 1916); "Port Sunlight War Memorial," *Builder* 116 (May 16, 1919): 482, plate; Christopher Hussey, "The Port Sunlight War Memorial," *Country Life* 50 (December 17, 1921): 817; E. S. Draper, "Two European Industrial Village Developments," *Landscape Architecture* 21 (July 1931): 300–312; Catherine Bauer, *Modern Housing* (Boston and New York: Houghton Mifflin, 1934), 90; G. G. Kirkpatrick, "Port Sunlight," *Town and Country Planning* 20 (February 1952): 87–89; Walter L. Creese, *The Search for Environment*, exp. ed. (New Haven, Conn.: Yale University Press, 1966; Baltimore and London: Johns Hopkins University Press, 1992), 108–43; Colin and Rose Bell, *City Fathers: Town Planning in Britain from Roman Times to 1900* (New York: Preager, 1969), 208–13; Norman T. Newton, *Design on the Land: The Development of Landscape Architecture* (Cambridge, Mass.: Belknap Press of Harvard University Press, 1971), 449–51; J. N. Tarn, *Working-Class Housing in 19th-Century Britain* (London: Lund Humphries for the Architectural Association, 1971), 34–36, 84; A. E. J. Morris, "Philanthropic Housing," *Official Architecture and Planning* 34 (August 1971): 600; John Nelson Tarn, *Five Per Cent Philanthropy: An Account of Housing in Urban Areas between 1840 and 1914* (Cambridge: Cambridge University Press, 1973), 156–58; H. J. Dyos and Michael Wolff, ed., *The Victorian City: Images and Realities, Volume 1* (London and Boston: Routledge & Kegan Paul, 1973), 884–85; R. R. Morton, "Housing Renewal at Port Sunlight," *Town Planning Review* 44 (October 1973): 319–36; Gordon E. Cherry, *The Evolution of British Town Planning* (New York and Toronto: John Wiley & Sons, 1974), 19–20, 23; Enid Gauldie, *Cruel Habitations: A History of Working-Class Housing, 1780–1918* (London: Allen & Unwin, 1974), 192–94; Stephen Bayley, *The Garden City* (Milton Keynes: Open University Press, 1975), 16–17; Gillian Darley, *Villages of Vision* (London: Architectural Press, 1975), 70–76; Stern with Massengale, *The Anglo-American Suburb*, 53–54; Arthur S. Edwards, *The Design of Suburbia* (London: Pembridge Press, 1981), 79–82; Myles Wright, *Lord Leverhulme's Unknown Venture* (London: Hutchinson Benham, 1982), 29–32; Ailsa Bowers, "Port Sunlight," *Heritage Outlook* 5 (July/August 1985): 81; Christopher Crouch, "Village Soap," *RIBA Journal* 95 (November 1988): 52–53; Edward Hubbard, *The Work of John Douglas* (London: The Victorian Society, 1991), 168–71; Peter Burman, Keith Gardner, and Leo Schmidt, eds., *The Conservation of Twentieth Century Historic Buildings* (York: Institute of Advanced Architectural Studies, University of York, 1996), 97–103; Joseph Sharples, *Charles Reilly & the Liverpool School of Architecture, 1904–1933* (Liverpool: Liverpool University Press, 1996), 43–48, 56; Standish Meacham, *Regaining Paradise: Englishness and the Early Garden City Movement* (New Haven, Conn., and London: Yale University Press, 1999), 11–43; Ruth Eaton, *Ideal Cities: Utopianism and the (Un)Built Environment* (London and New York: Thames & Hudson, 2001), 131; Peter Richmond, *Marketing Modernisms: The Architecture and Influence of Charles Reilly* (Liverpool: Liverpool University Press, 2001), 100–101, fig. 8; Edward Hubbard and Michael Shippobottom, *A Guide to Port Sunlight Village*, 2nd rev. ed. (1988; Liverpool: Liverpool University Press, 2005); Joseph Sharples, *Liverpool* (New Haven, Conn., and London: Yale University Press, 2004), 299–301; Mervyn Miller, *Hampstead Garden Suburb: Arts and Crafts Utopia?* (Chichester, Sussex: Phillimore, 2006), 43, 48; James Stevens Curl, *Victorian Architecture: Diversity & Invention* (Reading: Spire, 2007), 505–7; Allan Greenberg, *Lutyens and the Modern Movement* (London: Papadakis Publisher, 2007), 83–84; Janet Waymark, *Thomas Mawson: Life, Gardens and Landscapes* (London: Francis Lincoln, 2009), 198–202; Vittorio Magnago Lampugnani, *Die Stadt im 20. Jahrhundert* (Berlin: Verlag Klaus Wagenbach, 2010), 21–24.
80 Hubbard and Shippobottom, *A Guide to Port Sunlight Village*, 17.
81 George Augustus Sala, *Illustrated London News* (1890), quoted in Kirkpatrick, "Port Sunlight": 88.
82 Creese, *The Search for Environment*, 123.
83 Creese, *The Search for Environment*, 122.
84 Muthesius, *Das englische Haus*, 199, translated by Alan Johnson, quoted in Hubbard and Shippobottom, *A Guide to Port Sunlight Village*, 63. Also see Muthesius, *The English House, Volume I: Development*, trans. by Janet Seligman, 199–201.
85 Muthesius, *Das englische Haus*, 200–201, translated by Alan Johnson, quoted in Hubbard and Shippobottom, *A Guide to Port Sunlight Village*, 63.
86 Cornes, *Modern Housing in Town and Country*, 77.
87 Creese, *The Search for Environment*, 137.
88 Darley, *Villages of Vision*, 75–76.
89 Bayley, *The Garden City*, 17.
90 *The Factory in a Garden*, promotional brochure (n.d.); "Bournville: A Worcestershire Eden," *Black and White* 11 (February 15, 1896): 215–16; G. L. Morris, "The Evolution of Village Architecture," *International Studio* 1 (May 1897): 177–87; Lona Bartlett, "The Bournville Village Trust," *House and Garden* 4 (1903): 297–306; Georges Benoît-Lévy, *La Cité-Jardin* (Paris: Editions des Cités-Jardins de France, 1904), 103–60; Hermann Muthesius, *The English House, Volume I: Development*, trans. by Janet Seligman, (1904; London: Frances Lincoln, 2007), 201–4; Budgett Meakin, *Model Factories and Villages: Ideal Conditions of Labour and Housing* (London: T. Fisher Unwin, 1905), 433–43; James Cornes, *Modern Housing in Town and Country* (London: B. T. Batsford, 1905), 70–75; J. H. Barlow, "The Village of Bournville," *The Garden City* 1 (April 1905): 34–37; W. Alexander Harvey, *The Model Village and Its Cottages: Bournville* (London: B. T. Batsford, 1906); Sydney Hungerford, "Inexpensive English Houses that Might be Adapted to American Uses," *American Homes and Gardens* 2 (February 1906): 107–10; "Bournville," *The Garden City* 1 (March 1906): 44–45; Mabel Tuke Priestman, "A Co-operative Village for Working People—Beautiful and Practical and a Four Per Cent Investment," *Craftsman* 10 (July 1906): 494–506; "Bournville," *The Garden City* 1 (January 1907): 257; "Bournville," *The Garden City* 2 (April 1907): 319; Patrick Abercrombie, "Modern Town Planning in England: A Comparative Review of 'Garden City' Schemes in England," *Town Planning Review* 1 (April 1910): 35–37, plates 10–11; Patrick Abercrombie, "A Tour of the Garden Cities," *Town Planning Review* 2 (October 1911), 230–33; Perry R. MacNeille, *The Industrial Village* (New York: Standard Buildings, 1913), 2–8; Henry D. Aldridge, *The Case for Town Planning* (London: National Housing and Town Planning Council, c. 1915), 399–402; *Bournville—1924* (Bournville: Cadbury Brothers, 1924); Catherine Bauer, *Modern Housing* (Boston and New York: Houghton Mifflin, 1934), 90; "Bournville Village Trust," *RIBA Journal* (October 1949): 517–21; Walter L. Creese, *The Search for Environment*, exp. ed. (New Haven, Conn.: Yale University Press, 1966; Baltimore and London: Johns Hopkins University Press, 1992), 108–43; Nikolaus Pevsner and Alexandra Wedgwood, *Warwickshire* (Harmondsworth: Penguin, 1966; New Haven, Conn., and London: Yale University Press, 2003), 47, 154–63; Colin and Rose Bell, *City Fathers: Town Planning in Britain from Roman Times to 1900* (New York: Praeger, 1969), 199–209; Norman T. Newton, *Design on the Land: The Development of Landscape Architecture* (Cambridge, Mass.: Belknap Press of Harvard University Press, 1971), 448–49, 451–52; J. N. Tarn, *Working-Class Housing in 19th-Century Britain* (London: Lund Humphries for the Architectural Association, 1971), 35–36; A. E. J. Morris, "Philanthropic Housing," *Official Architecture and Planning* 34 (August 1971): 598–600; John Nelson Tarn, *Five Per Cent Philanthropy: An Account of Housing in Urban Areas between 1840 and 1914* (Cambridge: Cambridge University Press, 1973), 161; H. J. Dyos and Michael Wolff, ed., *The Victorian City: Images and Realities, Volume 1* (London and Boston: Routledge & Kegan Paul, 1973), 884–85; Gordon E. Cherry, *The Evolution of British Town Planning* (New York and Toronto: John Wiley & Sons, 1974), 19, 21–23; Enid Gauldie, *Cruel Habitations: A History of Working-Class Housing, 1780–1918* (London: Allen & Unwin, 1974), 192–94; Stephen Bayley, *The Garden City* (Milton Keynes: Open University Press, 1975), 17–18; Gillian Darley, *Villages of Vision* (London: Architectural Press, 1975), 70–76; Stern with Massengale, *The Anglo-American Suburb*, 56–57; Arthur S. Edwards, *The Design of Suburbia* (London: Pembridge Press, 1981), 79–82; Joel M. Hoffman, "Imaging the Industrial Village: Architecture, Art, and Visual Culture in the Garden Community of Bournville, England: Volume I" (Ph.D. diss., Yale University, May 1993); Michael Harrison, "Bournville, 1919–1939," *Planning History* 17 (1995): 22–31; Gordon E. Cherry, "Bournville, England, 1895–1995," *Journal*

of Urban History 22 (May 1996): 493–508; Michael Harrison, *Bournville: Model Village to Garden Suburb* (Chichester, Sussex: Phillimore, 1999); Standish Meacham, *Regaining Paradise: Englishness and the Early Garden City Movement* (New Haven, Conn., and London: Yale University Press, 1999), 11–43; John Bryson, "Bournville: Model Village to Garden Suburb," book review, *Planning Perspectives* 15 (October 2000): 395–97; Ruth Eaton, *Ideal Cities: Utopianism and the (Un)Built Environment* (London and New York: Thames & Hudson, 2001), 131–32; Andrés Duany, Elizabeth Plater-Zyberk, and Robert Alminana, *The New Civic Art: Elements of Town Planning* (New York: Rizzoli International Publications, 2003), 38; Andy Foster, *Birmingham* (New Haven, Conn., and London: Yale University Press, 2005), 255–68; Mervyn Miller, *Hampstead Garden Suburb: Arts and Crafts Utopia?* (Chichester, Sussex: Phillimore, 2006), 48; Della Hooke, *England's Landscape: The West Midlands* (London: Collins, 2006), 197–98; James Stevens Curl, *Victorian Architecture: Diversity & Invention* (Reading: Spire, 2007), 507–14; Michael Harrison, "William Alexander Harvey," in Phillada Ballard, ed., *Birmingham's Victorian and Edwardian Architects* (Wetherby: Oblong Creative for the Birmingham and West Midlands Group of the Victorian Society, 2009), 527–53; Vittorio Magnago Lampugnani, *Die Stadt im 20. Jahrhundert* (Berlin: Verlag Klaus Wagenbach, 2010), 18–21.

91 Harrison, *Bournville: Model Village to Garden Suburb*, 26 (n.33).

92 *Bournville Village Trust* (Bournville: Bournville Trust, 1907), 3.

93 Tarn, *Five Per Cent Philanthropy*, 160.

94 Harrison, "Bournville, 1919–1939": 22–31.

95 Creese, *The Search for Environment*, 118.

96 Ebenezer Howard, quoted in Harrison, *Bournville: Model Village to Garden Suburb*, 87 (n.190).

97 Tarn, *Working-class Housing in 19th-Century Britain*, 35–36.

98 Bayley, *The Garden City*, 17–18.

99 Budgett Meakin, *Model Factories and Villages: Ideal Conditions of Labour and Housing* (London: T. Fisher Unwin, 1905), 423–26; Raymond Unwin, *Town Planning in Practice* (London: T. Fisher Unwin, 1909; New York: Princeton Architectural Press, 1994), 230, 233, 308–10, 320, 376; "The Joseph Rowntree Village Trust," *Garden Cities and Town Planning* 4 (May 1909): 197; Patrick Abercrombie, "Modern Town Planning in England," *Town Planning Review* 1 (April 1910): 37–38; Barry Parker, "Country Homes in England: By Barry Parker: Number Twenty," *Craftsman* 21 (December 1911): 290–303; Barry Parker, "Modern Country Homes in England: By Barry Parker: Number Twenty-two," *Craftsman* 21 (February 1912): 508–20; Joseph Rowntree Village Trust, *New Earswick* (1913); Ewart G. Culpin, *The Garden City Movement Up-to-Date* (London: Garden Cities and Town Planning Association, 1913), 39; Henry R. Aldridge, *The Case for Town Planning* (London: National Housing and Town Planning Council, 1915), 410–11; Barry Parker, "The Planning of Non-Parlour Cottages," *Garden Cities and Town Planning* 9 (November 1919): 203–7; C. H. James and F. R. Yerbury, *Small Houses for the Community* (London: Crosby Lockwood and Son, 1924), plates 77, 81–82; Lawrence Weaver, "Cottages at Earswick," *Country Life* 58 (October 31, 1925): 680–81; Barry Parker, "Site Planning as Exemplified at New Earswick," *Town Planning Review* 17 (February 1937): 79–102; Walter Creese, "Parker and Unwin: Architects of Totality," *Journal of the Society of Architectural Historians* 22 (October 1963): 61–70; Nikolaus Pevsner, *Yorkshire, The North Riding* (Harmondsworth, England: Penguin, 1966; New Haven, Conn., and London: Yale University Press, 2002), 266–68; Walter L. Creese, *The Search for Environment*, exp. ed. (New Haven, Conn.: Yale University Press, 1966; Baltimore and London: Johns Hopkins University Press, 1992), 191–202; Gordon E. Cherry, *The Evolution of British Town Planning* (New York and Toronto: John Wiley & Sons, 1974), 23–24; Stephen Bayley, *The Garden City* (Milton Keynes: Open University Press, 1975), 18; Michael G. Day, "The Contribution of Sir Raymond Unwin (1863–1940) and R. Barry Parker (1867–1947) to the Development of Site-Planning Theory and Practice," in Anthony Sutcliffe, ed., *British Town Planning: the Formative Years* (New York: St. Martin's Press; Leicester: Leicester University Press, 1981), 168–73; Rupert Hebblethwaite, "The Housing Programme in Sheffield Before 1914," *Architectural History* 30 (1987): 143–79; Mervyn Miller, *Raymond Unwin: Garden Cities and Town Planning* (Leicester: Leicester University Press, 1992), 35–48; Mervyn Miller and A. Stuart Gray, *Hampstead Garden Suburb* (Chichester, Sussex: Phillimore, 1992), 41–43; Paolo Bertozzi, "The Experiment: New Earswick," in Gabriele Tagliaventi, ed., *Garden City* (Rome: Gangemi Editore, 1994), 192–99; Chris Coates, ed., *Utopia Britannica: Volume I, British Utopian Experiments: 1325–1945* (London: Diggers and Dreamers, 2001), 211; Mervyn Miller, "Garden Cities and Suburbs: at Home and Abroad," *Journal of Planning History* (February 2002): 6–28; Mervyn Miller, "The Origins of the Garden City Neighborhood," in Kermit C. Parsons and David Schuyler, eds., *From Garden City to Green City: The Legacy of Ebenezer Howard* (Baltimore and London: Johns Hopkins University Press, 2002), 109–10, 125; F. H. A. Allen with Colm O'Brien, eds., *England's Landscape: The North East* (London: Collins, 2006), 176; Mervyn Miller, *Hampstead Garden Suburb: Arts and Crafts Utopia?* (Chichester, Sussex: Phillimore, 2006), 44, 46–49, 140.

100 Quoted in Pevsner, *Yorkshire, The North Riding*, 267.

101 David Gebhard, *Charles F. A. Voysey Architect* (Los Angeles: Hennessey & Ingalls, 1975), 27–28, 156; Duncan Simpson, *CFA Voysey: An Architect of Individuality* (New York: Whitney Library of Design, 1981), 65, 67, 95–96; Stuart Durant, *CFA Voysey* (London: Academy Editions, 1992), 15, 141; Wendy Hitchmough, *CFA Voysey* (London: Phaidon, 1995), 182–83, 232; Alice Shirley Schofield, *C. F. A. Voysey's Buildings at Whitwood* (West Yorkshire, 1997); Creese, *The Search for Environment*, 191–93.

102 Day, "The Contribution of Sir Raymond Unwin and R. Barry Parker," in Sutcliffe, ed., *British Town Planning: The Formative Years*, 170.

103 Barry Parker, quoted in Creese, *The Search for Environment*, 192.

104 Bayley, *The Garden City*, 18.

105 Miller, *Hampstead Garden Suburb: Arts and Crafts Utopia?*, 48–49.

106 Harrison, *Bournville: Model Village to Garden Suburb*, 88. Also see M. G. Day, "The Contribution of Sir Raymond Unwin and R. Barry Parker," in A. Sutcliffe, ed., *British Town Planning: The Formative Years* (New York: St. Martin's Press; Leicester: Leicester University Press, 1981), 172.

107 James Cornes, *Modern Housing in Town and Country* (London: B. T. Batsford, 1905), 63–69, 124–31; M. H. H. Macartney, "The First Garden City-I," *Architectural Review* 18 (July 1905): 14–21; H. Kempton Dyson, "Cheap Cottages and the Exhibition at Letchworth-I," *Architectural Review* 18 (September 1905): 108–15; Raymond Unwin, "The Improvement of Towns," *The Craftsman* 8 (September 1905): 809–16; H. Kempton Dyson, "Cheap Cottages and the Exhibition at Letchworth-II," *Architectural Review* 18 (October 1905): 154–69; Lucy M. Salmon, "The Garden City Cheap Cottages Exhibition," *The Craftsman* 9 (November 1905): 166–79; Samuel Swift, "The Garden City—I," *Indoors & Out* 1 (November 1905): 90–95; Samuel Swift, "The Garden City—II," *Indoors & Out* 1 (December 1905): 137–45; "The Cloisters, Letchworth," *Architectural Review* 23 (March 1908): 198–207; Raymond Unwin, *Town Planning in Practice* (London: T. Fisher Unwin, 1909; New York: Princeton University Press, 1994), 225–28, 309–10, 346–51; Frederick Law Olmsted, "Through American Spectacles: an Expert's View of English 'Garden City' Schemes," *Garden Cities and Town Planning* 4 (May 1909): 198–200; "An Artist's Studio Cottage," *Architectural Review* 27 (January 1910): 35–37; *Letchworth Garden City in Fifty-five Pictures* (Letchworth: First Garden City Ltd.; London: Halton House, 1911); Barry Parker, "Modern Country Homes in England: Number Twelve," *The Craftsman* 20 (April 1911): 69–79; Barry Parker, "Modern Country Homes in England: Number Fourteen," *The Craftsman* 20 (June 1911): 278–88; Barry Parker, "Modern Country Homes in England: Number Twenty," *The Craftsman* 21 (December 1911): 290–303; Barry Parker, "Modern Country Homes in England: Number Twenty-two," *The Craftsman* 21 (February 1912): 508–20; C. B. Purdom, *The Garden City: A Study in the Development of a Modern Town* (London: J. M. Dent & Sons, 1913), esp. pp. 41–119, 154–65, 222–94; W. H. Gaunt, "The Town Square at Letchworth," *Garden Cities and Town Planning* (March 1913): 75–79; William H. Schuchardt, "The Fibre of the Nation: Part III," *American Architect* 104 (July 23, 1913): 33–37; "The Progress of Letchworth," *Garden Cities and Town Planning* 10 (1920): 167–73; Mrs. E. B. Pearsall, "Co-operative Houses at Letchworth," *Garden Cities and Town Planning* 10 (1920): 174–75; Charles Harris Whitaker, "An American View of Letchworth," *Garden Cities and Town Planning* 10 (1920): 179–80; "Modern Domestic Architecture: 24—The Boys' Club, Letchworth," *Architects' Journal* 53 (January 5, 1921): 221–23; Lawrence Veiller, "Are Great Cities a Menace? The Garden City as a Way Out," *Architectural Record* 51 (February 1922): 175–84; C. B. Purdom, *The Building of Satellite Towns*, rev. ed. (London: J. M. Dent & Sons, 1925, 1949), 49–178, plates I–XV; "The Meaning of Letchworth," *Garden Cities and Town Planning* 16 (July 1926): 127–28; Harold Craske, "Garden City Pioneer Company," *Garden Cities and Town Planning* 16 (July 1926): 135–36; Henry B. Harris, "Letchworth as a Model Manufacturing and Industrial Town," *Garden Cities and Town Planning* 16 (July 1926): 137–38; William L. Hare, "Residential Letchworth: The Town without a Slum," *Garden Cities and Town Planning* 16 (July 1926): 144–46; Dugald Macfadyen, "The Outdoor Life of Letchworth," *Garden Cities and Town Planning* 16 (July 1926): 147–48; Thomas Adams, *The Design of Residential Areas: Basic Considerations, Principles, and Methods* (Cambridge, Mass.: Harvard University Press, 1934), 250–54; *Industrial Letchworth* (Hertfordshire, England: First Garden City Ltd., 1937); *Letchworth: The Well-Planned Beautiful Town* (Hertfordshire, England: First Garden City Ltd., 1937); Patrick Abercrombie, *Town and Country Planning* (London: Oxford University Press, 1943), 98–99; Frederick James Osborn, *Green-belt Cities, the British Contribution* (London: Faber and Faber, 1946), 56–128; Eric Macfadyen, "Letchworth (Herts): First New Town," *Town and Country Planning* 19 (January 1951): 16–18; Sir Edgar Bonham-Carter, "Planning and Development of Letchworth Garden City," *Town Planning Review* 21 (January 1951): 362–76; Nikolaus Pevsner, *Hertfordshire* (Melbourne, London, and Baltimore: Penguin Books, 1953), 26–27, 153–55; "The Jubilee of Letchworth," *RIBA Journal* 60 (September 1953): 442–45; "The Letchworth Jubilee," *Town and Country Planning* 21 (September 1953): entire issue; "The Letchworth Dividend Limit," *Town and Country Planning* 24 (May 1956): 248–51; Walter Creese, "Parker and Unwin: Architects of Totality," *Journal of the Society of Architectural Historians* 22 (October 1963): 161–70; Walter L. Creese, *The Search for Environment*, exp. ed. (New Haven, Conn.: Yale University Press, 1966; Baltimore and London: Johns Hopkins University Press, 1992), 203–18; James D. Kornwolf, *M. H. Baillie Scott and the Arts and Crafts Movement* (Baltimore and London: Johns Hopkins Press, 1972), 288–305; Nikolaus Pevsner and Bridget Cherry, *Hertfordshire*, rev. ed. (New Haven, Conn., and London: Yale University Press, 1977), 224–35; Mervyn Miller, "'In Search of the £150 Cottage,'" *Town and Country Planning* 49 (February 1980): 48–50; "Parsimonious Philanthropy: The Minor Architecture of F. W. Troup," *RIBA Journal* 92 (June 1985): 36–37; Dennis J. De Witt and Elizabeth R. De Witt, *Modern Architecture in Europe* (New York: E. P. Dutton, 1987), 190–91; Mervyn Miller, *Letchworth: The First Garden City* (Chichester, Sussex: Phillimore, 1989); Mervyn Miller, "Letchworth Garden City: An Architectural View," in *Garden Cities and New Towns: Five Lectures* (Hertford, England: Hertfordshire Publications, 1990), 48–87; Iain Borden, "Social Space and Cooperative Housekeeping in the English Garden City," *Journal of Architectural and Planning Research* 16 (Autumn 1990): 242–57; Mervyn Miller, "Homesgarth—Howard's Model for Co-operative Living," *Town and Country Planning* 60 (April 1991): 119–20; Mervyn Miller, *Raymond Unwin: Garden Cities and Town Planning* (Leicester: Leicester University Press, 1992), 49–77; Mervyn Miller and A. Stuart Gray, *Hampstead Garden Suburb* (Chichester, Sussex: Phillimore, 1992), 41–44; Petra Hagen-Hodgson, "Die gesunde Stadt," *Werk, Bauen + Wohnen* 76 (April 1992): 6–21, 74; Paolo Bertozzi, "The First Garden-City: Letchworth Garden-City," in Gabriele Tagliaventi, ed., *Garden City* (Rome: Gangemi Editore, 1994), 200–209; Diane Haight, *Baillie Scott: The Artistic House* (London: Academy Editions, 1995), 94, 127; Margaret Crawford, "The 'New' Company Town," *Perspecta* 30 (1999): 48–57; Chris Coates, *Utopia Britannica*, vol. 1 (London: Diggers & Dreamers Publications, 2001), 212–15; Mervyn Miller, "The Origins of the Garden City Residential Neighborhood," in Kermit C. Parsons and David Schuyler, eds., *From Garden City to Green City: The Legacy of Ebenezer Howard* (Baltimore and London: Johns Hopkins University Press, 2002), 109–13; Mervyn Miller, "Garden Cities and Suburbs: At Home and Abroad," *Journal of Planning History* 1 (February 2002): 6–28; Dennis Hardy, "Letchworth—A Ticket to Utopia," *Town and Country Planning* 71 (March 2002): 76–77; Andrés Duany, Elizabeth Plater-Zyberk, and Robert Alminana, *The New Civic Art: Elements of Town Planning* (New York: Rizzoli International Publications, 2003), 44, 140, 288; Jonathan Meades, "Paradox of the Picturesque," *Country Life* 197 (October 2003): 78–81; Brian Short, *England's Landscape: The*

South East (London: Collins, 2006), 99, 229; Vittorio Magnago Lampugnani, *Die Stadt im 20. Jahrhundert* (Berlin: Verlag Klaus Wagenbach, 2010), 28–31.

108 Pevsner, *Hertfordshire* (1953), 153.

109 Swift, "The Garden City—II": 141.

110 Miller, "Letchworth Garden City," in *Garden Cities and New Towns: Five Lectures*, 83.

111 Unwin, *Town Planning in Practice*, 225. Also see Camillo Sitte, *The Art of Building Cities: City Building According to Its Artistic Fundamentals*, trans. by Charles T. Stewart (New York: Reinhold, 1945); George R. Collins and Christiane Crasemann Collins, *Camillo Sitte and the Birth of Modern City Planning* (New York: Random House, 1965), 138–39.

112 Pevsner, *Hertfordshire* (1953), 154.

113 Raymond Unwin, "The Improvement of Towns," paper read at the Conference of the National Union of Women Workers of Great Britain and Ireland (November 8, 1904): 3, quoted in Creese, *The Search for Environment*, 207.

114 Barry Parker and Raymond Unwin, *The Art of Building a Home* (London: Longams, Green & Co., 1901), plate 11.

115 Miller, *Letchworth*, 68, 71–72.

116 *The Book of the Cheap Cottages Exhibition* (London: The County Gentleman and Land & Water, 1905). Also see James Cornes, *Modern Housing in Town and Country* (London: B. T. Batsford, 1905).

117 Barry Parker and Raymond Unwin, "The Cheap Cottage: What Is Really Needed," *Garden City* (July 1905): 55, quoted in Meacham, *Regaining Paradise*, 115.

118 C. B. Purdom, quoted in Miller, "Letchworth Garden City," in *Garden Cities and New Towns: Five Lectures*, 57.

119 Ebenezer Howard, quoted in Miller, "Homesgarth—Howard's Model for Co-operative Living": 120.

120 Meades, "Paradox of the Picturesque": 78–81.

121 *Welwyn Garden City, a New Town in Hertfordshire on the Great Northern Railway Main Line* (Welwyn Garden City, Herts: G. S. Herne); R. L. Reiss, "Welwyn Garden City," *Town Planning Review* 8 (December 1920): 179–82; "Welwyn Garden City," *Garden Cities and Town Planning* 10 (December 1920): 245–46; E. W. Martin, "Some Differences Between English and American Architectural Office Practice," *Builder* 120 (February 18, 1921): 227–28; Lawrence Veiller, "Are Great Cities a Menace?" *Architectural Record* 51 (February 1922): 175–84; "Architects' Working Drawings; Proposed Studio at Welwyn Garden City," *Architects' Journal* 55 (March 8, 1922): 374–75; C. B. Purdom, *The Place of the Welwyn Stores in the Welwyn Garden City* (Welwyn Garden City: Welwyn Garden City Bookshop, 1923); C. Murray Hennell and C. H. James, "Welwyn Garden City, Herts," *Architects' Journal* 57 (January 2, 1923): 18–22; "Welwyn Garden City," *Builder* 124 (April 20, 1923): 647–58; "Bauten in der Gartenstadt Welwyn," *Wasmuths Monatshefte für Baukunst* 8 (1924): 190–92; C. H. James and F. R. Yerbury, *Small Houses for the Community* (London: Crosby Lockwood and Son, 1924), plates 28–52; "Arbeiten von Louis de Soissons und Anderen für die Gartenstadt Welwyn," *Wasmuths Monatshefte für Baukunst* 9 (1925): 285–303; C. B. Purdom, *The Building of Satellite Towns*, rev. ed. (London: J. M. Dent & Sons, 1925, 1949), 179–360, plates XVII–XXXIV; "Shredded Wheat Factory, Welwyn," *Builder* 128 (June 26, 1925): 976–79; "Welwyn Garden City," *Builder* 128 (June 26, 1925), 979; Louis de Soissons, "Recent Work at Welwyn Garden City," *Architects' Journal* 62 (August 19, 1925): 268–75; "A Design for a New Factory," *Architect & Building News* 116 (July 23, 1926): 103–5; "A Group of Concrete Cottages at Welwyn Garden City," *Builder* 131 (September 17, 1926): 444–45; S. C. Ramsey, "Church of St. Bonaventure, Welwyn Garden City," *Architect & Building News* 116 (September 24, 1926): 347–49; "Editorial Comments," *Garden Cities & Town Planning* 16 (December 1926): 239–41; "Gardens of Welwyn Garden City," *Garden Cities & Town Planning* 16 (December 1926): 275–76; "The Local Government of Welwyn Garden City," *Garden Cities & Town Planning* 16 (December 1926): 259–61; Sir Theodore Chambers, "The Growth of Welwyn Garden City," *Garden Cities & Town Planning* 16 (December 1926): 244–47; F. J. Osborn, "Welwyn Garden City as an Industrial Centre," *Garden Cities & Town Planning* 16 (December 1926): 247–50; C. H. James, "The Architecture of Welwyn Garden City," *Garden Cities & Town Planning* 16 (December 1926): 250–54; F. H. Masters, "Garden Cities and Electricity Supply," *Garden Cities & Town Planning* 16 (December 1926): 255–58; C. B. Purdom, "An Account of the Organisation of the Welwyn Garden City Stores," *Garden Cities & Town Planning* 16 (December 1926): 262–67; Arthur E. Brown, "The Brickmaking Plant at Welwyn Garden City," *Garden Cities & Town Planning* 16 (December 1926): 268–71; William L. Hare, "Religious Life in Welwyn Garden City," *Garden Cities & Town Planning* 16 (December 1926): 272–73; R. L. Reiss, "Educational, Recreational, and Social Life at Welwyn Garden City," *Garden Cities & Town Planning* 16 (December 1926): 274–75; "The Kindergarten School, Welwyn Garden City," *Architect & Building News* 116 (December 10, 1926): 691; Louis de Soissons and Arthur Wm. Kenyon, *Site Planning in Practice at Welwyn Garden City* (London: Ernest Benn Limited, 1927); R. L. Reiss, "The Significance of Welwyn Garden City," *Architectural Review* 61 (May 1927): 177–82; Ronald Orfeur, "New Wine: The Theatre at Welwyn," *Architectural Review* 63 (April 1928): 138–44; "The Theatre at Welwyn," *Architect & Building News* 119 (April 20, 1928): 563–69; "The Free Church Hall at Welwyn," *Architect & Building News* 121 (April 26, 1929): 546–48; *Welwyn Garden City: Twenty-four Views* (Welwyn Garden City, 1930); "The Howard Memorial, Welwyn Garden City, Herts," *Architects' Journal* 72 (July 9, 1930): 37–38; "Housing Scheme, Welwyn Garden City," *Architects' Journal* 86 (July 29, 1937): 184–86; "The Community Centre, Welwyn Garden City," *Builder* 155 (July 22, 1938): 159–61; "Factory, Welwyn Garden City, by Professor O. R. Salvisberg in Association with C. Stanley Brown," *Architects' Journal* 89 (January 19, 1939): 126–32; "Factory at Welwyn, O. R. Salvisberg, Architect, C. Stanley Brown, Associate," *Architectural Review* 85 (April 1939): 193–96; "Welwyn Stores," *Architect & Building News* 159 (August 25, 1939): 211–15; "House, Welwyn Garden City, Designed by Eugen C. Kaufmann," *Architects' Journal* 90 (December 28, 1939): 762–64; F. J. Osborn, "Welwyn Revisited," letter to the editor, *Architects' Journal* 93 (May 1, 1941): 290; "The Welwyn Experiment," *Architects' Journal* 93 (May 1, 1941): 286; F. J. Osborn, "The Welwyn Experiment," letter to the editor, *Architects' Journal* 93 (May 29, 1941): 352–53; Frederick James Osborn, *Green-belt Cities, the British Contribution* (London: Faber and Faber, 1946), 56–128; Nikolaus Pevsner, *Hertfordshire* (London: Penguin Books, 1951), 26, 270–72; "Welwyn Garden City—50 Years,"

Town and Country Planning 38 (May 1970): 244–51; Stephen Bayley, *History of Architecture and Design, 1890–1939* (Milton Keynes: Open University Press, 1975), 39–43, plates 42–52; Nikolaus Pevsner, *Hertfordshire*, rev. ed. by Bridget Cherry (New Haven, Conn., and London: Yale University Press, 1977), 36–37, 396–401; Maurice de Soissons, *Welwyn Garden City: A Town Designed for Healthy Living* (Cambridge: Publications for Companies, 1988), esp. chs. 1–7; William Allen, "The Architecture of the Garden Cities and New Towns," in *Garden Cities and New Towns: Five Lectures* (Hertford: Hertfordshire Publications, 1990), 88–112; Stanley Buder, *Visionaries and Planners: The Garden City Movement and the Modern Community* (New York and Oxford: Oxford University Press, 1990), 117–32; Standish Meacham, *Regaining Paradise: Englishness and the Early Garden City Movement* (New Haven, Conn., and London: Yale University Press, 1999), 180–81; Iain Borden, "Social Space and Cooperative Housekeeping in the English Garden City," *Journal of Architectural and Planning Research* 16 (Autumn 1999): 242–57; Tony Rook, *Welwyn Garden City Past* (Chichester: Phillimore, 2001); Mervyn Miller, "The Origins of the Garden City Neighborhood," in Kermit C. Parsons and David Schuyler, eds., *From Garden City to Green City: The Legacy of Ebenezer Howard* (Baltimore and London: Johns Hopkins University Press, 2002), 124–27; Mervyn Miller, "Garden Cities and Suburbs: At Home and Abroad," *Journal of Planning History* 1 (February 2002): 6–28; Andrés Duany, Elizabeth Plater-Zyberk, and Robert Alminana, *The New Civic Art: Elements of Town Planning* (New York: Rizzoli International Publications, 2003), 200, 231, 299; Vittorio Magnago Lampugnani, *Die Stadt im 20. Jahrhundert* (Berlin: Verlag Klaus Wagenbach, 2010), 31–33.

122 For the Shredded Wheat Company, see "Shredded Wheat Factory, Welwyn": 976–79; Pevsner, *Hertfordshire*, 396, 398; De Soissons, *Welwyn Garden City: A Town Designed for Healthy Living*, 58–62. For the Hoffman La Roche factory, see "Factory, Welwyn Garden City, by Professor O. R. Salvisberg in Association with C. Stanley Brown": 126–32; "Factory at Welwyn, O. R. Salvisberg, Architect, C. Stanley Brown, Associate": 193–96; Dennis Sharp, "Salvisberg in England," *Werk-Archithese* 64 (October 1977): 26–28; De Soissons, *Welwyn Garden City: A Town Designed for Healthy Living*, 58–62; Claude Lichtenstein, *O. R. Salvisberg: die Andere Moderne* (Zurich: GTA, 1995), 102–3, 266.

123 Rook, *Welwyn Garden City Past*, 85.

124 Pevsner, *Hertfordshire* (1951), 272.

125 Clough Williams-Ellis, quoted in Sharp, "Salvisberg in England": 28.

126 Buder, *Visionaries and Planners*, 125, 127.

127 Barry Parker, "Highways, Parkways and Freeways," *Town and Country Planning* 1 (February 1933): 38–43; E. D. Simon and J. Inman, *The Rebuilding of Manchester* (London: Longmans, Green and Co., 1935), 36–53; Wesley Dougill, "Wythenshawe: A Modern Satellite Town," *Town Planning Review* 16 (June 1935): 209; Alfred P. Simon, *Manchester Made Over* (London: P.S. King & Son, 1936), 81–94; Norman Worral, "Wythenshawe: Observations on the Development of a Rural Area as a Community Unit," *Journal of the Town Planning Institute* 23 (November 1936): 235–38; N. F. Cachemaille-Day, "Church of St. Michael and All Angels—Wythenshawe," *Architect and Building News* 153 (January 1938): 41–44; "'Mitchell Gardens,' Wythenshawe: Dwellings for Aged Persons," *Builder* 154 (April 22, 1938): 784–86; R. Nicholas, *City of Manchester Plan, Abridged Edition* (Norwich and London: Jarrold & Sons, 1945), 24–25, plate 7; Norman Jordan Moss, "Wythenshawe: An Experiment in Town Planning," *South African Architectural Record* 31 (August 1946): 210–12; C. B. Purdom, *The Building of Satellite Towns*, rev. ed. (London: J.M. Dent & Sons, 1949), 46–47; Walter L. Creese, *The Search for Environment*, exp. ed. (New Haven, Conn.: Yale University Press, 1966; Baltimore and London: Johns Hopkins University Press, 1992), 255–72; Stephen Bayley, *History of Architecture and Design, 1890–1939* (Milton Keynes: Open University Press, 1975), 43–44, plates 53–57; Clare Hartwell, Matthew Hyde, and Nikolaus Pevsner, *Lancashire: Manchester and the South-East* (1969; New Haven, Conn., and London: Yale University Press, 2004), 488–506; Derick Deakin, *Wythenshawe: The Story of a Garden City* (Chichester: Phillimore, 1989); Mervyn Miller, "The Origins of the Garden City Neighborhood," in Kermit C. Parsons and David Schuyler, ed., *From Garden City to Green City: The Legacy of Ebenezer Howard* (Baltimore and London: Johns Hopkins University Press, 2002), 125–30.

128 Hartwell, Hyde, and Pevsner, *Lancashire: Manchester and the South-East*, 488.

129 Creese, *The Search for Environment*, 261.

130 Creese, *The Search for Environment*, 255–56.

131 Creese, *The Search for Environment*, 271–72. Also see Barry Parker, "Where We Stand," Presidential Address, Town Planning Institute (November 1929), 8–9.

132 A. E. J. Morris, "Public Health and Social Reform," *Official Architecture + Planning* 34 (June 1971): 460–62; Leland M. Roth, *American Architecture: A History* (Boulder, Col.: Icon Editions/Westview Press, 2001), 202.

133 "Metropolitan Annexation and Consolidation," editorial, *New York Times* (July 20, 1869): 4; "The Hempstead Plains," *Harper's Weekly* 13 (August 7, 1869): 503; William M. Laffan, *The New Long Island: A Handbook of Summer Travel* (New York: Rogers & Sherwood, 1879), 65–68; M., "A Millionaire's Cathedral City—I," *American Architect and Building News* 6 (September 20, 1879): 91; M., "A Millionaire's Cathedral City—II," *American Architect and Building News* 6 (September 27, 1879): 102–3; James C. Brierley, "A Millionaire's Cathedral," letter to the editor, *American Architect and Building News* 6 (October 25, 1879): 135; "Stewart's Garden City," *New York Herald* (January 20, 1880): 3; W. G. Marshall, *Through America; or Nine Months in the United States* (London: Sampson, Low, Marston, Searle & Rivington, 1881), 16–19; Montgomery Schuyler, "Some Suburbs of New York: Part II—Westchester and Long Island," *Lippincott's Magazine* 8 (August 1884): 113–26; "The Garden City Competition for Inexpensive Cottages," *Indoors and Out* 3 (December 1906): 144–48; "Garden City Competition," *American Architect* 90 (December 22, 1906): 199–200; "The Garden City Competition for Inexpensive Cottages: The Second Prize Designs," *Indoors and Out* 3 (January 1907): 196–201; *Garden City*, promotional brochure, Garden City Company (1910); Grosvenor Atterbury, "Model Towns in America," *Scribner's* 52 (July 1912): 25; "Franklin Court, Garden City, L.I.," *Architecture* 32 (November 1915): 305–6; "Group of Houses, Franklin Court, Garden City, L.I.," *Architecture* 32 (December 1915): 305–8; Nelson P. Lewis, *The Planning of the Modern City* (New York: John Wiley & Sons, 1916), 301–2, plate 84; Harriet Sisson Gillespie, "An English Cottage Group," *House Beautiful* 46 (August 1919): 74–76; Arthur C. Comey and Max S. Wehrly,

"A Study of Planned Communities" (Department of Regional Planning of Harvard University, November 1936): 385–86; M. H. Smith, *History of Garden City*, rev. ed. (Garden City, N.Y.: Garden City Historical Society, 1963, 1980); Vincent F. Seyfried, *The Founding of Garden City: 1869–1893* (Uniondale, N.Y.: published by the author, 1969); Deborah S. Gardner, "The Architecture of Commercial Capitalism: John Kellum and the Development of New York, 1840–1875" (Ph.D. diss., Columbia University, 1979): 261–313, figs. 114–34; Bette S. Weidman and Linda B. Martin, *Nassau County, Long Island in Early Photographs, 1869–1940* (New York: Dover, 1981), figs. 82–83; Kenneth T. Jackson, *Crabgrass Frontier: The Suburbanization of the United States* (New York: Oxford University Press, 1985), 81–84; M. H. Smith, *Garden City, Long Island, in Early Photographs, 1869–1919* (New York: Dover, 1987); Richard Plunz, *A History of Housing in New York City* (New York: Columbia University Press, 1990), 113–14; Stephen N. Elias, *Alexander T. Stewart: The Forgotten Merchant Prince* (Westport, Conn.: Praeger, 1992), 177–88; Vivien Kellerman, "If You're Thinking of Living In/Garden City: From 'Stewart's Folly' to Thriving Suburb," *New York Times* (October 24, 1993), X: 5; John Rather, "If You're Thinking of Living In/Garden City: A Model Village with a Rare Squabble," *New York Times* (February 22, 2004), XI: 5.
134 Jackson, *Crabgrass Frontier*, 81.
135 M., "A Millionaire's Cathedral City—I": 91.
136 Alexander T. Stewart, quoted in "Stewart's Garden City": 3.
137 "Stewart's Garden City": 3.
138 M. "A Millionaire's Cathedral City—I": 91.
139 Alexander T. Stewart, quoted in "Stewart's Garden City": 3.
140 "Stewart's Garden City": 3.
141 Quoted in M., "A Millionaire's Cathedral City—I": 91.
142 "The Hempstead Plains": 503.
143 Quoted in Smith, *History of Garden City*, 21.
144 M., "A Millionaire's Cathedral City—I": 91.
145 Schuyler, "Some Suburbs of New York: Part II—Westchester and Long Island": 113–26.
146 "Franklin Court, Garden City, L.I.": 305–6; "Group of Houses, Franklin Court, Garden City, L.I.": 305–8; Gillespie, "An English Cottage Group": 74–76.
147 "The Arcadian City of Pullman," *Agricultural Review* 3 (January 1883): 69–87; Richard T. Ely, "Pullman: A Social Study," *Harper's New Monthly Magazine* 70 (February 1885): 452–65; Mrs. Duane Doty, *The Town of Pullman, Illustrated: Its Growth with Brief Accounts of Its Industries* (Pullman: T. P. Struhsacker, 1893); "The Failure of Philanthropic Commercialism at Pullman and Saltaire," *American Architect and Building News* 45 (September 22, 1894): 105; Theodore Dreiser, "The Town of Pullman," *Ainslee's Magazine* 3 (March 1899): 189–200; Budgett Meakin, *Model Factories and Villages* (London: T. Fisher Unwin, 1905), 385–89; "Market Building, Pullman, Ill.," *American Architect and Building News* 91 (February 23, 1907): plate, n.p.; "Market Square, Pullman, Ill.," *American Architect and Building News* 91 (February 23, 1907): plate; George C. Nimmons, "Model Industrial Plants, Part I," *Architectural Record* 44 (November 1918): 414–21; Irving K. Pond, "Pullman—America's First Planned Industrial Town," *Illinois Society of Architects Monthly Bulletin* 18–19 (June-July 1934): 6–8; Arthur C. Comey and Max S. Wehrly, "A Study of Planned Communities" (Department of Regional Planning of Harvard University, November 1936): 194–202; Almont Lindsey, "Paternalism and the Pullman Strike," *American Historical Review* 44 (January 1939): 272–89; Christopher Tunnard and Henry Hope Reed, *American Skyline: The Growth and Form or Our Cities and Towns* (New York: New American Library, 1953), 130–31; Robert M. Lillibridge, "Pullman: Town Development in the Era of Eclecticism," *Journal of the Society of Architectural Historians* 12 (October 1953): 17–22; William T. W. Morgan, "The Pullman Experiment in Review," *Journal of the American Institute of Planners* 20 (Winter 1954): 26–30; John W. Reps, *The Making of Urban America: A History of City Planning in the United States* (Princeton: Princeton University Press, 1965), 421–24; Stanley Buder, *Pullman: An Experiment in Industrial Order and Community Planning, 1880–1930* (New York: Oxford University Press, 1967), esp. ch. 6; Harold M. Mayer and Richard C. Wade, *Chicago: Growth of a Metropolis* (Chicago and London: University of Chicago Press, 1969), 186, 188–91; Norbert J. Pointner II, "Pullman: a New Town Takes Shape on the Illinois Prairie," *Historic Preservation* 22 (April–June 1970): 26–35; Daniel J. Boorstin, *The Americans: The Democratic Experience* (New York: Vintage Books, 1974), 281–83; Perry Duis, *Chicago: Creating New Traditions* (Chicago: Chicago Historical Society, 1976), 42–43; Francesco Dal Co, "From Parks to the Region: Progressive Ideology and the Reform of the American City," in Giorgio Ciucci et al., *The American City: From the Civil War to the New Deal* (Cambridge, Mass.: MIT Press, 1979), 196–200; Stern with Massengale, *The Anglo-American Suburb*, 51; Theresa Ducato, "Pulling for Pullman," *Inland Architect* 26 (March/April 1982): 6–19; Thomas J. Schlereth, "Solon Spencer Beman, 1853–1914: The Social History of a Midwest Architect," *Chicago Architectural Journal* 5 (1985): 8–31; Richard E. Foglesong, *Planning the Capitalist City: The Colonial Era to the 1920s* (Princeton: Princeton University Press, 1986), 190–94; Robert A. M. Stern with Thomas Mellins and Raymond W. Gastil, *Pride of Place: Building the American Dream* (Boston: Houghton Mifflin; New York: American Heritage, 1986), 135–38; Thomas J. Schlereth, "Solon Spencer Beman, Pullman, and the European Influence on and Interest in his Chicago Architecture," in John Zukowsky, ed., *Chicago Architecture, 1872–1922* (Munich: Prestel-Verlag in association with the Art Institute of Chicago, 1987), 173–87; Christian Laine, "Renewing a Remarkable Planned Community," *Architecture: The AIA Journal* 76 (November 1987): 60–65; James Burkhart Gilbert, *Perfect Cities: Chicago's Utopias of 1893* (Chicago and London: University of Chicago Press, 1991), 131–68; John S. Garner, *The Company Town: Architecture and Society in the Early Industrial Age* (New York: Oxford University Press, 1992), 6–8; Margaret Crawford, *Building the Workingman's Paradise: The Design of American Company Towns* (London and New York: Verso, 1995), 37–45; Margaret Crawford, "The 'New' Company Town," *Perspecta* 30 (1999): 48–57; Neal Vogel, "When Company Comes to Town," *Old-House Journal* 27 (December 1999): 48–53.
148 Ely, "Pullman: A Social Study": 460.
149 Pullman Palace Car Company brochure, quoted in Boorstin, *The Americans: The Democratic Experience*, 282.
150 Reps, *The Making of Urban America*, 421.
151 Buder, *Pullman: An Experiment in Industrial Order and Community Planning, 1880–1930*, 70.
152 Lillibridge, "Pullman: Town Development in the Era of Eclecticism": 20.
153 Mark Hanna, quoted in Thomas Beer, *Hanna* (New York: Knopf, 1929), 132–33.
154 Ely, "Pullman: A Social Study": 457.
155 See Schlereth, "Solon Spencer Beman," in Zukowsky, ed., *Chicago Architecture, 1872–1922*, 176, 187(n.13).
156 Schlereth, "Solon Spencer Beman, 1853–1914: The Social History of a Midwest Architect": 10, 12.
157 Reps, *The Making of Urban America*, 422.
158 Albert Kimsey Owen, *Integral Co-operation at Work* (New York: John W. Lovell, 1890); Albert K. Owen, "Pacific City," *Lend a Hand* IX (November 1892): 344–52; Mark Holloway, *Heavens on Earth: Utopian Communities in America, 1680–1880* (New York: Library Publishers, 1951), 216; Dolores Hayden, *The Grand Domestic Revolution: A History of Feminist Designs for American Homes, Neighborhoods, and Cities* (Cambridge, Mass.: MIT Press, 1981), 103–13; Stanley Buder, *Visionaries and Planners: The Garden City Movement and the Modern Community* (New York: Oxford University Press, 1990), 39–47; Robert S. Fogarty, *All Things New: American Communes and the Utopian Movements, 1860–1914* (Chicago and London: University of Chicago Press, 1990), 121–34; Daniel W. Hollis III, *The ABC-CLIO World History Companion to Utopian Movements* (Santa Barbara, Calif.: ABC-CLIO, 1998), 245–47; Richard C. S. Trahair, *Utopias and Utopians: An Historical Dictionary* (Westport, Conn.: Greenwood Press, 1999), 301, 405–6; Charles Postel, *The Populist Vision* (New York: Oxford University Press, 2007), 239–41.
159 Albert Kimsey Owen, *Dream of an Ideal City* (London, 1897), quoted in Buder, *Visionaries and Planners*, 44.
160 Albert Kimsey Owen, quoted in Fogarty, *All Things New*, 122.
161 Buder, *Visionaries and Planners*, 44.
162 Hayden, *The Grand Domestic Revolution*, 106.
163 Hayden, *The Grand Domestic Revolution*, 106, 109.
164 John W. Reps, *The Making of Urban America* (Princeton: Princeton University Press, 1965), 472–74. Also see "Bird's-Eye View of the Proposed Zion from Lake Michigan," *Chicago Daily Tribune* (July 16, 1901): 3; Budgett Meakin, *Model Factories and Villages* (London: T. Fisher Unwin, 1905; New York and London: Garland Publishing, 1985), 411–13; Thomas Adams, *Outline of Town and City Planning, a Review of Past Efforts and Modern Aims* (New York: Russell Sage, 1936), 178; *Supplementary Report of the Urbanism Committee to the National Resources Committee* (Washington, D.C.: U. S. Government Printing Office, 1939), 504–6; Philip L. Cook, *Zion City, Illinois, Twentieth-Century Utopia* (Syracuse, NY: Syracuse University Press, 1996), esp. chs. 3–6; Robert Rhodes, "Zion City, Illinois: Twentieth Century Utopia," book review, *Communities* 105 (Winter 1999): 68; Robert P. Sutton, *Heartland Utopias* (DeKalb, Ill.: Northern Illinois University Press, 2009), 131–42.
165 Quoted in Reps, *The Making of Urban America*, 474.
166 Reps, *The Making of Urban America*, 474.
167 J. R. Snavely, "The Industrial Community Development of Hershey, Pennsylvania," *American Landscape Architect* 3 (November 1930): 24–36; Alexander Stoddart and J. Horace McFarland, "Pennsylvania's Chocolate Town," *Planning and Civic Comment* 3 (April–June 1937): 9–11, plates; "The Town that Chocolate Built: Hershey's 'Industrial Utopia,'" *New York Times* (May 23, 1937): 158; Arthur C. Comey and Max S. Wehrly, "A Study of Planned Communities" (Department of Regional Planning of Harvard University, November 1936): 104–10; Joseph Richard Snavely, *The Story of Hershey: The Chocolate Town* (Hershey, Pa., 1953); John W. Reps, *The Making of Urban America: A History of City Planning in the United States* (Princeton: Princeton University Press, 1965), 428, 430; Donald Janson, "Chocolate Town, Pa.: A Sweet Smell of Success," *New York Times* (February 27, 1977), X: 1, 20; Stern with Massengale, *The Anglo-American Suburb*, 56; John S. Garner, *The Model Company Town* (Amherst: University of Massachusetts Press, 1984), 43; Mary Davidoff Houts and Pamela Cassidy Whitenack, *Images of America: Hershey* (Charleston, S.C.: Arcadia Publishing, 2000); Michael D'Antonio, *Hershey: Milton S. Hershey's Extraordinary Life of Wealth, Empire, and Utopian Dreams* (New York: Simon and Schuster, 2006), 107–26.
168 Reps, *The Making of Urban America*, 428.
169 Milton S. Hershey, quoted in "The Town that Chocolate Built": 158.
170 "Hershey, Pennsylvania, USA," July 31, 2001, www.bbc.co.uk.
171 "The Best!" *St. Louis Post Dispatch* (December 13, 1902): 3; "Making a Park," *St. Louis Globe Democrat* (December 28, 1902); "The Building of a City," advertisement, *St. Louis Republic* (December 28, 1902): 13; "Isometric View of University Heights," advertisement, *St. Louis Republic* (May 17, 1903): 21; Sidney Morse, *The Siege of University City, the Dreyfus Case of America* (University City: University City Publishing Company, 1912), 211–26; "Studio Building, University City, Mo. Messrs. Eames & Young," *American Architect* 104 (December 24, 1913): n.p.; *Urban Oasis: 75 Years in Parkview a St. Louis Private Place* (St. Louis: Boar's Head Press, 1979), esp. chs. 1–2; Frank Peters and George McCue, *A Guide to the Architecture of St. Louis* (Columbia: University of Missouri Press, 1989), 123–25; Allen Freeman, "Remarkable Relic Of a Tarnished Utopia," *Architecture* 78 (April 1989): 88–91; David T. Beito and Bruce Smith, "The Formation of Urban Infrastructure through Nongovernmental Planning: The Private Places of St. Louis, 1869–1920," *Journal of Urban History* 16 (May 1990): 263–303; John Wright, *University City, Missouri* (Chicago: Arcadia, 2002), 7–8, 24, 32, 33, 63; Esley Hamilton, "Ernest W. Bowditch: Designer of University Heights Number One," *Society of Architectural Historians Missouri Valley Chapter Newsletter* IX (Spring 2003): 4–5; *City Hall Plaza Historic District, National Register of Historic Places Inventory—Nomination Form* (Washington, D. C.: National Park Service, n.d.); "St. Louis County Designated Landmarks in University City," in http://www.stlouisco.com/parks/landmarks/universitycity-landmark.pdf.
172 Edward Gardner Lewis, quoted in Morse, *The Siege of University City; the Dreyfus Case of America*, 212.
173 Edward Gardner Lewis, quoted in Morse, *The Siege of University City; the Dreyfus Case of America*, 212, 215.
174 Edward Gardner Lewis, quoted in Morse, *The Siege of University City; the Dreyfus Case of America*, 216.

175 "Making a Park."
176 Quoted in John W. Snyder, *The Planning and Development of Atascadero, California* (Hilliard, Ohio: Society for American City and Regional Planning History, 1990), n.p. Also see "A Model Civic Center for the Woman's Republic Community, Atascadero," *Architect and Engineer of California* 35 (November 1913): 69–74; "'Back to The Soil' Problem Solved by Scientific Development," *Los Angeles Times* (January 1, 1914), V: 155; "A Model City," *Architect and Engineer of California* 41 (May 1915): 109; "Getting the Best Out of Life," *Illustrated Review* (June 1919): 29; "Atascadero the Beautiful," *San Francisco Chronicle* (January 14, 1920): 110–11; *Atascadero, California, "The Beautiful,"; The Long Life Town* (Atascadero: Atascadero Press, 1923); "Justice Catches Up," *Los Angeles Times* (September 16, 1927): 4; *Atascadero: Brightest and Whitest Spot in California* (Atascadero, Calif.: Western Publishers, 1929), Charles W. Moore, "You Have to Pay for the Public Life," *Perspecta* 9/10 (1965): 58–59; David Gebhard and Robert Winter, *A Guide to Architecture in Los Angeles & Southern California* (Santa Barbara and Salt Lake City: Peregrine Smith, 1977), 584; *WPA Guide to California* (1939; New York: Pantheon Books, 1984), 390; Cheryl Robertson, "The Resort to the Rustic: Simple Living and the California Bungalow," in Kenneth R. Trapp, ed., *The Arts and Crafts Movement in California: Living the Good Life* (Oakland, Calif.: Oakland Museum, 1993), 84–87; Fukuo Akimoto, "California Garden Suburbs: St. Francis Wood and Palos Verdes Estates," *Journal of Urban Design* 12 (February 2007): 43–72.
177 "Dominguez Industrial Center Looks Likely," *Los Angeles Times* (November 28, 1911): 6; "Huge Fee for Laying Out Industrial City," *Los Angeles Times* (December 23, 1911), II: 1, 3; "Modern City Takes Shape," *Los Angeles Times* (December 27, 1911), II: 6; "Alladin Like: Company Plans Thousand Homes," *Los Angeles Times* (April 14, 1912), VI: 20; "Big Campaign on For New Town," *Los Angeles Times* (April 28, 1912), VI: 8; "Present Appearance of Union Tool Company's Shops at Torrance," *Los Angeles Times* (June 30, 1912), VI: 13; "Will Find Town Ready," *Los Angeles Times* (December 1, 1912), V: 12; "Torrance, The Modern Industrial City," advertisement, *Los Angeles Times* (January 26, 1913), II: 4; "Large Manufacturing Plant for Thriving Industrial City," *Los Angeles Times* (February 9, 1913), VI: 4; Dana W. Bartlett, "Torrance," *American City* 9 (October 1913): 310–14; "Homes for Children," *Los Angeles Times* (October 2, 1913), II: 11; "Homes for Workers," *Los Angeles Times* (January 26, 1916), II: 2; Edith Elmer Wood, *Housing of the Unskilled Wage Earner* (New York: Macmillan Company, 1919), 108–9; *The WPA Guide to California* (1939; New York: Pantheon Books, 1984), 419; Arthur C. Comey and Max S. Wehrly, "Planned Communities," (November 1936) in *Supplementary Report of the Urbanism Committee to the National Resources Committee* (Washington, D.C.: U. S. Government Printing Office, 1939), vol. 2: 46–47, 111, 122, 130, 146; Esther McCoy, *Five California Architects* (New York: Reinhold Publishing Corporation, 1960), 86–87; Reyner Banham, *Los Angeles: The Architecture of Four Ecologies* (New York: Harper and Row, 1971; Berkeley: University of California Press, 2000), 46; Charles Moore, Peter Becker, and Regula Campbell, *The City Observed: Los Angeles* (Santa Monica: Hennessey & Ingalls, 1984), 121, 282–85; Dennis F. Shanahan and Charles Elliott Jr., *Historic Torrance: A Pictorial History of Torrance, California* (Redondo Beach, CA: Legends Press, 1984), esp. pp. 55–75; Bruce Kamerling, *Irving J. Gill, Architect* (San Diego: San Diego Historical Society, 1993), 88, 92, 93, 132; Margaret Crawford, *Building the Workingman's Paradise* (London and New York: Verso, 1995), 89–93; Margaret Crawford, "The 'New' Company Town," *Perspecta* 30 (1999): 48–57; Thomas H. Hines, *Irving Gill and the Architecture of Reform: A Study in Modernist Architectural Culture* (New York: Monacelli Press, 2000), 141, 183–93, 290; William Alexander McClung, *Landscapes of Desire: Anglo Mythologies of Los Angeles* (Berkeley: University of California Press, 2000), 159–62; David Gebhard and Robert Winter, *An Architectural Guidebook to Los Angeles*, edited and updated edition (Salt Lake City: Gibbs Smith, 2003), 97–99; Natalie Shivers, "Architecture: A New Creative Medium," in Victoria Dailey, Natalie Shivers, and Michael Dawson, *LA's Early Moderns: Art/Architecture/Photography* (Los Angeles: Balcony Press, 2003), 139; Bonnie Mae Barnard and Save Historic Old Torrance, *Old Torrance: Olmsted Districts* (Charleston, S.C.: Arcadia, 2005), esp. chs. 1–3; Robert M. Fogelson, *Bourgeois Nightmares: Suburbia, 1870–1930* (New Haven, Conn.: Yale University Press, 2005), 79–80; Marvin Rand, *Irving J. Gill, Architect, 1870–1936* (Salt Lake City: Gibbs Smith, 2006), 140–43, 234–35.
178 Frederick Law Olmsted Jr., File 5354.1, Olmsted Collection, Manuscript Division, Library of Congress, as quoted in Crawford, *Building the Workingman's Paradise*, 91.
179 McCoy, *Five California Architects*, 86.
180 Crawford, *Building the Workingman's Paradise*, 92.
181 Hines, *Irving Gill and the Architecture of Reform*, 190.
182 For the Wheaton House, see Hines, *Irving Gill and the Architecture of Reform*, 108.
183 *Mossmain, Montana* (Billings, Mont.: Yellowstone Garden City Holding Corporation, c. 1915). Also see "A Garden City Project," *American City* 14 (June 1916): 633; Mark L. Peisch, "The Chicago School and Walter Burley Griffin, 1893–1914" (Ph.D. diss., Columbia University, 1959): 138; Mark L. Peisch, *The Chicago School of Architecture: Early Followers of Sullivan and Wright* (New York: Random House, 1964), 102–3; Donald Leslie Johnson, *The Architecture of Walter Burley Griffin* (Melbourne, Australia: Macmillan Company of Australia, 1977), 30–31, 33–34; Peter Harrison, *Walter Burley Griffin: Landscape Architect* (Canberra: National Library of Australia, 1995), 53–54.
184 *Mossmain, Montana*, 4.
185 Peisch, "The Chicago School and Walter Burley Griffin, 1893–1914": 138.
186 S. Herbert Hare, "The Planning of a New Industrial City," *American City* 29 (August 1923): 501–3; "Longview—A City-Planned Community," *Architect and Engineer* 81 (April 1925): 99–104; B. L. Lambuth, "A Small City Whose Growth Is Aided and Controlled by a Plan," *American City* 33 (August 1926): 186–91; "Longview, Washington, the New Industrial City of the Pacific Northwest," *Städtebau* 24 (1929): 26–32; "American Small Towns II, Longview, Washington," *Town Planning Review* 16 (December 1935): 279–86, plates 56–59; S. Herbert Hare, "Longview, Washington," *Architectural Record* 80 (July 1936): 23–28; Arthur C. Comey and Max S. Wehrly, "Planned Communities," (November 1936) in *Supplementary Report of the Urbanism Committee to the National Resources Committee* (Washington, D.C.: U. S. Government Printing Office, 1939), vol. 2: 41–44, 111, 117, 122, 130, 135–36, 146; John M. McClelland Jr., *Longview...the Remarkable Beginnings of a Modern Western City* (Portland, Ore.: Binfords & Mort, 1949), passim; Kenneth A. Erickson, "The Morphology of Lumber Settlements in Western Oregon and Washington" (Ph.D. diss., University of California, Berkeley, 1966): 267–75; Mel Scott, *American City Planning Since 1890* (Berkeley and Los Angeles: University of California Press, 1969), 234; Norman T. Newton, *Design on the Land: The Development of Landscape Architecture* (Cambridge, Mass.: Belknap Press of Harvard University Press, 1971), 480–82; Steven Dotterrer, "Cities and Towns," in Thomas Vaughan, ed., *Space, Style and Structure: Building in Northwest America* (Portland: Oregon Historical Society, 1974), 463–66; Sally B. Woodbridge and Roger Montgomery, *A Guide to Architecture in Washington State: An Environmental Perspective* (Seattle: University of Washington Press, 1980), 24–26, 353–55; Margaret Ripley Wolfe, *Kingsport, Tennessee: A Planned American City* (Lexington: University Press of Kentucky, 1987), 56–57; Leland M. Roth, "Company Towns in the Western United States," in John S. Garner, ed., *The Company Town: Architecture and Society in the Early Industrial Age* (New York: Oxford University Press, 1992), 188–91; Cydney E. Millstein, "Sidney J. Hare and S. Herbert Hare," in Charles A. Birnbaum and Robin Karson, eds., *Pioneers of American Landscape Design* (New York: McGraw-Hill, 2000), 162–68; Abraham Ott, "Boulevards in the Forest: Progressive Urban Planning, Environment and Labor in Longview, Washington" (Master's thesis, University of Washington, Seattle, 2008).
187 Jesse Clyde Nichols, speech, 1925, quoted in Ott, "Boulevards in the Forest: Progressive Urban Planning, Environment and Labor in Longview, Washington": 49.
188 Jesse Clyde Nichols, quoted in McClelland Jr., *Longview . . .The Remarkable Beginnings of a Modern Western City*, 22.
189 Hare, "American Small Towns; II: Longview, Washington": 285.
190 Hare, "Longview, Washington": 27.
191 Hare, "American Small Towns; II: Longview, Washington": 281.
192 Roth, "Company Towns in the Western United States," in Garner, ed., *The Company Town: Architecture and Society in the Early Industrial Age*, 190.
193 Ott, "Boulevards in the Forest: Progressive Urban Planning, Environment and Labor in Longview, Washington": 95.
194 Wesley Vandercook, letter to Samuel Morris, December 1, 1923, quoted in Ott,"Boulevards in the Forest: Progressive Urban Planning, Environment and Labor in Longview, Washington": 92.
195 Geddes Smith, quoted in Dotterrer, "Cities and Towns," in Vaughan, ed., *Space, Style and Structure*, 466.
196 S. R. DeBoer, "Boulder City," *American City* 44 (February 1931): 146–49; S. R. DeBoer, "The City Plan of Boulder City," *National Civic Review* 20 (May 1931): 253–55; Arthur C. Comey and Max S. Wehrly, "Planned Communities," (November 1936) in *Supplementary Report of the Urbanism Committee to the National Resources Committee* (Washington, D.C.: U. S. Government Printing Office, 1939), vol. 2: 69–70, 145–46; Stanley L. McMichael, *Real Estate Subdivisions* (New York: Prentice-Hall, 1949), 50; Julie Nicoletta, *Buildings of Nevada* (New York: Oxford University Press, 2000), 206, 234–38; Mimi Garat Rodden, *Images of America: Boulder City, Nevada* (Chicago: Arcadia Publishing, 2000); http://www.benv.org/history.asp.
197 DeBoer, "The City Plan of Boulder City": 253.
198 Saco Rienk DeBoer, quoted in *Supplementary Report of the Urbanism Committee to the National Resources Committee*, 145–46.
199 Dean Thrift Sinclair, "'A New Town Will Appear on Charleston Neck': North Charleston and the Creation of the New South Garden City" (Ph.D. diss., Louisiana State University and Agricultural and Mechanical College, 2001): 3. Also see Dean Sinclair, "William Bell Marquis," in Charles A. Birnbaum and Robin Karson, eds., *Pioneers of American Landscape Design* (New York: McGraw Hill, 2000), 242–26; Donald Wilkinson, *North Charleston* (Charleston, S.C.: Arcadia, 2002), 28.
200 Sinclair, "William Bell Marquis," in Birnbaum and Karson, eds., *Pioneers of American Landscape Design*, 242.
201 Charles C. May, "Indian Hill: An Industrial Village at Worcester, Mass.," *Architectural Record* 41 (January 1917): 20–35; Lawrence Veiller, "Industrial Housing Developments in America: A Colony in the Blue Ridge Mountains at Erwin, Tennessee," *Architectural Record* 43 (June 1918): 547–59, partially reprinted in *Homes for Workmen: A Presentation of Leading Examples of Industrial Community Development* (New Orleans: Southern Pine Association, 1919), 135–39; John Burchard and Albert Bush-Brown, *The Architecture of America: A Social and Cultural History* (Boston: Little, Brown and Company, 1961), 360; Leland M. Roth, *A Concise History of American Architecture* (New York: Harper & Row, 1979), 224–25; Gwendolyn Wright, *Building the Dream: A Social History of Housing in America* (New York: Pantheon Books, 1981), 182; John S. Garner, *The Model Company Town: Urban Design through Private Enterprise in Nineteenth-Century New England* (Amherst: University of Massachusetts Press, 1984), 43; Margaret Duncan Binnicker, "Erwin, Tennessee: Transformation of Work and Place in an Appalachian Community, 1900–1960" (Ph.D. diss., Middle Tennessee State University, 1999): esp. ch. 3; Margaret Duncan Binnicker, "A Garden City in Appalachia Tennessee; Grosvenor Atterbury's Design for Erwin," *Tennessee Historical Quarterly* 59 (Winter 2000): cover, 274–89; Leland M. Roth, *American Architecture: A History* (Boulder, Colo.: Icon Editions/Westview Press, 2001), 328; Linda Davis March, *Images of America: Erwin and Unicoi County* (Charleston, S.C.: Arcadia, 2007), 63; Peter Pennoyer and Anne Walker, *The Architecture of Grosvenor Atterbury*, foreword by Robert A. M. Stern (New York: W. W. Norton, 2008), 190, 199–204, 264.
202 Veiller, "Industrial Housing Developments in America: A Colony in the Blue Ridge Mountains at Erwin, Tennessee": 548.
203 Veiller, "Industrial Housing Developments in America: A Colony in the Blue Ridge Mountains at Erwin, Tennessee": 554.
204 Clinton Mackenzie, *Industrial Housing* (New York: Knickerbocker Press, 1920), 1–41, excerpts published in *Western Architect* 35 (November 1926): 139–40; Isaac Shuman, "Kingsport, an Unusual City, Built to Make Business for a Railroad: How Vision Backed by Science Is Creating a Model Community in the Tennessee Mountains," *American City* 22 (May 1920): 471–73; Rexford Newcomb, "The New Industrial City of Kingsport, Tennessee," *Western Architect* 35 (November 1926): 137–38, plates 161–76; John Nolen, *New Towns for Old* (Boston: Marshall Jones, 1927; Amherst and Boston: University of Massachusetts Press, 2005), 50–65; John Nolen, "Kingsport, Tennessee: An Industrial City Built

to Order," *American Review of Reviews* 75 (March 1927): 286–92; Howard Long, *Kingsport: A Romance of Industry* (Kingsport: Sevier Press, 1928); Mary Frances Hughes, "Where Planned Beauty Blossoms in an Industrial Community," *American City* 43 (December 1930): 140–41; John Nolen, "American Small Towns," *Town Planning Review* (July 1934): 16–24; *Kingsport: The Planned Industrial City* (Kingsport: The Rotary Club, 1946), esp. pp. 32–35; John Loretz Hancock, "John Nolen and the American City Planning Movement: A History of Culture Change and Community Response, 1900–1940" (Ph.D. diss., University of Pennsylvania, 1964): 448–86; Walter L. Creese, *The Search for Environment*, exp. ed. (New Haven, Conn.: Yale University Press, 1966; Baltimore and London: Johns Hopkins University Press, 1992), 302; Stewart Jerome Wilson, "John Nolen: An Overview of His Career" (Masters thesis, University of Oregon, 1982): 60–66, plates 30–31; Keller Easterling, "Kingsport, Tennessee," (unpublished study, National Endowment of the Arts Grant, 1986); John Hancock, "'What Is Fair Must Be Fit,'" *Lotus International* 50 (1986): 30–45; Margaret Ripley Wolfe, *Kingsport, Tennessee: A Planned American City* (Lexington: University Press of Kentucky, 1987); Carl Abbott, "Model Cities," book review, *Reviews in American History* 16 (December 1988): 599–603; David L. Ames, book review, *Winterthur Portfolio* 24 (Summer–Autumn 1989): 204–6; Andrés Duany, Elizabeth Plater-Zyberk, and Robert Alminana, *The New Civic Art: Elements of Town Planning* (New York: Rizzoli International Publications, 2003), 93; Margaret Crawford, *Building the Workingman's Paradise: The Design of American Company Towns* (London and New York: Verso, 1995), 165–68; Margaret Crawford, "John Nolen, the Design of the Company Town," *Rassegna* 19 (1997): 46–53; Millard F. Rogers, Jr., *John Nolen & Mariemont: Building a New Town in Ohio* (Baltimore and London: Johns Hopkins University Press, 2001), 53–54; Charles D. Warren, "Introduction," in Nolen, *New Towns for Old* (2005), lxvi–lxxiii; Peter Pennoyer and Anne Walker, *The Architecture of Grosvenor Atterbury*, foreword by Robert A.M. Stern (New York: W. W. Norton, 2009), 190, 204–7; Tom Martinson, *The Atlas of American Architecture: 2000 Years of Architecture, City Planning, Landscape Architecture and Civil Engineering* (New York: Rizzoli International Publications, 2009), 369.

205 Ames, book review, *Winterthur Portfolio*: 204–6.

206 Mackenzie, *Industrial Housing*, 4.

207 Nolen, *New Towns for Old*, 52.

208 Warren, "Introduction," in Nolen, *New Towns for Old* (2005), lxvii.

209 Hancock, "John Nolen and the American City Planning Movement: A History of Culture Change and Community Response, 1900–1940": 455.

210 Long, *Kingsport: A Romance of Industry*, 94–95.

211 Easterling, "Kingsport, Tennessee," (unpublished study, National Endowment of the Arts Grant, 1986).

212 Warren, "Introduction," in Nolen, *New Towns for Old* (2005), lxvi.

213 Mackenzie, "A New Factor in Planning of Homes for Industrial Workers": 140.

214 John Nolen, quoted in Hancock, "John Nolen and the American City Planning Movement: A History of Culture Change and Community Response, 1900–1940": 466.

215 Easterling, "Kingsport, Tennessee," (unpublished study, National Endowment of the Arts Grant, 1986).

216 "Mariemont, America's Demonstration Town," *American City* 27 (October 1922): 309–10; Walter Brinkman, "Mariemont—A Model Village," *Popular Mechanics* 38 (December 1922): 893–94; "Preliminary Studies, Group of Houses, Mariemont, Ohio," *The Architect* 4 (June 1924): 208; H. I. Brock, "The City Set at the Crossroads," *New York Times* (August 24, 1924): 8; *A Descriptive and Pictured Story of Mariemont: A New Town: "A National Exemplar"* (Cincinnati, Ohio: The Mariemont Co., 1925); "A Two-Family House at Mariemont, O.," *Architectural Forum* 43 (September 1925): 176; *J. Walter Thompson News Bulletin Describing Mariemont: The New Town* (Cincinnati: Mariemont Press, 1926); Warren E. Leavitt, "'The Romance of Mariemont,'" (March 19, 1926–November 26, 1926), reprinted as *Mariemont Souvenir Edition* (April 19, 1973); "Mariemont—New Town: A Complete Residential Village Near Cincinnati, Ohio," *Architecture* 54 (September 1926): 247–74, plates 171–85; "Mariemont–'A National Exemplar,'" editorial, *Architecture* 54 (September 1926): 277–78; John Nolen, *New Towns for Old* (Boston: Marshall Jones, 1927; Amherst and Boston: University of Massachusetts Press, 2005), 111–32; Frank Chouteau Brown, "Some Recent Apartment Buildings," *Architectural Record* 63 (March 1928): 242; Lewis Mumford, "American Architecture To-day," part 2, *Architecture* 57 (September 1928): 301–8; John Nolen, "Mariemont, Ohio—A New Town Built to Produce Local Happiness," *American Civic Annual* 1 (1929): 235–37; Arthur C. Holden, "Realty Developments and the Architect," *Architectural Record* 69 (April 1931): 342–45; "Mariemont, Ohio," *Architectural Forum* 56 (March 1932): 245–48; Thomas Adams, *The Design of Residential Areas: Basic Considerations, Principles, and Methods* (Cambridge, Mass.: Harvard University Press, 1934), 243; *Monograph of the Work of Robert Rodes McGoodwin, 1910–1940* (Philadelphia: William F. Fell, 1942), plates 113–14; John L. Hancock, "John Nolen and the American City Planning Movement: A History of Culture Change and Community Response, 1900–1940" (Ph.D. diss., University of Pennsylvania, 1964): 367–81; Walter L. Creese, *The Search for Environment*, exp. ed. (New Haven, Conn.: Yale University Press, 1966; Baltimore and London: Johns Hopkins University Press, 1992), 302; Warren Wright Parks, *The Mariemont Story* (Cincinnati: Creative Writers & Publishers, 1967); Mel C. Scott, *American City Planning Since 1890* (Berkeley: University of California, 1969), 233; Stanley Buder, "The Mariemont Story," book review, *Journal of American History* 57 (June 1970): 197; Norman T. Newtown, *Design on the Land: The Development of Landscape Architecture* (Cambridge, Mass., and London: Harvard University Press, 1971), 482–86; Judith Paine, "Pioneer Women Architects," in Susan Torre, ed., *Women in Architecture: A Historic and Contemporary Perspective* (New York: Whitney Library of Design, 1977), 66; Stewart Jerome Wilson, "John Nolen: An Overview of His Career" (Master's thesis, University of Oregon, 1982): 73–75, plate 33; Elaine D. Engst and H. Thomas Hickerson, *Urban America: Documenting the Planners*, exhibition catalogue (Ithaca, N.Y.: Department of Manuscripts and University Archives, Cornell University Libraries, 1985), 10, 13–14; Keller Easterling, "Mariemont, Ohio," (unpublished study, National Endowment of the Arts Grant, 1986); John L. Hancock, "'What is Fair Must Be Fit,'": Drawings and Plans by John Nolen, American City Planner," *Lotus International* 50 (1986): 31–45; Witold Rybczynski, *City Life: Urban Expectations in a New World* (New York: Scribner, 1995), 188–89; Bradley D. Cross, "New Jerusalems for a New World: The Garden City Idea in Modern Planning Thought and Practice in Britain, Canada, and the United States, 1900–1970" (Ph.D. diss., University of Cincinnati, 1997): 158–80, 350, 357; Robert A. M. Stern, "In Praise of Invented Towns," Seaside Prize Acceptance Speech, Seaside, Florida, May 15, 1999, in Cynthia Davidson, ed., *Tradition and Invention in Architecture: Conversations and Essays, Robert A. M. Stern* (New Haven, Conn., and London: Yale University Press, 2011), 39–46; Millard F. Rogers Jr., *John Nolen & Mariemont: Building a New Town in Ohio* (Baltimore: Johns Hopkins University Press, 2001); Bruce Stephenson, "The Roots of the New Urbanism: John Nolen's Garden City Ethic," *Journal of Planning History* 1 (May 2002): 99–123; Cliff Ellis, book review, *APA Journal* 69 (Spring 2003): 205; Kristin M. Szylvian, book review, *Planning Perspectives* 18 (October 2003): 429–31; Mary Corbin Sies, book review, *Journal of the Society of Architectural Historians* 62 (December 2003): 533–35; Randall Arendt, *Crossroads, Hamlet, Village, Town: Design Characteristics of Traditional Neighborhoods, Old and New (Revised Edition)* (Chicago: American Planning Association, Planning Advisory Service, 2004), 32, 34–36; Bradley D. Cross, "'On a Business Basis': An American Garden City," *Planning Perspectives* 19 (January 2004): 57–77; Joseph L. Arnold, book review, *Journal of American History* (March 2004): 1498; Charles D. Warren, "Introduction," in Nolen, *New Towns for Old* (2005), xcii–xcvii; Witold Rybczynski, *Last Harvest: How a Cornfield Became new Daleville* (New York: Scribner, 2007), 87; Witold Rybczynski, "Scatteration," *Wilson Quarterly* 31 (Spring 2007): 24; Christiane Crasemann Collins, "Camillo Sitte across the Atlantic: Raymond Unwin, John Nolen, and Werner Hegemann," in Charles C. Bohl and Jean-François Lejeune, eds., *Sitte, Hegemann and the Metropolis: Modern Civic Art and International Exchanges* (London: Routledge, 2009), 179; Peter Pennoyer and Anne Walker, *The Architecture of Grosvenor Atterbury*, foreword by Robert A. M. Stern (New York: W. W. Norton, 2009), 190, 208–9, 265.

217 *A Descriptive and Pictured Story of Mariemont: A New Town: "A National Exemplar"*, 1, 13.

218 Quoted in Nolen, *New Towns for Old*, 113, 115.

219 Charles J. Livingood, letter to John Nolen, January 19, 1927, quoted in Warren, "Introduction," in Nolen, *New Towns for Old* (2005), xciii.

220 Warren, "Introduction," in Nolen, *New Towns for Old* (2005), xciv.

221 Warren, "Introduction," in Nolen, *New Towns for Old* (2005), xciii.

222 Werner Hegemann, *Amerikanische Architektur und Stadtbaukunst* (Berlin: Wasmuth, 1925), quoted in Collins, "Camillo Sitte across the Atlantic," in Bohl and Lejeune, eds., *Sitte, Hegemann and the Metropolis*, 179.

223 *A Descriptive and Pictured Story of Mariemont: A New Town: "A National Exemplar"*, 29.

224 Warren, "Introduction," in Nolen, *New Towns for Old* (2005), xcvi.

225 Robert Rodes McGoodwin, quoted in "Mariemont—A New Town": 258. Also see *Monograph of the Work of Robert Rodes McGoodwin*, plates 113–14.

226 Mumford, "American Architecture To-Day," part 2: 301–8.

227 *A Descriptive and Pictured Story of Mariemont: A New Town: "A National Exemplar"*, 31.

228 Thomas Adams, *Proposed Farm City in Pender County, North Carolina* (New York: Farm Cities Corporation, 1921); *The Farm Cities Corporation of America*, booklet (Washington, D.C.: The Corporation, c. 1921); "Farm Cities," *Housing Betterment* (January 1922): 395–96; George H. Ball, "Making Farm Life Profitable and Pleasant," *National Real Estate Journal* 24 (May 21, 1923): 29–32; Frank Bohn, "New South's Farmers Have a New Teacher," *New York Times* (May 16, 1926), IX: 24; John Nolen, *New Towns for Old* (Boston: Marshall Jones, 1927; Amherst and Boston: University of Massachusetts Press, 2005), 12, 200; Gordon Van Schaack, "Penderlea Homesteads," *Landscape Architecture* 25 (January 1935): 75–80; Arthur C. Comey and Max S. Wehrly, "A Study of Planned Communities" (Department of Regional Planning of Harvard University, November 1936): 356–57; Arthur C. Comey and Max S. Wehrly, "Planned Communities," (November 1936) in *Supplementary Report of the Urbanism Committee to the National Resources Committee* (Washington, D.C.: U. S. Government Printing Office, 1939), vol. 2: 114, 159; "Penderlea Homesteads," *Architectural Forum* 66 (June 1937): 490–91; Paul K. Conklin, *Tomorrow a New World: The New Deal Community Program* (Ithaca, N.Y.: Cornell University Press, 1959), 277–93; John Loretz Hancock, "John Nolen and the American City Planning Movement: A History of Culture Change and Community Response, 1900–1940" (Ph.D. diss., University of Pennsylvania, 1964): 362–67, 581–82, 616; Stewart Jerome Wilson, "John Nolen: An Overview of His Career" (Master's thesis, University of Oregon, 1982): 72, 87–89; Marcia G. Synnott, "Hugh MacRae, Penderlea, and the Model Farm Communities Movement," *Proceedings of the South Carolina Historical Association* 54 (1987): 53–65; Daniel T. Rodgers, *Atlantic Crossings: Social Politics in a Progressive Age* (Cambridge, Mass., and London: Belknap Press of Harvard University Press, 1998), 352; Charles D. Warren, "Introduction," in Nolen, *New Towns for Old* (2005), lii–liii; Ann S. Cottle, *The Roots of Penderlea: A Memory of a New Deal Homestead Community* (Wilmington: University of North Carolina Wilmington, 2008); Robert H. Kargon and Arthur P. Molella, *Invented Edens: Techno-Cities of the Twentieth Century* (Cambridge, Mass.: MIT Press, 2008), 31. Also see www.penderleahomesteadmuseum.org.

229 Warren, "Introduction," in Nolen, *New Towns for Old* (2005), lii.

230 John Nolen, quoted in *The Farm Cities Corporation of America*, 10–11.

231 John Nolen, "What Florida Can Teach and Learn," *American City* 34 (June 1926): 65–66; John Nolen, *New Towns for Old* (Boston: Marshall Jones, 1927; Amherst and Boston: University of Massachusetts Press, 2005), 153; "Neue Siedlungsplane und Neue Lebensbedingungen," *Städtebau* 22 (April 1927): 50–54; Arthur C. Comey and Max S. Wehrly, "A Study of Planned Communities" (Department of Regional Planning of Harvard University, November 1936): 397–98; John Loretz Hancock, "John Nolen and the American City Planning Movement: A History of Culture Change and Community Response, 1900–1940" (Ph.D. diss., University of Pennsylvania, 1964): 394; Mel Scott, *American City Planning Since 1890* (Berkeley and Los Angeles: University of California Press, 1969), 234–35; "Planning Pioneer Honored by City He Designed in 1925," *Practicing Planner* 6 (September 1976): 37; Stewart Jerome Wilson, "John Nolen: An Overview of His Career" (Master's thesis, University of Oregon, 1982): 77, plate 35; James Arthur Glass, "John Nolen and the Planning of New Towns: Three Case Studies" (Ph.D. diss., Cornell University, 1984): 10–11, 250–393; Elaine D. Engst and H. Thomas Hickerson, *Urban America: Documenting the Planners*, exhibition catalog (Ithaca, N.Y.: Department of Manuscripts and University Archives, Cornell University Libraries, 1985), 15–18; John Hancock, "'What Is Fair Must Be Fit,'" *Lotus International* 50 (1986): 30–45; Janet Snyder Matthews, *Sarasota: Journey to Centennial* (Sarasota, Fla.: Pine Level Press, 1989), 95–103; Janet Snyder Matthews, *Venice: Journey from Horse to Chaise* (Sarasota, Fla.: Pine Level Press, 1989), 224–48; John F. Eades, "City Planning in West Palm Beach, Florida, During the 1920s," (Master's thesis, Florida Atlantic University, 1991): 96, 136; John Hancock, "John Nolen: New Towns in Florida," *The New City* 1 (Fall 1991): 68–87; Jean-François Lejeune, "The Grid, the Park, and the Model-T—Searching for Paradise: Garden Cities in Florida," in Gabriele Tagliaventi, ed., *Garden City* (Rome: Gangemi Editore, 1994), 247–56; Thomas E. Low, "The Chautauquans and Progressives in Florida," *Journal of Decorative and Propaganda Arts* 23 (1998): 306–21; Gregg M. Turner, *Venice in the 1920s* (Charleston, S.C.: Arcadia Publishing, 2000); Michael Zimny, "Venice," *Florida Trend* 31 (January 2001): 6–11; Bruce Stephenson, "The Roots of the New Urbanism: John Nolen's Garden City Ethic," *Journal of Planning History* 1 (May 2002): 99–123; Andrés Duany, Elizabeth Plater-Zyberk, and Robert Alminana, *The New Civic Art: Elements of Town Planning* (New York: Rizzoli International Publications, 2003), 43; Charles D. Warren, "Introduction," in Nolen, *New Towns for Old* (2005), xcvii–xcix.

232 Stephenson, "The Roots of the New Urbanism: John Nolen's Garden City Ethic": 108–9.

233 John Nolen, quoted in *Venice News* (June 1927), also quoted in Stephenson, "The Roots of the New Urbanism: John Nolen's Garden City Ethic": 108.

234 Nolen, "What Florida Can Teach and Learn": 66.

235 Lejeune, "The Grid, the Park, and the Model-T—Searching for Paradise: Garden Cities in Florida," in Tagliaventi, ed., *Garden City*, 248.

236 Stephenson, "The Roots of the New Urbanism: John Nolen's Garden City Ethic": 110. Also see Nolen, *New Towns for Old*, 110.

237 Lejeune, "The Grid, the Park, and the Model-T—Searching for Paradise: Garden Cities in Florida," in Tagliaventi, ed., *Garden City*, 287.

238 Stephenson, "The Roots of the New Urbanism: John Nolen's Garden City Ethic": 111.

239 John Nolen, *New Towns for Old* (Boston: Marshall Jones, 1927; Amherst and Boston: University of Massachusetts Press, 2005), 193, 196; Arthur C. Comey and Max S. Wehrly, "A Study of Planned Communities" (Department of Regional Planning of Harvard University, November 1936): 380–81; John Loretz Hancock, "John Nolen and the American City Planning Movement: A History of Culture Change and Community Response, 1900–1940" (Ph.D. diss., University of Pennsylvania, 1964): 396–98; Mel Scott, *American City Planning Since 1890* (Berkeley and Los Angeles: University of California Press, 1969), 237; John Hancock, "John Nolen: New Towns in Florida," *The New City* 1 (Fall 1991): 68–87; Kathleen LaFrank, "Seaside, Florida: 'The New Town—The Old Ways,'" *Perspectives in Vernacular Architecture* 6 (1997): 111–21. Also see www.clewiston.org/city.htm.

240 "Model Town to Rise in Jersey to Meet Needs of Motor Age," *New York Times* (January 25, 1928): 1, 13; "Garden Cities and Model Towns," editorial, *New York Times* (January 26, 1928): 22; "Many Old Holdings in Model Town Site," *New York Times* (February 12, 1928): 169; "A Town for Moderns," *Survey* 59 (February 15, 1928): 621; "Radburn, N.J., a Town of Modern Plan," *Architecture* 57 (March 1928): 135–36; "New York's First Satellite Town: An Interview with Mr. Alexander M. Bing," *National Municipal Review* 17 (March 1928): 142–46; Geddes Smith, "A Town for the Motor Age," *Survey* 59 (March 1, 1928): 694–98; Stuart Chase, "A Suburban Garden City for the Motor Age," *New York Times* (June 24, 1928), XX: 4; "First Radburn Industry," *New York Times* (July 13, 1928): 33; "Break Ground for Radburn Project," *New York Times* (July 31, 1928): 44; "Radburn," *New York Times* (August 4, 1928): 12; "Second Industry for Radburn," *New York Times* (September 26, 1928): 53; "Rockefeller to Help Finance Radburn, N.J.," *New York Times* (February 19, 1929): 58; "Model Town of Radburn," *New York Times* (February 19, 1929): 58; Henry Wright, "Planning a Town for Wholesome Living," *Playground* (March 1929): 684; "Model Town of Radburn," *New York Times* (March 17, 1929), XII: 13; "Application of Closed-End Street Plan at Radburn," *American City* 40 (April 1929): 142; "Making Radburn City for Safety," *New York Times* (May 26, 1929), XII: 1; "First Settlers Move Into Radburn Homes," *New York Times* (June 23, 1929), XI: 1; Charles S. Ascher, "The Extra-Municipal Administration of Radburn: An Experiment in Government By Contract," *National Muncipal Review* 18 (July 1929): 442–46; "167 New Dwellings to Rise in Radburn," *New York Times* (July 7, 1929): 157; "Radburn Apartment," *New York Times* (August 18, 1929), XI: 16; "Model Town to Try Religious Unity," *New York Times* (September 30, 1929): 23; Henry M. Propper, "Radburn's Unique Plan Shows Results," *American City* 41 (November 1929): 142–44; "Radburn House Wins Duplex Home Award," *New York Times* (November 24, 1929): XIII: 1; "Radburn, N.J.: A Suburban Town Planned for the Motor Age," *Architecture* 60 (December 1929): 317–24; "Radburn: A Town Planned for Safety," *American Architect* 137 (January 1930): 42–45, 128, 130; Louis Brownlow, "Radburn: A New Town Planned for the Motor Age," *International Housing and Town Planning Bulletin* 21 (February 1930): 4–27; Lewis Mumford, "Mass-Production and the Modern House," *Architectural Record* 67 (February 1930): 110–16; "Abbott Court Apartments, Radburn, N.J.," *Architectural Record* 67 (March 1930): 269; "One Year of Radburn," *New York Times* (April 27, 1930): 172; Alexander M. Bing, "American Garden Colonies," *Housing and Building* (May–June 1930): 99–113; "'Town for the Motor Age' Finds Public Ready for Innovations," *Business Week* (July 9, 1930): 19; Henry Wright, "The Autobiography of Another Idea," *Western Architect* 39 (September 1930): 137–41, 153, plates 129–32; *Radburn Garden Homes* (New York: City Housing Corporation, September 1, 1930); M. S. Cautley, "Planting at Radburn," *Landscape Architecture* 21 (October 1930): 23–29; "Safe Streets at Radburn," *New York Times* (October 19, 1930): 181; Robert Lederer, "Die Stadt Radburn," *Wasmuths Monatshefte für Baukunst* 14 (November 1930): 529–30; "Work for Idle Men and Dollars," *Survey* 65 (December 15, 1930): 308; Tracy B. Augur, "Radburn: The Challenge of a New Town," *Michigan Municipal Review* 4 (February–March 1931): 19–22, 30, 39–41; "Model Housing Wins Architects' Award," *New York Times* (February 20, 1931): 43; Arthur C. Holden, "Realty Developments and the Architect," *Architectural Record* 69 (April 1931): 343; "Town of Radburn Is Two Years Old," *New York Times* (April 19, 1931): 151; "Radburn Observes Its Third Birthday," *New York Times* (April 10, 1932), XI: 1; "A Planned Town," *Review of Reviews* 85 (June 1932): 39–41; Leo Levine, "A Neighborhood Unit for Radburn, N.J.," *Architectural Record* 73 (March 1933): 230–31; Thomas Adams, *The Design of Residential Areas* (Cambridge, Mass.:

Harvard University Press, 1934), 245–49; "Refuge for Radburn," *Architectural Forum* 61 (October 1934): 28; "Community Patterns: Radiant Valley, U.S.A., Radburn, N.J., Clarence S. Stein, Henry Wright, Architects," *Architectural Forum* 64 (April 1936): 244–47; Arthur C. Comey and Max S. Wehrly, "Planned Communities," (November 1936) in *Supplementary Report of the Urbanism Committee to the National Resources Committee* (Washington, D.C.: U. S. Government Printing Office, 1939), vol. 2: 97–101; Elbert Peets, "Greendale," in Werner Hegemann, *City Planning and Housing* (New York: Architectural Book Publishing Co., 1937), 407–14, reprinted in Paul D. Speiregen, ed., *On the Art of Designing Cities: Selected Essay of Elbert Peets* (Cambridge, Mass.: MIT Press, 1968), 216–22; Lewis Mumford, *The Culture of Cities* (New York: Harcourt, Brace and Co, 1938), 437; Lewis Mumford, *City Development: Studies in Disintegration and Renewal* (New York: Harcourt, Brace and Company, 1945), 74; Christopher Tunnard and Henry Hope Reed, *American Skyline* (New York: New American Library, 1953), 169; Lewis Mumford, *The Brown Decades* (New York: Dover Publications, 1955), 93; Clarence S. Stein, *Toward New Towns for America* (Cambridge, Mass., and London: MIT Press, 1957), 36–73; Lewis Mumford, *The City in History: Its Origins, Its Transformations, and Its Prospects* (New York: Harcourt, Brace & World, 1961), 450–51; Lewis Mumford, "Yesterday's City of Tomorrow," *Architectural Record* 132 (November 1962): 139–44, reprinted in Lewis Mumford, *The Urban Prospect* (New York: Harcourt, Brace & World, 1968), 116–27; Alden Christie, "Radburn Reconsidered," *Connection* 7 (May 1964): 36–41; Anthony Bailey, "Radburn Revisited," *Regional Plan News* 76 (December 1964): 1–5; Walter L. Creese, *The Search for Environment*, exp. ed. (New Haven, Conn.: Yale University Press, 1966; Baltimore and London: Johns Hopkins University Press, 1992), 2, 194–95, 266–70; "Radburn Estates Revisted," *Architects' Journal* 146 (November 1, 1967): 1075–82; A. Miller, "Radburn and Its Validity Today," *Architect and Building News* 2 (March 13, 1969): 40–46, (March 27, 1969): 30–34; A. E. J. Morris, "Radburn Revited," *Official Architecture and Planning* 32 (April 1969): 402–4; A. E. J. Morris, "Private Sector Housing: The Radburn Dilemma," *Official Architecture and Planning* 33 (May 1970): 416–24; Norman T. Newton, *Design on the Land: The Development of Landscape Architecture* (Cambridge, Mass., and London: Belknap Press of Harvard University Press, 1971), 490–95; Henry N. Wright, "Radburn Revisited," *Architectural Forum* 135 (July–August 1971): 52–57; Penny Schwartz, "Radburn, a Planned Community, Still Living Up to Its Plan," *New York Times* (September 3, 1972): 52; Michael Fagence, "The Radburn Idea," *Built Environment* 2 (August 1973): 467–70, (October 1973): 587–80; Michael T. Fagence, "Let's Be Fair to Radburn," *Town and Country Planning* 42 (September 1974): 415–18; Mark B. Lapping, "Radburn: Planning the American Community," *New Jersey History* 95 (Summer 1977): 92; Agis Salpukas, "Planners Rediscover Radburn," *New York Times* (August 14, 1977), XI: 3; Fred Ferretti, "Radburn, 'Town for Motor Age,' Is Still Running Smoothly at 50," *New York Times* (April 19, 1979), B: 1, 4; Paul Goldberger, "Model Designed on Dreams of Utopia," *New York Times* (April 19, 1979), B: 1, 5; Eugenie Ladner Birch, "Radburn and the American Planning Movement: The Persistence of an Idea," *Journal of the American Planning Association* 46 (October 1980): 424–39; Stern with Massengale, *The Anglo-American Suburb*, 84; Paul Goldberger, "To Utopia by Bus and Subway," *New York Times* (April 17, 1981), C: 1, 4; Jan Gehl, "Planeando Para Peatones," *Cuadernos de Arquitectura y Conservacion del Patrimonio Artistico* 17 (September–October 1981): 23–28; Daniel Schaffer, *Garden Cities for America: The Radburn Experience* (Philadelphia: Temple University Press, 1982); Martin Filler, "Planning for a Better World: The Lasting Legacy of Clarence Stein," *Architectural Record* 170 (August 1982): 122–27; David Schuyler, "Garden Cities for America: The Radburn Experience," book review, *Journal of the Society of Architectural Historians* 42 (May 1983): 192–93; Elaine D. Engst and H. Thomas Hickerson, *Urban America: Documenting the Planners*, exhibition catalogue (Ithaca, N.Y.: Department of Manuscripts and University Archives, Cornell University Libraries, 1985), cover, 20–22; Robert Fishman, *Bourgeois Utopias: The Rise and Fall of Suburbia* (New York: Basic Books, 1987), 49–50, 204; Rachelle Garbarine, "Change on Horizon for a 20's Community," *New York Times* (May 24, 1987), VIII: 8; Robert J. Salgado, "'Motor Age' Town Thrives in the Space Age," *New York Times* (October 4, 1987), XI: 2; Stanley Buder, *Visionaries and Planners: The Garden City Movement and the Modern Community* (New York: Oxford University Press, 1990), 168–69; Suzanne DiGeronimo, "A Vision for the Town: Radburn," *Architecture New Jersey* 27 (No. 4, 1991): 9, 21; Robert A. M. Stern and Thomas Mellins, "1920/1929: Housing America," *Architectural Record* 179 (July 1991): 158–61, reprinted in Cynthia Davidson, ed., *Tradition and Invention in Architecture: Conversations and Essays, Robert A. M. Stern* (New Haven, Conn., and London: Yale University Press, 2011), 16–22; Kermit C. Parsons, "British and American Community Design: Clarence Stein's Manhattan Transfer," *Planning Pespectives* 7 (April 1992): 181–210; Cynthia Girling, "The Pedestrian Pocket: Reorienting Radburn," *Landscape Journal* 12 (Spring 1993): 40–50; Randall Arendt, *Rural by Design: Maintaining Small Town Character* (Chicago and Washington, D. C.: American Planning Association, 1994), 318–21; Jean-François Lejeune, "The Grid, the Park, and the Model-T—Searching for Paradise: Garden Cities in Florida," in Gabriele Tagliaventi, ed., *Garden City* (Rome: Gangemi Editore, 1994), 223; Cynthia L. Girling and Kenneth I. Helphand, *Yard, Street, Park: The Design of Suburban Open Space* (New York: Wiley, 1994), 54–69; Peter Walker and Melanie Simo, *Invisible Gardens: The Search for Modernism in the American Landscape* (Cambridge, Mass., and London: MIT Press, 1994), 32–35, 39, 43, 45–49, 52–54, Ross Woodward, "Paradise Lost: Reflections on Some Failings of Radburn," *Journal of the Royal Australian Planning Institute* 34 (No. 1, 1997): 25–29; Andrew A. Meyers, "Invisible Cities," *Colloqui* 13 (Spring 1998): 14–32; Allen Freeman, "Suburb on the Green," *Preservation* 52 (September–October 2000): 58–63, 87; Ann Marie T. Cammarota, *Pavements in the Garden* (Madison, N.J.: Fairleigh Dickinson University Press, 2001), 180–81; David Michael Martin, "Returning to Radburn," *Landscape Journal* 20 (No. 1, 2001): 156–75; Chang-Moo Lee and Barbara Stabin-Nesmith, "The Continuing Value of a Planned Community: Radburn in the Evolution of Suburban Development," *Journal of Urban Design* 6 (No. 2, 2001): 151–84; Alexander Garvin, *The American City: What Works, What Doesn't*, 2nd ed. (New York: McGraw-Hill, 2002), 26–27, 325–31, 338–40; Nicholas N. Patricios, "Urban Design Principles of the Original Neighbourhood Concepts," *Urban Morphology* 6 (No. 1, 2002): 21–32; Mervyn Miller, "Garden Cities and Suburbs: At Home and Abroad," *Journal of Planning History* 1 (February 2002): 18–19; Andrés Duany, Elizabeth Plater-Zyberk, and

Robert Alminana, *The New Civic Art: Elements of Town Planning* (New York: Rizzoli International Publications, 2003), 46, 89, 175, 300; Chang-Moo Lee and Kun-Hyuck Ahn, "Is Kentlands Better than Radburn? The American Garden City and New Urbanist Paradigms," *Journal of the American Planning Association* 69 (Winter 2003): 50–71; Steve Chambers, "Radburn Residents Divide on Proposed Parkland Sale," *Planning* 70 (November 2004): 38–39; "Radburn Designated National Historic Landmark," *Planning* 71 (June 2005): 47; Jane Roy Brown, "Four for the Record: Landscapes Are Among Newly Designated Historic Landmarks," *Landscape Architecture* 95 (August 2005): 20, 22; Tom Martinson, *The Atlas of American Architecture: 2000 Years of Architecture, City Planning, Landscape Architecture and Civil Engineering* (New York: Rizzoli International Publications, 2009), 369–70; Thaïsa Way, *Unbounded Practice: Women and Landscape Architecture in the Early Twentieth Century* (Charlottesville and London: University of Virginia Press, 2009), 239–42, 245–48, 250–52; Vittorio Magnago Lampugnani, *Die Stadt im 20. Jahrhundert* (Berlin: Verlag Klaus Wagenbach, 2010), 518–21.

241 Stein, *Toward New Towns for America*, 44.

242 Smith, "A Town for the Motor Age": 695.

243 Stein, *Toward New Towns for America*, 44.

244 "First Radburn Industry": 33; "Second Industry for Radburn": 53.

245 "Garden Cities and Model Towns": 22.

246 Mumford, *The City in History*, 450.

247 Mumford, "Mass-Production and the Modern House": 110.

248 Christie, "Radburn Reconsidered": 38–39.

249 Schaffer, *Garden Cities for America: The Radburn Experience*, 4, 9.

250 Goldberger, "Model Designed on Dreams of Utopia": 1.

251 Clarence S. Stein, *Toward New Towns for America* (Cambridge, Mass., and London: MIT Press, 1957), 114–17; Ellen K. Popper, "Living with the Automobile: Variations on the Radburn Idea," http://www.millbrookcivic.com. Also see "Building on Old Airport," *New York Times* (May 22, 1936): 43; "Green Acres Building," *New York Times* (December 24, 1939): 104.

252 Stein, *Toward New Towns for America*, 114–15.

253 Earle S. Draper, "The New TVA Town of Norris, Tennessee," *American City* 48 (December 1933): 67–68; Earle S. Draper and Tracy B. Augur, "The Regional Approach to the Housing Problem," *Law and Contemporary Problems* 1 (March 1934): 168–75; "TVA Houses, Norris, Tennessee," *American Architect* 144 (May 1934): 55–58; Tracy B. Augur, "The Planning of the Town of Norris," *American Architect* 148 (April 1936): 19–26; Arthur C. Comey and Max S. Wehrly, "Planned Communities," (November 1936) in *Supplementary Report of the Urbanism Committee to the National Resources Committee* (Washington, D.C.: U. S. Government Printing Office, 1939), vol. 2: 70–74, 111, 121; James Dahir, *Communities for Better Living* (New York: Harper & Brothers, 1950), 199–201; Mel Scott, *American City Planning Since 1890* (Berkeley and Los Angeles: University of California Press, 1969), 313–15, 335; Norman T. Newton, *Design on the Land: The Development of Landscape Architecture* (1971; Cambridge, Mass., and London: Belknap Press of Harvard University Press, 1978), 500–503; Aelred J. Gray, "The Maturing of a Planned New Town: Norris, Tennessee," *Tennessee Planner* 32 (1974): 1–25; *Norris District, National Register of Historic Places Inventory-Nomination Form* (Washington, D.C.: National Park Service, 1975); Marian Moffett and Lawrence Wodehouse, "Noble Structures Set in Handsome Parks: Public Architecture of the TVA," *Modulus* 17 (1984): 74–83; Earle Sumner Draper Jr., "The TVA's Forgotten Town: Norris, Tennessee," *Landscape Architecture* 78 (March 1988): 96–100; Walter L. Creese, *TVA's Public Planning: The Vision, the Reality* (Knoxville: University of Tennessee Press, 1990), 239–63; K. C. Parsons, "Clarence Stein and the Greenbelt Towns: Settling for Less," *Journal of the American Planning Association* 56 (Spring 1990): 164; William H. Jordy, "'A Wholesome Environment Through Plain, Direct Means': The Planning of Norris by the Tennessee Valley Authority," *Arris: Journal of the Southeast Chapter of the Society of Architectural Historians* 5 (1994): 6–30; Margaret Crawford, *Building the Workingman's Paradise: The Design of American Company Towns* (London: Verso, 1995), 196–99; Neal Vogel, "When Company Comes to Town," *Old-House Journal* 27 (December 1999): 48–53; Michael Sorkin, "Critique/Sorkin Finds a Model in a Tennessee Small Town with a Genuine Sense of Purpose," *Architectural Record* 189 (July 2001): 63–64; Peter Hall, *Cities of Tomorrow: An Intellectual History of Urban Planning and Design in the Twentieth Century*, 3rd ed. (Oxford and Malden, Mass.: Blackwell Publishers, 2002), 177–78; "An American Ideal," in www.tva.gov/heritage/norris/index.htm.

254 Draper and Augur, "The Regional Approach to the Housing Problem": 173.

255 Draper, "The New TVA Town of Norris, Tennessee": 67.

256 Jordy, "A Wholesome Environment": 23.

257 Jordy, "A Wholesome Environment": 24.

258 Jordy, "A Wholesome Environment": 24.

259 Newton, *Design on the Land*, 502.

260 Lewis Mumford, letter to Frederic J. Osborn, August 25, 1945, quoted in Jordy, "A Wholesome Environment": 14, 15.

261 Draper Jr., "The TVA's Forgotten Town: Norris, Tennessee": 100.

262 Creese, *TVA's Public Planning: The Vision, the Reality*, 248–49.

263 Comey and Wehrly, "Planned Communities," in *Supplementary Report of the Urbanism Committee to the National Resources Committee*, vol. 2: 74.

264 Newton, *Design on the Land*, 500–502.

265 Newton, *Design on the Land*, 502.

266 Jordy, "A Wholesome Environment": 18.

267 Jordy, "A Wholesome Environment": 12, 28–29.

268 Intended as the fourth of the Greenbelt towns, but abandoned as the result of legal difficulties, Greenbrook was to have been located at Bound Brook, five miles west of New Brunswick, New Jersey, where it had excellent access to New York and Philadelphia via main line rail service as well as to a large number of industrial jobs located in the area. Planned by Henry Wright and Allan Kamstra, with architects Albert Mayer (1897–1981), Henry S. Churchill (1893–1962) and Carl Vollmer (1890–1973), for a 3,800-acre site, of which 1,400 acres were to be developed, the town of approximately 4,000 families proposed a Radburn-like arrangement of cul-de-sac streets and continuous linked greenswards bounded by duplex and rowhouses.

269 Clarence S. Stein, *Toward New Towns for America* (Cambridge, Mass., and London: MIT Press, 1957), 118.

270 John Dreier, "Greenbelt Planning," *Pencil Points* 17 (August 1936): 400–19; "Greenbelt Towns," *Architectural Record* 80 (September 1936): 215–34; "Comparative Architectural Details in the Greenbelt Housing," *American Architect & Architecture* 149 (October 1936): 20–25; Arthur C. Comey and Max S. Wehrly, "Planned Communities," (November 1936) in *Supplementary Report of the Urbanism Committee to the National Resources Committee* (Washington, D.C.: U. S. Government Printing Office, 1939), vol. 2: 75–76, 126–27; Felix Belair Jr., "Greenbelt—an Experimental Town—Starts Off," *New York Times* (October 10, 1937), 135; Frances Fink, "Cooperative Corners," *Literary Digest* (October 16, 1937); Frances Fink, "Moving Day," *Literary Digest* (November 6, 1937); "American Housing: a Failure, a Problem, a Potential Boon and Boom," *Life* (November 15, 1937), 45; Hale J. Walker, "Some Major Technical Problems Encountered in the Planning of Greenbelt, Maryland," *Planner's Journal* 4 (March/April 1938): 34–37; "F. S. A. Farm Security Administration," *Architectural Forum* 68 (May 1938): 415–17, 424; Cedric Larson, "Greenbelt, Maryland: a Federally Planned Community," *National Municipal Review* (August 1938): 413–20; O. Kline Fulmer, "Greenbelt Lends Its Experience to the Solution of the Housing Problem," *Real Estate Record* 142 (October 1, 1938): 15–17; Christine Sadler, "Greenbelt, One Year Old, Pays Social Dividends as Test-Tube City," *Washington Post* (October 9, 1938), B: 7; John O. Walker, "Life in a Greenbelt Community," *Shelter* 5 (December 1938): 16–23; "A Planned Community Appraised," *Architectural Forum* 72 (January 1940): 34, 62–63; Farm Security Administration, *Greenbelt Communities* (Washington, D.C.: Farm Security Administration, U.S. Department of Agriculture, 1940); O. Kline Fulmer, *Greenbelt* (Washington, D.C.: American Council on Public Affairs, 1941), passim; Lewis Mumford, "Introduction," in Fulmer, *Greenbelt*, 1–3; Frederick Gutheim, "Greenbelt Revisited," *Magazine of Art* 40 (January 1947): 16–20; James Dahir, *Communities for Better Living* (New York: Harper & Brothers, 1950), 201–8; George A. Warner, *Greenbelt: The Cooperative Community* (New York: Exposition Press, 1954); J. S. Lansill, "Introduction," in Warner, *Greenbelt: The Cooperative Community*, 13–22; Clarence Stein, *Toward New Towns for America* (Cambridge, Mass., and London: MIT Press, 1957), 119–76; Paul K. Conkin, *Tomorrow a New World: The New Deal Community Program* (Ithaca, N.Y.: Cornell University Press, 1959), 305–25; Albert Mayer, "Greenbelt Towns Revisited, part I," *Journal of Housing* 24 (January 1967): 12–26; Albert Mayer, "Greenbelt Towns Revisited, part II," *Journal of Housing* 24 (February/March 1967): 80–85; Albert Mayer, "Greenbelt Towns Revisited, part III," *Journal of Housing* 24 (April 1967): 151–66; Vincent Scully, *American Architecture and Urbanism* (New York: Praeger, 1969), 161–65; Joseph L. Arnold, *The New Deal in the Suburbs: A History of the Greenbelt Town Program, 1935–1954* (Columbus, OH: Ohio State University Press, 1971), esp. ch. 5; Norman T. Newton, *Design on the Land: The Development of Landscape Architecture* (Cambridge, Mass., and London: Belknap Press of Harvard University Press, 1971), 502–7; Phoebe Cutler, *The Public Landscape of the New Deal* (New Haven, Conn., and London: Yale University Press, 1985), ch. 9; David Margolick, "A Suburb Recalls Its New Deal Mission," *New York Times* (June 9, 1985): 52; Laurence E. Coffin Jr. and Beatriz de Winthuysen Coffin, "Greenbelt: A Maryland 'New Town' Turns 50," *Landscape Architecture* 78 (June 1988): 48–53; K. C. Parsons, "Clarence Stein and the Greenbelt Towns: Settling for Less," *Journal of the American Planning Association* 56 (Spring 1990): 161–83; "American Modern," *Perspecta* 30 (1999): 40–41; Cathy D. Knepper, *Greenbelt, Maryland: A Living Legacy of the New Deal* (Baltimore and London: Johns Hopkins University Press, 2001), esp. ch. 1; Eugenie L. Birch, "Five Generations of the Garden City," in Kermit C. Parsons and David Schuyler, eds., *From Garden City to Green City: The Legacy of Ebenezer Howard* (Baltimore and London: Johns Hopkins University Press, 2002), 175, 177; Mervyn Miller, "Garden Cities and Suburbs: At Home and Abroad," *Journal of Planning History* 1 (February 2002): 6–28; Andrés Duany, Elizabeth Plater-Zyberk, and Robert Alminana, *The New Civic Art* (New York: Rizzoli International Publications, 2003), 141, 292; Dolores Hayden, *Building Suburbia: Green Fields and Urban Growth, 1820–2000* (New York: Pantheon Books, 2003), 126–27; Isabelle Gournay and Mary Corbin Sies, "Greenbelt, Maryland," in Richard Longstreth, ed., *Housing Washington: Two Centuries of Residential Development and Planning in the National Capitol Area* (Chicago: Center for American Places at Columbia College Chicago, 2010), 203–28.

271 Lewis Mumford, "Introduction," in Fulmer, *Greenbelt*, 1–2.

272 John Dreier, "Greenbelt Planning," *Pencil Points* 17 (August 1936): 400–19; "Comparative Architectural Details in the Greenbelt Housing," *American Architect & Architecture* 149 (October 1936): 20, 26–29; Justin R. Hartzog, "Planning of Suburban Resettlement Towns: Greenhills," *Planner's Journal* 4 (March/April 1938): 29–33; "F. S. A. Farm Security Administration," *Architectural Forum* 68 (May 1938): 418–19, 424; John O. Walker, "A Demonstration in Community Planning," *Shelter* 3 (February 1939): 29–36; J. S. Lansill, "Introduction," in George A. Warner, *Greenbelt: The Cooperative Community* (New York: Exposition Press, 1954), 13–22; Clarence Stein, *Toward New Towns for America* (Cambridge, Mass., and London: MIT Press, 1957), 178–81; Paul K. Conkin, *Tomorrow a New World: The New Deal Community Program* (Ithaca, N.Y.: Cornell University Press, 1959), 312–15; Albert Mayer, "Greenbelt Towns Revisited, part I," *Journal of Housing* 24 (January 1967): 12–26; Albert Mayer, "Greenbelt Towns Revisited, part II," *Journal of Housing* 24 (February/March 1967): 80–85; Albert Mayer, "Greenbelt Towns Revisited, part III," *Journal of Housing* 24 (April 1967): 151–66; Arthur B. Gallion and Simon Eisner, *The Urban Pattern: City Planning and Design* (New York: D. Van Nostrand Company, 1975), 158; Charles Bradley Leach, "Greenhills, Ohio: The Evolution of an American New Town" (Ph.D. diss., Case Western Reserve University, January 1978); K. C. Parsons, "Clarence Stein and the Greenbelt Towns: Settling for Less," *Journal of the American Planning Association* 56 (Spring 1990): 161–83.

273 Conkin, *Tomorrow a New World: The New Deal Community Program*, 312.

274 John Dreier, "Greenbelt Planning," *Pencil Points* 17 (August 1936): 400–19; "Greenbelt Towns," *Architectural Record* 80 (September 1936): 215–34; "Comparative Architectural Details in the Greenbelt Housing," *American Architect & Architecture* 149 (October 1936): 20, 30–33; Elbert Peets, "Greendale," in Werner Hegemann, *City Planning and Housing* (New York: Architectural Book Publishing Co., 1937), 407–14, reprinted in Paul D. Speiregen, ed., *On the Art of Designing Cities: Selected Essay of Elbert Peets* (Cambridge, Mass.:

MIT Press, 1968), 216–22; Jacob Crane, "Greendale—The General Plan," *Planners' Journal* 3 (July–August 1937): 89–90; "F. S. A. Farm Security Administration," *Architectural Forum* 68 (May 1938): 420–24; John O. Walker, "Greenbelt Towns," *Shelter* 3 (January 1939): 20–24; Farm Security Administration, *Greenbelt Communities* (Washington, D.C.: Farm Security Administration, U.S. Department of Agriculture, 1940); Wisconsin Historical Records Survey, Division of Community Service Programs, Work Projects Administration, *Inventory of the Local Government Archives of Wisconsin, Village Series, No. 141, Greendale* (Madison: Wisconsin Historical Records Survey, July 1941), 1–6; Elbert Peets, "Studies in Planning Texture, for Housing in a Greenbelt Town," *Architectural Record* 106 (September 1949): 130–37, reprinted in Speiregen, ed., *On the Art of Designing Cities: Selected Essay of Elbert Peets*, 202–15; James Dahir, *Communities for Better Living* (New York: Harper & Brothers, 1950), 208–9; Clarence Stein, *Toward New Towns for America* (Cambridge, Mass., and London: MIT Press, 1957), 184–87; James Dahir, *Greendale Comes of Age* (Milwaukee: Milwaukee Community Development Corporation, 1958); 6–31; Paul K. Conkin, *Tomorrow a New World: The New Deal Community Program* (Ithaca, N.Y.: Cornell University Press, 1959), 305–25; Albert Mayer, "Greenbelt Towns Revisited, part I," *Journal of Housing* 24 (January 1967): 12–26; Albert Mayer, "Greenbelt Towns Revisited, part II," *Journal of Housing* 24 (February/March 1967): 80–85; Albert Mayer, "Greenbelt Towns Revisited, part III," *Journal of Housing* 24 (April 1967): 151–66; Joseph L. Arnold, *The New Deal in the Suburbs: A History of the Greenbelt Town Program, 1935–1954* (Columbus: Ohio State University Press, 1971), esp. ch. 5; Caroline Shillaber, "Elbert Peets, Champion of the Civic Form," *Landscape Architecture* 72 (November 1982): 54–59, 100; Joseph A. Eden and Arnold R. Alanen, "Looking Backward at a New Deal Town, Greendale, Wisconsin, 1935–1980," *Journal of the American Planning Association* 49 (Winter 1983): 40–58; Phoebe Cutler, *The Public Landscape of the New Deal* (New Haven, Conn., and London: Yale University Press, 1985), ch. 9; Arnold R. Alanen and Joseph A. Eden, *Main Street Ready-Made: The New Deal Community of Greendale, Wisconsin* (Madison: The State Historical Society of Wisconsin, 1987), passim; Gregory C. Randall, *America's Original GI Town: Park Forest, Illinois* (Baltimore and London: Johns Hopkins University Press, 2000), 74–77; Arnold R. Alanen, "Elbert Peets: History as Precedent in Midwestern Landscape Design," in William H. Tishler, ed., *Midwestern Landscape Architecture* (Chicago: University of Illinois Press, 2000), 193–214; Andrés Duany, Elizabeth Plater-Zyberk, and Robert Alminana, *The New Civic Art* (New York: Rizzoli International Publications, 2003), 212; Tom Martinson, *The Atlas of American Architecture: 2000 Years of Architecture, City Planning, Landscape Architecture and Civil Engineering* (New York: Rizzoli International Publications, 2009), 370; http://www.greendale.org/history.htm.

275 Peets, "Greendale," in Speiregen, ed., *On the Art of Designing Cities: Selected Essays of Elbert Peets*, 220–22.

276 Elbert Peets, "Report of the Town Planning Section of the Greendale Planning Staff," vol. 2 of *Final Report of the Greendale Project of the Greenbel Town Program* (1938), as quoted in Alanen and Eden, *Main Street Ready-Made*, 38.

277 Eden and Alanen, "Looking Backward at New Deal Town": 43.

278 Peets, "Greendale," in Hegemann, *City Planning and Housing*, 414, also quoted in Eden and Alanen, "Looking Backward at New Deal Town": 43–44.

279 Dahir, *Greendale Comes of Age*, 8.

280 Tony Garnier, *Une Cité Industrielle, etude pour la construction des villes*, trans. by Marguerite E. McGoldrick (1917; New York: Princeton Architectural Press, 1989); Nikolaus Pevsner, *Pioneers of Modern Design: From William Morris to Walter Gropius*, 4th ed. (1936; New Haven, Conn., and London: Yale University Press, 2005), 148–49; Sigfried Giedion, *Space, Time and Architecture: The Growth of a New Tradition*, 5th ed., rev. and enlarged (1941; Cambridge, Mass.: Harvard University Press, 1967), 332–33, 787–93; Lewis Mumford, "The Modern City," *Form and Functions of Twentieth Century Architecture, Volume 4* (New York: Columbia University Press, 1952), reprinted as Lewis Mumford, "The Ideal Form of the Modern City," in Donald L. Miller, ed., *The Lewis Mumford Reader* (New York: Pantheon, 1986), 166; Reyner Banham, *Theory and Design in the First Machine Age* (1960; Cambridge, Mass.: MIT Press, 1980), 35–38; Dora Wiebenson, "Utopian Aspects of Tony Garnier's Cité Industrielle," *Journal of the Society of Architectural Historians* 19 (March 1960): 16–24; Christophe Pawlowski, *Tony Garnier et les débuts de l'urbanisme fonctionnel en France* (Paris: Centre de Recherche d'Urbanisme, 1967), esp. ch. 3; Dora Wiebenson, *Tony Garnier: The Cité Industrielle* (New York: George Braziller, 1969); Anthony Vidler, "The New World: The Reconstruction of Urban Utopian in Late Nineteenth Century France," *Perspecta* 13 (1971): 243–56; Catherine Diederichs, "Les realizations de Tony Garnier à Lyon," *Monuments Historique* 3 (1977): 69–73; Ian Tod and Michael Wheeler, *Utopia* (New York: Harmony Books, 1978), 128–30; Kenneth Frampton, *Modern Architecture: A Critical History*, rev. ed. (1980; New York and London: Thames & Hudson, 1985), 100–104; Anthony Sutcliffe, *Towards the Planned City: Germany, Britain, the United States and France, 1780–1914* (Oxford: Basil Blackwell, 1981), 155–56; Dennis J. De Witt and Elizabeth R. De Witt, *Modern Architecture in Europe: A Guide to Buildings Since the Industrial Revolution* (New York: E. P. Dutton, 1987), 164–65; Peter Hall, *Cities of Tomorrow* (Cambridge, Mass.: Basil Blackwell, 1988), 113; René Jullian, *Tony Garnier: Constructeur et Utopiste* (Paris: Philippe Sers Editeur, 1989); Riccardo Mariani, ed., *Tony Garnier: Une Cité Industrielle* (New York: Rizzoli International Publications, 1990); Ruth Eaton, *Ideal Cities: Utopianism and the (Un) Built Environment* (New York and London: Thames & Hudson, 2002), 196–99; Peter Hall, *Urban and Regional Planning*, 4th ed. (London and New York: Routledge, 2002), 48–49; Wolfgang Förster, *Housing in the 20th and 21st Centuries* (München: Prestel, 2006), 44–46; Le Corbusier, *Toward an Architecture* (1924; Los Angeles: Getty Institute, 2007), 120–23; Vittorio Magnago Lampugnani, *Die Stadt im 20. Jahrhundert* (Berlin: Verlag Klaus Wagenbach, 2010), 79–83; Jean-François Lejeune and Michelangelo Sabatino, "North Versus South," in Jean-François Lejeune and Michelangelo Sabatino, eds., *Modern Architecture and the Mediterranean* (London and New York: Routlege, 2010), 1–4.

281 Garnier, *Une Cité Industrielle*, 13.

282 Garnier, *Une Cité Industrielle*, 14.

283 Pevsner, *Pioneers of Modern Design*, 148–49.

284 Wiebenson, "Utopian Aspects of Tony Garnier's Cité Industrielle": 17.

285 Garnier, *Une Cité Industrielle*, 14.

286 Banham, *Theory and Design in the First Machine Age*, 36–37.

287 Garnier, *Une Cité Industrielle*, 14.

288 Frampton, *Modern Architecture: A Critical History*, 103.

289 Le Corbusier, *Toward an Architecture*, 122.

290 Eaton, *Ideal Cities*, 116.

291 Le Corbusier, *Toward an Architecture*, 121–22.

292 Frampton, *Modern Architecture: A Critical History*, 104.

293 Wiebenson, "Utopian Aspects of Tony Garnier's Cité Industrielle": 16.

294 For the Quartier Etats-Unis, see Edith Elmer Wood, "The Cités-Jardins of Lyon and Rheims," *American City* 28 (March 1923): 228–34; Christophe Pawlowski, *Tony Garnier et les débuts de l'urbanisme fonctionnel en France* (Paris: Centre de Recherche d'Urbanisme, 1967), 160–62, 168–70; Dennis J. De Witt and Elizabeth R. De Witt, *Modern Architecture in Europe: A Guide to Buildings Since the Industrial Revolution* (New York: E. P. Dutton, 1987), 165; Wolfgang Förster, *Housing in the 20th and 21st Centuries* (München: Prestel, 2006), 44–46. For Garnier's work in Lyon, see Pawlowski, *Tony Garnier et les débuts de l'urbanisme fonctionnel en France*, esp. ch. 4; René Jullian, *Tony Garnier: Constructeur et Utopiste* (Paris: Philippe Sers Editeur, 1989).

295 Bernard Kampffmeyer, "The Garden City at Helleran[*sic*]," *Garden Cities and Town Planning*, new series 3 (December 1908): 141–42; "Rundschau Gartenstadt Hellerau," *Gartenstadt* 3 (No. 3, 1909): 60; Harry S. Stewart, "Garden City Work in Germany," *Garden Cities and Town Planning*, new series 4 (July 1910): 297–99; Patrick Abercrombie, "Some Notes on German Garden Villages," *Town Planning Review* 1 (October 1910): 246–50, plates 75–76; *Gartenstadt Hellerau, Ein Bericht über den Zweck, die Organisation, die Ansiedlungs-Bedingungen, die bisherigen Erfolge und Ziele* (Hellerau: Verlag der Gartenstadt Hellerau, 1911); Robert Breuer, "Die Gartenstadt Hellerau," *Deutsche Kunst und Dekoration* 6 (No. 4, 1911): 453; "German Town Planning Tour," *Garden Cities and Town Planning* 1 (June 1911): 112–28; Ewart G. Culpin, "Hellerau, Germany's First Garden City," *Garden Cities and Town Planning* 1 (July 1911): 142, 152–55; Eva Elise Vom Baur, "Hellerau, the City of the Future," *The Craftsman* 21 (February 1912): 536–46; Hermann Muthesius, "Die Gartenstadt Hellerau," *Über Land und Meer* 54 (No. 3, 1912): 86–87; Ewart G. Culpin, *The Garden City Movement Up-to-Date* (London: Garden Cities and Town Planning Association, 1913), 61–65; John T. Klaber, "The Garden City of Hellerau," *Architectural Record* 35 (February 1914): 151–61; Richard T. Watrous, "Personal Observations of Some Development in Housing in Europe," *Journal of the American Institute of Architects* 2 (July 1914): 332–43; Nelson P. Lewis, *The Planning of the Modern City* (New York: John Wiley & Sons, 1916), 302; "Erweiterungsbauten, Der Deutschen Werkstätten AG., Hellerau," *Moderne Bauformen* 40 (April 1941): 157–78; Franziska Bollerey and Kristiana Hartmann, "Wünsche und Wirklichkeit," *Bauwelt* 65 (February 18, 1974): 285–91; Gerda Wangerin and Gerhard Weiss, *Heinrich Tessenow: Ein Baumeister, 1876–1950, Leben Lehre Werk* (Essen: Verlag Richard Bacht, 1976), 190; Franziska Bollerey and Kristiana Hartmann, "A Patriarchal Utopia: The Garden City and Housing Reform at the Turn of the Century," in Anthony Sutcliffe, ed., *The Rise of Modern Urban Planning 1800–1914* (New York: St. Martin's Press, 1980), 151–54; Norbert Borrmann, *Paul Schultze-Naumburg, 1869–1949: Maler, Publizist, Architekt* (Essen: Verlag Richard Bacht, 1989), 134; Marco De Michelis, "Modernity and Reform, Heinrich Tessenow and the Institut Dalcroze at Hellerau," *Perspecta* 26 (1990): 143–70; "Hellerau: Ein Neuer Anfang," *Bauwelt* 81 (December 1990): 2286; Marco De Michelis, "In the First German Garden City; Tessenow in Hellerau," *Lotus International* 69 (1991): 54–71; Marco De Michelis, *Heinrich Tessenow* (Milan: Electa, 1991), 201–19, 264, 267; Françoise Rogier, "German Garden City Rediscovered," *Architectural Review* 189 (February 1991): 4; Hans-Jürgen Sarfert, *Hellerau: Die Gartenstadt und Künstlerkolonie* (Dresden: Hellerau-Verlag, 1993); Wilfried Wang, "Elusive Ideals: Manu-facture and Small Towns," *Modulus* 22 (1993): 40–55; Jean-François Lejeune, "From Hellerau to the Bauhaus: Memory and Modernity of the Germany Garden City," *The New City* 3 (Fall 1996): 50–69; Marco De Michelis, "Tessenow e Hellerau," *Domus* 751 (July 1993): n.p.; Uta Wight, "On Experiences of Hellerau," *Transition* 61/61 (2000): 63–67; Peter Hall, *Cities of Tomorrow: An Intellectual History of Urban Planning and Design in the Twentieth Century*, 3rd ed. (Oxford and Malden, Mass.: Blackwell Publishers, 2002), 120–21; "Festspielhaus Hellerau/Refurbishment of Hellerau Festival Theatre," *Detail* 43 (October 2003): 1102; John V. Maciuika, *Before the Bauhaus: Architecture, Politics, and the German State, 1890–1920* (Cambridge: Cambridge University Press, 2005), 217–47; W. Owen Harrod, "The Deutsche Werkstätten and the Dissemination of Mainstream Modernity," *Studies in the Decorative Arts* 10 (Spring–Summer 2003): 21–41; Clemens Galonska and Frank Elstner, *Gartenstadt/Garden City of Hellerau* (Chemnitz: Palisander Verlag, 2007); Claudia Beger, *Gartenstadt Hellerau: Architekturführer/Architectural Guide*, trans. by Christopher Wynne with Robert McInnes (Munich: Deutsche Verlags-Anstalt, 2008); Didem Ekici, "'The Laboratory of a New Humanity': The Concept of Type, Life Reform, and Modern Architecture in Hellerau Garden City, 1900–1914" (Ph.D. diss., University of Michigan, 2008); Ralph Lindner and Hans-Peter Lühr, eds., *Gartenstadt Hellerau: Die Geschichte ihrer Bauten* (Dresden: Sandstein Verlag, 2008); Gert Kähler, *The Path of Modernism: Architecture 1900–1930: From the World Heritage of Wroclow to that of Dessau* (Berlin: Jovis, 2009), 66–73; Wolfgang Sonne, "Political Connotations of the Picturesque," in Charles C. Bohl and Jean-François Lejeune, eds., *Sitte, Hegemann and the Metropolis: Modern Civic Art and International Exchanges* (London and New York: Routledge, 2009), 132; Maiken Umbach, *German Cities and Bourgeois Modernism, 1890–1924* (New York: Oxford University Press, 2009), 20, 113–19; Vittorio Magnago Lampugnani, *Die Stadt im 20. Jahrhundert* (Berlin: Verlag Klaus Wagenbach, 2010), 255–57.

296 Culpin, "Hellerau, Germany's First Garden City": 152.

297 Umbach, *German Cities and Bourgeois Modernism, 1890–1924*, 118.

298 Vom Baur, "Hellerau, The City of the Future": 536.

299 E. Haenel, "Die Gartenstadt Hellerau," *Die Kunst* 24 (1911): 327, quoted in De Michelis, "In the First German Garden City: Tessenow in Hellerau": 66.

300 De Michelis, "In the First German Garden City: Tessenow in Hellerau": 64.

301 See Muthesius, "Die Gartenstadt Hellerau": 86–87; Ekici, "'The Laboratory of a New Humanity': The Concept of Type, Life Reform, and Modern Architecture in Hellerau Garden City, 1900–1914": 80.

Chapter 4

1 "Tuxedo Park," *Real Estate Record and Builders' Guide* 37 (March 27, 1886): 383–84; "Shooting-Box at Tuxedo Park, New York," *American Architect and Building News* 21 (May 28, 1887): 260, plate 596; "House of Pierre Lorillard, Esq., Tuxedo Park, New York, Mr. James Brown Lord, Architect, New York," *American Architect and Building News* 22 (September 10, 1887): 123, plate 616; "Gate Lodge, Tuxedo Park," *Building* 7 (September 17, 1887): 12; "Annex to Club House, Tuxedo Park, N.Y.," *American Architect and Building News* 22 (October 15, 1887): 182, plate 616; "Tuxedo Park," *The Daily Graphic* (March 16, 1889): 9–10; James Smith Haring, "Art and Engineering at Tuxedo Park," *Engineering Magazine* 2 (January 1892): 459–75; "Residence of A.D. Juilliard, Tuxedo Park, N.Y.," *Inland Architect and News Record* 32 (October 1898): plates; "House of William R. Garrison, Esq., Tuxedo Park, N.Y.," *American Architect and Building News* 64 (June 3, 1899): 79, plate 1223; "House of H. Casimir de Rham, Esq., Tuxedo Park, N.Y.," *American Architect and Building News* 65 (July 1, 1899): 7, plate 1227; "House of Mrs. Alexander T. Van Nest, Tuxedo Park, N.Y.," *American Architect and Building News* 65 (July 8, 1899): 15, plate 1228; "House of Charles H. Coster, Esq., Tuxedo Park, N.Y.," *American Architect and Building News* 65 (July 22, 1899): 31, plate 1230; "House of Robert McMaster Gillespie, Esq., Tuxedo Park, N.Y.," *American Architect and Building News* 66 (November 18, 1899): 55, plate 1247; Samuel Swift, "Community Life in Tuxedo (American Suburban Communities—V)," *House and Garden* 8 (August 1905): 60–71; Emily Post, "Tuxedo Park, an American Rural Community," *Century Magazine* 82 (October 1911): 795–805; Edwin Clark Kent, *The Story of Tuxedo Park* (Rhinebeck, N.Y., privately published, 1937); Works Project Administration, *New York: A Guide to the Empire State* (New York: Oxford University Press, 1940), 384–85; Cleveland Amory, *The Last Resorts* (New York: Harper & Brothers, 1948), 79–99; Vincent Scully, *The Shingle Style and The Stick Style: Architectural Theory and Design from Downing to the Origins of Wright*, rev. ed. (New Haven, Conn.: Yale University Press, 1955; rev. ed. 1971), 128–29; George M. Rushmore, *The World With a Fence Around It: Tuxedo Park, the Early Days* (New York: Pageant, 1957); Frank Kintrea, "Tuxedo Park: An Exclusive Preserve of New York's Social Elite," *American Heritage Magazine* 29 (August–September 1978): 69–77; Stern with Massengale, *The Anglo-American Suburb*, 68; Clay Lancaster, *The Japanese Influence in America*, rev. ed. (New York: Abbeville Press, 1983), 59–60; Laura Furman, "All the Best Places: Tuxedo Park," *House and Garden* 156 (May 1984): 98, 102, 104, 109; Wendy Insinger, "The Greening of Tuxedo Park," *Town and Country* 138 (May 1984): 187–97, 261–65; Clay Lancaster, *The American Bungalow: 1880–1930* (New York: Abbeville Press, 1985), 67–68, 111, 170; Stern, *Pride of Place: Building the American Dream*, 160–61; Norma Skurka, "Tuxedo Park," *House Beautiful* 128 (May 1986): 68–77; Kevin Wolfe, "Visible City: Tuxedo Park," *Metropolis* 6 (July/August 1986): 48–51; James D. Kornwolf, "Tuxedo Park," *Orange County Historical Society Journal* 15 (November 1986): 23–32; Kara Cathleen Hamley, "Cleveland's Park Allotment: Euclid Heights, Cleveland Heights, Ohio, and Its Designer, Ernest W. Bowditch" (Master's thesis, Cornell University, 1996): 43–53; Dolores Hayden, *Building Suburbia: Green Fields and Urban Growth, 1820–2000* (New York: Pantheon Books, 2003), 67; *Tuxedo Park: The Historic Houses*, eds. Christian R. Sonne and Chiu yin Hempel (Tuxedo Park, N.Y.: Tuxedo Park Historical Society, 2007); Thomas Bender, "Introduction: A Place Apart," in *Tuxedo Park: The Historic Houses*, 2–15; Christian R. Sonne, "The Making of Tuxedo Park," in *Tuxedo Park: The Historic Houses*, 18–69; Gwendolyn Wright, "Architectural Explorations: 1886–1945," in *Tuxedo Park: The Historic Houses*, 73–83; Tom Martinson, *The Atlas of American Architecture: 2000 Years of Architecture, City Planning, Landscape Architecture and Civil Engineering* (New York: Rizzoli International Publications, 2009), 367.

2 Lancaster, *The American Bungalow: 1880–1930*, 67.

3 Swift, "Community Life in Tuxedo": 69–70.

4 Bruce Price, quoted in Amory, *The Last Resorts*, 84.

5 "Tuxedo Park," *Real Estate Record and Builders' Guide*: 383.

6 "New York Men Buy Great Bixby Ranch," *Los Angeles Times* (November 1, 1913): 1–2; "Highway May Open the Palos Verdes," *Los Angeles Times* (December 3, 1913), II: 2; "Splendid Country Club Will Overlook Ocean," *Los Angeles Times* (May 17, 1914), V: 2; "Planning Great Things on Palos Verdes Ranch," *Los Angeles Times* (October 14, 1914), II: 8; "Begin Boulevards on Palos Verdes," *Los Angeles Times* (August 3, 1916): 6; "Great Rancho to Be Cut Up," *Los Angeles Times* (August 31, 1921), II: 1; Mary Eva Thacker, "A History of Los Palos Verdes Rancho, 1542–1923" (Master's thesis, University of Southern California, 1923): 65–73; Werner Hegemann, *Amerikanische Architektur & Stadtbaukunst* (Berlin: Ernst Wasmuth, 1927), 117; Charles H. Cheney, "Palos Verdes Estates—a Model Residential Suburb," *Pacific Coast Architect* 31 (April 1927): 21–22, 53, 55; Myron Hunt, "Palos Verdes—Where Bad Architecture is Eliminated," *Pacific Coast Architect* 31 (April 1927): 1, 10–20; Frederick Law Olmsted, "Palos Verdes Estates," *Landscape Architecture* 17 (July 1927): 255–79; Werner Hegemann, "Kalifornische Einfamilienhäuser," *Wasmuths Monatshefte für Baukunst* 12 (1928): 358–75; Charles H. Cheney, "Where Poor Architecture Cannot Come," *Western Architect* 37 (April 1928): 75–85, plates 55–72; Rexford Newcomb, "Palos Verdes Estates: an Ideal Residential Community," *Western Architect* 37 (April 1928): 79–82; Frances Duncan, "The Landscaping at Palos Verdes," *Palos Verdes Bulletin* 4 (December 1928): 1–6; "Palos Verdes Public Library," *Architectural Forum* 56 (June 1932): 597–98; Frank A. Vanderlip, *From Farm Boy to Financier* (New York: D. Appleton-Century Company, 1935), 249–54; "Rancho Los Palos Verdes," *Architectural Forum* 62 (May 1935): 470–71; Charles H. Cheney, "Palos Verdes Drive," *Planning and Civic Comment* 2 (January–March 1936): 20–24; Arthur C. Comey and Max S. Wehrly, "Planned Communities," (November 1936) in *Supplementary Report of the Urbanism Committee to the National Resources Committee* (Washington, D.C.: U. S. Government Printing Office, 1939), vol. 2: 85–89; Augusta Fink, *Time and the Terraced Land* (Berkeley, CA: Howell-North Books, 1966); Robert Fogelson, *The Fragmented Metropolis: Los Angeles, 1850–1930* (Cambridge, Mass.: Harvard University Press, 1967), 157–59; Mel Scott, *American City Planning Since 1890* (Berkeley and Los Angeles: University of California Press, 1969), 233; Reyner Banham, *Los Angeles: The Architecture of Four Ecologies* (Berkeley: University of California Press, 1971), 123–26; Arthur B. Gallion and Simon Eisner, *The Urban Pattern: City Planning and Design, 3rd edition* (New York: D. Van Nostrand Co., 1975), 128, 261; Robert A.M. Stern with John Montague Massengale, *The Anglo-American Suburb* (London: Architectural Design, 1981), 80; Delane Morgan, *The Palos Verdes Story* (Palos Verdes, Calif.: Palos Verdes Peninsula Library Foundation, 1983); Robert John Pierson, *The Beach Towns: a Walker's Guide to L.A.'s Beach Communities* (San Francisco: Chronicle Books, 1985), 99–119; John W. Snyder, *The Planning and Development of Atascadero, California* (Hillier, Ohio: Society for American City and Regional Planning History, 1990), 6–7; Kevin Starr, *Material Dreams: Southern California Through the 1920's* (New York: Oxford University Press, 1990), 84, 198–200, 202–3; Arleyn A. Levee, "The Olmsted Brothers' Residential Communities: A Preview of a Career Legacy," in Charles A. Birnbaum, ed., *The Landscape Universe: Historic Designated Districts in Context* (Bronx: Wave Hill, 1993), 42–45; David Gebhard and Robert Winter, *Los Angeles: An Architectural Guide* (Salt Lake City: Gibbs-Miller, 1994), 53–57; Richard Longstreth, *City Center to Regional Mall: Architecture, the Automobile, and Retailing in Los Angeles, 1920–1950* (Cambridge, Mass.: MIT Press, 1997), 153–59; Henry Mathews, *Kirtland Cutter: Architect in the Land of Promise* (Seattle and London: University of Washington Press; Spokane: Eastern Washington State Historical Society, 1998), 329–54; Alexander Garvin, *The American City: What Works, What Doesn't*, 2nd ed. (New York: McGraw-Hill, 2002), 391–95; Andrés Duany, Elizabeth Plater-Zyberk, and Robert Alminana, *The New Civic Art: Elements of Town Planning* (New York: Rizzoli International Publications, 2003), 254; Dolores Hayden, *Building Suburbia: Green Fields and Urban Growth, 1820–2000* (New York: Pantheon Books, 2003), 68; Fukuo Akimoto, "Charles H. Cheney of California," *Planning Perspectives* 18 (July 2003): 253–75; Cheryl Lynn Caldwell Ferguson, "Upscale Suburban Architecture and Development in Dallas and Houston, Texas, 1890–1930" (Ph.D. diss.: University of Delaware, 2004): 287–90; Robert M. Fogelson, *Bourgeois Nightmares: Suburbia, 1870–1930* (New Haven, Conn.: Yale University Press, 2005), 5–6, 12–19, 208–10; Robert M. Fogelson, "Protecting Palos Verdes: The Dark Side of the Bourgeois Utopia," in Eran Ben-Joseph and Terry S. Szold, eds., *Regulating Place: Standards and the Shaping of Urban America* (New York: Routledge, 2005), 233–47; Robert Winter and Alexander Vertikoff, *The Architecture of Entertainment: LA in the Twenties* (Salt Lake City: Gibbs Smith, 2006), 54–56; Sally Sims Stokes, "In a Climate Like Ours: The California Campuses of Allison & Allison," *California History* 84 (Fall 2007): 56–57, 60; Fukuo Akimoto, "California Garden Suburbs: St. Francis Wood and Palos Verdes Estates," *Journal of Urban Design* 12 (February 2007): 43–72; Tom Martinson, *The Atlas of American Architecture: 2000 Years of Architecture, City Planning, Landscape Architecture and Civil Engineering* (New York: Rizzoli International Publications, 2009), 368; Maureen Megowan, "History of Palos Verdes Estates," in http://www.maureenmegowan.com.

7 Vanderlip, *From Farm Boy to Financier*, 250.

8 See Fogelson, *Bourgeois Nightmares*, 7, 14, 169; Fogelson, "Protecting Palos Verdes," in Ben-Joseph and Szold, *Regulating Place*, 234.

9 *Boston Evening Transcript* (July 18, 1914): 249–51, quoted in Fink, *Time and the Terraced Land*, 109, and Fogelson, "Protecting Palos Verdes," in Ben-Joseph and Szold, eds., *Regulating Place*, 236.

10 Cheney, "Palos Verdes Estates—a Model Residential Suburb": 21.

11 Newcomb, "Palos Verdes Estates: an Ideal Residential Community": 81.

12 Frederick Law Olmsted Jr., quoted in Fogelson, "Protecting Palos Verdes: The Dark Side of the Bourgeois Utopia," in Ben-Joseph and Szold, *Regulating Place*, 238.

13 Hunt, "Palos Verdes—Where Bad Architecture Is Eliminated": 1.

14 Myron Hunt, quoted in Matthews, *Kirtland Cutter: Architect in the Land of Promise*, 353–54.

15 Olmsted, "Palos Verdes Estates": 264.

16 Frederick Law Olmsted Jr., quoted in Megowan, "History of Palos Verdes Estates": 9–10.

17 See Ferguson, "Upscale Suburban Architecture and Development in Dallas and Houston, Texas, 1890–1930": 289. For Cutter's work in Palos Verdes, see Mathews, *Kirtland Cutter: Architect in the Land of Promise*, 329–54.

18 Megowan, "History of Palos Verdes Estates": 11.

19 Olmsted, "Palos Verdes Estates": 256, 258.

20 Charles H. Cheney, quoted in Fogelson, "Protecting Palos Verdes: The Dark Side of the Bourgeois Utopia," in Ben-Joseph and Szold, *Regulating Place*, 238.

21 Promotional brochure, quoted in Fogelson, "Protecting Palos Verdes: The Dark Side of the Bourgeois Utopia," in Ben-Joseph and Szold, *Regulating Place*, 238.

22 Olmsted, "Palos Verdes Estates": 258.

23 Akimoto, "California Garden Suburbs: St. Francis Wood and Palos Verdes Estates": 67–68.

24 Elizabeth Church, "Pasatiempo," *California Arts and Architecture* 39 (June 1931): 40–42, 54–55; Elizabeth Church, "Week-end in California," *California Arts and Architecture* 41 (May 1932): 26–27, 44; "Mr. and Mrs. Thomas D. Church Home," *California Arts and Architecture* 42 (July/August 1932): 23; Daniel P. Gregory, "Pasatiempo," in John Chase, *The Sidewalk Companion to Santa Cruz Architecture*, rev. ed. (Santa Cruz, Calif.: Paper Vision Press, 1979), 293–309.

25 Gregory, "Pasatiempo," in Chase, *The Sidewalk Companion to Santa Cruz Architecture*, 295–96.

26 Moses Foster Sweetser, *New England: A Handbook for Travellers* (Boston: J. R. Osgood & Co., 1875), 59–60; Oramel S. Senter, "Civic and Scenic New England, Part II—The Cape Region and Martha's Vineyard," *Potter's American Monthly* 9 (August 1877): 81–95; "Martha's Vineyard," *Frank Leslie's Sunday Magazine* 12 (July 1882): 3; Joseph C. Hazen Jr., "Jigsaw City," *Architectural Forum* 112 (May 1960): 134–39; John W. Reps, *The Making of Urban America* (Princeton, N.J.: Princeton University Press, 1965), 346, 348; Henry Beetle Hough, *Martha's Vineyard, Summer Resort* (1936; Rutland, Vt.: Academy Books, 1966), 55–83; Ellen Weiss, "Robert Morris Copeland's Plans for Oak Bluffs," *Journal of the Society of Architectural Historians* 34 (March 1975): 60–66; Ellen Weiss, "Introducing S. F. Pratt," *Nineteenth Century* 4 (Autumn 1978): 88–93; Chris Stoddard, *A Centennial History of Cottage City* (Oak Bluffs: Oak Bluffs Historical Commission, 1980); Robert A. M. Stern with John Montague Massengale, *The Anglo-American Suburb* (London: Architectural Design, 1981), 22; Ellen Barbara Weiss, "Wesleyan Grove and Oak Bluffs: From Camp Meeting to Summer Resort" (Ph.D. diss., University of Illinois at Urbana-Champaign, 1984): esp. ch. 5; Robert A. M. Stern with Thomas Mellins and Raymond Gastil, *Pride of Place: Building the American Dream* (Boston: Houghton Mifflin; New York: American Heritage, 1986), 129, 132–33, 144–45; Ellen Weiss, *City in the Woods: The Life and Design of an American Camp Meeting* on *Martha's Vineyard* (New York: Oxford University Press, 1987), 76–109; Dona Brown, *Inventing New England: Regional Tourism in the Nineteenth Century* (Washington, D.C., and London: Smithsonian Institution Press, 1995), 96–101; Michael Wayne Miller, "The American Camp Ground Community: An Urban Nucleus as Basis for Modern Community Planning" (Master's thesis, Mississippi State University, 1996): 117–22; Philip Pregill and Nancy Volkman, *Landscapes in History: Design and Planning in the Eastern and Western Traditions* (New York: John Wiley, 1999), 539–40; Peter A. Jones, *Oak Bluffs: the Cottage City Years on Martha's Vineyard* (Portsmouth, N.H.: Arcadia, 2007); Tom Martinson, *The Atlas of American Architecture: 2000 Years of Architecture, City Planning, Landscape Architecture and Civil Engineering* (New York: Rizzoli International Publications, 2009), 317.

27 Weiss, *City in the Woods*, 37–38. Also see Henry Beetle Hough, *Martha's Vineyard, Summer Resort* (1936; Rutland, Vermont: Academy Books, 1966), 32–55; Ellen Weiss, "The Wesleyan Grove Campground," *Architecture Plus* 1 (November 1973): 44–49; William Nathaniel Banks, "The Wesleyan Grove Campground on Martha's Vineyard," *Antiques* 124 (July 1983): 104–15.

28 Quoted in Weiss, *City in the Woods*, 82.

29 Weiss, "Wesleyan Grove and Oak Bluffs: From Camp Meeting to Summer Resort": 92–93.

30 Weiss, "Wesleyan Grove and Oak Bluffs: From Camp Meeting to Summer Resort": 93.

31 Weiss, "Wesleyan Grove and Oak Bluffs: From Camp Meeting to Summer Resort": 100.

32 Hough, *Martha's Vineyard, Summer Resort*, 80.

33 Senter, "Civic and Scenic New England, Part II—The Cape Region and Martha's Vineyard": 90; Weiss, "Robert Morris Copeland's Plans for Oak Bluffs": 61, 65, 66; Weiss, *City in the Woods*, 80, 88, 90–92; Pregill and Volkman, *Landscapes in History: Design and Planning in the Eastern and Western Traditions*, 540.

34 Weiss, "Wesleyan Grove and Oak Bluffs: From Camp Meeting to Summer Resort": 100–101.

35 Stewart W. Herman, *The Smallest Village: The Story of Dering Harbor, Shelter Island, New York, 1874–1974* (Shelter Island, NY: Shelter Island Historical Society, 1976), 33. Also see Weiss, *City in the Woods*, 92, 94; Pregill and Volkman, *Landscapes in History: Design and Planning in the Eastern and Western Traditions*, 540; www.shelter-island.org.

36 Weiss, *City in the Woods*, 92, 94; National Register of Historic Places, *Shelter Island Heights Historic District Survey* (Washington, D.C.: United States Department of the Interior, National Park Service, 1993); www.shelter-island.org.

37 See Jeffrey Simpson, *Chautauqua: An American Utopia* (New York: Harry N. Abrams, 1999).

38 Andrew W. Young, *History of Chautauqua County, New York, From Its First Settlement to the Present Time* (Buffalo: Matthews & Warren, 1875), 664–65; Frederick Law Olmsted, letter to the Rev. J. H. Miller, February 28, 1876, in Charles Capen McLaughlin, ed., *The Papers of Frederick Law Olmsted* (Baltimore: Johns Hopkins University Press, 1977), 179–82; Laura Wood Roper, *FLO: A Biography of Frederick Law Olmsted* (Baltimore and London: Johns Hopkins University Press, 1973), 348; Phyllis Lambert, ed., *Viewing Olmsted: Photographs by Robert Burley, Leo Friedlander and Geoffrey James* (Montreal: Canadian Centre for Architecture, 1996), 54; Charles E. Beveridge and Paul Rocheleau, *Frederick Law Olmsted: Designing the American Landscape* (New York: Universe, 1998), 103; Edgar C. Conklin, *Frederick Law Olmsted's Point Chautauqua: The Story of an Historic Lakeside Community* (Buffalo: Canisius College Press, 2001); Kathleen Crocker and Jane Currie, *Images of America: Chautauqua Lake Region* (Charleston, S.C.: Arcadia Publishing, 2002), 43–44, 53–58.

39 Reps, *The Making of Urban America*, 410–13.

40 Quoted in Conklin, *Frederick Law Olmsted's Point Chautauqua*, 38.

41 Conklin, *Frederick Law Olmsted's Point Chautauqua*, 43.

42 Conklin, *Frederick Law Olmsted's Point Chautauqua*, 44.

43 *Cushing's Island Company, Summer Homes: Cushing's Island, Portland Harbor*, pamphlet (New York: Hosford & Sons, 1883); Frederick Law Olmsted, *Report and Advice of Frederick Law Olmsted for the Development and Improvement of Cushing's Island, Maine* (May 10, 1883); Edward H. Elwell, *Portland and Vicinity* (Portland, Me.: Loring, Short & Harmon, 1886; Portland, Me.: Greater Portland Landmarks, 1975), 92–93; William A.M. Sargent, *An Historic Sketch, Guide Book, and Prospectus to Cushing's Island, Casco Bay, Coast of Maine* (New York: American Photo Engraving Company, 1886); John Calvin Stevens and Albert Winslow Cobb, *Examples of American Domestic Architecture* (New York: William T. Comstock, 1889; Watkins Glen, N.Y.: Library of Victorian Culture, 1978), plate xvii; Deborah Thompson, ed., *Maine Forms of American Architecture* (Camden, Me.: Colby Museum of Art and Downeast Magazine, 1976), 192, 194; John Calvin Stevens II and Earl G. Shettleworth, Jr., *John Calvin Stevens: Domestic Architecture, 1890–1930* (Portland, Me.: Greater Portland Landmarks, 1995), 52–59; Elizabeth Igleheart, "Cushing's Island: A Planned Summer Colony," *Maine Olmsted Alliance for Parks & Landscapes Journal* (Fall 1996): 7–10; Earle G. Shettleworth Jr., and Scott T. Hanson, *The Architecture of Cushing's Island* (Cushing's Island, Me.: Cushing's Island Association, 2012).

44 Igleheart, "Cushing's Island: A Planned Summer Colony": 7–10.

45 Gouldsboro Land Improvement Company, *A Description of Its Property Upon Grindstone Neck and the Schoodic Peninsula, in Frenchman's Bay, Near Bar Harbor* (New York, 1890); Charles Edward Hooper, *The Country House: A Practical Manual of the Planning and Construction of the American Country Home and Its Surroundings* (New York: Doubleday, Page & Co., 1905), 237; Nathalie White Hahn, *A History of Winter Harbor Maine* (privately published, 1974), 8–9, 18–20; Clay Lancaster, *The American Bungalow: 1880–1930* (New York: Abbeville, 1985), 82–83; "Lindley Johnson, 1854–1937," in Earle G. Shettleworth, Jr., ed., *A Biographical Dictionary of Architects in Maine* 6 (Portland, Me.: Maine Citizens for Historic Preservation, 1991), n.p.; Philip Pregill and Nancy Volkman, *Landscapes in History: Design and Planning in the Eastern and Western Traditions* (New York: John Wiley, 1999), 537; Allan Smallidge, *Musquito Harbor: A Narrative History of Winter Harbor, Maine, 1790–2005* (Winter Harbor, Me.: Ironbound Press, 2006), 109–24.

46 Nathan F. Barrett, quoted in *A Description of Its Property Upon Grindstone Neck and the Schoodic Peninsula, in Frenchman's Bay, Near Bar Harbor*, 24–25.

47 Smallidge, *Musquito Harbor: A Narrative History of Winter Harbor, Maine, 1790–2005*, 112.

48 Catherine Mahan, "Sudbrook Park: Olmsted's Hidden Community in Baltimore," *Design Action* 1 (September/October 1982): 6; James F. Waesche, *Crowning the Gravelly Hill: A History of the Roland Park-Guilford-Homeland District* (Baltimore: Maclay & Associates, 1987), 41; Arleyn A. Levee, "The Olmsted Brothers' Residential Communities: Preview of a Legacy," in *The Landscape Universe: Designed Landscapes in Context* (Bronx: Catalog of Landscape Records in the U.S. at Wave Hill, 1993); Michael Watkins, ed., *A Guidebook to Old and New Urbanism in the Baltimore/Washington Region* (San Francisco: Congress for the New Urbanism, 1993), 113; Charles E. Beveridge and Paul Rocheleau, *Frederick Law Olmsted: Designing the American Landscape* (New York: Rizzoli International Publications, 1995), 124–25; Gianni Pettena, *Olmsted: L'origine del parco urbano e del parco naturale contemporaneo* (Firenze: Centro Di, 1996), 148–49, 203; Melanie D. Anson, *Olmsted's Sudbrook: The Making of a Community* (Baltimore: Sudbrook Park, Inc., 1997); John Dorsey and James D. Dilts, *A Guide to Baltimore Architecture*, 3rd ed. (Centreville, Md.: Tidewater Publishers, 1997), 24, 393–94; Beryl Frank, *Way Back When in Sudbrook Park* (Baltimore: Sudbrook Park, 1997), passim; Charles E. Beveridge and Paul Rocheleau, *Frederick Law Olmsted: Designing the American Landscape* (New York: Universe, 1998), 107; Alexander Garvin, *Parks, Recreation, and Open Space: A Twenty-first Century Agenda* (Chicago: American Planning Association, 2000), 15; Alexander Garvin, *The American City: What Works, What Doesn't*, 2nd ed. (New York: McGraw-Hill, 2002), 320–21; Andrés Duany, Elizabeth Plater-Zyberk, and Robert Alminana, *The New Civic Art: Elements of Town Planning* (New York: Rizzoli International Publications, 2003), 140; Dolores Hayden, *Building Suburbia: Green Fields and Urban Growth, 1820–2000* (New York: Pantheon Books, 2003), 65; Mary Ellen Hayward and Frank R. Shivers, Jr., eds., *The Architecture of Baltimore: An Illustrated History* (Baltimore and London: Johns Hopkins University Press, 2004), 231. Also see Melanie Anson, "Sudbrook Park: A Brief History," www.sudbrookpark.com.

49 Quoted in Beveridge and Rocheleau, *Frederick Law Olmsted: Designing the American Landscape*, 125.

50 John Charles Olmsted, letter to Hugh Lennox Bond Jr., April 16, 1889, quoted in Anson, *Olmsted's Sudbrook: The Making of a Community*, 14.

51 Anson, "Sudbrook Park: A Brief History," www.sudbrookpark.com.

52 Garvin, *The American City: What Works, What Doesn't*, 320.

53 Victor Mays, *Pathway to a Village: A History of Bronxville* (Bronxville, N.Y.: Nebko Press, 1961), quoted in Tessa Melvin, "A Bastion Against Urban Encroachment," *New York Times* (September 12, 1993), X: 5. Also see Alice Wellington Rollins, *The Story of Lawrence Park* (New York: Douglas Robinson & Co., 1895); Theodore Tuttle, "A Picturesque American Suburb," *Architectural Record* 16 (September 1904): 167–77; Frederick E. Partington, "A Unique Suburb," *Indoors and Out* 23 (July 1906): 153–60, and (August 1906): 223–30; Alvah P. French, ed., *History of Westchester County, New York*, vol. 2 (New York and Chicago: Lewis Historical Publishing Co., 1925), 687–88; Frank E. Sanchis, *American Architecture: Westchester County, New York: Colonial to Contemporary* (Croton-on-Hudson, N.Y.: North River Press, 1977), 119–25; Stern with Massengale, *The Anglo-American Suburb*, 31; Anita Inman Comstock, *Bronxville: In the Good 'Ol Days* (Bronxville, N.Y.: Nicholas T. Smith, Publisher, 1982); Kenneth T. Jackson, *Crabgrass Frontier: The Suburbanization of the United States* (New York: Oxford University Press, 1985), 95–97; Loretta Hoagland, *Lawrence Park: Bronxville's Turn-of-the-Century Art Colony* (Bronxville, N.Y.: Lawrence Park Hilltop Association, 1992); *Building a Suburban Village: Bronxville, New York, 1898–1998* (Bronxville, N.Y.: Bronxville Centennial Celebration, 1998); Gray Williams, "Westchester County: Historic Suburban Neighborhoods," in Roger Panetta, ed., *Westchester: The American Suburb* (New York: Fordham University Press; Yonkers, N.Y.: Hudson River Museum, 2006), 187–91.

54 Tuttle, "A Picturesque American Suburb": 167, 172–73.

55 For typical early work of Bates, see Tuttle, "A Picturesque Suburb": 167–77; Partington, "A Unique Suburb," (July 1906): 153–60, and (August 1906): 223–30. Also see "The Casino, Lawrence Park," *American Architect and Building News* 70 (October 27, 1900): plate; "Gray Arches, Lawrence Park, Bronxville, New York," *American Architect and Building News* 70 (September 22, 1900): 95, plate 1291; "House of Will H. Low, Esq., Lawrence Park, Bronxville, N.Y.," *Architectural Record* 14 (July 1903): 137–39; "House for C. Rushton, Jr., Esq., Lawrence Park," *American Architect and Building News* 99 (April 12, 1911): plates; "House at Lawrence Park, N.Y.," *American Architect and Building News* 99 (June 7, 1911): plates; "Two Bronxville Residences and Another in Lawrence Park West," *Architectural Record* 32 (October 1912): 366–69; "House of Mr. Ward Leonard, Bronxville, N.Y.," *American Architect* 103 (June 11, 1913): plate; "House, Charles Ruston, Jr., Lawrence Park, Bronxville, N.Y.," *Architecture* 29 (March 1914): 68–69; "House of Robert O. Hayward, Esq., Bronxville, N.Y.," *American Architect* 107 (May 12, 1915): plates; "The Architect's Scrap-Book—Houses in Bronxville, N.Y.," *Architecture* 33 (January 1916): 18–19; "House of Mr. Chapin S. Pratt, Lawrence Park, Bronxville, N.Y.," *American Architect* 119 (April 20, 1921): plate; "House of Chapin S. Pratt, Lawrence Park, N.Y.," *American Architect* 120 (October 12, 1921): 277. Other architects who worked at Lawrence Park pursued a similar style in the early years. See, for example, "House at Lawrence Park, Bronxville, W. W. Kent, Architect," *American Architect and Building News* 43 (January 6, 1894): plate.

56 "Hotel Gramatan," *American Architect* 91 (June 1, 1907): plates; "Hotel Gramatan, Bronxville, N.Y.," *American Architect and Building News* 96 (October 13, 1909): plate; "Hotel Gramatan, Bronxville, N.Y.," *Architectural Review* 19 (April 1913): 146.

57 Partington, "A Unique Suburb": 159.

58 "Alger Court, Lawrence Park, Bronxville, New York," *American Architect* 109 (January 5, 1916): plates; "Alger Court Apartments, Bronxville, N.Y.," *Architecture and Building* 55 (February 1923): plates 27–28.

59 Kenneth G. How, "Housing Problems in Small Suburban Developments," *American Architect* 110 (August 16, 1916): 91–97, plates.

60 "Garden Cottage Group, Bronxville, N.Y.," *Architecture* 32 (August 1915): 200–201; How, "Housing Problems in Small Suburban Developments": 91–97, plates.

61 "Oak Court Terrace Cottages, Bronxville, N.Y.," *Architecture* 35 (April 1917): 76; "Oak Court Terrace," *Architectural Forum* 43 (September 1925): 161–62. Bates & How also built at least one double house independent of a larger grouping. See "Two House Group at Bronxville, N.Y.," *Architectural Forum* 43 (September 1925): 171–72.

62 Kenneth G. How, "Gramatan Court: A Fire Proof Suburban Apartment," *Architectural Record* 35 (February 1914): 140–50.

63 "Apartment House, Bronxville, N.Y.," *Architecture* 43 (June 1921): plates 77–79.
64 John Taylor Boyd, Jr., "The Suburban Apartment House," *Architectural Forum* 43 (September 1925): 131–36.
65 The Bronxville Public Library has monographs published for publicity by Bowman, Stout, and R. H. Scannell. Also see "Grassy Sprayn Manor: A Proposed Apartment Group at Bronxville, N.Y., Carrere & Hastings, Architects—Shreve, Lamb & Blake, Associates," *Architectural Review* 12 (January 1921): 1–6; Frank Chouteau Brown, "Some Recent Apartment Buildings," *Architectural Record* 63 (March 1928): 193–278; "The Colonnade Apartment, Bronxville, N.Y.," *Architectural Record* 65 (March 1929): 278.
66 Boyd, "The Suburban Apartment House": 131–36; "Study, Community House Development, Bronxville, N.Y.," *The Architect* 8 (April 1927): plate; "Merestone Community Houses, Bronxville, N.Y.," *American Architect* 135 (April 20, 1929): 543.
67 Arthur C. Holden, "Realty Development and the Architect," *Architectural Record* 69 (April 1931): 331–57.
68 B. A. Goodridge, "A New England Village in the Southern Pines," *New England Magazine* (November 1896): 321–26; "Our New Store Building," *Pinehurst Outlook* (October 22, 1897): 1; "A Glimpse of Pinehurst," *Pinehurst Outlook* (November 12, 1897): 1; "Moore County: Description of the Shire in which Pinehurst Is Located," *Pinehurst Outlook* (March 18,1898): 1; "Open Letter," *Pinehurst Outlook* (March 25, 1898): 1; "The Making of Pinehurst," *Pinehurst Outlook* (October 28, 1898): 1; "The Berkshire Opens," *Pinehurst Outlook* (December 16, 1898): 1; "Pinehurst Golf Links," *Pinehurst Outlook* (February 24, 1899): 1; "The Carolina Hotel," *Pinehurst Outlook* (November 3, 1899): 4; "Golf at Pinehurst," *Pinehurst Outlook* (November 3, 1899): 5; "Changes of the Year," *Pinehurst Outlook* (November 3, 1899): 9; "Holly Inn Opens," *Pinehurst Outlook* (December 8, 1899): 1–2; "The Carolina Hotel," *Pinehurst Outlook* (November 9, 1900): 4; "The Mystic," *Pinehurst Outlook* (November 9, 1900): 11; Harry Redan, "Pinehurst Today," *New England Magazine* (October 19, 1901): 256–58; Bertrand E. Taylor, "A Southern Village Among the Pines," *Indoors & Out* 1 (January 1906): 167–73; Edwin A. Denham, "The New Home of the Pinehurst Country Club," *Pinehurst Outlook* 26 (November 1922): 1, 4, 13; Bion Butler, "The Summer's Growth," *Pinehurst Outlook* 29 (November 1925): 1; Donald J. Ross, "Pinehurst Personalities," *Pinehurst Outlook* (March 21, 1931): 7, 12; Andrew Hepburn, *Great Resorts of North America* (Garden City, N.Y.: Doubleday & Co., 1965), 53–62, figs. 15–18; Gianni Pettena, *Olmsted: L'origine del parco urbano e del parco naturale contemporaneo* (Firenze: Centro Di, 1996), 147; Richard J. Moss, "Constructing Eden: The Early Days of Pinehurst, North Carolina," *New England Quarterly* 72 (September 1999): 388–414; Margaret Huffadine, *Resort Design: Planning, Architecture, and Interiors* (New York: McGraw-Hill, 2000), 31–34; Orin Starn, "Caddying for the Dalai Lama: Golf, Heritage Tourism, and the Pinehurst Resort," *South Atlantic Quarterly* 105 (Spring 2006): 447–63; Stephen Wells, "Havens: Pinehurst, N.C.: A Genteel Setting with World-Class Golf," *New York Times* (August 22, 2008), F: 3. Also see Audrey Moriarity, "Pinehurst Beginnings," www.themooreexchange.com.
69 Quoted in Hepburn, *Great Resorts of North America*, 54.
70 Moss, "Constructing Eden: The Early Days of Pinehurst, North Carolina": 394.
71 James Walker Tufts, quoted in Hepburn, *Great Resorts of North America*, 56.
72 Moss, "Constructing Eden: The Early Days of Pinehurst, North Carolina": 392.
73 Quoted in Moss, "Constructing Eden: The Early Days of Pinehurst, North Carolina": 397.
74 Samuel Parsons Jr., *How to Plan the Home Grounds* (New York: Doubleday & McClure, 1901), 174–83; Albemarle Park-Manor Grounds Association, *The Manor, Albemarle Park, Asheville, N.C.* (New York: J. C and W. E. Powers, c. 1905); Samuel Parsons, *Landscape Gardening Studies* (New York: John Lane Company, 1910), 32–36; Richard Schermerhorn Jr., "Samuel Parsons," obituary, *Landscape Architecture* 14 (July 1924): 231–34; Jane Gianvito Mathews and Richard A. Mathews, eds., *The Manor and Cottages: Albemarle Park, Asheville, North Carolina: A Historic Planned Residential Community* (Asheville, N.C.: Albemarle-Park-Manor Grounds Association, 1991); Charles A. Birnbaum, "Making Educated Decisions on the Treatment of Historic Landscapes," *APT Bulletin* 24 (1992): 42–51; "The Manor and Cottages: Albemarle Park," *Landscape Architecture* 84 (April 1994): 89; Charles A. Birnbaum, *Samuel Parsons Jr.: The Art of Landscape Architecture* (Bronx: Wave Hill, 1995), 29–30; Eve M. Kahn, "Perpetuating Parsons," *Landscape Architecture* 85 (April 1995): 24; Catherine W. Bishir, Michael T. Southern, and Jennifer F. Martin, *A Guide to the Historic Architecture of Western North Carolina* (Chapel Hill: University of North Carolina Press, 1999), 279–80; Charles A. Birnbaum, "Samuel Parsons, Jr.," in Charles A. Birnbaum and Robin Karson, eds., *Pioneers of American Landscape Design* (New York, McGraw Hill, 2000), 287–91; "Manor and Cottages (Albemarle Park)," in www.nps.gove/history/nr/travel/asheville/man.htm.
75 Albemarle Park-Manor Grounds Association, *The Manor, Albemarle Park, Asheville, N.C.*, 12.
76 Albemarle Park-Manor Grounds Association, *The Manor, Albemarle Park, Asheville, N.C.*, 3.
77 Parsons, *How to Plan the Home Grounds*, 176.
78 Quoted in Catherine W. Bishir, Michael T. Southern, and Jennifer F. Martin, *A Guide to the Historic Architecture of Western North Carolina* (Chapel Hill and London: University of North Carolina Press, 1999), 293–94. Also see "Biltmore Forest Country Club, Biltmore, N.C.," *American Architect* 127 (May 20, 1925): 431–66; John M. Bryan, *Biltmore Estate: The Most Distinguished Private Place* (New York: Rizzoli International Publications, 1994), 147–48; Robin Karson, *Fletcher Steele, Landscape Architect: An Account of the Gardenmaker's Life, 1885–1971*, rev. ed. (Amherst, Mass.: Library of American Landscape History, 2003), 98–100; Douglas Stuart McDaniel, *Asheville* (Charleston, S.C.: Arcadia, 2004), 63; Howard E. Covington Jr., *Lady on the Hill: How Biltmore Estate Became an American Icon* (Hoboken, N.J.: John Wiley & Sons, 2006), 50; Bill Alexander, *Around Biltmore Village* (Charleston, S.C.: Arcadia, 2008), 113–25.
79 James Pooton, Jr., "Henry O. Havemeyer's 'Venice,'" *New York Times* (May 23, 1897), illustrated weekly magazine: 14. Also see *Moorish Houses at Bayberry Point, Islip, L.I., Built for Mr. H. O. Havemeyer* (1897); Pittsburgh Architectural Club, *Catalogue of the Annual Exhibition of the Pittsburgh Architectural Club* (Pittsburgh: The Club, 1900): 20; Pittsburgh Architectural Club, *Catalogue of the Annual Exhibition of the Pittsburgh Architectural Club* (Pittsburgh: The Club, 1903): 29, 70; "Bayberry Point," *American Architect* 96 (September 8, 1909): 98–101; "The Pittsburgh Architectural Club's Exhibition," *American Architect and Building News* 92 (November 30, 1907): plate; Aymar Embury, *One Hundred Country Houses* (New York: Century Co., 1909), 96, 98; "Some Work at Bayberry Point, L.I. By Grosvenor Atterbury, F.A.I.A.," *American Architect* 96 (September 8, 1909): 94, 96; Russell F. Whitehead, "American Seaside Homes," *Architectural Record* 28 (August 1910): 79–87; Pittsburgh Architectural Club, *Catalogue of the Annual Exhibition of the Pittsburgh Architectural Club* (Pittsburgh: The Club, 1910); Oswald C. Hering, *Concrete and Stucco Houses* (New York: McBride, Nast & Co., 1912), plates; Grosvenor Atterbury, Stowe Phelps, and John A. Tompkins, Architects, *Architectural Catalog* (April 1918): plates; "Bayberry Point Homes," *New York Times* (July 7, 1930): 39; Frances Weitzenhoffer, *The Havemeyers: Impressionism Comes to America* (New York: Harry N. Abrams, 1986), 121, 144, 148–50; *AIA Architectural Guide to Nassau and Suffolk Counties, Long Island* (New York: Dover, 1992), figs. 160–160A; Alice Cooney Frelinghuysen et al., *Splendid Legacy: The Havemeyer Collection* (New York: Metropolitan Museum of Art, 1993), 195, 221; Harry W. Havemeyer, *Along the Great South Bay: From Oakdale to Babylon, the Story of a Summer Spa, 1840–1940* (Mattituck, N.Y.: Amereon House, 1996), 224–31, 240, 385–89, 401; Donald Dwyer, "Grosvenor Atterbury, 1869–1956," in Robert B. Mackay, Anthony K. Baker, and Carol A. Traynor, eds., *Long Island Country Houses and Their Architects, 1860–1940* (New York: W. W. Norton in association with the Society for the Preservation of Long Island Antiquities, 1997), 51; Raymond E. and Judith A. Spinzia, *Long Island's Prominent South Shore Families: Their Estates and Their Country Homes in the Towns of Babylon and Islip* (College Station, Tx.: Virtual Bookworm, 2007), 102–4, 371–72; Peter Pennoyer and Anne Walker, *The Architecture of Grosvenor Atterbury*, foreword by Robert A. M. Stern (New York: W. W. Norton & Company, 2009), 77–81, 260.
80 For 1 East Sixty-sixth Street, see Stern, Mellins, and Fishman, *New York 1880*, 654, 658–61.
81 Pooton, "Henry O. Havemeyer's 'Venice'": 14.
82 Pennoyer and Walker, *The Architecture of Grosvenor Atterbury*, 78–80.
83 "Belle-Terre: the Tuxedo of Long Island," *Country Life in America* 4 (September 1903): 351–52; "Beautifying Vast Park Overlooking the Sound," *New York Times* (May 31, 1908): 10; Belle Terre Estates, Inc., *Belle Terre* (New York: William Darling, 1910); Belle Terre Estates, Inc., *Cottages, Belle Terre, Port Jefferson, Long Island* (New York, 1910); "Developing Long Island's North Shore," *New York Times* (February 13, 1910), VI: 10; "Beauties of Belle Terre," *New York Times* (April 24, 1910), VI: 4; "Opening Day at Belle Terre," *New York Times* (June 12, 1910): 12; "House at Belle Terre, Long Island, N.Y.," *Brickbuilder* 19 (December 1910): 275–78, plates 166–70; Henry H. Saylor, *Bungalows* (Philadelphia: John C. Winston Company, 1911), 55, 60, 68; "Alvord Companies Pass to Receiver," *New York Times* (January 11, 1913): 1; *Statement of Board of Trustees of Village of Belle Terre* (Belle Terre, 1935); Robert B. Mackay, Anthony K. Baker, and Carol A. Traynor, eds., *Long Island Country Houses and Their Architects, 1860–1940* (New York: W.W. Norton, 1997), 237–38; Andrew Scott Dolkart, *The Row House Reborn: Architecture and Neighborhoods in New York City, 1908–1929* (Baltimore, Md.: Johns Hopkins University Press, 2009), 37–39.
84 Belle Terre Estates, Inc., *Belle Terre*, 8.
85 Elizabeth Mary Delude, "Jamestown, Rhode Island: A Nineteenth Century Resort and Shoreby Hill, a Resort Suburb" (Master's thesis: Columbia University, 1986), esp. pp. 50–84; Charles C. Savage, *Architecture of the Private Streets of St. Louis: The Architects and the Houses They Designed* (Columbia: University of Missouri Press, 1987), 12; Kara Cathleen Hamley, "Cleveland's Park Allotment: Euclid Heights, Cleveland Heights, Ohio, and Its Designer, Ernest W. Bowditch" (Master's thesis, Cornell University, 1996): 72–76; James C. Buttrick, *Jamestown* (Charleston, S.C.: Arcadia, 2003), 7–8, 15, 29, 42–44, 65, 71–72, 95–96; William H. Jordy, *Buildings of Rhode Island* (New York: Oxford University Press, 2004), 602–4; Rhode Island Historical Preservation Commission, *Historic Architectural Resources of Jamestown, Rhode Island* (Providence: Rhode Island Historical Preservation Commission, 2005).
86 "Great Hotel Planned," *Los Angeles Times* (June 25, 1905), V: 20; "Thousands Go to See Venice," *Los Angeles Times* (July 3, 1905), I: 4; "Fair Venice of America," *Los Angeles Times* (July 20, 1905), III: 1; "Still as Tomb Venice 'Boom,'" *Los Angeles Times* (September 21, 1905), II: 7; "Notes & Comments/An American Venice," *Architectural Record* 20 (October 1906): 347–50; Hoon L. Izzy, "Why is Venice-of-America?" *Los Angeles Times* (April 16, 1916), II: 14; "Old Landmarks Downed," *Los Angeles Times* (November 8, 1925), B: 8; Bill Murphy, *The Dolphin Guide to Los Angeles and Southern California* (Garden City, NY: Doubleday, 1962), 104–5; Lynn Craig Cunningham, "Venice, California: From City to Suburb" (Ph.D. diss., University of California, Los Angeles, 1976), esp. ch. 1; David Gebhard and Robert Winter, *A Guide to Architecture in Los Angeles and Southern California* (Santa Barbara: Peregrine Smith, 1977), 60–63; Tom Moran and Tom Sewell, *Fantasy by the Sea: A Visual History of the American Venice* (Culver City, Calif.: Peace Press, 1979), passim; David Gebhard and Robert Winter, *Architecture in Los Angeles: A Compleat Guide* (Salt Lake City: Gibbs M. Smith, 1985), 64–68; Robert John Pierson, *The Beach Towns: A Walker's Guide to L.A.'s Beach Communities* (San Francisco: Chronicle Books, 1985), 54–74; Kevin Starr, *Inventing the Dream: California Through the Progressive Era* (New York: Oxford University Press, 1985), 79–80; Charles Moore, Peter Becker, and Regula Campbell, *The City Observed: Los Angeles* (Santa Monica, Calif.: Hennessey & Ingalls, 1998), 122–24; David Gebhard and Robert Winter, *An Architectural Guidebook to Los Angeles*, rev. ed. (Salt Lake City: Gibbs Smith, 2003), 68–75; www.betsysellsvenice.com/pagemanager/default.aspx?pageid=182649.
87 Starr, *Inventing the Dream*, 79–80.
88 Starr, *Inventing the Dream*, 79–80.
89 "Rancho Santa Fe an Unusual Undertaking," *Los Angeles Times* (March 4, 1923): 8, 12; "Rancho Santa Fe Opened," *Los Angeles Times* (March 11, 1923): 12; "Plan Perfect Land Project," *Los Angeles Times* (March 26, 1923): 1; "It Sounds Like Utopia," *Los Angeles Times* (April 23, 1923): 16; Lilian Rice, "Rancho Santa Fe—A Vision," *The Modern Clubwoman* (January–February 193): 5; M. Urmy Seares, "The Village of Rancho Santa Fe," *California Arts & Architecture* 38 (September 1930): 38–39, 66; L.G. Sinnard, *Rancho Santa Fe: California Yesterday-Today*, promotional brochure (c. 1934), Edith Elmer Wood Collection, Avery Library, Columbia University; S. R. Nelson, "Rancho Santa Fe," *Architect and Engineer* 168 (January 1947): 20–27; David Gebhard and Robert Winter, *A Guide to the Architecture of Los Angeles and Southern California* (Santa Barbara: Peregrine Smith,

1977), 493–94; Judith Payne, "Lilian Rice," in Susana Torre, ed., *Women in American Architecture: A Historic and Contemporary Perspective* (New York: Whitney Library of Design, 1977), 108–10; Kevin Starr, *Material Dreams: Southern California Through the 1920s* (New York: Oxford University Press, 1990), 202–3; Lauren V. Farber, "Rancho Santa Fe, California: Architecture, Planning, and Community Development, 1922–1991" (Masters thesis, University of Delaware, 1993); Cheryl Lynn Caldwell Ferguson, "Upscale Suburban Architecture and Development in Dallas and Houston, Texas, 1890–1930" (Ph.D. diss., University of Delaware, 2004): 289–90, 732; Vonn Marie May, *Images of America: Rancho Santa Fe* (Charleston, S.C.: Arcadia Publishing, 2010); Diane Y. Welch, *Lilian J. Rice: Architect of Rancho Santa Fe, California* (Atglen, Penn.: Schiffer, 2010), esp. chs. 4–6.

90 Sinnard, *Rancho Santa Fe: California Yesterday–Today*, 1.

91 Thomas Murphy Dowler, *On Sunset Highways: A Book of Motor Rambles in California* (Boston: Page, 1915), 181; *Santa Barbara: A Guide to the Channel City and Its Environs* (New York: Hastings House, 1941), 166, 167; Harold S. Chase, *Hope Ranch, a Rambling Record* (Santa Barbara, Calif.: Santa Barbara Historical Society, 1963), passim; Kevin Starr, *Material Dreams: Southern California Through the 1920s* (New York: Oxford University Press, 1990), 278; Alson Clark, "Reginald D. Johnson: Regionalism and Recognition," in *Johnson, Kaufmann, Coate: Partners in the California Style* (Santa Barbara, Calif.: Capra, 1992), 22–23; Richard J. Orsi, *Sunset Limited: The Southern Pacific Railroad and the Development of the American West* (Berkeley: University of California Press, 2005), 117, 203.

92 C. L. Sonnichsen, *Tucson: The Life and Times of an American City* (Norman: University of Oklahoma Press, 1982), 217; Wendy Laird, *El Encanto Estates Residential Historic District, National Register of Historic Places Registration Form* (National Park Service, January 1988); Joe Burchell, "El Encanto Becomes 6th Neighborhood in Tucson to Gain National Historic Status," *Arizona Daily Star* (April 15, 1988); *Joesler & Murphey: An Architectural Legacy for Tucson* (Tucson: City of Tucson Planning Department, 1994), 4–5; Virginia and Lee McAlester, *A Field Guide to America's Historic Neighborhoods and Museum Houses: The Western States* (New York: Alfred A. Knopf, 1998), xxxix, 24; Anne M. Nequette and R. Brooks Jeffery, *A Guide to Tucson Architecture* (Tucson: University of Arizona Press, 2002), 194, 26–27.

93 Wendy Laird, *El Encanto Estates Residential Historic District, National Register of Historic Places Registration Form* (National Park Service, January 1988).

94 Stephen Child, "Colonia Solana: A Subdivision on the Arizona Desert," *Landscape Architecture* 19 (October 1928): 6–13. Also see C.L. Sonnichsen, *Tucson: The Life and Times of an American City* (Norman: University of Oklahoma Press, 1982), 217; Ralph Comey Architects, *Colonia Solana Residential Historic District, National Register of Historic Places Registration Form* (National Park Service, April 1, 1988); Ralph Comey Architects, *Colonia Solana Residential Historic District, National Register of Historic Places Continuation Sheet* (National Park Service, January 1, 1989); Mary Blaine Korff, "Stephen Child: Visionary Landscape Architect" (Master's thesis, University of Arizona, 1991): 6–9, 22–43; *Joesler & Murphey: An Architectural Legacy for Tucson* (Tucson: City of Tucson Planning Department, 1994), 4–5; Virginia and Lee McAlester, *A Field Guide to America's Historic Neighborhoods and Museum Houses: The Western States* (New York: Alfred A. Knopf, 1998), 24; Mary Blaine Korff, "Stephen Child," in Charles A. Birnbaum and Robin Karson, eds., *Pioneers of American Landscape Design* (New York: McGraw Hill, 2000), 50–52; Anne M. Nequette and R. Brooks Jeffery, *A Guide to Tucson Architecture* (Tucson: University of Arizona Press, 2002), 26–27, 194.

95 McAlester, *A Field Guide to America's Historic Neighborhoods and Museum Houses*, 24.

96 Child, "Colonia Solana: A Subdivision on the Arizona Desert": 8, 11.

97 McAlester, *A Field Guide to America's Historic Neighborhoods and Museum Houses*, 24.

98 Child, "Colonia Solana: A Subdivision on the Arizona Desert": 11.

99 C.L. Sonnichsen, *Tucson: The Life and Times of an American City* (Norman: University of Oklahoma Press, 1982), 218–19; *Joesler & Murphey: An Architectural Legacy for Tucson* (Tucson: City of Tucson Planning Department, 1994), 12–16; Anne M. Nequette and R. Brooks Jeffery, *A Guide to Tucson Architecture* (Tucson: University of Arizona Press, 2002), 26–27; Michael F. Logan, *Desert Cities* (Pittsburgh: University of Pittsburgh Press, 2006), 175–76. For Joelser, see "Josias Joesler: an Architectural Eclectic," in http://parentseyes.arizona.edu/josiasjoesler/bio.html.

100 Henry V. Hubbard, "The Golf Course and the Land Subdivision," *Landscape Architecture* 17 (April 1927): 211–19.

101 Hubbard, "The Golf Course and the Land Subdivision": 217; "Gibson Island," advertisement, *Washington Post* (July 22, 1927): 2; "H. Clay Primrose," *Landscape Architecture* 42 (January 1952): 84–85; William B. Cronin, *The Disappearing Islands of the Chesapeake* (Baltimore: Johns Hopkins University Press, 2005), 33–37; Marianne Kyriakos, "A Special Island Unto Themselves: Wary Bay Community Thinks Private Makes More Perfect," *Washington Post* (October 8, 2005), G: 1. Also see "History of Gibson Island," www.gibsonisland.com; www.olmstedmaryland.org/history.cfm.

102 Hubbard, "The Golf Course and the Land Subdivision": 218; Robert Goodwyn Rhett, *Charleston: An Epic of Carolina* (Richmond, Va.: Garrett and Massie, 1940), 337; Martha R. Severens, *The Charleston Renaissance* (Spartanburg, S. C. Garland, 1998), 19–20; Aaron Betsky, *James Gamble Rogers and the Architecture of Pragmatism* (New York: Architectural History Foundation, 1994), 35–36; Michael J. Heitzle and Nancy Paul Kirchner, *Good Creek: A Definitive History* (Charleston, S. C.: History Press, 2006), 163; Charlton deSaussure Jr., *The Cottages and Architects of Yeamans Hall* (Charleston, S. C.: Yeamans Hall, Inc., 2010).

103 Frederick Law Olmsted Jr., quoted in Severens, *The Charleston Renaissance*, 19–20.

104 Betsky, *James Gamble Rogers and the Architecture of Pragmatism*, 36.

105 Peter Pennoyer and Anne Walker, *The Architecture of Grosvenor Atterbury*, foreword by Robert A. M. Stern (New York: W. W. Norton & Company, 2009), 226–27, 266.

106 Hubbard, "The Golf Course and the Land Subdivision": 219; Arthur C. Holden, "Realty Developments and the Architect," *Architectural Record* 69 (April 1931): 332–33; "Oyster Harbors," www.falgen.org.

107 "Developing Fishers Island," *New York Times* (June 28, 1925), XI: 2; Hubbard, "The Golf Course and the Land Subdivision": 215; "The New Fishers Island Club," *Golf Illustrated* 29 (April 1928): 49–50; "Hamlet Study—Fishers Island Strategic Plan," www.southoldtown.northfork.net.

108 *Montauk Beach on Long Island: The Miami Beach of the North* (Montauk, N.Y.: Montauk Beach Realty, 1926); "Plan to Develop Montauk," *New York Times* (July 7, 1926): 3; Robert Tappan, "The Unit System as a Factor in Economical Construction," *American Architect* 130 (November 5, 1926): 365–76; "Big Hotel Opened at Montauk Beach," *New York Times* (June 19, 1927), X: 18; Jane Fisher, *Fabulous Hoosier: A Story of American Achievement* (New York: Robert M. McBride & Co., 1947), 120, 213–28; Albert Farwell Bemis, *The Evolving House, Volume III: Rational Design* (Cambridge, Mass.: MIT Press, 1956), 552–57; John Heilig, "Montauk's Master Planner," *On the Sound* 4 (May 1974): 27–31; Ralph Hausrath, "Carl G. Fisher and Montauk," *Long Island Forum* 44 (November 1981): 224–31, and (December 1981): 254–60; Cecil Roseberry, *From Niagara to Montauk: The Scenic Pleasures of New York State* (Albany, N.Y.: SUNY Press, 1982), 315; Diana Shaman, "On Long Island: Reviving a Grandiose Vision for Montauk," *New York Times* (April 22, 1984), VIII: 10; Alastair Gordon, "Fisher's Montauk Legacy Getting a New Look," *New York Times* (December 23, 1984), XXI: 1, 4; Robert B. Mackay, Anthony K. Baker, and Carol A. Traynor, eds., *Long Island Country Houses and Their Architects, 1860–1940* (New York: Society for the Preservation of Long Island Antiquities in association with W.W. Norton, 1997), 384; Mark S. Foster, *Castles in the Sand: The Life and Times of Carl Graham Fisher* (Gainesville: University Press of Florida, 2000), 248–61; Alastair Gordon, *Weekend Utopia: Modern Living in the Hamptons* (New York: Princeton Architectural Press, 2001), 19, 21–23; Marianne Lamonaca and Jonathan Mogul, eds., *Grand Hotels of the Jazz Age: The Architecture of Schultze & Weaver* (New York: Princeton Architectural Press, 2005), 184–89.

109 *Arcady* (New York: Arcady Executives, 1929), cover. Also see "Main Hotel of a Beach Club," *Architecture* 60 (July 1929): 52; Walter H. Kilham, *Raymond Hood, Architect: Form Through Function in the American Skyscraper* (New York: Architectural Book Publishing, 1973), 106–7; Rosemarie Bletter, "King Kong en Arcadie," *Archithese* 20 (1976): 25–34; Giorgio Ciucci et al., *The American City: From the Civil War to the New Deal* (Cambridge, Mass.: MIT Press, 1979), 521; Robert A. M. Stern with Thomas Catalano, *Raymond M. Hood* (New York: Institute for Architecture and Urban Studies; New York: Rizzoli International Publications, 1982), 19, 70–72; Barbara F. Stokes, *Myrtle Beach: A History, 1900–1980* (Columbia, S.C.: University of South Carolina Press, 2007), 29–31, 41.

110 Seth Bramson, *Speedway to Sunshine: The Story of the Florida East Coast Railway* (Ontario: Boston Mills, 1984), 17.

111 Herbert Croly, "Notes and Comments: A National Winter Suburb," *Architectural Record* 58 (December 1925): 605–6.

112 For a general discussion of Flagler's role, see Jane Fisher, *Fabulous Hoosier: A Story of American Achievement* (New York: Robert M. McBride & Company, 1947), 93–106, 126–45; John Ney, *Palm Beach* (Boston: Little, Brown, 1966), 75–79; Donald W. Curl, *Mizner's Florida: American Resort Architecture* (New York: Architectural History Foundation; Cambridge, Mass., and London: MIT Press, 1984), 39–41; Stuart B. McIver, *Yesterday's Palm Beach, Including Palm Beach County* (Miami: E. A. Seemann Publishing, 1976), 35–40; Mark S. Foster, *Castles in the Sand: The Life and Times of Carl Graham Fisher* (Gainesville: University Press of Florida, 2000), 136–99. Also see "Via Mizner, Palm Beach, Fla.," *Architecture* 55 (March 1927): 161–64; *The WPA Guide to Florida: The Federal Writers' Project Guide to 1930s Florida* (New York: Oxford University Press, 1939; New York: Pantheon, 1984), 227–31; Stern with Massengale, *The Anglo-American Suburb*, 69–72.

113 Addison Mizner, quoted in Christina Orr, *Addison Mizner: Architect of Dreams and Realities* (Palm Beach: Norton Gallery, 1977), 18. For views of Shingle Style Palm Beach, see Polly Anne Earl, *Palm Beach: The Way We Were* (Palm Beach: Preservation Foundation of Palm Beach, 2001). For discussions of Addison Mizner, see Ida Tarbell, *The Florida Architecture of Addison Mizner* (New York: Helburn, 1928); Barbara D. Hoffstot, *Landmark Architecture of Palm Beach* (Pittsburgh, Pa.: Ober Park, 1947), 11; McIver, *Yesterday's Palm Beach, Including Palm Beach County*; Ada Louise Huxtable, "The Maverick Who Created Palm Beach," *New York Times* (March 20, 1977), II: 27–28; Curl, *Mizner's Florida: American Resort Architecture*.

114 "Everglades Club, Palm Beach, Fla.," *Architecture* 54 (November 1926): 361–64; Curl, *Mizner's Florida*, 38–133.

115 Quoted in Hoffstot, *Landmark Architecture of Palm Beach*, 11.

116 Orr, *Addison Mizner: Architect of Dreams and Realities*, 18.

117 "The Florida House," an interview of Addison Mizner by John Taylor Boyd, *Arts and Decoration* 32 (January 1930): 39–40, quoted in Orr, *Addison Mizner: Architect of Dreams and Realities*, 38.

118 "'House of the Palms,' Mr. Paris E. Singer, Palm Beach, Florida," *The Architect* 5 (March 1926): 624–34.

119 Theodore Pratt, *The Story of Boca Raton* (Boca Raton, Fla.: Roy S. Patten, 1953), 6–11; Orr, *Addison Mizner: Architect of Dreams and Realities*, 40–45; *The Spanish River Papers* 5 (February 1977); *The Spanish River Papers* 7 (October 1978); Jeffrey Limerick, Nancy Ferguson, and Richard Oliver, *America's Grand Resort Hotels* (New York: Random House, 1979), 181–85; *The Spanish River Papers* 11 (Fall 1982); Curl, *Mizner's Florida: American Resort Architecture*, 39–41; Stern, *Pride of Place: Building the American Dream*, 163–66; Donald W. Curl and John P. Johnson, *Boca Raton: A Pictorial History* (Virginia Beach, Va.: Donning Company Publishers, 1990); Caroline Seebohm, *Boca Rococo: How Addison Mizner Invented Florida's Gold Coast* (New York: Clarkson Potter, 2001), 110, 212–21.

120 Addison Mizner, quoted in Curl, *Mizner's Florida*, 138.

121 Curl, *Mizner's Florida*, 164.

122 Virginia Robie, "A Spanish City in Florida," *International Studio* 81 (May 1925): 107–12; Matlack Price, "Coral Gables—Miami," *Arts and Decoration* 22 (January 1925): 2–18; "Indications of Florida's Growth," *Bankers' Magazine* (January 1926): 60; "Something New in Waterfronts," *The Architect* 5 (January 1926): 438, 440; Richard Peck, "Is it Déjà Vu? No, It's the Return of the Palazzo," *New York Times* (September 11, 1977), VIII: 1, 3; Woodrow W. Wilkins, "Coral Gables: 1920s New Town," *Historic Preservation* 30 (January–March 1978): 6–9; Metro-Dade Office of Community and Economic Development, Historic Preservation Division, *Survey Findings in the City of Coral Gables* (September 1980); Stern with Massengale, *The Anglo-American Suburb*, 73–74; Stern, *Pride of Place: Building the American Dream*, 161–63; Roberto M. Behar and Maurice G. Culot, eds., *Coral Gables: An American Garden City* (Paris: Norma Editions, 1997), 31–61; Robert A. M. Stern, "In Praise of Invented Towns," in Cynthia Davidson, ed., *Tradition and Invention in Architecture: Conversations and Essays, Robert A. M. Stern* (New Haven, Conn., and London: Yale University Press, 2011), 39–46; Aristides J. Millas and Ellen J. Uguccioni, *Coral Gables, Miami Riviera: An Architectural Guide* (Miami: Dade Heritage Trust, 2003). Also see *The Story of Coral Gables*, promotional brochure (no date); Tom Martinson, *The Atlas of American Architecture: 2000 Years of Architecture, City Planning, Landscape Architecture and Civil Engineering* (New York: Rizzoli International Publications, 2009), 365.

123 Thomas Adams, "Housing and Community Planning: The Plan for Coconut Grove," *Journal of the American Institute of Architects* 9 (April 1921): 110; John Irwin Bright, "The Town of Coconut Grove, Florida," *Journal of the American Institute of Architects* 9 (April 1921): 110–27; Nicholas N. Patricios, *Building Marvelous Miami* (Gainesville, Fla: University Press of Florida, 1994), 24–28.

124 Witold Rybczynski and Laurie Olin, *Vizcaya: An American Villa and Its Makers* (Philadelphia: University of Pennsylvania Press, 2007).

125 Frank M. Button, quoted in Millas, "Coral Gables, the Chronological Development," in Millas and Uguccioni, *Coral Gables, Miami Riviera*, 26.

126 Scully, "A Dream of Coral Gables," in Behar and Culot, eds., *Coral Gables: An American Garden City*, 39.

127 Quoted in Peck, "Is It Deju Vu? No, It's the Return of the Palazzo": 1, 3.

128 Ellen J. Uguccioni, "Coral Gables, the City Inspired," in Millas and Uguccioni, *Coral Gables, Miami Riviera*, 13.

129 "Interview with George E. Merrick," *Jacksonville Times Union* (January 28, 1925).

130 Millas and Uguccioni, *Coral Gables, Miami Riviera*, 16.

131 These villages are described in *Historic Coral Gables: Self-Guided Tour* (Miami: Junior League of Miami, 1986) and Millas and Uguccioni, *Coral Gables, Miami Riviera*, 79–81. Also see "Study, Group of Houses, Miami, Fla.," *The Architect* 5 (December 1925): 262; Philip Lippincott Goodwin, "Small Houses in the Formal French Style," *Architectural Forum* 44 (March 1926): 169–75; Mark Alan Hewitt, *The Architecture of Mott B. Schmidt* (New York: Rizzoli International Publications, 1991), n.p.

132 For Murphy's work in China, see Jeffrey W. Cody, *Building in China: Henry K. Murphy's "Adaptive Architecture" 1914–1935* (Hong Kong: The Chinese University Press, 2001).

133 Jeffrey W. Cody, *Building in China: Henry K. Murphy's "Adaptive Architecture" 1914–1935* (Hong Kong: The Chinese University Press, 2001), 188–89; Jeffrey W. Cody, *Exporting American Architecture, 1870–2000* (London and New York: Routledge, 2003), 114, 118.

134 Howell Taylor and Theodore J. Moreau, "Municipal Golf Courses, Those in Chicago District and Elsewhere," *Architectural Forum* 42 (March 1925): 161–64; "Coral Gables Inn, Coral Gables, Miami, Florida," *Architectural Record* 57 (April 1925): plates; "Study, Miami Biltmore Hotel, Coral Gables, Fla.," *The Architect* 5 (January 1926): 372; "Coral Gables Elementary School," *Architectural Forum* 48 (March 1928): 380, plate 70.

135 *Coral Gables: America's Finest Suburb* (1927), quoted in Millas, "Coral Gables, the Chronological Development," in Millas and Uguccioni, *Coral Gables, Miami Riviera*, 42.

136 Vincent Scully, "A Dream of Coral Gables," in Behar and Culot, eds., *Coral Gables: An American Garden City*, 34, 36.

137 "Florida Becomes Year Round State," *Wall Street Journal* (September 17, 1925): 11; "Enjoy a Tour of South-Sea-Isle Charm Plus Modern Seaside-Resort Comfort," advertisement, *New York Times* (September 20, 1925): 19; "Hollywood Absorbs Dania," *Wall Street Journal* (January 20, 1926): 6; Jack Kofoed, *The Florida Story* (Garden City, N.Y.: Doubleday, 1960), 111–21; Harold Mehling, *The Most of Everything: The Story of Miami Beach* (New York: Harcourt, Brace and Company, 1960), 45–46; Virginia Elliott TenEick, *History of Hollywood (1920–1950)* (Hollywood, Fla.: City of Hollywood, 1966); Stuart B. McIver, *Dreamers, Schemers and Scalawags* (Sarasota, Fla.: Pineapple Press, 1994), 60–61; Jean-François Lejeune, "The Grid, the Park, and the Model-T—Searching for Paradise: Garden Cities in Florida," in Gabriele Tagliaventi, ed., *Garden City* (Rome: Gangemi Editore, 1994), 240; Douglas Waitley, *Roadside History of Florida* (Missoula, MT: Mountain Press Publishing Company, 1997), 269–71; Mike Sheridan, "Hollywood Beach Revival," *Urban Land* 62 (October 2003): 60–61; Joan Mickelson, *A Guide to Historic Hollywood: A Tour Through Place and Time* (Charleston, S.C.: History Press, 2005).

138 Joseph Wesley Young Jr., quoted in TenEick, *History of Hollywood (1920–1950)*, xviii.

139 Bernhardt E. Muller, "Bernhardt Muller's Dream of Arabian City in Florida Is Reality," *Opa-locka Times* (February 23, 1927): 1; H. Sayre Wheeler, "Opa-locka, Created from the Arabian Nights," *Journal of the American Institute of Architects* 16 (April 1928): 157–58; Metro-Dade Office of Community and Economic Development, Historic Preservation Division, *Survey Findings in the City of Opa-locka* (September 1980); Michel Marriott, "Opa-Locka Journal/Grimy Reality Invades Fantasyland," *New York Times* (February 2, 1989): 16; Suzanne Stephens, "Currents/Old Drawings of a Dream Deferred," *New York Times* (November 5, 1992), C: 3; Catherine Lynn, "Dream and Substance: Araby and the Planning of Opa-locka," *Journal of Decorative and Propaganda Arts* 23 (1998): 163–89; Seth H. Bramson, *The Curtiss-Bright Cities: Hialeah, Miami Springs & Opa Locka* (Charleston, S.C.: History Press, 2008), 115–34; Tom Martinson, *The Atlas of American Architecture: 2000 Years of Architecture, City Planning, Landscape Architecture and Civil Engineering* (New York: Rizzoli International Publications, 2009), 321.

140 For Hialeah and Miami Springs, see *From Wilderness to Metropolis: The History and Architecture of Dade County, Florida, 1825–1940* (Miami: Metropolitan Dade County, 1982), 103–6; Lynn, "Dream and Substance: Araby and the Planning of Opa-locka": 164–65; Seth H. Bramson, *The Curtiss-Bright Cities: Hialeah, Miami Springs & Opa Locka*, 25–68, 81–114.

141 Muller, "Bernhardt Muller's Dream of Arabian City in Florida Is Reality": 1, quoted in Lynn, "Dream and Substance: Araby and the Planning of Opa-locka": 164.

142 For examples of Muller's work in the northeast, see "Gate Lodge, Estate of Carl L. Schweinler, West Orange, New Jersey," *American Architect* 141 (June 1932): 55–56; "House of Arthur R. Rule, Westfield, New Jersey," *American Architect* 141 (June 1932): 54; "House of C. J. Goodman, Old Short Hills, New Jersey," *American Architect* 142 (September 1932): 63; "House of A. J. Travers, Short Hills, New Jersey," *American Architect* 142 (November 1932): 52–54.

143 Quoted in Lynn, "Dream and Substance: Araby and the Planning of Opa-locka": 170.

144 Federal Writers' Project of the Works Progress Administration, *The WPA Guide to Florida* (Florida and New York: Oxford University Press, 1939; New York: Pantheon Books, 1984), 269; Gene Plowden, *Those Amazing Ringlings and Their Circus* (Caldwell, Id.: Caxton Printers, 1967), 142–58; David C. Weeks, *Ringling: The Florida Years, 1911–1936* (Gainesville: University Press of Florida, 1993), 89–105; Pat Ringling Buck, *The Ringling Legacy* (self published, 1995), 15–17; John Howey, *The Sarasota School of Architecture: 1941–1966* (Cambridge, Mass.: MIT Press, 1995), 15–19; Amy A. Elder, *Sarasota* (Charleston, S.C.: Arcadia, 2003), 114–18; Jeff LaHurd, *Quintessential Sarasota: Stories and Pictures from the 1920s to the 1950s* (Charleston, S.C.: History Press, 2004), 44–46; Jeff LaHurd, *Sarasota: A Sentimental Journey in Vintage Images* (Charleston, S.C.: History Press, 2004), 49; Jeff LaHurd, *Gulf Coast Chronicles: Remembering Sarasota's Past* (Charleston, S.C.: History Press, 2005), 29, 33–35.

145 John Nolen, *New Towns for Old* (Boston: Marshall Jones, 1927; Amherst and Boston: University of Massachusetts Press, 2005), 197, 199; John Loretz Hancock, "John Nolen and the American City Planning Movement: A History of Culture Change and Community Response, 1900–1940" (Ph.D. diss., University of Pennsylvania, 1964): 394, 398–99; Stewart Jerome Wilson, "John Nolen: An Overview of His Career" (Master's thesis, University of Oregon, 1982): 77; James Arthur Glass, "John Nolen and the Planning of New Towns: Three Case Studies" (Ph.D. diss., Cornell University, 1984): 258 (n.11); John Hancock, "John Nolen: New Towns in Florida," *The New City* 1 (Fall 1991): 68–87; Lejeune, "The Grid, the Park, and the Model-T—Searching for Paradise: Garden Cities in Florida," in Tagliaventi, ed., *Garden City*, 246–47; Thomas E. Low, "The Chautauquans and Progressives in Florida," *Journal of Decorative and Propaganda Arts* 23 (1998): 306–21.

146 *Comprehensive City Plan: Sarasota, Florida* (1925), reprinted at www.sarasotagov.com; Nolen, *New Towns for Old*, 193, 196–97; Hancock, "John Nolen and the American City Planning Movement": 394–97; Janet Snyder Matthews, *Sarasota: Journey to Centennial* (Sarasota, Fla.: Pine Level Press, 1989), 113–20; John F. Eades, "City Planning in West Palm Beach, Florida, During the 1920s," (Master's thesis, Florida Atlantic University, 1991): 56–68, 64–90, 102–14, 127; Hancock, "John Nolen: New Towns in Florida": 86–87; Lejeune, "The Grid, the Park, and the Model-T—Searching for Paradise: Garden Cities in Florida," in Tagliaventi, ed., *Garden City*, 242–44; R. Bruce Stephenson, *Visions of Eden: Environmentalism, Urban Planning, and City Building in St. Petersburg, Florida, 1900–1995* (Columbus: Ohio State University Press, 1997), 46–69, 70–85; Bruce Stephenson, "The Roots of the New Urbanism: John Nolen's Garden City Ethic," *Journal of Planning History* 1 (May 2002): 99–123.

147 Nolen, *New Towns for Old*, 138, 195–96; "Neue Siedlungsplane und Neue Lebensbedingungen," *Der Städtebau* 22 (April 1927): 50–54; Nolen, *New Towns for Old*, 138; Wilson, "John Nolen: An Overview of His Career": 77, plate 34; Hancock, "John Nolen: New Towns in Florida": 81; Lejeune, "The Grid, the Park, and the Model-T—Searching for Paradise: Garden Cities in Florida," in Tagliaventi, ed., *Garden City*, 241; Low, "The Chautauquans and Progressives in Florida": 317–19.

148 Low, "The Chautauquans and Progressives in Florida": 316–17. Also see "Neue Siedlungsplane und Neue Lebensbedingungen": 52; Hancock, "John Nolen: New Towns in Florida": 86; Lejeune, "The Grid, the Park, and the Model-T—Searching for Paradise: Garden Cities in Florida," in Tagliaventi, ed., *Garden City*, 241.

149 Nolen, *New Towns for Old*, 196; Wayne W. Wood, *Jacksonville's Architectural Heritage: Landmarks for the Future*, rev. ed. (Gainesville, Fla.: University Press of Florida, 1996), 270–81. Also see John Nolen, "What Florida Can Teach and Learn," *American City* 34 (June 1926): 65–66; "Neue Siedlungsplane und Neue Lebensbedingungen": 53; Hancock, "John Nolen: New Towns in Florida": 84–85; Lejeune, "The Grid, the Park, and the Model-T—Searching for Paradise: Garden Cities in Florida," in Tagliaventi, ed., *Garden City*, 241; Low, "The Chautauquans and Progressives in Florida": 317–18.

150 Quoted in Wood, *Jacksonville's Architectural Heritage: Landmarks for the* Future, 274.

Chapter 5

1 Raymond Unwin, *Town Planning in Practice* (London: T. Fisher Unwin, 1909; New York: Princeton University Press, 1994), 320, 376, 379, 393, fig. 169; Bridget Cherry and Nikolaus Pevsner, *London 3: North West* (London: Penguin Books, 1991, 1999), 178–79, fig. 74; John Delafons, "Brentham Estate—A New Community, 1901," *Town & Country Planning* 61 (November–December 1992): 317–19; Peter Hall, "Brentham—London's Forgotten Garden Suburb," *Town & Country Planning* 68 (June 1999): 180–81; Aileen Reid, *Brentham: A History of the Pioneer Garden Suburb 1901–2001* (London: Brentham Heritage Society, 2000); Tanis Hinchcliffe, "Brentham," book review, *London Journal* 27 (No. 2, 2000): 98–99; Chris Coates, *Utopia Britannica, vol. 1: British Utopian Experiments: 1325 to 1945* (London: Diggers & Dreamers Publications, 2001), 210–11; Dennis Hardy, "A Success Story of Housing and Community," *Built Environment* (27 (No. 1, 2001): 59–60; Mervyn Miller, "Brentham," book review, *Newsletter of the Charles Rennie Mackintosh Society* 80 (Spring 2001): 8; Anne Riches, "Brentham," book review, *Newsletters of the Society of Architectural Historians of Great Britain* 74 (Autumn 2001): 18–19; Peter Hall, *Cities of Tomorrow*, 3rd ed. (Oxford: Blackwell Publishing 2002), 104–6; Mervyn Miller, "The Origins of the Garden City Residential Neighborhood," in Kermit C. Parsons and David Schuyler, eds., *From Garden City to Green City: The Legacy of Ebenezer Howard* (Baltimore and London: Johns Hopkins University Press, 2002), 120, fig. 38; Mervyn Miller, "Garden Cities and Suburbs: At Home and Abroad," *Journal of Planning History* 1 (February 2002): 6–28.

2 Cherry and Pevsner, *London 3: North West*, 178.

3 Cherry and Pevsner, *London 3: North West*, 178.

4 William Webb, *Garden First in Land Development* (London: Longmans, Green and Co., 1919); Bridget Cherry and Nikolaus Pevsner, *London 2: South* (London: Penguin, 1983), 235–36.

5 Webb, *Garden First in Land Development*, 11, 15.

6 Walter L. Creese, *The Search for Environment*, expanded edition (New Haven, Conn.: Yale University Press, 1966; Baltimore and London: Johns Hopkins University Press, 1992), 235. Also see Mrs. S. A. Barnett, "The Hampstead Garden Suburb," *Garden City* (May 1907): 326–28; *Town Planning and Modern Architecture at the Hampstead Garden*

Suburb (London: Garden Suburb Development Co. Ltd., 1908); Raymond Unwin, *Town Planning in Practice* (London: T. Fisher Unwin, 1909; New York: Princeton University Press, 1994), 227–28; "Die Neue Gartenvorstadt in London-Hampstead," *Der Städtebau* (1909): 99–103, figs. 57–64; H. E. von Berlepsch-Valendas, "Hampstead," *Kunst und Kunsthandwerk* 12 (1909): 241–84; Francis S. Swales, "Notes from Europe," *American Architect* 96 (September 1, 1909): 77–82; "Rapid Growth of the Garden City Movement, Which Promises to Reorganize Social Conditions All Over the World," *The Craftsman* 17 (December 1909): 296–310; *Garden Suburbs: Town Planning and Modern Architecture* (London: T. Fisher Unwin, 1910), 1–37, 83–90, 98–116; R. Randal Phillips, "The Hampstead Garden Suburb," *The Brickbuilder* (January 1910): 9–12; Barry Parker, "Modern Country Homes in England: Number Twelve," *The Craftsman* 20 (April 1911): 69–79; Barry Parker, "Modern Country Homes in England: Number Fourteen," *The Craftsman* 20 (June 1911): 278–88; Barry Parker, "Modern Country Homes in England: Number Twenty," *The Craftsman* 21 (December 1911): 290–303; "The New Hampstead Garden Suburb," *Architectural Review* 18 (November 1912): 126–28; Lawrence Weaver, *Houses and Gardens By Sir Edwin Lutyens* (London: Country Life, 1913), 284–90; Lawrence Veiller, "Industrial Housing Developments in America," *Architectural Record* 44 (August 1918): 140–51; William L. Hare, "Hampstead Garden Suburb," *Town and Country Planning* 4 (June 1936): 86–93; Christopher Hussey, "Hampstead Garden Suburb," *Country Life* 80 (October 17, 1936): 408–14; *The Hampstead Garden Suburb: Its Achievements and Significance* (London: Hampstead Garden Suburb Trust, Ltd., 1937); P. T. Harrison, "Planning a Suburb," *Journal of the Town Planning Institute* 24 (June 1938): 260–73; A. S. G. Butler, *The Architecture of Sir Edwin Lutyens, vol. 2* (London: Country Life, 1950), 18–22, plates xi–xix, figs. 79–98; Christopher Hussey, *The Life of Sir Edwin Lutyens* (London: Country Life, 1950), 186–92; Nikolaus Pevsner and Bridget Cherry, *London 4: North* (1951; New Haven, Conn. and London: Yale University Press, 1998), 139–55; R. L. Reiss, "Henrietta Octavia Barnett and Hampstead Garden Suburb," *Town and Country Planning* 25 (July 1957): 277–82; Percy Johnson-Marshall, "Hampstead Garden Suburb," *Architects' Journal* 126 (July 11, 1957): 83, 85–86; W. A. Eden, "Hampstead Garden Suburb 1907–1957," *RIBA Journal* 64 (October 1957): 489–95; Walter Creese, "Parker and Unwin: Architects of Totality," *Journal of the Society of Architectural Historians* 22 (October 1963): 161–70; James D. Kornwolf, *M. H. Baillie Scott and the Arts and Crafts Movement* (Baltimore: Johns Hopkins Press, 1972), 288–94, 305–16; Geoffrey Lee, "London's Edwardian Village," *Country Life* 156 (September 19, 1974): 754–56; Brigid Grafton Green, *Hampstead Garden Suburb 1907–1977* (London: Hampstead Garden Suburb Residents' Association, 1977); Susan Beattie, *A Revolution in London Housing: LCC Housing Architects and Their Work 1893–1914* (London: Architectural Press, 1980), 110–20; Gérard Bauer, Gildas Baudez, Jean-Michel Roux, *Banlieues de charme, ou, L'art des quartiers-jardins* (Aix-en-Provence: Pandora, 1980), 179–203; Robert A. M. Stern with John Massengale, *The Anglo-American Suburb* (London: Architectural Design, 1981), 41–44; Robert Kornfeld Jr., "Hampstead Garden Suburb and the Leading Players in Its Creation," (unpublished paper, Columbia University, January 1985); Mervyn Miller, *Raymond Unwin: Garden Cities and Town Planning* (Leicester: Leicester University Press, 1992), 78–103; Mervyn Miller and A. Stuart Gray, *Hampstead Garden Suburb* (Chichester, Sussex: Phillimore, 1992); Paolo Bertozzi, "The Extension of the Pattern: Hampstead Garden Suburb," in Gabriele Tagliaventi, ed., *Garden City* (Rome: Gangemi Editore, 1994), 210–19; Diane Haight, *Baillie Scott: The Artistic House* (London: Academy Editions, 1995), 54–59; 96–101, 128; Atsushi Katagi, "Quadrangles in Hampstead Garden Suburb," *Nihon Kenchiku Gakkai Keikakukei ronbun hokoku shu* (April 1996): 239–48; Standish Meacham, *Regaining Paradise: Englishness and the Early Garden City Movement* (New Haven, Conn., and London: Yale University Press, 1999), 146–77; Elizabeth Wilhide, *Sir Edwin Lutyens: Designing in the English Tradition* (New York: Harry N. Abrams, 2000), 38; Peter Hall, *Cities of Tomorrow*, 3rd ed. (Oxford, England: Blackwell Publishing 2002), 104–10; Mervyn Miller, "The Origins of the Garden City Residential Neighborhood," in Kermit C. Parsons and David Schuyler, eds., *From Garden City to Green City: The Legacy of Ebenezer Howard* (Baltimore and London: Johns Hopkins University Press, 2002), 99–130; Mervyn Miller, "Garden Cities and Suburbs: At Home and Abroad," *Journal of Planning History* 1 (February 2002): 6–28; Andrés Duany, Elizabeth Plater-Zyberk, and Robert Alminana, *The New Civic Art: Elements of Town Planning* (New York: Rizzoli International Publications, 2003), 39, 165, 189; William Palin, "St. Jude's Vicarage," *Country Life* 198 (March 25, 2004): 86–89; Briant Short, *England's Landscape: The South East* (London: Collins, 2006), 99, 229; Mervyn Miller, *Hampstead Garden Suburb: Arts and Crafts Utopia?* (Chichester, Sussex: Phillimore, 2006); Vittorio Magnago Lampugnani, *Die Stadt im 20. Jahrhundert* (Berlin: Verlag Klaus Wagenbach, 2010), 33–36.

7 Miller and Gray, *Hampstead Garden Suburb* (1992), 7, 19.

8 Barnett, "The Hampstead Garden Suburb": 326–28.

9 Unwin, *Columbia University Lectures 1936–1937*, 46, quoted in Creese, *The Search for Environment* (1992), 239.

10 Creese, *The Search for Environment* (1992), 239.

11 Steen Eiler Rasmussen, "A Great Planning Achievement," *Town and Country Planning* (July 1957): 286, quoted in Creese, *The Search for Environment* (1992), 239.

12 Miller, "The Origins of the Garden City Residential Neighborhood," in Parsons and Schuyler, eds., *From Garden City to Green City*, 115.

13 Creese, *The Search for Environment* (1992), 240.

14 Unwin, *Town Planning in Practice*, 154, quoted in Miller and Gray, *Hampstead Garden Suburb* (1992), 62.

15 Raymond Unwin, "Building and Natural Beauty," in Barry Parker and Raymond Unwin, *The Art of Building a Home* (London: Longmans, 1901), 85, quoted in Miller and Gray, *Hampstead Garden Suburb* (1992), 62.

16 Kornwolf, *Baillie Scott and the Arts and Crafts Movement*, 308–12.

17 Raymond Unwin, "Preface," in *Town Planning and Modern Architecture at the Hampstead Garden Suburb*, 3, quoted in Miller and Gray, *Hampstead Garden Suburb* (1992), 72.

18 J. D. Kornwolf, quoted in Kornfeld Jr., "Hampstead Garden Suburb and the Leading Players in its Creation," 9–10. Originally published as Kornwolf, *Baillie Scott and the Arts and Crafts Movement*, 305.

19 Hussey, *The Life of Sir Edwin Lutyens*, 189.

20 Butler, *The Architecture of Sir Edwin Lutyens, vol. 2*, 18, plate X.

21 Edwin Lutyens, quoted in Hussey, *The Life of Sir Edwin Lutyens*, 187, also quoted in Miller and Gray, *Hampstead Garden Suburb* (1992), 77.

22 Kornfeld., "Hampstead Garden Suburb and the Leading Players in Its Creation": 1–2.

23 Miller and Gray, *Hampstead Garden Suburb* (1992), 99.

24 Phillips, "The Hampstead Garden Suburb": 9–12, quoted in Kornfeld, "Hampstead Garden Suburb and the Leading Players in Its Creation": 6. Phillips's books included *The Book of Bungalows* (New York: Scribner's, 1922) and *The Modern English Interior* (London: Country Life, 1928).

25 Steen Eiler Rasmussen, quoted in Creese, *The Search for Environment*, 247. Originally published as S. E. Rasmussen, "A Great Planning Achievement," *Town and Country Planning* (July 1957): 285.

26 "Knebworth Garden Village," *Garden Cities and Town Planning* 1 (May 1911): 94, 97–98. Also see "A Recent Example of Town Planning: Knebworth," *Architectural Review* 27 (April 1910): 252–55; Patrick Abercrombie, "A Comparative Review of 'Garden City' Schemes in England," *Town Planning Review* 1 (July 1910): 116, plate 40; "Notes and Comments," *Architectural Record* 29 (February 1911): 190; "Opening of Knebworth Garden Village," *Garden Cities and Town Planning* 2 (May 15, 1912): 104–8; Ewart G. Culpin, *The Garden City Movement Up-to-Date* (London: Garden Cities and Town Planning Association, 1913), 35–36; Werner Hegemann and Elbert Peets, *The American Vitruvius: An Architect's Handbook of Civic Art* (New York: Architectural Book Publishing, 1922), 264; Nikolaus Pevsner and Bridget Cherry, *Hertfordshire*, rev. ed. (New Haven, Conn., and London: Yale University Press, 1977), 221; Frank A. Richardson, *Knebworth, the Story of a Hertfordshire Village* (Knebworth: Knebworth Village Association Committee, 1982), 81; Michael Simpson, *Thomas Adams and the Modern Planning Movement* (London: Mansell, 1985), 48–50; Ann Judge, "Knebworth Garden Village: An Idea That Never Materialised" (January 2006), http://www.hertsmemories.org.uk; "Deards End Lane Conservation Area Appraisal" (February 2008), http://www.north-herts.gov.uk.

27 For the clubhouse, see *The Smaller House: Being Selected Examples of the Latest Practice in Modern English Domestic Architecture* (London: Architectural Press, 1924), 33–34; Lawrence Weaver, *Houses and Gardens by Sir Edwin Lutyens, R.A.* (London: Country Life; New York: Charles Scribner's Sons, 1925), 236–37; Christopher Hussey, *The Life of Sir Edwin Lutyens* (London: Country Life; New York: Charles Scribner's Sons, 1950), 135–36; Pevsner and Cherry, *Hertfordshire*, 221; Jane Brown, *Lutyens and the Edwardians: An English Architect and His Clients* (London and New York: Viking Press, 1996), 121, 126–27; Jane Ridley, *A Life of Sir Edwin Lutyens: The Architect and His Wife* (London: Chatto & Windus, 2002), 174.

28 "A Recent Example of Town Planning: Knebworth": 254.

29 Abercrombie, "A Comparative Review of 'Garden City' Schemes in England": 116.

30 Simpson, *Thomas Adams and the Modern Planning Movement*, 48, 50.

31 Pevsner and Cherry, *Hertfordshire*, 221; A.S.G. Butler, *The Architecture of Sir Edwin Lutyens I: Country Houses* (Woodbridge, Suffolk: Antique Collectors' Club, 1984), 59, plate 97.

32 Hussey, *The Life of Sir Edwin Lutyens*, 326; Pevsner and Cherry, *Hertfordshire*, 221; Gavin Stamp, *Edwin Lutyens: Country Houses: From the Archives of Country Life* (London: Aurum Press, 2001), 14.

33 R.W. Johnson, "Cinderella Estate," *Journal of the Town Planning Institute* 57 (December 1971): 461–62. Also see J. S. Nettlefold, "Town Planning Experiment at Harborne," *Town Planning Review* 2 (July 1911): 111, plate 57; J. S. Nettlefold, *Practical Town Planning* (London: St. Catherine Press, 1914), 98–102; Nikolaus Pevsner and Alexandra Wedgewood, *Warwickshire* (New Haven, Conn., and London: Yale University Press, 1966), 186; Barbara Shackley, "Frederick William Martin," in Phillada Ballard, ed., *Birmingham's Victorian and Edwardian Architects* (Wetherby: Oblong Creative for the Birmingham and West Midlands Group of the Victorian Society, 2009), 352–57; Mervyn Miller, *Moore Pool Conservation Area Report* (June 30, 2009); http://www.moorpool.com.

34 Nettlefold, *Practical Town Planning*, 99–100.

35 Pevsner and Wedgewood, *Warwickshire*, 186.

36 Miller, *Moore Pool Conservation Area Report*, 4.

37 http://www.english-heritage.org.uk/discover/people-and-places/womens-history/visible-in-stone/architects-builders-garden-cities. Also see "Oldham," *Garden Cities and Town Planning* 4 (May 1909): 197; "Oldham's Garden Suburb," *Garden Cities and Town Planning* 4 (August 1909): 233; "Oldham," *Town Planning Review* 1 (July 1910): 124, plate 47; "Notes and Comments," *Architectural Record* 29 (February 1911): 190; Ewart G. Culpin, *The Garden City Movement Up-to-Date* (London: Garden Cities and Town Planning Association, 1913), 40; Gillian Darley, *Villages of Vision* (London: Architectural Press, 1975), 141; Clare Hartwell, Matthew Hyde and Nikolaus Pevsner, *Lancashire: Manchester and the South-East* (New Haven, Conn., and London: Yale University Press, 2004), 549; Karen Doherty, "Vapour Trails of Pilot's Past," http://www.oldham-chronicle.co.uk/news-features/8/news-headlines/44043; http://www.oldhamgardensuburb.co.uk.

38 "Oldham," *Town Planning Review*: 124.

39 "Oldham," *Town Planning Review*: 124.

40 "Warrington," *The Garden City* 1 (January 1907): 258; "An Interesting Scheme; A Girdle of Garden Suburbs," *The Garden City* 2 (August 1907): 396–98; "Warrington," *The Garden City* 2 (January 1908): 498; "The Warrington Garden Suburbs Scheme," *Garden Cities and Town Planning* 3 (December 1908): 156–60; Patrick Abercrombie, "A Comparative Review of 'Garden City' Schemes in England," *Town Planning Review* 1 (July 1910): 112–13, plates 34–35; Ewart G. Culpin, *The Garden City Movement Up-to-Date* (London: Garden Cities and Town Planning Association, 1913), 44–46; Richard Pollard and Nikolaus Pevsner, *Lancashire: Liverpool and the South-West* (1969; New Haven, Conn., and London: Yale University Press, 2006), 87, 633–34.

41 Richard Pollard and Nikolaus Pevsner, *Lancashire: Liverpool and the South-West* (1969; New Haven, Conn., and London: Yale University Press, 2006), 87, 252, 500. Also see "The Liverpool Garden Suburb Tenants, Limited," *Town Planning Review* 1 (July 1910): 174; "Liverpool Garden Suburb," *Town Planning Review* 2 (January 1911): 333–34, plate 112;

"Liverpool Garden Suburb, Wavertree," *Town Planning Review* 2 (October 1911): 243, plate 99; "Progress at Liverpool," *Garden Cities and Town Planning* 2 (May 1912): 111–12; G. L. Sutcliffe, "The Liverpool Garden Suburb," *Garden Cities and Town Planning* 2 (August 1912): 182–84; Ewart G. Culpin, *The Garden City Movement Up-to-Date* (London: Garden Cities and Town Planning Association, 1913), 54, 55–56; Perry R. MacNeille, *The Industrial Village* (New York: Standard Buildings, 1913), 7; Michael Simpson, *Thomas Adams and the Modern Planning Movement* (London and New York: Mansell, 1985), 51–52; Christopher Crouch, "Village Soap," *RIBA Journal* 95 (November 1988): 52–53.

42 "Alkrington Hall Estate," *Garden Cities and Town Planning* 1 (November 1906): 214–15; "Alkrington, near Manchester," *Garden Cities and Town Planning* 4 (May 1909): 207; "A Recent Example of Town Planning: Alkrington," *Architectural Review* 27 (June 1910): 370–71; Patrick Abercrombie, "A Comparative Review of 'Garden City' Schemes in England, Part II," *Town Planning Review* 1 (July 1910): 111; "Alkrington Garden Village, Middleton, Manchester," *Garden Cities and Town Planning* (May 1911): 95, 98–99; "The Alkrington Garden Village," *Garden Cities and Town Planning* (September 1911): 195; Ewart G. Culpin, *The Garden City Movement Up-to-Date* (London: Garden Cities and Town Planning Association, 1913), 22, 23; Nelson D. Lewis, *The Planning of the Modern City* (New York: Wiley, 1916), 304–5, plate 85; Clare Hartwell, Matthew Hyde, and Nikolaus Pevsner, *Lancashire: Manchester and the South-East* (1969; New Haven and London: Yale University Press, 2004), 82, 517–18; Gordon E. Cherry, "George Pepler, 1882–1959," in Gordon E. Cherry, ed., *Pioneers in British Planning* (London: Architectural Press, 1981), 132; Michael Simpson, "Thomas Adams, 1871–1940," in Cherry, ed., *Pioneers in British Planning*, 22–23; Michael Simpson, *Thomas Adams and the Modern Planning Movement* (London and New York: Mansell, 1985), 47–48; Angus J. L. Winchester, ed., *England's Landscape: The North West* (London: Collins, 2006), 184.

43 Michael Simpson, *Thomas Adams and the Modern Planning Movement* (London: Mansell, 1985), 42–44. Also see Thomas Adams, "A Garden City in the Black Country," *The Garden City* 2 (June 1907): 348–49; "Fallings Park Estate," *The Garden City* 2 (July 1907): 370–71; "Fallings Park Garden Suburb," *The Garden City* 2 (January 1908): 496–98; Thomas Adams, "Some New Garden Suburb Schemes," *Garden Cities and Town Planning* 4 (May 1909): 206–7; Patrick Abercrombie, "A Comparative Review of Examples of Modern Town Planning and 'Garden City' Schemes in England, Part II," *Town Planning Review* 1 (July 1910): 122, plate 46; Ewart G. Culpin, *The Garden City Movement Up-to-Date* (London: Garden Cities and Town Planning Association, 1913), 28; Nikolaus Pevsner, *Staffordshire* (New Haven, Conn., and London: Yale University Press, 1974), 321; Mervyn Miller, "Garden Cities and Suburbs: At Home and Abroad," *Journal of Planning History* 1 (February 2002): 11.

44 "Fallings Park Garden Suburb": 496.

45 Adams, "Some New Garden Suburb Schemes": 206.

46 Simpson, *Thomas Adams and the Modern Planning Movement*, 42.

47 Simpson, *Thomas Adams and the Modern Planning Movement*, 44.

48 Pevsner, *Staffordshire*, 321.

49 "A Garden City near Bristol," *The Garden City* 1 (February 1906): 5; "At Home and Abroad: Bristol," *Garden Cities and Town Planning* 4 (January–February 1909): 168; "A Bristol Garden Suburb," *Garden Cities and Town Planning* 4 (May 1909): 195; Patrick Abercrombie, "A Comparative Review of 'Garden City' Schemes in England, Part II," *Town Planning Review* 1 (July 1910): 114, plate 37; "Bristol Garden Suburb," *Garden Cities and Town Planning* (August 1911): 177; Ewart G. Culpin, *The Garden City Movement Up-to-Date* (London: Garden Cities and Town Planning Association, 1913), 25; Michael Simpson, "Thomas Adams, 1871–1940," in Gordon E. Cherry, ed., *Pioneers in British Planning* (London: Architectural Press, 1981), 132; Michael Simpson, *Thomas Adams and the Modern Planning Movement* (London and New York: Mansell, 1985), 50–51.

50 *Garden Suburbs, Town Planning and Modern Architecture* (London: T. Fisher Unwin, 1910), 38–58; S. D. Adshead, "Romford Garden Suburb, Gidea Park: Cottage Exhibition and Town Plan," *Town Planning Review* 2 (July 1911): 124–27; Patrick Abercrombie, "A Tour of the Garden Cities," *Town Planning Review* 2 (October 1911): 230–33, plate 96; "Town Planning at Gidea Park," *Garden Cities and Town Planning* 2 (July 15, 1912): 154–56; Ewart G. Culpin, *The Garden City Movement Up-to-Date* (London: Garden Cities and Town Planning Association, 1913), 30; R. Randal Phillips, "Gidea Park: The Newest English Garden Suburb," *Brickbuilder* 22 (October 1913): 229–32; Richard B. Watrous, "Personal Observations of Some Developments in Housing in Europe," *Journal of the American Institute of Architects* 2 (July 1914): 332–43; "An English Competition for a Low-Cost Housing Exhibition in Connection with the Opening of 'Gidea Park,' a London 'Garden City' Suburb," *Architectural Review* 5 (April 1917): 78–82; Frank Chouteau Brown, "Gidea Park: A Typical English 'Garden City' Development," *Architectural Review* 5 (April 1917): 73–77; Roderick Gradidge and David Prout, *Worlds Apart* (London: The Victorian Society, 1989); Diane Haight, *Baillie Scott: The Artistic House* (London: Academy Editions, 1995), 95, 128; John East, *The Hundred Best Houses: An Afternoon Walk in Gidea Park, July 1998* (London: The Twentieth Century Society, 1998); *London Suburbs* (London: Merrell Holberton, 1999), 204; Mervyn Miller, "Garden Cities and Suburbs: At Home and Abroad," *Journal of Planning History* 1 (February 2002): 6–28; David Davidson, *Return to Gidea Park: A Walk Led by David Davidson and Nick Collins* (London: The Victorian Society, 2004); Bridget Cherry, Charles O'Brien, and Nikolaus Pevsner, *London 5: East* (1954; New Haven, Conn., and London: Yale University Press, 2005), 61, 202–5.

51 Phillips, "Gidea Park: The Newest English Garden Suburb": 230.

52 East, *The Hundred Best Houses: An Afternoon Walk in Gidea Park, July 1998*, n.p.

53 Cherry, O'Brien, and Pevsner, *London 5: East*, 202.

54 M. H. Baillie Scott, quoted in James D. Kornwolf, *M. H. Baillie Scott and the Arts and Crafts Movement* (Baltimore: Johns Hopkins Press, 1972), 424, also quoted in East, *The Best Hundred Houses: An Afternoon Walk in Gidea Park, July 1998*, n.p.

55 "Ruislip Manor Estate: Competition Award," *Town Planning Review* 1 (January 1911): 334–38; "The Ruislip Manor Competition: A Study in Comparative Town Planning," *Architectural Review* 29 (March 1911): 171–80; "Ruislip Manor," *Garden Cities and Town Planning* 1 (April 1911): 63; Ewart G. Culpin, *The Garden City Movement Up-To-Date* (London: Garden Cities and Town Planning Association, 1913), 41–43; W. Thompson, "Ruislip Manor Town Planning Scheme," *Garden Cities and Town Planning* 3 (January 1913): 7–15; W. Thompson, "The Ruislip-Northwood and Ruislip-Manor Joint Town Planning Scheme," *Town Planning Review* 4 (July 1913): 133–44, plate 32; Henry R. Aldridge, *The Case for Town Planning* (London: National Housing and Town Planning Council, 1915), 529–612; E. R. Abbott and F. M. Elgood, "The Ruislip-Northwood Scheme," *Town Planning Institute, British Papers & Discussions, 1914–15* 1 (1915): 1–26; Frank Chouteau Brown, "'Ruislip Manor': A Typical English Housing Suburb and Its Development," *Architectural Review* 6 (January 1918): 6–10; A.C. Holliday, "The Site Planning of Housing Schemes," *Town Planning Review* 8 (December 1920): 135–38; C. H. James and F. R. Yerbury, *Small Houses for the Community* (London: Crosby Lockwood & Son, 1924), plates 19–27; Clarence S. Stein, "Post-War Housing at Ruislip-Northwood," *Journal of the American Institute of Architects* 12 (May 1924): 225–29; Bridget Cherry and Nikolaus Pevsner, *London 3, North West* (1991; London: Penguin, 2001), 350–51; Mervyn Miller and A. Stuart Gray, *Hampstead Garden Suburb* (Chichester, Sussex: Phillimore, 1992), 103–4.

56 "The Ruislip Manor Competition: A Study in Comparative Town Planning": 171, 179.

57 Stein, "Post-War Housing at Ruislip-Northwood": 225.

58 Ewart G. Culpin, *The Garden City Movement Up-to-Date* (London: Garden Cities and Town Planning Association, 1913), 45; "A New Co-Partnership Suburb," *Garden Cities and Town Planning* 3 (July 15, 1913): 191–92; Aileen Reid, *Brentham: A History of the Pioneer Garden Suburb, 1901–2001* (London: Brentham Heritage Society, 2000), 162; "Sutton's Garden Suburb," *Sutton Scene* (June/July 2004): 12; *Sutton Garden Suburb Conservation Area Character Appraisal* (London Borough of Sutton, June 2006).

59 "Whiteley Village," http://www.artsandcraftsmovementinsurrey.org.uk. Also see R. Randal Phillips, "Whiteley Village, at Burhill, Surrey," *Architectural Forum* 36 (March 1922): 85–90, plates 38–39; Maurice E. Webb, "Whiteley Village, near Walton-on-Thames, Surrey," *Architectural Review* 56 (October 1924): 126–34; Ian Nairn and Nikolaus Pevsner, *Surrey*, rev. ed. by Bridget Cherry (London: Penguin Books, 1962; New Haven, Conn., and London: Yale University Press, 1971), 520–21; Gillian Darley, *Villages of Vision* (London: Architectural Press, 1975), 125–27; http://www.whiteleyvillage.org.uk.

60 Quoted in Phillips, "Whiteley Village, at Burhill, Surrey": 86–87.

61 Quoted in http://www.whiteleyvillage.org.uk.

62 Phillips, "Whiteley Village, at Burhill, Surrey": 88–89.

63 Webb, "Whiteley Village, near Walton-on-Thames, Surrey": 128.

64 Darley, *Villages of Vision*, 126–27.

65 Bridget Cherry and Nikolaus Pevsner, *London 4, North* (1998; London: Penguin, 1999), 558; *London Suburbs* (London: Merrell Holberton, 1999), 201.

66 Stewart Gillies and Pamela Taylor, *Finchley & Friern Barnet: A Pictorial History* (Chichester, Sussex: Phillimore, 1992), fig. 86; Cherry and Pevsner, *London 4: North*, 42, 129; *London Suburbs*, 179.

67 "Ilford Garden Suburb," *Garden Cities and Town Planning* 4 (July 1910): 300–301; Mary V. Fuller, "Gleanings: London's Newest Garden Suburb," *American City* 3 (November 1910): 248; Ewart G. Culpin, *The Garden City Movement Up-to-Date* (London: Garden Cities and Town Planning Association, 1913), 34; Bridget Cherry, Charles O'Brien, and Nikolaus Pevsner, *London 5: East* (New Haven, Conn., and London: Yale University Press, 2005), 350; Mervyn Miller, "Garden Cities and Suburbs: At Home and Abroad," *Journal of Planning History* 1 (February 2002): 11.

68 Culpin, *The Garden City Movement Up-to-Date*, 34.

69 Miller, "Garden Cities and Suburbs: At Home and Abroad": 11.

70 "Municipal Aid at Hereford," *Garden Cities and Town Planning* 4 (November 1909): 264; Patrick Abercrombie, "A Comparative Review of 'Garden City' Schemes in England," *Town Planning Review* 1 (July 1910): 124–25, plate 48; "Notes and Comments," *Architectural Record* 29 (February 1911): 190; Ewart G. Culpin, *The Garden City Movement Up-to-Date* (London: Garden Cities and Town Planning Association, 1913), 33–34; J. S. Nettlefold, "Hereford Garden Suburb: The Value of Co-operation," *Town Planning Review* 2 (July 1913): 145–49, plate 33; J. S. Nettlefold, *Practical Town Planning* (London: St. Catherine Press, 1914), 102–5; Nikolaus Pevsner, *Herefordshire* (Harmondsworth: Penguin Books, 1963), 190–91; Mervyn Miller, "Garden Cities and Suburbs: At Home and Abroad," *Journal of Planning History* 1 (February 2002): 10.

71 Abercrombie, "A Comparative Review of 'Garden City' Schemes in England": 125.

72 Abercrombie, "A Comparative Review of 'Garden City' Schemes in England": 125.

73 Culpin, *The Garden City Movement Up-to-Date*, 33.

74 Nettlefold, *Practical Town Planning*, 103.

75 Patrick Abercrombie, "A Comparative Review of Examples of Modern Town Planning and 'Garden City' Schemes in England, Part II," *Town Planning Review* 1 (July 1910): 120–21, plates 43–44; Ewart G. Culpin, *The Garden City Movement Up-to-Date* (London: Garden Cities and Town Planning Association, 1913), 53; Gillian Darley, *Villages of Vision* (London: Architectural Press, 1975), 141; Michael Harrison, "Burnage Garden Village: An Ideal Life for Manchester," *Town Planning Review* 47 (July 1976): 256–68; Michael Harrison, "Housing and Town Planning in Manchester before 1914," in Anthony Sutcliffe, ed., *British Town Planning: The Formative Years* (New York: St. Martin's Press; Leicester: Leicester University Press, 1981), 123–32; Clare Hartwell, Matthew Hyde, and Nikolaus Pevsner, *Lancashire: Manchester and the South East* (New Haven, Conn., and London: Yale University Press, 2004), 409–11; Angus J. L. Winchester, ed., *England's Landscape: The North West* (London: Collins, 2006), 184.

76 Patrick Abercrombie, quoted in Harrison, "Burnage Garden Village": 262.

77 Winchester, ed., *England's Landscape: The North West*, 184. Also see Harrison, "Burnage Garden Village": 266; Harrison, "Housing and Town Planning in Manchester before 1914," in Sutcliffe, ed., *British Town Planning: The Formative Years*, 132–40; Hartwell, Hyde, and Pevsner, *Lancashire: Manchester and the South-East*, 82, 418.

78 *Manchester Evening Chronicle* (November 7, 1911), quoted in Winchester, ed., *England's Landscape: The North West*, 184.

79 John H.G. Archer, *Edgar Wood (1860–1935), a Manchester 'Art Nouveau' Architect* (Manchester: H. Rawson & Co., 1966), partially excerpted in David Boardman, "The Fairfield Housing Estate," http://manchesterhistory.net; John H.G. Archer, *Partnership* *in Style: Edgar Wood & J. Henry Sellers*, exhibition catalogue (Manchester: Manchester City Art Gallery, 1975), 67; Clare Hartwell, Matthew Hyde, and Nikolaus Pevsner, *Lancashire: Manchester and the South-East* (London: Penguin Books, 1969; New Haven, Conn., and London: Yale University Press, 2004), 206–7; "Fairfield Tenants Ltd," http://www.utopia-britannica.org.uk.

80 John H. G. Archer, "An Introduction to Two Manchester Architects: Edgar Wood and James Henry Sellers," *Journal of the Royal Institute of British Architects* 62 (December 1954): 50–53. Also see John H. G. Archer, "Edgar Wood: A Notable Manchester Architect," *Transactions of the Lancashire and Cheshire Antiquarian Society* 73–74 (1963–1964): 153–87; Archer, *Edgar Wood (1860–1935), a Manchester 'Art Nouveau' Architect*; J. H. G. Archer, "Edgar Wood and the Architecture of the Arts and Crafts and Art Nouveau Movements in Britain" (Master's thesis, University of Manchester, 1968); Archer, *Partnership in Style: Edgar Wood & J. Henry Sellers*; Jill Seddon, "The Furniture Design of Edgar Wood (1860–1935)," *Burlington Magazine* 117 (December 1975): 859–67; David Morris, *The Buildings of Edgar Wood: Architect, Designer, Artist & Craftsman in Middleton Town Centre* (Rochdale: Rochdale Metropolitan Borough Council), http://manchesterhistory.net.

81 Archer, *Partnership in Style: Edgar Wood & J. Henry Sellers*, 67; Archer, *Edgar Wood (1860–1935), a Manchester 'Art Nouveau' Architect*, quoted in Boardman, "The Fairfield Housing Estate," http://manchesterhistory.net.

82 Hartwell, Hyde, and Pevsner, *Lancashire: Manchester and the South-East*, 206–7.

83 John Newman and Nikolaus Pevsner, *Dorset* (London: Penguin Books, 1972), 57, 108–9; Gillian Darley, *Villages of Vision* (London: Architectural Press, 1975), 124, 139; Campbell de Burgh and John Snoxell, *The Story of Briantspuddle: Dorset's 20th Century Model Village* (Briantspuddle, 1983); Trevor Rowley, *The English Landscape in the Twentieth Century* (London: Hambledon Continuum, 2006), 239; "Briantspuddle, Dorset, England," www.thedorsetpage.com; www.briantspuddle.info.

84 Jeremy Musson, "Debenham House," *Country Life* 199 (February 17, 2005): 52–57.

85 Newman and Pevsner, *Dorset*, 108.

86 Nikolaus Pevsner and Bridget Cherry, *Hertfordshire*, rev. ed. (New Haven, Conn., and London: Yale University Press, 1977), 73. Also see Gillian Darley, *Villages of Vision* (London: Architectural Press, 1975), 124–25; Trevor Rowley, *The English Landscape in the Twentieth Century* (London: Hambledon Continuum, 2006), 239; "Ardeley," http://www.visitoruk.com.

87 Darley, *Villages of Vision*, 125.

88 Cherry and Pevsner, *London 4, North*, 415–16. Also see *London Suburbs*, 187; Isobel Watson, "Rebuilding London: Abraham Davis and his Brothers," *London Journal* 29 (2004): 62–84.

89 Cherry and Pevsner, *London 3: North West*, 128; *London Suburbs*, 182; *Homestead Park Conservation Area: Character Appraisal* (Brent Council, 2005).

90 Cherry and Pevsner, *London 3, North West*, 128.

91 Bridget Cherry and Nikolaus Pevsner, *London 2, South* (1983; London: Penguin, 1999), 76–77, 367–68. Also see A. Trystan Edwards, "The Duchy of Cornwall Estate, Kennington," *Architects' & Builders' Journal* 39 (March 4, 1914): 151–54; Lawrence Weaver, "The Prince of Wales as Landowner: Duchy of Cornwall, Kennington Estate," *Country Life* 6 (June 26, 1915), supplement: 2–8; R. Randal Phillips, "An English Housing Scheme: Duchy of Cornwall Estate at Kennington, London; Adshead & Ramsey, Architects," *Brickbuilder* 25 (March 1916): 69–74; Patrick Abercrombie, "The Duchy of Cornwall Estate at Kennington," in *Houses for Workers* (London: Technical Journals, 1917), 99–101, 103, 105, 107, 109, 111, 115, 119, 121, 125, 127, 129, 131, 133, 135; C. H. James and F. R. Yerbury, *Small Houses for the Community* (London: Crosby Lockwood & Son, 1924), plates 67–70; Simon Pepper and Mark Swenarton, "Neo-Georgian Maison-type," *Architectural Review* 168 (August 1980): 87–92; Alan Powers, "'Architects I Have Known': The Architectural Career of S. D. Adshead," *Architectural History* 24 (1981): 104, 105, 117–19, 122–23, plates 40a–40b.

92 Peter Richmond, *Marketing Modernisms: The Architecture and Influence of Charles Reilly* (Liverpool: Liverpool University Press, 2001).

93 Abercrombie, "The Duchy of Cornwall Estate at Kennington," in *Houses for Workers*, 100.

94 Susan Beattie, *A Revolution in London Housing: LCC Architects and Their Work* (London: Architectural Press, 1980), 97.

95 Frederick Law Olmsted, "Through American Spectacles: an Expert's View of English 'Garden City' Schemes," *Garden Cities and Town Planning* 4 (May 1909): 198–200; London County Council, *Housing of the Working Classes of London* (London: London County Council, 1913), 70–72, 125–30; Richard B. Watrous, "Personal Observations of Some Developments in Housing in Europe," *Journal of the American Institute of Architects* 2 (July 1914): 332–43; "Municipal Housing. No. 1.—the London County Council," *Builder* 114 (March 15, 1918): 173–74; London County Council, *Housing* (London: Hodder & Stoughton; London: University of London Press, 1924), 9; London County Council, *London Housing* (London: London County Council, 1937), 129–30; Alan A. Jackson, *Semi-Detached London* (London: George Allen & Unwin, 1973), 54–56; Judith Lever, *Home Sweet Home: Housing Designed by the London County Council and Greater London Council Architects, 1888–1975* (London: Academy Editions for the Greater London Council, 1976), 12–13, 28–29; Beattie, *A Revolution in London Housing: LCC Architects and Their Work*, 89–96; Bridget Cherry and Nikolaus Pevsner, *London 2, South* (1983; London: Penguin, 1999), 76, 700; *London Suburbs* (London: Merrell Holberton, 1999), 232; "Totterdown Fields Estate," *Wandsworth Borough Council: Conservation Area Character Statements* (Conservation and Design Group, Borough Planner's Service).

96 London County Council, *Housing of the Working Classes of London* (1913), 72–76, 131–37; Richard B. Watrous, "Personal Observations of Some Developments in Housing in Europe," *Journal of the American Institute of Architects* 2 (July 1914): 332–43; "Municipal Housing: No. 1.—The London County Council," *The Builder* 114 (March 15, 1918): 173–74; London County Council, *Housing* (1924), 9, 12; London County Council, *London Housing* (1937), 132–35; Jackson, *Semi-Detached London*, 57–58; Lever, *Home Sweet Home*, 12–13, 28–29; Beattie, *A Revolution in London Housing*, 98–105; Cherry and Pevsner, *London 2: South*, 76; Mervyn Miller, *Letchworth: The First Garden City* (London: Phillimore, 1989), 7; Andrzej Olechnowicz, *Working-Class Housing in England Between the Wars: The Becontree Estate* (Oxford: Clarendon; New York: Oxford University Press, 1997), 20–21; Bridget Cherry and Nikolaus Pevsner, *London 4: North* (London: Penguin Books, 1998), 42, 588–89; Chris Coates, *Utopia Britannica, vol. 1: British Utopian Experiments: 1325 to 1945* (London: Diggers & Dreamers Publications, 2001), 214.

97 London County Council, *Housing of the Working Classes of London* (1913), 76–78, 138–41; "Municipal Housing: The London County Council: No. 2," *Builder* 114 (March 22, 1918): 187; London County Council, *Housing* (1924), 8; London County Council, *London Housing* (1937), 130–32; Jackson, *Semi-Detached London*, 56–57; Lever, *Home Sweet Home*, 12–13, 31; Beattie, *A Revolution in London Housing:*, 105–7, 109–10; Cherry and Pevsner, *London 2, South*, 76, 226; Olechnowicz, *Working-Class Housing in England Between the Wars: The Becontree Estate*, 20.

98 Beattie, *A Revolution in London Housing: LCC Architects and Their Work*, 105.

99 London County Council, *Housing of the Working Classes of London* (1913), 82–83; "Municipal Housing: The London County Council: No. 2," *The Builder* 114 (March 22, 1918): 187; London County Council, *Housing* (1924), 6, 9; London County Council, *London Housing* (1937), 135–38; Jackson, *Semi-Detached London*, 58; Lever, *Home Sweet Home*, 12–13, 28, 30; Beattie, *A Revolution in London Housing*, 106, 108, 111–20; Bridget Cherry and Nikolaus Pevsner, *London 3: Northwest* (London: Penguin Books, 1991, 1999), 50, 223; Coates, *Utopia Britannica, vol. 1: British Utopian Experiments: 1325 to 1945*, 214.

100 Beattie, *A Revolution in London Housing*, 113.

101 London County Council, *London Housing* (1937), 155–56; Jackson, *Semi-Detached London*, 308; Cherry and Pevsner, *London 3: Northwest*, 223–24; *London Suburbs*, 198–99.

102 Cherry and Pevsner, *London 3: Northwest*, 224; *London Suburbs*, 198–99.

103 Susan Beattie, *A Revolution in London Housing: LCC Housing Architects and Their Work 1893–1914* (London: Architectural Press, 1980), 101.

104 G. Topham Forrest, "London County Council Housing Schemes," *Architects' Journal* (January 3, 1923): 8, 10, 14–17; London County Council, *Housing* (1924), 7, 27–29; Lawrence Weaver, *Cottages: Their Planning, Design and Materials* (London: Country Life; New York: Charles Scribner's Sons, 1926), 357–65; London County Council, *London Housing* (1937), 139–42; Paul Davies, "Comparing Two Estates," *Architect* 77 (October 1972): 77–80; Jackson, *Semi-Detached London*, 302–3; Lever, *Home Sweet Home*, 12–13, 32–33; Eugenie Ladner Birch, "Woman-made America: The Case of Early Public Housing Policy," in Donald A. Krueckeberg, ed., *The American Planner* (New York and London: Methuen, 1983), 163; Cherry and Pevsner, *London 2: South*, 688; Darrin Bayliss, "Revisiting the Cottage Council Estates: England, 1919–1939," *Planning Perspectives* 16 (2001): 169–200.

105 Forrest, "London County Council Housing Schemes": 8.

106 Davies, "Comparing Two Estates": 77.

107 "The London County Council Housing Estate at Bellingham," *Builder* 123 (September 15, 1922), 373–76; Forrest, "London County Council Housing Schemes": 8–17; London County Council, *Housing* (1924), 26–27; Weaver, *Cottages: Their Planning, Design and Materials*, 357–65; London County Council, *London Housing* (1937), 143–45; Jackson, *Semi-Detached London*, 299–301; Lever, *Home Sweet Home*, 12–13, 32–33; Cherry and Pevsner, *London 2: South*, 82–83, 428; *London Suburbs*, 108–9, 217.

108 London County Council, *Housing* (1924), 30; London County Council, *London Housing* (1937), 147–49, plan facing page 146; Jackson, *Semi-Detached London*, 301–2; Lever, *Home Sweet Home*, 12–13, 32, 34–35; Cherry and Pevsner, *London 2: South*, 82–83, 428; *London Suburbs*, 108–9, 217; Alistair Black, "Downham Estate: Its Origins and Early History," in www.ideal-homes.org.uk/lewisham/main/downham-estate.htm.

109 London County Council, *London Housing* (1937), 166–71, plan facing page 166; Jackson, *Semi-Detached London*, 308–10; Cherry and Pevsner, *London 2: South*, 654.

110 London County Council, *London Housing* (1937), 165–66, plan facing page 164; Ruth Durant, *Watling: A Survey of Social Life on a New Housing Estate* (London: P. S. King & Son, 1939), esp. pp. 1–3, 91–93; Caroline. F. Ware, "Watling," book review, *American Journal of Sociology* 45 (March 1940): 813–14; Jackson, *Semi-Detached London*, 303–7; Cherry and Pevsner, *London 4: North*, 168; *London Suburbs*, 179; Bayliss, "Revisiting the Cottage Council Estates: England, 1919–39": 169–200.

111 "The L. C. C. Housing Estate at Becontree," *Architects' Journal* 52 (December 29, 1920): 708–13; "London County Council Becontree Housing Scheme," *Builder* 121 (July 1921): 44–46; London County Council, *Housing* (1924), 22–25; Weaver, *Cottages: Their Planning, Design and Materials*, 12–13, 32, 36–37; London County Council, *London Housing* (1937), 154, 157–65, plan facing page 158; Terence Young, *Becontree and Dagenham* (London: Becontree Social Survey Committee, 1934); Harold S. Buttenheim, "Urban Land Policies," in *Supplementary Report of the Urbanism Committee to the National Resources Committee* (Washington, D.C.: U.S. Government Printing Office, 1939), 276; Nikolaus Pevsner, *Essex* (1954; London, Penguin, 1965), 18, 79–80; Jackson, *Semi-Detached London*, 291–99; Lever, *Home Sweet Home*, 12–13, 32, 36–37; Olechnowicz, *Working-Class Housing in England Between the Wars: The Becontree Estate*; *London Suburbs*, 108–9, 177; Mervyn Miller, "Garden Cities and Suburbs: At Home and Abroad," *Journal of Planning History* 1 (February 2002): 20.

112 Pevsner, *Essex*, 79.

113 Pevsner, *Essex*, 18.

114 "Our Record of Progress: Coryville," *The Garden City* 1 (February 1906): 5; "Coryville," *The Garden City* 1 (March 1906): 45; "Coryndon," *The Garden City* 3 (February 1908): 12–13; Thomas Adams, "Some New Garden Suburb Schemes," *Garden Cities and Town Planning* (May 1909): 207; Patrick Abercrombie, "Modern Town Planning in England: A Comparative Review of 'Garden City' Schemes in England, Part II," *Town Planning Review* 1 (July 1910): 113–14, plate 26; Thomas Mawson, *Civic Art: Studies in Town Planning, Parks, Boulevards, and Open Spaces* (London: B. T. Batsford; New York: Charles Scribner's Sons, 1911), 286–98; Ewart G. Culpin, *The Garden City Movement Up-to-Date* (London: Garden Cities and Town Planning Association, 1913), 30; Gillian Darley, *Villages of Vision* (London: Architectural Press, 1975), 147; Michael Simpson, "Thomas Adams, 1871–1940," in Gordon E. Cherry, ed., *Pioneers in British Planning* (London: Architectural Press, 1981), 22–23; Michael Simpson, *Thomas Adams and the Modern Planning Movement* (London and New York: Mansell, 1985), 45–46; John Newman, *Glamorgan (Mid Glamorgan, South Glamorgan and West Glamorgan)* (London: Penguin; Cardiff: University of Wales Press, 1995), 113; Janet Waymark, *Thomas Mawson: Life, Gardens and Landscapes* (London: Francis Lincoln, 2009), 198–99.

115 Ewart G. Culpin, *The Garden City Movement Up-to-Date* (London: Garden Cities and

Town Planning Association, 1913), 25–26, 29; "Co-Operative Housing in Wales," *Garden Cities and Town Planning* (August 15, 1913): 206–9; "The Cardiff Garden Suburb," *Garden Cities and Town Planning* (October 15, 1913): 261–62); "A Concrete Tea-Garden House," *Architects' and Builders' Journal* 44 (August 16, 1916): 8–82; "Rhiwbina Garden Village," *Architects' Journal* 57 (January 1923): 53–56; "Two Housing Estates, S. Wales," *Builder* 45 (November 17, 1933): 778, 785; T. Alwyn Lloyd, "The Welsh Town Planning and Housing Trust and Its Affiliated Societies," *Town Planning Review* 23 (April 1952): 40–51; John Newman, *Glamorgan (Mid Glamorgan, South Glamorgan and West Glamorgan)* (London: Penguin; Cardiff: University of Wales Press, 1995), 113, 295–97, fig. 106; Mervyn Miller, "Garden Cities and Suburbs: At Home and Abroad," *Journal of Planning History* 1 (February 2002): 6–28.

116 Edgar L. Chappell, "Welsh Housing Schemes: I," *Garden Cities and Town Planning* (October 1914): 229–34.

117 Culpin, *The Garden City Movement Up-to-Date*, 26.

118 Edgar L. Chappell, "Welsh Housing Schemes—I," *Garden Cities and Town Planning* (October 1914): 229–34; "Opening of Barry Garden Suburb," *Garden Cities and Town Planning* (October 1917): 59–60; "Barry Garden Suburb," *Town Planning Review* 8 (December 1920): 139, plate 28; "Two Housing Estates, S. Wales," *Builder* 45 (November 17, 1933): 778, 785; T. Alwyn Lloyd, "The Welsh Town Planning and Housing Trust and Its Affiliated Societies," *Town Planning Review* 23 (April 1952): 40–51; John Newman, *Glamorgan (Mid Glamorgan, South Glamorgan and West Glamorgan)* (London: Penguin; Cardiff: University of Wales Press, 1995), 113, 151.

119 Ewart G. Culpin, *The Garden City Movement Up-to-Date* (London: Garden Cities and Town Planning Association, 1913), 47; Edgar L. Chappell, "Welsh Housing Schemes—I," *Garden Cities and Town Planning* (October 1914): 229–34; T. Alwyn Lloyd, "The Welsh Town Planning and Housing Trust and Its Affiliated Societies," *Town Planning Review* 23 (April 1952): 40–51; Edward Hubbard, *Clwyd (Denbighshire and Flintshire)* (London: Penguin Books; Cardiff: University of Wales Press, 1986), 84–85, 312–13.

120 Ewart G. Culpin, *The Garden City Movement Up-to-Date* (London: Garden Cities and Town Planning Association, 1913), 35, 38–39; Edgar L. Chappell, "Welsh Housing Schemes—I," *Garden Cities and Town Planning* (October 1914): 229–34; T. Alwyn Lloyd, "The Welsh Town Planning and Housing Trust and Its Affiliated Societies," *Town Planning Review* 23 (April 1952): 40–51; Richard Haslam, *Powys (Montgomeryshire, Radnorshire, Breconshire)* (New Haven, Conn., and London: Yale University Press, 2003), 66, 145, 157.

121 Lloyd, "The Welsh Town Planning and Housing Trust and Its Affiliated Societies": 43.

122 Ewart G. Culpin, *The Garden City Movement Up-to-Date* (London: Garden Cities and Town Planning Association, 1913), 29–30; Raymond Unwin, "Glasgow Garden Suburb," *Garden Cities and Town Planning* (May 1913): 138–41; Mervyn Miller, *Raymond Unwin: Garden Cities and Town Planning* (Leicester: Leicester University Press, 1992), 48; Maureen Whitelaw, *A Garden Suburb for Glasgow: The Story of Westerton* (Glasgow: M. Whitelaw, 1992); K. Barrett, *Westerton: A Village Story* (Glasgow: Westerton's Women's Group, 1993), 16–32; John Gifford and Frank Arneil Walker, *Stirling and Central Scotland* (New Haven, Conn., and London: Yale University Press, 2002), 222. Also see T. R. Marr, *Housing Conditions in Manchester & Salford* (Manchester: Sherratt and Hughes, University Press, 1904).

123 *Prospectus, Glasgow Garden Suburb Tenants Ltd.*, quoted in Barrett, *Westerton: A Village Story*, 18.

124 Whitelaw, *A Garden Suburb for Glasgow: The Story of Westerton*, 5.

125 *Prospectus, Glasgow Garden Suburb Tenants Ltd.*, quoted in Whitelaw, *A Garden Suburb for Glasgow: The Story of Westerton*, 9–10.

126 Whitelaw, *A Garden Suburb for Glasgow: The Story of Westerton*, 5.

127 Unwin, "Glasgow Garden Suburb": 139.

128 Murray Fraser, *John Bull's Other Homes: State Housing and British Policy in Ireland, 1883–1922* (Liverpool: Liverpool University Press, 1996), 132. Also see Murray Fraser, "Home Rule and Garden Suburb Ideals in Ireland before 1914," *Planning History* 12 (1990): 15–24.

129 John Clancy, quoted in F.H.A. Aalen, "The Working-Class Housing Movement in Dublin, 1850–1920," in Michael J. Bannon, ed., *The Emergence of Irish Planning, 1880–1920* (Dublin: Turoe Press, 1985), 174–75. Also see "Dublin Topics," *Irish Times* (October 29, 1910): 4; "Dublin Corporation," *Irish Times* (November 19, 1910): 11.

130 Aalen, "The Working-Class Housing Movement in Dublin, 1850–1920," in Bannon, ed., *The Emergence of Irish Planning, 1880–1920*, 175.

131 Fraser, *John Bull's Other Homes: State Housing and British Policy in Ireland, 1883–1922*, 132.

132 Patrick Geddes, quoted in *Report of the Departmental Inquiry on Housing Conditions of the Working Classes in the City of Dublin* (London, 1914), 210, also quoted in Mervyn Miller, "Raymond Unwin and the Planning of Dublin," in Bannon, ed., *The Emergence of Irish Planning, 1880–1920*, 265. For a biography of Geddes, see Philip Boardman, *Patrick Geddes: Maker of the Future*, with an introduction by Lewis Mumford (Chapel Hill: University of North Carolina Press, 1944).

133 *Irish Builder and Engineer* 56 (April 11, 1914): 213; Miller, "Raymond Unwin and the Planning of Dublin," in Bannon, ed., *The Emergence of Irish Planning, 1880–1920*, 264–66.

134 *Report of the Housing Committee, Reports and Printed Documents of The Corporation of Dublin* 1 (1915): 707, quoted in Miller, "Raymond Unwin and the Planning of Dublin," in Bannon, ed., *The Emergence of Irish Planning, 1880–1920*, 266. Also see "Editorial," *Irish Times* (July 7, 1914): 6; "Dublin Housing: Corporation Committee's Report," *Irish Times* (April 7, 1915): 6; Aalen, "The Working-Class Housing Movement in Dublin, 1850–1920," in Bannon, ed., *The Emergence of Irish Planning, 1880–1920*, 174–80; Miller, "Raymond Unwin and the Planning of Dublin," in Bannon, ed., *The Emergence of Irish Planning, 1880–1920*, 263–67, 270–75; Helen Elizabeth Meller, *Patrick Geddes: Social Evolutionist and City Planner* (London and New York: Routledge, 1990), 182–89; Mervyn Miller, *Raymond Unwin: Garden Cities and Town Planning* (Leicester: Leicester University Press, 1992), 131, 152; Fraser, *John Bull's Other Homes: State Housing and British Policy in Ireland, 1883–1922*, 132–43; Ruth McManus, *Dublin, 1910–1940: Shaping the City & Suburbs* (Portland: Four Courts Press, 2002), 50–53, 182–83; Mervyn Miller, "The Origins of the Garden City Residential Neighborhood," in Kermit C. Parsons and David Schuyler, eds., *From Garden City to Green City: The Legacy of Ebenezer Howard* (Baltimore and London: Johns Hopkins University Press, 2002), 120, 123; Andrew Kincaid, *Postcolonial Dublin: Imperial Legacies and the Built Environment* (Minneapolis and London: University of Minnesota Press, 2006), 12–13.

135 For Chambers' Marino Casino, see John Redmill and Ian Christopher Bristow, "The Casino at Marino, Dublin," *Association for Studies in the Conservation of Historic Buildings Transactions* 9 (1984): 29–44.

136 Patrick Geddes and Raymond Unwin, "Memorandum No. 3," in *Reports and Printed Documents of Dublin Corporation* (1915), quoted in Miller, "Raymond Unwin and the Planning of Dublin," in Bannon, ed., *The Emergence of Irish Planning, 1880–1920*, 270.

137 Miller, "Raymond Unwin and the Planning of Dublin," in Bannon, ed., *The Emergence of Irish Planning, 1880–1920*, 272.

138 Miller, "The Origins of the Garden City Residential Neighborhood," in Parsons and Schuyler, eds., *From Garden City to Green City: The Legacy of Ebenezer Howard*, 123.

139 Miller, "Raymond Unwin and the Planning of Dublin," in Bannon, ed., *The Emergence of Irish Planning, 1880–1920*, 271–75.

140 "Dublin Housing Schemes," *Irish Times* (November 23, 1918): 2; "Housing in Dublin: Marino Housing Scheme," *The Builder* 118 (February 27, 1920): 247–49; Miller, "Raymond Unwin and the Planning of Dublin," in Bannon, ed., *The Emergence of Irish Planning, 1880–1920*, 272–74; McManus, *Dublin, 1910–1940: Shaping the City & Suburbs*, 168–69, 183–86; Miller, *Raymond Unwin: Garden Cities and Town Planning*, 152.

141 Miller, "Raymond Unwin and the Planning of Dublin," in Bannon, ed., *The Emergence of Irish Planning, 1880–1920*, 274.

142 "Building & Reconstruction," *Irish Times* (May 21, 1925): 5; "4,400 Applications for 243 Houses," *Irish Times* (June 13, 1925): 6; "A Labour-Saving House: Marino Estate Exhibit," *Irish Times* (June 27, 1925): 10; "Slums and Other Housing Problems: Tremendous Task of the Dublin Corporation," *Irish Times* (June 21, 1939): 34, 36; Aalen, "The Working-Class Housing Movement in Dublin, 1850–1920," in Bannon, ed., *The Emergence of Irish Planning, 1880–1920*, 151, 171–72, 175, 177; Miller, "Raymond Unwin and the Planning of Dublin," in Bannon, ed., *The Emergence of Irish Planning, 1880–1920*, 274; Miller, "The Origins of the Garden City Residential Neighborhood," in Parsons and Schuyler, eds., *From Garden City to Green City: The Legacy of Ebenezer Howard*, 120.

143 Aalen, "The Working-Class Housing Movement in Dublin, 1850–1920," in Bannon, ed., *The Emergence of Irish Planning, 1880–1920*, 177.

144 "County Borough of Dublin," *Irish Times* (January 18, 1915): 4; "Dublin Corporation Agenda," *Irish Times* (October 1, 1915): 2; "Housing Schemes in Dublin," *Irish Times* (October 21, 1915): 3; "Housing Schemes in Dublin," *Irish Times* (April 5, 1917): 3; Joseph V. O'Brien, *Dear, Dirty Dublin: A City in Distress, 1899–1916* (Berkeley: University of California Press, 1982), 148; Fraser, *John Bull's Other Homes: State Housing and British Policy in Ireland, 1883–1922*, 159–62; Christine Casey, *Dublin: The City within the Grand and Royal Canals and the Circular Road with the Phoenix Park* (New Haven, Conn.: Yale University Press, 2005), 74.

145 Fraser, *John Bull's Other Homes: State Housing and British Policy in Ireland, 1883–1922*, 160.

146 "Fairbrothers' Fields," *Irish Times* (September 19, 1913): 7; "Dublin Housing Scheme," *Irish Times* (June 2, 1915): 3; "Housing Schemes in Dublin," *Irish Times* (April 5, 1917): 3; "Dublin Housing Schemes," *Irish Times* (September 11, 1917): 2; "Plotholders and Tillage," *Irish Times* (February 12, 1918): 7; "Dublin," *Architect* 100 (November 29, 1918): 299; "Slums and Other Housing Problems: Tremendous Task of the Dublin Corporation": 34; O'Brien, *Dear, Dirty Dublin: A City in Distress, 1899–1916*, 148; Aalen, "The Working-Class Housing Movement in Dublin, 1850–1920," in Bannon, ed., *The Emergence of Irish Planning, 1880–1920*, 176; Fraser, *John Bull's Other Homes: State Housing and British Policy in Ireland, 1883–1922*, 159, 162–69; Casey, *Dublin: The City within the Grand and Royal Canals and the Circular Road with the Phoenix Park*, 74.

147 *Reports and Printed Documents of the Corporation of Dublin* 2 (No. 109, 1917): 285–95, quoted in Aalen, "The Working-Class Housing Movement in Dublin, 1850–1920," in Bannon, ed., *The Emergence of Irish Planning, 1880–1920*, 176.

148 Fraser, *John Bull's Other Homes: State Housing and British Policy in Ireland, 1883–1922*, 164–65.

149 "New Dublin Housing Scheme," *Irish Times* (March 10, 1927): 4; "Slums and Other Housing Problems: Tremendous Task of the Dublin Corporation": 34; McManus, *Dublin, 1910–1940: Shaping the City & Suburbs*, 196–205.

150 McManus, *Dublin, 1910–1940: Shaping the City & Suburbs*, 204.

151 "421 Houses at Donnycarney," *Irish Times* (August 22, 1929): 8; "Electric Wiring of Donnycarney Houses," *Irish Times* (December 5, 1929): 3; "The Donnycarney Housing Scheme," *Irish Times* (December 31, 1929): 11; "Slums and Other Housing Problems: Tremendous Task of the Dublin Corporation": 34; Fraser, *John Bull's Other Homes: State Housing and British Policy in Ireland, 1883–1922*, 421; McManus, *Dublin, 1910–1940: Shaping the City & Suburbs*, 207–10; Kincaid, *Postcolonial Dublin: Imperial Legacies and the Built Environment*, 74.

152 Quoted in "A Historical Note," http://www.killestervillage.com. Also see F.H.A. Aalen, "Homes for Irish Heroes," *Town Planning Review* 59 (July 1988): 305–23; Fraser, *John Bull's Other Homes: State Housing and British Policy in Ireland, 1883–1922*, 247–71; Joseph Brady and Patrick Lynch, "The Irish Sailors' and Soldiers' Land Trust and Its Killester Nemesis," *Irish Geography* 42 (November 2009): 261–92.

153 "Killester Garden City for Ex-Soldiers," *Irish Times* (April 7, 1921): 7; "Killester Garden Suburb," *Irish Times* (October 19, 1921): 4; "Killester," *Irish Times* (October 4, 1922): 6; "Killester Garden Suburb," *Parliamentary Debates: Official Report* 1 (1922): 1016; "Killester Garden Suburb," *Dublin Magazine* 2–3 (1924): 346; "Dublin Bungalows," *Irish Times* (October 21, 1925): 5; "Ex-Service Men's Houses," *Irish Times* (July 14, 1926): 3; "An Irishman's Diary: Suburban Buildings," *Irish Times* (July 25, 1928): 4; "Town Planners' Impressions," *Irish Times* (August 23, 1928): 5; "Killester: Its History and Meaning," *Irish Times* (August 5, 1933): 13; Michael J. Bannon, "Irish Planning from 1921 to 1945: An Overview," in Bannon, ed., *The Emergence of Irish Planning, 1880–1920*, 33, 67; Aalen, "Homes for Irish Heroes": 305–23; Fraser, *John Bull's Other Homes: State Housing and British Policy in Ireland, 1883–1922*, 249–55;

McManus, *Dublin, 1910–1940: Shaping the City & Suburbs*, 82–83; Brady and Lynch, "The Irish Sailors' and Soldiers' Land Trust and Its Killester Nemesis": 261–92; "The Irish Sailors' and Soldiers' Land Trust," http://www.nationalarchives.gov.uk/records/research-guides/irish-genealogy.htm; http://www.killestervillage.com.

154 Aalen, "Homes for Irish Heroes": 312, 316.

155 Lady Aberdeen, letter to F. C. Mears, May 10, 1922, quoted in Fraser, *John Bull's Other Homes: State Housing and British Policy in Ireland, 1883–1922*, 252.

156 "Mount Merrion," *Irish Times* (September 11, 1925): 4; "Mount Merrion Estate Development," *Irish Times* (December 3, 1925): 5; "Mount Merrion Estate," *Irish Times* (February 1, 1927): 3; "Architects' Competition," *Irish Times* (August 18, 1928): 8; "Housing Development in County Dublin," *Irish Times* (June 5, 1929): 11; Gerard O'Kelly, "Continuing the Mount Merrion Connection," *Dublin Historical Record* 52 (Spring 1999): 4–14; McManus, *Dublin, 1910–1940: Shaping the City & Suburbs*, 379, 381; http://www.mountmerrion300.ie/housing_development.html.

157 "Mount Merrion Estates," *Irish Times* (May 27, 1933): 11; "Mount Merrion Estates," *Irish Times* (July 31, 1933): 4; "Mount Merrion Estate," *Irish Times* (January 16, 1934): 2; "Mount Merrion Estate," *Irish Times* (February 1, 1934): 4; "Mount Merrion Estates," *Irish Times* (February 23, 1934): 11; "The Private Builder," *Irish Times* (October 13, 1934): 4; "Irish Homes Mount Merrion Park," *Irish Times* (December 12, 1934): 4; "Mount Merrion Fete," *Irish Times* (July 15, 1935): 2; "The Private Builder: Irish Homes, at Ireland's Garden Suburb, Mount Merrion Park," *Irish Times* (March 14, 1936): 5; "Home Builders Page," *Irish Times* (December 10, 1936): 3; O'Kelly, "Continuing the Mount Merrion Connection": 4–14; McManus, *Dublin, 1910–1940: Shaping the City & Suburbs*, 327, 379–82; http://www.mountmerrion300.ie/housing_development.html.

158 http://www.mountmerrion300.ie/housing_development.html.

159 McManus, *Dublin, 1910–1940: Shaping the City & Suburbs*, 382.

Chapter 6

1 Jean-François Lejeune, "From Hellerau to Bauhaus: Memory and Modernity in the German Garden City," *The New City* 3 (Fall 1996): 50–69. Also see Patrick Abercrombie, "Some Notes on German Garden Villages," *Town Planning Review* 1 (October 1910): 246–50; Franziska Bollerey and Kristiana Hartmann, "A Patriarchal Utopia: The Garden City and Housing Reform in Germany at the Turn of the Century," in Anthony Sutcliffe, ed., *The Rise of Modern Urban Planning, 1800–1914* (New York: St. Martin's Press, 1980), 135–65; Gerhard Fehl and Juan Rodriguez-Lores, "La 'città giardino' in Germania tra il 1910 e il 1918," *Casabella* 57 (January 1993): 12–16, 117–18; Kristina Hartmann, "Garden City Experiences in Germany," in Gabriele Tagliaventi, ed., *Garden City* (Rome: Gangemi Editore, 1994), 267–83.

2 Lejeune, "From Hellerau to Bauhaus: Memory and Modernity in the German Garden City": 53.

3 Muthesius's report was published as *Das englische Haus: Entwicklung, Bedingungen, Anlage, Aufbau, Einrichtung und Innenraum*, 3 vols. (Berlin: E. Wasmuth, 1904–5). Also see Hermann Muthesius, *The English House*, trans. by Janet Seligman (London: Crosby Lockwood Staples, 1979); Hermann Muthesius, *The English House, Volume I: Development*, trans. by Janet Seligman (London: Frances Lincoln, 2007).

4 Lejeune, "From Hellerau to Bauhaus: Memory and Modernity in the German Garden City": 54.

5 Abercrombie, "Some Notes on German Garden Villages": 246–50.

6 Lejeune, "From Hellerau to Bauhaus: Memory and Modernity in the German Garden City": 54. Also see Paul Mebes, *Um 1800: Architektur und Handwerk im letzten Jahrhundert ihrer traditionellen Entwicklung* (Munich: F. Bruckmann, 1908); Paul Schultze-Naumberg, *Kulturarbeiten* (Munich: G. D. W. Callwey, 1901–17); Norbert Borrmann, *Paul Schultze-Naumburg, 1869–1949: Maler, Publizist, Architekt* (Essen: Verlag Richard Bacht, 1989), 27–58; Kai K. Gutschow, "The Anti-Mediterranean in the Literature of Modern Architecture: Paul Schultze-Naumburg's Kulturarbeiten," in Jean-François Lejeune and Michelangelo Sabatino, eds., *Modern Architecture and the Mediterranean: Vernacular Dialogues and Contested Identities* (London and New York: Routledge, 2010), 148–73.

7 Harry S. Stewart, "Garden City Work in Germany," *Garden Cities and Town Planning* 4 (July 1910): 297–99; Patrick Abercrombie, "Some Notes on German Garden Villages," *Town Planning Review* 1 (October 1910): 246–47, plate 71; "German Town Planning Tour," *Garden Cities & Town Planning* 1 (June 1911): 112–15; "Hellerau, Germany's First Garden City," *Garden Cities & Town Planning* 1 (July 1911): 152; Nelson P. Lewis, *The Planning of the Modern City: A Review of the Principles Governing City Planning* (New York: John Wiley & Sons, 1916), 391–92; J. Stübben, *Der Städtebau* (Leipzig: J. M. Gebhardt, 1924), 115, 117; Thomas Adams, *The Design of Residential Areas: Basic Considerations, Principles, and Methods* (Cambridge, Mass.: Harvard University Press, 1934), 240; Daniel T. Rodgers, *Atlantic Crossings: Social Politics in a Progressive Age* (Cambridge, Mass., and London: Belknap Press of Harvard University Press, 1998), 163, 176, 191.

8 Adams, *The Design of Residential Areas: Basic Considerations, Principles, and Methods*, 240.

9 Winfried Nerdinger, *Theodor Fischer: Architekt und Städtebauer* (Berlin: Ernst, 1988), 50, 162, 189; Gabriele Tagliaventi, "The Romantic Tradition in 20th Century Town Planning," in Gabriele Tagliaventi, ed., *Garden City* (Rome: Gangemi Editore, 1994), 40–42; John V. Maciuika, *Before the Bauhaus: Architecture, Politics, and the German State, 1890–1920* (New York: Cambridge University Press, 2005), 32–33.

10 Winfried Nerdinger, *Theodor Fischer: Architekt und Städtebauer* (Berlin: Ernst, 1988), 134–35, 137; "Siedlung Stadlohner Strasse," www.muenchen.de.

11 Winfried Nerdinger, *Theodor Fischer: Architekt und Städtebauer* (Berlin: Ernst, 1988), 134–35, 137; Karl Kiem, *Die Gartenstadt Staaken* (Berlin: Gebr. Mann Verlag, 1997). 157–58, 160–61, 165; Winfried Nerdinger, *Architectural Guide to Munich* (Berlin: Dietrich Reimer Verlag, 2007), 171; "Grunzenlehastrasse in München," www.sueddeutsche.de.

12 W.F. Storck, "Die Gartenstadt Mannheim—Waldorf," *Deutsche Kunst und Dekoration* 40 (April–September 1917): 308–14; Andreas Schenk, *Architekturführer Mannheim* (Berlin: Dietrich Reimer Verlag, 1999), 234–35; http://www.gartenstadt-genossenschaft.de/?site=mitgliederzeitung/ausgaben/20040600.

13 Hans Eduard von Berlepsch-Valendas, *Die Garten-Stadt München-Perlach* (München: C. Reinhardt, 1910); Harry S. Stewart, "Garden City Work in Germany," *Garden Cities and Town Planning* 4 (July 1910): 297–99; Patrick Abercrombie, "Some Notes on German Garden Villages," *Town Planning Review* 1 (October 1910): 246–50; "Die Garten Stadt Munchen-Perlach," *Town Planning Review* 1 (October 1910): 255–56; George Benoit-Lévy, *La Cité-Jardin* (Paris: Éditions des Cités-jardins de France, 1911), 115.

14 Annette Ciré, "'Beyond the Metropolis': Urban Design and Architecture of the 'Country House Colonies' and Garden Cities in Berlin Suburbs before 1914," in Thorsten Scheer, Josef Paul Kleihues, and Paul Kahlfeldt, eds., *City of Architecture, Architecture of the City: Berlin 1900–2000* (Berlin: Nicolai, 2000), 61–62; Michael Bienert and Elke Linda Buchholz, *Kaiserzeit und Moderne: Ein Wegwiser durch Berlin* (Berlin: Berlin Story Verlag, 2007), 164; "Preussensiedulung," http://www.altglienicke24.de.

15 Hermann Muthesius, letter, August 6, 1912, Akte Preussensiedlung, Archives of the Bauaufsichtsamt Treptow, quoted in Ciré, "'Beyond the Metropolis': Urban Design and Architecture of the 'Country House Colonies' and Garden Cities in Berlin Suburbs before 1914," in Scheer, Kleihues, and Kahlfeldt, eds., *City of Architecture, Architecture of the City: Berlin 1900–2000*, 61.

16 Ciré, "'Beyond the Metropolis': Urban Design and Architecture of the 'Country House Colonies' and Garden Cities in Berlin Suburbs before 1914," in Scheer, Kleihues, and Kahlfeldt, eds., *City of Architecture, Architecture of the City: Berlin 1900–2000*, 61–62.

17 Bruno Taut, "Die Gartenstadt Falkenberg bei Berlin," *Gartenstadt* 7 (May 1913): 88; "Stadtbaurat Bruno Taut, Magdeburg," *Moderne Bauformen* 21 (October 1922): 294–97; Kristiana Hartmann, *Deutsche Gartenstadtbewegung: Kulturpolitik und Gesellschaftsreform* (Munich: Heinz Moos Verlag, 1976), 108–12; Franziska Bollerey and Kristiana Hartmann, "A Patriarchal Utopia: The Garden City and Housing Reform in Germany at the Turn of the Century," in Anthony Sutcliffe, ed., *The Rise of Modern Urban Planning, 1800–1914* (New York: St. Martin's Press, 1980), 155–58; Iain Boyd Whyte, *Bruno Taut and the Architecture of Activism* (Cambridge: Cambridge University Press, 1982), 29–32, 38–39; Kurt Junghanns, *Bruno Taut: 1880–1938* (Berlin: Elefanten Press Verlag, 1983), 25, figs. 39–45; Rosemarie Haag Bletter, "Revising Modernist History: The Architecture of the 1920s and 1930s," *Art Journal* 43 (Summer 1983): 108–20; Norbert Borrmann, *Paul Schultze-Naumburg, 1869–1949: Maler, Publizist, Architekt* (Essen: Verlag Richard Bacht, 1989), 133; Vittorio Magnago Lampugnani, "From the New Community to the Horseshoe Estate: A History of German Modern Architecture—Part 4," trans. by Chris Charlesworth, *Architecture + Urbanism* (December 1992): 49, 52; Kristiana Hartmann, "Garden-Cities' Experiences in Germany," in Gabriele Tagliaventi, ed., *Garden City* (Rome: Gangemi Editore, 1994), 267–83; "Im Osten tauts," *Deutsche Bauzeitung* 129 (April 1995): 88–92, 201; Winfried Nerdinger and Cornelius Tafel, *Architectural Guide Germany: 20th Century* (Basel: Birkhäuser, 1996), 184; Jean-François Lejeune, "From Hellerau to Bauhaus: Memory and Modernity in the German Garden City," *The New City* 3 (Fall 1996): 50–69; Karl Kiem, *Die Gartenstadt Staaken* (Berlin: Gebr. Mann Verlag, 1997), 168; Annette Ciré, "'Beyond the Metropolis': Urban Design and Architecture of the 'Country House Colonies' and Garden Cities in Berlin Suburbs before 1914," in Thorsten Scheer, Josef Paul Kleihues, and Paul Kahlfeldt, eds., *City of Architecture, Architecture of the City: Berlin 1900–2000* (Berlin: Nicolai, 2000), 59–61; "Garden City Falkenberg," *Architecture + Urbanism* (September 2002): 124–27; Arne Ehmann, "Wohnarchitektur des Mitteleuropäischen: Traditionalismus um 1910 in Ausgewählten Beispielen" (Ph.D. diss., University of Hamburg, 2006): 312; Jörg Haspel and Annemarie Jaeggi, *Siedlungen der Berliner Moderne* (Munich: Deutscher Kunstverlag, 2007), 29–37; Wolfgang Sonne, "Political Connotations of the Picturesque," in Charles C. Bohl and Jean-François Lejeune, eds., *Sitte, Hegemann and the Metropolis: Modern Civic Art and International Exchanges* (London and New York: Routledge, 2009), 128–29; Maiken Umbach, *German Cities and Bourgeois Modernism, 1890–1924* (New York: Oxford University Press, 2009), 132; Vittorio Magnago Lampugnani, *Die Stadt im 20. Jahrhundert* (Berlin: Verlag Klaus Wagenbach, 2010), 256–57. Also see http://www.osun.org/falkenberg+taut-pdf.html.

18 Bruno Taut, quoted in Whyte, *Bruno Taut and the Architecture of Activism*, 31.

19 Bruno Taut, quoted in Whyte, *Bruno Taut and the Architecture of Activism*, 31.

20 Taut, "Die Gartenstadt Falkenberg bei Berlin": 88, quoted in Bollerey and Hartmann, "A Patriarchal Utopia: The Garden City and Housing Reform in Germany at the Turn of the Century," in Sutcliffe, ed., *The Rise of Modern Urban Planning, 1800–1914*, 156.

21 Lampugnani, "From the New Community to the Horseshoe Estate: A History of German Modern Architecture—Part 4": 49.

22 Kurt Junghanns, *Bruno Taut: 1880–1938* (Berlin: Elefanten Press Verlag, 1983), 25, figs. 45–46; Rosemarie Haag Bletter, "Revising Modernist History: The Architecture of the 1920s and 1930s," *Art Journal* 43 (Summer 1983): 108–20; Kristiana Hartmann, "Garden-Cities' Experiences in Germany," in Gabriele Tagliaventi, ed., *Garden City* (Rome: Gangemi Editore, 1994), 267–83; "Im Osten tauts," *Deutsche Bauzeitung* 129 (April 1995): 88–92, 201; Winfried Nerdinger and Cornelius Tafel, *Architectural Guide Germany: 20th Century* (Basel: Birkhäuser, 1996), 91.

23 Bruno Taut, *Die Stadtkrone* (Jena: Eugen Diederichs, 1919).

24 Jean-François Lejeune, "From Hellerau to Bauhaus: Memory and Modernity in the German Garden City," *The New City* 3 (Fall 1996): 50–69; Frank Rattay, "Die Gartenstadt Zehlendorf 1913–1930," *Zehlendorfer Chronik* 11 (1999): 6; Annette Ciré, "'Beyond the Metropolis': Urban Design and Architecture of the 'Country House Colonies' and Garden Cities in Berlin Suburbs before 1914," in Thorsten Scheer, Josef Paul Kleihues, and Paul Kahlfeldt, eds., *City of Architecture, Architecture of the City: Berlin 1900–2000* (Berlin: Nicolai, 2000), 62–63; Vittorio Magnago Lampugnani, *Die Stadt im 20. Jahrhundert* (Berlin: Verlag Klaus Wagenbach, 2010), 256–57.

25 Ciré, "'Beyond the Metropolis': Urban Design and Architecture of the 'Country House Colonies' and Garden Cities in Berlin Suburbs before 1914," in Scheer, Kleihues, and Kahlfeldt, eds., *City of Architecture, Architecture of the City: Berlin 1900–2000*, 62–63.

26 *Gartenstadt Gablenzsiedlung Chemnitz: Entstehung, Geschichte und Sanierung einer Genossenschaftssiedlung* (Chemnitz: Verlag Heimatland Sachsen, 2002); "Die Gartenstadt Gablenzsiedlung," *Chemnitz: Magazin der City-Management und Tourismus* (Winter 2008): 20–21; Gert Kähler, *The Path of Modernism, Architecture 1900–1930: From the World Heritage of Wroclaw to that of Dessau* (Berlin: Jovis, 2009), 96, 98; "Gablenz," www.chemnitzgeschichte.de.

27 Gérard Bauer, Gildas Baudez, and Jean-Michel Roux, *Banlieues de charme* (Aix-en-Provence: Pandora Editions, 1980), 144–57; "Am Winterberg," www.ruhrnachritchten.de.

28 Walter Curt Behrendt, "Über die Deutsche Baukunst der Gegenwart," *Kunst und Künstler* 12 (1914): 331; "Vorstadthäuser bei Breslau," *Der Baumeister* 13 (April 1915): 53–60; "Schmitthenners Breslauer Bauten," *Moderne Bauformen* 21 (1922): 14–26; Jean-François Lejeune, "From Hellerau to Bauhaus: Memory and Modernity in the German Garden City," *The New City* 3 (Fall 1996): 50–69; Konstanze Beelitz and Niclas Förster, *Die Architektur der Moderne: Breslau/Wroclaw* (Berlin: Ernst Wasmuth Verlag Tübingen, 2006), 136–37; "Villenkolonie Carlowitz," http://www.breslau-wroclaw.de.

29 Gabriele Tagliaventi, "The Romantic Tradition in 20th Century Town Planning," in Gabriele Tagliaventi, ed., *Garden City* (Rome: Gangemi Editore, 1994), 44–47, 51; Karl Kiem, *Die Gartenstadt Staaken* (Berlin: Gebr. Mann Verlag, 1997), 213; Wolfgang Voigt and Hartmut Frank, *Paul Schmitthenner, 1884–1972* (Tübingen: Wasmuth, 2003), 16–17, 131–32.

30 Jeannette Redensek, "Manufacturing Gemeinschaft: Architecture, Tradition, and the Sociology of Community in Germany, 1890–1920" (Ph.D. diss., City University of New York, 2007): 264 (n.71).

31 Jean-François Lejeune, "From Hellerau to Bauhaus: Memory and Modernity in the German Garden City," *The New City* 3 (Fall 1996): 50–69. Also see Harald Kegler, "Gartenstadt 'Hohe Lache' in Dessau," in *Villa und Eigenheim: Suburbaner Städtebau in Deutschland* (Stuggart: Deutsche Verlags-Anstalt, 2001), 209–17; Jeannette Redensek, "Manufacturing Gemeinschaft: Architecture, Tradition, and the Sociology of Community in Germany, 1890–1920" (Ph.D. diss., City University of New York, 2007): 30, 242, 262–66; David H. Haney, *When Modern Was Green: Life and Work of Landscape Architect Leberecht Migge* (London and New York: Routledge, 2010), 165–66.

32 Redensek, "Manufacturing Gemeinschaft: Architecture, Tradition, and the Sociology of Community in Germany, 1890–1920": 266.

33 Leberecht Migge, "Siedlung Hof Hammer bei Kiel," *Sparsamer Bauweise* 3 (1921): 37–42; Dieter-Jürgen Mehlhorn, *Architekturführer Kiel*, trans. by Angelika Salomon (Berlin: Dietrich Reimer Verlag, 1997), 143; Dörte Beier, *Kiel in der Weimarer Republik: Die städtebauliche Entwicklung unter der Leitung Willy Hahns* (Kiel: Ludwig: 2004), 179–84; David H. Haney, *When Modern Was Green: Life and Work of Landscape Architect Leberecht Migge* (London and New York: Routledge, 2010), 149–54; "Gartendenkmalpflege in Schleswig-Holstein," www.historischegaerten. de; www.russee-hammer.info.

34 Haney, *When Modern Was Green: Life and Work of Landscape Architect Leberecht Migge*, 154.

35 David H. Haney, *When Modern Was Green: Life and Work of Landscape Architect Leberecht Migge* (London and New York: Routledge, 2010), 148–49; http://www.birkut.strefa.pl/ogrod%20w%20zielonej.pdf.

36 "Siedlungen und Andere Bauten von Architekt Wilhelm Riphahn, Köln," *Moderne Bauformen* 22 (January 1923): 21–27; Wolfram Hagspiel, *Der Kölner Architket Wilhelm Riphahn: sein Lebenswerk von 1913 bis 1945* (Cologne: W. König, 1982), 27–40; Werner Heinen and Anne-Marie Pfeffer, *Köln: Siedlungen 1888–1938* (Cologne: Verlag J. P. Bachem, 1988), 91–97; Alexander Kierdorf, *Architectural Guide to Cologne*, trans. by Jean-Marie Clarke and Jeanne Haunschild (Berlin: Dietrich Reimer Verlag, 1999), 135; Britta Funck, *Wilhelm Riphahn: Architekt in Köln* (Cologne: W. König, 2004), 40–50; http://www.bilderbuch-koeln.de; http://www.gag-koeln.de; http://www.koelnergartensiedlung.de/bickendorf.htm.

37 D. Stuart, "Architekt Wilhelm Riphahn, Köln," *Moderne Bauformen* 26 (December 1927): 476–85; Wolfram Hagspiel, *Der Kölner Architket Wilhelm Riphahn: sein Lebenswerk von 1913 bis 1945* (Cologne: W. König, 1982), 155–63; Werner Heinen and Anne-Marie Pfeffer, *Köln: Siedlungen 1888–1938* (Cologne: Verlag J. P. Bachem, 1988), 174–80; Helmut Fussbroich, *Architekturführer Köln: Profane Architektur nach 1900* (Cologne: J. P. Bachem Verlag, 1997), 82; Alexander Kierdorf, *Architectural Guide to Cologne*, trans. by Jean-Marie Clarke and Jeanne Haunschild (Berlin: Dietrich Reimer Verlag, 1999), 135; Britta Funck, *Wilhelm Riphahn: Architekt in Köln* (Cologne: W. König, 2004), 50–59; http://www.bilderbuch-koeln.de; www.gag-koeln.de.

38 Werner Heinen and Anne-Marie Pfeffer, *Köln: Siedlungen 1888–1938* (Cologne: Verlag J. P. Bachem, 1988), 104–8; http://www.bilderbuch-koeln.de; www.gag-koeln.de; http://www.k-poll.de/index_2.html.

39 Werner Heinen and Anne-Marie Pfeffer, *Köln: Siedlungen 1888–1938* (Cologne: Verlag J. P. Bachem, 1988), 121–25; Alexander Kierdorf, *Architectural Guide to Cologne*, trans. by Jean-Marie Clarke and Jeanne Haunschild (Berlin: Dietrich Reimer Verlag, 1999), 194; http://www.bilderbuch-koeln.de; http://www.diemaerchensiedlung.de; www.gag-koeln.de.

40 Alexander Kierdorf, *Architectural Guide to Cologne*, trans. by Jean-Marie Clarke and Jeanne Haunschild (Berlin: Dietrich Reimer Verlag, 1999), 194; http://www.fritz-august-breuhaus.com.

41 "Siedlung am Nordfriedhof," *Wasmuths Monatshefte für Baukunst* 6 (1922): 286–97; "Siedlungen und Andere Bauten von Architekt Wilhelm Riphahn, Köln," *Moderne Bauformen* 22 (January 1923): 17–19; Wolfram Hagspiel, *Der Kölner Architket Wilhelm Riphahn: sein Lebenswerk von 1913 bis 1945* (Cologne: W. König, 1982), 40–59; Werner Heinen and Anne-Marie Pfeffer, *Köln: Siedlungen 1888–1938* (Cologne: Verlag J. P. Bachem, 1988), 98–103; Britta Funck, *Wilhelm Riphahn: Architekt in Köln* (Cologne: W. König, 2004), 40–50; http://www.bilderbuch-koeln.de; www.gag-koeln.de.

42 Wolfram Hagspiel, *Der Kölner Architket Wilhelm Riphahn: sein Lebenswerk von 1913 bis 1945* (Cologne: W. König, 1982), 73–80; Werner Heinen and Anne-Marie Pfeffer, *Köln: Siedlungen 1888–1938* (Cologne: Verlag J. P. Bachem, 1988), 167–73; Helmut Fussbroich, *Architekturführer Köln: Profane Architektur nach 1900* (Cologne: J. P. Bachem Verlag, 1997), 55; Alexander Kierdorf, *Architectural Guide to Cologne*, trans. by Jean-Marie Clarke and Jeanne Haunschild (Berlin: Dietrich Reimer Verlag, 1999), 145; Britta Funck, *Wilhelm Riphahn: Architekt in Köln* (Cologne: W. König, 2004), 50–59; http://www. bilderbuch-koeln.de; http://www.gag-koeln.de.

43 Wolfram Hagspiel, *Der Kölner Architket Wilhelm Riphahn: sein Lebenswerk von 1913 bis 1945* (Cologne: W. König, 1982), 181–92; Werner Heinen and Anne-Marie Pfeffer, *Köln: Siedlungen 1888–1938* (Cologne: Verlag J. P. Bachem, 1988), 206–11; Helmut Fussbroich, *Architekturführer Köln: Profane Architektur nach 1900* (Cologne: J. P. Bachem Verlag, 1997), 61; Alexander Kierdorf, *Architectural Guide to Cologne*, trans. by Jean-Marie Clarke and Jeanne Haunschild (Berlin: Dietrich Reimer Verlag, 1999), 185; Britta Funck, *Wilhelm Riphahn: Architekt in Köln* (Cologne: W. König, 2004), 60–70; http://www. bilderbuch-koeln.de; http://www.gag-koeln.de.

44 Wolfram Hagspiel, *Der Kölner Architket Wilhelm Riphahn: sein Lebenswerk von 1913 bis 1945* (Cologne: W. König, 1982), 245–63; Werner Heinen and Anne-Marie Pfeffer, *Köln: Siedlungen 1888–1938* (Cologne: Verlag J. P. Bachem, 1988), 243–49; Helmut Fussbroich, *Architekturführer Köln: Profane Architektur nach 1900* (Cologne: J. P. Bachem Verlag, 1997), 74; Alexander Kierdorf, *Architectural Guide to Cologne*, trans. by Jean-Marie Clarke and Jeanne Haunschild (Berlin: Dietrich Reimer Verlag, 1999), 185; http://www.bilderbuch-koeln.de; http://www.gag-koeln.de.

45 Jörg A. E. Heimeshoff, *Denkmalgeschützte Häuser in Düsseldorf: mit Garten- und Bodendenkmälern* (Essen: Nobel, 2001), vol. 1: 13–19, 114–15; Roland Kanz and Jürgen Wiener, eds., *Architekturführer Düsseldorf* (Berlin: Dietrich Reimer Verlag, 2001), 115; Jürgen Wiener, *Die Gesolei und di Düsseldorfer Architektur der 20er Jahre* (Cologne: Bachem, 2001), 146; http://www.bilderbuch-duesseldorf.de; http://www.duesseldorf.de.

46 Roland Kanz and Jürgen Wiener, eds., *Architekturführer Düsseldorf* (Berlin: Dietrich Reimer Verlag, 2001), 97; Jürgen Wiener, *Die Gesolei und di Düsseldorfer Architektur der 20er Jahre* (Cologne: Bachem, 2001), 146; http://www.bilderbuch-duesseldorf.de; http://www.duesseldorf.de.

47 Jürgen Wiener, *Die Gesolei und di Düsseldorfer Architektur der 20er Jahre* (Cologne: Bachem, 2001), 146–47; http://www.bilderbuch-duesseldorf.de.

48 Roland Kanz and Jürgen Wiener, eds., *Architekturführer Düsseldorf* (Berlin: Dietrich Reimer Verlag, 2001), 159; Jürgen Wiener, *Die Gesolei und di Düsseldorfer Architektur der 20er Jahre* (Cologne: Bachem, 2001), 180; http://www.bilderbuch-duesseldorf.de; http://www.duesseldorf.de.

49 Roland Kanz and Jürgen Wiener, eds., *Architekturführer Düsseldorf* (Berlin: Dietrich Reimer Verlag, 2001), 99; Jürgen Wiener, *Die Gesolei und di Düsseldorfer Architektur der 20er Jahre* (Cologne: Bachem, 2001), 142, 144; http://www.bilderbuch-duesseldorf.de.

50 "Der Nordpark in Düsseldorf, der Ausklang einer Ausstellung," *Deutsche Bauzeitung* 74 (September 4, 1940), K: 133–40; Roland Kanz and Jürgen Wiener, eds., *Architekturführer Düsseldorf* (Berlin: Dietrich Reimer Verlag, 2001), 130–31; Jürgen Wiener, *Die Gesolei und di Düsseldorfer Architektur der 20er Jahre* (Cologne: Bachem, 2001), 26.

51 Dirk Schubert, *Hamburger Wohnquartiere* (Berlin: Dietrich Reimer Verlag, 2005), 132–35; "Wandsbek Garden City," http://www.fredriks.de; http://www.wandsbek-gartenstadt.de.

52 Ralf Lange, *Architekturführer Hamburg* (Stuttgart: Edition Axel Menges, 1995), 237; Dirk Schubert, *Hamburger Wohnquartiere* (Berlin: Dietrich Reimer Verlag, 2005), 136–39; Nataly Bombeck, "Eine Dorf-Idylle wie vor 85 Jahren," http://www.abendblatt.de; Holmer Stahnck, "Ein Wohn-Ensemble im Wandel der Zeit," http://www.aandblatt.de; "Friedrich Ostermeyer," http://www.architekten-portrait.de; "Jugendzentrum Notkestrasse," http://www.juno-hamburg.de; "Steenkamp Settlement," http://www.gustav-oelsner.de; http://hamburg-bildrchiv.de.

53 Hugo Koch, *Gartenkunst im Städtebau* (Berlin: Verlag Ernest Wasmuth, 1921), 273; Manfred F. Fischer, *Fritz Schumacher: Das Hamburger Stadtbild und die Denkmalpflege, Nr. 4* (Hamburg: Hans Christians Verlag, 1977), 63–64; Dirk Schubert and Hans Harms, *Wohnen in Hamburg* (Hamburg: Hans Christians Verlag, 1989), 276–80; Hermann Hipp, "Fritz Schumachers Hamburg: Die reformierte Grossstadt," in Vittorio Magnago Lampugnani and Romana Schneider, eds., *Moderne Architektur in Deutschland 1900 bis 1950: Reform und Tradition* (Stuttgart: Verlag Gerd Hatje, 1992), 162; Ralf Lange, *Architekturführer Hamburg* (Stuttgart: Edition Axel Menges, 1995), 182; Dirk Schubert, *Hamburger Wohnquartiere* (Berlin: Dietrich Reimer Verlag, 2005), 146–49; Dirk Meyhöfer, *Hamburg: Der Architekturführer* (Berlin: Verlagshaus Braun, 2007), 93; www.genossenschaft-fss-langenhorn.de.

54 For Schumacher's Hamburg work, see Gerhard Langmaack, *Fritz Schumacher: Vortrag in der Reihe 'Bedeutende Hamburger'* (Hamburg: H. Christian, 1964); *Schumacher und Hamburg* (Hamburg: Christians, 1969); Manfred F. Fischer, *Fritz Schumacher: Das Hamburger Stadtbild und die Denkmalpflege, Nr. 4* (Hamburg: Hans Christians Verlag, 1977).

55 "Die Neugestaltung eines Bebauungsplanes: Dulsberg-Gelände in Hamburg," *Städtebau* 20 (September–October 1925): 132–34; Manfred F. Fischer, *Fritz Schumacher: Das Hamburger Stadtbild und die Denkmalpflege* (Hamburg: H. Christians, 1977), 48, 57–62; "Amburgo Rossa: Dulsberg-Siedlung," *Abitare* 298 (July–August 1991): 168–70; Hermann Hipp, "Fritz Schumachers Hamburg: Die reformierte Grossstadt," in Vittorio Magnago Lampugnani and Romana Schneider, eds., *Moderne Architektur in Deutschland 1900 bis 1950: Reform und Tradition* (Stuttgart: Verlag Gerd Hatje, 1992), 155–56; Susanne Harth, "Stadt und Region," in Hartmut Frank, ed., *Fritz Schumacher: Reformkultur und Moderne*, exhibition catalogue (Stuttgart: Hatje, 1994), 160–61; Ralf Lange, *Architekturführer Hamburg* (Stuttgart: Edition Axel Menges, 1995), 189–90; Winfried Nerdinger and Cornelius Tafel, *Architectural Guide Germany: 20th Century* (Basel: Birkhäuser, 1996), 27; Jean-François Lejeune, "From Hellerau to Bauhaus: Memory and Modernity in the German Garden City," *The New City* 3 (Fall 1996): 50–69; Dirk Schubert, *Hamburger Wohnquartiere* (Berlin: Dietrich Reimer Verlag, 2005), 150–53; Dirk Meyhöfer, *Hamburg: Der Architekturführer* (Berlin: Verlagshaus Braun, 2007), 122–23; Zineb Braunig, "Emergence of Dulsberg," www.architekturarchiv-web.de/dulsberg.htm.

56 "Die Siedlung Laatzen bei Hannover," *Wasmuths Monatshefte für Baukunst* 5 (1920–21): 299–310; Isa Baumgart, Jens Giesecke, and Hartmut Millarg, *Urban Design in Hannover*, trans. Johann Bernhardt (Berlin: Dietrich Reimer Verlag, 2000), 68–69; Andrés Duany, Elizabeth Plater-Zyberk, and Robert Alminana, *The New Civic Art: Elements of Town Planning* (New York: Rizzoli International Publications, 2003), 297; http://www.hannover.de/region/naherholung/gruenerring/tour4/staedts.html.

57 Karl Elkart, *Neues Bauen in Hannover* (Hannover: Verkehrs-Verein, 1929), 20–21; Isa Baumgart, Jens Giesecke, and Hartmut Millarg, *Urban Design in Hannover*, trans. by Johann Bernhardt (Berlin: Dietrich Reimer Verlag, 2000), 76–77; Martin Wörner, Ulrich Hägele, and Sabine Kirchof, *Architectural Guide to Hannover*, trans. by Margaret Marks (Berlin: Dietrich Reimer Verlag, 2000), 162; "Gartenstadt Kleefeld," http://www.stadthistorie.info.

58 Paul Sigel et al., *Architectural Guide to Potsdam*, trans. by Lucinda Rennison (Berlin: Dietrich Reimer Verlag, 2006), 140; http://www. gewoba.com/downloads/1115138086_ieterzeitung_05_052.pdf.

59 Martin Neitzke, "Perspektiven eines aufgeklärten Traditionalismus," *Archithese* 19 (November–December 1989): 18–24; Martin Neitzke, *Gustav Wolf: bauen für das Leben: Neues Wohnen zwischen Tradition und Moderne* (Tübingen and Berlin: Ernst Wasmuth Verlag, 1993), 26–35; Winfried Nerdinger and Cornelius Tafel, *Architectural Guide Germany: 20th Century*, trans. by Ingrid Taylor and Ralph Stern (Basel: Birkhäuser, 1996), 262–63; Jörg Kirchner, "Traditionalismus in der Architektur der frühen DDR," in Bernfried Lichtnau, ed., *Architketur und Städtebau: im südlichen Ostseeraum zwischen 1936 und 1980* (Berlin: Lukas Verlag, 2002), 289–90; Sylvaine Hänsel and Stefan Rethfeld, *Architectural Guide to Münster*, trans. by Lucinda Rennison (Berlin: Dietrich Reimer Verlag, 2008), 243.
60 Hänsel and Rethfeld, *Architectural Guide to Münster*, 243.
61 Vittorio Magnago Lampugnani, "Modernism, Lifestyle Reforms, City and Nature Experiments in Urban Design in Berlin from 1900 to 1914," in Thorsten Scheer, Josef Paul Kleihues, and Paul Kahlfeldt, eds., *City of Architecture, Architecture of the City: Berlin 1900–2000* (Berlin: Nicolai, 2000), 36–37. Also see Theodor Fischer, "Wie stellt sich der Architekt zur Normalisierung und Typisierung," in *Süddeutsche Bauzeitung* 12 (June 15, 1919): 50; John Robert Mullin, "City Planning in Frankfurt, 1925–1932: A Study in Practical Utopianism," *Journal of Urban History* 4 (1977): 25 (n.24); Richard Pommer, "The Architecture of Urban Housing in the United States During the Early 1930s," *Journal of the Society of Architectural Historians* 37 (December 1978): 259, 261; Winfried Nerdinger, "Theodor Fischer," trans. by Peter Blundell Jones, *Architectural Review* 180 (November 1986): 61–65; Winfried Nerdinger, *Theodor Fischer: Architekt und Städtebauer* (Berlin: Ernst, 1988), 93, 120–21, 286–87; Gabriele Schickel, "Theodor Fischer als Lehrer der Avantgarde," in Vittorio Magnago Lampugnani and Romana Schneider, eds., *Moderne Architektur in Deutschland 1900 bis 1950: Reform und Tradition* (Stuttgart: Verlag Gerd Hatje, 1992), 62–63; Winfried Nerdinger and Cornelius Tafel, *Architectural Guide Germany: 20th Century* (Basel: Birkhäuser, 1996), 454; Winfried Nerdinger, *Architectural Guide to Munich* (Berlin: Dietrich Reimer Verlag, 2007), 144; Vittorio Magnago Lampugnani, *Die Stadt im 20. Jahrhundert* (Berlin: Verlag Klaus Wagenbach, 2010), 312–13; www.kulturverein-alteheide.de/ah/alteheide.htm.
62 Nerdinger, "Theodor Fischer," *Architectural Review*: 64.
63 Fischer, "Wie stellt sich der Architekt zur Normalisierung und Typisierung": 50, quoted in Lampugnani, "Modernism, Lifestyle Reforms, City and Nature Experiments in Urban Design in Berlin from 1900 to 1914," in Scheer, Kleihues, and Kahlfeldt, eds., *City of Architecture, Architecture of the City: Berlin 1900–2000*, 37.
64 Lampugnani, "Modernism, Lifestyle Reforms, City and Nature Experiments in Urban Design in Berlin from 1900 to 1914," in Scheer, Kleihues, and Kahlfeldt, eds., *City of Architecture, Architecture of the City: Berlin 1900–2000*, 36.
65 Georg Haberland, *40 Jahre Berlinische Boden-Gesellschaft* (Berlin, 1930), 140–41; "Die neue Siedlung Lindenhof in Berlin," *Wasmuths Monatschefte für Baukunst* 15 (January 1931): 17–24; Ronald Wiedenhoeft, "Workers' Housing as Social Politics," *Via* 4 (1980): 112–25; Rosemarie Haag Bletter, "Revising Modernist History: The Architecture of the 1920s and 1930s," *Art Journal* 43 (Summer 1983): 108–20; *Martin Wagner: 1885–1957*, exhibition catalog (Berlin: Akademie der Künste, 1985), 165; Ronald Wiedenhoeft, *Berlin's Housing Revolution: German Reform in the 1920s* (Ann Arbor: UMI Research Press, 1985), 59, 64–65; Ludovica Scarpa, *Martin Wagner und Berlin* (Braunschweig: F. Vieweg & Sohn, 1986), 27–28, 173–76; Manfredo Tafuri, *The Sphere and the Labyrinth: Avant-Gardes and Architecture From Piranesi to the 1970s*, trans. by Pellegrino d'Acierno and Robert Connolly (Cambridge, Mass.: MIT Press, 1987), 200, figs. 214–16; Vittorio Magnago Lampugnani, "From the New Community to the Horseshoe Estate: A History of German Modern Architecture—Part 4," trans. by Chris Charlesworth, *Architecture + Urbanism* (December 1992): 51–52, 54; Jean-François Lejeune, "From Hellerau to Bauhaus: Memory and Modernity in the German Garden City," *The New City* 3 (Fall 1996): 50–69; Karl Kiem, *Die Gartenstadt Staaken* (Berlin: Gebr. Mann Verlag, 1997), 208; Annette Ciré, "'Beyond the Metropolis': Urban Design and Architecture of the 'Country House Colonies' and Garden Cities in Berlin Suburbs before 1914," in Thorsten Scheer, Josef Paul Kleihues, and Paul Kahlfeldt, eds., *City of Architecture, Architecture of the City: Berlin 1900–2000* (Berlin: Nicolai, 2000), 64; Vittorio Magnago Lampugnani, "Modernism, Lifestyle Reforms, City and Nature Experiments in Urban Design in Berlin from 1900 to 1914," in Scheer, Kleihues, and Kahlfeldt, eds., *City of Architecture, Architecture of the City: Berlin 1900–2000*, 38; Pamela E. Swett, *Neighbors and Enemies: The Culture of Radicalism in Berlin, 1929–1933* (Cambridge and New York: Cambridge University Press, 2004), 48; Jeannette Redensek, "Manufacturing Gemeinschaft: Architecture, Tradition, and the Sociology of Community in Germany, 1890–1920" (Ph.D. diss., City University of New York, 2007): 271, 298–99; David H. Haney, *When Modern Was Green: Life and Work of Landscape Architect Leberecht Migge* (London and New York: Routledge, 2010), 180–82; Vittorio Magnago Lampugnani, *Die Stadt im 20. Jahrhundert* (Berlin: Verlag Klaus Wagenbach, 2010), 318–19.
66 Lampugnani, "From the New Community to the Horseshoe Estate: A History of German Modern Architecture—Part 4": 51.
67 Wiedenhoeft, *Berlin's Housing Revolution*, 65.
68 Werner Hegemann, "Die Rettung des Tempelhofer Feldes," *Wasmuths Monatshefte für Baukunst* 8 (November–December 1924): 333–45; Paul Wolf, *Wohnung und Siedlung* (Berlin: Wasmuth, 1926), 212; Albert Gut, *Der Wohnungsbau in Deutschland* (Munich: Verlag F. Bruckmann, 1928), 536; Friedrich Schmidt and Martin Ebel, *Wohnungsbau der Nachkriegszeit in Deutschland* (Berlin: Eulen-Verlag, 1928), 174; Georg Haberland, *40 Jahre Berlinische Boden-Gesellschaft* (Berlin, 1930), 33, 80; Ronald Wiedenhoeft, *Berlin's Housing Revolution: German Reform in the 1920s* (Ann Arbor: UMI Research Press, 1985), 65–71; Peter Güttler et al., *Berlin-Brandenburg: An Architectural Guide* (Berlin: Ernst & Sohn, 1990), 124; Gerhard Fehl and Juan Rodriguez-Lores, "La 'città giardino' in Germania tra il 1910 e il 1918," *Casabella* 57 (January 1993): 12–16, 117–18; Jean-François Lejeune, "From Hellerau to Bauhaus: Memory and Modernity in the German Garden City," *The New City* 3 (Fall 1996): 50–69; Karl Kiem, *Die Gartenstadt Staaken* (Berlin: Gebr. Mann Verlag, 1997), 208–9; Vittorio Magnago Lampugnani, "Modernism, Lifestyle Reforms, City and Nature Experiments in Urban Design in Berlin from 1900 to 1914," in Thorsten Scheer, Josef Paul Kleihues, and Paul Kahlfeldt, eds., *City of Architecture, Architecture of the City: Berlin 1900–2000* (Berlin: Nicolai, 2000), 34; Christiane Crasemann Collins, *Werner Hegemann and the Search for Universal Urbanism* (New York: W. W. Norton, 2005), 171. Also see www.berlin.de/ba-tempelhof-schoeneberg; www.templhofer-feld.de.
69 Wiedenhoeft, *Berlin's Housing Revolution*, 71.
70 Wiedenhoeft, *Berlin's Housing Revolution*, 70.
71 *Neuere arbeiten von O.R. Salvisberg* (Berlin: Friedrich Ernst Hübsch, 1927; Berlin: Gebr. Mann Verlag, 2000), 39–43; Martin Wörner, Doris Mollenschott, and Karl-Heinz Hütter, *Architekturführer Berlin*, trans. by Claus Warren Offerman (Berlin: Dietrich Reimer Verlag, 1991, 1994), 440; *Berlin/Brandenburg: An Architectural Guide* (Berlin: Ernst & Sohn, 1993), 194; Kristiana Hartmann, "Von der Gartenstadt zur Grossiedlung," in *O.R. Salvisberg: Die Andere Moderne* (Zurich: GTA, 1995), 170–79; Claude Lichtenstein, "Werkkatalog," in *O.R. Salvisberg: Die Andere Moderne*, 260; Karl Kiem, *Die Gartenstadt Staaken* (Berlin: Gebr. Mann Verlag, 1997), 208, 210.
72 Walter Lehwess, "Kleinhassiedlung in Berlin Dahlem," *Stadtbaukunst alter und neuer Zeit* 2 (1921): 213–20; *40 Jahre: Berlinische Boden-Gesellschaft* (Berlin, 1930), 72; Ronald Wiedenhoeft, *Berlin's Housing Revolution: German Reform in the 1920s* (Ann Arbor: UMI Research Press, 1985), 55, 59–61; "Lentze Settlement," www.berlin.de.
73 Jakob Schallenberger and Hans Kraffert, *Berliner Wohnungsbauten aus öffentlichen Mitteln* (Berlin: Bauwelt, 1926), 48–52; Albert Gut, *Der Wohnungsbau in Deutschland nach dem Weltkriege* (Munich: Bruckmann, 1928), plate X; Ronald Wiedenhoeft, *Berlin's Housing Revolution: German Reform in the 1920s* (Ann Arbor: UMI Research Press, 1985), 74–77; Norbert Borrmann, *Paul Schultze-Naumburg, 1869–1949: Maler, Publizist, Architekt* (Essen: Verlag Richard Bacht, 1989), 136; Winfried Nerdinger and Cornelius Tafel, *Architectural Guide Germany: 20th Century* (Basel: Birkhäuser, 1996), 110; "'Am Heidehof' Siedlung," www.berlin.de. Also see Jakob Schallenberger, *Der Wohnungsneubau in Berlin* (Berlin: Berliner Wohnungsfürsorgegesellschaft, n.d.,), 10.
74 Ronald Wiedenhoeft, *Berlin's Housing Revolution: German Reform in the 1920s* (Ann Arbor: UMI Research Press, 1985), 77–81. Also see Jakob Schallenberger and Erwin Gutkind, *Berliner Wohnbauten der letzten jahre* (Berlin: Verlag W. & S. Loewenthal, 1931), 102; Rosemarie Haag Bletter, "Bruno Taut and Paul Scheerbart's Vision: Utopian Aspects of German Expressionist Architecture" (Ph.D. diss., Columbia University, 1973): 504–5; Kurt Junghanns, *Bruno Taut: 1880–1938* (Berlin: Elefanten Press Verlag, 1983), figs. 131–38; Rosemarie Haag Bletter, "Revising Modernist History: The Architecture of the 1920s and 1930s," *Art Journal* 43 (Summer 1983): 108–20; Martin Wörner, Doris Mollenschott, and Karl-Heinz Hütter, *Architekturführer Berlin*, trans. by Claus Warren Offerman (Berlin: Dietrich Reimer Verlag, 1991, 1994), 401; Vittorio Magnago Lampugnani, "From the New Community to the Horseshoe Estate: A History of German Modern Architecture—Part 4," trans. by Chris Charlesworth, *Architecture + Urbanism* (December 1992): 52; Kristina Hartmann, "Garden City Experiences in Germany," in Gabriele Tagliaventi, ed., *Garden City* (Rome: Gangemi Editore, 1994), 278; Winfried Brenne ed., *Bruno Taut: Meister des farbigen Bauens in Berlin* (Berlin: Verlagshaus Braun, 2005), 68–73; Jörg Haspel and Annemarie Jaeggi, *Siedlungen der Berliner Moderne* (Munich: Deutscher Kunstverlag, 2007), 38–47; Gerrit Engel and Detlef Jessen-Klingenberg, *Berlin Photographs: 234 Berlin Buildings in Chronological Order from 1230 to 2008* (Munich: Schirmer/Mosel, 2009), 122; Rolf Rave, *Modern Architecture in Berlin*, trans. by Karl Edward Johnsen (Stuttgart: Edition Axel Menges, 2009), 450; *Siedlungen der Berliner Moderne: Eintragung in die Welterbeliste der UNESCO* (Berlin: Braun, 2009), 37, 42–45, 74–78, 107–9, 129–31, 156–57, 169–71, 220–21, 235–36, 271–72. Also see Jakob Schallenberger, *Der Wohnungsneubau in Berlin* (Berlin: Berliner Wohnungsfürsorgegesell-schaft, n.d.,), 5–6; "Schiller Park Village," www.berlin.de.
75 Bletter, "Bruno Taut and Paul Scheerbart's Vision: Utopian Aspects of German Expressionist Architecture": 504–5.
76 Kurt Junghanns, *Bruno Taut: 1880–1938* (Berlin: Elefanten Press Verlag, 1983), figs. 234–44; Martin Wörner, Doris Mollenschott, and Karl-Heinz Hütter, *Architekturführer Berlin*, trans. by Claus Warren Offerman (Berlin: Dietrich Reimer Verlag, 1991, 1994), 270; Vittorio Magnago Lampugnani, "From the New Community to the Horseshoe Estate: A History of German Modern Architecture—Part 4," trans. by Chris Charlesworth, *Architecture + Urbanism* (December 1992): 48, 52; Kristina Hartmann, "Garden City Experiences in Germany," in Gabriele Tagliaventi, ed., *Garden City* (Rome: Gangemi Editore, 1994), 278; Jean-François Lejeune, "From Hellerau to Bauhaus: Memory and Modernity in the German Garden City," *The New City* 3 (Fall 1996): 50–69; Rolf Rave, *Modern Architecture in Berlin*, trans. by Karl Edward Johnsen (Stuttgart: Edition Axel Menges, 2009), 455; "Freie Scholle," www.capitalieuropee.altervista.org; "Settlement Tegel," www.freischolle.de.
77 Lejeune, "From Hellerau to Bauhaus: Memory and Modernity in the German Garden City": 61.
78 Winfried Nerdinger and Cornelius Tafel, *Architectural Guide Germany: 20th Century* (Basel: Birkhäuser, 1996), 114–15. Also see Bruno Taut, *Die neue Baukunst in Europa und Amerika* (Stuttgart: J. Hoffmann, 1929), 7; "Housing, Berlin-Britz: Horseshoe Plan Surrounding Lake," *Architecture* (New York) 60 (December 1929): 337; Jakob Schallenberger and Erwin Gutkind, *Berliner Wohnbauten der letzten jahre* (Berlin: Verlag W. & S. Loewenthal, 1931), 62–63; Rosemarie Haag Bletter, "Bruno Taut and Paul Scheerbart's Vision: Utopian Aspects of German Expressionist Architecture" (Ph.D. diss., Columbia University, 1973): 507–11; Francesco Dal Co and Manfredo Tafuri, *Modern Architecture*, trans. by Robert Erich Wolf (New York: Harry N. Abrams, 1979), 186, 196; Ronald Wiedenhoeft, "Workers' Housing as Social Politics," *Via* 4 (1980): 112–25; Helge Pitz, "Gelb-weiss-schwarz-oder…? Gespräch mit einen Siedlungsarchitekten," *Daidalos* 6 (December 1982): 89–97; Kurt Junghanns, *Bruno Taut: 1880–1938* (Berlin: Elefanten Press Verlag, 1983), figs. 145–60; Rosemarie Haag Bletter, "Revising Modernist History: The Architecture of the 1920s and 1930s," *Art Journal* 43 (Summer 1983): 108–20; Annemarie Jaeggi, "Hufeisensiedlung Britz," in Norbert Huse, ed., *Siedlungen der zwanziger jahre—heute. Vier Berliner Grossiedlungen 1924–1984* (Berlin: Bauahu-Archiv, 1985), 111–36; Ronald Wiedenhoeft, *Berlin's Housing Revolution: German Reform in the 1920s* (Ann Arbor: UMI Research Press, 1985), 84–91; *Martin Wagner: 1885–1957*, exhibition catalog (Berlin: Akademie der Künste, 1985), 166–67; Ludovica Scarpa, *Martin Wagner und Berlin* (Braunschweig: F. Vieweg & Sohn, 1986), 177–79; Dennis J. De Witt and Elizabeth R. De

Witt, *Modern Architecture in Europe: A Guide to Buildings Since the Industrial Revolution* (New York: E. P. Dutton, 1987), 70; Joachim Fait, *Berlin* (Munich: Prestel, 1992), 127; Vittorio Magnago Lampugnani, "From the New Community to the Horseshoe Estate: A History of German Modern Architecture—Part 4," trans. by Chris Charlesworth, *Architecture + Urbanism* (December 1992): 48–59; Nicholas Bullock, "Searching for the New Dimensions of the City," in Josef Paul Kleihues and Christina Rathgeber, eds., *Berlin/New York: Like and Unlike* (New York: Rizzoli International Publications, 1993), 242–44; *Berlin/Brandenburg: An Architectural Guide* (Berlin: Ernst & Sohn, 1993), 201; Jorge Sainz, "Bruno Taut: Colonia Hufeisen, Berlin-Britz, 1925–1927," *AV Monographs* 56 (November–December 1995): 22–23; Jean-François Lejeune, "From Hellerau to Bauhaus: Memory and Modernity in the German Garden City," *The New City* 3 (Fall 1996): 50–69; Nike Bätzner, "Housing Projects of the 1920s: A Laboratory of Social Ideas and Formal Experiment," in Thorsten Scheer, Josef Paul Kleihues, and Paul Kahlfeldt, eds., *City of Architecture, Architecture of the City: Berlin 1900–2000* (Berlin: Nicolai, 2000), 150–51; Winfried Brenne, ed., *Bruno Taut: Meister des farbigen Bauens in Berlin* (Berlin: Verlagshaus Braun, 2005), 158; Wolfgang Förster, *Housing in the 20th and 21st Centuries* (Munich: Prestel, 2006), 41; Rainer Haubrich, Hans Wolfgang Hoffmann, and Philipp Meuser, *Berlin: The Architecture Guide* (Berlin: Braun, 2006), 121–23; Jörg Haspel and Annemarie Jaeggi, *Siedlungen der Berliner Moderne* (Munich: Deutscher Kunstverlag, 2007), 48–61; Jeannette Redensek, "Manufacturing Gemeinschaft: Architecture, Tradition, and the Sociology of Community in Germany, 1890–1920" (Ph.D. diss., City University of New York, 2007): 267–73; Eric D. Weitz, *Weimar Germany: Promise and Tragedy* (Princeton, N.J.: Princeton University Press, 2007), 179–83; Gerrit Engel and Detlef Jessen-Klingenberg, *Berlin Photographs: 234 Berlin Buildings in Chronological Order from 1230 to 2008* (Munich: Schirmer/Mosel, 2009), 121; Rolf Rave, *Modern Architecture in Berlin*, trans. by Karl Edward Johnsen (Stuttgart: Edition Axel Menges, 2009), 169–71; *Siedlungen der Berliner Moderne: Eintragung in die Welterbeliste der UNESCO* (Berlin: Braun, 2009), 46–51, 131–33, 158, 225–26, 236–38, 275; Harald Bodenschatz, *Berlin Urban Design: A Brief History*, trans. by Sasha Disko (Berlin: DOM Publishers, 2010), 41–43; David H. Haney, *When Modern Was Green: Life and Work of Landscape Architect Leberecht Migge* (London and New York: Routledge, 2010), 180, 182–88; Vittorio Magnago Lampugnani, *Die Stadt im 20. Jahrhundert* (Berlin: Verlag Klaus Wagenbach, 2010), 310, 326–29; Celina Kress, *Adolf Sommerfeld/Andrew Sommerfield: Bauen für Berlin 1910–1970* (Berlin: Lukas Verlag, 2011), 138–39; http://www.hufeisensiedlung-berlin.de; http://www.neubritz.de.

79 Redensek, "Manufacturing Gemeinschaft: Architecture, Tradition, and the Sociology of Community in Germany, 1890–1920": 268–69.

80 Lampugnani, "From the New Community to the Horseshoe Estate: A History of German Modern Architecture—Part 4": 53.

81 Taut, *Die neue Baukunst in Europa und Amerika*, 7, quoted in Lampugnani, "From the New Community to the Horseshoe Estate: A History of German Modern Architecture—Part 4": 53.

82 "Housing, Berlin-Zehlendorf, Germany," *Architecture* (New York) 60 (December 1929): 338–39; Jakob Schallenberger and Erwin Gutkind, *Berliner Wohnbauten der letzten jahre* (Berlin: Verlag W. & S. Loewenthal, 1931), 62; Rosemarie Haag Bletter, "Bruno Taut and Paul Scheerbart's Vision: Utopian Aspects of German Expressionist Architecture" (Ph.D. diss., Columbia University, 1973): 512–16; Helge Pitz, "Gelb-weiss-schwarz-oder…? Gespräch mit einen Siedlungsarchitekten," *Daidalos* 6 (December 1982): 89–97; Kurt Junghanns, *Bruno Taut: 1880–1938* (Berlin: Elefanten Press Verlag, 1983), figs. 194–203; Rosemarie Haag Bletter, "Revising Modernist History: The Architecture of the 1920s and 1930s," *Art Journal* 43 (Summer 1983): 108–20; Richard Pommer, "The Flat Roof: A Modernist Controversy in Germany," *Art Journal* 43 (Summer 1983): 158–69; "Nel quartiere Onkel-Toms-Hütte," *Abitare* 226 (July–August 1984): 24–26; Ronald Wiedenhoeft, *Berlin's Housing Revolution: German Reform in the 1920s* (Ann Arbor: UMI Research Press, 1985), 105, 115–17, figs. 48–56; "Siedlungen der zwanziger Jahre: Vier Berliner Grosssiedlungen," *Bauforum* 19 (1986): 41–45; Dennis J. De Witt and Elizabeth R. De Witt, *Modern Architecture in Europe: A Guide to Buildings Since the Industrial Revolution* (New York: E. P. Dutton, 1987), 69; Joachim Fait, *Berlin* (Munich: Prestel, 1992), 138–39; *Berlin/Brandenburg: An Architectural Guide* (Berlin: Ernst & Sohn, 1993), 214; Jan-Olaf Moed, "Waldsiedlung Zehlendorf," (1993), http://content.grin.com/document/v105206.pdf; "Les cités-jardins de Berlin," *L'Architecture d'Aujourd'hui* 287 (June 1993): 49; Winfried Nerdinger and Cornelius Tafel, *Architectural Guide Germany: 20th Century* (Basel: Birkhäuser, 1996), 116; Jean-François Lejeune, "From Hellerau to Bauhaus: Memory and Modernity in the German Garden City," *The New City* 3 (Fall 1996): 50–69; Nike Bätzner, "Housing Projects of the 1920s: A Laboratory of Social Ideas and Formal Experiment," in Thorsten Scheer, Josef Paul Kleihues, and Paul Kahlfeldt, eds., *City of Architecture, Architecture of the City: Berlin 1900–2000* (Berlin: Nicolai, 2000), 152–53; Peter Blundell-Jones, "Delight: Waldsiedlung Onkel Toms Hütte, Berlin," *Architectural Review* 211 (May 2002): 98; Winfried Brenne and Franz Jaschke, "Städtebau und Architektur bei Bruno Taut," in Winfried Brenne ed., *Bruno Taut: Meister des farbigen Bauens in Berlin* (Berlin: Verlagshaus Braun, 2005), 156–64; Rainer Haubrich, Hans Wolfgang Hoffmann, and Philipp Meuser, *Berlin: The Architecture Guide* (Berlin: Braun, 2006), 137; Jeannette Redensek, "Manufacturing Gemeinschaft: Architecture, Tradition, and the Sociology of Community in Germany, 1890–1920" (Ph.D. diss., City University of New York, 2007): 216–17; Eric D. Weitz, *Weimar Germany: Promise and Tragedy* (Princeton, N.J.: Princeton University Press, 2007), 177–79; Gerrit Engel and Detlef Jessen-Klingenberg, *Berlin Photographs: 234 Berlin Buildings in Chronological Order from 1230 to 2008* (Munich: Schirmer/Mosel, 2009), 132; Rolf Rave, *Modern Architecture in Berlin*, trans. by Karl Edward Johnsen (Stuttgart: Edition Axel Menges, 2009), 300–301; Maiken Umbach, *German Cities and Bourgeois Modernism, 1890–1924* (New York: Oxford University Press, 2009), 203; David H. Haney, *When Modern Was Green: Life and Work of Landscape Architect Leberecht Migge* (London and New York: Routledge, 2010), 185, 189–90; Vittorio Magnago Lampugnani, *Die Stadt im 20. Jahrhundert* (Berlin: Verlag Klaus Wagenbach, 2010), 328–31; Celina Kress, *Adolf Sommerfeld/Andrew Sommerfield: Bauen für Berlin 1910–1970* (Berlin: Lukas Verlag, 2011), 134, 138–40, 155–57; "Waldsiedlung Zehlendorf," www.berlin.de; "Waldsiedlung Zehlendorf," www.hyke.wordpress.com.

83 Bätzner, "Housing Projects of the 1920s: A Laboratory of Social Ideas and Formal Experiment," in Scheer, Kleihues, and Kahlfeldt, eds., *City of Architecture, Architecture of the City: Berlin 1900–2000*, 152.

84 Bletter, "Bruno Taut and Paul Scheerbart's Vision: Utopian Aspects of German Expressionist Architecture": 513.

85 Bletter, "Revising Modernist History: The Architecture of the 1920s and 1930s": 117.

86 Jeannette Redensek, "Manufacturing Gemeinschaft: Architecture, Tradition, and the Sociology of Community in Germany, 1890–1920" (Ph.D. diss., City University of New York, 2007): 217. Also see Rolf Rave, *Modern Architecture in Berlin*, trans. by Karl Edward Johnsen (Stuttgart: Edition Axel Menges, 2009), 302–4; Vittorio Magnago Lampugnani, *Die Stadt im 20. Jahrhundert* (Berlin: Verlag Klaus Wagenbach, 2010), 330.

87 Leo Adler, *Neuzeitliche Miethäuser und Siedlungen* (Berlin-Charlottenburg: Ernst Pollack, 1931; Munich: Kraus Reprint, 1981), 158; Heinz Johannes, *Neues Bauen in Berlin* (Berlin: Deutscher Kunstverlag, 1931), 79; "GEHAG Gross-Siedlung Carl Legien Stadt an der Carmen Sylva Strasse," *Die Bauwelt* 22 (1931): issue 19; "German and Austrian Architecture: Carl Legien, Berlin," *Builder* 142 (January 1932): 384; Ronald Wiedenhoeft, *Berlin's Housing Revolution: German Reform in the 1920s* (Ann Arbor: UMI Research Press, 1985), 135–36, figs. 64–66; *Berlin/Brandenburg: An Architectural Guide* (Berlin: Ernst & Sohn, 1993), 111; "Les cites-jardins de Berlin," *L'Architecture d'Aujourd'hui* 287 (June 1993): 49; Winfried Nerdinger and Cornelius Tafel, *Architectural Guide Germany: 20th Century* (Basel: Birkhäuser, 1996), 114–15; Nike Bätzner, "Housing Projects of the 1920s: A Laboratory of Social Ideas and Formal Experiment," in Thorsten Scheer, Josef Paul Kleihues, and Paul Kahlfeldt, eds., *City of Architecture, Architecture of the City: Berlin 1900–2000* (Berlin: Nicolai, 2000), 153–54; Winfried Brenne and Franz Jaschke, "Städtebau und Architektur bei Bruno Taut," in Winfried Brenne ed., *Bruno Taut: Meister des farbigen Bauens in Berlin* (Berlin: Verlagshaus Braun, 2005), 156–64; Jörg Haspel and Annemarie Jaeggi, *Siedlungen der Berliner Moderne* (Munich: Deutscher Kunstverlag, 2007), 62–71; Gerrit Engel and Detlef Jessen-Klingenberg, *Berlin Photographs: 234 Berlin Buildings in Chronological Order from 1230 to 2008* (Munich: Schirmer/Mosel, 2009), 133; Rolf Rave, *Modern Architecture in Berlin*, trans. by Karl Edward Johnsen (Stuttgart: Edition Axel Menges, 2009), 98; *Siedlungen der Berliner Moderne: Eintragung in die Welterbeliste der UNESCO* (Berlin: Braun, 2009), 37, 52–55, 83–87, 112–14, 133–35, 150, 159–60, 174–75, 181–82, 188, 195, 226–27, 272; Vittorio Magnago Lampugnani, *Die Stadt im 20. Jahrhundert* (Berlin: Verlag Klaus Wagenbach, 2010), 331–32.

88 "Gross-Siedlung Berlin Reinickendorf, Schiller-Promenade," *Die Bauwelt* 21 (1930): issue 48; Leo Adler, *Neuzeitliche Miethäuser und Siedlungen* (Berlin-Charlottenburg: Ernst Pollack, 1931; Munich: Kraus Reprint, 1981), 175; Heinz Johannes, *Neues Bauen in Berlin* (Berlin: Deutscher Kunstverlag, 1931), 79; Jakob Schallenberger and Erwin Gutkind, *Berliner Wohnbauten der letzten jahre* (Berlin: Verlag W. & S. Loewenthal, 1931), 110–14; "Das Fernheizwerk am Schillerring in Berlin-Reinickendorf," *Deutsche Bauzeitung* 65 (1931): 236–38; Ronald Wiedenhoeft, *Berlin's Housing Revolution: German Reform in the 1920s* (Ann Arbor: UMI Research Press, 1985), 136, 144–46, figs. 67–72; *Berlin/Brandenburg: An Architectural Guide* (Berlin: Ernst & Sohn, 1993), 169; Claude Lichtenstein, "Werkkatalog," in *O.R. Salvisberg: Die Andere Moderne* (Zurich: GTA, 1995), 66–69; Winfried Nerdinger and Cornelius Tafel, *Architectural Guide Germany: 20th Century* (Basel: Birkhäuser, 1996), 119; Philipp Meuser, "Die Weisse Stadt," *Bauwelt* 87 (November 1, 1996): 2348–53; Nike Bätzner, "Housing Projects of the 1920s: A Laboratory of Social Ideas and Formal Experiment," in Thorsten Scheer, Josef Paul Kleihues, and Paul Kahlfeldt, eds., *City of Architecture, Architecture of the City: Berlin 1900–2000* (Berlin: Nicolai, 2000), 155–56; Jörg Haspel and Annemarie Jaeggi, *Siedlungen der Berliner Moderne* (Munich: Deutscher Kunstverlag, 2007), 72–83; Rolf Rave, *Modern Architecture in Berlin*, trans. by Karl Edward Johnsen (Stuttgart: Edition Axel Menges, 2009), 52; *Siedlungen der Berliner Moderne: Eintragung in die Welterbeliste der UNESCO* (Berlin: Braun, 2009), 37, 58–59, 86–90, 115, 160–61, 176–77, 188, 227–28, 239–40, 272–73; Vittorio Magnago Lampugnani, *Die Stadt im 20. Jahrhundert* (Berlin: Verlag Klaus Wagenbach, 2010), 334.

89 Wiedenhoeft, *Berlin's Housing Revolution: German Reform in the 1920s*, 144.

90 Wiedenhoeft, *Berlin's Housing Revolution: German Reform in the 1920s*, 146.

91 Susan Rose Henderson, "The Work of Ernst May, 1919–1930" (Ph.D. diss., Columbia University, 1990): 178–295; Susan R. Henderson, "Ernst May and the Campaign to Resettle the Countryside: Rural Housing in Silesia, 1919–1925," *Journal of the Society of Architectural Historians* 61 (June 2002): 188–211; Beate Störtkuhl, "Ernst May and the Schlesische Heimstäte," trans. by Jane Michael, in *Ernst May: 1886–1970*, eds. Claudia Quiring, Wolfgang Voigt, Peter Cachola Schmal, and Eckhard Herrel (Munich: Prestel, 2011), 33–49.

92 *Bericht über die geschäftliche Lage der schlesischen Heimstätte Breslau* (1922), quoted in Störtkuhl, "Ernst May and the Schlesische Heimstäte," in *Ernst May: 1886–1970*, 34.

93 Störtkuhl, "Ernst May and the Schlesische Heimstäte," in *Ernst May: 1886–1970*, 33.

94 Henderson, "The Work of Ernst May, 1919–1930": 74–87; Claudia Quiring, "Catalogue Raisonné," in *Ernst May: 1886–1970*, 251; Störtkuhl, "Ernst May and the Schlesische Heimstäte," in *Ernst May: 1886–1970*, 36–38.

95 Ernst May, "Wohnungsfürsorgegesellschaften und Baukultur," *Das Schlesische Heim* 1 (No. 12, 1920): 3, quoted in Störtkuhl, "Ernst May and the Schlesische Heimstäte," in *Ernst May: 1886–1970*, 36.

96 Störtkuhl, "Ernst May and the Schlesische Heimstäte," in *Ernst May: 1886–1970*, 37.

97 Henderson, "The Work of Ernst May, 1919–1930": 86–87; Quiring, "Catalogue Raisonné," in *Ernst May: 1886–1970*, 256; Störtkuhl, "Ernst May and the Schlesische Heimstäte," in *Ernst May: 1886–1970*, 38.

98 Ernst May, "Stadterweiterungsplan für den Westteil von Leobschütz," *Das Schlesische Heim* 4 (1923): 194, quoted in Störtkuhl, "Ernst May and the Schlesische Heimstäte," in *Ernst May: 1886–1970*, 38.

99 Quiring, "Catalogue Raisonné," in *Ernst May: 1886–1970*, 249.

100 Henderson, "The Work of Ernst May, 1919–1930": 235–38; Quiring, "Catalogue Raisonné," in *Ernst May: 1886–1970*, 251; Störtkuhl, "Ernst May and the Schlesische Heimstäte," in *Ernst May: 1886–1970*, 38–39.

101 Henderson, "The Work of Ernst May, 1919–1930": 229–35; Henderson, "Ernst May and the Campaign to Resettle the Countryside: Rural Housing in Silesia, 1919–1925": 199–201,

206–7; Quiring, "Catalogue Raisonné," in *Ernst May: 1886–1970*, 257–58; Störtkuhl, "Ernst May and the Schlesische Heimstäte," in *Ernst May: 1886–1970*, 38.

102 Henderson, "The Work of Ernst May, 1919–1930": 192–95; Henderson, "Ernst May and the Campaign to Resettle the Countryside: Rural Housing in Silesia, 1919–1925": 195–96, 206–7; Quiring, "Catalogue Raisonné," in *Ernst May: 1886–1970*, 253; Störtkuhl, "Ernst May and the Schlesische Heimstäte," in *Ernst May: 1886–1970*, 41, 43.

103 Henderson, "The Work of Ernst May, 1919–1930": 213–18; Henderson, "Ernst May and the Campaign to Resettle the Countryside: Rural Housing in Silesia, 1919–1925": 197, 206–7; Quiring, "Catalogue Raisonné," in *Ernst May: 1886–1970*, 253; Störtkuhl, "Ernst May and the Schlesische Heimstäte," in *Ernst May: 1886–1970*, 40, 42.

104 Störtkuhl, "Ernst May and the Schlesische Heimstäte," in *Ernst May: 1886–1970*, 40.

105 Störtkuhl, "Ernst May and the Schlesische Heimstäte," in *Ernst May: 1886–1970*, 46.

106 Ernst May, "Das Neue Frankfurt," *Das Neue Frankfurt* 1 (October 1926): 2–11; "Modern Architecture in Frankfort, Germany," *Architecture* (New York) 59 (January 1929): 51–53; "Reformschule am Bornheimer Hang, Frankfurt am Main," *Wasmuths Monatshefte für Baukunst* 13 (April 1929): 164; "Housing, Frankfort, Germany," *Architecture* (New York) 60 (December 1929): 341–42; Catherine Bauer, *Modern Housing* (Boston: Houghton Mifflin, 1934), 148–49; Lewis Mumford, letter to Frank Lloyd Wright (June 25, 1935), in Bruce Brooks Pfeiffer and Robert Wojtowicz, eds., *Frank Lloyd Wright & Lewis Mumford Thirty Years of Correspondence* (New York: Princeton Architectural Press, 2001), 165; Henry Wright, *Rehousing Urban America* (New York: Columbia University Press, 1936), 95; Werner Hegemann, *City Planning: Housing, Volume III* (New York: Architectural Book Publishing Co., 1938), 110–11; Lewis Mumford, *The Culture of Cities* (New York: Harcourt, Brace & Jovanovich, 1938), 453; Reyner Banham, *Theory and Design in the First Machine Age* (London: Architectural Press, 1960), 266; Lewis Mumford, *The City in History: Its Origins, Its Transformations, and Its Prospects* (New York: Harcourt, Brace & World, 1961), 314; Justus Buekschmitt, *Ernst May* (Stuttgart: Verlagsanstalt Alexander Koch, 1963), 42–51; Catherine Bauer Wurster, "The Social Front of Modern Architecture in the 1930s," *Journal of the Society of Architectural Historians* 24 (March 1965): 48–52; Sigfried Giedeon, *Space, Time and Architecture*, 5th ed. (Cambridge, Mass.: Harvard University Press, 1967), 795; Manfredo Tafuri, *Architecture and Utopia: Design and Capitalist Development*, trans. by Barbara Luigia La Penta (Cambridge, Mass., and London: MIT Press, 1976), 109, 114–21; Karin Carmen Jung and Dietrich Worbs, "Mythos und Wirklichkeit—Ernst Mays Wohnungs- und Städtebau, 1920–1970," *Bauwelt* 198 (July 25, 1977): 1050–75; John Robert Mullin, "City Planning in Frankfurt, Germany, 1925–1932: A Study in Practical Utopianism," *Journal of Urban History* 4 (November 1977): 3–28; Manfredo Tafuri, *The Sphere and the Labyrinth: Avant-Gardes and Architecture from Piranesi to the 1970s*, trans. by Pellegrino d'Acierno and Robert Connolly (Cambridge, Mass., and London: MIT Press, 1978), 206–11, figs. 224–33; Nicholas Bullock, "Housing in Frankfurt: 1925 to 1931 and the New Wohnkultur," *Architectural Review* 163 (June 1978): 335–42; John Robert Mullin, "Ideology, Planning Theory and the German City in the Inter-War Years: Part I," *Town Planning Review* 53 (April 1982): 124, 126; Heike Risse, *Frühe moderne in Frankfurt am Main, 1920–1933* (Frankfurt am Main: Societäts-Verlag, 1984), 227–29, 243–99; Christian Borngräber, "Dispute attorno a un pannello," *Rassegna* 7 (December 1985): 67–75; Rosemarie Höpfner and Volker Fischer, eds., *Ernst May und das Neue Frankfurt, 1925–1930* (Berlin: Ernst & Sohn, 1986); Barbara Miller Lane, "Architects in Power: Politics and Ideology in the Work of Ernst May and Albert Speer," *Journal of Interdisciplinary History* 17 (Summer 1986): 283–310; Francesco Collotti, "Ernst May a Francoforte," *Domus* 682 (April 1987): 4–5; D.W. Dreysse, *Ernst May Housing Estates*, trans. by Patricia Grossmann (Frankfurt am Main: Fricke, 1988); Peter Hall, *Cities of Tomorrow: An Intellectual History of Urban Planning and Design in the Twentieth Century* (Oxford: Basil Blackwell, 1988), 117–18, 120; Susan Rose Henderson, "The Work of Ernst May, 1919–1930" (Ph.D. diss., Columbia University, 1990): 296–416; Peter G. Rowe, *Modernity and Housing* (Cambridge, Mass., and London: MIT Press, 1993), 128–44; "Ampliamento della città mediante nuclei satellite," *Storia urbana* 17 (October–December 1993): 109–19; Christoph Mohr, "Modernität in Not: der Römerstadt in Frankfurt am Main droht die Privatisierung," *Deutsche Bauzeitung* 128 (1994): 44–46; John Zukowsky, "Das Neue Frankfurt," in John Zukowsky, ed., *The Many Faces of Modern Architecture: Building in Germany between the World Wars* (Munich and New York: Prestel, 1994), 56–60; Hubertus von Allwörden, "Siedlungen in Gefahr: Ernst Mays Siedlungswerk in Frankfurt," *Architekt* (July 1994): 368; Susan R. Henderson, "A Setting for Mass Culture: Life and Leisure in the Nidda Valley," *Planning Perspectives* 10 (April 1995): 199–222; Jorge Sainz, "Ernst May: Colonia Römerstadt, Frankfurt," *AV Monografias* 56 (November–December 1995): 30–31; Winfried Nerdinger and Cornelius Tafel, *Architectural Guide Germany: 20th Century* (Basel: Birkhäuser, 1996), 280; Jean-François Lejeune, "From Hellerau to Bauhaus: Memory and Modernity in the German Garden City," *The New City* 3 (Fall 1996): 50–69; Bernard Leupen et al., *Design and Analysis* (New York: Van Nostrand Reinhold, 1997), 146–49; Hilde Heynen, *Architecture and Modernity: A Critique* (Cambridge, Mass.: MIT Press, 1999), 43–70; Barbara Miller Lane, *National Romanticism and Modern Architecture in Germany and the Scandinavian Countries* (Cambridge: Cambridge University Press, 2000), 274–79; Eric Paul Mumford, *The CIAM Discourse on Urbanism, 1928–1960* (Cambridge, Mass.: MIT Press, 2000), 30; Wolf-Christian Setzepfandt, *Frankfurt am Main: Architectural Guide*, trans. by Christian Setzepfandt (Berlin: Dietrich Reimer Verlag, 2002), 45, 140, 149, 169, 206; Dennis Sharp, *Twentieth Century Architecture: A Visual History* (Mulgrave, Australia: Images Publishing, 2002), 105; Jean Castex et al., *Urban Forms: Death and Life of the Urban Block*, trans. by Olga Vitale Samuels (Oxford and Boston: Architectural Press, 2004), 90–113; Wolfgang Förster, *Housing in the 20th and 21st Centuries* (Munich: Prestell, 2006), 38–39; Christopher Wilk, ed., *Modernism: Designing a New World, 1914–1939* (London: V&A Publications, 2006), 180; Susan R. Henderson, "Housing the Single Woman: The Frankfurt Experiment," *Journal of the Society of Architectural Historians* 68 (September 2009): 358–77; David H. Haney, *When Modern Was Green: Life and Work of Landscape Architect Leberecht Migge* (London and New York: Routledge, 2010), 197–99; Vittorio Magnago Lampugnani, *Die Stadt im 20.*

Jahrhundert (Berlin: Verlag Klaus Wagenbach, 2010), 344–55; Christoph Mohr, "The New Frankfurt," trans. by James R. O'Donovan, in *Ernst May: 1886–1970*, eds. Claudia Quiring, Wolfgang Voigt, Peter Cachola Schmal, and Eckhard Herrel (Munich: Prestel, 2011), 50–67; David H. Haney, "Birds and Fishes Versus Potatoes and Cabbages: Max Bromme and Leberecht Migge's Attitudes Towards Green Space Planning in the New Frankfurt," in *Ernst May: 1886–1970*, 68–77; Michael Stöneberg, "Through Focusing Screen and Viewfinder: The Photographers of the New Frankfurt," trans. by Jane Michael, in *Ernst May: 1886–1970*, 78–89; Helen Barr and Ulrike May, "'Apart from the Content, the Form Matters Too': On Designing a City: The New Frankfurt," trans. by Jane Michael, in *Ernst May: 1886–1970*, 90–97; Wolfgang Pehnt, "The New Man and the Old Adam: On the Image of Man and the New Building," trans. by Jane Michael, in *Ernst May: 1886–1970*, 98–109; D.W. Dreysse, "May's Siedlungen—Today and Tomorrow," trans. by Steven Lindberg, in *Ernst May: 1886–1970*, 110–17; François Claessens, "Mapping Urban and Social Space," www.tudelft.nl; Owen Hatherley, "Revolution in the Garden," www.audacity.org; Hilde Heynen, "Ernst May," www.asro.kuleuven.ac.be/CAADPUBS/files/306.doc; "May Settlements," www.frankfurt.de; "Ernst May and the New Frankfurt," www.ernst-museum.de. Also see monthly issues of *Das Neue Frankfurt*, from October 1926 to December 1931.

107 Heynen, "Ernst May": 2–3. Also see Heynen, *Architecture and Modernity: A Critique*, 51–56.

108 Lane, "Architects in Power: Politics and Ideology in the Work of Ernst May and Albert Speer": 293.

109 May, "Das Neue Frankfurt": 4, quoted in Lane, "Architects in Power: Politics and Ideology in the Work of Ernst May and Albert Speer": 293.

110 Buekschmitt, *Ernst May*, 42–43; Mullin, "City Planning in Frankfurt, Germany, 1925–1932: A Study in Practical Utopianism": 10; Tafuri, *The Sphere and the Labyrinth: Avant-Gardes and Architecture from Piranesi to the 1970s*, 207, fig. 225; Bullock, "Housing in Frankfurt: 1925 to 1931 and the New Wohnkultur": 337; Höpfner and Fischer, eds., *Ernst May und das Neue Frankfurt, 1925–1930*, 139–43; Dreysse, *Ernst May Housing Estates*, 35–38, plan; Henderson, "The Work of Ernst May, 1919–1930": 313–21; Rowe, *Modernity and Housing*, 131; Zukowsky, "Das Neue Frankfurt," in Zukowsky, ed., *The Many Faces of Modern Architecture: Building in Germany between the World Wars*, 58–59; Nerdinger and Tafel, *Architectural Guide Germany: 20th Century*, 281; Lejeune, "From Hellerau to Bauhaus: Memory and Modernity in the German Garden City": 61; Mumford, *The CIAM Discourse on Urbanism, 1928–1960*, 30; Setzepfandt, *Frankfurt am Main: Architectural Guide*, 206; Quiring, "Catalogue Raisonné," in *Ernst May: 1886–1970*, 264, 66; Owen Hatherley, "Revolution in the Garden," www.audacity.org; www.ernst-may-museum.de/zickzackhausen.htm.

111 "Reformschule am Bornheimer Hang, Frankfurt am Main": 164; Hegemann, *City Planning: Housing, Volume III*, 110; Buekschmitt, *Ernst May*, 42; Tafuri, *The Sphere and the Labyrinth: Avant-Gardes and Architecture from Piranesi to the 1970s*, 207, fig. 230; Höpfner and Fischer, eds., *Ernst May und das Neue Frankfurt, 1925–1930*, 127; Dreysse, *Ernst May Housing Estates*, 23–26, plan; Henderson, "The Work of Ernst May, 1919–1930": 353–60; Lejeune, "From Hellerau to Bauhaus: Memory and Modernity in the German Garden City": 61; Setzepfandt, *Frankfurt am Main: Architectural Guide*, 182–83; Quiring, "Catalogue Raisonné," in *Ernst May: 1886–1970*, 263–65; Owen Hatherley, "Revolution in the Garden," www.audacity.org; www.ernst-may-museum.de/zickzackhausen.htm; www.ernst-may-museum.de/bornheimerhang.htm.

112 Heynen, "Ernst May": 3. Also see Bauer, *Modern Housing*, 148–49; Mumford, letter to Wright (June 25, 1935), in Pfeiffer and Wojtowicz, eds., *Frank Lloyd Wright & Lewis Mumford Thirty Years of Correspondence*, 165; Mumford, *The Culture of Cities*, 453; Buekschmitt, *Ernst May*, 44–46, 50–51; Tafuri, *Architecture and Utopia: Design and Capitalist Development*, 118; Mullin, "City Planning in Frankfurt, Germany, 1925–1932: A Study in Practical Utopianism": 11–14; Tafuri, *The Sphere and the Labyrinth: Avant-Gardes and Architecture from Piranesi to the 1970s*, 207–8, figs. 227–29; Bullock, "Housing in Frankfurt: 1925 to 1931 and the New Wohnkultur": 336; Höpfner and Volker Fischer, eds., *Ernst May und das Neue Frankfurt, 1925–1930*, 111–15; Dreysse, *Ernst May Housing Estates*, 13–18, plan; Hall, *Cities of Tomorrow: An Intellectual History of Urban Planning and Design in the Twentieth Century*, 118, 120; Henderson, "The Work of Ernst May, 1919–1930": 325–34; Rowe, *Modernity and Housing*, 132–42; Zukowsky, "Das Neue Frankfurt," in Zukowsky, ed., *The Many Faces of Modern Architecture: Building in Germany between the World Wars*, 58; Mohr, "Modernität in Not: der Römerstadt in Frankfurt am Main droht die Privatisierung": 44–46; Allwörden, "Siedlungen in Gefahr: Ernst Mays Siedlungswerk in Frankfurt": 368; Sainz, "Ernst May: Colonia Römerstadt, Frankfurt": 30–31; Nerdinger and Tafel, *Architectural Guide Germany: 20th Century*, 282–83; Lejeune, "From Hellerau to Bauhaus: Memory and Modernity in the German Garden City": 61; Leupen et al., *Design and Analysis*, 146–49; Heynen, *Architecture and Modernity: A Critique*, 55–57; Mumford, *The CIAM Discourse on Urbanism, 1928–1960*, 30; Setzepfandt, *Frankfurt am Main: Architectural Guide*, 169; Castex et al., *Urban Forms: Death and Life of the Urban Block*, 94–100; Förster, *Housing in the 20th and 21st Centuries*, 38–39; Haney, *When Modern Was Green: Life and Work of Landscape Architect Leberecht Migge*, 197–99; Quiring, "Catalogue Raisonné," in *Ernst May: 1886–1970*, 269–70; Hatherley, "Revolution in the Garden," www.audacity.org; http://www.ernst-may-museum.de/roemerstadtnidda.htm.

113 Heynen, *Architecture and Modernity: A Critique*, 56–57.

114 Bauer, *Modern Housing*, 148–49. Bauer is referring to the Deutscher Werkbund's 1929 exhibition in Breslau (now Wroclaw, Poland) titled "Wohnung und Werkraum" (apartment and work space). See *Auf dem Weg zum neuen Wohnen: Die Werkbundsiedlung Breslau, 1929*, exhibition catalogue (Basel: Birkhäuser, 1996).

115 Mumford, *The Culture of Cities*, 453.

116 Hegemann, *City Planning: Housing, Volume III*, 111; Wurster, "The Social Front of Modern Architecture in the 1930s": 51; Buekschmitt, *Ernst May*, 44–45; Mullin, "City Planning in Frankfurt, Germany, 1925–1932: A Study in Practical Utopianism": 14–16; Tafuri, *The Sphere and the Labyrinth: Avant-Gardes and Architecture from Piranesi to the 1970s*, 207, fig. 226; Bullock, "Housing in Frankfurt: 1925 to 1931 and the New Wohnkultur": 339; Höpfner and Fischer, eds., *Ernst May und das Neue Frankfurt, 1925–1930*, 107; Lane, "Architects in Power: Politics and Ideology in the Work of Ernst May and Albert Speer": 290–91; Dreysse, *Ernst May Housing Estates*, 7–12, plan; Henderson, "The Work of Ernst May, 1919–1930": 334–46; Rowe, *Modernity and Housing*, 132–33; Zukowsky, "Das Neue Frankfurt," in Zukowsky, ed., *The Many Faces of Modern Architecture: Building in*

Germany between the World Wars, 58; Nerdinger and Tafel, *Architectural Guide Germany: 20th Century*, 281; Lejeune, "From Hellerau to Bauhaus: Memory and Modernity in the German Garden City": 61; Setzepfandt, *Frankfurt am Main: Architectural Guide*, 140; Haney, *When Modern Was Green: Life and Work of Landscape Architect Leberecht Migge*, 197–99; Quiring, "Catalogue Raisonné," in *Ernst May: 1886–1970*, 266–68; http://www.ernst-may-museum.de/praunheim. html.

117 Mullin, "City Planning in Frankfurt, Germany, 1925–1932: A Study in Practical Utopianism": 15.

118 Henderson, "The Work of Ernst May, 1919–1930": 345.

119 Hegemann, *City Planning: Housing, Volume III*, 110; Mullin, "City Planning in Frankfurt, Germany, 1925–1932: A Study in Practical Utopianism": 16–19; Tafuri, *The Sphere and the Labyrinth: Avant-Gardes and Architecture from Piranesi to the 1970s*, 207; Mullin, "Ideology, Planning Theory and the German City in the Inter-War Years: Part I": 124, 126; Höpfner and Fischer, eds., *Ernst May und das Neue Frankfurt, 1925–1930*, 116–17; Dreysse, *Ernst May Housing Estates*, 19–22, plan; Henderson, "The Work of Ernst May, 1919–1930": 381–86; Rowe, *Modernity and Housing*, 132–34; Zukowsky, "Das Neue Frankfurt," in Zukowsky, ed., *The Many Faces of Modern Architecture: Building in Germany between the World Wars*, 58; Lejeune, "From Hellerau to Bauhaus: Memory and Modernity in the German Garden City": 61; Heynen, *Architecture and Modernity: A Critique*, 59–63; Setzepfandt, *Frankfurt am Main: Architectural Guide*, 140; Quiring, "Catalogue Raisonné," in *Ernst May: 1886–1970*, 273–74; Claessens, "Mapping Urban and Social Space": 8; http://www.ernst-may-museum.de/westhausen.htm.

120 Mullin, "City Planning in Frankfurt, Germany, 1925–1932: A Study in Practical Utopianism": 17.

121 Lejeune, "From Hellerau to Bauhaus: Memory and Modernity in the German Garden City": 61.

122 Sven Markelius, "Bostadsområde vid Dessau-Törten," *Byggmästaren* 21 (1927): 238, 243; "Habitations, à Dessau-Torten, 1926," *Architecture Vivante* (August 1931): 18–20, plate 23; Walter Gropius, *The New Architecture and the Bauhaus*, trans. by P. Morton Shand (London: Faber and Faber, 1935; Cambridge, Mass.: MIT Press, 1965), 72, plate 13; Siegfried Giedion, *Walter Gropius: Work and Teamwork* (New York: Reinhold Publishing Corp., 1954), 86–87, 210–11, 233; James Marston Fitch, *Walter Gropius* (New York: George Braziller, 1960), 26, figs. 70–72; Barbara Miller Lane, *Architecture and Politics in Germany, 1918–1945* (Cambridge, Mass.: Harvard University Press, 1968), 117–19; Francesco Dal Co and Manfredo Tafuri, *Modern Architecture*, trans. by Robert Erich Wolf (New York: Harry N. Abrams, 1979), 149; Winfried Nerdinger, *Walter Gropius* (Berlin: Mann Verlag, 1985), 240–41; Norbert Borrmann, *Paul Schultze-Naumburg, 1869–1949: Maler, Publizist, Architekt* (Essen: Verlag Richard Bacht, 1989), 148; Thomas P. Hughes, *American Genesis: A Century of Invention and Technological Enthusiasm, 1870–1970* (New York: Viking, 1989), 317–19; Reginald Isaacs, *Gropius: An Illustrated Biography of the Creator of the Bauhaus* (Boston: Little, Brown, and Co., 1991), 127–28; Stephen Kinzer, "Bauhaus at the Source," *New York Times* (June 21, 1992), V: 15, 34; Magdalena Droste, *Bauhaus, 1919–1933* (Cologne: Benedikt Taschen, 1993), 132–34; Paolo Berdini, *Walter Gropius* (Barcelona: G. Gili, 1994), 76–79; Winfried Nerdinger and Cornelius Tafel, *Architectural Guide Germany: 20th Century* (Basel: Birkhäuser, 1996), 84–85; Chup Friemert, *Neues Bauen in Dessau*, trans. by Peter Craven (Dessau: Bauhaus Dessau, 1996), chapter 7; Jean-François Lejeune, "From Hellerau to Bauhaus: Memory and Modernity in the German Garden City," *The New City* 3 (Fall 1996): 50–69; Andreas Schwarting, "Die Siedlung Dessau-Törten: Bauhistorische Aspekte und Folgerungen für den Umgang mit einem Baudenkmal der klassischen Moderne," *Architectura: Zeitschrift für Geschichte der Baukunst* 31 (No. 1, 2001): 27–48; Karel Teige, *The Minimum Dwelling*, trans. by Eric Dluhosch (Cambridge, Mass.: MIT Press, 2002), 201–2; Gilbert Lupfer and Paul Sigel, *Walter Gropius, 1883–1969: The Promoter of a New Form* (Cologne: Taschen, 2004), 54–57; Magdalena Droste, *The Bauhaus, 1919–1933: Reform and Avant-Garde* (Cologne: Taschen, 2006), 52–53; *Architektouren durch Sachsen-Anhalt: Bauten des 20. Jahrhunderts* (Petersberg: Michael Imhof Verlag, 2006), 48–50; Jeannette Redensek, "Manufacturing Gemeinschaft: Architecture, Tradition, and the Sociology of Community in Germany, 1890–1920" (Ph.D. diss., City University of New York, 2007): 264 (n.71); Gretchen Gasterland-Gustafsson, "Design for Living: German and Swedish Design in the Early Twentieth Century" (Ph.D. diss., University of Minnesota, 2008): 166–70; Gert Kähler, *The Path of Modernism, Architecture 1900–1930: From the World Heritage of Wroclaw to that of Dessau* (Berlin: Jovis, 2009), 148–51; Celina Kress, *Adolf Sommerfeld/Andrew Sommerfield: Bauen für Berlin 1910–1970* (Berlin: Lukas Verlag, 2011), 150–51; http://www. bauhaus-dessau.de; www.creen.demon.co.uk/travel/dessau.html.

123 Friemert, *Neues Bauen in Dessau*, chapter 7: 3–4, 6.

124 Markelius, "Bostadsområde vid Dessau-Törten": 238, 243, quoted and translated in Gasterland-Gustafsson, "Design for Living: German and Swedish Design in the Early Twentieth Century": 168–69.

125 Lejeune, "From Hellerau to Bauhaus: Memory and Modernity in the German Garden City": 65–66.

126 Leopold Fischer, "Die Siedlung Dessau-Ziebigk," *Siedlungs-Wirtschaft* 9/10 (1926): 61–63; Jeannine Fiedler, ed., *Social Utopias of the Twenties* (Wuppertal, Germany: Müller + Busman Press, 1995), fig. 94; Jean-François Lejeune, "From Hellerau to Bauhaus: Memory and Modernity in the German Garden City," *The New City* 3 (Fall 1996): 50–69; David H. Haney, "Leberecht Migge's 'Green Manifesto': Envisioning a Revolution of Gardens," *Landscape Journal* 26 (February 2007): 213–14; David H. Haney, *When Modern Was Green: Life and Work of Landscape Architect Leberecht Migge* (London and New York: Routledge, 2010), 164–70, plate 3.2; Frank Walter, "Die Siedlung Knarrberg in Dessau," in *Leopold Fischer: Architekt Moderne* (Dessau-Rosslau: Funk Verlag Bernhard Hein, 2010), 28–39; Fritz Becker, "Aus den erinnerungen eines Erstbewohners der Siedlung Knarrberg," in *Leopold Fischer: Architekt Moderne*, 40–51; http://www.dessau-ziebigk.de.

127 Lejeune, "From Hellerau to Bauhaus: Memory and Modernity in the German Garden City": 65.

128 *Bau und Wohnung: Die Bauten der Weissenhofsiedlung in Stuttgart errichtet 1927* (Stuttgart: F. Wedekind, 1927); Philip C. Johnson, *Mies van der Rohe*, 3rd rev. ed. (New York: The Museum of Modern Art, 1947, 1978), 44–49, 193; Francesco Dal Co and Manfredo Tafuri, *Modern Architecture*, trans. by Robert Erich Wolf (New York: Harry N. Abrams, 1979), 153, 188–89; Kenneth Frampton and Yukio Futagawa, *Modern Architecture: 1920–1940* (New York: Rizzoli International Publications, 1983), 296–97; Dennis J. De Witt and Elizabeth R. De Witt, *Modern Architecture in Europe: A Guide to Buildings Since the Industrial Revolution* (New York: E. P. Dutton, 1987), 95–96; Norbert Borrmann, *Paul Schultze-Naumburg, 1869–1949: Maler, Publizist, Architekt* (Essen: Verlag Richard Bacht, 1989), 130, 147–48, 154; Karin Kirsch, *The Weissenhofsiedlung: Experimental Housing Built for the Deutscher Werkbund, Stuttgart, 1927* (New York: Rizzoli International Publications, 1989); Helge Classen, *Dies Weissenhofsiedlung: Beginn eines neuen Bauens* (Dortmund: Harenberg, 1990); Richard Pommer and Christian F. Otto, *Weissenhof 1927 and the Modern Movement in Architecture* (Chicago and London: University of Chicago Press, 1991); Winfried Nerdinger and Cornelius Tafel, *Architectural Guide Germany: 20th Century* (Basel: Birkhäuser, 1996), 402–5; Deborah Gans, *The Le Corbusier Guide*, 3rd ed. (New York: Princeton Architectural Press, 2006), 173–77; Martin Wörner, Gilbert Lupfer and Ute Schulz, *Architekturführer Stuttgart* (Berlin: Dietrich Reimer Verlag, 2006), 124–29; Jean-Louis Cohen, *Ludwig Mies van der Rohe*, 2nd rev. ed. (Basel: Birkhäuser, 2007), 51–55; Maiken Umbach, *German Cities and Bourgeois Modernism, 1890–1924* (New York: Oxford University Press, 2009), 199; Vittorio Magnago Lampugnani, *Die Stadt im 20. Jahrhundert* (Berlin: Verlag Klaus Wagenbach, 2010), 340–43; Kai K. Gutschow, "The Anti-Mediterranean in the Literature of Modern Architecture," in Jean-François Lejeune and Michelangelo Sabatino, eds., *Modern Architecture and the Mediterranean* (London and New York: Routlege, 2010), 148–51.

129 Ludwig Mies van der Rohe, "Vorwort," in *Bau und Wohnung: Die Bauten der Weissenhofsiedlung in Stuttgart errichtet 1927*, 7, quoted and translated in Pommer and Otto, *Weissenhof 1927 and the Modern Movement in Architecture*, 61.

130 Paul Schmitthenner, *Die 25 Einfamilienhäuser der Holzsiedlung am Kochenhof* (Stuttgart: J. Hoffmann, 1933); "Ein Richtungsweisendes Beispiel der neuen Baugesinnung: die Ausstellung 'Deutsche Holz für Hausbau und Wohnung Stuttgart 1933,'" *Bauzeitung* 30 (October 5, 1933): 333–36; "Die konstruktionen und holzbausysteme der kochenhofsiedlung in Stuttgart," *Bauzeitung* 30 (October 15, 1933): 345–48; "Am Kochenhof Siedlung, Stuttgart," *Moderne Bauformen* 32 (November 1933): 11; Richard Pommer and Christian F. Otto, *Weissenhof 1927 and the Modern Movement in Architecture* (Chicago and London: University of Chicago Press, 1991), 153–57, figs. 262–69; Winfried Nerdinger and Cornelius Tafel, *Architectural Guide Germany: 20th Century* (Basel: Birkhäuser, 1996), 404; Stefanie Plarre, *Die Kochenhofsiedlung: das Gegenmodell zur Wiessenhofsiedlung* (Stuttgart: Hohenheim, 2001); Wolfgang Voigt and Hartmut Frank, *Paul Schmitthenner, 1884–1972* (Tübingen: Wasmuth, 2003), 21, 24, 75–79, 153, 197; Maiken Umbach, "The Deutscher Werkbund, Globalization and the Invention of Modern Vernaculars," in Maiken Umbach and Bernd Hüppauf, eds., *Vernacular Modernism: Heimat, Globalization, and the Built Environment* (Stanford: Stanford University Press, 2005), 136–38; Martin Wörner, Gilbert Lupfer, and Ute Schulz, *Architekturführer Stuttgart* (Berlin: Dietrich Reimer Verlag, 2006), 122; Vittorio Magnago Lampugnani, *Die Stadt im 20. Jahrhundert* (Berlin: Verlag Klaus Wagenbach, 2010), 340–41; Wolfgang Voit and Roland May, eds., *Paul Bonatz: 1877–1956* (Berlin: Ernst Wasmuth Verlag Tübingen, 2011), 235–36; www.kochenhof-siedlung.de.

131 "Die konstruktionen und holzbausysteme der kochenhofsiedlung in Stuttgart": 345–48, quoted and translated in Umbach, "The Deutscher Werkbund, Globalization and the Invention of Modern Vernaculars," in Umbach and Hüppauf, eds., *Vernacular Modernism*, 136–37.

132 "Die Siedlung München-Ramersdorf," *Baumeister* 32 (September 1934): 289–324; "Die deutsche Siedlungsausstellung in München," *Zentralblatt der Bauverwaltung* 54 (September 1934): 549–56; "La Citè Modèle de Ramersdorf," *L'Architecture d'Aujourd'hui* 6 (January 1935): 82; "Housing Scheme at Ramersdorf," *Architect and Building News* 144 (December 20, 1935): 353–55; *The New International Year Book* (New York: Dodd, Mead and Co., 1936): 44; Robert R. Taylor, *The Word in Stone: The Role of Architecture in the National Socialist Ideology* (Berkeley: University of California Press, 1974), 232; Roswitha Mattausch-Schirmbeck, *Siedlungsbau und Stadtneugründungen im deutschen Faschismus: dargestellt anhand exemplarischen Beispiele* (Frankfurt: Haag + Herchen, 1981), 19–28, 298; Ursula Henn, *Die Mustersiedlung Ramersdorf in München: Ein Siedlungskonzept zwischen Tradition und Moderne* (Munich: Kommissionsverlag UNI-Druck, 1987); Werner Durth and Winfried Nerdinger, *Architektur und Städtebau der 30er/40er Jahre* (Bonn: Deutsches Nationalkomitee für Denkmalschutz, 1992), 74–75; Carsten Jonas, *Die Stadt und ihr Grundriss* (Tübingen: Wasmuth, 2006), 113; Winfried Nerdinger, *Architectural Guide to Munich*, trans. by Claus Warren Offermann, Margaret Marks, and Lucinda Rennison (Berlin: Dietrich Reiomer Verlag, 2007), 184; "Ramersdorf—Ramersdorfer Geschichte," http://www.wochenanzeiger.de/article/61748.html; "The Exemplary Settlement at Ramersdorf," http://www.muenchen.de/Rathaus/plan/stadtentwicklung/flaechennutzplan/stadt_bau_plan_index/160830/section4.html.

133 "Housing Scheme at Ramersdorf," *Architect and Building News*: 355.

134 "Housing Scheme at Ramersdorf," *Architect and Building News*: 353. For Siedlung Neu-Ramersdorf, see Nerdinger, *Architectural Guide to Munich*, 185.

135 Nerdinger, *Architectural Guide to Munich*, 184.

136 "The Exemplary Settlement at Ramersdorf," http://www.muenchen.de/Rathaus/plan/stadtentwicklung/flaechennutzplan/stadt_bau_plan_index/160830/section4.html.

137 "Hamburger Einfamilienhäuser des Architekten Willy Eggers," *Moderne Bauformen* 41 (February 1942): 55–60; John Zukowsky, "Hamburg, Hanover, and Expressionist Architecture in North Germany," in John Zukowsky, ed., *The Many Faces of Modern Architecture: Building in Germany between the World Wars* (Munich and New York: Prestel, 1994), 138–39; Ralf Lange, *Architekturführer Hamburg* (Stuttgart: Edition Axel Menges, 1995), 174; Dirk Schubert, *Hamburger Wohnquartiere* (Berlin: Dietrich Reimer Verlag, 2005), 184–87; http://www.alsterdorfer-bv.de.

138 Jean Pierre Gaudin, "The French Garden City," in Stephen V. Ward, ed., *The Garden City: Past, Present and Future* (London: E and FN Spon, 1992), 63.

139 Gaudin, "The French Garden City," in Ward, ed., *The Garden City: Past, Present and Future*, 55, 68.

140 Gaudin, "The French Garden City," in Ward, ed., *The Garden City: Past, Present and Future*, 55.
141 Stanley Buder, *Visionaries and Planners: The Garden City Movement and the Modern Community* (New York: Oxford University Press, 1990), 138.
142 Anthony Sutcliffe, *Towards the Planned City: Germany, Britain, the United States and France, 1780–1914* (Oxford: Basil Blackwell, 1981), 193.
143 Sutcliffe, *Towards the Planned City: Germany, Britain, the United States and France, 1780–1914*, 192.
144 Stanley Buder, *Visionaries and Planners: The Garden City Movement and the Modern Community* (New York: Oxford University Press, 1990), 138–39. For Soria y Mata's Linear City, see George R. Collins, "The Ciudad Lineal of Madrid," *Journal of the Society of Architectural Historians* 18 (May 1959): 38–53; Waclaw Ostrowski, *Contemporary Town Planning: From the Origins to the Athens Charter* (Hague, Netherlands: International Federation for Housing and Planning, 1970), 24–32.
145 "Progress with the Housing Problem in France," *Architect* 110 (September 14, 1923): 166. Also see Bryant Hall, "French Railroad Builds Model Towns," *Housing Betterment* 11 (January 1922): 36; W. P. Mitchell, "Garden Cities and Model Dwellings as Conceived by the French," *Engineering and Contracting* 57 (June 28, 1922): 613–14; René Chavance, "Les Cités Jardins de la Compagnie du Nord," *Art et Décoration* 42 (October 1922): 111–28; Edith Elmer Wood, "Recent Housing Work in Western Europe," *Architectural Record* 53 (February 1923): 173–83; Jacques Boyer, "Les Cités-Jardins de la Compagnie du Chemin de Fer du Nord," *La Nature* no. 2641 (November 15, 1924), 310–16; B. S. Townroe, "France Re-builds: Garden Cities in the War Zone, for Eleven Thousand Railroad Employees," *American Review of Reviews* 74 (September 1926): 293–97; J. P. Farré, "Urbanisme et Rail: Les Cités de la Compagnie du Nord," *L'amour de L'art* 10 (November 1929): 428–33; John M. Sherwood, "Rationalization and Railway Workers in France: Raoul Dautry and Les Chemins de Fer de l'Etat, 1928–1937," *Journal of Contemporary History* 15 (July 1980): 443–74; Jean Pierre Gaudin, "The French Garden City," in Stephen V. Ward, ed., *The Garden City: Past, Present and Future* (London: E and FN Spon, 1992), 57.
146 Gwendolyn Wright, *The Politics of Design in French Colonial Urbanism* (Chicago and London: University of Chicago Press, 1991), 47.
147 Bryant Hall, "French Railroad Builds Model Towns," *Housing Betterment* 11 (January 1922): 36.
148 Georges Benoit-Lévy, "Garden Villages of France and Belgium," *New York Times Current History* XVI (September 1922): 964–65. Also see Bryant Hall, "French Railroad Builds Model Towns," *Housing Betterment* 11 (January 1922): 35–37; W. P. Mitchell, "Garden Cities and Model Dwellings as Conceived by the French," *Engineering and Contracting* 57 (June 28, 1922): 613–14; René Chavance, "Les Cités Jardins de la Compagnie du Nord," *Art et Décoration* 42 (October 1922): 111–28; "Progress with the Housing Problem in France," *Architect* 110 (September 14, 1923): 166–67; B. S. Townroe, "France Re-builds: Garden Cities in the War Zone, for Eleven Thousand Railroad Employees," *American Review of Reviews* 74 (September 1926): 293–97; J. P. Farré, "Urbanisme et Rail: Les Cités de la Compagnie du Nord," *L'amour de L'art* 10 (November 1929): 428–33; Werner Hegemann, *City Planning, Housing, Volume III* (New York: Architectural Book Publishing Company, 1938), 7; Walter Kieβ, *Urbanismus im Industriezeitalter* (Berlin: Ernst & Sohn, 1991), 446–47; Bertrand Lemoine, *Birkhäuser Architectural Guide to France; 20th Century* (Basel: Birkhäuser, 2000), 256.
149 Mitchell, "Garden Cities and Model Dwellings as Conceived by the French": 614.
150 Hall, "French Railroad Builds Model Towns": 36.
151 Jean Bossu, "Reconstruction de Tergnier (Aisne); Une Cité de Cheminots," *L'Architecture d'Aujourd'hui* 17 (November 1946): 26–30.
152 René Chavance, "Les Cités Jardins de la Compagnie du Nord," *Art et Décoration* 42 (October 1922): 111–28; "Progress with the Housing Problem in France," *Architect* 110 (September 14, 1923): 166–67; B. S. Townroe, "France Re-builds: Garden Cities in the War Zone, for Eleven Thousand Railroad Employees," *American Review of Reviews* 74 (September 1926): 293–97; J. P. Farré, "Urbanisme et Rail: Les Cités de la Compagnie du Nord," *L'amour de L'art* 10 (November 1929): 428–33; Werner Hegemann, *City Planning, Housing, Volume III* (New York: Architectural Book Publishing Company, 1938), 7; Gwendolyn Wright, *The Politics of Design in French Colonial Urbanism* (Chicago and London: University of Chicago Press, 1991), 47, 48; *Le Patrimoine des Communes du Nord, Tome II* (Paris: Flohic Editions, 2001), 1095–96.
153 Edith Elmer Wood, "Recent Housing Work in Western Europe," *Architectural Record* 53 (February 1923): 177; "Progress with the Housing Problem in France," *Architect* 110 (September 14, 1923): 166–67; B. S. Townroe, "France Re-builds: Garden Cities in the War Zone, for Eleven Thousand Railroad Employees," *American Review of Reviews* 74 (September 1926): 293–97; J. P. Farré, "Urbanisme et Rail: Les Cités de la Compagnie du Nord," *L'amour de L'art* 10 (November 1929): 430, 431; M. Süe, "L'Oeuvre de la Compagnie du Chemin de Fer du Nord, La Cité-Jardin de Lens Méricourt (Pas-de-Calais)," *La Construction Moderne* (April 2, 1933): 402–11; Susan Day, *Louis Süe, Architectures* (Mardaga: Institut Français D'Architecture, 1986), 55, 186; Bertrand Lemoine, *Birkhäuser Architectural Guide to France; 20th Century* (Basel: Birkhäuser, 2000), 224, 225.
154 "Progress with the Housing Problem in France," *Architect* 110 (September 14, 1923): 166–67.
155 "Progress with the Housing Problem in France," *Architect* 110 (September 14, 1923): 166–67.
156 René Chavance, "Les Cités Jardins de la Compagnie du Nord," *Art et Décoration* 42 (October 1922): 111–28.
157 Centre de recherche d'urbanisme, *Urbanization and Planning in France* (La Haye: I.F.H.P.; Paris: C.R.U., 1968), 52–55.
158 Maurice Guillemot, "Une Cité-Jardin à Draveil," *Art et Décoration* 35 (February 1914): 49–54; Jean Walter, "La Première Cité-Jardin de France," *L'Architecture* 27 (July 11, 1914): 237–41; "A Draveil (Essonne) La Curieuse Histoire d'un Domaine," *Sites et Monuments* no.107 (1984): 40–41.
159 Georges Benoit-Lévy, *La Cité-Jardin* (Paris: Editions des Cités-Jardins de France, 1904), 193; Benoît Pouvreau et al., *Les cités-jardins de la banlieue nord-est parisien* (Paris: Groupe Moniteur, 2007), 42–43.
160 *Urbanization and Planning in France*, 55.
161 Henri Sellier, quoted in Harris, "Housing Development in the Department of the Seine": 153.
162 Henri Sellier, quoted in Gaudin, "The French Garden City," in Ward, ed., *The Garden City: Past, Present, and Future*, 58.
163 Harris, "Housing Development in the Department of the Seine": 154.
164 Henri Sellier, *La crise du logement et l'intervention publique en matière d'habitation populaire dans l'agglomération parisienne* (Paris: Éditions de l'Office Public d'Habitation à Bon Marché du Départment de la Seine, 1921), 99–100, 767–94; Eugene H. Klaber, "The Housing Crisis in Paris," *Journal of the American Institute of Architects* 11 (January 1923): 19–24; Eugene H. Klaber, "Two French Garden Suburbs," *Journal of the American Institute of Architects* 11 (May 1923): 210–12; "A Short Street, 'La Cité-Jardin Des Lilas', a new Garden Suburb near Paris," *Landscape Architecture* 14 (July 1924): 269; *Réalisations de l'Office public d'habitations du département de la Seine* (Strasbourg: Edari, Édition d'architecture et d'industrie et d'économie rurale S.A.R. L., 1933), 12–13, 46–47; Paul Chemetov, Marie-Jeanne Dumont, and Bernard Marrey, *Paris-Banlieue, 1919–1939, Architectures domestiques* (Paris: Dunod, 1989), 138–39, 175; Jean Pierre Gaudin, "The French Garden City," in Stephen V. Ward, ed., *The Garden City: Past, Present and Future* (London: E and FN Spon, 1992), 58; Benoît Pouvreau et al., *Les cités-jardins de la banlieue nord-est parisien* (Paris: Groupe Moniteur, 2007), 31, 57, 59, 108, 115, 129.
165 Henri Sellier, *La crise du logement et l'intervention publique en matière d'habitation populaire dans l'agglomération parisienne* (Paris: Éditions de l'Office Public d'Habitation à Bon Marché du Départment de la Seine, 1921), 739–66; Werner Hegemann, "France," in *International Cities and Town Planning Exhibition. English Catalogue. Jubilee Exhibition, Gothenburg, Sweden, 1923* (Göteborg, Wezäta, W. Zachrissons boktyrckeri a.-b., 1923), 117, 120; "A 'Place' Street in 'Drancy,' A Garden Suburb near Paris," *Landscape Architecture* 14 (July 1924): 268; *Réalisations de l'Office public d'habitations du département de la Seine* (Strasbourg: Edari, Édition d'architecture et d'industrie et d'économie rurale S.A.R.L., 1933), 12, 35–36; Olivier Nicoulaud, "Cite Jardins," *Architecture, Mouvement, Continuité* 34 (July 1974): 10–25; Ann Caroll Werquin and Alain Demangeon, "Un Heureux Moment Dans La Fabrication du Paysage de la Banlieue: Les Cités-Jardins," *Bulletin d'Informations Architecturales*, supplement to no. 96 (June 1985); Paul Chemetov, Marie-Jeanne Dumont, and Bernard Marrey, *Paris-Banlieue, 1919–1939, Architectures domestiques* (Paris: Dunod, 1989), 138–39; Jean Pierre Gaudin, "The French Garden City," in Stephen V. Ward, ed., *The Garden City: Past, Present and Future* (London: E and FN Spon, 1992), 59; Benoît Pouvreau et al., *Les cités-jardins de la banlieue nord-est parisien* (Paris: Groupe Moniteur, 2007), 16, 18, 57, 59, 60, 61, 68, 92, 108, 128.
166 Henri Sellier, *La crise du logement et l'intervention publique en matière d'habitation populaire dans l'agglomération parisienne* (Paris: Éditions de l'Office Public d'Habitation à Bon Marché du Départment de la Seine, 1921), 837–48; Werner Hegemann, "France," in *International Cities and Town Planning Exhibition. English Catalogue. Jubilee Exhibition, Gothenburg, Sweden, 1923* (Göteborg, Wezäta, W. Zachrissons boktyrckeri a.-b., 1923), 118, 120; Paul Chemetov, Marie-Jeanne Dumont, and Bernard Marrey, *Paris-Banlieue, 1919–1939, Architectures domestiques* (Paris: Dunod, 1989), 138–39; Benoît Pouvreau et al., *Les cités-jardins de la banlieue nord-est parisien* (Paris: Groupe Moniteur, 2007), 34, 35, 56, 59, 116, 119.
167 Henri Sellier, *La crise du logement et l'intervention publique en matière d'habitation populaire dans l'agglomération parisienne* (Paris: Éditions de l'Office Public d'Habitation à Bon Marché du Départment de la Seine, 1921), 849–63; Albert Devienne, "La Cité-Jardin d'Arcueil," *L'Architecture* 36 (December 25, 1923): 391–96; Paul Chemetov, Marie-Jeanne Dumont, and Bernard Marrey, *Paris-Banlieue, 1919–1939, Architectures domestiques* (Paris: Dunod, 1989), 138–39, 229.
168 Henri Sellier, *La crise du logement et l'intervention publique en matière d'habitation populaire dans l'agglomération parisienne* (Paris: Éditions de l'Office Public d'Habitation à Bon Marché du Départment de la Seine, 1921), 864–79; Jean Virette, *La Cité Jardin* (Paris: Éditions S. de Bonadona, 1931), plates 10–18; *Paris-Banlieue, 1919–1939, Architectures domestiques* (Paris: Dunod, 1989), 138–39, 219.
169 Henri Sellier, *La crise du logement et l'intervention publique en matière d'habitation populaire dans l'agglomération parisienne* (Paris: Éditions de l'Office Public d'Habitation à Bon Marché du Départment de la Seine, 1921), 615; *Réalisations de l'Office public d'habitations du département de la Seine* (Strasbourg: Edari, Édition d'architecture et d'industrie et d'économie rurale S.A.R. L., 1933), 12, 41–45; Ann Caroll Werquin and Alain Demangeon, "Un Heureux Moment Dans La Fabrication du Paysage de la Banlieue: Les Cités-Jardins," *Bulletin d'Informations Architecturales*, supplement to no. 96 (June 1985): n.p.; *Paris-Banlieue, 1919–1939, Architectures domestiques* (Paris: Dunod, 1989), 138–39, 162–64, 223, 225.
170 G. Montagu Harris, "Housing Development in the Department of the Seine," *Garden Cities and Town Planning* 9 (August 1919), 152–53; Henri Sellier, *La crise du logement et l'intervention publique en matière d'habitation populaire dans l'agglomération parisienne* (Paris: Éditions de l'Office Public d'Habitation à Bon Marché du Départment de la Seine, 1921), 89–92, 696–729; Jean Virette, *La Cité Jardin* (Paris: Éditions S. de Bonadona, 1931), plates 40–56; *Réalisations de l'Office public d'habitations du département de la Seine* (Strasbourg: Edari, Édition d'architecture et d'industrie et d'économie rurale S.A.R.L., 1933), 14, 72–76; Paul Chemetov, Marie-Jeanne Dumont, and Bernard Marrey, *Paris-Banlieue, 1919–1939, Architectures domestiques* (Paris: Dunod, 1989), 138–39, 192–94, 195, 224; Bertrand Lemoine, *Birkhäuser Architectural Guide to France; 20th Century* (Basel: Birkhäuser, 2000), 110, 111; Benoît Pouvreau et al., *Les cités-jardins de la banlieue nord-est parisien* (Paris: Groupe Moniteur, 2007), 16–20, 28–31, 44–51, 68–69.
171 G. Montagu Harris, "Housing Development in the Department of the Seine," *Garden Cities and Town Planning* 9 (August 1919), 152–53; Henri Sellier, *La crise du logement et l'intervention publique en matière d'habitation populaire dans l'agglomération parisienne* (Paris: Éditions de l'Office Public d'Habitation à Bon Marché du Départment de la Seine, 1921), 683, 686–87, 690; Edith Elmer Wood, "Recent Housing in Western Europe," *Architectural Record* 53 (February 1923): 173–83; "Suresnes," *Urbanisme* 4 (January 1935): 1–72; Andre Menabrea, "Urbanisme ed Deuil: Henri Sellier, Maire de Suresnes," *Urbanisme* 13 (January 1944): 1–20; Henri Sellier, *Une Cité pour Tous* (Paris: Editions du Linteau,

1998), 144–45; *La Banlieue Oasis: Henri Sellier et les cités-jardins, 1900–1940* (Saint-Denis: Presses Universitaires de Vincennes, 1987), 68; Paul Chemetov, Marie-Jeanne Dumont, and Bernard Marrey, *Paris-Banlieue, 1919–1939, Architectures domestiques* (Paris: Dunod, 1989), 138–39, 194; Jean Pierre Gaudin, "The French Garden City," in Stephen V. Ward, ed., *The Garden City: Past, Present and Future* (London and New York: E & FN Spon, 1992), 68; Stephen V. Ward, "The Howard Legacy," in Kermit C. Parsons and David Schuyler, eds., *From Garden City to Green City: The Legacy of Ebenezer Howard* (Baltimore and London: Johns Hopkins University Press, 2002), 225–26; Mervyn Miller, "Garden Cities and Suburbs: At Home and Abroad," *Journal of Planning History* 1 (February 2002): 6–28; www.ville-suresnes.fr; Andrés Duany, Elizabeth Plater-Zyberk, and Robert Alminana, *The New Civic Art: Elements of Town Planning* (New York: Rizzoli International Publications, 2003), 293.

172 For Grand Street Houses, see Stern, Gilmartin, and Mellins, *New York 1930*, 421, 422.

173 Gaudin, "The French Garden City," in Ward, ed., *The Garden City: Past, Present, and Future*, 59.

174 François Laisney, "Quand le HLM étaint roses," *Architecture, Mouvement, Continuité* no. 35 (April 1974): 79–104; Benoît Pouvreau et al., *Les cités-jardins de la banlieue nord-est parisien* (Paris: Groupe Moniteur, 2007), 52–54.

175 G. Montagu Harris, "Housing Development in the Department of the Seine," *Garden Cities and Town Planning* 9 (August 1919): 152–53; Joseph Bassompierre-Sewrin, "L'Urbanisme en France," *L'Architecture d'Aujourd'hui* no. 8 (November 1931): 57–58; *Réalisations de l'Office public d'habitations du département de la Seine* (Strasbourg: Edari, Édition d'architecture et d'industrie et d'économie rurale S.A.R. L., 1933), 29–30; Paul Sirvin, "La Cité-Jardin de Chatenay-Malabry," *Construction Moderne* 69 (February 1953): 59–68; François Laisney, "Quand le HLM étaint roses," *Architecture, Mouvement, Continuité* no. 35 (April 1974): 79–104; Paul Chemetov, Marie-Jeanne Dumont, and Bernard Marrey, *Paris-Banlieue, 1919–1939, Architectures domestiques* (Paris: Dunod, 1989), 134, 138–39, 148–50; Jean Pierre Gaudin, "The French Garden City," in Stephen V. Ward, ed., *The Garden City: Past, Present and Future* (London: E and FN Spon, 1992), 58–59, 66; Bertrand Lemoine, *Birkhäuser Architectural Guide to France; 20th Century* (Basel: Birkhäuser, 2000), 66–67.

176 G. Montagu Harris, "Housing Development in the Department of the Seine," *Garden Cities and Town Planning* 9 (August 1919): 152–53; Friedrich Klein, "Die Gartenstadt Plessis-Robinson Bei Paris," *Städtebau* 23 (1928): 70–73; Jean Virette, *La Cité Jardin* (Paris: Éditions S. de Bonadona, 1931), plate 28; *Réalisations de l'Office public d'habitations du département de la Seine* (Strasbourg: Edari, Édition d'architecture et d'industrie et d'économie rurale S.A.R.L., 1933), 55–62; Olivier Nicoulaud, "Cite Jardins," *Architecture, Mouvement, Continuité* no.34 (July 1974): 22–23; "Au Plessis-Robinson: Maurice Payret-Dortail," *Sites et Monuments* no. 126 (1988): 25–28; Paul Chemetov, Marie-Jeanne Dumont, and Bernard Marrey, *Paris-Banlieue, 1919–1939, Architectures domestiques* (Paris: Dunod, 1989), 138–39, 170–72; Gwendolyn Wright, *The Politics of Design in French Colonial Urbanism* (Chicago and London: University of Chicago Press, 1991), 36, 37; Jean Pierre Gaudin, "The French Garden City," in Stephen V. Ward, ed., *The Garden City: Past, Present and Future* (London: E and FN Spon, 1992), 58–59, 66.

177 Edith Elmer Wood, "Recent Housing Work in Western Europe," *Architectural Record* 53 (February 1923): 176; Edith Elmer Wood, "The Cités-Jardins of Lyons and Rheims," *American City* 28 (March 1923): 228–34; "Le Foyer Rémois, J.-M. Auburtin, architecte," *L'architecte* 3 (1926): 52–56, plates 37–42; Pierre Vago, "Lotissement du Chemin-Vert du Foyer Rémois a Reims," *L'Architecture d'Aujourd'hui* 50 (February 1934): 23; Gwendolyn Wright, *The Politics of Design in French Colonial Urbanism* (Chicago and London: University of Chicago Press, 1991), 38, 39; Bertrand Lemoine, *Birkhäuser Architectural Guide to France; 20th Century* (Basel: Birkhäuser, 2000), 46; http://www.foyer-remois.fr/-Notre-histoire-semee-de-.

178 Vago, "Lotissement du Chemin-Vert du Foyer Rémois a Reims": 23.

179 Theodor Goecke, "Gartenvorstadt Stockfeld in Strassburg-Neuhof," *Der Städtebau* 8 (April 1911): 37–39, plates 19–22; Gordon E. Cherry, *The Evolution of British Town Planning* (New York and Toronto: John Wiley & Sons, 1974), 39; Stéphane Jonas, "La Création de la Cité-Jardin de Stockfeld à Strasbourg, 1907–1912," in *Stadtentwicklung im deutsch-französisch-luxemburgischen Grenzraum* (Saarbrücken: Saarbrücker Druckerei und Verlag, 1991), 199–236; Théodore Rieger, *Strasbourg Architecture: 1871–1918* (Illkirch-Graffenstaden: Le Verger, 1991), 28–29, 170, 171; Stéphane Jonas, "La cite-jardin du Stockfeld: de la ville à la campagne," in *Strasbourg 1900: naissance d'une capitale* (Strasbourg: Musées de Strasbourg, 2000), 244–52.

180 Alfred Dachert, "Positive Eugenics in Practice," *The Eugenics Review* XXIII (April 1931): 15–18. Also see Jean Virette, *La Cité Jardin* (Paris: Éditions S. de Bonadona, 1931), plates 1–9; "A Eugenic Experiment," *British Medical Journal* 1 (May 9, 1931): 808–9; "Notes of Science: Eugenics Get a Test," *New York Times* (August 30, 1931), XX: 4; Lansing Warren, "Success Has Come to Eugenic Village," *New York Times* (September 27, 1931), E: 4; Charles Matthias Goethe, *War profits…and better babies…* (Sacramento and San Francisco: Keystone Press, 1946), IV–XI, 1–21; Gérard Bauer, Gildas Baudez, Jean-Michel Roux, *Banlieues de Charme ou l'art des quartiers-jardins* (Paris: Pandora editions, 1980), 110–21; William H. Schneider, *Quality and Quantity: The Quest for Biological Regeneration in Twentieth Century France* (Cambridge and New York: Cambridge University Press, 1990), 124–28; Gwendolyn Wright, *The Politics of Design in French Colonial Urbanism* (Chicago and London: University of Chicago Press, 1991), 35, 37; Stéphane Jonas, "Les Jardins d'Ungemach à Strasbourg: une cité-jardin d'origine nataliste," in *Cités, Cités-Jardins: Une Histoire Européenne* (Talence: Editions de la maison des sciences de l'homme d'aquitaine, 1996), 66–85.

181 Schneider, *Quality and Quantity: The Quest for Biological Regeneration in Twentieth Century France*, 127.

182 Dachert, "Positive Eugenics in Practice": 16.

183 Alfred Dachert, quoted in Goethe, *War profits…and better babies…*, 5.

184 Dachert, "Positive Eugenics in Practice": 15.

185 Georges Benoît-Lévy, "A French Garden Hamlet," *Town Planning Review* 7 (April 1918): 251–52; Brian Brace Taylor, *Le Corbusier at Pessac, 1914–1928* (Paris: Spadem, 1972), 5; H. Allen Brooks, *Le Corbusier's Formative Years* (Chicago and London: The University of Chicago Press, 1997), 481–85, 486; Stanislaus von Moos and Arthur Rüegg, *Le Corbusier before Le Corbusier: Applied Arts, Architecture, Painting, Photography, 1907–1922* (New Haven, Conn., and London: Yale University Press, 2002), 21; Mervyn Miller, "Garden Cities and Suburbs: At Home and Abroad," *Journal of Planning History* 1 (February 2002): 21; Andrés Duany, Elizabeth Plater-Zyberk, and Robert Alminana, *New Civic Art* (New York: Rizzoli International Publications; London: Troika, 2003), 201; Deborah Gans, *The Le Corbusier Guide, Third Edition* (New York: Princeton Architectural Press, 2006), 139.

186 Brooks, *Le Corbusier's Formative Years*, 481.

187 Brooks, *Le Corbusier's Formative Years*, 482.

188 Brooks, *Le Corbusier's Formative Years*, 484.

189 Henri Frugès, quoted in Thomas Matthews, "Le Corbusier's Pessac: An Experiment in Urbanism Continues," *Architectural Record* 175 (November 1987): 87–89. Also see Henry-Russell Hitchcock, *Modern Architecture: Romanticism and Reintegration* (New York: Payson & Clarke, 1929), 168–69; Henry-Russell Hitchcock, *Architecture: Nineteenth and Twentieth Centuries* (Baltimore: Penguin Books, 1958), 372; Philippe Boudon, *Lived-in Architecture: Le Corbusier's Pessac Revisited* (Cambridge, Mass.: MIT Press, 1972); Brian Brace Taylor, *Le Corbusier at Pessac, 1914–1928* (Paris: Spadem, 1972); Ada Louise Huxtable, "Architecture View/Le Corbusier's Housing Project—Flexible Enough to Endure," *New York Times* (March 15, 1981), D: 27; Dennis J. De Witt and Elizabeth R. De Witt, *Modern Architecture in Europe: A Guide to Buildings Since the Industrial Revolution* (New York: E. P. Dutton, 1987), 167; W. Boesiger and O. Stonorov, eds., *Le Corbusier Œuvre Complète, Volume 1, 1910–29* (Basel: Birkhäuser, 1995), 78–86; Marylène Ferrand et al., *Le Corbusier: Le Quartiers Modernes Frugès* (Paris: Fondation Le Corbusier; Basel: Birkhäuser, 1998); Carl Fredrik Svenstedt, "Corbu Comeback," *Metropolis* 18 (February/March 1999): 66–69; Bernard Lemoine, *Birkhäuser Architectural Guide: France, 20th Century* (Basel: Birkhäuser, 2000), 18; Mervyn Miller, "Garden Cities and Suburbs: At Home and Abroad," *Journal of Planning History* 1 (February 2002): 6–28; Jean-Louis Cohen, *Le Corbusier, 1887–1965: The Lyricism of Architecture in the Machine Age* (Köln and Los Angeles: Taschen, 2004), 28–29.

190 Boudon, *Lived-in Architecture: Le Corbusier's Pessac Revisited*, 7–8; Ferrand et al., *Le Corbusier: Le Quartiers Modernes Frugès*, 52–63.

191 Miller, "Garden Cities and Suburbs": 21.

192 Ferrand et al., *Le Corbusier: les quartiers modernes Frugès*, 84.

193 Le Corbusier, quoted in Matthews, "Le Corbusier's Pessac: An Experiment in Urbanism Continues": 87, 89.

194 Hitchcock, *Modern Architecture: Romanticism and Reintegration*, 168–69.

195 Boudon, *Lived-in Architecture*, 161.

196 Huxtable, "Architecture View/Le Corbusier's Housing Project—Flexible Enough to Endure": 27.

197 *La Côte d'Opale: Architectures des Années 20 et 30* (Paris: Norma Éditions, 1998).

198 Aurélie Pirotte, "Wissant," in *La Côte d'Opale: Architectures des Années 20 et 30* (Paris: Norma Éditions, 1998), 41–60.

199 Richard Klein, *Le Touquet Paris-Plage* (Paris: Norma Éditions, 1994), passim; Richard Klein, "Le Touquet," in *La Côte d'Opale: Architectures des Années 20 et 30* (Paris: Norma Éditions, 1998), 99–120, 182.

200 Quoted in Richard Klein, "Le Touquet," in *La Côte d'Opale: Architectures des Années 20 et 30* (Paris: Norma Éditions, 1998), 101. Also see "Obituary/Thomas William Cutler," *Royal Institute of British Architects Journal* 17 (1909–1910): 176; Richard Klein, *Le Touquet Paris-Plage* (Paris: Norma Éditions, 1994), 24, 26, 27.

201 Charles Lowe, quoted in *John R. Whitley: A Sketch of His Life and Work* (London: Dryden Press, J. Davy & Sons, 1912), 43–52. Also see "Cottages Modernes d'une Robuste Structure," *La Vie à la Campagne* 13 (June 15, 1913): 380–96; Richard Klein, "Hardelot," in *La Côte d'Opale: Architectures des Années 20 et 30* (Paris: Norma Éditions, 1998), 89–98; Bernard Toulier, *Villes d'eaux: Architecture publique des stations thermals et balnéaires* (Paris: Dexia and Imprimerie Nationale, 2002), 29.

202 Klein, "Hardelot," in *La Côte d'Opale: Architectures des Années 20 et 30*, 91.

203 Caroline Dupuich, "Stella-Plage," in *La Côte d'Opale: Architectures des Années 20 et 30* (Paris: Norma Éditions, 1998), 121–32, 183–84; Bernard Toulier, *Villes d'eaux: Architecture publique des stations thermals et balnéaires* (Paris : Dexia and Imprimerie Nationale, 2002), 21, 30, 32, 98.

204 Dominique Rouillard, *Le Site Balneaire* (Liège : Pierre Mardaga, 1984), 13–14.

205 Karl Baedeker, *Belgium and Holland including the Grand-duchy of Luxembourg* (Leipzig: Karl Baedeker, 1905), 19–20; *Histoire d'eaux: stations thermals et balnéaires en Belgique XVIe–XXe siècle* (Bruxelles: Caisse générale d'épargne et de retraite, 1987), 282–84; Amy F. Ogata, *Art Nouveau and the Social Vision of Modern Living: Belgian Artists in a European Context* (Cambridge: Cambridge University Press, 2001), 150.

206 Claude Laroche, *Hossegor: 1920–1940, La Station des Sports Élégants* (Paris: Norma Editions, 1991); Claude Laroche, *Architecture et identité régionale: Hossegor, 1923–1939* (Bordeaux: A. P. I. A; Le Festin, 1993); Claude Laroche, "La Station des Sports Élégants," *Vieilles Maisons Françaises* no. 207 (April 2005): 32–37.

207 *Architectures de Biarritz et de La Cote Basque: de la belle epoque aux années trente* (Liège: P. Mardaga, 1990), 74–76; *Le Pays Basque: Architectures des Années 20 et 30* (Paris: Norma Editions, 1993), 166–77; *Hendaye, Irún, Fontarabie: Villes de la frontière* (Paris: Norma Editions, 1998), esp. pp. 153–218; Bernard Toulier, *Villes d'eaux: Architecture publique des stations thermals et balnéaires* (Paris: Dexia and Imprimerie Nationale, 2002), 12, 30, 91, 99, 100–101, 116, 137, 138–39, 153.

208 "Amenagement du Port d'Hendaye," *Architecture méditerranéenne* 42 (April 1994): 143–46.

209 *Hendaye, Irún, Fontarabie: Villes de la frontière* (Paris: Norma Editions, 1998), esp. pp. 133–53, 301–42.

210 *Hendaye, Irún, Fontarabie: Villes de la frontière* (Paris: Norma Editions, 1998), 120, 121, 122–23.

211 Pieter Uyttenhove, "The Garden City Education of Belgian Planners around the First World War," *Planning Perspectives* 5 (1990): 271–83.

212 Charles Didier, quoted in Ewart G. Culpin, *The Garden City Movement Up-to-Date* (London: Garden Cities and Town Planning Association, 1913), 66.

213 Ewart G. Culpin, *The Garden City Movement Up-to-Date* (London: Garden Cities and Town Planning Association, 1913), 66; Patrick Burniat, Pierre Puttemans, and Jos Vandenbreeden, *L'architecture Moderne à Bruxelles, Modern Architecture in Brussels*, trans. by Christopher Bourne (Brussels: Les Éditions L'Octogone, 2000), 39–41; Edith Elmer Wood, "Recent Housing Work in Western Europe," *Architectural Record* 53 (February 1923), 177–78; Marcel Smets, "Stedebouw in België, 1920–1940, Algemene Ontwikkeling; Urbanistic Thinking in Belgium, 1920–1940, General Development," *Forum* (Amsterdam) 24, no. 4 (1972); Marcel Smets, "Stedebouw in België, 1920–1940, Tuinwijken; Urbanistic Thinking in Belgium, 1920–1940, Garden Districts," *Forum* (Amsterdam) 24, no. 5 (1972); Pierre Puttemans, *Modern Architecture in Belgium*, trans. by Mette Willert (Brussels: Marc Vokaer, 1976), 111–37; Jan Maes, "L'expérience des cites-jardins dans le contexte de la reconstruction de la Belgique après 1918," in Marcel Smets, ed., *Resurgam: la reconstruction en Belgique après 1914: Passage 44, Bruxelles, 27 Mars-30 Juin 1985* (Bruxelles: Crédit communal, 1985), 189–213; Pieter Uyttenhove, "The Garden City Education of Belgian Planners around the First World War," *Planning Perspectives* 5 (1990): 271–83; Eric Hennaut, "La Cité-Jardin Dans L'entre-Deux-Guerres," in *Cités-Jardins, 1920–1940, en Belgique* (Bruxelles: Archives d'Architecture Moderne, 1994), 35–38.

214 Gabriele Tagliaventi, "Garden-Cities within the City: Begiunages-Begijnhofe," in Gabriele Tagliaventi, ed., *Garden City* (Rome: Gangemi Editore, 1994), 156–65. Also see Anna Barozzi, "The Morphology of the Garden City," in Tagliaventi, ed., *Garden City*, 108; Gabriele Tagliaventi, "The Garden City's Archetype," in Tagliaventi, ed., *Garden City*, 116, 134.

215 Marcel Smets, "Stedebouw in België, 1920–1940, Algemene Ontwikkeling; Urbanistic Thinking in Belgium, 1920–1940, General Development," *Forum* (Amsterdam) 24, no. 4 (1972), 11, 13.

216 Louis Van der Swaelmen, "Cité-Jardin 'Floréal,'" *L'Habitation à Bon Marché* 1 (January 1921), quoted in Betta Latis, "Dal Béguinage alla Ville Radieuse," *Spazio e Società* 17 (January–March 1994): 39–40.

217 "Le Foyer Anderlechtois," *L'Habitation à Bon Marché* 3 (July 1923): 158–64; *Brussels, 1890–1971: Guide to the Architecture* (Bruxelles: Ministére de la Culture française a l'initiative de la Société Belge des Urbanistes et Architectes Modernistes, 1972), 42; Jacques Gubler, "Two Early Works: The House a Campo and the Architect's Own House," in *Louis Herman de Koninck: Architect of Modern Times* (Brussels: Archives d'Architecture Moderne, 1989), 74–75; Maurizio Cohen, "Città-giardino anni 20 a Bruxelles: itinerario n.99," *Domus* 758 (March 1994): 86–90; Patrick Burniat, Pierre Puttemans, and Jos Vandenbreeden, *L'architecture Moderne à Bruxelles, Modern Architecture in Brussels* trans. by Christopher Bourne (Brussels: Les Éditions L'Octogone, 2000), 271; Maurice Culot, ed., *J.-J. Eggericx: Gentleman Architecte Créateur de Cités-Jardins* (Brussels: AAM Éditions, CFC Éditions, 2013), 68, 71.

218 "Le Foyer Anderlechtois," *L'Habitation à Bon Marché* 3 (July 1923): 158–64; Maurizio Cohen, "Città-giardino anni 20 a Bruxelles: itinerario n.99," *Domus* 758 (March 1994): 86–90.

219 Maurizio Cohen, "Città-giardino anni 20 a Bruxelles: itinerario n.99," *Domus* 758 (March 1994): 86–90; Patrick Burniat, Pierre Puttemans, and Jos Vandenbreeden, *L'architecture Moderne à Bruxelles, Modern Architecture in Brussels* trans. by Christopher Bourne (Brussels: Les Éditions L'Octogone, 2000), 273.

220 Maurizio Cohen, "Città-giardino anni 20 a Bruxelles: itinerario n.99," *Domus* 758 (March 1994): 86–90. Also see *Joseph Diongre: Een Huis, een Kerk, en een geluidsfabriek* (Brussels: Sint. Lukasarchief, 1989), project list on back jacket flap; François Aubry, Jos Vandenbreeden, and France Vanlaethem, *L'architecture en Belgique: Art Nouveau, Art Déco & Modernisme* (Bruxelles: Éditions Racine, 2006), 312.

221 *Brussels, 1890–1971: Guide to the Architecture* (Bruxelles: Ministére de la Culture française a l'initiative de la Société Belge des Urbanistes et Architectes Modernistes, 1972), 42.

222 Maurizio Cohen, "Città-giardino anni 20 a Bruxelles: itinerario n.99," *Domus* 758 (March 1994): 86–90.

223 Maurizio Cohen, "Città-giardino anni 20 a Bruxelles: itinerario n.99," *Domus* 758 (March 1994): 86–90.

224 "Cité=Jardin Kersbeek à Forest," *L'Habitation à Bon Marché* 3 (May 1923): 87–96; Maurizio Cohen, "Città-giardino anni 20 a Bruxelles: itinerario n.99," *Domus* 758 (March 1994): 86–90.

225 Maurizio Cohen, "Città-giardino anni 20 a Bruxelles: itinerario n.99," *Domus* 758 (March 1994): 86–90.

226 Maurizio Cohen, "Città-giardino anni 20 a Bruxelles: itinerario n.99," *Domus* 758 (March 1994): 86–90.

227 *Cités-Jardins, 1920–1940, en Belgique* (Bruxelles: Archives d'Architecture Moderne, 1994), 31; Maurizio Cohen, "Città-giardino anni 20 a Bruxelles: itinerario n.99," *Domus* 758 (March 1994): 86–90.

228 Maurizio Cohen, "Città-giardino anni 20 a Bruxelles: itinerario n.99," *Domus* 758 (March 1994): 86–90.

229 Carlos Thirion, "Le Quartier-Jardin des Hougnes a Verviers," *L'Habitation à Bon Marché* 5 (July 1925): 121–30; Marcel Smets, *L'avenement de la Cité-Jardin en Belgique: Histoire de l'habitat social en Belgique de 1830 à 1930* (Bruxelles: P. Mardaga, 1977), 122.

230 Patrick Burniat, Pierre Puttemans, and Jos Vandenbreeden, *L'architecture Moderne à Bruxelles, Modern Architecture in Brussels*, trans. by Christopher Bourne (Brussels: Les Éditions L'Octogone, 2000), 259. Also see *Cités-Jardins, 1920–1940, en Belgique* (Bruxelles: Archives d'Architecture Moderne, 1994), 84–87; Maurizio Cohen, "Città-giardino anni 20 a Bruxelles: itinerario n.99," *Domus* 758 (March 1994): 86–90.

231 "Cité-Jardin 'Floreal,'" *L'Habitation à Bon Marché* 5 (January 1925): 1–18; *Brussels, 1890–1971: Guide to the Architecture* (Bruxelles: Ministére de la Culture française a l'initiative de la Société Belge des Urbanistes et Architectes Modernistes, 1972), 40, 41; Marcel Smets, "Stedebouw in België, 1920–1940, Algemene Ontwikkeling; Urbanistic Thinking in Belgium, 1920–1940, General Development," *Forum* (Amsterdam) 24, no. 4 (1972): 11, 13, 15, 17; Marcel Smets, "Stedebouw in België, 1920–1940, Tuinwijken; Urbanistic Thinking in Belgium, 1920–1940, Garden Districts," *Forum* (Amsterdam) 24, no. 5 (1972); Serge Goyens de Heusch, *"7 Arts" Bruxelles 1922–1929, un front de jeunesse pour la revolution artistique* (Bruxelles: Ministere de la Culture Française de Belgique, 1976), 76; Marcel Smets, *L'avenement de la Cité-Jardin en Belgique: Histoire de l'habitat social en Belgique de 1830 à 1930* (Bruxelles: P. Mardaga, 1977), 112–13, 128, 130, 131, 136–39, 140–43; Herman Stynen, *Urbanisme et Société: Louis van der Swaelmen, 1883–1929: animateur du movement moderne en Belgique* (Bruxelles: P. Mardaga, 1979), 94–101, 128; Gérard Bauer, Gildas Baudez, and Jean-Michel Roux, *Banlieues de charme ou l'art des quartiers-jardins* (Aix-en-Provence: Pandora Éditions, 1980), 158–77; "Un Heureux Moment Dans la Fabrications du Paysage de la Banlieue: Les Cités-Jardin," *Bulletin D'Informations Architecturales* supplement to no. 96 (June 1985): n.p.; Dennis J. De Witt and Elizabeth R. De Witt, *Modern Architecture in Europe: A Guide to Buildings Since the Industrial Revolution* (New York: E. P. Dutton, 1987), 48; "Le cités-jardins di Le Logis e Floréal," *Rassegna* 34 (June 1988): 47–52; *Cités-Jardins, 1920–1940, en Belgique* (Bruxelles: Archives d'Architecture Moderne, 1994), 55–65; Anna Barozzi, "The Morphology of the Garden City," in Gabriele Tagliaventi, ed., *Garden City* (Rome: Gangemi Editore, 1994), 108; Betta Latis, "Dal Béguinage alla Ville Radieuse," *Spazio e Società* 17 (January–March 1994): 34–49; Maurizio Cohen, "Città-giardino anni 20 a Bruxelles: itinerario n.99," *Domus* 758 (March 1994): 86–90; Herman van Bergeijk and Otakar Máčel, *Birkhäuser Architectural Guide: Belgium, The Netherlands, Luxembourg, 20th Century* (Basel: Birkäuser, 1998), 71; Patrick Burniat, Pierre Puttemans, and Jos Vandenbreeden, *L'architecture Moderne à Bruxelles, Modern Architecture in Brussels* trans. by Christopher Bourne (Brussels: Les Éditions L'Octogone, 2000), 209; Michiel Heirman and Linda Van Santvoort, *Le Guide de L'architecture en Belgique* (Brussels: Éditions Racine, 2000), 180; *Brussels* (Watford, England: Michelin Travel Publications, 2001), 194; Geert Bekaert, "Introduction," in Mil De Kooning, ed., *Horta and After: 25 Masters of Modern Architecture in Belgium*, 2nd rev. ed. (Ghent: Department of Architecture and Urbanism, Ghent University, 2001), 17; Hellen Meller, *European Cities, 1890–1930s: History, Culture and the Built Environment* (New York: John Wiley & Sons, 2001), 120–21; Dorothée Imbert, "Counting Trees and Flowers: The Reconstructed Landscapes of Belgium and France," in Marc Treib, ed., *The Architecture of Landscape, 1940–1960* (Philadelphia: University of Pennsylvania Press, 2002), 83–84; Andrés Duany, Elizabeth Plater-Zyberk, and Robert Alminana, *The New Civic Art: Elements of Town Planning* (New York: Rizzoli International Publications, 2003), 287; François Aubry, Jos Vandenbreeden, and France Vanlaethem, *L'architecture en Belgique: Art Nouveau, Art Déco & Modernisme* (Bruxelles: Éditions Racine, 2006), 304, 314–15, 316, 317; Maurice Culot, ed., *J.-J. Eggericx: Gentleman Architecte Créateur de Cités-Jardins* (Brussels: AAM Éditions, CFC Éditions, 2013), 70, 71–75; Lauréline Tissot, "Le Logis et Floréal," in Culot, ed., *J.-J. Eggericx: Gentleman Architecte Créateur de Cités-Jardins*, 96–139.

232 Meller, *European Cities, 1890–1930s*, 121.

233 Louis van der Swaelmen, "Cite-Jardin Floreal," *L'Habitation à Bon Marché* (1921): 1, quoted in Latis, "Dal Béguinage alla Ville Radieuse": 39.

234 Victor Bourgeois, "La Cité Moderne," *L'Habitation à Bon Marché* 3 (October 1923): 245–54; Pierre Bourgeois, "La Cité Moderne," *L'Habitation à Bon Marché* 5 (October 1925): 182–90; *Victor Bourgeois: Architectures, 1922–1952* (Brussels: Editions Art et Techniques, 1952), 14–18; George Linze, *Victor Bourgeois* (Brussels: Édité par les Éditions et ateliers d'art graphique Elsevier, pour le Ministère de l'instruction publique, 1960), plates 1, 2; *Brussels, 1890–1971: Guide to the Architecture* (Bruxelles: Ministére de la Culture française a l'initiative de la Société Belge des Urbanistes et Architectes Modernistes, 1972), 40, 41; Marcel Smets, "Stedebouw in België, 1920–1940, Algemene Ontwikkeling; Urbanistic Thinking in Belgium, 1920–1940, General Development," *Forum* (Amsterdam) 24, no. 4 (1972): 11, 13, 15; Marcel Smets, "Stedebouw in België, 1920–1940, Tuinwijken; Urbanistic Thinking in Belgium, 1920–1940, Garden Districts," *Forum* (Amsterdam) 24, no. 5 (1972); Serge Goyens de Heusch, *"7 Arts" Bruxelles 1922–1929, un front de jeunesse pour la revolution artistique* (Bruxelles: Ministere de la Culture Française de Belgique, 1976), 74, 76; Marcel Smets, *L'avenement de la Cité-Jardin en Belgique: Histoire de l'habitat social en Belgique de 1830 à 1930* (Bruxelles: P. Mardaga, 1977), 126, 133–37, 140–41; Dennis J. De Witt and Elizabeth R. De Witt, *Modern Architecture in Europe: A Guide to Buildings Since the Industrial Revolution* (New York: E. P. Dutton, 1987), 49; Francis Strauven, "De Koninck and the Legacy of Horta: From the Hotel Dubois to the Dotremont House," in *Louis Herman De Koninck: Architecte Des Années Modernes, Architect of Modern Times* (Bruxelles: Archives d'Architecture Moderne, 1989), 106; "Victor Bourgeois, La Cité Moderne," *Rassegna* 34 (June 1988): 44–46; *Cités-Jardins, 1920–1940, en Belgique* (Bruxelles: Archives d'Architecture Moderne, 1994), 66–75; Maurizio Cohen, "Città-giardino anni 20 a Bruxelles: itinerario n.99," *Domus* 758 (March 1994): 86–90; Els Claessens, "La Cite Moderne," *Monumenten en Landschappen: M & L* 15 (March–April 1996): 45–62, 63; Patrick Burniat, Pierre Puttemans, and Jos Vandenbreeden, *L'architecture Moderne à Bruxelles, Modern Architecture in Brussels*, trans. by Christopher Bourne (Brussels: Les Éditions L'Octogone, 2000), 288; Michiel Heirman and Linda Van Santvoort, *Le Guide de L'architecture en Belgique* (Brussels: Éditions Racine, 2000), 178; Iwan Strauven, "Victor Bourgeois, 1897–1962," in Mil De Kooning, ed., *Horta and After: 25 Masters of Modern Architecture in Belgium*, 2nd rev. ed. (Ghent: Department of Architecture and Urbanism, Ghent University, 2001), 76–84; François Aubry, Jos Vandenbreeden, and France Vanlaethem, *L'architecture en Belgique: Art Nouveau, Art Déco & Modernisme* (Bruxelles: Éditions Racine, 2006), 314–15, 318, 319.

235 Geert Bekaert, "Introduction," in Mil De Kooning, ed., *Horta and After: 25 Masters of Modern Architecture in Belgium*, 2nd rev. ed. (Ghent: Department of Architecture and Urbanism, Ghent University, 2001), 17–18. Also see "La Cité-Jardin du 'Kapelleveld' à Woluwe-St-Lambert," *L'Habitation à Bon Marché* 4 (June 1924): 123–46; A. I. Petrov, "Notes and News/II.—La Cité-Jardin de Kapelleveld," *Garden Cities and Town Planning* 15 (April 1925): 94–95; *Brussels, 1890–1971: Guide to the Architecture* (Bruxelles: Ministére de la Culture française a l'initiative de la Société Belge des Urbanistes et Architectes Modernistes, 1972), 42, 43; Marcel Smets, *Huib Hoste: propagateur d'une architecture renouvelée* (Bruxelles: Confédération Nationale de la Construction in collaboration with Librairie Simon Stevin, 1972), 64–68, 101, 102, 103; Marcel Smets, "Stedebouw in België, 1920–1940, Algemene Ontwikkeling; Urbanistic Thinking in Belgium, 1920–1940, General Development," *Forum* (Amsterdam) 24, no. 4 (1972): 11, 13, 15, 17; Marcel Smets, "Stedebouw in België, 1920–1940, Tuinwijken; Urbanistic Thinking in Belgium, 1920–1940, Garden Districts," *Forum* (Amsterdam) 24, no. 5 (1972); Serge Goyens de Heusch, *"7 Arts" Bruxelles*

1922–1929, un front de jeunesse pour la revolution artistique (Bruxelles: Ministere de la Culture Française de Belgique, 1976), 76; Marcel Smets, *L'avenement de la Cité-Jardin en Belgique: Histoire de l'habitat social en Belgique de 1830 à 1930* (Bruxelles: P. Mardaga, 1977), 130, 138–43; Herman Stynen, *Urbanisme et Société: Louis van der Swaelmen, 1883–1929: animateur du movement moderne en Belgique* (Bruxelles: P. Mardaga, 1979), 88–91, 128–29; Aleks A. M. Deseyne, *Huib Hoste: 1881–1957, en de wederopbouw te Zonnebeke* (Zonnebeke: Zonnebekse Heemvrienden, 1981), 50, 52; Dennis J. De Witt and Elizabeth R. De Witt, *Modern Architecture in Europe: A Guide to Buildings Since the Industrial Revolution* (New York: E. P. Dutton, 1987), 48; "La Cité-Jardin di Kapelleveld, 1922–26," *Rassegna* 34 (June 1988): 53–55; *Cités-Jardins, 1920–1940, en Belgique* (Bruxelles: Archives d'Architecture Moderne, 1994), 76–83; Anna Barozzi, "The Morphology of the Garden City," in Gabriele Tagliaventi, ed., *Garden City* (Rome: Gangemi Editore, 1994), 103; Maurizio Cohen, "Città-giardino anni 20 a Bruxelles: itinerario n.99," *Domus* 758 (March 1994): 86–90; Patrick Burniat, Pierre Puttemans, and Jos Vandenbreeden, *L'architecture Moderne à Bruxelles, Modern Architecture in Brussels*, trans. by Christopher Bourne (Brussels: Les Éditions L'Octogone, 2000), 210; Michiel Heirman and Linda Van Santvoort, *Le Guide de L'architecture en Belgique* (Brussels: Éditions Racine, 2000), 178–79; *Brussels* (Watford, England: Michelin Travel Publications, 2001), 199; Marcel Smets, "Huib Hoste, 1881–1957," in De Kooning, ed., *Horta and After: 25 Masters of Modern Architecture in Belgium*, 102–6; Dorothée Imbert, "Counting Trees and Flowers: The Reconstructed Landscapes of Belgium and France," in Marc Treib, ed., *The Architecture of Landscape, 1940–1960* (Philadelphia: University of Pennsylvania Press, 2002), 83–84; Andrés Duany, Elizabeth Plater-Zyberk, and Robert Alminana, *The New Civic Art: Elements of Town Planning* (New York: Rizzoli International Publications, 2003), 176; Liesbeth De Winter, Marcel Smets, and Ann Verdonck, *Huib Hoste: 1881–1957* (Antwerp: Vlaams Architectuurinstituut, 2005), 131–33; François Aubry, Jos Vandenbreeden, and France Vanlaethem, *L'architecture en Belgique: Art Nouveau, Art Déco & Modernisme* (Bruxelles: Éditions Racine, 2006), 314–15, 317, 320, 321.

236 Smets, "Huib Hoste, 1881–1957," in De Kooning, ed., *Horta and After: 25 Masters of Modern Architecture in Belgium*, 104.

237 Georges Benoît-Lévy, "Garden Villages of France and Belgium," *New York Times Current History* XVI (September 1922): 966–67. Also see Marcel Smets, *L'avenement de la Cité-Jardin en Belgique: Histoire de l'habitat social en Belgique de 1830 à 1930* (Bruxelles: P. Mardaga, 1977), 166–67.

238 Edward Leonard, "Unitas Tuinwijk," *L'Habitation à Bon Marché* 6 (August 1926): 140–47; *Eduard Van Steenbergen, Bouwmeester en Binnenhuiskunstenaar (1889–1952)* (Antwerpen: De Sikkel, 1955), 12, 46, 47, 48, plates 33–41; "Edward Van Steenbergen, cite-jardin Unitas, Deurne, 1923–32," *Rassegna* 34 (June 1988): 41; Michiel Heirman and Linda Van Santvoort, *Le Guide de L'architecture en Belgique* (Brussels: Éditions Racine, 2000), 52; François Aubry, Jos Vandenbreeden, and France Vanlaethem, *L'architecture en Belgique: Art Nouveau, Art Déco & Modernisme* (Bruxelles: Éditions Racine, 2006), 322.

239 Marcel Smets, *L'avenement de la Cité-Jardin en Belgique: Histoire de l'habitat social en Belgique de 1830 à 1930* (Bruxelles: P. Mardaga, 1977), 32, 105, 123; Andrés Duany, Elizabeth Plater-Zyberk, and Robert Alminana, *The New Civic Art: Elements of Town Planning* (New York: Rizzoli International Publications, 2003), 219.

240 "Belgium's Recovery," *Housing Betterment* 12 (July 1923): 252; Marcel Smets, *L'avenement de la Cité-Jardin en Belgique: Histoire de l'habitat social en Belgique de 1830 à 1930* (Bruxelles: P. Mardaga, 1977), 122–23; Jan Maes, "L'expérience des cites-jardins dans le contexte de la reconstruction de la Belgique après 1918," in Marcel Smets, ed., *Resurgam: la reconstruction en Belgique après 1914: Passage 44, Bruxelles, 27 Mars–30 Juin 1985* (Bruxelles: Crédit communal, 1985), 200, 203–5.

241 Herman Stynen, *Urbanisme et Société: Louis van der Swaelmen, 1883–1929: animateur du movement moderne en Belgique* (Bruxelles: P. Mardaga, 1979), 34; Jan Maes, "L'expérience des cites-jardins dans le contexte de la reconstruction de la Belgique après 1918," in Marcel Smets, ed., *Resurgam: la reconstruction en Belgique après 1914: Passage 44, Bruxelles, 27 Mars–30 Juin 1985* (Bruxelles: Crédit communal, 1985), 209–10.

242 J. Bruinwold Riedel, *Tuinsteden* (Utrecht: J. Van Boekhoven, 1906). Also see Donald I. Grinberg, *Housing in the Netherlands, 1900–1940* (Delft: Delft University Press, 1977), 54–55; Rudy Schreijnders, *De Droom van Howard: verleden en toekomst van de tuindorpen* (Rijswijk: Elmar, 1991), 274.

243 Rudy Schreijnders, *De Droom van Howard: verleden en toekomst van de tuindorpen* (Rijswijk: Elmar, 1991), 178–80; Cor Wagenaar, *Town Planning in the Netherlands since 1800* (Rotterdam: 010 Publishers, 2011), 298, 299.

244 Henri Polak, quoted in Nancy Steiber, *Housing Design and Society in Amsterdam: Reconfiguring Urban Order and Identity, 1900–1920* (Chicago and London: University of Chicago Press, 1998), 146.

245 R. De Clercq, quoted in Ewart G. Culpin, *The Garden City Movement Up-to-Date* (London: Garden Cities and Town Planning Association, 1913), 66.

246 Hans Ibelings, *20th Century Urban Design in the Netherlands* (Rotterdam: NAi Publishers, 1999), 20.

247 Sh. Rg. Hofstee, "Housing Built by Industrialists in the Netherlands," in *L'Étude et la mise en valeur du patrimoine industriel : 4e conférence internationale, Lyon, Grenoble, septembre 1981* (Paris: Editions du Centre national de la recherche scientifique, 1985), 319.

248 Nancy Stieber, *Housing Design and Society in Amsterdam: Reconfiguring Urban Order and Identity, 1900–1920* (Chicago and London: University of Chicago Press, 1998), 61, 62.

249 Daniele Baroni, "Leaders of the Modern Movement: Jan Wils," *Ottagono* 22 (March 1987): 49.

250 Wim de Wagt, *Architectuurgids Haarlem* (Rotterdam: 010, 2005), 78–79.

251 Wim de Wagt, *Architectuurgids Haarlem* (Rotterdam: 010, 2005), 82–83.

252 Chris Kolman et al., *Monumenten in Nederland: Utrecht* (Zeist: Rijksdienst voor de Monumentenzorg; Zwolle: Waanders Uitgevers, 1996), 322; Constance D. H. Moes, *L.A. Springer: Tuinarchitect Dendroloog* (Rotterdam: de Hef, 2002), 268.

253 Moes, *L.A. Springer: Tuinarchitect Dendroloog*, 268.

254 Moes, *L.A. Springer Tuinarchitect Dendroloog*, 82–83.

255 Maurits Van Rooijen, "Open Space, Urban Planning and the Evolution of the Green City," in Robert Freestone, ed., *Urban Planning in a Changing World: The Twentieth Century Experience* (London: E & FN Spon, 2000), 217.

256 For Wilhelminapark, see Constance D. H. Moes, *L.A. Springer: Tuinarchitect Dendroloog* (Rotterdam: de Hef, 2002), 266–68. For Oud-Bussum, see Hans Ibelings, *20th Century Urban Design in the Netherlands* (Rotterdam: NAi Publishers, 1999), 10.

257 Annette Koenders, *Hilversum: Architectuur en Stedenbouw, 1850–1940* (Zwolle: Waanders Uitgevers; Gemeente Hilversum, 2001), 50–51.

258 Annette Koenders, *Hilversum: Architectuur en Stedenbouw, 1850–1940* (Zwolle: Waanders Uitgevers; Gemeente Hilversum, 2001), 57–58.

259 E. C. M. Cremers, "Het Villa Park Overbeek: het onstaan van een villapark aan de Veluwezoom," *Bijdragen en Mededelingen Vereniging Gelre* 73 (1982): 124–43; "Villapark Overbeek," in http://library.wur.nl/tuin/.

260 Dennis J. De Witt and Elizabeth R. De Witt, *Modern Architecture in Europe: A Guide to the Buildings Since the Industrial Revolution* (New York: E. P. Dutton, 1987), 258–59. Also see Dennis Sharp, "Park Meerwijk: An Expressionist Experiment in Holland," *Perspecta* 13 (1971): 177–89; Wim de Wit, ed., *The Amsterdam School: Dutch Expressionist Architecture, 1915–1930* (New York: Cooper-Hewitt Museum; Cambridge, Mass.: MIT Press, 1983), 30–31, 58–59; Joseph Buch, *A Century of Architecture in the Netherlands, 1880–1990* (Rotterdam: NAi Publishers, 1993), 64–65; Maristella Casciato, *The Amsterdam School* (Rotterdam: 010 Publishers, 1996), 54–65; Paul Groenendijk and Piet Vollaard, *Gids voor moderne architectuur in Nederland; Guide to modern architecture in the Netherlands* (Rotterdam: Uitgeverij 010, 1998), 126–27.

261 Donald I. Grinberg, *Housing in the Netherlands, 1900–1940* (Delft: Delft University Press, 1977), 42, 59; *Hendrik Petrus Berlage: disegni/Biennale di Venezia, in collaborazione con Rijksdienst Beeldende Kunst, Den Haage/Amsterdam* (Venice: Arsenale Editrice, 1986), 129–35; Sergio Polano, *Hendrik Petrus Berlage: Complete Works* (New York: Rizzoli International Publications, 1988), 165–68; Vincent van Rossem, "Berlage and the Culture of City Planning," in Polano, *Hendrik Petrus Berlage: Complete Works*, 45–49; Manfred Bock, "Berlage and Amsterdam," in Manfred Bock, Jet Collee, and Hester Coucke, *Berlage in Amsterdam* (Amsterdam: Achitectura & Natura Press in conjunction with ARCAM, 1992), 38, 43; Maristella Casciato, *The Amsterdam School* (Rotterdam: 010 Publishers, 1996), 122–28; Paul Groenendijk and Piet Vollaard, *Gids voor moderne architectuur in Nederland; Guide to modern architecture in the Netherlands* (Rotterdam: Uitgeverij 010, 1998), 184–85; Hans Ibelings, *20th Century Urban Design in the Netherlands* (Rotterdam: NAi Publishers, 1999), 7, 14; Jean-Paul Baeten, "Social Housing as 'Community Art,'" in *Living in the Lowlands: the Dutch Domestic Scene, 1850–2004* (Rotterdam: Netherlands Architecture Institute; NAi Publishers, 2004), 63–83; Mieke Dings, "Historical Perspective, 1900–2010," in Henk Ovink and Elien Wierenga, eds., *Ontwerp en Politiek; Design and Politics* (Rotterdam: Uitgeverij 010, 2009), 13–17; Cor Wagenaar, *Town Planning in the Netherlands since 1800* (Rotterdam: 010 Publishers, 2011), 222, 224.

262 "Snarepijperij," *De Kroniek* 3 no. 113 (March 7, 1897): 78, quoted in Stieber, *Housing Design and Society in Amsterdam*, 55.

263 H. P. Berlage, "Stedenbouw," *De Beweging* 10 (June 1914): 271, quoted in Stieber, *Housing Design and Society in Amsterdam*, 57.

264 *Hendrik Petrus Berlage: disegni/Biennale di Venezia, in collaborazione con Rijksdienst Beeldende Kunst, Den Haage/Amsterdam* (Venice: Arsenale Editrice, 1986), 148–57; Sergio Polano, *Hendrik Petrus Berlage: Complete Works* (New York: Rizzoli International Publications, 1988), 186; Vincent van Rossem, "Berlage and the Culture of City Planning," in Polano, *Hendrik Petrus Berlage: Complete Works*, 53–57; Manfred Bock, "Berlage and Amsterdam," in Manfred Bock, Jet Collee, and Hester Coucke, *Berlage in Amsterdam* (Amsterdam: Achitectura & Natura Press in conjunction with ARCAM, 1992), 44; Mieke Dings, "Historical Perspective, 1900–2010," in Henk Ovink and Elien Wierenga, eds., *Ontwerp en Politiek; Design and Politics* (Rotterdam: Uitgeverij 010, 2009), 17–18; Cor Wagenaar, *Town Planning in the Netherlands since 1800* (Rotterdam: 010 Publishers, 2011), 224–25, 226–27.

265 Polano, *Hendrik Petrus Berlage: Complete Works*, 186.

266 Donald I. Grinberg, *Housing in the Netherlands, 1900–1940* (Delft: Delft University Press, 1977), 38–39, 59; A. W. Reinink, *K. P. C. De Bazel* (Rotterdam: 010, 1993), 114–16; Polano, *Hendrik Petrus Berlage: Complete Works*, 186.

267 H. P. Berlage et al., *Arbeiderswoningen in Nederland* (Rotterdam: W. L. & J. Brusse, 1921), 40–45; *International Cities and Town Planning Exhibition. English Catalogue. Jubilee Exhibition, Gothenburg, Sweden, 1923* (Göteborg, Wezäta, W. Zachrissons boktyrckeri a.-b., 1923), 171–72, 173, 174, 175; Edith Elmer Wood, "Housing in the Netherlands," *Housing Betterment* 12 (January 1923): 350–56; S. J. Fockema Andreae, "The Garden City Idea in the Netherlands Before 1930," *Stedebouw en Volkshuisvesting* 44 (1963): 104–5; Waclaw Ostrowski, *Contemporary Town Planning: From the origins to the Athens Charter* (Hague, Netherlands: International Federation for Housing and Planning, 1970), 97, 98; Donald I. Grinberg, *Housing in the Netherlands, 1900–1940* (Delft: Delft University Press, 1977), 59, 60, 61, 62; Gérard Bauer, Gildas Baudez, and Jean-Michel Roux, *Banlieues de charme ou l'art des quartiers-jardins* (Aix-en-Provence: Pandora Éditions, 1980), 122–43; Donald I. Grinberg, "Modernist Housing and Its Critics: The Dutch Contributions," *Harvard Architecture Review* 1 (Spring 1980): 148–49; Sergio Polano, *Hendrik Petrus Berlage: Complete Works* (New York: Rizzoli International Publications, 1988), 214; Koos Bosma, "Town and Regional Planning in the Netherlands, 1920–1945," *Planning Perspectives* 5 (1990): 136–37; Rudy Schreijnders, *De Droom van Howard : verleden en toekomst van de tuindorpen* (Rijswijk: Elmar, 1991), 122–35, 226–33; Masaki Yashiro, "Garden City as a Source of 20th Century Ways of Living," *Process: Architecture* 112 (September 1993): 120, 124; Paul Groenendijk and Piet Vollaard, *Gids voor moderne architectuur in Nederland; Guide to modern architecture in the Netherlands* (Rotterdam: Uitgeverij 010, 1998), 302; Hans Ibelings, *20th Century Urban Design in the Netherlands* (Rotterdam: NAi Publishers, 1999), 21, 55; Gerritjan Deunk, *20th Century Garden and Landscape Architecture in the Netherlands* (Rotterdam: NAi Publishers, 2002), 32–33; Willemijn Wilms Floet, "Vreewijk Garden Village," in S. Umberto Barbieri and Leen van Duin, eds., *A Hundred Years of Dutch Architecture, 1901–2000, Trends, Highlights* (Amsterdam: Uitgeverij SUN, 2003), 93–104; Leen Van Duin, "Traditionalism," in Barbieri and van Duin, eds., *A Hundred Years of*

Dutch Architecture, 1901–2000, Trends, Highlights, 18–19; Harm Jan Korthals Altes, *Tuinsteden: tussen utopie en realitet* (Bussum: Thoth, 2004), 122–25; Willem Frijhoff and Marijke Spies, *Dutch Culture in a European Perspective: 1900, The Age of Bourgeois Culture* (Assen, Netherlands: Royal Van Gorcum, 2004), 134–35; Paul Groenendijk and Piet Vollaard, *Architectuurgids Rotterdam; Architectural Guide to Rotterdam* (Rotterdam: Uitgeverij 010, 2007), 11, 258; Mieke Dings, "Historical Perspective, 1900–2010," in Henk Ovink and Elien Wierenga, eds., *Ontwerp en Politiek; Design and Politics* (Rotterdam: Uitgeverij 010, 2009), 20–25; Cor Wagenaar, *Town Planning in the Netherlands since 1800* (Rotterdam: 010 Publishers, 2011), 232–33, 238, 274–78.

268 Donald I. Grinberg, "Modernist Housing and Its Critics: The Dutch Contributions," *Harvard Architecture Review* 1 (Spring 1980): 148–49.

269 A. C. Burgdorffer, quoted in Dings, "Historical Perspective, 1900–2010," in Ovink and Wierenga, eds., *Ontwerp en Politiek; Design and Politics*, 21.

270 Dings, "Historical Perspective, 1900–2010," in Ovink and Wierenga, eds., *Ontwerp en Politiek; Design and Politics*, 21.

271 Grinberg, *Housing in the Netherlands, 1900–1940*, 62.

272 Floet, "Vreewijk Garden Village," in Barbieri and van Duin, *A Hundred Years of Dutch Architecture*, 94–95.

273 Wood, "Housing in the Netherlands": 356.

274 Marinus Jan Granpré Molière, quoted in Groenendijk and Vollaard, *Architectural Guide to Rotterdam*, 258.

275 Dings, "Historical Perspective, 1900–2010," in Ovink and Wierenga, eds., *Ontwerp en Politiek; Design and Politics*, 25.

276 Mart Stam, quoted in Grinberg, "Modernist Housing and Its Critics": 149.

277 Dings, "Historical Perspective, 1900–2010," in Ovink and Wierenga, eds., *Ontwerp en Politiek; Design and Politics*, 25.

278 H. P. Berlage et al., *Arbeiderswoningen in Nederland* (Rotterdam: W. L. & J. Brusse, 1921), 31–33; Edith Elmer Wood, "Housing in the Netherlands," *Housing Betterment* 12 (January 1923), 353–55; G. F., "Een Nieuw Arbeiderswoning-complex van Dudok," *Bouwen* 1 (April–September 1924): 132–38; J. P. Mieras and F. R. Yerbury, *Hollandische Architektur des 20. Jahrhunderts* (Berlin: Verlag Ernst Wasmuth, 1926), plates XXX–XXXIV; Sir Selwyn Fremantle, "Hilversum," *Town and Country Planning* 3 (December 1934): 19–21; R. M. H. Magnee, *Willem M. Dudok* (Amsterdam: G. van Saane, 1954), 10–11; Donald I. Grinberg, *Housing in the Netherlands, 1900–1940* (Delft: Delft University Press, 1977), 63, 122; Max Cramer, Hans van Grieken, and Heleen Pronk, *W. M. Dudok, 1884–1974* (Amsterdam: Stichting Architectuur Museum, 1981), 91–98, 122–23; Joseph Buch, *A Century of Architecture in the Netherlands, 1880–1990* (Rotterdam: NAi Publishers, 1993), 143–49; Herman van Bergeijk, *Willem Marinus Dudok: Architect-stedebouwkundige, 1884–1974* (Inmerc, Naarden: V+K Publishing, 1995), 142–71, 198–200, 205, 212–13, 222–23, 225, 227, 284, 285–89, 298–99, 302–3; Paola Jappelli and Givoanni Menna, *Willem Marinus Dudok: Architetture e città, 1884–1974* (Naples: Clean Edizioni, 1997), 79–97, 324, 325, 326, 327, 328, 329, 332, 333; Herman van Bergeijk, "Willem Marinus Dudok, an Architect and a Government Official," *Rassegna* 75 (1998), 52–69; Paul Groenendijk and Piet Vollaard, *Gids voor moderne architectuur in Nederland; Guide to modern architecture in the Netherlands* (Rotterdam: Uitgeverij 010, 1998), 110–11; Hans Ibelings, *20th Century Urban Design in the Netherlands* (Rotterdam: NAi Publishers, 1999), 40, 45; Jos Smit, *Architectuur in Hilversum: Bouwkunst uit de twintigste eeuw in kaart gebracht* (Hilversum: Dudok Centrum, 2000), 21, 37; Herman van Bergeijk, *W. M. Dudok* (Rotterdam: 010 Publishers, 2001), 7–11, 36–37, 50–51, 56–57, 62–63, 94, 123, 143, 144, 145, 146, 147, 149, 150; Annette Koenders, *Hilversum: Architectuur en Stedenbouw, 1850–1940* (Zwolle: Waanders Uitgevers; Gemeente Hilversum, 2001), 63–71, 76; Harm Jan Korthals Altes, *Tuinsteden: tussen utopie en realitet* (Bussum: Thoth, 2004), 134–36; Herman van Bergeijk, "Dudok and the Image of Hilversum," in *Living in the Lowlands: the Dutch Domestic Scene, 1850–2004* (Rotterdam: Netherlands Architecture Institute; NAi Publishers, 2004), 85–95; Cor Wagenaar, *Town Planning in the Netherlands since 1800* (Rotterdam: 010 Publishers, 2011), 281–84.

279 Buch, *A Century of Architecture in the Netherlands, 1880–1990*, 145.

280 H. P. Berlage et al., *Arbeiderswoningen in Nederland* (Rotterdam: W. L. & J. Brusse, 1921), 34–36; Gunther Stamm, *The Architecture of J. J. P. Oud, 1906–1963* (Tallahassee: University Presses of Florida, 1978), 16–17; Max Cramer, Hans van Grieken, and Heleen Pronk, *W. M. Dudok, 1884–1974* (Amsterdam: Stichting Architectuur Museum, 1981), 121; B. Colenbrander, "J. J. P. Oud, Restrained and Careful," in *Het Nieuwe Bouwen* (Delft: Delft University Press; Nederlands Dokumentatiecentrum voor de Bouwkunst, 1982), 154; Herman van Bergeijk, *W. M. Dudok* (Rotterdam: 010 Publishers, 2001), 34–35; Ed Taverne, Cor Wagenaar, and Martien de Vletter, *J. J. P. Oud: Poetic Functionalist, The Complete Works, 1890–1963* (Rotterdam: NAi Publishers, 2001), 15, 96–97.

281 Taverne, Wagenaar, and de Vletter, *J. J. P. Oud: Poetic Functionalist, The Complete Works, 1890–1963*, 96–97.

282 W. M. Dudok, quoted in Fremantle, "Hilversum": 19.

283 W. M. Dudok, quoted in Fremantle, "Hilversum": 19.

284 W. M. Dudok, quoted in van Bergeijk, "Dudok and the Image of Hilversum," in *Living in the Lowlands: the Dutch Domestic Scene, 1850–2004*, 94.

285 Buch, *A Century of Architecture in the Netherlands, 1880–1990*, 143.

286 Van Bergeijk, "Dudok and the Image of Hilversum," in *Living in the Lowlands: the Dutch Domestic Scene, 1850–2004*, 93.

287 Van Bergeijk, *W. M. Dudok*, 62.

288 Wood, "Housing in the Netherlands": 355.

289 R. M. H. Magnee, *Willem M. Dudok* (Amsterdam: G. van Saane, 1954), 104–5; Hans Ibelings, *20th Century Urban Design in the Netherlands* (Rotterdam: NAi Publishers, 1999), 58–59; Herman van Bergeijk, *W. M. Dudok* (Rotterdam: 010 Publishers, 2001), 109.

290 A. T. Pike, "Housing and Town Planning Tour No. 19 to Holland/I.—Amsterdam," *Town and Country Planning* 3 (December 1934): 9–13; S. J. Fockema Andreae, "The Garden City Idea in the Netherlands Before 1930," *Stedebouw en Volkshuisvesting* 44 (1963): 105; "Het Betondorp," *Forum* (Amsterdam) 19 (1965–66): whole issue; P.K.A. Pennink, "Concrete Suburb," *Forum* 19 (1965–66): 9–23; J. van de Beek and G. Smienk, "ir j.b. van loghem b.i. architect," *Plan* 2 no. 12 (1971): 28–30; Donald I. Grinberg, *Housing in the Netherlands, 1900–1940* (Delft: Delft University Press, 1977), 90–92; J. B. van Loghem, *Bouwen = Bauen = Bâtir = Building Holland: een dokumentatie van de hoogtepunten van de moderne architektuur in Nederland van 1900 tot 1932* (Nijmegen, Netherlands: Socialistiese Uitgeverij Nijmegen, 1980), 95, 96; Tracy Metz, "Amsterdam Restores Its 'Concrete Village' and a Way of Life," *Architectural Record* 174 (February 1986): 79; Paul Broers et al., *Amsterdam Architecture: A Guide* (Amsterdam: Uitgeverij Thoth, 1987), 20, 104; Helen Searing, "Betondorp: Amsterdam's Concrete Garden Suburb," *Assemblage* 3 (July 1987): 108–43; Rudy Schreijnders, *De Droom van Howard : verleden en toekomst van de tuindorpen* (Rijswijk: Elmar, 1991), 157–64; Joseph Buch, *A Century of Architecture in the Netherlands, 1880–1990* (Rotterdam: NAi Publishers, 1993), 140–43; Masaki Yashiro, "Garden City as a Source of 20th Century Ways of Living," *Process: Architecture* 112 (September 1993): 120–23; Erik Mattie, *Functionalism in the Netherlands* (Amsterdam: Architectura & Natura, 1994), 18, 20; Hans Ibelings, *20th Century Architecture in the Netherlands* (Rotterdam: NAi Publishers, 1995), 40–41, 50; Maristella Casciato, *The Amsterdam School* (Rotterdam: 010 Publishers, 1996), 200, 209–13; Herman van Bergeijk and Otakar Máčel, *Birkhäuser Architectural Guide: Belgium, The Netherlands, Luxembourg, 20th Century* (Basel: Birkhäuser, 1998), 102; Paul Groenendijk and Piet Vollaard, *Gids voor moderne architectuur in Nederland; Guide to modern architecture in the Netherlands* (Rotterdam: Uitgeverij 010, 1998), 196–97; *Living in the Lowlands: The Dutch Domestic Scene, 1850–2004* (Rotterdam: NAi Publishers, 2004), 50–58; Harm Jan Korthals Altes, *Tuinsteden: tussen utopie en realitet* (Bussum: Thoth, 2004), 127–30; Marieke Kuipers, "A Concrete Test Plot," in *Living in the Lowlands: The Dutch Domestic Scene, 1850–2004* (Rotterdam: NAi Publishers, 2004), 59–61.

291 Searing, "Betondorp: Amsterdam's Concrete Garden Suburb": 118.

292 Kuipers, "A Concrete Test Plot": 59.

293 Pennink, "Concrete-suburb": 12.

294 Mattie, *Functionalism in the Netherlands*, 20.

295 Searing, "Betondorp: Amsterdam's Concrete Garden Suburb": 133.

296 Searing, "Betondorp: Amsterdam's Concrete Garden Suburb": 136.

297 Pennink, "Concrete Suburb": 22.

298 Searing, "Betondorp: Amsterdam's Concrete Garden Suburb": 109.

299 *Nieuw-Nederlandsche bouwkunst; architecture moderne en Hollande* (Amsterdam: Uitgevers-Maatschij "Kosmos", 1929), plate 25; S. J. Fockema Andreae, "The Garden City Idea in the Netherlands Before 1930," *Stedebouw en Volkshuisvesting* 44 (1963): 95–107; Donald I. Grinberg, *Housing in the Netherlands, 1900–1940* (Delft: Delft University Press, 1977), 85, 86; Jouke van der Werf, "The History of a Densely Populated City," in Guus Kemme, ed., *Amsterdam Architecture: A Guide* (Amsterdam: Uitgeverij Thoth, 1987), 20; Rudy Schreijnders, *De Droom van Howard : verleden en toekomst van de tuindorpen* (Rijswijk: Elmar, 1991), 152–57, 193–94; Maristella Casciato, *The Amsterdam School* (Rotterdam: 010 Publishers, 1996), 190; Paul Groenendijk and Piet Vollaard, *Gids voor moderne architectuur in Amsterdam; Guide to modern architecture in Amsterdam* (Rotterdam: Uitgeverij 010, 1996), 35; Paul Groenendijk and Piet Vollaard, *Gids voor moderne architectuur in Nederland; Guide to modern architecture in the Netherlands* (Rotterdam: Uitgeverij 010, 1998), 165; Hans Ibelings, *20th Century Urban Design in the Netherlands* (Rotterdam: NAi Publishers, 1999), 29.

300 Ir. L. H. J. Angenot and Drs. W. J. Bruyn, "The Garden City Idea in the Netherlands since 1930," *Stedebouw en Volkshuisvesting* 44 (1963): 108–15; Rudy Schreijnders, *De Droom van Howard : verleden en toekomst van de tuindorpen* (Rijswijk: Elmar, 1991), 168–71; Nancy Stieber, *Housing Design and Society in Amsterdam: Reconfiguring Urban Order and Identity, 1900–1920* (Chicago and London: University of Chicago Press, 1998), 234–35, 274–75, 304 (n.48), 337 (n.88).

301 A. T. Pike, "Housing and Town Planning Tour No. 19 to Holland, I.—Amsterdam," *Town and Country Planning* 3 (December 1934): 9; Maristella Casciato, *The Amsterdam School* (Rotterdam: 010 Publishers, 1996), 190–95; Hans Ibelings, *20th Century Urban Design in the Netherlands* (Rotterdam: NAi Publishers, 1999), 40.

302 J. van de Beek and G. Smienk, "ir j.b. van loghem b.i. architect," *Plan* 2 no. 12 (1971): 27–29; Donald I. Grinberg, *Housing in the Netherlands, 1900–1940* (Delft: Delft University Press, 1977), 71–74, 86; Bernard Colenbrander, "J. B. van Loghem: a Combative Architect," in *Het Nieuwe Bouwen: Voorgeschiedenis/Previous History* (Delft: Delft University Press; Nederlands Dokumentatiecentrum voor de Bouwkunst, 1982), 122, 132; Dennis J. De Witt and Elizabeth R. De Witt, *Modern Architecture in Europe: A Guide to Buildings Since the Industrial Revolution* (New York: E. P. Dutton, 1987), 259; Jeroen Schilt, "Documentatiecentrum ABC ontfermt zich over 'alles wat met het bouwen in Haarlem samenhangt,'" *Archis* (May 1989): 7; Rudy Schreijnders, *De Droom van Howard : verleden en toekomst van de tuindorpen* (Rijswijk: Elmar, 1991), 205–10; Joseph Buch, *A Century of Architecture in the Netherlands, 1880–1990* (Rotterdam: NAi Publishers, 1993), 138–39; Olga van der Klooster, "Tuinwijk-Zuid (Van Loghem, 1919–1922)," *Journal / International Working-Party for Documentation and Conservation of Buildings, Sites and Neighbourhoods of the Modern Movement* 8 (January 1993): 43–45; Wim de Wagt, *J. B. Van Loghem: 1881–1940: Landhuizen, Stadswoonhuizen en Woningbouwprojecten* (Haarlem: Schuyt & Co., 1995), 25–29, 221–28; Herman van Bergeijk and Otakar Máčel, *Birkhäuser Architectural Guide: Belgium, The Netherlands, Luxembourg, 20th Century* (Basel: Birkhäuser, 1998), 120; Paul Groenendijk and Piet Vollaard, *Gids voor moderne architectuur in Nederland; Guide to modern architecture in the Netherlands* (Rotterdam: Uitgeverij 010, 1998), 135; Wim de Wagt, *Architectuurgids Haarlem* (Rotterdam: 010, 2005), 112–13.

303 Buch, *A Century of Architecture in the Netherlands, 1880–1990*, 139.

304 Grinberg, *Housing in the Netherlands, 1900–1940*, 71.

305 Donald I. Grinberg, *Housing in the Netherlands, 1900–1940* (Delft: Delft University Press, 1977), 71; Bernard Colenbrander, "J. B. van Loghem: a Combative Architect," in *Het Nieuwe Bouwen: Voorgeschiedenis/Previous History* (Delft: Delft University Press; Nederlands Dokumentatiecentrum voor de Bouwkunst, 1982), 122; Wim de Wagt, *J. B. Van Loghem: 1881–1940: Landhuizen, Stadswoonhuizen en Woningbouwprojecten* (Haarlem: Schuyt & Co., 1995), 247–50.

306 Groenendijk and Vollaard, *Gids voor moderne architectuur in Nederland; Guide to* modern architecture in the Netherlands, 133. Also see J. van de Beek and G. Smienk, "ir j.b. van loghem b.i. architect," Plan 2 no. 12 (1971): 25–26; Bernard Colenbrander, "J. B. van Loghem: a Combative Architect," in Het Nieuwe Bouwen: Voorgeschiedenis/Previous History (Delft: Delft University Press; Nederlands Dokumentatiecentrum voor de Bouwkunst, 1982), 122, 131; Wim de Wagt, J. B. Van Loghem: 1881–1940: Landhuizen, Stadswoonhuizen en Woningbouwprojecten (Haarlem: Schuyt & Co., 1995), 251, 252, 253, 254, 255, 256, 276, 277, 278; Wim de Wagt, Architectuurgids Haarlem (Rotterdam: 010, 2005), 114.

307 Niels Prak and Hugo Priemus, "The Netherlands," in Colin G. Pooley, ed., Housing Strategies in Europe, 1880–1930 (Leicester and New York: Leicester University Press; New York: St. Martin's Press, 1992), 179, 185.

308 Donald I. Grinberg, "Modernist Housing and Its Critics: The Dutch Contributions," Harvard Architecture Review 1 (Spring 1980): 147–60. Also see Norbert Schoenauer, 6,000 Years of Housing, revised and expanded edition (New York: W. W. Norton, 2000), 401–2.

309 Bernard Colenbrander, "Illusions of Zeitgeist and Eternity, Twentieth Century," in Bernard Colenbrander, ed., Style: Standard and Signature in Dutch Architecture of the Nineteenth and Twentieth Centuries (Rotterdam: NAi Publishers, 1993), 57–92, 252, 255. Also see Koos Bosma, "Town and Regional Planning in the Netherlands, 1920–1945," Planning Perspectives 5 (1990): 137; Coen Van der Wal, In Praise of Common Sense: Planning the ordinary. A physical planning history of the new town in the IJsselmeerpolders (Rotterdam: 010 Publishers, 1997), 71–84; Hans Ibelings, 20th Century Urban Design in the Netherlands (Rotterdam: NAi Publishers, 1999), 56–57; Gerritjan Deunk, 20th Century Garden and Landscape Architecture in the Netherlands (Rotterdam: NAi Publishers, 2002), 43–44, 53; Gerrie Andela, J. T. P. Bijhouwer: Grensverleggend Landschapsarchitect (Rotterdam: 010, 2011), 56–79, 243; Cor Wagenaar, Town Planning in the Netherlands since 1800 (Rotterdam: 010 Publishers, 2011), 310–16.

310 Quoted in Colenbrander, "Illusions of Zeitgeist and Eternity, Twentieth Century," in Colenbrander, ed., Style, 57.

311 Colenbrander, "Illusions of Zeitgeist and Eternity, Twentieth Century," in Colenbrander, ed., Style, 62.

312 Colenbrander, "Illusions of Zeitgeist and Eternity, Twentieth Century," in Colenbrander, ed., Style, 62–63.

313 Gustav Linden, "Town Planning in Sweden after 1850," Town Planning Review 10 (February 1924): 273.

314 Eva Eriksson, "International Impulses and National Tradition," in Claes Caldenby, Jöran Lindvall, and Wilfried Wang, eds., 20th Century Architecture: Sweden (Munich: Prestel, 1998), 32.

315 Olof Hultin et al., The Complete Guide to Architecture in Stockholm, 3rd ed. rev. ed. (Stockholm: Arkitektur Förlag, 2009), 88.

316 Henrik O. Andersson and Fredric Bedoire, Stockholm Architecture and Townscape (Stockholm: Bokförlaget Prisma, 1988), 16; Hultin et al., The Complete Guide to Architecture in Stockholm, 88.

317 Henrik O. Andersson and Fredric Bedoire, Stockholm Architecture and Townscape (Stockholm: Bokförlaget Prisma, 1988), 16; Hultin et al., The Complete Guide to Architecture in Stockholm, 179.

318 The Garden Suburbs of the City of Stockholm. Retrospective Survey and Prospects of the Future (Stockholm: O. Eklunds Boktryckeri, 1937), 3.

319 "Bebauungsplan für einen Teil von Enskede bei Stockholm (Sweden)," Der Städtebau 5 (1908): 109–10, plate 64; Garden Suburbs of the City of Stockholm; Some Official Data (Stockholm, 1934); The Garden Suburbs of the City of Stockholm. Retrospective Survey and Prospects of the Future (Stockholm: O. Eklunds Boktryckeri, 1937), 3–4; Henrik O. Andersson and Fredric Bedoire, Stockholm Architecture and Townscape (Stockholm: Bokförlaget Prisma, 1988), 275; Thomas Hall, "Urban Planning in Sweden," in Thomas Hall, ed., Planning and Urban Growth in the Nordic Countries (London: E & FN Spon, 1991), 191–92, 211, 212; Walter Creese, The Search for Environment (1966; Baltimore and London: Johns Hopkins University Press, 1992), 300; Heleni Porfyriou, "Artistic Urban Design and Cultural Myths: the Garden City Idea in Nordic Countries, 1900–1925," Planning Perspectives 7 (1992): 270, 271–72; Johan Rådberg, Den Svenska Trädgårdsstaden (Stockholm: Byggforskningsrådet, 1994), 26–27, 74, 75–96; Eva Eriksson, "International Impulses and National Tradition," in Claes Caldenby, Jöran Lindvall, and Wilfried Wang, eds., 20th Century Architecture: Sweden (Munich: Prestel, 1998), 43; Barbara Miller Lane, National Romanticism and Modern Architecture in Germany and the Scandinavian Countries (Cambridge: Cambridge University Press, 2000), 121, 123, 156, 222, 258, 370 (n.19); Rasmus Waern et al., A Guide to Swedish Architecture (Stockholm: The Swedish Institute, 2001), 177; Stephen V. Ward, "The Howard Legacy," in Kermit C. Parsons and David Schuyler, eds., From Garden City to Green City: The Legacy of Ebenezer Howard (Baltimore and London: Johns Hopkins University Press, 2002), 237–38; Olof Hultin et al., The Complete Guide to Architecture in Stockholm, 3rd ed. rev. ed. (Stockholm: Arkitektur Förlag, 2009), 180.

320 Porfyriou, "Artistic Urban Design and Cultural Myths: the Garden City Idea in Nordic Countries, 1900–1925": 272.

321 Quoted in Porfyriou, "Artistic Urban Design and Cultural Myths: the Garden City Idea in Nordic Countries, 1900–1925": 272.

322 The Housing Question in Sweden (London: Swedish Delegation at the Interallied Housing and Town Planning Congress, 1920), figs. 1, 25; International Cities and Town Planning Exhibition. English Catalogue. Jubilee Exhibition, Gothenburg, Sweden, 1923 (Göteborg, Wezäta, W. Zachrissons boktyrckeri a.-b., 1923), 290; Stockholm: med omgivningar, with surroundings (Stockholm: Svenska Turistföreningens Förlag, 1928), 6; The Garden Suburbs of the City of Stockholm. Retrospective Survey and Prospects of the Future (Stockholm: O. Eklunds Boktryckeri, 1937), 4; Henrik O. Andersson and Fredric Bedoire, Stockholm Architecture and Townscape (Stockholm: Bokförlaget Prisma, 1988), 276–77; Johan Rådberg, Den Svenska Trädgårdsstaden (Stockholm: Byggforskningsrådet, 1994), 31; Björn Linn, "The Architect in Focus During the First Half of the Twentieth Century," in Cecilia Widenheim, ed., Utopia & Reality: Modernity in Sweden, 1900–1960 (New Haven and London: Yale University Press in association with the Bard Graduate Center for Studies in the Decorative Arts, Design, and Culture, New York, 2002), 177; Olof Hultin et al., The Complete Guide to Architecture in Stockholm, 3rd ed. rev. ed. (Stockholm: Arkitektur Förlag, 2009), 191.

323 The Housing Question in Sweden (London: Swedish Delegation at the Interallied Housing and Town Planning Congress, 1920), 25; International Cities and Town Planning Exhibition. English Catalogue. Jubilee Exhibition, Gothenburg, Sweden, 1923 (Göteborg, Wezäta, W. Zachrissons boktyrckeri a.-b., 1923), 290; Johan Rådberg, Den Svenska Trädgårdsstaden (Stockholm: Byggforskningsrådet, 1994), 30, 31; Hultin et al., The Complete Guide to Architecture in Stockholm, 191.

324 Kell Åström, City Planning in Sweden (Stockholm: Swedish Institute for Cultural Relations with Foreign Countries, 1967), 30, 31; Thomas Hall, "Urban Planning in Sweden," in Thomas Hall, ed., Planning and Urban Growth in the Nordic Countries (London: E & FN Spon, 1991), 192; Torsten Westman, "Town-Planning in the 20th Century," in Jöran Lindvall, ed., The Swedish Art of Building (Stockholm: The Swedish Institute and the Swedish Museum of Architecture, 1992), 52–53, 227; Heleni Porfyriou, "Artistic Urban Design and Cultural Myths: the Garden City Idea in Nordic Countries, 1900–1925," Planning Perspectives 7 (1992): 272; Johan Rådberg, Den Svenska Trädgårdsstaden (Stockholm: Byggforskningsrådet, 1994), 24–25; Eva Eriksson, "Rationalism and Classicism 1915–30," in Claes Caldenby, Jöran Lindvall, and Wilfried Wang, eds., 20th Century Architecture: Sweden (Munich: Prestel, 1998), 49; Caldenby, Lindvall, Wang, eds., 20th Century Architecture: Sweden, 254, 384, 392; Rasmus Waern et al., A Guide to Swedish Architecture (Stockholm: The Swedish Institute, 2001), 105.

325 "Entwurf zum Bebauungslplan eines Teiles on Gothenburg in Schweden," Der Städtebau 7 (1910): plate 531; The Housing Question in Sweden (London: Swedish Delegation at the Interallied Housing and Town Planning Congress, 1920), figs. 11, 16, 18; International Cities and Town Planning Exhibition. English Catalogue. Jubilee Exhibition, Gothenburg, Sweden, 1923 (Göteborg, Wezäta, W. Zachrissons boktyrckeri a.-b., 1923), 262; Eriksson, "International Impulses and National Tradition, 1900–1915," in Caldenby, Lindvall, and Wang, eds., 20th-Century Architecture: Sweden, 33–34.

326 Eva Eriksson, "Rationalism and Classicism, 1915–30," in Caldenby, Lindvall, and Wang, eds., 20th-Century Architecture: Sweden, 63. Also see The Housing Question in Sweden (London: Swedish Delegation at the Interallied Housing and Town Planning Congress, 1920), fig. 3.

327 International Cities and Town Planning Exhibition. English Catalogue. Jubilee Exhibition, Gothenburg, Sweden, 1923 (Göteborg, Wezäta, W. Zachrissons boktyrckeri a.-b., 1923), 272, 273; Johan Rådberg, "Trädgårdsstadens Mönster," Arkitektur: the Swedish Review of Architecture 93 (October 1993): 4–15; Johan Rådberg, Den Svenska Trädgårdsstaden (Stockholm: Byggforskningsrådet, 1994), 20–23.

328 Heleni Porfyriou, "Artistic Urban Design and Cultural Myths: the Garden City Idea in Nordic Countries, 1900–1925," Planning Perspectives 7 (1992): 273. Also see The Housing Question in Sweden (London: Swedish Delegation at the Interallied Housing and Town Planning Congress, 1920), figs. 2, 28, 38; Henrik O. Andersson and Fredric Bedoire, Stockholm Architecture and Townscape (Stockholm: Bokförlaget Prisma, 1988), 560; Johan Rådberg, Den Svenska Trädgårdsstaden (Stockholm: Byggforskningsrådet, 1994), 28–29.

329 Johan Rådberg, Den Svenska Trädgårdsstaden (Stockholm: Byggforskningsrådet, 1994), 18.

330 The Housing Question in Sweden (London: Swedish Delegation at the Interallied Housing and Town Planning Congress, 1920), 12, 18, fig. 6; International Cities and Town Planning Exhibition. English Catalogue. Jubilee Exhibition, Gothenburg, Sweden, 1923 (Göteborg, Wezäta, W. Zachrissons boktyrckeri a.-b., 1923), 312; Heleni Porfyriou, "Artistic Urban Design and Cultural Myths: the Garden City Idea in Nordic Countries, 1900–1925," Planning Perspectives 7 (1992): 276.

331 International Cities and Town Planning Exhibition. English Catalogue. Jubilee Exhibition, Gothenburg, Sweden, 1923 (Göteborg, Wezäta, W. Zachrissons boktyrckeri a.-b., 1923), 313; Heleni Porfyriou, "Artistic Urban Design and Cultural Myths: the Garden City Idea in Nordic Countries, 1900–1925," Planning Perspectives 7 (1992): 276.

332 Stockholms Stads Småstugebygge 1935 (Stockholm, 1935); The Garden Suburbs of the City of Stockholm. Retrospective Survey and Prospects of the Future (Stockholm: O. Eklunds Boktryckeri, 1937); Werner Hegemann, City Planning: Housing, Volume III (New York: Architectural Book Publishing Co., 1938), 135; Elizabeth Sloan Chesser, "Garden Homes in Scandinavia," Town and Country Planning 6 (January 1938): 32–33; Heleni Porfyriou, "Artistic Urban Design and Cultural Myths: the Garden City Idea in Nordic Countries, 1900–1925," Planning Perspectives 7 (1992): 270; Eva Eriksson, "Rationalism and Classicism 1915–30," in Claes Caldenby, Jöran Lindvall, and Wilfried Wang, eds., 20th Century Architecture: Sweden (Munich: Prestel, 1998), 62.

333 Stockholm: med omgivningar, with surroundings (Stockholm: Svenska Turistföreningens Förlag, 1928), n.p.; The Garden Suburbs of the City of Stockholm. Retrospective Survey and Prospects of the Future (Stockholm: O. Eklunds Boktryckeri, 1937), 9, 11; Henrik O. Andersson and Fredric Bedoire, Stockholm Architecture and Townscape (Stockholm: Bokförlaget Prisma, 1988), 276–77; Olof Hultin et al., The Complete Guide to Architecture in Stockholm, 3rd ed. rev. ed. (Stockholm: Arkitektur Förlag, 2009), 194.

334 The Garden Suburbs of the City of Stockholm. Retrospective Survey and Prospects of the Future (Stockholm: O. Eklunds Boktryckeri, 1937), 10; Werner Hegemann, City Planning: Housing, Volume III (New York: Architectural Book Publishing Co., 1938), 135; Henrik O. Andersson and Fredric Bedoire, Stockholm Architecture and Townscape (Stockholm: Bokförlaget Prisma, 1988), 278; Olof Hultin et al., The Complete Guide to Architecture in Stockholm, 3rd ed. rev. ed. (Stockholm: Arkitektur Förlag, 2009), 210.

335 Werner Hegemann, City Planning: Housing, Volume III (New York: Architectural Book Publishing Co., 1938), 135; Henrik O. Andersson and Fredric Bedoire, Stockholm Architecture and Townscape (Stockholm: Bokförlaget Prisma, 1988), 277–78; Lars Nilsson with Stuart Burch, "The Stockholm Style, 1930s–60s," in Peter Clark, ed., The European City and Green Space: London, Stockholm, Helsinki, and St. Petersburg, 1850–2000 (Aldershot, England and Burlington, Vt: Ashgate, 2006), 146–47; Olof Hultin et al., The Complete Guide to Architecture in Stockholm, 3rd ed. rev. ed. (Stockholm: Arkitektur Förlag, 2009), 207, 228.

336 Hultin et al., The Complete Guide to Architecture in Stockholm, 229. Also see Nilsson with Burch, "The Stockholm Style, 1930s–60s," in Peter Clark, ed., in The European City and Green Space, 146.

337 Lars Sonck, quoted in Kolbe, "Garden Suburb Planners, 1900–1914": 10–16. Also see Asko Salokorpi, "Lars Sonck's Town Plans," in Lars Sonck, Architect: 1870–1956 (Helsinki: Suomen Rakennustaiteen Museon, 1981), 128–29.

338 For Töölö, see Bertel Jung, "Från Stadsbyggnadskonstens Genombrottsår, Finland," *Arkitekten* (no.4, 1941): 55–59; Otto-I. Meurman, "Town Planning in Finland in the Early 20th Century," *Arkitekten* (no. 7–8, 1967): 59–63; Kirmo Mikkola, *Architecture in Finland in the 20th Century* (Helsinki: Finnish-American Cultural Institute, 1981), 18–19; Asko Salokorpi, "Lars Sonck's Town Plans," in *Lars Sonck, Architect: 1870–1956* (Helsinki: Suomen Rakennustaiteen Museon, 1981), 129, 130, 133–44; Riitta Nikula, "The Myths of Nature and City in Finnish Housing," in *Seminar on Architecture and Urban Planning in Finland, 1987; Urbanism with Identity: Towards New Integrations in Finnish Housing Architecture* (Helsinki: SAFA, 1987), 13; Arvi Ilonen, *Helsinki, Espoo, Kauniainen, Vantaa: an Architectural Guide* (Helsinki: Otava Publishing Company, 1990), 89–90; Mikael Sundman, "Urban Planning in Finland after 1850," in Thomas Hall, ed., *Planning and Urban Growth in the Nordic Countries* (London: E & FN Spon, 1991), 71–72; Riitta Nikula, *Architecture and Landscape: the Building of Finland* (Helsinki: Otava, 1993), 112; Riitta Nikula, "Bertel Jung: The Pioneer of Modern Town Planning in Helsinki," in *Icon to Cartoon: a Tribute to Sixten Ringbom* (Helsinki: Taidehistorian Seura, 1995), 193–212; Barbara Miller Lane, *National Romanticism and Modern Architecture in Germany and the Scandinavian Countries* (Cambridge: Cambridge University Press, 2000), 199–200; Marja-Riitta Norri, Elina Standertskjöld, and Wilfried Wang, eds., *20th Century Architecture: Finland* (Helsinki: Museum of Finnish Architecture, 2000), 150–51; Roger Connah, *Finland* (London: Reaktion Books, 2005), 40–41; Riitta Nikula, *Wood, Stone and Steel: Contours of Finnish Architecture* (Helsinki: Otava Publishing Company, 2005), 114.

339 Mikael Sundman, "Urban Planning in Finland after 1850," in Thomas Hall, ed., *Planning and Urban Growth in the Nordic Countries* (London: E & FN Spon, 1991), 72.

340 Nikula, *Wood, Stone and Steel: Contours of Finnish Architecture*, 114.

341 Ilonen, *Helsinki, Espoo, Kauniainen, Vantaa: an Architectural Guide*, 89.

342 Otto-I. Meurman, "Town Planning in Finland in the Early 20th Century," *Arkitekten* (no. 7–8, 1967): 59–63; J. M. Richards, *800 Years of Finnish Architecture* (Newton Abbot and London: David & Charles, 1978), 122, 123; Asko Salokorpi, "Lars Sonck's Town Plans," in *Lars Sonck, Architect: 1870–1956* (Helsinki: Suomen Rakennustaiteen Museon, 1981), 129, 131, 137; Marc Treib, "Urban Fabric by the Bold: Eliel Saarinen at Munkkiniemi-Haaga," *AAQ: Architectural Association Quarterly* 13 (January–June 1982): 45, 58 (n.24); *Lars Sonck, 1870–1956, Tradizione e Modernità* (Milan: Electa, 1990), 93, 94; Arvi Ilonen, *Helsinki, Espoo, Kauniainen, Vantaa: an Architectural Guide* (Helsinki: Otava Publishing Company, 1990), 73–74; Mikael Sundman, "Urban Planning in Finland after 1850," in Thomas Hall, ed., *Planning and Urban Growth in the Nordic Countries* (London: E & FN Spon, 1991), 71, 73–74; Riitta Nikula, *Architecture and Landscape: the Building of Finland* (Helsinki: Otava, 1993), 113–14; Riitta Nikula, *Wood, Stone and Steel: Contours of Finnish Architecture* (Helsinki: Otava Publishing Company, 2005), 113, 116–17.

343 Riitta Nikula, quoted in Sundman, "Urban Planning in Finland after 1850," in Hall, ed., *Planning and Urban Growth in the Nordic Countries*, 74.

344 Sundman, "Urban Planning in Finland after 1850," in Hall, ed., *Planning and Urban Growth in the Nordic Countries*, 74.

345 Gustaf Strengell, quoted in Nikula, *Wood, Stone and Steel*, 117.

346 Nikula, *Architecture and Landscape*, 114.

347 Asko Salokorpi, "Lars Sonck's Town Plans," in *Lars Sonck, Architect: 1870–1956* (Helsinki: Suomen Rakennustaiteen Museon, 1981), 137.

348 Asko Salokorpi, "Lars Sonck's Town Plans," in *Lars Sonck, Architect: 1870–1956* (Helsinki: Suomen Rakennustaiteen Museon, 1981), 137; Mikael Sundman, "Urban Planning in Finland after 1850," in Thomas Hall, ed., *Planning and Urban Growth in the Nordic Countries*, 73, 74.

349 For Talsola Manor, see Salokorpi, "Lars Sonck's Town Plans," in *Lars Sonck, Architect: 1870–1956*, 137. For Alberga mansion, see Kirmo Mikkola, "Eliel Saarinen and Town Planning," in Marika Hausen et al., *Eliel Saarinen: Projects, 1896–1923* (Cambridge, Mass.: MIT Press, 1990), 192.

350 Otto-I. Meurman, "Town Planning in Finland in the Early 20th Century," *Arkitekten* (no. 7–8, 1967): 59–63; Asko Salokorpi, "Lars Sonck's Town Plans," in *Lars Sonck, Architect: 1870–1956* (Helsinki: Suomen Rakennustaiteen Museon, 1981), 130, 137–38; Marc Treib, "Urban Fabric by the Bold: Eliel Saarinen at Munkkiniemi-Haaga," *AAQ: Architectural Association Quarterly* 13 (January–June 1982): 48, 58 (n.33); Riitta Nikula, "The Myths of Nature and City in Finnish Housing," in *Seminar on Architecture and Urban Planning in Finland, 1987; Urbanism with Identity: Towards New Integrations in Finnish Housing Architecture* (Helsinki: SAFA, 1987), 11–12; Riitta Nikula, *Armas Lindgren, 1874–1929: arkkitehti/architect* (Helsinki: Museum of Finnish Architecture, 1988), 47–56, 158–60; Arvi Ilonen, *Helsinki, Espoo, Kauniainen, Vantaa: an Architectural Guide* (Helsinki: Otava Publishing Company, 1990), 135–36; *Lars Sonck, 1870–1956, Tradizione e Modernità* (Milan: Electa, 1990), 93; Mikael Sundman, "Urban Planning in Finland after 1850," in Thomas Hall, ed., *Planning and Urban Growth in the Nordic Countries* (London: E & FN Spon, 1991), 74–76; Heleni Porfyriou, "Artistic Urban Design and Cultural Myths: the Garden City Idea in Nordic Countries, 1900–1925," *Planning Perspectives* 7 (1992): 276–77; Riitta Nikula, *Architecture and Landscape: the Building of Finland* (Helsinki: Otava, 1993), 114–15; Roger Connah, *Finland* (London: Reaktion Books, 2005), 41; Riitta Nikula, *Wood, Stone and Steel: Contours of Finnish Architecture* (Helsinki: Otava Publishing Company, 2005), 118–19.

351 Sundman, "Urban Planning in Finland after 1850," in Hall, ed., *Planning and Urban Growth in the Nordic Countries*, 76.

352 Sundman, "Urban Planning in Finland after 1850," in Hall, ed., *Planning and Urban Growth in the Nordic Countries*, 76.

353 Eliel Saarinen, *Munkkiniemi-Haaga ja Suur-Helsinki* (Helsinki: Lilius & Hertzberg, 1915); "Views of Model for Development of Munknas-Haga, a Suburb of Helsingfors, Finland," *Western Architect* 32 (July 1923): plate 16; Kenneth Reid, "Eliel Saarinen—Master of Design," *Pencil Points* XXII (September 1936): 468–69; Albert Christ-Janer, *Eliel Saarinen* (Chicago: University of Chicago Press, 1948), 38–39, 128, 134; Otto-I. Meurman, "Town Planning in Finland in the Early 20th Century," *Arkitekten* (no. 7–8, 1967): 59–63; Kirmo Mikkola, *Architecture in Finland in the 20th Century* (Helsinki: Finnish-American Cultural Institute, 1981), 19–20; Marc Treib, "Urban Fabric by the Bold: Eliel Saarinen at Munkkiniemi-Haaga," *AAQ: Architectural Association Quarterly* 13 (January–June 1982): 43–59; *Saarinen in Finland, Gesellius, Lindgren, Saarinen, 1896–1907, Saarinen 1907–1923*, exhibition catalogue (Helsinki: Museum of Finnish Architecture, 1984), 102–7; Kirmo Mikkola, "The Roots of Eliel Saarinen's Town Plans," in *Saarinen in Finland, Gesellius, Lindgren, Saarinen, 1896–1907, Saarinen 1907–1923*, exhibition catalogue (Helsinki: Museum of Finnish Architecture, 1984), 88–91; Leo Aario, "The Original Garden Cities in Britain and the Garden City Ideal in Finland," *Fennia* 164 (no. 2, 1986): 186–91; Riitta Nikula, "The Myths of Nature and City in Finnish Housing," in *Seminar on Architecture and Urban Planning in Finland, 1987; Urbanism with Identity: Towards New Integrations in Finnish Housing Architecture* (Helsinki: SAFA, 1987), 11; Kirmo Mikkola, "Eliel Saarinen and Town Planning," in Marika Hausen et al., *Eliel Saarinen: Projects, 1896–1923* (Cambridge, Mass.: MIT Press, 1990), 187–95, 203–11; Tytti Valto, "Catalogue of Works—Architecture and Urban Planning," Marika Hausen et al., *Eliel Saarinen: Projects, 1896–1923* (Cambridge, Mass.: MIT Press, 1990), 316, 318–20, 325, 329–30; Mikael Sundman, "Urban Planning in Finland after 1850," in Thomas Hall, ed., *Planning and Urban Growth in the Nordic Countries* (London: E & FN Spon, 1991), 76–79; Heleni Porfyriou, "Artistic Urban Design and Cultural Myths: the Garden City Idea in Nordic Countries, 1900–1925," *Planning Perspectives* 7 (1992): 280–83; Riitta Nikula, *Architecture and Landscape: the Building of Finland* (Helsinki: Otava, 1993), 112, 113; Gabriele Tagliaventi, "The Romantic Tradition in 20th Century Town Planning," in Gabriele Tagliaventi, ed., *Garden City* (Rome: Gangemi Editore, 1994), 34, 56–58; Riitta Nikula, "Bertel Jung: The Pioneer of Modern Town Planning in Helsinki," in *Icon to Cartoon: a Tribute to Sixten Ringbom* (Helsinki: Taidehistorian Seura, 1995), 193–212; Marja-Riitta Norri, Elina Standertskjöld, and Wilfried Wang, eds., *20th Century Architecture: Finland* (Helsinki: Museum of Finnish Architecture, 2000), 170–71; Riitta Nikula, "The Inter-War Period: the Architecture of the Young Republic," in Marja-Riitta Norri, Elina Standertskjöld, and Wilfried Wang, eds., *20th Century Architecture: Finland* (Helsinki: Museum of Finnish Architecture, 2000), 45–48; Andrés Duany, Elizabeth Plater-Zyberk, and Robert Alminana, *The New Civic Art: Elements of Town Planning* (New York: Rizzoli International Publications, 2003), 269; Roger Connah, *Finland* (London: Reaktion Books, 2005), 44; Riitta Nikula, *Wood, Stone and Steel: Contours of Finnish Architecture* (Helsinki: Otava Publishing Company, 2005), 115, 116.

354 Nikula, *Architecture and Landscape*, 113.

355 Eliel Saarinen quoted in Mikkola, "The Roots of Eliel Saarinen's Town Plans," in *Saarinen in Finland, Gesellius, Lindgren, Saarinen, 1896–1907, Saarinen 1907–1923*, 98.

356 Sundman, "Urban Planning in Finland after 1850," in Hall, ed., *Planning and Urban Growth in the Nordic Countries*, 77.

357 Bertel Jung, *"Suur-Helsingin" Asemakaavan Ehdotus, Laatineet Eliel Saarinen* (Helsinki: Osakeyhtiö Lilius & Hertzberg, 1918); Albert Christ-Janer, *Eliel Saarinen* (Chicago: University of Chicago Press, 1948), 39, 40, 41, 43; Kirmo Mikkola, *Architecture in Finland in the 20th Century* (Helsinki: Finnish-American Cultural Institute, 1981), 20; *Saarinen in Finland, Gesellius, Lindgren, Saarinen, 1896–1907, Saarinen 1907–1923*, exhibition catalogue (Helsinki: Museum of Finnish Architecture, 1984), 108–11; Kirmo Mikkola, "The Roots of Eliel Saarinen's Town Plans," in *Saarinen in Finland, Gesellius, Lindgren, Saarinen, 1896–1907, Saarinen 1907–1923* (Helsinki: Museum of Finnish Architecture, 1984), 88–91; Kirmo Mikkola, "Eliel Saarinen and Town Planning," in Marika Hausen et al., *Eliel Saarinen: Projects, 1896–1923* (Cambridge, Mass.: MIT Press, 1990), 187–95, 214–17; Tytti Valto, "Catalogue of Works—Architecture and Urban Planning," in Marika Hausen et al., *Eliel Saarinen: Projects, 1896–1923* (Cambridge, Mass.: MIT Press, 1990), 327–28; Mikael Sundman, "Urban Planning in Finland after 1850," in Thomas Hall, ed., *Planning and Urban Growth in the Nordic Countries* (London: E & FN Spon, 1991), 78–79; Heleni Porfyriou, "Artistic Urban Design and Cultural Myths: the Garden City Idea in Nordic Countries, 1900–1925," *Planning Perspectives* 7 (1992): 278–80; Riitta Nikula, *Architecture and Landscape: the Building of Finland* (Helsinki: Otava, 1993), 113; Gabriele Tagliaventi, "The Romantic Tradition in 20th Century Town Planning," in Gabriele Tagliaventi, ed., *Garden City* (Rome: Gangemi Editore, 1994), 58–60; Riitta Nikula, "Bertel Jung: The Pioneer of Modern Town Planning in Helsinki," in *Icon to Cartoon: a Tribute to Sixten Ringbom* (Helsinki: Taidehistorian Seura, 1995), 193–212; Marja-Riitta Norri, Elina Standertskjöld, and Wilfried Wang, eds., *20th Century Architecture: Finland* (Helsinki: Museum of Finnish Architecture, 2000), 172; Riitta Nikula, "The Inter-War Period: the Architecture of the Young Republic," in Marja-Riitta Norri, Elina Standertskjöld, and Wilfried Wang, eds., *20th Century Architecture: Finland* (Helsinki: Museum of Finnish Architecture, 2000), 45–48; Andrés Duany, Elizabeth Plater-Zyberk, and Robert Alminana, *The New Civic Art: Elements of Town Planning* (New York: Rizzoli International Publications, 2003), 87, 134; Roger Connah, *Finland* (London: Reaktion Books, 2005), 44, 50–51; Riitta Nikula, *Wood, Stone and Steel: Contours of Finnish Architecture* (Helsinki: Otava Publishing Company, 2005), 115–16.

358 Nikula, *Architecture and Landscape*, 113.

359 Eliel Saarinen, quoted in Mikkola, "Eliel Saarinen and Town Planning," in Hausen et al., *Eliel Saarinen: Projects, 1896–1923*, 195.

360 Eliel Saarinen, "Lausunto eräistä Helsingin kaupungin asemakaavakysymyksistä," *Helsingin kaupungin keskiosien yleisasemakaavaehdotus* (Helsinki, 1932), quoted in Mikkola, "Eliel Saarinen and Town Planning," in Hausen et al., *Eliel Saarinen: Projects, 1896–1923*, 214.

361 Eliel Saarinen, *The City: It's Growth, It's Decay, It's Future* (New York: Reinhold Publishing, 1943), esp. ch. 6.

362 Porfyriou, "Artistic Urban Design and Cultural Myths: the Garden City Idea in Nordic Countries, 1900–1925": 280.

363 Kenneth Reid, "Eliel Saarinen—Master of Design," *Pencil Points* XXII (September 1936): 470–71; J. M. Richards, *800 Years of Finnish Architecture* (Newton Abbot and London: David & Charles, 1978), 138, 141; Kirmo Mikkola, *Architecture in Finland in the 20th Century* (Helsinki: Finnish-American Cultural Institute, 1981), 22–23; *Nordic Classicism, 1910–1930* (Helsinki: Museum of Finnish Architecture, 1982), 103–4; Leo Aario,

"The Original Garden Cities in Britain and the Garden City Ideal in Finland," *Fennia* 164 (no. 2, 1986): 190–91; Riitta Nikula, "The Myths of Nature and City in Finnish Housing," in *Seminar on Architecture and Urban Planning in Finland, 1987; Urbanism with Identity: Towards New Integrations in Finnish Housing Architecture* (Helsinki: SAFA, 1987), 15–17; Arvi Ilonen, *Helsinki, Espoo, Kauniainen, Vantaa: an Architectural Guide* (Helsinki: Otava Publishing Company, 1990), 113; Kirmo Mikkola, "Eliel Saarinen and Town Planning," in Marika Hausen et al., *Eliel Saarinen: Projects, 1896–1923* (Cambridge, Mass.: MIT Press, 1990), 190, 192; Mikael Sundman, "Urban Planning in Finland after 1850," in Thomas Hall, ed., *Planning and Urban Growth in the Nordic Countries* (London: E & FN Spon, 1991), 83–84; Karl-Erik Michelsen, "On the Borderline of the Modern Architects vs. Master-Buiders," in Pekka Korvenmaa, ed., *The Work of Architects: The Finnish Association of Architects, 1892–1992* (Helsinki: Finnish Association of Architects; The Finnish Building Centre, 1992), 98; Heleni Porfyriou, "Artistic Urban Design and Cultural Myths: the Garden City Idea in Nordic Countries, 1900–1925," *Planning Perspectives* 7 (1992): 277–78; *Martti Välikangas, 1893–1973, arkkitehti* (Helsinki: Suomen Rakennustaiteen Museo, 1993), 7–23; Riitta Nikula, *Architecture and Landscape: the Building of Finland* (Helsinki: Otava, 1993), 125; Johan Rådberg, *Den Svenska Trädgårdsstaden* (Stockholm: Byggforskningsrådet, 1994), 46–49; Pertti Solla, "Lachende Streichholschachteln: die Holzbausiedlung Käpylä," *Deutsche Bauzeitung* 128 (February 1994): 112–15; Pertti Solla and Pentti Peurasuo, "Käpylä 1923—Dessau 1993: The New Idea of Building," *Topos: European Landscape Magazine* 7 (June 1994): 91–97; Malcolm Quantrill, *Finnish Architecture and the Modernist Tradition* (London: E & FN Spon, 1995), 29–32; Barbara Miller Lane, *National Romanticism and Modern Architecture in Germany and the Scandinavian Countries* (Cambridge: Cambridge University Press, 2000), 258; Marja-Riitta Norri, Elina Standertskjöld, and Wilfried Wang, *20th Century Architecture: Finland* (Helsinki: Museum of Finnish Architecture, 2000), 176–77; Roger Connah, *Finland* (London: Reaktion Books, 2005), 58–60; Riitta Nikula, *Wood, Stone and Steel: Contours of Finnish Architecture* (Helsinki: Otava Publishing Company, 2005), 132; Katri Lento, "The Role of Nature in the City: Green Space in Helsinki, 1917–1960," in Peter Clark, ed., *The European City and Green Space: London, Stockholm, Helsinki, and St. Petersburg, 1850–2000* (Aldershot, England and Burlington, VT: Ashgate, 2006), 190–92.

364 Connah, *Finland*, 59, 60.

365 Ulla Salmela, "Happy Homes and Stable Society. Otto-Iivari Meurman and *Omakoti* in Interwar Finland," *Planning Perspectives* 22 (October 2007): 451–52.

366 Heleni Porfyriou, "Artistic Urban Design and Cultural Myths: the Garden City Idea in Nordic Countries, 1900–1925," *Planning Perspectives* 7 (1992): 289.

367 "Magnus Poulsson, Architekt, Siedlung Lille Töien bei Kristiania," *Wasmuths Monatshefte für Baukunst* 7 (1922/23): 107–8; Sverre Pedersen, "Norway," in *International Cities and Town Planning Exhibition. English Catalogue. Jubilee Exhibition, Gothenburg, Sweden, 1923* (Göteborg, Wezäta, W. Zachrissons boktyrckeri a.-b., 1923), 206, 228; Heleni Porfyriou, "Artistic Urban Design and Cultural Myths: the Garden City Idea in Nordic Countries, 1900–1925," *Planning Perspectives* 7 (1992): 290–91.

368 Christian Gierlöff, "Housing in Norway," *Garden Cities and Town Planning* 10 (March 1920): 55–60; "Harald Hals and Ad. Jensen, Architekten, Kristiania, Gartenstadt Ullevaal bei Kristiania," *Wasmuths Monatshefte für Baukunst* 7 (1922/23): 98–105; Harald Aars, "Welcome to Oslo," *Garden Cities and Town Planning* XX (September–October 1930): 232; Elizabeth Sloan Chesser, "Garden Homes in Scandinavia," *Town and Country Planning* 6 (January 1938): 32–33; Pål Henry Engh and Arne Gunnarsjaa, *Oslo en Arkitekturguide* (Oslo: Universitetsforlaget, 1984), 155–56; Erik Lorange and Jan Eivind Myhre, "Urban Planning in Norway," in Thomas Hall, ed., in *Planning and Urban Growth in the Nordic Countries* (London: E & FN Spon, 1991), 138; Heleni Porfyriou, "Artistic Urban Design and Cultural Myths: the Garden City Idea in Nordic Countries, 1900–1925," *Planning Perspectives* 7 (1992): 290, 291; Christian Norberg-Schulz, *Nightlands: Nordic Building* (Cambridge, Mass.: MIT Press, 1996), 144, 145; Gabrielle Tagliaventi, ed., *A Vision of Europe: L'Altra Modernità, 1900–2000* (Savona, Italia: Dogma, 2000), 374–75; Helen Meller, *European Cities, 1890–1930s* (New York: John Wiley & Sons, 2001), 127.

369 Norberg-Schulz, *Nightlands*, 144.

370 "Harald Hals and Ad. Jensen, Architeten, Kristiania, Linderen bei Kristiania, Teilansicht des Abschnitts I und Lageplan," *Wasmuths Monatshefte für Baukunst* 7 (1922–23): 106; Sverre Pedersen, "Norway," in *International Cities and Town Planning Exhibition. English Catalogue. Jubilee Exhibition, Gothenburg, Sweden, 1923* (Göteborg, Wezäta, W. Zachrissons boktyrckeri a.-b., 1923), 206, 229. Heleni Porfyriou, "Artistic Urban Design and Cultural Myths: the Garden City Idea in Nordic Countries, 1900–1925," *Planning Perspectives* 7 (1992): 290.

371 Christian Gierlöff, "Housing in Norway," *Garden Cities and Town Planning* 10 (March 1920): 58; Sverre Pedersen, "Norway," in *International Cities and Town Planning Exhibition. English Catalogue. Jubilee Exhibition, Gothenburg, Sweden, 1923* (Göteborg, Wezäta, W. Zachrissons boktyrckeri a.-b., 1923), 229.

372 Sverre Pedersen, "Planning Unbuilt Areas—Plotting and Planning of Building Sites," *Proceedings of the International Town Planning Conference* (New York, 1925), 343–61; Werner Hegemann, *City Planning: Housing, Volume III* (New York: Architectural Book Publishing Co., 1938), 22–23; *Nordic Classicism, 1910–1930* (Helsinki: Museum of Finnish Architecture, 1982), 110, 119; Unnleiv Bergsgard, "Sverre Pedersen (1882–1971), Un Urbaniste Norvegien Classique," *Archives d'architecture moderne* no. 29 (1985): 84–99; Heleni Porfyriou, "Artistic Urban Design and Cultural Myths: the Garden City Idea in Nordic Countries, 1900–1925," *Planning Perspectives* 7 (1992): 291–93.

373 Sverre Pedersen, "Planning Unbuilt Areas—Plotting and Planning of Building Sites," *Proceedings of the International Town Planning Conference* (New York, 1925), 350.

374 Pedersen, "Norway," in *International Cities and Town Planning Exhibition. English Catalogue. Jubilee Exhibition, Gothenburg, Sweden, 1923*, 207.

375 Sverre Pedersen, "Planning Unbuilt Areas—Plotting and Planning of Building Sites," *Proceedings of the International Town Planning Conference* (New York, 1925), 350.

376 Sverre Pedersen, "Planning Unbuilt Areas—Plotting and Planning of Building Sites," *Proceedings of the International Town Planning Conference* (New York, 1925), 357–58.

377 Hegemann, *City Planning, Housing, Volume III*, 23.

378 Sverre Pedersen, "An Example of Town Planning in Norway," *Garden Cities and Town Planning* 10 (March 1920): 47–54; Sverre Pedersen, "Norway," in *International Cities and Town Planning Exhibition. English Catalogue. Jubilee Exhibition, Gothenburg, Sweden, 1923* (Göteborg, Wezäta, W. Zachrissons boktyrckeri a.-b., 1923), 206, 208–12, 213, 215; Knut Larsen, "By-og Boligplanlegging I Norge 1900–20 Og Arkitekt Sverre Pedersen," *Byggenkunst* 53 (1972): 140–43; Unnleiv Bergsgard, "Sverre Pedersen (1882–1971), Un Urbaniste Norvegien Classique," *Archives d'architecture moderne* no. 29 (1985): 84–99.

379 Sverre Pedersen, "Planning Unbuilt Areas—Plotting and Planning of Building Sites," *Proceedings of the International Town Planning Conference* (New York, 1925), 355.

380 Sverre Pedersen, "Norway," in *International Cities and Town Planning Exhibition. English Catalogue. Jubilee Exhibition, Gothenburg, Sweden, 1923* (Göteborg, Wezäta, W. Zachrissons boktyrckeri a.-b., 1923), 213, 216, 222; Sverre Pedersen, "Planning Unbuilt Areas—Plotting and Planning of Building Sites," *Proceedings of the International Town Planning Conference* (New York, 1925), plates following page 350; Werner Hegemann, *City Planning: Housing, Volume III* (New York: Architectural Book Publishing Co., 1938), 22–23.

381 Sverre Pedersen, "Norway," in *International Cities and Town Planning Exhibition. English Catalogue. Jubilee Exhibition, Gothenburg, Sweden, 1923* (Göteborg, Wezäta, W. Zachrissons boktyrckeri a.-b., 1923), 215, 220; Sverre Pedersen, "Planning Unbuilt Areas—Plotting and Planning of Building Sites," *Proceedings of the International Town Planning Conference* (New York, 1925), plate before page 353; Bergsgard, "Sverre Pedersen (1882–1971), Un Urbaniste Norvegien Classique": 86; Werner Hegemann, *City Planning: Housing, Volume III* (New York: Architectural Book Publishing Co., 1938), 22.

382 Sverre Pedersen, "Planning Unbuilt Areas—Plotting and Planning of Building Sites," *Proceedings of the International Town Planning Conference* (New York, 1925), plate following page 352, 355.

383 Werner Hegemann, *City Planning: Housing, Volume III* (New York: Architectural Book Publishing Co., 1938), 22–23.

384 Werner Hegemann, *City Planning: Housing, Volume III* (New York: Architectural Book Publishing Co., 1938), 22.

385 Olaf Lind, *Jutland Architecture Guide* (Copenhagen: Danish Architectural Press, 2002), 94.

386 Tim Knudsen, "International Influences and Professional Rivalry in Early Danish Planning," *Planning Perspectives* 3 (1988): 302; Bo Larsson and Ole Thomassen, "Urban Planning in Denmark," in Thomas Hall, ed., in *Planning and Urban Growth in the Nordic Countries* (London: E & FN Spon, 1991), 17–18; Jørgen Sestoft and Jørgen Hegner Christiansen, *Guide to Danish Architecture 1, 1000–1960* (Copenhagen: Arkitektens Forlag, 1995), 199; Olaf Lind and Annemarie Lund, *Copenhagen Architecture Guide* (Copenhagen: Arkitektens Forlag, 2001), 23–24.

387 Bo Larsson and Ole Thomassen, "Urban Planning in Denmark," in Thomas Hall, ed., in *Planning and Urban Growth in the Nordic Countries* (London: E & FN Spon, 1991), 17.

388 Leuning Borch, *Stationsbyen: Landsudstillingen I Aarhus 1909* (Copenhagen, 1909); Fred L. Levy, "Stationsbyen I," *Architekten* 12 (October 2, 1909): 1–8; "Stationsbyen II," *Architekten* 12 (October 9, 1909): 9–13; Tim Knudsen, "International Influences and Professional Rivalry in Early Danish Planning," *Planning Perspectives* 3 (1988): 302–3; Olaf Lind, *Jutland Architecture Guide* (Copenhagen: Danish Architectural press, 2002), 94.

389 Heleni Porfyriou, "Artistic Urban Design and Cultural Myths: the Garden City Idea in Nordic Countries, 1900–1925," *Planning Perspectives* 7 (1992): 288; Jørgen Sestoft and Jørgen Hegner Christiansen, *Guide to Danish Architecture 1, 1000–1960* (Copenhagen: Arkitektens Forlag, 1995), 199; Olaf Lind and Annemarie Lund, *Copenhagen Architecture Guide* (Copenhagen: Arkitektens Forlag, 2001), 104.

390 Steen Eiler Rasmussen, "Neighbourhood Planning," *Town Planning Review* 27 (January 1957): 205, 206–7; Tobias Faber, *A History of Danish Architecture* (Denmark: De Danske Selskab in cooperation with the American-Scandinavian Foundation, 1963), 160; *Nordic Classicism, 1910–1930* (Helsinki: Museum of Finnish Architecture, 1982), 62, 63; Jørgen Sestoft and Jørgen Hegner Christiansen, *Guide to Danish Architecture 1, 1000–1960* (Copenhagen: Arkitektens Forlag, 1995), 198, 199; Christopher Woodward, *The Buildings of Europe: Copenhagen* (Manchester and New York: Manchester University Press, 1998), 69; Olaf Lind and Annemarie Lund, *Copenhagen Architecture Guide* (Copenhagen: Arkitektens Forlag, 2001), 25, 104, 105; *Dansk Arkitektur 250 År; 250 Years of Danish Architecture* (Copenhagen: Danish Architectural Press, 2004), 107–8.

391 Rasmussen, "Neighbourhood Planning": 207.

392 Woodward, *The Buildings of Europe: Copenhagen*, 69.

393 Charles J.[*sic*] Schou, "Vigerslev Haveforstad," *Architekten* 17 (November 7, 1914): 41–47; Tim Knudsen, "International Influences and Professional Rivalry in Early Danish Planning," *Planning Perspectives* 3 (1988): 303; Bo Larsson and Ole Thomassen, "Urban Planning in Denmark," in Thomas Hall, ed., *Planning and Urban Growth in the Nordic Countries* (London: E & FN Spon, 1991), 16; Heleni Porfyriou, "Artistic Urban Design and Cultural Myths: the Garden City Idea in Nordic Countries, 1900–1925," *Planning Perspectives* 7 (1992): 289, 290; Olaf Lind and Annemarie Lund, *Copenhagen Architecture Guide*, rev. ed. (Copenhagen: Arkitektens Forlag, 1996, 2001), 240.

394 "Denmark," in *International Cities and Town Planning Exhibition. English Catalogue. Jubilee Exhibition, Gothenburg, Sweden, 1923* (Göteborg, Wezäta, W. Zachrissons boktyrckeri a.-b., 1923), 70; Hans Helge Madsen and Otto Käszner, *The Award-Winning City* (Copenhagen: Arkitektens Forlag, 2003), 176.

395 "Denmark," in *International Cities and Town Planning Exhibition. English Catalogue. Jubilee Exhibition, Gothenburg, Sweden, 1923* (Göteborg, Wezäta, W. Zachrissons boktyrckeri a.-b., 1923), 70; *Lokalplan Nr. 2-448 for Gerthasminde* (Odense: Odense Kommune, 1990); Jørgen Sestoft and Jørgen Hegner Christiansen, *Guide to Danish Architecture 1, 1000–1960* (Copenhagen: Arkitektens Forlag, 1995), 189, 190; Lone Jensen, "Gerthasminde," in *Anton Rosen: arkitekt og kunster* (Silkeborg, Denmark: KunstCentret Silkeborg Bad, 2003), 55–58.

396 Heleni Porfyriou, "Artistic Urban Design and Cultural Myths: the Garden City Idea in Nordic Countries, 1900–1925," *Planning Perspectives* 7 (1992): 284–86. Also see "Konkurrencer," *Architekten* 21 (1919): 425–31; "Denmark," in *International Cities and Town Planning Exhibition. English Catalogue. Jubilee Exhibition, Gothenburg, Sweden, 1923* (Göteborg, Wezäta, W. Zachrissons boktyrckeri a.-b., 1923), 71, 74; *Nordic Classicism,*

1910–1930 (Helsinki: Museum of Finnish Architecture, 1982), 74; Tim Knudsen, "International Influences and Professional Rivalry in Early Danish Planning," *Planning Perspectives* 3 (1988): 304; Bo Larsson and Ole Thomassen, "Urban Planning in Denmark," in Thomas Hall, ed., in *Planning and Urban Growth in the Nordic Countries* (London: E & FN Spon, 1991), 29; Andrés Duany, Elizabeth Plater-Zyberk, and Robert Alminana, *The New Civic Art: Elements of Town Planning* (New York: Rizzoli International Publications, 2003), 98. For Unwin, see Raymond Unwin, *Nothing Gained by Overcrowding* (London: Garden Cities and Town Planning Association, 1912).

397 "Konkurrence om Byplan for Ringsted," *Architekten* 21 (1919): 391–98; Bo Larsson and Ole Thomassen, "Urban Planning in Denmark," in Thomas Hall, ed., in *Planning and Urban Growth in the Nordic Countries* (London: E & FN Spon, 1991), 28–29.

398 Albert Baur, "Bergheim bei Zürich," *Schweizerische Baukunst* 2 (1910): 5–15; "Kolonie Bergheim in Zürich-Hirslanden," *Schweizerische Bauzeitung* 55 (April 1910): 200–201, plates 47–50; Quintus Miller, "Der Kolonie Bergheim (1908–09) und die Gartenstadt Kapf (1910–11) in Zürich Hirslanden," *Archithese* 23 (January/February 1993): 24–29; Mercedes Daguerre, *Birkhäuser Architectural Guide: Switzerland, 20th Century*, trans. by David Kerr et al. (Basel: Birkhäuser, 1997), 36–37; Dominique von Burg, *Gebrüder Pfister: Architektur für Zürich 1907–1950* (Zurich: Niggli, 2000), 110–15; Vittorio Magnago Lampugnani and Matthias Noell, *Stadtformen: Die Architektur der Stadt Zwischen Imagination und Konstruktion* (Zurich: gta Verlag, 2005), 215; http://www.pfister-arch.ch/gebr-pfister.html.

399 Quintus Miller, "Der Kolonie Bergheim (1908–09) und die Gartenstadt Kapf (1910–11) in Zürich Hirslanden," *Archithese* 23 (January/February 1993): 24–29; Mercedes Daguerre, *Birkhäuser Architectural Guide: Switzerland, 20th Century*, trans. by David Kerr et al. (Basel: Birkhäuser, 1997), 36–37; Dominique von Burg, *Gebrüder Pfister: Architektur für Zürich 1907–1950* (Zurich: Niggli, 2000), 110–15; Vittorio Magnago Lampugnani and Matthias Noell, *Stadtformen: Die Architektur der Stadt Zwischen Imagination und Konstruktion* (Zurich: gta Verlag, 2005), 215; http://www.pfister-arch.ch/gebr-pfister.html.

400 "Wohnsiedlung Riedtli," http://www.stadt-zuerich.ch; http://www.muellerund-schmidt. ch/pro-riedtli.html?projecte.

401 Mary Patricia May Sekler, "Le Corbusier, Ruskin, the Tree, and the Open Hand," in Russell Walden, ed., *The Open Hand: Essays on Le Corbusier* (Cambridge, Mass.: MIT Press, 1977), 53; H. Allen Brooks, "Jeanneret and Sitte: Le Corbusier's Earliest Ideas on Urban Design," in Helen Searing, ed., *In Search of Modern Architecture: A Tribute to Henry-Russell Hitchcock* (Cambridge, Mass.: MIT Press, 1982), 278–97; H. Allen Brooks, "Le Corbusier's Formative Years at La Chaux-de-Fonds," in H. Allen Brooks, ed., *Le Corbusier* (Princeton, N.J.: Princeton University Press, 1987), 35; *La Chaux-de-Fonds et Jeanneret avant Le Corbusier* (La Chaux-de Fonds, Switzerland: Musée des Beaux-Arts, 1987), 103; *Le Corbusier, Architect of the Century*, exhibition catalogue (London: Arts Council of Great Britain, 1987), 201; Ivan Zaknic, "Le Corbusier's Epiphany on Mount Athos," *Journal of Architectural Education* 43 (Summer 1990): 27–36; H. Allen Brooks, *Le Corbusier's Formative Years* (Chicago and London: The University of Chicago Press, 1997), 368–70, 481; Stanislaus von Moos and Arthur Rüegg, *Le Corbusier before Le Corbusier: Applied Arts, Architecture, Painting, Photography, 1907–1922* (New Haven, Conn., and London: Yale University Press, 2002), 20; Andrés Duany, Elizabeth Plater-Zyberk, and Robert Alminana, *The New Civic Art: Elements of Town Planning* (New York: Rizzoli International Publications, 2003), 47; Jean-Louis Cohen, *Le Corbusier, 1887–1965: The Lyricism of Architecture in the Machine Age* (Cologne and Los Angeles: Taschen, 2004), 19, 91; Emma Dummett, "Rethinking Le Corbusier's Urban Plans: The Influence of His Early Years in La-Chaux-de-Fonds," *Scroope: Cambridge Architectural Journal* 18 (June 2006): 128–33; Emma Dummett, "Green Space and Cosmic Order: Le Corbusier's Understanding of Nature" (Ph.D. diss., University of Edinburgh, 2007): 62–68; Martin Filler, *Makers of Modern Architecture* (New York: New York Review of Books, 2007), 79; Stanislaus von Moos, *Le Corbusier: Elements of a Synthesis*, rev. ed. (Rotterdam: 010 Publishers, 2009), 140, 142; www.fondation-lecorbusier.fr.

402 Brooks, *Le Corbusier's Formative Years*, 368–69.

403 Johann Friedrich Schär, Henri Faucherre, and Hannes Meyer, *Die Siedlung Freidorf* (Basel: Buchhandlung VSK, 1921); Hannes Meyer, "Die Siedlung Freidorf," *Das Werk* 12 (No. 2, 1925): 40–51; Alexander Klein and Werner Hegemann, "Siedlungs-Genossenschaft 'Friedorf' bei Basel," *Wasmuths Monatshefte für Baukunst und Städtebau* 10 (1926): 1–10; Paul Artaria, "Die Entwicklung des Wohnungsbaus von 1908 bis 1930," *Das Werk* 45 (1958): 300–303; Claude Schnaidt, ed., *Hannes Meyer: Buildings, Projects and Writings*, trans. by D. Q. Stephenson (Teufen AR, Switzerland: Arthur Niggli Ltd., 1965), 2–15; Jacques Gubler, "Hannes Meyer's Freidorf-Siedlung Muttenz," trans. by J. Hull, *Das Werk* 60 (No. 4, 1973): 462–74, 487; Jacques Gubler, *Nationalisme et internationalisme dans l'architecture moderne de la Suisse*, rev. ed. (Geneva: Editions Archigraphie, 1988), 86–100; K. Michael Hays, *Modernism and the Posthumanist Subject: The Architecture of Hannes Meyer and Ludwig Hilberseimer* (Cambridge, Mass.: MIT Press, 1992), 47–48, 85–89; Christa Zeller, *Guide to Swiss Architecture* (Zurich: Werk-Verlag, 1992), vol. 2: 80; Emma Dummett, "Green Space and Cosmic Order: Le Corbusier's Understanding of Nature" (Ph.D. diss., University of Edinburgh, 2007): 68.

404 Hannes Meyer, "Freidorf Housing Estate, near Basle, 1919–21," in Schnaidt, ed., *Hannes Meyer: Buildings, Projects and Writings*, 5.

405 Hannes Meyer, "Wie ich arbeite," *Architektura CCCP* 6 (1933), translated and quoted in Claude Schnaidt, "Introduction," in Schnaidt, ed., *Hannes Meyer: Buildings, Projects and Writings*, 19, 21.

406 Meyer, "Freidorf Housing Estate, near Basle, 1919–21," in Schnaidt, ed., *Hannes Meyer: Buildings, Projects and Writings*, 13.

407 "Genossenschafts-Wohnbauten in Prélaz bei Lausanne," *Schweizerische Bauzeitung* 81/82 (April 7, 1923): 171–73; Arthur Freymond, "A propos d'un anniversaire," *Habitation* 18 (1945): 111–14; Francesco Dal Co and Manfredo Tafuri, *Modern Architecture*, trans. by Robert Erich Wolf (New York: Harry N. Abrams, 1979), 268; Christa Zeller, *Guide to Swiss Architecture* (Zurich: Werk-Verlag, 1992), vol. 3: 92; Mercedes Daguerre, *Birkhäuser Architectural Guide: Switzerland, 20th Century*, trans. by David Kerr et al. (Basel: Birkhäuser, 1997), 231; Anita Frei, "Signes Extérieurs de Coopération," *Habitation* 69 (No. 3, 1997): 11–14; Isabelle Charollais and Bruno Marchand, "Cité-Jardins ou Blocs Locatifs?" *Habitation* 69 (No. 3, 1997): 15–16; "Cité-Jardin de Prélaz," http://www.lausanne.ch.

408 Zeller, *Guide to Swiss Architecture*, vol. 3: 92.

409 "Gartenvorstadt Avenue D'aïre, Genf.," *Wasmuths Monatshefte für Baukunst und Städtebau* 8 (1924): 360–64; Arnold Hoechel, "L'habitation à Genève," *Werk* 30 (October 1952): 309–14; Paul Artaria, "Die Entwicklung des Wohnungsbaus von 1908 bis 1930," *Das Werk* 45 (1958): 300–303; "Arnold Hoechel, 1889–1974," *Das Werk* 62 (1975): 108; Françoise et Jean-Pierre Lewerer, "La crepuscule de la cite-jardin d'Aïre," *Archithese* 15 (May 1986): 79–82; Isabelle Charollais et al., *L'architecture à Genève, 1919–1975* (Lausanne: Payot Lausanne, 1990), 129–31; Christa Zeller, *Guide to Swiss Architecture* (Zurich: Werk-Verlag, 1992), vol. 3: 146; Mercedes Daguerre, *Birkhäuser Architectural Guide: Switzerland, 20th Century*, trans. by David Kerr et al. (Basel: Birkhäuser, 1997), 250–51; "Genève, Cités-jardins d'Aïre et de Nouvel-Aïre," www.nike-kulture.ch.

410 Paul Artaria, "Die Entwicklung des Wohnungsbaus von 1908 bis 1930," *Das Werk* 45 (1958): 300–303; Christa Zeller, *Guide to Swiss Architecture* (Zurich: Werk-Verlag, 1992), vol. 2: 24–25; Karl and Maya Nägelin-Gschwind, *Hans Bernoulli: Architekt und Städtebauer* (Basel: Birkhäuser, 1993), 59, 66, 195–97; Mercedes Daguerre, *Birkhäuser Architectural Guide: Switzerland, 20th Century*, trans. by David Kerr et al. (Basel: Birkhäuser, 1997), 122–23; Martina Desax and Dorette Paraventi-Gempp, *Bauen in Basel* (Basel: C. Merian, 2007), 228–35.

411 Hans Bernoulli, "Vom Kleinwohnungsbau: was man darf und was man nicht darf," *Das Werk* 11 (December 1924): 311–17; Claude Lichtenstein, "Bernoulli-Häuser," *Archithese* (November–December 1981): 38–41; Christoph Luchsinger, "Adolf Kellermüller (1895–1981)," *Archithese* (November–December 1983): 35–41; Gianfranco Agazzi, "L'edilizia Sociale Negli Anni '20," *Parametro* 140 (October 1985): 32–39; Helmut Winter, *Zum Wandel der Schoenheitsvorstellungen im modernen Staedtebau* (Zurich: Verlag der Fachvereine Zurich, 1988), 215; Christa Zeller, *Guide to Swiss Architecture* (Zurich: Werk-Verlag, 1992), vol. 1: 162–63; Karl and Maya Nägelin-Gschwind, *Hans Bernoulli: Architekt und Städtebauer* (Basel: Birkhäuser, 1993), 73, 215; Mercedes Daguerre, *Birkhäuser Architectural Guide: Switzerland, 20th Century*, trans. by David Kerr et al. (Basel: Birkhäuser, 1997), 40–41; Heinz Bächinger, "Bernoulli, Hans, architect, 1876–1959," http://www.winterthur-glossar.ch.

412 Zeller, *Guide to Swiss Architecture*, 163.

413 A. Bodmer, "Winterthur," *Das Werk* 15 (1928): 204–5; Christoph Luchsinger and Thomas Schönbächler, "Ausgewählte Bauten von Adolf Kellermüller," *Archithese* (November–December 1983): 42; Hans-Peter Bärtschi, *Die Siedlungsstadt Winterthur* (Bern: Gesellschaft für Schweizerische Kunstgeschichte, 1989), 34; Christa Zeller, *Guide to Swiss Architecture* (Zurich: Werk-Verlag, 1992), vol. 1: 144; Karl and Maya Nägelin-Gschwind, *Hans Bernoulli: Architekt und Städtebauer* (Basel: Birkhäuser, 1993), 209–10; Gilbert Brossard and Daniel Oederlin, *Architekturführer Winterthur* (Zurich: Vdf, 1997), 198–99; Mercedes Daguerre, *Birkhäuser Architectural Guide: Switzerland, 20th Century*, trans. by David Kerr et al. (Basel: Birkhäuser, 1997), 26–27.

414 Christoph Luchsinger, "Adolf Kellermüller (1895–1981)," *Archithese* (November–December 1983): 38; Christoph Luchsinger and Thomas Schönbächler, "Ausgewählte Bauten von Adolf Kellermüller," *Archithese* (November–December 1983): 42; Christa Zeller, *Guide to Swiss Architecture* (Zurich: Werk-Verlag, 1992), vol. 1: 144; Karl and Maya Nägelin-Gschwind, *Hans Bernoulli: Architekt und Städtebauer* (Basel: Birkhäuser, 1993), 211; Mercedes Daguerre, *Birkhäuser Architectural Guide: Switzerland, 20th Century*, trans. by David Kerr et al. (Basel: Birkhäuser, 1997), 26–27; Siedlung Eichliacker," http://bau.winterthur.ch.

415 A. Bodmer, "Winterthur," *Das Werk* 15 (1928): 204–5; Christoph Luchsinger, "Adolf Kellermüller (1895–1981)," *Archithese* (November–December 1983): 37–39; Christoph Luchsinger and Thomas Schönbächler, "Ausgewählte Bauten von Adolf Kellermüller," *Archithese* (November–December 1983): 43; Hans-Peter Bärtschi, *Die Siedlungsstadt Winterthur* (Bern : Gesellschaft für Schweizerische Kunstgeschichte, 1989), 43; Christa Zeller, *Guide to Swiss Architecture* (Zurich: Werk-Verlag, 1992), vol. 1: 144; Gilbert Brossard and Daniel Oederlin, *Architekturführer Winterthur* (Zurich: Vdf, 1997), 202–3; Mercedes Daguerre, *Birkhäuser Architectural Guide: Switzerland, 20th Century*, trans. by David Kerr et al. (Basel: Birkhäuser, 1997), 26–27; Martin Steinmann, *Forme forte: ecrits, 1972–2002* (Boston: Birkhauser Verlag für Architektur, 2004), 36.

416 "Kreuzreihenhäuser der Heimstätten-Genossenschaft Winterthur," *Das Werk* (1933): 145–50; Christoph Luchsinger, "Adolf Kellermüller (1895–1981)," *Archithese* (November–December 1983): 39–41; Christoph Luchsinger and Thomas Schönbächler, "Ausgewählte Bauten von Adolf Kellermüller," *Archithese* (November–December 1983): 44–45; Irma Noseda and Martin Steinmann, *Zeitzeichen: Schweizer Baukultur im 19. und 20. Jahrhundert* (Zurich: Verlags-AG der Akademischen Technischen Vereine, 1988), 98; Hans-Peter Bärtschi, *Die Siedlungsstadt Winterthur* (Bern: Gesellschaft für Schweizerische Kunstgeschichte, 1989), 36–39; Christa Zeller, *Guide to Swiss Architecture* (Zurich: Werk-Verlag, 1992), vol. 1: 146; Mercedes Daguerre, *Birkhäuser Architectural Guide: Switzerland, 20th Century*, trans. by David Kerr et al. (Basel: Birkhäuser, 1997), 26–27.

417 K. Hippenmeier, "Blockpläne," *Das Werk* (1928): 74–76; "Wohnkolonie Erismannhof," *Das Werk* (1929): 134–35; W. Ruf, "Die Finanzierung der gemeinnützigen Baugenossenschaften der Schweiz," *Das Wohnen* 4 (1929): 248–50; H. Oetiker, "Maisons collectives ou maisons familiales," *Habitation* 3 (1930): 1–2; "Vom Kleinwohnungsbau in Zürich," *Schweizerische Bauzeitung* 95/96 (1930): 22–23, plates 1–2; Gianfranco Agazzi, "L'edilizia Sociale Negli Anni '20," *Parametro* 140 (October 1985): 32–39; Mercedes Daguerre, *Birkhäuser Architectural Guide: Switzerland, 20th Century*, trans. by David Kerr et al. (Basel: Birkhäuser, 1997), 40–41; "Erismannhof," http://www.stadt-zuerich.ch.

418 "Die Frage Hochbau-Flachbau," *Das Werk* (1929): 136–39; W. Ruf, "Die Finanzierung der gemeinnützigen Baugenossenschaften der Schweiz," *Das Wohnen* 4 (1929): 251–53; H. Oetiker, "Maisons collectives ou maisons familiales," *Habitation* 3 (1930): 1–2; "Vom Kleinwohnungsbau in Zürich," *Schweizerische Bauzeitung* 95/96 (1930): 35–36, plates 3–4.

419 "Die Werkbundsiedlung Neubühl in Zürich-Wollishofen," *Das Werk* 17 (1930): 182–87; "Die Werkbundsiedlung Neubühl in Zürich-Wollishofen," *Das Werk* 18 (1931): 257–79; Leonardo Benevolo, *History of Modern Architecture, vol. two: The Modern Movement*, trans. by H.J. Landry (Bari: Giuseppe Laterza & Figli, 1960; Cambridge, Mass.: MIT Press, 1971), 618–19, 622–23; Gianfranco Agazzi, "L'edilizia Sociale Negli Anni '20," *Parametro* 140 (October 1985): 32–39; Lore Kelly, "Sanierung der Werkbundsiedlung Neubühl/Zürich," *Bauwelt* 79 (January 29, 1988): 218; Ueli Marbach and Arthur

Rüegg, *Werkbundsiedlung Neubühl* (Zurich: GTA Verlag, 1990); Giancarlo Rosa, "Il Werkbundsiedlung 'Neubühl' a Zurigo (1928–32)," *Frames, porte & finestre* 33 (August–September 1991): 34–41, xiii; Christa Zeller, *Guide to Swiss Architecture* (Zurich: Werk-Verlag, 1992), vol. 1: 168–69; Mercedes Daguerre, *Birkhäuser Architectural Guide: Switzerland, 20th Century*, trans. by David Kerr et al. (Basel: Birkhäuser, 1997), 44–45; http://www.neubuehl.ch.

420 Benevolo, *History of Modern Architecture, vol. two: The Modern Movement*, 619.

421 "La Cité Vieusseux, Genève," *Das Werk* 20 (May 1933): 130–39; Arnold Hoechel, "L'habitation à Genève," *Werk* 30 (October 1952): 309–14; André Corboz, Jacques Gubler et Jean-Marc Lamunière, *Guide d'architecture moderne de Genève* (Lausanne: Payot, 1969), 18–19; Susan Kent, *Domestic Architecture and the Use of Space: An Interdisciplinary Cross-Cultural Study* (Cambridge, England and New York: Cambridge University Press, 1990), 83; Christa Zeller, *Guide to Swiss Architecture* (Zurich: Werk-Verlag, 1992), vol. 2: 147; Mercedes Daguerre, *Birkhäuser Architectural Guide: Switzerland, 20th Century*, trans. by David Kerr et al. (Basel: Birkhäuser, 1997), 250–51.

422 "Siedlungsbauten in Bern-Bümpliz," *Das Werk* 31 (1944): xxvi; E.E. Strasser, "Ensemble des colonies Bethlehemacker," *Habitation* 18 (1945): 12–13; "Siedlung Bethlehemacker, Bern," *Das Werk* 36 (March 1949): 67–71; "Die Siedlungsgenossenschaft der Holzarbeiter-Zimmerleute des SBHV Bern," *Das Wohnen* 24 (December 1949): 347–50; Christa Zeller, *Guide to Swiss Architecture* (Zurich: Werk-Verlag, 1992), vol. 2: 197; Werner Huber and Dominique Uldry, *Building Bern* (Zurich: Verlag Hochparterre and Scheidegger & Spiess, 2009), 189; http://rp-architekten.ch.

423 Zeller, *Guide to Swiss Architecture*, vol. 2: 197.

424 See Eve Blau, *The Architecture of Red Vienna, 1919–1934* (Cambridge, Mass., and London: MIT Press, 1999), 422 (n.3). Also see Wilfried Posch, "Die Gartenstadtbewegung in Wien: Persönlichkeiten, Ziele, Erfolge und Misserfolge," *Bauforum* 77/78 (1980): 9–24; Manfredo Tafuri, *Vienna Rossa: La politica residenziale nella Vienna socialista, 1919–1933* (Milan: Electra Editrice, 1980); Wilfried Posch, *Die Wiener Gartenstadt-bewegung: Reformversuch Zwischen erster und zweiter Gründerzeit* (Vienna: Edition Tusch, 1981); Klaus Novy and Wolfgang Förster, *Einfach Bauen* (Vienna: Picus Verlag, 1991); Willem Korthals Altes and Andreas Faludi, "Why the Greening of Red Vienna Did Not Come to Pass: An Unknown Chapter of the Garden City Movement, 1919–1934," *European Planning Studies* 3 (June 1995): 205–25; Helmut Weihsmann, *Das Rote Wien* (Vienna: Promedia, 2002); www.dasortewien.at.

425 Dietmar Steiner, *Architecture in Vienna* (Vienna: Georg Prachner Verlag, 1990), 32.

426 Hans Kampffmeyer, "Die Siedlungsbewegung in Wien," *Kommunale Praxis* 22 (1922): 719–20, quoted and translated in Klaus Novy, "The Rosenhügel Pioneers: On the Real Revolution of Workers' Housing by the Viennese Settlers," *9H* 6 (1983): 45–51.

427 Werner Hegemann, "Kritisches zu den Wohnbauten der Stadt Wien," *Wasmuths Monatshefte für Baukunst und Städtebau* 10 (1926): 365–66, translated and quoted in Blau, *The Architecture of Red Vienna, 1919–1934*, 342.

428 Heinrich Goldemund, *Die Kaiser Karl-Kriegerheimstätte in Aspern* (Vienna: Gerlach und Wiedlung, 1918); Klaus Novy and Wolfgang Förster, *Einfach Bauen* (Vienna: Picus Verlag, 1991), 20; Eve Blau, *The Architecture of Red Vienna, 1919–1934* (Cambridge, Mass., and London: MIT Press, 1999), 110.

429 Hans Hafner, "Die Bautätigkeit der Gemeinde Wien," *Zeitschrift des Österreichischen Ingenieur- und Architekten-Veriens* 15–16 (April 18, 1924): 127; Felix Czeike, *Wiener Bezirkskulturführer Rudolfsheim-Fünfhaus* (Vienna: Jugend und Volk, 1980), 23, 25; Catherine Cooke, "Map Guide: Vienna 1870–1930," in Hans Hollein and Catherine Cooke, eds., *Vienna: Dream and Reality* (London: AD Editions, 1986), 74–76; Katharina Schild, "Siedlung Schmelz: Freiräume einer Wiener Wohnhausanlage der Ersten Republik" (Diplomarbeit, Technische Universität, Munich, 1989); Renate Banik-Schwitzer, "Vienna," in M. J. Daunton, ed., *Housing the Workers, 1850–1914: A Comparative Perspective* (London: Leicester University Press, 1990), 117; Dietmar Steiner, *Architecture in Vienna* (Vienna: Georg Prachner Verlag, 1990), 131; Klaus Novy and Wolfgang Förster, *Einfach Bauen* (Vienna: Picus Verlag, 1991), 131; August Sarnitz, ed., *Architecture in Vienna* (Vienna: Springer, 1998), 266; Eve Blau, *The Architecture of Red Vienna, 1919–1934* (Cambridge, Mass., and London: MIT Press, 1999), 110–11; Eva Berger, *Historische Gärten Österreichs, 1: Niederösterreich, Burgenland* (Vienna: Böhlau, 2002), 345; Mark Steinmetz and Sandy Panek, *Wien: Der Architektur Führer* (Berlin: Verlagshaus Braun, 2007), 140; August Sarnitz, *Architecture Vienna: 700 Buildings*, trans. by Susan Siegle (Vienna: Springer, 2008), 373; www.siedlung-schmelz.at.

430 Blau, *The Architecture of Red Vienna, 1919–1934*, 110.

431 Hugo Mayer, "Die Kleingartensiedlung Rosenhügel," *Der Siedler* 1 (January 1921): 12–13; Manfredo Tafuri, *Vienna Rossa: La politica residenziale nella Vienna socialista, 1919–1933* (Milan: Electra Editrice, 1980), 18; Klaus Novy, "The Rosenhügel Pioneers: On the Real Revolution of Workers' Housing by the Viennese Settlers," *9H* 6 (1983): 45–51; Catherine Cooke, "Map Guide: Vienna 1870–1930," in Hans Hollein and Catherine Cooke, eds., *Vienna: Dream and Reality* (London: AD Editions, 1986), 73, 74–76; Dietmar Steiner, *Architecture in Vienna* (Vienna: Georg Prachner Verlag, 1990), 132; Klaus Novy and Wolfgang Förster, *Einfach Bauen* (Vienna: Picus Verlag, 1991), 155–57; August Sarnitz, ed., *Architecture in Vienna* (Vienna: Springer, 1998), 224; Eve Blau, *The Architecture of Red Vienna, 1919–1934* (Cambridge, Mass., and London: MIT Press, 1999), 110, 112–14; Helmut Weihsmann, *Das Rote Wien* (Vienna: Promedia, 2002), 290–91; August Sarnitz, *Architecture Vienna: 700 Buildings*, trans. by Susan Siegle (Vienna: Springer, 2008), 313; www.ah-rosenhuegel.net.

432 Mayer, "Die Kleingartensiedlung Rosenhügel": 12–13, translated and quoted in Novy, "The Rosenhügel Pioneers": 47, also partially quoted in Blau, *The Architecture of Red Vienna, 1919–1934*, 112.

433 Friedrich Bauermeister, "Lehrsiedlung Heubert," *Der Siedler* (June 1921): 91; Benedetto Gravagnuolo, *Adolf Loos: Theory and Works*, trans. by C. H. Evans (New York: Rizzoli International Publications, 1982), 168–69; Burkhard Rukschcio and Roland Schachel, *Adolf Loos: Leben und Werk* (Salzburg: Residenz Verlag, 1982), 283–84, 539–40; Catherine Cooke, "Map Guide: Vienna 1870–1930," in Hans Hollein and Catherine Cooke, eds., *Vienna: Dream and Reality* (London: AD Editions, 1986), 73; Dietmar Steiner, *Architecture in Vienna* (Vienna: Georg Prachner Verlag, 1990), 99; Klaus Novy and Wolfgang Förster, *Einfach Bauen* (Vienna: Picus Verlag, 1991), 166–67; Robert Rotenberg, *Landscape and Power in Vienna* (Baltimore and London: Johns Hopkins University Press, 1995), 242–43; August Sarnitz, ed., *Architecture in Vienna* (Vienna: Springer, 1998), 279; Eve Blau, *The Architecture of Red Vienna, 1919–1934* (Cambridge, Mass., and London: MIT Press, 1999), 107–9, 128; Norbert Schoenauder, *6,000 Years of Housing*, rev. ed. (New York: W. W. Norton, 2000), 399; Helmut Weihsmann, *Das Rote Wien* (Vienna: Promedia, 2002), 382–85; Mark Steinmetz and Sandy Panek, *Wien: Der Architektur Führer* (Berlin: Verlagshaus Braun, 2007), 141; August Sarnitz, *Architecture Vienna: 700 Buildings*, trans. by Susan Siegle (Vienna: Springer, 2008), 393; www.dasrotewien.at.

434 Adolf Loos, patent application, quoted in Gravagnuolo, *Adolf Loos: Theory and Works*, 171.

435 Benedetto Gravagnuolo, *Adolf Loos: Theory and Works*, trans. by C. H. Evans (New York: Rizzoli International Publications, 1982), 168–69; Burkhard Rukschcio and Roland Schachel, *Adolf Loos: Leben und Werk* (Salzburg: Residenz Verlag, 1982), 260–63; Klaus Novy and Wolfgang Förster, *Einfach Bauen* (Vienna: Picus Verlag, 1991), 140–43; Eve Blau, *The Architecture of Red Vienna, 1919–1934* (Cambridge, Mass., and London: MIT Press, 1999), 102–6.

436 Blau, *The Architecture of Red Vienna, 1919–1934*, 102, 105.

437 Christopher Long, "The Wayward Heir: Josef Frank's Vienna Years, 1885–1933," in Nina Stritzler-Levine, ed., *Josef Frank, Architect and Designer*, exhibition catalogue (New York: Bard Graduate Center for Studies in the Decorative Arts; New Haven, Conn., and London: Yale University Press, 1996), 58.

438 Josef Frank, Hugo Fuchs, and Franz Zettinig, "Wohnhäuser aus Gußbeton: Ein Vorschlag zur Lösung der Wohnungsfrage," *Der Architect* 22 (1919): 33–37; Johannes Spalt and Hermann Czech, *Josef Frank, 1885–1967: Zusammenstellung und Gestaltung* (Vienna: Hochschule für Angewandte Kunst, 1981), 112–15; Long, "The Wayward Heir: Josef Frank's Vienna Years, 1885–1933," in Stritzler-Levine, ed., *Josef Frank, Architect and Designer*, 49–50; Eve Blau, *The Architecture of Red Vienna, 1919–1934* (Cambridge, Mass., and London: MIT Press, 1999), 432 (n.121); Christopher Long, *Josef Frank: Life and Work* (Chicago and London: University of Chicago Press, 2002), 52–53.

439 Otto Neurath, *Österreichs Kleingärten- und Siedlerorganisation* (Vienna: Wiener Volksbuchhandlung, 1923), 34; Werner Hegemann, "Kritisches zu den Wohnbauten der Stadt Wien," *Wasmuths Monatshefte für Baukunst und Städtebau* 10 (1926): 365–66; Manfredo Tafuri, *Vienna Rossa: La politica residenziale nella Vienna socialista, 1919–1933* (Milan: Electra Editrice, 1980), 17; Johannes Spalt and Hermann Czech, *Josef Frank, 1885–1967: Zusammenstellung und Gestaltung* (Vienna: Hochschule für Angewandte Kunst, 1981), 124–25; Otto Kapfinger, "Josef Frank—Siedlungen und Siedlungsprojekte 1919–1932," *Um Bau* 10 (August 1986): 48; Dietmar Steiner, *Architecture in Vienna* (Vienna: Georg Prachner Verlag, 1990), 147; Christopher Long, "Space for Living: The Architecture of Josef Frank," in Nina Stritzler-Levine, ed., *Josef Frank, Architect and Designer*, exhibition catalogue (New York: Bard Graduate Center for Studies in the Decorative Arts; New Haven, Conn., and London: Yale University Press, 1996), 81–82; August Sarnitz, ed., *Architecture in Vienna* (Vienna: Springer, 1998), 222; Eve Blau, *The Architecture of Red Vienna, 1919–1934* (Cambridge, Mass., and London: MIT Press, 1999), 114–17; Christopher Long, *Josef Frank: Life and Work* (Chicago and London: University of Chicago Press, 2002), 58–61; Helmut Weihsmann, *Das Rote Wien* (Vienna: Promedia, 2002), 289–90; Mark Steinmetz and Sandy Panek, *Wien: Der Architektur Führer* (Berlin: Verlagshaus Braun, 2007), 142–43; August Sarnitz, *Architecture Vienna: 700 Buildings*, trans. by Susan Siegle (Vienna: Springer, 2008), 307.

440 Long, *Josef Frank: Life and Work*, 59–60.

441 Blau, *The Architecture of Red Vienna, 1919–1934*, 117.

442 Neurath, *Österreichs Kleingärten- und Siedlerorganisation*, 34, translated and quoted in Long, *Josef Frank: Life and Work*, 60–61.

443 Johannes Spalt and Hermann Czech, *Josef Frank, 1885–1967: Zusammenstellung und Gestaltung* (Vienna: Hochschule für Angewandte Kunst, 1981), 126; Christopher Long, *Josef Frank: Life and Work* (Chicago and London: University of Chicago Press, 2002), 61–62.

444 Long, *Josef Frank: Life and Work*, 61.

445 Johannes Spalt and Hermann Czech, *Josef Frank, 1885–1967: Zusammenstellung und Gestaltung* (Vienna: Hochschule für Angewandte Kunst, 1981), 127; Christopher Long, *Josef Frank: Life and Work* (Chicago and London: University of Chicago Press, 2002), 68–69.

446 Josef Frank, "Einzelmöbel und Kunsthandwerk," *Innen-Dekoration* 34 (November 1923): 336–38; Spalt and Czech, *Josef Frank, 1885–1967: Zusammenstellung und Gestaltung*, 122–29; Christopher Long, "Space for Living: The Architecture of Josef Frank," in Nina Stritzler-Levine, ed., *Josef Frank, Architect and Designer*, exhibition catalogue (New York: Bard Graduate Center for Studies in the Decorative Arts; New Haven, Conn., and London: Yale University Press, 1996), 82; Long, *Josef Frank: Life and Work*, 68, 70–73.

447 "Bautätigkeit der Wiener Stadtverwaltung: Die Siedlungen: Am Flötzersteig und Weissenböckstrasse," *Österreichs Bau- und Werkkunst* (1925/1926): 277–83; Guenter Hirschel-Protsch, "Die Gemeindebauten der Stadt Wien," *Wasmuths Monatshefte für Baukunst und Städtebau* 10 (1926): 363–64; "Wiener Siedlungen," *Moderne Bauformen* 26 (May 1927): 186–96; "Siedlung Flötzersteig und Volksschule Sieggraben," *Moderne Bauformen* 33 (June 1934): 293–95; Klaus Novy and Wolfgang Förster, *Einfach Bauen* (Vienna: Picus Verlag, 1991), 151; Eve Blau, *The Architecture of Red Vienna, 1919–1934* (Cambridge, Mass., and London: MIT Press, 1999), 127–28; Helmut Weihsmann, *Das Rote Wien* (Vienna: Promedia, 2002), 330–32; www.dasrotewien.at.

448 Blau, *The Architecture of Red Vienna, 1919–1934*, 128.

449 Guenter Hirschel-Protsch, "Die Gemeindebauten der Stadt Wien," *Wasmuths Monatshefte für Baukunst und Städtebau* 10 (1926): 363–64; "Wiener Siedlungen," *Moderne Bauformen* 26 (May 1927): 186–96; Manfredo Tafuri, *Vienna Rossa: La politica residenziale nella Vienna socialista, 1919–1933* (Milan: Electra Editrice, 1980), 17; Catherine Cooke, "Map Guide: Vienna 1870–1930," in Hans Hollein and Catherine Cooke, eds., *Vienna: Dream and Reality* (London: AD Editions, 1986), 80; Dietmar Steiner, *Architecture in Vienna* (Vienna: Georg Prachner Verlag, 1990), 170; Klaus Novy and Wolfgang Förster, *Einfach Bauen* (Vienna: Picus Verlag, 1991), 80, 83, 119, 149–50; August Sarnitz, ed., *Architecture in Vienna* (Vienna: Springer, 1998), 211; Eve Blau, *The Architecture of Red*

Vienna, 1919–1934 (Cambridge, Mass., and London: MIT Press, 1999), 127–28; Helmut Weihsmann, *Das Rote Wien* (Vienna: Promedia, 2002), 268–71; Mark Steinmetz and Sandy Panek, *Wien: Der Architektur Führer* (Berlin: Verlagshaus Braun, 2007), 143; August Sarnitz, *Architecture Vienna: 700 Buildings*, trans. by Susan Siegle (Vienna: Springer, 2008), 287; www.dasrotewien.at.

450 Karl Ehn, "Bautätigkeit der Wiener Stadtverwaltung: Dies Siedlung Hermeswiese," *Österreichs Bau- und Werkkunst* (1925): 73–80; "Planverfassung: Wiener Stadtbauamt (Architekt Karl Ehn)," *Moderne Bauformen* 24 (1925): 355–56; Manfredo Tafuri, *Vienna Rossa: La politica residenziale nella Vienna socialista, 1919–1933* (Milan: Electra Editrice, 1980), 60, 156; Klaus Novy and Wolfgang Förster, *Einfach Bauen* (Vienna: Picus Verlag, 1991), 83, 162–63; Willem Korthals Altes and Andreas Faludi, "Why the Greening of Red Vienna Did Not Come to Pass: An Unknown Chapter of the Garden City Movement, 1919–1934," *European Planning Studies* 3 (June 1995): 205–25; Eve Blau, *The Architecture of Red Vienna, 1919–1934* (Cambridge, Mass., and London: MIT Press, 1999), 128–30; Helmut Weihsmann, *Das Rote Wien* (Vienna: Promedia, 2002), 294; www.dasortewien.at; www.gebietsbetreuung.wien.at; www.hietzing.at.

451 For Karl Marx Hof, see Donald Brooke, "The Karl Marx Hof, Vienna," *Journal of the Royal Institute of British Architects* 38 (1931): 671–77; Giovani Denti, *Karl Ehn: Il Karl Marx-Hof* (Florence: Alinea, 1997); Blau, *The Architecture of Red Vienna, 1919–1934*, 320–30.

452 "Arbeiten von Franz Schuster und Franz Schacherl, Wien," *Wasmuths Monatshefte für Baukunst und Städtebau* 10 (1926): 153–56; "Eine Einfamilienkolonie an der Stadtgrenze," *Die Neue Wirtschaft* (February 15, 1926): 10–11; Franz Shuster, "Die Siedlung 'Am Wasserturm,'" *Der Aufbau* (Nos. 8–9, 1926): 152–59; "Wiener Siedlungen," *Moderne Bauformen* 26 (May 1927): 186–96; Dietmar Steiner, *Architecture in Vienna* (Vienna: Georg Prachner Verlag, 1990), 148; August Sarnitz, ed., *Architecture in Vienna* (Vienna: Springer, 1998), 201; Eve Blau, *The Architecture of Red Vienna, 1919–1934* (Cambridge, Mass., and London: MIT Press, 1999), 119, 121–26; Mark Steinmetz and Sandy Panek, *Wien: Der Architektur Führer* (Berlin: Verlagshaus Braun, 2007), 148; August Sarnitz, *Architecture Vienna: 700 Buildings*, trans. by Susan Siegle (Vienna: Springer, 2008), 267; www.architektenlexikon.at/de/530.htm; www.dasrotewien.at.

453 Tessenow, in collaboration with Hugo Mayer and Engelbert Mang (1883–1955), designed only one modest residential project in Vienna, Kolonie Rannersdorf (1921), consisting of one row of six two-story stucco-and-timber-clad houses for officials of a city-owned brewery. See Marco De Michelis, *Heinrich Tessenow: 1876–1950* (Milan: Electa, 1991), 263; Klaus Novy and Wolfgang Förster, *Einfach Bauen* (Vienna: Picus Verlag, 1991), 132; Blau, *The Architecture of Red Vienna, 1919–1934*, 121–22.

454 Blau, *The Architecture of Red Vienna, 1919–1934*, 122.

455 "Arbeiten von Franz Schuster und Franz Schacherl, Wien," *Wasmuths Monatshefte für Baukunst und Städtebau* 10 (1926): 153–56; "Wiener Siedlungen," *Moderne Bauformen* 26 (May 1927): 186–96; www.architektenlexikon.at/de/530.htm; www.dasrotewien.at; www.wien.gv.at/stadtentwicklung/flaechenwidmung/aktuell/rtf/7904-eb.rtf.

456 Manfredo Tafuri, *Vienna Rossa: La politica residenziale nella Vienna socialista, 1919–1933* (Milan: Electra Editrice, 1980), 182–83; Catherine Cooke, "Map Guide: Vienna 1870–1930," in Hans Hollein and Catherine Cooke, eds., *Vienna: Dream and Reality* (London: AD Editions, 1986), 80; Dietmar Steiner, *Architecture in Vienna* (Vienna: Georg Prachner Verlag, 1990), 119; Klaus Novy and Wolfgang Förster, *Einfach Bauen* (Vienna: Picus Verlag, 1991), 73, 172–73; Helmut Weihsmann, *Das Rote Wien* (Vienna: Promedia, 2002), 451–53; August Sarnitz, ed., *Architecture in Vienna* (Vienna: Springer, 1998), 335; Mark Steinmetz and Sandy Panek, *Wien: Der Architektur Führer* (Berlin: Verlagshaus Braun, 2007), 145; August Sarnitz, *Architecture Vienna: 700 Buildings*, trans. by Susan Siegle (Vienna: Springer, 2008), 492; www.dasrotewein.at.

457 Steiner, *Architecture in Vienna*, 119.

458 Manfredo Tafuri, *Vienna Rossa: La politica residenziale nella Vienna socialista, 1919–1933* (Milan: Electra Editrice, 1980), 124–25, 208; Catherine Cooke, "Map Guide: Vienna 1870–1930," in Hans Hollein and Catherine Cooke, eds., *Vienna: Dream and Reality* (London: AD Editions, 1986), 73; Dietmar Steiner, *Architecture in Vienna* (Vienna: Georg Prachner Verlag, 1990), 132; Klaus Novy and Wolfgang Förster, *Einfach Bauen* (Vienna: Picus Verlag, 1991), 74, 182; Robert Rotenberg, *Landscape and Power in Vienna* (Baltimore and London: Johns Hopkins University Press, 1995), 245; August Sarnitz, ed., *Architecture in Vienna* (Vienna: Springer, 1998), 243; Eve Blau, *The Architecture of Red Vienna, 1919–1934* (Cambridge, Mass., and London: MIT Press, 1999), 129–30, 132; Helmut Weihsmann, *Das Rote Wien* (Vienna: Promedia, 2002), 300–301; Mark Steinmetz and Sandy Panek, *Wien: Der Architektur Führer* (Berlin: Verlagshaus Braun, 2007), 164; August Sarnitz, *Architecture Vienna: 700 Buildings*, trans. Susan Siegle (Vienna: Springer, 2008), 340; www.dasrotewein.at; www.gebietsbetreuung.wien.at.

459 Sarnitz, *Architecture Vienna: 700 Buildings*, 340.

460 Steiner, *Architecture in Vienna*, 132.

461 Cooke, "Map Guide: Vienna 1870–1930," in Hollein and Cooke, eds., *Vienna: Dream and Reality*, 73.

462 Josef Frank, ed., *Die internationale Werkbundsiedlung: Wien, 1932*, exhibition catalogue (Vienna: Anton Schroll & Co., 1932); Otto Neurath, "Glückliches Wohnen: Die Bedeutung der Werkbundsiedlung für die Zukunft," *Arbeiter-Zeitung* (June 19, 1932): 5; Wilhelm Lotz, "Die Wiener Werkbundsiedlung," *Die Form* 7 (July 15, 1932): 201–4; Guido Harbers, "'Moderne Linie,' Wohnkultur und Stagnation: Abschliessende Randbemerkungen zur Werkbundsiedlung," *Der Baumeister* 30 (October 1932): 367–73; Wolfdieter Dreibolz, "Die internationale Werkbundsiedlung: Wien, 1932," *Bauforum* 10 (No. 61, 1977): 19–22; Johannes Spalt and Hermann Czech, *Josef Frank, 1885–1967: Zusammenstellung und Gestaltung* (Vienna: Hochschule für Angewandte Kunst, 1981), 126; Jan Tabor, "Die erneuerte Vision: Die Wiener Werkbundsiedlung, 1932–1984," in Viktor Hufnagl, ed., *Reflexionen und Aphorismen zur österreichischen Architektur* (Vienna: Georg Prachner, 1984), 346–52; Astrid Gmeiner and Gottfried Pirhofer, *Der Österreichische Werkbund* (Salzburg: Residenz, 1985), 155–79; Adolf Krischanitz and Otto Kapfinger, *Die Wiener Werkbundsiedlung: Dokumentation einer Erneuerung* (Vienna: Compress, 1985); Catherine Cooke, "Map Guide: Vienna 1870–1930," in Hans Hollein and Catherine Cooke, eds., *Vienna: Dream and Reality* (London: AD Editions,

1986), 72; "Werkbund Siedlung 1932," *Arquitectura 70* (May–August 1989): 74–87; Dietmar Steiner, *Architecture in Vienna* (Vienna: Georg Prachner Verlag, 1990), 134–35; Christopher Long, "The Wayward Heir: Josef Frank's Vienna Years, 1885–1933," in Nina Stritzler-Levine, ed., *Josef Frank, Architect and Designer*, exhibition catalogue (New York: Bard Graduate Center for Studies in the Decorative Arts; New Haven, Conn., and London: Yale University Press, 1996), 52–58; August Sarnitz, ed., *Architecture in Vienna* (Vienna: Springer, 1998), 244–45; Eve Blau, *The Architecture of Red Vienna, 1919–1934* (Cambridge, Mass., and London: MIT Press, 1999), 132–33; Christopher Long, *Josef Frank: Life and Work* (Chicago and London: University of Chicago Press, 2002), 178–87; Helmut Weihsmann, *Das Rote Wien* (Vienna: Promedia, 2002), 307; Mark Steinmetz and Sandy Panek, *Wien: Der Architektur Führer* (Berlin: Verlagshaus Braun, 2007), 172–73; August Sarnitz, *Architecture Vienna: 700 Buildings*, trans. by Susan Siegle (Vienna: Springer, 2008), 336–37; www.werkbundsiedlung.at.

463 Quoted in Long, "The Wayward Heir: Josef Frank's Vienna Years, 1885–1933," in Stritzler-Levine, ed., *Josef Frank, Architect and Designer*, 54.

464 For Frank's apartment building projects, see Long, *Josef Frank: Life and Work*, 75–84, 168–76.

465 Long, *Josef Frank: Life and Work*, 178.

466 Frank, ed., *Die internationale Werkbundsiedlung: Wien, 1932*, 8.

467 Long, *Josef Frank: Life and Work*, 182.

468 Blau, *The Architecture of Red Vienna, 1919–1934*, 132.

469 *Second Annual Report of the Homestead Commission, 1914* (Boston: Wright & Potter, 1915), 141; "Unione Cooperativa, Milan," *Monthly Review of the U.S. Bureau of Labor Statistics* 4 (January 1917): 646; *Consumers' Co-operative Societies* (New York: Haskell House, 1921), 115; Orazio Marcheselli, *Milanino: la prima città-giardino italiana* (Milan: Cordani, 1935); Anthony Sutcliffe, *Towards the Planned City: Germany, Britain, the United States and France, 1780–1914* (Oxford: Basil Blackwell, 1981), 187; Carlo Santi, "The Italian Garden City," *Abitare* 227 (September 1984): 71–73; Virgilio Vercelloni, *Il giardino a Milano, per pochi e per tutti, 1288–1945* (Milan: L'Archivolto, 1986), 306; Maurizio Boriani and Susanna Bortolotto, *Origini e sviluppo di una città giardino: L'esperienza del Milanino* (Milan: Guerini e associate, 1991); Jonathan Morris, *The Political Economy of Shopkeeping in Milan, 1886–1922* (Cambridge and New York: Cambridge University Press, 1993), 148; Alberto Corlaita, "Garden Cities in Italy: A Possible Future?" in Gabriele Tagliaventi, ed., *Garden City* (Rome: Gangemi Editore, 1994), 299; Benedetto Gravagnuolo, *Historia del Urbanismo en Europa, 1750–1960* (Madrid: Ediciones Akal, 1998), 129–30, 191; Manfredi Nicoletti, "Art Nouveau in Italy," in Nikolaus Pevsner, J. M. Richards, and Dennis Sharp, eds., *The Anti-Rationalists and the Rationalists* (Oxford: Architectural Press, 2000), 59; Giuseppe De Finetti, *Milano: Costruzione di una città* (Milan: Editore Ulrico Hoepli, 2002), 178–80; John Haywood, "A Garden Suburb in Milan," *Hampstead Garden Suburb News* 100 (Spring 2009): 11; www.comune.cusano-milanino.mi.it; www.provincia.milano.it.

470 Santi, "The Italian Garden City": 73.

471 Haywood, "A Garden Suburb in Milan": 11.

472 Enrico Coen-Cagli, *Il Porto di Venezia* (Venice: La Poligrafica Italiana, 1925); *Chambers's Encyclopedia* (Oxford: Pergamon Press, 1963), vol. 14: 276; Alvise Zorzi, *Venezia Scomparsa, volume primo: Storia di una secolare degradazione* (Milan: Electa Editrice, 1972), 242–44; Cesco Chinellis, *Porto Marghera, 1902–1926: alle origin del 'Problem di Venezia'* (Venice: Marsilio, 1979); Paola Somma, *Venezia nuova: la politica della casa, 1893–1941* (Venice: Marsilio, 1983), 101–6; Alessandro Filippo Nappi, *Storia de Marghera da periferia a città* (Mestre and Venice: Cetid, 1994); Valeria Farinati, "L'esperienza di Venezia," *Rassegna* 20 (1998): 97–98; B. De Marchi, "Learning from Citizens: A Venetian Experience," *Journal of Hazardous Materials* 78 (2000): 247–59; Deborah Howard, *The Architectural History of Venice*, rev. ed. (New Haven, Conn., and London: Yale University Press, 2002), 276, 280; Margaret Plant, *Venice: Fragile City, 1797–1997* (New Haven, Conn., and London: Yale University Press, 2002), 276–79; George Taylor, "Porto Marghera," www.nuovevie.vegapark.it; "Rise and Decline of the Venetian Industrial Site of Porto Marghera," www.decon.unipd.it/assets/pdf/ dp/0017.pdf; www.slideshare.net/VivaVenezia/alberi-a-marghera.

473 Howard, *The Architectural History of Venice*, 280.

474 Howard, *The Architectural History of Venice*, 280.

475 Irene De Guttry, *Guide to Modern Rome: From 1870 Until Today* (Rome: De Luca, 2001), 24.

476 Christopher Woodward, *The Buildings of Europe: Rome* (Manchester and New York: Manchester University Press, 1995), 25. Also see Marcello Piacentini, *Sulla conservazione della bellezza di Roma e sullo sviluppo della Città moderna* (Rome: Stabilimento Tipografico Aternum, 1916).

477 "Concorsi per tipo di case popolari da erigersi in Roma," *Architettura e Arti Decorative* 3 (March 1924): 330; Richard A. Etlin, *Modernism in Italian Architecture, 1890–1940* (Cambridge, Mass., and London: MIT Press, 1991), 102, 134, 142–50; Mario Sanfilippo, *La Costruzione di una Capitale: Roma, 1911–1945* (Milan: Silvana, 1992), 32, 92–93; Diane Ghirardo, "City and Suburb in Fascist Italy: Rome 1922–43," in Malcolm Quantrill and Bruce Webb, eds., *Urban Forms, Suburban Dreams* (College Station: Texas A&M University Press, 1993), 55; Steven Brooke, *Views of Rome* (New York: Rizzoli International Publications, 1995), 210; Woodward, *The Buildings of Europe: Rome*, 25, 138; Paolo Rosa, *La Città Antica Tra Storia e Urbanistica (1913–1957)* (Rome: Editrice Librerie Dedalo, 1998), 27–28, 44–45, 62; P. Misino, "Città Giardino Aniene," in *Il moderno attraverso Roma: 200 architetture scelte*, ed. Gaia Remiddi et al. (Rome: Palombi Editori, 2000), 168; De Guttry, *Guide to Modern Rome: From 1870 Until Today*, 25; Romana Stabile, *Regionalismo a Roma* (Roma : Librerie Dedalo, 2001), 123–26; Claudio Marsilio, *Montesacro: città giardino Aniene: memoria e identità di un quartiere di Roma* (Latina: Novecento, 2003); Ettore Maria Mazzola, ed., *"A Counter History" of Modern Architecture: Rome 1900–1940*, trans. by Philip Rand (Florence: Alinea Editrice, 2004), 32–37, 50, 134–35, 148; Dianne Bennett and William Graebner, *Rome: The Second Time* (Nashville: Curious Traveler Press, 2009), 140–41; Antonella De Michelis, "The Garden Suburb of the Garbatella, 1920–1929: Defining Community and Identity Through Planning in Post-War Rome," *Planning Perspectives* 24 (October 2009): 509–20; Simona Benedetti, "Contaminazione di tradizione e modernità nei quartieri popolari a Roma: 1920–30," in Marina Docci and Maria Grazia Turco, eds., *L'Architettura dell' "altra" modernità* (Rome: Gangemi Editore, 2010), 350–52; Michelangelo Sabatino, *Pride in Modesty: Modernist Architecture and the Vernacular Tradition in Italy* (Toronto: University of Toronto Press, 2010), 70–72; www.domuscittagiardino.it.

478 Comme di Roma, *Il problema edilizio: Per la costruzionde di nuove case* (Rome: Ufficio Municipale del Lavoro, 1920), 132–33, quoted in Etlin, *Modernism in Italian Architecture, 1890–1940*, 147.

479 Etlin, *Modernism in Italian Architecture, 1890–1940*, 147, 149. Also see Comme di Roma, *Il problema edilizio: Per la costruzionde di nuove case* (Rome: Ufficio Municipale del Lavoro, 1920), 221–22.

480 De Michelis, "The Garden Suburb of the Garbatella, 1920–1929: Defining Community and Identity Through Planning in Post-War Rome": 510.

481 Ghirardo, "City and Suburb in Fascist Italy: Rome 1922–43," in Quantrill and Webb, eds., *Urban Forms, Suburban Dreams*, 55.

482 Innocenzo Costantini, "Le Nuove Costruzioni dell'Istituto per le Case Popolari in Roma: La Borgata Giardino 'Garbatella,'" *Architettura e Arti Decorative* 2 (November 1922): 119–37; Dario Barbieri and M. Crosland Seabrooke, "The Urban Problem of Modern Rome," *Town Planning Review* 10 (September 1923): 145; "Concorsi per tipo di case popolari da erigersi in Roma," *Architettura e Arti Decorative* 3 (March 1924): 330; Fulvio Leoni and Guglielmo Monti, "Garbatella: Cité jardin et 'hôtels suburbains' dans la Rome fasciste," *L'Architecture d'Aujourd'hui* 189 (1977): 85–93; Dennis P. Doordan, *Building Modern Italy: Italian Architecture, 1914–1936* (New York: Princeton Architectural Press, 1988), 68, fig. 36; Jens Mollerup, "Garbatella," *Arkitekten* 90 (May 1988): 321–34; Diane Ghirardo, *Building New Communities: New Deal America and Fascist Italy* (Princeton, N.J.: Princeton University Press, 1989), 66; Richard A. Etlin, *Modernism in Italian Architecture, 1890–1940* (Cambridge, Mass., and London: MIT Press, 1991), 102, 134, 142, 145–49, 227, 272; Mario Sanfilippo, *La Costruzione di una Capitale: Roma, 1911–1945* (Milan: Silvana, 1992), 32, 94–95; Ilaria Armocida, *La Garbatella a Roma: da borgata a quartiere residenziale* (Rome: Dipartimento di planificazione territoriale e urbanistica, 1993); Andrés Duany, Elizabeth Plater-Zyberk, and Robert Alminana, *The New Civic Art: Elements of Town Planning* (New York: Rizzoli International Publications, 2003), 294; Diane Ghirardo, "City and Suburb in Fascist Italy: Rome 1922–43," in Malcolm Quantrill and Bruce Webb, eds., *Urban Forms, Suburban Dreams* (College Station: Texas A&M University Press, 1993), 55; Christopher Woodward, *The Buildings of Europe: Rome* (Manchester and New York: Manchester University Press, 1995), 138; Manuela Semmelmann, "La Garbatella," *Bauwelt* 89 (April 3, 1998): 700–713; Irene De Guttry, *Guide to Modern Rome: From 1870 Until Today* (Rome: De Luca, 2001), 68–72; Ettore Maria Mazzola, ed., *"A Counter History" of Modern Architecture: Rome 1900–1940*, trans. by Philip Rand (Florence: Alinea Editrice, 2004), 36, 40, 42, 44, 46, 48, 50, 52, 54, 56, 58, 166, 177–78, 226–29; Steven Brooke, *Views of Rome* (New York: Rizzoli International Publications, 1995), 208–9; Terry Kirk, *The Architecture of Modern Italy, Volume 2: Visions of Utopia, 1900–Present* (New York: Princeton Architectural Press, 2005), 124; Borden W. Painter Jr, *Mussolini's Rome: Rebuilding the Eternal City* (New York: Palgrave Macmillan, 2005), 96–97; Monica Sinatra, *La Garbatella a Roma: 1920–1940* (Milan: FrancoAngeli, 2006); Antonella De Michelis, "The Garden Suburb of the Garbatella, 1920–1929: Defining Community and Identity Through Planning in Post-War Rome," *Planning Perspectives* 24 (October 2009): 509–20; Simona Benedetti, "Contaminazione di tradizione e modernità nei quartieri popolari a Roma: 1920–30," in Marina Docci and Maria Grazia Turco, eds., *L'Architettura dell' "altra" modernità* (Rome: Gangemi Editore, 2010), 350–52; Michelangelo Sabatino, *Pride in Modesty: Modernist Architecture and the Vernacular Tradition in Italy* (Toronto: University of Toronto Press, 2010), 70–72; www.mimoa.eu/Italy/Rome/Garbatella; www.romeartlover.it/Garbatel.html.

483 Etlin, *Modernism in Italian Architecture, 1890–1940*, 147. Also see Comme di Roma, *Il problema edilizio: Per la costruzionde di nuove case* (Rome: Ufficio Municipale del Lavoro, 1920), 132, 207–8, 222.

484 De Michelis, "The Garden Suburb of the Garbatella, 1920–1929: Defining Community and Identity Through Planning in Post-War Rome": 511. Also see Ebenezer Howard, *Garden Cities of To-morrow* (London: S. Sonnenschein & Co., 1902; Cambridge, Mass.: MIT Press, 1965), 46.

485 Wesley Dougill, "Two New Towns in Italy: Littoria and Sabaudia," *Town Planning Review* 17 (June 1936): 43–50; Riccardo Mariani, "Le 'citta nuove' del periodo fascista," *Abitare* (October 1978): 76–91, 94–95; Henry A. Millon, "Some New Towns in Italy in the 1930s," in Henry Millon and Linda Nochlin, eds., *Art and Architecture in the Service of Politics* (Cambridge, Mass.: MIT Press, 1978), 326–41; Manfredo Tafuri and Francesco Dal Co, *Modern Architecture*, trans. by Robert Erich Wolf (New York: Harry N. Abrams, 1979), 415 (n.5); Ellen Ruth Shapiro, "Building Under Mussolini" (Ph.D. diss., Yale University, 1985): 199–215; Diane Ghirardo, *Building New Communities: New Deal America and Fascist Italy* (Princeton, N.J.: Princeton University Press, 1989), 26–28, 37, 40–88; David Watkin, *A History of Western Architecture*, 3rd ed. (New York: Watson-Guptill, 2000), 629–30; Borden W. Painter Jr., *Mussolini's Rome: Rebuilding the Eternal City* (New York: Palgrave Macmillan, 2005), 84–90; Federico Caprotti, *Mussolini's Cities: Internal Colonialism in Italy, 1930–1939* (Youngstown, N.Y.: Cambria Press, 2007), 115–53; Wolfgang Schivelbusch, *Three New Deals: Reflections on Roosevelt's America, Mussolini's Italy, and Hitler's Germany, 1933–1939* (New York: Picador, 2007), 142–53; Helga Tvinnereim, *Agro Pontino: Urbanism and Regional Development in Lazio Under Benito Mussolini*, trans. by Viviann Hansen-Aarones (Oslo: Solum Forlag, 2007); Vittorio Magnago Lampugnani, *Die Stadt im 20. Jahrhundert* (Berlin: Verlag Klaus Wagenbach, 2010), 477–78; Michelangelo Sabatino, "The Politics of *Mediterraneità* in Italian Modernist Architecture," in Jean-François Lejeune and Michelangelo Sabatino, eds., *Modern Architecture and the Mediterranean* (London and New York: Routlege, 2010), 57, 61–62; Alan Berger and Case Brown, "A New Systemic Nature for Mussolini's Landscape Urbanism," http://www.columbia.edu/~hom2104/Berger_PENNVIA_DIRT.pdf. Previous to his efforts to build in the Agro Pontino, Mussolini failed in his attempt to build a garden city (1923–25) in Sicily. See Salvatore Venezia, "Mussolinia di Sicilia," in Giorgio Pellegrini, ed., *Città di fondazione italiane: 1928–1942* (Latina: Novecento, 2005), 71–78.

486 Quoted in Arrigo Serpieri, "Bonifica," *Encyclopedia Italian* (1938), appendix I: 299.

487 Schivelbusch, *Three New Deals: Reflections on Roosevelt's America, Mussolini's Italy, and Hitler's Germany, 1933–1939*, 148.

488 Schivelbusch, *Three New Deals: Reflections on Roosevelt's America, Mussolini's Italy, and Hitler's Germany, 1933–1939*, 142.

489 Emmanuel de Thubert, "Littoria," *La Construction Moderne* 50 (June 1935): 758–71; M. Schmitt, "Littoria: die Eroberung einer Provinz," *Deutsche Bauzeitung* 69 (December 1935): 1022–32; Wesley Dougill, "Two New Towns in Italy: Littoria and Sabaudia," *Town Planning Review* 17 (June 1936): 43–50; Karl Ernst Rimbach, "Die vier neuen Städte Italiens," *Deutsche Bauzeitung* 70 (June 3, 1936): 475–80; A. Muñoz, "Le Corbusier parla di urbanistica romana," *L'Urbe* 1 (November 1936): 34; "The Post-Office, Littoria, Italy: Architect Angilo Mazzoni," *Architect and Building News* 149 (January 1937): 7–9; Giuseppe Nicolosi, "Le case popolari di Littoria nel quadro degli attuali orientamenti della edilizia popolare in Italia," *Architettura* 16 (January 1937): 21–35; "Casa di abitazione a Littoria," *Architettura* 19 (August 1940): 387–92; Nikolaus Pevsner, *Outline of European Architecture* (Baltimore: Penguin Books, 1960), 611; A. Mioni, "Littoria et Sabaudia," *Architecture* 395 (February 1976): 58–60; Henry A. Millon, "Some New Towns in Italy in the 1930s," in Henry Millon and Linda Nochlin, eds., *Art and Architecture in the Service of Politics* (Cambridge, Mass.: MIT Press, 1978), 327–30, 332, 335, 337, 340; Riccardo Mariani, "Le 'citta nuove' del periodo fascista," *Abitare* (October 1978): 76–91, 94–95; Manfredo Tafuri and Francesco Dal Co, *Modern Architecture*, trans. by Robert Erich Wolf (New York: Harry N. Abrams, 1979), 415 (n.5); Ellen Ruth Shapiro, "Building Under Mussolini" (Ph.D. diss., Yale University, 1985): 202–4, 209–12; Diane Ghirardo, *Building New Communities: New Deal America and Fascist Italy* (Princeton, N.J.: Princeton University Press, 1989), 26, 53, 60, 62–64, 67–75; Richard A. Etlin, *Modernism in Italian Architecture, 1890–1940* (Cambridge, Mass., and London: MIT Press, 1991), 294, 317, 593; Jean-Louis Cohen, "Gaston Bardet and 'Mussolini's Rome,'" *Zodiac* 17 (1997): 70–85; Massimiliano Vittori, Claudio Galeazzi, and Giorgio Muratore, eds., *Littoria, Latina: la storia, le architetture* (Latina: Novecento, 1999); David Watkin, *A History of Western Architecture*, 3rd ed. (New York: Watson-Guptill, 2000), 629; Carlo Fabrizio Carli and Massimiliano Vittori, *Oriolo Frezzotti, 1888–1965: Un Architetto in Territorio Pontino* (Latina: Novecento, 2002), 27, 58–59, 64–65; Hanne Storm Ofteland, "Sabaudia, 1934: Materialzing the Fascist, Corporate Town" (Ph.D. diss., University of Oslo-Institute for Art History, 2002): 46–47; Massimiliano Vittori, "Littoria," in Renato Besana, Carlo Fabrizio Carli, Leonardo Devoti, and Luigi Prisco, eds., *Metafisica Costruita* (Milan: Touring Club Italiano, 2002), 7, 25, 29, 37, 44, 77–81; Marcello Trabucco, *Latina: Segni, Forme e Volumi dal Cielo* (Latina: Arti Grafiche Archimio, 2004); Borden W. Painter Jr., *Mussolini's Rome: Rebuilding the Eternal City* (New York: Palgrave Macmillan, 2005), 85–89; Giorgio Pellegrini, ed., *Città di fondazione italiane: 1928–1942* (Latina: Novecento, 2005), 156–91; Flavio Mangione and Andrea Soffitta, eds., *L'architettura delle Case del Fascio nella Regione Lazio* (Florence: Alinea Editrice, 2006), 14–16, 44–45, 65, 67; Federico Caprotti, *Mussolini's Cities: Internal Colonialism in Italy, 1930–1939* (Youngstown, N.Y.: Cambria Press, 2007), 118, 124, 128, 131–34; Wolfgang Schivelbusch, *Three New Deals: Reflections on Roosevelt's America, Mussolini's Italy, and Hitler's Germany, 1933–1939* (New York: Picador, 2007), 146, 148, 150–52; Helga Tvinnereim, *Agro Pontino: Urbanism and Regional Development in Lazio Under Benito Mussolini*, trans. by Viviann Hansen-Aarones (Oslo: Solum Forlag, 2007), 50–51, fig. 10; Vittorio Magnago Lampugnani, *Die Stadt im 20. Jahrhundert* (Berlin: Verlag Klaus Wagenbach, 2010), 478–81; Michelangelo Sabatino, *Pride in Modesty: Modernist Architecture and the Vernacular Tradition in Italy* (Toronto: University of Toronto Press, 2010), 141–42.

490 Benito Mussolini, *Opera Omnis*, 44 vols. (Florence: La Fenice, 1951–78), vol. 3: 184–85, quoted and translated in Painter, *Mussolini's Rome: Rebuilding the Eternal City*, 87.

491 Dougill, "Two New Towns in Italy: Littoria and Sabaudia": 44.

492 Ghirardo, *Building New Communities: New Deal America and Fascist Italy*, 67. Giovannoni's book represented an expansion of ideas first published in 1913. See Gustavo Giovannoni, "Vecchie città ed edilizia nuova," *Nuova Antologia* 165 (June 1913): 449–72; Gustavo Giovannoni, *Veccie città ed edilizia nouva* (Turin: Unione tipografico-editrice torinese, 1931).

493 Ghirardo, *Building New Communities: New Deal America and Fascist Italy*, 64, 68, 71.

494 Ghirardo, *Building New Communities: New Deal America and Fascist Italy*, 70–71.

495 Dougill, "Two New Towns in Italy: Littoria and Sabaudia": 44, 46.

496 Le Corbusier, quoted in Muñoz, "Le Corbusier parla di urbanistica romana": 34, also quoted and translated in Etlin, *Modernism in Italian Architecture, 1890–1940*, 294.

497 Marcello Piacentini, "Sabaudia," *Architettura* 13 (June 1934): 321–57; Pierre Vago, "Sabaudia," *L'Architecture d'Aujourd'hui* 5 (September 1934): 17–30; Angelo Vicario, "Nuovi Edifici a Sabaudia," *Architettura* 14 (April 1935): 205–12; "Nuovi Edifici a Sabaudia," *Architettura* 14 (September 1935): 513–22; "Mercato coperto di Sabaudia," *Architettura* 14 (September 1935): 523–24; M. Schmitt, "Littoria: die Eroberung einer Provinz," *Deutsche Bauzeitung* 69 (December 1935): 1022–32; S. Gille-Delafon, "Le XIII Congrès International des Architectes," *La Construction Moderne* 51 (February 23, 1936): 428–36; Karl Ernst Rimbach, "Die vier neuen Städte Italiens," *Deutsche Bauzeitung* 70 (June 3, 1936): 475–80; Wesley Dougill, "Two New Towns in Italy: Littoria and Sabaudia," *Town Planning Review* 17 (June 1936): 43–50; "Alcuni recenti edifice sacri italiani," *Rassegna de Architettura* 10 (January 1938): 5–22; "L'église et le baptistère de Sabaudia," *L'Architecture d'Aujourd'hui* 9 (July 1938): 39; Nikolaus Pevsner, *Outline of European Architecture* (Baltimore: Penguin Books, 1960), 611; Silvia Danesi and Luciano Patetta, eds., *Il Razionalismo e L'Architettura in Italia durante il Fascismo* (Venice: La Biennale di Venezia, 1976), 162–64; A. Mioni, "Littoria et Sabaudia," *Architecture* 395 (February 1976): 58–60; Henry A. Millon, "Some New Towns in Italy in the 1930s," in Henry A. Millon and Linda Nochlin, eds., *Art and Architecture in the Service of Politics* (Cambridge, Mass.: MIT Press, 1978), 327, 330, 332, 334–37; Riccardo Mariani, "Le 'citta nuove' del periodo fascista," *Abitare* (October 1978): 76–91, 94–95; Manfredo Tafuri and Francesco Dal Co, *Modern Architecture*, trans. by Robert Erich Wolf (New York: Harry N. Abrams, 1979), 289, 415 (n.5); Richard Burdett, ed., *Sabaudia 1933: Città nuova fascista* (London: Architectural Association, 1981); David Wild, "Sabaudia—Città Nuova Fascista," *AA Files* 1 (July 1982): 71–73; Ellen Ruth Shapiro, "Building Under Mussolini" (Ph.D. diss., Yale University, 1985): 203–7, 416–20; Gerrit Confurius, "Rationalismus im Faschismus," *Bauwelt* 77 (February 21, 1986): 248–59; Dennis P. Doordan, *Building Modern Italy: Italian Architecture, 1914–1936* (New York: Princeton Architectural Press, 1988), 105–9; Diane Ghirardo, *Building New Communities:*

New Deal America and Fascist Italy (Princeton, N.J.: Princeton University Press, 1989), 74–79; Richard A. Etlin, *Modernism in Italian Architecture, 1890–1940* (Cambridge, Mass., and London: MIT Press, 1991), 228, 429–30, 486–87; Alberto Corlaita, "Garden Cities in Italy: A Possible Future," in Gabriele Tagliaventi, ed., *Garden City* (Rome: Gangemi Editore, 1994), 304–5; Lars Marcus, "Sabaudia Och Det Modernas Skugga," *Arkitektur* 95 (November/December 1995): 4–13; Michael McNamara, "Sensuous Motion, Sensuous Boundaries, Sensuous Place: Angiolo Mazzoni's Blue Building," *Oz* 19 (1997): 40–45; Jean-Louis Cohen, "Gaston Bardet and 'Mussolini's Rome,'" *Zodiac* 17 (1997): 70–85; Claudio Galeazzi, ed., *Sabaudia: quando la cronaca diventa storia* (Latina: Novecento, 1998); Giorgio Muratore, "Sabaudia," *Abitare* 408 (July 2001): 218–23; Renato Besana, Carlo Fabrizio Carli, Leonardo Devoti, and Luigi Prisco, eds., *Metafisica Costruita* (Milan: Touring Club Italiano, 2002), 9, 28, 61, 83–86, 110–14; Hanne Storm Ofteland, "Sabaudia, 1934: Materialzing the Fascist, Corporate Town" (Ph.D. diss., University of Oslo-Institute for Art History, 2002); Andrés Duany, Elizabeth Plater-Zyberk, and Robert Alminana, *The New Civic Art: Elements of Town Planning* (New York: Rizzoli International Publications, 2003), 49; Borden W. Painter Jr., *Mussolini's Rome: Rebuilding the Eternal City* (New York: Palgrave Macmillan, 2005), 88–89; Terry Kirk, *The Architecture of Modern Italy, Volume 2: Visions of Utopia, 1900–Present* (New York: Princeton Architectural Press, 2005), 125–27; Giorgio Pellegrini, ed., *Città di fondazione italiane: 1928–1942* (Latina: Novecento, 2005), 192–207; Flavio Mangione and Andrea Soffitta, eds., *L'architettura delle Case del Fascio nella Regione Lazio* (Florence: Alinea Editrice, 2006), 46; Federico Caprotti, *Mussolini's Cities: Internal Colonialism in Italy, 1930–1939* (Youngstown, N.Y.: Cambria Press, 2007), 118, 128, 135–37, 143–48, 152–53; Wolfgang Schivelbusch, *Three New Deals: Reflections on Roosevelt's America, Mussolini's Italy, and Hitler's Germany, 1933–1939* (New York: Picador, 2007), 146–47; Helga Tvinnereim, *Agro Pontino: Urbanism and Regional Development in Lazio Under Benito Mussolini*, trans. by Viviann Hansen-Aarones (Oslo: Solum Forlag, 2007), 50–56, 113–62, 260–84; Vittorio Magnago Lampugnani, *Die Stadt im 20. Jahrhundert* (Berlin: Verlag Klaus Wagenbach, 2010), 481–83; Michelangelo Sabatino, "The Politics of *Mediterraneità* in Italian Modernist Architecture," in Jean-François Lejeune and Michelangelo Sabatino, eds., *Modern Architecture and the Mediterranean* (London and New York: Routlege, 2010), 57, 61–62; Michelangelo Sabatino, *Pride in Modesty: Modernist Architecture and the Vernacular Tradition in Italy* (Toronto: University of Toronto Press, 2010), 141–42; Diane Ghirardo, *Italy: Modern Architectures in History* (London: Reaktion Books, 2013), 109–16; http://www.handtomouth.net/Sabaudia; www.sabaudia.net.

498 Quoted and translated in Burdett, ed., *Sabaudia 1933: Città nuova fascista*, 12.

499 "Come sorgerà Sabaudia: la mostra dei progetti del nuovo Commune Pontino," *Il Popolo d'Italia* (July 27, 1933), 6, quoted and translated in Ofteland, "Sabaudia, 1934: Materialzing the Fascist, Corporate Town": 51.

500 Piacentini, "Sabaudia," quoted and translated in Burdett, ed., *Sabaudia 1933: Città nuova fascista*, 28, also quoted in Ofteland, "Sabaudia, 1934: Materialzing the Fascist, Corporate Town": 60.

501 Ofteland, "Sabaudia, 1934: Materialzing the Fascist, Corporate Town": 56–57.

502 Kirk, *The Architecture of Modern Italy, Volume 2: Visions of Utopia, 1900–Present*, 127.

503 Gaston Bardet, *Une nouvelle ère romaine sous le signe du Faisceau: La Rome de Mussolini* (Paris: Massin, 1937), 308–9, quoted and translated in Cohen, "Gaston Bardet and 'Mussolini's Rome'": 81.

504 Richard Burdett, "Introduction," in Burdett, ed., *Sabaudia 1933: Città nuova fascista*, 3.

505 Tafuri and Dal Co, *Modern Architecture*, 415 (n.5).

506 Valentino Orsolini Cencelli, "Littoria provincial rurale," *La Conquista della Terra* 5 (December 1934): 5; Karl Ernst Rimbach, "Die vier neuen Städte Italiens," *Deutsche Bauzeitung* 70 (June 3, 1936): 475–80; Riccardo Mariani, *Fascismo e città nuove* (Milan: Feltrinelli, 1976), 260–61; Henry A. Millon, "Some New Towns in Italy in the 1930s," in Henry A. Millon and Linda Nochlin, eds., *Art and Architecture in the Service of Politics* (Cambridge, Mass.: MIT Press, 1978), 327, 331–32, 338, 340; Riccardo Mariani, "Le 'citta nuove' del periodo fascista," *Abitare* (October 1978): 76–91, 94–95; Manfredo Tafuri and Francesco Dal Co, *Modern Architecture*, trans. by Robert Erich Wolf (New York: Harry N. Abrams, 1979), 415 (n.5); Claudio Galeazzi, *Pontinia: Tra storia e cronaca* (Latina: Comune di Pontinia, 1985); Ellen Ruth Shapiro, "Building Under Mussolini" (Ph.D. diss., Yale University, 1985): 199, 212, 427–29; Diane Ghirardo, *Building New Communities: New Deal America and Fascist Italy* (Princeton, N.J.: Princeton University Press, 1989), 67, 79–80; Hanne Storm Ofteland, "Sabaudia, 1934: Materialzing the Fascist, Corporate Town" (Ph.D. diss., University of Oslo-Institute for Art History, 2002): 47–49, 123–24, plate 9; Borden W. Painter Jr., *Mussolini's Rome: Rebuilding the Eternal City* (New York: Palgrave Macmillan, 2005), 85–87, 89–90; Giorgio Pellegrini, ed., *Città di fondazione italiane: 1928–1942* (Latina: Novecento, 2005), 208–17; Flavio Mangione and Andrea Soffitta, eds., *L'architettura delle Case del Fascio nella Regione Lazio* (Florence: Alinea Editrice, 2006), 50–52; Federico Caprotti, *Mussolini's Cities: Internal Colonialism in Italy, 1930–1939* (Youngstown, N.Y.: Cambria Press, 2007), 131, 133–34, 148; Wolfgang Schivelbusch, *Three New Deals: Reflections on Roosevelt's America, Mussolini's Italy, and Hitler's Germany, 1933–1939* (New York: Picador, 2007), 146; www.pontiniaweb.it; www.sabaudia.net.

507 Ofteland, "Sabaudia, 1934: Materialzing the Fascist, Corporate Town": 47.

508 Giuseppe Pagano, quoted in Mariani, "Le 'citta nuove' del periodo fascista": 90.

509 Alfredo Giarratana, "Inchiesta su Aprilia," *Quadrante* 33 (1936); Karl Ernst Rimbach, "Aprilia," *Deutsche Bauzeitung* 70 (April 8, 1936): 317–20; Marcello Piacentini, "Aprilia," *Architettura* 15 (May 1936): 193–212; Karl Ernst Rimbach, "Die vier neuen Städte Italiens," *Deutsche Bauzeitung* 70 (June 3, 1936): 475–80; "Aprilia," *Architettura* 17 (July 1938): 393–416; "Église paroissiale à aprilia," *L'Architecture d'Aujourd'hui* 9 (July 1938): 40; "Un centro rurale dell'agro pontino, Aprilia," *Architettura Italiana* 33 (August 1938): 237–49; "Iglesia parroquial de Aprilia, Italia," *Arquitectura* 9 (November 1943): 225; Silvia Danesi and Luciano Patetta, eds., *Il Razionalismo e L'Architettura in Italia durante il Fascismo* (Venice: La Biennale di Venezia, 1976), 164–66; Riccardo Mariani, *Fascismo e città nuove* (Milan: Feltrinelli, 1976), 62; Henry A. Millon, "Some New Towns in Italy in the 1930s," in Henry Millon and Linda Nochlin, eds., *Art and Architecture in the Service of Politics* (Cambridge, Mass.: MIT Press, 1978), 327, 332–33, 335, 339–40; Riccardo Mariani, "Le 'citta nuove' del periodo fascista," *Abitare* (October 1978): 76–91, 94–95; Manfredo Tafuri and Francesco Dal Co, *Modern Architecture*, trans. by Robert Erich Wolf (New York: Harry N. Abrams, 1979), 415 (n.5); Ellen Ruth Shapiro, "Building Under Mussolini" (Ph.D. diss., Yale University, 1985): 207–9, 421–22; Diane Ghirardo, *Building New Communities: New Deal America and Fascist Italy* (Princeton, N.J.: Princeton University Press, 1989), 80, 183; Giovanni Papi, "Aprilia ritrovata," in Renato Besana, Carlo Fabrizio Carli, Leonardo Devoti, and Luigi Prisco, eds., *Metafisica Costruita* (Milan: Touring Club Italiano, 2002), 120–27; Hanne Storm Ofteland, "Sabaudia, 1934: Materialzing the Fascist, Corporate Town" (Ph.D. diss., University of Oslo-Institute for Art History, 2002): 16, 46, 48–49; Borden W. Painter Jr., *Mussolini's Rome: Rebuilding the Eternal City* (New York: Palgrave Macmillan, 2005), 86, 90; Giovanni Papi, ed., *Aprilia: Arte, Architettura, Urbanistica* (Rome: Gangemi Editore, 2005); Giorgio Pellegrini, ed., *Città di fondazione italiane: 1928–1942* (Latina: Novecento, 2005), 218–28; Arturo Cucciolla, *Vecchie Città/Città Nuove: Concezio Petrucci, 1926–1946* (Bari: Edizioni Dedalo, 2006), 213–45; Flavio Mangione and Andrea Soffitta, eds., *L'architettura delle Case del Fascio nella Regione Lazio* (Florence: Alinea Editrice, 2006), 47–48; Federico Caprotti, *Mussolini's Cities: Internal Colonialism in Italy, 1930–1939* (Youngstown, N.Y.: Cambria Press, 2007), 118, 131, 133–34; Vittorio Magnago Lampugnani, *Die Stadt im 20. Jahrhundert* (Berlin: Verlag Klaus Wagenbach, 2010), 484–85.

510 Shapiro, "Building Under Mussolini": 207. Also see Mariani, *Fascismo e città nuove*, 62.

511 Ofteland, "Sabaudia, 1934: Materialzing the Fascist, Corporate Town": 48.

512 Shapiro, "Building Under Mussolini": 207.

513 Shapiro, "Building Under Mussolini": 207.

514 Ghirardo, *Building New Communities: New Deal America and Fascist Italy*, 80.

515 Millon, "Some New Towns in Italy in the 1930s," in Millon and Nochlin, eds., *Art and Architecture in the Service of Politics*, 332, 335.

516 Caprotti, *Mussolini's Cities: Internal Colonialism in Italy, 1930–1939*, 134.

517 Giarratana, "Inchiesta su Aprilia," *Quadrante*, quoted and translated in Ofteland, "Sabaudia, 1934: Materialzing the Fascist, Corporate Town": 48.

518 "Concorso per il Piano Regolatore di Pomezia," *Architettura* 17 (September 1938): 551–66; Henry A. Millon, "Some New Towns in Italy in the 1930s," in Henry Millon and Linda Nochlin, eds., *Art and Architecture in the Service of Politics* (Cambridge, Mass.: MIT Press, 1978), 327, 332–33, 335, 340; Riccardo Mariani, "Le 'citta nuove' del periodo fascista," *Abitare* (October 1978): 76–91, 94–95; Manfredo Tafuri and Francesco Dal Co, *Modern Architecture*, trans. by Robert Erich Wolf (New York: Harry N. Abrams, 1979), 415 (n.5); Diane Ghirardo, *Building New Communities: New Deal America and Fascist Italy* (Princeton, N.J.: Princeton University Press, 1989), 40, 53, 81, 183; Hanne Storm Ofteland, "Sabaudia, 1934: Materialzing the Fascist, Corporate Town" (Ph.D. diss., University of Oslo-Institute for Art History, 2002): 16, 46, 48–49, 126–27; Borden W. Painter Jr., *Mussolini's Rome: Rebuilding the Eternal City* (New York: Palgrave Macmillan, 2005), 86, 89–90; Giorgio Pellegrini, ed., *Città di fondazione italiane: 1928–1942* (Latina: Novecento, 2005), 146–54; Arturo Cucciolla, *Vecchie Città/Città Nuove: Concezio Petrucci, 1926–1946* (Bari: Edizioni Dedalo, 2006), 245–56; Federico Caprotti, *Mussolini's Cities: Internal Colonialism in Italy, 1930–1939* (Youngstown, N.Y.: Cambria Press, 2007), 118, 131, 133–34; Vittorio Magnago Lampugnani, *Die Stadt im 20. Jahrhundert* (Berlin: Verlag Klaus Wagenbach, 2010), 485.

519 Ghirardo, *Building New Communities: New Deal America and Fascist Italy*, 183.

520 Buenaventura Bassegoda, "Cuestiones artísticas, el parque Güell," *El Diario de Barcelona* (January 14, 1903): 69–70; Joan Rubió, "Dificultats per a arribar a la síntesi arquetectònica," *Anuario: Asociacion de Arquitectos de Cataluña* (1913): 63–79; C. M. Villies-Stuart, *Spanish Gardens, Their History, Types, and Features* (London: B. T. Batsford, 1929), 132; George R. Collins, *Antonio Gaudí* (New York: George Braziller, 1960), 9, 17–19, 31, figs. 3, 66–71; Carola Giedion-Welcker, *Park Güell de A. Gaudí* (Barcelona: Ediciones La Poligrafa, 1966); Arleen Pabon-Charneco, "The Architectural Collaborators of Antoni Gaudí" (Ph.D. diss., Northwestern University, 1983): 116–22, figs. 153–59; Dennis J. De Witt and Elizabeth R. De Witt, *Modern Architecture in Europe: A Guide to Buildings Since the Industrial Revolution* (New York: E. P. Dutton, 1987), 120–21; Michael Jacobs, *Blue Guide: Barcelona* (London: A & C Black; New York: W.W. Norton, 1992), 149–50; Christopher Woodward, *The Buildings of Europe: Barcelona* (Manchester and New York: Manchester University Press, 1992), 74–75; Conrad Kent and Dennis Prindle, *Park Güell* (New York: Princeton Architectural Press, 1993); Josep M. Carandell, *Park Güell: Gaudí's Utopia* (Sant Lluis, Spain: Triangle Postals, 1998); Gijs Van Hensbergen, *Gaudí* (London: HarperCollins, 2001), 142–51; Maria Antonietta Crippa, ed., *Living Gaudí: The Architects Complete Vision* (New York: Rizzoli International Publications, 2002), 50, 72–80, 198–227; Manuel Gausa, Marta Cervelló, and Maurici Pla, *Barcelona: A Guide to Its Modern Architecture, 1860–2002* (Barcelona: Actar, 2002), D: 10; José Antonio Martínez Lapeña and Elías Torres, *Park Güell* (Barcelona: Gustavo Gili, 2002); Alejandro Lapunzina, *Architecture of Spain* (Westport, Conn., and London: Greenwood Press, 2005), 176–82; Damien Simonis, *Barcelona* (London: Lonely Planet Publications, 2006), 111; Carlos Giordano, *Park Güell: A Magical Place Originally Conceived as a Select Garden City* (Barcelona, Dos de Arte, 2010).

521 De Witt and De Witt, *Modern Architecture in Europe: A Guide to Buildings Since the Industrial Revolution*, 120.

522 Van Hensbergen, *Gaudí*, 143.

523 Pabon-Charneco, "The Architectural Collaborators of Antoni Gaudí": 118.

524 Kent and Prindle, *Park Güell*, 90.

525 Simonis, *Barcelona*, 111.

526 De Witt and De Witt, *Modern Architecture in Europe: A Guide to Buildings Since the Industrial Revolution*, 120.

527 Quoted in Van Hensbergen, *Gaudí*, 144.

528 Róbert Fleischl, *Munkáslakótelepek: A Kispesti munkástelep tervezése tárgyában* (Budapest: Magyar Építőművészek Szövetsége, 1908); Charles Scott, "Hungarian Paradigm for Urban Design," *Inland Architect* 37 (March–April 1993): 63–64; Gergely Nagy, *Kertvárosunk, a Wekerle* (Budapest: Szelényi Ház, 1994); János Gerle et al., *Architectural Guide: Architecture in Budapest from the Turn of the Century to the Present* (Budapest: 6 BT Kiadása, 1997), 107; Edwin Heathcote, *Budapest: A Guide to Twentieth-Century Architecture* (London:

Ellipsis, 1997), 212–13; János Gerle, "Hungarian Architecture from 1900 to 1918," in Dora Wiebenson and Jósef Sisa, eds., *The Architecture of Historic Hungary* (Cambridge, Mass., and London: MIT Press, 1998), 236–39; Anthony Gall, "Kós a Budapest e in Transilvania," *Domus* 804 (May 1998): 117–24; Gergely Nagy, *Wekerle Estate, Budapest* (Budapest: Magyar Kepek, 2000); Anthony Gall, *The Workshop of Károly Kós: Essays and Archives* (Budapest: Mundus Magyar Egyetemi Kiadó, 2002), 63–68, 248–59; Anita Poletti-Anderson, "The Search for a Hungarian National Style: The Fiatalok and the National Folk Movement" (Ph.D. diss., University of Virginia, 2002): 83–87, 315–21; Paul Reuber, "Transylvanian Treat," *Canadian Architect* 47 (January 2002): 27; Mervyn Miller, "Garden Cities and Suburbs: At Home and Abroad," *Journal of Planning History* 1 (February 2002): 6–28; Edward R. Bosley, "The Workshop of Károly Kós: Essays and Archives," book review, *Centropa* 4 (September 2004): 293–94; Gergely Nagy, *Garden Cities: The British Example in Hungary* (Budapest: Magyar Képek, 2008); András Nagy, "Wekerle Estate—A Village in the City," http://www.spottedbylocal.com/budapest/wekerle-estate; "Wekerle Estate," http://budapestpocketguide.com.

529 Heathcote, *Budapest: A Guide to Twentieth-Century Architecture*, 212.

530 Miller, "Garden Cities and Suburbs: At Home and Abroad": 11–13.

531 See Jaromir Štván, "Town Planning in Czechoslovakia: I," *Town & Country Planning* 26 (January 1958): 69–72; Jaromir Štván, "Town Planning in Czechoslovakia: II," *Town & Country Planning* 26 (March 1958): 121–24; Jiří Musil, Vladimír Šlapeta, and Jaroslav Novak, "Czech Mate for Letchworth," *Town & Country Planning* 53 (November 1984): 314–15; Cliff Hague and Alan Prior, "Planning in Czechoslovakia: Retrospect and Prospects," *Planning Practice & Research* 6 (Summer 1991): 19–24; Jane Pavitt, "The Bata Project: A Social and Industrial Experiment," *Twentieth Century Architecture* 1 (Summer 1994): 37; Rostislav Švácha, *The Architecture of New Prague, 1895–1945*, trans. by Alexandra Büchler (Cambridge, Mass., and London: MIT Press, 1995), 153–58; Jane Pavitt, "From the Garden to the Factory: Urban Visions in Czechoslovakia Between the Wars," in Macolm Gee, Tim Kirk, and Jill Steward, eds., *The City in Central Europe: Culture and Society from 1800 to the Present* (Aldershot, England, and Brookfield, Vt.: Ashgate, 1999), 27–40; Pavel Šopák, "Workers' Housing Colonies," in *Jan Kotěra, 1871–1923: The Founder of Modern Czech Architecture*, trans. by Karolina Vočadlová (Prague: Municipal House, 2001), 352–69.

532 Jan Kotěra, quoted in Vladimír Šlapeta and Wojciech Leśnikowski, "Functionalism in Czechoslovakian Architecture," in Wojciech Leśnikowski, ed., *East European Modernism: Architecture in Czechoslovakia, Hungary, and Poland Betweeen the Wars* (New York: Rizzoli International Publications, 1996), 59.

533 Jiří Musil, Vladimír Šlapeta, and Jaroslav Novak, "Czech Mate for Letchworth," *Town & Country Planning* 53 (November 1984): 314–15; Cliff Hague and Alan Prior, "Planning in Czechoslovakia: Retrospect and Prospects," *Planning Practice & Research* 6 (Summer 1991): 19–24; Jane Pavitt, "The Bata Project: A Social and Industrial Experiment," *Twentieth Century Architecture* 1 (Summer 1994): 37; Rostislav Švácha, *The Architecture of New Prague, 1895–1945*, trans. by Alexandra Büchler (Cambridge, Mass., and London: MIT Press, 1995), 154–56; Ákos Moravánsky, *Competing Visions: Aesthetic Invention and Social Imagination in Central European Architecture, 1867–1918* (Cambridge, Mass., and London: MIT Press, 1998), 60; Jane Pavitt, "From the Garden to the Factory: Urban Visions in Czechoslovakia Between the Wars," in Macolm Gee, Tim Kirk, and Jill Steward, eds., *The City in Central Europe: Culture and Society from 1800 to the Present* (Aldershot, England, and Brookfield, Vt.: Ashgate, 1999), 32–33, fig. 2.2; Jane Pavitt, *Prague* (Manchester and New York: Manchester University Press, 2000), 101–2; *Prague, 20th Century Architecture*, 2nd ed. (Prague: Zlatý řez, 2008), 119; Marek Lehmann, "Garden City," www.archinet.cz; http://www.radio.cz/cz/clanek/99732.

534 Pavitt, "From the Garden to the Factory: Urban Visions in Czechoslovakia Between the Wars," in Gee, Kirk, and Steward, eds., *The City in Central Europe*, 33.

535 Pavitt, "From the Garden to the Factory: Urban Visions in Czechoslovakia Between the Wars," in Gee, Kirk, and Steward, eds., *The City in Central Europe*, 32–33.

536 Jaromir Štván, "Town Planning in Czechoslovakia: I," *Town & Country Planning* 26 (January 1958): 69–72; Jiří Musil, Vladimír Šlapeta, and Jaroslav Novak, "Czech Mate for Letchworth," *Town & Country Planning* 53 (November 1984): 314–15; Vladimir Scheufler, "The Apartment Building in Prague Suburbs," *Urban Anthropology* 13 (Winter 1984): 368; Rostislav Švácha, *Od moderny k funkcionalismu* (Prague: Odeon, 1985), 170; Jaroslava Staňková, Jiři Štursa, and Svatopluk Voděra, *Prague: Eleven Centuries of Architecture* (Prague: PAV, 1992), 298; Rostislav Švácha, *The Architecture of New Prague, 1895–1945*, trans. by Alexandra Büchler (Cambridge, Mass., and London: MIT Press, 1995), 155; Jane Pavitt, "From the Garden to the Factory: Urban Visions in Czechoslovakia Between the Wars," in Macolm Gee, Tim Kirk, and Jill Steward, eds., *The City in Central Europe: Culture and Society from 1800 to the Present* (Aldershot, England, and Brookfield, Vt.: Ashgate, 1999), 33–34, fig. 2.3; Jane Pavitt, *Prague* (Manchester and New York: Manchester University Press, 2000), 105; Marek Lehmann, "Garden City," www.archinet.cz; http://www.radio.cz/cz/clanek/99732; "Spořilov," www.prostor-ad.cz; www.sporilov.info.

537 Vladimir Scheufler, "The Apartment Building in Prague Suburbs," *Urban Anthropology* 13 (Winter 1984): 368; Rostislav Švácha, *The Architecture of New Prague, 1895–1945*, trans. by Alexandra Büchler (Cambridge, Mass., and London: MIT Press, 1995), 155; Jane Pavitt, "From the Garden to the Factory: Urban Visions in Czechoslovakia Between the Wars," in Macolm Gee, Tim Kirk, and Jill Steward, eds., *The City in Central Europe: Culture and Society from 1800 to the Present* (Aldershot, England, and Brookfield, Vt.: Ashgate, 1999), 33–34.

538 Pavitt, "From the Garden to the Factory: Urban Visions in Czechoslovakia Between the Wars," in Gee, Kirk, and Steward, eds., *The City in Central Europe*, 34.

539 Władysław Dobrzyński, "The Movement in Poland," *Garden Cities and Town Planning* 1 (September 1911): 178–80. Also see Edward Ewing Pratt, "The Foreign Department: A Garden Cities Association for Poland," *American City* 8 (June 1913): 626–27.

540 Dobrzyński, "The Movement in Poland": 179.

541 David Turnock, *The Economy of East Central Europe, 1815–1989: Stages of Transformation in a Peripheral Region* (London and New York: Routledge, 2006), 247; Anna Żukowska-Maziarska, *A Guide to the Garden-City Podkowa Leśna "Horseshoe Grove"*, trans. by Philip Earl Steele (Podkowa Leśna: Friends of Podkowa Leśna, 2008); Magdalena Prosińska, "Architecture," in www.otwarteogrody.pl; http://free.art.pl/podkowa.magazyn/nr49/jawornicki.htm; www.architektura.info/index.php/wydarzenia_architektoniczne/antoni_jawornicki_architekt_i_urbanista_1886_1950; www.ckiopodkowa.pl; www.intbau.org/podkowalesna2008.htm; www.moja-warszawa.waw.pl/str/Maz_Podkowa_Lesna.html; www.podkowalesna.pl.

Chapter 7

1 "Canada," *American Architect and Building News* 61 (September 24, 1898): 102; Donald Campbell Masters, *The Rise of Toronto, 1850–1900* (Toronto: University of Toronto Press, 1947), 170; Liz Lundell, *The Estates of Old Toronto* (Erin, Canada: Boston Mills Press, 1997), 94–95; Philip Pregill and Nancy Volkman, *Landscapes in History: Design and Planning in the Eastern and Western Traditions* (New York: John Wiley, 1999), 534; Tom Cruickshank, *Old Toronto Houses* (Toronto: Firefly Books, 2003), 59, 212–13.

2 Pregill and Volkman, *Landscapes in History: Design and Planning in the Eastern and Western Traditions*, 534.

3 "Canada": 102.

4 William Dendy and William Kilbourn, *Toronto Observed: Its Architecture, Patrons and History* (Toronto: Oxford University Press, 1986), 175–77; *The Revised Wychwood Park Heritage Conservation District Plan* (Toronto: Toronto Historical Board, November 1994); Liz Lundell, *The Estates of Old Toronto* (Erin, Canada: Boston Mills Press, 1997), 84–85; John Blumenson, "Wychwood Park," in Nancy Byrtus, Mark Fram, and Michael McClelland, eds., *East/West: A Guide to Where People Live in Downtown Toronto* (Toronto: Couch House Toronto, 1998), 78, 79; Philip Pregill and Nancy Volkman, *Landscapes in History: Design and Planning in the Eastern and Western Traditions* (New York: John Wiley, 1999), 537.

5 *The Revised Wychwood Park Heritage Conservation District Plan*, 1.

6 *The Revised Wychwood Park Heritage Conservation District Plan*, 7.

7 "Prince Rupert to Be the City Beautiful," *The Globe* (Toronto) (November 24, 1906); "Prince Rupert," *Canadian Life and Resources* V (March 1907): 9–11; "Projected Plan of the Future City of Prince Rupert," *Victoria Daily Colonist* (September 8, 1908): 16; Raymond Unwin, *Town Planning in Practice: An Introduction to the Art of Designing Cities and Suburbs* (1909; New York: Princeton Architectural Press, 1994), 89; "City Built to Order; Prince Rupert, B. C. Is About Ready for Business," *Washington Post* (April 11, 1909), E: 2; George D. Hall, "The Future Prince Rupert as Conceived by the Landscape Architects," *Architectural Record* 26 (August 1909): 97–106; "A City Made to Order," *Canadian Life and Resources* VIII (March 1910): 18–20; "Prince Rupert, B. C.—A City Built to Order," *American Review of Reviews* 41 (April 1910): 475–76; Anthony A. Barrett and Rhodri Windsor Liscombe, *Francis Rattenbury and British Columbia: Architecture and Challenge in the Imperial Age* (Vancouver: University of British Columbia Press, 1983), 181, 225, 226, 245; Gerald Hodge, *Planning Canadian Communities: An Introduction to the Principles, Practice and Participants* (Scarborough, Ontario: Nelson Canada, 1989), 63; Harold Kalman, *A History of Canadian Architecture, Volume 2* (New York: Oxford University Press, 1994), 655–57; Alan Emmet, *So Fine a Prospect: Historic New England Gardens* (Hanover, N. H.: University Press of New England, 1996), 221; Meredith Kaplan, "George Duffield Hall," in Charles Birnbaum and Robin Karson, eds., *Pioneers of American Landscape Design* (New York: McGraw Hill, 2000), 156–58; *Prince Rupert: An Illustrated History* (Prince Rupert, B. C.: Prince Rupert City & Regional Archives Society, 2010), esp. pp. 26–43.

8 Hall, "The Future Prince Rupert as Conceived by the Landscape Architects": 104–5.

9 Hall, "The Future Prince Rupert as Conceived by the Landscape Architects": 105.

10 Hall, "The Future Prince Rupert as Conceived by the Landscape Architects": 106.

11 Kalman, *A History of Canadian Architecture, Volume 2*, 657.

12 Kalman, *A History of Canadian Architecture, Volume 2*, 656.

13 Deryck W. Holdsworth, "House and Home in Vancouver: Images of West Coast Urbanism, 1886–1929," in Gilbert A. Stelter and Alan F. J. Artibise, eds., *The Canadian City: Essays in Urban History* (1966; Toronto: Macmillan of Canada, 1979), 201–2; L. D. McCann, "Planning and Building the Corporate Suburb of Mount Royal, 1910–1925," *Planning Perspectives* 11 (1996): 270, 271; Lance Berelowitz, *Dream City: Vancouver and the Global Imagination* (Vancouver: Douglas & McIntyre, 2005), 97, 100; "Walking Tour: Shaughnessy," in http://vancouver.ca/COMMSVCS/planning/heritage/walks/w_sh_in.htm.

14 John Sewell, *The Shape of the City: Toronto Struggles with Modern Planning* (Toronto: University of Toronto Press, 1993), 50, 52; Witold Rybczynski, *City Life: Urban Expectations in a New World* (New York: Scribner, 1995), 190; L. D. McCann, "Planning and Building the Corporate Suburb of Mount Royal, 1910–1925," *Planning Perspectives* 11 (1996): 259–301.

15 Frederick G. Todd, quoted in McCann, "Planning and Building the Corporate Suburb of Mount Royal, 1910–1925": 279.

16 Sewell, *The Shape of the City: Toronto Struggles with Modern Planning*, 50.

17 McCann, "Planning and Building the Corporate Suburb of Mount Royal, 1910–1925": 283.

18 John Sewell, *The Shape of the City: Toronto Struggles with Modern Planning* (Toronto: University of Toronto Press, 1993), 51, 52; Nancy Byrtus, Mark Fram, and Michael McClellan, *East/West: A Guide to Where People Live in Downtown Toronto* (Toronto: Coach House Books, 1998), 156–57.

19 Sewell, *The Shape of the City: Toronto Struggles with Modern Planning*, 52.

20 John Sewell, *The Shape of the City: Toronto Struggles with Modern Planning* (Toronto: University of Toronto Press, 1993), 44–45. Also see Ian Ellingham, "Ontario Places: Lawrence Park Lessons," *Perspectives: The Journal of the Ontario Association of Architects* 6 (Spring 1998): 30; Eric Ross Arthur and Stephen A. Otto, *Toronto: No Mean City*, 3rd ed. (Toronto: University of Toronto Press, 2003), 243.

21 *Tuxedo, Detailed Area Plan* (Winnipeg: Metropolitan Corporation of Greater Winnipeg Planning Division, November 1970); Ian McDonald and Rosemary Malaher, "History and Walking Tour of Tuxedo," (Manitoba Historical Society, May 1991), in http://www.mhs.mb.ca/docs/features/walkingtours/tuxedo/index.shtml; Harold Kalman, *A History of Canadian Architecture, Volume 2* (New York: Oxford University Press,

1994), 658; L. D. McCann, "Planning and Building the Corporate Suburb of Mount Royal, 1910–1925," *Planning Perspectives* 11 (1996): 270; Nancy D. Pollock-Ellwand, "The Olmsted Firm in Canada: A Correction of the Record," *Planning Perspectives* 21 (July 2006): 280, 290, 293.

22 John Charles Olmsted, quoted in Pollock-Ellwand, "The Olmsted Firm in Canada: A Correction of the Record": 290.

23 Nancy D. Pollock-Ellwand, "The Olmsted Firm in Canada: A Correction of the Record," *Planning Perspectives* 21 (July 2006): 292. For South Mount Royal, see Elise A. Corbet and Lorne G. Simpson, *Calgary's Mount Royal: A Garden Suburb* (Calgary: Planning and Building Department and the Heritage Advisory Board, City of Calgary, September 1994).

24 Martin Segger and Douglas Franklin, *Victoria: A Primer for Regional History in Architecture* (Victoria: Milestone Publications, 1979): 308–11; Arleyn A. Levee, "The Olmsted Brothers' Residential Communities: Preview of a Legacy," in Charles A. Birnbaum, ed., *The Landscape Universe: Historic Designed Landscapes in Context* (Bronx, New York: Catalog of Landscape Records in the United States at Wave Hill, 1993), 30, 33; Harold Kalman, *A History of Canadian Architecture, Volume 2* (New York: Oxford University Press, 1994), 658; Larry McCann, "Suburbs of Desire: The Suburban Landscape of Canadian Cities, c. 1900–1950," in Richard Harris and Peter J. Larkham, eds., *Changing Suburbs: Foundation, Form and Function* (London: E & FN Spon, 1999), 117, 120, 127, 135; Robert M. Fogelson, *Bourgeois Nightmares: Suburbia, 1870–1930* (New Haven, Conn., and London, 2005), 75, 85, 93, 107, 172; Nancy D. Pollock-Ellwand, "The Olmsted Firm in Canada: A Correction of the Record," *Planning Perspectives* 21 (July 2006): 277–310; Joan Hockaday, *Greenscapes: Olmsted's Pacific Northwest* (Pullman: Washington State University Press, 2009), 65, 76, 124–28, 130–33; Jim Hume, "Raise a Toast to the Uplands," *Victoria Times Colonist* (August 22, 2009).

25 Segger and Franklin, *Victoria: A Primer for Regional History in Architecture*, 311.

26 Arthur C. Comey and Max S. Wehrly, "A Study of Planned Communities" (Department of Regional Planning of Harvard University, November 1936): 400–402; *Capilano Estates Limited*, promotional brochure (1937); Lance Berelowitz, *Dream City: Vancouver and the Global Imagination* (Vancouver: Douglas & McIntyre, 2005), 123–25; Nancy D. Pollock-Ellwand, "The Olmsted Firm in Canada: A Correction of the Record," *Planning Perspectives* 21 (July 2006): 280, 290, 292, 293, 297.

27 Jeffrey Turnbull and Peter Y. Navaretti, eds., *The Griffins in Australia and India* (Melbourne, Australia: Miegunyah Press, 1998), 109; Dustin Griffin, ed., *The Writings of Walter Burley Griffin* (New York: Cambridge University Press, 2008), 163, 215.

28 Walter Burley Griffin, "Architecture," in Dustin Griffin, ed., *The Writings of Walter Burley Griffin*, 215.

29 For Meadlands, see E. G. Vandermeulen, "Mawson – A Landscape Architect at the Turn of the Century," *Architecture Canada* 43 (September 1966): 36–38; Janet Waymark, *Thomas Mawson: Life, Gardens and Landscapes* (London: Frances Lincoln Ltd. Publishers, 2009), 145–46, 236. For James Estate, see Waymark, *Thomas Mawson: Life, Gardens and Landscapes*, 145–46, 236.

30 Vandermeulen, "Mawson – A Landscape Architect at the Turn of the Century": 38; Waymark, *Thomas Mawson: Life, Gardens and Landscapes*, 147–48, 149, 236.

31 Thomas Mawson, *Regina: A Preliminary Report on the Development of the City*, 4, quoted in Anthony Rasporich, "The City Yes, The City No: Perfection by Design in the Western City," in R. Douglas Francis and Chris Kitzan, eds., *The Prairie West as Promised Land* (Calgary: University of Calgary Press, 2007), 183–85. Also see Waymark, *Thomas Mawson: Life, Gardens and Landscapes*, 149–56, 236.

32 Thomas Mawson, *The City of Calgary: Past, Present and Future* (Calgary: City Planning Commission, 1914), esp. pp. 36, 50, 51, 52, 54; Max Foran, "The Mawson Report in Historical Perspective," *Alberta History* 28 (Summer 1980): 31–39; Gorden E. Cherry, "Gardens, Civic Art and Town Planning: The Work of Thomas H. Mawson," *Planning Perspectives* 8 (July 1993): 318–19; Anthony Rasporich, "The City Yes, The City No: Perfection by Design in the Western City," in R. Douglas Francis and Chris Kitzan, eds., *The Prairie West as Promised Land* (Calgary: University of Calgary Press, 2007), 181–83; Janet Waymark, *Thomas Mawson: Life, Gardens and Landscapes* (London: Frances Lincoln Ltd. Publishers, 2009), 157–63, 236.

33 Mawson, *The City of Calgary: Past, Present and Future*, 54.

34 Foran, "The Mawson Report in Historical Perspective": 36.

35 Thomas Adams, "The True Meaning of Town Planning: A Reply to Mr. C. F. A. Voysey," *Architectural Review* 46 (September 1919): 75–77; Michael Simpson, "Thomas Adams, 1871–1940," in Gordon E. Cherry, ed., *Pioneers in British Planning* (London: Architectural Press, 1981), 28–29; Jill Delaney, "The Garden Suburb of Lindenlea, Ottawa: A Model Project for the First Federal Housing Policy, 1918–1924," *Urban History Review/Revue d'Histoire Urbaine* 19 (February 1991): 151–65; John Sewell, *The Shape of the City: Toronto Struggles with Modern Planning* (Toronto: University of Toronto Press, 1993), 12, 13; Harold Kalman, *A History of Canadian Architecture, Volume 2* (New York: Oxford University Press, 1994), 660–61; Larry McCann, "Suburbs of Desire: The Suburban Landscape of Canadian Cities, c. 1900–1950," in Richard Harris and Peter J. Larkham, eds., *Changing Suburbs: Foundation, Form and Function* (London: E & FN Spon, 1999), 129.

36 McCann, "Suburbs of Desire," in Harris and Larkham, *Changing Suburbs*, 129.

37 Delaney, "The Garden Suburb of Lindenlea": 151, 164.

38 Simpson, "Thomas Adams, 1871–1940," in Cherry, ed., *Pioneers in British Planning*, 28.

39 Thomas Adams, quoted in Simpson, "Thomas Adams, 1871–1940," in Cherry, ed., *Pioneers in British Planning*, 28.

40 Thomas Adams, "The Planning of the New Halifax," *Contract Record* 32 (August 28, 1918): 680–81; George A. Ross, "The Halifax Disaster and the Re-Housing," *Construction* XII (October 19, 1919): 293–307; Michael Simpson, "Thomas Adams, 1871–1940," in Gordon E. Cherry, ed., *Pioneers in British Planning* (London: Architectural Press, 1981), 27; "The Hydrostone Neighbourhood, early 1920s," *Trace* 1 (January/March 1981): 23–24; Joann Latremouille, "The Hydrostone District, Halifax, Canada's Public Housing Began with a Bang," *Landscape Architectural Review* 4 (September 1983): 5–7; Gerald Hodge, *Planning Canadian Communities: An Introduction to the Principles, Practice and Participants* (Scarborough, Ontario: Nelson Canada, 1989), 63; John Sewell, *The Shape of the City: Toronto Struggles with Modern Planning* (Toronto: University of Toronto Press, 1993), 12, 14; Harold Kalman, *A History of Canadian Architecture, Volume 2* (New York: Oxford University Press, 1994), 660; Larry McCann, "Suburbs of Desire: The Suburban Landscape of Canadian Cities, c. 1900–1950," in Richard Harris and Peter J. Larkham, eds., *Changing Suburbs: Foundation, Form and Function* (London: E & FN Spon, 1999), 129; "'A Vision of Regeneration': Reconstruction after the Halifax Explosion, 1917–1921," in http://www.gov.ns.ca/nsarm/virtual/explosion.

41 Simpson, "Thomas Adams, 1871–1940," in Cherry, ed., *Pioneers in British Planning*, 27.

42 Kalman, *A History of Canadian Architecture, Volume 2*, 660.

43 T. Philip Terry, *Terry's Guide to Mexico* (Boston and New York: Houghton Mifflin Company, 1923), 390a–b, 391. Also see Kurt Culbertson, "George Edward Kessler: Landscape Architect of the American Renaissance," in William H. Tishler, ed., *Midwestern Landscape Architecture* (Urbana and Chicago: University of Illinois Press, 2000), 114; John M. Hurt, *Empire and Revolution: The Americans in Mexico since the Civil War* (Berkeley: University of California Press, 2002), 244–46; Carol McMichael Reese, "The Urban Development of Mexico City, 1850–1930," in Arturo Almandoz, ed., *Planning Latin America's Capital Cities, 1850–1950* (London and New York: Routledge, 2002), 160–62; David F. Marley, *Historic Cities of the Americas: An Illustrated Encyclopedia, Volume 1* (Santa Barbara: ABC-CLIO, 2005), 266; Patrice Elizabeth Olsen, *Artifacts of Revolution: Architecture, Society, and Politics in Mexico City, 1920–1940* (Plymouth, England: Rowman & Littlefield Publishers, 2008), 32–33, 55–56; Alfonso Valenzuela Aguilera, "Green and Modern: Planning Mexico City, 1900–1940," in Dorothee Brantz and Sonja Dümpelmann, eds., *Greening the City: Urban Landscapes in the Twentieth Century* (Charlottesville: University of Virginia Press, 2011), 40–43.

44 Terry, *Terry's Guide to Mexico*, 390b.

45 Reese, "The Urban Development of Mexico City, 1850–1930," in Almandoz, ed., *Planning Latin America's Capital Cities, 1850–1950*, 162.

46 Olsen, *Artifacts of Revolution: Architecture, Society, and Politics in Mexico City, 1920–1940*, 32.

47 Hurt, *Empire and Revolution: The Americans in Mexico since the Civil War*, 245.

48 Keith L. Eggener, *Luis Barragán's Gardens of El Pedregal* (New York: Princeton Architectural Press, 2001).

49 Francis Violich, *Cities of Latin America: Housing and Planning to the South* (New York: Reinhold Publishing, 1944), 115; Silvia Ferreira Santos Wolff, *Jardim América: o primeiro bairro-jardim de São Paulo e sua arquitetura* (São Paulo: Imprensa Oficial SP: Edusp: FAPESP, 2000); Margareth da Silva Pereira, "The Time of the Capitals: Rio de Janeiro and São Paulo: Words, Actors and Plans," in Arturo Almandoz, ed., *Planning Latin America's Capital Cities, 1850–1950* (London: Routledge, 2002), 8, 30, 95–96; Arturo Almandoz, "The Garden City in Early Twentieth-Century Latin America," *Urban History* 31 (no. 3, 2004), 437–52; Maria Cristina da Silva Leme, ed., *Urbanismo no Brasil, 1895–1965* (Salvador, Brazil: EDUFBA, PPGAU/FAUFBA, 2005), 300–303; Hugo Segawa, "Jardim América: o Primeiro Bairro-jardim de São Paulo e sua Arquitetura," book review, *Planning Perspectives* 21 (July 2006): 321–22; Hugo Segawa, *Architecture of Brazil: 1900–1990* (New York: Springer, 2012), 6.

50 Pereira, "The Time of the Capitals: Rio de Janeiro and São Paulo," in Almandoz, ed., *Planning Latin America's Capital Cities, 1850–1950*, 95–96.

51 Pereira, "The Time of the Capitals: Rio de Janeiro and São Paulo," in Almandoz, ed., *Planning Latin America's Capital Cities, 1850–1950*, 95; Hugo Segawa, *Architecture of Brazil: 1900–1990* (New York: Springer, 2012), 8.

52 For Macedo Vieira, see Antonio Carlos Bonfato, *Macedo Vieira: Ressonâncias do modelo cidade-jardim* (São Paulo: Editora Senac São Paulo, 2008); George Dantas et al., "The Diffusion of the Term 'Garden City': Some Issues on the Transfer of Town Planning Models in Brazil," in http://www.etsav.upc.es/personals/iphs2004/pdf/043_p.pdf; Renato Rego, "Travelling Ideas: British Town & Country Planning Models and the Transformation of Brazilian Tropical Hinterlands," lecture, 14th International Planning History Society Conference (Istanbul, July 2010) in http://iphs2010.com/abs/ID52.pdf.

53 Bonfato, *Macedo Vieira: Ressonâncias do modelo cidade-jardim*, 79–80.

54 Bonfato, *Macedo Vieira: Ressonâncias do modelo cidade-jardim*, 81–82.

55 Bonfato, *Macedo Vieira: Ressonâncias do modelo cidade-jardim*, 82.

56 Bonfato, *Macedo Vieira: Ressonâncias do modelo cidade-jardim*, 80–81.

57 Bonfato, *Macedo Vieira: Ressonâncias do modelo cidade-jardim*, 82, 83.

58 Bonfato, *Macedo Vieira: Ressonâncias do modelo cidade-jardim*, 85, 86, 87.

59 Bonfato, *Macedo Vieira: Ressonâncias do modelo cidade-jardim*, 82, 84, 85.

60 Bonfato, *Macedo Vieira: Ressonâncias do modelo cidade-jardim*, 87–88.

61 Bonfato, *Macedo Vieira: Ressonâncias do modelo cidade-jardim*, 89.

62 Bonfato, *Macedo Vieira: Ressonâncias do modelo cidade-jardim*, 90–91.

63 For Vila Nova Campinos, Vila Medeiros, Vila Campesina, Vila Formosa (1947), and Jardim Rolinópolis, see Antonio Carlos Bonfato, *Macedo Vieira: Ressonâncias do modelo cidade-jardim* (São Paulo: Editora Senac São Paulo, 2008), 91–98.

64 Renato Rego, "Travelling Ideas: British Town & Country Planning Models and the Transformation of Brazilian Tropical Hinterlands," lecture, 14th International Planning History Society Conference (Istanbul, July 2010) in http://iphs2010.com/abs/ID52.pdf: 2. Also see Bonfato, *Macedo Vieira*, 106–14; Joseli Macedo, "Maringá: A British Garden City in the Tropics," *J. Cities* (2011), doi:10.1016/j.cities.2010.11.003.

65 Francis Violich, *Cities of Latin America: Housing and Planning to the South* (New York: Reinhold Publishing, 1944), 115, 168. Also see Elisabete França, ed., *Guarapiranga: recuperação urbana e ambiental no município de Sao Paulo* (Sao Paulo: M. Carrilho Arquitetos, 2000), 52–58.

66 Francis Violich, *Cities of Latin America: Housing and Planning to the South* (New York: Reinhold Publishing, 1944), 114–15. Also see Henry Stephens, *South American Travels* (New York: Knickerbocker Press, 1915), 562–63.

67 Lincoln Continentino, quoted in Dantas et al., "The Diffusion of the Term 'Garden City': Some Issues on the Transfer of Town Planning Models in Brazil": 7–8. Also see Lincoln Continentino, *Saneamento e urbanismo* (Belo Horizonte: 1937); Telma de Barros Correia, "De Vila Operária a Cidade-Companhia: as Aglomerações Criadas Por Empresas No Vacabulário Especializado e Vernacular," *R. B. Estudos Urbanos e Regionais*

4 (Maio 2001): 89; F. J. M. de Lima, "Por uma cidade moderna: Ideários de urbanismo em jogo no concurso para Monlevade e nos projetos destacados da trajetória dos técnicos concorrentes (1931–1943)" (Ph.D. diss., FAUUSP, São Paulo, 2003).

68 Walter Burley Griffin, "Commonwealth of Australia Federal Capitol Competition," *Western Architect* 18 (September 1912): n.p.; John Nolen, "Australian Federal Capital Plan," *National Municipal Review* 1 (October 1912): 718–22; Werner Hegemann and Elbert Peets, *The American Vitruvius: An Architects' Handbook of Civic Art* (1922; New York: Benjamin Blom, 1972), 249–50; Benjamin Higgins, "Canberra: A Garden Without a City," *Journal of the Royal Architectural Institute of Canada* 28 (September 1951): 245–56; A.J. Brown, "Some Notes on the Plan of Canberra, Federal Capital of Australia," *Town Planning Review* 23 (July 1952): 163–65; James Birrell, *Walter Burley Griffin* (St. Lucia: University of Queensland Press, 1964), ch. 6; Mark L. Peisch, *The Chicago School of Architecture: Early Followers of Sullivan and Wright* (New York: Random House, 1964), chapter 7; Robin Boyd, "Australia," *World Architecture* 4 (1967): 202–5; Donald Leslie Johnson, *The Architecture of Walter Burley Griffin* (South Melbourne: Macmillan Company of Australia, 1977), 11–34; M. M. B. Latham, "The City in the Park," *Landscape Australia* 4 (August 1982): 241–45, 247–49; Romaldo Giurgola, "A Splendid Place," *Urban Design International* 4 (Winter 1983): 10–14; Jaquelin Robertson, "The Griffin Plan," *Urban Design International* 4 (Winter 1983), 15–18; David Van Zanten, "Walter Burley Griffin's Design for Canberra, the Capital of Australia," in John Zukowsky, ed., *Chicago Architecture, 1872–1922, Birth of a Metropolis* (Munich: Prestel in association with the Art Institute of Chicago, 1987), 318–43; *Walter Burley Griffin: a Re-view* (Clayton, Victoria, Australia: Monash University Gallery, 1988), 7–10, 36–37; Robert Freestone, *Model Communities: The Garden City Movement in Australia* (Melbourne: Thomas Nelson, 1989), 115–24; Peter Proudfoot, "Symbolism and Axiality in Canberra," *Architecture Australia* 80 (August 1991): 45–49; Peter Harrison, *Walter Burley Griffin, Landscape Architect* (Canberra: National Library of Australia, 1995), 27–75; Peter Proudfoot, "Geomancy: The Basis of the Initial Plan for Canberra," *Planning History* 17 (1995): 7–13; Peter Proudfoot, "The Symbolism of the Crystal in the Planning and Geometry of the Design for Canberra," *Planning Perspectives* 11 (1996): 225–57; John W. Reps, *Canberra 1912: Plans and Planners of the Australian Capital Competition* (Melbourne, Melbourne University Press, 1997); Jeffrey Turnbull and Peter Y. Navaretti, eds., *The Griffins in Australia and India* (Melbourne, Australia: Miegunyah Press, 1998), 19–36, 101–3, 142–44, 164–65; Jeffrey Turnbull, "Dreams of Equity, 1911–1924," in Anne Watson, ed., *Beyond Architecture: Marion Mahony and Walter Burley Griffin, America, Australia, India* (Sydney: Powerhouse, 1998), 106–9; James Weirick, "Spirituality and Symbolism in the Work of the Griffins," in Anne Watson, ed., *Beyond Architecture: Marion Mahony and Walter Burley Griffin, America, Australia, India* (Sydney: Powerhouse, 1998), 63–68; Robert Freestone, "The City Beautiful: Towards an Understanding of the Australian Experience," *Journal of Architectural and Planning Research* 15 (Summer 1998): 91–104; Paul Reid, *Canberra Following Griffin: A Design History of Australia's National Capital* (Canberra: National Archives of Australia, 2002); Andreas Volwahsen, *Imperial Delhi: The British Capital of the Indian Empire* (Munich: Prestel, 2002), 51–54; Peter Hall, *Cities of Tomorrow: An Intellectual History of Urban Planning and Design in the Twentieth Century*, 3rd ed. (Oxford: Blackwell Publishing, 2003), 206–10; Wolfgang Sonne, *Representing the State: Capital City Planning the Early Twentieth Century* (Munich: Prestel, 2003), 149–88; Christopher Vernon, "Canberra: Where Landscape is Pre-eminent," in David L. A. Gordon, ed., *Planning Twentieth Century Capital Cities* (London and New York: Routledge, 2006), 130–49.

69 William Hardy Wilson, quoted in Freestone, *Model Communities*, 118.

70 Albert Agache, quoted in Freestone, *Model Communities*, 118.

71 *Town Planning Review* 3 (October 1912), 166, quoted in Peisch, *The Chicago School of Architecture*, 113–14.

72 William Davidge, quoted in Freestone, *Model Communities*, 119–21.

73 Higgins, "Canberra: A Garden without a City": 251, 254.

74 Walter Burley Griffin, quoted in Hall, *Cities of Tomorrow*, 210.

75 Hall, *Cities of Tomorrow*, 210.

76 Brown, "Some Notes on the Plan of Canberra, Federal Capital of Australia": 165.

77 Peter Harrison, *Walter Burley Griffin: Landscape Architect* (Canberra: National Library of Australia, 1995), 54.

78 John Oxley, quoted in "History of Griffith," in www.griffith.nsw.gov.au/page/page.asp?page_id=239&p=1.

79 James Birrell, *Walter Burley Griffin* (St. Lucia, Brisbane: University of Queensland Press, 1964), 130, 132–33; Donald Leslie Johnson, *The Architecture of Walter Burley Griffin* (South Melbourne: Macmillan Company of Australia, 1977), 33–34; Robert Freestone, *Model Communities: The Garden City Movement in Australia* (Melbourne: Nelson, 1989), 130–31; Peter Harrison, *Walter Burley Griffin: Landscape Architect* (Canberra: National Library of Australia, 1995), 55–57; John R. Newland, "Griffin and the Town Planning of Leeton and Griffith," *Walter Burley Griffin Society Incorporated Newsletter* (March 1997): 3–4; Donald Dunbar, "Of Social Concern: Towns and Buildings for Ordinary Australians," in Jeff Turnbull and Peter Y. Navaretti, eds., *The Griffins in Australia and India* (Melbourne: Miegunyah Press, 1998), 29–31, 104–6; "History of Griffith," in www.griffith.nsw.gov.au/page/page.asp?page_id=239&p=1.

80 Harrison, *Walter Burley Griffin: Landscape Architect*, 55.

81 Freestone, *Model Communities*, 130. Also see James Birrell, *Walter Burley Griffin* (St. Lucia, Brisbane: University of Queensland Press, 1964), 131, 132; Donald Leslie Johnson, *The Architecture of Walter Burley Griffin* (South Melbourne: Macmillan Company of Australia, 1977), 33–34; Robert Freestone, *Model Communities: The Garden City Movement in Australia* (Melbourne: Nelson, 1989), 130, 131; Peter Harrison, *Walter Burley Griffin: Landscape Architect* (Canberra: National Library of Australia, 1995), 54–55; John R. Newland, "Griffin and the Town Planning of Leeton and Griffith," *Walter Burley Griffin Society Incorporated Newsletter* (March 1997): 3–4; Donald Dunbar, "Of Social Concern: Towns and Buildings for Ordinary Australians," in Jeff Turnbull and Peter Y. Navaretti, eds., *The Griffins in Australia and India* (Melbourne: Miegunyah Press, 1998), 29–31, 106–8.

82 Harrison, *Walter Burley Griffin: Landscape Architect*, 55.

83 Harrison, *Walter Burley Griffin: Landscape Architect*, 55.

84 Harrison, *Walter Burley Griffin: Landscape Architect*, 56.

85 Peter Harrison, *Walter Burley Griffin: Landscape Architect* (Canberra: National Library of Australia, 1995), 58; Jeffrey Turnbull and Peter Y. Navaretti, eds., *The Griffins in Australia and India* (Melbourne, Australia: Miegunyah Press, 1998), 158.

86 Donald Leslie Johnson, *The Architecture of Walter Burley Griffin* (South Melbourne: Macmillan Company of Australia, 1977), 33; Meredith Walker, Adrienne Kabos, and James Weirick, *Building for Nature: Walter Burley Griffin and Castlecrag* (Castlecrag: Walter Burley Griffin Society, 1994), 9–10; Peter Harrison, *Walter Burley Griffin: Landscape Architect* (Canberra: National Library of Australia, 1995), 57–58; James Weirick, "Beyond the Garden Suburb: The Mythopoeic Landscape of Castlecrag," *Planning History* 17 (1995): 17; Jeff Turnbull and Peter Y. Navaretti, *The Griffins in Australia and India* (Melbourne, Australia: The Miegunyah Press, 1998), 112; Andrew Ward and Ian Wight, *Heritage Guidelines for the Mount Eagle Estate, Eaglemont* (Banyule City Council, May 16, 2005).

87 Jeffrey Turnbull and Peter Y. Navaretti, eds., *The Griffins in Australia and India* (Melbourne, Australia: Miegunyah Press, 1998), 176.

88 Peter Harrison, *Walter Burley Griffin: Landscape Architect* (Canberra: National Library of Australia, 1995), 58; Jeffrey Turnbull and Peter Y. Navaretti, eds., *The Griffins in Australia and India* (Melbourne, Australia: Miegunyah Press, 1998), 219; www.griffinsociety.org/education/tours.html#ranelagh.

89 James Birrell, *Walter Burley Griffin* (St. Lucia: Brisbane, University of Queensland Press, 1964), 133–47; Mark L. Peisch, *The Chicago School of Architecture: Early Followers of Sullivan and Wright* (London: Phaidon Press, 1964), 128, 131; Donald L. Johnson, "Castlecrag: A Physical and Social Planning Experiment," *Prairie School Review* 8 (3rd Quarter, 1971): 5–13; Donald Leslie Johnson, *The Architecture of Walter Burley Griffin* (South Melbourne: Macmillan Company of Australia, 1977), 80–95; *Walter Burley Griffin—a Re-view* (Victoria, Australia: Monash University Gallery, 1988), 10–14, 34–35; Robert Freestone, *Model Communities: The Garden City Movement in Australia* (Melbourne: Nelson, 1989), 185–87; Meredith Walker, Adrienne Kabos, and James Weirick, *Building for Nature: Walter Burley Griffin and Castlecrag* (Castlecrag: Walter Burley Griffin Society, 1994), passim; James Weirick, "Beyond the Garden Suburb: The Mythopoeic Landscape of Castlecrag," *Planning History* 17 (1995): 13–18; Peter Harrison, *Walter Burley Griffin: Landscape Architect* (Canberra: National Library of Australia, 1995), 76–84; Tempe Macgowan, "Castlecrag/Building for Nature," book review, *Fabrications* 6 (June 1995): 132–34; Meredith Walker, "The Development of Castlecrag," in Jeff Turnbull and Peter Y. Navaretti, *The Griffins in Australia and India* (Melbourne, Australia: The Miegunyah Press, 1998), 74–85, 178–79.

90 Walter Burley Griffin, quoted in Johnson, "Castlecrag: A Physical and Social Planning Experiment": 8.

91 Johnson, "Castlecrag: A Physical and Social Planning Experiment": 8.

92 Ewart G. Culpin, *The Garden City Movement Up-to-Date* (London: Garden Cities and Town Planning Association, 1913), 64; Robert Freestone, *Model Communities: The Garden City Movement in Australia* (Melbourne: Thomas Nelson, 1989), 164–68; Peter Harrison, *Walter Burley Griffin: Landscape Architect* (Canberra: National Library of Australia, 1995), 54; *Development Control Plan No 36: Daceyville Garden Suburb* (City of Botany Bay, April 2005).

93 Culpin, *The Garden City Movement Up-to-Date*, 64.

94 Donald Langmead, "Foreword," in Christine Garnaut, *Colonel Light Gardens: Model Garden Suburb* (Darlinghurst, New South Wales: Crossing Press, 1999), xi. Also see Alan Hutchings, "Comprehensive Town Planning Comes to South Australia," in Alan Hutchings and Raymond Bunker, eds., *With Conscious Purpose: A History of Town Planning in South Australia* (Netley, South Australia: Wakefield Press in association with Royal Australian Planning Institute, South Australian Division, 1986), 65, 66, 73–76; Robert Freestone, *Model Communities: The Garden City Movement in Australia* (Melbourne: Nelson, 1989), 169–72; Brian Y. Harper, "Colonel Light Gardens—Seventy Years of a Garden Suburb," *Australian Planner* 29 (June 1991): 62–69; Christine Garnaut, "Of Passion, Publicity and Planning: Charles Reade and the Mitcham Garden Suburb," *Australian Planner* 32 (1995): 181–89; Christine Garnaut, "Model Intentions," *Australian Planner* 35 (1998): 81–89; Christine Garnaut, *Colonel Light Gardens: Model Garden Suburb* (Darlinghurst, New South Wales: Crossing Press, 1999); Mervyn Miller, "Colonel Light Gardens: Model Garden Suburb," book review, *Planning Perspectives* 15 (2000): 397–98; Christine Garnaut and Alan Hutchings, "The Colonel Light Gardens Garden Suburb Commission: Building a Planned Community," *Planning Perspectives* 18 (July 2003): 277–93; "Colonel Light Gardens State Heritage Area," in http://www.environment.sa.gov.au/heritage/shas/sha_cl_gardens.html; *Suburb History* (Colonel Light Gardens Historical Society, 2006), in http://www.clghs.org.au/; *Charles Reade, 1880–1933* (Colonel Light Gardens Historical Society, 1999), in http://www.clghs.org.au/.

95 Garnault, *Colonel Light Gardens: Model Garden Suburb*, 39–53.

96 For these proposals, see Alan Hutchings, "Comprehensive Town Planning Comes to South Australia," in Alan Hutchings and Raymond Bunker, eds., *With Conscious Purpose: A History of Town Planning in South Australia* (Netley, South Australia: Wakefield Press in association with Royal Australian Planning Institute, South Australian Division, 1986), 61–83; Robert Freestone, *Model Communities: The Garden City Movement in Australia* (Melbourne: Nelson, 1989), 205–8.

97 Robert Freestone, *Model Communities: The Garden City Movement in Australia* (Melbourne: Nelson, 1989), 205–8; Robert Freestone, "The Australian Garden City," in Stephen V. Ward, ed., *The Garden City: Past, Present and Future* (London: E & FN Spon, 1992), 118; Christine Garnaut, "Towards Metropolitan Organisation: Town Planning and the Garden City Idea," in Stephen Hamnett and Robert Freestone, eds., *The Australian Metropolis: A Planning History* (London: E & FN Spon, 2000), 59, 60.

98 Garnaut, "Towards Metropolitan Organisation: Town Planning and the Garden City Idea," in Hamnett and Freestone, eds., *The Australian Metropolis: A Planning History*, 59.

99 Robert Freestone, *Model Communities: The Garden City Movement in Australia* (Melbourne: Nelson, 1989), 94, 124–29, 204; Robert Freestone, "The Australian Garden City," in Stephen V. Ward, ed., *The Garden City: Past, Present and Future* (London: E & FN Spon, 1992), 121.

100 Freestone, *Model Communities*, 124.

101 Alan La Gerche, quoted in Freestone, *Model Communities*, 125.

102 Freestone, *Model Communities*, 125.
103 Quoted in Freestone, *Model Communities*, 128.
104 Robert Freestone, *Model Communities: The Garden City Movement in Australia* (Melbourne: Nelson, 1989), 142; Robert Freestone, "The Australian Garden City," in Stephen V. Ward, ed., *The Garden City: Past, Present and Future* (London: E & FN Spon, 1992), 117, 118.
105 Alan Hutchings, "Comprehensive Town Planning Comes to South Australia," in Alan Hutchings and Raymond Bunker, eds., *With Conscious Purpose: A History of Town Planning in South Australia* (Netley, South Australia: Wakefield Press in association with Royal Australian Planning Institute, South Australian Division, 1986), 72, 77; Robert Freestone, *Model Communities: The Garden City Movement in Australia* (Melbourne: Nelson, 1989), 151–55.
106 Ben Schrader, "Avoiding the Mistakes of the 'Mother Country': The New Zealand Garden City Movement, 1900–1926," *Planning Perspectives* 14 (1999): 395–411.
107 Schrader, "Avoiding the Mistakes of the 'Mother Country': The New Zealand Garden City Movement, 1900–1926": 409.
108 S. Hurst Seager, "Town Planning in New Zealand," *Garden Cities and Town Planning* 11 (May 1921): 120–24; Ben Schrader, "Garden Cities and Planning," *New Zealand Historic Places* no.43 (September 1993): 30–33; Ben Schrader, "Avoiding the Mistakes of the 'Mother Country': The New Zealand Garden City Movement, 1900–1926," *Planning Perspectives* 14 (1999): 395–411; Caroline L. Miller, "Theory Poorly Practised: The Garden Suburb in New Zealand," *Planning Perspectives* 19 (January 2004): 37–55.
109 *Official volume of proceedings of the first New Zealand town-planning conference and exhibition* (Wellington: Government Printer, 1919), opp. p. 114; Gael Ferguson, *Building the New Zealand Dream* (Palmerston North, N.Z.: Dunmore Press with the assistance of the Historical Branch, Dept. of Internal Affairs, 1994), 74–77.
110 Schrader, "Avoiding the Mistakes of the 'Mother Country': The New Zealand Garden City Movement, 1900–1926": 405.
111 Eric C. Franklin, "The Bottleneck Nuisance," *Garden Cities and Town Planning* XX (January 1930): 43–45; Gael Ferguson, *Building the New Zealand Dream* (Palmerston North, N.Z.: Dunmore Press with the assistance of the Historical Branch, Dept. of Internal Affairs, 1994), 79; Ben Schrader, "Avoiding the Mistakes of the 'Mother Country': The New Zealand Garden City Movement, 1900–1926," *Planning Perspectives* 14 (1999): 395–411; Caroline L. Miller, "Theory Poorly Practised: The Garden Suburb in New Zealand," *Planning Perspectives* 19 (January 2004): 37–55.
112 Robert Grant Irving, *Indian Summer: Lutyens, Baker, and Imperial Delhi* (New Haven and London: Yale University Press, 1981), 88. Also see "Planning and Imperial Capital," *Garden Cities and Town Planning* 2 (April 1912): 78; "The Planning of Delhi," *Architectural Review* 31 (April 1912): 240–41; "The New Capital City at Delhi," editorial, *Town Planning Review* 4 (October 1913): 185; "Imperial Delhi," *Architect* 107 (May 5, 1922), four plates following p. 338; T. Salkield, "Delhi, the Imperial City and Capital of India," *Architect* 110 (1923): 7–10; "The New Delhi," *Architectural Review* 60 (December 1926): 216–25; Robert Byron, "New Delhi," *Architectural Review* 69 (January 1931); A. S. G. Butler, *The Architecture of Sir Edwin Lutyens, vol. 2* (London: Country Life, 1950), 28–44, plate XXXV, photographs 188, 120–25, 127; Christopher Hussey, *The Life of Sir Edwin Lutyens* (London: Country Life, 1950), esp. pp. 238–325; Walter George, "The Roadside Planting of Lutyens' New Delhi," in *Journal of Urban and Planning Thought* 1 (April 1958): 77–93; Mark L. Peisch, *The Chicago School of Architecture: Early Followers of Sullivan and Wright* (New York: Random House, 1964), 120; Philip Davies, *Splendours of the Raj: British Architecture in India, 1660–1947* (Middlesex: Penguin, 1985), 222–26; Norma Everson, *The Indian Metropolis: A View Toward the West* (New Haven and London: Yale University Press, 1989), 104–9; Allan Greenberg, *Lutyens and the Modern Movement* (London: Papadakis, 2007), originally published as Allan Greenberg, "Lutyens's Architecture Restudied," *Perspecta* 12 (1969): 129–52; Jane Ridley, "Edwin Lutyens, New Delhi, and the Architecture of Imperialism," in Peter Burroughs and A. J. Stockwell, eds., *Managing the Business of Empire: Essays in Honour of David Fieldhouse* (London and Portland, Oregon: Frank Cass, 1998), 67–81; Peter Hall, *Cities of Tomorrow*, 3rd ed. (Oxford: Blackwell, 2002), 198–202; Andrew Hopkins and Gavin Stamp, eds., *Lutyens Abroad: The Work of Sir Edwin Lutyens Outside the British Isles* (London: British School at Rome, 2002), passim; Jane Ridley, *Architect and His Wife: A Life of Edwin Lutyens* (London: Chatto & Windus, 2002), passim; Andreas Volwahsen, *Imperial Delhi: The British Capital of the Indian Empire* (Munich: Prestel, 2002), passim; Patwant Singh, "Sir Edwin Lutyens and the Building of New Delhi," *World Monuments Icon* (Winter 2002–2003): 38–43; Andrés Duany, Elizabeth Plater-Zyberk, and Robert Alminana, *The New Civic Art: Elements of Town Planning* (New York: Rizzoli International Publications, 2003), 137; Wolfgang Sonne, *Representing the State: Capital City Planning in the Early Twentieth Century* (Munich: Prestel, 2003), chapter 5; David L. A. Gordon, ed., *Planning Twentieth Century Capital Cities* (London and New York: Routledge, 2006), 181–87.
113 George Swinton, quoted in "Planning an Imperial Capital," as quoted in Peisch, *The Chicago School of Architecture*, 120.
114 Greenberg, *Lutyens and the Modern Movement*, 66.
115 Irving, *Indian Summer*, 88.
116 Sonne, *Representing the State: Capital City Planning in the Early Twentieth Century*, 190.
117 Greenberg, *Lutyens and the Modern Movement*, 81.
118 Greenberg, *Lutyens and the Modern Movement*, 83–84.
119 Thomas Sharp, *Town and Countryside: Some Aspects of Urban and Rural Development* (London: Oxford University Press, 1932), 163, quoted in Irving, *Indian Summer*, 88–89.
120 Irving, *Indian Summer*, 227.
121 Irving, *Indian Summer*, 230–31.
122 Irving, *Indian Summer*, 88.
123 Singh, "Sir Edwin Lutyens and the Building of New Delhi": 41.
124 Robert Byron, "New Delhi," *The Architectural Review* 69 (January 1931): 1, as quoted in Greenberg, *Lutyens and the Modern Movement*, 75.
125 Volwahsen, *Imperial Delhi*, 51.
126 Kenneth Bradley, *Lusaka, The New Capital of Northern Rhodesia, Opened Jubilee Week, 1935* (London: Produced for private circulation by Jonathan Cape, 1935); John Collins, "Lusaka: The Myth of the Garden City," in *Zambian Urban Studies, no. 2* (Lusaka: University of Zambia, Institute for Social Research, 1969): 1–32; D. Hywel Davies, "Lusaka, Zambia: Some Town Planning Problems in an African Capital City at Independence," in *Zambian Urban Studies no. 2* (Lusaka: University of Zambia, Institute for Social Research, 1969): 1–18; John Collins, "Lusaka: Urban Planning in a British Colony," in Gordon E. Cherry, ed., *Shaping an Urban World* (New York: St. Martin's Press, 1980), 227–41; Karsten Thøgersen and Jørgen Eskemose Andersen, *Urban Planning in Zambia—the case of Lusaka* (Copenhagen: Royal Danish Academy of Fine Arts, School of Architecture, 1983); John Collins, "Lusaka: the Historical Development of a Planned Capital, 1931–1970," in Geoffrey J. Williams, ed., *Lusaka and Its Environs* (Lusaka: The Zambia Geographical Association, 1986), 95–137; Geoffrey J. Williams, "The Early Years of the Township," in Williams, ed., *Lusaka and Its Environs*, 71–94; Karen Tranberg Hansen, *Keeping House in Lusaka* (New York: Columbia University Press, 1997), 21–46; Robert K. Home, *Of Planting and Planning: The Making of British Colonial Cities* (London: Spon, 1997), 161–62; Dixon Bwalya, "Zambia: Lusaka City—What Has Gone Wrong?" *Times of Zambia* (May 25, 2012), in http://allafrica.com/stories/201205250829.html; Paul Makasa, "Lusaka City: What Went Wrong?" *Times of Zambia* (November 2, 2012), in www.times.co.zm/?p=18114; Nakubiana Shabongo, "What Happened to House Numbers?" *Times of Zambia* (January 25, 2013), in www.times.co.zm/?p=28095.
127 Bradley, *Lusaka, The New Capital of Northern Rhodesia, Opened Jubilee Week, 1935*, 60.
128 Collins, "Lusaka: The Myth of the Garden City": 9, 20.
129 Stanley D. Adshead, quoted in Bradley, *Lusaka, The New Capital of Northern Rhodesia, Opened Jubilee Week, 1935*, 28.
130 Bradley, *Lusaka, The New Capital of Northern Rhodesia, Opened Jubilee Week*, 27–28.
131 Collins, "Lusaka: The Myth of the Garden City": 12, 18, 23, 29.
132 Collins, "Lusaka: The Myth of the Garden City": 5.
133 John Muller, "Influence and Experience: Albert Thompson and South Africa's Garden City," *Planning History* 17 (no. 3, 1995): 14–21. Also see J. W. P. Logan, "Garden Cities for Africa: Pinelands, a venture at Cape Town," *Town and Country Planning* 4 (December 1935): 26–28; Eric Rosenthal, *A History of Pinelands, South Africa's First Garden City* (c. 1950), in http://dvdmerwe.bravehost.com/history_of_pinelands.htm; Robert K. Home, *Of Planting and Planning: The Making of British Colonial Cities* (London: Spon, 1997), 163–65; Vivian Bickford Smith, Elizabeth van Heyningen, and Nigel Worden, *Cape Town in the Twentieth Century: An Illustrated Social History* (Claremont: South Africa: D. Philip Publishers, 1999), 144–45; Nicholas Coetzer, "Langa Township in the 1920s—an (extra)ordinary Garden Suburb," *South African Journal of Art History* 24 (no. 1, 2009): 1–19.
134 Muller, "Influence and Experience: Albert Thompson and South Africa's Garden City": 16.
135 H. de Saint-Omer, *Les enterprises belges en Égypt* (Brussels: G. Piquart, 1907); H. G. Hunting, "City Built on Desert Sands," *Technical World Magazine* (December 1909): 371–73; Sydney A. Clark, "Heliopolis: A Suburban Miracle," *Suburban Life: The Countryside Magazine* 17 (August 1913): 65; "Heliopolis, 'A Suburban Miracle,'" *American Review of Reviews* 48 (September 1913): 366–68; Wilfrid Scawen Blunt, *My Diaries: Being a Personal Narrative of Events, 1888–1914* (New York: Alfred A. Knopf, 1921), 132; Michel Roux-Spitz, "Héliopolis," *L'Art vivant* 5 (1929): 100–101; Robert Ilbert, *Héliopolis: le Caire, 1905–1922: genèse d'une ville* (Paris: Editions du Centre national de la recherche scientifique, 1981); Robert Ilbert, "From Alexandria to Cairo, 1830–1930," *UIA International Architect* 7 (1985): 14–15; André Raymond, *Cairo*, trans. by Willard Wood (Cambridge, Mass.: Harvard University Press, 2000), 324, 329–33; Khaled Adham, "Heliopolis: A European Vision of the Orient," in Yasser Elsheshtawy, ed., *Planning Middle Eastern Cities: An Urban Kaleidoscope in a Globalizing World* (London: Routledge, 2004), 144–51; Andrew Beattie, *Cairo: A Cultural History* (New York: Oxford University Press, 2005), 182–87; Deba Rashed, "Celebration of a Suburb," *Al-Ahram Weekly* (April 21–27, 2005), http://weekly.ahram.org.eg; Samir Raafat, "Once, We Hosted Kings," *Egypt Today* (June 2005), http://www. egypttoday.com; Agnieszka Dobrowolska and Jaroslaw Dobrowolski, *Heliopolis: Rebirth of the City of the Sun* (Cairo and New York: American University in Cairo Press, 2006); Anne Van Loo and Marie-Cécile Bruwier, eds., *Heliopolis* (Brussels: Fonds Mercator, 2010); Nadine el Sayed, "City of the Sun Under Destruction," *Egypt Today* (July 2010), http://www.egypttoday.com; http://www.amicale-csf.com/documents/Heliopolis.doc; "Héliopolis," http://passion-egyptienne.fr; "L'identification d'un ensemble urbain du XXème siècle en Egypte Héliopolis, Le Caire," http://www.revue. inventaire.culture.gouv.fr.
136 "Heliopolis, 'A Suburban Miracle,'" *American Review of Reviews*: 377.
137 Adham, "Heliopolis: A European Vision of the Orient," in Elsheshtawy, ed., *Planning Middle Eastern Cities*, 147.
138 Hunting, "City Built on Desert Sands": 373.
139 Adham, "Heliopolis: A European Vision of the Orient," in Elsheshtawy, ed., *Planning Middle Eastern Cities*, 150.
140 Clark, "Heliopolis: A Suburban Miracle": 65, quoted in *American Review of Reviews*: 367–68.
141 Beattie, *Cairo*, 186.
142 James Aldridge, *Cairo* (Boston: Little, Brown, 1969), 215–16; Marianne Guillet, "Mythe et limites: Garden-City ou l'espace réinventé," *Égypte/Monde arabe* 22 (1995): 123–42; Paul Reuber, "Travel Diary: Cairo: Garden City," *Canadian Architect* 44 (January 1999): 32–33; André Raymond, *Cairo*, trans. by Willard Wood (Cambridge, Mass.: Harvard University Press, 2000), 328; Andrew Beattie, *Cairo: A Cultural History* (New York: Oxford University Press, 2005), 171–76; Mercedes Volait, *Architects et Architectures de l'Égypte Moderne (1830–1950)* (Paris: Maisonneuve et Larose, 2005), 202–4; Linda Lambert, *Cairo Diary* (Bloomington, Ind.: AuthorHouse, 2010), 122–23; Samir Raafat, "Garden City," (August 6, 1998), http://egy.com/gardencity; Lobna Sherif, "Architecture as a System of Appropriation: Colonization in Egypt," http://www.sea1917.org/heritage/UIA-WPAHR-V/Papers-PDF/Dr.%20Lobna %20Sherif.pdf.
143 Raafat, "Garden City," (August 6, 1998), http://egy.com/gardencity.
144 Reuber, "Travel Diary: Cairo: Garden City": 33.
145 Samir W. Raafat, *Maadi 1904–1962: Society and History in a Cairo Suburb* (Cairo: Palm Press, 1994); Andrew Beattie, *Cairo: A Cultural History* (New York: Oxford University Press, 2005), 182–84; Lobna Sherif, "Architecture as a System of Appropriation:

Colonization in Egypt," http://www.sea1917.org/heritage/UIA-WPAHR-V/Papers-PDF/Dr.%20Lobna%20Sherif.pdf; http://www.egy.com/maadi.

146 U. Brettholz, "Zur anlage einer Kolonie im Heiligen Lande oder einem seiner Nebenländer von k.k. Baurat Wilhelm Stiassny," *Allgemeine Zeitung des Judenthums* (May 20, 1909): 238; "Danksagung an Wilhelm Stiassny," *Die Welt* 25 (June 18, 1909): 545; Mordekhai Na'or, *Tel-aviv be-reshitah, 1909–1934* (Jerusalem: Yad Yitshak Ben-Tsevi, 1984), 17, 34, 37, 43, 48–53, 159, 182; Yossi Katz, "Ahuzat Bayit Association, 1906–1909: Laying the Foundation for Tel Aviv," *Cathedra* 33 (October 1984): 161–92; Gideon Biger, "European Influence on Town Planning and Town Building in Palestine 1850–1920," *Urbanism Past & Present* 9 (Winter–Spring 1984): 30–35; Yossi Katz, "Ideology and Urban Development: Zionism and the Origins of Tel-Aviv, 1906–1914," *Journal of Historical Geography* 12 (October 1986): 402–24; Yossi Katz, "The Establishment of Tel Aviv with the Assistance of the Jewish National Fund," *Jewish Social Studies* 49 (Summer–Autumn 1987): 293–302; Ruth Kark, *Jaffa: A City in Evolution, 1799–1917* (Jerusalem: Yad Izhak Ben-Zvi Press, 1990), 107, 124; Edina Meyer-Maril, "Europäische Städtebauideen in Palästina 1909–1939: das Bespiel Tel Aviv," *Architectura: Zeitschrift für Geschichte der Baukunst* 22 (1992): 135–48; Yossi Katz, "The Extension of Ebenezer Howard's Ideas on Urbanization Outside the British Isles: The Example of Palestine," *GeoJournal* 34 (No. 4, 1994): 467–73; Joachim Schlör, *Tel Aviv: From Dream to City*, trans. by Helen Atkins (London: Reaktion Books, 1999), 14–19, 40–57; S. Ilan Troen, *Imagining Zion: Dreams, Designs, and Realities in a Century of Jewish Settlement* (New Haven, Conn.: Yale University Press, 2003), 91–93; Mark LeVine, "Land, Law and the Planning of Empire: Jaffa and Tel Aviv During the Late Ottoman and Mandate Periods," in Huri Islamoglu, ed., *Constituting Modernity: Private Property in the East and West* (London: I. B. Tauris, 2004), 112–14; Mark LeVine, *Overthrowing Geography: Jaffa, Tel Aviv, and the Struggle for Palestine, 1880–1948* (Berkeley: University of California Press, 2005), 60–72; Helen Berman, "The Birth of Tel Aviv" (October 31, 2005), http://www.jpost.com/Travel; Maoz Azaryahu, *Tel Aviv: Mythography of a City* (Syracuse, N.Y.: Syracuse University Press, 2007), 33–38; Vittorio Magnago Lampugnani, *Die Stadt im 20. Jahrhundert* (Berlin: Verlag Klaus Wagenbach, 2010), 356–57; Ines Sonder, "Wilhelm Stiassny and the Development Plan for Tel Aviv (1909)," http://www.david.juden.at; http://lib.stanford.edu/eliasaf-robinson-tel-aviv-collection/ahuzat-bayit-and-founding-tel-aviv-1909.

147 Katz, "The Extension of Ebenezer Howard's Ideas on Urbanization Outside the British Isles: The Example of Palestine": 469.

148 *The Company for the Founding of the Model Moshava and Garden City in Eretz Israel (Palestine)* (Warsaw, 1917); Yossi Katz, "The Extension of Ebenezer Howard's Ideas on Urbanization Outside the British Isles: The Example of Palestine," *GeoJournal* 34 (No. 4, 1994): 467–73; Ruth Kark and Michal Oren-Nordheim, *Jerusalem and Its Environs: Quarters, Neighborhoods, Villages, 1800–1948* (Detroit: Wayne State University Press; Jerusalem: Hebrew University Magnes Press, 2001), 169.

149 Ruth Kark, *Jerusalem Neighborhoods: Planning and By-laws, 1855–1930*, trans. by Michael Gordon (Jerusalem: Magnes Press, 1991), 95, 167–68; Yossi Katz, "The Extension of Ebenezer Howard's Ideas on Urbanization Outside the British Isles: The Example of Palestine," *GeoJournal* 34 (No. 4, 1994): 467–73; Ruth Kark and Michal Oren-Nordheim, *Jerusalem and Its Environs: Quarters, Neighborhoods, Villages, 1800–1948* (Detroit: Wayne State University Press; Jerusalem: Hebrew University Magnes Press, 2001), 160, 169–71; David Kroyanker, *Jerusalem Architecture* (New York: Vendome Press, 2002), 157; S. Ilan Troen, *Imagining Zion: Dreams, Designs, and Realities in a Century of Jewish Settlement* (New Haven, Conn.: Yale University Press, 2003), 144; Myra Warhaftig, *They Laid the Foundation: Lives and Works of German-Speaking Jewish Architects in Palestine 1918–1948*, trans. by Andrea Lerner (Berlin: Ernst Wasmuth Verlag Tübingen, 2007), 37, 43; "Talpiot," http://www. jerusalem.muni.il; http://www.biu.ac.il/js/rennert/history_12.html.

150 Ruth Kark, *Jerusalem Neighborhoods: Planning and By-laws, 1855–1930*, trans. by Michael Gordon (Jerusalem: Magnes Press, 1991), 93, 96, 134–36, 154; Martin Gilbert, *Jerusalem in the Twentieth Century* (New York: John Wiley & Sons, 1996), 110, 117; Ruth Kark and Michal Oren-Nordheim, *Jerusalem and Its Environs: Quarters, Neighborhoods, Villages, 1800–1948* (Detroit: Wayne State University Press; Jerusalem: Hebrew University Magnes Press, 2001), 160, 169, 171; David Kroyanker, *Jerusalem Architecture* (New York: Vendome Press, 2002), 157–61; Viorica Feler-Morgan, "Jerusalem's International Style Under Pressure," *Docomomo* 37 (September 2007): 72–78; Lili Eylon, "Jerusalem: Architecture in the British Mandate Period," http://www. jewishvirtuallibrary.org; "Rehavia," http://www.jerusalem.muni.il; http://www.biu.ac.il/js/rennert/history_12.html.

151 *Rehavia*, brochure (Palestine Land Development Company, 1930), quoted in Kark, *Jerusalem Neighborhoods: Planning and By-laws, 1855–1930*, 93.

152 "Modern Town-Planning in Palestine," *Architects' Journal* 62 (September 23, 1925): 447–48; Ruth Kark, *Jerusalem Neighborhoods: Planning and By-laws, 1855–1930*, trans. by Michael Gordon (Jerusalem: Magnes Press, 1991), 92, 94, 152–53, 160–61; Ruth Kark and Michal Oren-Nordheim, *Jerusalem and Its Environs: Quarters, Neighborhoods, Villages, 1800–1948* (Detroit: Wayne State University Press; Jerusalem: Hebrew University Magnes Press, 2001), 160, 169, 171; David Kroyanker, *Jerusalem Architecture* (New York: Vendome Press, 2002), 157; S. Ilan Troen, *Imagining Zion: Dreams, Designs, and Realities in a Century of Jewish Settlement* (New Haven, Conn.: Yale University Press, 2003), 144; Lili Eylon, "Jerusalem: Architecture in the British Mandate Period," http://www.jewishvirtuallibrary.org; "Beit Hakerem," http://www.jerusalem.muni.il; http://www.biu.ac.il/js/rennert/history_12.html.

153 "Modern Town-Planning in Palestine," *Architects' Journal* 62 (September 23, 1925): 447–48; "Jews from the World's Cities Now Farm Palestine," *Life* (July 5, 1937): 54–55; S. Ilan Troen, *Imagining Zion: Dreams, Designs, and Realities in a Century of Jewish Settlement* (New Haven, Conn.: Yale University Press, 2003), 64–67; Myra Warhaftig, *They Laid the Foundation: Lives and Works of German-Speaking Jewish Architects in Palestine 1918–1948*, trans. by Andrea Lerner (Berlin: Ernst Wasmuth Verlag Tübingen, 2007), 36–37, 39–40; "Nahalal," http://www.jafi.org.il.

154 Troen, *Imagining Zion: Dreams, Designs, and Realities in a Century of Jewish Settlement*, 64, 67.

155 Erich Mendelsohn, *Erich Mendelsohn: Complete Works of the Architect*, trans. by Antje Fritsch (Berlin: R. Mosse, 1930; New York: Princeton Architectural Press, 1992), 100–101; Ita Heinze-Greenberg, "'Around Noon Land in Sight': Travels to Holland, Palestine, the United States, and Russia," in Regina Stephan, ed., *Eric Mendelsohn: Architect 1887–1953* (New York: Monacelli Press, 1999), 60–65; Myra Warhaftig, *They Laid the Foundation: Lives and Works of German-Speaking Jewish Architects in Palestine 1918–1948*, trans. by Andrea Lerner (Berlin: Ernst Wasmuth Verlag Tübingen, 2007), 210–13; http://bezalel.secured.co.il/8/rapoport14.htm; http://www.slideshare.net/kienviet/tel-aviv-turner.

156 For Mendelsohn's work in Palestine between 1933 and 1941, see *Erich Mendelsohn in Palestine*, exhibition catalogue (Haifa: Israel Institute of Technology, 1994).

157 "Tel Aviv, Palästina," *Städtebau* 24 (1929): 48–50; Ruth Kark, *Jaffa: A City in Evolution, 1799–1917* (Jerusalem: Yad Izhak Ben-Zvi Press, 1990), 124; Gideon Biger, "Uno scozzese nella prima città ebraica," *Spazio e società* 14 (October–December 1991): 98–103; Edina Meyer-Maril, "Europäische Städtebauideen in Palästina 1909–1939: das Bespiel Tel Aviv," *Architectura: Zeitschrift für Geschichte der Baukunst* 22 (1992): 135–48; Catherine Weill-Rochant, "Tel-Aviv des années trente; béton sur la terre promise," *L'Architecture d'Aujourd'hui* 293 (June 1994): 40–47; Frank G. Novak, Jr., ed., *Lewis Mumford and Patrick Geddes: The Correspondence* (London and New York Routledge, 1995), 225–27; Neal I. Payton, "The Machine in the Garden City: Patrick Geddes' Plan for Tel Aviv," *Planning Perspectives* 10 (1995): 359–81; Neal I. Payton, "Patrick Geddes (1854–1932) and the Plan of Tel Aviv," *The New City* 3 (Fall 1996): 5–23; Rachel Kallus, "Patrick Geddes and the Evolution of a Housing Type in Tel-Aviv," *Planning Perspectives* 12 (1997): 281–320; S. Ilan Troen, *Imagining Zion: Dreams, Designs, and Realities in a Century of Jewish Settlement* (New Haven, Conn.: Yale University Press, 2003), 144–45; Mark LeVine, "Land, Law and the Planning of Empire: Jaffa and Tel Aviv During the Late Ottoman and Mandate Periods," in Huri Islamoglu, ed., *Constituting Modernity: Private Property in the East and West* (London: I. B. Tauris, 2004), 100–101; Mark LeVine, *Overthrowing Geography: Jaffa, Tel Aviv, and the Struggle for Palestine, 1880–1948* (Berkeley: University of California Press, 2005), 171–72; Maoz Azaryahu, *Tel Aviv: Mythography of a City* (Syracuse, N.Y.: Syracuse University Press, 2007), 39–51; Hanna Ram and Shaked Gilboa, "Tel Aviv-Jaffa," *Encyclopedia Judaica*, 2nd ed. (Farmington Hills, Mi.: Thomson Gale, 2009), vol. 19: 589–93; Volker M. Welter, "The 1925 Master Plan for Tel-Aviv by Patrick Geddes," *Israel Studies* 14 (Fall 2009): 94–119; Vittorio Magnago Lampugnani, *Die Stadt im 20. Jahrhundert* (Berlin: Verlag Klaus Wagenbach, 2010), 338, 355–61; Noah Hysler-Rubin, *Patrick Geddes and Town Planning: A Critical View* (London and New York: Routledge, 2011), 32, 84–87, 90–93, 115–18; "Tel Aviv (Israel), No. 1096," http://www.unesco.org; http://www.slideshare.net/kienviet/tel-aviv-turner.

158 Although the master plan was rejected, three buildings envisioned by Geddes and Mears were built. See "New Hebrew University in Jerusalem for the Zionist Organization," *Building News* 119 (1920): 161, 284; Hysler-Rubin, *Patrick Geddes and Town Planning: A Critical View*, 100–103; Diana Dolev, "Architectural Orientalism in the Hebrew University—The Patrick Geddes and Frank Mears Master-Plan," http://arts.tau.ac.il.

159 Payton, "The Machine in the Garden City: Patrick Geddes' Plan for Tel Aviv": 364–65.

160 Lewis Mumford, letter to Sophia Wittenberg, July 7, 1920, quoted in Novak, ed., *Lewis Mumford and Patrick Geddes: The Correspondence*, 6.

161 Kiki Kafkoula, "The Replanning of the Destroyed Villages of Eastern Macedonia after World War I: The Influence of the Garden City Tradition on an Emergency Programme," *Planning History* 14 (No. 2, 1992): 4–11; Gordon E. Cherry, Harriet Jordan, and Kiki Kafkoula, "Gardens, Civic Art and Town Planning: The Work of Thomas H. Mawson (1861–1933)," *Planning Perspectives* 8 (1993): 321–25; Kiki Kafkoula, "In Search of Urban Reform: Co-operative Housing in Inter-War Athens," *Urban History* 21 (April 1994): 49–60; Kiki Kafkoula, *The Garden City Adventure: Social and Environmental Reform in Europe and Greece during the 20th Century* (Thessaloniki: University Studio Press, 2007), 251–92, 477–78, 497–98; Janet Waymark, *Thomas Mawson: Life, Gardens and Landscapes* (London: Frances Lincoln, 2009), 181–82.

162 John William Mawson, "Address to the Central Council for the Installation of Refugees in the Destroyed Areas of Macedonia (1919)," quoted in Kafkoula, "The Replanning of the Destroyed Villages of Eastern Macedonia after World War I": 10 (n.11).

163 Kafkoula, *The Garden City Adventure: Social and Environmental Reform in Europe and Greece during the 20th Century*, 477.

164 Kafkoula, "The Replanning of the Destroyed Villages of Eastern Macedonia after World War I": 8.

165 Kiki Kafkoula, "The Replanning of the Destroyed Villages of Eastern Macedonia after World War I: The Influence of the Garden City Tradition on an Emergency Programme," *Planning History* 14 (No. 2, 1992): 4–11; Kiki Kafkoula, *The Garden City Adventure: Social and Environmental Reform in Europe and Greece during the 20th Century* (Thessaloniki: University Studio Press, 2007), 478–80; Kiki Kafkoula, "Philothei in Inter-War Athens: A Co-Operative Garden Suburb Par Excellence" (unpublished paper, School of Architecture, Aristotle University of Thessaloniki): 1–5.

166 Kiki Kafkoula, *The Garden City Adventure: Social and Environmental Reform in Europe and Greece during the 20th Century* (Thessaloniki: University Studio Press, 2007), 365–69, 480–81, 500.

167 Dimitri Philippides, "A Tale of Two Suburbs in Athens," *AARP: Art and Archaeology Research Papers* 14 (December 1978): 46–53; Kiki Kafkoula, "In Search of Urban Reform: Co-operative Housing in Inter-War Athens," *Urban History* 21 (April 1994): 49–60; Dimitri Philippides, "Town Planning in Greece," in Savas Condaratos and Wilfried Wang, eds., *20th Century Architecture: Greece* (Munich: Prestel, 1999), 68, 280; Richard Stoneman, *A Traveller's History of Athens* (New York: Interlink Books, 2004), 278; Dimitri Philippides, *Athens Suburbs & Countryside in the 1930s: Architecture and Urban Planning* (Athens: Olkos, 2006), 6–7, 22–23, 46–53; Kiki Kafkoula, *The Garden City Adventure: Social and Environmental Reform in Europe and Greece during the 20th Century* (Thessaloniki: University Studio Press, 2007), 302–7, 478–80, 482, 499; http://www.fhw.gr/chronos/14/en/1923_1940/civilization/choros/index.html.

168 Philippides, "A Tale of Two Suburbs in Athens": 46.

169 Philippides, "A Tale of Two Suburbs in Athens": 46.

170 Dimitri Philippides, "A Tale of Two Suburbs in Athens," *AARP: Art and Archaeology Research Papers* 14 (December 1978): 46–53; Kiki Kafkoula, "In Search of Urban Reform: Co-operative Housing in Inter-War Athens," *Urban History* 21 (April 1994): 49–60; Kiki

Kafkoula, *The Garden City Adventure: Social and Environmental Reform in Europe and Greece during the 20th Century* (Thessaloniki: University Studio Press, 2007), 480, 520.
171 Philippides, "A Tale of Two Suburbs in Athens": 49.
172 Philippides, "A Tale of Two Suburbs in Athens": 50.
173 Dimitri Philippides, "A Tale of Two Suburbs in Athens," *AARP: Art and Archaeology Research Papers* 14 (December 1978): 52 (n.3); Kiki Kafkoula, "In Search of Urban Reform: Co-operative Housing in Inter-War Athens," *Urban History* 21 (April 1994): 49–60; Richard Stoneman, *A Traveller's History of Athens* (New York: Interlink Books, 2004), 278; Dimitri Philippides, *Athens Suburbs & Countryside in the 1930s: Architecture and Urban Planning* (Athens: Olkos, 2006), 54–64; Kiki Kafkoula, *The Garden City Adventure: Social and Environmental Reform in Europe and Greece during the 20th Century* (Thessaloniki: University Studio Press, 2007), 353–59, 480, 482, 500; Kiki Kafkoula, "Philothei in Inter-War Athens: A Co-Operative Garden Suburb Par Excellence" (unpublished paper, School of Architecture, Aristotle University of Thessaloniki): 1–5; http://www.philothei.gr/municipality.
174 Kafkoula, "Philothei in Inter-War Athens: A Co-Operative Garden Suburb Par Excellence": 3–4.
175 Kiki Kafkoula, "In Search of Urban Reform: Co-operative Housing in Inter-War Athens," *Urban History* 21 (April 1994): 49–60; Dimitri Philippides, "Town Planning in Greece," in Savas Condaratos and Wilfried Wang, eds., *20th Century Architecture: Greece* (Munich: Prestel, 1999), 68; Ioannis N. Koumanoudis, *I Ekali pou efyge* (Athens: Technical Chamber of Greece, 2001); Richard Stoneman, *A Traveller's History of Athens* (New York: Interlink Books, 2004), 278; Kiki Kafkoula, *The Garden City Adventure: Social and Environmental Reform in Europe and Greece during the 20th Century* (Thessaloniki: University Studio Press, 2007), 307–10, 478–79, 499; Nikos Vatopoulos, "A Meticulous Biography of Ekali," book review, http://www. ekathimerini. com; http://www.fhw.gr/chronos/14/en/1923_1940/civilization/choros/index.html.
176 Vatopoulos, "A Meticulous Biography of Ekali," http://www.ekathimerini.com.
177 Dimitri Philippides, "Town Planning in Greece," in Savas Condaratos and Wilfried Wang, eds., *20th Century Architecture: Greece* (Munich: Prestel, 1999), 68; Richard Stoneman, *A Traveller's History of Athens* (New York: Interlink Books, 2004), 278; Panos Totsikas, *Edo kapote* (Athens: Kapsimi, 2005); Kiki Kafkoula, *The Garden City Adventure: Social and Environmental Reform in Europe and Greece during the 20th Century* (Thessaloniki: University Studio Press, 2007), 311–12, 330, 499; http://www.mlahanas.de/Greece/Cities/Ilioupoli.html.
178 A. Ensh, "Pervyi gorod-sad v Rossii," *Gorodskoe delo* (No. 22, 1922): 1571–75; Etienne De Groër, "Town Planning in Russia," *Garden Cities and Town Planning* 12 (July–August 1922): 117–23; W. Irschick, "A Forest Settlement at Riga," *Garden Cities and Town Planning* 12 (September–October 1922): 146–48; E. Kupffer, "Die Villenkolnie 'Kaiserwald' bei Riga," *Jahrbuch für bildende Kunst in den Ostseeprovinzen* (1928): 126; S. Frederick Starr, "The Revival and Schism of Urban Planning in Twentieth-Century Russia," in Michael F. Hamm, ed., *The City in Russian History* (Lexington: University Press of Kentucky, 1976), 231–32, 234; Catherine Cooke, "Russian Responses to the Garden City Idea," *Architectural Review* 163 (June 1978): 353–63; R. A. Krastinich, *Stili Moderni v Arxiekturye Rigi* (Moscow: Stroiizdat, 1988), 30; Stanley Buder, *Visionaries and Planners: The Garden City Movement and the Modern Community* (New York: Oxford University Press, 1990), 139; Irene Bakule, "Riga Garden Suburb," *Planning History* 17 (No. 2, 1995): 6–11; Helen Meller, *European Cities, 1890–1930s: History, Culture and the Built Environment* (Chichester: John Wiley & Sons, 2001), 125; Anita Kaze, "Mežaparks: The Garden Suburb," http://www.bestriga.com.
179 See A. J. Downing, *Cottage Residences, or, a Series of Designs for Rural Cottages and Cottage-Villas, and Their Gardens and Grounds Adapted to North America* (New York: Wiley and Putnam, 1842).
180 Buder, *Visionaries and Planners*, 139.
181 Starr, "The Revival and Schism of Urban Planning in Twentieth-Century Russia," in Hamm, ed., *The City in Russian History*, 234.
182 "Goroda sady," *Zodchii* (No. 17, 1904): 209–11. For the beginnings of the Russian Garden City movement, see D. Protopopof and A. Bloch, "The Housing Question and the Garden City Movement in Russia," *Garden Cities and Town Planning* 4 (July 1914): 167–69; Etienne De Groër, "Town Planning in Russia," *Garden Cities and Town Planning* 12 (July–August 1922): 117–23; Dr. J. Guelman, "Garden Cities for Russia," *Garden Cities and Town Planning* 13 (February 1923): 21–23; Catherine Cooke, "Activities of the Garden City Movement in Russia," *Transactions of the Martin Centre for Architecture and Urban Studies, University of Cambridge* 1 (1976): 225–49; S. Frederick Starr, "The Revival and Schism of Urban Planning in Twentieth-Century Russia," in Michael F. Hamm, ed., *The City in Russian History* (Lexington: University Press of Kentucky, 1976), 230–35; Catherine Cooke, "Russian Responses to the Garden City Idea," *Architectural Review* 163 (June 1978): 353–63; Catherine Cooke, "Le mouvement pour la cité-jardin en Russie," in Jean-Louis Cohen, Marco De Michelis, and Manfredo Tafuri, eds., *URSS, 1917–1978* (Paris: L'Équerre, 1979), 200–233; R. A. French, "Moscow, the Socialist Metropolis," in Anthony Sutcliffe, *Metropolis, 1890–1940* (London: Mansell, 1984), 366; Stanley Buder, *Visionaries and Planners: The Garden City Movement and the Modern Community* (New York: Oxford University Press, 1990), 139–40; Catherine Cooke, "The Vesnins' Palace of Labour," in Neil Leach, ed., *Architecture and Revolution: Contemporary Perspectives on Central and Eastern Europe* (London and New York: Routledge, 1999), 38; Helen Meller, *European Cities, 1890–1930s: History, Culture and the Built Environment* (Chichester: John Wiley & Sons, 2001), 125–26; Stephen Lovell, "Between Arcadia and Suburbia: Dachas in Late Imperial Russia," *Slavic Review* 61 (Spring 2002): 66–87; Boris Anan'ich and Alexander Kobak, "St. Petersburg and Green Space, 1850–2000: An Introduction," in Peter Clark, ed., *The European City and Green Space* (Aldershot, England, and Burlington, Vt.: Ashgate, 2006), 258–60; Robert H. Kargon and Arthur P. Molella, *Invented Edens: Techno-Cities of the Twentieth Century* (Cambridge, Mass., and London: MIT Press, 2008), 25–26.
183 M.G. Dikanskii, *Kvartirnyĭ vopros I sotsial'nye opyty ego reshenilia (The Housing Question and Social Experiments to Solve It)* (St. Petersburg, 1908), 125, quoted in Cooke, "Russian Responses to the Garden City Idea": 355.
184 Cooke, "Russian Responses to the Garden City Idea": 355.
185 D. Protopopov, "Goroda budushchego," *Gorodskoe Delo* (No. 17, 1909): 855–86, quoted in Lovell, "Between Arcadia and Suburbia: Dachas in Late Imperial Russia": 82.
186 Ebenezer Howard, introduction to the 1911 Russian translation of *Garden Cities of To-morrow*, quoted in Anan'ich and Kobak, "St. Petersburg and Green Space, 1850–2000: An Introduction," in Clark, ed., *The European City and Green Space*, 260.
187 Cooke, "Russian Responses to the Garden City Idea": 355. Also see V. N. Semionov, *Blagoustroistvo Gorodov* (Moscow, 1912); V. N. Beloussov, "V. N. Semenov," in O.A. Shvidkovsky, *Building in the USSR, 1917–1932* (New York: Praeger, 1971), 67–71.
188 N. A. Sytenko, "O gorode-sade Moskovskogo-Kazanskoi zheleznoi dorogi," *Zodchii* (No. 47, 1913): 483–87; D. Protopopof and A. Bloch, "The Housing Question and the Garden City Movement in Russia," *Garden Cities and Town Planning* 4 (July 1914): 167–69; Etienne De Groër, "Town Planning in Russia," *Garden Cities and Town Planning* 12 (July–August 1922): 117–23; Vigdaria E. Khazanova, *Sovetskaia arkhitektura pervykh let Oktiabria, 1917–25* (Moscow: Nauka, 1970), 44–45; V. N. Beloussov, "V. N. Semenov," in O. A. Shvidkovsky, *Building in the USSR, 1917–1932* (New York: Praeger, 1971), 67; Milka Bliznakov, "Urban Planning in the USSR: Integrative Theories," in Michael F. Hamm, ed., *The City in Russian History* (Lexington: University Press of Kentucky, 1976), 244; Michael F. Hamm, "The Breakdown of Urban Modernization: A Prelude to the Revolutions of 1917," in Hamm, ed., *The City in Russian History*, 196; S. Frederick Starr, "The Revival and Schism of Urban Planning in Twentieth-Century Russia," in Hamm, ed., *The City in Russian History*, 234–35; Catherine Cooke, "Activities of the Garden City Movement in Russia," *Transactions of the Martin Centre for Architecture and Urban Studies, University of Cambridge* 1 (1976): 237–38; Catherine Cooke, "Russian Responses to the Garden City Idea," *Architectural Review* 163 (June 1978): 353–63; Francesco Dal Co and Manfredo Tafuri, *Modern Architecture*, trans. by Robert Erich Wolf (New York: Harry N. Abrams, 1979), 210; Stanley Buder, *Visionaries and Planners: The Garden City Movement and the Modern Community* (New York: Oxford University Press, 1990), 139–40; Timothy J. Colton, *Moscow: Governing the Socialist Metropolis* (Cambridge, Mass.: Belknap Press of Harvard University Press, 1995), 63, 112–16, 221; David C. Goodman and Colin Chant, *European Cities and Technology: Industrial to Post-Industrial Cities* (London: Routledge, 1999), 308; Michael H. Lang, *Designing Utopia: John Ruskin's Urban Vision for Britain and America* (Montreal and New York: Black Rose Books, 1999), 57; Helen Meller, *European Cities, 1890–1930s: History, Culture and the Built Environment* (Chichester: John Wiley & Sons, 2001), 125–26; Kathleen Berton Murrell, *Discovering the Moscow Countryside: A Travel Guide to the Heart of Russia* (London and New York: I. B. Tauris, 2001), 141–42; Ivan V. Nevzgodine, "The Impact of the Trans-Siberian Railway on the Architecture and Urban Planning of Russian Cities," in Ralf Roth and Marie-Noëlle Polino, eds., *The City and the Railway in Europe* (Aldershot England, and Burlington, Vt.: Ashgate, 2003), 97–98; Boris Anan'ich and Alexander Kobak, "St. Petersburg and Green Space, 1850–2000: An Introduction," in Peter Clark, ed., *The European City and Green Space* (Aldershot, England, and Burlington, Vt.: Ashgate, 2006), 258–60; Robert H. Kargon and Arthur P. Molella, *Invented Edens: Techno-Cities of the Twentieth Century* (Cambridge, Mass., and London: MIT Press, 2008), 26; "Pioneers of the Railroad," http://phoebetaplin.com; "Prozorovka," http://www.utopia-britannica.org.uk.
189 Colton, *Moscow: Governing the Socialist Metropolis*, 63.
190 M. G. Dikanskii, *Postroila gorodov: Ikh plan I krasota* (Petrograd, 1915), quoted in Cooke, "Russian Responses to the Garden City Idea": 357.
191 Cooke, "Russian Responses to the Garden City Idea": 357.
192 Buder, *Visionaries and Planners: The Garden City Movement and the Modern Community*, 140.
193 Protopopof and Bloch, "The Housing Question and the Garden City Movement in Russia": 169.
194 De Groër, "Town Planning in Russia": 120.
195 Colton, *Moscow: Governing the Socialist Metropolis*, 221.
196 G. Vegman, "Rabochie stroitelstva v Moskve," *Sovremmennaia Arkhitektura* 1 (1926): 9; "Sokol," *Vechernyaya Moskva* (August 13, 1928): 2; "Einfamilienhaus der Siedlung 'Sokol,' Moskau, 1926," *Wasmuths Monatshefte für Baukunst* 13 (March 1929): 131; N. Markovnikov, "Poselok 'Sokol,'" *Stroitel'naya Promyshlennost'* 12 (December 1929): 1069–76; S. Frederick Starr, "OSA: The Union of Contemporary Architects," in George Gibian and H. W. Tjalsma, eds., *Russian Modernism: Culture and the Avant-Garde, 1900–1930* (Ithaca, N.Y., and London: Cornell University Press, 1976), 201 (n.47); Kathleen Berton, *Moscow: An Architectural History* (London: Studio Vista, 1977), 209; Catherine Cooke, "Russian Responses to the Garden City Idea," *Architectural Review* 163 (June 1978): 353–63; Francesco Dal Co and Manfredo Tafuri, *Modern Architecture*, trans. by Robert Erich Wolf (New York: Harry N. Abrams, 1979), 209–10; Serge Fauchereau, *Moscow, 1900–1930* (New York: Rizzoli International Publications, 1988), 197; Timothy J. Colton, *Moscow: Governing the Socialist Metropolis* (Cambridge, Mass.: Belknap Press of Harvard University Press, 1995), 221; Michael Lang and Leonid Rapoutov, "Capital City as Garden City: The Planning of Post-Revolutionary Moscow," in Vilma Hastaoglou, ed., *The Planning of Capital Cities* (Thessaloniki, Greece: Aristotle University, 1996), 795–812; Michael H. Lang, *Designing Utopia: John Ruskin's Urban Vision for Britain and America* (Montreal and New York: Black Rose Books, 1999), 57; Helen Meller, *European Cities, 1890–1930s: History, Culture and the Built Environment* (Chichester: John Wiley & Sons, 2001), 118, 126; Richard Anderson, "USA/USSR: Architecture and War," *Grey Room* 34 (Winter 2009): 80–103; Luke Harding, "Demolition Ball Threatens Moscow Artists' Colony," *The Guardian* (February 5, 2010): 27; Caldor Loth, "Moscow's Skyline: Handle with Care," *www.maps-moscow.com/userdata/part_01.pdf*; Phoebe Taplin, "Living in Moscow's Endangered Utopia," http://rbth.ru/articles/2010/02/24/240210_utopia.html; "Sokol," http://www.utopia-britannica.org.uk.
197 Meller, *European Cities, 1890–1930s: History, Culture and the Built Environment*, 118, 126.
198 John B. Powell, *My Twenty-five Years in China* (New York: Macmillan, 1945), 15–17; Jeffrey Cody, "Columbia Circle—an Obscured Shanghai Suburb, 1928–1932," *Dialogue: architecture + design + culture* 23 (Feb/March 1999): 130–35; Jeffrey W. Cody, *Exporting American Architecture, 1870–2000* (London and New York: Routledge, 2003), 118; Thomas J. Campanella, *The Concrete Dragon: China's Urban Revolution and What It Means for the World* (New York: Princeton Architectural Press, 2008), 207–8.

199 Quoted in Cody, "Columbia Circle—an Obscured Shanghai Suburb, 1928–1932": 132.
200 Gwendolyn Wright, *The Politics of Design in French Colonial Urbanism* (Chicago and London: University of Chicago Press, 1991), 228, 230–33; Robert R. Reed, "Constructing Highland Cities in Southeast Asia: Baguio (Philippines) and Dalat (Vietnam) as Scenes of Environmental Degradation," in Carla Chifos and Ruth Yabes, eds., *Southeast Asian Urban Environment: Structured and Spontaneous* (Tempe, Arizona: Arizona State University Program for Southeast Asian Studies Monograph Series Press, 2000), 227–46; Eric T. Jennings, "From Indochine to Indochic: The Lang Bian/Dalat Palace Hotel and French Colonial Leisure, Power and Culture," *Modern Asian Studies* 37 (no. 1, 2003): 159–94; Eric T. Jennings, *Imperial Heights: Dalat and the Making and Undoing of French Indochina* (Berkeley and Los Angeles: University of California Press, 2011), esp. chapter 7. For France's architectural endeavors in Indochina, see Wright, *The Politics of Design in French Colonial Urbanism*, chapter 4.
201 Reed, "Constructing Highland Cities in Southeast Asia: Baguio (Philippines) and Dalat (Vietnam) as Scenes of Environmental Degradation": 236.
202 Jennings, "From Indochine to Indochic": 166.
203 Reed, "Constructing Highland Cities in Southeast Asia: Baguio (Philippines) and Dalat (Vietnam) as Scenes of Environmental Degradation": 236.
204 Wright, *The Politics of Design in French Colonial Urbanism*, 232.
205 Wright, *The Politics of Design in French Colonial Urbanism*, 232.
206 Wright, *The Politics of Design in French Colonial Urbanism*, 232.
207 Gordon E. Cherry, "Introduction: Aspects of Twentieth-Century Planning," in Gordon E. Cherry, ed., *Shaping an Urban World* (New York: St. Martin's Press, 1980), 11; Shun-ichi J. Watanabe, "Garden City Japanese Style: The Case of Den-en Toshi Company Ltd., 1918–28," in Cherry, ed., *Shaping an Urban World*, 129–43; Shun-ichi J. Watanabe, "Metropolitanism as a Way of Life: The Case of Tokyo, 1868–1930," in Anthony Sutcliffe, ed., *Metropolis, 1890–1940* (London: Mansell, 1984), 423–25; Christine Chapman, "An Oasis of Spacious Living," *Look Japan* (August 1987): 39; Shun-ichi J. Watanabe, "The Japanese Garden City," in Steven V. Ward, ed., *The Garden City: Past, Present and Future* (London: E & FN Spon, 1992), 69–87; Ken Tadashi Oshima, "Denenchōfu: Building the Garden City in Japan," *Journal of the Society of Architectural Historians* 55 (June 1996): 140–51; Roman Cybriwsky, *Tokyo: The Shogun's City at the Twenty-first Century* (Chichester and New York: John Wiley & Sons, 1998), 135; Stephen V. Ward, "The Garden City as a Global Project," *Town & Country Planning* 67 (October 1998), special supplement: 28–32; Philip Pregill and Nancy Volkman, *Landscapes in History: Design and Planning in the Eastern and Western Traditions* (New York: John Wiley & Sons, 1999), 372; André Sorensen, *The Making of Urban Japan: Cities and Planning from Edo to the Twenty-first Century* (London and New York: Routledge, 2002), 137–38; Jordan Sand, *House and Home in Modern Japan: Architecture, Domestic Space and Bourgeois Culture, 1880–1930* (Cambridge, Mass., and London: Harvard University Press, 2003), 237–45; Angela Yiu, "'Beautiful Town': The Discovery of the Suburbs and the Vision of the Garden City in Late Meiji and Taishō Literature," *Japan Forum* 18 (No. 3, 2006): 315–38; Yorifusa Ishida, "The Concept of *Machi-Sodate* and Urban Planning," in André Sorensen and Carolin Funck, eds., *Living Cities in Japan* (London and New York: Routledge, 2007), 131 (n.5); Sumiko Enbutsu, "Meandering in Time Beside the Tama," *Japan Times* (November 7, 2003), http://search.japantimes.co.jp; "Garden Suburb, Japanese Style," http://jieunyverse.files.wordpress.com; http://homepage3.nifty.com/katodb/doc/text/2618.html; http://living-in-tokyo.com/en/area/denenchofu.html; http://www.tokyu-land.co.jp/english /company/history/index.html.
208 Hideo Shibusawa, *Waga Machi* (Tokyo: Ensen Shinbun-sha, 1971), 6, quoted in Watanabe, "Garden City Japanese Style: The Case of Den-en Toshi Company Ltd., 1918–28," in Cherry, ed., *Shaping an Urban World*, 141.
209 Hideo Shibusawa, quoted in Oshima, "Denenchōfu: Building the Garden City in Japan": 144.
210 Oshima, "Denenchōfu: Building the Garden City in Japan": 145–46.
211 Sand, *House and Home in Modern Japan: Architecture, Domestic Space and Bourgeois Culture, 1880–1930*, 241.
212 Pregill and Volkman, *Landscapes in History: Design and Planning in the Eastern and Western Traditions*, 372.
213 Oshima, "Denenchōfu: Building the Garden City in Japan": 146–47.
214 Quoted in Sand, *House and Home in Modern Japan: Architecture, Domestic Space and Bourgeois Culture, 1880–1930*, 242.
215 Quoted in Oshima, "Denenchōfu: Building the Garden City in Japan": 146.
216 Oshima, "Denenchōfu: Building the Garden City in Japan": 149.
217 Watanabe, "The Japanese Garden City," in Ward, ed., *The Garden City: Past, Present and Future*, 83.
218 Sorensen, *The Making of Urban Japan: Cities and Planning from Edo to the Twenty-first Century*, 137.
219 Jeffrey Eldon Hanes, "Seki Hajime and the Making of Modern Osaka" (Ph.D. diss., University of California, Berkeley, 1988): 344.
220 Hanes, "Seki Hajime and the Making of Modern Osaka": 343–50; Shun-ichi J. Watanabe, "The Japanese Garden City," in Steven V. Ward, ed., *The Garden City: Past, Present and Future* (London: E & FN Spon, 1992), 74–76, 79–80; Kuniaki Ito and Masatsugu Chiba, "Railway Stations and Local Communities in Japan," *Japan Railway & Transport Review* 28 (September 2001): 4–17; André Sorensen, *The Making of Urban Japan: Cities and Planning from Edo to the Twenty-first Century* (London and New York: Routledge, 2002), 137–39; http://homepage3.nifty.com/katodb/doc/text/2618.html.
221 Hajime Seki, *Jutaku mondai to toshi keikaku* (Kyoto: Kobundo shobo, 1923), 6, 65, quoted in Hanes, "Seki Hajime and the Making of Modern Osaka": 348.
222 Quoted in http://homepage3.nifty.com/katodb/doc/text/2618.html.

Chapter 8

1 John Nelson Tarn, *Five Per Cent Philanthropy* (Cambridge: Cambridge University Press, 1973), 144, 145. Also see G. L. Morris, "The Evolution of Village Architecture in England," *International Studio* 1 (May 1897): 177–84; "Robert Owen's Scheme," *Garden Cities and Town Planning* 4 (August 1909): 231–32; Lewis Mumford, *The Story of Utopias* (New York: Boni and Liveright, 1922), 123–24; Catherine Bauer, *Modern Housing* (Boston and New York: Houghton Mifflin, 1934), 69–73; Lewis Mumford, *The Culture of Cities* (New York: Harcourt, Brace & Co., 1938), 392–93; J. Bronowski and Bruce Mazlish, *The Western Intellectual Tradition* (New York: Harper Perennial, 1960), 450–71; W. H. G. Armytage, *Heavens Below: Utopian Experiments in England, 1560–1960* (Toronto: University of Toronto Press, 1961), 77–87; G. D. H. Cole, *The Life of Robert Owen* (London: Frank Cass, 1965), 90–115, 179–85; Gerald Burke, *Towns in the Making* (London: Edward Arnold, 1971), 137; Norman T. Newton, *Design on the Land: The Development of Landscape Architecture* (Cambridge, Mass., and London: Harvard University Press, 1971), 447–48; J. N. Tarn, *Working-Class Housing in 19th-Century Britain* (London: Lund Humphries for the Architectural Association, 1971), 30; A. E. J. Morris, "Public Health and Social Reform," *Official Architecture and Planning* 34 (June 1971): 460–62; Enid Gaulde, *Cruel Habitations: A History of Working-Class Housing, 1780–1918* (London: Allen & Unwin, 1974), 58–62; Arthur B. Gallion and Simon Eisner, *The Urban Pattern: City Planning and Design* (New York: D. Van Nostrand Company, 1975), 76; Stephen Bayley, *The Garden City* (Milton Keynes: Open University Press, 1975), 11–12; Michael Reed, *The Landscape of Britain from the Beginnings to 1914* (London: Routledge, 1990), 300–301; Gregory Claeys, ed., *Selected Works of Robert Owen, Volume 1: Early Writings* (London: William Pickering, 1993), 13–21; Ian Donnachie and George Hewitt, *Historic New Lanark* (Edinburgh: Edinburgh University Press, 1999), especially chapters 4, 5, and 6; Roland Schaer, Gregory Claeys, and Lyman Tower Sargen, eds., *Utopia: The Search for the Ideal Society in the Western World* (New York: New York Public Library and Oxford University Press, 2000), 208–9; Ruth Eaton, *Ideal Cities: Utopianism and the (Un)Built Environment* (New York and London: Thames & Hudson, 2001), 128–30.
2 For Cromford, see Nikolaus Pevsner, *The Buildings of England: Derbyshire* (1953; London: Penguin, 2000), 48–51, 157–60; Michael Reed, *The Landscape of Britain from the Beginnings to 1914* (London: Routledge, 1990), 263; John S. Garner, "The Company Town. Industry and Territory in the 19th Century," *Rassegna* 70 (1997): 30; Ian Donnachie and George Hewitt, *Historic New Lanark* (Edinburgh: Edinburgh University Press, 1999), 6, 19. For Belper, see Nikolaus Pevsner, *The Buildings of England: Derbyshire* (1953; London: Penguin, 2000), 49–51, 87–90. For Milford and Derby, see Nikolaus Pevsner, *The Buildings of England: Derbyshire* (1953; London: Penguin, 2000), 49–51, 87–88.
3 Pevsner, *The Buildings of England: Derbyshire*, 49.
4 J. D. Porteous, "Goole: A Pre-Victorian Company Town," *Industrial Archaeology* 6 (May 1969): 105–13, 137, 138. Also see Nikolaus Pevsner, *The Buildings of England: Yorkshire, The West Riding* (1959; New Haven, Conn., and London: Yale University Press, 2003), 223–24; Michael Reed, *The Landscape of Britain* (London: Routledge, 1990), 299.
5 Porteous, "Goole: A Pre-Victorian Company Town": 109.
6 Gilbert Camblin, *The Town in Ulster* (Mullan: Belfast, 1951), quoted in Gerald Burke, *Towns in the Making* (London: Edward Arnold, 1971), 137. Also see Budgett Meakin, *Model Factories and Villages* (London: T. Fisher Unwin, 1905; New York and London: Garland Publishing, 1985), 419–20; W. Ashworth, "British Industrial Villages in the Nineteenth Century," *Economic History Review* new series 3 (1951): 378–87; J. N. Tarn, *Working-Class Housing in 19th-Century Britain* (London: Lund Humphries for the Architectural Association, 1971), 32; John Nelson Tarn, *Five Per Cent Philanthropy* (Cambridge: Cambridge University Press, 1973), 145; Gordon E. Cherry, *The Evolution of British Town Planning* (New York: John Wiley & Sons, 1974), 18; John S. Garner, *The Company Town: Architecture and Society in the Early Industrial Age* (New York: Oxford University Press, 1992), 8; James Stevens Curl, *Victorian Architecture: Diversity & Invention* (Reading: Spire Books, 2007), 501.
7 John Herapath, "Wolverton Establishment," *Herapath's Railway Magazine* (November 20, 1841): 989–90; Colin and Rose Bell, *City Fathers: Town Planning in Britain from Roman Times to 1900* (New York and Washington: Frederick A. Praeger, 1969), 146, 147–48; J. N. Tarn, *Working-Class Housing in 19th-Century Britain* (London: Lund Humphries for the Architectural Association, 1971), 33, 79; John Nelson Tarn, *Five Per Cent Philanthropy* (Cambridge: Cambridge University Press, 1973), 148–49; Michael Reed, *The Landscape of Britain* (London: Routledge, 1990), 283–84; John Cattell and Keith Falconer, *Swindon: The Legacy of a Railway Town* (London: HMSO, 1995), 12–13; Nikolaus Pevsner and Elizabeth Williamson, *The Buildings of England: Buckinghamshire* (New Haven, Conn., and London: Yale University Press, 2003), 564–66.
8 Colin and Rose Bell, *City Fathers: Town Planning in Britain from Roman Times to 1900* (New York and Washington: Frederick A. Praeger, 1969), 148–55; Gavin Gibbons, *The Welsh Border: From the Wirral to the Wye* (London: Geographia, 1970), 33–34; J. N. Tarn, *Working-Class Housing in 19th-Century Britain* (London: Lund Humphries for the Architectural Association, 1971), 33; Nikolaus Pevsner and Edward Hubbard, *The Buildings of England: Cheshire* (1971; New Haven, Conn., and London: Yale University Press, 2003), 186–90; John Nelson Tarn, *Five Per Cent Philanthropy* (Cambridge: Cambridge University Press, 1973), 148–49; M. J. Daunton, *House and Home in the Victorian City: Working-Class Housing 1850–1914* (London and Baltimore, MD: Edward Arnold, 1983), 185; Michael Reed, *The Landscape of Britain from the Beginnings to 1914* (London: Routledge, 1990), 299–300; Diane K. Drummond, *Crewe: Railway Town, Company and People, 1840–1914* (Aldershot, Hants, England; Brookfield, VT: Scolar Press, 1995), 9–34; Jonathan Glancey, "The Beauty of Crewe," *Guardian* (December 6, 2005), in guardian.co.uk.
9 L. V. Grinsell, H. B. Wells, H. S. Tallamy, and John Betjeman, *Studies in the History of Swindon* (Swindon: Borough Council, 1950), 93–130; Colin and Rose Bell, *City Fathers: Town Planning in Britain from Roman Times to 1900* (New York and Washington: Frederick A. Praeger, 1969), 147; J. N. Tarn, *Working-Class Housing in 19th-Century Britain* (London: Lund Humphries for the Architectural Association, 1971), 33; John Nelson Tarn, *Five Per Cent Philanthropy* (Cambridge: Cambridge University Press, 1973), 148–49; John Cattell and Keith Falconer, *Swindon: The Legacy of a Railway Town* (London: HMSO, 1995).
10 Nikolaus Pevsner, *The Buildings of England: North Lancashire* (1969; New Haven, Conn., and London: Yale University Press, 2002), 55–59. Also see Colin and Rose Bell, *City Fathers: Town Planning in Britain from Roman Times to 1900* (New York and Washington: Frederick A. Praeger, 1969), 155–62; M. J. Daunton, *House and Home in the Victorian City: Working-Class Housing 1850–1914* (London and Baltimore, MD: Edward Arnold, 1983), 185.
11 "Copley," part 1, Turner Clippings of the Halifax Public Library, 4 (June 19, 1880), 222,

quoted in Walter L. Creese, *The Search for Environment*, expanded edition (New Haven, Conn.: Yale University Press, 1966; Baltimore and London: Johns Hopkins University Press, 1992), 23. Also see James Hole, *The Homes of the Working Classes* (London: Longmans, Green & Co., 1866), 69–73, plates 7–9; Nikolaus Pevsner and Enid Radcliffe, *The Buildings of England: Yorkshire, The West Riding* (1959; New Haven and London: Yale University Press, 2003), 64, 170; Creese, *The Search for Environment*, 22–29; John L. Berbiers, "The Planned Villages of Halifax," *Building* 211 (July 15, 1966): 79–80; Colin and Rose Bell, *City Fathers: Town Planning in Britain from Roman Times to 1900* (New York: Praeger, 1969), 198; Vanessa Parker, *The English House in the Nineteenth Century* (London: Historical Association, 1970), 35–37; J. N. Tarn, *Working-Class Housing in 19th-Century Britain* (London: Lund Humphries for the Architectural Association, 1971), 32, figs. 45, 46; John Nelson Tarn, *Five Per Cent Philanthropy* (Cambridge: Cambridge University Press, 1973), 147; Stephen Bayley, *The Garden City* (Milton Keynes: Open University Press, 1975), 12–13; John S. Garner, *The Model Company Town: Urban Design Though Private Enterprise in Nineteenth-Century New England* (Amherst: University of Massachusetts Press, 1984), 102, 103, 104; Rupert Hebblethwaite, "Housing Programme in Sheffield before 1914," *Architectural History* 30 (1987): 143–79; Walter Kieß, *Urbanismus im Industriezeitalter* (Berlin: Ernst & Sohn, 1991), 262–64; Ruth Eaton, *Ideal Cities: Utopianism and the (Un)Built Environment* (New York and London: Thames & Hudson, 2002), 131; James Stevens Curl, *Victorian Architecture: Diversity & Invention* (Reading: Spire Books, 2007), 504.

12 Edward Akroyd, quoted in Parker, *The English House in the Nineteenth Century*, 36.

13 Bayley, *The Garden City*, 12–13.

14 Hole, *The Homes of the Working Classes*, 66–69, plates 5–6; Robert Balgarnie, *Sir Titus Salt, Baronet: His Life and Its Lessons* (London: Hodder & Stoughton, 1878), 113–22; *Saltaire: Yorkshire, England, A Sketch-History, with Brief Descriptions of Its Origin and Later Developments* (Saltaire: Sir Titus Salt, Bart., Sons & Co., 1895); Budgett Meakin, *Model Factories and Villages: Ideal Conditions of Labour and Housing* (London: T. Fisher Unwin, 1905), 416–17; Catherine Bauer, *Modern Housing* (Boston and New York: Houghton Mifflin, 1934), 89; J. M. Richards, "Minor Masters of the XIXth Century: Notes on Some Lesser-Known Architects, VII. Sir Titus Salt or The Lord of Saltaire," *Architectural Review* 80 (November 1936): 213–18; "The Congregational Church at Saltaire Built as Part of the Planning Scheme," *Country Life* 96 (October 13, 1944): 649; "Yorkshire Model Town," letter to the editor, *Country Life* 96 (October 13, 1944): 649; Pevsner and Radcliffe, *The Buildings of England: Yorkshire, The West Riding*, 427–28; Robert K. Dewhirst, "Saltaire," *Town Planning Review* 31 (July 1960): 135–44; Creese, *The Search for Environment*, 30–40; Colin and Rose Bell, *City Fathers: Town Planning in Britain from Roman Times to 1900* (New York: Praeger, 1969), 188–95; Gerald Burke, *Towns in the Making* (London: Edward Arnold, 1971), 140–41; Tarn, *Working-Class Housing in 19th-Century Britain*, 22, 32; A. E. J. Morris, "Philanthropic Housing," *Official Architecture and Planning* 34 (August 1971): 598–600; James Stevens Curl, "A Victorian Model Town: Saltaire, Yorkshire," *Country Life* 151 (March 9, 1972): 542–44; H. J. Dyos and Michael Wolff, ed., *The Victorian City: Images and Realities, Volume 1* (London and Boston: Routledge & Kegan Paul, 1973), 883; Enid Gauldie, *Cruel Habitations: A History of Working-Class Housing, 1780–1918* (London: Allen & Unwin, 1974), 62–63; Bayley, *The Garden City*, 13; Gillian Darley, *Villages of Vision* (London: The Architectural Press, 1975), 66, 67; John Nelson Tarn, *Five Per Cent Philanthropy* (Cambridge: Cambridge University Press, 1973), 145–46; *Titus of Salts* (Bradford, Yorkshire: Watmoughs, Ltd., 1976); Jack Reynolds, *Saltaire: An Introduction to the Village of Sir Titus Salt* (Bradford: City of Bradford Metropolitan Council Art Galleries and Museums, 1977), 5–28; Robert A. M. Stern with John Massengale, *The Anglo-American Suburb* (London: Architectural Design, 1981), 51; Ian Campbell Bradley, "Titus Salt: Enlightened Entrepreneur," *History Today* 37 (May 1987): 30–36; Walter Kieß, *Urbanismus im Industriezeitalter* (Berlin: Ernst & Sohn, 1991), 264–70; F. H. A. Aalen and Colm O'Brien, eds., *England's Landscape: The North East* (London: Collins, 2006), 176; Tim Lynch, "Saltaire: the Town That Titus Built," *British Heritage* 27 (July 2006): 50–52; James Stevens Curl, *Victorian Architecture: Diversity & Invention* (Reading: Spire Books, 2007), 502–4; Neil Jackson, Jo Lintonbon, and Bryony Staples, *Saltaire: The Making of a Model Town* (Reading: Spire Books, 2010); Vittorio Magnago Lampugnani, *Die Stadt im 20. Jahrhundert* (Berlin: Verlag Klaus Wagenbach, 2010), 15–17.

15 Creese, *The Search for Environment*, 31.

16 In 1851 the English critic Robert Baker in his book *The Present Condition of the Working Classes* (Longman Brown, London) urged that English reformers look to Lowell as their model. But Walter L. Creese suggests in *The Search for Environment* (p.1) that the first attempt at model industrial housing was at New Lanark, Scotland in 1793.

17 Bradley, "Titus Salt: Enlightened Entrepreneur": 33.

18 Morris, "Philanthropic Housing": 598.

19 J. S. Fletcher, *Picturesque History of Yorkshire* (London: Dent, 1899), 397, quoted in Creese, *The Search for Environment*, 36. Also see Creese, *The Search for Environment*, 35.

20 J. M. Richards, "Sir Titus Salt," *Architectural Review* LXXX (November 1936): 213–18, quoted in Morris, "Philanthropic Housing": 599.

21 Curl, "A Victorian Model Town": 544.

22 Henry S. Simmonds, *All About Battersea* (London: Ashfield Printer, 1882), 62; William Hulme Lever Leverhulme, *Viscount Leverhulme, by His Son* (London: George Allen & Unwin, 1927), 87; Eric Hardwicke Rideout, *The Growth of Wirral* (Liverpool, E. A. Bryant, 1927), 84–85, 87; W. Ashworth, "British Industrial Villages in the Nineteenth Century," *Economic History Review* new series 3 (1951): 379; J. N. Tarn, "The Model Village at Bromborough Pool," *Town Planning Review* 35 (January 1965): 329–36; Alan Watson, *Price's Village: A Study of a Victorian Industrial and Social Experiment* (Bromborough Pool: Price's (Bromborough) Limited, 1966); Colin and Rose Bell, *City Fathers: Town Planning in Britain from Roman Times to 1900* (New York and Washington: Frederick A. Praeger, 1969), 195; Nikolaus Pevsner and Edward Hubbard, *The Buildings of England: Cheshire* (1971; New Haven, Conn., and London: Yale University Press, 2003), 37, 116–17; J. N. Tarn, *Working-Class Housing in 19th-Century Britain* (London: Lund Humphries for the Architectural Association, 1971), 32; Enid Gaulde, *Cruel Habitations: A History of Working-Class Housing, 1780–1918* (London: Allen & Unwin, 1974), 62; Gillian Darley, *Villages of Vision* (London: The Architectural Press, 1975), 65–66; Gerald Burke, *Towns in the Making* (London: Edward Arnold, 1971), 137; Stephen Bayley, *The Garden City* (Milton Keynes: Open University Press, 1975), 14–15.

23 Watson, *Price's Village: A Study of a Victorian Industrial and Social Experiment*, 56–57.

24 Tarn, "The Model Village at Bromborough Pool": 336.

25 "Akroydon, Improved Dwellings for the Working Classes," *Builder* 21 (February 14, 1863): 109–12, 116, 117; Hole, *The Homes of the Working Classes*, 72–75; Nikolaus Pevsner and Enid Radcliffe, *The Buildings of England: Yorkshire, The West Riding* (1959; New Haven, Conn., and London: Yale University Press, 2003), 64, 239–40; Walter L. Creese, *The Search for Environment*, expanded edition (New Haven, Conn.: Yale University Press, 1966; Baltimore and London: Johns Hopkins University Press, 1992), 40–46; John L. Berbiers, "The Planned Villages of Halifax," *Building* 211 (July 15, 1966): 79–80; Colin and Rose Bell, *City Fathers: Town Planning in Britain from Roman Times to 1900* (New York: Praeger, 1969), 198; Vanessa Parker, *The English House in the Nineteenth Century* (London: Historical Association, 1970), 35–39; J. N. Tarn, *Working-Class Housing in 19th-Century Britain* (London: Lund Humphries for the Architectural Association, 1971), 32–33, figs. 47–49; John Nelson Tarn, *Five Per Cent Philanthropy* (Cambridge: Cambridge University Press, 1973), 147–48; Gillian Darley, *Villages of Vision* (London: Architectural Press, 1975), 63, 67–68; Garner, *The Model Company Town*, 104; Dyos and Wolff, ed., *The Victorian City: Images and Realities, Volume 1*, 883; Walter Kieß, *Urbanismus im Industriezeitalter* (Berlin: Ernst & Sohn, 1991), 271–73; Ruth Eaton, *Ideal Cities: Utopianism and the (Un)Built Environment* (New York and London: Thames & Hudson, 2002), 130, 131; F. H. A. Aalen and Colm O'Brien, eds., *England's Landscape: The North East* (London: Collins, 2006), 176; James Stevens Curl, *Victorian Architecture: Diversity & Invention* (Reading: Spire Books, 2007), 504–5; Vittorio Magnago Lampugnani, *Die Stadt im 20. Jahrhundert* (Berlin: Verlag Klaus Wagenbach, 2010), 17–19.

26 "Akroydon, Improved Dwellings for the Working Classes": 110.

27 Edward Akroyd, *On Improved Dwellings for the Working Classes* (London: Shaw, 1862), 8, quoted in Creese, *The Search for Environment*, 43 (n.9).

28 Creese, *The Search for Environment*, 43.

29 Edward Akroyd, quoted in Creese, *The Search for Environment*, 44.

30 Bayley, *The Garden City*, 14.

31 Walter L. Creese, *The Search for Environment*, expanded edition (New Haven, Conn.: Yale University Press, 1966; Baltimore and London: Johns Hopkins University Press, 1992), 46–48, 50. Also see James Hole, *The Homes of the Working Classes, with Suggestions for their Improvement* (London: Longmans, Green & Co., 1866), 75–79; H. J. Dyos and Michael Wolff, *The Victorian City: Images and Realities, Volume 1* (London and Boston: Routledge & Kegan Paul, 1973), 883; John Nelson Tarn, *Five Per Cent Philanthropy* (Cambridge: Cambridge University Press, 1973), 148.

32 Creese, *The Search for Environment*, 48.

33 Tarn, *Five Per Cent Philanthropy*, 148.

34 Sir Francis Crossley, quoted in H. J. Dyos and Michael Wolff, *The Victorian City: Images and Realities, Volume 1* (London and Boston: Routledge & Kegan Paul, 1973), 883. Also see Kate Colquhoun, *"The Busiest Man in England": A Life of Joseph Paxton* (Boston: David R. Godine, 2003), 228; Walter L. Creese, *The Search for Environment*, expanded edition (New Haven, Conn.: Yale University Press, 1966; Baltimore and London: Johns Hopkins University Press, 1992), 48–55.

35 Budgett Meakin, *Model Factories and Villages* (London: T. Fisher Unwin, 1905; New York and London: Garland Publishing, 1985), 422. Also see "Competitions/Aintree," *Building News* 55 (July 6, 1888): 29; "A Model Village," *Builder* 55 (July 7, 1888): 16; "Design for Model Village, Aintree," *Builder* 55 (August 25, 1888): 140–41; "Model Village at Aintree, near Liverpool: Selected Design," *Building News* 55 (September 7, 1888): 314, 315, 324; "Workmen's Dwellings at Aintree," *Building News* 55 (September 21, 1888): 390–91; Stephen Bayley, *The Garden City* (Milton Keynes: Open University Press, 1975), 15; Walter L. Creese, *The Search for Environment*, expanded edition (New Haven, Conn.: Yale University Press, 1966; Baltimore and London: Johns Hopkins University Press, 1992), 126–27, 184; J. N. Tarn, *Working-Class Housing in 19th-Century Britain* (London: Lund Humphries for the Architectural Association, 1971), 36.

36 Martin Gaskell, "Model Industrial Villages in S. Yorkshire/N. Derbyshire and the Early Town Planning Movement," *Town Planning Review* 50 (October 1979): 437–58.

37 Emerson Bainbridge, quoted in Gaskell, "Model Industrial Villages in S. Yorkshire/N. Derbyshire and the Early Town Planning Movement": 446.

38 Nikolaus Pevsner, *The Buildings of England: Derbyshire*, rev. by Elizabeth Williamson (Harmondsworth; New York: Penguin, 1986), 92, 101. Also see Walter L. Creese, *The Search for Environment*, expanded edition (New Haven, Conn.: Yale University Press, 1966; Baltimore and London: Johns Hopkins University Press, 1992), 184; Martin Gaskell, "Model Industrial Villages in S. Yorkshire/N. Derbyshire and the Early Town Planning Movement," *Town Planning Review* 50 (October 1979): 437–58; Robin Thornes, *Images of Industry: Coal* (Swindon: Royal Commission on the Historical Monuments of England, 1994), 80–81; *New Bolsover Model Village Planning Guidelines: Supplementary Planning Guidance* (Bolsover: Bolsover District Council, October 2008); Philip Riden and Dudley Fowkes, *Bolsover: Castle, Town and Colliery* (Chichester, England: Phillimore, 2008), 128–36.

39 "Evolution of Village Architecture in England," *International Studio* 1 (May 1897): 177–84. Also see Catherine Bauer, *Modern Housing* (Boston and New York: Houghton Mifflin, 1934), 7, 89–90; Walter L. Creese, *The Search for Environment*, expanded edition (New Haven, Conn.: Yale University Press, 1966; Baltimore and London: Johns Hopkins University Press, 1992), 184; Gordon E. Cherry, *The Evolution of British Town Planning* (New York: John Wiley & Sons, 1974), 23; Martin Gaskell, "Model Industrial Villages in S. Yorkshire/N. Derbyshire and the Early Town Planning Movement," *Town Planning Review* 50 (October 1979): 437–58; Nikolaus Pevsner, *The Buildings of England: Derbyshire*, rev. by Elizabeth Williamson (Harmondsworth; New York: Penguin, 1986), 156; Philip Riden and Dudley Fowkes, *Bolsover: Castle, Town and Colliery* (Chichester, England: Phillimore, 2008), 133.

40 Bauer, *Modern Housing*, 89–90.

41 P. B. Houfton, "A Model Mining Village," *Garden Cities and Town Planning* 3 (November 1908): 125–28; Patrick Abercrombie, "Modern Town Planning in England: A Comparative Review of 'Garden City' Schemes in England," *Town Planning Review* 1 (July 1910): 111–12; Patrick Abercrombie, "A Tour of the Garden Cities," *Town Planning Review* 2 (October 1911): 230–33; Ewart G. Culpin, *The Garden City Movement Up-to-Date* (London: Garden Cities and Town Planning Association, 1913), 46–47; Henry R. Aldridge, *The Case for Town*

Planning (London: National Housing and Town Planning Council, c. 1915), 413, 415; Nelson P. Lewis, *The Planning of the Modern City* (New York: Wiley, 1916), 304–5; Nikolaus Pevsner, *The Buildings of England: Yorkshire, The West Riding* (1959; New Haven, Conn., and London: Yale University Press, 2003), 557; Walter L. Creese, *The Search for Environment*, expanded edition (New Haven, Conn.: Yale University Press, 1966; Baltimore and London: Johns Hopkins University Press, 1992), 184; John Nelson Tarn, *Five Per Cent Philanthropy* (Cambridge: Cambridge University Press, 1973), 172–74; Martin Gaskell, "Model Industrial Villages in S. Yorkshire/N. Derbyshire and the Early Town Planning Movement," *Town Planning Review* 50 (October 1979): 437–58; Robin Thornes, *Images of Industry: Coal* (Swindon: Royal Commission on the Historical Monuments of England, 1994), 84–86.

42 Gaskell, "Model Industrial Villages in S. Yorkshire/N. Derbyshire and the Early Town Planning Movement": 447.

43 Gaskell, "Model Industrial Villages in S. Yorkshire/N. Derbyshire and the Early Town Planning Movement": 448.

44 Ebenezer Howard, quoted in Tarn, *Five Per Cent Philanthropy*, 173.

45 Abercrombie, "A Tour of the Garden Cities": 232.

46 Abercrombie, "A Tour of the Garden Cities": 232.

47 Abercrombie, "A Tour of the Garden Cities": 231.

48 Percy Houfton, "The Raw Material of Town Planning," *Garden Cities and Town Planning* 4 (1910): 294, as quoted in Gaskell, "Model Industrial Villages in S. Yorkshire/N. Derbyshire and the Early Town Planning Movement": 448.

49 Robert Brown, "Progress of the Garden City Movement in England," *The Arena* 40 (November 1908): 459–60; Patrick Abercrombie, "A Comparative Review of 'Garden City' Schemes in England, Part II," *Town Planning Review* 1 (July 1910): 114–15, plate 38; "The Shopping Centre, the Garden Village, Hull," *Building News* 99 (October 14, 1910): 545; Ewart G. Culpin, *The Garden City Movement Up-to-Date* (London: Garden Cities and Town Planning Association, 1913), 34; "The Garden Village, Hull," *Builder* 104 (February 7, 1913): 183–85; Nikolaus Pevsner and David Neave, *The Buildings of England: Yorkshire: York and the East Riding* (1972; New Haven, Conn., and London: Yale University Press, 1995), 102, 563–64; John Nelson Tarn, *Five Per Cent Philanthropy* (Cambridge: Cambridge University Press, 1973), 173; Gordon E. Cherry, *The Evolution of British Town Planning* (New York: John Wiley & Sons, 1974), 23; M. J. Daunton, *House and Home in the Victorian City: Working-Class Housing 1850–1914* (London and Baltimore, MD: Edward Arnold, 1983), 28–29; "Reinforcing Humberside's Heritage," *Heritage Outlook* 5 (September 1985): 104; Mervyn Miller, "Garden Cities and Suburbs: At Home and Abroad," *Journal of Town Planning History* 1 (February 2002): 6–28; David and Susan Neave, *Hull* (New Haven, Conn., and London: Yale University Press, 174–77.

50 Letter to T. R. Ferens, quoted in Pevsner and Neave, *The Buildings of England: Yorkshire: York and the East Riding*, 563.

51 Pevsner and Neave, *The Buildings of England: Yorkshire: York and the East Riding*, 564.

52 "The Garden Village, Hull": 183.

53 Ewart G. Culpin, "Housing Organization," *Garden Cities and Town Planning* 6 (May 1916): 61–73; *Houses for Workers* (London: Technical Journals, 1917), 58–65, 71, 73, 79, 83, 85, 87, 89, 91, 93; "Government Housing Scheme, Well Hall, Eltham, Kent," *Journal of the American Institute of Architects* 5 (September 1917): 425–40; Gordon Allen, *The Cheap Cottage and Small House: A Manual of Economical Building* (London: B. T. Batsford, 1919), frontispiece, figs. 27–30; S. L. G. Beaufoy, "Well Hall Estate, Eltham," *Town Planning Review* (October 1950): 259–71; Bridget Cherry and Nikolaus Pevsner, *The Buildings of England: London 2, South* (1983; London: Penguin, 1999), 242, 305–6; Michael H. Lang, "The Design of Yorkship Garden Village," in Mary Corbin Sies and Christopher Silver, eds., *Planning the Twentieth-Century American City* (Baltimore: Johns Hopkins University Press, 1996), 120–44; Miller, "Garden Cities and Suburbs: At Home and Abroad": 17; Chris Coates, *Utopia Britannica: Volume I, British Utopian Experiments: 1325–1945* (London: Diggers & Dreamers, 2001), 216.

54 Mark Swenarton, "Well Hall Estate," in Cherry and Pevsner, *The Buildings of England: London 2, South*, 305–6.

55 G. E. Phillips, quoted in Beaufoy, "Well Hall Estate, Eltham": 260.

56 Ewart G. Culpin, quoted in "Government Housing Scheme, Well Hall, Eltham, Kent": 425.

57 Culpin, "Housing Organization": 70.

58 "A Government Housing Scheme; Roe Green Village Scheme, Kingsbury," *Builder* 114 (January 4, 1918): 5–8; J. F. McR, "Roe Green Garden Hamlet," *Architectural Review* 49 (February 1921): 27–33; Allen, *The Cheap Cottage and Small House*, figs. 54, 57, 74, 101; "Roe Green Village, Hendon," *Garden Cities and Town Planning* 10 (April 1920): 84; Mark Swenarton, "Roe Green Village," in Bridget Cherry and Nikolaus Pevsner, *The Buildings of England: London 3, North West* (1991; London: Penguin, 2001), 138; *London Suburbs* (London: Merrell Holberton, 1999), 103, 182; Miller, "Garden Cities and Suburbs: At Home and Abroad": 17.

59 Swenarton, "Roe Green Village," in Cherry and Pevsner, *The Buildings of England: London 3, North West*, 138.

60 McR, "Roe Green Garden Hamlet": 28.

61 Ewart G. Culpin, "Housing Organization," *Garden Cities and Town Planning* 6 (May 1916): 61–73; Gordon Allen, *The Cheap Cottage and Small House: A Manual of Economical Building* (London: B. T. Batsford, 1919), 2–3, 18–19, 23–24, 26–27, 50; "Crayford Village Extension," *The Builder* (June 20, 1919): 612–13; Simon Pepper and Mark Swenarton, "Garden Suburbs for Munition Workers," *Architectural Review* 162 (1978): 366–75; Malcolm Barr-Hamilton, *From Country to Suburb: The Development of the Bexley Area from 1800 to the Present Day* (Bexley, Kent: Bexley London Borough Leisure Services, 1996), 47–52; Bridget Cherry and Nikolaus Pevsner, *London 2: South* (London: Penguin, 1999), 82, 143.

62 "Dormanstown: A New Industrial Village," *Architect* 101 (May 2, 1919): 295–96, plates; "Dormanstown: An Industrial Village," *Architects' Journal* 49 (May 28, 1919): 370–71; H. J. Birnstingl, "Notes from England, with Special References to Post-War Housing Developments," *Architectural Forum* 31 (November 1919): 163–69; "The Industrial Village of Dormanstown, Redcar, Yorks," *Architects' Journal* 49 (December 31, 1919): 812–15; C. H. James and F. R. Yerbury, *Small Houses for the Community* (London: Crosby Lockwood & Son, 1924), plates 56–64; Lawrence Weaver, *Cottages: Their Planning, Design and Materials* (London: Country Life; New York: Charles Scribner's Sons, 1926), 328–30, 333–35; Nikolaus Pevsner, *The Buildings of England: Yorkshire, The North Riding* (London: Penguin, 1966; New

Haven, Conn., and London: Yale University Press, 2002), 138; Gillian Darley, *Villages of Vision* (London: Architectural Press, 1975), 146; Simon Pepper and Mark Swenarton, "Neo-Georgian Maison-type," *Architectural Review* 168 (August 1980): 87–92; Alan Powers, "'Architects I Have Known': The Architectural Career of S. D. Adshead," *Architectural History* 24 (1981): 105.

63 Pepper and Mark Swenarton, "Neo-Georgian Maison-type": 87.

64 "Some Public Utility Societies' Schemes," *Garden Cities and Town Planning* 9 (May 1919): 89–92; "Swanpool Garden Suburb, Lincoln," *Architects' Journal* 50 (July 16, 1919): 90–95; Birnstingl, "Notes from England, with Special References to Post-War Housing Developments": 163–69; A. C. Holliday, "The Site Planning of Housing Schemes," *Town Planning Review* 8 (December 1920): 133; "Swanpool Garden Suburb, Lincoln," *Architects' Journal* 55 (May 24, 1922): 749–58; C. H. James and F. R. Yerbury, *Small Houses for the Community* (London: Crosby Lockwood & Son, 1924), plates XC–CI; Nikolaus Pevsner and John Harris, revised by Nicholas Antram, *The Buildings of England: Lincolnshire* (1964; New Haven, Conn., and London: Yale University Press, 1989), 31, 526; David Stocker, *England's Landscape: The East Midlands* (London: Collins, 2006), 101.

65 See Gordon Cherry, "Homes for Heroes," *New Society* 47 (February 1, 1979): 238–40; Mark Swenarton, *Homes Fit for Heroes: The Politics and Architecture of Early State Housing in Britain* (London: Heinemann Educational, 1981).

66 Bridget Cherry and Nikolaus Pevsner, *The Buildings of England: London 2, South* (1983; London: Penguin, 1994), 553; *London Suburbs*, 224.

67 Bridget Cherry and Nikolaus Pevsner, *The Buildings of England: London 3, North West* (London: Penguin, 1999), 163. Also see "G. W. R. Garden Villages, Middlesex," *Builder* 145 (November 17, 1933): 778, 782; *London Suburbs*, 192.

68 "Fairholme Estate at Bedford, Middlesex," *Architects' Journal* 83 (February 6, 1936): 238–40; Bridget Cherry and Nikolaus Pevsner, *The Buildings of England: London 3, North West* (London: Penguin, 1999), 69, 415.

69 Thomas Lloyd, Julian Orbach, and Robert Scourfield, *The Buildings of Wales: Pembrokeshire* (New Haven, Conn., and London: Yale University Press, 2004), 107, 196.

70 W. Ashworth, "British Industrial Villages in the Nineteenth Century," *Economic History Review* new series 3 (1951): 385; Richard Haslam, *The Buildings of Wales: Powys (Montgomeryshire, Radnorshire, Breconshire)* (New Haven, Conn., and London: Yale University Press, 2003), 318; Mary Worsfold, "Buckland and Farmer," in Phillada Ballard, ed., *Birmingham's Victorian and Edwardian Architects* (Wetherby: Oblong Creative for the Birmingham and West Midlands Group of the Victorian Society, 2009), 516–17, 518.

71 Edward Hubbard, *The Buildings of Wales: Clwyd (Denbighshire and Flintshire)* (London: Penguin; Cardiff: University of Wales Press, 1994), 85, 421.

72 "A Swansea Garden Village," *Garden Cities and Town Planning* 4 (July 1910): 304; Ewart G. Culpin, *The Garden City Movement Up-to-Date* (London: Garden Cities and Town Planning Association, 1913), 28, 30; Gordon E. Cherry, "George Pepler, 1882–1959," in Gordon E. Cherry, ed., *Pioneers in British Planning* (London: Architectural Press, 1981), 132; John Newman, *The Buildings of Wales: Glamorgan (Mid Glamorgan, South Glamorgan and West Glamorgan)* (London: Penguin; Cardiff: University of Wales Press, 1995), 113, 622.

73 John Newman, *The Buildings of Wales: Glamorgan (Mid Glamorgan, South Glamorgan and West Glamorgan)* (London: Penguin; Cardiff: University of Wales Press, 1995), 113, 131.

74 John Newman, *The Buildings of Wales: Gwent/Monmouthshire* (New Haven, Conn., and London: Yale University Press, 2002), 73, 459–60; www.oakdalevillage.net.

75 Newman, *The Buildings of Wales: Gwent/Monmouthshire*, 459.

76 Newman, *The Buildings of Wales: Gwent/Monmouthshire*, 73.

77 John Newman, *The Buildings of Wales: Gwent/Monmouthshire* (New Haven, Conn., and London: Yale University Press, 2002), 73, 514–15.

78 John Newman, *The Buildings of Wales: Gwent/Monmouthshire* (New Haven, Conn. and London: Yale University Press, 2002), 73, 225.

79 Newman, *The Buildings of Wales: Gwent/Monmouthshire*, 225.

80 "Burry Port Garden Suburb," *Architects' Journal* 51 (February 25, 1920): 252–53; A. C. Holliday, "The Site Planning of Housing Schemes," *Town Planning Review* 8 (December 1920): 139–40, pl. 29; T. Alwyn Lloyd, "The Welsh Town Planning and Housing Trust and Its Affiliated Societies," *Town Planning Review* 23 (April 1952): 40–51; Thomas Lloyd, Julian Orbach, and Robert Scourfield, *The Buildings of Wales: Carmarthenshire and Ceredigion* (New Haven, Conn., and London: Yale University Press, 2006), 105, 124.

81 "Chepstow Housing Scheme," *Architects Journal* 49 (May 28, 1919): 372–77; William Dunn and W. Curtis Green, "A Chepstow Housing Scheme," *Journal of the Royal Institute of British Architects* 27 (November 1918): 25–38; "Discussion of the Foregoing Paper," *Journal of the Royal Institute of British Architects* 27 (November 1918): 38–41; H. J. Birnstingl, "Notes from England," *Architectural Forum* 33 (November 1920): 167–70; John Newman, *The Buildings of Wales: Gwent/Monmouthshire* (New Haven, Conn., and London: Yale University Press, 2002), 73, 162–64, 188.

82 Dunn and Green, "A Chepstow Housing Scheme": 28.

83 Birnstingl, "Notes from England": 167, 169.

84 Dunn and Green, "A Chepstow Housing Scheme": 29.

85 Newman, *The Buildings of Wales: Gwent/Monmouthshire*, 73, 188.

86 Birnstingl, "Notes from England": 167–70; Holliday, "The Site Planning of Housing Schemes": 134, pl. 25; Newman, *The Buildings of Wales: Gwent/Monmouthshire*, 73, 162–64, 188.

87 "Eastriggs: An Industrial Town Built by the British Government," *Journal of the American Institute of Architects* 5 (October 1917): 499–514; "H.M. Factory Settlement at Gretna," *Architect and Contract Reporter* 100 (October 1918): 201–4; Gordon Allen, *The Cheap Cottage and Small House: A Manual of Economical Building* (London: B. T. Batsford, 1919), 31, 70, figs. 23–24, 51–52; Sir Robert Lorimer, "Gretna, the Home of an Industrial Army," *Country Life* (August 17, 1919): 132–38; "The Future of Gretna," *Garden Cities and Town Planning* (September 1919): 172–74; A. T. Pike, "Gretna and East Riggs," *Garden Cities and Town Planning* (May 1923): 76–77; Lawrence Weaver, *Cottages: Their Planning, Design and Materials* (London: Country Life, 1926), 322–28, 331, 333; Mervyn Miller, *Raymond Unwin: Garden Cities and Town Planning* (Leicester: Leicester University Press, 1992), 156–59, 226, figs. 56–58; John Gifford, *Dumfries and Galloway* (New Haven, Conn., and London: Yale University Press, 1996), 300–301; Chris Coates, *Utopia Britannica*, vol. 1 (London: Diggers & Dreamers Publications,

2001), 216–17; Mervyn Miller, "Garden Cities and Suburbs: At Home and Abroad," *Journal of Planning History* 1 (February 2002): 6–28.

88 Miller, *Raymond Unwin: Garden Cities and Town Planning*, 156, 159.

89 Miller, *Raymond Unwin: Garden Cities and Town Planning*, 156.

90 Lorimer, "Gretna, the Home of an Industrial Army": 137.

91 John Gifford, *The Buildings of Scotland: Fife* (New Haven, Conn., and London: Yale University Press in association with the Buildings of Scotland Trust, 2003), 354; Norma Aldred, "New Acquisitions to the RCAHMS Rare Books Collection," *The Architectural Heritage Society of Scotland* (Spring 2010): 18–19.

92 "The Rosyth Naval Base," *Garden Cities and Town Planning* 3 (August 1908): 110–11; "The Rosyth Naval Base," *Garden Cities and Town Planning* 3 (September 1908): 130–31; "The Rosyth Naval Base," *Garden Cities and Town Planning* 3 (December 1908): 152–53.

93 Gifford, *The Buildings of Scotland: Fife*, 354.

94 Edward Hubbard, *The Buildings of Wales: Clwyd (Denbighshire and Flintshire)* (London: Penguin; Cardiff: University of Wales Press, 1994), 421.

95 Helen Rosenau, "Stylistic Changes and Their Social Background, 1780–1830," *Town Planning Review* 22 (January 1952): 311–19; Anthony Vidler, *Claude-Nicolas Ledoux: Architecture and Social Reform at the End of the Ancien Régime* (Cambridge, Mass.: MIT Press, 1990), 75–132, 255–361; John S. Garner, "Introduction," in John S. Garner, ed., *The Company Town: Architecture and Society in the Early Industrial Age* (New York: Oxford University Press, 1992), 10; Ruth Eaton, *Ideal Cities: Utopianism and the (Un)Built Environment* (New York and London: Thames & Hudson, 2001), 106–17; *Visionary Architects: Boullee Ledoux Lequeu* (Santa Monica: Hennessey + Ingalls, 2002), 109–49; Ulrich Maximilian Schumann, "The Hidden Roots of the Garden City Idea: From John Sinclair to John Claudius Loudon," *Journal of Planning History* 2 (November 2003): 301.

96 Eaton, *Ideal Cities: Utopianism and the (Un)Built Environment*, 115–16.

97 Vidler, *Claude-Nicolas Ledoux: Architecture and Social Reform at the End of the Ancien Régime*, 95.

98 Vidler, *Claude-Nicolas Ledoux: Architecture and Social Reform at the End of the Ancien Régime*, 263.

99 Eaton, *Ideal Cities: Utopianism and the (Un)Built Environment*, 115–16.

100 Cyril Connolly and Jerome Zerbe, *Les Pavillons: French Pavilions of the Eighteenth Century* (New York: Macmillan, 1962), 108–9; Pierre Lemoine, *Versailles and Trianon* (Paris: Editions de la Réunion des musées nationaux, 1990), 266–67; Anthony Vidler, *Claude-Nicolas Ledoux: Architecture and Social Reform at the End of the Ancien Régime* (Cambridge, Mass.: MIT Press, 1990), 298, 302; Pierre Arizzoli-Clémentel, *Views and Plans of the Petit Trianon at Versailles* (Paris: Alain de Gourcuff Éditeur, 1998), 14–15, 99–103.

101 Émile Muller, *Habitations Ouvrières et Agricoles, Cités, Bains et Lavoirs* (Paris: Librairie Scientifique-Industrielle et Agricole, 1856), 48–49; John S. Garner, "Noisiel-sur-Marne and the Ville Industrielle in France," in John S. Garner, ed., *The Company Town: Architecture and Society in the Early Industrial Age* (New York: Oxford University Press, 1992), 44–73.

102 Edith Elmer Wood, *The Housing of the Unskilled Wage Earner: America's Next Problem* (New York: Macmillan, 1919), 185.

103 C. H. Blackall, "The Workingmen's Colony at Essen, Germany," *American Architect and Building News* 19 (May 1, 1886): 207–9; E. R. L. Gould, *The Housing of the Working People* (Washington: Government Printing Office, 1895), 382–84, plans no. 72–73; Edith Elmer Wood, *The Housing of the Unskilled Wage Earner: America's Next Problem* (New York: Macmillan, 1919), 185; Georges Risler, *Better Housing for Workers in France* (Paris: Centre d'Informations Documetaires, 1937), 3–4; Anthony Sutcliffe, *Towards the Planned City: Germany, Britain, the United States and France, 1780–1914* (Oxford: Basil Blackwell, 1981), 146–47; Walter Kieß, *Urbanismus im Industriezeitalter* (Berlin: Ernst & Sohn, 1991), 308–16; John S. Garner, "Noisiel-sur-Marne and the Ville Industrielle in France," in John S. Garner, ed., *The Company Town: Architecture and Society in the Early Industrial Age* (New York: Oxford University Press, 1992), 44–73; *Noisiel: La Chocolaterie Menier, Seine-et-Marne* (l'Association pour le Patrimoine d'Ile-de-France, 1994), 56–57.

104 John S. Garner, "Noisiel-sur-Marne and the Ville Industrielle in France," in John S. Garner, ed., *The Company Town: Architecture and Society in the Early Industrial Age* (New York: Oxford University Press, 1992), 48. Also see E. R. L. Gould, *The Housing of the Working People* (Washington: Government Printing Office, 1895), 351–53, plans 62A–62C; Budgett Meakin, *Model Factories and Villages* (1905; New York & London: Garland Publishing, 1985), 355–56; "The Model Village of Noisiel," *The Garden City* 1 (March 1906): 41–42; John S. Garner, *The Model Company Town: Urban Design through Private Enterprise in Nineteenth-Century New England* (Amherst, Mass.: University of Massachusetts Press, 1984), 105, 106, 107; Dennis J. De Witt and Elizabeth R. De Witt, *Modern Architecture in Europe: A Guide to Buildings Since the Industrial Revolution* (New York: E. P. Dutton, 1987), 155; *Noisiel: La Chocolaterie Menier, Seine-et-Marne* (l'Association pour le Patrimoine d'Ile-de-France, 1994); John S. Garner, "The Company Town. Industry and Territory in the 19th Century," *Rassegna* 70 (no. 2, 1997), 30–37.

105 Sigfried Giedion, *Space, Time and Architecture: The Growth of a New Tradition*, fifth edition, revised and enlarged (1941; Cambridge, Mass.: Harvard University Press, 1967), 204–7.

106 Michael Honhart, "Company Housing as Urban Planning in Germany," *Central European History* 23 (March 1990): 3; Walter Kieß, *Urbanismus im Industriezeitalter* (Berlin: Ernst & Sohn, 1991), 351–55; http://www.route-industriekultur.de/eisenheim2.

107 James Henry Smith, "Homes of the German Working People," in *U. S. Consular Report No. 98* (1888), 253–54; *Cost of Living in German Towns: Report of an Enquiry by the Board of Trade into Working Class Rents, Housing and Retail Prices, Together with the Rates of Wages in Certain Occupations in the Principal Industrial Towns of the German Empire* (London: Printed for His Majesty's Stationery Office by Darling & Son, 1908), 88; S. H. F. Hickey, *Workers in Imperial Germany: The Miners of the Ruhr* (Oxford: Clarendon Press, 1985), 54–55, 60, 62; Walter Kieß, *Urbanismus im Industriezeitalter* (Berlin: Ernst & Sohn, 1991), 365–67; Yasemin Utku, "Siedlung Stahlhausen," in *Historische Siedlungen in Bochum: Ein Querschnitt von 1868 bis 1918* (Bochum: Stadt Bochum, 2010), 18–21, in www.bochum.de.

108 Cedric Bolz, "Constructing *Heimat* in the Ruhr Valley: Assessing the Historical Significance of Krupp Company Housing from its Origins through the National Socialist Era, 1855–1941" (Ph.D. diss., Simon Fraser University, 2003): 123–25.

109 Gainsborough Commission, *Life and Labour in Germany* (London, 1906), 25–26, as quoted in Hickey, *Workers in Imperial Germany: The Miners of the Ruhr*, 55.

110 Roland Kanz and Jürgen Wiener, eds., *Architekturführer Düsseldorf* (Berlin: Dietrich Reimer Verlag, 2001), 160; http://www.bilderbuch-duesseldorf.de.

111 William Mayner, "German Model Houses for Workmen, III.—Spindlersfeld," *House and Garden* 10 (November 1906): 229–32.

112 William Mayner, "German Model Houses for Workmen, IV.—Colony Wildau," *House and Garden* 10 (December 1906): 267–71.

113 "German Town Planning Tour," *Garden Cities & Town Planning Magazine* 1 (June 1911): 113, 128; Ewart G. Culpin, "Promoting Cottage Building," *Garden Cities & Town Planning Magazine* 1 (July 1911): 153–54; Stephen Child, "Production, Not Reconstruction, the Order of the Day in Germany," *American City* 26 (May 1922): 437–41; Stephen Child, "A German Garden City," *Architect and Engineer* 105 (June 1931): 53–56; V. Deznai, "Essai d'Une Chronologie Urbaine," *La Vie Urbaine* 20 (March 15, 1934): 107; Alexander Kierdof, *Architectural Guide to Cologne*, trans. by Jean-Marie Clarke and Jeanne Haunschild (Berlin: Dietrich Reimer Verlag, 1999), 199; "Gronauer Waldsiedlung," www.bgv-rhein-berg.de.

114 Culpin, "Promoting Cottage Building": 154.

115 Werner Heinen and Anne-Marie Pfeffer, *Köln: Siedlungen 1888–1938* (Cologne: Verlag J. P. Bachem, 1988), 57–61; Alexander Kierdof, *Architectural Guide to Cologne*, trans. by Jean-Marie Clarke and Jeanne Haunschild (Berlin: Dietrich Reimer Verlag, 1999), 146; http://www. bilderbuch-koeln.de.

116 Harry S. Stewart, "Garden City Work in Germany," *Garden Cities and Town Planning* 4 (July 1910): 297–99; "Ninth International Housing Congress at Vienna," *Town Planning Review* 1 (July 1910): 166–67; Patrick Abercrombie, "Some Notes on German Garden Villages," *Town Planning Review* 1 (October 1910): 247–48, plates 72–73; Theodor Fischer, "Gmindersdorf bei Reutlingen, Arbeiterkolonie von Ulrich Gminder G.m.b.H. in Reutlingen," in C. H. Baer, ed., *Kleinbauten und Siedelungen* (Stuttgart: Julius Hoffman, c. 1919), 1–44; Gabriele Howaldt, "Gmindersdorf in Reutlingen, Baden-Württemberg," *Deutsche Kunst und Denkmalpflege* 35 (1977): 75–88; John Robert Mullin, "City Planning in Frankfurt, Germany, 1925–1932: A Study in Practical Utopianism," *Journal of Urban History* 4 (November 1977): 25 (n.24); Rosemarie Haag Bletter, "Revising Modernist History: The Architecture of the 1920s and 1930s," *Art Journal* 43 (Summer 1983): 108–20; Winfried Nerdinger, *Theodor Fischer: Architekt und Städtebauer* (Berlin: Ernst, 1988), 115–17; Gabriele Schickel, "Theodor Fischer als Lehrer der Avantgarde," in Vittorio Magnago Lampugnani and Romana Schneider, eds., *Moderne Architektur in Deutschland 1900 bis 1950: Reform und Tradition* (Stuttgart: Verlag Gerd Hatje, 1992), 58–60; Gabriele Tagliaventi, "The Romantic Tradition in 20th Century Town Planning," in Gabriele Tagliaventi, ed., *Garden City* (Rome: Gangemi Editore, 1994), 40–41, 45; Jean-François Lejeune, "From Hellerau to Bauhaus: Memory and Modernity in the German Garden City," *The New City* 3 (Fall 1996): 54, 56, 63; Karl Kiem, *Die Gartenstadt Staaken* (Berlin: Gebr. Mann Verlag, 1997), 154, 161; Vittorio Magnago Lampugnani, "Modernism, Lifestyle Reforms, City and Nature Experiments in Urban Design in Berlin from 1900 to 1914," in Thorsten Scheer, Josef Paul Kleihues, and Paul Kahlfeldt, eds., *City of Architecture, Architecture of the City: Berlin 1900–2000* (Berlin: Nicolai, 2000), 36–37; Andrés Duany, Elizabeth Plater-Zyberk, and Robert Alminana, *The New Civic Art: Elements of Town Planning* (New York: Rizzoli International Publications, 2003), 295; Martina Schröder et al., *Arbeiter—Siedlung Gmindersdorf* (Reutlingen: Heimatmuseum Reutlingen, 2003); John V. Maciuika, *Before the Bauhaus: Architecture, Politics, and the German State, 1890–1920* (New York: Cambridge University Press, 2005), 234–35; Jeannette Redensek, "Manufacturing Gemeinschaft: Architecture, Tradition, and the Sociology of Community in Germany, 1890–1920" (Ph.D. diss., City University of New York, 2007): 214, 268, 271.

117 Lampugnani, "Modernism, Lifestyle Reforms, City and Nature Experiments in Urban Design in Berlin from 1900 to 1914": 36.

118 John Robert Mullin, "City Planning in Frankfurt, Germany, 1925–1932: A Study in Practical Utopianism," *Journal of Urban History* 4 (November 1977): 25 (n.24); Winfried Nerdinger, *Theodor Fischer: Architekt und Städtebauer* (Berlin: Ernst, 1988), 121, 264, 323; Karl Kiem, *Die Gartenstadt Staaken* (Berlin: Gebr. Mann Verlag, 1997), 157–58, 160, 162, 165.

119 "Marga Garden City," www.erih.net. Also see "Die Gartenstadt Marga in Brieske," *Architekt* 10 (October 1996): 600; Andrea Höber and Karl Ganser, *IndustrieKulture: Mythos und Moderne im Ruhrgebiet* (Essen: Klartext Verlag, 1999), 100; Peter Paulhans, *Marga: Bergarbeiter-Kolonie in der Lausitz* (Munich: Dölling und Galitz, 2002); Andrés Duany, Elizabeth Plater-Zyberk, and Robert Alminana, *The New Civic Art: Elements of Town Planning* (New York: Rizzoli International Publications, 2003), 44; http://www.iba-see2010.de/en/projekte/projekt2.

120 Lejeune, "From Hellerau to Bauhaus: Memory and Modernity in the German Garden City": 65, 69. Also see Jochen Wittmann, "Vineta in Sachsen-Anhalt," *Deutsche Bauzeitschrift* 41 (November 1993): 1851–56; Herlind Reiss, *Kraftwerk und Kolonie Zschornewitz* (Dessau: Bauhaus Dessau, 1995); www.zschornewitz.de.

121 "The Teutoburgia Housing Estate," in http://www.route-industriekultur.de/en/workers-settlement/teutoburgia/; "The Teutoburgia settlement in Herne," in http://www.lwl.org/LWL/Kultur/fremde-impulse/die_impulse/Impuls-Gartenstadt/?lang=en; "Teutoburgia Estates, Herene," in http://www.mai-nrw.de/Teutoburgia-Estates.33.0.html?&L=1.

122 C. H. Baer, ed., *Kleinbauten und Siedelungen* (Stuttgart: Julius Hoffmann, c. 1919), 167–71; Christine Breig, *Die "Falterau" in Stuttgart-Degerloch: Baugeschichte einer Arbeitersiedlung* (Tübingen: Silberburg-Verlag, 1992), 143–52; Silke Schwarz and Clemens Daum, "Die Arbeitersiedlung Zeppelindorf," *Der Architekt* (no. 12, 1992): 618–20; Wolfgang Voigt and Roland May, eds., *Paul Bonatz, 1877–1956* (Berlin: Ernst Wasmuth Verlag Tübingen, 2010), 196–97; Gabriele Tagliaventi, "The Romantic Tradition in 20th Century Town Planning," www.avoe.org/cityplanart3.html.

123 Ursula V. Petz, "Margarethenhöhe Essen: Garden City, Workers' Colony or Satellite Town?" *Planning History* 12 (1990): 3.

124 Bauer, *Modern Housing*, 89.

125 C. H. Blackall, "The Workingmen's Colony at Essen, Germany," *American Architect and Building News* 19 (May 1, 1886): 207–9; E. R. L. Gould, *The Housing of the Working People* (Washington: Government Printing Office, 1895), 384–87; Budgett Meakin, "The

Evolution of Ideal Industrial Housing," *Garden City* 1 (April 1905): 41–43; William Mayner, "German Model Houses for Workmen," *House and Garden* 10 (September 1906): 123–29; Will Darville, "Les Maisons Ouvrières de Usines Krupp," *La Construction Moderne* 25 (December 18, 1909): 137–40, plates 29–30; Krupp Works, ed., *Krupp: A Century's History of the Krupp Works, 1812–1912* (1912), 171–73, 303–10; Ewart G. Culpin, *The Garden City Movement Up-to-Date* (London: Garden Cities and Town Planning Association, 1913), 61–65; L. Deubner, "The Workmen's Colonies of the Krupp Company," *International Studio* 50 (September 1913): 199–206; Frank Koester, *Modern City Planning and Maintenance* (New York: McBride, Nast and Company, 1914), 189–93; Wm. H. Schuchardt, "The Fibre of the Nation. Part VI: Some Observations of the Housing Problem in This Country and in Europe," *American Architect* 105 (March 18, 1914): 113–17; Nelson P. Lewis, *The Planning of the Modern City* (New York: John Wiley & Sons, 1916), 197–98, 300–301, plates 52–55; A. E. Brinckmann, "Kruppsche Arbeitersiedelungen erbaut von dem Kruppschen Baubüro Essen," in C. H. Baer, ed., *Kleinbauten und Siedelungen* (Stuttgart: Julius Hoffman, c. 1919), 45–58; Frank Koester, "Garden Cities," in *Encyclopedia Americana* 12 (New York: Encyclopedia Americana Corp., 1919), 282–86; Stephen Child, "Production, Not Reconstruction, the Order of the Day in Germany," *American City* 26 (May 1922): 437–41; Catherine Bauer, *Modern Housing* (Boston and New York: Houghton Mifflin, 1934), 89; John S. Garner, *The Model Company Town* (Amherst: University of Massachusetts Press, 1984), 106, 108, 109; Stanford Anderson, "Critical Conventionalism: The History of Architecture," *Midgård* 1 (1987): 33–47; Walter Kieß, *Urbanismus im Industriezeitalter* (Berlin: Ernst & Sohn, 1991), 373–92; Theodor Böll, "Essen: Steel, Cannons and Workers' Houses," *Rassegna* 70 (Spring 1997): 38–41; Cedric Bolz, "Constructing *Heimat* in the Ruhr Valley: Assessing the Historical Significance of Krupp Company Housing from its Origins through the National Socialist Era, 1855–1941" (Ph.D. diss., Simon Fraser University, 2003): esp. ch. 3.

126 Krupp Works, ed., *Krupp: A Century's History of the Krupp Works, 1812–1912* (1912), 310.

127 Budgett Meakin, "The Evolution of Ideal Industrial Housing," *Garden City* 1 (April 1905): 41–43.

128 Cedric Bolz, "Constructing *Heimat* in the Ruhr Valley: Assessing the Historical Significance of Krupp Company Housing from its Origins through the National Socialist Era, 1855–1941" (Ph.D. diss., Simon Fraser University, 2003): 115.

129 Budgett Meakin, "The Evolution of Ideal Industrial Housing," *Garden City* 1 (April 1905): 41–43. Also see William Mayner, "German Model Houses for Workmen," *House and Garden* 10 (September 1906): 123–29; Krupp Works, ed., *Krupp: A Century's History of the Krupp Works, 1812–1912* (1912), 171–73, 303–10; Frank Koester, "Garden Cities," in *Encyclopedia Americana* 12 (New York: Encyclopedia Americana Corp., 1919), 282–86; Stanford Anderson, "Critical Conventionalism: The History of Architecture," *Midgård* 1 (1987): 33–47; Walter Kieß, *Urbanismus im Industriezeitalter* (Berlin: Ernst & Sohn, 1991), 373–92; Theodor Böll, "Essen: Steel, Cannons and Workers' Houses," *Rassegna* 70 (Spring 1997): 38–41; Bolz, "Constructing *Heimat* in the Ruhr Valley": 128–29.

130 Bolz, "Constructing *Heimat* in the Ruhr Valley": 126.

131 Budgett Meakin, "The Evolution of Ideal Industrial Housing," *Garden City* 1 (April 1905): 41–43; William Mayner, "German Model Houses for Workmen," *House and Garden* 10 (September 1906): 123–29; Krupp Works, ed., *Krupp: A Century's History of the Krupp Works, 1812–1912* (1912), 171–73, 303–10; Frank Koester, "Garden Cities," in *Encyclopedia Americana* 12 (New York: Encyclopedia Americana Corp., 1919), 282–86; Stanford Anderson, "Critical Conventionalism: The History of Architecture," *Midgård* 1 (1987): 33–47; Walter Kieß, *Urbanismus im Industriezeitalter* (Berlin: Ernst & Sohn, 1991), 373–92; Theodor Böll, "Essen: Steel, Cannons and Workers' Houses," *Rassegna* 70 (Spring 1997): 38–41; Bolz, "Constructing *Heimat* in the Ruhr Valley": 128–29.

132 For Nordhof, see C. H. Blackall, "The Workingmen's Colony at Essen, Germany," *American Architect and Building News* 19 (May 1, 1886): 207–9. For Nordhof, see Budgett Meakin, "The Evolution of Ideal Industrial Housing," *Garden City* 1 (April 1905): 41–43; William Mayner, "German Model Houses for Workmen," *House and Garden* 10 (September 1906): 123–29; Krupp Works, ed., *Krupp: A Century's History of the Krupp Works, 1812–1912* (1912), 171–73, 303–10; Walter Kieß, *Urbanismus im Industriezeitalter* (Berlin: Ernst & Sohn, 1991), 379. For Schederhof, see Budgett Meakin, "The Evolution of Ideal Industrial Housing," *Garden City* 1 (April 1905): 41–43; William Mayner, "German Model Houses for Workmen," *House and Garden* 10 (September 1906): 123–29; Krupp Works, ed., *Krupp: A Century's History of the Krupp Works, 1812–1912* (1912), 171–73, 303–10; Stanford Anderson, "Critical Conventionalism: The History of Architecture," *Midgård* 1 (1987): 33–47; Walter Kieß, *Urbanismus im Industriezeitalter* (Berlin: Ernst & Sohn, 1991), 380–81; Bolz, "Constructing *Heimat* in the Ruhr Valley": 130.

133 C. H. Blackall, "The Workingmen's Colony at Essen, Germany," *American Architect and Building News* 19 (May 1, 1886): 207–9; Budgett Meakin, "The Evolution of Ideal Industrial Housing," *Garden City* 1 (April 1905): 41–43. Also see E. R. L. Gould, *The Housing of the Working People* (Washington: Government Printing Office, 1895), 384–87; William Mayner, "German Model Houses for Workmen," *House and Garden* 10 (September 1906): 123–29; Krupp Works, ed., *Krupp: A Century's History of the Krupp Works, 1812–1912* (1912), 171–73, 303–10; John S. Garner, *The Model Company Town* (Amherst: University of Massachusetts Press, 1984), 106, 108, 109; Stanford Anderson, "Critical Conventionalism: The History of Architecture," *Midgård* 1 (1987): 33–47; Walter Kieß, *Urbanismus im Industriezeitalter* (Berlin: Ernst & Sohn, 1991), 381; Bolz, "Constructing *Heimat* in the Ruhr Valley": 132–33.

134 Garner, ed., *The Model Company Town*, 109.

135 C. H. Blackall, "The Workingmen's Colony at Essen, Germany," *American Architect and Building News* 19 (May 1, 1886): 207–9; Budgett Meakin, "The Evolution of Ideal Industrial Housing," *Garden City* 1 (April 1905): 41–43; William Mayner, "German Model Houses for Workmen," *House and Garden* 10 (September 1906): 123–29; Krupp Works, ed., *Krupp: A Century's History of the Krupp Works, 1812–1912* (1912), 171–73, 303–10; Frank Koester, *Modern City Planning and Maintenance* (New York: McBride, Nast and Company, 1914), 189–93; Wm. H. Schuchardt, "The Fibre of the Nation. Part VI: Some Observations of the Housing Problem in This Country and in Europe," *American Architect* 105 (March 18, 1914): 113–17; Frank Koester, "Garden Cities," in *Encyclopedia Americana* 12 (New York: Encyclopedia Americana Corp., 1919), 282–86; Werner Hegemann, *City Planning: Housing, Volume III* (New York: Architectural Book Publishing

Co., 1938), 106; Walter Kieß, *Urbanismus im Industriezeitalter* (Berlin: Ernst & Sohn, 1991), 382–84; Bolz, "Constructing *Heimat* in the Ruhr Valley": 130–32.

136 Mayner, "German Model Houses for Workmen": 124.

137 Blackall, "The Workingmen's Colony at Essen, Germany": 207.

138 Blackall, "The Workingmen's Colony at Essen, Germany": 208.

139 Krupp Works, ed., *Krupp: A Century's History of the Krupp Works, 1812–1912*, 307.

140 Budgett Meakin, "The Evolution of Ideal Industrial Housing," *Garden City* 1 (April 1905): 41–43; William Mayner, "German Model Houses for Workmen," *House and Garden* 10 (September 1906): 123–29; "German Town Planning Tour," *Garden Cities and Town Planning* 1 (June 1911): 120; Krupp Works, ed., *Krupp: A Century's History of the Krupp Works, 1812–1912* (1912), 171–73, 303–10; Ewart G. Culpin, *The Garden City Movement Up-to-Date* (London: Garden Cities and Town Planning Association, 1913), 65; L. Deubner, "The Workmen's Colonies of the Krupp Company," *International Studio* 50 (September 1913): 199–206; Frank Koester, *Modern City Planning and Maintenance* (New York: McBride, Nast and Company, 1914), 189–93; A. E. Brinckmann, "Kruppsche Arbeitersiedelungen erbaut von dem Kruppschen Baubüro Essen," in Baer, ed., *Kleinbauten und Siedelungen*, 45–58; Wm. H. Schuchardt, "The Fibre of the Nation. Part VI: Some Observations of the Housing Problem in This Country and in Europe," *American Architect* 105 (March 18, 1914): 113–17; Nelson P. Lewis, *The Planning of the Modern City* (New York: John Wiley & Sons, 1916), 197–98, 300–301, plates 52–55; Stephen Child, "Production, Not Reconstruction, the Order of the Day in Germany," *American City* 26 (May 1922): 437–41; Werner Hegemann, *City Planning: Housing, Volume III* (New York: Architectural Book Publishing Co., 1938), 106; Kenneth Hudson, *World Industrial Archaeology* (Cambridge, England: Cambridge University Press, 1979), 23–25; Walter Kieß, *Urbanismus im Industriezeitalter* (Berlin: Ernst & Sohn, 1991), 373–92; Bolz, "Constructing *Heimat* in the Ruhr Valley": 139–44.

141 Böll, "Essen: Steel, Cannons and Workers' Houses": 40.

142 Schuchardt, "The Fibre of the Nation. Part VI: Some Observations of the Housing Problem in This Country and in Europe": 114.

143 Child, "Production, Not Reconstruction, the Order of the Day in Germany": 441.

144 Budgett Meakin, "The Evolution of Ideal Industrial Housing," *Garden City* 1 (April 1905): 41–43. Also see William Mayner, "German Model Houses for Workmen," *House and Garden* 10 (September 1906): 123–29; Krupp Works, ed., *Krupp: A Century's History of the Krupp Works, 1812–1912* (1912), 171–73, 303–10; L. Deubner, "The Workmen's Colonies of the Krupp Company," *International Studio* 50 (September 1913): 199–206; Frank Koester, *Modern City Planning and Maintenance* (New York: McBride, Nast and Company, 1914), 189–93; Wm. H. Schuchardt, "The Fibre of the Nation. Part VI: Some Observations of the Housing Problem in This Country and in Europe," *American Architect* 105 (March 18, 1914): 113–17; Nelson P. Lewis, *The Planning of the Modern City* (New York: John Wiley & Sons, 1916), 301, plates 54–55; A. E. Brinckmann, "Kruppsche Arbeitersiedelungen erbaut von dem Kruppschen Baubüro Essen," in C. H. Baer, ed., *Kleinbauten und Siedelungen* (Stuttgart: Julius Hoffman, c. 1919), 45–58; Frank Koester, "Garden Cities," in *Encyclopedia Americana* 12 (New York: Encyclopedia Americana Corp., 1919), 282–86; L. Jahn, "Der Alfredshof, Der Firma Friedr. Krupp in Essen-Ruhr," *Wasmuths Monatshefte für Baukunst* 5 (1920–21): 206–23; Werner Hegemann and Elbert Peets, *The American Vitruvius: An Architects' Handbook of Civic Art* (1922; New York: Benjamin Blom, 1972), 212, 269; Stephen Child, "Production, Not Reconstruction, the Order of the Day in Germany," *American City* 26 (May 1922): 437–41; Stanford Anderson, "Critical Conventionalism: The History of Architecture," *Midgård* 1 (1987): 33–47; Walter Kieß, *Urbanismus im Industriezeitalter* (Berlin: Ernst & Sohn, 1991), 373–92.

145 L. Jahn, "Der Alfredshof, Der Firma Friedr. Krupp in Essen-Ruhr," *Wasmuths Monatshefte für Baukunst* 5 (1920–21): 206–23.

146 Hegemann and Peets, *Civic Art*, 269.

147 William Mayner, "German Model Houses for Workmen," *House and Garden* 10 (September 1906): 123–29; Will Darville, "Les Maisons Ouvrières de Usines Krupp," *La Construction Moderne* 25 (December 18, 1909): 137–40, plates 29–30; "German Town Planning Tour," *Garden Cities and Town Planning* 1 (June 1911): 119; Krupp Works, ed., *Krupp: A Century's History of the Krupp Works, 1812–1912* (1912), 171–73, 303–10; Frank Koester, *Modern City Planning and Maintenance* (New York: McBride, Nast and Company, 1914), 189–93; Frank Koester, "Garden Cities," in *Encyclopedia Americana* 12 (New York: Encyclopedia Americana Corp., 1919), 282–86; Walter Kieß, *Urbanismus im Industriezeitalter* (Berlin: Ernst & Sohn, 1991), 373–92.

148 "German Town Planning Tour," *Garden Cities and Town Planning* 1 (June 1911): 121; A. E. Brinckmann, "Kruppsche Arbeitersiedelungen erbaut von dem Kruppschen Baubüro Essen," in C. H. Baer, ed., *Kleinbauten und Siedelungen* (Stuttgart: Julius Hoffman, c. 1919), 46, 47.

149 Georg Biskup, "Kolonie Hannover (1874–1890)," in *Historische Siedlungen in Bochum: Ein Querschnitt von 1868 bis 1918* (Bochum: Stadt Bochum, 2010), 26–29, at www.bochum.de.

150 Bolz, "Constructing *Heimat* in the Ruhr Valley": 145. Also see "German Town Planning Tour," *Garden Cities and Town Planning* 1 (June 1911): 122; Frank Koester, *Modern City Planning and Maintenance* (New York: McBride, Nast and Company, 1914), 189, 190; A. E. Brinckmann, "Kruppsche Arbeitersiedelungen erbaut von dem Kruppschen Baubüro Essen," in C. H. Baer, ed., *Kleinbauten und Siedelungen* (Stuttgart: Julius Hoffman, c. 1919), 46, 56, 57, 58; Hermann Muthesius, *Kleinhaus und Kleinsiedlung* (Munich: F. Bruckmann, 1920); S. H. F. Hickey, *Workers in Imperial Germany: The Miners of the Ruhr* (Oxford: Clarendon Press, 1985), 57–58; Andrés Duany, Elizabeth Plater-Zyberk, and Robert Alminana, *The New Civic Art: Elements of Town Planning* (New York: Rizzoli International Publications, 2003), 295; Jeannette Redensek, "Manufacturing Gemeinschaft: Architecture, Tradition, and the Sociology of Community in Germany, 1890–1920" (Ph.D. diss., City University of New York, 2007), xii, 184; Patrick Voss, "Siedlung Dahlhauser Heide (1906–1915)," in *Historische Siedlungen in Bochum: Ein Querschnitt von 1868 bis 1918* (Bochum: Stadt Bochum, 2010), 34–37, at www.bochum.de.

151 Duany, Plater-Zyberk, and Alminana, *The New Civic Art*, 295.

152 "German Town Planning Tour," *Garden Cities and Town Planning* 1 (June 1911): 119; A. E. Brinckmann, "Kruppsche Arbeitersiedelungen erbaut von dem Kruppschen Baubüro Essen," in C. H. Baer, ed., *Kleinbauten und Siedelungen* (Stuttgart: Julius Hoffman, c. 1919), 46, 53, 54, 55, 57; Bolz, "Constructing *Heimat* in the Ruhr Valley": 116, 144–46.

153 "A German Bournville," *Garden Cities and Town Planning* 1 (June 1911): 129–30; Krupp

Works, ed., *Krupp: A Century's History of the Krupp Works, 1812–1912* (1912), 303; Ewart G. Culpin, *The Garden City Movement Up-to-Date* (London: Garden Cities and Town Planning Association, 1913), 61–63; L. Deubner, "The Workmen's Colonies of the Krupp Company," *International Studio* 50 (September 1913): 199–206; Wm. H. Schuchardt, "The Fibre of the Nation. Part VI: Some Observations of the Housing Problem in This Country and in Europe," *American Architect* 105 (March 18, 1914): 113–17; Richard B. Watrous, "Personal Observations of Some Developments in Housing in Europe," *Journal of the American Institute of Architects* 2 (July 1914): 337, 338, 339, 340, 341, 342–43; Elsa Rehmann, "Margarethenhöhe bei Essen — the Krupp Foundation Suburb," *Architectural Record* 36 (October 1914): 372–78; Frank Chouteau Brown, "A German 'Garden City' Suburb," *Architectural Review* 3 (September 1915): 69–74; A. E. Brinckmann, "Kruppsche Arbeitersiedelungen erbaut von dem Kruppschen Baubüro Essen," in C. H. Baer, ed., *Kleinbauten und Siedelungen* (Stuttgart: Julius Hoffman, c. 1919), 45–58; Georg Metzendorf, *Kleinwohnungs-Bauten und Siedlungen* (Darmstadt: Alexander Koch, 1920), 1–109; Stephen Child, "Production, Not Reconstruction, the Order of the Day in Germany," *American City* 26 (May 1922): 437–41; Earle S. Draper, "Two European Industrial Village Developments," *Landscape Architecture* 21 (July 1931): 300–312; Walter L. Creese, *The Search for Environment*, expanded edition (New Haven, Conn.: Yale University Press, 1966; Baltimore and London: Johns Hopkins University Press, 1992), 311; Roland Günter, "Krupp und Essen," in Martin Warnke, *Das Kunstwerk zwischen Wissenschaft und Weltanschauung* (Gütersloh: Bertelsmann, 1970), 128–74; Gérard Bauer, Gildas Baudaz, and Jean-Michel Roux, *Banlieues de Charme ou l'Art des Quartiers-Jardins* (Aix-en-Provence: Pandora éditions, 1980), 76–93; Stanford Anderson, "Critical Conventionalism: The History of Architecture," *Midgård* 1 (1987): 33–47; Ursula V. Petz, "Margarethenhöhe Essen: Garden City, Workers' Colony or Satellite Town?" *Planning History* 12 (1990): 3–9; Walter Kieß, *Urbanismus im Industriezeitalter* (Berlin: Ernst & Sohn, 1991), 373–92; Rainer Metzendorf, *Georg Metzendorf, 1874–1934, Siedlungen und Bauten* (Darmstadt: Selbstverlag der Hessischen Historischen Kommission Darmstadt; Marburg: Historischen Kommission für Hessen, 1994), 80–131; Maria Rosa Ronzoni, "A Garden-City Between the River and the Factory: Margarethenhöhe," in Gabriele Tagliaventi, ed., *Garden City* (Rome: Gangemi Editore, 1994), 284–94; Winfried Nerdinger and Cornelius Tafel, *Architectural Guide: Germany, 20th Century* (Basel: Birkhauser, 1996), 224; Jean-François Lejeune, "From Hellerau to the Bauhaus: Memory and Modernity of the German Garden City," *The New City* 3 (Fall 1996): 50–69; Theodor Böll, "Essen: Steel, Cannons and Workers' Houses," *Rassegna* 70 (Spring 1997): 38–41; Andreas Helfrich, *Die Margarethenhöhe Essen* (Weimar: VDG, 2000); Peter Hall, *Cities of Tomorrow*, 3rd ed. (1988; Oxford: Blackwell Publishing, 2002), 119–21; Andrés Duany, Elizabeth Plater-Zyberk, and Robert Alminana, *The New Civic Art: Elements of Town Planning* (New York: Rizzoli International Publications, 2003), 132, 298.

154 "A German Bournville": 129.

155 Rehmann, "Margarethenhohe bei Essen—The Krupp Foundation Suburb": 375.

156 Draper, "Two European Industrial Village Developments": 307.

157 Rehmann, "Margarethenhöhe bei Essen — the Krupp Foundation Suburb": 378, 374.

158 "A German Bournville," *Garden Cities and Town Planning* 1 (June 1911): 129–30; Peter Hall, *Cities of Tomorrow*, 3rd ed. (1988; Oxford: Blackwell Publishing, 2002), 119–21; Ursula V. Petz, "Margarethenhöhe Essen: Garden City, Workers' Colony or Satellite Town?" *Planning History* 12 (1990): 3–9.

159 Hall, *Cities of Tomorrow*, 119–20.

160 "German Town Planning Tour," *Garden Cities and Town Planning* 1 (June 1911): 126; Otto Albert Schneider, "Die Gartenstadt Hüttenau bei Blankenstein a. Ruhr," in C. H. Baer, ed., *Kleinbauten und Siedelungen* (Stuttgart: Julius Hoffmann, c. 1919), 69–88; Georg Metzendorf, *Kleinwohnungs-Bauten und Siedlungen* (Darmstadt: Alexander Koch, 1920), 113–43; Gerhard Fehl and Juan Rodriguez-Lores, "La 'città giardino' in Germania tra il 1910 e il 1918," *Casabella* 57 (January 1993): 12–16, 117–18.

161 Cedric Bolz, "Constructing *Heimat* in the Ruhr Valley: Assessing the Historical Significance of Krupp Company Housing from its Origins through the National Socialist Era, 1855–1941" (Ph.D. diss., Simon Fraser University, 2003): 26–27, 117–18, 151–58. Also see Theodor Suhnel, *Theodor Suhnel* (Berlin: F. E. Hübsch, 1929), XII–XIII: 22–34.

162 Bolz, "Constructing *Heimat* in the Ruhr Valley": 151, 154.

163 Albert Gut, *Wohnungsbau in Deutschland nach dem Weltkriege* (Munich: Verlag F. Bruckmann, 1928), 460; *Neue Werkkunst: Theodore Suhnel* (Berlin: F.E. Hübsch, 1929), 35–44; Rolf Glasmeier, *Essen: Architekturführer* (Essen: Bund Deutscher Architekten, 1983), 29; "Kleinhaussiedlung Altendorf," *Denkmalliste Stadt Essen* (1995); Alexandra Döll, "Die Kleinhaussiedlung in Essen-Altendorf" (February 2, 2011), http://suite101.de; Berger Bergmann and Peter Brdenk, *Architektur in Essen 1900–1960* (Essen: Klartext Verlag, 2012), 185.

164 Fritz Stahl, *Die Gartenstadt Staaken* (Berlin: Wasmuth, 1917); "Industrial Colonies in Switzerland and Germany," *Städtebau* 16 (1919): 32–33, plates 19–25; Norbert Borrmann, *Paul Schultze-Naumburg, 1869–1949: Maler, Publizist, Architekt* (Essen: Verlag Richard Bacht, 1989), 135; Vittorio Magnago Lampugnani, "From the New Community to the Horseshoe Estate: A History of German Modern Architecture—Part 4," trans. by Chris Charlesworth, *Architecture + Urbanism* (December 1992): 48–59; Gabriele Tagliaventi, "The Romantic Tradition in 20th Century Town Planning," in Gabriele Tagliaventi, ed., *Garden City* (Rome: Gangemi Editore, 1994), 44–47; Winfried Nerdinger and Cornelius Tafel, *Architectural Guide Germany: 20th Century* (Basel: Birkhäuser, 1996), 107; Lejeune, "From Hellerau to Bauhaus: Memory and Modernity in the German Garden City": 56–60; Karl Kiem, *Die Gartenstadt Staaken* (Berlin: Gebr. Mann Verlag, 1997); Annette Ciré, "'Beyond the Metropolis': Urban Design and Architecture of the 'Country House Colonies' and Garden Cities in Berlin Suburbs before 1914," in Thorsten Scheer, Josef Paul Kleihues, and Paul Kahlfeldt, eds., *City of Architecture, Architecture of the City: Berlin 1900–2000* (Berlin: Nicolai, 2000), 63–65; Wolfgang Voigt and Hartmut Frank, *Paul Schmitthenner, 1884–1972* (Tübingen: Wasmuth, 2003), 8–15, 110–11, 128–30; Arne Ehmann, "Wohnarchitektur des Mitteleuropäischen: Traditionalismus um 1910 in Ausgewählten Beispielen" (Ph.D. diss., University of Hamburg, 2006): 301–9; Jeannette Redensek, "Manufacturing Gemeinschaft: Architecture, Tradition, and the Sociology of Community in Germany, 1890–1920" (Ph.D. diss., City University of New York, 2007): 205–9; Wolfgang Sonne, "Political Connotations of the Picturesque," in Charles C. Bohl and Jean-François Lejeune, eds., *Sitte, Hegemann and the Metropolis: Modern Civic Art and International Exchanges* (London and New York: Routledge, 2009), 128–29; Maiken Umbach, *German Cities and Bourgeois Modernism, 1890–1924* (New York: Oxford University Press, 2009), 199–200; Harald Bodenschatz, *Berlin Urban Design: A Brief History*, trans. by Sasha Disko (Berlin: DOM Publishers, 2010), 32; Piergiacomo Bucciarelli, "Schmitthenner, Muthesius, Behrens: l'uso 'progressista' della tradizione," in Marina Docci and Maria Grazia Turco, eds., *L'Architettura dell' "altra" modernità* (Rome: Gangemi Editore, 2010), 130–32; Vittorio Magnago Lampugnani, *Die Stadt im 20. Jahrhundert* (Berlin: Verlag Klaus Wagenbach, 2010), 257–59.

165 Ciré, "'Beyond the Metropolis': Urban Design and Architecture of the 'Country House Colonies' and Garden Cities in Berlin Suburbs before 1914," in Scheer, Kleihues, and Kahlfeldt, eds., *City of Architecture, Architecture of the City: Berlin 1900–2000*, 63.

166 Lejeune, "From Hellerau to Bauhaus: Memory and Modernity in the German Garden City": 57.

167 Ciré, "'Beyond the Metropolis': Urban Design and Architecture of the 'Country House Colonies' and Garden Cities in Berlin Suburbs before 1914," in Scheer, Kleihues, and Kahlfeldt, eds., *City of Architecture, Architecture of the City: Berlin 1900–2000*, 63–64.

168 Lampugnani, "Modernism, Lifestyle Reforms, City and Nature Experiments in Urban Design in Berlin from 1900 to 1914": 49.

169 Robert R. Taylor, *The Word in Stone: The Role of Architecture in the National Sociologist Ideology* (Berkeley: University of California Press, 1974), 104–18; Heinz Sunker, "Community's Discontent: The Ideology of the 'Volk' Community in National Socialism," *Policy Futures in Education* 4 (No. 3, 2006): 306–19. Also see Paul Schmitthenner, *Die Baukunst im neuen Reich* (Munich: G.D.W. Callwey, 1934).

170 Sonne, "Political Connotations of the Picturesque," in Bohl and Lejeune, eds., *Sitte, Hegemann and the Metropolis: Modern Civic Art and International Exchanges*, 128. Also see Franz Oppenheimer, "Einleitung," in Fritz Stahl, *Die Gartenstadt Staaken*, 3–4.

171 *Berlin/Brandenburg: An Architectural Guide* (Berlin: Ernst & Sohn, 1993), 292; Gabriele Tagliaventi, "The Romantic Tradition in 20th Century Town Planning," in Gabriele Tagliaventi, ed., *Garden City* (Rome: Gangemi Editore, 1994), 44–45, 47–48; Lejeune, "From Hellerau to Bauhaus: Memory and Modernity in the German Garden City": 56; Karl Kiem, *Die Gartenstadt Staaken* (Berlin: Gebr. Mann Verlag, 1997), 187, 202; Wolfgang Voigt and Hartmut Frank, *Paul Schmitthenner, 1884–1972* (Tübingen: Wasmuth, 2003), 106, 108–9, 130–31.

172 Lejeune, "From Hellerau to Bauhaus: Memory and Modernity in the German Garden City": 56; Karl Kiem, *Die Gartenstadt Staaken* (Berlin: Gebr. Mann Verlag, 1997), 187, 204; Wolfgang Voigt and Hartmut Frank, *Paul Schmitthenner, 1884–1972* (Tübingen: Wasmuth, 2003), 107, 131–32.

173 Lejeune, "From Hellerau to Bauhaus: Memory and Modernity in the German Garden City": 64–66. Also see *40 Jahre: Berlinische Boden-Gesellschaft* (Berlin, 1930), 44–50; Florian von Buttlar, "Zwischen Piesteritz und Königsweg," *Bauwelt* 77 (July 1986): 1020–29; Gerhard Fehl and Juan Rodriguez-Lores, "La 'città giardino' in Germania tra il 1910 e il 1918," *Casabella* 57 (January 1993): 12–16, 117–18; Kristina Hartmann, "Garden City Experiences in Germany," in Gabriele Tagliaventi, ed., *Garden City* (Rome: Gangemi Editore, 1994), 272–74; Claude Lichtenstein, "Werkkatalog," in *O.R. Salvisberg: Die Andere Moderne* (Zurich: GTA, 1995), 26–27; "Die Neue Werkssiedlung: Piesteritz," *Bauwelt* 90 (August 1999): 1646–53. Also see "Piesteritz Housing Estate," http://www.erih.net; http://www.uni-kiel.de/anorg/lagaly/group/klausSchiver/piesteritz3.pdf; http://fantastisch-reisen.de/sachsen-anhalt/werkssiedlung-piesteritz.htm.

174 Harald Kegler, *Die Piesteritzer Werksiedlung* (Dessau: Bauhaus Dessau, Werkssiedlung GmbH, Stadtverwaltung Wittenber, 1992), 26, quoted and translated in Lejeune, "From Hellerau to Bauhaus: Memory and Modernity in the German Garden City": 64–65.

175 Werner Heinen and Anne-Marie Pfeffer, *Köln: Siedlungen 1888–1938* (Cologne: Verlag J. P. Bachem, 1988), 130–33; Alexander Kierdorf, *Architectural Guide to Cologne*, trans. by Jean-Marie Clarke and Jeanne Haunschild (Berlin: Dietrich Reimer Verlag, 1999), 158; Knut Stegmann and Philippe von Glisczynski, "Die Eisenbahnersiedlung Gremberghoven," *Denkmalpflege im Rheinland* 21 (2004): 177–83; http://www.bilderbuch-koeln.de.

176 Thomas Freytag and Ulrich Peickert, "Die Siedlung 'Am schmalen Rain' in Gotha: Aspekte des Städtebaus der 20er Jahre," *Architektur der DDR* 35 (December 1986): 758–61; Winfried Nerdinger and Cornelius Tafel, *Architectural Guide Germany: 20th Century*, trans. by Ingrid Taylor and Ralph Stern (Basel: Birkhäuser, 1996), 322–23; Ulrich Wieler et al., *Architekturführer Thüringen* (Weimar: Bauhaus-Universität, Universitätsverlag, 2001), 99; "Am Schmalen Rain," http://www.gotha.de; "Am Schmalen Rain," http://www.thueringen-tourismus.de; "Am Schmalen Rain Gotha," http://www.mdm-online.de; http://www.am-schmalen-rain.de; http://www.architekturkonsulat.de/michael_bender_projekte.html.

177 Hans Hertlein, *Siemensbauten: Neue Fabrik- und Verwaltungsgebäude Wohlfahrtsanlagen des Siemenskonzerns* (Berlin: Verlag Ernst Wasmuth, 1928), 106–23; "Neue Bauten der Siedlung Siemensstadt," *Wasmuths Monatshefte für Baukunst* 14 (1930): 186–88; Ronald Wiedenhoeft, *Berlin's Housing Revolution: German Reform in the 1920s* (Ann Arbor: UMI Research Press, 1985), 71–74; Dietrich Worbs, "Die Denkmalschutzkonzeption für die Siemensstadt in Berlin," *Denkmalpflege* 52 (No. 1, 1996): 2–14; Rolf Rave, *Modern Architecture in Berlin*, trans. by Karl Edward Johnsen (Stuttgart: Edition Axel Menges, 2009), 381–86; David H. Haney, *When Modern Was Green: Life and Work of Landscape Architect Leberecht Migge* (London and New York: Routledge, 2010), 187.

178 Wiedenhoeft, *Berlin's Housing Revolution*, 71.

179 Werner Hegemann, "Martin Wagner gewinnt Scharoun," *Wasmuths Monatshefte für Baukunst* 13 (1929): 84; Carl Gorgas, "Gross-Siedlung Siemensstadt, Berlin," *Bauwelt* 21 (no. 46, 1930): 1–24; Leberecht Migge, "Gross-Berliner Siedlungsfreiraum," *Die Wohnung* 5 (no. 4, 1930): 97–108; Leo Adler, *Neuzeitliche Miethäuser und Siedlungen* (Berlin-Charlottenburg: Ernst Pollack, 1931; Munich: Kraus Reprint, 1981), 144–57; Heinz Johannes, *Neues Bauen in Berlin* (Berlin: Deutscher Kunstverlag, 1931), 90–91; Jakob Schallenberger and Erwin Gutkind, *Berliner Wohnbauten der letzten jahre* (Berlin: Verlag W. & S. Loewenthal, 1931), 114–23; "La Cité Siemensstadt à Berlin," *La Construction Moderne* 46 (no. 23, 1931): 358–63, 365; Fred Forbat, "Gross-Siedlung Siemensstadt," *Bauwelt* 22 (no. 47, 1931): 33–38; "Habitations Siemenstadt à Berlin," *Architecture Vivante* (Autumn 1931): plates 3–6; Sigfried Giedion, *Walter Gropius: Work and Teamwork* (New York: Reinhold Publishing Corporation, 1954), 87, 218–20; "Groupe d'habitations à Berlin-Siemensstadt," *L'Architecture d'Aujourd'hui* 33 (no. 104, 1962): 36–39; "40 Jahre Grosssiedlung Siemensstadt," *Bauwelt* 62 (November 29, 1971): 1907–11; Peter Pfankuch, *Hans Scharoun: Bauten, Entwürfe, Texte* (Berlin: Gebr. Mann, 1974), 249, 394; Manfredo Tafuri, *Architecture and Utopia: Design and Capitalist Development*, trans. by Barbara Luigia La Penta (Cambridge, Mass.: MIT Press, 1976), 116–17;

Ronald Wiedenhoeft, *Berlin's Housing Revolution: German Reform in the 1920s* (Ann Arbor: UMI Research Press, 1985), 123, 132–35, figs. 58–63; "Siedlungen der zwanziger Jahre: Vier Berliner Grosssiedlungen," *Bauforum* 19 (1986): 41–45; Dennis J. De Witt and Elizabeth R. De Witt, *Modern Architecture in Europe: A Guide to Buildings Since the Industrial Revolution* (New York: E. P. Dutton, 1987), 75–76; Karl-Heinz Hüter, *Architektur in Berlin, 1900–1933* (Stuttgart: Kohlhammer, 1988), 224–36; Reginald Isaacs, *Gropius: An Illustrated Biography of the Creator of the Bauhaus* (Boston: Little, Brown and Co., 1991), 153–55; J. Christoph Bürkle, *Hans Scharoun* (Zurich: Artemis, 1993), 76–79; *Berlin/Brandenburg: An Architectural Guide* (Berlin: Ernst & Sohn, 1993), 155; J.S. Marcus, "Visionary Design for Berlin's Workers," *New York Times* (June 6, 1993), V: 23, 37; Peter Blundell Jones, *Hans Scharoun* (London: Phaidon, 1995), 64–67; Winfried Nerdinger and Cornelius Tafel, *Architectural Guide Germany: 20th Century* (Basel: Birkhäuser, 1996), 118–19; Peter Blundell Jones, *Hans Häring: The Organic Versus the Geometric* (Stuttgart: Ed. Axel Menges, 1999), 120–21; Nike Bätzner, "Housing Projects of the 1920s: A Laboratory of Social Ideas and Formal Experiment," in Thorsten Scheer, Josef Paul Kleihues, and Paul Kahlfeldt, eds., *City of Architecture, Architecture of the City: Berlin 1900–2000* (Berlin: Nicolai, 2000), 157; Jörg Haspel and Annemarie Jaeggi, *Siedlungen der Berliner Moderne* (Munich: Deutscher Kunstverlag, 2007), 84–94; Gerrit Engel and Detlef Jessen-Klingenberg, *Berlin Photographs: 234 Berlin Buildings in Chronological Order from 1230 to 2008* (Munich: Schirmer/Mosel, 2009), 139–40; *Siedlungen der Berliner Moderne: Eintragung in die Welterbeliste der UNESCO* (Berlin: Braun, 2009), 37, 60–65, 91–97, 116–17, 137–38, 178–79, 188, 228–29, 240–41, 273; Haney, *When Modern Was Green: Life and Work of Landscape Architect Leberecht Migge*, 187, 190–93; Vittorio Magnago Lampugnani, *Die Stadt im 20. Jahrhundert* (Berlin: Verlag Klaus Wagenbach, 2010), 334–36.

180 "Architektenvereinigung 'Der Ring,'" *Form* 1 (1926): 225.

181 Jones, *Hans Häring: The Organic Versus the Geometric*, 120.

182 De Witt and De Witt, *Modern Architecture in Europe*, 75–76.

183 "Lehrsiedlung Braunschweig-Mascherode," *Deutsche Bauzeitung* 74 (January 10, 1940), K: 1–4, 21; Roswitha Mattausch-Schirmbeck, *Siedlungsbau und Stadtneugründungen im deutschen Faschismus: dargestellt anhand exemplarischen Beispiele* (Frankfurt: Haag + Herchen, 1981), 89–97, 299; Werner Durth and Winfried Nerdinger, *Architektur und Städtebau der 30er/40er Jahre* (Bonn: Deutsches Nationalkomitee für Denkmalschutz, 1992), 64–65; Winfried Nerdinger and Cornelius Tafel, *Architectural Guide Germany: 20th Century*, trans. by Ingrid Taylor and Ralph Stern (Basel: Birkhäuser, 1996), 74–75; Markus Mittmann, *Bauen im Nationalsozialismus: Braunschweig, die 'Deutsche Siedlungsstadt' und die 'Mustersiedlung der Deutschen Arbeitsfront' Braunschweig-Mascherode: Ursprung, Gestaltung, Analyse* (Haemeln: Niemeyer, 2003); Carsten Jonas, *Die Stadt und ihr Grundriss* (Tübingen: Wasmuth, 2006), 114; Friederike Hansell, "Commemorating the Past," in Sam Merrill and Leo Schmidt, eds., *A Reader in Uncomfortable Heritage and Dark Tourism* (2009), http://www.tu-cottbus.de.

184 Nerdinger and Tafel, *Architectural Guide Germany: 20th Century*, 74.

185 Erich Bauer, "Baulicher Luftschutz und Städtebau," *Zentralblatt der Bauverwaltung* 63 (Nos. 5–6, 1943): 49–57; Gerda Wangerin and Gerhard Weiss, *Heinrich Tessenow: Ein Baumeister, 1876–1950* (Essen: Verlag Richard Bacht, 1976), 259–60; Marco De Michelis, *Heinrich Tessenow: 1876–1950* (Milan: Electa, 1991), 322–23; Andrés Duany, Elizabeth Plater-Zyberk, and Robert Alminana, *The New Civic Art: Elements of Town Planning* (New York: Rizzoli International Publications, 2003), 309.

186 Andrés Duany, "Mosigkau," in Duany, Plater-Zyberk, and Alminana, *The New Civic Art*, 309.

187 E. R. L. Gould, *The Housing of the Working People* (Washington: Government Printing Office, 1895), 370; Marinette Bruwier, Anne Meurant, and Christiane Piérard, "Le Grand-Hornu," *Industrial Archaeology* 6 (November 1969): 354–68; Kenneth Hudson, *World Industrial Archaeology* (Cambridge, England: Cambridge University Press, 1979), 58–62; Walter Kieß, *Urbanismus im Industriezeitalter* (Berlin: Ernst & Sohn, 1991), 291–97; Martin Dunford and Phil Lee, *The Rough Guide to Belgium & Luxembourg* (London: Rough Guides, 2008), 326.

188 Henri de Gorge, quoted in Bruwier, Meurant, and Piérard, "Le Grand-Hornu": 359.

189 Phillipe Vandermaelen, *Dictionnaire géographique de la Province de Hainaut* (1833), quoted in Bruwier, Meurant, and Piérard, "Le Grand-Hornu": 359.

190 Stephen Child, "Winterslag; Belgium's Unique Garden City Near Genck," *Landscape Architecture* 11 (July 1921): 180–85; Georges Benoit-Levy, "Garden Villages of France and Belgium," *New York Times Current History* XVI (September 1922): 967; Edith Elmer Wood, "Recent Housing Work in Western Europe," *Architectural Record* 53 (February 1923): 178; Marcel Smets, *L'avenement de la Cité-Jardin en Belgique: Histoire de l'habitat social en Belgique de 1830 à 1930* (Bruxelles: P. Mardaga, 1977), 82, 83; Frieda Schlusmans et al., *Bouwen door de eeuwen heen. Inventaris van het cultuurbezit in België: Architectuur. Deel 6n 1 (A-Ha), Provincie Limburg. Arrondissement Hasselt* (Gent: Snoeck-Ducaju & Zoon, 1981), 133–37, 138; Bert van Doorslaer, "Zwarte monumenten in groen Limburg," *Monumenten en landschappen: M & L* 4 (July–August 1990): 38, 39; Michiel Heirman and Linda Van Santvoort, *Le Guide de L'architecture en Belgique* (Brussels: Éditions Racine, 2000), 244; Geert Bekaert, "Introduction," in Mil De Kooning, ed., *Horta and After: 25 Masters of Modern Architecture in Belgium*, 2nd rev. ed. (Ghent: Department of Architecture and Urbanism, Ghent University, 2001), 17; François Aubry, Jos Vandenbreeden, and France Vanlaethem, *L'architecture en Belgique: Art Nouveau, Art Déco & Modernisme* (Bruxelles: Éditions Racine, 2006), 307; https://inventaris.onroerenderfgoed.be/dibe/geheel/22165.

191 Frieda Schlusmans et al., *Bouwen door de eeuwen heen. Inventaris van het cultuurbezit in België: Architectuur. Deel 6n 1 (A-Ha), Provincie Limburg. Arrondissement Hasselt* (Gent: Snoeck-Ducaju & Zoon, 1981), 125–26; Herman van Bergeijk and Otakar Máčel, *Birkhäuser Architectural Guide: Belgium, The Netherlands, Luxembourg, 20th Century* (Basel: Birkhäuser, 1998), 53; "UiT in Genk/Waterschei Garden Suburb," in http://www.uitingenk.be/en/uig_content/record/3037/waterschei-garden-suburb.html; https://inventaris.onroerenderfgoed.be/dibe/geheel/22160.

192 Frieda Schlusmans et al., *Bouwen door de eeuwen heen. Inventaris van het cultuurbezit in België: Architectuur. Deel 14n 3, Provincie Limburg. Arrondissement Tongeren, Kantons Bilzen-Maasmechelen* (Turnhout: Brepols, 1996), 387–90; https://inventaris.onroerenderfgoed.be/dibe/geheel/22141.

193 Frieda Schlusmans et al., *Bouwen door de eeuwen heen. Inventaris van het cultuurbezit in België: Architectuur. Deel 6n 1 (A-Ha), Provincie Limburg. Arrondissement Hasselt* (Gent: Snoeck-Ducaju & Zoon, 1981), 51–60; https://inventaris.onroerenderfgoed.be/dibe/geheel/22201.

194 Huib Hoste, "La Cité de Selzaete," *L'Habitation à Bon Marché* 9 (September 1923): 213–15; Marcel Smets, *Huib Hoste: propagateur d'une architecture renouvelée* (Bruxelles: Confédération Nationale de la Construction in collaboration with Librairie Simon Stevin, 1972), 63, 64, 97–100; Marcel Smets, "Stedebouw in België, 1920–1940, Algemene Ontwikkeling; Urbanistic Thinking in Belgium, 1920–1940, General Development," *Forum* (Amsterdam) 24, no. 4 (1972): 11, 13, 15; Marcel Smets, "Stedebouw in België, 1920–1940, Tuinwijken; Urbanistic Thinking in Belgium, 1920–1940, Garden Districts," *Forum* (Amsterdam) 24, no. 5 (1972); Marcel Smets, *L'avenement de la Cité-Jardin en Belgique: Histoire de l'habitat social en Belgique de 1830 à 1930* (Bruxelles: P. Mardaga, 1977), 114, 124–27, 132, 134, 135, 140; Herman Stynen, *Urbanisme et Société: Louis van der Swaelmen, 1883–1929: animateur du movement moderne en Belgique* (Bruxelles: P. Mardaga, 1979), 83–87, 128; Aleks A. M. Deseyne, *Huib Hoste: 1881–1957, en de wederopbouw te Zonnebeke* (Zonnebeke: Zonnebeekse Heemvrienden, 1981), 50, 51, 52, 53; Anna Barozzi, "The Morphology of the Garden City," in Gabriele Tagliaventi, ed., *Garden City* (Rome: Gangemi Editore, 1994), 108; Herman van Bergeijk and Otakar Máčel, *Birkhäuser Architectural Guide: Belgium, The Netherlands, Luxembourg, 20th Century* (Basel: Birkhäuser, 1998), 37; Michiel Heirman and Linda Van Santvoort, *Le Guide de L'architecture en Belgique* (Brussels: Éditions Racine, 2000), 480; Marcel Smets, "Huib Hoste, 1881–1957," in Mil De Kooning, ed., *Horta and After: 25 Masters of Modern Architecture in Belgium*, 2nd rev. ed. (Ghent: Department of Architecture and Urbanism, Ghent University, 2001), 102–6; Liesbeth De Winter, Marcel Smets, and Ann Verdonck, *Huib Hoste: 1881–1957* (Antwerp: Vlaams Architectuurinstituut, 2005), 53, 115–18; François Aubry, Jos Vandenbreeden, and France Vanlaethem, *L'architecture en Belgique: Art Nouveau, Art Déco & Modernisme* (Bruxelles: Éditions Racine, 2006), 314–15, 318.

195 Smets, "Urbanistic Thinking in Belgium, 1920–1940, General Development": 15.

196 "A Dutch Employer's Experiment: The 'Agneta Park' Village at Delft," *The Review of Reviews* 3 (June 1891): 486–87; "A Dutch Co-operative Town," *American Architect and Building News* XLVI (December 1, 1894): 91; S. J. Fockema Andreae, "The Garden City Idea in the Netherlands Before 1930," *Stedebouw en Volkshuisvesting* 44 (1963): 95–107; François Choay, *The Modern City: Planning in the 19th Century* (New York: George Braziller, 1969), 30; Gillian Darley, *Villages of Vision* (London: Architectural Press, 1975), 75; Donald I. Grinberg, *Housing in the Netherlands, 1900–1940* (Delft: Delft University Press, 1977), 24–26; Donald I. Grinberg, "Modernist Housing and Its Critics: The Dutch Contributions," *Harvard Architecture Review* 1 (Spring 1980): 148; Sh. Rg. Hofstee, "Housing Built by Industrialists in the Netherlands," in *L'Étude et la mise en valeur du patrimoine industriel: 4e conférence internationale, Lyon, Grenoble, septembre 1981* (Paris: Editions du Centre national de la recherche scientifique, 1985), 318–29; Rudy Schreijnders, *De Droom van Howard: verleden en toekomst van de tuindorpen* (Rijswijk: Elmar, 1991), 81–82; Niels Prak and Hugo Priemus, "The Netherlands," in Colin G. Pooley, *Housing Strategies in Europe, 1880–1930* (Leicester: Leicester University Press; New York: St. Martin's Press, 1992), 181–82; Paul Groenendijk and Piet Vollaard, *Gids voor moderne architectuur in Nederland; Guide to modern architecture in the Netherlands* (Rotterdam: Uitgeverij 010, 1998), 211; Hans Ibelings, *20th Century Urban Design in the Netherlands* (Rotterdam: NAi Publishers, 1999), 20; Harm Jan Korthals Altes, *Tuinsteden: tussen utopie en realitet* (Bussum: Thoth, 2004), 93–94; Cor Wagenaar, *Town Planning in the Netherlands since 1800* (Rotterdam: 010 Publishers, 2011), 231–32.

197 Choay, *The Modern City: Planning in the 19th Century*, 30.

198 Grinberg, "Modernist Housing and Its Critics: The Dutch Contributions": 148.

199 Sh. Rg. Hofstee, "Housing Built by Industrialists in the Netherlands," in *L'Étude et la mise en valeur du patrimoine industriel: 4e conférence internationale, Lyon, Grenoble, septembre 1981* (Paris: Editions du Centre national de la recherche scientifique, 1985), 318–29; Rutger Dinger, "Snouck van Loosenpark in Enkhuizen erfstuk van sociale woningbouw," *Heemschut* 63 (May–June 1986): 97–98.

200 G. Feenstra, *Tuinsteden en Volkshuisvesting in Nederland en Buitenland* (Amsterdam: Van Mantgem & De Does, 1920), 240–58; *International Cities and Town Planning Exhibition. English Catalogue. Jubilee Exhibition, Gothenburg, Sweden, 1923* (Göteborg, Wezäta, W. Zachrissons boktyrckeri a.-b., 1923), 185, 192–93; S. J. Fockema Andreae, "The Garden City Idea in the Netherlands Before 1930," *Stedebouw en Volkshuisvesting* 44 (1963): 102–3; Donald I. Grinberg, *Housing in the Netherlands, 1900–1940* (Delft: Delft University Press, 1977), 40–41, 56; Sh. Rg. Hofstee, "Housing Built by Industrialists in the Netherlands," in *L'Étude et la mise en valeur du patrimoine industriel: 4e conférence internationale, Lyon, Grenoble, septembre 1981* (Paris: Editions du Centre national de la recherche scientifique, 1985), 323; Hilda van der Iest, "Volkshuisvestingscomplexen waard te blijven," *Heemschut* 64 (September 1987): 18–19; Rudy Schreijnders, *De Droom van Howard: verleden en toekomst van de tuindorpen* (Rijswijk: Elmar, 1991), 86; Hans Ibelings, *20th Century Urban Design in the Netherlands* (Rotterdam: NAi Publishers, 1999), 20, 37; Maarten Piek, *K. J. Muller (1857–1942): sportcomplexen, buitenplaatsen en tuindorpen – gezondheid als leidraad in architectuur* (Rotterdam: BONAS, 2000), 8, 9, 10–11, 23–26, 57–97; Pieter Van Wesemael, "Calendar of Dutch 20th-century Architecture," in S. Umberto Barbieri and Leen van Duin, *A Hundred Years of Dutch Architecture, 1901–2000, Trends, Highlights* (Amsterdam: Uitgeverij SUN, 2003), 367; Harm Jan Korthals Altes, *Tuinsteden: tussen utopie en realitet* (Bussum: Thoth, 2004), 108–10; Mieke Dings, "Historical Perspective, 1900–2010," in Henk Ovink and Elien Wierenga, eds., *Ontwerp en Politiek; Design and Politics* (Rotterdam: Uitgeverij 010, 2009), 24; Cor Wagenaar, *Town Planning in the Netherlands since 1800* (Rotterdam: 010 Publishers, 2011), 231–32, 233; http://www.tuindorplansink.nl.

201 *International Cities and Town Planning Exhibition. English Catalogue. Jubilee Exhibition, Gothenburg, Sweden, 1923* (Göteborg, Wezäta, W. Zachrissons boktyrckeri a.-b., 1923), 175; Edith Elmer Wood, "Housing in the Netherlands," *Housing Betterment* 12 (January 1923): 356; S. J. Fockema Andreae, "The Garden City Idea in the Netherlands Before 1930," *Stedebouw en Volkshuisvesting* 44 (1963): 102–3; Donald I. Grinberg, *Housing in the Netherlands, 1900–1940* (Delft: Delft University Press, 1977), 56, 58, 59; Sh. Rg. Hofstee, "Housing Built by Industrialists in the Netherlands," in *L'Étude et la mise en valeur du patrimoine industriel: 4e conférence internationale, Lyon, Grenoble, septembre 1981* (Paris: Editions du Centre national de la recherche scientifique, 1985), 323; Rudy Schreijnders, *De Droom van Howard: verleden en toekomst van de tuindorpen* (Rijswijk: Elmar, 1991), 83–85; Hans Ibelings, *20th Century Urban Design in the Netherlands* (Rotterdam: NAi Publishers, 1999), 20, 31; Harm Jan Korthals Altes, *Tuinsteden: tussen utopie en realitet* (Bussum: Thoth, 2004), 101–3; Paul Groenendijk and Piet Vollaard, *Architectuurgids Rotterdam; Architectural Guide to Rotterdam* (Rotterdam: Uitgeverij 010, 2007), 11, 225.

202 Grinberg, *Housing in the Netherlands, 1900–1940*, 58.

203 Hofstee, "Housing Built by Industrialists in the Netherlands": 323.

204 Rudy Schreijnders, *De Droom van Howard: verleden en toekomst van de tuindorpen* (Rijswijk: Elmar, 1991), 85–86; Hans Ibelings, *20th Century Urban Design in the Netherlands* (Rotterdam: NAi Publishers, 1999), 20; Maarten Piek, *K. J. Muller (1857–1942): sportcomplexen, buitenplaatsen en tuindorpen – gezondheid als leidraad in architectuur* (Rotterdam: BONAS, 2000), 107–11; Catja Edens and Bettina van Santen, *Gids voor architectuur en stedenbouw in Utrecht, 1900–2005* (Bussum: Thoth, 2004), 203; Zoeken.nai.nl/CIS/project/18692; http://www.bonas.nl/tud/sites/kj_muller/main.swf.

205 Adriaan Wessel Reinink, *K. P. C. de Bazel—Architect* (1965; Rotterdam: Uitgeverij 010, 1993), 213–14; Donald I. Grinberg, *Housing in the Netherlands, 1900–1940* (Delft: Delft University Press, 1977), 56, 57, 58; A. Heerding, *The History of N. V. Philips' Gloeilampenfabrieken: Volume 2, A Company of Many Parts* (Cambridge; New York: Cambridge University Press, 1988), 263–65; Rudy Schreijnders, *De Droom van Howard: verleden en toekomst van de tuindorpen* (Rijswijk: Elmar, 1991), 86–87; Hans Ibelings, *20th Century Urban Design in the Netherlands* (Rotterdam: NAi Publishers, 1999), 20, 32–33; Vladimir Stissi, "Eternal Boredom, Happily," in *Living in the Lowlands: the Dutch Domestic Scene, 1850–2004* (Rotterdam: Netherlands Architecture Institute; NAi Publishers, 2004), 38–49; Mieke Dings, "Historical Perspective, 1900–2010," in Henk Ovink and Elien Wierenga, eds., *Ontwerp en Politiek; Design and Politics* (Rotterdam: Uitgeverij 010, 2009), 24.

206 Stissi, "Eternal Boredom, Happily," in *Living in the Lowlands: the Dutch Domestic Scene, 1850–2004*, 49.

207 Stissi, "Eternal Boredom, Happily," in *Living in the Lowlands: the Dutch Domestic Scene, 1850–2004*, 49.

208 Herman van Bergeijk and Otakar Máčel, *Birkhäuser Architectural Guide: Belgium, The Netherlands, Luxembourg, 20th Century* (Basel: Birkhäuser, 1998), 132; Marloes Eskens, Leo van der Laan, and Bé Lamberts, *Willem Cornelis de Groot (1853–1939), Architect in Friesland* (Leeuwarden: Friese Pers Boekerij, 2009), 41, 79, 83–85, 102; http://www.wcdegroot.nl.

209 Sh. Rg. Hofstee, "Housing Built by Industrialists in the Netherlands," in *L'Étude et la mise en valeur du patrimoine industriel : 4e conférence internationale, Lyon, Grenoble, septembre 1981* (Paris : Editions du Centre national de la recherche scientifique, 1985), 324; Rudy Schreijnders, *De Droom van Howard : verleden en toekomst van de tuindorpen* (Rijswijk: Elmar, 1991), 88–89, 220–25; Paul Groenendijk and Piet Vollaard, *Gids voor moderne architectuur in Nederland; Guide to modern architecture in the Netherlands* (Rotterdam: Uitgeverij 010, 1998), 77; Hans Ibelings, *20th Century Urban Design in the Netherlands* (Rotterdam: NAi Publishers, 1999), 20, 25.

210 H. P. Berlage et al., *Arbeiderswoningen in Nederland* (Rotterdam: W. L. & J. Brusse, 1921), 73–75; Rudy Schreijnders, *De Droom van Howard: verleden en toekomst van de tuindorpen* (Rijswijk: Elmar, 1991), 89; Margriet Panman and Jans Possel, *Architectuur en stedebouw in Groningen, 1850–1940* (Zwolle: Waanders; Zeist, Rijksdienst voor de Monumentenzorg, 1992), 77; Harm Jan Korthals Altes, *Tuinsteden: tussen utopie en realitet* (Bussum: Thoth, 2004), 98–101.

211 H. P. Berlage et al., *Arbeiderswoningen in Nederland* (Rotterdam: W. L. & J. Brusse, 1921), 105–7; Harm Jan Korthals Altes, *Tuinsteden: tussen utopie en realitet* (Bussum: Thoth, 2004), 117, 132–34.

212 H. P. Berlage et al., *Arbeiderswoningen in Nederland* (Rotterdam: W. L. & J. Brusse, 1921), 148–50; *International Cities and Town Planning Exhibition. English Catalogue. Jubilee Exhibition, Gothenburg, Sweden, 1923* (Göteborg, Wezäta, W. Zachrissons boktyrckeri a.-b., 1923), 187–88; Hilda van der Iest, "Volkshuisvestingscomplexen waard te blijven," *Heemschut* 64 (September 1987): 18–19; Herman van Bergeijk and Otakar Máčel, *Birkhäuser Architectural Guide: Belgium, The Netherlands, Luxembourg, 20th Century* (Basel: Birkhäuser, 1998), 182; Paul Groenendijk and Piet Vollaard, *Gids voor moderne architectuur in Nederland; Guide to modern architecture in the Netherlands* (Rotterdam: Uitgeverij 010, 1998), 65; Hans Ibelings, *20th Century Urban Design in the Netherlands* (Rotterdam: NAi Publishers, 1999), 30.

213 Gunther Stamm, *The Architecture of J. J. P. Oud, 1906–1963* (Tallahassee: University Presses of Florida, 1978), 10, 29.

214 Bernard Colenbrander, "J. J. P. Oud: Restrained and Careful," in *Het Nieuwe Bouwen: Voorgeschiedenis=Previous History* (Delft: Delft University Press; Nederlands Dokumentatiecentrum voor de Bouwkunst, 1982), 155.

215 J. J. P. Oud, quoted in Colenbrander, "J. J. P. Oud: Restrained and Careful": 155.

216 Ed Taverne, Cor Wagenaar, and Martien de Vletter, *Poetic Functionalist: J. J. P. Oud, 1890–1963: The Complete Works* (Rotterdam: NAi Publishers, 2001), 192.

217 J. J. P. Oud, "Semi-Permanente Woningbouw 'Oud-Mathenesse' Rotterdam," *Bouwkundig Weekblad Architectura* 45 (1924): 418–21, reprinted in English in Ed Taverne, Cor Wagenaar, and Martien de Vletter, *Poetic Functionalist: J. J. P. Oud, 1890–1963: The Complete Works* (Rotterdam: NAi Publishers, 2001), 255; J. P. Mieras and F. R. Yerbury, *Holländische Architektur des 20. Jahrhunderts* (Berlin: Ernst Wasmuth, 1926), plate LXXVIII–LXXIX; J. J. P. Oud, "Architecture and the Future," *Creative Art* 3 (December 1928): 403–6; Henry Russell Hitchcock Jr., *J. J. P. Oud* (Paris: Editions Cahiers D'art, 1931), 13–18; Henry-Russell Hitchcock Jr., "J. J. P. Oud," in *Modern Architecture; International Exhibition, New York Feb. 10 to March 23, 1932*, reprint edition (New York: 1932; Arno Press, 1969), 94–95, 105; Giulia Veronesi, *J. J. Pieter Oud* (Milano: Il Balcone, 1953), 78–83; Donald I. Grinberg, *Housing in the Netherlands, 1900–1940* (Delft: Delft University Press, 1977), 79, 84, 85; Gunther Stamm, *The Architecture of J. J. P. Oud, 1906–1963* (Tallahassee: University Presses of Florida, 1978), 16–17; Umberto Barbieri, ed., *J. J. P. Oud* (Bologna: Zanichelli, 1986), 86–93; Bernard Colenbrander, *Oud-Mathenesse: het Witte Dorp, 1923–1987* (Rotterdam: De Hef, 1987), passim; Rudy Schreijnders, *De Droom van Howard: verleden en toekomst van de tuindorpen* (Rijswijk: Elmar, 1991), 193–94, 233–39; Joseph Buch, *A Century of Architecture in the Netherlands, 1880–1990* (Rotterdam: NAi, 1993), 206–7; Paul Groenendijk and Piet Vollaard, *Gids voor moderne architectuur in Nederland; Guide to modern architecture in the Netherlands* (Rotterdam: Uitgeverij 010, 1998), 277; Ed Taverne, Cor Wagenaar, and Martien de Vletter, *Poetic Functionalist: J. J. P. Oud, 1890–1963: The Complete Works* (Rotterdam: NAi Publishers, 2001), 192, 195, 247–54; Harm Jan Korthals Altes, *Tuinsteden: tussen utopie en realitet* (Bussum: Thoth, 2004), 130–32; Paul Groenendijk and Piet Vollaard, *Architectuurgids Rotterdam; Architectural Guide to Rotterdam* (Rotterdam: Uitgeverij 010, 2007), 212.

218 Hitchcock, "J. J. P. Oud," in *Modern Architecture; International Exhibition*, 94.

219 Taverne, Wagenaar, and de Vletter, *Poetic Functionalist: J. J. P. Oud, 1890–1963: The Complete Works*, 247.

220 Taverne, Wagenaar, and de Vletter, *Poetic Functionalist: J. J. P. Oud, 1890–1963: The Complete Works*, 250.

221 "The New Architecture: J. J. P. Oud—Holland," *Creative Art* 3 (December 1928): 401–2; J. J. P. Oud, "Architecture and the Future," *Creative Art* 3 (December 1928): 403–6, 453; *Nieuw-Nederlandsche bouwkunst; architecture moderne en Hollande* (Amsterdam: Uitgevers-Maatschij "Kosmos", 1929), plates 201, 202; Henry Russell Hitchcock Jr., *J. J. P. Oud* (Paris: Editions Cahiers d'Art, 1931), 20–23; Henry-Russell Hitchcock Jr., "J. J. P. Oud," in *Modern Architecture; International Exhibition, New York Feb. 10 to March 23, 1932*, reprint edition (New York: 1932; Arno Press, 1969), 95, 106; Giulia Veronesi, *J. J. Pieter Oud* (Milano: Il Balcone, 1953), 88–89; Donald I. Grinberg, *Housing in the Netherlands, 1900–1940* (Delft: Delft University Press, 1977), 79, 93–94; Gunther Stamm, *The Architecture of J. J. P. Oud, 1906–1963* (Tallahassee: University Presses of Florida, 1978), 35–38; J. B. van Loghem, *Bouwen = Bauen = Bâtir = Building Holland: een dokumentatie van de hoogtepunten van de moderne architektuur in Nederland van 1900 tot 1932* (Nijmegen, Netherlands: Socialistiese Uitgeverij Nijmegen, 1980), 114; Umberto Barbieri, ed., *J. J. P. Oud* (Bologna: Zanichelli, 1986), 98–103; Joseph Buch, *A Century of Architecture in the Netherlands, 1880–1990* (Rotterdam: NAi, 1993), 207; Hans Ibelings, *20th Century Architecture in the Netherlands* (Rotterdam: NAi Publishers, 1995), 40, 48; Erik Mattie, *Functionalism in the Netherlands* (Amsterdam: Architectura & Natura, 1995), 67–68; Herman van Bergeijk and Otakar Máčel, *Birkhäuser Architectural Guide: Belgium, The Netherlands, Luxembourg, 20th Century* (Basel: Birkhäuser, 1998), 204; Paul Groenendijk and Piet Vollaard, *Gids voor moderne architectuur in Nederland; Guide to modern architecture in the Netherlands* (Rotterdam: Uitgeverij 010, 1998), 216–17; Ed Taverne, Cor Wagenaar, and Martien de Vletter, *Poetic Functionalist: J. J. P. Oud, 1890–1963: The Complete Works* (Rotterdam: NAi Publishers, 2001), 192, 196, 260–73; Wolfgang Förster, *Housing in the 20th and 21st Centuries* (Munich: Prestel, 2006), 34–35; Paul Groenendijk and Piet Vollaard, *Architectuurgids Rotterdam; Architectural Guide to Rotterdam* (Rotterdam: Uitgeverij 010, 2007), 276–77.

222 Taverne, Wagenaar, and de Vletter, *Poetic Functionalist: J. J. P. Oud, 1890–1963: The Complete Works*, 262.

223 J. J. P. Oud, "Woningbouw te Hoek van Holland," in I. M. Dugteren, H. Dekking, eds., *Het Groen-Wit-Groene Boek* (Rotterdam, 1927), 38–41, quoted in Taverne, Wagenaar, and de Vletter, *Poetic Functionalist: J. J. P. Oud, 1890–1963: The Complete Works*, 263.

224 Henry Russell Hitchcock Jr., *J. J. P. Oud* (Paris: Editions Cahiers D'art, 1931), 34–45; Henry-Russell Hitchcock Jr., "J. J. P. Oud," in *Modern Architecture; International Exhibition, New York Feb. 10 to March 23, 1932*, reprint edition (New York: 1932; Arno Press, 1969), 96–107; Giulia Veronesi, *J. J. Pieter Oud* (Milano: Il Balcone, 1953), 92–107; Waclaw Ostrowski, *Contemporary Town Planning: From the origins to the Athens Charter* (Hague, Netherlands: International Federation for Housing and Planning, 1970), 100–101; Donald I. Grinberg, *Housing in the Netherlands, 1900–1940* (Delft: Delft University Press, 1977), 44–45; Gunther Stamm, *The Architecture of J. J. P. Oud, 1906–1963* (Tallahassee: University Presses of Florida, 1978), 42–43; J. B. van Loghem, *Bouwen = Bauen = Bâtir = Building Holland: een dokumentatie van de hoogtepunten van de moderne architektuur in Nederland van 1900 tot 1932* (Nijmegen, Netherlands: Socialistiese Uitgeverij Nijmegen, 1980), 109, 110, 111; Umberto Barbieri, ed., *J. J. P. Oud* (Bologna: Zanichelli, 1986), 104–9; Joseph Buch, *A Century of Architecture in the Netherlands, 1880–1990* (Rotterdam: NAi Publishers, 1993), 140–43, 207; *De Kiefhoek: Een Woonwijk in Rotterdam* (Rotterdam: Stichting Museumwoning De Kiefhoek; Laren: V & K Publishing, 1990); Erik Mattie, *Functionalism in the Netherlands* (Amsterdam: Architectura & Natura, 1995), 69–70; Hans Ibelings, *20th Century Architecture in the Netherlands* (Rotterdam: NAi Publishers, 1995), 40, 49; Paul Groenendijk and Piet Vollaard, *Gids voor moderne architectuur in Nederland; Guide to modern architecture in the Netherlands* (Rotterdam: Uitgeverij 010, 1998), 300–301; Ed Taverne, Cor Wagenaar, and Martien de Vletter, *Poetic Functionalist: J. J. P. Oud, 1890–1963: The Complete Works* (Rotterdam: NAi Publishers, 2001), 192, 274–89; S. Umberto Barbieri, "Rationalism," in Umberto Barbieri and Leen van Duin, eds., *A Hundred Years of Dutch Architecture, 1901–2000, Trends, Highlights* (Amsterdam: Uitgeverij SUN, 2003), 56–57; Martien de Vletter, "The 'Dwelling-Ford': Cutting and Contriving for 2,740 Guilders per House," in *Living in the Lowlands: the Dutch Domestic Scene, 1850–2004* (Rotterdam: Netherlands Architecture Institute; NAi Publishers, 2004), 96–107; Jean-Yves Andrieux and Fabienne Chevallier, eds., *The Reception of Architecture of the Modern Movement: Image, Usage, and Heritage* (Saint-Ettiene: Publications de l'Universite de Saint Etienne, 2005), 211–13; Wolfgang Förster, *Housing in the 20th and 21st Centuries* (Munich: Prestel, 2006), 36; Paul Groenendijk and Piet Vollaard, *Architectuurgids Rotterdam; Architectural Guide to Rotterdam* (Rotterdam: Uitgeverij 010, 2007), 12, 256–57.

225 De Jonge van Ellemeet, quoted in Taverne, Wagenaar, and de Vletter, *Poetic Functionalist: J. J. P. Oud, 1890–1963: The Complete Works*, 276.

226 De Vletter, "The 'Dwelling-Ford': Cutting and Contriving for 2,740 Guilders per House," in *Living in the Lowlands*, 105.

227 De Vletter, "The 'Dwelling-Ford': Cutting and Contriving for 2,740 Guilders per House," in *Living in the Lowlands*, 106.

228 Hjalmar Lundbohm, *Kiruna* (Stockholm: Norstedt & Söner, 1910); Frederic Bedoire, *En arkitekt och hans verksamhetsfält kring sekelskiftet, Gustaf Wickmans arbeten*

1884–1916 (Stockholm: AB Draken, 1974), 11, 20, 21, 22, 35–37, 62, 66, 67, 98, 101–2, 143–47; Thomas Hall, "Urban Planning in Sweden," in Thomas Hall, ed., *Planning and Urban Growth in the Nordic Countries* (London: E & FN Spon, 1991), 191; Mats Ahnlund and Lasse Brunnström, "The Company Town in Scandinavia," in John S. Garner, *The Company Town: Architecture and Society in the Early Industrial Age* (New York: Oxford University Press, 1992), 91–94; Claes Caldenby, Jöran Lindvall, and Wilfried Wang, eds., *20th Century Architecture: Sweden* (Munich: Prestel, 1998), 246–47; Rasmus Waern et al., *A Guide to Swedish Architecture* (Stockholm: The Swedish Institute, 2001), 379; *Utopia & Reality: Modernity in Sweden, 1900–1960* (New Haven and London: Yale University Press in association with the Bard Graduate Center for Studies in the Decorative Arts, Design, and Culture, New York, 2002), 392–93; "Kiruna—a city in transformation," in http://www.kommun.kiruna.se/Om-kommunen/English/City-in-Transformation/; http://www.kommun.kiruna.se/Om-kommunen/English/History/.

229 Janne Ahlin, *Sigurd Lewerentz, architect, 1885–1975* (Cambridge, Mass.: MIT Press, 1987), 22–23, 25, 185. Also see *Sigurd Lewerentz, 1885–1975* (Madrid: Secretaría General Técnica, Centro de Publicaciones, Ministerio de Obras Públicas y Urbanismo, 1987), 52; Wilfried Wang, "Architecture as an Extension of Life," in Claes Dymling, ed., *Architect Sigurd Lewerentz, Vol. I Photographs of the Work* (Stockholm: Byggförlaget, 1997), 13; Nicola Flora, Paolo Giardello, and Gennaro Postiglione, *Sigurd Lewerentz, 1885–1975* (Milan: Electa, 2001), 85.

230 *Sigurd Lewerentz, 1885–1975* (Madrid: Secretaría General Técnica, Centro de Publicaciones, Ministerio de Obras Públicas y Urbanismo, 1987), 53; Janne Ahlin, *Sigurd Lewerentz, architect, 1885–1975* (Cambridge, Mass.: MIT Press, 1987), 26–27, 185; Claes Dymling, ed., *Architect Sigurd Lewerentz, Vol. I Photographs of the Work* (Stockholm: Byggförlaget, 1997), 46–49; Claes Dymling, ed., *Architect Sigurd Lewerentz, Vol. II Drawings* (Stockholm: Byggförlaget, 1997), 8–9; Eva Eriksson, "Rationalism and Classicism 1915–30," in Claes Caldenby, Jöran Lindvall, and Wilfried Wang, eds., *20th Century Architecture: Sweden* (Munich: Prestel, 1998), 49–50; Wilfried Wang, "Architecture as an Extension of Life," in Dymling, ed., *Architect Sigurd Lewerentz, Vol. I Photographs of the Work*, 13; Nicola Flora, Paolo Giardello, and Gennaro Postiglione, *Sigurd Lewerentz, 1885–1975* (Milan: Electa, 2001), 68–71.

231 Janne Ahlin, *Sigurd Lewerentz, architect, 1885–1975* (Cambridge, Mass.: MIT Press, 1987), 24, 25, 185; Nicola Flora, Paolo Giardello, and Gennaro Postiglione, *Sigurd Lewerentz, 1885–1975* (Milan: Electa, 2001), 72–73.

232 *Sigurd Lewerentz, 1885–1975* (Madrid: Secretaría General Técnica, Centro de Publicaciones, Ministerio de Obras Públicas y Urbanismo, 1987), 56; Janne Ahlin, *Sigurd Lewerentz, architect, 1885–1975* (Cambridge, Mass.: MIT Press, 1987), 186; Nicola Flora, Paolo Giardello, and Gennaro Postiglione, *Sigurd Lewerentz, 1885–1975* (Milan: Electa, 2001), 106.

233 Mats Ahnlund and Lasse Brunnström, "The Company Town in Scandinavia," in John S. Garner, ed., *The Company Town: Architecture and Society in the Early Industrial Age* (New York: Oxford University Press, 1992), 101–2, 103.

234 Ahnlund and Brunnström, "The Company Town in Scandinavia," in Garner, ed., *The Company Town*, 102.

235 Heleni Porfyriou, "Artistic Urban Design and Cultural Myths: the Garden City Idea in Nordic Countries, 1900–1925," *Planning Perspectives* 7 (1992): 275–76; Eva Eriksson, "Rationalism and Classicism 1915–30," in Claes Caldenby, Jöran Lindvall, and Wilfried Wang, eds., *20th Century Architecture: Sweden* (Munich: Prestel, 1998), 49; Caldenby, Lindvall, and Wang, eds., *20th Century Architecture: Sweden*, 264.

236 Eriksson, "Rationalism and Classicism, 1915–30," in Caldenby, Lindvall, and Wang, eds., *20th Century Architecture: Sweden*, 49.

237 Marika Hausen et al., *Eliel Saarinen: Projects, 1896–1923* (Cambridge, Mass.: MIT Press, 1990), 332–33.

238 Marika Hausen et al., *Eliel Saarinen: Projects, 1896–1923* (Cambridge, Mass.: MIT Press, 1990), 334.

239 Ulla Salmela, "Happy Homes and Stable Society. Otto-Iivari Meurman and *Omakoti* in Interwar Finland," *Planning Perspectives* 22 (October 2007): 452–53.

240 Otto-Iivari Meurman, quoted in Salmela, "Happy Homes and Stable Society": 453.

241 *International Cities and Town Planning Exhibition. English Catalogue. Jubilee Exhibition, Gothenburg, Sweden, 1923* (Göteborg, Wezäta, W. Zachrissons boktyrckeri a.-b., 1923), 205; Mats Ahnlund and Lasse Brunnström, "The Company Town in Scandinavia," in John S. Garner, ed., *The Company Town: Architecture and Society in the Early Industrial Age* (New York: Oxford University Press, 1992), 100. Also see Sverre Pedersen, "Norway," in *International Cities and Town Planning Exhibition. English Catalogue. Jubilee Exhibition, Gothenburg, Sweden, 1923* (Göteborg, Wezäta, W. Zachrissons boktyrckeri a.-b., 1923), 205, 206; Stig Andersen, "En Industriby Blir Til," *Byggekunst* 62 (no.1, 1980): 25–38, 56; Erik Lorange and Jan Eivind Myhre, "Urban Planning in Norway," in Thomas Hall, ed., in *Planning and Urban Growth in the Nordic Countries* (London: E & FN Spon, 1991), 140; "1906: The Next Gigantic Step," in www.hydro.com/en/about-hydro/our-history/1900-1917/1906-the-next-gigantic-step/.

242 Bernardetta Ricatti, "The New Workers' Neighborhood in Schio," www.schioindustrialheritage.com/uk. Also see Department of State, *Cotton and Woolen Mills of Europe* (Washington: Government Printing Office, 1882), 255–72; C. H. Blackall, "The Workingmen's Colony at Essen, Germany," *American Architect and Building News* 19 (May 1, 1886): 207–9; Horatio Forbes Brown, *In and Around Venice* (New York: Scribner, 1905), 229–32; Alberto Abriani, "Getting to the Roots of Modern Architecture, Through the Analysis of a Workers' Village: Borgata Leumann," *Lotus International* 9 (1975): 138, 229; Elisa and Leonardo Mariani Travi, *Il paesaggio italiano della rivoluzione industriale: Crespi d'Adda e Schio* (Bari : Dedalo libri, 1979); G.L. Fontana, ed., *Schio e Alessandro Rossi*, 2 vols. (Rome: Edizioni di Stori e Letteratura, 1985–86); David LoRomer, "Schio e Alessandro Rossi," book review, *Journal of Modern History* 61 (March 1989): 177–79; Vera Zamagni, *The Economic History of Italy, 1869–1990: Recovery After Decline* (Oxford: Clarendon Press, 1993), 183; George Holmes, *The Oxford Illustrated History of Italy* (Oxford and New York: Oxford University Press, 2001), 240; Luca Valente, "Schio," www.comune.schio.vi.it; "Schio," http://workingheritage.european-heritage.net/uk.

243 Ricatti, "The New Workers' Neighborhood in Schio": 1.

244 Alessandro Rossi, quoted in Ricatti, "The New Workers' Neighborhood in Schio": 3.

245 Brown, *In and Around Venice*, 230–32.

246 S.B. Crespi, "Il villaggio operaio Crespi a Capriate," *L'Edilizia Moderna* (August 1894), reprinted and translated in Lorenzo Lotesto, "Crespi d'Adda: The Village of an Industrial Dynasty," *Rassegna* 19 (1997): 20–23; Jürgen Zänker, "Non Amor, sed 'Labor omnia vincit': Crespi d'Adda, eine Industriesiedlung des 19. Jahrhunderts in Oberitalien," *Archithese* 8 (1973): 27–38; Alberto Abriani, "Getting to the Roots of Modern Architecture, Through the Analysis of a Workers' Village: Borgata Leumann," *Lotus International* 9 (1975): 138, 229; Leonardo and Elisa Mariani Travi, "Un paesaggio Lombardo della prima rivoluzion industriale: Crespi d'Adda," *Architettura cronache e storia* 24 (December 1978): 467–74; Elisa and Leonardo Mariani Travi, *Il paesaggio italiano della rivoluzione industriale: Crespi d'Adda e Schio* (Bari: Dedalo libri, 1979); Edo Bricchetti, "Crespi d'Adda: Un Villaggio operaio fine Ottocento," *Spazio e societa* 5 (September 1982): 58–71; Enzo Quarenghi and Carlo Leidi, *Crespi d'Adda: la fabbrica e il villaggio* (Milan: Il Filo di Arianna, 1984); Vera Zamagni, *The Economic History of Italy, 1869–1990: Recovery After Decline* (Oxford: Clarendon Press, 1993), 183; Luigi Cortesi, *Crespi d'Adda: Villaggio ideale del laboro* (Bergamo: Grafica e arte, 1995); Giancarlo Consonni, "Crespi d'Adda," *Ottagono* 31 (June–August 1996): 73–88; Federico Bucci, *Company Towns* (Bologna: Editrice Composition, 1997), 17; www.crespidadda.it; "Crespi d'Adda," www.lifeinitaly.com; "The Working Village of Crespi d'Adda," http://www.sitiunesco.it; www.villaggiocrespi.it.

247 *Il cotonificio N. Leumann e le sue istituzioni d'igiene, di educazione e di previdenza* (Aarau, Switzerland: Officine d'Arti Grafiche, 1911); Alberto Abriani, "Getting to the Roots of Modern Architecture, Through the Analysis of a Workers' Village: Borgata Leumann," *Lotus International* 9 (1975): 136–45, 229–31; "Un caso vivo da discutere: il villaggio Leumann," *Abitare* 158 (October 1977): 76–87, 95; Riccardo Nelva and Bruno Signorelli, *Le opera di Pietro Fenoglio nel clima dell'art nouveau internazionale* (Bari: Dedalo libri, 1979), 43–46, 56–68; Sergio Polano and Marco Mulazzani, *Guida all'architettura italiana del Novecento* (Milan: Electa, 1991), 32; Piero Ventura, *Houses: Structures, Methods, and Ways of Living* (Boston: Houghton Mifflin, 1993), 45; Vera Zamagni, *The Economic History of Italy, 1869–1990: Recovery After Decline* (Oxford: Clarendon Press, 1993), 183; Florence Vidal, *Histoire industrielle de l'Italie: de 1860 à nos jours* (Paris: Seli Arslan, 1998), 62; Sergio Pace, "Leumann Workers' Village," in Lorenzo Capellini, Vera Comoli, and Carlo Olmo, eds., *Torino Architectural Guide* (Rome: Umberto Allemandi & Company, 1999), 171; Carla Federica Gütermann, *Leumann: storia di un imprenditore e del suo villaggio modello* (Turin: D. Piazza, 2006); Annalisa Dameri, *Tradizione e sperimentazione costruire nel piemonte del xix secolo* (2010), 98–109, http://www.lulu.com/items/volume_68/8672000/8672801/1/print/8672801.pdf; "Stazionetta Leumann: La Storia," www.axmedia.it/download/collegno/stazionetta-collegno.pdf; "Village Leumann," www.provincia.torino.it; "Villagio Leumann," www.collegno.net; "Villaggio Leumann," www.nbts.it/torino/leumann.htm.

248 Abriani, "Getting to the Roots of Modern Architecture, Through the Analysis of a Workers' Village: Borgata Leumann": 230.

249 Abriani, "Getting to the Roots of Modern Architecture, Through the Analysis of a Workers' Village: Borgata Leumann": 230.

250 Werner Oechslin and Sonja Hildebrand, eds., *Karl Moser: Architektur für eine neue Zeit 1880 bis 1936* (Zurich: gta Verlag, 2010), vol. 1: 327–33, vol. 2: 207–9, 376.

251 Oechslin and Hildebrand, eds., *Karl Moser: Architektur für eine neue Zeit 1880 bis 1936*, vol. 2: 230–32, 383.

252 Oechslin and Hildebrand, eds., *Karl Moser: Architektur für eine neue Zeit 1880 bis 1936*, vol. 2: 265–66, 390.

253 Oechslin and Hildebrand, eds., *Karl Moser: Architektur für eine neue Zeit 1880 bis 1936*, vol. 2: 267–69, 390.

254 Otti Gmür, *Spaziergänge durch Raum und Zeit: Architekturführer Luzern* (Lucerne: Quart Verlag, 2003), 206.

255 Jan Kotěra, "Dělnické kolonie," *Stavitel* 2 (1921): 65–84; Karel B. Mádl, *Jan Kotěra* (Prague: Jan Štenc, 1922), 22–23; "Z dopisů Jana Kotěra svému příteli R.G. ve Vidni," *Stavitel* 5 (1924): 61–65; Manfredo Tafuri and Francesco Dal Co, *Modern Architecture*, trans. by Robert Erich Wolf (New York: Harry N. Abrams, 1979), 414 (n.16); Jiří Musil, Vladimír Šlapeta, and Jaroslav Novak, "Czech Mate for Letchworth," *Town & Country Planning* 53 (November 1984): 314–15; Rostislav Švácha, "Jan Kotěra," *Domov* 25 (No. 1, 1985): 49–53; Cliff Hague and Alan Prior, "Planning in Czechoslovakia: Retrospect and Prospects," *Planning Practice & Research* 6 (Summer 1991): 19–24; Petr Krajči and Rostislav Švácha, "The Architectural Avant-Garde in Prague," in Eve Blau and Monika Platzer, eds., *Shaping the Great City: Modern Architecture in Central Europe, 1890–1937* (Munich: Prestel, 1999), 117; Jane Pavitt, "From the Garden to the Factory: Urban Visions in Czechoslovakia Between the Wars," in Macolm Gee, Tim Kirk, and Jill Steward, eds., *The City in Central Europe: Culture and Society from 1800 to the Present* (Aldershot, England, and Brookfield, Vt.: Ashgate, 1999), 31–32, fig. 2.1; Jane Pavitt, *Prague* (Manchester and New York: Manchester University Press, 2000), 101; Pavel Šopák, "Workers' Housing Colonies," in *Jan Kotěra, 1871–1923: The Founder of Modern Czech Architecture*, trans. by Karolina Vočadlová (Prague: Municipal House, 2001), 352–65; *Jan Kotěra, 1871–1923: The Founder of Modern Czech Architecture*, 30, 85, 154, 171; Martin Vostřel, "Kotěra's Settlement in Louny," http://ff.osu.cz/chd/dokumenty/publ/summaries-mesto-a-mestska.pdf.

256 Šopák, "Workers' Housing Colonies," in *Jan Kotěra, 1871–1923: The Founder of Modern Czech Architecture*, 360.

257 Kotěra, "Dělnické kolonie": 65, quoted and translated in Šopák, "Workers' Housing Colonies," in *Jan Kotěra, 1871–1923: The Founder of Modern Czech Architecture*, 359–60.

258 Z. Rossman, *Zlín, mesto zivotni aktivity* (Zlín: Tisk, 1935); *Zavody Baťa a.s. ve Zlíne, urbanismus, architektura* (Prague: Stavitel, 1935); Göran Sidenbladh, "Zlín," *Byggmästaren* 12 (1936): 142–50; "La 'città delle scarpe,'" *Casabella* 9 (June–July 1936): 24–27; Jirí Voženílek, "Nová Vystavba Zlína," *Architektura ČSR* 6 (1947): 69–84; Jan Pokorny and Elizabeth Hird, "From a Quaint Provincial Town, Zlin, Czechoslovakia, Developed Into a Completely Integrated Industrial City Because—They Planned It That Way," *Architectural Record* 102 (August 1947): 68–75; Jiří Voženílek, "Obytné Stavby 2lp ve Zlíně," *Architektura ČSR* 7 (1948): 219–22; Jean-Lous Cohen, "Nostro cliente è il nostro padrone, Le Corbusier e Baťa," *Rassegna* 3 (June 1980): 47–60; Jiri Musil, Vladimir Slapeta, and Jaroslav Novak, "Czech Mate for Letchworth," *Town & Country Planning* 53 (November 1984): 314–15; Vladimir

Slapeta, "Baťa Architecture," *Rassegna* 12 (September 1990): 70–79; "Die Baťa-architektur, oder die Architektur eines unternehmens," *Bauforum* 136 (1990): 19–48; Koji Chikugo, "Tomáš Baťa: The Czech Example of Welfare Capitalism" (Master's thesis, State University of New York at Albany, 1991): 95–107; Vladimír Šlapeta, *Baťa: Architektura a Urbanismus, 1910–1950* (Zlín: Státní Galerie ve Zlíně, 1991); Cliff Hague and Alan Prior, "Planning in Czechoslovakia: Retrospect and Prospects," *Planning Practice & Research* 6 (Summer 1991): 19–24; Jan Sedlák, "The Bata Company: Czechslovakian Architecture and Town Planning in 1910–1950," *Docomomo Newsletter* 6 (November 1991): 14–15; Pavel Novák, *Zlínská Architektura, 1900–1950* (Zlín: Čas: Ve spolupráci s Nadací Studijního ústavu Tomáše Bati, 1993); Susanne Ostertag, "Zlin, die Musterstadt der Bata-Brüder in der Tschenechischen Republik," *Deutsche Bauzeitung* 128 (April 1994): 34–36; Jane Pavitt, "The Bata Project: A Social and Industrial Experiment," *Twentieth Century Architecture* 1 (Summer 1994): 31–44; Wojciech Leśnikowski, "Functionalism in Czechoslovakian, Hungarian, and Polish Architecture from the European Perspective," in Wojciech Leśnikowski, ed., *Eastern European Modernism* (New York: Rizzoli International Publications, 1996), 21–22; Jean-Louis Cohen, "Zlin: An Industrial Republic," *Rassegna* 19 (1997): 42–45; Eric J. Jenkins, "Utopia, Inc.: Czech Culture and Bata Shoe Company: Architecture and Garden Cities," *Thresholds* 18 (1999): 60–66; Jane Pavitt, "From the Garden to the Factory: Urban Visions in Czechoslovakia Between the Wars," in Macolm Gee, Tim Kirk, and Jill Steward, eds., *The City in Central Europe: Culture and Society from 1800 to the Present* (Aldershot, England, and Brookfield, Vt.: Ashgate, 1999), 34–39; Rostislav Švácha, "Architecture and Society," in Eve Blau and Monika Platzer, eds., *Shaping the Great City: Modern Architecture in Central Europe, 1890–1937* (Munich: Prestel, 1999), 218, 225; Reinhard Seiss and Philipp Krebs, "La città del futor compie 100 anni," *L'Arca* 151 (September 2000): 94; Helen Meller, *European Cities, 1890–1930s: History, Culture and the Built Environment* (Chichester, England: John Wiley & Sons, 2001), 128–48; Pavel Šopák, "Workers' Housing Colonies," in *Jan Kotěra, 1871–1923: The Founder of Modern Czech Architecture*, trans. by Karolina Vočadlová (Prague: Municipal House, 2001), 364–66; *Une Ville Industrielle Modèle: Zlín* (Paris: Ecomusee le Creusot Montceau, 2002); Gillian Darley, *Factory* (London: Reaktion Books, 2003), 92–97; Pavel Simek and Jitka Trevisan, "Weiterentwicklung einer Gartenstadt," *Garten + Landschaft* 114 (November 2004): 33–36; Henrieta Moravčíková, Slávka Doricová, and Mária Topolčanská, "Baťa's Architecture: A Problematic Cultural Heritage?" *Docomomo Journal* 32 (March 2005): 54–58; "Partizanske: réinventer la ville fonctionnelle," *L'Architecture d'aujoud'hui* 357 (March–April 2005): 14–15; William Shaw, "Design for Living: A Czech Workers' Utopia Is Becoming an Architectural Mecca," *New York Times* (March 25, 2007), F: 54–56; Michael Webb, "Workers' Playtime," *Architectural Review* 223 (March 2008): 30–31; Katrin Klingan, ed., *A Utopia of Modernity: Zlín: Revisiting Baťa's Functional City* (Berlin: Jovis, 2009); *Zlín: Modellstadt der Moderne* (Berlin: Jovis, 2009); http://www.zlin.eu/en/.

259 Darley, *Factory*, 92.

260 Pavitt, "The Bata Project: A Social and Industrial Experiment": 36.

261 Tomáš Baťa, *How I Began*, trans. by Jan Baros (Batanagar, India: Club for Graduates of Bata School, 1941), 204, quoted in Pavitt, "The Bata Project: A Social and Industrial Experiment": 36.

262 Hague and Prior, "Planning in Czechoslovakia: Retrospect and Prospects": 19.

263 Cohen, "Zlin: An Industrial Republic": 42.

264 Le Corbusier, quoted in Antonín Cekota, *Entrepreneur Extraordinary: The Biography of Tomas Bata* (Rome: Edizioni Internazionali Sociali, 1968), 232, also quoted in Chikugo, "Tomáš Baťa: The Czech Example of Welfare Capitalism": 104.

265 See Sharon Ricketts, "Batawa," *Society for the Study of Architecture in Canada: Bulletin* 18 (September 1993): 80–87.

266 Meller, *European Cities, 1890–1930s: History, Culture and the Built Environment*, 145. Also see Hague and Prior, "Planning in Czechoslovakia: Retrospect and Prospects": 19; Pavitt, "The Bata Project: A Social and Industrial Experiment": 36.

Chapter 9

1 John Coolidge, *Mill and Mansion: A Study of Architecture and Society in Lowell, Massachusetts, 1820–1865* (New York: Columbia University Press, 1942; Amherst: University of Massachusetts Press, 1993); John W. Reps, *The Making of Urban America: A History of City Planning in the United States* (Princeton, N.J.: Princeton University Press, 1965), 414–20; Francesco Dal Co, "From Parks to the Region: Progressive Ideology and the Reform of the American City," in Giorgio Ciucci et al., *The American City: From the Civil War to the New Deal* (Cambridge, Mass.: MIT Press, 1979), 191–95; Stern with Massengale, *The Anglo-American Suburb*, 51; John S. Garner, ed., *The Company Town: Architecture and Society in the Early Industrial Age* (New York: Oxford University Press, 1992), 11, 113–14; Margaret Crawford, *Building the Workingman's Paradise: The Design of American Company Towns* (London and New York: Verso, 1995), 22–27.

2 Reps, *The Making of Urban America*, 415.

3 Dal Co, "From Parks to the Region: Progressive Ideology and the Reform of the American City," in Ciucci et al., *The American City: From the Civil War to the New Deal*, 192.

4 Michael Chevalier, *Society, Manners and Politics in the United States* (Boston: Weeks Jordan and Company, 1839), 128–29.

5 Randolph Langenbach, "A City No One Knew," *Architectural Forum* 130 (January–February 1969): 84–91. Also see John W. Reps, *The Making of Urban America: A History of City Planning in the United States* (Princeton, N.J.: Princeton University Press, 1965), 417–18, 420; Randolph Langenbach, "Amoskeag Millyard Remembered," *Historic Preservation* 27 (July–September, 1975): 26–29; Randolph Langenbach, "Amoskeag Mills: A Sense of Place," *Nineteenth Century* 2 (Summer 1976): 30–34; Coolidge, *Mill and Mansion: A Study of Architecture and Society in Lowell, Massachusetts, 1820–1865*, 97, 172–73 (n.37), 239; John Mayer, "The Mills and Machinery of the Amoskeag Manufacturing Company of Manchester, New Hampshire," *IA: The Journal of the Society for Industrial Archaeology* 20 (1994): 69–79.

6 Langenbach, "Amoskeag Millyard Remembered": 26.

7 Langenbach, "A City No One Knew": 88.

8 John S. Garner, *The Model Company Town: Urban Design through Private Enterprise in Nineteenth-Century New England* (Amherst, Mass.: University of Massachusetts Press, 1984), 30–35. Also see Budgett Meakin, *Model Factories and Villages* (London: T. Fisher Unwin, 1905), 397; Margaret Crawford, *Building the Workingman's Paradise: The Design of American Company Towns* (London and New York: Verso, 1995), 32–33, 35–36.

9 Meakin, *Model Factories and Villages*, 397.

10 Quoted in Meakin, *Model Factories and Villages*, 397.

11 Garner, *The Model Company Town*, 37–39; Allen D. Hodgdon, "Fairbanks, Lambert," in John J. Duffy, Samuel B. Hand, and Ralph H. Orth, eds., *The Vermont Encyclopedia* (Lebanon, N.H.: University Press of New England, 2003), 226.

12 Grosvenor Atterbury, quoted in Crawford, *Building the Workingman's Paradise*, 112. Also see Meakin, *Model Factories and Villages*, 398–400; Arthur C. Comey and Max S. Wehrly, "A Study of Planned Communities" (Department of Regional Planning of Harvard University, November 1936): 243–48; Garner, *The Model Company Town*, 61; Leland M. Roth, *A Concise History of American Architecture* (New York: Harper & Row, 1979), 224.

13 Meakin, *Model Factories and Villages*, 400. Also see Leland M. Roth, *A Concise History of American Architecture* (New York: Harper & Row, 1979), 138, 224; Crawford, *Building the Workingman's Paradise*, 33–34, 39, 58.

14 John Maass, *The Victorian Home in America* (New York: Hawthorn Books, 1972), 203; Roth, *A Concise History of American Architecture*, 138; Earle J. Shettleworth Jr., "Turn-of-the-Century Architecture: From about 1880–1920," in Deborah Thompson, ed., *Maine Forms of American Architecture* (Camden, Maine: Downeast Magazine, 1976), 189.

15 Budgett Meakin, *Model Factories and Villages* (London: T. Fisher Unwin, 1905), 395; Robert Leavitt Davison, "A Check List of the Principal Housing Developments in the United States," *Architectural Review* 5 (April 1917): 91; Steven Kibert, *WABCO General Office Building, Pennsylvania Historic Resource Survey Form* (Harrisburg, Pa., 1981); Steven Kibert, *Borough of Wilmerding, Allegheny County Survey Zone Form* (Harrisburg, Pa., 1981); *History of Wilmerding, Pennsylvania, 1890–2004* (Wilmerding, 2004); Quentin R. Skrabec Jr., *George Westinghouse: Gentle Genius* (New York: Algora Publishing, 2007), 147–60; http://www.wilmerdingrenewed.org/history.html.

16 Skrabec Jr., *George Westinghouse: Gentle Genius*, 152–53.

17 "Niagara Falls in Harness," *New York Times* (July 31, 1892): 15; John Bogart, "The Industrial Village of Echota at Niagara," *Cassier's Magazine* 8 (July 1895): 307–21; "Flagstaff for the Cataract Construction Company, Niagara Falls, N.Y.," *American Architect and Building News* 49 (September 28, 1895): plate 1031; Charles Mulford Robinson, "'Echota': A Village Color Scheme," *Architects' and Builders' Magazine* 3 (1902): 241–43; G.W.W. Hangar, "Housing of the Working People by Employers," *Bulletin of the Bureau of Labor* 54 (Washington, D. C: Government Printing Office, 1904), 1218–20; Budgett Meakin, *Model Factories and Villages* (London: T. Fisher Unwin, 1905; New York and London: Garland Publishing, 1985), 411; F. C. Howe, "Industrial Villages in America," *Garden City* 1 (July 1906): 142–50; William A. Tolman, "Workmen's Cities in the United States," *Bericht, 9th International Housing Congress* (Vienna, 1910), 1084–85; R. L. Davison, "A Check List of the Principal Housing Developments in the United States," *Architectural Review* 5 (1917): 83–92; Leifur Magnusson, "Housing by Employers in the United States," *Bulletin of the United States Bureau of Labor Statistics, no. 263* (October 1920): 267; Edward Dean Adams, *Niagara Power: History of the Niagara Falls Power Company, 1886–1918*, 2 vols (Niagara Falls, N.Y., 1927), vol. 1: 323–31; Charles Baldwin, *Stanford White* (New York: Dodd Mead, 1931), 321; Leland Roth, "The Urban Architecture of McKim, Mead and White: 1870–1910" (Ph.D. diss., Yale University, 1973): 407–13; Leland Roth, "McKim, Mead & White Reappraised," in *A Monograph of the Work of McKim, Mead & White, 1879–1915* (New York: Arno Press, 1973), 25–28; Leland Roth, *The Architecture of McKim, Mead and White: A Building List* (New York: Garland, 1978), nos. 182–85; Leland Roth, "Three Industrial Towns by McKim, Mead & White," *Journal of the Society of Architectural Historians* 38 (December 1979): 317–47; Stern with Massengale, *The Anglo-American Suburb*, 9, 55; Leland M. Roth, *McKim, Mead & White, Architects* (New York: Harper & Row, 1983), 204–7; Lawrence Woodhouse, "McKim, Mead & White," book review, *Winterthur Portfolio* 20 (Spring 1985): 94–98; Paul R. Baker, *Stanny: The Gilded Life of Stanford White* (New York: Free Press, 1989), 436 (n.38); Margaret Crawford, *Building the Workingman's Paradise: The Design of American Company Towns* (London and New York: Verso, 1995), 53, 78–80.

18 For the Villard Houses, see Stern, Mellins, and Fishman, *New York 1880*, 601–8.

19 Roth, "Three Industrial Towns by McKim, Mead & White": 324.

20 Bogart, "The Industrial Village of Echota at Niagara": 321.

21 Robinson, "'Echota': A Village Color Scheme": 242.

22 Meakin, *Model Factories and Villages*, 411.

23 Crawford, *Building the Workingman's Paradise*, 80.

24 "Mills at Roanoke Rapids," *Washington Post* (April 1, 1895): 1; Zeb R. Denny, ed., *A City's Heritage* (Roanoke Rapids, N.C.: Roanoke Rapids Diamond Jubilee, 1972), 17–19; Leland Roth, *The Architecture of McKim, Mead and White: A Building List* (New York: Garland, 1978), nos. 724–726; Leland Roth, "Three Industrial Towns by McKim, Mead & White," *Journal of the Society of Architectural Historians* 38 (December 1979): 317–47; Leland M. Roth, *McKim, Mead & White, Architects* (New York: Harper & Row, 1983), 208–9; Lawrence Woodhouse, "McKim, Mead & White," book review, *Winterthur Portfolio* 20 (Spring 1985): 94–98; Paul R. Baker, *Stanny: The Gilded Life of Stanford White* (New York: Free Press, 1989), 256–57; Mats Ahnlund and Lasse Brunnström, "The Company Town in Scandinavia," in John S. Garner, ed., *The Company Town: Architecture and Society in the Early Industrial Age* (New York: Oxford University Press, 1992), 93; Catherine W. Bishir, *North Carolina Architecture* (Chapel Hill: University of North Carolina Press, 2005), 502.

25 Roth, "Three Industrial Towns by McKim, Mead & White": 331.

26 John Armstrong Chanler, letter to Charles McKim, July 31, 1895, McKim, Mead & White Archive, Correspondence, Box M-13, quoted in Roth, "Three Industrial Towns by McKim, Mead & White": 330.

27 Arthur Reed Kimbal, "The Story of Leclaire," *Harper's Weekly* 38 (March 24, 1894): 278; Nellie Bly, "Nellie Bly Finds a Model Town," *World* (July 29, 1894): 21; Frank W. Blackmar, "Two Examples of Successful Profit-Sharing," *Forum* (March 1895): 57–67; G.W.W. Hanger,

"Housing of the Working People in the United States by Employers," *Bulletin of the Bureau of Labor* 21 (September 1904): 1215–18; Budgett Meakin, *Model Factories and Villages* (London: T. Fisher Unwin, 1905; New York and London: Garland Publishing, 1985), 382–84; George W. Eads, "N. O. Nelson, Practical Cooperator, and the Great Work He Is Accomplishing for Human Upliftment," *Arena* 36 (November 1906): 463–85; N. O. Nelson, "The Leclaire Idea," *The Independent* 67 (August 19, 1909): 411; Grosvenor Atterbury, "Model Towns in America," *Scribner's* 52 (July 1912): 25; Edith Elmer Wood, *The Housing of the Unskilled Wage Earner: America's Next Problem* (New York: MacMillan Company, 1919), 118–19; John S. Garner, "Leclaire, Illinois: A Model Company Town (1890–1934)," *Journal of the Society of Architectural Historians* 30 (October 1971): 219–27; Kim McQuaid, "The Businessman as Social Innovator: Nelson O. Nelson as Promoter of Garden Cities and the Consumer Cooperative Movement," *American Journal of Economics and Sociology* 34 (1975): 411–22; Margaret Crawford, *Building the Workingman's Paradise: The Design of American Company Towns* (London and New York: Verso, 1995), 219 (n.60); John S. Garner, "The Company Town. Industry and Territory in the 19th Century," *Rassegna* 19 (1997): 30–37; Cindy Reinhardt, *Leclaire* (Charleston, S.C.: Arcadia, 2010); http://www.historic-leclaire.org/4.html.

28 For Leclaire, see L. A., "The Labor Problem; The Maison Leclaire," *Christian Union* 33 (February 18, 1886): 9; "The Father of Profit Sharing, and His House," in Nicholas Paine Gilman, *Profit Sharing Between Employer and Employee: a Study in the Evolution of the Wages System* (Boston and New York: Houghton Mifflin, 1889), 66–105.

29 Edward Everett Hale, quoted in "The Story of Leclaire": 278.

30 N. O. Nelson, quoted in Meakin, *Model Factories and Villages*, 384.

31 For Nellie Bly, see Brooke Kroeger, *Nellie Bly: Daredevil, Reporter, Feminist* (New York: Times Books, 1994).

32 Bly, "Nellie Bly Finds a Model Town": 21.

33 John J. McLaurin, *Sketches in Crude Oil* (Harrisburg, Pa.: John J. McLaurin, 1896), 276; "Vandergrift, PA., a New Industrial Town," *American Architect and Building News* 43 (August 1, 1896): 2; R. E. Phillips, "Self-Help to Employees," in *The World's Work: a History of Our Time, Volume 1, November 1900–April 1901* (New York: Doubleday, 1901), 392–94; Budgett Meakin, *Model Factories and Villages* (London: T. Fisher Unwin, 1905; New York and London: Garland Publishing, 1985), 393–95; "The Town of Vandergrift, an Industrial Settlement Owned and Governed by Workmen," *The Craftsman* 17 (February 1910): 562–76; Ida M. Tarbell, *New Ideals in Business* (New York: MacMillan Company, 1917), 146–54; Arthur C. Comey and Max S. Wehrly, "Planned Communities," (November 1936) in *Supplementary Report of the Urbanism Committee to the National Resources Committee* (Washington, D.C.: U. S. Government Printing Office, 1939), vol. 2: 47–51, 111, 122, 124, 127; John W. Reps, *The Making of Urban America* (Princeton, N.J.: Princeton University Press, 1965), 348, 424, 426, 427; Leland M. Roth, *A Concise History of American Architecture* (New York: Harper & Row, 1979), 221; Stern with Massengale, *The Anglo-American Suburb*, 9; Arleyn A. Levee, "The Olmsted Brothers' Residential Communities: Preview of a Legacy," in Charles A. Birnbaum, ed., *The Landscape Universe: Historic Designed Landscapes in Context* (Bronx, New York: Catalog of Landscape Records in the United States at Wave Hill, 1993), 33; Margaret Crawford, *Building the Workingman's Paradise: The Design of American Company Towns* (London and New York: Verso, 1995), 43, 52–53, 56, 78, 80, 82; Anne E. Mosher, "'Something Better than the Best': Industrial Restructuring, George McMurtry and the Creation of the Model Industrial Town of Vandergrift, Pennsylvania, 1883–1901," *Annals of the Association of American Geographers* 85 (1995): 84–107; Randall Arendt, *Crossroads, Hamlet, Village, Town: Design Characteristics of Traditional Neighborhoods, Old and New (Revised Edition)* (Chicago: American Planning Association/Planning Advisory Service, 2004), 28; Anne E. Mosher, *Capital's Utopia: Vandergrift, Pennsylvania, 1855–1916* (Baltimore: Johns Hopkins University Press, 2004), esp. introduction and chs. 3–4; Arnold R. Alanen, *Morgan Park: Duluth, U.S. Steel, and the Forging of a Company Town* (Minneapolis and London: University of Minnesota Press, 2007), 5–6.

34 Wallace P. Bache, letter to Frederick Law Olmsted Sr., April 25, 1895, quoted in Mosher, *Capital's Utopia*, 76.

35 Frederick Law Olmsted Sr., letter to Frederick Law Olmsted Jr., July 23, 1895, quoted in Mosher, *Capital's Utopia*, 81.

36 Quoted in Mosher, *Capital's Utopia*, 80.

37 Mosher, *Capital's Utopia*, 75.

38 John C. Olmsted, quoted in Mosher, *Capital's Utopia*, 89.

39 John C. Olmsted, quoted in Mosher, *Capital's Utopia*, 88.

40 Mosher, *Capital's Utopia*, 84.

41 Quoted in Mosher, *Capital's Utopia*, 88.

42 Mosher, *Capital's Utopia*, 89, 93.

43 Mosher, *Capital's Utopia*, 2–3.

44 Reps, *The Making of Urban America*, 424, 427.

45 "The Town of Vandergrift, an Industrial Settlement Owned and Governed by Workmen": 565.

46 Tarbell, *New Ideals in Business*, 146, 151, 154.

47 Comey and Wehrley, "Planned Communities," in *Supplementary Report of the Urbanism Committee to the National Resources Committee*, 49.

48 Washington A. Roebling, "An Illuminating Account of the John A. Roebling's Sons Co.," (c. 1907), in www.inventionfactory.com; "The Industrial Village at Roebling, N.J.," *Iron Age* (August 6, 1908); William H. Tolman, *Social Engineering: A Record of Things Done by American Industrialists Employing Upwards of One and One-Half Million of People* (New York: McGraw Publishing Co., 1909), 346–49; *Garden City Movement Hearing Before the Subcommittee of the Committee on Agriculture and Forestry, United States Senate, Sixty-fourth Congress, Second Session* (Washington, D.C.: Government Printing Office, 1917), 16; Edith Elmer Wood, *The Housing of the Unskilled Wage Earner: America's Next Problem* (New York: Macmillan, 1919), 121–22; "Industrial Village on Sound Basis," *Iron Age* 113 (January 3, 1924); Federal Writers' Project of the Works Progress Administration, *New Jersey, a Guide to Its Present and Past* (New York: Viking, 1939), 72–73, 76, 122; David McCullough, *The Great Bridge* (New York: Simon and Schuster, 1972), 556; Martha T. Moore, "Our Town: Company Paternalism and Community Participation in Roebling, New Jersey," (unpublished paper, 1982), in www.inventionfactory.com; Ilene Dube, "Men of Steel," *The Princeton Packet* (August 13, 2008). Also see Jon Blackwell, "1905: Model of a Company Town," in www.

capitalcentury. com. For a history of the company, see Clifford W. Zinc and Dorothy White Hartman, *Spanning the Industrial Age: The John A. Roebling's Sons Company, Trenton, New Jersey, 1848–1974* (Trenton, N.J.: Trenton Roebling Community Development Corp., 1992). For the Brooklyn Bridge, see Stern, Mellins, and Fishman, *New York 1880*, 110–20.

49 Washington A. Roebling, quoted in Tolman, *Social Engineering*, 346.

50 Roebling, "An Illuminating Account of the John A. Roebling's Sons Co."

51 Roebling, "An Illuminating Account of the John A. Roebling's Sons Co."

52 McCullough, *The Great Bridge*, 556.

53 Arthur C. Comey and Max S. Wehrly, "Planned Communities," (November 1936) in *Supplementary Report of the Urbanism Committee to the National Resources Committee* (Washington, D.C.: U. S. Government Printing Office, 1939), vol. 2: 117–18; John W. Reps, *The Making of Urban America* (Princeton, N.J.: Princeton University Press, 1965), 427–29; Harold M. Mayer and Richard C. Wade, *Chicago: Growth of a Metropolis* (Chicago and London: University of Chicago Press, 1969), 241–46; Raymond A. Mohl and Neil Betten, "The Failure of Industrial City Planning: Gary Indiana, 1906–1910," *Journal of the American Institute of Planners* 38 (July 1972): 202–15; James B. Lane, *City of the Century: A History of Gary, Indiana* (Bloomington: Indiana University Press, 1978), esp. chs. 2–3; Margaret Crawford, *Building the Workingman's Paradise: The Design of American Company Towns* (London and New York: Verso, 1995), 43–44; Dean Thrift Sinclair, "'A New Town Will Appear on Charleston Neck': North Charleston and the Creation of the New South Garden City" (Ph.D. diss.: Louisiana State University and Agricultural and Mechanical College, 2001): 107–14; Arnold R. Alanen, *Morgan Park: Duluth, U.S. Steel, and the Forging of a Company Town* (Minneapolis and London: University of Minnesota Press, 2007), 6–7; Steve McShane, "The Magic City of Steel," in http://www.dlib.indiana.edu/collections/stee/context/essay3.html.

54 For a history of U.S. Steel, see Kenneth Warren, *Big Steel: The First Century of the United States Steel Corporation, 1901–2001* (Pittsburgh: University of Pittsburgh Press, 2001). For Elbert H. Gary, see Ida M. Tarbell, *The Life of Elbert H. Gary: The Story of Steel* (New York: D. Appleton & Co., 1925).

55 Reps, *The Making Of Urban America*, 428.

56 Lane, *City of the Century*, 30.

57 Crawford, *Building the Workingman's Paradise*, 44.

58 Comey and Wehrly, "Planned Communities," in *Supplementary Report of the Urbanism Committee to the National Resources Committee*, vol. 2: 117.

59 George H. Miller, "Fairfield, a Town with a Purpose," *American City* 9 (September 1913): 213–19; C. J. Stark, "Steel Corporation's Industrial Community Development, with Particular Reference to the Creation of Fairfield, Ala." *Iron Trade Review* 54 (January 1, 1914): 74–83; Graham Romeyn Taylor, *Satellite Cities: A Study of Industrial Suburbs* (New York: D. Appleton and Company, 1915), 237–58; Southern Pine Association, *Homes for Workmen; a Presentation of Leading Examples of Industrial Community Development* (New Orleans: Southern Pine Association, 1919), 103–10; Arthur C. Comey and Max S. Wehrly, "Planned Communities," (November 1936) in *Supplementary Report of the Urbanism Committee to the National Resources Committee* (Washington, D.C.: U. S. Government Printing Office, 1939), vol. 2: 27–30, 111, 117, 121–23, 130; John W. Reps, *The Making of Urban America* (Princeton, N.J.: Princeton University Press, 1965), 430, 431; Marjorie Longenecker White, *The Birmingham District: An Industrial History and Guide* (Birmingham: Birmingham Historical Society, 1981), 116–25; Marjorie Longenecker White, "The Grid and the Garden," in Philip A. Morris and Marjorie Longenecker White, *Designs on Birmingham: A Landscape History of a Southern City and Its Suburbs* (Birmingham: Birmingham Historical Society, 1989), 15–19; Robert Gamble, *Historic Architecture in Alabama: A Guide to Styles and Types, 1810–1930* (Tuscaloosa and London: University of Alabama Press, 1990), 150–51; Margaret Crawford, *Building the Workingman's Paradise: The Design of American Company Towns* (London and New York: Verso, 1995), 84–89; Henry M. McKiven Jr., *Iron and Steel: Class, Race, and Community in Birmingham, Alabama, 1875–1920* (Chapel Hill: University of North Carolina Press, 1995), 138–39; Arnold R. Alanen, *Morgan Park: Duluth, U.S. Steel, and the Forging of a Company Town* (Minneapolis and London: University of Minnesota Press, 2007), 9–10.

60 Crawford, *Building the Workingman's Paradise*, 84.

61 "Mrs. Corey is Free, Wife of Steel Man Gets Divorce and Custody of Son," *Washington Post* (July 31, 1906): 1; "W. E. Corey, a 'Free' Man," editorial, *New York Times* (August 1, 1906): 8.

62 Miller, "Fairfield, a Town with a Purpose": 218.

63 Miller, "Fairfield, a Town with a Purpose": 217.

64 Crawford, *Building the Workingman's Paradise*, 86.

65 Comey and Wehrly, "Planned Communities," in *Supplementary Report of the Urbanism Committee to the National Resources Committee*, vol. 2: 27, 29.

66 Comey and Wehrly, "Planned Communities," in *Supplementary Report of the Urbanism Committee to the National Resources Committee*, vol. 2: 29.

67 Crawford, *Building the Workingman's Paradise*, 87.

68 "A Model Industrial Village," *Coal Age* 12 (August 18, 1917), 289; George H. Miller, "Kaulton, Alabama: A Southern Pine Manufacturing Town Built Along Model Lines," in Southern Pine Association, *Homes for Workmen; a Presentation of Leading Examples of Industrial Community Development* (New Orleans: Southern Pine Association, 1919), 8–15; John L. Kaul, "Kaulton from an Investment Standpoint," in Southern Pine Association, *Homes for Workmen*, 16; George M. Cruikshank, *A History of Birmingham and Its Environs, Volume II* (Chicago and New York: Lewis Publishing Co., 1920), 79–81; Arthur C. Comey and Max S. Wehrly, "A Study of Planned Communities" (Department of Regional Planning of Harvard University, November 1936): 125–28; Arthur C. Comey and Max S. Wehrly, "Planned Communities," (November 1936) in *Supplementary Report of the Urbanism Committee to the National Resources Committee* (Washington, D.C.: U. S. Government Printing Office, 1939), vol. 2: 111, 117, 122, 130, 146; John W. Reps, *The Making of Urban America* (Princeton, N.J.: Princeton University Press, 1965), 430; Gwendolyn Wright, *Building the Dream: A Social History of Housing in America* (New York: Pantheon Books, 1981), 180–81.

69 Comey and Wehrly, "A Study of Planned Communities": 127.

70 Reps, *The Making of Urban America*, 430.

71 George D. McCarthy, "Morgan Park—A New Type of Industrial Community," *American City* 14 (February 1916): 150–53; Leifur Magnusson, "A Modern Industrial Suburb," *Monthly Review of U.S. Bureau of Labor Statistics* 6 (April 1918): 729–53; Dean & Dean, Architects,

"Morgan Park, Minn.: An Industrial Suburb for the Minnesota Steel Company," *American Architect* 113 (June 5, 1918): 743–61; Arthur C. Comey and Max S. Wehrly, "A Study of Planned Communities" (Department of Regional Planning of Harvard University, November 1936): 175–81; Arthur C. Comey and Max S. Wehrly, "Planned Communities," (November 1936) in *Supplementary Report of the Urbanism Committee to the National Resources Committee* (Washington, D.C.: U. S. Government Printing Office, 1939), vol. 2: 111, 117–18, 122, 126–27, 130, 136, 158; John W. Reps, *The Making of Urban America* (Princeton, N.J.: Princeton University Press, 1965), 430, 433; Arnold R. Alanen, "The Planning of Company Communities in the Lake Superior Mining Region," *Journal of the American Planning Association* 45 (July 1979): 266–67; Gregory Kopischke, "Anthony Morell and Arthur Nichols," in Charles A. Birnbaum and Robin Karson, *Pioneers of American Landscape Design* (New York: McGraw-Hill, 2000), 253–57; Arnold R. Alanen, *Morgan Park: Duluth, U. S. Steel, and the Forging of a Company Town* (Minneapolis and London: University of Minnesota Press, 2007), passim.
72 United States Steel Corporation Bureau of Safety, Sanitation and Welfare (1918), quoted in Comey and Wehrly, "A Study of Planned Communities": 178.
73 Comey and Wehrly, "A Study of Planned Communities": 179–80.
74 "Garden Village Is Promising," *Christian Science Monitor* (November 15, 1913): 13; John Nolen, *More Houses for Bridgeport* (Cambridge, Mass., August 1916), 59–60; Walpole Town Planning Committee, *Town Planning for Small Communities* (New York and London: D. Appleton and Company, 1917), 173–231, 263–81, 370–91; John Nolen, "Report," in Walpole Town Planning Committee, *Town Planning for Small Communities*, 283–99; John Nolen, *The Industrial Village* (New York: National Housing Association, 1918), 10, 19; Charles C. May, "Some Aspects of Industrial Housing," *Architectural Forum* 28 (January 1918): 7–14; John Nolen, *New Towns for Old* (Boston: Marshall Jones, 1927; Amherst and Boston: University of Massachusetts Press, 2005), 31–49; John Loretz Hancock, "John Nolen and the American City Planning Movement: A History of Culture Change and Community Response, 1900–1940" (Ph.D. diss., University of Pennsylvania, 1964): 258–61, 272; Stewart Jerome Wilson, "John Nolen: An Overview of His Career" (Master's thesis, University of Oregon, 1982): 52–56, plates 20–25; John Hancock, "'What Is Fair Must Be Fit,'" *Lotus International* 50 (1986): 30–45; Margaret Crawford, *Building the Workingman's Paradise: The Design of American Company Towns* (London and New York: Verso, 1995), 156–59; Margaret Crawford, "John Nolen, the Design of the Company Town," *Rassegna* 19 (1997): 46–53; Charles D. Warren, "Introduction," in Nolen, *New Towns for Old* (2005), lx–lxvi.
75 John Nolen, quoted in "Garden Village Is Promising": 13, also quoted in Crawford, *Building the Workingman's Paradise: The Design of American Company Towns*, 156.
76 Walpole Town Planning Committee, *Town Planning for Small Communities*, 200, quoted in Crawford, "John Nolen, the Design of the Company Town": 48.
77 John Nolen, *More Houses for Bridgeport* (Cambridge, Mass., August 1916), 56–57; "Bound Brook, N.J.: Westerly Gardens," *Architectural Review* 22 (April 1917): 84; John Nolen, *A Good Home for Every Wage-Earner*, pamphlet (Cambridge, Mass., 1917).
78 "Bound Brook, N.J.: Westerly Gardens": 84.
79 "Allwood—An Industrial Village," *Journal of the American Institute of Architects* 4 (December 1916): 499; John Nolen, *The Industrial Village* (New York: National Housing Association, 1918), 4, 19; Charles C. May, "Some Aspects of Industrial Housing," *Architectural Forum* 28 (January 1918): 7–14; Ralph F. Warner, "Allwood: An American 'Garden Village' Near Passaic, N.J.," *Architectural Review* 6 (February 1918): 21–24; Arthur C. Comey and Max S. Wehrly, "A Study of Planned Communities" (Department of Regional Planning of Harvard University, November 1936): 65–68; Margaret Crawford, *Building the Workingman's Paradise: The Design of American Company Towns* (London and New York: Verso, 1995), 164–65.
80 Perry MacNeille, "Industrial Housing—What Types of Houses to Build," *Housing Problems in America: Proceedings of the Fifth National Congress on Housing* (1916): 67–79; Frank J. Mulvihill, "Kistler Industrial Village," *Wildwood Magazine* 3 (Autumn 1916): 14–15, 36; John Nolen, *The Industrial Village* (New York: National Housing Association, 1918), 6, 19; Charles C. May, "Some Aspects of Industrial Housing," *Architectural Forum* 28 (January 1918): 7–14; Edith Elmer Wood, *The Housing of the Unskilled Wage Earner: America's Next Problem* (New York: Macmillan Company, 1919), 122; John Nolen, *New Towns for Old* (Boston: Marshall Jones, 1927; Amherst and Boston: University of Massachusetts Press, 2005), 66–74; Arthur C. Comey and Max S. Wehrly, "A Study of Planned Communities" (Department of Regional Planning of Harvard University, November 1936): 146–49; Arthur C. Comey and Max S. Wehrly, "Planned Communities," (November 1936) in *Supplementary Report of the Urbanism Committee to the National Resources Committee* (Washington, D.C.: U. S. Government Printing Office, 1939), vol. 2: 123, 126, 136; John Loretz Hancock, "John Nolen and the American City Planning Movement: A History of Culture Change and Community Response, 1900–1940" (Ph.D. diss., University of Pennsylvania, 1964): 273; John W. Reps, *The Making of Urban America* (Princeton, N.J.: Princeton University Press, 1965), 436, fig. 259; Stewart Jerome Wilson, "John Nolen: An Overview of His Career" (Master's thesis, University of Oregon, 1982): 60–61, plate 29; Margaret Crawford, *Building the Workingman's Paradise: The Design of American Company Towns* (London and New York: Verso, 1995), 160–64; Margaret Crawford, "John Nolen, the Design of the Company Town," *Rassegna* 19 (1997): 46–53; Christine Tate, "Viscose Village: Model Industrial Workers' Housing in Marcus Hook, Delaware County, Pennsylvania" (Ph.D. diss., University of Pennsylvania, 2002): 148–49 (n.32); Charles D. Warren, "Introduction," in Nolen, *New Towns for Old* (2005), lxxiii–lxxviii. Also see ww.livingplaces/com/PA/Mifflin_County/Kistler_Borough.html.
81 Nolen, *New Towns for Old*, 68–69.
82 Crawford, *Building the Workingman's Paradise: The Design of American Company Towns*, 160.
83 Nolen, *New Towns for Old*, 73.
84 MacNeille, "Industrial Housing—What Types of Houses to Build": 72.
85 John Nolen, *The Industrial Village* (New York: National Housing Association, 1918), 2, 19; Charles C. May, "Some Aspects of Industrial Housing," *Architectural Forum* 28 (January 1918): 7–14; John Nolen, "The Essential Principles of Industrial Village Development," *Architectural Forum* 28 (April 1918): 97–102; "Loveland Farms," *The City Plan* 3 (April 1918), 3–5; "Community Planning for Peace-Time Industries," *American Architect* 113 (May 15, 1918): 635–38; A. D. F. Hamlin, "The Workingman and His House," *Architectural Record* 44 (October 1918): 307, 309; Morris Knowles, *Industrial Housing* (New York: McGraw-Hill, 1920), 61–62, 84, 96, 113–14, 135–36; 179–80, 291–92; John Nolen, *New Towns for Old* (Boston: Marshall Jones, 1927; Amherst and Boston: University of Massachusetts Press, 2005), 189; Arthur C. Comey and Max S. Wehrly, "A Study of Planned Communities" (Department of Regional Planning of Harvard University, November 1936): 274–76; Thomas W. Brunk, *Leonard B. Willeke: Excellence in Architecture and Design* (Detroit: University of Detroit Press, 1986), 141; Ford R. Bryan, *Beyond the Model T: The Other Ventures of Henry Ford* (Detroit: Wayne State University Press, 1997), 80. Also see "Youngstown Sheet and Tube Company's Loveland Farms," http://ohsweb.ohiohistory.org.
86 "Community Planning for Peace-Time Industries," *American Architect* 113 (May 15, 1918): 635–38; F. J. Herding, "Workingmen's Colony, East Youngstown," *American Architect* 114 (October 2, 1918): 383–97; Arthur C. Comey and Max S. Wehrly, "Planned Communities," (November 1936) in *Supplementary Report of the Urbanism Committee to the National Resources Committee* (Washington, D.C.: U. S. Government Printing Office, 1939), vol. 2: 155. Also see "Youngstown Sheet and Tube Company's Blackburn Plat," http://ohsweb.ohiohistory.org.
87 John Nolen, *The Industrial Village* (New York: National Housing Association Publications, 1918), 8, 19; Charles C. May, "Some Aspects of Industrial Housing," *Architectural Forum* 28 (January 1918): 7–14; "Housing Development at Claymont, Delaware," *Building Age* (September 1918): 435; William Phillips Comstock, *The Housing Book* (New York: William T. Comstock, 1919), 65–70; "Overlook Colony, Claymont, Del.," *Architecture and Building* 51 (January 1919): 3–5, plates; Lee K. Frankel and Alexander Fleisher, *The Human Factor in Industry* (New York: Macmillan, 1920), 274; "Overlook Colony," *Architectural Forum* 36 (May 1922): 197–200, plates 74–75; John Nolen, *New Towns for Old* (Boston: Marshall Jones, 1927; Amherst and Boston: University of Massachusetts Press, 2005), 5, 189; Arthur C. Comey and Max S. Wehrly, "A Study of Planned Communities" (Department of Regional Planning of Harvard University, November 1936): 183–87; John Loretz Hancock, "John Nolen and the American City Planning Movement: A History of Culture Change and Community Response, 1900–1940" (Ph.D. diss., University of Pennsylvania, 1964): 273, plate XI; Margaret Crawford, *Building the Workingman's Paradise: The Design of American Company Towns* (London and New York: Verso, 1995), 165; Millard F. Rogers, Jr., *John Nolen & Mariemont: Building a New Town in Ohio* (Baltimore and London: Johns Hopkins University Press, 2001), 54; Charles D. Warren, "Introduction," in Nolen, *New Towns for Old* (2005), lxxxv.
88 May, "Some Aspects of Industrial Housing": 12, 14.
89 Emile G. Perrot, *Discussion on Garden Cities: An Industrial Village on Garden City Lines* (Philadelphia: G. L. Mitchell, 1912; rev. and exp., Philadelphia: G. L. Mitchell, 1915); "An Industrial Village at Marcus Hook, Pa.," *Brickbuilder* 25 (December 1916): 329–30; William E. Groben, *Modern Industrial Housing* (Philadelphia: Ballinger & Perrot, 1918), 15–17; Emile G. Perrot, "Marcus Hook, Pa.," *The City Plan* 3 (April 1918): 5–6; "Development of Marcus Hook, Pa.," *Architectural Review* 23 (June 1918): 40; William E. Groben, "The Recreation Building of the Viscose Company, Marcus Hook, Pa.," *The Architect* 38 (September 1918): 256; Ballinger & Perrot, *An Industrial Village* (Philadelphia: Ballinger & Perrot, 1919); Edith Elmer Wood, *The Housing of the Unskilled Wage Earner: America's Next Problem* (New York: Macmillan, 1919), 122–23; Margaret Crawford, *Building the Workingman's Paradise: The Design of American Company Towns* (London and New York: Verso, 1995), 171–72; Christine Tate, "Viscose Village: Model Industrial Workers' Housing in Marcus Hook Delaware County, Pennsylvania" (Ph.D. diss., University of Pennsylvania, 2002). Also see www.marcushookboro.com.
90 Perrot, "Marcus Hook, Pa.," *The City Plan*: 5.
91 Perrot, *Discussion on Garden Cities: An Industrial Village on Garden City Lines*, n.p.
92 "Houses for Operatives at Hopedale, Mass.," *Architecture and Building* (November 6, 1897): 174; Grosvenor Atterbury, "Model Towns in America," *Scribner's* 52 (July 1912): 25; James Church Alvord, "What the Neighbors Did in Hopedale," *Country Life in America* 25 (January 1914): 61–62, 80; Paul R. Smith, "An Instance of Practical and Esthetic Industrial Housing," *American City* 13 (December 1915): 474–76; Frank Chouteau Brown, "Workmen's Housing at Hopedale, Mass," *Architectural Review* (Boston) 4 (April 1916): 64–67; "A Suburban Development at Hopedale, Mass, Arthur A. Shurtleff, Landscape Architect," *American Architect* 117 (January 28, 1920): 112; "Community Building, Hopedale, Mass.," *Architect* 1 (December 1923): plate LIII; Budgett Meakin, *Model Factories and Villages* (London: T. Fisher Unwin, 1905; New York and London: Garland Publishing, 1985), 405–9; Edith Elmer Wood, *The Housing of the Unskilled Wage Earner: America's Next Problem* (New York: Macmillan Company, 1919), 121; Arthur C. Comey and Max S. Wehrly, "Planned Communities," (November 1936) in *Supplementary Report of the Urbanism Committee to the National Resources Committee* (Washington, D.C.: U. S. Government Printing Office, 1939), vol. 2: 30–32, 111, 122; Leland M. Roth, *A Concise History of American Architecture* (New York: Harper & Row, 1979), 221, 222; Stern with Massengale, *The Anglo-American Suburb*, 9; John S. Garner, *The Model Company Town: Urban Design through Private Enterprise in Nineteenth-Century New England* (Amherst, Mass.: University of Massachusetts Press, 1984), esp. chs. 1, 5–8; Edward K. Spann, *Hopedale: From Commune to Company Town, 1840–1920* (Columbus: Ohio State University Press, 1992), passim; John S. Garner, "The Company Town. Industry and Territory in the 19th Century," *Rassegna* 19 (1997): 30–37; *Hopedale National Register Historic District Designation Report* (Washington, D. C.: National Park Service, 2002); Elaine Malloy, Daniel Malloy, and Alan J. Ryan, *Hopedale* (Charleston, S.C.: Arcadia, 2002), esp. ch. 3.
93 Meakin, *Model Factories and Villages*, 404.
94 Arthur A. Shurtleff, quoted in Garner, *The Model Company Town*, 158.
95 Garner, *The Model Company Town*, 160–61.
96 Comey and Wehrly, "Planned Communities," in *Supplementary Report of the Urbanism Committee to the National Resources Committee*, vol. 2: 31.
97 W. E. Freedland, "New Housing Development at Worcester," *Iron Age* 97 (May 18, 1916): 1188; "Housing Plans of the Norton Companies," *The Review* 13 (August 1916): 353–65; Ida Tarbell, *New Ideals in Business* (New York: Macmillan Company, 1917), 155–62; George B. Ford, "Town-Planning and Housing," *Journal of the American Institute of Architects* 5 (January 1917): 28–29; Charles C. May, "Indian Hill: An Industrial Village at Worcester, Mass.," *Architectural Record* 41 (January 1917): 20–35, partially reprinted in *Homes for Workmen: A Presentation of Leading Examples of Industrial Community Development* (New Orleans: Southern Pine Association, 1919), 117–24; "Worcester, Mass.: Indian Hill Development: The Norton Grinding Co.," *Architectural Review* 22 (April 1917): 91; "Giving the People What They Want:

Number Two: Beautiful Homes for Working People Designed by Grosvenor Atterbury," *The Touchstone* 1 (June 1917): 179–87, 209–10; *Grosvenor Atterbury, Stowe Phelps, John A. Tompkins: Architects, New York. Architectural Catalog* (New York: Architectural Catalog Co., 1918), n.p.; Edith Elmer Wood, *The Housing of the Unskilled Wage Earner: America's Next Problem* (New York: Macmillan, 1919), 120–21; Arthur C. Comey and Max S. Wehrly, "Planned Communities," (November 1936) in *Supplementary Report of the Urbanism Committee to the National Resources Committee* (Washington, D.C.: U. S. Government Printing Office, 1939), vol. 2: 53–55; *Indian Hill: An Ideal Village* (Worcester, Mass.: Norton Company, 1953); John Burchard and Albert Bush-Brown, *The Architecture of America: A Social and Cultural History* (Boston: Little, Brown and Company, 1961), 360; *Yearbook* (Philadelphia: American Swedish Historical Foundation, 1963), 33; Leland M. Roth, *A Concise History of American Architecture* (New York: Harper & Row, 1979), 224, 228; John S. Garner, *The Model Company Town: Urban Design through Private Enterprise in Nineteenth-Century New England* (Amherst: University of Massachusetts Press, 1984), 177; Elliott B. Knowlton, ed., *Worcester's Best: A Guide to the City's Architectural Heritage* (Worcester, Mass.: Commonwealth Press, 1984), 205–6; Charles R. Wolfe, "Streets Regulating Neighborhood Form," in Anne Vernez Mondon, ed., *Public Streets for Public Use* (New York: Van Nostrand Reinhold, 1987), 114; Margaret Crawford, *Building the Workingman's Paradise: The Design of American Company Towns* (London and New York: Verso, 1995), 101–28; Leland M. Roth, *American Architecture: A History* (Boulder: Icon Editions/Westview Press, 2001), 328, 339; Susan L. Klaus, *A Modern Arcadia: Frederick Law Olmsted Jr. and the Plan for Forest Hills* (Amherst: University of Massachusetts Press, 2002), 50; Peter Pennoyer and Anne Walker, *The Architecture of Grosvenor Atterbury*, foreword by Robert A. M. Stern (New York: W. W. Norton & Company, 2009), 190, 193–99, 264.

98 May, "Indian Hill: An Industrial Village at Worcester, Mass.": 25.

99 Quoted in May, "Indian Hill: An Industrial Village at Worcester, Mass.": 35.

100 Tarbell, *New Ideals in Business*, 156.

101 Arthur C. Comey, "Plans for an American Garden Suburb," *American City* 11 (July 1914): 35–37; Arthur C. Comey, "Billerica Garden Suburb," *Landscape Architecture* 4 (July 1914): 145–49; "Billerica Garden Suburb," *Town Planning Review* 5 (October 1914): 255; Nelson P. Lewis, *The Planning of the Modern City* (New York: John Wiley & Sons, 1916), 312–13, plate 87; Porter E. Sargent, *A Handbook of New England* (Boston: Porter E. Sargent, 1917), 531; Arthur C. Comey and Max S. Wehrly, "A Study of Planned Communities" (Department of Regional Planning of Harvard University, November 1936): 249; Margaret Crawford, *Building the Workingman's Paradise: The Design of American Company Towns* (London and New York: Verso, 1995), 75–77; Robert Campbell, "Forgotten Utopias," *Boston Globe* (May 21, 1995): 18; Ruth Eckdish Knack, "Lots to Learn from Billerica, Arnstein," *Planning* 71 (March 2005): 24–25; Robin Karson, *A Genius for Place: American Landscapes of the Country Place Era* (Amherst: University of Massachusetts Press, 2007), 42.

102 Crawford, *Building the Workingman's Paradise*, 76.

103 Newton A. Fuessle, "The Seven-League Loom," *Outlook* (June 22, 1921): 341–48; "American Woolen Sells $5,500,000 Note Issue," *New York Times* (October 16, 1921): 99; "W. M. Wood in Good Health," *Wall Street Journal* (October 18, 1923): 9; *Shawsheen: The Model Community and the Home of the Offices and Staff of the American Woolen Co.* (Providence, N.Y.: Livermore & Knight, 1924); "School Building, Shawsheen Village, Andover, Mass.," *American Architect* 132 (August 5, 1927): 187–90; Edward G. Roddy, *Mills, Mansions, and Mergers: The Life of William M. Wood* (North Andover, Mass.: Merrimack Valley Textile Museum, 1982), esp. ch. 5; Mary J. Oates, "Mills, Mansions, and Mergers," book review, *Journal of American History* 70 (September 1983): 426–27; Leland M. Roth, "Mills, Mansions and Mergers," book review, *Journal of the Society of Architectural Historians* 42 (December 1983): 404–5; Susan Diesenhouse, "Andover, Mass.: A Facelift for a Historic Mill," *New York Times* (August 23, 1987), VIII: 21; Margaret Crawford, *Building the Workingman's Paradise: The Design of American Company Towns* (London and New York: Verso, 1995), 200. Also see http://beautifulshawsheen.com.

104 John W. Reps, *The Making of Urban America* (Princeton, N.J.: Princeton University Press, 1965), 430, 434, 436. Also see A. T. Luce, "Kincaid, Illinois—A Model Mining Town," *American City* 13 (July 1915): 10–13; Arthur C. Comey and Max S. Wehrly, "A Study of Planned Communities" (Department of Regional Planning of Harvard University, November 1936): 130; Mara Gelbloom, "Ossian Simonds: Prairie Spirit in Landscape Gardening," *Prairie School Review* 12 (1975): 8; Julia Sniderman Bachrach, "Ossian Cole Simonds: Conservation Ethic in the Prairie Style," in William H. Tishler, ed., *Midwestern Landscape Architecture* (Urbana and Chicago: University of Illinois Press, 2000), 92; John S. Garner, "The Garden City and Planned Industrial Suburb," in John F. Bauman, Roger Biles, and Kristin Szylvian, eds., *From Tenements to the Taylor Homes: In Search of an Urban Housing Policy in Twentieth-Century America* (University Park: Pennsylvania State University Press, 2000), 54, 56–58.

105 Paul Underwood Kellogg, ed., *Wage-Earning Pittsburgh: The Pittsburgh Survey, Findings in Six Volumes* (New York: Survey Associates, 1914), 410–13; J. E. Wright, "An Industrial Town That's Fit to Live In," *American City* (town and county edition) 13 (November 1915): 388–90; Albert H. Spahr, "The Town of Midland, Pa.: A New Development in Housing near Pittsburgh," *Architectural Review* 4 (March 1916): 33–36; Arthur C. Comey and Max S. Wehrly, "A Study of Planned Communities" (Department of Regional Planning of Harvard University, November 1936): 113–14; Leland M. Roth, "Company Towns in the Western United States," in John S. Garner, ed., *The Company Town: Architecture and Society in the Early Industrial Age* (New York: Oxford University Press, 1992), 179; Margaret Crawford, *Building the Workingman's Paradise* (London and New York: Verso, 1995), 128.

106 Spahr, "The Town of Midland, Pa.": 33.

107 Spahr, "The Town of Midland, Pa.": 36.

108 For Edison's single pour concrete system, see Barry Bergdoll and Peter Christensen, *Home Delivery: Fabricating the Modern Dwelling* (New York: Museum of Modern Art, 2008), 42–47.

109 Wright, "An Industrial Town That's Fit to Live In": 389.

110 Edith Elmer Wood, *Housing of the Unskilled Wage Earner* (New York: MacMillan Company, 1919), 130. Also see William S. Millener, "An Industrial Village in Williamsport," *American City* 17 (July 1917): 58–59; "Citizen Housing Development at Williamsport," *Housing Betterment* 7 (February 1918): 40–42; Lawrence Veiller, "Industrial Housing Developments in America: Part III—A Development of Group Houses, Sawyer Park, Williamsport, Pa.," *Architectural Record* 43 (May 1918): 447–69; "Sawyer Park—An Industrial Development at Williamsport, Pa.," *American Architect* 113 (May 15, 1918): 639–42; "Supplement Showing the Best Homes Planned for Recent Industrial Housing Operations," *Building Age* 40 (September 1918): 439; "Correction in Architect's Name," *Building Age* 40 (October 1918): 502; Arthur C. Comey and Max S. Wehrly, "A Study of Planned Communities" (Department of Regional Planning of Harvard University, November 1936): 438–39.

111 Promotional brochure, quoted in "Citizen Housing Development at Williamsport": 41–42.

112 Veiller, "Industrial Housing Developments in America: Part III—A Development of Group Houses, Sawyer Park, Williamsport, Pa.": 448.

113 Veiller, "Industrial Housing Developments in America: Part III—A Development of Group Houses, Sawyer Park, Williamsport, Pa.": 447.

114 Veiller, "Industrial Housing Developments in America: Part III—A Development of Group Houses, Sawyer Park, Williamsport, Pa.": 448, 459.

115 Veiller, "Industrial Housing Developments in America: Part III—A Development of Group Houses, Sawyer Park, Williamsport, Pa.": 448, 469.

116 Veiller, "Industrial Housing Developments in America: Part III—A Development of Group Houses, Sawyer Park, Williamsport, Pa.": 462.

117 Comey and Wehrly, "A Study of Planned Communities": 439.

118 Ralph F. Warner, "The Town of Mark, Indiana: A Manufacturer's Housing Enterprise," *Architectural Review* 7 (November 1918): 97–100, plates LXXXIII–LXXXV; "Industrial Housing Development, Mark, Indiana," *Western Architect* 28 (April 1919): plate 14; Richard Morrisroe, *Marktown Historic District. National Register of Historic Places Nomination Form* (January 13, 1975); Gene Mustain and Doreen Weisenhaus, "Marktown: This Community of Contradictions Lives and Dies a Little Each Day," *Chicago Sun-Times* (August 31, 1980): 3–7; Virginia A. Greene, *The Architecture of Howard Van Doren Shaw* (Chicago: Chicago Review Press, 1998), 29–30, 129–30; Jim Guelcher, "Industrial Legacy Survives in Historic Company Town," *Indiana Preservationist* no.6 (November/December 2002): 12; Wilbert R. Hasbrouck, *The Chicago Architectural Club: Prelude to the Modern* (New York: Monacelli Press, 2005), 471; http://www.marktown.org/tour.

119 For the Clayton Mark residence, see Greene, *The Architecture of Howard Van Doren Shaw*, 82, 162.

120 For Ragdale, see Greene, *The Architecture of Howard Van Doren Shaw*, 12–19, 60–61.

121 Warner, "The Town of Mark, Indiana": 100.

122 "Kohler, Wisconsin," *Architectural Review* 22 (April 1917): plates XX–XXII; "The American Club at Kohler, Wis.," *American Architect* CXIV (October 2, 1918): 401–2; "Typical Cottage, Kohler Village, Wis.," *Architect* 2 (May 1924): plate 30; "The Town of Kohler, Wisconsin: A Model Industrial Development, Brust & Philipp, Architects," *Architecture* 51 (April 1925): 149–53; *Moderne Amerikanische Landhäuser* (Berlin: E. Wasmuth, 1926), 16, 18, 19; Rhys G. Thackwell, "An Industrial Village of Home Owners," *American City* 36 (May 1927): 669–71; "Reducing Building Costs: Materials and Equipment," *American Architect* 129 (March 5, 1926): 335; George L. Geiger, "Kohler: A Planned Village of Beauty and Neighborliness," *American City* 43 (August 1930): 134–36; L. L. Smith, "The Industrial Garden City of Kohler, Wisconsin," *American Landscape Architect* 3 (September 1930): 11–18; James C. Young, "A Model Town that Grew on a Prairie," *New York Times* (October 11, 1931): 6; Arthur C. Holden, "Realty Developments and the Architect," *Architectural Record* 69 (April 1931): 331–58; Arthur C. Comey and Max S. Wehrly, "Planned Communities," (November 1936) in *Supplementary Report of the Urbanism Committee to the National Resources Committee* (Washington, D.C.: U. S. Government Printing Office, 1939), vol. 2: 39–41, 111, 126, 130, 146; John W. Reps, *The Making of Urban America* (Princeton, N.J.: Princeton University Press, 1965), 430, 432; Richard H. Lemmerhirt, *Kohler Co.: Bold Craftsmen* (Kohler, Wis.: Kohler Co., 1973); Arnold R. Alanen and Thomas J. Peltin, "Kohler, Wisconsin: Planning and Paternalism in a Model Industrial Village," *Journal of the American Institute of Planners* 44 (April 1978): 145–59; Leland Roth, *A Concise History of American Architecture* (New York: Harper & Row, 1979), 221; Stern with Massengale, *The Anglo-American Suburb*, 60; Caroline Shillaber, "Elbert Peets, Champion of the Civic Form," *Landscape Architecture* 72 (November–December 1982): 54–59, 100; Margaret Crawford, *Building the Workingman's Paradise: The Design of American Company Towns* (London and New York: Verso, 1995), 127, 203, 207; Arnold R. Alanen, "Elbert Peets: History as Precedent in Midwestern Landscape Design," in William H. Tishler, ed., *Midwestern Landscape Architecture* (Urbana and Chicago: University of Illinois Press, 2000), 195–96; Christiane Crasemann Collins, *Werner Hegemann and the Search for Universal Urbanism* (New York: W. W. Norton & Company, 2005), 118–25; James Miara, "ULX: The Burbs' Best," *Urban Land* 65 (February 2006): 41; Christiane Crasemann Collins, "Camillo Sitte across the Atlantic: Raymond Unwin, John Nolen, and Werner Hegemann," in Charles C. Bohl and Jean-François Lejeune, eds., *Sitte, Hegemann and the Metropolis: Modern Civic Art and International Exchanges* (London and New York: Routledge, 2009), 185–86; *Kohler of Kohler News: Kohler Village Issue* (Kohler, Wis.: Kohler Co., n.d.).

123 Werner Hegemann, quoted in Collins, *Werner Hegemann and the Search for Universal Urbanism*, 122.

124 "Kohler, Wisconsin: Planning and Paternalism in a Model Industrial Village": 150.

125 Werner Hegemann, quoted in Collins, *Werner Hegemann and the Search for Universal Urbanism*, 122.

126 Crawford, *Building the Workingman's Paradise*, 127.

127 Young, "A Model Town that Grew on a Prairie": 6.

128 Walter J. Kohler, quoted in Collins, *Werner Hegemann and the Search for Universal Urbanism*, 124.

129 Walter J. Kohler, quoted in Alanen, "Elbert Peets: History as Precedent in Midwestern Landscape Design," in Tishler, ed., *Midwestern Landscape Architecture*, 212 (n.14). For a more detailed discussion of the correspondence between Hegemann and Kohler, see Alanen and Peltin, "Kohler, Wisconsin: Planning and Paternalism in a Model Industrial Village": 149.

130 For a history of the company, see Hugh Allen, *The House of Goodyear, a Story of Rubber and of Modern Business* (Cleveland: Corday & Gross, 1943).

131 Warren H. Manning, "A Step Towards Solving the Industrial Housing Problem," *American City* 7 (April 1915): 321–25; "Rubber Company Builds Town for Its Workmen," *New York Times* (January 23, 1916): 6; "Goodyear Heights," *Architectural Review* 22 (April 1917): 83; *Which Shall It Be: Home or Hovel*, brochure (Akron: Goodyear Heights Realty

Company, 1918); "Two Housing Propositions," *American Architect* 113 (January 30, 1918): 121; Ralph F. Warner, "Goodyear Heights: A Garden Suburb for Wage-Earners at Akron, Ohio," *Architectural Review* 23 (March 1918): 41–44; "Goodyear Heights, Akron, Ohio," *Architectural Forum* 28 (April 1918): 140–42; Edith Elmer Wood, *The Housing of the Unskilled Wage Earner: America's Next Problem* (New York: Macmillan Company, 1919), 119–20; Frederick M. Davenport, "Treating Men White in Akron Town," *The Outlook* 126 (November 3, 1920): 407–11; "Busses Meet All Demands," *Los Angeles Times* (October 1, 1922): 18; Arthur C. Comey and Max S. Wehrly, "Planned Communities," (November 1936) in *Supplementary Report of the Urbanism Committee to the National Resources Committee* (Washington, D.C.: U. S. Government Printing Office, 1939), vol. 2: 51–53; Leland M. Roth, *A Concise History of American Architecture* (New York: Harper & Row, 1979), 228; Gwendolyn Wright, *Building the Dream: A Social History of Housing in America* (New York: Pantheon Books, 1981), 185; John S. Garner, *The Model Company Town: Urban Design through Private Enterprise in Nineteenth-Century New England* (Amherst: University of Massachusetts Press, 1984), 43–44, 222; Charles R. Wolfe, "Streets Regulating Neighborhood Form," in Anne Vernez Mondon, ed., *Public Streets for Public Use* (New York: Van Nostrand Reinhold, 1987), 114; Margaret Crawford, *Building the Workingman's Paradise: The Design of American Company Towns* (London and New York: Verso, 1995), 83, 95–97; Frances McGovern, *Written on the Hills: The Making of the Akron Landscape* (Akron: University of Akron Press, 1996), 88, 125–26; Robin Karson, *A Genius for Place: American Landscapes of the Country Place Era* (Amherst: University of Massachusetts Press, 2007), 41, 93–94, 111; *Akron History Trails: Our Historic Neighborhoods* (Akron, 2008), 16.

132 For Stan Hywet, see Karson, *A Genius for Place*, 89–115.

133 Manning, "A Step Towards Solving the Industrial Housing Problem": 323.

134 Wood, *The Housing of the Unskilled Wage Earner: America's Next Problem*, 119.

135 "Rubber Company Builds Town for Its Workmen": 6.

136 "Two Housing Propositions": 121; Warner, "Goodyear Heights: A Garden Suburb for Wage-Earners at Akron, Ohio": 41–44; "Goodyear Heights, Akron, Ohio," *Architectural Forum*: 140–42; Comey and Wehrly, "Planned Communities," in *Supplementary Report of the Urbanism Committee to the National Resources Committee*, vol. 2: 51–53.

137 Karson, *A Genius for Place*, 42–43, 111. Also see McGovern, *Written on the Hills: The Making of the Akron Landscape*, 88; *Akron History Trails: Our Historic Neighborhoods*, 14.

138 William Phillips Comstock, *The Housing Book* (New York: William T. Comstock Co., 1919), 101–5; H. S. Firestone, "Firestone Park, Akron, Ohio," in *Homes for Workmen: A Presentation of Leading Examples of Industrial Community Development* (New Orleans: Southern Pine Association, 1919), 199–202; "Industrial Housing," *Architecture and Building* 51 (January 1919): 5, plates 14–15; "Firestone Park, Akron, Ohio," *Architecture* 40 (December 1919): 327–31; Frederick M. Davenport, "Treating Men White in Akron Town," *The Outlook* 126 (November 3, 1920): 407–11; Arthur C. Comey and Max S. Wehrly, "A Study of Planned Communities" (Department of Regional Planning of Harvard University, November 1936): 254–57; Leland M. Roth, *A Concise History of American Architecture* (New York: Harper & Row, 1979), 228; Gwendolyn Wright, *Building the Dream: A Social History of Housing in America* (New York: Pantheon Books, 1981), 185; John S. Garner, *The Model Company Town: Urban Design through Private Enterprise in Nineteenth-Century New England* (Amherst: University of Massachusetts Press, 1984), 43, 222; Jean Czerkas, "Alling Stephen DeForest," in Charles A. Birnbaum and Robin Karson, eds., *Pioneers of American Landscape Design* (New York: McGraw-Hill, 2000), 88–91; Margaret Crawford, *Building the Workingman's Paradise: The Design of American Company Towns* (London and New York: Verso, 1995), 226 (n.37); Frances McGovern, *Written on the Hills: The Making of the Akron Landscape* (Akron: University of Akron Press, 1996), 88, 126; Robin Karson, *A Genius for Place: American Landscapes of the Country Place Era* (Amherst: University of Massachusetts Press, 2007), 370 (n. 28); *Akron History Trails: Our Historic Neighborhoods* (Akron, 2008), 15.

139 Comey and Wehrly, "A Study of Planned Communities": 254.

140 Lawrence Veiller, "Industrial Housing Developments in America: Eclipse Park, Beloit, Wisconsin," *Architectural Record* 43 (March 1918): 231–56; Ralph F. Warner, "A Wage Earners' Community Development at Beloit, Wisconsin," *American Architect* 113 (May 22, 1918): 657–66; "Industrial Housing Developments in America," *The Survey* (May 25, 1918): 210; Ralph F. Warner, "Industrial Housing in War Time," *Bankers* 96 (June 1918): 703–8; William Phillips Comstock, *The Housing Book* (New York: William T. Comstock Co., 1919), 16–26; *Homes for Workmen: A Presentation of Leading Examples of Industrial Community Development* (New Orleans: Southern Pine Association, 1919), 69–77; "American Society of Landscape Architects," *Landscape Architecture* 9 (July 1919): 185; Lee K. Frankel and Alexander Fleisher, *The Human Factor in Industry* (New York: Macmillan Company, 1920), 274–75, 277; John Burchard and Albert Bush-Brown, *The Architecture of America: A Social and Cultural History* (Boston: Little, Brown and Co., 1961), 360; Leland M. Roth, *A Concise History of American Architecture* (New York: Harper & Row, 1979), 228–29; Leland Roth, "Three Industrial Towns by McKim, Mead & White," *Journal of the Society of Architectural Historians* 38 (December 1979): 317–47; Stern with Massengale, *The Anglo-American Suburb*, 9; John S. Garner, *The Model Company Town: Urban Design through Private Enterprise in Nineteenth-Century New England* (Amherst: University of Massachusetts Press, 1984), 43; Charles R. Wolfe, "Streets Regulating Neighborhood Form," in Anne Vernez Mondon, ed., *Public Streets for Public Use* (New York: Van Nostrand Reinhold, 1987), 114; Margaret Crawford, *Building the Workingman's Paradise: The Design of American Company Towns* (London and New York: Verso, 1995), 127–28; Sarah Bradford Landau, *George B. Post: Picturesque Designer & Determined Realist* (New York: Monacelli Press, 1998), 177–79; John S. Garner, "The Garden City and Planned Industrial Suburbs: Housing and Planning on the Eve of World War I," in John F. Bauman, Roger Biles, and Kristin Szylvian, eds., *From Tenements to the Taylor Homes: In Search of an Urban Housing Policy in Twentieth-Century America* (University Park: Pennsylvania State University Press, 2000), 44, 53–57; Leland M. Roth, *American Architecture: A History* (Boulder: Icon Editions/Westview Press, 2001), 338, 340–41.

141 For the Wisconsin State Capitol, see Landau, *George B. Post: Picturesque Designer & Determined Realist*, 163–70, plates 22–23.

142 Comstock, *The Housing Book*, 17.

143 Veiller, "Industrial Housing Developments in America: Eclipse Park, Beloit, Wisconsin": 256.

144 For Fairbanks Flats, see Nancy C. Curtis, *Black Heritage Sites* (Chicago: American Library Association, 1996), 523.

145 Garner, "The Garden City and Planned Industrial Suburbs: Housing and Planning on the Eve of World War I," in Bauman, Biles, and Szylvian, eds., *From Tenements to the Taylor Homes: In Search of an Urban Housing Policy in Twentieth-Century America*, 53.

146 H. E. Davis, "The Civic Building Company's Development at Flint, Michigan," *Architectural Review* 5 (April 1917): 92–94; "Housing Developments in Flint, Michigan," *Journal of the American Institute of Architects* 5 (April 1917): 180–81; "Industrial Housing Development for the Civic Building Co, at Flint, Michigan," *American Architect* 113 (May 15, 1918): 623–34; *Homes for Workmen: A Presentation of Leading Examples of Industrial Community Development* (New Orleans: Southern Pine Association, 1919), 142–48; Lucy Tilden Stewart, "A Big Scheme Done in a Big Way," *Housing Betterment* 8 (June 1919): 16–19; Kathryn Bishop Eckert, *Buildings of Michigan* (New York: Oxford University Press, 1993), 337–38. Also see "Civic Park Historic District," www.mcgi.state.mi.us.

147 Davis, "The Civic Building Company's Development at Flint, Michigan": 93–94.

148 Ford R. Bryan, "Concrete Homes for Dearborn," *Dearborn Historian* 24 (Summer 1984): 87–92; Thomas W. Brunk, *Leonard B. Willeke: Excellence in Architecture and Design* (Detroit: University of Detroit Press, 1986), 137–47, 181; Ford R. Bryan, *Beyond the Model T: The Other Ventures of Henry Ford* (Detroit: Wayne State University Press, 1997), 78–83; Carolyn S. Loeb, *Entrepreneurial Vernacular: Developers' Subdivisions in the 1920s* (Baltimore and London: Johns Hopkins University Press, 2001), 23.

149 Brunk, *Leonard B. Willeke: Excellence in Architecture and Design*, 140, 144.

150 "Ford Housing Project Is Started," *Detroit News* (July 6, 1939): 42; Dean R. Luedders, "Springwells Park," *Dearborn Historian* 14 (Winter 1974): 15–21; "Oral History Interview with William Bostick, August 11–19, 1981," www.aaa.si.edu; Brunk, *Leonard B. Willeke: Excellence in Architecture and Design*, 232 (n.11); Bryan, *Beyond the Model T: The Other Ventures of Henry Ford*, 83 (n.16).

151 Milton D. Morrill, "Standardized Small Houses," *Building Age* 42 (June 1920): 19–25, 41–43; Joseph Oldenburg, "Ford Homes Historic District," *Dearborn Historian* 20 (Spring 1980): 31–50; Kathryn Bishop Eckert, *Buildings of Michigan* (New York: Oxford University Press, 1993), 119–20; Bryan, *Beyond the Model T: The Other Ventures of Henry Ford*, 82–83; Donn P. Werling, *Henry Ford: A Hearthside Perspective* (Warrendale, Pa.: Society of Automotive Engineers, 2000), 73; Loeb, *Entrepreneurial Vernacular: Developers' Subdivisions in the 1920s*, 11–12, 19–54; Craig Hutchinson and Kimberly Rising, *Images of America: Dearborn, Michigan* (Charleston, S.C.: Arcadia Publishing, 2003), 82, 94–95; Alison K. Hoagland, "Entrepreneurial Vernacular," book review, *Journal of the Society of Architectural Historians* 62 (March 2003): 148–49. Also see "Ford Homes Historic District," www.fordhomes.org.

152 Eckert, *Buildings of Michigan*, 120.

153 "Solvay Companies Promote Improved Housing," *Housing Betterment* 6 (December 1917): 33; "Jefferson Rouge, the Development of Solvay Process Company, Detroit, Mich.," *Architectural Forum* 28 (April 1918): 121–23; Brunk, *Leonard B. Willeke: Excellence in Architecture and Design*, 137, 141; Margaret Crawford, *Building the Workingman's Paradise: The Design of American Company Towns* (London and New York: Verso, 1995), 163.

154 Brunk, *Leonard B. Willeke: Excellence in Architecture and Design*, 141.

155 Huger Elliott, "An Ideal City in the West," *Architectural Review* 15 (September 1908): 137–42, plate 59; Leland M. Roth, *A Concise History of American Architecture* (New York: Harper & Row, 1979), 221–22; John Pastier, "Roots of Regionalism: Mining Towns," *Journal of the American Institute of Architects* 73 (March 1984): 106–11; Leland M. Roth, "Company Towns in the Western United States," in John S. Garner, ed., *The Company Town: Architecture and Society in the Early Industrial Age* (New York: Oxford University Press, 1992), 177, 180–82; Margaret Crawford, *Building the Workingman's Paradise: The Design of American Company Towns* (London and New York: Verso, 1995), 130; Leland M. Roth, *American Architecture: A History* (Boulder: Icon Editions/Westview Press, 2001), 326; Dixie Leger, "The Forgotten City Beautiful: Warren, Ariz.," *American Bungalow* 40 (Winter 2003): 125–30. Also see www.ghosttowns.com/states/az/warren.html.

156 Elliott, "An Ideal City in the West": 142.

157 Warren H. Manning, "Villages and Homes for Working Men," *Western Architect* 16 (August 1910): 84–88; Arnold R. Alanen, "The Planning of Company Communities in the Lake Superior Mining Region," *Journal of the American Planning Association* 45 (July 1979): 264–65; Katherine Eckert, *Buildings of Michigan* (New York: Oxford University Press, 1993), 498–99; Arnold R. Alanen, "Gwinn: a Model Town 'Without Equal,'" *Michigan History* 78 (November/December 1994): 33–35; Arnold R. Alanen and Lynn Bjorkman, "Plats, Parks, Playgrounds, and Plants: Warren H. Manning's Landscape Designs for the Mining Districts of Michigan's Upper Peninsula, 1899–1932," *IA: The Journal for the Society of Industrial Archaeology* 24 (No. 1, 1998): 41–60; Arnold R. Alanen, *Morgan Park: Duluth, U.S. Steel, and the Forging of a Company Town* (Minneapolis and London: University of Minnesota Press, 2007), 9–10. For Manning's work at the Gwinn estate, see Robin Karson, *A Genius for Place: American Landscapes of the Country Place Era* (Amherst: University of Massachusetts Press in association with Library of American Landscape History, 2007), 61–88.

158 Alanen, "Gwinn: a Model Town 'Without Equal'": 35.

159 Alanen and Bjorkman, "Plats, Parks, Playgrounds, and Plants": 49.

160 "Tyrone, New Mexico, the Development of Phelps-Dodge Corporation," *Architectural Forum* 28 (April 1918): 131–34; "The New Mining Community of Tyrone, N.M.," *Architectural Review* 6 (April 1918): 59–62, plates 52–56; Marcia Mead, "The Architecture of the Small House," *Architecture* 37 (June 1918): 145–54; Leifur Magnusson, "A Modern Copper Mining Town," *Monthly Labor Review* 7 (September 1918): 278–84; A. D. F. Hamlin, "The Workingman and His House," *Architectural Record* 44 (October 1918): 309, 311, 314–16; Charles F. Willis, "Housing at Tyrone, New Mexico," *Chemical and Metallurgical Engineering* 19 (October 15, 1918): 629–30; "Best Known Examples of Goodhue's Work," *Los Angeles Times* (December 25, 1921), V: 1; Werner Hegemann and Elbert Peets, *The American Vitruvius: An Architect's Handbook of Civic Art* (New York: Architectural Book Publishing Co., 1922), 108–9; Arthur C. Comey and Max S. Wehrly, "A Study of Planned Communities" (Department of Regional Planning of Harvard University, November 1936): 226–29; Christopher Tunnard and Henry Hope Reed, *American Skyline: The Growth and Form of Our Cities and Towns* (Boston: Houghton Mifflin, 1955), 221–22; Ian Nairn, *The American Landscape: A Critical View* (New

York: Random House, 1965), 54–55; John W. Reps, *The Making of Urban America: A History of City Planning in the United States* (Princeton, N.J.: Princeton University Press, 1965), 436, fig. 258; James B. Allen, *The Company Town in the American West* (Norman: University of Oklahoma Press, 1966), 84, 115–16; Don Branning, "The Rebirth and Death of Tyrone," *Los Angeles Times* (May 21, 1967), N: 36; Robert B. Riley, "Gone Forever: Goodhue's Beaux Arts Ghost Town," *Journal of the American Institute of Architects* 50 (August 1968): 67–70; Vincent Scully, *American Architecture and Urbanism* (New York: Praeger, 1969), 162–63; Leland M. Roth, *A Concise History of American Architecture* (New York: Harper & Row, 1979), 222–24; Stern with Massengale, *The Anglo-American Suburb*, 61; Richard Oliver, *Bertram Grosvenor Goodhue* (New York: Architectural History Foundation; Cambridge, Mass., and London: MIT Press, 1983), 151–54; John Pastier, "Roots of Regionalism: Mining Towns," *Journal of the American Institute of Architects* 73 (March 1984): 106–11; David Gebhard, "Ajo, Arizona's Garden City," *Triglyph* 4 (Summer 1986): 33–44; Charles Moore, "Hispanic Lecture," previously unpublished lecture delivered at Columbia University, 1987, in Kevin Keim, ed., *You Have to Pay for the Public Life: Selected Essays of Charles W. Moore* (Cambridge, Mass., and London: MIT Press, 2001), 357, 359–60; Leland M. Roth, "Company Towns in the Western United States," in John S. Garner, ed., *The Company Town: Architecture and Society in the Early Industrial Age* (New York: Oxford University Press, 1992), 177, 184–87; Margaret Crawford, *Building the Workingman's Paradise: The Design of American Company Towns* (London and New York: Verso, 1995), 129–45; C. J. Haggard, "Reading the Landscape: Phelps Dodge's Tyrone, New Mexico, in Time and Space," *Journal of the West* 35 (October 1996): 29–39; Neal Vogel, "When Company Comes to Town," *Old-House Journal* 27 (December 1999): 48–53; Romy Wyllie, *Bertram Goodhue: His Life and Residential Architecture* (New York: W. W. Norton, 2007), 90, 113–17.

161 Goodhue was selected in 1911 as supervisory architect of the exposition. See Oliver, *Bertram Grosvenor Goodhue*, 109–19; Richard W. Amero, "The Making of the Panama-California Exposition, 1909–1915," *Journal of San Diego History* 36 (Winter 1990): 1–47.

162 Oliver, *Bertram Grosvenor Goodhue*, 152.

163 Bertram Grosvenor Goodhue, letter to George W. Horsefield, February 6, 1919, quoted in Crawford, *Building the Workingman's Paradise: The Design of American Company Towns*, 140.

164 Oliver, *Bertram Grosvenor Goodhue*, 152.

165 "Tyrone, New Mexico, the Development of Phelps-Dodge Corporation," *Architectural Forum*: 134.

166 "Town Site, New Cornelia Copper Company, Ajo, Arizona," *Building Review* 18 (1919): 17, plates 8–12; William M. Kenyon, "The Town Site of the New Cornelia Copper Company," *Architecture* 39 (January 1919): 7–10, plates 11–14; Werner Hegemann and Elbert Peets, *The American Vitruvius: An Architect's Handbook of Civic Art* (New York: Architectural Book Publishing Co., 1922), 188, 193; Christopher Tunnard and Henry Hope Reed, *American Skyline: The Growth and Form of Our Cities and Towns* (Boston: Houghton Mifflin, 1955), 222; James B. Allen, *The Company Town in the American West* (Norman: University of Oklahoma Press, 1966), 5, 83–84, 119–20, 146; Stern with Massengale, *The Anglo-American Suburb*, 61; John Pastier, "Roots of Regionalism: Mining Towns," *Journal of the American Institute of Architects* 73 (March 1984): 106–11; David Gebhard, "Ajo, Arizona's Garden City," *Triglyph* 4 (Summer 1986): 33–44; Leland M. Roth, "Company Towns in the Western United States," in John S. Garner, ed., *The Company Town: Architecture and Society in the Early Industrial Age* (New York: Oxford University Press, 1992), 181, 183–84; Margaret Crawford, *Building the Workingman's Paradise: The Design of American Company Towns* (London and New York: Verso, 1995), 145–48; Patricia Gebhard, *George Washington Smith: Architect of the Spanish Colonial Revival* (Salt Lake City: Gibbs Smith, 2005), 101–5.

167 Gebhard, "Ajo, Arizona's Garden City": 37–38.

168 Crawford, *Building the Workingman's Paradise: The Design of American Company Towns*, 147.

169 Gebhard, "Ajo, Arizona's Garden City": 41.

170 Esther McCoy, *Five California Architects* (New York: Reinhold Publishing Corporation, 1960), 46, 48; Kenneth A. Erickson, "The Morphology of Lumber Settlements in Western Oregon and Washington" (Ph.D. diss., University of California, Berkeley, 1966): 267–75; Kenneth H. Cardwell, *Bernard Maybeck: Artisan, Architect, Artist* (Salt Lake City: Gibbs M. Smith, 1977), 191–93; Leland M. Roth, "Company Towns in the Western United States," in John S. Garner, ed., *The Company Town: Architecture and Society in the Early Industrial Age* (New York: Oxford University Press, 1992), 177, 190–92; Sally B. Woodbridge, *Bernard Maybeck: Visionary Architect* (New York: Abbeville Press, 1992), 12, 214, 232; B. J. Novitski, "Maybeck Returns to Oregon," *Architecture Week* (May 31, 2000), B: 2; Lawrence Kreisman and Glenn Mason, *The Arts and Crafts Movement in the Pacific Northwest* (Portland, Ore.: Timber Press, 2007), 122–23; Mark Anthony Wilson, *Bernard Maybeck: Architect of Elegance* (Layton, Utah: Gibbs-Smith, 2011), 185.

171 Cardwell, *Bernard Maybeck: Artisan, Architect, Artist*, 192.

172 "San Francisco, Cal.," *Housing Betterment* 6 (December 1917): 62–63; Ralph Warner, "Bay Point Garden Suburb: A Manufacturer's Housing Project on the Pacific Coast," *Architectural Review* 7 (August 1918): 35–38; Frank Moore Colby, ed., *The New International Year Book: A Compendium of the World's Progress for the Year 1918* (New York: Dodd, Mead & Co., 1919), 48; National Housing Association, *Housing Problems in America: Proceedings of the Eighth National Conference on Housing, Bridgeport, Connecticut* (New York: National Housing Association, 1920), 350; "Navy Wins Its Long Battle to Level California Town," *Wall Street Journal* (April 1, 1968): 10; Dean L. McLeod, *Bay Point* (Charleston, S.C.: Arcadia Publishing, 2005), 47.

173 Warner, "Bay Point Garden Suburb: A Manufacturer's Housing Project on the Pacific Coast": 36.

174 "San Francisco, Cal.," *Housing Betterment*: 62.

175 Dean Thrift Sinclair, "'A New Town Will Appear on Charleston Neck': North Charleston and the Creation of the New South Garden City" (Ph.D. diss., Louisiana State University, 2001): 523.

176 Leifer Magnusson, *Housing By Employers in the United States* (Washington, D.C.: Government Printing Office, 1920), photograph opposite page 144; Federal Writers' Project of the Work Projects Administrations for the State of Tennessee, *Tennessee: A Guide to the State* (New York: Viking Press, 1939), 414; James A. Spencer, "Bemis, Tennessee—The Oldest 'New Town,'" *Tennessee Planner* 26 (Autumn 1966): 20–25; John Linn Hopkins, *Bemis Historic District, National Register of Historic Places Registration Form* (July 15, 1991); Judith B. Tankard, "Shurcliff, Arthur Asahel (Shurtleff)," in Charles A. Birnbaum and Robin Karson, eds., *Pioneers of American Landscape Design* (New York: McGraw-Hill, 2000), 351–56; "Bemis," *Tennessee Encyclopedia of History and Culture* in http://tennesseeencyclopedia.net/imagegallery.php? EntryID=B032.

177 Albert Farwell Bemis and John Ely Burchard, *The Evolving House*, 3 vols. (Cambridge, Mass.: The Technology Press, Massachusetts Institute of Technology, 1933–36).

178 Hopkins, *Bemis Historic District, National Register of Historic Places Registration Form*, 7: 2.

179 Hopkins, *Bemis Historic District, National Register of Historic Places Registration Form*, 8: 38.

180 Hopkins, *Bemis Historic District, National Register of Historic Places Registration Form*, 7: 8

181 Spencer, "Bemis, Tennessee—The Oldest 'New Town'": 20, 23, 25.

182 Margaret Crawford, "Earle S. Draper and the Company Town in the American South," in John S. Garner, ed., *The Company Town: Architecture and Society in the Early Industrial Age* (New York and Oxford: Oxford University Press, 1992), 139.

183 Earle S. Draper, quoted in Thomas W. Hanchett, "Earle Sumner Draper: City Planner of the New South," in Catherine W. Bishir and Lawrence S. Earley, *Early Twentieth-Century Suburbs in North Carolina: Essays on History, Architecture and Planning* (Raleigh: North Carolina Department of Cultural Resources, 1985), 79.

184 Earle S. Draper, "Southern Textile Village Planning," *Landscape Architecture* 18 (October 1927): 4.

185 Crawford, "Earle S. Draper and the Company Town in the American South," in Garner, ed., *The Company Town*, 161.

186 Draper, "Southern Textile Village Planning": 3.

187 Earle S. Draper, "Southern Textile Village Planning," *Landscape Architecture* 18 (October 1927): 1–28; Catherine W. Bishir and Michael T. Southern, *A Guide to the Historic Architecture of Piedmont North Carolina* (Chapel Hill and London: University of North Carolina Press, 2003), 409; *Erlanger Mill Village National Register Historic District Designation Report* (Washington, D.C.: National Park Service, 2008).

188 Earle S. Draper, "Southern Textile Village Planning," *Landscape Architecture* 18 (October 1927): 1–28; Margaret Crawford, *Building the Workingman's Paradise: The Design of American Company Towns* (London and New York: Verso, 1995), 184; *Pacolet Mills National Register Historic District Designation Report* (Washington, D.C.: National Park Service, 2007).

189 Quoted in Betsy Wakefield Teter, ed., *Textile Town: Spartanburg County, South Carolina* (Spartanburg, S.C.: Hub City Writers Project, 2002), 140, in *Pacolet Mills National Register Historic District Designation Report*, 8: 34.

190 Earle S. Draper, "Southern Textile Village Planning," *Landscape Architecture* 18 (October 1927): 1–28; Arthur C. Comey and Max S. Wehrly, "Planned Communities," (November 1936) in *Supplementary Report of the Urbanism Committee to the National Resources Committee* (Washington, D.C.: U. S. Government Printing Office, 1939), vol. 2: 24–27, 111, 117, 121–22, 136; Mel Scott, *American City Planning Since 1890* (Berkeley and Los Angeles: University of California Press, 1969), 234; Norman T. Newton, *Design on the Land: The Development of Landscape Architecture* (Cambridge, Mass.: Belknap Press of Harvard University Press, 1971), 486–89; Thomas W. Hanchett, "Earle Sumner Draper: City Planner of the New South," in Catherine W. Bishir and Lawrence S. Earley, *Early Twentieth-Century Suburbs in North Carolina: Essays on History, Architecture and Planning* (Raleigh: North Carolina Department of Cultural Resources, 1985), 79; Margaret Crawford, "Earle S. Draper and the Company Town in the American South," in John S. Garner, ed., *The Company Town: Architecture and Society in the Early Industrial Age* (New York and Oxford: Oxford University Press, 1992), 139–72; Margaret Crawford, *Building the Workingman's Paradise: The Design of American Company Towns* (London and New York: Verso, 1995), 189–93, 195, 197–98, 204; Frank B. Burggraff and Charles E. Aguar, "Draper, Earle Sumner," in Charles A. Birnbaum and Robin Karson, eds., *Pioneers of American Landscape Design* (New York: McGraw-Hill, 2000), 100–103; Dean Thrift Sinclair, "'A New Town Will Appear on Charleston Neck': North Charleston and the Creation of the New South Garden City" (Ph.D. diss., Louisiana State University, 2001), 526–36.

191 Draper, "Southern Textile Village Planning": 18.

192 Newton, *Design on the Land*, 487.

193 Crawford, *Building the Workingman's Paradise*, 189.

194 Draper, "Southern Textile Village Planning": 6.

195 Crawford, "Earle S. Draper and the Company Town in the American South," in Garner, ed., *The Company Town*, 161.

196 Crawford, *Building the Workingman's Paradise*, 190.

197 Newton, *Design on the Land*, 487.

198 Crawford, *Building the Workingman's Paradise*, 193.

199 Newton, *Design on the Land*, 489.

200 Comey and Wehrly, "Planned Communities," in *Supplementary Report of the Urbanism Committee to the National Resources Committee*, vol. 2: 24–26.

201 Scott, *American City Planning Since 1890*, 234.

202 *Housing the Shipbuilders* (Philadelphia: United States Shipping Board, Emergency Fleet Corporation, Passenger Transportation and Housing Division, 1920), 1. Also see "To Build Nation's Ships," *New York Times* (April 18, 1917): 12; "Shipbuilders Need Workmen's Houses," *New York Times* (December 17, 1917): 6; Frederick L. Ackerman, "The Government, the Architects, and the Artisan in Relation to Government Housing," *Proceedings of the American Institute of Architects* 6 (1918): 88; "Housing for Shipyard Workers," *The Survey* 39 (January 5, 1918): 399–400; "Fleet Corporation to Seize Houses," *New York Times* (March 2, 1918): 8; Frederick L. Ackerman, "The Real Meaning of the Housing Problem," *Journal of the American Institute of Architects* 6 (May 1918): 231; "Model Towns for Uncle Sam's Shipworkers," *New York Times* (July 14, 1918), VII: 7; Edward N. Hurley, "How Shipyard Housing Work Is Organized and Operated," *Engineering News-Record* 44 (July 18, 1918): 122–24; F. L. Ackerman, "Houses and Ships," *American City* 19 (August 1918): 85–86; "A Brief Record of Progress in the Government's War Housing Program," *Journal of the American Institute of Architects* 6

(September 1918): 445–47; William Morris Houghton, "Says the Pastor Please Work Faster," *World Outlook* 4 (October 1918): 24–25; Sylvester Baxter, "The Government's Housing Activities," *Architectural Record* 44 (November 1918): 561–65; Ernest Cawcroft, "The Present and Future Government of War Communities," *National Municipal Review* 8 (January 1919): 52–60; Edith Elmer Wood, *The Housing of the Unskilled Wage Earner: America's Next Problem* (New York: Macmillan Company, 1919), 234–37; George Gove, "Housing the Workers—An Unfinished Job," *American City* 20 (January 1919): 23–25; "Notes on the Government Housing Developments," *Architectural Forum* 30 (January 1919): 29; Robert D. Kohn, "Letter, Editors, The Architectural Forum," *Architectural Forum* 30 (January 1919): 30; Richard S. Childs, "What Will Become of the Government Housing?" *National Municipal Review* 8 (January 1, 1919): 50; C. Grant LaFarge, "The Case of Government Housing," *New Republic* 15 (January 18, 1919): 337; "War Housing in the United States," *Housing Betterment* 8 (February 1919); Richard S. Childs, "The Government's Model Villages," *The Survey* (February 1, 1919): 585–92; John Ihlder, "Uncle Sam as Auctioneer: What Is the Federal Government Going to Do With Its Housing Projects," *The Survey* 41 (February 8, 1919): 659–60; Clarence Wilson Brazer, "The Future of Government Villages," *American Architect* 115 (February 12, 1919): 219–21; Charles Piez, "Labor and Ships," *North American Review* 209 (March 1919): 352–61; "Quantity House Production Methods, Construction Branch, Emergency Fleet Corporation," *American Architect* 115 (March 5, 1919): 353–58, and (March 12, 1919): 393–98; Curtice N. Hitchcock, "The War Housing Program and Its Future," *Journal of Political Economy* 27 (April 1919): 241–79; Karl B. Lohmann, "The Gains in Town Planning from the Building of Emergency Towns," *American City* 20 (May 1919): 421–25; Robert D. Kohn, "Housing in a Reconstruction Program," *The Survey* 42 (May 31, 1919): 341, 392, 394; Sylvester Baxter, "The Future of Industrial Housing," *Architectural Record* 45 (June 1919): 567–72; W. G. Tucker, "Plumbing Standards for the Housing Projects of the Emergency Fleet Corporation," *Architectural Record* 46 (July 1919): 47–56; "Disposal of Emergency Fleet Corporation's Surplus and Salvage Property," *Scientific American* 121 (August 16, 1919): 159; Morris Knowles, *Industrial Housing* (New York: McGraw-Hill, 1920), 9–10, 45–46, 57–58; William Courtney Mattox, *Building the Emergency Fleet* (Cleveland: Penton Publishing, 1920), esp. pp. 139–48; John Taylor Boyd Jr., "Industrial Housing Reports," *Architectural Record* 47 (January 1920): 89–92; *Sixth Annual Report of the United States Shipping Board* (Washington, D.C., 1922), 201–6; Edith Elmer Wood, *Recent Trends in American Housing* (New York: Macmillan Company, 1931), 66–82; Lewis Mumford, *The Culture of Cities* (New York: Harcourt, Brace and Co., 1938), 373; Miles L. Colean, *Housing for Defense: A Review of the Role of Housing in Relation to America's Defense and a Program for Action* (New York: Twentieth Century Fund, 1940), 7–16; Frederick Lee Ackerman, "An Appraisal of War Housing," *Pencil Points* 21 (September 1940): 534–35; John L. Tierney, "War Housing: The Emergency Fleet Corporation Experience, Parts 1 and 2," *Journal of Land & Public Utility Economics* 17 (May 1941): 151–64, and (August 1941): 303–12; Lewis Mumford, "Frederick Lee Ackerman, F.A.I.A., 1878–1950," *Journal of the American Institute of Architects* 14 (December 1950): 249–54; Electus D. Litchfield, "Frederick Lee Ackerman, F.A.I.A.," *Journal of the American Institute of Architects* 15 (February 1951): 98–99; Roy Lubove, "Homes and 'A Few Well Placed Fruit Trees': An Object Lesson in Federal Housing," *Social Research* 27 (Winter 1960): 469–86; Paul D. Spreiregen, *Urban Design: The Architecture of Towns and Cities* (New York: McGraw-Hill, 1965), 192; Mel Scott, *American City Planning Since 1890* (Berkeley and Los Angeles: University of California Press, 1969), 171–74; Francesco Dal Co, "From Parks to the Region: Progressive Ideology and the Reform of the American City," in Giorgio Ciucci et al., *The American City: From the Civil War to the New Deal*, trans. by Barbara Luigia La Penta (Rome: Guis, Laterza & Figli, 1973; Cambridge, Mass.: MIT Press, 1979), 222–31; Stern with Massengale, *The Anglo-American Suburb*, 9; Kenneth T. Jackson, *Crabgrass Frontier: The Suburbanization of the United States* (New York: Oxford University Press, 1985), 191–92; Christian Topalov, "Scientific Urban Planning and the Ordering of Daily Life: The First 'War Housing' in the United States, 1917–1919," *Journal of Urban History* 17 (November 1990): 14–45; Ronald Schaffer, *America in the Great War: The Rise of the War Welfare State* (New York: Oxford University Press, 1991), 69–72; Bruce I. Bustard, "Homes for War Workers: Federal Housing Policy During World War I," *Prologue* 24 (Spring 1992): 33–43; Margaret Crawford, *Building the Workingman's Paradise: The Design of American Company Towns* (London and New York: Verso, 1995), 168–70; Michael H. Lang, "The Design of Yorkship Garden Village," in Mary Corbin Sies and Christopher Silver, eds., *Planning the Twentieth-Century American City* (Baltimore: Johns Hopkins University Press, 1996), 124–27; Kristin M. Szylvian, "Industrial Housing Reform and the Emergency Fleet Corporation," *Journal of Urban History* 25 (July 1999): 647–89; Leland M. Roth, *American Architecture: A History* (Boulder: Icon Editions/ Westview Press, 2001), 340–42; Emily Talen, *New Urbanism and American Planning: The Conflict of Cultures* (New York: Routledge, 2005), 181–83.

203 Baxter, "The Government's Housing Activities": 561.

204 "A Brief Record of Progress in the Government's War Housing Program": 445.

205 "Fleet Corporation to Seize Houses": 8.

206 Ackerman, "Houses and Ships": 86. Also see Frederick L. Ackerman, "What Is a House? IV," *Journal of the American Institute of Architects* 5 (January 1917): 591–639.

207 Woodrow Wilson, letter to Edward N. Hurley, March 1, 1919, quoted in Tierney, "War Housing: The Emergency Fleet Corporation Experience": 305.

208 Electus D. Litchfield, quoted in "Model Towns for Uncle Sam's Shipworkers": 7.

209 Kohn, "Housing in a Reconstruction Program": 341.

210 Tierney, "War Housing: The Emergency Fleet Corporation Experience": 306.

211 Szylvian, "Industrial Housing Reform and the Emergency Fleet Corporation": 676–77.

212 Lohmann, "The Gains in Town Planning from the Building of Emergency Towns": 425.

213 Mumford, "Frederick Lee Ackerman, F.A.I.A., 1878–1950": 251, 253.

214 Dal Co, "From Parks to the Region: Progressive Ideology and the Reform of the American City," in Ciucci et al., *The American City: From the Civil War to the New Deal*, 224, 231.

215 Richard S. Childs, "The First Emergency Government Towns for Shipyard Workers, I. 'Yorkship Village' at Camden, N.J.," *Journal of the American Institute of Architects* 6 (May 1918): 237–44, 249–51; Charles C. May, "Yorkship Village, a Development for the New York Shipbuilding Corporation, Camden, N.J.," *Architectural Forum* 28 (June 1918): 205–10; Ralph F. Warner, "Yorkship, a New War Town for the Emergency Fleet Corporation, near Camden, N.J.," *Architectural Review* 6 (June 1918): 91–94; "Housing Development for New York Shipbuilding Corporation, Camden, N.J.," *American Architect* 113 (June 5, 1918): plates 195–98;

Richard S. Childs, "Building a War Town," *Independent* (June 22, 1918): 469, 487; "Model Towns for Uncle Sam's Shipworkers," *New York Times* (July 14, 1918), VII: 7; C. W. Moores, "The Greatest Landlord in America," *House Beautiful* 44 (December 1918): 379–81, 395; *Types of Housing for Shipbuilders: Constructed as a War Necessity Under the Direction of United States Shipping Board Emergency Fleet Corporation Passenger Transportation and Housing Division* (Washington, D.C.: U.S. Shipping Board, 1919), n.p.; William Phillips Comstock, *The Housing Book* (New York: William T. Comstock, 1919), 71–78; "Industrial Housing; Yorkship Village, West Collingswood, Camden, N.J.," *Architecture and Building* 51 (January 1919): 5, plates 16–18; Electus D. Litchfield, "Yorkship Village," *The American Review of Reviews* 60 (December 1919): 599–602; *Housing the Shipbuilders* (Philadelphia: United States Shipping Board, Emergency Fleet Corporation, Passenger Transportation and Housing Division, 1920), 4–11; Morris Knowles, *Industrial Housing* (New York: McGraw-Hill, 1920), 114–17; George Gove, "Community Values in Government Housing," *American City* 22 (January 1920): 1–7; "U. S. Government to Sell 1,898 Dwellings at Auction," *New York Times* (November 27, 1921), IX: 1; "World's Greatest Auction Sale Ends," *New York Times* (December 15, 1921): 21; Werner Hegemann and Elbert Peets, *The American Vitruvius: An Architects' Handbook of Civic Art* (New York: Architectural Book Publishing Co., 1922; New York: Benjamin Blom, 1972), 273; Electus D. Litchfield, "The Model Village That Is," *House Beautiful* 51 (June 1922): 533–36; "A Six-store Building at Yorkship Village, N. J.," *Architectural Forum* 42 (February 1925): 115–18; Werner Hegemann, *Amerikanische Architektur & Stadtbaukunst* (Berlin: Wasmuth, 1927), 122; "A Pictorial Plea for City Beautification," *American City* 36 (April 1927): 480–81; Electus D. Litchfield, "Housing Projects," letter to the editor, *New York Times* (August 29, 1936): 12; Arthur C. Comey and Max S. Wehrly, "Planned Communities," (November 1936) in *Supplementary Report of the Urbanism Committee to the National Resources Committee* (Washington, D.C.: U. S. Government Printing Office, 1939), vol. 2: 64–67, 111, 124, 126, 128–34, 136; James Dahir, *Communities for Better Living* (New York: Harper & Brothers, 1950), 192, 196–98; Mel Scott, *American City Planning Since 1890* (Berkeley and Los Angeles: University of California Press, 1969), 172–73; Francesco Dal Co, "From Parks to the Region: Progressive Ideology and the Reform of the American City," in Giorgio Ciucci et al., *The American City: From the Civil War to the New Deal* (Cambridge, Mass.: MIT Press, 1979), 226, 228–30; Stern with Massengale, *The Anglo-American Suburb*, 62; Charles R. Wolfe, "Streets Regulating Neighborhood Form: A Selective History," in Anne Vernez Moudon, ed., *Public Streets for Public Use* (New York: Van Nostrand Reinhold, 1987), 114–15; Witold Rybczynski, *City Life: Urban Expectations in a New World* (New York: Scribner, 1995), 191; Michael H. Lang, "The Design of Yorkship Garden Village," in Mary Corbin Sies and Christopher Silver, eds., *Planning the Twentieth-Century American City* (Baltimore: Johns Hopkins University Press, 1996), 120–44; Steven Lagerfeld, "The Old Urbanism," *Preservation* 48 (November–December 1996): 52–59; Michael H. Lang, *Designing Utopia: John Ruskin's Urban Vision for Britain and America* (Montreal and New York: Black Rose Books, 1999), 144–52; Kristin M. Szylvian, "Industrial Housing Reform and the Emergency Fleet Corporation," *Journal of Urban History* 25 (July 1999): 647–89; Leland M. Roth, *American Architecture: A History* (Boulder: Icon Editions/Westward Press, 2001), 341–42; Alexander Garvin, *The American City: What Works, What Doesn't*, 2nd ed. (New York: McGraw-Hill, 2002), 406–7; Rachelle Garbarine, "A Plan to Revitalize a Historic Enclave in Camden," *New York Times* (January 6, 2002), J: 7; Mervyn Miller, "Garden Cities and Suburbs: At Home and Abroad," *Journal of Planning History* 1 (February 2002): 17; Randall Arendt, *Crossroads, Hamlet, Village, Town: Design Characteristics of Traditional Neighborhoods, Old and New (Revised Edition)* (Chicago: American Planning Association, Planning Advisory Service, 2004), 29–30; Emily Talen, *New Urbanism and American Planning: The Conflict of Cultures* (New York and London: Routledge, 2005), 181–83, 209–10.

216 Litchfield, "The Model Village That Is": 535.

217 See Electus Litchfield, architect, to Frederick L. Ackerman, chief, Bureau of Design, Philadelphia, PA, July 2, 1918, NARA, EFC, RG 32, Entry 288, PI-97, Box 1, as cited in Szylvian, "Industrial Housing Reform and the Emergency Fleet Corporation": 686 (n.75).

218 Electus D. Litchfield, quoted in "Model Towns for Uncle Sam's Shipworkers": 7.

219 "Model Towns for Uncle Sam's Shipworkers": 7.

220 Electus D. Litchfield, quoted in "Model Towns for Uncle Sam's Shipworkers": 7.

221 Electus D. Litchfield, quoted in Childs, "Building a War Town": 469.

222 "Model Towns for Uncle Sam's Shipworkers": 7.

223 Litchfield, "Yorkship Village": 601.

224 Litchfield, "Yorkship Village": 601.

225 Comey and Wehrly, "Planned Communities," in *Supplementary Report of the Urbanism Committee to the National Resources Committee*, vol. 2: 65–66.

226 Dal Co, "From Parks to the Region: Progressive Ideology and the Reform of the American City": 226.

227 Comey and Wehrly, "Planned Communities," in *Supplementary Report of the Urbanism Committee to the National Resources Committee*, vol. 2: 66.

228 Comey and Wehrly, "Planned Communities," in *Supplementary Report of the Urbanism Committee to the National Resources Committee*, vol. 2: 66–67.

229 Lang, *Designing Utopias*, 147–48, 151.

230 *Types of Housing for Shipbuilders: Constructed as a War Necessity Under the Direction of United States Shipping Board Emergency Fleet Corporation Passenger Transportation and Housing Division* (Washington, D.C.: U.S. Shipping Board, 1919), n.p.; "Quantity Housing Production Methods, Construction Branch, Emergency Fleet Corporation," *American Architect* 115 (March 5, 1919): 355; "Buckman Village, Chester, PA," *American Architect* 116 (August 20, 1919): 242; *Housing the Shipbuilders* (Philadelphia: United States Shipping Board, Emergency Fleet Corporation, Passenger Transportation and Housing Division, 1920), 19–25; George Gove, "Community Values in Government Housing," *American City* 22 (January 1920): 1–7; "Buckman Village; U.S. Shipping Board Housing Development at Chester, PA.," *Architectural Forum* 32 (May 1920): 183–88; "Shipping Board to Sell Houses," *New York Times* (January 27, 1922): 8; "To Sell More War Houses," *New York Times* (February 19, 1922): 106; "War Town to Be Sold at Public Auction," *New York Times* (February 26, 1922): 100.

231 "Buckman Village; U.S. Shipping Board Housing Development at Chester, PA.": 185.

232 "Buckman Village; U.S. Shipping Board Housing Development at Chester, PA.": 184.

233 Gove, "Community Values in Government Housing": 4.

234 Ernest Flagg, "Housing of the Workingmen," *Architect* 38 (October 1918): 269–70, plate 172; *Types of Housing for Shipbuilders: Constructed as a War Necessity Under the Direction of United States Shipping Board Emergency Fleet Corporation Passenger Transportation and Housing Division* (Washington, D.C.: U.S. Shipping Board, 1919), n.p.; "Quantity Housing Production Methods, Construction Branch, Emergency Fleet Corporation," *American Architect* 115 (March 5, 1919): 355; "Sun Village, Chester, PA," *American Architect* 116 (August 20, 1919): 242; *Housing the Shipbuilders* (Philadelphia: United States Shipping Board, Emergency Fleet Corporation, Passenger Transportation and Housing Division, 1920), 26–33; Morris Knowles, *Industrial Housing* (New York: McGraw-Hill, 1920), 64; "Rapid Economical Construction," advertisement, *American City* 23 (October 1920): 460; Mardges Bacon, *Ernest Flagg: Beaux-Arts Architect and Urban Reformer* (New York: Architectural History Foundation; Cambridge, Mass.: MIT Press, 1986), 288–89; Dan Hardy, "Fixing Up Chester, Block to Block," *Philadelphia Inquirer* (December 6, 1998), MD: 3; Kristin M. Szylvian, "Industrial Housing Reform and the Emergency Fleet Corporation," *Journal of Urban History* 25 (July 1999): 647–89.

235 Bacon, *Ernest Flagg*, 288. Also see Ernest Flagg, *Small Houses: Their Economic Design and Construction* (New York: Scribner's Sons, 1921).

236 Flagg, "Housing of the Workingmen": 269.

237 Flagg, "Housing of the Workingmen": 269.

238 Bacon, *Ernest Flagg*, 289.

239 *Types of Housing for Shipbuilders: Constructed as a War Necessity Under the Direction of United States Shipping Board Emergency Fleet Corporation Passenger Transportation and Housing Division* (Washington, D.C.: U.S. Shipping Board, 1919), n.p.; William Phillips Comstock, *The Housing Book* (New York: William T. Comstock, 1919), 37–46; "Industrial Housing; The Westinghouse Group at South Philadelphia, Pa.," *Architecture and Building* 51 (January 1919): 4, plates 12–13; "Westinghouse Village at South Philadelphia," *American Architect* 115 (February 12, 1919): 222–29; "Quantity Housing Production Methods, Construction Branch, Emergency Fleet Corporation," *American Architect* 115 (March 5, 1919): 356, 358; *Housing the Shipbuilders* (Philadelphia: United States Shipping Board, Emergency Fleet Corporation, Passenger Transportation and Housing Division, 1920), 48; "Westinghome[*sic*] Village, South Philadelphia, PA.," *Architectural Forum* 56 (March 1932): 237–38; "C. W. Brazer, 76, Architect Here," *New York Times* (May 8, 1956): 33; Francesco Dal Co, "From Parks to the Region: Progressive Ideology and the Reform of the American City," in Giorgio Ciucci et al., *The American City: From the Civil War to the New Deal* (Cambridge, Mass.: MIT Press, 1979), 226–28.

240 "Harriman to Build Forty Freight Ships," *New York Times* (August 28, 1917): 16; C. Stanley Taylor, "Bristol, America's Greatest Single Industrial Housing Development," *American Architect* 114 (May 15, 1918): 599–615; "A Brief Record of Progress in the Government's War Housing Program," *Journal of the American Institute of Architects* 6 (September 1918): 447; *Types of Housing for Shipbuilders: Constructed as a War Necessity Under the Direction of United States Shipping Board Emergency Fleet Corporation Passenger Transportation and Housing Division* (Washington, D.C.: U.S. Shipping Board, 1919), n.p.; William Phillips Comstock, *The Housing Book* (New York: William T. Comstock, 1919), 47–64; Caroll H. Pratt, "Bristol, Pennsylvania," in Southern Pine Association, *Homes for Workmen; a Presentation of Leading Examples of Industrial Community Development* (New Orleans: Southern Pine Association, 1919), 126–31; "Industrial Housing; the Bristol, Pennsylvania, Development," *Architecture and Building* 51 (January 1919): 3–4, plates 1–6; "U. S. Government to Sell 1,898 Dwellings at Auction," *New York Times* (November 27, 1921), IX: 1; *Sixth Annual Report of the United States Shipping Board* (Washington, D.C.: Government Printing Office, 1922), 202–4, 206; Patrick W. O'Bannon, *Harriman Historic District National Register of Historic Places Inventory—Nomination Form* (December 1986); Rudy Abramson, *Spanning the Century: The Life of W. Averell Harriman, 1891–1986* (New York: W. Morrow, 1992), 118–23; D. A. Hamer, *History in Urban Places: The Historic Districts of the United States* (Columbus: Ohio State University Press, 1998), 50–51; "Harriman," in http://www.livingplaces.com/PA/Bucks_County/Bristol_Borough/Harriman.html.

241 "Industrial Housing; the Bristol, Pennsylvania, Development": 4.

242 Taylor, "Bristol, America's Greatest Single Industrial Housing Development": 599.

243 Taylor, "Bristol, America's Greatest Single Industrial Housing Development": 606.

244 Comstock, *The Housing Book*, 48.

245 John Nolen, *The Industrial Village* (New York: National Housing Association, 1918), 19–20; Emile G. Perrot, "Recent Government Housing Developments: Union Park Gardens, Wilmington, Delaware," in *Housing Problems in America: Proceedings of the Seventh National Conference on Housing* (Boston: National Housing Association, 1918), 101–17; M. S. Franklin, "Union Park Gardens, Wilmington, Del.: A Government Housing Project for Ship-Workers," *Architectural Review* 7 (September 1918): 56–58; William E. Groben, "Union Park Gardens: A Model Garden City for Industrial Workers at Wilmington, Del.," *Architecture* 38 (September 1918): 248–50; *Types of Housing for Shipbuilders: Constructed as a War Necessity Under the Direction of United States Shipping Board Emergency Fleet Corporation Passenger Transportation and Housing Division* (Washington, D.C.: U.S. Shipping Board, 1919), n.p.; William E. Groben, "Union Park Gardens," *Architectural Record* 45 (January 1919): 45–64; "Department of Architectural Engineering: Quantity House Production Methods, Construction Branch, Emergency Fleet Corporation," *American Architect* 115 (March 5, 1919): 353–58; *Housing the Shipbuilders* (Philadelphia: United States Shipping Board, Emergency Fleet Corporation, Passenger Transportation and Housing Division, 1920), 34–35; John Nolen, *New Towns for Old* (Boston: Marshall Jones, 1927; Amherst and Boston: University of Massachusetts Press, 2005), 89–99; John Loretz Hancock, "John Nolen and the American City Planning Movement: A History of Culture Change and Community Response, 1900–1940" (Ph.D. diss., University of Pennsyvlania, 1964): 278, 287–94, plate XV; Walter L. Creese, *The Search for Environment*, exp. ed. (New Haven, Conn.: Yale University Press, 1966; Baltimore and London: Johns Hopkins University Press, 1992), 302; Francesco Dal Co, "From Parks to the Region: Progressive Ideology and the Reform of the American City," in Giorgio Ciucci et al., *The American City: From the Civil War to the New Deal*, trans. by Barbara Luigia La Penta (Rome: Guis, Laterza & Figli, 1973; Cambridge, Mass.: MIT Press, 1979), 226; Leland M. Roth, *A Concise History of American Architecture* (New York: Harper & Row, 1979), 230; Stewart Jerome Wilson, "John Nolen: An Overview of His Career" (Master's thesis, University of Oregon, 1982): 67–69, plate 32; Margaret Crawford, *Building the Workingman's Paradise: The Design of American Company Towns* (London and New York: Verso, 1995), 170–73; Kristin M. Szylvian, "Industrial Housing Reform and the Emergency Fleet Corporation," *Journal of Urban History* 25 (July 1999): 647–89; Millard F. Rogers, Jr., *John Nolen & Mariemont: Building a New Town in Ohio* (Baltimore and London: Johns Hopkins University Press, 2001), 54; Charles D. Warren, "Introduction," in Nolen, *New Towns for Old* (2005), lxxxiv–lxxxvii.

246 Emile G. Perrot, quoted in Szylvian, "Industrial Housing Reform and the Emergency Fleet Corporation": 667.

247 Groben, "Union Park Gardens": 46.

248 Groben, "Union Park Gardens": 44.

249 Nolen, *New Towns for Old*, 93.

250 Crawford, *Building the Workingman's Paradise: The Design of American Company Towns*, 172.

251 Crawford, *Building the Workingman's Paradise: The Design of American Company Towns*, 171.

252 Warren, "Introduction," in Nolen, *New Towns for Old* (2005), lxxxvi.

253 "Cleland Heights Housing Development, Wilmington, Del.," *Architecture* 38 (September 1918): frontispiece, 243, plates 156–57.

254 *Types of Housing for Shipbuilders: Constructed as a War Necessity Under the Direction of United States Shipping Board Emergency Fleet Corporation Passenger Transportation and Housing Division* (Washington, D.C.: U.S. Shipping Board, 1919), n.p.; "Quantity House Production Methods, Construction Branch, Emergency Fleet Corporation," *American Architect* (March 12, 1919): 397; Karl B. Lohmann, "The Gains in Town Planning from the Building of Emergency Towns," *American City* 20 (May 1919): 421–25; *Housing the Shipbuilders* (Philadelphia: United States Shipping Board, Emergency Fleet Corporation, Passenger Transportation and Housing Division, 1920), 17–18; George Gove, "Community Values in Government Housing," *American City* 22 (January 1920): 1–7; "Shipping Board Homes Are Sold at Auction," *New York Times* (May 23, 1923): 23; "Sells Wartime Houses," *New York Times* (May 28, 1923): 24; "Shipping Board Saves War Village in Crisis," *New York Times* (October 22, 1931): 25; Arthur C. Comey and Max S. Wehrly, "Planned Communities," (November 1936) in *Supplementary Report of the Urbanism Committee to the National Resources Committee* (Washington, D. C.: U. S. Government Printing Office, 1939), vol. 2: 56–59, 111, 124, 126–27, 130, 136; James Dahir, *Communities for Better Living* (New York: Harper & Brothers, 1950), 192–94.

255 Lohmann, "The Gains in Town Planning from the Building of Emergency Towns": 424.

256 Comey and Wehrly, "Planned Communities," in *Supplementary Report of the Urbanism Committee to the National Resources Committee*, vol. 2: 56–57.

257 Comey and Wehrly, "Planned Communities," in *Supplementary Report of the Urbanism Committee to the National Resources Committee*, vol. 2: 57.

258 Comey and Wehrly, "Planned Communities," in *Supplementary Report of the Urbanism Committee to the National Resources Committee*, vol. 2: 58.

259 Comey and Wehrly, "Planned Communities," in *Supplementary Report of the Urbanism Committee to the National Resources Committee*, vol. 2: 58.

260 Walter H. Kilham, "Recent Government Housing Developments: Atlantic Heights at Portsmouth, N. H.," in *Housing Problems in America* (New York: National Housing Association, 1918), 94–100; "The First War Emergency Government Towns: Atlantic Heights," *Journal of the American Institute of Architects* 6 (September 1918): 427–34; "A Brief Record of Progress in the Government's War Housing Program," *Journal of the American Institute of Architects* 6 (September 1918): 445–47; William Roger Greeley, "Portsmouth and the War: Notes on the Development at Atlantic Heights, N. H.," *American Architect* 114 (October 16, 1918): 447–56; *Types of Housing for Shipbuilders: Constructed as a War Necessity Under the Direction of United States Shipping Board Emergency Fleet Corporation Passenger Transportation and Housing Division* (Washington, D. C.: U.S. Shipping Board, 1919), n.p.; Morris Knowles, *Industrial Housing* (New York: McGraw-Hill, 1920), 290–92; *Housing the Shipbuilders* (Philadelphia: United States Shipping Board, Emergency Fleet Corporation, Passenger Transportation and Housing Division, 1920), 40–42; Arthur C. Comey and Max S. Wehrly, "A Study of Planned Communities" (Department of Regional Planning of Harvard University, November 1936): 314–17; Frederick Lee Ackerman, "An Appraisal of War Housing," *Pencil Points* 21 (September 1940): 534–45; Francesco Dal Co, "From Parks to the Region: Progressive Ideology and the Reform of the American City," in Giorgio Ciucci et al., *The American City: From the Civil War to the New Deal*, trans. by Barbara Luigia La Penta (Rome: Guis, Laterza & Figli, 1973; Cambridge, Mass.: MIT Press, 1979), 226, 228–29; Stern with Massengale, *The Anglo-American Suburb*, 9; Richard M. Candee, *Atlantic Heights, a World War I Shipbuilders' Community* (Portsmouth, N. H.: Portsmouth Marine Society and P. E. Randall, 1985); Thomas W. Harvey, "Atlantic Heights," book review, *Journal of the Society for Industrial Archeology* (No. 1, 1987): 72–73; Richard M. Candee and Greer Hardwicke, "Early Twentieth-Century Reform Housing by Kilham and Hopkins, Architects of Boston," *Winterthur Portfolio* 22 (Spring 1987): 47–80; Sam Bass Warner, Jr., "Suburbia Felix," book review, *Design Book Review* 11 (Winter 1987): 14–19; Richard M. Candee, *Building Portsmouth: The Neighborhoods & Architecture of New Hampshire's Oldest City* (Portsmouth, N. H.: Portsmouth Advocates, 1992), 184–87. Also see J. Dennis Robinson, "Atlantic Heights Was Architecture for the Poor," www.seacostnh.com.

261 *Portsmouth Daily Chronicle* (August 15, 1918), quoted in Candee and Hardwicke, "Early Twentieth-Century Reform Housing by Kilham and Hopkins, Architects of Boston": 69.

262 *Types of Housing for Shipbuilders: Constructed as a War Necessity Under the Direction of United States Shipping Board Emergency Fleet Corporation Passenger Transportation and Housing Division* (Washington, D. C.: U.S. Shipping Board, 1919), n.p.; *Housing the Shipbuilders* (Philadelphia: United States Shipping Board, Emergency Fleet Corporation, Passenger Transportation and Housing Division, 1920), 45–47; John L. Tierney, "War Housing: The Emergency Fleet Corporation Experience, Part 1," *Journal of Land and Public Utility Economics* 17 (May 1941): 151–64.

263 "Ship Output of Year Only 3,000,000 Tons; Poor Prospect Due to Lack of Housing for Workers, Builder Ferguson Declares," *New York Times* (January 9, 1918): 3; "Millions for Houses," *New York Times* (January 10, 1918): 4; "Houses for Ship Workers," *New York Times* (January 11, 1918): 8; Henry V. Hubbard, "Some Preliminary Considerations in Government Industrial War Housing," *Landscape Architecture* 8 (July 1918): 156–68; Henry V. Hubbard and Frances Y. Joannes, "The First Emergency Government Towns: II. Hilton, Virginia," *Journal of the American Institute of Architects* 6 (July 1918): 333–45; "Government Industrial Housing a Business Proposition," *American Architect* 114 (August 7, 1918):

157–66; *Types of Housing for Shipbuilders: Constructed as a War Necessity Under the Direction of United States Shipping Board Emergency Fleet Corporation Passenger Transportation and Housing Division* (Washington, D. C.: U.S. Shipping Board, 1919), n.p.; United States Department of Labor, Bureau of Industrial Housing and Transportation, *Report of the United States Housing Corporation, Volume II: Houses, Site-Planning, Utilities* (Washington, D. C.: Government Printing Office, 1919), 253–55; Werner Hegemann, *Amerikanische Architecktur & Stadtbaukunst* (Berlin: Wasmuth, 1927), 123; Arthur C. Comey and Max S. Wehrly, "Planned Communities," (November 1936) in *Supplementary Report of the Urbanism Committee to the National Resources Committee* (Washington, D. C.: U. S. Government Printing Office, 1939), vol. 2: 61–64, 111, 121–24, 126, 130; James Dahir, *Communities for Better Living* (New York: Harper & Brothers, 1950), 193–96; *National Register of Historic Places, Hilton Village Historic District Nomination Form* (National Park Service, 1969); Francesco Dal Co, "From Parks to the Region: Progressive Ideology and the Reform of the American City," in Giorgio Ciucci et al., *The American City: From the Civil War to the New Deal* (Cambridge, Mass.: MIT Press, 1979), 226–27; Karen Madsen, "Henry Vincent Hubbard," in Charles A. Birnbaum and Robin Karson, eds., *Pioneers of American Landscape Design* (New York: McGraw-Hill, 2000), 177–80; Richard Guy Wilson, ed., *Buildings of Virginia: Tidewater and Piedmont* (Oxford and New York: Oxford University Press, 2002), 389–90; Andrés Duany, Elizabeth Plater-Zyberk, and Robert Alminana, *The New Civic Art: Elements of Town Planning* (New York: Rizzoli International Publications, 2003), 90.

264 Homer L. Ferguson, quoted in "Ship Output of Year Only 3,000,000 Tons": 3.

265 Henry Vincent Hubbard and Theodora Kimball, *An Introduction to the Study of Landscape Design* (New York: Macmillan Company, 1917).

266 "Governmental Industrial Housing a Business Proposition": 164.

267 Joannes, "The First Emergency Government Towns: II. Hilton, Virginia": 342.

268 "Governmental Industrial Housing a Business Proposition": 165.

269 Comey and Wehrly, "Planned Communities," in *Supplementary Report of the Urbanism Committee to the National Resources Committee*, vol. 2: 63.

270 Comey and Wehrly, "Planned Communities," in *Supplementary Report of the Urbanism Committee to the National Resources Committee*, vol. 2: 63.

271 *Report of the United States Housing Corporation* (Washington, D. C.: Government Printing Office, 1919), vol. 1: 70, vol. 2: 253–55.

272 "Baltimore and Sparrows Point," *Housing Betterment* 7 (February 1918): 10–12; "A Brief Record of Progress in the Government's War Housing Program," *Journal of the American Institute of Architects* 6 (September 1918): 445–47; *Types of Housing for Shipbuilders: Constructed as a War Necessity Under the Direction of United States Shipping Board Emergency Fleet Corporation Passenger Transportation and Housing Division* (Washington, D. C.: U.S. Shipping Board, 1919), n.p.; Ernest Cawcroft, "The Present and Future Government of War Communities," *National Municipal Review* 8 (January 1919): 52–60; "Dundalk, Baltimore," *American Architect* 115 (February 19, 1919): 17; "To Sell Up-to-Date Town," *New York Times* (July 21, 1919): 14; "United States Shipping Board Emergency Fleet Corporation: A Housing Development Located in Baltimore County, Maryland," *Washington Post* (July 21, 1919): 4; "Village on Sale by Government," *Washington Post* (July 22, 1919): 5; "United States to Sell a Town," *American Architect* 116 (August 6, 1919): 180; "Solving the Problem of the Low Cost House," *American Architect* 116 (August 20, 1919): 229–34; *Housing the Shipbuilders* (Philadelphia: United States Shipping Board, Emergency Fleet Corporation, Passenger Transportation and Housing Division, 1920), 36–39; Daniel Bloomfield, *Labor Maintenance: A Practical Handbook of Employees' Service Work* (New York: Ronald Press Co., 1920), 316–17; Morris Knowles, *Industrial Housing* (New York: McGraw-Hill, 1920), 45, 92, 95, 100; William Courtney Mattox, *Building the Emergency Fleet* (Cleveland: Penton Publishing, 1920), 141, 144; "Shipping Board May Evict 200," *New York Times* (April 7, 1921): 3; *Sixth Annual Report of the United States Shipping Board* (Washington, D. C., 1922), 202, 205–6; Miles L. Colean, *Housing for Defense: A Review of the Role of Housing in Relation to America's Defense and a Program for Action* (New York: Twentieth Century Fund, 1940), 155; John L. Tierney, "War Housing: The Emergency Fleet Corporation Experience, Part 1," *Journal of Land & Public Utility Economics* 17 (May 1941): 151–64; Neal A. Brooks, Eric G. Rockel, and William C. Hughes, *A History of Baltimore County* (Towson, Md.: Friends of the Towson Library, 1979), 329; Sue Anne Pressley, "Improving Dundalk's Image Is No Joke," *Washington Post* (July 25, 1985), MD: 1, 13; James Waesche, *Crowning the Gravelly Hill: A History of the Roland Park-Guilford-Homeland District* (Baltimore: Maclay, 1987), 102–3, 107; Michael Watkins, *A Guidebook to Old and New Urbanism in the Baltimore/Washington Region* (San Francisco: Congress for the New Urbanism, 1993), 53; John Dorsey and James D. Dilts, *A Guide to Baltimore Architecture*, 3rd rev. ed. (Centreville, Md.: Tidewater Publishers, 1997), 368; Sherry H. Olson, *Baltimore: The Building of an American City* (Baltimore: Johns Hopkins University Press, 1997), 292–94; Randall Arendt, *Crossroads, Hamlet, Village, Town: Design Characteristics of Traditional Neighborhoods, Old and New (Revised Edition)* (Chicago: American Planning Association, Planning Advisory Service, 2004), 29, 31; Mary Ellen Hayward and Frank R. Shivers Jr., eds., *The Architecture of Baltimore* (Baltimore and London: Johns Hopkins University Press, 2004), 234, 259; Christopher Niedt, "Gentrification and the Grassroots: Popular Support in the Revanchist Suburb," *Journal of Urban Affairs* 28 (No. 2, 2006): 104–5. Also see "Dundalk Historic District," http://marylandhistoricaltrust.net.

273 Dorsey and Dilts, *A Guide to Baltimore Architecture*, 368.

274 Dorsey and Dilts, *A Guide to Baltimore Architecture*, 368.

275 *Types of Housing for Shipbuilders: Constructed as a War Necessity Under the Direction of United States Shipping Board Emergency Fleet Corporation Passenger Transportation and Housing Division* (Washington, D. C.: U. S. Shipping Board, 1919), n.p.; "Quantity Housing Production Methods, Construction Branch, Emergency Fleet Corporation," *American Architect* 115 (March 5, 1919): 354; "Solving the Problem of the Low Cost House," *American Architect* 116 (August 20, 1919): 229–35; *Housing the Shipbuilders* (Philadelphia: United States Shipping Board, Emergency Fleet Corporation, Passenger Transportation and Housing Division, 1920), 49–50; Wayne W. Wood, *Jacksonville's Architectural Heritage: Landmarks for the Future* (Gainesville: University of Florida Press, 1996), 232–33; Robert C. Broward, *The Architecture of Henry John Klutho: The Prairie School in Jacksonville*, rev. 2nd ed. (Jacksonville: University of North Florida Press, 1983; Jacksonville: Jacksonville Historical Society, 2003), 209–13.

276 "Pacific Coast Shipbuilding," *San Francisco Chronicle* (May 29, 1918): 18; *Types of Housing for Shipbuilders: Constructed as a War Necessity Under the Direction of United States Shipping Board Emergency Fleet Corporation Passenger Transportation and Housing Division* (Washington, D. C.: U. S. Shipping Board, 1919), n.p.; Harris Allen, "Clyde, California: The Housing Colony of the Pacific Coast Shipbuilding Company," *Building Review* 18 (October 1919): 64–66, 71–73, 79, plates 49–64; *Housing the Shipbuilders* (Philadelphia: United States Shipping Board, Emergency Fleet Corporation, Passenger Transportation and Housing Division, 1920), 56; Railroad Commission of the State of California, *Decisions of the Railroad Commission of the State of California* (June 1, 1920): 289–90; *Sixth Annual Report of the United States Shipping Board* (Washington, D.C., 1922), 203; Miles L. Colean, *Housing for Defense: A Review of the Role of Housing in Relation to America's Defense and a Program for Action* (New York: Twentieth Century Fund, 1940), 155; John L. Tierney, "War Housing: The Emergency Fleet Corporation Experience, Part 1," *Journal of Land & Public Utility Economics* 17 (May 1941): 151–64; Esther McCoy, *Five California Architects* (New York: Reinhold Publishing Co., 1960), 46, 48–49; Kenneth H. Cardwell, *Bernard Maybeck: Artisan, Architect, Artist* (Salt Lake City: Peregrine Smith Books, 1977), 181, 193–96, 244; Sally B. Woodbridge, *Bernard Maybeck: Visionary Architect* (New York: Abbeville Press, 1992), 233; Stacy Finz, "Navy Wins Building Battle with Contra Costa Town," *San Francisco Chronicle* (February 8, 1999): 16; Mildred Brooke Hoover et al., *Historic Spots in California*, 5th ed. (Palo Alto, Calif.: Stanford University Press, 2002), 68; Dean L. McLeod, *Bay Point* (Charleston, S. C.: Arcadia Publishing, 2005), 9, 37, 96; Mark Anthony Wilson, *Bernard Maybeck: Architect of Elegance* (Layton, Utah: Gibbs-Smith, 2011), 185. Also see "George A. Applegarth Collection," www.ced.berkeley.edu.

277 Allen, "Clyde, California: The Housing Colony of the Pacific Coast Shipbuilding Company": 64, 66.

278 *Types of Housing for Shipbuilders: Constructed as a War Necessity Under the Direction of United States Shipping Board Emergency Fleet Corporation Passenger Transportation and Housing Division* (Washington, D. C.: U. S. Shipping Board, 1919), n.p.; "Newburgh, New York, United States Shipping Board, Emergency Fleet Corporation," *Architecture* 39 (June 1919): 172–75; *Housing the Shipbuilders* (Philadelphia: United States Shipping Board, Emergency Fleet Corporation, Passenger Transportation and Housing Division, 1920), 54–55; Miles L. Colean, *Housing for Defense: A Review of the Role of Housing in Relation to America's Defense and a Program for Action* (New York: Twentieth Century Fund, 1940), 155; John L. Tierney, "War Housing: The Emergency Fleet Corporation Experience, Part 1," *Journal of Land & Public Utility Economics* 17 (May 1941): 151–64; Brian Flannery, "A Neo-Traditional Link With the Past," letter to the editor, *New York Times* (April 2, 1995), IX: 12; Kevin Barrett, *Newburgh* (Charleston, S. C.: Arcadia, 2000), 28, 90–91, 112. Also see Brian Flannery, "Colonial Terraces Walking Tour," in www.ctna.info.

279 Alfred C. Bossom, "The Emergency Fleet Corporation Project for the Bayles Shipyard, Inc., at Port Jefferson, Long Island," *Architecture* 38 (September 1918): 255, plates 151–55. Also see "A Brief Record of Progress in the Government's War Housing Program," *Journal of the American Institute of Architects* 6 (September 1918): 445–47; *Types of Housing for Shipbuilders: Constructed as a War Necessity Under the Direction of United States Shipping Board Emergency Fleet Corporation Passenger Transportation and Housing Division* (Washington, D. C.: U. S. Shipping Board, 1919), n.p.; "Department of Architectural Engineering: Quantity House Production Methods, Construction Branch, Emergency Fleet Corporation," *American Architect* 115 (March 5, 1919): 353–58; "Solving the Problem of the Low Cost House," *American Architect* 116 (August 20, 1919): 229–34; "$2,000,000 for Port Jefferson Yard," *New York Times* (January 15, 1920): 11; Miles L. Colean, *Housing for Defense: A Review of the Role of Housing in Relation to America's Defense and a Program for Action* (New York: Twentieth Century Fund, 1940), 155; John L. Tierney, "War Housing: The Emergency Fleet Corporation Experience, Part 1," *Journal of Land & Public Utility Economics* 17 (May 1941): 151–64; Roy Lubove, "Homes and 'A Few Well Placed Fruit Trees': An Object Lesson in Federal Housing," *Social Research* 27 (Winter 1960): 479; Michael Adams, "Sir Alfred C. Bossom, 1881–1965," in Robert B. Mackay, Anthony K. Baker, and Carol A. Traynor, eds., *Long Island Country Houses and Their Architects, 1860–1940* (Setauket, N. Y.: Society for the Preservation of Long Island Antiquities; New York: W. W. Norton & Co., 1997), 73.

280 "The First War Emergency Government Towns, IV. Groton, Connecticut," *Journal of the American Institute of Architects* 6 (November 18, 1918): 510–17; "Shipworkers' Homes at Groton, Conn.," *Architecture* 38 (November 1918): 306–9; *Types of Housing for Shipbuilders: Constructed as a War Necessity Under the Direction of United States Shipping Board Emergency Fleet Corporation Passenger Transportation and Housing Division* (Washington, D. C.: U. S. Shipping Board, 1919), n.p.; "Solving the Problem of the Low Cost House," *American Architect* 116 (August 20, 1919): 229, 231, 235; *Sixth Annual Report of the United States Shipping Board* (Washington, D. C.: Government Printing Office, 1922), 202, 206; John L. Tierney, "War Housing: The Emergency Fleet Corporation Experience, Part 1," *Journal of Land and Public Utility Economics* 17 (May 1941): 151–64; Carol W. Kimball, James L. Streeter, and Marilyn J. Comrie, *Groton Revisited* (Charleston, S. C.: Arcadia, 2007), 113.

281 *Types of Housing for Shipbuilders: Constructed as a War Necessity Under the Direction of United States Shipping Board Emergency Fleet Corporation Passenger Transportation and Housing Division* (Washington, D. C.: U. S. Shipping Board, 1919), n.p.; "Quantity Housing Production Methods, Construction Branch, Emergency Fleet Corporation," *American Architect* 115 (March 5, 1919): 354; "Solving the Problem of the Low Cost House," *American Architect* 116 (August 20, 1919): 232; *Housing the Shipbuilders* (Philadelphia: United States Shipping Board, Emergency Fleet Corporation, Passenger Transportation and Housing Division, 1920), 51; *Sixth Annual Report of the United States Shipping Board* (Washington, D. C.: Government Printing Office, 1922), 202, 206; John L. Tierney, "War Housing: The Emergency Fleet Corporation Experience, Part 1," *Journal of Land and Public Utility Economics* 17 (May 1941): 151–64.

282 *Types of Housing for Shipbuilders: Constructed as a War Necessity Under the Direction of United States Shipping Board Emergency Fleet Corporation Passenger Transportation and Housing Division* (Washington, D. C.: U. S. Shipping Board, 1919), n.p.; "Quantity Housing Production Methods, Construction Branch, Emergency Fleet Corporation," *American Architect* 115 (March 12, 1919): 394 *Housing the Shipbuilders* (Philadelphia: United States Shipping Board, Emergency Fleet Corporation, Passenger Transportation and Housing Division, 1920), 52–53; John L. Tierney, "War Housing: The Emergency Fleet Corporation Experience, Part 1," *Journal of Land and Public Utility Economics* 17 (May 1941): 151–64.

283 *Types of Housing for Shipbuilders: Constructed as a War Necessity Under the Direction* *of United States Shipping Board Emergency Fleet Corporation Passenger Transportation and Housing Division* (Washington, D. C.: U. S. Shipping Board, 1919), n.p.; "Quantity Housing Production Methods, Construction Branch, Emergency Fleet Corporation," *American Architect* 115 (March 5, 1919): 354; "Solving the Problem of the Low Cost House," *American Architect* 116 (August 20, 1919): 232; *Housing the Shipbuilders* (Philadelphia: United States Shipping Board, Emergency Fleet Corporation, Passenger Transportation and Housing Division, 1920), 43–44; *Sixth Annual Report of the United States Shipping Board* (Washington, D. C.: Government Printing Office, 1922), 202.

284 "Atlas Building Nitrate Plant," *Wall Street Journal* (February 20, 1918): 8; "A Brief Record of Progress in the Government's War Housing Program," *Journal of the American Institute of Architects* 6 (September 1918): 445; "Industrial Housing at Perryville, Md.," *American Architect* 114 (October 30, 1918): 503–10, plates 129, 131–32; C. Stanley Taylor, "A Modern Industrial Housing Development at Perryville, MD.," in Southern Pine Association, *Homes for Workmen; a Presentation of Leading Examples of Industrial Community Development* (New Orleans: Southern Pine Association, 1919), 188–95; "The Town of Perry Point, Md.: A Development by the U.S. Ordnance Department," *Architectural Review* 8 (February 1919): 45–50; Martha Candler, "The Community House as a War Memorial," *American Architect* 116 (August 13, 1919): 195–201, 205–7; "Restoring Shell-Shocked Soldiers to Health," *Washington Post* (September 5, 1920): 51; Leland M. Roth, *A Concise History of American Architecture* (New York: Icon Editions, 1979), 230.

285 "The Town of Perry Point, Md.": 50.

286 Charles C. May, "Housing Development for the Air Nitrate Corporation, Sheffield, Alabama," *Architectural Forum* 29 (September 1918): 69–74, plates 46–48; "Ordnance Re-Creates Town," *Washington Post* (September 9, 1918): 4; United States Army, Ordnance Department, *Report on the Fixation and Utilization of Nitrogen* (Washington, D. C.: Government Printing Office, 1922), 323.

287 May, "Housing Development for the Air Nitrate Corporation, Sheffield, Alabama": 69.

288 May, "Housing Development for the Air Nitrate Corporation, Sheffield, Alabama": 74.

289 May, "Housing Development for the Air Nitrate Corporation, Sheffield, Alabama": 72–73.

290 "A Brief Record of Progress in the Government's War Housing Program," *Journal of the American Institute of Architects* 6 (September 1918): 445; Ralph F. Warner, "Muscle Shoals—A New Industrial Town in Alabama," *Architectural Review* 8 (January 1919): 18–20; J. O. Hammitt, "Managing a Temporary Town," *National Municipal Review* 8 (June 1919): 311–17; "United States Nitrate Plant No. 2, Muscle Shoals, Alabama," *Architecture and Building* 51 (September 1919): 71–72, plates 137–40; United States Army, Ordnance Department, *Report on the Fixation and Utilization of Nitrogen* (Washington, D. C.: Government Printing Office, 1922), 331.

291 Warner, "Muscle Shoals—A New Industrial Town in Alabama": 18.

292 "A Brief Record of Progress in the Government's War Housing Program," *Journal of the American Institute of Architects* 6 (September 1918): 445; "Nitro, West Virginia, U.S. Government Explosives Plant 'C,' Graham, Anderson, Probst & White, Designing Engineers," in Southern Pine Association, *Homes for Workmen; a Presentation of Leading Examples of Industrial Community Development* (New Orleans: Southern Pine Association, 1919), 78–87; "The Nation's Industrial Progress: Building a Complete Powder City with Motor Trucks," *Outlook* 121 (February 19, 1919): 320–21; "Government Has a City for Sale," *New York Times* (August 23, 1919): 12; "To Sell Town of Nitro, West Virginia," *Wall Street Journal* (August 25, 1919): 9; "Nitro, West Virginia, For Sale," advertisement, *New York Times* (August 29, 1919): 13; "United States Explosives Plant 'C,' Nitro, West Virginia," *Architecture and Building* 51 (September 1919): 70–71, plates 133–34; "Nitro, W. VA., Sold for 8 1–2 Millions," *Washington Post* (October 26, 1919): 10; H. F. Driver, "Cities for Sale," *Nation's Business* 7 (November 1919): 28, 81–82; Helen A. Ballard, "Even a City Can Be Marketed by Advertising; Nitro, West Virginia, Put on Sale as Any Trade-Marked Article," *Printers' Ink* 110 (February 26, 1920): 149–50, 152; Writers' Program of the Work Projects Administration in the State of West Virginia, *West Virginia: A Guide to the Mountain State* (New York: Oxford University Press, 1941), 185, 418; Leland M. Roth, *A Concise History of American Architecture* (New York: Icon Editions, 1979), 230; Donna Sammons, "Making Chemicals in Nitro, W. Va.," *New York Times* (July 20, 1980), F: 9; William D. Wintz, *Nitro: The World War I Boom Town* (Charleston, W. Va.: Pictorial Histories Publishing Co., 1985), esp. prologue and chs. 9, 13; Sally A. Kitt Chappell, *Architecture and Planning of Graham, Anderson, Probst and White, 1912–1936: Transforming Tradition* (Chicago and London: University of Chicago Press, 1992), 290; S. Allen Chambers, Jr., *Buildings of West Virginia* (New York: Oxford University Press, 2004), 101–2.

293 *West Virginia: A Guide to the Mountain State*, 418.

294 Victor F. Hammel, *Construction and Operation of a Shell Loading Plant and the Town of Amatol, New Jersey, for the United States Government Ordnance Department, U. S. Army* (New York: Atlantic Loading Company, 1918), passim; Clinton Mackenzie, *Industrial Housing* (New York: Knickerbocker Press, 1920), 43–48; http://venus.atlantic.edu/amatol.

295 *Construction and Operation of a Shell-Loading Plant and the Town of Amatol, New Jersey*, 15.

296 Mackenzie, *Industrial Housing*, 43.

297 *Construction and Operation of a Shell-Loading Plant and the Town of Amatol, New Jersey*, 181.

298 *Report of the United States Housing Corporation*, 2 vols. (Washington, D. C.: Government Printing Office, 1919).

299 John Taylor Boyd Jr., "Industrial Housing Reports," *Architectural Record* 47 (January 1920): 89–92.

300 *United States Housing Corporation: Hearings Before a Subcommittee of the Committee on Public Buildings and Grounds* (Washington, D. C.: Government Printing Office, 1919).

301 William E. Shannon, "Some Observations on Government Housing at Home and Abroad," address before the Convention of National Association of Real Estate Boards, Atlantic City, June 27, 1919," as reprinted in *United States Housing Corporation: Hearings Before a Subcommittee of the Committee on Public Buildings and Grounds* (Washington, D. C.: Government Printing Office, 1919), 84–88.

302 A. D. F. Hamlin, "The Workingman and His House," *Architectural Record* 44 (October 1918): 302–25; Sylvester Baxter, "The Government's Housing Activities," *Architectural Record* 44 (November 1918): 561–65; *Report of the United States Housing Corporation* (Washington, D. C.: Government Printing Office, 1919), vol. 1: 54–55, 62–63, 82–83, vol. 2: frontispiece, 120–36; Arthur A. Shurtleff, "The Development of a Street Plan," *Landscape Architecture* 9 (January 1919): 67–75; "Government Houses at Quincy, Bath and Bridgeport Will Be Completed," *Boston Daily Globe* (January 19, 1919): 17; Sylvester Baxter, "The Government's Housing at Bridgeport, Connecticut," *Architectural Record* 45 (February 1919): 123–41; Frederick Law Olmsted Jr., "Lessons from Housing Developments of the United States Housing Corporation," *Monthly Labor Review* 8 (May 1919): 27–38; Sylvester Baxter, "The Future of Industrial Housing," *Architectural Record* 45 (June 1919): 567–72; "Where Workers Live as Comfortably as Rich Men," *New York Times* (August 17, 1919): 71; W. Stanley Parker, "Government Housing Work at Bridgeport, Conn.," *Architectural Forum* 31 (October 1919): 111–18; W. H. Ham, "Lessons from Housing Work in Bridgeport," in *Housing Problems in America: Proceedings of the Eighth National Conference on Housing* (Bridgeport, 1920), 95–118; John Taylor Boyd Jr., "Industrial Housing Reports," *Architectural Record* 47 (January 1920): 89–92; "Housing Corporation Replies to Senatorial Criticism," *American Architect* 117 (March 17, 1920): 343; Werner Hegemann and Elbert Peets, *The American Vitruvius: An Architects' Handbook of Civic Art* (New York: Architectural Book Publishing Co., 1922; New York: Benjamin Blom, 1972), 274–75; Frank Chouteau Brown, "Low Rental Housing: Community Planning and the Unit Suburban Group Apartment," *Architectural Record* 56 (October 1924): 353–67; William T. Benslyn, "Recent Developments in Apartment Housing in America," *Journal of the Royal Institute of British Architects* 32 (June 27, 1925): 507; Thomas Adams, "Housing Conditions in the New York Region," in *Buildings: Their Uses and the Spaces About Them* (New York: Regional Plan of New York and Its Environs, 1931), vol. 6: 307–11; Edith Elmer Wood, *Recent Trends in American Housing* (New York: Macmillan Company, 1931), 77, illustration between pp. 80–81; Arthur C. Holden, "Realty Developments and the Architect," *Architectural Record* 69 (April 1931): 338–39; Thomas Adams, *The Design of Residential Areas: Basic Considerations, Principles, and Methods* (Cambridge, Mass.: Harvard University Press, 1934), 241–43; Frederick Lee Ackerman, "An Appraisal of War Housing," *Pencil Points* 21 (September 1940): 534–45; Mel Scott, *American City Planning Since 1890* (Berkeley and Los Angeles: University of California Press, 1969), 172; Francesco Dal Co, "From Parks to the Region: Progressive Ideology and the Reform of the American City," in Giorgio Ciucci et al., *The American City: From the Civil War to the New Deal*, trans. by Barbara Luigia La Penta (Rome: Guis, Laterza & Figli, 1973; Cambridge, Mass.: MIT Press, 1979), 223; Stern with Massengale, *The Anglo-American Suburb*, 63–64; Stern, Gilmartin, and Massengale, *New York 1900*, 488 (n.598); Kenneth T. Jackson, *Crabgrass Frontier: The Suburbanization of the United States* (New York: Oxford University Press, 1985), 192; Robert Leon Maciesky, "A Place in Time: The Shaping of City Space in Bridgeport, Connecticut, 1890–1919" (Ph.D. diss., Boston College, 1994): esp. chs. 6–8; Vincent Scully, "America at the Millennium: Architecture and Community," *The Pritzker Architecture Prize, 1998: Presented to Renzo Piano* (Los Angeles: Jensen & Walker, 1999), reprinted in Vincent Scully, *Modern Architecture and Other Essays*, ed. Neil Levine (Princeton, N. J., and Oxford: Princeton University Press, 2003), 358–67; Elizabeth Hope Cushing, "Arthur Asahel Shurcliff (Shurtleff)," in Charles Birnbaum and Robin Karson, eds., *Pioneers of American Landscape Design* (New York: McGraw Hill, 2000), 352, 355; Robert Maciesky, "'The Home of the Workingman Is the Balance Wheel of Democracy': Housing Reform in Wartime Bridgeport," *Journal of Urban History* 26 (September 2000): 715–39.

303 Federal Writers' Project of the Works Progress Administration, "Bridgeport During the World War: Housing," interviews conducted between 1938–1940, quoted in Macieski, "'The Home of the Workingman Is the Balance Wheel of Democracy': Housing Reform in Wartime Bridgeport": 722.

304 John Nolen, *More Houses for Bridgeport: Report to the Chamber of Commerce* (Cambridge, Mass., 1916); John Nolen, *Better City Planning for Bridgeport* (Bridgeport: Brewer Colgan, 1916); Baxter, "The Government's Housing at Bridgeport, Connecticut": 123–24; John Loretz Hancock, "John Nolen and the American City Planning Movement: A History of Culture Change and Community Response, 1900–1940" (Ph.D. diss., University of Pennsylvania, 1964): 240, 261–65; Stewart Jerome Wilson, "John Nolen: An Overview of His Career" (Master's thesis, University of Oregon, 1982): 52, 56–60, plates 26–28; Elaine D. Engst and H. Thomas Hickerson, *Urban America: Documenting the Planners*, exhibition catalogue (Ithaca, N. Y.: Department of Manuscripts and University Archives, Cornell University Libraries, 1985), 7–8; Maciesky, "A Place in Time: The Shaping of City Space in Bridgeport, Connecticut, 1890–1919": 357–59; Maciesky, "'The Home of the Workingman Is the Balance Wheel of Democracy': Housing Reform in Wartime Bridgeport": 726–27; Charles D. Warren, "Introduction," in John Nolen, *New Towns for Old* (Boston: Marshall Jones, 1927; Amherst and Boston: University of Massachusetts Press, 2005), xlvi–xlviii.

305 Ham, "Lessons from Housing Work in Bridgeport," in *Housing Problems in America*, 114.

306 Alfred C. Bossom, "The Housing of Employees," *Architectural Forum* 27 (August 1917): 43–54; Baxter, "The Government's Housing at Bridgeport, Connecticut": 124; Dennis Sharp, ed., *Alfred C. Bossom's American Architeture, 1903–1926* (London: Book Art, 1984), 48.

307 "The Bridgeport Housing Development," *American Architect* 113 (February 6, 1918): 129–41; Marcia Mead, "The Architecture of the Small House," *Architecture* 37 (June 1918): 145–54; "The War-Boom City: Housing in Bridgeport," *Woman Citizen* (July 20, 1918): 150–51; Hamlin, "The Workingman and His House": 303–4, 307, 309–12; Baxter, "The Government's Housing at Bridgeport, Connecticut": 124; Parker, "Government Housing Work at Bridgeport, Conn.": 111; Ham, "Lessons from Housing Work in Bridgeport," in *Housing Problems in America*, 104–5; Judith Paine, "Pioneer Women Architects," in Susana Torre, ed., *Women in American Architecture: A Historic and Contemporary Perspective* (New York: Whitney Library of Design, 1977), 68; Margaret Crawford, *Building the Workingman's Paradise: The Design of American Company Towns* (London and New York: Verso, 1995), 170; Sarah Allaback, *The First American Women Architects* (Urbana: University of Illinois Press, 2008), 135–37. For the Neighborhood Center Competition, see "Women Architects Win Chicago Prize," *New York Times* (March 6, 1915): 5; "Mrs. Schenck Wins Competition," *Construction News* (March 13, 1915): 6; Anna Pendleton Schenck, "The Need for Neighborhood Centers in American Cities," *American City* 7 (April 1915): 337–39; Paine, "Pioneer Women Architects," in Torre, ed., *Women in Architecture: A Historic and Contemporary Perspective*, 68–69; Allaback, *The First American Women Architects*, 135–37.

308 Baxter, "The Government's Housing at Bridgeport, Connecticut": 126, 129–30, 134; Olmsted, "Lessons from Housing Developments of the United States Housing Corporation": 27–38; Parker, "Government Housing Work at Bridgeport, Conn.": 111–13; *Report* of the United States Housing Corporation, vol. 1: 54–55, vol. 2: 121–23, 135–36; Ham, "Lessons from Housing Work in Bridgeport," in Housing Problems in America, 106; Hegemann and Peets, The American Vitruvius: An Architects' Handbook of Civic Art, 274–75; Brown, "Low Rental Housing: Community Planning and the Unit Suburban Group Apartment": 353–67; Benslyn, "Recent Developments in Apartment Housing in America": 507.

309 Brown, "Low Rental Housing: Community Planning and the Unit Suburban Group Apartment": 364.

310 Benslyn, "Recent Developments in Apartment Housing in America": 507.

311 Baxter, "The Government's Housing at Bridgeport, Connecticut": 127, 129–30, 134; Olmsted, "Lessons from Housing Developments of the United States Housing Corporation": 27–38; Parker, "Government Housing Work at Bridgeport, Conn.": 111, 113; Report of the United States Housing Corporation, vol. 2: 123; Ham, "Lessons from Housing Work in Bridgeport," in Housing Problems in America, 106; Hegemann and Peets, The American Vitruvius: An Architects' Handbook of Civic Art, 275; Brown, "Low Rental Housing: Community Planning and the Unit Suburban Group Apartment": 353–67.

312 Baxter, "The Government's Housing at Bridgeport, Connecticut": 134.

313 Baxter, "The Government's Housing at Bridgeport, Connecticut": 128–31, 134–35; Olmsted, "Lessons from Housing Developments of the United States Housing Corporation": 27–38; Parker, "Government Housing Work at Bridgeport, Conn.": 114–18; Report of the United States Housing Corporation, vol. 1: 82, vol. 2: frontispiece, 127–29; Ham, "Lessons from Housing Work in Bridgeport," in Housing Problems in America, 105.

314 Olmsted, "Lessons from Housing Developments of the United States Housing Corporation": 27–38.

315 Baxter, "The Government's Housing at Bridgeport, Connecticut": 130–31, 135; Parker, "Government Housing Work at Bridgeport, Conn.": 116, 118; Report of the United States Housing Corporation, vol. 2: 126–27, 129; Ham, "Lessons from Housing Work in Bridgeport," in Housing Problems in America, 105; Hegemann and Peets, The American Vitruvius: An Architects' Handbook of Civic Art, 274; Rita Papazian, Remembering Fairfield (Charleston, S.C.: History Press, 2007), 29–30.

316 Report of the United States Housing Corporation, vol. 2: 126–27, 129.

317 Shurtleff, "The Development of a Street Plan": 67–75; Baxter, "The Government's Housing at Bridgeport, Connecticut": 132–41; Karl B. Lohmann, "The Gains in Town Planning from the Building of Emergency Towns," American City 20 (May 1919): 421–25; Parker, "Government Housing Work at Bridgeport, Conn.": 117–18; Report of the United States Housing Corporation, vol. 1: 62–63, vol. 2: 123–25, 131–36; Ham, "Lessons from Housing Work in Bridgeport," in Housing Problems in America, 106; Nolen, New Towns for Old, 95–96; Adams, "Housing Conditions in the New York Region," in Buildings: Their Uses and the Spaces About Them, 308–9; Holden, "Realty Developments and the Architect": 338; "Bridgeport Housing Development," Architectural Forum 56 (March 1932): 264–65; Adams, The Design of Residential Areas: Basic Considerations, Principles, and Methods, 241–42; Roy Lubove, "Homes and 'A Few Well Placed Fruit Trees': An Object Lesson in Federal Housing," Social Research 27 (Winter 1960): 481; Mark Alden Branch, "Two Villages, Two Worlds: Traditional and Modern Planning, Side by Side in Bridgeport, Connecticut," Progressive Architecture 74 (December 1993): 50–53; Scully, "America at the Millennium: Architecture and Community," in Scully, Modern Architecture and Other Essays, 365–67; Cushing, "Arthur Asahel Shurcliff (Shurtleff)," in Birnbaum and Karson, eds., Pioneers of American Landscape Design, 352; Christopher Wigren, "Unnecessary Excellence: Seaside Village, Bridgeport," Connecticut Preservation News 23 (May–June 2000): 16; Randall Arendt, Crossroads, Hamlet, Village, Town: Design Characteristics of Traditional Neighborhoods, Old and New (Revised Edition) (Chicago: American Planning Association, Planning Advisory Service, 2004), 29–32.

318 Baxter, "The Government's Housing at Bridgeport, Connecticut": 138.

319 Report of the United States Housing Corporation, vol. 2: 124.

320 Branch, "Two Villages, Two Worlds: Traditional and Modern Planning, Side by Side in Bridgeport, Connecticut": 50.

321 Scully, "America at the Millennium: Architecture and Community," in Scully, Modern Architecture and Other Essays, 367.

322 Baxter, "The Government's Housing at Bridgeport, Connecticut": 130.

323 Adams, "Housing Conditions in the New York Region," in Buildings: Their Uses and the Spaces About Them, vol. 6: 307.

324 "The Americanization of Our Industrial Aliens," American Architect 113 (February 27, 1918): 239; "Building News: Connecticut," American Architect 114 (September 11, 1918): 24; A. D. F. Hamlin, "The Workingman and His House," Architectural Record 44 (October 1918): 307; Report of the United States Housing Corporation (Washington, D. C.: Government Printing Office, 1919), vol. 1: 74, 211, 236–38, 279, 288–89, 346–47, vol. 2: 78, 369–74; United States Housing Corporation: Hearings Before a Subcommittee of the Committee on Public Buildings and Grounds (Washington, D. C.: Government Printing Office, 1919), 585, 600; "War Housing in the United States," Housing Betterment 8 (February 1919): 6–13; Ralph F. Warner, "Industrial Housing in War Time," Bankers 96 (June 1918): 703–8; "Development for the United States Housing Corporation at Waterbury, Conn.," Architectural Review 9 (December 1919): 171–74; Talbot Hamlin, The American Spirit in Architecture (New Haven, Conn.: Yale University Press, 1926), 273; Miles L. Colean, Housing for Defense: A Review of the Role of Housing in Relation to America's Defense and a Program for Action (New York: Twentieth Century Fund, 1940), 156; Robert Gutman, The Design of American Housing: A Reappraisal of the Architect's Role (New York: Publishing Center for Cultural Resources, 1985), 3; Margaret Crawford, Building the Workingman's Paradise: The Design of American Company Towns (London and New York: Verso, 1995), 170.

325 Report of the United States Housing Corporation, vol 2: 370.

326 Hamlin, The American Spirit in Architecture, 273.

327 Report of the United States Housing Corporation, vol 2: 370.

328 "Development for the United States Housing Corporation at Waterbury, Conn.": 174.

329 John P. Leo, "Department of Architectural Engineering," American Architect 115 (June 4, 1919): 800; Report of the United States Housing Corporation (Washington, D. C.: Government Printing Office, 1919), vol. 1: 1, 29, 69–70, 95, 101–3, 109, 155, 175, 211, 234, 279, 285, 289, vol. 2: 241–45; United States Housing Corporation: Hearings Before a Subcommittee of the Committee on Public Buildings and Grounds (Washington, D. C.: Government

Printing Office, 1919), 585, 599; "War Housing in the United States," Housing Betterment 8 (February 1919): 6–13; "New London," American Architect 115 (May 14, 1919): 686; Miles L. Colean, Housing for Defense: A Review of the Role of Housing in Relation to America's Defense and a Program for Action (New York: Twentieth Century Fund, 1940), 156.

330 Report of the United States Housing Corporation, vol 2: 241–42.

331 George S. Welsh and Ruth Dean, "A Community for Workingmen, Bethlehem, Pa.," Architecture 35 (April 1917): 69; Ralph F. Warner, "Elmwood Park: An Housing Enterprise at Bethlehem, Pa.," Architectural Review 6 (April 1918): 63–65; Nicholas Adams, "The United States Housing Corporation's Munitions Worker Suburb in Bethlehem, Pennsylvania (1918) and Its Architectural Context," Pennsylvania Magazine of History and Biography 108 (January 1984): 67–69; James G. Whildin Jr. and Philip Michael Clark, Elmwood Park Historic District, National Register of Historic Places Registration Form (1987); Eve F. W. Linn, "Ruth Bramley Dean," in Charles A. Birnbaum and Robin Karson, eds., Pioneers of Landscape Architecture (New York: McGraw-Hill, 2000), 338–43.

332 Ruth Dean, The Livable House: Its Garden (New York: Moffat Yard and Co., 1917).

333 Welsh and Dean, "A Community for Workingmen, Bethlehem, Pa.": 69.

334 Welsh and Dean, "A Community for Workingmen, Bethlehem, Pa.": 69.

335 Whildin Jr. and Clark, Elmwood Park Historic District, National Register of Historic Places Registration Form, 4.

336 Report of the United States Housing Corporation (Washington, D. C.: Government Printing Office, 1919), vol. 1: 91, 300, 307, 313, 482, 488–89, 581–82, 585, vol. 2: 111–19; Nicholas Adams, "The United States Housing Corporation's Munitions Worker Suburb in Bethlehem, Pennsylvania (1918) and Its Architectural Context," Pennsylvania Magazine of History and Biography 108 (January 1984): 59–86; James G. Whildin Jr. and Philip Michael Clark, Pembroke Village Historic District, National Register of Historic Places Registration Form (1987); D. A. Hamer, History in Urban Places: The Historic Districts of the United States (Columbus: Ohio State University Press, 1998), 50; Catherine Howett, "Thomas W. Sears," in Charles A. Birnbaum and Robin Karson, eds., Pioneers of Landscape Architecture (New York: McGraw-Hill, 2000), 338–43.

337 Report of the United States Housing Corporation, vol. 2: 112.

338 Report of the United States Housing Corporation, vol. 2: 113.

339 Adams, "The United States Housing Corporation's Munitions Worker Suburb in Bethlehem, Pennsylvania (1918) and Its Architectural Context": 86 (n.52).

340 Whildin and Clark, Pembroke Village Historic District, National Register of Historic Places Registration Form, 2.

341 Adams, "The United States Housing Corporation's Munitions Worker Suburb in Bethlehem, Pennsylvania (1918) and Its Architectural Context": 77–78, 86.

342 Report of the United States Housing Corporation, vol. 2: 304.

343 William Phillips Comstock, The Housing Book (New York: William T. Comstock Co., 1919), 129; Report of the United States Housing Corporation (Washington, D. C.: Government Printing Office, 1919), vol. 1: 100–101, vol. 2: 16, 167–77, 405; United States Housing Corporation: Hearings Before a Subcommittee of the Committee on Public Buildings and Grounds (Washington, D. C.: Government Printing Office, 1919), 143–44, 275–76, 302–3, 585, 600, 608; "War Housing in the United States," Housing Betterment 8 (February 1919): 6–13; "The Report of the United States Housing Corporation," The American 116 (September 24, 1919): 399–412; Morris Knowles, Industrial Housing (New York: McGraw-Hill, 1920), 325; Francesco Dal Co, "From Parks to the Region: Progressive Ideology and the Reform of the American City," in Giorgio Ciucci et al., The American City: From the Civil War to the New Deal, trans. by Barbara Luigia La Penta (Rome: Guis, Laterza & Figli, 1973; Cambridge, Mass.: MIT Press, 1979), 226; Laurie E. Hempton, "Charles Downing Lay," in Charles A. Birnbaum and Robin Karson, eds., Pioneers of American Landscape Design (New York: McGraw-Hill, 2000), 221–23.

344 Report of the United States Housing Corporation, vol. 2: 167.

345 Comstock, The Housing Book, 79–87; "Housing Development of American Brake Shoe & Foundry Company, Erie, Pa.," Architecture and Building 51 (January 1919): 4, plates 7–9.

346 Report of the United States Housing Corporation (Washington, D. C.: Government Printing Office, 1919), vol. 1: 5, 66, 99, 383, vol. 2: 137–40; United States Housing Corporation: Hearings Before a Subcommittee of the Committee on Public Buildings and Grounds (Washington, D. C.: Government Printing Office, 1919), 290, 313, 585, 599; Morris Knowles, Industrial Housing (New York: McGraw-Hill, 1920), 46.

347 Report of the United States Housing Corporation (Washington, D. C.: Government Printing Office, 1919), vol. 1: 7, 70, 165, 211, 285, 289, vol. 2: 260–65; "War Housing in the United States," Housing Betterment 8 (February 1919): 6–13; John Nolen, New Towns for Old (Boston: Marshall Jones, 1927; Amherst and Boston: University of Massachusetts Press, 2005), 190; John Loretz Hancock, "John Nolen and the American City Planning Movement: A History of Culture Change and Community Response, 1900–1940" (Ph.D. diss., University of Pennsylvania, 1964): 278–81; Francesco Dal Co, "From Parks to the Region: Progressive Ideology and the Reform of the American City," in Giorgio Ciucci et al., The American City: From the Civil War to the New Deal, trans. by Barbara Luigia La Penta (Rome: Guis, Laterza & Figli, 1973; Cambridge, Mass.: MIT Press, 1979), 226; Stewart Jerome Wilson, "John Nolen: An Overview of His Career" (Master's thesis, University of Oregon, 1982): 67; Margaret Crawford, Building the Workingman's Paradise: The Design of American Company Towns (London and New York: Verso, 1995), 170; Margaret Crawford, "John Nolen, the Design of the Company Town," Rassegna 19 (1997): 46–53; Charles D. Warren, "Introduction," in Nolen, New Towns for Old (2005), lxxxv.

348 John Nolen, "Planning Problems of Industrial Cities—Niagara Falls as an Illustration," Proceedings of the Eleventh National Conference on City Planning (Cambridge, Mass.: University Press, 1920), 22–31. Also see Nolen, New Towns for Old, 189; Hancock, "John Nolen and the American City Planning Movement: A History of Culture Change and Community Response, 1900–1940": 279.

349 Report of the United States Housing Corporation, vol. 1: 67, 159, vol. 2: 151–55; Nolen, New Towns for Old, 190; Hancock, "John Nolen and the American City Planning Movement: A History of Culture Change and Community Response, 1900–1940": 278, 281–83, 285, 287; Wilson, "John Nolen: An Overview of His Career": 67; Crawford, Building the Workingman's Paradise: The Design of American Company Towns, 170; Crawford, "John Nolen, the Design of the Company Town": 52; Warren, "Introduction," in Nolen, New Towns for Old (2005), lxxxv.

350 Report of the United States Housing Corporation, vol. 1: 67, 159, vol. 2: 151, 156–58; Nolen,

New Towns for Old, 190; Hancock, "John Nolen and the American City Planning Movement: A History of Culture Change and Community Response, 1900–1940": 278, 281–84, 287; Wilson, "John Nolen: An Overview of His Career": 67; Crawford, Building the Workingman's Paradise: The Design of American Company Towns, 170; Crawford, "John Nolen, the Design of the Company Town": 52; Warren, "Introduction," in Nolen, New Towns for Old (2005), lxxxv.

351 "Housing Development at New Brunswick, N.J. for the United States Housing Corporation," Architectural Forum 29 (December 1918): 163–65; Report of the United States Housing Corporation (Washington, D. C.: Government Printing Office, 1919), vol. 1: 7, 69, 112–14, 172, 175, 179, 225–26, 233–34, 285, vol. 2: 230–40; United States Housing Corporation: Hearings Before a Subcommittee of the Committee on Public Buildings and Grounds (Washington, D. C.: Government Printing Office, 1919), 585; "War Department Villages," National Municipal Review 8 (January 1919): 51; "War Housing in the United States," Housing Betterment 8 (February 1919): 6–13; "The Report of the United States Housing Corporation," The American 116 (September 24, 1919): 399–412; Frank Julian Warne, The Workers at War (New York: Century Co., 1920), 143; Thomas Adams, Outline of Town and City Planning: A Review of Past Efforts and Modern Aims (New York: Russell Sage Foundation, 1935), 231.

352 "Housing Development at New Brunswick, N. J. for the United States Housing Corporation": 163.

353 Report of the United States Housing Corporation, vol. 2: 230; "Housing Development at New Brunswick, N.J. for the United States Housing Corporation": 165.

354 "Housing Development at New Brunswick, N. J. for the United States Housing Corporation": 165.

355 Report of the United States Housing Corporation, vol. 2: 231.

356 Report of the United States Housing Corporation (Washington, D.C.: Government Printing Office, 1919), vol. 1: 4, 66, vol. 2: 97–103.

357 Report of the United States Housing Corporation, vol. 2: 97.

358 Report of the United States Housing Corporation, vol. 2: 98.

359 "An Housing Development at Watertown, N. Y., for the United States Housing Corporation," Architectural Review 7 (December 1918): 129–31; Report of the United States Housing Corporation (Washington, D. C.: Government Printing Office, 1919), vol. 1: 74–75, 175, 216, 227–29, vol. 2: 375–82; Laurie E. Hempton, "Ferruccio Vitale," in Charles A. Birnbaum and Robin Karson, eds., Pioneers of American Landscape Design (New York: McGraw-Hill, 2000), 418; R. Terry Schnadelbach, Ferruccio Vitale: Landscape Architect of the Country Place Era (New York: Princeton Architectural Press, 2001), 34, 38, 223.

360 Report of the United States Housing Corporation, vol. 2: 375.

361 Report of the United States Housing Corporation, vol. 2: 375.

362 "An Housing Development at Watertown, N. Y., for the United States Housing Corporation": 131.

363 Report of the United States Housing Corporation, vol. 2: 376.

364 Report of the United States Housing Corporation (Washington, D. C.: Government Printing Office, 1919), vol. 1: 67, 183, vol. 2: 159–66; R. Terry Schnadelbach, Ferruccio Vitale: Landscape Architect of the Country Place Era (New York: Princeton Architectural Press, 2001), 34, 38, 223.

365 H. F. Driver, "Cities for Sale," Nation's Business 7 (November 1911): 28, 81–82; William Phillips Comstock, The Housing Book (New York: William T. Comstock Co., 1919), 27–36; Report of the United States Housing Corporation (Washington, D. C.: Government Printing Office, 1919), vol. 1: 45, 48, 70, 184, 376–77, vol. 2: 270–85; "Uncle Sam, Landlord, He Built and Owns the Town of Cradock, Va.," New York Times (June 29, 1919): 82; Arthur C. Comey and Max S. Wehrly, "Planned Communities," (November 1936) in Supplementary Report of the Urbanism Committee to the National Resources Committee (Washington, D.C.: U. S. Government Printing Office, 1939), vol. 2: 59–61, 111, 121–23, 126, 130, 137; James Dahir, Communities for Better Living (New York: Harper & Brothers, 1950), 194; "James Otis Post, 77, Architect, Is Dead," New York Times (April 22, 1951): 89; Sarah Bradford Landau, George B. Post, Architect, Picturesque Designer and Determined Realist (New York: Monacelli Press, 1998), 178; Calder Loth, ed., The Virginia Landmarks Register, 4th ed. (Charlottesville and London: University Press of Virginia, 1999), 387; Richard Guy Wilson, ed., Buildings of Virginia: Tidewater and Piedmont (New York: Oxford University Press, 2002), 450–51.

366 Driver, "Cities for Sale": 82.

367 Comey and Wehrly, "Planned Communities," in Supplementary Report of the Urbanism Committee to the National Resources Committee, vol. 2: 60.

368 Comey and Wehrly, "Planned Communities," in Supplementary Report of the Urbanism Committee to the National Resources Committee, vol. 2: 61.

369 Comey and Wehrly, "Planned Communities," in Supplementary Report of the Urbanism Committee to the National Resources Committee, vol. 2: 61.

370 Report of the United States Housing Corporation (Washington, D. C.: Government Printing Office, 1919), vol. 2: 285–87.

371 William Phillips Comstock, The Housing Book (New York: William T. Comstock Co., 1919), 106–9; Report of the United States Housing Corporation (Washington, D. C.: Government Printing Office, 1919), vol. 2: 287–89; "Uncle Sam Opens Model Village for Negroes," Housing Betterment 8 (December 1919): 47; Calder Loth, ed., The Virginia Landmarks Register, 4th ed. (Charlottesville and London: University Press of Virginia, 1999), 390; Richard Guy Wilson, ed., Buildings of Virginia: Tidewater and Piedmont (New York: Oxford University Press, 2002), 450–51; Andrés Duany, Elizabeth Plater-Zyberk, and Robert Alminana, The New Civic Art: Elements of Town Planning (New York: Rizzoli International Publications, 2003), 298.

372 Report of the United States Housing Corporation (Washington, D. C.: Government Printing Office, 1919), vol. 2: 288.

373 Report of the United States Housing Corporation (Washington, D. C.: Government Printing Office, 1919), vol. 2: 289.

374 Report of the United States Housing Corporation (Washington, D. C.: Government Printing Office, 1919), vol. 1: 65, 182, 211, 289, vol. 2: 81–88; United States Housing Corporation: Hearings Before a Subcommittee of the Committee on Public Buildings and Grounds (Washington, D.C.: Government Printing Office, 1919), 291, 348; Mary Blaine Korff, "Stephen Child," in Charles A. Birnbaum and Robin Karson, eds., Pioneers of American Landscape Design (New York: McGraw-Hill, 2000), 51.

375 Report of the United States Housing Corporation, vol. 2: 82.

376 Report of the United States Housing Corporation (Washington, D. C.: Government Printing Office, 1919), vol. 1: 68, vol. 2: 191–98; United States Housing Corporation: Hearings Before a Subcommittee of the Committee on Public Buildings and Grounds (Washington, D.C.: Government Printing Office, 1919), 357, 585; "The Report of the United States Housing Corporation," The American (September 24, 1919): 401; Charles A. Birnbaum and Robin Karson, eds., Pioneers of American Landscape Design (New York: McGraw-Hill, 2000), 51.

377 Report of the United States Housing Corporation, vol. 2: 191.

378 Report of the United States Housing Corporation, vol. 2: 192.

379 Report of the United States Housing Corporation, vol. 2: 192.

380 Report of the United States Housing Corporation (Washington, D. C.: Government Printing Office, 1919), vol. 2: 199–201; Charles A. Birnbaum and Robin Karson, eds., Pioneers of American Landscape Design (New York: McGraw-Hill, 2000), 51.

381 Report of the United States Housing Corporation, vol. 2: 200.

382 Report of the United States Housing Corporation (Washington, D. C.: Government Printing Office, 1919), vol. 1: 6, 68, vol. 2: 183–88; United States Housing Corporation: Hearings Before a Subcommittee of the Committee on Public Buildings and Grounds (Washington, D. C.: Government Printing Office, 1919), 313; Charles A. Birnbaum and Robin Karson, eds., Pioneers of American Landscape Design (New York: McGraw-Hill, 2000), 51.

383 "Building News: California," American Architect 114 (September 11, 1918): 24; "The Local Housing Situation," Architect and Engineer of California 55 (December 1918): 108; Report of the United States Housing Corporation (Washington, D. C.: Government Printing Office, 1919), vol. 1: 7, 69, 79, 101, 112–13, 128–29, 136–37, 154, 211, 251, 285, 288–89, 378, vol. 2: 211–21; United States Housing Corporation: Hearings Before a Subcommittee of the Committee on Public Buildings and Grounds (Washington, D. C.: Government Printing Office, 1919), 521, 585, 599, 685; William C. Hayes, "The Vallejo Housing Scheme," Architect and Engineer of California 56 (January 1919): 39–47; Stephen E. Kieffer, "Data on Utilities for Project No. 581: Vallejo, California, United States Housing Corporation," Architect and Engineer of California 56 (January 1919): 46, 48–49; "War Housing in the United States," Housing Betterment 8 (February 1919): 6–13; "Mare Island Houses of Government Open," Los Angeles Times (May 23, 1919): 11; "The Report of the United States Housing Corporation," The American 116 (September 24, 1919): 399–412; "Attacks U. S. Housing," Washington Post (December 19, 1919): 3; Arthur C. Comey and Max S. Wehrly, "A Study of Planned Communities" (Department of Regional Planning of Harvard University, November 1936): 303–5; Federal Writers' Project, The WPA Guide to California (New York: Hastings House, 1939; New York: Pantheon Books, 1984), 413–14; Miles L. Colean, Housing for Defense: A Review of the Role of Housing in Relation to America's Defense and a Program for Action (New York: Twentieth Century Fund, 1940), 157; Greg Hise, Magnetic Los Angeles: Planning the Twentieth-Century Metropolis (Baltimore: Johns Hopkins University Press, 1997), 36.

384 Comey and Wehrly, "A Study of Planned Communities": 303–4.

385 "Attacks U. S. Housing," Washington Post: 3.

386 Report of the United States Housing Corporation, vol. 2: 214.

387 Comey and Wehrly, "A Study of Planned Communities": 303–4.

388 Report of the United States Housing Corporation (Washington, D. C.: Government Printing Office, 1919), vol. 1: 79, 184–85, 204–5, 211, 234, 285, 378, 381, vol. 2: 26, 72, 319–22; United States Housing Corporation: Hearings Before a Subcommittee of the Committee on Public Buildings and Grounds (Washington, D. C.: Government Printing Office, 1919), 585, 599; James Ford, "Government Housing at Bremerton, Washington," Architect and Engineer of California 56 (January 1919): 50–56; "War Housing in the United States," Housing Betterment 8 (February 1919): 6–13; "The Report of the United States Housing Corporation," The American 116 (September 24, 1919): 399–412; Miles L. Colean, Housing for Defense: A Review of the Role of Housing in Relation to America's Defense and a Program for Action (New York: Twentieth Century Fund, 1940), 157.

389 Report of the United States Housing Corporation, vol. 2: 320.

390 Charles C. May, "Housing Development for the United States Naval Ordnance Plant Near Charleston, West Virginia," Architectural Forum 29 (November 1918): 131–35. Also see Report of the United States Housing Corporation (Washington, D. C.: Government Printing Office, 1919), vol. 1: 67, vol. 2: 144–50; "A Housing Development that Solves the Lodger Problem," American Architect 115 (April 23, 1919): 565–69, plates 133–39; S. Allen Chambers Jr., Buildings of West Virginia (New York: Oxford University Press, 2004), 96–97.

391 Report of the United States Housing Corporation, vol. 2: 144.

392 Report of the United States Housing Corporation, vol. 2: 145.

393 Report of the United States Housing Corporation (Washington, D. C.: Government Printing Office, 1919), vol. 1: 68, vol. 2: 178–82; "The Work of the United States Housing Corporation: Project No. 457—Hammond, Indiana," Architecture 39 (February 1919): 52–55; Federal Writers Project, West Virginia: A Guide to the Mountain State (New York: Oxford University Press, 1941), 448.

394 Report of the United States Housing Corporation, vol. 2: 178.

395 Report of the United States Housing Corporation, vol. 2: 181–82.

396 Report of the United States Housing Corporation (Washington, D. C.: Government Printing Office, 1919), vol. 1: 4–5, 66, 288, vol. 2: 104–10; United States Housing Corporation: Hearings Before a Subcommittee of the Committee on Public Buildings and Grounds (Washington, D. C.: Government Printing Office, 1919), 292, 574, 585; "The United States Housing Corporation: Project No. 59 at Bath, Maine," Architectural Record 45 (January 1919): 21–25.

397 Report of the United States Housing Corporation, vol. 2: 104.

398 Report of the United States Housing Corporation, vol. 2: 105.

399 Report of the United States Housing Corporation, vol. 2: 105.

400 Report of the United States Housing Corporation (Washington, D. C.: Government Printing Office, 1919), vol. 1: 7–8, 70, vol. 2: 266–69; United States Housing Corporation: Hearings Before a Subcommittee of the Committee on Public Buildings and Grounds (Washington, D. C.: Government Printing Office, 1919), 361, 500, 585.

401 Report of the United States Housing Corporation, vol. 2: 266.

402 Report of the United States Housing Corporation, vol. 2: 266.

403 Report of the United States Housing Corporation (Washington, D. C.: Government Printing Office, 1919), vol. 1: 9, 72–73, vol. 2: 345–46.

404 *Report of the United States Housing Corporation*, vol. 2: 345.

405 *Report of the United States Housing Corporation* (Washington, D. C.: Government Printing Office, 1919), vol. 1: 66, 175, 211, vol. 2: 93–96; *United States Housing Corporation: Hearings Before a Subcommittee of the Committee on Public Buildings and Grounds* (Washington, D. C.: Government Printing Office, 1919), 349, 585, 600.

406 *Report of the United States Housing Corporation*, vol. 2: 93.

407 *Report of the United States Housing Corporation*, vol. 2: 94.

408 *Report of the United States Housing Corporation* (Washington, D. C.: Government Printing Office, 1919), vol. 1: 47, 70, 175, 211, vol. 2: 249–52; *United States Housing Corporation: Hearings Before a Subcommittee of the Committee on Public Buildings and Grounds* (Washington, D. C.: Government Printing Office, 1919), 585, 594; "War Housing in the United States," *Housing Betterment* 8 (February 1919): 6–13; Miles L. Colean, *Housing for Defense: A Review of the Role of Housing in Relation to America's Defense and a Program for Action* (New York: Twentieth Century Fund, 1940), 156.

409 *Report of the United States Housing Corporation*, vol 2: 250.

410 *Report of the United States Housing Corporation* (Washington, D. C.: Government Printing Office, 1919), vol. 1: 8, 72, 167, 211, vol. 2: 314–18; *United States Housing Corporation: Hearings Before a Subcommittee of the Committee on Public Buildings and Grounds* (Washington, D. C.: Government Printing Office, 1919), 289–90, 314, 585.

411 *Report of the United States Housing Corporation*, vol. 2: 314.

412 "Uncle Sam Builds 256 Houses for Quincy Shipbuilders," *Boston Daily Globe* (September 29, 1918): 31; "Will Open Fore River Dormitories Saturday," *Boston Daily Globe* (December 30, 1918): 14; *Report of the United States Housing Corporation* (Washington, D. C.: Government Printing Office, 1919), vol. 1: 182, 184, 234–35, 256–57, 274–75, 292–93, vol. 2: 323–31; "Government Houses at Quincy, Bath and Bridgeport Will Be Completed," *Boston Daily Globe* (January 19, 1919): 17; Sylvester Baxter, "The Government's Housing Project at Quincy, Mass.," *Architectural Record* 44 (March 1919): 242–61; "Need for Housing Workers Still Great," *American Architect* 115 (March 12, 1919): 391; "Development for the United States Housing Corporation," *Architectural Review* 8 (June 1919): 21–23; "U. S. Tenants at Quincy Seek Change in Lease," *Boston Daily Globe* (August 23, 1919): 12; "Government-Owned Houses Being Sold: Thirty Are Disposed Of at Quincy," *Boston Daily Globe* (July 4, 1920): 10; "Quincy Tenants Won't Be Ousted," *Boston Daily Globe* (November 20, 1920): 14; "U. S. Will Not Oust Tenants at Quincy," *Boston Daily Globe* (November 24, 1920): 1; "Some Limitations on Government Housing," *Housing Betterment* 10 (June 1921): 110–11; Carl Rust Parker, Bremer W. Pond, and Theodora Kimball, eds., *Transactions of the American Society of Landscape Architects, 1909–1921* (Amsterdam, N.Y.: Recorder Press, 1922), 76; "U. S. Turns Over Deeds to 135 Dwellings in Quincy," *Boston Daily Globe* (October 10, 1922): 17; "Quincy," *Boston Daily Globe* (January 13, 1925): 10; Robert Campbell, "Forgotten Utopias," *Boston Globe Sunday Magazine* (May 21, 1995): 18; Lawrence J. Vale, *From the Puritans to the Projects: Public Housing and Public Neighbors* (Cambridge, Mass.: Harvard University Press, 2000), 135–39. Also see Richard Heath, "Architecture as Public Policy," http://www.jphs.org.

413 "Development for the United States Housing Corporation": 21–22.

414 *Report of the United States Housing Corporation*, vol. 2: 323.

415 "Will Open Fore River Dormitories Saturday": 14.

416 James E. McLaughlin, quoted in "Uncle Sam Builds 256 Houses for Quincy Shipbuilders": 31.

417 Baxter, "The Government's Housing Project at Quincy, Mass.": 253, 261.

418 "Development for the United States Housing Corporation": 22–23.

419 Campbell, "Forgotten Utopias": 18.

420 *Report of the United States Housing Corporation* (Washington, D. C.: Government Printing Office, 1919), vol. 1: 71, vol. 2: 308–13; Carl Rust Parker, Bremer W. Pond, and Theodora Kimball, eds., *Transactions of the American Society of Landscape Architects, 1909–1921* (Amsterdam, N.Y.: Recorder Press, 1922), 76.

421 *Report of the United States Housing Corporation* (Washington, D. C.: Government Printing Office, 1919), vol. 1: 71, vol. 2: 292–95; *United States Housing Corporation: Hearings Before a Subcommittee of the Committee on Public Buildings and Grounds* (Washington, D. C.: Government Printing Office, 1919), 284, 290, 585.

422 *Report of the United States Housing Corporation* (Washington, D. C.: Government Printing Office, 1919), vol. 1: 70, vol. 2: 246–48; *United States Housing Corporation: Hearings Before a Subcommittee of the Committee on Public Buildings and Grounds* (Washington, D. C.: Government Printing Office, 1919), 284, 290, 585.

423 *Report of the United States Housing Corporation* (Washington, D. C.: Government Printing Office, 1919), vol. 1: 67, 139, vol. 2: 141–43; *United States Housing Corporation: Hearings Before a Subcommittee of the Committee on Public Buildings and Grounds* (Washington, D. C.: Government Printing Office, 1919), 88, 284, 290, 585.

424 *Report of the United States Housing Corporation* (Washington, D. C.: Government Printing Office, 1919), vol. 2: 141.

425 "Government Plans Big Housing Project," *Wall Street Journal* (September 17, 1918): 5; *Report of the United States Housing Corporation* (Washington, D. C.: Government Printing Office, 1919), vol. 1: 69, vol. 2: 224–27.

426 *Report of the United States Housing Corporation*, vol. 2: 224.

427 *Report of the United States Housing Corporation*, vol. 2: 226.

428 *Report of the United States Housing Corporation*, vol. 2: 226.

429 "Architects and Engineers for U. S. Housing Contracts," *American Architect* 114 (August 28, 1918): 265; "Chamber Assists in Appraisal of Real Estate," *Bulletin of the Chamber of Commerce of the State of New York* (September 1918): 64; "Real Estate Field," *New York Times* (October 24, 1918): 19; *Report of the United States Housing Corporation* (Washington, D. C.: Government Printing Office, 1919), vol. 1: 73, 175, 383, vol. 2: 347–49; *United States Housing Corporation: Hearings Before a Subcommittee of the Committee on Public Buildings and Grounds* (Washington, D. C.: Government Printing Office, 1919), 599; "American Small Houses Lead the World's," *American Architect* 116 (September 24, 1919): 415–25; Carl Rust Parker, Bremer W. Pond, and Theodora Kimball, eds., *Transactions of the American Society of Landscape Architects, 1909–1921* (Amsterdam, N.Y.: Recorder Press, 1922), 75; "Suburban Homes in Active Demand," *New York Times* (September 17, 1926): 36; Miles L. Colean, *Housing for Defense: A Review of the Role of Housing in Relation to America's Defense and*

a Program for Action (New York: Twentieth Century Fund, 1940), 156; Richard Plunz, *A History of Housing in New York City* (New York: Columbia University Press, 1990), 125–26.

430 *Report of the United States Housing Corporation*, vol. 2: 347.

431 *Report of the United States Housing Corporation* (Washington, D. C.: Government Printing Office, 1919), vol. 1: 71, 95, 118, vol. 2: 296–97; *United States Housing Corporation: Hearings Before a Subcommittee of the Committee on Public Buildings and Grounds* (Washington, D. C.: Government Printing Office, 1919), 315, 585; "The Report of the United States Housing Corporation," *The American* 116 (September 24, 1919): 399–412; Lee K. Frankel and Alexander Fleisher, *The Human Factor in Industry* (New York: Macmillan Company, 1920), 264.

432 *Report of the United States Housing Corporation* (Washington, D. C.: Government Printing Office, 1919), vol. 2: 350.

433 "Housing for War Workers, Washington, D. C., United States Housing Corporation," *Architecture* 38 (October 1918): 295–96; *Report of the United States Housing Corporation* (Washington, D. C.: Government Printing Office, 1919), vol. 1: 9, 51, 73–74, 211, 297–99, 306, vol. 2: 350–67; *United States Housing Corporation: Hearings Before a Subcommittee of the Committee on Public Buildings and Grounds* (Washington, D. C.: Government Printing Office, 1919), 33–61, 113–16, 204–10, 600; "War Housing in the United States," *Housing Betterment* 8 (February 1919): 6–13; "The Report of the United States Housing Corporation," *The American* 116 (September 24, 1919): 399–412; C. Ford Peatross, ed., *Capital Drawings: Architectural Designs for Washington, D. C., from the Library of Congress* (Baltimore: Johns Hopkins University Press; Washington, D. C.: Library of Congress, 2005), 156–62, 223–24, 226–30.

434 "Housing for War Workers, Washington, D. C., United States Housing Corporation": 295.

435 "The Russell Senate Office Building," http://www.senate.gov.

436 Judith Paine, "Pioneer Women Architects," in Susana Torre, ed., *Women in American Architecture: A Historic and Contemporary Perspective* (New York: Whitney Library of Design, 1977), 68; Sarah Allaback, *The First American Women Architects* (Urbana: University of Illinois Press, 2008), 136.

437 *Report of the United States Housing Corporation*, vol. 2: 356, 361.

438 Jeffrey P. Ward, "'White Coal': The Birth of a Company Town 100 Years Ago," *Plan Canada* 45 (Autumn 2005): 32–35.

439 Ward, "'White Coal': The Birth of a Company Town 100 Years Ago": 34.

440 "A Canadian Model Industrial Town: Temiskaming, Quebec, Canada," *Garden Cities and Town Planning* 20 (December 1930): 307–8; A. K. Grimmer, "The Development and Operation of a Company-Owned Industrial Town," *Engineering Journal* 17 (May 1934): 219–23; Arthur C. Comey and Max S. Wehrly, "A Study of Planned Communities" (Department of Regional Planning of Harvard University, November 1936): 215–20; Michael Simpson, "Thomas Adams, 1871–1940," in Gordon E. Cherry, ed., *Pioneers in British Planning* (London: Architectural Press, 1981), 27; Gerald Hodge, *Planning Canadian Communities: An Introduction to the Principles, Practice and Participants* (Scarborough, Ontario: Nelson Canada, 1989), 63, 64, 65; Harold Kalman, *A History of Canadian Architecture, Volume 2* (New York: Oxford University Press, 1994), 671–72; Paul Trépanier, "Témiscaming: Une cité-jardin du Nord," in Robert Fortier, ed., *Villes Industrielles Planifiées* (Montréal: Boréal, 1996), 117–52; Richard Symonds, *The Architecture and Planning of the Townsite Development of Corner Brook, 1923–25* (St. John's, Newfoundland: Heritage Foundation of Newfoundland and Labrador, 2001), 4, 6.

441 Comey and Wehrly, "A Study of Planned Communities": 217.

442 Grimmer, "The Development and Operation of a Company-Owned Industrial Town": 223.

443 Thomas Adams, *Recent Advances in Town Planning* (London: J. & A. Churchill, 1932), 162–63; Thomas Adams, *The Design of Residential Areas: Basic Considerations, Principles, and Methods* (Cambridge, Mass.: Harvard University Press, 1934), 258; Jean B. Weir, *Rich in Interest and Charm: The Architecture of Andrew Randall Cobb, 1876–1943* (Halifax, Nova Scotia: Art Gallery of Nova Scotia, 1990), 37–43, 60, 63, 65; Richard Symonds, *The Architecture and Planning of the Townsite Development of Corner Brook, 1923–25* (St. John's, Newfoundland: Heritage Foundation of Newfoundland and Labrador, 2001).

444 Adams, *Recent Advances in Town Planning*, 162.

445 Adams, *Recent Advances in Town Planning*, 163.

446 Arthur C. Comey and Max S. Wehrly, "Planned Communities," (November 1936) in *Supplementary Report of the Urbanism Committee to the National Resources Committee* (Washington, D. C.: U. S. Government Printing Office, 1939), vol. 2: 32–35, 111, 122, 126–27, 130, 145–46; Gilbert A. Stelter and Alan F. J. Artibise, eds., *Power and Place: Canadian Urban Development in the North American Context* (Vancouver: University of British Columbia Press, 1986), 238–43, 244; Gerald Hodge, *Planning Canadian Communities: An Introduction to the Principles, Practice and Participants* (Scarborough, Ontario: Nelson Canada, 1989), 10, 63; John Sewell, *The Shape of the City: Toronto Struggles with Modern Planning* (Toronto: University of Toronto Press, 1993), 46, 48; Harold Kalman, *A History of Canadian Architecture, Volume 2* (New York: Oxford University Press, 1994), 672; *Kapuskasing—Garden City and Model Town* (Ontario: Ontario Heritage Trust, 2007) in http://www.heritagefdn.on.ca/userfiles/page_attachments/Library/1/1528671_Kapuskasing_ENG.pdf.

447 *The First Fifty Years, 1921–1971: A Golden Jubilee History of Kapuskasing* (Kapuskasing: Kapuskasing Golden Jubilee Souvenir Book Committee, 1971), 1, quoted in *Kapuskasing—Garden City and Model Town*, 3.

448 Comey and Wehrly, "Planned Communities," in *Supplementary Report of the Urbanism Committee to the National Resources Committee*, vol. 2: 33, 146.

449 Sewell, *The Shape of the City: Toronto Struggles with Modern Planning*, 46.

450 J. P. Mertz, "Townsite Planning at Pine Falls, Man.," *Canadian Engineer* 57 (July 2, 1929): 109–10; Arthur C. Comey and Max S. Wehrly, "A Study of Planned Communities" (Department of Regional Planning of Harvard University, November 1936): 191–93; Robert Robson, "Manitoba's Resource Towns: The Twentieth Century Frontier," *Manitoba History* no. 16 (August 1988): n.p.

451 Mertz, "Townsite Planning at Pine Falls, Man.": 109.

452 Mertz, "Townsite Planning at Pine Falls, Man.": 109.

453 H. R. Wake, "Building the City of Arvida," *Engineering Journal* 9 (November 1926): 461–64; "Model City Built by Aluminum Industry," *Engineering and Contract Record* 58 (July 1945): 60–65, 108, 110, 112; Fergus Cronin, "Arvida: Ace Company Town," *Saturday Night* 65

(December 13, 1949): 10; Harold Kalman, *A History of Canadian Architecture, Volume 2* (New York: Oxford University Press, 1994), 672; José Igartua, "Vivre à Arvida," in Robert Fortier, ed., *Villes Industrielles Planifiées* (Montréal: Boréal, 1996), 153–73; Lucie K. Morisset and Luc Noppen, "La Ville de l'Aluminum," in Robert Fortier, ed., *Villes Industrielles Planifiées* (Montréal: Boréal, 1996), 174–239; Lucie K. Morisset, "The Washington of the North: The Design and Creation of an Industrial Metropolis," *Society for the Study of Architecture in Canada* 22 (March 1997): 11–18; Lucie K. Morisset, "Non-Fiction Utopia," *Journal of the Society for the Study of Architecture in Canada* 36 (no. 1, 2011): 3–40.

454 Morisset, "The Washington of the North: The Design and Creation of an Industrial Metropolis": 18.

455 Hjalmar E. Skougor, "Rosita, Mexico, a Carefully Planned City; Pleasing, Comfortable and Hygienic—I," *Coal Age* 19 (June 2, 1921): 983–87; Hjalmar E. Skougor, "Rosita, Mexico, a Carefully Planned City; Pleasing, Comfortable and Hygienic—II," *Coal Age* 19 (June 9, 1921): 1037–40; Arthur C. Comey and Max S. Wehrly, "A Study of Planned Communities" (Department of Regional Planning of Harvard University, November 1936): 204–8.

Epilogue

1 Mel C. Scott, *American City Planning Since 1890* (Berkeley: University of California Press, 1969), 540.

2 Frank Lloyd Wright, *The Disappearing City* (New York: W. F. Payson, 1932), reprinted in Bruce Brooks Pfeiffer, ed., *The Essential Frank Lloyd Wright: Critical Writings on Architecture* (Princeton, N.J.: Princeton University Press, 2008), 235–75; Frank Lloyd Wright, "'Broadacre City': An Architect's Vision," *New York Times* (March 20, 1932), V: 8–9; Frank Lloyd Wright, "America Tomorrow," *American Architect* 141 (May 1932): 14–17, 76; Frank Lloyd Wright, "Broadacre City: A New Community Plan," *Architectural Record* 77 (April 1935): 243–54; "Exhibit Model City," *New York Times* (April 14, 1935), X: 2; "Arts in Industry Glorified in Show," *New York Times* (April 16, 1935): 23; Lewis Mumford, "The Sky Line: Mr. Wright's City—Downtown Dignity," *New Yorker* 11 (April 27, 1935): 79–81; "Broadacre City: Frank Lloyd Wright, Architect," *American Architect* 146 (May 1935): 55–62; Baker Brownell and Frank Lloyd Wright, *Architecture and Modern Life* (New York: Harper and Brothers, 1937), 298–35; Meyer Schapiro, "Architect's Utopia," book review, *Partisan Review* 4 (February 1938): 42–47; Frank Lloyd Wright, *An Organic Architecture: The Architecture of Democracy* (London: Lund Humphries & Co., 1939), 26–29; Roy Kantorowich "The Modern Theorists of Planning; Le Corbusier, Frank Lloyd Wright etc.," *South African Architectural Record* 27 (January 1942): 6–15; Paul Goodman and Percival Goodman, "Frank Lloyd Wright on Architecture," *Kenyon Review* 4 (Winter 1942): 7–28; Arthur C. Comey, "When Democracy Builds," book review, *Landscape Architecture* 36 (October 1945): 38–39; Arthur B. Gallion and Simon Eisner, *The Urban Pattern: City Planning and Design* (New York: Van Nostrand, 1951), 126; Frank Lloyd Wright, interview with Oskar Stonorov, January 1951, published in Patrick J. Meehan, ed., *The Master Architect: Conversations with Frank Lloyd Wright* (New York: Wiley, 1984), 119–27; Frank Lloyd Wright, *The Living City* (New York: Horizon Press, 1958), 66–69, 94–96; Carl Feiss, "Broadacre City Revisited: FLW's Restatement, with Embellishments," *Progressive Architecture* 40 (July 1959): 181–82, 188; Peter Blake, *The Master Builders* (New York: Knopf, 1960), 369–71; Robert C. Weinberg, book review, *Journal of the American Institute of Planners* 27 (November 1961): 352–54; Lewis Mumford, "Megalopolis as Anti-City," *Architectural Record* 132 (December 1962): 101–8; George R. Collins, "Broadacre City: Wright's Utopia Reconsidered," in *Four Great Makers of Modern Architecture: Gropius, Le Corbusier, Mies van der Rohe, Wright* (New York: Columbia University, 1963), 55–75; Norris Kelly Smith, *Frank Lloyd Wright: A Study in Architectural Content* (Englewood Cliffs, N. J.: Prentice-Hall, 1966), 148–55; Olgivanna Lloyd Wright, *Frank Lloyd Wright: His Life, His Work, His Words* (New York: Horizon, 1966), 110–20; Vincent Scully, *American Architecture and Urbanism* (New York: Praeger, 1969), 161, 171; Lionel March, "An Architect in Search of Democracy: Broadacre City (1970)," in H. Allen Brooks, ed., *Writings on Wright: Selected Comment on Frank Lloyd Wright* (Cambridge, Mass., and London: MIT Press, 1981), 195–206; Robert C. Twombly, "Undoing the City: Frank Lloyd Wright's Planned Communities," *American Quarterly* 24 (October 1972): 538–49, discussion largely repeated in Robert C. Twombly, *Frank Lloyd Wright: An Interpretative Biography* (New York: Harper & Row, 1973), 177–85; Stephen Grabow, "Frank Lloyd Wright and the American City: The Broadacres Debate," *Journal of the American Institute for Architects* 43 (April 1977): 115–24; Paul Goldberger, "He Had an Answer for Everything," book review, *New York Times* (June 19, 1977), VII: 13, 43; Donald Hoffmann, *Frank Lloyd Wright's Fallingwater: The House and Its History* (New York: Dover, 1978), 12–16; Diane R. Blum, "American Modernism: Suburban Groupings," student paper, c. 1978, Architecture 4375, Columbia University; Giorgio Ciucci, "The City in Agrarian Ideology and Frank Lloyd Wright," in Giorgio Ciucci et al., *The American City: From the Civil War to the New Deal* (Cambridge, Mass.: MIT Press, 1979), 352–75; Stern with Massengale, *The Anglo-American Suburb*, 86; Robert Fishman, *Urban Utopias in the Twentieth Century: Ebenezer Howard, Frank Lloyd Wright, and Le Corbusier* (Cambridge, Mass.: MIT Press, 1982), 122–34; Herbert Muschamp, *Man About Town: Frank Lloyd Wright in New York City* (Cambridge, Mass.: MIT Press, 1983), 175–77, 185–88; John Sergeant, *Frank Lloyd Wright's Usonian Houses* (New York: Whitney Library of Design, 1984), 121–36; Walter L. Creese, *The Crowning of the American Landscape* (Princeton, N.J.: Princeton University Press, 1985), 271–78; Bruce Brooks Pfeiffer, *Frank Lloyd Wright Monograph, 1924–36, vol. 6* (Tokyo: A. D. A. Edita, 1985), 140–49; Robert Fishman, *Bourgeois Utopias: The Rise and Fall of Suburbia* (New York: Basic Books 1987), 188, 203–5; Brendan Gill, *Many Masks: A Life of Frank Lloyd Wright* (New York: G. P. Putnam's Sons, 1987), 334, 336–38; Anthony Alofsin, "Visions and Revisions," *Center* 5 (1989): 5–43; Donald Leslie Johnson, *Frank Lloyd Wright Versus America: The 1930s* (Cambridge, Mass., and London: MIT Press, 1990), 108–41; Alvin Rosenbaum, *Usonia: Frank Lloyd Wright's Design for America* (Washington, D. C.: Preservation Press, 1993), 111–22; Denise Scott Brown, "Wright in the Rear-View Mirror," *New York Times* (September 12, 1993), II: 56; Cynthia L. Girling and Kenneth I. Helphand, *Yard, Street, Park: The Design of Suburban Open Space* (New York: Wiley, 1994), 69–76; Jon Lang, *Urban Design: The American Experience* (New York: Van Nostrand Reinhold, 1994), 49–50; Paul Goldberger, "Not an Urbanist, Only a Genius," *New York Times* (February 13, 1994), VI: 48–49; Witold Rybczynski, "Not an Urbanist, Only a Genius," letter to the editor, *New York Times* (March 13, 1994), VI: 10; Lionel March, "Broadacre City: Intellectual Sources," *Frank Lloyd Wright: The Phoenix Papers, Vol. 1: Broadacre City* (Tempe, Ariz.: Herberger Center, 1995), 80–117; John Sergeant, "Broadacre City: Looking Backward 1991–1935," in *Frank Lloyd Wright: The Phoenix Papers, Vol. 1: Broadacre City*, 68–77; K. Paul Zygas, "Broadacre City as Artifact," in *Frank Lloyd Wright: The Phoenix Papers, Vol. 1: Broadacre City*, 18–30; Arthur C. Nelson, "The Planning of Exurban America: Lessons from Frank Lloyd Wright's Broadacre City," *Journal of Architectural and Planning Research* 12 (Winter 1995): 337–56; Robert McCarter, *Frank Lloyd Wright* (London: Phaidon, 1997), 243–47; Patricia M. Young, "Frank Lloyd Wright: His Search for the Perfect Blend of Nature and City in His Model of Broadacre City" (Master's thesis, California State University Dominguez Hills, 1997); Jean-Louis Cohen, "Wright's Ideas of Twentieth-Century Urbanism and Their European Echoes," in David G. De Long, ed., *Frank Lloyd Wright and the Living City* (Milan: Skira, 1998), 280–93; David G. De Long, "Frank Lloyd Wright and the Evolution of City Living," in De Long, ed., *Frank Lloyd Wright and the Living City*, 25–42; Peter Zellner, "'The Big City Is No Longer Modern,'" *Daidalos* 69–70 (December 1998–January 1999): 68–75; Michael J. Lewis, "The American View of Landscape," *New Criterion* 18 (April 2000): 4–13; Charles E. Aguar and Berdeana Aguar, *Wrightscapes* (New York: McGraw-Hill, 2002), 222, 226–28; Michiel Dehaene, "Broadacre City: The City in the Eye of the Beholder," *Journal of Architectural and Planning Research* 19 (Summer 2002): 91–109; Ada Louise Huxtable, *Frank Lloyd Wright* (New York: Penguin, 2004), 201–2; Donald Leslie Johnson, "Frank Lloyd Wright's Community Planning," *Journal of Planning History* 3 (February 2004): 3–28; Tom Martinson, *The Atlas of American Architecture: 2000 Years of Architecture, City Planning, Landscape Architecture and Civil Engineering* (New York: Rizzoli International Publications, 2009), 485–86; Vittorio Magnago Lampugnani, *Die Stadt im 20. Jahrhundert* (Berlin: Verlag Klaus Wagenbach, 2010), 500–503, 514–18.

3 Johnson, "Frank Lloyd Wright's Community Planning": 3–28.

4 Quoted in Collins, "Broadacre City: Wright's Utopia Reconsidered," in *Four Great Makers of Modern Architecture: Gropius, Le Corbusier, Mies van der Rohe, Wright*, 71.

5 Quoted in Wright, *Frank Lloyd Wright: His Life, His Work, His Words*, 110.

6 Blum, "American Modernism: Suburban Groupings": 3.

7 For Wright's St. Mark's-in-the-Bouwerie proposal, see Stern, Gilmartin, and Mellins, assisted by Fishman and Gastil, *New York 1930*, 40–41, 167–69, 447–49.

8 Wright, *The Disappearing City*, reprinted in Pfeiffer, ed., *The Essential Frank Lloyd Wright: Critical Writings on Architecture*, 266.

9 Stern, Gilmartin, and Mellins, assisted by Fishman and Gastil, *New York 1930*, 742–45, 748–49, 751.

10 Feiss, "Broadacre City Revisited: FLW's Restatement, with Embellishments": 188.

11 Fishman, *Urban Utopias in the Twentieth Century: Ebenezer Howard, Frank Lloyd Wright, and Le Corbusier*, 127–28.

12 Anthony C. Antoniades, "Architecture From Inside Lens: Jokes and Stories About Celebrated Architects," *A + U* 106 (July 1979): 3–22.

13 Leon Neyfakh, "Green Building," *Boston Globe* (January 30, 2011), K: 1. Also see Andres Duany, Elizabeth Plater-Zyberk, and Jeff Speck, *Suburban Nation: The Rise of Sprawl and the Decline of the American Dream* (New York: North Point Press, 2000); Dolores Hayden, *A Field Guide to Sprawl* (New York: W. W. Norton, 2004); Robert Bruegmann, *Sprawl: A Compact History* (Chicago: University of Chicago Press, 2005); William S. Saunders, ed., *Sprawl and Suburbia: A Harvard Design Magazine Reader* (Minneapolis: University of Minnesota Press, 2005); Galina Tachieva, *Sprawl Repair Manual* (Washington, D. C.: Island Press, 2010).

14 Charles Siegel, *Unplanning: Livable Cities and Political Choices* (Berkeley, Calif.: Preservation Institute, 2010), 32–33. Also see Herbert J. Gans, *The Levittowners: Ways of Life and Politics in a New Suburban Community* (New York: Pantheon Books, 1967).

15 Vincent Scully, "The Threat and Promise of Urban Redevelopment in New Haven," *Zodiac* 17 (1967): 171–75; Vincent Scully, "RIBA Discourse 1969: A Search for Principle between Two Wars," *RIBA Journal* 76 (June 1969): 240–47, reprinted in Vincent Scully, *Modern Architecture and Other Essays* (Princeton, N. J.: Princeton University Press, 2003), 142–57; Vincent Scully, *American Architecture and Urbanism*, new rev. ed. (New York: Henry Holt and Co., 1988), 246–55; Neil Levine, "Introduction," in Scully, *Modern Architecture and Other Essays*, 24–25.

16 Jerry Hulse, "Dream Realized—Disneyland Opens," *Los Angeles Times* (July 18, 1955), A: 1, 26; Ruth P. Shellhorn, "Disneyland: Dream Built in One Year Through Teamwork of Many Artists," *Landscape Architecture* 46 (April 1956): 125–36; Charles W. Moore, "You Have to Pay for the Public Life," *Perspecta* 9 (1965): 57–106; Reyner Banham, *Los Angeles: The Architecture of Four Ecologies* (London: Allen Lane, 1971; Berkeley and Los Angeles: University of California Press, 2001), 108–11; Martin A. Sklar, *Walt Disney's Disneyland* (Anaheim, Calif.: Walt Disney Productions, 1969); *Disneyland* (New York: Crescent Books, 1985); Robert A. M. Stern, *Pride of Place: Building the American Dream* (Boston: Houghton Mifflin; New York: American Heritage, 1986), 211–12; Kevin Starr, *Golden Dreams: California in an Age of Abundance, 1950–1963* (New York: Oxford University Press, 2009), 15–16; Kathy Merlock Jackson and Mark I. West, eds., *Disneyland and Culture: Essays on the Parks and Their Influence* (Jefferson, N. C.: P McFarland & Co., 2011).

17 James Rouse, quoted in Joshua Olsen, *Better Places, Better Lives: A Biography of James Rouse* (Washington, D.C.: Urban Land Institute, 2003), 241, and "A Moment with Walt Disney," http://samlanddisney.blogspot.com/2010/03/moment-with-walt-disney.html.

18 Moore, "You Have to Pay for the Public Life": 65.

19 Robert Venturi, Denise Scott Brown, and Steven Izenour, *Learning from Las Vegas* (Cambridge, Mass.: MIT Press, 1972), 176–79. For Stern's early advocacy of the garden suburb model, see Robert A. M. Stern, "The Suburban Alternative for the 'Middle City,'" *Architectural Record* 164 (August 1978): 93–100; Peter Arnell and Ted Bickford, eds., *Robert A. M. Stern: Buildings and Projects 1965–1980* (New York: Rizzoli International Publications, 1981), 118–21; Stern with Massengale, *The Anglo-American Suburb*.

20 See Peter M. Wolf, *Another Chance for Cities* (New York: Whitney Museum of American Art, 1970).

21 Robert A. M. Stern, "New Directions in American Architecture," Preston Thomas Memorial Lectures, Cornell University College of Art, Architecture, and Planning, Ithaca, NY, October 23, 1976, revised in 1993 and reprinted in Cynthia Davidson, ed., *Architecture on the*

Edge of Postmodernism: Collected Essays, 1964–1988, Robert A. M. Stern (New Haven, Conn.: Yale University Press, 2009), 51–54; Robert A. M. Stern, "The Suburban Alternative for the 'Middle City,'" *Architectural Record* 164 (August 1978): 93–100; Franco Raggi, ed., *Europa-America: architetture urbane, alternative suburbane* (Venice: La Biennale di Venezia, 1978); Barbaralee Diamonstein, *American Architecture Now* (New York: Rizzoli International Publications, 1980), 245–46; Robert A. M. Stern, "Architecture, History, and Historiography at the End of the Modernist Era," in John E. Hancock, ed., *History in, of, and for Architecture* (Cincinnati: The School of Architecture and Interior Design, 1981), 34–43; Stern with Massengale, *The Anglo-American Suburb*, 92; Peter Arnell and Ted Bickford, eds., *Robert A. M. Stern: Buildings and Projects 1965–1980* (New York: Rizzoli International Publications, 1981), 118–21; Stan Pinkwas, "Suburbia's Cutting Edge," *Metropolis* 2 (June 1983): cover, 10–14, 26; Vincent Scully, "Buildings without Souls," *New York Times* (September 8, 1985), VI: 43, 62, 64, 66, 109–10, 116; Vincent Scully, *American Architecture and Urbanism*, new rev. ed. (New York: Henry Holt and Co., 1988), 279; Peter G. Rowe, *Making a Middle Landscape* (Cambridge, Mass., and London: MIT Press, 1991), 271–72; Walter Creese, *The Search for Environment: The Garden City Before and After*, rev. ed. (Baltimore: Johns Hopkins University Press, 1992), 359–63; Vincent Scully, "The Architecture of Community," in Peter Katz, *The New Urbanism: Toward an Architecture of Community* (New York: McGraw-Hill, 1994), 229–30; Jon T. Lang, *Urban Design: The American Experience* (New York: Van Nostrand Reinhold, 1994), 96; Jonathan Barnett, *The Fractured Metropolis* (New York: HarperCollins, 1995), 145–47; Stern, Mellins, and Fishman, *New York 1960*, 925–26; Robert A. M. Stern, "In Praise of Invented Towns," in Cynthia Davidson, ed., *Tradition and Invention in Architecture: Conversations and Essays, Robert A. M. Stern* (New Haven, Conn., and London: Yale University Press, 2011), 39–46; Andrés Duany, Elizabeth Plater-Zyberk, and Robert Alminana, *The New Civic Art: Elements of Town Planning* (New York: Rizzoli International Publications, 2003), 63; Robert A. M. Stern, "Garden City Suburbs," *Wharton Real Estate Review* XI (Fall 2007): 84–93.

22 Creese, *The Search for Environment*, 362.

23 Barnett, *The Fractured Metropolis*, 134, 135, 145–47. Also see "In Progress: Ghent Square," *Progressive Architecture* 57 (May 1976): 44.

24 Marta Gutman and Richard Plunz, "Anatomy of Insurrection," in Richard Oliver, ed., *The Making of an Architect, 1881–1981* (New York: Rizzoli International Publications, 1981), 260–61; Stern, "Architecture, History, and Historiography at the End of the Modernist Era," in Hancock, ed., *History in, of, and for Architecture*, 34–43.

25 Scully, "Buildings without Souls": 63. For Charlotte Gardens, see Stern, Fishman, and Tilove, *New York 2000*, 1215–16.

26 Blair Kamin, "Public Housing in 1999: A Hard Assessment," *Architectural Record* 187 (November 1999): 76–83, 200–201; Peter Calthorpe and William Fulton, *The Regional City* (Washington, D. C.: Island Press, 2001), 253–70; Kim A. O'Connell, "A Change of Address," *Journal of Housing & Community Development* (March–April 2004): 45–48; Robert Fishman, ed., *New Urbanism Peter Calthorpe vs. Lars Lerup, Michigan Debates on Urbanism, vol. II* (Ann Arbor: University of Michigan, 2005), 25–31; Henry Cisneros and Lora Engdahl, eds., *From Despair to Hope: HOPE VI and the New Promise of Public Housing in America's Cities* (Washington, D.C.: Brookings Institution Press, 2009); "Hope VI Projects," http://www.calthorpe.com; http://bladesandgoven. com.

27 Vincent Scully, *American Architecture and Urbanism*, new rev. ed. (New York: Henry Holt and Company, 1988), 263–65; Philip Langdon, "A Good Place to Live," *Atlantic Monthly* (March 1988): 39–60; HRH The Prince of Wales, *A Vision of Britain: A Personal View of Architecture* (New York: Doubleday, 1989), 143–46; Robert A. M. Stern, "Planned Communities: They Reflect the Search for the Ideal," in Lisa Taylor, ed., *Housing: Symbol, Structure, Site* (New York: Rizzoli International Publications, 1990), 68–69; Alex Krieger, ed., *Andres Duany and Elizabeth Plater-Zyberk: Towns and Town-Making Principles* (New York: Rizzoli International Publications, 1991); Vincent Scully, "Seaside and New Haven," in Krieger, ed., *Andres Duany and Elizabeth Plater-Zyberk: Towns and Town-Making Principles*, 17–20; David Mohney and Keller Easterling, *Seaside: Making a Town in America* (New York: Princeton Architectural Press, 1991); Andres Duany and Elizabeth Plater-Zyberk, "The Second Coming of the American Small Town," *Wilson Quarterly* 16 (Winter 1992): 19–48; James Howard Kunstler, *The Geography of Nowhere: The Rise and Decline of America's Man-Made Landscape* (New York: Simon and Schuster, 1993), 257; Philip Langdon, *A Better Place to Live* (Amherst: University of Massachusetts Press, 1994), 107–16; *Seaside: Text and Photography by Steven Brooke* (Gretna, La.: Pelican Publishing Company, 1995); Witold Rybczynski, "This Old House: The Rise of Family Values Architecture," *New Republic* (May 8, 1995): 14–16; Julie V. Iovine, "Boom vs. Bungalow in Seaside," *New York Times* (June 10, 1997), C: 1; Kathleen LaFrank, "Seaside, Florida: 'The New Town–The Old Ways,'" *Perspectives in Vernacular Architecture* 6 (1997): 111–21; Robert A. M. Stern, "In Praise of Invented Towns," in Cynthia Davidson, ed., *Tradition and Invention in Architecture,Conversations and Essays, Robert A. M. Stern* (New Haven, Conn., and London: Yale University Press, 2011), 39–46; Jean François Lejeune, "Verso Nuove Cittá per L'America: Le Fonti Del New Urbanism," in Gabriele Tagliaventi, ed., *Rinascimento Urbano: La Cittá nel Terzo Millennio* (Milan: Teleura, 2000), 55–57; Todd W. Bressi, ed., *The Seaside Debates* (New York: Rizzoli International Publications, 2002); Susan Klaus, *A Modern Arcadia* (Amherst: University of Massachusetts Press, 2002), 159–61; Alexander Garvin, *The American City: What Works, What Doesn't*, 2nd ed. (New York: McGraw-Hill, 2002), 386–89; Andrés Duany, Elizabeth Plater-Zyberk, and Robert Alminana, *The New Civic Art: Elements of Town Planning* (New York: Rizzoli International Publications, 2003), 91; Dolores Hayden, *Building Suburbia* (New York: Pantheon Books, 2003), 203–9; Witold Rybczynski, "Seaside Revisited: A Model Town, 25 Years Later," (February 28, 2007), www.slate.com; Tom Martinson, *The Atlas of American Architecture: 2000 Years of Architecture, City Planning, Landscape Architecture and Civil Engineering* (New York: Rizzoli International Publications, 2009), 320; Vittorio Magnago Lampugnani, *Die Stadt im 20. Jahrhundert* (Berlin: Verlag Klaus Wagenbach, 2010), 798–801; Dhiru A. Thadani, *Visions of Seaside: Foundation/Evolution/Imagination: Built & Unbuilt Architecture* (New York: Rizzoli International Publications, 2013).

28 Robert S. Davis, quoted in *Seaside: Text and Photography by Steven Brooke*, 15.

29 Kunstler, *The Geography of Nowhere*, 257.

30 Andres Duany and Elizabeth Plater-Zyberk, *Towns and Town-Making Principles* (New York: Rizzoli International Publications, 1991), 52–57; Beth Dunlop, "Our Towns," *Architectural Record* 179 (October 1981): 110–19; Peter Katz, *The New Urbanism: Toward an Architecture of Community* (New York: McGraw-Hill, 1994), 30–45; Witold Rybczynski, "This Old House: The Rise of Family Values Architecture," *New Republic* (May 8, 1995): 14–16.

31 Witold Rybczynski, *Last Harvest: How a Cornfield Became New Daleville* (New York: Scribner, 2007). Also see Robert A. M. Stern, "Garden City Suburbs," *Wharton Real Estate Review* XI (Fall 2007), 84–93.

32 "Prince Charles and the Architectural Debate," *Architectural Design* 59 (1989): 46–55; Dan Cruickshank, "Model Vision," *Architects' Journal* 189 (June 28, 1989): 24–29; Dan Cruickshank, "Village Vision," *Architects' Journal* 194 (October 1991): 10–11; Richard Economakis, ed., *Leon Krier: Architecture and Urban Design, 1967–1992* (London: Academy Editions, 1992), 261–73; *Demetri Porphyrios* (London: Academy Editions, 1993), 50–51; Robert Thorne, "Town Design That Puts Buildings Before Traffic," *Architects' Journal* 197 (January 1993): 23; "Leon Krier: Poundbury," *Architectural Design* 63 (May–June 1993): 42–49; Leon Krier, "Poundbury Masterplan: Dorchester, Dorset, 1988–91," *Architectural Design* 63 (September–October 1993): 70–81; Rosemary Hill, "A Breath of Life," *Perspectives on Architecture* 3 (October–November 1996): 58–61; Andreas Papadakis, *Classical Modern Architecture* (Paris: Terrail, 1997), 188–96; John Walker, "Prince Charming?" *Architectural Review* 202 (July 1997): 68–72; Michele Thompson-Fawcett, "Leon Krier and the Organic Revival with Urban Policy and Practice," *Planning Perspectives* 13 (1998): 180–85; Gabriele Tagliaventi, *Rinascimento Urbano: La Città nel Terzo Millenio* (Milan: Teleura, 2000), 31–33; Jo Allen Gouse, ed., *Great Planned Communities* (Washington, D. C.: Urban Land Institute, 2002), 160–69, 281; Mervyn Miller, "Garden Cities and Suburbs: At Home and Abroad," *Journal of Planning History* 1 (February 2002): 24–25; Clive Aslet, "In Praise of Poundbury," *Country Life* 197 (June 26, 2003): 84–89; Robert Campbell, "Getting It Right (Maybe a Little Too Right) in Well-Behaved England," *Architectural Record* 192 (November 2004): 75–76; Dennis Hardy, *Poundbury: The Town that Charles Built* (London: Town and Country Planning Association, 2006); His Royal Highness The Prince of Wales, "On Civitas," *Clem Labine's Traditional Building* 19 (February 2006): 240–42; Lawrence O. Houstoun, "Place Making at Poundbury," *Urban Land* 65 (July 2006): 78–81; Gillian Darley, "Poundbury Unpicked," *Architects' Journal* 228 (November 13, 2008): 41–42; Leon Krier, *The Architecture of Community* (Washington, D. C.: Island Press, 2009), 99–101, 151–67, 420–35; Michael Z. Wise, "Preservation: Poundbury," *Travel and Leisure* (November 2009): 60–66; Vittorio Magnago Lampugnani, *Die Stadt im 20. Jahrhundert* (Berlin: Verlag Klaus Wagenbach, 2010), 830–32; *Three Classicists* (Oxford: Bardwell Press, 2010), 37, 44–45, 50–52.

33 Krier, "Poundbury Masterplan: Dorchester, Dorset, 1988–91": 71. Also see HRH The Prince of Wales, *A Vision of Britain: A Personal View of Architecture* (New York: Doubleday, 1989).

34 Cruickshank, "Village Vision": 11.

35 Cruickshank, "Model Vision": 24, 29.

36 Quoted in Wise, "Preservation: Poundbury": 62.

37 Quoted in Gouse, ed., *Great Planned Communities*, 161.

38 Stephen Bayley, quoted in Wise, "Preservation: Poundbury": 66.

39 HRH Prince Charles, The Prince of Wales, quoted in Gouse, ed., *Great Planned Communities*, 163.

40 Miller, "Garden Cities and Suburbs: At Home and Abroad": 24–25.

41 Andres Duany, "In Celebration," *Urban Land* 61 (January 2002): 57–61. Also see Beth Dunlop, *Building a Dream: The Art of Disney Architecture* (New York: Henry N. Abrams, 1996); Witold Rybczynski, "Tomorrowland," *New Yorker* 72 (July 22, 1996): 36–39; The Celebration Company, *Celebration Pattern Book*, 2nd ed. (1997); Ada Louise Huxtable, *The Unreal America: Architecture and Illusion* (New York: New Press, 1997), 64–67; Reed Kroloff, "Disney Builds a Town," *Architecture* (August 1997): 114–18; Peter Morris Dixon, ed., *Robert A. M. Stern: Buildings and Projects, 1993–1998* (New York: Monacelli Press, 1998), 90–98; Robert A. M. Stern, "In Praise of Invented Towns," in Cynthia Davidson, ed., *Tradition and Invention in Architecture: Conversations and Essays, Robert A. M. Stern* (New Haven, Conn., and London: Yale University Press, 2011), 39–46; Douglas Frantz and Catherine Collins, *Celebration, U. S. A.* (New York: Henry Holt and Company, 1999); Andrew Ross, *The Celebration Chronicles: Life, Liberty, and the Pursuit of Property Value in Disney's New Town* (New York: Ballantine Books, 1999); Jo Allen Gause, ed., *Great Planned Communities* (Washington, D. C.: Urban Land Institute, 2002), 50–60; Alexander Garvin, *The American City: What Works, What Doesn't*, 2nd ed. (New York: McGraw-Hill, 2002), 417–20; Eugenie L. Birch, "Five Generations of the Garden City," in Kermit C. Parsons and David Schuyler, eds., *From Garden City to Green City: The Legacy of Ebenezer Howard* (Baltimore: The Johns Hopkins University Press, 2002), 186–88; Andrés Duany, Elizabeth Plater-Zyberk, and Robert Alminana, *The New Civic Art: Elements of Town Planning* (New York: Rizzoli International Publications, 2003), 91; Dolores Hayden, *Building Suburbia: Green Fields and Urban Growth, 1820–2000* (New York: Pantheon Books, 2003), 208–15; Michael Lassell, *Celebration: The Story of a Town* (New York: Disney Editions, 2004); Michael Bierut, *Seventy-Nine Short Essays on Design* (New York: Princeton Architectural Press, 2007), 200–203; Karrie Jacobs, "Paradise, U. S. A.," *Travel and Leisure* (February 2007): 151–78; Tom Martinson, *The Atlas of American Architecture: 2000 Years of Architecture, City Planning, Landscape Architecture and Civil Engineering* (New York: Rizzoli International Publications, 2009), 374–75; Vittorio Magnago Lampugnani, *Die Stadt im 20. Jahrhundert* (Berlin: Verlag Klaus Wagenbach, 2010), 803–8.

42 Walt Disney, quoted in Dunlop, *Building a Dream*, 55.

43 Duany, "In Celebration": 58–59.

44 Kroloff, "Disney Builds a Town": 116.

45 Michael Eisner, quoted in Frantz and Collins, *Celebration, U. S. A.*, 59.

46 Huxtable, *The Unreal America*, 65.

47 Vincent Scully, quoted in Frantz and Collins, *Celebration, U. S. A.*, 8.

48 Peter Katz, "Notes on the History of the New Urbanism," in *The Seaside Debates: A Critique of the New Urbanism* (New York: Rizzoli International Publications, 2002), 35.

49 "The Charter of the New Urbanism," in Peter Calthorpe and William Fulton, *The Regional City: Planning for the End of Sprawl* (Washington, D. C.: Island Press, 2001), 282–85.

50 Andres Duany, quoted in Katz, "Notes on the History of New Urbanism": 34.

51 For a discussion of landscape urbanism seen from the point of view of New Urbanism, see *Landscape Urbanism and its Discontents: Dissimulating the Sustainable City*, eds. Andrés Duany and Emily Talen (Gabriola, BC: New Society Publishers, 2013).

PHOTOGRAPHERS

Aaron: Peter Aaron
Adkisson: Dale Adkisson
Ames: David Ames
Andersen: Line Andersen
Andrew: citizenandrew,
    licensed under Creative Commons
    Attribution-NoDerivs 3.0 Unported
Angeles: Los Angeles,
    licensed under Creative Commons
    Attribution-ShareAlike 3.0 Unported
Anoldent: Anoldent,
    licensed under Creative Commons
    Attribution-ShareAlike 2.0 Generic
Anom: Anomalous_A
Antony: Doris Antony,
    licensed under Creative Commons
    Attribution-ShareAlike 3.0 Unported
Aquitaine: GTD Aquitaine/
    public domain
Arild: ArildV, licensed under Creative
    Commons Attribution-ShareAlike
    3.0 Unported
Arl: Arlington County,
    licensed under Creative Commons
    Attribution-ShareAlike 2.0 Generic
Arm: army.arch, licensed under
    Creative Commons Attribution-
    ShareAlike 2.0 Generic
Arnold: Arnoldius,
    licensed under Creative Commons
    Attribution 3.0 Unported
Asseline: Stéphane Asseline,
    ADAGP, 2003
Augustsson: Jan Augustsson
Averette: Marc Averette,
    licensed under Creative Commons
    Attribution-ShareAlike 3.0 Unported
Avery: John Avery
Ayumi: taylorandayumi
Azambuja: Paulo Azambuja
Bächinger: Rosmarie Bächinger
Baer: Plan drawn by Pat Hays Baer
Bakker: A. Bakker,
    licensed under Creative Commons
    Attribution-NoDerivs 3.0 Unported
Barnett: A. L. Barnett
Bartlett: Brian Bartlett
Beall: Jeffrey Beall,
    licensed under Creative Commons
    Attribution-ShareAlike 3.0 Unported
Beck: Vivienne Beck
Ben: Ben2, licensed under Creative
    Commons Attribution-NoDerivs
    3.0 Unported
Ben-Joseph: Eran Ben-Joseph
Benkid: Benkid77, licensed under
    GNU Free Documentation
Bergman: Ronald Bergman
Berman: Dan Berman
Bernoully: Moritz Bernoully
Best: Andy Best
Betts: Helen Betts
Bidgee: Bidgee,
    licensed under Creative
    Commons Attribution-ShareAlike
    2.0 Generic
Birchall: Copyright Eugene Birchall
    and licensed for reuse under
    Creative Commons Attribution-
    ShareAlike 2.0 Generic
Bird: Copyright Richard Bird and
    licensed for reuse under Creative
    Commons Attribution-ShareAlike
    2.0 Generic
Blanc: Bernard Blanc
Blenkin: Copyright Des
    Blenkinsopp and licensed
    for reuse under Creative
    Commons Attribution-
    ShareAlike 2.0 Generic
Blöss: Christian Blöss
Boardman: David Boardman
Boehl: Emil Boehl

Böhringer: Friedrich Böhringer,
    licensed under Creative Commons
    Attribution-ShareAlike 2.5 Generic
Bolton: Humphrey Bolton
Bombieri: Giorgio Bombieri
Boozer: Mark Boozer
Bossi: Andrew Bossi,
    licensed under Creative Commons
    Attribution-ShareAlike 2.5 Generic
Boucher: Jack E. Boucher
Bouvet: Hubert Bouvet © 2010
Brooke: Steven Brooke
Brown: Elliott Brown,
    licensed under Creative Commons
    Attribution-ShareAlike 2.0 Generic
Buchhändler: Buchhändler,
    licensed under Creative
    Commons Attribution-
    ShareAlike 3.0 Unported
Bunjes: Alex Bunjes
Burgert: Burgert Brothers
Bürgmann: Peter Bürgmann
Cabezos: Julian Cabezos
Cadman: Steve Cadman,
    licensed under Creative Commons
    Attribution-ShareAlike 2.0 Generic
Caldwell: Geoff Caldwell
Canaan: Canaan,
    licensed under Creative Commons
    Attribution-ShareAlike 3.0 Unported
Cardwell: Kenneth Cardwell
CCaldwell: Charlotte Caldwell
Chamberlain: Oliver Chamberlain
Cheek: Richard Cheek
Childs: C. R. Childs
Chroustchoff: Natasha de Chroustchoff
Clarke: Diane Clarke
Clemens: Clemens,
    licensed under Creative Commons
    Attribution-ShareAlike 3.0 Austria
Clinco: Demion Clinco
Col: Colros,
    licensed under Creative Commons
    Attribution-ShareAlike 2.0 Generic
Collischonn: Hermann Collischonn
Comellec: Didier Comellec
Coyne: Michael Coyne
CPSmith: C P Smith, licensed under
    Creative Commons Attribution-
    ShareAlike 2.0 Generic
Crews: David Robert Crews
Cschirp: Cschirp, licensed under
    Creative Commons Attribution-
    ShareAlike 3.0 Germany
Cuan: David Cuan
Currlin: Wolfgang Currlin
Dalbéra: Jean-Pierre Dalbéra,
    licensed under Creative Commons
    Attribution 2.0 Generic
Dark: darkblue
Deul: C. A. Deul
Dezidor: Dezidor,
    licensed under Creative Commons
    Attribution-ShareAlike 3.0 Unported
Dias: Michele Dias
Dixon: Oliver Dixon, licensed for
    reuse under Creative Commons
    Attribution-ShareAlike 2.0 Generic
Dobrowolski: Jaroslaw Dobrowolski
Dogs: Wolf-Rüdiger Dogs
Dorrell: Copyright Richard Dorrell
    and licensed for reuse under
    Creative Commons Attribution-
    ShareAlike 2.0 Generic
Doug: Dougtone
Doyle: Miles Doyle
Drews: Ralf-Dieter Drews
Dukker: Gerrard Dukker
DWilson: David Wilson, licensed
    under Creative Commons
    Attribution 2.0 Generic
Dzikowski: Francis Dzikowski
Ebyabe: Ebyabe, licensed under
    Creative Commons Attribution-
    ShareAlike 3.0 Unported

Eccles: Copyright Pauline Eccles and
    licensed for reuse under Creative
    Commons Attribution-ShareAlike
    2.0 Generic
Eckhardt: Juergen Eckhardt
Eddy: Eddy1988, licensed under
    Creative Commons Attribution-
    ShareAlike 3.0 Unported
Egermann: Heinz Egermann
Eino: Heinonen Eino
Eklund: Calle Eklund/V-wolf,
    licensed under Creative Commons
    Attribution-ShareAlike 3.0 Unported
Ellgaard: Holger.Ellgaard,
    licensed under Creative Commons
    Attribution-ShareAlike 3.0 Unported
Elliott: Clyde Elliott
Emerson: Brad Emerson
EMunro: Ewan Munro,
    licensed under Creative Commons
    Attribution-ShareAlike 2.0 Generic
Eskens: Marloes Eskens
Ewing: M. Keith Ewing
Fairchild: Sherman M. Fairchild
Feigenbaum: David Feigenbaum
Felix: Sludgegulper,
    licensed under Creative Commons
    Attribution-ShareAlike 2.0 Generic
Ferguson: Cheryl Caldwell
    Ferguson, Ph.D.
Fischer: William E. Fischer Jr.
Fishbaugh: W. A. Fishbaugh
Fleck: Clare Fleck, Knebworth
    House Archive
Fleger: Hans-Dieter Fleger
Ford: Bruce S. Ford
Franck: Charles L.
    Franck Photographers
Free: Freekee
Frerichs: Stefan Frerichs,
    licensed under Creative Commons
    Attribution-ShareAlike 2.0 Generic
Gagnon: Bernard Gagnon
Gardner: Rev. Stephen Gardner
Garvin: Alexander Garvin
Gehrmann: Marek Gehrmann,
    licensed under Creative Commons
    Attribution-ShareAlike 3.0 Unported
Gerlach: Martin Gerlach
Giacomelli: Pietro Giacomelli
Gottscho-Schleisner: Samuel H.
    Gottscho; William H. Schleisner
Gougeon: Aurélie Gougeon
Gräfe: Ulrich Gräfe
Graham: Julian P. Graham
Grayson: Copyright J Grayson
    and licensed for reuse under
    Creative Commons Attribution-
    ShareAlike 2.0 Generic
Green: Tim Green,
    licensed under Creative Commons
    Attribution 2.0 Generic
Greene: A. S. Greene
Guerra: Marcos Guerra
Gugerell: Peter Gugerell
Ha'Eri: Bobak Ha'Eri,
    licensed under Creative Commons
    Attribution-ShareAlike 2.5 Generic
Haeferl: Haeferl,
    licensed under Creative Commons
    Attribution-ShareAlike 3.0 Austria
Hagemann: Otto Hagemann
Halama: Rainer Halama
Haley: Chris Haley
Hamilton: Maxwell Hamilton,
    licensed under Creative Commons
    Attribution-ShareAlike 2.0 Generic
Hansa: Hansa Luftbild
Harris: Harris & Ewing
Heard: heardjoin
Heegmann: Jürgen Heegmann
Heinrich: Rolf Heinrich
Heisey: Greg Heisey
Henschen: Patricia Henschen
Holzheimer: Nadine Holzheimer

Honegger: Mark Honegger
Hope-Fitch: Christopher Hope-Fitch
Horn: Markus Horn
Hornung: Piotr Hornung
Houghton: John Houghton
Houlton: Walter Houlton
HSmith: Harold Smith
Hubacher: Max Hubacher
Hunt: Gene Hunt,
    licensed under Creative Commons
    Attribution-ShareAlike 2.0 Generic
Icema: Iceman93,
    licensed under Creative Commons
    Attribution-NoDerivs 3.0 Unported
Igor: Raphael Igor/GNU
    Free Documentation License
Indech: Indech
Invis: Invisigoth67,
    licensed under Creative Commons
    Attribution-ShareAlike 3.0 Unported
Irid: Iridescent,
    licensed under GNU Free
    Documentation License
Ives/Townsend: Thomas Ives and
    Mike Townsend
Jack: Harry Jack, Edinburgh, Scotland
Jackson: Jackson-fu
Jahn: Harald A. Jahn
Jameson: Andrew Jameson,
    licensed under Creative Commons
    Attribution-ShareAlike 3.0 Unported
Jasmine: JasmineElias,
    licensed under Creative Commons
    Attribution-ShareAlike 3.0 Unported
JBrown: Jay E. Brown
JJackson: Joel Jackson
JLowe: Jet Lowe
Joevare: Joevare on flickr, licensed for
    reuse under Attribution-NoDerivs 2.0
    Generic
Johnson: T. S. Johnson
Joly: Michel Joly
Jord: Jordgubbe,
    licensed under Creative Commons
    Attribution-ShareAlike 3.0 Unported
JSmith: Jeremai Smith
JSutton: Copyright John Sutton
    and licensed for reuse under
    Creative Commons Attribution-
    ShareAlike 2.0 Generic
JTurner: John S Turner,
    licensed for reuse under
    Creative Commons
    Attribution-ShareAlike
    2.0 Generic
Jumb: jumbo
Jünger: Daniel Jünger
JWeiss: Juri Weiss
JWTaylor: J. W. Taylor
Kadar: © Martin Kadar
Kafkoula: Kiki Kafkoula
Kantokari: Petteri Kantokari
Kereshun: Alyona Kereshun
KGGucwa: KGGucwa,
    licensed under Creative Commons
    Attribution-ShareAlike 3.0 Unported
Kleemann: Stefanie Kleemann
Klumper: Martin Klumper
Knight: Philip Knight
Knuth: Karsten Knuth
Kochi: Kochi,
    licensed under Creative Commons
    Attribution-ShareAlike 3.0 Unported
Koerber: Celia Koerber
Koltsov: Evgeniy Koltsov
Konoy: Peter Konoy
Korten: Henry Otto Korten
Koslowski: Paul Koslowski
Köster: Arthur Köster © Artists
    Rights Society, New York/VG
    Bild-Kunst, Bonn
Kreupeling: Carl Kreupeling,
    Utrecht, Netherlands
Kublins: Ikars Kublins
Kühne: Ralf Kühne

SOURCES

A15: Architecture (1915)

A16: Architecture (1916)

A17: Architecture (1917)

A18: Architecture (1918)

A19: Architecture (1919)

A21: Architecture (1921)

A29: Architecture (1929)

AA15: American Architect (1915)

AA16: American Architect (1916)

AA18: American Architect (1918)

AA19: American Architect (1919)

AA26: American Architect (1926)

AAAR: *Academy Architecture and Architectural Review* (January 1920)

AAF: Alinari Archives, Florence

AAM: Archives d'Architecture Moderne

AASL: Associazione Amici della Scuola Leumann

AB: Andy Best

ABH: Barry Parker and Raymond Unwin, *The Art of Building a Home* (New York: Longmans, Green & Co., 1901)

ABJ16: *The Architects' & Builders' Journal* (1916)

ABN00: *American Architect and Building News, International Edition* (1900)

ABN07: *American Architect and Building News, International Edition* (1907)

ABN09: *American Architect and Building News* (1909)

ABR: abracus GmbH

AC: *Atlanta Constitution* (August 23, 1908)

AC15: *American City* (1915)

AC16: *American City* (1916)

ACA: Amsterdam City Archives

ACB: Antonio Carlos Bonfato, *Macedo Vieira: Ressonâncias do modelo cidade-jardim* (São Paulo: Editora Senac São Paulo, 2008)

ACC: Ajo Chamber of Commerce

ACL: Archives communales de Lomme

ACP: Archives of the City of Prague

ACR18: *Architect and Contract Reporter* (1918)

AD22: *Architettura e Arti Decorative* (1922)

AD33: *Architettura e Arti Decorative* (1933)

AD34: *Architettura e Arti Decorative* (1934)

AD38: *Architettura e Arti Decorative* (1938)

ADA: *L'Architecture d'Aujourd'hui* (1950)

ADL: Archives départementales des Landes, 3 O 535

ADS: Archives de Strasbourg

ADVM: © Archives départementales du Val-de-Marne

AED14: *Art et Décoration* (1914)

AF17: *Architectural Forum* (1917)

AF18: *Architectural Forum* (1918)

AF19: *Architectural Forum* (1919)

AF20: *Architectural Forum* (1920)

AFC: From the Adrian Farmer Collection

AFP: Courtesy Anthony F. Pinto III

AG: Photographs ©Alexander Garvin

AGL: Archiv der Gemeinde Limburgerhof

AH: Courtesy of Andover Historical Society

AHG06: *American Homes and Gardens* (1906)

AHMW: © Crown copyright: Royal Commission on the Ancient and Historical Monuments of Wales

AHP: Office of Archaeology and Historic Preservation, Denver, Colorado

AHS: Arizona Historical Society/Tucson

AISI: *Bulletin of the American Iron and Steel Institute* (1913)

AJ: Courtesy of Andrew Johnston

AJ20: *Architects' Journal* (1920)

AJ23: *Architects' Journal* (1923)

AJDC: Agnieszka and Jaroslaw Dobrowolski Collection

AJMV: Acervo Jorge Macedo Vieira/ Arquivo Municipal Washington Luís/DPH

AK: Alyona Kereshun

AKA: Akademie der Künste, Berlin, Arthur-Köster-Archiv

AKR: Edward Akroyd, *On Improved Dwellings for the Working Classes with a Plan for Building Them in Connection with Benefit Building Societies* (London: Shaw, 1862). Courtesy of Central Reference Library, Halifax UK.

AL: Aberdare Library

ALB: Albertina, Vienna; Loos work © 2013 Artists Rights Society, New York/VBK, Vienna

ALC: Archivi Luigi Cortesi - Marco Pedroncelli

ALT: Courtesy of Robert Altman

ALZ: Archiv der Luftschiffbau Zeppelin GmbH

AM: Associazione Amici del Milanino, including Archivio Pulga and Archivio Zanelli

AMA29: *American Architect* (1929)

AMAT: Victor F. Hammel, *Construction and Operation of a Shell Loading Plant and the Town of Amatol, New Jersey, for the United States Government Ordnance Department, U. S. Army* (New York: Atlantic Loading Company, 1918)

AMC: *Atlas of Middlesex County* (Boston: G. H. Walker, 1889)

AMI1: Archivo Municipal Irun 1250/1

AMI2: Archivo Municipal Irun foto 25791

AMMB: Archives municipales de Marcq-en-Baroeul

AMP: Arva Moore Parks

AMPR: © Archives municipales du Plessis-Robinson

AN: Aerofototeca Nazionale, ICCD; and British School at Rome

ANMT: Archives Nationales du Monde de Travail

AOM: Courtesy Archives of Michigan

APD: City of Akron Planning Department

APL: Courtesy Anaheim Public Library

APMG: Courtesy Albemarle Park and the Manor Grounds

APT: *Grosvenor Atterbury, Stowe Phelps [and] John A. Tompkins: Architects, New York. Architectural Catalog* (New York, Architectural Catalog Co., 1918)

AR09: *Architectural Record* (1909)

AR10: *Architectural Record* (1910)

AR13: *Architectural Record* (1913)

AR14: *Architectural Record* (1914)

AR18: *Architectural Record* (1918)

AR19: *Architectural Record* (1919)

AR20: *Architectural Record* (1920)

AR24: *Architectural Record* (1924)

AR28: *Architectural Record* (1928)

AR31: *Architectural Record* (1931)

ARA: *Anton Rosen: arkitekt og kunster* (Silkeborg, Denmark: KunstCentret Silkeborg Bad, 2003)

ARB08: *Architectural Review* (Boston) (1908)

ARB13: *Architectural Review* (Boston) (1913)

ARB15: *Architectural Review* (Boston) (1915)

ARB16: *Architectural Review* (Boston) (1916)

ARB17: *Architectural Review* (Boston) (1917)

ARB18: *Architectural Review* (Boston) (1918)

ARB19: *Architectural Review* (Boston) (1919)

ARB24: *Architectural Review* (Boston) (1924)

ARB99: *Architectural Review* (Boston) (1899)

ARC: *Arcady* (New York: Arcady Executives, 1929)

ARCH: Courtesy of ARCH, Inc.

ARKM: Arkitekturmuseet

AS: Arthur Schankler

ASC: *Atlas of Suffolk County, Long Island, New York* (Brooklyn: E. Belcher Hyde, 1909)

ASCW: Rev. Stephen Gardner © All Saints Church, Woodlands and Highfields

ASG: © Archive stad Genk (Belgium)

ASGB: A. S. G. Butler, *The Architecture of Sir Edwin Lutyens, vol. 2* (London: Country Life, 1950)

ASM: © 2013 Alex S. MacLean/ Landslides - www.alexmaclean.com

AST: Andrew Steel, fforestfachhistory.com

ATER: Azienda Territoriale per l'Edilizia Residenziale Pubblica del Comune di Roma

ATHM: American Textile History Museum, Lowell, MA

ATL: Alexander Turnbull Library, Wellington, N.Z.

ATL1: F. J. Denton Collection, Alexander Turnbull Library, Wellington, N.Z.

ATL2: *Official volume of proceedings of the first New Zealand town-planning conference and exhibition* (Wellington: Government Printer, 1919), opp. p. 114 (B-K 926-114), Alexander Turnbull Library, Wellington, N.Z.

ATL3: Whites Aviation, Alexander Turnbull Library, Wellington, N.Z.

ATU: Architekturmuseum der TU München

AU: Archivio Urbani, courtesy Ed. Novecento

AV: Amelie Varzi

AVB: Archives de la Ville de Bruxelles

AVL: Archives de la Ville de Lausanne, Service d'Architecture, Plans de la Police des constructions

AW: Aaron Walton

AWR: Alice Wellington Rollins, *The Story of Lawrence Park* (New York: Douglas Robinson & Co, 1895)

B30: *Bauwelt* (1930)

BA08: *British Architect* (1908)

BAB: © 2013 Artists Rights Society, New York/VG Bild-Kunst, Bonn/ Bauhaus-Archiv Berlin

BAN: H. P. Berlage et al., *Arbeiderswoningen in Nederland* (Rotterdam: W. L. & J. Brusse, 1921)

BAR15: *Berliner Architekturwelt* (1915)

BARA: Bruce Anderson of rusholmearchive.org

BAU34: *Baumeister* (1934)

BBG: Georg Haberland, *40 Jahre Berlinische Boden-Gesellschaft* (Berlin, 1930)

BCPL: Baltimore County Public Library

BE: Brad Emerson

BEHI: Bemis Historical Society

BEL: Beloit Historical Society

BEM: Biblioteca Estense, Modena, On concession of the Ministry of Heritage and Culture

BETT: © Bettmann/Corbis

BF: Bezirksmuseum Favoriten

BG: Bernard Gagnon

BGO: Blades and Goven, LLC

BHAM: Bildarchiv Hamburg

BHC: Burton Historical Collection, Detroit Public Library

BHL: Bentley Historical Library, University of Michigan

BHPL: Beverly Hills Public Library

BHS: The Brooklyn Historical Society

BHVP: Bibliothèque Historique de la Ville de Paris

BIB: Barnet Image Bank, London Borough of Barnet - Local Studies

BIRD: Paul Bird

BK: Borlange Kommun, City architect's office

BL: Brandenburgisches Landeshauptarchiv

BLDT: Benedito Lima de Toledo, *Prestes Maia e as origens do urban ismo moderno de São Paulo* (São Paulo: Empresa dos Artes Projetos e Edições Artísticas, 1996)

BLP: BL Press LLC

BLS: Reproduced by permission of Bradford Libraries

BLUCB: The Bancroft Library, University of California, Berkeley

BMC: Bernard Maybeck Collection, Environmental Design Archives, University of California, Berkeley

BMGA: © Bristol's Museums, Galleries & Archives

BN77: *Building News* (1877)

BNUS: Collection et photographie BNU Strasbourg (1910)

BOD1: The Bodleian Libraries, The University of Oxford, MS. Top. Gen. a. 22, fol. 27r

BODPT: The Bodleian Libraries, The University of Oxford, with permission of the Park Town Trustees

BODR: The Bodleian Libraries, The University of Oxford, with permission of the Radcliffe Trust

BON: Bildarchiv der Österreichische Nationalbibliothek

BP: Ballinger & Perrot, *An Industrial Village* (Philadelphia: Ballinger & Perrot, 1919)

BP11: *Building Progress* (1911)

BPA: Ben Pentreath & Associates

BPK: bpk, Berlin/Art Resource, NY

BPL: Norman B. Leventhal Map Center at the Boston Public Library

BPLA: Birmingham, Alabama Public Library Archives

BR: Brent Roberts

BR10: *The Brickbuilder* (1910)

BR13: *The Brickbuilder* (1913)

BRB: General Collection, Beinecke Rare Book and Manuscript Library, Yale University

BRENT: Brent Archives

BRHS: Boca Raton Historical Society & Museum

BRL: By kind permission of Birkenhead Reference Library

BRO: Bristol Record Office

BRRL: Courtesy of Bristol Reference Library

BRV19: *Building Review* (1919)

BSA: Brentham Society Archive

BT: Brian Tunnard

BTDS: Bruno Taut, *Die Stadtkrone* (Jena: Eugen Diederichs, 1919)

BTS: Akademie der Künste, Berlin, Bruno-Taut-Sammlung

BUN: Alex Bunjes

BURL: Burlingame Historical Society

BUX: Buxton Museum

BVT: Bournville Village Trust

BVTB: Bournville Village Trust,

The Bournville Village Trust (Birmingham, c. 1927)

CA21: *Coal Age* (1921)

CAHS: Courtesy of Atascadero Historical Society

CAL: Courtesy Andrew Liptak

CALS: Image courtesy of Cumbria Archive and Local Studies Centre, Barrow

CAM: Courtesy of the Campbell family, Fforestfach

CAN: City Archives of Norrköping

CAWG: Chemnitzer Allgemeine Wohnungsbaugenossenschaft eG

CB: Christian Blöss

CBMA: Courtesy of the Corner Brook Museum and Archives

CBP: C. B. Purdom, *The Building of Satellite Towns*, rev. ed. (London: J. M. Dent & Sons, 1925, 1949)

CC: Charlotte Caldwell

CCA: Canadian Center for Architecture

CCC: Cumbria County Council, Carlisle Library

CCF: Cheryl Caldwell Ferguson, Ph.D.

CCG: City of Coral Gables

CCHM: Collection of the Campbell House Museum, Saint Louis, Mo. (Including the Robert Campbell family album)

CCHS: Courtesy of the Chevy Chase Historical Society

CDAP: City Development Authority Prague

CDV: Comune di Venezia, Archivio della Comunicazione

CEH: *Constitution of Evergreen Hamlet* (1851)

CEL: www.celebration.fl.us

CFG: Collection Familistère de Guise

CFH: Collectie Fotoarchief Hollanderwijk

CFL: Courtesy of Friends of Leclaire

CFS: Circolo Fotografico Scledense/Biblioteca Civica Schio/Alfredo Talin

CFVW: Jonathan Beecher, *Charles Fourier: The Visionary and His World* (Berkeley: University of California Press, 1986)

CG: Càtedra Gaudí

CHB: C. H. Baer, ed., *Kleinbauten und Siedelungen* (Stuttgart: Julius Hoffmann, 1919)

CHC: City Housing Corporation, *Sunnyside Gardens: A Home Community* (1929)

CHG: Catena-Historic Gardens and Landscapes Archive, Bard Graduate Center: Decorative Arts, Design History, Material Culture: New York

CHHS: Chestnut Hill Historical Society

CHM: Chicago History Museum

CHOR: Chorltonville.org

CHS1: Courtesy California Historical Society, CHS-7537

CHS2: Courtesy California Historical Society, CHS-33257

CIA: Cia. City Archive

CIG: Centre d'Iconographie Genevoise

CJCM: Office public d'habitations du Département de la Seine, *Cité-jardins de Chatenay-Malabry* (1937)

CK: Christoph Kuras

CLH: Collection of the Lowell Historical Society

CLLC: Courtesy of Chiswick Library Local Collection

CLM: Courtesy of Larry McCann

CLS: Conservative Land Society, Saint Margaret's, poster (1854)

CLSLA: Reproduced by kind permission of Croydon Local Studies Library and Archives Service

CM: Clewiston Museum

CM17: *Cassier's Magazine* (July 1895)

CMC: Cincinnati Museum Center - Cincinnati History Library

CME: Chris Mead, East Yorkshire Local History Society

CMU: Courtesy of Colum Mulhern

CN: © Chris Naffziger, St. Louis, Missouri

CNG: *Colbran's New Guide for Tunbridge Wells* (London : A. H. Bailey and Co., 1840)

CNH: Courtesy of Nicholas Hartley

CNL: Claude-Nicolas Ledoux, *L'architecture de C. N. Ledoux* (Paris: Lenoir, 1847)

COM: William Phillips Comstock, *The Housing Book* (New York: William T. Comstock, 1919)

COP: City of Olmos Park

COR: Cornell University, Division of Rare and Manuscript Collections

COWL: Cowlitz County Historical Museum

CPB: Courtesy Patrick Bonaventure

CPCS: Raymond Unwin, *Cottage Plans and Common Sense* (London: The Fabian Society, 1902)

CPG: Collection of Philippe Gallois

CPHV: Werner Hegemann, *City Planning, Housing, Volume III* (New York: Architectural Book Publishing Co., 1938)

CPL: Cleveland Public Library Map Collection

CPR: City of Prince Rupert

CPT: Collection P. Thillaud

CR: Ryan Mortgage, courtesy of Carol Roark

CRA: Calumet Regional Archives, Indiana University Northwest, Gary, Indiana

CRAA: Collection Regional Archive Alkmaar, the Netherlands

CRAAT: P. S. Teeling/Collection Regional Archive Alkmaar, the Netherlands

CRLD: Alfred B. Yeomans, ed., *City Residential Land Development: Studies in Planning: Competitive Plans for Subdividing a Typical Quarter Section of Land in the Outskirts of Chicago* (Chicago: University of Chicago Press, 1916)

CRO: Cheshire Record Office

CRS: Collection of Robert A. M. Stern Architects

CRT: © CRT Franche-Comté/Michel Joly

CSAS: Centre of South Asian Studies

CSU: Cleveland State University. Michael Schwartz Library. Special Collections

CTA1: City of Toronto Archives, Fonds 1231, Item 1503

CTA2: City of Toronto Archives, Fonds 1478, Item 1

CTIA: Connecticut Image Archive

CTPL: Courtesy of Toronto Public Library

CU: Avery Library, Columbia University

CUA: David Cuan

CUCAP: Cambridge University Collection of Aerial Photography

CUL: Courtesy Maurice Culot

CUR: Wolfgang Currlin

CV: Courtesy of Camilo Vergara

CVA: City of Vancouver Archives

CVA1: City of Vancouver Archives, Map 329

CVA2: City of Vancouver Archives, Major Matthews Collection, Item CVA 371-2857

CVA3: City of Vancouver Archives, Stuart Thomson fonds, Item CVA 99-5416

CVA4: City of Vancouver Archives,

Map contained in Pamphlet 1937-51, Thompson-Jones and Company Golf Architects

CVD: Collection Ville de Drancy

CW: Caroline Walker

CWH: Courtesy Walter Houlton

CZA: Central Zionist Archives, Jerusalem

DA: Dale Adkisson

DA19: *Der Architect* (1919)

DAC: Directions des Archives du Calvados

DB: Dan Berman

DBA28: *Deutsche Bauzeitung* (1928)

DBF: Courtesy of the Debenham Family

DBK: Leberecht Migge, *Deutsche Binnen-Kolonisation* (Berlin: Deutscher Kommunal-Verlag, 1926)

DBO: David Boardman

DC: Demion Clinco

DCA: Dublin City Library & Archive

DCHM: Davidson County Historical Museum

DCI: Development Corporation for Israel

DDPW: Durham, N.C., Department of Public Works

DEN: Denenchōfu Association

DF: David Feigenbaum

DFP1: Archives of Ontario. Dinnick family papers. F 175-1-0-2.1 and F175-1-0-2.3

DGS: Fritz Stahl, *Die Gartenstadt Staaken* (Berlin: Wasmuth, 1917)

DHS: Dallas Historical Society

DIAS: Michele Dias

DIS: © 1965 Disney

DIW: Josef Frank, ed., *Die internationale Werkbundsiedlung: Wien, 1932,* exhibition catalogue (Vienna: Anton Schroll & Co., 1932)

DJ: Daniel Jünger

DK: Daniel Karatzas Collection

DK02: *Dekorative Kunst* (1902)

DKD17: *Deutsche Kunst und Dekoration* (1917)

DKR: *De Kiefhoek: een woonwijk in Rotterdam* (Rotterdam: Stichting Museumwoning De Kiefhoek; Laren: V & K Publishing, 1990)

DL: Dru Lamb

DLF: Louis Paul Zocher/Archives Delft, 1038

DLF1: Archives Delft, 118

DLSL: Derbyshire Local Studies Library

DM: D. P. Munro

DNF30: *Das Neue Frankfurt* (1930)

DNW26: *Das Neue Wien* (1926)

DPL: Dallas Public Library

DPL41: Denver Public Library, Western History Collection, L.C. McClure, MCC-1641

DPL5: Denver Public Library, Western History Collection, L.C. McClure, MCC-2605

DPL77: Denver Public Library, Western History Collection, Parks Album 111, X-20277

DPZ: Courtesy of Duany Plater-Zyberk & Company

DS: Daniel Schechter

DS08: *Der Städtebau* (1908)

DS11: *Der Städtebau* (1911)

DSCH: David Schalliol

DSH20: *Das Schlesische Heim* (1920)

DSH22: *Das Schlesische Heim* (1922)

DSH23: *Das Schlesische Heim* (1923)

DSTW: J. Britton, *Descriptive sketches of Tunbridge Wells and the Calverley estate: With brief notices of the picturesque scenery, seats, and antiquities in the vicinity* (London, 1832)

DSU: © David Sundberg/Esto

DW19: *Daimler-Werkszeitung*

(1919/1920)

DWD: D. W. Dreysse, *Ernst May Housing Estates* (Frankfurt am Main: Fricke, 1988)

DWO26: *Die Wohnungswirtschaft* (1926)

ECTM: © Entre Ciel Terre et Mer - www.ectm.fr

EDA: Environmental Design Archives, University of California, Berkeley

EDC: East Dunbartonshire Council

EDLCT: East Dunbartonshire Leisure and Culture Trust

EEH: El Encanto Estates Homeowners Association

EFC: *Housing the Shipbuilders* (Philadelphia: United States Shipping Board, Emergency Fleet Corporation, Passenger Transportation and Housing Division, 1920)

EGC: Ewart G. Culpin, *The Garden City Movement Up-to-Date* (London: Garden Cities and Town Planning Association, 1913)

EGM: Ernst Michalek, www.egm.at

EGP: Emile G. Perrot, *Discussion on Garden Cities: An Industrial Village on Garden City Lines* (Philadelphia: G. L. Mitchell, 1912; rev. and exp., 1915)

EH: Reproduced by permission of English Heritage

EHAC: © English Heritage (Aerofilms Collection)

EHC: © English Heritage

EIM: A. Soskin Collection, Eretz Israel Museum, Tel Aviv

EK: Evgeniy Koltsov

EM92: *Engineering Magazine* (January 1892)

EMBC: E. M. Ball Collection, D. H. Ramsey Library Special Collections, UNC Asheville

EMG: ernst-may-gesellschaft e.v.

ENSC: Elachee Nature Science Center

EP: Elizabeth Porterfield, City of San Antonio, Office of Historic Preservation

ESK: Marloes Eskens

ESML: Earth Sciences and Map Library, University of California, Berkeley

ESP: Marika Hausen et al., *Eliel Saarinen: Projects, 1896–1923* (Cambridge, Mass.: MIT Press, 1990)

ETH: ETH-Bibliothek, Zürich, Bildarchiv

ETSAV: http://www.etsav.upc.es/personals/iphs2004/pdf/043_p.pdf

ETU: © www.etudedumilieu.be

EV: Courtesy of Edwin Venn Architectural Artist

EVW: Ebbw Vale Works Archival Trust and Ebbw Vale Works Museum

EW: *The Electrical World* (1893)

FAWA: Sarah Allaback, *The First American Women Architects* (Urbana: University of Illinois Press, 2008)

FBA: Fondation Braillard Architects

FBAH: Fonds Bétons armés Hennebique. CNAM/SIAF/Cité de l'architecture et du patrimoine/Archives d'architecture du XXe siècle

FCR: Forsyth County Register of Deeds Office

FDE: *Führer durch die Essener Wohnsiedlungen der Firma Krupp* (Essen : Graphische Anstalt der Fried. Krupp Aktiengesellschaft, 1930)

FDZ: © Francis Dzikowski/Esto

FG: Fotosammlung Gerlach, Wiener Stadt- und Landesarchiv

FGC: © First Garden City Heritage Museum

FH: Flanders Heritage

FHC: From the Fenton History Center collections, Jamestown, N.Y.

FHG: The Sage Foundation Homes Company, *Forest Hills Gardens* (December 1913)

FHHO: Forest Hill Home Owners

FHS: The Filson Historical Society

FICA: Fundación ICA

FL: Flickr

FLC: © 2013 Artists Rights Society, New York/ADAGP, Paris/FLC

FLO: Courtesy of the National Park Service, Frederick Law Olmsted National Historic Site

FLW: © Frank Lloyd Wright Foundation, AZ/Artists Rights Society, NY/Art Resource, NY

FM: Foto Marburg/Art Resource, NY; Riemerschmid work © 2013 Artists Rights Society, New York/VG Bild-Kunst, Bonn

FML: Fonds Marcel Lods. Académie d'architecture/Cité de l'architecture et du patrimoine/Archives d'architecture du XXe siècle

FP: Friends of Pittville

FRO: Flintshire Record Office

FS: The Finchley Society

FSRM: Friends of Swindon Railway Museum

FW: Falk Weihmann

FWB: F. W. Beers & Company/Historic Map Works

GA: Gwent Archives

GAI: Glenbow-Alberta Institute, Calgary, Canada

GAP: G. + A. Pfister Architektur

GARN: John S. Garner, *The Company Town* (New York: Oxford University Press, 1992)

GBL: Georges Benoît-Lévy, *La Cité-Jardin* (Paris: Editions des Cités-Jardins de France, 1911)

GC: Geoff Caldwell

GCT: Ebenezer Howard, *Garden Cities of To-morrow* (London: S. Sonnen-schein, 1902)

GCTP10: *Garden Cities and Town Planning* (1910)

GCTP11: *Garden Cities and Town Planning* (1911)

GCTP13: *Garden Cities and Town Planning* (1913)

GCTP14: *Garden Cities and Town Planning* (1914)

GCTP22: *Garden Cities and Town Planning* (1922)

GE: Google Earth

GEIS: Wohngenossenschaft Geissenstein - EBG

GEO: Geograph Britain and Ireland

GES: Geert Sommer

GF: Geschichtswerkstatt Forstfeld

GH: Goldschmidt & Howland

GHI: Grand-Hornu Images

GI: *Golf Illustrated* (1925)

GJM: Glenn and Joanne Mellor

GKA: The Gallen-Kallela Museum

GM: Goole Museum (East Riding of Yorkshire Museums & Galleries)

GMG: Courtesy of Gavin Macrae-Gibson

GN: Gergely Nagy

GPHA: Greenway Parks Homeowners Association

GPL: Courtesy of Gary Public Library

GRT: Graham Romeyn Taylor, *Satellite Cities: A Study of Industrial Suburbs* (New York: D. Appleton, 1915)

GS: Göteborgs Stad

GS28: *Garten Schönheit* (1928)

GSGK: Photograph by Göteborgs Konstförlag, AB, courtesy of Göteborgs Stadsmuseum

GSM: Göteborgs Stadsmuseum

GSTP: *Garden Suburbs, Town Planning and Modern Architecture* (London: T. F. Unwin, 1910)

GT: Gabriel Tilove

GTA: gta Archive

GUAR: Promotional brochure of S/A Auto-estradas, published in Elisabete França, ed., *Guarapiranga : recuperação urbana e ambiental no município de Sao Paulo* (Sao Paulo: M. Carrilho Arquitetos, 2000)

GUL: Ghent University Library

GWR11: *Great Western Railway Magazine* (1911)

HA: Hinsdale Archives

HAG03: *House and Garden* (1903)

HAK: Historisches Archiv Krupp

HALC: homesandland.com

HALS: Hertfordshire Archives and Local Studies

HAM: Harvard Art Museums/ Busch-Reisinger Museum, Gift of Ise Gropius, BRGA.22.31. Photo: Imaging Department © President and Fellows of Harvard College

HAM1: Harvard Art Museums/Fogg Museum, Transfer from the Carpenter Center for the Visual Arts, Social Museum Collection, 3.2002.1801. Photo: Imaging Department © President and Fellows of Harvard College

HAM2: Harvard Art Museums/Fogg Museum, Transfer from the Carpenter Center for the Visual Arts, Social Museum Collection, 3.2002.507.5. Photo: Imaging Department © President and Fellows of Harvard College

HAM3: Harvard Art Museums/Fogg Museum, Transfer from the Carpenter Center for the Visual Arts, Social Museum Collection, 3.2002.3330.3. Photo: Imaging Department © President and Fellows of Harvard College

HAM4: Harvard Art Museums/Fogg Museum, Transfer from the Carpenter Center for the Visual Arts, Social Museum Collection, 3.2002.2001.1. Photo: Imaging Department © President and Fellows of Harvard College

HB: Humphrey Bolton

HB18: *House Beautiful* (1918)

HBAA: Helen Beneki and Argiro Aggelopoulou

HBE: Helen Betts

HBM: Henri Sellier, *Habitations à bon marché du département de la Seine* (Paris: Ch. Massin, 1921)

HBM23: *L'Habitation à Bon Marché* (1923)

HBM24: *L'Habitation à Bon Marché* (1924)

HBM25: *L'Habitation à Bon Marché* (1925)

HCA: Courtesy of Hershey Community Archives, Hershey, PA

HCL: Hennepin County Library

HCM: Helsinki City Museum (Helsingen kaupunginmuseo)

HCPD: Helsinki City Planning Department

HDF: Hans-Dieter Fleger

HDG: Haus der Geschichte Baden-Württemberg, Sammlung Metz Nr. 47613

HE: Heinz Egermann

HEBV: Hans Eduard von Berlepsch-Valendas, *Die Garten-Stadt München-Perlach* (Munich: C. Reinhardt, 1910)

HELS: Helsinki City Archives

HERM: Gil Herman, *Three Decades: The Story of the State Electricity Commission of Victoria from Its Inception to December 1948* (Hutchinson & Co., 1948)

HESC: Henning Schröder

HF: From the Collections of The Henry Ford

HFW: *Homes for Workmen: A Presentation of Leading Examples of Industrial Community Development* (New Orleans: Southern Pine Association, 1919)

HG05: *House and Garden* (1905)

HG06: *House and Garden* (1906)

HGDK: Heinrich Goldemund, *Die Kaiser Karl-Kriegerbeimstätte in Aspern* (Vienna: Gerlach und Wiedlung, 1918)

HGRA: Hans und Gret Reinhard, Architects, and reinhardtpartner AG, Architects and Planners

HGS: *The Hampstead Garden Suburb: Its Achievements and Significance* (London: Hampstead Garden Suburb Trust, Ltd., 1937)

HH: www.hidden-helsinki.com

HHCR: Hare and Hare Company Records (KO206), The State Historical Society of Missouri

HHS: Hinsdale Historical Society

HIGH: The Highlands, Inc.

HJ: Courtesy of Henry Jessup

HJES: Harry Jack, Edinburgh, Scotland

HLW: Haines, Lundberg & Waehler

HM: HistoryMiami

HMF: Historisches Museum Frankfurt, Foto: Horst Ziegenfusz

HML: Hagley Museum and Library

HMRC: Houston Metropolitan Research Center, Houston Public Library, Houston, Texas

HMW: Hazel M. Wyle

HN: © Hamish Niven

HNE: Historic New England

HNOC: The Charles L. Franck Studio Collection at The Historic New Orleans Collection, Acc. No. 1979.325.4831

HOL: © Hans-Otto Lindgreen

HOLL: Collection of the Hollywood Historical Society

HQS: *The Housing Question in Sweden* (London: Swedish Delegation at the Interallied Housing and Town Planning Congress, 1920)

HRO: Hampshire Record Office: Ordnance Survey County Series, 1:2500: Hampshire sheet 33.8, First edition (c1870)

HS: © Crown Copyright reproduced courtesy of Historic Scotland. www.historicscotlandimages.gov.uk

HSO: H. de Saint-Omer, *Les enterprises belges en Égypt* (Brussels: G. Piquart, 1907)

HSUC: The Archives of the Historical Society of University City

HTS: Heinrich-Tessenow-Stiftung/ John H. Clorius

HW: Hannah Wisniowski

HWC: James Hole, *The Homes of the Working Classes, with Suggestions for Their Improvement* (London: Longmans, Green, 1866). Courtesy of Central Reference Library, Halifax UK.

HWP: E. R. L. Gould, *The Housing of the Working People* (Washington, D.C.: Government Printing Office, 1895)

HWTJ: *Houses for Workers* (London: Technical Journals, 1917)

IAA: Irish Architectural Archive

IAO06: *Indoors and Out* (1906)

ICTP: *International Cities and Town Planning Exhibition. English Catalogue. Jubilee Exhibition, Gothenburg, Sweden, 1923* (Göteborg, Wezäta: W. Zachrissons boktyrckeri a.-b., 1923)

ID: Andreas Volwahsen, *Imperial Delhi: The British Capital of the Indian Empire* (Munich: Prestel, 2002)

IEP: Stadsarchief Ieper

IEPA: Stadsarchief Ieper, Archief Richard Acke 3

IEPF: Stadsarchief Ieper, Fotocollectie B 180

IFA: Cité de l'architecture et du patri moine/Institut français d'archives

IGN38: © IGN 1938

IGN49: © IGN 1949

IHS: Irvington Historical Society

IHS1: Indiana Historical Society, Bass #208903-F

IHS2: Indiana Historical Society, Bass #208902-F

IK: Ikars Kublins, Photoriga.com

IKK: Ikeuchi Kazuta

ILL23: *l'Illustration* (1923)

ISSLT: *The Irish Sailors' and Soldiers' Land Trust: First Report* (January 1, 1924-March 31, 1926)

ISUL: Iowa State University Library/ Special Collections Department

IT: Thomas Ives and Mike Townsend

JAIA17: *Journal of the American Institute of Architects* (1917)

JAIA18: *Journal of the American Institute of Architects* (1918)

JAIA21: *Journal of the American Institute of Architects* (1921)

JAJ: James Andrew Jarvis

JBBG: Georg Haberland, *40 Jahre Berlinische Boden-Gesellschaft* (Berlin, 1930)

JBR: J. Bruinwold Riedel, *Tuinsteden* (Utrecht: J. Van Boekhoven, 1906)

JC: James Cornes, *Modern Housing in Town and Country* (London: B. T. Batsford, 1905)

JCM: James C. Massey

JEKP: John Ellis Kordes photography

JGA: John Gordon Allen, *The Cheap Cottage and Small House: A Manual of Economical Building* (London, B. T. Batsford, 1919)

JH: John Houghton

JHS: Jamestown Historical Society

JHU: The John Work Garrett Library, The Sheridan Libraries of the Johns Hopkins University (from S. Y. Griffith, *Griffith's New Historical Description of Cheltenham and its Vicinity*, 1826)

JJ: Joel Jackson

JM: Joel Mendelson

JMA: Joe Mabel

JRB: Jane Raoul Bingham

JRF: Joseph Rowntree Foundation Archive

JS: John Summerson, *John Nash, Architect to King George IV* (London: G. Allen & Unwin, 1935)

JSB: James Silk Buckingham, *National evils and practical remedies, with the plan of a model town* (London: P. Jackson, Late Fisher, 1849)

JSHK: Jakob Schallenberger and Hans Kraffert, *Berliner Wohnungsbauten aus öffentlichen Mitteln* (Berlin: Bauwelt, 1926)

JSL: John Scott Lansill papers, University of Kentucky Special Collections and Archives

JSN: J. S. Nettlefold, *Practical Town Planning* (London: St. Catherine Press, 1914)

JSSC: John Sewell, *Shape of the City*

(Toronto: University of Toronto Press, 1993)

JV: Jean Virette, *La Cité Jardin* (Paris: Éditions S. de Bonadona, 1931)

JVA: Johann Valentin Andreae, *Reipublicae Christianopolitanae descriptio* (Strasbourg: Héritiers de Lazare Zetzher, 1619), reprinted in Roland Schaer, Gregory Claeys, and Lyman Tower Sargent, eds., *Utopia: The Search for the Ideal Society in the Western World* (New York: New York Public Library/ Oxford University Press, 2000)

JWTM: Janet Waymark, *Thomas Mawson: Life, Gardens and Landscapes* (London: Frances Lincoln, 2009)

KB: Klaus Beneke

KBL: Kenneth Bradley, *Lusaka, The New Capital of Northern Rhodesia, Opened Jubilee Week, 1935* (London: Produced for private circulation by Jonathan Cape, 1935)

KC: Kohler Co.

KCC: Kenneth Cardwell Collection, Visual Resources Center Environmental Design Archives, University of California Berkeley

KHA: Knebworth House Archive

KJM: Maarten Piek, *K. J. Muller (1857-1942): sportcomplexen, buitenplaatsen en tuindorpen – gezondheid als leidraad in architectuur* (Rotterdam: BONAS, 2000)

KK: Kiki Kafkoula, with the permission of the University Studio Press, Thessaloniki, Greece

KKS: KØBENHAVNS KOMMUNE/ Stadsarkivet

KLU: Robert C. Broward, *The Architecture of Henry John Klutho: The Prairie School in Jacksonville*, rev. 2nd ed. (Jacksonville: University of North Florida Press, 1983; Jacksonville: Jacksonville Historical Society, 2003)

KRC: Kenan Research Center at the Atlanta History Center

KT: Kendra Taylor

KUL: K. U. Leuven - Fonds Verwilghen

KUS: Kratovo Urban Settlement

LA14: *Landscape Architecture* (1914)

LA27: *Landscape Architecture* (1927)

LA28: *Landscape Architecture* (1928)

LAB: *Laburnum Park*, promotional brochure (Richmond, Va.: Laburnum Corporation, 1919), courtesy of Sarah Driggs

LAPC: Los Angeles Public Library Photo Collection

LAPL: Security Pacific National Bank Collection/Los Angeles Public Library

LAR: Lars Börner

LAS: Lasse Brunnström

LB: Landesarchiv Berlin

LBE: Landesdenkmalamt Berlin

LBH: Local Studies, Archives and Museums Service, London Borough of Hillingdon

LC24: *La Cité* (1924)

LCC37: London County Council, *London Housing* (London: London County Council, 1937)

LCDL: Office d'Habitation à Bon Marché, *La crise du logement et l'intervention publique en matière d'habitation populaire dans l'agglomération parisienne* (Paris: Éditions de l'Office Public d'Habitation à Bon Marché du Départment de la Seine, 1921)

LCDM: Lake County

Discovery Museum

LCNC: Lavin Collection, North Carolina Department of Cultural Resources, Division of Archives and History, Raleigh, North Carolina

LDS: Louis de Soissons and Arthur William Kenyon, *Site Planning in Practice at Welwyn Garden City* (London: Ernest Benn, 1927)

LFC: Donnelley Library, Susan Dart Collection, Lake Forest College

LFD: Landesamt für Denkmalpflege und Archäologie Sachsen-Anhalt

LHS: Julian P. Graham/Loon Hilll Studios

LI: Luce Institute/Alinari Archives Management, Florence

LINC: Lincolnshire Archives

LK: Courtesy of Leon Krier

LLFH: Courtesy Leeds Local and Family History Library

LMA: City of London, London Metropolitan Archives

LNW: Landesarchiv Nordrhein-Westfalen

LOC1: Library of Congress, Prints & Photographs Division, Detroit Publishing Company Collection, LC-D4-16329

LOC2: Library of Congress, Prints & Photographs Division, Detroit Publishing Company Collection, LC-D4-33063

LOC3: Library of Congress, Prints & Photographs Division, Detroit Publishing Company Collection, LC-D4-12562

LOC4: Library of Congress, Prints & Photographs Division, Detroit Publishing Company Collection, LC-D4-10885

LOC5: Library of Congress, Prints & Photographs Division, Detroit Publishing Company Collection, LC-D4-34735

LOC6: Library of Congress, Prints & Photographs Division, Detroit Publishing Company Collection, LC-D4-34736

LOC7: Library of Congress, Prints & Photographs Division, Detroit Publishing Company Collection, LC-D4-10819

LOC8: Library of Congress, Prints & Photographs Division, Detroit Publishing Company Collection, LC-D4-18672

LOCCA: Library of Congress, Chronicling America, Historic American Newspapers

LOCG: Library of Congress, Geography & Map Division

LOCP: Library of Congress, Prints & Photographs Division

LOCPF: Library of Congress, Prints & Photographs Division, FSA/OWI Collection

LOCPG: Library of Congress, Prints & Photographs Division, Gottscho-Schleisner Collection

LOCPH: Library of Congress, Prints & Photographs Division, HABS NH,6-MANCH,2--47

LOCPH1: Library of Congress, Prints & Photographs Division, HABS NH,6-MANCH,2--105

LOCPM: Library of Congress, Prints & Photographs Division, G. Eric and Edith Matson Photograph Collection

LRO: Liverpool Record Office

LS: Laurence Scales, www.allertonoak.com

LSM: Courtesy of the Collections of the Louisiana State Museum

LUL: Stadsarkivet Luleå

LUTT: Ben Luttermoser

LVR: Library of Virginia, Richmond, Virginia

LVRI: LVR-Industriemuseum

LVRZ: LVR-Zentrum für Medien und Bildung

LW: Lawrence Weaver, *Houses and Gardens by Sir Edwin Lutyens, R.A.* (London: Country Life; New York: Charles Scribner's Sons, 1925)

LWCF: Lawrence Weaver, *The 'Country Life' Book of Cottages* (London: Country Life, 1919)

MAG: Stadtarchiv Magdeburg

MAN: Courtesy of Manchester Libraries, Information and Archives, Manchester City Council

MAR: From the collection of Homme Martinus, Hengelo, Netherlands

MAW: Thomas Mawson, *The City of Calgary: Past, Present and Future* (Calgary: City Planning Commission, 1914)

MB: Moritz Bernoully

MB22: *Moderne Bauformen* (1922)

MB27: *Moderne Bauformen* (1927)

MB34: *Moderne Bauformen* (1934)

MBG: Missouri Botanical Garden [*Plat Book of Property Owned by Henry Shaw in the City of St. Louis* (St. Louis: Sterling & Webster Abstract Co., c. 1884)]

MC: Michael Coyne

MCHS: Courtesy of the Madison County Historical Society (IL)

MCNY: Museum of the City of New York

MCRO: Marion County Recorder's Office

MD: Miles Doyle

MDN: © Mairie de Noisiel

MDN1: © Mairie de Noisiel/IGN

MDV: Musées de Verviers

MEND: Erich Mendelsohn, *Erich Mendelsohn: Das Gesamtschaffen des Architekten* (Berlin: R. Mosse, 1930)

METZ: Georg Metzendorf, *Klein wohnungs-Bauten und Siedlungen* (Darmstadt: Alexander Koch, 1920)

MFA: Museum of Finnish Architecture

MFV: Budgett Meakin, *Model Factories and Villages* (London: T. Fisher Unwin, 1905)

MH: Markus Horn

MHM: Missouri History Museum, St. Louis, Missouri

MHP: Midland Heritage Project

MHPC: Courtesy of Maine Historic Preservation Commission

MHS: Musée Historique de Strasbourg, photo M. Bertola

MHSL: Montana Historical Society- Library, Helena

MHZ: Mark Honegger - Zurich

MI: James Elmes. *Metropolitan improvements : or, London in the nineteenth century. . . from original drawings by Thos. H. Shepherd* (London: Jones, 1827)

MJP: Metro Jacksonville Photographs

MLA: Miroslaw Lanowiecki

MM: Maureen Megowan

MMA: Metropolitan Museum of Art, New York, N.Y.

MME: Martin Meek

MMN: Maine Memory Network

MNA: Mezaparks Neighbourhood Association

MOG: Mayor's Office, Gerlafingen, Switzerland

MOSS: *Mossmain, Montana* (Billings, Mont.: Yellowstone Garden City Holding Corporation, c. 1915)

MOU: © Moulin Studios

MP: Mariemont Preservation Foundation

MPA: Marc Perrey Aeromedias

MPF: Myers Park Foundation

MPR: Mark Preuschl

MPRA: Moor Pool Residents' Association

MR: Courtesy Martin Rogers

MRWV: Courtesy of Mike Roycroft, Whiteley Village

MSA: Maryland State Archives

MSCL: Mandeville Special Collections Library, UC San Diego

MSHHS: Millburn-Short Hills Historical Society

MSL: Marcel Smets, *L'avenement de la Cité-Jardin en Belgique: Histoire de l'habitat social en Belgique de 1830 à 1930* (Bruxelles: P. Mardaga, 1977)

MSP: Mark Sunderland Photography

MT: Museum Treptow

MTD: www.mtdavidson.org

MTL: Manchester Tenants Ltd.

MUL: Mulhouse Archives

MUS: © MUS-Musée d'Histoire Urbaine et Sociale de Suresnes

MVC: Mercedes Volait Collection

MVM: From the Collections of the Martha's Vineyard Museum

MVSC: Missouri Valley Special Collections, Kansas City Public Library, Kansas City, Missouri

MWA: Akademie der Künste, Berlin, Martin-Wagner-Archiv

MZR: Collection Sincfala, Museum of the Zwin Region (Knokke-Heist, Belgium) - www.sincfala.be and www.zwinregio.eu

NAA: National Archives of Australia: A710, 8

NACP: National Archives at College Park, College Park, MD

NAF: National Archives of Finland

NAI: Netherlands Architecture Institute, Rotterdam

NAI22: NAi Collection/HAME_ph22

NAI26: NAi Collection/HAME_ph26

NAIO: © 2013 Artists Rights Society, New York/Courtesy of Pictoright Amsterdam/NAI Collection

NAIZ: NAI Collection/De Bazel archive

NBH: Karl Elkart, *Neues Bauen in Hannover* (Hannover: Verkehrs-Verein, 1929)

NCA: Norton Company Archives/ Worcester Historical Museum/ Worcester, MA

NCCP: North Carolina County Photographic Collection #P0001, North Carolina Photographic Archives, The Wilson Library, University of North Carolina at Chapel Hill

NCP: Nassau County Dept. of Parks, Recreation & Museums, Photo Archives Center

NCSA: North Carolina State Archives

NEMHC: NEMHC, Univ. of Minnesota Duluth

NF: NotreFamille.com

NG: National Grid

NGAL: Goode-Phillips Collection, Department of Image Collections, National Gallery of Art Library, Washington, DC

NGBO: Raymond Unwin, *Nothing Gained by Overcrowding! How the Garden City type of Development May Benefit Both Owner and Occupier* (London: Garden Cities and Town Planning Association, 1912)

NH: Nadine Holzheimer

NHA: Noord-Hollands Archief, Haarlem, The Netherlands

NJIC: New Jersey Information Center, New Jersey Public Library

NK: Nacka Kommun

NLA00: National Library of Australia, BibID: 4180000

NLA14: National Library of Australia, BibID: 3704514

NLA15: National Library of Australia, BibID: 3943215

NLA17: National Library of Australia, BibID: 3698217

NLA23: National Library of Australia, BibID: 3698223

NLA29: National Library of Australia, BibID: 3721929

NLA37: National Library of Australia, BibID: 3721214

NLA39: National Library of Australia, BibID: 3919541

NLA41: National Library of Australia, BibID: 3701541

NLA53: National Library of Australia, BibID: 1909753

NLA54: National Library of Australia, BibID: 4180454

NLA55: National Library of Australia, BibID: 3660155

NLA75: National Library of Australia, BibID: 3660675

NLA82: National Library of Australia, BibID: 4184682

NLA85: National Library of Australia, BibID: 3791585

NLA97: National Library of Australia, BibID: 3701697

NLW: Supplied by National Library of Wales

NM: Neill Menneer

NMS: Leo Adler, *Neuzeitliche Miethäuser und Siedlungen* (Berlin-Charlottenburg: Ernst Pollack, 1931)

NNPL: Virginiana Collection, Main Street Library, Newport News Public Library System, Newport News, VA

NPL: Nashville Public Library, The Nashville Room

NRE26: *National Real Estate and Building Journal* (1926)

NRHA: Norfolk Redevelopment and Housing Authority Photo Archive

NRM: National Railway Museum/ Science & Society Picture Library

NRPL: New Rochelle Public Library

NRW: North Rhine-Westphalia State Archives

NSA: Courtesy of Nova Scotia Archives

NTM: Archives of Architecture and Civil Engineering, National Technical Museum, Czech Republic

NTNU: NTNU University Library

NVO: © Norbert van Onna Architectural Photography

NW: Nicholas Warner

NWTS: *Neue Werkkunst: Theodore Suhnel* (Berlin: F. E. Hübsch, 1929)

NYHS: Collection of the New-York Historical Society

NYPL: New York Public Library

NYPLM: New York Public Library, Milstein Division

NYPLMD: New York Public Library, Map Division

NYSA: New York State Archives, Fairchild Aerial Surveys Collection

NYSC: New York Shipbuilding Corporation

NYT: The New York Times/Redux

OC: Oliver Chamberlain

OCA: Odense City Archives

OGS: Open Garden Squares Weekend, Photo by Gavin Gardiner

OHS: Ohio Historical Society

OHS1: Ohio Historical Society [*Sessions Village: The Development of an Ideal* (Converse & Fulton, 1927)]

OHS6: Oregon Historical Society, #bb003006

OHS28: Oregon Historical Society, #bb009728

OHS40: Oregon Historical Society, #bb009760

OHS47: Oregon Historical Society, #bb009747

OHS71: Oregon Historical Society, #bb000871

OHS73: Oregon Historical Society, # bb002973

OHS85: Oregon Historical Society, # bb008785

OLSA: Oldham Local Studies and Archives

OMCL: Osaka Municipal Central Library, Osaka Historical Archives

OMH: Office for Metropolitan History

ONT: Archives of Ontario

OR: Courtesy Olivier Rigaud

ORFR: Archives du Foyer Rémois, Courtesy Olivier Rigaud

ORS: *Neuere Arbeiten von O. R. Salvisberg* (Berlin: Friedrich Ernst Hübsch, 1927)

OS: Ordnance Survey

OSG: Öffentlichkeitsarbeit & Stadtmarketing Gemeindeverwaltung Wildau

OSI: Ordnance Survey Ireland

OSL: Omega Segurança Ltda

OSLO: Oslo City Archives/ photographer unknown

OSNI: Ordnance Survey of Northern Ireland

PA: Portsmouth Athenaeum

PA76: *Progressive Architecture* (1976)

PALD: Charles A. Birnbaum and Robin Karson, eds., *Pioneers of American Landscape Design* (New York: McGraw-Hill, 2000)

PAN: Panoramio

PAO: Peter Aaron/OTTO

PB: Peter Bürgmann

PC05: *Plan Canada* (2005)

PCR: Polk County Recorder

PCSE: Pitzmans Co. of Surveyors and Engineers

PDC: Archives départementales du Pas-de-Calais/BHB 1122

PDC1: Archives départementales du Pas-de-Calais/1997 W 13

PDC2: Archives départementales du Pas-de-Calais/1 W 13185

PDS: Paul D. Spreiregen, ed., *On the Art of Designing Cities: Selected Essays of Elbert Peets* (Cambridge, Mass.: MIT Press, 1968)

PDSA: Charles Reade, *Planning and Development of Towns and Cities in South Australia* (Adelaide: R.R.E. Rogers, 1919)

PE: *Paisajes Españoles*

PENC: *Pencil Points* (1936)

PITT: Stefan Lorant, *Pittsburgh: The Story of an American City* (Garden City, N.Y.: Doubleday, 1964)

PK: Philip Knight

PL: Society of Friends of the Garden City Podkowa Leśna

PLC: Courtesy of the Robinson-Spangler Carolina Room - Public Library of Charlotte & Mecklenburg County

PM: Paul Murrain

PMG: Courtesy of Peter McGahey

PMM: Assessoria de Comuicação/PMM

POB: Patricia O'Brien

POE: Pictures of England

PPC: Courtesy of Derbyshire Local Studies Libraries and www.picturethepast.org.uk

PRIJ: *Prijsvraag voor het ontwerpen van een tuinstadwijk* (Amsterdam, 1915)

PRO: Pembrokeshire Record Office, part of Pembrokeshire County Council

PS: Patrick Shiels

PSL: Richard Compton and Camille Dry, *Pictorial St. Louis* (St. Louis: Compton & Co., 1876)

PSS: American Illustrating Company, *Pen and Sunlight Sketches of Greater New Orleans: The Gateway to the Panama Canal* (New Orleans: American Illustrating Company, n.d.)

PT: Panos Totsikas, Architect-Urbanist and Writer

PV: Palisander Verlag; *Garden City of Hellerau: One Hundred Years of Germany's First Garden City*

PVLD: Palos Verdes Library District, Local History Collection

QEL: File 20.02.001, Coll-137 Geography Collection-Historical Photographs of Newfoundland and Labrador, Archives and Special Collections, Queen Elizabeth II Library, Memorial University, St. John's, Newfoundland and Labrador

RA: © Region Alsace - Inventaire general

RA34: *Rassegna di Architettura* (1934)

RAC: Rockefeller Archive Center

RAMSA: Robert A. M. Stern Architects

RATP: Thomas Adams, *Recent Advances in Town Planning* (London: J. & A. Churchill, 1932)

RB: Rheinisches Bildarchiv, Konservator Stadt Köln

RBA1: Chatham Fields, Chicago, IL, 1914. Edward H. Bennett, architect. Archival Image Collection, Ryerson and Burnham Archives, The Art Institute of Chicago. Digital File # 197301.080530-07. Courtesy of The Art Institute of Chicago

RBA2: Historic Architecture and Land scape Image Collection, Ryerson and Burnham Archives, The Art Institute of Chicago. Digital File # 46167 Courtesy of The Art Institute of Chicago

RBA3: Historic Architecture and Landscape Image Collection, Ryerson and Burnham Archives, The Art Institute of Chicago. Digital File # 46168 Courtesy of The Art Institute of Chicago

RBA4: Historic Architecture and Landscape Image Collection, Ryerson and Burnham Archives, The Art Institute of Chicago. Digital File # 46144 Courtesy of The Art Institute of Chicago

RBA5: Historic Architecture and Landscape Image Collection, Ryerson and Burnham Archives, The Art Institute of Chicago. Digital File # 46145 Courtesy of The Art Institute of Chicago

RBA6: Historic Architecture and Landscape Image Collection, Ryerson and Burnham Archives, The Art Institute of Chicago. Digital File # 46152. Courtesy of The Art Institute of Chicago

RBA7: Historic Architecture and Landscape Image Collection, Ryerson and Burnham Archives, The Art Institute of Chicago. Digital File # 46165 Courtesy of The Art Institute of Chicago

RBG: Robert Bosch GmbH – FCM-Rt-Archiv

RBH: Ring Brothers History

RC: Richard Cheek

RCA: © RCAHMS (Aerofilms Collection). Licensor www.rcahms.gov.uk

RCE: Rijksdienst voor het Cultureel Erfgoed

RCHS: Ramsey County Historical Society

RDD: Ralf-Dieter Drews

RDL: Robert D. Loversidge

REPS: John W. Reps, *The Making of Urban America: A History of City Planning in the United States* (Princeton, N.J.: Princeton University Press, 1965)

RERG: *Real Estate Record and Builders' Guide* (1913)

RES: Stanley L. McMichael, *Real Estate Subdivisions* (New York: Prentice-Hall, 1949)

RFP: Raoul Family Papers, The Special Collections Division, Robert W. Woodruff Library, Emory University, Atlanta, Georgia

RGFA: Regional Gallery of Fine Arts, Zlín

RGV: Debbie Nyman, Roe Green Village Residents' Association

RH: Rijksarchief Hasselt

RHM: Riverside Historical Museum

RI: Reflective Images

RIAS: Courtesy of RCAHMS (RIAS Collection)

RIBA10: *Journal of the Royal Institute of British Architects* (1910)

RIBA18: *Journal of the Royal Institute of British Architects* (1918)

RIBAD: RIBA Library Drawings & Archives Collection

RIBAP: RIBA Library Photographs Collection

RIKS: Riksantikvarieämbetet

RL: Risca Library

RLS: Courtesy of Richmond Local Studies Collection

RM: Courtesy Roebling Museum, Ferdinand Roebling III Archives

RMN: © Ministère de la Culture/ Médiathèque du Patrimoine, Dist. RMN-Grand Palais/Art Resource, NY

RNPC: Région Nord-Pas de Calais

ROE: Martin Roe, meerstone.co.uk

ROL: Ralf Roletschek

RPA: Regional Plan Association

RPD: Thomas Adams, *Rural Planning and Development* (Ottawa, 1917)

RPM: The Royal Pavilion and Museums, Brighton & Hove

RR: Rory Rae

RRM: *Monograph of the Work of Robert Rodes McGoodwin 1910-1940* (Philadelphia: William F. Fell, 1942)

RRPC: L. M. Roth, based on Roanoke Rapids Power Company map of 1900, supplied by A. Edwin Akers

RS: Ruth Sharville

RSFHS: Rancho Santa Fe Historical Society

RSG: Region- och Stadsarkivet Göteborg

RSL: Richard S. Lane

RV: Rainer Voltmer

S11: *Scribner's Magazine* (1911)

S12: *Scribner's Magazine* (1912)

SAA: Southeastern Architectural Archive, Special Collections Division, Tulane University Libraries

SACS: San Antonio Conservation Society Foundation

SAF: State Archives of Florida

SAP: Smith Aerial Photos

SAR: Giorgio Sarto, co-author, *Mestre Novecento: il secolo breve della città di terraferma* (Venice: Marsilio, 2007)

SATP: Archives de la Société Académique du Touquet-Paris-Plage

SAV: Charles C. Savage, *Architecture of the Private Streets of St. Louis: The Architects and the Houses They Designed* (Columbia: University of

Missouri Press, 1987)

SB: Stadt Bochum

SB05: *Der Städtebau* (1905)

SBG: Stadtarchiv Bergisch Gladbach

SBHM: Santa Barbara Historical Museum

SBPI: Stadt Bochum, Presse- und Informationsamt

SBS: © Steven Brooke Studios

SC: Steve Clicque

SCA: Siemens Corporate Archives, Munich

SCB10: *Schweizerische Bauzeitung* (1910)

SCB30: *Schweizerische Bauzeitung* (1930)

SCDO: Geoffrey Baker and Bruno Funaro, *Shopping Centers: Design and Operation* (New York: Reinhold, 1951)

SCH: Dirk Schubert

SCHL: Société Coopérative d'Habitation Lausanne

SCPD: Stockholm City Planning Department

SCPL: Photograph courtesy of the Herald-Journal Willis Collection Spartanburg County (SC) Public Libraries

SCWH: Seaver Center for Western History Research, Museum of Natural History of Los Angeles County

SD: Steven Date

SDC: Sokol District Council

SDO: Stadt Dortmund

SDR: Stadtarchiv Dessau-Rosslau/Landesarchiv NRW-Abteilung Rheinland

SEC: State Electricity Commission of Victoria, *Establishment of Township at Yallourn* (1921), courtesy of Philip Knight

SF: Siedlungsgenossenschaft Freidorf (Philipp Potocki)

SFHC: San Francisco History Center, San Francisco Public Library

SG: Courtesy of Sheila Geary

SGV0: Streekarchief Gooi en Vechtstreek, Hilversum/gooienvechthistorisch.nl Collection SAGV032

SGV1: Streekarchief Gooi en Vechtstreek, Hilversum/gooienvechthistorisch.nl Collection SAGV169

SHC: C. H. James and F. R. Yerbury, *Small Houses for the Community* (London: Lockwood, 1924)

SHDS: Société historique du Saguenay

SHG: Société historique P.E. Gendreau, courtesy Musée de la Gare, Témiscaming

SHLGP: Stanley C. Ramsey, *Small Houses of the Late Georgian Period, 1750-1820* (London: Technical Journals, 1919-23)

SHS: Shaker Historical Society

SHSM: J. C. Nichols Company Scrapbooks (K0054), The State Historical Society of Missouri

SHV: Société d'Histoire du Vésinet

SIAF: SIAF/Cité de l'architecture et du patrimoine/Archives d'architecture du XXe siècle

SIHS: Shelter Island Historical Society

SIM: From the Collection of the Staten Island Museum

SJC1: St. John's College Archive, EST III. MP.183; By permission of the President and Fellows of St. John's College, Oxford

SJC2: St. John's College Archive, MUN V.C.7; By permission of the President and Fellows of St. John's College, Oxford

SJC3: St. John's College Archive, MUN

V.C.8; By permission of the President and Fellows of St. John's College, Oxford

SJH: Library and Archives Division, Sen. John Heinz History Center

SJS: By courtesy of the Trustees of Sir John Soane's Museum, Photo: Ardon Bar-Hama

SK: Stadtarchiv Kiel

SKB: Staatskanzlei des Kantons Basel-Stadt

SKV: Andrei Skvortsov

SLD: Stadtarchiv Landeshauptstadt Düsseldorf

SLMA: AN11413 Stockholms läns museum (Stockholm county museum), Alf Nordström

SLML: Ld970702 Stockholms läns museum (Stockholm county museum), Ingvar Lundkvist

SLMX: X990307 Stockholms läns museum (Stockholm county museum)

SLSA: Sutton Local Studies & Archives Service

SLV: State Library of Victoria

SM: Stadtarchiv München

SMA: Seattle Municipal Archives

SMCHM: San Mateo County History Museum

SMLW: Santa Monica Land & Water Company Archives

SNCF: Centre des Archives Historiques de la SNCF

SNHB: Swedish National Heritage Board

SOR: André Sorensen

SPA: Springwells Park Association

SPJ: Samuel Parsons Jr., *How to Plan the Home Grounds* (New York: Doubleday & McClure, 1901)

SPVM: Service Patrimoine de la Ville de Marcq-en-Baroeul

SRV: Siedlung Rosenhügel, Vienna

SRW: Stiftung Rheinisch-Westfälisches Wirtschaftsarchiv zu Köln

SS: Stadtarchiv Stuttgart

SSD: Archives départementales de la Seine-Saint-Denis

SSDB: Archives Municipales du Blanc-Mesnil, Service du patrimoine culturel, Département de la Seine-Saint-Denis

SSDI: © Inventaire général, Département de la Seine-Saint-Denis, ADAGP

SSDJ: Emmanuelle Jacquot, Service du patrimoine culturel, Département de la Seine-Saint-Denis

SSDO: OPHBMDS, Service du patrimoine culturel, Département de la Seine-Saint-Denis

SSL: Stadtarchiv - Stadt Luzern

SSM: Stadtarchiv, Stadt Münster

STBR: Stadtarchiv Braunschweig

STK: Stadtkonservator Köln

STS: Stockholms Stadsmuseum

SU: Stadtarchiv Ulm

SUITA: Suita City

SUL: John Sulman, *An Introduction to the Study of Town Planning in Australia* (William Applegate Gullick, Government Printer, 1919), courtesy of Philip Knight

SUN13: *Sunset* (1913)

SW: Stadtarchiv Winterthur

SW27: *Siedlungs-Wirtschaft* (1927)

SWJA: Silvia Ferreira Santos Wolff, *Jardim América: o primeiro bairro-jardim de São Paulo e sua arquitetura* (São Paulo: Imprensa Oficial SP: Edusp: FAPESP, 2000)

SWLD: Stephen Williams/Lauren Diliberto

SZ: Amt für Städtebau der Stadt Zürich,

Baugeschichtliches Archiv

TA22: *The Architect* (1922)

TA26: *The Architect* (1926)

TAHO: Tasmanian Archive and Heritage Office: Miscellaneous Collection of Photographs. 1860-1992 Item PH30-2-3940

TAY: Tel Aviv-Yafo Municipal Archives

TB12: *The Builder* (1912)

TB19: *The Builder* (1919)

TB20: *The Builder* (1920)

TB83: *The Builder* (1883)

TB88: *The Builder* (1888)

TBC: The Biltmore Company, Asheville, North Carolina

TBF: Town of Biltmore Forest

TC: Tom Clemett

TCA: Trondheim City Archive (Trondheim byarkiv)

TCHS: The Connecticut Historical Society, Hartford, Connecticut

TCI: Touring Club Italiano

TCP33: *Town and Country Planning* (1933)

TCPL: Courtesy, Tampa-Hillsborough County Public Library System

TDP10: *The Daily Picayune* (1910)

TDP91: *The Daily Picayune* (1891)

TEK09: *Architekten* (1909)

TEK14: *Architekten* (1914)

TEK19: *Architekten* (1919)

TERR: Terraplan

TH: Sir Timothy Harford, Bt.

THM: Thomas H. Mawson, *Civic Art: Studies in Town Planning, Parks, Boulevards, and Open Spaces* (London. B. T. Batsford, 1911)

THS: Torrance Historical Society

TIW: © Jacques Boyer/Roger-Viollet/The Image Works

TL: Courtesy of Theodore Liebman

TLSAC: Tameside Local Studies and Archives Centre

TM: Tony Murray Photography

TMBC: Tameside Metropolitan Borough Council

TMRA: Courtesy of Town of Mount Royal Archives

TNA: The National Archives of the UK: ref. MPE 1/911

TNA1: The National Archives of the UK: ref. AP 7/171/1

TNA2: The National Archives of the UK: ref. MPD 1/17

TNT: Clarence S. Stein, *Toward New Towns for America* (Cambridge, Mass.: MIT Press, 1957)

TOM: *Ebenezer Howard, To-morrow: a Peaceful Path to Real Reform* (London: Swan Sonnenschein & Co., 1898)

TOP: Town of Pacolet

TPL: Tuxedo Park Library

TPMA: *Garden Suburbs, Town Planning and Modern Architecture* (London: T. Fisher Unwin, 1910)

TPP: Raymond Unwin, *Town Planning in Practice* (London: T. Fisher Unwin, 1909)

TPR10: *Town Planning Review* (1910)

TPR11: *Town Planning Review* (1911)

TPR13: *Town Planning Review* (1913)

TPR16: *Town Planning Review* (1916)

TPR52: *Town Planning Review* (1952)

TPR60: *Town Planning Review* (1960)

TPR76: *Town Planning Review* (1976), Courtesy of G. MacQueen

TRC: Peter Calthorpe and William Fulton, *The Regional City* (Washington, D.C.: Island Press, 2001)

TS: Theodor Suhnel, *Theodor Suhnel* (Berlin: F. E. Hübsch, 1929)

TTA: John Avery, The Teddington Architect

TUCK: tuckdb.org, licensed under Creative Commons Attribution-ShareAlike 3.0 Unported

TUIN: *Rapport van de Commissie ter bestudeering van het vraagstuk van den bouw eener tuinstad of van tuindorpen in de omgeving van Amsterdam*, 1929)

TVA: Tennessee Valley Authority Archives

TW: Image courtesy of Tunbridge Wells Museum & Art Gallery

TW94: *The World* (July 29, 1894)

TWB: Thomas W. Brunk, *Leonard B. Willeke: Excellence in Architecture and Design* (Detroit: University of Detroit Press, 1986)

TWS: Courtesy Mike Chitty, The Wavertree Society

UA: University Libraries at The University of Akron

UAK: Universität für angewandte Kunst Wien, Kunstsammlung und Archiv

UCHS: Unicoi County Historical Society

UCLA: Special Collections, University of California, Los Angeles

UCPL: The Archives of the University City Public Library

UDC: Universidade da Coruña

UG: Ulrich Gräfe

UHL: Courtesy of Special Collections, University of Houston Libraries

UM: Courtesy of the Northwest Architectural Archives, part of the Special Collections, Rare Books, and Manuscripts Unit, University of Minnesota, Minneapolis

UMAS: University of Manitoba, Archives & Special Collections

UML: Bernhardt E. Muller Collection, Courtesy of Special Collections, University of Miami Libraries, Coral Gables, Florida

UNI: Reproduced with kind permission of Unilever from an original in Unilever Archives

UOL: © University of London (Victoria County History)

UOM: Art, Architecture & Engineering Library Lantern Slide Collection, University of Michigan (image 006999)

URB35: *Urbanisme* (1935)

USC: Courtesy of University of Southern California, on behalf of the USC Libraries Special Collections

USHC: *Report of the United States Housing Corporation*, 2 vols. (Washington, D.C.: Government Printing Office, 1919)

USNA: U.S. National Archives and Records Administration

USSB: *Types of Housing for Shipbuilders: Constructed as a War Necessity Under the Direction of United States Shipping Board Emergency Fleet Corporation Passenger Transportation and Housing Division* (Washington, D.C.: U.S. Shipping Board, 1919)

UU: Rare Books Division, Special Collections, J. Willard Marriott Library, University of Utah

UVL: University of Victoria Libraries, László Hudec Architectural Drawings

UWL: Special Collections Division, University of Washington Libraries

UWM: University of Wisconsin-Madison Archives

VA: Venice Archives and Area Historical Collection

VB: Vivienne Beck

VDG: Ville de Gennevilliers

VDS: Ville de Saguenay

VG: Village of Glendale, Ohio

VGA: Verein für Geschichte der Arbeiterbewegung, Vienna

VPF: *Brooklyn's Garden: Views of Picturesque Flatbush* (Brooklyn: C. A. Ditmas, c. 1908), digital image by Avery Library, Columbia University

VS: ©www.viennaslide.com

VU20: *Vie Urbaine* (1920)

WA13: *Western Architect* (1913)

WA18: *Western Architect* (1918)

WAC: City of Westminster Archives Centre

WALS: Image reproduced with the permission of Wolverhampton Archives & Local Studies

WAS: Wirral Archives Service

WB: Winterthurer Bibliotheken

WC: Wikimedia Commons

WCA: Westchester County Archives

WCAR: Western Cape Archives and Records Service

WCHS: Westchester County Historical Society

WCRO: Warwickshire County Record Office; photo of Newbold Comyn from *Leamington Spa Courier*

WDDC: Courtesy of West Dorset District Council

WEFJ: William E. Fischer Jr.

WEL: Courtesy Webb Estate Limited

WEN: Wohnungsgenossenschaft Essen-Nord eG

WG: Winterthur Glossar

WGK: *Wohlfahrtseinrichtungen der Gussstahlfabrik von Fried. Krupp zu Essen a.d. Ruhr* (Essen: Buchdruckerei der gusstahlfabrik von F. Krupp, 1902)

WHHS: Winter Harbor Historical Society

WHL: W. H. Lever, *The Buildings Erected at Port Sunlight and Thornton Hough: Paper Read by W. H. Lever, at a Meeting of the Architectural Association, London, March 21st, 1902* (1905)

WID: Albert Gut, *Wohnungsbau in Deutschland nach dem Weltkriege* (Munich: Verlag F. Bruckmann, 1928)

WIE: Hunter Wieczorek

WL: Warrington Library, reproduced with the permission of LiveWire, working in partnership with Warrington Borough Council

WLC: Woodlands Library and Customer Service Centre

WM: Wien Museum

WM20: *Wasmuths Monatshefte für Baukunst und Städtebau* (1920/21)

WM24: *Wasmuths Monatshefte für Baukunst und Städtebau* (1924)

WM26: *Wasmuths Monatshefte für Baukunst und Städtebau* (1926)

WO: Winston Owen

WP: WingPics

WRD: Wolf-Rüdiger Dogs

WUR: Special Collections, Wageningen UR library

WVSA: West Virginia State Archives

WXAS: Wrexham Archives Service

YHC: Courtesy of Yeamans Hall Club

YKLB: Courtesy of Professor Yossi Katz and Dr. Liora Bigon

YOR: Yvan & Olowine Rogg

YY: Yiorgis Yerolymbos

ZB: Zeitschrift fur Baukunde

ZE: Zuiderzeemuseum Enkhuizen, Netherlands

ZOI: *Zeitschrift des Österreichischen Ingenieur- und Architekten-Veriens* (1924)

ZUS: John Collins, "Lusaka: The Myth of the Garden City," *Zambian Urban Studies*, no. 2 (Lusaka: University of Zambia, Institute for Social Research, 1969)

De Ligne, Jean, 496, 498, *500*
Delisle, Oscar, 460
Delk, Edward Buehler, 174
Del Mue, Maurice, 882
De Michelis, Antonella, 600, 602
Deming, William I., 916
De Miranda, S. R., 507
Democracy in America (Tocqueville), 48
Denenchōfu, 694, *695*, 696
Denker, Charles, 157
Denmark, 565–69
Dennis, John Stoughton, 619
Dennison, Ethan A., *931*, 932
Denver, Colo., 67–68
Derby, 700, *701*
Derée, Henri, 498, *500*
De Renzi, Mario, 602
Dering Harbor, N.Y., 305, *306*
De Roos, J. H., 516
de Rousiers, Paul, 248
Der Städtebau (Hegemann), 82
de Rutté, Paul, *469*, 470–71, *471*, *472*, 475–76, *476*, *481*, 482
Description of a Christian Republic, The (Andreae), 204–5
Desmond, Thomas, 882
de Soissons, Louis, 228, 236, *236*, 238
Dessez, Leon E., 148
Detroit, Mich., 86, 105
Detroit Shipbuilding Co., 884
Deutsche Arbeitsfront (German Labor Front), 764
Deutsche Gartenstadtgesellschaft (DGG; German Garden City Association), 409, 427, 614
Deutscher Werkbund, 409, 458, 579, 595
Deutsche Werkstätten für Handwerkskunst, 292
de Vletter, Martien, 776–77, *778*, *779*, 780
Devonshire, William Cavendish, sixth Duke of, 33
de Wijs, W. K., 775–76, *777*
De Witt, Dennis J. and Elizabeth R., 512, 610, 762, 764
Diamandidis, D., 682
Dickson, Joseph, Jr., 101
Didier, Charles, 494
Diergaardepark, 510, *512*
Dietrich, E. G. W., 107
Dikanskii, M. G., 688, 689
Dilts, James, 881
Dings, Mieke, 516
Dinnick, Wilfred, 625
Diongre, Joseph, 496
Disney, Walt, 957, *958*
Disneyland, 944, *944*
Disraeli, Benjamin, 706
Ditmas Park, Brooklyn, 108–9, *111*
Dixon, Thomas, 51
Dixon's Hill, 51, *52*
Dizengoff, Meir, 680
Djursholm, 536, *536*
Dobrzyński, Władysław, 616
Döcker, Richard, 458
Dohnberg, Rudolf, 687
Dollfuss, Jean, 729
Domènech, Martín Trías, 610
Domnarvet Ironworks, 783
Dondorff, Jakob, 422
Donn, Edward Wilton, Jr., 916
Donnycarney, 404, *405*
Donohue, J., 835, 837
Dorfsiedlung Geissenstein, 792, *792*
Dormanstown, 716–17, *716*
Dorpsbelant Housing Association, 518
Dorsey, John, 881
Doubleday, Page and Doran, 244
Dougill, Wesley, 603–4
Douglas, Walter, 850
Douglas & Fordham, 220
Dowie, John Alexander, 250–51
Downham Estate, 387–88, *388*
Downing, Andrew Jackson, 49, *50*, 120, 128, 131, 303, 687

Dozier, A. W., 324, *324*
Drane, F. N., 89, 90
Draper, Earle, Jr., 282
Draper, Earle S., 87, 155–56, *156*, 266, 280–82, 750, 857–61, *858*, *859*, *860*
Draper, Ebenezer, 824, 826
Draper, George, 824, 826
Driving Park Addition, Fort Wayne, 102
Druid Hills, 150–51, *151*, *152*
Druid Hills Company, 151
Drumcondra, 402, 404, *404*
Drummond, William, 162–63, *164*
Duany, Andrés, 13, 81, 88, 765, 951. 952, 957, 958, 961
Duany, Douglas 953
Dublin Citizens' Housing League, 399, 405
Dublin Corporation, 399–402, 404
Dudok, Willem Marinus, 516, 518–22, *518*, *519*, *521*, 523, *524*, 525, *525*, 776
Dufour, Lucien, 489, *489*
Duhring, H. Louis, 138
Duhring, Okie & Ziegler, 138–39, *139*
Duiker, Jan, 516
Duinbergen, 489, *490*, 491
Duke, James Buchanan, 937
Duke University, 87
Dumail, Félix, 473, *474*
Dundalk, Md., 880–81, *880*
Dunkerley, F. B., 374–75, *375*
Dunn, Watson & Curtis Green, 722–23, *723*
Dunn, William, 722–23
DuPont, 83–84
DuPont Engineering Company, 888
Dupuy, Léopold, 492, *493*
Durandeau, Edmond, 492
Durham, N.C., 87
Durie Hill, 660–61, *660*
Dutch Garden City Association, 508
Dzierżanowski, Juliusz, 617, *617*
Eagle, Pilkington & McQueen, 668
Ealing Tenants Limited, 349
Eames, William Sylvester, 95–96, *96*
Eames & Young, 253
Earle, William, 659, *659*
East, John, 367
Easterling, Keller, 266
East Lake Land Company, 180
East Pittsburgh Improvement Company, 801
Eastriggs, 724, *725*, 726
East Stratton, 19, *20*
Eaton, Ruth, 289, 727, 729
Ebbett, Charles, 108
Ebbw Vale Steel, Iron and Coal Company, 721
Eberlein, Harold D., 138
Echota, 801, *803*
Eckert, Kathryn, 845
Eclipse Park, Wisc., 86, 840–42, *841*
Economy, Pa., 207
Eddystone, 908, *908*
Eden, F. C., 378–79
Eden, Joseph A., 287
Edison, Thomas, 831, 833, 843
Edwards, Albert F., 907
Effner, Joseph, 17
Eggericx, Jean-Jules, 495, 496, 498, 501, *502*, 505
Eggers, Willy, 460
Egypt, 669–74
Egyptian Delta Land and Investment Company, 674
E. H. Fleming & Company, 115
Eigen Haard housing association, 527
Eigenheim Baugesellschaft für Deutschland, 416
Eighteenth Municipal Housing Complex, Hilversum, 522, *524*
Eira, 548–49, *548*
Eisden, 766–67, *768*
Eisenheim, 733, *733*

Eisenman, Peter, 946
Eisner, Michael, 957, 960
Ekali, 686–87, *686*
Ekeburg, 560, *561*
Ekelund, Hilding, 785
Elan Valley Estate Village, 719, *719*
Electrona, 659, *659*
Elektryczne, 617
El Encanto Estates, 325, *325*
Eleventh Municipal Housing Complex, Hilversum, 522, *524*
Eliot, Charles, 806
Elkart, Karl, 431, *432*
Ellington, Douglas D., 283
Elliott, Huger, 846
Ellis, Harvey, 97
Ellis, John Joseph, 154
Elmwood Park, 902–3, *903*
Elsässer, Martin, 453
Eluère, Alfred, 491
Ely, Richard T., 245, 247, 248
Embury, Aymar, II, 320, *320*
Emergency Fleet Corporation (EFC), 274, 822, 856, 861–85, 892
Emery, Mary M., 267, 269, 270
Emmer, Pietro Emilio, 599–600, *599*
Emmerich, Herbert, 193, 275
Emmerich, Paul, 415, *415*, 437
Emory Hills, Wheaton, 80–81, *81*
Empain, Baron Édouard, 669–71, *670*, 672
Emscher-Lippe, 747, 749, *750*
Eneborg, 782, *782*
Engelske Haveby, Den, 567, *568*
Engineering Service Company, 78, 325
England, 17–42, 220–41, 349–91, 700–719
Engström, Edvin, 544, *546*
Enke, Fritz, 737
Enskede, 537, *538*, *539*, 542
Enskededalen, 542–43, *542*
Enskede Gård, 544, *546*
Entrada Court, 73, *73*
EPCOT, 957, *958*
Erhard, V., 492, *493*
Erichs, Malte, 540
Erie, Pa., 905–7, *906*
Eriksson, Eva, 536, 542
Erlanger Mills, 857, *858*
Erwin, Tenn., 263–64, *264*
Esch, Hermann, 411–12
Esch & Anke, 411–12, *412*
Etlin, Richard, 600, 601
Euclid Golf Club, 150
Euclid Heights, Ohio, 149, *149*
European Cities, 1890–1930s (Meller), 501
Evanston, Ill., 81
Everett Place, 111, *114*
Evergreen Hamlet, Pa., 121–22, *122*
Evolving House, The (Bemis and Burchard), 856
Ewald, Sigfrid, 782
Ewing, Charles, 888
Ewing & Allen, 888
Exall, Henry, 159
Eyde, Sam, 785
Eyre, Wilson, 309
Eyre Estate, 21, *22*, 27
Ezelbrugwijk, 505, *506*
Faber, Erich, 587–88
Faber, Manfred, 422
Fair & Myer, 368
Fairbairn, Walter, 727
Fairbanks, Douglas, 159
Fairbanks, Morse & Co., 840, 842
Fairbanks Flats, 841–42, *841*
Fairbanks Village, 800, *800*
Fairbrothers' Fields Estate, 402, *403*
Fairfield, Ala., 810–12, *812*, *813*, 814
Fairfield Housing Estate, 376–78, *377*
Fairfield Tenants' Association, 376
Fairholme Estate, 718–19, *718*
Fairlawn Heights, 839, *839*
Fairview Realty Company, 863

Falkenberg, *408*, 413, *414*, 442
Fallings Park Garden Suburb, 364, *365*, 366
Fallings Park Garden Suburb Tenants' Society, 366
Familistère, *206*, 207, 250
Fanning, J. J., 801, *803*
F. A. Pease Engineering Company, 175
Farmer, Henry E., 724, *724*
Farquhar, Robert D., 256, 298
Farrell, James A., 811
Fatio, Maurice T., 334
Faville, William B., 255, *255*
Favrot, Charles Allen, 111, 928–29, *929*
Fawcett, Waldon, 145
Fechheimer, Ihorst & McCoy, 269
Federal Capital Advisory Committee, Australia, 646
Federal Housing Administration (FHA), 195
Federal Housing Scheme, Canada, 632
Feiss, Carl, 942
Fenhagen, G. Corner, 915, *915*
Fenoglio, Pietro, 788–89, *789*
Ferguson, Alfred L. and Henry L., 330
Ferguson, Cheryl Lynn Caldwell, 160
Ferguson, Homer L., 878
Fernández de Casadevante, José Ángel, 492, *494*
Fernhill Garden Village, 719, *721*
Ferry, George B., 158
Few Hints on Landscape Gardening in the West (Cleveland), 52–53
Fforestfach Miners' Village, 719, *720*
Ficken, Richard, 107
Fieldston, Bronx, N.Y., 59–61, *61*
Fieldston Hill, 60
Fieldston Property Owners Association, 59–60
Fifth Municipal Housing Complex, Hilversum, 519–20, *519*, *521*
Finchley Garden Village, *372*, 373
Fink, Denman, *338*, *339*, 340–41, 342
Fink, H. George, 341
Finke, Albert, 419
Finland, 546–58, 784–85
Firestone, Harvey, 839
Firestone Park, 839–40, *840*
First Garden City, see Letchworth, England
First Garden City Ltd., 233
First Municipal Housing Complex, Hilversum, 519, *519*, 520
Fischer, Theodor, 290, 409, 410–11, *410*, *411*, 413, 434, *434*, 441, 446, 459, 507, 567, 676, 737, *738*, *739*, 741, 776
Fisher, Arthur A., 68
Fisher, Carl G., 330, 333
Fisher, Francis, 61
Fisher, Oscar, 196
Fisher, William Ellsworth, 68
Fisher Hill, Brookline, 60–62, *62*, 63
Fishers Island Club, 330, *330*
Fishman, Robert, 31, 124, 139–40, 170, 214, 942
Fiske Terrace, Brooklyn, 109, *111*
Fissler, Friedrich, 570
Flagg, Ernest, 868, *869*, 870
Flagler, Henry, 333
Flatbush Congregational Church, 109, *111*
Fleischl, Róbert, 611
Fletcher Park, 881–82, *881*
Flewelling, Ralph C., 159
Flint, Mich., 842, *842*
Flippen, Edgar, 159, 161
Floet, Willemijn Wilms, 516
Flora Boulevard, 97, *98*
Florapark, 508, *509*
Fogelson, Robert, 80
Foggitt, William H., 653, *655*
Foltz, Osler & Thompson, 182
Fontaine, Pierre-François-Léonard, 765
Fontaine de Laveleye, Edouard, 635
Fontarabie, 492, *494*
Fooshee & Cheek, 90, 161